β	beta coefficient, a measure of an asset's systematic riskiness.	£	pound (United Kingdom currency).
C	call option value.	OAS	option-adjusted spread.
CAPM	capital asset pricing model.	P	price of a share of stock or put option; P_o is the current price.
CAR	cumulative average residuals.		
CF	cash flow; CF_t is cash flow in period t.	P/BV	price/book value ratio.
CML	capital market line.	P/E	price/earnings ratio.
COV_{ij}	covariance of the returns between assets i and j.	PPP	purchasing power parity.
		P/S	price/sales ratio.
		PV	present value.
D	dividend per share of stock; D_t is dividend per share during period t.	PVIF	present value interest factor for a lump sum.
		PVIFA	present value interest factor for an annuity.
DDM	dividend discount model.	r_{ij}	correlation coefficient between assets i and j.
DM	deutschemark (German currency).	RFR	rate of return on a risk-free asset.
EBIT	earnings before interest and taxes.	ROA	return on assets.
EBITDA	earning before interest, taxes, depreciation, and amortization.	ROE	return on equity.
		RR	fraction of a firm's earnings retained rather than paid out. It is equal to $(1 - D/E)$, where D/E is the ratio of dividends (D) to earnings (E).
EMH	efficient market hypothesis.		
EPS	earnings per share.		
E(R)	expected return; $E(R_t)$ is the expected return during period t.		
		SML	security market line.
F	futures contract delivery price.	Σ	summation sign (capital sigma).
FV	future value.	σ	standard deviation (lowercase sigma).
FVIF	future value interest factor for a lump sum.	σ_{ij}	covariance between returns for security i and j.
FVIFA	future value interest factor for an annuity.		
FX	foreign exchange.	t	tax rate.
G	geometric mean.	time when used as a subscript (e.g., D_t-the dividend in year t).	
g	growth rate in earnings, dividends, or stock prices.		
		T	time to expiration.
h	hedge ratio.	V	value of an asset; V_j is the value of asset j.
HPR	holding period return.	WACC	weighted average cost of capital.
HPY	holding period yield.	X	option exercise price.
I	rate of inflation. $E(I)$ is the expected rate of inflation.	¥	yen (Japanese currency).
		YTC	yield to call.
k	required rate of return.	YTM	yield to maturity.

INVESTMENT ANALYSIS AND PORTFOLIO MANAGEMENT

Seventh Edition

INVESTMENT
ANALYSIS AND PORTFOLIO
MANAGEMENT

Seventh Edition

FRANK K. REILLY
University of Notre Dame

KEITH C. BROWN
University of Texas at Austin

THOMSON

SOUTH-WESTERN

Australia · Canada · Mexico · Singapore · Spain · United Kingdom · United States

Investment Analysis and Portfolio Management, 7e

Frank K. Reilly and Keith C. Brown

VP/Team Director:
Mike Roche

Executive Editor:
Mike Reynolds

Developmental Editor:
Elizabeth Thomson

Production Editor:
Tamborah Moore

Sr. Marketing Manager:
Charlie Stutesman

Editorial Assistant:
Joe Squance

Manufacturing Coordinator:
Sandee Milewski

Media Technology Editor:
Vicky True

Media Development Editor:
John Barans

Media Production Editor:
Mark Sears

Design Project Manager:
Rik Moore

Internal Designer:
Jody Johnson Gittinger,
Gittinger Graphics

Cover Designer:
Chris Miller

Cover Illustrator:
Jeff Brice

Production House and Compositor:
Shepherd, Inc.

Printer:
QuebecorWorld, Versailles

PCN 2002108659
ISBN 0-324-17173-0

To my best friend & wife,
Therese,
and the greatest gifts and
sources of our happiness,
Frank K. III, Charlotte, and Lauren
Clarence R. II and Michelle
Therese B., and Denise
Edgar B., Michele, Kayleigh, and Madison J. T.
F. K. R.

To Sheryl, Alexander, and Andrew
who make it all worthwhile
K. C. B.

Preface

The pleasure of authoring a textbook comes from writing about a subject that you enjoy and find exciting. As an author, you hope that you can pass on to the reader not only knowledge but also the excitement that you feel for the subject. In addition, writing about investments brings an added stimulant because the subject can affect the reader during his or her entire business career and beyond. We hope what readers derive from this course will help them enjoy better lives through managing their financial resources properly.

The purpose of this book is to help you learn how to manage your money so that you will derive the maximum benefit from what you earn. To accomplish this purpose, you need to learn about the investment alternatives that are available today and, what is more important, to develop a way of analyzing and thinking about investments that will remain with you in the years ahead when new and different investment opportunities become available.

Because of its dual purpose, the book mixes description and theory. The descriptive material discusses available investment instruments and considers the purpose and operation of capital markets in the United States and around the world. The theoretical portion details how you should evaluate current investments and future opportunities to develop a portfolio of investments that will satisfy your risk-return objectives.

Preparing this seventh edition has been challenging for two reasons. First, many changes have occurred in the securities markets during the last few years in terms of theory, new financial instruments, and trading practices. Second, as mentioned in prior editions, capital markets have become increasingly global in nature. Consequently, very early in the book we present the compelling case for global investing. Subsequently, to ensure that you are prepared to function in this new global environment, almost every chapter discusses how investment practice or theory is influenced by the globalization of investments and capital markets. This completely integrated treatment is to ensure that you leave this course with a sufficiently broad mindset on investments that will serve you well in the 21st century.

Intended Market

This text is addressed to both graduate and advanced undergraduate students who are looking for an in-depth discussion of investments and portfolio management. The presentation of the material is intended to be rigorous and empirical, without being overly quantitative. A proper discussion of the modern developments in investments and portfolio theory must be rigorous. The detailed discussion of numerous empirical studies reflects the belief that it is essential for alternative investment theories to be exposed to the real world and be judged on the basis of how well they help us understand and explain reality.

Key Features of the Seventh Edition

When planning the seventh edition of *Investment Analysis and Portfolio Management,* we wanted to retain its traditional strengths and capitalize on new developments in the investments area to make it the most comprehensive investments textbook available.

First, the current edition maintains its unparalleled international coverage. Investing knows no borders, and although the total integration of domestic and global investment opportunities may seem to contradict the need for separate discussions of international issues, it in fact makes the need for specific information on non-U.S. markets, instruments, conventions, and techniques even more compelling. Sections of chapters that deal with international topics are designated by this global icon for easy identification.

Second, today's investing environment includes derivative securities not as exotic anomalies but as standard investment instruments. We felt that *Investment Analysis and Portfolio Management* must reflect that reality. Consequently, our four chapters on derivatives have been revised and rearranged to provide an even more intuitive, clear discussion of the different instruments, their markets, valuation, trading strategies, and general use as risk management/return enhancement tools.

vii

The introductory derivatives chapter, which now appears as Chapter 21 in the section titled "Derivative Security Analysis," continues to provide an overview of the purpose and nature of derivative contracting, as well as the important role that these instruments have come to play in the investment management process. We kept this overview from the previous edition because we are still committed to the philosophy that every investments student needs to be exposed to the basics of derivative instruments, markets, and usage.

For instructors who want to get into more detail on derivative pricing, valuation, and strategies, we have three additional chapters in the same section. Chapter 22 discusses forwards and futures contracts first, before options, because typically investors consider forward/futures positions before they turn to options to hedge risk. Chapter 23 then covers option contracts, which are variations of forwards and futures. Part 6 concludes with a chapter on swaps, warrants, convertibles, and structured notes. Chapter 24 is an in-depth discussion of these more "advanced" derivative types, including a section on how investors can view many potential investments from a "real options" perspective.

Third, Chapter 9, "Multifactor Models of Risk and Return," follows immediately after the introductory chapter on single-factor asset pricing models. This material, which includes the progression from the Arbitrage Pricing Theory to the empirical forms of the relationship between multiple systematic risk factors and investment return, has been completely rewritten for this edition. We felt that instructors who wanted to teach this chapter would do so in this order.

Fourth, we have added many new questions and problems to the end-of-chapter material, including a significant number of CFA exercises through the 2001 exam, to provide more student practice on executing computations concerned with more sophisticated investment problems. These are designated by the CFA icon.

Web Site Listings

To reflect the growing use of the World Wide Web as a learning tool and a source of information, each chapter contains an annotated list of the Web sites that relate to the chapter's topic. Students will want to "surf the net" using these applications to gain further insight into the practice of investments and the textbook discussions.

Major Content Changes in the Seventh Edition

The text has been thoroughly updated for currency. In addition to these time-related revisions, we have also made the following specific changes to individual chapters:

Chapter 2 In this asset allocation chapter there is a discussion of several tax changes and how they impact the asset allocation decision, as well as consideration of several new studies on the importance of this allocation decision. Finally, we consider how the asset allocation differs among foreign countries and is changing.

Chapter 3 The updated evidence of returns (especially 2000–2001) continues to support the notion of global diversification. Also, there is a consideration of new investment instruments available for global investors, including global index funds and, notably, exchange-traded funds (ETFs) for numerous countries that trade continuously.

Chapter 4 Significant market changes discussed include decimal pricing and its effects, the continued growth of 144A security issues, and growth in share trading on the secondary equity markets (to over a billion shares a day on the NYSE and on the Nasdaq market). We also demonstrate that global markets and exchanges continue to consolidate.

Chapter 5 Contains a new discussion of growth and value style stock indexes.

Chapter 6   Considers several new studies that both support the efficient market hypothesis but also provide new evidence of anomalies. There is also a new section that explains *behavioral finance* and discusses how it explains many of the anomalies. There is an expanded discussion of the implications of the recent findings related to the efficient market hypothesis.

Chapter 9   Contains a completely revised discussion of the theory and practice of using multifactor models of risk and expected return in the evaluation of securities and the management of portfolios. Particular emphasis is given to the transition from the conceptual underpinnings of the Arbitrage Pricing Theory (APT) to the empirical manifestations of the APT, such as the BARRA and Fama-French models.

Chapter 10   Contains a fairly major rewrite of the "Analysis of Financial Statements" to include further examination of alternative cash flow specifications that are used in valuation models and credit analysis. There is also a detailed discussion of how to analyze operating leases and a demonstration of how the capitalization of these leases and the implied interest dramatically impacts the financial risk ratios for a firm like Walgreens.

Chapter 11   We continue to emphasize the two alternative approaches to valuation (present value of cash flows and relative valuation) with additional discussions of how and when they should be implemented.

Chapter 12   The cyclical indicator series are now maintained by The Conference Board with updated timing results. There is a more detailed analysis of the relationship among inflation, interest rates, and stock returns.

Chapter 13   In line with a growing concern with the equity market risk premium, there is additional discussion of alternative estimates and consideration of recent studies that provide new empirical estimates. The updated aggregate stock market valuations consider the end of our longest economic expansion as well as the impact of the September 11, 2001 terrorist attack.

Chapter 14   There was a significant reorganization of the industry analysis presentation wherein we increased the emphasis on the macroanalysis of an industry and concentrated the several analytical techniques related to this analysis in the early part of the chapter. This macroanalysis has a large impact on the subsequent microanalysis (valuation) of the industry.

Chapter 15   The numerous valuations of the stock of Walgreens using the alternative techniques emphasize a key point of this chapter that an outstanding *company* like Walgreens can have a fully valued or overvalued *stock*. There is also an expanded discussion dealing with the importance of quarterly earnings estimates. We conclude the chapter with a consideration of the numerous unique factors that must be considered when analyzing foreign companies.

Chapter 17   Contains a revised discussion on the merits of passive versus active asset management. Also includes extensive new sections that discuss the various equity portfolio management philosophies, consider the issue of a portfolio's tracking error relative to a benchmark, explain the merits of "style" investing, illustrate the topic of style analysis, and present asset allocation strategies.

Chapter 18   The updated global bond market data considers the recent creation of the Euroland Sector.

Chapter 19   Contains additional discussion of the calculation and use of empirical duration. There is also consideration of the relationship between static yield spreads and option-adjusted spreads (OAS) and what variables affect the option-adjusted spreads.

Chapter 20   Contains a new discussion of the core-plus bond portfolio management technique and some of the "plus" strategies. There is an update and analysis of an expanded set of cumulative default rates for bonds across rating classes.

Chapter 21   Includes greatly expanded coverage of the basic payoffs and trading mechanics of forwards, futures, and options, with new examples based on actual market data. Also contains a substantially revised section on using derivatives to manage portfolio risk.

Chapter 22   Includes revised examples throughout the chapter emphasizing actual market data, and revised sections on the mechanics of futures trading and index arbitrage and the management of currency risk.

Chapter 23   Contains extensive revisions to the section on the binomial option pricing model and the option strategies section. There are also revised discussions of the role volatility plays in option valuation and trading and of option trading fundamentals. Finally, an extended discussion of the Black-Scholes model in practice is included.

Chapter 24   Includes a revised discussion of the interest-rate-swap valuation, an expanded and revised discussion of convertible bonds and structured notes, and a new section on using a "real options" approach to asset valuation.

Chapter 25   Includes discussions of all forms of professional asset management, comparing the various forms of private and public professional asset management. There is also an expanded section on ethics and regulation in the professional asset management industry, which includes discussions of soft dollars and compensation arrangements.

Chapter 26   Includes extensively revised sections on peer group comparisons, on the traditional risk-adjusted performance measures, and on reporting investment performance, including a discussion of time-weighted versus dollar-weighted returns and AIMR's Performance Presentation Standards. The chapter also contains updated examples of performance measurement using actual market data and a revised treatment of bond portfolio measurement.

Supplement Package   The preparation of the seventh edition provided the opportunity to enhance the supplement products offered to instructors and students who use *Investment Analysis and Portfolio Management.* The result of this examination is a greatly improved package that provides more than just basic answers and solutions. We are indebted to the supplement writers who devoted their time, energy, and creativity to making this supplement package the best it has ever been.

The Instructor's Manual and Test Bank   The *Instructor's Manual,* written by Narendar Rao at Northeastern Illinois University, and *Test Bank,* written by Murli Rajan at the University of Scranton, contains a brief outline of each chapter's key concepts and equations that can be easily copied and distributed to students as a reference tool. The *Test Bank* includes an extensive set of new questions and problems and complete solutions to the testing material.

For instructors who would like to prepare their exams electronically, there is a *Computerized Test Bank* available in Word format that contains all the test questions found in the printed version.

The Solutions Manual This separate volume, which can be purchased by students if instructors wish, contains all the answers to the end-of-chapter questions and solutions to end-of-chapter problems. David Leahigh at King's College was ever diligent in the preparation of these materials, ensuring the most error-free solutions possible.

Lecture Presentation Software A comprehensive set of PowerPoint slides created by Narendar Rao at Northeastern Illinois University is available. Each chapter has a self-contained presentation that covers all the key concepts, equations, and examples within the chapter. The files can be used as is for an innovative, interactive class presentation. Instructors who have access to Microsoft PowerPoint can modify the slides in any way they wish, adding or deleting materials to match their needs.

Web Site The text's *Web Site* can be accessed through *http://reilly.swcollege.com* and includes up-to-date teaching and learning aids for instructors and students. The Instructor's Manual, Test Bank, and PowerPoint slides are available to instructors for download and students can download the PowerPoint presentation.

Acknowledgments

So many people have helped us in so many ways that we hesitate to list them, fearing that we may miss someone. Accepting this risk, we will begin with the University of Notre Dame and the University of Texas at Austin because of their direct support. Also, we must thank the Bernard J. Hank Family, who have endowed the Chair that helped bring Frank Reilly back to Notre Dame and that has provided support for our work.

Reviewers for this edition were:

Charles Q. Cao
Penn State University

Ananth Madhaven
University of Southern California

Paul Bolster
Northeastern University

Russell R. Wermers
University of Maryland

Linda Martin
Arizona State University

Heber Farnsworth
Washington University, St. Louis

We were fortunate to have the following excellent reviewers for earlier editions:

John Alexander
Clemson University

John Clinebell
University of Northern Colorado

Robert Angell
East Carolina University

James D'Mello
Western Michigan University

George Aragon
Boston College

Eugene F. Drzycimski
University of Wisconsin—Oshkosh

Brian Belt
University of Missouri—Kansas City

William Dukes
Texas Tech University

Omar M. Benkato
Ball State University

John Dunkelberg
Wake Forest University

Arand Bhattacharya
University of Cincinnati

Eric Emory
Sacred Heart University

Carol Billingham
Central Michigan University

Thomas Eyssell
University of Missouri—St. Louis

Susan Block
University of California—Santa Barbara

James Feller
Middle Tennessee State University

Gerald A. Blum
Babson College

Eurico Ferreira
Clemson University

Robert E. Brooks
University of Alabama

Michael Ferri
John Carroll University

Robert J. Brown
Harrisburg, Pennsylvania

Greg Filbeck
University of Toledo

Charles Cao
Pennsylvania State University

Joseph E. Finnerty
University of Illinois

Atreya Chakraborty
Brandeis University

Harry Friedman
New York University

Dosoung Choi
University of Tennessee

R. H. Gilmer
University of Mississippi

Robert Clark
University of Vermont

Stephen Goldstein
University of South Carolina

Steven Goldstein
Robinson-Humphrey/American Express

Keshav Gupta
Oklahoma State University

Sally A. Hamilton
Santa Clara University

Eric Higgins
Drexel University

Ronald Hoffmeister
Arizona State University

Ron Hutchins
Eastern Michigan University

A. James Ifflander
Arizona State University

Stan Jacobs
Central Washington University

Kwang Jun
Michigan State University

Jaroslaw Komarynsky
Northern Illinois University

Danny Litt
Century Software Systems/UCLA

Miles Livingston
University of Florida

Christopher Ma
Texas Tech University

Davinder Malhotra
Philadelphia College of Textiles and Science

Stephen Mann
University of South Carolina

Iqbal Mansur
Widener University

George Mason
University of Hartford

John Matthys
DePaul University

Michael McBain
Marquette University

Dennis McConnell
University of Maine

Jeanette Medewitz
University of Nebraska—Omaha

Jacob Michaelsen
University of California—Santa Cruz

Nicholas Michas
Northern Illinois University

Thomas W. Miller Jr.
University of Missouri—Columbia

Lalatendu Misra
University of Texas—San Antonio

Michael Murray
LaCrosse, Wisconsin

Henry Oppenheimer
University of Rhode Island

John Peavy
Southern Methodist University

George Philippatos
University of Tennessee

George Pinches
University of Kansas

Rose Prasad
Central Michigan University

Laurie Prather
University of Tennessee at Chattanooga

George A. Racette
University of Oregon

Murli Rajan
University of Scranton

Narendar V. Rao
Northeastern Illinois University

Steve Rich
Baylor University

Bruce Robin
Old Dominion University

James Rosenfeld
Emory University

Stanley D. Ryals
Investment Counsel, Inc.

Katrina F. Sherrerd
Association of Investment Management and Research

Shekar Shetty
University of South Dakota

Frederic Shipley
DePaul University

Douglas Southard
Virginia Polytechnic Institute

Harold Stevenson
Arizona State University

Kishore Tandon
The City University of New York—Baruch College

Donald Thompson
Georgia State University

David E. Upton
Virginia Commonwealth University

E. Theodore Veit
Rollins College

Premal Vora
King's College

Bruce Wardrep
East Carolina University

Robert Weigand
University of South Florida

Rolf Wubbels
New York University

Valuable comments and data support has come from my frequent co-author David Wright, University of Wisconsin—Parkside. Once more, we were blessed with bright, dedicated research assistants when we needed them the most. This includes Victor Agrigoroae Bolos, Larry Cao, Vincent Lu, and Emma Wu, who have been extremely careful, dependable, and creative.

Current and former colleagues have been very helpful: Yu-Chi Chang, Rob Batallio, Mike Hemler, Jerry Langley, and Paul Schultz, University of Notre Dame; C. F. Lee, Rutgers University; and John M. Wachowicz, University of Tennessee. As always, some of the best insights and most stimulating comments continue to come during too-infrequent walks with a very good friend, Jim Gentry of the University of Illinois.

We are convinced that professors who want to write a book that is academically respectable and relevant, as well as realistic, require help from the "real world." We have been fortunate to develop relationships with a number of individuals (including a growing number of former students) whom we consider our contacts with reality.

We especially want to thank Robert Conway, who was the managing director of the London office of Goldman, Sachs and Company, for suggesting many years ago that it was essential to have the book reflect the rapidly evolving global market. This important advice has had a profound effect on this book over time.

The following individuals have graciously provided important insights and material:

Sharon Athey
Brown Brothers Harriman

David G. Booth
Dimensional Fund Advisors, Inc.

Gary Brinson
UBS Brinson

David Chapman
University of Texas

Dwight D. Churchill
Fidelity Management and Research

Abby Joseph Cohen
Goldman, Sachs and Company

Robert Conway
Goldman, Sachs and Company

Robert J. Davis
Crimson Capital Company

Robert J. Davis Jr.
Merrill Lynch Pierce Fenner and Smith

Philip Delaney Jr.
Northern Trust Bank

Sam Eisenstadt
Value Line

Frank J. Fabozzi
Journal of Portfolio Management

Kenneth Fisher
Forbes

John J. Flanagan Jr.
Lawrence, O'Donnell, Marcus and Company

H. Gifford Fong
Gifford Fong Associates

Martin S. Fridson
Merrill, Lynch, Pierce, Fenner & Smith

Khalid Ghayur
Morgan Stanley

Richard A. Grasso
New York Stock Exchange

William J. Hank
Moore Financial Corporation

Rick Hans
Walgreens

Lea B. Hansen
Greenwich Associates

W. Van Harlow
Fidelity Management and Research

Joanne Hill
Goldman, Sachs and Company

John W. Jordan II
The Jordan Company

Andrew Kalotay
Kalotay Associates

Luke Knecht
Dresdner RCM Capital Management

Warren N. Koontz Jr.
Loomis, Sayles and Company

Mark Kritzman
Windham Capital Management

C. Prewitt Lane
Morgan Keegan & Co.

Martin Leibowitz
TIAA-CREF

Douglas R. Lempereur
Templeton Investment Counsel, Inc.

Robert Levine
Nomura Securities

Amy Lipton
Bankers Trust

George W. Long
Long Investment Management Ltd.

Scott Lummer
Lummer Investment Consulting

John Maginn
Maginn Associates

Scott Malpass
University of Notre Dame

Jack Malvey
Lehman Brothers

Andras Marosi
University of Alberta

Dominic Marshall
Benson Associates

Frank Martin
Martin Capital

Todd Martin
Martin Capital

Joseph McAlinden
Morgan Stanley

Richard McCabe
Merrill, Lynch, Pierce, Fenner & Smith

Michael McCowin
State of Wisconsin Investment Board

Terrence J. McGlinn
McGlinn Capital Markets

Mitch Merin
Morgan Stanley

Kenneth Meyer
Lincoln Capital Management

Janet T. Miller
Rowland and Company

Brian Moore
McDonald's Corporation

Salvator Muoio
SM Investors, LP

Gabrielle Napolitano
Goldman, Sachs and Company

Ian Rossa O'Reilly
Wood Gundy, Inc.

Robert Parrino
University of Texas

Philip J. Purcell III
Morgan Stanley

Jack Pycik
Consultant

Chet Ragavan
Merrill, Lynch, Pierce, Fenner & Smith

John C. Rudolf
Summit Capital Management

Guy Rutherford
Morgan Stanley

Ron Ryan
Ryan Labs, Inc.

Mark Rypzinski
Henry & Co.

Sean St. Clair
Lehman Brothers

Robert F. Semmens Jr.
Semmens Consultants

Brian Singer
UBS Brinson

Clay Singleton
Rollins College

Donald J. Smith
Boston University

Fred H. Speece Jr.
Speece, Thorson Capital Group

William M. Stephens
Husic Capital Management

James Stork
Uitermarkt & Associates

Kevin Terhaar
UBS Brinson

William M. Wadden
Stein, Roe and Farnham

Sushi Wadhwani
Goldman, Sachs and Company

Ken Wiles
Fulcrum Financial Group

Robert Wilmouth
National Futures Association

Richard S. Wilson
Ryan Labs, Inc.

Hong Yan
University of Texas

We continue to benefit from the help and consideration of the dedicated people who are or have been associated with the Institute of Chartered Financial Analysts, which is a part of the Association for Investment Management and Research:, Tom Bowman, Whit Broome, Bob Johnson, Bob Luck, Pete Morley, Sue Martin, Katie Sherrerd, and Donald Tuttle.

Professor Reilly would like to thank his assistant, Rachel Karnafel, who had the unenviable task of keeping his office and his life in some sort of order during this project.

As always, our greatest gratitude is to our families—past, present, and future. Our parents gave us life and helped us understand love and how to give it. Most important are our wives who provide love, understanding, and support throughout the day and night. We thank God for our children and grandchildren who ensure that our lives are full of love, laughs, and excitement.

Frank K. Reilly
Notre Dame, Indiana

Keith C. Brown
Austin, Texas
September 2002

About the Authors

Frank K. Reilly is the Bernard J. Hank Professor of Finance and former dean of the Mendoza College of Business at the University of Notre Dame. Holding degrees from the University of Notre Dame (B.B.A.), Northwestern University (M.B.A.), and the University of Chicago (Ph.D.), Professor Reilly has taught at the University of Illinois, the University of Kansas, and the University of Wyoming in addition to the University of Notre Dame. He has several years of experience as a senior securities analyst, as well as experience in stock and bond trading. A Chartered Financial Analyst (CFA), he has been a member of the Council of Examiners, the Council on Education and Research, the grading committee, and was Chairman of the Board of Trustees of the Institute of Charted Financial Analysts and Chairman of the Board of the Association of Investment Management and Research (AIMR). Professor Reilly has been president of the Financial Management Association, the Midwest Business Administration Association, the Eastern Finance Association, the Academy of Financial Services, and the Midwest Finance Association. He is or has been on the board of directors of the First Interstate Bank of Wisconsin, Norwest Bank of Indiana, the Investment Analysts Society of Chicago, UBS Brinson Global Funds (chairman), Fort Dearborn Income Securities, Discover Bank, NIBCO, Inc., International Board of Certified Financial Planners, Battery Park High Yield Bond Fund, Inc., Morgan Stanley Trust FSB, the AIMR Research Foundation, the Financial Analysts Seminar, and the Association for Investment Management and Research.

As the author of more than 100 articles, monographs, and papers, his work has appeared in numerous publications including *Journal of Finance, Journal of Financial and Quantitative Analysis, Journal of Accounting Research, Financial Management, Financial Analysts Journal, Journal of Fixed Income,* and *Journal of Portfolio Management.* In addition to *Investment Analysis and Portfolio Management,* Seventh Edition, Professor Reilly is the co-author of another textbook, *Investments,* Sixth Edition (South-Western, 2003) with Edgar A. Norton.

Professor Reilly was named on the list of *Outstanding Educators in America* and has received the University of Illinois Alumni Association Graduate Teaching Award, the Outstanding Educator Award from the M.B.A. class at the University of Illinois, and the Outstanding Teacher Award from the M.B.A. class and the Senior Class at Notre Dame. He also received from the Association of Investment Management and Research (AIMR) both the C. Stewart Sheppard Award for his contribution to the educational mission of the Association and the Daniel J. Forrestal III Leadership Award for Professional Ethics and Standards of Investment Practice. Recently he was part of the inaugural group selected as a Fellow of the Financial Management Association International. He is editor of *Readings and Issues in Investments, Ethics and the Investment Industry,* and *High Yield Bonds: Analysis and Risk Assessment,* and is or has been a member of the editorial boards of *Financial Management, The Financial Review, International Review of Economics and Finance, Journal of Financial Education, Quarterly Review of Economics and Finance,* and the *European Journal of Finance.* He is included in the *Who's Who in Finance and Industry, Who's Who in America, Who's Who in American Education,* and *Who's Who in the World.*

Keith C. Brown holds the position of Allied Bancshares Centennial Fellow and Professor of Finance at the Graduate School of Business, University of Texas. He received his B.A. in Economics from San Diego State University, where he was a member of the Phi Beta Kappa, Phi Kappa Phi, and Omicron Delta Epsilon honor societies. He received his M.S. and Ph.D. in Financial Economics from the Krannert Graduate School of Management at Purdue University. Since leaving school in 1981, he has specialized in teaching Investments, Derivatives, and Capital Markets courses at the M.B.A. and Ph.D. levels and has received ten awards for teaching innovation and excellence. In addition to his academic responsibilities, he is also President and Chief Executive Officer of The MBA Investment Fund, L.L.C., a privately funded investment company managed by graduate students at the University of Texas.

Professor Brown has published more than 40 articles, monographs, chapters, and papers on topics ranging from asset pricing and investment strategy to financial risk management. His publications have appeared in such journals as *Journal of Finance, Journal of Financial Economics, Journal of Financial and Quantitative Analysis, Review of Economics and Statistics, Financial Analysts Journal, Financial Management, Advances in Futures and Options Research, Journal of Fixed Income, Journal of Applied Corporate Finance,* and *Journal of Portfolio Management.* In addition to his contributions to *Investment Analysis and Portfolio Management,* Seventh Edition, he is a coauthor of *Interest Rate and Currency Swaps: A Tutorial,* a textbook published in 1995 through the Association for Investment Management and Research (AIMR). He received a Graham and Dodd Award from the Financial Analysts Federation as an author of one of the best articles published by *Financial Analysts Journal* in 1990, and a Smith-Breeden Prize from the *Journal of Finance* in 1996.

In August 1988, Professor Brown received his charter from the Institute of Chartered Financial Analysts (ICFA). He has served as a member of AIMR's CFA Candidate Curriculum Committee and Education Committee, and on the CFA Examination Grading staff. For 5 years, he was the research director of the Research Foundation of the ICFA, from which position he guided the development of the research portion of the organization's worldwide educational mission. For the past several years, he has also been associate editor for *Financial Analysts Journal* and *Journal of Psychology and Financial Markets.* In other professional service, Professor Brown has been a regional director for the Financial Management Association and has served as the applied research track chairman for that organization's annual conference.

Professor Brown is the cofounder and senior partner of Fulcrum Financial Group, a portfolio management and investment advisory firm located in Austin, Texas, and Atlanta, Georgia, that currently oversees portfolios holding a total of $60 million in fixed-income securities. From May 1987 to August 1988 he was based in New York as a senior consultant to the Corporate Professional Development Department at Manufacturers Hanover Trust Company. He has lectured extensively throughout the world on investment and risk management topics in the executive development programs for such companies as JP Morgan Chase, BMO Nesbitt Burns, Merrill Lynch, Chase Manhattan Bank, Chemical Bank, Lehman Brothers, Union Bank of Switzerland, Shearson, Chase Bank of Texas, The Beacon Group, Motorola, and Halliburton. He also spent 13 months as a senior planner with a California-based financial planning firm.

Contents In Brief

Contents

INVESTMENT
ANALYSIS AND PORTFOLIO
MANAGEMENT

Seventh Edition

Part 1

The Investment Background

*T*he chapters in this section will provide a background for your study of investments by answering the following questions:

➤ Why do people invest?
➤ How do you measure the returns and risks for alternative investments?
➤ What factors should you consider when you make asset allocation decisions?
➤ What investments are available?
➤ How do securities markets function?
➤ How and why are securities markets in the United States and around the world changing?
➤ What are the major uses of security market indexes?
➤ How can you evaluate the market behavior of common stocks and bonds?
➤ What factors cause differences among stock-and-bond market indexes?

In the first chapter, we consider why an individual would invest, how to measure the rates of return and risk for alternative investments, and what factors determine an investor's required rate of return on an investment. The latter point will be important in subsequent analyses when we work to understand investor behavior, the markets for alternative securities, and the valuation of various investments.

Because the ultimate decision facing an investor is the makeup of his or her portfolio, Chapter 2 deals with the all-important asset allocation decision. This includes specific steps in the portfolio management process and factors that influence the makeup of an investor's portfolio over his or her life cycle.

To minimize risk, investment theory asserts the need to diversify. Chapter 3 begins our exploration of investments available to investors by making an overpowering case for investing globally rather than limiting choices to only U.S. securities. Building on this premise, we discuss several investment instruments found in global markets. We conclude the chapter with a review of the historical rates of return and measures of risk for a number of alternative asset groups.

In Chapter 4, we examine how markets work in general, and then specifically focus on the purpose and function of primary and secondary bond and stock markets. During the 1980s and 1990s, significant changes occurred in the operation of the securities market, including a trend toward a global market. After discussing these changes, the globalization of existing markets, and the rapid development of new capital markets around the world, we speculate about how global markets will continue to expand available investment alternatives.

Investors, market analysts, and financial theorists often gauge the behavior of securities markets by evaluating changes in various market indexes and evaluate portfolio performance by comparing a portfolio's results to an appropriate benchmark. In Chapter 5, we examine and compare a number of stock-market and bond-market indexes that can be used for these purposes for the domestic and global markets.

This initial section provides the framework for you to understand various securities, how to allocate among alternative asset classes, the markets where they are bought and sold, the indexes that reflect their performance, and how you might manage a collection of investments in a portfolio. Specific portfolio management techniques are described in later chapters.

Chapter 1

The Investment Setting

After you read this chapter, you should be able to answer the following questions:

➤ Why do individuals invest?
➤ What is an investment?
➤ How do investors measure the rate of return on an investment?
➤ How do investors measure the risk related to alternative investments?
➤ What factors contribute to the rates of return that investors require on alternative investments?
➤ What macroeconomic and microeconomic factors contribute to changes in the required rates of return for individual investments and investments in general?

This initial chapter discusses several topics basic to the subsequent chapters. We begin by defining the term *investment* and discussing the returns and risks related to investments. This leads to a presentation of how to measure the expected and historical rates of returns for an individual asset or a portfolio of assets. In addition, we consider how to measure risk not only for an individual investment but also for an investment that is part of a portfolio.

The third section of the chapter discusses the factors that determine the required rate of return for an individual investment. The factors discussed are those that contribute to an asset's *total* risk. Because most investors have a portfolio of investments, it is necessary to consider how to measure the risk of an asset when it is a part of a large portfolio of assets. The risk that prevails when an asset is part of a diversified portfolio is referred to as its *systematic risk.*

The final section deals with what causes *changes* in an asset's required rate of return over time. Changes occur because of both macroeconomic events that affect all investment assets and microeconomic events that affect the specific asset.

WHAT IS AN INVESTMENT?

For most of your life, you will be earning and spending money. Rarely, though, will your current money income exactly balance with your consumption desires. Sometimes, you may have more money than you want to spend; at other times, you may want to purchase more than you can afford. These imbalances will lead you either to borrow or to save to maximize the long-run benefits from your income.

When current income exceeds current consumption desires, people tend to save the excess. They can do any of several things with these savings. One possibility is to put the money under a mattress or bury it in the backyard until some future time when consumption desires exceed current income. When they retrieve their savings from the mattress or backyard, they have the same amount they saved.

Another possibility is that they can give up the immediate possession of these savings for a future larger amount of money that will be available for future consumption. This tradeoff of *present* consumption for a higher level of *future* consumption is the reason for saving. What you do with the savings to make them increase over time is *investment*.[1]

Those who give up immediate possession of savings (that is, defer consumption) expect to receive in the future a greater amount than they gave up. Conversely, those who consume more than their current income (that is, borrow) must be willing to pay back in the future more than they borrowed.

The rate of exchange between *future consumption* (future dollars) and *current consumption* (current dollars) is the *pure rate of interest*. Both people's willingness to pay this difference for borrowed funds and their desire to receive a surplus on their savings give rise to an interest rate referred to as the *pure time value of money*. This interest rate is established in the capital market by a comparison of the supply of excess income available (savings) to be invested and the demand for excess consumption (borrowing) at a given time. If you can exchange $100 of certain income today for $104 of certain income one year from today, then the pure rate of exchange on a risk-free investment (that is, the time value of money) is said to be 4 percent (104/100 − 1).

The investor who gives up $100 today expects to consume $104 of goods and services in the future. This assumes that the general price level in the economy stays the same. This price stability has rarely been the case during the past several decades when inflation rates have varied from 1.1 percent in 1986 to 13.3 percent in 1979, with an average of about 5.4 percent a year from 1970 to 2001. If investors expect a change in prices, they will require a higher rate of return to compensate for it. For example, if an investor expects a rise in prices (that is, he or she expects inflation) at the rate of 2 percent during the period of investment, he or she will increase the required interest rate by 2 percent. In our example, the investor would require $106 in the future to defer the $100 of consumption during an inflationary period (a 6 percent nominal, risk-free interest rate will be required instead of 4 percent).

Further, if the future payment from the investment is not certain, the investor will demand an interest rate that exceeds the pure time value of money plus the inflation rate. The uncertainty of the payments from an investment is the *investment risk*. The additional return added to the nominal, risk-free interest rate is called a *risk premium*. In our previous example, the investor would require more than $106 one year from today to compensate for the uncertainty. As an example, if the required amount were $110, $4, or 4 percent, would be considered a risk premium.

Investment Defined

From our discussion, we can specify a formal definition of investment. Specifically, an **investment** is the current commitment of dollars for a period of time in order to derive future payments that will compensate the investor for (1) the time the funds are committed, (2) the expected rate of inflation, and (3) the uncertainty of the future payments. The "investor" can be an individual, a government, a pension fund, or a corporation. Similarly, this definition includes all types of investments, including investments by corporations in plant and equipment and investments by individuals in stocks, bonds, commodities, or real estate. This text emphasizes investments by individual investors. In all cases, the investor is trading a *known* dollar amount today for some *expected* future stream of payments that will be greater than the current outlay.

At this point, we have answered the questions about why people invest and what they want from their investments. They invest to earn a return from savings due to their deferred consumption. They want a rate of return that compensates them for the time, the expected rate of inflation, and the uncertainty of the return. This return, the investor's **required rate of return**, is discussed throughout this book. A central question of this book is how investors select investments that will give them their required rates of return.

---

[1]In contrast, when current income is less than current consumption desires, people borrow to make up the difference. Although we will discuss borrowing on several occasions, the major emphasis of this text is how to invest savings.

The next section of this chapter describes how to measure the expected or historical rate of return on an investment and also how to quantify the uncertainty of expected returns. You need to understand these techniques for measuring the rate of return and the uncertainty of these returns to evaluate the suitability of a particular investment. Although our emphasis will be on financial assets, such as bonds and stocks, we will refer to other assets, such as art and antiques. Chapter 3 discusses the range of financial assets and also considers some nonfinancial assets.

MEASURES OF RETURN AND RISK

The purpose of this book is to help you understand how to choose among alternative investment assets. This selection process requires that you estimate and evaluate the expected risk-return trade-offs for the alternative investments available. Therefore, you must understand how to measure the rate of return and the risk involved in an investment accurately. To meet this need, in this section we examine ways to quantify return and risk. The presentation will consider how to measure both *historical* and *expected* rates of return and risk.

We consider historical measures of return and risk because this book and other publications provide numerous examples of historical average rates of return and risk measures for various assets, and understanding these presentations is important. In addition, these historical results are often used by investors when attempting to estimate the *expected* rates of return and risk for an asset class.

The first measure is the historical rate of return on an individual investment over the time period the investment is held (that is, its holding period). Next, we consider how to measure the *average* historical rate of return for an individual investment over a number of time periods. The third subsection considers the average rate of return for a *portfolio* of investments.

Given the measures of historical rates of return, we will present the traditional measures of risk for a historical time series of returns (that is, the variance and standard deviation).

Following the presentation of measures of historical rates of return and risk, we turn to estimating the *expected* rate of return for an investment. Obviously, such an estimate contains a great deal of uncertainty, and we present measures of this uncertainty or risk.

Measures of Historical Rates of Return

When you are evaluating alternative investments for inclusion in your portfolio, you will often be comparing investments with widely different prices or lives. As an example, you might want to compare a $10 stock that pays no dividends to a stock selling for $150 that pays dividends of $5 a year. To properly evaluate these two investments, you must accurately compare their historical rates of returns. A proper measurement of the rates of return is the purpose of this section.

When we invest, we defer current consumption in order to add to our wealth so that we can consume more in the future. Therefore, when we talk about a return on an investment, we are concerned with the *change in wealth* resulting from this investment. This change in wealth can be either due to cash inflows, such as interest or dividends, or caused by a change in the price of the asset (positive or negative).

If you commit $200 to an investment at the beginning of the year and you get back $220 at the end of the year, what is your return for the period? The period during which you own an investment is called its *holding period,* and the return for that period is the **holding period return (HPR)**. In this example, the HPR is 1.10, calculated as follows:

➤1.1
$$HPR = \frac{\text{Ending Value of Investment}}{\text{Beginning Value of Investment}}$$
$$= \frac{\$220}{\$200} = 1.10$$

This value will always be zero or greater—that is, it can never be a negative value. A value greater than 1.0 reflects an increase in your wealth, which means that you received a positive rate of return during the period. A value less than 1.0 means that you suffered a decline in wealth, which indicates that you had a negative return during the period. An HPR of zero indicates that you lost all your money.

Although HPR helps us express the change in value of an investment, investors generally evaluate returns in *percentage terms on an annual basis*. This conversion to annual percentage rates makes it easier to directly compare alternative investments that have markedly different characteristics. The first step in converting an HPR to an annual percentage rate is to derive a percentage return, referred to as the **holding period yield (HPY)**. The HPY is equal to the HPR minus 1.

➤1.2 $$HPY = HPR - 1$$

In our example:

$$HPY = 1.10 - 1 = 0.10$$
$$= 10\%$$

To derive an *annual* HPY, you compute an *annual* HPR and subtract 1. Annual HPR is found by:

➤1.3 $$\text{Annual HPR} = HPR^{1/n}$$

where:

n = number of years the investment is held

Consider an investment that cost $250 and is worth $350 after being held for two years:

$$HPR = \frac{\text{Ending Value of Investment}}{\text{Beginning Value of Investment}} = \frac{\$350}{\$250}$$
$$= 1.40$$
$$\text{Annual HPR} = 1.40^{1/n}$$
$$= 1.40^{1/2}$$
$$= 1.1832$$
$$\text{Annual HPY} = 1.1832 - 1 = 0.1832$$
$$= 18.32\%$$

If you experience a decline in your wealth value, the computation is as follows:

$$HPR = \frac{\text{Ending Value}}{\text{Beginning Value}} = \frac{\$400}{\$500} = 0.80$$
$$HPY = 0.80 - 1.00 = -0.20 = -20\%$$

A multiple year loss over two years would be computed as follows:

$$HPR = \frac{\text{Ending Value}}{\text{Beginning Value}} = \frac{\$750}{\$1,000} = 0.75$$
$$\text{Annual HPR} = (0.75)^{1/n} = 0.75^{1/2}$$
$$= 0.866$$
$$\text{Annual HPY} = 0.866 - 1.00 = -0.134 = -13.4\%$$

In contrast, consider an investment of $100 held for only six months that earned a return of $12:

$$\text{HPR} = \frac{\$112}{\$100} = 1.12 (n = 0.5)$$

$$\text{Annual HPR} = 1.12^{1/.5}$$

$$= 1.12^{2}$$

$$= 1.2544$$

$$\text{Annual HPY} = 1.2544 - 1 = 0.2544$$

$$= 25.44\%$$

Note that we made some implicit assumptions when converting the HPY to an annual basis. This annualized holding period yield computation assumes a constant annual yield for each year. In the two-year investment, we assumed an 18.32 percent rate of return each year, compounded. In the partial year HPR that was annualized, we assumed that the return is compounded for the whole year. That is, we assumed that the rate of return earned during the first part of the year is likewise earned on the value at the end of the first six months. The 12 percent rate of return for the initial six months compounds to 25.44 percent for the full year.[2] Because of the uncertainty of being able to earn the same return in the future six months, institutions will typically not compound partial year results.

Remember one final point: The ending value of the investment can be the result of a positive or negative change in price for the investment alone (for example, a stock going from $20 a share to $22 a share), income from the investment alone, or a combination of price change and income. Ending value includes the value of everything related to the investment.

Computing Mean Historical Returns

Now that we have calculated the HPY for a single investment for a single year, we want to consider **mean rates of return** for a single investment and for a portfolio of investments. Over a number of years, a single investment will likely give high rates of return during some years and low rates of return, or possibly negative rates of return, during others. Your analysis should consider each of these returns, but you also want a summary figure that indicates this investment's typical experience, or the rate of return you should expect to receive if you owned this investment over an extended period of time. You can derive such a summary figure by computing the mean annual rate of return for this investment over some period of time.

Alternatively, you might want to evaluate a portfolio of investments that might include similar investments (for example, all stocks or all bonds) or a combination of investments (for example, stocks, bonds, and real estate). In this instance, you would calculate the mean rate of return for this portfolio of investments for an individual year or for a number of years.

Single Investment   Given a set of annual rates of return (HPYs) for an individual investment, there are two summary measures of return performance. The first is the arithmetic mean return, the second the geometric mean return. To find the **arithmetic mean (AM)**, the sum (Σ) of annual HPYs is divided by the number of years (n) as follows:

➤1.4
$$\text{AM} = \Sigma\text{HPY}/n$$

where:

ΣHPY = the sum of annual holding period yields

---

[2]To check that you understand the calculations, determine the annual HPY for a three-year HPR of 1.50. (Answer: 14.47 percent.) Compute the annual HPY for a three-month HPR of 1.06. (Answer: 26.25 percent.)

An alternative computation, the **geometric mean (GM)**, is the nth root of the product of the HPRs for n years.

➤1.5
$$GM = [\pi \ HPR]^{1/n} - 1$$

where:

π = **the product of the annual holding period returns as follows:**

$$(HPR_1) \times (HPR_2) \cdots (HPR_n)$$

To illustrate these alternatives, consider an investment with the following data:

YEAR	BEGINNING VALUE	ENDING VALUE	HPR	HPY
1	100.0	115.0	1.15	0.15
2	115.0	138.0	1.20	0.20
3	138.0	110.4	0.80	−0.20

$$AM = [(0.15) + (0.20) + (-0.20)]/3$$
$$= 0.15/3$$
$$= 0.05 = 5\%$$

$$GM = [(1.15) \times (1.20) \times (0.80)]^{1/3} - 1$$
$$= (1.104)^{1/3} - 1$$
$$= 1.03353 - 1$$
$$= 0.03353 = 3.353\%$$

Investors are typically concerned with long-term performance when comparing alternative investments. GM is considered a superior measure of the long-term mean rate of return because it indicates the compound annual rate of return based on the ending value of the investment versus its beginning value.[3] Specifically, using the prior example, if we compounded 3.353 percent for three years, $(1.03353)^3$, we would get an ending wealth value of 1.104.

Although the arithmetic average provides a good indication of the expected rate of return for an investment during a future individual year, it is biased upward if you are attempting to measure an asset's long-term performance. This is obvious for a volatile security. Consider, for example, a security that increases in price from $50 to $100 during year 1 and drops back to $50 during year 2. The annual HPYs would be:

YEAR	BEGINNING VALUE	ENDING VALUE	HPR	HPY
1	50	100	2.00	1.00
2	100	50	0.50	−0.50

---

[3]Note that the GM is the same whether you compute the geometric mean of the individual annual holding period yields or the annual HPY for a three-year period, comparing the ending value to the beginning value, as discussed earlier under annual HPY for a multiperiod case.

This would give an AM rate of return of:

$$[(1.00) + (-0.50)]/2 = .50/2$$
$$= 0.25 = 25\%$$

This investment brought no change in wealth and therefore no return, yet the AM rate of return is computed to be 25 percent.

The GM rate of return would be:

$$(2.00 \times 0.50)^{1/2} - 1 = (1.00)^{1/2} - 1$$
$$= 1.00 - 1 = 0\%$$

This answer of a 0 percent rate of return accurately measures the fact that there was no change in wealth from this investment over the two-year period.

When rates of return are the same for all years, the GM will be equal to the AM. If the rates of return vary over the years, the GM will always be lower than the AM. The difference between the two mean values will depend on the year-to-year changes in the rates of return. Larger annual changes in the rates of return—that is, more volatility—will result in a greater difference between the alternative mean values.

An awareness of both methods of computing mean rates of return is important because published accounts of investment performance or descriptions of financial research will use both the AM and the GM as measures of average historical returns. We will also use both throughout this book. Currently most studies dealing with long-run historical rates of return include both AM and GM rates of return.

A Portfolio of Investments   The mean historical rate of return (HPY) for a portfolio of investments is measured as the weighted average of the HPYs for the individual investments in the portfolio, or the overall change in value of the original portfolio. The weights used in computing the averages are the relative *beginning* market values for each investment; this is referred to as *dollar-weighted* or *value-weighted* mean rate of return. This technique is demonstrated by the examples in Exhibit 1.1. As shown, the HPY is the same (9.5 percent) whether you compute the weighted average return using the beginning market value weights or if you compute the overall change in the total value of the portfolio.

Although the analysis of historical performance is useful, selecting investments for your portfolio requires you to predict the rates of return you *expect* to prevail. The next section discusses how you would derive such estimates of expected rates of return. We recognize the great uncertainty regarding these future expectations, and we will discuss how one measures this uncertainty, which is referred to as the risk of an investment.

Calculating Expected Rates of Return   **Risk** is the uncertainty that an investment will earn its expected rate of return. In the examples in the prior section, we examined *realized* historical rates of return. In contrast, an investor who is evaluating a future investment alternative expects or anticipates a certain rate of return. The investor might say that he or she *expects* the investment will provide a rate of return of 10 percent, but this is actually the investor's most likely estimate, also referred to as a *point estimate*. Pressed further, the investor would probably acknowledge the uncertainty of this point estimate return and admit the possibility that, under certain conditions, the annual rate of return on this investment might go as low as −10 percent or as high as 25 percent. The point is, the specification of a larger range of possible returns from an investment reflects the investor's uncertainty regarding what the actual return will be. Therefore, a larger range of expected returns makes the investment riskier.

EXHIBIT 1.1 *COMPUTATION OF HOLDING PERIOD YIELD FOR A PORTFOLIO*

INVESTMENT	NUMBER OF SHARES	BEGINNING PRICE	BEGINNING MARKET VALUE	ENDING PRICE	ENDING MARKET VALUE	HPR	HPY	MARKET WEIGHT[a]	WEIGHTED HPY
A	100,000	$10	$ 1,000,000	$12	$ 1,200,000	1.20	20%	0.05	0.01
B	200,000	20	4,000,000	21	4,200,000	1.05	5	0.20	0.01
C	500,000	30	15,000,000	33	16,500,000	1.10	10	0.75	0.075
Total			$20,000,000		$21,900,000				0.095

$$HPR = \frac{21,900,000}{20,000,000} = 1.095$$

$$HPY = 1.095 - 1 = 0.095$$
$$= 9.5\%$$

[a]Weights are based on beginning values.

An investor determines how certain the expected rate of return on an investment is by analyzing estimates of expected returns. To do this, the investor assigns probability values to all *possible* returns. These probability values range from zero, which means no chance of the return, to one, which indicates complete certainty that the investment will provide the specified rate of return. These probabilities are typically subjective estimates based on the historical performance of the investment or similar investments modified by the investor's expectations for the future. As an example, an investor may know that about 30 percent of the time the rate of return on this particular investment was 10 percent. Using this information along with future expectations regarding the economy, one can derive an estimate of what might happen in the future.

The *expected* return from an investment is defined as:

$$\text{Expected Return} = \sum_{i=1}^{n} (\text{Probability of Return}) \times (\text{Possible Return})$$

➤1.6
$$E(R_i) = [(P_1)(R_1) + (P_2)(R_2) + (P_3)(R_3) + \cdots + (P_n R_n)]$$

$$E(R_i) = \sum_{i=1}^{n} (P_i)(R_i)$$

Let us begin our analysis of the effect of risk with an example of perfect certainty wherein the investor is absolutely certain of a return of 5 percent. Exhibit 1.2 illustrates this situation.

Perfect certainty allows only one possible return, and the probability of receiving that return is 1.0. Few investments provide certain returns. In the case of perfect certainty, there is only one value for $P_i R_i$:

$$E(R_i) = (1.0)(0.05) = 0.05$$

In an alternative scenario, suppose an investor believed an investment could provide several different rates of return depending on different possible economic conditions. As an example, in a strong economic environment with high corporate profits and little or no inflation, the investor might expect the rate of return on common stocks during the next year to reach as high as 20 percent. In contrast, if there is an economic decline with a higher-than-average rate of inflation, the investor might expect the rate of return on common stocks during the next year to be –20 percent. Finally, with no major change in the economic environment, the rate of return during the next year would probably approach the long-run average of 10 percent.

EXHIBIT 1.2 ▸   *PROBABILITY DISTRIBUTION FOR RISK-FREE INVESTMENT*

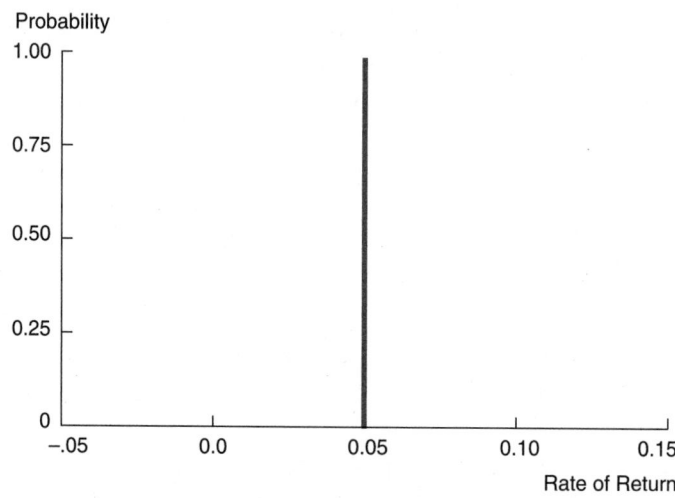

The investor might estimate probabilities for each of these economic scenarios based on past experience and the current outlook as follows:

Economic Conditions	Probability	Rate of Return
Strong economy, no inflation	0.15	0.20
Weak economy, above-average inflation	0.15	–0.20
No major change in economy	0.70	0.10

This set of potential outcomes can be visualized as shown in Exhibit 1.3.

The computation of the expected rate of return $[E(R_i)]$ is as follows:

$$E(R_i) = [(0.15)(0.20)] + [(0.15)(-0.20)] + [(0.70)(0.10)]$$
$$= 0.07$$

Obviously, the investor is less certain about the expected return from this investment than about the return from the prior investment with its single possible return.

A third example is an investment with 10 possible outcomes ranging from –40 percent to 50 percent with the same probability for each rate of return. A graph of this set of expectations would appear as shown in Exhibit 1.4.

In this case, there are numerous outcomes from a wide range of possibilities. The expected rate of return $[E(R_i)]$ for this investment would be:

$$E(R_i) = (0.10)(-0.40) + (0.10)(-0.30) + (0.10)(-0.20) + (0.10)(-0.10) + (0.10)(0.0)$$
$$+ (0.10)(0.10) + (0.10)(0.20) + (0.10)(0.30) + (0.10)(0.40) + (0.10)(0.50)$$
$$= (-0.04) + (-0.03) + (-0.02) + (-0.01) + (0.00) + (0.01) + (0.02) + (0.03)$$
$$+ (0.04) + (0.05)$$
$$= 0.05$$

EXHIBIT 1.3   *PROBABILITY DISTRIBUTION FOR RISKY INVESTMENT WITH THREE POSSIBLE RATES OF RETURN*

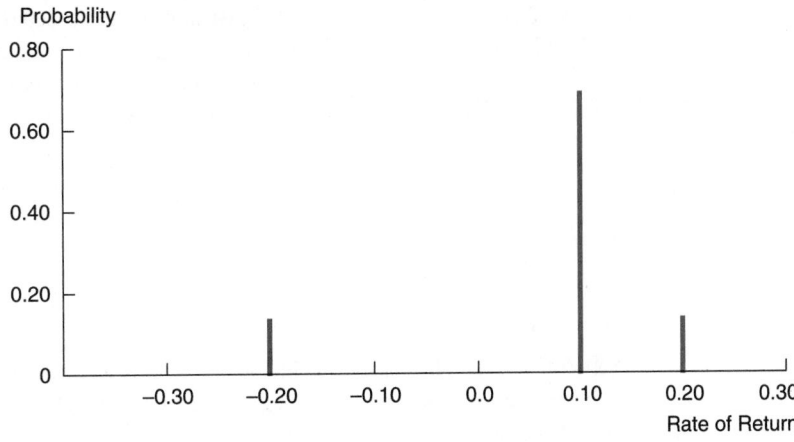

EXHIBIT 1.4   *PROBABILITY DISTRIBUTION FOR RISKY INVESTMENT WITH 10 POSSIBLE RATES OF RETURN*

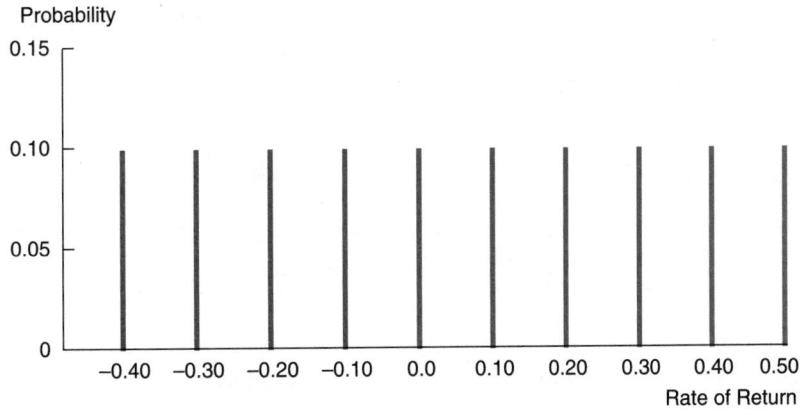

The *expected* rate of return for this investment is the same as the certain return discussed in the first example; but, in this case, the investor is highly uncertain about the *actual* rate of return. This would be considered a risky investment because of that uncertainty. We would anticipate that an investor faced with the choice between this risky investment and the certain (risk-free) case would select the certain alternative. This expectation is based on the belief that most investors are **risk averse**, which means that if everything else is the same, they will select the investment that offers greater certainty.

Measuring the Risk of Expected Rates of Return   We have shown that we can calculate the expected rate of return and evaluate the uncertainty, or risk, of an investment by identifying the range of possible returns from that investment and assigning each possible return a weight based on the probability that it will occur. Although the graphs help us visualize the dispersion of possible returns, most investors want to quantify this dispersion using statistical techniques. These statistical measures allow you to compare the return and risk measures for alternative investments directly. Two possible measures of risk (uncertainty) have received support in theoretical work on portfolio theory: the *variance* and the *standard deviation* of the estimated distribution of expected returns.

In this section, we demonstrate how variance and standard deviation measure the dispersion of possible rates of return around the expected rate of return. We will work with the examples discussed earlier. The formula for variance is as follows:

➤1.7
$$\text{Variance } (\sigma^2) = \sum_{i=1}^{n} (\text{Probability}) \times \left(\begin{array}{c} \text{Possible} \\ \text{Return} \end{array} - \begin{array}{c} \text{Expected} \\ \text{Return} \end{array} \right)^2$$

$$= \sum_{i=1}^{n} (P_i)[R_i - E(R_i)]^2$$

Variance   The larger the **variance** for an expected rate of return, the greater the dispersion of expected returns and the greater the uncertainty, or risk, of the investment. The variance for the perfect-certainty example would be:

$$(\sigma^2) = \sum_{i=1}^{n} P_i [R_i - E(R_i)]^2$$
$$= 1.0(0.05 - 0.05)^2 = 1.0(0.0) = 0$$

Note that, in perfect certainty, there is *no variance of return* because there is no deviation from expectations and, therefore, *no risk* or *uncertainty*. The variance for the second example would be:

$$(\sigma^2) = \sum_{i=1}^{n} P_i [R_i - E(R_i)]^2$$
$$= [(0.15)(0.20 - 0.07)^2 + (0.15)(-0.20 - 0.07)^2 + (0.70)(0.10 - 0.07)^2]$$
$$= [0.010935 + 0.002535 + 0.00063]$$
$$= 0.0141$$

Standard Deviation   The **standard deviation** is the square root of the variance:

➤1.8
$$\text{Standard Deviation} = \sqrt{\sum_{i=1}^{n} P_i [R_i - E(R_i)]^2}$$

For the second example, the standard deviation would be:

$$\sigma = \sqrt{0.0141}$$
$$= 0.11874 = 11.874\%$$

Therefore, when describing this example, you would contend that you expect a return of 7 percent, but the standard deviation of your expectations is 11.87 percent.

A Relative Measure of Risk   In some cases, an unadjusted variance or standard deviation can be misleading. If conditions for two or more investment alternatives are not similar—that is, if there are major differences in the expected rates of return—it is necessary to use a measure of *relative variability* to indicate risk per unit of expected return. A widely used relative measure of risk is the **coefficient of variation (CV)**, calculated as follows:

➤1.9

$$\text{Coefficient of Variation (CV)} = \frac{\text{Standard Deviation of Returns}}{\text{Expected Rate of Return}}$$

$$= \frac{\sigma_i}{E(R)}$$

The *CV* for the preceding example would be:

$$CV = \frac{0.11874}{0.07000}$$

$$= 1.696$$

This measure of relative variability and risk is used by financial analysts to compare alternative investments with widely different rates of return and standard deviations of returns. As an illustration, consider the following two investments:

	INVESTMENT A	INVESTMENT B
Expected return	0.07	0.12
Standard deviation	0.05	0.07

Comparing absolute measures of risk, investment B appears to be riskier because it has a standard deviation of 7 percent versus 5 percent for investment A. In contrast, the *CV* figures show that investment B has less relative variability or lower risk per unit of expected return because it has a substantially higher expected rate of return:

$$CV_A = \frac{0.05}{0.07} = 0.714$$

$$CV_B = \frac{0.07}{0.12} = 0.583$$

Risk Measures for Historical Returns

To measure the risk for a series of historical rates of returns, we use the same measures as for expected returns (variance and standard deviation) except that we consider the historical holding period yields (HPYs) as follows:

➤1.10

$$\sigma^2 = \sum_{i=1}^{n} \left[\text{HPY}_i - E(\text{HPY}) \right]^2 / n$$

where:

σ^2 = **the variance of the series**
HPY_i = **the holding period yield during period *i***
$E(\text{HPY})$ = **the expected value of the holding period yield that is equal to the arithmetic mean of the series**
n = **the number of observations**

EXHIBIT 1.5	PROMISED YIELDS ON ALTERNATIVE BONDS						
TYPE OF BOND	1995	1996	1997	1998	1999	2000	2001
U.S. government 3-month Treasury bills	5.49%	5.01%	5.06%	4.78%	4.64%	5.82%	3.80%
U.S. government long-term bonds	6.93	6.80	6.67	5.69	6.14	6.41	6.18
Aaa corporate bonds	7.59	7.37	7.27	6.53	7.05	7.62	7.32
Baa corporate bonds	7.83	8.05	7.87	7.22	7.88	8.36	8.19

Source: *Federal Reserve Bulletin*, various issues.

The standard deviation is the square root of the variance. Both measures indicate how much the individual HPYs over time deviated from the expected value of the series. An example computation is contained in the appendix to this chapter. As is shown in subsequent chapters where we present historical rates of return for alternative asset classes, presenting the standard deviation as a measure of risk for the series or asset class is fairly common.

DETERMINANTS OF REQUIRED RATES OF RETURN

In this section, we continue our consideration of factors that you must consider when selecting securities for an investment portfolio. You will recall that this selection process involves finding securities that provide a rate of return that compensates you for: (1) the time value of money during the period of investment, (2) the expected rate of inflation during the period, and (3) the risk involved.

The summation of these three components is called the *required rate of return*. This is the minimum rate of return that you should accept from an investment to compensate you for deferring consumption. Because of the importance of the required rate of return to the total investment selection process, this section contains a discussion of the three components and what influences each of them.

The analysis and estimation of the required rate of return are complicated by the behavior of market rates over time. First, a wide range of rates is available for alternative investments at any time. Second, the rates of return on specific assets change dramatically over time. Third, the difference between the rates available (that is, the spread) on different assets changes over time.

The yield data in Exhibit 1.5 for alternative bonds demonstrate these three characteristics. First, even though all these securities have promised returns based upon bond contracts, the promised annual yields during any year differ substantially. As an example, during 1999 the average yields on alternative assets ranged from 4.64 percent on T-bills to 7.88 percent for Baa corporate bonds. Second, the changes in yields for a specific asset are shown by the three-month Treasury bill rate that went from 4.64 percent in 1999 to 5.82 percent in 2000. Third, an example of a change in the difference between yields over time (referred to as a spread) is shown by the Baa–Aaa spread.[4] The yield spread in 1995 was only 24 basis points (7.83 – 7.59), but the spread in 1999 was 83 basis points (7.88 – 7.05). (A basis point is 0.01 percent.)

---

[4]Bonds are rated by rating agencies based upon the credit risk of the securities, that is, the probability of default. Aaa is the top rating Moody's (a prominent rating service) gives to bonds with almost no probability of default. (Only U.S. Treasury bonds are considered to be of higher quality.) Baa is a lower rating Moody's gives to bonds of generally high quality that have some possibility of default under adverse economic conditions.

Because differences in yields result from the riskiness of each investment, you must understand the risk factors that affect the required rates of return and include them in your assessment of investment opportunities. Because the required returns on all investments change over time, and because large differences separate individual investments, you need to be aware of the several components that determine the required rate of return, starting with the risk-free rate. The discussion in this chapter considers the three components of the required rate of return and briefly discusses what affects these components. The presentation in Chapter 11 on valuation theory will discuss the factors that affect these components in greater detail.

The Real Risk-Free Rate	The **real risk-free rate (RRFR)** is the basic interest rate, assuming no inflation and no uncertainty about future flows. An investor in an inflation-free economy who knew with certainty what cash flows he or she would receive at what time would demand the RRFR on an investment. Earlier, we called this the *pure time value of money,* because the only sacrifice the investor made was deferring the use of the money for a period of time. This RRFR of interest is the price charged for the exchange between current goods and future goods.

Two factors, one subjective and one objective, influence this exchange price. The subjective factor is the time preference of individuals for the consumption of income. When individuals give up $100 of consumption this year, how much consumption do they want a year from now to compensate for that sacrifice? The strength of the human desire for current consumption influences the rate of compensation required. Time preferences vary among individuals, and the market creates a composite rate that includes the preferences of all investors. This composite rate changes gradually over time because it is influenced by all the investors in the economy, whose changes in preferences may offset one another.

The objective factor that influences the RRFR is the set of investment opportunities available in the economy. The investment opportunities are determined in turn by the *long-run real growth rate of the economy.* A rapidly growing economy produces more and better opportunities to invest funds and experience positive rates of return. A change in the economy's long-run real growth rate causes a change in all investment opportunities and a change in the required rates of return on all investments. Just as investors supplying capital should demand a higher rate of return when growth is higher, those looking for funds to invest should be willing and able to pay a higher rate of return to use the funds for investment because of the higher growth rate. Thus, a *positive* relationship exists between the real growth rate in the economy and the RRFR.

Factors Influencing the Nominal Risk-Free Rate (NRFR)	Earlier, we observed that an investor would be willing to forgo current consumption in order to increase future consumption at a rate of exchange called the *risk-free rate of interest.* This rate of exchange was measured in real terms because the investor wanted to increase the consumption of actual goods and services rather than consuming the same amount that had come to cost more money. Therefore, when we discuss rates of interest, we need to differentiate between *real* rates of interest that adjust for changes in the general price level, as opposed to *nominal* rates of interest that are stated in money terms. That is, nominal rates of interest that prevail in the market are determined by real rates of interest, plus factors that will affect the nominal rate of interest, such as the expected rate of inflation and the monetary environment. It is important to understand these factors.

As noted earlier, the variables that determine the RRFR change only gradually over the long term. Therefore, you might expect the required rate on a risk-free investment to be quite stable over time. As discussed in connection with Exhibit 1.5, rates on three-month T-bills were *not* stable over the period from 1995 to 2001. This is demonstrated with additional observations in Exhibit 1.6, which contains yields on T-bills for the period 1980 to 2001.

Investors view T-bills as a prime example of a default-free investment because the government has unlimited ability to derive income from taxes or to create money from which to pay

| EXHIBIT 1.6 | THREE-MONTH TREASURY BILL YIELDS AND RATES OF INFLATION |

YEAR	3-MONTH T-BILLS	RATE OF INFLATION	YEAR	3-MONTH T-BILLS	RATE OF INFLATION
1980	11.43%	7.70%	1991	5.38%	3.06%
1981	14.03	10.40	1992	3.43	2.90
1982	10.61	6.10	1993	3.33	2.75
1983	8.61	3.20	1994	4.25	2.67
1984	9.52	4.00	1995	5.49	2.54
1985	7.48	3.80	1996	5.01	3.32
1986	5.98	1.10	1997	5.06	1.70
1987	5.78	4.40	1998	4.78	1.61
1988	6.67	4.40	1999	4.64	2.70
1989	8.11	4.65	2000	5.82	3.40
1990	7.50	6.11	2001	3.80	1.55

Source: *Federal Reserve Bulletin,* various issues; *Economic Report of the President,* various issues.

interest. Therefore, rates on T-bills should change only gradually. In fact, the data show a highly erratic pattern. Specifically, there was an increase from about 11.4 percent in 1980 to more than 14 percent in 1981 before declining to less than 6 percent in 1987 and 3.33 percent in 1993. In sum, T-bill rates increased almost 23 percent in one year and then declined by almost 60 percent in six years. Clearly, the nominal rate of interest on a default-free investment is *not* stable in the long run or the short run, even though the underlying determinants of the RRFR are quite stable. The point is, two other factors influence the *nominal risk-free rate (NRFR):* (1) the relative ease or tightness in the capital markets, and (2) the expected rate of inflation.

Conditions in the Capital Market   You will recall from prior courses in economics and finance that the purpose of capital markets is to bring together investors who want to invest savings with companies or governments who need capital to expand or to finance budget deficits. The cost of funds at any time (the interest rate) is the price that equates the current supply and demand for capital. A change in the relative ease or tightness in the capital market is a short-run phenomenon caused by a temporary disequilibrium in the supply and demand of capital.

As an example, disequilibrium could be caused by an unexpected change in monetary policy (for example, a change in the growth rate of the money supply) or fiscal policy (for example, a change in the federal deficit). Such a change in monetary policy or fiscal policy will produce a change in the NRFR of interest, but the change should be short-lived because, in the longer run, the higher or lower interest rates will affect capital supply and demand. As an example, a decrease in the growth rate of the money supply (a tightening in monetary policy) will reduce the supply of capital and increase interest rates. In turn, this increase in interest rates (for example, the price of money) will cause an increase in savings and a decrease in the demand for capital by corporations or individuals. These changes in market conditions will bring rates back to the long-run equilibrium, which is based on the long-run growth rate of the economy.

Expected Rate of Inflation   Previously, it was noted that if investors expected the price level to increase during the investment period, they would require the rate of return to include compensation for the expected rate of inflation. Assume that you require a 4 percent real rate of return on a risk-free investment but you expect prices to increase by 3 percent during the investment period. In this case, you should increase your required rate of return by this expected rate of inflation to about 7 percent $[(1.04 \times 1.03) - 1]$. If you do not increase your required return, the $104 you receive at the end of the year will represent a real return of about 1 percent, not 4 percent. Because prices have increased by 3 percent during the year, what previously cost $100 now costs $103, so you can consume only about 1 percent more at the end of the year $[(\$104/103) - 1]$. If you had required a 7.12 percent nominal return, your real consumption could have increased by 4 percent $[(\$107.12/103) - 1]$. Therefore, an investor's nominal required rate of return on a risk-free investment should be:

➤1.11 $$NRFR = (1 + RRFR) \times (1 + \text{Expected Rate of Inflation}) - 1$$

Rearranging the formula, you can calculate the RRFR of return on an investment as follows:

➤1.12 $$RRFR = \left[\frac{(1 + NRFR \text{ of Return})}{(1 + \text{Rate of Inflation})} \right] - 1$$

To see how this works, assume that the nominal return on U.S. government T-bills was 9 percent during a given year, when the rate of inflation was 5 percent. In this instance, the RRFR of return on these T-bills was 3.8 percent, as follows:

$$RRFR = [(1 + 0.09)/(1 + 0.05)] - 1$$
$$= 1.038 - 1$$
$$= 0.038 = 3.8\%$$

This discussion makes it clear that the nominal rate of interest on a risk-free investment is not a good estimate of the RRFR, because the nominal rate can change dramatically in the short run in reaction to temporary ease or tightness in the capital market or because of changes in the expected rate of inflation. As indicated by the data in Exhibit 1.6, the significant changes in the average yield on T-bills typically were caused by large changes in the rates of inflation.

The Common Effect   All the factors discussed thus far regarding the required rate of return affect all investments equally. Whether the investment is in stocks, bonds, real estate, or machine tools, if the expected rate of inflation increases from 2 percent to 6 percent, the investor's required rate of return for *all* investments should increase by 4 percent. Similarly, if a decline in the expected real growth rate of the economy causes a decline in the RRFR of 1 percent, the required return on all investments should decline by 1 percent.

Risk Premium   A risk-free investment was defined as one for which the investor is certain of the amount and timing of the expected returns. The returns from most investments do not fit this pattern. An investor typically is not completely certain of the income to be received or when it will be received. Investments can range in uncertainty from basically risk-free securities, such as T-bills, to highly speculative investments, such as the common stock of small companies engaged in high-risk enterprises.

Most investors require higher rates of return on investments if they perceive that there is any uncertainty about the expected rate of return. This increase in the required rate of return over the NRFR is the **risk premium (RP)**. Although the required risk premium represents a composite of all uncertainty, it is possible to consider several fundamental sources of uncertainty. In this section, we identify and discuss briefly the major sources of uncertainty, including: (1) business risk, (2) financial risk (leverage), (3) liquidity risk, (4) exchange rate risk, and (5) country (political) risk.

Business risk is the uncertainty of income flows caused by the nature of a firm's business. The less certain the income flows of the firm, the less certain the income flows to the investor. Therefore, the investor will demand a risk premium that is based on the uncertainty caused by the basic business of the firm. As an example, a retail food company would typically experience stable sales and earnings growth over time and would have low business risk compared to a firm in the auto industry, where sales and earnings fluctuate substantially over the business cycle, implying high business risk.

Financial risk is the uncertainty introduced by the method by which the firm finances its investments. If a firm uses only common stock to finance investments, it incurs only business risk. If a firm borrows money to finance investments, it must pay fixed financing charges (in the form of interest to creditors) prior to providing income to the common stockholders, so the uncertainty of returns to the equity investor increases. This increase in uncertainty because of fixed-cost financing is called *financial risk* or *financial leverage* and causes an increase in the stock's risk premium.[5]

Liquidity risk is the uncertainty introduced by the secondary market for an investment.[6] When an investor acquires an asset, he or she expects that the investment will mature (as with a bond) or that it will be salable to someone else. In either case, the investor expects to be able to convert the security into cash and use the proceeds for current consumption or other investments. The more difficult it is to make this conversion, the greater the liquidity risk. An investor must consider two questions when assessing the liquidity risk of an investment: (1) How long will it take to convert the investment into cash? (2) How certain is the price to be received? Similar uncertainty faces an investor who wants to acquire an asset: How long will it take to acquire the asset? How uncertain is the price to be paid?

Uncertainty regarding how fast an investment can be bought or sold, or the existence of uncertainty about its price, increases liquidity risk. A U.S. government Treasury bill has almost no liquidity risk because it can be bought or sold in minutes at a price almost identical to the quoted price. In contrast, examples of illiquid investments include a work of art, an antique, or a parcel of real estate in a remote area. For such investments, it may require a long time to find a buyer and the selling prices could vary substantially from expectations. Investors will increase their required rates of return to compensate for liquidity risk. Liquidity risk can be a significant consideration when investing in foreign securities depending on the country and the liquidity of its stock and bond markets.

Exchange rate risk is the uncertainty of returns to an investor who acquires securities denominated in a currency different from his or her own. The likelihood of incurring this risk is becoming greater as investors buy and sell assets around the world, as opposed to only assets within their own countries. A U.S. investor who buys Japanese stock denominated in yen must consider not only the uncertainty of the return in yen but also any change in the exchange value of the yen relative to the U.S. dollar. That is, in addition to the foreign firm's business and financial risk and the security's liquidity risk, the investor must consider the additional uncertainty of the return on this Japanese stock when it is converted from yen to U.S. dollars.

As an example of exchange rate risk, assume that you buy 100 shares of Mitsubishi Electric at 1,050 yen when the exchange rate is 115 yen to the dollar. The dollar cost of this investment would be about $9.13 per share (1,050/115). A year later you sell the 100 shares at 1,200 yen

---

[5]For a discussion of financial leverage, see Eugene F. Brigham, *Fundamentals of Financial Management,* 9th ed. (Hinsdale, Ill.: The Dryden Press, 2001), 232–236.

[6]You will recall from prior courses that the overall capital market is composed of the primary market and the secondary market. Securities are initially sold in the primary market, and all subsequent transactions take place in the secondary market. These concepts are discussed in Chapter 4.

when the exchange rate is 130 yen to the dollar. When you calculate the HPY in yen, you find the stock has increased in value by about 14 percent (1,200/1,050), but this is the HPY for a Japanese investor. A U.S. investor receives a much lower rate of return, because during this period the yen has weakened relative to the dollar by about 13 percent (that is, it requires more yen to buy a dollar—130 versus 115). At the new exchange rate, the stock is worth $9.23 per share (1,200/130). Therefore, the return to you as a U.S. investor would be only about 1 percent ($9.23/$9.13) versus 14 percent for the Japanese investor. The difference in return for the Japanese investor and U.S. investor is caused by the decline in the value of the yen relative to the dollar. Clearly, the exchange rate could have gone in the other direction, the dollar weakening against the yen. In this case, as a U.S. investor, you would have experienced the 14 percent return measured in yen, as well as a gain from the exchange rate change.

The more volatile the exchange rate between two countries, the less certain you would be regarding the exchange rate, the greater the exchange rate risk, and the larger the exchange rate risk premium you would require.[7]

There can also be exchange rate risk for a U.S. firm that is extensively multinational in terms of sales and components (costs). In this case, the firm's foreign earnings can be affected by changes in the exchange rate. As will be discussed, this risk can generally be hedged at a cost.

Country risk, also called *political risk,* is the uncertainty of returns caused by the possibility of a major change in the political or economic environment of a country. The United States is acknowledged to have the smallest country risk in the world because its political and economic systems are the most stable. Nations with high country risk include Russia, because of the several changes in the government hierarchy and its currency crises during 1998, and Indonesia, where there were student demonstrations, major riots, and fires prior to the resignation of President Suharto in May 1998. In both instances, the stock markets experienced significant declines surrounding these events.[8] Individuals who invest in countries that have unstable political-economic systems must add a country risk premium when determining their required rates of return.

When investing globally (which is emphasized throughout the book), investors must consider these additional uncertainties. How liquid are the secondary markets for stocks and bonds in the country? Are any of the country's securities traded on major stock exchanges in the United States, London, Tokyo, or Germany? What will happen to exchange rates during the investment period? What is the probability of a political or economic change that will adversely affect your rate of return? Exchange rate risk and country risk differ among countries. A good measure of exchange rate risk would be the absolute variability of the exchange rate relative to a composite exchange rate. The analysis of country risk is much more subjective and must be based on the history and current environment of the country.

This discussion of risk components can be considered a security's *fundamental risk* because it deals with the intrinsic factors that should affect a security's standard deviation of returns over time. In subsequent discussion, the standard deviation of returns is referred to as a measure of the security's *total risk,* which considers the individual stock by itself—that is, it is not considered as part of a portfolio.

Risk Premium = f (Business Risk, Financial Risk, Liquidity Risk, Exchange Rate Risk, Country Risk)

---

[7]An article that examines the pricing of exchange rate risk in the U.S. market is Philippe Jorion, "The Pricing of Exchange Rate Risk in the Stock Market," *Journal of Financial and Quantitative Analysis* 26, no. 3 (September 1991): 363–376.

[8]Carlotta Gall, "Moscow Stock Market Falls by 11.8%," *Financial Times,* 19 May 1998, 1; "Russian Contagion Hits Neighbours," *Financial Times,* 29 May 1998, 17; John Thornhill, "Russian Stocks Fall 10% over Lack of Support from IMF," *Financial Times,* 2 June 1998, 1; Robert Chote, "Indonesia Risks Further Unrest as Debt Talks Falter," *Financial Times,* 11 May 1998, 1; Sander Thoenes, " Suharto Cuts Visit as Riots Shake Jakarta," *Financial Times,* 14 May 1998, 12; Sander Thoenes, "Economy Hit as Jakarta Is Paralysed," *Financial Times,* 15 May 1998, 17.

Risk Premium and Portfolio Theory

An alternative view of risk has been derived from extensive work in portfolio theory and capital market theory by Markowitz, Sharpe, and others.[9] These theories are dealt with in greater detail in Chapter 7 and Chapter 8 but their impact on the risk premium should be mentioned briefly at this point. These prior works by Markowitz and Sharpe indicated that investors should use an *external market* measure of risk. Under a specified set of assumptions, all rational, profit-maximizing investors want to hold a completely diversified market portfolio of risky assets, and they borrow or lend to arrive at a risk level that is consistent with their risk preferences. Under these conditions, the relevant risk measure for an individual asset is its *comovement with the market portfolio.* This comovement, which is measured by an asset's covariance with the market portfolio, is referred to as an asset's **systematic risk**, the portion of an individual asset's total variance attributable to the variability of the total market portfolio. In addition, individual assets have variance that is unrelated to the market portfolio (that is, it is nonmarket variance) that is due to the asset's unique features. This nonmarket variance is called *unsystematic risk,* and it is generally considered unimportant because it is eliminated in a large, diversified portfolio. Therefore, under these assumptions, *the risk premium for an individual earning asset is a function of the asset's systematic risk with the aggregate market portfolio of risky assets.* The measure of an asset's systematic risk is referred to as its *beta:*

$$\text{Risk Premium} = f \text{ (Systematic Market Risk)}$$

Fundamental Risk versus Systematic Risk

Some might expect a conflict between the market measure of risk (systematic risk) and the fundamental determinants of risk (business risk, and so on). A number of studies have examined the relationship between the market measure of risk (systematic risk) and accounting variables used to measure the fundamental risk factors, such as business risk, financial risk, and liquidity risk. The authors of these studies have generally concluded that *a significant relationship exists between the market measure of risk and the fundamental measures of risk.*[10] Therefore, the two measures of risk can be complementary. This consistency seems reasonable because, in a properly functioning capital market, the market measure of the risk should reflect the fundamental risk characteristics of the asset. As an example, you would expect a firm that has high business risk and financial risk to have an above average beta. At the same time, as we discuss in Chapter 8, it is possible that a firm that has a high level of fundamental risk and a large standard deviation of return on stock can have a lower level of systematic risk because its variability of earnings and stock price is not related to the aggregate economy or the aggregate market. Therefore, one can specify the risk premium for an asset as:

$$\text{Risk Premium} = f \text{ (Business Risk, Financial Risk, Liquidity Risk, Exchange Rate Risk, Country Risk)}$$

or

$$\text{Risk Premium} = f \text{ (Systematic Market Risk)}$$

---

[9]These works include Harry Markowitz, "Portfolio Selection," *Journal of Finance* 7, no. 1 (March 1952): 77–91; Harry Markowitz, *Portfolio Selection—Efficient Diversification of Investments* (New Haven, Conn.: Yale University Press, 1959); and William F. Sharpe, "Capital Asset Prices: A Theory of Market Equilibrium under Conditions of Risk," *Journal of Finance* 19, no. 3 (September 1964): 425–442.

[10]A brief review of some of the earlier studies is contained in Donald J. Thompson II, "Sources of Systematic Risk in Common Stocks," *Journal of Business* 49, no. 2 (April 1976): 173–188. There is a further discussion of specific variables in Chapter 10.

**Summary
of Required Rate
of Return**

The overall required rate of return on alternative investments is determined by three variables: (1) the economy's RRFR, which is influenced by the investment opportunities in the economy (that is, the long-run real growth rate); (2) variables that influence the NRFR, which include short-run ease or tightness in the capital market and the expected rate of inflation (notably, these variables, which determine the NRFR, are the same for all investments); and (3) the risk premium on the investment. In turn, this risk premium can be related to fundamental factors, including business risk, financial risk, liquidity risk, exchange rate risk, and country risk, or it can be a function of systematic market risk (beta).

Measures and Sources of Risk   In this chapter, we have examined both measures and sources of risk arising from an investment. The *measures* of risk for an investment are:

➤ Variance of rates of return
➤ Standard deviation of rates of return
➤ Coefficient of variation of rates of return (standard deviation/means)
➤ Covariance of returns with the market portfolio (beta)

The *sources* of risk are:

➤ Business risk
➤ Financial risk
➤ Liquidity risk
➤ Exchange rate risk
➤ Country risk

RELATIONSHIP BETWEEN RISK AND RETURN

Previously, we showed how to measure the risk and rates of return for alternative investments and we discussed what determines the rates of return that investors require. This section discusses the risk-return combinations that might be available at a point in time and illustrates the factors that cause *changes* in these combinations.

Exhibit 1.7 graphs the expected relationship between risk and return. It shows that investors increase their required rates of return as perceived risk (uncertainty) increases. The line that reflects the combination of risk and return available on alternative investments is referred to as the **security market line (SML)**. The SML reflects the risk-return combinations available for all risky assets in the capital market at a given time. Investors would select investments that are consistent with their risk preferences; some would consider only low-risk investments, whereas others welcome high-risk investments.

Beginning with an initial SML, three changes can occur. First, individual investments can change positions on the SML because of changes in the perceived risk of the investments. Second, the slope of the SML can change because of a change in the attitudes of investors toward risk; that is, investors can change the returns they require per unit of risk. Third, the SML can experience a parallel shift due to a change in the RRFR or the expected rate of inflation—that is, a change in the NRFR. These three possibilities are discussed in this section.

**Movements along
the SML**

Investors place alternative investments somewhere along the SML based on their perceptions of the risk of the investment. Obviously, if an investment's risk changes due to a change in one of its risk sources (business risk, and such), it will move along the SML. For example, if a firm increases its financial risk by selling a large bond issue that increases its financial leverage, investors will perceive its common stock as riskier and the stock will move up the SML to a

| EXHIBIT 1.7 | *RELATIONSHIP BETWEEN RISK AND RETURN* |

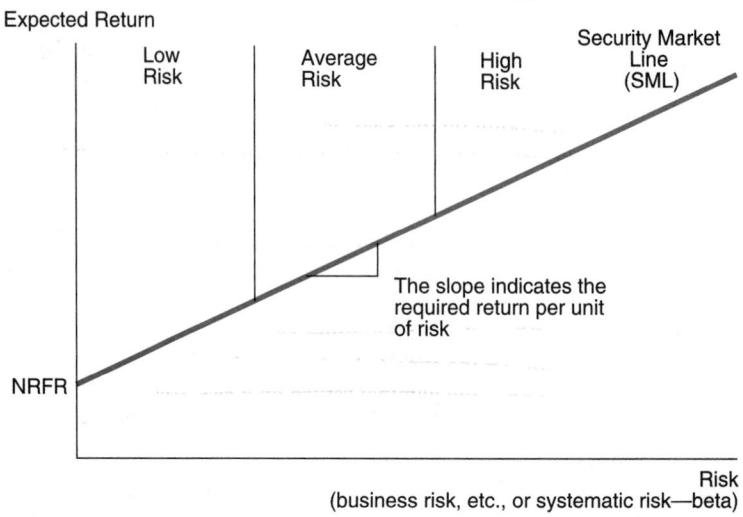

| EXHIBIT 1.8 | *CHANGES IN THE REQUIRED RATE OF RETURN DUE TO MOVEMENTS ALONG THE SML* |

higher risk position. Investors will then require a higher rate of return. As the common stock becomes riskier, it changes its position on the SML. Any change in an asset that affects its fundamental risk factors or its market risk (that is, its beta) will cause the asset to move *along* the SML as shown in Exhibit 1.8. Note that the SML does not change, only the position of assets on the SML.

Changes in the Slope of the SML   The slope of the SML indicates the return per unit of risk required by all investors. Assuming a straight line, it is possible to select any point on the SML and compute a risk premium (RP) for an asset through the equation:

➤1.13 $$RP_i = E(R_i) - NRFR$$

where:

> RP_i = **risk premium for asset i**
> $E(R_i)$ = **the expected return for asset i**
> **NRFR = the nominal return on a risk-free asset**

If a point on the SML is identified as the portfolio that contains all the risky assets in the market (referred to as the *market portfolio*), it is possible to compute a market RP as follows:

➤1.14
$$RP_m = E(R_m) - \text{NRFR}$$

where:

> RP_m = **the risk premium on the market portfolio**
> $E(R_m)$ = **the expected return on the market portfolio**
> **NRFR = the nominal return on a risk-free asset**

This market RP is *not constant* because the slope of the SML changes over time. Although we do not understand completely what causes these changes in the slope, we do know that there are changes in the *yield* differences between assets with different levels of risk even though the inherent risk differences are relatively constant.

These differences in yields are referred to as **yield spreads**, and these yield spreads change over time. As an example, if the yield on a portfolio of Aaa-rated bonds is 7.50 percent and the yield on a portfolio of Baa-rated bonds is 9.00 percent, we would say that the yield spread is 1.50 percent. This 1.50 percent is referred to as a credit risk premium because the Baa-rated bond is considered to have higher credit risk—that is, greater probability of default. This Baa–Aaa yield spread is *not* constant over time. For an example of changes in a yield spread, note the substantial changes in the yield spreads on Aaa-rated bonds and Baa-rated bonds shown in Exhibit 1.9.

Although the underlying risk factors for the portfolio of bonds in the Aaa-rated bond index and the Baa-rated bond index would probably not change dramatically over time, it is clear from the time-series plot in Exhibit 1.9 that the difference in yields (i.e., the yield spread) has experienced changes of more than 100 basis points (1 percent) in a short period of time (for example, see the yield spread increase in 1974 to 1975 and the dramatic yield spread decline in 1983 to 1984). Such a significant change in the yield spread during a period where there is no major change in the risk characteristics of Baa bonds relative to Aaa bonds would imply a change in the market RP. Specifically, although the risk levels of the bonds remain relatively constant, investors have changed the yield spreads they demand to accept this relatively constant difference in risk.

This change in the RP implies a change in the slope of the SML. Such a change is shown in Exhibit 1.10. The exhibit assumes an increase in the market risk premium, which means an increase in the slope of the market line. Such a change in the slope of the SML (the risk premium) will affect the required rate of return for all risky assets. Irrespective of where an investment is on the original SML, its required rate of return will increase, although its individual risk characteristics remain unchanged.

Changes in Capital Market Conditions or Expected Inflation

The graph in Exhibit 1.11 shows what happens to the SML when there are changes in one of the following factors: (1) expected real growth in the economy, (2) capital market conditions, or (3) the expected rate of inflation. For example, an increase in expected real growth, temporary tightness in the capital market, or an increase in the expected rate of inflation will cause the SML to experience a parallel shift upward. The parallel shift occurs because changes in expected real growth or in capital market conditions or a change in the expected rate of inflation affect all investments, no matter what their levels of risk are.

PLOT OF MOODY'S CORPORATE BOND YIELD SPREADS (BAA–AAA): MONTHLY 1966–2000

CHANGE IN MARKET RISK PREMIUM

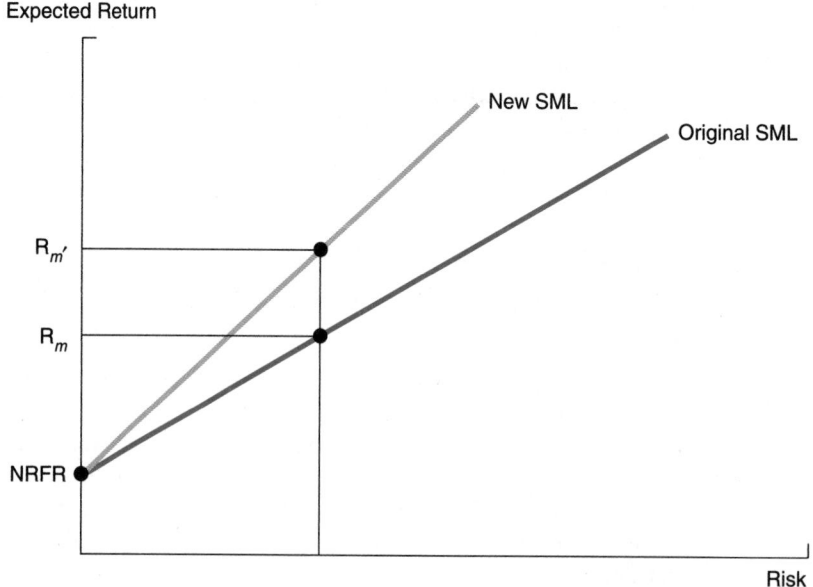

EXHIBIT 1.11 *CAPITAL MARKET CONDITIONS, EXPECTED INFLATION, AND THE SECURITY MARKET LINE*

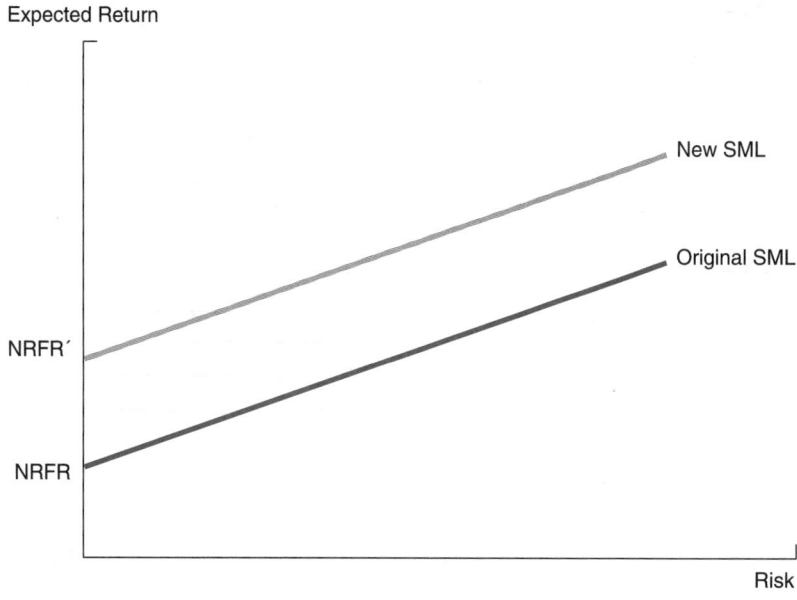

Summary of Changes in the Required Rate of Return

The relationship between risk and the required rate of return for an investment can change in three ways:

1. A movement *along* the SML demonstrates a change in the risk characteristics of a specific investment, such as a change in its business risk, its financial risk, or its systematic risk (its beta). This change affects only the individual investment.
2. A change in the *slope* of the SML occurs in response to a change in the attitudes of investors toward risk. Such a change demonstrates that investors want either higher or lower rates of return for the same risk. This is also described as a change in the market risk premium (R_m − NRFR). A change in the market risk premium will affect all risky investments.
3. A *shift* in the SML reflects a change in expected real growth, a change in market conditions (such as ease or tightness of money), or a change in the expected rate of inflation. Again, such a change will affect all investments.

The Internet *Investments Online*

There are a great many Internet sites that are set up to assist the beginning or novice investor. Because they cover the basics, have helpful links to other Internet sites, and sometimes allow users to calculate items of interest (rates of return, the size of an investment necessary to meet a certain goal, and so on), these sites are useful for the experienced investor, too.

http://www.finpipe.com The Financial Pipeline is an excellent site for those just starting to learn about investments or who need a quick refresher. A site focused on financial education, it contains information and links on a variety of investment topics such as bonds, stocks, strategy, retirement, and consumer finance.

(continued)

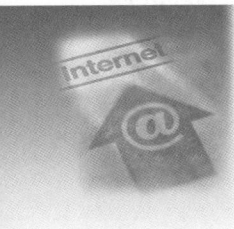

The Internet *Investments Online (cont.)*

http://www.investorguide.com This is another site offering a plethora of information that is useful to both the novice and seasoned investor. It contains links to pages with market summaries, news research, and much more. It offers users a glossary of investment terms. Basic investment education issues are taught in the "University " section. There are links to personal financial help pages, including sites dealing with buying a home or car, retirement, loans, and insurance. It offers links to a number of calculator functions to help users make financial decisions.

http://finance.yahoo.com Yahoo's finance portal is an excellent site for the beginning investor because of the information and data it contains. The site covers a number of investing and personal finance topics and gives visitors access to much financial data and charts.

Here are some other sites that may be of interest:
http://www.finweb.com Focuses on electronic publishing, databases, working papers, links to other Web sites.

http://fisher.osu.edu/fin Contains links to numerous finance sites.

http://www.aaii.com The home page for the American Association of Individual Investors, a group dealing with investor education.

Many representatives of the financial press have Internet sites:
http://www.wsj.com *The Wall Street Journal*
http://www.ft.com *Financial Times*
http://www.economist.com *The Economist* magazine
http://www.fortune.com *Fortune* magazine
http://www.money.cnn.com *Money* magazine
http://www.forbes.com *Forbes* magazine
http://www.worth.com *Worth* magazine
http://www.smartmoney.com *SmartMoney* magazine
http://www.barrons.com *Barron's* newspaper

Summary

The purpose of this chapter is to provide background that can be used in subsequent chapters. To achieve that goal, we covered several topics:

- We discussed why individuals save part of their income and why they decide to invest their savings. We defined *investment* as the current commitment of these savings for a period of time to derive a rate of return that compensates for the time involved, the expected rate of inflation, and the uncertainty.
- We examined ways to quantify historical return and risk to help analyze alternative investment opportunities. We considered two measures of mean return (arithmetic and geometric) and applied these to a historical series for an individual investment and to a portfolio of investments during a period of time.
- We considered the concept of uncertainty and alternative measures of risk (the variance, standard deviation, and a relative measure of risk—the coefficient of variation).
- Before discussing the determinants of the required rate of return for an investment, we noted that the estimation of the required rate of return is complicated because the rates on individual investments change over time, because there is a wide range of rates of return available on alternative investments, and because the differences between required returns on alternative investments (for example, the yield spreads) likewise change over time.
- We examined the specific factors that determine the required rate of return: (1) the real risk-free rate, which is based on the real rate of growth in the economy, (2) the nominal risk-free rate, which is influenced by capital market conditions and the expected rate of inflation, and (3) a risk premium, which is a function of fundamental factors, such as business risk, or the systematic risk of the asset relative to the market portfolio (that is, its beta).
- We discussed the risk-return combinations available on alternative investments at a point in time (illustrated by the SML) and the three factors that can cause changes in this relationship. First, a change in the inherent risk of an investment (that is, its fundamental risk or market risk) will cause a movement along the SML. Second, a change in investors' attitudes toward risk will cause a change in the required return per unit of risk—that is, a change in the market risk premium. Such a change will cause a

change in the slope of the SML. Finally, a change in expected real growth, in capital market conditions, or in the expected rate of inflation will cause a parallel shift of the SML.

Based on this understanding of the investment environment, you are prepared to consider the asset allocation decision. This is the subject of Chapter 2.

Questions

1. Discuss the overall purpose people have for investing. Define investment.
2. As a student, are you saving or borrowing? Why?
3. Divide a person's life from ages 20 to 70 into 10-year segments and discuss the likely saving or borrowing patterns during each period.
4. Discuss why you would expect the saving-borrowing pattern to differ by occupation (for example, for a doctor versus a plumber).
5. *The Wall Street Journal* reported that the yield on common stocks is about 2 percent, whereas a study at the University of Chicago contends that the annual rate of return on common stocks since 1926 has averaged about 12 percent. Reconcile these statements.
6. Some financial theorists consider the variance of the distribution of expected rates of return to be a good measure of uncertainty. Discuss the reasoning behind this measure of risk and its purpose.
7. Discuss the three components of an investor's required rate of return on an investment.
8. Discuss the two major factors that determine the market nominal risk-free rate (NRFR). Explain which of these factors would be more volatile over the business cycle.
9. Briefly discuss the five fundamental factors that influence the risk premium of an investment.
10. You own stock in the Gentry Company, and you read in the financial press that a recent bond offering has raised the firm's debt/equity ratio from 35 percent to 55 percent. Discuss the effect of this change on the variability of the firm's net income stream, other factors being constant. Discuss how this change would affect your required rate of return on the common stock of the Gentry Company.
11. Draw a properly labeled graph of the security market line (SML) and indicate where you would expect the following investments to fall along that line. Discuss your reasoning.
    a. Common stock of large firms
    b. U.S. government bonds
    c. U.K. government bonds
    d. Low-grade corporate bonds
    e. Common stock of a Japanese firm
12. Explain why you would change your nominal required rate of return if you expected the rate of inflation to go from 0 (no inflation) to 4 percent. Give an example of what would happen if you did not change your required rate of return under these conditions.
13. Assume the long-run growth rate of the economy increased by 1 percent and the expected rate of inflation increased by 4 percent. What would happen to the required rates of return on government bonds and common stocks? Show graphically how the effects of these changes would differ between these alternative investments.
14. You see in *The Wall Street Journal* that the yield spread between Baa corporate bonds and Aaa corporate bonds has gone from 350 basis points (3.5 percent) to 200 basis points (2 percent). Show graphically the effect of this change in yield spread on the SML and discuss its effect on the required rate of return for common stocks.
15. Give an example of a liquid investment and an illiquid investment. Discuss why you consider each of them to be liquid or illiquid.

Problems

1. On February 1, you bought 100 shares of a stock for $34 a share and a year later you sold it for $39 a share. During the year, you received a cash dividend of $1.50 a share. Compute your HPR and HPY on this stock investment.
2. On August 15, you purchased 100 shares of a stock at $65 a share and a year later you sold it for $61 a share. During the year, you received dividends of $3 a share. Compute your HPR and HPY on this investment.

3. At the beginning of last year, you invested $4,000 in 80 shares of the Chang Corporation. During the year, Chang paid dividends of $5 per share. At the end of the year, you sold the 80 shares for $59 a share. Compute your total HPY on these shares and indicate how much was due to the price change and how much was due to the dividend income.

4. The rates of return computed in Problems 1, 2, and 3 are nominal rates of return. Assuming that the rate of inflation during the year was 4 percent, compute the real rates of return on these investments. Compute the real rates of return if the rate of inflation were 8 percent.

5. During the past five years, you owned two stocks that had the following annual rates of return:

Year	Stock T	Stock B
1	0.19	0.08
2	0.08	0.03
3	−0.12	−0.09
4	−0.03	0.02
5	0.15	0.04

a. Compute the arithmetic mean annual rate of return for each stock. Which stock is most desirable by this measure?

b. Compute the standard deviation of the annual rate of return for each stock. (Use Chapter 1 Appendix if necessary.) By this measure, which is the preferable stock?

c. Compute the coefficient of variation for each stock. (Use the Chapter 1 Appendix if necessary.) By this relative measure of risk, which stock is preferable?

d. Compute the geometric mean rate of return for each stock. Discuss the difference between the arithmetic mean return and the geometric mean return for each stock. Relate the differences in the mean returns to the standard deviation of the return for each stock.

6. You are considering acquiring shares of common stock in the Madison Beer Corporation. Your rate of return expectations are as follows:

MADISON BEER CORP.

Possible Rate of Return	Probability
−0.10	0.30
0.00	0.10
0.10	0.30
0.25	0.30

Compute the expected return $[E(R_i)]$ on your investment in Madison Beer.

7. A stockbroker calls you and suggests that you invest in the Lauren Computer Company. After analyzing the firm's annual report and other material, you believe that the distribution of rates of return is as follows:

LAUREN COMPUTER CO.

Possible Rate of Return	Probability
−0.60	0.05
−0.30	0.20
−0.10	0.10
0.20	0.30
0.40	0.20
0.80	0.15

Compute the expected return [$E(R_i)$] on Lauren Computer stock.

8. Without any formal computations, do you consider Madison Beer in Problem 6 or Lauren Computer in Problem 7 to present greater risk? Discuss your reasoning.

9. During the past year, you had a portfolio that contained U.S. government T-bills, long-term government bonds, and common stocks. The rates of return on each of them were as follows:

U.S. government T-bills	5.50%
U.S. government long-term bonds	7.50
U.S. common stocks	11.60

During the year, the consumer price index, which measures the rate of inflation, went from 160 to 172 (1982–1984 = 100). Compute the rate of inflation during this year. Compute the real rates of return on each of the investments in your portfolio based on the inflation rate.

10. You read in *Business Week* that a panel of economists has estimated that the long-run real growth rate of the U.S. economy over the next five-year period will average 3 percent. In addition, a bank newsletter estimates that the average annual rate of inflation during this five-year period will be about 4 percent. What nominal rate of return would you expect on U.S. government T-bills during this period?

11. What would your required rate of return be on common stocks if you wanted a 5 percent risk premium to own common stocks given what you know from Problem 10? If common stock investors became more risk averse, what would happen to the required rate of return on common stocks? What would be the impact on stock prices?

12. Assume that the consensus required rate of return on common stocks is 14 percent. In addition, you read in *Fortune* that the expected rate of inflation is 5 percent and the estimated long-term real growth rate of the economy is 3 percent. What interest rate would you expect on U.S. government T-bills? What is the approximate risk premium for common stocks implied by these data?

References

Fama, Eugene F., and Merton H. Miller. *The Theory of Finance.* New York: Holt, Rinehart and Winston, 1972.

Fisher, Irving. *The Theory of Interest.* New York: Macmillan, 1930; reprinted by Augustus M. Kelley, 1961.

APPENDIX
Chapter 1

Computation of Variance and Standard Deviation

Variance and standard deviation are measures of how actual values differ from the expected values (arithmetic mean) for a given series of values. In this case, we want to measure how rates of return differ from the arithmetic mean value of a series. There are other measures of dispersion, but variance and standard deviation are the best known because they are used in statistics and probability theory. Variance is defined as:

$$\text{Variance } (\sigma^2) = \sum_{i=1}^{n} (\text{Probability})(\text{Possible Return} - \text{Expected Return})^2$$

$$= \sum_{i=1}^{n} (P_i)\big[R_i - E(R_i)\big]^2$$

Consider the following example, as discussed in the chapter:

Probability of Possible Return (P_i)	Possible Return (R_i)	P_iR_i
0.15	0.20	0.03
0.15	−0.20	−0.03
0.70	0.10	0.07
		$\Sigma = 0.07$

This gives an expected return $[E(R_i)]$ of 7 percent. The dispersion of this distribution as measured by variance is:

Probability (P_i)	Return (R_i)	$R_i - E(R_i)$	$[R_i - E(R_i)]^2$	$P_i[R_i - E(R_i)]^2$
0.15	0.20	0.13	0.0169	0.002535
0.15	−0.20	−0.27	0.0729	0.010935
0.70	0.10	0.03	0.0009	0.000630
				$\Sigma = 0.014100$

The variance (σ^2) is equal to 0.0141. The standard deviation is equal to the square root of the variance:

$$\text{Standard Deviation } (\sigma^2) = \sqrt{\sum_{i=1}^{n} P_i \left[R_i - E(R_i) \right]^2}$$

Consequently, the standard deviation for the preceding example would be:

$$\sigma_i = \sqrt{0.0141} = 0.11874$$

In this example, the standard deviation is approximately 11.87 percent. Therefore, you could describe this distribution as having an expected value of 7 percent and a standard deviation of 11.87 percent.

In many instances, you might want to compute the variance or standard deviation for a historical series in order to evaluate the past performance of the investment. Assume that you are given the following information on annual rates of return (HPY) for common stocks listed on the New York Stock Exchange (NYSE):

Year	Annual Rate of Return
2003	0.07
2004	0.11
2005	−0.04
2006	0.12
2007	−0.06

In this case, we are not examining expected rates of return but actual returns. Therefore, we assume equal probabilities, and the expected value (in this case the mean value, R) of the series is the sum of the individual observations in the series divided by the number of observations, or 0.04 (0.20/5). The variances and standard deviations are:

Year	R_i	$R_i - \bar{R}$	$(R_i - \bar{R})^2$	
2003	0.07	0.03	0.0009	$\sigma^2 = 0.0286/5$
2004	0.11	0.07	0.0049	$= 0.00572$
2005	−0.04	−0.08	0.0064	
2006	0.12	0.08	0.0064	$\sigma = \sqrt{0.00572}$
2007	−0.06	−0.10	0.0110	$= 0.0756$
			$\Sigma = 0.0286$	

We can interpret the performance of NYSE common stocks during this period of time by saying that the average rate of return was 4 percent and the standard deviation of annual rates of return was 7.56 percent.

Coefficient of Variation

In some instances, you might want to compare the dispersion of two different series. The variance and standard deviation are *absolute* measures of dispersion. That is, they can be influenced by the magnitude of the original numbers. To compare series with greatly different values, you need a *relative* measure of dispersion. A measure of relative dispersion is the coefficient of variation, which is defined as:

$$\text{Coefficient of Variation }(CV) = \frac{\text{Standard Deviation of Returns}}{\text{Expected Rate of Return}}$$

A larger value indicates greater dispersion relative to the arithmetic mean of the series. For the previous example, the CV would be:

$$CV_1 = \frac{0.0756}{0.0400} = 1.89$$

It is possible to compare this value to a similar figure having a markedly different distribution. As an example, assume you wanted to compare this investment to another investment that had an average rate of return of 10 percent and a standard deviation of 9 percent. The standard deviations alone tell you that the second series has greater dispersion (9 percent versus 7.56 percent) and might be considered to have higher risk. In fact, the relative dispersion for this second investment is much less.

$$CV_1 = \frac{0.0756}{0.0400} = 1.89$$

$$CV_2 = \frac{0.0900}{0.1000} = 0.90$$

Considering the relative dispersion and the total distribution, most investors would probably prefer the second investment.

Problems

1. Your rate of return expectations for the common stock of Gray Disc Company during the next year are:

GRAY DISC CO.

Possible Rate of Return	Probability
–0.10	0.25
0.00	0.15
0.10	0.35
0.25	0.25

   a. Compute the expected return $[E(R_i)]$ on this investment, the variance of this return (σ^2), and its standard deviation (σ).
   b. Under what conditions can the standard deviation be used to measure the relative risk of two investments?
   c. Under what conditions must the coefficient of variation be used to measure the relative risk of two investments?

2. Your rate of return expectations for the stock of Kayleigh Computer Company during the next year are:

KAYLEIGH COMPUTER CO.

Possible Rate of Return	Probability
–0.60	0.15
–0.30	0.10
–0.10	0.05
0.20	0.40
0.40	0.20
0.80	0.10

a. Compute the expected return $[E(R_i)]$ on this stock, the variance (σ^2) of this return, and its standard deviation (σ).
b. On the basis of expected return $[E(R_i)]$ alone, discuss whether Gray Disc or Kayleigh Computer is preferable.
c. On the basis of standard deviation (σ) alone, discuss whether Gray Disc or Kayleigh Computer is preferable.
d. Compute the coefficients of variation (*CVs*) for Gray Disc and Kayleigh Computer and discuss which stock return series has the greater relative dispersion.

3. The following are annual rates of return for U.S. government T-bills and U.K. common stocks.

Year	U.S. Government T-Bills	U.K. Common Stock
2003	.063	.150
2004	.081	.043
2005	.076	.374
2006	.090	.192
2007	.085	.106

a. Compute the arithmetic mean rate of return and standard deviation of rates of return for the two series.
b. Discuss these two alternative investments in terms of their arithmetic average rates of return, their absolute risk, and their relative risk.
c. Compute the geometric mean rate of return for each of these investments. Compare the arithmetic mean return and geometric mean return for each investment and discuss this difference between mean returns as related to the standard deviation of each series.

Chapter 2 ▷ The Asset Allocation Decision*

After you read this chapter, you should be able to answer the following questions:

➤ What is asset allocation?
➤ What are the four steps in the portfolio management process?
➤ What is the role of asset allocation in investment planning?
➤ Why is a policy statement important to the planning process?
➤ What objectives and constraints should be detailed in a policy statement?
➤ How and why do investment goals change over a person's lifetime and circumstances?
➤ Why do asset allocation strategies differ across national boundaries?

The previous chapter informed us that *risk drives return.* Therefore, the practice of investing funds and managing portfolios should focus primarily on managing risk rather than on managing returns.

This chapter examines some of the practical implications of risk management in the context of asset allocation. **Asset allocation** is the process of deciding how to distribute an investor's wealth among different countries and asset classes for investment purposes. An **asset class** is comprised of securities that have similar characteristics, attributes, and risk/return relationships. A broad asset class, such as "bonds," can be divided into smaller asset classes, such as Treasury bonds, corporate bonds, and high-yield bonds. We will see that, in the long run, the highest compounded returns will most likely accrue to those investors with larger exposures to risky assets. We will also see that although there are no shortcuts or guarantees to investment success, maintaining a reasonable and disciplined approach to investing will increase the likelihood of investment success over time.

The asset allocation decision is not an isolated choice; rather, it is a component of a portfolio management process. In this chapter, we present an overview of the four-step portfolio management process. As we will see, the first step in the process is to develop an investment policy statement, or plan, that will guide all future decisions. Much of an asset allocation strategy depends on the investor's policy statement, which includes the investor's goals or objectives, constraints, and investment guidelines.

What we mean by an "investor" can range from an individual to trustees overseeing a corporation's multibillion-dollar pension fund, a university endowment, or invested premiums for an insurance company. Regardless of who the investor is or how simple or complex the investment needs, he or she should develop a policy statement before making long-term investment decisions. Although most of our examples will be in the context of an individual investor, the concepts we introduce here—investment objectives, constraints, benchmarks, and so on—apply to any investor, individual or institutional. We'll review historical data to show the importance of the asset allocation decision and discuss the need for investor education, an important issue for

---

*The authors acknowledge the collaboration of Professor Edgar Norton of Illinois State University on this chapter.

individuals or companies who offer retirement or savings plans to their employees. The chapter concludes by examining asset allocation strategies across national borders to show the effect of market environment and culture on investing patterns; what is appropriate for a U.S.-based investor is not necessarily appropriate for a non-U.S.-based investor.

INDIVIDUAL INVESTOR LIFE CYCLE

Financial plans and investment needs are as different as each individual. Investment needs change over a person's life cycle. How individuals structure their financial plan should be related to their age, financial status, future plans, risk aversion characteristcs, and needs.

The Preliminaries Before embarking on an investment program, we need to make sure other needs are satisfied. No serious investment plan should be started until a potential investor has adequate income to cover living expenses and has a safety net should the unexpected occur.

Insurance Life insurance should be a component of any financial plan. Life insurance protects loved ones against financial hardship should death occur before our financial goals are met. The death benefit paid by the insurance company can help pay medical bills and funeral expenses and provide cash that family members can use to maintain their lifestyle, retire debt, or invest for future needs (for example, children's education, spouse retirement). Therefore, one of the first steps in developing a financial plan is to purchase adequate life insurance coverage.

Insurance can also serve more immediate purposes, including being a means to meet long-term goals, such as retirement planning. On reaching retirement age, you can receive the cash or surrender value of your life insurance policy and use the proceeds to supplement your retirement lifestyle or for estate planning purposes.

You can choose among several basic life insurance contracts. *Term life insurance* provides only a death benefit; the premium to purchase the insurance changes every renewal period. Term insurance is the least expensive life insurance to purchase, although the premium will rise as you age to reflect the increased probability of death. *Universal* and *variable life policies,* although technically different from each other, are similar in that they each provide both a death benefit and a savings plan to the insured. The premium paid on such policies exceeds the cost to the insurance company of providing the death benefit alone; the excess premium is invested in a number of investment vehicles chosen by the insured. The policy's cash value grows over time, based on the size of the excess premium and on the performance of the underlying investment funds. Insurance companies may restrict the ability to withdraw funds from these policies before the policyholder reaches a certain age.

Insurance coverage also provides protection against other uncertainties. *Health* insurance helps to pay medical bills. *Disability* insurance provides continuing income should you become unable to work. *Automobile and home* (or rental) insurances provide protection against accidents and damage to cars or residences.

Although nobody ever expects to use his or her insurance coverage, a first step in a sound financial plan is to have adequate coverage "just in case." Lack of insurance coverage can ruin the best-planned investment program.

Cash Reserve Emergencies, job layoffs, and unforeseen expenses happen, and good investment opportunities emerge. It is important to have a cash reserve to help meet these occasions. In addition to providing a safety cushion, a cash reserve reduces the likelihood of being forced to sell investments at inopportune times to cover unexpected expenses. Most experts recommend

EXHIBIT 2.1 *RISE AND FALL OF PERSONAL NET WORTH OVER A LIFETIME*

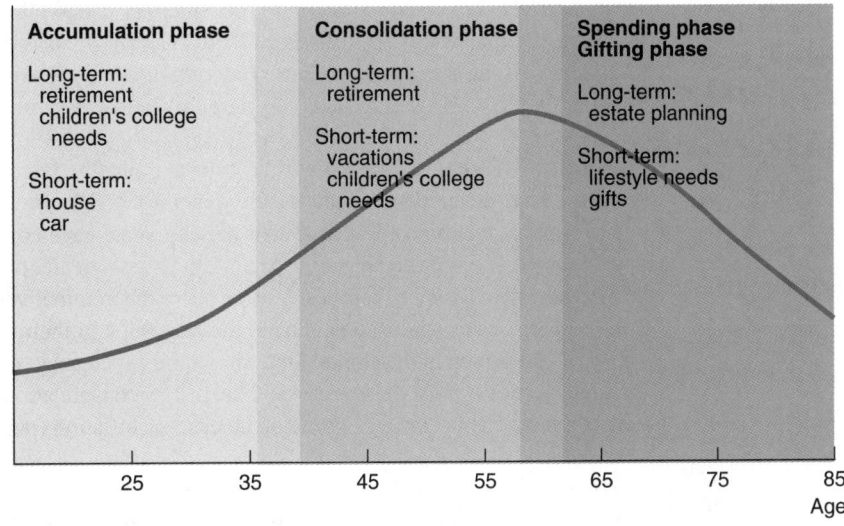

a cash reserve equal to about six months' living expenses. Calling it a "cash" reserve does not mean the funds should be in cash; rather, the funds should be in investments you can easily convert to cash with little chance of a loss in value. Money market mutual funds and bank accounts are appropriate vehicles for the cash reserve.

Similar to the financial plan, an investor's insurance and cash reserve needs will change over his or her life. We've already mentioned how a retired person may "cash out" a life insurance policy to supplement income. The need for disability insurance declines when a person retires. In contrast, other insurance, such as supplemental Medicare coverage or long-term care insurance, may become more important.

Life Cycle Net Worth and Investment Strategies

Assuming the basic insurance and cash reserve needs are met, individuals can start a serious investment program with their savings. Because of changes in their net worth and risk tolerance, individuals' investment strategies will change over their lifetime. In the following sections, we review various phases in the investment life cycle. Although each individual's needs and preferences are different, some general traits affect most investors over the life cycle. The four life cycle phases are shown in Exhibit 2.1 (the third and fourth phases are shown as concurrent) and described here.

Accumulation Phase   Individuals in the early-to-middle years of their working careers are in the **accumulation phase**. As the name implies, these individuals are attempting to accumulate assets to satisfy fairly immediate needs (for example, a down payment for a house) or longer-term goals (children's college education, retirement). Typically, their net worth is small, and debt from car loans or their own past college loans may be heavy. As a result of their typically long investment time horizon and their future earning ability, individuals in the accumulation phase are willing to make relatively high-risk investments in the hopes of making above-average nominal returns over time.

Consolidation Phase   Individuals in the **consolidation phase** are typically past the mid-point of their careers, have paid off much or all of their outstanding debts, and perhaps have paid, or have the assets to pay, their children's college bills. Earnings exceed expenses, so the excess can be invested to provide for future retirement or estate planning needs. The typical investment horizon for this phase is still long (20 to 30 years), so moderately high risk investments are attractive. At the same time, because individuals in this phase are concerned about capital preservation, they do not want to take very large risks that may put their current nest egg in jeopardy.

Spending Phase   The **spending phase** typically begins when individuals retire. Living expenses are covered by social security income and income from prior investments, including employer pension plans. Because their earning years have concluded (although some retirees take part-time positions or do consulting work), they seek greater protection of their capital. At the same time, they must balance their desire to preserve the nominal value of their savings with the need to protect themselves against a decline in the *real* value of their savings due to inflation. The average 65-year-old person in the United States has a life expectancy of about 20 years. Thus, although their overall portfolio may be less risky than in the consolidation phase, they still need some risky growth investments, such as common stocks, for inflation (purchasing power) protection.

Gifting Phase   The **gifting phase** is similar to, and may be concurrent with, the spending phase. In this stage, individuals believe they have sufficient income and assets to cover their expenses while maintaining a reserve for uncertainties. Excess assets can be used to provide financial assistance to relatives or friends, to establish charitable trusts, or to fund trusts as an estate planning tool to minimize estate taxes.

Life Cycle Investment Goals

During the investment life cycle, individuals have a variety of financial goals. **Near-term, high-priority goals** are shorter-term financial objectives that individuals set to fund purchases that are personally important to them, such as accumulating funds to make a house down payment, buy a new car, or take a trip. Parents with teenage children may have a near-term, high-priority goal to accumulate funds to help pay college expenses. Because of the emotional importance of these goals and their short time horizon, high-risk investments are not usually considered suitable for achieving them.

Long-term, high-priority goals typically include some form of financial independence, such as the ability to retire at a certain age. Because of their long-term nature, higher-risk investments can be used to help meet these objectives.

Lower-priority goals are just that—it might be nice to meet these objectives, but it is not critical. Examples include the ability to purchase a new car every few years, redecorate the home with expensive furnishings, or take a long, luxurious vacation.

A well-developed policy statement considers these diverse goals over an investor's lifetime. The following sections detail the process for constructing an investment policy, creating a portfolio that is consistent with the policy and the environment, managing the portfolio, and monitoring its performance relative to its goals and objectives over time.

THE PORTFOLIO MANAGEMENT PROCESS

The process of managing an investment portfolio never stops. Once the funds are initially invested according to the plan, the real work begins in monitoring and updating the status of the portfolio and the investor's needs.

The first step in the portfolio management process, as seen in Exhibit 2.2, is for the investor, either alone or with the assistance of an investment advisor, to construct a **policy statement**. The

EXHIBIT 2.2   *THE PORTFOLIO MANAGEMENT PROCESS*

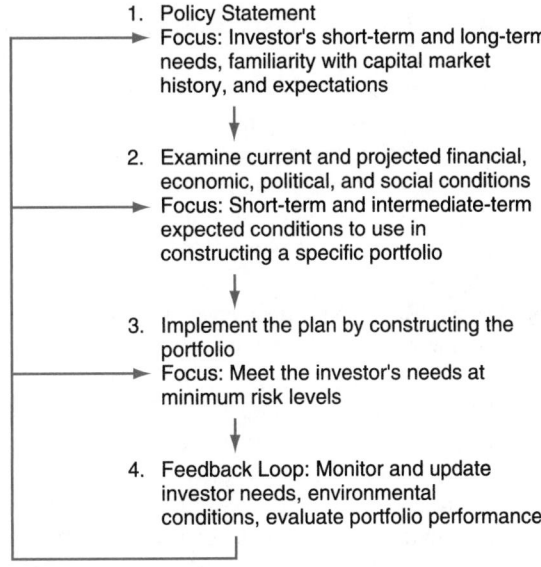

1. Policy Statement
   Focus: Investor's short-term and long-term needs, familiarity with capital market history, and expectations

2. Examine current and projected financial, economic, political, and social conditions
   Focus: Short-term and intermediate-term expected conditions to use in constructing a specific portfolio

3. Implement the plan by constructing the portfolio
   Focus: Meet the investor's needs at minimum risk levels

4. Feedback Loop: Monitor and update investor needs, environmental conditions, evaluate portfolio performance

policy statement is a road map; in it, investors specify the types of risks they are willing to take and their investment goals and constraints. All investment decisions are based on the policy statement to ensure they are appropriate for the investor. We examine the process of constructing a policy statement later in this chapter. Because investor needs change over time, the policy statement must be periodically reviewed and updated.

The process of investing seeks to peer into the future and determine strategies that offer the best possibility of meeting the policy statement guidelines. In the second step of the portfolio management process, the manager should study current financial and economic conditions and forecast future trends. The investor's needs, as reflected in the policy statement, and financial market expectations will jointly determine **investment strategy**. Economies are dynamic; they are affected by numerous industry struggles, politics, and changing demographics and social attitudes. Thus, the portfolio will require constant monitoring and updating to reflect changes in financial market expectations. We examine the process of evaluating and forecasting economic trends in Chapter 12.

The third step of the portfolio management process is to **construct the portfolio**. With the investor's policy statement and financial market forecasts as input, the advisors implement the investment strategy and determine how to allocate available funds across different countries, asset classes, and securities. This involves constructing a portfolio that will minimize the investor's risks while meeting the needs specified in the policy statement. Financial theory frequently assists portfolio construction, as is discussed in Part 2. Some of the practical aspects of selecting investments for inclusion in a portfolio are discussed in Part 4 and Part 5.

The fourth step in the portfolio management process is the **continual monitoring** of the investor's needs and capital market conditions and, when necessary, updating the policy statement. Based upon all of this, the investment strategy is modified accordingly. A component of the monitoring process is to evaluate a portfolio's performance and compare the relative results to the expectations and the requirements listed in the policy statement. The evaluation of portfolio performance is discussed in Chapter 26.

THE NEED FOR A POLICY STATEMENT

As noted in the previous section, a policy statement is a road map that guides the investment process. Constructing a policy statement is an invaluable planning tool that will help the investor understand his or her needs better as well as assist an advisor or portfolio manager in managing a client's funds. While it does not guarantee investment success, a policy statement will provide discipline for the investment process and reduce the possibility of making hasty, inappropriate decisions. There are two important reasons for constructing a policy statement: First, it helps the investor decide on realistic investment goals after learning about the financial markets and the risks of investing. Second, it creates a standard by which to judge the performance of the portfolio manager.

Understand and Articulate Realistic Investor Goals

When asked about their investment goal, people often say, "to make a lot of money," or some similar response. Such a goal has two drawbacks: First, it may not be appropriate for the investor, and second, it is too open-ended to provide guidance for specific investments and time frames. Such an objective is well suited for someone going to the racetrack or buying lottery tickets, but it is inappropriate for someone investing funds in financial and real assets for the long term.

An important purpose of writing a policy statement is to help investors understand their own needs, objectives, and investment constraints. As part of this, investors need to learn about financial markets and the risks of investing. This background will help prevent them from making inappropriate investment decisions in the future and will increase the possibility that they will satisfy their specific, measurable financial goals.

Thus, the policy statement helps the investor to specify realistic goals and become more informed about the risks and costs of investing. Market values of assets, whether they be stocks, bonds, or real estate, can fluctuate dramatically. For example, during the October 1987 crash, the Dow Jones Industrial Average (DJIA) fell more than 20 percent in one day; in October 1997, the Dow fell "only" 7 percent. A review of market history shows that it is not unusual for asset prices to decline by 10 percent to 20 percent over several months—for example, the months following the market peak in March 2000, and the major decline when the market reopened after September 11, 2001. Investors will typically focus on a single statistic, such as an 11 percent average annual rate of return on stocks, and expect the market to rise 11 percent every year. Such thinking ignores the risk of stock investing. Part of the process of developing a policy statement is for the investor to become familiar with the risks of investing, because we know that a strong positive relationship exists between risk and return.

➤ One expert in the field recommends that investors should think about the following set of questions and explain their answers as part of the process of constructing a policy statement:

1. What are the real risks of an adverse financial outcome, especially in the short run?
2. What probable emotional reactions will I have to an adverse financial outcome?
3. How knowledgeable am I about investments and markets?
4. What other capital or income sources do I have? How important is this particular portfolio to my overall financial position?
5. What, if any, legal restrictions may affect my investment needs?
6. What, if any, unanticipated consequences of interim fluctuations in portfolio value might affect my investment policy?

Adapted from Charles D. Ellis, *Investment Policy: How to Win the Loser's Game* (Homewood, Ill.: Dow Jones–Irwin, 1985), 25–26. Reproduced with permission of The McGraw-Hill Companies.

In summary, constructing a policy statement is mainly the investor's responsibility. It is a process whereby investors articulate their realistic needs and goals and become familiar with financial markets and investing risks. Without this information, investors cannot adequately communicate their needs to the portfolio manager. Without this input from investors, the portfolio manager cannot construct a portfolio that will satisfy clients' needs; the result of bypassing this step will most likely be future aggravation, dissatisfaction, and disappointment.

Standards for Evaluating Portfolio Performance

The policy statement also assists in judging the performance of the portfolio manager. Performance cannot be judged without an objective standard; the policy statement provides that objective standard. The portfolio's performance should be compared to guidelines specified in the policy statement, not on the portfolio's overall return. For example, if an investor has a low tolerance for risky investments, the portfolio manager should not be fired simply because the portfolio does not perform as well as the risky S&P 500 stock index. Because risk drives returns, the investor's lower-risk investments, as specified in the investor's policy statement, will probably earn lower returns than if all the investor's funds were placed in the stock market.

The policy statement will typically include a **benchmark portfolio,** or comparison standard. The risk of the benchmark, and the assets included in the benchmark, should agree with the client's risk preferences and investment needs. Notably, both the client and the portfolio manager must agree that the benchmark portfolio reflects the risk preferences and appropriate return requirements of the client. In turn, the investment performance of the portfolio manager should be compared to this benchmark portfolio. For example, an investor who specifies low-risk investments in the policy statement should compare the portfolio manager's performance against a low-risk benchmark portfolio. Likewise, an investor seeking high-risk, high-return investments should compare the portfolio's performance against a high-risk benchmark portfolio.

Because it sets an objective performance standard, the policy statement acts as a starting point for periodic portfolio review and client communication with managers. Questions concerning portfolio performance or the manager's faithfulness to the policy can be addressed in the context of the written policy guidelines. Managers should mainly be judged by whether they consistently followed the client's policy guidelines. The portfolio manager who makes unilateral deviations from policy is not working in the best interests of the client. Therefore, even deviations that result in higher portfolio returns can and should be grounds for the manager's dismissal.

Thus, we see the importance of the client constructing the policy statement: The client must first understand his or her own needs before communicating them to the portfolio manager. In turn, the portfolio manager must implement the client's desires by following the investment guidelines. As long as policy is followed, shortfalls in performance should not be a major concern. Remember that the policy statement is designed to impose an investment discipline on the client and portfolio manager. The less knowledgeable they are, the more likely clients are to inappropriately judge the performance of the portfolio manager.

Other Benefits

A sound policy statement helps to protect the client against a portfolio manager's inappropriate investments or unethical behavior. Without clear, written guidance, some managers may consider investing in high-risk investments, hoping to earn a quick return. Such actions are probably counter to the investor's specified needs and risk preferences. Though legal recourse is a possibility against such action, writing a clear and unambiguous policy statement should reduce the possibility of such innappropriate manager behavior.

Just because one specific manager currently manages your account does not mean that person will always manage your funds. As with other positions, your portfolio manager may be promoted or dismissed or take a better job. Therefore, after a while, your funds may come under the management of an individual you do not know and who does not know you. To prevent costly delays during this transition, you can ensure that the new manager "hits the ground running" with a clearly written policy statement. A policy statement should prevent delays in monitoring and rebalancing your portfolio and will help create a seamless transition from one money manager to another.

To sum up, a clearly written policy statement helps avoid future potential problems. When the client clearly specifies his or her needs and desires, the portfolio manager can more effectively construct an appropriate portfolio. The policy statement provides an objective measure for evaluating portfolio performance, helps guard against ethical lapses by the portfolio manager, and aids in the transition between money managers. Therefore, the first step before beginning any investment program, whether it is for an individual or a multibillion-dollar pension fund, is to construct a policy statement.

➤ An appropriate policy statement should satisfactorily answer the following questions:

1. Is the policy carefully designed to meet the specific needs and objectives of this particular investor? (Cookie-cutter or one-size-fits-all policy statements are generally inappropriate.)
2. Is the policy written so clearly and explicitly that a competent stranger could use it to manage the portfolio in conformance with the client's needs? In case of a manager transition, could the new manager use this policy statement to handle your portfolio in accordance with your needs?
3. Would the client have been able to remain committed to the policies during the capital market experiences of the past 60 to 70 years? That is, does the client fully understand investment risks and the need for a disciplined approach to the investment process?
4. Would the portfolio manager have been able to maintain the policies specified over the same period? (Discipline is a two-way street; we do not want the portfolio manager to change strategies because of a disappointing market.)
5. Would the policy, if implemented, have achieved the client's objectives? (Bottom line: Would the policy have worked to meet the client's needs?)

Adapted from Charles D. Ellis, *Investment Policy: How to Win the Loser's Game* (Homewood, Ill.: Dow Jones–Irwin, 1985), 62. Reproduced with permission of The McGraw-Hill Companies.

INPUT TO THE POLICY STATEMENT

Before an investor and advisor can construct a policy statement, they need to have an open and frank exchange of information, ideas, fears, and goals. To build a framework for this information-gathering process, the client and advisor need to discuss the client's investment objectives and constraints. To illustrate this framework, we discuss the investment objectives and constraints that may confront "typical" 25-year-old and 65-year-old investors.

Investment Objectives
The investor's **objectives** are his or her investment goals expressed in terms of both risk and returns. The relationship between risk and returns requires that goals not be expressed only in terms of returns. Expressing goals only in terms of returns can lead to inappropriate investment practices by the portfolio manager, such as the use of high-risk investment strategies or account "churning," which involves moving quickly in and out of investments in an attempt to buy low and sell high.

For example, a person may have a stated return goal such as "double my investment in five years." Before such a statement becomes part of the policy statement, the client must become

| EXHIBIT 2.3 | RISK CATEGORIES AND SUGGESTED ASSET ALLOCATIONS FOR MERRILL LYNCH CLIENTS |

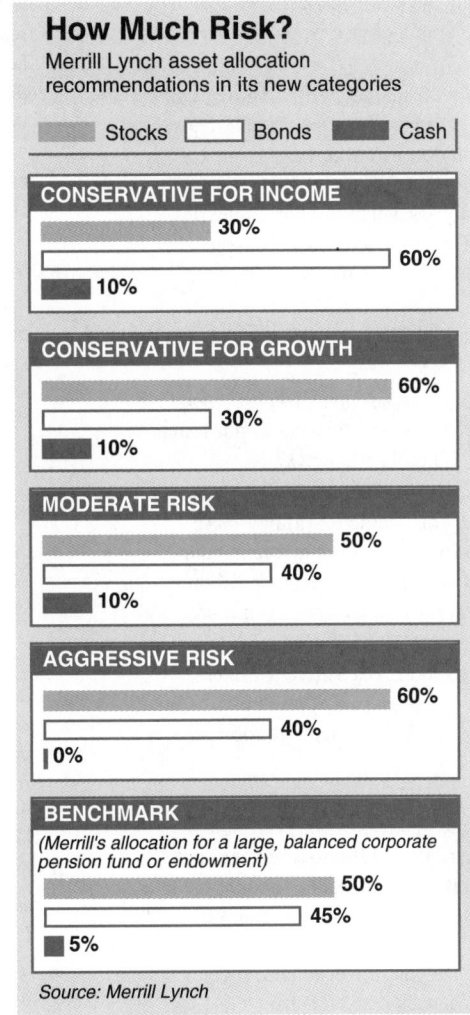

Source: Merrill Lynch

Source: William Power, "Merrill Lynch to Ask Investors to Pick a Risk Category," *The Wall Street Journal,* 2 July 1990, C1. Reprinted with permission of *The Wall Street Journal,* Dow Jones and Co., Inc. All rights reserved.

fully informed of investment risks associated with such a goal, including the possibility of loss. *A careful analysis of the client's risk tolerance should precede any discussion of return objectives.* It makes little sense for a person who is risk averse to invest funds in high-risk assets. Investment firms survey clients to gauge their risk tolerance. For example, Merrill Lynch has asked its clients to place themselves in one of the four categories in Exhibit 2.3. Sometimes investment magazines or books contain tests that individuals can take to help them evaluate their risk tolerance (see Exhibit 2.4).

Risk tolerance is more than a function of an individual's psychological makeup; it is affected by other factors, including a person's current insurance coverage and cash reserves. Risk tolerance is also affected by an individual's family situation (for example, marital status and the number and ages of children) and by his or her age. We know that older persons generally have

EXHIBIT 2.4 ▶ *HOW MUCH RISK IS RIGHT FOR YOU?*

You've heard the expression "no pain, no gain"? In the investment world, the comparable phrase would be "no risk, no reward."

How you feel about risking your money will drive many of your investment decisions. The risk-comfort scale extends from very conservative (you don't want to risk losing a penny regardless of how little your money earns) to very aggressive (you're willing to risk much of your money for the possibility that it will grow tremendously). As you might guess, most investors' tolerance for risk falls somewhere in between.

If you're unsure of what your level of risk tolerance is, this quiz should help.

1. You win $300 in an office football pool. You: (a) spend it on groceries, (b) purchase lottery tickets, (c) put it in a money market account, (d) buy some stock.

2. Two weeks after buying 100 shares of a $20 stock, the price jumps to over $30. You decide to: (a) buy more stock; it's obviously a winner, (b) sell it and take your profits, (c) sell half to recoup some costs and hold the rest, (d) sit tight and wait for it to advance even more.

3. On days when the stock market jumps way up, you: (a) wish you had invested more, (b) call your financial advisor and ask for recommendations, (c) feel glad you're not in the market because it fluctuates too much, (d) pay little attention.

4. You're planning a vacation trip and can either lock in a fixed room-and-meals rate of $150 per day or book standby and pay anywhere from $100 to $300 per day. You: (a) take the fixed-rate deal, (b) talk to people who have been there about the availability of last-minute accommodations, (c) book standby and also arrange vacation insurance because you're leery of the tour operator, (d) take your chances with standby.

5. The owner of your apartment building is converting the units to condominiums. You can buy your unit for $75,000 or an option on a unit for $15,000. (Units have recently sold for close to $100,000, and prices seem to be going up.) For financing, you'll have to borrow the down payment and pay mortgage and condo fees higher than your present rent. You: (a) buy your unit, (b) buy your unit and look for another to buy, (c) sell the option and arrange to rent the unit yourself, (d) sell the option and move out because you think the conversion will attract couples with small children.

6. You have been working three years for a rapidly growing company. As an executive, you are offered the option of buying up to 2% of company stock: 2,000 shares at $10 a share. Although the company is privately owned (its stock does not trade on the open market), its majority owner has made handsome profits selling three other businesses and intends to sell this one eventually. You: (a) purchase all the shares you can and tell the owner you would invest more if allowed, (b) purchase all the shares, (c) purchase half the shares, (d) purchase a small amount of shares.

7. You go to a casino for the first time. You choose to play: (a) quarter slot machines, (b) $5 minimum-bet roulette, (c) dollar slot machine, (d) $25 minimum-bet blackjack.

8. You want to take someone out for a special dinner in a city that's new to you. How do you pick a place? (a) read restaurant reviews in the local newspaper, (b) ask coworkers if they know of a suitable place, (c) call the only other person you know in this city, who eats out a lot but only recently moved there, (d) visit the city sometime before your dinner to check out the restaurants yourself.

9. The expression that best describes your lifestyle is: (a) no guts, no glory, (b) just do it!, (c) look before you leap, (d) all good things come to those who wait.

10. Your attitude toward money is best described as: (a) a dollar saved is a dollar earned, (b) you've got to spend money to make money, (c) cash and carry only, (d) whenever possible, use other people's money.

SCORING SYSTEM: Score your answers this way: (1) a-1, b-4, c-2, d-3 (2) a-4, b-1, c-3, d-2 (3) a-3, b-4, c-2, d-1 (4) a-2, b-3 c-1, d-4 (5) a-3, b-4, c-2, d-1 (6) a-4, b-3, c-2, d-1 (7) a-1, b-3, c-2, d-4 (8) a-2, b-3, c-4, d-1 (9), a-4, b-3, c-2, d-1 (10) a-2, b-3, c-1, d-4.

What your total score indicates:

■ 10–17: You're not willing to take chances with your money, even though it means you can't make big gains.

■ 18–25: You're semi-conservative, willing to take a small chance with enough information.

■ 24–32: You're semi-aggressive, willing to take chances if you think the odds of earning more are in your favor.

■ 33–40: You're aggressive, looking for every opportunity to make your money grow, even though in some cases the odds may be quite long. You view money as a tool to make more money.

---

shorter investment time frames within which to make up any losses; they also have years of experience, including living through various market gyrations and "corrections" (a euphemism for downtrends or crashes) that younger people have not experienced or whose effect they do not fully appreciate. Risk tolerance is also influenced by one's current net worth and income expectations. All else being equal, individuals with higher incomes have a greater propensity to undertake risk because their incomes can help cover any shortfall. Likewise, individuals with larger net worths can afford to place some assets in risky investments while the remaining assets provide a cushion against losses.

A person's return objective may be stated in terms of an absolute or a relative percentage return, but it may also be stated in terms of a general goal, such as capital preservation, current income, capital appreciation, or total return.

Capital preservation means that investors want to minimize their risk of loss, usually in real terms: They seek to maintain the purchasing power of their investment. In other words, the return needs to be no less than the rate of inflation. Generally, this is a strategy for strongly risk-averse investors or for funds needed in the short-run, such as for next year's tuition payment or a down payment on a house.

Capital appreciation is an appropriate objective when the investors want the portfolio to grow in real terms over time to meet some future need. Under this strategy, growth mainly occurs through capital gains. This is an aggressive strategy for investors willing to take on risk to meet their objective. Generally, longer-term investors seeking to build a retirement or college education fund may have this goal.

When **current income** is the return objective, the investors want the portfolio to concentrate on generating income rather than capital gains. This strategy sometimes suits investors who want to supplement their earnings with income generated by their portfolio to meet their living expenses. Retirees may favor this objective for part of their portfolio to help generate spendable funds.

The objective for the **total return** strategy is similar to that of capital appreciation; namely, the investors want the portfolio to grow over time to meet a future need. Whereas the capital appreciation strategy seeks to do this primarily through capital gains, the total return strategy seeks to increase portfolio value by both capital gains and reinvesting current income. Because the total return strategy has both income and capital gains components, its risk exposure lies between that of the current income and capital appreciation strategies.

Investment Objective: 25-Year-Old

What is an appropriate investment objective for our typical 25-year-old investor? Assume he holds a steady job, is a valued employee, has adequate insurance coverage, and has enough money in the bank to provide a cash reserve. Let's also assume that his current long-term, high-priority investment goal is to build a retirement fund. Depending on his risk preferences, he can select a strategy carrying moderate to high amounts of risk because the income stream from his job will probably grow over time. Further, given his young age and income growth potential, a low-risk strategy, such as capital preservation or current income, is inappropriate for his retirement fund goal; a total return or capital appreciation objective would be most appropriate. Here's a possible objective statement:

> Invest funds in a variety of moderate- to higher-risk investments. The average risk of the equity portfolio should exceed that of a broad stock market index, such as the NYSE stock index. Foreign and domestic equity exposure should range from 80 percent to 95 percent of the total portfolio. Remaining funds should be invested in short- and intermediate-term notes and bonds.

Investment Objective: 65-Year-Old

Assume our typical 65-year-old investor likewise has adequate insurance coverage and a cash reserve. Let's also assume she is retiring this year. This individual will want less risk exposure than the 25-year-old investor, because her earning power from employment will soon be ending; she will not be able to recover any investment losses by saving more out of her paycheck. Depending on her income from social security and a pension plan, she may need some current income from her retirement portfolio to meet living expenses. Given that she can be expected to live an average of another 20 years, she will need protection against inflation. A risk-averse investor will choose a combination of current income and capital preservation strategy; a more risk-tolerant investor will choose a combination of current income and total return in an attempt to have principal growth outpace inflation. Here's an example of such an objective statement:

> Invest in stock and bond investments to meet income needs (from bond income and stock dividends) and to provide for real growth (from equities). Fixed-income securities should comprise 55–65 percent of the total portfolio; of this, 5–15 percent should be invested in short-term securities for extra liquidity and safety. The remaining 35–45 percent of the portfolio should be invested in high-quality stocks whose risk is similar to the S&P 500 index.

More detailed analyses for our 25-year-old and our 65-year-old would make more specific assumptions about the risk tolerance of each, as well as clearly enumerate their investment goals, return objectives, the funds they have to invest at the present, the funds they expect to invest over time, and the benchmark portfolio that will be used to evaluate performance.

Investment Constraints

In addition to the investment objective that sets limits on risk and return, certain other constraints also affect the investment plan. Investment constraints include liquidity needs, an investment time horizon, tax factors, legal and regulatory constraints, and unique needs and preferences.

Liquidity Needs

An asset is **liquid** if it can be quickly converted to cash at a price close to fair market value. Generally, assets are more liquid if many traders are interested in a fairly standardized product. Treasury bills are a highly liquid security; real estate and venture capital are not.

Investors may have liquidity needs that the investment plan must consider. For example, although an investor may have a primary long-term goal, several near-term goals may require available funds. Wealthy individuals with sizable tax obligations need adequate liquidity to pay their taxes without upsetting their investment plan. Some retirement plans may need funds for shorter-term purposes, such as buying a car or a house or making college tuition payments.

Our typical 25-year-old investor probably has little need for liquidity as he focuses on his long-term retirement fund goal. This constraint may change, however, should he face a period of unemployment or should near-term goals, such as honeymoon expenses or a house down payment, enter the picture. Should any changes occur, the investor needs to revise his policy statement and financial plans accordingly.

Our soon-to-be-retired 65-year-old investor has a greater need for liquidity. Although she may receive regular checks from her pension plan and social security, it is not likely that they will equal her working paycheck. She will want some of her portfolio in liquid securities to meet unexpected expenses or bills.

Time Horizon

Time horizon as an investment constraint briefly entered our earlier discussion of near-term and long-term high-priority goals. A close (but not perfect) relationship exists between an investor's time horizon, liquidity needs, and ability to handle risk. Investors with long investment horizons generally require less liquidity and can tolerate greater portfolio risk: less liquidity because the funds are not usually needed for many years; greater risk tolerance because any shortfalls or losses can be overcome by returns earned in subsequent years.

Investors with shorter time horizons generally favor more liquid and less risky investments because losses are harder to overcome during a short time frame.

EXHIBIT 2.5 *INDIVIDUAL MARGINAL TAX RATES, 2001*

	TAXABLE INCOME	TAX	PERCENT ON EXCESS
Married Filing Jointly	$ 0	$ 0.00	15%
	45,200	6,780.00	28
	109,250	24,714.00	31
	166,450	42,446.00	36
	297,300	89,552.00	39.6
Single	$ 0	$ 0.00	15%
	27,050	4,057.50	28
	65,550	14,837.50	31
	136,750	36,909.50	36
	297,300	94,707.50	39.6
Head of Household	$ 0	$ 0.00	15%
	36,250	5,437.50	28
	93,600	21,495.50	31
	151,600	39,475.50	36
	297,300	91,927.50	39.6
Married Filing Separately	$ 0	$ 0.00	15%
	22,600	3,390.00	28
	54,625	12,357.00	31
	83,225	21,223.00	36
	148,650	44,776.00	39.6

Because of life expectancies, our 25-year-old investor has a longer investment time horizon than our 65-year-old investor. But, as discussed earlier, this does not mean the 65-year-old should put all her money in short-term CDs; she needs the inflation protection that long-term investments, such as common stock, can provide. Still, because of the differing time horizons, the 25-year-old will probably have a greater proportion of his portfolio in equities, including stocks in growth companies, small firms, or international firms, than the 65-year-old.

Tax Concerns   Investment planning is complicated by the tax code; taxes complicate the situation even more if international investments are part of the portfolio. Taxable income from interest, dividends, or rents is taxable at the investor's marginal tax rate. The marginal tax rate is the proportion of the next one dollar in income paid as taxes. Exhibit 2.5 shows the marginal tax rates for different levels of taxable income. As of 2001, the top federal marginal tax rate was 39.6 percent. Under the provisions of the 2001 tax relief act, the top marginal rate will decline to 35 percent by 2006. State taxes make the tax bite even higher.

Capital gains or losses arise from asset price changes. They are taxed differently than income. Income is taxed when it is received; capital gains or losses are taxed only when the asset is sold and the gain or loss is realized. **Unrealized capital gains** reflect the price appreciation of currently held assets that have *not* been sold; the tax liability on unrealized capital gains can be deferred indefinitely. Capital gains only become taxable after the asset has been sold for a price higher than its cost, or **basis**. If appreciated assets are passed on to an heir upon the investor's death, the basis of the assets is considered to be their value on the date of the holder's death. The heirs can then sell the assets and not pay capital gains tax. Capital gains taxes are paid on **realized capital gains.** Beginning in 2001, gains on assets purchased after January 1, 2001, and held for at least five years will be only 18 percent. For taxpayers in the 15 percent income tax bracket, the capital gains tax rate fell to 8 percent on assets held longer than five years.

Sometimes it is necessary to make a trade-off between taxes and diversification needs. If entrepreneurs concentrate much of their wealth in equity holdings of their firm, or if employees purchase substantial amounts of their employer's stock through payroll deduction plans during their working life, their portfolios may contain a large amount of unrealized capital gains. In addition, the risk position of such a portfolio may be quite high because it is concentrated in a single company. The decision to sell some of the company stock in order to diversify the portfolio's risk by reinvesting the proceeds in other assets must be balanced against the resulting tax liability. To attain the prudent diversification, one should consider making the change over time.

Some find the difference between average and marginal income tax rates confusing. The **marginal tax rate** is the part of each additional dollar in income that is paid as tax. Thus, a married person, filing jointly, with an income of $50,000 will have a marginal tax rate of 28 percent. The 28 percent marginal tax rate should be used to determine after-tax returns on investments.

The **average tax rate** is simply a person's total tax payment divided by his or her total income. It represents the average tax paid on each dollar the person earned. From Exhibit 2.5, a married person, filing jointly, will pay $8,124 in tax on a $50,000 income [$6,780 plus 0.28($50,000 − $45,200)]. His or her average tax rate is $8,124/$50,000 or 16.25 percent.

Note that the average tax rate is a weighted average of the person's marginal tax rates paid on each dollar of income. The first $45,200 of income has a marginal tax rate of 15 percent; the next $4,800 has a 28 percent marginal tax rate:

$$\frac{\$45,200}{\$50,000} \times 0.15 + \frac{\$\ 4,800}{\$50,000} \times .28 = 0.1625, \text{ or the Average Tax Rate of } 16.25\%$$

Another tax factor is that some sources of income are exempt from federal and state taxes. Interest on federal securities, such as Treasury bills, notes, and bonds, is exempt from state taxes. Interest on municipal bonds (bonds issued by a state or other local governing body) are exempt from federal taxes. Further, if the investor purchases municipal bonds issued by a local governing body of the state in which they live, the interest is usually exempt from both state and federal income tax. Thus, high-income individuals have an incentive to purchase municipal bonds to reduce their tax liabilities.

The after-tax return on a taxable investment is:

$$\text{After-Tax Return} = \text{Pre-Tax Return} (1 - \text{Marginal Tax Rate})$$

Thus, the after-tax return on a taxable investment should be compared to that on municipals before deciding which should be purchased by a tax-paying investor. Alternatively, a municipal's equivalent taxable yield can be computed. The equivalent taxable yield is what a taxable bond investment would have to offer to produce the same after-tax return as the municipal. It is given by:

$$\text{Equivalent Taxable Yield} = \frac{\text{Municipal Yield}}{1 - \text{Marginal Tax Rate}}$$

To illustrate, if an investor is in the 28 percent marginal tax bracket, a taxable investment yield of 8 percent has an after-tax yield of 8 percent × (1 − 0.28), or 5.76 percent; an equivalent-risk municipal security offering a yield greater than 5.76 percent offers the investor greater after-tax returns. On the other hand, a municipal bond yielding 6 percent has an equivalent taxable yield of

$$6\%/(1 - 0.28) = 8.33\%$$

To earn more money after taxes, an equivalent-risk taxable investment has to offer a return greater than 8.33 percent.

Other means to reduce tax liabilities are available. Contributions to an individual retirement account (IRA) may qualify as a tax deduction if certain income limits are met. The investment returns of the IRA investment, including any income, are deferred until the funds are withdrawn from the account. Any funds withdrawn from an IRA are taxable as current income, regardless of whether growth in the IRA occurs as a result of capital gains, income, or both. The benefits of deferring taxes can dramatically compound over time. Exhibit 2.6 illustrates how $1,000 invested in an IRA at a tax-deferred rate of 8 percent grows compared to funds invested in a taxable investment that returns (from bond income) 8 percent pre-tax. For an investor in the 28 percent bracket, this taxable investment grows at an after-tax rate of 5.76 percent. After 30 years, the value of the tax-deferred investment is nearly twice that of the taxable investment.

Tax-deductible contributions of up to $2,000 (which is raised, in phases, to $5,000 under the 2001 tax act) can made to a regular IRA. The Tax Reform Act of 1997 created the Roth IRA. The Roth IRA contribution, although not tax deductible, allows up to $2,000 (to be raised to $5,000) to be invested each year; the returns on this investment will grow on a tax-deferred basis and can be withdrawn, tax-free, if the funds are invested for at least five years and are withdrawn

| EXHIBIT 2.6 | *EFFECT OF TAX DEFERRAL ON INVESTOR WEALTH OVER TIME* |

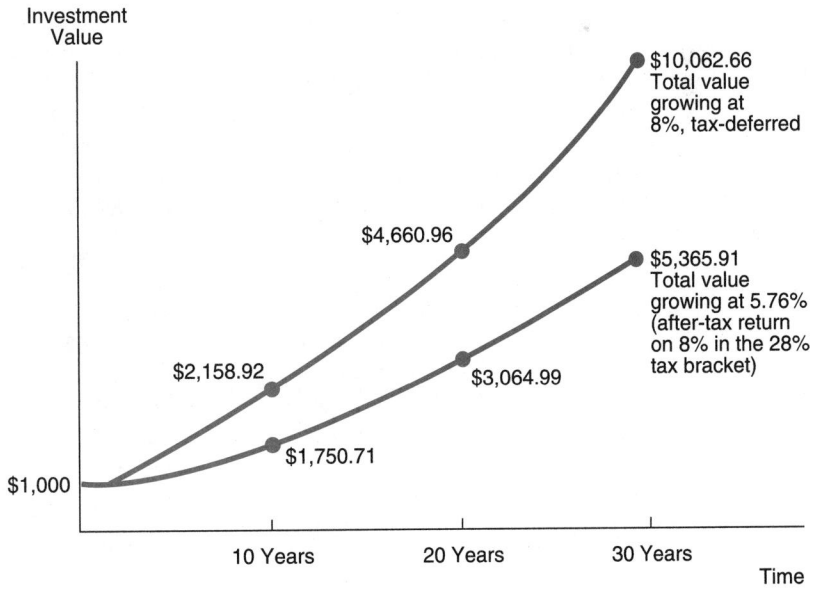

after the investor reaches age 59½.[1] The Roth IRA is subject to limitations based on the investor's annual income, but the income ceiling is much higher than that for the regular IRA.

For money you intend to invest in some type of IRA, the advantage of the Roth IRA's tax-free withdrawals will outweigh the tax-deduction benefit from the regular IRA—unless you expect your tax rate when the funds are withdrawn to be substantially less than when you initially invest the funds.[2]

Tax questions can puzzle the most astute minds. For example, depending on one's situation, it may be best to hold stock in taxable rather than in tax-deferred accounts, such as IRAs, company retirement plans, and variable annuities, mainly because earnings on such tax-deferred accounts are taxed as ordinary income when the funds are withdrawn. Even if most of the growth in a tax-deferred equity investment arises from capital gains, the withdrawals will be taxed at the higher ordinary income tax rate. Stocks held in taxable accounts will likely have large capital gains tax liability over the years; thus, after the 1997 Tax Reform Act's slashing of realized capital gains tax rates, taxable equity accounts may offer better after-tax return potential than tax-deferred investments. This will not be true in all cases. The point is, any analysis must consider each investor's return, time horizon, and tax assumptions.[3]

Other tax-deferred investments include cash values of life insurance contracts that accumulate tax-free until the funds are withdrawn. Employers may offer employees 401(k) or 403(b) plans, which allow the employee to reduce taxable income by making tax-deferred investments; many times employee contributions are matched by employer donations (up to a specified limit), thus allowing the employees to double their investment with little risk!

Our typical 25-year-old investor probably is in a fairly low tax bracket, so detailed tax planning will not be a major concern, and tax-exempt income, such as that available from municipals, will also not be a concern. Nonetheless, he should still invest as much as possible into tax-deferred plans, such as an IRA or a 401(k). The drawback to such investments, however, is that early withdrawals (before age 59½) are taxable and subject to an additional 10 percent early withdrawal tax. Should the liquidity constraint of these plans be too restrictive, the young investor should probably consider total-return- or capital-appreciation-oriented mutual funds.

Our 65-year-old retiree may face a different situation. If she is in a high tax bracket prior to retiring—and therefore has sought tax-exempt income and tax-deferred investments—her situation may change shortly after retirement. Without large, regular paychecks, the need for tax-deferred investments or tax-exempt income becomes less. Taxable income may now offer higher after-tax yields than tax-exempt municipals due to the investor's lower tax bracket. Should her employer's stock be a large component of her retirement account, careful decisions must be made regarding the need to diversify versus the cost of realizing large capital gains (in her lower tax bracket).

Legal and Regulatory Factors As you might expect, the investment process and financial markets are highly regulated. At times, these legal and regulatory factors constrain the investment strategies of individuals and institutions.

In our discussion about taxes, we mentioned one such constraint: Funds removed from a regular IRA account or 401(k) plan before age 59½ are taxable and subject to an additional

---

[1]Earlier tax-free withdrawals are possible if the funds are to be used for educational purposes or first-time home purchases.

[2]For additional insights, see Jonathan Clements, "Jam Today or Jam Tomorrow? Roth IRA Will Show Many Investors It Pays to Wait," *The Wall Street Journal,* 16 September 1997, C1.

[3]Terry Sylvester Charron, "Tax Efficient Investing for Tax-Deferred and Taxable Accounts," *Journal of Private Portfolio Management* 2, no. 2 (Fall 1999): 31–37.

10 percent withdrawal penalty. You may also be familiar with the tag line in many bank CD advertisements—"substantial interest penalty upon early withdrawal." Such regulations may make such investments unattractive for investors with substantial liquidity needs in their portfolios.

Regulations can also constrain the investment choices available to someone in a **fiduciary** role. A fiduciary, or trustee, supervises an investment portfolio of a third party, such as a trust account or discretionary account.[4] The fiduciary must make investment decisions in accordance with the owner's wishes; a properly written policy statement assists this process. In addition, trustees of a trust account must meet the "prudent-man" standard, which means that they must invest and manage the funds as a prudent person would manage his or her own affairs. Notably, the prudent-man standard is based on the composition of the entire portfolio, not each individual asset in the portfolio.[5]

All investors must respect some laws, such as insider trading prohibitions. Insider trading involves the purchase and sale of securities on the basis of important information that is not publicly known. Typically, the people possessing such private or inside information are the firm's managers, who have a fiduciary duty to their shareholders. Security transactions based on access to inside information violate the fiduciary trust the shareholders have placed with management, because the managers seek personal financial gain from their privileged position as agents for the shareholders.

For our typical 25-year-old investor, legal and regulatory matters will be of little concern, with the possible exception of insider trading laws and the penalties associated with early withdrawal of funds from tax-deferred retirement accounts. Should he seek a financial advisor to assist him in constructing a financial plan, the financial advisor would have to obey the regulations pertinent to a client-advisor relationship.

Similar concerns confront our 65-year-old investor. In addition, as a retiree, if she wants to do some estate planning and set up trust accounts, she should seek legal and tax advice to ensure her plans are properly specified and implemented.

Unique Needs and Preferences   This category covers the individual concerns of each investor. Some investors may want to exclude certain investments from their portfolio solely on the basis of personal preferences. For example, they may request that no firms that manufacture or sell tobacco, alcohol, pornography, or environmentally harmful products be included in their portfolio. As of 2001, over 200 mutual funds include at least one social-responsibility criterion.

Another example of a personal constraint is the time and expertise a person has for managing his or her portfolio. Busy executives may prefer to relax during nonworking hours and let a trusted advisor manage their investments. Retirees, on the other hand, may have the time but believe they lack the expertise to choose and monitor investments, so they may also seek professional advice.

Some of the constraints we previously discussed can also be considered as unique needs and preferences. For example, consider the businessperson with a large portion of his wealth tied up in his firm's stock. Though it may be financially prudent to sell some of the firm's stock and reinvest the proceeds for diversification purposes, it may be hard for the individual to approve such a strategy due to emotional ties to the firm. Further, if the stock holdings are in a private company, it may be difficult to find a buyer except if shares are sold at a discount from their fair market value.

---

[4]A discretionary account is one in which the fiduciary, many times a financial planner or stockbroker, has the authority to purchase and sell assets in the owner's portfolio without first receiving the owner's approval.

[5]As we will discuss in Chapter 7, it is sometimes wise to hold assets that are individually risky in the context of a well-diversified portfolio, even if the investor is strongly risk averse.

Because each investor is unique, the implications of this final constraint differ for each person; there is no "typical" 25-year-old or 65-year-old investor. Each individual will have to communicate specific goals in a well-constructed policy statement.

Institutional investors (endowments, pension funds, and the like) also need to have investment policy statements. Factors considered by institutional investors when developing policy statements are found in the chapter appendix.

Constructing the Policy Statement

A policy statement allows the investor to determine what factors are personally important for the investor's objectives (risk and return) and constraints (liquidity, time horizon, tax factors, legal and regulatory constraints, and unique needs and preferences). To do without a policy statement is to place the success of the financial plan in jeopardy. In contrast, having a policy statement allows the investor to communicate these needs to the advisor who can do a better job of constructing an investment strategy to satisfy the investor's objectives and constraints.

Surveys show that fewer than 40 percent of employees who participate in their firm's retirement savings plan have a good understanding of the value of diversification, the harmful effect of inflation on one's savings, or the relationship between risk and return. Because of this lack of investment expertise, the market for financial planning services and education is a growth industry.

Participants in employer-sponsored retirement plans have invested an average of 30–40 percent of their retirement funds in their employer's stock. Having so much money invested in one asset violates diversification principles. To put this in context, most mutual funds are limited to having no more than 5 percent of their assets in any one company's stock; a firm's pension plan can invest no more than 10 percent of its funds in the firm's stock. Thus, individuals are unfortunately doing what government regulations prevent many institutional investors from doing.[6] Other studies point out that the average stock allocation in retirement plans is lower than it should be to allow for growth of principal over time.

Studies of retirement plans show that Americans are not saving enough to finance their retirement years and they are not planning sufficiently for what will happen to their savings after they retire.[7] Americans are saving at about one-half the rate needed to finance their retirement. This poor savings rate, coupled with lack of diversification and lack of equity growth potential in their portfolios, can lead to disappointments in one's retirement years.

THE IMPORTANCE OF ASSET ALLOCATION

A major reason why investors develop policy statements is to determine an overall investment strategy. Though a policy statement does not indicate which specific securities to purchase and when they should be sold, it should provide guidelines as to the asset classes to include and the relative proportions of the investor's funds to invest in each class. How the investor divides funds into different asset classes is the process of asset allocation. Rather than present strict percentages, asset allocation is usually expressed in ranges. This allows the investment manager some freedom, based on his or her reading of capital market trends, to invest toward the upper or lower end of the ranges. For example, suppose a policy statement requires that common stocks be 60 percent to 80 percent of the value of the portfolio and that bonds should be 20 percent to 40 percent of

---

[6]Ellen R. Schultz, "Workers Put Too Much in Their Employer's Stock," *The Wall Street Journal,* 13 September 1996, C1, C25.

[7]Glenn Ruffenach, "Fewer Americans Save for Their Retirement, *"The Wall Street Journal,* 10 May 2001, A2; Jonathan Clements, "Retirement Honing: How Much Should You Have Saved for a Comfortable Life?" *The Wall Street Journal,* 28 January 1997, C1; Jonathan Clements, "Squeezing the Right Amount from a Retirement Stash," *The Wall Street Journal,* 25 February 1997, C1.

the portfolio's value. If a manager is particularly bullish about stocks, she will increase the allocation of stocks toward the 80 percent upper end of the equity range and decrease bonds toward the 20 percent lower end of the bond range. Should she be more optimistic about bonds, that manager may shift the allocation closer to 40 percent of the funds invested in bonds with the remainder in equities.

A review of historical data and empirical studies provides strong support for the contention that the asset allocation decision is a critical component of the portfolio management process. In general, four decisions are made when constructing an investment strategy:

➤ What asset classes should be considered for investment?
➤ What normal or policy weights should be assigned to each eligible asset class?
➤ What are the allowable allocation ranges based on policy weights?
➤ What specific securities should be purchased for the portfolio?

The asset allocation decision comprises the first two points. How important is the asset allocation decision to an investor? In a word, *very*. Several studies have examined the effect of the normal policy weights on investment performance, using data from both pension funds and mutual funds, from periods of time extending from the early 1970s to the late 1990s.[8] The studies all found similar results: About 90 percent of a fund's returns over time can be explained by its target asset allocation policy. Exhibit 2.7 shows the relationship between returns on the target or policy portfolio allocation and actual returns on a sample mutual fund.

Rather than looking at just one fund and how the target asset allocation determines its returns, some studies have looked at how much the asset allocation policy affects returns on a variety of funds with different target weights. For example, Ibbotson and Kaplan (see Footnote 8) found that, across a sample of funds, about 40 percent of the difference in fund returns is explained by differences in asset allocation policy. And what does asset allocation tell us about the *level* of a particular fund's returns? The studies by Brinson and colleagues and Ibbotson and Kaplan (Footnote 8) answered that question as well. They divided the policy return (what the fund return would have been had it been invested in indexes at the policy weights) by the actual fund return (which includes the effects of varying from the policy weights and security selection). Thus, a fund that was passively invested at the target weights would have a ratio value of 1.0, or 100 percent. A fund managed by someone with skill in market timing (for moving in and out of asset classes) and security selection would have a ratio less than 1.0 (or less than 100 percent); the manager's skill would result in a policy return less than the actual fund return. The studies showed the opposite: The policy return/actual return ratio averaged over 1.0, showing that asset allocation explains slightly more than 100 percent of the level of a fund's returns. Because of market efficiency, fund managers practicing market timing and security selection, on average, have difficulty surpassing passively invested index returns, after taking into account the expenses and fees of investing.

Thus, asset allocation is a very important decision. Across all funds, the asset allocation decision explains an average of 40 percent of the variation in fund returns. For a single fund, asset allocation explains 90 percent of the fund's variation in returns over time and slightly more than 100 percent of the average fund's level of return.

Good investment managers may add some value to portfolio performance, but the major source of investment return—and risk—over time is the asset allocation decision. Investors who

[8]Findings discussed in this section are based on Roger G. Ibbotson and Paul D. Kaplan, "Does Asset Allocation Policy Explain 40, 90, or 100 Percent of Performance?" *Financial Analysts Journal* 56, no. 1 (January–February 2000): 26–33; Gary P. Brinson, Brian D. Singer, and Gilbert L. Beebower, "Determinants of Portfolio Performance II: An Update," *Financial Analysts Journal* 47, no. 3 (May–June 1991): 40–48; Gary P. Brinson, L. Randolph Hood, and Gilbert L. Beebower, "Determinants of Portfolio Performance," *Financial Analysts Journal* 42, no. 4 (July–August 1986): 39–48.

EXHIBIT 2.7

TIME-SERIES REGRESSION OF MONTHLY FUND RETURN VERSUS FUND POLICY RETURN: ONE MUTUAL FUND, APRIL 1988–MARCH 1998

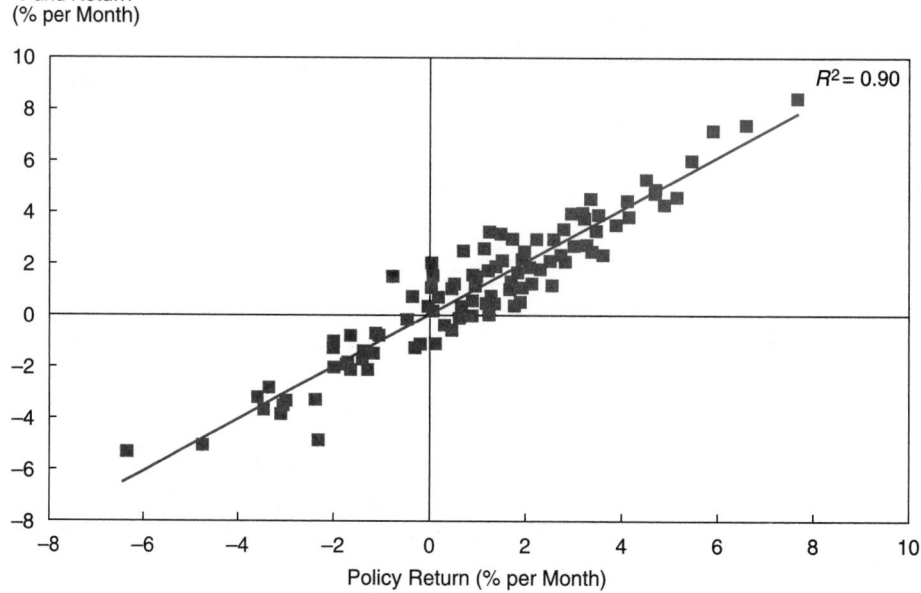

Note: The sample fund's policy allocations among the general asset classes were 52.4 percent U.S. large-cap stocks, 9.8 percent U.S. small-cap stocks, 32 percent non-U.S. stocks, 20.9 percent U.S. bonds, and 13.7 percent cash.

thought asset allocation was an outmoded concept during the bull market of the late 1990s found they were mistaken in the market declines of 2000–2001.[9] A number of studies have shown that individual investors frequently trade stocks too often—driving up commissions—and sell stocks with gains too early (prior to further price increases), while they hold onto losers too long (as the price continues to fall).[10] These results are especially true for men and online traders.[11] The desire to "get rich quick" by trading in the stock market may lead to a few success stories; but, for most investors, implementing a prudent asset allocation strategy and investing over time are a more likely means of investment success. A well-constructed policy statement can go a long way toward ensuring that an appropriate asset allocation decision is implemented and maintained.

[9]Ken Brown, "Fund Diversification Dies a Not Very Slow Death," *The Wall Street Journal,* 7 February 2000, R1, R5.

[10]Brad Barber and Terrance Odean, "Trading is Hazardous to Your Wealth: The Common Stock Investment Performance of Individual Investors," *Journal of Finance* 55, no. 2 (April 2000): 773–806; Terrance Odean, "Do Investors Trade Too Much?" *American Economic Review* 89 (December 1999): 1279–1298; Brad Barber and Terrance Odean, "The Courage of Misguided Convictions: The Trading Behavior of Individual Investors, *Financial Analyst Journal* 55, no. 6 (November–December 1999): 41–55; Terrance Odean, "Are Investors Reluctant to Realize Their Losses?" *Journal of Finance* 53, no. 5 (October 1998): 1775–1798.

[11]Brad Barber and Terrance Odean, "Boys Will Be Boys: Gender, Overconfidence, and Common Stock Investment," *Quarterly Journal of Economics* 116, no. 1 (February 2001): 261–292; Brad Barber and Terrance Odean, "Online Investors: Do the Slow Die First?" University of California at Davis working paper.

EXHIBIT 2.8 ▶ *THE EFFECT OF TAXES AND INFLATION ON INVESTMENT RETURNS, 1926–2001*

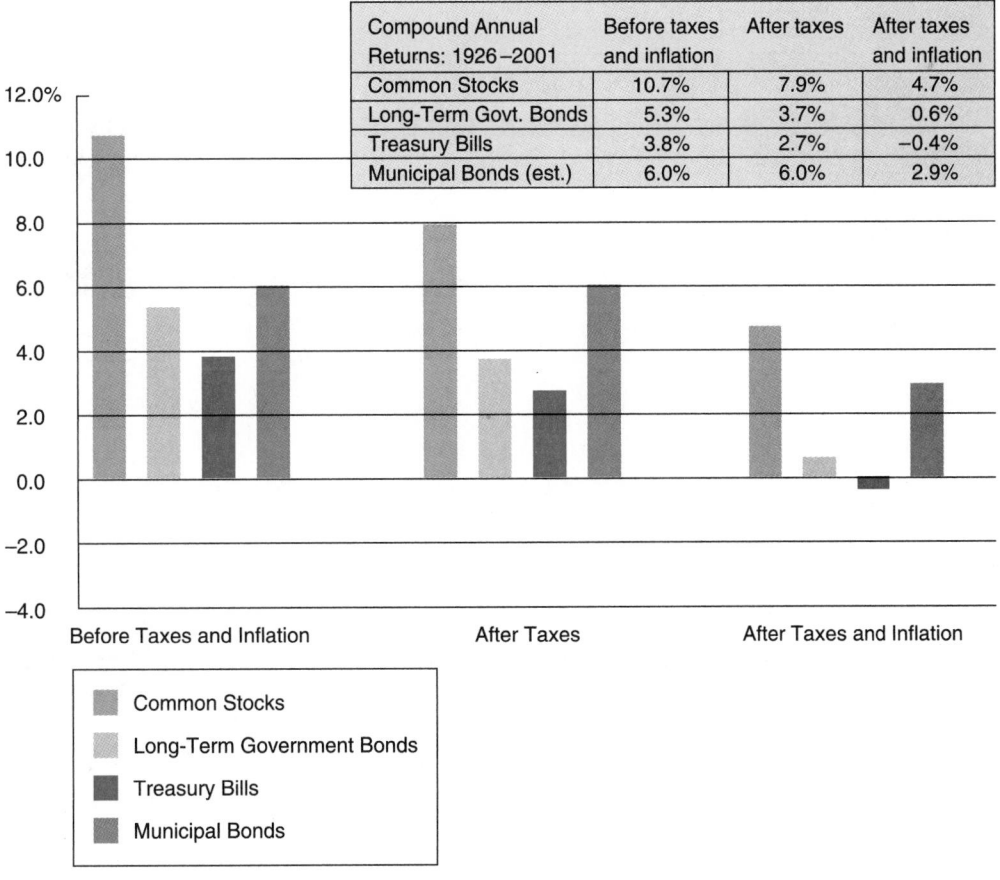

Compound Annual Returns: 1926–2001	Before taxes and inflation	After taxes	After taxes and inflation
Common Stocks	10.7%	7.9%	4.7%
Long-Term Govt. Bonds	5.3%	3.7%	0.6%
Treasury Bills	3.8%	2.7%	−0.4%
Municipal Bonds (est.)	6.0%	6.0%	2.9%

Legend:
- Common Stocks
- Long-Term Government Bonds
- Treasury Bills
- Municipal Bonds

Note: A 28 percent marginal tax rate was used for income across all years, and we assumed a 20 percent capital gains tax rate with gains realized after 20 years.

Source: *Stocks, Bonds, Bills, and Inflation,*® *2002 Yearbook,* © 2002 Ibbotson Associates, Inc. Based on copyrighted works by Ibbotson and Sinquefield. All rights reserved. Used with permission.

Real Investment Returns after Taxes and Costs

Exhibit 2.8 provides additional historical perspectives on returns. It indicates how an investment of $1 would have grown over the 1926 to 2001 period and, using fairly conservative assumptions, examines how investment returns are affected by taxes and inflation.

Focusing first on stocks, funds invested in 1926 in the S&P 500 would have averaged a 10.7 percent annual return by the end of 2001. Unfortunately, this return is unrealistic because if the funds were invested over time, taxes would have to be paid and inflation would erode the real purchasing power of the invested funds.

Except for tax-exempt investors and tax-deferred accounts, annual tax payments reduce investment returns. Incorporating taxes into the analysis lowers the after-tax average annual return of a stock investment to 7.9 percent.

But the major reduction in the value of our investment is caused by inflation. The real after-tax average annual return on a stock over this time frame was only 4.7 percent, which is quite a bit less than our initial unadjusted 10.7 percent return!

| EXHIBIT 2.9 | HISTORICAL AVERAGE ANNUAL RETURNS AND RETURN VARIABILITY, 1926–2001 |

Series	Geometric Mean	Arithmetic Mean	Standard Deviation	Distribution
Large company stocks	10.7%	12.7%	20.2%	
Small company stocks[*]	12.5	17.3	33.2	
Long-term corporate bonds	5.8	6.1	8.6	
Long-term government bonds	5.3	5.7	9.4	
Intermediate-term government bonds	5.3	5.5	5.7	
U.S. Treasury bills	3.8	3.9	3.2	
Inflation	3.1	3.1	4.4	

[*]The 1933 Small Company Stock Total Return was 142.9 percent. —90%   0%   90%

Source: *Stocks, Bonds, Bills, and Inflation,*® *2002 Yearbook,* © Ibbotson Associates, Inc. Based on copyrighted works by Ibbotson and Sinquefield. All rights reserved. Used with permission.

This example shows the long-run impact of taxes and inflation on the real value of a stock portfolio. For bonds and bills, however, the results in Exhibit 2.8 show something even more surprising. After adjusting for taxes, long-term bonds barely maintained their purchasing power; T-bills *lost* value in real terms. One dollar invested in long-term government bonds in 1926 gave the investor an annual average after-tax real return of 0.6 percent. An investment in Treasury bills lost an average of 0.4 percent after taxes and inflation. Municipal bonds, because of the protection they offer from taxes, earned an average annual real return of almost 3 percent during this time.

This historical analysis demonstrates that, for taxable investments, the only way to maintain purchasing power over time when investing in financial assets is to invest in common stocks. An asset allocation decision for a taxable portfolio that does not include a substantial commitment to common stocks makes it difficult for the portfolio to maintain real value over time.[12]

---

[12]Of course other equity-oriented investments, such as venture capital or real estate, may also provide inflation protection after adjusting for portfolio costs and taxes. Future studies of the performance of Treasury inflation-protected securities (TIPs) will likely show their usefulness in protecting investors from inflation as well.

EXHIBIT 2.10 ▶ *OVER LONG TIME PERIODS, EQUITIES OFFER HIGHER RETURNS*

Stocks far outperformed Treasury bills during the 34 years through 2001, but stocks often did worse than T-bills when held for shorter periods during those 34 years.

	COMPOUND ANNUAL TOTAL RETURN[a]	
S&P 500 stock index	12.1%	
Treasury bills	6.6	
	LENGTH OF HOLDING PERIOD (CALENDAR YEARS)	PERCENTAGE OF PERIODS THAT STOCKS TRAILED BILLS
	1	38%
	5	21
	10	16
	20	0

[a]Price change plus reinvested income.

Source: *Stocks, Bonds, Bills, and Inflation,*® 2002 Yearbook, © Ibbotson Associates, Inc. Based on copyrighted works by Ibbotson and Sinquefield. All rights reserved. Used with permission.

Returns and Risks of Different Asset Classes

By focusing on returns, we have ignored its partner—risk. Assets with higher long-term returns have these returns to compensate for their risk. Exhibit 2.9 illustrates returns (unadjusted for costs and taxes) for several asset classes over time. As expected, the higher returns available from equities come at the cost of higher risk. This is precisely why investors need a policy statement and why the investor and manager must understand the capital markets and have a disciplined approach to investing. Safe Treasury bills will sometimes outperform equities, and, because of their higher risk, common stocks sometimes lose significant value. These are times when undisciplined and uneducated investors sell their stocks at a loss and vow never to invest in equities again. In contrast, these are times when disciplined investors stick to their investment plan and position their portfolio for the next bull market.[13] By holding on to their stocks and perhaps purchasing more at depressed prices, the equity portion of the portfolio will experience a substantial increase in the future.

The asset allocation decision determines to a great extent both the returns and the volatility of the portfolio. Exhibit 2.9 indicates that stocks are riskier than bonds or T-bills. Exhibit 2.10 and Exhibit 2.11 illustrate the year-by-year volatility of stock returns and show that stocks have sometimes earned returns lower than those of T-bills for extended periods of time. Sticking with an investment policy and riding out the difficult times can earn attractive long-term rates of return.[14]

One popular way to measure risk is to examine the variability of returns over time by computing a standard deviation or variance of annual rates of return for an asset class. This measure, which is contained in Exhibit 2.9, indicates that stocks are risky and T-bills are not. Another intriguing measure of risk is the probability of *not* meeting your investment return objective. From this perspective, based on the results shown in Exhibit 2.10, if the investor has a long time horizon (i.e. approaching 20 years), the risk of equities is small and that of T-bills is large because of their differences in expected returns.

[13]Newton's law of gravity seems to work two ways in financial markets. What goes up must come down; it also appears over time that what goes down may come back up. Contrarian investors and some "value" investors use this concept of reversion to the mean to try to outperform the indexes over time.

[14]The added benefits of diversification—combining different asset classes in the portfolio—may reduce overall portfolio risk without harming potential return. The topic of diversification is discussed in Chapter 7.

EXHIBIT 2.11 *EQUITY RISK: LONG-TERM AND SHORT-TERM PERSPECTIVES: 1940–2001*

Historically, the S&P 500 has posted healthy gains . . .
Total returns, by decade, including share price gains and reinvested dividends, in percent

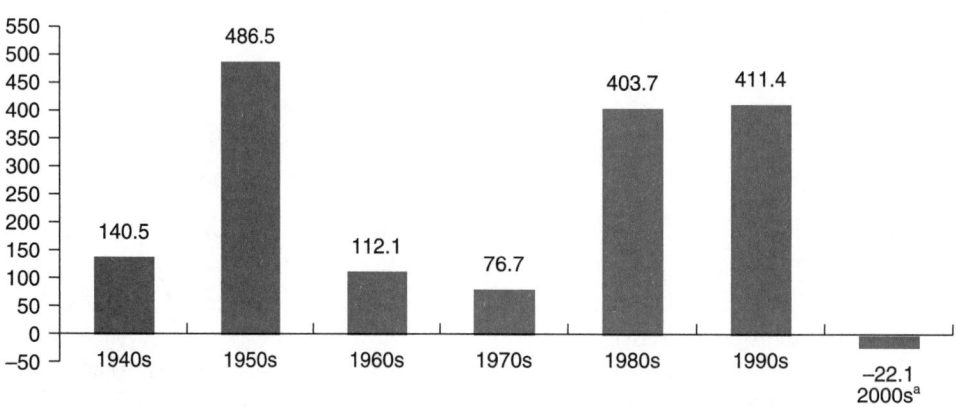

aThrough Dec. 31, 2001.

. . . but getting there can be rough
Annual total returns including share price gains and reinvested dividends, in percent

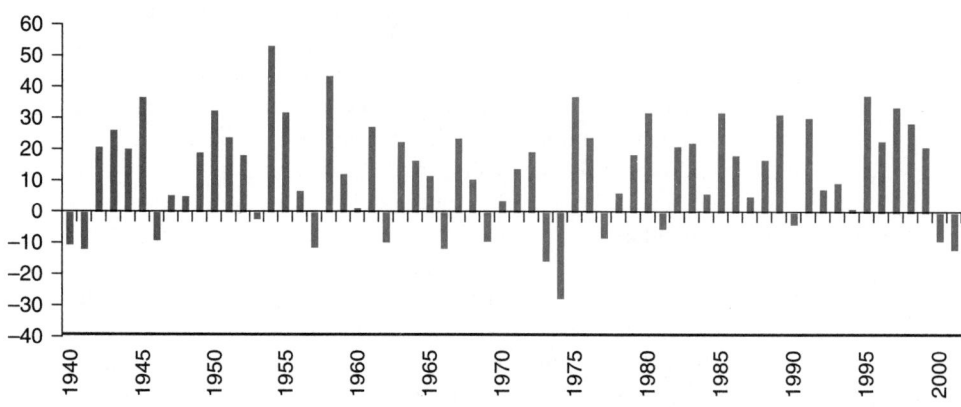

Focusing solely on return variability as a measure of risk ignores a significant risk for income-oriented investors, such as retirees or endowment funds. "Safe," income-oriented investments, such as Treasury bills or certificates of deposit, suffer from *reinvestment risk*—that is, the risk that interim cash flows or the principal paid at maturity will be reinvested in a lower-yielding security. The year of 1992 was particularly hard on investors in "safe" T-bills, because their T-bill income fell 37 percent from 1991 levels due to lower interest rates. Exhibit 2.12 compares the variability of income payouts from common stocks (measured by the dividends from the S&P 500) and T-bills. Over the 1926 to 2001 time frame, dividend income from stocks rose 59 times compared to 44 times for T-bills. The income from stocks fell only 17 times, while

EXHIBIT 2.12	*COMPARISON OF INCOME PAYOUTS FROM COMMON STOCKS AND TREASURY BILLS, 1926–2001*

During the past 76 years, stocks have been a more reliable source of income than either bonds or Treasury bills. The following figures presume that each year an investor spent all dividend and interest income kicked off by the securities but left the capital intact.

	Years When Payout Rose	Years When Payout Fell	Worst One-Year Drop in Income	1926 TO 2001 Change in Value of Income	1926 TO 2001 Change in Value of Principal
Stocks	59	17	–39%	1,891.8%	4,409.9%
20-Year Treasury bonds	41	35	–15.0	93.1	–13.3
5-Year Treasury bonds	44	32	–36.9	75.5	26.1
Treasury bills	44	32	–76.6	70.1	—

Exhibit data source: Ibbotson Associates, Inc.

Source: "T-Bill Trauma and the Meaning of Risk," *The Wall Street Journal,* 12 February 1993, C1. Reprinted with permission of *The Wall Street Journal.* ©1993 Dow Jones and Co., Inc. All rights reserved. Updated by the authors, using Ibbotson data.

T-bill rollovers resulted in an income loss 32 times. The worst one-year drop in stock income, 39.0 percent in 1932, was not as severe as the largest decline, 76.6 percent, in T-bill income, which occurred in 1940. In addition, the growth rate of income from stocks far outpaced that of inflation and the growth of income from T-bills. During the 1926 through 2001 period, stock dividends rose almost 1,900 percent, inflation rose 886 percent, and T-bill income rose only 70 percent. When one considers the growth in principal that stocks offer, we see that "conservative," income-oriented T-bill investors are in fact exposed to substantial amounts of risk.

Asset Allocation Summary

A carefully constructed policy statement determines the types of assets that should be included in a portfolio. The asset allocation decision, not the selection of specific stocks and bonds, determines most of the portfolio's returns over time. Although seemingly risky, investors seeking capital appreciation, income, or even capital preservation over long time periods will do well to include a sizable allocation to the equity portion in their portfolio. As noted in this section, a strategy's risk may depend on the investor's goals and time horizon. At times, investing in T-bills may be a riskier strategy than investing in common stocks due to reinvestment risks and the risk of not meeting long-term investment return goals after considering inflation and taxes.

ASSET ALLOCATION AND CULTURAL DIFFERENCES

Thus far, our analysis has focused on U.S. investors. Non-U.S. investors make their asset allocation decisions in much the same manner; but because they face different social, economic, political, and tax environments, their allocation decisions differ from those of U.S. investors. Exhibit 2.13 shows the equity allocations of pension funds in several countries. As shown, the equity allocations vary dramatically from 79 percent in Hong Kong to 37 percent in Japan and only 8 percent in Germany.

National differences can explain much of the divergent portfolio strategies. Of these six nations, the average age of the population is highest in Germany and Japan and lowest in the United States and the United Kingdom, which helps explain the greater use of equities in the latter countries. Government privatization programs during the 1980s in the United Kingdom encouraged equity ownership among individual and institutional investors. In Germany, regulations prevent insurance firms from having more than 20 percent of their assets in equities. Both Germany and Japan have banking sectors that invest privately in firms and whose officers sit on corporate boards. Since

EXHIBIT 2.13

EQUITY ALLOCATIONS IN PENSION FUND PORTFOLIOS

COUNTRY	PERCENTAGE IN EQUITIES
Hong Kong	79%
United Kingdom	78
Ireland	68
United States	58
Japan	37
Germany	8

EXHIBIT 2.14

ASSET ALLOCATION AND INFLATION FOR DIFFERENT COUNTRIES EQUITY ALLOCATION AS OF DECEMBER 1997; AVERAGE INFLATION MEASURED OVER 1980–1997

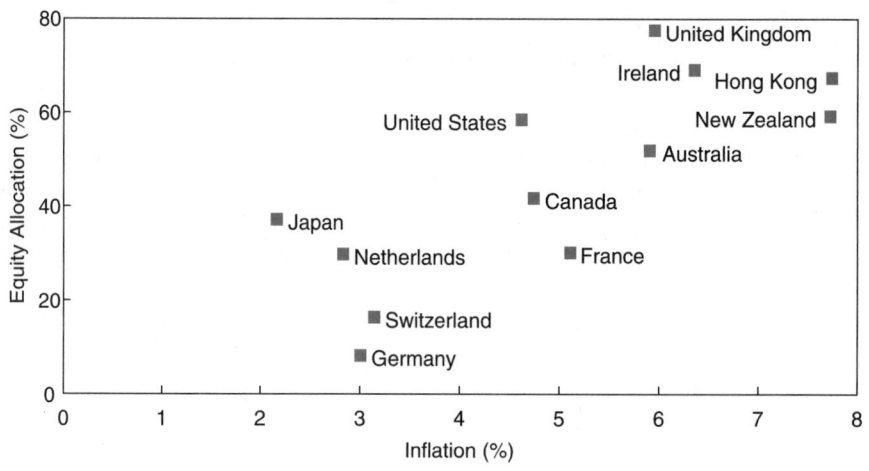

1960, the cost of living in the United Kingdom has increased at a rate more than 4.5 times that of Germany; this inflationary bias in the U.K. economy favors equities in U.K. asset allocations. Exhibit 2.14 shows the positive relationship between the level of inflation in a country and pension fund allocation to equity in the country. These results indicate that the general economic environment, as well as demographics, has an effect on the asset allocation in a country.

The need to invest in equities for portfolio growth is less in Germany, where workers receive generous state pensions. Germans tend to show a cultural aversion to the stock market: Many Germans are risk averse and consider stock investing a form of gambling. Although this attitude is changing, the German stock market is rather illiquid, with only a handful of stocks accounting for 50 percent of total stock trading volume.[15] New legislation that encourages 401(k)-like plans in Germany may encourage citizens to invest more in equities, but in mid-2001, less than 10 percent of Germans over the age of 14 owned stocks either directly or indirectly.[16]

---

[15]Peter Gumbel, "The Hard Sell: Getting Germans to Invest in Stocks," *The Wall Street Journal,* 4 August 1995, p. A2.

[16]Christopher Rhoads, "Germany Is Poised for a Pension Overhaul," *The Wall Street Journal,* 10 May 2001, p. A13.

Other Organization for Economic Cooperation and Development (OECD) countries place regulatory restrictions on institutional investors. For example, pension funds in Austria must have at least 50 percent of their assets in bank deposits or schilling-denominated bonds. Belgium limits pension funds to a minimum 15 percent investment in government bonds. Finland places a 5 percent limit on investments outside its borders by pension funds, and French pension funds must invest a minimum of 34 percent in public debt instruments.[17]

Asset allocation policy and strategy are determined in the context of an investor's objectives and constraints. Among the factors that explain differences in investor behavior across countries, however, are their political and economic environments.

The Internet *Investments Online*

Many inputs go into an investment policy statement as an investor maps out his or her objectives and constraints. Some inputs and helpful information are available in the following Web sites. Many of the sites mentioned in Chapter 1 contain important information and insights about asset allocation decisions, as well.

http://www.ssa.gov Information on a person's expected retirement funds from Social Security can be obtained by using the Social Security Administration's Web site.

http://www.ibbotson.com Much of the data in this chapter's charts and tables came from Ibbotson's published sources. Many professional financial planners use Ibbotson's data and education resources.

http://www.mfea.com/ InvestmentStrategies/Calculators/ default.asp This site contains links to calculators on Web sites of mutual fund families.

Sites with information and sample Monte Carlo simulations for spending plans in retirement include: **http://www.financialengines.com, http://www.troweprice.com** (click on investment tools and select the investment strategy planner); **http://www3.troweprice.com/ retincome/RIC/** (for a retirement income calculator), and **http://www.decisioneering.com.**

Many professional organizations have Web sites for use by their members, those interested in seeking professional finance designations, and those interested in seeking advice from a professional financial adviser. These sites include:

http://www.aimr.org Association for Investment Management and Research home page. AIMR awards the CFA (Chartered Financial Analyst) designation. This site provides information about the CFA designation, AIMR publications, investor education, and various Internet resources.

http://www.amercoll.edu This is the Web site for The American College, which is the training arm of the insurance industry. The American College offers the CLU and ChFC designations, which are typically earned by insurance professionals.

http://www.cfp-board.org The home page of Certified Financial Planner Board of Standards. Contains links to find a CFP™ mark holder and other information about the financial planning profession.

http://www.napfa.org This is the home page for the National Association of Personal Financial Advisors. This is the trade group for fee-only financial planners. Fee-only planners do not sell products on commission, or, should they recommend a commission-generating product, they pass the commission on to the investor. This site features press releases, finding a fee-only planner in your area, a list of financial resources on the Web and position openings in the financial planning field.

http://www.fpanet.org The Financial Planning Association's Web site. The site offers features and topics of interest to financial planners including information on earning the CFP designation and receiving the *Journal of Financial Planning.*

http://www.asec.org The home page of the American Saving Education Council.

---

[17]Daniel Witschi, "European Pension Funds: Turning More Aggressive?" in *Asset Allocation in a Changing World,* edited by Terence E. Burns (Charlottesville, Va., Association for Investment Management and Research, 1998): 72–84; Joel Chernoff, "OECD Eyes Pension Rules," *Pensions and Investments* (December 23, 1996): 2, 34.

Summary

- In this chapter, we saw that investors need to prudently manage risk within the context of their investment goals and preferences. Income, spending, and investing behavior will change over a person's lifetime.
- We reviewed the importance of developing an investment policy statement before implementing a serious investment plan. By forcing investors to examine their needs, risk tolerance, and familiarity with the capital markets, policy statements help investors correctly identify appropriate objectives and constraints. In addition, the policy statement becomes a standard by which to judge the performance of the portfolio manager.
- We also reviewed the importance of the asset allocation decision in determining long-run portfolio investment returns and risks. Because the asset allocation decision follows setting the objectives and constraints, it is clear that the success of the investment program depends on the first step, the construction of the policy statement.

Questions

1. "Young people with little wealth should not invest money in risky assets such as the stock market, because they can't afford to lose what little money they have." Do you agree or disagree with this statement? Why?

2. Your healthy 63-year-old neighbor is about to retire and comes to you for advice. From talking with her, you find out she was planning on taking all the money out of her company's retirement plan and investing it in bond mutual funds and money market funds. What advice should you give her?

3. Discuss how an individual's investment strategy may change as he or she goes through the accumulation, consolidation, spending, and gifting phases of life.

4. Why is a policy statement important?

5. Use the questionnaire "How much risk is right for you?" (Exhibit 2.4) to determine your risk tolerance. Use this information to help write a policy statement for yourself.

6. Your 45-year-old uncle is 20 years away from retirement; your 35-year-old older sister is about 30 years away from retirement. How might their investment policy statements differ?

7. What information is necessary before a financial planner can assist a person in constructing an investment policy statement?

8. Use the Internet to find the home pages for some financial-planning firms. What strategies do they emphasize? What do they say about their asset allocation strategy? What are their firms' emphases: value investing, international diversification, principal preservation, retirement and estate planning, and such?

9. *CFA Examination Level III*

Mr. Franklin is 70 years of age, is in excellent health, pursues a simple but active lifestyle, and has no children. He has interest in a private company for $90 million and has decided that a medical research foundation will receive half the proceeds now; it will also be the primary beneficiary of his estate upon his death. Mr. Franklin is committed to the foundation's well-being because he believes strongly that, through it, a cure will be found for the disease that killed his wife. He now realizes that an appropriate investment policy and asset allocations are required if his goals are to be met through investment of his considerable assets. Currently, the following assets are available for use in building an appropriate portfolio:

$45.0 million cash (from sale of the private company interest, net of pending
$45 million gift to the foundation)
10.0 million stocks and bonds ($5 million each)
9.0 million warehouse property (now fully leased)
1.0 million Franklin residence
$65.0 million total available assets

a. Formulate and justify an investment policy statement setting forth the appropriate guidelines within which future investment actions should take place. Your policy statement must encompass all relevant objective and constraint considerations.

b. Recommend and justify a long-term asset allocation that is consistent with the investment policy statement you created in Part a. Briefly explain the key assumptions you made in generating your allocation.

Problems

1. Suppose your first job pays you $28,000 annually. What percentage should your cash reserve contain? How much life insurance should you carry if you are unmarried? If you are married with two young children?

2. What is the marginal tax rate for a couple, filing jointly, if their taxable income is $20,000? $40,000? $60,000? What is their tax bill for each of these income levels? What is the average tax rate for each of these income levels?

3. What is the marginal tax rate for a single individual if her taxable income is $20,000? $40,000? $60,000? What is her tax bill for each of these income levels? What is her average tax rate for each of these income levels?

4. a. Someone in the 36 percent tax bracket can earn 9 percent annually on her investments in a tax-exempt IRA account. What will be the value of a one-time $10,000 investment in five years? Ten years? Twenty years?

   b. Suppose the preceding 9 percent return is taxable rather than tax-deferred and the taxes are paid annually. What will be the after-tax value of her $10,000 investment after 5, 10, and 20 years?

5. a. Someone in the 15 percent tax bracket can earn 10 percent on his investments in a tax-exempt IRA account. What will be the value of a $10,000 investment in 5 years? 10 years? 20 years?

   b. Suppose the preceding 10 percent return is taxable rather than tax-deferred. What will be the after-tax value of his $10,000 investment after 5, 10, and 20 years?

References

Bhatia, Sanjiv, ed. *Managing Assets for Individual Investors.* Charlottesville, Va.: Association for Investment Management and Research, 1995.

Burns, Terence E., ed. *Investment Counseling for Private Clients.* Charlottesville, Va.: Association for Investment Management and Research, 1999.

Ellis, Charles D. *Investment Policy: How to Win the Loser's Game.* Homewood, Ill.: Dow Jones–Irwin, 1985.

Miller, Janet T. ed. *Investment Counseling for Private Clients, III.* Charlottesville, Va.: Associate for Investment Management and Research, 2001.

Mitchell, Roger S. ed. *Investment Counseling for Private Clients, II.* Charlottesville, Va.: Association for Investment Management and Research, 2000.

Peavy, John. *Cases in Portfolio Management.* Charlottesville, Va.: Association for Investment Management and Research, 1990.

Peavy, John W., ed. *Investment Counsel for Private Clients.* Charlottesville, Va.: Association for Investment Management and Research, 1993.

APPENDIX
Chapter 2

Objectives and Constraints of Institutional Investors

Institutional investors manage large amounts of funds in the course of their business. They include mutual funds, pension funds, insurance firms, endowments, and banks. In this appendix, we review the characteristics of various institutional investors and discuss their typical investment objectives and constraints.

Mutual Funds

A mutual fund pools sums of money from investors, which are then invested in financial assets. Each mutual fund has its own investment objective, such as capital appreciation, high current income, or money market income. A mutual fund will state its investment objective, and investors choose the funds in which to invest. Two basic constraints face mutual funds: those created by law to protect mutual fund investors and those that represent choices made by the mutual fund's managers. Some of these constraints will be discussed in the mutual fund's prospectus, which must be given to all prospective investors before they purchase shares in a mutual fund. Mutual funds are discussed in more detail in Chapter 25.

Pension Funds

Pension funds are a major component of retirement planning for individuals. As of March 2001, U.S. pension assets were nearly $10 trillion. Basically, a firm's pension fund receives contributions from the firm, its employees, or both. The funds are invested with the purpose of giving workers either a lump-sum payment or the promise of an income stream after their retirement. **Defined benefit pension**

plans promise to pay retirees a specific income stream after retirement. The size of the benefit is usually based on factors that include the worker's salary, or time of service, or both. The company contributes a certain amount each year to the pension plan; the size of the contribution depends on assumptions concerning future salary increases and the rate of return to be earned on the plan's assets. Under a defined benefit plan, the company carries the risk of paying the future pension benefit to retirees; should investment performance be poor, or should the company be unable to make adequate contributions to the plan, the shortfall must be made up in future years. "Poor" investment performance means the actual return on the plan's assets fell below the assumed **actuarial rate of return**. The actuarial rate is the discount rate used to find the present value of the plan's future obligations and thus determines the size of the firm's annual contribution to the pension plan.

Defined contribution pension plans do not promise set benefits; rather, employees' benefits depend on the size of the contributions made to the pension fund and the returns earned on the fund's investments. Thus, the plan's risk is borne by the employees. Unlike a defined benefit plan, employees' retirement income is not an obligation of the firm.

A pension plan's objectives and constraints depend on whether the plan is a *defined benefit plan* or a *defined contribution plan*. We review each separately below.

Defined Benefit

The plan's risk tolerance depends on the plan's funding status and its actuarial rate. For **underfunded plans** (where the present value of the fund's liabilities to employees exceeds the value of the fund's assets), a more conservative approach toward risk is taken to ensure that the funding gap is closed over time. This may entail a strategy whereby the firm makes larger plan contributions and assumes a lower actuarial rate. **Overfunded plans** (where the present value of the pension liabilities is less than the plan's assets) allow a more aggressive investment strategy in which the firm reduces its contributions and increases the risk exposure of the plan. The return objective is to meet the plan's actuarial rate of return, which is set by actuaries who estimate future pension obligations based on assumptions about future salary increases, current salaries, retirement patterns, worker life expectancies, and the firm's benefit formula. The actuarial rate also helps determine the size of the firm's plan contributions over time.

The liquidity constraint on defined benefit funds is mainly a function of the average age of employees. A younger employee base means less liquidity is needed; an older employee base generally means more liquidity is needed to pay current pension obligations to retirees. The time horizon constraint is also affected by the average age of employees, although some experts recommend using a 5- to 10-year horizon for planning purposes. Taxes are not a major concern to the plan, because pension plans are exempt from paying tax on investment returns. The major legal constraint is that the plan must be run in accordance with the Employee Retirement and Income Security Act (ERISA), and investments must satisfy the "prudent-expert" standard when evaluated in the context of the overall pension plan's portfolio.

Defined Contribution

As the individual worker decides how his contributions to the plan are to be invested, the objectives and constraints for defined contribution plans depend on the individual. Because the worker carries the risk of inadequate retirement funding rather than the firm, defined contribution plans are generally more conservatively invested (some suggest that employees tend to be too conservative). If, however, the plan is considered more of an estate planning tool for a wealthy founder or officer of the firm, a higher risk tolerance and return objective are appropriate because most of the plan's assets will ultimately be owned by the individual's heirs.

The liquidity and time horizon needs for the plan differ depending on the average age of the employees and the degree of employee turnover within the firm. Similar to defined benefit plans, defined contribution plans are tax-exempt and are governed by the provisions of ERISA.

Endowment Funds

Endowment funds arise from contributions made to charitable or educational institutions. Rather than immediately spending the funds, the organization invests the money for the purpose of providing a future stream of income to the organization. The investment policy of an endowment fund is the result of a "tension" between the organization's need for current income and the desire to plan for a growing stream of income in the future to protect against inflation.

To meet the institution's operating budget needs, the fund's return objective is often set by adding the spending rate (the amount taken out of the funds each year) and the expected inflation rate. Funds that have more risk-tolerant trustees may have a higher spending rate than those overseen by more risk-averse trustees. Because a total return approach usually serves to meet the return objective over time, the organization is generally withdrawing both income and capital gain returns to meet budgeted needs. The risk tolerance of an endowment fund is largely affected by the collective risk tolerance of the organization's trustees.

Due to the fund's long-term time horizon, liquidity requirements are minor except for the need to spend part of the endowment each year and maintain a cash reserve for emergencies. Many endowments are tax-exempt, although income from some private foundations can be taxed at either a 1 percent or 2 percent rate. Short-term capital gains are taxable, but long-term capital gains are not. Regulatory and legal constraints arise on the state level, where most endowments are regulated. Unique needs and preferences may affect investment strategies, especially among college or religious endowments, which sometimes have strong preferences about social investing issues.

Insurance Companies

The investment objectives and constraints for an insurance company depend on whether it is a life insurance company or a nonlife (such as a property and casualty) insurance firm.

Life Insurance Companies

Except for firms dealing only in term life insurance, life insurance firms collect premiums during a person's lifetime that must be invested until a death benefit is paid to the insurance contract's beneficiaries. At any time, the insured can turn in her policy and receive its cash surrender value. Discussing investment policy for an insurance firm is also complicated by the insurance industry's proliferation of insurance and quasi-investment products.

Basically, an insurance company wants to earn a positive "spread," which is the difference between the rate of return on investment minus the rate of return it credits its various policyholders. This concept is similar to a defined benefit pension fund that tries to earn a rate of return in excess of its actuarial rate. If the spread is positive, the insurance firm's surplus reserve account rises; if not, the surplus account declines by an amount reflecting the negative spread. A growing surplus is an important competitive tool for life insurance companies. Attractive investment returns allow the company to advertise better policy returns than those of its competitors. A growing surplus also allows the firm to offer new products and expand insurance volume.

Because life insurance companies are quasi-trust funds for savings, fiduciary principles limit the risk tolerance of the invested funds. The National Association of Insurance Commissioners (NAIC) establishes risk categories for bonds and stocks; companies with excessive investments in higher-risk categories must set aside extra funds in a mandatory securities valuation reserve (MSVR) to protect policyholders against losses.

Insurance companies' liquidity needs have increased over the years due to increases in policy surrenders and product-mix changes. A company's time horizon depends upon its specific product mix. Life insurance policies require longer-term investments, whereas guaranteed insurance contracts (GICs) and shorter-term annuities require shorter investment time horizons.

Tax rules changed considerably for insurance firms in the 1980s. For tax purposes, investment returns are divided into two components: first, the policyholder's share, which is the return portion covering the actuarially assumed rate of return needed to fund reserves; and second, the balance that is transferred to reserves. Unlike pensions and endowments, life insurance firms pay income and capital gains taxes at the corporate tax rates on this second component of return.

Except for the NAIC, most insurance regulation is on the state level. Regulators oversee the eligible asset classes and the reserves (MSVR) necessary for each asset class and enforce the "prudent-expert" investment standard. Audits ensure that various accounting rules and investment regulations are followed.

Nonlife Insurance Companies

Cash outflows are somewhat predictable for life insurance firms, based on their mortality tables. In contrast, the cash flows required by major accidents, disasters, and lawsuit settlements are not as predictable for nonlife insurance firms.

Due to their fiduciary responsibility to claimants, risk exposures are low to moderate. Depending on the specific company and competitive pressures, premiums may be affected both by the probability of a claim and the investment returns earned by the firm. Typically, casualty insurance firms invest their insurance reserves in bonds for safety purposes and to provide needed income to pay claims; capital and surplus funds are invested in equities for their growth potential. As with life insurers, property and casualty firms have a stronger competitive position when their surplus accounts are larger than those of their competitors. Many insurers now focus on a total return objective as a means to increase their surplus accounts over time.

Because of uncertain claim patterns, liquidity is a concern for property and casualty insurers who also want liquidity so they can switch between taxable and tax-exempt investments as their underwriting activities generate losses and profits. The time horizon for investments is typically shorter than that of life insurers, although many invest in long-term bonds to earn the higher yields available on these instruments. Investing strategy for the firm's surplus account focuses on long-term growth.

Regulation of property and casualty firms is more permissive than for life insurers. Similar to life companies, states regulate classes and quality of investments for a certain percentage of the firm's assets. But beyond this restriction, insurers can invest in many different types and qualities of instruments, except that some states limit the proportion of real estate assets.

Banks

Pension funds, endowments, and insurance firms obtain virtually free funds for investment purposes. Not so with banks. To have funds to lend, they must attract investors in a competitive interest rate environment. They compete against other banks and also against companies that offer other investment vehicles, from bonds to common stocks. A bank's success relies primarily on its ability to generate returns in excess of its funding costs.

A bank tries to maintain a positive difference between its cost of funds and its returns on assets. If banks anticipate falling interest rates, they will try to invest in longer-term assets to lock in the returns while seeking short-term deposits, whose interest cost is expected to fall over time. When banks expect rising rates, they will try to lock in longer-term deposits with fixed-interest costs, while investing funds short term to capture rising interest rates. The risk of such strategies is that losses may occur should a bank incorrectly forecast the direction of interest rates. The aggressiveness of a bank's strategy will be related to the size of its capital ratio and the oversight of regulators.

Banks need substantial liquidity to meet withdrawals and loan demand. A bank has two forms of liquidity. *Internal liquidity* is provided by a bank's investment portfolio that includes highly liquid assets that can be sold to raise cash. A bank has *external liquidity* if it can borrow funds in the federal funds markets (where banks lend reserves to other banks), from the Federal Reserve Bank's discount window, or by selling certificates of deposit at attractive rates.

Banks have a short time horizon for several reasons. First, they have a strong need for liquidity. Second, because they want to maintain an adequate interest revenue–interest expense spread, they generally focus on shorter-term investments to avoid interest rate risk and to avoid getting "locked in" to a long-term revenue source. Third, because banks typically offer short-term deposit accounts (demand deposits, NOW accounts, and such), they need to match the maturity of their assets and liabilities to avoid taking undue risks.[18]

Banks are heavily regulated by numerous state and federal agencies. The Federal Reserve Board, the Comptroller of the Currency, and the Federal Deposit Insurance Corporation all oversee various components of bank operations. The Glass-Steagall Act restricts the equity investments that banks can make. Unique situations that affect each bank's investment policy depend on their size, market, and management skills in matching asset and liability sensitivity to interest rates. For example, a bank in a small community may have many customers who deposit their money with it for the sake of convenience. A bank in a more populated area will find its deposit flows are more sensitive to interest rates and competition from nearby banks.

Institutional Investor Summary

Among the great variety of institutions, each institution has its "typical" investment objectives and constraints. This discussion has given us a taste of the differences that exist among types of institutions and some of the major issues confronting them. Notably, just as with individual investors, "cookie-cutter" policy statements are inappropriate for institutional investors. The specific objectives, constraints, and investment strategies must be determined on a case-by-case basis.

---

[18]An asset/liability mismatch caused the ultimate downfall of savings and loan associations. They attracted short-term liabilities (deposit accounts) and invested in long-term assets (mortgages). When interest rates became more volatile in the early 1980s and short-term rates increased dramatically, S&Ls suffered large losses.

Chapter 3 ▶ Selecting Investments in a Global Market*

After you read this chapter, you should be able to answer the following questions:

➤ Why should investors have a global perspective regarding their investments?
➤ What has happened to the relative size of U.S. and foreign stock and bond markets?
➤ What are the differences in the rates of return on U.S. and foreign securities markets?
➤ How can changes in currency exchange rates affect the returns that U.S. investors experience on foreign securities?
➤ Is there additional advantage to diversifying in international markets beyond the benefits of domestic diversification?
➤ What alternative securities are available? What are their cash flow and risk properties?
➤ What are the historical return and risk characteristics of the major investment instruments?
➤ What is the relationship among the returns for foreign and domestic investment instruments? What is the implication of these relationships for portfolio diversification?

Individuals are willing to defer current consumption for many reasons. Some save for their children's college tuition or their own; others wish to accumulate down payments for a home, car, or boat; others want to amass adequate retirement funds for the future. Whatever the reason for an investment program, the techniques we used in Chapter 1 to measure risk and return will help you evaluate alternative investments.

But what are those alternatives? Thus far, we have said little about the investment opportunities available in financial markets. In this chapter, we address this issue by surveying investment alternatives. This is essential background for making the asset allocation decision discussed in Chapter 2 and for later chapters where we analyze several individual investments, such as bonds, common stock, and other securities. It is also important when we consider how to construct and evaluate portfolios of investments.

As an investor in the 21st century, you have an array of investment choices unavailable a few decades ago. Together, the dynamism of financial markets, technological advances, and new regulations have resulted in numerous new investment instruments and expanded trading opportunities.[1] Improvements in communications and relaxation of international regulations have made it easier for investors to trade in both domestic and global markets. Telecommunications networks enable U.S. brokers to reach security exchanges in London, Tokyo, and other European and Asian cities as easily as those in New York, Chicago, and other U.S. cities. The competitive environment in the brokerage industry and the deregulation of the banking sector have made it

*The authors acknowledge data collection help on this chapter from Edgar Norton of Illinois State University and David J. Wright from University of Wisconsin–Parkside.

[1]For an excellent discussion of the reasons for the development of numerous financial innovations and the effect of these innovations on world capital markets, see Merton H. Miller, *Financial Innovations and Market Volatility* (Cambridge, Mass.: Blackwell Publishers, 1991).

possible for more financial institutions to compete for investor dollars. This has spawned investment vehicles with a variety of maturities, risk-return characteristics, and cash flow patterns. In this chapter, we examine some of these choices.

As an investor, you need to understand the differences among investments so you can build a properly diversified **portfolio** that conforms to your objectives. That is, you should seek to acquire a group of investments with different patterns of returns over time. If chosen carefully, such portfolios minimize risk for a given level of return because low or negative rates of return on some investments during a period of time are offset by above-average returns on others. The goal is to build a balanced portfolio of investments with relatively stable overall rates of return. A major goal of this text is to help you understand and evaluate the risk-return characteristics of investment portfolios. An appreciation of alternative security types is the starting point for this analysis.

This chapter is divided into three main sections. As noted earlier, investors can choose securities from financial markets around the world. Therefore, in the first section, we look at a combination of reasons why investors *should* include foreign as well as domestic securities in their portfolios. Taken together, these reasons provide a compelling case for global investing.

In the second section of this chapter, we discuss securities in domestic and global markets, describing their main features and cash flow patterns. You will see that the varying risk-return characteristics of alternative investments suit the preferences of different investors. Some securities are more appropriate for individuals, whereas others are better suited for financial institutions.

The third and final section contains the historical risk and return performance of several investment instruments from around the world and examines the relationship among the returns for many of these securities, which provides further support for global investing.

THE CASE FOR GLOBAL INVESTMENTS

Twenty years ago, the bulk of investments available to individual investors consisted of U.S. stocks and bonds. Now, however, a call to your broker gives you access to a wide range of securities sold throughout the world. Currently, you can purchase stock in General Motors or Toyota, U.S. Treasury bonds or Japanese government bonds, a mutual fund that invests in U.S. biotechnology companies, a global growth stock fund or a German stock fund, or options on a U.S. stock index.

Several changes have caused this explosion of investment opportunities. For one, the growth and development of numerous foreign financial markets, such as those in Japan, the United Kingdom, and Germany, as well as in emerging markets, such as China, have made these markets accessible and viable for investors around the world. Numerous U.S. investment firms have recognized this opportunity and established and expanded facilities in these countries. This expansion was aided by major advances in telecommunications technology that made it possible to maintain constant contact with offices and financial markets around the world. In addition to the efforts by U.S. firms, foreign firms and investors undertook counterbalancing initiatives, including significant mergers of firms and security exchanges. As a result, investors and investment firms from around the world can trade securities worldwide. Thus, investment alternatives are available from security markets around the world.[2]

---

[2]In this regard, see Scott E. Pardee, "Internationalization of Financial Markets," Federal Reserve Bank of Kansas City, *Economic Review* (February 1987): 3–7.

Three interrelated reasons U.S. investors should think of constructing global investment portfolios can be summarized as follows:

1. When investors compare the absolute and relative sizes of U.S. and foreign markets for stocks and bonds, they see that ignoring foreign markets reduces their choices to less than 50 percent of available investment opportunities. Because more opportunities broaden your range of risk-return choices, it makes sense to evaluate foreign securities when selecting investments and building a portfolio.
2. The rates of return available on non-U.S. securities often have substantially exceeded those for U.S.-only securities. The higher returns on non-U.S. *equities* can be justified by the higher growth rates for the countries where they are issued. These superior results typically prevail even when the returns are risk-adjusted.
3. One of the major tenets of investment theory is that investors should diversify their portfolios. Because the relevant factor when diversifying a portfolio is low correlation between asset returns, diversification with foreign securities that have very low correlation with U.S. securities can help to substantially reduce portfolio risk.

In this section, we analyze these reasons to demonstrate the advantages to a growing role of foreign financial markets for U.S. investors and to assess the benefits and risks of trading in these markets. Notably, the reasons that global investing is appropriate for U.S. investors are generally even more compelling for non-U.S. investors.

Relative Size of U.S. Financial Markets

Prior to 1970, the securities traded in the U.S. stock and bond markets comprised about 65 percent of all the securities available in world capital markets. Therefore, a U.S. investor selecting securities strictly from U.S. markets had a fairly complete set of investments available. Under these conditions, most U.S. investors probably believed that it was not worth the time and effort to expand their investment universe to include the limited investments available in foreign markets. That situation has changed dramatically over the past 33 years. Currently, investors who ignore foreign stock and bond markets limit their investment choices substantially.

Exhibit 3.1 shows the breakdown of securities available in world capital markets in 1969 and 2000. Not only has the overall value of all securities increased dramatically (from $2.3 trillion to $64 trillion), but the composition has also changed. Concentrating on proportions of bond and equity investments, the exhibit shows that U.S. dollar bonds and U.S. equity securities made up 53 percent of the total value of all securities in 1969 versus 28.4 percent for the total of nondollar bonds and equity. By 2000, U.S. bonds and equities accounted for 43.5 percent of the total securities market versus 46.7 percent for nondollar bonds and stocks. These data indicate that if you consider only the stock and bond market, the U.S. proportion of this combined market has declined from 65 percent of the total in 1969 to about 48 percent in 2000.

The point is, the U.S. security markets now include a smaller proportion of the total world capital market, and it is likely that this trend will continue. The faster economic growth of many other countries compared to the United States will require foreign governments and individual companies to issue debt and equity securities to finance this growth. Therefore, U.S. investors should consider investing in foreign securities because of the growing importance of these foreign securities in world capital markets. Not investing in foreign stocks and bonds means you are ignoring almost 52 percent of the securities that are available to you.

Rates of Return on U.S. and Foreign Securities

An examination of the rates of return on U.S. and foreign securities not only demonstrates that many non-U.S. securities provide superior rates of return but also shows the impact of the exchange rate risk discussed in Chapter 1.

EXHIBIT 3.1 *TOTAL INVESTABLE ASSETS IN THE GLOBAL CAPITAL MARKET*

Source: UBS Global Asset Management.

EXHIBIT 3.2 *INTERNATIONAL BOND MARKET COMPOUND ANNUAL RATES OF RETURN: 1990–2000*

	COMPONENTS OF RETURN		
	TOTAL DOMESTIC RETURN	TOTAL RETURN IN U.S. $	EXCHANGE RATE EFFECT
Canada	10.36	8.17	–2.19
France	9.51	8.30	–1.21
Germany	8.12	6.76	–1.36
Japan	5.82	8.67	2.85
United Kingdom	13.10	12.94	–0.17
United States	9.78	9.78	—

Source: Calculated using data presented in *Stocks, Bonds, Bills, and Inflation*® *2002 Yearbook,* © Ibbotson Associates, Inc. Based on copyrighted works by Ibbotson and Sinquefield. All rights reserved. Used with permission.

Global Bond Market Returns Exhibit 3.2 reports compound annual rates of return for several major international bond markets for 1990–2000. The *domestic return* is the rate of return an investor within the country would earn. In contrast, the return in U.S. dollars is what a U.S. investor would earn after adjusting for changes in the currency exchange rates during the period.

An analysis of the domestic returns in Exhibit 3.2 indicates that the performance of the U.S. bond market ranked third out of the six countries. When the impact of exchange rates is considered, the U.S. experience was the second out of six. The difference in performance for domestic versus U.S. dollar returns means that the exchange rate effect for a U.S. investor who invested in foreign bonds was almost always negative (that is, the U.S. dollar was strong against all currencies except the yen) and detracted from the domestic performance.

As an example, the domestic return on Canadian bonds was 10.36 percent compared with the return for U.S. bonds of 9.78 percent. The Canadian foreign exchange effect was –2.19 percent, which decreased the return on Canadian bonds converted to U.S. dollars to 8.17 percent, which was below the return for U.S. bonds. The point is, a U.S. investor who invested in non-U.S. bonds from several countries experienced rates of return close to those of U.S. investors who limited themselves to the U.S. bond market after the negative effects of a strong dollar.

Global Equity Market Returns   Exhibit 3.3 shows the rates of return in local currencies and in U.S. dollars for 34 major equity markets for the four years 1997–2000. The performance in local currency indicated that the U.S. market on average was ranked 15th of the total 34 countries. The performance results in U.S. dollars indicate that during this four-year period the currency effect was almost always negative for U.S. investors who acquired foreign securities (the U.S. dollar was strong relative to these countries). Overall, in U.S. dollar returns, the U.S. market was ranked 13th of the 34 countries.

Like the bond market performance, these results for equity markets around the world indicate that investors who limited themselves to the U.S. market experienced rates of return below those in several other countries (the U.S. market returns were seldom in the top 10 countries). This is true for comparisons that considered both domestic returns and rates of return adjusted for exchange rates. Notably, during three of these years (1996–1999), the U.S. equity market experienced above average returns and the dollar was quite strong.

Individual Country Risk and Return   As shown, several countries experienced higher compound returns on bonds and stocks than the United States. A natural question is whether these superior rates of return are attributable to higher levels of risk for securities in these countries.

Exhibit 3.4 contains the returns and risk measures for six major bond markets in local currency and U.S. dollars, along with a composite ratio of return per unit of risk. The results in local currency are similar to the results with only the rates of return—the U.S. bond market ranked fourth of the six countries. The results when returns and risk are measured in U.S. dollars were quite different. Specifically, as noted previously, the returns in U.S. dollars generally decreased because of the strong dollar. In addition, the risk measures increased dramatically (that is, the average risk for the five non-U.S. countries almost doubled, going from 6.33 percent to 11.72 percent). As a result, the returns per unit of risk for these countries declined signifcantly and the U.S. return-risk performance ranked first. Beyond the impact on the relative results in U.S. dollars, these significant increases in the volatility for returns of foreign stocks in U.S. dollars (which almost always happens) are evidence of significant exchange rate risk discussed in Chapter 1.

Exhibit 3.5 contains the scatter plot of local currency equity returns and risk for 12 individual countries, during the period 1990–2000. The risk measure is the standard deviation of daily returns as discussed in Chapter 1. Notably, the U.S. market experienced one of the lowest risk values. The return-on-risk position for the U.S., which plots above the line of best fit, indicates that the U.S. performance in local currency was first out of 12 mainly because of low risk. The results in U.S. dollars in Exhibit 3.6 show similar risk results wherein the U.S. return-risk performance is ranked first of 12. While most countries experience lower returns in U.S. dollars, similar to the bond results, the risk measures increased substantially again due to the exchange rate risk.

While these results for the decade of the 1990s makes U.S. stocks look very strong relative to other countries, it should be recognized that these were unusual years for the United States. Specifically, the five years 1995–1999 provided the five best years for equities in the 20th century—the fact is, it will be hard to match these results going forward. The results in 2000 and 2001 reflect a movement back to the long-run "normal" results for U.S. equities. In addition, the

EXHIBIT 3.3   ANNUAL RETURNS IN U.S. DOLLARS AND LOCAL CURRENCY: 1997–2000

Country	Year 2000 Returns				Year 1999 Returns				Year 1998 Returns				Year 1997 Returns			
	U.S. Dollar Returns	Rank	Local Currency Returns	Rank	U.S. Dollar Returns	Rank	Local Currency Returns	Rank	U.S. Dollar Returns	Rank	Local Currency Returns	Rank	U.S. Dollar Returns	Rank	Local Currency Returns	Rank
United States	-10.15%	11	-10.15%	17	18.90%	21	18.90%	24	26.78%	13	26.78%	9	31.69%	7	31.69%	11
Australia	-10.03	10	5.72	5	20.53	20	12.45	26	5.40	19	12.03	16	-10.31	21	9.48	21
Austria	-15.40	17	-9.72	16	-6.97	30	8.40	28	-3.00	22	-9.84	25	-1.72	19	13.74	19
Belgium	-13.95	13	-8.17	14	-17.29	34	-3.66	34	62.73	4	51.16	4	11.85	14	30.70	12
Brazil	-10.25	12	-3.04	12	50.99	10	134.82	2	-46.19	33	-44.04	33				
Britain	-14.60	14	-7.44	13	14.26	22	17.45	25	13.40	16	12.68	14	17.79	12	22.01	16
Canada	0.85	6	4.59	6	42.98	11	34.65	19	-5.10	24	1.91	20	13.44	13	18.31	18
Chile	-17.61	20	-10.69	19	32.91	17	48.88	13	-28.50	28	-23.15	30				
Denmark	22.23	1	17.80	2	5.38	26	22.13	22	3.26	20	-3.79	21	34.05	6	54.86	5
Finland	-15.23	16	-9.53	15	153.14	1	193.79	1	94.63	2	82.14	2	11.53	16	31.75	10
France	-7.89	8	-1.70	10	32.18	18	53.50	11	40.26	7	30.94	8	22.67	10	43.08	8
Germany	-15.96	18	-10.31	18	20.87	19	40.74	17	28.38	12	19.14	12	21.20	11	41.67	9
Greece	-42.09	29	-42.89	32	39.30	15	62.99	8	86.24	3	83.89	1	39.27	3	61.43	2
Hong Kong	-14.98	15	-14.67	21	73.20	5	73.81	6	-10.34	25	-10.38	26	-25.06	24	-24.92	25
Indonesia	-56.44	33	-39.88	30	77.31	4	58.05	9	-41.94	32	7.52	18	-63.25	28	-34.74	27
Ireland	7.38	4	14.59	3	-13.24	33	1.19	32	38.05	8	37.18	7	24.05	9	28.49	14
Italy	-5.46	7	0.89	8	6.45	25	24.33	21	50.57	5	40.44	5	36.95	5	59.66	3
Japan	-31.15	27	-22.95	28	67.26	7	50.12	12	5.42	18	-8.05	24	-26.39	25	-17.01	24
Malaysia	-20.81	23	-20.82	26	42.30	12	42.31	15	-2.19	21	-4.35	22	-70.03	30	-53.92	30
Mexico	-22.25	24	-20.84	27	91.01	3	82.52	4	-38.16	31	-24.08	31	54.21	1	57.73	4
Netherlands	-8.03	9	-1.86	11	7.24	24	24.92	20	29.95	11	20.61	11	24.19	8	44.56	7
New Zealand	-31.62	28	-19.25	23	9.27	23	10.37	27	-23.57	27	-15.78	27	-17.98	23	-0.52	22
Norway	2.43	5	1.43	7	33.29	16	41.04	16	-31.87	30	-29.90	32	6.55	18	21.71	17
Philippines	-43.70	30	-30.12	29	2.59	28	5.75	31	14.47	15	12.17	15	-62.36	27	-43.01	29
Portugal	-20.45	22	-15.10	22	-7.17	31	8.18	29	30.91	10	21.75	10	51.04	2	79.31	1
Singapore	-23.75	25	-20.59	25	56.18	9	57.60	10	-4.82	23	-6.64	23	-37.83	26	-25.30	26
South Africa	-19.20	21	-0.22	9	64.35	8	71.52	7	-31.43	29	-17.03	28	-11.52	22	-8.00	23
South Korea	-58.77	34	-54.12	34	110.63	2	99.06	3	117.12	1	54.29	3	-68.68	29	-37.33	28
Spain	-25.29	26	-20.27	24	4.58	27	21.87	23	48.09	6	37.36	6	10.46	17	28.06	15
Sweden	-17.15	19	-13.92	20	70.72	6	78.85	5	6.23	17	8.77	17	11.56	15	28.55	13
Switzerland	16.21	2	10.13	4	-6.70	29	7.84	30	21.13	14	13.91	13	38.36	4	50.97	6
Taiwan	-45.43	31	-42.49	31	42.30	13	38.82	18	-19.45	26	-20.49	29	-4.73	20	13.14	20
Thailand	-50.96	32	-43.24	33	39.46	14	43.28	14	31.89	9	2.83	19	-75.83	31	-55.90	31
Venezuela	11.93	3	20.68	1	-12.57	32	0.45	33	-55.46	34	-50.11	34				

EXHIBIT 3.4 ▶ *INTERNATIONAL BOND MARKET RETURN-RISK RESULTS: LOCAL CURRENCY AND U.S. DOLLARS, 1990–2000*

	LOCAL CURRENCY			U.S. DOLLARS		
COUNTRY	RETURN	RISK	RETURN-RISK	RETURN	RISK	RETURN-RISK
Canada	10.36	7.00	1.48	8.17	9.16	0.89
France	9.51	5.20	1.83	8.30	10.97	0.76
Germany	8.12	5.31	1.53	6.76	11.23	0.60
Japan	5.82	5.88	0.99	8.67	13.92	0.62
United Kingdom	13.10	8.26	1.59	12.94	13.34	0.97
United States	9.78	8.03	1.22	9.78	8.03	1.22

EXHIBIT 3.5 ▶ *ANNUAL RATES OF RETURN AND RISK FOR MAJOR STOCK MARKETS IN LOCAL CURRENCY, 1990–2000*

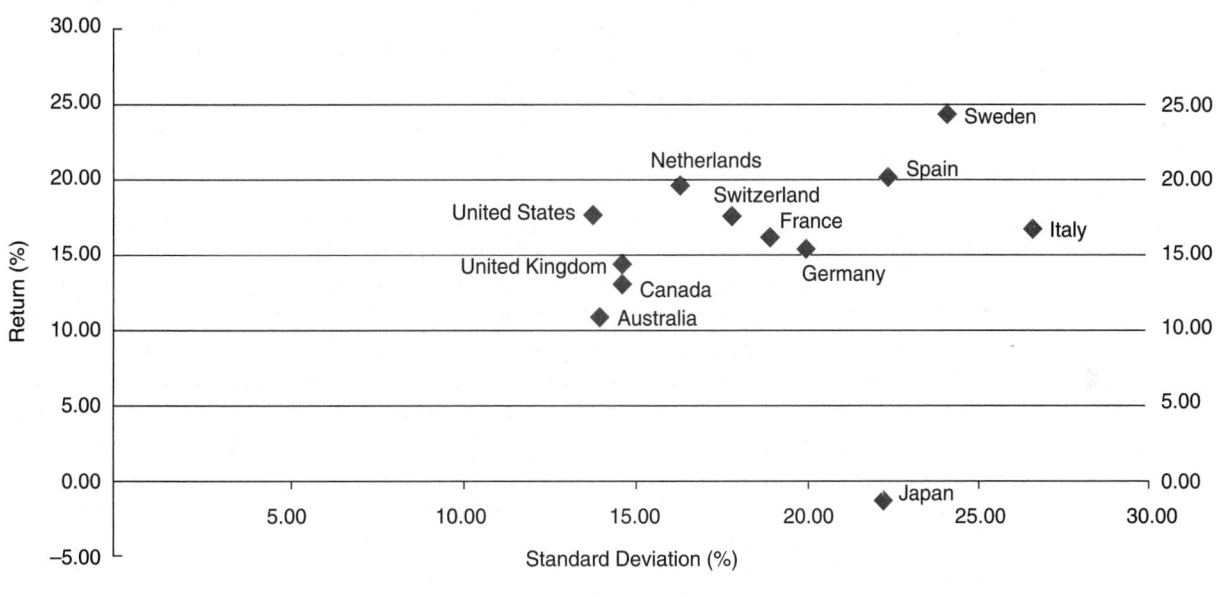

performance of the dollar has been quite strong due to our strong economy and the low rate of inflation, and, as noted, this has had a negative impact on dollar returns for foreign stocks. One must question how long this strength in the dollar can last and be mindful of the cyclical nature of currencies.

Risk of Combined Country Investments

Thus far, we have discussed the risk and return results for individual countries. In Chapter 1, we considered the idea of combining a number of assets into a portfolio and noted that investors should create diversified portfolios to reduce the variability of the returns over time. We discussed how proper diversification reduces the variability (our measure of risk) of the portfolio

EXHIBIT 3.6 ▶ *ANNUAL RATES OF RETURN AND RISK FOR MAJOR STOCK MARKETS IN U.S. DOLLARS, 1990–2000*

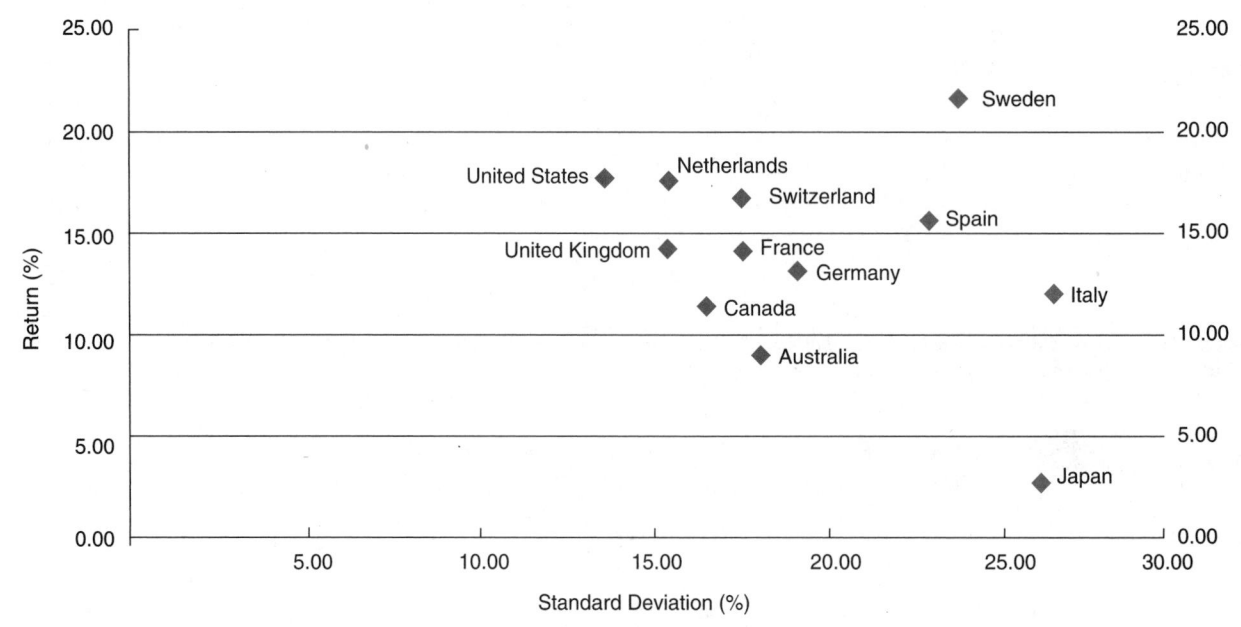

because alternative investments have different patterns of returns over time. Specifically, when the rates of return on some investments are negative or below average, other investments in the portfolio will be experiencing above-average rates of return. Therefore, if a portfolio is properly diversified, it should provide a more stable rate of return for the total portfolio (that is, it will have a lower standard deviation and therefore less risk). Although we will discuss and demonstrate portfolio theory in detail in Chapter 7, we need to consider the concept at this point to fully understand the benefits of global investing.

The way to measure whether two investments will contribute to diversifying a portfolio is to compute the correlation coefficient between their rates of return over time. Correlation coefficients can range from +1.00 to −1.00. A correlation of +1.00 means that the rates of return for these two investments move exactly together. Combining investments that move together in a portfolio would not help diversify the portfolio because they have identical rate-of-return patterns over time. In contrast, a correlation coefficient of −1.00 means that the rates of return for two investments move exactly opposite to each other. When one investment is experiencing above-average rates of return, the other is suffering through similar below-average rates of return. Combining two investments with large negative correlation in a portfolio would contribute much to diversification because it would stabilize the rates of return over time, reducing the standard deviation of the portfolio rates of return and hence the risk of the portfolio. Therefore, if you want to diversify your portfolio and reduce your risk, you want an investment that has either *low positive* correlation, *zero* correlation, or, ideally, *negative correlation* with the other investments in your portfolio. With this in mind, the following discussion considers the correlations of returns among U.S. bonds and stocks with the returns on foreign bonds and stocks.

EXHIBIT 3.7

CORRELATION COEFFICIENTS BETWEEN RATES OF RETURN ON BONDS IN THE UNITED STATES AND MAJOR FOREIGN MARKETS: 1990–2000 (MONTHLY DATA)

	DOMESTIC RETURNS	RETURNS IN U.S. DOLLARS
Canada	0.58	0.47
France	0.44	0.28
Germany	0.42	0.29
Japan	0.32	0.15
United Kingdom	0.50	0.41
Average	0.45	0.32

Source: Frank K. Reilly and David J. Wright, "Global Bond Markets: Alternative Benchmarks and Risk-Return Performance" (May 1997). Updated using International Monetary Fund data.

Global Bond Portfolio Risk   Exhibit 3.7 lists the correlation coefficients between rates of return for bonds in the United States and bonds in major foreign markets in domestic and U.S. dollar terms from 1990 to 2000. Notice that only one correlation between domestic rates of return is above 0.50. For a U.S. investor, the important correlations are between the rates of return in U.S. dollars. In this case, all the correlations between returns in U.S. dollars are substantially lower than the correlations among domestic returns and only two correlations are above 0.40. Notably, while the individual volatilities increased substantially when returns were converted to U.S. dollars, the correlations among returns in U.S. dollars always declined.

These low positive correlations among returns in U.S. dollars mean that U.S. investors have substantial opportunities for risk reduction through global diversification of bond portfolios. A U.S. investor who bought bonds in any market would substantially reduce the standard deviation of the well-diversified portfolio.

Why do these correlation coefficients for returns between U.S. bonds and those of various foreign countries differ? That is, why is the U.S.–Canada correlation 0.47 whereas the U.S.–Japan correlation is only 0.15? The answer is because the international trade patterns, economic growth, fiscal policies, and monetary policies of the countries differ. We do not have an integrated world economy but, rather, a collection of economies that are related to one another in different ways. As an example, the U.S. and Canadian economies are closely related because of these countries' geographic proximity, similar domestic economic policies, and the extensive trade between them. Each is the other's largest trading partner. In contrast, the United States has less trade with Japan and the fiscal and monetary policies of the two countries differ dramatically. For example, the U.S. economy was growing during much of the 1990s while the Japanese economy was in a recession.

The point is, macroeconomic differences cause the correlation of bond returns between the United States and each country to likewise differ. These differing correlations make it worthwhile to diversify with foreign bonds, and the different correlations indicate which countries will provide the greatest reduction in the standard deviation (risk) of returns for a U.S. investor.

Also, *the correlation of returns between a single pair of countries changes over time* because the factors influencing the correlations, such as international trade, economic growth, fiscal policy, and monetary policy, change over time. A change in any of these variables will produce a change in how the economies are related and in the relationship between returns on bonds. For example, the correlation in U.S. dollar returns between U.S. and Japanese bonds was 0.07 in the late 1980s and 1970s; it was 0.25 in the 1980s and 0.15 in the early 1990s but only 0.03 in the 1995–2000 time frame.

EXHIBIT 3.8   *RISK-RETURN TRADE-OFF FOR INTERNATIONAL BOND PORTFOLIOS*

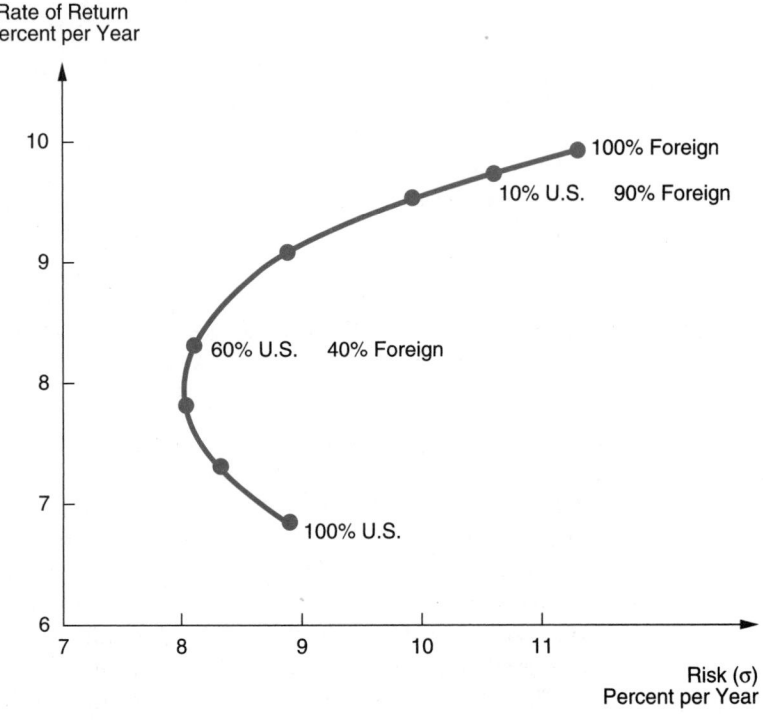

Source: Kenneth Cholerton, Pierre Piergerits, and Bruno Solnik, "Why Invest in Foreign Currency Bonds?" *Journal of Portfolio Management* 12, no. 4 (Summer 1986): 4–8. This copyrighted material is reprinted with permission from *Journal of Portfolio Management,* a publication of Institutional Investor, Inc.

Exhibit 3.8 shows what happens to the risk–return trade-off when we combine U.S. and foreign bonds. A comparison of a completely non-U.S. portfolio (100 percent foreign) and a 100 percent U.S. portfolio indicates that the non-U.S. portfolio has both a higher rate of return and a higher standard deviation of returns than the U.S. portfolio. Combining the two portfolios in different proportions provides an interesting set of points.

As we will discuss in Chapter 7, the expected rate of return is a weighted average of the two portfolios. In contrast, the risk (standard deviation) of the combination is *not* a weighted average but also depends on the correlation between the two portfolios. In this example, the risk levels of the combined portfolios decline below those of the individual portfolios. Therefore, by adding noncorrelated foreign bonds to a portfolio of U.S. bonds, a U.S. investor is able to not only increase the expected rate of return but also reduce the risk of a total U.S. bond portfolio.

Global Equity Portfolio Risk   The correlation of world equity markets resembles that for bonds. Exhibit 3.9 lists the correlation coefficients between monthly equity returns of each country and the U.S. market (in both domestic and U.S. dollars) for the period from 1990 to 2000. Most of the correlations between local currency returns (8 of 11) topped 0.50. The correlations among rates of return adjusted for exchange rates were always lower; 5 of the 11 correlations between U.S. dollar returns were 0.50 or less, and the average correlation was only 0.50.

EXHIBIT 3.9 *CORRELATION COEFFICIENTS BETWEEN TOTAL RETURNS ON COMMON STOCKS IN THE UNITED STATES AND MAJOR FOREIGN STOCK MARKETS: 1990–2000*

	LOCAL CURRENCY TOTAL RETURNS	U.S. DOLLAR TOTAL RETURNS
Australia	0.55	0.50
Canada	0.73	0.72
France	0.57	0.54
Germany	0.53	0.49
Italy	0.30	0.28
Japan	0.35	0.32
Netherlands	0.61	0.58
Spain	0.53	0.51
Sweden	0.43	0.45
Switzerland	0.63	0.54
United Kingdom	0.66	0.61

Source: Correlation table computed by the author using monthly FT-Actuaries return data from Goldman, Sachs & Co.

These relatively small positive correlations between U.S. stocks and foreign stocks have similar implications to those derived for bonds. Investors can reduce the overall risk of their stock portfolios by including foreign stocks.

Exhibit 3.10 demonstrates the impact of international equity diversification. These curves demonstrate that, as you increase the number of randomly selected securities in a portfolio, the standard deviation will decline due to the benefits of diversification *within your own country.* This is referred to as *domestic diversification.* After a certain number of securities (30 to 40), the curve will flatten out at a risk level that reflects the basic market risk for the domestic economy. The lower curve illustrates the benefits of international diversification. This curve demonstrates that adding foreign securities to a U.S. portfolio to create a global portfolio enables an investor to experience lower overall risk because the non-U.S. securities are not correlated with our economy or our stock market, allowing the investor to eliminate some of the basic market risks of the U.S. economy.

To see how this works, consider, for example, the effect of inflation and interest rates on all U.S. securities. As discussed in Chapter 1, all U.S. securities will be affected by these variables. In contrast, a Japanese stock is mainly affected by what happens in the Japanese economy and will typically not be affected by changes in U.S. variables. Thus, adding Japanese, German, and French stocks to a U.S. stock portfolio reduces the portfolio risk of the global portfolio to a level that reflects only worldwide systematic factors.

Summary on Global Investing   At this point, we have considered the relative size of the market for non-U.S. bonds and stocks and found that it has grown in size and importance, becoming too big to ignore. We have also examined the rates of return for foreign bond and stock investments and determined that, when considering domestic results, their rates of return per unit of risk were superior to those in the U.S. market. This did not carry over for returns in U.S. dollars because the returns in U.S. dollars were typically lower during the 1990s because of the strength of the dollar and the risk was always higher, and this had a major impact on the return-risk results. Finally, we discussed constructing a portfolio of investments and the importance of diversification in reducing the variability of returns over time, which reduces the risk of

EXHIBIT 3.10 *RISK REDUCTION THROUGH NATIONAL AND INTERNATIONAL DIVERSIFICATION*

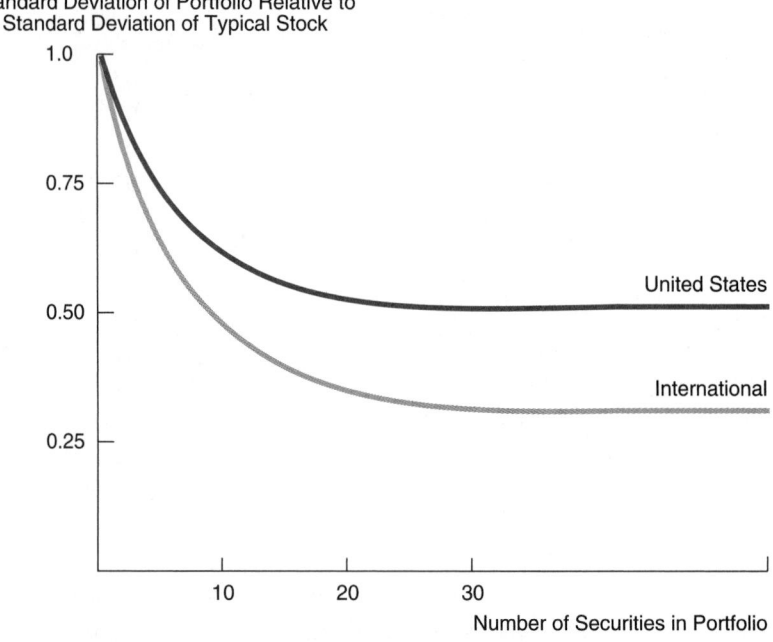

the portfolio. As noted, to have successful diversification, an investor should combine investments with low positive or negative correlations between rates of return. An analysis of the correlation between rates of return on U.S. and foreign bonds and stocks indicated a consistent pattern of low positive correlations. Therefore, the existence of similar rates of return on foreign securities combined with low correlation coefficients indicates that adding foreign stocks and bonds to a U.S. portfolio *will almost certainly reduce the risk of the portfolio and can possibly increase its average return.*

As promised, several rather compelling reasons exist for adding foreign securities to a U.S. portfolio. Therefore, developing a global investment perspective is important because such an approach has been shown to be justified, and this current trend in the investment world is expected to continue. Implementing this new global investment perspective will not be easy because it requires an understanding of new terms, instruments (such as Eurobonds), and institutions (such as non-U.S. stock and bond markets). Still, the effort is justified because you are developing a set of skills and a way of thinking that will enhance your investing results.

The next section presents an overview of investment alternatives from around the world, beginning with fixed-income investments and progressing through numerous alternatives.

GLOBAL INVESTMENT CHOICES

This section provides an important foundation for subsequent chapters in which we describe techniques to value individual investments and combine alternative investments into properly diversified portfolios that conform to your risk-return objectives. In this section, we briefly describe the numerous investment alternatives available and provide an overview of each. The purpose of this survey is to briefly introduce each of these investment alternatives so you can appreciate the full spectrum of opportunities.

The investments are divided by asset classes. First, we describe fixed-income investments, including bonds and preferred stocks. In the second subsection, we discuss equity investments, and the third subsection contains a discussion of special equity instruments, such as warrants and options, which have characteristics of both fixed-income and equity instruments. In subsection four, we consider futures contracts that allow for a wide range of return-risk profiles. The fifth subsection considers investment companies.

All these investments are called *financial assets* because their payoffs are in money. In contrast, *real assets,* such as real estate, are discussed in the sixth subsection. We conclude with assets that are considered *low liquidity investments* because of the relative difficulty in buying and selling them. This includes art, antiques, coins, stamps, and precious gems.

The final section of the chapter describes the historical return and risk patterns for many individual investment alternatives and the correlations among the returns for these investments. This additional background and perspective will help you evaluate individual investments in order to build a properly diversified portfolio of global investments.

Fixed-Income Investments

Fixed-income investments have a contractually mandated payment schedule. Their investment contracts promise specific payments at predetermined times, although the legal force behind the promise varies and this affects their risks and required returns. At one extreme, if the issuing firm does not make its payment at the appointed time, creditors can declare the issuing firm bankrupt. In other cases (for example, income bonds), the issuing firm must make payments only if it earns profits. In yet other instances (for example, preferred stock), the issuing firm does not have to make payments unless its board of directors votes to do so.

Investors who acquire fixed-income securities (except preferred stock) are really lenders to the issuers. Specifically, you lend some amount of money, the *principal,* to the borrower. In return, the borrower promises to make periodic interest payments and to pay back the principal at the maturity of the loan.

Savings Accounts

You might not think of savings accounts as fixed-income investments, yet an individual who deposits funds in a savings account at a bank or savings and loan association (S&L) is really lending money to the institution and, as a result, earning a fixed payment. These investments are generally considered to be convenient, liquid, and low risk because almost all are insured. Consequently, their rates of return are generally low compared with other alternatives. Several versions of these accounts have been developed to appeal to investors with differing objectives.

The passbook savings account has no minimum balance, and funds may be withdrawn at any time with little loss of interest. Due to its flexibility, the promised interest on passbook accounts is relatively low.

For investors with larger amounts of funds who are willing to give up liquidity, banks and S&Ls developed **certificates of deposit (CDs)**, which require minimum deposits (typically $500) and have fixed durations (usually three months, six months, one year, two years). The promised rates on CDs are higher than those for passbook savings, and the rate increases with the size and the duration of the deposit. An investor who wants to cash in a CD prior to its stated expiration date must pay a heavy penalty in the form of a much lower interest rate.

Investors with large sums of money ($10,000 or more) can invest in Treasury bills (T-bills)—short-term obligations (maturing in 3 to 12 months) of the U.S. government. To compete against T-bills, banks and S&Ls issue money market certificates, which require minimum investments of $10,000 and have minimum maturities of six months. The promised rate on these certificates fluctuates at some premium over the weekly rate on six-month T-bills. Investors can redeem these certificates only at the bank of issue, and they incur penalties if they withdraw their funds before maturity.

Capital Market Instruments Capital market instruments are fixed-income obligations that trade in the secondary market, which means you can buy and sell them to other individuals or institutions. Capital market instruments fall into four categories: (1) U.S. Treasury securities, (2) U.S. government agency securities, (3) municipal bonds, and (4) corporate bonds.

U.S. Treasury Securities All government securities issued by the U.S. Treasury are fixed-income instruments. They may be bills, notes, or bonds depending on their times to maturity. Specifically, bills mature in one year or less, notes in over one to 10 years, and bonds in more than 10 years from time of issue. U.S. government obligations are essentially free of credit risk because there is little chance of default and they are highly liquid.

U.S. Government Agency Securities Agency securities are sold by various agencies of the government to support specific programs, but they are not direct obligations of the Treasury. Examples of agencies that issue these bonds include the Federal National Mortgage Association (FNMA or Fannie Mae), which sells bonds and uses the proceeds to purchase mortgages from insurance companies or savings and loans; and the Federal Home Loan Bank (FHLB), which sells bonds and loans the money to its 12 banks, which in turn provide credit to savings and loans and other mortgage-granting institutions. Other agencies are the Government National Mortgage Association (GNMA or Ginnie Mae), Banks for Cooperatives, Federal Land Banks (FLBs), and the Federal Housing Administration (FHA).

Although the securities issued by federal agencies are not direct obligations of the government, they are virtually default-free because it is inconceivable that the government would allow them to default. Also, they are fairly liquid. Because they are not officially guaranteed by the Treasury, they are not considered riskless. Also, because they are not as liquid as Treasury bonds, they typically provide slightly higher returns than Treasury issues.

Municipal Bonds Municipal bonds are issued by local government entities as either general obligation or revenue bonds. General obligation bonds (GOs) are backed by the full taxing power of the municipality, whereas revenue bonds pay the interest from revenue generated by specific projects (e.g., the revenue to pay the interest on sewer bonds comes from water taxes).

Municipal bonds differ from other fixed-income securities because they are tax-exempt. The interest earned from them is exempt from taxation by the federal government and by the state that issued the bond, provided the investor is a resident of that state. For this reason, municipal bonds are popular with investors in high tax brackets. For an investor having a marginal tax rate of 35 percent, a regular bond with an interest rate of 8 percent yields a net return after taxes of only 5.20 percent [$0.08 \times (1 - 0.35)$]. Such an investor would prefer a tax-free bond of equal risk with a 6 percent yield. This allows municipal bonds to offer yields that are generally 20 to 30 percent lower than yields on comparable taxable bonds.

Corporate Bonds Corporate bonds are fixed-income securities issued by industrial corporations, public utility corporations, or railroads to raise funds to invest in plant, equipment, or working capital. They can be broken down by issuer, in terms of credit quality (measured by the ratings assigned by an agency on the basis of probability of default), in terms of maturity (short term, intermediate term, or long term), or based on some component of the indenture (sinking fund or call feature).

All bonds include an **indenture**, which is the legal agreement that lists the obligations of the issuer to the bondholder, including the payment schedule and features such as call provisions and sinking funds. **Call provisions** specify when a firm can issue a call for the bonds prior to their maturity, at which time current bondholders must submit the bonds to the issuing firm, which redeems them (that is, pays back the principal and a small premium). A **sinking fund** provision specifies payments the issuer must make to redeem a given percentage of the outstanding issue prior to maturity.

Corporate bonds fall into various categories based on their contractual promises to investors. They will be discussed in order of their seniority.

Secured bonds are the most senior bonds in a firm's capital structure and have the lowest risk of distress or default. They include various secured issues that differ based on the assets that are pledged. **Mortgage bonds** are backed by liens on specific assets, such as land and buildings. In the case of bankruptcy, the proceeds from the sale of these assets are used to pay off the mortgage bondholders. **Collateral trust bonds** are a form of mortgage bond except that the assets backing the bonds are financial assets, such as stocks, notes, and other high-quality bonds. Finally, **equipment trust certificates** are mortgage bonds that are secured by specific pieces of transportation equipment, such as locomotives and boxcars for a railroad and airplanes for an airline.

Debentures are promises to pay interest and principal, but they pledge no specific assets (referred to as *collateral*) in case the firm does not fulfill its promise. This means that the bondholder depends on the success of the borrower to make the promised payment. Debenture owners usually have first call on the firm's earnings and any assets that are not already pledged by the firm as backing for senior secured bonds. If the issuer does not make an interest payment, the debenture owners can declare the firm bankrupt and claim any unpledged assets to pay off the bonds.

Subordinated bonds are similar to debentures, but, in the case of default, subordinated bondholders have claim to the assets of the firm only after the firm has satisfied the claims of all senior secured and debenture bondholders. That is, the claims of subordinated bondholders are secondary to those of other bondholders. Within this general category of subordinated issues, you can find senior subordinated, subordinated, and junior subordinated bonds. Junior subordinated bonds have the weakest claim of all bondholders.

Income bonds stipulate interest payment schedules, but the interest is due and payable only if the issuers earn the income to make the payment by stipulated dates. If the company does not earn the required amount, it does not have to make the interest payment and it cannot be declared bankrupt. Instead, the interest payment is considered in arrears and, if subsequently earned, it must be paid off. Because the issuing firm is not legally bound to make its interest payments except when the firm earns it, an income bond is not considered as safe as a debenture or a mortgage bond, so income bonds offer higher returns to compensate investors for the added risk. There are a limited number of corporate income bonds. In contrast, income bonds are fairly popular with municipalities because municipal revenue bonds are basically income bonds.

Convertible bonds have the interest and principal characteristics of other bonds, with the added feature that the bondholder has the option to turn them back to the firm in exchange for its common stock. For example, a firm could issue a $1,000 face-value bond and stipulate that owners of the bond could turn the bond in to the issuing corporation and convert it into 40 shares of the firm's common stock. These bonds appeal to investors because they combine the features of a fixed-income security with the option of conversion into the common stock of the firm, should the firm prosper.

Because of their desirable conversion option, convertible bonds generally pay lower interest rates than nonconvertible debentures of comparable risk. The difference in the required interest rate increases with the growth potential of the company because this increases the value of the option to convert the bonds into common stock. These bonds are almost always subordinated to the nonconvertible debt of the firm, so they are considered to have higher credit risk and receive a lower credit rating from the rating firms.

An alternative to convertible bonds is a debenture with warrants attached. The **warrant** is an option that allows the bondholder to purchase the firm's common stock from the firm at a specified price for a given time period. The specified purchase price for the stock set in the warrant is typically above the price of the stock at the time the firm issues the bond but below the expected future stock price. The warrant makes the debenture more desirable, which lowers its required yield. The warrant also provides the firm with future common stock capital when the holder exercises the warrant and buys the stock from the firm.

Unlike the typical bond that pays interest every six months and its face value at maturity, a **zero coupon bond** promises no interest payments during the life of the bond but only the payment of the principal at maturity. Therefore, the purchase price of the bond is the present value of the principal payment at the required rate of return. For example, the price of a zero coupon bond that promises to pay $10,000 in five years with a required rate of return of 8 percent is $6,756. To find this, assuming semiannual compounding (which is the norm), use the present value factor for 10 periods at 4 percent, which is 0.6756.

Preferred Stock

Preferred stock is classified as a fixed-income security because its yearly payment is stipulated as either a coupon (for example, 5 percent of the face value) or a stated dollar amount (for example, $5 preferred). Preferred stock differs from bonds because its payment is a dividend and therefore not legally binding. For each period, the firm's board of directors must vote to pay it, similar to a common stock dividend. Even if the firm earned enough money to pay the preferred stock dividend, the board of directors could theoretically vote to withhold it. Because most preferred stock is cumulative, the unpaid dividends would accumulate to be paid in full at a later time.

Although preferred dividends are not legally binding, as are the interest payments on a bond, they are considered *practically* binding because of the credit implications of a missed dividend. Because corporations can exclude 80 percent of intercompany dividends from taxable income, preferred stocks have become attractive investments for financial corporations. For example, a corporation that owns preferred stock of another firm and receives $100 in dividends can exclude 80 percent of this amount and pay taxes on only 20 percent of it ($20). Assuming a 40 percent tax rate, the tax would only be $8 or 8 percent versus 40 percent on other investment income. Due to this tax benefit, the yield on high-grade preferred stock is typically lower than that on high-grade bonds.

International Bond Investing

As noted earlier, more than half of all fixed-income securities available to U.S. investors are issued by firms in countries outside the United States. Investors identify these securities in different ways: by the country or city of the issuer (for example, United States, United Kingdom, Japan); by the location of the primary trading market (for example, United States, London); by the home country of the major buyers; and by the currency in which the securities are denominated (for example, dollars, yen, pounds sterling). We identify foreign bonds by their country of origin and include these other differences in each description.

A **Eurobond** is an international bond denominated in a currency not native to the country where it is issued. Specific kinds of Eurobonds include Eurodollar bonds, Euroyen bonds, Eurodeutschemark bonds, and Eurosterling bonds. A Eurodollar bond is denominated in U.S. dollars and sold outside the United States to non-U.S. investors. A specific example would be a U.S. dollar bond issued by General Motors and sold in London. Eurobonds are typically issued in Europe, with the major concentration in London.

Eurobonds can also be denominated in yen. For example, Nippon Steel can issue Euroyen bonds for sale in London. Also, if it appears that investors are looking for foreign currency bonds, a U.S. corporation can issue a Euroyen bond in London.

Yankee bonds are sold in the United States, denominated in U.S. dollars, but issued by foreign corporations or governments. This allows a U.S. citizen to buy the bond of a foreign firm or government but receive all payments in U.S. dollars, eliminating exchange rate risk.

An example would be a U.S. dollar–denominated bond issued by British Airways. Similar bonds are issued in other countries, including the Bulldog Market, which involves British sterling–denominated bonds issued in the United Kingdom by non-British firms, or the Samurai Market, which involves yen-denominated bonds issued in Japan by non-Japanese firms.

International domestic bonds are sold by an issuer within its own country in that country's currency. An example would be a bond sold by Nippon Steel in Japan denominated in yen. A U.S. investor acquiring such a bond would receive maximum diversification but would incur exchange rate risk.

Equity Instruments This section describes several equity instruments, which differ from fixed-income securities because their returns are not contractual. As a result, you can receive returns that are much better or much worse than what you would receive on a bond. We begin with common stock, the most popular equity instrument and probably the most popular investment instrument.

Common stock represents *ownership* of a firm. Owners of the common stock of a firm share in the company's successes and problems. If, like Wal-Mart Stores, Home Depot, Microsoft, or Intel, the company prospers, the investor receives high rates of return and can become wealthy. In contrast, the investor can lose money if the firm does not do well or even goes bankrupt, as the once formidable K-Mart, Enron, W. T. Grant, and Interstate Department Stores all did. In these instances, the firm is forced to liquidate its assets and pay off all its creditors. Notably, the firm's preferred stockholders and common stock owners receive what is left, which is usually little or nothing. Investing in common stock entails all the advantages and disadvantages of ownership and is a relatively risky investment compared with fixed-income securities.

Common Stock Classifications

When considering an investment in common stock, people tend to divide the vast universe of stocks into categories based on general business lines and by industry within these business lines. The division includes broad classifications for industrial firms, utilities, transportation firms, and financial institutions. Within each of these broad classes are industries. The most diverse industrial group includes such industries as automobiles, industrial machinery, chemicals, and beverages. Utilities include electrical power companies, gas suppliers, and the water industry. Transportation includes airlines, trucking firms, and railroads. Financial institutions include banks, savings and loans, insurance companies, and investment firms.

An alternative classification scheme might separate domestic (U.S.) and foreign common stocks. We avoid this division because the business line–industry breakdown is more appropriate and useful when constructing a diversified portfolio of global common stock investments. With a global capital market, the focus of analysis should include all the companies in an industry viewed in a global setting. The point is, it is not relevant whether a major chemical firm is located in the United States or Germany, just as it is not releveant whether a computer firm is located in Michigan or California. Therefore, when considering the automobile industry, it is necessary to go beyond pure U.S. auto firms like General Motors and Ford and consider auto firms from throughout the world, such as Honda Motors, Porsche, Daimler-Chrysler, Nissan, and Fiat.

Acquiring Foreign Equities

We begin our discussion on foreign equities regarding how you buy and sell these securities because this procedural information has often been a major impediment. Many investors may recognize the desirability of investing in foreign common stock because of the risk and return characteristics, but they may be intimidated by the logistics of the transaction. The purpose of this section is to alleviate this concern by explaining the alternatives available. Currently, there are several ways to acquire foreign common stock:

1. Purchase or sale of American Depository Receipts (ADRs)
2. Purchase or sale of American shares
3. Direct purchase or sale of foreign shares listed on a U.S. or foreign stock exchange
4. Purchase or sale of international or global mutual funds

Purchase or Sale of American Depository Receipts   The easiest way to acquire foreign shares directly is through **American Depository Receipts (ADRs)**. These are certificates of ownership issued by a U.S. bank that represent indirect ownership of a certain number of shares of a specific foreign firm on deposit in a bank in the firm's home country. ADRs are a convenient way to own foreign shares because the investor buys and sells them in U.S. dollars and receives all dividends in U.S. dollars. Therefore, the price and returns reflect both the domestic returns for the stock and the exchange rate effect. Also, the price of an ADR can reflect the fact that it represents multiple shares—for example, an ADR can be for 5 or 10 shares of the foreign stock. ADRs can be issued at the discretion of a bank based on the demand for the stock. The shareholder absorbs the additional handling costs of an ADR through higher transfer expenses, which are deducted from dividend payments.

ADRs are quite popular in the United States because of their diversification benefits.[3] By the end of 2000, 434 foreign companies had stocks listed on the New York Stock Exchange (NYSE) and 345 of these were available through ADRs, including all the stock listed from Japan, the United Kingdom, Australia, Mexico, and the Netherlands.

Purchase or Sale of American Shares   American shares are securities issued in the United States by a transfer agent acting on behalf of a foreign firm. Because of the added effort and expense incurred by the foreign firm, a limited number of American shares are available.

Direct Purchase or Sale of Foreign Shares   The most difficult and complicated foreign equity transaction takes place in the country where the firm is located because it must be carried out in the foreign currency and the shares must then be transferred to the United States. This routine can be cumbersome. A second alternative is a transaction on a foreign stock exchange outside the country where the securities originated. For example, if you acquired shares of a French auto company listed on the London Stock Exchange (LSE), the shares would be denominated in pounds and the transfer would be swift, assuming your broker has a membership on the LSE.

Finally, you could purchase foreign stocks listed on the NYSE or AMEX. This is similar to buying a U.S. stock, but only a limited number of foreign firms qualify for—and are willing to accept—the cost of listing. Still, this number is growing. At the end of 2000, more than 96 foreign firms (mostly Canadian) were directly listed on the NYSE, in addition to the firms that were available through ADRs. Also, many foreign firms are traded on the National Association of Securities Dealers Automatic Quotations (Nasdaq) system.

Purchase or Sale of International or Global Mutual Funds   Numerous investment companies invest all or a portion of their funds in stocks of firms outside the United States. The alternatives range from *global funds,* which invest in both U.S. stocks and foreign stocks, to *international funds,* which invest almost wholly outside the United States. In turn, international funds can (1) diversify across many countries, (2) concentrate in a segment of the world (for example, Europe, South America, the Pacific basin), (3) concentrate in a specific country (for

---

[3]For evidence of this, see Mahmoud Wahab and Amit Khandwala, "Why Not Diversify Internationally with ADRs?" *Journal of Portfolio Management* 19, no. 2 (Winter 1993): 75–82.

example, the Japan Fund, the Germany Fund, the Italy Fund, or the Korea Fund), or (4) concentrate in types of markets (for example, emerging markets, which would include stocks from countries such as Thailand, Indonesia, India, and China). A mutual fund is a convenient path to global investing, particularly for a small investor, because the purchase or sale of one of these funds is similar to a transaction for a comparable U.S. mutual fund.[4]

Special Equity Instruments: Options

In addition to common stock investments, it is also possible to invest in equity-derivative securities, which are securities that have a claim on the common stock of a firm. This would include **options**—rights to buy or sell common stock at a specified price for a stated period of time. The two kinds of option instruments are (1) warrants and (2) puts and calls.

Warrants   As mentioned earlier, a warrant is an option issued by a corporation that gives the holder the right to acquire a firm's common stock from the company at a specified price within a designated time period. The warrant does not constitute ownership of the stock, only the option to buy the stock.

Puts and Calls   A **call option** is similar to a warrant because it is an option to buy the common stock of a company within a certain period at a specified price called the *striking price*. A call option differs from a warrant because it is not issued by the company but by another investor who is willing to assume the other side of the transaction. Options also are typically valid for a shorter time period than warrants. Call options are generally valid for less than a year, whereas warrants extend more than five years. The holder of a **put option** has the right to sell a given stock at a specified price during a designated time period. Puts are useful to investors who expect a stock price to decline during the specified period or to investors who own the stock and want protection from a price decline.

Futures Contracts

Another instrument that provides an alternative to the purchase of an investment is a **futures contract.** This agreement provides for the future exchange of a particular asset at a specified delivery date (usually within nine months) in exchange for a specified payment at the time of delivery. Although the full payment is not made until the delivery date, a good-faith deposit, the **margin**, is made to protect the seller. This is typically about 10 percent of the value of the contract.

The bulk of trading on the commodity exchanges is in futures contracts. The current price of the futures contract is determined by the participants' beliefs about the future for the commodity. For example, in July of a given year, a trader could speculate on the Chicago Board of Trade for wheat in September, December, March, and May of the next year. If the investor expected the price of a commodity to rise, he or she could buy a futures contract on one of the commodity exchanges for later sale. If the investor expected the price to fall, he or she could sell a futures contract on an exchange with the expectation of buying similar contracts later when the price had declined to cover the sale.

Several differences exist between investing in an asset through a futures contract and investing in the asset itself. One is the use of a small good-faith deposit, which increases the volatility of returns. Because an investor puts up only a small portion of the total value of the futures contract (10 to 15 percent), when the price of the commodity changes, the change in the total value of the contract is large compared to the amount invested. Another unique aspect is the term of the investment: Although stocks can have infinite maturities, futures contracts typically expire in less than a year.

---

[4]Mutual funds in general and those related to global investing are discussed in Chapter 25.

Financial Futures   In addition to futures contracts on commodities, there also has been the development of futures contracts on financial instruments, such as T-bills, Treasury bonds, and Eurobonds. For example, it is possible to buy or sell a futures contract that promises future delivery of $100,000 of Treasury bonds at a set price and yield. The major exchanges for financial futures are the Chicago Mercantile Exchange (CME) and the Chicago Board of Trade (CBOT). These futures contracts allow individual investors, bond portfolio managers, and corporate financial managers to protect themselves against volatile interest rates. Certain currency futures allow individual investors or portfolio managers to speculate on or to protect against changes in currency exchange rates. Finally, futures contracts pertain to stock market series, such as the S&P (Standard & Poor's) 500, the *Value Line* Index, and the Nikkei Average on the Tokyo Stock Exchange.

Investment Companies   The investment alternatives described so far are individual securities that can be acquired from a government entity, a corporation, or another individual. However, rather than directly buying an individual stock or bond issued by one of these sources, you may choose to acquire these investments indirectly by buying shares in an investment company, also called a **mutual fund**, that owns a portfolio of individual stocks, bonds, or a combination of the two. Specifically, an **investment company** sells shares in itself and uses the proceeds of this sale to acquire bonds, stocks, or other investment instruments. As a result, an investor who acquires shares in an investment company is a partial owner of the investment company's portfolio of stocks or bonds. We will distinguish investment companies by the types of investment instruments they acquire.

Money Market Funds   **Money market funds** are investment companies that acquire high-quality, short-term investments (referred to as *money market* instruments), such as T-bills, high-grade commercial paper (public short-term loans) from various corporations, and large CDs from the major money center banks. The yields on the money market portfolios always surpass those on normal bank CDs because the investment by the money market fund is larger and the fund can commit to longer maturities than the typical individual. In addition, the returns on commercial paper are above the prime rate. The typical minimum initial investment in a money market fund is $1,000, it charges no sales commission, and minimum additions are $250 to $500. You can always withdraw funds from your money market fund without penalty (typically by writing a check on the account), and you receive interest to the day of withdrawal.

Individuals tend to use money market funds as alternatives to bank savings accounts because they are generally quite safe (although they are not insured, they typically limit their investments to high-quality, short-term investments), they provide yields above what is available on most savings accounts, and the funds are readily available. Therefore, you might use one of these funds to accumulate funds to pay tuition or for a down payment on a car. Because of relatively high yields and extreme flexibility and liquidity, the total value of these funds reached more than $1.8 trillion in 2000.

Bond Funds   Bond funds generally invest in various long-term government, corporate, or municipal bonds. They differ by the type and quality of the bonds included in the portfolio as assessed by various rating services. Specifically, the bond funds range from those that invest only in risk-free government bonds and high-grade corporate bonds to those that concentrate in lower-rated corporate or municipal bonds, called **high-yield bonds** or *junk bonds*. The expected rate of return from various bond funds will differ, with the low-risk government bond funds paying the lowest returns and the high-yield bond funds expected to pay the highest returns.

Common Stock Funds   Numerous common stock funds invest to achieve stated investment objectives, which can include aggressive growth, income, precious metal investments, and international stocks. Such funds offer smaller investors the benefits of diversification and professional management. They include different investment styles, such as growth or value, and concentrate in alternative-sized firms, including small-cap, mid-cap, and large-capitalization stocks. To meet the diverse needs of investors, numerous funds have been created that concentrate in one industry or sector of the economy, such as chemicals, electric utilities, health, housing, and technology. These funds are diversified within a sector or an industry, but are not diversified across the total market. Investors who participate in a sector or an industry fund bear more risk than investors in a total market fund because the sector funds will tend to fluctuate more than an aggregate market fund that is diversified across all sectors. Also, international funds that invest outside the United States and global funds that invest in the United States and in other countries offer opportunities for global investing by individual investors.[5]

Balanced Funds   Balanced funds invest in a combination of bonds and stocks of various sorts depending on their stated objectives.

Index Funds   Index funds are mutual funds created to equal the performance of a market index like the S&P 500. Such funds appeal to *passive* investors who want to simply experience returns equal to some market index either because they do not want to try to "beat the market" or they believe in efficient markets and do not think it is possible to do better than the market in the long run. Given the popularity of these funds, they have been created to emulate numerous stock indexes including very broad indexes like the Wilshire 5000, broad foreign indexes like the EAFE index, and nonstock indexes including various bond indexes for those who want passive bond investing.

Exchange-Traded Funds (ETFs)   A problem with mutual funds in general and index funds in particular is that they are only priced daily at the close of the market and all transactions take place at that price. As a result, if you are aware of changes taking place for the aggregate market due to some economic event during the day and want to buy or sell to take advantage of this, you can put in an order but it will not be executed until the end of the day at closing prices. In response to this problem, the AMEX in 1993 created an indexed fund tied to the S&P 500—that is, an exchange-traded fund, ETF—that could be traded continuously because the prices for the 500 stocks are updated continuously so it is possible to buy and sell this ETF like a share of stock. This concept of an ETF has been applied to other foreign and domestic indexes including the Morgan Stanley Capital International (MSCI) indexes. Barclay's Global Investors (BGI) have created "i shares" using the MSCI indexes for numerous individual countries.[6]

Real Estate   Like commodities, most investors view real estate as an interesting and profitable investment alternative but believe that it is only available to a small group of experts with a lot of capital to invest. In reality, some feasible real estate investments require no detailed expertise or large capital commitments. We will begin by considering low-capital alternatives.

---

[5]For a study that examines the diversification of individual country funds, see Warren Bailey and Joseph Lim, "Evaluating the Diversification Benefits of the New Country Funds," *Journal of Portfolio Management* 18, no. 3 (Spring 1992): 74–80.

[6]For an analysis of these funds, see Ajay Khorana, Edward Nelling, and Jeffrey Trester, "The Emergence of Country Index Funds," *Journal of Portfolio Management* 24, no. 4 (Summer 1998): 78–84.

Real Estate Investment Trusts (REITS)   A **real estate investment trust** is an investment fund designed to invest in various real estate properties. It is similar to a stock or bond mutual fund, except that the money provided by the investors is invested in property and buildings rather than in stocks and bonds. There are several types of REITs.

Construction and development trusts lend the money required by builders during the initial construction of a building. *Mortgage trusts* provide the long-term financing for properties. Specifically, they acquire long-term mortgages on properties once construction is completed. *Equity trusts* own various income-producing properties, such as office buildings, shopping centers, or apartment houses. Therefore, an investor who buys shares in an equity real estate investment trust is buying part of a portfolio of income-producing properties.

REITs have experienced periods of great popularity and significant depression in line with changes in the aggregate economy and the money market. Although they are subject to cyclical risks depending on the economic environment, they offer small investors a way to participate in real estate investments.[7]

Direct Real Estate Investment   The most common type of direct real estate investment is the purchase of a home, which is the largest investment most people ever make. Today, according to the Federal Home Loan Bank, the average cost of a single family house exceeds $115,000. The purchase of a home is considered an investment because the buyer pays a sum of money either all at once or over a number of years through a mortgage. For most people, those unable to pay cash for a house, the financial commitment includes a down payment (typically 10 to 20 percent of the purchase price) and specific mortgage payments over a 20- to 30-year period that include reducing the loan's principal and paying interest on the outstanding balance. Subsequently, a homeowner hopes to sell the house for its cost plus a gain.

Raw Land   Another direct real estate investment is the purchase of raw land with the intention of selling it in the future at a profit. During the time you own the land, you have negative cash flows caused by mortgage payments, property maintenance, and taxes. An obvious risk is the possible difficulty of selling it for an uncertain price. Raw land generally has low liquidity compared to most stocks and bonds. An alternative to buying and selling the raw land is the development of the land.

Land Development   Land development can involve buying raw land, dividing it into individual lots, and building houses on it. Alternatively, buying land and building a shopping mall would also be considered land development. This is a feasible form of investment but requires a substantial commitment of capital, time, and expertise. Although the risks can be high because of the commitment of time and capital, the rates of return from a successful housing or commercial development can be significant.[8]

---

[7]See Eric S. Hardy, "The Ground Floor," *Forbes,* 14 August 1995, 185; and Susan E. Kuhn, "Real Estate: A Smart Alternative to Stocks," *Fortune,* 27 May 1996, 186.

[8]For a review of studies that have examined returns on real estate, see William Goetzmann and Roger Ibbotson, "The Performance of Real Estate as an Asset Class," *Journal of Applied Corporate Finance* 3, no. 1 (Spring 1990): 65–76; C. F. Myer and James Webb, "Return Properties of Equity REITs, Common Stocks, and Commercial Real Estate: A Comparison," *Journal of Real Estate Research* 8, no. 1 (1993): 87–106; and Stephen Ross and Randall Zisler, "Risk and Return in Real Estate," *Journal of Real Estate Financial Economics* 4, no. 2 (1991): 175–190. For an analysis of the diversification possibilities, see Susan Hudson-Wilson and Bernard L. Elbaum, "Diversification Benefits for Investors in Real Estate," *Journal of Portfolio Management* 21, no. 3 (Spring 1995): 92–99.

Rental Property   Many investors with an interest in real estate investing acquire apartment buildings or houses with low down payments, with the intention of deriving enough income from the rents to pay the expenses of the structure, including the mortgage payments. For the first few years following the purchase, the investor generally has no reported income from the building because of tax-deductible expenses, including the interest component of the mortgage payment and depreciation on the structure. Subsequently, rental property provides a cash flow and an opportunity to profit from the sale of the property.[9]

Low-Liquidity Investments   Most of the investment alternatives we have described thus far are traded on securities markets and except for real estate, have good liquidity. In contrast, the investments we discuss in this section have very poor liquidity and financial institutions do not typically acquire them because of the illiquidity and high transaction costs compared to stocks and bonds. Many of these assets are sold at auctions, causing expected prices to vary substantially. In addition, transaction costs are high because there is generally no national market for these investments, so local dealers must be compensated for the added carrying costs and the cost of searching for buyers or sellers. Therefore, many financial theorists view the following low-liquidity investments more as hobbies than investments, even though studies have indicated that some of these assets have experienced substantial rates of return.

Antiques   The greatest returns from antiques are earned by dealers who acquire them at estate sales or auctions to refurbish and sell at a profit. If we gauge the value of antiques based on prices established at large public auctions, it appears that many serious collectors enjoy substantial rates of return. In contrast, the average investor who owns a few pieces to decorate his or her home finds such returns elusive. The high transaction costs and illiquidity of antiques may erode any profit that the individual may expect to earn when selling these pieces.

Art   The entertainment sections of newspapers or the personal finance sections of magazines often carry stories of the results of major art auctions, such as when Van Gogh's *Irises* and *Sunflowers* sold for $59 million and $36 million, respectively.

Obviously, these examples and others indicate that some paintings have increased significantly in value and thereby generated large rates of return for their owners. However, investing in art typically requires substantial knowledge of art and the art world, a large amount of capital to acquire the work of well-known artists, patience, and an ability to absorb high transaction costs. For investors who enjoy fine art and have the resources, these can be satisfying investments; but, for most small investors, it is difficult to get returns that compensate for the uncertainty and illiquidity.[10]

Coins and Stamps   Many individuals enjoy collecting coins or stamps as a hobby and as an investment. The market for coins and stamps is fragmented compared to the stock market, but it is more liquid than the market for art and antiques as indicated by the publication of weekly and monthly price lists.[11] An investor can get a widely recognized grading specification on a coin or

---

[9]For a discussion of this alternative, see Diane Harris, "An Investment for Rent," *Money,* April 1984, 87–90.

[10]For a discussion of art sold at auction, see "Market Is Picture of Optimism in Flux," *The Wall Street Journal,* 26 April 1996, C1.

[11]A weekly publication for coins is *Coin World,* published by Amos Press, Inc., 911 Vandermark Rd., Sidney, OH 45367. There are several monthly coin magazines, including *Coinage,* published by Behn-Miller Publications, Inc., Encino, Calif. Amos Press also publishes several stamp magazines, including *Linn's Stamp News* and *Scott Stamp Monthly.* These magazines provide current prices for coins and stamps.

stamp, and, once graded, a coin or stamp can usually be sold quickly through a dealer.[12] It is important to recognize that the percentage difference between the bid price the dealer will pay to buy the stamp or coin and the asking or selling price the investor must pay the dealer is going to be substantially larger than the bid-ask spread on stocks and bonds.

Diamonds Diamonds can be and have been good investments during many periods. Still, investors who purchase diamonds must realize that (1) diamonds can be highly illiquid, (2) the grading process that determines their quality is quite subjective, (3) most investment-grade gems require substantial investments, and (4) they generate no positive cash flow during the holding period until the stone is sold. In fact, during the holding period, the investor must cover costs of insurance and storage and there are appraisal costs before selling.

In this section, we have briefly described the most common investment alternatives. We will discuss many of these in more detail when we consider how you evaluate them for investment purposes.

In our final section, we will present data on historical rates of return and risk measures, as well as correlations among several of these investments. This should give you some insights into future expected returns and risk characteristics for these investment alternatives.

HISTORICAL RISK-RETURNS ON ALTERNATIVE INVESTMENTS

How do investors weigh the costs and benefits of owning investments and make decisions to build portfolios that will provide the best risk-return combinations? To help individual or institutional investors answer this question, financial theorists have examined extensive data to provide information on the return and risk characteristics of various investments.

There have been numerous studies of the historical rates of return on common stocks, and there has been a growing interest in bonds. Because inflation has been so pervasive, many studies include both nominal and real rates of return on investments. Still other investigators have examined the performance of such assets as real estate, foreign stocks, art, antiques, and commodities. The subsequent review of these results should help you to make decisions on building your investment portfolio and on the allocation to the various asset classes.

Stocks, Bonds, and T-Bills A set of studies by Ibbotson and Sinquefield (I&S) examined historical nominal and real rates of return for seven major classes of assets in the United States: (1) large-company common stocks, (2) small-capitalization common stocks,[13] (3) long-term U.S. government bonds, (4) long-term corporate bonds, (5) intermediate-term U.S. government bonds, (6) U.S. Treasury bills, and (7) consumer goods (a measure of inflation).[14] For each asset, the authors calculated total rates of return before taxes or transaction costs.

---

[12]For an article that describes the alternative grading services, see Diana Henriques, "Don't Take Any Wooden Nickels," *Barron's,* 19 June 1989, 16, 18, 20, 32. For an analysis of commemorative coins, see R. W. Bradford, "How to Lose a Mint," *Barron's,* 6 March 1989, 54, 55.

[13]Small-capitalization stocks were broken out as a separate class of asset because several studies have shown that firms with relatively small capitalization (stock with low market value) have experienced rates of return and risk significantly different from those of stocks in general. Therefore, they were considered a unique asset class. We will discuss these studies in Chapter 6, which deals with the efficient markets hypothesis. The large-company stock returns are based upon the S&P Composite Index of 500 stocks—the S&P 500 (described in Chapter 5).

[14]The original study was by Roger G. Ibbotson and Rex A. Sinquefield, "Stocks, Bonds, Bills, and Inflation: Year-by-Year Historical Returns (1926–1974)," *Journal of Business* 49, no. 1 (January 1976): 11–47. Although this study was updated in several monographs, the current update is contained in *Stocks, Bonds, Bills, and Inflation: 2002 Yearbook* (Chicago: Ibbotson Associates, 2002).

These investigators computed geometric and arithmetic mean rates of return and computed nine series derived from the basic series. Four of these series were net returns reflecting different premiums: (1) a *risk premium,* which I&S defined as the difference in the rate of return that investors receive from investing in large-company common stocks rather than in risk-free U.S. Treasury bills; (2) a *small-stock premium,* which they defined as the return on small-capitalization stocks minus the return on large-company stocks; (3) a *horizon premium,* which they defined as the difference in the rate of return received from investing in long-term government bonds rather than short-term U.S. Treasury bills; and (4) a *default premium,* which they defined as the difference between the rates of return on long-term risky corporate bonds and long-term risk-free government bonds. I&S also computed the real inflation-adjusted rates of return for the six major classes of assets (not including inflation).

A summary of the rates of return, risk premiums, and standard deviations for the basic and derived series appears in Exhibit 3.11. As discussed in Chapter 1, the geometric means of the rates of return are always lower than the arithmetic means of the rates of return, and the difference between these two mean values increases with the standard deviation of returns.

During the period from 1926 to 2001, large-company common stocks returned 10.7 percent a year, compounded annually. To compare this to other investments, the results show that common stock experienced a risk premium of 6.6 percent and inflation-adjusted real returns of 7.4 percent per year. In contrast to all common stocks, the small-capitalization stocks (which are represented by the smallest 20 percent of stocks listed on the NYSE measured by market value) experienced a geometric mean return of 12.5 percent, which was a premium compared to all common stocks of 1.6 percent.

EXHIBIT 3.11   *BASIC AND DERIVED SERIES: HISTORICAL HIGHLIGHTS (1926–2001)*

SERIES	ANNUAL GEOMETRIC MEAN RATE OF RETURN	ARITHMETIC MEAN OF ANNUAL RETURNS	STANDARD DEVIATION OF ANNUAL RETURNS
Large-company stocks	10.7%	12.7%	20.2%
Small-capitalization stocks	12.5	17.3	33.2
Long-term corporate bonds	5.8	6.1	8.6
Long-term government bonds	5.3	5.7	9.4
Intermediate-term government bonds	5.3	5.5	5.7
U.S. Treasury bills	3.8	3.9	3.2
Consumer price index	3.1	3.1	4.4
Equity risk premium	6.6	8.6	19.9
Small-stock premium	1.6	3.3	18.4
Default premium	0.4	0.5	3.1
Horizon premium	1.4	1.8	8.5
Large-company stock—inflation adjusted	7.4	9.4	20.2
Small-capitalization stock—inflation adjusted	8.7	13.3	32.1
Long-term corporate bonds—inflation adjusted	2.6	3.1	9.8
Long-term government bonds—inflation adjusted	2.2	2.7	10.5
Intermediate-term government bonds—inflation adjusted	2.2	2.4	6.9
U.S. Treasury bills—inflation adjusted	0.7	0.8	4.1

Although large-cap common stocks and small-capitalization stocks experienced higher rates of return than the other asset groups, their returns were also more volatile as measured by the standard deviations of annual returns.

Long-term U.S. government bonds experienced a 5.3 percent annual return, a real return of 2.2 percent, and a horizon premium (compared to Treasury bills) of 1.4 percent. Although the returns on these bonds were lower than those on stocks, they were also far less volatile.

The annual compound rate of return on long-term corporate bonds was 5.8 percent, the default premium compared to U.S. government bonds was 0.4 percent, and the inflation-adjusted return was 2.6 percent. Although corporate bonds provided a higher return, as one would expect, the volatility of corporate bonds was slightly lower than that experienced by long-term government bonds.

The nominal return on U.S. Treasury bills was 3.8 percent a year, whereas the inflation-adjusted return was 0.7 percent. The standard deviation of nominal returns for T-bills was the lowest of the series examined, which reflects the low risk of these securities and is consistent with the lowest rate of return.

This study reported the rates of return, return premiums, and risk measures on various asset groups in the United States. As noted, the rates of return were generally consistent with the uncertainty (risk) of annual returns as measured by the standard deviations of annual returns.

World Portfolio Performance

Expanding this analysis from domestic to global securities, Reilly and Wright examined the performance of numerous assets, not only in the United States, but around the world.[15] Specifically, for the period from 1980 to 1999, they examined the performance of stocks, bonds, cash (the equivalent of U.S. T-bills), real estate, and commodities from the United States, Canada, Europe, Japan, and the emerging markets. He computed annual returns, risk measures, and correlations among the returns for alternative assets. Exhibit 3.12 shows the geometric and arithmetic average annual rates of return, the standard deviations of returns, and the systematic risk (beta) for the 20-year period.

Asset Return and Risk   The results in Exhibit 3.12 generally confirm the expected relationship between annual rates of return and the risk of these securities. The riskier assets—those that had higher standard deviations—experienced higher returns. For example, the MSCI, EAFE, and Frankfurt FAZ indexes had relatively high returns (16.74 and 14.31 percent) and very large standard deviations (20.64 and 23.48 percent). It is not a surprise that the highest-risk asset class (without commodities) was emerging market stock at 28.87 percent, whereas risk-free U.S. cash equivalents (one-year government bonds) had low returns (8.14 percent) and the smallest standard deviation (3.78 percent).

Relative Asset Risk   The coefficients of variation (CVs), which measure relative variability, indicated a wide range of values. The lowest CV was experienced by the low-risk one-year government bond. Japanese stocks had the highest CV value because of their large standard deviation and relatively low returns during this period. The CVs for stocks ranged from 0.69 to 2.74, with U.S. stocks toward the low end due to the strong rates of return during this period. Finally, the Brinson Global Security Market index had a very low CV (0.63), demonstrating the benefits of global diversification.

---

[15]Frank K. Reilly and David J. Wright, "An Analysis of Global Capital Market Risk-Adjusted Returns," Mimeo (July 2001).

EXHIBIT 3.12 ▶ *SUMMARY RISK-RETURN RESULTS FOR ALTERNATIVE CAPITAL MARKET ASSETS: 1980–1999*

INDEX	ARITHMETIC RETURN	GEOMETRIC RETURN	STANDARD DEVIATION	COEFFICIENT OF VARIATION[a]	BETA 20 YEARS[b]
S&P 500	18.41	17.71	12.69	0.69	1.34
Ibbotson Small Cap	16.89	15.46	17.68	1.05	1.37
Wilshire 5000	17.77	17.02	13.04	0.73	1.38
Russell 1000	18.04	17.30	12.97	0.72	1.36
Russell 1000 Value	17.45	16.78	12.33	0.71	1.22
Russell 1000 Growth	18.93	17.82	16.04	0.85	1.49
Russell 2000	15.10	13.83	16.72	1.11	1.52
Russell 2000 Value	16.26	14.92	17.01	1.05	1.27
Russell 2000 Growth	14.25	12.50	20.05	1.41	1.77
Russell 3000	17.72	16.99	12.92	0.73	1.37
Russell 3000 Value	17.31	16.63	12.36	0.71	1.22
Russell 3000 Growth	18.44	17.33	15.98	0.87	1.52
IFC Emerg. Mkt.	12.43	8.79	28.87	2.32	0.76
MSCI EAFE	16.74	14.98	20.64	1.23	1.22
Toronto Stock Exch. 300	8.94	7.98	14.36	1.61	1.27
Financial Times All Shares	14.80	14.15	11.64	0.79	1.07
Frankfurt (FAZ) Index	14.31	11.93	23.48	1.64	0.98
Nikkei Index	7.66	5.44	20.98	2.74	1.00
Tokyo Stk. Exch. Index	9.34	6.83	22.80	2.44	0.85
M-S World Index	16.47	14.83	19.67	1.19	1.27
Brinson GSMI	14.63	14.26	9.23	0.63	1.00
LB Government Bond	9.96	9.71	7.35	0.74	0.23
LB Corporate Bond	10.96	10.53	9.92	0.91	0.35
LB Aggregate Bond	10.27	9.98	8.14	0.79	0.27
LB High-Yield Bond	13.10	12.47	12.18	0.93	0.43
ML World Gov't Bond[c]	9.31	9.07	7.30	0.78	0.18
ML World Gov't Bond except U.S.	10.72	10.10	11.91	1.11	0.27
Wilshire Real Estate	11.18	9.78	17.76	1.59	0.85
Goldman Commodities Index	9.23	7.22	20.07	2.17	0.07
Goldman Energy Commodities Sub-Index[d]	16.84	10.34	38.65	2.29	−0.24
Goldman Non-Energy Commodities Sub-Index	5.92	5.06	13.17	2.23	0.23
Goldman Ind. Metals Commodities Sub-Index	12.66	6.87	42.49	3.36	0.41
Goldman Metals Commodities Sub-Index	−2.59	−3.68	14.20	−5.48	0.34
Goldman Agriculture Commodities Sub-Index	2.68	1.10	17.65	6.60	0.20
Goldman Livestock Commodities Sub-Index	10.71	9.05	19.04	1.78	0.22
Treasury-Bill (1 year)	8.14	8.07	3.78	0.46	0.05
Inflation	4.03	4.00	2.54	0.63	−0.02

[a]Coefficient of Variation = Standard Deviation / Arithmetic Mean of Return

[b]The Beta is calculated using monthly rates of return for 20 years (240 observations) of the Brinson GSMI.

[c]Statistics for the ML World Government Bond indexes were based upon 1986–1999 data only.

[d]Statistics for the Goldman Energy Commodities Sub-Index were based upon 1983–1999 data only.

Source: Frank K. Reilly and David J. Wright, "An Analysis of Global Capital Market Risk-Adjusted Returns," Mimeo (July 2001).

Correlations between Asset Returns   Exhibit 3.13 is a correlation matrix of selected U.S. and world assets. The first column shows that U.S. equities have a reasonably high correlation with Canadian and U.K. stocks (.769 and .641) but low correlation with emerging market stocks and Japanese stocks (.347 and .306). Also, U.S. equities show almost zero correlation with world government bonds except U.S. bonds (.005). Recall from our earlier discussion that you can use this information to build a diversified portfolio by combining those assets with low positive or negative correlations.

Art and Antiques   Unlike financial securities, where the results of transactions are reported daily, art and antique markets are fragmented and lack any formal transaction reporting system. This makes it difficult to gather data. The best-known series that attempt to provide information about the changing value of art and antiques were developed by Sotheby's, a major art auction firm. These value indexes cover 13 areas of art and antiques and a weighted aggregate series that is a combination of the 13.

Reilly examined these series for the period from 1976 to 1991 and computed rates of return, measures of risk, and the correlations among the various art and antique series.[16] Exhibit 3.14 shows these data and compares them with returns for one-year Treasury bonds, the Lehman Brothers Government/Corporate Bond Index, the Standard & Poor's 500 Stock Index, and the annual inflation rate.

Because the results vary so much, it is impossible to generalize about the performance of art and antiques. As shown, the average annual compound rates of return (measured by the geometric means) ranged from a high of 16.8 percent (modern paintings) to a low of 9.99 percent (English silver). Similarly, the standard deviations varied from 21.67 percent (Impressionist-Postimpressionist paintings) to 8.74 percent (American furniture). The relative risk measures (the coefficients of variation) varied from a high of 1.33 (Continental silver) to a low value of 0.71 (English furniture). The annual rankings likewise changed over time.

Although there was a wide range of mean returns and risk, the risk-return plot in the exhibit indicates a fairly consistent relationship between risk and return during this 16-year period. Comparing the art and antique results to the bond and stock indexes indicates that the stocks and bonds experienced results in the middle of the art and antique series.

Analysis of the correlations among these assets using annual rates of return reveals several important relationships. First, the correlations among alternative antique and art categories vary substantially from above 0.90 to negative correlations. Second, the correlations between rates of return on art/antiques and bonds are generally negative. Third, the correlations of art/antiques with stocks are typically small positive values. Finally, the correlation of art and antiques with the rate of inflation indicates that several of the categories were fairly good inflation hedges since they were positively correlated with inflation and they were clearly superior inflation hedges compared to long bonds and common stocks.[17] This would suggest that a properly diversified portfolio of art, antiques, stocks, and bonds should provide a fairly low-risk portfolio. The reader should recall our earlier observation that most art and antiques are quite illiquid and the transaction costs are fairly high compared to financial assets.

---

[16]Frank K. Reilly, "Risk and Return on Art and Antiques: The Sotheby's Indexes," Eastern Finance Association Meeting, May 1987. The results reported are a summary of the study results and have been updated through September 1991.

[17]These results for stocks are consistent with several prior studies that likewise found a negative relationship between inflation and returns on stocks, which indicates that common stocks have been poor inflation hedges. See Eugene F. Fama, "Stock Returns, Real Activity, Inflation and Money," *American Economic Review* 71, no. 2 (June 1991): 545–565; and Jeffrey Jaffe and Gershon Mandelker, "The 'Fisher Effect' for Risky Assets: An Empirical Investigation," *Journal of Finance* 31, no. 2 (June 1976): 447–458.

| EXHIBIT 3.13 | CORRELATIONS AMONG GLOBAL CAPITAL MARKET ASSETS: 1980–1999 (MONTHLY) | | | | | |

INDEX	S&P 500	WILSHIRE 5000	IFC EMERGING MARKET STOCK	MSCI EAFE	M-S WORLD STOCK	BRINSON GSMI
S&P 500	1.000	0.989	0.347	0.497	0.555	0.911
Ibbotson Small Cap	0.775	0.844	0.352	0.413	0.459	0.763
Wilshire 5000	0.989	1.000	0.361	0.499	0.560	0.919
Russell 1000	0.997	0.996	0.350	0.494	0.553	0.916
Russell 1000 Value	0.960	0.954	0.366	0.480	0.538	0.881
Russell 1000 Growth	0.972	0.975	0.315	0.476	0.533	0.894
Russell 2000	0.838	0.901	0.356	0.443	0.496	0.822
Russell 2000 Value	0.814	0.866	0.352	0.430	0.480	0.797
Russell 2000 Growth	0.824	0.891	0.344	0.433	0.488	0.808
Russell 3000	0.993	0.999	0.354	0.495	0.555	0.918
Russell 3000 Value	0.958	0.958	0.370	0.482	0.541	0.885
Russell 3000 Growth	0.969	0.979	0.322	0.479	0.536	0.897
IFC Emerg. Mkt.	0.347	0.361	1.000	0.348	0.354	0.359
MSCI EAFE	0.497	0.499	0.348	1.000	0.986	0.719
Toronto Stock Exch. 300	0.769	0.800	0.383	0.529	0.591	0.784
Financial Times All Shares	0.641	0.654	0.419	0.549	0.563	0.662
Frankfurt (FAZ) Index	0.518	0.513	0.399	0.461	0.475	0.521
Nikkei Index	0.389	0.387	0.356	0.727	0.716	0.507
Tokyo Stk. Exch. Index	0.306	0.305	0.313	0.692	0.677	0.428
M-S World Index	0.555	0.560	0.354	0.986	1.000	0.760
Brinson GSMI	0.911	0.919	0.359	0.719	0.760	1.000
LB Government Bond	0.278	0.250	–0.127	0.184	0.187	0.393
LB Corporate Bond	0.338	0.320	–0.064	0.205	0.216	0.448
LB Aggregate Bond	0.301	0.278	–0.091	0.196	0.201	0.419
LB High-Yield Bond	0.462	0.482	0.142	0.337	0.352	0.547
ML World Gov't Bond[a]	0.055	0.027	–0.229	0.433	0.430	0.281
ML World Gov't Bond except U.S.	0.005	–0.006	–0.127	0.507	0.502	0.259
Wilshire Real Estate	0.640	0.688	0.281	0.388	0.432	0.672
Goldman Commodities Index	0.044	0.052	0.026	0.084	0.103	0.048
Goldman Energy Commodities Sub-Index[b]	–0.059	–0.065	–0.006	–0.011	0.003	–0.074
Goldman Non-Energy Commodities Sub-Index	0.193	0.210	0.099	0.238	0.248	0.216
Goldman Ind. Metals Commodities Sub-Index	0.123	0.145	–0.063	0.142	0.155	0.169
Goldman Metals Commodities Sub-Index	0.110	0.134	0.037	0.203	0.242	0.179
Goldman Agriculture Commodities Sub-Index	0.130	0.154	0.067	0.129	0.142	0.132
Goldman Livestock Commodities Sub-Index	0.123	0.122	0.057	0.160	0.160	0.145
Treasury-Bill (1 year)	0.116	0.101	–0.080	0.114	0.106	0.244
Inflation	–0.159	–0.164	–0.005	–0.192	–0.199	–0.212

[a]Statistics for the ML World Government Bond indexes were based upon 1986–1999 data only.
[b]Statistics for the Goldman Energy Commodities Sub-Index were based upon 1983–1999 data only.

Source: Frank K. Reilly and David J. Wright, "An Analysis of Global Capital Market Risk-Adjusted Returns," Mimeo (July 2001).

EXHIBIT 3.14 *GEOMETRIC MEAN RATES OF RETURN AND STANDARD DEVIATION FOR SOTHEBY'S INDEXES, S&P 500, BOND MARKET SERIES, ONE-YEAR BONDS, AND INFLATION: 1976–1991*

Source: Adapted from Frank K. Reilly, "Risk and Return on Art and Antiques: The Sotheby's Indexes," Eastern Finance Association Meeting, May 1987. (Updated through September 1991.)

Real Estate Somewhat similar to art and antiques, returns on real estate are difficult to derive because of the limited number of transactions and the lack of a national source of data for the transactions that allows one to accurately compute rates of return. In the study by Goetzmann and Ibbotson, the authors gathered data on commercial real estate through REITs and Commingled Real Estate Funds (CREFs) and estimated returns on residential real estate from a series created by Case and Shiller.[18] The summary of the real estate returns compared to various stock, bond, and an inflation series is contained in Exhibit 3.15. As shown, the two commercial real estate series reflected strikingly different results. The CREFs had lower returns and low volatility, while the REIT index had higher returns and risk. Notably, the REIT returns were higher than those of common stocks, but the risk measure for real estate was lower (there was a small difference in the time period). The residential real estate series reflected lower returns and low risk. The longer-term results indicate that all the real estate series experienced lower returns than common stock, but they also had much lower risk.

The correlations in Exhibit 3.16 among annual returns for the various asset groups indicate a relatively low positive correlation between commercial real estate and stocks. In contrast, there was negative correlation between stocks and residential and farm real estate. This negative rela-

---

[18]William N. Goetzmann and Roger G. Ibbotson, "The Performance of Real Estate as an Asset Class," *Journal of Applied Corporate Finance* 3, no 1 (Spring 1990): 65–76; Carl Case and Robert Shiller, "Price of Single Family Homes Since 1970; New Indexes for Four Cities," National Bureau of Economic Research, Inc., Working Paper No. 2393 (1987).

EXHIBIT 3.15 *SUMMARY STATISTICS OF COMMERCIAL AND RESIDENTIAL REAL ESTATE SERIES COMPARED TO STOCKS, BONDS, T-BILLS, AND INFLATION*

SERIES	DATE	GEOMETRIC MEAN	ARITHM. MEAN	STANDARD DEVIATION
Annual Returns 1969–1987				
CREF (Comm.)	1969–87	10.8%	10.9%	2.6%
REIT (Comm.)	1972–87	14.2	15.7	15.4
C&S (Res.)	1970–86	8.5	8.6	3.0
S&P (Stocks)	1969–87	9.2	10.5	18.2
LTG (Bonds)	1969–87	7.7	8.4	13.2
TBILL (Bills)	1969–87	7.6	7.6	1.4
CPI (Infl.)	1969–87	6.4	6.4	1.8
Annual Returns over the Long Term				
I&S (Comm.)	1960–87	8.9%	9.1%	5.0%
CPIHOME (Res.)	1947–86	8.1	8.2	5.2
USDA (Farm)	1947–87	9.6	9.9	8.2
S&P (Stocks)	1947–87	11.4	12.6	16.3
LTG (Bonds)	1947–87	4.2	4.6	9.8
TBILL (Bills)	1947–87	4.9	4.7	3.3
CPI (Infl.)	1947–87	4.5	4.6	3.9

Source: William N. Goetzmann and Roger G. Ibbotson, "The Performance of Real Estate as an Asset Class," *Journal of Applied Corporate Finance* 3, no. 1 (Spring 1990): 65–76. Reprinted with permission.

EXHIBIT 3.16 *CORRELATIONS OF ANNUAL REAL ESTATE RETURNS WITH THE RETURNS ON OTHER ASSET CLASSES*

	I&S	CREF	CPI Home	C&S	Farm	S&P	20-Yr. Gvt.	1-Yr. Gvt.	Infl.
I&S	1								
CREF	0.79	1							
CPI Home	0.52	0.12	1						
C&S	0.26	0.16	0.82	1					
Farm	0.06	–0.06	0.51	0.49	1				
S&P	0.16	0.25	–0.13	–0.20	–0.10	1			
20-Yr. Gvt.	–0.04	0.01	–0.22	–0.54	–0.44	0.11	1		
1-Yr. Gvt.	0.53	0.42	0.13	–0.56	–0.32	–0.07	0.48	1	
Infl.	0.70	0.35	0.77	0.56	0.49	–0.02	–0.17	0.26	1

Note: Correlation coefficient for each pair of asset classes uses the maximum number of observations, that is, the minimum length of the two series in the pair.

Source: William N. Goetzmann and Roger G. Ibbotson, "The Performance of Real Estate as an Asset Class," *Journal of Applied Corporate Finance* 3, no. 1 (Spring 1990): 65–76. Reprinted with permission.

tionship with real estate was also true for 20-year government bonds. Several studies that considered international commercial real estate and REITs indicated the returns were correlated with stock prices but also provided significant diversification.[19]

These results imply that returns on real estate are equal to or slightly lower than returns on common stocks, but real estate possesses favorable risk results. Specifically, real estate had much lower standard deviations as unique assets and either low positive or negative correlations with other asset classes in a portfolio context.

The Internet   *Investments Online*

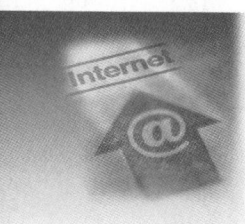

As this chapter describes, the variety of financial products is huge and potentially confusing to the novice (not to mention the experienced professional). Two good rules of investing are (1) stick to your risk tolerance; unfortunately, some people will try to sell instruments that may not be appropriate for the typical individual investor, even when taken in the context of their overall portfolio, and (2) don't invest in something if you don't understand it. Web sites mentioned in Chapters 1 and 2 provide useful information on a variety of investments. Below we list a few others that may be of interest.

http://www.site-by-site.com This site features global financial news including market information and economic reports for a variety of countries with developed, developing, and emerging markets. Some company research is available on this site as is information on derivatives markets worldwide.

http://www.global-investor.com This site contains information on ADRs, global financial information, and allows users to follow the performance of the world's major markets. It provides a number of links to global, regional, and country markets.

http://www.nfsn.com The home page of the National Financial Services Network offers information on personal and commercial financial products and services, in addition to news, interest rate updates, and stock price quotes.

http://www.emgmkts.com The Emerging Markets Companion home page contains information on emerging markets in Asia, Latin America, Africa, and Eastern Europe. Available information and links includes news, prices, market information, and research.

http://www.law.duke.edu/globalmark Duke University's Global Capital Markets Center includes information and studies on a variety of financial market topics, most written from a legal perspective.

http://sothebys.ebay.com Home page of Sotheby's Inc., the auction house. This site contains auction updates and information on collectibles, Internet resources, and featured upcoming sales.

Summary

- Investors who want the broadest range of choices in investments must consider foreign stocks and bonds in addition to domestic financial assets. Many foreign securities offer investors higher risk-adjusted returns than do domestic securities. In addition, the low positive or negative correlations between foreign and U.S. securities make them ideal for building a diversified portfolio.
- Exhibit 3.17 summarizes the risk and return characteristics of the investment alternatives described in this chapter. Some of the differences are due to unique factors that we discussed. Foreign bonds are

---

[19]P. A. Eichholtz, "Does International Diversification Work Better for Real Estate than for Stocks and Bonds?" *Financial Analysts Journal* 52, no. 1 (January–February 1996): 56–62; S. R. Mull and L. A. Socnen, "U.S. REITs as an Asset Class in International Investment Portfolios," *Financial Analysts Journal* 53, no. 2 (March–April 1997): 55–61; and D. C. Quan and S. Titman, "Commercial Real Estate Prices and Stock Market Returns: An International Analysis," *Financial Analysts Journal* 53, no. 3 (May–June 1997): 21–34.

EXHIBIT 3.17 *ALTERNATIVE INVESTMENT RISK AND RETURN CHARACTERISTICS*

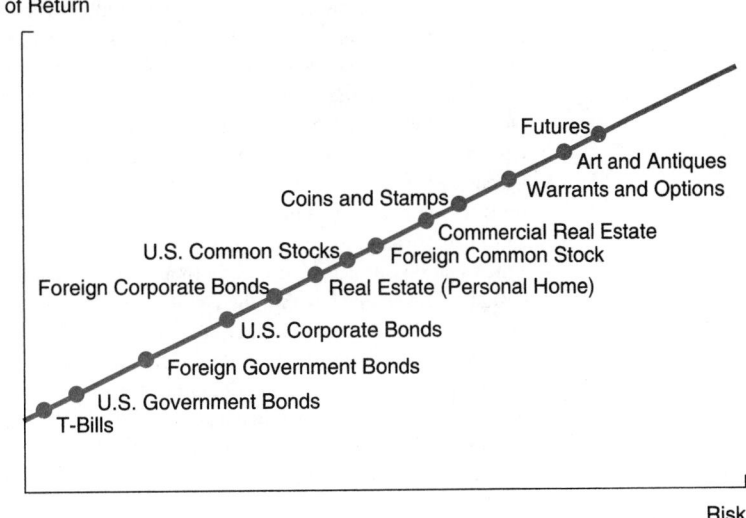

considered riskier than domestic bonds because of the unavoidable uncertainty due to exchange rate risk and country risk. The same is true for foreign and domestic common stocks. Such investments as art, antiques, coins, and stamps require heavy liquidity risk premiums. You should divide consideration of real estate investments between your personal home, on which you do not expect as high a return because of nonmonetary factors, and commercial real estate, which requires a much higher rate of return due to cash flow uncertainty and illiquidity.

- Studies on the historical rates of return for investment alternatives (including bonds, commodities, real estate, foreign securities, and art and antiques) point toward two generalizations.[20]

1. A positive relationship typically holds between the rate of return earned on an asset and the variability of its historical rate of return. This is expected in a world of risk-averse investors who require higher rates of return to compensate for more uncertainty.

2. The correlation among rates of return for selected alternative investments is typically quite low, especially for U.S. and foreign stocks and bonds and between these financial assets and real assets, as represented by art, antiques, and real estate. This confirms the advantage of diversification among investments from around the world.

- In addition to describing many direct investments, such as stocks and bonds, we also discussed investment companies that allow investors to buy investments indirectly. These can be important to investors who want to take advantage of professional management but also want instant diversification with a limited amount of funds. With $10,000, you may not be able to buy many individual stocks or bonds, but you could acquire shares in a mutual fund, which would give you a share of a diversified portfolio that might contain 100 to 150 different U.S. and international stocks or bonds.

- Now that we know the range of domestic and foreign investment alternatives, our next task is to learn about the markets in which they are bought and sold. That is the objective of the next chapter.

---

[20]An excellent discussion of global investing and extensive analysis of returns and risks for alternative asset classes is Roger G. Ibbotson and Gary P. Brimson, *Global Investing* (New York: McGraw-Hill, 1993).

Questions

1. What are the advantages of investing in the common stock rather than the corporate bonds of a company? Compare the certainty of returns for a bond with those for a common stock. Draw a line graph to demonstrate the pattern of returns you would envision for each of these assets over time.

2. Discuss three factors that cause U.S. investors to consider including global securities in their portfolios.

3. Discuss why international diversification reduces portfolio risk. Specifically, why would you expect low correlation in the rates of return for domestic and foreign securities?

4. Discuss why you would expect a *difference* in the correlation of returns between securities from the United States and from alternative countries (for example, Japan, Canada, South Africa).

5. Discuss whether you would expect any *change* in the correlations between U.S. stocks and the stocks for different countries. For example, discuss whether you would expect the correlation between U.S. and Japanese stock returns to change over time.

6. When you invest in Japanese or German bonds, what major additional risks must you consider besides yield changes within the country?

7. Some investors believe that international investing introduces additional risks. Discuss these risks and how they can affect your return. Give an example.

8. What alternatives to direct investment in foreign stocks are available to investors?

9. You are a wealthy individual in a high tax bracket. Why might you consider investing in a municipal bond rather than a straight corporate bond, even though the promised yield on the municipal bond is lower?

10. You can acquire convertible bonds from a rapidly growing company or from a utility. Speculate on which convertible bond would have the lower yield and discuss the reason for this difference.

11. Compare the liquidity of an investment in raw land with that of an investment in common stock. Be specific as to why and how they differ. (Hint: Begin by defining *liquidity*.)

12. What are stock warrants and call options? How do they differ?

13. Discuss why financial analysts consider antiques and art to be illiquid investments. Why do they consider coins and stamps to be more liquid than antiques and art? What must an investor typically do to sell a collection of art and antiques? Briefly contrast this procedure to the sale of a portfolio of stocks listed on the New York Stock Exchange.

14. You have a fairly large portfolio of U.S. stocks and bonds. You meet a financial planner at a social gathering who suggests that you diversify your portfolio by investing in emerging market stocks. Discuss whether the correlation results in Exhibit 3.13 support this suggestion.

15. You are an avid collector/investor of American paintings. Based on the information in Exhibit 3.14, describe your risk-return results during the period from 1976 to 1991 compared to U.S. common stocks.

 16. *CFA Examination Level 1*
Chris Smith of XYZ Pension Plan has historically invested in the stocks of only U.S.-domiciled companies. Recently, he has decided to add international exposure to the plan portfolio.
a. Identify and briefly discuss *three* potential problems that Smith may confront in selecting international stocks that he did not face in choosing U.S. stocks.

 17. *CFA Examination Level III*
TMP has been experiencing increasing demand from its institutional clients for information and assistance related to international investment management. Recognizing that this is an area of growing importance, the firm has hired an experienced analyst/portfolio manager specializing in international equities and market strategy. His first assignment is to represent TMP before a client company's investment committee to discuss the possibility of changing their present "U.S. securities-only" investment approach to one including international investments. He is told that the committee wants a presentation that fully and objectively examines the basic, substantive considerations on which the committee should focus its attention, including both theory and evidence. The company's pension plan has no legal or other barriers to adoption of an international approach; no non-U.S. pension liabilities currently exist.
a. Identify and briefly discuss *three* reasons for adding international securities to the pension portfolio and *three* problems associated with such an approach.
b. Assume that the committee has adopted a policy to include international securities in its pension portfolio. Identify and briefly discuss *three* additional *policy-level* investment decisions the committee must make *before* management selection and actual implementation can begin.

Problems

1. Calculate the current horizon (maturity) premium on U.S. government securities based on data in *The Wall Street Journal*. The long-term security should have a maturity of at least 20 years.

2. Using a source of international statistics, compare the percentage change in the following economic data for Japan, Germany, Canada, and the United States for a recent year. What were the differences, and which country or countries differed most from the United States?
   a. Aggregate output (GDP)
   b. Inflation
   c. Money supply growth

3. Using a recent edition of *Barron's*, examine the weekly percentage change in the stock price indexes for Japan, Germany, Italy, and the United States. For each of three weeks, which foreign series moved most closely with the U.S. series? Which series diverged most from the U.S. series? Discuss these results as they relate to international diversification.

4. Using published sources (for example, *The Wall Street Journal, Barron's, Federal Reserve Bulletin*), look up the exchange rate for U.S. dollars with Japanese yen for each of the past 10 years (you can use an average for the year or a specific time period each year). Based on these exchange rates, compute and discuss the yearly exchange rate effect on an investment in Japanese stocks by a U.S. investor. Discuss the impact of this exchange rate effect on the risk of Japanese stocks for a U.S. investor.

CFA

5. *CFA Examination Level I* (Adapted)
   The following information is available concerning the historical risk and return relationships in the U.S. capital markets:

U.S. CAPITAL MARKETS TOTAL ANNUAL RETURNS, 1960–1984

Investment Category	Arithmetic Mean	Geometric Mean	Standard Deviation of Return[a]
Common stocks	10.28%	8.81%	16.9%
Treasury bills	6.54	6.49	3.2
Long-term government bonds	6.10	5.91	6.4
Long-term corporate bonds	5.75	5.35	9.6
Real estate	9.49	9.44	3.5

[a]Based on arithmetic mean.

Source: Adapted from R. G. Ibbotson, Laurence B. Siegel, and Kathryn S. Love, "World Wealth: Market Values and Returns," *Journal of Portfolio Management* 12, no. 1 (Fall 1985): 4–23. Copyright *Journal of Portfolio Management*, a publication of Institutional Investor, Inc. Used with permission.

   a. Explain why the geometric and arithmetic mean returns are not equal and whether one or the other may be more useful for investment decision making. [5 minutes]
   b. For the time period indicated, rank these investments on a risk-adjusted basis from most to least desirable. Explain your rationale. [6 minutes]
   c. Assume the returns in these series are normally distributed.
      (1) Calculate the range of returns that an investor would have expected to achieve 95 percent of the time from holding common stocks. [4 minutes]
      (2) Suppose an investor holds real estate for this time period. Determine the probability of at least breaking even on this investment. [5 minutes]
   d. Assume you are holding a portfolio composed entirely of real estate. Discuss the justification, if any, for adopting a mixed asset portfolio by adding long-term government bonds. [5 minutes]

6. You are given the following long-run annual rates of return for alternative investment instruments:

U.S. Government T-bills	4.50%
Large-cap common stock	12.50
Long-term corporate bonds	5.80
Long-term government bonds	5.10
Small-capitalization common stock	14.60

a. On the basis of these returns, compute the following:
   (1) The common stock risk premium
   (2) The small-firm stock risk premium
   (3) The horizon (maturity) premium
   (4) The default premium
b. The annual rate of inflation during this period was 4 percent. Compute the real rate of return on these investment alternatives.

References

Fisher, Lawrence, and James H. Lorie. *A Half Century of Returns on Stocks and Bonds.* Chicago: University of Chicago Graduate School of Business, 1977.

Grabbe, J. Orlin. *International Financial Markets.* New York: Elsevier Science Publishing, 1986.

Hamao, Yasushi. "Japanese Stocks, Bonds, Inflation, 1973–1987." *Journal of Portfolio Management* 16, no. 2 (Winter 1989).

Ibbotson, Roger G., and Gary P. Brinson. *Global Investing.* New York: McGraw-Hill, 1993.

Lessard, Donald R. "International Diversification." In *The Financial Analyst's Handbook,* 2d ed., ed. Sumner N. Levine. Homewood, Ill.: Dow Jones-Irwin, 1988.

Malvey, Jack. "Global Corporate Bond Portfolio Management." In *The Handbook of Fixed-Income Securities,* 6th ed., ed. Frank J. Fabozzi. New York: McGraw-Hill, 2001.

Reilly, Frank K., and David J. Wright. "Global Bond Markets: An Analysis of Alternative Benchmarks and Risk-Return Performance." Midwest Finance Association Meeting (March 1995).

Rosenberg, Michael R. " International Fixed-Income Investing: Theory and Practice." In *The Handbook of Fixed-Income Securities,* 6th ed., ed. Frank J. Fabozzi. New York: McGraw-Hill, 2001.

Siegel, Laurence B., and Paul D. Kaplan. "Stocks, Bonds, Bills, and Inflation Around the World." In *Managing Institutional Assets,* ed. Frank J. Fabozzi. New York: Harper & Row, 1990.

Solnik, Bruno. *International Investments,* 4th ed. Reading, Mass.: Addison-Wesley, 2000.

Steward, Christopher. "International Bond Markets and Instruments." In *The Handbook of Fixed-Income Securities,* 6th ed., ed. Frank J. Fabozzi. New York: McGraw-Hill, 2001.

Van der Does, Rein W. "Investing in Foreign Securities." In *The Financial Analyst's Handbook,* 2d ed., ed. Sumner N. Levine. Homewood, Ill.: Dow Jones-Irwin, 1988.

APPENDIX
Chapter 3

Covariance and Correlation

Covariance

Because most students have been exposed to the concepts of covariance and correlation, the following discussion is set forth in intuitive terms with examples to help the reader recall the concepts.[21]

Covariance is an absolute measure of the extent to which two sets of numbers move together over time, that is, how often they move up or down together. In this regard, *move together* means they are generally above their means or below their means at the same time. Covariance between i and j is defined as

$$\text{Cov}_{ij} = \frac{\Sigma(i - \bar{i})(j - \bar{j})}{n}$$

If we define $(i - \bar{i})$ as i' and $(j - \bar{j})$ as j', then

$$\text{COV}_{ij} = \frac{\Sigma i'j'}{n}$$

---

[21]A more detailed, rigorous treatment of the subject can be found in any standard statistics text, including S. Christian Albright, *Statistics for Business and Economics* (New York: Macmillan, 1987), 63–67.

EXHIBIT 3A.1 ▶ CALCULATION OF COVARIANCE

OBSERVATION	i	j	$i - \bar{i}$	$j - \bar{j}$	$i'j'$
1	3	8	−4	−4	16
2	6	10	−1	−2	2
3	8	14	+1	+2	2
4	5	12	−2	0	0
5	9	13	+2	+1	2
6	11	15	+4	+3	12
Σ	42	72			34
Mean	7	12			

$$\text{Cov}_{ij} = \frac{34}{6} = +5.67$$

Obviously, if both numbers are consistently above or below their individual means at the same time, their products will be positive, and the average will be a large positive value. In contrast, if the i value is below its mean when the j value is above its mean or vice versa, their products will be large negative values, giving negative covariance.

Exhibit 3A.1 should make this clear. In this example, the two series generally moved together, so they showed positive covariance. As noted, this is an *absolute* measure of their relationship and, therefore, can range from $+\infty$ to $-\infty$. Note that the covariance of a variable with itself is its *variance*.

Correlation

To obtain a relative measure of a given relationship, we use the **correlation coefficient** (r_{ij}), which is a measure of the relationship:

$$r_{ij} = \frac{\text{COV}_{ij}}{\sigma_i \sigma_j}$$

You will recall from your introductory statistics course that

$$\sigma_i = \sqrt{\frac{\Sigma(i - \bar{i})^2}{N}}$$

If the two series move completely together, then the covariance would equal $\sigma_i \sigma_j$ and

$$\frac{\text{COV}_{ij}}{\sigma_i \sigma_j} = 1.0$$

The correlation coefficient would equal unity in this case, and we would say the two series are perfectly correlated. Because we know that

$$r_{ij} = \frac{\text{COV}_{ij}}{\sigma_i \sigma_j}$$

we also know that $\text{COV}_{ij} = r_{ij}\sigma_i\sigma_j$. This relationship may be useful when computing the standard deviation of a portfolio, because in many instances the relationship between two securities is stated in terms of the correlation coefficient rather than the covariance.

Continuing the example given in Exhibit 3A.1, the standard deviations are computed in Exhibit 3A.2, as is the correlation between i and j. As shown, the two standard deviations are rather large and similar but not exactly the same. Finally, when the positive covariance is normalized by the product of the two standard deviations, the results indicate a correlation coefficient of 0.898, which is obviously quite large and close to 1.00. Apparently, these two series are highly related.

EXHIBIT 3A.2   *CALCULATION OF CORRELATION COEFFICIENT*

OBSERVATION	$i - \bar{\imath}^a$	$(i - \bar{\imath})^2$	$j - \bar{\jmath}^a$	$(j - \bar{\jmath})^2$
1	−4	16	−4	16
2	−1	1	−2	4
3	+1	1	+2	4
4	−2	4	0	0
5	+2	4	+1	1
6	+4	16	+3	9
		42		34

$$\sigma_i^2 = 42 / 6 = 7.00 \qquad\qquad \sigma_j^2 = 34 / 6 = 5.67$$

$$\sigma_i = \sqrt{7.00} = 2.65 \qquad\qquad \sigma_j = \sqrt{5.67} = 2.38$$

$$r_{ij} = COV_{ij} / \sigma_i \sigma_j = \frac{5.67}{(2.65)(2.38)} = \frac{5.67}{6.31} = 0.898$$

Problems

1. As a new analyst, you have calculated the following annual rates of return for both Lauren Corporation and Kayleigh Industries.

Year	Lauren's Rate of Return	Kayleigh's Rate of Return
1996	5	5
1997	12	15
1998	−11	5
1999	10	7
2000	12	−10

Your manager suggests that because these companies produce similar products, you should continue your analysis by computing their covariance. Show all calculations.

2. You decide to go an extra step by calculating the coefficient of correlation using the data provided in Problem 1. Prepare a table showing your calculations and explain how to interpret the results. Would the combination of Lauren and Kayleigh be good for diversification?

Chapter 4 ▷ Organization and Functioning of Securities Markets*

After you read this chapter, you should be able to answer the following questions:

➤ What is the purpose and function of a market?
➤ What are the characteristics that determine the quality of a market?
➤ What is the difference between a primary and secondary capital market and how do these markets support each other?
➤ What are the national exchanges and how are the major securities markets around the world becoming linked (what is meant by "passing the book")?
➤ What are regional stock exchanges and over-the-counter (OTC) markets?
➤ What are the alternative market-making arrangements available on the exchanges and the OTC market?
➤ What are the major types of orders available to investors and market makers?
➤ What are the major functions of the specialist on the NYSE and how does the specialist differ from the central market maker on other exchanges?
➤ What are the significant changes in markets around the world during the past 15 years?
➤ What are the major changes in world capital markets expected over the next decade?

The stock market, the Dow Jones Industrials, and the bond market are part of our everyday experience. Each evening on the television news broadcasts, we find out how stocks and bonds fared; each morning we read in our daily newspapers about expectations for a market rally or decline. Yet most people have an imperfect understanding of how domestic and world capital markets actually function. To be a successful investor in a global environment, you must know what financial markets are available around the world and how they operate.

In Chapter 1, we considered why individuals invest and what determines their required rate of return on investments. In Chapter 2, we discussed the life cycle for investors and the alternative asset allocation decisions by investors during different phases. In Chapter 3, we learned about the numerous alternative investments available and why we should diversify with securities from around the world. This chapter takes a broad view of securities markets and provides a detailed discussion of how major stock markets function. We conclude with a consideration of how global securities markets are changing.

We begin with a discussion of securities markets and the characteristics of a good market. Two components of the capital markets are described: primary and secondary. Our main emphasis in this chapter is on the secondary stock market. We consider the national stock exchanges around the world and how these markets, separated by geography and by time zones, are becoming linked into a 24-hour market. We also consider regional stock markets and the over-the-counter markets and provide a detailed analysis of how alternative exchange markets operate.

*The authors acknowledge helpful comments on this chapter from Robert Battalio and Paul Schultz of the University of Notre Dame.

The final section considers numerous historical changes in financial markets, additional current changes, and significant future changes expected. These numerous changes in our securities markets will have a profound effect on what investments are available to you from around the world and how you buy and sell them.

WHAT IS A MARKET?

This section provides the necessary background for understanding different securities markets around the world and the changes that are occurring. The first part considers the general concept of a market and its function. The second part describes the characteristics that determine the quality of a particular market. The third part of the section describes primary and secondary capital markets and how they interact and depend on one another.

A **market** is the means through which buyers and sellers are brought together to aid in the transfer of goods and/or services. Several aspects of this general definition seem worthy of emphasis. First, a market need not have a physical location. It is only necessary that the buyers and sellers can communicate regarding the relevant aspects of the transaction.

Second, the market does not necessarily own the goods or services involved. For a good market, ownership is not involved; the important criterion is the smooth, cheap transfer of goods and services. In most financial markets, those who establish and administer the market do not own the assets but simply provide a physical location or an electronic system that allows potential buyers and sellers to interact. They help the market function by providing information and facilities to aid in the transfer of ownership.

Finally, a market can deal in any variety of goods and services. For any commodity or service with a diverse clientele, a market should evolve to aid in the transfer of that commodity or service. Both buyers and sellers will benefit from the existence of a smooth functioning market.

Characteristics of a Good Market

Throughout this book, we will discuss markets for different investments, such as stocks, bonds, options, and futures, in the United States and throughout the world. We will refer to these markets using various terms of quality, such as *strong, active, liquid,* or *illiquid.* There are many financial markets, but they are not all equal—some are active and liquid; others are relatively illiquid and inefficient in their operations. To appreciate these discussions, you should be aware of the following characteristics that investors look for when evaluating the quality of a market.

One enters a market to buy or sell a good or service quickly at a price justified by the prevailing supply and demand. To determine the appropriate price, participants must have timely and accurate information on the volume and prices of past transactions and on all currently outstanding bids and offers. Therefore, one attribute of a good market is **timely and accurate information**.

Another prime requirement is **liquidity**, the ability to buy or sell an asset quickly and at a known price—that is, a price not substantially different from the prices for prior transactions, assuming no new information is available. An asset's likelihood of being sold quickly, sometimes referred to as its *marketability,* is a necessary, but not a sufficient, condition for liquidity. The expected price should also be fairly certain, based on the recent history of transaction prices and current bid-ask quotes.[1]

---

[1]For a more formal discussion of liquidity, see Puneet Handa and Robert A. Schwartz, "How Best to Supply Liquidity to a Securities Market," *Journal of Portfolio Management* 22, no. 2 (Winter 1996): 44–51. For a recent set of articles that consider liquidity and all components of trade execution, see *Best Execution and Portfolio Performance* (Charlottesville, Va.: Association for Investment Management and Research, 2000).

A component of liquidity is **price continuity**, which means that prices do not change much from one transaction to the next unless substantial new information becomes available. Suppose no new information is forthcoming and the last transaction was at a price of $20; if the next trade were at $20.05, the market would be considered reasonably continuous.[2] A continuous market without large price changes between trades is a characteristic of a liquid market.

A market with price continuity requires *depth,* which means that numerous potential buyers and sellers must be willing to trade at prices above and below the current market price. These buyers and sellers enter the market in response to changes in supply and demand or both and thereby prevent drastic price changes. In summary, liquidity requires marketability and price continuity, which, in turn, requires depth.

Another factor contributing to a good market is the **transaction cost**. Lower costs (as a percent of the value of the trade) make for a more efficient market. An individual comparing the cost of a transaction between markets would choose a market that charges 2 percent of the value of the trade compared with one that charges 5 percent. Most microeconomic textbooks define an efficient market as one in which the cost of the transaction is minimal. This attribute is referred to as *internal efficiency.*

Finally, a buyer or seller wants the prevailing market price to adequately reflect all the information available regarding supply and demand factors in the market. If such conditions change as a result of new information, the price should change accordingly. Therefore, participants want prices to adjust quickly to new information regarding supply or demand, which means that prices reflect all available information about the asset. This attribute is referred to as **external efficiency** or **informational efficiency**. This attribute is discussed extensively in Chapter 6.

In summary, a good market for goods and services has the following characteristics:

1. Timely and accurate information is available on the price and volume of past transactions and the prevailing bid and ask prices.
2. It is liquid, meaning an asset can be bought or sold quickly at a price close to the prices for previous transactions (has price continuity), assuming no new information has been received. In turn, price continuity requires depth.
3. Transactions entail low costs, including the cost of reaching the market, the actual brokerage costs, and the cost of transferring the asset.

4. Prices rapidly adjust to new information; thus, the prevailing price is fair because it reflects all available information regarding the asset.

Decimal Pricing Common stocks in the United States have always been quoted in fractions prior to the change in late 2000. Specifically, prior to 1997, they were quoted in eighths (e.g., 1/8, 2/8, . . . 7/8), with each eighth equal to $0.125. This was modified in 1997 when the fractions for most stocks went to sixteenths (e.g., 1/16, 2/16, . . . 15/16) equal to $0.0625. The Securities and Exchange Commission (SEC) has been pushing for a change to decimal pricing for a number of years and eventually set a deadline for the early part of 2001. The NYSE started the transition with seven stocks as of August 28, 2000, included an additional 52 stocks on September 25, and added 94 securities effective December 4, 2000. The final deadline for all stocks on the NYSE and the AMEX to go "decimal" was April 9, 2001. The Nasdaq market deferred the change until late April 2001.

---

[2]You should be aware that common stocks are currently sold in decimals (dollars and cents), which is a significant change from the pre-2000 period when they were priced in eighths and sixteenths. This change to decimals is discussed at the end of this subsection.

The espoused reasons for the change to decimal pricing were threefold. The first reason was the ease with which investors could understand the prices and compare them. Second, decimal pricing was expected to save investors money since it would almost certainly reduce the size of the bid-ask spread from a minimum of 6.25 cents when prices are quoted in 16ths to possibly 1 cent when prices are in decimals. Of course, this is also why many brokers and investment firms were against the change since the bid-ask spread is the price of liquidity for the investor and the compensation to the dealer. Third, this change is also expected to make the U.S. markets more competitive on a global basis since other countries already price on a comparable basis and, as noted, this would cause our transaction costs to be lower.

Organization of the Securities Market

Before discussing the specific operation of the securities market, you need to understand its over-all organization. The principal distinction is between **primary markets**, where new securities are sold, and **secondary markets**, where outstanding securities are bought and sold. Each of these markets is further divided based on the economic unit that issued the security. The following discussion considers each of these major segments of the securities market with an emphasis on the individuals involved and the functions they perform.

PRIMARY CAPITAL MARKETS

The primary market is where new issues of bonds, preferred stock, or common stock are sold by government units, municipalities, or companies to acquire new capital.[3]

Government Bond Issues

All U.S. government bond issues are subdivided into three segments based on their original maturities. **Treasury bills** are negotiable, non-interest-bearing securities with original maturities of one year or less. **Treasury notes** have original maturities of 2 to 10 years. Finally, **Treasury bonds** have original maturities of more than 10 years.

To sell bills, notes, and bonds, the Treasury relies on Federal Reserve System auctions. (The bidding process and pricing are discussed in detail in Chapter 18.)

Municipal Bond Issues

New municipal bond issues are sold by one of three methods: competitive bid, negotiation, or private placement. **Competitive bid** sales typically involve sealed bids. The bond issue is sold to the bidding syndicate of underwriters that submits the bid with the lowest interest cost in accordance with the stipulations set forth by the issuer. **Negotiated sales** involve contractual arrangements between underwriters and issuers wherein the underwriter helps the issuer prepare the bond issue and set the price and has the exclusive right to sell the issue. **Private placements** involve the sale of a bond issue by the issuer directly to an investor or a small group of investors (usually institutions).

Note that two of the three methods require an *underwriting* function. Specifically, in a competitive bid or a negotiated transaction, the investment banker typically underwrites the issue, which means the investment firm purchases the entire issue at a specified price, relieving the issuer from the risk and responsibility of selling and distributing the bonds. Subsequently, the underwriter sells the issue to the investing public. For municipal bonds, this underwriting function is performed by both investment banking firms and commercial banks.

---

[3] For an excellent set of studies related to the primary market, see Michael C. Jensen and Clifford W. Smith, Jr., eds., "Symposium on Investment Banking and the Capital Acquisition Process," *Journal of Financial Economics* 15, no. 1/2 (January–February 1986).

The underwriting function can involve three services: origination, risk bearing, and distribution. Origination involves the design of the bond issue and initial planning. To fulfill the risk-bearing function, the underwriter acquires the total issue at a price dictated by the competitive bid or through negotiation and accepts the responsibility and risk of reselling it for more than the purchase price. Distribution means selling it to investors, typically with the help of a selling syndicate that includes other investment banking firms and/or commercial banks.

In a negotiated bid, the underwriter will carry out all three services. In a competitive bid, the issuer specifies the amount, maturities, coupons, and call features of the issue and the competing syndicates submit a bid for the entire issue that reflects the yields they estimate for the bonds. The issuer may have received advice from an investment firm on the desirable characteristics for a forthcoming issue, but this advice would have been on a fee basis and would not necessarily involve the ultimate underwriter who is responsible for risk bearing and distribution. Finally, a private placement involves no risk bearing, but an investment banker could assist in locating potential buyers and negotiating the characteristics of the issue.

Corporate Bond Issues

Corporate bond issues are almost always sold through a negotiated arrangement with an investment banking firm that maintains a relationship with the issuing firm. In a global capital market that involves an explosion of new instruments, the origination function, which involves the design of the security in terms of characteristics and currency, is becoming more important because the corporate chief financial officer (CFO) will probably not be completely familiar with the availability and issuing requirements of many new instruments and the alternative capital markets around the world. Investment banking firms compete for underwriting business by creating new instruments that appeal to existing investors and by advising issuers regarding desirable countries and currencies. As a result, the expertise of the investment banker can help reduce the issuer's cost of new capital.

Once a stock or bond issue is specified, the underwriter will put together an underwriting syndicate of other major underwriters and a selling group of smaller firms for its distribution as shown in Exhibit 4.1.

EXHIBIT 4.1 *THE UNDERWRITING ORGANIZATION STRUCTURE*

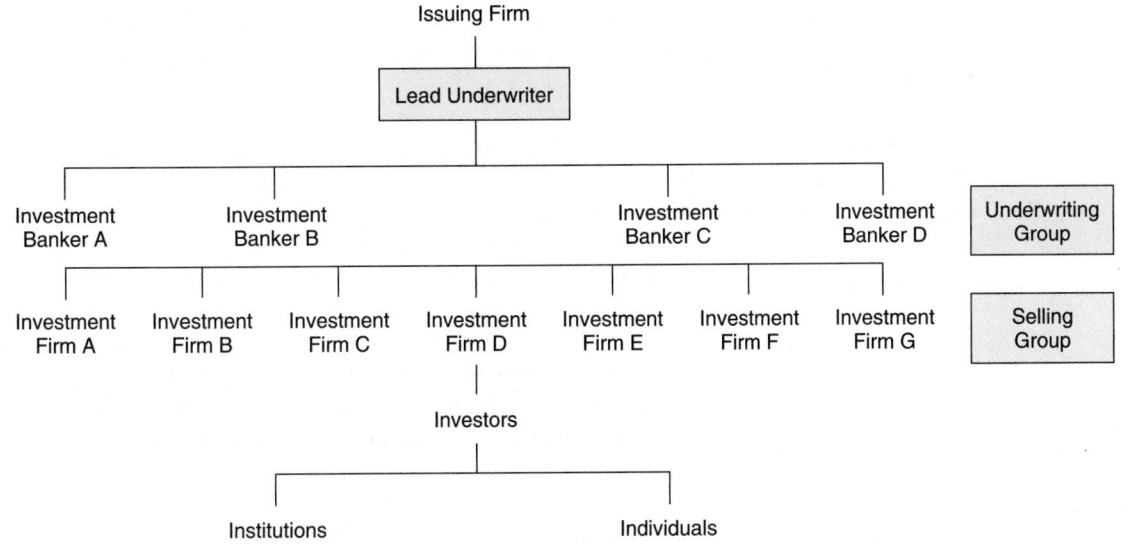

Corporate Stock Issues In addition to the ability to issue fixed-income securities to get new capital, corporations can also issue equity securities—generally common stock. For corporations, new stock issues are typically divided into two groups: (1) seasoned equity issues and (2) initial public offerings (IPOs).

Seasoned equity issues are new shares offered by firms that already have stock outstanding. An example would be General Electric, which is a large, well-regarded firm that has had public stock trading on the NYSE for over 50 years. If General Electric decided that it needed new capital, it could sell additional shares of its common stock to the public at a price very close to the current price of the firm's stock.

Initial public offerings (IPOs) involve a firm selling its common stock to the public for the first time. At the time of an IPO offering, there is no existing public market for the stock, that is, the company has been closely held. An example would be an IPO by Polo Ralph Lauren in 1997, at $26 per share. The company is a leading manufacturer and distributor of men's clothing. The purpose of the offering was to get additional capital to expand its operations.

New issues (seasoned or IPOs) are typically underwritten by investment bankers, who acquire the total issue from the company and sell the securities to interested investors. The underwriter gives advice to the corporation on the general characteristics of the issue, its pricing, and the timing of the offering. The underwriter also accepts the risk of selling the new issue after acquiring it from the corporation.[4]

Relationships with Investment Bankers

The underwriting of corporate issues typically takes one of three forms: negotiated, competitive bids, or best-efforts arrangements. As noted, negotiated underwritings are the most common, and the procedure is the same as for municipal issues.

A corporation may also specify the type of securities to be offered (common stock, preferred stock, or bonds) and then solicit competitive bids from investment banking firms. This is rare for industrial firms but is typical for utilities, which may be required by law to sell the issue via a competitive bid. Although competitive bids typically reduce the cost of an issue, it also means that the investment banker gives less advice but still accepts the risk-bearing function by underwriting the issue and fulfills the distribution function.

Alternatively, an investment banker can agree to support an issue and sell it on a *best-efforts basis*. This is usually done with speculative new issues. In this arrangement, the investment banker does not underwrite the issue because it does not buy any securities. The stock is owned by the company, and the investment banker acts *as a broker* to sell whatever it can at a stipulated price. The investment banker earns a lower commission on such an issue than on an underwritten issue.

Introduction of Rule 415

The typical practice of negotiated arrangements involving numerous investment banking firms in syndicates and selling groups has changed with the introduction of Rule 415, which allows large firms to register security issues and sell them piecemeal during the following two years. These issues are referred to as *shelf registrations* because, after they are registered, the issues lie on the shelf and can be taken down and sold on short notice whenever it suits the issuing firm. As an example, General Electric could register an issue of 5 million shares of common stock during 2003 and sell a million shares in early 2003, another million shares late in 2003, 2 million shares in early 2004, and the rest in late 2004.

Each offering can be made with little notice or paperwork by one underwriter or several. In fact, because relatively few shares may be involved, the lead underwriter often handles the whole

---

[4]For an extended discussion of the underwriting process, see Richard A. Brealey and Stewart C. Myers, *Principles of Corporate Finance,* 7th ed. (New York: McGraw-Hill, 2001), Chapter 15.

deal without a syndicate or uses only one or two other firms. This arrangement has benefited large corporations because it provides great flexibility, reduces registration fees and expenses, and allows firms issuing securities to request competitive bids from several investment banking firms.

On the other hand, some observers fear that shelf registrations do not allow investors enough time to examine the current status of the firm issuing the securities. Also, the follow-up offerings reduce the participation of small underwriters because the underwriting syndicates are smaller and selling groups are almost nonexistent. Shelf registrations have typically been used for the sale of straight debentures rather than common stock or convertible issues.[5]

Private Placements and Rule 144A

Rather than a public sale using one of these arrangements, primary offerings can be sold privately. In such an arrangement, referred to as a *private placement,* the firm designs an issue with the assistance of an investment banker and sells it to a small group of institutions. The firm enjoys lower issuing costs because it does not need to prepare the extensive registration statement required for a public offering. The institution that buys the issue typically benefits because the issuing firm passes some of these cost savings on to the investor as a higher return. In fact, the institution should require a higher return because of the absence of any secondary market for these securities, which implies higher liquidity risk.

The private placement market changed dramatically when Rule 144A was introduced by the SEC. This rule allows corporations—including non-U.S. firms—to place securities privately with large, sophisticated institutional investors without extensive registration documents. It also allows these securities to be subsequently traded among these large, sophisticated investors (those with assets in excess of $100 million). The SEC intends to provide more financing alternatives for U.S. and non-U.S. firms and possibly increase the number, size, and liquidity of private placements.[6] Presently, a large percent of high-yield bonds are issued as 144A issues.

SECONDARY FINANCIAL MARKETS

In this section, we consider the purpose and importance of secondary markets and provide an overview of the secondary markets for bonds, financial futures, and stocks. Next, we consider national stock markets around the world. Finally, we discuss regional and over-the-counter stock markets and provide a detailed presentation on the functioning of stock exchanges.

Secondary markets permit trading in outstanding issues; that is, stocks or bonds already sold to the public are traded between current and potential owners. The proceeds from a sale in the secondary market do not go to the issuing unit (the government, municipality, or company) but, rather, to the current owner of the security.

Why Secondary Markets Are Important

Before discussing the various segments of the secondary market, we must consider its overall importance. Because the secondary market involves the trading of securities initially sold in the primary market, *it provides liquidity to the individuals who acquired these securities.* After acquiring securities in the primary market, investors want the ability to sell them again to acquire other securities, buy a house, or go on a vacation. The primary market benefits greatly from the liquidity provided by the secondary market because investors would hesitate to acquire securities

---

[5]For further discussion of Rule 415, see Robert J. Rogowski and Eric H. Sorensen, "Deregulation in Investment Banking: Shelf Registration, Structure and Performance," *Financial Management* 14, no. 1 (Spring 1985): 5–15.

[6]For a discussion of some reactions to Rule 144A, see John W. Milligan, "Two Cheers for 144A," *Institutional Investor* 24, no. 9 (July 1990): 117–119; and Sara Hanks, "SEC Ruling Creates a New Market," *The Wall Street Journal,* 16 May 1990, A12.

in the primary market if they thought they could not subsequently sell them in the secondary market. That is, without an active secondary market, potential issuers of stocks or bonds in the primary market would have to provide a much higher rate of return to compensate investors for the substantial liquidity risk.

Secondary markets are also important to those selling seasoned securities because the prevailing market price of the securities is determined by transactions in the secondary market. New issues of outstanding stocks or bonds to be sold in the primary market are based on prices and yields in the secondary market.[7] Even forthcoming IPOs are priced based on the prices and values of comparable stocks or bonds in the public secondary market.

Secondary Bond Markets

The secondary market for bonds distinguishes among those issued by the federal government, municipalities, or corporations.

Secondary Markets for U.S. Government and Municipal Bonds

U.S. government bonds are traded by bond dealers that specialize in either Treasury bonds or agency bonds. Treasury issues are bought or sold through a set of 35 primary dealers, including large banks in New York and Chicago and some of the large investment banking firms (for example, Merrill Lynch, Goldman Sachs, Morgan Stanley). These institutions and other firms also make markets for government agency issues, but there is no formal set of dealers for agency securities.

The major market makers in the secondary municipal bond market are banks and investment firms. Banks are active in municipal bond trading and underwriting of general obligation issues since they invest heavily in these securities. Also, many large investment firms have municipal bond departments that underwrite and trade these issues.

Secondary Corporate Bond Markets

Historically, the secondary market for corporate bonds included two major segments: security exchanges and an over-the-counter (OTC) market. The major exchange for corporate bonds was the NYSE Fixed-Income Market where about 10 percent of the trading took place. In contrast, about 90 percent of trading, including all large transactions, took place on the over-the-counter market. This mix of trading changed in early 2001 when the NYSE announced that it was shutting down its Automated Bond System (ABS), which had been a fully automated trading and information system for small bond trades—that is, the exchange market for bonds was considered the "odd-lot" bond market. As a result, currently all corporate bonds are traded over the counter by dealers who buy and sell for their own accounts.

The major bond dealers are the large investment banking firms that underwrite the issues such as Merrill Lynch, Goldman Sachs, Salomon Brothers, Lehman Brothers, and Morgan Stanley. Because of the limited trading in corporate bonds compared to the fairly active trading in government bonds, corporate bond dealers do not carry extensive inventories of specific issues. Instead, they hold a limited number of bonds desired by their clients and, when someone wants to do a trade, they work more like brokers than dealers.

Financial Futures

In addition to the market for the bonds, a market has developed for futures contracts related to these bonds. These contracts allow the holder to buy or sell a specified amount of a given bond issue at a stipulated price. The two major futures exchanges are the Chicago Board of Trade

---

[7]In the literature on market microstructure, it is noted that the secondary markets also have an effect on market efficiency, the volatility of security prices, and the serial correlation in security returns. In this regard, see F. D. Foster and S. Viswanathan, "The Effects of Public Information and Competition on Trading Volume and Price Volatility," *Review of Financial Studies* 6, no. 1 (spring 1993): 23–56; C. N. Jones, G. Kaul, and M. L. Lipson, "Information, Trading and Volatility," *Journal of Financial Economics* 36, no. 1 (August 1994): 127–154.

(CBOT) and the Chicago Mercantile Exchange (CME). These futures contracts and the futures market are discussed in Chapter 21.

Secondary Equity Markets

The secondary equity market is usually been broken down into three major segments: (1) the major national stock exchanges, including the New York, the Tokyo, and the London stock exchanges; (2) regional stock exchanges in such cities as Chicago, San Francisco, Boston, Osaka and Nagoya in Japan, and Dublin in Ireland; and (3) the over-the-counter (OTC) market, which involves trading in stocks not listed on an organized exchange. These segments differ in importance in different countries.

Securities Exchanges The first two segments, referred to as *listed securities exchanges,* differ only in size and geographic emphasis. Both are composed of formal organizations with specific members and specific securities (stocks or bonds) that have qualified for listing. Although the exchanges typically consider similar factors when evaluating firms that apply for listing, the level of requirement differs (the national exchanges have more stringent requirements). Also, the prices of securities listed on alternative stock exchanges are determined using several different trading (pricing) systems that will be discussed in the next subsection.

Alternative Trading Systems Although stock exchanges are similar in that only qualified stocks can be traded by individuals who are members of the exchange, they can differ in their *trading systems.* There are two major trading systems, and an exchange can use one of these or a combination of them. One is a *pure auction market,* in which interested buyers and sellers submit bid and ask prices for a given stock to a central location where the orders are matched by a broker who does not own the stock but who acts as a facilitating agent. Participants refer to this system as *price-driven* because shares of stock are sold to the investor with the highest bid price and bought from the seller with the lowest offering price. Advocates of the auction system argue for a very centralized market that ideally will include all the buyers and sellers of the stock.

The other major trading system is a *dealer market* where individual dealers provide liquidity for investors by buying and selling the shares of stock for themselves. Ideally, with this system there will be numerous dealers who will compete against each other to provide the highest bid prices when you are selling and the lowest asking price when you are buying stock. When we discuss the various exchanges, we will indicate the trading system used.

Call versus Continuous Markets Beyond the alternative trading systems for equities, the operation of exchanges can differ in terms of when and how the stocks are traded.

In **call markets**, trading for individual stocks takes place at specified times. The intent is to gather all the bids and asks for the stock and attempt to arrive at a single price where the quantity demanded is as close as possible to the quantity supplied. Call markets are generally used during the early stages of development of an exchange when there are few stocks listed or a small number of active investors/traders. If you envision an exchange with only a few stocks listed and a few traders, you would call the roll of stocks and ask for interest in one stock at a time. After determining all the available buy and sell orders, exchange officials attempt to arrive at a single price that will satisfy *most* of the orders, and all orders are transacted at this one price.

Notably, call markets also are used at the opening for stocks on the NYSE if there is an overnight buildup of buy and sell orders, in which case the opening price can differ from the prior day's closing price. Also, this concept is used if trading is suspended during the day because of some significant new information. In either case, the specialist or market maker would attempt to derive a new equilibrium price using a call-market approach that would reflect the imbalance and take care of most of the orders. For example, assume a stock had been trading at about $42 per share and some significant, new, positive information was released overnight or during the day. If it was overnight, it would affect the opening; if it happened during the day, it would affect the price established after trading was suspended. If the buy orders were three or four times as numerous as the sell orders, the price based on the call market might be $44, which is the specialists' estimate of a new equilibrium price that reflects the supply-demand caused by the new information. Several studies have shown that this temporary use of the call-market mechanism contributes to a more orderly market and less volatility in such instances.

In a **continuous market**, trades occur at any time the market is open. Stocks in this continuous market are priced either by auction or by dealers. If it is a dealer market, dealers are willing to make a market in the stock, which means that they are willing to buy or sell for their own account at a specified bid and ask price. If it is an auction market, enough buyers and sellers are trading to allow the market to be continuous; that is, when you come to buy stock, there is another investor available and willing to sell stock. A compromise between a pure dealer market and a pure auction market is a combination structure wherein the market is basically an auction market, but there exists an intermediary who is willing to act as a dealer if the pure auction market does not have enough activity. These intermediaries who act as brokers and dealers provide temporary liquidity to ensure that the market will be liquid as well as continuous.

An appendix at the end of this chapter contains two exhibits that list the characteristics of stock exchanges around the world and indicate whether each of the exchanges provides a continuous market, a call-market mechanism, or a mixture of the two. Notably, although many exchanges are considered continuous, they also employ a call-market mechanism on specific occasions such as at the open and during trading suspensions. The NYSE is such a market.

National Stock Exchanges   Two U.S. securities exchanges are generally considered national in scope: the New York Stock Exchange (NYSE) and the American Stock Exchange (AMEX). Outside the United States, each country typically has had one national exchange, such as the Tokyo Stock Exchange (TSE), the London Exchange, the Frankfurt Stock Exchange, and the Paris Bourse. These exchanges are considered national because of the large number of listed securities, the prestige of the firms listed, the wide geographic dispersion of the listed firms, and the diverse clientele of buyers and sellers who use the market. As we discuss in a subsequent section on changes, there is a clear trend toward consolidation of these exchanges into global markets.

New York Stock Exchange (NYSE)   The New York Stock Exchange (NYSE), the largest organized securities market in the United States, was established in 1817 as the New York Stock and Exchange Board. The Exchange dates its founding to when the famous Buttonwood Agreement was signed in May 1792 by 24 brokers.[8] The name was changed to the New York Stock Exchange in 1863.

At the end of 2000, approximately 3,000 companies had stock issues listed on the NYSE, for a total of about 3200 stock issues (common and preferred) with a total market value of more than $13.0 trillion. The specific listing requirements for the NYSE appear in Exhibit 4.2.

The average number of shares traded daily on the NYSE has increased steadily and substantially, as shown in Exhibit 4.3. Prior to the 1960s, the daily volume averaged less than 3 million shares, compared with current average daily volume in excess of 1 billion shares and numerous days when volume is over 1.3 billion shares.

The NYSE has dominated the other exchanges in the United States in trading volume. During the past decade, the NYSE has consistently accounted for about 85 percent of all shares traded on U.S.-listed exchanges, as compared with about 5 percent for the American Stock Exchange and about 10 percent for all regional exchanges combined. Because share prices on

---

[8]The NYSE considers the signing of this agreement the birth of the Exchange and celebrated its 200th birthday during 1992. For a pictorial history, see *Life,* collectors' edition, Spring 1992.

EXHIBIT 4.2 — *PARTIAL CRITERIA OF LISTING REQUIREMENTS FOR STOCKS ON THE NYSE AS OF 2001*

Pretax earnings most recent fiscal year	$ 2,500,000
Pretax earnings prior two fiscal years	2,000,000
Shares publicly held	1,100,000
Market value of publicly held shares[a]	100,000,000
Minimum number of holders of round lots (100 shares or more)	2,000

[a]This minimum required market value is $60 million for spin-offs, carve-outs, or IPOs. For specifics, see the 2001 *NYSE Fact Book,* 37–42.

Source: *NYSE Fact Book* 2001, New York Stock Exchange. Reprinted with permission.

EXHIBIT 4.3 — *AVERAGE DAILY REPORTED SHARE VOLUME TRADED ON SELECTED STOCK MARKETS (× 1,000)*

YEAR	NYSE	NASDAQ	TSE
1955	2,578	N.A.	8,000
1960	3,042	N.A.	90,000
1965	6,176	N.A.	116,000
1970	11,564	N.A.	144,000
1975	18,551	5,500	183,000
1980	44,871	26,500	359,000
1985	109,169	82,100	428,000
1990	156,777	131,900	500,000
1995	346,101	401,400	369,600
1996	411,953	543,700	405,500
1997	526,925	650,324	439,000
1998	673,590	801,747	498,000
1999	809,183	1,077,500	633,000
2000	1,041,578	1,759,900	702,000

N.A. = not available.

Source: *NYSE Fact Book* 2001, New York Stock Exchange. Reprinted with permission.

the NYSE tend to be higher than those on other exchanges, the dollar value of trading on the NYSE has averaged about 87 percent of the total value of U.S. trades, compared with less than 3 percent for the AMEX and about 10 percent for the regional exchanges.[9]

The volume of trading and relative stature of the NYSE is reflected in the price of a membership on the exchange (referred to as a seat). As shown in Exhibit 4.4, the price of membership has fluctuated in line with trading volume and other factors that influence the profitability of membership.

[9]For a discussion of trading volume and membership prices, see Greg Ip, "Prices Soften for Exchange Seats," *The Wall Street Journal,* 27 May 1998, C1, C17.

EXHIBIT 4.4 *MEMBERSHIP PRICES ON THE NYSE ($000)*

YEAR	HIGH	LOW	YEAR	HIGH	LOW
1925	$150	$ 99	1985	$ 480	$ 310
1935	140	65	1990	430	250
1945	95	49	1995	1,050	785
1955	90	80	1996	1,450	1,050
1960	162	135	1997	1,750	1,175
1965	250	190	1998	2,000	1,225
1970	320	130	1999	2,650	2,000
1975	138	55	2000	2,000	1,650
1980	275	175			

Source: *NYSE Fact Book* 2001, New York Stock Exchange. Reprinted with permission.

American Stock Exchange (AMEX)   The American Stock Exchange (AMEX) was begun by a group who traded unlisted shares at the corner of Wall and Hanover Streets in New York. It was originally called the Outdoor Curb Market. In 1910, it established formal trading rules and changed its name to the New York Curb Market Association. The members moved inside a building in 1921 and continued to trade mainly in unlisted stocks (stocks not listed on one of the registered exchanges) until 1946, when its volume in listed stocks finally outnumbered that in unlisted stocks. The current name was adopted in 1953.

The AMEX is a national exchange, distinct from the NYSE because, except for a short period in the late 1970s, no stocks have been listed on both the NYSE and AMEX at the same time. The AMEX has emphasized foreign securities, and warrants were listed on the AMEX for a number of years before the NYSE listed them.

The AMEX has become a major stock options exchange since January 1975 and subsequently added options on interest rates and stock indexes. The AMEX and the Nasdaq merged in 1998, although they continued to operate as separate markets. There was some discussion in early 2001 that the two entities might split up.

Tokyo Stock Exchange (TSE)   The TSE dominates its country's market much as the NYSE does the United States. Specifically, about 87 percent of trades in volume and 83 percent of value occur on the TSE. The Tokyo Stock Exchange Co., Ltd., established in 1878, was replaced in 1943 by the Japan Securities Exchange, a quasi-governmental organization that absorbed all existing exchanges in Japan. The Japan Securities Exchange was dissolved in 1947, and the Tokyo Stock Exchange in its present form was established in 1949. The trading mechanism is a price-driven system wherein investors submit bid and ask prices for stocks. At the end of 1999, there were about 1,700 companies listed with a total market value of 300.2 trillion yen (this equals about 2.4 trillion dollars at an exchange rate of 125 yen to the dollar). As shown in Exhibit 4.3, average daily share volume has increased from 90 million shares per day in 1960 to about 700 million shares in 2000.

Both domestic and foreign stocks are listed on the Tokyo Exchange. The domestic stocks are further divided between the First and Second Sections. The First Section contains about 1,200 stocks and the Second Section about 450 stocks. The 150 most active stocks on the First Section are traded on the trading floor. Trading in all other domestic stocks and all foreign stocks is conducted by computer.

London Stock Exchange (LSE)   The largest established securities market in the United Kingdom is the London Stock Exchange, which has served as the stock exchange of Great Britain and Ireland, with operating units in London, Dublin, and six other cities. Both listed securities (bonds and equities) and unlisted securities are traded on the LSE. The listed equity segment involves more than 2,600 companies with a market value in excess of 374 billion pounds (approximately $561 billion at an exchange rate of $1.50/pound). Of the 2,600 companies listed on the LSE, about 600 are foreign firms—the largest number on any exchange.

The stocks listed on the LSE are divided into three groups: Alpha, Beta, and Gamma. The Alpha stocks are the 65 most actively traded stocks, and the Betas are the 500 next most active stocks. In Alpha and Beta stocks, market makers are required to offer firm bid-ask quotes to all members of the exchange. For the rest of the stocks (Gamma stocks), market quotations are only indicative and must be confirmed before a trade. All equity trades must be reported to the Stock Exchange Automated Quotation (SEAQ) system within minutes, although only trades in Alpha stocks are reported in full on the trading screen.

The pricing system on the LSE is done by competing dealers who communicate via computers in offices away from the stock exchange. This system is similar to the Nasdaq system used in the OTC market in the United States, which is described in the next section.

Divergent Trends—New Exchanges and Consolidations   The global secondary equity market has been experiencing two trends that appear divergent yet are reasonable in a dynamic global equity market with economies that range from being very developed to newly emerging. The first trend is the creation of a number of *new* stock exchanges around the world in emerging economies, including China, Russia, Sri Lanka, Poland, Hungary, and Peru. The second trend is toward *consolidation* of existing exchanges in developed countries through mergers, partnerships, or strong affiliations.

The creation of numerous new exchanges in emerging economies is based upon the need in these countries for capital to help foster growth. The point was made early in the chapter that a strong secondary market for securities is necessary to provide the liquidity that investors require if they are going to buy securities in the primary market from which firms acquire new capital. Put another way, if companies in emerging countries need new capital and want to get it by selling stock, it is necessary to have a liquid secondary equity market—that is, a stock exchange.

The second trend toward the consolidation of existing exchanges in developed markets, such as London, Frankfurt, and Paris, can be explained by the economies of scale required by these exchanges, including the need for significant expenditures for technology to remain globally competitive. To acquire and maintain the necessary technology is extremely expensive, and a smaller exchange may not be able to afford this outlay. Further, once an exchange is created, there are substantial economies of scale—a trading system can probably handle 4,000 stocks as easily and cheaply as 400 stocks. The cost of, and the economies of scale related to, technology are the major reasons for most of the mergers and affiliations being proposed.

Another reason is the added liquidity provided by adding members to the exchange. Assume two exchanges, each with 200 members and 1,000 different stocks listed. If you combine the exchanges into 400 members and 2,000 stocks, each stock should benefit in terms of potential liquidity because there are more members (dealers) who are available to buy and sell the stocks and bring clients to the exchange.

Therefore, the normal evolution in the global economy with global capital markets should be the creation of new stock exchanges in emerging economies followed by the subsequent consolidation of these exchanges into regional exchanges (e.g., Pan-European) to meet the need for expensive technology and enhanced liquidity.

The following section discusses some of the recent consolidations to document this trend.

Recent Consolidations   Although the rate of consolidations has increased recently, they began in 1995 when Germany's three largest exchanges merged into the one in Frankfurt.

The recent merger movement of exchanges began when the NASD merged with the AMEX in 1998. Another combination in the United States occurred in July 1998 when the Chicago Board Options Exchange (CBOE) agreed to merge with the Pacific Exchange. These two exchanges account for about 60 percent of options trading in the United States.

The major move toward consolidation in Europe occurred in July 1998 when the London Stock Exchange and the Frankfurt Stock Exchange proposed a pan-European market by announcing a potential merger that was eventually called off. In the process, it stimulated other merger discussions.

This initial announcement prompted several smaller exchanges in Europe to form alliances. In November 1998, the Dutch, Belgian, and Luxembourg stock exchanges indicated an alliance. This was followed in December by an alliance of the Stockholm, Copenhagen, and Oslo exchanges.

In March 2000, the French, Dutch, and Belgian exchanges talked seriously about a merger. Following a concern that mergers were moving rapidly, the NYSE proposed a partnership with nine other exchanges around the world to create a Global Equity market (GEM).[10]

Exhibit 4.5 shows some of the recent changes in the overall security market structure. Notably, in an earlier version, it appeared certain that the London and Frankfurt exchanges would merge, but this was canceled following extensive negotiations with members of the two exchanges. It is also possible that the prior merger of the AMEX and the Nasdaq may be reversed.

The Global 24-Hour Market   Our discussion of the global securities market will tend to emphasize the three markets in New York, London, and Tokyo because of their relative size and importance, and because they represent the major segments of a world-wide 24-hour stock market. You will often hear about a continuous market where investment firms "pass the book" around the world. This means the major active market in securities moves around the globe as trading hours for these three markets begin and end. Consider the individual trading hours for each of the three exchanges, translated into a 24-hour eastern standard time (EST) clock:

	Local Time (24-Hour Notations)	24-Hour EST
New York Stock Exchange	0930–1600	0930–1600
Tokyo Stock Exchange	0900–1100	2300–0100
	1300–1500	0300–0500
London Stock Exchange	0815–1615	0215–1015

Imagine trading starting in New York at 0930 and going until 1600 in the afternoon, being picked up by Tokyo late in the evening and going until 0500 in the morning, and continuing in London (with some overlap) until it begins in New York again (with some overlap) at 0930. Alternatively, it is possible to envision trading as beginning in Tokyo at 2300 hours and continuing until 0500, when it moves to London, then ends the day in New York. This latter model seems the most relevant because the first question a London trader asks in the morning is "What happened in Tokyo?" and the U.S. trader asks "What happened in Tokyo and what *is* happening

---

[10]Terzah Ewing and Silvia Ascarelli, "One World, How Many Stock Exchanges?" *The Wall Street Journal,* 15 May 2000, C1; Elena Cherney and Thom Beal, "As NYSE Plans for Global Market, Nasdaq Gets Left Out in the Cold," *The Wall Street Journal,* 8 June 2000, C1.

EXHIBIT 4.5 *THE MOVE TOWARD CONSOLIDATION AND AFFILIATION IN THE SECONDARY EQUITY MARKET*

in London?" The point is, the markets operate almost continuously and are related in their response to economic events. Therefore, as an investor you are not dealing with three separate and distinct exchanges but with one interrelated world market.[11] Clearly, this interrelationship is growing daily because of numerous multiple listings where stocks are listed on several exchanges around the world (such as the NYSE and TSE) and the availability of sophisticated telecommunications.

REGIONAL EXCHANGES AND THE OVER-THE-COUNTER MARKET

Within most countries, regional stock exchanges compete with and supplement the national exchanges by providing secondary markets for the stocks of smaller companies. Beyond these exchanges, trading off the exchange (the over-the-counter [OTC] market) includes all stocks not

---

[11]In response to this trend toward global trading, the International Organization of Securities Commissions (IOSCO) has been established. For a discussion of it, see David Lascelles, "Calls to Bring Watchdogs into Line," *Financial Times,* 14 August 1989, 10.

listed on one of the formal exchanges. The size, significance, and the relative impact of these two sectors on the overall secondary stock markets vary among countries. Initially, we discuss the rationale for and operation of regional stock exchanges. Subsequently, we describe the OTC market, including heavy emphasis on the OTC market in the United States where it is a growing part of the total secondary stock market.

Regional Securities Exchanges

Regional exchanges typically have the same operating procedures as the national exchanges in the same countries, but they differ in their listing requirements and the geographic distributions of the listed firms. Regional stock exchanges exist for two main reasons: First, they provide trading facilities for local companies not large enough to qualify for listing on one of the national exchanges. Their listing requirements are typically less stringent than those of the national exchanges.

Second, regional exchanges in some countries list firms that also list on one of the national exchanges to give local brokers who are not members of a national exchange access to these securities. As an example, American Telephone & Telegraph and General Motors are listed on both the NYSE and several regional exchanges. This dual listing or the use of unlisted trading privileges (UTP) allows a local brokerage firm that is not large enough to purchase a membership on the NYSE to buy and sell shares of a dual-listed stock (such as General Motors) without going through the NYSE and giving up part of the commission. The regional exchanges in the United States are

➤ Chicago Stock Exchange
➤ Pacific Stock Exchange (San Francisco–Los Angeles)
➤ Philadelphia Exchange
➤ Boston Stock Exchange
➤ Cincinnati Stock Exchange

The Chicago, Pacific, and Philadelphia exchanges account for about 90 percent of all regional exchange volume. In turn, total regional exchange volume is 9 to 10 percent of total exchange volume in the United States.

In Japan, seven regional stock exchanges supplement the Tokyo Stock Exchange. The United Kingdom has one stock exchange in London with operating units in seven cities. Germany has five stock exchanges, including its national exchange in Frankfurt where approximately 80 percent of the trading occurs.

Without belaboring the point, each country typically has one national exchange that accounts for the majority of trading and several regional exchanges that have less-stringent listing requirements to allow trading in smaller firms. Recently, several national exchanges have created second-tier markets that are divisions of the national exchanges to allow smaller firms to be traded as part of the national exchanges.[12]

Over-the-Counter (OTC) Market

The over-the-counter (OTC) market includes trading in all stocks not listed on one of the exchanges. It can also include trading in listed stocks, which is referred to as the *third market,* and is discussed in the following section. The OTC market is not a formal organization with membership requirements or a specific list of stocks deemed eligible for trading.[13] In theory, any security can be traded on the OTC market as long as a registered dealer is willing to make a market in the security (willing to buy and sell shares of the stock).

---

[12]An example of a second-tier market is the Second Section on the TSE. The exchange is attempting to provide trading facilities for smaller firms without changing its listing requirements for the national exchange.

[13]The requirements of trading on different segments of the OTC trading system are discussed later in this section.

EXHIBIT 4.6 ▶ *NUMBER OF COMPANIES AND ISSUES TRADING ON NASDAQ: 1980–2000*

YEAR	NUMBER OF COMPANIES	NUMBER OF ISSUES
1980	2,894	3,050
1985	4,136	4,784
1990	4,132	4,706
1995	5,122	5,955
1996	5,556	6,384
1997	5,487	6,208
1998	5,068	5,583
1999	4,829	5,210
2000	4,734	5,053

Source: *Nasdaq Research datalink* (Washington, D.C.: National Association of Securities Dealers).

Size of the OTC Market The U.S. OTC market is the largest segment of the U.S. secondary market in terms of the number of issues traded. It is also the most diverse in terms of quality. As noted earlier, there are about 3,000 issues traded on the NYSE and about 600 issues on the AMEX. In contrast, almost 5,000 issues are actively traded on the OTC market's Nasdaq National Market System (NMS).[14] Another 1,000 stocks are traded on the Nasdaq system independent of the NMS. Finally, 1,000 OTC stocks are regularly quoted in *The Wall Street Journal* but not in the Nasdaq system. Therefore, a total of almost 7,000 issues are traded on the OTC market—substantially more than on the NYSE and AMEX combined.

Exhibit 4.6 sets forth the growth in the number of companies and issues on Nasdaq. The growth in average daily trading is shown in Exhibit 4.3 relative to some national exchanges. As of the end of 2000, almost 600 issues on Nasdaq were either foreign stocks or American Depository Receipts (ADRs). Trading in foreign stocks and ADRs represented over 8 percent of total Nasdaq share volume in 2001. About 300 of these issues trade on both Nasdaq and a foreign exchange such as Toronto. In 1988, Nasdaq developed a link with the Singapore Stock Exchange that allows 24-hour trading from Nasdaq in New York to Singapore to a Nasdaq/London link and back to New York.

Although the OTC market has the greatest number of issues, the NYSE has a larger total value of trading. In 2000, the approximate value of equity trading on the NYSE was over $11,200 billion, and Nasdaq was about $7,400 billion. Notably, the Nasdaq value substantially exceeded what transpired on the LSE ($900 billion) and on the TSE ($1,100 billion).

There is tremendous diversity in the OTC market because it imposes no minimum requirements. Stocks that trade on the OTC range from those of small, unprofitable companies to large, extremely profitable firms (such as Microsoft, Intel). On the upper end, all U.S. government bonds are traded on the OTC market as are the majority of bank and insurance stocks. Finally, about 100 exchange-listed stocks are traded on the OTC—the third market.

Operation of the OTC As noted, any stock can be traded on the OTC as long as someone indicates a willingness to make a market whereby the party buys or sells for his or her own account acting as a dealer.[15] This differs from most transactions on the listed exchanges, where

---

[14]Nasdaq is an acronym for National Association of Securities Dealers Automated Quotations. The system is discussed in detail in a later section. To be traded on the NMS, a firm must have a certain size and trading activity and at least four market makers. A specification of requirements for various components of the Nasdaq system is contained in Exhibit 4.7.

[15]*Dealer* and *market maker* are synonymous.

some members act as brokers who attempt to match buy and sell orders. Therefore, the OTC market is referred to as a *negotiated market,* in which investors directly negotiate with dealers.

The Nasdaq System   (currently named The Nasdaq Stock Market, Inc) is an automated, electronic quotation system for the vast OTC market. Any number of dealers can elect to make markets in an OTC stock. The actual number depends on the activity in the stock. The average Nasdaq stock has over 10 market makers, according to Nasdaq.

Nasdaq makes all dealer quotes available immediately. The broker can check the quotation machine and call the dealer with the best market, verify that the quote has not changed, and make the sale or purchase. The Nasdaq system has three levels to serve firms with different needs and interests.

Level 1 provides a single median representative quote for the stocks on Nasdaq. This quote system is for firms that want current quotes on OTC stocks but do not consistently buy or sell OTC stocks for their customers and are not market makers. This composite quote changes constantly to adjust for any changes by individual market makers.

Level 2 provides instantaneous current quotations on Nasdaq stocks by all market makers in a stock. This quotation system is for firms that consistently trade OTC stocks. Given an order to buy or sell, brokers check the quotation machine, call the market maker with the best market for their purposes (highest bid if they are selling, lowest offer if buying), and consummate the deal.

Level 3 is for OTC market makers. Such firms want Level 2, but they also need the capability to change their own quotations, which Level 3 provides.

Listing Requirements for the Nasdaq Stock Market   Quotes and trading volume for the OTC market are reported in two lists: a National Market System (NMS) list and a regular Nasdaq list. As of 2001, alternative standards exist (see Exhibit 4.7) for initial listing and continued listing on the Nasdaq National Market System. A company must meet all of the requirements under at least one of the three listing standards for initial listing and meet at least one continued listing standard to maintain its listing on the National Market. For stocks on this system, reports include up-to-the-minute volume and last-sale information for the competing market makers as well as end-of-the-day information on total volume and high, low, and closing prices.

A Sample Trade   Assume you are considering the purchase of 100 shares of Intel. Although Intel is large enough and profitable enough to be listed on a national exchange, the company has never applied for listing because it enjoys an active market on the OTC. (It is one of the volume leaders with daily volume typically above 1 million shares and often in excess of 5 million shares.) When you contact your broker, he or she will consult the Nasdaq electronic quotation machine to determine the current dealer quotations for INTC, the trading symbol for Intel.[16] The quote machine will show that about 35 dealers are making a market in INTC. An example of differing quotations might be as follows:

Dealer	Bid	Ask
1	30.50	30.75
2	30.35	30.65
3	30.25	20.65
4	30.35	30.75

---

[16]Trading symbols are one- to four-letter codes used to designate stocks. Whenever a trade is reported on a stock ticker, the trading symbol appears with the figures. Many symbols are obvious, such as GM (General Motors), F (Ford Motors), GE (General Electric), GS (Goldman Sachs), HD (Home Depot), AMGN (Amgen), and DELL (Dell).

EXHIBIT 4.7 ▶ *NASDAQ NATIONAL MARKET REQUIREMENTS*

REQUIREMENTS	INITIAL LISTING			CONTINUED LISTING	
	STANDARD 1	STANDARD 2	STANDARD 3	STANDARD 1	STANDARD 2
Net Tangible Assets[a]	$6 million	$18 million	N/A	$4 million	N/A
Market capitalization[b]			$75 million		$50 million
			or		or
Total assets	N/A	N/A	$75 million	N/A	$50 million
			and		and
Total revenue			$75 million		$50 million
Pretax income (in latest fiscal year or 2 of last 3 fiscal years)	$1 million	N/A	N/A	N/A	N/A
Public float (shares)[c]	1.1 million	1.1 million	1.1 million	750,000	1.1 million
Operating history	N/A	2 years	N/A	N/A	N/A
Market value of public float	$8 million	$18 million	$20 million	$5 million	$15 million
Minimum bid price	$5	$5	$5	$1	$5
Shareholders (round lot holders)[d]	400	400	400	400	400
Market makers[e]	3	3	4	2	4
Corporate governance	Yes	Yes	Yes	Yes	Yes

[a]Net tangible assets equals total assets minus total liabilities minus goodwill minus redeemable securities.
[b]For initial listing under Standard 3, or continued listing under Standard 2, a company must satisfy one of the following for compliance: (1) the market capitalization requirement or (2) the total assets and the total revenue requirement.
[c]Public float is defined as shares outstanding less any shares held by officers, directors, or beneficial owners of 10 percent.
[d]Round lot holders are holders of 100 shares or more.
[e]An Electronic Communications Network (ECN) is not considered an active market maker.

Source: *The Nasdaq Stock Market* web site.

Assuming these are the best markets available from the total group, your broker would call either Dealer 2 or Dealer 3 because they have the lowest offering prices. After verifying the quote, your broker would give one of these dealers an order to buy 100 shares of INTC at $30.65 a share. Because your firm was not a market maker in the stock, the firm would act as a broker and charge you $3,065 plus a commission for the trade. If your firm had been a market maker in INTC, with an asking price of $30.65, the firm would have sold the stock to you at 30.65 net (without commission). If you had been interested in selling 100 shares of Intel instead of buying, the broker would have contacted Dealer 1, who made the highest bid.

Changing Dealer Inventory   Let us consider the price quotations by an OTC dealer who wants to change his or her inventory on a given stock. For example, assume Dealer 4, with a current quote of 30.35 bid–30.75 ask, decides to increase his or her holdings of INTC. The Nasdaq quotes indicate that the highest bid is currently 30.50. Increasing the bid to 30.50 would bring some of the business currently going to Dealer 1. Taking a more aggressive action, the dealer might raise the bid to 30.65 and buy all the stock offered, including some from Dealers 2 and 3, who are offering it at 30.65. In this example, the dealer raises the bid price but does not change the asking price, which was above those of Dealers 2 and 3. This dealer will buy stock but probably will not sell any. A dealer who had excess stock would keep the bid below the market (lower than 30.50) and reduce the asking price to 30.65 or less. Dealers constantly change their bid and ask prices or both, depending on their current inventories or changes in the outlook based on new information for the stock.

Third Market

As mentioned, the term **third market** describes OTC trading of shares listed on an exchange. Although most transactions in listed stocks take place on an exchange, an investment firm that is not a member of an exchange can make a market in a listed stock. Most of the trading on the third market is in well-known stocks such as General Electric, IBM, and Merck. The success or failure of the third market depends on whether the OTC market in these stocks is as good as the exchange market and whether the relative cost of the OTC transaction compares favorably with the cost on the exchange. This market is critical during the relatively few periods when trading is not available on the NYSE either because trading is suspended or the exchange is closed.[17]

Fourth Market

The term **fourth market** describes direct trading of securities between two parties with no broker intermediary. In almost all cases, both parties involved are institutions. When you think about it, a direct transaction is really not that unusual. If you own 100 shares of AT&T Corp. and decide to sell it, there is nothing wrong with simply offering it to your friends or associates at a mutually agreeable price (for example, based on exchange transactions) and making the transaction directly.

Investors typically buy or sell stock through brokers because it is faster and easier. Also, you would expect to get a better price for your stock because the broker has a good chance of finding the best buyer. You are willing to pay a commission for these liquidity services. The fourth market evolved because of the substantial fees charged by brokers to institutions with large orders. At some point, it becomes worthwhile for institutions to attempt to deal directly with each other and bypass the brokerage fees. Assume an institution decides to sell 100,000 shares of AT&T, which is selling for about $25 per share, for a total value of $2.5 million. The average commission on such a transaction prior to the advent of negotiated rates in 1975 was about 1 percent of the value of the trade, or about $25,000. This cost made it attractive for a selling institution to spend some time and effort finding another institution interested in increasing its holdings of AT&T and negotiating a direct sale. Currently, such transactions cost about 5 cents per share, which implies a cost of $5,000 for the 100,000-share transactions. This is lower but still not trivial. Because of the diverse nature of the fourth market and the lack of reporting requirements, no data are available regarding its specific size or growth.

DETAILED ANALYSIS OF EXCHANGE MARKETS

The importance of listed exchange markets requires that we discuss them at some length. In this section, we discuss several types of membership on the exchanges, the major types of orders, and the role and function of exchange market makers—a critical component of a good exchange market.

---

[17]Craig Torres, "Third Market Trading Crowds Stock Exchanges," *The Wall Street Journal,* 8 March 1990, C1, C9. For an analysis of the effect of this trading, see Robert H. Battalio, "Third-Market Broker-Dealers: Cost Competitors or Cream Skimmers," *Journal of Finance* 52, no. 1 (March 1997): 341–352.

Exchange Membership   Listed U.S. securities exchanges typically offer four major categories of membership: (1) specialist, (2) commission broker, (3) floor broker, and (4) registered trader. Specialists (or exchange market makers), who constitute about 25 percent of the total membership on exchanges, will be discussed after a description of types of orders.

Commission brokers are employees of a member firm who buy or sell for the customers of the firm. When you place an order to buy or sell stock through a brokerage firm that is a member of the exchange, in many instances the firm contacts its commission broker on the floor of the exchange. That broker goes to the appropriate post on the floor and buys or sells the stock as instructed.

Floor brokers are independent members of an exchange who act as brokers for other members. As an example, when commission brokers for Merrill Lynch become too busy to handle all of their orders, they will ask one of the floor brokers to help them. At one time, these people were referred to as *$2 brokers* because that is what they received for each order. Currently, they receive about $4 per 100-share order.[18]

Registered traders are allowed to use their memberships to buy and sell for their own accounts. They therefore save commissions on their own trading, and observers believe they have an advantage because they are on the trading floor. The exchanges and others are willing to allow these advantages because these traders provide the market with added liquidity, but regulations limit how they trade and how many registered traders can be in a trading crowd around a specialist's booth at any time. In recent years, registered traders have become **registered competitive market makers (RCMMs)**, who have specific trading obligations set by the exchange. Their activity is reported as part of the specialist group.[19]

Types of Orders   It is important to understand the different types of orders entered by investors and the specialist as a dealer.

Market Orders   The most frequent type of order is a **market order**, an order to buy or sell a stock at the best current price. An investor who enters a market sell order indicates a willingness to sell immediately at the highest bid available at the time the order reaches a specialist on the exchange or an OTC dealer. A market buy order indicates that the investor is willing to pay the lowest offering price available at the time the order reaches the floor of the exchange or an OTC dealer. Market orders provide immediate liquidity for someone willing to accept the prevailing market price.

Assume you are interested in General Electric (GE) and you call your broker to find out the current "market" on the stock. The quotation machine indicates that the prevailing market is 45 bid—45.25 ask. This means that the highest current bid on the books of the specialist is 45; that is, $75 is the most that anyone has offered to pay for GE. The lowest offer is 45.25, that is, the lowest price anyone is willing to accept to sell the stock. If you placed a market buy order for 100 shares, you would buy 100 shares at $45.25 a share (the lowest ask price) for a total cost of $4,525 plus commission. If you submitted a market sell order for 100 shares, you would sell the shares at $45 each and receive $4,500 less commission.

---

[18]These brokers received some unwanted notoriety in 1998: Dean Starkman and Patrick McGeehan, "Floor Brokers on Big Board Charged in Scheme," *The Wall Street Journal,* 26 February 1998, C1, C21; and Suzanna McGee, " '$2 Brokers' Worried about Notoriety from Charges of Illegal Trading Scheme," *The Wall Street Journal,* 5 March 1998, C1, C22.

[19]Prior to the 1980s, there also were odd-lot dealers who bought and sold to individuals with orders for less than round lots (usually 100 shares). Currently, this function is handled by either the specialist or some large brokerage firm.

Limit Orders   The individual placing a **limit order** specifies the buy or sell price. You might submit a bid to purchase 100 shares of Coca-Cola stock at $50 a share when the current market is 60 bid–60.25 ask, with the expectation that the stock will decline to $50 in the near future.

You must also indicate how long the limit order will be outstanding. Alternative time specifications are basically boundless. A limit order can be instantaneous ("fill or kill," meaning fill the order instantly or cancel it). It can also be good for part of a day, a full day, several days, a week, or a month. It can also be open-ended, or good until canceled (GTC).

Rather than wait for a given price on a stock, your broker will give the limit order to the specialist, who will put it in a limit-order book and act as the broker's representative. When and if the market reaches the limit-order price, the specialist will execute the order and inform your broker. The specialist receives a small part of the commission for rendering this service.

Short Sales   Most investors purchase stock ("go long") expecting to derive their return from an increase in value. If you believe that a stock is overpriced, however, and want to take advantage of an expected decline in the price, you can sell the stock short. A **short sale** is the sale of stock that you do not own with the intent of purchasing it back later at a lower price. Specifically, you would borrow the stock from another investor through your broker, sell it in the market, and subsequently replace it at (you hope) a price lower than the price at which you sold it. The investor who lent the stock has the proceeds of the sale as collateral. In turn, this investor can invest these funds in short-term, risk-free securities. Although a short sale has no time limit, the lender of the shares can decide to sell the shares, in which case your broker must find another investor willing to lend the shares.[20]

Three technical points affect short sales. First, a short sale can be made only on an *uptick trade,* meaning the price of the short sale must be higher than the last trade price. This is because the exchanges do not want traders to force a profit on a short sale by pushing the price down through continually selling short. Therefore, the transaction price for a short sale must be an uptick or, without any change in price, the previous price must have been higher than its previous price (a zero uptick). For an example of a zero uptick, consider the following set of transaction prices: 42, 42.25, 42.25. You could sell short at 42.25 even though it is no change from the previous trade at 42.25 because that prior trade was an uptick trade.

The second technical point concerns dividends. The short seller must pay any dividends due to the investor who lent the stock. The purchaser of the short-sale stock receives the dividend from the corporation, so the short seller must pay a similar dividend to the lender.

Finally, short sellers must post the same margin as an investor who had acquired stock. This margin can be in any unrestricted securities owned by the short seller.

Special Orders   In addition to these general orders, there are several special types of orders. A *stop loss order* is a conditional market order whereby the investor directs the sale of a stock if it drops to a given price. Assume you buy a stock at 50 and expect it to go up. If you are wrong, you want to limit your losses. To protect yourself, you could put in a stop loss order at 45. In this case, if the stock dropped to 45, your stop loss order would become a market sell order, and the stock would be sold at the prevailing market price. The stop loss order does not guarantee that you will get the $45; you can get a little bit more or a little bit less. Because of the possibility of

---

[20]For a discussion of negative short-selling results, see William Power, "Short Sellers Set to Catch Tumbling Overhead Stocks," *The Wall Street Journal,* 28 December 1993, C1, C2. For a discussion of short-selling events, see Carol J. Loomis. "Short Sellers and the Seamy Side of Wall Street," *Fortune,* 22 July 1996, pp. 66–72; and Gary Weiss, "The Secret World of Short Sellers," *Business Week,* 5 August 1996, pp. 62–68. For a discussion of short selling during 2000–2001, see Allison Beard, "Short Selling Goes from Strength to Strength," *Financial Times,* 16 March 2001, p. 29.

market disruption caused by a large number of stop loss orders, exchanges have, on occasion, canceled all such orders on certain stocks and not allowed brokers to accept further stop loss orders on those issues.

A related type of stop loss tactic for short sales is a *stop buy order.* An investor who has sold stock short and wants to minimize any loss if the stock begins to increase in value would enter this conditional buy order at a price above that at which the investor sold the stock short. Assume you sold a stock short at 50, expecting it to decline to 40. To protect yourself from an increase, you could put in a stop buy order to purchase the stock using a market buy order if it reached a price of 55. This conditional buy order would hopefully limit any loss on the short sale to approximately $5 a share.

Margin Transactions   On any type of order, an investor can pay for the stock with cash or borrow part of the cost, leveraging the transaction. Leverage is accomplished by buying on **margin**, which means the investor pays for the stock with some cash and borrows the rest through the broker, putting up the stock for collateral.

As shown in Exhibit 4.8, the dollar amount of margin credit extended by members of the NYSE has increased consistently since 1992 and exploded in late 1999–2000 prior to a decline in late 2000 when the overall market value fell dramatically. Exhibit 4.9 relates this debt to the

EXHIBIT 4.8   *NYSE MEMBER FIRM CUSTOMERS' MARGIN DEBTS, BILLION $, 1992–2000*

Source: Goldman Sachs.

EXHIBIT 4.9 ➤ *NYSE MARGIN DEBT AS A PERCENT OF U.S. MARKET CAPITALIZATION (1993–2000)*

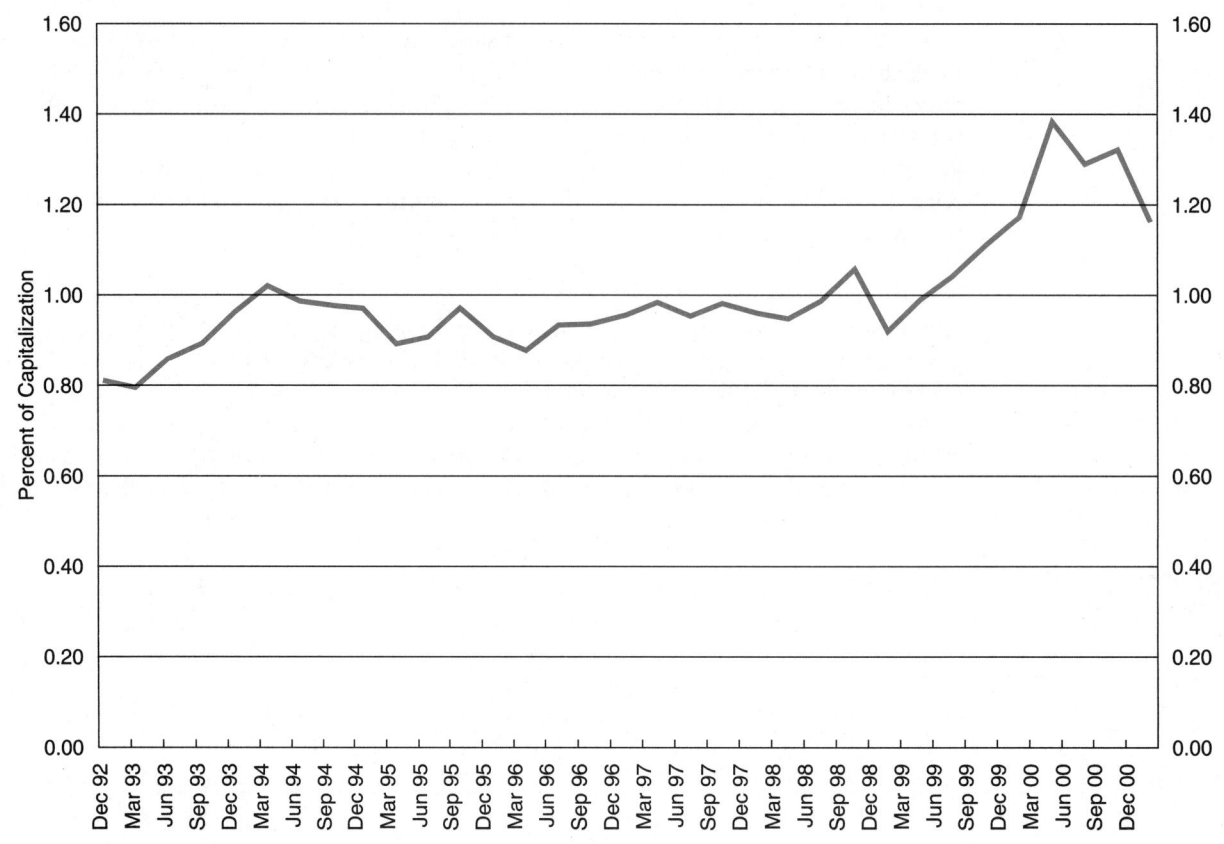

Source: Goldman Sachs.

market value of stocks and the increase is still clear but not as sharp. Again, there is a decline at the end of 2000. The interest rate charged on these loans by the investment firms is typically 1.50 percent above the rate charged by the bank making the loan. The bank rate, referred to as the *call money rate,* is generally about 1 percent below the prime rate. For example, in July, 2002, the prime rate was 4.75 percent, and the call money rate was 3.50 percent.

Federal Reserve Board Regulations T and U determine the maximum proportion of any transaction that can be borrowed. This *margin requirement* (the proportion of total transaction value that must be paid in cash) has varied over time from 40 percent (allowing loans of 60 percent of the value) to 100 percent (allowing no borrowing). As of July 2002, the initial margin requirement specified by the Federal Reserve was 50 percent, although individual investment firms can require higher rates.

After the initial purchase, changes in the market price of the stock will cause changes in the *investor's equity,* which is equal to the market value of the collateral stock minus the amount borrowed. Obviously, if the stock price increases, the investor's equity as a proportion of the total market value of the stock increases; that is, the investor's margin will exceed the initial margin requirement.

Assume you acquired 200 shares of a $50 stock for a total cost of $10,000. A 50 percent initial margin requirement allowed you to borrow $5,000, making your initial equity $5,000. If the stock price increases by 20 percent to $60 a share, the total market value of your position is

$12,000 and your equity is now $7,000 or 58 percent ($7,000/$12,000). In contrast, if the stock price declines by 20 percent to $40 a share, the total market value would be $8,000 and your investor's equity would be $3,000 or 37.5 percent ($3,000/$8,000).

This example demonstrates that buying on margin provides all the advantages and the disadvantages of leverage. Lower margin requirements allow you to borrow more, increasing the percentage of gain or loss on your investment when the stock price increases or decreases. The leverage factor equals 1/percent margin. Thus, as in the example, if the margin is 50 percent, the leverage factor is 2, that is, 1/.50. Therefore, when the rate of return on the stock is plus or minus 10 percent, the return on your equity is plus or minus 20 percent. If the margin declines to 33 percent, you can borrow more (67 percent) and the leverage factor is 3(1/.33). When you acquire stock or other investments on margin, you are increasing the financial risk of the investment beyond the risk inherent in the security itself. You should increase your required rate of return accordingly.[21]

The following example shows how borrowing by using margin affects the distribution of your returns before commissions and interest on the loan. When the stock increased by 20 percent, your return on the investment was as follows:

1. The market value of the stock is $12,000, which leaves you with $7,000 after you pay off the loan.
2. The return on your $5,000 investment is:

$$\frac{7,000}{5,000} - 1 = 1.40 - 1$$
$$= 0.40 = 40\%$$

In contrast, if the stock declined by 20 percent to $40 a share, your return would be as follows:

1. The market value of the stock is $8,000, which leaves you with $3,000 after you pay off the loan.
2. The return on your $5,000 investment is:

$$\frac{3,000}{5,000} - 1 = 0.60 - 1$$
$$= -0.40 = -40\%$$

You should also recognize that this symmetrical increase in gains and losses is only true prior to commissions and interest. Obviously, if we assume a 6 percent interest on the borrowed funds (which would be $5,000 × .06 = $300) and a $100 commission on the transaction, the results would indicate a lower increase and a larger negative return as follows:

$$20\% \text{ Increase:} \frac{\$12,000 - \$5,000 - \$300 - \$100}{5,000} - 1$$
$$= \frac{6,600}{5,000} - 1 = 1.32 - 1.00$$
$$= 0.32 = 32\%$$

$$20\% \text{ Decline:} \frac{\$8,000 - \$5,000 - \$300 - \$100}{5,000} - 1$$
$$= \frac{2,600}{5,000} - 1 = 0.52 - 1.00$$
$$= -0.48 = -48\%$$

---

[21]For a discussion of the investment environment in early 2000, see Greg Ip, "Margin Debt Set a Record in January, Sparking Fresh Fears Over Speculation," *The Wall Street Journal,* 15 February 2000, C1, C2.

In addition to the initial margin requirement, another important concept is the **maintenance margin**, which is the required proportion of your equity to the total value of the stock; the maintenance margin protects the broker if the stock price declines. At present, the minimum maintenance margin specified by the Federal Reserve is 25 percent, but, again, individual brokerage firms can dictate higher margins for their customers. If the stock price declines to the point where your equity drops below 25 percent of the total value of the position, the account is considered undermargined and you will receive a **margin call** to provide more equity. If you do not respond with the required funds in time, the stock will be sold to pay off the loan. The time allowed to meet a margin call varies between investment firms and is affected by market conditions. Under volatile market conditions, the time allowed to respond to a margin call can be shortened drastically.

Given a maintenance margin of 25 percent, when you buy on margin you must consider how far the stock price can fall before you receive a margin call. The computation for our example is as follows: If the price of the stock is P and you own 200 shares, the value of the position is $200P$ and the equity in the account is $200P - \$5,000$. The percentage margin is $(200P - 5,000)/200P$. To determine the price, P, that is equal to 25 percent (0.25), we use the equation:

$$\frac{200P - \$5,000}{200P} = 0.25$$
$$200P - 5,000 = 50P$$
$$P = \$33.3$$

Therefore, when the stock price declines to $33.33 (from the original cost of $50), the equity value is exactly 25 percent; so if the stock goes below $33.33, the investor will receive a margin call.

To continue the previous example, if the stock declines to $30 a share, its total market value would be $6,000 and your equity value would be $1,000, which is only about 17 percent of the total value ($1,000/$6,000). You would receive a margin call for approximately $667, which would give you equity of $1,667, or 25 percent of the total value of the account ($1,667/$6,667).

Exchange Market Makers   Now that we have discussed the overall structure of the exchange markets and the orders that are used to buy and sell stocks, we can discuss the role and function of the market makers on the exchange. These people and the role they play differ among exchanges. For example, on U.S. exchanges these people are called **specialists**; on the TSE they are a combination of the *Saitori* and regular members. Most exchanges do not have a single market maker but have competing dealers such as the Nasdaq Stock Market. On exchanges that have central market makers, these individuals are critical to the smooth and efficient functioning of these markets.

As noted, a major requirement for a good market is liquidity, which depends on how the market makers do their job. Our initial discussion centers on the specialist's role in U.S. markets, followed by a consideration of comparable roles on exchanges in other countries.

U.S. Markets   The specialist is a member of the exchange who applies to the exchange to be assigned stocks to handle.[22] The typical specialist will handle about 15 stocks. The minimum capital requirement for specialists was raised in 1998 to $1 million or the value of 15,000 shares of each stock assigned, whichever is greater.

---

[22]Each stock is assigned to one specialist. Most specialists are part of a specialist firm where partners join together to spread the work load and the risk of the stock assigned to the firm. As of mid-2002, a total of 460 individual specialists were in 10 specialist firms—seven that traded equities and three that only traded Exchange Traded Funds (ETFs).

Functions of the Specialist Specialists have two major functions. First, they serve as *brokers* to match buy and sell orders and to handle special limit orders placed with member brokers. As noted earlier, an individual broker who receives a limit order (or stop loss or stop buy order) leaves it with the specialist, who executes it when the specified price occurs.

The second major function of a specialist is to act as a *dealer* to maintain a fair and orderly market by providing liquidity when the normal flow of orders is not adequate. As a dealer, the specialist must buy and sell for his or her own account (like an OTC dealer) when public supply or demand is insufficient to provide a continuous, liquid market.

Consider the following example. If a stock is currently selling for about $40 per share, the current bid and ask in an auction market (without the intervention of the specialist) might be a 40 bid–41 ask. Under such conditions, random market buy and sell orders might cause the stock price to fluctuate between 40 and 41 constantly—a movement of 2.5 percent between trades. Most investors would probably consider such a price pattern too volatile; the market would not be considered continuous. Under such conditions, the specialist is expected to provide "bridge liquidity" by entering alternative bids and asks or both to narrow the spread and improve the stock's price continuity. In this example, the specialist could enter a bid of 40.40 or 40.50 or an ask of 40.60 or 40.70 to narrow the spread to about $0.20.

Specialists can enter either side of the market, depending on several factors, including the trend of the market. Notably, they are expected to buy or sell against the market when prices are clearly moving in one direction. Specifically, they are required to buy stock for their own inventories when there is a clear excess of sell orders and the market is definitely declining. Alternatively, they must sell stock from their inventories or sell it short to accommodate an excess of buy orders when the market is rising. Specialists are not expected to prevent prices from rising or declining, but only to ensure that *prices change in an orderly fashion* (that is, to maintain price continuity). Evidence that they have fulfilled this requirement is that during recent years NYSE stocks traded unchanged from, or within 10 cents of, the price of the previous trade about 97 percent of the time.

Assuming that there is not a clear trend in the market, a factor affecting specialists' decisions on how to narrow the spread is their current inventory position in the stock. For example, if they have large inventories of a given stock, all other factors being equal, they would probably enter on the ask (sell) side to reduce these heavy inventories. In contrast, specialists who have little or no inventory of shares because they had been selling from their inventories, or selling short, would tend toward the bid (buy) side of the market to rebuild their inventories or close out their short positions.

Finally, the position of the limit order book will influence how they narrow the spread. Numerous limit buy orders (bids) close to the current market and few limit sell orders (asks) might indicate a tendency toward higher prices because demand is apparently heavy and supply is limited. Under such conditions, a specialist who is not bound by one of the other factors would probably opt to accumulate stock in anticipation of a price increase. The specialists on the NYSE have historically participated as dealers in about 15 percent of the trades, but this percent has been increasing in recent years—from about 18 percent in 1996 to 27 percent in 2000.[23]

Specialist Income The specialist derives income from the broker and the dealer functions. The actual breakdown between the two sources depends on the specific stock. In an actively traded stock such as IBM, a specialist has little need to act as a dealer because the substantial public interest in the stock creates a tight market (that is, a small bid-ask spread). In such a case,

---

[23]For a discussion of this trend and its effect on specialists' income, see Greg Ip, "Big Board Specialists: A Profitable Anachronism, *The Wall Street Journal,* 12 March 2001, A10.

the main source of income would come from maintaining the limit orders for the stock. The income derived from acting as a broker for a high-volume stock such as IBM can be substantial, and it is basically without risk.

In contrast, a stock with low trading volume and substantial price volatility would probably have a fairly wide bid-ask spread, and the specialist would have to be an active dealer. The specialist's income from such a stock would depend on his or her ability to trade it profitably. Specialists have a major advantage when trading because of their limit order books. Officially, only specialists are supposed to see the limit order book, which means that they would have a monopoly on very important information regarding the current supply and demand for a stock. The fact is, most specialists routinely share the limit order book with other brokers, so it is not a competitive advantage.[24]

Most specialists attempt to balance their portfolios between strong broker stocks that provide steady, riskless income and stocks that require active dealer roles. Notably, it is pointed out in the article referenced in footnote 23 that the increase in dealer activity has been matched with an increase in return on capital for specialists.[25]

Tokyo Stock Exchange (TSE)   As of 2001, the TSE has a total of 124 "regular members" (100 Japanese members and 24 foreign members) and 1 *Saitori* member (4 *Saitori* firms merged during 1992). For each membership, the firm is allowed several people on the floor of the exchange, depending on its trading volume and capital position (the average number of employees on the floor is 20 per firm for a regular member). The employees of a regular member are called *trading clerks,* and the employees of the *Saitori* member are called *intermediary clerks.*

Regular members buy and sell securities on the TSE either as agents or principals (brokers or dealers). *Saitori* members specialize in acting as intermediaries (brokers) for transactions among regular members, and they maintain the books for limit orders. (Stop loss and stop buy orders as well as short selling are not allowed.) Therefore, *Saitori* members have some of the characteristics of the U.S. exchange specialists because they match buy and sell orders for customers, handle limit orders, and are not allowed to deal with public customers. They *differ* from the U.S. exchange specialists because they do not act as dealers to maintain an orderly market. Only regular members are allowed to buy and sell for their own accounts. Therefore, the TSE is a two-way, continuous auction, order-driven market where buy and sell orders directly interact with one another with the *Saitori* acting as the auctioneer (intermediary) between firms submitting the orders.

Also, although there are about 1,700 listed domestic stocks and 100 foreign stocks on the First Section, only the largest 150 stocks are traded on the floor of the exchange. Trading on the floor is enhanced by an electronic trading system called the Floor Order Routing and Execution System (FORES). All other stocks on the TSE are traded through a computer system called CORES, which stands for Computer-assisted Order Routing and Execution System. With CORES, after an order is entered into the central processing unit, it becomes part of an electronic "book," which is monitored by a *Saitori* members who matches all buy and sell orders on the computer in accordance with trading rules.

---

[24]If a major imbalance in trading arises due to new information, the specialist can request a temporary suspension of trading. For an analysis of what occurs during these trading suspensions, see Michael H. Hopewell and Arthur L. Schwartz, Jr., "Temporary Trading Suspensions in Individual NYSE Securities," *Journal of Finance* 33, no. 5 (December 1978): 1355–1373; and Frank J. Fabozzi and Christopher K. Ma, "The Over-the-Counter Market and New York Stock Exchange Trading Halts," *The Financial Review* 23, no. 4 (November 1988): 427–437.

[25]For a rigorous analysis of specialist trading, see Ananth Madhaven and George Sofianos, "An Empirical Analysis of NYSE Specialist Trading," *Journal of Financial Economics* 48, no. 2 (May 1998): 189–210.

TSE membership is available to corporations licensed by the Minister of Finance. Member applicants may request any of four licenses: (1) to trade securities as a dealer, (2) to trade as a broker, (3) to underwrite new securities, or (4) to handle retail distribution of new or outstanding securities.

London Stock Exchange (LSE)   Historically, members on the LSE were either brokers who could trade shares on behalf of customers or jobbers who bought and sold shares as principals. Following a major deregulation (the "Big Bang") on October 27, 1986, brokers are allowed to make markets in various equities and gilts (British government bonds) and jobbers can deal with non-stock-exchange members, including the public and institutions.

Membership in the LSE includes more than 5,000 individual memberships that are held by 214 broker firms and 22 jobbers. Although individuals gain membership, the operational unit is a member firm that pays an annual charge equal to 1 percent of its gross revenues.

CHANGES IN THE SECURITIES MARKETS

Since 1965, numerous changes have emerged prompted by the significant growth of trading by large financial institutions such as banks, insurance companies, pension funds, and investment companies because the trading requirements of these institutions differ from those of individual investors. Additional changes have transpired because of capital market globalization. In this section, we discuss why these changes occurred, consider their impact on the market, and speculate about future changes.

Evidence and Effect of Institutionalization   The growing influence of large financial institutions is shown by data on block trades (transactions involving at least 10,000 shares) and the size of trades in Exhibit 4.10.

Financial institutions are the main source of large block trades, and the number of block trades on the NYSE has grown steadily from a daily average of 9 in 1965 to almost 22,000 a day in 2000. On average, such trades constitute more than half of all the volume on the exchange. Institutional involvement is also reflected in the average size of trades, which has grown from about 200 shares in 1965 to about 1,200 shares per trade in 2000.[26]

Several major effects of this institutionalization of the market have been identified:

1. Negotiated (competitive) commission rates
2. The influence of block trades
3. The impact on stock price volatility
4. The development of a National Market System (NMS)

In the following sections, we discuss how each of these effects has affected the operation of the U.S. securities market.

Negotiated Commission Rates   **Background**   When the NYSE was formally established in 1792, it was agreed that members would carry out all trades in designated stocks on the exchange and that they would charge nonmembers on the basis of a *minimum commission schedule* that outlawed price cutting. The minimum commission schedule was initially developed to compensate for handling small orders and made no allowance for the trading of large orders by institutions. As a result, institutional investors had to pay substantially more in commissions than the costs of the transactions justified.

---

[26]Although the influence of institutional trading is greatest on the NYSE, it is also a major factor on the Nasdaq-NMS, where block trades accounted for almost 50 percent of share volume in 2000.

EXHIBIT 4.10 *BLOCK TRANSACTIONS[a] AND AVERAGE SHARES PER SALE ON THE NYSE*

YEAR	TOTAL NUMBER OF BLOCK TRANSACTIONS	TOTAL NUMBER OF SHARES IN BLOCK TRADES (× 1,000)	PERCENTAGE OF REPORTED VOLUME	AVERAGE NUMBER OF BLOCK TRANSACTIONS PER DAY	AVERAGE SHARES PER SALE
1965	2,171	48,262	3.1%	9	224
1970	17,217	450,908	15.4	68	388
1975	34,420	778,540	16.6	136	495
1980	133,597	3,311,132	29.2	528	872
1985	539,039	14,222,272	51.7	2,139	1,878
1990	843,365	19,681,849	49.6	3,333	2,082
1995	1,963,889	49,736,912	57.0	7,793	1,489
1996	2,348,457	58,510,323	55.9	9,246	1,392
1997	2,831,321	67,832,129	50.9	11,191	1,300
1998	3,518,200	82,656,678	48.7	13,961	1,250
1999	4,195,721	102,293,458	50.2	16,650	1,205
2000	5,529,152	135,772,004	51.7	21,941	1,187

[a]Trades of 10,000 shares or more.

Source: *NYSE Fact Book* 2001, New York Stock Exchange. Reprinted by permission.

The initial reaction to the excess commissions was "give-ups," whereby brokers agreed to pay part of their commissions (sometimes as much as 80 percent) to other investment firms designated by the institution making the trade that provided services to the institution. These commission transfers were referred to as *soft dollars*. Another response was the increased use of the third market, where commissions were not fixed as they were on the NYSE. The fixed commission structure also fostered the development and use of the fourth market.

Negotiated Commissions   In 1970, the SEC began a program of negotiated commissions on large transactions and finally allowed negotiated commissions on all transactions on May 1, 1975 ("May Day").

The effect on commissions charged has been dramatic. Currently, commissions for institutions are approximately 5 cents per share regardless of the price of the stock, which implies a large discount on high-priced shares. Individuals also receive discounts from numerous competing discount brokers who charge a straight transaction fee and provide no research advice or safekeeping services. These discounts vary depending on the size of the trade.

The reduced commissions caused numerous mergers and liquidations by smaller investment firms after May Day. Also, with fixed minimum commissions, it was cheaper for most institutions to buy research using soft dollars from large brokerage firms that had good trading and research capabilities. As a result, many independent research firms disappeared.

Some observers expected regional exchanges to be adversely affected by competitive rates. Apparently, the unique trading capabilities on these exchanges prevented this because the relative trading on these exchanges has been maintained and increased.[27]

---

[27]Three papers examine the impact of regional exchanges and the practice of purchasing order flow that would normally go to the NYSE; see Robert H. Battalio, "Third Market Broker-Dealers: Cost Competitors or Cream Skimmers?" *Journal of Finance* 52, no. 1 (March 1997). 341–352. Robert Battalio, Jason Greene, and Robert Jennings, "How Do Competing Specialists and Preferencing Dealers Affect Market Quality?" *Review of Financial Studies* 10 (1997): 969–993; and David Easley, Nicholas Kiefer, and Maureen O'Hara, "Cream-Skimming or Profit Sharing? The Curious Role of Purchased Order Flow," *Journal of Finance* 51, no. 3 (July 1996): 811–833.

Total commissions paid have shown a significant decline, and the size and structure of the industry have changed as a result. Although independent research firms contracted, the third market and regional stock exchanges have survived.

The Impact of Block Trades Because the increase in institutional trading has caused an increase in block trades, it is important to consider how block trades influence the market and understand how they are transacted.

Block Trades on the Exchanges

The increase in block trading by institutions has strained the specialist system because some specialists did not have the capital needed to acquire blocks of 10,000 or 20,000 shares. Also, because of Rule 113, specialists were not allowed to directly contact institutions to offer a block brought by another institution. Therefore, specialists were cut off from the major source of demand for blocks.

Block Houses

This lack of capital and contacts by specialists on the exchange created a vacuum in block trading that resulted in the development of block houses. *Block houses* are investment firms (also referred to as *upstairs traders* because they are away from the exchange floor) that help institutions locate other institutions interested in buying or selling blocks of stock. A good block house has (1) the capital required to position a large block, (2) the willingness to commit this capital to a block transaction, and (3) contacts among institutions.

Example of a Block Trade

Assume a mutual fund decides to sell 50,000 of its 250,000 shares of Ford Motors. The fund decides to do it through Goldman Sachs (GS), a large block house and lead underwriter for Ford that knows institutions interested in the stock. After being contacted by the fund, the traders at Goldman Sachs contact several institutions that own Ford to see if any of them want to add to their position and to determine their bids. Assume that the previous sale of Ford on the NYSE was at 35.75 and GS receives commitments from four different institutions for a total of 40,000 shares at an average price of 35.65. Goldman Sachs returns to the mutual fund and bids 35.50 minus a negotiated commission for the total 50,000 shares. Assuming the fund accepts the bid, Goldman Sachs now owns the block and immediately sells 40,000 shares to the four institutions that made prior commitments. It also "positions" 10,000 shares; that is, it owns the 10,000 shares and must eventually sell them at the best price possible. Because GS is a member of the NYSE, the block will be processed ("crossed") on the exchange as one transaction of 50,000 shares at 35.50. The specialist on the NYSE might take some of the stock to fill limit orders on the book at prices between 35.50 and 35.75.

For working on this trade, GS receives a negotiated commission, but it has committed almost $355,000 to position the 10,000 shares. The major risk to GS is the possibility of a subsequent price change on the 10,000 shares. If it can sell the 10,000 shares for 35.50 or more, it will just about break even on the position and have the commission as income. If the price of the stock weakens, GS may have to sell the position at 35.25 and take a loss on it of about $2,500, offsetting the income from the commission.

This example indicates the importance of institutional contacts, capital to position a portion of the block, and willingness to commit that capital to the block trade. Without all three, the transaction would not take place.

Institutions and Stock Price Volatility Some stock market observers speculate there should be a strong positive relationship between institutional trading and stock price volatility because institutions trade in large blocks, and it is contended that they tend to trade together. Empirical studies of the relationship between the proportion of trading by large financial institutions and stock price volatility have never supported

EXHIBIT 4.11 ▸ *CONSOLIDATED TAPE VOLUME (THOUSANDS OF SHARES)*

1976	6,281,008
1980	12,935,607
1985	32,988,595
1990	48,188,072
1995	106,554,583
1996	126,340,065
1997	159,451,717
1998	203,727,877
1999	247,453,423
2000	316,760,429

Source: *NYSE Fact Book* 2001, New York Stock Exchange. Reprinted by permission.

the folklore.[28] In a capital market where trading is dominated by institutions, the best environment is one where all institutions are actively involved because they provide liquidity for one another and for noninstitutional investors.

National Market System (NMS) The development of a National Market System (NMS) has been advocated by financial institutions because it is expected to provide greater efficiency, competition, and lower cost of transactions. Although there is no generally accepted definition of an NMS, four major characteristics are generally expected:

1. Centralized reporting of all transactions
2. Centralized quotation system
3. Centralized limit order book (CLOB)
4. Competition among all qualified market makers

Centralized Reporting Centralized reporting requires a composite tape to report all transactions in a stock regardless of where the transactions took place. On the tape you might see a trade in GM on the NYSE, another trade on the Chicago Exchange, and a third on the OTC.

The NYSE has been operating a central tape since 1975 that includes all NYSE stocks traded on other exchanges and on the OTC. The volume of shares reported on the consolidated tape is shown in Exhibit 4.11. The recent breakdown among the seven exchanges and two OTC markets appears in Exhibit 4.12. Therefore, this component of a National Market System (NMS) is available for stocks listed on the NYSE. As shown, although the volume of trading is dispersed among the exchanges and the NASD, the NYSE is clearly dominant.[29]

---

[28]In this regard, see Neil Berkman, "Institutional Investors and the Stock Market," *New England Economic Review* (November–December 1977): 60–77; and Frank K. Reilly and David J. Wright, "Block Trades and Aggregate Stock Price Volatility," *Financial Analysts Journal* 40, no. 2 (March–April 1984): 54–60.

[29]For a discussion of these changes, see Janet Bush, "Hoping for a New Broom at the NYSE," *Financial Times,* 16 August 1990, 13; William Power, "Big Board, at Age 200, Scrambles to Protect Grip on Stock Market," *The Wall Street Journal,* 13 May 1992, A1, A8; and Pat Widder, "Nasdaq Has Its Eyes Set on the Next 100 Years," *Chicago Tribune,* 17 May 1992, Section 7, pp. 1, 4.

EXHIBIT 4.12 *EXCHANGES AND MARKETS INVOLVED IN CONSOLIDATED TAPE WITH PERCENTAGE OF TRADES DURING 2001*

	PERCENTAGE		PERCENTAGE
Boston	2.36	NASD	7.02
Chicago	3.67	NYSE	84.61
Cincinnati	1.25	Pacific	0.46
Instinet	0.00	Philadelphia	0.64

Source: *NYSE Fact Book* 2001, New York Stock Exchange. Reprinted by permission.

EXHIBIT 4.13 *INTERMARKET TRADING SYSTEM ACTIVITY*

		DAILY AVERAGE		
YEAR	ISSUES ELIGIBLE	SHARE VOLUME	EXECUTED TRADES	AVERAGE SIZE OF TRADE
1980	884	1,565,900	2,868	546
1985	1,288	5,669,400	5,867	966
1990	2,126	9,397,114	8,744	1,075
1995	3,542	12,185,064	10,911	1,117
1996	4,001	12,721,968	11,426	1,113
1997	4,535	15,429,377	14,057	1,098
1998	4,844	18,136,472	17,056	1,063
1999	5,056	21,617,723	19,315	1,119
2000	4,664	28,176,178	23,972	1,175

Source: *NYSE Fact Book* 2001, New York Stock Exchange. Reprinted by permission.

Centralized Quotation System   A centralized quotation system would list the quotes for a given stock (say, General Electric, GE) from all market makers on the national exchanges, the regional exchanges, and the OTC. With such a system, a broker who requested the current market quota for GE would see all the prevailing quotes and should complete the trade on the market with the best quote.

Intermarket Trading System   A centralized quotation system is currently available—the Intermarket Trading System (ITS), developed by the American, Boston, Chicago, New York, Pacific, and Philadelphia Stock Exchanges and the NASD. ITS consists of a central computer facility with interconnected terminals in the participating market centers. As shown in Exhibit 4.13, the number of issues included, the volume of trading, and the size of trades have all grown substantially.

With ITS, brokers and market makers in each market center indicate specific buying and selling commitments through a composite quotation display that shows the current quotes for each stock in every market center. A broker is expected to go to the best market to execute a customer's order by sending a message committing to a buy or sell at the price quoted. When this commitment is accepted, a message reports the transaction. The following example illustrates how ITS works.

A broker on the NYSE has a market order to sell 100 shares of GE stock. Assuming the quotation display at the NYSE shows that the best current bid for GE is on the Pacific Stock Exchange (CSE), the broker will enter an order to sell 100 shares at the bid on the PSE. Within seconds, the commitment flashes on the computer screen and is printed out at the PSE specialist's post where it is executed against the PSE bid. The transaction is reported back to New York and on the consolidated tape. Both brokers receive immediate confirmation, and the results are transmitted at the end of each day. Thereafter, each broker completes his or her own clearance and settlement procedure.

The ITS system currently provides centralized quotations for stocks listed on the NYSE and specifies whether a bid or ask *away* from the NYSE market is superior to that *on* the NYSE. Note, however, that the system lacks several characteristics. It does not automatically execute at the best market. Instead, you must contact the market maker and indicate that you want to buy or sell, at which time the bid or ask may be withdrawn. Also, it is not mandatory that a broker go to the best market. Although the best price may be at another market center, a broker might consider it inconvenient to trade on that exchange if the price difference is not substantial. It is almost impossible to audit such actions. Still, even with these shortcomings, substantial technical and operational progress has occurred on a central quotation system.

Central Limit Order Book (CLOB) Substantial controversy has surrounded the idea of a central limit order book (CLOB) that would contain all limit orders from all exchanges. Ideally, the CLOB would be visible to everyone and all market makers and traders could fill orders on it. Currently, most limit orders are placed with specialists on the NYSE and filled when a transaction on the NYSE reaches the stipulated price. The NYSE specialist receives some part of the commission for rendering this service. The NYSE has opposed a CLOB because its specialists do not want to share this lucrative business. Although the technology for a CLOB is available, it is difficult to estimate when it will become a reality.

Competition Among Market Makers (Rule 390) Market makers have always competed on the OTC market, but competition has been opposed by the NYSE. The competition argument contends that it forces dealers to offer better bids and asks or they will not do any business. Several studies have indicated that competition among dealers (as in the OTC market) results in a smaller spread. In contrast, the NYSE argues that a central auction market forces all orders to one central location where the orders are exposed to all interested participants and this central auction results in the best market and execution, including many transactions at prices between the current bid and ask.

To help create a centralized auction market, the NYSE's Rule 390 requires members to obtain the permission of the exchange before carrying out a transaction in a listed stock off the exchange. The exchange contends that Rule 390 is necessary to protect the auction market, arguing that its elimination would fragment the market, tempting members to trade off the exchange and to internalize many orders (that is, members would match orders from their own customers, which would keep these orders from exposure to the full auction market). Due to the controversy, progress in achieving this final phase of the NMS has been slow.[30]

New Trading Systems As daily trading volume has gone from about 5 million shares to more than a billion shares, it has become necessary to introduce new technology into the trading process. Currently, the NYSE routinely handles days with volume over one billion. The following discussion considers some technological innovations that assist in the trading process.

---

[30]See Hans R. Stoll, "Organization of the Stock Market: Competition or Fragmentation," *Journal of Applied Corporate Finance* 5, no. 4 (Winter 1993): 89–93.

Super Dot   Super Dot is an electronic order-routing system through which member firms transmit market and limit orders in NYSE-listed securities directly to the posts where securities are traded or to the Exchange's order management system, referred to as the Broker Booth Support System (BBSS), which is at the firm's trading booth on the floor of the Exchange. After the order has been executed, a report of execution is returned directly to the member firm office over the same electronic circuit and the execution is submitted directly to the comparison systems. Member firms can enter market orders up to 2,099 shares and limit orders in round or odd lots up to 30,099 shares. An estimated 85 percent of all market orders enter the NYSE through the Super Dot system.

Display Book   The Display Book is an electronic workstation that keeps track of all limit orders and incoming market orders. This includes incoming Super Dot limit orders. The Display Book sorts the limit orders and displays them in price/time priority.

Opening Automated Report Service (OARS)   OARS, the opening feature of the Super Dot system, accepts member firms' preopening market orders up to 30,099 shares. OARS automatically and continuously pairs buy and sell orders and presents the imbalance to the specialist prior to the opening of a stock. This system helps the specialist determine the opening price and the potential need for a preopening call market.

Market Order Processing   Super Dot's postopening market order system is designed to accept member firms' postopening market orders up to 3 million shares. The system provides rapid execution and reporting of market orders. During 2000, the average time for an execution and report back to a member firm for eligible market orders was 15–16 seconds.

Limit Order Processing   The limit order processing system provides an overnight file for orders with a specified price so they can be executed when and if a specific price is reached. The system accepts limit orders up to 3 million shares and electronically updates the specialists' Display Book. Good-until-canceled orders that are not executed on the day of submission are automatically stored until executed or canceled.

Global Market Changes

NYSE Off-Hours Trading   One of the major concerns of the NYSE is the continuing erosion of its market share for stocks listed on the NYSE due to global trading. Specifically, the share of trading of NYSE-listed stock has declined from about 85 percent during the early 1980s to about 80 percent in 2000. This reflects an increase in trading on regional exchanges and the third market, some increase in fourth-market trading, but mainly an increase in trading in foreign markets in London and Tokyo. The NYSE has attempted to respond to this by expanding its trading hours and listing more non-U.S. stocks. The expansion of hours involves two NYSE crossing sessions.

Crossing Session I (CSI) provides the opportunity to trade individual stocks at the NYSE closing prices after the regular session—from 4:15 P.M. to 5:00 P.M. Crossing Session II (CSII) allows trading a collection of at least 15 NYSE stocks with a market value of at least $1 million. This session is from 4:00 P.M. to 5:15 P.M.

Listing Foreign Stocks on the NYSE   A major goal and concern for the NYSE is the ability to list foreign stocks on the exchange. The NYSE chairman, Richard A. Grasso, has stated on several occasions that the exchange recognizes that much of the growth in the coming decades will be in foreign countries and their stocks. As a result, the exchange wants to list a number of these stocks. The problem is that current SEC regulations will not allow the NYSE to list these firms because they follow less-stringent foreign accounting and disclosure standards. Specifically, many foreign companies issue financial statements less frequently and with less information than what is required by the SEC. As a result, about 434 foreign firms currently have shares traded on the NYSE (mainly through ADRs), but it is contended that 2,000 to 3,000 foreign companies would qualify for listing on the NYSE except for the accounting rules. The exchange contends that, unless the rules are adjusted and the NYSE is allowed to compete with other world exchanges (the LSE lists more than 600 foreign stocks), it will eventually become a regional exchange in the global market. The view of the SEC is that they have an obligation to ensure that investors receive adequate disclosure. This difference hopefully will be resolved in favor of allowing additional foreign listings.[31]

London Stock Exchange   As noted, the London Stock Exchange initiated several major changes with the *Big Bang,* such as allowing being brokers to act as market makers, jobbers being allowed to deal with the public and with institutions, and all commissions being fully negotiable.

The gilt market was restructured to resemble the U.S. government securities market. This new arrangement has created a more competitive environment.

Trades are reported on a system called *Stock Exchange Automated Quotations (SEAQ) International,* which is an electronic market-price information system similar to Nasdaq. In addition, real-time prices are being shared with the NYSE while the NASD provides certain U.S. OTC prices to the London market.[32]

Tokyo Stock Exchange (TSE)   The TSE experienced a "big bang" during 1998 that introduced more competition in trading commissions and also encouraged competition among market participants.

Currently, 25 foreign firms are members of the TSE, although Japanese investment firms dominate the Japanese financial market: Nomura, Daiwa, and Nikko.

Future Developments   In addition to the expected effects of the NMS and a global capital market, there are other changes that you should understand.

Creation and Consolidation of Stock Exchanges   Earlier in this chapter, we discussed two major trends that appeared to be inconsistent. The first was the creation of new exchanges in many emerging markets because these countries needed the new capital from primary equity markets, but these primary markets needed to be supported by the liquidity provided by the secondary stock exchange markets. The second trend was the consolidation of the exchanges in many developed countries because of the added liquidity provided by size and the financial resources provided by the mergers that would be used to develop the technology required to compete in the current and future environment. The fact is, we expect both of these trends to continue. Specifically, the new exchanges will be created to help an emerging country develop its full capital market but, subsequently, these exchanges will merge or affiliate with other exchanges after the markets become more developed in order to provide additional liquidity and concentrate the resources needed for technology.

[31]The NYSE argument is supported in the following articles: William J. Baumol and Burton Malkiel, "Redundant Regulation of Foreign Security Trading and U.S. Competitiveness," *Journal of Applied Corporate Finance* 5, no. 4 (Winter 1993): 19–27; and Franklin Edwards, "Listing of Foreign Securities on U.S. Exchanges," *Journal of Applied Corporate Finance* 5, no. 4 (Winter 1993): 28–36.

[32]For a recent discussion of the challenges facing the London Stock Exchange (LSE), see Vincent Boland, "Securing a Future," *Financial Times* (March 5, 2001).

More Specialized Investment Companies Although more individuals want to own stocks and bonds, they have increasingly acquired this ownership through investment companies because most individuals find it too difficult and time-consuming to do their own analysis. This increase in fund sales has caused an explosion of new funds (discussed in Chapter 3 and Chapter 25) that provide numerous opportunities to diversify in a wide range of asset classes.

This trend toward specialized funds will continue and could possibly include other investment alternatives such as stamps, coins, and art. Because of the lower liquidity of foreign securities, stamps, coins, and art, many of these new mutual funds will be closed-end and will be traded on an exchange.

Changes in the Financial Services Industry The financial services industry is experiencing a major change in makeup and operation. Prior to 1960, the securities industry was composed of specialty firms that concentrated in specific investments such as stocks, bonds, commodities, real estate, or insurance. During the early 1980s, some firms focused on creating financial supermarkets that considered all these investment alternatives around the world. Prime examples would be Merrill Lynch, which acquired insurance and real estate subsidiaries, and Travelers Insurance, which acquired Salomon Brothers and Smith Barney. A subset includes firms that are global in coverage but limit their product line to mainstream investment instruments, such as bonds, stocks, futures, and options. Firms in this category would include Merrill Lynch, Goldman Sachs, and Morgan Stanley, among others. At the other end of the spectrum, large banks such as Citicorp and UBS (formerly Union Bank of Switzerland) are entering the investment banking and money management business.

In contrast to financial supermarkets, some firms are going the specialty, or "boutique," route, attempting to provide unique, superior financial products. Examples include discount brokers, investment firms that concentrate on institutional or individual investors, or firms that concentrate on an industry such as banking.

It appears we are moving toward a world with two major groups. Specifically, one group would include a few global investment firms that deal in almost all the asset classes available, while the second group would include numerous firms that provide specialized services in unique products.

Trading in Cybermarkets Beyond these firm changes, the advances in technology continue to accelerate and promise to affect how the secondary market will be organized and operated. Specifically, computerized trading has made tremendous inroads during the past five years and promises to introduce numerous additional changes into the 21st century in markets around the world. The 24-hour market will require extensive computerized trading. It is envisioned that the markets of the future will be floorless, global, and highly automated.[33]

---

[33]This includes the "Market 2000" report, prepared by the SEC, which is concerned with the organization and operation of securities markets in the United States. Notably, many emerging market exchanges are able to "leapfrog" to the latest technology. This also includes the technology innovations related to the merger of the NASD and the AMEX, discussed earlier. This is discussed in Paula Dwyer, A. Osterland, K. Capell, and S. Reier, "The 21st Century Stock Market," *Business Week,* 10 August 1998, 66–72. Also, Greg Ip, "Instinet Expands Its Presence," *The Wall Street Journal,* 28 July 1999, C1, discusses a new electronic market that will compete with the NYSE and the Nasdaq. For a set of articles on this topic, see Kathryn D. Jost, ed., *Best Execution and Portfolio Performance* (Charlottesville, Va.: The Association of Investment Management and Research, 2001). The presentation by Erik Sirri entitled "The Future of Stock Exchanges" is very relevant.

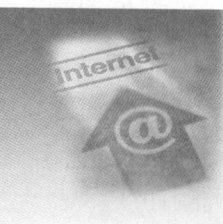

The Internet *Investments Online*

Many Internet sites deal with different aspects of investing. Earlier site suggestions led you to information and prices of securities traded both in the U.S. and around the globe. Here are some additional sites of interest:

http://finance.yahoo.com One of the best sites for a variety of investment information including market quotes, commentary, and research, both domestic and international.

http://www.quote.com This site offers substantial market information, including price quotes on stocks, selected bonds, and options. Price charts are available.

http://www.sec.gov The Web site of the SEC (Securities and Exchange Commission) offers news and information, investor assistance and complaint handling, SEC rules, enforcement, and data. **http://www.nyse.com** New York Stock Exchange; **http://www.amex.com** American Stock Exchange; **www.nasdaq.com** National Association of Securities Dealers Automated Quotation (Nasdaq)

The Web sites offer information about the relevant market, price quotes, listings of firms, and investor services. The AMEX site includes price quotes for SPDRs (S&P Depository Receipts, which represent ownership in the S&P 500 index or the S&P Midcap 400 index) and iShares MSCI Index Funds, which track the Morgan Stanley Capital International (MSCI) indexes of over 20 countries and regions.

Several Nasdaq-related sites are of special interest. **http://www.nasdaqtrader.com** pre-

sents useful statistics about trading in individual stocks. **http://www.academic.nasdaq.com** has a feature, "Nasdaq Head Trader," which allows a visitor to pretend to be a market maker.

http://www.etrade.com E*Trade Financial **http://www.schwab.com** Charles Schwab Co. **http://www.ml.com** Merrill Lynch & Co., Inc. Many brokerage houses have Web pages. These are three examples of such sites. E*Trade Securities is an example of an on-line brokerage firm that allows investors to trade securities over the Internet. Schwab is a discount broker, whereas Merrill Lynch is a full-service broker with a reputation for good research.

Links to country stock and other financial markets are available at

http://www.internationalist.com/ business, http://biz.yahoo.com/ifc/, http://www.gwdg.de/~ifbg/stock1.htm, and links available on **http://finance.wat.ch.**

Web sites of regional stock exchanges in the U.S. include **http://www.bostonstock.com, http://www.chicagostock.com, http://www.cincinnatistock.com, http://www.pacificex.com,** and **http://www.phlx.com.**

The NASD's Web site is **http://www. nasd.com;** other industry organizations include the Securities Industry Association **http://www. sia.com** and the Securities Traders Association **http://www.securitiestraders.com**.

Summary

- The securities market is divided into primary and secondary markets. Secondary markets provide the liquidity that is critical for primary markets. The major segments of the secondary markets include listed exchanges (the NYSE, AMEX, TSE, LSE, and regional exchanges), the over-the-counter market, the third market, and the fourth market. Because you will want to invest across these secondary markets within a country as well as among countries, you need to understand how the markets differ and how they are similar.

- Many of the dramatic changes in our securities markets during the past 30 years are due to an increase in institutional trading and to rapidly evolving global markets. It is important to understand what has happened and why it happened because numerous changes have occurred—and many more are yet to come. You need to understand how these changes will affect your investment alternatives and opportunities. You must look not only for the best investment but also for the best securities market to buy and/or sell the investment. This discussion should provide the background to help you make that trading decision.

Questions

1. Define *market* and briefly discuss the characteristics of a good market.
2. You own 100 shares of General Electric stock and you want to sell it because you need the money to make a down payment on a stereo. Assume there is absolutely no secondary market system in common stocks. How would you go about selling the stock? Discuss what you would have to do to find a buyer, how long it might take, and the price you might receive.
3. Define *liquidity* and discuss the factors that contribute to it. Give examples of a liquid asset and an illiquid asset, and discuss why they are considered liquid and illiquid.
4. Define a primary and secondary market for securities and discuss how they differ. Discuss why the primary market is dependent on the secondary market.
5. Give an example of an initial public offering (IPO) in the primary market. Give an example of a seasoned equity issue in the primary market. Discuss which would involve greater risk to the buyer.
6. Find an advertisement for a recent primary offering in *The Wall Street Journal.* Based on the information in the ad, indicate the characteristics of the security sold and the major underwriters. How much new capital did the firm derive from the offering before paying commissions?
7. Briefly explain the difference between a competitive bid underwriting and a negotiated underwriting.
8. The figures in Exhibit 4.4 reveal a major change over time in the price paid for a membership (seat) on the NYSE. How would you explain this change over time?
9. What are the major reasons for the existence of regional stock exchanges? Discuss how they differ from the national exchanges.
10. Which segment of the secondary stock market (listed exchanges or the OTC) is larger in terms of the number of issues? Which is larger in terms of the value of the issues traded?
11. Discuss the three levels of Nasdaq in terms of what each level provides and who would subscribe to each of these levels.
12. a. Define the third market. Give an example of a third-market stock.
    b. Define the fourth market. Discuss why a financial institution would use the fourth market.
13. Briefly define each of the following terms and give an example:
    a. Market order
    b. Limit order
    c. Short sale
    d. Stop loss order
14. Briefly discuss the two major functions and sources of income for the NYSE specialist.
15. Describe the duties of the *Saitori* member on the TSE. Discuss how these duties differ from those of the NYSE specialist.
16. Discuss why the U.S. equity market has experienced major changes since 1965.
17. What were give-ups? What are "soft dollars"? Discuss why soft dollars and give-ups existed when there were fixed commissions.
18. Describe block houses and explain why they evolved. Describe what is meant by *positioning* part of a block.
19. a. Describe the major attributes of the National Market System (NMS).
    b. Briefly describe the ITS and what it contributes to the NMS. Discuss the growth of the ITS.
20. The chapter includes a discussion of expected changes in world capital markets. Discuss one of the suggested changes in terms of what has been happening or discuss an evolving change that was not mentioned.

Problems

1. The initial margin requirement is 60 percent. You have $40,000 to invest in a stock selling for $80 a share. Ignoring taxes and commissions, show in detail the impact on your rate of return if the stock rises to $100 a share and if it declines to $40 a share assuming (a) you pay cash for the stock, and (b) you buy it using maximum leverage.

2. Lauren has a margin account and deposits $50,000. Assuming the prevailing margin requirement is 40 percent, commissions are ignored, and The Gentry Shoe Corporation is selling at $35 per share:
   a. How many shares of Gentry Shoe can Lauren purchase using the maximum allowable margin?
   b. What is Lauren's profit (loss) if the price of Gentry's stock
      (1) Rises to $45?
      (2) Falls to $25?
   c. If the maintenance margin is 30 percent, to what price can Gentry Shoe fall before Lauren will receive a margin call?

3. Suppose you buy a round lot of Maginn Industries stock on 55 percent margin when the stock is selling at $20 a share. The broker charges a 10 percent annual interest rate, and commissions are 3 percent of the total stock value on both the purchase and sale. A year later, you receive a $0.50 per share dividend and sell the stock for 27. What is your rate of return on the investment?

4. You decide to sell short 100 shares of Charlotte Horse Farms when it is selling at its yearly high of 56. Your broker tells you that your margin requirement is 45 percent and that the commission on the sale is $155. While you are short the stock, Charlotte pays a $2.50 per share dividend. At the end of one year, you buy 100 shares of Charlotte at 45 to close out your position and are charged a commission of $145 and 8 percent interest on the money borrowed. What is your rate of return on the investment?

5. You own 200 shares of Shamrock Enterprises that you bought at $25 a share. The stock is now selling for $45 a share.
   a. If you put in a stop loss order at $40, discuss your reasoning for this action.
   b. If the stock eventually declines in price to $30 a share, what would be your rate of return with and without the stop loss order?

6. Two years ago, you bought 300 shares of Kayleigh Milk Co. for $30 a share with a margin of 60 percent. Currently, the Kayleigh stock is selling for $45 a share. Assuming no dividends and ignoring commissions, (a) compute the annualized rate of return on this investment if you had paid cash and (b) your rate of return with the margin purchase.

7. The stock of the Michele Travel Co. is selling for $28 a share. You put in a limit buy order at $24 for one month. During the month, the stock price declines to $20, then jumps to $36. Ignoring commissions, what would have been your rate of return on this investment? What would be your rate of return if you had put in a market order? What if your limit order was at $18?

References

Amihad, Y., and H. Mendelson. "Trading Mechanisms and Stock Returns. An Empirical Investigation." *Journal of Finance* 42, no. 3 (July 1987).

Barclay, Michael J., William G. Christie, Jeffrey H. Harris, Eugene Kandel, and Paul Schultz. "The Effects of Market Reform on the Trading Costs and Depth of Nasdaq Stocks." *Journal of Finance* 54, no. 1 (March, 1999).

Blume, Marshall E., and Jeremy J. Siegel. "The Theory of Security Pricing and Market Structure." *Financial Markets, Institutions and Instruments* 1, no. 3 (1992). New York University Salomon Center.

Christie, William, and Paul Schultz. "Why Do Nasdaq Market Makers Avoid Odd-Eighth Quotes?" *Journal of Finance* 49, no. 5 (December 1994).

Dutts, Prajit, and Ananth Madhaven. "Competition and Collusion in Dealer Markets." *Journal of Finance* 52, no. 1 (March 1997).

Economides, Nicholas, and Robert A. Schwartz. "Electronic Call Market Trading." *Journal of Portfolio Management* 21, no. 3 (Spring 1995).

Grossman, S. J., and Merton H. Miller. "Liquidity and Market Structure." *Journal of Finance* 43, no. 2 (June 1988).

Harris, Jeffrey, and Paul Schultz. "The Trading Profits of SOES Bandits." *Journal of Financial Economics* 50, no. 1 (October 1998).

Hasbrouck, Joel. "Assessing the Quality of a Security Market: A New Approach to Transaction-Cost Measurement." *Review of Financial Studies* 6, no. 1 (1993).

Huang, Roger, and Hans Stoll. "Dealer versus Auction Markets: A Paired Comparison of Execution Costs on Nasdaq and the NYSE." *Journal of Financial Economics* 41, no. 3 (July 1996).

Ibbotson, Roger G., and Gary P. Brinson. *Global Investing.* New York: McGraw-Hill, 1993.

Jost, Kathryn Dixon, ed. *Best Execution and Portfolio Performance* (Charlottesville, Va.: The Association for Investment Management and Research, 2001).

Kee, C. "Market Integration and Price Execution for NYSE-Listed Securities." *Journal of Finance* 48, no. 2 (June 1993).

Madhaven, Ananth. "Trading Mechanisms in Securities Markets." *Journal of Finance* 47, no. 2 (June 1992).

Nasdaq Fact Book. Washington, D.C.: National Association of Securities Dealers, published annually.

Neal, Robert. "A Comparison of Transaction Cost between Competitive Market Maker and Specialist Market Structures." *Journal of Business* 65, no. 3 (July 1992).

NYSE Fact Book. New York: NYSE, published annually.

Pagano, M. "Trading Volume and Asset Liquidity." *Quarterly Journal of Economics* 104, no. 2 (1989).

Sherrerd, Katrina F., ed. *Execution Techniques, True Trading Costs, and the Microstructure of Markets.* Charlottesville, Va.: Association for Investment Management and Research, 1993.

Solnik, Bruno. *International Investments,* 4th ed. Reading, Mass.: Addison-Wesley, 2000.

Stoll, Hans. *The Stock Exchange Specialist System: An Economic Analysis.* Monograph Series in Financial Economics 1985, 2. New York University, 1985.

Stoll, Hans, and Robert Whaley. "Stock Market Structure and Volatility." *Review of Financial Studies* 3, no. 1 (1990).

Tokyo Stock Exchange Fact Book. Tokyo: TSE, published annually.

APPENDIX
Chapter 4

Characteristics of Stock Exchanges in Developed and Developing Markets around the World

(Exhibits 4A.1 and 4A.2 on the following pages)

EXHIBIT 4A.1

CHARACTERISTICS OF STOCK EXCHANGES IN DEVELOPED MARKETS AROUND THE WORLD

Country	Principal Exchange	Other Exchanges	Total Market Capitalization ($ Billions)	Available Market Capitalization ($ Billions)	Trading Volume ($ Billions)	Domestic Issues Listed	Total Issues Listed	Auction Mechanism	Official Specialists	Options/Futures Trading	Price Limits	Principal Market Indexes
Australia	Sydney	5	82.3	53.5	39.3	N.A.	1,496	Continuous	No	Yes	None	All ordinaries—324 issues
Austria	Vienna	—	18.7	8.3	37.2	125	176	Call	Yes	No	5%	GZ Aktienindex—25 issues
Belgium	Brussels	3	48.5	26.2	6.8	186	337	Mixed	No	Few	10%	Brussels Stock Exchange Index—186 issues
Canada	Toronto	4	186.8	124.5	71.3	N.A.	1,208	Continuous	Yes	Yes	None	TSE 300 Composite Index
Denmark	Copenhagen	—	29.7	22.2	11.1	N.A.	284	Mixed	No	No	None	Copenhagen Stock Exchange Index—38 issues
Finland	Helsinki	—	9.9	1.7	5.2	N.A.	125	Mixed	N.A.	N.A.	N.A.	KOP (Kansallis-Osake-Pannki) Price Index
France	Paris	6	256.5	137.2	129.0	463	663	Mixed	Yes	Yes	4%	CAC General Index—240 issues
Germany	Frankfurt	7	297.7	197.9	1,003.7	N.A.	355	Continuous	Yes	Options	None	DAX; FAZ (Frankfurter Allgemeine Zeitung)
Hong Kong	Hong Kong	—	67.7	37.1	34.6	N.A.	479	Continuous	No	Futures	None	Hang Seng Index—33 issues
Ireland	Dublin	—	8.4	6.4	5.5	N.A.	N.A.	Continuous	No	No	None	J&E Davy Total Market Index
Italy	Milan	9	137.0	73.2	42.6	N.A.	317	Mixed	No	No	10–20%	Banca Commerziale—209 issues
Japan	Tokyo	7	2,754.6	1,483.5	1,602.4	N.A.	1,576	Continuous	Yes	No	10% down	TOPIX—1,097 issues; TSE II—423 issues; Nikkei 225
Luxembourg	Luxembourg	—	1.5	0.9	0.1	61	247	Continuous	N.A.	N.A.	N.A.	Domestic Share Price Index—9 issues
Malaysia	Kuala Lumpur	—	199.3	95.0	126.4	430	478	Continuous	No	No	None	Kuala Lumpur Composite Index—83 issues
The Netherlands	Amsterdam	—	112.1	92.4	80.4	279	569	Continuous	Yes	Options	Variable	ANP-CBS

Country	Principal Exchange	Other Exchanges	Total Market Capitalization ($ Billions)	Available Market Capitalization ($ Billions)	Trading Volume ($ Billions)	Domestic Issues Listed	Total Issues Listed	Auction Mechanism	Official Specialists	Options/Futures Trading	Price Limits	Principal Market Indexes
New Zealand	Wellington	—	6.7	5.3	2.0	295	451	Continuous	No	Futures	None	Barclay's International Price Index—40 issues
Norway	Oslo	9	18.4	7.9	14.1	N.A.	128	Call	No	No	None	Oslo Bors Stock Index—50 issues
Singapore	Singapore	—	28.6	15.6	8.2	N.A.	324	Continuous	No	No	None	Straits Times Index—30 issues; SES—32 issues
South Africa	Johannesburg	—	72.7	N.A.	8.2	N.A.	N.A.	Continuous	No	Options	None	JSE Actuaries Index—141 issues
Spain	Madrid	3	86.6	46.8	41.0	N.A.	368	Mixed	No	No	10%	Madrid Stock Exchange Index—72 issues
Sweden	Stockholm	—	59.0	24.6	15.8	N.A.	151	Mixed	No	Yes	None	Jacobson & Ponsbach—30 issues
Switzerland	Zurich	6	128.5	75.4	376.6	161	380	Mixed	No	Yes	5%	Société de Banque Suisse—90 issues
United Kingdom	London	5	756.2	671.1	280.7	1,911	2,577	Continuous	No	Yes	None	Financial Times (FT) Ordinaries—750 issues; FTSE 100; FT 33
United States	New York	6	9,431.1	8,950.3	5,778.7	N.A.	3,358	Continuous	Yes	Yes	None	S&P 500; Dow Jones Industrial Average; Wilshire 5000; Russel 3000

Notes: Market capitalizations (both total and available) are as of December 31, 1990, except for South African market capitalization, which is from 1988. Available differs from total market capitalization by subtracting cross holdings, closely held and government-owned shares, and takes into account restrictions on foreign ownership. Number of issues listed are from 1988 except for Malaysia, which is from 1994. Trading volume data are 1990 except for Switzerland, which are from 1988. Trading institutions data are from 1987. Market capitalizations (both total and available) for all countries except the United States and South Africa are from the Salomon-Russel Global Equity Indices. U.S. market capitalization (both total and available) is from the Frank Russell Company. All trading volume information (except for Switzerland) and Malaysian total issues listed are from the *Emerging Stock Markets Factbook: 1991,* International Finance Corp., 1991. Trading institutions information is from Richard Roll, "The International Crash of 1987," *Financial Analysts Journal,* September/October 1988. South African market capitalization, number of issues listed for all countries (except Malaysia), and Swiss trading volume are reproduced courtesy of Euromoney Books, extracted from *The G.T. Guide to World Equity Markets: 1989, 1988.*

Source: Roger G. Ibbotson and Gary P. Brinson, *Global Investing* (New York: McGraw-Hill, 1993): 109–111. Reproduced with permission of The McGraw-Hill Companies.

EXHIBIT 4A.2 CHARACTERISTICS OF STOCK EXCHANGES IN EMERGING MARKETS AROUND THE WORLD

COUNTRY	PRINCIPAL EXCHANGE	OTHER EXCHANGES	MARKET CAPITALIZATION ($ BILLIONS)	TRADING VOLUME ($ BILLIONS)	TOTAL ISSUES LISTED	AUCTION MECHANISM	PRINCIPAL MARKET INDEXES
Argentina	Buenos Aires	4	36.9	11.4	156	N.A.	Buenos Aires Stock Exchange Index
Brazil	São Paulo	9	189.2	109.5	544	Continuous	BOVESPA Share Price Index—83 issues
Chile	Santiago	—	68.2	5.3	279	Mixed	IGPA Index—180 issues
China	Shanghai	1	43.5	97.5	291	Continuous	Shanghai Composite Index
Colombia	Bogotá	1	14.0	2.2	90	N.A.	Bogotá General Composite Index
Greece	Athens	—	14.9	5.1	216	Continuous	Athens Stock Exchange Industrial Price Index
India	Bombay	14	127.5	27.3	4,413	Continuous	Economic Times Index—72 issues
Indonesia	Jakarta	—	47.2	11.8	216	Mixed	Jakarta Stock Exchange Index
Israel	Tel Aviv	—	10.6	5.5	267	Call	General Share Index—all listed issues
Jordan	Amman	—	4.6	0.6	95	N.A.	Amman Financial Market Index
Mexico	Mexico City	—	130.2	83.0	206	Continuous	Bolsa de Valores Index—49 issues
Nigeria	Lagos	—	2.7	N.A.	177	Call	Nigerian Stock Exchange General Index
Pakistan	Karachi	—	12.2	3.2	724	Continuous	State Bank of Pakistan Index
Philippines	Makati	1	55.5	13.9	189	N.A.	Manila Commercial & Industrial Index—25 issues
Portugal	Lisbon	1	16.2	5.2	195	Call	Banco Totta e Acores Share Index—50 issues
South Korea	Seoul	—	191.8	286.0	699	Continuous	Korea Composite Stock Price Index
Taiwan	Taipei	—	247.3	711.0	313	Continuous	Taiwan Stock Exchange Index
Thailand	Bangkok	—	131.4	80.2	389	Continuous	Securities Exchange of Thailand Price Index
Turkey	Istanbul	—	21.6	21.7	176	Continuous	Istanbul Stock Exchange Index—50 issues
Venezuela	Caracas	1	4.1	0.9	90	Continuous	Indice de Capitalization de la BVC
Zimbabwe	N.A.	—	1.8	0.2	64	N.A.	Zimbabwe S.E. Industrial Index

Notes: Market capitalizations, trading volume, and total issues listed are as of 1994. Market capitalization, trading volume, and total issues listed for Brazil and São Paulo only. Trading volume for the Philippines is for both Manila and Makati. Total issues listed for India is Bombay only. Trading institutions information is from 1987 and 1988. Market capitalizations, trading volume, and total issues listed are from the *Emerging Stock Markets Factbook: 1995*, International Finance Corp., 1995. Trading institutions information is from Richard Roll, "The International Crash of 1987," *Financial Analysis Journal*, September/October 1988.

Source: Roger G. Ibbotson and Gary P. Brinson, *Global Investing* (New York: McGraw-Hill, 1993): 125–126. Reproduced with permission of The McGraw-Hill Companies.

Chapter 5 ⟩ Security Market Indicator Series

After you read this chapter, you should be able to answer the following questions:

➤ What are some major uses of security market indicator series (indexes)?
➤ What are the major characteristics that cause alternative indexes to differ?
➤ What are the major stock market indexes in the United States and globally, and what are their characteristics?
➤ What are the major bond market indexes for the United States and the world?
➤ What are some of the composite stock–bond market indexes?
➤ Where can you get historical and current data for all these indexes?

A fair statement regarding **security market indicator series**—especially those outside the United States—is that everybody talks about them but few people understand them. Even those investors familiar with widely publicized stock market series, such as the Dow Jones Industrial Average (DJIA), usually know little about indexes for the U.S. bond market or for non-U.S. stock markets such as Tokyo or London.

Although portfolios are obviously composed of many different individual stocks, investors typically ask, "What happened to the market today?" The reason for this question is that if an investor owns more than a few stocks or bonds, it is cumbersome to follow each stock or bond individually to determine the composite performance of the portfolio. Also, there is an intuitive notion that most individual stocks or bonds move with the aggregate market. Therefore, if the overall market rose, an individual's portfolio probably also increased in value. To supply investors with a composite report on market performance, some financial publications or investment firms have developed stock market and bond market indexes.[1]

The initial section discusses several ways that investors use market indicator series. An awareness of these significant functions should provide an incentive for becoming familiar with these series and indicates why we present a full chapter on this topic. The second section considers what characteristics cause alternative indexes to differ. In this chapter, we discuss numerous stock market and bond market indexes. You should understand their differences and why one of them is preferable for a given task because of its characteristics. The third section presents the most well-known U.S. and global stock market series separated into groups based on the weighting scheme used. The fourth section considers bond market indexes, which is a relatively new topic, because the creation and maintenance of total return bond indexes are new. Again, we consider international bond indexes following the domestic indexes. In the fifth section, we consider composite stock market–bond market series. With this background, you should be able to make an intelligent choice of the indicator series based upon how you want to use the index.

---

[1]Throughout this chapter and the book, we will use *indicator series* and *indexes* interchangeably, although *indicator series* is the more correct specification because it refers to a broad class of series; one popular type of series is an index, but there can be other types and many different indexes.

USES OF SECURITY MARKET INDEXES

Security market indexes have at least five specific uses. A primary application is to use the index values to compute total returns and risk for an aggregate market or some component of a market over a specified time period and use the rates of return and risk measures computed as a *benchmark* to judge the performance of individual portfolios. A basic assumption when evaluating portfolio performance is that any investor should be able to experience a risk-adjusted rate of return comparable to the market by randomly selecting a large number of stocks or bonds from the total market; hence, a superior portfolio manager should consistently do better than the market. Therefore, *an aggregate stock or bond market index can be used as a benchmark to judge the performance of professional money managers.*

Indicator series are also used to develop an index portfolio. As we will discuss later, it is difficult for most money managers to consistently outperform specified market indexes on a risk-adjusted basis over time. If this is true, an obvious alternative is to invest in a portfolio that will emulate this market portfolio. This notion led to the creation of *index funds,* whose purpose is to track the performance of the specified market series (index) over time.[2] The original index fund concept was related to common stocks. Subsequently, development of comprehensive, well-specified bond market indexes and similar inferior performance relative to the bond market by most bond portfolio managers have led to a similar phenomenon in the fixed-income area (bond index funds).[3]

Securities analysts, portfolio managers, and others use security market indexes to examine the factors that influence aggregate security price movements (that is, the indexes are used to measure aggregate market movements).

Another group interested in an aggregate market series is "technicians," who believe past price changes can be used to predict future price movements. For example, to project future stock price movements, technicians would plot and analyze price and volume changes for a stock market series like the Dow Jones Industrial Average.

Finally, work in portfolio and capital market theory has implied that the relevant risk for an individual risky asset is its *systematic risk,* which is the relationship between the rates of return for a risky asset and the rates of return for a market portfolio of risky assets.[4] Therefore, in this case, an aggregate market index is used as a proxy for the market portfolio of risky assets.

In summary, security market indexes are used:

➤ As benchmarks to evaluate the performance of professional money managers
➤ To create and monitor an index fund
➤ To measure market rates of return in economic studies
➤ For predicting future market movements by technicians
➤ As a proxy for the market portfolio of risky assets when calculating the systematic risk of an asset

---

[2]For a discussion of indexing, see "New Ways to Play the Indexing Game," *Institutional Investor* 22, no. 13 (November 1988): 92–98; and Sharmin Mossavar-Rahmani, "Indexing Fixed-Income Assets," in *The Handbook of Fixed Income Securities,* 6th ed., ed. Frank J. Fabozzi (New York: McGraw-Hill, 2001).

[3]See Fran Hawthorne, "The Battle of the Bond Indexes," *Institutional Investor* 20, no. 4 (April 1986), and Chris P. Dialynas. "The Active Decisions in the Selection of Passive Management and Performance Bogeys," in *The Handbook of Fixed Income Securities,* 6th ed., ed. Frank J. Fabozzi (New York: McGraw-Hill, 2001).

[4]This concept and its justification are discussed in Chapter 7 and Chapter 8. Subsequently, in Chapter 26, we consider the difficulty of finding an index that is an appropriate proxy for the market portfolio of risky assets.

DIFFERENTIATING FACTORS IN CONSTRUCTING MARKET INDEXES

Because the indicator series are intended to reflect the overall movements of a group of securities, it is necessary to consider which factors are important when constructing an index that is intended to represent a total population.

The Sample   The size of the sample, the breadth of the sample, and the source of the sample used to construct a series are all important.

A small percentage of the total population will provide valid indications of the behavior of the total population *if* the sample is properly selected. In fact, at some point the costs of taking a larger sample will almost certainly outweigh any benefits of increased size. The sample should be *representative* of the total population; otherwise, its size will be meaningless. A large biased sample is no better than a small biased sample. The sample can be generated by completely random selection or by a nonrandom selection technique that is designed to incorporate the characteristics of the desired population. Finally, the *source* of the sample is important if there are any differences between segments of the population, in which case samples from each segment are required.

Weighting Sample Members   Our second concern is with the weight given to each member in the sample. Three principal weighting schemes are used: (1) a price-weighted series, (2) a market-value-weighted series, and (3) an unweighted series, or what would be described as an equally weighted series.

Computational Procedure   Our final consideration is selecting the computational procedure. One alternative is to take a simple arithmetic average of the various members in the series. Another is to compute an index and have all changes, whether in price or value, reported in terms of the basic index. Finally, some prefer using a geometric average of the components rather than an arithmetic average.

STOCK MARKET INDICATOR SERIES

As mentioned previously, we hear a lot about what happens to the Dow Jones Industrial Average (DJIA) each day. In addition, you might also hear about other stock indexes, such as the S&P 500 index, the Nasdaq composite, or even the Nikkei Average. If you listen carefully, you will realize that these indexes change by differing amounts. Reasons for some differences are obvious, such as the DJIA versus the Nikkei Average, but others are not. In this section, we briefly review how the major series differ in terms of the characteristics discussed in the prior section, which will help you understand why the movements over time for alternative indexes *should* differ.

The discussion of the indexes is organized by the weighting of the sample of stocks. We begin with the price-weighted series because some of the most popular indexes are in this category. The next group is the market-value-weighted series, which is the technique currently used for most indexes. Finally, we will examine the unweighted series.

Price-Weighted Series   A **price-weighted series** is an arithmetic average of current prices, which means that index movements are influenced by the differential prices of the components.

Dow Jones Industrial Average   The best-known price-weighted series is also the oldest and certainly the most popular stock market indicator series, the Dow Jones Industrial Average (DJIA). The DJIA is a price-weighted average of 30 large, well-known industrial stocks that are generally the leaders in their industry (blue chips). The DJIA is computed by totaling the current

EXHIBIT 5.1		EXAMPLE OF CHANGE IN DJIA DIVISOR WHEN A SAMPLE STOCK SPLITS	

	BEFORE SPLIT	AFTER THREE-FOR-ONE SPLIT BY STOCK A	
	Prices	Prices	
A	30	10	
B	20	20	
C	10	10	
	$\overline{60 \div 3 = 20}$	$\overline{40 \div X = 20}$	X = 2 (New Divisor)

prices of the 30 stocks and dividing the sum by a divisor that has been adjusted to take account of stock splits and changes in the sample over time.[5] The divisor is adjusted so that the index value will be the same before and after the split. An adjustment of the divisor is demonstrated in Exhibit 5.1.

$$DJIA_t = \sum_{i=1}^{30} p_{it}/D_{adj}$$

where:

$DJIA_t$ = the value of the DJIA on day t
p_{it} = the closing price of stock i on day t
D_{adj} = the adjusted divisor on day t

In Exhibit 5.1, three stocks are employed to demonstrate the procedure used to derive a new divisor for the DJIA when a stock splits. When stocks split, the divisor becomes smaller as shown. The cumulative effect of splits can be derived from the fact that the divisor was originally 30.0; but, as of July 2002, it was 0.14445222.

The adjusted divisor ensures that the new value for the series is the same as it would have been without the split. In this example, the pre-split index value was 20. Therefore, after the split, given the new sum of prices, the divisor is adjusted downward to maintain this value of 20. The divisor is also changed when there is a change in the sample makeup of the series.

Because the series is price weighted, a high-priced stock carries more weight than a low-priced stock, so, as shown in Exhibit 5.2, a 10 percent change in a $100 stock ($10) will cause a larger change in the series than a 10 percent change in a $30 stock ($3). In Case A, when the $100 stock increases by 10 percent, the average rises by 5.5 percent; in Case B, when the $30 stock increases by 10 percent, the average rises by only 1.7 percent.

The DJIA has been criticized on several counts. First, the sample used for the series is limited to 30 nonrandomly selected blue-chip stocks that cannot be representative of the thousands of U.S. stocks. Further, the stocks included are large, mature, blue-chip firms rather

---

[5]A complete list of all events that have caused a change in the divisor since the DJIA went to 30 stocks on October 1, 1928, is contained in Phyllis S. Pierce, ed., *The Business One Irwin Investor's Handbook* (Burr Ridge, Ill.: Dow Jones Books, annual). In May 1996 the DJIA celebrated its 100th birthday, which was acknowledged with two special sections entitled "A Century of Investing" and "100 Years of the DJIA," *The Wall Street Journal,* 28 May 1996.

| EXHIBIT 5.2 | DEMONSTRATION OF THE IMPACT OF DIFFERENTLY PRICED SHARES ON A PRICE-WEIGHTED INDICATOR SERIES |

		PERIOD $T + 1$	
	PERIOD T	CASE A	CASE B
A	100	110	100
B	50	50	50
C	30	30	33
Sum	180	190	183
Divisor	3	3	3
Average	60	63.3	61
Percentage change		5.5	1.7

than the typical company. Several studies have shown that the DJIA has not been as volatile as other market indexes and its long-run returns are not comparable to other NYSE stock indexes.

In addition, because the DJIA is price weighted, when companies have a stock split, their prices decline, and therefore their weight in the DJIA is reduced—even though they may be large and important. Therefore, the weighting scheme causes a downward bias in the DJIA, because high-growth stocks will have higher prices; and, because such stocks tend to split, they will consistently lose weight within the index.[6] Dow Jones also publishes an average of 20 stocks in the transportation industry and 15 utility stocks. Detailed reports of the averages are contained daily in *The Wall Street Journal* and weekly in *Barron's,* including hourly figures.

Nikkei–Dow Jones Average   Also referred to as the Nikkei Stock Average Index, the Nikkei–Dow Jones Average is an arithmetic average of prices for 225 stocks on the First Section of the Tokyo Stock Exchange (TSE). This best-known series in Japan shows stock price trends since the reopening of the TSE. Notably, it was formulated by Dow Jones and Company, and, similar to the DJIA, it is a price-weighted series. It is also criticized because the 225 stocks that are included comprise only about 15 percent of all stocks on the First Section. It is reported daily in *The Wall Street Journal* and the *Financial Times* and weekly in *Barron's.*

Market-Value-Weighted Series   A market-value-weighted series is generated by deriving the initial total market value of all stocks used in the series (Market Value = Number of Shares Outstanding × Current Market Price). This initial figure is typically established as the base and assigned an index value (the most popular beginning index value is 100, but it can vary—say, 10, 50). Subsequently, a new

---

[6]For several articles that consider the origin and performance of the DJIA during its 100 years, see "100 Years of the DJIA," section in *The Wall Street Journal,* 28 May 1996, R29–R56. For a discussion of differing results, see Greg Ip, "What's Behind the Trailing Performance of the Dow Industrials vs. the S & P 500?" *The Wall Street Journal,* 20 August 1998, C1, C17.

EXHIBIT 5.3		*EXAMPLE OF A COMPUTATION OF A MARKET-VALUE-WEIGHTED INDEX*	

STOCK	SHARE PRICE	NUMBER OF SHARES	MARKET VALUE
December 31, 2002			
A	$10.00	1,000,000	$ 10,000,000
B	15.00	6,000,000	90,000,000
C	20.00	5,000,000	100,000,000
Total			$200,000,000
			Base Value Equal to an Index of 100
December 31, 2003			
A	$12.00	1,000,000	$ 12,000,000
B	10.00	12,000,000[a]	120,000,000
C	20.00	5,500,000[b]	110,000,000
Total			$242,000,000

$$\begin{aligned} \frac{\text{New}}{\text{Index Value}} &= \frac{\text{Current Market Value}}{\text{Base Value}} \times \frac{\text{Beginning}}{\text{Index Value}} \\ &= \frac{\$242,000,000}{\$200,000,000} \times 100 \\ &= 1.21 \times 100 \\ &= 121 \end{aligned}$$

[a]Stock split two-for-one during the year.
[b]Company paid a 10 percent stock dividend during the year.

market value is computed for all securities in the index, and the current market value is compared to the initial "base" value to determine the percentage of change, which in turn is applied to the beginning index value.

$$\text{Index}_t = \frac{\Sigma P_t Q_t}{\Sigma P_b Q_b} \times \text{Beginning Index Value}$$

where:

Index$_t$ = index value on day t
 P_t = ending prices for stocks on day t
 Q_t = number of outstanding shares on day t
 P_b = ending price for stocks on base day
 Q_b = number of outstanding shares on base day

A simple example for a three-stock index in Exhibit 5.3 indicates that there is an *automatic adjustment* for stock splits and other capital changes with a value-weighted index because the decrease in the stock price is offset by an increase in the number of shares outstanding.

In a market-value-weighted index, the importance of individual stocks in the sample depends on the market value of the stocks. Therefore, a specified percentage change in the value of a large company has a greater impact than a comparable percentage change for a small company. As shown in Exhibit 5.4, assuming the only change is a 20 percent increase in the value of Stock A,

EXHIBIT 5.4 ▶ *DEMONSTRATION OF THE IMPACT OF DIFFERENT VALUES ON A MARKET-VALUE-WEIGHTED STOCK INDEX*

| | | DECEMBER 31, 2002 | | DECEMBER 31, 2003 | | | |
| | | | | CASE A | | CASE B | |
STOCK	NUMBER OF SHARES	PRICE	VALUE	PRICE	VALUE	PRICE	VALUE
A	1,000,000	$10.00	$ 10,000,000	$12.00	$ 12,000,000	$10.00	$ 10,000,000
B	6,000,000	15.00	90,000,000	15.00	90,000,000	15.00	90,000,000
C	5,000,000	20.00	100,000,000	20.00	100,000,000	24.00	120,000,000
			$200,000,000		$202,000,000		$220,000,000
Index Value			100.00		101.00		110.00

which has a beginning value of $10 million, the ending index value would be $202 million, or an index of 101. In contrast, if only Stock C increases by 20 percent from $100 million, the ending value will be $220 million or an index value of 110. The point is, price changes for the large market value stocks in a market-value-weighted index will dominate changes in the index value over time. This value-weighting effect was prevalent during 1998 when the market was being driven by large-growth stocks—that is, almost all of the gain for the year was attributable to the largest 50 of the S&P 500 Index.

Exhibit 5.5 is a summary of the characteristics of the major price-weighted, market-value-weighted, and equal-weighted stock price indexes for the United States and the major foreign countries. As shown, the major differences are the number of stocks in the index, but more important, the *source* of the sample (stocks from the NYSE, the Nasdaq OTC, all U.S. stocks, or stocks from a foreign country, such as the United Kingdom or Japan).

Exhibit 5.6 shows the "Stock Market Data Bank" from *The Wall Street Journal* of July 13, 2001, which contains values for many of the U.S. stock indexes we have discussed. To gain an appreciation of the differences among indexes, you should examine the different 12-month percentage changes of alternative indexes in the third column from the left. Exhibit 5.7 shows a similar table for alternative indexes created and maintained by the *Financial Times*.

Unweighted Price Indicator Series

In an unweighted index, all stocks carry equal weight regardless of their price or market value. A $20 stock is as important as a $40 stock, and the total market value of the company is unimportant. Such an index can be used by individuals who randomly select stock for their portfolio and invest the same dollar amount in each stock. One way to visualize an unweighted series is to assume that equal dollar amounts are invested in each stock in the portfolio at the beginning of the period (for example, an equal $1,000 investment in each stock would work out to 50 shares of a $20 stock, 100 shares of a $10 stock, and 10 shares of a $100 stock). In fact, the actual movements in the index are typically based on *the arithmetic average of the percent changes in price or value for the stocks in the index.* The use of percentage price changes means that the price level or the market value of the stock does not make a difference—each percentage change has equal weight. This arithmetic average of percent changes procedure is used in academic studies when the authors specify equal weighting.

In contrast to computing an arithmetic average of percentage changes, both Value Line and the *Financial Times* Ordinary Share Index compute a *geometric* mean of the holding period

EXHIBIT 5.5 ▶   *SUMMARY OF STOCK MARKET INDEXES*

Name of Index	Weighting	Number of Stocks	Source of Stocks
Dow Jones Industrial Average	Price	30	NYSE, OTC
Nikkei–Dow Jones Average	Price	225	TSE
S&P Industrials	Market value	400	NYSE, OTC
S&P Transportation	Market value	20	NYSE, OTC
S&P Utilities	Market value	40	NYSE, OTC
S&P Financials	Market value	40	NYSE, OTC
S&P 500 Composite	Market value	500	NYSE, OTC
NYSE			
Industrial	Market value	1,601	NYSE
Utility	Market value	253	NYSE
Transportation	Market value	55	NYSE
Financial	Market value	909	NYSE
Composite	Market value	2,818	NYSE
Nasdaq			
Composite	Market value	5,575	OTC
Industrial	Market value	3,394	OTC
Banks	Market value	375	OTC
Insurance	Market value	103	OTC
Other finance	Market value	610	OTC
Transportation	Market value	104	OTC
Telecommunications	Market value	183	OTC
Computer	Market value	685	OTC
Biotech	Market value	121	OTC
AMEX Market Value	Market value	900	AMEX
Dow Jones Equity Market Index	Market value	2,300	NYSE, AMEX, OTC
Wilshire 5000 Equity Value	Market value	5,000	NYSE, AMEX, OTC
Russell Indexes			
3,000	Market value	3,000	NYSE, AMEX, OTC
1,000	Market value	1,000 largest	NYSE, AMEX, OTC
2,000	Market value	2,000 smallest	NYSE, AMEX, OTC
Financial Times Actuaries Index			
All share	Market value	700	LSE
FT100	Market value	100 largest	LSE
Small cap	Market value	250	LSE
Mid cap	Market value	250	LSE
Combined	Market value	350	LSE
Tokyo Stock Exchange			
Price Index (TOPIX)	Market value	1,800	TSE
Value Line Averages			
Industrials	Equal (geometric average)	1,499	NYSE, AMEX, OTC
Utilities	Equal	177	NYSE, AMEX, OTC
Rails	Equal	19	NYSE, AMEX, OTC
Composite	Equal	1,695	NYSE, AMEX, OTC
Financial Times Ordinary Share Index	Equal (geometric average)	30	LSE
FT-Actuaries World Indexes	Market value	2,275	24 countries, 3 regions (returns in $, £, ¥, DM, and local currency)
Morgan Stanley Capital International (MSCI) Indexes	Market value	1,375	19 countries, 3 international, 38 international industries (returns in $ and local currency)
Dow Jones World Stock Index	Market value	2,200	13 countries, 3 regions, 120 industry groups (returns in $, £, ¥, DM, and local currency)
Euromoney—First Boston Global Stock Index	Market value	—	17 countries (returns in $ and local currency)
Salomon-Russell World Equity Index	Market value	Russell 1000 and S-R PMI of 600 non-U.S. stocks	22 countries (returns in $ and local currency)

| EXHIBIT 5.6 | *STOCK MARKET DATA BANK* |

STOCK MARKET DATA BANK 7/12/01

MAJOR INDEXES

†12-MO HIGH	LOW		DAILY HIGH	LOW	CLOSE	NET CHG	% CHG	†12-MO CHG	% CHG	FROM 12/31	% CHG
DOW JONES AVERAGES											
11337.92	9389.48	30 Industrials	10496.64	10269.31	10478.99	+ 237.97	+ 2.32	− 309.72	− 2.87	− 307.86	− 2.85
3145.65	2368.65	20 Transportation	2902.72	2822.95	x2902.34	+ 82.55	+ 2.93	+ 13.74	+ 0.48	− 44.26	− 1.50
416.11	325.01	15 Utilities	367.24	361.11	362.60	− 3.61	− 0.99	+ 35.11	+ 10.72	− 49.56	− 12.02
3392.23	2882.28	65 Composite	3163.73	3112.91	x3161.91	+ 53.80	+ 1.73	+ 20.70	+ 0.66	− 155.50	− 4.69
358.00	252.46	DJ US Total Mkt	280.04	273.05	279.61	+ 6.56	+ 2.40	− 71.21	− 20.30	− 27.27	− 8.89
STANDARD & POOR'S INDEXES											
1520.77	1103.25	500 Index	1210.25	1180.18	1208.14	+ 27.96	+ 2.37	− 287.70	− 19.23	− 112.14	− 8.49
1874.50	1260.17	Industrials	1392.43	1354.97	1390.03	+ 35.06	+ 2.59	− 463.04	− 24.99	− 137.83	− 9.02
353.03	272.98	Utilities	309.67	305.10	306.56	− 2.48	− 0.80	+ 32.56	+ 11.88	− 44.05	− 12.56
548.60	433.70	400 MidCap	507.38	496.00	506.96	+ 10.96	+ 2.21	− 8.02	− 1.56	− 9.80	− 1.90
236.76	192.86	600 SmallCap	225.77	219.74	225.77	+ 6.00	+ 2.73	+ 5.98	+ 2.72	+ 6.18	+ 2.81
324.40	237.80	1500 Index	262.51	256.03	262.10	+ 6.07	+ 2.37	− 55.96	− 17.59	− 22.00	− 7.74
NASDAQ STOCK MARKET											
4274.67	1638.80	Composite	2080.13	2031.84	2075.74	+ 103.70	+ 5.26	−2099.12	− 50.28	− 394.78	− 15.98
4099.30	1370.75	Nasdaq 100	1757.29	1700.41	1750.13	+ 108.57	+ 6.61	−2206.54	− 55.77	− 591.57	− 25.26
2319.28	1114.27	Industrials	1460.00	1421.55	1457.93	+ 59.75	+ 4.27	− 805.40	− 35.58	− 25.06	− 1.69
2314.75	1740.33	Insurance	2285.15	2247.16	2281.61	+ 29.45	+ 1.31	+ 487.55	+ 27.18	+ 88.24	+ 4.02
2105.97	1549.11	Banks	2102.74	2065.17	2102.74	+ 37.79	+ 1.83	+ 527.47	+ 33.48	+ 163.29	+ 8.42
2538.43	779.72	Computer	1058.00	1029.19	1054.36	+ 74.22	+ 7.57	−1394.85	− 56.95	− 240.61	− 18.58
935.90	275.94	Telecommunications	291.18	283.82	290.48	+ 14.54	+ 5.27	− 625.80	− 68.30	− 172.96	− 37.32
NEW YORK STOCK EXCHANGE											
677.58	566.35	Composite	613.44	603.21	612.76	+ 9.54	+ 1.58	− 46.95	− 7.12	− 44.11	− 6.72
851.94	696.58	Industrials	754.88	741.97	753.95	+ 11.98	+ 1.61	− 79.41	− 9.53	− 49.34	− 6.14
504.91	365.58	Utilities	378.23	375.34	377.94	+ 2.10	+ 0.56	− 119.35	− 24.00	− 62.60	− 14.21
494.71	379.37	Transportation	475.71	468.24	475.18	+ 5.59	+ 1.19	+ 59.94	+ 14.44	+ 12.42	+ 2.68
657.52	542.16	Finance	614.23	601.77	613.73	+ 11.96	+ 1.99	+ 56.71	+ 10.18	− 33.22	− 5.13
OTHERS											
974.18	832.24	Amex Composite	894.17	888.23	891.70	− 1.13	− 0.13	− 47.73	− 5.08	− 6.05	− 0.67
813.71	577.85	Russell 1000	637.43	621.65	636.43	+ 14.78	+ 2.38	− 157.80	− 19.87	− 63.66	− 9.09
545.18	425.74	Russell 2000	489.12	475.83	489.04	+ 13.21	+ 2.78	− 53.72	− 9.90	+ 5.51	+ 1.14
841.47	601.74	Russell 3000	665.85	649.31	664.92	+ 15.61	+ 2.40	− 157.87	− 19.19	− 60.83	− 8.38
439.78	346.50	Value-Line	389.23	379.72	389.15	+ 9.43	+ 2.48	− 38.12	− 8.92	− 4.32	− 1.10
14329.94	10068.63	Wilshire 5000	....	....	11208.21	+ 263.66	+ 2.41	−2877.63	− 20.43	− 967.67	− 7.95

†-Based on comparable trading day in preceding year.

Source: *The Wall Street Journal,* 13 July 2001, C2. Reprinted with permission from *The Wall Street Journal,* Dow Jones Co., Inc.

returns *and* derive the holding period yield from this calculation. Exhibit 5.8 contains an example of an arithmetic average and a geometric average. This demonstrates the downward bias of the geometric calculation. Specifically, the geometric mean of holding period yields (HPY) shows an average change of only 5.3 percent versus the actual change in wealth of 6 percent.

Style Indexes   Financial service firms such as Dow Jones, Moody's, Standard & Poor's, Russell, and Wilshire Associates are generally very fast in responding to changes in investment practices. One example is the growth in popularity of small-cap stocks following the academic research in the early 1980s that suggested that, over long-term periods, small-cap stocks outperformed large-cap stocks on a risk-adjusted basis. In response to this, Ibbotson Associates created the first small-cap stock index and this was followed by small-cap indexes by Frank Russell Associates (the Russell 2000 Index), the Standard & Poor's 600, the Wilshire 1750, and the Dow Jones

EXHIBIT 5.7 ▶ *FINANCIAL TIMES ACTUARIES SHARE INDICES*

FTSE Actuaries Share Indices   **UK Series**
Produced in conjunction with the Faculty and Institute of Actuaries

	£ Stlg Jul 6	Day's chge%	Euro Index	£ Stlg Jul 5	Year ago	Actual yld%	Cover	P/E ratio	Xd adj. ytd	Total Return	2001 High		2001 Low		Since Compilation High		Low	
FTSE 100	5479.2	-1.3	7121.4	5549.6	6497.5	2.44	2.02	20.29	78.10	2572.05	6334.5	30/1	5314.8	22/3	6930.2	30/12/99	986.9	23/7/84
FTSE 250	6138.2	-1.0	7977.9	6201.7	6626.6	2.85	1.78	19.73	98.73	2851.66	6788.3	8/2	5929.7	22/3	7149.6	4/9/00	1379.4	21/1/86
FTSE 250 ex Inv Co	6254.6	-1.0	8129.1	6314.9	6652.9	3.00	1.84	18.15	105.43	2927.73	6873.6	8/2	6037.6	22/3	7166.2	4/9/00	1378.3	21/1/86
FTSE 350	2702.4	-1.2	3512.4	2736.3	3164.1	2.49	1.98	20.21	39.17	2595.66	3103.7	30/1	2620.1	22/3	3327.0	30/12/99	664.5	14/1/86
FTSE 350 ex Inv Co	2697.5	-1.2	3506.0	2730.8	3154.5	2.51	1.99	19.96	39.36	1329.60	3093.8	30/1	2614.7	22/3	3324.4	30/12/99	2211.6	3/6/97
FTSE 350 Higher Yield	3144.1	-1.2	4086.3	3183.4	2904.9	3.40	1.88	15.61	61.37	2655.00	3344.2	8/6	2900.3	22/3	3344.2	8/6/01	674.2	14/1/86
FTSE 350 Lower Yield	2219.6	-1.2	2884.8	2247.3	3451.4	1.34	2.31	32.23	14.79	1686.80	2944.0	30/1	2219.6	6/7	3843.1	6/3/00	669.6	20/1/86
FTSE SmallCap	2819.88	-1.5	3665.00	2862.55	3373.64	2.54	1.37	28.61	42.16	2666.86	3326.82	31/1	2794.94	4/4	3629.06	4/9/00	1363.79	31/12/92
FTSE SmallCap ex Inv Co	2784.30	-1.5	3618.75	2826.24	3334.66	2.57	1.51	25.70	41.72	2671.66	3292.45	8/2	2776.23	4/4	3575.63	4/9/00	1363.79	31/12/92
FTSE All-Share	2649.60	-1.2	3443.68	2683.00	3104.49	2.50	1.96	20.42	38.43	2583.93	3045.55	30/1	2573.07	22/3	3265.95	4/9/00	61.92	13/12/74
FTSE All-Share ex Inv Co	2644.33	-1.2	3436.83	2677.14	3094.33	2.51	1.98	20.08	38.59	1327.53	3035.02	30/1	2567.48	22/3	3248.90	4/9/00	2172.42	4/6/97
FTSE All-Share ex Multinational	922.97	-1.5	994.24	937.39	1049.48	2.65	1.75	21.58	15.02	964.83	1070.50	30/1	886.60	22/3	1160.20	6/3/00	886.60	22/3/01
FTSE Fledgling	2171.68	-1.0	2822.53	2193.50	2201.62	3.23	0.3880.00†		35.64	2624.30	2383.79	13/2	2061.23	4/4	2463.91	10/3/00	31.14	12/12/94
FTSE Fledgling ex Inv Co	2312.47	-0.9	3005.51	2332.41	2240.82	3.08	0.2280.00†		37.28	2816.16	2512.25	13/2	2173.09	4/4	2554.54	10/3/00	26.13	12/12/94
FTSE All-Small	1728.86	-1.4	2247.00	1753.09	1998.60	2.69	1.11	33.34	26.40	2088.11	2007.14	31/1	1697.63	4/4	2158.65	4/9/00	991.35	23/11/98
FTSE All-Small ex Inv Co	1753.88	-1.4	2279.52	1778.06	2020.47	2.67	1.22	30.71	26.66	2140.68	2039.40	8/2	1728.71	4/4	2177.07	4/9/00	986.74	23/11/98
FTSE AIM	1096.0	-1.0	1424.4	1107.0	1687.0	0.64	‡	‡	3.42	1020.34	1451.9	25/1	1096.0	6/7	2924.9	3/3/00	761.3	14/10/98

Source: *Financial Times*, 7/8 July 2001, 34.

EXHIBIT 5.8 ▶ *EXAMPLE OF AN ARITHMETIC AND GEOMETRIC MEAN OF PERCENTAGE CHANGES*

	SHARE PRICE			
STOCK	T	T + 1	HPR	HPY
X	10	12	1.20	0.20
Y	22	20	.91	−0.09
Z	44	47	1.07	0.07

$\Pi = 1.20 \times 0.91 \times 1.07$

$= 1.168$

$1.168^{1/3} = 1.0531$

$\Sigma = 0.18$

$0.18/3 = 0.06$

$= 6\%$

Index Value $(T) \times 1.0531 =$ Index Value $(T + 1)$

Index Value $(T) \times 1.06 =$ Index Value $(T + 1)$

Small-Cap Index.[7] Eventually there were sets of size indexes, including large-cap, mid-cap, small-cap, and micro-cap, and these new size indexes were used to evaluate the performance of money managers who concentrated in those size sectors.

The next innovation was for money managers to concentrate in *types* of stocks, that is, *growth* stocks or *value* stocks. The financial services firms again responded by creating indexes of growth stocks and value stocks based upon relative price/earnings ratios, price/book value ratios, price/cash flow ratios, and other metrics such as return on equity (ROE) and revenue growth rates.

Finally, they have combined these two styles (size and type) to identify six categories:

Small-cap growth	Small-cap value
Mid-cap growth	Mid-cap value
Large-cap growth	Large-cap value

---

[7]For an analysis and comparison of these small-cap stock indexes, see Frank K. Reilly and David J. Wright, "Alternative Small-Cap Stock Benchmarks," *The Journal of Portfolio Management* 28, no. 3 (Spring 2002): 82–95.

EXHIBIT 5.9 ▷ *FINANCIAL TIMES ACTUARIES WORLD INDEXES*

FTSE All-World Index Series

Jul 05	US Dollar index	Day %	Mth %	YTD %	Gross Div Yield
FTSE All-World Index (2271)	164.06	-1.4	-5.8	-11.9	1.6
FTSE World Index (1903)	294.53	-1.4	-5.8	-12.0	1.6
FTSE World Europe (592)	301.00	-1.6	-7.3	-19.5	2.2
All-World Developed (1707)	164.51	-1.4	-5.8	-12.2	1.5
All-World All Emerging (564)	153.32	-0.6	-3.7	-0.2	2.7
All-World Adv Emerging (196)	156.68	-0.9	-3.5	1.7	2.6
All-World Emerging (368)	144.83	0.1	-4.2	-5.4	2.8
All-World ex US (1762)	155.92	-1.5	-6.7	-15.9	1.9
All-World ex UK (2130)	163.75	-1.4	-5.7	-11.5	1.5
All-World ex Japan (1935)	166.66	-1.4	-5.7	-12.1	1.6
All-World Dev ex US (1198)	157.69	-1.5	-6.9	-16.6	1.9
All-World ex Eurobloc (1945)	165.88	-1.3	-5.5	-10.3	1.5
All-World Nordic (109)	107.73	-3.2	-15.2	-34.7	1.8
All-World Euro-Pacific (1456)	154.53	-1.5	-6.9	-16.3	1.9
Americas (717)	171.21	-1.3	-5.2	-8.6	1.3
Argentina (12)	261.08	-3.6	-14.4	-9.4	4.0
Brazil (39)	146.87	-1.0	-9.9	-22.0	3.7
Chile (25)	310.04	0.0	-6.7	-0.7	4.4
Colombia (9)	342.32	0.2	1.9	24.5	4.8
Mexico (18)	2144.81	-0.7	3.3	25.4	2.0
Peru (6)	352.61	0.9	1.4	21.9	1.4
Venezuela (6)	332.01	0.0	-3.9	7.7	2.9
North America (602)	170.97	-1.3	-5.2	-8.8	1.3
Canada (93)	246.58	-0.7	-5.3	-16.0	1.8
USA (509)	501.09	-1.3	-5.2	-8.4	1.3

	US Dollar index	Day %	Mth %	YTD %	Gross Div Yield
Europe (663)	158.04	-1.6	-7.3	-19.4	2.2
United Kingdom (141)	311.79	-1.4	-6.9	-15.9	2.5
Europe ex UK (522)	152.23	-1.8	-7.5	-21.2	2.0
Czech Republic (6)	63.60	-1.2	-5.9	-24.7	5.5
Denmark (27)	489.85	-1.0	-2.3	-9.8	1.4
Hungary (8)	63.82	-1.2	-3.2	-19.1	1.5
Norway (34)	254.95	-1.2	-5.0	-9.5	1.9
Poland (23)	71.95	-1.4	-14.1	-25.5	2.0
Russia (9)	89.55	1.1	-4.8	34.6	2.3
Sweden (39)	475.68	-3.1	-9.3	-31.4	2.1
Switzerland (25)	321.67	-2.0	-8.0	-22.5	1.7
Turkey (25)	37.33	0.8	-10.0	-34.5	1.9
Eurobloc (326)	153.86	-1.7	-7.5	-20.7	2.0
Austria (20)	146.81	-0.7	-3.3	1.2	2.4
Belgium / Luxembourg (23)	257.55	0.0	0.9	-14.1	2.8
Finland (9)	644.41	-4.9	-28.4	-49.3	1.6
France (51)	319.34	-2.2	-8.3	-20.8	2.1
Germany (40)	239.88	-1.4	-5.3	-16.2	1.9
Greece (74)	187.46	-1.0	-11.6	-33.0	3.0
Ireland (13)	444.25	-1.6	-2.1	0.3	1.5
Italy (42)	134.70	-1.0	-4.6	-22.5	2.2
Netherlands (19)	431.03	-0.8	-4.1	-17.4	2.1
Portugal (13)	143.39	-1.3	-7.3	-25.6	2.6
Spain (22)	282.04	-2.1	-9.9	-14.3	1.9

	US Dollar index	Day %	Mth %	YTD %	Gross Div Yield
Asia Pacific (793)	150.25	-1.3	-6.0	-9.6	1.3
Japan (336)	108.00	-1.2	-7.2	-10.9	0.8
Asia Pacific ex Japan (457)	166.69	-1.3	-2.5	-5.9	2.6
Australia (67)	209.87	-2.2	0.6	0.9	3.1
China (45)	598.35	-2.5	-9.9	56.5	3.9
Hong Kong - China (50)	366.31	-1.5	-4.6	-11.4	2.5
India (40)	251.78	0.2	-6.5	-18.4	1.7
Indonesia (25)	31.44	0.9	7.2	-11.4	4.3
Korea South (27)	229.15	-1.0	-3.1	12.4	2.7
Malaysia (31)	235.36	3.6	10.6	-11.6	1.9
New Zealand (19)	43.75	-0.8	-2.9	0.8	4.1
Pakistan (16)	224.81	-1.8	-10.9	-23.6	7.9
Philippines (22)	44.74	1.4	-3.7	-6.9	1.0
Singapore (41)	201.08	-0.5	-0.6	-20.0	1.9
Taiwan (40)	167.83	-0.5	-6.2	-3.6	1.7
Thailand (34)	17.10	-0.8	2.1	14.2	2.2
Middle East & Africa (98)	207.91	-1.4	-3.6	-0.8	3.3
Egypt (18)	63.97	-0.3	1.0	-9.7	6.1
Israel (21)	86.75	-0.3	0.9	-18.5	2.6
Morocco (8)	72.80	-1.3	-8.9	-17.4	3.8
South Africa (51)	294.33	-1.7	-4.6	3.0	3.3
Europe ex Eurobloc (337)	160.61	-1.6	-7.1	-18.0	2.3
Europe ex Ebloc ex UK (196)	146.95	-2.0	-7.7	-22.6	1.8

Source: *Financial Times,* 6 July 2001, 36.

Currently, the majority of money managers identify their investment style as one of these six categories and consultants generally identify money managers using these categories.

The most recent addition to style indexes are those created to track ethical funds referred to as "socially responsible investment" (SRI) funds. These SRI indexes are further broken down by country and include a global ethical stock index.

The best source of style stock indexes (both size and type of stock) is *Barron's.*

Global Equity Indexes

As noted in this chapter's appendix, there are stock market indexes available for most individual foreign markets similar to those we described for Japan (the Nikkei and TOPIX) and the United Kingdom (the several *Financial Times* indexes) described in Exhibit 5.5. While these local indexes are closely followed within each country, a problem arises in comparing the results implied by these indexes across countries because of a lack of consistency among them in sample selection, weighting, or computational procedure. To solve these comparability problems, several groups have computed a set of consistent country stock indexes. As a result, these indexes can be directly compared and can be combined to create various regional indexes (for example, Pacific Basin). We will describe the three sets of global equity indexes.

FT/S&P-Actuaries World Indexes The FT/S&P-Actuaries World Indexes are jointly compiled by the Financial Times Limited, Goldman Sachs and Company, and Standard and Poor's (the "compilers") in conjunction with the Institute of Actuaries and the Faculty of Actuaries. Approximately 2,271 equity securities in 30 countries are measured, covering at least 70 percent of the total value of all listed companies in each country. All securities included must allow direct holdings of shares by foreign nationals.

The indexes are market-value weighted and have a base date of December 31, 1986 = 100. The index results are reported in U.S. dollars, U.K. pound sterling, Japanese yen, German marks, and the local currency of the country. In addition to the individual countries and the world index, there are several geographic subgroups, as shown in Exhibit 5.9.

| EXHIBIT 5.10 | MARKET COVERAGE OF MORGAN STANLEY CAPITAL INTERNATIONAL INDEXES AS OF JUNE 29, 2001 |

| | GDP WEIGHTS[a] | | | | WEIGHT AS PERCENT OF INDEX | |
	PERCENT EAFE	PERCENT WORLD	COMPANIES IN INDEX	MARKET CAP. U.S. $ BILLION	FREE EAFE[b]	WORLD
Austria	1.4	0.8	16	19.6	0.2	0.1
Belgium	1.7	0.9	16	144.6	0.9	0.4
Denmark	1.2	0.7	19	99.5	1.0	0.4
Finland	0.9	0.5	27	166.9	1.8	0.8
France	9.5	5.3	52	1,210.7	11.1	4.9
Germany	13.8	7.8	47	1,103.3	8.7	3.9
Greece	0.8	0.5	24	80.1	0.3	0.1
Ireland	0.7	0.4	14	75.9	0.7	0.3
Italy	7.9	4.4	40	576.4	4.4	2.0
The Netherlands	2.7	1.5	23	603.8	5.6	2.5
Norway	1.2	0.7	20	58.0	0.5	0.2
Portugal	0.8	0.4	10	51.6	0.5	0.2
Spain	4.1	2.3	31	339.8	3.0	1.3
Sweden	1.7	0.9	34	278.6	2.2	1.0
Switzerland	1.8	1.0	35	615.2	6.7	3.0
United Kingdom	10.5	5.9	112	2,327.2	21.7	9.7
Europe	60.7	34.0	520	7,751.1	69.4	31.0
Australia	2.9	1.6	55	375.7	3.2	1.4
Hong Kong	1.2	0.7	28	276.1	2.1	0.9
Japan	34.1	19.1	277	3,239.3	24.3	10.9
New Zealand	0.4	0.2	10	17.7	0.1	0.1
Singapore	0.7	0.4	29	125.6	0.9	0.4
Pacific	39.3	22.0	399	4,034.4	30.6	13.7
Pacific ex Japan	5.2	2.9	122	795.1	6.3	2.8
EAFE	100.0	56.0	919	17,785.5	100.0	44.7
Canada	—	2.8	67	658.4	—	2.2
United States	—	41.1	324	15,563.7	—	53.1
The World Index	—	100.0	1,310	28,007.6	—	100.0
EMU	44.4	24.9	300	4,372.6	—	16.7
Europe ex UK	50.3	28.2	408	5,423.9	—	21.3
Far East	36.0	20.2	334	3,641.0	27.3	12.2
North America	—	44.0	391	16,222.1	—	55.3
Kokusai Index (World ex Japan)	—	80.9	1,033	24,768.3	—	89.1

[a]GDP weight figures represent the initial weights applicable for the first month. They are used exclusively in the MSCI "GDP weighted" indexes.
[b]Free indicates that only stocks that can be acquired by foreign investors are included in the index. If the number of companies is the same and the value is different, it indicates that the stocks available to foreigners are priced differently from domestic shares.

Source: Morgan Stanley Capital International (New York: Morgan Stanley & Co., 2001).

Morgan Stanley Capital International (MSCI) Indexes   The Morgan Stanley Capital International Indexes consist of 3 international, 19 national, and 38 international industry indexes. The indexes consider some 1,375 companies listed on stock exchanges in 19 countries with a combined market capitalization that represents approximately 60 percent of the aggregate market value of the stock exchanges of these countries. All the indexes are market-value weighted. Exhibit 5.10 contains the countries included, the number of stocks, and market values for stocks in the various countries and groups.

In addition to reporting the indexes in U.S. dollars and the country's local currency, the following valuation information is available: (1) price-to-book value (P/BV) ratio, (2) price-to-cash earnings (earnings plus depreciation) (P/CE) ratio, (3) price-to-earnings (P/E) ratio, and (4) dividend yield (YLD). These ratios help in analyzing different valuation levels among countries and over time for specific countries.

Notably, the Morgan Stanley group index for Europe, Australia, and the Far East (EAFE) is being used as the basis for futures and options contracts on the Chicago Mercantile Exchange and the Chicago Board Options Exchange. Several of the MSCI country indexes, the EAFE index, and a world index are reported daily in *The Wall Street Journal,* as shown in Exhibit 5.11.

Dow Jones World Stock Index   In January 1993, Dow Jones introduced its World Stock Index with results beginning December 31, 1991. Composed of more than 2,200 companies worldwide and organized into 120 industry groups, the index includes 33 countries representing more than 80 percent of the combined capitalization of these countries. In addition to the 34 countries shown in Exhibit 5.12, the countries are grouped into three major regions: Asia/Pacific, Europe/Africa, and the Americas. Finally, each country's index is calculated in its own currency as well as in the U.S. dollar. The index is reported daily in *The Wall Street Journal* (domestic), in *The Wall Street Journal Europe,* and in *The Asian Wall Street Journal.* It is published weekly in *Barron's.*

Comparison of World Stock Indexes   A correlation analysis between the three world stock series for the period December 31, 1991 (when the DJ series became available) to December 31, 2000, indicates an average correlation coefficient among them in excess of 0.99. Clearly, the results with the alternative world stock indexes are quite comparable.

EXHIBIT 5.11   *LISTING OF MORGAN STANLEY CAPITAL INTERNATIONAL STOCK INDEX VALUES FOR JULY 10 AND JULY 11, 2001.*

MSCI INDEXES			
	July 11	**July 10**	**%FROM 12-00**
U.S.	1123.4	1124.5	− 10.1
Britain	1609.8	1632.8	− 12.6
Canada	952.8	950.7	− 17.6
Japan	766.3	780.8	− 5.2
France	1590.3	1610.0	− 16.4
Germany	725.4	727.7	− 11.3
Hong Kong	6327.9	6340.5	− 17.7
Switzerland	845.4	855.6	− 16.9
Australia	688.8	683.7	+ 7.6
World Index	**1045.7**	**1049.8**	**− 14.4**
EAFE MSCI-p	**1212.9**	**1221.9**	**− 18.7**

As calculated by Morgan Stanley Capital International Perspective, Geneva. Each index, calculated in local currencies, is based on the close of 1969 equaling 100.

Source: *The Wall Street Journal,* 13 July 2001, C16. Reprinted with permission from *The Wall Street Journal,* Dow Jones Co., Inc.

EXHIBIT 5.12   *DOW JONES GLOBAL STOCK INDEX LISTING*

DOW JONES GLOBAL INDEXES

5:30 P.M., Thursday, July 12, 2001

IN U.S. DOLLARS

REGION/COUNTRY	DJ GLOBAL INDEXES, LOCAL CURRENCY	% CHG.	5:30 P.M. INDEX	CHG.	% CHG.	12-MO HIGH	12-MO LOW	12-MO CHG.	% CHG.	FROM 12/31	% CHG.
Americas			271.40	+ 6.04	+ 2.28	350.42	245.99	− 71.38	− 20.82	− 27.72	− 9.27
Brazil†	1517.13	+ 1.08	234.48	− 2.22	− 0.94	378.86	234.48	− 125.60	− 34.88	− 97.15	− 29.30
Canada	247.24	+ 1.37	186.82	+ 2.15	+ 1.16	290.99	176.62	− 85.17	− 31.31	− 38.62	− 17.13
Chile	246.81	− 1.05	139.07	− 1.69	− 1.20	159.27	136.13	− 18.39	− 11.68	− 4.32	− 3.02
Mexico	481.52	− 1.47	157.88	− 4.37	− 2.69	181.35	124.12	− 21.43	− 11.95	+ 25.65	+ 19.40
U.S.	279.61	+ 2.40	279.61	+ 6.56	+ 2.40	358.00	252.46	− 71.21	− 20.30	− 27.27	− 8.89
Venezuela	479.24	− 1.05	40.97	+ 0.35	+ 0.86	49.29	36.30	− 1.15	− 2.74	+ 1.90	+ 4.86
Latin America			155.32	− 2.60	− 1.65	209.03	155.32	− 50.51	− 24.54	− 17.91	− 10.34
Europe			191.76	+ 1.49	+ 0.78	263.18	190.27	− 69.16	− 26.51	− 49.30	− 20.45
Austria	134.13	+ 0.71	89.15	− 0.03	− 0.03	96.78	75.77	+ 4.93	+ 5.86	+ 3.04	+ 3.53
Belgium	254.99	+ 0.96	169.57	+ 0.35	+ 0.21	201.51	156.78	− 26.73	− 13.62	− 27.09	− 13.78
Denmark	300.48	− 0.83	203.86	− 3.24	− 1.56	259.65	189.61	− 37.05	− 15.38	− 40.04	− 16.42
Finland	1244.23	+ 4.27	739.66	+ 25.00	+ 3.50	1987.51	714.66	− 1187.57	− 61.62	− 796.35	− 51.85
France	292.57	+ 0.81	197.10	+ 0.11	+ 0.06	283.64	196.99	− 82.46	− 29.50	− 55.47	− 21.96
Germany	268.23	+ 1.53	177.72	+ 1.37	+ 0.78	254.08	171.84	− 68.86	− 27.93	− 41.10	− 18.78
Greece	229.04	+ 3.08	112.37	+ 2.54	+ 2.31	219.00	109.83	− 98.48	− 46.71	− 56.91	− 33.62
Ireland	496.30	+ 1.21	322.26	+ 1.45	+ 0.45	326.56	253.57	+ 53.22	+ 19.78	+ 10.31	+ 3.31
Italy	269.51	− 0.14	147.18	− 1.30	− 0.88	209.49	147.18	− 62.31	− 29.74	− 44.81	− 23.34
Netherlands	413.94	+ 0.64	274.42	− 0.29	− 0.11	357.41	266.83	− 82.78	− 23.17	− 60.92	− 18.17
Norway	214.16	+ 0.46	137.19	− 0.05	− 0.04	187.14	132.23	− 37.51	− 21.47	− 30.26	− 18.07
Portugal	231.67	+ 0.13	133.69	− 0.82	− 0.61	215.73	133.69	− 75.56	− 36.11	− 50.59	− 27.45
Spain	314.80	− 1.14	157.27	− 3.00	− 1.87	230.37	157.27	− 68.52	− 30.35	− 36.02	− 18.64
Sweden	408.66	+ 2.55	222.56	+ 5.42	+ 2.50	505.16	217.14	− 267.95	− 54.63	− 116.33	− 34.33
Switzerland	389.43	+ 1.65	298.25	+ 3.99	+ 1.36	415.56	292.13	− 92.22	− 23.62	− 117.24	− 28.22
United Kingdom	223.41	+ 1.54	168.24	+ 2.44	+ 1.47	212.11	164.14	− 39.59	− 19.05	− 31.58	− 15.81
Euro Zone			191.52	+ 0.15	+ 0.08	277.92	191.37	− 83.07	− 30.25	− 55.10	− 22.34
Europe (ex. U.K.)			202.50	+ 0.77	+ 0.38	293.98	201.73	− 88.16	− 30.33	− 60.57	− 23.02
South Africa	285.27	+ 0.26	94.58	+ 0.08	+ 0.08	106.90	82.19	− 3.34	− 3.41	+ 0.69	+ 0.74
Asia/Pacific			85.02	+ 1.54	+ 1.84	118.49	83.09	− 32.94	− 27.93	− 8.03	− 8.63
Australia	228.08	+ 0.48	151.66	+ 0.75	+ 0.50	168.64	133.82	− 13.47	− 8.16	− 4.51	− 2.89
Hong Kong	220.80	+ 0.97	220.16	+ 2.12	+ 0.97	311.28	203.21	− 82.55	− 27.27	− 25.41	− 10.35
Indonesia	161.26	+ 1.09	28.28	+ 0.26	+ 0.93	43.99	21.12	− 10.55	− 27.17	− 2.97	− 9.50
Japan	79.01	+ 1.76	79.65	+ 1.74	+ 2.23	111.90	75.67	− 31.54	− 28.37	− 8.64	− 9.79
Malaysia	111.28	− 0.99	79.68	− 0.80	− 0.99	116.42	71.97	− 36.74	− 31.56	− 8.82	− 9.97
New Zealand	130.47	+ 0.66	97.78	+ 0.89	+ 0.92	120.97	86.94	− 22.32	− 18.58	+ 1.11	+ 1.14
Philippines	133.51	+ 0.66	65.33	+ 0.42	+ 0.65	87.10	61.27	− 17.99	− 21.59	− 8.19	− 11.13
Singapore	124.94	+ 0.87	110.39	+ 1.04	+ 0.95	153.92	103.21	− 29.11	− 20.87	− 24.93	− 18.42
South Korea	101.71	+ 1.24	59.41	+ 1.11	+ 1.90	105.26	49.86	− 45.85	− 43.56	+ 6.27	+ 11.80
Taiwan	121.75	+ 1.93	89.79	+ 1.71	+ 1.94	177.34	88.08	− 82.00	− 47.73	− 6.10	− 6.36
Thailand	56.62	+ 0.57	29.31	+ 0.16	+ 0.55	36.14	24.81	− 6.83	− 18.90	+ 2.12	+ 7.79
Asia/Pacific (ex. Japan)			130.16	+ 1.12	+ 0.87	178.48	124.86	− 47.59	− 26.77	− 8.19	− 5.92
World (ex. U.S.)			131.41	+ 1.40	+ 1.08	181.58	130.01	− 48.99	− 27.16	− 25.47	− 16.23
DOW JONES WORLD STOCK INDEX			185.16	+ 3.33	+ 1.83	244.35	176.60	− 57.04	− 23.55	− 25.74	− 12.20

Indexes based on 12/31/91=100. †Local Currency index shown in 000s.

Source: *The Wall Street Journal,* 13 July 2001, C16. Reprinted with permission from *The Wall Street Journal,* Dow Jones Co., Inc.

BOND MARKET INDICATOR SERIES[8]

Investors know little about the several bond market series because these bond series are relatively new and not widely published. Knowledge regarding these bond series is becoming more important because of the growth of fixed-income mutual funds and the consequent need to have a reliable set of benchmarks to use in evaluating performance.[9] Also, because the performance of many fixed-income money managers has been unable to match that of the aggregate bond market, interest has been growing in bond index funds, which requires the development of an index to emulate.[10]

Notably, the creation and computation of bond market indexes is more difficult than a stock market series for several reasons. First, the universe of bonds is much broader than that of stocks, ranging from U.S. Treasury securities to bonds in default. Second, the universe of bonds is changing constantly because of new issues, bond maturities, calls, and bond sinking funds. Third, the volatility of prices for individual bonds and bond portfolios changes because bond price volatility is affected by duration, which is likewise changing constantly because of changes in maturity, coupon, and market yield (see Chapter 19). Finally, significant problems can arise in correctly pricing the individual bond issues in an index (especially corporate and mortgage bonds) compared to the current and continuous transactions prices available for most stocks used in stock indexes.

The subsequent discussion is divided into three subsections: (1) U.S. investment-grade bond indexes, including Treasuries; (2) U.S. high-yield bond indexes; and (3) global government bond indexes. Notably, all of these indexes indicate total rates of return for the portfolio of bonds and most of the indexes are market-value weighted. Exhibit 5.13 contains a summary of the characteristics for the indexes available for these three segments of the bond market.

Investment-Grade Bond Indexes

As shown in Exhibit 5.13, four investment firms have created and maintain indexes for Treasury bonds and other bonds considered investment grade; that is, the bonds are rated BBB or higher. As demonstrated in Reilly and Wright and shown in Chapter 4, the relationship among the returns for these investment-grade bonds is strong (that is, the correlations among the returns average about 0.95), regardless of the segment of the market.

High-Yield Bond Indexes

One of the fastest-growing segments of the U.S. bond market during the past 15 years has been the high-yield bond market, which includes bonds that are not investment grade—that is, they are rated BB, B, CCC, CC, and C. Because of this growth, four investment firms created indexes related to this market. A summary of the characteristics for these indexes is included in Exhibit 5.13. As shown in studies by Reilly and Wright, the relationship among the alternative high-yield bond indexes is weaker than among the investment-grade indexes, and this is especially true for the bonds rated CCC.[11]

Exhibit 5.14 contains the Bond Market Data Bank, which provides recent returns for a wide range of domestic bonds from Treasuries to high-yield and including municipal bonds.

---

[8]The discussion in this section draws heavily from Frank K. Reilly and David J. Wright, "Bond Market Indexes," *The Handbook of Fixed-Income Securities,* 6th ed., ed. Frank J. Fabozzi (New York: McGraw-Hill, 2001).

[9]For a discussion of benchmark selection, see Chris P. Dialynas, "The Active Decisions in the Selection of Passive Management and Performance Bogeys," in *The Handbook of Fixed-Income Securities,* 6th ed., ed. Frank J. Fabozzi (New York: McGraw-Hill, 2001).

[10]For a discussion of this phenomenon, see Kenneth E. Volpert, "Managing Indexed and Enhanced Indexed Bond Portfolios," in *The Handbook of Fixed-Income Securities,* 6th ed., ed. Frank J. Fabozzi (New York: McGraw-Hill, 2001).

[11]Frank K. Reilly and David J. Wright, "An Analysis of High-Yield Bond Benchmarks," *Journal of Fixed Income* 3, no. 4 (March 1994): 6–24. The uniqueness of CCC bonds is demonstrated in Frank K. Reilly and David J. Wright, "The Unique Risk-Return Characteristics of High-Yield Bonds," *The Journal of Fixed Income* 11, no. 2 (September 2001): 65–82.

EXHIBIT 5.13   *SUMMARY OF BOND MARKET INDEXES*

NAME OF INDEX	NUMBER OF ISSUES	MATURITY	SIZE OF ISSUES	WEIGHTING	PRICING	REINVESTMENT ASSUMPTION	SUBINDEXES AVAILABLE
U.S. Investment-Grade Bond Indexes							
Lehman Brothers	5,000+	Over 1 year	Over $100 million	Market value	Trader priced and model priced	No	Government, gov./corp., corporate, mortgage-backed, asset-backed
Merrill Lynch	5,000+	Over 1 year	Over $50 million	Market value	Trader priced and model priced	In specific bonds	Government, gov./corp., corporate, mortgage
Ryan Treasury	300+	Over 1 year	All Treasury	Market value and equal	Market priced	In specific bonds	Treasury
Salomon Smith Barney	5,000+	Over 1 year	Over $50 million	Market value	Trader priced	In one-month T-bill	Broad inv. grade, Treas.-agency, corporate, mortgage
U.S. High-Yield Bond Indexes							
C.S. First Boston	423	All maturities	Over $75 million	Market value	Trader priced	Yes	Composite and by rating
Lehman Brothers	624	Over 1 year	Over $100 million	Market value	Trader priced	No	Composite and by rating
Merrill Lynch	735	Over 1 year	Over $25 million	Market value	Trader priced	Yes	Composite and by rating
Salomon Smith Barney	299	Over 7 years	Over $50 million	Market value	Trader priced	Yes	Composite and by rating
Global Government Bond Indexes							
Lehman Brothers	800	Over 1 year	Over $200 million	Market value	Trader priced	Yes	Composite and 13 countries, local and U.S. dollars
Merrill Lynch	9,736	Over 1 year	Over $50 million	Market value	Trader priced	Yes	Composite and 9 countries, local and U.S. dollars
J. P. Morgan	445	Over 1 year	Over $100 million	Market value	Trader priced	Yes in index	Composite and 11 countries, local and U.S. dollars
Salomon Smith Barney	400	Over 1 year	Over $250 million	Market value	Trader priced	Yes at local short-term rate	Composite and 14 countries, local and U.S. dollars

EXHIBIT 5.14   *BOND MARKET DATA BANK*

BOND MARKET DATA BANK   7/12/01

BOND YIELDS

	TREASURY ISSUES*			MUNICIPAL ISSUES (Comparable Maturities)†				
				Aaa	TAX	MUNI/TREAS	52-WEEK RATIO	
MATURITY	COUPON	PRICE	YIELD	YIELD	EQUIV.	YIELD RATIO	HIGH	LOW
06/30/03	3.875	99.22	4.041	3.04	4.40	75.2	85.6	68.0
08/15/03	5.750	103.07	4.125	3.08	4.46	74.6	84.2	69.0
05/15/06	4.625	99.15	4.748	3.68	5.33	77.4	88.0	72.3
02/15/11	5.000	98.06	5.242	4.33	6.27	82.6	89.6	78.6
02/15/31	5.375	96.01	5.652	5.18	7.50	91.6	98.9	90.0

*Most recent auctions.   †From Delphis Hanover. Tax equiv. based on 31% bracket.

MAJOR INDEXES

12 MONTHS HIGH	LOW		CLOSE	NET CHG	% CHG	12-MO CHG	% CHG	FROM 12/31	% CHG
U.S. Treasury Securities (Lehman Brothers indexes)									
6466.28	5839.98	Intermediate	6458.39 +	8.93 +	0.14 +	596.96 +	10.18 +	245.46 +	3.95
9884.78	8614.54	Long-term	9643.44 +	31.29 +	0.33 +	925.18 +	10.61 +	129.16 +	1.36
1693.82	1540.04	Long-term (price)	1619.93 +	4.98 +	0.31 +	59.57 +	3.82 –	32.16 –	1.95
7177.55	6439.37	Composite	7147.79 +	14.66 +	0.21 +	667.46 +	10.30 +	207.81 +	2.99
U.S. Corporate Debt Issues (Merrill Lynch)									
1162.40	1021.21	Corporate Master	1159.47 +	2.52 +	0.22 +	132.34 +	12.88 +	70.75 +	6.50
843.99	745.05	1-10 Yr Maturities	842.65 +	1.31 +	0.16 +	93.94 +	12.55 +	48.04 +	6.05
903.71	784.15	10+ Yr Maturities	899.10 +	3.56 +	0.40 +	108.78 +	13.76 +	63.96 +	7.66
528.89	477.60	High Yield	513.92 –	0.21 –	0.04 +	9.81 +	1.95 +	25.37 +	5.19
854.31	749.68	Yankee Bonds	851.59 +	1.30 +	0.15 +	97.94 +	13.00 +	44.91 +	5.57
Tax-Exempt Securities (Bond Buyer Muni Index; Dec. 22, 1999)									
105– 19	97-08	Bond Buyer 6% Muni	104-07 +	0-06 +	0.18 +	6-17 +	6.69 +	0-30 +	0.91
164.84	151.10	7-12 yr G.O.	164.74 +	0.05 +	0.03 +	13.31 +	8.79 +	4.95 +	3.10
172.93	156.13	12-22 yr G.O.	172.93 +	0.15 +	0.09 +	15.87 +	10.10 +	4.32 +	2.56
163.63	145.66	22+ yr Revenue	163.63 +	0.32 +	0.20 +	16.98 +	11.58 +	4.21 +	2.64
Mortgage-Backed Securities (current coupon; Merrill Lynch: Dec. 31, 1986 = 100)									
363.38	327.96	Ginnie Mae (GNMA)	361.61 +	0.51 +	0.14 +	31.17 +	9.43 +	10.96 +	3.13
356.66	320.85	Fannie Mae (FNMA)	356.12 +	0.40 +	0.11 +	33.37 +	10.34 +	11.61 +	3.37
218.24	196.60	Freddie Mac (FHLMC)	217.27 +	0.25 +	0.12 +	19.49 +	9.85 +	6.46 +	3.06
Broad Market (Merrill Lynch)									
959.60	853.85	Domestic Master	957.31 +	1.69 +	0.18 +	97.64 +	11.36 +	39.86 +	4.34
1066.93	948.30	Corporate/Government	1063.24 +	2.34 +	0.22 +	108.82 +	11.40 +	43.97 +	4.31

Source: *The Wall Street Journal,* 13 July 2001, C14. Reprinted with permission from *The Wall Street Journal,* Dow Jones Co., Inc.

Merrill Lynch Convertible Securities Indexes   In March 1988, Merrill Lynch introduced a convertible bond index with data beginning in January 1987. This index includes 600 issues in three major subgroups: U.S. domestic convertible bonds, Eurodollar convertible bonds issued by U.S. corporations, and U.S. domestic convertible preferred stocks. The issues included must be public U.S. corporate issues, have a minimum par value of $25 million, and have a minimum maturity of one year.

Global Government Bond Market Indexes

Similar to the high-yield bond market, the global bond market has experienced significant growth in size and importance during the recent 10-year period. Unlike the high-yield bond market, this global segment is completely dominated by government bonds because few non-U.S. countries have a corporate bond market. Once again, several major investment firms have created indexes that reflect the performance for the global bond market. As shown in Exhibit 5.13, the various indexes have several similar characteristics, such as measuring total rates of return, using market-value weighting, and using trader pricing. At the same time, the total sample sizes and the number of countries included differ.

An analysis of performance in this market indicates that the differences mentioned have caused some large differences in the long-term risk-return performance by the alternative indexes.[12] Also, the low correlation among the various countries is similar to stocks. Finally, there was a significant exchange rate effect on volatility and correlations.

COMPOSITE STOCK–BOND INDEXES

Beyond separate stock indexes and bond indexes for individual countries, a natural step is the development of a composite series that measures the performance of all securities in a given country. A composite series of stocks and bonds makes it possible to examine the benefits of diversifying with a combination of asset classes such as stocks and bonds in addition to diversifying within the asset classes of stocks or bonds. There are two such series available.

Merrill Lynch–Wilshire U.S. Capital Markets Index (ML–WCMI)

First a market-value-weighted index called Merrill Lynch–Wilshire Capital Markets Index (ML–WCMI) measures the total return performance of the combined U.S. taxable fixed-income and equity markets. It is basically a combination of the Merrill Lynch fixed-income indexes and the Wilshire 5000 common-stock index. As such, it tracks more than 10,000 stocks and bonds. The makeup of the index is as follows (as of July 2001):

Security	Percent of Total
Treasury bonds	10.05%
Agency bonds	4.40
Mortgage bonds	10.25
Corporate bonds	8.05
OTC stocks	7.74
AMEX stocks	2.10
NYSE stocks	57.41
	100.00%

Brinson Partners Global Security Market Index (GSMI)

The second composite series is the Brinson Partners Global Security Market Index (GSMI) series that contains both U.S. stocks and bonds but also includes non-U.S. equities and nondollar bonds. The specific breakdown is as follows (as of July 2001):

---

[12]Frank K. Reilly and David J. Wright, "Global Bond Markets: Alternative Benchmarks and Risk-Return Performance," mimeo (June 2000).

SECURITIES	PERCENT
Equities	
U.S. large capitalization	28
U.S. small and mid-cap	12
Non-U.S. developed country	22
Emerging markets	3
Fixed Income	
U.S. domestic investment grade	21
U.S. high yield	3
Nondollar developed country	9
Emerging markets	2
Total	100

Although related to the relative market values of these asset classes, the weights specified are not constantly adjusted. The construction of the GSMI used optimization techniques to identify the portfolio mix of available global asset classes that match the risk level of a typical U.S. pension plan. The index is balanced to the policy weights monthly.

Because the GSMI contains both U.S. and international stocks and bonds, it is clearly the most diversified benchmark available with a weighting scheme that approaches market values. As such, it is closest to the theoretically specified "market portfolio of risky assets" referred to in the CAPM literature.[13]

MEAN ANNUAL SECURITY RISK-RETURNS AND CORRELATIONS

The use of security indexes to measure returns and risk was demonstrated in Chapter 3 where we showed the average annual price change or rate of return and risk measure for a large set of asset indexes. As one would expect, there were clear differences among the series due to the different asset classes (e.g., stocks versus bonds) and when there were different samples within asset classes (e.g., the results for NYSE stocks versus Nasdaq stocks versus non-U.S. stocks). Equally important, the results were generally consistent with what one should expect in a risk-averse world—that is, there was a positive relationship between the average rate of return for an asset and its measure of risk—for example, the return-risk results for T-bills versus the results for the S&P 500 stocks. The point is, these security market indexes can be used to measure the historical performance of an asset class but can also be used as benchmarks to evaluate the performance of a money manager for a mutual fund, a personal trust, or a pension plan.

We also considered the correlation of monthly returns among the asset classes, which indicated a wide range of correlations. Because diversification requires combining assets with low positive or ideally negative correlation, these results indicated which assets are optimal for investors depending upon the current portfolio. Finally, the correlation of asset returns with the rate of inflation implied good and poor inflation hedge assets.

---

[13]This GSMI series is used in a study that examines the effect of alternative benchmarks on the estimate of the security market and estimates of individual stock betas. See Frank K. Reilly and Rashid A. Akhtar, "The Benchmark Error Problem with Global Capital Markets," *Journal of Portfolio Management* 22, no. 1 (Fall 1995). Brinson Partners has a Multiple Markets Index (MMI) that also contains venture capital and real estate. Because these assets are not actively traded, the value and rate of return estimates tend to be relatively stable, which reduces the standard deviation of the series.

The Internet *Investments Online*

We've seen several previous Web sites that offer online users a look at current market conditions in the form of a time-delayed market index (some sites offer real-time stock and index prices, but only at a cost to their customers). Here are a few others:

http://www.bloomberg.com The site is somewhat of an Internet version of the "Bloomberg machine," which is prevalent in many brokerage house offices. It offers both news and current data on a wide variety of global market securities and indexes, including historical charts. The site contains information on interest rates, commodities, and currencies.

http://www.barra.com Barra offers downloadable historical data on several S&P/Barra equity indexes, including S&P 500, midcap, and small cap indexes as well as Canadian equity indexes. Also included is information about the characteristics of the indexes.

http://www.msci.com Morgan Stanley Capital International contains links to sites which offer downloadable data on several of its international equity indexes. Information and graphics on several fixed income indexes are available, too.

http://www.barcap.com/euroidx/data/ Summary.shtml and the home page of Barclays Capital, **http://www.barcap.com**, offer information on European bond market indexes.

Additional global bond index performance information can be found at **http://www.datastream.com/product/ investor/index.htm.** Information on Japanese bond indexes are available at a Daiwa Institute of Research site, **http://www.dir.co.jp/ InfoManage/datarsc.html**.

http://www.world-exchanges.org The Web site of the World Federation of Exchanges contains many links and much data related to global securities markets.

Summary

- Given the several uses of security market indicator series, you should know how they are constructed and the differences among them. If you want to use one of the many series to learn how the "market" is doing, you should be aware of what market you are dealing with so you can select the appropriate index. As an example, are you only interested in the NYSE or do you also want to consider the AMEX and the OTC? Beyond the U.S. market, are you interested in Japanese or U.K. stocks, or do you want to examine the total world market?[14]

- Indexes are also used as benchmarks to evaluate portfolio performance.[15] In this case, you must be sure the index (benchmark) is consistent with your investing universe. If you are investing worldwide, you should not judge your performance relative to the DJIA, which is limited to 30 U.S. blue-chip stocks. For a bond portfolio, the index should match your investment philosophy. Finally, if your portfolio contains both stocks and bonds, you must evaluate your performance against an appropriate combination of indexes or one of the indexes that specifically combines the indexes for you.

- Whenever you invest, you examine numerous market indexes to tell you what has happened and how successful you have been. The selection of the appropriate indexes for information or evaluation will depend on how knowledgeable you are regarding the various series. The purpose of this chapter is to help you understand what to look for and how to make the right decision.

Questions

1. Discuss briefly several uses of security market indicator series.
2. What major factors must be considered when constructing a market index? Put another way, what characteristics differentiate indexes?

---

[14]For a readable discussion on this topic, see Anne Merjos, "How's the Market Doing?" *Barron's,* 20 August 1990, 18–20, 27, 28.

[15]Chapter 26 includes an extensive discussion of the purpose and construction of benchmarks and considers the evaluation of portfolio performance.

3. Explain how a market indicator series is price weighted. In such a case, would you expect a $100 stock to be more important than a $25 stock? Why or why not?

4. Explain how to compute a market-value-weighted series.

5. Explain how a price-weighted series and a market-value-weighted series adjust for stock splits.

6. Describe an unweighted price indicator series and describe how you would construct such a series. Assume a 20 percent price change in GM ($40/share; 50 million shares outstanding) and Coors Brewing ($25/share and 15 million shares outstanding). Explain which stock's change will have the greater impact on such an index.

7. If you correlated percentage changes in the Wilshire 5000 equity index with percentage changes in the NYSE composite and the Nasdaq composite index, would you expect a difference in the correlations? Why or why not?

8. There are high correlations among the monthly percentage price changes for the alternative NYSE indexes. Discuss the reason for this similarity: Is it size of sample, source of sample, or method of computation?

9. You learn that the Wilshire 5000 market-value-weighted series increased by 16 percent during a specified period, whereas a Wilshire 5000 equal-weighted series increased by 23 percent during the same period. Discuss what this difference in results implies.

10. Why is it contended that bond market indexes are more difficult to construct and maintain than stock market indexes?

11. The Wilshire 5000 market-value-weighted index increased by 5 percent, whereas the Merrill Lynch–Wilshire Capital Markets Index increased by 15 percent during the same period. What does this difference in results imply?

12. The Russell 1000 increased by 8 percent during the past year, whereas the Russell 2000 increased by 15 percent. Discuss the implication of these results.

13. Based on what you know about the *Financial Times* (FT) World Index, the Morgan Stanley Capital International World Index, and the Dow Jones World Stock Index, what level of correlation would you expect among monthly rates of return? Discuss the reasons for your answer based on the factors that affect indexes.

Problems

1. You are given the following information regarding prices for stocks of the following firms:

		PRICE	
Stock	Number of Shares	T	$T + 1$
Lauren Corp.	1,000,000	60	80
Kayleigh Co.	10,000,000	20	35
Madison Ltd.	30,000,000	18	25

a. Construct a *price-weighted* index for these three stocks, and compute the percentage change in the series for the period from T to $T + 1$.

b. Construct a *market-value-weighted* index for these three stocks, and compute the percentage change in the series for the period from T to $T + 1$.

c. Briefly discuss the difference in the results for the two stock indexes.

2. a. Given the data in Problem 1, construct an equal-weighted index by assuming $1,000 is invested in each stock. What is the percentage change in wealth for this equal-weighted portfolio?

b. Compute the percentage of price change for each of the stocks in Problem 1. Compute the arithmetic average of these percentage changes. Discuss how this answer compares to the answer in 2a.

c. Compute the geometric average of the three percentage changes in 2b. Discuss how this result compares to the answer in 2b.

3. For the past five trading days, on the basis of figures in *The Wall Street Journal,* compute the daily percentage price changes for the following stock indexes:

a. DJIA

b. S&P 500

c. Nasdaq Composite Index

d. FT-100 Share Index

e. Nikkei Stock Price Average

Discuss the difference in results for a and b, a and c, a and d, a and e, d and e. What do these differences imply regarding diversifying within the United States versus diversifying between countries?

4.

	PRICE			SHARES		
Company	A	B	C	A	B	C
Day 1	12	23	52	500	350	250
Day 2	10	22	55	500	350	250
Day 3	14	46	52	500	175[a]	250
Day 4	13	47	25	500	175	500[b]
Day 5	12	45	26	500	175	500

[a]Split at close of Day 2
[b]Split at close of Day 3

a. Calculate a Dow Jones Industrial Average for Days 1 through 5.

b. What effects have the splits had in determining the next day's index? (Hint: Think of the relative weighting of each stock.)

c. From a copy of *The Wall Street Journal,* find the divisor that is currently being used in calculating the DJIA. (Normally this value can be found on pages C2 and C3.)

5. Utilizing the price and volume data in Problem 4.

a. Calculate a Standard & Poor's Index for Days 1 through 5 using a beginning index value of 10.

b. Identify what effects the splits had in determining the next day's index. (Hint: Think of the relative weighting of each stock.)

6. Based on the following stock price and shares outstanding information, compute the beginning and ending values for a price-weighted index and a market-value-weighted index.

	DECEMBER 31, 2002		DECEMBER 31, 2003	
	Price	Shares Outstanding	Price	Shares Outstanding
Stock K	20	100,000,000	32	100,000,000
Stock L	80	2,000,000	45	4,000,000[a]
Stock M	40	25,000,000	42	25,000,000

[a]Stock split two-for-one during the year

a. Compute the percentage change in the value of each index.

b. Explain the difference in results between the two indexes.

c. Compute the results for an unweighted index and discuss why these results differ from the others.

References Fisher, Lawrence, and James H. Lorie. *A Half Century of Returns on Stocks and Bonds.* Chicago: University of Chicago Graduate School of Business, 1997.

Ibbotson Associates. *Stocks, Bonds, Bills and Inflation.* Chicago: Ibbotson Associates, annual.

Reilly, Frank K., and David J. Wright, "Bond Market Indexes." In *The Handbook of Fixed-Income Securities,* 6th ed., ed. Frank J. Fabozzi. New York: McGraw-Hill, 2001.

APPENDIX Foreign Stock Market Indexes
Chapter 5

Index Name	Number of Stocks	Weights of Stocks	Calculation Method	History of Index
ATX-index (Vienna)	All stocks listed on the exchange	Market capitalization	Value weighted	Base year 1967, 1991 began including all stocks (Value = 100)
Swiss Market Index	18 stocks	Market capitalization	Value weighted	Base year 1988, stocks selected from the Basle, Geneva, and Zurich Exchanges (Value = 1,500)
Stockholm General Index	All stocks (voting) listed on exchange	Market capitalization	Value weighted	Base year 1979, continuously updated (Value = 100)
Copenhagen Stock Exchange Share Price Index	All stocks traded	Market capitalization	Value weighted	Share price is based on average price of the day
Oslo SE Composite Index (Sweden)	25 companies			Base year 1972 (Value = 100)
Johannesburg Stock Exchange Actuaries Index	146 companies	Market capitalization	Value weighted	Base year 1959 (Value = 100)
Mexican Market Index	Variable number, based on capitalization and liquidity		Value weighted (adjustment for value of paid-out dividends)	Base year 1978, high dollar returns in recent years
Milan Stock Exchange MIB	Variable number, based on capitalization and liquidity		Weighted arithmetic average	Change base at beginning of each year (Value = 1,000)
Belgium BEL-20 Stock Index	20 companies	Market capitalization	Value weighted	Base year 1991 (Value = 1,000)
Madrid General Stock Index	92 stocks	Market capitalization	Value weighted	Change base at beginning of each year
Hang Seng Index (Hong Kong)	33 companies	Market capitalization	Value weighted	Started in 1969, accounts for 75 percent of total market
FT-Actuaries World Indexes	2,212 stocks	Market capitalization	Value weighted	Base year 1986
FT-SE 100 Index (London)	100 companies	Market capitalization	Value weighted	Base year 1983 (Value = 1,000)
CAC General Share Index (French)	212 companies	Market capitalization	Value weighted	Base year 1981 (Value = 100)
Morgan Stanley World Index	1,482 stocks	Market capitalization	Value weighted	Base year 1970 (Value = 100)
Singapore Straits Times Industrial Index	30 stocks	Unweighted		
German Stock Market Index (DAX)	30 companies (Blue Chips)	Market capitalization	Value weighted	Base year 1987 (Value = 1,000)
Frankfurter Allgemeine Zeitung Index (FAZ) (German)	100 companies (Blue Chips)	Market capitalization	Value weighted	Base year 1958 (Value = 100)
Australian Stock Exchange Share Price Indices	250 stocks (92 percent of all shares listed)	Market capitalization	Value weighted	Introduced in 1979
Dublin ISEQ Index	71 stocks (54 official, 17 unlisted); all stocks traded	Market capitalization	Value weighted	Base year 1988 (Value = 1,000)

APPENDIX   **Foreign Stock Market Indexes** *(continued)*
Chapter 5

Index Name	Number of Stocks	Weights of Stocks	Calculation Method	History of Index
Dublin ISEQ Index	71 stocks (54 official, 17 unlisted); all stocks traded	Market capitalization	Value weighted	Base year 1988 (Value = 1,000)
HEX Index (Helsinki)	Varies with different share price indexes	Market capitalization	Value weighted	Base changes every day
Jakarta Stock Exchange	All listed shares (148 currently)	Market capitalization	Value weighted	Base year 1982 (Value = 100)
Taiwan Stock Exchange Index	All ordinary stocks (listed for at least a month)	Market capitalization	Value weighted	Base year 1966 (Value = 100)
TSE 300 Composite Index (Toronto)	300 stocks (comprised of 14 subindexes)	Market capitalization (adjusted for major shareholders)	Value weighted	Base year 1975 (Value = 1,000)
KOSPI (Korean Composite Stock Price Index)	All common stocks listed on exchange	Market capitalization (adjusted for major shareholders)	Value weighted	Base year 1980 (Value = 100)

Part 2

Developments in Investment Theory

The chapters in Part 1 provided background on why individuals invest their funds and what they expect to derive from this activity. We also argued very strongly for a global investment program, described the major instruments and capital markets in a global investment environment, and showed the relationship among these instruments and markets.

We now are ready to discuss how to analyze and value the various investment instruments available. In turn, valuation requires the estimation of expected returns (cash flows) and a determination of the risk involved in the securities. Before we can begin the analysis, we need to understand several major developments in investment theory that have influenced how we specify and measure risk in the valuation process. The purpose of the four chapters in Part 2 is to provide this background on risk and asset valuation.

Chapter 6 describes the concept of efficient capital markets, which hypothesizes that security prices reflect the effect of all information. This chapter considers why markets should be efficient, discusses how one goes about testing this hypothesis, describes the results of numerous tests that both support the hypotheses and indicate the existence of anomalies that are inconsistent with the hypotheses. There is also a consideration of behavioral finance, which provides a rationale for some of the results. We conclude the chapter with a discussion of the implications of the results for those engaged in technical and fundamental analysis as well as portfolio management.

Chapter 7 provides an introduction to portfolio theory, which was developed by Harry Markowitz. This theory provided the first rigorous measure of risk for investors and showed how one selects alternative assets to diversify and reduce the risk of a portfolio. Markowitz also derived a risk measure for individual securities within the context of an efficient portfolio.

Following the development of the Markowitz portfolio model, William Sharpe and several other academicians extended the Markowitz model into a general equilibrium asset pricing model that included an alternative risk measure for all risky assets. Chapter 8 contains a detailed description of these developments and an explanation of the relevant risk measure implied by this valuation model, referred to as the *capital asset pricing model* (CAPM). We introduce the CAPM at this early point in the book because the risk measure implied by this model has been used extensively in various valuation models. Although the CAPM has long been the preeminent theoretical explanation in finance for the connection between risk and expected return, the past several decades have seen the rise of several competing models.

Chapter 9 is devoted to exploring several alternative asset pricing models, which differ from the CAPM primarily by specifying multiple risk factors in lieu of a single market portfolio-based variable. The chapter begins with an examination of the *arbitrage pricing theory* (APT), which is the conceptual foundation for virtually all of the subsequent multi-factor asset pricing models. The APT, which was developed by Steve Ross in response to criticisms of the CAPM, suggests a linear relationship between a stock's expected return and many systematic risk factors. After presenting the conceptual development of the theory, we discuss numerous studies that have empirically tested the APT. As with the CAPM, the results of this research are mixed in terms of supporting the model, including some observations that question whether it is even possible to test the APT.

One severe challenge for investors attempting to use the APT in practice is that it offers no theoretical guidance as to either the number or the identity of the risk factors. To overcome this problem, researchers have developed several *multi-factor models*, which attempt to link a stock's realized returns to market data on a collection of pre-specified variables that are believed to proxy for the APT risk factors. In specifying these variables, both macroeconomic and microeconomic approaches and risk factors have been adopted. After explaining these various approaches, we demonstrate how they are used by investors to both evaluate individual companies and assess the investment styles of money managers and mutual funds.

Chapter 6 ▶ Efficient Capital Markets

After you read this chapter, you should be able to answer the following questions:

➤ What does it mean to say that capital markets are efficient?
➤ Why *should* capital markets be efficient?
➤ What factors contribute to an efficient market?
➤ Given the overall efficient market hypothesis (EMH), what are the three subhypotheses and what are the implications of each of them?
➤ How do you test the three efficient market subhypotheses and what are the results of the tests?
➤ For each set of tests, which results support the EMH and which results indicate an anomaly related to the hypothesis?
➤ What is behavioral finance and how does it relate to the EMH?
➤ What are some of the major findings of behavioral finance and what are the implications of these findings for the EMH?
➤ What are the implications of the test results for the following?
  • Technical analysis
  • Fundamental analysis
  • Portfolio managers with superior analysts
  • Portfolio managers with inferior analysts
➤ What is the evidence related to the EMH for markets in foreign countries?

An **efficient capital market** is one in which security prices adjust rapidly to the arrival of new information and, therefore, the current prices of securities reflect all information about the security. Some of the most interesting and important academic research during the past 20 years has analyzed whether our capital markets are efficient. This extensive research is important because its results have significant real-world implications for investors and portfolio managers. In addition, the question of whether capital markets are efficient is one of the most controversial areas in investment research. Recently, a new dimension has been added to the controversy because of the rapidly expanding research in behavioral finance that likewise has major implications regarding the concept of efficient capital markets.

Because of its importance and controversy, you need to understand the meaning of the terms *efficient capital markets* and the *efficient market hypothesis (EMH)*. You should understand the analysis performed to test the EMH and the results of studies that either support or contradict the hypothesis. Finally, you should be aware of the implications of these results when you analyze alternative investments and work to construct a portfolio.

We are considering the topic of efficient capital markets at this point for two reasons. First, the prior discussion indicated how the capital markets function, so now it seems natural to consider the efficiency of the market in terms of how security prices react to new information. Second, the overall evidence on capital market efficiency is best described as mixed; some studies support the hypothesis, and others do not. The implications of these diverse results are important for you as an investor involved in analyzing securities and building a portfolio.

This chapter contains five major sections. The first discusses why we would expect capital markets to be efficient and the factors that contribute to an efficient market where the prices of securities reflect available information.

The efficient market hypothesis has been divided into three subhypotheses to facilitate testing. The second section describes these three subhypotheses and the implications of each of them.

The third section is the largest section because it contains a discussion of the results of numerous studies. This review of the research reveals that a large body of evidence supports the EMH, but a growing number of other studies do not support the hypotheses.

In the fourth section, we discuss the concept of behavioral finance, the studies that have been done in this area related to efficient markets, and the conclusions as they relate to the EMH.

The final section discusses what these results imply for an investor who uses either technical analysis or fundamental analysis or what they mean for a portfolio manager who has access to superior or inferior analysts. We conclude with a brief discussion of the evidence for markets in foreign countries.

WHY SHOULD CAPITAL MARKETS BE EFFICIENT?

As noted earlier, in an efficient capital market, security prices adjust rapidly to the infusion of new information, and, therefore, current security prices fully reflect all available information. To be absolutely correct, this is referred to as an **informationally efficient market**. Although the idea of an efficient capital market is relatively straightforward, we often fail to consider *why* capital markets *should* be efficient. What set of assumptions imply an efficient capital market?

An initial and important premise of an efficient market requires that *a large number of profit-maximizing participants analyze and value securities,* each independently of the others.

A second assumption is that *new information regarding securities comes to the market in a random fashion,* and the timing of one announcement is generally independent of others.[1]

The third assumption is especially crucial: *profit-maximizing investors adjust security prices rapidly to reflect the effect of new information.* Although the price adjustment may be imperfect, it is unbiased. This means that sometimes the market will overadjust and other times it will underadjust, but you cannot predict which will occur at any given time. Security prices adjust rapidly because of the many profit-maximizing investors competing against one another.

The combined effect of (1) information coming in a random, independent, unpredictable fashion and (2) numerous competing investors adjusting stock prices rapidly to reflect this new information means that one would expect price changes to be independent and random. You can see that the adjustment process requires a large number of investors following the movements of the security, analyzing the impact of new information on its value, and buying or selling the security until its price adjusts to reflect the new information. This scenario implies that informationally efficient markets require some minimum amount of trading and that more trading by numerous competing investors should cause a faster price adjustment, making the market more efficient. We will return to this need for trading and investor attention when we discuss some anomalies of the EMH.

Finally, because security prices adjust to all new information, these security prices should reflect all information that is publicly available at any point in time. Therefore, the security prices that prevail at any time should be an unbiased reflection of all currently available

---

[1]New information, by definition, must be information that was not known before and it is not predictable because if it was predictable it would have been impounded in the security price.

information, including the risk involved in owning the security. Therefore, in an efficient market, *the expected returns implicit in the current price of the security should reflect its risk,* which means that investors who buy at these informationally efficient prices should receive a rate of return that is consistent with the perceived risk of the stock. Put another way, in terms of the CAPM, all stocks should lie on the SML such that their expected rates of return are consistent with their perceived risk.

ALTERNATIVE EFFICIENT MARKET HYPOTHESES

Most of the early work related to efficient capital markets was based on the *random walk hypothesis,* which contended that changes in stock prices occurred randomly. This early academic work contained extensive empirical analysis without much theory behind it. An article by Fama attempted to formalize the theory and organize the growing empirical evidence.[2] Fama presented the efficient market theory in terms of a *fair game model,* contending that investors can be confident that a current market price fully reflects all available information about a security and the expected return based upon this price is consistent with its risk.

In his original article, Fama divided the overall efficient market hypothesis (EMH) and the empirical tests of the hypothesis into three subhypotheses depending on the information set involved: (1) weak-form EMH, (2) semistrong-form EMH, and (3) strong-form EMH.

In a subsequent review article, Fama again divided the empirical results into three groups but shifted empirical results between the prior categories.[3] Therefore, the following discussion uses the original categories but organizes the presentation of results using the new categories.

In the remainder of this section, we describe the three subhypotheses and the implications of each of them. As will be noted, the three subhypotheses are based on alternative information sets. In the following section, we briefly describe how researchers have tested these hypotheses and summarize the results of these tests.

Weak-Form Efficient Market Hypothesis

The **weak-form EMH** assumes that current stock prices fully reflect *all security market information,* including the historical sequence of prices, rates of return, trading volume data, and other market-generated information, such as odd-lot transactions, block trades, and transactions by exchange specialists. Because it assumes that current market prices already reflect all past returns and any other security market information, this hypothesis implies that past rates of return and other historical market data should have no relationship with future rates of return (that is, rates of return should be independent). Therefore, this hypothesis contends that you should gain little from using any trading rule that decides whether to buy or sell a security based on past rates of return or any other past market data.

Semistrong-Form Efficient Market Hypothesis

The **semistrong-form EMH** asserts that security prices adjust rapidly to the release of *all public information;* that is, current security prices fully reflect all public information. The semistrong hypothesis encompasses the weak-form hypothesis, because all the market information considered by the weak-form hypothesis, such as stock prices, rates of return, and trading volume, is public. Public information also includes all nonmarket information, such as earnings and dividend announcements, price-to-earnings (P/E) ratios, dividend-yield (D/P) ratios, price-book value (P/BV) ratios, stock splits, news about the economy, and political news. This

---

[2]Eugene F. Fama, "Efficient Capital Markets: A Review of Theory and Empirical Work," *Journal of Finance* 25, no. 2 (May 1970): 383–417.

[3]Eugene F. Fama, "Efficient Capital Markets: II," *Journal of Finance* 46, no. 5 (December 1991): 1575–1617.

hypothesis implies that investors who base their decisions on any important new information *after it is public* should not derive above-average risk-adjusted profits from their transactions, considering the cost of trading because the security price already reflects all such new public information.

Strong-Form Efficient Market Hypothesis

The **strong-form EMH** contends that stock prices fully reflect *all information from public and private sources.* This means that no group of investors has monopolistic access to information relevant to the formation of prices. Therefore, this hypothesis contends that no group of investors should be able to consistently derive above-average risk-adjusted rates of return. The strong-form EMH encompasses both the weak-form and the semistrong-form EMH. Further, the strong-form EMH extends the assumption of efficient markets, in which prices adjust rapidly to the release of new public information, to assume perfect markets, in which all information is cost-free and available to everyone at the same time.

TESTS AND RESULTS OF EFFICIENT MARKET HYPOTHESES

Now that you understand the three components of the EMH and what each of them implies regarding the effect on security prices of different sets of information, we can consider the tests used to see whether the data support the hypotheses. Therefore, in this section we discuss the specific tests and summarize the results of these tests.

Like most hypotheses in finance and economics, the evidence on the EMH is mixed. Some studies have supported the hypotheses and indicate that capital markets are efficient. Results of other studies have revealed some **anomalies** related to these hypotheses, indicating results that do not support the hypotheses.

Weak-Form Hypothesis: Tests and Results

Researchers have formulated two groups of tests of the weak-form EMH. The first category involves statistical tests of independence between rates of return. The second entails a comparison of risk-return results for trading rules that make investment decisions based on past market information relative to the results from a simple buy-and-hold policy, which assumes that you buy stock at the beginning of a test period and hold it to the end.

Statistical Tests of Independence
As discussed earlier, the EMH contends that security returns over time should be independent of one another because new information comes to the market in a random, independent fashion and security prices adjust rapidly to this new information. Two major statistical tests have been employed to verify this independence.

First, **autocorrelation tests** of independence measure the significance of positive or negative correlation in returns over time. Does the rate of return on day t correlate with the rate of return on day $t - 1$, $t - 2$, or $t - 3$?[4] Those who believe that capital markets are efficient would expect insignificant correlations for all such combinations.

Several researchers have examined the serial correlations among stock returns for several relatively short time horizons including 1 day, 4 days, 9 days, and 16 days. The results typically indicated insignificant correlation in stock returns over time. Some recent studies that considered portfolios of stocks of different market size have indicated that the autocorrelation is stronger for portfolios of small market size stocks. Therefore, although the older results tend to support the hypothesis, the more recent studies cast doubt on it for portfolios of small firms, although these

---

[4]For a discussion of tests of independence, see S. Christian Albright, *Statistics for Business and Economics* (New York: Macmillan Publishing, 1987), 515–517.

results could be affected by transaction costs of small-cap stocks and nonsynchronous trading for small-firm stocks.

The second statistical test of independence is the **runs test**.[5] Given a series of price changes, each price change is either designated a plus (+) if it is an increase in price or a minus (–) if it is a decrease in price. The result is a set of pluses and minuses as follows: +++–+––++––++. A run occurs when two consecutive changes are the same; two or more consecutive positive or negative price changes constitute one run. When the price changes in a different direction, such as when a negative price change is followed by a positive price change, the run ends and a new run may begin. To test for independence, you would compare the number of runs for a given series to the number in a table of expected values for the number of runs that should occur in a random series.

Studies that have examined stock price runs have confirmed the independence of stock price changes over time. The actual number of runs for stock price series consistently fell into the range expected for a random series. Therefore, these statistical tests of stocks on the NYSE and on the OTC market have likewise confirmed the independence of stock price changes over time.

Although short-horizon stock returns have generally supported the weak-form EMH, several studies that examined price changes for individual *transactions* on the NYSE found significant serial correlations. Notably, none of these studies attempted to show that the dependence of transaction price movements could be used to earn above-average risk-adjusted returns after considering the trading rule's substantial transactions costs.

Tests of Trading Rules The second group of tests of the weak-form EMH were developed in response to the assertion that the prior statistical tests of independence were too rigid to identify the intricate price patterns examined by technical analysts. As we will discuss in Chapter 16, technical analysts do not expect a set number of positive or negative price changes as a signal of a move to a new equilibrium in the market. They typically look for a general consistency in the price trends over time. Such a trend might include both positive and negative changes. For this reason, technical analysts believed that their trading rules were too sophisticated and complicated to be properly tested by rigid statistical tests.

In response to this objection, investigators attempted to examine alternative technical trading rules through simulation. Advocates of an efficient market hypothesized that investors could not derive abnormal profits above a buy-and-hold policy using any trading rule that depended solely on past market information.

The trading rule studies compared the risk-return results derived from trading-rule simulations, including transactions costs, to the results from a simple buy-and-hold policy. Three major pitfalls can negate the results of a trading-rule study:

1. The investigator should *use only publicly available data* when implementing the trading rule. As an example, the trading activities of specialists as of December 31 may not be publicly available until February 1, so you should not factor in information about specialist trading activity until then.
2. When computing the returns from a trading rule, you should *include all transactions costs* involved in implementing the trading strategy because most trading rules involve many more transactions than a simple buy-and-hold policy.
3. You must *adjust the results for risk* because a trading rule might simply select a portfolio of high-risk securities that should experience higher returns.

Researchers have encountered two operational problems in carrying out these tests of specific trading rules. First, some trading rules require too much subjective interpretation of data to

---

[5]For the details of a runs test, see Albright, *Statistics for Business and Economics,* 695–699.

simulate mechanically. Second, the almost infinite number of potential trading rules makes it impossible to test all of them. As a result, only the better-known technical trading rules have been examined.

Another factor that you should recognize is that the studies have typically been restricted to relatively simple trading rules, which many technicians contend are rather naïve. In addition, many of these studies employed readily available data from the NYSE, which is biased toward well-known, heavily traded stocks that certainly should trade in efficient markets. Recall that markets should be more efficient when there are numerous aggressive, profit-maximizing investors attempting to adjust stock prices to reflect new information, so market efficiency will be related to trading volume. Specifically, *more trading in a security should promote market efficiency*. Alternatively, for securities with relatively few stockholders and little trading activity, the market could be inefficient simply because fewer investors would be analyzing the effect of new information, and this limited interest would result in insufficient trading activity to move the price of the security quickly to a new equilibrium value that would reflect the new information. Therefore, using only active, heavily traded stocks when testing a trading rule could bias the results toward finding efficiency.

Results of Simulations of Specific Trading Rules

In the most popular trading technique, **filter rule**, an investor trades a stock when the price change exceeds a filter value set for it. As an example, an investor using a 5 percent filter would envision a positive breakout if the stock were to rise 5 percent from some base, suggesting that the stock price would continue to rise. A technician would acquire the stock to take advantage of the expected continued rise. In contrast, a 5 percent decline from some peak price would be considered a breakout on the downside, and the technician would expect a further price decline and would sell any holdings of the stock and possibly even sell the stock short.

Studies of this trading rule have used a range of filters from 0.5 percent to 50 percent. The results indicated that small filters would yield above-average profits *before* taking account of trading commissions. However, small filters generate numerous trades and, therefore, substantial trading costs. When these trading commissions were considered, all the trading profits turned to losses. Alternatively, trading using larger filters did not yield returns above those of a simple buy-and-hold policy.

Researchers have simulated other trading rules that used past market data other than stock prices.[6] Trading rules have been devised that consider advanced-decline ratios, short sales, short positions, and specialist activities. These simulation tests have generated mixed results. Most of the early studies suggested that these trading rules generally would not outperform a buy-and-hold policy on a risk-adjusted basis after commissions, although several recent studies have indicated support for specific trading rules. Therefore, most evidence from simulations of specific trading rules indicates that most trading rules tested have not been able to beat a buy-and-hold policy. Therefore, these results generally support the weak-form EMH, but the results are not unanimous.

Semistrong-Form Hypothesis: Tests and Results

Recall that the semistrong-form EMH asserts that security prices adjust rapidly to the release of all public information; that is, security prices fully reflect all public information. Studies that have tested the semistrong-form EMH can be divided into the following sets of studies:

1. *Studies to predict future rates of return using available public information beyond pure market information such as prices and trading volume considered in the weak-form tests.* These studies can involve either *time-series analysis* of returns or the *cross-section distribution* of returns for individual stocks. Advocates of the EMH would contend that it would

---

[6]Many of these trading rules are discussed in Chapter 16 on technical analysis.

not be possible to predict *future* returns using past returns or to predict the distribution of future returns using public information.

2. *Event studies that examine how fast stock prices adjust to specific significant economic events.* A corollary approach would be to test whether it is possible to invest in a security after the public announcement of a significant event and experience significant abnormal rates of return. Again, advocates of the EMH would expect security prices to adjust rapidly, such that it would not be possible for investors to experience superior risk-adjusted returns by investing after the public announcement and paying normal transactions costs.

Adjustment for Market Effects   For any of these tests, you need to adjust the security's rates of return for the rates of return of the overall market during the period considered. The point is, a 5 percent return in a stock during the period surrounding an announcement is meaningless until you know what the aggregate stock market did during the same period and how this stock normally acts under such conditions. If the market had experienced a 10 percent return during this period, the 5 percent return for the stock may be lower than expected.

Authors of studies undertaken prior to 1970 generally recognized the need to make such adjustments for market movements. They typically assumed that the individual stocks should experience returns equal to the aggregate stock market. This assumption meant that the market-adjustment process simply entailed subtracting the market return from the return for the individual security to derive its **abnormal rate of return**, as follows:

➤6.1
$$AR_{it} = R_{it} - R_{mt}$$

where:

> AR_{it} = **abnormal rate of return on security i during period t**
> R_{it} = **rate of return on security i during period t**
> R_{mt} = **rate of return on a market index during period t**

In the example where the stock experienced a 5 percent increase while the market increased 10 percent, the stock's abnormal return would be minus 5 percent.

Since the 1970s, many authors have adjusted the rates of return for securities by an amount different from the market rate of return because they recognize that, based on work with the CAPM, all stocks do not change by the same amount as the market. That is, as will be discussed in Chapter 8, some stocks are more volatile than the market, and some are less volatile. These possibilities mean that you must determine an **expected rate of return** for the stock based on the market rate of return *and* the stock's relationship with the market (its beta). As an example, suppose a stock is generally 20 percent more volatile than the market (that is, it has a beta of 1.20). In such a case, if the market experiences a 10 percent rate of return, you would expect this stock to experience a 12 percent rate of return. Therefore, you would determine the abnormal return by computing the difference between the stock's actual rate of return and its *expected rate of return* as follows:

➤6.2
$$AR_{it} = R_{it} - E(R_{it})$$

where:

> $E(R_{it})$ = **the expected rate of return for stock i during period t based on the market rate of return and the stock's normal relationship with the market (its beta)**

Continuing with the example, if the stock that was expected to have a 12 percent return (based on a market return of 10 percent and a stock beta of 1.20) had only a 5 percent return, its abnormal rate of return during the period would be minus 7 percent. Over the normal long-run period, you would expect the abnormal returns for a stock to sum to zero. Specifically, during one period the returns may exceed expectations and the next period they may fall short of expectations.

To summarize, there are two sets of tests of the semistrong-form EMH. The first set of studies are referred to as **return prediction studies**. For this set of studies, investigators attempt to predict the time series of future rates of return for individual stocks or the aggregate market using public information. For example, is it possible to predict abnormal returns over time for the market based on public information such as specified values or changes in the aggregate dividend yield or the risk premium spread for bonds? Another example would be **event studies** that examine abnormal rates of return for a period immediately after an announcement of a significant economic event, such as a stock split, a proposed merger, or a stock or bond issue, to determine whether an investor can derive above-average risk-adjusted rates of return by investing after the release of public information.

The second set of studies are those that predict cross-sectional returns. In these studies, investigators look for public information regarding individual stocks that will allow them to predict the cross-sectional distribution of future risk-adjusted rates of return. For example, they test whether it is possible to use variables such as the price-earnings ratio, market value size, the price/book-value ratio, the P/E/growth rate (PEG) ratio, or the dividend yield to predict which stocks will experience above-average or below-average risk-adjusted rates of return in the future.

In both sets of tests, the emphasis is on the analysis of abnormal rates of return that deviate from long-term expectations or returns that are adjusted for a stock's specific risk characteristics and overall market rates of return during the period.

Results of Return Prediction Studies

The **time-series analysis** assumes that in an efficient market the best estimate of *future* rates of return will be the long-run *historical* rates of return. The point of the tests is to determine whether any public information will provide superior estimates of returns for a short-run horizon (one to six months) or a long-run horizon (one to five years).

The results of these studies have indicated limited success in predicting short-horizon returns, but the analysis of long-horizon returns has been quite successful. A prime example is dividend yield studies. After postulating that the aggregate dividend yield (D/P) was a proxy for the risk premium on stocks, they found a positive relationship between the D/P and future stock market returns. Subsequent authors found that the predictive power of this relationship increases with the horizon, that is, dividend yields were better at predicting long-run returns.

In addition, several studies have considered two variables related to the term structure of interest rates: (1) a *default spread,* which is the difference between the yields on lower-grade and Aaa-rated long-term corporate bonds (this spread has been used in earlier chapters of this book as a proxy for a market risk premium), and (2) the *term structure spread,* which is the difference between the long-term Aaa yield and the yield on one-month Treasury bills. These variables have been used to predict stock returns and bond returns. Similar variables in foreign countries have also been useful for predicting returns for foreign common stocks.

The reasoning for these empirical results is as follows: When the two most significant variables—the dividend yield (D/P) and the default spread—are high, it implies that investors are expecting or requiring a high return on stocks and bonds. Notably, this occurs during poor economic environments, as reflected in the growth rate of output. A poor economic environment also implies a low-wealth environment wherein investors perceive higher risk for investments. As a result, for investors to invest and shift consumption from the present to the future, they will require a high rate of return. It is suggested that, if you invest during this risk-averse period, your subsequent returns will be above normal. In contrast, when these values are small, it implies that investors have reduced their risk premium and required rates of return and future returns will be below normal.

Quarterly Earnings Reports   Studies that address quarterly reports are considered part of the times-series analysis. Specifically, these studies question whether it is possible to predict future returns for a stock based on publicly available quarterly earnings reports. The typical test examined firms that experienced changes in quarterly earnings that differed from expectations. The results generally indicated abnormal returns during the 13 or 26 weeks *following* the announcement of a large unanticipated earnings change—referred to as an **earnings surprise**. These results suggest that an earnings surprise is *not* instantaneously reflected in security prices.

An extensive analysis by Rendleman, Jones, and Latané (RJL) using a large sample and daily data from 20 days before a quarterly earnings announcement to 90 days after the announcement indicated that 31 percent of the total response in stock returns came before the announcement, 18 percent on the day of the announcement, and 51 percent afterward.[7]

Several studies examined reasons for the earnings drift following earnings announcements and found that unexpected earnings explained more than 80 percent of the subsequent stock price drift for the total time period. Several authors who reviewed the prior studies contended that the reason for the stock price drift was the *earnings revisions* that followed the earnings surprises and contributed to the positive correlations of prices.

In summary, these results indicate that the market has not adjusted stock prices to reflect the release of quarterly earnings surprises as fast as expected by the semistrong EMH, which implies that earnings surprises and earnings revisions can be used to predict returns for individual stocks. These results are evidence against the EMH.[8]

The final set of calendar studies questioned whether some regularities in the rates of return during the calendar year would allow investors to predict returns on stocks. These studies include numerous studies on "the January anomaly" and studies that consider a variety of other daily and weekly regularities.

The January Anomaly   Several years ago, Branch proposed a unique trading rule for those interested in taking advantage of tax selling.[9] Investors (including institutions) tend to engage in tax selling toward the end of the year to establish losses on stocks that have declined. After the new year, the tendency is to reacquire these stocks or to buy other stocks that look attractive. This scenario would produce downward pressure on stock prices in late November and December and positive pressure in early January. Such a seasonal pattern is inconsistent with the EMH since it should be eliminated by arbitrageurs who would buy in December and sell in early January.

A supporter of the hypothesis found that December trading volume was abnormally high for stocks that had declined during the previous year and that significant abnormal returns occurred during January for stocks that had experienced losses during the prior year. It was concluded

[7]Richard J. Rendleman, Jr., Charles P. Jones, and Henry A. Latané, "Empirical Anomalies Based on Unexpected Earnings and the Importance of Risk Adjustments," *Journal of Financial Economics* 10, no. 3 (November 1982): 269–287; and C. P. Jones, R. J. Rendleman, Jr., and H. A. Latané, "Earnings Annoucements: Pre- and Post-Responses," *Journal of Portfolio Management* 11, no. 3 (Spring 1985): 28–32.

[8]Academic studies such as these that have indicated the importance of earnings surprises have led *The Wall Street Journal* to publish a section on "earnings surprises" in connection with regular quarterly earnings reports.

[9]Ben Branch, "A Tax Loss Trading Rule," *Journal of Business* 50, no. 2 (April 1977): 198–207. These results were generally confirmed in Ben Branch and Kyun Chun Chang, "Tax-Loss Trading—Is the Game Over or Have the Rules Changed?" *Financial Review* 20, no. 1 (February 1985): 55–69.

that, because of transaction costs, arbitrageurs must not be eliminating the January tax-selling anomaly. Subsequent analysis showed that most of the January effect was concentrated in the first week of trading, particularly on the first day of the year.

Several studies provided support for a January effect inconsistent with the tax-selling hypothesis by examining what happened in foreign countries that did not have our tax laws or a December year-end. They found abnormal returns in January, but the results could not be explained by tax laws. It has also been shown that the classic relationship between risk and return is strongest during January and there is a year-end trading volume bulge in late December–early January.

In summary, despite numerous studies, the January anomaly poses as many questions as it answers.[10]

Other Calendar Effects   Several other "calendar" effects have been examined, including a monthly effect, a weekend/day-of-the-week effect, and an intraday effect. One study found a significant monthly effect wherein all the market's cumulative advance occurred during the first half of trading months.

An analysis of the weekend effect found that the mean return for Monday was significantly negative during five-year subperiods and a total period. In contrast, the average return for the other four days was positive.

A study decomposed the Monday effect that is typically measured from Friday close to Monday close into a *weekend effect* (from Friday close to Monday open), and a *Monday trading effect* (from Monday open to the Monday close). It was shown that the negative Monday effect found in prior studies actually occurs from the Friday close to the Monday open (it is really a weekend effect). After adjusting for the weekend effect, the Monday trading effect was positive. Subsequently, it was shown that the Monday effect was on average positive in January and negative for all other months.

Finally, for *large firms,* the negative Monday effect occurred before the market opened (it was a weekend effect), whereas for *smaller firms* most of the negative Monday effect occurred during the day on Monday (it was a Monday trading effect).

Predicting Cross-Sectional Returns   Assuming an efficient market, *all securities should have equal risk-adjusted returns* because security prices should reflect all public information that would influence the security's risk. Therefore, studies in this category attempt to determine if you can use public information to predict what stocks will enjoy above-average or below-average risk-adjusted returns.

These studies typically examine the usefulness of alternative measures of size or quality to rank stocks in terms of risk-adjusted returns. Notably, all of these tests involve *a joint hypothesis* because they not only consider the efficiency of the market but also are dependent on the asset pricing model that provides the measure of risk used in the test. Specifically, if a test determines that it is possible to predict risk-adjusted returns, these results could occur because the market is not efficient, *or* they could be because the measure of risk is faulty and, therefore, the measures of risk-adjusted returns are wrong.

Price-Earnings Ratios   Several studies have examined the relationship between the historical **price-earnings (P/E) ratios** for stocks and the returns on the stocks. Some have suggested that low P/E stocks will outperform high P/E stocks because growth companies enjoy high P/E ratios, but the market tends to overestimate the growth potential and thus overvalues these growth companies, while undervaluing low-growth firms with low P/E ratios. A relationship

---

[10]An article that reviews these studies and others is Donald B. Keim, "The CAPM and Equity Return Regularities," *Financial Analysts Journal* 42, no. 3 (May–June 1986): 19–34.

between the historical P/E ratios and subsequent risk-adjusted market performance would constitute evidence against the semistrong EMH, because it would imply that investors could use publicly available information regarding P/E ratios to predict future abnormal returns.

Performance measures that consider both return and risk indicated that low P/E ratio stocks experienced superior risk-adjusted results relative to the market, whereas high P/E ratio stocks had significantly inferior risk-adjusted results.[11] Subsequent analysis concluded that publicly available P/E ratios possess valuable information regarding future returns, which is inconsistent with semistrong efficiency.

Another study examined P/E ratios with adjustments for firm size, industry effects, and infrequent trading and likewise found that the risk-adjusted returns for stocks in the lowest P/E ratio quintile were superior to those in the highest P/E ratio quintile.

Price-Earnings/Growth Rate (PEG) Ratios   During the past decade, there has been a significant increase in the use of the ratio of a stock's price-earnings ratio divided by the firm's expected growth rate of earnings (referred to as the PEG ratio) as a relative valuation tool, especially for stocks of growth companies that have P/E ratios substantially above average. Advocates of the PEG ratio hypothesize an inverse relationship between the PEG ratio and subsequent rates of return—that is, they expect that stocks with relatively low PEG ratios (i.e., less than one) will experience above-average rates of return while stocks with relatively high PEG ratios (i.e., in excess of three or four) will have below-average rates of return. A study by Peters using quarterly rebalancing supported the hypothesis of an inverse relationship.[12] These results would constitute an anomaly and would not support the EMH. A subsequent study by Reilly and Marshall assumed annual rebalancing and divided the sample on the basis of a risk measure (beta), market value size, and by expected growth rate.[13] Except for stocks with low betas and very low expected growth rates, the results were not consistent with the hypothesis of an inverse relationship between the PEG ratio and subsequent rates of return.

In summary, the results related to using the PEG ratio to select stocks are mixed—several studies that assume either monthly or quarterly rebalancing indicate an anomaly because the authors use public information and derive above-average rates of return. In contrast, a study with annual rebalancing indicated that no consistent relationship exists between the PEG ratio and subsequent rates of return.

The Size Effect   Several authors have examined the impact of size (measured by total market value) on the risk-adjusted rates of return. The risk-adjusted returns for extended periods (20 to 35 years) indicated that the small firms consistently experienced significantly larger risk-adjusted returns than the larger firms. It was contended that it was the size, not the P/E ratio, that caused the results discussed in the prior subsection, but this contention was disputed.

Recall that abnormal returns may occur because the markets are inefficient or because the market model provides incorrect estimates of risk and expected returns.

It was suggested that the riskiness of the small firms was improperly measured because small firms are traded less frequently. An alternative risk measure technique confirmed that the small firms had much higher risk, but the difference in beta did not account for the large difference in rates of return.

A study that examined the impact of transaction costs confirmed the size effect but also found that firms with small market value have low stock prices. Because transaction costs vary

---

[11]Composite performance measures are discussed in Chapter 26.

[12]Donald J. Peters, "Valuing a Growth Stock," *Journal of Portfolio Management* 17, no. 3 (Spring 1991): 49–51.

[13]Frank K. Reilly and Dominic R. Marshall, "Using P/E/Growth Ratios to Select Stocks," Financial Management Association Meeting (October 1999).

inversely with price per share, these costs must be considered when examining the small-firm effect. It was shown that there was a significant difference in the percentage total transaction cost for large firms (2.71 percent) versus small firms (6.77 percent). This differential in transaction costs, with frequent trading, can have a significant impact on the results. Assuming daily transactions, the original small-firm effects are reversed. The point is, size-effect studies must consider realistic transaction costs and specify holding period assumptions. Studies that have considered both factors over long periods have demonstrated that infrequent rebalancing (about once a year) is almost ideal—the results are better than long-run buy-and-hold and avoids frequent rebalancing that experiences excess costs. In summary, the small firms outperformed the large firms after considering risk and transaction costs, assuming annual rebalancing.

Most studies on the size effect employed large databases and long time periods (over 50 years) to show that this phenomenon has existed for many years. In contrast, a study that examined the performance over various intervals of time concluded that *the small-firm effect is not stable.* During most periods they found the negative relationship between size and return; but, during others (such as 1967 to 1975), they found that large firms outperformed the small firms. Notably, this positive relationship held during the following recent periods: 1984–87; 1989–90; and 1995–99. A study by Reinganum acknowledges this instability but contends that the small-firm effect is still a long-run phenomenon.[14]

In summary, firm size is a major efficient market anomaly. Numerous attempts to explain the size anomaly indicate that the two strongest explanations are the risk measurements and the higher transaction costs. Depending on the frequency of trading, these two factors may account for much of the differential. These results indicate that the size effect must be considered in any event study that uses long intervals and contains a sample of firms with significantly different market values.

Neglected Firms and Trading Activity   Arbel and Strebel considered an additional influence beyond size—attention or neglect.[15] They measured attention in terms of the number of analysts who regularly follow a stock and divided the stocks into three groups: (1) highly followed, (2) moderately followed, and (3) neglected. They confirmed the small-firm effect but also found a neglected-firm effect caused by the lack of information and limited institutional interest. The neglected-firm concept applied across size classes. Contrary results are reported by Beard and Sias who found no evidence of a neglected firm premium after controlling for capitalization[16]

Another study examined the impact of trading volume by considering the relationship between returns, market value, and trading activity. The results confirmed the relationship between size and rates of return, but the results indicated no significant difference between the mean returns of the highest and lowest trading activity portfolios. A subsequent study hypothesized that firms with less information require higher returns. Using the period of listing as a proxy for information, they found a negative relationship between returns and the period of listing after adjusting for firm size and the January effect.

Book Value–Market Value Ratio   This ratio relates the book value (BV) of a firm's equity to the market value (MV) of its equity. Roseberg, Reid, and Lanstein found a significant positive relationship between current values for this ratio and future stock returns and contended that

[14]Marc R. Reinganum, "A Revival of the Small-Firm Effect," *Journal of Portfolio Management* 18, no. 3 (Spring 1992): 55–62.

[15]Avner Arbel and Paul Strebel, "Pay Attention to Neglected Firms!" *Journal of Portfolio Management* 9, no. 2 (Winter 1983): 37–42.

[16]Craig Beard and Richard Sias, "Is There a Neglected-Firm Effect?" *Financial Analysts Journal* 53, no. 5 (September–October 1997): 19–23.

such a relationship between available public information on the BV/MV ratio and future returns was evidence against the EMH.[17]

Strong support for this ratio was provided by Fama and French who evaluated the joint effects of market beta, size, E/P ratio, leverage, and the BV/MV ratio (referred to as BE/ME) on a cross section of average returns.[18] They analyzed the hypothesized positive relationship between beta and expected returns and found that this positive relationship held pre-1969 but disappeared during the period 1963 to 1990. In contrast, the negative relationship between size and average return was significant by itself and significant after inclusion of other variables.

In addition, they found a significant positive relationship between the BV/MV ratio and average return that persisted even when other variables are included. Most importantly, *both* size and the BV/MV ratio are significant when included together and they dominate other ratios. Specifically, although leverage and the E/P ratio were significant by themselves or with size, they become insignificant when *both* size and the BV/MV ratio are considered.

The results in Exhibit 6.1 show the separate and combined effect of the two variables. As shown, going across the Small-ME (small size) row, BV/MV captures strong variation in average returns (0.70 to 1.92 percent). Alternatively, controlling for the BV/MV ratio leaves a size effect in average returns (the high BV/MV results decline from 1.92 to 1.18 percent when going from small to large). These positive results for the BV/MV ratio were replicated for returns on Japanese stocks.

In summary, studies that have used publicly available ratios to predict the cross section of expected returns for stocks have provided substantial evidence in conflict with the semistrong-form EMH. Significant results were found for P/E ratios, market value size, neglected firms, and BV/MV ratios. Although the Fama/French work indicated that the optimal combination appears to be size and the BV/MV ratio, a study by Jensen, Johnson, and Mercer indicates that this combination only works during periods of expansive monetary policy.[19]

Results of Event Studies

Recall that the intent of event studies is to examine abnormal rates of return surrounding significant economic information. Those who advocate the EMH would expect returns to adjust quickly to announcements of new information such that investors cannot experience positive abnormal rates of return by acting after the announcement. Because of space constraints, we can only summarize the results for some of the more popular events considered.

The discussion of results is organized by event or item of public information. Specifically, we will examine the price movements and profit potential surrounding stock splits, the sale of initial public offerings, exchange listings, unexpected world or economic events, and the announcements of significant accounting changes. Notably, the results for most of these studies have supported the semistrong-form EMH.

Stock Split Studies Many investors believe that the prices of stocks that split will increase in value because the shares are priced lower, which increases demand for them. In contrast, advocates of efficient markets would not expect a change in value because the firm has simply issued additional stock and nothing fundamentally affecting the value of the firm has occurred.

---

[17]Barr Rosenberg, Kenneth Reid, and Ronald Lanstein, "Persuasive Evidence of Market Inefficiency," *Journal of Portfolio Management* 11, no. 3 (Spring 1985): 9–17. Many studies define this ratio as "book-to-market value" (BV/MV) because it implies a positive relationship, but most practitioners refer to it as the "price-to-book value" (P/B) ratio. Obviously the concept is the same, but the sign changes.

[18]Eugene F. Fama and Kenneth R. French, "The Cross Section of Expected Stock Returns," *Journal of Finance* 47, no. 2 (June 1992): 427–465.

[19]Gerald R. Jensen, Robert R. Johnson, and Jeffrey M. Mercer, "New Evidence on Size and Price-to-Book Effects in Stock Returns," *Financial Analysts Journal* 53 no. 6 (November–December 1997): 34–42.

| EXHIBIT 6.1 ▶ | *AVERAGE MONTHLY RETURNS ON PORTFOLIOS FORMED ON SIZE AND BOOK-TO-MARKET EQUITY; STOCKS SORTED BY ME (DOWN) AND THEN BE/ME (ACROSS); JULY 1963 TO DECEMBER 1990* |

In June of each year *t*, the NYSE, AMEX, and Nasdaq stocks that meet the CRSP-COMPUSTAT data requirements are allocated to 10 size portfolios using the NYSE size (ME) breakpoints. The NYSE, AMEX, and Nasdaq stocks in each size decile are then sorted into 10 BE/ME portfolios using the book-to-market ratios for year $t-1$. BE/ME is the book value of common equity plus balance-sheet deferred taxes for fiscal year $t-1$, over market equity for December of year $t-1$. The equal-weighted monthly portfolio returns are then calculated for July of year *t* to June of year $t+1$.

Average monthly return is the time-series average of the monthly equal-weighted portfolio returns (in percent).

The All column shows average returns for equal-weighted size decile portfolios. The All row shows average returns for equal-weighted portfolios of the stocks in each BE/ME group

					BOOK-TO-MARKET PORTFOLIOS						
	ALL	LOW	2	3	4	5	6	7	8	9	HIGH
All	1.23	0.64	0.98	1.06	1.17	1.24	1.26	1.39	1.40	1.50	1.63
Small-ME	1.47	0.70	1.14	1.20	1.43	1.56	1.51	1.70	1.71	1.82	1.92
ME-2	1.22	0.43	1.05	0.96	1.19	1.33	1.19	1.58	1.28	1.43	1.79
ME-3	1.22	0.56	0.88	1.23	0.95	1.36	1.30	1.30	1.40	1.54	1.60
ME-4	1.19	0.39	0.72	1.06	1.36	1.13	1.21	1.34	1.59	1.51	1.47
ME-5	1.24	0.88	0.65	1.08	1.47	1.13	1.43	1.44	1.26	1.52	1.49
ME-6	1.15	0.70	0.98	1.14	1.23	0.94	1.27	1.19	1.19	1.24	1.50
ME-7	1.07	0.95	1.00	0.99	0.83	0.99	1.13	0.99	1.16	1.10	1.47
ME-8	1.08	0.66	1.13	0.91	0.95	0.99	1.01	1.15	1.05	1.29	1.55
ME-9	0.95	0.44	0.89	0.92	1.00	1.05	0.93	0.82	1.11	1.04	1.22
Large-ME	0.89	0.93	0.88	0.84	0.71	0.79	0.83	0.81	0.96	0.97	1.18

Source: Eugene F. Fama and Kenneth French, "The Cross Section of Expected Stock Returns," *Journal of Finance* 47, no. 2 (June 1992): 446. Reprinted with permission of Blackwell Publishing.

The classic FFJR study hypothesized no significant price change following a stock split because any relevant information (such as earnings growth) that caused the split would have already been discounted.[20]

The FFJR study analyzed abnormal price movements surrounding the time of the split and divided the stock split sample into those stocks that did or did not raise their dividends. Both groups experienced positive abnormal price changes prior to the split. Stocks that split but did *not* increase their dividend experienced abnormal price *declines* following the split and within 12 months lost all their accumulated abnormal gains. In contrast, stocks that split and also increased their dividend experienced no abnormal returns after the split.

These results support the semistrong EMH because they indicate that investors cannot gain from the information on a stock split after the public announcement. These results were confirmed by most (but not all) subsequent studies.

In summary, most studies found no short-run or long-run positive impact on security returns because of a stock split, although the results are not unanimous.

---

[20]E. F. Fama, L. Fisher, M. Jensen, and R. Roll, "The Adjustment of Stock Prices to New Information," *International Economic Review* 10, no. 1 (February 1969): 1–21.

Initial Public Offerings (IPOs)   During the past 20 years, a number of closely held companies have gone public by selling some of their common stock. Because of uncertainty about the appropriate offering price and the risk involved in underwriting such issues, it has been hypothesized that the underwriters would tend to underprice these new issues.

Given this general expectation of underpricing, the studies in this area have generally considered three sets of questions: (1) How great is the underpricing on average? Does the underpricing vary over time? If so, why? (2) What factors cause different amounts of underpricing for alternative issues? (3) How fast does the market adjust the price for the underpricing?

The answer to the first question is an average underpricing of almost 18 percent, but it varies over time as shown by the results in Exhibit 6.2. The major variables that cause differential underpricing seem to be: various risk measures, the size of the firm, the prestige of the underwriter, and the status of the firm's accounting firms. Finally, on the question of direct interest to the EMH, results indicate that the price adjustment to the underpricing takes place within one day after the offering.[21] Therefore, it appears that some underpricing occurs based on the original offering price, but the only ones who benefit from this underpricing are investors who receive allocations of the original issue. Further, a more recent study showed that institutional investors captured most (70 percent) of the short-term profits. This rapid adjustment of the initial underpricing would support the semistrong EMH. Finally, several studies that examined the long-run returns on IPOs indicate that investors who acquire the stock after the initial adjustment do *not* experience positive long-run abnormal returns.[22]

Exchange Listing   A significant economic event for a firm is its stock being listed on a national exchange, especially the NYSE. Such a listing is expected to increase the market liquidity of the stock and add to its prestige. An important question is, can an investor derive abnormal returns from investing in the stock when a new listing is announced or around the time of the actual listing? The results regarding abnormal returns from such investing were mixed. All the studies agreed that (1) the stocks' prices increased before any listing announcements, and (2) stock prices consistently declined after the actual listing. The crucial question is, what happens between the announcement of the application for listing and the actual listing (a period of four to six weeks)? Recent studies point toward profit opportunities immediately after the announcement that a firm is applying for listing and the possibility of excess returns from price declines after the actual listing.[23] Finally, studies that have examined the impact of listing on the risk of the securities found no significant change in systematic risk or the firm's cost of equity.

In summary, these listing studies that provide some evidence of short-run profit opportunities for investors using public information would not support the semistrong-form EMH.

Unexpected World Events and Economic News   The results of several studies that examined the response of security prices to world or economic news have supported the semistrong-form EMH. An analysis of the reaction of stock prices to unexpected world events, such as the Eisenhower heart attack, the Kennedy assassination, and military events, found that prices

---

[21]In this regard, see Robert E. Miller and Frank K. Reilly, "An Examination of Mispricing, Returns, and Uncertainty for Initial Public Offerings," *Financial Management* 16, no. 2 (January 1987): 33–38. For an excellent review of the research on this topic, see Roger G. Ibbotson, Jody L. Sindelar, and Jay R. Ritter, "The Market Problems with the Pricing of Initial Public Offerings," *Journal of Applied Corporate Finance* 7, no. 1 (Spring 1994): 66–74.

[22]This is documented in Jay R. Ritter, "The Long-Run Performance of Initial Public Offerings," *Journal of Finance* 46, no. 1 (March 1991): 3–27; Richard B. Carter, Frederick Dark, and Asah Singh, "Underwriter Reputation, Initial Returns, and the Long-Run Performance of IPO Stocks," *Journal of Finance,* 53, no. 1 (February 1998): 285–311; and Timothy Loughran and Jay Ritter "The New Issues Puzzle," *Journal of Finance* 50, no. 1 (March 1995).

[23]See John J. McConnell and Gary Sanger, "A Trading Strategy for New Listings on the NYSE," *Financial Analysts Journal* 40, no. 1 (January–February 1989): 38–39.

EXHIBIT 6.2 ▶ *NUMBERS OF OFFERINGS, AVERAGE FIRST-DAY RETURNS, AND GROSS PROCEEDS OF INITIAL PUBLIC OFFERINGS IN 1975–2000*

Year	Number of Offerings[a]	Average First-Day Return, %[b]	Gross Proceeds, $ Millions[c]
1975	12	−1.5	262
1976	26	1.9	214
1977	15	3.6	127
1978	20	11.2	209
1979	39	8.5	312
1980	78	15.2	962
1981	202	6.4	2,386
1982	83	10.6	1,081
1983	523	8.8	12,047
1984	227	2.6	3,012
1985	215	6.2	5,488
1986	464	6.0	16,195
1987	322	5.5	12,160
1988	121	5.6	4,053
1989	113	7.8	5,212
1990	111	10.5	4,453
1991	287	11.7	15,765
1992	396	10.0	22,198
1993	503	12.6	29,232
1994	412	9.7	18,103
1995	464	21.1	28,866
1996	664	16.7	41,916
1997	483	13.7	33,216
1998	318	20.1	34,856
1999	491	69.0	65,471
2000	385	55.5	66,100
1975–79	112	5.7	1,124
1980–89	2,348	6.8	62,596
1990–99	4,129	20.9	294,076
2000	385	55.5	66,100
Total	6,974	17.8	423,896

[a]The number of offerings excludes IPOs with an offer price of less than $5.00, ADRs, best efforts offers, unit offers, Regulation A offerings (small issues, raising less than $1.5 million during the 1980s), real estate investment trusts (REITs), partnerships, and closed-end funds.

[b]First-day returns are computed as the percentage return from the offering price to the first closing market price.

[c]Gross proceeds data are from Securities Data Co. and exclude overallotment options but include the international tranche, if any. No adjustments for inflation have been made.

Source: Jay R. Ritter, "Summary Statistics on 1975–2000 Initial Public Offerings with an Offer Price of $5.00 or More" (University of Florida, January 29, 2001).

adjusted to the news before the market opened or before it reopened after the announcement (generally, as with the World Trade Center attack, the Exchanges are closed immediately for various time periods—e.g., 1–4 days). A study that examined the response to announcements about money supply, inflation, real economic activity, and the discount rate found either no impact or an impact that did not persist beyond the announcement day. Finally, an analysis of hourly stock returns and trading volume response to surprise announcements about money supply, prices, industrial production, and the unemployment rate found that unexpected information about money supply and prices impacted stock prices within one hour.

Announcements of Accounting Changes   Numerous studies have analyzed the impact of announcements of accounting changes on stock prices. In efficient markets, security prices should react quickly and predictably to announcements of accounting changes. An announcement of an accounting change that affects the economic value of the firm should cause a rapid change in stock prices. An accounting change that affects reported earnings but has no economic significance should not affect stock prices. For example, when a firm changes its depreciation accounting method for reporting purposes from accelerated to straight line, the firm should experience an increase in reported earnings, but there is no economic consequence. An analysis of stock price movements surrounding this accounting change supported the EMH because there were no positive price changes following the change, and there were some negative price changes because firms making such an accounting change are typically performing poorly.

During periods of high inflation, many firms will change their inventory method from first-in, first-out (FIFO) to last-in, first-out (LIFO), which causes a decline in reported earnings but benefits the firm because it reduces its taxable earnings and, therefore, tax expenses. Advocates of efficient markets would expect positive price changes because of the tax savings, and study results confirmed this expectation.

Therefore, these studies indicate that the securities markets react quite rapidly to accounting changes and adjust security prices as expected on the basis of changes in true value (that is, analysts pierce the accounting veil and value securities on the basis of economic events).[24]

Corporate Events   Corporate finance events such as mergers and acquisitions, reorganization, and various security offerings (common stock, straight bonds, convertible bonds) have been examined, relative to two general questions: (1) What is the market impact of these alternative events? (2) How fast does the market adjust the security prices?

Regarding the reaction to corporate events, the answer is very consistent—stock prices react as one would expect based on the underlying economic impact of the action. For example, the reaction to mergers is that the stock of the firm being acquired increases in line with the premium offered by the acquiring firm, whereas the stock of the acquiring firm typically declines because of the concern that they overpaid for the firm. On the question of speed of reaction, the evidence indicates fairly rapid adjustment—that is, the adjustment period declines as shorter interval data is analyzed (using daily data, most studies find that the price adjustment is completed in about three days). Studies related to financing decisions are reviewed by Smith.[25] Studies on corporate control that consider mergers and reorganizations are reviewed by Jensen and Warner.[26]

---

[24]For a review of studies on this contention, see V. Bernard and J. Thomas, "Evidence That Stock Prices Do Not Fully Reflect the Implications of Current Earnings for Future Earnings," *Journal of Accounting and Economics* (December 1990): 305–341.

[25]Clifford W. Smith, Jr., "Investment Banking and the Capital Acquisition Process," *Journal of Financial Economics* 15, no. 1–2 (January–February 1986): 3–29.

[26]Michael C. Jensen and Jerald B. Warner, "The Distribution of Power among Corporate Managers, Shareholders, and Directors," *Journal of Financial Economics* 20, no. 1–2 (January–March 1988): 3–24.

Summary on the Semistrong-Form EMH   Clearly, the evidence from tests of the semistrong EMH is mixed. The hypothesis receives almost unanimous support from the numerous event studies on a range of events including stock splits, initial public offerings, world events and economic news, accounting changes, and a variety of corporate finance events. About the only mixed results come from exchange listing studies.

In sharp contrast, the numerous studies on predicting rates of return over time or for a cross section of stocks presented evidence counter to semistrong efficiency. This included time-series studies on risk premiums, calender patterns, and quarterly earnings surprises. Similarly, the results for cross-sectional predictors such as size, the BV/MV ratio (when there is expansive monetary policy), P/E ratios, and some neglected firm studies indicated nonefficiencies.

Strong-Form Hypothesis: Tests and Results   The strong-form EMH contends that stock prices fully reflect *all information,* public and private. This implies that no group of investors has access to *private information* that will allow them to consistently experience above-average profits. This extremely rigid hypothesis requires not only that stock prices must adjust rapidly to new public information but also that no group has access to private information.

Tests of the strong-form EMH have analyzed returns over time for different identifiable investment groups to determine whether any group consistently received above-average risk-adjusted returns. Such a group must have access to and act upon important private information or an ability to act on public information before other investors, which would indicate that security prices were not adjusting rapidly to *all* new information.

Investigators have tested this form of the EMH by analyzing the performance of the following four major groups of investors: (1) *corporate insiders,* (2) *stock exchange specialists,* (3) *security analysts* at Value Line and elsewhere, and (4) *professional money managers.*

Corporate Insider Trading   Corporate insiders are required to report monthly to the SEC on their transactions (purchases or sales) in the stock of the firm for which they are insiders. Insiders include major corporate officers, members of the board of directors, and owners of 10 percent or more of any equity class of securities. About six weeks after the reporting period, this insider trading information is made public by the SEC. These insider trading data have been used to identify how corporate insiders have traded and determine whether they bought on balance before abnormally good price movements and sold on balance before poor market periods for their stock.[27] The results of these studies have generally indicated that corporate insiders consistently enjoyed above-average profits, especially on purchase transactions. This implies that many insiders had private information from which they derived above-average returns on their company stock.

In addition, an early study found that *public* investors who consistently traded with the insiders based on announced insider transactions would have enjoyed excess risk-adjusted returns (after commissions), although a subsequent study concluded that the market had eliminated this inefficiency after considering total transaction costs.

Overall, these results provide mixed support for the EMH because several studies indicate that insiders experience abnormal profits, while subsequent studies indicate it is no longer possible for noninsiders to use this information to generate excess returns. Notably, because of investor interest in these data as a result of academic research, *The Wall Street Journal* currently publishes a monthly column entitled "Inside Track" that discusses the largest insider transactions.

---

[27]Studies on this topic include M. Chowdhury, J. S. Howe, and J. C. Lin, "The Relation between Aggregate Insider Transactions and Stock Market Returns," *Journal of Financial and Quantitative Analysis* 28, no. 3 (September 1993): 431–437; and R. R. Pettit and P. C. Venkatesh, "Insider Trading and Long-Run Return Performance," *Financial Management* 24, no. 2 (Summer 1995): 88–103.

Stock Exchange Specialists   Several studies have determined that specialists have monopolistic access to certain important information about unfilled limit orders, and they should be able to derive above-average returns from this information. This expectation is generally supported by the data. First, specialists generally make money because they typically sell shares at higher prices than their purchased price. Also, they apparently make money when they buy or sell after unexpected announcements and when they trade in large blocks of stock. A recent article in *The Wall Street Journal* supported this belief; it contended that specialists are doing more trading as dealers and the return on their capital during 2000 was 26%.[28]

Security Analysts   Several tests have considered whether it is possible to identify a set of analysts who have the ability to select undervalued stocks. The analysis involves determining whether, after a stock selection by an analyst is made known, a significant abnormal return is available to those who follow these recommendations. These studies and those that discuss performance by money managers are more realistic and relevant than those that considered corporate insiders and stock exchange specialists because these analysts and money managers are full-time investment professionals with no obvious advantage except emphasis and training. If anyone should be able to select undervalued stocks, it should be these "pros." We initially examine Value Line rankings and then analyze what returns investors experience when they follow the recommendations by individual analysts.

The Value Line Enigma   Value Line (VL) is a large well-known advisory service that publishes financial information on approximately 1,700 stocks. Included in its report is a timing rank, which indicates Value Line's expectation regarding a firm's common stock performance over the coming 12 months. A rank of 1 is the most favorable performance and 5 the worst. This ranking system, initiated in April 1965, assigns numbers based on four factors:

1. An earnings and price rank of each security relative to all others
2. A price momentum factor
3. Year-to-year relative changes in quarterly earnings
4. A quarterly earnings "surprise" factor (actual quarterly earnings compared with VL estimated earnings)

The firms are ranked based on a composite score for each firm. The top and bottom 100 are ranked 1 and 5, respectively; the next 300 from the top and bottom are ranked 2 and 4; and the rest (approximately 900) are ranked 3. Rankings are assigned every week based on the latest data. Notably, all the data used to derive the four factors are public information.

Several years after the ranking was started, Value Line contended that the stocks rated 1 substantially outperformed the market and the stocks rated 5 seriously underperformed the market (the performance figures did not include dividend income but also did not charge commissions).

Studies on the Value Line enigma indicate that there is information in the VL rankings (especially either rank 1 or 5) and in changes in the rankings (especially going from 2 to 1). Further, recent evidence indicates that the market is fairly efficient, because the abnormal adjustments appear to be complete by Day + 2. An analysis of study results over time indicates a faster adjustment to the rankings during recent years. Also, despite statistically significant price changes, mounting evidence indicates that it is not possible to derive abnormal returns from these announcements after considering realistic transaction costs. The strongest evidence regarding not being able to use this information is that Value Line's Centurion Fund, which concentrates on investing in rank-1 stocks, has consistently underperformed the market over the past decade.

---

[28]Greg Ip, "If Big Board Specialists Are an Anachronism, They're a Profitable One," *The Wall Street Journal* (12 March 2001), A1, A10.

Analysts' Recommendations   There is evidence in favor of the existence of superior analysts who apparently possess private information. This evidence is provided in two studies where the authors found that the prices of stocks mentioned in *The Wall Street Journal* column "Heard on the Street" experience a significant change on the day that the column appears. A study by Womach found that analysts appear to have both market timing and stock-picking ability, especially in connection with relatively rare sell recommendations.[29]

Performance of Professional Money Managers   The studies of professional money managers are more realistic and widely applicable than the analysis of insiders and specialists because money managers typically do not have monopolistic access to important new information but are highly trained professionals who work full time at investment management. Therefore, if any "normal" set of investors should be able to derive above-average profits, it should be this group. Also, if any noninsider should be able to derive inside information, professional money managers should, because they conduct extensive management interviews.

Most studies on the performance of money managers have examined mutual funds because performance data is readily available for them. Recently, data have become available for bank trust departments, insurance companies, and investment advisers. The original mutual fund studies indicated that most funds did not match the performance of a buy-and-hold policy.[30] When risk-adjusted returns were examined *without* considering commission costs, slightly more than half of the money managers did better than the overall market. When commission costs, load fees, and management costs were considered, approximately two-thirds of the mutual funds did *not* match aggregate market performance. It was also found that successful funds during individual years were inconsistent in their performance.

Now that it is possible to get performance data for pension plans and endowment funds, several studies have documented that the performances of pension plans and endowments did not match that of the aggregate market.

The figures in Exhibit 6.3 provide a rough demonstration of these results for recent periods. These data are collected by Frank Russell Analytical Services as part of its performance evaluation service. Exhibit 6.3 contains the median rates of return for several investment groups compared to the Standard & Poor's 500 Index.[31] These results show that for short-term periods (1–2–4 years) the majority of groups beat the S&P 500, but for the long 6-year horizon only 3 of 10 outperformed. Assuming we are more concerned with long-run performance, this would support the EMH.

Conclusions Regarding the Strong-Form EMH   The tests of the strong-form EMH generated mixed results, but the bulk of relevant evidence supported the hypothesis. The results for two unique groups of investors (corporate insiders and stock exchange specialists) did not support the hypothesis because both groups apparently have monopolistic access to important information and use it to derive above-average returns.

Tests to determine whether there are any analysts with private information concentrated on the Value Line rankings and publications of analysts' recommendations. The results for Value Line rankings have changed over time and currently tend toward support for the EMH. Specifically, the adjustment to rankings and ranking changes is fairly rapid, and it appears that trading

---

[29]Kent L. Womach, "Do Brokerage Analysts' Recommendations Have Investment Value?" *Journal of Finance* 51, no. 1 (March 1996): 137–167.

[30]These studies and others on this topic are reviewed in Chapter 25.

[31]The results for these individual accounts have an upward bias because they consider only accounts retained (for example, if a firm or bank does a poor job on an account and the client leaves, those results would not be included).

ANNUALIZED RATES OF RETURN DURING ALTERNATIVE PERIODS ENDING DECEMBER 31, 2000

	1 Year	2 Years	4 Years	6 Years
U.S. Equity Broad Universe Medians				
Equity accounts	−17.6	−0.4	13.6	17.2
Equity pooled accounts	−20.3	−1.0	13.1	16.5
Equity-oriented separate accounts	−17.0	0.0	13.8	17.6
Special equity pooled accounts	−6.2	16.1	12.3	15.0
Mutual Fund Universe Medians				
Balanced mutual funds	−7.2	1.8	9.2	11.4
Equity mutual funds	−13.8	2.4	11.5	14.4
U.S. Equity Style Universe Medians				
Growth equity accounts	−39.6	−6.7	13.9	16.8
Small capitalization accounts	−6.9	15.9	13.3	15.3
Value equity accounts	10.4	6.7	12.9	16.6
Market-oriented accounts	−19.2	−1.2	13.9	17.7
S&P 500 Index	−21.7	−3.9	12.8	17.0
Number of universes with returns above the S&P 500	9	9	7	3

is not profitable after transactions costs. Alternatively, individual analysts' recommendations seem to contain significant information.

Finally, the performance by professional money managers generally provided support for the strong-form EMH. The vast majority of money manager performance studies have indicated that these highly trained, full-time investors could not consistently outperform a simple buy-and-hold policy on a risk-adjusted basis. This has been consistently true for mutual funds, pension plans, and endowment funds over long-term periods. Because money managers are similar to most investors who do not have access to inside information, these latter results are considered more relevant to the hypothesis. Therefore, it appears that there is support for the strong-form EMH as applied to most investors.

BEHAVIORAL FINANCE

The discussion up to this point in the chapter has dealt with standard finance theory, how this theory assumes that the capital markets function, and how to test within this theoretical context whether capital markets are informationally efficient. Notably, during the last decade, a new branch of financial economics has been developed referred to as **behavioral finance**, which is concerned with the analysis of various psychological traits of individuals and how these traits affect how they act as investors, analysts, and portfolio managers. As noted by Olsen, behavioral finance recognizes that the standard finance model of rational behavior and profit maximization can be true within specific boundaries, but advocates of behavioral finance assert that this model is *incomplete* since it does not consider individual behavior.[32] Specifically, behavioral finance

---

[32]Robert A. Olsen, "Behavioral Finance and Its Implications for Stock-Price Volatility," *Financial Analysts Journal* 54, no. 2 (March/April 1998): 10–18.

Seeks to understand and predict systematic financial market implications of psychological decision processes. . . . Behavioral finance is focused on the implication of psychological and economic principles for the improvement of financial decision making.[33]

While it is acknowledged that currently there is no unified theory of behavioral finance, the emphasis has been on identifying portfolio anomalies that can be explained by various psychological traits in individuals or groups or pinpointing instances where it is possible to experience above-normal rates of return by exploiting the biases of analysts or portfolio managers. The following subsection discusses some anamolies that can be explained by psychology or some biased actions that can be exploited.

Explaining Biases   Over time, it has been noted that investors have a number of biases that negatively affect their investment performance. Advocates of behavioral finance have been able to explain a number of these biases based on psychological characteristics. A major documented bias is the propensity of investors to hold on to losing positions too long and sell "winners" too soon.[34] The point is, investors fear losses much more than they value gains. This is explained by prospect theory, which contends that utility depends on deviations from moving reference points rather than absolute wealth. Another bias they mention is overconfidence in forecasts, which causes analysts to overestimate growth rates for growth companies. In addition, they overemphasize good news for firms evaluated and ignore negative news items—that is, they generally believe that the stocks of the growth companies they have analyzed will be "good" stocks. This is referred to as "confirmation bias," where investors look for information that supports their prior opinion and decision. As a result, they tend to misvalue the stocks of these generally popular companies.

A study by Brown examined the effect of "noise traders" (nonprofessionals with no special information) on the volatility of closed-end mutual funds.[35] When there is a shift in sentiment, these traders move heavily, which increases the prices and the volatility of these securities during trading hours. Also, Clark and Statman find that noise traders tend to follow newsletter writers, who in turn tend to "follow the herd"; and these writers and "the herd" are almost always wrong, which contributes to excess volatility.[36]

There is also "escalation bias," which causes investors to put more money into a failure that they feel responsible for rather than into a success.[37] This leads to the relatively popular investor practice of "averaging down" on an investment that has declined in value since the initial purchase rather than consider selling the stock if it was a mistake—for example, if it was a buy at $40, it is a screaming bargain at $30. Obviously, the appropriate action is to go through a revaluation of the stock to determine if you missed some important bad news in your initial valuation (therefore, sell it and accept your loss) or confirm your initial valuation and acquire more of the "bargain." The difficult psychological factor is to seriously look for the bad news and consider the effects of that negative information on your prior valuation.[38]

---

[33]Ibid.: 11.

[34]This is discussed in J. Scott, M. Stumpp, and P. Xu, "Behavioral Bias Valuation and Active Management," *Financial Analysts Journal* 55, no. 4 (July–August 1999): 49–57.

[35]Gregory Brown, "Volatility, Sentiment, and Noise Traders," *Financial Analysts Journal* 55, no. 2 (March–April 1999): 82–90.

[36]R. G. Clark and M. Statman, "Bullish or Bearish," *Financial Analysts Journal* 54, no. 3 (May–June 1998): 63–72.

[37]Hersh Shefrin, "Behavioral Corporate Finance," *Journal of Applied Corporate Finance* 14, no. 3 (Fall 2001): 113–124.

[38]For an extended presentation on this topic, see Hersh Shefrin, *Beyond Greed and Fear: Understanding Behavioral Finance and the Psychology of Investing* (Boston: Harvard Business School Press, 1999).

> IMPLICATIONS OF EFFICIENT CAPITAL MARKETS

Having reviewed the results of numerous studies related to different facets of the EMH, the important question is, What does this mean to individual investors, financial analysts, portfolio managers, and institutions? Overall, the results of many studies indicate that the capital markets are efficient as related to numerous sets of information. At the same time, research has uncovered a substantial number of instances where the market fails to adjust prices rapidly to public information. Given these mixed results regarding the existence of efficient capital markets, it is important to consider the implications of this contrasting evidence of market efficiency.

The following discussion considers the implications of both sets of evidence. Specifically given results that support the EMH, we consider what techniques will not work and what you should do if you cannot beat the market. In contrast, because of the evidence that fails to support the EMH, we discuss what information and psychological biases should be considered when attempting to derive superior investment results through active security valuation and portfolio management.

Efficient Markets and Technical Analysis

The assumptions of technical analysis directly oppose the notion of efficient markets. A basic premise of technical analysis is that stock prices move in trends that persist.[39] Technicians believe that when new information comes to the market, it is not immediately available to everyone but is typically disseminated from the informed professional to the aggressive investing public and then to the great bulk of investors. Also, technicians contend that investors do not analyze information and act immediately. This process takes time. Therefore, they hypothesize that stock prices move to a new equilibrium after the release of new information in a gradual manner, which causes trends in stock price movements that persist.

Technical analysts believe that nimble traders can develop systems to detect the beginning of a movement to a new equilibrium (called a "breakout"). Hence, they hope to buy or sell the stock immediately after its breakout to take advantage of the subsequent, gradual price adjustment.

The belief in this pattern of price adjustment directly contradicts advocates of the EMH who believe that security prices adjust to new information very rapidly. These EMH advocates do not contend, however, that prices adjust perfectly, which implies a chance of overadjustment or underadjustment. Still, because it is uncertain whether the market will over- or underadjust at any time, you cannot derive abnormal profits from adjustment errors.

If the capital market is weak-form efficient as indicated by most of the results, then prices fully reflect all relevant market information so technical trading systems that depend only on past trading data *cannot* have any value. By the time the information is public, the price adjustment has taken place. Therefore, a purchase or sale using a technical trading rule should not generate abnormal returns after taking account of risk and transaction costs.

Efficient Markets and Fundamental Analysis

As you know from our prior discussion, fundamental analysts believe that, at any time, there is a basic intrinsic value for the aggregate stock market, various industries, or individual securities and that these values depend on underlying economic factors. Therefore, investors should determine the intrinsic value of an investment asset at a point in time by examining the variables that determine value such as current and future earnings or cash flows, interest rates, and risk variables. If the prevailing market price differs from the estimated intrinsic value by enough to cover transaction costs, you should take appropriate action: You buy if the market price is substantially below intrinsic value and sell if it is above. Investors who engaged in fundamental analysis believe that, occasionally, market price and intrinsic value differ but, eventually, investors recognize the discrepancy and correct it.

---

[39]Chapter 16 contains an extensive discussion of technical analysis.

If you can do a superior job of *estimating* intrinsic value, you can consistently make superior market timing (asset allocation) decisions or acquire undervalued securities and generate above-average returns. Fundamental analysis involves aggregate market analysis, industry analysis, company analysis, and portfolio management. The divergent results from the EMH research have important implications for all of these components.

Aggregate Market Analysis with Efficient Capital Markets   Chapter 11 makes a strong case that intrinsic value analysis should begin with aggregate market analysis. Still, the EMH implies that if you examine only *past* economic events, it is unlikely that you will be able to outperform a buy-and-hold policy because the market rapidly adjusts to known economic events. Evidence suggests that the market experiences long-run price movements; but, to take advantage of these movements in an efficient market, you must do a superior job of *estimating* the relevant variables that cause these long-run movements. Put another way, if you only use *historical* data to estimate future values and invest on the basis of these estimates, you will *not* experience superior, risk-adjusted returns.

Industry and Company Analysis with Efficient Capital Markets   As discussed in Chapter 11, the wide distribution of returns from different industries and companies clearly justifies industry and company analysis. Again, the EMH does not contradict the potential value of such analysis but implies that you need to (1) understand the relevant variables that affect rates of return and (2) do a superior job of *estimating future* values for these relevant valuation variables. To demonstrate this, Malkiel and Cragg developed a model that did an excellent job of explaining past stock price movements using historical data. When this valuation model was employed to project *future* stock price changes using *past* company data, however, the results were consistently inferior to a buy-and-hold policy.[40] This implies that, even with a good valuation model, you cannot select stocks that will provide superior future returns using only past data as inputs. The point is, most analysts are aware of the several well-specified valuation models, so the factor that differentiates superior from inferior analysts is the ability to *provide more accurate estimates* of the critical inputs to the valuation models.

Another study showed that the crucial difference between the stocks that enjoyed the best and worst price performance during a given year was the relationship between expected earnings of professional analysts and actual earnings (that is, it was *earnings surprises*). Specifically, stock prices increased if actual earnings substantially exceeded expected earnings and stock prices fell if actual earnings did not reach expected levels. Thus, if you can do a superior job of projecting earnings and your expectations *differ from the consensus,* you will have a superior stock selection record.[41] Put another way, there are two factors that are required to be superior: (1) you must be *correct* in your estimates, and (2) you must be *different* from the consensus. Remember that, if you are only correct and not different, that assumes you were predicting the consensus and the consensus was correct, which implies no surprise and no abnormal price movement.

The quest to be a superior analyst holds some good news and some suggestions. The good news is related to the strong-form tests that indicated the likely existence of superior analysts. It was shown that the rankings by Value Line contained information value, even though it might not be possible to profit from the work of these analysts after transaction costs. Also, the price adjustments to the publication of analyst recommendations also point to the existence of

---

[40]Burton G. Malkiel and John G. Cragg, "Expectations and the Structure of Share Prices," *American Economic Review* 60, no. 4 (September 1970): 601–617.

[41]This is a major point made in H. Russell Fogler, "A Modern Theory of Security Analysis," *Journal of Portfolio Management* 19, no. 3 (Spring 1993): 6–14.

superior analysts. The point is, there are some superior analysts, but a limited number, and it is *not* an easy task to be among this select group. Most notably, to be a superior analyst you must do a superior job of *estimating* the relevant valuation variables and *predicting earning surprises.*

The suggestions for those involved in fundamental analysis are based on the studies that considered the cross section of future returns. As noted, these studies indicated that P/E ratios, size, and the BV/MV ratios were able to differentiate future return patterns with size and the BV/MV ratio appearing to be the optimal combination. Therefore, these factors should be considered when selecting a universe or analyzing firms. In addition, the evidence suggests that neglected firms should be given extra consideration. Although these ratios and characteristics have been shown to be useful in isolating superior stocks from a large sample, it is our suggestion that they are best used to derive a viable sample to analyze from the total universe (e.g., select 200 stocks to analyze from a universe of 3,000). Then the 200 stocks should be rigorously valued using the techniques discussed in this text.

How to Evaluate Analysts or Investors

If you want to determine if an individual is a superior analyst or investor, you should examine the performance of numerous securities that this analyst or investor recommends over time in relation to the performance of a set of randomly selected stocks of the same risk class. The stock selections of a superior analyst or investor should *consistently* outperform the randomly selected stocks. The consistency requirement is crucial because you would expect a portfolio developed by random selection to outperform the market about half the time.

Conclusions about Fundamental Analysis

A text on investments can indicate the relevant variables that you should analyze and describe the important analysis techniques, but actually estimating the relevant variables is as much an art and a product of hard work as it is a science. If the estimates could be done on the basis of some mechanical formula, you could program a computer to do it, and there would be no need for analysts. Therefore, the superior analyst or successful investor must understand what variables are relevant to the valuation process and have the ability and work ethic to do a superior job of *estimating* these variables. Alternatively, one can be superior if he or she has the ability to interpret the impact or estimate the effect of some public information better than others.

Efficient Markets and Portfolio Management

As noted, studies have indicated that the majority of professional money managers cannot beat a buy-and-hold policy on a risk-adjusted basis. One explanation for this generally inferior performance is that there are no superior analysts and the cost of research and trading forces the results of merely adequate analysis into the inferior category. Another explanation, which is favored by the author and has some empirical support from the Value Line and analyst recommendation results, is that money management firms employ both superior and inferior analysts and the gains from the recommendations by the few superior analysts are offset by the costs and the poor results derived from the recommendations of the inferior analysts.

This raises the question, Should a portfolio be managed actively or passively? The point of the following discussion is that the decision of how one manages the portfolio (actively or passively) should depend on whether the manager has access to superior analysts. A portfolio manager with superior analysts or an investor who believes that he or she has the time and expertise to be a superior investor can manage a portfolio actively by attempting to time major market trends or looking for undervalued securities and trading accordingly. In contrast, without access to superior analysts or the time and ability to be a superior investor, you should manage passively and assume that all securities are properly priced based on their levels of risk.

Portfolio Management with Superior Analysts   A portfolio manager with access to superior analysts who have unique insights and analytical ability should follow their recommendations. The superior analysts should make investment recommendations for a certain proportion of the portfolio, and the portfolio manager should ensure that the risk preferences of the client are maintained.

Also, the superior analysts should be encouraged to concentrate their efforts in mid-cap stocks that possess the liquidity required by institutional portfolio managers; but, because they do not receive the attention given the top-tier stocks, the markets for these neglected stocks may be less efficient than the market for large well-known stocks.

Recall that capital markets are expected to be efficient because many investors receive new information and analyze its effect on security values. If the number of analysts following a stock differ, one could conceive of differences in the efficiency of the markets. New information on top-tier stocks is well publicized and rigorously analyzed so the price of these securities should adjust rapidly to reflect the new information. In contrast, middle-tier firms receive less publicity and fewer analysts follow these firms, so prices might be expected to adjust less rapidly to new information. Therefore, the possibility of finding temporarily undervalued securities among these neglected stocks is greater. Again, in line with the cross-section study results, these superior analysts should pay particular attention to the BV/MV ratio, to the size of stocks being analyzed, and to the monetary policy environment.

Portfolio Management without Superior Analysts   If you do not have access to superior analysts, your procedure should be as follows. First, you should *measure your risk preferences* or those of your clients. Then build a portfolio to match this risk level by investing a certain proportion of the portfolio in risky assets and the rest in a risk-free asset as discussed in Chapter 8.

You must *completely diversify* the risky asset portfolio on a global basis so it moves consistently with the world market. In this context, proper diversification means eliminating all unsystematic (unique) variability. In our prior discussion, it was estimated that it required about 20 securities to gain most of the benefits (more than 90 percent) of a completely diversified portfolio. More than 100 stocks are required for complete diversification. To decide how many securities to actually include in your global portfolio, you must balance the added benefits of complete worldwide diversification against the costs of research for the additional stocks.

Finally, you should *minimize transaction costs.* Assuming that the portfolio is completely diversified and is structured for the desired risk level, excessive transaction costs that do not generate added returns will detract from your expected rate of return. Three factors are involved in minimizing total transaction costs:

1. *Minimize taxes.* Methods of accomplishing this objective vary, but it should receive prime consideration.
2. *Reduce trading turnover.* Trade only to liquidate part of the portfolio or to maintain a given risk level.
3. *When you trade, minimize liquidity costs by trading relatively liquid stocks.* To accomplish this, submit limit orders to buy or sell several stocks at prices that approximate the specialist's quote. That is, you would put in limit orders to buy stock at the bid price or sell at the ask price. The stock bought or sold first is the most liquid one; all other orders should be withdrawn.

In summary, if you lack access to superior analysts, you should do the following:

1. Determine and quantify your risk preferences.
2. Construct the appropriate risk portfolio by dividing the total portfolio between risk-free assets and a risky asset portfolio.

3. Diversify completely on a global basis to eliminate all unsystematic risk.
4. Maintain the specified risk level by rebalancing when necessary.
5. Minimize total transaction costs.

The Rationale and Use of Index Funds

As the prior discussion indicates, efficient capital markets and a lack of superior analysts imply that many portfolios should be managed *passively* so that their performance matches that of the aggregate market, minimizing the costs of research and trading. In response to this demand, several institutions have introduced *market funds,* also referred to as *index funds,* which are security portfolios designed to duplicate the composition and, therefore, the performance of a selected market index series.

Notably, this concept of stock market index funds has been extended to other areas of investments. Index bond funds attempt to emulate the bond market indexes discussed in Chapter 5. Also, some index funds focus on specific segments of the market such as international bond index funds, international stock index funds that target specific countries, and index funds that target small-capitalization stocks in the United States and Japan.[42] The point is, when portfolio managers decide that they want a given asset class in their portfolio, they often look for index funds to fulfill this need. The use of index funds is less costly in terms of research and commission; and, during almost all time periods, it has provided the same or better performance than what is available from the vast majority of active portfolio managers.

Insights from Behavioral Finance

As noted, the major contributions of behavioral finance are both explanations for some of the anomalies discovered by prior academic research and opportunities to derive abnormal rates of return by acting upon some of the deeply ingrained biases of investors. Clearly, their findings support the notion that the stocks of growth companies will typically not be growth stocks because analysts become overconfident in their ability to predict future growth rates and eventually derive valuations that either fully value or overvalue future growth. Behavioral findings also support the notion of contrary investing, since they confirm the notion of the "herd mentality" of analysts in stock recommendations or quarterly earning estimates and the recommendations by newsletter writers. Also, it is important to recall the "loss aversion" and "escalation bias" that cause investors to hold losers too long and, in some cases, cause investors to acquire additional shares to average down the cost. Before you engage in this practice, be sure that you reevaluate the stock and consider all the potential bad news we tend to ignore.

Efficiency in European Equity Markets

The discussion in this chapter has addressed generally the efficiency of U.S. markets. The growing importance of world markets raises a natural question about the efficiency of securities markets outside the United States. Numerous studies have dealt with this set of questions, and a discussion of them would substantially lengthen the chapter. Fortunately, a monograph by Hawawini contains a review of numerous studies that examined the behavior of European stock prices and evaluated the efficiency of European equity markets.[43] The monograph lists more than 280 studies covering 14 Western European countries from Austria to the United Kingdom classified by country; and, within each country, the studies are divided into five categories:

1. Market model, beta estimation, and diversification
2. Capital asset pricing model and arbitrage pricing model

[42]For a discussion of some of these indexes, see James A. White, "The Index Boom: It's No Longer Just the S&P 500 Stock Index," *The Wall Street Journal,* 19 May 1991, C1, C3.

[43]Gabriel Hawawini, *European Equity Markets: Price Behavior and Efficiency,* Monograph 1984-4/5, Monograph Series in Finance and Economics, Salomon Brothers Center for the Study of Financial Institutions, Graduate School of Business, New York University, 1984.

3. Weak-form test of market efficiency
4. Semistrong-form tests of market efficiency
5. Strong-form tests of market efficiency

Hawawini offers the following overall conclusion after acknowledging that European markets are smaller and less active than U.S. markets:

> Our review of the literature indicates that despite the peculiarities of European equity markets, the behavior of European stock prices is, with few exceptions, surprisingly similar to that of U.S. common stocks. That is true even for countries with extremely narrow equity markets such as Finland. The view that most European equity markets, particularly those of smaller countries, are informationally inefficient does not seem to be borne out by the data. We will see that most of the results of empirical tests performed on European common stock prices are generally in line with those reported by researchers who used U.S. data.

This implies that when one considers securities outside the United States, it is appropriate to assume a level of efficiency similar to that for U.S. markets.

The Internet *Investments Online*

Capital market prices reflect current news items fairly quickly. On the other hand, a portfolio manager should not ignore news just because prices adjust quickly. News provides information he/she can use to structure portfolios and allows the managers to update potential future scenarios.

A number of news sources are available on the Internet. Some of them, such as **http://www.bloomberg.com, www.ft.com,** and **http://www.wsj.com,** were listed in previous chapters. Other sites include:

http://www.infogate.com This system allows you to have news sent directly to your PC.

http://finance.yahoo.com contains links to a number of news, information, commentary, and finance-related sites

http://money.cnn.com The financial network site for the Cable News Network and Money magazine. The CNN Web site is **http://www.cnn.com.**

http://www.cnbc.com The Web site of the CNBC cable TV station.

http://www.foxnews.com, http://www.abcnews.com, http://www.cbsnews.com, and **http://www.msnbcnews.com** are the URLs for news from Fox, ABC, CBS, and MSNBC.

Meir Statman (**http://lsb.scu.edu/finance/faculty/statman/default.htm**) and Richard Thaler (**http://gsb.uchicago.edu/fac/richard.thaler/**) are two leading researchers in the area of behavioral finance. These pages contain links to their research.

Summary

- The efficiency of capital markets has implications for the investment analysis and management of your portfolio. Capital markets should be efficient because numerous rational, profit-maximizing investors react quickly to the release of new information. Assuming prices reflect new information, they are unbiased estimates of the securities' true, intrinsic value, and there should be a consistent relationship between the return on an investment and its risk.
- The voluminous research on the EMH has been divided into three segments that have been tested separately. The weak-form EMH states that stock prices fully reflect all market information, so any trading rule that uses past market data to predict future returns should have no value. The results of most studies consistently supported this hypothesis.

- The semistrong-form EMH asserts that security prices adjust rapidly to the release of all public information. The tests of this hypothesis either examine the opportunities to predict future rates of return (either a time series or a cross section) or they involve event studies in which investigators analyzed whether investors could derive above-average returns from trading on the basis of public information. The test results for this hypothesis were clearly mixed. On the one hand, the results for almost all the event studies related to economic events such as stock splits, initial public offerings, and accounting changes consistently supported the semistrong hypothesis. In contrast, several studies that examined the ability to predict rates of return on the basis of unexpected quarterly earnings, P/E ratios, size, neglected stocks, and the BV/MV ratio, as well as several calendar effects, generally did not support the hypothesis.

- The strong-form EMH states that security prices reflect all information. This implies that nobody has private information, so no group should be able to derive above-average returns consistently. Studies that examined the results for corporate insiders and stock exchange specialists do not support the strong-form hypothesis. An analysis of individual analysts as represented by Value Line or by recommendations published in *The Wall Street Journal* give mixed results. The results indicated that the Value Line rankings have significant information but it may not be possible to profit from it, whereas the recommendations by analysts indicated the existence of private information. In contrast, the performance by professional money managers supported the EMH because their risk-adjusted investment performance (whether mutual funds, pension funds, or endowment funds) was typically inferior to results achieved with buy-and-hold policies.

- During the past decade, there has been significant research in behavioral finance by investigators who contend that the standard finance theory model is incomplete since it does not consider implications of psychological decisions made by individuals that both help explain many anomalies and the existence of several biases and provide opportunities for excess returns. It is important to be aware of a number of biases for two reasons: first, they can lead to inferior performance as an analyst and portfolio manager; second, it is possible to exploit them for excess returns.

- Given the mixed results, it is important to consider the implications of all of this for technical or fundamental analysts and for portfolio managers. The EMH indicates that technical analysis should be of no value. All forms of fundamental analysis are useful, but they are difficult to implement because they require the ability *to estimate future values* for relevant economic variables. Superior analysis is possible but difficult because it requires superior projections. Those who manage portfolios should constantly evaluate investment advice to determine whether it is superior.

- Without access to superior analytical advice, you should run your portfolio like an index fund. In contrast, those with superior analytical ability should be allowed to make decisions, but they should concentrate their efforts on mid-cap firms and neglected firms where there is a higher probability of discovering misvalued stocks. The analysis should be particularly concerned with a firm's BV/MV ratio, its size, and the monetary environment.

- This chapter contains some good news and some bad news. The good news is that the practice of investment analysis and portfolio management is not an art that has been lost to the great computer in the sky. Viable professions still await those willing to extend the effort and able to accept the pressures. The bad news is that many bright, hardworking people with extensive resources make the game tough. In fact, those competitors have created a fairly efficient capital market in which it is extremely difficult for most analysts and portfolio managers to achieve superior results.

Questions

1. Discuss the rationale for expecting an efficient capital market. What factor would you look for to differentiate the market efficiency for two alternative stocks?
2. Define and discuss the weak-form EMH. Describe the two sets of tests used to examine the weak-form EMH.
3. Define and discuss the semistrong-form EMH. Describe the two sets of tests used to examine the semistrong-form EMH.
4. What is meant by the term *abnormal rate of return?*

5. Describe how you would compute the abnormal rate of return for a stock for a period surrounding an economic event. Give a brief example for a stock with a beta of 1.40.

6. Assume you want to test the EMH by comparing alternative trading rules to a buy-and-hold policy. Discuss the three common mistakes that can bias the results against the EMH.

7. Describe the results of a study that supported the semistrong-form EMH. Discuss the nature of the test and specifically why the results support the hypothesis.

8. Describe the results of a study that did *not* support the semistrong-form EMH. Discuss the nature of the test and specifically why the results did not support the hypothesis.

9. For many of the EMH tests, it is really a test of a "joint hypothesis." Discuss what is meant by this concept. What are the joint hypotheses being tested?

10. Define and discuss the strong-form EMH. Why do some observers contend that the strong-form hypothesis really requires a perfect market in addition to an efficient market? Be specific.

11. Discuss how you would test the strong-form EMH. Why are these tests relevant? Give a brief example.

12. Describe the results of a study that did *not* support the strong-form EMH. Discuss the test involved and specifically why the results reported did not support the hypothesis.

13. Describe the results of a study that supported the strong-form EMH. Discuss the test involved and specifically why these results support the hypothesis.

14. Describe the general goal of behavioral finance.

15. Why do the advocates of behavioral finance contend that the standard finance theory is incomplete?

16. What does the EMH imply for the use of technical analysis?

17. What does the EMH imply for fundamental analysis? Discuss specifically what it does not imply.

18. In a world of efficient capital markets, what do you have to do to be a superior analyst? How would you test whether an analyst was superior?

19. What advice would you give to your superior analysts in terms of the set of firms to analyze and variables that should be considered in the analysis? Discuss your reasoning for this advice.

20. How should a portfolio manager without any superior analysts run his or her portfolio?

21. Describe the goals of an index fund. Discuss the contention that index funds are the ultimate answer in a world with efficient capital markets.

22. At a social gathering, you meet the portfolio manager for the trust department of a local bank. He confides to you that he has been following the recommendations of the department's six analysts for an extended period and has found that two are superior, two are average, and two are clearly inferior. What would you recommend that he do to run his portfolio?

23. Discuss your reaction to Hawawini's summary of findings related to the EMH for the European equity markets. Were you surprised?

24. Describe a test of the weak-form EMH for the Japanese stock market and indicate where you would get the required data.

25. *CFA Examination Level I*
    a. List and briefly define the *three* forms of the efficient market hypothesis. [6 minutes]
    b. Discuss the role of a portfolio manager in a perfectly efficient market. [9 minutes]

26. *CFA Examination Level II*
    Tom Max, TMP's quantitative analyst, has developed a portfolio construction model about which he is excited. To create the model, Max made a list of the stocks currently in the S&P 500 Stock Index and obtained annual operating cash flow, price, and total return data for each issue for the past five years. As of each year-end, this universe was divided into five equal-weighted portfolios of 100 issues each, with selection based solely on the price/cash flow rankings of the individual stocks. Each portfolio's average annual return was then calculated.

    During this five-year period, the linked returns from the portfolios with the lowest price/cash flow ratio generated an annualized total return of 19.0 percent, or 3.1 percentage points better than the 15.9 percent return on the S&P 500 Stock Index. Max also noted that the lowest price–cash-flow portfolio had a below-market beta of 0.91 over this same time span.
    a. Briefly comment on Max's use of the beta measure as an indicator of portfolio risk in light of recent academic tests of its explanatory power with respect to stock returns. [5 minutes]
    b. You are familiar with the literature on market anomalies and inefficiencies. Against this background, discuss Max's use of a single-factor model (price–cash flow) in his research. [8 minutes]

c. Identify and briefly describe *four* specific concerns about Max's test procedures and model design. (The issues already discussed in your answers to Parts a and b may *not* be used in answering Part c.) [12 minutes]

27. *CFA Examination Level III*

a. Briefly explain the concept of the *efficient market hypothesis* (EMH) and each of its three forms—*weak, semistrong, and strong*—and briefly discuss the degree to which existing empirical evidence supports each of the three forms of the EMH. [8 minutes]

b. Briefly discuss the implications of the efficient market hypothesis for investment policy as it applies to:
  (i) technical analysis in the form of charting, and
  (ii) fundamental analysis. [4 minutes]

c. Briefly explain *two* major roles or responsibilities of portfolio managers in an efficient market environment. [4 minutes]

d. Briefly discuss whether active asset allocation among countries could consistently outperform a world market index. Include a discussion of the implications of *integration versus segmentation* of international financial markets as it pertains to portfolio diversification, but ignore the issue of stock selection. [6 minutes]

Problems

1. Compute the abnormal rates of return for the following stocks during period t (ignore differential systematic risk):

Stock	R_{it}	R_{mt}
B	11.5%	4.0%
F	10.0	8.5
T	14.0	9.6
C	12.0	15.3
E	15.9	12.4

R_{it} = return for stock i during period t

R_{mt} = return for the aggregate market during period t

2. Compute the abnormal rates of return for the five stocks in Problem 1 assuming the following systematic risk measures (betas):

Stock	β_i
B	0.95
F	1.25
T	1.45
C	0.70
E	–0.30

3. Compare the abnormal returns in Problems 1 and 2 and discuss the reason for the difference in each case.

4. You are given the following data regarding the performance of a group of stocks recommended by an analyst and a set of stocks with matching betas:

Stock	Beginning Price	Ending Price	Dividend
C	43	47	1.50
C-match	22	24	1.00
R	75	73	2.00
R-match	42	38	1.00
L	28	34	1.25
L-match	18	16	1.00
M	52	57	2.00
M-match	38	44	1.50
S	63	68	1.75
S-match	32	34	1.00

Based on the composite results for these stocks (assume equal weights), would you judge this individual to be a superior analyst? Discuss your reasoning.

5. Look up the daily trading volume for the following stocks during a recent five-day period:

- Merck
- Anheuser Busch
- Intel
- McDonald's
- General Electric

Randomly select five stocks from the NYSE and examine their daily trading volume for the same five days.

a. What are the average daily volumes for the two samples?

b. Would you expect this difference to have an impact on the efficiency of the markets for the two samples? Why or why not?

References

Ball, Ray. "The Theory of Stock Market Efficiency: Accomplishments and Limitations." *Journal of Applied Corporate Finance* 8, no. 1 (Spring 1995).

Banz, R. W. "The Relationship between Return and Market Value of Common Stocks." *Journal of Financial Economics* 9, no. 1 (March 1981).

Barry, Christopher B., and Stephen J. Brown. "Differential Information and the Small Firm Effect." *Journal of Financial Economics* 13, no. 2 (June 1984).

Basu, Senjoy. "Investment Performance of Common Stocks in Relation to Their Price-Earnings Ratios: A Test of the Efficient Market Hypothesis." *Journal of Finance* 32, no. 3 (June 1977).

Berkowitz, Stephen A., Louis D. Finney, and Dennis Logue. *The Investment Performance of Corporate Pension Plans.* New York: Quorum Books, 1988.

Bernard, Victor. "Capital Markets Research in Accounting During the 1980s: A Critical Review," in *The State of Accounting Research as We Enter the 1990s,* Thomas J. Frecka, Ed. Urbana: University of Illinois Press, 1989.

Bernard, Victor L., and Jacob K. Thomas. "Post-Earnings–Announcements Drift: Delayed Price Response or Risk Premium?" *Journal of Accounting Research* 27, Supplement (1989).

Fama, Eugene F. "Efficient Capital Market: II." *Journal of Finance* 46, no. 5 (December 1991).

Hawawini, Gabriel. *European Equity Markets: Price Behavior and Efficiency,* Monograph 1984-4/5. Monograph Series in Finance and Economics, Salomon Brothers Center for the Study of Financial Institutions, Graduate School of Business, New York University, 1984.

Huberman, Gur, and Shmuel Kandel. "Market Efficiency and Value Line's Record." *Journal of Business* 63, no. 2 (April 1990).

Ibbotson, Roger G., Jody Sindelar, and Jay R. Ritter. "Initial Public Offerings." *Journal of Applied Corporate Finance* 1, no. 3 (Summer 1988).

Jain, Prom C. "Response of Hourly Stock Prices and Trading Volume to Economic News." *Journal of Business* 61, no. 2 (April 1988).

Keim, Donald B. "Size-Related Anomalies and Stock Return Seasonality." *Journal of Financial Economics* 12, no. 1 (June 1983).

Keim, Donald B., and Robert F. Stambaugh. "Predicting Returns in Stock and Bond Markets." *Journal of Financial Economics* 17, no. 2 (December 1986).

Lev, Baruch. "On the Usefulness of Earnings and Earning Research: Lessons and Directions from Two Decades of Empirical Research." *Journal of Accounting Research* (Supplement, 1989).

Loughran, Timothy, and Jay Ritter. "The New Issues Puzzle." *Journal of Finance* 50, no. 1 (March 1995).

Malkiel, Burton G. *A Random Walk Down Wall Street.* New York: Norton, 2000.

Miller, Robert E., and Frank K. Reilly. "Examination of Mispricing, Returns, and Uncertainty for Initial Public Offerings." *Financial Management* 16, no. 2 (January 1987).

Ou, J., and S. Penman. "Financial Statement Analysis and the Prediction of Stock Returns." *Journal of Accounting and Economics* (November 1989).

Seyhun, H. Nejat. "Insider Profits, Costs of Trading, and Market Efficiency." *Journal of Financial Economics* 16, no. 2 (June 1986).

Shafrin, Hersh. *Beyond Greed and Fear: Understanding Behavioral Finance and the Psychology of Investing.* Boston: Harvard Business School Press, 1999.

Shafrin, Hersh, and Meir Statman. "Behavioral Capital Asset Pricing Theory." *Journal of Financial and Quantitative Analysis* 30, no. 3 (September 1995).

Wood, Arnold S., ed. *Behavioral Finance and Decision Theory in Investment Management.* Charlottesville, Va.: Association for Investment Management and Research, April 1995.

Chapter 7 An Introduction to Portfolio Management

After you read this chapter, you should be able to answer the following questions:

➤ What do we mean by *risk aversion,* and what evidence indicates that investors are generally risk averse?
➤ What are the basic assumptions behind the Markowitz portfolio theory?
➤ What do we mean by *risk,* and what are some of the alternative measures of risk used in investments?
➤ How do you compute the expected rate of return for an individual risky asset or a portfolio of assets?
➤ How do you compute the standard deviation of rates of return for an individual risky asset?
➤ What do we mean by the *covariance* between rates of return, and how do you compute covariance?
➤ What is the relationship between covariance and correlation?
➤ What is the formula for the standard deviation for a portfolio of risky assets, and how does it differ from the standard deviation of an individual risky asset?
➤ Given the formula for the standard deviation of a portfolio, why and how do you diversify a portfolio?
➤ What happens to the standard deviation of a portfolio when you change the correlation between the assets in the portfolio?
➤ What is the risk-return–efficient frontier of risky assets?
➤ Is it reasonable for alternative investors to select different portfolios from the portfolios on the efficient frontier?
➤ What determines which portfolio on the efficient frontier is selected by an individual investor?

One of the major advances in the investment field during the past few decades has been the recognition that the creation of an optimum investment portfolio is not simply a matter of combining a lot of unique individual securities that have desirable risk-return characteristics. Specifically, it has been shown that you must consider the relationship *among* the investments if you are going to build an optimum portfolio that will meet your investment objectives. The recognition of what is important in creating a portfolio was demonstrated in the derivation of portfolio theory.

This chapter explains portfolio theory step by step. It introduces you to the basic portfolio risk formula that you must understand when you are combining different assets. When you understand this formula and its implications, you will increase your understanding of not only why you should diversify your portfolio but also *how* you should diversify. The subsequent chapters introduce asset pricing models including capital market theory and multifactor models with an emphasis on determining the appropriate risk measure for individual assets.

◀ **SOME BACKGROUND ASSUMPTIONS** ▶

Before presenting portfolio theory, we need to clarify some general assumptions of the theory. This includes not only what we mean by an *optimum portfolio* but also what we mean by the terms *risk aversion* and *risk.*

One basic assumption of portfolio theory is that as an investor you want to maximize the returns from your investments for a given level of risk. To adequately deal with such an assumption, certain ground rules must be laid. First, your portfolio should *include all of your assets and liabilities,* not only your stocks or even your marketable securities but also such items as your car, house, and less-marketable investments, such as coins, stamps, art, antiques, and furniture. The full spectrum of investments must be considered because the returns from all these investments interact, and *this relationship between the returns for assets in the portfolio is important.* Hence, a good portfolio is *not* simply a collection of individually good investments.

Risk Aversion   Portfolio theory also assumes that investors are basically **risk averse**, meaning that, given a choice between two assets with equal rates of return, they will select the asset with the lower level of risk. Evidence that most investors are risk averse is that they purchase various types of insurance, including life insurance, car insurance, and health insurance. Buying insurance basically involves an outlay of a given amount to guard against an uncertain, possibly larger outlay in the future. When you buy insurance, this implies that you are willing to pay the current known cost of the insurance policy to avoid the uncertainty of a potentially large future cost related to a car accident or a major illness. Further evidence of risk aversion is the difference in promised yield (the required rate of return) for different grades of bonds that supposedly have different degrees of credit risk. Specifically, the promised yield on bonds increases as you go from AAA (the lowest-risk class) to AA to A, and so on—that is, investors require a higher rate of return to accept higher risk.

This does not imply that everybody is risk averse or that investors are completely risk averse regarding all financial commitments. The fact is, not everybody buys insurance for everything. Some people have no insurance against anything, either by choice or because they cannot afford it. In addition, some individuals buy insurance related to some risks such as auto accidents or illness, but they also buy lottery tickets and gamble at race tracks or in casinos, where it is known that the expected returns are negative, which means that participants are willing to pay for the excitement of the risk involved. This combination of risk preference and risk aversion can be explained by an attitude toward risk that depends on the amount of money involved. Friedman and Savage speculate that this is the case for people who like to gamble for small amounts (in lotteries or slot machines) but buy insurance to protect themselves against large potential losses, such as fire or accidents.[1]

While recognizing this diversity of attitudes, our basic assumption is that most investors committing large sums of money to developing an investment portfolio are risk averse. Therefore, we expect a positive relationship between expected return and expected risk. Notably, this is also what we generally find in terms of long-run historical results—that is, there is generally a positive relationship between the rates of return on various assets and their measures of risk as shown in Chapter 3.

Definition of Risk   Although there is a difference in the specific definitions of *risk* and *uncertainty,* for our purposes and in most financial literature the two terms are used interchangeably. In fact, one way to define

---

[1]Milton Friedman and Leonard J. Savage, "The Utility Analysis of Choices Involving Risk," *Journal of Political Economy* 56, no. 3 (August 1948): 279–304.

risk is *the uncertainty of future outcomes.* An alternative definition might be *the probability of an adverse outcome.* Subsequently, in our discussion of portfolio theory, we will consider several measures of risk that are used when developing the theory.

MARKOWITZ PORTFOLIO THEORY

In the early 1960s, the investment community talked about risk, but there was no specific measure for the term. To build a portfolio model, however, investors had to quantify their risk variable. The basic portfolio model was developed by Harry Markowitz, who derived the expected rate of return for a portfolio of assets and an expected risk measure.[2] Markowitz showed that the variance of the rate of return was a meaningful measure of portfolio risk under a reasonable set of assumptions, and he derived the formula for computing the variance of a portfolio. This portfolio variance formula indicated the importance of diversifying your investments to reduce the total risk of a portfolio but also showed *how* to effectively diversify. The Markowitz model is based on several assumptions regarding investor behavior:

1. Investors consider each investment alternative as being represented by a probability distribution of expected returns over some holding period.
2. Investors maximize one-period expected utility, and their utility curves demonstrate diminishing marginal utility of wealth.
3. Investors estimate the risk of the portfolio on the basis of the variability of expected returns.
4. Investors base decisions solely on expected return and risk, so their utility curves are a function of expected return and the expected variance (or standard deviation) of returns only.
5. For a given risk level, investors prefer higher returns to lower returns. Similarly, for a given level of expected return, investors prefer less risk to more risk.

Under these assumptions, *a single asset or portfolio of assets is considered to be efficient if no other asset or portfolio of assets offers higher expected return with the same (or lower) risk, or lower risk with the same (or higher) expected return.*

Alternative Measures of Risk

One of the best-known measures of risk is the *variance,* or *standard deviation of expected returns.*[3] It is a statistical measure of the dispersion of returns around the expected value whereby a larger variance or standard deviation indicates greater dispersion. The idea is that the more disperse the expected returns, the greater the uncertainty of future returns.

Another measure of risk is the *range of returns.* It is assumed that a larger range of expected returns, from the lowest to the highest return, means greater uncertainty and risk regarding future expected returns.

Instead of using measures that analyze all deviations from expectations, some observers believe that when you invest you should be concerned only with *returns below expectations,* which means that you only consider deviations below the mean value. A measure that only considers deviations below the mean is the *semivariance.* Extensions of the semivariance measure only computed expected returns *below zero* (that is, negative returns), or returns below some

---

[2]Harry Markowitz, "Portfolio Selection," *Journal of Finance* 7, no. 1 (March 1952): 77–91; and Harry Markowitz, *Portfolio Selection—Efficient Diversification of Investments* (New York: John Wiley & Sons, 1959).

[3]We consider the variance and standard deviation as one measure of risk because the standard deviation is the square root of the variance.

specific asset such as T-bills, the rate of inflation, or a benchmark. These measures of risk implicitly assume that investors want to *minimize the damage* from returns less than some target rate. Assuming that investors would welcome returns above some target rate, the returns above a target return are not considered when measuring risk.

Although there are numerous potential measures of risk, we will use the variance or standard deviation of returns because (1) this measure is somewhat intuitive, (2) it is a correct and widely recognized risk measure, and (3) it has been used in most of the theoretical asset pricing models.

Expected Rates of Return

The expected rate of return for *an individual investment* is computed as shown in Exhibit 7.1. The expected return for an individual risky asset with the set of potential returns and an assumption of equal probabilities used in the example would be 11 percent.

The expected rate of return for a *portfolio* of investments is simply the weighted average of the expected rates of return for the individual investments in the portfolio. The weights are the proportion of total value for the investment.

The expected rate of return for a hypothetical portfolio with four risky assets is shown in Exhibit 7.2. The expected return for this portfolio of investments would be 11.5 percent. The effect of adding or dropping any investment from the portfolio would be easy to determine because you would use the new weights based on value and the expected returns for each of the investments. This computation of the expected return for the portfolio [$E(R_{port})$] can be generalized as follows:

➤7.1
$$E(R_{port}) = \sum_{i=1}^{n} W_i E(R_i)$$

where:

W_i = the percent of the portfolio in asset i
$E(R_i)$ = the expected rate of return for asset i

EXHIBIT 7.1 ▶ *COMPUTATION OF EXPECTED RETURN FOR AN INDIVIDUAL RISKY ASSET*

PROBABILITY	POSSIBLE RATE OF RETURN (PERCENT)	EXPECTED RETURN (PERCENT)
.25	.08	.0200
.25	.10	.0250
.25	.12	.0300
.25	.14	.0350
		$E(R) = .1100$

EXHIBIT 7.2 ▶ *COMPUTATION OF THE EXPECTED RETURN FOR A PORTFOLIO OF RISKY ASSETS*

WEIGHT (W_i) (PERCENT OF PORTFOLIO)	EXPECTED SECURITY RETURN $E(R_i)$	EXPECTED PORTFOLIO RETURN [$W_i \times E(R_i)$]
.20	.10	.0200
.30	.11	.0330
.30	.12	.0360
.20	.13	.0260
		$E(R_{port}) = .1150$

Variance (Standard Deviation) of Returns for an Individual Investment

As noted, we will be using the variance or the standard deviation of returns as the measure of risk (recall that the standard deviation is the square root of the variance). Therefore, at this point, we will demonstrate how you would compute the standard deviation of returns for an individual investment. Subsequently, after discussing some other statistical concepts, we will consider the determination of the standard deviation for a *portfolio* of investments.

The variance, or standard deviation, is a measure of the variation of possible rates of return, R_i, from the expected rate of return $[E(R_i)]$ as follows:

➤7.2
$$\text{Variance } (\sigma^2) = \sum_{i=1}^{n} [R_i - E(R_i)]^2 P_i$$

where

P_i is the probability of the possible rate of return, R_i

➤7.3
$$\text{Standard Deviation } (\sigma) = \sqrt{\sum_{i=1}^{n} [R_i - E(R_i)]^2 P_i}$$

The computation of the variance and standard deviation of the expected rate of return for the individual risky asset in Exhibit 7.1 is set forth in Exhibit 7.3.

Variance (Standard Deviation) of Returns for a Portfolio

Two basic concepts in statistics, covariance and correlation, must be understood before we discuss the formula for the variance of the rate of return for a portfolio.

Covariance of Returns In this section, we discuss what the covariance of returns is intended to measure, give the formula for computing it, and present an example of the computation. **Covariance** is a measure of the degree to which two variables "move together" relative to their individual mean values over time. In portfolio analysis, we usually are concerned with the covariance of *rates of return* rather than prices or some other variable.[4] A positive covariance

---

EXHIBIT 7.3 *COMPUTATION OF THE VARIANCE OF THE EXPECTED RATE OF RETURN FOR AN INDIVIDUAL RISKY ASSET*

POSSIBLE RATE OF RETURN (R_i)	EXPECTED RETURN $E(R_i)$	$R_i - E(R_i)$	$[R_i - E(R_i)]^2$	P_i	$(R_i - E(R_i))^2 P_i$
.08	.11	−.03	.0009	.25	.000225
.10	.11	−.01	.0001	.25	.000025
.12	.11	.01	.0001	.25	.000025
.14	.11	.03	.0009	.25	.000225
					.000500

Variance (σ^2) = .00050
Standard Deviation (σ) = .02236

---

[4]Returns, of course, can be measured in a variety of ways, depending on the type of asset. You will recall that we defined returns (R_i) in Chapter 1 as:

$$R_i \frac{EV - BV + CF}{BV}$$

where EV is ending value, BV is beginning value, and CF is the cash flow during the period.

| EXHIBIT 7.4 | COMPUTATION OF MONTHLY RATES OF RETURN: 2001 |

	COCA-COLA			HOME DEPOT		
DATE	CLOSING PRICE	DIVIDEND	RATE OF RETURN (%)	CLOSING PRICE	DIVIDEND	RATE OF RETURN (%)
Dec-00	60.938			45.688		
Jan-01	58.000		−4.82	48.200		5.50
Feb-01	53.030		−8.57	42.500		−11.83
Mar-01	45.160	0.18	−14.50	43.100	0.04	1.51
Apr-01	46.190		2.28	47.100		9.28
May-01	47.400		2.62	49.290		4.65
Jun-01	45.000	0.18	−4.68	47.240	0.04	−4.08
Jul-01	44.600		−0.89	50.370		6.63
Aug-01	48.670		9.13	45.950	0.04	−8.70
Sep-01	46.850	0.18	−3.37	38.370		−16.50
Oct-01	47.880		2.20	38.230		−0.36
Nov-01	46.960	0.18	−1.55	46.650	0.05	22.16
Dec-01	47.150		0.40	51.010		9.35
			$E(R_{\text{Coca-Cola}}) = -1.81$			$E(R_{\text{Home Depot}}) = 1.47$

means that the rates of return for two investments tend to move in the same direction relative to their individual means during the same time period. In contrast, a negative covariance indicates that the rates of return for two investments tend to move in different directions relative to their means during specified time intervals over time. The *magnitude* of the covariance depends on the variances of the individual return series, as well as on the relationship between the series.

Exhibit 7.4 contains the monthly closing prices and dividends for Coca-Cola and Home Depot. You can use these data to compute monthly rates of return for these two stocks during 2001. Exhibit 7.5 and Exhibit 7.6 contain a time-series plot of the monthly rates of return for the two stocks during 2001. Although the rates of return for the two stocks moved together during some months, in other months they moved in opposite directions. The covariance statistic provides an *absolute* measure of how they moved together over time.

For two assets, i and j, the covariance of rates of return is defined as:

➤7.4 $$\text{Cov}_{ij} = E\{[R_i - E(R_i)][R_j - E(R_j)]\}$$

When we apply this formula to the monthly rates of return for Coca-Cola and Home Depot during 2001, it becomes:

$$\frac{1}{12}\sum_{i=1}^{n}[R_i - E(R_i)][R_j - E(R_j)]$$

As can be seen, if the rates of return for one stock are above (below) its mean rate of return during a given period and the returns for the other stock are likewise above (below) its mean rate of return during this same period, then the *product* of these deviations from the mean is positive. If this happens consistently, the covariance of returns between these two stocks will be some

EXHIBIT 7.5   *TIME SERIES OF MONTHLY RATES OF RETURN FOR COCA-COLA: 2001*

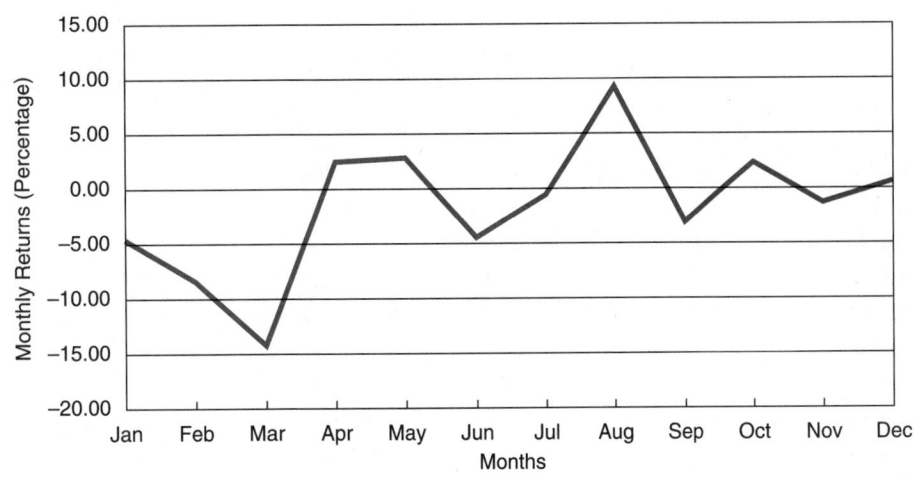

EXHIBIT 7.6   *TIME SERIES OF MONTHLY RATES OF RETURN FOR HOME DEPOT: 2001*

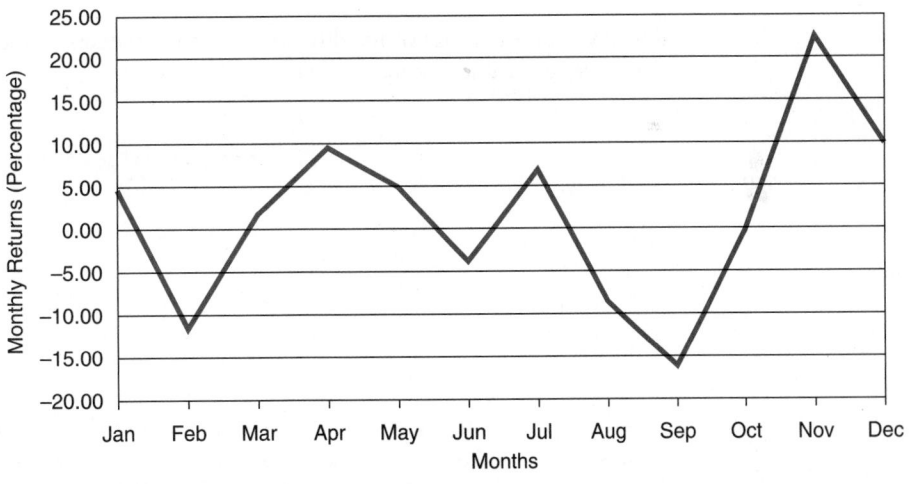

large positive value. If, however, the rate of return for one of the securities is above its mean return while the return on the other security is below its mean return, the product will be negative. If this contrary movement happened consistently, the covariance between the rates of return for the two stocks would be a large negative value.

Exhibit 7.7 contains the monthly rates of return during 2001 for Coca-Cola and Home Depot as computed in Exhibit 7.4. One might expect the returns for the two stocks to have reasonably

EXHIBIT 7.7 *COMPUTATION OF COVARIANCE OF RETURNS FOR COCA-COLA AND HOME DEPOT: 2001*

	MONTHLY RETURN		COCA-COLA	HOME DEPOT	COCA-COLA		HOME DEPOT
DATE	COCA-COLA (R_i)	HOME DEPOT (R_j)	$R_i - E(R_i)$	$R_j - E(R_j)$	$[R_i - E(R_i)]$	$\times$	$[R_j - E(R_j)]$
Jan-01	−4.82	5.50	−3.01	4.03			−12.13
Feb-01	−8.57	−11.83	−6.76	−13.29			89.81
Mar-01	−14.50	1.51	−12.69	0.04			−0.49
Apr-01	2.28	9.28	4.09	7.81			31.98
May-01	2.62	4.65	4.43	3.18			14.11
Jun-01	−4.68	−4.08	−2.87	−5.54			15.92
Jul-01	−0.89	6.63	0.92	5.16			4.76
Aug-01	9.13	−8.70	10.94	−10.16			−111.16
Sep-01	−3.37	−16.50	−1.56	−17.96			27.97
Oct-01	2.20	−0.36	4.01	−1.83			−7.35
Nov-01	−1.55	22.16	0.27	20.69			5.52
Dec-01	0.40	9.35	2.22	7.88			17.47
	$E(R_i) = -1.81$	$E(R_j) = 1.47$				Sum =	76.42

$$Cov_{ij} = 76.42/12 = 6.37$$

low covariance because of the differences in the products of these firms. The expected returns $E(R)$ were the arithmetic mean of the monthly returns:

$$E(R_i) = \frac{1}{12} \sum_{i=1}^{12} R_{it}$$

and

$$E(R_j) = \frac{1}{12} \sum_{j=1}^{12} R_{jt}$$

All figures (except those in the last column) were rounded to the nearest hundredth of 1 percent. As shown in Exhibit 7.4, the average monthly return was −1.81 percent for Coca-Cola and 1.47 percent for Home Depot stock. The results in Exhibit 7.7 show that the covariance between the rates of return for these two stocks was:

$$Cov_{ij} = \frac{1}{12} \times 76.42$$
$$= 6.37$$

Interpretation of a number such as 6.37 is difficult; is it high or low for covariance? We know the relationship between the two stocks is generally positive, but it is not possible to be more

| EXHIBIT 7.8 | *SCATTER PLOT OF MONTHLY RATES OF RETURN FOR COCA-COLA AND HOME DEPOT: 2001* |

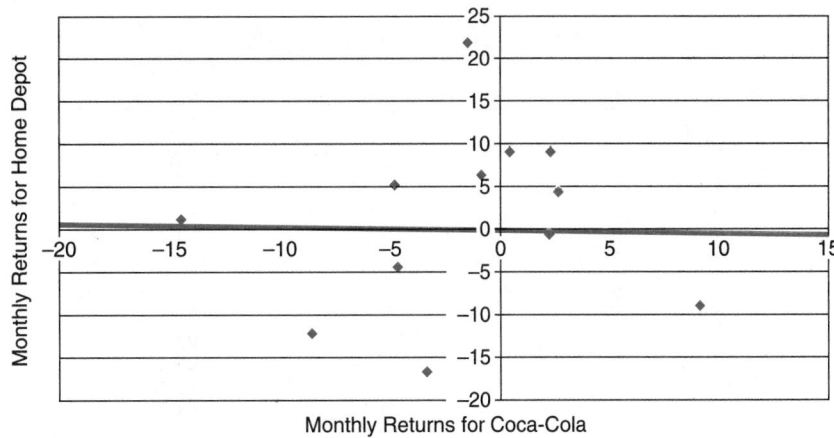

Monthly Returns for Coca-Cola

specific. Exhibit 7.8 contains a scatter diagram with paired values of R_{it} and R_{jt} plotted against each other. This plot demonstrates the linear nature and strength of the relationship and shows several instances during 2001 when Coca-Cola experienced negative returns relative to its mean return when Home Depot had positive rates of return relative to its mean.

Covariance and Correlation Covariance is affected by the variability of the two individual return series. Therefore, a number such as the 6.37 in our example might indicate a weak positive relationship if the two individual series were volatile but would reflect a strong positive relationship if the two series were very stable. Obviously, you want to "standardize" this covariance measure taking into consideration the variability of the two individual return series, as follows:

➤ 7.5
$$r_{ij} = \frac{Cov_{ij}}{\sigma_i \sigma_j}$$

where:

    r_{ij} = **the correlation coefficient of returns**
    σ_i = **the standard deviation of R_{it}**
    σ_j = **the standard deviation of R_{jt}**

Standardizing the covariance by the individual standard deviations yields the **correlation coefficient** (r_{ij}), which can vary only in the range –1 to +1. A value of +1 would indicate a perfect positive linear relationship between R_i and R_j, meaning the returns for the two stocks move together in a completely linear manner. A value of –1 indicates a perfect negative relationship between the two return series such that when one stock's rate of return is above its mean, the other stock's rate of return will be below its mean by the comparable amount.

To calculate this standardized measure of the relationship, you need to compute the standard deviation for the two individual return series. We already have the values for $R_{it} - E(R_i)$ and

EXHIBIT 7.9	COMPUTATION OF STANDARD DEVIATION OF RETURNS FOR COCA-COLA AND HOME DEPOT: 2001

	COCA-COLA		HOME DEPOT	
DATE	$R_i - E(R_i)$	$[R_i - E(R_i)]^2$	$R_i - E(R_i)$	$[R_i - E(R_i)]^2$
Jan-01	−3.01	9.05	4.03	16.26
Feb-01	−6.76	45.65	−13.29	176.69
Mar-01	−12.69	161.01	0.04	0.00
Apr-01	4.09	16.75	7.81	61.06
May-01	4.43	19.64	3.18	10.13
Jun-01	−2.87	8.24	−5.54	30.74
Jul-01	0.92	0.85	5.16	26.61
Aug-01	10.94	119.64	−10.16	103.28
Sep-01	−1.56	2.42	−17.96	322.67
Oct-01	4.01	16.09	−1.83	3.36
Nov-01	0.27	0.07	20.69	428.01
Dec-01	2.22	4.92	7.88	62.08
		Sum = 404.34		Sum = 1240.90
	Variance$_j$ = 404.34/12 =	33.69	Variance$_j$ = 240.90/12 =	103.41
	Standard Deviation$_j$ = (33.69)$^{1/2}$ =	5.80	Standard Deviation$_j$ = (103.41)$^{1/2}$ =	10.17

$R_{jt} - E(R_j)$ in Exhibit 7.7. We can square each of these values and sum them as shown in Exhibit 7.9 to calculate the variance of each return series.

$$\sigma = \frac{1}{12}(404.34) = 33.69$$

and

$$\sigma = \frac{1}{12}(1240.90) = 103.41$$

The standard deviation for each series is the square root of the variance for each, as follows:

$$\sigma_i = \sqrt{33.69} = 5.80$$
$$\sigma_j = \sqrt{103.41} = 10.17$$

Thus, based on the covariance between the two series and the individual standard deviations, we can calculate the correlation coefficient between returns for Coca-Cola and Home Depot as

$$r_{ij} = \frac{Cov_{ij}}{\sigma_i \sigma_j} = \frac{6.37}{(5.80)(10.17)} = \frac{6.37}{58.99} = 0.108$$

Obviously, this formula also implies that

$$Cov_{ij} = r_{ij}\,\sigma_i\sigma_j\,(.108)(5.80)(10.17) = 6.37$$

as computed in Exhibit 7.7.

Standard Deviation of a Portfolio

As noted, a correlation of +1.0 would indicate perfect positive correlation, and a value of –1.0 would mean that the returns moved in a completely opposite direction. A value of zero would mean that the returns had no linear relationship, that is, they were uncorrelated statistically. That does *not* mean that they are independent. The value of $r_{ij} = 0.108$ is quite low. This relatively low correlation is not unusual for stocks in diverse industries (i.e., beverages and building materials). Correlation between stocks of companies *within* some industries approaches 0.85.

Portfolio Standard Deviation Formula   Now that we have discussed the concepts of covariance and correlation, we can consider the formula for computing the standard deviation of returns for a *portfolio* of assets, our measure of risk for a portfolio. As noted, Harry Markowitz derived the formula for computing the standard deviation of a portfolio of assets.[5]

In Exhibit 7.2, we showed that the expected rate of return of the portfolio was the weighted average of the expected returns for the individual assets in the portfolio; the weights were the percentage of value of the portfolio.

One might assume it is possible to derive the standard deviation of the portfolio in the same manner, that is, by computing the weighted average of the standard deviations for the individual assets. This would be a mistake. Markowitz derived the general formula for the standard deviation of a portfolio as follows:[6]

➤ 7.6
$$\sigma_{\text{port}} = \sqrt{\sum_{i=1}^{n} w_i^2 \sigma_i^2 + \sum_{i=1}^{n} \sum_{\substack{j=1 \\ i \neq j}}^{n} w_i w_j \, \text{Cov}_{ij}}$$

where:

> σ_{port} = **the standard deviation of the portfolio**
> w_i = **the weights of the individual assets in the portfolio, where weights are determined by the proportion of value in the portfolio**
> σ_i^2 = **the variance of rates of return for assets i**
> Cov_{ij} = **the covariance between the rates of return for assets i and j, where $\text{Cov}_{ij} = r_{ij}\sigma_i\sigma_j$**

This formula indicates that the standard deviation for a portfolio of assets is a function of the weighted average of the individual variances (where the weights are squared), *plus* the weighted covariances between all the assets in the portfolio. The standard deviation for a portfolio of assets encompasses not only the variances of the individual assets but *also* includes the covariances between pairs of individual assets in the portfolio. Further, it can be shown that, in a portfolio with a large number of securities, this formula reduces to the sum of the weighted covariances.

Although most of the subsequent demonstration will consider portfolios with only two assets because it is possible to show the effect in two dimensions, we will demonstrate the computations for a three-asset portfolio. Still, it is important at this point to consider what happens in a large portfolio with many assets. Specifically, what happens to the portfolio's standard deviation when you add a new security to such a portfolio? As shown by the formula, we see two effects. The first is the asset's own variance of returns, and the second is the covariance between the returns of this new asset and the returns of *every other asset that is already in the portfolio*. The relative weight of these numerous covariances is substantially greater than the asset's unique variance; and the more assets in the portfolio, the more this is true. This means that the important factor to consider when adding an investment to a portfolio that contains a number of other

---

[5]Markowitz, *Portfolio Selection*.

[6]For the detailed derivation of this formula, see Markowitz, *Portfolio Selection*.

investments is *not* the investment's own variance but *its average covariance with all the other investments in the portfolio.*

In the following examples, we will consider the simple case of a two-asset portfolio. We do these relatively simple calculations and provide graphs with two assets to demonstrate the impact of different covariances on the total risk (standard deviation) of the portfolio.

Demonstration of the Portfolio Standard Deviation Calculation Because of the assumptions used in developing the Markowitz portfolio model, any asset or portfolio of assets can be described by two characteristics: the expected rate of return and the expected standard deviation of returns. Therefore, the following demonstrations can be applied to two *individual* assets with the indicated return–standard deviation characteristics and correlation coefficients, two *portfolios* of assets, or two *asset classes* with the indicated return–standard deviation characteristics and correlation coefficients.

Equal Risk and Return—Changing Correlations Consider first the case in which both assets have the same expected return and expected standard deviation of return. As an example, let us assume

$$E(R_1) = 0.20$$
$$\sigma_1 = 0.10$$
$$E(R_2) = 0.20$$
$$\sigma_2 = 0.10$$

To show the effect of different covariances, assume different levels of correlation between the two assets. Consider the following examples where the two assets have equal weights in the portfolio ($W_1 = 0.50$; $W_2 = 0.50$). Therefore, the only value that changes in each example is the correlation between the returns for the two assets.

Recall that

$$\text{Cov}_{ij} = r_{ij}\sigma_i\sigma_j$$

Consider the following alternative correlation coefficients and the covariances they yield. The covariance term in the equation will be equal to $r_{1,2}$ (0.10)(0.10) because both standard deviations are 0.10.

a. $r_{1,2} = 1.00$; $\text{Cov}_{1,2} = (1.00)(0.10)(0.10) = 0.010$
b. $r_{1,2} = 0.50$; $\text{Cov}_{1,2} = (0.50)(0.10)(0.10) = 0.005$
c. $r_{1,2} = 0.00$; $\text{Cov}_{1,2} = 0.000(0.10)(0.10) = 0.000$
d. $r_{1,2} = -0.50$; $\text{Cov}_{1,2} = (-0.50)(0.10)(0.10) = -0.005$
e. $r_{1,2} = -1.00$; $\text{Cov}_{1,2} = (-1.00)(0.10)(0.10) = -0.01$

Now let us see what happens to the standard deviation of the portfolio under these five conditions. Recall from Equation 7.6 that

$$\sigma_{\text{port}} = \sqrt{\sum_{i=1}^{n} w_i^2\sigma_i^2 + \sum_{i=1}^{n}\sum_{\substack{j=1 \\ i\neq i}}^{n} w_i\, w_j\, \text{Cov}_{ij}}$$

When this general formula is applied to a two-asset portfolio, it is

➤7.7
$$\sigma_{\text{port}} = \sqrt{w_1^2\sigma_1^2 + w_2^2\sigma_2^2 + 2w_1 w_2 r_{1,2}\sigma_1\sigma_2}$$

or

$$\sigma_{port} = \sqrt{w_1^2\sigma_1^2 + w_2^2\sigma_2^2 + 2w_1w_2\text{Cov}_{1,2}}$$

Thus, in Case a,

$$\begin{aligned}
\sigma_{port(a)} &= \sqrt{(0.5)^2(0.10)^2 + (0.5)^2(0.10)^2 + 2(0.5)(0.5)(0.01)} \\
&= \sqrt{(0.25)(0.01) + (0.25)(0.01) + 2(0.25)(0.01)} \\
&= \sqrt{0.01} \\
&= 0.10
\end{aligned}$$

In this case, where the returns for the two assets are perfectly positively correlated ($r_{1,2} = 1.0$), the standard deviation for the portfolio is, in fact, the weighted average of the individual standard deviations. The important point is that we get no real benefit from combining two assets that are perfectly correlated; they are like one asset already because their returns move together.

Now consider Case b, where $r_{1,2}$ equals 0.50:

$$\begin{aligned}
\sigma_{port(b)} &= \sqrt{(0.5)^2(0.10)^2 + (0.5)^2(0.10)^2 + 2(0.5)(0.5)(0.005)} \\
&= \sqrt{(0.0025)(0.0025) + 2(0.25)(0.005)} \\
&= \sqrt{0.0075} \\
&= 0.0868
\end{aligned}$$

The only term that changed from Case a is the last term, $\text{Cov}_{1,2}$, which changed from 0.01 to 0.005. As a result, the standard deviation of the portfolio declined by about 13 percent, from 0.10 to 0.0868. Note that *the expected return did not change* because it is simply the weighted average of the individual expected returns; it is equal to 0.20 in both cases.

You should be able to confirm through your own calculations that the standard deviations for Portfolios c and d are as follows:

c. 0.0707
d. 0.05

The final case where the correlation between the two assets is –1.00 indicates the ultimate benefits of diversification:

$$\begin{aligned}
\sigma_{port(e)} &= \sqrt{(0.5)^2(0.10)^2 + (0.5)^2(0.10)^2 + 2(0.5)(0.5)(-0.01)} \\
&= \sqrt{(0.0050) + (-0.0050)} \\
&= \sqrt{0} \\
&= 0
\end{aligned}$$

Here, the negative covariance term exactly offsets the individual variance terms, leaving an overall standard deviation of the portfolio of zero. *This would be a risk-free portfolio.*

Exhibit 7.10 illustrates a graph of such a pattern. Perfect negative correlation gives a mean combined return for the two securities over time equal to the mean for each of them, so the returns for the portfolio show no variability. Any returns above and below the mean for each of the assets are *completely offset* by the return for the other asset, so there is *no variability* in total returns, that is, *no risk,* for the portfolio. This combination of two assets that are completely negatively correlated provides the maximum benefits of diversification—it completely eliminates risk.

EXHIBIT 7.10　*TIME PATTERNS OF RETURNS FOR TWO ASSETS WITH PERFECT NEGATIVE CORRELATION*

The graph in Exhibit 7.11 shows the difference in the risk-return posture for these five cases. As noted, the only effect of the change in correlation is the change in the standard deviation of this two-asset portfolio. Combining assets that are not perfectly correlated does *not* affect the expected return of the portfolio, but it *does* reduce the risk of the portfolio (as measured by its standard deviation). When we eventually reach the ultimate combination of perfect negative correlation, risk is eliminated.

Combining Stocks with Different Returns and Risk　The previous discussion indicated what happens when only the correlation coefficient (covariance) differs between the assets. We now consider two assets (or portfolios) with different expected rates of return and individual standard deviations.[7] We will show what happens when we vary the correlations between them. We will assume two assets with the following characteristics:

ASSET	$E(R_i)$	W_i	σ^2_i	σ_i
1	.10	.50	.0049	.07
2	.20	.50	.0100	.10

The previous set of correlation coefficients gives a different set of covariances because the standard deviations are different. For example, the covariance in Case b where $r_{1,2} = 0.50$ would be $(0.50)(0.07)(0.10) = 0.0035$.

---

[7]As noted, these could be two asset classes. For example, Asset 1 could be low risk–low return bonds and Asset 2 could be higher-return–higher-risk stocks.

| EXHIBIT 7.11 | RISK-RETURN PLOT FOR PORTFOLIOS WITH EQUAL RETURNS AND STANDARD DEVIATIONS BUT DIFFERENT CORRELATIONS |

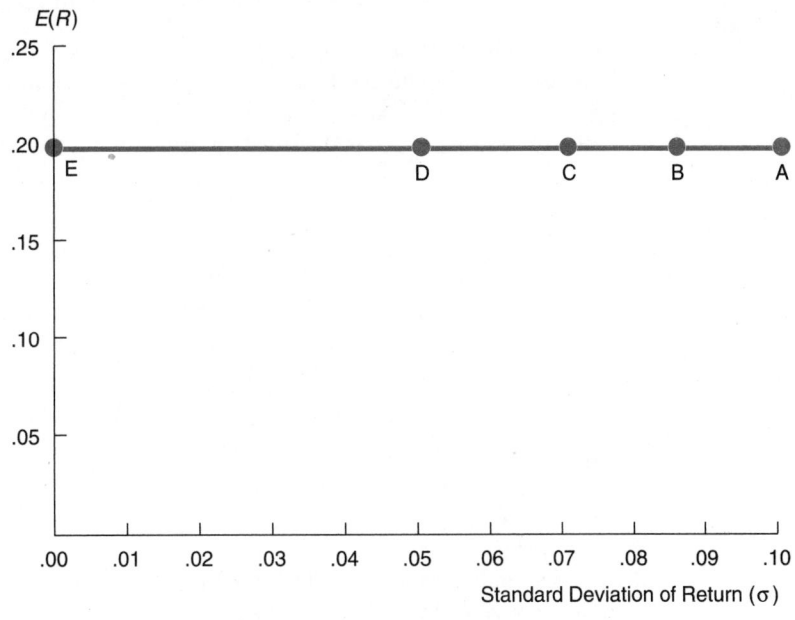

CASE	CORRELATION COEFFICIENT	COVARIANCE $(R_{ij}\sigma_i\sigma_j)$
a	+1.00	.0070
b	+0.50	.0035
c	0.00	.0000
d	−0.50	−.0035
e	−1.00	−.0070

Because we are assuming the same weights in all cases (0.50 − 0.50), the expected return in every instance will be

$$E(R_{\text{port}}) = 0.50(0.10) + 0.50(0.20)$$
$$= 0.15$$

The standard deviation for Case a will be

$$\sigma_{\text{port(a)}} = \sqrt{(0.5)^2 (0.07)^2 + (0.5)^2 (0.10)^2 + 2(0.5)(0.5)(0.0070)}$$
$$= \sqrt{(0.001225) + (0.0025) + (0.5)(0.0070)}$$
$$= \sqrt{0.007225}$$
$$= 0.085$$

Again, with perfect positive correlation, the standard deviation of the portfolio is the weighted average of the standard deviations of the individual assets:

$$(0.5)(0.07) + (0.5)(0.10) = 0.085$$

As you might envision, changing the weights with perfect positive correlation causes the standard deviation for the portfolio to change in a linear fashion. This is an important point to remember when we discuss the capital asset pricing model (CAPM) in the next chapter.

For Cases b, c, d, and e, the standard deviation for the portfolio would be as follows:[8]

$$\sigma_{port(b)} = \sqrt{(0.001225) + (0.0025) + (0.5)(0.0035)}$$
$$= \sqrt{(0.005475)}$$
$$= 0.07399$$

$$\sigma_{port(c)} = \sqrt{(0.001225) + (0.0025) + (0.5)(0.00)}$$
$$= 0.0610$$

$$\sigma_{port(d)} = \sqrt{(0.001225) + (0.0025) + (0.5)(-0.0035)}$$
$$= 0.0444$$

$$\sigma_{port(e)} = \sqrt{(0.003725) + (0.5)(-0.0070)}$$
$$= 0.015$$

Note that, in this example, with perfect negative correlation the standard deviation of the portfolio is not zero. This is because the different examples have equal weights, but the individual standard deviations are not equal.[9]

Exhibit 7.12 shows the results for the two individual assets and the portfolio of the two assets assuming the correlation coefficients vary as set forth in Cases a through e. As before, the expected return does not change because the proportions are always set at $0.50 - 0.50$, so all the portfolios lie along the horizontal line at the return, $E(R) = 0.15$.

Constant Correlation with Changing Weights If we changed the weights of the two assets while holding the correlation coefficient constant, we would derive a set of combinations that trace an ellipse starting at Asset 2, going through the $0.50 - 0.50$ point, and ending at Asset 1. We can demonstrate this with Case c, in which the correlation coefficient of zero eases the computations. We begin with 100 percent in Asset 2 (Case f) and change the weights as follows, ending with 100 percent in Asset 1 (Case m):

CASE	W_1	W_2	$E(R_i)$
f	.00	1.00	.20
g	.20	.80	.18
h	.40	.60	.16
i	.50	.50	.15
j	.60	.40	.14
k	.80	.20	.12
m	1.00	.00	.10

[8] In all the following examples, we will skip some steps because you are now aware that only the last term changes. You are encouraged to work out the individual steps to ensure that you understand the computational procedure.

[9] The two appendixes to this chapter show proofs for equal weights with equal variances and solve for the appropriate weights to get zero standard deviation when standard deviations are not equal.

EXHIBIT 7.12 ▶ *RISK-RETURN PLOT FOR PORTFOLIOS WITH DIFFERENT RETURNS, STANDARD DEVIATIONS, AND CORRELATIONS*

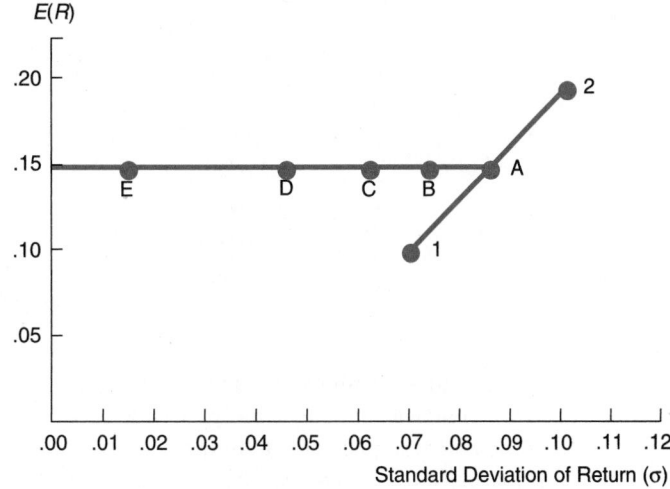

We already know the standard deviation (σ) for Portfolio i. In Cases f, g, h, j, k, and m, the standard deviations would be[10]

$$\sigma_{\text{port(g)}} = \sqrt{(0.20)^2 (0.07)^2 + (0.80)^2 (0.10)^2 + 2(0.20)(0.80)(0.00)}$$

$$= \sqrt{(0.04)(0.0049) + (0.64)(0.01) + (0)}$$

$$= \sqrt{(0.006596)}$$

$$= 0.0812$$

$$\sigma_{\text{port(h)}} = \sqrt{(0.40)^2 (0.07)^2 + (0.60)^2 (0.10)^2 + 2(0.40)(0.60)(0.00)}$$

$$= \sqrt{(0.004384)}$$

$$= 0.0662$$

$$\sigma_{\text{port(j)}} = \sqrt{(0.60)^2 (0.07)^2 + (0.40)^2 (0.10)^2 + 2(0.60)(0.40)(0.00)}$$

$$= \sqrt{(0.003364)}$$

$$= 0.0580$$

$$\sigma_{\text{port(k)}} = \sqrt{(0.80)^2 (0.07)^2 + (0.20)^2 (0.10)^2 + 2(0.80)(0.20)(0.00)}$$

$$= \sqrt{(0.003536)}$$

$$= 0.0595$$

---

[10]Again, you are encouraged to fill in the steps we skipped in the computations.

These alternative weights with a constant correlation would yield the following risk-return combinations:

CASE	W_1	W_2	$E(R_i)$	σ_{PORT}
f	0.00	1.00	0.20	0.1000
g	0.20	0.80	0.18	0.0812
h	0.40	0.60	0.16	0.0662
i	0.50	0.50	0.15	0.0610
j	0.60	0.40	0.14	0.0580
k	0.80	0.20	0.12	0.0595
m	1.00	0.00	0.10	0.0700

A graph of these combinations appears in Exhibit 7.13 for the curve with $r_{1,2} = +0.00$. You could derive a complete curve by simply varying the weighting by smaller increments.

A notable result is that with low, zero, or negative correlations, it is possible to derive portfolios that have *lower risk than either single asset*. In our set of examples where $r_{ij} = 0.00$, this occurs in Cases h, i, j, and k. This ability to reduce risk is the essence of diversification. As shown in Exhibit 7.13, assuming the normal risk-return relationship where assets with higher risk (larger standard deviation of returns) provide high rates of return, it is possible for a conservative investor to experience *both* lower risk *and* higher return by diversifying into a higher-risk–higher-return asset assuming the correlation between the two assets is fairly low. As shown in Exhibit 7.13, in the case where it is assumed that the correlation was zero (0.00), the low-risk investor at Point 1 who would receive a return of 10 percent and risk of 7 percent could *increase* his/her return to 14 percent *and* experience a *decline* in risk to 5.8 percent by investing (diversifying) 40 percent of the portfolio in riskier Asset 2. As noted, the benefits of diversification are

EXHIBIT 7.13   *PORTFOLIO RISK-RETURN PLOTS FOR DIFFERENT WEIGHTS WHEN $r_{i,j} = +1.00$; +0.50; 0.00; −0.50; −1.00*

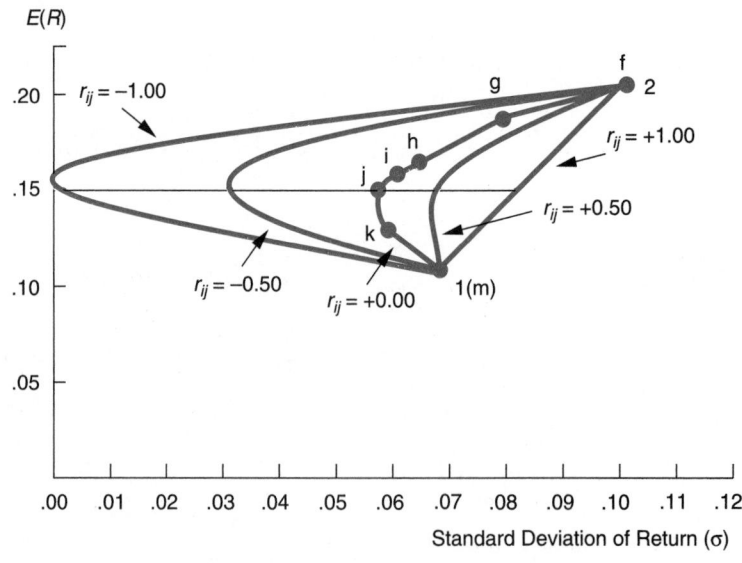

critically dependent on the correlation between assets; but, even if the correlation is not zero, you still derive some benefit as shown in Exhibit 7.13 when the correlation is 0.50.

As shown in Exhibit 7.13, the curvature in the graph depends on the correlation between the two assets or portfolios. With $r_{ij} = +1.00$, the combinations lie along a straight line between the two assets. When $r_{ij} = 0.50$, the curve is to the right of our $r_{ij} = 0.00$ curve, while the $r_{ij} = -0.50$ is to the left. Finally, when $r_{ij} = -1.00$, the graph would be two straight lines that would touch at the vertical line (zero risk) with some combination. As discussed in Appendix B of this chapter, it is possible to solve for the specified set of weights that would give a portfolio with zero risk. In this case, it is $W_1 = 0.412$ and $W_2 = 0.588$.

A Three-Asset Portfolio

A demonstration of what occurs with a three-asset class portfolio is useful because it shows the dynamics of the portfolio process when we add additional assets to a portfolio. It also shows the rapid growth in the computations required, which is why we will stop at three assets.

In this example, we will combine three asset classes we have been discussing: stocks, bonds, and cash equivalents.[11] We will assume the following characteristics for these assets:

Asset Classes	$E(R_i)$	σ_i	W_i
Stocks (S)	.12	.20	.60
Bonds (B)	.08	.10	.30
Cash equivalent (C)	.04	.03	.10

The correlations are as follows:

$$r_{S,B} = 0.25; \ r_{S,C} = -0.08; \ r_{B,C} = 0.15$$

Given the weights specified, the $E(R_p)$ is:

$$E(R_p) = (0.60)(0.12) + (0.30)(0.08) + (0.10)(0.04)$$
$$= (0.072 + 0.024 + 0.004) = 0.100 = 10.00\%$$

When we apply the generalized formula to the expected standard deviation of a three-asset class, it is as follows:

$$\sigma_p^2 = [W_S^2 \ \sigma_S^2 + W_B^2 \ \sigma_B^2 + W_C^2 \ \sigma_C^2] + [2W_S \ W_B \ \sigma_S \ \sigma_B \ r_{S,B} + 2W_S \ W_C \ \sigma_S\sigma_C \ r_{S,C} + 2W_B \ W_C \ \sigma_B \ \sigma_C \ r_{B,C}]$$

Using the characteristics specified, the standard deviation of this three-asset class portfolio (σ_p) would be:

$$\sigma_p^2 = [(0.6)^2(0.20)^2 + (0.3)^2(0.10)^2 + (0.1)^2(0.03)^2]$$
$$+ \{[2(0.6)(0.3)(0.20)(0.10)(0.25)] + [2(0.6)(0.1)(0.20)(0.03)(-0.08)]$$
$$+ [2(0.3)(0.1)(0.10)(0.03)(0.15)]\}$$
$$= [0.015309] + \{[0.0018] + [-0.0000576] + [0.000027]\}$$
$$= 0.0170784$$
$$\sigma_p = (0.0170784)^{1/2} = 0.1306 = 13.06\%$$

---

[11]The asset allocation articles regularly contained in *The Wall Street Journal* generally refer to these three asset classes.

Estimation Issues

It is important to keep in mind that the results of this portfolio asset allocation depend on the accuracy of the statistical inputs. In the current instance, this means that for every asset (or asset class) being considered for inclusion in the portfolio, you must estimate its expected returns and standard deviation. In addition, the correlation coefficient among the entire set of assets must also be estimated. The number of correlation estimates can be significant—for example, for a portfolio of 100 securities, the number is 4,950 (that is, 99 + 98 + 97 + . . .). The potential source of error that arises from these approximations is referred to as *estimation risk*.

It is possible to reduce the number of correlation coefficients that must be estimated by assuming that stock returns can be described by a single index market model as follows:

➤7.8
$$R_i = a_i + b_i R_m + \varepsilon_i$$

where:

b_i = **the slope coefficient that relates the returns for security *i* to the returns for the aggregate stock market**
R_m = **the returns for the aggregate stock market**

If all the securities are similarly related to the market and a slope coefficient (b_i) is derived for each one, it can be shown that the correlation coefficient between two securities *i* and *j* is given as:

➤7.9
$$r_{ij} = b_i b_j \frac{\sigma_m^2}{\sigma_i \sigma_j}$$

where:

σ_m^2 = **the variance of returns for the aggregate stock market**

This reduces the number of estimates from 4,950 to 100—that is, once you have derived a slope estimate (b_i) for each security, the correlation estimates can be computed. Keep in mind that this assumes that the single index market model provides a good estimate of security returns.

The Efficient Frontier

If we examined different two-asset combinations and derived the curves assuming all the possible weights, we would have a graph like that in Exhibit 7.14. The envelope curve that contains the best of all these possible combinations is referred to as the **efficient frontier**. Specifically, *the efficient frontier represents that set of portfolios that has the maximum rate of return for every given level of risk, or the minimum risk for every level of return.* An example of such a frontier is shown in Exhibit 7.15. Every portfolio that lies on the efficient frontier has either a higher rate of return for equal risk or lower risk for an equal rate of return than some portfolio beneath the frontier. Thus, we would say that Portfolio A in Exhibit 7.15 *dominates* Portfolio C because it has an equal rate of return but substantially less risk. Similarly, Portfolio B dominates Portfolio C because it has equal risk but a higher expected rate of return. Because of the benefits of diversification among imperfectly correlated assets, we would expect the efficient frontier to be made up of *portfolios* of investments rather than individual securities. Two possible exceptions arise at the end points, which represent the asset with the highest return and that asset with the lowest risk.

EXHIBIT 7.14   *NUMEROUS PORTFOLIO COMBINATIONS OF AVAILABLE ASSETS*

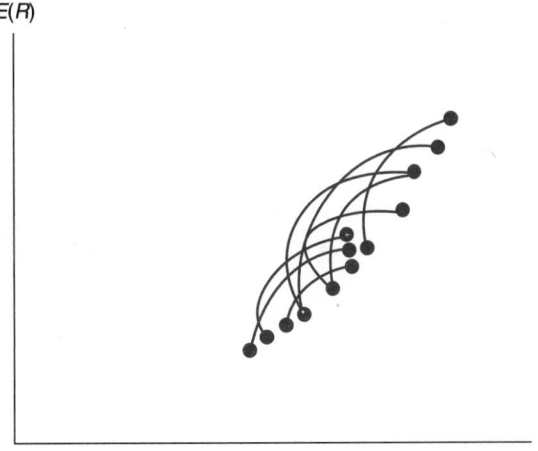

EXHIBIT 7.15   *EFFICIENT FRONTIER FOR ALTERNATIVE PORTFOLIOS*

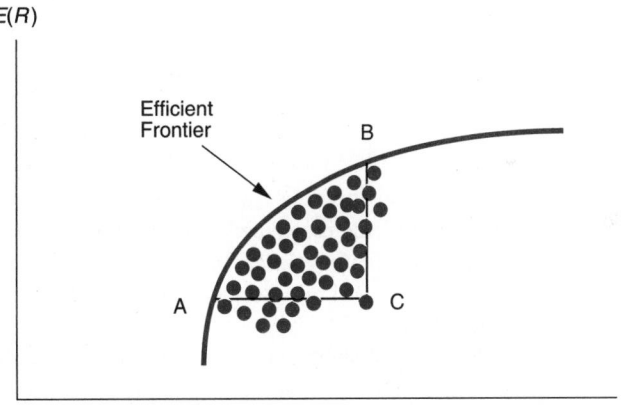

As an investor, you will target a point along the efficient frontier based on your utility function and your attitude toward risk. No portfolio on the efficient frontier can dominate any other portfolio on the efficient frontier. All of these portfolios have different return and risk measures, with expected rates of return that increase with higher risk.

The Efficient Frontier and Investor Utility

The curve in Exhibit 7.15 shows that the slope of the efficient frontier curve decreases steadily as you move upward. This implies that adding equal increments of risk as you move up the efficient frontier gives you diminishing increments of expected return. To evaluate this slope, we calculate the slope of the efficient frontier as follows:

EXHIBIT 7.16 ➤ *SELECTING AN OPTIMAL RISKY PORTFOLIO ON THE EFFICIENT FRONTIER*

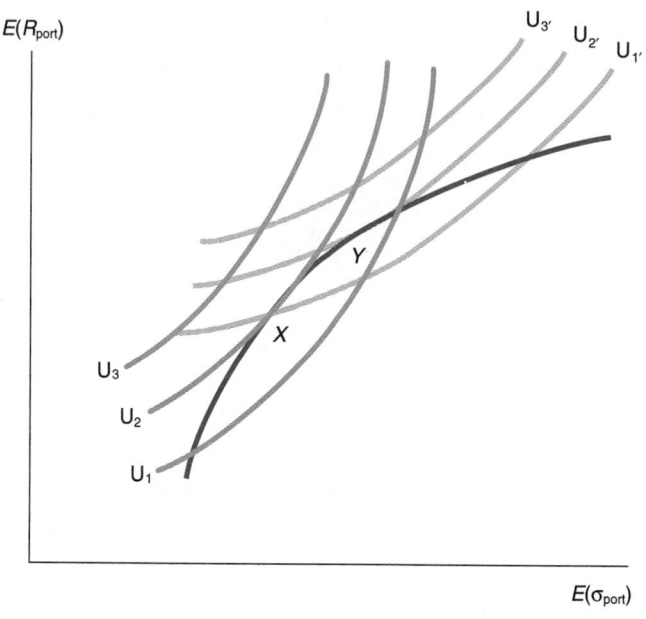

➤ 7.10

$$\frac{\Delta E(R_{port})}{\Delta \sigma_{port}}$$

An individual investor's utility curves specify the trade-offs he or she is willing to make between expected return and risk. In conjunction with the efficient frontier, these utility curves determine which *particular* portfolio on the efficient frontier best suits an individual investor. Two investors will choose the same portfolio from the efficient set only if their utility curves are identical.

Exhibit 7.16 shows two sets of utility curves along with an efficient frontier of investments. The curves labeled U_1 are for a strongly risk-averse investor (with U_3 U_2 U_1). These utility curves are quite steep, indicating that the investor will not tolerate much additional risk to obtain additional returns. The investor is equally disposed toward any $E(R)$, σ combinations along a specific utility curve, such as U_1.

The curves labeled $U_{1'}$ ($U_{3'}$ $U_{2'}$ $U_{1'}$) characterize a less-risk-averse investor. Such an investor is willing to tolerate a bit more risk to get a higher expected return.

The **optimal portfolio** is the portfolio on the efficient frontier that has the highest utility for a given investor. It lies at *the point of tangency between the efficient frontier and the curve with the highest possible utility.* A conservative investor's highest utility is at point X in Exhibit 7.16, where the curve U_2 just touches the efficient frontier. A less-risk-averse investor's highest utility occurs at point Y, which represents a portfolio with a higher expected return and higher risk than the portfolio at X.

The Internet *Investments Online*

By seeking to operate on the efficient frontier, portfolio managers try to minimize risk for a certain level of return, or maximize return for a given level of risk. Software programs, called optimizers, are used by portfolio managers to determine the shape of the efficient frontier as well as to determine some of the portfolios that lie on it. Financial planners use information on past returns and manager performance, in addition to optimizers, to make recommendations to their clients. Some interesting Web sites for money managers include:

http://www.pionline.com This is the home page for *Pensions and Investments,* a newspaper for money managers. Items on the home page include links to news of interest to managers and ePIPER performance data on a number of equity,

fixed income, real estate, and global portfolios from money manager and pension funds. Contains many links to organizations such as central banks, consultants, and sellers of investment-related products.

http://www.investmentnews.com *Investment News* is a sister publication to *Pensions and Investments,* with a focus toward the financial advisor. This site includes information on financial planning, the mutual fund industry, regulation, equity performance, and industry trends.

Software for creating efficient frontiers are available from firms such as Ibbotson Associates (**http://www.ibbotson.com**), Zephyr Associates (**http://www.styleadvisor.com**), Wagner Associates (**http://www.wagner.com**), and Efficient Solutions, Inc. (**http://www.effisols.com**).

Summary

- The basic Markowitz portfolio model derived the expected rate of return for a portfolio of assets and a measure of expected risk, which is the standard deviation of expected rate of return. Markowitz shows that the expected rate of return of a portfolio is the weighted average of the expected return for the individual investments in the portfolio. The standard deviation of a portfolio is a function not only of the standard deviations for the individual investments but *also* of the covariance between the rates of return for all the pairs of assets in the portfolio. In a large portfolio, these covariances are the important factors.
- Different weights or amounts of a portfolio held in various assets yield a curve of potential combinations. Correlation coefficients among assets are the critical factor you must consider when selecting investments because you can maintain your rate of return while reducing the risk level of your portfolio by combining assets or portfolios that have low positive or negative correlation.
- Assuming numerous assets and a multitude of combination curves, the efficient frontier is the envelope curve that encompasses all of the best combinations. It defines the set of portfolios that has the highest expected return for each given level of risk or the minimum risk for each given level of return. From this set of dominant portfolios, you select the one that lies at the point of tangency between the efficient frontier and your highest utility curve. Because risk-return utility functions differ among investors, your point of tangency and, therefore, your portfolio choice will probably differ from those of other investors.
- At this point, we understand that an optimum portfolio is a combination of investments, each having desirable individual risk–return characteristics that also fit together based on their correlations. This deeper understanding of portfolio theory should lead you to reflect back on our earlier discussion of global investing. Because many foreign stock and bond investments provide superior rates of return compared with U.S. securities *and* have low correlations with portfolios of U.S. stocks and bonds as shown in Chapter 3, including these foreign securities in your portfolio will help you to reduce the overall risk of your portfolio while possibly increasing your rate of return.

Questions

1. Why do most investors hold diversified portfolios?
2. What is covariance, and why is it important in portfolio theory?
3. Why do most assets of the same type show positive covariances of returns with each other? Would you expect positive covariances of returns between *different* types of assets such as returns on Treasury bills, General Electric common stock, and commercial real estate? Why or why not?
4. What is the relationship between covariance and the correlation coefficient?
5. Explain the shape of the efficient frontier.
6. Draw a properly labeled graph of the Markowitz efficient frontier. Describe the efficient frontier in exact terms. Discuss the concept of dominant portfolios and show an example of one on your graph.
7. Assume you want to run a computer program to derive the efficient frontier for your feasible set of stocks. What information must you input to the program?
8. Why are investors' utility curves important in portfolio theory?
9. Explain how a given investor chooses an optimal portfolio. Will this choice always be a diversified portfolio, or could it be a single asset? Explain your answer.
10. Assume that you and a business associate develop an efficient frontier for a set of investments. Why might the two of you select different portfolios on the frontier?
11. Draw a hypothetical graph of an efficient frontier of U.S. common stocks. On the same graph, draw an efficient frontier assuming the inclusion of U.S. bonds as well. Finally, on the same graph, draw an efficient frontier that includes U.S. common stocks, U.S. bonds, and stocks and bonds from around the world. Discuss the differences in these frontiers.
12. Stocks K, L, and M each have the same expected return and standard deviation. The correlation coefficients between each pair of these stocks are:

K and L	correlation coefficient = +0.8
K and M	correlation coefficient = +0.2
L and M	correlation coefficient = −0.4

Given these correlations, a portfolio constructed of which pair of stocks will have the lowest standard deviation? Explain.

Problems

1. Considering the world economic outlook for the coming year and estimates of sales and earnings for the pharmaceutical industry, you expect the rate of return for Lauren Labs common stock to range between −20 percent and +40 percent with the following probabilities:

Probability	Possible Returns
0.10	−0.20
0.15	−0.05
0.20	0.10
0.25	0.15
0.20	0.20
0.10	0.40

Compute the expected rate of return $[E(R_i)]$ for Lauren Labs.

2. Given the following market values of stocks in your portfolio and their expected rates of return, what is the expected rate of return for your common stock portfolio?

Stock	Market Value ($ Mil.)	$E(R_i)$
Morgan Stanley	$15,000	0.14
Starbucks	17,000	−0.04
General Electric	32,000	0.18
Intel	23,000	0.16
Walgreens	7,000	0.12

3. The following are the monthly rates of return for Madison Software Corp. and for Kayleigh Electric during a six-month period.

Month	Madison Software	Kayleigh Electric
1	−.04	.07
2	.06	−.02
3	−.07	−.10
4	.12	.15
5	−.02	−.06
6	.05	.02

Compute the following:

a. Expected monthly rate of return $[E(R_i)]$ for each stock

b. Standard deviation of returns for each stock

c. The covariance between the rates of return

d. The correlation coefficient between the rates of return

What level of correlation did you expect? How did your expectations compare with the computed correlation? Would these two stocks offer a good chance for diversification? Why or why not?

4. You are considering two assets with the following characteristics:

$$E(R_1) = .15 \qquad \sigma_1 = .10 \qquad W_1 = .5$$
$$E(R_2) = .20 \qquad \sigma_2 = .20 \qquad W_2 = .5$$

Compute the mean and standard deviation of two portfolios if $r_{1,2} = 0.40$ and -0.60, respectively. Plot the two portfolios on a risk-return graph and briefly explain the results.

5. Given: $E(R_1) = .10$

$$E(R_2) = .15$$
$$\sigma_1 = .03$$
$$\sigma_2 = .05$$

Calculate the expected returns and expected standard deviations of a two-stock portfolio in which Stock 1 has a weight of 60 percent under the following conditions:

a. $r_{1,2} = 1.00$

b. $r_{1,2} = 0.75$

c. $r_{1,2} = 0.25$

d. $r_{1,2} = 0.00$

e. $r_{1,2} = -0.25$

f. $r_{1,2} = -0.75$

g. $r_{1,2} = -1.00$

Calculate the expected returns and expected standard deviations of a two-stock portfolio having a correlation coefficient of 0.70 under the following conditions:

a. $w_1 = 1.00$

b. $w_1 = 0.75$

c. $w_1 = 0.50$

d. $w_1 = 0.25$

e. $w_1 = 0.05$

6. Given: $E(R_1) = 0.12$

$$E(R_2) = 0.16$$
$$\sigma_1 = 0.04$$
$$\sigma_2 = 0.06$$

Plot the results on a return-risk graph. Without calculations, draw in what a curve with varying weights would look like if the correlation coefficient had been 0.00, or if it had been −0.70.

7. The following are monthly percentage price changes for four market indexes:

Month	DJIA	S&P 500	Russell 2000	NIKKEI
1	.03	.02	.04	.04
2	.07	.06	.10	−.02
3	−.02	−.01	−.04	.07
4	.01	.03	.03	.02
5	.05	.04	.11	.02
6	−.06	−.04	−.08	.06

Compute the following:
a. Expected monthly rate of return for each series.
b. Standard deviation for each series.
c. Covariance between the rates of return for the following indexes:
   DJIA—S&P 500
   S&P 500—Russell 2000
   S&P 500—NIKKEI
   Russell 2000—NIKKEI
d. The correlation coefficients for the same four combinations.
e. Using the answers from Parts a, b, and d, calculate the expected return and standard deviation of a portfolio consisting of equal parts of (1) the S&P and the Russell 2000 and (2) the S&P and the NIKKEI. Discuss the two portfolios.

8. The standard deviation of Shamrock Corp. stock is 19 percent. The standard deviation of Baron Co. stock is 14 percent. The covariance between these two stocks is 100. What is the correlation between Shamrock and Baron stock?

References

Elton, Edwin J., and Martin J. Gruber. *Modern Portfolio Theory and Investment Analysis,* 5th ed. New York: John Wiley & Sons, Inc., 1995.

Farrell, James L., Jr. *Portfolio Management: Theory and Application,* 2d ed. New York: McGraw-Hill, 1997.

Harrington, Diana R. *Modern Portfolio Theory, the Capital Asset Pricing Model, and Arbitrage Pricing Theory: A User's Guide,* 2d ed. Englewood Cliffs, N.J.: Prentice-Hall, 1987.

Maginn, John L., and Donald L. Tuttle, eds. *Managing Investment Portfolios: A Dynamic Process,* 2d ed. Sponsored by The Institute of Chartered Financial Analysts. Boston: Warren, Gorham & Lamont, 1990.

Markowitz, Harry. "Portfolio Selection." *Journal of Finance* 7, no. 1 (March 1952).

Markowitz, Harry. *Portfolio Selection: Efficient Diversification of Investments.* New York: John Wiley & Sons, 1959.

APPENDIX
Chapter 7

A. Proof That Minimum Portfolio Variance Occurs with Equal Weights When Securities Have Equal Variance

When $\sigma_1 = \sigma_2$, we have:

$$\sigma_{port}^2 = w_1^2(\sigma_1)^2 + (1 - w_1)^2(\sigma_1)^2 - 2w_1(1 - w_1)r_{1,2}(\sigma_1)^2$$
$$= (\sigma_1)^2[w_1^2 + 1 - 2w_1 + w_1^2 + 2w_1r_{1,2} - 2w_1^2 r_{1,2}]$$
$$= (\sigma_1)^2 [2w_1^2 + 1 - 2w_1 + 2w_1 r_{1,2} - 2w_1^2 r_{1,2}]$$

For this to be a minimum,

$$\frac{\partial(\sigma_{port}^2)}{\partial w_1} = 0 = (\sigma_1)^2 \left[4w_1 \times 2 + 2r_{1,2} \times 4w_1 r_{1,2} \right]$$

Assuming $(\sigma_1)^2 > 0$,

$$4w_1 - 2 + 2r_{1,2} - 4w_1 r_{1,2} = 0$$
$$4w_1(1 - r_{1,2}) - 2(1 - r_{1,2}) = 0$$

from which

$$w_1 \frac{2(1 - r_{1,2})}{4(1 - r_{1,2})} = \frac{1}{2}$$

regardless of $r_{1,2}$. Thus, if $\sigma_1 = \sigma_2$, σ_{port}^2 will *always* be minimized by choosing $w_1 = w_2 = 1/2$, regardless of the value of $r_{1,2}$, except when $r_{1,2} = +1$ (in which case $\sigma_{port} = \sigma_1 = \sigma_2$. This can be verified by checking the second-order condition

$$\frac{\partial(\sigma_{port}^2)}{\partial w_1^2} > 0$$

Problems

1. The following information applies to Questions 1a and 1b. The general equation for the weight of the first security to achieve minimum variance (in a two-stock portfolio) is given by

$$w_1 = \frac{(\sigma_2)^2 - r_{1,2}(\sigma_1)(\sigma_2)}{(\sigma_1)^2 + (\sigma_2)^2 - 2r_{1,2}(\sigma_1)(\sigma_2)}$$

1a. Show that $w_1 = 0.5$ when $\sigma_1 = \sigma_2$.

1b. What is the weight of Security 1 that gives minimum portfolio variance when $r_{1,2} = 0.5$, $\sigma_1 = 0.04$, and $\sigma_2 = 0.06$?

APPENDIX
Chapter 7

B. Derivation of Weights That Will Give Zero Variance When Correlation Equals −1.00

$$\sigma^2_{port} = w_1^2(\sigma_1)^2 + (1 - w_1)^2(\sigma_2)^2 + 2w_1(1 - w_1)r_{1,2}(\sigma_1)(\sigma_2)$$
$$= w_1^2(\sigma_1)^2 + (\sigma_2)^2 - 2w_1(\sigma_2) - w_1^2(\sigma_2)^2 + 2w_1r_{1,2}(\sigma_1)(\sigma_2) - 2w_1^2r_{1,2}(\sigma_1)(\sigma_2)$$

If $r_{1,2} = 1$, this can be rearranged and expressed as

$$\sigma^2_{port} = w_1^2[(\sigma_1)^2 + 2(\sigma_1)(\sigma_2) + (\sigma_2)^2] - 2w[(\sigma_2)^2 + (\sigma_1)(\sigma_2)] + (\sigma_2)^2$$
$$= w_1^2[(\sigma_1) + (\sigma_2)]^2 - 2w_1(\sigma_2)[(\sigma_1) - (\sigma_2)] + (\sigma_2)^2$$
$$= \{w_1[(\sigma_1) + (\sigma_2)] - (\sigma_2)\}^2$$

We want to find the weight, w_1, which will reduce (σ^2_{port}) to *zero;* therefore,

$$w_1[(\sigma_1) + (\sigma_2)] - (\sigma_2) = 0$$

which yields

$$w_1 = \frac{(\sigma_2)}{(\sigma_1) + (\sigma_2)}, \text{ and } w_2 = 1 - w_1 = \frac{(\sigma_1)}{(\sigma_1) + (\sigma_2)}$$

Problem

1. Given two assets with the following characteristics:

$E(R_1) = .12 \qquad \sigma_1 = .04$

$E(R_2) = .16 \qquad \sigma_2 = .06$

Assume that $r_{1,2} = -1.00$. What is the weight that would yield a zero variance for the portfolio?

Chapter 8 — An Introduction to Asset Pricing Models

After you read this chapter, you should be able to answer the following questions:

➤ What are the assumptions of the capital asset pricing model?

➤ What is a risk-free asset and what are its risk-return characteristics?

➤ What is the covariance and correlation between the risk-free asset and a risky asset or portfolio of risky assets?

➤ What is the expected return when you combine the risk-free asset and a portfolio of risky assets?

➤ What is the standard deviation when you combine the risk-free asset and a portfolio of risky assets?

➤ When you combine the risk-free asset and a portfolio of risky assets on the Markowitz efficient frontier, what does the set of possible portfolios look like?

➤ Given the initial set of portfolio possibilities with a risk-free asset, what happens when you add financial leverage (that is, borrow)?

➤ What is the market portfolio, what assets are included in this portfolio, and what are the relative weights for the alternative assets included?

➤ What is the capital market line (CML)?

➤ What do we mean by complete diversification?

➤ How do we measure diversification for an individual portfolio?

➤ What are systematic and unsystematic risk?

➤ Given the CML, what is the separation theorem?

➤ Given the CML, what is the relevant risk measure for an individual risky asset?

➤ What is the security market line (SML), and how does it differ from the CML?

➤ What is *beta,* and why is it referred to as a standardized measure of systematic risk?

➤ How can you use the SML to determine the expected (required) rate of return for a risky asset?

➤ Using the SML, what do we mean by an undervalued and overvalued security, and how do we determine whether an asset is undervalued or overvalued?

➤ What is an asset's characteristic line, and how do you compute the characteristic line for an asset?

➤ What is the impact on the characteristic line when you compute it using different return intervals (such as weekly versus monthly) and when you employ different proxies (that is, benchmarks) for the market portfolio (for example, the S&P 500 versus a global stock index)?

➤ What happens to the capital market line (CML) when you assume there are differences in the risk-free borrowing and lending rates?

➤ What is a zero-beta asset and how does its use impact the CML?

➤ What happens to the security line (SML) when you assume transactions costs, heterogeneous expectations, different planning periods, and taxes?

➤ What are the major questions considered when empirically testing the CAPM?

> ➤ What are the empirical results from tests that examine the stability of beta?
> ➤ How do alternative published estimates of beta compare?
> ➤ What are the results of studies that examine the relationship between systematic risk and return?
> ➤ What other variables besides beta have had a significant impact on returns?
> ➤ What is the theory regarding the "market portfolio" and how does this differ from the market proxy used for the market portfolio?
> ➤ Assuming there is a benchmark problem, what variables are affected by it?

Following the development of portfolio theory by Markowitz, two major theories have been put forth that derive a model for the valuation of risky assets. In this chapter, we introduce one of these two models—that is, the capital asset pricing model (CAPM). The background on the CAPM is important at this point in the book because the risk measure implied by this model is a necessary input for our subsequent discussion on the valuation of risky assets. The presentation concerns capital market theory and the capital asset pricing model that was developed almost concurrently by three individuals. Subsequently, an alternative multifactor asset valuation model was proposed, the arbitrage pricing theory (APT). This has led to the development of numerous other multifactor models that are the subject of the following chapter.

CAPITAL MARKET THEORY: AN OVERVIEW

Because capital market theory builds on portfolio theory, this chapter begins where the discussion of the Markowitz efficient frontier ended. We assume that you have examined the set of risky assets and derived the aggregate efficient frontier. Further, we assume that you and all other investors want to maximize your utility in terms of risk and return, so you will choose portfolios of risky assets on the efficient frontier at points where your utility maps are tangent to the frontier as shown in Exhibit 7.16. When you make your investment decision in this manner, you are referred to as a *Markowitz efficient investor.*

Capital market theory extends portfolio theory and develops a model for pricing all risky assets. The final product, the **capital asset pricing model (CAPM)**, will allow you to determine the required rate of return for any risky asset.

We begin with the background of capital market theory that includes the underlying assumptions of the theory and a discussion of the factors that led to its development following the Markowitz portfolio theory. This includes an analysis of the effect of assuming the existence of a risk-free asset.

Notably, assuming the existence of a risk-free rate has significant implications for the potential return and risk and alternative risk-return combinations. This discussion implies a central portfolio of risky assets on the efficient frontier, which we call the **market portfolio**. We discuss the market portfolio in the third section and what it implies regarding different types of risk.

The fourth section considers which types of risk are relevant to an investor who believes in capital market theory. Having defined a measure of risk, we consider how you determine your required rate of return on an investment. You can then compare this required rate of return to your estimate of the asset's expected rate of return during your investment horizon to determine whether the asset is undervalued or overvalued. The section ends with a demonstration of how to calculate the risk measure implied by capital market theory.

Background for Capital Market Theory

When dealing with any theory in science, economics, or finance, it is necessary to articulate a set of assumptions that specify how the world is expected to act. This allows the theoretician to concentrate on developing a theory that explains how some facet of the world will respond to changes in the environment. In this section, we consider the main assumptions that underlie the development of capital market theory.

Assumptions of Capital Market Theory Because capital market theory builds on the Markowitz portfolio model, it requires the same assumptions, along with some additional ones:

1. All investors are Markowitz efficient investors who want to target points on the efficient frontier. The exact location on the efficient frontier and, therefore, the specific portfolio selected will depend on the individual investor's risk-return utility function.

2. Investors can borrow or lend any amount of money at the risk-free rate of return *(RFR)*. Clearly, it is always possible to lend money at the nominal risk-free rate by buying risk-free securities such as government T-bills. It is not always possible to borrow at this risk-free rate, but we will see that assuming a higher borrowing rate does not change the general results.

3. All investors have homogeneous expectations; that is, they estimate identical probability distributions for future rates of return. Again, this assumption can be relaxed. As long as the differences in expectations are not vast, their effects are minor.

4. All investors have the same one-period time horizon such as one month, six months, or one year. The model will be developed for a single hypothetical period, and its results could be affected by a different assumption. A difference in the time horizon would require investors to derive risk measures and risk-free assets that are consistent with their investment horizons.

5. All investments are infinitely divisible, which means that it is possible to buy or sell fractional shares of any asset or portfolio. This assumption allows us to discuss investment alternatives as continuous curves. Changing it would have little impact on the theory.

6. There are no taxes or transaction costs involved in buying or selling assets. This is a reasonable assumption in many instances. Neither pension funds nor religious groups have to pay taxes, and the transaction costs for most financial institutions are less than 1 percent on most financial instruments. Again, relaxing this assumption modifies the results, but it does not change the basic thrust.

7. There is no inflation or any change in interest rates, or inflation is fully anticipated. This is a reasonable initial assumption, and it can be modified.

8. Capital markets are in equilibrium. This means that we begin with all investments properly priced in line with their risk levels.

You may consider some of these assumptions unrealistic and wonder how useful a theory we can derive with these assumptions. In this regard, two points are important. First, as mentioned, relaxing many of these assumptions would have only a minor effect on the model and would not change its main implications or conclusions. Second, a theory should never be judged on the basis of its assumptions but, rather, on how well it explains and helps us predict behavior in the real world. If this theory and the model it implies help us explain the rates of return on a wide variety of risky assets, it is useful, even if some of its assumptions are unrealistic. Such success implies that the questionable assumptions must be unimportant to the ultimate objective of the model, which is to explain asset pricing and rates of return on assets.

Development of Capital Market Theory   The major factor that allowed portfolio theory to develop into capital market theory is the concept of a risk-free asset. Following the development of the Markowitz portfolio model, several authors considered the implications of assuming the existence of a **risk-free asset**, that is, an asset with *zero variance*. As we will show, such an asset would have zero correlation with all other risky assets and would provide the *risk-free rate of return (RFR)*. It would lie on the vertical axis of a portfolio graph.

This assumption allows us to derive a generalized theory of capital asset pricing under conditions of uncertainty from the Markowitz portfolio theory. This achievement is generally attributed to William Sharpe, for which he received the Nobel Prize, but Lintner and Mossin derived similar theories independently.[1] Consequently, you may see references to the Sharpe-Lintner-Mossin (SLM) capital asset pricing model.

Risk-Free Asset

As noted, the assumption of a risk-free asset in the economy is critical to asset pricing theory. Therefore, this section explains the meaning of a risk-free asset and shows the effect on the risk and return measures when this risk-free asset is combined with a portfolio on the Markowitz efficient frontier.

We have defined a **risky asset** as one from which future returns are uncertain, and we have measured this uncertainty by the variance, or standard deviation, of expected returns. Because the expected return on a risk-free asset is entirely certain, the standard deviation of its expected return is zero ($\sigma_{RF} = 0$). The rate of return earned on such an asset should be the risk-free rate of return *(RFR)*, which, as we discussed in Chapter 1, should equal the expected long-run growth rate of the economy with an adjustment for short-run liquidity. The next sections show what happens when we introduce this risk-free asset into the risky world of the Markowitz portfolio model.

Covariance with a Risk-Free Asset   Recall that the covariance between two sets of returns is

➤ 8.1
$$\text{Cov}_{ij} = \sum_{i=1}^{n} [R_i - E(R_i)][R_j - E(R_j)]/n$$

Because the returns for the risk-free asset are certain, $\sigma_{RF} = 0$, which means that $R_i = E(R_i)$ during all periods. Thus, $R_i - E(R_i)$ will also equal zero, and the product of this expression with any other expression will equal zero. Consequently, the covariance of the risk-free asset with any risky asset or portfolio of assets will always equal zero. Similarly, the correlation between any risky asset *i*, and the risk-free asset, RF, would be zero because it is equal to

$$r_{RF,i} = \text{Cov}_{RF,i}/\sigma_{RF}\sigma_j$$

Combining a Risk-Free Asset with a Risky Portfolio   What happens to the average rate of return and the standard deviation of returns when you combine a risk-free asset with a portfolio of risky assets such as those that exist on the Markowitz efficient frontier?

---

[1] William F. Sharpe, "Capital Asset Prices: A Theory of Market Equilibrium under Conditions of Risk," *Journal of Finance* 19, no. 3 (September 1964): 425–442; John Lintner, "Security Prices, Risk and Maximal Gains from Diversification," *Journal of Finance* 20, no. 4 (December 1965): 587–615; and J. Mossin, "Equilibrium in a Capital Asset Market," *Econometrica* 34, no. 4 (October 1966): 768–783.

Expected Return   Like the expected return for a portfolio of two risky assets, the expected rate of return for a portfolio that includes a risk-free asset is the weighted average of the two returns:

$$E(R_{port}) = w_{RF}(RFR) + (1 - w_{RF})E(R_i)$$

where:

> w_{RF} = the proportion of the portfolio invested in the risk-free asset
> $E(R_i)$ = the expected rate of return on risky Portfolio i

Standard Deviation   Recall from Chapter 7 (Equation 7.7) that the expected variance for a two-asset portfolio is

$$\sigma^2_{port} = w_1^2\sigma_1^2 + w_2^2\sigma_2^2 + 2w_1w_2r_{1,2}\sigma_1\sigma_2$$

Substituting the risk-free asset for Security 1, and the risky asset portfolio for Security 2, this formula would become

$$\sigma^2_{port} = w_{RF}^2\sigma_{RF}^2 + (1 - w_{RF})^2\sigma_i^2 + 2w_{RF}(1 - w_{RF})r_{RFi}\sigma_{RF}\sigma_i$$

We know that the variance of the risk-free asset is zero, that is, $\sigma^2_{RF} = 0$. Because the correlation between the risk-free asset and any risky asset, i, is also zero, the factor $r_{RF,i}$ in the preceding equation also equals zero. Therefore, any component of the variance formula that has either of these terms will equal zero. When you make these adjustments, the formula becomes

$$\sigma^2_{port} = (1 - w_{RF})^2\sigma_i^2$$

The standard deviation is

$$\sigma_{port} = \sqrt{(1 - w_{RF})^2 \sigma_i^2}$$
$$= (1 - w_{RF})\sigma_i$$

Therefore, the standard deviation of a portfolio that combines the risk-free asset with risky assets is *the linear proportion of the standard deviation of the risky asset portfolio.*

The Risk-Return Combination   Because both the expected return *and* the standard deviation of return for such a portfolio are linear combinations, a graph of possible portfolio returns and risks looks like a straight line between the two assets. Exhibit 8.1 shows a graph depicting portfolio possibilities when a risk-free asset is combined with alternative risky portfolios on the Markowitz efficient frontier.

You can attain any point along the straight line *RFR*-A by investing some portion of your portfolio in the risk-free asset w_{RF} and the remainder $(1 - w_{RF})$ in the risky asset portfolio at Point A on the efficient frontier. This set of portfolio possibilities dominates all the risky asset portfolios on the efficient frontier below Point A because some portfolio along Line *RFR*-A has equal variance with a higher rate of return than the portfolio on the original efficient frontier. Likewise, you can attain any point along the Line *RFR*-B by investing in some combination of the risk-free asset and the risky asset portfolio at Point B. Again, these potential combinations dominate all portfolio possibilities on the original efficient frontier below Point B (including Line *RFR*-A).

EXHIBIT 8.1 *PORTFOLIO POSSIBILITIES COMBINING THE RISK-FREE ASSET AND RISKY PORTFOLIOS ON THE EFFICIENT FRONTIER*

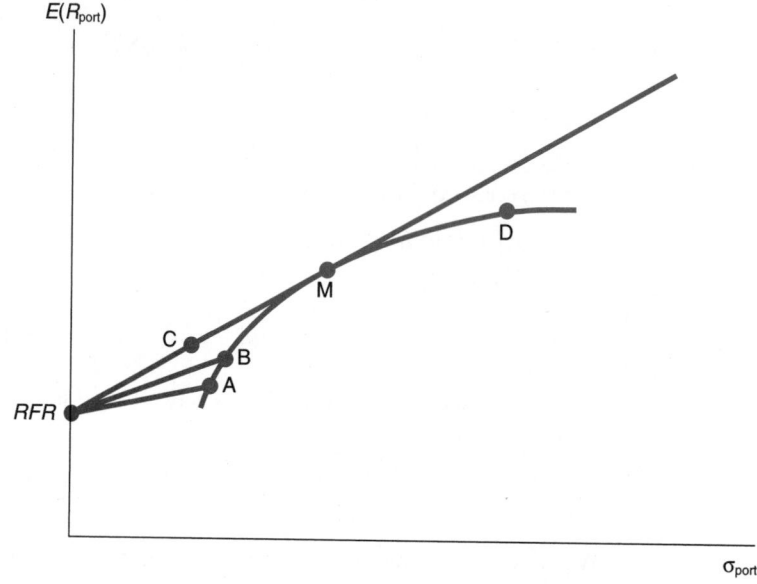

You can draw further lines from the *RFR* to the efficient frontier at higher and higher points until you reach the point where the line is tangent to the frontier, which occurs in Exhibit 8.1 at Point M. The set of portfolio possibilities along Line *RFR*-M dominates *all* portfolios below Point M. For example, you could attain a risk and return combination between the *RFR* and Point M (Point C) by investing one-half of your portfolio in the risk-free asset (that is, lending money at the *RFR*) and the other half in the risky portfolio at Point M.

Risk-Return Possibilities with Leverage An investor may want to attain a higher expected return than is available at Point M in exchange for accepting higher risk. One alternative would be to invest in one of the risky asset portfolios on the efficient frontier beyond Point M such as the portfolio at Point D. A second alternative is to add *leverage* to the portfolio by *borrowing* money at the risk-free rate and investing the proceeds in the risky asset portfolio at Point M. What effect would this have on the return and risk for your portfolio?

If you borrow an amount equal to 50 percent of your original wealth at the risk-free rate, w_{RF} will not be a positive fraction but, rather, a negative 50 percent ($w_{RF} = -0.50$). The effect on the expected return for your portfolio is:

$$E(R_{port}) = w_{RF}(RFR) + (1 - w_{RF})E(R_M)$$
$$= -0.50(RFR) + [1 - (-0.50)]E(R_M)$$
$$= -0.50(RFR) + 1.50E(R_M)$$

The return will increase in a *linear* fashion along the Line *RFR*-M because the gross return increases by 50 percent, but you must pay interest at the *RFR* on the money borrowed. For example, assume that $E(RFR) = .06$ and $E(R_M) = .12$. The return on your leveraged portfolio would be:

$$E(R_{port}) = -0.50(0.06) + 1.5(0.12)$$
$$= -0.03 + 0.18$$
$$= 0.15$$

EXHIBIT 8.2 ▶ *DERIVATION OF CAPITAL MARKET LINE ASSUMING LENDING OR BORROWING AT THE RISK-FREE RATE*

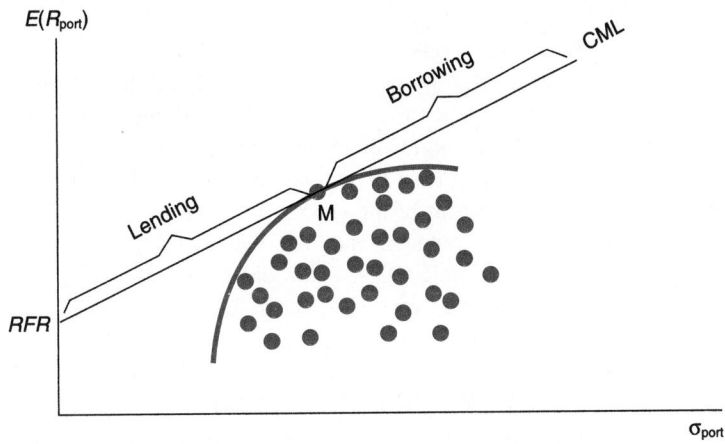

The effect on the standard deviation of the leveraged portfolio is similar.

$$\sigma_{port} = (1 - w_{RF})\sigma_M$$
$$= [1 - (-0.50)]\sigma_M = 1.50\sigma_M$$

where:

σ_M = the standard deviation of the M portfolio

Therefore, *both return and risk increase in a linear fashion along the original Line RFR-M,* and this extension dominates everything below the line on the original efficient frontier. Thus, you have a new efficient frontier: the straight line from the *RFR* tangent to Point M. This line is referred to as the **capital market line (CML)** and is shown in Exhibit 8.2.

Our discussion of portfolio theory stated that, when two assets are perfectly correlated, the set of portfolio possibilities falls along a straight line. Therefore, because the CML is a straight line, it implies that all the portfolios on the CML are perfectly positively correlated. This positive correlation appeals to our intuition because all these portfolios on the CML combine the risky asset Portfolio M and the risk-free asset. You either invest part of your portfolio in the risk-free asset (i.e., you *lend* at the *RFR*) and the rest in the risky asset Portfolio M, or you *borrow* at the risk-free rate and invest these funds in the risky asset portfolio. In either case, all the variability comes from the risky asset M portfolio. The only difference between the alternative portfolios on the CML is the magnitude of the variability, which is caused by the proportion of the risky asset portfolio in the total portfolio.

The Market Portfolio

Because Portfolio M lies at the point of tangency, it has the highest portfolio possibility line, and everybody will want to invest in Portfolio M and borrow or lend to be somewhere on the CML. This portfolio must, therefore, include *all risky assets.* If a risky asset were not in this portfolio in which everyone wants to invest, there would be no demand for it and therefore it would have no value.

Because the market is in equilibrium, it is also necessary that all assets are included in this portfolio *in proportion to their market value.* If, for example, an asset accounts for a higher proportion of the M portfolio than its market value justifies, excess demand for this asset will increase its price until its relative market value becomes consistent with its proportion in the M portfolio.

This portfolio that includes all risky assets is referred to as the **market portfolio**. It includes not only U.S. common stocks but *all* risky assets, such as non-U.S. stocks, U.S. and non-U.S. bonds, options, real estate, coins, stamps, art, or antiques. Because the market portfolio contains all risky assets, it is a **completely diversified portfolio**, which means that all the risk unique to individual assets in the portfolio is diversified away. Specifically, the unique risk of any single asset is offset by the unique variability of all the other assets in the portfolio.

This unique (diversifiable) risk is also referred to as **unsystematic risk**. This implies that only **systematic risk**, which is defined as the variability in all risky assets caused by macroeconomic variables, remains in the market portfolio. This systematic risk, measured by the standard deviation of returns of the market portfolio, can change over time if and when there are changes in the macroeconomic variables that affect the valuation of all risky assets.[2] Examples of such macroeconomic variables would be variability of growth in the money supply, interest rate volatility, and variability in such factors as industrial production, corporate earnings, and corporate cash flow.

How to Measure Diversification

As noted earlier, all portfolios on the CML are perfectly positively correlated, which means that all portfolios on the CML are perfectly correlated with the completely diversified market Portfolio M. This implies a measure of complete diversification.[3] Specifically, a completely diversified portfolio would have a correlation with the market portfolio of +1.00. This is logical because complete diversification means the elimination of all the unsystematic or unique risk. Once you have eliminated all unsystematic risk, only systematic risk is left, which cannot be diversified away. Therefore, completely diversified portfolios would correlate perfectly with the market portfolio because it has only systematic risk.

Diversification and the Elimination of Unsystematic Risk

As discussed in Chapter 7, the purpose of diversification is to reduce the standard deviation of the total portfolio. This assumes imperfect correlations among securities.[4] Ideally, as you add securities, the average covariance for the portfolio declines. An important question is, about how many securities must be included to arrive at a completely diversified portfolio? To discover the answer, you must observe what happens as you increase the sample size of the portfolio by adding securities that have some positive correlation. The typical correlation among U.S. securities is about 0.5 to 0.6.

One set of studies examined the average standard deviation for numerous portfolios of randomly selected stocks of different sample sizes. Specifically, the authors computed the standard deviation for portfolios of increasing numbers up to 20 stocks. The results indicated a large initial impact wherein the major benefits of diversification were achieved rather quickly. Specifically, about 90 percent of the maximum benefit of diversification was derived from portfolios of 12 to 18 stocks. Exhibit 8.3 shows a graph of the effect.

A subsequent study compared the benefits of lower risk from diversification to the added transaction costs with more securities. It concluded that a well-diversified stock portfolio must include at least 30 stocks for a borrowing investor and 40 stocks for a lending investor.

---

[2]For an analysis of changes in the standard deviation (volatility) of returns for stocks and bonds in the United States, see G. William Schwert, "Why Does Stock Market Volatility Change over Time?" *Journal of Finance* 44, no. 5 (December 1989): 1115–1153; Peter S. Spiro, "The Impact of Interest Rate Changes on Stock Price Volatility," *Journal of Portfolio Management* 16, no. 2 (Winter 1990): 63–68; R. R. Officer, "The Variability of the Market Factor of the New York Stock Exchange," *Journal of Business* 46, no. 3 (July 1973): 434–453; and Frank K. Reilly, David J. Wright, and Kam C. Chan, "Bond Market Volatility Compared to Stock Market Volatility," *Journal of Portfolio Management* 27, no. 1 (Fall 2000): 82–92.

[3]James Lorie, "Diversification: Old and New," *Journal of Portfolio Management* 1, no. 2 (Winter 1975): 25–28.

[4]The discussion in Chapter 7 leads one to conclude that securities with negative correlation would be ideal. Although this is true in theory, it is difficult to find such assets in the real world.

| **EXHIBIT 8.3** | *NUMBER OF STOCKS IN A PORTFOLIO AND THE STANDARD DEVIATION OF PORTFOLIO RETURN* |

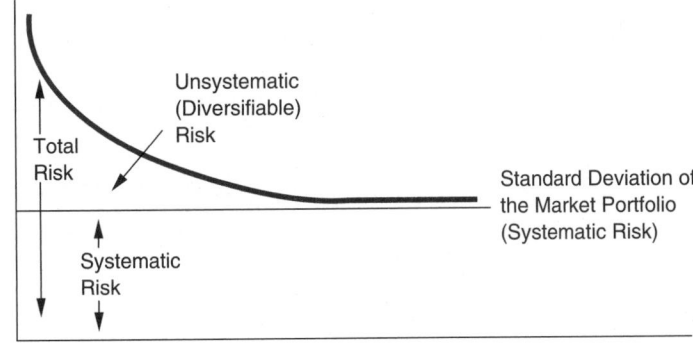

An important point to remember is that, by adding stocks to the portfolio that are not perfectly correlated with stocks in the portfolio, you can reduce the overall standard deviation of the portfolio but you *cannot eliminate variability.* The standard deviation of your portfolio will eventually reach the level of the market portfolio, where you will have diversified away all unsystematic risk, but you still have market or systematic risk. You cannot eliminate the variability and uncertainty of macroeconomic factors that affect all risky assets. At the same time, you will recall from the discussion in Chapter 3 that you can attain a lower level of systematic risk by diversifying globally versus only investing in the United States because some of the systematic risk factors in the U.S. market (such as U.S. monetary policy) are not correlated with systematic risk variables in other countries such as Germany and Japan. As a result, if you diversify globally you eventually get down to a world systematic risk level.

The CML and the Separation Theorem   The CML leads all investors to invest in the same risky asset portfolio, the M portfolio. Individual investors should only differ regarding their position on the CML, which depends on their risk preferences.

In turn, how they get to a point on the CML is based on their *financing decisions.* If you are relatively risk averse, you will lend some part of your portfolio at the *RFR* by buying some risk-free securities and investing the remainder in the market portfolio of risky assets. For example, you might invest in the portfolio combination at Point A in Exhibit 8.4. In contrast, if you prefer more risk, you might borrow funds at the *RFR* and invest everything (all of your capital plus what you borrowed) in the market portfolio, building the portfolio at Point B. This financing decision provides more risk but greater returns than the market portfolio. As discussed earlier, because portfolios on the CML dominate other portfolio possibilities, the CML becomes the efficient frontier of portfolios, and investors decide where they want to be along this efficient frontier. Tobin called this division of the investment decision from the financing decision the **separation theorem**.[5] Specifically, to be somewhere on the CML efficient frontier, you initially

---

[5]James Tobin, "Liquidity Preference as Behavior Towards Risk," *Review of Economic Studies* 25, no. 2 (February 1958): 65–85.

EXHIBIT 8.4 *CHOICE OF OPTIMAL PORTFOLIO COMBINATIONS ON THE CML*

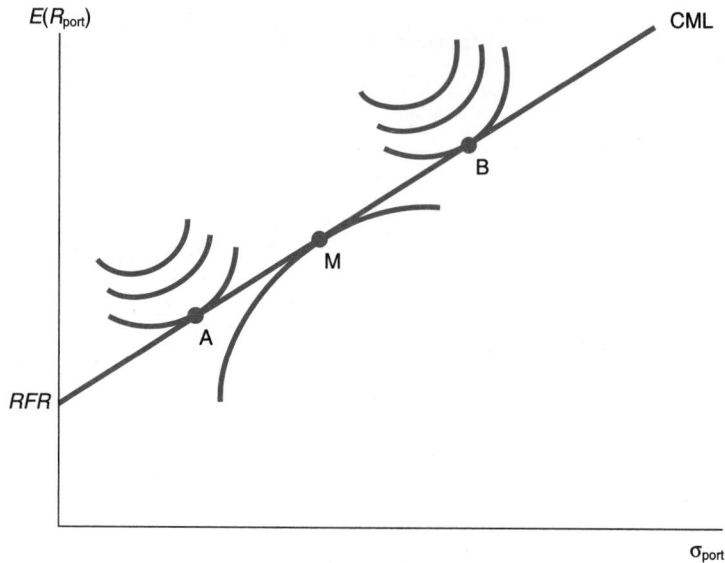

decide to invest in the market Portfolio M, which means that you will be on the CML. This is your *investment* decision. Subsequently, based on your risk preferences, you make a separate *financing* decision either to borrow or to lend to attain your preferred risk position on the CML.

A Risk Measure for the CML In this section, we show that the relevant risk measure for risky assets is *their covariance with the M portfolio,* which is referred to as their systematic risk. The importance of this covariance is apparent from two points of view.

First, in discussing the Markowitz portfolio model, we noted that the relevant risk to consider when adding a security to a portfolio is *its average covariance with all other assets in the portfolio.* In this chapter, we have shown that *the only relevant portfolio is the M portfolio.* Together, these two findings mean that the only important consideration for any individual risky asset is its average covariance with all the risky assets in the M portfolio or, simply, *the asset's covariance with the market portfolio.* This covariance, then, is the relevant risk measure for an individual risky asset.

Second, because all individual risky assets are a part of the M portfolio, one can describe their rates of return in relation to the returns for the M portfolio using the following linear model:

➤8.2 $$R_{it} = a_i + b_i R_{Mt} + \varepsilon$$

where:

$R_{i,t}$ = **return for asset *i* during period *t***
a_i = **constant term for asset *i***
b_i = **slope coefficient for asset *i***
R_{Mt} = **return for the M portfolio during period *t***
ε = **random error term**

The variance of returns for a risky asset could be described as

➤8.3
$$\text{Var}(R_{it}) = \text{Var}(a_i + b_iR_{Mt} + \varepsilon)$$
$$= \text{Var}(a_i) + \text{Var}(b_iR_{Mt}) + \text{Var}(\varepsilon)$$
$$= 0 + \text{Var}(b_iR_{Mt}) + \text{Var}(\varepsilon)$$

Note that $\text{Var}(b_iR_{Mt})$ is the variance of return for an asset related to the variance of the market return, or the *systematic variance or risk*. Also, $\text{Var}(\varepsilon)$ is the residual variance of return for the individual asset that is not related to the market portfolio. This residual variance is the variability that we have referred to as the unsystematic or *unique risk* or *variance* because it arises from the unique features of the asset. Therefore:

➤8.4 $$\text{Var}(R_{i,t}) = \text{Systematic Variance} + \text{Unsystematic Variance}$$

We know that a completely diversified portfolio such as the market portfolio has had all the unsystematic variance eliminated. Therefore, the unsystematic variance of an asset is not relevant to investors, because they can and do eliminate it when making an asset part of the market portfolio. Therefore, investors should not expect to receive added returns for assuming this unique risk. Only the systematic variance is relevant because it *cannot* be diversified away, because it is caused by macroeconomic factors that affect all risky assets.

THE CAPITAL ASSET PRICING MODEL: EXPECTED RETURN AND RISK

Up to this point, we have considered how investors make their portfolio decisions, including the significant effects of a risk-free asset. The existence of this risk-free asset resulted in the derivation of a capital market line (CML) that became the relevant efficient frontier. Because all investors want to be on the CML, an asset's covariance with the market portfolio of risky assets emerged as the relevant risk measure.

Now that we understand this relevant measure of risk, we can proceed to use it to determine an appropriate expected rate of return on a risky asset. This step takes us into the **capital asset pricing model (CAPM)**, which is a model that indicates what should be the expected or required rates of return on risky assets. This transition is important because it helps you to value an asset by providing an appropriate discount rate to use in any valuation model. Alternatively, if you have already estimated the rate of return that you think you will earn on an investment, you can compare this *estimated* rate of return to the *required* rate of return implied by the CAPM and determine whether the asset is undervalued, overvalued, or properly valued.

To accomplish the foregoing, we demonstrate the creation of a security market line (SML) that visually represents the relationship between risk and the expected or the required rate of return on an asset. The equation of this SML, together with estimates for the return on a risk-free asset and on the market portfolio, can generate expected or required rates of return for any asset based on its systematic risk. You compare this required rate of return to the rate of return that you estimate that you will earn on the investment to determine if the investment is undervalued or overvalued. After demonstrating this procedure, we finish the section with a demonstration of how to calculate the systematic risk variable for a risky asset.

The Security Market Line (SML)   We know that the relevant risk measure for an individual risky asset is its covariance with the market portfolio ($\text{Cov}_{i,M}$). Therefore, we can draw the risk-return relationship as shown in Exhibit 8.5 with the systematic covariance variable ($\text{Cov}_{i,M}$) as the risk measure.

EXHIBIT 8.5 ▶ *GRAPH OF SECURITY MARKET LINE*

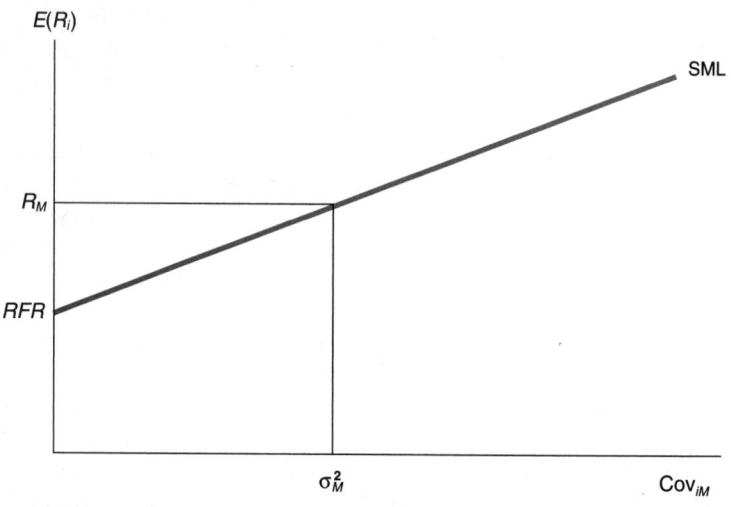

The return for the market portfolio (R_M) should be consistent with its own risk, which is the covariance of the market with itself. If you recall the formula for covariance, you will see that the covariance of any asset with itself is its variance, $\text{Cov}_{i,i} = \sigma_i^2$. In turn, the covariance of the market with itself is the variance of the market rate of return $\text{Cov}_{M,M} = \sigma_M^2$. Therefore, the equation for the risk-return line in Exhibit 8.5 is:

➤8.5
$$E(R_i) = RFR + \frac{R_M - RFR}{\sigma_M^2}(\text{Cov}_{i,M})$$
$$= RFR + \frac{\text{Cov}_{i,M}}{\sigma_M^2}(R_M - RFR)$$

Defining $\text{Cov}_{i,M}/\sigma_M^2$ as beta, (β_i), this equation can be stated:

➤8.6
$$E(R_i) = RFR + \beta_i(R_M - RFR)$$

Beta can be viewed as a *standardized* measure of systematic risk. Specifically, we already know that the covariance of any asset i with the market portfolio (Cov_{iM}) is the relevant risk measure. Beta is a standardized measure of risk because it relates this covariance to the variance of the market portfolio. As a result, the market portfolio has a beta of 1. Therefore, if the β_i for an asset is above 1.0, the asset has higher normalized systematic risk than the market, which means that it is more volatile than the overall market portfolio.

Given this standardized measure of systematic risk, the SML graph can be expressed as shown in Exhibit 8.6. This is the same graph as in Exhibit 8.5, except there is a different measure of risk. Specifically, the graph in Exhibit 8.6 replaces the covariance of an asset's returns with the market portfolio as the risk measure with the standardized measure of systematic risk (beta), which is the covariance of an asset with the market portfolio divided by the variance of the market portfolio.

Determining the Expected Rate of Return for a Risky Asset
The last equation and the graph in Exhibit 8.6 tell us that the expected (required) rate of return for a risky asset is determined by the *RFR* plus a risk premium for the individual asset. In turn, the risk premium is deter-

EXHIBIT 8.6   *GRAPH OF SML WITH NORMALIZED SYSTEMATIC RISK*

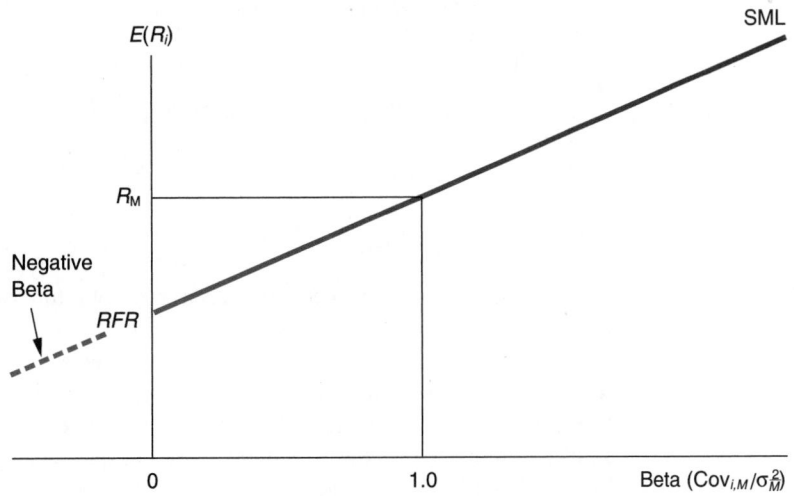

mined by the systematic risk of the asset (β_i), and the prevailing **market risk premium** ($R_M -$ *RFR*). To demonstrate how you would compute the expected or required rates of return, consider the following example stocks assuming you have already computed betas:

STOCK	BETA
A	0.70
B	1.00
C	1.15
D	1.40
E	−0.30

Assume that we expect the economy's *RFR* to be 6 percent (0.06) and the return on the market portfolio (R_M) to be 12 percent (0.12). This implies a market risk premium of 6 percent (0.06). With these inputs, the SML equation would yield the following expected (required) rates of return for these five stocks:

$$E(R_i) = RFR + \beta_i(R_M - RFR)$$
$$E(R_A) = 0.06 + 0.70\,(0.12 - 0.06)$$
$$= 0.102 = 10.2\%$$
$$E(R_B) = 0.06 + 1.00\,(0.12 - 0.06)$$
$$= 0.12 = 12\%$$
$$E(R_C) = 0.06 + 1.15\,(0.12 - 0.06)$$
$$= 0.129 = 12.9\%$$
$$E(R_D) = 0.06 + 1.40\,(0.12 - 0.06)$$
$$= 0.144 = 14.4\%$$
$$E(R_E) = 0.06 + (-0.30)\,(0.12 - 0.06)$$
$$= 0.06 - 0.018$$
$$= 0.042 = 4.2\%$$

| EXHIBIT 8.7 | PRICE, DIVIDEND, AND RATE OF RETURN ESTIMATES |

STOCK	CURRENT PRICE (P_t)	EXPECTED PRICE (P_{t+1})	EXPECTED DIVIDEND (D_{t+1})	ESTIMATED FUTURE RATE OF RETURN (PERCENT)
A	25	27	0.50	10.0%
B	40	42	0.50	6.2
C	33	39	1.00	21.2
D	64	65	1.10	3.3
E	50	54	—	8.0

As stated, these are the expected (required) rates of return that these stocks should provide based on their systematic risks and the prevailing SML.

Stock A has lower risk than the aggregate market, so you should not expect (require) its return to be as high as the return on the market portfolio of risky assets. You should expect (require) Stock A to return 10.2 percent. Stock B has systematic risk equal to the market's (beta = 1.00), so its required rate of return should likewise be equal to the expected market return (12 percent). Stocks C and D have systematic risk greater than the market's, so they should provide returns consistent with their risk. Finally, Stock E has a *negative* beta (which is quite rare in practice), so its required rate of return, if such a stock could be found, would be below the *RFR*.

In equilibrium, *all* assets and *all* portfolios of assets should plot on the SML. That is, all assets should be priced so that their **estimated rates of return**, which are the actual holding period rates of return that you anticipate, are consistent with their levels of systematic risk. Any security with an estimated rate of return that plots above the SML would be considered underpriced because it implies that you *estimated* you would receive a rate of return on the security that is above its *required* rate of return based on its systematic risk. In contrast, assets with estimated rates of return that plot below the SML would be considered overpriced. This position relative to the SML implies that your estimated rate of return is below what you should require based on the asset's systematic risk.

In an efficient market in equilibrium, you would not expect any assets to plot off the SML because, in equilibrium, all stocks should provide holding period returns that are equal to their required rates of return. Alternatively, a market that is "fairly efficient" but not completely efficient may misprice certain assets because not everyone will be aware of all the relevant information for an asset.

As we discussed in Chapter 6 on the topic of efficient markets, a superior investor has the ability to derive value estimates for assets that are consistently superior to the consensus market evaluation. As a result, such an investor will earn better rates of return than the average investor on a risk-adjusted basis.

Identifying Undervalued and Overvalued Assets   Now that we understand how to compute the rate of return one should expect or require for a specific risky asset using the SML, we can compare this *required* rate of return to the asset's *estimated* rate of return over a specific investment horizon to determine whether it would be an appropriate investment. To make this comparison, you need an independent estimate of the return outlook for the security based on either fundamental or technical analysis techniques, which will be discussed in subsequent chapters. Let us continue the example for the five assets discussed in the previous section.

Assume that analysts in a major trust department have been following these five stocks. Based on extensive fundamental analysis, the analysts provide the expected price and dividend estimates contained in Exhibit 8.7. Given these projections, you can compute the estimated rates of return the analysts would anticipate during this holding period.

EXHIBIT 8.8   *COMPARISON OF REQUIRED RATE OF RETURN TO ESTIMATED RATE OF RETURN*

Stock	Beta	Required Return $E(R_i)$	Estimated Return	Estimated Return Minus $E(R_i)$	Evaluation
A	0.70	10.2	10.0	–0.2	Properly valued
B	1.00	12.0	6.2	–5.8	Overvalued
C	1.15	12.9	21.2	8.3	Undervalued
D	1.40	14.4	3.3	–11.1	Overvalued
E	–0.30	4.2	8.0	3.8	Undervalued

EXHIBIT 8.9   *PLOT OF ESTIMATED RETURNS ON SML GRAPH*

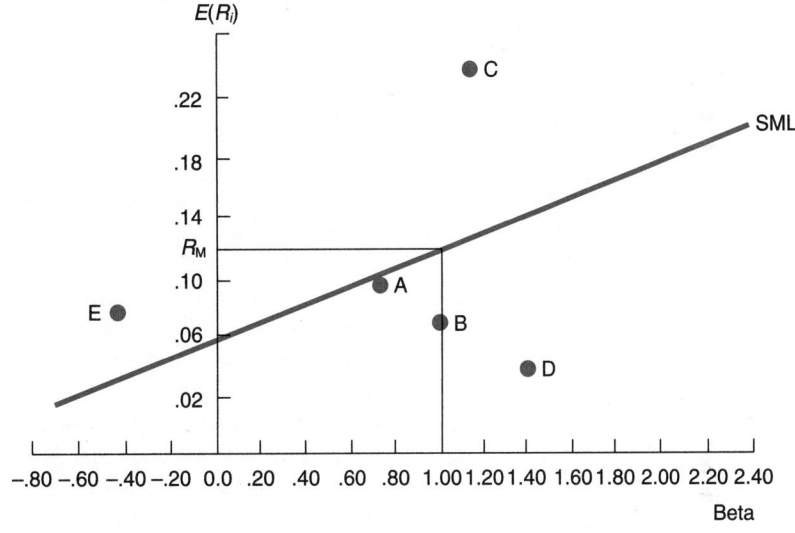

Exhibit 8.8 summarizes the relationship between the required rate of return for each stock based on its systematic risk as computed earlier, and its estimated rate of return (from Exhibit 8.7) based on the current and future prices, and its dividend outlook. This difference between estimated return and expected (required) return is sometimes referred to as a stock's *alpha* or its excess return. This alpha can be positive (the stock is undervalued) or negative (the stock is overvalued). If the alpha is zero, the stock is on the SML and is properly valued in line with its systematic risk.

Plotting these estimated rates of return and stock betas on the SML we specified earlier gives the graph shown in Exhibit 8.9. Stock A is almost exactly on the line, so it is considered properly valued because its estimated rate of return is almost equal to its required rate of return. Stocks B and D are considered overvalued because their estimated rates of return during the coming period are below what an investor should expect (require) for the risk involved. As a result, they plot below the SML. In contrast, Stocks C and E are expected to provide rates of return greater than we would require based on their systematic risk. Therefore, both stocks plot above the SML, indicating that they are undervalued stocks.

Assuming that you trusted your analyst to forecast estimated returns, you would take no action regarding Stock A, but you would buy Stocks C and E and sell Stocks B and D. You might even sell Stocks B and D short if you favored such aggressive tactics.

Calculating Systematic Risk: The Characteristic Line

The systematic risk input for an individual asset is derived from a regression model, referred to as the asset's **characteristic line** with the market portfolio:

➤8.7
$$R_{i,t} = \alpha_i + \beta_i R_{M,t} + \varepsilon$$

where:

$R_{i,t}$ = **the rate of return for asset *i* during period *t***
$R_{M,t}$ = **the rate of return for the market portfolio M during period *t***
α_i = **the constant term, or intercept, of the regression, which equals $\bar{R}_i - \beta_i \bar{R}_M$**
β_i = **the systematic risk (beta) of asset *i* equal to $\text{Cov}_{i,M}/\sigma_M^2$**
ε = **the random error term**

The characteristic line (Equation 8.7) is the regression line of best fit through a scatter plot of rates of return for the individual risky asset and for the market portfolio of risky assets over some designated past period, as shown in Exhibit 8.10.

The Impact of the Time Interval   In practice, the number of observations and the time interval used in the regression vary. Value Line Investment Services derives characteristic lines for common stocks using weekly rates of return for the most recent five years (260 weekly observations). Merrill Lynch, Pierce, Fenner & Smith uses monthly rates of return for the most recent five years (60 monthly observations). Because there is no theoretically correct time interval for analysis, we must make a trade-off between enough observations to eliminate the impact of random rates of return and an excessive length of time, such as 15 or 20 years, over which the subject company may have changed dramatically. Remember that what you really want is the *expected* systematic risk for the potential investment. In this analysis, you are analyzing historical data to help you derive a reasonable estimate of the asset's expected systematic risk.

A couple of studies have considered the effect of the time interval used to compute betas (weekly versus monthly). Statman examined the relationship between Value Line (VL) betas and Merrill Lynch (ML) betas and found a relatively weak relationship.[6] Reilly and Wright

EXHIBIT 8.10 ➤   *SCATTER PLOT OF RATES OF RETURN*

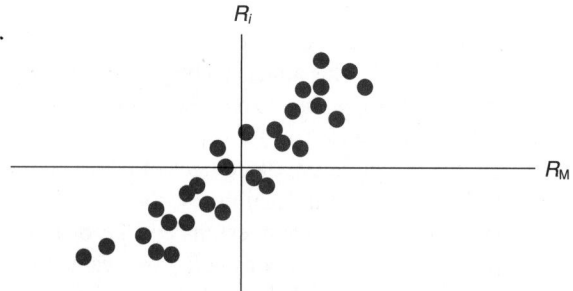

[6]Meir Statman, "Betas Compared: Merrill Lynch vs. Value Line," *Journal of Portfolio Management* 7, no. 2 (Winter 1981): 41–44.

analyzed the differential effects of return computation, market index, and the time interval and showed that the major cause of the differences in beta was the use of monthly versus weekly return intervals.[7] Also, the interval effect depended on the sizes of the firms. The shorter weekly interval caused a larger beta for large firms and a smaller beta for small firms. For example, the average beta for the smallest decile of firms using monthly data was 1.682, but the average beta for these small firms using weekly data was only 1.080. The authors concluded that the return time interval makes a difference, and its impact increases as the firm size declines.

The Effect of the Market Proxy   Another significant decision when computing an asset's characteristic line is which indicator series to use as a proxy for the market portfolio of all risky assets. Most investigators use the Standard & Poor's 500 Composite Index as a proxy for the market portfolio, because the stocks in this index encompass a large proportion of the total market value of U.S. stocks and it is a value-weighted series, which is consistent with the theoretical market series. Still, this series contains only U.S. stocks, most of them listed on the NYSE. Previously, it was noted that the market portfolio of all risky assets should include U.S. stocks and bonds, non-U.S. stocks and bonds, real estate, coins, stamps, art, antiques, and any other marketable risky asset from around the world.[8]

Example Computations of a Characteristic Line

The following examples show how you would compute characteristic lines for Coca-Cola based on the monthly rates of return during 2001.[9] Twelve is not enough observations for statistical purposes, but it provides a good example. We demonstrate the computations using two different proxies for the market portfolio. First, we use the standard S&P 500 as the market proxy. Second, we use the Morgan Stanley (M-S) World Equity Index as the market proxy. This analysis demonstrates the effect of using a complete global proxy of stocks.

The monthly price changes are computed using the closing prices for the last day of each month. These data for Coca-Cola, the S&P 500, and the M-S World Index are contained in Exhibit 8.11. Exhibit 8.12 contains the scatter plot of the percentage price changes for Coca-Cola and the S&P 500. During this 12-month period, except for August, Coca-Cola had returns that varied positively when compared to the aggregate market returns as proxied by the S&P 500. Still, as a result of the negative August effect, the covariance between Coca-Cola and the S&P 500 series was a fairly small positive value (10.57). The covariance divided by the variance of the S&P 500 market portfolio (30.10) indicates that Coca-Cola's beta relative to the S&P 500 was equal to a relatively low 0.35. This analysis indicates that during this limited time period Coca-Cola was clearly less risky than the aggregate market proxied by the S&P 500. When we draw the computed characteristic line on Exhibit 8.12, the scatter plots are reasonably close to the characteristic line except for two observations, which is consistent with the correlation coefficient of 0.33.

---

[7]Frank K. Reilly and David J. Wright, "A Comparison of Published Betas," *Journal of Portfolio Management* 14, no. 3 (Spring 1988): 64–69.

[8]Substantial discussion surrounds the market index used and its impact on the empirical results and usefulness of the CAPM. This concern is discussed further and demonstrated in the subsequent section on computing an asset's characteristic line. The effect of the market proxy is also considered when we discuss the arbitrage pricing theory (APT) in Chapter 9 and in Chapter 26 when we discuss the evaluation of portfolio performance.

[9]These betas are computed using only monthly price changes for Coca-Cola, the S&P 500, and the M-S World Index (dividends are not included). This is done for simplicity but is also based on a study indicating that betas derived with and without dividends are correlated 0.99: William Sharpe and Guy M. Cooper, "Risk-Return Classes of New York Stock Exchange Common Stocks," *Financial Analysts Journal* 28, no. 2 (March–April 1972): 35–43.

EXHIBIT 8.11   COMPUTATION OF BETA FOR COCA-COLA WITH SELECTED INDEXES

	INDEX		RETURN			$R_{S\&P} - E(R_{S\&P})$ S&P 500 (1)	$R_{M\text{-}S} - E(R_{M\text{-}S})$ M-S WORLD (2)	$R_{KO} - E(R_{RO})$ COCA-COLA (3)	(4)[a]	(5)[b]
DATE	S&P 500	M-S WORLD	S&P 500	M-S WORLD	COCA-COLA					
Dec-00	1320.28	1221.253								
Jan-01	1366.01	1244.222	3.46	1.88	−4.82	4.47	3.38	−3.01	−13.44	−10.15
Feb-01	1239.94	1137.879	−9.23	−8.55	−8.57	−8.22	−7.05	−6.76	55.56	47.64
Mar-01	1160.33	1061.262	−6.42	−6.73	−14.50	−5.41	−5.24	−12.69	68.70	66.46
Apr-01	1249.46	1138.087	7.68	7.24	2.28	8.69	8.73	4.09	35.56	35.74
May-01	1255.82	1121.088	0.51	−1.49	2.62	1.51	0.00	4.43	6.71	0.005
Jun-01	1224.38	1084.788	−2.50	−3.24	−4.68	−1.50	−1.74	−2.87	4.30	5.00
Jul-01	1211.23	1069.669	−1.07	−1.39	−0.89	−0.07	0.10	0.92	−0.06	0.09
Aug-01	1133.58	1016.732	−6.41	−4.95	9.13	−5.40	−3.45	10.94	−59.12	−37.77
Sep-01	1040.94	926.023	−8.17	−8.92	−3.37	−7.17	−7.43	−1.56	11.16	11.56
Oct-01	1059.78	943.2	1.81	1.85	2.20	2.82	3.35	4.01	11.29	13.43
Nov-01	1139.45	997.928	7.52	5.80	−1.55	8.52	7.30	0.27	2.27	1.94
Dec-01	1148.08	1003.516	0.76	0.56	0.40	1.76	2.05	2.22	3.91	4.55
Average			−1.01	−1.49	−1.81			TOTAL =	126.85	138.54
Standard Deviation			5.49	5.03	5.80					

$Cov_{KO,S\&P} = 126.85/12 = 10.57$ $Var_{S\&P} = St.Dev._{S\&P}^2 = 5.49^2 = 30.10$ $Beta_{KO,S\&P} = 10.57/30.10 = 0.35$ $Alpha_{KO,S\&P} = -1.81 - (0.35 * -1.01) = -1.46$

$Cov_{KO,M\text{-}S} = 138.54/12 = 11.54$ $Var_{M\text{-}S} = St.Dev._{,M\text{-}S}^2 = 5.03^2 = 25.31$ $Beta_{KO,M\text{-}S} = 11.54/25.31 = 0.46$ $Alpha_{KO,M\text{-}S} = -1.81 - (0.46 * -1.49) = -1.13$

Correlation coef._{KO,S\&P} = 10.57/(5.49 * 5.80) = 0.33   Correlation coef._{KO,M\text{-}S} = 11.54/(5.03 * 5.80) = 0.40

[a] Column 4 is equal to Column 1 multiplied by Column 3
[b] Column 5 is equal to Column 2 multiplied by Column 3

EXHIBIT 8.12   *SCATTER PLOT OF COCA-COLA AND THE S&P 500 WITH CHARACTERISTIC LINE FOR COCA-COLA: 2001*

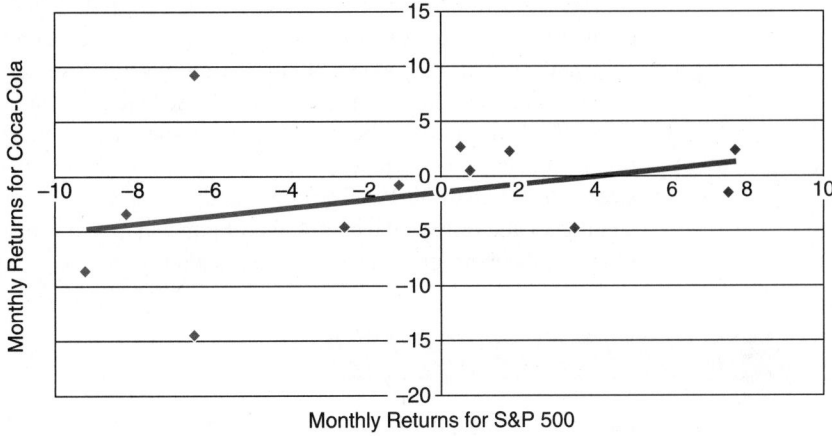

EXHIBIT 8.13   *SCATTER PLOT OF COCA-COLA AND THE M-S WORLD WITH CHARACTERISTIC LINE FOR COCA-COLA: 2001*

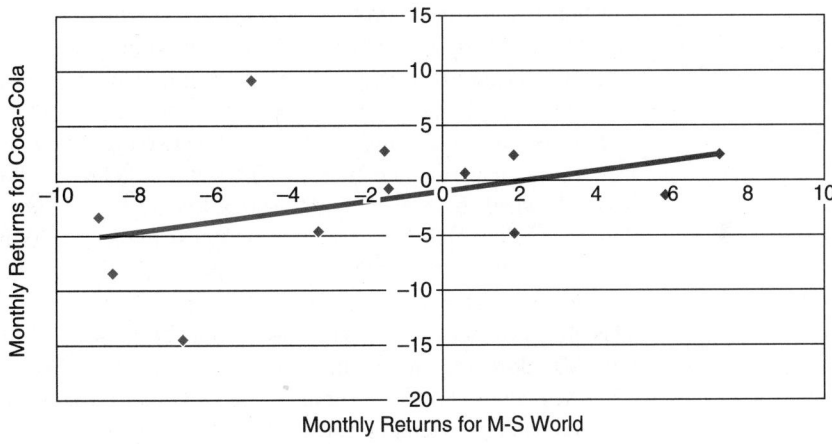

The computation of the characteristic line for Coca-Cola using the M-S World Index as the proxy for the market is contained in Exhibit 8.11, and the scatter plots are in Exhibit 8.13. At this point, it is important to consider what one might expect to be the relationship between the beta relative to the S&P 500 versus the betas with the M-S World Index. This requires a consideration of the two components that go into the computation of beta: (1) the covariance between the stock and the benchmark and (2) the variance of returns for the benchmark series. Notably, there is no obvious answer regarding what will happen for either series because one would expect both components to change. Specifically, the covariance of Coca-Cola with the S&P 500 will probably be higher than the covariance with the global series because you are matching a U.S. stock with a U.S. market index rather than a world index. Thus, one would expect the covariance with the global index to be smaller. At the same time, the variance of returns for the world stock index should also be smaller than the variance for the S&P 500 because it is a more diversified stock portfolio.

Therefore, the direction of change for the beta will depend on the relative change in the two components. Empirically, the beta is typically smaller with the world stock index because the covariance is definitely lower, but the variance is only slighter smaller.[10] The results of this example were not consistent with expectations. The beta of Coca-Cola with the world stock index was larger (0.46 versus 0.35) because the covariance with the global index was unexpectedly larger (11.54 versus 10.57), whereas the variance of the global market proxy was smaller as hypothesized (25.31 versus 30.10). The fact that the betas with the alternative market proxies differed is significant and reflects the potential problem in a global investment environment, which involves selecting the appropriate proxy for the market portfolio.

RELAXING THE ASSUMPTIONS

Earlier in the chapter, several assumptions were set forth related to the CAPM. In this section, we discuss the impact on the capital market line (CML) and the security market line (SML) when we relax several of these assumptions.

Differential Borrowing and Lending Rates

One of the first assumptions of the CAPM was that investors could borrow and lend any amount of money at the risk-free rate. It is reasonable to assume that investors can *lend* unlimited amounts at the risk-free rate by buying government securities (e.g., T-bills). In contrast, one may question the ability of investors to borrow unlimited amounts at the T-bill rate because most investors must pay a premium relative to the prime rate when borrowing money. For example, when T-bills are yielding 5 percent, the prime rate will probably be about 7 percent, and most individuals would have to pay about 8 percent to borrow at the bank.

Because of this differential, there will be two different lines going to the Markowitz efficient frontier, as shown in Exhibit 8.14. The segment *RFR–F* indicates the investment opportunities available when an investor combines risk-free assets (i.e., lending at the *RFR*) and Portfolio F on the Markowitz efficient frontier. It is not possible to extend this line any farther if it is assumed that you cannot borrow at this risk-free rate to acquire further units of Portfolio F. If it is assumed that you can borrow at R_b, the point of tangency from this rate would be on the curve at Point K. This indicates that you could borrow at R_b and use the proceeds to invest in Portfolio K to extend the CML along the line segment *K–G*. Therefore, the CML is made up of *RFR–F–K–G*; that is, a line segment (*RFR–F*), a curve segment (*F–K*), and another line segment (*K–G*). This implies that you can either lend or borrow, but the borrowing portfolios are not as profitable as when it was assumed that you could borrow at the *RFR*. In this instance, because you must pay a borrowing rate that is higher than the *RFR,* your net return is less—that is, the slope of the borrowing line (*K–G*) is below that for *RFR–F*.[11]

Zero-Beta Model

If the market portfolio (M) is mean-variance efficient (i.e., it has the lowest risk for a given level of return among the attainable set of portfolios), an alternative model, derived by Black, does not

---

[10]For a demonstration of this effect for a large sample that confirms these expectations, see Frank K. Reilly and Rashid A. Akhtar, "The Benchmark Error Problem with Global Capital Markets," *Journal of Portfolio Management* 22, no. 1 (Fall 1995): 33–52.

[11]For a detailed discussion, see Michael Brennan, "Capital Market Equilibrium with Divergent Borrowing and Lending Rules," *Journal of Financial and Quantitative Analysis* 4, no. 1 (March 1969): 4–14.

EXHIBIT 8.14 *INVESTMENT ALTERNATIVES WHEN THE COST OF BORROWING IS HIGHER THAN THE COST OF LENDING*

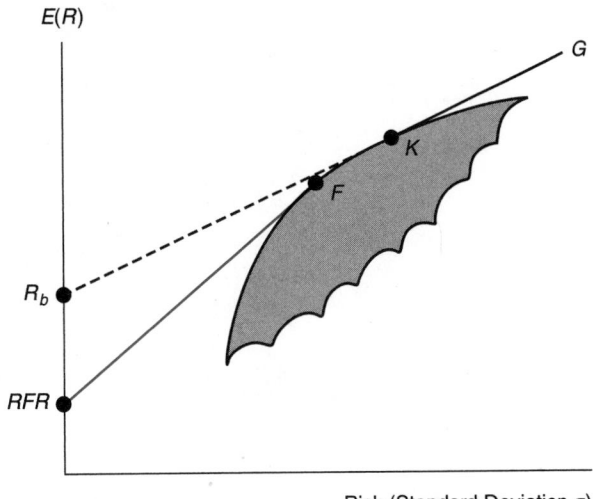

require a risk-free asset.[12] Specifically, within the set of feasible alternative portfolios, several portfolios exist where the returns are completely uncorrelated with the market portfolio; the beta of these portfolios with the market portfolio is zero. From among the several zero-beta portfolios, you would select the one with minimum variance. Although this portfolio does not have any systematic risk, it does have some unsystematic risk. The availability of this zero-beta portfolio will not affect the CML, but it will allow construction of a linear SML, as shown in Exhibit 8.15. In the model, the intercept is the expected return for the zero-beta portfolio. Similar to the earlier proof in this chapter, the combinations of this zero-beta portfolio and the market portfolio will be a linear relationship in return and risk because the covariance between the zero-beta portfolio (R_z) and the market portfolio likewise is similar to the risk-free asset. Assuming the return for the zero-beta portfolio is greater than that for a risk-free asset, the slope of the line through the market portfolio would not be as steep; that is, the market risk premium would be smaller. The equation for this zero-beta CAPM line would be

➤8.8
$$E(R_i) = E(R_z) + B_i[E(R_M) - E(R_z)]$$

Obviously, the risk premiums for individual assets would be a function of the beta for the individual security and the market risk premium:

$$[E(R_M) - E(R_z)]$$

Some of the empirical results discussed in the next section support this model with its higher intercept and flatter slope. Alternatively, several studies have specifically tested this model and

---

[12]Fischer Black, "Capital Market Equilibrium with Restricted Borrowing," *Journal of Business* 45, no. 3 (July 1972): 444–445.

EXHIBIT 8.15 ▶   *SECURITY MARKET LINE WITH A ZERO-BETA PORTFOLIO*

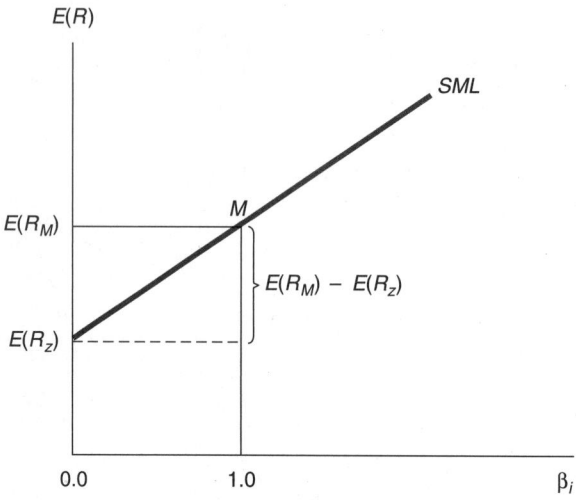

had conflicting results. Specifically, studies by Gibbons and Shanken rejected the model, while a study by Stambaugh supported the zero-beta CAPM.[13]

Transaction Costs   The basic assumption is that there are no transaction costs, so investors will buy or sell mispriced securities until they again plot on the SML. For example, if a stock plots above the SML, it is underpriced so investors should buy it and bid up its price until its estimated return is in line with its risk—that is, until it plots on the SML. With transaction costs, investors will not correct all mispricing because in some instances the cost of buying and selling the mispriced security will offset any potential excess return. Therefore, securities will plot very close to the SML—but not exactly on it. Thus, the SML will be a band of securities, as shown in Exhibit 8.16, rather than a single line. Obviously, the width of the band is a function of the amount of the transaction costs. In a world with a large proportion of trading by institutions at pennies per share and with discount brokers available for individual investors, the band should be quite narrow.

The existence of transaction costs also will affect the extent of diversification by investors. Earlier in the chapter, we discussed the relationship between the number of stocks in a portfolio and the variance of the portfolio (see Exhibit 8.3). Initially, the variance declined rapidly, approaching about 90 percent of complete diversification with about 15 to 18 securities. An important question is, How many securities must be added to derive the last 10 percent? Because of transaction costs, at some point the additional cost of diversification would exceed its benefit, especially when considering the costs of monitoring and analyzing the added securities.[14]

---

[13]Michael Gibbons, "Multivariate Tests of Financial Models: A New Approach," *Journal of Financial Economics* 10, no. 1 (March 1982): 3–28; Jay Shanken, "Multivariate Tests of the Zero Beta CAPM," *Journal of Financial Economics* 14, no. 3 (September 1985): 327–348; and Robert Stambaugh, "On the Exclusion of Assets from Tests of the Two-Parameter Model: A Sensitivity Analysis," *Journal of Financial Economics* 10, no. 4 (November 1982): 237–268.

[14]The impact of transaction costs and illiquidity is considered in E. Dimson, "Risk Management When Shares Are Subject to Infrequent Trading," *Journal of Financial Economics* 7, no. 2 (June 1979): 197–226; M. J. Brennan and A. Subramanyam, "Market Microstructure and Asset Pricing on the Compensation for Illiquidity in Stock Returns," *Journal of Financial Economics* 41, no. 3 (July 1996): 341–344.

EXHIBIT 8.16 ▶   *SECURITY MARKET LINE WITH TRANSACTION COSTS*

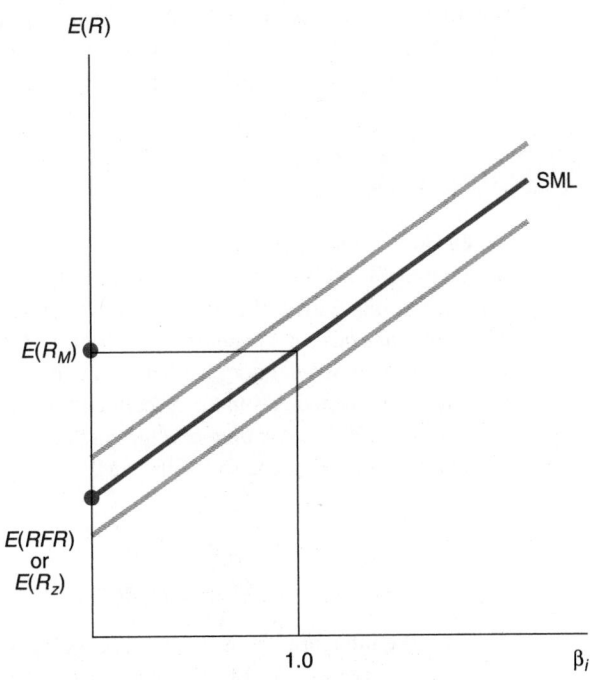

Heterogeneous Expectations and Planning Periods

If all investors had different expectations about risk and return, each would have a unique CML and/or SML, and the composite graph would be a set (band) of lines with a breadth determined by the divergence of expectations. If all investors had similar information and background, the band would be reasonably narrow.

The impact of *planning periods* is similar. Recall that the CAPM is a one-period model, corresponding to the planning period for the individual investor. Thus, if you are using a one-year planning period, your CML and SML could differ from mine, which assumes a one-month planning period.

Taxes

The rates of return that we normally record and that were used throughout the model were pretax returns. In fact, the actual returns for most investors are affected as follows:

▶8.9
$$E(R_i)(AT) = \frac{(P_e - P_b) \times (1 - T_{cg}) + (Div) \times (1 - T_i)}{P_b}$$

where:

$R_i(AT)$ = **after-tax rate of return**
P_e = **ending price**
P_b = **beginning price**
T_{cg} = **tax on capital gain or loss**
Div = **dividend paid during period**
T_i = **tax on ordinary income**

Clearly, tax rates differ between individuals and institutions. For institutions that do not pay taxes, the original pretax model is correctly specified—that is, T_{cg} and T_i take on values of zero. Alternatively, because investors have heavy tax burdens, this could cause major differences in the CML and SML among investors.[15] Several recent studies have examined the effect of the differential taxes on dividends versus capital gains but the evidence is not unanimous.[16]

EMPIRICAL TESTS OF THE CAPM

When we discussed the assumptions of capital market theory, we pointed out that a theory should not be judged on the basis of its assumptions, but on *how well it explains the relationships that exist in the real world.* When testing the CAPM, there are two major questions. First, *How stable is the measure of systematic risk (beta)?* Because beta is our principal risk measure, it is important to know whether past betas can be used as estimates of future betas. Also, how do the alternative published estimates of beta compare? Second, *Is there a positive linear relationship as hypothesized between beta and the rate of return on risky assets?* More specifically, how well do returns conform to the following SML equation, discussed earlier as Equation 8.6.

$$E(R_i) = RFR + \beta_i(R_M - RFR)$$

Some specific questions might include:

➤ Does the intercept approximate the prevailing *RFR?*
➤ Was the slope of the line positive and was it consistent with the slope implied by the prevailing risk premium $(R_M - RFR?)$

We consider these two major questions in the following section.

Stability of Beta   Numerous studies have examined the stability of beta and generally concluded that the risk measure was *not* stable for individual stocks but the stability of the beta for *portfolios* of stocks increased dramatically. Further, the larger the portfolio of stocks (e.g., over 50 stocks) and the longer the period (over 26 weeks), the more stable the beta of the portfolio. Also, the betas tended to regress toward the mean. Specifically, high-beta portfolios tended to decline over time toward unity (1.00), whereas low-beta portfolios tended to increase over time toward unity.

Another factor that affects the stability of beta is how many months are used to estimate the original beta and the test beta. Roenfeldt, Griepentrog, and Pflamm (RGP) compared betas derived from 48 months of data to subsequent betas for 12, 24, 36, and 48 months.[17] The 48-month betas were not good for estimating subsequent 12-month betas but were quite good for estimating 24-, 36-, and 48-month betas.

---

[15]For a detailed consideration of this, see Fischer Black and Myron Scholes, "The Effects of Dividend Yield and Dividend Policy on Common Stock Prices and Returns," *Journal of Financial Economics* 1, no. 1 (March 1979): 1–22; and Robert Litzenberger and K. Ramaswamy, "The Effect of Personal Taxes and Dividends on Capital Asset Prices: Theory and Empirical Evidence," *Journal of Financial Economics* 7, no. 2 (June 1979): 163–196.

[16]Edwin Elton, Martin Gruber, and Joel Rentzler, "A Single Examination of the Empirical Relationship between Dividend Yields and Deviations from the CAPM," *Journal of Banking and Finance* 7, no. 1 (March 1983): 135–146; Merton Miller and Myron Scholes, "Dividends and Taxes: Some Empirical Evidence," *Journal of Political Economy* 90, no. 4 (December 1982): 1118–1141; and William Christie, "Dividend Yield and Expected Returns," *Journal of Financial Economics* 28, no. 1 (November–December 1990): 95–125.

[17]Rodney L. Roenfeldt, Gary L. Griepentrog, and Christopher C. Pflamm, "Further Evidence on the Stationarity of Beta Coefficients," *Journal of Financial and Quantitative Analysis* 13, no. 1 (March 1978): 117–121.

Chen concluded that portfolio betas would be biased if individual betas were unstable, so he suggested a Bayesian approach to estimating these time-varying betas.[18]

Carpenter and Upton considered the influence of the trading volume on beta stability and contended that the predictions of betas were slightly better using the volume-adjusted betas.[19] This impact of volume on beta estimates is related to small-firm effect which noted that the beta for low-volume securities was biased downward as confirmed by Ibbotson, Kaplan, and Peterson.[20]

To summarize, individual betas were generally volatile over time whereas large portfolio betas were stable. Also, it is important to use at least 36 months of data to estimate beta and be conscious of the stock's trading volume and size.

Comparability of Published Estimates of Beta

In contrast to deriving your own estimate of beta for a stock, you may want to use a published source for speed or convenience, such as Merrill Lynch's *Security Risk Evaluation Report* (published monthly) and the weekly *Value Line Investment Survey*. Both services use the following market model equation:

$$(R_{i,t}) = RFR + \beta_i R_{M,t} + E_t$$

Notably, they differ in the data used. Specifically, Merrill Lynch uses *60 monthly observations* and the S&P 500 as the market proxy, whereas the *Value Line* estimates beta using *260 weekly observations* and the NYSE composite series as the market proxy. They both use an adjustment process because of the regression tendencies.

Given these relatively minor differences, one would probably expect the published betas to be quite comparable. In fact, Statman found a small but significant difference between the betas for both individual and portfolios of stocks.[21]

Reilly and Wright examined over 1,100 securities for three nonoverlapping periods and confirmed the difference in beta found by Statman.[22] They also indicated that the reason for the difference was the alternative time intervals (i.e., weekly versus monthly observations) and the security's market value affected both the size and the direction of the interval effect. Therefore, when estimating beta or using a published source, you must consider the return interval used and the firm's relative size.

RELATIONSHIP BETWEEN SYSTEMATIC RISK AND RETURN

The ultimate question regarding the CAPM is whether it is useful in explaining the return on risky assets. Specifically, is there a positive linear relationship between the systematic risk and the rates of return on these risky assets? Sharpe and Cooper found a positive relationship between return and risk, although it was not completely linear.[23]

---

[18]Son-Nan Chen, "Beta Nonstationarity, Portfolio Residual Risk, and Diversification," *Journal of Financial and Quantitative Analysis* 16, no. 1 (March 1981): 95–111.

[19]Michael D. Carpenter and David E. Upton, "Trading Volume and Beta Stability," *Journal of Portfolio Management* 7, no. 2 (Winter 1981): 60–64.

[20]Roger G. Ibbotson, Paul D. Kaplan, and James D. Peterson, "Estimates of Small-Stock Betas Are Much Too Low," *Journal of Portfolio Management* 23, no. 4 (Summer 1997): 104–111.

[21]Meir Statman, "Betas Compared: Merrill Lynch vs. Value Line," *Journal of Portfolio Management* 7, no. 2 (Winter 1981): 41–44.

[22]Frank K. Reilly and David J. Wright, "A Comparison of Published Betas," *Journal of Portfolio Management* 14, no. 3 (Spring 1988): 64–69.

[23]William F. Sharpe and Guy M. Cooper, "Risk-Return Classes of New York Stock Exchange Common Stocks: 1931–1967," *Financial Analysis Journal* 28, no. 2 (March–April 1972): 46–54.

Douglas examined the relationship, and his results indicated intercepts that were larger than the prevailing risk-free rates and the coefficients for the systematic risk variables were typically not significant.[24]

Because of the statistical problems with individual stocks, Black, Jensen, and Scholes examined the risk and return for portfolios of stocks and found a positive linear relationship between monthly excess return and portfolio beta, although the intercept was higher than the zero value expected.[25] Exhibit 8.17 contains charts from this study, which show that (1) most of the measured SMLs had a positive slope, (2) the slopes change between periods, (3) the intercepts are not zero, and (4) the intercepts likewise change between periods.

Effect of Skewness on the Relationship

Beyond the analysis of return and beta, several authors also have considered the impact of skewness on expected returns. You will recall from your statistics course that skewness reflects the presence of too many large positive or negative observations in a distribution. A normal distribution is symmetric, which means that balance exists between positive and negative observations. In contrast, positive skewness indicates an abnormal number of large positive price changes.

Investigators considered skewness as a means to possibly explain the prior results wherein the model appeared to underprice low-beta stocks (so investors received returns above expectations) and overprice high-beta stocks (so investors received returns lower than expected). Some early results confirmed these expectations, but also found that high-beta stocks had high-positive skewness, which implied that investors prefer stocks with high-positive skewness that provide an opportunity for very large returns.

Kraus and Litzenberger tested a CAPM with a skewness term and confirmed that investors are willing to pay for positive skewness.[26] They concluded that their three-moment CAPM corrects for the apparent mispricing of high- and low-risk stocks encountered with the standard CAPM. The importance of skewness was supported in studies by Sears and Wei and subsequently by Lim.[27]

Effect of Size, P/E, and Leverage

In the efficient markets hypothesis (EMH) chapter, there was extensive analysis of the size effect (the small-firm anomaly) and the P/E effect. Both of these variables were shown to have an inverse impact on returns after considering the CAPM. These results imply that these variables (size and P/E) are additional risk factors that need to be considered along with beta (similar to the skewness argument). Specifically, expected returns are a positive function of beta, but investors also require higher returns from relatively small firms and for stocks with relatively low P/E ratios.

Bhandari found that financial leverage (measured by the debt/equity ratio) also helps explain the cross section of average returns after both beta and size are considered.[28] This implies a multivariate CAPM with three risk variables: beta, size, and financial leverage.

---

[24]G. W. Douglas, "Risk in the Equity Markets: An Empirical Appraisal of Market Efficiency," *Yale Economic Essays* 9, no. 1 (1969): 3–48.

[25]Fischer Black, Michael Jensen, and Myron Scholes, "The Capital Asset Pricing Model: Some Empirical Tests," in *Studies in the Theory of Capital Markets,* ed. Michael Jensen (New York: Praeger, 1972).

[26]Alan Kraus and Robert Litzenberger, "Skewness Preference and the Valuation of Risky Assets," *Journal of Finance* 31, no. 4 (September 1976): 1085–1094.

[27]R. Stephen Sears and John Wei, "The Structure of Skewness Preferences in Asset Pricing Models with Higher Moments," *Financial Review* 23, no. 1 (February 1988): 25–38; and Kian-Guan Lim, "A New Test of the Three-Moment Capital Asset Pricing Model," *Journal of Financial and Quantitative Analysis* 24, no. 2 (June 1989): 205–216.

[28]Laxims Chand Bhandari, "Debt/Equity Ratio and Expected Common Stock Returns: Empirical Evidence," *Journal of Finance* 43, no. 2 (June 1988): 507–528.

EXHIBIT 8.17

AVERAGE EXCESS MONTHLY RATES OF RETURN COMPARED TO SYSTEMATIC RISK DURING ALTERNATIVE TIME PERIODS

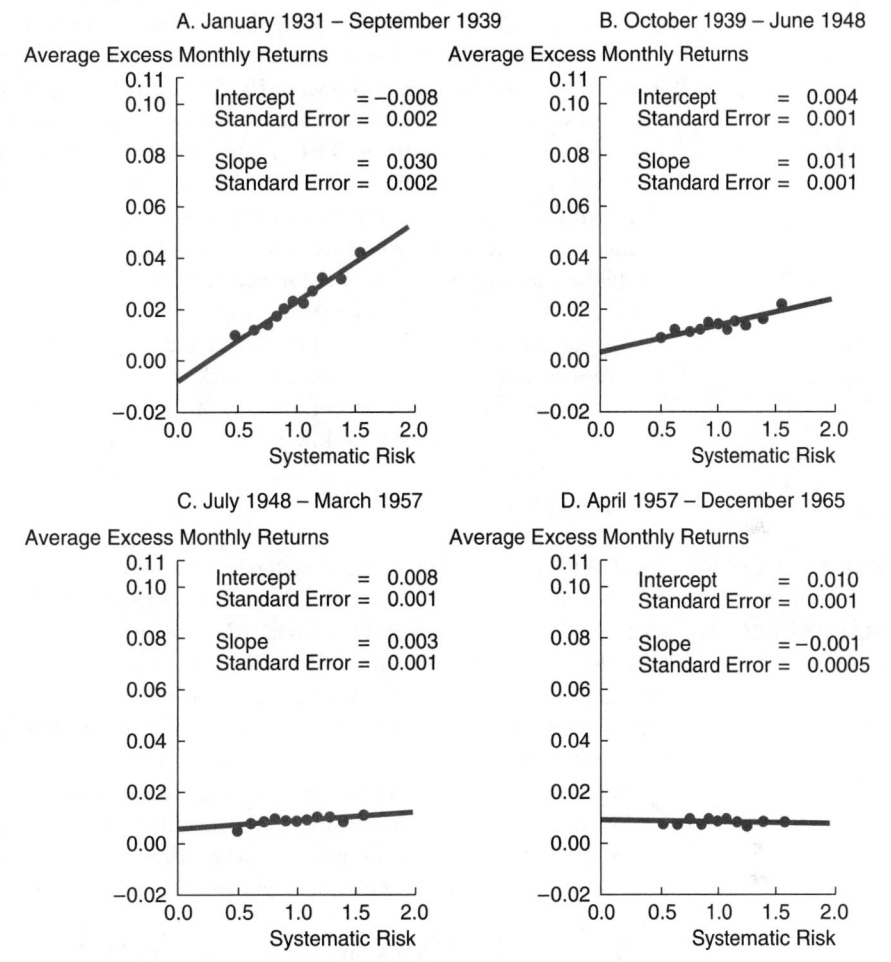

Source: Michael C. Jensen, ed., *Studies in the Theory of Capital Markets* (New York: Praeger Publishers, 1972): 96–97. Reprinted with permission.

Effect of Book-to-Market Value: The Fama-French Study

A study by Fama and French attempted to evaluate the joint roles of market beta, size, E/P, financial leverage, and the book-to-market equity ratio in the cross section of average returns on the NYSE, AMEX, and Nasdaq stocks.[29] While some earlier studies found a significant positive relationship between returns and beta, this study finds that the relationship between beta and the average rate of return disappears during the recent period 1963 to 1990, even when beta is used alone to explain average returns. In contrast, univariate tests between average returns and size, leverage, E/P, and book-to-market equity (BE/ME) indicate that all of these variables are significant and have the expected sign.

[29]Eugene F. Fama and Kenneth French, "The Cross Section of Expected Stock Returns," *Journal of Finance* 47, no. 2 (June 1992): 427–465.

In the multivariate tests, the results contained in Exhibit 8.18 show that the negative relationship between size [In (ME)] and average returns is robust to the inclusion of other variables. Further, the positive relation between BE/ME and average returns also persists when the other variables are included. Interestingly, when both of these variables are included, the book-to-market value ratio (BE/ME) has the consistently stronger role in explaining average returns. The joint effect of size and BE/ME is shown in Exhibit 8.18. The top row confirms the positive relationship between return versus the book-to-market ratio—that is, as the book-to-market ratio increases, the returns go from 0.64 to 1.63. The left-hand column shows the negative relationship between return and size—that is, as the size declines, the returns increase from 0.89 to 1.47. Even within a size class, the returns increase with the BE/ME ratio. Similarly, within a BE/ME decile, there is generally a negative relationship for size. Hence, it is not surprising that the single highest average return is in the upper, right-hand corner (1.92), which is the portfolio with the smallest size and highest BE/ME stocks.

The authors conclude that between 1963 and 1990, size and book-to-market equity capture the cross-sectional variation in average stock returns associated with size, E/P, book-to-market equity, and leverage. Moreover, of the two variables, the book-to-market equity ratio appears to subsume E/P and leverage.[30] Following these results, Fama-French suggested the use of a three-factor CAPM model and used this model in a subsequent study to explain a number of the anomalies from prior studies.[31]

Summary of CAPM Risk-Return Empirical Results

Most of the early evidence regarding the relationship between rates of return and systematic risk of portfolios supported the CAPM; there was evidence that the intercepts were generally higher than implied by the *RFR* that prevailed, which is either consistent with a zero-beta model or the existence of higher borrowing rates. In a search for other variables that could explain these unusual returns, additional variables were considered including the third moment of the distribution (skewness). The results indicated that positive skewness and high betas were correlated.

The efficient markets literature provided extensive evidence that size, the P/E ratio, financial leverage, and the book-to-market value ratio have explanatory power regarding returns beyond beta.

The Fama-French study considered most of the variables suggested and concluded that beta was not related to average returns on stocks when included with other variables or when considered alone. Moreover, the two dominant variables were size and the book value to market value ratio.

A subsequent study by Dennis, Perfect, Snow, and Wiles[32] confirmed the Fama-French results and showed that this superiority of the three-factor model prevailed after assuming 1 percent transaction costs and annual rebalancing (the optimal results were derived rebalancing every four years). Alternatively, in contrast to Fama-French who measure beta with monthly returns, Kothari, Shanken, and Sloan (KSS) measured beta with annual returns to avoid trading problems and found substantial compensation for beta risk.[33] They suggested that the Fama-French results

---

[30]A prior study that documented the importance of the BE/ME ratio was Barr Rosenberg, Kenneth Reid, and Ronald Lanstein, "Persuasive Evidence of Market Inefficiency," *Journal of Portfolio Management* 11, no. 3 (Spring 1985): 9–17.

[31]The three-factor model was suggested in Eugene F. Fama and Kenneth French, "Common Risk Factors in the Returns on Stocks and Bonds," *Journal of Financial Economics* 33, no. 1 (February 1993): 3–56. The model was used in Eugene F. Fama and Kenneth French, "Multifactor Explanations of Asset Pricing Anomalies," *Journal of Finance* 51, no. 1 (March 1996): 55–84.

[32]Patrick Dennis, Steven Perfect, Karl Snow, and Kenneth Wiles, "The Effects of Rebalancing on Size and Book-to-Market Ratio Portfolio Returns," *Financial Analysts Journal* 51, no. 3 (May–June 1995): 47–57.

[33]S. P. Kothari, Jay Shanken, and Richard G. Sloan, "Another Look at the Cross Section of Expected Stock Returns," *Journal of Finance* 50, no. 2 (March 1995): 185–224.

EXHIBIT 8.18

AVERAGE SLOPES (t-STATISTICS) FROM MONTH-BY-MONTH REGRESSIONS OF STOCK RETURNS ON β, SIZE, BOOK-TO-MARKET EQUITY, LEVERAGE, AND E/P: JULY 1963 TO DECEMBER 1990

Stocks are assigned the post-ranking β of the size-β portfolio they are in at the end of June of year t. BE is the book value of common equity plus balance-sheet deferred taxes, A is total book assets, and E is earnings (income before extraordinary items, plus income-statement deferred taxes, minus preferred dividends). BE, A, and E are for each firm's latest fiscal year ending in calendar year $t - 1$. The accounting ratios are measured using market equity ME in December of year $t - 1$. Firm size ln(ME) is measured in June of year t. In the regressions, these values of the explanatory variables for individual stocks are matched with returns for the CRSP tapes from the University of Chicago for the months from July of year t to June of year $t + 1$. The gap between the accounting data and the returns ensures that the accounting data are available prior to the returns. If earnings are positive, E(+)/P is the ratio of total earnings to market equity and E/P dummy is 0. If earnings are negative, E(+)/P is 0 and E/P dummy is 1.

The average slope is the time-series average of the monthly regression slopes for July 1963 to December 1990, and the t-statistic is the average slope divided by its time-series standard error.

On average, there are 2,267 stocks in the monthly regressions. To avoid giving extreme observations heavy weight in the regressions, the smallest and largest 0.5% of the observations of E(+)/P, BE/ME, A/ME, and A/BE are set equal to the next largest or smallest values of the ratios (the 0.005 and 0.995 fractiles). This has no effect on inferences.

β	ln(ME)	ln(BE/ME)	ln(A/ME)	ln(A/BE)	E/P Dummy	E(+)/P
0.15						
(0.46)						
	−0.15					
	(−2.58)					
−0.37	−0.17					
(−1.21)	(−3.41)					
		0.50				
		(5.71)				
			0.50	−0.57		
			(5.69)	(−5.34)		
					0.57	4.72
					(2.28)	(4.57)
	−0.11	0.35				
	(−1.99)	(4.44)				
	−0.11		0.35	−0.50		
	(−2.06)		(4.32)	(−4.56)		
	−0.16				0.06	2.99
	(−3.06)				(0.38)	(3.04)
	−0.13	0.33			−0.14	0.87
	(−2.47)	(4.46)			(−0.90)	(1.23)
	−0.13		0.32	−0.46	−0.08	1.15
	(−2.47)		(4.28)	(−4.45)	(−0.56)	(1.57)

Source: Eugene F. Fama and Kenneth French, "The Cross Section of Expected Stock Returns," *Journal of Finance* 47, no. 2 (June 1992): 439. Reprinted with permission of Blackwell Publishing.

may have been periodic to this time frame and might not be significant over a longer period. Pettengill, Dundaram, and Matthur noted that empirical studies typically use realized returns to test the CAPM model when theory specifies expected returns.[34] When the authors adjust for negative market excess returns, they find a consistent and significant relationship between beta and rates of return. When Jagannathan and Wang employed a conditional CAPM that allows for changes in betas and the market risk premium, this model performed well in explaining the cross section of returns.[35] Grundy and Malkiel also contend that beta is a very useful measure of risk during declining markets, which is when it is important.[36]

THE MARKET PORTFOLIO: THEORY VERSUS PRACTICE

Throughout our presentation of the CAPM, we noted that the market portfolio included *all* the risky assets in the economy. Further, in equilibrium, the various assets would be included in the portfolio in proportion to their market value. Therefore, this market portfolio should contain not only U.S. stocks and bonds but also real estate, options, art, stamps, coins, foreign stocks and bonds, and so on, with weights equal to their relative market value.

Although this concept of a market portfolio is reasonable in theory, it is difficult—if not impossible—to implement when testing or using the CAPM. The easy part is getting a stock series for the NYSE, the AMEX, and major world stock exchanges, such as Tokyo, London, and Germany. There are stock series for the OTC market, too, but these series generally are incomplete. Also, as noted in Chapter 5, there is a growing number of world stock indexes. There also are some well-regarded U.S. bond series available (e.g., from Lehman Brothers, Merrill Lynch, Ryan Labs, and Salomon Brothers) and several world bond series (e.g., from J. P. Morgan, Salomon Brothers, and Merrill Lynch). Because of the difficulty in deriving series that are available monthly in a timely fashion for the numerous other assets mentioned, most studies have limited themselves to using a stock or bond series alone. In fact, the vast majority of studies have chosen the S&P 500 series or some other NYSE stock series that is obviously limited to only U.S. stocks, which constitutes *less than 20 percent* of a truly global risky asset portfolio (see Exhibit 3.1). At best, it was assumed that the particular series used as a proxy for the market portfolio was highly correlated with the true market portfolio.

Most academicians recognize this potential problem but assume that the deficiency is not serious. Several articles by Roll, however, concluded that, on the contrary, the use of these indexes as a proxy for the market portfolio had very serious implications for tests of the model and especially for using the model when evaluating portfolio performance.[37] Roll referred to it as a **benchmark error** because the practice is to compare the performance of a portfolio manager to the return of an unmanaged portfolio of equal risk—that is, the market portfolio

---

[34]Glenn Pettengill, Sridhar Dundaram, and Ike Matthur, "The Conditional Relation between Beta and Returns," *Journal of Financial and Quantitative Analysis* 30, no. 1 (March 1995): 101–115.

[35]Ravi Jagannathan and Zhenyu Wang, "The Conditional CAPM and the Cross Section of Expected Returns," *Journal of Finance* 51, no. 1 (March 1996): 3–53.

[36]Kevin Grundy and Burton Malkiel, "Reports of Beta's Death Have Been Greatly Exaggerated," *Journal of Portfolio Management* 22, no. 3 (Spring 1996): 36–44.

[37]Richard Roll, "A Critique of the Asset Pricing Theory's Tests," *Journal of Financial Economics* 4, no. 4 (March 1977): 129–176; Richard Roll, "Ambiguity When Performance Is Measured by the Securities Market Line," *Journal of Finance* 33. no. 4 (September 1978): 1051–1069; Richard Roll, "Performance Evaluation and Benchmark Error I," *Journal of Portfolio Management* 6, no. 4 (Summer 1980): 5–12; and Richard Roll, "Performance Evaluation and Benchmark Error II," *Journal of Portfolio Management* 7, no. 2 (Winter 1981): 17–22. This discussion draws heavily from these articles.

EXHIBIT 8.19   *DIFFERENTIAL PERFORMANCE BASED ON AN ERROR IN ESTIMATING SYSTEMATIC RISK*

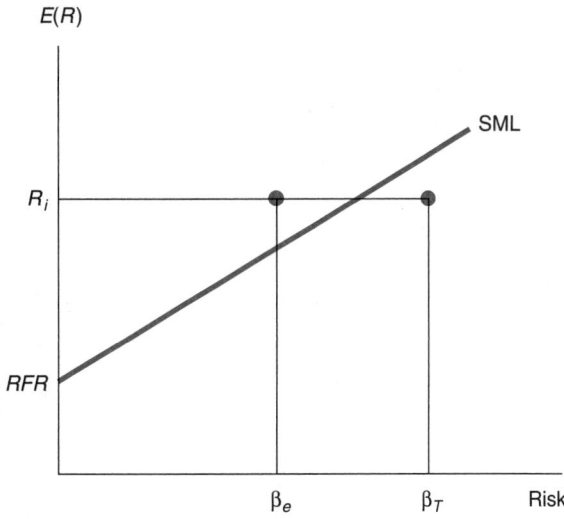

adjusted for risk would be the benchmark. Roll's point is that, if the benchmark is mistakenly specified, you cannot measure the performance of a portfolio manager properly. A mistakenly specified market portfolio can have two effects. First, the beta computed for alternative portfolios would be wrong because the market portfolio used to compute the portfolio's systematic risk is inappropriate. Second, the SML derived would be wrong because it goes from the *RFR* through the improperly specified M portfolio. Exhibit 8.19 shows an example where the true portfolio risk (β_T) is underestimated (β_e) possibly because of the proxy market portfolio used in computing the estimated beta. As shown, the portfolio being evaluated may appear to be above the SML using β_e, which would imply superior management. If, in fact, the true risk (β_T) is greater, the portfolio will shift to the right and be below the SML, which would indicate inferior performance.

Exhibit 8.20 indicates that the intercept and slope will differ if (1) there is an error in selecting a proper risk-free asset and (2) if the market portfolio selected is not the correct mean-variance efficient portfolio. Obviously, it is very possible that under these conditions, a portfolio judged to be superior relative to the first SML (i.e., the portfolio plotted above the measured SML) could be inferior relative to the true SML (i.e., the portfolio would plot below the true SML).

Roll contends that a test of the CAPM requires an analysis of whether the proxy used to represent the market portfolio is mean-variance efficient (on the Markowitz efficient frontier) and whether it is the true optimum market portfolio. Roll showed that if the proxy market portfolio (e.g., the S&P 500 index) is mean-variance efficient, it is mathematically possible to show a linear relationship between returns and betas derived with this portfolio. Unfortunately, this is not a true test of the CAPM because you are not working with the true SML (see Exhibit 8.21).

A demonstration of the impact of the benchmark problem is provided in a study by Reilly and Akhtar.[38] Exhibit 8.22 shows the substantial difference in average beta for the 30 stocks in the

---

[38]Frank K. Reilly and Rashid A. Akhtar, "The Benchmark Error Problem with Global Capital Markets," *Journal of Portfolio Management* 22, no. 1 (Fall 1995): 33–52.

EXHIBIT 8.20   *DIFFERENTIAL SML BASED ON MEASURED RISK-FREE ASSET AND PROXY MARKET PORTFOLIO*

EXHIBIT 8.21   *DIFFERENTIAL SML USING MARKET PROXY THAT IS MEAN-VARIANCE EFFICIENT*

EXHIBIT 8.22 ▶ *AVERAGE BETA FOR THE 30 STOCKS IN THE DOW JONES INDUSTRIAL AVERAGE DURING ALTERNATIVE TIME PERIODS USING DIFFERENT PROXIES FOR THE MARKET PORTFOLIOS*

	ALTERNATIVE MARKET PROXIES		
TIME PERIOD	S&P 500	M-S WORLD	BRINSON GSMI
1983–1988			
Average beta	0.820	0.565	1.215
Mean index return	0.014	0.017	0.014
Standard deviation of index returns	0.049	0.043	0.031
1989–1994			
Average beta	0.991	0.581	1.264
Mean index return	0.010	0.004	0.008
Standard deviation of index returns	0.036	0.043	0.026
1983–1994			
Average beta	0.880	0.606	1.223
Mean index return	0.012	0.011	0.011
Standard deviation of index returns	0.043	0.043	0.029

Source: Frank K. Reilly and Rashid A. Akhtar, "The Benchmark Error Problem with Global Capital Markets," *Journal of Portfolio Management* 22, no. 1 (Fall 1995): 33–52.

DJIA during three alternative periods using three different proxies for the market portfolio: (1) the S&P 500 Index, (2) the Morgan Stanley World Stock Index, and (3) the Brinson Partners Global Security Market Index (GSMI). The GSMI includes not only U.S. and international stocks but also U.S. and international bonds. The results in Exhibit 8.22 are as one would expect because, as we know from earlier in this chapter (Equations 8.5 and 8.6), beta is equal to:

$$\text{Beta} = \frac{\text{Cov}_{i,M}}{\sigma_M^2}$$

where:

> $\text{Cov}_{i,M}$ = **the covariance between asset** *i* **and the M portfolio**
> σ_M^2 = **the variance of the M portfolio**

As we change from an all–U.S. stock index to a world stock index (M-S World) or a world stock and bond index (GSMI), we would expect the covariance with U.S. stocks to decline. The other component of beta is the standard deviation for the market portfolio. As shown in Exhibit 8.22, typically the M-S World Stock Index has a smaller variance than the S&P 500 because it is more diversified with international stocks. Therefore, while both covariance and market variance decline, the covariance effect dominates, so the beta is smaller with the M-S World Stock Index. In contrast, although the covariance between the U.S. stocks and the GSMI also is lower, the variance of the GSMI market portfolio, which is highly diversified with stocks *and* bonds from around the world, is substantially lower (about 25 to 33 percent). As a result, the beta is substantially larger (about 27 to 48 percent larger) when the Brinson Partners Index is used rather than the S&P 500 Index. Notably, the Brinson Index has a composition of assets that is substantially closer to the "true" M portfolio than either of the other proxies that contain only U.S. stocks or global stocks.

EXHIBIT 8.23 ▶ *COMPONENTS OF SECURITY MARKET LINES USING ALTERNATIVE MARKET PROXIES*

	1983–1988			1989–1994			1983–1994		
	R_M	RFR	$(R_M - RFR)$	R_M	RFR	$(R_M - RFR)$	R_M	RFR	$(R_M - RFR)$
S&P 500	18.20	8.31	9.90	13.07	5.71	7.36	15.61	7.01	8.60
Nikkei	26.05	5.35	20.70	−3.62	4.70	−8.32	10.30	5.02	5.28
FAZ	16.36	5.01	11.35	7.97	7.83	0.14	12.09	6.42	5.67
FT AllShare	18.01	10.00	8.01	10.09	10.07	0.02	13.99	10.03	3.95
M-S World	22.64	8.31	14.33	5.18	5.71	−0.52	13.60	7.01	6.60
Brinson GSMI	18.53	8.31	10.22	10.18	5.71	4.48	14.28	7.01	7.28

RFR = risk-free return.

Source: Frank K. Reilly and Rashid Akhtar, "The Benchmark Error Problem with Global Capital Markets," *Journal of Portfolio Management* 22, no. 1 (Fall 1995): 33–52.

EXHIBIT 8.24 ▶ *THE AVERAGE EXPECTED RETURNS FOR STOCKS IN THE DJIA BASED ON DIFFERENT BETAS AND SECURITY MARKET LINES DERIVED WITH ALTERNATIVE BENCHMARKS*

	MEAN EXPECTED RATE OF RETURN		
TIME PERIOD	S&P 500	M-S WORLD	BRINSON GSMI
1983–1988	16.41	17.72	20.75
1989–1994	13.00	5.40	11.36

Source: Frank K. Reilly and Rashid A. Akhtar, "The Benchmark Error Problem with Global Capital Markets," *Journal of Portfolio Management* 22, no. 1 (Fall 1995): 33–52.

There also was a difference in the SMLs implied by each of the market proxies. Exhibit 8.23 contains the average *RFR,* the market returns, and the slope of the SML during the three time periods for the three indexes and for market series from Japan (Nikkei), Germany (FAZ), and the United Kingdom (FT All-Share). Clearly, the slopes differ dramatically among the alternative indexes and over time. Needless to say, the benchmark used does make a difference.

Finally, it is necessary to combine the estimate of systematic risk (beta) with the estimated SML to determine the combined effect on the required rate of return for an asset. Exhibit 8.24 shows that during specific time periods the difference between the highest and the lowest expected (required) return ranges from about 4 percent to 7.5 percent, with the highest expected returns when the market proxy was the Brinson GSMI because of the high betas. There were also large differences in the expected (required) returns for individual stocks (i.e., a range of about 4 to 5 percent), which can have a substantial impact on valuation.

In summary, an incorrect market proxy will affect both the beta risk measures and the position and slope of the SML that is used to evaluate portfolio performance. In general, the errors will tend to overestimate the performance of portfolio managers because the proxy used for the market portfolio is probably not as efficient as the true market portfolio, so the slope of the SML will be underestimated. Also, the beta measure generally will be underestimated because the true market portfolio will have a lower variance than the typical market proxy due to greater diversification.

Roll's benchmark problems, however, do not invalidate the value of the CAPM as *a normative model of asset pricing;* they only indicate a problem in *measurement* when attempting to test the theory and when using this model for evaluating portfolio performance. Therefore, it is necessary to develop a better market portfolio proxy similar to the Brinson GSMI and/or adjust the portfolio performance measures to reflect this measurement problem.

At this point, we have discussed the basic theory of the CAPM, the impact of changing some of its major assumptions, the empirical evidence that does and does not support the theory, and its dependence on a market portfolio of all risky assets. In addition, the model assumes that investors have quadratic utility functions and that the distribution of security prices is normal (symmetrically distributed), with a variance term that can be estimated.

The tests of the CAPM indicated that the beta coefficients for individual securities were not stable, but the portfolio betas generally were stable assuming long enough sample periods and adequate trading volume. There was mixed support for a positive linear relationship between rates of return and systematic risk for portfolios of stock, with some recent evidence indicating the need to consider additional risk variables or a need for different risk proxies. In addition, several papers have criticized the tests of the model and the usefulness of the model in portfolio evaluation because of its dependence on a market portfolio of risky assets that is not currently available.

Consequently, the academic community has considered alternative asset pricing models, which are considered in the following chapter.

The Internet *Investments Online*

Asset pricing models show how risk measures or underlying return-generating factors will affect asset returns. Estimates from such models are usually proprietary and are available from providers only by buying their research. Of course, users can always purchase their raw data elsewhere (see some of our earlier Internet discussions) and develop their own estimates of beta and factor sensitivities.

http://www.valueline.com The Value Line Investment Survey has been a longtime favorite of investors and many local and college/university libraries subscribe to it. It is a popular source of finding a stock's beta. Value Line Publishing, Inc's Web site contains useful information for the online researcher and student of investments. Its site features investment-related articles, sample pages from the ValueLine Investment Survey, and a product directory that lists the venerable investment survey as well as Value Line's mutual fund, options, and convertibles survey.

http://www.barra.com For subscribers, Barra's Web site offers a gold mine of data and analytical analysis. Links offer information on portfolio management, investment data, market indices, and research. Barra offers its clients data, software, consulting, as well as money management services

for equity, fixed income, currency, and other global financial instruments. Barra estimates multiple factor models and their global and single country equity models provide risk analysis on over 25,000 globally traded securities, including predicted and historical beta values. Explore this data to discover its data resources, charts, and graphs.

http://www.wsharpe.com William F. Sharpe, the 1990 winner of the Nobel prize in Economics because of his development of the Capital Asset Pricing Model, has a home page on the Internet. Web surfers can read drafts of a sophisticated textbook in progress, some of his published papers, and case studies he has written. Sharpe's site offers monthly returns data on a number of mutual funds, stock indices, and bond indices, and links to other finance sites.

http://gsb.uchicago.edu/fac/eugene. fama/ The home page of Eugena Fama, whose empirical work first found support . . . and then lack of support . . . for beta as a risk measure.

http://www.moneychimp.com This is an informative education site on investments and includes CAPM calculators for estimating a stock's return and a "market simulator" to show the effect of randomness on a portfolio's return over time.

Summary

- The assumptions of capital market theory expand on those of the Markowitz portfolio model and include consideration of the risk-free rate of return. The correlation and covariance of any asset with a risk-free asset are zero, so that any combination of an asset or portfolio with the risk-free asset generates a linear return and risk function. Therefore, when you combine the risk-free asset with any risky asset on the Markowitz efficient frontier, you derive a set of straight-line portfolio possibilities.
- The dominant line is the one that is tangent to the efficient frontier. This dominant line is referred to as the *capital market line (CML)*, and all investors should target points along this line depending on their risk preferences.
- Because all investors want to invest in the risky portfolio at the point of tangency, this portfolio—referred to as the market portfolio—must contain all risky assets in proportion to their relative market values. Moreover, the investment decision and the financing decision can be separated because, although everyone will want to invest in the market portfolio, investors will make different financing decisions about whether to lend or borrow based on their individual risk preferences.
- Given the CML and the dominance of the market portfolio, the relevant risk measure for an individual risky asset is its covariance with the market portfolio, that is, its *systematic risk*. When this covariance is standardized by the covariance for the market portfolio, we derive the well-known beta measure of systematic risk and a security market line (SML) that relates the expected or required rate of return for an asset to its beta. Because all individual securities and portfolios should plot on this SML, you can determine the expected (required) return on a security based on its systematic risk (its beta).
- Alternatively, assuming security markets are not always completely efficient, you can identify undervalued and overvalued securities by comparing your estimate of the rate of return to be earned on an investment to its expected (required) rate of return. The systematic risk variable (beta) for an individual risky asset is computed using a regression model that generates an equation referred to as the asset's *characteristic line.*
- When we relax several of the major assumptions of the CAPM, the required modifications are reasonably minor and do not change the overall concept of the model. Empirical studies have indicated stable portfolio betas, especially when enough observations were used to derive the betas and there was adequate volume. Although the early tests confirmed the expected relationship between returns and systematic risk (with allowance for the zero-beta model), several subsequent studies indicated that the univariate beta model needed to be supplemented with additional variables that considered skewness, size, P/E, leverage, and the book value/market value ratio. A study by Fama and French contended that during the period 1963 to 1990, beta was not relevant. In their study, the most significant variables were book-to-market value (BE/ME) and size. Subsequent studies both supported their findings and differed with them because some more recent authors have found a significant relationship between beta and rates of return on stocks.
- Another problem has been raised by Roll, who contends that it is not possible to empirically derive a true market portfolio, so it is not possible to test the CAPM model properly or to use the model to evaluate portfolio performance. A study by Reilly and Akhtar provided empirical support for this contention by demonstrating significant differences in betas, SMLs, and expected returns with alternative benchmarks.

Questions

1. Explain why the set of points between the risk-free asset and a portfolio on the Markowitz efficient frontier is a straight line.
2. Draw a graph that shows what happens to the Markowitz efficient frontier when you combine a risk-free asset with alternative risky asset portfolios on the Markowitz efficient frontier. Explain this graph.
3. Draw and explain why the line from the *RFR* that is tangent to the efficient frontier defines the dominant set of portfolio possibilities.
4. Discuss what risky assets are in Portfolio M and why they are in it.
5. Discuss leverage and its effect on the CML.
6. Discuss and justify a measure of diversification for a portfolio in terms of capital market theory.

7. What changes would you expect in the standard deviation for a portfolio of between 4 and 10 stocks, between 10 and 20 stocks, and between 50 and 100 stocks?
8. Discuss why the investment and financing decisions are separate when you have a CML.
9. Given the CML, discuss and justify the relevant measure of risk for an individual security.
10. Capital market theory divides the variance of returns for a security into systematic variance and unsystematic or unique variance. Describe each of these terms.
11. The capital asset pricing model (CAPM) contends that there is systematic and unsystematic risk for an individual security. Which is the relevant risk variable and why is it relevant? Why is the other risk variable not relevant?
12. How does the SML differ from the CML?

13. *CFA Examination Level I*
    Identify and briefly discuss *three* criticisms of beta as used in the capital asset pricing model (CAPM). [6 minutes]

14. *CFA Examination Level I*
    Briefly explain whether investors should expect a higher return from holding Portfolio A versus Portfolio B under capital asset pricing theory (CAPM). Assume that both portfolios are fully diversified. [6 minutes]

	Portfolio A	Portfolio B
Systematic risk (beta)	1.0	1.0
Specific risk for each individual security	High	Low

15. *CFA Examination Level II*
    You have recently been appointed chief investment officer of a major charitable foundation. Its large endowment fund is currently invested in a broadly diversified portfolio of stocks (60 percent) and bonds (40 percent). The foundation's board of trustees is a group of prominent individuals whose knowledge of modern investment theory and practice is superficial. You decide a discussion of basic investment principles would be helpful.
    a. Explain the concepts of *specific risk, systematic risk, variance, covariance, standard deviation,* and *beta* as they relate to investment management. [12 minutes]
    You believe that the addition of other asset classes to the endowment portfolio would improve the portfolio by reducing risk and enhancing return. You are aware that depressed conditions in U.S. real estate markets are providing opportunities for property acquisition at levels of expected return that are unusually high by historical standards. You believe that an investment in U.S. real estate would be both appropriate and timely, and have decided to recommend a 20 percent position be established with funds taken equally from stocks and bonds.
    Preliminary discussions revealed that several trustees believe real estate is too risky to include in the portfolio. The board chairman, however, has scheduled a special meeting for further discussion of the matter and has asked you to provide background information that will clarify the risk issue.
    To assist you, the following expectational data have been developed:

Asset Class	Return	Standard Deviation	CORRELATION MATRIX			
			U.S. Stocks	U.S. Bonds	U.S. Real Estate	U.S. T-Bills
U.S. Stocks	12.0%	21.0%	1.00			
U.S. Bonds	8.0	10.5	0.14	1.00		
U.S. Real Estate	12.0	9.0	−0.04	−0.03	1.00	
U.S. Treasury Bills	4.0	0.0	−0.05	−0.03	0.25	1.00

b. Explain the effect on *both* portfolio risk *and* return that would result from the addition of U.S. real estate. Include in your answer *two* reasons for any change you expect in portfolio risk. (Note: It is *not* necessary to compute expected risk and return.) [8 minutes]

c. Your understanding of capital market theory causes you to doubt the validity of the expected return and risk for U.S. real estate. Justify your skepticism. [5 minutes]

16. In the empirical testing of the CAPM, what are two major concerns? Why are they important?

17. Briefly discuss why it is important for beta coefficients to be stationary over time.

18. Discuss the empirical results relative to beta stability for individual stocks and portfolios of stocks.

19. In the tests of the relationship between systematic risk (beta) and return, what are you looking for?

20. Draw an ideal SML. Based on the early empirical results, what did the actual risk-return relationship look like relative to the ideal relationship implied by the CAPM?

21. According to the CAPM, what assets are included in the market portfolio, and what are the relative weightings? In empirical studies of the CAPM, what are the typical proxies used for the market portfolio?

22. Assuming that the empirical proxy for the market portfolio is not a good proxy, what factors related to the CAPM will be affected?

23. Some studies related to the efficient market hypothesis generated results that implied additional factors beyond beta should be considered to estimate expected returns. What are these other variables and why should they be considered?

24. According to the Fama-French study, discuss what variables you should consider when selecting a cross section of stocks.

Problems

1. Assume that you expect the economy's rate of inflation to be 3 percent, giving an *RFR* of 6 percent and a market return (R_M) of 12 percent.
   a. Draw the SML under these assumptions.
   b. Subsequently, you expect the rate of inflation to increase from 3 percent to 6 percent. What effect would this have on the *RFR* and the R_M? Draw another SML on the graph from Part a.
   c. Draw an SML on the same graph to reflect an *RFR* of 9 percent and an R_M of 17 percent. How does this SML differ from that derived in Part b? Explain what has transpired.

2. You expect an *RFR* of 10 percent and the market return (R_M) of 14 percent. Compute the expected (required) return for the following stocks, and plot them on an SML graph.

Stock	Beta	$E(R_i)$
U	0.85	
N	1.25	
D	−0.20	

3. You ask a stockbroker what the firm's research department expects for the three stocks in Problem 2. The broker responds with the following information:

Stock	Current Price	Expected Price	Expected Dividend
U	22	24	0.75
N	48	51	2.00
D	37	40	1.25

Plot your estimated returns on the graph from Problem 2 and indicate what actions you would take with regard to these stocks. Discuss your decisions.

4. Select a stock from the NYSE and collect its month-end prices for the latest 13 months to compute 12 monthly percentage of price changes ignoring dividends. Do the same for the S&P 500 series.

Prepare a scatter plot of these series on a graph and draw a visual characteristic line of best fit (the line that minimizes the deviations from the line). Compute the slope of this line from the graph.

5. Given the returns derived in Problem 4, compute the beta coefficient using the formula and techniques employed in Exhibit 8.11. How many negative products did you have for the covariance? How does this computed beta compare to the visual beta derived in Problem 4?

6. Look up the index values and compute the monthly rates of return for either the FT World Index or the Morgan Stanley World Index.

   a. Compute the beta for your NYSE stock from Problem 4 using one of these world stock indexes as the proxy for the market portfolio.

   b. How does this world stock index beta compare to your S&P beta? Discuss the difference.

7. Look up this stock in *Value Line* and record the beta derived by *VL*. How does this *VL* beta compare to the beta you computed using the S&P 500? Discuss reasons why the betas might differ.

8. Select a stock that is listed on Nasdaq and plot the returns during the past 12 months relative to the S&P 500. Compute the beta coefficient. Did you expect this stock to have a higher or lower beta than the NYSE stock? Explain your answer.

9. Given the returns for the Nasdaq stock in Problem 8, plot the stock returns relative to monthly rates of return for the Nasdaq composite index and compute the beta coefficient. Does this beta differ from that derived in Problem 8? If so, how can you explain this? (Hint: Analyze the specific components of the formula for the beta coefficient. How did the components differ between Problems 8 and 9?)

10. Using the data from the prior questions, compute the beta coefficient for the Nasdaq composite index relative to the S&P 500 Index. A priori, would you expect a beta less than or greater than 1.00? Discuss your expectations and the actual results.

11. Based on five years of monthly data, you derive the following information for the companies listed:

Company	a_i (Intercept)	σ_i	r_{iM}
Intel	0.22	12.10%	0.72
Ford	0.10	14.60	0.33
Anheuser Busch	0.17	7.60	0.55
Merck	0.05	10.20	0.60
S&P 500	0.00	5.50	1.00

   a. Compute the beta coefficient for each stock.

   b. Assuming a risk-free rate of 8 percent and an expected return for the market portfolio of 15 percent, compute the expected (required) return for all the stocks and plot them on the SML.

   c. Plot the following estimated returns for the next year on the SML and indicate which stocks are undervalued or overvalued.

   - Intel—20 percent
   - Ford—15 perent
   - Anheuser Busch—19 percent
   - Merck—10 percent

12. Calculate the expected (required) return for each of the following stocks when the risk-free rate is 0.08 and you expect the market return to be 0.14.

Stock	Beta
A	1.72
B	1.14
C	0.76
D	0.44
E	0.03
F	−0.79

13. The following are the historic returns for the Chelle Computer Company:

Year	Chelle Computer	General Index
1	37	15
2	9	13
3	−11	14
4	8	−9
5	11	12
6	4	9

Based on this information, compute the following:
a. The correlation coefficient between Chelle Computer and the General Index.
b. The standard deviation for the company and the index.
c. The beta for the Chelle Computer Company.

14. *CFA Examination Level II*
The following information describes the expected return and risk relationship for the stocks of two of WAH's competitors.

	Expected Return	Standard Deviation	Beta
Stock X	12.0%	20%	1.3
Stock Y	9.0	15	0.7
Market Index	10.0	12	1.0
Risk-free rate	5.0		

Using only the data shown in the preceding table:
a. Draw and label a graph showing the security market line and position stocks X and Y relative to it. [5 minutes]
b. Compute the alphas *both* for Stock X *and* for Stock Y. Show your work. [4 minutes]
c. Assume that the risk-free rate increases to 7 percent with the other data in the preceding matrix remaining unchanged. Select the stock providing the higher expected risk-adjusted return and justify your selection. Show your calculations. [6 minutes]

15. *CFA Examination Level II*
An analyst expects a risk-free return of 4.5 percent, a market return of 14.5 percent, and the returns for Stocks A and B that are shown in the following table.

STOCK INFORMATION		
Stock	Beta	Analyst's Estimated Return
A	1.2	16%
B	0.8	14%

a. Show on the graph provided in the answer book:
   (1) Where Stock A and B would plot on the security market line (SML) if they were fairly valued using the capital asset pricing model (CAPM)
   (2) Where Stock A and B actually plot on the same graph according to the returns estimated by the analyst and shown in the table [6 minutes]
b. State whether Stock A and B are undervalued or overvalued if the analyst uses the SML for strategic investment decisions. [4 minutes]

16. Given the following results, indicate what will happen to the beta for Stock E, relative to the market proxy, compared to the beta relative to the true market portfolio:

| | YEARLY RATES OF RETURN | | |
| | Stock E | Market Proxy | True Market |
Year	(Percent)	(Percent)	(Percent)
1	10	8	6
2	20	14	11
3	−14	−10	−7
4	−20	−18	−12
5	15	12	10

Discuss the reason for the differences in measured beta. Does the suggested relationship appear reasonable? Why or why not?

17. Draw the implied SMLs for the following two sets of conditions:
    a. $RFR = 0.07$; R_M (S + P 500) = 0.16
    b. $R_z = 0.09$; R_M (True) = 0.18
    Under which set of conditions would it be more difficult for a portfolio manager to be superior?

18. Using the graph and equations from Problem 17, which of the following portfolios would be superior?
    a. $R_a = 11\%$; $\beta = 0.09$
    b. $R_b = 14\%$; $\beta = 1.00$
    c. $R_c = 12\%$; $\beta = -0.40$
    d. $R_d = 20\%$; $\beta = 1.10$
    Does it matter which SML you use?

19. Draw the security market line for each of the following conditions:
    a. (1) $RFR = 0.08$ R_M(proxy) = 0.12
       (2) $R_z = 0.06$ R_M(true) = 0.15
    b. Rader Tire has the following results for the last six periods. Calculate and compare the betas using each index.

Period	Return of Rader (Percent)	Proxy Specific Index (Percent)	True General Index (Percent)
1	29	12	15
2	12	10	13
3	−12	−9	−8
4	17	14	18
5	20	25	28
6	−5	−10	0

c. If the current period return for the market is 12 percent and for Rader is 11 percent, are superior results being obtained for either index beta?

References   Black, Fischer. "Capital Market Equilibrium with Restricted Borrowing." *Journal of Business* 45, no. 3 (July 1972).

Brinson, Gary P., Jeffrey J. Diermeier, and Gary Schlarbaum. "A Composite Portfolio Benchmark for Pension Plans." *Financial Analysts Journal* 42, no. 2 (March–April 1986).

Campbell, John Y., and John Ammer. "What Moves the Stock and Bond Markets? A Variance Decomposition for Long-Term Asset Returns." *Journal of Finance* 48, no. 1 (March 1993).

Elton, Edwin J., and Martin J. Gruber. *Modern Portfolio Theory and Investment Analysis,* 5th ed. New York: John Wiley & Sons, 1995.

Farrell, James L., Jr. *Portfolio Management Theory and Application,* 2d ed. New York: McGraw-Hill, 1997.

Handa, Puneet, S. P. Kothari, and Charles Wasley. "The Relation between the Return Interval and Betas: Implications of the Size Effect." *Journal of Financial Economics* 23, no. 1 (June 1989).

Hawawini, Gabriel A. "Why Beta Shifts as the Return Interval Changes." *Financial Analysts Journal* 39, no. 3 (May–June 1983).

Reilly, Frank K., and Rashid A. Akhtar. "The Benchmark Error Problem with Global Capital Markets." *Journal of Portfolio Management* 22, no. 1 (Fall 1995).

Chapter 9 Multifactor Models of Risk and Return

After you read this chapter, you should be able to answer the following questions:

➤ What are the deficiencies of the capital asset pricing model (CAPM) as an explanation of the relationship between risk and expected asset returns?

➤ What is the arbitrage pricing theory (APT) and what are its similarities and differences relative to the CAPM?

➤ What are the major assumptions *not* required by the APT model compared to the CAPM?

➤ What are the strengths and weaknesses of the APT as a theory of how risk and expected return are related?

➤ How can the APT be used in the security valuation process?

➤ How do you test the APT by examining anomalies found with the CAPM and why do some authors contend that the APT model is untestable?

➤ What are multifactor models and how are they related to the APT?

➤ What are the steps necessary in developing a usable multifactor model?

➤ What are the two primary approaches employed in defining common risk factors?

➤ What are the main macroeconomic variables used in practice as risk factors?

➤ What are the main security characteristic-oriented variables used in practice as risk factors?

➤ How can multifactor models be used to identify the investment "bets" that an active portfolio manager is making relative to a benchmark?

➤ How are multifactor models used to estimate the expected risk premium of a security or portfolio?

Chapter 7 and Chapter 8 introduced in detail the Markowitz portfolio theory and the capital asset pricing model (CAPM), which collectively represent the foundation for understanding the connection between risk and expected return in financial markets. This chapter considers several important extensions of this framework. Specifically, whereas the CAPM designated a single risk factor to account for the volatility inherent in an individual security or portfolio of securities, in this chapter we develop the intuition and application of *multifactor* explanations of risk and return. In particular, we begin with an explanation of the leading alternative to the CAPM—the arbitrage pricing theory (APT), which was developed by Stephen Ross. The chief difference between the CAPM and the APT is that the latter specifies several risk factors, thereby allowing for a more expansive definition of systematic investment risk than that implied by the CAPM's single market portfolio.

After developing the conceptual basis for the APT in the next section and contrasting its major assumptions with those of the CAPM, we also examine the empirical evidence supporting the theory. Despite several appealing features, one of the practical challenges that an investor faces when attempting to implement the APT is that the risk factors in the model are not defined in terms of their quantity (i.e., how many there are) or their identity (i.e., what they are). We conclude the chapter by discussing how investors use **multifactor models,** which can be viewed as attempts to convert the APT into a tractable working tool in the area of security analysis, thus turning theory into practice. A wide variety of factor models are currently in use. These models differ primarily in how they define the risk factors and can be grouped broadly into those models that use *macroeconomic* factor definitions and those that specify *microeconomic* factors. Several examples of the different approaches that have been taken in developing multifactor explanations of risk and return are given to illustrate the myriad forms these important models can assume.

ARBITRAGE PRICING THEORY

The last chapter highlighted many of the ways in which the CAPM has contributed to the investment management field. Indeed, in many respects, the CAPM has been one of the most useful—and frequently used—financial economic theories ever developed. However, many of the empirical studies cited also point out some of the deficiencies in the model as an explanation of the link between risk and return. For example, tests of the CAPM indicated that the beta coefficients for individual securities were not stable but that portfolio betas generally were stable assuming long enough sample periods and adequate trading volume. There was mixed support for a positive linear relationship between rates of return and systematic risk for portfolios of stock, with some recent evidence indicating the need to consider additional risk variables or a need for different risk proxies. In addition, several papers criticized the tests of the model and the usefulness of the model in portfolio evaluation because of its dependence on a market portfolio of risky assets that is not currently available.

One especially compelling challenge to the efficacy of the CAPM was the set of results suggesting that it is possible to use knowledge of certain firm or security characteristics to develop profitable trading strategies, even after adjusting for investment risk as measured by beta. Typical of this work were the findings of Banz, who showed that portfolios of stocks with low market capitalizations (i.e., "small" stocks) outperformed "large" stock portfolios on a risk-adjusted basis, and Basu, who documented that stocks with low price-earnings (P-E) ratios similarly outperformed high P-E stocks.[1] More recent work by Fama and French also demonstrates that "value" stocks (i.e., those with high book value-to-market price ratios) tend to produce larger risk-adjusted returns than "growth" stocks (i.e., those with low book-to-market ratios).[2] Of course, in an efficient market, these return differentials should not occur, which in turn leads to one of two conclusions: (1) markets are not particularly efficient for extended periods of time (i.e., investors have been ignoring profitable investment opportunities for decades), or (2) market prices are efficient but there is something wrong with the way the single-factor models such as the CAPM measure risk.

Given the implausibility of the first possibility, in the early 1970s, financial economists began to consider in earnest the implications of the second. In particular, the academic community searched for an alternative asset pricing theory to the CAPM that was reasonably intuitive, required only limited assumptions, and allowed for multiple dimensions of investment risk. The

---

[1]See R. W. Banz, "The Relationship between Return and Market Value of Common Stocks," *Journal of Financial Economics* 9, no. 1 (March 1981): 3–18; and S. Basu, "Investment Performance of Common Stocks in Relation to Their Price-Earnings Ratios: A Test of the Efficient Market Hypothesis," *Journal of Finance* 32, no. 3 (June 1977): 663–682.

[2]Eugene F. Fama and Kenneth French, "The Cross Section of Expected Stock Returns," *Journal of Finance* 47, no. 2 (June 1992): 427–465.

result was the **arbitrage pricing theory (APT)**, which was developed by Ross in the mid-1970s and has three major assumptions:[3]

1. Capital markets are perfectly competitive.
2. Investors always prefer more wealth to less wealth with certainty.
3. The stochastic process generating asset returns can be expressed as a linear function of a set of K risk factors (or indexes).

Equally important, the following major assumptions—which were used in the development of the CAPM—are *not* required: (1) Investors possess quadratic utility functions, (2) normally distributed security returns, and (3) a market portfolio that contains all risky assets and is mean-variance efficient. Obviously, if such a model is both simpler and can explain differential security prices, it will be considered a superior theory to the CAPM.

Prior to discussing the empirical tests of the APT, we provide a brief review of the basics of the model. As noted, the theory assumes that the stochastic process generating asset returns can be represented as a K factor model of the form:

➤9.1
$$R_i = E(R_i) + b_{i1}\delta_1 + b_{i2}\delta_2 + \ldots + b_{ik}\delta_k + \varepsilon_i \text{ for } i = 1 \text{ to } n$$

where:

R_i = **the actual return on asset *i* during a specified time period, $i = 1, 2, 3, \ldots n$**
$E(R_i)$ = **the expected return for asset *i* if all the risk factors have zero changes**
b_{ij} = **the reaction in asset *i*'s returns to movements in a common risk factor *j***
δ_k = **a set of common factors or indexes with a zero mean that influences the returns on all assets**
ε_i = **a unique effect on asset *i*'s return (i.e., a random error term that, by assumption, is completely diversifiable in large portfolios and has a mean of zero)**
n = **number of assets**

Two terms require elaboration: δ_j and b_{ij}. As indicated, δ terms are the multiple risk factors expected to have an impact on the returns of *all* assets. Examples of these factors might include inflation, growth in gross domestic product (GDP), major political upheavals, or changes in interest rates. The APT contends that there are many such factors that affect returns, in contrast to the CAPM, where the only relevant risk to measure is the covariance of the asset with the market portfolio (i.e., the asset's beta).

Given these common factors, the b_{ij} terms determine how each asset reacts to the *j*th particular common factor. To extend the earlier intuition, although all assets may be affected by growth in GDP, the impact (i.e., reaction) to a factor will differ. For example, stocks of cyclical firms will have larger b_{ij} terms for the "growth in GDP" factor than will noncyclical firms, such as grocery store chains. Likewise, you will hear discussions about interest-sensitive stocks. All stocks are affected by changes in interest rates; however, some experience larger impacts. For example, an interest-sensitive stock would have a b_j interest of 2.0 or more, whereas a stock that is relatively insensitive to interest rates would have a b_j of 0.5. Other examples of common factors include changes in unemployment rates, exchange rates, and yield curve shifts. It is important to note, however, that when we apply the theory, *the factors are not identified*. That is, when we

[3]Stephen Ross, "The Arbitrage Theory of Capital Asset Pricing," *Journal of Economic Theory* 13, no. 2 (December 1976): 341–360; and Stephen Ross, "Return, Risk, and Arbitrage," in *Risk and Return in Finance,* edited by I. Friend and J. Bicksler (Cambridge: Ballinger, 1977), 189–218.

EXHIBIT 9.1 ▶   *COMPARING THE CAPITAL ASSET PRICING MODEL (CAPM) AND THE ARBITRAGE PRICING THEORY (APT)*

	CAPM	APT
Form of Equation	Linear	Linear
Number of Risk Factors	1	$K \ (\geq 1)$
Factor Risk Premium	$[E(R_m) - RFR]$	$\{\lambda_j\}$
Factor Risk Sensitivity	β_i	$\{b_{ij}\}$
"Zero-Beta" Return	RFR	λ_0

discuss the empirical studies of the APT, the investigators will note that they found three, four, or five factors that affect security returns, but *they will give no indication of what these factors represent.*

Similar to the CAPM model, the APT assumes that the unique effects (ε_i) are independent and will be diversified away in a large portfolio. Specifically, the APT requires that in equilibrium the return on a zero-investment, zero-systematic-risk portfolio is zero when the unique effects are diversified away. This assumption (and some theoretical manipulation using linear algebra) implies that the expected return on any asset i (i.e., $E(R_i)$), can be expressed as:

$$E(R_i) = \lambda_0 + \lambda_1 b_{i1} + \lambda_2 b_{i2} + \ldots + \lambda_k b_{ik} \qquad \text{(APT)}$$

where:

λ_0 = **the expected return on an asset with zero systematic risk**
λ_j = **the risk premium related to the *j*th common risk factor**
b_{ij} = **the pricing relationship between the risk premium and the asset; that is, how responsive asset *i* is to the *j*th common factor. (These are called factor betas or factor loadings.)**

This equation represents the fundamental result of the APT. It is useful to compare the form of the APT's specification of the expected return-risk relationship with that of the CAPM. Recall from Chapter 8 that the comparable result for the CAPM is:

$$E(R_i) = RFR + \beta_i[E(R_m) - RFR] \qquad \text{(CAPM)}$$

Exhibit 9.1 compares the relevant features of the two models. From this summary, it should be clear that the ultimate difference between these two theories lies in the way systematic investment risk is defined: a single, market-wide risk factor for the CAPM versus a few (or several) factors in the APT that capture the salient nuances of that market-wide risk. It is important to recognize, though, that both theories specify linear models based on the common belief that investors are compensated for performing two functions: committing capital and bearing risk. Finally, notice that the equation for the APT suggests a relationship that is analogous to the security market line associated with the CAPM. However, instead of a line connecting risk and expected return, the APT implies a *security market plane* with $(K + 1)$ dimensions—K risk factors and one additional dimension for the security's expected return. Exhibit 9.2 illustrates this relationship for two risk factors (i.e., $K = 2$).

Using the APT   As noted earlier, the primary challenge in using the APT in security valuation involves the identification of the risk factors. The complexities of this issue are addressed later, so in order to illustrate how the model works we will assume that there are two common factors: one related to unexpected changes in the level of inflation and another related to unanticipated changes in the real

EXHIBIT 9.2 *THE RELATIONSHIP BETWEEN EXPECTED RETURN AND TWO COMMON RISK FACTORS ($\lambda_0 = 4\%$, $\lambda_1 = 2\%$, $\lambda_2 = 3\%$)*

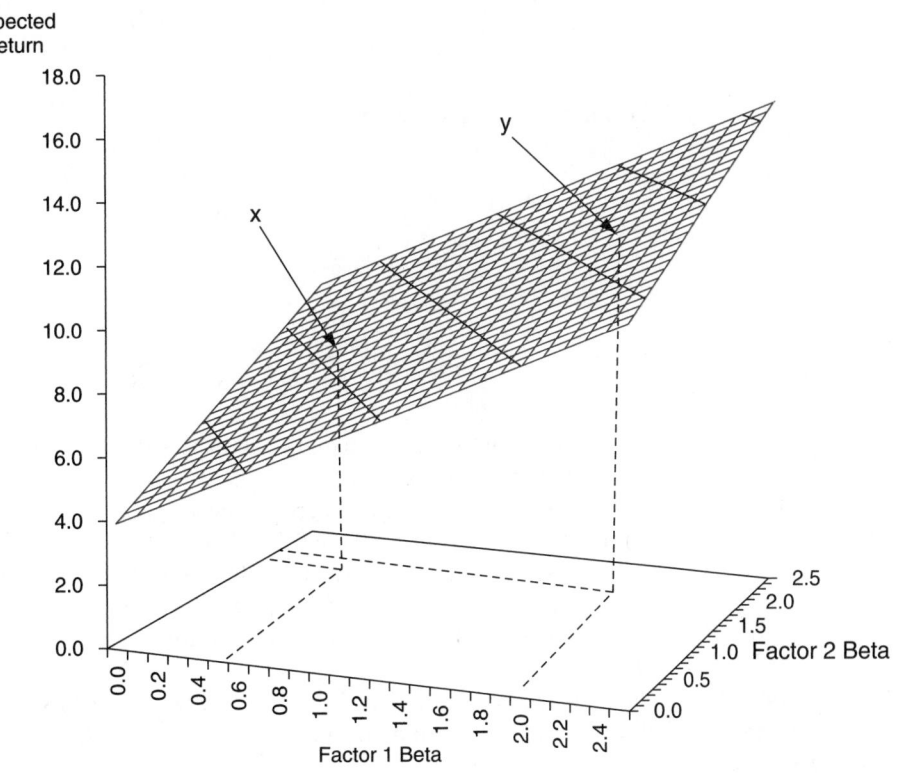

level of GDP. If we further assume that the risk premium related to GDP sensitivity is 0.03 and a stock that is sensitive to GDP has a b_j (where j represents the GDP factor) of 1.5, this means that this factor would cause the stock's expected return to increase by 4.5 percent (= 1.5×0.03).

To develop this notion further, consider the following example of two stocks and a two-factor model. First, consider these risk factor definitions and sensitivities:

> δ_1 = **unanticipated changes in the rate of inflation. The risk premium related to this factor is 2 percent for every 1 percent change in the rate ($\lambda_1 = 0.02$)**
>
> δ_2 = **unexpected changes in the growth rate of real GDP. The average risk premium related to this factor is 3 percent for every 1 percent change in the rate of growth ($\lambda_2 = 0.03$)**
>
> λ_0 = **the rate of return on a zero-systematic risk asset (i.e., zero beta) is 4 percent ($\lambda_0 = 0.04$)**

Assume also that there are two assets (x and y) that have the following response coefficients to these common risk factors:

> b_{x1} = **the response of asset x to changes in the inflation factor is 0.50 ($b_{x1} = 0.50$)**
> b_{x2} = **the response of asset x to changes in the GDP factor is 1.50 ($b_{x2} = 1.50$)**
> b_{y1} = **the response of asset y to changes in the inflation factor is 2.00 ($b_{y1} = 2.00$)**
> b_{y2} = **the response of asset y to changes in the GDP factor is 1.75 ($b_{y2} = 1.75$)**

These factor sensitivities can be interpreted in much the same way as beta in the CAPM; that is, the higher the level of b_{ij}, the greater the sensitivity of asset i to changes in the jth risk factor. Thus, the response coefficients listed indicate that if these are the major factors influencing asset returns, asset y is a higher risk asset than asset x, and, therefore, its expected return should be greater. The overall expected return equation will be:

$$E(R_i) = \lambda_0 + \lambda_1 b_{i1} + \lambda_2 b_{i2}$$
$$= 0.04 + (0.02)b_{i1} + (0.03)b_{i2}$$

Therefore, for assets x and y:

$$E(R_x) = 0.04 + (0.02)(0.50) + (0.03)(1.50)$$
$$= 0.0950 = 9.50\%$$

and

$$E(R_y) = 0.04 + (0.02)(2.00) + (0.03)(1.75)$$
$$= 0.1325 = 13.25\%$$

The positions of the factor loadings and expected returns for these two assets are illustrated in Exhibit 9.2. If the prices of the two assets do not reflect these expected returns, we would expect investors to enter into arbitrage arrangements whereby they would sell overpriced assets short and use the proceeds to purchase the underpriced assets until the relevant prices were corrected. Given these linear relationships, it should be possible to find an asset or a combination of assets with equal risk to the mispriced asset, yet providing a higher expected return. A detailed example of how the APT can be used in the security valuation process follows.

Security Valuation with the APT: An Example

Suppose that three stocks (A, B, and C) and two common systematic risk factors (1 and 2) have the following relationship (for simplicity, it is assumed that the zero-beta return (λ_0) equals zero):

$$E(R_A) = (0.80) \lambda_1 + (0.90) \lambda_2$$
$$E(R_B) = (-0.20) \lambda_1 + (1.30) \lambda_2$$
$$E(R_C) = (1.80) \lambda_1 + (0.50) \lambda_2$$

If $\lambda_1 = 4\%$ and $\lambda_2 = 5\%$, then the returns expected by the market over the next year can be expressed:

$$E(R_A) = (0.80) (4\%) + (0.90) (5\%) = 7.7\%$$
$$E(R_B) = (-0.20) (4\%) + (1.30) (5\%) = 5.7\%$$
$$E(R_C) = (1.80) (4\%) + (0.50) (5\%) = 9.7\%$$

which, assuming that all three stocks are currently priced at $35 and will not pay a dividend over the next year, implies the following expected prices a year from now:

$$E(P_A) = \$35 \ (1.077) = \$37.70$$
$$E(P_B) = \$35 \ (1.057) = \$37.00$$
$$E(P_C) = \$35 \ (1.097) = \$38.40$$

Now, suppose you "know" that in one year the actual prices of stocks A, B, and C will be $37.20, $37.80, and $38.50. How can you best take advantage of what you consider to be a market mispricing?

The first thing to note is that, according to your forecasts of future prices, Stock A will not achieve a price level in one year consistent with investor return expectations. Accordingly, you conclude that at a current price of $35 a share, Stock A is *overvalued*. Similarly, Stock B is *undervalued* and Stock C is (slightly) *undervalued*. Consequently, any investment strategy designed to take advantage of these discrepancies will, at the very least, need to consider purchasing Stocks B and C while short selling Stock A.

The idea of *riskless arbitrage* is to assemble a portfolio that: (1) requires no net wealth invested initially and (2) will bear no systematic or unsystematic risk but (3) still earns a profit. Letting w_i represent the percentage investment in security i, the conditions that must be satisfied can be written formally as follows:

1. $\sum_i w_i = 0$ [i.e., no net wealth invested]
2. $\sum_i w_i b_{ij} = 0$ for all K factors [i.e., no systematic risk]
   and w_i is "small" for all i [i.e., unsystematic risk is fully diversified]
3. $\sum_i w_i R_i > 0$ [i.e., the actual portfolio return is positive]

In this example, since Stock A is the only one that is overvalued, assume that it is the only one that actually is short sold. The proceeds from the short sale of Stock A can then be used to purchase the two undervalued securities, Stocks B and C. To illustrate this process, consider the following investment proportions:

$$w_A = -1.0$$
$$w_B = +0.5$$
$$w_C = +0.5$$

These investment weights imply the creation of a portfolio that is *short two shares of Stock A for each one share of Stock B and one share of Stock C held long*. Notice that this portfolio meets the net investment and risk mandates of an arbitrage-based trade:

Net Initial Investment:

Short 2 shares of A:	+70
Purchase 1 share of B:	−35
Purchase 1 share of C:	−35
Net investment:	0

Net Exposure to Risk Factors:

	Factor 1	Factor 2
Weighted exposure from Stock A:	(−1.0)(0.8)	(−1.0)(0.9)
Weighted exposure from Stock B:	(0.5)(−0.2)	(0.5)(1.3)
Weighted exposure from Stock C:	(0.5)(1.8)	(0.5)(0.5)
Net risk exposure:	0	0

Assuming prices in one year actually rise to the levels that you initially "knew" they would, your net profit from covering the short position and liquidating the two long holdings will be:

Net Profit:

$$[2(35) - 2(37.20)] + [37.80 - 35] + [38.50 - 35] = \$1.90$$

Thus, from a portfolio in which you invested no net wealth and assumed no net risk, you have realized a positive profit. This is the essence of arbitrage investing and is an example of the "long-short" trading strategies often employed by hedge funds.

Finally, if everyone else in the market today begins to believe the way you do about the future price levels of A, B, and C—but do not revise their forecasts about the expected factor returns or factor betas for the individual stocks—then the current prices for the three stocks will be adjusted by the resulting volume of arbitrage trading to:

$$P_A = (\$37.20) \div (1.077) = \$34.54$$
$$P_B = (\$37.80) \div (1.057) = \$35.76$$
$$P_C = (\$38.50) \div (1.097) = \$35.10$$

Thus, the price of Stock A will be bid down while the prices of Stocks B and C will be bid up until arbitrage trading in the current market is no longer profitable.

Empirical Tests of the APT   Although the APT is considerably newer than the CAPM, it has undergone numerous empirical studies. Before we begin discussing the empirical tests, remember the crucial earlier caveat that when applying the theory, we do not know what the factors generated by the formal model actually represent. This becomes a major point in some discussions of test results.

Roll-Ross Study

Roll-Ross Study   Roll and Ross produced one of the first large-scale empirical tests of the APT.[4] Their methodology followed a two-step procedure:

1. Estimate the expected returns and the factor coefficients from time-series data on individual asset returns.
2. Use these estimates to test the basic cross-sectional pricing conclusion implied by the APT. Specifically, are the expected returns for these assets consistent with the common factors derived in Step 1?

In particular, the authors tested the following pricing relationship:

H_0: There exist nonzero constants $(\lambda_0, \lambda_i, \ldots \lambda_k)$ such that for any asset i:
$$[E(R_i) - \lambda_0] = \lambda_1 b_{i1} + \lambda_2 b_{i2} + \ldots + \lambda_k b_{ik}$$

The specific b_i coefficients were estimated using the statistical technique of factor analysis. The authors pointed out that the estimation procedure was generally appropriate for the model involved, but there is very little known about the small sample properties of the results. Therefore, they emphasized the tentative nature of the conclusions.

Their database consisted of daily returns for the period from 1962 through 1972. Stocks were put into 42 portfolios of 30 stocks each (1,260 stocks) by alphabetical order. The initial estimation of the factor model indicated that the maximum reasonable number of factors was five. The factors derived were applied to all 42 portfolios, with the understanding that the importance of the various factors might differ among portfolios (e.g., the first factor in Portfolio A might not be first in Portfolio B). Assuming a risk-free rate of 6 percent ($\lambda_0 = 0.06$), the subsequent analysis revealed the existence of at least three meaningful factors but probably not more than four. However, when they allowed the model to estimate the risk-free rate (λ_0), only two factors were consistently significant.

[4]Richard Roll and Stephen A. Ross, "An Empirical Investigation of the Arbitrage Pricing Theory," *Journal of Finance* 35, no. 5 (December 1980): 1073–1103.

A subsequent test related returns to a security's own standard deviation, which should not affect expected return if the APT is valid because a security's unsystematic component would be eliminated by diversification, and the nondiversifiable components should be explained by the factor sensitivities (or "loadings"). The test analyzed returns against the five factors plus the security's own standard deviation. The primary results showed that the security's own standard deviation was statistically significant, which provided evidence against the APT. Subsequently, they adjusted the results for skewness and found that the security's own standard deviation was insignificant, which supports the APT.

Finally, Roll and Ross tested whether the three or four factors that affect Group A were the same as the factors that affect Group B. The analysis involved testing for cross-sectional consistency by examining whether the λ_0 terms for the 42 groups are similar. The results yielded no evidence that the intercept terms were different, although the test was admittedly weak. The authors concluded that the evidence generally supported the APT but acknowledged that their tests were not conclusive.

Extensions of the Roll-Ross Tests   Cho, Elton, and Gruber tested the APT by examining the number of factors in the return-generating process that were priced.[5] Because the APT model contends that more factors affect stock returns than are implied by the CAPM, they examined different sets of data to determine what happened to the number of factors priced in the model compared to prior studies that found between three and five significant factors. They simulated returns using the zero-beta CAPM with betas derived from Wilshire's fundamental beta estimates and with betas derived from historical data. They found that five factors were required using the Roll-Ross procedures, six factors were present when using historical beta, and the fundamental betas indicated a need for three factors. The authors concluded that even when returns were generated by a two-factor model, two or three factors are required to explain the returns. These results support the APT model because it allows for the consideration of these additional factors, which is not possible with the classical CAPM.

Dhrymes, Friend, and Gultekin reexamined the techniques used in prior studies and contended that these techniques have several major limitations.[6] Although the division of the total sample of stocks into numerous portfolios of 30 stocks was necessary because of computer limitations, this practical constraint produced results that differed from large-sample results, especially for the total sample of over 1,000 stocks. Specifically, they found *no* relationship between the factor loadings for groups of 30 stocks and for a group of 240 stocks. Also, they could not identify the actual number of factors that characterize the return-generating process. When they applied the model to portfolios of different sizes, the number of factors changed. For example, for 15 securities, it is a two-factor model; for 30 securities, a three-factor model; for 45, a four-factor model; for 60, a six-factor model; and for 90, a nine-factor model.

Roll and Ross acknowledged that the number of risk factors differ with 30 stocks versus 240 but contended that the important consideration is whether the resulting estimates are *consistent* because it is not feasible to consider all of the stocks together.[7] When they tested for consistency, the APT was generally supported. They point out that the number of factors is a secondary issue compared to how well the model explains expected security returns compared to alternative

---

[5]D. Chinhyung Cho, Edwin J. Elton, and Martin J. Gruber, "On the Robustness of the Roll and Ross Arbitrage Pricing Theory," *Journal of Financial and Quantitative Analysis* 19, no. 1 (March 1984): 1–10.

[6]Phoebus J. Dhrymes, Irwin Friend, and N. Bulent Gultekin, "A Critical Re-Examination of the Empirical Evidence on the Arbitrage Pricing Theory," *Journal of Finance* 39, no. 2 (June 1984): 323–346.

[7]Richard Roll and Stephen A. Ross, "A Critical Re-Examination of the Empirical Evidence on the Arbitrage Pricing Theory," *Journal of Finance* 39, no. 2 (June 1984): 347–350.

models. Also, one would *expect* the number of factors to increase with the sample size because more potential relationships would arise (e.g., you would introduce industry effects). The relevant question is: How many of these factors are significant in a diversified portfolio?

Dhrymes, Friend, Gultekin, and Gultekin repeated the prior tests for larger groups of securities.[8] When they increased the number of securities in each group (30, 60, and 90 securities), both the number of factors that entered the model and the number of statistically significant (i.e., "priced") factors increased, although most factors are not priced. These results confirmed their results. In addition, they found that the unique or total standard deviation for a period was as good at predicting subsequent returns as the factor loadings. Also, the number of time-series observations affected the number of factors discovered, and the group size of securities affected the model's intercept. These findings are not favorable to the empirical relevance of APT because they indicate extreme instability in the relationships and suggest that the risk-free rate implied by the model depends on group size and the number of observations.

Finally, Connor and Korajczyk argued that most tests for the number of priced risk factors are valid only for strict factor models in which diversifiable returns are uncorrelated across the set of stocks in the sample.[9] They developed a test that identifies the number of factors in a less-restrictive model that does allow the unsystematic components of risk to be correlated across assets. Using this framework, they showed that between one and six priced factors exist in their sample of stock returns for NYSE- and ASE-listed stocks.

The APT and Stock Market Anomalies

An alternative set of tests of the APT considers how well the theory explains pricing anomalies that are not explained by a competing model (i.e., the CAPM). Two anomalies considered are the **small-firm effect** and the **January effect**.

APT Tests of the Small-Firm Effect

Reinganum addressed the APT's ability to account for the differences in average returns between small firms and large firms.[10] He contended that this anomaly, which could not be explained by the CAPM, should be explained by the APT if the latter was to be considered a superior theory. Reinganum's test is conducted in two stages:

1. During Year Y-1, factor loadings are estimated for all securities, and securities with similar factor loadings are put into common control portfolios. (The author tests models with three, four, and five factors.) During Year Y, excess security returns are derived for each control portfolio from the daily returns of the individual stocks in the portfolio. Assuming that all stocks within a control portfolio have equal risk according to the APT, they should have similar average returns and the average excess returns should be zero.
2. All the stocks were ranked on the basis of their market value at the end of Year Y-1, and the excess returns of the firms in the bottom 10 percent of the size distribution were combined (equal weights) to form the average excess returns for Portfolio MV1. Similarly, nine other portfolios were formed, with MV10 containing excess returns for the largest firms. These size portfolios were rebalanced annually.

According to the APT, the 10 size-based portfolios should possess identical average excess returns, which should be insignificantly different from zero. If the 10 portfolios do not have identical average excess returns, this evidence would be inconsistent with the APT.

---

[8] Phoebus J. Dhrymes, Irwin Friend, Mustofa N. Gultekin, and N. Bulent Gultekin, "New Tests of the APT and Their Implications," *Journal of Finance* 40, no. 3 (July 1985): 659–674.

[9] Gregory Connor and Robert A. Korajczyk, "A Test for the Number of Factors in an Approximate Factor Model," *Journal of Finance* 48, no. 4 (September 1993): 1263–1291.

[10] Mark R. Reinganum, "The Arbitrage Pricing Theory: Some Empirical Results," *Journal of Finance* 36, no. 2 (May 1981): 313–321.

The test results were clearly inconsistent with the APT. Specifically, the average excess returns of the 10 portfolios were not equal to zero for either a three-, four-, or five-factor model. The small-firm portfolio, MV1, experienced a positive and statistically significant average excess return, whereas Portfolio MV10 had a statistically significant negative average excess return. The mean difference in excess returns between the small and large firms was about 25 percent a year. Also, the mean excess returns of MV1 through MV10 were perfectly inversely ordered with firm size.

Reinganum also tested for significant differences between individual portfolio returns and the difference between the high and low portfolio each year. Both tests confirmed that the low-market-value portfolios outperformed the high-market-value portfolios regardless of whether excess returns were derived from the three-, four-, or five-factor model. The author concluded that these results did not support the APT, but he acknowledged that the analysis involved a joint test of several hypotheses implicit in the theory and that it was impossible to pinpoint the error.

In contrast to Reinganum's work, Chen compared the APT model to the CAPM and provided contrary evidence related to the small-firm effect.[11] Prior to discussing the tests, the author contended that problems caused by the need for a limited sample and the existence of multiple factors were related to the *testing* of the theory and should not reflect on the theory itself. The analysis employed 180 stocks and 5 factors. The cross-sectional results indicated that the first factor was highly correlated with the CAPM beta. Chen's test of the two models for performance measurement was based on the contention that if the CAPM does not capture all the information related to returns, this remaining information will be in the residual series. In turn, if the APT can provide factors to explain these residual returns, it will be superior. He concluded that the CAPM was misspecified and that the missing price information was picked up by the APT.

The final tests Chen produced examined whether some major variables have explanatory power after the factor loadings from the APT model. If so, it would cause one to reject the APT. The two variables considered based on prior CAPM studies were a stock's own variance and firm size. The results supported the APT because neither a stock's own variance nor a firm's size had explanatory power after adjusting for risk based on factor loadings. Again, these results are in contrast to the earlier results by Reinganum.

APT Tests of the January Effect   Given the so-called *January effect,* where returns in January are significantly larger than in any other month, Gultekin and Gultekin tested the ability of the APT model to adjust for this anomaly.[12] The APT model was estimated separately for each month, and risk premia were *always* significant in January but rarely priced in other months. It was concluded that the APT model, like the CAPM, can explain the risk-return relation only in January, which indicates that the APT model does not explain this anomaly any better than the CAPM.

Burmeister and McElroy estimated a linear factor model (LFM), the APT, and a CAPM.[13] They found a significant January effect that was not captured by any of the models. When they moved beyond the January effect, however, they rejected the CAPM in favor of the APT. More recently, Kramer shows that an empirical form of the APT accounts for the January seasonal effect in average stock returns while the CAPM cannot.[14]

---

[11]Nai-fu Chen, "Some Empirical Tests of the Theory of Arbitrage Pricing," *Journal of Finance* 38, no. 5 (December 1983): 1393–1414.

[12]Mustofa N. Gultekin and N. Bulent Gultekin, "Stock Return Anomalies and the Tests of APT," *Journal of Finance* 42, no. 5 (December 1987): 1213–1224.

[13]Edwin Burmeister and Marjorie B. McElroy, "Joint Estimation of Factor Sensitivities and Risk Premia for the Arbitrage Pricing Theory," *Journal of Finance* 43, no. 3 (July 1988): 721–733.

[14]Charles Kramer, "Macroeconomic Seasonality and the January Effect," *Journal of Finance* 49, no. 5 (December 1994): 1883–1891.

Is the APT Even Testable?   Similar to Roll's critique of the CAPM, Shanken challenged whether it is possible for the APT to be empirically verified at all.[15] Rather than question specific tests or methods, Shanken questioned whether the APT is more susceptible to testing than the CAPM based on the usual empirical test that determines whether asset returns conform to a *K* factor model. One problem is that if stock returns are not explained by such a model, it is not considered a rejection of the model; however, if the factors do explain returns, it is considered support. Also, it is contended that APT has no advantage because the factors need not be observable, which means that equivalent sets of securities may conform to different factor structures. Therefore, the empirical formulation of the APT may yield different implications regarding the expected returns for a given set of securities. Unfortunately, this implies that the theory cannot explain differential returns between securities because it cannot identify the relevant factor structure that explains the differential returns. This need to identify the relevant factor structure that affects asset returns is similar to the CAPM benchmark problem. In summary, each of the models has a problem with testing. Specifically, before you can test the CAPM, you must identify and use the true market portfolio; whereas, before you can test the APT, you must identify the relevant factor structure that affects security returns.

Dybvig and Ross replied by suggesting that the APT is testable as an equality rather than the "empirical APT" proposed by Shanken.[16] Shanken responded that what has developed is a set of equilibrium APT pricing models that are testable but that arbitrage-based models are not testable as originally specified.[17]

Alternative Techniques for Testing the APT   In addition to the test procedures just described, several other articles have proposed alternative statistical techniques for testing the APT model. Jobson proposes that the APT be tested using a multivariate linear regression model.[18] Brown and Weinstein propose an approach to estimating and testing asset pricing models using a bilinear paradigm.[19] Geweke and Zhou produce an exact Bayesian framework for testing the APT and conclude that there is little reduction in pricing error from including additional factors beyond the first one.[20] A number of subsequent papers have proposed new methodologies for testing the APT.[21]

---

[15]Jay Shanken, "The Arbitrage Pricing Theory: Is It Testable?" *Journal of Finance* 37, no. 5 (December 1982: 1129–1140.

[16]Philip H. Dybvig and Stephen A. Ross, "Yes, The APT Is Testable," *Journal of Finance* 40, no. 4 (September 1985): 1173–1188.

[17]Jay Shanken, "Multi-Beta CAPM or Equilibrium APT?: A Reply," *Journal of Finance* 40, no. 4 (September 1985): 1189–1196.

[18]J. D. Jobson, "A Multivariate Linear Regression Test for the Arbitrage Pricing Theory," *Journal of Finance* 37, no. 4 (September 1982): 1037–1042.

[19]Stephen J. Brown and Mark I. Weinstein, "A New Approach to Testing Asset Pricing Models: The Bilinear Paradigm," *Journal of Finance* 38, no. 3 (June 1983): 711–743.

[20]John Geweke and Guofu Zhou, "Measuring the Price of the Arbitrage Pricing Theory," *Review of Financial Studies* 9, no. 2 (Summer 1996): 557–587.

[21]Among the papers are Chinhyang Cho, "On Testing the Arbitrage Pricing Theory: Inter-Battery Factor Analysis," *Journal of Finance* 39, no. 5 (December 1984): 1485–1502; Robert McCulloch and Peter Rossi, "Posterior, Predictive, and Utility-Based Approaches to Testing the Arbitrage Pricing Theory," *Journal of Financial Economics* 28, no. 1 and 2 (November–December 1990): 7–38; and Ravi Shakla and Charles Trzcinka, "Sequential Tests of the Arbitrage Pricing Theory: A Comparison of Principle Components and Maximum Likelihood Factors," *Journal of Finance* 45, no. 5 (December 1990): 1542–1564.

MULTIFACTOR MODELS AND RISK ESTIMATION

When it comes to putting theory into practice, one advantage of the CAPM framework is that the identity of the single risk factor (i.e., the excess return to the market portfolio) is well specified. Thus, as noted earlier, the empirical challenge in implementing the CAPM successfully is to accurately estimate the market portfolio, a process that first requires identifying the relevant investment universe. As we saw in the last chapter, however, this is not a trivial problem as an improperly chosen proxy for the market portfolio (e.g., using the S&P 500 index to represent the market when evaluating a fixed-income portfolio) can lead to erroneous judgments. However, we also saw that once the returns to an acceptable surrogate for the market portfolio are identified (i.e., R_m), the process for estimating the parameters of the CAPM is straightforward and can be accomplished by either of the following regression equations:

1. A security or portfolio's *characteristic line* can be estimated via regression techniques using the *single-index market model:*

$$R_{it} = a_i + b_i R_{mt} + e_t$$

2. Alternatively, this equation can also be estimated in *excess return form* by netting the risk-free rate from the period t returns to security i and the market portfolio:

$$(R_{it} - RFR_t) = \alpha_i + b_i(R_{mt} - RFR_t) + e_{it}$$

In contrast to the CAPM, we have seen that the primary practical problem associated with implementing the APT is that neither the identity nor the exact number of the underlying risk factors are developed by theory and therefore must be specified in an ad hoc manner. Said differently, before the APT can be used to value securities or measure investment performance, the investor must fill in a considerable amount of missing information about the fundamental relationship between risk and expected return.

As discussed earlier, the first attempts to implement a usable form of the APT relied on multivariate statistical techniques, wherein many periods of realized returns for a large number of securities are analyzed simultaneously in order to detect recognizable patterns of behavior.[22] A consistent finding of these studies is that there appear to be as many as three or four "priced" (i.e., statistically significant) factors, although researchers were not able to establish that the same set of factors was generated by different subsets of their sample. Indeed, we also saw that other researchers noted that the inability to identify the risk factors is a major limitation to the usefulness of the APT.[23]

A different approach to developing an empirical model that captures the essence of the APT relies on the direct specification of the form of the relationship to be estimated. That is, in a *multifactor model,* the investor chooses the exact number and identity of risk factors in the following equation:

▶9.2 $$R_{it} = a_i + [b_{i1}F_{1t} + b_{i2}F_{2t} + \ldots + b_{iK}F_{Kt}] + e_{it}$$

---

[22]See, for instance, Richard Roll and Stephen A. Ross, "An Empirical Investigation of the Arbitrage Pricing Theory," *Journal of Finance* 35, no. 5 (December 1980): 1073–1103; and Nai-fu Chen, "Some Empirical Tests of the Arbitrage Pricing Theory," *Journal of Finance* 38, no. 5 (December 1983): 1393–1414.

[23]See Jay Shanken, "The Arbitrage Pricing Theory: Is It Testable," *Journal of Finance* 37, no. 5 (December 1982): 1129–1140.

where F_{jt} is the period t return to the jth designated risk factor and R_{it} can be measured as either a nominal or excess return to security i. The advantage of this approach, of course, is that the investor knows precisely how many and what things need to be estimated to fit the regression equation. On the other hand, the major disadvantage of a multifactor model is that it is developed with little theoretical guidance as to the true nature of the risk-return relationship. In this sense, developing a useful factor model is as much an art form as it is a theoretical exercise.

Multifactor Models in Practice

A wide variety of empirical factor specifications have been employed in practice. A hallmark of each alternative model that has been developed is that it attempts to identify a set of economic influences that is simultaneously broad enough to capture the major nuances of investment risk but small enough to provide a workable solution to the analyst or investor. Two general approaches have been employed in this factor identification process. First, risk factors can be *macroeconomic* in nature; that is, they can attempt to capture variations in the underlying reasons an asset's cash flows and investment returns might change over time (e.g., changes in inflation or real GDP growth in the example discussed earlier). On the other hand, risk factors can also be identified at a *microeconomic* level by focusing on relevant characteristics of the securities themselves, such as the size of the firm in question or some of its financial ratios. A few examples representative of both of these approaches to the problem are discussed in the following sections.

Macroeconomic-Based Risk Factor Models   One particularly influential model was developed by Chen, Roll, and Ross, who hypothesized that security returns are governed by a set of broad economic influences in the following fashion:[24]

➤9.3 $$R_{it} = a_i + [b_{i1}R_{mt} + b_{i2}MP_t + b_{i3}DEI_t + b_{i4}UI_t + b_{i5}UPR_t + b_{i6}UTS_t] + e_{it}$$

where:

R_m = **the return on a value-weighted index of NYSE-listed stocks**
MP = **the monthly growth rate in U.S. industrial production**
DEI = **the change in inflation, measured by the U.S. consumer price index**
UI = **the difference between actual and expected levels of inflation**
UPR = **the unanticipated change in the bond credit spread (Baa yield – *RFR*)**
UTS = **the unanticipated term structure shift (long-term less short-term *RFR*)**

In estimating this model, the authors used a series of monthly returns for a large collection of securities from the Center for Research in Security Prices (CRSP) database over the period 1958–1984. Exhibit 9.3 shows the factor sensitivities (along with the associated *t*-statistics in parentheses) that they established. Notice two things about these findings. First, the economic significance of the designated risk factors changed dramatically over time. For instance, the inflation factors (*DEI* and *UI*) appear to only be relevant during the 1968–1977 period. Second, the parameter on the stock market proxy is never significant, suggesting that it contributes little to the explanation beyond the information contained in the other macroeconomic risk factors.

Burmeister, Roll, and Ross analyzed the predictive ability of a model based on a different set of macroeconomic factors.[25] Specifically, they define the following five risk exposures: (1) *con-*

---

[24]Nai-fu Chen, Richard Roll, and Stephen A. Ross, "Economic Forces and the Stock Market," *Journal of Business* 59, no. 3 (April 1986): 383–404.

[25]Edwin Burmeister, Richard Roll, and Stephen A. Ross, "A Practitioner's Guide to Arbitrage Pricing Theory," in John Peavy, ed., *A Practitioner's Guide to Factor Models* (Charlottesville, Va.: Research Foundation of the Institute of Chartered Financial Analysts, 1994.

| EXHIBIT 9.3 | *ESTIMATING A MULTIFACTOR MODEL WITH MACROECONOMIC RISK FACTORS* |

PERIOD	CONSTANT	R_M	MP	DEI	UI	UPR	UTS
1958–84	10.71	–2.40	11.76	–0.12	–0.80	8.27	–5.91
	(2.76)	(–0.63)	(3.05)	(–1.60)	(–2.38)	(2.97)	(–1.88)
1958–67	9.53	1.36	12.39	0.01	–0.21	5.20	–0.09
	(1.98)	(0.28)	(1.79)	(0.06)	(–0.42)	(1.82)	(–0.04)
1968–77	8.58	–5.27	13.47	–0.26	–1.42	12.90	–11.71
	(1.17)	(–0.72)	(2.04)	(–3.24)	(–3.11)	(2.96)	(–2.30)
1978–84	15.45	–3.68	8.40	–0.12	–0.74	6.06	–5.93
	(1.87)	(–0.49)	(1.43)	(–0.46)	(–0.87)	(0.78)	(–0.64)

Source: Nai-fu Chen, Richard Roll, and Stephen A. Ross, "Economic Forces and the Stock Market," *Journal of Business* 59, no. 3 (April 1986).

fidence risk, based on unanticipated changes in the willingness of investors to take on investment risk; (2) *time horizon risk,* which is the unanticipated changes in investors' desired time to receive payouts; (3) *inflation risk,* based on a combination of the unexpected components of short-term and long-term inflation rates; (4) *business cycle risk,* which represents unanticipated changes in the level of overall business activity; and (5) *market-timing risk,* defined as the part of the Standard & Poor's 500 total return that is not explained by the other four macroeconomic factors. Using monthly data through the first quarter of 1992, the authors estimated risk premia (i.e. the market "price" of risk) for these factors:

RISK FACTOR	RISK PREMIUM
Confidence	2.59%
Time horizon	–0.66
Inflation	–4.32
Business cycle	1.49
Market timing	3.61

They also compared the factor sensitivities for several different individual stocks and stock portfolios. Panel A and Panel B of Exhibit 9.4 show these factor beta estimates for a particular stock (Reebok International Ltd.) versus the S&P 500 index and for a portfolio of small-cap firms versus a portfolio of large-cap firms. Also included in these graphs is the security's or portfolio's exposure to the BIRR composite risk index, which is designed to indicate which position has the most overall systematic risk. These comparisons highlight how a multifactor model can help investors distinguish the nature of the risk they are assuming when they hold with a particular position. For instance, notice that Reebok has greater exposures to all sources of risk than the S&P 500, with the incremental difference in the business cycle exposure being particularly dramatic. Additionally, smaller firms are more exposed to business cycle and confidence risk than larger firms but less exposed to horizon risk.

Microeconomic-Based Risk Factor Models In contrast to macroeconomic-based explanations of the connection between risk and expected return, it is also possible to specify

EXHIBIT 9.4   *MACROECONOMIC RISK EXPOSURE PROFILES*

A. Reebok International LTD. versus S&P 500 Index

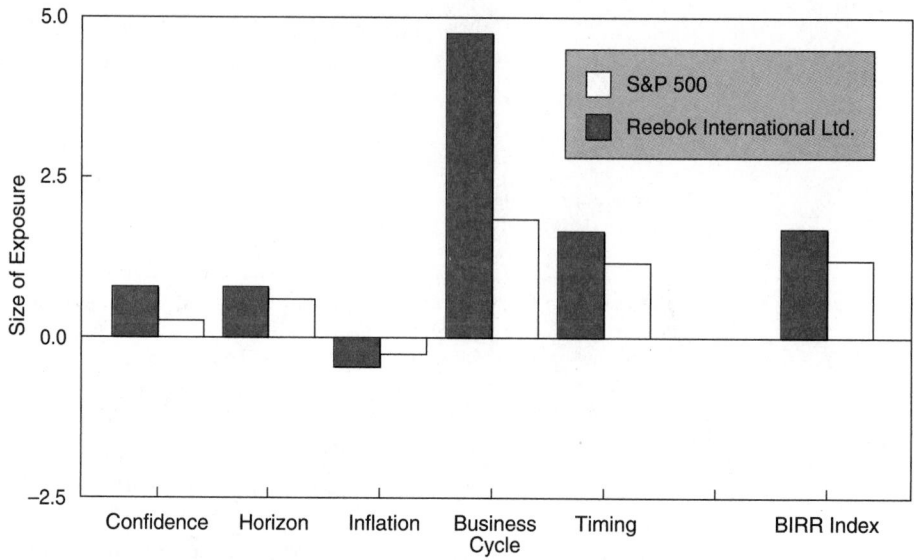

B. Large-Cap versus Small-Cap Firms

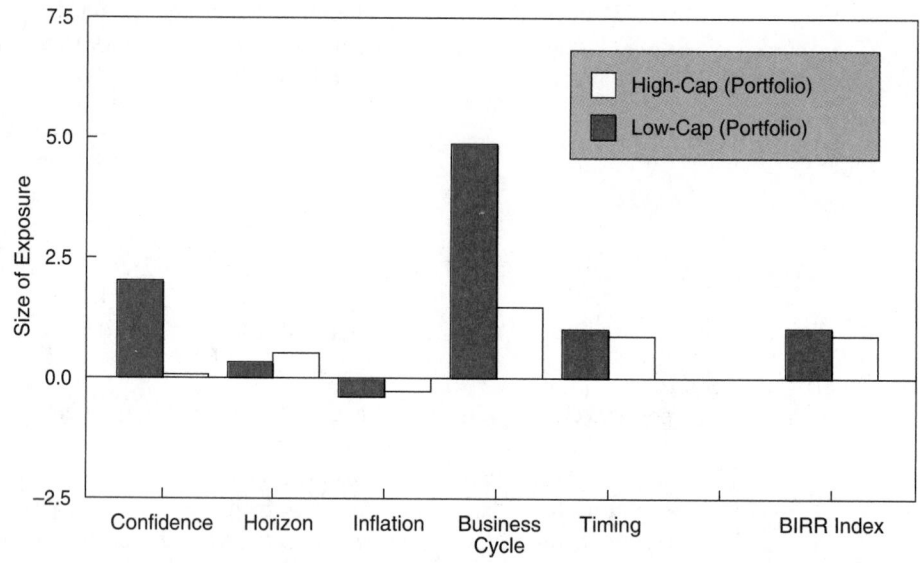

| **EXHIBIT 9.5** | *ESTIMATING A MULTIFACTOR MODEL WITH CHARACTERISTIC-BASED RISK FACTORS* |

PORTFOLIO	CONSTANT	MARKET	SMB	HML	R^2
		(1) SINGLE-INDEX MODEL			
Lowest P-E	0.46	0.94	—	—	0.78
	(3.69)	(34.73)			
Highest P-E	–0.20	1.10	—	—	0.91
	(–2.35)	(57.42)			
		(2) MULTIFACTOR MODEL			
Lowest P-E	0.08	1.03	0.24	0.67	0.91
	(1.01)	(51.56)	(8.34)	(19.62)	
Highest P-E	0.04	0.99	–0.01	–0.50	0.96
	(0.70)	(66.78)	(–0.55)	(–19.73)	

Reprinted from Eugene F. Fama and Kenneth R. French, "Common Risk Factors in the Returns on Stocks and Bonds," *Journal of Financial Economics* 33, no. 1 (January 1993), with permission from Elsevier Science.

risk in microeconomic terms using certain characteristics of the underlying sample of securities. Typical of this *characteristic-based approach* to forming a multifactor model is the work of Fama and French, who use the following functional form:[26]

➤9.4 $$(R_{it} - RFR_t) = \alpha_i + b_{i1}(R_{mt} - RFR_t) + b_{i2}SMB_t + b_{i3}HML_t + e_{it}$$

where, in addition to the excess return on a stock market portfolio, two other risk factors are defined:

> *SMB* (i.e., small minus big) is the return to a portfolio of small capitalization stocks less the return to a portfolio of large capitalization stocks
> *HML* (i.e., high minus low) is the return to a portfolio of stocks with high ratios of book-to-market values less the return to a portfolio of low book-to-market value stocks

In this specification, *SMB* is designed to capture elements of risk associated with firm size while *HML* is intended to distinguish risk differentials associated with "growth" (i.e., low book-to-market ratio) and "value" (i.e., high book-to-market) firms. As we saw earlier, these are two dimensions of a security—or portfolio of securities—that have consistently been shown to matter when evaluating investment performance. Also, notice that without the *SMB* and *HML* factors this model simply reduces to the excess returns form of the single-index market model.

As part of their analysis of the role that *SMB* and *HML* play in the return-generating process, Fama and French examined the behavior of a broad sample of stocks grouped into quintile portfolios by their price-earnings (P-E) ratios on a yearly basis over the period from July 1963 to December 1991. The results for both the single-index and multifactor versions of the model for the two extreme quintiles are shown in Exhibit 9.5 (*t*-statistics for the estimated coefficients are listed parenthetically). There are several important things to note about these findings. First, while the estimated beta from the single-factor model indicates that there are substantial differences between low and high P-E stocks (i.e., 0.94 versus 1.10), this gap is dramatically reduced

---

[26]Eugene F. Fama and Kenneth R. French, "Common Risk Factors in the Returns on Stocks and Bonds," *Journal of Financial Economics* 33, no. 1 (January 1993): 3–56.

in the multifactor specification (i.e., 1.03 versus 0.99). This suggests that the market portfolio in a one-factor model serves as a proxy for some, but not all, of the additional risk dimensions provided by *SMB* and *HML*. Second, it is apparent that low P-E stocks tend to be positively correlated with the small-firm premium, but the reverse is not reliably true for high P-E stocks. Finally, low P-E stocks also tend to have high book-to-market ratios while high P-E stocks tend to have low book-to-market ratios (i.e., estimated *HML* parameters of 0.67 and –0.50, respectively). Not surprisingly, relative levels of P-E and book-to-market ratios are both commonly employed in practice to classify growth and value stocks.

Extensions of Characteristic-Based Risk Factor Models

There have been other interesting characteristic-based approaches to estimating a multifactor model of risk and return. Three of those approaches are described here. First, Carhart directly extends the Fama-French three-factor model by including a fourth common risk factor that accounts for the tendency for firms with positive (negative) past returns to produce positive (negative) future returns.[27] He calls this additional risk dimension a *momentum factor* and estimates it by taking the average return to a set of stocks with the best performance over the prior year minus the average return to stocks with the worst returns. In this fashion, Carhart defines the momentum factor—which he labels *PR1YR*—in a fashion similar to *SMB* and *HML*. Formally, the model he proposes is:

➤9.5 $$(R_{it} - RFR_t) = \alpha_i + b_{i1}(R_{mt} - RFR_t) + b_{i2}SMB_t + b_{i3}HML_t + b_{i4}PR1YR_t + e_{it}$$

He demonstrates that the typical factor sensitivity (i.e., factor beta) for the momentum variable is positive and its inclusion into the Fama-French model increases explanatory power by as much as 15 percent.

A second type of security characteristic-based method for defining systematic risk exposures involves the use of index portfolios (e.g., S&P 500, Wilshire 5000) as common factors. The intuition behind this approach is that, if the indexes themselves are designed to emphasize certain investment characteristics, they can act as proxies for the underlying exposure that determines returns to that characteristic. Examples of this include the Russell 1000 Growth index, which emphasizes large-cap stocks with low book-to-market ratios, or the EAFE (Europe, Australia, and the Far East) index that selects a variety of companies that are domiciled outside the United States. Typical of these index-based factor models is the work of Elton, Gruber, and Blake, who rely on four indexes: the S&P 500, the Lehman Brothers aggregate bond index, the Prudential Bache index of the difference between large- and small-cap stocks, and the Prudential Bache index of the difference between value and growth stocks.[28] Ferson and Schadt have developed an interesting variation on this approach, which, in addition to using stock and bond indexes as risk factors, also includes other "public information" variables, such as the shape of the yield curve and dividend payouts.[29]

BARRA, a leading risk forecasting and investment consulting firm, provides a final example of the microeconomic approach to building a multifactor model. In its most expansive form, the BARRA model for analyzing U.S. equities includes as risk factors 13 characteristic-based variables and more than 50 industry indexes.[30] Exhibit 9.6 provides a brief description of the 13 characteristic-

[27]Mark M. Carhart, "On Persistence in Mutual Fund Performance," *Journal of Finance* 52, no. 1 (March 1997): 57–82.

[28]Edwin J. Elton, Martin J. Gruber, and Christopher R. Blake, "The Persistence of Risk-Adjusted Mutual Fund Performance," *Journal of Business* 69, no. 2 (April 1996): 133–157.

[29]Wayne R. Ferson and Rudi W. Schadt, "Measuring Fund Strategy and Performance in Changing Economic Conditions," *Journal of Finance* 51, no. 2 (June 1996): 425–462.

[30]A more complete description of the BARRA approach to analyzing investment risk can be found in Richard Grinold and Ronald N. Kahn, "Multiple-Factor Models for Portfolio Risk," in John Peavy, ed., *A Practitioner's Guide to Factor Models* (Charlottesville, Va.: Research Foundation of the Institute of Chartered Financial Analysts, 1994.

EXHIBIT 9.6

DESCRIPTION OF BARRA CHARACTERISTIC-BASED RISK FACTORS

- **Volatility (VOL)**   Captures both long-term and short-term dimensions of relative return variability
- **Momentum (MOM)**   Differentiates between stocks with positive and negative excess returns in the recent past
- **Size (SIZ)**   Based on a firm's relative market capitalization
- **Size Nonlinearity (SNL)**   Captures deviations from linearity in the relationship between returns and firm size
- **Trading Activity (TRA)**   Measures the relative trading in a stock, based on the premise that more actively traded stocks are more likely to be those with greater interest from institutional investors
- **Growth (GRO)**   Uses historical growth and profitability measures to predict future earnings growth
- **Earnings Yield (EYL)**   Combines current and historical earnings-to-price ratios with analyst forecasts under the assumption that stocks with similar earnings yields produce similar returns
- **Value (VAL)**   Based on relative book-to-market ratios
- **Earnings Variability (EVR)**   Measures the variability in earnings and cash flows using both historical values and analyst forecasts
- **Leverage (LEV)**   Measures the relative financial leverage of a company
- **Currency Sensitivity (CUR)**   Based on the relative sensitivity of a company's stock return to movements in a basket of foreign currencies
- **Dividend Yield (YLD)**   Computes a measure of the predicted dividend yield using a firm's past dividend and stock price history
- **Nonestimation Indicator (NEU)**   Uses returns to firms outside the equity universe to account for risk dimensions not captured by the other risk factors

Source: BARRA.

based factors that form the heart of the BARRA approach to decomposing investment risk. One useful application for this model is to understand where the investment "bets" in an actively managed portfolio are being placed relative to a performance benchmark. Exhibit 9.7 illustrates this sort of comparison for a small-cap-oriented mutual fund (POOL2) versus the S&P 500 index (SAP500). As you would expect, there are dramatic differences between the fund and the benchmark in terms of the firm-size risk factors (i.e., size, SIZ, and size nonlinearity, SNL). However, it also appears that POOL2 contains more highly leveraged companies (LEV) with more emphasis on earnings momentum (MOM).

Conner has analyzed the ability of the BARRA model to explain the returns generated by a sample of U.S. stocks over the period from 1985 to 1993.[31] Interestingly, he found that the industry indexes, taken collectively, provided about four times the explanatory power as any single characteristic-based factor, followed in importance by volatility, growth, dividend yield, and momentum. Overall, the BARRA model was able to explain slightly more return variability than the other models to which it was compared, in part because of the large number of factors it employs.

---

[31]Gregory Connor, "The Three Types of Factor Models: A Comparison of Their Explanatory Power," *Financial Analysts Journal* 51, no. 3 (May/June 1995): 42–46.

EXHIBIT 9.7 *BARRA RISK DECOMPOSITION FOR A SMALL-CAP FUND VERSUS S&P 500*

Estimating Risk in a Multifactor Setting: Examples

Estimating Expected Returns for Individual Stocks One direct way in which to employ a multifactor risk model is to use it to estimate the expected return for an individual stock position. In order to accomplish this task, the following steps must be taken: (1) a specific set of K common risk factors must be identified, (2) the risk premia (F_j) for the factors must be estimated, (3) the sensitivities (b_{ij}) of the ith stock to each of those K factors must be estimated, and (4) the expected returns can be calculated by combining the results of the previous steps in the appropriate way.

As an example of this process, we will use the Fama-French model discussed earlier. This immediately solves the first step by designating the following three common risk factors: the excess return on the market portfolio (R_m), the return differential between small and large capitalization stocks *(SMB),* and the return differential between high and low book-to-market stocks *(HML).* The second step is often addressed in practice by using historical return data to calculate the average values for each of the risk factors. However, it is important to recognize that these averages can vary tremendously depending on the time period the investor selects. For example, for the three-factor model, the top panel of Exhibit 9.8 lists the average annual risk premia over three different time frames: a five-year period ending in June 2000, a 20-year period ending in December 2000, and a 73-year period ending in December 2000.[32] Notice that, while data for the longest time frame confirm that small stocks earn higher returns than large stocks and value stocks outperform growth stocks (i.e., positive risk premia for the *SMB* and *HML* factors), this is not true over shorter periods. In particular, during the most recent five years, the opposite occurred in both cases.

To illustrate the final steps involved in estimating expected stock returns, risk factor sensitivities were estimated by regression analysis for three different stocks using monthly return data

[32]The data used in these calculations are available from Professor Kenneth French's Web site at http://mba.tuck.dartmouth.edu/pages/faculty/ken.french

EXHIBIT 9.8 ▶ *ESTIMATES FOR RISK FACTOR PREMIA AND FACTOR SENSITIVITIES*

A. Risk Factor Premia Estimates Using Historical Data

	RISK PREMIUM ESTIMATE		
RISK FACTOR	1996–2000	1981–2000	1928–2000
Market	11.50%	9.09%	7.02%
SMB	−1.44	−1.10	3.09
HML	−5.40	4.48	4.39

B. Regression Estimates of Risk Factor Sensitivities

STOCK	MARKET	*SMB*	*HML*
INTC	0.615	−0.640	−1.476
	(1.63)	(−1.74)	(−2.55)
JPM	1.366	−0.387	0.577
	(7.15)	(−2.07)	(1.96)
WFMI	1.928	0.817	1.684
	(4.33)	(1.88)	(2.46)

over the period from July 1995 to June 2000. The three stocks were Intel (INTC), a large semi-conductor manufacturer; JP Morgan Chase (JPM), a large global banking firm; and Whole Foods Market (WFMI), a small specialty food retailer. The estimated factor betas are listed in Panel B of Exhibit 9.8, with the *t*-statistics associated with the various sensitivities estimates reported in parentheses. These factor betas provide some interesting comparisons between the three stocks. First, the positive coefficients on the market factor indicate that all of these stocks are positively correlated with general movement in the stock market. The coefficients on the *SMB* factor confirm that JPM and INTC produce returns consistent with large-cap stocks (i.e, negative *SMB* exposures), while WFMI acts like a small-cap stock. Finally, JPM and WFMI are more likely to be considered value stocks (i.e., positive *HML* exposures) while the technology company INTC can be considered a growth-oriented stock.

Whichever specific factor risk estimates are used, the expected return for any stock in excess of the risk-free rate (i.e., the expected risk premium) can be calculated with the formula:

$$\blacktriangleright 9.6 \qquad [E(R_i) - RFR] = b_{im}\lambda_m + b_{iSMB}\,\lambda_{SMB} + b_{iHML}\,\lambda_{HML}.$$

Using the data for the most recent five-year period reported in Exhibit 9.8, the expected excess returns for the three stocks are as follows:

$$\text{INTC: } [E(R) - RFR] = (0.615)(11.50) + (-0.640)(-1.44) + (-1.476)(-5.40)$$
$$= 15.96\%$$
$$\text{JPM: } [E(R) - RFR] = (1.366)(11.50) + (-0.387)(-1.44) + (0.577)(-5.40)$$
$$= 13.15\%$$
$$\text{WFMI: } [E(R) - RFR] = (1.928)(11.50) + (0.817)(-1.44) + (1.684)(-5.40)$$
$$= 11.90\%$$

Notice that while these values are high relative to longer-term historical norms—especially the market factor premium—they reflect the conditions that prevailed in the capital markets at the time.

Comparing Mutual Fund Risk Exposures   To get a better sense of how risk factor sensitivity is estimated at the portfolio level, consider the returns produced by two popular mutual funds: Fidelity's Magellan Fund (FMAGX) and Gabelli's Asset Fund (GABAX). Morningstar Inc., an independent stock and mutual fund advisory service, classifies FMAGX's investment style into the *large-cap blend* category. This means that the typical equity holding of FMAGX is characterized as a large-market capitalization firm whose P-E and book-to-market ratios place it somewhere in the spectrum between a value and a growth company. Exhibit 9.9 shows a sample page for FMAGX from Morningstar's public-access Web site and shows graphically where the fund fits into the investment "style box" as of August 2001. Conversely, as shown in Exhibit 9.10, Morningstar puts GABAX into the *mid-cap blend* category, meaning that the fund generally emphasizes smaller companies than does FMAGX. This implies that, assuming Morningstar's classification system makes a meaningful distinction, there should be measurable differences in the relative sensitivities on the *SMB* factor.

Using monthly returns over the period July 1995 to June 2000, the risk parameters for both funds were estimated relative to three different specifications: (1) a single-factor model using the Standard & Poor's 500 index as proxy for the market portfolio, (2) a single-factor model using a broader composite index of the U.S. stock market as a market proxy, and (3) the Fama-French three-factor model using the U.S. market composite. The results of these estimations are summarized in Exhibit 9.11.

Looking first at the findings for the two versions of the one-factor market model, it is apparent that there are important differences in the systematic risk levels of FMAGX and GABAX. In particular, the beta coefficient of FMAGX is essentially identical to that of the overall market (i.e., 1.00). Given its size, this is not particularly surprising: with more than $75 billion in assets under management as of August 2001, it is necessarily a broad-based, well-diversified portfolio. On the other hand, with just under $2 billion of assets, GABAX's manager has more flexibility to implement his active stock and sector selection decisions. A consequence of this flexibility is a portfolio beta that can differ from the market average; 18 percent lower (i.e., 0.82) in this case. Additionally, notice that during the July 1995–June 2000 sample period, the beta estimates for the two funds do not vary appreciably when estimated relative to different proxies of the market portfolio.

The multifactor model gives a much better sense of how the risk exposures of the FMAGX and GABAX portfolios actually differ from one another. First, notice that once the additional explanatory power of the *SMB* and *HML* factors is added, the systematic market risks of these funds are basically the same (i.e., 0.97 and 0.96, respectively). This indicates that the difference in beta levels from the single-factor model is itself "explained" by the size and book-to-market risk variables in the three-factor specification.

A second implication of the multifactor equation involves the differential sensitivities to the *SML* variable. As suggested by the Morningstar style categories, FMAGX is more oriented toward large capitalization stocks; its *SMB* sensitivity of –0.16 is statistically significant and shows that FMAGX's returns move inversely to a risk factor that, by its construction, is implicitly long in small-cap stocks and short in large-cap stocks. Conversely, the *SMB* coefficient is positive (i.e., 0.07) but of marginal statistical reliability, which is as expected for a fund that tends to hold stocks that are neither overly small nor overly large.

Finally, although not implied by the Morningstar classification system that places them both in the *blend* category, FMAGX and GABAX also differ in their sensitivity to the *HML* risk factor. Specifically, while not significant at conventional levels, the negative parameter for FMAGX (i.e., –0.10) indicates that the portfolio is slightly tilted toward stocks that have lower book-to-market ratios. Recall that a low book-to-market ratio, like a high P-E ratio, is a characteristic of a growth-oriented stock. GABAX's sensitivity to the *HML* risk factor shows the opposite tendency in that its estimated parameter is positive (i.e., 0.30) and significant. This suggests that, on balance, the GABAX portfolio is tilted toward value-oriented stocks that have higher book-to-market—and lower P-E—ratios.

EXHIBIT 9.9   *MORNINGSTAR REPORT FOR FIDELITY MAGELLAN (FMAGX) FUND*

Snapshot
Fidelity Magellan FMAGX

How Has This Fund Performed?
Growth of $10,000
● Fund: Fidelity Magellan
● Category: Large Blend
○ Index: S&P 500

Annual Returns

	1998	1999	2000	08–01
Fund	33.6	24.0	−9.3	−13.5
+/– Cat	11.5	4.0	−2.7	1.4
+/– Index	5.1	3.0	−0.2	−0.2

Data through 08-31-01

View additional performance information

Category Rating What is this?

Worst   Best

Return
Above Avg

Risk
Average

Data through 08-31-01

Fund Details
Sales Charge %
   Front: Closed
   Deferred   Closed
Expense Ratio%   0.89

Manager Name: Robert E. Stansky
Manager Start Date: 06-03-96

View additional fund details

Quick Stats

NAV (09-28-01)	$94.03
Day Change	$2.01
YTD Return	−20.53%
Morningstar Rating	★★★
Morningstar Category	Large Blend
Net Assets ($mil)	78,834

View ratings details

Inside Scoop
As the largest mutual fund around, this isn't a nimble portfolio. But management has used solid stock-picking and well-timed sector calls to put up good numbers here. With low expenses and a broadly diversified portfolio, this is a great core holding

▶ Read full analysis

What Does This Fund Own?
Style Box What is this?
Compare investment-style returns

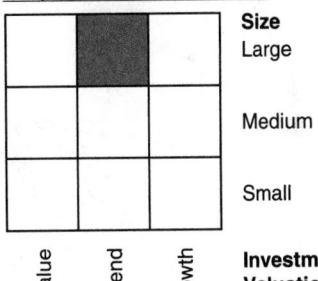

Style Box as of 03-31-01

View Style Box details

Asset allocation %

Cash	5.6
Stocks	94.4
Bonds	0.0
Other	0.0

Top 3 Stock Sectors %

Financials	21.7
Technology	14.4
Health	13.7

Asset data through 03-31-01
Sector data through 03-31-01

Source: Morningstar.com, October 1, 2001.

EXHIBIT 9.10 ▶ *MORNINGSTAR REPORT FOR GABELLI ASSET (GABAX) FUND*

Snapshot
Gabelli Asset GABAX

How Has This Fund Performed?
Growth of $10,000
● Fund: Gabelli Asset
◐ Category: Mid-Cap Blend
○ Index: S&P 500

| | 1998 | 1999 | 2000 | 2001 |

Annual Returns

	1998	1999	2000	08–01
Fund	15.9	28.5	−2.4	−0.9
+/− Cat	9.0	6.7	−5.3	7.7
+/− Index	−12.6	7.5	−6.7	−14.3

Data through 08-31-01

View additional performance information

Category Rating What is this?

Return
Above Avg

Risk
Average

Worst   Best

Data through 08-31-01

Fund Details
Sales Charge %
   Front: None
   Deferred: None
Expense Ratio%   0.77

Manager Name: Mario J Gabelli
Manager Start Date: 03-03-86

View additional fund details

Quick Stats

NAV (09-28-01)	$30.70
Day Change	$0.66
YTD Return	−9.44%
Morningstar Rating	★★★★★
Morningstar Category	Mid-Cap Blend
Net Assets ($mil)	1,938

View ratings details

Inside Scoop
Among its mid-blend rivals, this fund is tough to beat. A value approach and diversification across names helps limit risk. Great stock picking and a willingness to play bold themes also make for top-notch returns. Can have dry spells, but is well worth it ▶ Read full analysis

What Does This Fund Own?
Style Box What is this?
Compare investment-style returns

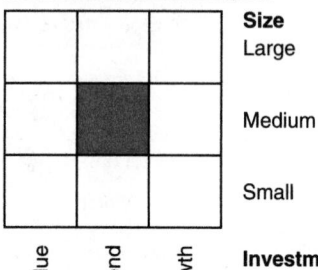

Style Box as of 03-31-01
View Style Box details

Asset allocation %

Cash	7.1
Stocks	89.2
Bonds	0.0
Other	3.7

Top 3 Stock Sectors %

Financials	35.3
Technology	20.3
Health	15.4

Asset data through 08-31-01
Sector data through 08-31-01

Source: Morningstar.com, October 1, 2001.

EXHIBIT 9.11 *RISK FACTOR ESTIMATES FOR FMAGX AND GABAX*

Mutual Fund	Constant	Market	SMB	HML	R^2
		(1) SINGLE-INDEX MODEL (MARKET = S&P 500)			
FMAGX	−0.23	1.00	—	—	0.91
	(−1.18)	(23.71)			
GABAX	0.00	0.82	—	—	0.83
	(0.01)	(16.60)			
		(2) SINGLE-INDEX MODEL (MARKET = U.S. COMPOSITE)			
FMAGX	−0.09	0.99	—	—	0.91
	(−0.49)	(24.27)			
GABAX	0.09	0.82	—	—	0.86
	(0.46)	(18.90)			
		(3) MULTIFACTOR MODEL (MARKET = U.S. COMPOSITE)			
FMAGX	−0.13	0.97	−0.16	−0.10	0.93
	(−0.77)	(20.82)	(−3.58)	(−1.45)	
GABAX	0.05	0.96	0.07	0.30	0.90
	(0.29)	(20.38)	(1.57)	(4.36)	

The Internet *Investments Online*

Asset pricing models show how risk measures or underlying return-generating factors will affect asset returns. Estimates from such models are usually proprietary and are available from providers by buying their research. Of course, users can always acquire the raw data elsewhere (see, for instance, some of our earlier Internet discussions) and develop their own factor definitions and sensitivity estimates.

http://www.barra.com For subscribers, Barra's Web site offers extensive data and analytical tools. Links offer information on portfolio management, investment data, market indices, risk estimation, and research. Barra offers its clients data, software, and consulting, as well as money management services for equity, fixed income, currency, and global financial instruments. Barra estimates multiple-factor models, and its global and country-specific models provide risk analysis on thousands of globally traded securities, including historical and predicted factor betas.

http://www.economy.com/dismal The Web site of The Dismal Scientist at Economy.com, which is the leading provider of economic information on the Internet, offering thorough and timely analysis, data, tools, and other features concerning macroeconomic trends and events. This is an excellent source of the type of raw data that would be necessary to construct a comprehensive set of macroeconomic risk factors.

http://www.federalreserve.gov/rnd.htm This link on the main Web site for the Federal Reserve Board permits access to a tremendous amount of staff research and raw data on the macroeconomy. The statistical releases that are available include daily, monthly, quarterly, and annual data on interest rates (e.g., Treasury bills, notes, and bonds; commercial paper), foreign exchange rates, monetary aggregates, industrial production, and consumer credit.

(continued)

The Internet *Investments Online (cont.)*

http://www.mba.tuck.dartmouth.edu/ pages/faculty/ken.french Maintained by Professor Kenneth French, this Web site gives users access to monthly, quarterly, and annual data series on the three Fama-French risk factors: the excess market return, the *SMB* factor return, and the *HML* factor return. The site also provides

excellent documentation as to how the risk factor portfolios are constructed and maintained. The data are offered in a downloadable format, making it easy for the user to customize the three-factor characteristic-based risk model to his or her own purposes.

Summary

- Although the CAPM is an elegant and appealing explanation for the way in which investment risk and expected return are related, a number of empirical anomalies—such as the small-firm effect—have caused financial economists to seek other answers. Ross subsequently devised an alternative asset pricing model—the APT—that makes fewer assumptions than the CAPM and does not specifically require the designation of a market portfolio. Instead, the APT posits that expected security returns are related in a linear fashion to multiple common risk factors. Unfortunately, however, the theory does not offer guidance as to how many factors exist or what their identities might be. The results from the empirical tests of the APT have thus far been mixed. On one hand, it appears that there are at least three risk factors that appear to be consistently "priced" by the capital markets. On the other hand, these factors may not be the same ones from one period to the next; and Shanken contends that the nature of many of the tests makes it impossible to credibly test the theory at all.

- Given that the common risk factors are not identified, the APT is difficult to put into practice in a theoretically rigorous fashion. Multifactor models of risk and return attempt to bridge this gap between theory and practice by specifying a set of variables that are thought to capture the essence of the systematic risk exposures that exist in the capital market. Over the past two decades, there have been a number of alternative risk factors suggested and tested by financial researchers. One general approach that has been adopted successfully has been to use macroeconomic variables—such as unexpected inflation, changes in consumer confidence, unanticipated shifts in the yield curve, or unexpected changes in real GDP—as surrogates for the types of exposures that will have an impact on all securities. Once selected, historical data are often employed to determine the risk premium (i.e., market "price") for each common factor.

- An equally successful second approach to identifying the risk exposures in a multifactor model has focused on the characteristics of the securities themselves. Typical of this sort of microeconomic approach is the work of Fama and French, who posit that three risk factors should be employed: the excess returns to a broad market index, the return difference between portfolios of small- and large-cap stocks, and the return difference between portfolios of value- and growth-oriented stocks. One immediate advantage of this specification is that it accounts directly for some of the anomalies that plagued the CAPM (i.e., the small-firm effect). Another advantage of the characteristic-based approach to forming factor models is the flexibility to modify the equation to changing market conditions. For instance, the Fama-French model has been expanded to include a factor accounting for stock return momentum, while the BARRA model incorporates almost 70 different risk and industry factors.

- In conclusion, it is probably safe to assume that both the CAPM and APT will continue to be used to price capital assets. Coincident with their use will be further empirical tests of both theories, the ultimate goal being to determine which theory does the best job of explaining current returns and predicting future ones. Notably, although the APT model requires fewer assumptions and considers multiple factors to explain the risk of an asset, the CAPM has an advantage in that its single risk factor is well defined. Future work in this area will continue to seek to identify the set of factors that best captures the relevant dimension of investment risk as well as explore the intertemporal dynamics of the models (e.g., factor betas and risk premia that change over time).

Questions

1. Both the capital asset pricing model and the arbitrage pricing theory rely on the proposition that a no-risk, no-wealth investment should earn, on average, no return. Explain why this should be the case, being sure to describe briefly the similarities and differences between the CAPM and the APT. Also, using either of these theories, explain how superior investment performance can be established.

2. *CFA Examination Level III*
   You are an investment officer at Pegasus Securities and are preparing for the next meeting of the investment committee. Several committee members are interested in reviewing two asset pricing models—the capital asset pricing theory (CAPM) and the arbitrage pricing theory (APT)—and their use in portfolio management and stock selection.
   a. Describe both the CAPM and the APT, and identify the factor(s) that determines returns in each.
   b. "The APT model is more general than the CAPM." Explain how this observation has meaning in the stock selection process.

3. The *small-firm effect* refers to the observed tendency for stock prices to behave in a manner that is contrary to normal expectations. Describe this effect and discuss whether it represents sufficient information to conclude that the stock market does not operate efficiently. In formulating your response, consider: (a) what it means for the stock market to be inefficient, and (b) what role the measurement of risk plays in your conclusions about each effect.

4. Some studies related to the efficient market hypothesis generated results that implied additional factors beyond beta should be considered to estimate expected returns. What are these other variables and why should they be considered?

5. *CFA Examination Level II*
   The arbitrage pricing theory (APT) and the capital asset pricing model (CAPM) have received much attention from practitioners and academicians for use in asset pricing and valuation.
   a. Explain the difference between APT and the CAPM with respect to:
      (1) investor utility functions
      (2) distribution of returns
      (3) the market portfolio
   b. Explain one conceptual difference between the APT and the CAPM other than those listed in Part a.

6. Suppose you are considering the purchase of shares in the XYZ mutual fund. As part of your investment analysis, you regress XYZ's monthly returns for the past five years against the three factors specified in the Fama-French models. This procedure generates the following coefficient estimates: market factor = 1.2, *SMB* factor = –0.3, *HML* factor = 1.4. Explain what each of these coefficient values means. What types of stocks is XYZ likely to be holding?

7. *CFA Examination Level III*
   As the manager of a large, broadly diversified portfolio of stocks and bonds, you realize that changes in certain macroeconomic variables may directly affect the performance of your portfolio. You are considering using an arbitrage pricing theory (APT) approach to strategic portfolio planning and want to analyze the possible impacts of the following four factors:
   • Industrial production
   • Inflation
   • Risk premia or quality spreads
   • Yield curve shifts
   Indicate how each of these four factors influences the cash flows and/or the discount rates in the traditional discounted cash flow model. Explain how unanticipated changes in each of these four factors could affect portfolio returns.

8. Describe the intuition underlying: (a) the macroeconomic approach to identifying risk factors, and (b) the microeconomic (i.e., characteristic-based) approach to identifying risk factors. Is it conceptually and practically possible for these two approaches to lead to the same estimate of expected return for any given security?

9. Describe the three risk factors specified by the Fama-French multifactor model. How do these factors differ from those used in macroeconomic-based approaches to risk factor development such as that used by Chen, Roll, and Ross?

10. How can multifactor models be used to help investors understand the relative risk exposures in their portfolios relative to a benchmark portfolio? Support your answer with examples using both macroeconomic and microeconomic approaches to factor identification.

11. Consider the following questions related to empirical tests of the APT:

a. Briefly discuss one study that does not support the APT. Briefly discuss a study that does support the APT. Which position seems more plausible?

b. Briefly discuss why Shanken contends that the APT is not testable. What is the contrary view to Shanken's position?

12. *CFA Examination Level III*

Multifactor models of security returns have received increased attention. The arbitrage pricing theory (APT) probably has drawn the most attention and has been proposed as a replacement for the capital asset pricing model (CAPM).

a. Briefly explain the primary differences between the APT and the CAPM.

b. Identify the *four* systematic factors suggested by Roll and Ross that determine an asset's riskiness. Explain how these factors affect an asset's expected rate of return.

13. *CFA Examination Level II*

Jeffrey Bruner, CFA, uses the capital asset pricing model (CAPM) to help identify mispriced securities. A consultant suggests Bruner use the arbitrage pricing theory (APT) instead. In comparing the CAPM and the APT, the consultant made the following arguments:

a. Both the CAPM and the APT require a mean-variance efficient market portfolio.

b. Neither the CAPM nor the APT assumes normally distributed security returns.

c. The CAPM assumes that one specific factor explains security returns, but the APT does not.

State whether *each* of the consultant's arguments is correct or incorrect. Indicate, for each incorrect argument, why the argument is incorrect.

Problems

1. Consider the following data for two risk factors (1 and 2) and two securities (J and L):

$\lambda_0 = 0.05$ $b_{J1} = 0.80$

$\lambda_1 = 0.02$ $b_{J2} = 1.40$

$\lambda_2 = 0.04$ $b_{L1} = 1.60$

                     $b_{L2} = 2.25$

a. Compute the expected returns for both securities.

b. Suppose that Security J is currently priced at $22.50 while the price of Security L is $15.00. Further, it is expected that both securities will pay a dividend of $0.75 during the coming year. What is the expected price of each security one year from now?

2. Earlier in the text, it was demonstrated how the Fama-French three-factor model could be used to estimate the expected risk compensation for a set of equities (INTC, JPM, and WFMI). Specifically, using return data from the 1996–2000 period, the following equations were estimated:

$$\text{INTC: } [E(R) - RFR] = (0.615)(\lambda_m) + (-0.640)(\lambda_{SMB}) + (-1.476)(\lambda_{HML})$$

$$\text{JPM: } [E(R) - RFR] = (1.366)(\lambda_m) + (-0.387)(\lambda_{SMB}) + (0.577)(\lambda_{HML})$$

$$\text{WFMI: } [E(R) - RFR] = (1.928)(\lambda_m) + (0.817)(\lambda_{SMB}) + (1.684)(\lambda_{HML})$$

Using the estimated factor risk premia of $\lambda_m = 11.50\%$, $\lambda_{SMB} = -1.44\%$, and $\lambda_{HML} = -5.40\%$, it was then shown that the expected excess returns for the three stocks were 15.96%, 13.15%, and 11.90%, respectively.

a. Exhibit 9.8 lists factor risk prices calculated over two different time frames: (1) 1981–2000 ($\lambda_m = 9.09\%$, $\lambda_{SMB} = -1.10\%$, and $\lambda_{HML} = 4.48\%$), and (2) 1928–2000 ($\lambda_m = 7.02\%$, $\lambda_{SMB} = 3.09\%$, and $\lambda_{HML} = 4.39\%$). Calculate the expected excess returns for INTC, JPM, and WFMI using both of these alternative sets of factor risk premia.

b. Do all of the expected excess returns you calculated in Part a make sense? If not, identify which ones seem inconsistent with asset pricing theory and discuss why.

c. Would you expect the factor betas to remain constant over time? Discuss how and why these coefficients might change in response to changing market conditions.

3. You have been assigned the task of estimating the expected returns for three different stocks: QRS, TUV, and WXY. Your preliminary analysis has established the historical risk premiums associated with three risk factors that could potentially be included in your calculations: the excess return on a proxy for the market portfolio (MKT), and two variables capturing general macroeconomic exposures (MACRO1 and MACRO2). These values are: $\lambda_{MKT} = 7.5\%$, $\lambda_{MACRO1} = -0.3\%$, and $\lambda_{MACRO2} = 0.6\%$. You have also estimated the following factor betas (i.e., loadings) for all three stocks with respect to each of these potential risk factors:

		Factor Loading	
Stock	MKT	MACRO1	MACRO2
QRS	1.24	–0.42	0.00
TUV	0.91	0.54	0.23
WXY	1.03	–0.09	0.00

a. Calculate expected returns for the three stocks using just the MKT risk factor. Assume a risk-free rate of 4.5%.
b. Calculate the expected returns for the three stocks using all three risk factors and the same 4.5% risk-free rate.
c. Discuss the differences between the expected return estimates from the single-factor model and those from the multifactor model. Which estimates are most likely to be more useful in practice?
d. What sort of exposure might MACRO2 represent? Given the estimated factor betas, is it really reasonable to consider it a common (i.e., systematic) risk factor?

4. Consider the following information about two stocks (D and E) and two common risk factors (1 and 2):

Stock	b_{i1}	b_{i2}	$E(R_i)$
D	1.2	3.4	13.1%
E	2.6	2.6	15.4%

a. Assuming that the risk-free rate is 5.0%, calculate the levels of the factor risk premia that are consistent with the reported values for the factor betas and the expected returns for the two stocks.
b. You expect that in one year the prices for Stocks D and E will be $55 and $36, respectively. Also, neither stock is expected to pay a dividend over the next year. What should the price of each stock be today to be consistent with the expected return levels listed at the beginning of the problem?
c. Suppose now that the risk premium for Factor 1 that you calculated in Part a suddenly increases by 0.25% (i.e., from x% to (x +0.25)%, where x is the value established in Part a). What are the new expected returns for Stocks D and E?
d. If the increase in the Factor 1 risk premium in Part c does not cause you to change your opinion about what the stock prices will be in one year, what adjustment will be necessary in the current (i.e., today's) prices?

5. Suppose that three stocks (A, B, and C) and two common risk factors (1 and 2) have the following relationship:

$$E(R_A) = (1.1) \lambda_1 + (0.8) \lambda_2$$
$$E(R_B) = (0.7) \lambda_1 + (0.6) \lambda_2$$
$$E(R_C) = (0.3) \lambda_1 + (0.4) \lambda_2$$

a. If $\lambda_1 = 4\%$ and $\lambda_2 = 2\%$, what are the prices expected next year for each of the stocks? Assume that all three stocks currently sell for $30 and will not pay a dividend in the next year.

b. Suppose that you know that next year the prices for Stocks A, B, and C will actually be $31.50, $35.00, and $30.50. Create and demonstrate a riskless, arbitrage investment to take advantage of these mispriced securities. What is the profit from your investment? You may assume that you can use the proceeds from any necessary short sale.

Problems 6–7 refer to the data contained in Exhibit 9.12, which lists 30 monthly excess returns to two different actively managed stock portfolios (A and B) and three different common risk factors (1, 2, and 3). (Note: You may find it useful to use a computer spreadsheet program (e.g., Microsoft Excel) to calculate your answers.)

6. a. Compute the average monthly return and monthly standard return deviation for each portfolio and all three risk factors. Also state these values on an annualized basis. (Hint: Monthly returns can be

EXHIBIT 9.12 ▶ *MONTHLY EXCESS RETURN DATA FOR TWO PORTFOLIOS AND THREE RISK FACTORS*

PERIOD	PORTFOLIO A	PORTFOLIO B	FACTOR 1	FACTOR 2	FACTOR 3
1	1.08%	0.00%	0.01%	−1.01%	−1.67%
2	7.58	6.62	6.89	0.29	−1.23
3	5.03	6.01	4.75	−1.45	1.92
4	1.16	0.36	0.66	0.41	0.22
5	−1.98	−1.58	−2.95	−3.62	4.29
6	4.26	2.39	2.86	−3.40	−1.54
7	−0.75	−2.47	−2.72	−4.51	−1.79
8	−15.49	−15.46	−16.11	−5.92	5.69
9	6.05	4.06	5.95	0.02	−3.76
10	7.70	6.75	7.11	−3.36	−2.85
11	7.76	5.52	5.86	1.36	−3.68
12	9.62	4.89	5.94	−0.31	−4.95
13	5.25	2.73	3.47	1.15	−6.16
14	−3.19	−0.55	−4.15	−5.59	1.66
15	5.40	2.59	3.32	−3.82	−3.04
16	2.39	7.26	4.47	2.89	2.80
17	−2.87	0.10	−2.39	3.46	3.08
18	6.52	3.66	4.72	3.42	−4.33
19	−3.37	−0.60	−3.45	2.01	0.70
20	−1.24	−4.06	−1.35	−1.16	−1.26
21	−1.48	0.15	−2.68	3.23	−3.18
22	6.01	5.29	5.80	−6.53	−3.19
23	2.05	2.28	3.20	7.71	−8.09
24	7.20	7.09	7.83	6.98	−9.05
25	−4.81	−2.79	−4.43	4.08	−0.16
26	1.00	−2.04	2.55	21.49	−12.03
27	9.05	5.25	5.13	−16.69	7.81
28	−4.31	−2.96	−6.24	−7.53	8.59
29	−3.36	−0.63	−4.27	−5.86	5.38
30	3.86	1.80	4.67	13.31	−8.78

annualized by multiplying them by 12, while monthly standard deviations can be annualized by multiplying them by the square root of 12.)

  b. Based on the return and standard deviation calculations for the two portfolios from Part a, is it clear whether one portfolio outperformed the other over this time period?

  c. Calculate the correlation coefficients between each pair of the common risk factors (i.e., 1 & 2, 1 & 3, and 2 & 3).

  d. In theory, what should be the value of the correlation coefficient between the common risk factors? Explain why.

  e. How close do the estimates from Part b come to satisfying this theoretical condition? What conceptual problem(s) is created by a deviation of the estimated factor correlation coefficients from their theoretical levels?

7. a. Using regression analysis, calculate the factor betas of each stock associated with each of the common risk factors. Which of these coefficients are statistically significant?

  b. How well does the factor model explain the variation in portfolio returns? On what basis can you make an evaluation of this nature?

  c. Suppose you are now told that the three factors in Exhibit 9.12 represent the risk exposures in the Fama-French characteristic-based model (i.e., excess market, *SMB*, and *HML*). Based on your regression results, which one of these factors is the most likely to be the market factor? Explain why.

  d. Suppose it is further revealed that Factor 3 is the *HML* factor. Which of the two portfolios is most likely to be a growth-oriented fund and which is a value-oriented fund? Explain why.

References

Campbell, John Y., and John Ammer. "What Moves the Stock and Bond Markets? A Variance Decomposition for Long-Term Asset Returns." *Journal of Finance* 48, no. 1 (March 1993).

Elton, Edwin J., and Martin J. Gruber. *Modern Portfolio Theory and Investment Analysis,* 5th ed. New York: John Wiley & Sons, 1995.

Fama, Eugene F. "Multifactor Portfolio Efficiency and Multifactor Asset Pricing." *Journal of Financial and Quantitative Analysis* 31, no. 4 (December 1996): 441–465.

Farrell, James L., Jr. *Portfolio Management Theory and Application,* 2d ed. New York: McGraw-Hill, 1997.

Grinold, Richard C., and Ronald N. Kahn. *Active Portfolio Management.* Chicago: Probus, 1995.

Handa, Puneet, and Scott C. Linn. "Arbitrage Pricing with Estimation Risk." *Journal of Financial and Quantitative Analysis* 28, no. 1 (March 1993).

Lehmann, B. N., and D. M. Modest. "The Empirical Foundations of the Arbitrage Pricing Theory." *Journal of Financial Economics* 21, no. 3 (September 1988).

Ross, Stephen A. "The Arbitrage Theory of Capital Asset Pricing." *Journal of Economic Theory* 13, no. 2 (December 1976).

Sharpe, William F. "Factor Models, CAPMs, and the APT." *Journal of Portfolio Management* 11, no. 1 (Fall 1984).

Part 3

Valuation Principles and Practices

In Parts 1 and 2 you learned the purpose of investing and the importance of an appropriate asset allocation decision. You also learned about the numerous investment instruments available on a global basis and the background regarding the institutional characteristics of the capital markets. In addition, you are now aware of the major developments in investment theory as they relate to efficient capital markets, portfolio theory, capital asset pricing, and multifactor valuation models. Therefore, at this point you are in a position to consider the theory and practice of estimating the value of various securities, which is the heart of investing and leads to the construction of a portfolio that is consistent with your risk-return objectives. You will recall that the investment decision is based on a comparison of an asset's intrinsic value and its market price.

The major source of information regarding a stock or bond is the corporation's financial statements. Chapter 10 considers what financial statements are available and what information they provide, followed by a discussion of the financial ratios used to answer several important questions about a firm's liquidity, its operating performance, its risk profile, and its growth potential.

Chapter 11 considers the basic principles of valuation and applies those principles to the valuation of bonds, preferred stock, and common stock. Because it is recognized that the valuation of common stock is the most challenging task, we present two general approaches to equity valuation (discounted cash flow models and relative valuation ratios) and several techniques for each of these approaches. We conclude this chapter by reviewing the basic factors that influence the two critical variables that determine the intrinsic value of an asset irrespective of the valuation model: (1) the required rate of return for an investment, and (2) the estimated growth rate of earnings, dividends, and cash flows for the investment.

Chapter 12 deals with a major question for the global investor that was introduced in Chapter 2—how to allocate assets across countries based on the state of their economies and the effect of alternative macroeconomic variables on a country's security markets. We initially examine some specific tools used in this macroeconomic analysis, including leading indicators and determinants of the monetary environment. Subsequently, it is demonstrated that within each country it is necessary to make a further allocation among available asset classes, including stocks, bonds, and cash.

Chapter 10 Analysis of Financial Statements

After you read this chapter, you should be able to answer the following questions:

➤ What are the major financial statements provided by firms, and what specific information does each of them contain?

➤ Why do we use financial ratios to examine the performance of a firm, and why is it important to examine performance relative to the economy and to a firm's industry?

➤ What are the major categories for financial ratios, and what questions are answered by the ratios in these categories?

➤ What specific ratios help determine a firm's internal liquidity, operating performance, risk profile, and growth potential?

➤ How can the DuPont analysis help evaluate a firm's past and future return on equity?

➤ What is a "quality" balance sheet or income statement?

➤ Why is financial statement analysis done if markets are efficient and forward-looking?

➤ What major financial ratios are used by analysts in the following areas: stock valuation, estimating and evaluating systematic risk, predicting the credit ratings on bonds, and predicting bankruptcy?

You have probably already flipped the pages of this chapter and recognized that it is a fairly long chapter with several financial statements and numerous financial ratios. A logical question is, What is the purpose of this extensive discussion of how to analyze financial statements? To answer this very reasonable question, we need to recall the process of investing. Early on, the point was made that our ultimate goal is to construct a portfolio of investments that will provide rates of return that are consistent with the risk involved with the portfolio. In turn, to determine the expected rates of return on alternative assets, it is necessary to *estimate the future value* of the asset since a major component of the rate of return is the change in value for the asset over time. Therefore, the crux of investments is valuation! While we will consider alternative valuation models in the next chapter, you are already aware from prior coursework that the value of any earning asset is the present value of the expected cash flows generated by the asset. Therefore, to estimate the value of an asset, you must derive an estimate of (1) the discount rate for the asset (your required rate of return) and (2) its expected cash flows. The point is, the main source of information that will help you make these two estimates is the financial statements. To derive an estimate of your required rate of return, you need to understand the business and financial risk of the firm, which is specifically considered in this chapter. To estimate future cash flows, you must understand the composition of cash flows and what will contribute to the short-run and long-run growth of this series. An analysis of the composition and growth of cash flow is a topic of this chapter. Put another way, a primary purpose of this chapter is to help you understand how to estimate the variables in alternative valuation models.

Financial statements are also the main source of information when deciding whether to lend money to a firm (invest in its bonds) or to buy warrants or options on a firm's stock. In this chapter, we first introduce a corporation's major financial statements and discuss why and how financial ratios are useful. In subsequent sections, we provide example computations of ratios that reflect internal liquidity, operating performance, risk analysis, and growth analysis. In the final section, we address four major areas in investments where financial ratios have been effectively employed.

Our example company in this chapter is Walgreen Co., the largest retail drugstore chain in the United States. It operates 3,165 drugstores in 43 states and Puerto Rico. General merchandise accounts for 26 percent and pharmacy generates over 55 percent of total sales. The firm leads its industry (retail drugstores) in sales, profit, and store growth. The firm's goal is to be America's most convenient and technologically advanced health care retailer. It takes great pride in its steady sales and earnings growth that has been reflected in outstanding stock performance—for example, dividends have been increased in each of the past 25 years and, since 1980, the stock has been split two-for-one seven times.

MAJOR FINANCIAL STATEMENTS

Financial statements are intended to provide information on the resources available to management, how these resources were financed, and what the firm accomplished with them. Corporate shareholder annual and quarterly reports include three required financial statements: the balance sheet, the income statement, and the statement of cash flows. In addition, reports that must be filed with the Securities and Exchange Commission (SEC) (for example, the 10-K and 10-Q reports) carry detailed information about the firm, such as information on loan agreements and data on product line and subsidiary performance. Information from the basic financial statements can be used to calculate financial ratios and to analyze the operations of the firm to determine what factors influence a firm's earnings, cash flows, and risk characteristics.

Generally Accepted Accounting Principles

Among the input used to construct the financial statements are **generally accepted accounting principles (GAAP)**, which are formulated by the Financial Accounting Standards Board (FASB). The FASB recognizes that it would be improper for all companies to use identical and restrictive accounting principles. Some flexibility and choice are needed because industries and firms within industries differ in their operating environments. Therefore, the FASB allows companies some flexibility to choose among appropriate GAAP. This flexibility allows the firm's managers to choose accounting standards that best reflect company practice. On the negative side, this flexibility can allow firms to appear healthier than they really are.[1] Given this possibility, the financial analyst must rigorously analyze the available financial information to separate those firms that *appear* attractive from those that actually are in good financial shape.

Fortunately, the FASB requires that financial statements include footnotes that inform analysts regarding which accounting principles were used by the firm. Because accounting principles frequently differ among firms, the footnote information assists the financial analyst in adjusting the financial statements of companies so the analyst can better compare "apples with apples."

Balance Sheet

The **balance sheet** shows what resources (assets) the firm controls and how it has financed these assets. Specifically, it indicates the current and fixed assets available to the firm *at a point in time* (the end of the fiscal year or the end of a quarter). In most cases, the firm owns these assets, but

---

[1]The recent Enron fiasco clearly makes this point. For a general discussion on this topic, see Nanette Byrnes and David Henry, "Confused About Earnings?" *Business Week* (26 November 2001): 77–84; David Henry, "The Numbers Game," *Business Week* (14 May 2001): 100–110; and Nanetta Byrnes, Mike McNamee, Diane Brady, Louis Lavelle, and Christopher Palmeri, "Accounting in Crises," *Business Week* (28 January 2002): 44–48.

EXHIBIT 10.1 *WALGREEN CO. AND SUBSIDIARIES CONSOLIDATED BALANCE SHEET ($ MILLIONS) YEARS ENDED AUGUST 31, 1999, 2000, AND 2001*

	2001	2000	1999
Assets			
Current Assets			
Cash and cash equivalents	$ 17	$ 13	$ 142
Trade accounts receivable—net of allowances	798	615	487
Inventories	3,482	2,831	2,463
Other current assets	96	92	131
Total Current Assets	4,393	3,550	3,222
Property, plant, and equipment	5,503	4,420	3,473
Less accumulated depreciation	1,158	992	879
Property—Net	4,345	3,428	2,594
Other noncurrent assets	95	125	91
Total Assets	$8,834	$7,104	$5,907
Liabilities and Shareholders' Equity			
Current Liabilities			
Short-term debt	$ 441	$ 0	$ 0
Current portion of long-term debt	0	0	0
Trade accounts payable	1,547	1,364	1,130
Accrued expenses and other liabilities	938	848	730
Income taxes payable	87	92	63
Other accrued liabilities	0	0	0
Total Current Liabilities	3,012	2,304	1,924
Long-term Debt	0	0	0
Other Noncurrent Liabilities	478	464	424
Deferred Income Taxes	137	102	75
Preferred Stock, $.0625 par value, authorized 32,000,000 shares; none issued			
Common Shareholders' Equity			
Common stock, $.078125 par value, authorized 3.2 billion shares; issued and outstanding 1,010,818,890 in 2000 and 1,004,022,258 in 1999	80	79	78
Paid-in capital	597	367	259
Retained earnings	4,531	3,788	3,147
Total Common Shareholders' Equity	5,207	4,234	3,484
Total Liabilities and Common Shareholders' Equity Co.	$8,834	$7,104	$5,907

Reprinted with permission from Walgreen Co., Deerfield, IL.

some firms lease assets on long-term bases. How the firm has financed the acquisition of these assets is indicated by its mixture of current liabilities (accounts payable or short-term borrowing), long-term liabilities (fixed-income debt), and owners' equity (preferred stock, common stock, and retained earnings).

The balance sheet for Walgreens in Exhibit 10.1 represents the *stock* of assets and its financing mix as of the end of Walgreens' fiscal year, August 31, 1999, 2000, and 2001.

EXHIBIT 10.2 ▶ *WALGREEN CO. AND SUBSIDIARIES CONSOLIDATED STATEMENT OF INCOME ($ MILLIONS, EXCEPT PER-SHARE DATA). YEARS ENDED AUGUST 31, 1999, 2000, AND 2001*

	2001	2000	1999
Net sales	$24,623	$21,207	$17,839
Cost of goods sold	18,049	15,466	12,979
Gross profit	6,574	5,741	4,860
Selling, general and administrative expenses	5,176	4,517	3,845
Operating profit (EBIT)	1,398	1,224	1,015
Interest income	(5)	(6)	(12)
Interest expense	3	0	0
Other Income	(22)	(34)	0
Gain on sale of long-term care pharmacies	0	0	0
Operating income before income taxes	1,422	1,263	1,027
Provision for income taxes	537	486	403
Operating income after taxes[b]	886	777	624
Cumulative effect of accounting change	0	0	0
Reported net income	886	777	624
Reported net income available for Common	886	777	624
Per Share Data[a]			
Operating income after taxes[b]	$ 0.86	$ 0.76	$ 0.62
Reported net income	$ 0.86	$ 0.76	$ 0.62
Dividends declared	$ 0.14	$ 0.14	$ 0.13
Average number of common shares outstanding (millions)[a]	1,029	1,020	1,014

[a]Adjusted for stock splits.

[b]Does not include gain on sale of pharmacies and effect of accounting changes.

Reprinted with permission from Walgreen Co., Deerfield, IL.

Income Statement

The **income statement** contains information on the profitability of the firm during some *period of time* (a quarter or a year). In contrast to the balance sheet, which indicates the firm's financial position at a fixed point in time, the income statement indicates the *flow* of sales, expenses, and earnings during a period of time. The income statement for Walgreens for the years 1999, 2000, and 2001 appears in Exhibit 10.2. We concentrate on earnings from operations after tax as the relevant net earnings figure. In the case of Walgreens, this is typically the same as net income; the firm generally has no nonrecurring or unusual income or expense items.

Statement of Cash Flows

Based upon our earlier discussion on valuation, you know that cash flows are a critical input. In response to a growing interest in this data, accountants now require firms to provide such information. The **statement of cash flows** integrates the information on the balance sheet and income statement. For a given period, it shows the effects on the firm's cash flow of income flows (based on the most recent year's income statement) and changes in various items on the balance sheet (based on the two most recent annual balance sheets). The result is a set of cash flow values that you can use to estimate the value of a firm and to evaluate the risk and return of the firm's bonds and stock.

The statement of cash flows has three sections: cash flows from operating activities, cash flows from investing activities, and cash flows from financing activities. The sum total of the cash flows from the three sections is the net change in the cash position of the firm. This bottom-line number should equal the difference in the cash balance between the ending and beginning balance sheets. The statements of cash flow for Walgreens for 1999, 2000, and 2001 appear in Exhibit 10.3

Cash Flow from Operating Activities

This section lists the sources and uses of cash that arise from the normal operations of a firm. In general, the net cash flow from operations is computed as the net income reported on the income statement, including changes in net working capital items (i.e., receivables, inventories, and so on) plus adjustments for noncash revenues and expenses (such as depreciation) or:

$$\text{Cash Flow from Operating Activities} = \text{Net Income} + \text{Noncash Revenue and Expenses} + \text{Changes in Net Working Capital Items}$$

Consistent with the preceding discussion, the cash account is not included in the calculations of cash flow from operations. Notably, Walgreens has been able to generate consistently large cash flows from operations even after accounting for consistent increases in receivables and inventory.

Cash Flows from Investing Activities

A firm makes investments in both its own non-current and fixed assets and the equity of other firms (which may be subsidiaries or joint ventures of the parent firm; they are listed in the "investment" account of the balance sheet). Increases and decreases in these noncurrent accounts are considered investment activities. The cash flow from investing activities is the change in gross plant and equipment plus the change in the investment account. The changes are positive if they represent a source of funds (e.g., sale of some plant and/or equipment); otherwise, they are negative. The dollar changes in these accounts are computed using the firm's two most recent balance sheets. Most firms (including Walgreens) experience negative cash flows from investments due to significant capital expenditures.

Cash Flows from Financing Activities

Cash flow from financing activities is computed as financing sources minus financing uses. Cash inflows are created by actions increasing notes payable and long-term liability and equity accounts, such as bond and stock issues. Financing uses (cash outflows) include decreases in such accounts (that is, the paydown of liability and debt accounts or the repurchase of common shares). Dividend payments to equityholders are a significant financing cash outflow.

The sum total of the cash flows from operating, investing, and financing activities is the net increase or decrease in the firm's cash. The statement of cash flows provides some of the cash flow detail that is lacking in the balance sheet and income statement.

Alternative Measures of Cash Flow

There are several cash flow measures an analyst can use to determine the underlying health of the corporation.

Cash Flow from Operations

This includes the traditional measure of cash flow, which is equal to net income plus depreciation expense and deferred taxes; but, as we have just seen, it is also necessary to adjust for changes in operating (current) assets and liabilities that either use or provide cash. For example, an increase in accounts receivable implies that either the firm is using cash to support this increase or the firm did not collect all the sales reported. In contrast, an increase in a current liability account, such as accounts payable, means that the firm acquired

EXHIBIT 10.3 ▶ *WALGREEN CO. AND SUBSIDIARIES CONSOLIDATED STATEMENT OF CASH FLOWS ($ MILLIONS): YEARS ENDED AUGUST 31, 1999, 2000, AND 2001*

	2001	2000	1999
Cash Flows from Operating Activities:			
Net Income	$ 886	$ 777	$ 624
Adjustments to Reconcile Net Income to Net Cash Provided by Operating Activities:			
Cumulative effect of accounting changes	0	0	0
Depreciation and amortization	269	230	210
Deferred income taxes and other items	47	21	(9)
Gain on sale of long-term care pharmacies	0	0	0
Income tax savings from employee stock plans	67	39	27
Other	2	14	12
Changes in Operating Assets and Liabilities (Used in) Provided from Continuing Operations:			
(Increase) decrease in trade accounts receivable	(177)	(135)	(106)
(Increase) decrease in inventories	(652)	(368)	(436)
(Increase) decrease in other current assets	0	0	0
Increase (decrease) in trade accounts payable	183	234	223
Increase (decrease) in other current liabilities	0	0	0
Accrued expenses and other liabilities	82	101	104
Income taxes	(5)	29	9
Other	17	32	(6)
Net Cash Provided by Operating Activities	$ 719	$ 972	$ 652
Cash Flows from Investing Activities:			
Additions to property, plant, and equipment	$(1,237)	$ (1119)	$(696)
Net borrowing against corporate-owned life insurance	59	11	9
Net proceeds from marketable securities	0	48	0
Disposition of property and equipment	44	23	42
Net Cash Used in Investing Activities	$(1,135)	$ (1037)	$(646)
Cash Flows from Financing Activities:			
Proceeds from short-term borrowings	$ 441	$ —	$ —
Cash dividends	(141)	(135)	(129)
Proceeds from employee stock plans	126	79	105
Other	(7)	(8)	15
Net Cash Used in Financing Activities	419	$ (63)	$(9)
Net increase (decrease) in cash and cash equivalents	4	(129)	(3)
Cash and cash equivalents—beginning of year	13	142	144
Cash and cash equivalents—end of year	$ 17	$ 13	$ 142

some assets but has not paid for them, which is a source (increase) of cash flow (that is, the firm's suppliers are implicitly providing financing to the firm). These changes in operating assets or liabilities can add to or subtract from the cash flow estimated from the traditional measure of cash flow: net income plus noncash expenses.

The following table compares the cash flow from operations figures (Exhibit 10.3) to the traditional cash flow figures for Walgreens from 1999 to 2001:

	TRADITIONAL CASH FLOW EQUALS NET INCOME + DEPRECIATION + CHANGE IN DEFERRED TAXES	CASH FLOW FROM OPERATIONS FROM STATEMENT OF CASH FLOWS
2001	1,045	719
2000	1,034	972
1999	820	652

In all three years, the cash flow from operations was less than the traditional cash flow estimate because of the several adjustments needed to arrive at cash flow from operations. Therefore, using this more exact measure of cash flow, the Walgreens ratios would not have been as strong. This is fairly typical because the effect of working-capital changes is often a large negative cash flow due to necessary increases in receivables or inventory to support sales growth (especially for high-growth companies like Walgreens).

Free Cash Flow   **Free cash flow** modifies cash flow from operations to recognize that some investing and financing activities are critical to the firm. It is assumed that these "necessary" expenditures must be made before a firm can use its cash flow for other purposes such as reducing debt outstanding or repurchasing common stock. Two additional items are considered: (1) capital expenditures (an investing expenditure) and (2) the disposition of property and equipment (a divestment source of cash). These two items are used to modify cash flow from operations for Walgreens as follows (some analysts only subtract capital expenditures, and those who are conservative also subtract dividends):

	CASH FLOW FROM OPERATIONS	−	CAPITAL EXPENDITURES	+	DISPOSITION OF PROPERTY AND EQUIPMENT	=	FREE CASH FLOW
2001	719	−	1,237	+	44	=	(474)
2000	972	−	1,119	+	23	=	(124)
1999	652	−	696	+	42	=	(2)

For firms involved in leveraged buyouts, this free cash flow number is critical because the new owners typically want to use the firm's free cash flow as funds available for retiring outstanding debt. As noted, it is not unusual for a firm's free cash flow to be a negative value. The free cash flow for Walgreens has been negative for these three years even though the firm has large cash flow from operations because the firm has committed to very heavy capital expenditures for new stores. Notably, this free cash flow value or a variation of it will be used in the subsequent cash flow valuations models.[2]

---

[2]As will be shown in the following chapter that deals with valuation, small modifications of this free cash flow, entitled free cash flow to equity (FCFE), free cash flow to the firm (FCFF), and NOPLAT are used in alternative valuation models and also in the well-regarded economic value added (EVA) model.

Purpose of Financial Statement Analysis

Financial statement analysis seeks to evaluate management performance in several important areas, including profitability, efficiency, and risk. Although we will necessarily analyze historical data, the ultimate goal of this analysis is to provide insights that will help you to *project* future management performance, including pro forma balance sheets, income statements, cash flows, and risk. It is the firm's *expected future* performance that determines whether you should lend money to a firm or invest in it.

ANALYSIS OF FINANCIAL RATIOS

Analysts use financial ratios because numbers in isolation typically convey little meaning. Knowing that a firm earned a net income of $100,000 is less informative than also knowing the sales figure that generated this income ($1 million or $10 million) and the assets or capital committed to the enterprise. Thus, ratios are intended to provide meaningful *relationships* between individual values in the financial statements.

Because the major financial statements include numerous individual items, it is possible to produce a vast number of potential ratios, many of which will have little value. Therefore, you want to limit your examination to the most relevant ratios and categorize them into groups that will provide information on important economic characteristics of the firm. It is also important to recognize the need for relative analysis.

Importance of Relative Financial Ratios

Just as a single number from a financial statement is of little use, an individual financial ratio has little value except in relation to comparable ratios for other entities. That is, *only relative financial ratios are relevant.* The important comparisons examine a firm's performance relative to

➤ The aggregate economy
➤ Its industry or industries
➤ Its major competitors within the industry
➤ Its past performance (time-series analysis)

The comparison to the aggregate economy is important because almost all firms are influenced by the economy's expansions and contractions (recessions) in the business cycle. For example, it is unreasonable to expect an increase in the profit margin for a firm during a recession; a stable margin might be encouraging under such conditions. In contrast, no change or a small increase in a firm's profit margin during a major business expansion may be a sign of weakness. Comparing a firm's financial ratios relative to a similar set of ratios for the economy will also help you to understand how a firm reacts to the business cycle and will help you *estimate* the future performance of the firm during subsequent business cycles.

Probably the most significant comparison relates a firm's performance to that of its industry. Different industries affect the firms within them differently, but this company-industry relationship is always significant. The industry effect is strongest for industries with homogeneous products, such as steel, rubber, glass, and wood products, because all firms within these industries experience coincidental shifts in demand. In addition, these firms employ fairly similar technology and production processes. For example, even the best-managed steel firm experiences a decline in sales and profit margins during a recession. In such a case, the relevant question is not whether sales and margins declined but how bad was the decline and how did the firm perform relative to other steel firms? As part of this, you should examine an industry's performance relative to aggregate economic activity to understand how the industry responds to the business cycle.

When comparing a firm's financial ratios to industry ratios, you may not feel comfortable using the average (mean) industry value when there is wide variation among individual firm ratios within the industry. Alternatively, you may believe that the firm being analyzed is not typical—that is, it has a unique component. Under these conditions, a **cross-sectional analysis** may be appropriate, in which you compare the firm to a subset of firms within the industry that are comparable in size or characteristics. As an example, if you were interested in Kroger, you would want to compare its performance to that of other national food chains rather than some regional chains or specialty food chains.

Another practical problem with comparing a firm's ratios to an industry average is that many large firms are multiproduct and multi-industry in nature. Inappropriate comparisons can arise when a multi-industry firm is evaluated against the ratios from a single industry. Two approaches can help mitigate this problem. First, you can use a cross-sectional analysis by comparing the firm against a rival that operates in many of the same industries. Second, you can construct composite industry average ratios for the firm. To do this, the firm's annual report or 10-K filing is used to identify each industry in which the firm operates and the proportion of total firm sales derived from each industry. Following this, composite industry average ratios are constructed by computing weighted average ratios based on the proportion of firm sales derived from each industry.

Finally, you should examine a firm's relative performance over time to determine whether it is progressing or declining. This **time-series analysis** is helpful when estimating future performance. For example, some analysts calculate the average of a ratio for a 5- or 10-year period without considering the trend. This can result in misleading conclusions. For example, an average rate of return of 10 percent can be based on rates of return that have increased from 5 percent to 15 percent over time, or it can be based on a series that begins at 15 percent and declines to 5 percent. Obviously, the difference in the trend for these series would have a major impact on your estimate for the future. Ideally, you want to examine a firm's time series of *relative* financial ratios compared to its industry and the economy.

COMPUTATION OF FINANCIAL RATIOS

We divide the financial ratios into five major categories that will help us understand the important economic characteristics of a firm. In this section, we focus on describing the various ratios and computing them using Walgreens data. Comparative analysis of Walgreens ratios with the economy and industry will be discussed in a later section. The five categories are

1. Common size statement
2. Internal liquidity (solvency)
3. Operating performance
   a. Operating efficiency
   b. Operating profitability
4. Risk analysis
   a. Business risk
   b. Financial risk
   c. Liquidity risk
5. Growth analysis

Common-Size Statements

Common-size statements "normalize" balance sheet and income statement items to allow easier comparison of different-size firms. A common-size balance sheet expresses all balance sheet accounts as a *percentage of total assets*. A common-size income statement expresses all income statement items as a *percentage of sales*. Exhibit 10.4 is the common-size balance sheet for Walgreens, and Exhibit 10.5 contains the common-size income statement. Common-size ratios are useful to quickly compare two different-size firms and to examine trends over time within a single firm. Common-size statements also give an analyst insight into the structure of a firm's finan-

EXHIBIT 10.4 ▶ *WALGREEN CO. AND SUBSIDIARIES COMMON-SIZE BALANCE SHEET[a]: YEARS ENDED AUGUST 31, 1997, 1998, 1999, 2000, AND 2001*

	2001	2000	1999	1998	1997
Assets					
Current Assets					
Cash and cash equivalents	0.19%	0.18%	2.40%	2.95%	1.74%
Trade accounts receivable—net of allowances	9.04	8.65	8.24	7.61	8.94
Inventories	39.42	39.85	41.69	41.35	41.19
Other Current assets	1.09	1.30	2.21	1.60	3.42
Total Current Assets	49.74	49.98	54.54	53.52	55.29
Property, plant, and equipment	62.30	62.22	58.79	60.39	59.47
Less accumulated depreciation	13.11	13.96	14.88	16.66	17.78
Property—Net	49.19	48.26	43.91	43.73	41.69
Other noncurrent assets	1.07	1.77	1.54	2.76	3.02
Total Assets	100.00%	100.00%	100.00%	100.00%	100.00%
Liabilities and Shareholders' Equity					
Current Liabilities					
Short-term debt	4.99%	0.00%	0.00%	0.00%	0.00%
Current portion of long-term debt	0.00	0.00	0.00	0.00	0.00
Trade accounts payable	17.51	19.20	19.14	18.50	19.32
Accrued expenses and other liabilities	10.62	11.93	12.36	12.62	13.17
Income taxes payable	0.98	1.30	1.07	1.12	1.71
Total Current Liabilities	34.09	32.43	32.57	32.24	34.20
Long-term Debt	0.00	0.00	0.00	0.00	0.00
Other Noncurrent Liabilities	5.41	6.54	7.17	7.82	6.70
Deferred Income Taxes	1.55	1.43	1.27	1.82	2.69
Preferred Stock, $.0625 par value, authorized 32,000,000 shares; none issued					
Common Shareholders' Equity					
Common stock, $.078125 par value, authorized 3.2 billion shares; issued and outstanding 1,010,818,890 in 2000 and 1,004,022,258 in 1999	0.91	1.11	1.33	1.59	1.83
Paid-in capital	6.76	5.17	4.38	2.41	0.71
Retained Earnings	51.32	53.32	53.28	54.13	53.86
Total Common Shareholders' Equity	58.95	59.60	58.99	58.12	56.41
Total Liabilities and Common Shareholders' Equity	100.00%	100.00%	100.00%	100.00%	100.00%

[a]Percentages may not add to 100% due to rounding.

cial statements—that is, the proportion of assets that are liquid, the proportion of liabilities that are short-term obligations, or the percentage of sales consumed by production costs. For example, for Walgreens, the common-size balance sheet shows a small decline in the percent of current assets and a steady increase in the proportion of net property. Alternatively, the common-size income statement in Exhibit 10.5 shows Walgreens' cost of goods sold was relatively stable

EXHIBIT 10.5   WALGREEN CO. AND SUBSIDIARIES COMMON-SIZE INCOME STATEMENT[a]: YEARS ENDED AUGUST 31, 1997, 1998, 1999, 2000, AND 2001

	2001	%	2000	%	1999	%	1998	%	1997	%
Net sales	$24,623	100.00%	$21,207	100.00%	$17,839	100.00%	$15,307	100.00%	$13,363	100.00%
Cost of goods sold	18,049	73.30	15,466	72.93	12,979	72.75	11,139	72.78	9,682	72.45
Gross profit	6,574	26.70	5,741	27.07	4,860	27.25	4,167	27.22	3,681	27.55
Selling, general and administrative expenses	5,176	21.02	4,517	21.30	3,845	21.55	3,332	21.77	2,973	22.25
Operating profit	1,398	5.68	1,224	5.77	1,015	5.69	835	5.46	708	5.30
Interest income	(5)	(0.02)	(6)	(0.03)	(12)	(0.07)	(6)	(0.04)	(6)	(0.04)
Interest expense	3	0.01	0	0.00	0	0.00	1	0.01	2	0.01
Other income	(22)	(0.09)	(34)	(0.16)						
Gain on sale of long-term care pharmacies							(37)	(0.24)		
Operating income before income taxes	1,423	5.78	1,263	5.96	1,027	5.76	877	5.73	712	5.33
Provision for income taxes	537	2.18	486	2.29	403	2.26	340	2.22	276	2.07
Operating income after taxes	886	3.60	777	3.66	624	3.50	537	3.51	436	3.26
Extraordinary loss (income)	0	–	0	–	0	–	0	–	0	–
Cumulative effect of accounting change	0	–	0	–	0	–	(26)	(0.17)	0	–
Reported net income	886	3.60	777	3.66	624	3.50	511	3.34	436	3.26
Operating income after taxes available for common	886	3.60	777	3.66	624	3.50	537	3.51	436	3.26
Reported net income available for common	886	3.60	777	3.66	624	3.50	511	3.34	436	3.26

[a]Percentages may not add to 100% due to rounding.

during the five years with a small increase overall in proportion to sales. As a result of this stability combined with a consistent small decline in the ratio for selling, general, and administrative (SG+A) expenses, the firm has experienced an overall increase in its operating profit margin before and after taxes. The ability of Walgreens to experience strong growth in sales (over 14 percent a year) *and* an overall increase in its profit margin is very impressive.

EVALUATING INTERNAL LIQUIDITY

Internal liquidity (solvency) ratios indicate the ability of the firm to meet future short-term financial obligations. They compare near-term financial obligations, such as accounts payable or notes payable, to current assets or cash flows that will be available to meet these obligations.

Internal Liquidity Ratios

Current Ratio   Clearly the best-known liquidity measure is the *current ratio,* which examines the relationship between current assets and current liabilities as follows:

$$\text{Current Ratio} = \frac{\text{Current Assets}}{\text{Current Liabilities}}$$

For Walgreens, the current ratios were (all ratios are computed using dollars in 1,000s):

$$2001: \frac{4394}{3012} = 1.46$$

$$2000: \frac{3550}{2304} = 1.54$$

$$1999: \frac{3222}{1924} = 1.67$$

These current ratios experienced a small decline during the three years and are consistent with the "typical' current ratio. As always, it is important to compare these values with similar figures for the firm's industry and the aggregate market. If the ratios differ from the industry results, it is necessary to determine what might explain it. This comparative analysis is considered in a subsequent section.

Quick Ratio   Some observers believe you should not consider total current assets when gauging the ability of the firm to meet current obligations because inventories and some other assets included in current assets might not be very liquid. As an alternative, they prefer the *quick ratio,* which relates current liabilities to only relatively liquid current assets (cash items and accounts receivable) as follows:

$$\text{Quick Ratio} = \frac{\text{Cash} + \text{Marketable Securities} + \text{Receivables}}{\text{Current Liabilities}}$$

Walgreens' quick ratios were:

$$2001: \frac{815}{3012} = 0.27$$

$$2000: \frac{627}{2304} = 0.27$$

$$1999: \frac{628}{1924} = 0.33$$

These quick ratios for Walgreens were small, but were fairly constant over the three years. As before, you should compare these values relative to other firms in the industry and to the aggregate economy. When possible, you should question management regarding the reason for these relatively low liquidity ratios (e.g., small receivables due to heavy cash sales?).

Cash Ratio The most conservative liquidity ratio is the *cash ratio*, which relates the firm's cash and short-term marketable securities to its current liabilities as follows:

$$\text{Cash Ratio} = \frac{\text{Cash} + \text{Marketable Securities}}{\text{Current Liabilities}}$$

Walgreens' cash ratios were:

$$2001: \frac{17}{3012} = 0.01$$

$$2000: \frac{13}{2304} = 0.01$$

$$1999: \frac{142}{1924} = 0.07$$

The cash ratios during these three years have been quite low and they would be cause for concern except that such cash ratios are typical for a fast-growing retailer with larger inventories being financed by accounts payable to its suppliers. In addition, the firm has strong lines of credit available on short notice at various banks. Still, as an investor, you would want to confirm how the firm can justify such a low ratio and how it is able to accomplish this.

Receivables Turnover In addition to examining total liquid assets relative to near-term liabilities, it is useful to analyze the quality (liquidity) of the accounts receivable. One way to do this is to calculate how often the firm's receivables turn over, which implies an average collection period. The faster these accounts are paid, the sooner the firm gets the funds that can be used to pay off its own current liabilities. Receivables turnover is computed as follows:

$$\text{Receivables Turnover} = \frac{\text{Net Annual Sales}}{\text{Average Receivables}}$$

Analysts typically derive the average receivables figure from the beginning receivables figure plus the ending value divided by two. Walgreens' receivables turnover ratios were:

$$2001: \frac{24,623}{(798 + 615)/2} = 34.9 \text{ Times}$$

$$2000: \frac{21,207}{(615 + 487)/2} = 38.5 \text{ Times}$$

It is not possible to compute a turnover value for 1999 because the tables used do not include a beginning receivables figure for 1999 (that is, we lack the ending receivables figure for 1998).

Given these annual receivables turnover figures, an average collection period is as follows:

$$\text{Average Receivable Collection Period} = \frac{365}{\text{Average Receivables Turnover}}$$

$$2001: \frac{365}{34.9} = 10.5 \text{ Days}$$

$$2000: \frac{365}{38.5} = 9.4 \text{ Days}$$

These results indicate that Walgreens currently collects its accounts receivable in about 10 days on average, and this collection period has increased slightly over the recent five years. To determine whether these receivable collection numbers are good or bad, it is essential that they be related to the firm's credit policy and to comparable collection figures for other firms in the industry. The point is, the receivable collection period value varies dramatically for different firms (e.g., from 10 to over 60) and it is mainly due to the product and the industry. Such an analysis would indicate similar rapid collection periods for other drugstore chains since this is basically a cash business for the majority of sales. Still, a significant change has occurred for drugstores because about 90 percent of pharmacy sales are to a third party (i.e., these pharmacy sales are reimbursed by a managed-care company), which, in turn, generates a receivable.

The receivables turnover is one of the ratios where *you do not want to deviate too much from the norm.* For example, in an industry where the "normal" collection period is 40 days, a collection period of 80 days would indicate slow-paying customers, which increases the capital tied up in receivables and the possibility of bad debts. Therefore, you would want the firm to be somewhat below the norm (for example, 35 days versus 40 days). At the same time, a figure *substantially below* the norm, such as 20 days, might indicate overly stringent credit terms relative to your competition, which could be detrimental to sales.

Inventory Turnover   Another current asset that should be examined in terms of its liquidity is inventory based upon the firm's inventory turnover and the implied processing time. Inventory turnover can be calculated relative to sales or cost of goods sold. The preferred turnover ratio is relative to cost of goods sold (CGS) because CGS does not include the profit implied in sales.

$$\text{Inventory Turnover} = \frac{\text{CGS}}{\text{Average Inventory}}$$

For Walgreens, the inventory turnover ratios are as follows:

$$2001: \frac{18,049}{(3,482 + 2,831)/2} = 5.7 \text{ Times}$$

$$2000: \frac{15,466}{(2,831 + 2,463)/2} = 5.8 \text{ Times}$$

Given the turnover values, you can compute the average inventory processing time as follows:

$$\text{Average Inventory Processing Period} = \frac{365}{\text{Average Annual Turnover}}$$

$$2001: \frac{365}{5.7} = 64 \text{ Days}$$

$$2000: \frac{365}{5.8} = 63 \text{ Days}$$

Although this seems like a low turnover figure, it is encouraging that the inventory processing period is very stable and has declined slightly compared to the longer run period. Still, it is essential to examine this figure relative to an industry norm and/or the firm's prime competition. Notably, it will also be affected by the products carried by the chain—for instance, if a drugstore chain adds high-profit-margin items, such as cosmetics and liquor, these products may have a lower turnover.

As with receivables, you do not want an extremely low inventory turnover value and long processing time because this implies that capital is being tied up in inventory and could signal obsolete inventory (especially for firms in the technology sector). Alternatively, an abnormally high inventory turnover and a very short processing time relative to competitors could mean inadequate inventory that could lead to outages, backorders, and slow delivery to customers, which would eventually have an adverse effect on sales.

Cash Conversion Cycle   A very useful measure of overall internal liquidity is the cash conversion cycle, which combines information from the receivables turnover, the inventory turnover, and the accounts payable turnover. The point is, cash is tied up in assets for a certain number of days. Specifically, cash is committed to receivables for the collection period and is also tied up for a number of days in inventory—the inventory processing period. At the same time, the firm receives an offset to this capital commitment from its own suppliers, who provide interest-free loans to the firm by carrying the firm's payables. Specifically, the payables payment period is equal to 365/the payables turnover ratio. In turn, the payables turnover ratio is equal to:

$$\text{Payables Turnover Ratio} = \frac{\text{Cost of Goods Sold}}{\text{Average Trade Payables}}$$

For Walgreens, the payables turnover ratio is:

$$2001: \frac{18,049}{(1,547 + 1,364)/2} = 12.4 \text{ Times}$$

$$2000: \frac{15,466}{(1,364 + 1,130)/2} = 12.4 \text{ Times}$$

$$\text{Payables Payment Period} = \frac{365}{\text{Payables Turnover}}$$

$$2001: \frac{365}{12.4} = 29 \text{ Days}$$

$$2000: \frac{365}{12.4} = 29 \text{ Days}$$

Therefore, the cash conversion cycle for Walgreens equals:

Year	Receivables Days	+	Inventory Processing Days	−	Payables Payment Period	=	Cash Conversion Cycle
2001	10	+	64	−	29	=	45 days
2000	9	+	63	−	29	=	43 days

Walgreens has experienced a small decline in its receivables days, it has been stable regarding its inventory processing days, and it is paying its bills at the same speed. Overall, the result has been a small decrease in its cash conversion cycle. Although the overall cash conversion cycle appears to be quite good (about 46 days), as always, you should examine the firm's long-term trend and compare it to other drugstore chains.

EVALUATING OPERATING PERFORMANCE

The ratios that indicate how well the management is operating the business can be divided into two subcategories: (1) **operating efficiency ratios** and (2) **operating profitability ratios**. Efficiency ratios examine how the management uses its assets and capital, measured in terms of the dollars of sales generated by various asset or capital categories. Profitability ratios analyze the profits as a percentage of sales and as a percentage of assets and capital employed.

Operating Efficiency Ratios

Total Asset Turnover   The total asset turnover ratio indicates the effectiveness of the firm's use of its total asset base (net assets equals gross assets minus depreciation on fixed assets). It is computed as follows:

$$\text{Total Asset Turnover} = \frac{\text{Net Sales}}{\text{Average Total Net Assets}}$$

Walgreens' total asset turnover values were:

$$2001: \frac{24,623}{(8,834+7,104)/2} = 3.09 \text{ Times}$$

$$2000: \frac{21,207}{(7,104+5,907)/2} = 3.3 \text{ Times}$$

It is essential that you compare this ratio to that of other firms in an industry because this particular ratio varies substantially between industries. For example, total asset turnover ratios range from about 1 (or less) for large, capital-intensive industries (steel, autos, and other heavy manufacturing companies) to over 10 for some retailing or service operations. This ratio can also be affected by the use of leased facilities.

Again, you should consider a *range* of turnover values consistent with the industry. It is poor management to have an exceedingly high asset turnover relative to your industry because this might imply too few assets for the potential business (sales), or it could be due to the use of outdated, fully depreciated assets. It is equally poor management to have a low relative asset turnover because this implies tying up capital in an excess of assets relative to the needs of the firm.

Beyond analyzing the firm's total assets, it is insightful to examine the utilization of some specific assets, such as receivables, inventories, and fixed assets. This is especially important to do if the firm has experienced a major decline or increase in total asset turnover because you want to know the cause of the change—that is, which of the component turnovers (receivables, inventory, fixed asset) contributed to the change. Because we have already examined the receivables and inventory turnover as part of our liquidity analysis, we will examine the fixed asset ratio.

Net Fixed Asset Turnover   The net fixed asset turnover ratio reflects the firm's utilization of fixed assets. It is computed as follows:

$$\text{Fixed Asset Turnover} = \frac{\text{Net Sales}}{\text{Average Net Fixed Assets}}$$

Walgreens' fixed asset turnover ratios were

$$2001: \frac{24,623}{(4,345+3,428)/2} = 6.3 \text{ Times}$$

$$2000: \frac{21,207}{(3,428+2,594)/2} = 7.0 \text{ Times}$$

These turnover ratios, which indicate a decline for Walgreens during the last few years, must be compared with those of firms in the same industry and should consider the impact of leased assets.[3] Also remember that an abnormally low turnover implies capital tied up in excessive fixed assets, while an abnormally high asset turnover ratio can indicate a lack of productive capacity to meet sales demand or it might imply the use of old, fully depreciated equipment that may be obsolete.[4]

Equity Turnover   In addition to specific asset turnover ratios, it is useful to examine the turnover for alternative capital components. An important one, equity turnover, is computed as follows:

$$\text{Equity Turnover} = \frac{\text{Net Sales}}{\text{Average Equity}}$$

Equity includes preferred and common stock, paid-in capital, and total retained earnings.[5] The difference between this ratio and total asset turnover is that it excludes current liabilities and long-term debt. Therefore, when examining this series, it is important to consider the firm's capital structure ratios because a firm can increase its equity turnover ratio by increasing its proportion of debt capital (that is, by having a higher debt/equity ratio).

Walgreens' equity turnover ratios were:

$$2001: \frac{24,623}{(5,207+4,234)/2} = 5.2 \text{ Times}$$

$$2000: \frac{21,207}{(4,234+3,484)/2} = 5.5 \text{ Times}$$

Walgreens has experienced a small decline in this ratio during the past several years. In our later analysis of sustainable growth, we examine the variables that affect the equity turnover ratio to understand what caused any changes.

Following an analysis of the firm's record of operating efficiency based upon its ability to generate sales from its assets and capital, the next step is to examine its profitability in relation to its sales and capital.

Operating Profitability Ratios   The ratios in this category indicate two facets of profitability: (1) the rate of profit on sales (profit margin) and (2) the percentage return on capital employed.

---

[3]The impact of leased assets is especially significant for retail firms that lease most of their stores and for airlines that lease their planes. We will consider this off-balance-sheet financing in the subsequent section on financial risk.

[4]There will be a longer-term analysis of the firm's total asset turnover ratio in the subsequent DuPont analysis section.

[5]Some investors prefer to consider only *owner's* equity, which would not include preferred stock.

Gross Profit Margin   Gross profit equals net sales minus the cost of goods sold. The gross profit margin is computed as:

$$\text{Gross Profit Margin} = \frac{\text{Gross Profit}}{\text{Net Sales}}$$

The gross profit margins for Walgreens were:

$$2001: \frac{6,574}{24,623} = 26.7\%$$

$$2000: \frac{5,741}{21,207} = 27.1\%$$

$$1999: \frac{4,860}{17,839} = 27.2\%$$

This ratio indicates the basic cost structure of the firm. An analysis of this ratio over time relative to a comparable industry figure shows the firm's relative cost-price position. Walgreens has experienced stability in this margin during the last several years. As always, it is important to compare these margins and any changes with the industry and strong competitors. Notably, this margin can be impacted by a change in the firm's product mix toward higher or lower profit margin items. In the case of Walgreens, the shift has been slightly negative because of the high rate of growth in the pharmacy business, which has a lower gross profit margin than other product sales.

Operating Profit Margin   Operating profit is gross profit minus sales, general, and administrative (SG&A) expenses. The operating profit margin is computed as:

$$\text{Operating Profit Margin} = \frac{\text{Operating Profit}}{\text{Net Sales}}$$

For Walgreens, the operating profit margins were:

$$2001: \frac{1,398}{24,623} = 5.7\%$$

$$2000: \frac{1,224}{21,207} = 5.8\%$$

$$1999: \frac{1,015}{17,839} = 5.7\%$$

The variability of the operating profit margin over time is a prime indicator of the business risk for a firm. As noted earlier for Walgreens, this margin has experienced an overall steady increase during the last several years. Because there has been a small decline in the gross profit margin, it is clearly the firm's ability to control its SG&A expense as it has experienced strong sales growth that has resulted in the higher operating profit margin.

There are two additional deductions from operating profit (also referred to as EBIT—earnings before interest rate and taxes)—interest expense and net foreign exchange loss. This indicates operating income before income taxes.

In some instances, investors add back to operating income depreciation expense and compute a profit margin that consists of earnings before interest, taxes, depreciation, and amortization

(EBITDA). This alternative operating profit margin reflects all controllable expenses and is used as a proxy for pre-tax cash flow.[6]

Net Profit Margin   This margin relates net income to sales. In the case of Walgreens, this is the same as operating income after taxes because the firm does not have any significant nonoperating adjustments. The net income used is earnings after taxes but before dividends on preferred and common stock. For most firms, this margin is equal to:

$$\text{Net Profit Margin} = \frac{\text{Net Income}}{\text{Net Sales}}$$

As noted, Walgreens' net profit margin is based on income after taxes as follows:

$$2001: \frac{886}{24,623} = 3.6\%$$

$$2000: \frac{777}{21,207} = 3.7\%$$

$$1999: \frac{624}{17,839} = 3.5\%$$

This ratio should be computed based on sales and earnings from *continuing* operations because our analysis seeks to derive insights about *future* expectations. Therefore, results for continuing operations are relevant rather than the profit or loss that considers earnings from discontinued operations, the gain or loss from the sale of these operations, or any truly nonrecurring income or expenses. Consistent with prior profit margins for Walgreens, this one also shows a small long-run increase.

Common-Size Income Statement   Beyond these ratios, an additional technique for analyzing operating profitability is a common-size income statement, which lists all expense and income items as a percentage of sales. Analyzing this statement for several years (five at least) will provide useful insights regarding the trends in cost figures and profit margins. Earlier, we discussed the common-size statement for Walgreens (Exhibit 10.5). Beyond the analysis of earnings related to sales, the ultimate measure of the success of management is the profits earned on the assets or the capital committed to the enterprise. Several ratios help us evaluate this important relationship.

Return on Total Capital   The return on total capital (ROTC) ratio relates the firm's earnings to all the capital involved in the enterprise (debt, preferred stock, and common stock). Therefore, the earnings figure used is the net income from continuing operations (before any dividends) *plus* the interest paid on debt.

$$\text{Return on Total Capital} = \frac{\text{Net Income} + \text{Gross Interest Expense}}{\text{Average Total Capital}}$$

---

[6]While this measure of "cash flow" has grown in popularity, there are a growing number of concerned observers who point out that this measure does *not* consider the necessary cash outflows for working capital items (which are considered in "cash flow from operations") or capital expenditures (which are considered in "free cash flow"). For a brief discussion, see Herb Greenberg, "Alphabet Dupe: Why EBITDA Falls Short," *Fortune* 10 July 2000): 240–241.

Walgreens incurred interest expense for long- and short-term debt. The gross interest expense value used in this ratio differs from the "net" interest expense item in the income statement, which is measured as gross interest expense minus interest income.

Walgreens' rate of return on total capital was:

$$2001: \frac{886 + 3}{(8,834 + 7,104)/2} = 11.2\%$$

$$2000: \frac{777 + 0.4}{(7,104 + 5,907)/2} = 11.9\%$$

This ratio indicates the firm's return on all the capital it employed. It should be compared with the ratio for other firms in the industry and the economy. If this rate of return does not match the perceived risk of the firm, one might question if the entity should continue to exist because the capital involved in the enterprise could be used more productively elsewhere in the economy. For Walgreens, the results are stable and indicate a small increase over the last several years.

ROTC Including Leases

An alternative computation of ROTC is appropriate for a firm such as Walgreens that employs operating leases for its stores. This treatment would be similar for most retail firms and for airlines that lease most of their aircraft. In such instances, it is appropriate to capitalize the lease payments and put the resulting value on the balance sheet as a fixed asset and as a long-term liability.[7]

An estimate of the discounted value of the future lease payments can be done one of two ways: (1) a multiple of the forthcoming minimum lease payments or (2) the discounted value of the future minimum lease payments provided in the annual report at the firm's cost of long-term debt. The traditional multiple technique multiplies the minimum lease payment in year $t + 1$ by 8. In the case of Walgreens, the future minimum lease payments in the annual report for the year 2001 are as follows:

Years relating to year end	2002	2003	2004	2005	2006	later
Minimum payments (in $millions)	783	826	817	805	785	9,010

Given these data, the estimate using the first technique (referred to as "the 8 times rule") would produce an estimate of *$6.26 billion* (8 × $783 million). To derive an estimate using the second technique, we need to estimate the firm's cost of long-term debt and consider how to handle the lump sum "later" payments. Our debt rate estimate is 8 percent, which is consistent with the prevailing rate on AA-A rated corporate bonds. Regarding the "later" lump sum payment, it is necessary to derive a reasonable estimate regarding how many years to assume for this amortization. A liberal assumption is that the later payment is amortized over 15 years based upon a typical building lease of 20 years (this assumption would imply $9,010/15 = $601 million per year). This assumption implies that the firm will have a lease payment of $601 million each year for the 15 years beginning in 2007. An alternative estimate of the amortization period is derived by dividing the lump sum payment by the payment in the latest year (2006), which implies a time estimate (9,010 ÷ 785 = 11.5 years). If we round this up to 12 years, it implies an annual payment of $751 million per year for 12 years ($9,010/12 = $751).

---

[7]In a subsequent section where we discuss measures for financial risk, we will include the capitalized value as part of the firm's debt and include an imputed interest expense in ratios that include interest expense—for example, fixed charge coverage ratios.

If we discount all the minimum annual flows and the amortized flows over 15 years at 8 percent, we derive an estimate of the lease debt of *$6.71 billion*. A similar computation using the 12-year amortization indicates an estimate of lease debt of *$7.06 billion*. The detailed calculations for these estimates are shown in Appendix A of this chapter. Therefore, we have the following three estimates:[8]

Eight times the $t + 1$ lease payment	$6.26 billion
Discounting the lease payments assuming a 15-year amortization	$6.71 billion
Discounting the lease payments assuming a 12-year amortization	$7.06 billion

We will use the $6.71 billion discounted value estimate, which assumes a 15-year amortization period since this provides an estimate that is more theoretically correct than the "8 times rule" but not as aggressive as assuming a 12-year amortization period—that is, it provides an estimate between the two alternatives.

If we add this amount to both fixed assets and long-term debt, we will have a better measure of the assets utilized by the firm and a better estimate of the complete financing of the assets. Notably, the value that we calculated using future minimum lease payments is an appropriate value to be included on the August 31, 2001, financial statement. To properly calculate several of the subsequent financial risk ratios, we need comparable estimates for each of the year ends of 1998, 1999, and 2000, which entails estimating the present value of minimum lease payments at the end of each of these years as shown in the annual reports. The calculation of these estimates is shown in Appendix B of this chapter.

Implied Interest for Leased Assets   When computing the return on total capital (ROTC) that considers these leased assets, it is also necessary to add the implied interest expense for the leases. Again, there are two estimating techniques: (1) a rule of thumb and (2) an interest rate applied to the discounted value of minimum lease payments. The interest expense component of a lease is estimated by some analysts using the rule-of-thumb technique, which contends interest is equal to one-third of the lease payment during the year in question. In the current example, if we wanted an estimate for the implied interest for the year 2001, we would use one-third of the lease payment in 2001, which was $730 million. Thus, the implied interest would be estimated at $243 million ($730/3).

An alternative to this "rule of thumb" would be to derive a specific estimate based on an estimate of the firm's cost of debt capital (8 percent) and the estimate of the present value (PV) of the lease obligation as follows:

ESTIMATING TECHNIQUE	PV OF LEASE OBLIGATION (BILLION $)	INTEREST EXPENSE @ 8 PERCENT (MILLION $)
8 times estimate of rent	6.26	501
P.V. with 15-year amortization	6.71	537
P.V. with 12-year amortization	7.06	565

Notably, all of these estimates of the implied interest expense that used the capitalized lease value are substantially higher than the "one-third of lease payment" rule-of-thumb estimate of $243 mil-

[8]Notably, the "8 times" estimate almost always provides the lowest estimate of debt value, which means that this "rule of thumb" will tend to underestimate the financial leverage for these firms and the resulting implied interest expense. Therefore, the authors prefer one of the specific discounted value estimates but feel that this relatively small underestimate is minor compared to not capitalizing these lease obligations.

lion. Again, the rule of thumb underestimates the financial leverage related to these lease obligations. For our calculations, we will apply the 8 percent debt cost to the present value of the lease payments assuming the 15-year amortization of the lump sum. Because the lease obligations are for future periods, it is necessary to use lagged values of the obligations—that is, the estimate for 2001 is 8 percent of the obligation estimated at the end of fiscal 2000. These values are as follows:

	ESTIMATE OF PV OF LEASE OBLIGATION (BILLION $)[a]	ESTIMATE OF INTEREST EXPENSE OF LEASE (MILLION $)[b]
2002	$6.71	$537
2001	5.76	461
2000	4.48	358
1999	3.65	292

[a]These are the capitalized lease payments on the books for year $t - 1$—for example, to get the 2002 value, we discount the minimum payments reported in the 2001 annual report, as shown in Appendix B of this chapter.
[b]Equal to 8 percent of the PV of lease obligation.

Adding these values to the prior ratios results in the following lease-adjusted return on total capital values:

$$2001: \frac{886 + 3 + 461}{(15,094 + 12,494)/2} = \frac{1,350}{13,454} = 10.03\%$$

$$2000: \frac{777 + 0.4 + 358}{(12,494 + 10.137)/2} = \frac{1,135.4}{11,315.5} = 10.03\%$$

As shown, the ROTCs that include the leased assets and lease debt are lower (about 10 percent versus 12 percent), but they are still quite reasonable.

Implied Depreciation on Leased Assets   Beyond the implied interest expense, another factor is the implied depreciation expense that would be taken if these were not leased assets. One alternative is to simply use the typical term of the lease or weighted average term. In the case of Walgreens, this is reasonably clear since almost all leases are for 20 years on buildings. A second alternative, if it is not clear, would be the depreciation expense as a percent of beginning of year net fixed assets. In the case of Walgreens, for 2000, this would be: depreciation—$230 million; net fixed assets at end of 1999—$2,594, which implies a percent of .089 (230/2,594), which is clearly higher than the 5 percent on buildings. Obviously, Walgreens has many assets being depreciated over shorter lives. For these calculations, we prefer to assume the 20-year life as follows:

	ESTIMATE OF PV OF LEASE OBLIGATION (BILLION $)	ESTIMATE OF IMPLIED DEPRECIATION EXPENSE OF LEASE (MILLION $)[a]
2001	5.76	288
2000	4.48	224
1999	3.65	183

[a]This assumes straight-line depreciation over a 20-year life.

These implied depreciation charges should be included in ratios that include depreciation expenses.

Return on Owner's Equity   The return on owner's equity (ROE) ratio is extremely important to the owner of the enterprise (the common stockholder) because it indicates the rate of return that management has earned on the capital provided by the owner after accounting for payments to all other capital suppliers. If you consider all equity (including preferred stock), this return would equal:

$$\text{Return on Total Equity} = \frac{\text{Net Income}}{\text{Average Total Equity}}$$

If an investor is concerned only with owner's equity (the common shareholder's equity), the ratio would be calculated

$$\text{Return on Owner's Equity} = \frac{\text{Net Income} - \text{Preferred Dividend}}{\text{Average Common Equity}}$$

Walgreens generated return on owner's equity of:

$$2001: \frac{886 - 0}{(5,207 + 4,234)/2} = 18.8\%$$

$$2000: \frac{777 - 0}{(4,234 + 3,484)/2} = 20.1\%$$

This ratio reflects the rate of return on the equity capital provided by the owners. It should correspond to the firm's overall business risk, but also the financial risk assumed by the common stockholder because of the prior claims of bondholders and store lessors.

The Dupont System   The importance of ROE as an indicator of performance makes it desirable to divide the ratio into several components that provide insights into the causes of a firm's ROE or any changes in it. This breakdown of ROE into component ratios is generally referred to as the **DuPont system**. To begin, the return on equity (ROE) ratio can be broken down into two ratios that we have discussed—net profit margin and equity turnover.

$$\text{ROE} = \frac{\text{Net Income}}{\text{Common Equity}} = \frac{\text{Net Income}}{\text{Net Sales}} \times \frac{\text{Net Sales}}{\text{Common Equity}}$$

This breakdown is an identity because we have both multiplied and divided by net sales. To maintain the identity, the common equity value used is the year-end figure rather than the average of the beginning and ending value. This identity reveals that ROE equals the net profit margin times the equity turnover, which implies that a firm can improve its return on equity by *either* using its equity more efficiently (increasing its equity turnover) or by becoming more profitable (increasing its net profit margin).

As noted previously, a firm's equity turnover is affected by its capital structure. Specifically, a firm can increase its equity turnover by employing a higher proportion of debt capital. We can see this effect by considering the following relationship:

$$\frac{\text{Net Sales}}{\text{Equity}} = \frac{\text{Net Sales}}{\text{Total Assets}} \times \frac{\text{Total Assets}}{\text{Equity}}$$

Similar to the prior breakdown, this is an identity because we have both multiplied and divided the equity turnover ratio by total assets. This equation indicates that the equity turnover ratio equals the firm's *total asset turnover* (a measure of efficiency) times the ratio of *total assets to equity,* a measure of financial leverage. Specifically, this latter ratio of total assets to equity indicates the proportion of total assets financed with debt. *All assets have to be financed by either equity or some form of debt* (either current liabilities or long-term debt). Therefore, the higher the ratio of assets to equity, the higher the proportion of debt to equity. A total asset/equity ratio of 2, for example, indicates that for every two dollars of assets there is a dollar of equity, which means the firm financed one-half of its assets with equity. This implies that it financed the other half with debt. A total asset/equity ratio of 3 indicates that only one third of total assets was financed with equity, so two-thirds must have been financed with debt. This breakdown of the equity turnover ratio implies that a firm can increase its equity turnover either by increasing its total asset turnover (becoming more efficient) or by increasing its financial leverage ratio (financing assets with a higher proportion of debt capital). This financial leverage ratio is also referred to as the *financial leverage multiplier* whereby the first two ratios (profit margin and total asset turnover) equal return on total assets (ROTA) and ROTA times the financial leverage multiplier equals ROE.

Combining these two breakdowns, we see that a firm's ROE is composed of three ratios as follows:

$$\frac{\text{Net Income}}{\text{Common Equity}} = \frac{\text{Net Income}}{\text{Net Sales}} \times \frac{\text{Net Sales}}{\text{Total Assets}} \times \frac{\text{Total Assets}}{\text{Common Equity}}$$

$$= \text{Profit Margin} \times \text{Total Asset Turnover} \times \text{Financial Leverage}$$

As an example of this important set of relationships, the figures in Exhibit 10.6 indicate what has happened to the ROE for Walgreens and the components of its ROE during the 20-year period from 1982 to 2001. As noted, these ratio values employ year-end balance sheet figures (assets and equity) rather than the average of beginning and ending data so they will differ from our individual ratio computations.

The DuPont results in Exhibit 10.6 indicate several significant trends:

1. The total asset turnover ratio experienced an overall decline with a total range of 2.79 to 3.31. Notably, the ratio declined to its lowest level in 2001.
2. The profit margin series experienced a stable increase from 2.75 to its peak value of 3.66 in 2000.
3. The product of the total asset turnover and the net profit margin is equal to return on total assets (ROTA), which experienced an overall increase from 9.09 percent to a peak of 10.94 percent in 2000.
4. The financial leverage multiplier (total assets/equity) experienced a steady decline from 2.06 to 1.68. Notably, most of this debt is trade credit, which is noninterest bearing. The fact is, the firm has almost no interest-bearing debt, except for the long-term leases on drugstores that were discussed and analyzed in the prior subsection and will be considered in the financial risk section.
5. Finally, as a result of the increasing ROTA and the declining financial leverage, the firm's ROE has experienced a small decline, beginning at 18.73 and ending at 17.07.

An Extended Dupont System[9]   Beyond the original DuPont system, some analysts have suggested using an extended DuPont system, which provides additional insights into the effect of

---

[9]The original DuPont system was the three-component breakdown discussed in the prior section. Because this extended analysis also involves the components of ROE, some still refer to it as the DuPont system. In our presentation, we refer to it as the extended DuPont system to differentiate it from the original three-component analysis.

EXHIBIT 10.6 *COMPONENTS OF RETURN ON TOTAL EQUITY FOR WALGREEN CO.[a]*

Year	1 Sales/Total Assets	2 Net Profit Margin (%)	3[b] Return on Total Assets	4 Total Assets/ Equity	5[c] Return on Equity (%)
1982	3.31	2.75	9.09	2.06	18.73
1983	3.29	2.96	9.72	2.04	19.84
1984	3.26	3.11	10.16	2.03	20.60
1985	3.29	2.98	9.79	2.00	19.58
1986	3.06	2.82	8.62	2.16	18.64
1987	3.14	2.42	7.60	2.19	16.63
1988	3.23	2.64	8.54	2.12	18.12
1989	3.20	2.87	9.18	2.04	18.74
1990	3.16	2.89	9.12	2.02	18.42
1991	3.21	2.90	9.31	1.94	18.04
1992	3.15	2.95	9.30	1.92	17.90
1993	3.27	2.67	8.74	1.84	16.07
1994	3.17	3.05	9.69	1.85	17.91
1995	3.20	3.09	9.86	1.81	17.85
1996	3.24	3.16	10.23	1.78	18.19
1997	3.18	3.26	10.37	1.77	18.35
1998	3.12	3.34	10.42	1.72	17.93
1999	3.02	3.50	10.57	1.70	17.91
2000	2.99	3.66	10.94	1.68	18.35
2001	2.79	3.60	10.04	1.70	17.07

[a]Ratios use year-end data for total assets and common equity rather than averages of the year.
[b]Column 3 is equal to Column 1 times Column 2.
[c]Column 5 is equal to Column 3 times Column 4.

financial leverage on the firm and also pinpoints the effect of income taxes on the firm's ROE. Because both financial leverage and tax rates have changed dramatically over the past decade, these additional insights are important.

In the prior presentation, we started with the ROE and divided it into components. In contrast, we now begin with the operating profit margin (EBIT divided by sales) and introduce additional ratios to derive an ROE value. Combining the operating profit margin and the total asset turnover ratio yields the following:

$$\frac{EBIT}{Net\ Sales} \times \frac{Net\ Sales}{Total\ Assets} = \frac{EBIT}{Total\ Assets}$$

This ratio is the operating profit return on total assets. To consider the negative effects of financial leverage, we examine the effect of interest expense as a percentage of total assets:

$$\frac{EBIT}{Total\ Assets} - \frac{Interest\ Expense}{Total\ Assets} = \frac{Net\ Before\ Tax\ (NBT)}{Total\ Assets}$$

We consider the positive effect of financial leverage with the financial leverage multiplier as follows:

$$\frac{\text{Net Before Tax (NBT)}}{\text{Total Assets}} \times \frac{\text{Total Assets}}{\text{Common Equity}} = \frac{\text{Net Before Tax (NBT)}}{\text{Common Equity}}$$

This indicates the pretax return on equity. To arrive at ROE, we must consider the tax-rate effect. We do this by multiplying the pre-tax ROE by a tax-retention rate as follows:

$$\frac{\text{Net Before Tax}}{\text{Common Equity}} \times \left(100\% - \frac{\text{Income Taxes}}{\text{Net Before Tax}} \right) = \frac{\text{Net Income}}{\text{Common Equity}}$$

In summary, we have the following five components:

1. $\dfrac{\text{EBIT}}{\text{Sales}}$ = Operating Profit Margin

2. $\dfrac{\text{Sales}}{\text{Total Assets}}$ = Total Asset Turnover

3. $\dfrac{\text{Interest Expense}}{\text{Total Assets}}$ = Interest Expense Rate

4. $\dfrac{\text{Total Assets}}{\text{Common Equity}}$ = Financial Leverage Multiplier

5. $\left(100\% - \dfrac{\text{Income Taxes}}{\text{Net Before Tax}} \right)$ = Tax Retention Rate

To demonstrate the use of this extended DuPont system, Exhibit 10.7 contains the calculations using the five components for the years 1982 through 2001. The first column indicates that the firm's operating profit margin peaked in 1985, subsequently declined to a low point in 1990, increased to a new peak of 5.77 percent in 2000 prior to a decline in 2001. We know from the prior discussion that the firm's total asset turnover (column 2) experienced an overall decline to a low point in 2001. The resulting operating return on assets increased prior to a decline in 2001. As discussed, because of virtually no interest-bearing debt (except off-balance sheet leases), Column 4 shows zero negative impact on leverage.

Column 5 reflects the firm's operating performance before the positive impact of financing (the leverage multiplier) and the impact of taxes. These results show strong performance by the firm overall. Column 6 reflects the steady decline in non-lease financial leverage. As a result of the reduced leverage multiplier, the before-tax ROE in Column 7 has declined since 1982. Column 8 shows the strong positive effect of lower tax rates, which caused a higher tax-retention rate that increased from the mid-50 percent range to the recent 62 percent rate.

In summary, this breakdown helps you to understand *what* happened to a firm's ROE and *why* it happened. The intent is to determine what happened to the firm's internal operating results, what has been the effect of its financial leverage policy, and what was the effect of external government tax policy. Although the two breakdowns should provide the same ending value, they typically differ by small amounts because of the rounding of components.

RISK ANALYSIS

Risk analysis examines the uncertainty of income flows for the total firm and for the individual sources of capital (that is, debt, preferred stock, and common stock). This involves examining

EXHIBIT 10.7 *EXTENDED DUPONT SYSTEM ANALYSIS FOR WALGREENS: 1982–2000[a]*

	1	2	3	4	5	6	7	8	9
YEAR	EBIT/SALES (PERCENT)	SALES/TOTAL ASSETS (TIMES)	EBIT/TOTAL ASSETS (PERCENT)[b]	INTEREST EXPENSE/TOTAL ASSETS (PERCENT)	NET BEFORE TAX/TOTAL ASSETS EQUITY (PERCENT)[c]	TOTAL ASSETS/ COMMON EQUITY (TIMES)	NET BEFORE TAX/COMMON EQUITY (PERCENT)[d]	TAX RETENTION RATE	RETURN ON EQUITY (PERCENT)[e]
1982	4.32	3.31	14.30	(0.85)	15.15	2.06	31.20	0.60	18.75
1983	5.16	3.29	17.00	0.25	16.75	2.04	34.20	0.56	19.30
1984	5.57	3.26	18.20	(0.24)	18.44	2.03	37.40	0.55	20.65
1985	5.63	3.29	18.50	0.43	18.07	2.00	36.10	0.54	19.57
1986	5.37	3.06	16.40	0.74	15.66	2.16	33.90	0.55	18.63
1987	4.92	3.14	15.50	1.22	14.28	2.19	31.30	0.53	16.69
1988	4.59	3.23	14.80	1.01	13.79	2.12	29.30	0.62	18.10
1989	4.71	3.20	15.10	0.57	14.53	2.04	29.70	0.63	18.79
1990	4.70	3.16	14.90	0.17	14.73	2.02	29.80	0.62	18.52
1991	4.77	3.21	15.30	0.44	14.86	1.94	28.80	0.63	18.00
1992	4.80	3.15	15.10	0.23	14.87	1.92	28.60	0.62	17.87
1993	4.90	3.31	16.20	0.26	15.94	1.82	29.00	0.61	17.80
1994	4.93	3.21	15.90	(0.10)	16.00	1.83	29.20	0.62	17.96
1995	5.00	3.20	15.99	0.04	15.95	1.81	28.90	0.61	17.70
1996	5.13	3.24	16.62	0.06	16.56	1.78	29.50	0.61	18.07
1997	5.30	3.18	16.85	0.05	16.80	1.77	29.74	0.61	18.14
1998	5.46	3.12	17.04	0.02	17.02	1.72	29.28	0.61	17.93
1999	5.69	3.02	17.19	0.00	17.19	1.70	29.22	0.61	17.83
2000	5.77	2.99	17.25	0.00	17.25	1.68	28.98	0.61	17.78
2001	5.08	2.79	15.84	0.00	16.11	1.70	27.33	0.62	17.07

[a]The percents in this table may not be the same as in Exhibit 10.6 due to rounding.
[b]Column 3 is equal to Column 1 times Column 2.
[c]Column 5 is equal to Column 3 minus Column 4.
[d]Column 7 is equal to Column 5 times Column 6.
[e]Column 9 is equal to Column 7 times Column 8.

the major factors that cause a firm's income flows to vary. More volatile income flows mean greater risk (uncertainty) facing the investor.

The total risk of the firm has two internal components: business risk and financial risk. The next section discusses the concept of business risk: how you measure it, what causes it, and how you measure its individual causes. The following section discusses financial risk and the several ratios used to measure it. After we examine the firm's internal risk factors, we discuss an important external risk factor, external liquidity risk—that is, the ability to buy or sell the firm's stock in the secondary equity market.

Business Risk[10]   Recall that **business risk** is the uncertainty of income caused by the firm's industry. In turn, this uncertainty is due to the firm's variability of sales caused by its products, customers, and the way it produces its products. Specifically, a firm's operating earnings vary over time because its sales

---

[10]For a further discussion on this general topic, see Eugene Brigham and Louis C. Gapenski, *Financial Management: Theory and Practice,* 9th ed. (Fort Worth, Tex.: Dryden, 2000), Chapters 6 and 10.

and production costs vary. As an example, the earnings for a steel firm will probably vary more than those of a grocery chain because (1) over the business cycle, steel sales are more volatile than grocery sales; and (2) the steel firm's large fixed production costs (operating leverage) make its earnings vary more than its sales.

Business risk is generally measured by the variability of the firm's operating income over time. In turn, the earnings variability is measured by the standard deviation of the historical operating earnings series. You will recall from Chapter 1 that the standard deviation is influenced by the size of the numbers, so investors standardize this measure of volatility by dividing it by the mean value for the series (i.e., the average operating earnings). The resulting ratio of the standard deviation of operating earnings divided by the average operating earnings is the coefficient of variation (CV) of operating earnings:

$$\text{Business Risk} = f(\text{Coefficient of Variation of Operating Earnings})$$

$$= \frac{\text{Standard Deviation of Operating Earnings (OE)}}{\text{Mean Operating Earnings}}$$

$$= \frac{\sqrt{\sum_{i=1}^{n}(OE_i - \overline{OE})^2/n}}{\sum_{i=1}^{n}OE_i/n}$$

The CV of operating earnings allows comparisons between standardized measures of business risk for firms of different sizes. To compute the CV of operating earnings, you need a minimum of 5 years up to about 10 years. Less than 5 years is not very meaningful, and data more than 10 years old are typically out of date. We cannot compute the CV of operating earnings of Walgreens because we have data for only 3 years.

Besides measuring overall business risk, it is very insightful to examine the two factors that contribute to the variability of operating earnings: sales variability and operating leverage.

Sales Variability Sales variability is the prime determinant of earnings variability. In turn, the variability of sales is mainly caused by a firm's industry and is largely outside the control of management. For example, sales for a firm in a cyclical industry, such as automobiles or steel, will be quite volatile over the business cycle compared to sales of a firm in a noncyclical industry, such as retail food or hospital supplies. Like operating earnings, the variability of a firm's sales is typically measured by the CV of sales during the most recent 5 to 10 years. The CV of sales equals the standard deviation of sales divided by the mean sales for the period.[11]

$$\text{Sales Volatility} = f(\text{Coefficient of Variation of Sales})$$

$$= \frac{\sqrt{\sum_{i=1}^{n}(S_i - \overline{S})^2/n}}{\sum_{i=1}^{n}S_i/n}$$

---

[11]Besides normalizing the standard deviation for size by computing the CV, it is also important to recognize that the standard deviation is measured relative to the mean value for the series—that is, it computes deviations from "expected value." The problem arises for firms that experience significant growth that will create very large deviations from the mean for the series even if it is *constant* growth. The way to avoid this bias is to measure deviations from the growth path of the series. For details see Appendix C of this chapter.

Operating Leverage   The variability of a firm's operating earnings also depends on its mixture of production costs. Total production costs of a firm with no *fixed* production costs would vary directly with sales, and operating profits would be a constant proportion of sales. In such an example, the firm's operating profit margin would be constant and its operating profits would have the same relative volatility as its sales. Realistically, firms always have some fixed production costs such as buildings, machinery, or relatively permanent personnel. Fixed production costs cause operating profits to vary more than sales over the business cycle. Specifically, during slow periods, operating profits will decline by a larger percentage than sales, while during an economic expansion, operating profits will increase by a larger percentage than sales.

The employment of fixed production costs is referred to as **operating leverage**. Clearly, greater operating leverage (caused by a higher proportion of fixed production costs) makes the operating earnings series more volatile relative to the sales series.[12] This basic relationship between operating profit and sales leads us to measure operating leverage as the percentage change in operating earnings relative to the percentage change in sales during a specified period as follows:

$$\text{Operating Leverage} = \frac{\sum_{i=1}^{n} \left| \frac{\% \Delta OE}{\% \Delta S} \right|}{n}$$

We take the absolute value of the percentage changes because the two series can move in opposite directions. The direction of the change is not important, but the relative size of the change is relevant. By implication, the more volatile the operating earnings as compared to the volatility of sales, the greater the firm's operating leverage.

Financial Risk   **Financial risk**, you will recall, is the additional uncertainty of returns to equity holders due to a firm's use of fixed obligation debt securities. This financial uncertainty is in addition to the firm's business risk. When a firm sells bonds to raise capital, the interest payments on this capital precede the computation of common stock earnings, and these interest payments are fixed contractual obligations. As with operating leverage, during an economic expansion, the net earnings available for common stock after the fixed interest payments will experience a larger percentage increase than operating earnings. In contrast, during a business decline, the earnings available to stockholders will decline by a larger percentage than operating earnings because of these fixed financial costs. Also, as a firm increases its relative debt financing with fixed contractual obligations, it increases its financial risk and the possibility of default and bankruptcy.

A very important point to remember is that *the acceptable level of financial risk for a firm depends on its business risk*. If the firm has low business risk (i.e., stable operating earnings), investors are willing to accept higher financial risk. For example, retail food companies typically have rather stable operating earnings over time and, therefore, relatively *low* business risk. As a result, investors and bond-rating firms will allow a firm in this industry to have *higher* financial risk.[13]

In our analysis of financial risk, we employ three sets of financial ratios to measure financial risk; and *all three* sets should be considered. First, there are balance sheet ratios that indicate the

---

[12]See C. F. Lee, Joseph Finnerty, and Edgar Norton, *Foundations of Financial MAnagement* (St. Paul, Minn. West Publishing, 1997).

[13]Support for this specific relationship is a set of tables published by Standard & Poor's Credit Rating division that suggests specific required financial risk ratios needed to be considered for a specific bond rating, and the required ratios differ based upon the perceived business risk of the firm. See *Corporate Ratings Criteria* (New York: Standard & Poor's, 55 Water Street, New York, NY 10041, 2002), p. 57.

proportion of capital derived from debt securities compared to equity capital. Second are ratios that compare the earnings available to pay fixed financial charges to the required interest payments. Third are ratios that compare the cash flows available to the financial charges or compare cash flows to the book value of the outstanding debt.

Proportion of Debt (Balance Sheet) Ratios

The proportion of debt ratios indicate what proportion of the firm's capital is derived from debt compared to other sources of capital, such as preferred stock, common stock, and retained earnings. A higher proportion of debt capital compared to equity capital makes earnings more volatile because of larger fixed financial charges and increases the probability that a firm will be unable to meet the required interest payments and will default on the debt. Therefore, higher proportion of debt ratios indicate greater financial risk. In this subsection, we describe the major proportion of debt ratios used to measure this risk.

Debt-Equity Ratio The debt-equity ratio is:

$$\text{Debt-Equity Ratio} = \frac{\text{Total Long-Term Debt}}{\text{Total Equity}}$$

The debt figure includes all long-term fixed obligations, including lease obligations and subordinated convertible bonds. The equity typically is the book value of equity and includes preferred stock, common stock, and retained earnings. Some analysts prefer to exclude preferred stock and consider only common equity. Total equity is preferable if you are examining an industry in which some of the firms being analyzed have preferred stock.

Notably, debt ratios can be computed *with and without deferred taxes.* Most balance sheets include an accumulated deferred tax figure, which comes just below long-term debt and other liabilities on the balance sheet. There is some controversy regarding whether you should treat these deferred taxes as a liability or as part of permanent capital. Some argue that if the deferred tax has accumulated because of the difference in accelerated and straight-line depreciation, this liability may never be paid. That is, as long as the firm continues to grow and add new assets, this total deferred tax account continues to grow and is never paid off. Alternatively, if the deferred tax account results from differences in the recognition of income on long-term contracts, such as government contracts, there will be a reversal, and this liability must eventually be paid. To resolve this question, you must determine the reason for the deferred tax account and examine its long-term trend.[14] Walgreens' deferred tax account is because of a depreciation difference and has grown over time.

A second factor that must be considered when computing debt ratios is the existence of operating leases, as mentioned previously. Given a firm like Walgreens with extensive leased facilities, it is necessary to estimate the present value of the lease payments as long-term debt.

To show the effect of these two significant items on the financial risk of Walgreens, we will be conservative and define the ratios to include both of these factors, but they will be broken out so that you can identify the effect of each of the components of total debt. Thus, the debt-equity ratio is:

$$\text{Debt-Equity Ratio} = \frac{\text{Total Long-Term Debt}}{\text{Total Equity}}$$
$$= \frac{\text{Noncurrent Liabilities} + \text{Deferred Taxes} + \text{PV of Lease Obligations}}{\text{Total Equity}}$$

---

[14]For a further discussion of this, see Gerald I. White, Ashwinpaul C. Sondhi, and Dov Fried, *The Analysis and Use of Financial Statements,* 2d ed. (New York: Wiley, 1997), 1017–1018.

Therefore, for Walgreens, the debt-equity ratios were:

$$2001: \frac{478 + 137 + 6,710}{5,207} = \frac{7,325}{5,207} = 140.68\%$$

$$2000: \frac{464 + 102 + 5,760}{4,234} = \frac{6,326}{4,234} = 149.41\%$$

$$1999: \frac{424 + 75 + 4,480}{3,484} = \frac{4,979}{3,484} = 142.91\%$$

These ratios demonstrate the significant impact of including the present value of the lease payments as part of long-term debt—for example, the debt-equity percent for 2001 went from less than 14 percent when only long-term debt on the balance sheet was considered to over 140 percent.

Long-Term Debt/Total Capital Ratio   The debt–total capital ratio indicates the proportion of long-term capital derived from long-term debt capital. It is computed as:

$$\text{Long-Term Debt / Total Long-Term Capital Ratio} = \frac{\text{Total Long-Term Debt}}{\text{Total Long-Term Capital}}$$

The total long-term debt values are the same as before. The total long-term capital would include all long-term debt, any preferred stock, and total equity. The debt–total capital ratios for Walgreens were:

INCLUDING DEFERRED TAXES AND LEASE OBLIGATIONS AS LONG-TERM DEBT

$$2001: \frac{7,325}{7,325 + 5,207} = \frac{7,325}{12,532} = 58.45\%$$

$$2000: \frac{6,326}{5,326 + 4,234} = \frac{6,326}{10,560} = 59.90\%$$

$$1999: \frac{4,979}{4,979 + 3,484} = \frac{4,979}{8,463} = 58.83\%$$

Again, this ratio, which includes the present value of lease obligations, shows that a significant percent of long-term capital for Walgreens is derived from debt obligations. This is very different from the impression without the lease obligations included.

Total Debt Ratios   In many cases, it is useful to compare *total* debt to *total* capital computed as:

$$\text{Total Debt Ratios} = \frac{\text{Current Liabilities} + \text{Total Long-Term Debt}}{\text{Total Debt} + \text{Total Equity}}$$

This ratio is especially revealing for a firm that derives substantial capital from short-term borrowing. The total debt/total capital ratios for Walgreens were:

INCLUDING DEFERRED TAXES AND LEASE OBLIGATIONS AS LONG-TERM DEBT

$$2001: \frac{3,012 + 7,325}{10,337 + 5,207} = \frac{10,337}{15,544} = 66.50\%$$

$$2000: \frac{2,304 + 6,326}{8,630 + 4,234} = \frac{8,630}{12,864} = 67.09\%$$

$$1999: \frac{1,924 + 4,979}{6,903 + 3,484} = \frac{6,903}{10,387} = 66.46\%$$

This ratio indicates that currently almost 67 percent of Walgreens assets are financed with debt. These ratios should be compared with those of other companies in the industry (after capitalizing leases) to evaluate their consistency with the business risk of this industry. Such a comparison with industry peers also would indicate how much higher this total debt ratio can go (i.e., the firm's unused debt capacity).

While this ratio indicates a relatively high proportion of total debt, some observers would consider it too conservative because it includes accounts payable and accrued expenses, which are *non-interest-bearing debt*. In the case of Walgreens, if this non-interest-bearing debt, along with deferred taxes, is excluded from debt and from total capital, the total debt ratio declines as follows:

$$\text{Total Interest-Bearing Debt / Total Funded Capital} = \frac{\text{Total Interest-Bearing Debt}}{\text{Total Capital} - \text{Non-Interest Liabilities}}$$

$$2001: \frac{919 + 6,710}{15,544 - 2,708} = \frac{7,629}{12,836} = 59.43\%$$

$$2000: \frac{464 + 5,760}{12,864 - 2,405} = \frac{6,224}{10,459} = 59.51\%$$

$$1999: \frac{424 + 4,480}{10,381 - 1,999} = \frac{4,904}{8,382} = 58.51\%$$

While these ratios are lower, the percents are still quite high, which confirms the importance of considering the impact of lease obligations on the financial risk of firms like Walgreens that employ this form of financing.

Earnings Flow Ratios In addition to ratios that indicate the proportion of debt on the balance sheet, investors are giving greater attention to ratios that relate the *flow* of earnings that is available to meet the required interest and lease payments. A higher ratio of available earnings relative to fixed financial charges indicates lower financial risk.

Interest Coverage The standard interest coverage ratio is computed as follows:

$$\text{Interest Coverage} = \frac{\text{Income Before Interest and Taxes (EBIT)}}{\text{Debt Interest Charges}}$$

$$= \frac{\text{Net Income} + \text{Income Taxes} + \text{Interest Expense}}{\text{Interest Expense}}$$

This ratio indicates how many times the fixed interest charges are earned, based on the earnings available to pay these expenses.[15] Alternatively, one minus the reciprocal of the coverage ratio indicates how far earnings could decline before it would be impossible to pay the interest charges from current earnings. For example, a coverage ratio of 5 means that earnings could decline by 80 percent (1 minus 1/5), and the firm could still pay its fixed financial charges. Again, it is necessary to consider the impact of the lease obligations on this ratio because if you only consider the firm's public interest-bearing debt, the interest cost is about one-half million

---

[15]The net income figure used in the analysis is the operating income after taxes because, once again, it is important to exclude earnings and cash flows that are considered nonrecurring. The idea is to consider only those earnings that should be available in the future (that is, those from ongoing operations).

dollars and the coverage ratio exceeds 3,000 times. In contrast, if we recognize the lease obligations as debt and use the estimated interest expenses derived earlier, the coverage ratio would be computed as follows:

$$\text{Interest Coverage} = \frac{\text{Earnings Before Interest and Taxes} + \text{Estimated Lease Interest Expense}}{\text{Gross Interest Expense} + \text{Estimated Lease Interest Expense}}$$

Hence, the coverage ratios for Walgreens were:

$$2001: \quad \frac{886 + 537 + (3 + 461)}{3 + 461} = \frac{1,887}{464} = 4.07 \text{ times}$$

$$2000: \quad \frac{777 + 486 + 358}{358} = \frac{1,621}{358} = 4.53 \text{ times}$$

$$1999: \quad \frac{624 + 403 + 292}{292} = \frac{1,319}{292} = 4.52 \text{ times}$$

These interest coverage ratios show a substantially different picture than the coverage ratios that do not consider the impact of the lease obligations. Still, these coverage ratios show reasonable financial risk for a firm with very low business risk.

The trend of Walgreens' coverage ratios has been consistent with the overall trend in the proportion of debt ratios. The proportion of debt ratios and the earnings flow ratios do not always give consistent results because the proportion of debt ratios is not sensitive to changes in earnings or to changes in the interest rates on the debt. For example, if interest rates increase or if the firm replaces old debt with new debt that has a higher interest rate, no change would occur in the proportion of debt ratios, but the interest coverage ratio would decline. Also, the interest coverage ratio is sensitive to an increase or decrease in earnings. Therefore, the indications regarding the financial risk of the firm using balance sheet ratios and coverage ratios can differ. Given a difference between the two sets of financial risk ratios, the authors have a strong preference for the coverage ratios that reflect the ability of the firm to meet its financial obligations.

Cash Flow Ratios   As an alternative to these earnings coverage ratios, analysts employ several cash flow ratios that relate the cash flow available from operations to either interest expense, total fixed charges, or the face value of outstanding debt. The first set of cash-flow-to-interest-expense ratios or cash-flow-to-total-fixed-charge ratios is an extension of the earnings coverage ratios. The second set of cash flow ratios is unique because it relates to the *flow* of earnings plus noncash expenses to the *stock* of outstanding debt. These cash-flow-to-outstanding-debt ratios have been significant variables in numerous studies concerned with predicting bankruptcies and bond ratings.

Cash Flow Coverage Ratios   These ratios are an alternative to the earnings coverage ratio. The motivation is that a firm's earnings and its cash flow typically will differ substantially (these differences have been noted and will be considered further in a subsequent section). To have ratios that can be compared to similar values for other firms in the industry, the measure of cash flow used is the "cash flow from operating activities" figure contained in the cash flow statement. As such, it includes depreciation expense, deferred taxes, and the impact of all working capital changes. Again, it is appropriate to specify the ratio in terms of total interest charges including estimated leases interest expense as follows:

$$\text{Cash Flow Coverage of Fixed Financial Costs} = \frac{\begin{array}{c}\text{Net Cash Flow Provided by Operating Activities} \\ + \text{Interest Expense} + \text{Estimated Lease Interest Expense}\end{array}}{\text{Interest Expense} + \text{Estimated Lease Interest Expense}}$$

Notably, the "change in deferred tax" component can be either a negative or positive value (positive cash flow is when deferred taxes increased; negative cash flow is when deferred taxes declined). The depreciation expense item can be found in the cash flow statement. The "change in deferred tax" item can be derived from changes in the balance sheet, or the change is reported in the cash flow statement. If the two approaches do not give the same number, we use the values given in the cash flow statement since we are specifically interested in the cash flow effect. The estimated lease interest expense was derived earlier, based on footnote data. The cash flow coverage ratios for Walgreens were:

$$2001: \quad \frac{719 + 3 + 461}{3 + 461} = \frac{1,183}{464} = 2.55 \text{ times}$$

$$2000: \quad \frac{972 + 358}{358} = \frac{1,330}{358} = 3.72 \text{ times}$$

$$1999: \quad \frac{652 + 292}{292} = \frac{944}{292} = 3.23 \text{ times}$$

These coverage ratios are clearly not overpowering but are respectable for a firm with low business risk and should be compared to other firms in the industry after adjusting for leases.

Cash Flow/Long-Term Debt Ratio   Beyond relating cash flow to the required financing expense, several studies have used a ratio that relates cash flow to a firm's outstanding long-term debt as a predictor of bankruptcy and have found that this ratio was an excellent explanatory variable (these studies are listed in the references). The cash flow figure used in most of these studies was the traditional measure of cash flow (net income plus noncash expenses) that prevailed at the time the studies were done. In the current analysis, as shown earlier, we use the "cash flow from operating activities," which goes beyond the traditional measure and also considers the effect of working capital changes. This is a more conservative measure of cash flow because working capital changes typically have a negative impact on cash flow for a growing firm like Walgreens. Therefore, this ratio would be computed as:

$$\text{Cash Flow/Long-Term Debt} = \frac{\text{Cash Flow Provided by Operating Activities}}{\text{Book Value of Long-Term Debt} + \text{Present Value of Lease Obligations}}$$

Again, we computed these ratios assuming that deferred taxes and lease obligations were included as long-term debt as follows:

$$2001: \quad \frac{719}{615 + 6,710} = \frac{719}{7,325} = 9.82\%$$

$$2000: \quad \frac{972}{566 + 5,760} = \frac{972}{6,326} = 15.37\%$$

$$1999: \quad \frac{652}{499 + 4,480} = \frac{652}{4,979} = 13.09\%$$

Cash Flow/Total Debt Ratio Investors also should consider the relationship of cash flow to *total* interest-bearing debt to check that a firm has not had a significant increase in its short-term borrowing. For Walgreens, these ratios were:

$$\text{Cash Flow/Total Interest-Bearing Debt} = \frac{\text{Cash Flow Provided by Operating Activities}}{\text{Total Long-Term Debt} + \text{Current Interest-Bearing Liabilities}}$$

$$2001: \frac{719}{7,325+441} = \frac{719}{7,766} = 9.26\%$$

$$2000: \frac{972}{6,326+0} = \frac{972}{6,326} = 15.37\%$$

$$1999: \frac{652}{4,979+0} = \frac{652}{4,979} = 13.09\%$$

When you compare these ratios to those with only long-term debt (that includes deferred taxes), they reflect the firm's proportion of short-term debt due to short-term borrowing. In this analysis we exclude accounts payable and accrued expenses because they are non-interest-bearing. In the case of Walgreens, this eliminates almost all current liabilities. As before, it is important to compare these flow ratios with similar ratios for other companies in the industry and with the overall economy to gauge the firm's relative performance.

Alternative Measures of Cash Flow[16] As noted, many past studies that included a cash flow variable used the traditional measure of cash flow. The requirement that companies must prepare and report the statement of cash flows to stockholders has raised interest in other exact measures of cash flow. The first alternative is the *cash flow from operations,* which is taken directly from the statement of cash flows and is the one we have used. A second alternative measure is *free cash flow,* which is a modification of the cash flow from operations—that is, capital expenditures are also deducted. Some analysts are very conservative and also subtract dividends. The following table summarizes the values derived earlier in the chapter.

| | | | | FREE CASH FLOW | |
| | TRADITIONAL | CASH FLOW | NET CAPITAL | BEFORE | AFTER |
YEAR	CASH FLOW	FROM OPERATIONS	EXPENDITURES*	DIVIDENDS	DIVIDENDS
2001	1,045	719	1,193	(474)	(615)
2000	1,034	972	1,096	(124)	(259)
1999	820	652	654	(2)	(131)

*Net Capital Expenditures = Property and Equipment Additions minus Dispositions

As shown, Walgreens has strong and growing cash flow from operations after considering working capital requirements, but the firm experiences small or negative free cash flow because of substantial capital expenditures related to growth.

External Liquidity Risk

External Liquidity Defined In Chapter 4, we discussed *external market liquidity* as the ability to buy or sell an asset quickly with little price change from a prior transaction assuming no new information. AT&T and IBM are examples of liquid common stocks because you can sell them quickly with little price change from the prior trade. You might be able to sell an illiquid

---

[16]A list of studies in which ratios or cash flow variables are used to predict bankruptcies or bond ratings is included in the reference section.

stock quickly, but the price would be significantly different from the prior price. Alternatively, the broker might be able to get a specified price but could take several days doing so.

Determinants of Market Liquidity   As an investor, you should know the liquidity characteristics of the securities you currently own or may buy because liquidity can be important if you want to change the composition of your portfolio. Although the major determinants of market liquidity are reflected in market trading data, several internal corporate variables are good proxies for these market variables. The most important determinant of external market liquidity is the number of shares or dollar value of shares traded (the dollar value adjusts for different price levels). More trading activity indicates a greater probability that you can find someone to take the other side of a desired transaction.

A measure that is usually available is **trading turnover** (the percentage of outstanding shares traded during a period of time), which indicates relative trading activity. During calendar year 2001, about 705 million Walgreens shares were traded, which indicates turnover of approximately 70 percent (705 million/1,020 million).[17] This compares with the average turnover of the NYSE of about 68 percent.

Another measure of market liquidity is the bid-ask spread (a smaller spread indicates greater liquidity). In addition, there are certain internal corporate variables that correlate highly with these market trading variables:

1. Total market value of outstanding securities (number of common shares outstanding times the market price per share)
2. Number of security owners

Numerous studies have shown that the main determinant of the bid-ask spread (besides price) is the dollar value of trading.[18] In turn, the value of trading correlates highly with the market value of the outstanding securities and the number of security holders. This relationship holds because, with more shares outstanding, there will be more stockholders to buy or sell at any time for a variety of purposes. Numerous buyers and sellers provide liquidity.

You can estimate the market value of Walgreens' outstanding stock as the average number of shares outstanding during the year (adjusted for stock splits) times the average market price for the year (equal to the high price plus the low price divided by two) as follows:[19]

$$2001: 1{,}029 \times [(45 + 28)/2] = \$37.56 \text{ Billion}$$
$$2000: 1{,}017 \times [(46 + 23)/2] = \$35.09 \text{ Billion}$$
$$1999: 1{,}010 \times [(33 + 23)/2] = \$28.28 \text{ Billion}$$

These market values would place Walgreens in the large-capitalization category, which usually begins at about \$6 billion. Walgreens stockholders number 88,000, including more than 650 institutions that own approximately 56 percent of the outstanding stock. These large values for market value, the number of stockholders and institutional holders, along with the high trading turnover indicate a highly liquid market in the common stock of Walgreens. That is, Walgreens has extremely low external liquidity risk.

---

[17]An excellent source of information on shares traded during the calendar year for stocks on the NYSE, the AMEX, and the Nasdaq National Market System is the "Year-End Review" section of *The Wall Street Journal,* which is published on the first business day of the new year—for example, data for calendar 2001 were in the review published January 2, 2002.

[18]Studies on this topic were discussed in Chapter 4.

[19]These values are for Walgreens' fiscal year. Stock prices are rounded to the nearest whole dollar.

ANALYSIS OF GROWTH POTENTIAL

Importance of Growth Potential

The analysis of **sustainable growth potential** examines ratios that indicate how fast a firm should grow. Analysis of a firm's growth potential is important for both lenders and owners. Owners know that the value of the firm depends on its future growth in earnings, cash flow, and dividends. In the following chapter, we discuss various valuation models that determine the value of the firm based on your required rate of return for the stock and the expected growth rate of the firm's alternative cash flows.

Creditors also are interested in a firm's growth potential because the firm's future success is the major determinant of its ability to pay obligations, and the firm's future success is influenced by its growth. Some financial ratios used in credit analysis measure the book value of a firm's assets relative to its financial obligations, assuming the firm can sell these assets to pay off the loan in case of default. Selling assets in a forced liquidation will typically yield only about 10 to 15 cents on the dollar. Currently, it is widely recognized that the more relevant analysis is the ability of the firm to pay off its obligations as an ongoing enterprise, and its growth potential indicates its future status as an ongoing enterprise. This analysis is also relevant if you are interested in changes of bond ratings.

Determinants of Growth

The growth of business, like the growth of any economic entity, including the aggregate economy, depends on

1. the amount of resources retained and reinvested in the entity, and
2. the rate of return earned on the resources retained and reinvested.

The greater the proportion of earnings that a firm reinvests, the greater its potential for growth. Alternatively, for a given level of reinvestment, a firm will grow faster if it earns a higher rate of return on the resources reinvested. Therefore, the growth of equity earnings is a function of two variables: (1) the percentage of net earnings retained and reinvested into the business (the firm's retention rate) and (2) the rate of return earned on the firm's equity capital (the firm's ROE) because when earnings are retained they become part of the firm's equity (i.e., its retained earnings). This can be summarized as follows:

$$g = \text{Percentage of Earnings Retained} \times \text{Return on Equity}$$
$$= \text{RR} \times \text{ROE}$$

where:

g = **potential (i.e., sustainable) growth rate**
RR = **the retention rate of earnings**
ROE = **the firm's return on equity**

The retention rate is a decision by the board of directors based on the investment opportunities available to the firm. Theory suggests that the firm should retain earnings and reinvest them as long as the expected rate of return on the investment exceeds the firm's cost of capital.

As discussed earlier in the chapter, using the DuPont system, the firm's ROE is a function of three components:

➤ Net profit margin
➤ Total asset turnover
➤ Financial leverage (total assets/equity)

Therefore, a firm can increase its ROE by increasing its profit margin, by becoming more efficient (increasing its total asset turnover), or by increasing its financial leverage and financial risk.

As discussed, you should examine and estimate each of these components when estimating the ROE for a firm.

An analysis of the sustainable growth potential for Walgreens begins with the retention rate (RR):

$$\text{Retention Rate} = 1 - \frac{\text{Dividends Declared}}{\text{Operating Income After Taxes}}$$

Walgreens' RR figures were:

$$2001: 1 - \frac{0.14}{0.86} = 0.84$$

$$2000: 1 - \frac{0.14}{0.76} = 0.82$$

$$1999: 1 - \frac{0.13}{0.62} = 0.79$$

The historical results shown in Exhibit 10.8 indicate that the retention rate for Walgreens has been relatively stable during the 20-year period at an average rate in excess of 70 percent.

Exhibit 10.6 contains the three components of ROE for the period 1982–2001. Exhibit 10.8 contains the two factors that determine a firm's growth potential and the implied growth rate during

EXHIBIT 10.8   *WALGREEN CO. COMPONENTS OF GROWTH AND THE IMPLIED SUSTAINABLE GROWTH RATE*

YEAR	1 RETENTION RATE	2 RETURN ON EQUITY[a]	3[b] SUSTAINABLE GROWTH RATE
1982	0.72	18.73	13.49
1983	0.74	19.84	14.68
1984	0.74	20.60	15.24
1985	0.71	19.58	13.90
1986	0.70	18.64	13.05
1987	0.68	16.63	11.31
1988	0.71	18.12	12.87
1989	0.73	18.74	13.68
1990	0.72	18.42	13.26
1991	0.71	18.04	12.81
1992	0.71	17.90	12.71
1993	0.67	16.07	10.77
1994	0.70	17.91	12.54
1995	0.69	17.89	12.34
1996	0.71	18.19	12.91
1997	0.73	18.35	13.40
1998	0.75	17.92	13.44
1999	0.79	17.91	14.13
2000	0.82	18.35	15.09
2001	0.84	17.07	14.29

[a]From Exhibit 10.6.

[b]Column 3 is equal to Column 1 times Column 2.

the past 20 years. Overall, Walgreens experienced a slight decline in its growth potential during the early 1990s, but since 1995 the firm increased its potential growth rate to over 15 percent prior to a small decline in 2001.

Exhibit 10.8 reinforces the importance of the firm's ROE. Walgreens' retention rate was quite stable throughout the period with an increase during the last six years. Even with this, it has been the firm's ROE that has mainly determined its sustainable growth rate. This analysis indicates that the important consideration is *the long-run outlook for the components of sustainable growth.* As an investor, you need to *project* changes in each of the components of ROE and employ these projections to estimate an ROE to use in the growth model along with an estimate of the firm's long-run retention rate. We will come back to these concepts on numerous occasions when valuing the market, alternative industries, and individual firms. This detailed analysis of ROE is extremely important for growth companies where the ROEs are notably above average for the economy and vulnerable to competition.

COMPARATIVE ANALYSIS OF RATIOS

We have discussed the importance of comparative analysis, but so far we have concentrated on the selection and computation of specific ratios. Exhibit 10.9 contains most of the ratios discussed for Walgreens, the retail drug store industry (as derived from the S&P *Analysts Handbook*), and the S&P Industrials Index. The three-year comparison should provide some insights, although you typically would want to examine data for a 5-to 10-year period. It is necessary to do the comparison for the period 1998 to 2000 because industry and market data from Standard and Poors were not available for 2001 until late 2002.

Internal Liquidity   The three basic ratios (current ratio, quick ratio, and cash ratio) provided mixed results regarding liquidity for Walgreens relative to the industry and market. The current ratio is above the industry and market. The firm's receivables turnover has declined due to a high percentage of the pharmacy sales being paid by a third party. Still, its collection period is substantially less than the S&P Industrials and the retail drug store industry (9 days versus 12 and 78 in 2000). Because the collection period has been fairly steady, the difference is because of the firm's basic credit policy.

Overall, the comparisons indicate reasonably strong internal liquidity. An additional positive factor related to liquidity is the firm's ability to sell high-grade commercial paper and the existence of several major bank credit lines.

Operating Performance   This segment of the analysis considers efficiency ratios (turnovers) and profitability ratios. Given the nature of the analysis, the major comparison is relative to the industry. Walgreens turnover ratios were consistently substantially above those of the retail drug store (RDS) industry.

The comparison of profitability from sales was mixed. Operating profit margins were consistently below the industry, but net margins beat the industry performance. The lower operating profit margin is due to the higher growth rate of new stores for Walgreens relative to the competition. The fact is, new stores require 18 to 24 months to reach the firm's "normal" profit rate.

The profit performance related to invested capital was historically strong. The return on total capital (including capitalized leases) for Walgreens was above both the S&P Industrials and the RDS industry in all three years. Walgreens likewise consistently attained higher ROEs than its industry and the market.

Risk Analysis   Walgreens' financial risk ratios, measured in terms of proportion of debt, were consistently much higher than its industry and the market when both deferred taxes and capitalized leases were

	2000			1999			1998		
	WALGREENS[a]	DRUGSTORES	S&P INDUSTRIALS	WALGREENS	DRUGSTORES	S&P INDUSTRIALS	WALGREENS	DRUGSTORES	S&P INDUSTRIALS
Internal Liquidity									
Current ratio	1.54	1.26	1.02	1.67	1.18	1.07	1.66	1.28	1.37
Quick ratio	0.27	0.26	0.72	0.33	0.24	0.75	0.33	0.26	0.93
Cash ratio	0.01	0.04	0.18	0.07	0.05	0.18	0.09	0.05	0.20
Receivables turnover	38.52	29.86	4.70	41.50	28.35	4.59	40.86	31.89	4.43
Average collection period	9.46	12.22	77.66	8.80	12.87	79.56	8.93	11.44	82.41
Working capital/sales	0.06	0.04	0.01	0.07	0.03	0.03	0.07	0.05	0.12
Operation Performance									
Total asset turnover	3.26	2.92	0.84	3.30	2.22	0.88	3.36	2.24	0.91
Inventory turnover (sales)[b]	8.01	6.59	12.09	7.95	6.17	11.17	8.14	5.62	10.31
Working capital turnover	17.01	27.95	30.50	13.74	30.21	33.33	14.68	19.06	8.33
Net fixed asset turnover	7.04	7.98	3.10	7.53	7.58	2.81	7.85	7.57	2.58
Equity turnover	5.49	5.27	2.72	5.63	5.52	3.06	5.86	5.34	3.15
Profitability									
Gross profit margin	27.07	—	—	27.25	—	—	27.22	—	—
Operating profit margin	5.77	6.18	16.42	5.69	6.82	15.92	5.46	7.00	16.70
Net profit margin	3.66	3.00	6.32	3.50	2.70	6.27	3.34	2.58	5.14
Return on total capital	10.03	7.75	7.10	8.86	7.10	7.17	8.62	7.11	6.40
Return on owner's equity	20.13	16.05	17.14	19.71	14.90	19.19	19.56	13.77	16.21
Financial Risk									
Debt/equity ratio	149.41	7.96	100.87	135.73	46.44	116.98	140.51	49.25	129.09
Long-term debt/long-term capital	59.90	7.38	50.22	57.58	34.11	71.66	58.42	35.77	76.07
Total debt/total capital[c]	67.09	48.38	67.39	65.63	58.70	68.39	66.21	58.52	62.29
Interest coverage	4.53	28.57	6.26	6.82	9.79	6.05	6.77	8.06	5.10
Cash flow/long-term debt	15.37	295.56	38.99	17.34	58.55	51.70	16.91	46.45	44.16
Cash flow/total debt[c]	15.36	25.11	12.77	12.33	14.88	14.57	12.31	12.41	13.61
Growth Analysis[d]									
Retention rate	0.82	0.64	0.69	0.79	0.75	0.65	0.75	0.71	0.55
Return on equity	18.35	17.22	16.22	17.91	14.08	17.46	17.93	13.12	16.26
Total asset turnover	2.99	2.92	0.84	3.02	2.09	0.84	3.12	2.04	0.85
Total assets/equity	1.67	1.94	3.07	1.70	2.49	3.32	1.72	2.49	3.70
Net profit margin	3.66	3.00	6.32	3.50	2.70	6.27	3.34	2.58	5.14
Sustainable growth rate	15.09	11.02	11.19	14.13	10.57	11.42	13.45	9.32	8.94

[a]Ratios for Walgreens are consistent with calculations in the chapter.

[b]Computed using sales since cost of sales not available for industry and S&P Industrials.

[c]Total debt equal to total assets minus (common stock plus retained earnings).

[d]Calculated using year-end data.

included as long-term debt for Walgreens, because it was not possible to do a comparable adjustment for the S&P Industrials or the RDS industry. The lack of such an adjustment would have a significant impact on the industry results. Similarly, the financial risk flow ratios for Walgreens were always below the market and its industry. These comparisons indicate that Walgreens has a reasonable amount of financial risk, but it is not a major concern because the firm has very low business risk based upon a high stable growth rate in sales and operating profit. While there are no specific comparative ratios available for both business and external liquidity risk, it is noteworthy that in both cases the prior analysis concluded that Walgreens had very low business and liquidity risk.

Growth Analysis   Walgreens has generally maintained a sustainable growth rate above its industry and the aggregate market based upon both a higher ROE and a consistently higher retention rate.

In sum, Walgreens has adequate liquidity; a good operating record, including a consistent growth record that implies low business risk; "reasonable" financial risk, even when you consider the leases on stores; and above-average growth performance. Your success as an investor depends on how well you use these historical numbers to derive meaningful *estimates* of future performance for use in a valuation model. Remember the point made in the efficient market chapter—everybody is generally aware of the valuation models, so it is the individual who can provide the best *estimates* of relevant valuation variables who will experience superior risk-adjusted performance.

ANALYSIS OF NON-U.S. FINANCIAL STATEMENTS

As noted previously, your portfolio should encompass other economies and markets, numerous global industries, and many foreign firms in these global industries. You should recognize, however, that non-U.S. financial statements will differ widely from those in this chapter and be different from what you will see in a typical accounting course because accounting conventions differ substantially among countries. While it is beyond the scope of this book to discuss alternative accounting conventions in detail, we encourage the reader to examine the references at the end of the chapter on international accounting topics.

THE QUALITY OF FINANCIAL STATEMENTS

Analysts sometimes speak of the quality of a firm's earnings, or the quality of a firm's balance sheet. In general, **quality financial statements** are a good reflection of reality; accounting tricks and one-time charges are not used to make the firm appear stronger than it really is. Some factors that lead to lower-quality financial statements were mentioned previously when we discussed ratio analysis. Other quality influences are discussed in the following sections.[20]

Balance Sheet   A high-quality balance sheet typically has a conservative use of debt and leverage. Therefore, the potential of experiencing financial distress resulting from the need to service debt is quite low. Little use of debt also implies the firm has unused borrowing capacity; should an attractive investment opportunity arise, the firm can draw on that unused capacity to invest wisely for the shareholders' benefit.

---

[20]For additional discussion, see K. G. Palepu, Victor L. Bernard, and P. M. Healy, *Business Analysis and Valuation* (Cincinnati, Ohio: South-Western Publishing Co., 1996), Chapter 3.

A quality balance sheet contains assets with a market value greater than their book value. The capacity of management and the existence of intangible assets, such as goodwill, trademarks, or patents, will make the market value of the firm's assets exceed their book values. In general, as a result of inflation and historical cost accounting, we might expect the market value of assets to exceed their book values. Some situations in which the opposite may occur include the use of outdated, technologically inferior assets; unwanted or out-of-fashion inventory; and the presence of nonperforming assets on the firm's books (an example would be a bank that has not written off nonperforming loans).

The presence of off-balance-sheet liabilities also harms the quality of a balance sheet. Such liabilities may include joint ventures and loan commitments or guarantees to subsidiaries.[21]

Income Statement   High-quality earnings are *repeatable* earnings. For example, they arise from sales to customers who are expected to do repeat business with the firm and from costs that are not artificially low as a result of unusual or temporary price reductions. One-time and nonrecurring items, such as accounting changes, mergers, and asset sales, should be ignored when examining earnings. Unexpected exchange rate fluctuations that raise revenues or reduce costs should also be viewed as nonrecurring.

High-quality earnings result from the use of conservative accounting principles that do not result in overstated revenues and understated costs. The closer the earnings are to cash, the higher the quality of the income statement. Suppose a firm sells furniture "on time" by allowing customers to make monthly payments. A higher-quality income statement will recognize revenue using the "installment" principle; that is, as the cash is collected each month, in turn, annual sales will reflect only the cash collected from sales during the year. A lower-quality income statement will recognize 100 percent of the revenue from a sale at the time of sale, even though payments may stretch well into the next year.[22]

Footnotes   A word to the wise—READ THE FOOTNOTES! The purpose of the footnotes (that have come to include three or more pages in most annual reports) is to provide information on how the firm handles balance sheet and income items. While the footnotes may not reveal everything you should know (e.g., Enron), if you do not read them you cannot hope to be informed.

THE VALUE OF FINANCIAL STATEMENT ANALYSIS

Financial statements, by their nature, are backward-looking. They report the firm's assets, liabilities, and equity as of a certain (past) date; they report a firm's revenues, expenses, or cash flows over some (past) time period. An efficient capital market will have already incorporated this past information into security prices; so it may seem, at first glance, that the analysis of a firm's financial statements and ratios is a waste of the analyst's time.

The fact is, the opposite is true. Analysis of financial statements allows the analyst to gain knowledge of a firm's operating and financial strategy and structure. This, in turn, assists the analyst in determining the effect of *future* events on the firm's cash flows. Likely future scenarios can be analyzed and a knowledge of the firm's operating and financial leverage can help the analyst gauge the risk and expected cash flows of the firm. Combining knowledge of the firm's strategy, operating and financial leverage, and possible macro- and microeconomic scenarios is

---

[21]For detailed analysis of these items, see Clyde P. Stickney, *Financial Reporting and Statement Analysis,* 3d ed. (Fort Worth, Tex.: Dryden, 1996), Chapter 6.

[22]For detailed analysis of income items, see Stickney, *Financial Reporting and Statement Analysis,* 3d ed., Chapter 5.

necessary to determine an appropriate market price for the firm's stock. Combining what is known about the firm, based on the analysis of historical data, with potential future scenarios allows analysts to evaluate the risks facing the firm and then to develop an expected return forecast based on these risks. The final outcome of the process, as future chapters will detail, is a determination of the firm's current value based on expected cash flows and an appropriate discount rate that is compared to the firm's security price. The point is, the detailed analysis of the historical results will help you estimate the required discount rate and the expected cash flows and, thus, derive a superior valuation of the firm.

SPECIFIC USES OF FINANCIAL RATIOS

We have discussed the role of financial ratios in measuring firm performance and risk. Financial ratios have been used in four major areas in investments: (1) stock valuation, (2) the identification of internal corporate variables that affect a stock's systematic risk (beta), (3) assigning credit quality ratings on bonds, and (4) predicting insolvency (bankruptcy) of firms. In this section, we discuss how ratios have been used in each of these four areas and the specific ratios found to be most useful.

Stock Valuation Models

As will be discussed in the following chapter, most valuation models attempt to derive a value based upon one of several cash flow models or relative valuation ratios for a stock. As we will discuss, all the valuation models are influenced by the expected growth rate of earnings, cash flows, or dividends and the required rate of return on the stock. Clearly, financial ratios can help in estimating these critical inputs. The estimate of the growth rate for earnings, cash flow, or dividends employs the ratios discussed in the potential growth rate section—the retention rate and the return on investments (either equity or total assets).

When estimating the required rate of return on an investment (i.e., either the cost of equity, k, or the weighted average cost of capital, WACC), you will recall from Chapter 1 that these estimates depend on the risk premium for the security, which is a function of business risk, financial risk, and liquidity risk. Business risk typically is measured in terms of earnings variability; financial risk is identified by either the debt proportion ratios or the earnings or cash flow ratios; insights regarding a stock's liquidity risk can be derived from the external liquidity measures discussed.

The typical empirical valuation model has examined a cross section of companies and has used a multivariate statistical model that relates one of the relative valuation ratios (i.e., P/E; P/sales; P/book value) for the sample firms to some of the following corporate variables (the averages generally consider the past 5 or 10 years):[23]

Financial Ratios
1. Average debt/equity
2. Average interest coverage
3. Average dividend payout
4. Average return on equity
5. Average retention rate
6. Average market price to book value
7. Average market price to cash flow
8. Average market price to sales

---

[23]A list of studies in this area appears in the reference section at the end of the chapter.

Variability Measures
1. Coefficient of variation of operating earnings
2. Coefficient of variation of sales
3. Coefficient of variation of net income
4. Systematic risk (beta)

Nonratio Variables
1. Average growth rate of sales and earnings
2. Average growth rate of cash flow

Estimating Systematic Risk

As discussed in Chapter 8, the capital asset pricing model (CAPM) asserts that the relevant risk variable for an asset should be its systematic risk, which is its beta coefficient related to the market portfolio of all risky assets. In efficient markets, a relationship should exist between internal corporate risk variables and market-determined risk variables, such as beta. Numerous studies have tested the relationship between a stock's systematic risk (beta) and the firm's internal corporate variables intended to reflect business risk and financial risk.[24] Some of the significant variables (usually five-year averages) included were:

Financial Ratios
1. Dividend payouts
2. Total debt/total assets
3. Cash flow/total debt
4. Fixed charge (interest) coverage
5. Working capital/total assets
6. Current ratio

Variability Measures
1. Variance of operating earnings
2. Coefficient of variation of operating earnings
3. Coefficient of variation of operating profit margins
4. Operating earnings beta (company earnings related to aggregate earnings)

Nonratio Variables
1. Asset size of firm
2. Market value of stock outstanding

Estimating the Credit Ratings on Bonds

As will be discussed in the initial bond chapter, three financial service firms assign credit ratings to bonds on the basis of the issuing company's ability to meet all its obligations related to the bond. An AAA or Aaa rating indicates high quality and almost no chance of default, whereas a C rating indicates the bond is already in default. Studies have used financial ratios to predict the credit rating to be assigned to a bond.[25] The major financial variables considered in these studies (again, typically five-year averages) were as follows:

Financial Ratios
1. Long-term debt/total assets
2. Total debt/total capital
3. Net income plus depreciation (cash flow)/long-term senior debt
4. Cash flow/total debt
5. Earnings before interest and taxes (EBIT)/interest expense (fixed charge coverage)
6. Cash flow from operations plus interest/interest expense

---

[24]A list of studies in this area appears in the reference section at the end of the chapter.

[25]A list of studies in this area appears in the reference section at the end of the chapter.

   7. Market value of stock/par value of bonds
   8. Net operating profit/sales
   9. Net income/owners' equity (ROE)
  10. Net income plus interest/total assets
  11. Working capital/sales
  12. Sales/owners' equity (equity turnover)

Variability Measures
   1. Coefficient of variation (CV) of sales
   2. Coefficient of variation of operating earnings
   3. Coefficient of variation of net earnings
   4. Coefficient of variation of return on assets

Nonratio Variables
   1. Subordination of the bond issue
   2. Size of the firm (total assets)
   3. Issue size
   4. Par value of all publicly traded bonds of the firm

Predicting Insolvency (Bankruptcy)

Analysts have always been interested in using financial ratios to identify which firms might default on a loan or declare bankruptcy. Several studies have attempted to identify a set of ratios for this purpose.[26] The typical study examines a sample of firms that have declared bankruptcy against a matched sample of firms in the same industry and of comparable size that have not failed. The analysis involves examining a number of financial ratios or cash flow variables expected to reflect declining liquidity for several years (usually five years) prior to the declaration of bankruptcy. The goal is to determine which ratios or set of ratios provides the best predictions of bankruptcy—that is, correctly predicts that the firm will be in the bankrupt or nonbankrupt group. The models have typically been able to properly classify more than 80 percent of the firms one year prior to failure, and some achieve high classification results three to five years before failure. The financial ratios typically included in successful models were:[27]

Financial Ratios
   1. Cash flow/total debt
   2. Cash flow/long-term debt
   3. Sales/total assets*
   4. Net income/total assets
   5. EBIT/total assets*
   6. Total debt/total assets
   7. Market value of stock/book value of debt*
   8. Working capital/total assets*
   9. Retained earnings/total assets*
  10. Current ratio
  11. Cash/current liabilities
  12. Working capital/sales

---

[26]A list of studies on this topic appears in the reference section at the end of the chapter.

[27]In addition to the several studies that have used financial ratios to predict bond ratings and failures, other studies have used cash flow variables or a combination of financial ratios and cash flow variables for these predictions, and the results have been quite successful. These studies are listed in the reference section at the end of the chapter. The five ratios designated by an asterisk (*) are the ratios used in the well-known Altman Z-score model following. Edward I. Altman, "Financial Ratios, Discriminant Analysis and the Prediction of Corporate Bankruptcy," *Journal of Finance* 23, no. 4 (September 1968): 589–609.

Limitations of Financial Ratios

We must reinforce the earlier point that you should always consider *relative* financial ratios. In addition, you should be aware of other questions and limitations of financial ratios:

1. Are alternative firms' accounting treatments comparable? As you know from prior accounting courses, there are several generally accepted methods of treating various accounting items, and the alternatives can cause a difference in results for the same event. Therefore, you should check on the accounting treatment of significant items and adjust the values for major differences. This becomes a critical consideration when dealing with non-U.S. firms.
2. How homogeneous is the firm? Many companies have several divisions that operate in different industries. This may make it difficult to derive comparable industry ratios.
3. Are the implied results consistent? It is important to develop a total profile of the firm and not depend on only one set of ratios (for example, internal liquidity ratios). As an example, a firm may be having short-term liquidity problems but be very profitable, and the profitability will eventually alleviate the short-run liquidity problems.
4. Is the ratio within a reasonable range for the industry? As noted on several occasions, you typically want to consider a *range* of appropriate values for the ratio because a value that is either too high or too low for the industry can be a cause for concern.

The Internet *Investments Online*

Many publicly traded companies have Web sites which, among other pieces of information, contain financial information. Sometimes complete copies of the firm's annual report and SEC filings are on their home page. Since the focus of this chapter has been Walgreen's financial statements, here are some relevant sites:

http://www.walgreens.com Walgreen's home page, with financial information available through links from this page. At least three of Walgreen's competitors have Web sites featuring financial information. These include:

http://www.cvs.com The home page for CVS Pharmacy.

http://www.riteaid.com The Rite Aid Corporation's home page.

http://www.longs.com The Web site for Longs Drug Stores.

http://www.duanereade.com Duane Reade's home page.

Commercially oriented and government-sponsored databases are also available through the Web:

http://www.sec.gov The Web home page for the Securities and Exchange Commission allows entrance into the SEC's EDGAR (electronic data gathering, analysis, and retrieval) database. Most firm's SEC filings are accessible through EDGAR, including filings for executive compensation, 10-K, and 10-Q forms.

http://www.hoovers.com Hoovers Online is a commercial source of company-specific information, including financial statements and stock performance. Some data are available for free, including a company profile, news, stock price and chart of recent stock price performance. It contains links to a number of sources, including the firm's annual report, SEC filings, and earnings per share estimates by First Call.

http://www.dnb.com Dun & Bradstreet is a well-known gatherer of financial information. Corporations use its business credit reporting services. D&B publishes industry average financial ratios are useful in equity and fixed income analysis.

Summary

- The overall purpose of financial statement analysis is to help you make decisions on investing in a firm's bonds or stocks. Financial ratios should be examined relative to the economy, the firm's industry, the firm's main competitors, and the firm's past relative ratios.
- The specific ratios can be divided into four categories, depending on the purpose of the analysis: internal liquidity, operating performance, risk analysis, and growth analysis.

- When analyzing the financial statements for non-U.S. firms, you must consider differences in format and in accounting principles that cause different values for specific ratios in alternative countries.
- An important consideration for domestic or international financial statements is to READ THE FOOTNOTES to ensure that you understand how the GAAP was applied and the accounting philosophy of the firm.
- Four major uses of financial ratios are (1) stock valuations, (2) the identification of variables affecting a stock's systematic risk (beta), (3) assigning credit quality ratings on bonds, and (4) predicting insolvency (bankruptcy).
- A final caveat: You can envision a large number of potential financial ratios through which to examine almost every possible relationship. The trick is not to come up with more ratios but to attempt to limit the number of ratios so you can examine them in a meaningful way. This entails an analysis of the ratios over time relative to the economy, the industry, or the past. Any additional effort should be spent on deriving better comparisons for a limited number of ratios that provide insights into the questions of interest to you (for example, the firm's future operating performance or its business and financial risk).

Questions
1. Discuss briefly two decisions that require the analysis of financial statements.
2. Why do analysts use financial ratios rather than the absolute numbers? Give an example.
3. Besides comparing a company's performance to its total industry, discuss what other comparisons should be considered *within* the industry.
4. How might a jewelry store and a grocery store differ in terms of asset turnover and profit margin? Would you expect their return on total assets to differ assuming equal business risk? Discuss.
5. Describe the components of business risk, and discuss how the components affect the variability of operating earnings.
6. Would you expect a steel company or a retail food chain to have greater business risk? Discuss this expectation in terms of the components of business risk.
7. When examining a firm's financial structure, would you be concerned with the firm's business risk? Why or why not?
8. Give an example of how a cash flow ratio might differ from a proportion of debt ratio. Assuming these ratios differ for a firm (for example, the cash flow ratios indicate high financial risk, while the proportions of debt ratio indicates low risk), which ratios would you follow? Justify your choice.
9. Why is the analysis of growth potential important to the common stockholder? Why is it important to the debt investor?
10. Discuss the general factors that determine the rate of growth of *any* economic unit.
11. A firm is earning 24 percent on equity and has low business and financial risk. Discuss why you would expect it to have a high or low retention rate.
12. The Orange Company earned 18 percent on equity, whereas the Blue Company earned only 14 percent on equity. Does this mean that Orange will grow faster than Blue? Explain.
13. In terms of the factors that determine market liquidity, why do investors consider real estate to be a relatively illiquid asset?
14. Discuss some internal company factors that would indicate a firm's market liquidity.
15. Select one of the limitations of ratio analysis and indicate why you believe it is a major limitation.

Problems
1. The Shamrock Vegetable Company has the following results:

Net sales	$6,000,000
Net total assets	4,000,000
Depreciation	160,000
Net income	400,000
Long-term debt	2,000,000
Equity	1,160,000
Dividends	160,000

a. Compute Shamrock's ROE directly. Confirm this using the three Du Pont components.
b. Using the ROE computed in Part a, what is the expected sustainable growth rate for Shamrock?
c. Assuming the firm's net profit margin went to 0.04, what would happen to Shamrock's ROE?
d. Using the ROE in Part c, what is the expected sustainable growth rate? What if dividends were only $40,000?

2. Three companies have the following results during the recent period.

	K	L	M
Net profit margin	.04	.06	.10
Total asset turnover	2.20	2.00	1.40
Total assets/equity	2.40	2.20	1.50

a. Derive for each its return on equity based on the three DuPont components.
b. Given the following earnings and dividends, compute the estimated sustainable growth rate for each firm.

	K	L	M
Earnings/share	2.75	3.00	4.50
Dividends/share	1.25	1.00	1.00

3. Given the following balance sheet, fill in the ratio values for 2003 and discuss how these results compare with both the industry average and Eddies' past performance.

EDDIES ENTERPRISES CONSOLIDATED BALANCE SHEET: YEARS ENDED DECEMBER 31, 2002 AND 2003

ASSETS (DOLLARS IN THOUSANDS)		
	2003	2002
Cash	$ 100	$ 90
Receivables	220	170
Inventories	330	230
Total current assets	650	490
Property, plant, and equipment	1,850	1,650
Depreciation	350	225
Net properties	1,500	1,425
Intangibles	150	150
Total assets	2,300	2,065

LIABILITIES AND SHAREHOLDERS' EQUITY		
	2003	2002
Accounts payable	$ 85	$ 105
Short-term bank notes	125	110
Current portion of long-term debt	75	—
Accruals	65	85
Total current liabilities	350	300
Long-term debt	625	540
Deferred taxes	100	80
Preferred stock (10%, $100 par)	150	150
Common stock ($2 par, 100,000 issued)	200	200
Additional paid-in capital	325	325
Retained earnings	550	470
Common shareholders' equity	1,075	995
Total liabilities and shareholders' equity	2,300	2,065

EDDIES ENTERPRISES CONSOLIDATED STATEMENT OF INCOME:
YEARS ENDED DECEMBER 31, 2002 AND 2003

(DOLLARS IN THOUSANDS)

	2003	2002
Net sales	$3,500	$2,990
Cost of goods sold	2,135	1,823
Selling, general, and administrative expenses	1,107	974
Operating profit	258	193
Net interest expense	62	54
Income from operations	195	139
Income taxes	66	47
Net income	129	91
Preferred dividends	15	15
Net income available for common shares	114	76
Dividends declared	40	30

	Eddies (2003)	Eddies' Average	Industry Average
Current ratio	_____	2.00	2.20
Quick ratio	_____	1.00	1.10
Receivable turnover	_____	18.00	18.00
Average collection period	_____	20.00	21.00
Total asset turnover	_____	1.50	1.40
Inventory turnover	_____	11.00	12.50
Fixed-asset turnover	_____	2.50	2.40
Equity turnover	_____	3.20	3.00
Gross profit margin	_____	.40	.35
Operating profit margin	_____	8.00	7.50
Return on capital	_____	.107	.120
Return on equity	_____	.118	.126
Return on common equity	_____	.128	.135
Debt/equity ratio	_____	.60	.50
Debt/total capital ratio	_____	.40	.37
Interest coverage	_____	4.00	4.50
Fixed charge coverage	_____	3.00	4.00
Cash flow/long-term debt	_____	.40	.45
Cash flow/total debt	_____	.25	.30
Retention rate	_____	.35	.40

4. *CFA Examination Level I (adapted)*
   [Question 4 is composed of two parts, for a total of 20 minutes.]
   The DuPont formula defines the net return on shareholders' equity as a function of the following components:

   - Operating margin
   - Asset turnover
   - Interest burden
   - Financial leverage
   - Income tax rate

   Using *only* the data in the following table:
   a. Calculate *each* of the *five* components listed for 1999 *and* 2003, and calculate the return on equity (ROE) for 1999 *and* 2003, using all of the *five* components. Show calculations. [15 minutes]

b. Briefly discuss the impact of the changes in asset turnover *and* financial leverage on the change in ROE from 1999 to 2003. [5 minutes]

	1999	2003
Income Statement Data		
Revenues	$542	$979
Operating income	38	76
Depreciation and amortization	3	9
Interest expense	3	0
Pretax income	32	67
Income taxes	13	37
Net income after tax	19	30
Balance Sheet Data		
Fixed assets	$ 41	$ 70
Total assets	245	291
Working capital	123	157
Total debt	16	0
Total shareholders' equity	159	220

References

General

Beaver, William H. *Financial Reporting: An Accounting Revolution.* Englewood Cliffs, N.J.: Prentice-Hall, 1989.

Bernstein, Leopold A., and John J. Wild. *Financial Statement Analysis: Theory, Application, and Interpretation,* 6th ed. Homewood, Ill.: Irwin/McGraw-Hill, 1998.

Frecka, Thomas J., and Cheng F. Lee. "Generalized Financial Ratio Adjustment Processes and Their Implications." *Journal of Accounting Research* 27, no. 1 (Spring 1983).

Heckle, Kenneth S., and Joshua Livnat. *Cash Flow and Security Analysis,* 2d ed. Burr Ridge, Ill.: Business One Irwin, 1996.

Helfert, Erich A. *Techniques of Financial Analysis,* 10th ed. New York: McGraw-Hill, 2000.

Higgins, Robert C. *Analysis of Financial Management,* 5th ed. Chicago: Irwin, 1998.

Lev, Baruch, and S. Ramu Thiagarajan. "Fundamental Information Analysis." *Journal of Accounting Research* 37, no. 2 (Fall 1993).

White, Gerald I., Ashwinpaul Sondhi, and Dov Fried. *The Analysis and Use of Financial Statements,* 2d ed. New York: Wiley, 1998.

Analysis of International Financial Statements

Choi, Frederick D. S., Carol Ann Frost, and Gary Meek. *International Accounting.* Englewood Cliffs, N.J.: Prentice-Hall, 2000.

Evans, Thomas G., Martin E. Taylor, and Oscar Holzmann. *International Accounting and Reporting.* New York: Macmillan, 1985.

Iqbal, M. Zafar, *International Accounting: A Global Approach* (Cincinnati, OH: South-Western, 2002).

Rueschhoff, Norlin, and David Strupeck, "Equity Returns: Local GAAP versus US GAAP for Foreign Issuers from Developing Countries," *Journal of International Accounting* 33, no. 3 (Spring 2000).

Saudagaran, Shakrokh, *International Accounting: A User Perspective* (Cincinnati, OH: South-Western College Publishing, 2001).

Financial Ratios and Stock Valuations Models

Babcock, Guilford. "The Concept of Sustainable Growth." *Financial Analysts Journal* 26, no. 3 (May–June 1970).

Beaver, William, and Dale Morse. "What Determines Price-Earnings Ratios?" *Financial Analysts Journal* 34, no. 4 (July–August 1978).

Copeland, Tom, Tim Koller, and Jack Murrin. *Valuation: Measuring and Managing the Value of Companies,* 3d ed. New York: John Wiley & Co., 2000.

Damodaran, Aswath. *Damodaran on Valuation.* New York: John Wiley & Co., 1994.

Danielson, M. G., "A Simple Valuation Model and Growth Expectations," *Financial Analysts Journal* 54, no. 3 (May–June 1998).

Fairfield, Patricia M. "P/E, P/B and the Present Value of Future Dividends." *Financial Analysts Journal* 50, no. 4 (July–August 1994).

Farrell, James L. "The Dividend Discount Model: A Primer." *Financial Analysts Journal* 41, no. 6 (November–December 1985).

Hickman, Kent, and Glenn Petry. "A Comparison of Stock Price Predictions Using Court Accepted Formulas, Dividend Discount, and P/E Models." *Financial Management* (Summer 1990).

Kaplan, S. N., and R. S. Ruback. "The Valuation of Cash Flow Forecasts: An Empirical Analysis," *Journal of Finance* 50, no. 4 (September 1995).

Leibowitz, M. L., and S. Kogelman. "Inside the P/E Ratio: The Franchise Factor." *Financial Analysts Journal* 46, no. 6 (November–December 1990).

Palepu, Krishna G., Victor L. Bernard, and Paul M. Healy. *Business Analysis and Valuation.* Cincinnati, Ohio: South-Western Publishing Co., 1996.

Penman, S. H. "The Articulation of Price-Earnings Ratios and Market-to-Book Ratios and the Evaluation of Growth." *Journal of Accounting Research* 34, no. 2 (Spring 1996).

Wilcox, Jarrod W. "The P/B-ROE Valuation Model." *Financial Analysts Journal* 40, no. 1 (January–February 1984).

Financial Ratios and Systematic Risk (Beta)

Beaver, William H., Paul Kettler, and Myron Scholes. "The Association between Market-Determined and Accounting-Determined Risk Measures." *Accounting Review* 45, no. 4 (October 1970).

Gahlon, James M., and James A. Gentry. "On the Relationship between Systematic Risk and the Degrees of Operating and Financial Leverage." *Financial Management* 11, no. 2 (Summer 1982).

Mandelker, Gershon M., and S. Ghon Rhee. "The Impact of Degrees of Operating and Financial Leverage on the Systematic Risk of Common Stock." *Journal of Financial and Quantitative Analysis* 19, no. 1 (March 1984).

Rosenberg, Barr. "Prediction of Common Stock Investment Risk." *Journal of Portfolio Management* 11, no. 1 (Fall 1984).

Rosenberg, Barr. "Prediction of Common Stock Betas." *Journal of Portfolio Management* 11, no. 2 (Winter 1985).

Financial Ratios and Bond Ratings

Cantor, R., and F. Packer. "The Credit Rating Industry." *The Journal of Fixed Income* 5, no. 3 (December 1995).

Fisher, Lawrence. "Determinants of Risk Premiums on Corporate Bonds." *Journal of Political Economy* 67, no. 3 (June 1959).

Fons, Jerome S. "An Approach to Forecasting Default Rates." New York: Moody's Investors Services (August 1991).

Gentry, James A., David T. Whitford, and Paul Newbold. "Predicting Industrial Bond Ratings with a Probit Model and Funds Flow Components." *Financial Review* 23, no. 3 (August 1988).

Kaplan, Robert S., and Gabrial Urwitz. "Statistical Models of Bond Ratings: A Methodological Inquiry." *Journal of Business* 52, no. 2 (April 1979).

Standard and Poor's Corporation. "Corporate Ratings Criteria," 2000.

Zhou, Chunsheng. "Credit Rating and Corporate Defaults." *Journal of Fixed Income* 11, no. 3 (December 2001).

Financial Ratios and Corporate Bankruptcy

Altman, Edward I. *Corporate Financial Distress and Bankruptcy,* 2d ed. New York: Wiley, 1993.

Altman, Edward I. "Financial Ratios, Discriminant Analysis, and the Prediction of Corporate Bankruptcy." *Journal of Finance* 23, no. 4 (September 1968).

Altman, Edward I., Robert G. Haldeman, and P. Narayanan. "Zeta Analysis: A New Model to Identify Bankruptcy Risk of Corporations." *Journal of Banking and Finance* 1, no. 2 (June 1977).

Aziz, A., and G. H. Lawson. "Cash Flow Reporting and Financial Distress Models: Testing of Hypothesis." *Financial Management* 18, no. 1 (Spring 1989).

Beaver, William H. "Financial Ratios as Predictors of Failure." *Empirical Research in Accounting: Selected Studies,* 1966, supplement to vol. 4, *Journal of Accounting Research.*

Beaver, William H. "Market Prices, Financial ratios, and the Prediction of Failure." *Journal of Accounting Research* 6, no. 2 (Autumn 1968).

Casey, Cornelius, and Norman Bartczak. "Using Operating Cash Flow Data to Predict Financial Distress: Some Extensions." *Journal of Accounting Research* 23, no. 1 (Spring 1985).

Dumbolena, I. G., and J. M. Shulman. "A Primary Rule of Detecting Bankruptcy: Watch the Cash." *Financial Analysts Journal* 44, no. 5 (September–October 1988).

Gentry, James A., Paul Newbold, and David T. Whitford. "Classifying Bankrupt Firms with Funds Flow Components." *Journal of Accounting Research* 23, no. 1 (Spring 1985).

Gentry, James A., Paul Newbold, and David T. Whitford. "Predicting Bankruptcy: If Cash Flow's Not the Bottom Line, What Is?" *Financial Analysts Journal* 41, no. 5 (September–October 1985).

Gombola, M. F., M. E. Haskins, J. E. Katz, and D. D. Williams. "Cash Flow in Bankruptcy Prediction." *Financial Management* 16, no. 4 (Winter 1987).

Helwege, J., and P. Kleiman. "Understanding High Yield Bond Default Rates." *Journal of Fixed Income* 7, no. 1 (June 1997).

Jonsson, J. G., and M. S. Fidson. "Forecasting Default Rates on High Yield Bonds." *Journal of Fixed Income* 6, no. 1 (June 1996).

Largay, J. A., and C. P. Stickney. "Cash Flows Ratio Analysis and the W. T. Grant Company Bankruptcy." *Financial Analysts Journal* 36, no. 4 (July–August 1980).

Ohlson, J. A. "Financial Ratios and the Probabalistic Prediction of Bankruptcy." *Journal of Accounting Research* 18, no. 2 (Spring 1980).

Reilly, Frank K. "Using Cash Flows and Financial Ratios to Predict Bankruptcies." In Thomas A. Bowman, ed., *Analyzing Investment Opportunities in Distressed and Bankrupt Companies.* Charlottesville, Va.: The Institute of Chartered Financial Analysts, 1991.

APPENDIX **A. Computation of Present Value of Lease Payments for Walgreens as of**
Chapter 10 **September 1, 2001 (Discount rate of 8%)**

	Present Value assuming 15-Year Spread of Lump Sum		Present Value assuming 12-Year Spread of Lump Sum	
Year	Payment $ Mil.	Present Value of Payment $ Mil.	Payment $ Mil.	Present Value of Payment $ Mil.
2002	782.7	724.7	782.7	724.7
2003	826.3	708.4	826.3	708.4
2004	817.0	648.6	817.0	648.6
2005	804.7	591.5	804.7	591.5
2006	785.4	534.5	785.4	534.5
2007	600.7	378.5	750.9	473.2
2008	600.7	350.5	750.9	438.1
2009	600.7	324.5	750.9	405.7
2010	600.7	300.5	750.9	375.6
2011	600.7	278.2	750.9	347.8
2012	600.7	257.6	750.9	322.0
2013	600.7	238.5	750.9	298.2
2014	600.7	220.9	750.9	276.1
2015	600.7	204.5	750.9	255.7
2016	600.7	189.4	750.9	236.7
2017	600.7	175.3	750.9	219.2
2018	600.7	162.4	750.9	202.9
2019	600.7	150.3		
2020	600.7	139.2		
2021	600.7	128.9		
Total		**6707.1**		**7059.0**

APPENDIX B. Computation of Operating Lease Obligations for Walgreens for 1998, 1999, 2000, 2001 (8% Debt Rate, 15-year Amortization Period)
Chapter 10

2001			2000			1999			1998		
Year	Payment $ Mil.	Present Value of Payment $ Mil.	Year	Payment $ Mil.	Present Value of Payment $ Mil.	Year	Payment $ Mil.	Present Value of Payment $ Mil.	Year	Payment $ Mil.	Present Value of Payment $ Mil.
2002	782.7	724.7	2001	673.7	623.8	2000	528.8	489.6	1999	441.0	408.3
2003	826.3	708.4	2002	715.2	613.2	2001	567.0	486.1	2000	473.0	405.5
2004	817.0	648.6	2003	704.0	558.9	2002	553.6	439.5	2001	460.0	365.2
2005	804.7	591.5	2004	691.3	508.1	2003	540.1	397.0	2002	446.0	327.8
2006	785.4	534.5	2005	679.8	462.7	2004	528.2	359.5	2003	432.0	294.0
2007	600.7	378.5	2006	513.5	323.6	2005	396.1	249.6	2004	318.1	200.5
2008	600.7	350.5	2007	513.5	299.6	2006	396.1	231.1	2005	318.1	185.6
2009	600.7	324.5	2008	513.5	277.4	2007	396.1	214.0	2006	318.1	171.9
2010	600.7	300.5	2009	513.5	256.9	2008	396.1	198.1	2007	318.1	159.1
2011	600.7	278.2	2010	513.5	237.9	2009	396.1	183.5	2008	318.1	147.4
2012	600.7	257.6	2011	513.5	220.2	2010	396.1	169.9	2009	318.1	136.4
2013	600.7	238.5	2012	513.5	203.9	2011	396.1	157.3	2010	318.1	126.3
2014	600.7	220.9	2013	513.5	188.8	2012	396.1	145.6	2011	318.1	117.0
2015	600.7	204.5	2014	513.5	174.8	2013	396.1	134.9	2012	318.1	108.3
2016	600.7	189.4	2015	513.5	161.9	2014	396.1	124.9	2013	318.1	100.3
2017	600.7	175.3	2016	513.5	149.9	2015	396.1	115.6	2014	318.1	92.9
2018	600.7	162.3	2017	513.5	138.8	2016	396.1	107.1	2015	318.1	86.0
2019	600.7	150.3	2018	513.5	128.5	2017	396.1	99.1	2016	318.1	79.6
2020	600.7	139.2	2019	513.5	119.0	2018	396.1	91.8	2017	318.1	73.7
2021	600.7	128.9	2020	513.5	110.2	2019	396.1	85.0	2018	318.1	68.3
Total		6706.9	Total		5758.1	Total		4479.1	Total		3654.1

APPENDIX
Chapter 10

C. As indicated in footnote 11, when computing the volatility of sales and/or operating earnings it is important to consider the effect of growth on the volatility of a series. For example, if you are analyzing the sales data for a company that is growing at a constant 15 percent a year and you compute the standard deviation of the series, you will derive a large measure of volatility because the deviations are being measured from the overall mean of the series. Therefore, the firm's sales during the initial years will be substantially below the mean and the firm's sales in the latter years will be substantially above the mean. The way to avoid this problem is to examine the deviations from a "growth series" that takes account of either linear growth or compound growth, as shown in Exhibit 10C.1. Notably, in all three calculations the variability measures are compared to the mean value for the series to derive a relative measure of volatility. As shown with the Walgreen example for sales in Exhibit 10C.1, the coefficient of variation based on the standard deviation from the mean indicates a significant level of sales volatility (42%), in contrast to the volatility assuming linear growth, where the relative measure of volatility declines to 15 percent. Finally, when you compute the firm's sales deviation from a compound growth curve of about 14 percent, the relative volatility is only 5 percent, which indicates fairly low sales volatility when the measurement considers growth.

The results when we measure the volatility of operating earnings (EBIT) are similar. Specifically, the relative volatility is 48 percent when compared to the mean, 17 percent when examined relative to the linear growth curve, and only 5 percent when computed relative to the compound growth curve of almost 20 percent a year. This implies what can be seen in the graphs—the growth rates for sales and operating earnings are fairly high, but they are also quite constant, which means that there is not the uncertainty (risk) implied if the volatility is measured relative to the overall mean.

EXHIBIT 10C.1 ▶ *CALCULATION OF SALES AND OPERATING EARNINGS VOLATILITY FOR WALGREENS FROM ARITHMETIC MEAN, FROM LINEAR GROWTH CURVE, AND FROM A COMPOUND GROWTH CURVE*

	1992	1993	1994	1995	1996	1997	1998	1999	2000	2001	
Sales	7,475.0	8,295.0	9,235.0	10,395.0	11,778.0	13,363.0	15,307.0	17,839.0	21,207.0	24,623.0	
EBIT	358.5	406.2	455.6	520.0	604.1	708.0	835.0	1,015.4	1,224.1	1,398.0	
	1992	1993	1994	1995	1996	1997	1998	1999	2000	2001	
Sales	7,475.0	8,295.0	9,235.0	10,395.0	11,778.0	13,363.0	15,307.0	17,839.0	21,207.0	24,623.0	
Linear	7,475.0	9,380.3	11,285.7	13,191.0	15,096.3	17,001.7	18,907.0	20,812.3	22,717.7	24,623.0	1,905.33
Constant Growth	7,475.0	8,533.7	9,742.3	11,122.1	12,697.4	14,495.7	16,548.7	18,892.5	21,568.3	24,623.0	1.14
vs. Mean	41%										
	0	1177948	4205234	7817616	11011336	13239895	12960000	8840711	2282114	0	
vs. Linear	15%										
	0	56972	257371	528711	845217	1282983	1541866	1109906	130520	0	
vs. C.G.	5%										

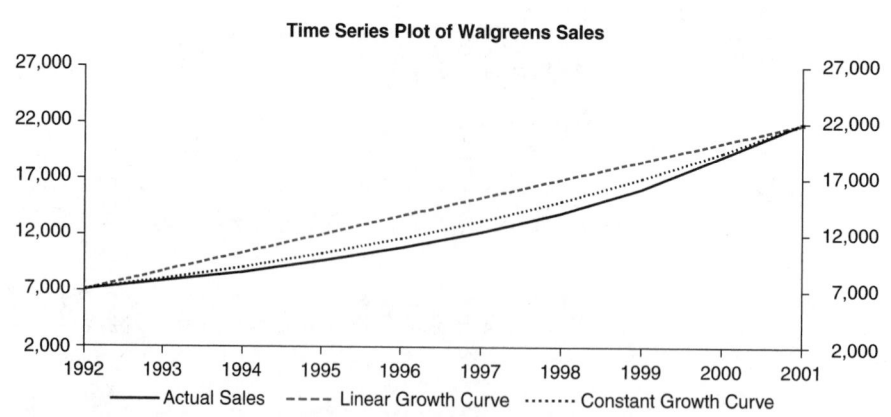

	1992	1993	1994	1995	1996	1997	1998	1999	2000	2001	
EBIT	358.5	406.2	455.6	520.0	604.1	708.0	835.0	1,015.4	1,224.1	1,398.0	
Linear	358.5	474.0	589.5	705.0	820.5	936.0	1,051.5	1,167.0	1,282.5	1,398.0	115.5
Constant Growth	358.5	417.0	485.1	564.3	656.4	763.5	888.2	1,033.2	1,201.8	1,398.0	1.2
vs. Mean	**48%**										
	0	4597	17929	34225	46829	51984	46872	22983	3411	0	
vs. Linear	**17%**										
	0	117	870	1961	2735	3085	2828	316	497	0	
vs. C.G.	**5%**										

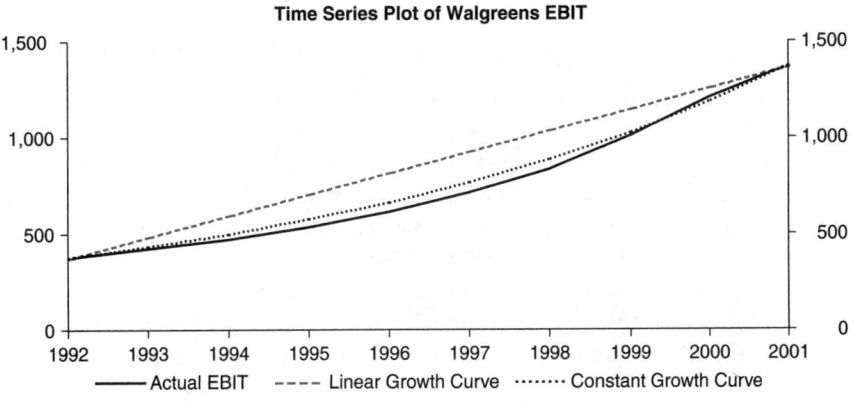

Time Series Plot of Walgreens EBIT

—— Actual EBIT   - - - - Linear Growth Curve   ········ Constant Growth Curve

Chapter 11 An Introduction to Security Valuation

After you read this chapter, you should be able to answer the following questions:

➤ What are the two major approaches to the investment process?

➤ What are the specifics and logic of the top-down (three-step) approach?

➤ What empirical evidence supports the usefulness of the top-down approach?

➤ When valuing an asset, what are the required inputs?

➤ After you have valued an asset, what is the investment decision process?

➤ How do you determine the value of bonds?

➤ How do you determine the value of preferred stock?

➤ What are the two primary approaches to the valuation of common stock?

➤ Under what conditions is it best to use the present value of cash flow approach for valuing a company's equity?

➤ Under what conditions is it best to use the relative valuation techniques for valuing a company's equity?

➤ How do you apply the discounted cash flow valuation approach, and what are the major discounted cash flow valuation techniques?

➤ What is the dividend discount model (DDM), and what is its logic?

➤ What is the effect of the assumptions of the DDM when valuing a growth company?

➤ How do you apply the DDM to the valuation of a firm that is expected to experience temporary supernormal growth?

➤ How do you apply the present value of operating cash flow technique?

➤ How do you apply the present value of free cash flow to equity technique?

➤ How do you apply the relative valuation approach?

➤ What are the major relative valuation ratios?

➤ How can you use the DDM to develop an earnings multiplier model?

➤ What does the DDM model imply are the factors that determine a stock's *P/E* ratio?

➤ What two general variables need to be estimated in any valuation approach?

➤ How do you estimate the major inputs to the stock valuation models: (1) the required rate of return and (2) the expected growth rate of earnings and dividends?

➤ What additional factors must be considered when estimating the required rate of return and growth rate for a foreign security?

At the start of this book, we defined an investment as a commitment of funds for a period of time to derive a rate of return that would compensate the investor for the time during which the funds are invested, for the expected rate of inflation during the investment horizon, and for the uncertainty involved. From this definition, we know that the first step in making an investment is determining your required rate of return.

Once you have determined this rate, some investment alternatives, such as savings accounts and T-bills, are fairly easy to evaluate because they provide stated cash flows. Most investments have expected cash flows and a stated market price (for example, common stock), and you must estimate a value for the investment to determine if its current market price is consistent with your required return. To do this, you must estimate the value of the security based on its expected cash flows and your required rate of return. This is the process of estimating the value of an asset. After you have completed estimating a security's intrinsic value, you compare this estimated intrinsic value to the prevailing market price to decide whether you want to buy the security or not.

This **investment decision process** is similar to the process you follow when deciding on a corporate investment or when shopping for clothes, a stereo, or a car. In each case, you examine the item and decide how much it is worth to you (its value). If the price equals its estimated value or is less, you would buy it. The same technique applies to securities except that the determination of a security's value is more formal.

We start our investigation of security valuation by discussing the **valuation process**. There are two general approaches to the valuation process: (1) the top-down, three-step approach; or (2) the bottom-up, stock valuation, stockpicking approach. Both of these approaches can be implemented by either fundamentalists or technicians. The difference between the two approaches is the perceived importance of the economy and a firm's industry on the valuation of a firm and its stock.

Advocates of the top-down, three-step approach believe that both the economy/market and the industry effect have a significant impact on the total returns for individual stocks. In contrast, those who employ the bottom-up, stockpicking approach contend that it is possible to find stocks that are undervalued relative to their market price, and these stocks will provide superior returns *regardless* of the market and industry outlook.

Both of these approaches have numerous supporters, and advocates of both approaches have been quite successful.[1] In this book, we advocate and present the top-down, three-step approach because of its logic and empirical support. Although we believe that a portfolio manager or an investor can be successful using the bottom-up approach, we believe that it is more difficult to be successful because these stockpickers are ignoring substantial information from the market and the firm's industry.

Although we know that the value of a security is determined by its quality and profit potential, we also believe that the economic environment and the performance of a firm's industry influence the value of a security and its rate of return. Because of the importance of these economic and industry factors, we present an overview of the valuation process that describes these influences and explains how they can be incorporated into the analysis of security value. Subsequently, we describe the theory of value and emphasize the factors that affect the value of securities.

Next, we apply these valuation concepts to the valuation of different assets—bonds, preferred stock, and common stock. In this section, we show how the valuation models help investors calculate how much they should pay for these assets. In the final section, we emphasize the estimation of the variables that affect value (the required rate of return and the expected rate of growth). We conclude with a discussion of additional factors that must be considered when we extend our analysis to the valuation of international securities.

AN OVERVIEW OF THE VALUATION PROCESS

Psychologists suggest that the success or failure of an individual can be caused as much by his or her social, economic, and family environment as by genetic gifts. Extending this idea to the valuation of securities means we should consider a firm's economic and industry environment

---

[1] For the history and selection process of a legendary stockpicker, see Robert G. Hagstrom, Jr., *The Essential Buffett* (New York: Wiley, 2001); or Roger Lowenstein, *Buffett: The Making of an American Capitalist* (New York: Random House, 1995).

during the valuation process. Regardless of the qualities or capabilities of a firm and its management, the economic and industry environment will have a major influence on the success of a firm and the realized rate of return on its stock.

As an example, assume you own shares of the strongest and most successful firm producing home furnishings. If you own the shares during a strong economic expansion, the sales and earnings of the firm will increase and your rate of return on the stock should be quite high. In contrast, if you own the same stock during a major economic recession, the sales and earnings of this firm (and probably most or all of the firms in the industry) would likely experience a decline and the price of its stock would be stable or decline. Therefore, when assessing the future value of a security, it is necessary to analyze the outlook for the aggregate economy and the firm's specific industry.

The valuation process is like the chicken-and-egg dilemma. Do you start by analyzing the macroeconomy and various industries before individual stocks, or do you begin with individual securities and gradually combine these firms into industries and the industries into the entire economy? For reasons discussed in the next section, we contend that the discussion should begin with an analysis of aggregate economies and overall securities markets and progress to different industries with a global perspective. Only after a thorough analysis of a global industry are you in a position to properly evaluate the securities issued by individual firms within the better industries. Thus, we recommend a three-step, top-down valuation process in which you first examine the influence of the general economy on all firms and the security markets, then analyze the prospects for various global industries with the best outlooks in this economic environment, and finally turn to the analysis of individual firms in the preferred industries and to the common stock of these firms. Exhibit 11.1 indicates the procedure recommended.

EXHIBIT 11.1 ▸ *OVERVIEW OF THE INVESTMENT PROCESS*

Analysis of Alternative Economies and Security Markets

Objective: Decide how to allocate investment funds among countries and within countries to bonds, stocks, and cash.

Analysis of Alternative Industries

Objective: Based upon the economic and market analysis, determine which industries will prosper and which industries will suffer on a global basis and within countries.

Analysis of Individual Companies and Stocks

Objective: Following the selection of the best industries, determine which companies within these industries will prosper and which stocks are undervalued.

WHY A THREE-STEP VALUATION PROCESS?

General Economic Influences

Monetary and fiscal policy measures enacted by various agencies of national governments influence the aggregate economies of those countries. The resulting economic conditions influence all industries and companies within the economies.

Fiscal policy initiatives, such as tax credits or tax cuts, can encourage spending, whereas additional taxes on income, gasoline, cigarettes, and liquor can discourage spending. Increases or decreases in government spending on defense, on unemployment insurance or retraining programs, or on highways also influence the general economy. All such policies influence the business environment for firms that rely directly on such government expenditures. In addition, we know that government spending has a strong *multiplier effect*. For example, increases in road building increase the demand for earthmoving equipment and concrete materials. As a result, in addition to construction workers, the employees in those industries that supply the equipment and materials have more to spend on consumer goods, which raises the demand for consumer goods, which affects another set of suppliers.

Monetary policy produces similar economic changes. A restrictive monetary policy that reduces the growth rate of the money supply reduces the supply of funds for working capital and expansion for all businesses. Alternatively, a restrictive monetary policy that targets interest rates would raise market interest rates and therefore firms' costs and make it more expensive for individuals to finance home mortgages and the purchase of other durable goods, such as autos and appliances. Monetary policy therefore affects all segments of an economy and that economy's relationship with other economies.

Any economic analysis requires the consideration of inflation. As we have discussed, inflation causes differences between real and nominal interest rates and changes the spending and savings behavior of consumers and corporations. In addition, unexpected changes in the rate of inflation make it difficult for firms to plan, which inhibits growth and innovation. Beyond the impact on the domestic economy, differential inflation and interest rates influence the trade balance between countries and the exchange rate for currencies.

In addition to monetary and fiscal policy actions, such events as war, political upheavals in foreign countries, or international monetary devaluations produce changes in the business environment that add to the uncertainty of sales and earnings expectations and therefore the risk premium required by investors. For example, the political uncertainty in Russia during 1995–1999 caused a significant increase in the risk premium for investors in Russia and a subsequent reduction in investment and spending in Russia. In contrast, the end of apartheid in South Africa and its open election in 1994 were viewed as positive events and led to a significant increase in economic activity in the country. Similarly, the peace accord in Northern Ireland in 1996 caused a major influx of investment and tourist dollars.

In short, it is difficult to conceive of any industry or company that can avoid the impact of macroeconomic developments that affect the total economy. Because aggregate economic events have a profound effect on all industries and companies within these industries, these macroeconomic factors should be considered before industries are analyzed.

Taking a global portfolio perspective, the asset allocation for a country within a global portfolio will be affected by its economic outlook. If a recession is imminent in a country, you would expect a negative impact on its security prices. Because of these economic expectations, investors would be apprehensive about investing in most industries in the country. Given these expectations, the country will be **underweighted** in portfolios relative to its weight based on its market value. Further, given these pessimistic expectations, any funds invested in the country would be directed to low-risk sectors of the economy.

In contrast, optimistic economic and stock market outlooks for a given country should lead an investor to increase the overall allocation to this country (**overweight** the country compared to its weights determined by its relative market value).[2] After allocating funds among countries, the investor looks for outstanding industries in each country. This search for the best industries is enhanced by the economic analysis because the future performance of an industry depends on the country's economic outlook *and* the industry's expected relationship to the economy during the particular phase of the business cycle.

Industry Influences

The second step in the valuation process is to identify global industries that will prosper or suffer in the long run or during the expected near-term economic environment. Examples of conditions that affect specific industries are strikes within a major producing country, import or export quotas or taxes, a worldwide shortage or an excess supply of a resource, or government-imposed regulations on an industry.

You should remember that alternative industries react to economic changes at different points in the business cycle. For example, firms typically increase capital expenditures when they are operating at full capacity at the peak of the economic cycle. Therefore, industries that provide plant and equipment will typically be affected toward the end of a cycle. In addition, alternative industries have different responses to the business cycle. As an example, cyclical industries, such as steel or autos, typically do much better than the aggregate economy during expansions, but they suffer more during contractions. In contrast, noncyclical industries, such as retail food, would not experience a significant decline during a recession but also would not experience a strong increase during an economic expansion.

Another factor that will have a differential effect on industries is demographics. For example, it is widely recognized that the U.S. population is weighted toward "baby boomers" entering their late 50s and that there has been a large surge in the number of citizens over age 65. These two groups have heavy demand for second homes and medical care and the industries related to these segments (e.g., home furnishings and pharmaceuticals).

Firms that sell in international markets can benefit or suffer as foreign economies shift. An industry with a substantial worldwide market might experience low demand in its domestic market but benefit from growing demand in its international market. As an example, much of the growth for Coca-Cola and Pepsi and the fast-food chains, such as McDonald's and Burger King, has come from international expansion in Europe and the Far East.

In general, an industry's prospects within the global business environment will determine how well or poorly an individual firm will fare, so industry analysis should precede company analysis. Few companies perform well in a poor industry, so even the best company in a poor industry is a bad prospect for investment. For example, poor sales and earnings in the farm equipment industry during the late 1980s had a negative impact on Deere and Co., a well-managed firm and probably the best firm in its industry. Though Deere performed better than other firms in the industry (some went bankrupt), its earnings and stock performance still fell far short of its past performance, and the company did poorly compared to firms in most other industries.

Notably, even money managers who are essentially "stockpickers" consider industry analysis important because it determines a firm's business risk due to sales volatility and operating leverage, and its profitability that is impacted by the competitive environment in the industry.

Company Analysis

After determining that an industry's outlook is good, an investor can analyze and compare individual firms' performance within the entire industry using financial ratios and cash flow values. As we discussed in Chapter 10, many financial ratios for firms are valid only when they are compared to the performance of their industries.

You undertake company analysis to identify the best company in a promising industry. This involves examining a firm's past performance, but more important, its future prospects. After you

---

[2]We will show an example of a global asset allocation in Chapter 12.

understand the firm and its outlook, you can determine its value. In the final step, you compare this estimated "intrinsic" value to the price of the firm's stock and decide whether its stock or bonds are good investments.

Your final goal is to select the best stock or bonds within a desirable industry and include it in your portfolio based on its relationship (correlation) with all other assets in your portfolio. As we discuss in more detail in Chapter 15, the best stock for investment purposes may not necessarily be issued by the best company because the stock of the finest company in an industry may be overpriced, which would cause it to be a poor investment. You cannot know whether a security is undervalued or overvalued until you have analyzed the company, estimated its intrinsic value, and compared your estimated intrinsic value to the market price of the firm's stock.

Does the Three-Step Process Work?
Although you might agree with the logic of the three-step investment process, you might wonder how well this process works in selecting investments. The results of several academic studies have supported this technique. First, studies indicated that most changes in an individual firm's *earnings* could be attributed to changes in aggregate corporate earnings and changes in the firm's industry, with the aggregate earnings changes being more important. Although the relative influence of the general economy and the industry on a firm's earnings varied among individual firms, the results consistently demonstrated that the economic environment had a significant effect on firm earnings.

Second, several studies have found a relationship between aggregate stock prices and various economic series, such as employment, income, or production. These results supported the view that a relationship exists between stock prices and economic expansions and contractions.[3]

Third, an analysis of the relationship between *rates of return* for the aggregate stock market, alternative industries, and individual stocks showed that most of the changes in rates of return for individual stocks could be explained by changes in the rates of return for the aggregate stock market and the stock's industry. Although the importance of the market effect tended to decline over time and the significance of the industry effect varied among industries, the combined market-industry effect on an individual stock's rate of return was still important.[4]

These results from academic studies support the use of the three-step investment process. This investment decision approach is consistent with the discussion in Chapter 2, which contended that the most important decision is the asset allocation decision.[5] The asset allocation specifies: (1) what proportion of your portfolio will be invested in various nations' economies; (2) within each country, how you will divide your assets among stocks, bonds, or other assets; and (3) your industry selections, based on which industries are expected to prosper in the projected economic environment. We provide an example of global asset allocation in Chapter 12.

Now that we have described and justified the three-step process, we need to consider the theory of valuation. The application of this theory allows us to compute estimated values for the market, for alternative industries, and for individual firms and stocks. Finally, we compare these estimated values to current market prices and decide whether we want to make particular investments.

---

[3]For a further discussion of this and empirical support, see Geoffrey Moore and John P. Cullity, "Security Markets and Business Cycles" in *The Financial Analysts Handbook,* 2d ed., ed. Sumner N. Levine (Homewood, Ill.: Dow Jones–Irwin, 1988); and Jeremy Siegel, "Does It Pay Stock Investors to Forecast the Business Cycle?" *Journal of Portfolio Management* 18, no. 1 (Fall 1991): 27–34.

[4]For an analysis, see Stephen L. Meyers, "A Re-Examination of Market and Industry Factors in Stock Price Behavior," *Journal of Finance* 28, no. 3 (June 1973): 695–705.

[5]The classic study that established the importance of asset allocation is Gary P. Brinson, L. R. Hood, and G. L. Beebower, "Determinants of Portfolio Performance," *Financial Analysts Journal* 42, no. 4 (July–August 1986): 35–43; followed by Gary P. Brinson, Brian D. Singer, and G. L. Beebower, "Determinants of Portfolio Performance II: An Update," *Financial Analysts Journal* 47, no. 3 (May–June 1991): 40–48. A subsequent well-regarded application of these concepts by Abby J. Cohen is contained in Abby J. Cohen, "Economic Forecasts and the Asset Allocation Decision," in *Economic Analysis for Investment Professionals* (Charlottesville, Va.: AIMR, November 1996).

THEORY OF VALUATION

You may recall from your studies in accounting, economics, or corporate finance that the value of an asset is the present value of its expected returns. Specifically, you expect an asset to provide a stream of returns during the period of time you own it. To convert this estimated stream of returns to a value for the security, you must discount this stream at your required rate of return. This process of valuation requires estimates of (1) the stream of expected returns and (2) the required rate of return on the investment.

Stream of Expected Returns (Cash Flows)

An estimate of the expected returns from an investment encompasses not only the size but also the form, time pattern, and the uncertainty of returns, which affect the required rate of return.

Form of Returns   The returns from an investment can take many forms, including earnings, cash flows, dividends, interest payments, or capital gains (increases in value) during a period. We will consider several alternative valuation techniques that use different forms of returns. As an example, one common stock valuation model applies a multiplier to a firm's earnings, whereas another valuation model computes the present value of a firm's operating cash flows, and a third model estimates the present value of dividend payments. Returns or cash flows can come in many forms, and you must consider all of them to evaluate an investment accurately.

Time Pattern and Growth Rate of Returns   You cannot calculate an accurate value for a security unless you can estimate when you will receive the returns or cash flows. Because money has a time value, you must know the time pattern and growth rate of returns from an investment. This knowledge will make it possible to properly value the stream of returns relative to alternative investments with a different time pattern and growth rate of returns or cash flows.

Required Rate of Return

Uncertainty of Returns (Cash Flows)   You will recall from Chapter 1 that the required rate of return on an investment is determined by (1) the economy's real risk-free rate of return, plus (2) the expected rate of inflation during the holding period, plus (3) a risk premium that is determined by the uncertainty of returns. All investments are affected by the risk-free rate and the expected rate of inflation because these two variables determine the nominal risk-free rate. Therefore, the factor that causes a difference in required rates of return is the risk premium for alternative investments. In turn, this risk premium depends on the uncertainty of returns or cash flows from an investment.

We can identify the sources of the uncertainty of returns by the internal characteristics of assets or by market-determined factors. Earlier, we subdivided the internal characteristics for a firm into business risk (BR), financial risk (FR), liquidity risk (LR), exchange rate risk (ERR), and country risk (CR). The market-determined risk measures are the systematic risk of the asset, its beta, or its multiple APT factors.

Investment Decision Process: A Comparison of Estimated Values and Market Prices

To ensure that you receive your required return on an investment, you must estimate the intrinsic value of the investment at your required rate of return and then compare this estimated intrinsic value to the prevailing market price. You should not buy an investment if its market price exceeds your estimated value because the difference will prevent you from receiving your required rate of return on the investment. In contrast, if the estimated value of the investment exceeds the market price, you should buy the investment. In summary:

If Estimated Value > Market Price, Buy

If Estimated Value < Market Price, Don't Buy

For example, assume you read about a firm that produces athletic shoes and its stock is listed on the NYSE. Using one of the valuation models we will discuss and making estimates of earnings, cash flow, and growth based on the company's annual report and other information, you estimate the company's stock value using your required rate of return as $20 a share. After estimating this value, you look in the paper and see that the stock is currently being traded at $15 a share. You would want to buy this stock because you think it is worth $20 a share and you can buy it for $15 a share. In contrast, if the current market price were $25 a share, you would not want to buy the stock because, based upon your valuation, it is overvalued.

The theory of value provides a common framework for the valuation of all investments. Different applications of this theory generate different estimated values for alternative investments because of the different payment streams and characteristics of the securities. The interest and principal payments on a bond differ substantially from the expected dividends and future selling price for a common stock. The initial discussion that follows applies the discounted cash flow method to bonds, preferred stock, and common stock. This presentation demonstrates that the same basic model is useful across a range of investments. Subsequently, because of the difficulty in estimating the value of common stock, we consider two general approaches and numerous techniques for the valuation of stock.

VALUATION OF ALTERNATIVE INVESTMENTS

Valuation of Bonds   Calculating the value of bonds is relatively easy because the size and time pattern of cash flows from the bond over its life are known. A bond typically promises

1. Interest payments every six months equal to one-half the coupon rate times the face value of the bond
2. The payment of the principal on the bond's maturity date

As an example, in 2003, a $10,000 bond due in 2018 with a 10 percent coupon will pay $500 every six months for its 15-year life. In addition, the bond issuer promises to pay the $10,000 principal at maturity in 2018. Therefore, assuming the bond issuer does not default, the investor knows what payments (cash flows) will be made and when they will be made.

Applying the valuation theory, which states that the value of any asset is the present value of its cash flows, the value of the bond is the present value of the interest payments, which we can think of as an annuity of $500 every six months for 15 years, and the present value of the principal payment, which in this case is the present value of $10,000 in 15 years. The only unknown for this asset (assuming the borrower does not default) is the required rate of return that should be used to discount the expected stream of returns (cash flows). If the prevailing nominal risk-free rate is 9 percent and the investor requires a 1 percent risk premium on this bond because there is some probability of default, the required rate of return would be 10 percent.

The present value of the interest payments is an annuity for 30 periods (15 years every six months) at one-half the required return (5 percent):[6]

$$\$500 \times 15.3725 = \$7,686$$

(Present Value of Interest Payments at 10 Percent)

The present value of the principal is likewise discounted at 5 percent for 30 periods:[7]

$$\$10,000 \times 0.2314 = \$2,314$$

(Present Value of the Principal Payment at 10 Percent)

---

[6]The annuity factors and present value factors are contained in Appendix C at the end of the book.

[7]If we used annual compounding, this would be 0.239 rather than 0.2314. We use semiannual compounding because it is consistent with the interest payments and is used in practice.

This can be summarized as follows:

Present Value of Interest Payments $500 × 15.3725	= $ 7,686
Present Value of Principal Payment $10,000 × 0.2314 =	2,314
Total Value of Bond at 10 Percent	= $10,000

This is the amount that an investor should be willing to pay for this bond, assuming that the required rate of return on a bond of this risk class is 10 percent. If the market price of the bond is above this value, the investor should not buy it because the promised yield to maturity at this higher price will be less than the investor's required rate of return.

Alternatively, assuming an investor requires a 12 percent return on this bond, its value would be:

$$\$500 \times 13.7648 = \$6,882$$
$$\$10,000 \times 0.1741 = \underline{1,741}$$
$$\text{Total Value of Bond at 12 Percent} = \$8,623$$

This example shows that if you want a higher rate of return, you will not pay as much for an asset; that is, a given stream of cash flows has a lower value to you. As before, you would compare this computed value to the market price of the bond to determine whether you should invest in it.[8]

Valuation of Preferred Stock

The owner of a preferred stock receives a promise to pay a stated dividend, usually each quarter, for an infinite period. Preferred stock is a **perpetuity** because it has no maturity. As was true with a bond, stated payments are made on specified dates although the issuer of this stock does not have the same legal obligation to pay investors as do issuers of bonds. Payments are made only after the firm meets its bond interest payments. Because this reduced legal obligation increases the uncertainty of returns, investors should require a higher rate of return on a firm's preferred stock than on its bonds. Although this differential in required return should exist in theory, it generally does not exist in practice because of the tax treatment accorded dividends paid to corporations. As described in Chapter 3, 80 percent of intercompany preferred dividends are tax-exempt, making the effective tax rate on them about 6.8 percent, assuming a corporate tax rate of 34 percent. This tax advantage stimulates the demand for preferred stocks by corporations; and, because of this demand, the yield on them has generally been below that on the highest-grade corporate bonds.

Because preferred stock is a perpetuity, its value is simply the stated annual dividend divided by the required rate of return on preferred stock (k_p) as follows:

$$V = \frac{\text{Dividend}}{k_p}$$

Assume a preferred stock has a $100 par value and a dividend of $8 a year. Because of the expected rate of inflation, the uncertainty of the dividend payment, and the tax advantage to you as a corporate investor, your required rate of return on this stock is 9 percent. Therefore, the value of this preferred stock to you is

$$V = \frac{\$8}{0.09}$$
$$= \$88.89$$

---

[8]To test your mastery of bond valuation, check that if the required rate of return were 8 percent, the value of this bond would be $11,729.

EXHIBIT 11.2   *COMMON STOCK VALUATION APPROACHES AND SPECIFIC TECHNIQUES*

Approaches to Equity Valuation

Discounted Cash Flow Techniques

- **Present Value of Dividends (DDM)**
- **Present Value of Operating Free Cash Flow**
- **Present Value of Free Cash Flow to Equity**

Relative Valuation Techniques

- **Price/Earning Ratio (*P/E*)**
- **Price/Cash Flow Ratio (*P/CF*)**
- **Price/Book Value Ratio (*P/BV*)**
- **Price/Sales Ratio (*P/S*)**

Given this estimated value, you would inquire about the current market price to decide whether you would want to buy this preferred stock. If the current market price is $95, you would decide against a purchase, whereas if it is $80, you would buy the stock. Also, given the market price of preferred stock, you can derive its promised yield. Assuming a current market price of $85, the promised yield would be

$$ k_p = \frac{\text{Dividend}}{\text{Price}} = \frac{\$8}{\$85.00} = 0.0941 $$

Approaches to the Valuation of Common Stock

Because of the complexity and importance of valuing common stock, various techniques for accomplishing this task have been devised over time. These techniques fall into one of two general approaches: (1) the discounted cash flow valuation techniques, where the value of the stock is estimated based upon the present value of some measure of cash flow, including dividends, operating cash flow, and free cash flow; and (2) the relative valuation techniques, where the value of a stock is estimated based upon its current price relative to variables considered to be significant to valuation, such as earnings, cash flow, book value, or sales. Exhibit 11.2 provides a visual presentation of the alternative approaches and specific techniques.

An important point is that *both of these approaches and all of these valuation techniques have several common factors.* First, all of them are significantly affected by the investor's *required rate of return* on the stock because this rate becomes the discount rate or is a major component of the discount rate. Second, all valuation approaches are affected by *the estimated growth rate of the variable* used in the valuation technique—for example, dividends, earnings, cash flow, or sales. As noted in the efficient market discussion, both of these critical variables must be *estimated*. As a result, different analysts using the same valuation techniques will derive different estimates of value for a stock because they have different estimates for these critical variable inputs.

The following discussion of equity valuation techniques considers the specific models and the theoretical and practical strengths and weaknesses of each of them. Notably, the authors' intent is to present these two approaches as complementary, *not* competitive, approaches—that is, you should learn and use both of them.

Why and When to Use the Discounted Cash Flow Valuation Approach

These discounted cash flow valuation techniques are obvious choices for valuation because they are the epitome of how we describe value—that is, the present value of expected cash flows. The major difference between the alternative techniques is how one specifies cash flow—that is, the measure of cash flow used.

The cleanest and most straightforward measure of cash flow is *dividends* because these are clearly cash flows that go directly to the investor, which implies that you should use *the cost of equity* as the discount rate. However, this dividend technique is difficult to apply to firms that do not pay dividends during periods of high growth, or that currently pay very limited dividends because they have high rate of return investment alternatives available. On the other hand, an advantage is that the reduced form of the dividend discount model (DDM) is very useful when discussing valuation for a stable, mature entity where the assumption of relatively constant growth for the long term is appropriate.

The second specification of cash flow is the *operating free cash flow,* which is generally described as cash flows after direct costs (cost of goods and S, G & A expenses) and before any payments to capital suppliers. Because we are dealing with the cash flows available for all capital suppliers, the discount rate employed is the firm's *weighted average cost of capital* (WACC). This is a very useful model when comparing firms with diverse capital structures because you determine the value of the total firm and then subtract the value of the firm's debt obligations to arrive at a value for the firm's equity.

The third cash flow measure is *free cash flow to equity,* which is a measure of cash flows available to the equity holder after payments to debt holders and after allowing for expenditures to maintain the firm's asset base. Because these are cash flows available to equity owners, the appropriate discount rate is the firm's *cost of equity.*

Beyond being theoretically correct, these models allow a substantial amount of flexibility in terms of changes in sales and expenses that implies changing growth rates over time. Once you understand how to compute each measure of cash flow, you can estimate cash flow for each year by constructing a pro forma statement for each year or you can estimate overall growth rates for the alternative cash flow values as we will demonstrate with the DDM.

A potential difficulty with these cash flow techniques is that they are very dependent on the two significant inputs—(1) the growth rates of cash flows (both the *rate* of growth and the *duration* of growth) and (2) the estimate of the discount rate. As we will show in several instances, a small change in either of these values can have a significant impact on the estimated value. This is a critical realization when using any theoretical model: Everyone knows and uses the same model, but it is the *inputs* that are critical—GIGO: garbage in, garbage out! This is similar to the discussion in Chapter 6 regarding being a superior analyst in a world with an efficient market.

Why and When to Use the Relative Valuation Techniques

As noted, a potential problem with the discounted cash flow valuation models is that it is possible to derive intrinsic values that are substantially above or below prevailing prices depending on how you adjust your estimated inputs to the prevailing environment. An advantage of the relative valuation techniques is that they provide information about how the market is *currently* valuing stock at several levels—that is, the aggregate market, alternative industries, and individual stocks within industries. Following this chapter, which provides the background for these two approaches, we will demonstrate the alternative relative valuation ratios for the aggregate market, for an industry relative to the market, and for an individual company relative to the aggregate market, to its industry, and to other stocks in its industry.

The good news is that this relative valuation approach provides information on how the market is currently valuing securities. The bad news is that it is providing information on current valuation. The point is, the relative valuation approach provides this information on current valuation, but it does not provide guidance on whether these current valuations are appropriate—that is, *all* valuations at a point in time could be too high or too low. For example, assume that the market becomes significantly overvalued. For example, if you compare the value for an industry to the very overvalued market, you might contend based on such a comparison that an industry is undervalued relative to the market. Unfortunately, your judgment may be wrong because of the benchmark you are using—that is, you might be comparing a fully valued industry to a *very* overvalued market.

Put another way, the relative valuation techniques are appropriate to consider under two conditions:

1. You have a good set of comparable entities—that is, comparable companies that are similar in terms of industry, size, and, it is hoped, risk.
2. The aggregate market and the company's industry are not at a valuation extreme—that is, they are not either seriously undervalued or overvalued.

Discounted Cash Flow Valuation Techniques

All of these valuation techniques are based on the basic valuation model, which asserts that the value of an asset is the present value of its expected future cash flows as follows:

$$V_j = \sum_{t=1}^{n} \frac{CF_t}{(1+k)^t}$$

where:

  V_j = **value of stock** j
  n = **life of the asset**
  CF_t = **cash flow in period** t
  k = **the discount rate that is equal to the investors' required rate of return for asset** j, **which is determined by the uncertainty (risk) of the stock's cash flows**

As noted, the specific cash flows used will differ between techniques. They range from dividends (the best-known model) to operating free cash flow and free cash flow to equity. We begin with a fairly detailed presentation of the present-value-of-dividend model, referred to as the dividend discount model (DDM), because it is intuitively appealing and is the best-known model. Also, its general approach is similar to the other discounted cash flow models.

The Dividend Discount Model (DDM)

The **dividend discount model** assumes that the value of a share of common stock is the present value of all future dividends as follows:[9]

$$V_j = \frac{D_1}{(1+k)} + \frac{D_2}{(1+k)^2} + \frac{D_3}{(1+k)^3} + \ldots + \frac{D_\infty}{(1+k)^\infty}$$

$$= \sum_{t=1}^{n} \frac{D_t}{(1+k)^t}$$

where:

  V_j = **value of common stock** j
  D_t = **dividend during period** t
  k = **required rate of return on stock** j

---

[9]This model was initially set forth in J. B. Williams, *The Theory of Investment Value* (Cambridge, Mass: Harvard, 1938). It was subsequently reintroduced and expanded by Myron J. Gordon, *The Investment, Financing, and Valuation of the Corporation* (Homewood, Ill.: Irwin, 1962).

An obvious question is: What happens when the stock is not held for an infinite period? A sale of the stock at the end of Year 2 would imply the following formula:

$$V_j = \frac{D_1}{(1+k)} + \frac{D_2}{(1+k)^2} + \frac{SP_{j2}}{(1+k)^2}$$

The value is equal to the two dividend payments during Years 1 and 2 plus the sale price (*SP*) for stock *j* at the end of Year 2. The expected selling price of stock *j* at the end of Year 2 (SP_{j2}) is simply the value of all remaining dividend payments.

$$SP_{j2} = \frac{D_3}{(1+k)} + \frac{D_4}{(1+k)^2} + \ldots + \frac{D_\infty}{(1+k)^\infty}$$

If SP_{j2} is discounted back to the present by $1/(1+k)^2$, this equation becomes

$$PV(SP_{j2}) = \frac{\dfrac{D_3}{(1+k)} + \dfrac{D_4}{(1+k)^2} + \ldots + \dfrac{D_\infty}{(1+k)^\infty}}{(1+k)^2}$$

$$= \frac{D_3}{(1+k)^3} + \frac{D_4}{(1+k)^4} + \ldots + \frac{D_\infty}{(1+k)^\infty}$$

which is simply an extension of the original equation. Whenever the stock is sold, its value (that is, the sale price at that time) will be the present value of all future dividends. When this ending value is discounted back to the present, you are back to the original dividend discount model.

What about stocks that pay no dividends? Again, the concept is the same, except that some of the early dividend payments are zero. Notably, there are expectations that *at some point* the firm will start paying dividends. If investors lacked such an expectation, nobody would be willing to buy the security. It would have zero value. A firm with a non-dividend-paying stock is reinvesting its capital in very profitable projects rather than paying current dividends so that its earnings and dividend stream will be larger and grow faster in the future. In this case, we would apply the DDM as:

$$V_j = \frac{D_1}{(1+k)} + \frac{D_2}{(1+k)^2} + \frac{D_3}{(1+k)^3} + \ldots + \frac{D}{(1+k)^\infty}$$

where:

$D_1 = 0$; $D_2 = 0$

The investor expects that when the firm starts paying dividends in Period 3, it will be a large initial amount and dividends will grow faster than those of a comparable stock that had paid out dividends. The stock has value because of these *future* dividends. We will apply this model to several cases having different holding periods that will show you how it works.

One-Year Holding Period Assume an investor wants to buy the stock, hold it for one year, and then sell it. To determine the value of the stock—that is, how much the investor should be willing to pay for it—using the DDM, we must estimate the dividend to be received during the period, the expected sale price at the end of the holding period, and the investor's required rate of return.

To estimate the dividend for the coming year, adjust the current dividend for expectations regarding the change in the dividend during the year. Assume the company we are analyzing earned $2.50 a share last year and paid a dividend of $1 a share. Assume further the firm has been fairly consistent in maintaining this 40 percent payout over time. The consensus of financial analysts is that the firm will earn about $2.75 during the coming year and will raise its dividend to $1.10 per share.

A crucial estimate is the expected selling price for the stock a year from now. You can estimate this expected selling price by either of two alternative procedures. In the first, you can apply the dividend discount model where you estimate the specific dividend payments for a number of years into the future and calculate the value of the stock from these estimates. In the second procedure, the earnings multiplier model, you multiply the future expected earnings for the stock by an earnings multiple, which you likewise estimate, to find an expected sale price. We will discuss the earnings multiple model in a later section of the chapter. For now, assume you prefer the DDM. Applying this model, you project the sale price of this stock a year from now to be $22.

Finally, you must determine the required rate of return. As discussed before, the nominal risk-free rate is determined by the real risk-free rate and the expected rate of inflation. A good proxy for this rate is the promised yield on one-year government bonds because your investment horizon (expected holding period) is one year. You estimate the stock's risk premium by comparing its risk level to the risk of other potential investments. In later chapters, we discuss how you can estimate this risk. For the moment, assume that one-year government bonds are yielding 10 percent, and you believe that a 4 percent risk premium over the yield of these bonds is appropriate for this stock. Thus, you specify a required rate of return of 14 percent.

In summary, you have estimated the dividend at $1.10 (payable at year end), an ending sale price of $22, and a required rate of return of 14 percent. Given these inputs, you would estimate the value of this stock as follows:

$$
\begin{aligned}
V_1 &= \frac{\$1.10}{(1+0.14)} + \frac{\$22}{(1+0.14)} \\
&= \frac{1.10}{1.14} + \frac{22.00}{1.14} \\
&= 0.96 + 19.30 \\
&= \$20.26
\end{aligned}
$$

Note that we have not mentioned the current market price of the stock. This is because the market price is not relevant to you as an investor except as a comparison to the independently derived value based on your estimates of the relevant variables. Once we have calculated the stock's value as $20.26, we can compare it to the market price and apply the investment decision rule: If the stock's market price is more than $20.26, do not buy; if it is equal to or less than $20.26, buy.

Multiple-Year Holding Period If you anticipate holding the stock for several years and then selling it, the valuation estimate is harder. You must forecast several future dividend payments and estimate the sale price of the stock several years in the future.

The difficulty with estimating future dividend payments is that the future stream can have numerous forms. The exact estimate of the future dividends depends on two projections. The first is your outlook for earnings growth because earnings are the source of dividends. The second projection is the firm's dividend policy, which can take several forms. A firm can have a constant percent payout of earnings each year, which implies a change in dividend each year, or the firm could follow a step pattern in which it increases the dividend rate by a constant dollar amount each year or every two or three years. The easiest dividend policy to analyze is one where the firm enjoys a constant growth rate in earnings and maintains a constant dividend payout. This set of assumptions implies that the dividend stream will experience a constant growth rate that is equal to the earnings growth rate.

Assume the expected holding period is three years, and you estimate the following dividend payments at the end of each year:

Year 1	$1.10/share
Year 2	$1.20/share
Year 3	$1.35/share

The next estimate is the expected sale price (*SP*) for the stock three years in the future. Again, if we use the DDM for this estimate, you would need to project the dividend growth pattern for this stock beginning three years from now. Assume an estimated sale price using the DDM of $34.

The final estimate is the required rate of return on this stock during this period. Assuming the 14 percent required rate is still appropriate, the value of this stock is

$$V = \frac{1.10}{(1+0.14)^1} + \frac{1.20}{(1+0.14)^2} + \frac{1.35}{(1+0.14)^3} + \frac{34.00}{(1+0.14)^3}$$

$$= \frac{1.10}{(1.14)} + \frac{1.20}{(1.30)} + \frac{1.35}{(1.4815)} + \frac{34.00}{(1.4815)}$$

$$= 0.96 + 0.92 + 0.91 + 22.95$$

$$= \$25.74$$

Again, to make an investment decision, you would compare this estimated value for the stock to its current market price to determine whether you should buy.

At this point, you should recognize that the valuation procedure discussed here is similar to that used in corporate finance when making investment decisions, except that the cash flows are from dividends instead of returns to an investment project. Also, rather than estimating the scrap value or salvage value of a corporate asset, we are estimating the ending sale price for the stock. Finally, rather than discounting cash flows using the firm's cost of capital, we use the individual's required rate of return on the company's equity. In both cases, we are looking for excess present value, which means that the present value of expected cash inflows—that is, the estimated intrinsic value of the asset—exceeds the present value of cash outflows, which is the market price of the asset.

Infinite Period Model We can extend the multiperiod model by extending our estimates of dividends 5, 10, or 15 years into the future. The benefits derived from these extensions would be minimal, however, and you would quickly become bored with this exercise. Instead, we will move to the infinite period dividend discount model, which assumes investors estimate future dividend payments for an infinite number of periods.

Needless to say, this is a formidable task! We must make some simplifying assumptions about this future stream of dividends to make the task viable. The easiest assumption is that *the future dividend stream will grow at a constant rate for an infinite period.* This is a rather heroic assumption in many instances, but where it does hold, we can use the model to value individual stocks as well as the aggregate market and alternative industries. This model is generalized as follows:

$$V_j = \frac{D_0(1+g)}{(1+k)} + \frac{D_0(1+g)^2}{(1+k)^2} + \ldots + \frac{D_0(1+g)^n}{(1+k)^n}$$

where:

V_j = the value of stock j
D_0 = the dividend payment in the current period
g = the constant growth rate of dividends
k = the required rate of return on stock j
n = the number of periods, which we assume to be infinite

In the appendix to this chapter, we show that with certain assumptions, this infinite period constant growth rate model can be simplified to the following expression:

$$V_j = \frac{D_1}{k-g}$$

You will probably recognize this formula as one that is widely used in corporate finance to estimate the cost of equity capital for the firm—that is, $k = D/V + g$.

To use this model for valuation, you must estimate (1) the required rate of return (k) and (2) the expected constant growth rate of dividends (g). After estimating g, it is a simple matter to estimate D_1, because it is the current dividend (D_0) times $(1 + g)$.

Consider the example of a stock with a current dividend of $1 a share, which you expect to rise to $1.09 next year. You believe that, over the long run, this company's earnings and dividends will continue to grow at 9 percent; therefore, your estimate of g is 0.09. For the long run, you expect the rate of inflation to decline, so you set your long-run required rate of return on this stock at 13 percent; your estimate of k is 0.13. To summarize the relevant estimates:

$$g = 0.09$$
$$k = 0.13$$
$$D_1 = 1.09(\$1.00 \times 1.09)$$
$$V = \frac{1.09}{0.13 - 0.09}$$
$$= \frac{1.09}{0.04}$$
$$= \$27.25$$

A small change in any of the original estimates will have a large impact on V, as shown by the following examples:

1. $g = 0.09$; $k = 0.14$; $D_1 = \$1.09$. (We assume an increase in k.)

$$V = \frac{\$1.09}{0.14 - 0.09}$$
$$= \frac{\$1.09}{0.05}$$
$$= \$21.80$$

2. $g = 0.10$; $k = 0.13$; $D_1 = \$1.10$. (We assume an increase in g.)

$$V = \frac{\$1.10}{0.13 - 0.10}$$
$$= \frac{\$1.10}{0.03}$$
$$= \$36.67$$

These examples show that as small a change as 1 percent in either g or k produces a large difference in the estimated value of the stock. The crucial relationship that determines the value of the stock is the *spread between the required rate of return* (k) *and the expected growth rate of dividends* (g). Anything that causes a decline in the spread will cause an increase in the computed value, whereas any increase in the spread will decrease the computed value of the stock.

Infinite Period DDM and Growth Companies

As noted in the appendix, the infinite period DDM has the following assumptions:

1. Dividends grow at a constant rate.
2. The constant growth rate will continue for an infinite period.
3. The required rate of return *(k) is greater than the infinite growth rate (g)*. If it is not, the model gives meaningless results because the denominator becomes negative.

What is the effect of these assumptions if you want to use this model to value the stock of growth companies, such as Intel, Merck, Microsoft, McDonald's, and Wal-Mart? **Growth companies** are firms that have the opportunities and abilities to earn rates of return on investments that are consistently above their required rates of return.[10] You will recall from corporate finance that the required rate of return for a corporation is its weighted average cost of capital (WACC). An example might be Intel, which has a WACC of about 12 percent, but is currently earning about 25 percent on its invested capital. Therefore, we would consider Intel a growth company. To exploit these outstanding investment opportunities, these growth firms generally retain a high percentage of earnings for reinvestment, and their earnings will grow faster than those of the typical firm. You will recall from the discussion in Chapter 10 that a firm's substainable growth is a function of its retention rate and its return on equity (ROE). Notably, as discussed subsequently, the earnings growth pattern for these growth companies is inconsistent with the assumptions of the infinite period DDM.

---

[10]Growth companies are discussed in Ezra Salomon, *The Theory of Financial Management* (New York: Columbia University Press, 1963); and Merton Miller and Franco Modigliani, "Dividend Policy, Growth, and the Valuation of Shares," *Journal of Business* 34, no. 4 (October 1961): 411–433. Models to value growth companies are discussed in Chapter 15.

First, the infinite period DDM assumes dividends will grow at a constant rate for an infinite period. This assumption seldom holds for companies currently growing at above average rates. As an example, both Intel and Wal-Mart have grown at rates in excess of 20 percent a year for several years. It is unlikely that they can maintain such extreme rates of growth because of the inability to continue earning the ROEs implied by this growth for an infinite period in an economy where other firms will compete with them for these high rates of return.

Second, during the periods when these firms experience abnormally high rates of growth, their rates of growth probably exceed their required rates of return. There is *no* automatic relationship between growth and risk; a high-growth company is not necessarily a high-risk company. In fact, a firm growing at a high *constant rate* would have lower risk (less uncertainty) than a low-growth firm with an unstable earnings pattern.

In summary, some firms experience periods of abnormally high rates of growth for some finite periods of time. The infinite period DDM cannot be used to value these true growth firms because these high-growth conditions are temporary and therefore inconsistent with the assumptions of the DDM. In the following section, we discuss how to supplement the DDM to value a firm with temporary supernormal growth. In Chapter 15 we will discuss additional models used for estimating the stock value of growth companies.

Valuation with Temporary Supernormal Growth

Thus far, we have considered how to value a firm with different growth rates for short periods of time (one to three years) and how to value a stock using a model that assumes a constant growth rate for an infinite period. As noted, the assumptions of the model make it impossible to use the infinite period constant growth model to value true growth companies. A company cannot permanently maintain a growth rate higher than its required rate of return because competition will eventually enter this apparently lucrative business, which will reduce the firm's profit margins and therefore its ROE and growth rate. Therefore, after a few years of exceptional growth—that is, a period of temporary supernormal growth—a firm's growth rate is expected to decline. Eventually its growth rate is expected to stabilize at a constant level consistent with the assumptions of the infinite period DDM.

To determine the value of a temporary supernormal growth company, you must combine the previous models. In analyzing the initial years of exceptional growth, you examine each year individually. If the company is expected to have two or three stages of supernormal growth, you must examine each year during these stages of growth. When the firm's growth rate stabilizes at a rate below the required rate of return, you can compute the remaining value of the firm assuming constant growth using the DDM and discount this lump-sum constant growth value back to the present. The technique should become clear as you work through the following example.

The Bourke Company has a current dividend (D_0) of $2 a share. The following are the expected annual growth rates for dividends.

YEAR	DIVIDEND GROWTH RATE
1–3	25%
4–6	20
7–9	15
10 on	9

EXHIBIT 11.3   *COMPUTATION OF VALUE FOR THE STOCK OF A COMPANY WITH TEMPORARY SUPERNORMAL GROWTH*

YEAR	DIVIDEND	DISCOUNT FACTOR (14 PERCENT)	PRESENT VALUE
1	$ 2.50	0.8772	$ 2.193
2	3.12	0.7695	2.401
3	3.91	0.6750	2.639
4	4.69	0.5921	2.777
5	5.63	0.5194	2.924
6	6.76	0.4556	3.080
7	7.77	0.3996	3.105
8	8.94	0.3506	3.134
9	10.28	0.3075[b]	3.161
10	11.21		
	$224.20[a]	0.3075[b]	68.941

Total value = $94.355

[a]Value of dividend stream for Year 10 and all future dividends (that is, $11.21/(0.14 − 0.09) = $224.20).
[b]The discount factor is the ninth-year factor because the valuation of the remaining stream is made at the end of Year 9 to reflect the dividend in Year 10 and all future dividends.

The required rate of return for the stock (the company's cost of equity) is 14 percent. Therefore, the value equation becomes

$$V_i = \frac{2.00(1.25)}{1.14} + \frac{2.00(1.25)^2}{(1.14)^2} + \frac{2.00(1.25)^3}{(1.14)^3}$$
$$+ \frac{2.00(1.25)^3(1.20)}{(1.14)^4} + \frac{2.00(1.25)^3(1.20)^2}{(1.14)^5}$$
$$+ \frac{2.00(1.25)^3(1.20)^3}{(1.14)^6} + \frac{2.00(1.25)^3(1.20)^3(1.15)}{(1.14)^7}$$
$$+ \frac{2.00(1.25)^3(1.20)^3(1.15)^2}{(1.14)^8} + \frac{2.00(1.25)^3(1.20)^3(1.15)^3}{(1.14)^9}$$
$$+ \frac{\dfrac{2.00(1.25)^3(1.20)^3(1.15)^3(1.09)}{(0.14-0.09)}}{(1.14)^9}$$

The computations in Exhibit 11.3 indicate that the total value of the stock is $94.36. As before, you would compare this estimate of intrinsic value to the market price of the stock when deciding whether to purchase the stock. The difficult part of the valuation is estimating the supernormal growth rates and determining *how long* each of the growth rates will last.

To summarize this section, the initial present value of cash flow stock valuation model considered was the dividend discount model (DDM). After explaining the basic model and the derivation of its reduced form, we noted that the infinite period DDM cannot be applied to the valuation of stock for growth companies because the abnormally high growth rate of earnings for the growth company is inconsistent with the assumptions of the infinite period constant growth DDM model. Subsequently we modified the DDM model to evaluate companies with temporary supernormal growth. In the following sections, we discuss the other present value of cash flow techniques assuming a similar set of scenarios.

**Present Value of
Operating Free
Cash Flows**

In this model, you are deriving the value of the total firm because you are discounting the operating free cash flows prior to the payment of interest to the debt holders but after deducting funds needed to maintain the firm's asset base (capital expenditures). Also, because you are discounting the total firm's operating free cash flow, you would use the firm's weighted average cost of capital (*WACC*) as your discount rate. Therefore, once you estimate the value of the total firm, you subtract the value of debt, assuming your goal is to estimate the value of the firm's equity. The total value of the firm is equal to:

$$V_j = \sum_{t=1}^{n} \frac{OFCF_t}{(1 + WACC_j)^t}$$

where:

V_j = value of firm j
n = number of periods assumed to be infinite
$OFCF_t$ = the firm's operating free cash flow in period t. The specification of operating free cash flow will be discussed in Chapter 15.
$WACC_j$ = firm j's weighted average cost of capital. The computation of the firm's *WACC* will be discussed in Chapter 15.

Similar to the process with the DDM, it is possible to envision this as a model that requires estimates for an infinite period. Alternatively, if you are dealing with a mature firm whereby its operating cash flows have reached a stage of stable growth, you can adapt the infinite period constant growth DDM model as follows:

$$V_j = \frac{OFCF_1}{WACC_j - g_{OFCF}}$$

where:

$OFCF_1$ = operating free cash flow in period 1 equal to $OFCF_0(1 + g_{OFCF})$
g_{OFCF} = long-term constant growth rate of operating free cash flow

Alternatively, assuming that the firm is expected to experience several different rates of growth for *OFCF*, these estimates can be divided into three or four stages, as demonstrated with the temporary supernormal dividend growth model. Similar to the dividend model, the analyst must estimate the *rate* of growth and the *duration* of growth for each of these periods of supernormal growth as follows:

YEAR	OFCF GROWTH RATE
1–4	20%
5–7	16
8–10	12
11 on	7

Therefore, the calculations would estimate the specific *OFCF*s for each year through Year 10 based on the expected growth rates, but you would use the infinite growth model estimate when the growth rate reached stability after Year 10. As noted, after determining the value of the total firm V_j, you must subtract the value of all nonequity items, including accounts payable, total interest-bearing debt, deferred taxes, and preferred stock, to arrive at the estimated value of the firm's equity. This calculation will be demonstrated in Chapter 15.

Present Value of Free Cash Flows to Equity

The third discounted cash flow technique deals with "free" cash flows to equity, which would be derived *after* operating free cash flows have been adjusted for debt payments (interest and principle). Also, these cash flows precede dividend payments to the common stockholder. Such cash flows are referred to as "free" because they are what is left after meeting all obligations to other capital suppliers (debt and preferred stock) and after providing the funds needed to maintain the firm's asset base (similar to operating free cash flow).

Notably, because these are cash flows available to equity owners, the discount rate used is the firm's cost of equity (*k*) rather than the firm's *WACC*.

$$V_j = \sum_{t=1}^{n} \frac{FCFE_t}{(1+k_j)^t}$$

where:

> V_j = **value of the stock of firm *j***
> n = **number of periods assumed to be infinite**
> $FCFE_t$ = **the firm's free cash flow to equity in period *t*. The specification of free cash flow to equity will be discussed in Chapter 15.**

Again, how an analyst would implement this general model depends upon the firm's position in its life cycle. That is, if the firm is expected to experience stable growth, analysts can use the infinite growth model. In contrast, if the firm is expected to experience a period of temporary supernormal growth, analysts should use the multistage growth model similar to the process used with dividends and for operating free cash flow.

RELATIVE VALUATION TECHNIQUES

In contrast to the various discounted cash flow techniques that attempt to estimate a specific value for a stock based on its estimated growth rates and its discount rate, the relative valuation techniques implicitly contend that it is possible to determine the value of an economic entity (i.e., the market, an industry, or a company) by comparing it to similar entities on the basis of several relative ratios that compare its stock price to relevant variables that affect a stock's value, such as earnings, cash flow, book value, and sales. Therefore, in this section, we discuss the following relative valuation ratios: (1) price/earnings (*P/E*), (2) price/cash flow (*P/CF*), (3) price/book value (*P/BV*), and price/sales (*P/S*). We begin with the *P/E* ratio, also referred to as the earnings multiplier model, because it is the most popular relative valuation ratio. In addition, we will show that the *P/E* ratio can be directly related to the DDM in a manner that indicates the variables that affect the *P/E* ratio.

Earnings Multiplier Model

As noted, many investors prefer to estimate the value of common stock using an **earnings multiplier model**. The reasoning for this approach recalls the basic concept that the value of any investment is the present value of future returns. In the case of common stocks, the returns that investors are entitled to receive are the net earnings of the firm. Therefore, one way investors can estimate value is by determining how many dollars they are willing to pay for a dollar of expected earnings (typically represented by the estimated earnings during the following 12-month period). For example, if investors are willing to pay 10 times expected earnings, they would value a stock they expect to earn $2 a share during the following year at $20. You can compute the prevailing earnings multiplier, also referred to as the **price/earnings (P/E) ratio**, as follows:

$$\text{Earnings Multiplier} = \text{Price / Earnings Ratio}$$

$$= \frac{\text{Current Market Price}}{\text{Expected 12-Month Earnings}}$$

This computation of the current earnings multiplier (*P/E* ratio) indicates the prevailing attitude of investors toward a stock's value. Investors must decide if they agree with the prevailing *P/E* ratio (that is, is the earnings multiplier too high or too low?) based upon how it compares to the *P/E* ratio for the aggregate market, for the firm's industry, and for similar firms and stocks.

To answer this question, we must consider what influences the earnings multiplier (*P/E* ratio) over time. For example, over time the aggregate stock market *P/E* ratio, as represented by the S&P Industrials Index, has varied from about 6 times earnings to about 30 times earnings.[11] The infinite period dividend discount model can be used to indicate the variables that should determine the value of the *P/E* ratio as follows:[12]

$$P_i = \frac{D_1}{k - g}$$

If we divide both sides of the equation by E_1 (expected earnings during the next 12 months), the result is

$$\frac{P_i}{E_1} = \frac{D_1/E_1}{k - g}$$

Thus, the *P/E* ratio is determined by

1. The *expected* dividend payout ratio (dividends divided by earnings)
2. The *estimated* required rate of return on the stock (k)
3. The *expected* growth rate of dividends for the stock (g)

As an example, if we assume a stock has an expected dividend payout of 50 percent, a required rate of return of 12 percent, and an expected growth rate for dividends of 8 percent, this would imply the following:

$$D/E = 0.50; k = 0.12; g = 0.08$$

$$P/E = \frac{0.50}{0.12 - 0.08}$$

$$= 0.50 / 0.04$$

$$= 12.5$$

---

[11]When computing historical *P/E* ratios, the practice is to use earnings for the past 12 months rather than expected earnings. Although this will influence the level, it demonstrates the changes in the *P/E* ratio over time. Although it is appropriate to use historical *P/E* ratios for past comparison, we strongly believe that investment decisions should emphasize future *P/E* ratios that use *expected* earnings.

[12]In this formulation of the model we use *P* rather than *V* (that is, the value is stated as the estimated price of the stock). Although the factors that determine the *P/E* are the same for growth companies, this formula cannot be used to estimate a specific value because these firms do not have dividends and the ($k - g$) assumptions don't apply.

Again, a small difference in either k or g or both will have a large impact on the earnings multiplier, as shown in the following three examples.

1. $D/E = 0.50$; $k = 0.13$; $g = 0.08$. (In this example, we assume a higher k for the stock.)

$$P/E = \frac{0.50}{0.13 - 0.08}$$
$$= \frac{0.50}{0.05}$$
$$= 10$$

2. $D/E = 0.50$; $k = 0.12$; $g = 0.09$. (In this example, we assume a higher g for the stock and the original k.)

$$P/E = \frac{0.50}{0.12 - 0.09}$$
$$= \frac{0.50}{0.03}$$
$$= 16.7$$

3. $D/E = 0.50$; $k = 0.11$; $g = 0.09$. (In this example, we assume a fairly optimistic scenario where the k for the stock is only 11 percent and there is a higher expected growth rate of dividends of 9 percent).

$$P/E = \frac{0.50}{0.11 - 0.09}$$
$$= \frac{0.50}{0.02}$$
$$= 25$$

As before, *the spread between* k *and* g *is the main determinant of the size of the* P/E *ratio.* Although the dividend payout ratio has an impact, we are generally referring to a firm's long-run target payout, which is typically rather stable with little effect on year-to-year changes in the *P/E* ratio (earnings multiplier).

After estimating the earnings multiple, you would apply it to your estimate of earnings for the next year (E_1) to arrive at an estimated value. In turn, E_1 is based on the earnings for the current year (E_0) and your expected growth rate of earnings. Using these two estimates, you would compute an estimated value of the stock and compare this estimated value to its market price.

Consider the following estimates for an example firm:

$$D/E = 0.50$$
$$k = 0.12$$
$$g = 0.09$$
$$E_0 = \$2.00$$

Using these estimates, you would compute an earnings multiple of:

$$P/E = \frac{0.50}{0.12 - 0.09} = \frac{0.50}{0.03} = 16.7$$

Given current earnings (E_0) of \$2.00 and a g of 9 percent, you would expect E_1 to be \$2.18. Therefore, you would estimate the value (price) of the stock as

$$V = 16.7 \times \$2.18$$
$$= \$36.41$$

As before, you would compare this estimated value of the stock to its current market price to decide whether you should invest in it. This estimate of value is referred to as a "two-step process" because it requires you to estimate future earnings (E_1) and a P/E ratio based on expectations of k and g. These two estimates are discussed in Chapter 15.

The Price/Cash Flow Ratio

The growth in popularity of this relative valuation ratio can be traced to concern over the propensity of some firms to manipulate earnings per share, whereas cash flow values are generally less prone to manipulation. Also, as noted, cash flow values are important in fundamental valuation (when computing the present value of cash flow), and they are critical when doing credit analysis where "cash is king." The price to cash flow ratio is computed as follows:

$$P/CF_j = \frac{P_t}{CF_{t+1}}$$

where:

> P/CF_j = **the price/cash flow ratio for firm** j
> P_t = **the price of the stock in period** t
> CF_{t+1} = **the expected cash flow per share for firm** j

Regarding what variables affect this valuation ratio, the factors are similar to the P/E ratio. Specifically, the main variables should be: (1) the expected growth rate of the cash flow variable used, and (2) the risk of the stock as indicated by the uncertainty or variability of the cash flow series over time. The specific cash flow measure used is typically EBITDA, but the measure will vary depending upon the nature of the company and industry and which cash flow specification (for example, operating cash flow or free cash flow) is the best measure of performance for this industry. An appropriate ratio can also be affected by the firm's capital structure.

The Price/Book Value Ratio

The price/book value (P/BV) ratio has been widely used for many years by analysts in the banking industry as a measure of relative value. The book value of a bank is typically considered a good indicator of intrinsic value because most bank assets, such as bonds and commercial loans, have a value equal to book value. This ratio gained in popularity and credibility as a relative valuation technique for all types of firms based upon a study by Fama and French that indicated a significant inverse relationship between P/BV ratios and excess rates of return for a cross section of stocks.[13] The P/BV ratio is specified as follows:

$$P/BV_j = \frac{P_t}{BV_{t+1}}$$

---

[13]Eugene Fama and Kenneth French, "The Cross Section of Expected Returns," *Journal of Finance* 47, no. 2 (June 1992). This study was discussed in Chapter 6.

where:

P/BV_j = **the price/book value ratio for firm** j
P_t = **the price of the stock in period** t
BV_{t+1} = **the estimated end-of-year book value per share for firm** j

As with other relative valuation ratios, it is important to match the current price with the future book value that is expected to prevail at the end of the year. The difficulty is that this future book value is not generally available. One can derive an estimate of the end-of-year book value based upon the historical growth rate for the series or use the growth rate implied by the sustainable growth formula: g = (ROE) (Retention Rate).

Regarding what factors determine the size of the P/BV ratio, it is a function of ROE relative to the firm's cost of equity since the ratio would be one if they were equal—that is, if the firm earned its required return on assets. In contrast, if the ROE is much larger, it is a growth company and investors are willing to pay a premium over book value for the stock.

The Price/Sales Ratio

The price/sales (P/S) ratio has a volatile history. It was a favorite of Phillip Fisher, a well-known money manager in the late 1950s, his son, and others.[14] Recently, the P/S ratio has been suggested as useful by Martin Leibowitz, a widely admired stock and bond portfolio manager.[15] These advocates consider this ratio meaningful and useful for two reasons. First, they believe that strong and consistent sales growth is a requirement for a growth company. Although they note the importance of an above-average profit margin, they contend that *the growth process must begin with sales.* Second, given all the data in the balance sheet and income statement, sales information is subject to less manipulation than any other data item. The specific P/S ratio is:

$$P/S_j = \frac{P_t}{S_{t+1}}$$

where:

P/S_j = **the price to sales ratio for firm** j
P_t = **the price of the stock in period** t
S_{t+1} = **the expected sales per share for firm** j

Again, it is important to match the current stock price with the firm's *expected* sales per share, which may be difficult to derive for a large cross section of stocks. Two caveats are relevant to the price to sales ratio. First, this particular relative valuation ratio varies dramatically by industry. For example, the sales per share for retail firms, such as Kroger or Wal-Mart, are typically much higher than sales per share for computer or microchip firms. The second consideration is the profit margin on sales. The point is, retail food stores have high sales per share, which will cause a low P/S ratio, which is considered good until one realizes that these firms have low net profit margins. Therefore, your relative valuation analysis using the P/S ratio should be between firms in the same or similar industries.

---

[14]Phillip A. Fisher, *Common Stock and Uncommon Profits,* rev. ed. (Woodside, Calif.: PSR Publications, 1984); Kenneth L. Fisher, *Super Stocks* (Homewood, Ill.: Dow Jones–Irwin, 1984); and A. J. Senchak, Jr., and John D. Martin, "The Relative Performance of the PSR and PER Investment Strategies," *Financial Analysts Journal* 43, no. 2 (March–April, 1987): 46–56.

[15]Martin L. Leibowitz, *Sales Driven Franchise Value* (Charlottesville, Va.: The Research Foundation of the Institute of Chartered Financial Analysts, 1997).

Implementing the Relative Valuation Technique

As noted, the relative valuation technique considers several valuation ratios—such as *P/E, P/BV*—to derive a value for a stock. To properly implement this technique, it is essential to compare the various ratios but also to recognize that the analysis needs to go beyond simply comparing the ratios—it is necessary to understand what factors affect each of the valuation ratios and, therefore, know why they should differ. The first step is to compare the valuation ratio (e.g., the *P/E* ratio) for a company to the comparable ratio for the market, for the stock's industry, and to other stocks in the industry to determine how it compares—that is, is it similar to these other *P/E*s, or is it consistently at a premium or discount? Beyond knowing the overall relationship to the market, industry, and competitors, the real analysis is involved in understanding *why* the ratio has this relationship or why it should *not* have this relationship and the implications of this mismatch. Specifically, the second step is to explain the relationship. To do this, you need to understand what factors determine the specific valuation ratio and then compare these factors for the stock versus the same factors for the market, industry, and other stocks.

To illustrate this process, consider the following example wherein you want to value the stock of a pharmaceutical company and, to help in this process, you decide to employ the *P/E* as a relative valuation technique. Assume that you compare the *P/E* ratios for this firm over time (e.g., the last 15 years) to similar ratios for the S&P Industrials, the pharmaceutical industry, and competitors. The results of this comparison indicate that the company *P/E* ratios are consistently above all the other sets. The obvious question leads you into the second part of the analysis—whether the fundamental factors that affect the *P/E* ratio (i.e., the firm's growth rate and required rate of return) justify the higher *P/E*. A positive scenario would be that the firm had a historical and expected growth rate that was substantially above all the comparables and a lower required rate of return. This would indicate that the higher *P/E* ratio is justified; the only question that needs to be considered is, How much higher should the *P/E* ratio be? Alternatively, the negative scenario would be if the company's expected growth rate was equal to or lower than the industry and competitors while the required *k* was higher than for the industry and competitors. This would signal a stock that is apparently overpriced based on the fundamental factors that determine a stock's *P/E* ratio.

In subsequent sections, we will discuss how an analyst arrives at estimates for *g* and *k,* and we will demonstrate the process in subsequent chapters. At this point, the idea is to understand the overall process required by the relative valuation technique.

ESTIMATING THE INPUTS: THE REQUIRED RATE OF RETURN AND THE EXPECTED GROWTH RATE OF VALUATION VARIABLES

This section deals with estimating two inputs that are critical to the valuation process irrespective of which approach or technique is being used: the required rate of return (*k*) and the expected growth rate of earnings and other valuation variables—that is, book value, cash flow, sales, and dividends.

We will review these factors and discuss how the estimation of these variables differs for domestic versus foreign securities. Although the valuation procedure is the same for securities around the world, *k* and *g* differ among countries. Therefore, we will review the components of the required rate of return for U.S. securities and then consider the components for foreign securities. Subsequently, we consider the estimation of the growth rate of earnings, cash flow, and dividends for domestic stocks and then for foreign stocks.

Required Rate of Return (*k*)

This discussion reviews the determinants of the nominal required rate of return on an investment, including a consideration of factors for non-U.S. markets. This required rate of return will be the discount rate for most cash flow models and affects all the relative valuation techniques. The only difference in the discount rate is between the present value of dividends and the present value of free cash flow techniques, which use the required rate of return on equity (*k*), and the present value of operating free cash flow technique, which uses the weighted average cost of capital (*WACC*), wherein the cost of equity is a critical input to estimating the firm's *WACC*.

Recall that three factors influence an investor's required rate of return:

1. The economy's real risk-free rate (*RRFR*)
2. The expected rate of inflation (*I*)
3. A risk premium (*RP*)

The Economy's Real Risk-Free Rate   This is the absolute minimum rate that an investor should require. It depends on the real growth rate of the investor's home economy because capital invested should grow at least as fast as the economy. As noted previously, this rate can be affected for short periods of time by temporary tightness or ease in the capital markets.

The Expected Rate of Inflation   Investors are interested in real rates of return that will allow them to increase their rate of consumption. Therefore, if investors expect a given rate of inflation, they should increase their required nominal risk-free rate of return (*NRFR*) to reflect any expected inflation as follows:

$$NRFR = [1 + RRFR]\,[1 + E(I)] - 1$$

where:

$E(I)$ = **expected rate of inflation**

The two factors that determine the *NRFR* affect all investments, from U.S. government securities to highly speculative land deals. Investors who hope to calculate security values accurately must carefully estimate the expected rate of inflation. Not only does the *NRFR* affect all investments, but its extreme volatility makes its estimation difficult.

The Risk Premium   The risk premium (*RP*) causes differences in the required rates of return among alternative investments that range from government bonds to corporate bonds to common stocks. The *RP* also explains the difference in the expected return among securities of the same type. For example, this is the reason corporate bonds with different ratings of Aaa, Aa, or A have different yields, and why different common stocks have widely varying earnings multipliers despite similar growth expectations.

In Chapter 1, we noted that investors demand a risk premium because of the uncertainty of returns expected from an investment. A measure of this uncertainty of returns was the dispersion of expected returns. We suggested several internal factors that influence a firm's variability of returns, such as its business risk, financial risk, and liquidity risk. We noted that securities of foreign firms or of domestic companies with significant foreign sales and earnings (e.g., Coca-Cola and McDonald's) bring additional risk factors, including exchange rate risk and country (political) risk.

Changes in the Risk Premium   Because different securities have different patterns of returns and different guarantees to investors, we expect their risk premiums to differ. In addition, the risk premiums for the same securities can *change over time*. For example, Exhibit 11.4 shows the spread between the yields to maturity for Aaa-rated corporate bonds and Baa-rated corporate bonds from 1974 through 2001. This yield spread, or difference in yield, is a measure of the risk

EXHIBIT 11.4 *TIME-SERIES PLOT OF MOODY'S CORPORATE BOND YIELD SPREADS (Baa–Aaa): MONTHLY 1974–2001*

Source: Lehman Brothers.

premium for investing in higher-risk bonds (Baa) compared to low-risk bonds (Aaa). As shown, the yield spread varied from about 0.40 percent to 2.69 percent (from less than one-half of 1 percent to almost 3 percent).

Exhibit 11.5 contains a plot of the *ratio* of the yields for the same period, which indicates the percentage risk premium of Baa bonds compared to Aaa bonds. You might expect a larger difference in yield between Baa and Aaa bonds if Aaa bonds are yielding 12 percent rather than 6 percent. The yield ratio in Exhibit 11.5 adjusts for this size difference. This shows that even adjusting for the yield level difference, the risk premium ratio varies from about 1.06 to 1.33—a 6 percent premium to a 33 percent premium over the base yield on Aaa bonds. This change in risk premium over time occurs because either investors perceive a change in the level of risk of Baa bonds compared to Aaa bonds or there is a change in the amount of return that investors require to accept the same risk differential. In either case, this change in the risk premium for a set of assets implies a change in the slope of the security market line (SML). This change in the slope of the SML was demonstrated in Chapter 1.

In Chapter 13, we will discuss the controversy regarding an appropriate equity market risk premium and the question of possible changes in the long-run equity risk premium.

Estimating the Required Return for Foreign Securities

Our discussion of the required rate of return for investments has been limited to the domestic market. Although the basic valuation model and its variables are the same around the world, there are significant differences in the values for specific variables. This section points out where these differences occur.

EXHIBIT 11.5 *TIME-SERIES PLOT OF MOODY'S CORPORATE BOND YIELD RATIO (Baa YIELD/Aaa YIELD): MONTHLY 1974–2001*

Source: Lehman Brothers.

Foreign Real RFR Because the *RRFR* in other countries should be determined by the real growth rate within the particular economy, the estimated rate can vary substantially among countries due to differences in an economy's real growth rate. An example of differences in the real growth rate of gross domestic product (GDP) can be seen in Exhibit 11.6. There is a range of estimates for 2003 of 2.0 percent (that is, 1.0 percent for Japan compared to 3.0 percent for the United States). This difference in the growth rates of real GDP implies a substantial difference in the RRFR for these countries.

Inflation Rate To estimate the *NRFR* for a country, you must also estimate its expected rate of inflation and adjust the *NRFR* for this expectation. Again, this rate of inflation typically varies substantially among countries. The price change data in Exhibit 11.7 show that the expected rate of inflation during 2003 varied from –0.7 percent in Japan to 2.6 percent in the United Kingdom. Assuming equal growth, this implies a difference in the nominal required rate of return between these two countries of 3.3 percent. Such a difference in *k* can have a substantial impact on estimated values, as demonstrated earlier. Again, you must make a separate estimate for each individual country in which you are evaluating securities.

To demonstrate the combined impact of differences in real growth and expected inflation, Exhibit 11.8 shows the results of the following computation for the six countries based on the year 2003 estimates:

$$NRFR = (1 + \text{Real Growth}) \times (1 + \text{Expected Inflation}) - 1$$

EXHIBIT 11.6   *GROWTH OF REAL GDP (PERCENTAGE CHANGES FROM PREVIOUS YEAR)*

PERIOD	UNITED STATES	JAPAN	GERMANY	FRANCE	UNITED KINGDOM	ITALY
1990	0.8%	5.6%	4.6%	2.5%	1.0%	1.9%
1991	0.1	3.6	3.3	1.2	−1.2	1.5
1992	2.1	1.5	1.5	1.2	−0.5	1.0
1993	3.0	0.1	−1.9	−0.7	1.9	−0.4
1994	3.5	0.5	2.9	2.8	4.0	2.1
1995	2.0	0.9	1.9	2.2	2.5	3.0
1996	2.8	3.9	1.4	1.6	2.5	0.7
1997	3.9	1.4	2.2	2.3	3.5	1.5
1998	3.8	−2.7	2.9	3.0	2.4	1.4
1999	3.8	1.1	1.8	3.2	2.5	2.0
2000	4.1	2.4	3.0	3.6	3.0	2.9
2001E	1.2	−0.4	0.6	2.0	2.4	1.9
2002E	1.9	−1.1	0.7	1.1	1.6	1.3
2003E	3.0	1.0	1.8	2.6	2.8	2.4

Source: *World Investment Strategy Highlights* by Neil Williams, Alain Kernels, and Joseph Hickey, employees of Goldman, Sachs & Co. Copyright March 2002 by Goldman, Sachs & Co. Used with permission.

EXHIBIT 11.7   *CHANGES IN CONSUMER OR RETAIL PRICES (PERCENTAGE CHANGES FROM PREVIOUS YEAR)*

PERIOD	UNITED STATES	JAPAN	GERMANY	FRANCE	UNITED KINGDOM	ITALY
1990	5.4%	3.0%	2.7%	3.4%	9.5%	6.1%
1991	4.7	3.2	3.5	3.1	6.0	6.0
1992	3.0	1.7	4.0	2.8	3.7	5.2
1993	3.0	1.3	4.2	2.1	1.6	4.2
1994	2.6	0.7	2.7	2.1	2.4	3.9
1995	2.8	0.0	1.8	1.6	2.8	5.4
1996	2.9	0.1	1.5	2.0	3.0	3.9
1997	2.3	1.7	1.8	1.2	2.8	1.7
1998	1.6	0.7	0.9	0.7	2.7	1.7
1999	1.9	−0.9	0.5	0.4	2.3	1.2
2000	3.4	−0.7	2.1	1.8	2.1	2.6
2001E	2.8	−0.7	2.4	1.8	2.1	2.7
2002E	1.2	−0.9	1.4	1.6	2.7	2.0
2003E	2.0	−0.7	1.3	1.5	2.6	1.4

Source: *World Investment Strategy Highlights* by Neil Williams, Alain Kernels, and Joseph Hickey, employees of Goldman, Sachs & Co. Copyright March 2002 by Goldman, Sachs & Co. Used with permission.

EXHIBIT 11.8 ▶ *ESTIMATES OF YEAR 2003 NOMINAL RFR FOR MAJOR COUNTRIES*

COUNTRY	REAL GROWTH IN GDP[a]	EXPECTED INFLATION[b]	NOMINAL RFR
United States	3.0%	2.0%	5.1%
Japan	1.0	−0.7	0.3
Germany	1.8	1.3	3.1
France	2.6	1.5	4.1
United Kingdom	2.8	2.6	5.5
Italy	2.4	1.4	3.8

[a]Taken from Exhibit 11.6.
[b]Taken from Exhibit 11.7.
Source: Reprinted by permission of Goldman, Sachs & Co.

Given the differences between countries in the two components, the range in the *NRFR* of 5.2 percent is not surprising (5.5 percent for the United Kingdom versus 0.3 percent for Japan). As demonstrated earlier, such a difference in *k* for an investment will have a significant impact on its value.

Risk Premium   You must also derive an equity risk premium for the investments in each country. Again, the five risk components differ substantially between countries: business risk, financial risk, liquidity risk, exchange rate risk, and country risk. *Business risk* can vary because it is a function of the variability of economic activity within a country and of the operating leverage used by firms within the country. Firms in different countries assume significantly different *financial risk* as well. For example, Japanese firms use substantially more financial leverage than U.S. or U.K. firms. Regarding *liquidity risk,* the U.S. capital markets are acknowledged to be the most liquid in the world, with Japan and the United Kingdom being close behind. In contrast, some emerging markets are quite illiquid and investors need to add a significant liquidity risk premium.

When investing globally, you also must estimate *exchange rate risk,* which is the additional uncertainty of returns caused by changes in the exchange rates for the currency of another country. This uncertainty can be small for a U.S. investor in a country such as Hong Kong because the currency is pegged to the U.S. dollar. In contrast, in some countries, substantial volatility in the exchange rate over time can mean significant differences in the domestic return for the country and return in U.S. dollars.[16] The level of volatility for the exchange rate differs between countries. The greater the uncertainty regarding future changes in the exchange rate, the larger the exchange rate risk for the country.[17]

Recall that country risk arises from unexpected events in a country, such as upheavals in its political or economic environment. An example of political and economic disruptions occurred in Russia during 1998 when there was substantial uncertainty about the potential devaluation of the ruble and the stock market declined over 60 percent between January and

---

[16]Although we generally refer to these as domestic and U.S. dollar returns, you will also see references to *hedged* returns (for example, domestic) and *unhedged* returns (returns in U.S. dollars). In some cases, the hedged returns will adjust for the cost of hedging.

[17]For a thorough analysis of exchange rate determination and forecasting models, see Michael Rosenberg, *Currency Forecasting* (Burr Ridge, Ill.: Irwin Professional Publishing, 1996).

August 1998. Similarly, unrest in Indonesia during 1998 led to riots and the eventual resignation of President Suharto. Such political unrest or a change in the economic environment creates uncertainties that increase the risk of investments in these countries. Before investing in such countries, investors must evaluate the additional returns they should require to accept this increased uncertainty.

Thus, when estimating required rates of return on foreign investments, you must assign a unique risk premium for each country.

Expected Growth Rates After arriving at a required rate of return, the investor must estimate the growth rate of cash flows, earnings, and dividends because the alternative valuation models for common stock depend heavily on good estimates of growth (g) for these variables. The initial procedure we describe here is similar to the presentation in Chapter 10, where we used financial ratios to measure a firm's growth potential. Subsequently, we discuss the use of historical growth rates as an input to the estimate.

Estimating Growth from Fundamentals

The growth rate of dividends is determined by the growth rate of earnings and the proportion of earnings paid out in dividends (the payout ratio). Over the short run, dividends can grow faster or slower than earnings if the firm changes its payout ratio. Specifically, if a firm's earnings grow at 6 percent a year and it pays out exactly 50 percent of earnings in dividends, then the firm's dividends will likewise grow at 6 percent a year. Alternatively, if a firm's earnings grow at 6 percent a year and the firm increases its payout, then during the period when the payout ratio increases, dividends will grow faster than earnings. In contrast, if the firm reduces its payout ratio, dividends will grow slower than earnings for a period of time. Because there is a limit to how long this difference in growth rates can continue, most investors assume that the long-run dividend payout ratio is fairly stable. Therefore, analysis of the growth rate of dividends typically concentrates on an analysis of the growth rate of equity earnings. Also, as will be shown in Chapter 15, these earnings are the major factor driving the operating cash flows or the free cash flows for the firm.

When a firm retains earnings and acquires additional assets, if it earns some positive rate of return on these additional assets, the total earnings of the firm will increase because its asset base is larger. How rapidly a firm's earnings increase depends on (1) the proportion of earnings it retains and reinvests in new assets and (2) the rate of return it earns on these new assets. Specifically, the growth rate (g) of equity earnings (that is, earnings per share) without any external financing is equal to the percentage of net earnings retained (the retention rate, which equals 1 – the payout ratio) times the rate of return on equity capital.

$$g = (\text{Retention Rate}) \times (\text{Return on Equity})$$
$$= RR \times ROE$$

Therefore, a firm can increase its growth rate by increasing its retention rate (reducing its payout ratio) and investing these added funds at its historic *ROE*. Alternatively, the firm can maintain its retention rate but increase its *ROE*. For example, if a firm retains 50 percent of net earnings and consistently has an *ROE* of 10 percent, its net earnings will grow at the rate of 5 percent a year, as follows:

$$g = RR \times ROE$$
$$= 0.50 \times 0.10$$
$$= 0.05$$

If, however, the firm increases its retention rate to 75 percent and invests these additional funds in internal projects that earn 10 percent, its growth rate will increase to 7.5 percent, as follows:

$$g = 0.75 \times 0.10$$
$$= 0.075$$

If, instead, the firm continues to reinvest 50 percent of its earnings but derives a higher rate of return on these investments, say 15 percent, it can likewise increase its growth rate, as follows:

$$g = 0.50 \times 0.15$$
$$= 0.075$$

Breakdown of ROE Although the retention rate is a management decision, changes in the firm's ROE result from changes in its operating performance or its financial leverage. As discussed in Chapter 10, we can divide the ROE ratio into three components:

$$ROE = \frac{\text{Net Income}}{\text{Sales}} \times \frac{\text{Sales}}{\text{Total Assets}} \times \frac{\text{Total Assets}}{\text{Equity}}$$

$$= \frac{\text{Profit}}{\text{Margin}} \times \frac{\text{Total Asset}}{\text{Turnover}} \times \frac{\text{Financial}}{\text{Leverage}}$$

This breakdown allows us to consider the three factors that determine a firm's ROE.[18] Because it is a multiplicative relationship, an increase in any of the three ratios will cause an increase in ROE. The first two of the three ratios reflect operating performance, and the third one indicates a firm's financing decision.

The first operating ratio, net profit margin, indicates the firm's profitability on sales. This ratio changes over time for some companies and is highly sensitive to the business cycle. For growth companies, this is one of the first ratios to decline because the increased competition increases the supply of the goods or services and forces price cutting, which leads to lower profit margins. Also, during recessions, profit margins decline because of price cutting or because of higher percentages of fixed costs due to lower sales.

The second component, total asset turnover, is the ultimate indicator of operating efficiency and reflects the asset and capital requirements of the business. Although this ratio varies dramatically by industry, within an industry it is an excellent indicator of management's operating efficiency.

The product of these first two components (profit margin and total asset turnover) equals the firm's return on assets (ROA), which reflects the firm's operating performance before the financing impact.[19]

The final component, total assets/equity, does not measure operating performance but, rather, financial leverage. Specifically, it indicates how management has decided to finance the firm. In turn, this management decision regarding the financing of assets can contribute to a higher ROE, but it also has financial risk implications for the stockholder.

Knowing this breakdown of ROE, you must examine past results and expectations for a firm and develop *estimates* of the three components and therefore an estimate of a firm's ROE. This

---

[18]You will recall from Chapter 10 (Exhibit 10.7) that it is possible to employ an extended DuPont system that involves eight ratios. For purposes of this discussion, the three ratios indicate the significant differences among countries.

[19]In Chapter 14, we will discuss a study that analyzes why and how alternative industries differ regarding the return on assets and the two components.

estimate of *ROE* combined with the firm's expected retention rate will indicate its future growth potential. Finally, it is important to note that when estimating growth, it is necessary to estimate, not only the *rate* of growth, but also the *duration* of growth (how long can the firm sustain this rate of growth?) Clearly, the higher the rate of growth the more significant the estimate of the duration of growth to the ultimate value of the stock.

Estimating Growth Based on History

Although the authors have a strong bias in favor of using the fundamentals to estimate future growth, which involves estimating the components of *ROE*, we also believe in using all the information available to make this critical estimate. Therefore, we suggest that analysts also consider the historical growth rate of sales, earnings, cash flow, and dividends in this process.

Although we will demonstrate these computations for the market, for an industry, and for a company in subsequent chapters, the following discussion considers some suggestions on alternative calculations. In terms of the relevant period to consider, one is struck by the cliché "more is better" as long as you recognize that "recent is relevant." Specifically, about 20 years of annual observations would be ideal, but it is important to consider subperiods as well as the total period—that is, 20 years, two 10-year periods, and four 5-year periods would indicate the overall growth rate but also would indicate if there were any *changes* in the growth rate in recent periods.

The specific measurement can be done using one or more of three techniques: (1) arithmetic or geometric average of annual percentage changes, (2) linear regression models, and (3) log-linear regression models. Irrespective of the measurement techniques used, we strongly encourage a time-series plot of the annual percentage changes.

The arithmetic or geometric average technique involves computing the annual percentage change and then computing either the simple arithmetic average or the geometric average of these values for the alternative periods. As you will recall from the discussion in Chapter 3, the arithmetic average will always be a higher value than the geometric average (except when the annual values are constant) and the difference between the arithmetic and geometric average values will increase with volatility. As noted previously, we generally prefer the geometric mean because it provides the average annual compound growth rate.

The linear regression model goes well with the suggested time-series plot and is as follows:

$$EPS_t = a + bt$$

where:

> EPS_t = **earnings per period in period** t
> t = **year** t **where** t **goes from 1 to** n
> b = **the coefficient that indicates the average absolute change in the series during the period**

It would be very informative to superimpose this regression line on the time-series plot because it would provide insights on changes in absolute growth.

The log-linear model considers that the series might be better described in terms of a constant *growth rate*. This model is as follows:

$$1n(EPS_t) = a + bt$$

where:

> $1n(EPS_t)$ = **the natural logarithm of earnings per share in period** t
> b = **the coefficient that indicates** *the average percentage change* **in the series during the period**

The analysis of these historical growth rates both visually with the time-series graph and the alternative calculations should provide you with significant insights into the trend of the growth rates as well as the *variability* of the growth rates over time. This could provide information on the unit's business risk with the analysis of sales and EBIT growth.

Estimating Dividend Growth for Foreign Stocks

The underlying factors that determine the growth rates for foreign stocks are similar to those for U.S. stocks, but the value of the equation's components may differ substantially from what is common in the United States. The differences in the retention rate or the components of *ROE* result from differences in accounting practices as well as alternative management performance or philosophy.

Retention Rates   The retention rates for foreign corporations differ within countries, but differences also exist among countries due to differences in the countries' investment opportunities. As an example, firms in Japan have a higher retention rate than firms in the United States, whereas the rate of retention in France is much lower. Therefore, you need to examine the retention rates for a number of firms in a country as a background for estimating the standard rate within a country.

Net Profit Margin   The net profit margin of foreign firms can differ because of different accounting conventions between countries. As noted in Chapter 10, foreign accounting rules allow firms to recognize revenue and allocate expenses differently from U.S. firms. For example, German firms are allowed to build up large reserves for various reasons. As a result, they report low earnings for tax purposes. Also, different foreign depreciation practices require adjustment of earnings and cash flows.

Total Asset Turnover   Total asset turnover can likewise differ among countries because of different accounting conventions on the reporting of asset values at cost or market values. For example, in Japan, a large part of the market values for some firms comes from their real estate holdings and their common stock investments in other firms. These assets are reported at cost, which typically has substantially understated their true value. This also means that the total asset turnover ratio for these firms is substantially overstated.

This ratio will also be impacted by leases that are not capitalized on the balance sheet—that is, both assets and liabilities are understated.

Total Asset/Equity Ratio   This ratio, a measure of financial leverage, differs among countries because of differences in economic environments, tax laws, management philosophies regarding corporate debt, and accounting conventions. In several countries, the attitude toward debt is much more liberal than in the United States. A prime example is Japan, where debt as a percentage of total assets is almost 50 percent higher than a similar ratio in the United States. Notably, most corporate debt in Japan entails borrowing from banks at fairly low rates of interest. Balance sheet debt ratios may be higher in Japan than in the United States or other countries; but, because of the lower interest rates in Japan, the fixed-charge coverage ratios, such as the times interest earned ratio, might be similar to those in other countries. The point is, it is important to consider the several cash flow financial risk ratios along with the balance sheet debt ratios.

Consequently, when analyzing a foreign stock market or an individual foreign stock that involves estimating the growth rate for earnings and dividends, you must consider the three components of the *ROE* just as you would for a U.S. stock. You must recognize that the financial ratios for foreign firms can differ from those of U.S. firms, as discussed in Chapter 10 references. Subsequent chapters on valuation applied to the aggregate market, to various industries, and to companies contain examples of these differences.

The Internet *Investments Online*

Several sites that we discussed in earlier chapters contained financial calculators. By inputting the required data, users can determine if it is better to buy or lease a car, calculate returns, and determine how much money they will have if funds are invested at a certain rate of return over time.

The sites listed all contain financial calculators that may be of use to investors and financial planners.
http://www.financenter.com
http://www.jamesko.com/FinCalc
http://www.numeraire.com

Summary

• As an investor, you want to select investments that will provide a rate of return that compensates you for your time, the expected rate of inflation, and the risk involved. To help you find these investments, this chapter considers the theory of valuation by which you derive the value of an investment using your required rate of return. We consider the two investment decision processes, which are the top-down, three-step approach and the bottom-up, stockpicking approach. Although it is recognized that either process can provide abnormal positive returns if the analyst is superior, we feel that a preferable approach is the top-down approach in which you initially consider the aggregate economy and market, then examine alternative global industries, and finally analyze individual firms and their stocks.

• We apply the valuation theory to a range of investments, including bonds, preferred stock, and common stock. Because the valuation of common stock is more complex and difficult, we suggest two alternative approaches (the present value of cash flows and the relative valuation approach) and several techniques for each of these approaches. Notably, we do *not* believe that these are competitive approaches but suggest that *both* approaches be used. Although we suggest using several different valuation models, the investment decision rule is always the same: If the estimated intrinsic value of the investment is greater than the market price, you should buy the investment; if the estimated intrinsic value of an investment is less than its market price, you should not invest in it.

• We conclude with a review of factors that you need to consider when estimating the value of stock with either approach—your required rate of return on an investment and the growth rate of earnings, cash flow, and dividends. Finally, we consider some unique factors that affect the application of these valuation models to foreign stocks.

Questions

1. Discuss the difference between the top-down and bottom-up approaches. What is the major assumption that causes the difference in these two approaches?
2. What is the benefit of analyzing the market and alternative industries before individual securities?
3. Discuss why you would not expect all industries to have a similar relationship to the economy. Give an example of two industries that have different relationships to the economy.
4. Discuss why estimating the value for a bond is easier than estimating the value for common stock.
5. Would you expect the required rate of return for a U.S. investor in U.S. common stocks to be the same as the required rate of return on Japanese common stocks? What factors would determine the required rate of return for stocks in these countries?
6. Would you expect the nominal *RFR* in the United States to be the same as in Germany? Discuss your reasoning.
7. Would you expect the risk premium for an investment in an Indonesian stock to be the same as that for a stock from the United Kingdom? Discuss your reasoning.
8. Would you expect the risk premium for an investment in a stock from Singapore to be the same as that for a stock from the United States? Discuss your reasoning.

9. Give an example of a stock where it would be appropriate to use the reduced form DDM for valuation and discuss why you feel that it is appropriate. Similarly, give an example and discuss a stock where it would not be appropriate to use the reduced form DDM.

10. Give an example of and discuss a stock that has temporary, supernormal growth where it would be appropriate (necessary) to use the modified DDM.

11. Under what conditions will it be ideal to use one or several of the relative valuation ratios to evaluate a stock?

12. Discuss a scenario where it would be appropriate to use one of the present value of cash flow techniques for the valuation.

13. Discuss why the two valuation approaches (present value of cash flows and the relative valuation ratios) are competitive or complementary.

Problems

1. What is the value to you of a 9 percent coupon bond with a par value of $10,000 that matures in 10 years if you want a 7 percent return? Use semiannual compounding.

2. What would be the value of the bond in Problem 1 if you wanted an 11 percent rate of return?

3. The preferred stock of the Clarence Radiology Company has a par value of $100 and a $9 dividend rate. You require an 11 percent rate of return on this stock. What is the maximum price you would pay for it? Would you buy it at a market price of $96?

4. The Baron Basketball Company (BBC) earned $10 a share last year and paid a dividend of $6 a share. Next year, you expect BBC to earn $11 and continue its payout ratio. Assume that you expect to sell the stock for $132 a year from now. If you require 12 percent on this stock, how much would you be willing to pay for it?

5. Given the expected earnings and dividend payments in Problem 4, if you expected a selling price of $110 and required an 8 percent return on this investment, how much would you pay for the BBC stock?

6. Over the long run, you expect dividends for BBC in Problem 4 to grow at 8 percent and you require 11 percent on the stock. Using the infinite period DDM, how much would you pay for this stock?

7. Based on new information regarding the popularity of basketball, you revise your growth estimate for BBC to 9 percent. What is the maximum P/E ratio you will apply to BBC, and what is the maximum price you will pay for the stock?

8. The Shamrock Dogfood Company (SDC) has consistently paid out 40 percent of its earnings in dividends. The company's return on equity is 16 percent. What would you estimate as its dividend growth rate?

9. Given the low risk in dog food, your required rate of return on SDC is 13 percent. What P/E ratio would you apply to the firm's earnings?

10. What P/E ratio would you apply if you learned that SDC had decided to increase its payout to 50 percent? (Hint: This change in payout has multiple effects.)

11. Discuss three ways a firm can increase its ROE. Make up an example to illustrate your discussion.

12. It is widely known that grocery chains have low profit margins—on average they earn about 1 percent on sales. How would you explain the fact that their ROE is about 12 percent? Does this seem logical?

13. Compute a recent five-year average of the following ratios for three companies of your choice (attempt to select diverse firms):
    a. Retention rate
    b. Net profit margin
    c. Equity turnover
    d. Total asset turnover
    e. Total assets/equity
    Based on these ratios, explain which firm should have the highest growth rate of earnings.

14. You have been reading about the Maddy Computer Company (MCC), which currently retains 90 percent of its earnings ($5 a share this year). It earns an *ROE* of almost 30 percent. Assuming a required rate of return of 14 percent, how much would you pay for MCC on the basis of the earnings multiplier model? Discuss your answer. What would you pay for Maddy Computer if its retention rate was 60 percent and its *ROE* was 19 percent? Show your work.

15. Gentry Can Company's (GCC) latest annual dividend of $1.25 a share was paid yesterday and maintained its historic 7 percent annual rate of growth. You plan to purchase the stock today because you believe that the dividend growth rate will increase to 8 percent for the next three years and the selling price of the stock will be $40 per share at the end of that time.
    a. How much should you be willing to pay for the GCC stock if you require a 12 percent return?
    b. What is the maximum price you should be willing to pay for the GCC stock if you believe that the 8 percent growth rate can be maintained indefinitely and you require a 12 percent return?
    c. If the 8 percent rate of growth is achieved, what will the price be at the end of Year 3, assuming the conditions in Part b?

16. In the *Federal Reserve Bulletin,* find the average yield of AAA and BBB bonds for a recent month. Compute the risk premium (in basis points) and the percentage risk premium on BBB bonds relative to AAA bonds. Discuss how these values compare to those shown in Exhibits 11.4 and 11.5.

References

Bhatia, Sanjiv, ed. *Global Equity Investing.* Proceedings of a seminar by the Association of Investment Management and Research. Charlottesville, Va.: AIMR, 1995.

Billingsley, Randall, ed. *Corporate Financial Decision Making and Equity Analysis.* Proceedings of a seminar by the Association of Investment Management and Research. Charlottesville, Va.: AIMR, 1995.

Copeland, T. E., Tim Koller, and Jack Murrin. *Valuation: Measuring and Managing the Value of Companies,* 3d ed. New York: Wiley, 2001.

Cornell, Bradford. *Corporate Valuation.* Burr Ridge, Ill.: Irwin Professional Publishing, 1993.

Damodaran, Aswath. *Damodaran on Valuation.* New York: Wiley, 1994.

Damodaran, Aswath. *Investment Valuation.* New York: Wiley, 1996.

Farrell, James L. "The Dividend Discount Model: A Primer." *Financial Analysts Journal* 41, no. 6 (November–December 1985).

Fogler, H. Russell, ed. *Blending Quantitative and Traditional Equity Analysis.* Proceedings of a seminar by the Association of Investment Management and Research. Charlottesville, Va.: AIMR, 1994.

Gastineau, Gary L., and Sanjiv Bhatia, eds. *Risk Management.* Proceedings of a seminar by the Association of Investment Management and Research. Charlottesville, Va.: AIMR, 1995.

Helfert, Erich A. *Techniques of Financial Analysis,* 10th ed. Burr Ridge, Ill.: Irwin McGraw-Hill, 2000.

Higgins, Robert C. *Analysis for Financial Management,* 5th ed. Chicago: Richard D. Irwin, Inc., 2000.

Levine, Sumner N., ed. *The Financial Analysts Handbook,* 2d ed. Homewood, Ill.: Dow Jones–Irwin, 1988.

Palepu, Krishna, Victor Bernard, and Paul Healy. *Business Analysis and Valuation.* Cincinnati, Ohio: SouthWestern Publishing, 1996.

Sharpe, William, and Katrina Sherrerd, eds. *Quantifying the Market Risk Premium Phenomenon for Investment Decision Making.* Proceedings of a seminar by the Association of Investment Management and Research. Charlottesville, Va.: AIMR, 1989.

Squires, Jan, ed. *Value and Growth Styles in Equity Investing.* Proceedings of a seminar by the Association of Investment Management and Research. Charlottesville, Va.: AIMR, 1995.

Squires, Jan, ed. *Equity Research and Valuation Techniques.* Proceedings of a seminar by the Association of Investment Management and Research. Charlottesville, Va.: AIMR, 1997.

Squires, Jan, ed. *Practical Issues in Equity Analysis.* Conference proceedings by the Association of Investment Management and Research. Charlottesville, Va.: AIMR, 2000.

APPENDIX
Chapter 11

Derivation of Constant Growth Dividend Discount Model (DDM)

The basic model is

$$P_0 = \frac{D_1}{(1+k)^1} + \frac{D_2}{(1+k)^2} + \frac{D_3}{(1+k)^3} + \ldots + \frac{D_n}{(1+k)^n}$$

where:

P_0 = current price
D_i = expected dividend in period i
k = required rate of return on asset j

If growth rate (g) is constant,

$$P_0 = \frac{D_0(1+g)^1}{(1+k)^1} + \frac{D_0(1+g)^2}{(1+k)^2} + \ldots + \frac{D_0(1+g)^n}{(1+k)^n}$$

This can be written

$$P_0 = D_0\left[\frac{(1+g)}{(1+k)} + \frac{(1+g)^2}{(1+k)^2} + \frac{(1+g)^3}{(1+k)^3} + \ldots + \frac{(1+g)^n}{(1+k)^n}\right]$$

Multiply both sides of the equation by $\dfrac{1+k}{1+g}$.

$$\left[\frac{(1+g)}{(1+k)}\right]P_0 = D_0\left[1 + \frac{(1+g)}{(1+k)} + \frac{(1+g)^2}{(1+k)^2} + \ldots + \frac{(1+g)^{n-1}}{(1+k)^{n-1}}\right]$$

Subtract the previous equation from this equation:

$$\left[\frac{(1+k)}{(1+g)} - 1\right]P_0 = D_0\left[1 - \frac{(1+g)^n}{(1+k)^n}\right]$$

$$\left[\frac{(1+k)-(1+g)}{(1+g)}\right]P_0 = D_0\left[1 - \frac{(1+g)^n}{(1+k)^n}\right]$$

Assuming $k > g$, as $n \to \infty$, the term in brackets on the right side of the equation goes to 1, leaving:

$$\left[\frac{(1+k)-(1+g)}{(1+g)}\right]P_0 = D_0$$

This simplifies to

$$\left[\frac{(1+k-1-g)}{(1+g)}\right]P_0 = D_0$$

which equals

$$\left[\frac{k-g}{(1+g)}\right]P_0 = D_0$$

This equals

$$(k-g)P_0 = D_0(1+g)$$
$$D_0(1+g) = D_1$$

so:

$$(k-g)P_0 = D_1$$
$$P_0 = \frac{D_1}{k-g}$$

Remember, this model assumes

- A constant growth rate
- An infinite time period
- The required return on the investment (k) is greater than the expected growth rate (g)

Chapter 12 Macroeconomic and Market Analysis: The Global Asset Allocation Decision

After you read this chapter, you should be able to answer the following questions:

➤ What are the expected and the empirical relationships between economic activity and security markets?

➤ What is the macroeconomic approach to estimating future market returns?

➤ What are the major macroeconomic techniques used to project the securities market?

➤ What is the leading economic indicator approach? What are its uses and shortcomings?

➤ What are the expected and the empirical relationships between the growth of the money supply and stock prices?

➤ What is meant by excess liquidity, and how is it measured?

➤ What is the effect of monetary policy on stock prices in the United States and around the world?

➤ What are the expected and the empirical relationships between inflation, interest rates, and bond prices?

➤ What are the expected and the empirical relationships between inflation and stock prices?

➤ When analyzing world security markets, what is the relationship between inflation and interest rates in alternative countries? What is the effect of inflation and interest rates on exchange rates?

➤ How do the basic valuation variables differ among countries?

➤ How do stock price returns among countries correlate when considering domestic returns and returns in U.S. dollars?

➤ What factors should be considered when analyzing the outlook for a foreign economy and its stock and bond market?

➤ What is the asset allocation procedure for a global portfolio?

➤ For a world asset allocation, what is meant by normal weighting, underweighting, and overweighting?

In Chapter 11, we introduced the three-step investment process and found that, although we are ultimately interested in securities markets, we analyze economies because of the strong link between the overall economic environment in a country and the performance of its security markets. *Security markets reflect what is expected to go on in an economy* because the value of an investment is determined by its expected cash flows and its future required rate of return, and both of these factors are influenced by its expected aggregate economic environment. Therefore, if you want to estimate cash flows, interest rates, and risk premiums for securities, you need to consider aggregate economic analysis.

From this interrelated economy–security market perspective, we begin by examining various techniques that relate economic variables to security markets. The first section discusses the expected relationship between economic activity and the security markets and provides empirical evidence of this relationship. Subsequently, we discuss several techniques that reflect this approach, including the use of leading economic indicators, the analysis of money supply growth, and other measures of monetary policy. Following this, we consider the effect of inflation on interest rates, bond prices, and stock returns.

Although most of the discussion focuses on the U.S. economy, we recognize the need to apply these techniques to other countries. To provide insights into this global investment process, we discuss an example of global investment analysis by an investment firm. The culmination of this analysis is a global asset allocation of investment funds among countries and further allocation within countries to specific asset classes: bonds, stocks, and cash equivalents.

In Chapter 11, we discussed analyzing the general economy as part of estimating future aggregate market values that imply future returns from investing in common stocks and/or bonds. Three major techniques are available for analyzing securities markets. First, the *macroeconomic approach* attempts to project the outlook for securities markets based on the underlying relationship between the aggregate economy and the securities markets. Second, the *micro-analysis approach* involves using the present value of cash flows and the relative valuation ratios to estimate a value for a country's aggregate stock market. Finally, the *technical analysis approach* assumes that the best way to determine future changes in security market values is to examine past movements in interest rates, security prices, and other market variables.

This chapter discusses the macroeconomic approach to security market analysis and considers the asset allocation decisions that flow from this analysis.

ECONOMIC ACTIVITY AND SECURITY MARKETS

Fluctuations in security markets are related to changes in the aggregate economy. The price of most bonds is determined by the level of interest rates, which are influenced by overall economic activity and Federal Reserve policy. Individual stock prices reflect investor expectations about an issuing firm's performance in terms of earnings, cash flow, and the investor's required rate of return. This performance is likewise affected by the overall performance of the economy.

In its monitoring of business cycles, the National Bureau of Economic Research (NBER) has examined the relationship of alternative economic series to the behavior of the entire economy and has classified numerous economic series into three groups: leading, coincident, and lagging indicator series. Further, extensive analysis of the relationship between the economy and the stock market has shown that stock prices are one of the better leading indicator series.

The evidence not only has indicated a strong relationship between stock prices and the economy but also has shown that stock prices consistently turn *before* the economy does.[1] The data in Exhibit 12.1 document this relationship, beginning in the 1950s including several instances of false signals given by the stock market.

---

[1] A detailed analysis of this relationship is contained in Geoffrey H. Moore and John P. Cullity, "Security Markets and Business Cycles," *The Financial Analysts Handbook,* 2d ed., ed. Sumner N. Levine (Homewood, Ill.: Dow Jones–Irwin, 1988). Also see Jeremy J. Siegel, "Does It Pay Stock Investors to Forecast the Business Cycle?" *Journal of Portfolio Management* 18. no. 1 (Fall 1991).

| EXHIBIT 12.1 ▶ | TIMING RELATIONSHIPS BETWEEN STOCK MARKET AND BUSINESS CYCLE PEAKS AND TROUGHS |

I. Stock Market Declines Associated with a Subsequent Recession

STOCK MARKET CYCLES[a]				BUSINESS CYCLES				LEAD OF STOCK MARKET OVER BUSINESS CYCLE	
PEAK		TROUGH		PEAK		TROUGH		PEAK	TROUGH
Jan.	1953	Sep.	1953	Jul.	1953	May	1954	6.0	8.0
Aug.	1956	Oct.	1957	Aug.	1957	Apr.	1958	11.0	6.0
Aug.	1959	Oct.	1960	Apr.	1960	Feb.	1961	8.0	4.0
Nov.	1968	May	1970	Dec.	1969	Nov.	1970	12.0	6.0
Jan.	1973	Oct.	1974	Nov.	1973	Mar.	1975	10.0	5.0
Feb.	1980	Aug.	1982	Jan.	1980	Nov.	1982	(1.0)	3.0
						Average		7.7	5.3

II. False Signals

Dec.	1961	Jan.	1962
Apr.	1971	Nov.	1971
Sep.	1976	Mar.	1978

III. Stock Market Declines Associated with a Subsequent Growth Recession

Feb.	1966	Mar.	1968

[a]Defined as market declines of approximately 15 percent or more.

Source: Jason Benderly and Edward McKelvey, "The Pocket Chartbook," *Economic Research,* Goldman, Sachs & Co., December 1987. Reprinted by permission of Goldman, Sachs & Co.

There are two possible reasons why stock prices lead the economy. One is that stock prices reflect *expectations* of earnings, dividends, and interest rates. As investors attempt to estimate these future variables, their stock price decisions reflect expectations for *future* economic activity, not current activity. A second possible reason is that the stock market reacts to various leading indicator series, the most important being corporate earnings, corporate profit margins, interest rates, and changes in the growth rate of the money supply. Because these series tend to lead the economy, when investors adjust stock prices to reflect expectations for these leading economic series, it makes stock prices a leading series as well.

Because stock prices lead the aggregate economy, our macroeconomic approach to market analysis concentrates on economic series that lead the economy by more than stock prices do. First, we discuss cyclical indicator approaches developed by various research groups. Next, we consider the money supply, as well as other measures of monetary liquidity and policy. Finally, we discuss the research related to a number of economic series expected to affect security returns (e.g., production, inflation, and risk premiums).

CYCLICAL INDICATOR APPROACH TO FORECASTING THE ECONOMY ▶

The *cyclical indicator approach* to forecasting the economy contends that the aggregate economy expands and contracts in discernible periods. The NBER, a nonprofit organization that

EXHIBIT 12.2 *COMPONENTS OF THE CONFERENCE BOARD LEADING INDEX*

	MEDIAN LEAD (−) OR LAG (+) (IN MONTHS)		
	Peaks	Troughs	All Turns
1. Average weekly hours of production workers (manufacturing)	−11	−½	−7
2. Average weekly initial claims for unemployment insurance (inverted)	−12	−1½	−4
3. Manufacturers' new orders in 1996 dollars—consumer goods and materials	−12	−½	−2
4. Index of raw private housing units authorized by local building permits	−11	−2½	−10
5. Index of stock prices, 500 common stocks	−8½	−4	−5
6. M2 money supply in 1996 dollars	−10	−3	−7
7. Vendor performance (percentage of firms receiving slower deliveries)	−4	−1½	−3
8. Manufacturers' new orders, nondefense capital goods	−8½	−½	−2½
9. Interest rate spread, 10-year Treasury yield less federal funds	−21	−12½	−21
10. Index of consumer expectations	−14	−4½	−6

Source: Marie P. Hertzberg and Barry A. Beckman, "Business Cycle Indicators: Revised Composite Indexes," *Business Conditions Digest* 17, no. 1 (January 1989); and The Conference Board (2002).

attempts to interpret important economic facts scientifically and impartially explains the business cycle as follows:

> The business cycle concept has been developed from the sequence of events discerned in the historical study of the movements of economic activity. Though there are many cross-currents and variations in the pace of business activity, periods of business expansion appear to cumulate to peaks. As they cumulate, contrary forces tend to gain strength, bringing about a reversal in business activity and the onset of a recession. As a recession continues, forces for an expansion gradually emerge until they become dominant and a recovery begins.[2]

The NBER examined the behavior of hundreds of economic time series in relation to past business cycles and grouped various economic series into three major categories based on their relationship to the business cycle.

Cyclical Indicator Categories

The first category, **leading indicators** of the business cycle, includes economic series that usually reach peaks or troughs before corresponding peaks or troughs in aggregate economic activity. The group currently includes the 10 series shown in Exhibit 12.2, which indicates the median lead or lag for each series relative to business cycle peaks or troughs. Included are common stock prices, which have a median lead of four months at peaks and troughs and the money supply in constant (1992) dollars, which has a median lead of five months at peaks and four months at troughs.

---

[2]Julius Shiskin, "Business Cycle Indicators: The Known and the Unknown," *Review of the International Statistical Institute* 31, no. 3 (1963): 361–383.

EXHIBIT 12.3	COMPONENTS OF THE CONFERENCE BOARD COINCIDENT AND LAGGING INDEXES

	MEDIAN LEAD (−) OR LAG (+) (IN MONTHS)		
	PEAKS	TROUGHS	ALL TURNS
A. Coincident Indicator Series			
1. Employees on nonagricultural payrolls	0	0	0
2. Personal income less transfer payments in 1996 dollars	0	−½	0
3. Index of industrial productions	−2	0	0
4. Manufacturing and trade sales in 1996 dollars	−3	−½	−1
B. Lagging Indicator Series			
1. Average duration of unemployment in weeks (inverted)	−2	+9	+5
2. Ratio of manufacturing and trade inventories to sales in 1996 dollars	+10	+20	+13
3. Average prime rate charged by banks	+2½	+20½	+5½
4. Commercial and industrial loans outstanding in 1996 dollars	+5	+12½	+9
5. Ratio of consumer installment credit outstanding to personal income	−4	+11	+5
6. Labor cost per unit of output in manufacturing, actual data as percentage of trend	+6	+7	+6½
7. Change in consumer price index for services	+3	+5	+5

Source: Moore, "The Leading Indicator Approach"; Hertzberg and Beckman, "Business Cycle Indicators," and The Conference Board (2002).

The second category, **coincident indicators**, includes economic time series that have peaks and troughs that roughly coincide with the peaks and troughs in the business cycle. As one might expect, many of these economic time series are used to define the different phases of the cycle.

The third category, **lagging indicators**, includes series that experience their peaks and troughs after those of the aggregate economy. A listing and the average timing relationships for the coincident and lagging series appear in Exhibit 12.3.

A final category, *selected series,* includes economic series that are expected to influence aggregate economic activity but do not fall neatly into one of the three main groups. This includes such series as U.S. balance of payments and federal surplus or deficit.

Composite Series and Ratio of Series   In addition to the individual economic series in each category, a composite time series combines these economic series—for example, the *composite leading indicator index.* This composite leading indicator series is widely reported in the press each month as an indicator of the current and future state of the economy. There also are composite coincident and lagging indicator series.

Some analysts have used a *ratio* of these composite series, contending that the ratio of the composite coincident series divided by the composite lagging series acts like a leading series, in some instances even leading the composite leading series. The rationale for expecting this leading relationship for the ratio is that the coincident series should turn before the lagging series, and the ratio of the two series will be quite sensitive to such changes. As a result, this ratio series is expected to lead both of the individual composite series, especially at turning points.

EXHIBIT 12.4   *INDICATOR SERIES PERFORMANCE*

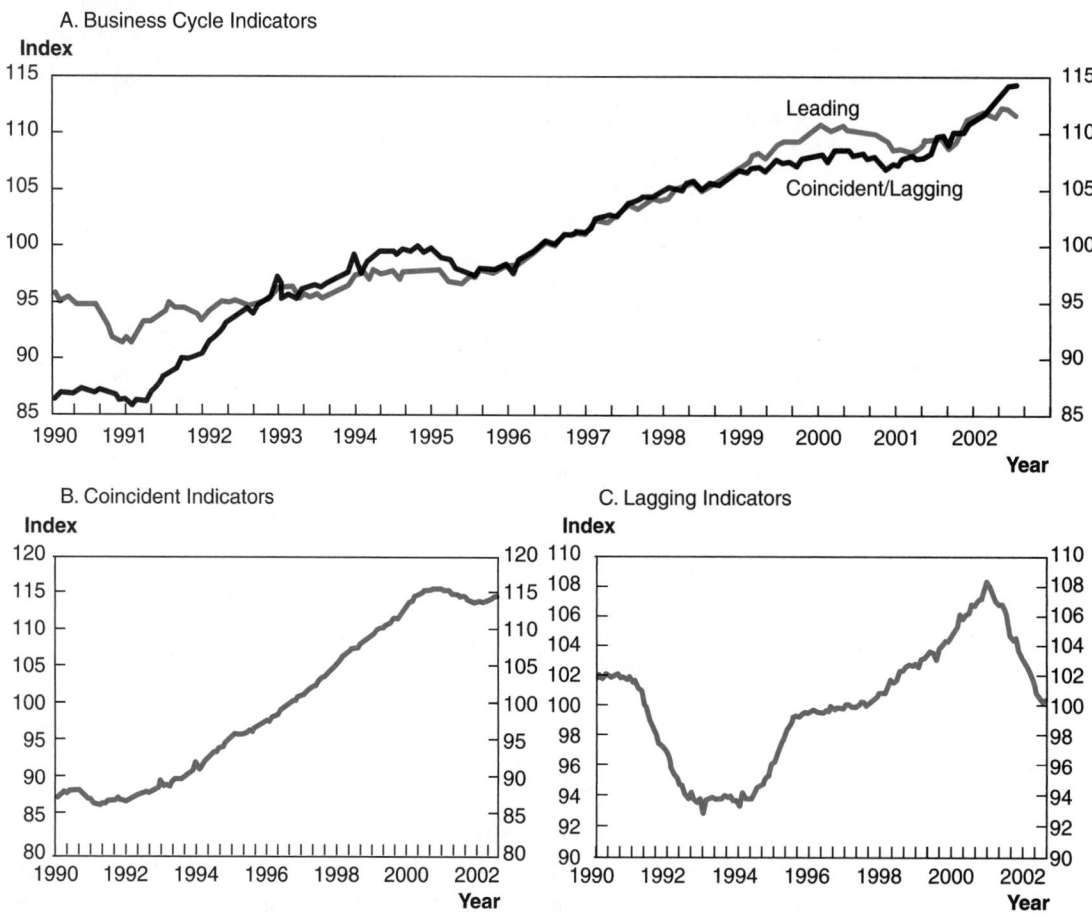

Source: Created by authors using data provided by The Conference Board from its *Business Cycle Indicators* database.

Although movements for this ratio series are generally parallel to those of the leading series, its real value comes when it diverges from the composite leading indicator series because this divergence signals a change in the normal relationship between the indicator series. For example, if the leading indicator series has been rising for a period of time, you would expect both the coincident and lagging series also to be rising, but the coincident series should be rising faster than the lagging series, so the ratio of the coincident to the lagging series should likewise be rising. In contrast, assume the composite leading indicator series is rising but the ratio of coincident to lagging series is flattening out or declining. This change in trend in the ratio series could occur because the coincident series is not rising as fast as the lagging indicator series or because the coincident series has turned down. Either scenario would indicate a possible end to an economic expansion or at least a less-robust expansion.

An example of such a divergence appears in Exhibit 12.4. The pattern indicates that between 1991 and mid-1994, the ratio series increased at a faster rate than the leading series because the coincident series was rising while the lagging series declined dramatically from 1991 to 1993 and was flat from 1993 to mid-1994. It appears that both the ratio series and the leading series experienced softness during 1995 and have increased together from 1996 to the beginning of 1999.

Analytical Measures of Performance

When predicting the future based on an economic series, it is important to consider more than the behavior of the series alone. Certain analytical measures have been suggested for examining behavior within an alternative economic series.

Diffusion Indexes   As the name implies, diffusion indexes indicate how pervasive a given movement is in a series. Diffusion index values are measured by computing the percentage of reporting units in a series that indicate a given result. For example, if 100 companies constitute the sample reporting new orders for equipment, the diffusion index for this series would indicate what proportion of the 100 companies was reporting higher orders during an expansion. In addition to knowing that aggregate new orders are increasing, it is helpful to know whether 55 percent or 95 percent of the companies in the sample are reporting higher orders. This information on the pervasiveness of the increase in new orders would help you project the future length and strength of an expansion.

You also would want to know the prevailing *trend* for a diffusion index. The diffusion index for a series almost always reaches its peak or trough before the peak or trough in the corresponding aggregate series. Therefore, you can use the diffusion index for a series to predict the behavior of the series itself. Assume that you are interested in the leading series, Manufacturers' New Orders in 1992 dollars—Consumer Goods. If the diffusion index for this series drops from 85 percent to 75 percent and then to 70 percent, it indicates a widespread receipt of new orders, but it also indicates a *diminishing* breadth to the increase and possibly a forthcoming decline in the series itself.

Besides creating diffusion indexes for individual series, there is also a diffusion index that shows the percentage of the 10 leading indicators rising or falling during a given period. This particular diffusion index is widely reported each month as an indicator of the future state of the economy.

Rates of Change   Knowing whether a series is increasing is useful, but more helpful is knowing that a 7 percent increase one month followed a 10 percent increase the previous month. The point is, the series is growing but at a declining rate. Similar to the diffusion index, the rate of change values for a series reaches peaks or troughs prior to the peak or trough in the aggregate series.

Direction of Change   Direction of change tables show which series rose or fell (indicated by plus or minus signs) during the most recent period and how long the movement in this direction has persisted.

Comparison with Previous Cycles   A set of tables and charts shows the movements of individual series during the current business cycle and compares these movements to previous cycles for the same economic series. This comparison reveals whether a given series is moving slower or faster than during prior cycles. This information can be useful because, typically, movements in the initial months of an expansion or contraction indicate their ultimate length and strength.[3]

Limitations of the Cyclical Indicator Approach

The NBER consistently has attempted to improve the usefulness of the cyclical indicators while acknowledging some limitations. The most obvious limitation is *false signals.* Past patterns might suggest that current indicator values signal a contraction, but then the indicator series turns up again and nullifies previous signals. A similar problem occurs when the indicators show

---

[3]Monthly presentations of all the series and analytical measures appear in the *Business Cycle Indicators* published by the Conference Board.

hesitancy that is difficult to interpret. Some economic series may exhibit *high variability,* diminishing confidence in short-run signals as compared to projecting longer-term trends.

Another limitation is the *currency of the data* and *revisions.* The problem is that you might not get the original data very soon and then you have to be aware of subsequent revisions that may actually change the sign or direction of a series. Many of the series are seasonally adjusted, so you also must watch for changes in the seasonal adjustment factors.

Also, no series adequately reflects the service sector, which has grown to be a major factor in our economy. Further, no series represents the very important global economy or world securities markets. Similarly, the whole import-export sector is represented only in the "other series" group when, in fact, the export sector was the fastest-growing sector of our economy in the 1990s. Finally, there are numerous political or international developments that significantly influence the economy, but these factors cannot be incorporated into a statistical system.[4]

Other Leading Indicator Series

The Center for International Business Conditions Research (CIBCR) at the Columbia Graduate School of Business has developed several additional leading indicator series. Monthly data for these series developed and maintained by the CIBCR are available in "The Leading Indicator Press Release." This release is published about the 10th day of each month with data as of 6 weeks prior to its release.

Long-Leading Index   The CIBCR has developed its *Long-Leading Index* to provide earlier signals of major turning points in the economy than other leading indexes. It includes the following four series: (1) Dow Jones bond prices (20 bonds by percentage of face value); (2) the ratio of price to unit labor cost in manufacturing (1982 = 100); (3) M2 money supply, deflated (billion 1992 dollars); and (4) new housing building permits (1967 = 100). This index has anticipated recessions by 14 months, on average, and always by at least 7 months.

Leading Employment Index   The purpose of the CIBCR's *Leading Employment Index* (1967 = 100) is to forecast future changes in U.S. employment. It includes the following six component series:

1. Average workweek in manufacturing
2. Overtime hours in manufacturing
3. Percentage layoff rate (inverted)
4. Voluntary/involuntary part-time employment
5. Percentage short duration unemployment rate (inverted)
6. Initial claims for unemployment insurance (inverted)

Leading Inflation Index   The CIBCR *Leading Inflation Index* is intended as a tool for forecasting inflation in the United States. It includes five variables:

1. The percentage employed of the working-age population
2. The growth rate of total debt (including business, consumer, and federal government debt)
3. The growth rate of industrial material prices
4. The growth rate of an index of import prices
5. The percentage of businesspeople anticipating an increase in their selling prices, as determined by a Dun and Bradstreet survey

---

[4]These problems are discussed in Evan Koenig and Kenneth Emery, "Misleading Indicators? Using the Composite Leading Indicators to Predict Cyclical Turning Points," Federal Reserve Bank of Dallas, *Economic Review* (July 1991): 1–14.

The leads for this series during the period 1950 to 1998 averaged seven months at troughs, four months at peaks, and five months at all turns.

Analysis of Alternative Leading Indicators of Inflation   A study by Garner examined the usefulness of the CIBCR series and four other series that have been suggested as leading indicators of inflation, including the price of gold and other composite series.[5] The results indicate that the composite indicators provide useful early indications of inflation turning points. Unfortunately, none of the series provides accurate estimates of the magnitude of inflation.

International Leading Indicator Series   In addition to developing leading indicators for the U.S. economy, the CIBCR also has developed a set of composite leading indicators for eight other major industrial countries: Canada, Germany, France, the United Kingdom, Italy, Japan, Australia, and Taiwan (Republic of China). These International Leading Indicator Series are part of an ongoing project to develop an international economic indicator (IEI) system. The series are comparable in data and analysis to the leading series for the United State.[6]

Surveys of Sentiment and Expectations   Consumer expectations seem to play a role as the economy approaches turning points in the business cycle. Two surveys of consumer expectations are reported monthly in the financial media. The University of Michigan Consumer Sentiment Index and the Conference Board Consumer Confidence Index both query a sample of households on their expectations over the next six months (Conference Board) or over the next year (Michigan). Although the two indexes sometimes deviate from each other month to month, over longer time periods they track each other fairly closely. Both indexes act as a leading indicator by rising and falling before the general level of economic activity does.

Other surveys of consumer and business expectations focus on the overall economy, and some focus on such areas as firms' capital spending or inventory investment plans. By subscribing to proprietary services or closely following the financial media, investment analysts can monitor how consumers and the business community feel about the economy and their spending plans. In general, the more optimistic they are, the better the prospects for increases in spending and economic growth. The more pessimistic they are, the worse the prospects for spending and growth. The problem with survey data is that individuals' and firms' reported plans may not come to fruition. Just because a survey reports that manufacturing firms expect to increase capital spending by a certain percentage does not mean they will actually do so.

Economic statistics released by the government are another source of helpful information about current economic trends, particularly concerning various economic sectors. Every Monday, *The Wall Street Journal* publishes a short commentary, "Tracking the Economy." The feature reports statistics that will be released during the coming week (for example, housing starts, agricultural production, GDP), their previous values, and their consensus forecasts. As you would expect from our discussion of efficient markets, investors react to economic "surprises" wherein the actual results deviate from the consensus forecasts (expectations).

---

[5]C. Alan Garner, "How Useful Are Leading Indicators of Inflation?" Federal Reserve Bank of Kansas City, *Economic Review* 80, no. 2 (Second Quarter 1995): 5–18.

[6]For an extended discussion, see Geoffrey H. Moore, "An Introduction to International Economic Indicators," *Business Cycles, Inflation, and Forecasting,* 2d ed. (New York: National Bureau of Economic Research, Studies in Business Cycles, No. 24, 1983).

MONETARY VARIABLES, THE ECONOMY, AND STOCK PRICES

Many academic and professional observers hypothesize a close relationship between stock prices and various monetary variables that are influenced by monetary policy. The best-known monetary variable in this regard is the *money supply*. You will recall from your economics course that the money supply can be measured in several ways, including currency plus demand deposits (referred to as the M1 money supply) and the M1 money supply plus time deposits (referred to as the M2 money supply). The government publishes other measures of the money supply, but M1 and M2 are the best known.[7] The Federal Reserve controls the money supply through various tools, the most useful of which is open market operations.

Money Supply and the Economy

In their classic work on the monetary history of the United States, Friedman and Schwartz thoroughly documented the relationship between changes in the growth rate of the money supply and subsequent changes in the economy.[8] Specifically, they demonstrated that declines in the rate of growth of the money supply have preceded business contractions by an average of 20 months, while increases in the growth rate of the money supply have preceded economic expansions by about 8 months.

Friedman suggests a transmission mechanism through which changes in the growth rate of the money supply affect the aggregate economy. He hypothesizes that, to implement planned changes in monetary policy, the Federal Reserve engages in open market operations, buying or selling Treasury bonds to adjust bank reserves and, eventually, the money supply. Because the Fed deals in government bonds, the initial liquidity impact when the Fed buys bonds affects the government bond market, creating excess liquidity for those who sold bonds to the Fed. The result is an increase in bond prices and lower interest rates. Rising or falling government bond prices subsequently filter down to corporate bonds, and this change in liquidity eventually affects common stocks and then the real goods market. The impact of money supply growth on stock prices is really part of the transmission process whereby money supply affects the aggregate economy. This liquidity transmission scenario implies that the effect of a change in monetary policy initially appears in financial markets (bonds and stocks) and only later in the aggregate economy.

Financial Conditions Index

In contrast to a specific monetary series (such as money supply or the monetary base) or an individual price series (like the federal funds rate or the discount rate), Goldman Sachs has created a composite financial condition series (the Goldman Sachs Financial Conditions Index—GSFCI).[9] The GSFCI is a combination of four variables that are expected to reflect the monetary policy environment. The four variables (with weights) are:

1. Real three-month LIBOR (.35)
2. Real A-rated corporate bond yield (.55)
3. Real Goldman Sachs Trade-Weighted Dollar Index (.05)
4. The equity market capitalization/GDP ratio (.05)

---

[7]For a discussion of alternative monetary series, see John R. Walter, "Monetary Aggregates: A User's Guide," Federal Reserve Bank of Richmond, *Economic Review* (January/February 1989): 53–61.

[8]Milton Friedman and Anna J. Schwartz, "Money and Business Cycles," *Review of Economics and Statistics* 45, no. 1, part 2, supplement (February 1963): 32–78, reprinted in Milton Friedman, *The Optimum Quantity of Money and Other Essays* (Chicago: Aldine Publishing, 1969): 189–235.

[9]For a full discussion, see William Dudley and Jan Hatzius, "The Goldman Sachs Financial Conditions Index: The Right Tool for a New Monetary Policy Regime," *Global Economics Paper,* no. 44 (New York: Goldman Sachs Global Research, June 8, 2000).

It is contended that this series is superior to any one series and also considers other relevant factors such as the strength of the dollar and the growing importance of the stock market in the economy. The empirical analysis of its relationship to the economy is strong—a one-point *increase* in the GSFCI is followed (with a three-quarter lag) by about a one-percentage-point *decrease* in the growth rate of real GDP. The point is, an increase in the GSFCI reflects a tightening of the monetary environment based upon a heavy weighting of interest rates—that is, the two interest rate variables constitute 90 percent of the index.

Money Supply and Stock Prices

Numerous studies have tested the relationship suggested by this transmission mechanism. Specifically, do changes in the growth rate of the money supply precede changes in stock prices? The results of these studies have tended to change over time. The initial studies done in the 1960s and early 1970s generally indicated a strong *leading* relationship between money supply changes and stock prices.[10] Such results implied that changes in the growth rate of the money supply could serve as a leading indicator of stock price changes.

Subsequent studies questioned these findings.[11] Although these studies likewise found a relationship between the money supply and stock prices, the timing of the relationship differed. These studies found that changes in the growth rate of the money supply did not lead stock prices but consistently *lagged* stock returns by about one to three months.

Studies in the 1980s examined the relationship of stock returns to anticipated and unanticipated money supply growth using weekly money supply data.[12] The results indicated that money changes affect stock prices but stock prices adjust very quickly to unexpected changes in money supply growth. Therefore, to enjoy superior returns, it is necessary to *forecast unanticipated changes* in money supply growth.

Following more than a decade of limited research on this topic, several recent studies have found that the monetary environment does have an impact on stock returns. A recent set of studies by Jensen, Johnson, and Mercer (JJM) showed that the results of several earlier studies that examined the relationship between some economic variables and stock returns or some company variables and stock returns can be significantly affected by the prevailing monetary environment.[13] Specifically, JJM showed that the business conditions proxies suggested by Fama and French[14] (i. e., the term spread, dividend yield, and default spread) have a different effect on

[10]Studies that generally support this view include Beryl W. Sprinkel, *Money and Markets: A Monetarist View* (Homewood, Ill.: Richard D. Irwin, 1971); Michael W. Keran, "Expectations, Money, and the Stock Market," Federal Reserve Bank of St. Louis, *Review* 53, no. 1 (January 1971): 16–31; and Kenneth Homa and Dwight Jaffee, "The Study of Money and Stock Prices," *Journal of Finance* 26, no. 5 (December 1971): 1015–1066.

[11]These studies include Richard V. L. Cooper, "Efficient Capital Markets and the Quantity Theory of Money," *Journal of Finance* 29, no. 3 (June 1974): 887–908; and M. S. Rozeff, "Money and Stock Prices: Market Efficiency and the Lag Effect of Monetary Policy," *Journal of Financial Economics* 1, no. 3 (September 1974): 245–302.

[12]These studies are found in Lawrence S. Davidson and Richard T. Froyen, "Monetary Policy and Stock Returns: Are Stock Markets Efficient?" Federal Reserve Bank of St. Louis, *Review* 64, no. 3 (March 1982): 3–12; and R. W. Hafer, "The Response of Stock Prices to Changes in Weekly Money and the Discount Rate," Federal Reserve Bank of St. Louis, *Review* 64, no. 3 (March 1985): 5–14.

[13]Gerald R. Jenson, Jeffrey Mercer, and Robert R. Johnson, "Business Conditions, Monetary Policy, and Expected Security Returns," *Journal of Financial Economics* 40, no. 2 (February 1996): 213–237; Gerald R. Jenson, Robert R. Johnson, and Jeffrey M. Mercer, "New Evidence on Size and Price-to-Book Effects in Stock Returns," *Financial Analysts Journal* 53, no. 6 (November–December 1997): 34–42; and Gerald R. Jenson, Robert R. Johnson, and Jeffrey M. Mercer, "The Inconsistency of Small Firm and Value Stock Premiums," *Journal of Portfolio Management* 24, no. 2 (Winter 1998): 27–36. This research is summarized in Gerald R. Jensen, Robert R. Johnson, and Jeffrey M. Mercer, *The Role of Monetary Policy in Investment Management* (Charlottesville, Va.: The Research Foundation of the Association of Investment Management and Research, 2000).

[14]Eugene F. Fama and Kenneth French, "Business Conditions and Expected Returns on Stocks and Bonds," *Journal of Financial Economics* 25, no. 1 (January 1989): 23–49.

EXHIBIT 12.5   *TIME-SERIES PLOT OF "EXCESS LIQUIDITY" IN THE UNITED STATES: 1980–2001*

stock returns depending on the prevailing monetary policy, where monetary policy is indicated by discount rate changes (i.e., declining discount rates imply an easy monetary policy, while rising discount rates imply a restrictive policy). The JJM studies also show that the relationship between stock price returns and both size and the price-to-book value ratio that was found in several studies only holds during periods of easy monetary policy.[15] A subsequent study by Thorbecke that examined how stock returns respond to monetary policy shocks indicated that expansionary monetary policy increases ex-post stock returns.[16] Patelis examined whether shifts in monetary policy affect the predictability of excess stock returns and found that monetary policy variables were significant predictors of future stock returns, although they were not the only relevant factors (i.e., dividend yield was also relevant).[17]

Excess Liquidity and Stock Prices   Some analysts contend that *excess liquidity* is the relevant monetary variable that influences stock prices. They define excess liquidity as the year-to-year percentage change in the M2 money supply adjusted for small time deposits minus the year-to-year percentage change in nominal GDP. It is reasoned that the growth rate of nominal GDP indicates the need for liquidity in the economy. If the money supply growth rate exceeds the GDP growth rate, this indicates there is excess money (liquidity) in the economy that is available for buying securities. Therefore, it is reasoned that positive excess liquidity should lead to higher security prices.

Exhibit 12.5 contains a time-series plot of excess liquidity in the United States since 1980. Our measure is somewhat different from that used by Goldman Sachs—ours is equal to the

[15]These prior studies include Eugene F. Fama and Kenneth French, "Size and Book-to-Market Factors in Earnings and Returns," *Journal of Finance* 50, no. 1 (March 1995): 131–155; and Patricia M. Fairfield, "P/E, P/B, and Present Value of Future Dividends," *Financial Analysts Journal* 50, no. 4 (July–August 1994): 23–31.

[16]Willem Thorbecke, "On Stock Market Returns and Monetary Policy," *Journal of Finance* 52, no. 2 (June 1997): 635–654.

[17]Alex D. Patelis, "Stock Returns Predictability and the Role of Monetary Policy," *Journal of Finance* 52, no. 5 (December 1997):1951–1972.

annual growth rate of the M2 money supply minus the annual growth rate of nominal GDP. As shown, it was almost always negative during the period 1991 into 1996, yet U.S. stocks experienced outstanding returns during 1995–1999. This inconsistency could be caused by the existence of positive excess liquidity in some of our major trading partner countries, such as the United Kingdom, Germany, and Japan, who tend to invest in our stocks. This significant non-U.S. liquidity helped the U.S. stock market continue to rise in 1995–1999.

Other Economic Variables and Stock Prices

Chen, Roll, and Ross examined equity returns relative to a set of macroeconomic variables.[18] They found the following variables to be significant in explaining stock returns:

➤ Growth in industrial production
➤ Changes in the risk premium
➤ Twists in the yield curve
➤ Measures of unanticipated inflation
➤ Changes in expected inflation during periods of volatile inflation

The authors did not attempt to use these variables to predict market returns, but suggested that these variables were important in explaining past stock market returns.

Inflation, Interest Rates, and Security Prices

Because this chapter is concerned with the macroeconomic analysis of security markets, we should examine the macroeconomic impact of inflation and interest rates. We have noted throughout the book the critical role of expected inflation and nominal interest rates in determining the required rate of return used to derive the value of all investments. We would expect these variables that are very important in microeconomic valuation to also affect changes in the aggregate markets.

Inflation and Interest Rates   Exhibit 12.6 contains a plot of long-term interest rates and the year-to-year percentage change in the consumer price index (CPI, a measure of inflation). This graph demonstrates the strong relationship between inflation and interest rates. We contended in our earlier discussion that when investors anticipated an increase in the rate of inflation, they would increase their required rates of return by a similar amount to derive constant real rates of return. The time-series graph of the promised yield of Aaa corporate bonds and the annual rate of inflation in Exhibit 12.6 confirms the expected relationship overall but also indicates an imperfect relationship between interest rates and inflation. If the relationship was perfect and investors were accurate in their *predictions* of future inflation, the difference between the interest rate and the inflation rate (the spread between them) would be fairly constant, reflecting the real return on corporate bonds. As shown, the spread between these two curves changes over time.

Exhibit 12.7 plots this spread between bond interest rates and inflation and demonstrates the following results. Although the two curves generally move together, during some periods (1975–1979) the inflation rate exceeded the yield on the bonds, which implies that during these periods investors received *negative* real returns on corporate bonds. In contrast, during 1983–1985, the real rates of return on these high quality bonds were in the 8 to 10 percent range, which clearly exceeds what most investors would expect on very low risk bonds.

This change in spread does not mean that there is not a relationship between inflation and interest rates; it only shows that *investors are not very good at predicting inflation*. Recall that the theoretical relationship is between *expected* inflation and interest rates, which is in contrast to these

---

[18]Nai-Fu Chen, Richard Roll, and Stephen A. Ross, "Economic Forces and the Stock Market," *Journal of Business* 59, no. 3 (July 1986).

EXHIBIT 12.6   *TIME-SERIES PLOT OF THE PROMISED YIELD OF MOODY'S AAA CORPORATE BONDS AND INFLATION: MONTHLY 1974–2000*

Reprinted with permission from Moody's Investors Service.

EXHIBIT 12.7   *SPREAD BETWEEN THE YIELD OF MOODY'S AAA CORPORATE BONDS AND INFLATION: MONTHLY 1974–2000*

Reprinted with permission from Moody's Investors Service.

data that reflect actual inflation. Apparently, investors underestimated the rapid increase in the rate of inflation during the period 1978–1980, which means that they employed a discount rate that was too low and, therefore, they overpaid for bonds and experienced negative real returns. In contrast, they overestimated the rate of inflation during 1980–1983 when inflation declined rapidly, so they underpaid for bonds and experienced abnormally high real rates of return.

Interest Rates and Bond Prices   The relationship between interest rates and bond prices is clearly negative because the only variable that changes in the valuation model is the discount factor. Specifically, the expected cash flows from a straight noncallable bond would not change, so an increase in interest rates will cause a decline in bond prices and a decline in interest rates will boost bond prices. For example, if you own a 10-year bond with a coupon of 10 percent, when interest rates go from 10 percent to 12 percent, the price of this bond will go from $1,000 (par) to $885. In contrast, if rates go from 10 percent to 8 percent, the price of the bond will go from $1,000 to $1,136.

The size of the price change will depend on the characteristics of the bond. A longer-term bond will experience a larger price change for a change in interest rates.[19] Therefore, we can anticipate a negative relationship between inflation and the rates of return on bonds because inflation generally has a direct effect on interest rates; and, in turn, interest rates have an inverse effect on bond prices and rates of return. One example of empirical verification for this negative relationship is provided in Exhibit 3.16, which shows a correlation of –0.17 between inflation and rates of return on long-term investment-grade bonds.

Inflation, Interest Rates, and Stock Prices   The relationship between inflation, interest rates, and stock prices is not direct and consistent. The reason is that the cash flows from stocks can change along with inflation and interest rates, and we cannot be certain whether this change in cash flows will augment or offset the change in interest rates. To demonstrate this, consider the following potential scenarios following an increase in the rate of inflation and the effect on stock prices based on the DDM.

1. *The Positive Scenario.* Interest rates rise due to an increase in the rate of inflation, and corporate earnings likewise experience an increase in growth because firms are able to increase prices in line with cost increases. In this case, stock prices might be fairly stable because the negative effect of an increase in the required rate of return (k) is partially or wholly offset by the increase in the growth rate of earnings and dividends (g), which means that the returns on stock increase in line with the rate of inflation.
2. *Mild Negative Scenario.* Interest rates increase due to inflation, but expected cash flows change very little or not at all because firms are not able to increase prices in response to higher costs. This would cause a decline in stock prices similar to what happens with a bond. The required rate of return (k) would increase, but the growth rate of dividends (g) would be constant. As a result, the k–g spread discussed in Chapter 11 would widen and stock prices would decline.
3. *Very Negative Scenario.* Interest rates increase due to inflation, while cash flows decline because the inflation that caused the rise in interest rates has a negative impact on earnings. For example, during 1981 to 1982, interest rates increased and remained high during a period of economic decline, which caused sales and earnings to decline. Alternatively, one can envision a period of inflation wherein the costs of production increase, but many firms are not able to increase prices, which causes a decline in profit margins. The impact of this set of events can be disastrous. Given this scenario, stock prices will experience a significant decline because k will increase as g declines, causing a large increase in the k–g spread.

In contrast to these scenarios, you can envision a comparable set of scenarios when inflation and interest rates decline. The relationship between inflation, interest rates, and stock prices is not as direct or consistent as the relationship between interest rates and bonds. The point is, the

---

[19]Chapter 19 contains a detailed discussion of the specific variables that influence bond price volatility.

effect of interest rate changes on stock prices will depend on what caused the change in interest rates and the effect of this event on the expected cash flows on common stock.

Notably, the actual relationship between inflation, interest rates, and stock prices is an empirical question and *the effect varies over time.* Therefore, although there has generally been a significant *negative* relationship between inflation, interest rates, and the returns on stock, as shown in Chapter 3 (Exhibit 3.16), this is not always true.[20] In addition, even when it is true for the overall market, certain industries may have earnings, cash flows, and dividends that react positively to inflation and interest rate changes. In such an instance, their stock prices would be positively correlated with inflation and interest rates.[21]

Summary of Macroeconomic Analysis

There is ample evidence of a strong and consistent relationship between economic activity and the stock market, although stock prices consistently seem to turn from four to nine months before the economy does. Therefore, to project the future direction of the stock market using the macroeconomic approach, you must either forecast economic activity about 12 months ahead or examine economic indicator series that lead the economy by more than stock prices do.

The results of a study with the leading indicator series indicated that they cannot be used to time stock selection. Past studies of the relationship between the money supply and stock prices have indicated a significant relationship but typically found that stock prices generally turn before the money supply does. Most recent research has indicated that the monetary environment does have a significant impact on stock market returns and impacts other relationships with stocks. Therefore, you should be aware of the monetary environment when projecting market returns.

Analysis of World Security Markets

Although we have focused on the U.S. market to demonstrate the macroeconomic approach to forecasting movements in the securities markets, you must also consider a similar analysis for numerous foreign markets, including those in Japan, Canada, the United Kingdom, and Germany. Although it is not feasible to analyze each of these markets in detail, we can provide an example of such an analysis by reviewing the extensive analysis done by Goldman, Sachs & Co. This analysis is contained in a quarterly Goldman Sachs publication, *World Investment Strategy Highlights,* as part of the firm's international research effort.

This publication draws on a number of other Goldman Sachs publications to provide a world and country portfolio strategy.[22]

---

[20]Studies on the topic of inflation and common stocks include Frank K. Reilly, "Companies and Common Stocks as Inflation Hedges," New York University, Center for the Study of Financial Institutions, *Bulletin* (April 1975); Jeffrey F. Jaffe and Gershon Mandelker, "The 'Fisher Effect' for Risky Assets: An Empirical Analysis," *Journal of Finance* 31, no. 2 (May 1976): 447–458; and Eugene F. Fama, "Stock Returns, Real Activity, Inflation and Money," *American Economic Review* 71, no. 4 (September 1981). For an analysis of the factors that cause this relationship between inflation and stock returns, see Frank K. Reilly, "The Impact of Inflation on ROE, Growth and Stock Prices," *Financial Services Review* 6, no. 1 (1997): 1–17.

[21]Studies that examined alternative industries as inflation hedges include Stephen P. Ferris and Anil K. Makhija, "A Search for Common Stock Inflation Hedges," *Review of Business and Economic Research* 22, no. 2 (Spring 1987): 27–36; and Frank K. Reilly, David J. Wright, and Robert R. Johnson, "An Analysis of the Interest Rate Sensitivity of Common Stocks," Financial Management Association Meeting (October 2000).

[22]The other Goldman Sachs publications used include *The International Economics Analyst, Financial Markets Perspectives, Investment Strategy Highlights, Japan Investment Strategy Highlights,* and *The U.K. Economics Analyst.*

| EXHIBIT 12.8 | FORECAST FOR WORLD ECONOMIC ACTIVITY—REAL GDP GROWTH |

COUNTRY	2000	2001E	2002E	2003E
United States	4.10	1.20	1.90	3.00
Japan	2.40	−0.40	−1.10	1.00
Germany	3.00	0.60	0.70	1.80
United Kingdom	3.00	2.40	1.60	2.80
France	3.60	2.00	1.10	2.60
Italy	2.90	1.90	1.30	2.40
Mexico	6.90	−0.30	1.70	3.90
Hong Kong	10.50	−0.20	2.00	5.50
Singapore	9.90	−2.00	3.50	5.80

E = estimate

Source: *World Investment Strategy Highlights* by Neil Williams, Alain Kernels, and Joseph Hickey, employees of Goldman, Sachs & Co. Copyright March 2002 by Goldman, Sachs & Co. Used with permission.

Goldman Sachs uses a version of the three-step process (also referred to as the *top-down approach*), initially examining a country's aggregate economy and its components that relate to the valuation of securities—GDP, inflation, and interest rates. Exhibit 12.8 contains the firm's forecast of real GDP growth for several major countries. Note the fairly substantial differences in outlook for real GDP growth during 2003 (e.g., 1.0 percent for Japan versus 5.8 percent for Singapore).

Inflation and Exchange Rates

An analysis of historical and expected price changes in Exhibit 12.9 also reveals differences in the outlook for inflation during 2003, ranging from –0.7 percent for Japan and 2.6 percent for the United Kingdom. These inflation estimates feed into an interest rate forecast for the end of 2002 in Exhibit 12.10. This combination of forecasts indicates the expected trend in interest rates. The forecast for interest rates was clearly mixed. The overall range for expected long-term rates for mid-2002 was from 1.5 percent (Japan) to 4.9 percent (United Kingdom).

Given these differences in inflation and interest rate levels and trends, you can expect major differences in the exchange rates. Exhibit 12.11 presents the firm's forecast for several currencies. The current rate and the forecast for 12 months imply trends during the year. These figures indicate that Goldman Sachs expects the U.S. dollar to become weaker against most of these major currencies during 2002–2003.

Based on this analysis of the underlying economies, Exhibit 12.12 contains estimates of corporate earnings growth rates for various countries. It also gives estimates of other stock market variables, including dividend growth, price/earnings ratios, and dividend yields. Again, all series show major differences among countries. The estimated earnings growth rates for 2002 vary from –1.0 percent for the United Kingdom to 24 percent for the United States. Likewise, the price/earnings ratio is expected to continue its historical variation, ranging in 2002 from about 17 times for Hong Kong to 59 times for Japan.

Correlations among Returns

These substantial differences in economic performance and major changes in the underlying valuation variables indicate that there should be fairly low correlations among stock market returns for alternative countries. The correlation matrix of price changes in local currencies in

EXHIBIT 12.9 *CONSUMER OR RETAIL PRICE CHANGES (PERCENTAGE CHANGES FROM PREVIOUS YEAR)*

Period	United States	Japan	Germany	France	United Kingdom	Italy	Hong Kong	Singapore
1988	4.1	0.7	1.3	2.7	4.9	5.0	NA	NA
1989	4.8	2.3	2.8	3.4	7.8	6.6	NA	NA
1990	4.4	3.0	2.7	3.5	9.5	6.1	NA	NA
1991	4.0	2.8	3.8	3.5	7.0	6.0	NA	NA
1992	3.0	1.7	4.0	2.8	3.7	5.2	NA	NA
1993	3.2	1.2	3.7	2.3	1.8	4.5	NA	NA
1994	2.6	0.7	2.7	2.1	2.4	3.9	8.1	3.1
1995	2.8	0.0	1.8	1.6	2.8	5.4	7.7	1.7
1996	2.6	0.0	1.8	1.8	2.9	3.8	6.8	2.0
1997	2.3	1.7	1.7	1.2	2.8	1.7	5.7	–0.3
1998	1.6	0.7	1.0	0.7	2.7	1.7	4.1	0.7
1999	1.9	–0.9	0.5	0.4	2.3	1.2	–1.5	1.2
2000	3.4	–0.7	2.1	1.8	2.1	2.6	–3.7	–1.3
2001E	2.8	–0.7	2.4	1.8	2.1	2.7	–1.6	–1.0
2002E	1.2	–0.9	1.4	1.6	2.7	2.0	–1.0	–0.7
2003E	2.0	–0.7	1.3	1.5	2.6	1.4	0.0	–1.5

E = estimate

Source: *World Investment Strategy Highlights* by Neil Williams, Alain Kernels, and Joseph Hickey, employees of Goldman, Sachs & Co. Copyright March 2002 by Goldman, Sachs & Co. Used with permission.

EXHIBIT 12.10 *INTEREST RATE FORECASTS (PERCENT PER ANNUM)*

Country	Current Rate	Short Term (3 Months)	Long Term (12 Months)
United States			
10 year	5.1	4.3	4.3
Eurozone			
10 year	5.1	4.3	4.8
Japan			
10 year	1.4	1.3	1.5
United Kingdom			
10 Year	5.2	4.4	4.9
Canada			
10 year	5.5	4.5	4.5

Source: *World Investment Strategy Highlights* by Neil Williams, Alain Kernels, and Joseph Hickey, employees of Goldman, Sachs & Co. Copyright March 2002 by Goldman, Sachs & Co. Used with permission.

EXHIBIT 12.11 ▶ *FORECAST OF EXCHANGE RATES AGAINST THE U.S. DOLLAR*

COUNTRY	CANADIAN DOLLAR	JAPANESE YEN	BRITISH POUND	EURO	SWISS FRANK
Current rate	1.58	132.90	1.43	0.88	1.66
3 month	1.58	138.00	1.42	0.91	1.60
12 month	1.52	128.00	1.45	1.03	1.50

Source: *World Investment Strategy Highlights* by Neil Williams, Alain Kernels, and Joseph Hickey, employees of Goldman, Sachs & Co. Copyright March 2002 by Goldman, Sachs & Co. Used with permission.

EXHIBIT 12.12 ▶ *COMPARATIVE STOCK MARKET STATISTICS*

	UNITED STATES	JAPAN	HONG KONG	UNITED KINGDOM	GERMANY	FRANCE	ITALY
Earnings Growth							
2000	5.0	146.0	24.0	14.0	13.0	31.0	21.0
2001E	−37.0	−44.0	−11.0	−18.0	−54.0	−40.0	−20.0
2002E	24.0	11.0	6.0	−1.0	10.0	3.0	
Dividend Growth							
2000	−3.0	−4.0	—	7.0	8.0	11.0	12.0
2001E	−3.0	—	—	−2.0	−6.0	−2.0	−4.0
2002E	2.0	7.0	—	−2.0	0.0	0.0	0.0
P/E							
2000	27.8	41.6	16.5	22.2	24.0	35.4	28.2
2001E	46.0	81.0	17.7	27.1	35.0	45.5	39.3
2002E	39.6	59.0	16.8	29.4	33.6	47.7	39.6
D/Y							
2000	1.2	0.8	—	2.8	2.0	1.7	1.7
2001E	1.4	0.9	—	3.0	2.3	2.0	2.0
2002E	1.4	1.0	—	3.2	2.6	2.2	2.3

Source: *World Investment Strategy Highlights* by Neil Williams, Alain Kernels, and Joseph Hickey, employees of Goldman, Sachs & Co. Copyright March 2002 by Goldman, Sachs & Co. Used with permission.

Exhibit 12.13 shows a fairly high correlation between the United States and the United Kingdom and between Germany and the United Kingdom, and the low correlation between the United States and Japan. Notably, the U.S.–Japan correlation increased during the early 1990s as our economies became more interdependent, but the correlations declined during the late 1990s when the Japanese economy and stock market experienced difficulty.

Exhibit 12.14, a similar correlation matrix in U.S. dollars, shows that most of the correlations of returns with the United States decline when one considers the exchange rate effect. Such comparisons justify and encourage worldwide diversification of investments.

Individual Country Stock Price Changes

The stock market impact of exchange rates is shown in Exhibit 12.15, which shows the percentage changes in stock prices in the local currency and adjusted for the U.S. dollar. The average annual percent price change in local currency from 1997–2001 ranges from −2.6 percent for Japan

EXHIBIT 12.13   *CORRELATION OF PRICE RETURNS IN LOCAL CURRENCY: 1997–2001*

	UNITED STATES	JAPAN	GERMANY	UNITED KINGDOM	FRANCE	ITALY
United States	—					
Japan	0.31	—				
Germany	0.86	0.47	—			
United Kingdom	0.84	0.56	0.99	—		
France	0.89	0.63	0.84	0.87	—	
Italy	0.78	0.14	0.93	0.89	0.67	—

Source: *World Investment Strategy Highlights* by Neil Williams, Alain Kernels, and Joseph Hickey, employees of Goldman, Sachs & Co. Copyright March 2002 by Goldman, Sachs & Co. Used with permission.

EXHIBIT 12.14   *CORRELATION OF PRICE RETURNS IN U.S. DOLLARS: 1997–2001*

	UNITED STATES	JAPAN	GERMANY	UNITED KINGDOM	FRANCE	ITALY
United States	—					
Japan	0.33	—				
Germany	0.79	0.41	—			
United Kingdom	0.75	0.47	0.98	—		
France	0.86	0.67	0.80	0.76	—	
Italy	0.82	0.49	0.98	0.94	0.90	—

Source: *World Investment Strategy Highlights* by Neil Williams, Alain Kernels, and Joseph Hickey, employees of Goldman, Sachs & Co. Copyright March 2002 by Goldman, Sachs & Co. Used with permission.

EXHIBIT 12.15   *WORLD STOCK MARKET PERFORMANCE: 1997–2001 (IN LOCAL CURRENCY AND U.S. DOLLARS)*

	1997		1998		1999		2000		2001		AVERAGE 1997–2001	
	LOCAL CURRENCY	U.S. DOLLARS	LOCAL CURRENCY	U.S. DOLLARS	LOCAL CURRENCY	U.S. DOLLARS	LOCAL CURRENCY	U.S. DOLLARS	LOCAL CURRENCY	U.S. DOLLARS	LOCAL CURRENCY	U.S. DOLLARS
United States	31.0	31.0	26.7	26.7	18.5	19.5	−10.1	−10.1	−18.9	−18.9	9.6	9.6
Japan	−20.1	−28.6	−8.9	−1.3	58.2	75.0	−25.5	−33.1	−16.6	−20.6	−2.6	−1.7
Germany	47.1	27.4	5.6	−11.2	38.3	19.7	−7.5	−13.6	−30.2	−32.0	10.7	−1.9
United Kingdom	19.7	17.7	−0.4	−11.5	20.3	14.5	−8.0	−14.8	−19.5	−20.1	2.4	−2.8
France	29.5	13.1	38.9	16.5	53.1	32.2	−0.6	−7.1	−29.7	−31.5	18.2	4.6
Italy	58.0	37.2	2.7	4.1	22.4	38.7	5.5	−1.3	−31.5	−33.2	11.4	9.1
World		17.7		20.9		24.2		−12.2		−17.5		6.6

Source: *World Investment Strategy Highlights* by Neil Williams, Alain Kernels, and Joseph Hickey, employees of Goldman, Sachs & Co. Copyright March 2002 by Goldman, Sachs & Co. Used with permission.

to 18.2 percent for France. The average annual percentage stock price change in U.S. dollars ranges from –2.8 percent (United Kingdom) to 9.6 percent (United States).

The significant impact of changes in exchange rates can be seen in two examples. Although the rate of change in Japan stock prices during 1999 was 58.2 percent, the change experienced by a U.S. citizen who invested in Japan during 1999 would have been 75.0 percent because of the significant strength of the yen. This increase in the rate of return due to exchange rate changes relative to the U.S. dollar varied between countries during 1999. In contrast, during 1997, the U.S. dollar was quite strong and all percentage stock price changes when converted to U.S. dollars were lower. For example, the stock price change in Germany during 1997 was over 47 percent in local currency but only about 27 percent in U.S. dollars.

Individual Country Analysis

Goldman Sachs provides a detailed analysis of major countries that includes the country's economy and equity market and culminates in a portfolio recommendation for investors in that country. Exhibit 12.16 shows the major economic indicators for the United Kingdom reflecting a continuation of the economic recession but some signs of a recovery.

There is an analysis of the U.K. equity market in Exhibit 12.17 following the economic projections. Goldman Sachs feels that the overall economic outlook for the United Kingdom is for

EXHIBIT 12.16   *ECONOMIC OUTLOOK FOR THE UNITED KINGDOM*

	CURRENT VALUE
GDP Growth	
2000	3.0
2001E	2.4
2002E	1.6
Earnings Growth	
2000	14.0
2001E	–18.0
2002E	–1.0
Dividend Growth	
2000	7.0
2001E	–2.0
2002E	–2.0
Inflation (Consumer Price Index) (Percent)	
2000	2.1
2001E	2.1
2002E	2.7

INTEREST RATE OUTLOOK

	CURRENT RATE	3 MONTHS	12 MONTHS
3-month CDs	4.1	4.3	4.7
10-year bond	5.2	4.4	4.9

E = estimate

Source: *World Investment Strategy Highlights* by Neil Williams, Alain Kernels, and Joseph Hickey, employees of Goldman, Sachs & Co. Copyright March 2002 by Goldman, Sachs & Co. Used with permission.

EXHIBIT 12.17	RECENT STOCK MARKET PERFORMANCE FOR UNITED KINGDOM RELATIVE TO WORLD MARKET AND EXPECTED RATES OF RETURN OVER NEXT 3 AND 12 MONTHS

	CURRENT PRICE	PERFORMANCE (PERCENT CHANGE)		52-WEEK RANGE	
		LAST 3 MONTHS	LAST 12 MONTHS	HIGH	LOW
FT-SE 100	5246	−1.6	−3.5		

	EXPECTED RETURN (PERCENT)	
	3 MONTHS	12 MONTHS
Equities	2.4	9.8
Bonds	4.4	4.9
Cash		4.6

Source: *World Investment Strategy Highlights* by Neil Williams, Alain Kernels, and Joseph Hickey, employees of Goldman, Sachs & Co. Copyright March 2002 by Goldman, Sachs & Co. Used with permission.

a recovery from the recession, but Goldman Sachs still expects U.K. equities to outperform bonds and short-term bonds (cash) during the next 12 months after inferior performance during the next 3 months.

World Asset Allocation

The final product of this analysis is a recommendation for an investor's world asset allocation. Exhibit 12.18 begins with a division among bonds, equities, and cash. As of early 2002, Goldman Sachs recommended that an investor should be at the lower end of the range for bonds; toward the upper end of the range for stocks; mid-range for commodities and cash; and the top of the range for convertibles.

For the equity segment of the portfolio, the firm specified a weighting for each country based on its relative market value, which is a country's equity value as a percentage of the total value of all world equities. For example, as shown in Exhibit 12.18, the market value of U.S. equities is 56.8 percent of the total value of all equities in the world, whereas Japanese equities account for 7.6 percent of the total. A completely neutral portfolio regarding all equity markets would invest a proportion in each country equal to the relative market values of that country's equities. For example, if the value of stocks in a country constituted 10 percent of the value of all stocks in the world, a neutral outlook would lead you to invest 10 percent of your equity portfolio in this country. If you were bullish toward this country relative to other markets, you would *overweight* it, investing more than 10 percent of your equity portfolio there. As of the publication date of this report (March 2002), Goldman Sachs was slightly bullish on the U.S. stock market because the expected returns were above those expected in some other countries, such as the United Kingdom, France, and Germany. Therefore, they recommended *overweighting* the United States (you should invest 58.5 percent of your equity portfolio in the United States versus a 56.8 percent market weighting). The firm was slightly bearish regarding Japan and recommended that you underweight Japanese stocks. Alternatively, the firm is recommending that you *overweight* other Asian countries.

After completing the global market analysis, the next step is to analyze alternative industries worldwide within specified countries. Finally, you should consider alternative firms and their stocks in the preferred industries. This analysis is the subject of Chapters 14 and 15.

EXHIBIT 12.18

ASSET ALLOCATION–WORLD PORTFOLIOS

	NORMAL RANGE (PERCENT)	WEIGHTING (PERCENT OF INDEX)	CURRENT SUGGESTED WEIGHTING[a] (PERCENT)
Bonds	20–40		23.0
Equities	45–65		60.0
United States		56.8	58.5
Canada		2.1	2.0
Japan		7.6	7.5
Other Asia		4.4	6.5
United Kingdom		10.1	7.5
Germany		2.9	2.5
France		3.8	3.5
Italy		1.4	1.3
The Netherlands		2.2	2.0
Switzerland		2.7	2.4
Spain		1.2	1.1
Sweden		0.9	0.8
Belgium		0.4	0.4
Norway		0.2	0.2
Finland		0.8	0.7
Other Europe		0.8	0.7
Latin America		0.9	1.3
EMEA		0.8	1.2
		100.0	100.0
Commodities	0–10		5.0
Cash	0–15		7.0
Convertibles	0–5		5.0

[a]It may not add up to 100 due to rounding.

Source: *World Investment Strategy Highlights* by Neil Williams, Alain Kernels, and Joseph Hickey, employees of Goldman, Sachs & Co. Copyright March 2002 by Goldman, Sachs & Co. Used with permission.

The Internet   *Investments Online*

The Internet contains a great many sources for economic and financial market information. Many banks, research firms, investment banks, stock brokerages, and government agencies feature data, analysis, or commentaries on their Web sites. Here are a few of the many Web resources you may wish to examine:

http://www.morganstanley.com The home page of Morgan Stanley includes the Global Economic Forum. The Forum is a compilation of reports filed by 15 economists located around the world and is updated daily. Prior reports are available in an archive. This site features daily updates of the MSCI indexes of international markets and links to Morgan Stanley Equity Research pages.

http://www.dri-wefa.com DRI-WEFA's home page features a number of links to resources. Items of interest include a feature that

(continued)

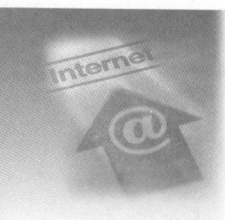

The Internet *Investments Online (cont.)*

gives a weekly analysis of international and U.S. economic news as well as current economic data.

http://www.cm1.prusec.com and **http://205.232.165.149** (formerly **www.yardeni.com**) Edward Yardeni is the Chief Investment Strategist of Prudential Financial. His home page contains links to market information, country information (including emerging markets), a weekly economic briefing, and studies of longer-term trends affecting the economy and financial markets. His site features a number of pull-down slides that provide links to Federal Reserve and U.S. Treasury information, as well as information about demographics, consumers, and marketing.

http://www.whitehouse.gov/fsbr/esbr.html This is the Economics Statistics Briefing Room of the White House Web site. It includes links to data produced by a number of Federal agencies.

http://www.federalreserve.gov The home page of the Board of Governors of the Federal Reserve System. This site features data and information on a number of Fed-related activities, including research, money supply trends, Board actions, consumer information, and reports to Congress. The site includes links to each of the 12 regional Federal Reserve Banks and to a number of foreign central banks. The Philadelphia Fed's site includes access to the Livingston Surveys and Surveys of Professional Forecasters; both provide professional economists' judgments about future economic trends. The URL is **http://www.phil.frb.org/econ/forecast/index.html**

Other sites of interest include:

http://www.worldbank.org Home page of the World Bank features data and articles.

http://www.bankofamerica.com From the Web site of the Bank of America, type "economic indicators" in the site's search function. Pages feature U.S. and global economic reviews, outlooks, and investment strategies.

http://www.spglobal.com/index.html This is a Standard & Poor's site for their index services; it contains current headlines, weekly features, and information on the S&P stock indexes.

http://www.bis.org/cbanks.htm This site includes links to more than 100 of the world's central banks.

Summary

In earlier chapters, we emphasized the importance of analyzing the aggregate markets before beginning any industry or company analysis. You must assess the economic and security market outlooks and their implications regarding the bond, stock, and cash components of your portfolio. Then you proceed to consider the best industry or company.

- Three techniques are used to make the market decision: (1) the macroeconomic technique, which is based on the relationship between the aggregate economy and the stock market; (2) the microeconomic technique, which determines future market values by applying the two valuation approaches discussed in Chapter 11 to the aggregate stock market; and (3) technical analysis, which estimates future returns based on recent past returns. This chapter concentrates on the macroeconomic approach. The microeconomic analysis of equity markets will be considered in Chapter 13 as a prelude to industry analysis in Chapter 14 followed by company and stock analysis in Chapter 15. Technical analysis is covered in Chapter 16.
- The economy and the stock market have a strong, consistent relationship, but the stock market generally turns before the economy does. Therefore, the best macroeconomic projection techniques use economic series that likewise lead the economy, and possibly the stock market. The Conference Board leading indicator series (which includes stock prices) is one possibility. Notably, the evidence does not support its use as a mechanical predictor of stock prices. Leading series for inflation and for other countries exist, but none of these series has been examined relative to stock prices.

- The money supply has been suggested as a predictor of aggregate market behavior based on its relationship to the economy. Some early studies indicated a strong relationship between the money supply and stock prices and suggested that money supply changes turned before stock prices. Subsequent studies confirmed the link between money supply and stock prices, but they indicated that stock prices turn with or before money supply changes. The most recent results show that monetary policy has an important impact on stock price movements and also affects how stocks relate to other variables.
- Although we emphasize the analysis of U.S. markets, we know it is also important to analyze foreign markets. Such an analysis is demonstrated by a Goldman Sachs application of the three-step, or top-down, approach to major countries. This includes an economic analysis and a market analysis for each country. The analysis culminates with a recommendation for a world portfolio allocation among bonds, stocks, and cash. It also recommends an allocation of equity investments among countries in comparison to the country's normal weighting based on its relative market value.

This aggregate market analysis should lead you to a decision as to how much of your portfolio should be committed to bonds, stocks, and cash during the forthcoming investment period.

Questions

1. Why would you expect a relationship between economic activity and stock price movements?
2. At a lunch with some business associates, you discuss the reason for the relationship between the economy and the stock market. One of your associates contends that she has heard that stock prices typically turn before the economy does. How would you explain this phenomenon?
3. Explain the following statements: (a) There is a strong, consistent relationship between money supply changes and stock prices, (b) Money supply changes cannot be used to predict stock price movements.
4. You are informed of the following estimates: nominal money supply is expected to grow at a rate of 7 percent, and GDP is estimated to grow at 4 percent. Explain what you think will happen to stock prices during this period and the reason for your expectation.
5. The current rate of inflation is 3 percent, and long-term Treasury bonds are yielding 7 percent. You estimate that the rate of inflation will increase to 6 percent. What do you expect to happen to long-term bond yields? Compute the effect of this change in inflation on the price of a 15-year, 10 percent coupon bond with a current yield to maturity of 8 percent.
6. Some observers contend that it is harder to estimate the effect of a change in interest rates on common stocks than on bonds. Discuss this contention.
7. Based on the economic projections in Exhibit 12.9 through Exhibit 12.12, would you expect the stock prices for the various countries to be highly correlated? Justify your answer with specific examples.
8. You are informed that a well-respected investment firm projects that the rate of return next year for the U.S. equity market will be 10 percent and returns for German stocks will be 13 percent. Assume that all risks except exchange rate risk are equal and you expect the Euro/U.S. dollar exchange rate to go from 0.90 to 0.75 during the year. Given this information, discuss where you would invest and why. Compute the effect if the exchange rate went from 0.90 to 1.10.

Problems

1. Prepare a table showing the percentage change for each of the last 10 years in (a) the Consumer Price Index (all items), (b) nominal GDP, (c) real GDP (in constant dollars), and (d) the GDP deflator. Discuss how much of nominal growth was due to *real* growth and how much was due to inflation.

2. *CFA Examination Level I*
   There has been considerable growth in recent years in the use of economic analysis in investment management. Further significant expansion may lie ahead as financial analysts develop greater skills in economic analysis and these analyses are integrated more into the investment decision-making

process. The following questions address the use of economic analysis in the investment decision-making process:

a. (1) Differentiate among leading, lagging, and coincident indicators of economic activity, and give an example of each.

(2) Indicate whether the leading indicators are one of the best tools for achieving above-average investment results. Briefly justify your conclusion.

b. Interest rate projections are used in investment management for a variety of purposes. Identify three significant reasons why interest rate forecasts may be important in reaching investment conclusions.

c. Assume you are a fundamental research analyst following the automobile industry for a large brokerage firm. Identify and briefly explain the relevance of *three* major economic time series, economic indicators, or economic data items that would be significant to automotive industry and company research.

3. *CFA Examination Level III*

A U.S. pension plan hired two offshore firms to manage the non-U.S. equity portion of its total portfolio. Each firm was free to own stocks in any country market included in Capital International's Europe, Australia, and Far East Index (EAFE) and free to use any form of dollar and/or nondollar cash or bonds as an equity substitute or reserve. After three years had elapsed, the records of the managers and the EAFE Index were as shown:

SUMMARY: CONTRIBUTIONS TO RETURN

	Currency	Country Selection	Stock Selection	Cash/Bond Allocation	Total Return Recorded
Manager A	(9.0%)	19.7%	3.1%	0.6%	14.4%
Manager B	(7.4)	14.2	6.0	2.8	15.6
Composite of A&B	(8.2)	16.9	4.5	1.7	15.0
EAFE Index	(12.9)	19.9	—	—	7.0

You are a member of the plan sponsor's pension committee, which will soon meet with the plan's consultant to review manager performance. In preparation for this meeting, you go through the following analysis:

a. Briefly describe the strengths and weaknesses of each manager, relative to the EAFE Index data.

b. Briefly explain the meaning of the data in the Currency column.

4. Each week in *Barron's* in the data section entitled "Market Week," there is a table in the pages for the "International Trader" for Global Stock Markets. Consult the latest available issue of this publication and the issue one year earlier to find the following information.

a. Show the closing value for five country indexes of your choice on each date relative to the yearly high for each year.

b. Which countries have markets in downtrends? Which countries are in uptrends?

c. Based on the percent range for the 52-week period $\frac{H-L}{(H+L)/2}$, which is the most volatile market?

d. For the five countries, calculate the percentage change over the one-year period in local currency and in U.S. dollars. Discuss how each country did relative to the World Index.

5. Using a source of financial data such as *Barron's* or *The Wall Street Journal*:

a. Plot the weekly percentage changes in the S&P Industrials index (*y* axis) versus comparable weekly percentage changes in the M2 money supply figures (*x* axis) for the past 10 weeks. Do you see a positive, negative, or zero correlation? (Monetary aggregates will lag the stock market aggregates.)

b. Examine the trend in money rates (e.g., federal funds, 90-day T-bills, etc.) over the past 10 weeks. Is there a correlation between these money rates? Estimate the correlation between the individual money rates and percentage changes in M2.

6. For the past 10 weeks, examine the relationship between the weekly percentage changes in the S&P Industrials Index and the DJIA. Plot the weekly percentage changes in each index using S&P as the *x* axis and DJIA as the *y* axis. Discuss your results as they relate to diversification. Do a similar comparison for the S&P Industrials and the Nikkei Index and discuss these results as they relate to diversification.

References

Baker, H. Kent, ed. *Improving the Investment Decision Process—Better Use of Economic Inputs in Security Analysis and Portfolio Management.* Charlottesville, Va.: Association for Investment Management and Research, 1992.

Belfer, Nathan. "Economic Indicators and Their Significance." In *The Financial Analysts Handbook,* 2d ed., ed. Sumner N. Levine. Homewood, Ill.: Dow Jones–Irwin, 1988.

Diermeier, Jeffrey J. "Capital Market Expectations: The Macro Factors." In *Managing Investment Portfolios: A Dynamic Process,* 2d ed., eds. John L. Maginn and Donald L. Tuttle. Boston: Warren Gorham and Lamont, 1990.

Droms, William G., ed. *Initiating and Managing a Global Investment Program.* Charlottesville, Va.: Association for Investment Management and Research, 1991.

Fogler, H. Russell, ed. *Developments in Quantitative Investment Models.* Charlottesville, Va.: Association for Investment Management and Research, 2001.

Implementing Global Equity Strategy: Spotlight on Asia. Charlottesville, Va.: Association for Investment Management and Research, 1997.

Investing Worldwide. An annual conference (started in 1990) sponsored by the Association for Investment Management and Research, Charlottesville, Va.

Jost, Kathryn Dixon, ed. *Evolution in Equity Markets: Focus on Asia.* Charlottesville, Va.: Association for Investment Management and Research, 2001.

Shackalford, Aaron L., ed. *Economic Analysis for Investment Professionals.* Charlottesville, Va.: Association for Investment Management and Research, 1997.

Solnik, Bruno. *Predictable Time-Varying Components of International Asset Returns.* Charlottesville, Va.: Association for Investment Management and Research, 1993.

Squires, Jan. ed. *Asset Allocation in a Changing World,* Charlottesville, VA: Association for Investment Management and Research, 1998.

Part 4

Analysis and Management of Common Stocks

In Part 3 we considered the basic valuation principles and practices applied to all securities and how this was applied to the global asset allocation decision. In Part 4, we apply these same valuation principles and practices to the analysis and management of common stocks. The objective is to be in position to make the critical risk-return decision at the market-industry-company stock level.

You will recall from Chapter 11 that successful investment requires several steps, beginning with a valuation of the aggregate economy and market and the examination of various industries and concluding with the analysis of individual companies and their securities. Globalization of the capital markets has definitely complicated this process wherein it is now necessary to consider markets on a worldwide basis followed by the analysis of *world* industries that involve numerous, complex foreign companies.

In Chapter 13, we begin the three-step, top-down approach and discuss how to analyze the aggregate stock market using the two general valuation approaches introduced in Chapter 11— the present value of cash flow models and the relative valuation ratios. In Chapter 14, we again demonstrate these two approaches to the valuation of an industry.

Chapter 15 on company analysis begins with a discussion of the difference between a company and its stock. In many instances, the common stock of a very fine company (possibly a true growth company) may not be a good investment, which is why we emphasize that company analysis and stock selection are two separate but dependent activities. Once again, the analysis procedure is built on the two valuation approaches employed for the market and alternative industries. We also consider other techniques, such as economic value added (EVA), that provide insights regarding the economic success of a firm and its management. The overall goal of this procedure is to select one of the best companies in a superior industry during a favorable market environment.

It was noted in Chapter 11 that it is not feasible to use the standard dividend discount model to value the stock of true growth companies. Therefore, in Chapter 15 we discuss several valuation models that have been specifically developed for the analysis and valuation of growth companies.

Throughout this section, we refer back to the semistrong efficient market hypothesis. Recall that, although many studies support this hypothesis, there is a growing literature dealing with anomalies related to this hypothesis. Therefore, in this section we provide a consistent and justifiable valuation process that can be used to find undervalued securities. You should never forget that the output of alternative valuation models is only as good as the estimated inputs and *the superior analyst is the one who provides the best estimates of the required rate of return on a security based upon its risk and expected growth rate of future cash flows.*

Chapter 16 deals with technical analysis, an alternative or supplement to the fundamental approach discussed in the prior chapters. Rather than estimating value based on fundamental variables, the technical analyst believes that it is possible to project future stock price movements based on past stock price changes or other stock market data. Various techniques used by technical analysts for U.S. and world markets are discussed and demonstrated.

Chapter 17 deals with equity portfolio management strategies. We begin with a general discussion of passive versus active management styles. This is followed by a specific discussion of indexing, including the selection of an appropriate benchmark index, and the various methods of index portfolio investing used in practice. The concept of *tracking error* is introduced as a means of assessing how well an investor has replicated the benchmark portfolio.

The overview of active equity portfolio management strategies includes a discussion of how one constructs a portfolio that reflects the client's risk-return objectives and constraints from three different perspectives: fundamental analysis (e.g., asset class and sector rotation, stock under- and overvaluation), technical analysis (e.g., overreaction, price momentum), and anomaly and attribute analysis (e.g., earnings momentum, firm size). In this discussion, we pay special attention to the conceptual and practical differences between forming portfolios based on both value-oriented and growth-oriented investment styles. Notably, all of these approaches should consider global opportunities.

We conclude Chapter 17 with a discussion of how the equity portfolio management decision fits into the investor's overall asset allocation strategy. After discussing the integrated approach to asset allocation, we also examine strategic, tactical, and insured allocation strategies. Finally, we present the basic intuition for how investors can use *derivative instruments* (such as futures and option contracts) to alter the risk and return characteristics of their equity portfolios.

Chapter 13 ▷ Stock Market Analysis

After you read this chapter, you should be able to answer the following questions:

➤ How do we apply the basic reduced form dividend discount model (DDM) to the valuation of the aggregate stock market?

➤ What would be the prevailing value of the market as represented by the S&P Industrials Index based upon the reduced form DDM?

➤ What would be the prevailing value of the aggregate stock market based upon the present value of free cash flow to equity (FCFE) model?

➤ What two components are involved in the two-part valuation procedure?

➤ Given the two components in the valuation procedure, which is more volatile?

➤ What steps are involved in estimating the earnings per share for an aggregate market series?

➤ What variables affect the aggregate operating profit margin and how do they affect it?

➤ What variables determine the level and changes in the market earnings multiplier?

➤ How do you arrive at an expected market value and an expected rate of return for the stock market?

➤ What has happened to the values for the other relative valuation ratios—that is, the *P/BV, P/CF,* and *P/S* ratios?

➤ What additional factors must be considered when you apply this microanalysis approach to the valuation of stock markets around the world?

➤ What are some differences between stock market statistics for the United States and those of other countries?

Interest in stock market movements has grown during the past decade. More individuals own stock than ever before, and significant mergers are increasingly frequent. In earlier chapters, we emphasized the importance of analyzing the aggregate economy and alternative security markets before an industry or a company analysis. As discussed in Chapter 11, it is very important to analyze the economy and the market before you consider which is the best industry or company.

There are three techniques for making the security market decision. The first is a macroanalysis approach, which is based on the strong relationship between the aggregate economy and alternative security markets. Chapter 12 was concerned with the macro techniques and discussed world asset allocation. The second technique presented in this chapter involves microanalysis, which applies basic valuation models introduced in Chapter 11 to the bond or equity markets. Chapter 19 contains a discussion of the microvaluation of bonds. The third technique is technical analysis, which assumes that past market series can be used to predict future market returns. This technique will be discussed in Chapter 16.

As noted, this chapter explains the microanalysis of a country's stock market. Your estimate of the fundamental value for the stock market in a country implies an estimate of the rate of return you expect as an equity investor in that country during the holding period.

This chapter begins the three-step valuation process introduced in Chapter 11. We initiate the fundamental analysis of stocks, which determines the future value of the aggregate stock market on the basis of sales, earnings, cash flows, and risk factors. In this chapter, we estimate the aggregate market outlook based on the outlook for the economy. This will be followed in Chapter 14 by a discussion of how one analyzes alternative industries. Finally, in Chapter 15, we consider how to analyze an individual firm and estimate the value of its stock.

The presentation of the fundamental valuation approaches to the aggregate stock market considers the two equity valuation approaches introduced in Chapter 11. Initially, we employ the present value of cash flow models. As before, we begin with a valuation using the present value of dividends—that is, the basic reduced form DDM. This is followed by a valuation using the present value of the free cash flow to equity (FCFE) model assuming the constant growth model. Subsequently, we demonstrate a valuation using the FCFE model assuming a three-stage growth scenario for a few years prior to constant growth. Notably, we do not employ the operating free cash flow model in this chapter due to space constraints but also because of the difficulty in estimating the debt for the S&P Industrials index.

After the present value of cash flow valuation, we move to the relative valuation techniques, beginning with the earnings multiple (*P/E* ratio) approach. Subsequently, we compute and analyze the trends for the other relative valuation ratios, *P/BV, P/CF,* and *P/S*. We do not attempt to use these ratios to derive a specific value of the market; rather, we discuss the trends for these ratios during the past 20 years to help you become familiar with them so that these relative valuation ratios can be used subsequently in industry and company stock analysis. Specifically, you will want to compare industry and company relative valuation ratios to the relative valuation ratios for the market. We finish the chapter with a discussion of unique factors that should be considered when applying these valuation techniques to foreign markets.

APPLYING THE DDM VALUATION MODEL TO THE MARKET

In Chapter 11, we worked with a valuation model that equated the value of an investment to

1. The stream of expected returns
2. The time pattern of expected returns
3. The required rate of return on the investment

Using this information, we employed the dividend discount model (DDM), which estimated the value of the stock (V_j) assuming a constant growth rate of dividends for an infinite period.

➤13.1
$$V_j = \frac{D_0(1+g)}{(1+k)} + \frac{D_0(1+g)^2}{(1+k)^2} + \ldots + \frac{D_0(1+g)^n}{(1+k)^n}.$$

where:

V_j = **the value of stock** j
D_0 = **the dividend payment in the current period**
g = **the constant growth rate of dividends**
k = **the required rate of return on stock** j
n = **the number of periods, which is assumed to be infinite**

This model, which was used for the fundamental analysis of common stock, can also be used to value a stock market series. In the appendix to Chapter 11, it was shown that this model can be simplified to the following reduced form expression:

➤13.2
$$V_j = P_j = \frac{D_1}{k - g}$$

where:

P_j = the price of stock j
D_1 = dividend in period 1, which is equal to: $D_0(1 + g)$
k = the required rate of return for stock j
g = the constant growth rate of dividends

This model suggests that the parameters to be estimated are (1) the required rate of return *(k)* and (2) the expected growth rate of dividends *(g)*. After estimating *g*, it is simple to estimate D_1 because it is equal to the current dividend (D_0) times $(1 + g)$.

Recall too that we can transform the dividend discount model into an earnings multiplier model by dividing both sides of the equation by E_1.

➤13.3
$$\frac{P_1}{E_1} = \frac{\frac{D_1}{E_1}}{k - g}$$

We call this *P/E* ratio the **earnings multiplier** or the *price/earnings ratio*. It is determined by

1. The expected dividend payout ratio (D_1/E_1)
2. The required rate of return on the stock *(k)*
3. The expected growth rate of dividends for the stock *(g)*

The estimation of this earnings multiplier is important because it varies between stocks and industries. Also, the multiplier for the aggregate stock market varies widely over time and has a big impact on changes in the value of the market.

We showed previously that the difficult parameters to estimate are *k* and *g*, or, more specifically, the *spread* between *k* and *g*. Recall that very small changes in either *k* or *g* can affect the spread and change the value of the aggregate market substantially.

Market Valuation Using the Reduced Form DDM

In this section we will apply the model to the valuation of the S&P Industrials Index as of mid-2002. As noted, the critical estimates are the prevailing *k* and *g* for the U.S. equity market. The estimate of D_1 is the current D_0 for the latest 52-week period times $(1 + g)$. As of mid-2002, the recent trailing 52-week dividend estimate in *Barron's* was $20.00.

As discussed previously, the estimate of *k* is a function of the nominal risk-free rate *(NRFR)* plus a market risk premium. Because both of these components are subject to interpretation, we will consider a range of values.

The Nominal Risk-Free Rate The alternatives for the *NRFR* are based upon the theoretical specifications that it should be a zero-coupon, default-free asset with a time to maturity that approximates the investor's holding period. The point is, such an asset would provide the asset's promised return (i.e., its yield to maturity) because there is no default risk, no reinvestment risk because it is a zero-coupon security, and no price risk because the asset matures at the end of the holding period. The range of suggested maturities goes from a three-month T-bill to an intermediate government bond (e.g., a 10-year Treasury), to the long-term government bond (e.g., a 30-year Treasury). As of mid-2002, these yields were:

3-month Treasury bill:	2.00%
10-year Treasury:	5.20%
30-year Treasury:	5.60%

The Equity Risk Premium   The attitude toward the estimation of the equity risk premium has undergone significant changes during the 1990s. The initial empirical estimate of an equity risk premium was provided by the pioneering work of Ibbotson and Sinquefield in their monograph for the *Financial Analysts Research Foundation.* They estimated the risk premium on common stock as the arithmetic mean of the difference in the annual rate of return from stocks minus the return on Treasury bills.[1] Although the original estimate was for 1926–1981, this estimated risk premium has been updated annually in a yearbook provided by Ibbotson Associates.[2] For example, the equity risk premium as of 2002 for 1926–2001 was 9.1 percent using the arithmetic mean of the annual values and 7.5 percent using the geometric mean of the annual values. The geometric mean is appropriate for long-run asset class comparisons, whereas the arithmetic mean is what you would use to estimate the premium for a given year (e.g., the *expected* performance next year). Because our application is to the long-term DDM model, the geometric mean value would probably be more appropriate, which implies using the 7.5 percent risk premium value.

An additional adjustment is suggested to reflect the belief that the typical investment horizon is longer than that implied by the T-bill rate. Assuming that most investors consider the intermediate time frame (5–10 years) a more appropriate investment horizon, the risk premium should be computed as the stock return less the return on intermediate government bonds. Given the typical upward-sloping yield curve, it is not surprising that this measure of the risk premium is about 1 percent less than the T-bill premium—that is, the arithmetic mean of the annual risk premiums relative to intermediate government bonds was 8.2 percent during 1926–2001, and the geometric mean of the annual risk premiums was 6.6 percent. In recent years, Ibbotson Associates has also provided a long-horizon risk premium estimate that employs the long-term government bond return. The arithmetic average for this series was 7.8 percent and the geometric average was 6.2 percent. Therefore, the long-term historical risk premium to use should be about *6.5 percent.*

Several authors have contended that there are problems with this estimate in a dynamic real-world environment. The major criticism is that it is *too long term* and assumes that the *market risk premium is almost a constant value.*[3] Given that we are dealing with an average value that encompasses almost 76 years, this technique will not reflect any changes over time. There are ways to adjust for this constant value problem, and there are other estimation approaches that have been suggested.

The first suggestion to adjust for the constant value is to use a constant period moving average for the Ibbotson-Sinquefield technique—for example, instead of using a single mean value for the total period since 1926, employ a 20-year moving average of the series. This would

---

[1]Roger G. Ibbotson and Rex A. Sinquefield, *Stocks, Bonds, Bills and Inflation: The Past and Future* (Charlottesville, Va.: Financial Analysts Research Foundation, 1982).

[2]*Stocks, Bonds, Bills and Inflation* (Chicago, Ill.: Ibbotson Associates, annual).

[3]This is the contention contained in Michael Rozeff, "Dividend Yields Are Equity Risk Premiums," *Journal of Portfolio Management* 11, no. 1 (Fall 1984): 68–75.

EXHIBIT 13.1 INTERMEDIATE-TERM EQUITY RISK PREMIUM: 20-YEAR MOVING ARITHMETIC AND GEOMETRIC AVERAGES

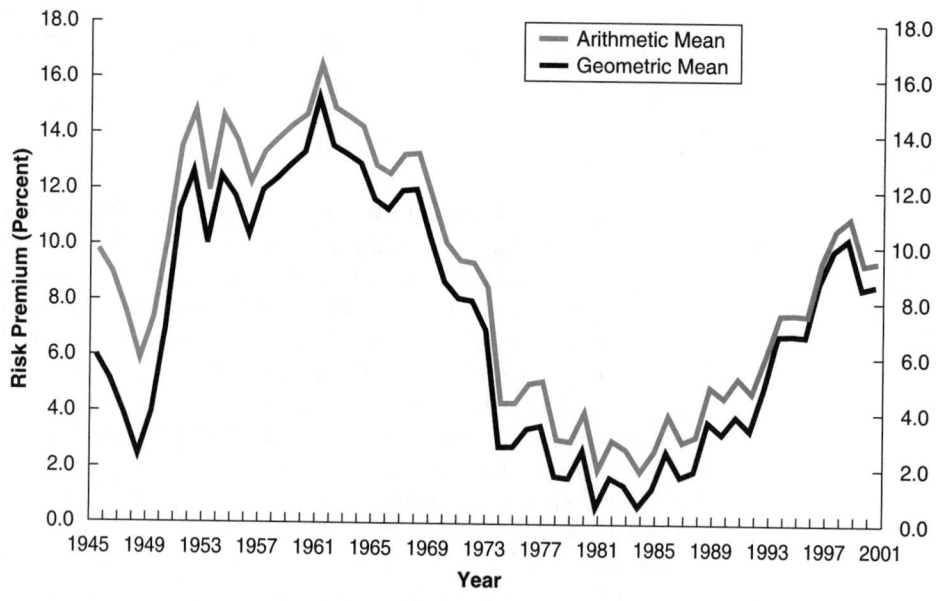

reflect any trends in the series over time. Exhibit 13.1 shows the impact of employing a moving average and using the intermediate bond return as the risk-free asset. These time-series plots also suggest that the risk premium series is not very stable since the 20-year moving average values vary from about 1 percent to 16 percent. Notably, given the computation of the risk premium, it increases during years when the market does well and declines during poor performing periods such as the late 1970s and early 1980s. This is clearly counterintuitive to expectations.

The paper by Rozeff discusses the equity risk premium concept similar to the presentation in this book.[4] This is followed by a review of alternative measures of the risk premium, including the Ibbotson-Sinquefield series, an estimate using the CAPM, and a brief consideration of the default risk premium (referred to as the credit risk series). Rozeff shows that, given some economic assumptions, the risk premium on equity is equal to the dividend yield. He further suggests that when the dividend yield exceeds 6 percent, it is an excellent time to buy stocks; when the yield is below 3 percent, it is generally a poor time to buy stocks. Some relatively casual empirical results were provided to support these contentions. The fact is, this decision rule has not worked during the period 1991–1999 and especially since 1995 because during the period 1995–1999, the dividend yield was consistently below 2.0 percent and yet, stocks experienced a rate of return that averaged over 20 percent (the highest five-year average since 1926).

The credit risk premium concept has been referred to on several occasions in this book when discussing changes in the capital market risk premium. The notion is that changes in the absolute or percentage spread between the yield on BAA and AAA bonds indicate a change in the required rate of return by investors for accepting credit risk. Further, this change in the credit risk premium implies a change in the slope of the security market line (SML). The percent yield spread is considered a preferable measure because it adjusts for the level of yields. An advantage of the credit risk measure is that it is based on current market results and reflects prevailing

---

[4]Ibid.

investor attitudes. For a recent plot of this credit yield spread, see Exhibit 1.9, which indicates a declining trend since 1985.

An alternative estimate of the equity risk premium is suggested by Reichenstein and Rich— namely, the Value Line forecast of dividends and capital gain.[5] This estimated total market return less the short-term government bond yield is shown to provide better and more consistent results than an earnings price value or dividend yield, although it provides consistently biased results that can be adjusted.

A comparison used by Woolridge to justify a change in the equity risk premium is the relative volatility of stocks versus bonds.[6] Woolridge argues that the risk premium for equity has declined from the 6 percent estimate based on the Ibbotson-Sinquefield data to about 2.5 percent because of the *increase* in bond market volatility relative to stock volatility.[7] Specifically, the equity risk premium spread has declined, not because stocks have become less volatile but because bonds have become more volatile. Thus, the difference in risk between the two asset classes is less than before, so the risk premium spread has declined. Finally, a recent study by Claus and Thomas derives an estimate of the equity risk premium from the discount rate that equates market valuations with prevailing expectations of future flows.[8] Their results indicate a risk premium between 1985 and 1998 of 3 percent or less.

In summary, if you use the current intermediate government bond rate as your estimate of the minimal *NRFR,* these studies indicate that the equity risk premium should be somewhere between 2.5 percent and 6.0 percent, depending on the current environment. In turn, you can derive an indicator of the current environment by examining the dividend yield, the prevailing credit risk spread, or the relative volatility of bonds versus stocks.

Once you have estimated the required rate of return for the current period, you must determine whether the expected rate of inflation or the risk premium on common stock will change during your investment horizon.

The Current Estimate of Risk Premium and *k*

Based upon the prior discussion, the total range for the equity risk premium is from about 1.5 percent (the prevailing dividend yield on the major market indexes) to about 6.0 percent (the long-run geometric average of the historical returns according to the Ibbotson data). For purposes of applying these results, we will employ three alternative risk premiums: 2, 4, and 6 percent. If we combine these risk premiums with the prior nominal risk-free rates for government bonds, we derive the following matrix of required rates of return *(k)* for the S&P Industrials Index:

	RISK PREMIUMS		
Nominal *RFR*	0.02	0.04	0.06
0.020	0.040	0.060	0.080
0.052	0.072	0.092	0.112
0.056	0.076	0.096	0.116

[5]William Reichenstein and Steven P. Rich, "The Market Risk Premium and Long-Term Stock Returns," *Journal of Portfolio Management* 19, no. 4 (Summer 1993): 63–72.

[6]Randall Woolridge, "Do Stock Prices Reflect Fundamental Values?" *Journal of Applied Corporate Finance* 8, no. 1 (Spring 1995): 64–69.

[7]For an analysis of relative volatility of bonds versus stocks that is consistent with the Woolridge contention, see Frank K. Reilly, David J. Wright, and Kam Chan, "Bond Market Volatility Compared to Stock Market Volatility," *Journal of Portfolio Management* 27, no. 1 (Fall 2000): 82–92.

[8]James Claus and Jacob Thomas, "Equity Premium as Low as 3 Percent? Evidence from Analysts Earnings Forecasts for Domestic and International Stock Markets," *Journal of Finance* 56, no. 5 (October 2001): 1629–1666.

The matrix indicates a range of k from 0.040 (4.0 percent) to 0.116 (11.6 percent). The low required rate of return assumes investors have a very short-run horizon and a very small risk premium, while the high required return implies a long-run horizon and the use of the long-run historical risk premium.

For purposes of our subsequent estimate, we will use the diagonal values from this matrix: 0.040, 0.092, and 0.116.

ESTIMATING THE GROWTH RATE OF DIVIDENDS (g)

The earnings multiple that is applied to next year's earnings must take into account the expected growth rate (g) for common dividends.[9] There is a positive relationship between the earnings multiplier and the growth rate of earnings and dividends—the higher the expected growth rate, the higher the multiple.[10] When estimating g, you should consider the current expected rate of growth and estimate any *changes* in the growth rate. Such changes in expectations indicate a change in the relationship between k and g and will have a profound effect on the earnings multiplier.

As discussed in Chapters 10 and 11, a firm's growth rate is equal to (1) the proportion of earnings retained and reinvested by the firm—that is, its retention rate (b)—times (2) the rate of return earned on investments (ROE). An increase in either or both of these variables causes an increase in the expected growth rate (g) and an increase in the earnings multiplier. Therefore, the growth rate can be stated as:

➤13.4
$$g = f(b, ROE)$$

where:

    g = **expected growth rate**
    b = **the expected retention rate equal to $1 - D/E$**
    ROE = **the expected return on equity investments**

Therefore, to estimate the growth rate, you need to estimate changes in the retention rate (b) and the return on equity (ROE). The plot in Exhibit 13.2 shows that the retention rate was relatively high (56 to 63 percent) during the 1970s, ranged between 45 and 62 percent during the 1980s, declined in 1991 because earnings declined but many firms did not cut their dividends, and it returned to over 55 percent during 1994–2000. Because the valuation model is a long-run model, you should estimate only relatively permanent changes, although short-run changes can affect expectations. Specifically, you should recognize that the annual retention rate, which has been quite volatile (between 45 and 60 percent), is heavily impacted by annual earnings changes (as will be discussed in the dividend payout section).

The second variable that affects g is changes in the return on equity (ROE) defined as

$$ROE = \frac{\text{Net Income}}{\text{Equity}}$$

---

[9]You know that the g in the valuation model is the expected growth rate for dividends. In our discussion, we assume a relatively constant dividend-payout ratio (dividend/earnings), so the growth of dividends is dependent on the growth in earnings.

[10]A paper that specifically examines this relationship is Patricia M. Fairfield, "*P/E, P/B,* and the Present Value of Future Dividends," *Financial Analysts Journal* 50, no. 4 (July/August 1994): 22–31.

EXHIBIT 13.2   *TIME-SERIES PLOT OF THE S&P INDUSTRIALS INDEX RETENTION RATE: 1977–2000*

You will recall from the discussion in Chapter 10 that *ROE* can be broken down using the three-component Du Pont analysis as follows:

➤13.5
$$ROE = \frac{\text{Net Income}}{\text{Equity}} = \frac{\text{Net Income}}{\text{Sales}} \times \frac{\text{Sales}}{\text{Total Assets}} \times \frac{\text{Total Assets}}{\text{Equity}}$$
$$= \frac{\text{Net Profit}}{\text{Margin}} \times \frac{\text{Total Asset}}{\text{Turnover}} \times \frac{\text{Financial}}{\text{Leverage}}$$

This equation shows that the *ROE* increases if either the total asset turnover or the profit margin increases. In addition, you can increase *ROE* by increasing financial leverage. Because the S&P Industrials series includes historical information on total assets only since 1977, we examine this three-component breakdown of *ROE* for this 23-year period.

As shown in Exhibit 13.3, the *ROE* for the S&P Industrials series experienced very little change over the 15-year period prior to the decline in 1991 and strong recovery in 1993–2000 to record levels. An analysis of the three components of *ROE* indicates what contributed to the overall change (or lack of change) over time. First, the profit margin (Exhibit 13.4) experienced a steady increase after 1993. The second component, total asset turnover (Exhibit 13.5) increased in 1980 and 1981 but then declined consistently to a low point in 2000. Combining these two variables *(PM* and *TATO)* equals return on total assets (Exhibit 13.3) that has increased since 1992 but has experienced a small decline during the total period from 1977 to 2000. Therefore, the major variable that contributed to the increase in *ROE* was the financial leverage ratio (Exhibit 13.6) that increased from about 2.00 to 3.10 in 2000.

The point is, an investor needs to estimate the long-term outlook for *ROE,* which in turn requires a long-term estimate for each of the three component ratios. Once established, multiply

EXHIBIT 13.3 *S&P INDUSTRIALS INDEX RETURN ON EQUITY AND RETURN ON ASSETS: 1977–2000*

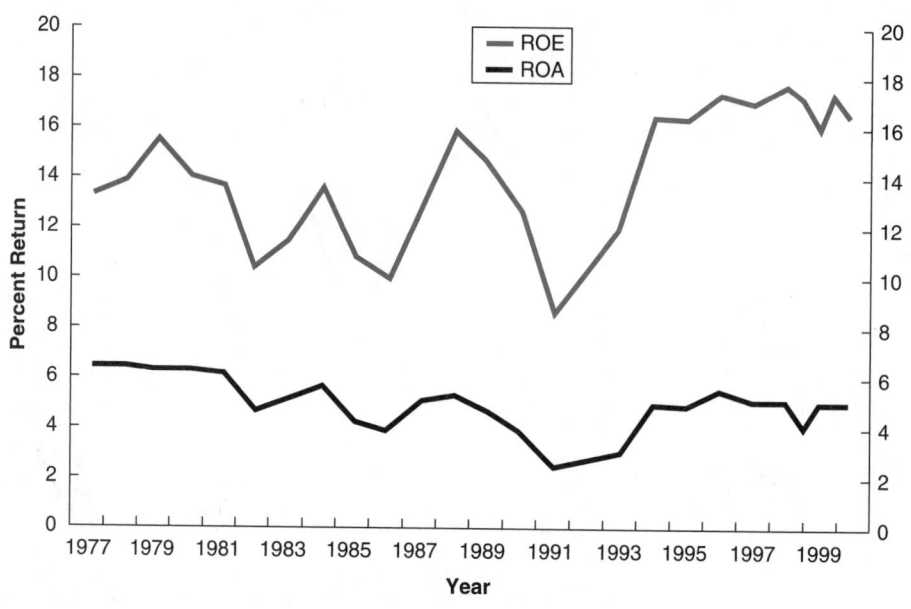

EXHIBIT 13.4 *S&P INDUSTRIALS INDEX NET PROFIT MARGIN: 1977–2000*

EXHIBIT 13.5 *S&P INDUSTRIALS INDEX TOTAL ASSET TURNOVER RATIO: 1977–2000*

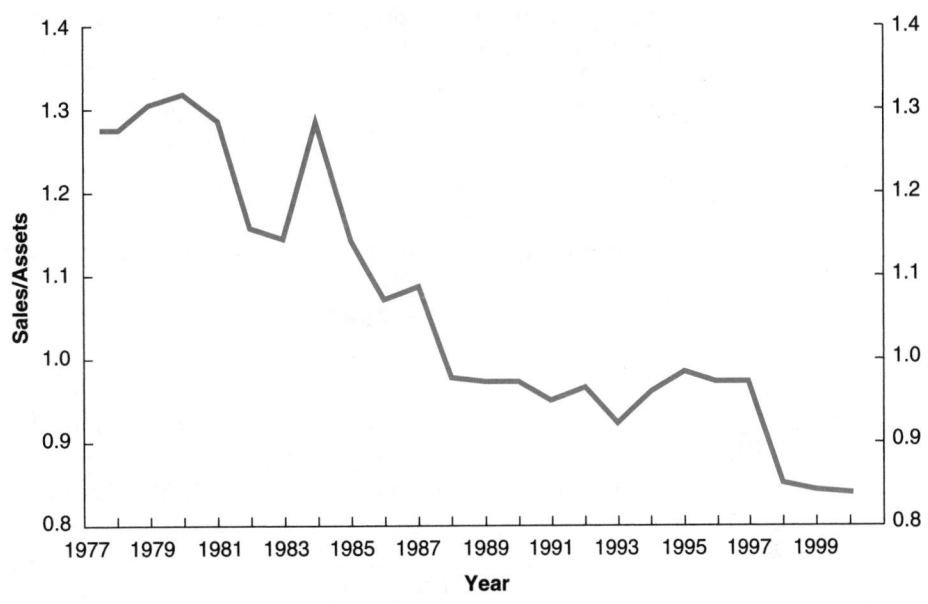

EXHIBIT 13.6 *S&P INDUSTRIALS INDEX ASSETS/EQUITY RATIO: 1977–2000*

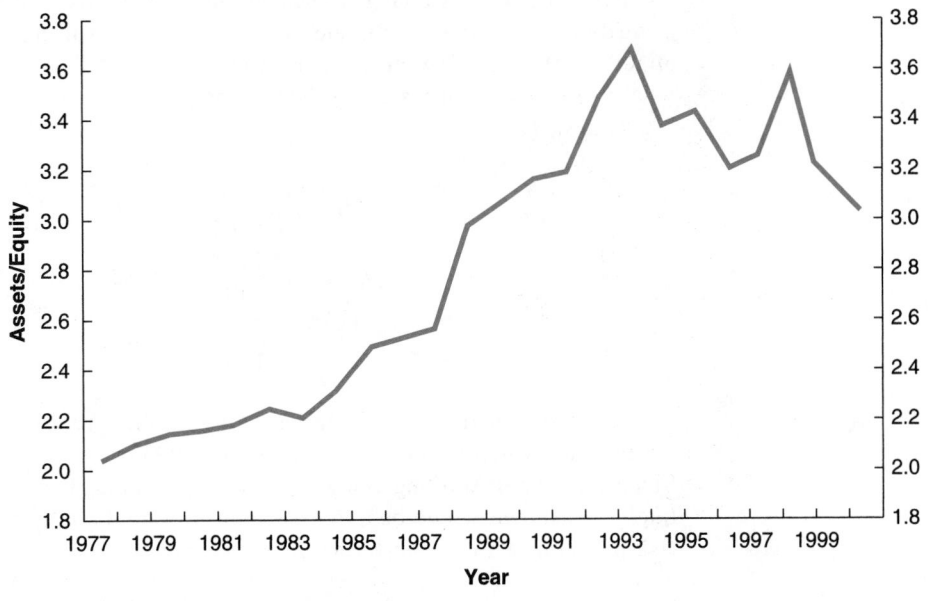

this long-term estimate of *ROE* by your estimate of *b,* the retention rate, to calculate an estimate of the long-term growth rate *(g)* of U.S. Industrial firms. As an example, if you estimate, the *long-run* retention rate of firms will be 55 percent and their *ROE* will be about 14 percent; this means you would expect the long-run growth rate of

➤13.6
$$g = b \times ROE$$
$$= 0.55 \times 0.14$$
$$= 0.077 = 7.7\%$$

Combining the Estimates   If we combine the several estimates, they are as follows:

$$D_0 = \$20.00$$
$$k = 0.064 \text{ or } 0.095 \text{ or } 0.117$$
$$g = 0.077$$
$$D_1 = 20.00(1 + g) = 20.00(1.077) = \$21.54$$

Using these inputs for the reduced form DDM indicates the following three-market value estimates:

1. $\dfrac{\$21.54}{0.064 - 0.077} = \dfrac{\$21.54}{-0.013} = \text{Meaningless } (g > k)$

2. $\dfrac{\$21.54}{0.095 - 0.077} = \dfrac{\$21.54}{0.018} = 1,196.67$

3. $\dfrac{\$21.54}{0.117 - 0.077} = \dfrac{\$21.54}{0.04} = 538.50$

These latter two estimated values, not including the one where the expected growth rate exceeds the very low *k* estimate, are below the prevailing index value in early 2002 of about 1,350. Assuming the dividend value of $21.54 is reasonable, one needs to consider what *k*–*g* spread is necessary to justify the prevailing market value. Consider the following values:

$$\frac{21.54}{0.017} = 1,267.06$$
$$\frac{21.54}{0.016} = 1,346.25$$
$$\frac{21.54}{0.015} = 1,436.00$$

It appears that the current market value implies (requires) a *k*–*g* spread very close to 1.6 percent, which means either a *k* below 0.095 or an expected growth rate above 0.077. Since the 7.7 percent long-run growth rate appears fairly aggressive (optimistic), the most likely adjustment would be a lower *k* approaching 0.093, which implies about a 3 percent risk premium with a long-term *NRFR* or a 4 percent risk premium with an intermediate *NRFR.*

EXHIBIT 13.7 ▶ *COMPONENTS OF FREE CASH FLOW TO EQUITY FOR THE S&P INDUSTRIALS INDEX: 1987–2000*

YEAR	NET INCOME	DEPRECIATION EXPENSE	CAPITAL EXPENDITURE	CHANGE IN WORKING CAPITAL	PRINCIPAL REPAYMENT	NEW DEBT ISSUES	TOTAL FCFE
1987	20.28	20.21	27.59	5.09	—	3.00	10.81
1988	26.59	23.59	35.43	–21.14	—	44.04	79.93
1989	26.83	24.21	40.98	–6.25	—	3.63	19.94
1990	24.77	26.31	43.93	–5.25	—	10.48	22.88
1991	16.91	27.50	40.33	–1.42	—	2.26	7.76
1992	19.05	29.48	39.36	–2.88	1.70	—	10.35
1993	21.93	28.72	39.28	6.63	2.42	—	2.32
1994	32.83	29.58	39.97	6.63	—	4.06	19.87
1995	35.44	33.06	46.16	6.63	—	10.90	26.61
1996	41.15	36.11	53.49	–3.85	—	10.17	41.64
1997	43.80	39.79	60.54	–0.94	—	11.04	35.03
1998	38.86	32.89	44.36	1.56	—	8.67	34.50
1999	50.88	41.70	56.62	23.61	—	16.35	28.70
2000	54.02	43.50	60.68	–41.42	—	5.66	83.92

Source: *Financial Analysts Handbook* (New York: Standard & Poor's, 2001). Reprinted with permission.

Market Valuation Using the Free Cash Flow to Equity (FCFE) Model

As indicated earlier, we will derive an estimate using this FCFE model under two scenarios: (1) a constant growth rate from the present and then (2) a two-stage growth rate assumption.

The Constant Growth FCFE Model   To begin, the FCFE is defined (measured) as follows:[11]

> *Net Income*
> *+ Depreciation expense*
> *– Capital expenditures*
> *– Δ in working capital*
> *– Principal debt repayments*
> *+ New debt issues*

This technique attempts to determine the free cash flow that is available to the stockholders after payments to all other capital suppliers and after providing for the continued growth of the firm. The FCFE data for the S&P Industrials Index for the period 1987–2000 is contained in Exhibit 13.7.

---

[11]For further discussion and detail, see Aswath Damodaran, *Damodaran on Valuation* (New York: John Wiley & Sons, 1994), Chapter 7.

Although there was overall growth in the series for the period 1987–1997 (13 percent a year) and for 1987–1998 (11 percent a year), there was also substantial variation, including the peak value in 1988 and the low value in 1993. Therefore, for the constant growth version of the model, we will use the growth values used in the DDM as follows:

$$g = 0.077$$
$$k = 0.095; 0.117$$
$$\text{FCFE} = 34.10 \text{ in } 1998 \ (\text{FCFE}_0)$$
$$= (34.10)(1.077) = 36.73 \text{ in } 1999 \ (\text{FCFE}_1)$$
$$\text{Equity Values} = \frac{36.73}{0.095 - 0.077} = \frac{36.73}{0.018} = 2,040$$
$$= \frac{36.73}{0.117 - 0.077} = \frac{36.73}{0.04} = 918.25$$

In contrast to the DDM results, this model indicates that the market at its current price of about 1,350 is undervalued if one assumes a cost of equity of 9.5 percent. In contrast, the market is overvalued assuming a cost of equity of 11.7 percent. Recall that the 9.5 percent cost of equity is based upon using the 10-year Treasury bond as the *NRFR* and assumes a 4 percent market risk premium.

Alternatively, if we assume a lower perpetual growth rate of 7.2 percent, the value declines to 1,597 (36.73/0.023), and if our growth estimate is only 7 percent, the value declines to 1,469. Needless to say, the estimated value is very sensitive to the estimates of k and g and the resulting spread.

The Two-Stage Growth FCFE Model   If one considers only the period 1994–1998 (no unusual working capital changes), the average annual percentage growth is about 15 percent. To demonstrate this model, we assumed the following above-average growth rates during the next five years (the first stage) followed by a second stage of constant growth at 7 percent.

2002–12%

2003–10%

2004–10%

2005–8%

2006–8%

2007 onward–7%

Assuming a k of 9.5 percent and an FCFE of 34.10 in 2001, the computations are as follows:

Year	FCFE	Discount Factor at 0.095	Present Value
2002	38.19	0.9132	34.88
2003	42.01	0.8340	35.04
2004	46.21	0.7616	35.19
2005	49.91	0.6954	34.71
2006	53.90	0.6353	34.24
Continuing Value[a]	2,307	0.6353	1,465.64
		Total *PV*	$1,639.70

[a] $\dfrac{57.67}{0.095 - 0.07} = 2,307$

As can be seen, this set of assumptions indicates an intrinsic market value very close to the current price of the market, which implies the following: (1) the market is properly valued at this time, and (2) investors who acquire a diversified portfolio of U.S. stocks at these prices should derive a long-run annual rate of return of about 9.5 percent. It is also possible to arrive at this market return estimate using the k estimate from the DDM as follows:

➤13.7
$$k = \frac{D}{P} + g$$

Combining the current dividend yield of about 1.4 percent and the expected g of 7.7 percent implies a return of 9.1 percent. Notably, this is higher than what is expected by Emmons from the St. Louis Federal Reserve who derives expected growth based on the growth of nominal GDP of about 6 percent plus a dividend yield of 1.3 percent to arrive at a return estimate of about 7 percent (he stipulates a range of 5 to 7 percent).[12]

The next section will discuss and demonstrate the four alternative relative valuation ratios as follows: (1) the price/earnings ratio (*P/E*), (2) the price/book value ratio (*P/BV*), (3) the price/cash flow ratio (*P/CF*), and (4) the price/sales ratio (*P/S*). We begin with the *P/E* ratio because it is the most well known and because it can be derived from the DDM. Finally, this model can be used to derive a specific market value, which implies an expected rate of return for the equity market.

VALUATION USING THE RELATIVE VALUATION APPROACH

Two-Part Valuation Procedure

We use the earnings multiplier version of the dividend discount model to value the stock market because it is a theoretically correct model of value assuming a constant growth of dividends for an infinite time period, which is a reasonable assumption for the aggregate stock market.[13] Also, this valuation technique is consistently used in practice.

Recall that k and g are independent variables because k depends heavily on risk, whereas g is a function of the retention rate and the *ROE*. Therefore, this spread between k and g can and does change over time. The following equations imply an estimate of this spread at a point in time equal to the prevailing dividend yield:

$$P_j = \frac{D_1}{k - g}$$
$$P_j/D_1 = 1/k - g$$
$$D_1/P_j = k - g$$

Although the dividend yield gives an estimate of the size of the prevailing spread, it does not indicate the values for the two individual components (k and g) or what caused the *change* in the spread. More important, it says nothing about what the spread *should* be, which is the critical value that must be determined based upon estimating values for k and g.

---

[12]William R. Emmons, "What Can 'Buy-and-Hold' Stock Investors Expect?" *Monetary Trends* (St. Louis: Federal Reserve Bank of St. Louis, June 1999).

[13]Recall that these assumptions may be unrealistic for many stocks, especially for stocks of growth companies. We will consider these problems and discuss alternative valuation models that consider such conditions in Chapter 15.

Importance of Both Components of Value

The ultimate objective of this microanalysis is to estimate the intrinsic market value for a major stock market series, such as the S&P Industrials Index. This estimation process has two equally important steps:

1. Estimating the future earnings per share for the stock market series
2. Estimating the appropriate earnings multiplier for the stock market series based on long-run estimates of k and g.[14]

Some analysts have concentrated on estimating the earnings for a market series with little consideration of changes in the earnings multiplier for the series. An investor who considers only the earnings for the series and ignores the earnings multiplier (i.e., the *P/E* ratio), assumes that the earnings multiplier will be relatively constant over time. If this were correct, stock prices would generally move in line with earnings. The fallacy of this assumption is obvious when one examines data for the two components during the period from 1975 to 2000, as shown in Exhibit 13.8.

The year-end stock price is the closing value for the S&P Industrials Index on the last trading day of the year. The next column is the percentage change in price for the year. The earnings figure is the earnings per share during the year for the S&P Industrials Index, and the next column shows the percentage change from the prior year. The fifth column is the historical earnings multiplier at the end of the year, which is equal to the year-end value for the S&P Industrials Index divided by the *historical* earnings for that year. As an example, at the end of 1975, the S&P Industrials Index was equal to 100.88 and the earnings per share for the firms that made up the series were 8.58 for the 12 months ending 12/31/75. This implies an earnings multiplier of 11.76 (100.88/8.58). Although this may not be the ideal measure of the multiplier, it is consistent in its measurement and shows the changes in the relationship between stock prices and earnings over time. An alternative measure is the forward multiplier using *next* year's earnings (i.e., stock price as of 12/31/75 versus earnings for the 12 months ending 12/31/76). This forward *P/E* series likewise experiences substantial annual changes and is the multiple we will be estimating. Typically, it is also a smaller multiple because it considers future earnings that are generally higher.

There have been numerous striking examples where annual stock price movements for the S&P Industrials Index were opposite to earnings changes during the same year as follows:

- ➤ 1975 profit *declined* by 10 percent; stock prices *increased* by 32 percent.
- ➤ 1977 profits *increased* by 7 percent; stock prices *declined* by 12 percent.
- ➤ 1980 profits *decreased* by 1 percent; stock prices *increased* by over 27 percent.
- ➤ 1982 profits *decreased* by 21 percent; stock prices *increased* by 15 percent.
- ➤ 1984 profits *increased* by almost 23 percent; stock prices were basically *unchanged.*
- ➤ 1985 profits *decreased* by 15 percent; stock prices *increased* by about 26 percent.
- ➤ 1989 profits were almost *unchanged;* stock prices *increased* by over 25 percent.
- ➤ 1991 profits *decreased* by almost 32 percent; stock prices *increased* by over 27 percent.
- ➤ 1994 profits *increased* by almost 50 percent; stock prices were basically *unchanged.*
- ➤ 1997 profits *increased* about 2 percent; stock prices *increased* almost 29 percent.
- ➤ 1998 profits *decreased* by 9 percent; stock prices *increased* almost 32 percent.

During each of these years, the major influences on stock price movements came from changes in the earnings multiplier. The greater volatility of the multiplier series compared to the earnings per share series can be seen from the summary figures at the bottom of Exhibit 13.8 and from the graph of the earnings multiplier in Exhibit 13.9. The standard deviation of annual changes for the earnings multiplier series is much larger than the standard deviation of earnings changes

---

[14]Our emphasis will be on *estimating future values* for EPS, as well as k and g. We will show the relevant variables and provide a procedural framework, but the final estimate depends on the ability of the analyst.

EXHIBIT 13.8 ANNUAL CHANGES IN STOCK PRICES, CORPORATE EARNINGS, AND THE EARNINGS MULTIPLIER FOR S&P INDUSTRIALS INDEX: 1975–2000

Year	Year-End Stock Prices	Percentage Change	Earnings per Share	Percentage Change	Year-End Earnings Multiple	Percentage Change	Earnings Multiple $t + 1$	Percentage Change
1975	100.88	31.9	8.58	−10.7	11.76	47.8	9.44	5.9
1976	119.46	18.4	10.69	24.6	11.17	−5.0	10.43	10.5
1977	104.71	−12.3	11.45	7.1	9.14	−18.2	8.03	−23.0
1978	107.21	2.4	13.04	13.9	8.22	−10.1	6.58	−18.1
1979	121.02	12.9	16.29	24.9	7.43	−9.6	7.51	14.1
1980	154.45	27.6	16.12	−1.0	9.58	28.9	9.23	22.9
1981	137.12	−11.2	16.74	3.8	8.19	−14.5	10.39	12.6
1982	157.62	15.0	13.20	−21.1	11.94	45.8	10.67	2.7
1983	186.17	18.1	14.77	11.9	12.60	5.5	10.28	−3.7
1984	186.36	0.1	18.11	22.6	10.29	−18.3	12.20	18.7
1985	234.56	25.9	15.28	−15.6	15.35	49.2	16.14	32.3
1986	269.93	15.1	14.53	−4.9	18.58	21.0	13.31	−17.5
1987	285.85	5.9	20.28	39.6	14.10	−24.1	10.75	−19.2
1988	321.26	12.4	26.59	31.1	12.08	−14.3	11.97	11.3
1989	403.49	25.6	26.83	0.9	15.04	24.5	16.29	36.1
1990	387.42	−4.0	24.77	−7.7	15.64	4.0	22.91	40.6
1991	492.72	27.2	16.91	−31.7	29.14	86.3	25.86	12.9
1992	507.46	3.0	19.05	12.7	26.64	−8.6	23.14	−10.5
1993	540.19	6.4	21.93	15.1	24.63	−7.5	16.45	−28.9
1994	547.51	1.4	32.83	49.7	16.68	−32.3	15.45	−6.1
1995	721.19	31.7	35.44	8.0	20.35	22.0	17.53	13.5
1996	869.97	20.6	41.15	16.1	21.14	3.9	20.65	17.8
1997	1,121.38	28.9	42.13	2.4	26.62	25.9	28.75	39.2
1998	1,479.16	31.9	38.37	−8.9	38.55	44.8	29.44	2.4
1999	1,841.92	24.5	50.25	31.0	36.66	−4.9	34.20	16.2
2000	1,527.86	−17.1	53.85	7.2	28.37	−22.6	NA	NA

With Signs

Mean		13.2		8.5	17.7	8.4	15.9	7.3
Standard deviation		14.6		18.9		29.0		19.6
Coefficient of variation		1.1		2.2		3.4		2.7

Without Signs

Mean		16.6		16.3		23.1		17.5
Standard deviation		10.4		12.5		19.1		11.0
Coefficient of variation		0.6		0.8		0.8		0.6

NA—not available

Source: *Financial Analysts Handbook* (New York: Standard & Poor's, 1998). Reprinted with permission.

EXHIBIT 13.9   *YEAR-END EARNINGS MULTIPLE FOR THE S&P INDUSTRIALS INDEX BASED ON HISTORICAL EARNINGS: 1975–2000*

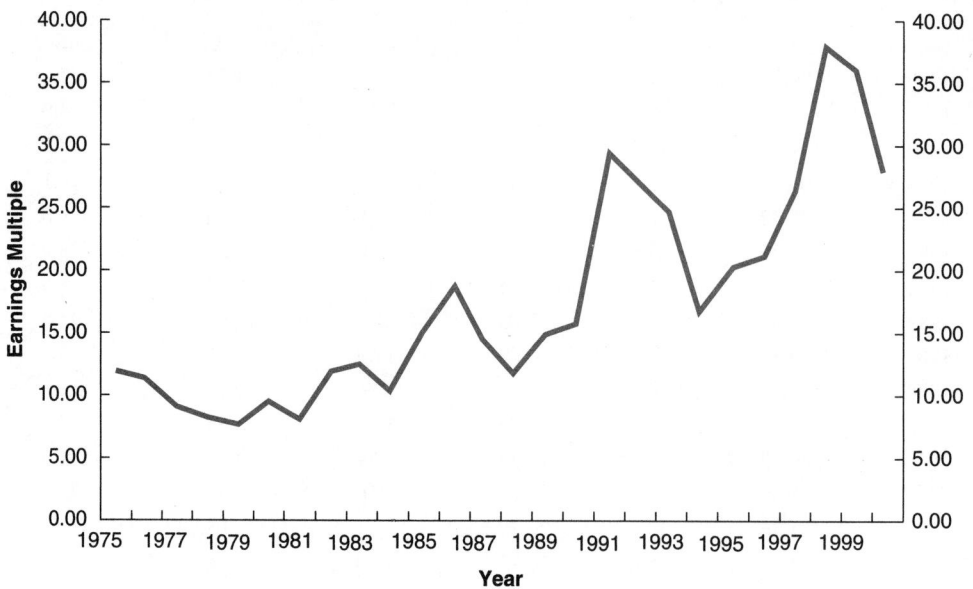

(29.0 versus 18.9). The same is true for the relative volatility measures of the coefficient of variability (3.4 versus 2.2). Also, the mean annual percentage change of the two multiplier series without signs has a larger mean annual percent change value (23.1 versus 16.3) and a larger standard deviation of annual percentage change (19.1 versus 12.5). Therefore, these figures show that, of the two estimates required for market valuation, *the earnings multiplier is the more volatile component.* This is also true for the forward multiplier.

The point of this discussion is not to reduce the importance of the earnings estimate but to note that the estimation of future market value requires two separate estimates and *both* are important and necessary. Therefore, we will begin by considering a procedure for estimating aggregate earnings. Later, we discuss the procedure for estimating the aggregate market earnings multiplier.

ESTIMATING EXPECTED EARNINGS PER SHARE

The estimate of expected earnings per share for the market series will consider the outlook for the aggregate economy and for the corporate sector. This requires the following steps:

1. Estimate sales per share for a stock market series, such as the S&P Industrials Index. This estimate of sales involves a prior estimate of gross domestic product (GDP) because of the relationship between the sales of major industrial firms and this measure of aggregate economic activity. Therefore, prior to estimating sales per share, we will consider sources for an estimate of GDP.
2. Estimate the operating profit margin for the series, which equals operating profit divided by sales. Given the data available from Standard and Poor's, we will define operating profit as earnings before interest, taxes, and depreciation (EBITDA).
3. Estimate depreciation per share for the next year.

EXHIBIT 13.10 ▶ *SCATTER PLOT OF ANNUAL PERCENTAGE CHANGES IN S&P INDUSTRIALS INDEX SALES AND GDP*

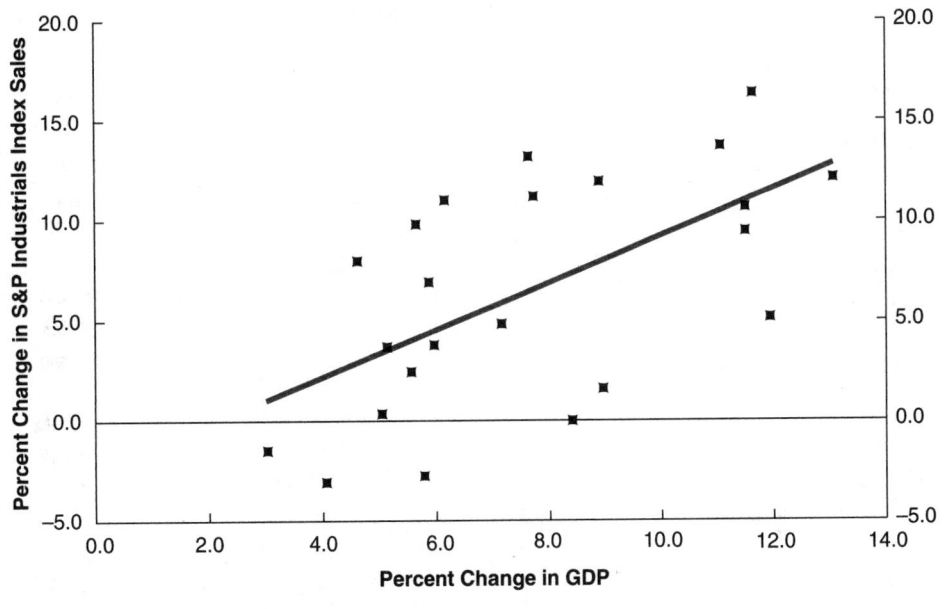

4. Estimate interest expense per share for the next year.

5. Estimate the corporate tax rate for the next year.

These steps will lead to an estimate of net earnings per share that will be combined with an estimate of the forward earnings multiplier to arrive at an estimate of the current intrinsic value for the stock market series.

Estimating Gross Domestic Product
GDP is a measure of aggregate economic output or activity. Therefore, one would expect aggregate corporate sales to be related to GDP. We begin our estimate of sales for a stock market series with a prediction of nominal GDP from one of several banks or financial service firms that regularly publish such estimates.[15] Using this estimate of nominal GDP, we can estimate corporate sales based on the historical relationship between S&P Industrials Index sales per share and aggregate economic activity (GDP).[16]

Estimating Sales per Share for a Market Series
As noted, we will use a sales figure for an existing stock market series—the S&P Industrials Index.[17] The plot in Exhibit 13.10 shows the relationship between the annual percentage changes in GDP and S&P Industrials Index sales per share contained in Exhibit 13.11. Generally, there

---

[15]This would include projections by Standard & Poor's appearing late in the year in *The Outlook;* and projections by several of the large investment firms, such as Goldman, Sachs, & Company ("The Pocket Chartroom") or Merrill Lynch, as well as by banks. *The Wall Street Journal* publishes a survey of over 50 economists every 6 months that includes estimates of various interest rates, GDP, inflation, and the value of the dollar versus the Japanese yen. For a sample survey, see Fred R. Bleakley, "Economy's Strength Is Seen Cooling in Second Half," *The Wall Street Journal,* 1 July 1996, A2.

[16]Because GDP includes imports and exports, we also considered a pure domestic series entitled "Final Sales of Domestic Product." Because an analysis of both series indicated that the GDP series provided superior regression results, it is used.

[17]Sales per share figures are available from 1945 in Standard & Poor's *Analysts Handbook* (New York: Standard & Poor's Corporation). Because the composite series include numerous companies of different sizes, all data are on a per-share basis. The book is updated annually, and some series are updated quarterly in a monthly supplement.

EXHIBIT 13.11   *NOMINAL GDP; FINAL SALES OF DOMESTIC PRODUCT, AND STANDARD AND POOR'S INDUSTRIALS INDEX SALES PER SHARE: 1975–2001*

YEAR	NOMINAL GDP (BILLIONS OF DOLLARS)	PERCENTAGE CHANGE	FINAL SALES TO DOMESTIC PURCHASERS (BILLIONS OF DOLLARS)	PERCENTAGE CHANGE	S&P INDUSTRIALS INDEX (DOLLAR VALUE OF SALES PER SHARE)	PERCENTAGE CHANGE
1975	1,635.2	8.9	1,627.9	9.2	185.2	1.7
1976	1,823.9	11.5	1,809.1	11.1	202.7	9.4
1977	2,031.4	11.4	2,032.7	12.4	224.2	10.6
1978	2,295.9	13.0	2,296.2	13.0	251.3	12.1
1979	2,566.4	11.8	2,572.4	12.0	292.4	16.3
1980	2,795.6	8.9	2,816.8	9.5	327.4	12.0
1981	3,131.3	12.0	3,116.5	10.6	344.3	5.2
1982	3,259.2	4.1	3,294.7	5.7	333.9	−3.0
1983	3,534.9	8.5	3,592.3	9.0	334.1	0.1
1984	3,932.7	11.3	3,969.3	10.5	379.7	13.7
1985	4,213.0	7.1	4,305.4	8.5	398.4	4.9
1986	4,452.9	5.7	4,578.2	6.3	387.8	−2.7
1987	4,742.5	6.5	4,857.6	6.1	430.4	11.0
1988	5,108.3	7.7	5,196.1	7.0	486.9	13.1
1989	5,489.1	7.5	5,542.1	6.7	541.4	11.2
1990	5,803.2	5.7	5,860.1	5.7	594.6	9.8
1991	5,986.2	3.2	6,007.1	2.5	586.9	−1.3
1992	6,318.9	5.6	6,331.7	5.4	601.4	2.5
1993	6,642.3	5.1	6,681.7	5.5	603.6	0.4
1994	7,054.3	6.2	7,078.9	5.9	626.3	3.8
1995	7,400.5	4.9	7,451.7	5.3	676.6	8.0
1996	7,813.2	5.6	7,872.1	5.6	701.9	3.7
1997	8,318.4	6.5	8,344.8	6.0	750.7	7.0
1998	8,781.5	5.6	8,860.1	6.2	755.5	0.6
1999	9,268.6	5.5	9,460.9	6.8	812.0	7.5
2000	9,872.9	6.5	10,187.5	7.7	853.9	5.2
2001	10,205.6	3.4	10,595.5	4.0	NA	NA
Average		7.4		7.6		6.3

Source: *Economic Report of the President, 2002* (Washington, DC: U.S. Government Printing Office, 2002); and *Financial Analysts Handbook* (New York: Standard & Poor's, 2001). Reprinted with permission.

is a strong relationship between the two series whereby a large proportion of the percentage changes in S&P Industrials Index sales per share can be explained by percentage changes in nominal GDP. The relationship is not stronger because (1) the S&P Industrials Index sales series is more volatile than the GDP series and (2) the GDP series never experienced a decline. The equation for the least-squares regression line relating annual percentage changes (% Δ) in the two series for the period 1975–2000 is

$$\$ \Delta \text{ S\&P Industrials Index Sales}_t = -2.40 + 1.16 \ (\% \ \Delta \text{ in Nominal GDP}_t)$$
$$(-0.85)(4.06)$$
$$\text{Adj. } R^2 = 0.36$$

These results indicate that about 36 percent of the variance in percentage changes in S&P Industrials Index sales can be explained by percentage changes in the nominal GDP. Thus, given an estimate of the expected percentage change in nominal GDP for next year, we can estimate the percentage change in sales for the S&P Industrials Index series and therefore the amount of sales per share. For example, assume the consensus estimate by economists is that nominal GDP next year will increase by approximately 6 percent (a 3 percent increase in real GDP plus 3 percent inflation). This estimate, combined with the regression results, would imply the following estimated increase in S&P Industrials Index sales:

$$\% \, \Delta \text{ S\&P Industrials Index Sales} = -0.024 + 1.16 \, (0.06)$$
$$= 0.046$$
$$= 4.6\%$$

Notably, this is referred to as a *point estimate of sales* because it is based on a point estimate of GDP. Although we know there is actually a *distribution* of estimates for GDP, we have used the mean value, or expected value, as our point estimate. In actual practice, you would probably consider several estimates and assign probabilities to each of them.

Alternative Estimates of Corporate Net Profits

Once sales per share for the market series have been estimated, the difficult estimate is the profit margin. Three alternative procedures are possible depending on the desired level of aggregation.

The first is a direct estimate of the *net* profit margin based on recent trends. As shown in Exhibit 13.12, the net profit margin series is quite volatile because of changes in depreciation, interest, and the tax rate over time. As such, it is the most difficult series to estimate.

The second procedure would attempt to estimate the *net before tax* (NBT) profit margin. Once the NBT margin is derived, a separate estimate of the tax rate is obtained based on recent tax rates and current government tax pronouncements.

The third method estimates an *operating* profit margin, defined as earnings before interest, taxes, and depreciation (EBITDA), as a percentage of sales. Because this measure of operating earnings as a percentage of sales is not influenced by changes in depreciation allowances, interest expense, or tax rates, it should be a more stable series compared to either the net profit margin or net before tax margin series. Our analysis begins with estimating this operating profit margin series.

After we estimate this operating profit margin, we will multiply it by the sales estimate to derive a dollar estimate of operating earnings (EBITDA). Subsequently, we will derive separate estimates of depreciation and interest expenses, which are subtracted from the EBITDA to arrive at earnings before taxes *(EBT.)* Finally, we estimate the expected tax rate *(T)* and multiply *EBT* times $(1 - T)$ to get our estimate of net income. The following sections discuss the details of estimating earnings per share beginning with the operating profit margin.

Estimating Aggregate Operating Profit Margin

Finkel and Tuttle hypothesized that the following four variables affected the aggregate profit margin:[18]

1. Capacity utilization rate
2. Unit labor costs
3. Rate of inflation
4. Foreign competition

---

[18]Sidney R. Finkel and Donald L. Tuttle, "Determinants of the Aggregate Profit Margin," *Journal of Finance* 26, no. 5 (December 1971): 1067–1075.

EXHIBIT 13.12 *S&P INDUSTRIALS INDEX SALES PER SHARE AND COMPONENTS OF OPERATING PROFIT MARGIN: 1977–2000*

YEAR	SALES PER SHARE	EBITDAª		DEPRECIATION		INTEREST		INCOME TAX		NET INCOME	
		PER SHARE	PERCENT OF SALES	PER SHARE	PERCENT OF SALES	PER SHARE	PERCENT OF SALES	PER SHARE	TAX RATE	PER SHARE	PERCENT OF SALES
1977	224.24	34.34	15.31	8.53	3.80	3.22	1.44	11.14	49.31	11.45	5.11
1978	251.32	38.63	15.37	9.64	3.84	3.81	1.52	12.14	48.21	13.04	5.19
1979	292.38	45.71	15.63	10.82	3.70	4.55	1.57	14.02	46.26	16.29	5.57
1980	327.36	48.11	14.70	12.37	3.78	5.95	1.82	13.67	45.89	16.12	4.92
1981	344.31	51.00	14.81	13.82	4.01	7.49	2.18	12.95	43.62	16.74	4.86
1982	333.86	47.68	14.28	15.30	4.58	5.23	2.47	10.95	45.34	13.20	3.95
1983	334.07	50.18	15.02	15.67	4.69	7.62	2.25	12.12	45.07	14.77	4.42
1984	379.70	57.11	15.04	16.31	4.30	8.54	2.25	14.15	43.86	18.11	4.77
1985	398.42	56.39	14.15	18.19	4.57	9.24	2.32	13.68	47.24	15.28	3.84
1986	387.76	54.70	14.11	19.41	5.01	9.75	2.51	11.01	43.11	14.53	3.75
1987	430.35	64.59	15.01	20.21	4.70	10.14	2.36	13.96	40.77	20.23	4.71
1988	486.92	80.02	16.43	23.59	4.84	14.84	3.05	15.00	36.07	26.59	5.46
1989	541.38	85.56	15.80	24.21	4.47	18.79	3.47	15.73	36.96	26.83	4.96
1990	594.55	87.52	14.72	26.31	4.43	20.17	3.39	16.27	39.64	24.77	4.17
1991	586.86	75.35	12.84	27.50	4.59	18.74	3.19	12.20	41.91	16.91	2.88
1992	601.39	76.74	12.76	29.48	4.90	16.20	2.69	12.01	38.61	19.05	3.17
1993	603.62	78.67	13.03	28.72	4.76	14.66	2.43	13.36	37.56	21.93	3.63
1994	626.26	94.06	15.02	29.58	4.72	12.77	2.04	18.88	36.51	32.83	5.24
1995	676.62	103.50	15.30	33.06	4.89	14.21	2.10	20.79	36.97	35.44	5.24
1996	701.91	115.45	16.45	36.11	5.14	14.32	2.04	23.87	36.71	41.15	5.86
1997	750.71	123.76	16.49	39.77	5.30	14.44	1.98	27.02	39.07	42.13	5.61
1998	755.48	106.68	14.12	32.89	4.35	14.56	1.93	20.86	35.22	38.37	5.08
1999	812.00	134.86	16.61	41.70	5.14	15.50	1.91	27.41	35.29	50.25	6.19
2000	853.86	146.03	17.10	43.50	5.09	16.39	1.92	32.29	37.49	53.85	6.31

ªThis is used as an estimate of operating earnings.

Source: *Financial Analysts Handbook* (New York: Standard & Poor's, 2001). Reprinted with permission.

Capacity Utilization Rate One would expect a positive relationship between the capacity utilization rate and the profit margin because if production increases as a proportion of total capacity, there is a decrease in per-unit fixed production costs and fixed financial costs. The relationship may not be completely linear at very high rates of capacity utilization because operating diseconomies are introduced as firms are forced to use marginal labor and/or older plant and equipment to reach the higher capacity. The figures in Exhibit 13.13 indicate that capacity utilization ranged from a peak of over 87 percent in 1978 to a trough of about 64 percent in 1982 and less than 70 percent during the recent recession of 2000–2002.

Unit Labor Cost The change in unit labor cost is a compound effect of two individual factors: (1) changes in wages per hour and (2) changes in worker productivity. Wage costs per hour typically increase every year by varying amounts depending on the economic environment. As shown in Exhibit 13.13, the annual percentage increase in compensation per hour varied from

EXHIBIT 13.13	VARIABLES THAT AFFECT THE AGGREGATE PROFIT MARGIN: CAPACITY UTILIZATION RATE, PERCENTAGE CHANGE IN COMPENSATION, PRODUCTIVITY, UNIT LABOR COST, AND CONSUMER PRICE INDEX: 1975–2001(P)

		COMPENSATION/ WORK HOURS	OUTPUT/ WORK HOURS	UNIT LABOR COSTS	
YEAR	UTILIZATION RATE (MFG)	PERCENTAGE CHANGE	PERCENTAGE CHANGE	PERCENTAGE CHANGE	RATE OF INFLATION
1975	72.2	10.1	2.7	7.2	6.9
1976	78.0	8.6	3.7	4.7	4.9
1977	82.1	8.0	1.5	6.4	6.7
1978	87.3	8.9	1.3	7.6	9.0
1979	83.0	9.5	−0.4	10.0	13.3
1980	78.6	10.8	−0.3	11.1	12.5
1981	71.9	9.7	1.2	8.3	8.9
1982	63.9	7.5	−0.6	8.1	3.8
1983	74.5	4.3	4.5	−0.2	3.8
1984	77.1	4.3	2.2	2.1	3.9
1985	76.0	4.7	1.3	3.3	3.8
1986	76.3	5.2	3.0	2.1	1.1
1987	80.3	3.8	0.4	3.4	4.4
1988	83.7	4.5	1.3	3.2	4.4
1989	80.3	2.7	0.8	1.9	4.6
1990	75.6	5.5	1.1	4.3	6.1
1991	74.9	4.9	1.2	3.6	3.1
1992	77.8	5.3	3.7	1.6	2.9
1993	80.5	2.2	0.5	1.7	2.7
1994	83.6	2.1	1.3	0.8	2.7
1995	81.0	2.1	0.9	1.2	2.5
1996	81.4	3.1	2.5	0.5	3.3
1997	82.5	3.0	2.0	0.9	1.7
1998	80.7	5.4	2.6	2.7	1.6
1999	81.2	4.4	2.3	2.0	2.7
2000	77.7	6.5	3.3	3.1	3.4
2001	69.7	4.5	1.1	3.3	1.6

Source: *Economic Report of the President, 2002* (Washington, D.C.: U.S. Government Printing Office, 2002).

2.1 percent to 10.8 percent. If workers did not become more productive, this increase in per-hour wage costs would be the increase in per-unit labor cost. Fortunately, because of advances in technology and greater mechanization, the worker units of output per hour (the measure of labor productivity) have increased over time—our labor force has become *more productive*. If wages per hour increase by 5 percent and labor productivity increases by 5 percent, there would be no increase in unit labor costs because the workers would offset wage increases by producing more. Therefore, the increase in *per-unit labor cost* is a function of the percentage change in hourly wages minus the increase in productivity during the period. The actual relationship typically is not this exact due to measurement problems, but it is quite close as indicated by the data in

Exhibit 13.13. For example, during 1983, productivity increased by slightly more than the hourly compensation did so there was basically no change in unit labor cost. In contrast, during 1980, wage rates increased by 10.8 percent, productivity *declined* by 0.3 percent because of the recession, and, therefore, unit labor costs increased by 11.1 percent. Because unit labor is the major variable cost of a firm, one would expect a *negative* relationship between the operating profit margin and percentage changes in unit labor cost—that is, a small (below-average) change in unit labor cost, similar to what we experienced during the mid-1990s (1994–97), should correspond to an above-average operating profit margin.

Rate of Inflation   The precise effect of inflation on the aggregate profit margin is unresolved. Finkel and Tuttle hypothesized a positive relationship between inflation and the profit margin for several reasons. First, it was contended that a higher level of inflation increases the ability of firms to pass higher costs on to the consumer and thereby raise their profit margin. Second, assuming the classic demand-pull inflation, the increase in prices would indicate an increase in general economic activity, which typically is accompanied by higher margins. Finally, an increase in the rate of inflation might stimulate consumption as individuals attempt to shift their holdings from financial assets to real assets, which would contribute to an expansion.

In contrast, many observers doubt that most businesses can consistently increase prices in line with rising costs. Assume a 5 percent rate of inflation that impacts labor and material costs. The question is whether all firms can *completely* pass these cost increases along to their customers. If a firm increases prices at the same rate as cost increases, the result will be a *constant* profit margin, *not* an increase. Only if a firm can raise prices by *more than* cost increases can it increase its margin. Many firms are not able to raise prices in line with increased costs because of the elasticity of demand for their products.[19] Such an environment will cause the profit margin to decline. Given the alternative scenarios, it is contended that most firms will not be able to increase their profit margins or even hold them constant. Because many firms will experience lower profit margins during periods of inflation, it is expected that the aggregate profit margin will probably decline when there is an increase in the rate of inflation.

Given the contrasting expectations, one would need to consider the empirical evidence to determine the relationship between inflation and the operating profit margin.

Foreign Competition   Finkel and Tuttle contend that export markets are more competitive than domestic markets so export sales are made at a lower margin. This implies that lower exports by U.S. firms would increase profit margins. In contrast, Gray believed that only exports between independent firms should be considered and they should be examined relative to total output exported.[20] Further, he felt that imports could have an important negative impact on the operating profit margin because they influence the selling price of all competing domestic products. Therefore, there is a divergence of expectations regarding the ultimate effect of foreign trade on the operating profit margin, so it is likewise an empirical question.

Analysis of the annual data for the period 1977 to 1997 by the authors confirmed that the relationship between the operating profit margin and the capacity utilization rate was always significant and positive, whereas the relationship between the unit labor cost and the operating profit margin was always negative and significant. Alternatively, the rate of inflation and foreign trade variables were never significant in the multiple regression. Finally, the simple correlation between the profit margin and inflation was consistently *negative*.

---

[19]An extreme example of this inability is regulated industries that may not be able to raise prices at all until after lengthy hearings before regulatory agencies. Even then, the increase in rates may not match the cost increase.

[20]H. Peter Gray, "Determinants of the Aggregate Profit Margin: A Comment," *Journal of Finance* 31, no. 1 (March 1976): 163–165.

Therefore, when estimating the operating profit margin, you should concentrate on the capacity utilization rate for the economy and the rate of change in unit labor cost. As an example, consider what will happen at two extremes of the business cycle. At the end of an economic recession, the capacity utilization rate will be very low. Therefore, during the early stages of an economic recovery, there should be a large increase in capacity utilization as firms increase production and sales. At the same time, workers will not be asking for large wage increases; and, as production increases, there will be large increases in labor productivity. As a result, unit labor costs will increase very slowly (or could decline). Therefore, as a result of an increase in capacity utilization and a very small increase (or a decline) in unit labor cost, there should be a large increase in the operating profit margin.

In contrast, at the peak of the business cycle, firms will be operating at full capacity, so there will be very small increases or possibly declines in capacity utilization. Also, one would expect a higher rate of inflation, which will prompt demands for large wage increases during a time when you would expect small increases in labor productivity because firms are using marginal labor and production facilities. The effect will be large increases in unit labor cost. Therefore, as a result of very small increases or possibly decreases in capacity utilization and large increases in unit labor cost, there should be a major decline in the operating profit margin at the peak of a business cycle.

How do you use this information to estimate an operating profit margin? The most important estimate is *the direction of the change from current levels.* Assuming that you know the recent operating profit margin, your primary analysis should be concerned with deciding whether the profit margin will increase, decrease, or stay about the same based on your expectation regarding capacity utilization and changes in unit labor cost. The size of the estimated change in the operating profit margin will depend on where the economy is in the business cycle and the direction and size of the expected changes in capacity utilization and unit labor cost.

After estimating the operating profit margin, you can calculate the dollar value of EBITDA by applying this operating profit margin estimate to the previously estimated sales-per-share figure. The next step is to estimate depreciation per share, which we subtract from operating profits to get EBIT. Exhibit 13.12 contains data on the operating earnings components for the period since 1977.

Estimating Depreciation Expense

As shown in Exhibit 13.14, the depreciation expense per share series has declined only twice since 1977 (in 1993 and 1998). This is not surprising because depreciation expense is an estimate of the fixed-cost expense related to the total fixed assets held by the S&P Industrials Index firms. Naturally, this fixed-asset base increases over time. Therefore, the relevant question when estimating depreciation expense is generally *not* whether it will increase or decrease but by *how much it will increase.*

There are two suggestions for estimating depreciation expense. First, you can use time-series analysis, which involves using the recent trend as a guide to the future increase. Probably the biggest external factor that could influence the rate of growth of the depreciation expense series is recent capital expenditures. If capital expenditures have been above normal, you would expect subsequent depreciation expense to grow at an above-average rate. Recently, the average annual percentage increase in depreciation expense has been in the range of 5 to 8 percent. Because a column in the exhibit indicates that depreciation is a percent of sales, you might consider this as an estimating approach—this would be a *mistake.* Depreciation is clearly a *fixed* expense, which means that generally it is independent of sales and so it should not be expected to vary with sales. As shown, depreciation as a percentage of sales has varied from 3.70 percent to over 5 percent, which is consistent with its fixed nature.

Second, you can derive an estimate of depreciation expense based upon an estimate of property, plant, and equipment *(PPE)* and then apply the historical depreciation rate relative to the

EXHIBIT 13.14 *TIME-SERIES PLOT OF DEPRECIATION EXPENSE FOR THE S&P INDUSTRIALS INDEX*

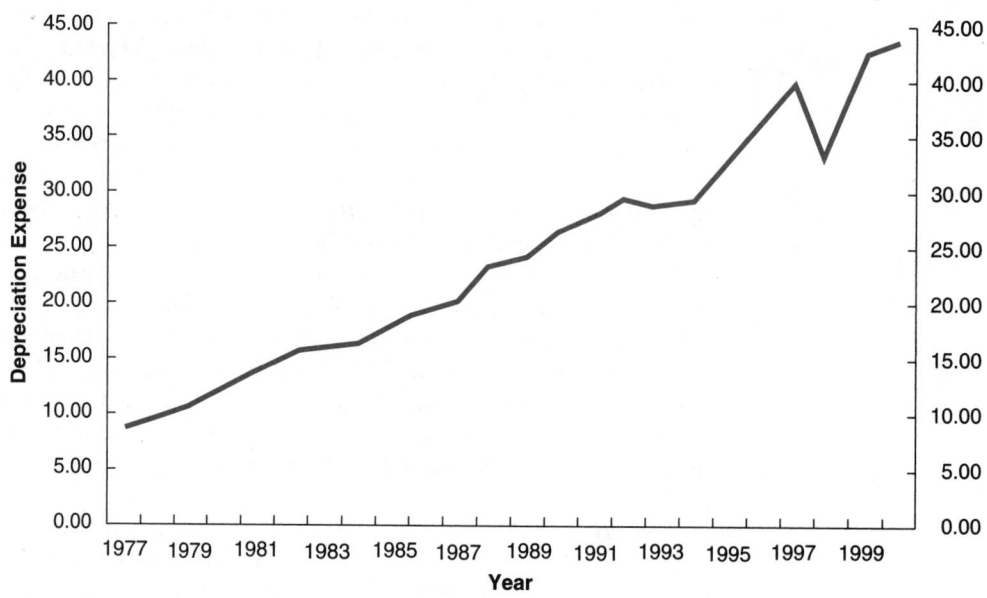

PPE account. This technique requires two steps. First, estimate the *PPE* account based on the relationship between sales (that have been estimated) and *PPE*—that is, the expected *PPE* turnover. Exhibit 13.15 contains the historical *PPE* turnover series, which was quite stable between 2.60 and 2.80 prior to increases in 1999 and 2000 (see Exhibit 13.16). Therefore, given your estimate for sales, it is possible to derive an estimate of *PPE*. The second estimate is the ratio of depreciation to *PPE*, which is in Exhibit 13.15 and plotted in Exhibit 13.17. As shown, this ratio has increased over time from about 10 percent in the late 1970s to almost 16 percent in 2000. This trend probably is the result of the increase in technology that has tended to reduce the useful life for productive machinery, which implies a higher annual depreciation rate. Therefore, one would derive an estimate of depreciation expense based upon an estimate of *PPE* and the estimated ratio of depreciation to *PPE*.

Based on these factors, you would estimate what you expect for this year. After you have estimated the depreciation expense, you subtract it from the operating profit estimate to get an estimate of EBIT.

Estimating Interest Expense

As shown in Exhibit 13.12, interest expense of the companies in the S&P Industrials Index series generally increased in absolute value until 1990 and increased as a percentage of sales from 1.44 percent in 1977 to a peak of 3.47 percent in 1989. This growth is consistent with an overall increase in debt financing and financial risk assumed by U.S. firms during the 1980s. This strong growth of interest expense was reversed after the 1989–1990 recession. Specifically, as shown in Exhibits 13.15 and 13.18, (1) corporations reduced their debt levels in 1992 and 1993 before resuming their growth in 1994, and (2) interest rates declined. The estimate of interest expense should be based on an estimate of debt outstanding (will it grow and by how much?) and the level of interest rates (do you expect interest rates to increase or decline in the future?)

A couple of examples should illustrate the point. In 1988, interest expense increased substantially to 15.01 from 10.14 in 1987. An analysis of the components indicates that this increase

EXHIBIT 13.15 ▶ *FOR THE S&P INDUSTRIALS INDEX: RATIO OF DEPRECIATION EXPENSE TO NET PPE AND RATIO OF INTEREST EXPENSE TO LONG-TERM DEBT: 1977–2000*

YEAR	DEPREC. EXPENSE	NET PPE	SALES/ NET PPE	DEPREC. EXP. NET PPE	INTEREST EXPENSE	TOTAL ASSET TURNOVER	L-T DEBT	L-T DEBT T. ASSETS	INT. EXP. L-T DEBT	L-T GOVT. BOND YIELD
1977	8.53	83.64	2.68	10.20	3.25	1.27	32.09		10.13	8.03
1978	9.64	94.15	2.67	10.24	3.84	1.27	36.23		10.60	8.98
1979	10.82	106.89	2.74	10.12	4.58	1.30	39.22		11.68	10.12
1980	12.37	120.03	2.73	10.31	5.95	1.31	43.27		13.75	11.99
1981	13.82	134.37	2.56	10.29	7.49	1.28	49.06		15.27	13.34
1982	15.30	144.06	2.49	10.62	8.23	1.17	52.72		15.61	10.95
1983	15.67	142.26	2.35	11.02	7.62	1.15	50.08		15.60	9.56
1984	16.31	138.79	2.74	11.75	8.54	1.22	53.25		16.04	11.70
1985	18.19	150.20	2.65	12.11	9.24	1.15	50.08		15.60	9.56
1986	19.41	154.64	2.51	12.55	9.75	1.07	66.89		14.58	7.89
1987	20.21	160.39	2.68	12.60	10.14	1.08	69.89		14.51	9.20
1988	23.59	175.31	2.78	13.46	15.01	0.98	113.93		13.17	9.18
1989	24.21	193.23	2.80	12.53	18.79	0.97	117.56		15.98	8.16
1990	26.31	212.30	2.80	12.39	20.17	0.97	123.04		15.75	8.44
1991	27.50	216.63	2.71	12.69	18.74	0.94	130.03		14.38	7.30
1992	29.48	219.19	2.74	13.45	16.20	0.95	128.60	0.20	12.60	7.26
1993	28.72	217.14	2.78	13.23	14.65	0.92	126.18	0.19	11.62	6.54
1994	29.58	223.46	2.80	13.24	12.77	0.95	130.24	0.20	9.80	7.99
1995	33.06	237.84	2.84	13.90	14.21	0.97	141.14	0.20	10.07	6.03
1996	36.11	264.21	2.66	13.67	14.32	0.93	151.31	0.20	9.46	6.73
1997	39.77	286.11	2.62	13.90	14.44	0.94	162.35	0.20	9.14	6.02
1998	32.89	299.02	2.53	11.00	14.56	0.85	170.02	0.19	8.56	
1999	41.70	277.92	2.92	15.00	15.50	0.84	186.37	0.19	8.32	
2000	43.50	275.80	3.10	15.77	16.39	0.84	192.03	0.19	8.54	
Mean										
1977–2000				12.34					12.53	
1991–2000				13.59					10.25	
1995–2000				13.87					8.80	

Source: *Financial Analysts Handbook* (New York: Standard & Poor's, 2001). Reprinted with permission.

was completely due to a substantial increase in debt outstanding (see Exhibits 13.15 and 13.18), that went from about 70 to almost 114 (a 63 percent increase), while the average interest rate, as shown in Exhibits 13.15 and 13.19, actually declined from 14.51 percent to 13.17 percent. In contrast, as shown in Exhibits 13.15 and 13.20, from 1990 to 1994, interest expense declined steadily from 20.17 to 12.77. In this case, the decline was mainly attributable to a decline in interest rates shown in Exhibit 13.19. Specifically, during this period, long-term debt outstanding *increased* from about 123 to 130, while interest rates declined steadily from 15.75 percent to 9.80 percent. The point is, to estimate interest expense you need to estimate both of these components (the amount of debt outstanding and the average interest rate on this debt) and determine the joint effect.

EXHIBIT 13.16

TIME-SERIES PLOT OF THE RATIO OF SALES TO PPE *(PPE TURNOVER) FOR THE S&P INDUSTRIALS INDEX*

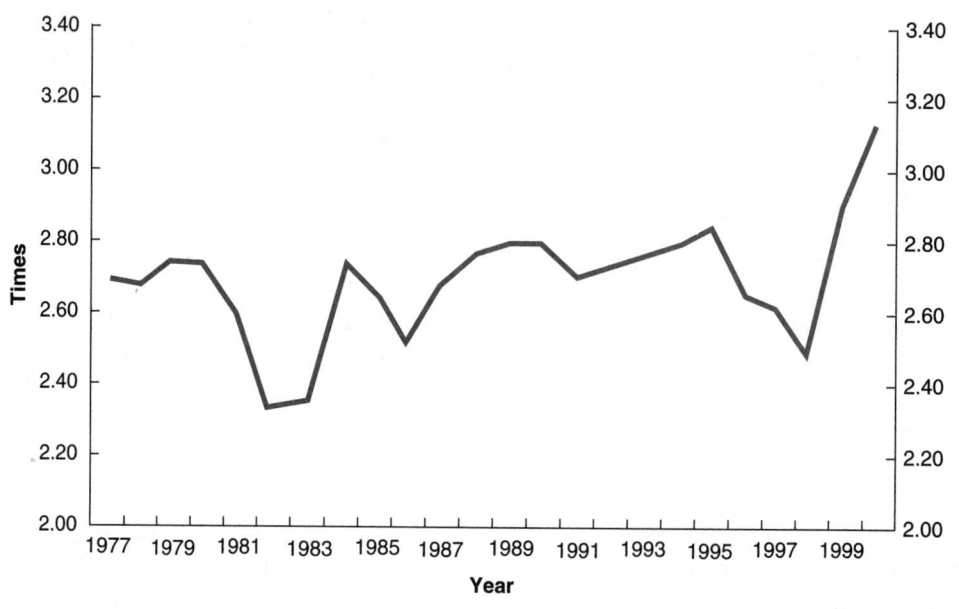

EXHIBIT 13.17

TIME-SERIES PLOT OF THE RATIO OF DEPRECIATION EXPENSES TO PPE *ACCOUNT FOR THE S&P INDUSTRIALS INDEX*

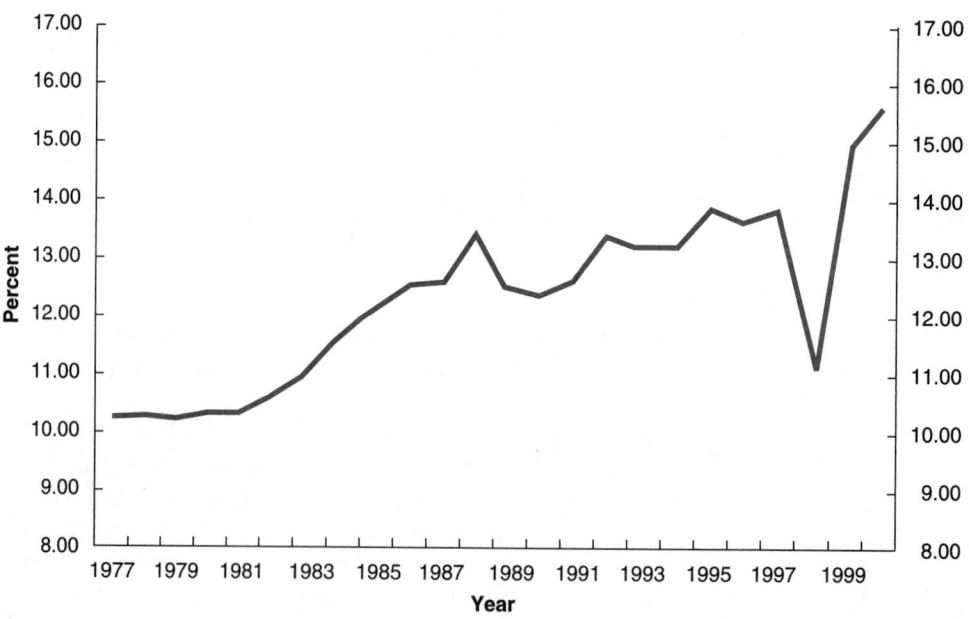

EXHIBIT 13.18 ▸ *TIME-SERIES PLOT OF DEBT OUTSTANDING FOR THE S&P INDUSTRIALS INDEX*

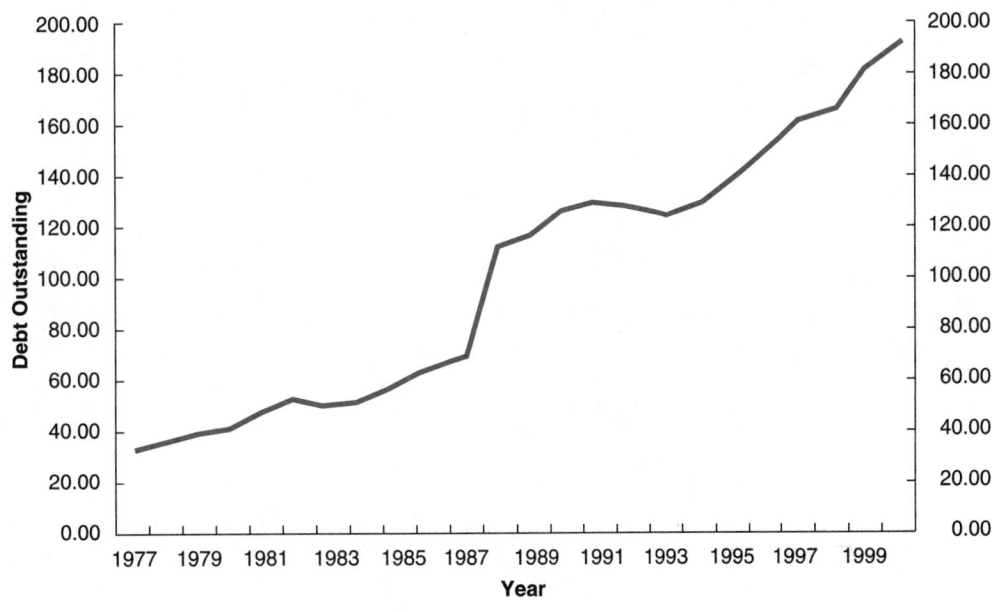

EXHIBIT 13.19 ▸ *TIME-SERIES PLOT OF THE INTEREST RATE ON DEBT OUTSTANDING FOR THE S&P INDUSTRIALS INDEX*

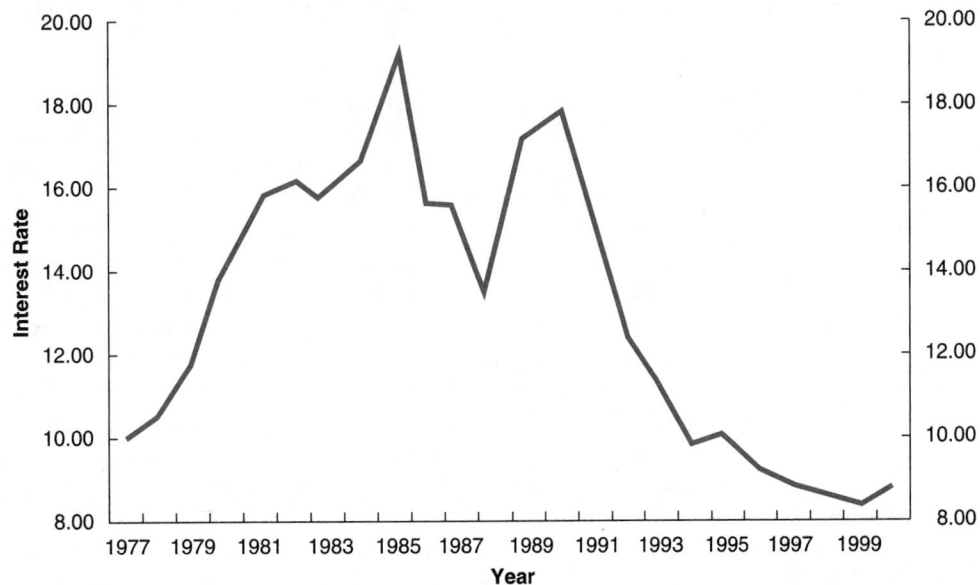

EXHIBIT 13.20 *TIMES-SERIES PLOT OF INTEREST EXPENSES FOR THE S&P INDUSTRIALS INDEX*

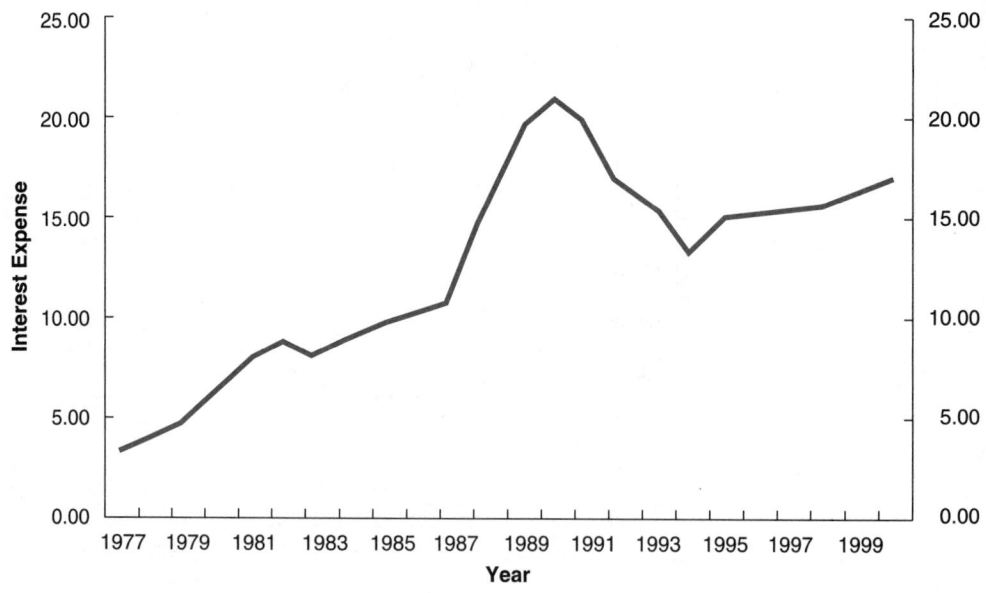

An estimate of debt outstanding requires two estimates: (1) the amount of total assets for the firm based upon the firm's expected total asset turnover and (2) the expected capital structure based upon the average total debt to total asset ratio. Both of these ratios are included in Exhibit 13.15.

Similar to depreciation, interest expense is a fixed expense that is impacted by corporate financing decisions and the cost of debt (i.e., interest rates). Therefore, interest expense as a percent of sales is a very unstable value and this percent value should *not* be used when estimating interest expense.

After you have estimated the interest expense figure, this value is subtracted from the EBIT per share value to estimate EBT.

Estimating the Tax Rate

This is the final step in estimating the earnings per share for the S&P Industrials Index series. As shown in Exhibit 13.12, the average tax rate for the firms in the S&P Industrials Index series during the late 1970s was in the 45 to 50 percent range. During the 1980s, it declined to almost 35 percent (in 1988) following the 1986 Tax Reform Act, then reversed and increased during the period 1989–1991, followed by rates in the 35–37 percent range except during 1997.

Estimating the future tax rate is difficult because it depends on political action. You must evaluate the current tax rate and recent tax legislation that affects business firms (e.g., tax credits). Once you have estimated the tax rate *(T)*, you multiply one minus this tax rate (1 – *T*) times the EBT per-share figure to derive an estimate of the net income per share for the S&P Industrials Index series.

At this point, we have derived an estimate of sales per share for an aggregate stock market series and discussed how to estimate an operating profit margin and several specific expense items on our way to an estimate of earnings per share. In the next section, we demonstrate this procedure by estimating earnings per share for 2002.

Calculating Earnings per Share: An Example

The following demonstration for estimating earnings per share emphasizes the procedure rather than the actual numbers. An analyst engaged in this exercise would provide a very long, detailed analysis. In this example, we estimate earnings per share for the S&P Industrials Index during 2002 using 2001 data (most of which is estimated).

Step 1   Nominal GDP for 2002 is based on an estimate for 2001 of approximately $10,200 billion. In 2001, the economy was in a recession following the longest expansion recorded for the United States (almost 10 years). The question at this point in 2002 is, How strong will the recovery be? Recent data have reversed earlier concern that it would be a slow, sluggish recovery—current expectations are for real GDP to increase by 2.0 percent and inflation will be approximately 2 percent. Therefore, nominal GDP in 2002 is estimated to increase by about 4.0 percent to $10,600 billion.

Step 2   Corporate sales have had a strong relationship with nominal GDP as shown in Exhibit 13.10. During 2001, when nominal GDP increased by about 3.3 percent, S&P sales were relatively flat, due to weak exports, at an estimated $875 per share. In 2002, with GDP rising only 4 percent, there is an expectation of strong foreign sales because of economic recoveries in many foreign countries. Therefore, the consensus is that S&P industrial sales should increase by almost 5 percent to $919 per share.

Step 3   The operating profit margin experienced an increase in 1999 and a new peak of 17.10 percent in 2000. We estimate a definite decline in the margin during the recession in 2001 to about 15.00 percent. In 2002, we expect some recovery in capacity utilization from the low point of 73 percent in the fourth quarter of 2001. In addition, unit labor cost will show little change with small wage increases and significant productivity gains as the economy recovers from the recession. The result should be an increase in the operating profit margin to about 16.00 percent, which implies operating profit for 2002 of $147 ($0.16 \times \$919$).

Step 4   The depreciation expense during 2001 was approximately $46.00 per share. As noted, we estimate sales in 2002 at $919 and the *PPE* turnover has been increasing steadily to over 3.00. We expect some stability in this value, so we will use 3.00 as the turnover, which implies *PPE* of $306.33. The depreciation/*PPE* ratio has also increased steadily to about 0.16 in 2001. We assume a small increase to 0.1625 in 2002, which implies depreciation expense for 2002 of 49.78 (0.1625×306.33). Thus, the estimated EBIT is $97.22 ($147 – 49.78$).

Step 5   Interest expense has experienced relatively small increases the last several years, mainly due to increases in debt outstanding, since the interest rate has been fairly steady. In 2002, given the sales estimate of $919 and a total asset turnover of 0.84, this implies total assets of $1,094. Further, a debt/total asset ratio of 0.19 indicates debt of $207.87 ($0.19 \times \$1,094$), which—combined with consistency in the interest rate of 8.50 percent (due to low steady inflation)—generates an interest expense estimate for 2002 of $17.67 ($0.085 \times \$207.87$). Therefore, EBT is estimated to be $79.55 ($97.22 – 17.67$).

Step 6   The tax rate was about 35 percent in 1998 and 1999, followed by an increase to over 37 percent in 2000. We estimate that it declined in 2001 to about 36 percent and we expect a 36 percent rate to be repeated in 2002. Using this rate, we get net income for 2002 of $50.91 ($79.55 \times 0.64$) For simplicity, we will round this to *$51.00*.

This per-share estimate can be summarized as follows:

Sales	$919.00	
EBITDA	147.00	(0.16)
Depreciation Expense	49.78	
EBIT	97.22	
Interest Expense	17.67	
EBT	79.55	
Taxes	28.64	(0.36)
Net Income (EPS)	$ 50.91	

Given our estimate of earnings per share, the next step is to estimate an earnings multiplier. A combination of the earnings per share estimate times the estimated earnings multiplier provides an estimate of the intrinsic value for the stock market series. Similar to the investment decision rule with the cash flow valuations, if the intrinsic value based on the *P/E* ratio and estimated EPS is greater than the current market price, we should overweight U.S. common stocks; if the value is below the market price we should underweight U.S. common stocks.

Our prior discussion related to Exhibit 13.8 indicated that the earnings multiplier (i.e., *P/E* ratio) over time has been more volatile than the earnings per share series because the multiplier is very sensitive to changes in the spread between *k* and *g*. Because of the significance of the earnings multiplier, we will examine each of the variables in the *P/E* ratio equation to determine what determines the value for them and why they change. Given this understanding, we can demonstrate how an investor would estimate a value for the earnings multiplier.

Determinants of the Earnings Multiplier

Recall the variables that influence the earnings multiplier or the *P/E* ratio based upon the dividend discount model:

➤ 13.8
$$P/E = \frac{D_1/E_1}{k - g}$$

where:

D_1 = **dividends expected in period 1, which is equal to $D_0(1 + g)$**
E_1 = **earnings expected in period 1**
D_1/E_1 = **the dividend-payout ratio expected in period 1**
k = **the required rate of return on the stock**
g = **the expected growth rate of dividends for the stock**

Therefore, the major variables that affect the earnings multiplier for common stocks in a country are

➤ The dividend-payout ratio
➤ The required rate of return on common stock in the country being analyzed
➤ The expected growth rate of dividends for the stocks in the country being analyzed

Because this equation is derived from the dividend discount model, it assumes constant growth for an infinite period. Also, the required rate of return is the long-term estimate. Therefore, the *k* and *g* projections are *long-term estimates*. Thus, although these variables can be impacted by near-term events, they should not experience major changes on a year-to-year basis.

It is easier to discuss the dividend-payout ratio after we have considered both *k* and *g*. Therefore, the order of discussion will be

➤ Estimating *k*, the required rate of return
➤ Estimating *g*, the growth rate of dividends
➤ Estimating D_1/E_1, the dividend-payout ratio

Estimating the Required Rate of Return (k)

The multiplier equation indicates that the earnings multiplier is inversely related to the required rate of return; the higher an investor's required rate of return, the less he or she will pay for a future earnings stream. Our prior discussions indicated that the required rate of return *(k)* is determined by (1) the economy's risk-free rate *(RFR)*; (2) the expected rate of inflation during the period of investment *(I)*; and (3) the risk premium for the specific investment.

Earlier in the chapter, we derived a range of estimates of k as follows:

NRFR	RISK PREMIUM	ESTIMATED K	DESCRIPTION
0.020	0.02	0.040	Short-term *RFR* and small risk premium
0.052	0.04	0.092	Intermediate *RFR* and midrange risk premium
0.056	0.06	0.116	Long-term *RFR* and historical risk premium

Estimating the Growth Rate of Dividends (g)

Earlier in the chapter, we discussed the estimated growth rate of earnings and dividends in connection with the present value of cash flow models. You will recall from Equation 13.6 that

$$g = b \times ROE$$

After a discussion of the pattern of dividend payouts over the business cycle, it was suggested that an appropriate long-run retention rate *(b)* was 55 percent.

We estimated a long-run *ROE* based upon an analysis of the three components of the Du Pont analysis, which showed an overall increase in the *ROE* for the S&P Industrials Index over the past 20 years as a result of recent strong profit margins combined with a decline in the total asset turnover that was offset by an increase in financial leverage. Long run, we estimated an *ROE* of 14 percent. The combined result was

$$g = 0.55 \times 0.14$$
$$= 0.077 = 7.7\%$$

Given these estimates of k, g, and dividend payout (1 minus the retention rate of 0.55), the following section discusses the estimation of the earnings multiples.

Estimating the Dividend-Payout Ratio (D_1/E_1)

Based on the *P/E* equation, there is a positive relationship between the dividend payout ratio and the *P/E* ratio. Therefore, if the $k - g$ spread is constant and this dividend-payout ratio increases, there will be an increase in the earnings multiplier. At the same time, you should recognize that the dividend-payout ratio is equal to one minus the earnings retention rate *(b)*. Therefore, if the dividend payout *increases,* there will be a *decline* in the earnings retention rate *(b),* which will cause a *decline* in the growth rate *(g).* Thus, there is at least a partial offset between changes in the dividend-payout rate and the expected growth rate *(g).*

In the discussion of the growth rate, we indicated that the retention rate was high in the 1970s, declined in the early 1980s, and has increased again since 1993. This increase in the retention rate implies that the payout ratio has declined recently.

Dividend Payout Rate—Active or Residual Decision?

When examining or attempting to estimate the dividend payout for the aggregate market or an individual firm, it is important to consider whether the dividend payout rate is (1) an active decision of management (and the board of directors) or (2) a residual outcome because the active decision is the dividend payment. Obviously, if the dividend payout rate is the active decision, the dividend payment would vary over time in line with earnings. In contrast, if the dividend payment is the active decision, this implies that the dividend payout rate is a residual decision. In this latter case, the dividend payments then would be reasonably stable and show fairly steady increases while the dividend payout ratio would be very volatile because it would be dictated by the earnings. That is, the dividend payout rate would increase dramatically during periods of low earnings and decline significantly during periods of abnormally high earnings growth.

EXHIBIT 13.21 ▶ *EARNINGS PER SHARE AND DIVIDENDS PER SHARE FOR S&P INDUSTRIALS INDEX: 1977–2000*

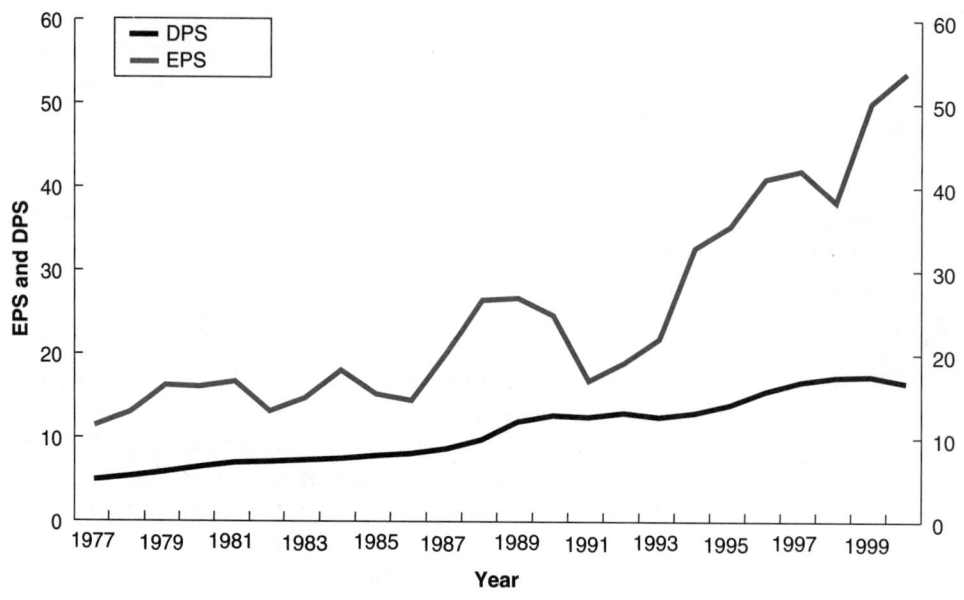

The time-series plots in Exhibit 13.21 and 13.22 support the residual payout theory because they show fairly constant changes in dividend payments (Exhibit 13.21) but high volatility for the dividend payout ratio in Exhibit 13.22 (the dividend payout was high during the recession in 1991 and was quite low during the expansion in 1993–2000). This discussion can be summarized as follows: the annual dividend payout is inversely related to earnings changes. Put another way, there is a positive relationship between the earnings retention rate and earnings changes. Therefore, when estimating the dividend payout ratio, it is necessary to estimate the dividend payment using time-series analysis and then relate this estimated dividend to the earnings estimate. Because of its volatility, it is important *not* to emphasize annual dividend payout changes but use a *long-run perspective* regarding the dividend payout ratio over the business cycle.

Beyond the *cyclical* pattern of the payout ratio, it is also useful to consider the *secular* trend, which appears to be declining for several reasons—that is, there is a tendency for corporations to increase their retention rate for the following reasons. First, given the generally rising *ROE* over the past decade, one could make the argument that corporations have more profitable investment opportunities, which justifies lower payouts. Second, corporations are taking advantage of an alternative way to pay dividends—that is, repurchase stock, which is a more tax-efficient way to reward the stockholder. The result is fewer shares, higher earnings per share, and higher valuation, which is not taxed like dividends to the shareholder.

Estimating an Earnings Multiplier: An Example

There are two ways to estimate the earnings multiplier based on our discussion of the multiplier variables. The first approach begins with the current earnings multiplier and attempts to estimate the direction and amount of any change based on your expectations for changes in the three major components. We will call this approach the *direction of change approach*.

In the second approach, you estimate a specific value for the earnings multiplier by deriving specific estimates for each of the three components in the *P/E* ratio equation. When using this approach, most analysts derive several estimates based on alternative optimistic or pessimistic scenarios. We will call this the *specific estimate approach*.

EXHIBIT 13.22   *TIME-SERIES PLOT FOR S&P INDUSTRIALS INDEX PAYOUT RATIO: 1977–2000*

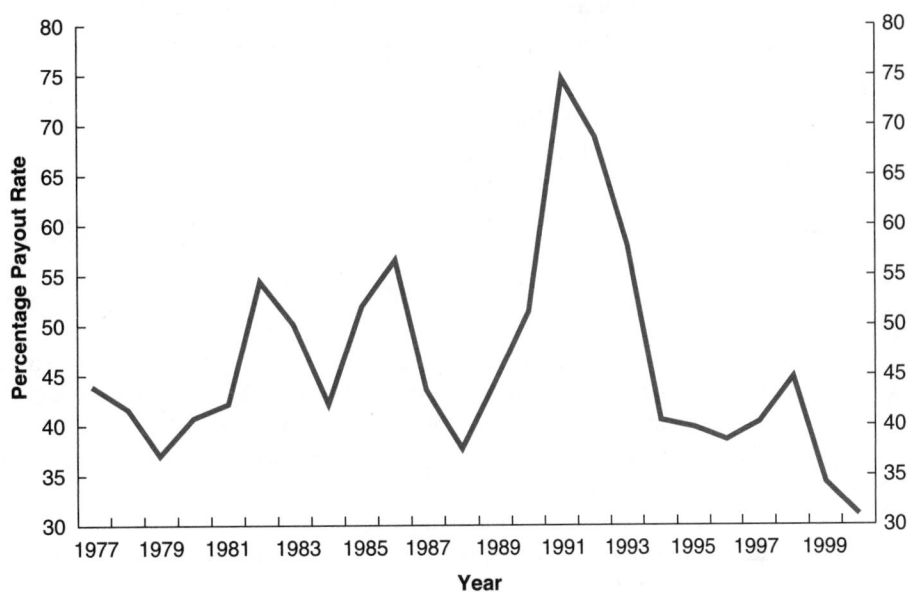

The Direction of Change Approach

Begin with the current earnings multiplier and estimate the direction and extent of change for the dividend payout and the variables that influence *k* and *g*. The direction of the change is more important than its size.

The variables that must be estimated are

1. Changes in the dividend-payout ratio
2. Changes in the real *RFR*   ⎫
3. Changes in the rate of inflation   ⎬ Changes in *k*
4. Changes in the risk premium for common stock ⎭
5. Changes in the earnings retention rate   ⎫ Changes in *g*
6. Changes in the return on equity *(ROE)*   ⎭

The dividend-payout ratio is expected to increase slightly in the near term because recent payout values have been lower than the historical average because of the strong earnings growth, which has resulted in a substantial increase in the retention rate.

Given the three variables that affect the required rate of return on common stocks *(k),* there will probably be very little change in the real *RFR* in 2002 because there will be almost no change in the rate of real growth caused by higher productivity. The rate of inflation was quite low during 2001 and is expected to experience very little change in 2002. Finally, the risk premium is expected to be fairly stable in 2002 after an increase during 2000 and especially 2001 due to the recession and the September 11 terrorist event. Therefore, given the trends in the three components, overall one would expect almost no change in *k* during 2002.

The last two factors in the earnings multiplier estimate relate to the growth rate. We expect a small increase in the payout rate, which implies a small decline in the long-run retention rate. The outlook is for a small increase in the aggregate *ROE* during 2002. Frist, the profit margin in 2002 is expected to increase slightly relative to the lower margin during the recession in 2001. Second, there should be a small increase in the total asset turnover at this time in the economic recovery. Finally, we envision a small decline in the financial leverage ratio during 2002 as firms continue to reduce their financial leverage. The result of a slightly higher profit margin, a small increase in asset turnover, and a decline in financial leverage should be a small increase in the *ROE* during 2002. Therefore, with a small decrease in the retention rate and a small increase in *ROE,* you would estimate virtually no change in the expected growth rate.[21] In summary, we expect

➤ An increase in the payout ratio
➤ No change in the required rate of return
➤ No change in the growth rate

Overall, this would imply almost *no change* in the earnings multiplier. The forward earnings multiplier early in 2002 is about 25 times. This discussion would indicate that the multiplier would remain at 25 times during 2002.

Specific Estimate Approach   This approach derives specific estimates for the earnings multiplier based on a range of estimates for the three variables: dividend payout (*D/E*), required rate of return *(k),* and growth *(g).* As indicated earlier, the retention rate has fluctuated between 45 and 65 percent during the past 10 years. Therefore, a reasonable dividend-payout ratio (*D/E*) would be 45 percent.

The required return *(k)* can be estimated using the interest rate on government bonds plus an estimate of the risk premium for common stocks. An appropriate risk premium could range from 2 percent to 6 percent, depending on the government security used to estimate a nominal risk-free rate. The 6 percent is based on the long-term geometric average risk premium as indicated by the Ibbotson-Sinquefield studies for the period 1926 to 2001, using T-bills as the risk-free investment. Notably, during the recent period (1977 to 2001), the risk premium has been in the range of 2.5 to 5.5 percent. As noted earlier, in early 2002, the rate on T-bills was about 2.00 percent, the rate on five-year government bonds was about 5.20 percent, and the rate on long-term bonds was 5.60 percent. Notably, these interest rates are at the low end of the range for the past 20 years, and most observers expect a small increase during the year. If there is an adjustment to reflect this, you could conceive of the following possibilities:

	EXPECTED AT YEAR END
A. Five-year government bonds	5.3%
Historical risk premium	6.0
Estimated *k*	11.3%
B. Five-year government bonds	5.3%
Low risk premium	2.0
Estimated *k*	7.3%
C. Five-year government bonds	5.3%
Medium risk premium	4.0
Estimated *k*	9.3%

Therefore, the required return *(k)* could be in the range of 7 to about 11 percent.

---

[21]This is the most reasonable scenario given the economic environment. At the same time, there have been changes in the value of common equity caused by asset write-offs and share repurchases. Both of these events can cause a significant decline in the equity account but have little impact on operating earnings. As a result, there has been a higher *ROE* simply because of a lower equity value.

The estimate of growth should be based on the current and expected return on equity *(ROE)* and the rate of retention. The graph in Exhibit 13.3 shows that the *ROE* for the S&P Industrials Index was in the 10 to 18 percent range during the period 1977 to 2000. Assuming that 2002 is at the start of an economic expansion that officially started in early 2002, a range of 12 to 16 percent for the *ROE* seems appropriate. As indicated earlier, the retention rate has been between 45 and 65 percent. Therefore, a conservative estimate of the growth rate would combine the 45 percent retention rate and an *ROE* of 12 percent: $0.45 \times 0.12 = 0.054$. An optimistic growth rate estimate would combine the 65 percent retention rate and a 16 percent *ROE:* $0.65 \times 0.16 = 0.104$. To summarize,

Dividend/earnings	0.35–0.55
Government securities	0.020–0.056
Equity risk premium	0.020–0.060
Required return *(k)*	0.07–0.11
ROE	0.120–0.160
Sustainable growth	0.06–0.08

By combining the most optimistic figures (with a positive $k - g$ spread), we can derive a reasonably generous estimate. Using the pessimistic estimates, we can derive a very conservative estimate. The dividend-payout *(D/E)* figure should be consistent with the retention rate.

High Estimate: $D/E = 0.45$

$$k = 0.09$$

$$g = 0.077 \, (0.55 \times 0.14)$$

$$P/E = \frac{0.45}{0.090 - 0.077} = \frac{0.45}{0.013} = 34.6 \text{ times}$$

Low Estimate: $D/E = 0.60$

$$k = 0.11$$

$$g = 0.06$$

$$P/E = \frac{0.60}{0.110 - 0.06} = \frac{0.60}{0.05} = 12 \text{ times}$$

Therefore, these data imply a range of earnings multipliers from about 12 times to 35 times with a midrange of about 24 times. The midrange is consistent with the expectation of a *P/E* ratio of 25 derived from the direction of change approach.

Calculating an Estimate of the Value for the Market Series

Previously, we estimated the earnings per share for Standard and Poor's Industrials Index of $51.00. Clearly, it would have been possible to derive additional earnings estimates.

In our work with the *P/E,* we developed several estimates for the price/earnings multiplier that varied from about 12 to 35. At this point, we can combine these estimates of an earnings per share of $51 and the several earnings multipliers and calculate the following estimates of intrinsic value for Standard & Poor's Industrials Index series:

$$12.0 \times \$51.00 = \quad 612.00$$
$$18.0 \times \$51.00 = \quad 918.00$$
$$24.0 \times \$51.00 = 1{,}224.00$$
$$30.0 \times \$51.00 = 1{,}530.00$$
$$36.0 \times \$51.00 = 1{,}836.00$$

This example is intended to help you understand the estimation procedure. The estimation of values for *D/E, k,* and *g* was not as extensive as the process used by professional analysts. In addition, we used a point estimate for earnings per share rather than a range of estimates (pessimistic, optimistic, most likely), which would have been preferable. Our discussion has provided the skeleton of the process that includes the theoretical background that forms the foundation for the fundamental analysis of stocks. It is important to understand *the relevant variables and how they relate to the critical estimates of earnings per share and the earnings multiplier.* Notably, the two critical estimates that are necessary for both the present value of cash flow models and the earnings multiplier approach are *k* and *g*—that is, the required rate of return discount rate and the expected growth rate of earnings, cash flow, and dividends.

CALCULATING THE ESTIMATED RATE OF RETURN ON COMMON STOCKS

Having estimated the intrinsic value for the stock market series, we can calculate the estimated rate of return that this intrinsic value implies by using the following equation and assuming that the market price will migrate towards its intrinsic value:

➤13.9
$$E(R_t) = \frac{IV - BV + Div}{BV}$$

where:

$E(R_t)$ = the estimated rate of return during period *t* (We will assume a one-year period.)
IV = the intrinsic value for the stock market series (We will use the several estimates of the intrinsic value of the S&P Industrials Index series derived in this section.)
BV = the beginning value for the stock market series (You would typically use the current value for the stock market series assuming you would be investing at this time.)
Div = the expected dividend payment on the stock market series during the investment horizon

We will compute six estimated rates of return based on the six intrinsic values calculated for the S&P Industrials Index series. We will always assume the same beginning value for the S&P Industrials Index that was the approximate closing value for 2001 (1,334) and an estimate of the dividend per share during the next 12 months (24.00).[22] Therefore, the six estimated rates of return are

$$\frac{612 - 1,334 + 24.00}{1,334} = -52.32\%$$

$$\frac{918 - 1,334 + 24.00}{1,334} = -29.39\%$$

$$\frac{1,224 - 1,334 + 24.00}{1,334} = -6.45\%$$

$$\frac{1,530 - 1,334 + 24.00}{1,334} = 16.49\%$$

$$\frac{1,836 - 1,334 + 24.00}{1,334} = 39.43\%$$

---

[22]This is an approximate estimate based on the expected earnings of $51.00 and a payout ratio of almost 50 percent, which is above the long-run payout.

As you would expect, there is a wide range of expected rates of return because of the range of intrinsic values for the S&P Industrials Index. At this point, you either select the most reasonable estimate and use this value and the implied rate of return to make the investment decision or you can assign probabilities to each of the estimates and derive an expected value estimate. In either case, you would compare this *estimated* rate of return on common stocks to your *required* rate of return on common stocks. If we assume the required k used in calculating the earnings multiplier, we know it is somewhere between 7 and 11 percent. Assuming that it is 9.0 percent, our investment decision would depend on whether the estimated return calculated was equal to or greater than 9.0 percent as follows:

ESTIMATE	ESTIMATED RATE OF RETURN	REQUIRED RATE OF RETURN	INVESTMENT DECISION
1	−52.32%	9.0%	Significant underweight
2	−29.39	9.0	Significant underweight
3	6.45	9.0	Underweight
4	16.49	9.0	Overweight
5	39.43	9.0	Significant overweight

Based on the discussion in Chapter 12, we know that this would cause us to underweight or overweight the U.S. equity market relative to either U.S. bonds or to stocks in other markets depending on the positive or negative excess returns.

One might want to compute the approximate market value that would provide the desired return as follows:

$$\frac{x + 24.00}{1,334} = 1.090$$

$$x = 1,430.00$$

This also implies that the market would have to sell at a 28 times multiple (1,430/51). Notably, this multiple is above our midrange estimate of 24 or the direction of change estimate of about 25.

Other Relative Valuation Ratios   In addition to the *P/E* ratio, several other ratios are used by investors as indicators of relative value. Specifically, when doing an industry and company stock analysis, analysts compare these valuation ratios to similar ratios for the aggregate market, other industries, and other stocks in an industry. Therefore, it is important to become familiar with the computation and historical movements for these ratios. The specific relative valuation ratios considered are

➤ The price-to-book-value ratio (*P/BV*)
➤ the price-to-cash-flow ratio (*P/CF*)
➤ the price-to-sales ratio (*P/S*)

Calculation of Relative Valuation Ratios   The calculation of each of these ratios is generally straightforward with some differences in the measurement of the valuation variable (i.e., *BV, CF,* or *S*). Again, it is necessary to decide whether one uses historical data or future values—that is, do you compare current price to the *historical* valuation variable (e.g., cash flow for the prior year) or the *future expected* variable (e.g., the expected cash flow for the industry or company). As before, the authors prefer future valuation ratios.

When computing the *price-to-book-value* (P/BV) *ratio* for current valuation purposes, it is equal to the current stock price divided by the equity book value per share of the entity. When

EXHIBIT 13.23 ▶ *RELATIVE VALUATION RATIOS FOR THE S&P INDUSTRIALS INDEX*

YEAR	PRICE/BOOK VALUE		PRICE/CASH FLOW (EBITDA)		PRICE/SALES		PRICE/EARNINGS	
	t	$t+1$	t	$t+1$	t	$t+1$	t	$t+1$
1977	1.33	1.22	5.49	4.83	0.49	0.44	9.55	8.39
1978	1.20	1.09	4.73	3.96	0.43	0.37	8.21	6.58
1979	1.17	1.07	4.28	4.07	0.40	0.35	7.11	7.18
1980	1.26	1.17	4.78	4.46	0.42	0.40	8.44	8.13
1981	1.22	1.19	4.64	4.97	0.41	0.42	8.45	10.72
1982	1.15	1.12	4.81	4.50	0.41	0.41	10.37	9.27
1983	1.43	1.41	5.75	5.08	0.52	0.46	11.84	9.66
1984	1.45	1.43	5.22	5.37	0.47	0.45	9.92	11.76
1985	1.66	1.67	6.25	6.16	0.52	0.54	13.68	14.38
1986	2.03	1.89	7.49	6.27	0.65	0.59	17.47	12.52
1987	2.42	2.32	8.02	6.47	0.75	0.67	15.99	12.20
1988	2.17	2.08	6.04	6.05	0.62	0.56	11.38	11.28
1989	2.51	2.39	7.29	7.14	0.67	0.61	13.59	14.72
1990	2.57	2.50	7.68	8.83	0.66	0.67	15.83	23.19
1991	2.73	3.01	9.66	8.84	0.73	0.71	25.36	22.51
1992	3.46	3.60	10.17	9.75	0.82	0.82	25.90	22.50
1993	3.80	3.45	10.28	8.33	0.86	0.83	23.72	15.85
1994	3.56	3.27	8.59	7.83	0.86	0.79	16.34	15.14
1995	3.90	3.80	9.33	8.24	0.94	0.91	18.03	15.53
1996	4.73	4.56	10.25	9.71	1.13	1.06	19.32	18.87
1997	5.78	5.40	12.28	14.05	1.34	1.33	23.88	26.22
1998	6.90	6.78	17.95	14.33	1.70	1.58	33.51	25.59
1999	8.71	8.08	18.41	16.76	2.03	1.93	32.87	30.67
2000	8.32	7.76E	17.28	15.90E	1.99	1.88E	31.61	29.25E

E = Estimate

computing any of the relative valuation ratios for historical exposition purposes, we use the average price each year, which is equal to the average of the high and low prices for the year. As noted, it is necessary to determine whether you want to use historical book value (i.e., compare the average stock price for Year t to the book value at the end of Year t) or use future book value (i.e., average stock price for Year t to *estimated* book value for Year $t+1$). Similar to the *P/E* ratio, when you compute a future ratio, the ratio will generally be lower and less volatile. Both sets of *P/BV* ratios are contained in Exhibit 13.23 and plotted in Exhibit 13.24. The future ratios are computed using *actual* values for Period $t+1$ except for the last year (2000) where we computed the value for the $t+1$ valuation variable assuming the average growth rate for the prior 20 years.

The *price-to-cash-flow* (P/CF) *ratio* is equal to the average stock price for Year t divided by either the historical or the estimated cash flow per share for the entity. Similar to most analysts, we use EBITDA as an imperfect measure of cash flow. Again, we use actual EBITDA in Period $t+1$ for the future ratio except for the final year where we estimate the components of EBITDA. The data are in Exhibit 13.23, and the two series are plotted in Exhibit 13.25.

EXHIBIT 13.24   *TIMES-SERIES PLOT OF THE PRICE-TO-BOOK-VALUE RATIO FOR THE S&P INDUSTRIALS INDEX: 1977–1999*

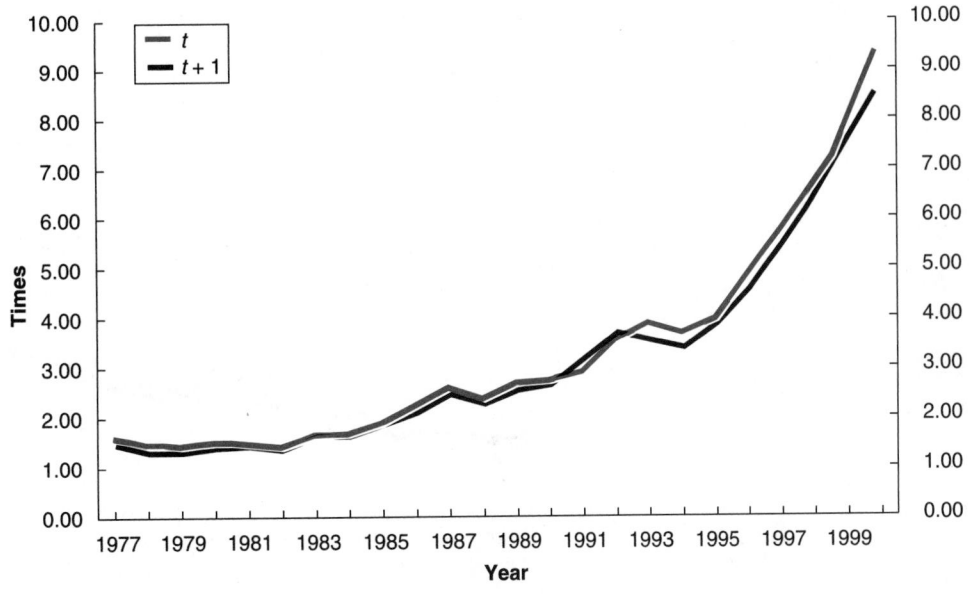

EXHIBIT 13.25   *TIMES-SERIES PLOT OF THE PRICE-TO-CASH-FLOW (EBITDA) RATIO FOR THE S&P INDUSTRIALS INDEX: 1977–1999*

EXHIBIT 13.26 *TIME-SERIES PLOT OF THE PRICE-TO-SALES RATIO FOR THE S&P INDUSTRIALS INDEX: 1977–1999*

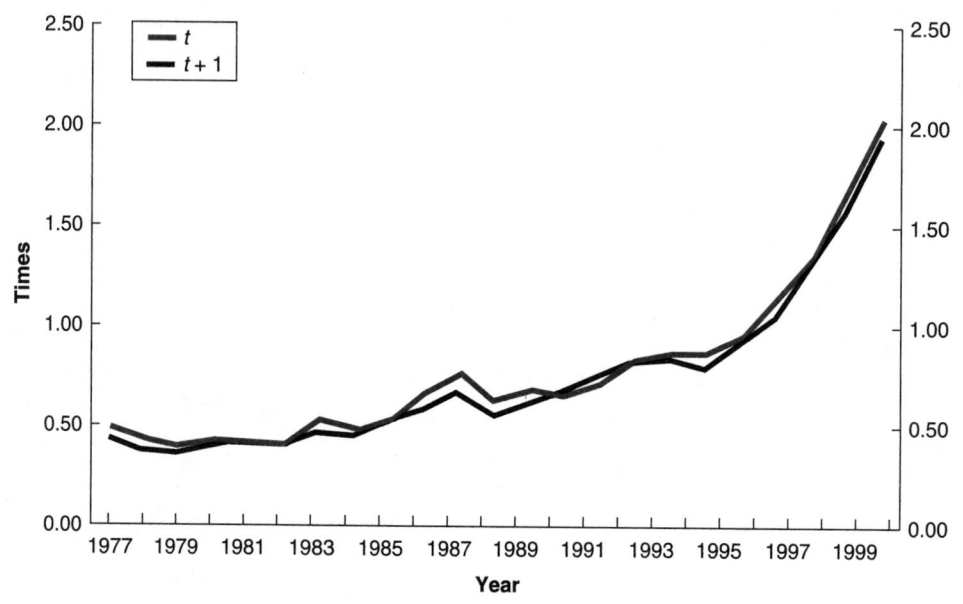

The *price-to-sales* (P/S) *ratio* is equal to the average stock price for Year t divided by net sales per share during Year t or an estimate of sales per share for Year $t + 1$. Again, for the future *P/S* ratio, we use actual sales per share during Period $t + 1$ except for the final year where we estimate sales based upon the average sales growth during the prior 20 years. The results are in Exhibit 13.23, and the two series are plotted in Exhibit 13.26.

As shown in the alternative time-series plots, all the ratios (using the $t + 1$ values) have experienced overall increases during the 23-year period as follows:

RELATIVE VALUATION RATIO	APPROXIMATE BEGINNING VALUE (1977)	APPROXIMATE ENDING VALUE (2000)
Price/Earnings	8.40	29.25
Price/Book Value	1.20	7.76
Price/Cash Flow	4.80	15.90
Price/Sales	0.40	1.88

To understand these higher valuation ratios, it is necessary to consider what factors drive the particular valuation ratio and whether these factors have changed over time. In the case of the *P/E* ratio, we know from DDM that the relevant variables are k and g for the economic unit. Therefore, when attempting to explain why the *P/E* ratio has gone from about 8 times to 29 times, you would consider what has happened to these two variables. Without going into detail, we know that k has declined over time due to lower inflation and some evidence that the market risk premium has declined. In addition, the aggregate *ROE* has been increasing so that the expected growth rate should have increased. In summary, the k–g spread has declined substantially so a higher *P/E* is justified. How much higher it should be is subject to estimation and debate. Subsequently, we will discuss the relevant factors for the other ratios.

The plots also show considerable consistency between the time series using historical data for Time *t* and future expected data for Time *t* + 1. Given the similarity, the authors have a definite preference for using the *future* valuation variables. The point is, we know that when investors buy a stock, they are actually buying future earnings, cash flows, book values, or sales. Therefore, we will always refer to *future P/E* ratios that relate price to *expected* earnings. Although it is not always easy to obtain estimates for these alternative valuation variables beyond earnings, it is important to think in these terms if you want to use these ratios for valuation. The point is, similar to valuation using the *P/E* ratio, you will estimate the valuation variable (i.e., *BV, CF,* or Sales) and then apply an appropriate *future* multiple to the valuation variable to derive an estimate of intrinsic value.

ANALYSIS OF WORLD MARKETS

Although we have worked with the U.S. market to demonstrate the procedure for analyzing a country's stock market, investors should perform a similar analysis for non-U.S. markets, especially the major world markets—Japan, Canada, the United Kingdom, and Germany. We do not have the space to carry out a detailed analysis of each of these markets, but we can provide an example of the extensive analysis by a major investment firm. Specifically, Goldman, Sachs & Company provides a publication entitled *World Investment Strategy Highlights* that contains a portfolio strategy for the world and for several individual countries.

Overall, it is a top-down approach in which Goldman Sachs initially examines the components of a country's economy that relate to the valuation of securities (i.e., GDP, capital investments, industrial production, inflation, and interest rates). In Chapter 12, we discussed the substantial difference in outlook for GDP growth during 2002 and 2003. Likewise, there are major differences among countries in the outlook for inflation, which leads to major differences in expectations for interest rates and exchange rates for alternative countries during 2002.

Given this approach, Exhibit 13.27 contains forecasts for real GDP growth and inflation for six major countries. These data provide insights regarding individual countries in two areas. First is the status of their new economic expansion, which is expected to start in 2002 following the 2001 recession. Goldman Sachs expected most countries, except Japan, to experience an economic expansion in 2002 and 2003.

Going from the economy to results for corporations, Exhibit 13.28 contains comparative results for firms in numerous countries regarding earnings and dividend growth. The range in results is substantial. For example, expected earnings growth in 2002 varies from 38 percent (Japan) to –10 percent (United Kingdom).

Because of the importance of interest rates in the valuation process, Exhibit 13.29 contains long-term bond interest rate forecasts for five countries and Euroland for the short term (3 months) and the long term (12 months). As one might expect, the range of expected yields on long-term bonds is quite large—from 1.5 percent (Japan) to 4.9 percent (United Kingdom).

Putting the earnings growth estimate and interest rates together brings us to market valuation variables, including *P/E* ratios and dividend yields. The prevailing values for various countries contained in Exhibit 13.30 indicate a wide range between countries (e.g., an estimated *P/E* during 2002 of about 29 for the United Kingdom versus 59 in Japan). The expected 2002 dividend yields range from 1.0 percent (Japan) to 3.2 percent for the United Kingdom.

Individual Country Analysis

Following the summary of market statistics for the major equity markets, Goldman Sachs provides a detailed analysis of each of the major countries. This begins with a discussion of the country's economy as part of an analysis of the country's equity market. Exhibit 13.31 contains estimates of the major economic indicators for the United Kingdom. These projections reflect an economy struggling to begin a new economic expansion. Currently, government authorities are concerned about the competitiveness of U.K. firms outside of the European economic community.

EXHIBIT 13.27

FORECASTS FOR COUNTRY REAL GDP GROWTH AND INFLATION (PERCENT PER ANNUM)

COUNTRY	2000	2001F	2002F	2003F
United States				
GDP	4.1	1.2	1.9	3.0
Inflation	3.4	2.8	1.2	2.0
Japan				
GDP	2.4	−0.4	−1.1	1.0
Inflation	−0.7	−0.7	−0.9	−0.7
Germany				
GDP	3.0	0.6	0.7	1.8
Inflation	2.1	2.4	1.4	1.3
United Kingdom				
GDP	3.0	2.4	1.6	2.8
Inflation	2.1	2.1	2.7	2.6
France				
GDP	3.6	2.0	1.1	2.6
Inflation	1.8	1.8	1.6	1.5
Italy				
GDP	2.9	1.9	1.3	2.4
Inflation	2.6	2.7	2.0	1.4

F = forecast

Source: *World Investment Strategy Highlights* by Neil Williams, Alain Kernels, and Joseph Hickey, employees of Goldman, Sachs & Co. Copyright March 2002 by Goldman, Sachs & Co. Used with permission.

EXHIBIT 13.28

COMPARATIVE CORPORATE GROWTH STATISTICS

	UNITED STATES	JAPAN	UNITED KINGDOM	GERMANY	FRANCE	ITALY
Earnings Growth						
2000	5	166	15	14	34	23
2001F	−47	−60	−18	−31	−22	−28
2002F	17	38	−10	1	−6	−2
Dividend Growth						
2000	−3	−4	7	8	11	12
2001F	−3	0	−2	−6	−2	−4
2002F	2	7	−2	0	0	0

Aggregates for earnings and dividend are based on an industrial sample of all the companies in each country.

F = forecast

Note: Figures for the United States refer to the S&P Industrials Index and pertain to operating earnings.

Source: *World Investment Strategy Highlights* by Neil Williams, Alain Kernels, and Joseph Hickey, employees of Goldman, Sachs & Co. Copyright March 2002 by Goldman, Sachs & Co. Used with permission.

EXHIBIT 13.29

INTEREST RATE FORECASTS (PERCENT PER ANNUM)

COUNTRY	CURRENT RATE[a]	SHORT TERM (3 MONTHS)	LONG TERM (12 MONTHS)
United States 10 year	5.1	4.3	4.3
Japan 10 year	1.4	1.3	1.5
Euroland 10 year	5.1	4.3	4.8
United Kingdom 10 year	5.2	4.4	4.9
Canada 10 year	5.5	4.5	4.5
Switzerland 10 year	3.6	2.8	2.6

[a]March 2002.

Source: *World Investment Strategy Highlights* by Neil Williams, Alain Kernels, and Joseph Hickey, employees of Goldman, Sachs & Co. Copyright March 2002 by Goldman, Sachs & Co. Used with permission.

EXHIBIT 13.30

WORLD MARKET EVALUATION MATRIX

	UNITED STATES	JAPAN	UNITED KINGDOM	GERMANY	FRANCE	ITALY
Industrial P/E						
2000	27.8	41.6	22.2	24.0	35.4	28.2
2001F	46.0	81.3	27.1	35.0	45.5	39.3
2002F	39.6	59.0	29.4	33.6	47.7	39.6
Div. Yield						
2000	1.2	0.8	2.8	2.0	1.7	1.7
2001F	1.4	0.9	3.0	2.3	2.0	2.0
2002F	1.4	1.0	3.2	2.6	2.2	2.3

Based on Datastream market indices.

F = forecast

U.S. figures refer to S&P Composite Index and pertain to operating earnings. U.K. figures refer to FT-500 Index.

Source: *World Investment Strategy Highlights* by Neil Williams, Alain Kernels, and Joseph Hickey, employees of Goldman, Sachs & Co. Copyright March 2002 by Goldman, Sachs & Co. Used with permission.

Following the discussion of the economy and the projections, Goldman Sachs analyzes the country's equity market. A summary for the United Kingdom is set forth in Exhibit 13.32. Goldman Sachs feels that the overall investment outlook for the United Kingdom is relatively weak because of the negative earnings growth outlook. Therefore, they recommend a slight underweighting of U.K. equities in a global portfolio—that is, they recommend a 2.5 percent weighting versus a neutral weighting of 2.9 percent, which implies a 0.4 percent underweighting.

EXHIBIT 13.31 ▸ *MAJOR U.K. ECONOMIC VARIABLES*

	CURRENT VALUE	HISTORICAL AVERAGE
GDP Growth		
2000	3.0	2.3
2001F	2.4	
2002F	1.6	
Earnings Growth (Industrials)		
2000	15	4.0
2001F	−18	
2002F	−10	
Dividend Growth (Industrials)		
2000	7	3.7
2001F	−2	
2002F	−2	
Inflation (Consumer Price Index) (%)		
2000	2.1	2.1
2001F	2.1	
2002F	2.7	

INTEREST RATE OUTLOOK

	CURRENT RATE	3 MONTHS	12 MONTHS
3 month	3.1	3.0	2.8
10 year	5.2	4.4	4.9

F = forecast

Source: *World Investment Strategy Highlights* by Neil Williams, Alain Kernels, and Joseph Hickey, employees of Goldman, Sachs & Co. Copyright March 2002 by Goldman, Sachs & Co. Used with permission.

EXHIBIT 13.32 ▸ *STOCK INDEXES FOR THE U.K. EQUITY MARKET AND EXPECTED RATES OF RETURN*

		PERFORMANCE (% CHANGE)		
		LAST MONTH	YTD	12 MONTHS
FTSE 100	5246	−3.3	−2.5	−3.5

	EXPECTED RETURNS (%)	
	3 MONTHS	12 MONTHS
Equities	2.4	9.8
Bonds	7.3	7.3
Cash	1.1	2.2

Source: *World Investment Strategy Highlights* by Neil Williams, Alain Kernels, and Joseph Hickey, employees of Goldman, Sachs & Co. Copyright March 2002 by Goldman, Sachs & Co. Used with permission.

The Internet *Investments Online*

As the economy goes, so goes the stock market; as we've seen in an earlier chapter, the stock market is a leading economic indicator. Good economic insight will help with analyzing the current state and likely future path of the stock market. A number of good Internet sites offer analysis on the market, too.

www.morganstanley.com Morgan Stanley's Web site has a link (or enter "global strategy bulletin" in the site's search function) to the Global Strategy Bulletin, which contains an analysis of the U.S. economy and the economies of several other countries.

www.cm1.prusec.com We've seen Edward Yardeni's site in an earlier chapter. Of special relevance to this chapter are the forecasts for the economy, earnings, and stock market, which appear on his site's pages. Information is available concerning the markets in a number of countries.

www.nabe.com The National Association of Business Economists home page includes links to a number of economic information-related sites and data sources. Links include the Bureau of Economic Analysis (**www.bea.doc.gov**), which contains information about GDP and its compo-

nents, and the U.S. government's publication, *Survey of Current Business.* Links to the Bureau of Labor Statistics (**stats.bls.gov**) provide data on various measures of inflation, unemployment, and productivity. Other links include the Census Bureau (**www.census.gov***)*, Congressional Budget Office (**www.cbo.gov***)*, Council of Economic Advisors (**www.whitehouse.gov/WH/EOP/ CEA/html/CEA.html***)*, The Conference Board, publishers of the Index of Leading Economic Indicators (**www.conference-board.org**), and links to a number of sources of international data, from both U.S. and overseas statistical agencies. The site contains helpful industry information, too, with links to the *U.S. Industrial Outlook,* Federal Trade Commission, and a number of industry trade association sites.

www.agedwards.com The home page of A. G. Edwards & Son, Inc., allows visitors to obtain specific research reports on different topics, companies, and stocks. The site contains pages with an analysis of economic trends, both in the U.S. and abroad. A separate site focuses on international perspectives. Web sites of many other brokerage houses will contain market analysis, too.

Summary

- We consistently emphasize the importance of analyzing the economies and security markets before analyzing alternative industries or companies. You should determine whether the economic and market outlooks indicate an underweighting or overweighting related to investing in stocks, bonds, or cash before you consider which is the best industry or company.
- There are three techniques available to help you make the market decision. The first are macrotechniques, which are based on the strong relationship between the economy and security markets. These models base their market projections on their outlook for the aggregate economy and certain components. The second are microtechniques, which estimate future market values by applying one of several basic valuation models to equity markets. The third is technical analysis, wherein you analyze past and recent market movements for indications of future performance. In Chapter 12, we examined the macrotechniques and discussed a world asset allocation. This chapter has been devoted to the microanalysis of equity markets in the United States and other countries. In Chapter 16 we will discuss numerous technical analysis tools.
- Our microanalysis of the U.S. equity market considered both approaches to equity analysis—the present value of cash flow techniques and the relative valuation ratio techniques. The cash flow techniques provided a range of estimates, most of which indicated that the market was fully valued, which implies that the rates of return on common stock in the near term will be lower than the long-run historical returns and certainly lower than during 1995–1999.

- We considered four relative valuation ratios, including the earnings multiple (*P/E*) approach where we discussed a two-step approach that included estimating EPS and the *P/E* ratio based upon the DDM. As a result, we generated a specific intrinsic market value and the expected rate of return implied by this fundamental market value. The other three ratios (*P/BV; P/CF;* and *P/S*) were defined and explained in anticipation of using them during industry and company analysis where the relative valuation technique compares an industry to the market and relates a company to both its industry and the aggregate market. The goal is to evaluate the relative value position of an industry or a stock. This initial analysis of the valuation ratios was intended to demonstrate the computations involved and show the consistent, substantial increase in all the ratios during the past 25 years. Subsequent analysis will need to consider what variables drive these relative valuation ratios and evaluate whether these variables have changed in a way that justifies these lofty ratio values.
- Finally, although we applied both sets of valuation techniques to the stock market in the United States, we know it is necessary to do a similar analysis for non-U.S. markets. An example of such an analysis by Goldman Sachs shows how the firm applied the top-down approach to several major countries.

Following this aggregate market analysis, the next step is industry analysis, which is considered in the following chapter.

Questions

1. An investor is convinced that the stock market will experience a substantial increase next year because corporate earnings are expected to rise by at least 12 percent. Do you agree or disagree? Why or why not?
2. Find at least three sources of historical information on nominal and real GDP. Find two sources of an annual estimate of nominal GDP.
3. To arrive at an estimate of the *net profit margin,* why would you spend time estimating the operating profit margin and work down?
4. You are convinced that capacity utilization next year will decline from 82 percent to about 79 percent. Explain what effect this change will have on the operating profit margin.
5. You see an estimate that hourly wage rates will increase by 6 percent next year. How does this affect your estimate of the operating profit margin? What other information do you need to determine the effect of this wage rate increase and why do you need it?
6. It is estimated that next year hourly wage rates will increase by 7 percent and productivity will increase by 5 percent. What would you expect to happen to unit labor cost? Discuss how this unit labor cost estimate would influence your estimate of the operating profit margin.
7. Assume that each of the following changes is independent (i.e., except for this change, all other factors remain unchanged). In each case, indicate what will happen to the earnings multiplier and explain why.
   a. The return on equity increases.
   b. The aggregate debt–equity ratio declines.
   c. Overall productivity of capital increases.
   d. The dividend-payout ratio declines.
8. Briefly discuss the two factors that must be considered (estimated) whether you are employing the present value of cash flow approaches or the relative valuation ratio approaches.
9. Discuss the difference between the constant growth DDM and the two-stage growth model. In your discussion, explain when you would use each of these models.
10. Based upon that data contained in Exhibit 13.27, what would be your estimate of nominal GDP growth for the United Kingdom versus Japan in 2003?
11. Based upon the data in Exhibits 13.27 and 13.29, what is the main reason for the current interest rate in the United States versus Japan?

Problems

1. You are told that nominal GDP will increase by about 10 percent next year. Using Exhibit 13.10 and the regression equation, what increase would you expect in corporate sales? How would this estimate change if you gave more weight to the recent observations in Exhibit 13.11?

2. Currently, the dividend-payout ratio (D/E) for the aggregate market is 60 percent, the required return (k) is 11 percent, and the expected growth rate for dividends (g) is 5 percent.
   a. Compute the current earnings multiplier.
   b. You expect the D/E ratio to decline to 50 percent, but you assume there will be no other changes. What will be the P/E?
   c. Starting with the initial conditions, you expect the dividend-payout ratio to be constant, the rate of inflation to increase by 3 percent, and the growth rate to increase by 2 percent. Compute the expected P/E.
   d. Starting with the initial conditions, you expect the dividend-payout ratio to be constant, the rate of inflation to decline by 3 percent, and the growth rate to decline by 1 percent. Compute the expected P/E.

3. *CFA Examination Level III*
   A U.S. pension plan hired two off-shore firms to manage the non-U.S. equity portion of its total portfolio. Each firm was free to own stocks in any country included in Capital International's Europe, Australia, and Far East Index (EAFE) and to use any form of dollar and/or nondollar cash or bonds as an equity substitute or reserve. After three years had elapsed, the records of the managers and the EAFE Index were as shown:

SUMMARY: CONTRIBUTIONS TO RETURN

	Currency	Country Selection	Stock Selection	Cash/Bond Allocation	Total Return Recorded
Manager A	(9.0%)	19.7%	3.1%	0.6%	14.4%
Manager B	(7.4)	14.2	6.0	2.8	15.6
Composite of A&B	(8.2)	16.9	4.5	1.7	15.0
EAFE Index	(12.9)	19.9	—	—	7.0

   You are a member of the plan sponsor's pension committee, which will soon meet with the plan's consultant to review manager performance. In preparation for this meeting, you go through the following analysis:
   a. Briefly describe the strengths and weaknesses of each manager, relative to the EAFE Index data. (5 minutes)
   b. Briefly explain the meaning of the data in the "Currency" column. (5 minutes)

4. As an analyst for Middle, Diddle, and O'Leary, you are forecasting the market P/E ratio using the dividend discount model. Because the economy has been expanding for 9 years, you expect the dividend-payout ratio will be at its low of 40 percent and that long-term government bond rates will rise to 7 percent. Because investors are becoming less risk averse, the equity risk premium will decline to 3 percent. As a result, investors will require a 10 percent return, and the return on equity will be 12 percent.
   a. What is the expected growth rate?
   b. What is your expectation of the market P/E ratio?
   c. What will be the value for the market index if the expectation is for earnings per share of $53.00?
   d. What will be your rate of return if you acquired the index at a value of 950, you sold the index at the value computed in Part c, and dividends during the year were $30.00?

5. You are given the following estimated per share data related to the S&P Industrials Index for the year 2004:

Sales	$1,020.00
Depreciation	45.00
Interest expense	18.00

You are also informed that the estimated operating profit margin is 0.152 and the tax rate is 32 percent.
a. Compute the estimated EPS for 2004.
b. Assume that a member of the research committee for your firm feels that it is important to consider a range of operating profit margin (OPM) estimates. Therefore, you are asked to derive both optimistic and pessimistic EPS estimates using 0.149 and 0.155 for the OPM and holding everything else constant.

6. Given the three EPS estimates in Problem 5, you are also given the following estimates related to the market earnings multiple:

	Pessimistic	Consensus	Optimistic
D/E	0.65	0.55	0.45
Nominal *RFR*	0.10	0.09	0.08
Risk premium	0.05	0.04	0.03
ROE	0.10	0.13	0.16

a. Based on the three EPS and *P/E* estimates, compute the high, low, and consensus intrinsic market value for the S&P Industrials Index in 2004.
b. Assuming that the S&P Industrials Index at the beginning of the year was priced at 1,600, compute your estimated rate of return under the three scenarios from Part a. Assuming your required rate of return is equal to the consensus, how would you weight the S&P Industrials Index in your global portfolio?

7. You are analyzing the U.S. equity market based upon the S&P Industrials Index and using the present value of free cash flow to equity technique. Your inputs are as follows:

Beginning FCFE: $40.00	
$k = 0.09$	
Growth Rates:	
Year 1–3:	9%
4–6:	8%
7 and beyond	7%

a. Assuming that the current value for the S&P Industrials Index is 1,600, would you underweight, overweight, or market weight the U.S. equity market?
b. Assume that there is a 1 percent increase in the rate of inflation—what would be the market's value and how would you weight the U.S. market? State your assumptions.

References   Copeland, Tom, Tim Koller, and Jack Murrin. *Valuation,* 3d ed. New York: John Wiley & Sons, 2001.

Damodaran, Aswath. *Investment Valuation.* New York: John Wiley & Sons, 1996.

Fama, Eugene F., and Kenneth French. "Business Conditions and Expected Returns on Stocks and Bonds." *Journal of Financial Economics* 25, no. 1 (November 1989).

Fama, Eugene F., and Kenneth R. French. "Common Risk Factors in the Returns on Stocks and Bonds." *Journal of Financial Economics* 33, no. 1 (February 1993).

Finnerty, John D., and Dean Leistikow. "The Behavior of Equity and Debt Risk Premiums." *Journal of Portfolio Management* 19, no. 4 (Summer 1993).

Haugen, Robert A., and Nardin L. Baker. "Commonality in the Determinants of Expected Stock Returns." *Journal of Financial Economics* 41, no. 3 (July 1996).

Palepu, Krishna, Victor Bernard, and Paul M. Healy. *Business Analysis and Valuation.* Cincinnati, Ohio: South-Western College Publishing, 1996.

Reichenstein, William, and Steven P. Rich. "The Market Risk Premium and Long-Term Stock Returns." *The Journal of Portfolio Management* 19, no. 4 (Summer 1993).

Reilly, Frank K., Frank T. Griggs, and Wenchi Wong. "Determinants of the Aggregate Stock Market Earnings Multiple." *Journal of Portfolio Management* 10, no. 1 (Fall 1983).

Shiller, Robert J., and John Campbell. "Stock Prices, Earnings, and Expected Dividends." *Journal of Finance* 43, no. 3 (July 1988).

Chapter 14 ⟩ Industry Analysis*

After you read this chapter, you should be able to answer the following questions:

➤ Is there a difference between the returns for alternative industries during specific time periods? What is the implication of these results?

➤ Is there consistency in the returns for individual industries over time? What do these results imply regarding industry analysis?

➤ Is the performance for firms within an industry consistent? What is the implication of these results for industry and company analysis?

➤ Is there a difference in risk among industries? What are the implications of these results for industry analysis?

➤ What happens to risk for individual industries over time? What does this imply for industry analysis?

➤ What are the stages in the industrial life cycle and how does the stage in an industry's life cycle affect the sales estimate for an industry?

➤ What are the five basic competitive forces that determine the intensity of competition in an industry and, thus, its rate of return on capital?

➤ What are the two variables that need to be estimated whether you use cash flow models or relative valuation ratios?

➤ How does an analyst determine the value of an industry using the DDM assuming constant growth or two-stage growth?

➤ How does an analyst determine the value of an industry using the free cash flow to equity (FCFE) model assuming constant growth or two-stage growth?

➤ What are the steps involved in estimating earnings per share for an industry?

➤ How does the procedure for estimating the operating profit margin differ for the aggregate market versus an industry?

➤ What are the two alternative procedures for estimating an industry earnings multiplier?

➤ What is involved in a macroanalysis of the industry earnings multiplier?

➤ What are the steps in the microanalysis of an industry earnings multiplier?

➤ After you estimate an industry earnings multiplier, how do you determine if the industry's multiplier is relatively high or low?

➤ How do analysts compare relative valuation ratios such as *P/BV, P/CF,* and *P/S* to comparable market ratios?

➤ How do industries differ in terms of what dictates their return on assets?

➤ What are some of the unique factors that must be considered in global industry analysis?

When asked about his or her job, a securities analyst typically will reply that he or she is an oil analyst, a retail analyst, or a computer analyst. A widely read trade publication, *The Institu-*

---

*The authors acknowledge inputs to the discussions on "The Business Cycle and Industry Sectors" and "Structural Economic Changes" provided by Professor Edgar Norton of Illinois State University.

tional Investor, selects an All-American analyst team each year based on industry groups. Investment managers talk about being in or out of the metals, the autos, or the utilities. This constant reference to industry groups is because most professional investors are extremely conscious of differences among alternative industries and organize their analyses and portfolio decisions according to industry groups.

We acknowledge the importance of industry analysis as a component of the three-step fundamental analysis procedure initiated in Chapter 11. Industry analysis is the second step as we progress toward selecting specific firms and stocks for our investment portfolio. As the first step, in Chapter 12, we discussed the macroanalysis of the stock market to decide whether the expected rate of return from investing in common stocks was equal to or greater than our required rate of return. Based on this comparison, we would decide to be overweighted, market weighted, or underweighted in stocks. We discussed the microanalysis of the market in Chapter 13 to support the macroanalysis. Following this economic/market decision, in this chapter we analyze different industries to determine if the expected rate of return for an industry is equal to or greater than our required rate of return for the industry. Based on this relationship, we decide how to weight the industry in our stock portfolio. We will take the final step in Chapter 15 when we analyze the individual companies and stocks within the alternative industries.

In the first section, we discuss the results of several studies that will help us identify the benefits and uses of industry analysis. Following that, we present two approaches for valuing industries that resemble the presentation in Chapter 13 for analyzing the aggregate stock market. We begin with the present value of cash flow models and then consider the several relative valuation ratios. Another section raises questions that are unique to industry analysis: What is the impact of the competitive environment within an industry and the effect of the intensity of competition on potential industry returns? We conclude the chapter with a demonstration of global industry analysis, which recognizes that many industries transcend U.S. borders and compete on a worldwide basis.

WHY DO INDUSTRY ANALYSIS?

Investment practitioners perform industry analysis because they believe it helps them isolate investment opportunities that have favorable return-risk characteristics. We likewise have recommended it as part of our three-step, top-down plan for valuing individual companies and selecting stocks for inclusion in our portfolio. What exactly do we learn from an industry analysis? Can we spot trends in industries that make them good investments? Are there unique patterns in the rates of return and risk measures over time in different industries? In this section, we survey the results of studies that addressed these questions.

In the research we describe, investigators asked the following set of questions designed to pinpoint the benefits and limitations of industry analysis:

➤ Is there a difference between the returns for alternative industries during specific time periods?
➤ Will an industry that performs well in one period continue to perform well in the future? That is, can we use past relationships between the market and an individual industry to predict future trends for the industry?
➤ Is the performance of firms within an industry consistent over time?

Several studies also considered questions related to risk:

➤ Is there a difference in the risk for alternative industries?
➤ Does the risk for individual industries vary, or does it remain relatively constant over time?

Based upon the results of these studies, we come to some general conclusions about the value of industry analysis. In addition, this assessment helps us interpret the results of our subsequent industry valuation.

Cross-Sectional Industry Performance

To find out if the rates of return among different industries varied during a given time period (e.g., during the year 2003), researchers compared the performance of alternative industries during a specific time period. Similar performance during specific time periods for different industries would indicate that industry analysis is not necessary. For example, assume that during 2003, the aggregate stock market experienced a rate of return of 10 percent and the returns for *all* industries were bunched between 9 percent and 11 percent. If this similarity in performance persisted for future periods, you might question whether it was worthwhile to do industry analysis to find an industry that would return 11 percent when random selection would provide a return of about 10 percent (the average return).

Studies of the annual industry performance have found that different industries have consistently shown *wide dispersion in their rates of return* (e.g., a typical range of rates of return during a year will be from minus 40 percent to plus 50 percent). A specific example is the year 2001. As shown in Exhibit 14.1, although the aggregate stock market experienced a total return of −11.88 percent (the S&P 500), the industry performance ranged from −71.60 percent (gas utilities) to 57.12 percent (consumer services). These results imply that *industry analysis is impor-*

EXHIBIT 14.1 ➤ *HOW THE DOW JONES U.S. INDUSTRY GROUPS FARED DURING 2001*

BEST PERFORMERS	% Change 12/31/2000 to 12/31/2001	WORST PERFORMERS	% Change 12/31/2000 to 12/31/2001
Consumer services	57.12	Food retailers	−14.49
Office equipment	50.38	Life insurers	−14.92
Advanced industrial equipment	46.85	Mining	−15.13
Toys	38.89	Drug retailers	−15.42
Water Utilities	37.07	Software	−15.94
Home construction	33.62	Aerospace	−16.18
Specialty retailers	31.41	Pharmaceuticals	−17.57
Auto parts	27.85	Full-line insurers	−17.94
Land transportation equipment	26.26	Biotechnology	−20.17
Furnish. & Appliances	25.31	Wireless communications	−21.96
Containers & packing	24.13	Auto manufacturers	−22.69
Household durables	21.87	Electric utilities	−23.22
Consumer electronics	18.43	Computers	−24.24
Precious metals	16.99	Securities brokers	−24.35
Steel	16.76	Electric components / equipment	−29.67
Railroads	16.47	Pipelines	−31.22
Medical supplies	16.12	Airlines	−34.13
Broadline retailers	14.33	Nonferous metals	−39.85
Pollution control	12.12	Communications technology	−56.58
Tires	11.74	Gas utilities	−71.60

Source: *The Wall Street Journal,* 2 January 2002. By permission of *The Wall Street Journal,* Dow Jones & Co., Inc.

tant and necessary to uncover these substantial performance differences that will help identify both unprofitable and profitable opportunities.

Industry Performance over Time

In another group of investigations, researchers questioned whether individual industries that perform well in one time period would continue to perform well in subsequent time periods or at least outperform the aggregate market in the later time period. In this case, investigators found *almost no association* in individual industry performance year to year or over sequential rising or falling markets.

These time-series studies imply that past performance alone does *not* help project future industry performance. The results do *not,* however, negate the usefulness of industry analysis. They simply confirm that variables that affect industry performance change over time and each year it is necessary to project the future performance for individual industries on the basis of future estimates of these relevant variables.

Performance of the Companies within an Industry

Other studies were designed to determine whether there is consistency in the performance of companies *within* an industry. If all the firms within an industry performed consistently during a specified time period, investors would not need company analysis. In such a case, industry analysis alone would be enough because once you selected a profitable industry, you would know that all the stocks in that industry would do well.

These studies typically have found *wide dispersion* in the performance among companies in most industries. Studies have also shown evidence of an industry effect in specific industries, such as oil or autos, but most stocks showed a small industry effect that has been declining over time.[1]

Implication of Dispersion within Industries

Some observers have contended that industry analysis is useless because all firms in an industry do not move together. Obviously, consistent firm performance in an industry would be ideal because you would not need to do company analysis. For industries that have a strong, consistent industry influence, such as oil, gold, steel, autos, and railroads, you can reduce the extent of your company analysis after your industry analysis.

Most analysts do not expect such a strong industry influence, which means that a thorough *company* analysis is still necessary. Even for industries that do not have a strong industry influence, industry analysis is valuable because it is much easier to select a superior company from a good industry than to find a good company in a poor industry. By selecting the best stocks within a strong industry, you avoid the risk that your analysis and selection of a good company will be offset by poor industry performance.

Differences in Industry Risk

Although a number of studies have focused on industry rates of return, few studies have examined industry risk measures. The studies on industry risk investigated two questions: (1) Does risk differ among industries during a given time period? (2) Are industry risk measures stable over time? The study results regarding the dispersion of risk found *a wide range of risk* among different industries at a point in time, and the differences in industry risk typically widened during rising and falling markets. The results on the analysis of risk stability were positive—an analysis of the risk measures for individual industries over time indicated that they were *reasonably stable over time.*

These findings indicate that although risk measures for different industries showed substantial dispersion during a period of time, individual industries' risk measures are stable over time.

---

[1]For example, see Stephen L. Meyers, "A Re-examination of Market and Industry Factors in Stock Price Behavior," *Journal of Finance* 28. no. 3 (June 1973): 695–705; and Miles Livingston, "Industry Movements of Common Stocks," *Journal of Finance* 32, no. 2 (June 1977): 861–874.

This means that the analysis of industry risk is necessary, but this anaysis of risk is useful when you attempt to estimate the future risk for an industry.

Summary of Research on Industry Analysis

The conclusions of the studies dealing with industry analysis are:

➤ During any time period, the returns for different industries vary within a wide range, which means that industry analysis is an important part of the investment process.

➤ The rates of return for individual industries vary over time, so we cannot simply extrapolate past industry performance into the future.

➤ The rates of return of firms within industries also vary, so analysis of individual companies in an industry is a necessary follow-up to industry analysis.

➤ During any time period, different industries' risk levels vary within wide ranges, so we must examine and estimate the risk factors for alternative industries.

➤ Risk measures for different industries remain fairly constant over time, so the historical risk analysis is useful when estimating future risk.

Industry Analysis Process

An important question is, How should you structure your industry analysis? In our previous analysis of the economy and the aggregate equity market for the United States or any other country, we contended that it is necessary to examine the macroeconomy for two related reasons. First, although the security markets tend to move ahead of the aggregate economy, it is recognized that the markets are driven by what happens in the economy—that is, security markets reflect the strength or weakness of the economy. Second, most of the variables that drive the valuation models for the security markets are macrovariables such as interest rates, GDP, and corporate earnings. Therefore, our analysis of the aggregate equity market was contained in two chapters—one dealing with macrovariables such as "leading indicators" and monetary policy and what these variables meant for the market and the global asset allocation decision. The second chapter was a microanalysis of specific variables that affect valuation. In this chapter, we derived specific values for the U.S. equity market using alternative valuation techniques—that is, cash flow models and relative valuation ratios.

The point is, the industry analysis process is similar—it contains first a *macroanalysis* of the industry in order to derive a very clear understanding of how this industry relates to the business cycle and what economic variables "drive" this industry in terms of success or failure. This part of the process will make the second component easier and better. The second component is a *microanalysis* of the industry that involves deriving a specific valuation for the industry using the several valuation techniques introduced earlier. As noted, if you have done your macroanalysis so that you thoroughly understand the industry, estimating the valuation inputs of a discount rate and expected growth for earnings and cash flows (both the rate and the duration of growth) should be relatively easy.

In summary, our industry analysis process includes both a macro- and a microanalysis. The specific macroanalysis topics are

1. The business cycle and industry sectors
2. Structural economic changes and alternative industries
3. Evaluating an industry's life cycle
4. Analysis of the competitive environment in an industry

THE BUSINESS CYCLE AND INDUSTRY SECTORS

Economic trends can and do affect industry performance. By identifying and monitoring key assumptions and variables, we can monitor the economy and gauge the implications of new

EXHIBIT 14.2 ▶ *THE STOCK MARKET AND THE BUSINESS CYCLE*

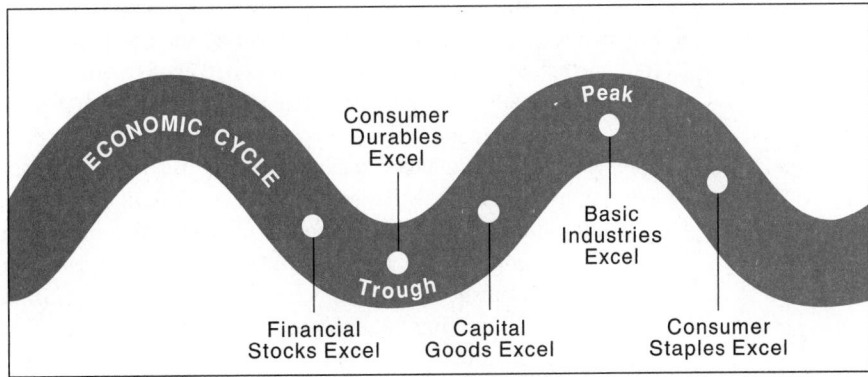

Source: Adapted from Susan E. Kuhn, "Stocks Are Still Your Best Buy," *Fortune,* 21 March 1994, 140. © 1994 Time Inc. All Rights Reserved. Source of data: Merrill Lynch.

information on our economic outlook and industry analysis. Recall that in order to "beat the market" on a risk-adjusted basis, we must have forecasts that differ from the market consensus *and* we must be correct more often than not.

Economic trends can take two basic forms: **cyclical changes** that arise from the ups and downs of the business cycle, and **structural changes** that occur when the economy is undergoing a major change in how it functions. For example, excess labor or capital may exist in some sectors whereas shortages of labor and capital exist elsewhere. The "downsizing" of corporate America during the 1990s, transitions from socialist to market economies in Eastern Europe, and the transition in the United States from a manufacturing to a service economy are all examples of structural change.[2] Industry analysts must examine structural economic changes for the implications they hold for the industry under review.

Most observers believe that industry performance is related to the stage of the business cycle. What makes industry analysis challenging is that every business cycle is different and those who look only at history miss the evolving trends that will determine future market performance.

Switching from one industry group to another over the course of a business cycle is known as a *rotation strategy.* When trying to determine which industry groups will benefit from the next stage of the business cycle, investors need to identify and monitor key variables related to economic trends and industry characteristics.

Exhibit 14.2 presents a stylized graphic of which industry groups typically perform well in the different stages of the business cycle. Toward the end of a recession, financial stocks rise in value because investors anticipate that banks' earnings will rise as both the economy and loan demand recover. Brokerage houses become attractive investments because their sales and earnings are expected to rise as investors trade securities, businesses sell debt and equity, and there is an increase in mergers during the economic recovery. These industry selections assume that when the recession ends there will be an increase in loan demand, housing construction, and security offerings.

Once the economy begins its recovery, consumer durable firms that produce expensive consumer items, such as cars, personal computers, refrigerators, lawn tractors, and snow blowers, become attractive investments because a reviving economy will increase consumer confidence and personal income. Once businesses recognize the economy is recovering, they begin to think about modernizing, renovating, or purchasing new equipment to satisfy rising demand and reduce costs. Thus, capital goods industries such as heavy equipment manufacturers, machine tool makers, and airplane manufacturers become attractive.

Cyclical industries whose sales rise and fall along with general economic activity are attractive investments during the early stages of an economic recovery because of their high degree of operating leverage, which means that they benefit greatly from the sales increases during an economic expansion.[3] Industries with high financial leverage likewise benefit from rising sales volume.[4]

Traditionally, toward the business cycle peak, the rate of inflation increases as demand starts to outstrip supply. Basic materials industries such as oil, metals, and timber, which transform raw materials into finished products, become investor favorites. Because inflation has little influence on the cost of extracting these products and they can increase prices, these industries experience higher profit margins.

During a recession, some industries do better than others. Consumer staples, such as pharmaceuticals, food, and beverages, outperform other sectors during a recession because, although overall spending may decline, people still spend money on necessities so these "defensive" industries generally maintain their values. Similarly, if a weak domestic economy causes a weak currency, industries with large export components to growing economies may benefit because their goods become more cost competitive in overseas markets.

We have identified certain industries that typically make attractive investments over the course of the business cycle. Generally, investors should not invest based upon the current economic environment because the efficient market has already incorporated current economic news into security prices. Rather, it is necessary to *forecast* important economic variables at least three to six months in the future and invest accordingly. The following subsections consider how changes in several important economic variables may affect different industries.

Inflation As noted in chapter 12, higher inflation is generally negative for the stock market, because it causes higher market interest rates, it increases uncertainty about future prices and costs, and it harms firms that cannot pass their cost increases on to consumers. Although these adverse effects are true for most industries, some industries benefit from inflation. Natural resource industries benefit *if* their production costs do not rise with inflation, because their output will likely sell at higher prices. Industries that have high operating leverage may benefit because many of their costs are fixed in nominal (current dollar) terms whereas revenues increase with inflation. Industries with high financial leverage may also gain because their debts are repaid in cheaper dollars.

Interest Rates Banks generally benefit from volatile interest rates, because stable interest rates lead to heavy competitive pressures that squeeze their interest margins. High interest rates clearly harm the housing and the construction industry, but they might benefit industries that supply the do-it-yourselfer. High interest rates also benefit retirees whose income is dependent on interest income.

---

[3]As discussed in Chapter 1, operating leverage arises from the existence of fixed costs in a firm's operating structure. Industries with large fixed expenses will have high degrees of operating leverage. This means a small percentage change in sales can result in a large percentage change in operating income.

[4]As noted in Chapter 10, financial leverage arises from fixed financial costs (that is, interest expense) in a firm's capital structure. Industries that have extensive debt financing (such as banks or utilities) will have net income that is sensitive to small changes in operating income.

International Economics

Both domestic and overseas events may cause the value of the U.S. dollar to fluctuate. A weaker U.S. dollar helps U.S. industries because their exports become comparatively cheaper in overseas markets while the goods of foreign competitors become more expensive in the United States. A stronger dollar has an opposite effect. Economic growth in world regions or specific countries benefits industries that have a large presence in those areas. The creation of free trade zones, such as the European Community and the North American Free Trade Zone, assist industries that produce goods and services that previously faced quotas or tariffs in partner countries.

Consumer Sentiment

Because it comprises about two-thirds of GDP, consumption spending has a large impact on the economy. Optimistic consumers are more willing to spend and borrow money for expensive goods, such as houses, cars, new clothes, and furniture. Therefore, the performance of consumer cyclical industries will be affected by changes in consumer sentiment and by consumers' willingness and ability to borrow and spend money.

STRUCTURAL ECONOMIC CHANGES AND ALTERNATIVE INDUSTRIES

Influences other than the economy are part of the business environment. Demographics, changes in technology, and political and regulatory environments will affect the cash flow and risk prospects of different industries.

Demographics

In the past 50 years, the United States has had a baby boom, a baby bust, and is now enjoying a baby boomlet as members of the baby-boom generation (those born between the end of World War II and the early 1960s) have children. The influx of the baby boom and "the graying of the baby boom" have had a large impact on U.S. consumption, from advertising strategies to house construction to concerns over social security and health care. The study of demographics includes much more than population growth and age distributions. Demographics also includes the geographical distribution of people, the changing ethnic mix in a society, and changes in income distribution. Wall Street industry analysts carefully study demographic trends and attempt to project their effect on different industries and firms.

In the 1990s, the fastest-growing age groups in the United States were those in their forties and fifties, teens, and those over 70; among the declining groups were those between ages 18 and 24. As of the early 2000s, more than one in eight Americans are 65 years of age or older. The changing age profile of Americans has implications for resource availability, namely, a possible shortage of entry-level workers leading to an increase in labor costs and difficulty in finding qualified persons to replace the retiring baby boomers. The aging U.S. population also affects U.S. savings patterns, as people in the 40 to 60 age bracket usually save more than younger people. This is good for the financial services industry, which offers assistance to those who want to invest their savings. Alternatively, fewer younger workers and more "saving seniors" may have a negative impact on some industries, such as the retailing industry.

Lifestyles

Lifestyles deal with how people live, work, form households, consume, enjoy leisure, and educate themselves. Consumer behavior is affected by trends and fads. The rise and fall of jeans, "designer" jeans, chinos, and other styles in clothes illustrate the sensitivity of some markets to changes in consumer tastes. The increase in divorce rates, dual-career families, population shifts away from cities, and computer-based education and entertainment have influenced numerous industries, including housing, automobiles, convenience and catalog shopping, services, and home entertainment. From an international perspective, some U.S.-brand goods—from blue jeans to movies—have a high demand overseas. They are perceived to be more "in style" and perhaps higher quality than items produced domestically. Sales in several industries have benefited from this exercise of consumer choice overseas.

Technology

Trends in technology can affect numerous industry factors including the product or service and how it is produced and delivered. There are literally dozens of examples of changes that have taken or are taking place due to technological innovations. For example, demand has fallen for carburetors on cars because of electronic fuel-injection technology. The engineering process has changed because of the advent of computer-aided design and computer-aided manufacturing. Perpetual improvement of designs in the semiconductor and microprocessor industry has made that industry a difficult one to evaluate. Innovations in process technology allowed steel mini-mills to grow at the expense of large steel producers. Advances in technology allow some plant sites and buildings to generate their own electricity, bypassing their need for power from the local electric utility. Trucks have reduced railroads' market share in the long-distance carrier industry, and planes, not trains, now mainly carry people long distances. The "information super-highway" is becoming a reality and may lead to linkages between telecommunications and cable television systems. Changes in technology have spurred capital spending in technological equipment as firms try to use microprocessors and software as a means to gain competitive advantages. The future effect of the Internet is astronomical.

The retailing industry is a user of new technology. Some forecasters envision "relationship merchandising," in which customer databases will allow closer links between retail stores and customer needs.[5] Rather than doing market research to focus on aggregate consumer trends, specialized retailers can offer products that particular consumer segments desire in the locations that consumers prefer. Technology may allow retailers to become more organizationally decentralized and geographically diversified.

Major retailers use bar-code scanning, which speeds the checkout process and allows the firm to track inventory. Use of customer credit cards allows firms to track customer purchases and send custom-made sales announcements. Electronic data interchange (EDI) allows the retailer to electronically communicate with suppliers to order new inventory and pay accounts payable. Electronic funds transfer allows retailers to move funds quickly and easily between local banks and headquarters.

Politics and Regulations

Because political change reflects social values, today's social trend may be tomorrow's law, regulation, or tax. The industry analyst needs to project and assess political changes relevant to the industry under study.

Some regulations and laws are based on economic reasoning. Due to utilities' positions as natural monopolies, their rates must be reviewed and approved by a regulatory body.[6] Some regulation involves social ends. For example, the Food and Drug Administration protects consumers by reviewing new drugs. Public and worker safety concerns spurred creation of the Consumer Product Safety Commission, the Environmental Protection Agency, and OSHA. Notably, heavy regulation of an industry can result in increasing a firm's costs and restricting entry into the industry.

---

[5]Carl E. Steidtmann, "General Trends in Retailing," in *The Retail Industry—General Merchandisers and Discounters,* ed. Charles Ingene (Charlottesville, Va.: Association for Investment Management and Research, 1993): 6–9.

[6]Technology can change natural monopolies. We mentioned earlier how some firms are generating their own electrical power. Advancing technology resulted in AT&T losing its monopoly in the early 1980s. Another example is that, currently, numerous states are allowing electric utilities to compete for customers.

Regulatory changes have affected numerous industries. A recent example is the numerous regulations and inspections following the September 11, 2001, attacks. Changing regulations and technology are bringing the various aspects of the financial services industry—banking, insurance, investment banking, and investment services—together.

Regulations and laws affect international commerce. International tax laws, tariffs, quotas, embargoes, and other trade barriers affect different industries and global commerce in various ways.

An interesting example is how the retail industry is affected by numerous regulatory factors. First is the minimum-wage law, which impacts many retail employees. A second factor is employer-paid health insurance, which would dramatically affect the labor costs of labor-intensive service industries, such as retailing. Third, because goods must first be delivered to the stores, regulations that affect the cost of shipping by airplane, ship, or truck will affect retailers' costs. Finally, trends toward the reduction of tariffs and quotas will allow retailers to offer imported goods at lower prices, which will expand their international marketing.

EVALUATING THE INDUSTRY LIFE CYCLE

An insightful analysis when predicting industry sales and trends in profitability is to view the industry over time and divide its development into stages similar to those that humans progress through as they move from birth to adolescence to adulthood to middle age to old age. The number of stages in this **industry life cycle analysis** can vary based on how much detail you want. A five-stage model would include

1. Pioneering development
2. Rapid accelerating growth
3. Mature growth
4. Stabilization and market maturity
5. Deceleration of growth and decline

Exhibit 14.3 shows the growth path of sales during each stage. The vertical scale in logs reflects *rates* of growth, whereas the arithmetic horizontal scale has different widths representing different, unequal time periods. To estimate industry sales, you must predict the length of time for each stage. This requires answers to such questions as: How long will an industry grow at an accelerating rate (Stage 2)? How long will it be in a mature growth phase (Stage 3) before its sales growth stabilizes (Stage 4) and then declines (Stage 5)?

Besides being useful when estimating sales, this analysis of an industry's life cycle also can provide some insights into profit margins and earnings growth, although these profit measures do not necessarily parallel the sales growth. The profit margin series typically peaks very early in the total cycle and then levels off and declines as competition is attracted by the early success of the industry.

To illustrate the contribution of life cycle stages to sales estimates, we briefly describe these stages and their effects on sales growth and profits:

1. *Pioneering development.* During this start-up stage, the industry experiences modest sales growth and very small or negative profit margins and profits. The market for the industry's product or service during this time period is small, and the firms involved incur major development costs.
2. *Rapid accelerating growth.* During this rapid growth stage, a market develops for the product or service and demand becomes substantial. The limited number of firms in the industry face little competition, and individual firms can experience substantial backlogs. The profit margins are very high. The industry builds its productive capacity as sales grow

EXHIBIT 14.3 *LIFE CYCLE FOR AN INDUSTRY*

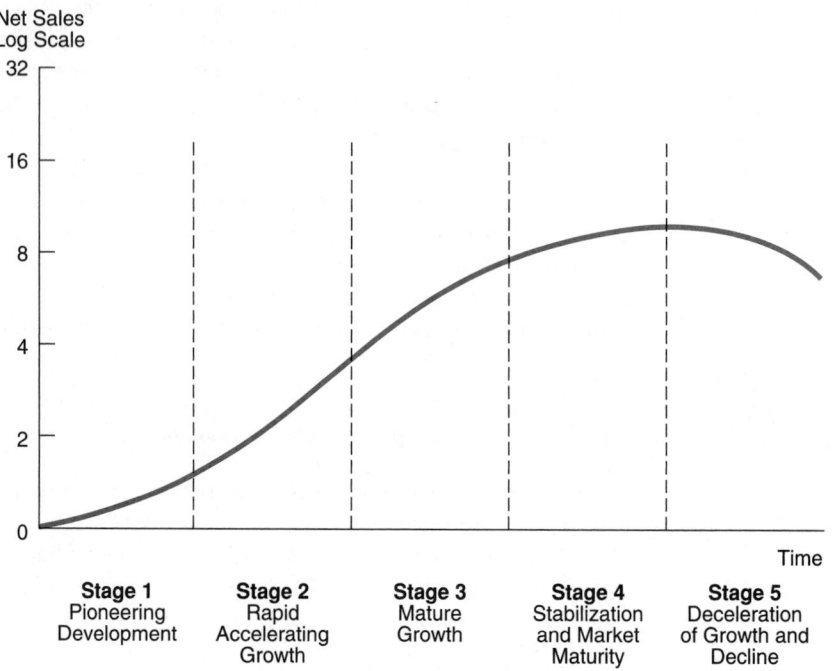

at an increasing rate as the industry attempts to meet excess demand. High sales growth and high profit margins that increase as firms become more efficient cause industry and firm profits to explode. During this phase, profits can grow at over 100 percent a year as a result of the low earnings base and the rapid growth of sales and net profit margins.

3. *Mature growth.* The success in Stage 2 has satisfied most of the demand for the industry goods or service. Thus, future sales growth may be above normal but it no longer accelerates. For example, if the overall economy is growing at 8 percent, sales for this industry might grow at an above normal rate of 15 percent to 20 percent a year. Also, the rapid growth of sales and the high profit margins attract competitors to the industry, which causes an increase in supply and lower prices, which means that the profit margins begin to decline to normal levels.

4. *Stabilization and market maturity.* During this stage, which is probably the longest phase, the industry growth rate declines to the growth rate of the aggregate economy or its industry segment. During this stage, investors can estimate growth easily because sales correlate highly with an economic series. Although sales grow in line with the economy, profit growth varies by industry because the competitive structure varies by industry, and by individual firms within the industry because the ability to control costs differs among companies. Competition produces tight profit margins, and the rates of return on capital (e.g., return on assets, return on equity) eventually become equal to or slightly below the competitive level.

5. *Deceleration of growth and decline.* At this stage of maturity, the industry's sales growth declines because of shifts in demand or growth of substitutes. Profit margins continue to be squeezed, and some firms experience low profits or even losses. Firms that remain profitable may show very low rates of return on capital. Finally, investors begin thinking about alternative uses for the capital tied up in this industry.

Although these are general descriptions of the alternative life cycle stages, they should help you identify the stage your industry is in, which should help you estimate its potential sales growth. Obviously, everyone is looking for an industry in the early phases of Stage 2 and hopes to avoid industries in Stage 4 or Stage 5. Comparing the sales and earnings growth of an industry to similar growth in the economy should help you identify the industry's stage within the industrial life cycle.

ANALYSIS OF INDUSTRY COMPETITION

Similar to the sales forecast that can be enhanced by the analysis of the industrial life cycle, an industry earnings forecast should be preceded by the analyses of the competitive structure for the industry. Specifically, a critical factor affecting the profit potential of an industry is the intensity of competition in the industry, as Porter has discussed in a series of books and articles.[7]

Competition and Expected Industry Returns

Porter's concept of **competitive strategy** is described as the search by a firm for a favorable competitive position in an industry. To create a profitable competitive strategy, a firm must first examine the basic competitive structure of its industry because the potential profitability of a firm is heavily influenced by the profitability of its industry. After determining the competitive structure of the industry, you examine the factors that determine the relative competitive position of a firm within its industry. In this section, we consider the competitive forces that determine the competitive structure of the industry. In the next chapter, our discussion of company analysis will cover the factors that determine the relative competitive position of a firm within its industry.

Basic Competitive Forces   Porter believes that the **competitive environment** of an industry (the intensity of competition among the firms in that industry) determines the ability of the firms to sustain above-average rates of return on invested capital. As shown in Exhibit 14.4, he suggests that five competitive forces determine the intensity of competition and that the relative effect of each of these five factors can vary dramatically among industries.

1. *Rivalry among the existing competitors.* For each industry analyzed, you must judge if the rivalry among firms is currently intense and growing, or if it is polite and stable. Rivalry increases when many firms of relatively equal size compete in an industry. When estimating the number and size of firms, be sure to include foreign competitors. Further, *slow growth* causes competitors to fight for market share and increases competition. *High fixed costs* stimulate the desire to sell at the full capacity, which can lead to price cutting and greater competition. Finally, look for *exit barriers,* such as specialized facilities or labor agreements. These can keep firms in the industry despite *below-average* or negative rates of return.
2. *Threat of new entrants.* Although an industry may have few competitors, you must determine the likelihood of firms entering the industry and increasing competition. *High barriers to entry,* such as low current prices relative to costs, keep the threat of new entrants low. Other barriers to entry include the need to invest large financial resources to compete and the availability of capital. Also, substantial economies of scale give a current industry member an advantage over a new firm. Further, entrants might be discouraged if success

---

[7]Michael E. Porter, *Competitive Strategy: Techniques for Analyzing Industries and Competitors* (New York: Free Press, 1980): Michael Porter, "Industry Structure and Competitive Strategy: Keys to Profitability," *Financial Analysts Journal* 36, no. 4 (July–August 1980); and Michael Porter, *Competitive Advantage: Creating and Sustaining Superior Performance* (New York: Free Press, 1985), Chapter 1.

EXHIBIT 14.4 *FORCE DRIVING INDUSTRY COMPETITION*

in the industry requires extensive distribution channels that are hard to build because of exclusive distribution contracts. Similarly, high costs of switching products or brands, such as those required to change a computer or telephone system, keep competition low. Finally, government policy can restrict entry by imposing licensing requirements or limiting access to materials (lumber, coal). Without some of these barriers, it might be very easy for competitors to enter an industry, increasing the competition and driving down potential rates of return.

3. *Threat of substitute products.* Substitute products limit the profit potential of an industry because they limit the prices firms in an industry can charge. Although almost everything has a substitute, you must determine how close the substitute is in price and function to the product in your industry. As an example, the threat of substitute glass containers hurts the metal container industry. Glass containers kept declining in price, forcing metal container prices and profits down. In the food industry, consumers constantly substitute between beef, pork, chicken, and fish. The more commoditylike the product, the greater the competition and the lower the profit margins.

4. *Bargaining power of buyers.* Buyers can influence the profitability of an industry because they can bid down prices or demand higher quality or more services by bargaining among competitors. Buyers become powerful when they purchase a large volume relative to the sales of a supplier (e.g., Wal-Mart, Home Depot). The most vulnerable firm is a one-customer firm that supplies a single large manufacturer, as is common for auto parts manufacturers or software developers. Buyers will be more conscious of the costs of items that represent a significant percentage of the firm's total costs. This consciousness increases if

the buying firm is feeling cost pressure from its customers. Also, buyers who know a lot about the costs of supplying an industry will bargain more intensely—for example, when the buying firm supplies some of its own needs and buys from the outside.

5. *Bargaining power of suppliers.* Suppliers can alter future industry returns if they increase prices or reduce the quality of the product or the services they provide. The suppliers are more powerful if they are few and if they are more concentrated than the industry to which they sell and if they supply critical inputs to several industries for which few, if any, substitutes exist. In this instance, the suppliers are free to change prices and services they supply to the firms in an industry. When analyzing supplier bargaining power, be sure to consider labor's power within each industry.

An investor needs to analyze these competitive forces to determine the intensity of the competition in an industry and assess the effect of this competition on the industry's long-run profit potential. You should examine each of these factors and develop a relative competitive profile for each industry. You need to update this analysis of an industry's competitive environment over time, because an industry's competitive structure can and will change over time.

ESTIMATING INDUSTRY RATES OF RETURN

At this point, we have determined that industry analysis helps an investor select profitable investment opportunities and we have completed a thorough macroanalysis of the industry. Our next question is, How do we go about valuing an industry and estimating the rate of return that an investment in it will provide? Again, we consider the two equity valuation approaches introduced in Chapter 12—the present value of cash flows and the relative valuation ratios. Beginning with the present value of cash flow models, we demonstrate the DDM with the two-stage growth assumption and then assume constant growth for the retail drugstore industry. Following this, we consider the present value of free cash flow (FCF) model. Subsequently, we will analyze the alternative relative valuation techniques with the price/earnings ratio and analysis of the *P/BV, P/CF,* and *P/S* ratios compared to the relative valuation ratios for the market presented in Chapter 13.

Although our investment decision is always the same, the form of the comparison depends on which valuation approach is being used. In the case of the present value of cash flow techniques, we derive a present value for the industry using our required rate of return for the industry—that is, we compare the present value of the specified cash flow versus the prevailing value of the index. If our estimated present value exceeds the prevailing index value, we should overweight the industry. Alternatively, if the *PV* of cash flows is less than the industry index, it implies that the industry is overvalued (i.e., the industry will not provide our required rate of return if acquired at the prevailing market price) and we should underweight this industry in our portfolio.

In contrast, if we use the two-step *P/E* ratio approach, we compute a current intrinsic value for the industry and compute an expected rate of return for the holding period based on this intrinsic value and the expected dividend return during the period compared to the current market price. If this expected rate of return exceeds the required rate of return *(k),* you should overweight the industry; if the return is below *k,* you should underweight the industry.

To demonstrate industry analysis, we use Standard and Poor's Retail Store–Drug index to represent industrywide data for this industry. This retail store–drug index (hereinafter referred to as the retail drugstore [RDS] industry) contains three companies: (1) Longs Drug Stores, (2) Rite-Aid, and (3) Walgreen Company. The industry should be reasonably familiar to most observers, and it is consistent with the subsequent company analysis of Walgreens.

Valuation Using the Reduced Form DDM

Recall that the reduced form DDM is

> 14.1

$$P_i = \frac{D_1}{k - g}$$

where:

P_i = the price of industry i at time t
D_1 = expected dividend for industry i in period 1 equal to D_0 $(1 + g)$
k = the required rate of return on the equity for industry i
g = the expected long-run growth rate of earnings and dividend for industry i

As always, *the two major estimates for any valuation model are* k *and* g. We will discuss each of these at this point in the chapter with the understanding that we will also use these estimates subsequently when applying the two-step, price/earnings ratio technique for valuation.

Estimating the Required Rate of Return *(k)*

Because the required rate of return *(k)* on all investments is influenced by the risk-free rate and the expected inflation rate, the differentiating factor in this case is the risk premium for the RDS industry versus the market. In turn, we discussed the risk premium in terms of fundamental factors, including business risk *(BR)*, financial risk *(FR)*, liquidity risk *(LR)*, exchange rate risk *(ERR)*, and country (political) risk *(CR)*. Alternatively, you can estimate the risk premium based on the CAPM, which implies that the risk premium is a function of the systematic risk (beta) of the asset. Therefore, to derive an estimate of the industry's risk premium, you should examine the *BR, FR, LR, ERR,* and *CR* for the industry and compare these industry risk factors to those of the aggregate market. Alternatively, you can compute the systematic risk (beta) for the industry and compare this to the market beta of 1.0. Prior to calculating a beta for the industry, we briefly discuss the fundamental risk factors for the industry.

Business risk is a function of relative sales volatility and operating leverage. As we will see when we examine the sales and earnings for the industry, the annual percentage changes in retail drugstore sales were less volatile than aggregate sales as represented by PCE. Also, the OPM (operating profit margin) for retail drugstores was less volatile than the S&P Industrials Index OPM. Therefore, because both sales and the OPM for the RDS industry have been less volatile than the market, operating profits are substantially less volatile. This implies that the business risk for the RDS industry is *below average.*

The *financial risk* for this industry is difficult to judge because of widespread use of building leases in the industry. Still, on the basis of the reported data on debt to total capital or interest coverage ratios, the *FR* for this industry is substantially below the market. Assuming substantial use of long-term lease contracts, when these are capitalized, this industry probably has financial risk *about equal* to the market.

To evaluate the market liquidity risk for an industry, it is necessary to estimate the liquidity risk for all the firms in the industry and derive a composite view. The fact is, there is substantial variation in market liquidity among the firms in this industry. Walgreens is very liquid, whereas Longs Drug Stores and Rite-Aid are relatively illiquid. A conservative view is that the RDS industry probably has *above-average* liquidity risk.

Exchange rate risk (ERR) is the uncertainty of earnings due to changes in exchange rates faced by firms in this industry that sell outside the United States. The amount of *ERR* is determined by what proportion of sales is non-U.S., how these sales are distributed among countries, and the exchange rate volatility for these countries. This risk could range from an industry with very limited international sales (e.g., a service industry that is not involved overseas) to an industry that is clearly worldwide (e.g., the chemical or pharmaceutical industry). For a truly global industry, you need to examine the distribution of sales among specific countries because we know that the exchange rate risk varies among countries based on the volatility of exchange rates with the U.S. dollar. The *ERR* for the RDS industry would be *quite low* because sales and earnings for these drugstore firms are almost wholly attributable to activity within the United States.

The existence of *country risk (CR)* is likewise a function of the proportion of foreign sales, the specific foreign countries involved, and the stability of the political/economic system in these countries. As noted, there is very little *CR* in the United Kingdom and Japan, but there can be substantial *CR* in China, Russia, or South Africa. Again, for the RDS industry, country risk would be very low because of limited foreign sales.

In summary, for the RDS industry, business risk is definitely below average, financial risk is at best equal to the market, liquidity risk is above average, and exchange rate risk and country risk are almost nonexistent. The consensus is that the overall risk for the RDS industry should be lower than for the aggregate market on the basis of fundamental characteristics.

The *systematic risk* for the retail drugstore industry is computed using the market model as follows:

➤ 14.2
$$\%\Delta \text{ RDS}_t = \alpha_i + \beta_i (\%\Delta \text{ S\&P } 500_t)$$

where:

$\%\Delta \text{ RDS}_t$ = the percentage price change in the retail drugstore (RDS) index during month t
α_i = the regression intercept for the RDS industry
β_i = the systematic risk measure for the RDS industry equal to $\text{Cov}_{i,m}/\sigma_m^2$

To derive an estimate for the RDS industry, the model specified was run with monthly data for the five-year period 1997 to 2001. The results for this regression are as follows:

$\alpha_t = 0.003$	$R^2 = 0.62$
$\beta_t = 0.82$	$DW = 1.83$
t-value $= 7.40$	$F = 68.37$

The systematic risk ($\beta = 0.82$) for the RDS industry is clearly below unity, indicating a low-risk industry (i.e., risk less than the market). These results are quite consistent with the prior analysis of fundamental risk factors *(BR, FR, LR, ERR, CR)*.

Translating this systematic risk into a required rate of return estimate *(k)* calls for using the security market line model as follows:

➤ 14.3
$$k_i = RFR + \beta_i (R_m - RFR)$$

Recall that in Chapter 13 we derived three estimates for the required market rate of return based upon alternative risk premiums (0.040–0.092–0.116). For our purposes here, it seems like the midpoint is reasonable—that is, a nominal *RFR* of 0.052 and an R_m of 0.092. This, combined with a beta for the industry at 0.82, indicates the following:

$$k = 0.052 + 0.82 (0.092 - 0.052)$$
$$= 0.052 + 0.82 (0.04)$$
$$= 0.052 + 0.0328$$
$$= 0.088 = 8.48\%$$

For ease of computation we will use a *k* of 8.5% A microestimate of fundamental risk below average and a risk estimate using the CAPM likewise below average implies an industry earnings multiple *above* the market multiple, all other factors being equal.

Estimating the Expected Growth Rate (*g*)   Recall that earnings and dividend growth are determined by the retention rate and the return on equity.

$$g = f \text{ (Retention Rate and Return on Equity)}$$

We have consistently broken down return on equity into the following three components:

$$\frac{\text{Net Profit}}{\text{Equity}} = \frac{\text{Net Income}}{\text{Sales}} \times \frac{\text{Sales}}{\text{Total Assets}} \times \frac{\text{Total Assets}}{\text{Equity}}$$

$$= \frac{\text{Profit}}{\text{Margin}} \times \frac{\text{Total Asset}}{\text{Turnover}} \times \frac{\text{Financial}}{\text{Leverage}}$$

Therefore, we need to examine each of these variables in Exhibit 14.5 to determine if they imply a difference in the expected growth rate for RDS as compared to the aggregate market (S&P Industrials Index).

Earnings Retention Rate   The retention rate data in Exhibit 14.5 indicate that the RDS industry has a higher retention rate (69 percent versus 55 percent). This means that the RDS industry would have a potentially *higher* growth rate, all else being the same (i.e., equal *ROE*).

Return on Equity   Because the return on equity is a function of the net profit margin, total asset turnover, and a measure of financial leverage, these three variables are examined individually.

Historically, the net profit margin for the S&P Industrials Index series has been consistently higher than the margin for the RDS industry. This is not surprising because retail firms typically have lower profit margins but higher turnover.

As noted, one would normally expect the total asset turnover *(TAT)* for a retail firm to be higher than the average industrial company. This expectation has typically been confirmed because the average *TAT* for the S&P Industrials Index was 1.06 versus 2.70 for the RDS industry. Beyond the overall difference, the spread between the two series changed over the period. This change occurred because the *TAT* for the S&P Industrials Index series declined steadily over the period while the *TAT* for the RDS industry experienced a secular decline from 1977 to 1999 but a major increase in 2000, as shown in Exhibit 14.6. Multiplying these two ratios indicates the industry's return on total assets *(ROTA)*.[8]

$$\frac{\text{Net Income}}{\text{Sales}} \times \frac{\text{Sales}}{\text{Total Assets}} = \frac{\text{Net Income}}{\text{Total Assets}}$$

When we do this for the two series, the results in Exhibit 14.5 indicate that the return on total assets *(ROTA)* for the S&P Industrials Index series went from 6.54 percent in 1977 to 5.29 percent in 2000 and averaged 5.06 percent, whereas the *ROTA* for the RDS industry went from 11.56 percent to 8.89 percent and averaged 8.35 percent. Clearly, the industry *ROTA* results were superior on average.

The final component is the financial leverage multiplier (total assets/equity). As shown in Exhibit 14.5 and Exhibit 14.7, the leverage multiplier for the S&P Industrials Index increased

---

[8]The reader is encouraged to read Appendix 14C to this chapter, which contains a discussion of an article by Selling and Stickney wherein they analyze the components of *ROA* and relate this to an industry's economics and its strategy: Thomas Selling and Clyde Stickney, "The Effects of Business Environment and Strategy on a Firm's Rate of Return on Assets," *Financial Analysts Journal* 39, no. 1 (January–February 1983).

EXHIBIT 14.5 EARNINGS MULTIPLIER FOR THE S&P INDUSTRIALS INDEX AND THE RDS INDUSTRY, AND INFLUENTIAL VARIABLES: 1977–2000

YEAR	EARNINGS MULTIPLIER (t + 1)		RETENTION RATE		NET PROFIT MARGIN		TOTAL ASSET TURNOVER		RETURN ON TOTAL ASSETS		TOTAL ASSETS/ EQUITY		RETURN ON EQUITY	
	S&P Ind	RDS	S&P Ind	RDS	S&P Ind	RDS	S&P Ind	RDS	S&P Ind	RDS	S&P Ind	RDS	S&P Ind	RDS
1977	8.39	9.42	56.80	79.90	5.15	4.07	1.27	2.84	6.54	11.56	2.08	1.53	13.60	17.68
1978	6.58	8.71	58.80	76.10	5.19	4.03	1.27	2.81	6.59	11.32	2.15	1.52	14.17	17.21
1979	7.18	7.61	63.70	72.60	5.57	3.47	1.30	3.00	7.24	10.41	2.20	1.65	15.93	17.18
1980	8.13	7.47	59.70	70.80	4.92	3.47	1.31	3.04	6.45	10.55	2.23	1.66	14.37	17.51
1981	10.72	9.21	58.10	69.00	4.86	3.45	1.28	3.03	6.22	10.45	2.25	1.65	14.00	17.25
1982	9.27	9.24	46.00	68.90	3.95	3.44	1.17	2.97	4.62	10.22	2.31	1.66	10.68	16.96
1983	9.66	13.83	50.40	70.70	4.42	3.79	1.15	2.86	5.08	10.84	2.28	1.88	11.59	20.38
1984	11.76	13.82	58.50	62.40	4.77	3.04	1.22	2.65	5.82	8.06	2.39	1.93	13.91	15.55
1985	14.38	13.93	48.50	59.20	3.84	2.96	1.15	2.68	4.42	7.93	2.54	1.88	11.22	14.91
1986	12.52	15.15	44.00	67.10	3.75	3.11	1.07	2.71	4.01	8.43	2.58	1.94	10.35	16.35
1987	12.20	15.70	57.00	68.40	4.77	2.88	1.08	2.80	5.15	8.06	2.62	2.04	13.50	16.45
1988	11.28	13.91	63.10	69.40	5.51	2.90	0.98	2.82	5.40	8.18	3.03	2.07	16.36	16.93
1989	14.72	14.01	55.97	67.71	5.01	2.79	0.97	2.82	4.86	7.87	3.16	2.03	15.36	15.97
1990	23.19	13.87	49.80	68.32	4.26	2.89	0.97	2.82	4.13	8.13	3.27	2.00	13.50	16.26
1991	22.51	15.59	28.19	67.19	2.97	2.91	0.94	2.85	2.80	8.31	3.24	1.83	9.09	15.25
1992	22.50	22.51	33.86	66.41	3.27	2.89	0.96	2.83	3.13	8.19	3.50	1.82	10.95	14.89
1993	15.85	15.43	41.96	53.17	3.73	2.15	0.92	2.79	3.42	6.00	3.76	1.88	12.86	11.27
1994	15.14	13.83	61.06	66.22	5.24	2.89	0.95	2.63	4.89	7.60	3.51	2.00	17.14	15.17
1995	15.53	15.46	60.61	66.33	5.24	2.84	0.97	2.66	5.08	7.55	3.32	2.03	16.87	15.33
1996	18.87	26.28	69.14	71.19	5.86	3.21	0.93	2.02	5.45	6.48	3.26	2.17	17.77	14.06
1997	26.22	26.36	60.31	59.05	5.61	1.96	0.94	2.23	5.27	4.37	3.33	2.18	17.55	9.53
1998	25.59	34.82	54.96	75.26	5.14	2.58	0.85	2.04	4.39	5.27	3.70	2.49	16.26	13.12
1999	30.67	43.00	65.37	75.09	6.27	2.70	0.84	2.09	5.26	5.65	3.32	2.49	17.46	14.08
2000			69.19	80.62	6.33	3.04	0.84	2.92	5.29	8.89	3.09	2.00	16.36	17.74
Mean	15.34	16.49	54.79	68.79	4.82	3.06	1.06	2.70	5.06	8.35	2.88	1.93	14.20	15.71

Source: *Financial Analysts Handbook* (New York: Standard & Poor's, 2001). Reprinted with permission.

EXHIBIT 14.6

TIME-SERIES PLOT OF TOTAL ASSET TURNOVER FOR THE S&P INDUSTRIALS INDEX AND THE RDS INDUSTRY: 1977–2000

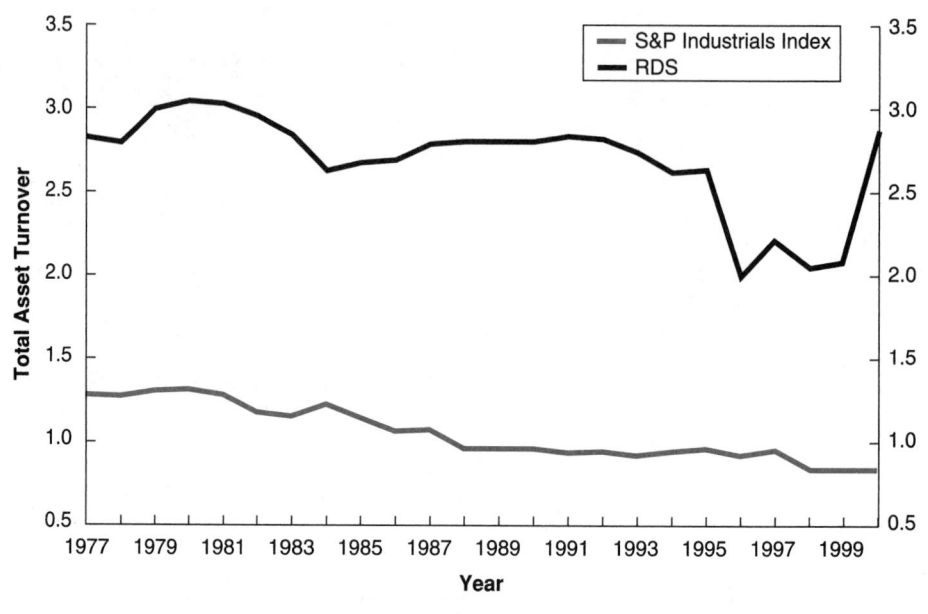

EXHIBIT 14.7

TIME-SERIES PLOT OF FINANCIAL LEVERAGE FOR THE S&P INDUSTRIALS INDEX AND THE RDS INDUSTRY: 1977–2000

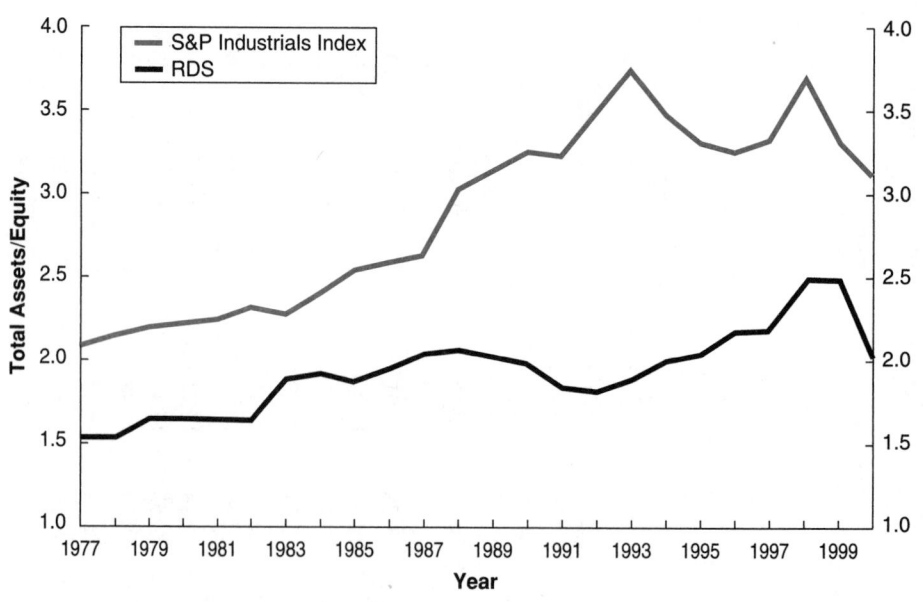

EXHIBIT 14.8   *TIME-SERIES PLOT OF THE RETURN ON EQUITY FOR THE S&P INDUSTRIALS INDEX AND THE RDS INDUSTRY: 1977–2000*

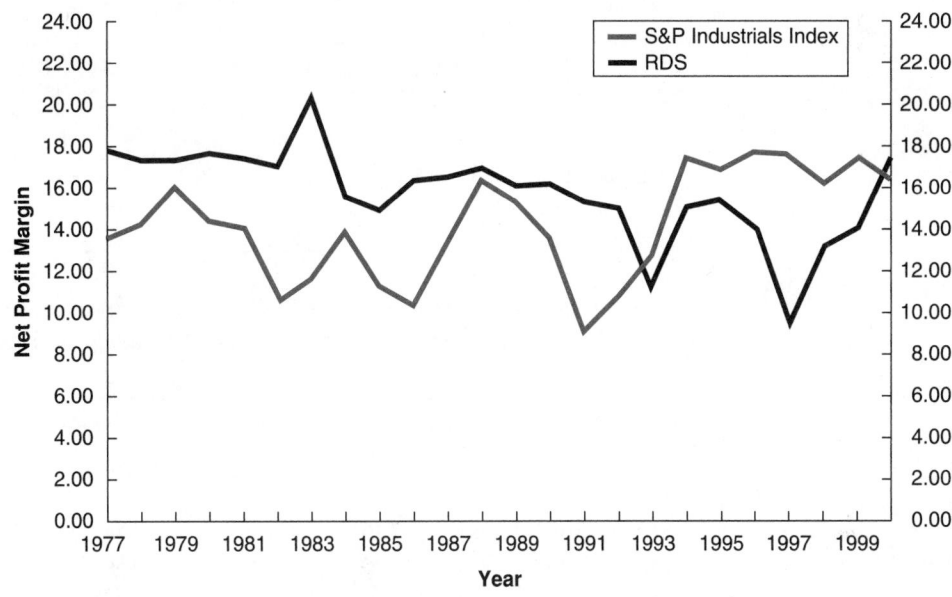

overall from 2.08 to 3.09, whereas the leverage multiplier for the RDS industry went from 1.53 to 2.00. Although these higher financial leverage multipliers imply greater financial risk for both the S&P Industrials Index series and the RDS industry, they also contribute to a higher *ROE,* all else being the same.

This brings us to the final value of *ROE,* which is the product of the three ratios (profit margin, total asset turnover, and financial leverage), or the product of return on total asset and the financial leverage multiplier. The data in Exhibit 14.5 and the plot in Exhibit 14.8 indicate that the *ROE* for the RDS industry was generally higher than the market except for the period 1993–1999. The average annual *ROE* was 15.71 percent for the RDS industry versus 14.20 percent for the S&P Industrials Index series. These average percentages are quite consistent with what would be derived from multiplying the averages of the components from Exhibit 14.5 as follows:

ROE ESTIMATE BASED ON TOTAL PERIOD AVERAGES (1977–2000)

	PROFIT MARGIN		TOTAL ASSET TURNOVER		TOTAL ASSETS/ EQUITY		ROE
S&P Industrials Index	4.82	×	1.06	×	2.88	=	14.71
RDS Industry	3.06	×	2.70	×	1.93	=	15.95

Although examining the historical trends and the averages for each of the components is important, you should not forget that expectations of *future* performance will determine the *ROE* value for the industry. In the current case, this analysis of expectations is very important because of the change in relative *ROE* during the period 1993–1999. As an analyst, it is necessary to determine whether the change during this period is a permanent change in the relative performance of this industry versus the market. In this case, you should be very concerned because of the inferior performance of the RDS industry during 1993–1999. Specifically, if you use the results for the recent five-year period (1996–2000), the *ROE* results are:

	PROFIT MARGIN		TOTAL ASSET TURNOVER		TOTAL ASSETS/ EQUITY		ROE
ROE ESTIMATE BASED ON RECENT FIVE-YEAR AVERAGES (1996–2000)							
S&P Industrials Index	5.84	×	0.88	×	3.34	=	17.16
RDS Industry	2.70	×	2.26	×	2.27	=	13.85

Notably, using the recent results, the *ROE* results are reversed. Combining these recent *ROE* results with alternative retention rates provides interesting growth estimates:

	RECENT* ROE	HISTORICAL** RR	ESTIMATED g	RECENT* ROE	RECENT* RR	ESTIMATED g
GROWTH ESTIMATES BASED ON RECENT *ROE* WITH HISTORICAL AND RECENT RETENTION RATES						
S&P Industrials Index	17.16	.55	9.44	17.16	.64	10.98
RDS Industry	13.85	.69	9.56	13.85	.72	9.97

*Recent five-year average.
**Total period average.

The point is, using full-period retention results indicates almost equal expected *g*. Alternatively, using the retention rates for the recent five-year period indicates a higher *g* for the market. Given the decline in *g* for the industry when we consider the recent results, it is probably appropriate to use a growth estimate for the RDS industry that is below the recent conservative estimate— that is, 9.5 percent. Obviously, the best estimate of *g* would be based upon an *estimate* of the three components of *ROE* for the *future* five years.

Combining the Estimates At this point, we have the following estimates:

$$k = 0.085$$
$$g = 0.095$$
$$D_0 = \$4.80 \text{ (Recent 12-Month Dividends)}$$
$$D_1 = \$4.80 \times 1.095 = \$5.26 \text{ (Estimated Dividend for 2002)}$$

Because of the inequality between *k* and *g* (this *g* is above *k* and above the long-run market norm of about 7 percent and probably cannot be sustained), we need to evaluate this industry using the temporary growth company model discussed in Chapter 12. We will assume the following growth pattern:

2003–2005	0.095
2006–2007	0.090
2008–2009	0.080
2010–onward	0.070

EXHIBIT 14.9	DIVIDEND DISCOUNT CALCULATIONS

YEAR	ESTIMATED DIVIDEND	DISCOUNT FACTOR @ 8.5%	PRESENT VALUE OF DIVIDEND
2002	5.26	—	—
2003	5.76	0.9217	5.31
2004	6.31	0.8495	5.36
2005	6.91	0.7829	5.41
2006	7.53	0.7216	5.43
2007	8.21	0.6650	5.46
2008	8.86	0.6129	5.43
2009	9.57	0.5649	5.41
Cont. Value[a]	682.67	0.5649	385.64
			Total Value $423.45

[a]Constant Growth Rate = 7%

$$\text{Continuing Value: } \frac{D_1}{k-g} = \frac{\$9.57(1.07)}{0.085 - 0.070} = \frac{\$10.24}{0.015} = \$682.67$$

Using these estimates of k and this growth pattern, the computation of value for the industry using the DDM is contained in Exhibit 14.9.

These computations imply a value of $423.45 compared to a price for the industry index of about $640.00 in mid-2002. Therefore, according to this valuation model and these k and g estimates, this industry is about 50 percent overvalued at this time. As will be shown, a fairly small change in the $k - g$ spread can have a large effect on the estimated value.

If we assumed a constant growth rate of 7 percent from the beginning and a D_1 of $5.76, the value would be even lower as follows:

$$P = \frac{5.76}{(0.085 - 0.070)} = \frac{5.76}{0.015} = 384.00$$

This is clearly a low estimate of value since it assumes the base growth rate of 7 percent from the beginning. To demonstrate the effect of a change in the $k - g$ spread, if we assume a decline in this spread from 0.015 to 0.01 because of either a lower k or a higher g or some combination of the two, the value of the industry would be:

$$P = \frac{5.76}{0.010} = \$576$$

This is still below the current price of $640, but if we reduce the spread to 0.009, the value becomes $640 (5.76/0.009), which exceeds the prevailing price. The question becomes: how do you justify such a $k - g$ spread in terms of the two components? The point is, using this constant growth model, if you cannot justify a lower k than 8.50 percent or a higher long-run growth rate (g) than 7.00 percent, you would conclude that this industry is overvalued and should be underweighted in your portfolio.

EXHIBIT 14.10 ▶ COMPONENTS OF FREE CASH FLOW TO EQUITY FOR THE RETAIL DRUG STORE INDUSTRY

YEAR	NET INCOME	DEPRECIATION EXPENSE	CAPITAL EXPENDITURE	CHANGE IN WORK. CAPITAL	PRINCIPAL REPAYMENT	NEW DEBT ISSUES	TOTAL FCFE
1987	5.53	2.63	5.80	2.37	—	2.00	1.99
1988	6.30	3.09	6.72	2.50	—	0.65	0.82
1989	6.69	3.39	6.02	9.36	—	7.00	1.70
1990	7.67	4.15	7.62	2.37	—	0.83	2.66
1991	8.26	4.03	7.73	0.16	1.20	—	3.20
1992	8.96	4.39	7.19	1.96	1.03	—	3.17
1993	7.09	4.75	9.24	0.14	—	2.71	5.17
1994	10.51	5.32	11.40	2.20	—	3.93	6.62
1995	11.76	6.02	13.97	3.30	—	4.16	4.67
1996	13.92	6.07	15.00	14.33	—	20.14	10.80
1997	10.77	8.45	17.40	–5.04	3.74	0.00	3.12
1998	15.81	9.66	24.95	0.65	—	20.58	20.45
1999	19.07	10.25	26.06	–4.93	—	3.39	11.58
2000	20.94	10.80	24.24	–19.06	30.50	—	–3.94
2001E	21.10	11.15	25.00	–5.00	—	—	12.25
5-Year Growth Rate	8.60	13.10	10.80	NM	NM	NM	2.60
10-Year Growth Rate	9.80	10.50	12.40	NM	NM	NM	14.35

E = estimate.

NM = not meaningful.

Industry Valuation Using the Free Cash Flow to Equity (FCFE) Model

Similar to the presentation in Chapter 13, we initially define the FCFE series and present the series for the recent 15-year period, including an estimate for 2001 in Exhibit 14.10. Given these data, we will consider the historical growth rates for the components and for the final FCFE series as inputs to estimating future growth for the valuation models. You will recall that FCFE is defined (measured) as follows:

Net Income
   + Depreciation expense

   – Capital expenditures

   – Δ in working capital

   – Principal debt repayments

   + New debt issues

As noted, the FCFE data inputs and final annual value of FCFE for the RDS industry for the period 1987–2001 is contained in Exhibit 14.10 along with 5-year and 10-year growth rates of the components. Using this data, we derive an estimate using the FCFE model under two scenarios: (1) a constant growth rate from the present, and (2) a two-stage growth rate assumption.

The Constant Growth Rate FCFE Model   We know that the constant growth rate model requires that the growth rate (g) be lower than the required rate of return (k), which we have specified as 8.50 percent. In the current case, this is difficult because the 10-year growth rate exceeds this. Still, in order to use the model, we assume a 10 percent growth in 2002 and 7 percent long-run growth in subsequent years. The result is as follows:

$$g = 0.07 \text{ (Long-Run Growth Beginning in 2003)}$$
$$k = 0.085$$
$$\text{FCFE (2001)} = \$12.25$$
$$\text{FCFE (2002)} = \$12.25 \,(1.10) = \$13.48 = \text{FCFE}_0$$
$$V = \frac{\text{FCFE}_1}{k - g}$$
$$= \frac{13.48 \,(1.07)}{0.085 - 0.070} = \frac{14.42}{0.015}$$
$$= 961$$

This $961 value exceeds the industry price of about $640 that prevailed in mid-2002. This implies that the industry is undervalued and should be overweighted in the portfolio.

The Two-Stage Growth FCFE Model As before, we assume a period of above-average growth for several years followed by a second period of constant growth at 7 percent. The period of above-average growth will be as follows based upon the 10 percent growth rate of FCFE experienced during the recent 10-year period.

2002	10%
2003	10%
2004	9%
2005	9%
2006	8%
2007	8%
2008–onward	7%

Assuming a k of 8.5 percent and an FCFE of $12.25 in 2001 and $13.48 in 2002, the value for the industry is as shown in Exhibit 14.11. These results are very encouraging for the industry because the computed value of $1,043 is substantially above the recent market price of about $640. This apparent undervaluation would indicate that the industry should be overweighted in the portfolio.

Notably, the alternative present value of cash flow models have generated a fairly wide range of intrinsic values as follows:

MODEL	COMPUTED VALUE
Constant growth DDM	$384
Two-stage growth DDM	$423
Constant growth FCFE	$961
Two-stage growth FCFE	$1,043

Because of this wide range of estimated values whereby two indicate overvaluation and two indicate undervaluation, it is clear that a critical variable is the $k - g$ spread. Specifically, the spread needs to be smaller for the DDM and could be larger for the FCFE models.

EXHIBIT 14.11   *COMPUTATION OF RDS INDUSTRY VALUE USING THE FCFE MODEL AND TWO-STAGE GROWTH*

YEAR	FCFE	DISCOUNT FACTOR @ 0.085	PRESENT VALUE
2003	14.83	0.9217	13.67
2004	16.16	0.8495	13.73
2005	17.62	0.7829	13.79
2006	19.03	0.7216	13.73
2007	20.55	0.6650	13.67
Cont. Value[a]	1,466.00	0.6650	974.89
		Total Present Value	$1,043.48

$$^{a}\ \frac{20.55(1.07)}{0.085-0.070} = \frac{21.99}{0.085-0.070} = 1,466$$

INDUSTRY ANALYSIS USING THE RELATIVE VALUATION APPROACH

This section contains a discussion and demonstration of the relative valuation ratio techniques: (1) price/earnings ratios (*P/E*), (2) the price to book value ratios (*P/BV*); (3) the price to cash flow ratios (*P/CF*), and (4) the price to sales ratios (*P/S*). Again, we will begin with the detailed demonstration of the *P/E* ratio approach, which provides a specific valuation and an estimated rate of return for the industry based upon its intrinsic value that equals an estimate of future earnings per share and an industry multiple.

The analysis of the other relative valuation ratios is also more meaningful because we can compare the industry valuation ratios to the market valuation ratios while considering what factors affect the specific valuation ratios.

The Earnings Multiple Technique   You will recall that the earnings multiple technique is a two-step process that involves (1) a detailed estimation of future earnings per share, and (2) an estimate of an appropriate earnings multiplier (*P/E* ratio) based upon a consideration of *P/E* determinants derived from the DDM.

Estimating Earnings per Share   To estimate earnings per share, you must start by estimating sales per share. The first part of this section describes three techniques that provide help and insights for the sales estimate. Next, we derive an estimate of earnings per share, which implies a net profit margin for the industry. As in Chapter 13 where we estimated earnings per share for a stock market series, we begin with the operating profit margin, which leads to an estimate of operating profits. Then we subtract estimates of depreciation expense and interest expense and apply a tax rate to arrive at an estimate of earnings per share.

Forecasting Sales per Share   Assuming an analyst has completed the macroanalysis of the industry that included (1) considering how the industry is impacted by the business cycle, (2) what structural changes have occurred within the industry, and (3) where the industry is in its life cycle, the analyst would have a strong start regarding a sales estimate for the industry. At this point, we would make suggestions regarding two minor estimation techniques (time series and input-output analysis) and one major technique that should be considered for almost all industries (a specific analysis of the industry-economy relationship).

Time-Series Analysis   A simple time-series plot of the sales for an industry versus time can be very informative regarding the pattern and the rate of growth for industry sales. Analyzing this series along with designations of business cycle periods (expansions and recessions) and notations regarding major events will provide further insights. Finally, for many industries, it is possible to extrapolate the time series to derive an estimate of sales. For industries that have experienced consistent growth, this can be a very useful estimate, especially if it is a new industry that has not developed a history with the economy. If the sales growth has been at a constant rate, you should do the time-series plot on semi-log paper where the constant growth shows as a straight line.

Input-Output Analysis   Input-output analysis is another way to gain insights regarding the outlook for an industry by separating industries that supply the input for a specific industry from those that get its output. In other words, we want to identify an industry's suppliers and customers. This will help us identify (1) the future demand from customers and (2) the ability of suppliers to provide the goods and services required by the industry. The goal is to determine the long-run sales outlook for the industry's suppliers and its major customers. To extend this analysis to global industries, we must include worldwide suppliers and customers.

Industry-Economy Relationships   The most rigorous and useful analysis involves comparing sales for an industry with one or several aggregate economic series that are related to the goods and services produced by the industry. The specific question is, What economic variables influence the demand for this industry? Notably, you should be thinking of numerous factors that will have an impact on industry sales, *how* these economic variables will impact demand, and how the factors might interact. In the following example, we will demonstrate this industry-economy technique for the retail drugstore industry (RDS).

Demonstrating a Sales Forecast   The retail drugstore (RDS) industry includes retailers of basic necessities, including pharmaceuticals and medical supplies and many nonmedical products, such as cosmetics, snacks, pop, and liquor. Therefore, we want a series that (1) reflects broad consumption expenditures and (2) gives weight to the impact of medical expenditures. The economic series we consider are personal consumption expenditures (PCE) and PCE medical care. Exhibit 14.12 contains the aggregate and per-capita values for the two series.

A casual analysis of these time series indicates that although personal consumption expenditures (PCE) have experienced reasonably steady growth of about 7.5 percent a year during this period, PCE medical care has grown at a faster rate of almost 10 percent. As a result, as shown in the exhibit's last column, medical care expenditures as a percentage of all PCE have grown from 9.6 percent in 1977 to almost 15 percent in 2000. Still, you would be concerned that this percent has declined steadily since 1995. Obviously, as an analyst, you would be pleased because it appears that retail drugstore sales had benefited from this growth in medical expenditures, as shown by the annual growth of drugstore sales of nearly 13 percent.

The scatter plot in Exhibit 14.13 indicates a strong linear relationship between retail drugstore sales per share and PCE medical care prior to the decline in RDS sales in 2000. Although not shown, there also is a good relationship with PCE. Therefore, if you can accurately estimate changes in these economic series, you should normally be able to derive a good estimate of expected sales for the RDS industry.

As the industry being analyzed becomes more specialized, you need a more individualized economic series that reflects the demand for the industry's product. The selection of an appropriate economic series is one place where an analyst can demonstrate knowledge and innovation. There also can be instances where industry sales are dependent on several components of the economy, in which case you should probably consider a multivariate model that would include two or more economic series. For example, if you were dealing with the tire industry, you might

| EXHIBIT 14.12 | | *S&P RETAIL DRUGSTORE SALES AND VARIOUS ECONOMIC SERIES: 1977–2000* | | | |

| | | | | PER CAPITA | | |
YEAR	RETAIL DRUGSTORE SALES ($/SHARE)	PERSONAL CONSUMPTION EXPENDITURES ($ BILLIONS)	PCE MEDICAL CARE ($ BILLIONS)	PERSONAL CONSUMPTION EXPENDITURES (DOLLARS)	PCE MEDICAL CARE (DOLLARS)	MEDICAL CARE AS A PERCENTAGE OF PCE
1977	43.99	1,278.40	122.60	5,804.6	556.7	9.59
1978	49.87	1,430.40	140.00	6,426.3	629.0	9.79
1979	73.39	1,596.30	158.10	7,092.9	702.5	9.90
1980	84.82	1,762.90	181.20	7,741.3	795.7	10.28
1981	95.50	1,944.20	213.00	8,454.3	926.2	10.96
1982	109.22	2,079.30	239.30	8,955.2	1,030.6	11.51
1983	118.85	2,286.40	267.90	9,758.1	1,143.4	11.72
1984	135.15	2,498.40	294.60	10,570.9	1,246.5	11.79
1985	153.30	2,712.60	322.50	11,375.2	1,352.4	11.89
1986	157.74	2,895.20	346.80	12,030.7	1,441.1	11.98
1987	191.72	3,105.30	381.80	12,789.3	1,572.5	12.30
1988	217.80	3,356.60	429.90	13,699.2	1,754.5	12.81
1989	239.68	3,596.70	479.20	14,541.4	1,937.4	13.32
1990	265.77	3,831.50	540.60	15,327.7	2,162.6	14.11
1991	283.50	3,971.20	591.00	15,717.3	2,339.1	14.88
1992	309.78	4,209.70	652.60	16,482.1	2,555.1	15.50
1993	329.20	4,454.70	700.60	17,258.3	2,714.3	15.73
1994	363.71	4,716.40	737.30	18,095.7	2,828.8	15.63
1995	413.52	4,969.00	780.70	18,887.6	2,967.5	15.71
1996	434.15	5,237.50	814.40	19,726.8	3,067.4	15.55
1997	549.51	5,529.30	854.60	20,628.0	3,188.2	15.46
1998	612.86	5,850.90	898.60	21,629.2	3,321.9	15.36
1999	706.21	6,268.70	943.60	22,966.9	3,457.1	15.05
2000	687.77	6,810.80	1,005.60	24,733.1	3,651.8	14.76
Mean Annual Growth	12.70%	7.54%	9.58%	6.50%	8.52%	1.89%

Source: *Financial Analysts Handbook* (New York: Standard & Poor's, 2001); and *Economic Report of the President* (Washington, DC: U.S. Government Printing Office, 1999). Reprinted with permission.

want to consider new-car production, new-truck production, and a series that would reflect the replacement tire demand.

You also should consider *per-capita* personal consumption expenditures—medical care. Although aggregate PCE medical care increases each year, there also is an increase in the aggregate population, so the increase in the PCE medical care per capita (the average PCE medical care for each adult and child) will be less than the increase in the aggregate series. As an example, during 2000, aggregate PCE medical care increased about 6.6 percent, but per-capita PCE medical care increased only 5.6 percent. Finally, an analysis of the relationship between changes in the economic variable and changes in industry sales will indicate how the two series move

EXHIBIT 14.13   *SCATTER PLOT OF RDS SALES PER SHARE AND PCE MEDICAL CARE: 1977–2000*

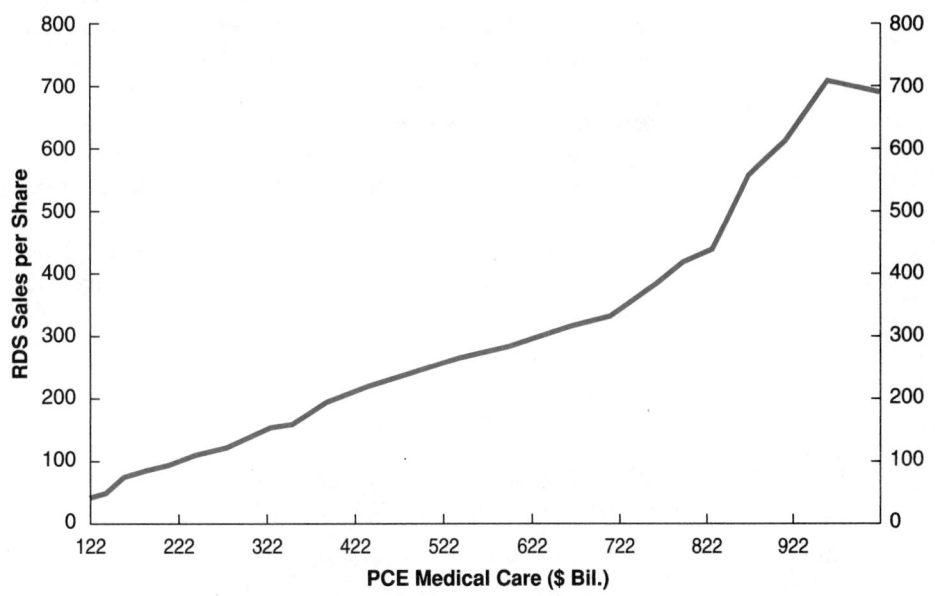

Source: International Monetary Fund, *International Financial Statistics.*

together and highlight any changes in the relationship. Using annual percentage changes provides the following regression model:

➤ 14.4   % Δ Industry Sales = α_i + β_i (% Δ in Economic Series)

The size of the β_i coefficient should indicate how closely the two series move together. Assuming the intercept (α_i) is close to zero, a slope (β_i) value of 1.00 would indicate relatively equal percentages of change (e.g., this would indicate that a 10 percent increase in PCE typically is associated with a 10 percent increase in industry sales). A β_i of less than unity would imply that industry sales are not as volatile annually as the economy is. This analysis and the levels relationship reflected in Exhibit 14.13 would help you find an economic series that closely reflects the demand for the industry's products; it also would indicate the form of the relationship.

As indicated in this analysis, the best relationship was between retail drugstore sales and PCE medical care. The specific regression result was

% Δ Retail Drugstore Sales = 5.40 + 0.55 (% Δ PCE Medical Care)

(*t* values)   (1.85) (1.98)

R^2 = 0.22

The specific sales estimate procedure would begin with an estimate of aggregate PCE for the coming year. Given the importance of the PCE series, it should be relatively easy to find one or several estimates. The next step would be to estimate a change in the proportion of PCE spent on medical care. As noted, this proportion has grown from 9.6 percent to 14.76 percent, but it has declined since 1995. Once you estimate this percentage spent on medical care, you apply it to the PCE estimate to arrive at an estimate of the percentage change in PCE medical care. Finally, you would use this PCE medical care estimate in a regression equation to derive a sales estimate for the industry. This procedure will be demonstrated in a subsequent section.

Forecasting Earnings per Share After the sales forecast, it is necessary to estimate the industry's profitability based on an analysis of the industry income statement. An analyst should also benefit from the prior macroanalysis that considered where the industry is in its life cycle, which impacts its profitability. How does this industry relate to the business cycle and what does this imply regarding profit margins at this point in the cycle? Most important, what did you conclude regarding the competitive environment in the industry and what does this mean for pricing and profitability of sales?

EXHIBIT 14.14 *PROFIT MARGINS AND COMPONENT EXPENSES FOR THE S&P INDUSTRIALS INDEX AND THE RDS INDUSTRY INDEX: 1977–2000*

YEAR	EBITDA ($) S&P IND	RDS	EBITDA MARGIN (%) S&P IND	RDS	DEPRECIATION EXPENSE ($) S&P IND	RDS	INTEREST EXPENSE ($) S&P IND	RDS	TAX RATE (%) S&P IND	RDS	NET PROFIT MARGIN (%) S&P IND	RDS
1977	32.20	3.94	14.36	8.96	8.53	0.41	3.22	0.13	48.90	48.60	5.15	4.07
1978	36.19	4.38	14.40	8.78	9.64	0.49	3.81	0.13	49.00	47.90	5.19	4.03
1979	42.01	5.31	14.37	7.40	10.82	0.71	4.58	0.23	46.00	45.70	5.57	3.47
1980	43.08	6.00	13.16	7.07	12.37	0.83	5.95	0.28	45.60	44.70	4.92	3.47
1981	44.50	6.85	12.92	7.17	13.82	1.02	7.49	0.39	43.30	44.20	4.86	3.45
1982	42.67	7.97	12.78	7.30	15.30	1.21	8.23	0.41	45.00	44.60	3.95	3.44
1983	45.57	9.48	13.64	7.98	15.67	1.40	7.62	0.43	44.60	45.00	4.42	3.79
1984	51.50	9.72	13.56	7.19	16.31	1.71	8.54	0.78	42.70	45.10	4.77	3.04
1985	53.23	10.73	13.36	7.00	18.19	2.02	9.24	0.73	46.70	45.90	3.84	2.96
1986	51.02	11.62	13.16	7.37	19.41	2.08	9.75	0.77	42.70	45.10	3.75	3.11
1987	58.89	13.57	13.68	7.08	20.21	2.63	10.14	1.17	40.50	43.90	4.77	2.88
1988	74.31	14.60	15.26	6.70	23.59	3.09	14.84	1.42	35.30	38.60	5.51	2.90
1989	79.52	16.08	14.69	6.71	24.21	3.39	18.79	1.65	37.00	37.80	5.01	2.79
1990	82.47	17.84	13.87	6.71	26.31	4.15	20.17	1.63	39.60	38.30	4.26	2.89
1991	75.10	18.49	12.80	6.52	27.50	4.03	18.74	1.32	41.19	36.70	2.97	2.91
1992	78.17	19.68	13.00	6.35	29.48	4.39	16.20	1.08	37.91	36.95	3.27	2.89
1993	82.16	20.56	13.61	6.25	28.72	4.75	14.66	0.80	37.27	39.29	3.73	2.15
1994	91.28	23.36	14.58	6.42	29.58	5.32	12.79	1.01	36.12	38.29	5.24	2.89
1995	104.67	26.93	15.47	6.51	33.06	6.02	14.21	1.57	36.62	38.62	5.24	2.84
1996	112.69	28.34	16.05	6.53	36.71	6.07	14.32	2.05	36.47	37.19	5.86	3.21
1997	123.15	38.81	16.40	7.06	39.77	8.45	14.84	3.08	35.62	45.11	5.61	1.96
1998	129.75	42.90	17.17	7.00	32.89	9.66	14.56	3.62	34.93	38.15	5.14	2.58
1999	135.72	48.56	16.71	6.88	41.70	10.25	15.50	3.55	35.01	38.92	6.27	2.70
2000	150.17	42.69	17.59	6.21	43.50	10.80	16.39	1.25	37.41	39.25	6.33	3.04

Source: *Financial Analysts Handbook* (New York: Standard & Poor's, 2001). Reprinted with permission.

Industry Profit Margin Forecast   Similar to the aggregate market, the net profit margin is the most volatile and the hardest margin to estimate directly. Alternatively, it is suggested that you begin with the operating profit margin (EBITDA/Sales) and then estimate depreciation expense, interest expense, and the tax rate.

The Industry's Operating Profit Margin   Recall that in the market analysis, we analyzed the factors that should influence the economy's operating profit margin, including capacity utilization, unit labor cost, inflation, and net exports. The most important variables were capacity utilization and unit labor cost. We cannot do such an analysis for most industries because the relevant variables typically are not available for individual industries. As an alternative, we can assume that movements in these industry profit margin variables are related to movements in similar economic variables. For example, when an increase in capacity utilization for the aggregate economy exists, there is probably a comparable increase in utilization for the auto industry or the chemical industry. The same could be true for unit labor cost and exports. If there is a stable relationship between these variables for the industry and the economy, you would expect a relationship to exist between the profit margins for the industry and the economy. Although it is not necessary that the relationship be completely linear, it is important for the relationship (whatever it is) to be generally stable.

The operating profit margin (OPM) for the S&P Industrials Index and the retail drugstore (RDS) index is presented in Exhibit 14.14. The time-series plot in Exhibit 14.15 indicates that the S&P Industrials Index *OPM* experienced a decline during the 1980s and early 1990s but increased steadily during the rest of the 1990s and ended the period with a record margin of over 17.50 percent. In contrast, the RDS *OPM* experienced a fairly steady decline with the exception of a small increase in 1997. The analysis of the relationship between the *OPM* for the market and industry using regression analysis was not useful, so it is not discussed. These results indicate that the best estimate for the RDS industry can be derived from the *OPM* time-series plot using

EXHIBIT 14.15 ▶ *TIME-SERIES PLOT OF OPERATING PROFIT MARGINS FOR THE S&P INDUSTRIALS INDEX AND THE RDS INDUSTRY: 1977–2000*

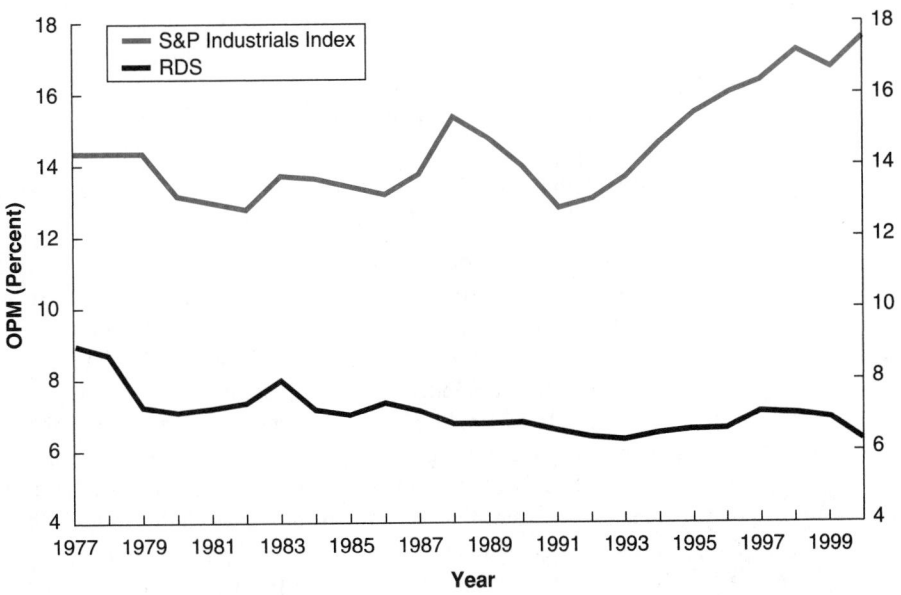

EXHIBIT 14.16   *TIME-SERIES PLOT OF DEPRECIATION FOR THE S&P INDUSTRIALS INDEX AND THE RDS INDUSTRY: 1977–2000*

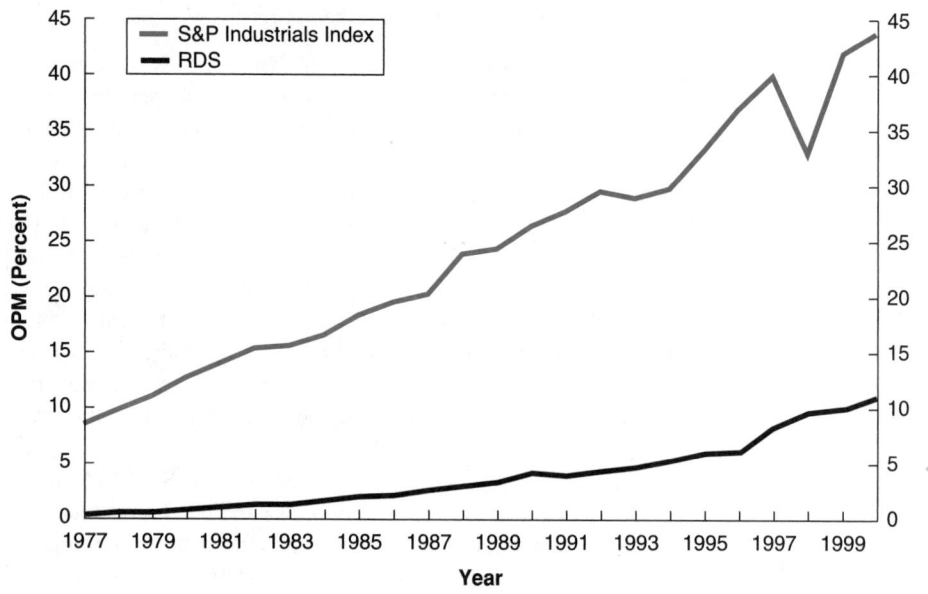

what we know about the changing competitive environment and profit trends in the retail drugstore business. It is a matter of judgment for each specific industry whether you use regression analysis and/or the time-series analysis. The point is, any such mathematical analysis should be considered a supplement to the economic analysis of the competitive environment for the industry.

Either regression analysis or time-series techniques can be useful tools, but *neither technique should be applied mechanically.* You should be aware of any unique factors affecting the specific industry, such as price wars, contract negotiations, building plans, or foreign competition. An analysis of these unique events is critical when estimating the final gross profit margin or when estimating a range of industry profit margins (optimistic, pessimistic, most likely).

Beyond this discussion, which is primarily concerned with an estimate of the near-term *OPM,* it also is important to consider the long-term profitability of the industry based on the competitive structure of the industry as discussed previously.

Industry Depreciation   The next step is estimating industry depreciation, which typically is easier because the series generally is increasing; the only question is by how much. As shown in Exhibit 14.14, except for 1993 and 1998, the depreciation series for RDS increased every year since 1977. The time-series plots in Exhibit 14.16 relate depreciation for the S&P Industrials Index and the RDS industry. To estimate depreciation expense, one can consider the two techniques used in the market analysis chapter (i.e., the time-series analysis and the specific estimate technique using the depreciation expense/*PPE* ratio) or an industry-market relationship.

An analysis of the graph, as well as regression analysis of levels and annual percentage changes, indicates that the relationship between this industry and the market is not good enough to use for an estimate. Alternatively, the depreciation expense series has been increasing at a fairly steady rate between 8 and 10 percent a year, so a time-series estimate could provide a viable estimate.

EXHIBIT 14.17 ▶ COMPONENTS FOR DERIVING SPECIFIC ESTIMATES FOR DEPRECIATION EXPENSE AND INTEREST EXPENSE FOR THE RDS INDUSTRY

YEAR	NET SALES	NET PPE	PPE TURNOVER	DEPREC. EXP.	DEPREC. EXP. PPE	TOTAL ASSETS	T. ASSET TURNOVER	L-T DEBT	L-T DEBT T. ASSETS	INT. EXP.	INT. EXP. L-T. DEBT
1977	43.99	3.32	13.25	0.41	0.12	15.51	2.84	1.25	0.08	0.13	0.10
1978	49.87	4.00	12.47	0.49	0.12	17.73	2.81	1.29	0.07	0.13	0.10
1979	73.39	6.18	11.88	0.71	0.11	24.49	3.00	2.69	0.11	0.23	0.09
1980	84.82	7.84	10.82	0.83	0.11	27.89	3.04	2.84	0.10	0.28	0.10
1981	95.50	9.68	9.87	1.02	0.11	31.53	3.03	2.48	0.08	0.39	0.16
1982	109.22	11.27	9.69	1.21	0.11	36.76	2.97	2.04	0.06	0.41	0.20
1983	118.85	12.90	9.21	1.40	0.11	41.61	2.86	1.82	0.04	0.43	0.24
1984	135.15	15.66	8.63	0.71	0.05	50.92	2.65	4.05	0.08	0.78	0.19
1985	153.30	18.56	8.26	2.02	0.11	56.74	2.70	8.25	0.15	1.14	0.14
1986	157.74	22.81	6.92	2.08	0.09	58.12	2.71	7.02	0.12	0.77	0.11
1987	191.72	26.45	7.25	2.63	0.10	68.54	2.80	8.76	0.13	1.17	0.13
1988	217.80	28.31	7.69	3.09	0.11	77.30	2.82	9.41	0.12	1.42	0.15
1989	239.68	38.80	7.78	3.39	0.11	85.50	2.80	16.41	0.19	1.65	0.10
1990	265.77	34.66	7.67	4.15	0.12	94.39	2.82	17.24	0.18	1.63	0.09
1991	283.50	37.55	7.55	4.03	0.11	99.34	2.85	12.84	0.13	1.32	0.10
1992	309.78	40.23	7.70	4.39	0.11	109.39	2.83	11.81	0.11	1.08	0.09
1993	329.20	43.63	7.55	4.75	0.11	118.19	2.79	14.52	0.12	0.80	0.06
1994	363.71	50.39	7.22	5.32	0.11	138.33	2.63	18.45	0.13	1.01	0.05
1995	413.52	58.69	7.05	6.02	0.10	155.38	2.66	22.61	0.15	1.57	0.07
1996	434.15	68.31	6.36	6.07	0.09	215.05	2.02	42.75	0.20	2.05	0.05
1997	549.51	73.01	7.53	8.45	0.12	246.75	2.23	39.01	0.16	3.08	0.08
1998	612.86	88.83	6.90	9.66	0.11	300.00	2.04	46.89	0.16	3.62	0.08
1999	706.21	97.40	7.25	10.25	0.11	337.42	2.09	50.35	0.15	3.55	0.07
2000	687.77	74.97	9.17	10.80	0.10	235.48	2.92	9.68	0.04	1.25	0.13

Source: *Financial Analysts Handbook* (New York: Standard & Poor's, 2001). Reprinted with permission.

Exhibit 14.17 contains the components needed to derive a specific depreciation expense estimate similar to what we did for the S&P Industrials Index using the following four steps:[9]

1. Calculate the annual *PPE* turnover for the RDS industry.
2. Based upon your sales estimate and your expected *PPE* turnover ratio, estimate the expected *PPE* for next year.
3. Calculate the annual depreciation expense as a percent of *PPE* for the RDS industry.
4. Estimate depreciation expense as follows:

$$(\text{Estimated } PPE) \times \text{Estimated}\left(\frac{\text{Depreciation Expense}}{PPE}\right)\text{Ratio}$$

---

[9]As noted previously, it is apparent that there has been an adjustment to this industry index in terms of makeup that has changed the data substantially in 2000. Therefore, the estimate will not use the data for this latest year.

For example, the *PPE* turnover had tended to decline during the recent period. A conservative estimate would be a *PPE* turnover of 7.40. This turnover value combined with a sales estimate for 2002 of $870 implies a *PPE* estimate of $117.57. In turn, the depreciation expense/*PPE* ratio was in the 10 percent range before 1996. Subsequently, it has been between 10 and 12 percent. Using the recent five-year average indicates an estimate of depreciation expense/*PPE* of about 10.60 percent. Applying this estimated percent to the *PPE* estimate of $117.57 implies a depreciation expense estimate of $12.46 ($117.57 × 0.1060).

Subtracting an estimate of depreciation expense from the operating profit figure indicates the industry's net income before interest and taxes (EBIT).

Industry Interest Expense   An industry's interest expense will be a function of its financial leverage and interest rates. As shown in Exhibit 14.18, interest expense for the RDS industry always has been relatively low when compared to the S&P Industrials Index and did not increase at the same rate during the 1980s. Therefore, looking for a relationship between the two interest expense series would not be fruitful. Your estimate for the future should be based on two separate estimates: (1) changes in the amount of debt outstanding for this industry during the year, and (2) an estimate of the level of interest rates (will they increase or decline?).

Estimating Interest Expense   The historical data needed to derive a specific estimate of interest expense are also in Exhibit 14.17. Recall the following steps used in Chapter 13:

1. Calculate the annual total asset turnover *(TAT)* for the RDS industry.
2. Use your 2002 sales estimate and an estimate of *TAT* to estimate total assets next year.
3. Calculate the annual long-term (interest-bearing) debt as a percentage of total assets for the RDS industry.
4. Use your estimate of total assets and the ratio of long-term debt as a percentage of total assets to estimate long-term debt for the next year.

EXHIBIT 14.18   *TIME-SERIES PLOT OF INTEREST EXPENSE FOR THE S&P INDUSTRIALS INDEX AND THE RDS INDUSTRY: 1977–2000*

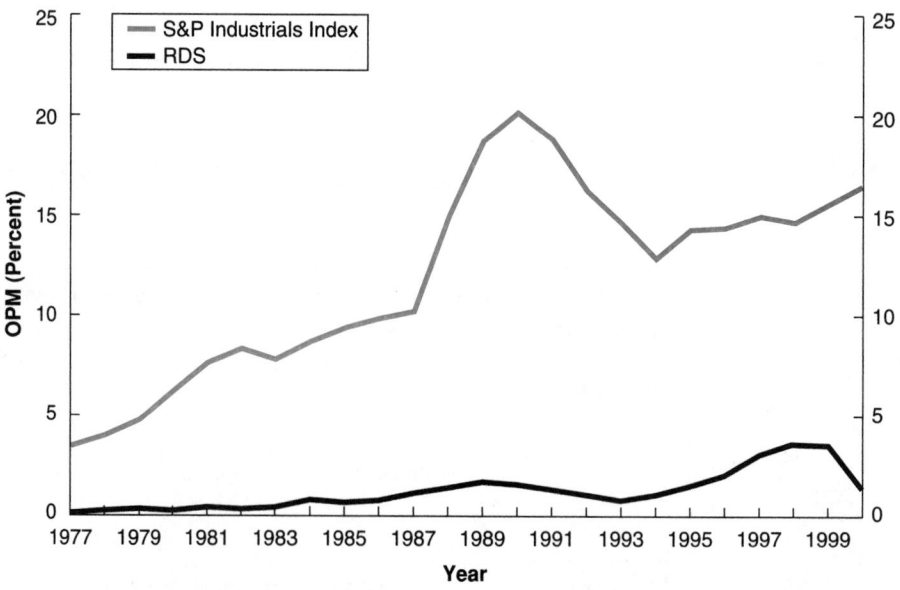

5. Calculate the annual interest cost as a percentage of long-term debt and analyze the trend of this series.
6. Estimate next year's interest cost of debt for this industry based upon your prior estimate of market yields.
7. Estimate interest expense based on the following:

(Estimated Interest Cost of Debt) × (Estimated Long-Term Debt)

For example, our sales estimate of $870 and a *TAT* that has averaged about 2.15 over the most recent years imply total assets of $405 next year. Long-term, interest-bearing debt has averaged about 15 percent of total assets for the RDS industry, which implies long-term debt next year of about $61 ($405 × 0.15). In turn, interest expense as a percentage of long-term debt during the recent period has averaged about 6.85 percent for this industry. Based upon the expectation of a small increase in market interest rates during 2002, we would estimate this interest rate to be 7.00 percent in 2002. This interest rate estimate combined with our long-term debt estimate of $61 implies interest expense of $4.27 (0.07 × $61).

Industry Tax Rate As you might expect, tax rates differ between industries. An extreme example would be the oil industry where heavy depletion allowances cause lower taxes. In some instances, however, you can assume that tax law changes have similar impacts on all industries. To see if this is valid, you need to examine the relationship of tax rates over time for your industry and the aggregate market to determine if you can use regression analysis in your estimation process. Alternatively, a time-series plot could provide a useful estimate.

As shown in Exhibit 14.19, except for 1997, the RDS tax rate has moved with the economy's tax rate. Therefore, the time-series plot in this figure is fairly informative, although you still need to consider pending national legislation and unique industry tax factors. Once you have

EXHIBIT 14.19 *TIME-SERIES PLOT OF THE TAX RATES FOR THE S&P INDUSTRIALS INDEX AND THE RDS INDUSTRY: 1977–2000*

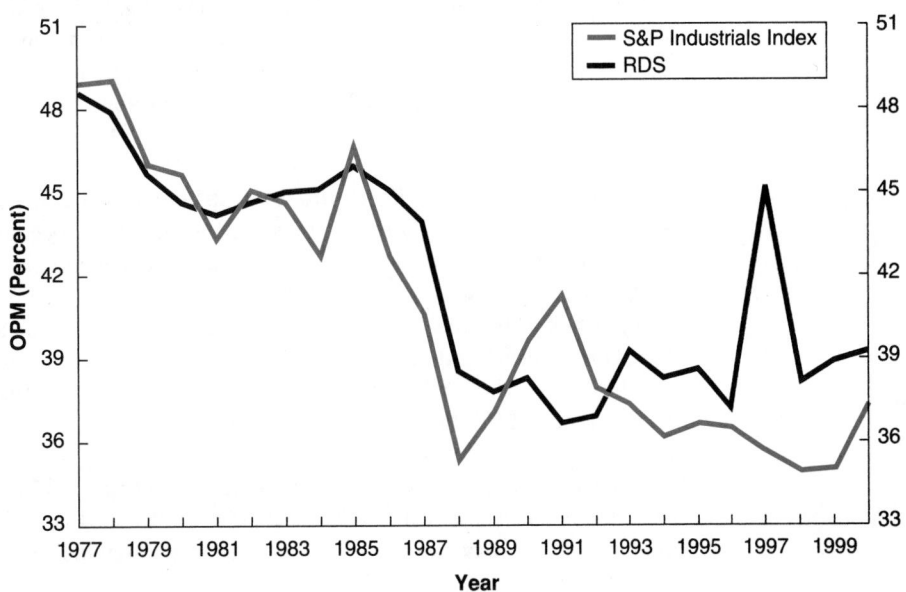

EXHIBIT 14.20   *TIME-SERIES PLOT OF NET PROFIT MARGIN FOR THE S&P INDUSTRIALS INDEX AND THE RDS INDUSTRY: 1977–2000*

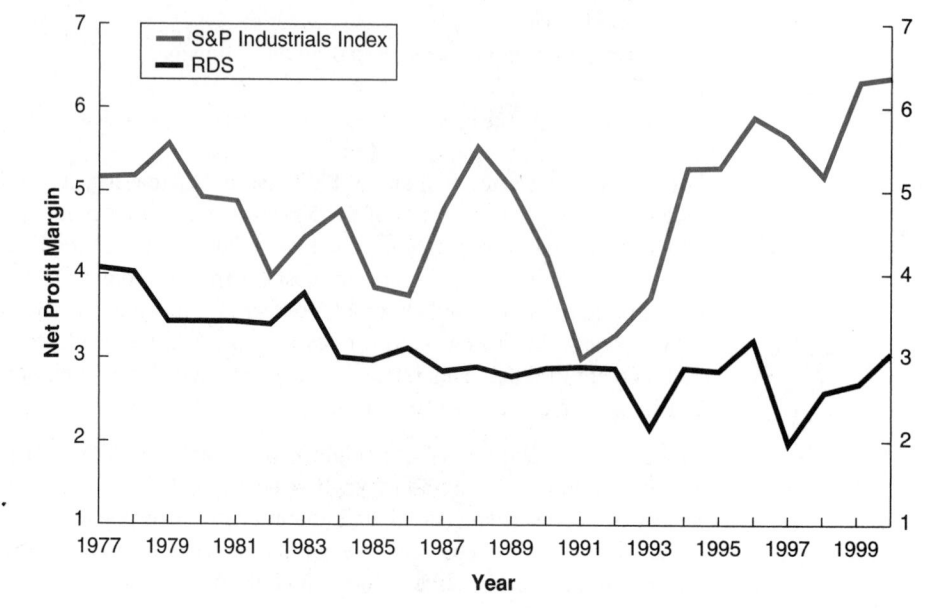

estimated the tax rate, you multiply the *EBT* per share value by (1 – tax rate) to get your estimate of earnings per share *(EPS).*

In addition to estimating *EPS,* you also should derive an estimate of the industry's net profit margin as a check on your *EPS* estimate. A time-series plot of the net profit margin series for the industry and the S&P Industrials Index is contained in Exhibit 14.20. Two important characteristics are notable. First, the S&P Industrials Index net profit margin series is much more volatile than that for RDS. Second, although both profit margin series showed an overall decline through 1993, the S&P Industrials Index has recovered since 1993 to a margin of over 6 percent, while the RDS margin started at about 4 percent and generally declined to about 3 percent.

An Industry Earnings Estimate Example   Now that we have described how to estimate each variable in the equation, to help you understand the procedure, the following is an estimate of earnings per share for the RDS industry using the economic forecasts from Chapter 13 and the relationship between the RDS industry and the market. Our results are not as exact as those of a practicing analyst who would use this example as an *initial* estimate that would be modified based on his or her industry knowledge, current events, and expectations of unique factors.

The regressions and the plots in Exhibit 14.13 indicated that the best relationship was between RDS sales and PCE medical care. The outlook for PCE is for an increase of 5.0 percent in 2001 (to about $7,100 billion) and a 3.6 percent increase in 2002 (to $7,355 billion). It is further estimated that medical care expenditures will be 14.8 percent of PCE in 2001 and 2002. This implies that PCE medical care will be about $1,050 billion in 2001 and $1,088 billion in 2002 (a 3.6 percent increase). Using these results in the earlier equation indicates that RDS sales in 2002 should be about $870.

The OPM for a retail drugstore was 6.88 percent in 1999. Although the OPM for the S&P Industrials Index declined during 2000, RDS margins were expected to experience stability at about 6.55. The aggregate OPM was expected to experience a small rebound during 2002. Based on the time-series plot in Exhibit 14.15, this would indicate that RDS margins should also increase to about 6.60 percent, which implies an operating profit share for the RDS industry of $57.42 (0.066 × $870).

Earlier we derived a specific estimate for industry depreciation expense of $12.46 for 2002. Therefore, earnings before interest and taxes would be $44.96 ($57.42 – $12.46).

Given the decline in yields during 2001 and the small increase in rates envisioned during 2002, our prior specific estimate of interest expense was $4.27 in 2002. Thus, *EBT* would be $40.69 ($44.96 – 4.27).

The tax rate for the RDS industry has been consistently higher than the aggregate during the last seven years. The aggregate tax rate was expected to be relatively stable in 2001 and 2002. Therefore, a rate of about 39 percent seems appropriate for the RDS industry. This implies taxes of 15.87 (40.69 × 0.39) and net income (earnings per share) of 24.82 (40.69 – 15.87). This indicates a net profit margin for the RDS industry of 2.83 percent (24.82/870.00), which is slightly below the recent experience.

Given an estimate of the industry's net income per share (for simplicity, we will round off the *EPS* estimate to $25 per share), your next step is to estimate the earnings multiplier for this industry. Together, the earnings per share and the earnings multiplier provide an estimate of the intrinsic value for the industry index. Given this intrinsic value and an estimate of dividends per share during the holding period, you can compute an estimated rate of return from investing in this industry.

Estimating an Industry Earnings Multiplier This section discusses how to estimate an industry earnings multiplier using two alternative techniques: macroanalysis and microanalysis. In macroanalysis, you examine the relationship between the multiplier for the industry and the market. In microanalysis, you estimate the industry earnings multiplier by examining the specific variables that influence it: (1) the dividend-payout ratio, (2) the required rate of return for the industry *(k),* and (3) the expected growth rate of earnings and dividends for the industry *(g).*

Macroanalysis of an Industry Multiplier

Why a Relationship? Given that this subsection considers the relationship between the earnings multiplier (*P/E* ratio) for an industry to the *P/E* for the aggregate market, a natural question is, Why do we *expect* a relationship? The reasons are based on the variables that influence the multiplier—the required rate of return, the expected growth rate of earnings and dividends, and the dividend-payout ratio. Specifically, as you know, the required rate of return *(k)* is a function of the nominal risk-free rate plus a risk premium. The fact is, the nominal risk-free rate is the same for all investment assets and is the major reason for changes in *k.* Also, though the level of the risk premium may differ between the market and an industry, any *changes* in the risk premium are probably related.

Although the rate of growth *(g)* for an industry may differ from that of the market, and this difference in *g* is a major reason for the difference in the level of the *P/E* ratio, *changes* in the growth expectations for many industries will be related to changes in *g* for the market and for other industries because they are driven by macroeconomic growth factors that affect the overall market and most industries. Therefore, since the major factor causing a change in the *P/E* ratio for the aggregate market and alternative industries is a change in the *k − g* spread and these two variables have several components that move together, it is not unreasonable to look for an overall (macro) relationship between changes in an industry's *P/E* and the market *P/E* ratio.

EXHIBIT 14.21 TIME-SERIES PLOT OF ANNUAL AVERAGE FUTURE EARNINGS MULTIPLIERS FOR THE S&P INDUSTRIALS INDEX AND THE RDS INDUSTRY: 1977–1999

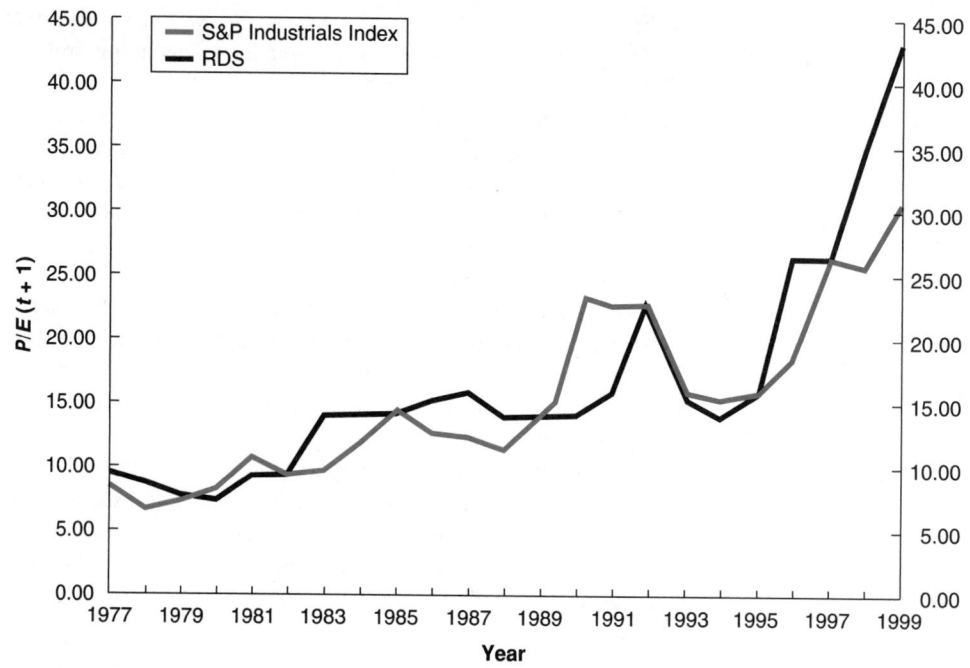

An examination of the relationship between the *P/E* ratios for 71 S&P industries and the S&P Industrials Index during four partially overlapping 21-year periods indicated a significant positive relationship between percentage changes in *P/E* ratios for most industries examined.[10] Notably, because there was a difference in the significance of the relationship between alternative industries and the market, it is necessary to evaluate the quality of the relationship between the *P/E* ratios for a specific industry and the market before using this technique.

The results in Exhibit 14.5 and Exhibit 14.21 for the RDS industry during the period 1977 to 1999 indicate a relatively close relationship between the market and the RDS industry. The *P/E* ratio for drugstores was generally above the market *P/E* ratio until 1989 when the market *P/E* increased while the *P/E* for drugstores was relatively stable. This was reversed again in 1996 when the RDS industry *P/E* ratios became larger. Notably, the industry *P/E* ratios are less volatile than the market *P/E* ratios. These results imply that the macroanalysis could be a useful input for this industry. Still, given the recent differences in *P/E* ratios a crucial question that the analyst must consider is, Why is the RDS multiplier larger and will this differential continue?

Microanalysis of an Industry Multiplier In Chapter 13, we estimated the future earnings multiplier for the stock market series in two ways. In the first, *the direction of change approach,* we estimated the changes for the three variables that determine the earnings multiplier—the dividend-payout ratio, the required rate of return, and the expected growth rate of earnings and dividends. Based on the consensus of changes, we estimated a direction of change for the multiplier from its current value. In the second approach, *the specific multiplier estimate,* we estimated

[10]Frank K. Reilly and Thomas Zeller, "An Analysis of Relative Industry Price-Earnings Ratios," *The Financial Review* (1974): 17–33.

a range of values for the three variables that determine the multiplier and derived a range of P/E ratio estimates. These two approaches provided several multiplier estimates that were used with our EPS estimate to compute a range of expected values for the market index that, in turn, provided estimated rates of return on common stocks.

Our microanalysis of the industry multiplier could use the same two approaches. Although this would certainly be reasonable, it would not take advantage of the prior work on the stock market multiplier. Because the variables that affect the stock market multiplier also determine the industry multiplier, it should be possible to compare the two sets of variables.

Therefore, in our microanalysis, we estimate the three variables that determine the industry earnings multiplier and compare them to the comparable values for the market P/E. This allows us to determine whether the industry earnings multiplier *should* be above, below, or equal to the market multiplier. Once we feel confident about this relationship, it is easier to derive a specific estimate for the industry P/E ratio. As a first step, we need to recall the long-run relationship between the industry and market P/E ratios.

Industry Multiplier versus the Market Multiplier   Recall from Exhibit 14.5 and Exhibit 14.21 that the P/E ratios for the RDS industry were larger than the P/E ratios for the stock market prior to 1989, generally lower than the market from 1989–1995, and then larger than the market from 1996–1999. The obvious question is: Why do the P/E ratios for this industry and the stock market differ over time? Specifically, why has the historical relationship that has prevailed between the P/E ratios for this industry and the stock market changed? A comparative analysis of the factors that determine the earnings multiplier should help us answer these questions.

Comparing Dividend-Payout Ratios   We can discuss the dividend-payout ratio directly or in terms of the retention rate because the retention rate is one minus the dividend-payout ratio. Analyzing the data in Exhibit 14.5 indicates that the retention rates of retail drugstores have consistently been higher than the retention rates for the market (69 percent versus 54 percent). This indicates a higher dividend payout (lower retention rate) for the S&P Industrials Index, which implies a higher multiplier for the S&P Industrials Index, holding all other variables constant.

Estimating the Required Rate of Return   Recall that we estimated the required rate of return (k) earlier in the chapter in connection with the present value of cash flow valuation models. The final estimate indicated a beta of 0.82 for the industry, which was generally consistent with the fundamental risk characteristics of the industry. In turn, this beta in the prevailing SML implied a k of 8.50 percent. This 8.50 percent compares to the k for the aggregate stock market derived in Chapter 13 of 9.50 percent, which implies that all else the same, the industry P/E should be higher than the market P/E.

Estimating the Expected Growth Rate (g)   You will recall that we likewise estimated a growth rate for the industry early in this chapter in connection with the present value of cash flow models. Using the relationship

$$g = \text{Retention Rate } (b) \times \text{Return on Equity } (ROE)$$
$$= (b) \times (ROE)$$

we estimated a g of over 10 percent based on long-run historical results, and a g of almost 10 percent using the results for the recent five-year period 1996–2000. Because of the steady deterioration of both b and ROE for the RDS industry, we decided upon an estimate of industry growth close to the lower bound—9.50 percent.

This 9.50 percent growth rate estimate compares to the growth rates for the S&P Industrials Index of between 8.10 percent (using the long-run retention rate) and 11.00 percent (using the recent five-year retention rate). The mean of these two growth rates for the market is about 9.50 percent. If we opted to be near the high value because of the steady improvement of the components that determine growth, we would be around 10.00 percent. All these growth estimates for the market exceed the industry g of about 8.50 percent, which implies that based on the growth factor, the industry multiple would be lower than the market multiple.

In summary, a comparison of the dividend-payout ratios indicates that the market P/E ratio should be higher; the required rate of return comparison indicates that the industry multiple should be higher; while the growth rate favors the market multiple. The consensus tends to favor a higher market multiple. Earlier it was discussed that the market multiple would need to be almost 30 times to justify the prevailing market price. This implies an industry multiplier in the mid-20s—that is, we will use an estimated industry P/E of 25 times.

Industry Estimated Value and Rate of Return   At this point, we have an estimate of the industry earnings per share ($25.00) and an estimate for an industry earnings multiple in the mid-20s based on a comparison of the industry and market components. It is not possible to derive a specific estimate using the DDM formula because the k and g for the industry are roughly equal—that is, both k and g are about 8.50 percent. Because the multiple estimate is necessarily not specific, it seems appropriate to consider an optimistic and a pessimistic estimate, with the initial estimate of intrinsic value as follows:

Optimistic Multiple:	$30 \times \$25.00 = \$750.00$
Expected Multiple:	$25 \times \$25.00 = \$625.00$
Pessimistic Multiple:	$20 \times \$25.00 = \$500.00$

Given a current market price for the industry index of about $640.00, these results indicate that the industry is overpriced based upon general expectations and the pessimistic estimate but is slightly underpriced if one favors the optimistic multiple. The specific calculation of rates of return during 2002 for the industry using these intrinsic values, an estimate of dividends, and an index value during early 2002 is as follows:

$$\text{Optimistic Rate of Return: } \frac{750.00 + 4.70}{640.00} = 1.057 - 1.0 = 5.7\%$$

$$\text{Expected Rate of Return: } \frac{625.00 + 4.70}{640.00} = 0.882 - 1.0 = -11.8\%$$

$$\text{Pessimistic Rate of Return: } \frac{500.00 + 4.70}{640.00} = 0.707 - 1.0 = -29.3\%$$

Comparing these estimated rates of return to the required rate of return for this industry of 8.50 percent indicates that, using this earnings multiple model, the industry is overpriced, even using an optimistic earnings multiple.

OTHER RELATIVE VALUATION RATIOS

Similar to the market analysis, we need to consider the other three relative valuation ratios (P/BV; P/CF; and P/S) and compare their performance over time relative to similar ratios for the aggregate stock market as represented by the S&P Industrials Index.

Again, the calculations will employ the average annual price and *future* book value, cash flow, and sales. The input data derived for the industry and the S&P Industrials Index (from Chapter 13) with 20-year and 10-year growth rates for each of these variables are contained in Exhibit 14.22.

EXHIBIT 14.22 INPUTS FOR RELATIVE VALUATION RATIOS: THE RETAIL DRUGSTORE INDUSTRY AND THE S&P INDUSTRIALS INDEX: 1977–2000

| | RETAIL DRUGSTORE INDUSTRY | | | | | | S&P INDUSTRIALS INDEX | | | | | |
YEAR	MEAN PRICE	EPS	CASH FLOW P/S	BOOK VALUE P/S	NET SALES P/S	DIVIDEND P/S	MEAN PRICE	EPS	CASH FLOW P/S	BOOK VALUE P/S	NET SALES P/S	DIVIDEND P/S
1977	18.93	1.79	2.20	9.35	43.99	0.36	109.40	11.45	19.94	82.21	224.23	4.95
1978	22.20	2.01	2.50	10.93	49.87	0.48	107.12	13.04	22.65	89.34	251.32	5.37
1979	22.38	2.55	3.26	13.95	73.39	0.70	115.79	16.29	27.06	98.71	292.38	5.92
1980	24.57	2.94	3.78	16.11	84.82	0.86	136.03	16.12	28.45	108.33	327.36	6.49
1981	34.62	3.29	4.31	18.45	95.50	1.02	141.48	16.74	30.52	116.06	344.31	7.01
1982	41.58	3.76	4.79	20.74	109.22	1.17	136.87	13.20	28.46	118.60	333.86	7.13
1983	56.70	4.50	5.90	23.34	118.85	1.32	174.90	14.77	30.41	122.32	334.07	7.32
1984	58.30	4.10	5.81	24.21	135.15	1.54	179.62	18.11	34.40	123.99	379.70	7.51
1985	68.28	4.22	6.24	26.82	153.30	1.72	208.99	15.28	33.44	125.89	398.42	7.87
1986	83.78	4.90	6.99	27.73	157.74	1.61	253.83	14.53	33.91	124.87	387.76	8.14
1987	98.93	5.53	8.16	30.79	191.72	1.75	324.30	20.28	40.46	134.19	430.35	8.72
1988	93.05	6.30	9.40	34.25	217.80	1.93	302.63	26.59	50.13	139.50	486.92	9.80
1989	107.46	6.69	10.07	38.31	239.68	2.16	364.58	26.83	50.02	145.34	541.38	11.85
1990	114.53	7.67	11.82	43.65	265.77	2.43	392.12	24.77	51.04	152.71	594.55	12.70
1991	139.70	8.26	12.29	50.94	283.50	2.71	428.81	16.91	44.41	157.05	586.86	12.51
1992	159.62	8.96	13.34	56.97	309.78	3.01	493.33	19.05	48.50	142.46	601.39	13.01
1993	162.19	7.09	11.84	60.04	329.20	3.32	520.21	21.93	50.61	136.91	603.62	12.51
1994	162.67	10.51	15.83	63.62	363.71	3.55	536.52	32.83	62.43	150.70	626.26	13.01
1995	215.26	11.76	17.77	68.93	413.52	3.96	638.97	35.44	68.51	163.94	676.62	13.96
1996	283.01	13.92	18.82	71.26	434.15	4.01	795.01	41.15	77.56	168.04	701.91	15.58
1997	411.75	10.77	19.22	70.88	549.51	4.41	1,006.12	42.13	81.90	174.21	750.71	16.72
1998	657.05	15.62	24.48	111.07	612.86	4.52	1,285.73	38.37	71.63	186.36	755.48	17.28
1999	718.90	18.87	29.20	126.36	706.21	4.70	1,651.82	50.25	89.71	189.54	812.00	17.40
2000	686.62	16.72	28.61	107.27	687.77	3.24	1,702.23	53.85	98.53	204.54	853.86	16.59
20-yr. G	**18.12**	**9.08**	**10.65**	**9.94**	**11.03**	**6.86**	**13.47**	**6.22**	**6.41**	**3.23**	**4.91**	**4.80**
10-yr. G	**19.61**	**8.10**	**9.24**	**9.41**	**9.97**	**2.92**	**15.81**	**8.08**	**6.80**	**2.97**	**3.69**	**2.71**

Source: *Financial Analysts Handbook* (New York: Standard & Poor's, 2001). Reprinted with permission.

EXHIBIT 14.23 ▶ *RELATIVE VALUATION RATIOS FOR THE RDS INDUSTRY COMPARED TO SIMILAR VALUATION RATIOS FOR THE S&P INDUSTRIALS INDEX: 1977–1999*

| | PRICE EARNINGS$_{t+1}$ | | | PRICE CASH FLOW$_{t+1}$ | | | PRICE BOOK VALUE$_{t+1}$ | | | PRICE SALES$_{t+1}$ | | |
Year	RDS	S&P Ind	Ratio Ind/Mkt	RDS	S&P Ind	Ratio Ind/Mkt	RDS	S&P Ind	Ratio Ind/Mkt	RDS	S&P Ind	Ratio Ind/Mkt
1977	9.42	8.39	1.12	7.57	4.83	1.57	1.73	1.22	1.41	0.38	0.44	0.87
1978	8.71	6.58	1.32	6.81	3.96	1.72	1.59	1.09	1.47	0.30	0.37	0.83
1979	7.61	7.18	1.06	5.92	4.07	1.45	1.39	1.07	1.30	0.26	0.35	0.75
1980	7.47	8.13	0.92	5.70	4.46	1.28	1.33	1.17	1.14	0.26	0.40	0.65
1981	9.21	10.72	0.86	7.23	4.97	1.45	1.67	1.19	1.40	0.32	0.42	0.75
1982	9.24	9.27	1.00	7.05	4.50	1.57	1.78	1.12	1.59	0.35	0.41	0.85
1983	13.83	9.66	1.43	9.76	5.08	1.92	2.34	1.41	1.66	0.42	0.46	0.91
1984	13.82	11.76	1.18	9.34	5.37	1.74	2.17	1.43	1.52	0.38	0.45	0.84
1985	13.93	14.38	0.97	9.77	6.16	1.58	2.46	1.67	1.47	0.43	0.54	0.80
1986	15.15	12.52	1.21	10.27	6.27	1.64	2.72	1.89	1.44	0.44	0.59	0.74
1987	15.70	12.20	1.29	10.52	6.47	1.63	2.89	2.32	1.24	0.45	0.67	0.68
1988	13.91	11.28	1.23	9.24	6.05	1.53	2.43	2.08	1.17	0.39	0.56	0.69
1989	14.01	14.72	0.95	9.09	7.14	1.27	2.46	2.39	1.03	0.40	0.61	0.66
1990	13.87	23.19	0.60	9.32	8.83	1.06	2.25	2.50	0.90	0.40	0.67	0.60
1991	15.59	22.51	0.69	10.47	8.84	1.18	2.45	3.01	0.81	0.45	0.71	0.63
1992	22.51	22.50	1.00	13.48	9.75	1.38	2.66	3.60	0.74	0.48	0.82	0.59
1993	15.43	15.85	0.97	10.25	8.33	1.23	2.55	3.45	0.74	0.45	0.83	0.54
1994	13.83	15.14	0.91	9.15	7.83	1.17	2.36	3.27	0.72	0.39	0.79	0.50
1995	15.46	15.53	1.00	11.44	8.24	1.39	3.02	3.80	0.79	0.50	0.91	0.54
1996	26.28	18.87	1.39	14.72	9.71	1.52	3.99	4.56	0.87	0.52	1.06	0.49
1997	26.36	26.22	1.01	16.82	14.05	1.20	3.71	5.40	0.69	0.67	1.33	0.50
1998	34.82	25.59	1.36	22.50	14.33	1.57	5.20	6.78	0.77	0.93	1.58	0.59
1999	43.00	30.67	1.40	25.13	16.76	1.50	6.70	8.08	0.83	1.05	1.93	0.54
20-yr.G	9.04	7.53	—	7.50	7.33	—	8.19	10.64	—	7.13	8.87	—
10-yr.G	11.87	7.62	—	10.70	8.91	—	10.53	12.96	—	9.96	12.18	—
Mean	16.49	15.34	1.08	10.94	7.65	1.46	2.69	2.81	1.12	0.46	0.73	0.68

Source: *Financial Analysts Handbook* (New York: Standard & Poor's, 2001). Reprinted with permission.

Exhibit 14.23 contains the four relative valuation ratios for the RDS industry and for the S&P Industrials Index along with the ratio of the annual industry valuation ratio divided by the market valuation ratio. The idea is to determine for each valuation ratio the long-run relationship between the industry and the market, including any changes in this relationship. Subsequently, the goal is to explain the overall relationship and consider any changes that have occurred and whether these changes can be explained based upon the factors that should affect the particular relative valuation ratio.

The Price/Book Value Ratio

The time-series plot in Exhibit 14.24 shows the overall increase in the price/book value ratio experienced by both the aggregate stock market and the RDS industry from less than two times to over six times. In addition, the relationship between the industry and the market has changed—that is, the industry *P/BV* ratio was larger from 1977 through 1989, after which the

EXHIBIT 14.24 ▶ *TIME-SERIES PLOT OF THE PRICE/BOOK VALUE RATIOS FOR THE S&P INDUSTRIALS INDEX AND THE RDS INDUSTRY: 1977–1999*

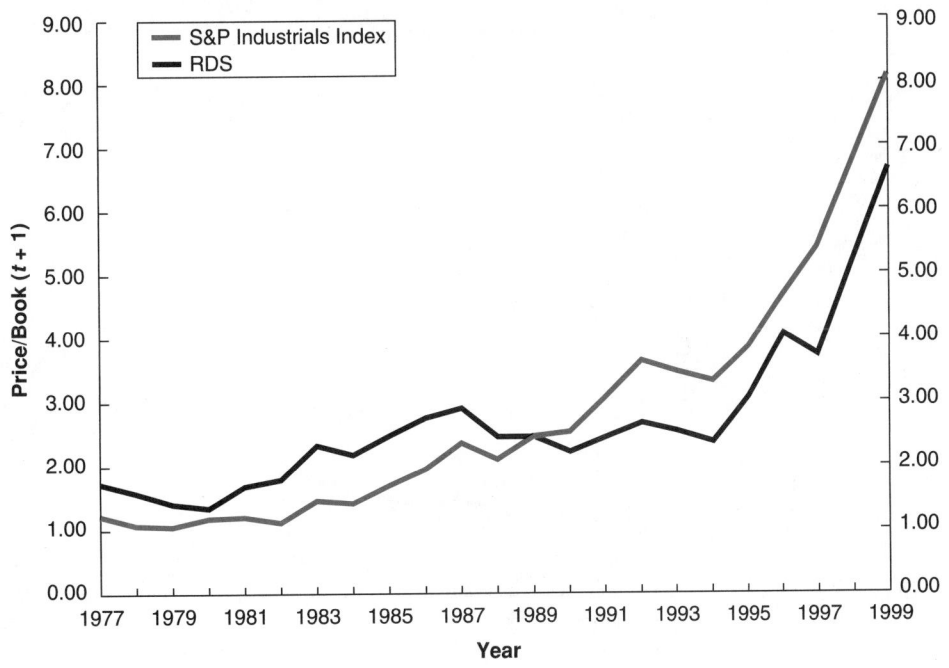

market *P/BV* ratio has been larger. The reason for this change in the relationship appears to be the change in *ROE* for the market and industry because the *P/BV* ratio should reflect the ability of the market, an industry, or a company to earn a return on capital that exceeds its cost of funds. In turn, this return on capital for the equity holder is the *ROE,* and we know from our earlier analysis that during the last decade, the *ROE* for the market has been increasing while the *ROE* for the RDS industry has steadily declined because of the decline in profit margin.

The Price/Cash Flow Ratio

As shown in Exhibit 14.23 and Exhibit 14.25, the *P/CF* ratio has increased for both the market and the RDS industry and the industry ratio has consistently been larger by almost 50 percent. The reason for the difference in the *P/CF* ratios is akin to the *P/E* ratio—that is, a difference in the growth rate of *CF* per share and the risk (volatility) of the *CF* series over time. As shown in Exhibit 14.22, the growth rate of the industry *CF* has been consistently higher than the growth of the market *CF,* and the industry *CF* series has also been more consistent in its growth. An important question is whether the industry *P/CF* ratio should be 50 percent higher than the *P/CF* ratio for the market—that is, does the difference in consistent growth of *CF* justify the fairly large difference in the *P/CF* ratios?

The Price/Sales Ratio

As shown in Exhibit 14.23 and Exhibit 14.26, the *P/S* ratio for the market has increased more than four times from about 0.40 to 1.93 while the industry *P/S* ratio has not quite tripled from 0.38 to 1.05. Because of this differential in the increase in the ratios, the industry-market ratio of *P/S* ratios has declined from 0.87 to 0.54. In terms of what should affect the *P/S* ratio, one can think of three factors: (1) sales growth rate; (2) the uncertainty (risk) of sales growth; and (3) the profitability of sales (i.e., the net profit margin). Because the industry experienced a *higher* rate

EXHIBIT 14.25

TIME-SERIES PLOT OF THE PRICE/CASH FLOW RATIOS FOR THE S&P INDUSTRIALS INDEX AND THE RDS INDUSTRY: 1977–1999

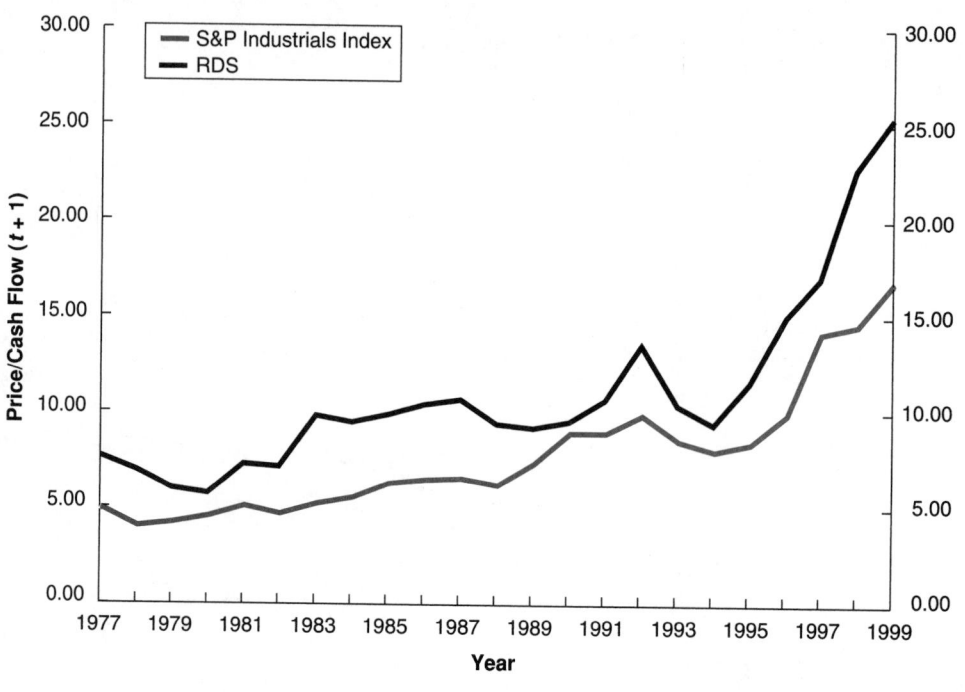

EXHIBIT 14.26

TIME-SERIES PLOT OF THE PRICE/SALES RATIOS FOR THE S&P INDUSTRIALS INDEX AND THE RDS INDUSTRY: 1977–1999

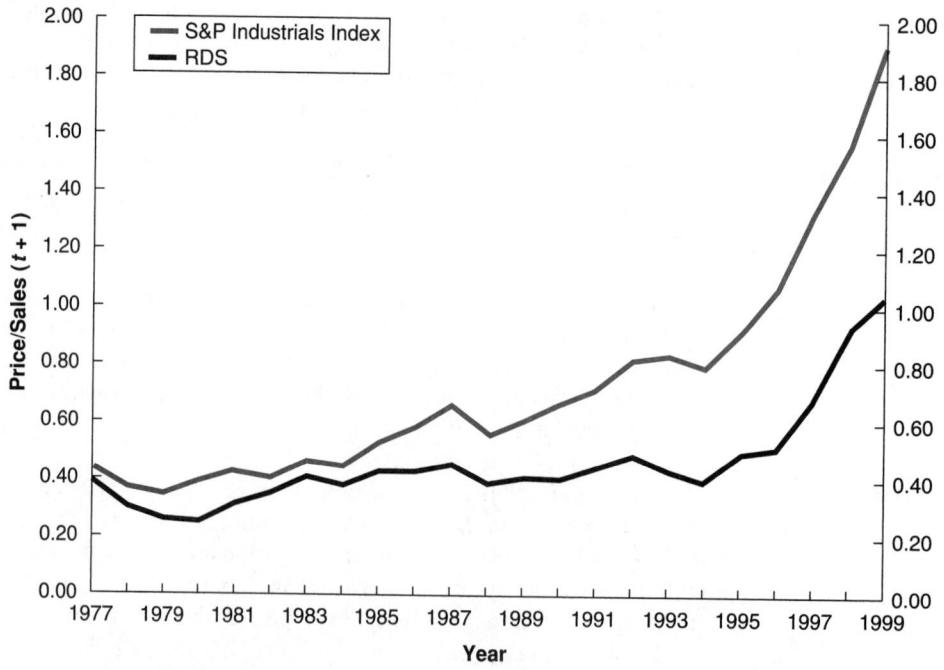

EXHIBIT 14.27 | TIME-SERIES PLOTS OF THE INDUSTRY-MARKET RELATIVE RATIO OF VALUATION RATIOS FOR THE S&P INDUSTRIALS INDEX AND THE RDS INDUSTRY: 1977–1999

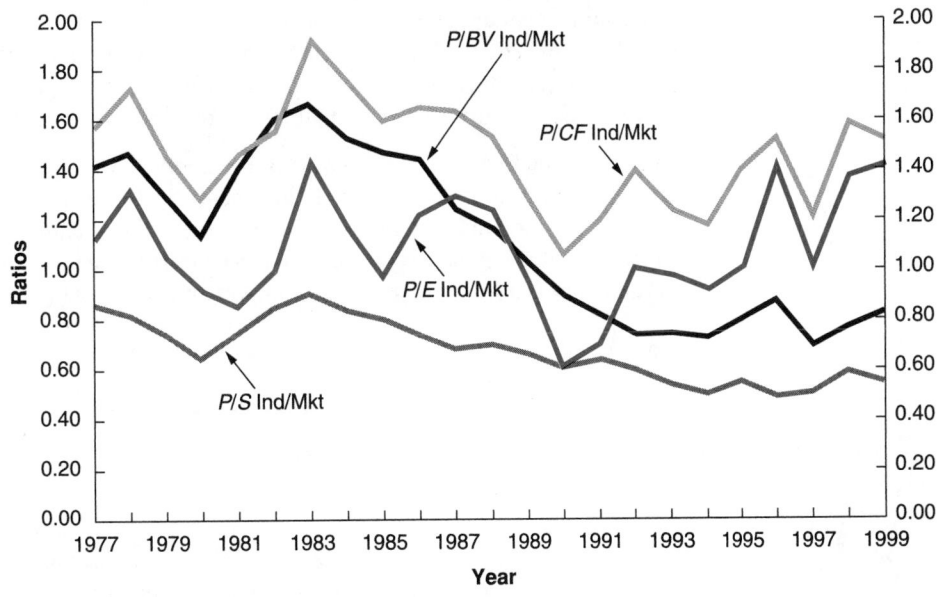

of growth for sales during both the 10-year and the 20-year period, it is not the rate of growth. Both have likewise experienced less volatility in sales growth. In contrast, the profit margin *(PM)* change is consistent with the difference in the *P/S* ratios—the *PM* for the market has increased recently while the *PM* for the industry has declined.

Exhibit 14.27 is a summary of the four industry-market ratios for each of the valuation ratios. In general, the results indicate that investors' assessment of this industry relative to the market has been somewhat mixed during this time period. While the relative *P/E* ratio increased over time, both the *P/BV* and the *P/S* declined as one would expect based on the underlying fundamentals.

GLOBAL INDUSTRY ANALYSIS

Because so many firms are active in foreign markets and because the proportion of foreign sales is growing for so many firms, it is necessary to consider the effects of foreign firms on industry returns. To see why this is so, consider the auto industry. Besides Ford and General Motors, the auto industry for a global investor includes numerous firms from Japan, Germany, Italy, and Korea, among others. Thus, we must extend the analysis described earlier to include global factors.

While space does not permit a complete example, the following major factors need to be analyzed in this context:

➤ The macroenvironment in the major producing and consuming countries for this industry. This will impact demand from these countries.
➤ An overall analysis of the significant companies in the industry, the products they produce, and how successful they are in terms of the DuPont three-component analysis.

➤ As part of the company analysis, what are the accounting differences by country and how do these differences impact the relative valuation ratios? Because of the accounting differences, it is typically not possible to directly compare such ratios across countries but only examine them over time within a country.

➤ What is the effect of currency exchange rate trends for the major countries? Significant changes can affect the demand for U.S. chemicals from specific countries and also costs assuming U.S. firms receive inputs from foreign firms.

This global industry analysis is growing in importance as documented in a study by Cavaglia, Brightman, and Aked (CBA), which documents that, historically, research showed that country factors dominated industry factors in terms of explaining equity returns.[11] The CBA study presented evidence that industry factors have been growing in importance and very likely now dominate country factors. In summary, it is important to carry out industry analysis on a global scale.

The Internet *Investments Online*

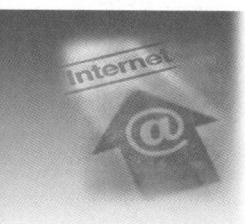

The Web can help researchers find information about an industry, but many industry analyses and studies are available on-line only to registered and paying clients of research firms, investment banks, and brokerage houses. You aren't likely to find up-to-date Porter-type analyses free on the Internet, at least not for a wide variety of industries. Web searches for industry information can focus on exploring Web sites of competitors in the industry. You may find trade group Web sites through key word searches using terms and phrases relevant to the industry you wish to study.

Because this chapter focuses on the retail drug store industry, a little investigation brought forth the sites described below; many more exist for your perusal.

www.lf.com The home page for Lebhar-Friedman, Inc., a publisher and provider of information about retailers.

www.nacds.org This page is sponsored by the National Association of Chain Drug Stores. It contains much data relevant to chain drugstores, from sales in different product categories to projected numbers of prescriptions. It offers news and links to related sites.

www.healthcaredistribution.org This is a site of the Healthcare Distribution Management Association. This page features links to managed-care issues, public policy issues, information for pharmacies, consumers, the press, manufacturers, analysts, and investors. Contains links to a number of related Web sites.

retailindustry.about.com A part of the about.com Web site, this site contains a number of links to other Web sites that deal with the retail industry and the analysis of the retail industry.

www.valuationresources.com This site contains links to industry information sources and economic information sources. Industry report information is segmented by SIC code.

Summary

- Several studies have examined industry performance and risk. They have found wide dispersion in the performance of alternative industries during specified time periods, implying that industry analysis can help identify superior investments. They also showed inconsistent industry performance over time, implying that looking at only past performance of an industry has little value in projecting future per-

---

[11]Stefano Cavaglia, Christopher Brightman, and Michael Aked, "The Increasing Importance of Industry Factors," *Financial Analysts Journal* 56, no. 5 (September–October 2000): 41–54.

formance. Also, the performance by firms within industries typically is not very consistent, so you must analyze individual companies in an industry following the industry analysis.

- The analysis of industry risk indicated wide dispersion in the measures of risk for different industries but a fair amount of consistency in the risk measure over time for individual industries. These results imply that risk analysis and measurement are useful in selecting industries. The good news is that past risk measures may be of some value when estimating future risk.
- We discussed and demonstrated both approaches to the valuation of the RDS industry. The present value of cash flow models indicated a fairly wide range of value wherein the DDM models indicated overvaluation of the industry, while the FCFE models indicated that the industry was undervalued.
- The four relative valuation ratio techniques also provided a range of results, including the two-step earnings multiple technique where the results generally pointed toward overvaluation. Two of the three relative valuation ratios showed a tendency to decline over time relative to the market with a major decline in the *P/BV* ratio caused by a deterioration in the industry profit margin and its *ROE*.
- Industry analysis needs to be carried out on a global scale and must evaluate the effects not only of world supply, demand, and cost components for an industry but also different valuation levels due to accounting conventions and, finally, the impact of exchange rates on the total industry and the firms within it.

Questions

1. Briefly describe the results of studies that examined the performance of alternative industries during specific time periods and discuss their implications for industry analysis.
2. Briefly describe the results of the studies that examined industry performance over time. Do these results complicate or simplify industry analysis?
3. Assume all the firms in a particular industry have consistently experienced similar rates of return. Discuss what this implies regarding the importance of industry and company analysis for this industry.
4. Discuss the contention that differences in the performance of various firms within an industry limit the usefulness of industry analysis.
5. Several studies have examined the difference in risk for alternative industries during a specified time period. Describe the results of these studies and discuss their implications for industry analysis.
6. What were the results when industry risk was examined during successive time periods? Discuss the implication of these results for industry analysis.
7. Assume the industry you are analyzing is in the fourth stage of the industrial life cycle. How would you react if your industry-economic analysis predicted that sales per share for this industry would increase by 20 percent? Discuss your reasoning.
8. Discuss at what stage in the industrial life cycle you would like to discover an industry. Justify your decision.
9. Give an example of an industry in Stage 2 of the industrial life cycle. Discuss your reasoning for putting the industry in Stage 2 and any evidence that caused you to select this industry.
10. Discuss an example of input-output analysis to predict the sales for the auto industry. Discuss how you would use input-output analysis to predict the costs of production for the auto industry.
11. Discuss the impact of the threat of substitute products on the steel industry's profitability.
12. Discuss the two variables that must be considered whether you are using the present value of cash flow approach or the relative valuation ratio approach to valuation. Why are these variables relevant for either valuation approach?
13. List the three variables that are relevant when attempting to determine whether the earnings multiple (*P/E* ratio) for an industry should be higher, equal to, or lower than the market multiple. Assuming you are analyzing the retail food industry, discuss which of these variables would be most important in explaining the difference in earnings multiple. Why is it relevant?
14. Discuss when you would use the two-stage growth FCFE model rather than the constant growth model.
15. You are examining the *P/CF* ratio for an industry compared to the market and find that the industry ratio has always been at a discount to the market—for example, the industry-market ratio of ratios is about 0.80. What variable(s) would you examine to explain this difference or to justify an increase in the industry-market ratio?

16. *CFA Examination Level II*

    Elizabeth Coronado, CFA, is analyzing Nelson Motors, Inc., one of the largest and most profitable automobile manufacturers in North America. Since the early 1990s, the fastest growing and most profitable product segment for Nelson has been its sport utility vehicles (SUV) line shown in the following exhibit.

    Coronado believes that applying the product life cycle model to Nelson's SUV product line will yield additional analytical insights into the company's recent rapid earnings growth.

    a. Identify the current product life cycle stage for the Raven, Hawk, and Eagle. Justify your choice of product life cycle stage by citing evidence from the following exhibit. [6 minutes]

    Because of the high expectations associated with the Eagle, Nelson Motors' current *P/E* is above its five-year historic range and above the auto industry *P/E*. An auto analyst states that "Nelson Motors has the best of both worlds:

    - increasing SUV profitability and
    - declining expected future earnings volatility."

    b. Evaluate *each* statement, using the data presented in the exhibit (6 minutes).

17. *CFA Examination Level II*

    Scott Kelly, a U.S.-based equity analyst, is analyzing the toy industry to determine which companies will be most competitive. He has determined that the U.S. toy industry is relatively mature and that revenue and earnings growth are slowing. His report contains the following statements:

    - I recommend that we invest in toy companies with a substantial percentage of revenues derived from non-U.S. sales.
    - Companies selected for the portfolio should derive a large portion of revenues from the largest discount toy retailer.

NELSON MOTORS ANNUAL SUV PRODUCTION AND FINANCIAL DATA

	1990	1991	1992	1993	1994	1995	1996	1997	1998	1999E	000E
SUV Units Sold in Thousands											
Raven	5	10	35	70	90	100	110	112	110	105	90
Hawk	—	—	—	—	3	10	20	45	63	68	69
Eagle	—	—	—	—	—	—	—	5	32	70	110
Profit per Vehicle in $ Thousands											
Raven	9	10	9	8	8	7	7	6	5	4	3
Hawk	—	—	—	—	6	7	8	7	7	8	7
Eagle	—	—	—	—	—	—	—	10	10	11	12
Profit per SUV Model in $ Millions											
Raven	45	100	315	560	720	700	770	672	550	420	270
Hawk	—	—	—	—	18	70	160	315	441	544	483
Eagle	—	—	—	—	—	—	—	50	320	770	1320
Total SUV Division profit in $ millions	45	100	315	560	738	770	930	1,037	1,311	1,734	2,073
Total Nelson Motors profit in $ millions	1,125	1,250	1,575	1,600	1,994	1,974	2,214	2,357	2,960	3,470	3,989
SUV Division profit % of Nelson Motors profit	4%	8%	20%	35%	37%	39%	42%	44%	44%	50%	52%
Year over year % change in total SUV profit	—	122%	215%	78%	32%	4%	21%	12%	26%	32%	20%
Model percent of SUV Division Profit											
Raven	100%	100%	100%	100%	98%	91%	83%	65%	42%	24%	13%
Hawk	—	—	—	—	2%	9%	17%	30%	34%	31%	23%
Eagle	—	—	—	—	—	—	—	5%	24%	44%	64%

- I am particularly interested in a start-up company that has an exciting new toy coming out based on a very popular television show.
- Although MasterToy has the dominant market share, I feel that smaller companies will have better opportunities for growth in a mature market.

State whether *each* of Kelly's statements is valid or not valid. Cite *two* industry characteristics by *number* from the following exhibit to support your decision. [16 minutes]

TOY INDUSTRY CHARACTERISTICS

Industry Life Cycle

1. U.S. toy sales grew by 5 percent compounded annually over the past 10 years. However, toy sales in the United States were down 4 percent last year. Growth of toy sales is expected to be 1.5–3.0 percent annually for the next five years.
2. Non-U.S. toy sales grew by 7 percent compounded annually over the past 10 years. Sales growth is expected to be 7–8 percent for the next five years.
3. The toy industry is in a period of rapid consolidation. Companies faced with slower internal growth are considering acquisitions to enhance growth.

Demographics

4. The birth rate in the United States is expected to decline by 3 percent annually for the next three years.
5. The birth rate in Europe and Asia is expected to increase by 2 percent annually for the next three years.
6. Age demographics are important drivers of demand both in the United States and in target non-U.S. markets (only 3 percent of the world's children live in the United States). Per capita consumption of toys in non-U.S. markets is lower than in the United States.

Consumer Preference

7. Brand names are one of the keys to success in both U.S. and non-U.S. markets. Consumers show a preference for products manufactured by well-regarded companies.
8. Marketing studies indicate that even technologically superior products will be hard to sell when manufactured by a company without a brand name or without a substantial advertising budget to support the product.
9. The top companies dedicate a large amount of money to focus groups and marketing studies in order to accurately gauge consumer preference.

Market Share

10. The world's two largest toy manufacturers (MasterToy and FunToyz) control more than 75 percent of the U.S. market. No other manufacturer represents more than 5 percent in market share. Economies of scale are important for production, advertisement, and promotion.
11. The larger companies in the industry have the ability to develop lucrative and cost-effective advertising in all media sectors. They have better bargaining power versus the competition and are more able to negotiate prime-time advertisements.
12. Marketing studies show that sales of products associated with hit movies and television shows are much higher than for competing products without the entertainment tie-in.

Retail Environment/Distribution

13. A major discount toy retailer's inventory-reduction program has negatively affected earnings for the group. This distribution channel has been critical to success in the past, accounting for a large percentage of sales. The company has adopted a new inventory control system in order to operate more efficiently.
14. To reduce dependence on traditional retail channels, companies are diversifying into direct mail and Internet commerce.
15. Global distribution of product is an essential component of long-term growth for industry leaders.

Diversification

16. Diversification is a key to success. A niche product can quickly lose its appeal. Typically, companies that rely on one or two key products fail when popularity fades.
17. The top two toy manufacturers have a highly diversified product mix.

Problems

1. Select three industries from the S&P *Analysts Handbook* with different demand factors. For each industry, indicate what economic series you would use to predict the growth for the industry. Discuss why the economic series selected is relevant for this industry.

2. Prepare a scatter plot for one of the industries in Problem 1 of industry sales per share and observations from the economic series you suggested for this industry. Do this for the most recent 10 years using information available in the *Analysts Handbook*. Based on the results of the scatter plot, discuss whether the economic series was closely related to this industry's sales.

3. Based on an analysis of the results in Problem 2, discuss the stage of your industry in its life cycle.

4. Evaluate your industry in terms of the five factors that determine an industry's intensity of competition. Based on this analysis, what are your expectations about the industry's profitability in the short run (1 or 2 years) and the long run (5–10 years)?

5. Using the S&P *Analysts Handbook,* plot the latest 10-year history of the operating profit margin for the S&P Industrials Index versus the S&P industry of your choice. Is there a positive, negative, or zero correlation?

6. Using the S&P *Analysts Handbook,* calculate the means for the following variables of the S&P Industrials Index and the industry of your choice during the last 10 years:
   a. Price/earnings multiplier
   b. Retention rate
   c. Return on equity
   d. Equity turnover
   e. Net profit margin
   Briefly comment on how your industry and the S&P Industrials Index differ for each of the variables.

7. Prepare a table listing the variables that influence the earnings multiplier for your chosen industry and the S&P Industrials Index series for the most recent 10 years.
   a. Do the average dividend-payout ratios for your industry and the S&P Industrials Index differ? How should the dividend payout influence the difference between the multipliers?
   b. Based on the fundamental factors, would you expect the risk for this industry to differ from that for the market? In what direction, and why? Calculate the industry beta using monthly data for five years. Based on the fundamental factors and the computed systematic risk, how does this industry's risk compare to the market? What effect will this difference in risk have on the industry multiplier relative to the market multiplier?
   c. Analyze and discuss the different components of growth (retention rate, total asset turnover, total assets/equity, and profit margin) for your chosen industry and the S&P Industrials Index during the most recent 10 years. Based on this analysis, how would you expect the growth rate for your industry to compare with the growth rate for the S&P Industrials Index? How would this difference in expected growth affect the multiplier?

8. *CFA Examination Level II*

   As a securities analyst, you have been asked to review a valuation of a closely held business. Wigwam Autoparts Heaven, Inc. (WAH), prepared by the Red Rocks Group (RRG). You are to give an opinion on the valuation and to support your opinion by analyzing each part of the valuation. WAH's sole business is automotive parts retailing.

   The RRG valuation includes a section called "Analysis of the Retail Autoparts Industry," based completely on the data in Table 1 and the following additional information.

   - WAH and its principal competitors each operated over 150 stores at year end 1994.
   - The average number of stores operated per company engaged in the retail auto parts industry is 5.3.
   - The major customer base for auto parts sold in retail stores consists of young owners of old vehicles. These owners do their own automotive maintenance out of economic necessity.

   a. One of RRG's conclusions is that the retail autoparts industry as a whole is in the stabilization stage of the industry life cycle. Discuss *three* relevant items of data from Table 1 that support this conclusion. [9 minutes]

TABLE 1 ▶ *SELECTED RETAIL AUTOPARTS INDUSTRY DATA*

	1994	1993	1992	1991	1990	1989	1988	1987	1986	1985
Population 18–29 years old (percentage change)	–1.8%	–2.0%	–2.1%	–1.4%	–0.8%	–0.9%	–1.1%	–0.9%	–0.7%	–0.3%
Number of households with income more than $35,000 (percentage change)	6.0%	4.0%	8.0%	4.5%	2.7%	3.1%	1.6%	3.6%	4.2%	2.2%
Number of households with income less than $35,000 (percentage (change)	3.0%	–1.0%	4.9%	2.3%	–1.4%	2.5%	1.4%	–1.3%	0.6%	0.1%
Number of cars 5–15 years old (percentage change)	0.9%	–1.3%	–6.0%	1.9%	3.3%	2.4%	–2.3%	–2.2%	–8.0%	1.6%
Automotive aftermarket industry retail sales (percentage change)	5.7%	1.9%	3.1%	3.7%	4.3%	2.6%	1.3%	0.2%	3.7%	2.4%
Consumer expenditures on automotive parts and accessories (percentage change)	2.4%	1.8%	2.1%	6.5%	3.6%	9.2%	1.3%	6.2%	6.7%	6.5%
Sales growth of retail auto parts companies with 100 or more stores	17.0%	16.0%	16.5%	14.0%	15.5%	16.8%	12.0%	15.7%	19.0%	16.0%
Market share of retail auto parts companies with 100 or more stores	19.0%	18.5%	18.3%	18.1%	17.0%	17.2%	17.0%	16.9%	15.0%	14.0%
Average operating margin of retail auto parts companies with 100 or more stores	12.0%	11.8%	11.2%	11.5%	10.6%	10.6%	10.0%	10.4%	9.8%	9.0%
Average operating margin of all retail auto parts companies	5.5%	5.7%	5.6%	5.8%	6.0%	6.5%	7.0%	7.2%	7.1%	7.2%

b. Another RRG conclusion is that WAH and its principal competitors are in the growth stage of their life cycle.

Cite *three* relevant items of data from Table 1 that support this conclusion.

Explain how WAH and its principal competitors can be in a growth stage while their industry as a whole is in the stabilization stage. [11 minutes]

9. You know the following about your industry (I) and the market (M):

ROE_I:	12%	ROE_M:	16%
RR_I:	0.60	RR_M:	0.55
$Beta_I$:	1.05	$Beta_M$:	1.00

Discuss what difference you would expect in the *P/E*s, and explain why you expect this difference.

References

Aber, John. "Industry Effects and Multivariate Stock Price Behavior." *Journal of Financial and Quantitative Analysis* 11, no. 5 (November 1976).

Fruhan, William E., Jr. *Financial Strategy.* Homewood, Ill.: Richard D. Irwin, 1979.

Goodman, D. A., and John W. Peavy III. "Industry Relative Price-Earnings Ratios as Indicators of Investment Returns." *Financial Analysts Journal* 39, no. 2 (March–April 1983): 60–66.

Porter, Michael E. *Competitive Advantage: Creating and Sustaining Superior Performance.* New York: Free Press, 1985.

Porter, Michael E. *Competitive Strategy: Techniques for Analyzing Industries and Competitors.* New York: Free Press, 1980.

Porter, Michael E. "How to Conduct an Industry Analysis." In *The Financial Analysts Handbook,* 2d ed., ed. Sumner N. Levine. Homewood, Ill.: Dow Jones–Irwin, 1988.

Stewart, Samuel S. "Forecasting Corporate Earnings." In *The Financial Analysts Handbook,* 2d ed., ed. Sumner N. Levine. Homewood, Ill.: Dow Jones–Irwin, 1988.

The following are proceedings from industry analysis seminars sponsored by the Association for Investment Management and Research:

Balog, James (ed.). *The Health Care Industry.* Charlottesville, Va.: Association for Investment Management and Research, 1993.

Bhatia, Sanjiv (ed.). *The Consumer Staples Industry.* Charlottesville, Va.: Association for Investment Management and Research, 1995.

Bhatia, Sanjiv (ed.). *The Media Industry.* Charlottesville, Va.: Association for Investment Management and Research, 1996.

Billingsley, Randall S. (ed.). *The Telecommunications Industry.* Charlottesville, Va.: Association for Investment Management and Research, 1994.

Petrie, Thomas A. (ed.). *The Oil and Gas Industries.* Charlottesville, Va.: Association for Investment Management and Research, 1993.

Shasta, Theodore (ed.). *The Automotive Industry.* Charlottesville, Va.: Association for Investment Management and Research, 1994.

APPENDIX
Chapter 14

A. Preparing an Industry Analysis: What Is an Industry?[12]

Identifying a company's industry can be difficult in today's business world. Although airlines, railroads, and utilities may be easy to categorize, what about manufacturing companies with three different divisions, none of which is dominant? Perhaps the best way to test whether a company fits into an industry grouping is to compare the operating results for the company and an industry. For our purposes, an industry is a group of companies with similar demand, supply, and operating characteristics.

The following is a set of guidelines for preparing an industry appraisal, including the topics to consider and some specific items to include.

Characteristics to Study

1. Price history reveals valuable long-term relationships.
   a. Price/earnings ratios
   b. Common stock yields
   c. Price/book value ratios
   d. Price/cash flow ratios
   e. Price/sales ratios
2. Operating data show comparisons of
   a. Return on total investment *(ROI)*
   b. Return on equity *(ROE)*
   c. Sales growth
   d. Trends in operating profit margin
   e. Evaluation of stage in industrial life cycle
   f. Book value per-share growth
   g. Earnings-per-share growth
   h. Profit margin trends (gross, operating, and net)
   i. Evaluation of exchange rate risk from foreign sales

---

[12]Reprinted and adapted with permission of Stanley D. Ryals, CFA; Investment Council, Inc.: La Crescenta, CA 91214.

3. Comparative results of alternative industries show
   a. Effects of business cycles on each industry group
   b. Secular trends affecting results
   c. Industry growth compared to other industries
   d. Regulatory changes
   e. Importance of overseas operations

Factors in Industry Analysis

Markets for Products

1. Trends in the markets for the industry's major products: historical and projected
2. Industry growth relative to GDP or other relevant economic series; possible changes from past trends
3. Shares of market for major products among domestic and global producers; changes in market shares in recent years; outlook for market share
4. Effect of imports on industry markets; share of market taken by imports; price and margin changes caused by imports; outlook for imports
5. Effect of exports on their markets; trends in export prices and units exported; outlook for exports
6. Expectations for the exchange rates in major non-U.S. countries; historical volatility of exchange rates; outlook for the level and volatility of exchange rates

Financial Performance

1. Capitalization ratios; ability to raise new capital; earnings retention rate; financial leverage
2. Ratio of fixed assets to capital invested; depreciation policies; capital turnover
3. Return on total capital; return on equity capital; components of *ROE*
4. Return on foreign investments; need for foreign capital

Operations

1. Degrees of integration; cost advantages of integration; major supply contracts
2. Operating rates as a percentage of capacity; backlogs; new-order trends
3. Trends of industry consolidation
4. Trends in industry competition
5. New-product development; research and development expenditures in dollars and as a percentage of sales
6. Diversification; comparability of product lines

Management

1. Management depth and ability to develop from within; organizational structure
2. Board of directors: internal versus external members; compensation package
3. Flexibility to deal with product demand changes; ability to identify and eliminate losing operations
4. Record and outlook regarding labor relations
5. Dividend policy and historical progression

Sources of Industry Information

1. Independent industry journals
2. Industry and trade associations
3. Government reports and statistics
4. Independent research organizations
5. Brokerage house research
6. Financial publishers (S&P; Moody's; Value Line)

APPENDIX
Chapter 14

B. Data Needs for an Industry Analysis

DATA NEEDS FOR AN INDUSTRY ANALYSIS

DATA CATEGORIES	COMPILATION
Product lines	By company
Buyers and their behavior	By year
Complementary products	By functional area
Substitute products	
Growth	
Rate	
Pattern (seasonal, cyclical)	
Determinants	
Technology of production and distribution	
Cost structure	
Economies of scale	
Value added	
Logistics	
Labor	
Marketing and selling	
Market segmentation	
Marketing practices	
Suppliers	
Distribution channels (if indirect)	
Innovation	
Types	
Sources	
Rate	
Economies of scale	
Competitors—strategy, goals, strengths and weaknesses, assumptions	
Social, political, legal environment	
Macroeconomic environment	

C. Insights on Analyzing Industry *ROAs*

Beyond the normal analysis of *ROA* as a component of *ROE* (*ROA* times Total Assets/Equity equals *ROE*), an article by Selling and Stickney provides some interesting insights for industry analysis based upon an analysis of the two components of the *ROA* ratio (profit margin and total asset turnover) and what these two components signal regarding the industry strategy.[13] Given the two components of the *ROA,* it is possible to graph each of these values as shown in Exhibit 14C.1 and determine what each component contributed to the *ROA* at the point of intersection. As shown, it is possible to draw a constant *ROA* curve, which demonstrates that it is possible to achieve an 8 percent (or 4 percent) *ROA* with numerous combinations of profit margin and asset turnover. The particular combination of profit margin and asset turnover is generally dictated by the nature of the industry and the strategy employed by management. For example, many industries necessarily require large capital inputs for equipment (e.g., steel, auto, heavy machinery manufacturers). Therefore, the asset turnover is necessarily low, which means the profit margin must be higher. The firms in such an industry are typically in the upper left segment of the graph (Segment *a*), and improvements of *ROA* in these industries are derived by increasing profit margins because it is difficult to increase asset turnover. In contrast, industries that have commodity-type products (e.g., retail food, paper, industrial chemicals) generally have low profit margins and succeed based upon high asset turnover. These industries are generally in the lower right segment of the graph (Segment *c*) and attempt to improve their *ROA* by increasing their asset turnover rather than the profit margin (i.e., they are constrained by price competition). Industries in the middle segment *(b)* are in a more balanced position and can attempt to improve the *ROA* by increasing *either* the profit margin or the asset turnover.

It is very important for an analyst to understand the nature of the industry and what contributes to the industry's *ROA* as well as what this implies about the constraints and opportunities facing the firms in the industry.

EXHIBIT 14C.1 ▶ ROA—*THE TRADE-OFF OF PROFIT MARGIN AND ASSET TURNOVER*

---

[13]Thomas Selling and Clyde P. Stickney, "The Effects of Business Environment and Strategy on a Firm's Rate of Return on Assets," *Financial Analysts Journal* 45, no. 1 (January–February 1989): 43–52.

Chapter 15 Company Analysis and Stock Valuation*

After you read this chapter, you should be able to answer the following questions:

➤ Why is it important to differentiate between company analysis and stock valuation?

➤ What is the difference between a true growth company and a growth stock?

➤ How do we apply the two valuation approaches and the several valuation techniques to Walgreens?

➤ What techniques are useful when estimating the inputs to alternative valuation models?

➤ What techniques are useful when estimating company sales?

➤ How do we estimate the profit margins and earnings per share for a company?

➤ What factors are considered when estimating the earnings multiplier for a firm?

➤ What two specific competitive strategies can a firm use to cope with the competitive environment in its industry?

➤ In addition to the earnings multiplier, what are some other relative valuation ratios?

➤ How do we apply the several present value of cash flow models to the valuation of a company?

➤ What value-added measures are available to evaluate the performance of a firm?

➤ How do we compute economic value added (EVA), market value added (MVA), and the franchise value for a firm?

➤ What is the relationship between these value-added measures and changes in the market value of firms?

➤ When should we consider selling a stock?

➤ What is meant by a true growth company?

➤ What is the relationship between positive EVA and a growth company?

➤ Why is it inappropriate to use the standard dividend discount model (DDM) to value a true growth company?

➤ What is the difference between no growth, simple growth, and dynamic growth?

➤ What is the growth duration model and what information does it provide when analyzing a true growth company and evaluating its stock?

➤ How can we use the growth duration model to derive an estimate of the *P/E* for Walgreens?

➤ What are some additional factors that should be considered when analyzing a company on a global basis?

At this point, you have made two decisions about your investment in equity markets. First, after analyzing the economy and stock markets for several countries, you have decided what percent of your portfolio should be invested in common stocks. Second, after analyzing various industries, you have identified those that appear to offer above-average risk-adjusted performance over your investment horizon. The final questions in the fundamental analysis procedure

---

*The authors acknowledge comments and suggestions on this chapter by Professor Edgar Norton of Illinois State University.

are: (1) Which are the best companies within these desirable industries? and (2) Are their stocks underpriced? Specifically, is the intrinsic value of the stock above its market value, or is the expected rate of return on the stock equal to or greater than its required rate of return?

This chapter begins with a discussion of the difference between company analysis and stock valuation. Company analysis should occur in the context of the prevailing economic and industry conditions. We discuss some competitive strategies that can help firms maximize returns in an industry's competitive environment. We demonstrate cash flow models and relative valuation ratios that can be used to determine a stock's intrinsic value and identify undervalued stocks. We also review factors that will help you determine when to sell a stock that you currently own and discuss the pressures and influences that affect professional stock analysts. We conclude with a discussion of important factors to consider when analyzing foreign stocks.

COMPANY ANALYSIS VERSUS THE VALUATION OF STOCK

This chapter is titled "Company Analysis and Stock Valuation" to convey the idea that the common stocks of good companies are not necessarily good investments. The point is, after analyzing a company and deriving an understanding of its strengths and risks, you need to compute the fundamental intrinsic value of the firm's stock and compare the intrinsic value of a stock to its market value to determine if the company's stock should be purchased. The stock of a wonderful firm with superior management and strong performance measured by sales and earnings growth can be priced so high that the intrinsic value of the stock is below its current market price and should not be acquired. In contrast, the stock of a company with less success based on its sales and earnings growth may have a stock market price that is below its intrinsic value. In this case, although the company is not as good, its stock could be the better investment.

The classic confusion in this regard concerns growth companies versus growth stocks. The stock of a growth company is not necessarily a growth stock. Recognition of this difference is absolutely essential for successful investing.

Growth Companies and Growth Stocks

Observers have historically defined growth companies as those that consistently experience above-average increases in sales and earnings. This definition has some limitations because many firms could qualify due to certain accounting procedures, mergers, or other external events.

In contrast, financial theorists define a growth company as a firm with the management ability and the opportunities to make investments that yield rates of return greater than the firm's required rate of return.[1] This required rate of return is the firm's weighted average cost of capital (WACC). As an example, a growth company might be able to acquire capital at an average cost of 10 percent and yet have the management ability and the opportunity to invest those funds at rates of return of 15 to 20 percent. As a result of these investment opportunities, the firm's sales and earnings grow faster than those of similar risk firms and the overall economy. In addition, a growth company that has above-average investment opportunities should, and typically does, retain a large portion of its earnings to fund these superior investment projects (i.e., they have low dividend payout ratios).

Growth stocks are *not* necessarily shares in growth companies. A growth stock is a stock with a higher rate of return than other stocks in the market with similar risk characteristics. The stock achieves this superior risk-adjusted rate of return because at some point in time the market

---

[1]Ezra Solomon, *The Theory of Financial Management* (New York: Columbia University Press, 1963), 55–68; and Merton Miller and Franco Modigliani, "Dividend Policy, Growth and the Valuation of Shares," *Journal of Business* 34, no. 4 (October 1961): 411–433.

undervalued it compared to other stocks. Although the stock market adjusts stock prices relatively quickly and accurately to reflect new information, available information is not always perfect or complete. Therefore, imperfect or incomplete information may cause a given stock to be undervalued or overvalued at a point in time.[2]

If the stock is undervalued, its price should eventually increase to reflect its true fundamental value when the correct information becomes available. During this period of price adjustment, the stock's realized return will exceed the required return for a stock with its risk, and, during this period of adjustment, it will be considered a growth stock. Growth stocks are not necessarily limited to growth companies. A future growth stock can be the stock of any type of company; the stock need only be undervalued by the market.

The fact is, if investors recognize a growth company and discount its future earnings stream properly, the current market price of the growth company's stock will reflect its future earnings stream. Those who acquire the stock of a growth company at this correct market price will receive a rate of return consistent with the risk of the stock, even when the superior earnings growth is attained. In many instances, overeager investors tend to overestimate the expected growth rate of earnings and cash flows for the growth company and, therefore, inflate the price of a growth company's stock. Investors who pay the inflated stock price will earn a rate of return below the risk-adjusted required rate of return, despite the fact that the growth company experiences the above-average growth of sales and earnings. Several studies that have examined the stock price performance for samples of growth companies have found that their stocks performed poorly—that is, the stocks of growth companies have generally *not* been growth stocks.[3]

Defensive Companies and Stocks

Defensive companies are those whose future earnings are likely to withstand an economic downturn. One would expect them to have relatively low business risk and not excessive financial risk. Typical examples are public utilities or grocery chains—firms that supply basic consumer necessities.

There are two closely related concepts of a **defensive stock**. First, a defensive stock's rate of return is not expected to decline during an overall market decline, or decline less than the overall market. Second, our CAPM discussion indicated that an asset's relevant risk is its covariance with the market portfolio of risky assets—that is, an asset's systematic risk. A stock with low or negative systematic risk (a small positive or negative beta) may be considered a defensive stock according to this theory because its returns are unlikely to be harmed significantly in a bear market.

Cyclical Companies and Stocks

A **cyclical company**'s sales and earnings will be heavily influenced by aggregate business activity. Examples would be firms in the steel, auto, or heavy machinery industries. Such companies will do well during economic expansions and poorly during economic contractions. This volatile earnings pattern is typically a function of the firm's business risk (both sales volatility and operating leverage) and can be compounded by financial risk.

A **cyclical stock** will experience changes in its rates of return greater than changes in overall market rates of return. In terms of the CAPM, these would be stocks that have high betas. The stock of a cyclical company, however, is not necessarily cyclical. A cyclical stock is the stock of any company that has returns that are more volatile than the overall market—that is, high-beta stocks that have high correlation with the aggregate market and greater volatility.

---

[2]An analyst is more likely to find such stocks outside the top tier of companies that are scrutinized by numerous analysts; in other words, look for "neglected" stocks.

[3]Michael Solt and Meir Statman, "Good Companies, Bad Stocks," *Journal of Portfolio Management* 15, no. 4 (Summer 1989): 39–44; Hersh Shafrin and Meir Statman, "Making Sense of Beta, Size, and Book-to-Market," *Journal of Portfolio Management* 21, no. 2 (Winter 1995): 26–34; and Michelle Clayman, "In Search of Excellence: The Investor's Viewpoint," *Financial Analysts Journal* 43, no. 3 (May–June 1987): 54–63.

Speculative Companies and Stocks

A speculative company is one whose assets involve great risk but that also has a possibility of great gain. A good example of a speculative firm is one involved in oil exploration.

A speculative stock possesses a high probability of low or negative rates of return and a low probability of normal or high rates of return. Specifically, a speculative stock is one that is overpriced, leading to a high probability that during the future period when the market adjusts the stock price to its true value, it will experience either low or possibly negative rates of return. Such an expectation might be the case for an excellent growth company whose stock is selling at an extremely high price/earnings ratio—i.e., it is substantially overvalued.

Value versus Growth Investing

Some analysts also divide stocks into "growth" stocks and "value" stocks. As we have discussed, growth stocks are companies that will have positive earnings surprises and above-average risk-adjusted rates of return because the stocks are undervalued. If the analyst does a good job in identifying such companies, investors in these stocks will reap the benefits of seeing their stock prices rise after other investors identify their earnings growth potential. Value stocks are those that appear to be undervalued for reasons other than earnings growth potential. Value stocks are usually identified by analysts as having low price-earning or price-book value ratios. Notably, in these comparisons between growth and value stocks, the specification of a growth stock is *not* consistent with our preceding discussion. In these discussions, a growth stock is generally specified as a stock of a company that is experiencing rapid growth of sales and earnings (e.g., Intel and Microsoft). As a result of this company performance, the stock typically has a high *P/E* and price-book-value ratio. Unfortunately, the specification does not consider the critical comparison between intrinsic value and market price. Exhibit 15.1 shows the recent performance of a growth and value stock index for the period 1991–2001. The two series were very close during 1991–1996. Growth outperformed during 1998–1999 but declined substantially in 2000–2001. Thus, for the total period, value stocks were superior.

EXHIBIT 15.1 ▶

A COMPARISON OF THE PERFORMANCE OF THE RUSSELL 3000 VALUE AND GROWTH STOCK INDEXES: 1991–2001

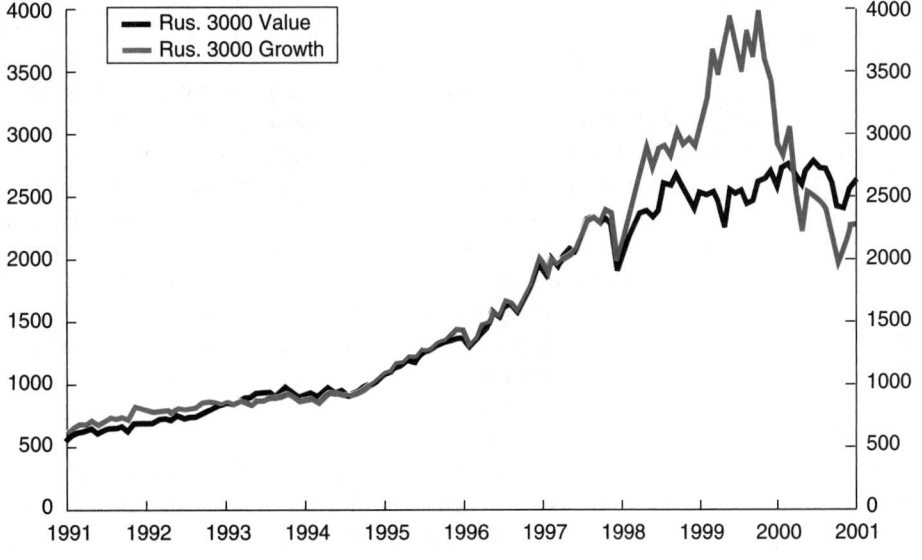

The major point of this section is that you must initially examine a company to determine its characteristics and subsequently derive an estimate of the intrinsic value of its stock. When you compare this intrinsic value of the stock to its current market price you decide whether you should acquire it—that is, will the stock provide a rate of return equal to or greater than what is consistent with its risk?

ECONOMIC, INDUSTRY, AND STRUCTURAL LINKS TO COMPANY ANALYSIS

The analysis of companies and their stocks is the final step in the top-down approach to investing. Rather than selecting stocks on the basis of company-specific factors (as with bottom-up analysis), top-down analysts review the current state and future outlook for domestic and international sectors of the economy. On the basis of this macroeconomic analysis, they identify industries that are expected to offer attractive returns in the expected future environment. Following this macroanalysis, we value the firms in the selected industries. Our analysis concentrates on the two significant determinants of a stock's intrinsic value: (1) growth of the firm's expected cash flows and (2) its risk and the appropriate discount rate.

Economic and Industry Influences

If economic trends are favorable for an industry, the company analysis should focus on firms in that industry that are well positioned to benefit from the economic trends. Research analysts should become familiar with the cash flow and risk attributes of the firms they are studying. In times of economic or industry growth, the most attractive candidates may be the firms in the industry with high levels of operating and financial leverage. A modest percentage increase in revenue can be magnified into a much larger percentage rise in earnings and cash flow for the highly leveraged firm. The point is, firms in an industry will have varying sensitivities to economic variables, such as economic growth, interest rates, input costs, and exchange rates. Because each firm is different, an investor must determine the best candidates for purchase under expected economic conditions.

Structural Influences

In addition to economic variables, other factors, such as social trends, technology, and political and regulatory influences, can have a major effect on some firms in an industry. Some firms in the industry can try to take advantage of demographic changes or shifts in consumer tastes and lifestyles, or invest in technology to lower costs and better serve their customers. Such firms may be able to grow and succeed despite unfavorable industry or economic conditions. For example, Wal-Mart became the nation's leading retailer in the 1990s because it benefited from smart management. The geographic location of many of its stores allowed it to benefit from rising regional population and lower labor costs. Its strategy, which emphasized everyday low prices, was appealing to consumers who had become concerned about the price and value of purchases. Wal-Mart's technologically advanced inventory and ordering systems and the logistics of its distribution system gave the retailer a competitive advantage.

During the initial stage of an industry's life cycle, the original firms in the industry can refine their technologies and move down the learning curve. Subsequent followers may benefit from these initial actions and can learn from the leaders' mistakes and take the market lead away from them. Investors need to be aware of such strategies so they can evaluate companies and their stocks accordingly.

Political and regulatory events can create opportunities in an industry even during weak economic periods. Deregulation in trucking, airlines, and the financial services industries in the 1980s led to the creation of new companies and innovative strategies. The point is, sharp price declines following bad industry news may be a good buying opportunity for astute investors. Some stocks in an industry may deserve lower prices following some political or regulatory events; but, if the market also punishes the stock prices of good companies with smaller exposures to the bad news, then an alert analyst will identify buying opportunities of underpriced stocks within an industry.

The bottom line is that, although the economy plays a major role in determining overall market trends and industry groups display sensitivity to economic variables, other structural changes may counterbalance the economic effects, or company management may be able to minimize the impact of economic events on a company. Analysts who are familiar with industry trends and company strategies can issue well-reasoned buy-and-sell recommendations irrespective of the economic forecast.

COMPANY ANALYSIS

This section groups various analysis components for discussion. "Firm Competitive Strategies" continues the Porter discussion of an industry's competitive environment. The basic SWOT analysis, is intended to articulate a firm's strengths, weaknesses, opportunities, and threats. These two analyses should provide a complete understanding of a firm's overall *strategic* approach. Given this background, we review the fundamental valuation models. In the rest of this chapter, we discuss estimating intrinsic value for Walgreens using the two valuation approaches: (1) the present value of cash flows, and (2) relative valuation ratio techniques. Following this, we discuss the significance of site visits to companies, how to prepare for an interview with management, and suggestions on when an investor should consider selling an asset. This is followed by a discussion of unique considerations regarding evaluation of international companies and their stocks. The final section of the chapter discusses the unique features of true growth companies and presents and demonstrates several models that can be used to value growth companies.

Firm Competitive Strategies

In describing competition within industries, we identified five competitive forces that could affect the competitive structure and profit potential of an industry. They are: (1) current rivalry, (2) threat of new entrants, (3) potential substitutes, (4) bargaining power of suppliers, and (5) bargaining power of buyers. After you have determined the competitive structure of an industry, you should attempt to identify the specific competitive strategy employed by each firm and evaluate these strategies in terms of the overall competitive structure of the industry.

A company's competitive strategy can either be *defensive* or *offensive*. A **defensive competitive strategy** involves positioning the firm so that its capabilities provide the best means to deflect the effect of the competitive forces in the industry. Examples may include investing in fixed assets and technology to lower production costs or creating a strong brand image with increased advertising expenditures.

An **offensive competitive strategy** is one in which the firm attempts to use its strengths to affect the competitive forces in the industry. For example, Microsoft dominated the personal computer software market by preempting, rivals and its early affiliation with IBM because it became the writer of operating system software for a large portion of the PC market. Similarly, Wal-Mart used its buying power to obtain price concessions from its suppliers. This cost advantage, coupled with a superior delivery system to its stores, allowed Wal-Mart to grow against larger competitors until it became the leading U.S. retailer.

As an investor, you must understand the alternative competitive strategies available, determine each firm's strategy, judge whether the firm's strategy is reasonable for its industry, and, finally, evaluate how successful the firm is in implementing its strategy.

In the following sections, we discuss analyzing a firm's competitive position and strategy. The analyst must decide whether the firm's management is correctly positioning the firm to take advantage of industry and economic conditions. The analyst's opinion about management's decisions should ultimately be reflected in, and be the basis for the analyst's estimates of the firm's growth of cash flow and earnings.

Porter suggests two major competitive strategies: low-cost leadership and differentiation.[4] These two competitive strategies dictate how a firm has decided to cope with the five competitive conditions that define an industry's environment. The strategies available and the ways of implementing them differ within each industry.

Low-Cost Strategy   The firm that pursues the low-cost strategy is determined to become *the* low-cost producer and, hence, the cost leader in its industry. Cost advantages vary by industry and might include economies of scale, proprietary technology, or preferential access to raw materials. In order to benefit from cost leadership, the firm must command prices near the industry average, which means that it must differentiate itself about as well as other firms. If the firm discounts price too much, it could erode the superior rates of return available because of its low cost. During the past decade, Wal-Mart was considered a low-cost source. The firm achieved this by volume purchasing of merchandise and lower-cost operations. As a result, the firm charged less but still enjoyed higher profit margins and returns on capital than many of its competitors.

Differentiation Strategy   With the differentiation strategy, a firm seeks to identify itself as unique in its industry in an area that is important to buyers. Again, the possibilities for differentiation vary widely by industry. A company can attempt to differentiate itself based on its distribution system (selling in stores, by mail order, or door-to-door) or some unique marketing approach. A firm employing the differentiation strategy will enjoy above-average rates of return only if the price premium attributable to its differentiation exceeds the extra cost of being unique. Therefore, when you analyze a firm using this strategy, you must determine whether the differentiating factor is truly unique, whether it is sustainable, its cost, and if the price premium derived from the uniqueness is greater than its cost (is the firm experiencing above-average rates of return?).

Focusing a Strategy   Whichever strategy it selects, a firm must determine where it will focus this strategy. Specifically, a firm must select segments in the industry and tailor its strategy to serve these specific groups. For example, a low-cost strategy would typically exploit cost advantages for certain segments of the industry, such as being the low-cost producer for the expensive segment of the market. Similarly, a differentiation focus would target the special needs of buyers in specific segments. For example, in the athletic shoe market, companies have attempted to develop shoes for unique sport segments, such as tennis, basketball, aerobics, or walkers and hikers, rather than offering only shoes for runners. Firms thought that participants in these activities needed shoes with characteristics different from those desired by joggers. Equally important, they believed that these athletes would be willing to pay a premium for these special shoes. Again, you must ascertain if special possibilities exist, if they are being served by another firm, and if they can be priced to generate abnormal returns to the firm. Exhibit 15.2 details some of Porter's ideas for the skills, resources, and company organizational requirements needed to successfully develop a cost leadership or differentiation strategy.

Next, you must determine which strategy the firm is pursuing and its success. Also, can the strategy be sustained? Further, you should evaluate a firm's competitive strategy over time, because strategies need to change as an industry evolves; different strategies work during differ-

---

[4]Michael E. Porter, *Competitive Strategy: Techniques for Analyzing Industries and Companies* (New York: The Free Press, 1980); Michael E. Porter, *Competitive Advantage: Creating and Sustaining Superior Performance* (New York: The Free Press, 1985).

EXHIBIT 15.2 *SKILLS, RESOURCES, AND ORGANIZATIONAL REQUIREMENTS NEEDED TO SUCCESSFULLY APPLY COST LEADERSHIP AND DIFFERENTIATION STRATEGIES*

GENERIC STRATEGY	COMMONLY REQUIRED SKILLS AND RESOURCES	COMMON ORGANIZATIONAL REQUIREMENTS
Overall cost leadership	Sustained capital investment and access to capital	Tight cost control
	Process engineering skills	Frequent, detailed control reports
	Intense supervision of labor	Structured organization and responsibilities
	Products designed for ease in manufacture	Incentives based on meeting strict quantitative targets
	Low-cost distribution system	
Differentiation	Strong marketing abilities	Strong coordination among functions in R&D, product development, and marketing
	Product engineering	
	Creative flair	Subjective measurement and incentives instead of quantitative measures
	Strong capability in basic research	
	Corporate reputation for quality or technological leadership	Amenities to attract highly skilled labor, scientists, or creative people
	Long tradition in the industry or unique combination of skills drawn from other businesses	
	Strong cooperation from channels	

Adapted with the permission of The Free Press, an imprint of Simon & Schuster Adult Publishing Group, from *Competitive Strategy: Techniques for Analyzing Industries and Competitors* by Michael E. Porter. Copyright ©1980, 1998 by The Free Press.

ent phases of an industry's life cycle. For example, differentiation strategies may work for firms in an industry during the growth stages. When the industry is in the mature stage, firms may try to lower their costs.

Through the analysis process, the analyst identifies what the company does well, what it doesn't do well, and where the firm is vulnerable to the five competitive forces. Some call this process developing a company's "story." This evaluation enables the analyst to determine the outlook and risks facing the firm. In summary, understanding the industry's competitive forces and the firm's strategy for dealing with them is the key to deriving an accurate estimate of the firm's long-run cash flows and risks of doing business.

Another framework for examining and understanding a firm's competitive position and its strategy is the following SWOT analysis.

SWOT Analysis   SWOT analysis involves an examination of a firm's *s*trengths, *w*eaknesses, *o*pportunities, and *t*hreats. It should help you evaluate a firm's strategies to exploit its competitive advantages or defend against its weaknesses. Strengths and weaknesses involve identifying the firm's *internal* abilities or lack thereof. Opportunities and threats include *external* situations, such as competitive forces, discovery and development of new technologies, government regulations, and domestic and international economic trends.

The *strengths* of a company give the firm a comparative advantage in the marketplace. Perceived strengths can include good customer service, high-quality products, strong brand image, customer loyalty, innovative R&D, market leadership, or strong financial resources. To remain strengths, they must continue to be developed, maintained, and defended through prudent capital investment policies.

Weaknesses result when competitors have potentially exploitable advantages over the firm. Once weaknesses are identified, the firm can select strategies to mitigate or correct the weaknesses. For example, a firm that is only a domestic producer in a global market can make investments that will allow it to export or produce its product overseas. Another example would be a firm with poor financial resources that would form joint ventures with financially stronger firms.

Opportunities, or environmental factors that favor the firm, can include a growing market for the firm's products (domestic and international), shrinking competition, favorable exchange rate shifts, a financial community that has confidence in the outlook for the industry or firm, or identification of a new market or product segment.

Threats are environmental factors that can hinder the firm in achieving its goals. Examples would include a slowing domestic economy (or sluggish overseas economies for exporters), additional government regulation, an increase in industry competition, threats of entry, buyers or suppliers seeking to increase their bargaining power, or new technology that can obsolete the industry's product. By recognizing and understanding opportunities and threats, an investor can make informed decisions about how the firm can exploit opportunities and mitigate threats.

Some Lessons from Lynch

Peter Lynch, the former portfolio manager of Fidelity Investments' highly successful Magellan Fund, looks for the following attributes when he analyzes firms.[5]

Favorable Attributes of Firms

The following attributes of firms may result in favorable stock market performance:

1. The firm's product is not faddish; it is one that consumers will continue to purchase over time.
2. The company should have some long-run comparative competitive advantage over its rivals that is sustainable.
3. The firm's industry or product has market stability. Therefore, it has little need to innovate or create product improvements or fear that it may lose a technological advantage. Market stability means less potential for entry.
4. The firm can benefit from cost reductions. An example would be a computer manufacturer that uses technology provided by suppliers competing to deliver a faster and less-expensive machine or computer chip.
5. Firms that buy back their shares or companies where management is buying shares, which indicates that its insiders are putting their money into the firm.

Tenets of Warren Buffett

The following tenets are from Hagstrom's *The Essential Buffett:*[6]

Business Tenets
➤ Is the business simple and understandable?
(This makes it easier to estimate future cash flows with a high degree of confidence.)
➤ Does the business have a consistent operating history?
(Again, cash flow estimates can be made with more confidence.)
➤ Does the business have favorable long-term prospects?
(Does the business have a "franchise"—meaning a product or service that is needed or desired without a close substitute and is not regulated? This implies the firm should have pricing flexibility.)

---

[5]See his two books: Peter Lynch, *One Up on Wall Street* (New York: Simon & Schuster, 1989); and Peter Lynch, *Beating the Street* (New York: Simon & Schuster, 1993).

[6]These tenets are from Robert G. Hagstrom, *The Essential Buffett* (New York: John Wiley, 2001). The parenthetical comments are based on discussions in this book and Berkshire Hathaway annual report letters.

Management Tenets
➤ Is management rational?
(Is the allocation of capital to projects that provide returns above the cost of capital? If not, do they pay capital to stockholders through dividends or repurchase stock?)
➤ Is management candid with its shareholders?
(Does management tell owners everything you would want to know?)
➤ Does management resist the institutional imperative?
(Does management not attempt to imitate the behavior of other managers?)

Financial Tenets
➤ Focus on return on equity, not earnings per share.
(Look for strong *ROE* with little or no debt.)
➤ Calculate "owner earnings."
("Owner earnings" are basically equal to "free cash flow" after capital expenditures.)
➤ Look for a company with relatively high profit margins for its industry.
➤ Make sure the company has created at least one dollar of market value for every dollar retained.

Market Tenets
➤ What is the value of the business?
(Value is equal to future free cash flows discounted at a government bond rate. Using this low rate is considered appropriate because the business owner is very confident of his/her cash flow estimates due to extensive analysis, and this confidence implies low risk.)
➤ Can the business be purchased at a significant discount to its fundamental intrinsic value?

The point is, investors should make use of research on the competitive forces in an industry, a firm's responses to those forces, SWOT analysis, Lynch's suggestions, and Buffet's tenets.

ESTIMATING INTRINSIC VALUE

Now that the analysis of the economy, structural forces, the industry, the company, and its competitors is completed, it is time to estimate the intrinsic value of the firm's common stock. If the intrinsic value estimate exceeds the stock's current market price, the stock should be purchased. In contrast, if the current market price exceeds our intrinsic value estimate, we should avoid the stock.

As noted in Chapter 11, analysts use two general approaches to valuation. The techniques that serve each of these approaches follow:

Present Value of Cash Flows (PVCF)
1. Present value of dividends (DDM)
2. Present value of free cash flow to equity (FCFE)
3. Present value of free operating cash flow to the firm (FCFF)

Relative Valuation Techniques
1. Price/earnings ratio (*P/E*)
2. Price/cash flow ratio (*P/CF*)
3. Price/book value ratio (*P/BV*)
4. Price/sales ratio (*P/S*)

This section contains a brief presentation for each of these techniques as applied to Walgreens, the largest retail drugstore (RDS) chain in the United States. It operates 3,520 drugstores in 43 states and Puerto Rico. General merchandise accounts for 23 percent of total sales, and its pharmacy operation generates 57.5 percent of sales.

EXHIBIT 15.3 ▶ *WALGREENS INPUT DATA FOR ALTERNATIVE PRESENT VALUE OF CASH FLOW MODELS (DOLLARS IN MILLIONS, EXCEPT PER SHARE DATA)[a]*

YEAR	DIVIDEND PER SHARE	NET INCOME	DEPRECIATION EXPENSE	CAPITAL SPENDING	CHANGE IN WORKING CAPITAL	PRINCIPAL REPAYMENT	NEW DEBT ISSUES	FCFE	EBIT	TAX RATE	FCFF	100% − TAX RATE	TIME
1983	0.02	70	25	−71	−15	−3	0	6	147	45%	19.7	55%	1
1984	0.03	85	29	−68	−56	−3	0	−13	181	45	4.6	55	2
1985	0.03	94	34	−97	−61	−3	20	−13	209	46	−11.0	54	3
1986	0.03	103	44	−156	−72	−5	92	6	229	45	−57.9	55	4
1987	0.04	104	54	−122	−118	−4	5	−81	243	46	−55.0	54	5
1988	0.04	129	59	−114	49	−4	31	150	263	38	156.9	62	6
1989	0.05	154	64	−121	−97	−4	0	−4	301	37	35.5	63	7
1990	0.05	175	70	−192	−69	−4	0	−20	344	38	22.1	62	8
1991	0.06	195	84	−202	−129	−24	0	−76	381	38	−10.6	62	9
1992	0.07	221	92	−145	−32	−6	0	130	429	37	185.2	63	10
1993	0.08	245	105	−185	−28	−112	0	25	483	39	186.7	61	11
1994	0.09	282	118	−290	−58	−6	0	46	550	38	111.3	62	12
1995	0.10	321	132	−310	−104	−7	0	32	629	39	101.5	61	13
1996	0.11	372	147	−364	−116	0	2	41	725	39	109.1	61	14
1997	0.12	436	164	−485	34	−1	0	148	842	39	226.8	61	15
1998	0.13	511	189	−641	−143	0	0	−84	878	39	−57.7	61	16
1999	0.13	624	210	−696	−206	0	0	−68	1028	39	−67	61	17
2000	0.14	777	230	−1119	−140	0	0	−252	1264	39	−252	61	18
2001	0.14	886	269	−1237	−569	0	0	−652	1426	38	−650	62	19
Annual compound growth rate 1983–2001	11.42%	15.14%	14.11%	17.21%							13.46%		
Annual compound growth rate 1991–2001	8.84%	16.34%	12.35%	19.87%							12.74%		
Compound sales per share growth rate 1991–2001	13.41%												
Compound BV/PS growth rate 1991–2001	16.60%												
ROE	18.80%												

[a]All per-share data are adjusted for prior stock splits, including the split that occurred in 1999.

Reprinted with permission from Walgreen Co., Deerfield, IL.

Although we limit our demonstration to Walgreens, your complete company analysis would cover all the firms in the RDS industry to determine which stocks should perform the best. The objective is to estimate the expected return and risk for all the individual firms in the industry over your investment horizon. The initial presentation considers the present value of cash flow (PVCF) models. Exhibit 15.3 contains historical data for Walgreens related to variables required for the PVCF models.

Present Value of Dividends

We learned in Chapter 11 that determining the present value of future dividends is a difficult task. Therefore, analysts apply one or more simplifying assumptions when employing the dividend discount models (DDMs). The typical assumption is that the stock's dividends will grow at a constant rate over time. Although unrealistic for fast-growing or cyclical firms, DDMs may be appropriate for some mature, slower-growing firms. More complex DDMs exist for more complicated growth forecasts. These include two-stage growth models (a period of fast growth followed by a period of constant growth) and three-stage growth models (a period of fast growth followed by a period of diminishing growth rates followed by a period of constant growth).[7]

For simplicity, we will initially discuss the constant growth DDM. We saw in Chapter 11 that when dividends grow at a constant rate, a stock's price should equal next year's dividend, D_1, divided by the difference between investors' required rate of return on the stock *(k)* and the dividend growth rate *(g)*:

➤15.1 $$\text{Intrinsic Value} = D_1 / (k - g)$$

With constant dividend growth, next year's dividend (D_1) should equal the current dividend, D_0, increased by the constant dividend growth rate: $D_1 = D_0 (1 + g)$. Because the current dividend is known, to estimate intrinsic value we need only estimate two parameters: the dividend growth rate and investors' required rate of return.

Growth Rate Estimates   If the stock has had fairly constant dividend growth over the past 5 to 10 years, one estimate of the constant growth rate is to use the actual growth of dividends over this period. The average compound rate of growth is found by computing

➤15.2 $$\text{Average Dividend Growth Rate} = \sqrt[n]{\frac{D_n}{D_0}} - 1$$

In the case of Walgreens, the 1983 dividend (D_0) was $0.02 a share and the 2001 dividend (D_{10}) was $0.140 a share. The average dividend growth rate was

$$\sqrt[10]{\frac{\$0.140}{\$0.02}} - 1 = \sqrt[18]{7.00} - 1 = 0.1142$$

or 11.42 percent. Clearly, it is inappropriate to blindly plug historical growth rates into our formulas because if we do, we've wasted our time analyzing economic, structural, industry, and company influences. Our analysis may have indicated that growth is expected to increase or decrease due to such factors as changes in government programs, demographic shifts, or changes in product mix. The historical growth rate may need to be raised or lowered to incorporate our findings.

In Chapter 10, we learned other ways to estimate future growth. The sustainable growth rate

➤15.3 $$g = RR \times ROE$$

assumes the firm will maintain a constant debt-equity ratio as it finances asset growth. We know from Chapter 10 and Chapter 14 that *ROA* can be expressed as the product of the firm's net profit margin and total asset turnover; *ROE* is the product of the net profit margin, total asset turnover, and the financial leverage multiplier. Thus, a firm's future growth rate and its components of

---

[7]These were discussed in Chapter 11. There is a detailed discussion of growth duration models later in this chapter.

ROE can be compared to those of its competitors, its industry, and the market. Although there is not necessarily a close relationship between the year-to-year growth in a firm's assets and its dividend cash flows, these calculations provide insight that, along with the rest of the top-down analysis, can assist the analyst in determining whether dividend growth may rise or fall in the future. For Walgreens, the sustainable growth rate calculation using 2001 data is[8]

$$g = RR \times ROE = 0.82 \times .1835$$
$$= 0.1509 = 15.09\%$$

The dividend growth rate will be influenced by the age of the industry life cycle, structural changes, and economic trends. Economic-industry-firm analysis provides valuable information regarding future trends in dividend growth. Information derived about management's plans to expand the firm, diversify into new areas, or change dividend policy can provide useful information about the firm's dividend policy. Averaging the historical growth rate of dividends (11.42 percent) and the implied sustainable growth estimate of 15.09 percent indicates a value of 13.24 percent. Although we feel that a firm's *ROE* is the critical growth factor and give this estimate more weight, we will use a conservative 13 percent for Walgreens' estimated *g*.

Required Rate of Return Estimate   We know an investor's required rate of return has two basic components: the nominal risk-free interest rate and a risk premium. If the market is efficient, over time the return earned by investors should compensate them for the risk of the investment.

Notably, we must estimate *future* risk premiums to determine the stock's current intrinsic value. Estimates of the nominal risk-free interest rate are available from the initial analysis of the economy during the top-down approach. The risk premium of the firm must rely on other information derived from the top-down company analysis, including evaluation of the financial statements and capital market relationships.

In Chapter 10, we examined ratios that measure several aspects of the risk of a firm and its stock. Business risk, financial risk, liquidity risk, exchange rate risk, and country risk are fundamental risk factors to be reviewed in the context of our economy-industry-firm analysis. These measures can be compared against the firm's major competitors, its industry, and the overall market. This fundamental comparison will tell the analyst if the firm should have a higher or lower risk premium than the overall market, other firms in the industry, or the firm's historical risk premium. Accounting-based risk measures use historical data, whereas investment analysis requires an estimate of the future. Investors need to incorporate into the risk analysis any information uncovered during the top-down process that would lead to higher or lower risk estimates.

For a market-based risk estimate, the firm's characteristic line is estimated by regressing market returns on the stock's returns. We know the slope of this regression line is the stock's beta, or measure of systematic risk. Estimates of the economy's risk-free rate, the future long-run market return, and an estimate of the stock's beta help estimate next year's required rate of return:

➤15.4 $$E(R_{stock}) = E(RFR) + \beta_{stock} [E(R_{market}) - E(RFR)]$$

Again, this estimate of beta begins with historical market information. Because beta is affected by changes in a firm's business and financial risks, as well as other influences, an investor should increase or lower the historical beta estimate based upon his or her analysis of the firm's *future* risk characteristics.

---

[8]This sustainable growth rate value differs from the one in Chapter 10 because this calculation uses year-end values for *ROE;* while, in Chapter 10, the equity value is an average of the beginning and ending values.

To demonstrate the estimate of the required rate of return equation for Walgreens, we make several assumptions regarding components of the security market line (SML) discussed in Chapter 8. First, the prevailing nominal risk-free rate *(RFR)* is estimated at about 5.0 percent—the current yield to maturity for the intermediate-term government bond. The expected equity market rate of return (R_M) depends on the expected market risk premium on stocks. As noted earlier, there is substantial controversy on the appropriate estimate for the equity market risk premium—that is, the estimates range from a high of about 8 percent (the arithmetic mean of the actual risk premium since 1926) to a low of about 3 percent, which is the risk premium suggested in several recent academic studies. The authors reject both of these extreme values and will use a 4.5 percent risk premium (0.045). The final estimate is the firm's systematic risk value (beta), which is typically derived based upon the following regression model (the characteristic line) noted in Chapter 8.

➤15.5 $$R_{WAG} = \alpha + \beta_{WAG} R_M$$

where:

R_{WAG} = **monthly rate of return for Walgreens**
α = **constant term**
β_{WAG} = **beta coefficient for Walgreens**

   equal to $\dfrac{\text{Cov}_{W,M}}{\sigma_M^2}$

R_M = **monthly rates of return for a market proxy—typically the S&P 500 Index**

When this regression was run using monthly rates of return during the five-year period 1997–2001 (60 observations), the beta coefficient was estimated at 0.90.

Putting together the RFR of 0.050 and the market risk premium of 0.045 implies an expected market return (R_M) of 0.095. This combined with the Walgreens beta of 0.90 indicates the following expected rate of return for Walgreens:

$$
\begin{aligned}
E(R) &= RFR + \beta_i(R_M - RFR) \\
&= 0.050 + 0.90\,(0.095 - 0.050) \\
&= 0.050 + 0.90\,(0.045) \\
&= 0.050 + 0.040 \\
&= 0.090 = 9.0\%
\end{aligned}
$$

Present Value of Dividends Model (DDM)

At this point, the analyst would face a problem: the intent was to use the basic DDM, which assumed a constant growth rate for an infinite period. You will recall that the model also required that $k > g$ (the required rate of return is larger than the expected growth rate), which is not true in this case because $k = 9.0$ percent and $g = 13$ percent (as computed earlier). Therefore, the analyst must employ a two- or three-stage growth model. Because of the fairly large difference between the current growth rate of 13 percent and the long-run constant growth rate of 8 percent, it seems reasonable to use a three-stage growth model, which includes a gradual transition period. We assume that the growth periods are as follows:

g_1 = **7 years (growing at 13 percent a year)**
g_2 = **5 years (during this period it is assumed that the growth rate declines 1 percent per year for 5 years)**
g_3 = **constant perpetual growth of 8 percent**

Therefore, beginning with 2002 when dividends were expected to be $0.15, the future dividend payments will be as follows (the growth rate is in parentheses):

Year	High-Growth Period		Year	Declining-Growth Period	
2003	(13%)	0.17	2010	(12%)	0.39
2004	(13%)	0.19	2011	(11%)	0.43
2005	(13%)	0.21	2012	(10%)	0.47
2006	(13%)	0.24	2013	(9%)	0.51
2007	(13%)	0.27	2014	(8%)	0.55
2008	(13%)	0.31			
2009	(13%)	0.35			

Constant Growth Period:

$$P_{2014} = \frac{0.55(1.08)}{0.09 - 0.08} = \frac{0.59}{0.09 - 0.08} = \frac{0.59}{0.01} = \$59.00$$

The total value of the stock is the sum of the three present value streams discounted at 9 percent:

1. Present value of high-growth period dividends	$1.20
2. Present value of declining-growth period dividends	1.00
3. Present value of constant-growth period dividends	20.91
Total present value of dividends	**$23.11**

The estimated value based on the DDM is substantially lower than the market price in mid-2002 of about $38.00. This estimated value also implies a *P/E* ratio based upon expected earnings in 2002 of about $0.98 per share (that is, about 23.6 times earnings) compared to the prevailing market *P/E* of almost 25 times 2002 earnings. In a subsequent section on relative valuation techniques, we compare Walgreens' *P/E* ratio to that of its industry and the market.

Present Value of Free Cash Flow to Equity

As noted in Chapter 11, this technique resembles a present value of earnings concept except that it considers the capital expenditures required to maintain and grow the firm and the change in working capital required for a growing firm (that is, an increase in accounts receivable and inventory). The specific definition of free cash flow to equity (FCFE) is:

Net Income + Depreciation Expense – Capital

Expenditures – Δ in Working Capital – Principal

Debt Repayments + New Debt Issues

This technique attempts to determine the free cash flow that is available to the stockholders after payments to all other capital suppliers and after providing for the continued growth of the firm. As noted in Chapter 11, given the current FCFE values, the alternative forms of the model are similar to those available for the DDM, which in turn depends on the firm's growth prospects. Specifically, if the firm is in its mature, constant-growth phase, it is possible to use a model similar to the reduced form DDM:

➤15.6

$$\text{Value} = \frac{\text{FCFE}_1}{k - g_{\text{FCFE}}}$$

where:

> FCFE = the expected free cash flow to equity in period 1
> k = the required rate of return on equity for the firm
> g_{FCFE} = the expected constant growth rate of free cash flow to equity for the firm

We already know from the prior dividend model that the firm's earnings are growing at a rate (about 13 percent) that exceeds the required rate of return. In the case of FCFE, it is necessary to consider the effect of capital expenditures relative to depreciation and changes in working capital as well as debt repayments and new debt issues. The historical data in Exhibit 15.3 shows a growth rate that exceeded 20 percent during some periods since 1983, in contrast to the negative values in 1998–2001. The reason for the dramatic change is evident—it is the very heavy capital expenditures that have grown at almost a 20 percent rate for the total period and the significant negative working capital items (including a special problem with inventories). The firm expects a reduction in the growth rate of stores—from a net increase (new stores minus closings) of about 475 stores per year. Based upon discussions with management, it appears that this slowdown in growth is due to the prevailing shortage of pharmacists. While Walgreens will continue adding stores, the slower rate of growth and the elimination of the inventory buildup problem will allow the firm to return to positive cash flows in 2003. Specifically, it is estimated that in 2003 the FCFE will be about $200 million and the FCFF (free cash flow to the firm) will be about $250 million. Such volatility makes it appropriate to use the conservative 13 percent growth rate going forward after 2003. Therefore, the following example again uses a three-stage growth model with characteristics similar to the dividend growth model.

> g_1 = 13 percent for the six years after 2003
> g_2 = a constantly declining growth rate to 8 percent over five years
> K = 9 percent cost of equity

The specific estimates of annual FCFE, beginning with the actual estimated value of $200 million in 2003, are as follows:

	HIGH-GROWTH PERIOD				DECLINING-GROWTH PERIOD		
YEAR	GROWTH	$ MILLION	PV @ 9%	YEAR	GROWTH	$ MILLION	PV @ 9%
2003	—	200	183	2010	(12%)	465	233
2004	(13%)	226	190	2011	(11%)	517	238
2005	(13%)	255	197	2012	(10%)	568	240
2006	(13%)	288	204	2013	(9%)	619	240
2007	(13%)	325	211	2014	(8%)	669	238
2008	(13%)	368	219			Total	1,189
2009	(13%)	416	228				
		Total	1,432				

$$\text{Constant Growth Period Value} = \frac{669(1.08)}{0.09 - 0.08} = \frac{723}{0.09 - 0.08} = 72,300$$

$$\text{PV @ 9\%} = 25,703$$

The total value of the stock is the sum of the three present value streams discounted at 9 percent:

	$ MILLION
1. Present value of high-growth cash flows	1,432
2. Present value of declining-growth cash flows	1,189
3. Present value of constant-growth cash flows	25,703
Total present value of FCFE	$28,324

The outstanding shares in 2001 were approximately 1,030 million. Therefore, the per share value based upon the present value of FCFE is $27.50 ($28,324/1,030). Again, this estimated value is lower than the prevailing market price of about $38.00. This estimated value implies a *P/E* ratio of about 28 times estimated 2002 earnings of $0.98 per share.

Present Value of Operating Free Cash Flow

This is also referred to as *free cash flow to the firm* (FCFF) by Damodaran and the *the entity DCF model* by Copeland, Koller, and Murrin.[9] The object is to determine a value for the total firm and subtract the value of the firm's debt obligations to arrive at a value for the firm's equity. Notably, in this valuation technique, we discount the firm's operating free cash flow to the firm (FCFF) at the firm's weighted average cost of capital (WACC) rather than its cost of equity.

Operating free cash flow or *free cash flow to the firm* is equal to

$$\text{EBIT (1 – Tax Rate) + Depreciation Expense}$$
$$\text{– Capital Expenditures – }\Delta\text{ in Working Capital}$$
$$\text{– }\Delta\text{ in other assets}$$

This is the cash flow generated by a company's operations and available to all who have provided capital to the firm—both equity and debt. As noted, because it is the cash flow from *all capital suppliers,* it is discounted at the firm's WACC.

Again, the alternative specifications of this operating FCF model are similar to the DDM—that is, the specification depends upon the firm's growth prospects. Assuming an expectation of constant growth, you can use the reduced form model:

➤15.7
$$\text{Firm Value} = \frac{\text{FCFF}_1}{\text{WACC} - g_{\text{FCFF}}} \text{ or } \frac{\text{OFCF}_1}{\text{WACC} - g_{\text{OFCF}}}$$

where:

> FCFF_1 = **the free cash flow for the firm in period 1**
> OFCF_1 = **the firm's operating free cash flow in period 1**
> WACC = **the firm's weighted average cost of capital**
> g_{FCFF} = **the constant infinite growth rate of free cash flow for the firm**
> g_{OFCF} = **the constant infinite growth rate of operating free cash flow**

As noted in Exhibit 15.3, the compound annual growth rate for operating free cash flow (free cash flow to the firm) during the 18-year period was negative due to the negative values starting in 1998, but it is anticipated that it will become positive in 2003. An alternative measure of long-run growth is the growth implied by the equation:

➤15.8
$$g = (RR)(ROIC)$$

where:

> *RR* = **the average retention rate**
> *ROIC* = **EBIT (1 – Tax Rate)/Total Capital**

---

[9]Aswath Damodaran, *Damodaran on Valuation* (New York: Wiley, 1994). Chapter 8; and Tom Copeland, Tim Koller, and Jack Murrin, *Valuation: Measuring and Managing the Value of Companies,* 3d ed. (New York: Wiley, 2001), Chapter 5.

For Walgreens, the recent retention rate is about 80 percent and

$$ROIC = \frac{\text{EBIT}(1 - \text{Tax Rate})}{\text{Total Capital}} = \frac{(1,423) \times (0.62)}{(4,800 + 5,822)/2} = \frac{882}{5,311} = 0.1660$$
$$= 16.60\%$$

Therefore,

$$g = (0.80)(0.1660)$$
$$= .1328 = 13.28\%$$

Since we expect the OFCF series to become positive in 2003, in the subsequent valuation calculation we will begin with a growth estimate for OFCF/FCFF of 13 percent.

Calculation of WACC   We calculate the discount rate (i.e., the firm's WACC) using the following formula:

➤15.9 $$\text{WACC} = W_E k + W_D i$$

where:

W_E = **the proportion of equity in total capital**
k = **the after-tax cost of equity (from the SML)**
W_D = **the proportion of debt in total capital**[10]
i = **the after-tax cost of debt**[11]

Recall from corporate finance courses that there are differences of opinion regarding how one should estimate the debt and equity weights—that is, using proportions based upon relative book values or based on relative market value weights. Without getting into the reasons for each choice, it is important to recognize that the use of market value weights will almost always result in a higher WACC because it will imply more equity financing since most firms have a P/BV ratio greater than one (for Walgreens the P/BV ratio is currently in excess of 5.0). To demonstrate this, we compute a WACC using both weightings. The cost of debt and cost of equity will be the same for both sets.

WACC Using Book Value Weights

---

k_e = 0.090 (from prior SML calculation)
k_d = 0.043 (current interest rate of 7% and recent tax rate of 38% for WAG)
     $0.07 \times (1 - 0.38) = 0.043$
W_d = 0.30 (including leases)
W_e = 0.70
     $\text{WACC} = (W_d \times k_d) + (W_e \times k_e)$
     $= (0.30 \times 0.043) + (0.70 \times 0.090)$
     $= 0.0129 + 0.063 = 0.0760 = 7.60\%$

---

[10]The proportions of debt and equity capital used in the WACC estimate will be computed using both book value weights that consider the value of capitalized lease payments as debt, and market value weights.

[11]For this estimate, we use the prevailing interest rate on corporate A-rated bonds (7 percent), and Walgreens' (ticker symbol WAG) recent tax rate of 38 percent.

WACC USING MARKET VALUE WEIGHTS	
$k_e = 0.090$	$W_e = 0.90$
$k_d = 0.043$	$W_d = 0.10$

$$\text{WACC} = (W_d \times k_d) + (W_e \times k_e)$$
$$= (0.10 \times 0.043) + (0.90 \times 0.090)$$
$$= 0.0043 + 0.081 = 0.0853 = 8.53\%$$

Therefore, we have a range of 7.60 percent to 8.53 percent and an average of 8.06 percent. We will use a WACC of 8 percent in the demonstration.

Again, because the expected growth rate of operating free cash flow (13 percent) is greater than the firm's WACC, we cannot use the reduced form model that assumes constant growth at this relatively high rate for an infinite period. Therefore, the following demonstration will employ the three-stage growth model with growth duration assumptions similar to the prior examples.

Given these inputs for recent growth and the firm's WACC, the growth estimates for a three-stage growth model are

g_1 = 13 percent for six years
g_2 = a constantly declining rate to 7 percent over six years.[12]

The specific estimates for future OFCF (or FCFF) are as follows, beginning from the 2003 value of $250 million.

	HIGH-GROWTH PERIOD				DECLINING-GROWTH PERIOD		
YEAR	GROWTH RATE	FCFF	PV @ 8%	YEAR	GROWTH RATE	FCFF	PV @ 8%
2003	—	250	231	2010	(12%)	583	315
2004	(13%)	282	242	2011	(11%)	647	324
2005	(13%)	319	253	2012	(10%)	712	330
2006	(13%)	361	265	2013	(9%)	776	333
2007	(13%)	408	278	2014	(8%)	838	333
2008	(13%)	461	291	2015	(7%)	897	330
2009	(13%)	520	303			Total	$1,965
	Total	$1,863					

$$\text{Constant Growth Period Value} = \frac{897(1.07)}{0.08 - 0.07} = \frac{960}{0.08 - 0.07} = \$96,000$$
$$\text{PV @ 8\%} = \$32,654$$

Thus, the total value of the firm is:

	$ MILLION
1. Present value of high-growth cash flows	$1,863
2. Present value of declining-growth cash flows	1,965
3. Present value of constant-growth cash flows	32,654
Total present value of operating FCF (FCFF)	$36,482

---

[12]This 7 percent long-run growth rate assumption implies that we do not believe that FCFF can grow as fast as FCFE. Given a beginning growth rate of 13 percent and a long-run rate of 7 percent means that the growth rate will decline by 0.01 per year as shown in the following example.

Recall that the value of equity is the total value of the firm (PV of OFCF) minus the current market value of debt, which is the present value of debt payments at the firm's cost of debt (0.07). The values are as follows:

Total present value of operating FCF	$ 36,482
Minus: value of debt[13]	6,710
value of equity	$29,772
Number of common shares	1,030 million
Value of equity per share	$ 28.90

Again, this estimated value compares to the recent market value of about $38.00. The $28.90 value implies a *P/E* of about 29 times estimated 2002 earnings of $0.98 per share.

To summarize, the valuations derived from the present value of cash flow techniques are as follows:

Present value of dividends	$23.11
Present value of FCFE	$27.50
Present value of OFCF	$28.90
(or the PV of FCFF)	

All of these prices must be compared to the prevailing market price of $38 to determine the investment decision.

Relative Valuation Ratio Techniques

In this section, we present the data required to compute the several relative valuation ratios and demonstrate the use of these relative valuation ratio techniques for Walgreens compared to the RDS industry and the S&P Industrials Index.

Exhibit 15.4 contains the basic data required to compute the relative valuation ratios, and Exhibit 15.5 contains the four sets of relative valuation ratios for Walgreens, its industry, and the aggregate market. This exhibit also contains a comparison of the company ratios to similar ratios for the company's industry and the market. Such a comparison helps the analyst determine changes in the relative valuation ratios over time and consider if the current valuation ratio for the company (Walgreens) is reasonable based on the financial characteristics of the firm versus its industry and the market. To aid in the analysis, four graphs contain the time series of the relative valuation ratios for the company, its industry, and the market. Four additional graphs show the relationship between the relative valuation ratios: for the company compared to its industry and for the company compared to the stock market. We begin with the *P/E* ratio approach where we derive an intrinsic value for the stock and a rate of return based upon an estimate of future EPS and an earnings multiple (*P/E*) for the stock.

ESTIMATING COMPANY EARNINGS PER SHARE

An estimate of the earnings per share for the company is a function of the sales forecast and the estimated profit margin. The sales forecast includes an analysis of the relationship of company sales to various relevant economic series and to the RDS industry series. These comparisons tell us how the company is performing relative to the economy and to its closest competition.

---

[13]This includes the present value of minimum lease payments discounted at the firm's cost of debt (7 percent).

EXHIBIT 15.4 INPUTS FOR RELATIVE VALUATION TECHNIQUE: WALGREENS, RETAIL DRUGSTORE INDUSTRY, S&P INDUSTRIALS INDEX: 1977–2000

	WALGREENS[a]					RETAIL DRUGSTORE INDUSTRY					S&P INDUSTRIALS INDEX				
YEAR	MEAN PRICE	EPS	CF PER SHARE	BV PER SHARE	SALES PER SHARE	MEAN PRICE	EPS	CF PER SHARE	BV PER SHARE	SALES PER SHARE	MEAN PRICE	EPS	CF PER SHARE	BV PER SHARE	SALES PER SHARE
1977	0.13	0.02	0.02	0.08	0.96	18.93	1.79	2.20	9.35	43.99	109.40	11.45	19.94	82.21	224.24
1978	0.18	0.03	0.02	0.09	1.09	22.20	2.01	2.50	10.93	49.87	107.12	13.04	22.65	89.34	251.32
1979	0.23	0.04	0.03	0.10	1.23	22.38	2.55	3.26	13.95	73.39	115.79	16.29	27.06	98.71	292.38
1980	0.27	0.04	0.03	0.12	1.55	24.57	2.94	3.78	16.11	84.82	136.03	16.12	28.45	108.33	327.36
1981	0.37	0.05	0.03	0.13	1.76	34.62	3.29	4.31	18.45	95.50	141.48	16.74	30.52	116.06	344.31
1982	0.63	0.06	0.08	0.31	1.94	41.58	3.76	4.79	20.74	109.22	136.87	13.20	28.46	118.60	333.86
1983	1.04	0.07	0.15	0.54	2.38	56.70	4.50	5.90	23.34	118.85	174.90	14.77	30.41	122.32	334.07
1984	1.15	0.08	0.11	0.42	2.77	58.30	4.10	5.81	24.21	135.15	179.62	18.11	34.40	123.99	379.70
1985	1.62	0.10	0.13	0.49	3.19	68.28	4.22	6.24	26.82	153.30	208.99	15.28	33.44	125.89	398.42
1986	2.17	0.11	0.16	0.61	3.70	83.78	4.90	6.99	27.73	157.74	253.83	14.53	33.91	124.87	387.76
1987	2.19	0.11	0.16	0.64	4.32	98.93	5.53	8.16	30.79	191.72	324.30	20.28	40.46	134.19	430.35
1988	2.03	0.13	0.19	0.73	4.93	93.05	6.30	9.40	34.25	217.80	302.63	26.59	50.13	139.50	486.92
1989	2.50	0.16	0.23	0.83	5.43	107.46	6.69	10.07	38.31	239.68	364.58	26.83	50.02	145.34	541.38
1990	2.91	0.18	0.26	1.00	6.10	114.53	7.67	11.82	43.65	265.77	392.12	24.77	51.04	152.71	594.55
1991	3.97	0.20	0.29	1.10	6.80	139.70	8.26	12.29	50.94	283.50	428.81	16.91	44.41	157.05	586.86
1992	4.69	0.22	0.39	1.25	7.54	159.62	8.96	13.34	56.97	309.78	493.33	19.05	48.50	142.46	601.39
1993	4.96	0.23	0.44	1.40	8.37	162.19	7.09	11.84	60.04	329.20	520.21	21.93	50.61	136.91	603.62
1994	5.06	0.29	0.50	1.60	9.32	162.67	10.51	15.83	63.62	363.71	536.52	32.83	62.43	150.70	626.26
1995	6.64	0.33	0.57	1.82	10.49	215.26	11.76	17.77	68.93	413.52	638.97	35.44	68.51	163.94	676.62
1996	9.10	0.38	0.65	2.08	11.85	283.01	13.92	18.82	71.26	434.15	795.01	41.15	77.56	168.04	701.91
1997	13.22	0.44	0.61	2.40	13.57	411.75	10.77	19.22	70.88	549.51	1006.12	42.13	81.90	174.21	750.71
1998	22.50	0.54	0.73	2.86	15.43	657.05	15.62	24.48	111.07	612.86	1285.73	38.37	71.63	186.36	755.48
1999	28.31	0.62	0.83	3.47	17.83	718.90	18.87	29.20	126.36	706.21	1651.82	50.25	89.71	169.54	812.00
2000	33.91	0.76	1.00	4.19	21.05	686.62	16.72	28.61	107.27	687.77	1702.23	53.85	98.53	204.54	853.86

[a]Adjusted for all stock splits through 2000.

Source: *Financial Analysts Handbook* (New York: Standard & Poor's, 2001). Reprinted with permission.

EXHIBIT 15.5 — RELATIVE VALUATION VARIABLES: WALGREENS[a], RETAIL DRUGSTORE INDUSTRY, S&P INDUSTRIALS INDEX: 1977–2000

	PRICE/EARNINGS RATIO					PRICE/CASH FLOW RATIO					PRICE/BOOK VALUE RATIO					PRICE/SALES RATIO				
Year	Walgreens	Retail Drug	Ratio Co/Ind	S&P Ind	Ratio Co/Mkt	Walgreens	Retail Drug	Ratio Co/Ind	S&P Ind	Ratio Co/Mkt	Walgreens	Retail Drug	Ratio Co/Ind	S&P Ind	Ratio Co/Mkt	Walgreens	Retail Drug	Ratio Co/Ind	S&P Ind	Ratio Co/Mkt
1977	7.43	10.58	0.70	9.55	0.78	8.67	8.60	1.01	5.49	1.58	1.58	2.02	0.78	1.33	1.18	0.14	0.43	0.31	0.49	0.28
1978	7.30	11.04	0.66	8.21	0.89	9.13	8.88	1.03	4.73	1.93	2.03	2.03	1.00	1.20	1.69	0.17	0.45	0.38	0.43	0.39
1979	6.57	8.78	0.75	7.11	0.92	9.20	6.87	1.34	4.28	2.15	2.24	1.60	1.40	1.17	1.91	0.19	0.30	0.61	0.40	0.47
1980	6.63	8.36	0.79	8.44	0.79	9.64	6.50	1.48	4.78	2.02	2.30	1.53	1.51	1.26	1.84	0.17	0.29	0.59	0.42	0.41
1981	8.11	10.52	0.77	8.45	0.96	11.23	8.03	1.40	4.64	2.42	2.75	1.88	1.47	1.22	2.26	0.21	0.36	0.57	0.41	0.51
1982	10.96	11.06	0.99	10.37	1.06	7.88	8.68	0.91	4.81	1.64	2.05	2.00	1.02	1.15	1.78	0.32	0.38	0.85	0.41	0.79
1983	14.31	12.60	1.14	11.84	1.21	7.16	9.61	0.74	5.75	1.24	1.93	2.43	0.79	1.43	1.35	0.44	0.48	0.91	0.52	0.83
1984	13.97	14.22	0.98	9.92	1.41	10.24	10.03	1.02	5.22	1.96	2.73	2.41	1.13	1.45	1.88	0.42	0.43	0.97	0.47	0.88
1985	17.03	16.18	1.05	13.68	1.24	12.44	10.94	1.14	6.25	1.99	3.30	2.55	1.30	1.66	1.99	0.51	0.45	1.14	0.52	0.97
1986	20.69	17.10	1.21	17.47	1.18	13.37	11.99	1.12	7.49	1.79	3.55	3.02	1.17	2.03	1.74	0.59	0.53	1.11	0.65	0.90
1987	20.81	17.89	1.16	15.99	1.30	13.66	12.12	1.13	8.02	1.70	3.44	3.21	1.07	2.42	1.42	0.51	0.52	0.98	0.75	0.67
1988	15.63	14.77	1.06	11.38	1.37	10.56	9.90	1.07	6.04	1.75	2.78	2.72	1.02	2.17	1.28	0.41	0.43	0.97	0.62	0.66
1989	15.87	16.06	0.99	13.59	1.17	11.11	10.67	1.04	7.29	1.52	3.00	2.81	1.07	2.51	1.20	0.46	0.45	1.03	0.67	0.68
1990	16.38	14.93	1.10	15.83	1.03	11.29	9.69	1.17	7.68	1.47	2.92	2.62	1.11	2.57	1.14	0.48	0.43	1.11	0.66	0.72
1991	20.10	16.91	1.19	25.36	0.79	13.93	11.37	1.23	9.66	1.44	3.62	2.74	1.32	2.73	1.32	0.58	0.49	1.19	0.73	0.80
1992	21.07	17.81	1.18	25.90	0.81	12.02	11.97	1.00	10.17	1.18	3.74	2.80	1.34	3.46	1.08	0.62	0.52	1.21	0.82	0.76
1993	22.02	22.88	0.96	23.72	0.93	11.33	13.70	0.83	10.28	1.10	3.54	2.70	1.31	3.80	0.93	0.59	0.49	1.20	0.86	0.69
1994	17.75	15.48	1.15	16.34	1.09	10.12	10.28	0.98	8.59	1.18	3.17	2.56	1.24	3.56	0.89	0.54	0.45	1.21	0.86	0.63
1995	20.42	18.30	1.12	18.03	1.13	11.75	12.11	0.97	9.33	1.26	3.65	3.12	1.17	3.90	0.94	0.63	0.52	1.22	0.94	0.67
1996	24.25	20.33	1.19	19.32	1.26	14.05	15.04	0.93	10.25	1.37	4.38	3.97	1.10	4.73	0.93	0.77	0.65	1.18	1.13	0.68
1997	30.03	38.23	0.79	23.88	1.26	21.69	21.42	1.01	12.28	1.77	5.51	5.81	0.95	5.78	0.95	0.97	0.75	1.30	1.34	0.73
1998	41.66	42.06	0.99	33.51	1.24	30.74	26.84	1.15	17.95	1.71	7.87	5.92	1.33	6.90	1.14	1.46	1.07	1.36	1.70	0.86
1999	45.65	38.10	1.20	32.87	1.39	33.94	24.62	1.38	18.41	1.84	8.16	5.69	1.43	8.71	0.94	1.59	1.02	1.56	2.03	0.78
2000	44.81	41.07	1.09	31.61	1.41	33.92	24.00	1.41	17.28	1.96	8.09	6.40	1.26	8.32	0.97	1.61	1.00	1.61	1.99	0.81
Mean	19.55	18.97	1.01	17.18	1.11	14.13	12.66	1.10	8.61	1.67	3.68	3.11	1.18	3.14	1.36	0.60	0.54	1.02	0.83	0.69

[a]Adjusted for all stock splits through 2000.

Source: *Financial Analysts Handbook* (New York: Standard & Poor's, 2001). Reprinted with permission.

EXHIBIT 15.6 ▶ *WALGREENS S&P RETAIL DRUGSTORE SALES, AND VARIOUS ECONOMIC SERIES: 1977–2001*

Year	Sales Walgreen Co. ($ Million)	Retail Drugstores ($/Share)	Personal Consumption Expenditures (PCE) ($ Billion)	PCE Medical Care ($ Billion)	Medical Care as a Percentage of PCE
1977	1,223.2	43.99	1,278.4	122.6	9.6
1978	1,192.9	49.87	1,430.4	140.0	9.8
1979	1,334.5	73.39	1,596.3	158.1	9.9
1980	1,530.7	84.82	1,762.9	181.2	10.3
1981	1,743.5	95.50	1,944.2	213.0	11.0
1982	2,039.5	109.22	2,079.3	239.3	11.5
1983	2,360.6	118.85	2,286.4	267.9	11.7
1984	2,744.6	135.15	2,498.4	294.6	11.8
1985	3,161.9	153.30	2,712.6	322.5	11.9
1986	3,660.6	157.74	2,895.2	346.8	12.0
1987	4,281.6	191.72	3,105.3	381.8	12.3
1988	4,883.5	217.80	3,356.6	429.9	12.8
1989	5,380.1	239.68	3,596.7	479.2	13.3
1990	6,047.5	265.77	3,831.5	540.6	14.1
1991	6,733.0	283.50	3,971.2	591.0	14.9
1992	7,475.0	309.78	4,209.7	652.6	15.5
1993	8,294.8	329.20	4,454.7	700.6	15.7
1994	9,235.0	363.71	4,716.4	737.3	15.6
1995	10,395.1	413.52	4,969.0	780.7	15.7
1996	11,778.4	434.15	5,237.5	814.4	15.5
1997	13,363.0	549.51	5,529.3	854.6	15.5
1998	15,307.0	612.86	5,856.0	899.0	15.4
1999	17,838.8	706.21	6,250.2	939.9	15.0
2000	21,206.9	687.77	6,728.4	996.5	14.8
2001	24,623.0	730.00	7,055.0	1044.1	14.8
CGR	13.33%	12.70%	7.38%	9.34%	1.82%

CGR = compound annual growth rate.
Source: *Financial Analysts Handbook* (New York: Standard & Poor's, 2001); and *Economic Report of the President* (Washington, DC: U.S. Government Printing Office, 2002). Reprinted with permission.

Company Sales Forecast

Besides providing background on the company, these relationships can help us develop specific sales forecasts for Walgreens.

Exhibit 15.6 contains data on sales for Walgreens from its annual report, sales per share for the RDS industry, and several personal consumption expenditure (PCE) series for the period 1977 to 2001.

To examine the relationship of Walgreens sales to the economy, we considered several alternative series. The series that had the strongest relationship was personal consumption expendi-

| EXHIBIT 15.7 | SCATTER PLOT OF WALGREENS SALES AND PCE MEDICAL CARE: 1977–2001 |

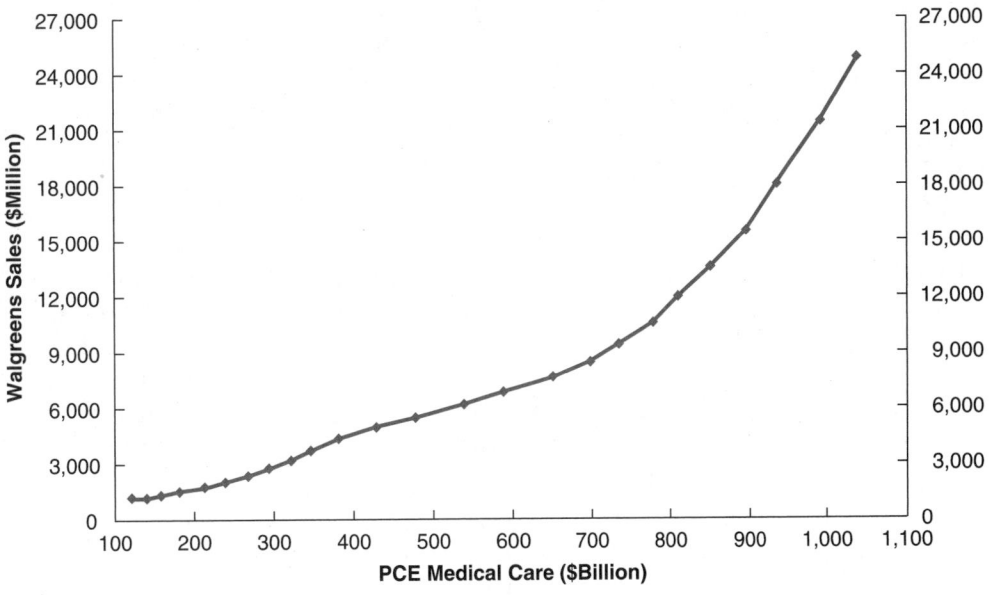

ture for medicine (PCE medical care).[14] The scatter plot of Walgreens sales and the PCE medical care expenditures contained in Exhibit 15.7 indicates a strong linear relationship, including the fact that Walgreens sales grew faster than PCE medical care (i.e., 13.33 percent versus 9.39 percent). As a result, Walgreens sales have gone from about 1.00 percent of PCE medical care to 2.36 percent.

We also compared Walgreens sales and sales per share for the RDS industry. Unfortunately, it did not reflect as strong a relationship and is not used subsequently.

The figures in the last column of Exhibit 15.6 indicate that during this period, the proportion of PCE allocated to medical care went from almost 10 percent in 1977 to almost 15 percent in 2001. The increasing proportion of PCE spent on medical care is a function of the growing proportion of the population over 65 and the rising cost of medical care. Because Walgreens sales are growing faster than medical expenditures, these increases should continue to be beneficial for Walgreens because over 55 percent of its sales is prescriptions. Notably, these increases in medical care expenditures continued during the economic recessions in 1981–1982 and in 1990–1991.

As shown in Exhibit 15.8, the internal sales growth for Walgreens resulted from an increase in the number of stores (from 633 in 1975 to 3,520 in 2001) and an increase in the annual sales per store because of the upgrading of stores. The net increase in stores includes numerous new, large stores and the closing of many smaller stores. As a result, the average size of stores has increased. More important, the firm has continued to increase its sales per thousand square feet at over 4 percent a year. This is a critical statistic in the retailing industry.

---

[14]The relationship between Walgreens sales and total PCE or per capital PCE was significant but not as strong as PCE medical care.

EXHIBIT 15.8 *SALES, NUMBER OF STORES, AND SALES AREA FOR WALGREENS: 1977–2001*

YEAR	SALES WALGREENS ($ MILLION)	NUMBER OF STORES	ANNUAL SALES PER STORE ($ MILLION)	STORE AREA (000 SQUARE FEET)	AREA PER STORE (000 SQUARE FEET)	AVERAGE SALES PER THOUSAND SQUARE FEET
1977	1,223.2	626	1.95	5,188	8.29	235.77
1978	1,192.9	641	1.86	5,390	8.41	221.32
1979	1,334.5	688	1.94	5,851	8.50	228.08
1980	1,530.7	739	2.07	6,305	8.53	242.78
1981	1,743.5	821	2.12	7,209	8.78	241.85
1982	2,039.5	883	2.31	7,815	8.85	260.97
1983	2,360.6	941	2.51	8,402	8.93	280.96
1984	2,744.6	1,002	2.74	9,002	8.98	304.89
1985	3,161.9	1,095	2.89	10,010	9.14	315.87
1986	3,660.6	1,273	2.88	11,895	9.34	307.74
1987	4,281.6	1,356	3.16	12,844	9.47	333.35
1988	4,883.5	1,416	3.45	13,549	9.57	360.43
1989	5,380.1	1,484	3.63	14,272	9.62	376.97
1990	6,047.5	1,564	3.87	15,105	9.66	400.36
1991	6,733.0	1,646	4.09	15,877	9.65	424.08
1992	7,475.0	1,736	4.31	16,811	9.68	444.65
1993	8,294.8	1,836	4.52	17,950	9.78	462.11
1994	9,235.0	1,968	4.69	19,342	9.83	477.46
1995	10,395.1	2,085	4.99	20,731	9.94	501.43
1996	11,778.4	2,193	5.37	22,124	10.09	532.38
1997	13,363.0	2,358	5.67	23,935	10.15	558.30
1998	15,307.0	2,549	6.01	26,024	10.21	588.19
1999	17,838.8	2,821	6.32	29,230	10.36	610.29
2000	21,206.9	3,165	6.70	33,684	10.64	629.58
2001	24,623.0	3,520	7.00	38,226	10.86	644.14
Average annual rate of growth (%)	13.3%	7.3%	5.6%	8.5%	1.1%	4.4%

Reprinted with permission from Walgreen Co., Deerfield, IL.

Sample Estimate of Walgreens Sales   The foregoing analysis indicates that you should use the Walgreens—PCE medical care graph. To estimate PCE medical care, you should initially project total PCE and then determine how much would be included in the medical care component. As noted in Chapter 14 in connection with the industry analysis, economists were forecasting an increase in PCE of 3 percent during 2002, which implied a 2002 estimate of $7,267 billion. In addition, it was estimated that the percentage of PCE spent on medical care in 2002 would be about 15.0 percent. This implies an estimate for PCE medical care of $1,090 billion, which is about a 4.4 percent increase from 2001. Based on the graph in Exhibit 15.7 which shows the historical relationship between PCE medical care and Walgreens sales, this would imply a 7.5 percent increase in Walgreens sales to about $26.50 billion (24.623 billion × 1.075). Notably, this is a conservative estimate that is below the firm's recent growth in sales.

Firms in this industry provide data on square footage and the number of stores. This allows us to compute an alternative sales estimate using these company data in Exhibit 15.8 to support the prior estimate that was based on macroeconomic data. If we assume an increase in store area during 2002 of about 4.5 million square feet (which is less than in most years), the firm's total sales area would be about 42.7 million square feet. As noted, sales per square foot have likewise increased. Assuming a conservative increase to $650 of sales per thousand square feet implies a sales forecast of about $27.75 billion for 2002, a 12.7 percent increase over 2001 sales of $24.62 billion.

Another internal estimate is possible by using the number of stores and sales per store. Walgreens is expected to open 475 stores during 2002. Assuming it closes 60, this would be a net addition of 415 to 3,935 stores at the end of 2002. Assuming sales per store likewise continue to increase from $7.00 million to $7.25 million implies an estimate of $28.53 billion (3,935 × 7.25), which is an increase of 16 percent over 2001.

Given the three estimates, the preference is for an estimate close to the high value because of the positive economic environment and the company's ability to increase sales between 16 and 18 percent a year during 2001 and 2000. Therefore, we will assume a 15 percent increase, which implies a final sales forecast for 2002 of $28 billion.

Estimating the Company Profit Margin

The next step in projecting earnings per share is to estimate the firm's net profit margin, which should include three considerations: (1) identification and evaluation of the firm's specific competitive strategy—that is, either low-cost or differentiation; (2) the firm's internal performance, including general company trends and consideration of any problems that might affect its future performance; and (3) the firm's relationship with its industry, which should indicate whether the company's past performance is attributable to its industry or if it is unique to the firm. These examinations should help us understand the firm's past performance but should also provide the background to make a meaningful estimate for the future. In this analysis, we do not consider the company-economy relationship because the significant economywide profit factors are reflected in the industry results. Since we have already discussed these strategies in general, we concentrate on how they affect Walgreens.

WALGREENS COMPETITIVE STRATEGIES

Over the years, has Walgreens pursued a low-cost strategy or has the firm attempted to differentiate itself from its competitors in some unique way? Based on its annual reports, Walgreens has pursued both strategies with different segments of its business. The firm's size and buying power allow it to be a cost leader for some of its nonprescription products, such as liquor, ice cream, candy, and soft drinks. These items are advertised heavily to attract customer traffic and to build consumer loyalty. At the same time, Walgreens has attempted to build a very strong franchise in the medical prescription business based on differentiation in service. Computer technology in the prescription area makes it possible for the firm to distinguish itself by providing outstanding service to its prescription customers. Specifically, the firm refers to itself as the nation's prescription druggist based on the number of prescriptions it fills and a nationwide computer system that allows customers to have their prescriptions filled at any of the 3,520 Walgreens drugstores in the country. This service leadership in the growing medical field is a major goal.

The Internal Performance

Profit margin figures for Walgreens and the RDS industry are in Exhibit 15.9. The profit margins for Walgreens increased from 1977 to the mid-1980s followed by a decline through 1988 and a recovery beginning in 1991. In contrast, the margins for the RDS industry experienced a relatively steady decline after a peak in 1983. Overall, Walgreens experienced a positive trend in its operating and net profit margins over the past 24 years. To predict future values, you need to

EXHIBIT 15.9 ▶ *PROFIT MARGINS AND COMPONENT EXPENSES FOR WALGREENS AND THE RETAIL DRUGSTORE INDUSTRY: 1977–2001*

YEAR	WALGREEN CO.			RETAIL DRUGSTORES		
	OPERATING MARGIN (%)	NBT MARGIN (%)	NET PROFIT MARGIN (%)	OPERATING MARGIN (%)	NBT MARGIN (%)	NET PROFIT MARGIN (%)
1977	3.11	2.66	1.46	8.96	7.92	4.07
1978	3.86	3.73	2.16	8.78	7.74	4.03
1979	3.86	3.79	2.25	7.24	6.39	3.47
1980	3.56	3.52	2.27	7.07	6.27	3.47
1981	3.40	3.54	2.42	7.17	6.18	3.45
1982	4.32	4.20	2.75	7.30	6.21	3.44
1983	5.16	5.11	2.96	7.98	6.89	3.79
1984	5.57	5.46	3.11	7.19	5.54	3.03
1985	5.63	5.49	2.98	7.00	5.47	2.96
1986	5.37	5.13	2.82	7.37	5.66	3.11
1987	4.92	4.54	2.42	7.08	5.13	2.88
1988	4.59	4.28	2.64	6.70	4.72	2.90
1989	4.71	4.53	2.87	6.71	4.49	2.79
1990	4.70	4.65	2.89	6.71	4.68	2.89
1991	4.77	4.63	2.90	6.52	4.60	2.91
1992	4.80	4.72	2.95	6.35	4.59	2.89
1993	4.90	4.82	2.96	6.25	4.67	2.80
1994	4.93	4.96	3.05	6.42	4.68	2.89
1995	5.00	5.04	3.09	6.51	4.63	2.84
1996	5.13	5.15	3.16	6.53	5.11	3.21
1997	5.30	5.33	3.84	7.06	3.57	1.96
1998	5.46	5.49	3.34	7.00	4.17	2.58
1999	5.69	5.69	3.43	6.82	4.42	2.70
2000	5.77	5.77	3.48	6.18	5.01	3.04
2001	5.68	5.67	3.48	NA	NA	NA

Source: *Financial Analysts Handbook* (New York: Standard & Poor's, 2001). Reprinted with permission.

determine the reason for the overall decline in the industry profit margin and, more important, what factors have contributed to Walgreens' strong positive performance.

Industry Factors   Industry profit margins have declined over the past two decades due to price discounting by aggressive regional drug chains.[15] The discussion in Chapter 14 suggested this as one of the competitive structure conditions that affect long-run profitability. Industry analysts have observed, however, that price cutting has subsided, and they foresee relative price stability. In addition, drugstores have tended toward a more profitable product mix featuring high-profit-margin items, such as cosmetics, and this has had a positive influence on profit margins.

---

[15]For a more complete discussion, see "Retailing—Drug Stores," *Standard & Poor's Industry Surveys* (New York: Standard & Poor's, 2001).

EXHIBIT 15.10 ▸ *TIME-SERIES PLOT OF NET PROFIT MARGIN FOR WALGREENS AND THE RETAIL DRUGSTORE INDUSTRY: 1977–2000*

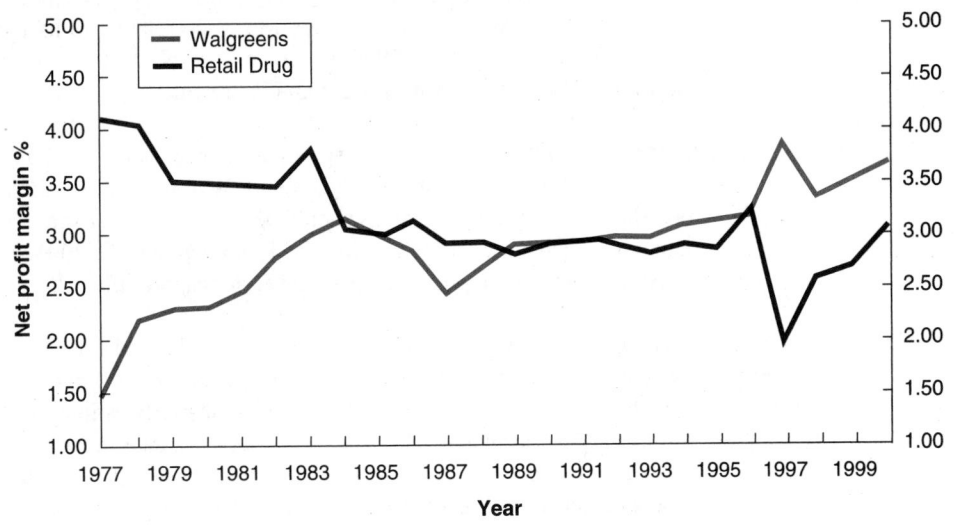

Company Performance   Walgreens' profit margin has shown consistent improvement, and a major reason has been the change in corporate structure. The outlook for profit margins is good because the firm has developed a strong position in the pharmacy business and has invested in service (including mail-order prescriptions) and inventory-control technology that will help the firm experience strong margins on this business. The firm also has emphasized high-profit-margin items, such as greeting cards, photofinishing, and cosmetics.

Specific estimates for Walgreens' future margins typically would begin with an analysis of the firm's relationship with drugstore industry margins using time-series plots, such as those in Exhibit 15.10.[16] This time-series plot for the period 1977–2000 showed good results for Walgreens versus its industry prior to 1997 followed by Walgreens outperforming through 2000. You should consider any unique factors that would influence this long-run relationship, such as price wars or an abnormal number of store openings or closings by the firm.

Following a consideration of the long-run company-industry profit margin relationship, you should analyze the firm's common-size income statement for several years. As discussed in Chapter 10, the breakdown of the income statement depends on the consistent detail provided by the firm. Exhibit 15.11 shows a common-size income statement for Walgreens during the period 1998–2001. An analysis of the main items of interest—cost of goods sold and SG&A expense—was encouraging. The cost-of-sales percentage increased slightly (less than 1 percent) while there was a larger decline in the percentage of SG&A expense through 2000. As a result, the operating profit margin increased from 5.46 percent to 5.68 percent. Interest expense was not a factor. Finally, the tax rate remained between 38 and 40 percent during the last several years.

---

[16]Both the operating margin and the net before tax margin were analyzed; the results indicated that the net profit margins yielded the best relationships. The long-run relationship cannot be very good because over the total period the industry margin was declining while Walgreens experienced fairly steady increases as shown in Exhibit 15.10.

Net Profit Margin Estimate The overall industry outlook is encouraging because of stable prices, an increase in mechanization within the industry, and the inclusion of more high-profit-margin items. Therefore, the industry profit margin is expected to increase slightly during 2002. Because of Walgreens' strong performance relative to its industry profit margin and the increase in its margin since 1995 as shown in Exhibit 15.11, it is estimated that the firm will show a small increase during 2002 to 3.55 percent.

Computing Earnings per Share This margin estimate, combined with the prior sales estimate of $28 billion, indicates net income of $994 million. Assuming about 1,030 million common shares outstanding, earnings should be about $0.97 per share for 2002, which is an increase of about 13 percent over the earnings of $0.86 per share in 2001. To find the value of Walgreen Co. stock, our next step is to estimate its earnings multiplier.

Importance of Quarterly Estimates

Once we have derived an estimate of next year's sales and net earnings, it is essential that we also derive an estimate of each of the quarterly results for two important reasons. First, this is a way to confirm our annual estimate—that is, do the quarterly estimates required to arrive at the annual estimate seem reasonable? If not, we need to reevaluate the annual forecast. Second, unless we have quarterly forecasts than confirm our annual forecast, we will not be in a position to determine whether the subsequent *actual* results are a positive surprise, negative surprise, or no surprise. Further, if the actual results are a surprise relative to our estimate, we will want to understand the reason for the surprise—for example, did we under- or overestimate sales growth and/or

EXHIBIT 15.11 *WALGREEN CO. AND SUBSIDIARIES COMMON-SIZE INCOME STATEMENT:[a]*
YEARS ENDED AUGUST 31, 1998, 1999, 2000, AND 2001

	2001	%	2000	%	1999	%	1998	%
Net sales	24,623	100.00	21,207	100.00	17,839	100.00	15,307	100.00
Cost of goods sold	18,049	73.30	15,466	72.93	12,979	72.75	11,140	72.78
Gross profit	6,574	26.70	5,741	27.07	4,860	27.25	4,167	27.22
Selling general, administrative expenses	5,176	21.02	4,517	21.30	3,845	21.55	3,332	21.77
Operating profit	1,398	5.68	1,224	5.77	1,015	5.69	835	5.46
Interest income	0	0.00	0	0.00	0	0.00	(6)	(0.04)
Interest expense	3	0.01	0	0.00	0	0.00	1	0.01
Operating income before income taxes	1,395	5.67	1,224	5.77	1,015	5.69	840	5.49
Provision for income taxes	537	2.18	486	2.29	403	2.26	340	2.22
Operating income after taxes	858	3.48	737	3.48	612	3.43	500	3.27
Extraordinary loss (income)	—	—	—	—	—	—	(37)	(0.24)
Cumulative effect of accounting change	—	—	—	—	—	—	26	0.17
Reported net income	858	3.48	737	3.48	612	3.43	511	3.34
Operating income after taxes available for common	858	3.48	737	3.48	612	3.43	500	3.27
Reported net income available for common	858	3.48	737	3.48	612	3.43	511	3.34

[a] Percentages may not add to 100.0% due to rounding.

was it due to differences in the profit margin from our estimates? This understanding is needed for an estimated *earnings revision* that reflects the new information from the company—we would probably revise each of our future quarterly estimates to arrive at a new annual estimate.

ESTIMATING COMPANY EARNINGS MULTIPLIERS

As in our analysis of industry multipliers in Chapter 14, we use two approaches to estimate a company multiplier. First, we estimate the *P/E* ratio from the relationships among Walgreens, its industry, and the market. This is the macroanalysis. Second, we estimate a multiplier based on its three components: the dividend-payout ratio, the required rate of return, and the rate of growth. We then resolve the estimates derived from each approach and settle on one estimate.

Macroanalysis of the Earnings Multiplier

Exhibit 15.5 and Exhibit 15.12 show the mean earnings multiple for the company, the RDS industry, and the aggregate market for the period 1977–2000. Notably, all these earnings multipliers are computed using future earnings. Walgreens' relationship to its industry has changed dramatically over time. During the late 1970s and early 1980s, Walgreens' multiplier was consistently below the industry's. After 1987, the Walgreens multiplier has generally followed the industry multiplier with a company/industry ratio between 1.00 and 1.15. Similarly, the Walgreens earnings multiplier was lower than the market multiplier until 1982 but they have been consistently higher since 1994 with a ratio between 1.10 and 1.40.

This pattern raises the question: Is the higher value for the Walgreens *P/E* relative to both its industry and the market that generally has prevailed since 1992 justified? The microanalyses should provide some insights regarding this question.

EXHIBIT 15.12

TIME-SERIES PLOT OF MEAN PRICE–EARNINGS RATIOS FOR WALGREENS, THE RETAIL DRUGSTORE INDUSTRY, AND THE S&P INDUSTRIALS INDEX: 1977–2000

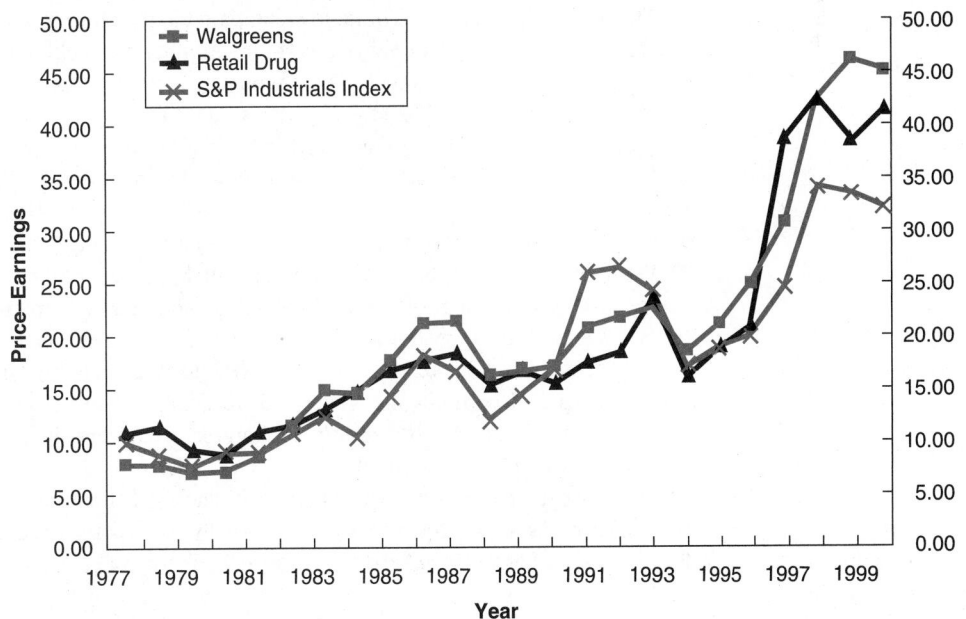

Microanalysis of the Earnings Multiplier

This historical data for the relevant series are contained in Exhibit 15.13.[17] The relevant question is, Why has the earnings multiplier for Walgreens been generally higher than the market and industry earnings multiplier since 1992? As before, we are looking for estimates of D/E, k, and g to find an earnings multiplier. We will use the historical data in Exhibit 15.13 to determine patterns for the data and to develop future projections.

Comparing Dividend-Payout Ratios   The dividend-payout ratio for Walgreens typically has been lower than its industry in recent years. The Walgreens-market comparison shows that Walgreens almost always had a lower payout, which by itself would imply a lower P/E ratio for Walgreens than for its industry and the market.

Estimating the Required Rate of Return   To find Walgreens' required rate of return (k), we need to analyze the firm's fundamental risk characteristics (BR, FR, LR, ERR, and CR) and also derive an estimate based on the SML and a measure of Walgreens' systematic risk (i.e., its beta).

Walgreens should have relatively low business risk due to its stable sales growth compared to its industry and the aggregate economy. As noted in Chapter 10, for a growth company like Walgreens it is necessary to adjust for both the growth and size factor by measuring variability around the growth trend and relating this volatility to the mean as in Exhibit 15.14. As shown in the appendix in Chapter 10, after adjusting for size and trend, the results indicated that Walgreens sales and EBIT experienced very stable growth, which indicates lower business risk.

Several financial risk variables for Walgreens, its industry, and the aggregate market are shown in Exhibit 15.15. Notably, these do not consider fairly large leases of stores. The firm's financial leverage ratio (notably, total assets/equity) has recently been less than 2.00, which is comparable to the industry and definitely lower than the aggregate market. Walgreens has a very large interest coverage ratio, a cash flow/long-term debt ratio of over 300 percent, and a cash flow/total debt ratio of about 30 percent. These financial risk ratios indicate that Walgreens has comparable financial risk to its industry and substantially lower financial risk than the aggregate stock market. In contrast, as shown in Chapter 10, when the leases are considered as they should be, the firm's financial risk is equal to, or somewhat higher than the market.

The firm's liquidity risk is quite low compared to its industry and the average firm in the market. Indicators of market liquidity are (1) the number of stockholders, (2) the number and market value of shares outstanding, (3) the number of shares traded, and (4) institutional interest in the stock. As of January 1, 2002, Walgreens had 30,000 holders of common stock—a relatively large number. At mid-2002, there were over one billion common shares outstanding (after the 1999 stock split) with a market value of over $35 billion. Clearly, Walgreens would qualify as an investment for institutions that require firms with large market value. Walgreens stock has an annual trading turnover of 55 percent, which is below average. Financial institutions own about 450 million shares of Walgreens, which is about 45 percent of the outstanding shares. Therefore, Walgreens' large number of stockholders, very large market capitalization, fairly active trading of its stock, and strong institutional interest indicate that Walgreen's has very little liquidity risk.

As discussed in Chapter 11, the exchange rate risk for companies depends on what proportion of sales and earnings are generated outside the United States and the volatility of the exchange rates in the specific countries. Walgreens has very little exchange rate risk or country risk because the firm has virtually no non-U.S. sales.

In summary, Walgreens has below-average business risk, financial risk higher than the market when we consider leases, low liquidity risk, and virtually no exchange rate and country risk. This implies that—based on fundamental factors—the overall risk for Walgreens should be lower than the market.

---

[17]Although some prior tables included data through 2001 using estimates for specific ratios, it is not possible to do this for all the variables in Exhibit 15.13 as of mid-2002. These data generally are not available until September.

EXHIBIT 15.13 VARIABLES THAT INFLUENCE THE EARNINGS MULTIPLIER FOR WALGREENS, THE RETAIL DRUGSTORE INDUSTRY, AND THE S&P INDUSTRIALS INDEX: 1977–2001

YEAR	WALGREENS						RETAIL DRUGSTORES						S&P INDUSTRIALS					
	D/E	NPM	TAT	ROA	TAE	ROE	D/E	NPM	TAT	ROA	TAE	ROE	D/E	NPM	TAT	ROA	TAE	ROE
1977	45.80	1.27	3.81	4.84	2.39	11.56	20.11	4.07	2.84	11.56	1.53	17.68	43.20	5.11	1.27	6.49	2.15	13.95
1978	30.31	2.16	3.45	7.45	2.34	17.44	23.90	4.03	2.81	11.32	1.52	17.21	41.20	5.19	1.27	6.59	2.22	14.63
1979	30.33	2.25	3.53	7.94	2.30	18.27	27.40	3.47	3.00	10.41	1.65	17.18	36.30	5.57	1.30	7.24	2.28	16.51
1980	30.47	2.27	3.60	8.17	2.16	17.65	29.20	3.47	3.04	10.55	1.66	17.51	40.30	4.92	1.31	6.45	2.30	14.82
1981	30.42	2.42	3.60	8.71	2.08	18.12	31.00	3.45	3.03	10.45	1.65	17.25	41.90	4.86	1.28	6.22	2.32	14.43
1982	26.93	2.75	3.59	9.87	2.06	20.34	31.10	3.44	2.97	10.22	1.66	16.96	54.00	3.95	1.17	4.62	2.40	11.09
1983	26.33	2.96	3.54	10.48	2.04	21.38	29.30	3.79	2.86	10.84	1.88	20.38	49.60	4.42	1.15	5.08	2.37	12.05
1984	25.84	3.11	3.52	10.95	2.03	22.22	37.60	3.04	2.65	8.06	1.93	15.55	41.50	4.77	1.22	5.82	2.51	14.61
1985	28.58	2.98	3.39	10.10	2.16	21.82	40.80	2.96	2.68	7.93	1.88	14.91	51.50	3.84	1.15	4.42	2.75	12.14
1986	29.81	2.82	3.39	9.56	2.16	20.65	31.90	3.11	2.71	8.43	1.94	16.35	56.00	3.75	1.07	4.01	2.90	11.64
1987	32.08	2.42	3.35	8.11	2.19	17.75	31.60	2.88	2.80	8.06	2.04	16.45	43.00	4.71	1.08	5.09	2.97	15.11
1988	28.59	2.64	3.40	8.98	2.12	19.03	30.60	2.90	2.82	8.18	2.07	16.93	36.90	5.46	0.98	5.35	3.56	19.06
1989	27.12	2.87	3.37	9.67	2.04	19.73	32.29	2.79	2.82	7.87	2.03	15.97	44.03	4.96	0.97	4.81	3.84	18.46
1990	28.19	2.89	3.16	9.13	2.02	18.45	31.68	2.89	2.82	8.13	2.00	16.26	50.20	4.17	0.97	4.04	4.01	16.22
1991	29.04	2.90	3.21	9.31	1.94	18.06	32.81	2.91	2.85	8.31	1.83	15.25	71.81	2.88	0.94	2.72	3.96	10.77
1992	29.21	1.95	3.15	9.29	1.92	17.89	33.59	2.89	2.83	8.19	1.82	14.89	66.14	3.17	0.96	3.03	4.41	13.37
1993	33.52	2.67	3.27	8.73	1.84	16.08	46.83	2.15	2.79	6.00	1.88	11.27	58.04	3.63	0.92	3.33	4.81	16.02
1994	29.82	3.05	3.17	9.67	1.85	17.92	33.78	2.89	2.63	7.60	2.00	15.17	38.94	5.24	0.95	4.98	4.38	21.79
1995	30.77	3.09	3.20	9.87	1.81	19.10	33.67	2.84	2.66	7.56	2.03	15.36	39.39	5.24	0.97	5.08	4.25	21.62
1996	28.95	3.16	3.24	10.24	1.78	19.40	28.81	3.21	2.02	6.48	2.17	14.06	37.86	5.86	0.93	5.45	4.49	24.49
1997	26.97	3.26	3.18	10.36	1.77	19.80	40.95	1.96	2.23	4.37	2.18	9.53	39.69	5.61	0.94	5.27	4.77	25.14
1998	24.27	3.51	3.12	10.95	1.72	19.60	24.74	2.58	2.04	5.27	2.70	14.23	45.04	5.08	0.85	4.33	4.75	20.59
1999	20.97	3.50	3.02	10.57	1.70	17.91	24.91	2.70	2.09	5.65	2.67	15.09	34.63	6.19	0.84	5.20	5.10	26.51
2000	18.18	3.66	2.99	10.94	1.68	18.35	19.38	3.04	2.92	8.89	2.20	19.52	30.81	6.31	0.84	5.27	4.99	26.33
2001	16.09	3.60	2.79	10.03	1.70	17.01	NA	NA	NA	NA	NA	NA	NA	NA	NA	NA	NA	NA
Mean	28.34	2.81	3.32	9.36	1.99	18.62	31.16	3.06	2.70	8.35	1.95	15.87	45.50	4.79	1.06	5.04	3.63	17.14

D/E = Dividend payout, equal to dividends/earnings.
NPM = Net profit margin, equal to net income/sales.
TAT = Total asset turnover, equal to sales/total assets.
ROA = Return on assets.
TAE = Leverage ratio, equal to total assets/equity.
ROE = Return on equity, equal to net income/equity.
NA = Data not available.

Source: *Financial Analysts Handbook* (New York: Standard & Poor's, 2001). Reprinted with permission.

EXHIBIT 15.14 ▶ TIME-SERIES PLOT OF WALGREENS SALES USED IN CALCULATION OF SALES VOLATILITY FOR WALGREENS FROM ARITHMETIC MEAN, FROM LINEAR GROWTH CURVE, AND FROM COMPOUND GROWTH CURVE

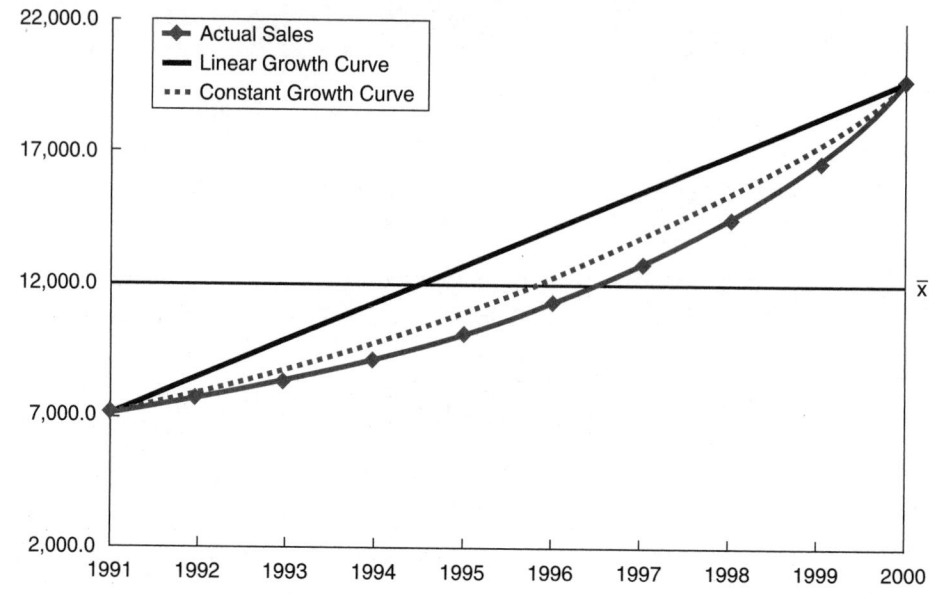

In addition to the consideration of fundamental factors, one should also consider market-determined risk (beta) based on the CAPM. As noted in connection with the cash flow models, the stock's beta derived from five years of monthly data relative to the S&P Industrials for the period 1997 to 2001 indicated a beta of 0.90.

These results are consistent with those derived from an analysis of the fundamental factors—both indicate that Walgreens' risk is below the aggregate market. This means that the risk premium and the required rate of return (k) for Walgreens stock should be lower than the market. By itself, this lower k would suggest an earnings multiplier above the market multiplier.

Estimating the Expected Growth Rate   Recall that the expected growth rate (g) is determined by the firm's retention rate and its expected return on equity (ROE). We have already noted Walgreens' low dividend payout compared to the industry and the aggregate market, which implies a higher retention rate.

As discussed using the DuPont model, a firm's ROE can be estimated in terms of the three ratios: (1) net profit margin (NPM), (2) total asset turnover (TAT), and (3) the financial leverage multiplier. We also know that NPM × TAT = Return on Assets (ROA). It is important to examine the relative impact of these two ratios and to compare the ROA of alternative firms as a measure of operating performance—that is, profitability and asset efficiency. Walgreens has experienced a small decline in TAT, but this has been offset by an increase in NPM, causing the firm's ROA to increase substantially from about 7 percent to over 10 percent, providing an ROA substantially above its industry and the market.

Finally, the firm's ROE equals the ROA times the financial leverage multiplier (total assets/equity). Notably since 1977 Walgreens has reduced its leverage multiplier from 2.39 to 1.68 while the industry and market have experienced increases (in particular, the market has

EXHIBIT 15.15 FINANCIAL RISK RATIOS FOR WALGREENS, THE RETAIL DRUGSTORE INDUSTRY, AND THE S&P INDUSTRIALS: 1977–2000

	WALGREENS[a]				RETAIL DRUGSTORES				S&P INDUSTRIALS			
YEAR	Total Assets/ Equity	Interest Coverage	Cash Flow/ Long-Term Debt[b]	Cash Flow/ Total Debt[c]	Total Assets/ Equity	Interest Coverage	Cash Flow/ Long-Term Debt	Cash Flow/ Total Debt	Total Assets/ Equity	Interest Coverage	Cash Flow/ Long-Term Debt	Cash Flow/ Total Debt
1977	2.39	6.91	0.36	0.13	1.53	28.90	1.76	0.41	2.15	8.00	0.63	0.22
1978	2.34	7.93	0.43	0.18	1.52	30.90	1.94	0.42	2.22	7.60	0.63	0.22
1979	2.30	8.83	0.50	0.19	1.65	21.20	1.21	0.34	2.28	7.70	0.70	0.22
1980	2.16	9.01	0.60	0.20	1.66	20.10	1.33	0.35	2.30	6.00	0.66	0.21
1981	2.08	10.44	0.91	0.22	1.65	16.20	1.74	0.36	2.32	5.00	0.63	0.21
1982	2.06	13.38	1.40	0.24	1.66	17.40	2.43	0.36	2.40	4.00	0.54	0.18
1983	2.04	19.61	1.76	0.26	1.88	20.20	3.24	0.35	2.37	4.60	0.61	0.19
1984	2.03	25.23	2.14	0.27	1.93	10.60	1.43	0.24	2.51	4.10	0.65	0.19
1985	2.16	28.65	1.79	0.27	1.88	12.10	0.75	0.22	2.75	4.20	0.51	0.16
1986	2.16	17.11	0.90	0.23	1.94	12.70	0.99	0.24	2.90	3.60	0.51	0.15
1987	2.19	11.76	0.94	0.21	2.04	9.40	0.93	0.23	2.97	4.40	0.58	0.17
1988	2.12	11.46	0.92	0.20	2.07	8.20	1.00	0.24	3.56	3.80	0.44	0.15
1989	2.04	13.94	1.23	0.22	2.03	7.10	0.61	0.23	3.84	3.70	0.43	0.13
1990	2.02	11.22	1.67	0.26	2.00	8.20	0.69	0.25	4.01	3.60	0.40	0.12
1991	1.94	18.18	2.27	0.28	1.83	10.30	0.96	0.27	3.96	3.40	0.34	0.10
1992	1.93	23.53	1.65	0.28	1.82	13.40	1.13	0.27	4.41	4.00	0.38	0.11
1993	1.84	15.59	2.50	0.29	1.88	15.80	0.82	0.21	4.81	4.50	0.40	0.10
1994	1.85	10.51	2.80	0.23	2.00	16.70	0.86	0.23	4.38	5.60	0.50	0.13
1995	1.94	12.14	3.15	0.31	2.03	13.20	0.79	0.23	4.25	3.40	0.49	0.14
1996	1.90	11.40	3.30	0.33	2.17	11.99	0.47	0.17	4.49	4.70	0.51	0.15
1997	1.91	11.75	3.35	0.33	2.18	7.37	0.49	0.14	4.77	5.63	0.52	0.15
1998	1.72	11.30	1.83	0.34	2.70	11.85	0.34	0.13	4.75	5.90	0.16	0.10
1999	1.70	11.40	1.97	0.34	2.67	13.57	0.38	0.14	5.10	5.95	0.20	0.12
2000	1.68	11.45	2.17	0.35	2.20	33.98	0.85	0.22	4.99	5.10	0.20	0.12

[a]These ratios do not reflect adjustment for capitalizing operating leases.
[b]Long-term debt does not include deferred taxes.
[c]Total debt is equal to total assets minus total equity, including preferred stock.

Source: *Financial Analysts Handbook*. (New York: Standard & Poor's, 2001). Reprinted with permission.

increased from 2.08 to 3.50). As a result, the *ROE*s are similar but the financial risk is different— that is, Walgreens has a higher *ROE* but lower financial risk (as noted, with leases the FR is higher than the market).

Using the results for the last three years (1998–2000), the *ROE*s would be approximately as follows:

	NPM	TAT	ROA	TOTAL ASSETS/ EQUITY	ROE
Walgreens	3.54	3.04	10.76	1.68	18.08
Retail drugstores	2.77	2.35	6.51	2.52	16.40
S&P Industrials	5.86	0.84	4.92	3.60	17.71

The foregoing is meant to highlight the difference among the three units based on history. An analyst would need to *estimate* future components and derive an expected *ROE* that reflects the firm's *future* performance.

The demonstration can be extended by combining the average annual *ROE*s derived in the preceding table and the average of recent retention rates from Exhibit 15.16 to derive expected growth rates:

	RETENTION RATE	ROE	EXPECTED GROWTH RATE
Walgreens	0.79	18.08	0.1428
Retail drugstores	0.77	16.40	0.1148
S&P Industrials	0.63	17.71	0.1116

Taken alone, these higher expected growth rates for Walgreens would indicate that it should definitely have a higher multiple than its industry and the market.

Computing the Earnings Multiplier   Comparing our estimates of *D/E, k,* and *g* to comparable values for the industry and the market, we find that Walgreens' earnings multiplier based on the microanalysis should be greater than the multiplier for its industry and the market. Specifically, the dividend-payout ratio points toward a lower multiplier for Walgreens, whereas both the lower risk analysis and the higher expected growth rate would indicate a multiplier for Walgreens above that of its industry and the market.

The macroanalysis indicated that Walgreens' multiplier typically has been above its industry and the market, and the microanalysis supported this relationship. Assuming a market multiple of about 23 and a retail drugstore multiplier of about 26, the multiplier for Walgreens should be between 28 and 30, with a tendency toward the upper end of the range and beyond (28–30–32 times). Alternatively, if we inserted some earlier estimated values for *D/E, k,* and *g* into the *P/E* ratio formula, we would not be able to derive an estimated multiplier for Walgreens because *g* is greater than *k*. As noted earlier in Chapter 11, because Walgreens is a true growth company, we cannot use the standard DDM formula to estimate a specific multiple. We would need to estimate a value based on the direction of change and the macroanalysis estimates of 28–30–32 times.

Estimate of the Future Value for Walgreens   Earlier, we estimated 2002 earnings per share for Walgreens of about $0.97 per share. Assuming multipliers of 28–30–32 implies the following estimated future values:

EXHIBIT 15.16 ▶ EXPECTED GROWTH RATE COMPONENTS FOR WALGREENS, THE RETAIL DRUGSTORE INDUSTRY, AND THE S&P INDUSTRIALS: 1977–2000

	WALGREENS			RETAIL DRUGSTORES			S&P INDUSTRIALS		
YEAR	RETENTION RATE	ROE	EXPECTED GROWTH RATE	RETENTION RATE	ROE	EXPECTED GROWTH RATE	RETENTION RATE	ROE	EXPECTED GROWTH RATE
1977	0.54	11.56	6.27	0.80	17.68	14.12	0.57	13.95	7.92
1978	0.70	17.44	12.15	0.76	17.21	13.10	0.59	14.63	8.60
1979	0.70	18.27	12.73	0.73	17.18	12.47	0.64	16.51	10.52
1980	0.70	17.65	12.27	0.71	17.51	12.40	0.60	14.82	8.85
1981	0.70	18.12	12.61	0.69	17.25	11.90	0.58	14.43	8.38
1982	0.73	20.34	14.86	0.69	16.96	11.69	0.46	11.09	5.10
1983	0.74	21.38	15.75	0.71	20.38	14.41	0.50	12.05	6.07
1984	0.74	22.22	16.48	0.62	15.55	9.70	0.59	14.61	8.55
1985	0.71	21.82	15.58	0.59	14.91	8.83	0.49	12.14	5.89
1986	0.70	20.65	14.49	0.68	16.35	11.13	0.44	11.64	5.12
1987	0.68	17.75	12.06	0.68	16.45	11.25	0.57	15.11	8.61
1988	0.71	19.03	13.59	0.69	16.93	11.75	0.63	19.06	12.03
1989	0.73	19.73	14.38	0.68	15.97	10.81	0.56	18.46	10.33
1990	0.72	18.45	13.25	0.68	16.26	11.11	0.50	16.22	8.08
1991	0.71	18.06	12.82	0.67	15.25	10.25	0.28	10.77	3.04
1992	0.71	17.89	12.66	0.66	14.89	9.89	0.34	13.37	4.53
1993	0.66	16.08	10.69	0.53	11.27	5.99	0.42	16.02	6.72
1994	0.70	17.92	12.58	0.66	15.17	10.05	0.61	21.79	13.30
1995	0.69	19.10	13.22	0.66	15.36	10.19	0.61	21.62	13.10
1996	0.71	19.40	13.78	0.71	14.06	10.01	0.62	24.49	15.22
1997	0.73	19.80	14.46	0.59	9.53	5.63	0.60	25.14	15.16
1998	0.76	19.60	14.84	0.75	14.23	10.71	0.55	20.59	11.32
1999	0.79	17.91	14.16	0.75	15.09	11.33	0.65	26.51	17.33
2000	0.82	18.35	15.01	0.81	19.52	15.74	0.69	26.33	18.22
Mean	0.71	18.69	13.36	0.69	15.87	11.02	0.55	17.14	9.67

$$28 \times \$0.97 = \$27.16$$
$$30 \times \$0.97 = \$29.10$$
$$32 \times \$0.97 = \$31.04$$

Making the Investment Decision

In our prior discussions of valuation, we set forth the investment decision in two forms:

1. Compute the estimated intrinsic value for an investment using your required rate of return as the discount rate. If this intrinsic value is equal to or greater than the current market price of the investment, buy it.
2. Compute the estimated intrinsic value for an investment using your required rate of return as one of the components. Given this intrinsic value, compute the expected rate of return you would receive if you bought the asset at the current market price and assume that this market price migrated to its intrinsic value plus the stocks dividend. If this expected rate of return is equal to or greater than your required rate of return, buy the investment; if the expected return is below your required rate of return, do not buy it.

The most obvious comparison is the estimated values derived using the present value of cash flow models and the values estimated using the earnings multiple model to the current market price of Walgreens of about $38 a share. The following is a summary of these estimated values. Recall that we could not calculate constant-growth models because Walgreens has consistently experienced growth rates above its required rates of return (it is a true growth company).

PRESENT VALUE OF CASH FLOW MODELS	
Three-stage DDM	$23.11
Three-stage FCFE	$27.50
Three-stage FCFF (OFCF)	$28.90

EARNINGS MULTIPLE MODELS	
28 times estimated earnings	$27.16
30 times estimated earnings	$29.10
32 times estimated earnings	$31.04

Because none of the computed values is equal to or larger than the current market price of $38.00, you would not recommend a purchase of the stock although Walgreens is clearly an outstanding firm. Stated in terms of our earlier discussion, Walgreens is obviously a true growth company, but apparently the firm's stock is not expected to be a growth stock at its current price.

Comparing Expected Rate of Return to Required Rate of Return   In past demonstrations of this decision rule, we have computed an expected rate of return using the intrinsic value and dividend. Although we will again use this technique, we also will introduce another technique for computing an expected rate of return based on the dividend discount model (DDM).

We can compute the expected rate of return, $E(R_i)$, based on our estimated intrinsic value using the formula

➤15.10
$$E(R_i) = \frac{IV - BV + Div}{BV}$$

where:

> IV = **the estimated intrinsic value of the stock**
> BV = **the beginning value of the stock (typically its current market price)**
> Div = **the expected dividend per share during the holding period**

In our case, these values would be

$$IV = \$31.00 \text{ (at best)}$$
$$BV = \text{(Assume \$38 a share)}$$
$$Div = \$0.16$$

Thus, we know that all the expected returns would be negative. Based on the k of 9.0 percent used in the valuation section, we would not buy this stock because its negative expected rates of return are below our required rate of return (9.0 percent).

The second technique used for deriving an expected rate of return is based on the dividend discount model. You will recall that the DDM states:

➤15.11
$$P_0 = \frac{D_1}{k - g}$$

Solving to estimate k:

➤15.12
$$k_i = \frac{D_1}{P_0} + g$$

In this equation, k serves as an estimate of the required rate of return when you assume that you know the firm's future growth rate. Alternatively, an investor can use this equation to estimate his or her *long-run* expected rate of return if you are estimating the future dividend and growth rate. For Walgreens, the P_0 would be the current price of the stock, D_1 would be the expected dividend during the investment horizon, and g would be the expected longer-run growth rate, as discussed in connection with Exhibit 15.16.

As an example, assume a current price of $38, an expected dividend of $0.16 per share, and a growth rate of 14 percent, which is the growth rate we used in the earlier microestimate of the multiplier. Notably, it is slightly below the g implied by the recent average values in Exhibit 15.16. This would imply the following estimate of your long-run expected rate of return on Walgreens common stock:

$$k = \frac{0.16}{38.00} + 0.140$$
$$= 0.004 + 0.140$$
$$= .144 = 14.4\%$$

This computation shows that you would expect a *long-run* rate of return from investing in Walgreens stock of 14.4 percent. If your required rate of return was 9.0 percent, you would buy this stock recognizing it is a *long-run* expectation.

ADDITIONAL MEASURES OF RELATIVE VALUE

The best-known measure of relative value for common stock is the price/earnings ratio or the earnings multiplier because it is derived from the dividend growth model and has stood the test of time as a useful measure of relative value. Analysts have also begun to calculate three additional measures of relative value for common stocks—the price/book value ratio, the price/cash flow ratio, and the price/sales ratio, which are demonstrated in this section.

Price/Book Value (P/BV) Ratio

The price-to-book-value ratio (*P/BV*) has gained prominence because of the studies by several authors.[18] The rationale is that book value can be a reasonable measure of value for firms that have consistent accounting practice (for example, firms in the same industry). Notably, this measure can apply to firms with negative earnings or negative cash flows. You should not attempt to use this ratio to compare firms with different levels of hard assets—for example, a heavy industrial firm to a service firm.

[18]Eugene F. Fama and Kenneth R. French, "The Cross Section of Expected Stock Returns," *Journal of Finance* 47, no. 2 (June 1992): 427–450; Barr Rosenberg, Kenneth Raid, and Ronald Lanstein, "Persuasive Evidence of Market Inefficiency," *Journal of Portfolio Management* 11, no. 3 (Spring 1985): 9–17; and Patricia Fairfield, "P/E, P/B and the Present Value of Future Dividends," *Financial Analysts Journal* 50, no. 4 (July–August 19): 23–31.

EXHIBIT 15.17 ▶ *TIME-SERIES PLOT OF MEAN PRICE–BOOK VALUE RATIOS FOR WALGREENS, THE RETAIL DRUGSTORE INDUSTRY, AND S&P INDUSTRIALS: 1977–2000*

The annual *P/BV* ratios for Walgreens, its industry, and the market are in Exhibit 15.5, along with the ratio of the company *P/BV* ratio relative to its industry and relative to the market ratio. In this instance, the major variable that should cause a difference in the *P/BV* ratio is the firm's return on investment *(ROI)* relative to its cost of capital (its WACC). Assuming that most firms in an industry have comparable WACCs, the major differential should be the firm's *ROI* because the larger the *ROI*-WACC difference, the greater the justified *P/BV* ratio. We will consider this in the subsequent section on EVA.

As shown in Exhibit 15.17, the *P/BV* ratios for the three components have increased from about 1.5–2.00 to 6.08–8.0. As shown in Exhibit 15.18, which contains a plot of relative valuation ratios, Walgreens has experienced a larger increase in its *P/BV* ratio than its industry as indicated by its Co/Ind ratio that has gone from about 0.80 to about 1.26. This seems reasonable based upon the difference in *ROE* for the Co versus the industry. In contrast, the Co/Mkt ratio for Walgreens has *declined* from about 1.18 to about 0.97 at the end of the period. This latter trend is interesting because the *ROE* for Walgreens has consistently been greater than for the S&P Industrials until 1995 when the *ROE* for the S&P Industrials rose substantially. One must question whether this declining trend in the Co/Mkt ratio is because the beginning relationship was too high.

Price/Cash Flow (*P/CF*) Ratio

As noted in Chapter 10, the price/cash flow ratio has grown in prominence and use because many observers contend that a firm's cash flow is less subject to manipulation than its earnings per share and because cash flows are widely used in the present value of cash flow models discussed earlier. An important question is, which of the several cash flow specifications should an analyst employ? In this analysis, we use the EBITDA cash flow measure equal to net income plus interest, depreciation, and taxes because this cash flow measure can be derived for both the RDS industry and the market. Although it is certainly legitimate to have a preference for one of the other cash flow measures discussed, a demonstration using this measure should provide a valid comparison for learning purposes.

EXHIBIT 15.18

TIME-SERIES PLOT OF RELATIVE PRICE–BOOK VALUE RATIOS FOR WALGREENS/INDUSTRY AND WALGREENS/MARKET: 1977–2000

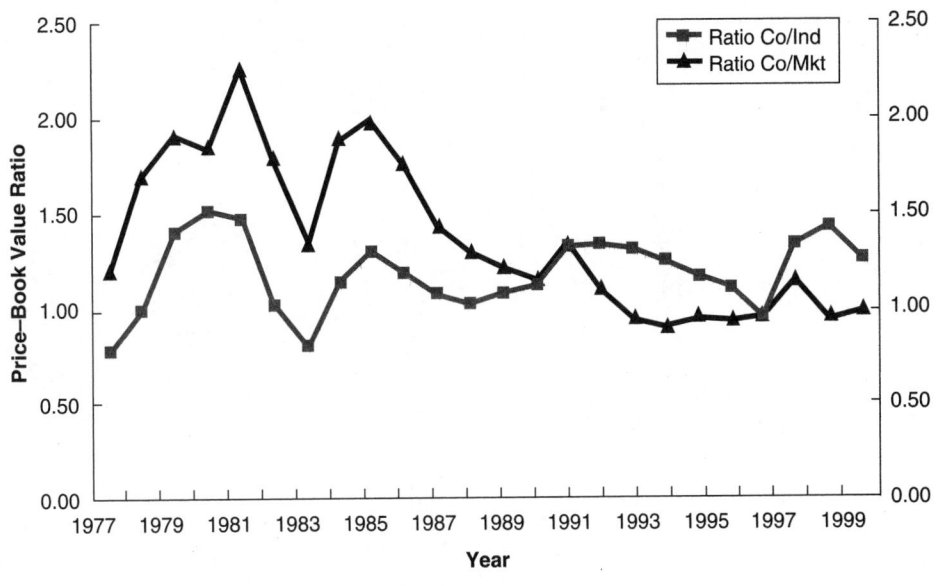

EXHIBIT 15.19

TIME-SERIES PLOT OF PRICE–CASH FLOW RATIOS FOR WALGREENS, THE RETAIL DRUGSTORE INDUSTRY, AND S&P INDUSTRIALS: 1977–2000

The time-series graph of the *P/CF* ratios in Exhibit 15.19 shows a general increase for Walgreens and its industry from about 7 times in 1977 to 35 for WAG and 25 for the industry while the market *P/CF* ratio went from 5 times to 18 times. Notably, not only did the absolute value of the ratios increase, the graphs in Exhibit 15.20 show that Walgreens *P/CF* ratios relative to its industry experienced an increase since a ratio of 0.83 in 1993 to and near its high value of 1.41

EXHIBIT 15.20

TIME-SERIES PLOT OF RELATIVE PRICE–CASH FLOW RATIOS FOR WALGREENS/INDUSTRY AND WALGREENS/MARKETS: 1977–2000

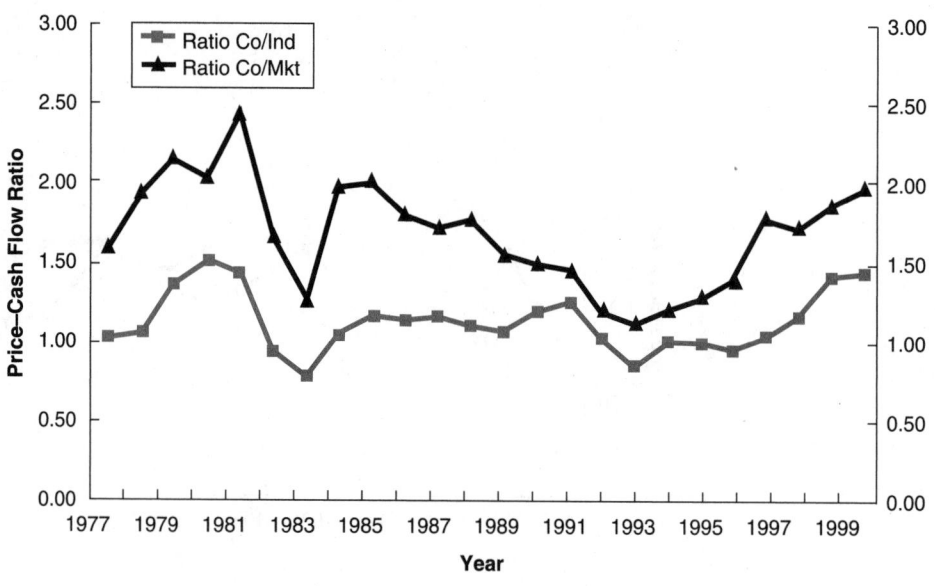

in 2000. Similarly, the Co/Mkt comparison experienced its low ratio of 1.10 in 1993 and has increased steadily to finish near its high at 1.96 in 2000. This indicates an overall increase in the *P/CF* ratio and a steady increase since 1993 in the *P/CF* ratio relative to the firm's industry and the overall market. In this case, the question becomes, What has happened to the firm's growth rate of cash flow and the risk of these cash flows that would justify this change in the relative *P/CF* ratio?

Price/Sales (P/S) Ratio

The price-to-sales ratio (*P/S*) has had a long but generally neglected existence followed by a recent reawakening. In the late 1950s, Phillip Fisher in his classic book suggested this ratio as a valuable tool when considering investments, including growth stocks.[19] Subsequently, his son Kenneth Fisher used the ratio as a major stock selection variable in his widely read book.[20] In the late 1990s, *P/S* has been suggested as a valuable tool in a monograph by award-winning author Martin Leibowitz, and this ratio was espoused by O'Shaughnessy in his book that compared several stock selection techniques.[21] Leibowitz makes the point that sales growth drives all subsequent earnings and cash flow, while those who are concerned with accounting manipulation point out that sales is one of the purest numbers available. Notably, this ratio is equal to the *P/E* ratio times the net profit margin (earnings/sales), which implies that it is heavily influenced by the profit margin of the entity being analyzed in addition to sales growth and sales volatility (risk).

---

[19]Phillip A. Fisher, *Common Stocks and Uncommon Profits* (Woodside, Calif.: PSR Publications, 1958, 1960 rev. ed., 1984).

[20]Kenneth L. Fisher, *SuperStocks* (Woodside, Calif.: Business Classics, 1984).

[21]Martin L. Leibowitz, *Sales-Driven Franchise Value* (Charlottesville, Va.: The Research Foundation of the Institute of Chartered Financial Analysis, 1997); and James P. O'Shaughnessy, *What Works on Wall Street* (New York: McGraw-Hill, 1997).

EXHIBIT 15.21 ▶ *TIME-SERIES PLOT OF MEAN PRICE–SALES RATIOS FOR WALGREENS, THE RETAIL DRUGSTORE INDUSTRY, AND THE S&P INDUSTRIALS: 1977–2000*

As shown in Exhibit 15.5 and Exhibit 15.21, the *P/S* ratio for Walgreens has experienced a significant increase from 0.14 to 1.61, compared to a moderate increase by its industry (0.43 to 1.00) and a healthy increase by the market (from 0.49 to 1.99). This substantial relative performance by Walgreens is reflected in Exhibit 15.22, which shows the plot of relative ratios wherein the Co/Ind ratio increased notably from 0.31 to almost 1.30, while the Co/Mkt ratio went from 0.30 to 0.67. Similar to prior comparisons, the question the analyst must ask is whether the growth of sales, the risk related to the sales growth, and the profit margin of Walgreens can justify a much higher *P/S* ratio than its industry. The positive news is that Walgreens' sales have experienced strong consistent growth relative to its industry and Walgreens has experienced a larger increase in its profit margin.

Summary of Relative Valuation Ratios

Notably, the four individual, relative valuation variables increased across the board—all four relative valuation ratios increased during the 20-year period for the firm, its industry, and the aggregate stock market. The widespread increases suggest that the relative valuation ratio changes are caused by changes in some aggregate economic variables, such as economic growth and economic risk factors. Interestingly, Dudley and McKelvey from Goldman, Sachs & Co. argued that the U.S. economy has experienced several significant changes during the past two decades that have caused an important change in the nature and length of our economic expansions and contractions.[22]

In addition to these overall increases for all three segments (firm, industry, and market), Walgreens has generally experienced a larger increase than its industry in terms of its *P/E* ratio, *P/BV* ratio, and *P/S* ratio, while lagging in terms of its *P/CF* ratio. Compared to the market, the firm's

---

[22]William C. Dudley and Edward F. McKelvey, *The Brave New Business Cycle* (New York: Goldman, Sachs & Co., October 1997).

EXHIBIT 15.22   *TIME-SERIES PLOT OF RELATIVE PRICE–SALES RATIOS FOR WALGREENS/INDUSTRY AND WALGREENS/MARKET: 1977–2000*

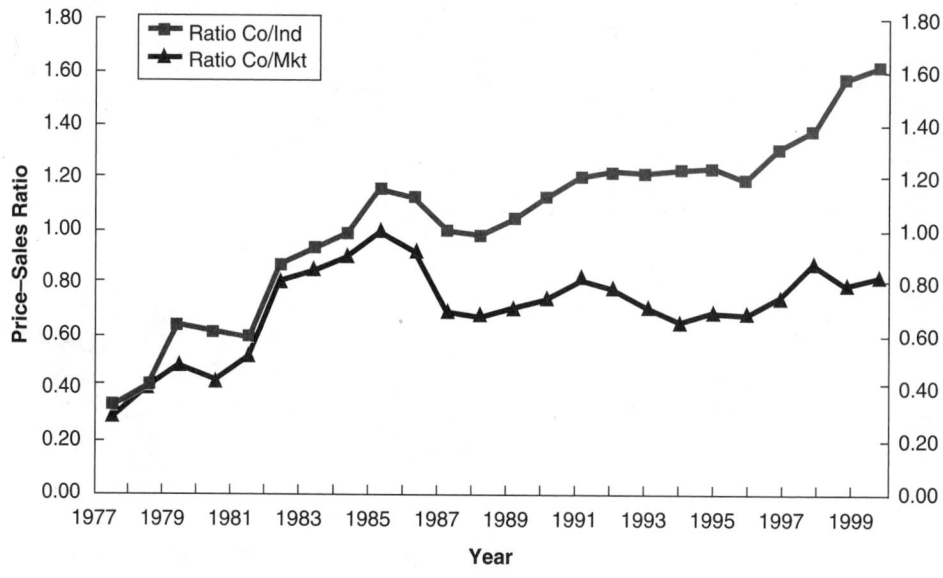

P/E ratio and *P/S* ratio increased more than the market, while its *P/CF* ratio and its *P/BV* ratios increased less than the market. Assuming that an investor wants to use these ratios to determine relative value or to make an investment decision, he or she needs to explain the differences based upon an analysis of the basic valuation factors that affect the ratios.

Now that we have considered the two major approaches to basic equity valuation, it is important to consider some techniques used to analyze and derive values for growth companies.

ANALYSIS OF GROWTH COMPANIES

Investment literature contains numerous accounts of the rapid growth of such companies as Wal-Mart, Cisco Systems, Intel, Merck, and Microsoft, along with stories about investors who became wealthy because of the timely acquisition of these stocks. These very high rates of return indicate that the early and proper valuation of true growth companies can be extremely rewarding. At the same time, for every successful Wal-Mart or Microsoft, there are numerous firms that did not survive. In addition, there are many instances where the stock price of a true growth company overcompensated for the firm's expected growth, and the subsequent returns to the stockholder were below expectations. As noted earlier, the common stock of a growth company is *not* always a growth stock.[23]

You are familiar with the dividend discount model and its basic assumptions—that is, that dividends are expected to grow at a *constant rate* for an *infinite time period*. As explained in Chapter 11. although these assumptions are reasonable when evaluating the aggregate market

---

[23]See Michael Solt and Meir Statman, "Good Companies, Bad Stocks," *Journal of Portfolio Management* 15, no. 4 (Summer 1989): 39–44.

and some large industries, they can be very tenuous when analyzing individual securities. *These assumptions are extremely questionable for a growth company.*

Growth Company Defined

A growth company has the opportunities and ability to invest capital in projects that generate rates of return greater than the firm's cost of capital. Such a condition is considered to be *temporary* because, in a competitive economy, all firms should produce at the point where marginal revenue equals marginal cost, which means that the returns to the producer will exactly compensate for the risks involved. If the returns earned in an industry are below what is expected for the risk involved, some participants will leave the industry. In contrast, if the rates of return for a given industry exceed the rates of return expected based on the risk involved, other companies will enter the industry, increase the supply, and eventually drive prices down until the rates of return earned are consistent with the risk involved, resulting in a state of equilibrium.

Actual Returns above Required Returns

The notion of a firm consistently earning rates of return above its required rate of return needs elaboration. Firms are engaged in business ventures that offer opportunities for investment of corporate capital, and these investments entail some risk. Investors determine their required return for owning a firm based on the risk of its investments compared to the risk of other firms. Based on the CAPM, one would expect the difference in the required rate of return to be a function of the difference in the stock's systematic risk. This required rate of return is referred to as the firm's *cost of equity*. If the market is in a state of equilibrium, the rates of return earned on risky investments by the firm should equal the rates of return required by investors. If a firm earns returns above those required for the systematic risk involved, these excess returns are referred to as *pure profits*.

One of the costs of production is the cost of the capital used. Therefore, in a competitive environment, marginal revenue should equal marginal costs (including capital costs), and there would be no excess returns or pure profits. Excess profits are possible only in a noncompetitive environment. Assume that a medical equipment firm is able to earn 20 percent on its capital, while investors require only 15 percent from the firm because of its systematic risk. The extra 5 percent is defined as pure profit, and numerous companies would enter the medical equipment field to enjoy the excess profits. These competitors would increase the supply of equipment and reduce the price that producers could charge for the equipment until the marginal returns equaled the marginal costs.

Because many firms have derived excess profits for a number of years, these excess returns are probably not due to a temporary disequilibrium but, rather, because of some noncompetitive factors that exist, such as patents or copyrights that provide a firm or person with monopoly rights to a process or a manuscript for a specified period. During this period of protection from competition, the firm can derive above-normal returns without fear of competition. Also, a firm could possess other strategies, such as those discussed by Porter, that provide added profits (e.g., a unique marketing technique or other organizational characteristics). Finally, there may be significant barriers to entry, such as capital requirements.

In a purely competitive economy with no frictions, true growth companies would not exist because competition would not allow continuing excess return investments. The fact is, our economy is not perfectly competitive (although this typically is the best model to use) because there are a number of frictions that restrict competition. Therefore, it is possible for *temporary* true growth companies to exist in our economy. The question is, How long can they earn these excess profits?

Growth Companies and Growth Stocks

Recall that a growth stock is expected to experience above-average risk-adjusted rates of return during some future period. This means that any undervalued stock can be a growth stock, regardless of the type of company. Alternatively, the stock of a growth company that is overvalued could be a speculative stock because the probability of below-normal returns would be very high.

In this section, we discuss models that are meant to help you evaluate the unique earnings stream of a growth company. As a result, you should derive a better estimate of the firm's value and be able to judge whether the stock of a growth company is (1) a growth stock, (2) a properly valued stock, or (3) a speculative overvalued stock.

Growth Companies and the Dividend Discount Model

We know that even in an economy with some noncompetitive factors, a true growth firm cannot exist for very long because patents and copyrights run out, unusual management practices can be copied, and competitors can enter the industry. Still, because these growth companies can experience abnormal growth for a finite period, the constant growth dividend discount growth model is *not* appropriate for the valuation of growth companies, and we must consider special valuation models that allow for the finite periods of abnormal growth and for the possibility of different rates of growth. The rest of the chapter deals with models for valuing growth companies.

Alternative Growth Models[24]

In this section, we consider the full range of growth models, from those of no growth and negative growth to dynamic true growth. Knowledge of the full range will help you understand why the dividend growth model is not always applicable. We assume the company is an all-equity firm to simplify the computations.

No-Growth Firm

The no-growth firm is a mythical company that is established with a specified portfolio of investments that generate a constant stream of earnings (E) equal to r times the value of assets. Earnings are calculated after allowing for depreciation expense used to maintain the assets at their original value. Therefore,

➤ 15.13
$$E = r \times \text{Assets}$$

It also is assumed that all earnings of the firm are paid out in dividends; if b is the rate of retention, $b = 0$. Hence,

➤ 15.14
$$E = r \times \text{Assets} = \text{Dividends}$$

Under these assumptions, the value of the firm is the discounted value of the perpetual stream of earnings (E). The discount rate (the required rate of return) is specified as k. In this case, it is assumed that $r = k$. The firm's rate of return on assets equals its required rate of return. Therefore, the value of the firm is

➤ 15.15
$$V = \frac{E}{k} = \frac{(1-b)E}{k}$$

In the no-growth case, the earnings stream never changes because the asset base never changes, and the rate of return (r) on the assets never changes. Therefore, the value of the firm never changes, and investors continue to receive k on their investment.

➤ 15.16
$$k = E/V$$

---

[24]The discussion in this section draws heavily from Ezra Solomon, *The Theory of Financial Management* (New York: Columbia University Press, 1963), 55–63; and M. Miller and F. Modigliani, "Dividend Policy, Growth, and the Valuation of Shares," *The Journal of Business* 34, no. 4 (October 1961): 411–433.

Long-Run Growth Models

Long-run models differ from the no-growth models because *they assume some of the earnings are reinvested.* In all cases, it is postulated that the market value *(V)* of an all-equity firm is the capitalized value of three component forms of returns discounted at the rate *k*.

➤ *E* = the level of (constant) net earnings expected from existing assets, without further net investments.

➤ *G* = the growth component that equals the present value of capital gains expected from reinvested funds. The return on reinvested funds is equal to *r,* which equals *mk* (*m* is the relative rate of return operator). If *m* is equal to 1, then *r = k.* If *m* is greater than 1, the projects that generate these returns are considered true growth investments *(r > k).* If *m* is less than 1, the investments are generating returns *(r)* below the cost of capital *(r < k).*

➤ *R* = the reinvestment of net earnings *(E)* and is equal to *bE,* where *b* is a percent of retention between zero (no reinvestment) and unity (total reinvestment; no dividends).

Simple Growth Model   This model assumes the firm has growth investment opportunities that provide rates of return equal to *r,* where *r* is greater than *k* (*m* is above 1). Further, it is assumed that the firm can invest *R* dollars a year at these rates and that *R = bE; R* is a *constant dollar amount* because *E* is the constant earnings at the beginning of the period.

The value of *G,* the capital gain component, is computed as follows: the first investment of *bE* dollars yields a stream of earnings equal to *bEr* dollars, and this is repeated every year. Each of these earnings streams has a present value, as of the year it begins, of *bEr/k,* which is the present value of a constant perpetual stream discounted at a rate consistent with the risk involved. Assuming the firm does this every year, it has a series of investments, each of which has a present value of *bEr/k.* The present value of all these series is *(bEr/k)/k,* which equals *bEr/k².* But because *r = mk,* this becomes

➤15.17
$$\frac{bEmk}{k^2} = \frac{bEm}{k} \text{ (Gross Present Value of Growth Investments)}$$

To derive these flows, the firm must invest *bE* dollars each year. The present value of these annual investments is equal to *bE/k.* Therefore, the *net* present value of growth investments is equal to

➤15.18
$$\frac{bEm}{k} - \frac{bE}{k} \text{ (Net Present Value of Growth Investments)}$$

The important variable is the value of *m,* which indicates the relationship of *r* to *k.* Combining this growth component with the capitalized value of the constant earnings stream indicates that the value of the firm is

➤15.19
$$V = \frac{E}{k} + \left[\frac{bEm}{k} - \frac{bE}{k} \right]$$

This equation indicates that the value of the firm is equal to the capitalized value of the constant earnings stream plus a growth component equal to the *net* present value of reinvestment in growth projects. By combining the first and third terms in Equation 15.19, it becomes

➤15.20
$$V = \frac{E(1-b)}{k} + \frac{bEm}{k}$$

Because $E(1 - b)$ is the dividend *(D)*, this model becomes

➤15.21 $$V = \frac{D}{k} + \frac{bEm}{k}$$ (Present Value of Constant Dividend Plus the Present Value of Growth Investments)

It can be stated as earnings only by rearranging Equation 15.19:

➤15.22 $$V = \frac{E}{k} + \frac{bE(m - 1)}{k}$$ (Present Value of Constant Earnings Plus the Present Value of Excess Earnings from Growth Investments)

Expansion Model The expansion model assumes a firm retains earnings to reinvest but receives a rate of return on its investments that is equal to its cost of capital ($m = 1$, so $r = k$). The effect of such a change can be seen in Equation 15.18, where the net present value of growth investments would be zero. Therefore, Equation 15.19 would become

➤15.23 $$V = \frac{E}{k}$$

Equation 15.20 would become

➤15.24 $$V = \frac{E(1 - b)}{k} + \frac{bE}{k} = \frac{E}{k}$$

Equation 15.21 is still valid, but the present value of the growth investment component would be smaller because *m* would be equal to 1. Finally, the last term in Equation 15.22 would disappear.

This discussion indicates that simply because a firm retains earnings and reinvests them, it is not necessarily beneficial to the stockholder *unless the reinvestment rate is above the required rate (r > k).* Otherwise, the investor in a tax-free world would be as well off with all earnings paid out in dividends. Either way, your return is *k*.

Negative Growth Model The negative growth model applies to a firm that retains earnings ($b > 0$) and reinvests these funds in projects that generate rates of return *below* the firm's cost of capital ($r < k$ or $m < 1$). The impact of this on the value of the firm can be seen from Equation 15.18, which indicates that with $m < 1$, the net present value of the growth investments would be *negative.* Therefore, the value of the firm in Equation 15.19 would be *less* than the value of a no-growth firm or an expansion firm. This also can be seen by examining the effect of $m < 1$ in Equation 15.22. The firm is withholding funds from the investor and investing them in projects that generate returns less than those available from comparable risk investments.

Such poor performance may be difficult to uncover because the firm's asset base will grow since it is retaining earnings and acquiring assets. Notably, the earnings of the firm will increase if it earns *any* positive rate of return on the new assets. The important point is, *the earnings will not grow by as much as they should,* so the value of the firm will decline over time when investors discount the cash flows from this reinvestment stream at the firm's cost of capital.

What Determines the Capital Gain Component? These equations highlight the factors that influence the capital gain component. All the equations beginning with 15.17 suggest that the gross present value of the growth investments is equal to

bEm/k

Therefore, three factors influence the size of this capital gain term. The first is *b*, the percentage of earnings retained for reinvestment. The greater the proportion of earnings retained, the larger the capital gain component. The second factor is *m*, which is critical because it indicates the relationship between the firm's rate of return on investments and the firm's required rate of return (i.e., its cost of capital). A value of 1 indicates the firm is earning only its required return. A firm with an *m* greater than 1 is a true growth company. The important question is, How much greater than *k* is the return? The final factor is the time period for the superior investments. How long can the firm make these superior return investments? This critical time factor often is overlooked because we have assumed an infinite horizon to simplify the computations. However, when analyzing growth companies, this time estimate is clearly a major consideration. In summary, the three factors that influence the capital gain component are

1. The amount of capital invested in growth investments *(b)*
2. The relative rate of return earned on the funds retained *(m)*
3. The time horizon for these growth investments

Dynamic True Growth Model   A dynamic true growth model applies to a firm that invests a constant *percentage of current* earnings in projects that generate rates of return above the firm's required rate ($r > k$, $m > 1$). In contrast to the simple growth model where the firm invests a *constant* dollar amount each year, in this model the amount invested is *growing* each year as earnings increase. As a result, the firm's earnings and dividends will grow at a *constant rate* that is equal to *br* (the percentage of earnings retained times the return on investments). In the current model, this would equal *bmk,* where *m* is greater than 1. Given these assumptions, the dynamic growth model for an infinite time period is the dividend discount model derived in the Appendix to Chapter 11:

►15.25

$$V = \frac{D_1}{k - g}$$

Applying this model to a true growth company means that earnings and dividends are growing at a constant rate and *the firm is investing larger and larger dollar amounts in projects that generate returns greater than* k. Moreover, the DDM model implicitly assumes that the firm can continue to do this for *an infinite time period.* If the growth rate *(g)* is greater than *k,* the model blows up and indicates that the firm should have an infinite value. Durand[25] considered this possibility and concluded that, although many firms had current growth rates above the normal required rates of return, very few of their stocks were selling for infinite values. He explained this by contending that investors expected the reinvestment rate to decline or they felt that the investment opportunities would not be available for an infinite time period. Exhibit 15.23 contains a summary of the alternative company characteristics.

The Real World   Because these models are simplified to allow us to develop a range of alternatives, several of them are extremely unrealistic. In the real world, companies generally would combine these models. Unfortunately, most firms have made some investments where $r < k$, and many firms invest in projects that generate returns about equal to their cost of capital. Finally, most firms invest in *some* projects that provide rates of return above the firm's cost of capital ($r > k$). The crucial questions are: (1) How much is invested in these true growth projects? and (2) How long do these true growth opportunities last?

---

[25]David Durand, "Growth Stocks and the Petersburg Paradox," *Journal of Finance* 12, no. 3 (September 1957): 348–363.

EXHIBIT 15.23 ▶ *SUMMARY OF COMPANY DESCRIPTIONS*

	RETENTION	RETURN ON INVESTMENTS
No-growth company	$b = 0$	$r = k$
Long-run growth (assumes reinvestment)		
Negative growth	$b > 0$	$r < k$
Expansion	$b > 0$	$r = k$
Simple long-run growth	$b > 0$	
	(constant $)	$r > k$
Dynamic long-run growth	$b > 0$	
	(constant %)	$r > k$

Given this understanding of growth companies and what creates their value, the rest of the chapter considers various models that help you understand how to identify a true growth company and estimate specific values for these growth companies. We begin with models that are intended to identify growth companies in terms of providing excess economic value, which some contend is due to franchise value. Subsequently, we consider several models that are intended to provide a valuation of these companies by concentrating on how long the superior growth can continue and, alternatively, the extent and length of the superior growth. This final model has some similarities to the three-stage cash flow models.

◀ *MEASURES OF VALUE ADDED*[26] ▶

In addition to the DDM, which feeds into the *P/E* ratio valuation technique and the supplementary *P/BV* and *P/CF,* ratios, there has been growing interest in a set of performance measures referred to as "value added." Notably, these value-added measures of performance are directly related to the capital budgeting techniques used in corporation finance. Specifically, they consider *economic profit,* which is analogous to the net present value (NPV) technique used in corporate capital budgeting. These value-added measures examine management performance based on the ability of managers to add value to the firm. They are also being used by security analysts as possible indicators of future equity returns, based on the logic that superior management performance should be reflected in a company's stock returns. In the subsequent discussion, we concentrate on three measures of value-added: **economic value added (EVA)** and **market value added (MVA)** pioneered by Stern and Stewart,[27] and the **franchise factor** developed by Leibowitz and Kogelman.[28]

[26]This section benefited from Pamela P. Peterson and David Peterson. "Company Performance Measures of Value-Added" (Charlottesville Va.: The Research Foundation of the Institute of Chartered Financial Analysis, 1996).

[27]These concepts are described in detail in G. Bennett Stewart III. *The Quest for Value* (New York: Harper Business, 1991).

[28]Martin L. Leibowitz and Staley Kogelman. *Franchise Value and the Price-Earnings Ratio* (Charlottesville, Va.: Research Foundation of the Institute of Chartered Financial Analysts, 1994).

Economic Value Added (EVA)[29]

As noted, EVA is closely related to the net present value (NPV) technique wherein you evaluate the expected performance of an investment by discounting its future cash flows at the firm's weighted average cost of capital (WACC) and compare this sum of discounted future cash flows to the cost of the project. If the discounted cash flows are greater than its cost, the project is expected to generate a positive NPV, which implies that it will add to the value of the firm and, therefore, it should be undertaken. In the case of EVA, you evaluate the annual performance of management by comparing the firm's net operating profit less adjusted taxes (NOPLAT) to the firm's total cost of capital in dollar terms, including the cost of equity. In this analysis, if the firm's NOPLAT during a specific year exceeds its dollar cost of capital, it has a positive EVA for the year and has added value for its stockholders. In contrast, if the EVA is negative, the firm has not earned enough during the year to cover its total cost of capital and the value of the firm has declined. Notably, NOPLAT indicates what the firm has earned for all capital suppliers and the dollar cost of capital is what all the capital suppliers required—including the firm's equity holders. The following summarizes the major calculations:[30]

EVA =

(A) Adjusted Operating Profits before Taxes

Minus (B) Cash Operating Taxes

Equals (C) Net Operating Profits Less Adjusted Taxes (NOPLAT)

Minus (D) The Dollar Cost of Capital

Equals (E) Economic Value Added (EVA)

In turn, these items are calculated as follows:

OPERATING PROFIT (AFTER DEPRECIATION AND AMORTIZATION)

Add: Implied Interest on Operating Leases

Add: An Increase in the LIFO Reserve

Add: Goodwill Amortization

Equals: (A) Adjusted Operating Profits before Taxes

INCOME TAX EXPENSE

Add: Decrease in Deferred Taxes

Add: Tax Benefit from Interest Expenses

Add: Tax Benefit from Interest on Leases

Less: Taxes on Nonoperating Income

Equals: (B) Cash Operating Taxes

---

[29]This is a registered trademark of Stern, Stewart & Co.

[30]For a detailed discussion, see Stewart, *The Quest for Value,* or Peterson and Peterson, *Company Performance Measures of Value Added.* For summary discussions, see Thomas P. Jones, "The Economic Value-Added Approach to Corporate Investments," in *Corporate Financial Decision Making and Equity Analysis* (Charlottesville, Va.: Association for Investment Management and Research, 1995); and S. Tully, "The Real Key to Creating Wealth," *Fortune* (September 1993):38–40, 44, 45, 48, 50.

(A) minus (B) equals: (C) Net Operating Profits Less Adjusted Taxes (NOPLAT)

Capital =

	Net Working Capital (current assets less non-interest-bearing liabilities)
Add:	LIFO Reserve
Add:	Net Plant, Property, and Equipment
Add:	Other Assets
Add:	Goodwill
Add:	Accumulated Goodwill Amortized
Add:	Present Value of Operating Leases
Equals:	*Capital*

Weighted Average Cost of Capital (WACC) =

	(Book Value of Debt/Total Book Value) × (the Market Cost of Debt) (1 − Tax Rate)
	(Book Value of Equity/Total Book Value) × (Cost of Equity)
	(Cost of equity is based on the CAPM using the prevailing 10-year Treasury bond as the *RFR,* a calculated beta, and a market risk premium between 3 and 6 percent.)
(D)	Dollar Cost of Capital = Capital × WACC
(E)	Economic Value Added (EVA) =
(C)	Net Operating Profits Less Adjusted Taxes (NOPLAT) Minus (D) Dollar Cost of Capital

---

EVA Return on Capital   The preceding calculations provide a positive or negative dollar value, which indicates whether the firm earned an excess above its cost of capital during the year analyzed. There are two problems with this annual dollar value for EVA. First, how does one judge over time if the firm is prospering relative to its past performance? Although you would want the absolute EVA to grow over time, the question is whether the rate of growth of EVA is adequate for the additional capital provided. Second, how does one compare alternative firms of different sizes? Both of these concerns can be met by calculating an EVA return on capital equal to

$$EVA/Capital$$

You would want this EVA rate of return on capital for a firm to remain constant over time, or, ideally, to grow, Also, using this ratio you can compare firms of different sizes and determine which firm has the largest *economic profit per dollar of capital.*

An Alternative Measure of EVA   An alternative but equal way to measure and think about EVA is to compare directly the firm's return on capital employed with the firm's average cost of capital (i.e., its WACC). As noted previously, it is this difference in the rates of return that identifies a company as a true growth company. Another way to measure EVA is to multiply this EVA spread (return on capital minus WACC) by the amount of capital employed. The appeal of this EVA spread approach is that it concentrates on the factors that create a growth company. Also, it helps the management and analysts recognize that true growth can be created either by increasing the firm's return on capital *or* by reducing its cost of capital.

An excellent example of this approach to the measurement and analysis of EVA is the work by Cohen and Napolitano of Goldman Sachs regarding EVA performance of the S&P Industrials.[31] As shown in Exhibit 15.24 and Exhibit 15.25, the EVA spread for the S&P Industrials has gone from a zero spread in 1986 to a negative spread during the 1990–1991 recession to a healthy estimated 3.0 percent spread in 2002 because of both an increase in the return on capital *and* a decline in the WACC for these firms.

Market Value Added (MVA)

In contrast to EVA, which generally is an evaluation of internal performance, MVA is a measure of external performance—how the market has evaluated the firm's performance in terms of the market value of debt and market value of equity compared to the capital invested in the firm.

$$\text{Market Value Added (MVA)} = (\text{Market Value of Firm}) - \text{Capital}$$
$$- \text{Market Value of Debt}$$
$$- \text{Market Value of Equity}$$

Again, to properly analyze this performance, it is necessary to look for positive changes over time—that is, the percent change each year. It is important to compare these changes in MVA each year to those for the aggregate stock and bond markets because these market values can be impacted by interest rates and general economic conditions.

Relationships between EVA and MVA

Although EVA is used primarily for evaluating management performance, it also is being used by external analysts to evaluate management with the belief that superior internal performance should be reflected in a company's stock performance. Several studies have attempted to determine the relationship between the two variables (EVA and MVA), and the results have not been encouraging. Although the stock of firms with positive EVAs has tended to outperform the stocks of negative EVA firms, the differences are typically insignificant and the relationship does not occur every year. This poor relationship may be due to the timing of the analysis (how fast EVA is reflected in stocks) or because the market values (MVAs) are affected by factors other than EVA—for example, MVA can be impacted by market interest rates and by changes in *future* expectations for a firm not considered by EVA—that is, it appears that EVA does an outstanding job of evaluating management's *past* performance in terms of adding value. While one would certainly hope that superior past performance will continue, there is nothing certain about this relationship.

The Franchise Factor

The franchise factor concept is similar to EVA since it recognizes that, to add value to a firm, it is necessary to invest in projects that provide excess NPV—that is, the firm must generate rates of return above its WACC. This technique is directly related to the valuation approach we have been using since the franchise value approach breaks a firm's observed *P/E* down into two components: (1) the *P/E* that based on the company's ongoing business (its base *P/E*); plus (2) a franchise *P/E* that the market assigns to *the expected value of new and profitable business opportunities.* This can be visualized as:

➤15.26
$$\text{Franchise } P/E = \text{Observed } P/E - \text{Base } P/E$$

---

[31]Abby Joseph Cohen and Gabrielle Napolitano, eds., *Investment Strategy Chartbook* (New York: Goldman, Sachs & Co. (October 2001).

EXHIBIT 15.24   *S&P INDUSTRIALS EVA® AND SPREAD ANALYSIS*

	1986	1987	1988	1989	1990	1991	1992	1993	1994	1995	1996	1997	1998	1999	2000E	2001E	2002E
Return on Capital Employed (r):																	
Nominal (a)	9.4%	11.2%	13.8%	11.5%	10.2%	7.1%	7.5%	8.4%	9.8%	11.8%	12.4%	12.5%	11.6%	12.3%	11.1%	9.6%	10.1%
Real	7.5	7.6	9.7	6.7	4.8	2.9	4.4	5.5	7.1	9.0	9.5	10.2	10.0	10.1	7.7	6.6	8.1
Cost of Capital (c*):																	
Nominal (b)	9.4%	10.1%	10.0%	9.7%	9.6%	9.3%	8.6%	7.7%	8.9%	8.4%	8.5%	8.0%	7.6%	8.7%	7.7%	7.8%	7.1%
Real	7.5	6.5	6.0	4.9	4.2	5.1	5.6	4.7	6.3	5.6	5.6	5.7	6.0	6.5	4.3	4.8	5.1
Spread (r − c*)	0.0%	1.1%	3.7%	1.8%	0.5%	(2.1%)	(1.1%)	0.7%	0.9%	3.4%	3.9%	4.5%	4.1%	3.6%	3.5%	1.8%	3.0%
EVA ($ per Share)	$0.00	$2.88	$10.66	$6.66	$2.23	($9.78)	($5.02)	$3.27	$4.09	$15.58	$18.68	$22.39	$21.07	$19.56	$20.58	$11.50	$19.97
Consumer Price Index	1.9%	3.7%	4.1%	4.8%	5.4%	4.2%	3.1%	3.0%	2.6%	2.8%	2.9%	2.3%	1.6%	2.2%	3.4%	3.0%	2.0%

(a) NOPAT/Beginning-period adjusted capital.

(b) Weighted-average after-tax cost of debt and equity capital.

Source: Standard & Poor's; Federal Reserve Board; Bureau of Labor Statistics; Goldman Sachs Research estimates.; Abby Joseph Cohen and Gabrielle Napolitano, eds., *Investment Strategy Chartbook* (New York: Goldman, Sachs & Co., October 2001).

EXHIBIT 15.25 ▶

TIME-SERIES PLOT OF RETURN ON CAPITAL, COST OF CAPITAL, AND EVA® SPREAD FOR S&P INDUSTRIALS: 1986–2002E

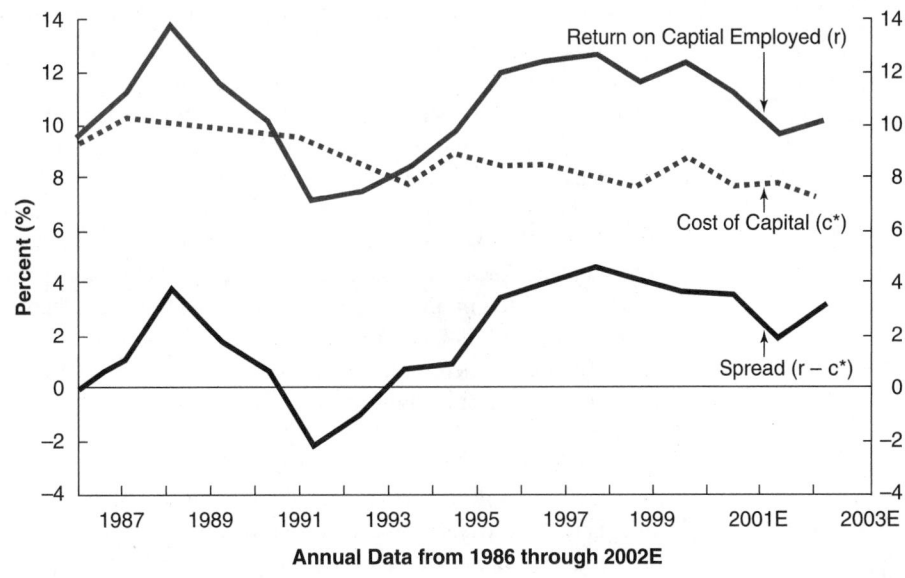

Source: Standard & Poor's; Federal Reserve Board; Goldman Sachs Research estimates.; Abby Joseph Cohen and Gabrielle Napolitano, eds., *Investment Strategy Chartbook* (New York: Goldman, Sachs & Co, October 2001).

The base *P/E* is the reciprocal of the market discount rate k (it is $1/k$). For example, if the stock's market discount rate is 12 percent, the base *P/E* would be about 8.5 times.

What determines the franchise *P/E?* Not surprising, it is a function of the relative rate of return on new business opportunities (the franchise factor) and the size of the superior return opportunities (the growth factor).

Incremental Franchise P/E = Franchise Factor × Growth Factor

▶15.27
$$= \frac{R-k}{rk} \times G$$

where:

    R = **the expected return on the new opportunities**
    k = **the current cost of equity**
    r = **the current *ROE* on investment**
    G = **the present value of the new growth projects relative to the current value of the firm**

The critical factors determining the franchise *P/E* are the difference between R and k and the size of these growth opportunities relative to the firm's current size (i.e., G).[32]

---

[32]For further detail and examples of the application, see Leibowitz and Kogelman, *Franchise Value and the Price/ Earnings Ratio.*

Growth Duration Model

The purpose of the growth duration model is to help you *evaluate* the high *P/E* ratio for the stock of a growth company by relating its *P/E* ratio to the firm's *rate* of growth and *duration* of growth. A stock's *P/E* ratio is a function of (1) the firm's expected rate of growth of earnings per share, (2) the stock's required rate of return, and (3) the firm's dividend-payout ratio. Assuming equal risk and no significant difference in the payout ratio for different firms, the principal variable affecting differences in the earnings multiple for two firms *is the difference in expected growth.* Notably, the growth estimate must consider both the *rate* of growth and how long this growth can be sustained—that is, the *duration* of expected growth. As noted earlier, no company can grow indefinitely at a rate substantially above normal. For example, Wal-Mart cannot continue to grow at 20 percent a year for an extended period, or it will eventually become the entire economy. In fact, Wal-Mart or any similar growth firm will eventually run out of high-profit investment projects. Recall that continued growth at a constant rate requires that larger amounts of money be invested in high-return projects. Eventually, competition will encroach on these high-return investments and the firm's growth rate will decline to a rate consistent with the rate for the overall economy. Therefore, a reasonable and accurate estimate of the duration of a firm's high-growth period becomes significant.

Computation of Growth Duration The growth duration concept was suggested by Holt, who showed that if you assume equal risk between a given security and a market security, such as the S&P Industrials, you can concentrate on the differential past growth rates for the market and the growth firm as a factor causing the alternative *P/E* ratios.[33] This allows you to compute the market's *implied growth duration* for the growth firm.

If $E'(0)$ is the firm's current earnings, then $E'(t)$ is earnings in Period t according to the expression

➤15.28
$$E'(t) = E(0)(1 + G)'$$

where G is the annual percentage growth rate for earnings. To adjust for dividend payments, it was assumed that all such payments are used to purchase further shares of the stock. This means the number of shares (N) will grow at the dividend rate (D). Therefore

➤15.29
$$N(t) = N(0)(1 + D)^t$$

To derive the total earnings for a firm, $E(t)$, the growth rate in per-share earnings and the growth rate in shares are combined as follows:

➤15.30
$$E(t) = E'(t)N(t) = E'(0)[(1 + G)(1 + D)]^t$$

Because G and D are small, this expression can be approximated by

➤15.31
$$E(t) \simeq E'(0)(1 + G + D)^t$$

Assuming the growth stock (g) and the nongrowth stock (a) have similar risk and payout, the market should value the two stocks in direct proportion to their earnings in year T, where T is the time when the growth company will begin to grow at the same rate as the market (i.e., the nongrowth stock). Put another way, T is the number of years the growth stock is expected to grow

---

[33]Charles C. Holt, "The Influence of Growth Duration on Share Prices," *Journal of Finance* 7, no. 3 (September 1962): 465–475.

at the high rate. In other words, *current prices should be in direct proportion to the expected future earnings ratio that will prevail in year* T. This relationship can be stated

➤15.32
$$\left(\frac{P_g(0)}{P_a(0)} \right) \simeq \left(\frac{E_g(0)(1+G_g+D_g)^T}{E_a(0)(1+G_a+D_a)^T} \right)$$

or

➤15.33
$$\left(\frac{P_g(0)/E_g(0)}{P_a(0)/E_a(0)} \right) \simeq \left(\frac{1+G_g+D_g}{1+G_a+D_a} \right)^T$$

As a result, the P/E *ratios of the two stocks are in direct proportion to the ratio of composite growth rates raised to the Tth power.* You can solve for T by taking the log of both sides as follows:

➤15.34
$$\ln \left(\frac{P_g(0)/E_g(0)}{P_a(0)/E_a(0)} \right) \simeq T\ln \left(\frac{1+G_g+D_g}{1+G_a+D_a} \right)$$

The growth duration model answers the question, How long must the earnings of the growth stock grow at this expected high rate, relative to the nongrowth stock, to justify its prevailing above-average *P/E* ratio? You must then determine whether the *implied* growth duration estimate is reasonable in terms of the company's potential.

Consider the following example. The stock of Walgreens is selling for $38 a share with expected per-share earnings of $0.97 (its future earnings multiple is 39). Walgreens' expected EPS growth rate is estimated to be 13 percent a year, and its dividend yield has been 1 percent and is expected to remain at this level. In contrast, the S&P Industrials Index has a future *P/E* ratio of 25 an average dividend yield of 2 percent, and an expected growth rate of 7 percent. Therefore, the comparison is as follows:

	S&P Industrials	Walgreens
P/E ratio	25.00	39.00
Expected growth rate	0.07	0.13
Dividend yield	0.01	0.01

Inserting these values into Equation 15.34 yields the following:

$$\ln \left(\frac{39.00}{25.00} \right) = T\ln \left(\frac{1+0.13+0.01}{1+0.07+0.01} \right)$$

$$\ln(1.56) = T\ln \left(\frac{1.14}{1.08} \right)$$

$$\ln(1.56) = T\ln(1.055)$$

$$T = \ln(1.56)/\ln(1.055)(\log \text{ base } 10)$$

$$= 0.1931/0.02325$$

$$= 8.31 \text{ Years}$$

These results indicate the market is implicitly assuming that Walgreens can continue to grow at this composite rate (14 percent) for about 8 more years, after which it is assumed Walgreens will grow at the same rate (8 percent) as the aggregate market (i.e., the S&P Industrials). You must now ask, Can this superior growth rate be sustained by Walgreens for at least this period? If the implied growth duration is greater than you believe is reasonable, you would advise against buying Walgreens stock. If the implied duration is below your expectations, you would recommend buying the stock.

Intraindustry Analysis   Besides comparing a company to a market series, you can directly compare two firms. For an intercompany analysis, you should compare firms in the same industry because the equal risk assumptions of this model are probably more reasonable.

Consider the following example from the computer software industry:

	COMPANY A	COMPANY B
P/E ratios	31.00	25.00
Expected annual growth rate	0.1700	0.1200
Dividend yield	0.0100	0.0150
Growth rate plus dividend yield	0.1800	0.1350
Estimate of T^a		5.53 years

[a]Readers should check to see that they get the same answer.

These results imply that the market expects Company A to grow at an annual total rate of 18 percent for about 5.5 years, after which it will grow at Company B's rate of 13.5 percent. If you believe the implied duration for growth at 18 percent is too long, you will prefer Company B; if you believe it is reasonable or low, you will recommend Company A.

An Alternative Use of *T*   Instead of solving for T and then deciding whether the figure derived is reasonable, you can use this formulation to compute a reasonable *P/E* ratio for a security relative to the aggregate market (or another stock) if the implicit assumptions are reasonable for the stock involved. Again, using Walgreens as an example, you estimate its expected composite growth to be 14 percent a year compared to the expected market growth of 8 percent. Further, you believe that Walgreens can continue to grow at this above-normal rate for about five years. Using Equation 15.34 this becomes

$$\ln(X) = 5 \times \ln \frac{1.14}{1.08}$$
$$= 5 \times \ln(1.055)$$
$$= 5 \times (0.02325)$$
$$= 0.11625$$

To determine what the *P/E* ratio should be given these assumptions, you must derive the antilog of 0.11625, which is approximately 1.3069. Therefore, assuming the market multiple is 25, the earnings multiple for Walgreens should be about 1.3069 times the market *P/E* ratio, or 33.

Alternatively, if you estimate that Walgreens can maintain a lower growth rate of .12 for a long time period of 10 years, you would derive the antilog for 1.5794 (10×0.01579). The answer is 1.4386, which implies a *P/E* ratio of 36 for Walgreens stock.

Factors to Consider   When using the growth duration technique, remember the following factors: First, the technique assumes equal risk, which may be acceptable when comparing two large, well-established firms or relating them to a market proxy (e.g., Merck and Pfizer to each other or to the S&P Industrials). It is probably *not* a valid assumption when comparing a small firm with a beta of 1.50 to the aggregate market.

Second, which growth estimate should be used? In the typical case, five-year historical growth rates are used. Actually, the authors prefer to use the *expected* rate of growth based on the factors that affect *g* (i.e., the retention rate and the components of *ROE*).

Third, the growth duration technique assumes that stocks with higher *P/E* ratios have the higher growth rates. However, there are cases in which the stock with the higher *P/E* ratio does not have a higher historical growth rate, which generates a useless negative growth duration value. Inconsistency between historical growth and the *P/E* ratio could be attributed to one of four factors:

1. A major difference in the risk involved.
2. Inaccurate growth rate estimates. Possibly the firm with the higher *P/E* ratio is *expected* to grow faster in the future. Consider the historical growth rate used and what you expect the firm's future growth rate to be.
3. The stock with a low *P/E* ratio relative to its expected growth rate is undervalued. (Before you accept this possibility, consider the first two factors.)
4. The stock with a high *P/E* and a low expected growth rate is overvalued. (Before this is accepted, consider both its risk and your estimated growth rate.)

The growth duration concept is valid, *given the assumptions made,* and can help you evaluate growth investments. It is not universally valid, though, because its answers are only as good as the data inputs (expected growth rates) and the applicability of the assumptions. The answer must be evaluated based on the analyst's knowledge.

The technique probably is most useful for helping spot overvalued growth companies with very high multiples. In such a case, the technique will highlight that the company must continue to grow at some very high rate for an extended period of time to justify its high *P/E* ratio (e.g., 15 to 20 years). Also, it can help you decide between two growth companies in the same industry by comparing each to the market, the industry, or directly to each other. Such a comparison has provided interesting insights wherein the new firms in an industry were growing faster than the large competitor but their *P/E* ratios were *substantially* higher and implied that these new firms had to maintain this large growth rate superiority for over *10 years* to justify the much higher *P/E* ratio.

SITE VISITS AND THE ART OF THE INTERVIEW

Brokerage house analysts and portfolio managers have access to persons that the typical small investor does not. Analysts frequently have contact with corporate personnel by telephone (conference calls), at formal presentations, or during plant site visits. Though insider trading laws restrict the analyst's ability to obtain material nonpublic information, these visits facilitate dialog between the corporation and the investor community. The analyst can gather information about the firm's plans and strategies, which helps the analyst understand the firm's prospects as an investment.

Interviewing is an art. The analyst wants information about the firm, and top management wants to put the firm in the best light possible. Thus, the analyst must be prepared to focus the interview on management's plans, strategies, and concerns. Analysts try to gauge the sensitivity of the firm's revenues, costs, and earnings to different scenarios by asking "what if" questions.

Analysts have frequent telephone contact with the firm's investor relations (IR) department regarding company pronouncements. The chief financial officer and chief executive officer of the firm also meet with security analysts and discuss the firm's planning process and major issues confronting the industry.

The analyst should talk to people other than top managers. Talking to middle managers or factory workers during a plant tour, visiting stores, and talking with customers provide insights beyond those of management. The firm's major customers can provide information regarding product quality and customer satisfaction. The firm's suppliers can furnish information about rising or falling supply orders and the timeliness of payments. Finally, an outstanding source of information is the firm's competitors who will be happy to point out the firm's weaknesses or possible problems.

The idea was always that analysts were able to create a mosaic regarding future expectations for the firm from numerous sources (including the company) and transmit this information to the market by sending research reports to brokerage clients and portfolio managers of pensions and mutual funds. This traditional way of doing research was changed by the SEC during the year 2000 when they issued the Fair Disclosure (FD) guidelines that required all disclosure of "material information" to be made public to all interested parties at the same time. The intent was to level the playing field by ensuring that professional analysts did not have a competitive advantage over nonprofessional investors. The result of this law is that many firms will not agree to interviews with analysts and will only provide information during large public presentations over the Internet.

The long-run impact of this FD requirement is not clear in terms of how firms will relate to the professional analyst community. One benefit is that analysts will spend more time with information sources beyond the firm such as trade shows, customers, suppliers, and competitors to build the mosaic.

WHEN TO SELL

Our analysis has focused on determining if a stock should be purchased. In fact, when we make a purchase, a subsequent question gains prominence: When should the stock be sold? Many times holding on to a stock too long leads to a return below expectations or less than what was available earlier. When stocks decline in value immediately following a portfolio manager's purchase, is this a further buying opportunity, or does the decline indicate that the stock analysis was incorrect?

The answer to the question of when to sell a stock is contained in the research that convinced the analyst to purchase the stock in the first place. The analyst should have identified the key assumptions and variables driving the expectations for the stock. Analysis of the stock doesn't end when intrinsic value is computed and the research report is written. Once the key value drivers are identified, the analyst must continually monitor and update his or her knowledge base about the firm. Notably, if the key value drivers appear to have weakened, it is time to reevaluate, and possibly sell, the stock.

The stock should also be closely evaluated when the current price approaches the intrinsic value estimate. When the stock becomes fairly priced, it may be time to sell it and reinvest the funds in other underpriced stocks. In short, if the "story" for buying the stock still appears to be true, continue to hold it. If the "story" changes, it may be time to sell the stock. If you know why you bought the stock, you'll be able to recognize when to sell it.

INFLUENCES ON ANALYSTS

Stock analysts and portfolio managers are, for the most part, highly trained individuals who possess expertise in financial analysis and background in their industry. A computer hardware analyst knows as much about industry trends and new product offerings as any industry insider. A pharmaceutical analyst is able to independently determine the market potential of drugs undergoing testing and the FDA approval process. So why don't more brokerage house customers and portfolio managers who receive the analysts' expert advice achieve investment success? The following subsections discuss several factors that make it difficult to "beat the market."

Efficient Markets

As noted in Chapter 6, the efficient market is difficult to outsmart, especially if you are considering actively traded and frequently analyzed companies. Information about the economy, a firm's industry, and the firm itself is reviewed by numerous bright analysts, investors, and portfolio managers. Because of the market's ability to review and absorb information, stock prices generally approximate fair market value. Investors look for situations where stocks may not be fairly valued. Notably, because there are numerous bright, hardworking analysts, it is difficult to successfully, frequently, and consistently find undervalued shares. Put another way, in most instances, the value estimated for a stock will be very close to its market price, which indicates that it is properly valued. The analyst's best place to seek attractive stocks is not among well-known companies and actively traded stocks, because they are analyzed by dozens of Wall Street analysts. Stocks with smaller market capitalizations, those not covered by many analysts, or those whose shares are mainly held by individual investors may be the best places to search for inefficiencies. Smaller capitalization stocks sometimes are too small for time-constrained analysts or too small for purchase by institutional investors.[34] The price of stocks not researched by many analysts ("neglected stocks") may not reflect all relevant information.[35]

Paralysis of Analysis

Analysts spend most of their time in a relentless search for one more contact or one more piece of information that will ensure the correct stock recommendation. Analysts need to develop a systematic approach for gathering, monitoring, and reviewing relevant information about economic trends, industry competitive forces, and company strategy. Analysts must evaluate the information as a whole to discern patterns that indicate the intrinsic value of the stock rather than searching for one more piece of information.

Because markets are generally efficient, the consensus view about the firm is already reflected in its stock price. To earn above-average returns, the analyst must have expectations that differ from the consensus *and* the analyst must be correct. Thus, the analyst should concentrate on identifying what is wrong with the market consensus or what surprises may upset the market consensus—that is, work at *estimating earning surprises*.

Analyst Conflicts of Interest

A potential conflict can arise if communication occurs between a firm's investment banking and equity research division. If the investment bankers assist a firm in a stock or bond offering, it will be difficult for an analyst to issue a negative evaluation of the company. Advisory fees have been lost because of a negative stock recommendation. Despite attempts to ensure the independence of stock analysts, firm politics may get in the way.

The analyst is in frequent contact with the top officers of the company he or she analyzes. Although there are guidelines about receiving gifts and favors, it is sometimes difficult to separate personal friendship and impersonal corporate relationships. Corporate officials may try to convince the analyst that his or her pessimistic report is in error or suggest that it glosses over

---

[34]According to SEC regulations, mutual funds cannot own more than 10 percent of a firm's shares. For some large funds, this constraint will make the resulting investment too small to have any significant impact on fund returns, so analysts do not bother to consider such stocks for purchase.

[35]Information on the number of analysts covering a stock is available from research firms, such as IBES and Zacks.

recent positive developments. To mitigate these problems, an analyst should call the company's investor relations department immediately *after* changing a recommendation to explain his or her perspective. The analyst needs to maintain independence and be objective in his or her analysis.

GLOBAL COMPANY AND STOCK ANALYSIS

As indicated on numerous occasions, a major goal of this text is to demonstrate investment technique that can be applied globally to markets, industries, and companies around the world. This chapter has been heavily concerned with presenting and demonstrating these techniques to U.S. firms. While space constraints do not allow a full demonstration to international firms, it is important to point out some of the major factors and constraints that analysts and portfolio managers need to acknowledge and adjust for when investing globally.

Availability of Data

In the United States, we suffer from information (data) overload, which is a blessing and a curse since we have more information than anywhere else in the world (which is good), but, as a result, there is a lot of information to digest and analyze. When you start analyzing international markets, industries, and stocks and cannot get the necessary data for valuation, you come to appreciate what is available in the United States. Beyond the limited amount of information, there is also the problem of timeliness (how long before you get the data?) and the reliability. (Can you believe and depend upon the data published in some countries and by some global industries?)

Differential Accounting Conventions

Even when the financial data for an industry and a firm are timely and reliable, it is necessary to recognize that the accounting rules and practices differ dramatically around the world. Not only are the financial statements very different in general presentation, but the accounting practices differ related to sales and expense recognition. The fact is, identical transactions in different countries can generate significant differences in income and cash flow. As a result, stocks in different countries will have very different *P/E* and *P/CF* ratios, not because investors differ in valuation but because the accounting numbers used are not the same. Notably, it is because of these accounting problems that many investors advocate using the price-to-sales ratio in valuations across countries since sales revenue is the least contaminated accounting figure.

Currency Differences (Exchange Rate Risk)

It is widely recognized that a significant factor that must be considered by global investors is currency risk caused by changes in exchange rates among countries. While these changes can work for or against you, the point is that it creates a major uncertainty that must be considered in your evaluation of the company and its stock.

Political (Country) Risk

Again, in the United States, we are blessed with the most stable political and economic environment in the world. Therefore, by definition, every other country will have greater political/country risk, which in some cases (e.g., Russia, Indonesia, North Korea) can be substantial. Therefore, it is necessary to acknowledge this factor and estimate its effect on the cost of equity for firms in these countries.

Transaction Costs

Higher transaction costs result from less-liquid markets—where it takes longer to trade and there is more prices volatility connected to a trade—or from a trade that costs more (e.g., higher commissions). Again, these costs vary dramatically among countries.

Valuation Differences

The point is, these individual differences among countries combine to cause a clear differential in the stock valuation for an international stock. Specifically, the earnings or cash flow numbers will differ and the required rate of return (the discount rate) for a non-U.S. stock will differ substantially because the nominal rate is different and there are additional risks that must be added such as exchange rate risk, political risk, and higher liquidity costs.

Summary

In summary, when investing globally, the *valuation process* is the same around the world and the investment decision in terms of the ultimate comparison of value and price is similar—the difference is in the *practice* of valuation that requires attention to these additional factors that must be considered by the global investor when valuing an international stock. Therefore, everything you have learned is relevant, but it must be applied differently (i.e., the inputs differ) depending on the country.

The Internet *Investments Online*

Many helpful sites have been reviewed in prior chapters, for example, examining individual firm sites and the SEC's EDGAR database for firm-specific information. Investment bank and brokerage house sites may also prove valuable, though they may expect payment for access to their published research on different firms. Still, many sites exist that allow users to examine free information and investing tips:

www.better-investing.org The home page for the National Association of Investment Clubs offers company information and investing ideas in addition to resources for those interested in setting up their own investment club.

www.fool.com This is the home page for the Motley Fool; despite its name, it is a well-known and popular site for investors to visit. It is chock full of data, articles, educational resources, news, and investing ideas.

www.cfonews.com Corporate Financials Online provides links to news about selected publicly traded firms.

www.firstcall.com and **www.thomsoninvest.net** are related corporate Web sites. Both maintain a database of analysts' earnings expectations on a variety of stocks. The

site offers selected screening ability to identify firms meeting various criteria and offers free reports on a selected number of firms.

www.zacks.com This is the Web site for Zacks Investment Research. When the user types in a ticker symbol, Zacks provides links to a company profile, financials, analysts' current stock ratings, consensus earnings estimates, and the number of analysts recommending strong buy, moderate buy, hold, moderate sell, and strong sell. Links allow the user to order brokerage reports. The site provides aggregate earnings growth estimates for the S&P 500, the market, and various economic sectors.

www.valueline.com This site was mentioned in an earlier chapter. The Value Line Investment Survey is a favorite source of information for many investors.

moneycentral.msn.com The site offers stock screens, price charts, and links to earnings estimates and analyst reports.

www.nyssa.org The home page of the New York Society of Security Analysts includes many financial links and sources of market and company information.

Summary

- This chapter demonstrates how to complete the fundamental analysis process by analyzing a company and deciding whether you should buy its stock. This requires a separate analysis of a company and its stock. A wonderful firm can have an overpriced stock, or a mediocre firm can have an underpriced stock.

- Although the chapter is mainly concerned with discussing and demonstrating several alternative valuation techniques, the initial section contained a discussion of the strategic alternatives available to firms in response to different competitive pressures in their industries. The alternative corporate strategies include low-cost leadership or differentiation which if properly implemented, should help the company attain above-average rates of return. In addition, we discussed SWOT analysis, which helps an analyst assess a firm's strengths and weaknesses as well as its external opportunities and threats. This strategic analysis of the firm's goals, objectives, and strategy should put you in a position to properly estimate the intrinsic value of the stock.

- When estimating a stock's intrinsic value, we can follow one or both of two approaches (the present value of cash flow, or the analysis of relative valuation ratios). We reviewed how to estimate the major inputs to the techniques and demonstrated results when these techniques are applied to Walgreens.

- We derived several estimated values for Walgreens based upon the present value of cash flow techniques and applied the relative valuation ratios beginning with *P/E* ratios and the other relative valuation ratios, including the price/book value ratio, the price/cash flow ratio, and the price/sales ratio, and compared these relative valuation ratios for the company to comparable ratios for both the retail drugstore industry and the aggregate market.

- The investment decision is based upon three comparisons. First, we compute the expected value of the stock discounted to the present and compare this intrinsic value to the prevailing market price. If the stock's intrinsic value exceeds the market price, we would buy the stock. Second, we compute the estimated rate of the return on the stock during our holding period on the basis of the expected value of the stock and the expected dividend. If this estimated rate of return exceeds our required rate of return, we would buy the stock. Finally, we compute the expected long-run rate of return based upon the stock's expected dividend yield plus the expected growth rate for the firm. Again, if this expected long-run rate of return exceeds our required rate of return, we would consider buying the stock for the long run.

- Because of the difficulty in estimating the intrinsic value of growth firms, we considered the concept of and alternative specifications for growth companies and several techniques that provide insights on the valuation of these firms. These techniques include economic value added (EVA), the franchise factor models, and a growth duration model that emphasizes the importance of estimating how long superior growth is expected to last. These models help the analyst concentrate attention on the relevant factors that determine "true" growth, which determines the intrinsic value of these growth companies. The critical question is, Is the stock of the growth company going to be a growth stock?

- We concluded the chapter with a discussion of several unique considerations an analyst must consider when analyzing and valuing global industries or firms. The importance of different accounting conventions and the impact of exchange rate differences were highlighted.

Questions

1. Give an example of a growth company and discuss why you identify it as such. Based on its *P/E,* do you think it is a growth stock? Explain.
2. Give an example of a cyclical stock and discuss why you have designated it as such. Is it issued by a cyclical company?
3. A biotechnology firm is growing at a compound rate of over 21 percent a year. (Its *ROE* is over 30 percent, and it retains about 70 percent of its earnings.) The stock of this company is priced at about 65 times next year's earnings. Discuss whether you consider this a growth company and/or a growth stock.
4. Select a company outside the retail drugstore industry and indicate what economic series you would use for a sales projection. Discuss why this is a relevant series.

5. Select a company outside the retail drugstore industry and indicate what industry series you would use in an industry analysis. (Use one of the industry groups designated by Standard & Poor's.) Discuss why this industry series is appropriate. Were there other possible alternatives?

6. Select a company outside the retail drugstore industry and, based on reading its annual report and other public information, discuss what you perceive to be its competitive strategy (i.e., low-cost producer or differentiation).

7. Discuss a company that is known to be a low-cost producer in its industry and consider why it is a cost leader. Do the same for a firm known for differentiating.

8. Under what conditions would you use a two- or three-stage cash flow model rather than the constant-growth model?

9. What is the rationale for using the price/book value (*P/BV*) ratio as a measure of relative value?

10. What would you look for to justify a price/book value ratio of 3.0? What would you expect to be the characteristics of a firm with a *P/BV* ratio of 0.6?

11. Why has the price/cash flow (*P/CF*) ratio become a popular measure of relative value during the recent past? What factors would help explain a difference in this ratio for two firms?

12. Assume that you uncover two stocks with substantially different price/sales ratios (e.g., 0.5 versus 2.5). Discuss the factors that might explain the difference.

13. Specify the major components for the calculation of economic value added (EVA) and describe what a positive EVA signifies.

14. Discuss why you would want to use EVA return on capital rather than absolute EVA to compare two companies or to evaluate a firm's performance over time.

15. Differentiate between EVA and MVA and discuss the relatively weak relationship between these two measures of performance. Is this relationship surprising to you? Explain.

16. Discuss the two factors that determine the franchise value of a firm. Assuming a firm has a base cost of equity of 11 percent and does not have a franchise value, what will be its *P/E*?

17. You are told that a company retains 80 percent of its earnings, and its earnings are growing at a rate of about 8 percent a year versus an average growth rate of 6 percent for all firms. Discuss whether you would consider this a growth company.

18. It is contended by some that in a completely competitive economy, there would never be a true growth company. Discuss the reasoning behind this contention.

19. Why is it not feasible to use the dividend discount model in the valuation of true growth companies?

20. Discuss the major assumptions of the growth duration model. Why could these assumptions present a problem?

21. You are told that a growth company has a *P/E* ratio of 13 times and a growth rate of 15 percent compared to the aggregate market, which has a growth rate of 8 percent and a *P/E* ratio of 16 times. What does this comparison imply regarding the growth company? What else do you need to know to properly compare the growth company to the aggregate market?

22. Given the alternative companies described in the chapter (negative growth, simple growth, dynamic growth), indicate what your label would be for Walgreens. Justify your label.

23. Indicate and justify a label for General Motors.

24. *CFA Examination Level I*

    Using book value to measure profitability and to value a company's stock has limitations. Discuss *five* such limitations from an accounting perspective. Be specific. [10 minutes]

25. *CFA Examination Level II*

    On your visit to Litchfield Chemical Corp. (LCC), you learned that the board of directors has periodically debated the company's dividend-payout policy.

    a. Briefly discuss *two* arguments *for* and *two* arguments *against* a high dividend-payout policy. [8 minutes]

       A director of LCC said that the use of dividend discount models by investors is "proof" that "the higher the dividend, the higher the stock price."

    b. Using a constant-growth dividend discount model as a basis of reference, evaluate the director's statement. [8 minutes]

c. Explain how an increase in dividend payout would affect *each* of the following (holding all other factors constant):
   (1) Internal (implied, normalized, or sustainable) growth rate; and
   (2) Growth in book value. [8 minutes]

26. *CFA Examination Level II*
    The Soft Corporation (SC) is planning to acquire a slower-growth competitor, which will materially increase SC's sales volume. The company to be acquired has pretax margins that are approximately the same as those of SC. SC plans to issue $300 million in long-term debt to finance the entire cost of the acquisition.
    a. Discuss how SC's potential acquisition might *decrease* its valuation based on a constant-growth dividend discount model. Be sure to comment on *each* of the three factors in such a model. [9 minutes]
    b. Discuss *two* reasons why SC's potential acquisition might *increase* the P/E multiple investors are willing to pay for SC. [4 minutes]

27. *CFA Examination Level II*
    A generalized model for the value of any asset is the present value of the expected cash flows:

$$\text{Value} = \sum_{t=1}^{N} \frac{CF_t}{(1+k)^t}$$

where:

N = life of the asset

CF_t = cash flow in period t

k = appropriate discount rate

Both stock and bond valuation models use a discounted cash flow approach, which includes the estimation of three factors (N, CF_t, k).

Explain why *each* of these *three* factors is generally more difficult to estimate for common stocks than for traditional corporate bonds. [12 minutes]

Problems

1. Select two stocks in an industry of your choice, and perform a common-size income statement analysis over a two-year period.
   a. Discuss which firm is more cost-effective.
   b. Discuss the relative year-to-year changes in gross profit margin, operating profit margin, and net profit margin for each company.
2. Select a company outside the retail drugstore industry, and examine its operating profit margin relative to the operating margin for its industry during the most recent 10-year period. Discuss the annual results in terms of levels and percentage changes.
3. Given Hitech's beta of 1.75 and a risk-free rate of 7 percent, what is the expected rate of return assuming
   a. a 15 percent market return?
   b. a 10 percent market return?
4. Select three companies from any industry except retail drugstores.
   a. Compute their P/E ratios using last year's average price [(high plus low)/2] and earnings.
   b. Compute their growth rate of earnings over the last five years.
   c. Look up the most recent beta reported in Value Line.
   d. Discuss the relationships between P/E, growth, and risk.

5. What is the implied growth duration of Kayleigh Industries given the following:

	S&P Industrials	Kayleigh Industries
P/E ratios	16	24
Expected growth	0.06	0.14
Dividend yield	0.04	0.02

6. Lauren Industries has an 18 percent annual growth rate compared to the market rate of 8 percent. If the market multiple is 18, determine P/E ratios for Lauren Industries, assuming its beta is 1.0 and you feel it can maintain its superior growth rate for
   a. the next 10 years.
   b. the next 5 years.

7. You are given the following information about two computer software firms and the S&P Industrials:

	Company A	Company B	S&P Industrials
P/E ratio	30.0	27.0	18.0
Expected annual growth rate	0.18	0.15	0.07
Dividend yield	0.00	0.01	0.02

   a. Compute the growth duration of each company stock relative to the S&P Industrials.
   b. Compute the growth duration of Company A relative to Company B.
   c. Given these growth durations, what determines your investment decision?

8. *CFA Examination Level II*
   The value of an asset is the present value of the expected returns from the asset during the holding period. An investment will provide a stream of returns during this period, and it is necessary to discount this stream of returns at an appropriate rate to determine the asset's present value. A dividend valuation model such as the following is frequently used:

$$P_i = \frac{D_1}{(k_i - g_i)}$$

where:

P_i = the current price of common stock i
D_1 = the expected dividend in period 1
k_i = the required rate of return on stock i
g_i = the expected constant growth rate of dividends for stock i

   a. *Identify* the three factors that must be estimated for any valuation model, and *explain* why these estimates are more difficult to derive for common stocks than for bonds. [9 minutes]
   b. *Explain* the principal problem involved in using a dividend valuation model to value
      (1) companies whose operations are closely correlated with economic cycles.
      (2) companies that are of giant size and are maturing.
      (3) companies that are of small size and are growing rapidly.
      Assume all companies pay dividends. [6 minutes]

TABLE 1	*ANNUAL CASH FLOW FROM LEASE*

End of Year		
1		$ -0-
2 Lease receipts		15,000
3 Lease receipts		25,000
3 Sale proceeds		$100,000

	PRESENT VALUE OF $1			
Period	6%	8%	10%	12%
1	0.943	0.926	0.909	0.893
2	0.890	0.857	0.826	0.797
3	0.840	0.794	0.751	0.712
4	0.792	0.735	0.683	0.636
5	0.747	0.681	0.621	0.567

9. *CFA Examination Level I*

   Your client is considering the purchase of $100,000 in common stock, which pays no dividends and will appreciate in market value by 10 percent per year. At the same time, the client is considering an opportunity to invest $100,000 in a lease obligation that will provide the annual year-end cash flows listed in Table 1. Assume that each investment will be sold at the end of three years and that you are given no additional information.

   Calculate the present value of each of the two investments assuming a 10 percent discount rate, and state which one will provide the higher return over the three-year period. Use the data in Table 1, and show your calculations. [10 minutes]

10. *CFA Examination Level I*

    The constant-growth dividend discount model can be used both for the valuation of companies and for the estimation of the long-term total return of a stock.

Assume:	$20 = The Price of a Stock Today
	8% = The Expected Growth Rate of Dividends
	$0.60 = The Annual Dividend One Year Forward

    a. Using *only* the preceding data, compute the expected long-term total return on the stock using the constant-growth dividend discount model. Show calculations.
    b. Briefly discuss *three* disadvantages of the constant-growth dividend discount model in its application to investment analysis.
    c. Identify *three* alternative methods to the dividend discount model for the valuation of companies. [10 minutes]

11. *CFA Examination Level I* (adapted)

    Mulroney recalled from her CFA studies that the constant-growth dividend discount model (DDM) was one way to arrive at a valuation for a company's common stock. She collected current dividend and stock price data for Eastover and Southampton, shown in Table 2.
    a. Using 11 percent as the required rate of return (i.e., discount rate) and a projected growth rate of 8 percent, compute a constant-growth DDM value for Eastover's stock and compare the computed value for Eastover to its stock price indicated in Table 2. Show calculations. [10 minutes]
    Mulroney's supervisor commented that a two-stage DDM may be more appropriate for companies such as Eastover and Southampton. Mulroney believes that Eastover and Southampton could grow more rapidly over the next three years and then settle in at a lower but sustainable rate of growth beyond 2004. Her estimates are indicated in Table 3.

TABLE 2

CURRENT INFORMATION

	Current Share Price	Current Dividends per Share	2002 EPS Estimate	Current Book Value per Share
Eastover (EO)	$ 28	$ 1.20	$ 1.60	$ 17.32
Southampton (SHC)	48	1.08	3.00	32.21
S&P Industrials	1100	16.00	48.00	423.08

TABLE 3

PROJECTED GROWTH RATES

	Next 3 Years (2002, 2003, 2004)	Growth Beyond 2004
Eastover (EO)	12%	8%
Southampton (SHC)	13%	7%

    b. Using 11 percent as the required rate of return, compute the two-stage DDM value of Eastover's stock and compare that value to its stock price indicated in Table 2. Show calculations. [15 minutes]

    c. Discuss *two* advantages and *three* disadvantages of using a constant-growth DDM. Briefly discuss how the two-stage DDM improves upon the constant-growth DDM. [10 minutes]

12. *CFA Examination Level I*

In addition to the dividend discount model (DDM) approach, Mulroney decided to look at the price/earnings ratio and price/book ratio, relative to the S&P Industrials, for both Eastover and Southampton. Mulroney elected to perform this analysis using 1997–2001 and current data.

    a. Using the data in Table 4 and Table 5, compute *both* the current and the five-year (1997–2001) average relative price/earnings ratios and relative price/book ratios for Eastover and Southampton. Discuss *each* company's current relative price/earnings ratio as compared to its five-year average relative price/earnings ratio and *each* company's current relative price/book ratio as compared to its five-year average relative price/book ratio. [10 minutes]

    b. Briefly discuss *one* disadvantage for *each* of the relative price/earnings and relative price/book approach to valuation. [5 minutes]

13. *CFA Examination Level I*

At year-end 1991, the Wall Street consensus was that Philip Morris' earnings and dividends would grow at 20 percent for five years after which growth would fall to a market-like 7 percent. Analysts also projected a required rate of return of 10 percent for the U.S. equity market.

    a. Using the data in Table 6 and the multistage dividend discount model, calculate the intrinsic value of Philip Morris stock at year-end 1991. Assume a similar level of risk for Philip Morris stock as for the typical U.S. stock. Show all work. [7 minutes]

    b. Using the data in Table 6, calculate Philip Morris' price/earnings ratio and the price/earnings ratio relative to the S&P Industrials Index as of December 31, 1991. [3 minutes]

    c. Using the data in Table 6, calculate Philip Morris' price/book ratio and the price/book ratio relative to the S&P Industrials Index as of December 31, 1991. [3 minutes]

14. *CFA Examination Level I*

    a. State *one* major advantage and *one* major disadvantage of *each* of the *three* valuation methodologies you used to value Philip Morris stock in Question 13. [6 minutes]

    b. State whether Philip Morris stock is undervalued or overvalued as of December 31, 1991. Support your conclusion using your answers to previous questions and any data provided. (The past 10-year average S&P Industrials Index relative price/earnings and price/book ratios for Philip Morris were 0.80 and 1.61, respectively.) [9 minutes]

TABLE 4

EASTOVER COMPANY (EO)						
	1996	1997	1998	1999	2000	2001
Earnings per share	$ 1.27	$ 2.12	$ 2.68	$ 1.56	$ 1.87	$ 0.90
Dividends per share	0.87	0.90	1.15	1.20	1.20	1.20
Book value per share	14.82	16.54	18.14	18.55	19.21	17.21
Stock price						
High	28	40	30	33	28	30
Low	20	20	23	25	18	20
Close	25	26	25	28	22	27
Average *P/E*	18.9×	14.2×	9.9×	18.6×	12.3×	27.8×
Average price/book	1.6×	1.8×	1.5×	1.6×	1.2×	1.5×

SOUTHAMPTON COMPANY (SHC)						
	1996	1997	1998	1999	2000	2001
Earnings per share	$1.66	$3.13	$3.55	$5.08	$2.46	$1.75
Dividends per share	0.77	0.79	0.89	0.98	1.04	1.08
Book value per share	24.84	27.47	29.92	30.95	31.54	32.21
Stock price						
High	34	40	38	43	45	46
Low	21	22	26	28	20	26
Close	31	27	28	39	27	44
Average *P/E*	16.6×	9.9×	9.0×	7.0×	13.2×	20.6×
Average price/book	1.1×	1.1×	1.1×	1.2×	1.0×	1.1×

S&P INDUSTRIALS							
	1996	1997	1998	1999	2000	2001	5-Year Average (1997–2001)
Average *P/E*	15.8×	16.0×	11.1×	13.9×	15.6×	19.2×	15.2×
Average price/book	1.8×	2.1×	1.9×	2.2×	2.1×	2.3×	2.1×

TABLE 5

CURRENT INFORMATION

	Current Share Price	Current Dividends per Share	2002 EPS Estimate	Current Book Value per Share
Eastover (EO)	$ 28	$ 1.20	$ 1.60	$ 17.32
Southampton (SHC)	48	1.08	3.00	32.21
S&P Industrials	1100	16.00	48.00	423.08

15. *CFA Examination Level II*

Your supervisor has asked you to evaluate the relative attractiveness of the stocks of two very similar chemical companies: Litchfield Chemical Corp. (LCC) and Aminochem Company (AOC). AOC also has a June 30 fiscal year end. You have compiled the data in Table 7 for this purpose. Use a one-year time horizon and assume the following:

* Real gross domestic product is expected to rise 5 percent;
* S&P Industrials expected total return of 20 percent;
* U.S. Treasury bills yield 5 percent; and
* 30-year U.S. Treasury bonds yield 8 percent.

a. Calculate the value of the common stock of LCC and AOC using the constant-growth dividend discount model. Show your work. [5 minutes]

TABLE 6	PHILIP MORRIS CORPORATION: SELECTED FINANCIAL STATEMENT AND OTHER DATA—YEARS ENDING DECEMBER 31 ($ MILLIONS EXCEPT PER-SHARE DATA)

	1991	1981
Income Statement		
Operating revenue	$56,458	$10,886
Cost of sales	25,612	5,253
Excise taxes on products	8,394	2,580
Gross profit	$22,452	$ 3,053
Selling, general, and administrative expenses	13,830	1,741
Operating income	$ 8,622	$ 1,312
Interest expense	1,651	232
Pretax earnings	$ 6,971	$ 1,080
Provision for income taxes	3,044	420
Net earnings	$ 3,927	$ 660
Earnings per share	$4.24	$0.66
Dividends per share	$1.91	$0.25
Balance Sheet		
Current assets	$12,594	$ 3,733
Property, plant, and equipment, net	9,946	3,583
Goodwill	18,624	634
Other assets	6,220	1,230
Total assets	$47,384	$ 9,180
Current liabilities	$11,824	$ 1,936
Long-term debt	14,213	3,499
Deferred taxes	1,803	455
Other liabilities	7,032	56
Stockholders' equity	12,512	3,234
Total liabilities and stockholders' equity	$47,384	$ 9,180
Other Data		
Philip Morris:		
Common shares outstanding (millions)	920	1,003
Closing price common stock	$80.250	$6.125
S&P Industrials Index:		
Closing price	417.09	122.55
Earnings per share	16.29	15.36
Book value per share	161.08	109.43

b. Calculate the expected return over the next year of the common stock of LCC and AOC using the capital asset pricing model. Show your work. [5 minutes]

c. Calculate the internal (implied, normalized, or sustainable) growth rate of LCC and AOC. Show your work. [5 minutes]

d. Recommend LCC *or* AOC for investment. Justify your choice by using your answers to a, b, and c and the information in Table 7. [10 minutes]

 16. *CFA Examination Level II*

Westfield Capital Management Company's equity investment strategy is to invest in companies with low price-to-book ratios, while taking into account differences in solvency and asset utilization. Westfield is considering investing in the shares of either Jerry's Department Stores (JDS) or Miller Stores (MLS).

a. Calculate *each* of the following ratios for *both* JDS and MLS. Use *only* the financial data in Table 8. Show your work. [6 minutes]

(1) Price-to-book ratio

(2) Total-debt-to-equity ratio

(3) Fixed-asset utilization (turnover)

TABLE 7

	Litchfield Chemical (LCC)	Aminochem (AOC)
Current stock price	$50	$30
Shares outstanding (millions)	10	20
Projected earnings per share (fiscal 1996)	$4.00	$3.20
Projected dividend per share (fiscal 1996)	$0.90	$1.60
Projected dividend growth rate	8%	7%
Stock beta	1.2	1.4
Investors' required rate of return	10%	11%
Balance sheet data (millions)		
Long-term debt	$100	$130
Stockholders' equity	$300	$320

TABLE 8

JERRY'S DEPARTMENT STORES AND MILLER STORES: SELECTED FINANCIAL DATA AT MARCH 31, 1997 (IN MILLIONS EXCEPT PER-SHARE DATA)

	JDS	MLS
Sales	$21,250	$18,500
PP&E	$ 5,700	$ 5,500
Short-term debt	$ 0	$ 1,000
Long-term debt	$ 2,700	$ 2,500
Common equity	$ 6,000	$ 7,500
Issued and outstanding shares as of 3/31/97	250	400
Per-share market price on 5/30/97	$ 51.50	$ 49.50

TABLE 9

JERRY'S DEPARTMENT STORES: DATA EXTRACTED FROM MARCH 31, 1997, FINANCIAL STATEMENT FOOTNOTES

1. The Company conducts the majority of its operations from leased premises, which include distribution centers, warehouses, offices, and retail stores. Future minimum lease payments for noncancelable real and personal property operating leases are as follows:

	Operating Leases ($ in Millions)
1997	$ 259
1998	213
1999	183
2000	160
2001	144
Thereafter	706
Total minimum lease payments	$1,665
Present value of lease payments	$1,000
Weighted-average interest rate	10%

2. During the fiscal year ended March 31, 1997, the Company sold $800 million of its accounts receivable with recourse, all of which were outstanding at year end.
3. Merchandise inventory. Substantially all merchandise inventory is valued at the lower of cost (first-in, first-out) or market.
4. Substantially all of the Company's employees are enrolled in Company-sponsored defined-contribution profit sharing and retirement savings plans.

TABLE 10 *MILLER STORES: DATA EXTRACTED FROM MARCH 31, 1997, FINANCIAL STATEMENT FOOTNOTES*

1. The Company's real estate policy is to own its stores; thus, the Company has no operating leases.
2. The Company does not sell or securitize its accounts receivable.
3. All inventories are valued on the last-in, first-out (LIFO) cost basis. As of March 31, 1997, inventories were $700 million lower than they would have been had the first-in, first-out (FIFO) cost basis been used.
4. Actuarial present value of accumulated (ABO) and projected (PBO) benefit obligation for its pension plan at March 31, 1997, was as follows ($ in millions):

	ABO	PBO
Vested	$1,550	$1,590
Nonvested	40	210
Total	$1,590	$1,800

Plan assets at fair value = $3,400
Accrued pension per 3/31/97 balance sheet = $0

b. Select, based on Part a, the company that best meets Westfield's investment criteria. Justify your choice. [4 minutes]
c. Describe, based on Table 9 and Table 10, the balance sheet adjustments in *each* of the following areas required to enhance the comparability of JDS and MLS. (A total of *four* adjustments is required.) [8 minutes]
   (1) Leases
   (2) Sale of receivables with recourse
   (3) Inventory valuation method
   (4) Pensions
d. Calculate each of the following ratios for *both* JDS and MLS using the adjusted financial data from Part c. Ignore any income tax effects. Show your work. [12 minutes]
   (1) Book value per common share
   (2) Total-debt-to-equity ratio
   (3) Fixed-asset utilization (turnover)
e. Select, based on Part d, the company that best meets Westfield's investment criteria. Justify your choice. [4 minutes]

> Note: Questions 17–21 are all related.

 17. *CFA Examination Level II*
Janet Ludlow is preparing a report on U.S.-based manufacturers in the electric toothbrush industry and has gathered the information shown in Table 11 and Exhibit 1.
Ludlow's report concludes that the electric toothbrush industry is in the maturity (i.e., late) phase of its industry life cycle.
a. Select and justify *three* factors from Table 11 that *support* Ludlow's conclusion. [6 minutes]
b. Select and justify *three* factors from Exhibit 1 that *refute* Ludlow's conclusion. [6 minutes]

> Note: Questions 18 through 21 relate to QuickBrush Company and SmileWhite Corporation. A total of 73 minutes is allocated to these questions. Use the first few minutes to review Table 12, Table 13, and Table 14; Exhibit 2 and Exhibit 3; and the questions themselves.

TABLE 11 *RATIOS FOR ELECTRIC TOOTHBRUSH INDUSTRY INDEX AND BROAD STOCK MARKET INDEX*

Year	1992	1993	1994	1995	1996	1997
Return on equity						
Electric toothbrush industry index	12.5%	12.0%	15.4%	19.6%	21.6%	21.6%
Market index	10.2	12.4	14.6	19.9	20.4	21.2
Average P/E						
Electric toothbrush industry index	28.5×	23.2×	19.6×	18.7×	18.5×	16.2×
Market index	10.2	12.4	14.6	19.9	18.1	19.1
Dividend payout ratio						
Electric toothbrush industry index	8.8%	8.0%	12.1%	12.1%	14.3%	17.1%
Market index	39.2	40.1	38.6	43.7	41.8	39.1
Average dividend yield						
Electric toothbrush industry index	0.3%	0.3%	0.6%	0.7%	0.8%	1.0%
Market index	3.8	3.2	2.6	2.2	2.3	2.1

EXHIBIT 1 *CHARACTERISTICS OF THE ELECTRIC TOOTHBRUSH MANUFACTURING INDUSTRY*

- *Industry Sales Growth*—Industry sales have grown at 15–20 percent per year in recent years and are expected to grow at 10–15 percent per year over the next three years.
- *Non-U.S. Markets*—Some U.S. manufacturers are attempting to enter fast-growing non-U.S. markets, which remain largely unexploited.
- *Mail Order Sales*—Some manufacturers have created a new niche in the industry by selling electric toothbrushes directly to customers through mail order. Sales for this industry segment are growing at 40 percent per year.
- *U.S. Market Penetration*—The current penetration rate in the United States is 60 percent of households and will be difficult to increase.
- *Price Competition*—Manufacturers compete fiercely on the basis of price, and price wars within the industry are common.
- *Niche Markets*—Some manufacturers are able to develop new, unexploited niche markets in the United States based on company reputation, quality, and service.
- *Industry Consolidation*—Several manufacturers have recently merged, and it is expected that consolidation in the industry will increase.
- *New Entrants*—New manufacturers continue to enter the market.

18. *CFA Examination Level II*

After describing the electric toothbrush industry, Janet Ludlow's report focuses on two companies, QuickBrush Company and SmileWhite Corporation. Her report concludes:

> QuickBrush is a more profitable company than SmileWhite, as indicated by the 40 percent sales growth and substantially higher margins it has produced over the last few years. SmileWhite's sales and earnings are growing at a 10 percent rate and produce much lower margins. We do not think SmileWhite is capable of growing faster than its recent growth rate of 10 percent whereas QuickBrush can sustain a 30 percent long-term growth rate.

a. Criticize Ludlow's analysis and conclusion that QuickBrush is more profitable (as defined by return on equity *(ROE)*) than SmileWhite and that it has a higher sustainable growth rate. Use

TABLE 12

QUICKBRUSH COMPANY: FINANCIAL STATEMENTS—YEARLY DATA ($000 EXCEPT PER-SHARE DATA)

	December 1995	December 1996	December 1997	
Income Statement				
Revenue	$3,480	$5,400	$7,760	
Cost of goods sold	2,700	4,270	6,050	
Selling, general, and admin. expense	500	690	1,000	
Depreciation and amortization	30	40	50	
Operating income (EBIT)	$ 250	$ 400	$ 660	
Interest expense	0	0	0	
Income before taxes	$ 250	$ 400	$ 660	
Income taxes	60	110	215	
Income after taxes	$ 190	$ 290	$ 445	
Diluted EPS	$ 0.60	$ 0.84	$ 1.18	
Average shares outstanding (000)	317	346	376	

	December 1995	December 1996	December 1997	3-Year Average
Financial Statistics				
COGS as % of sales	77.59%	79.07%	77.96%	78.24%
SG&A as % of sales	14.37	12.78	12.89	13.16
Operating margin	7.18	7.41	8.51	
Pretax income/EBIT	100.00	100.00	100.00	
Tax rate	24.00	27.50	32.58	

	December 1995	December 1996	December 1997
Balance Sheet			
Cash and cash equivalents	$ 460	$ 50	$ 480
Accounts receivable	540	720	950
Inventories	300	430	590
Net property, plant, and equipment	760	1,830	3,450
Total assets	$2,060	$3,030	$5,470
Current liabilities	$ 860	$1,110	$1,750
Total liabilities	$ 860	$1,110	$1,750
Stockholders' equity	1,200	1,920	3,720
Total liabilities and equity	$2,060	$3,030	$5,470
Market price per share	$21.00	$30.00	$45.00
Book value per share	$ 3.79	$ 5.55	$ 9.89
Annual dividend per share	$ 0.00	$ 0.00	$ 0.00

only the information provided in Table 12 and Table 13. Support your criticism by calculating and analyzing:

- the five components that determine *ROE*.
- the two ratios that determine sustainable growth. [20 minutes]

b. Explain how QuickBrush has produced an average annual earnings per share (EPS) growth rate of 40 percent over the last two years with an ROE that has been declining. Use only the information provided in Table 12. [8 minutes]

TABLE 13 ▶ *SMILEWHITE CORPORATION: FINANCIAL STATEMENTS—YEARLY DATA ($000 EXCEPT PER-SHARE DATA)*

	December 1995	December 1996	December 1997	
Income Statement				
Revenue	$104,000	$110,400	$119,200	
Cost of goods sold	72,800	75,100	79,300	
Selling, general, and admin. expense	20,300	22,800	23,900	
Depreciation and amortization	4,200	5,600	8,300	
Operating income	$6,700	$6,900	$7,700	
Interest expense	600	350	350	
Income before taxes	$6,100	$6,550	$7,350	
Income taxes	2,100	2,200	2,500	
Income after taxes	$4,000	$4,350	$4,850	
Diluted EPS	$2.16	$2.35	$2.62	
Average shares outstanding (000)	1,850	1,850	1,850	

	December 1995	December 1996	December 1997	3-Year Average
Financial Statistics				
COGS as % of sales	70.00%	68.00%	66.53%	68.10%
SG&A as % of sales	19.52	20.64	20.05	20.08
Operating margin	6.44	6.25	6.46	
Pretax income/EBIT	91.04	94.93	95.45	
Tax rate	34.43	33.59	34.01	

	December 1995	December 1996	December 1997	
Balance Sheet				
Cash and cash equivalents	$ 7,900	$ 3,300	$ 1,700	
Accounts receivable	7,500	8,000	9,000	
Inventories	6,300	6,300	5,900	
Net property, plant, and equipment	12,000	14,500	17,000	
Total assets	$33,700	$32,100	$33,600	
Current liabilities	$ 6,200	$ 7,800	$ 6,600	
Long-term debt	9,000	4,300	4,300	
Total liabilities	$15,200	$12,100	$10,900	
Stockholders' equity	18,500	20,000	22,700	
Total liabilities and equity	$33,700	$32,100	$33,600	
Market price per share	$23.00	$26.00	$30.00	
Book value per share	$10.00	$10.81	$12.27	
Annual dividend per share	$1.42	$1.53	$1.72	

EXHIBIT 2

FORECAST ASSUMPTIONS: QUICKBRUSH 1998 EPS

Revenue	Will rise 30% from 1997
Cost of goods sold (as % of sales)	3-year historical average
Selling, general, and administrative expense (as % of sales)	3-year historical average
Depreciation and amortization	2% of 1997 property, plant, and equipment
Interest expense	Zero
Tax rate	34%
Shares outstanding	No change

TABLE 14

VALUATION INFORMATION: DECEMBER 1997

	QuickBrush	SmileWhite
Beta	1.35	1.15
Market price	$45.00	$30.00
Intrinsic value	$63.00	?

Notes:

Risk-free rate	4.50%
Expected market return	14.50%

EXHIBIT 3

NOTES TO THE 1997 FINANCIAL STATEMENTS

	QuickBrush	SmileWhite
Goodwill	The company amortizes goodwill over 20 years.	The company amortizes goodwill over 5 years.
Property, plant, and equipment	The company uses a straight-line depreciation method over the economic lives of the assets, which range from 5 to 20 years for buildings.	The company uses an accelerated depreciation method over the economic lives of the assets, which range from 5 to 20 for buildings.
Accounts receivable	The company uses a bad debt allowance of 2 percent of accounts receivable.	The company uses a bad debt allowance of 5 percent of accounts receivable.

19. *CFA Examination Level II*
   In her forecast of 1998 earnings per share for QuickBrush Company, Janet Ludlow has made the assumptions shown in Exhibit 2:
   Construct a 1998 projected income statement for QuickBrush using the percent-of-sales forecasting method based on 1997 data in Table 12 and the assumptions in Exhibit 2 above. [6 minutes]

20. *CFA Examination Level II*
   Janet Ludlow's firm requires all its analysts to use a two-stage dividend discount model (DDM) and the capital asset pricing model (CAPM) to value stocks. Using the CAPM and DDM, Ludlow has valued QuickBrush Company at $63 per share. She now must value SmileWhite Corporation.
   a. Calculate the required rate of return for SmileWhite using the information in Table 14 and the CAPM. Show your work. [6 minutes]
   Ludlow estimates the following EPS and dividend growth rates for SmileWhite:

First 3 years:	12 percent per year
Years thereafter:	9 percent per year

b. Estimate the intrinsic value of SmileWhite using the data from Table 13 and Table 14 and the two-stage DDM. Show your work. [12 minutes]

c. Recommend QuickBrush or SmileWhite stock for purchase by comparing each company's intrinsic value with its current market price. Show your work. [6 minutes]

d. Describe *one* strength of the two-stage DDM in comparison with the constant-growth DDM. Describe *one* weakness inherent in all DDMs. [6 minutes]

21. *CFA Examination Level II*

The information in Exhibit 3 comes from the 1997 financial statements of QuickBrush Company and SmileWhite Corporation:

Determine which company has the higher quality of earnings by discussing *each* of the *three* notes. [9 minutes]

22. *CFA Examination Level II*

An analyst expects a risk-free return of 4.5 percent, a market return of 14.5 percent, and the returns for Stocks A and B that are shown in Table 15.

a. Show on a graph

(1) where Stocks A and B would plot on the security market line (SML) if they were fairly valued using the capital asset pricing model (CAPM).

(2) where Stocks A and B actually plot on the same graph according to the returns estimated by the analyst and shown in Table 15. [6 minutes]

b. State whether Stock A and Stock B are undervalued or overvalued if the analyst uses the SML for strategic investment decisions. [4 minutes]

23. *CFA Examination Level II*

Scott Kelly is reviewing MasterToy's financial statements in order to estimate its sustainable growth rate. Using the information presented in Table 16,

a. (1) Identify and calculate the *three* components of the DuPont formula.

(2) Calculate the *ROE* for 1999 using the three components of the DuPont formula.

(3) Calculate the sustainable-growth rate for 1999. [13 minutes]

Kelly has calculated actual and sustainable growth for each of the past four years and finds in each year that its calculated sustainable-growth rate substantially exceeds its actual growth rate.

b. Cite *two* courses of action (other than ignoring the problem) Kelly should encourage MasterToy to take, assuming the calculated sustainable-growth rate continues to exceed the actual growth rate. [6 minutes]

> Note: Questions 24 through 28 relate to Telluride and its subsidiaries.

24. *CFA Examination Level II*

The management of Telluride, an international diversified conglomerate based in the United States, believes that the recent strong performance of its wholly owned medical supply subsidiary, Sundanci, has gone unnoticed. In order to realize Sundanci's full value, Telluride has announced that it will divest Sundanci in a tax-free spin-off.

Sue Carroll, CFA, is the Director of Research at Kesson and Associates. In developing an investment recommendation for Sundanci, Carroll has directed four of her analysts to determine a valuation of Sundanci using various valuation disciplines. To assist her analysts, Carroll has gathered the information shown in Table 17 and Table 18.

Prior to determining Sundanci's valuation, Carroll analyzes Sundanci's return on equity *(ROE)* and sustainable growth.

a. (1) Calculate the *three* components of *ROE* in the duPont formula for the year 2000.

(2) Calculate *ROE* for the year 2000.

(3) Calculate the sustainable-growth rate. Show your work. [12 minutes]

| TABLE 15 | STOCK INFORMATION |

Stock	Beta	Analyst's Estimated Return
A	1.2	16%
B	0.8	14%

| TABLE 16 | MASTERTOY, INC.: ACTUAL 1998 AND ESTIMATED 1999 FINANCIAL STATEMENTS FOR FISCAL YEAR ENDING DECEMBER 31 ($ MILLIONS, EXCEPT PER-SHARE DATA) |

	1998	1999e	Change (%)
Income Statement			
Revenue	$4,750	$5,140	7.6
Cost of goods sold	$2,400	$2,540	
Selling, general, and administrative	1,400	1,550	
Depreciation	180	210	
Goodwill amortization	10	10	
Operating income	$ 760	$ 830	8.4
Interest expense	20	25	
Income before taxes	$ 740	$ 805	
Income taxes	265	295	
Net income	$ 475	$ 510	
Earnings per share	$ 1.79	$ 1.96	8.6
Average shares outstanding (millions)	265	260	
Balance Sheet			
Cash	$ 400	$ 400	
Accounts receivable	$ 680	$ 700	
Inventories	$ 570	$ 600	
Net property, plant, and equipment	$ 800	$ 870	
Intangibles	$ 500	$ 530	
Total assets	$2,950	$3,100	
Current liabilities	$ 550	$ 600	
Long-term debt	$ 300	$ 300	
Total liabilities	$ 850	$ 900	
Stockholders' equity	$2,100	$2,200	
Total liabilities and equity	$2,950	$3,100	
Book value per share	$ 7.92	$ 8.46	
Annual dividend per share	$ 0.55	$ 0.60	

TABLE 17	SUNDANCI ACTUAL 1999 AND 2000 FINANCIAL STATEMENTS FOR FISCAL YEARS ENDING MAY 31 ($ MILLION, EXCEPT PER-SHARE DATA)

	1999	2000
Income Statement		
Revenue	$474	$598
Depreciation	20	23
Other operating costs	368	460
Income before taxes	86	115
Taxes	26	35
Net income	60	80
Dividends	18	24
Earnings per share	$0.714	$0.952
Dividend per share	$0.214	$0.286
Common shares outstanding (millions)	84.0	84.0
Balance Sheet		
Current assets	$201	$326
Net property, plant and equipment	474	489
Total assets	675	815
Current liabilities	57	141
Long-term debt	0	0
Total liabilities	57	141
Shareholders' equity	618	674
Total liabilities and equity	675	815
Capital expenditures	34	38

TABLE 18	SELECTED FINANCIAL INFORMATION FOR SUNDANCI

Required rate of return on equity	14%
Growth rate of industry	13%
Industry *P/E* ratio	26

Carroll learns that Sundanci's Board of Directors is considering the following policy changes that will affect Sundanci's sustainable-growth rate:

- Director A proposes an increase in the quarterly dividend to $0.15 per share.
- Director B proposes a bond issue of $25 million, the proceeds of which would be used to increase production capacity.
- Director C proposes a 2-for-1 stock split.

b. Indicate the effect of *each* of these proposals on Sundanci's sustainable rate of growth, given that other factors remain unchanged. Identify which component of the sustainable-growth model, if any, is directly affected by *each* proposal. [9 minutes]

> Note: Answer Question 24b using the following template.

TEMPLATE FOR QUESTION 24b

Proposal	Effect on Sustainable-Growth Rate (Circle One)	Component Directly Affected (If Any)
Increase in quarterly dividend	Increase Decrease No effect	
Bond issue	Increase Decrease No effect	
Stock split	Increase Decrease No effect	

 25. *CFA Examination Level II*

Helen Morgan, CFA, has been asked by Carroll to determine the potential valuation for Sundanci, Inc., using the dividend discount model (DDM). Morgan anticipates that Sundanci's earnings and dividends will grow at 32 percent for two years and 13 percent thereafter.

Calculate the current value of a share of Sundanci stock using a two-stage dividend discount model and the data from Tables 17 and 18. Show your work. [8 minutes]

 26. *CFA Examination Level II*

Abbey Naylor, CFA, has been directed by Carroll to determine the value of Sundanci's stock using the free cash flow to equity (FCFE) model. Naylor believes that Sundanci's FCFE will grow at 27 percent for two years and 13 percent thereafter. Capital expenditures, depreciation, and working capital are all expected to increase proportionately with FCFE.

a. Calculate the amount of FCFE per share for the year 2000, using the data from Table 17. Show your work. [6 minutes]

b. Calculate the current value of a share of Sundanci stock based on the two-stage FCFE model. Show your work. [8 minutes]

c. (1) Describe *one* limitation of the two-stage DDM model that is addressed by using the two-stage FCFE model.

   (2) Describe *one* limitation of the two-stage DDM model that is *not* addressed by using the two-stage FCFE model. [6 minutes]

 27. *CFA Examination Level II*

Christie Johnson, CFA, has been assigned by Carroll to analyze Sundanci using the constant-growth dividend price/earnings (*P/E*) ratio model. Johnson assumes that Sundanci's earnings and dividends will grow at a constant rate of 13 percent.

a. Calculate the P/E ratio based on information in Tables 17 and 18 and on Johnson's assumptions for Sundanci. Show your work. [4 minutes]

b. Identify, within the context of the constant-growth dividend model, how *each* of the fundamental factors shown in the following template would affect the *P/E* ratio. [4 minutes]

   Note: A change in a fundamental factor is assumed to happen in isolation, and interactive effects between factors are ignored. Every other element of the firm is unchanged.

Note: Answer Question 27b using the following template.

TEMPLATE FOR QUESTION 27b

Fundamental Factor	Effect on *P/E* Ratio (Circle One)
The riskiness (beta) of Sundanci increases substantially.	Increase Decrease May increase or decrease
The estimated growth rate of Sundanci's earnings and dividends increases.	Increase Decrease May increase or decrease
The dividend-payout ratio of Sundanci increases.	Increase Decrease May increase or decrease
The market risk premium increases.	Increase Decrease May increase or decrease

c. Explain why an increase in the dividend-payout ratio may not have the effect that the constant-growth dividend *P/E* ratio model suggests. [4 minutes]

28. *CFA Examination Level II*

One week after the spin-off of Sundanci, Carroll asks analyst Jim Martin to use economic value added (EVA®) and market value added (MVA) to measure the performance of Sundanci. In addition to the information provided in Tables 17 and 18, Martin uses the following information in his analysis:

- Adjusted net operating profit after tax (NOPAT) is $100 million.
- Total adjusted capital is $700 million.
- Closing stock price is $26.

a. Calculate the following for Sundanci. Show your work. [6 minutes]
   (1) EVA for fiscal 2000
   (2) MVA as of fiscal year-end 2000
b. Discuss the *two* primary differences in calculating economic profit (as used in EVA) versus accounting profit. [6 minutes]

> Note: Use Tables 19, 20, and 21 for Questions 29 and 30.

29. *CFA Examination Level II*

A company that Jones is researching is Mackinac Inc., a U.S.-based manufacturing company. Mackinac has released its June 2001 financial statements, which are shown in Tables 19, 20, and 21. Jones is particularly interested in Mackinac's sustainable growth and sources of return.

a. Calculate Mackinac's sustainable growth rate. Show your calculations. [4 minutes]
   Note: Use June 30, 2001, year-end balanced sheet data rather than averages in ratio calculations.
b. Name *each* of the *five* components in the extended DuPont System and calculate a value for *each* component for Mackinac. [10 minutes]
   Note: Use June 30, 2001, year-end balance sheet data rather than averages in ratio calculations.

TABLE 19 ▶ MACKINAC INC. ANNUAL INCOME STATEMENT FOR THE YEAR ENDED JUNE 30, 2001 (IN THOUSANDS, EXCEPT PER-SHARE DATA)

Sales	$250,000
Cost of goods sold	125,000
Gross operating profit	$125,000
Selling, general, and administrative expenses	50,000
Earnings before interest, taxes, depreciation, and amortization (EBITDA)	$ 75,000
Depreciation and amortization	10,500
Earnings before interest and taxes (EBIT)	$ 64,500
Interest expense	11,000
Pretax income	$ 53,500
Income taxes	16,050
Net income	$ 37,450
Shares outstanding	13,000
Earnings per share (EPS)	$ 2.88

TABLE 20 ▶ MACKINAC INC. BALANCE SHEET AS OF JUNE 30, 2001 (IN THOUSANDS)

Current Assets			
Cash and equivalents		20,000	
Receivables		40,000	
Inventories		29,000	
Other current assets		23,000	
Total current assets			$112,000
Noncurrent Assets			
Property, plant, and equipment	$145,000		
Less: accumulated depreciation	(43,000)		
Net property, plant, and equipment		$102,000	
Investments		70,000	
Other noncurrent assets		36,000	
Total noncurrent assets			$208,000
Total assets			$320,000
Current Liabilities			
Accounts payable		$ 41,000	
Short-term debt		12,000	
Other current liabilities		17,000	
Total current liabilities			$ 70,000
Noncurrent Liabilities			
Long-term debt		$100,000	
Total noncurrent liabilities			$100,000
Total liabilities			$170,000
Shareholders' Equity			
Common equity		$ 40,000	
Retained earnings		110,000	
Total equity			$150,000
Total liabilities and equity			$320,000

| **TABLE 21** | **MACKINAC INC. CASH FLOW STATEMENT FOR THE YEAR ENDED JUNE 30, 2001 (IN THOUSANDS)** |

Cash Flow from Operating Activities		
Net income		$37,450
Depreciation and amortization		10,500
Change in Working Capital		
(Increase) decrease in receivables	($ 5,000)	
(Increase) decrease in inventories	(8,000)	
Increase (decrease) in payables	6,000	
Increase (decrease) in other current liabilities	1,500	
Net change in working capital		($ 5,500)
Net cash from operating activities		$42,450
Cash Flow from Investing Activities		
Purchase of property, plant, and equipment	($15,000)	
Net cash from investing activities		($15,000)
Cash Flow from Financing Activities		
Change in debt outstanding	$ 4,000	
Payment of cash dividends	(22,470)	
Net cash from financing activities		($18,470)
Net change in cash and cash equivalents		$8,980
Cash at beginning of period		11,020
Cash at end of period		$20,000

30. *CFA Examination Level II*

Mackinac has announced that it has finalized an agreement to handle North American production of a successful product currently marketed by a foreign company. Jones decides to value Mackinac using the dividend discount model (DDM) and the free cash flow to equity (FCFE) model. After reviewing Mackinac's financial statements in Tables 19, 20, and 21 and forecasts related to the new production agreement, Jones concludes the following:

- Mackinac's earnings and FCFE are expected to grow 17 percent per year over the next three years before stabilizing at an annual growth rate of 9 percent.
- Mackinac will maintain the current payout ratio.
- Mackinac's beta is 1.25.
- The government bond yield is 6 percent and the market equity risk premium is 5 percent.

a. Calculate the value of a share of Mackinac's common stock using the two-stage DDM. Show your calculations. [8 minutes]

b. Calculate the value of a share of Mackinac's common stock using the two-stage FCFE model. Show your calculations. [8 minutes]

Jones is discussing with a corporate client the possibility of that client acquiring a 70 percent interest in Mackinac.

c. Discuss whether the dividend discount model (DDM) or free cash flow to equity (FCFE) model is more appropriate for this client's valuation purposes. [3 minutes]

31. *CFA Examination Level II*

Peninsular has another client who has inquired about the valuation method best suited for comparison of companies in an industry that has the following characteristics:

- Principal competitors within the industry are located in the United States, France, Japan, and Brazil.
- The industry is currently operating at a cyclical low, with many firms reporting losses.
- The industry is subjected to rapid technological change.

Jones recommends that the client consider the following valuation ratios:

1. Price to earnings
2. Price to book value
3. Price to sales

a. Determine which *one* of the three valuation ratios is most appropriate for comparing companies in this industry. Support your answer with *two* reasons that make that ratio superior to *either* of the other two ratios. [5 minutes]

The client also has expressed interest in economic value added (EVA®) as a measure of company performance. Jones asks his assistant to prepare a presentation about EVA for the client. The assistant's presentation includes the following statements:

1. EVA is a measure of a firm's excess shareholder value generated over a long period of time.
2. In calculating EVA, the cost of capital is the weighted average of the after-tax yield on long-term bonds with similar risk and the cost of equity as calculated by the capital asset pricing model.
3. EVA provides a consistent measure of performance across firms.

b. Determine whether *each* of the statements is correct or incorrect and, if *incorrect,* explain why. [6 minutes]

Note: Explanations cannot repeat the statement in negative form but must indicate what is needed to make the statement correct.

> Note: Answer Question 31b in the following template.

TEMPLATE FOR QUESTION 31b

Statement	Determine Whether Correct or Incorrect (Circle One)	If Incorrect, Explain Why
1. EVA is a measure of a firm's excess shareholder value generated over a long period of time.	Correct Incorrect	
2. In calculating EVA, the cost of capital is the weighted average of the after-tax yield on long-term bonds with similar risk and the cost of equity as calculated by the capital asset pricing model.	Correct Incorrect	
3. EVA provides a consistent measure of performance across firms.	Correct Incorrect	

References

Bhatia, Sanjiv, ed. *Global Equity Investing.* Charlottesville, Va.: Association of Investment Management and Research, 1995.

Born, Jeffery, James Moses, and Dennis Officer. "Changes in Dividend Policy and Subsequent Earnings." *Journal of Portfolio Management* 14, no. 4 (Summer 1988).

Copeland, Tom, Tim Koller, and Jack Murrin. *Valuation: Measuring and Managing the Value of Companies,* 3d ed. New York: Wiley, 2000.

Damodaran, Aswath. *Damodaran on Valuation.* New York: Wiley, 1994.

Hackel, Kenneth S., and Joshua Livnat. *Cash Flow and Security Analysis,* 2d ed. Burr Ridge, Ill.: Irwin Professional Publishing, 1996.

Imhoff, Eugene, and G. Lobo. "Information Content of Analysts' Composite Forecast Revisions." *Journal of Accounting Research* 22, no. 3 (Autumn 1984).

Jaffe, Jeffery, Donald Keim, and Randolph Westerfield. "Earnings Yields, Market Values, Stock Returns." *Journal of Finance* 44, no. 1 (March 1989).

Jennings, Robert. *Reaction of Financial Analysts to Corporate Management Earnings per Share Forecasts.* New York: Financial Analysts Research Foundation, Monograph No. 20, 1984.

Johnson, R. S., Lyle Fiore, and Richard Zuber. "The Investment Performance of Common Stocks in Relation to Their Price-Earnings Ratios: An Update of the Basu Study." *Financial Review* 24, no. 3 (August 1989).

Levine, Sumner N., ed. *The Financial Analysts Handbook,* 2d ed. Homewood, Ill.: Dow Jones–Irwin, 1988.

Palepu, Krishna, Victor Bernard, and Paul Healy. *Business Analysis and Valuation.* Cincinnati, Ohio: Southwestern Publishing, 1996.

Porter, Michael E. *Competitive Advantage: Creating and Sustaining Superior Performance.* New York: The Free Press, 1985.

Squires, Jan R., ed. *Equity Research and Valuation Techniques.* Charlottesville, Va.: Association for Investment Management and Research, 1998.

Squires, Jan R., ed. *Practical Issues in Equity, Analysis.* Charlottesville, Va.: Association for Investment Management and Research, 2000.

Squires, Jan R., ed. *Value and Growth Styles in Equity Investing.* Charlottesville, Va.: Association for Investment Management and Research, 1995.

Waymire, G. "Additional Evidence on the Information Content of Management Earnings Forecasts." *Journal of Accounting Research* 22, no. 3 (Autumn 1984).

Chapter 16 ▷ Technical Analysis*

After you finish this chapter, you should be able to answer the following questions:

➤ How does technical analysis differ from fundamental analysis?
➤ What are the underlying assumptions of technical analysis?
➤ What major assumption causes a difference between technical analysis and the efficient market hypothesis?
➤ What are the major advantages of technical analysis compared to fundamental analysis?
➤ What are the major challenges to technical analysis and its rules?
➤ What is the logic for the major contrary opinion rules used by technicians?
➤ What are some of the significant rules used by technicians who want to follow the smart money and what is the logic of those rules?
➤ What is the breadth of market measures and what are they intended to indicate?
➤ What are the three types of price movements postulated in the Dow Theory and how are they used by a technician?
➤ Why is the volume of trading important and how do technicians use it in their analysis?
➤ What are support and resistance levels, when do they occur, and how are they used by technicians?
➤ What is the purpose of moving average lines and how do technicians use them to detect major changes in trends?
➤ What is the rationale behind the relative strength line for an industry or a stock?
➤ How are bar charts different from point-and-figure charts?
➤ What are some uses of technical analysis in foreign security markets?
➤ How is technical analysis used when analyzing bond markets?

> The market reacted yesterday to the report of a large increase in the short interest on the NYSE.
>
> Although the market declined today, it was not considered bearish because of the light volume.
>
> The market declined today after three days of increases due to profit taking by investors.

These and similar statements appear daily in the financial news. All of them have as their rationale one of numerous technical trading rules. Technical analysts develop technical trading rules from observations of past price movements of the stock market and individual stocks. The philosophy behind technical analysis is in sharp contrast to the efficient market hypothesis that we studied, which contends that past performance has no influence on future performance or market values. It also differs from what we learned about fundamental analysis, which involves making investment decisions based on the examination of the economy, an industry, and

---

*Richard T. McCabe, Chief Market Analyst at Merrill Lynch Capital Markets, provided helpful comments and material for this chapter.

company variables that lead to an estimate of value for an investment, which is then compared to the prevailing market price of the investment. In contrast to the efficient market hypothesis or fundamental analysis, **technical analysis** involves the examination of past market data such as prices and the volume of trading, which leads to an estimate of future price trends and, therefore, an investment decision. Whereas fundamental analysts use economic data that are usually separate from the stock or bond market, the technical analyst believes that using data *from the market itself* is a good idea because "the market is its own best predictor." Therefore, technical analysis is an alternative method of making the investment decision and answering the questions: What securities should an investor buy or sell? When should these investments be made?

Technical analysts see no need to study the multitude of economic, industry, and company variables to arrive at an estimate of future value because they believe that past price movements will signal future price movements. Technicians also believe that a change in the price trend may predict a forthcoming change in the fundamental variables such as earnings and risk before the change is perceived by most fundamental analysts. Are technicians correct? Many investors using these techniques claim to have experienced superior rates of return on many investments. In addition, many newsletter writers base their recommendations on technical analysis. Finally, even the major investment firms that employ many fundamental analysts also employ technical analysts to provide investment advice. Numerous investment professionals and individual investors believe in and use technical trading rules to make their investment decisions. Therefore, whether you are a fan of technical analysis or an advocate of the efficient market hypothesis, you should still have an understanding of the basic philosophy and reasoning behind technical approaches. To help you understand technical analysis, we begin this chapter with an examination of the basic philosophy underlying technical approaches to market analysis and company analysis. Subsequently, we consider the advantages and potential problems with the technical approach. Finally, we present alternative technical trading rules applicable to both U.S. and foreign securities markets.

UNDERLYING ASSUMPTIONS OF TECHNICAL ANALYSIS

Technical analysts base trading decisions on examinations of prior price and volume data to determine past market trends from which they predict future behavior for the market as a whole and for individual securities. Several assumptions lead to this view of price movements:

1. The market value of any good or service is determined solely by the interaction of supply and demand.
2. Supply and demand are governed by numerous rational and irrational factors. Included in these factors are those economic variables relied on by the fundamental analyst as well as opinions, moods, and guesses. The market weighs all these factors continually and automatically.
3. Disregarding minor fluctuations, *the prices for individual securities and the overall value of the market tend to move in trends, which persist for appreciable lengths of time.*
4. Prevailing trends change in reaction to shifts in supply and demand relationships. These shifts, no matter why they occur, *can be detected sooner or later in the action of the market itself.*[1]

Certain aspects of these assumptions are controversial, leading fundamental analysts and advocates of efficient markets to question their validity. Those aspects are emphasized in the preceding list.

---

[1]These assumptions are summarized in Robert A. Levy, "Conceptual Foundations of Technical Analysis," *Financial Analysts Journal* 22, no. 4 (July–August 1966): 83.

EXHIBIT 16.1   *TECHNICAL VIEW OF PRICE ADJUSTMENT TO NEW INFORMATION*

The first two assumptions are almost universally accepted by technicians and nontechnicians alike. Almost anyone who has had a basic course in economics would agree that, at any point in time, the price of a security (or any good or service) is determined by the interaction of supply and demand. In addition, most observers would acknowledge that supply and demand are governed by many variables. The only difference in opinion might concern the influence of the irrational factors. Certainly, everyone would agree that the market continually weighs all these factors.

A stronger difference of opinion arises over the assumption about the *speed of adjustment* of stock prices to changes in supply and demand. Technical analysts expect stock prices to move in trends that persist for long periods because they believe that new information does not come to the market at one point in time but, rather, enters the market *over a period of time.* This pattern of information access occurs because of different sources of information or because certain investors receive the information or perceive fundamental changes earlier than others. As various groups ranging from insiders to well-informed professionals to the average investor receive the information and buy or sell a security accordingly, its price moves gradually toward the new equilibrium. Therefore, technicians do not expect the price adjustment to be as abrupt as fundamental analysts and efficient market supporters do, but expect a *gradual price adjustment* to reflect the gradual flow of information.

Exhibit 16.1 shows this process wherein new information causes a decrease in the equilibrium price for a security, but the price adjustment is not rapid. It occurs as a trend that persists until the stock reaches its new equilibrium. Technical analysts look for the beginning of a movement from one equilibrium value to a new equilibrium value. Technical analysts do not attempt to predict the new equilibrium value. They look for the start of a change so that they can get on the bandwagon early and benefit from the move to the new equilibrium by buying if the trend is up or selling if the trend is down. Obviously, if there is a rapid adjustment of prices, as expected by those who espouse an efficient market, it would keep the ride on the bandwagon so short that investors could not get on board and benefit from the ride.

ADVANTAGES OF TECHNICAL ANALYSIS

Although technicians understand the logic of fundamental analysis, technical analysts see benefits in their approach compared to fundamental analysis. Most technical analysts admit that a fundamental analyst with good information, good analytical ability, and a keen sense of information's impact on the market should achieve above-average returns. However, this statement requires qualification. According to technical analysts, it is important to recognize that the fundamental analysts can experience superior returns *only* if they obtain new information before other investors and process it *correctly* and *quickly*. Technical analysts do not believe the vast majority of investors can consistently get new information before other investors and consistently process it correctly and quickly.

In addition, technical analysts claim that a major advantage of their method is that *it is not heavily dependent on financial accounting statements*—the major source of information about the past performance of a firm or industry. As you know from Chapters 14 and 15, the fundamental analyst evaluates such statements to help project future return and risk characteristics for industries and individual securities. The technician points out several major problems with accounting statements:

1. They lack a great deal of information needed by security analysts, such as information related to sales, earnings, and capital utilized by product line and customers.
2. According to GAAP (generally accepted accounting principles), corporations may choose among several procedures for reporting expenses, assets, or liabilities. Notably, these alternative procedures can produce vastly different values for expenses, income, return on assets, and return on equity. As a result, an investor can have trouble comparing the statements of two firms in the same industry, much less firms in different industries.
3. Many psychological factors and other nonquantifiable variables do not appear in financial statements. Examples include employee training and loyalty, customer goodwill, and general investor attitude toward an industry. Investor attitudes could be important when investors become concerned about the risk from restrictions or taxes on products such as tobacco or alcohol or when firms do business in countries that have significant political risk.

Therefore, because technicians are suspicious of financial statements, they consider it advantageous not to depend on them. As we will show, most of the data used by technicians, such as security prices, volume of trading, and other trading information, is derived from the stock market itself.

Also, a fundamental analyst must process new information correctly and *quickly* to derive a new intrinsic value for the stock or bond before the other investors can. Technicians, on the other hand, only need to quickly recognize a movement to a new equilibrium value *for whatever reason*—that is, they do not need to know about an event and determine the effect of the event on the value of the firm and its stock.

Finally, assume a fundamental analyst determines that a given security is under- or overvalued a long time before other investors. He or she still must determine *when* to make the purchase or sale. Ideally, the highest rate of return would come from making the transaction just before the change in market value occurs. For example, assume that based on your analysis in February, you expect a firm to report substantially higher earnings in June. Although you could buy the stock in February, you would be better off waiting until about May to buy the stock so your funds would not be tied up for an extra three months, but you may be reticent to wait that long. Because most technicians do not invest until the move to the new equilibrium is underway, they contend that they are more likely to experience ideal timing compared to the fundamental analyst.

CHALLENGES TO TECHNICAL ANALYSIS

Those who doubt the value of technical analysis for investment decisions question the usefulness of this technique in two areas. First, they challenge some of its basic assumptions. Second, they challenge some specific technical trading rules and their long-run usefulness. In this section, we consider both of these challenges.

Challenges to Technical Analysis Assumptions

The major challenge to technical analysis is based on the results of empirical tests of the efficient market hypothesis (EMH). As discussed in Chapter 6, for technical trading rules to generate superior risk-adjusted returns after taking account of transactions costs, the market would have to be slow to adjust prices to the arrival of new information, that is, it would have to be inefficient. (This is referred to as the weak-form efficient market hypothesis.) The two sets of tests of the weak-form EMH are: (1) the statistical analysis of prices to determine if prices moved in trends or were a random walk, and (2) the analysis of specific trading rules to determine if their use could beat a buy-and-hold policy after considering transactions costs and risk. Almost all the studies testing the weak-form EMH using statistical analysis have found that prices do not move in trends based on statistical tests of autocorrelation and runs. These results support the EMH.

Regarding the analysis of specific trading rules, as discussed in Chapter 6, numerous technical trading rules exist that have not been or cannot be tested. Still, the vast majority of the results for the trading rules tested support the EMH.

Challenges to Technical Trading Rules

An obvious challenge to technical analysis is that the past price patterns or relationships between specific market variables and stock prices may not be repeated. As a result, a technique that previously worked might miss subsequent market turns. This possibility leads most technicians to follow several trading rules and to seek a consensus of all of them to predict the future market pattern.

Other critics contend that many price patterns become self-fulfilling prophecies. For example, assume that many analysts expect a stock selling at $40 a share to go to $50 or more if it should rise above its current pattern and "break through" its channel at $45. As soon as it reaches $45, enough technicians will buy to cause the price to rise to $50, exactly as predicted. In fact, some technicians may place a limit order to buy the stock at such a breakout point. Under such conditions, the increase will probably be only temporary and the price will return to its true equilibrium.

Another problem with technical analysis is that the success of a particular trading rule will encourage many investors to adopt it. It is contended that this popularity and the resulting competition will eventually neutralize the technique. If numerous investors focus on a specific technical trading rule, some of them will attempt to anticipate the price pattern and either ruin the expected historical price pattern or eliminate profits for most traders by causing the price to change faster than expected. For example, suppose it becomes known that technicians who employ short selling data have been enjoying high rates of return. Based on this knowledge, other technicians will likely start using these data and thus accelerate the stock price pattern following changes in short selling. As a result, this profitable trading rule may no longer be profitable after the first few investors react.

Further, as we will see when we examine specific trading rules, *they all require a great deal of subjective judgment.* Two technical analysts looking at the same price pattern may arrive at widely different interpretations of what has happened and, therefore, will come to different investment decisions. This implies that the use of various techniques is neither completely mechanical nor obvious. Finally, as we will discuss in connection with several trading rules, *the standard values that signal investment decisions can change over time.* Therefore, technical analysts must adjust the specified values that trigger investment decisions over time to conform to the new environment. In other cases, trading rules are abandoned because it appears they no longer work.

TECHNICAL TRADING RULES AND INDICATORS

To help you understand the specific technical trading rules, Exhibit 16.2 shows a typical stock price cycle that could be an example for the overall stock market or for an individual stock. The graph shows a peak and trough, along with a rising trend channel, a flat trend channel, a declining trend channel, and indications of when a technical analyst would ideally want to trade.

EXHIBIT 16.2   *TYPICAL STOCK MARKET CYCLE*

The graph begins with the end of a declining (bear) market that finishes in a **trough** followed by an upward trend that breaks through the **declining trend channel**. Confirmation that the trend has reversed would be a buy signal. The technical analyst would buy stocks that showed this pattern.

The analyst would then look for the development of a **rising trend channel**. As long as the stock price stayed in this rising channel, the technician would hold the stock(s). Ideally, you want to sell at the **peak** of the cycle, but you cannot identify a peak until after the trend changes.

If the stock (or the market) begins trading in a flat pattern, it will necessarily break out of its rising trend channel. At this point, some technical analysts would sell, but most would hold to see if the stock experiences a period of consolidation and then breaks out of the **flat trend channel** on the upside and begins rising again. Alternatively, if the stock were to break out of the channel on the downside, the technician would take this as a sell signal and would expect a declining trend channel. The next buy signal would come after the trough when the price breaks out of the declining channel and establishes a rising trend. Subsequently, we will consider strategies to detect these changes in trend and the importance of volume in this analysis.

There are numerous technical trading rules and a range of interpretations for each of them, Almost all technical analysts watch many alternative rules and decide on a buy or sell decision based on a *consensus* of the signals, because complete agreement of all the rules is rare. This section discusses several well-known techniques. The presentation on domestic indicators is divided into four sections based on the attitudes of technical analysts. The first group includes trading rules used by analysts who like to trade against the crowd using contrary-opinion signals. The second group of rules attempts to emulate astute investors, that is, the smart money. The next section includes technical indicators that are very popular but not easily classified. The fourth section covers pure price and volume techniques, including the famous Dow Theory. The final sections describe how these technical trading rules have been applied to foreign securities markets and bond markets.

Contrary-Opinion Rules   Many technical analysts rely on technical trading rules that assume that the majority of investors are wrong as the market approaches peaks and troughs. Therefore, these technicians try to determine when the majority of investors is either strongly bullish or bearish and then trade in the opposite direction.

Mutual Fund Cash Positions   Mutual funds hold some part of their portfolio in cash for one of several reasons. One reason is that they need cash to liquidate shares submitted by fund-holders. Another reason is that new investments in the mutual fund may not have been invested. Third, the portfolio manager might be bearish on the market and want to increase the fund's defensive cash position.

Mutual funds' ratios of cash as a percentage of the total assets in their portfolios (the *cash ratio or liquid asset ratio*) are reported in the press, including monthly figures in *Barron's*.[2] This percentage of cash has varied in recent years from a low point of about 4 percent to a high point near 11 percent, although there appears to be a declining trend to the series.

Contrary-opinion technicians believe that mutual funds usually are wrong at peaks and troughs. Thus, they expect mutual funds to have a high percentage of cash near a market trough at the time that they should be fully invested to take advantage of the impending market rise. At the market peak, technicians expect mutual funds to be almost fully invested with a low percentage of cash when they should be selling stocks and realizing gains. Therefore, contrary-opinion technicians would watch for the mutual fund cash position to approach one of the extremes and act contrary to the mutual funds. Specifically, they would tend to buy when the cash ratio approaches 11 percent and to sell when the cash ratio approaches 4 percent.

A high cash position is also a bullish indicator because of potential buying power. Irrespective of the reason for the increase in cash balances, technicians believe these cash funds will eventually be invested and will cause stock prices to increase. Alternatively, a low cash ratio would mean that the institutions have bought heavily and are left with little potential buying power.

Credit Balances in Brokerage Accounts   Credit balances result when investors sell stocks and leave the proceeds with their brokers, expecting to reinvest them shortly. The amounts are reported by the SEC and the NYSE in *Barron's*. Because technical analysts view these credit balances as potential purchasing power, a decline in these balances is considered bearish because it indicates lower purchasing power as the market approaches a peak. Alternatively, a buildup of credit balances is an increase in buying power and a bullish signal.

Investment Advisory Opinions   Many technicians believe that if a large proportion of investment advisory services are bearish, this signals the approach of a market trough and the onset of a bull market. Because most advisory services tend to be trend followers, the number of bears usually is greatest when market bottoms are approaching. This trading rule is specific in terms of the ratio of the number of advisory services that are bearish/bullish as a percentage of the number of services expressing an opinion.[3] A 60 percent bearish and/or 20 percent bullish reading indicates a major market bottom (a bullish indicators), while a 60 percent bullish and/or 20 percent bearish reading suggests a major market top (a bearish signal). Exhibit 16.3 shows a time-series plot of the DJIA and both the bearish sentiment index and the bullish sentiment index. As of mid-2001, both indexes had moved away from the bearish boundary values back to the neutral territory.

OTC versus NYSE Volume   This ratio of trading volume is considered a measure of speculative activity. Speculative trading typically peaks at market peaks. Exhibit 16.4 contains a time-series plot of the Nasdaq Composite Average and the OTC/NYSE volume ratio.

---

[2]*Barron's* is a prime source for numerous technical indicators. For a readable discussion of relevant data and their use, see Martin E. Zweig, *Understanding Technical Forecasting* (New York: Dow Jones & Co., 1987).

[3]This ratio is compiled by Investors Intelligence, Larchmont, NY 10538. Richard McCabe at Merrill Lynch uses this series as one of his "Investor Sentiment Indicators."

| EXHIBIT 16.3 | *TIME-SERIES PLOT OF DOW JONES INDUSTRIAL AVERAGE AND THE BULLISH AND BEARISH ADVISORY SERVICES* |

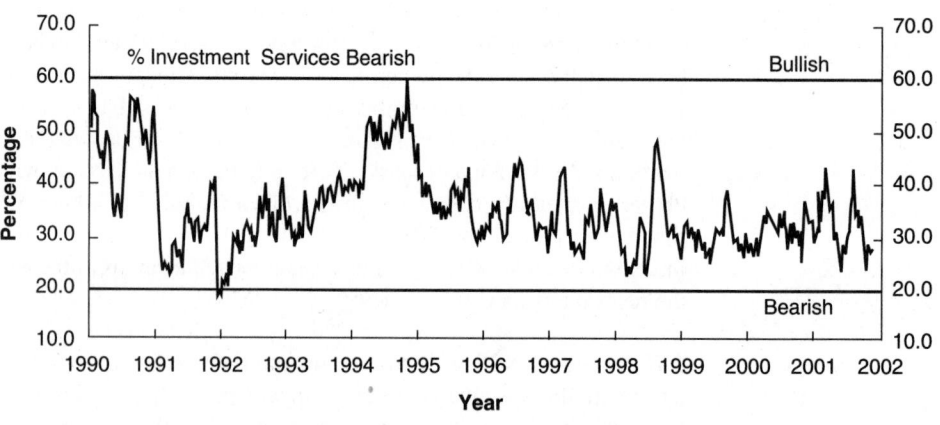

Source: *Where the Indicators Stand* (New York: Merrill Lynch, January 2002).

Source of data: Investors Intelligence, Larchmont NY 10538.

| EXHIBIT 16.4 | *TIME-SERIES PLOT OF NASDAQ COMPOSITE AVERAGE AND THE RATIO OF OTC VOLUME TO NYSE VOLUME (THREE-WEEK AVERAGE)* |

Source: *Where the Indicators Stand* (New York: Merrill Lynch, January 2002).

Notably, the interpretation of the ratio has changed—that is, the decision rules have changed. Specifically, in 1996, the decision rules were increased to 112 percent (i.e., heavy speculative trading and an over-bought market) and 87 percent (i.e., low speculative trading and an over-sold market). The source of this rising drift in the decision rules was faster growth in OTC trading volume and dominance of the OTC market by a few large-cap stocks. Subsequently, it was decided to detect excess speculative activity by using the *direction* of the volume ratio as a guide. As shown in Exhibit 16.4, the ratio peaked when the market peaked in early 2000.

The Chicago Board Options Exchange (CBOE) Put/Call Ratio

Contrary-opinion technicians use put options, which give the holder the right to sell stock at a specified price for a given time period, as signals of a bearish attitude. A higher put/call ratio indicates a pervasive bearish attitude, which technicians consider a bullish indicator.

This ratio fluctuates between .60 and .40, and it has typically been substantially less than 1 because investors tend to be bullish and avoid selling short or buying puts. The current decision rule states that a put/call ratio above .60—sixty puts are traded for every 100 calls—is considered bullish, while a relatively low put/call ratio of .40 or less is considered a bearish sign.

EXHIBIT 16.5 *TIME-SERIES PLOT OF DOW JONES INDUSTRIAL AVERAGE AND THE PERCENTAGE OF FUTURES TRADERS BULLISH ON STOCK INDEX FUTURES*

Source: *Where the Indicators Stand* (New York: Merrill Lynch, January 2002). Data courtesy of Market Vane.

Futures Traders Bullish on Stock Index Futures   Another relatively new contrary-opinion measure is the percentage of speculators in stock index futures who are bullish or bearish regarding stocks based on a survey of individual futures traders. These technicians would consider it a bearish sign when more than 70 percent of the speculators are bullish, and it is a bullish signal when this ratio declines to 30 percent or lower. The plot in Exhibit 16.5 shows that as of mid-2001 the series had been at the lower bound, which is bullish.

As shown, contrary-opinion technicians have several measures of how the majority of investors are investing, which prompts them to take the opposite action. They generally follow several of these series to provide a consensus regarding investors' attitudes.

Follow the Smart Money   Some technical analysts have created a set of indicators that they expect to indicate the behavior of smart, sophisticated investors and create rules to follow them. In this section, we discuss some of these indicators.

The Confidence Index   Published by *Barron's,* the Confidence Index is the ratio of *Barron's* average yield on 10 top-grade corporate bonds divided by the yield on the Dow Jones average of 40 bonds.[4] This index measures the difference in yield spread between high-grade bonds and a large cross section of bonds. Because the yields on high-grade bonds always should be lower than those on a large cross section of bonds, this ratio should approach 100 as the spread between the two sets of bonds gets smaller.

Technicians believe the ratio is a bullish indicator because, during periods of high confidence, investors are willing to invest in lower-quality bonds for the added yield, which causes a decrease in the average yield for the large cross section of bonds relative to the yield on high-grade bonds. Therefore, this ratio of yields, (the Confidence Index), will increase. In contrast, when investors are pessimistic, they avoid investing in low-quality bonds and this increases the yield spread between high-grade and average bonds, which causes the Confidence Index to decline.

Unfortunately, this interpretation assumes that changes in the yield spread are caused almost exclusively by changes in investor demand for different quality bonds. In fact, the yield differences have frequently changed because of changes in the supply of bonds. For example, a large issue of high-grade AT&T bonds could cause a temporary increase in yields on all high-grade bonds, reduce the yield spread, and increase the Confidence Index without any change in investors' attitudes. Such a change can generate a false signal of a change in confidence.

T-Bill–Eurodollar Yield Spread   An alternative measure of investor attitude or confidence on a global basis is the spread between T-bill yields and Eurodollar rates. It is reasoned that, at times of international crisis, this spread widens as money flows to safehaven U.S. T-bills, which causes a decline in this ratio. The stock market typically experiences a trough shortly thereafter.

Debit Balances in Brokerage Accounts (Margin Debt)   Debit balances in brokerage accounts represent borrowing (margin debt) by knowledgeable investors from their brokers. Hence, these balances indicate the attitude of sophisticated investors who engage in margin transactions. Therefore, an increase in debit balances implies buying and is considered a bullish sign, while a decline in debit balances would indicate selling by these sophisticated investors and would be a bearish indicator.

Monthly data on margin debt are reported in *Barron's*. Unfortunately, this series does not include borrowing by investors from other sources such as banks. Also, because it is an absolute value, technicians would look for changes in the trend of borrowing.

Other Market Environment Indicators   In addition to contrary opinion and smart money signals, there are several indicators of overall market sentiment that are used to make aggregate market decisions.

Breadth of Market   Breadth of market measures the number of issues that have increased each day and the number of issues that have declined. It helps explain the cause of a change of direction in a composite market series such as the DJIA. As discussed in Chapter 5, most stock market series are heavily influenced by the stocks of large firms because the indexes are value weighted. Therefore, a stock market series can increase, while the majority of the individual issues will not, which means that most stocks are not participating in the rising market. Such a divergence can be detected by examining the advance-decline figures for all stocks on the exchange, along with the overall market index.

The advance-decline series is typically a cumulative series of net advances or net declines. Specifically, each day major newspapers publish figures on the number of issues on the NYSE that advanced, declined, or were unchanged The figures for a five-day sample, as would be reported in *Barron's,* are shown in Exhibit 16.6. These figures, along with changes in the DJIA

---

[4]Historical data for this series are contained in the *Dow Jones Investor's Handbook* (Princeton, N.J.: Dow Jones Books, annual). Current figures appear in *Barron's*.

EXHIBIT 16.6 *DAILY ADVANCES AND DECLINES ON THE NEW YORK STOCK EXCHANGE*

	DAY				
	1	2	3	4	5
Issues traded	3,608	3,641	3,659	3,651	3,612
Advances	2,310	2,350	1,558	2,261	2,325
Declines	909	912	1,649	933	894
Unchanged	389	379	452	457	393
Net advances (advances minus declines)	+1,401	+1,438	−91	+1,328	+1,431
Cumulative net advances	+1,401	+2,839	+2,748	+4,076	+5,507
Changes in DJIA	+40.47	+43.99	−15.25	+60.50	+71.40

Sources: *NYSE* Fact Book 2001, New York Stock Exchange; and *Barron's*, 21 July 2001, Dow Jones & Co., Inc. Reprinted with permission.

at the bottom of the exhibit, indicate a strong market advance because the DJIA was increasing and the net advance figure was strong, indicating that the market increase was broadly based. Even the results on Day 3, when the market declined 15 points, were encouraging since it was a small decline and the individual stocks were split just about 50-50, which points toward a fairly even environment.

Short Interest The short interest is the cumulative number of shares sold short by investors and not covered. This means the investor has not purchased the shares sold short and returned them to the investor from whom they were borrowed. A relative measure of this activity is the short-interest ratio equal to the outstanding short interest divided by the average daily volume of trading on the exchange. For example, if the outstanding short interest on the NYSE was 5,000 million shares and the average daily volume of trading on the exchange was 1,200 million shares, the short-interest ratio would be 4.17 (5,000/1,200). This means the outstanding short interest equals about four days' trading volume.

Technicians probably interpret this ratio contrary to your initial intuition. Because short sales reflect investors' expectations that stock prices will decline, one would typically expect an increase in the short-interest ratio to be bearish. On the contrary, technicians consider a high short-interest ratio bullish because it indicates *potential demand* for the stock by those who previously sold short and have not covered the short sale.

A technician would be bullish when the short-interest ratio approached 5.0 and bearish if it declined toward 3.0. The short-interest position is calculated by the stock exchanges and the NASD as of the 20th of each month and is reported about two days later in *The Wall Street Journal*. Notably, this ratio—and any ratio that involves short selling—has been affected by new techniques for short selling such as options and futures.

Stocks above Their 200-Day Moving Average Technicians often compute moving averages of a series to determine its general trend. To examine individual stocks, the 200-day **moving average** of prices has been fairly popular. From these moving-average series for numerous stocks, Media General Financial Services calculates how many stocks currently are trading above their 200-day moving-average series, and this is used as an indicator of general investor sentiment. The market is considered to be *overbought* and subject to a negative correction when more than 80 percent of the stocks are trading above their 200-day moving average. In contrast, if less than 20 percent of the stocks are selling above their 200-day moving average, the market is considered to be *oversold,* which means investors should expect a positive correction. As shown

EXHIBIT 16.7

PERCENTAGE OF NYSE COMMON STOCKS ABOVE THEIR 200-DAY MOVING-AVERAGE PRICE

Sources: *Where the Indicators Stand* (New York: Merrill Lynch, January 2002).

in Exhibit 16.7, as of mid-2002, the percent of stocks selling above their 200-day moving average is about 60 percent, which is considered neutral.

Block Uptick-Downtick Ratio As we discussed in Chapter 6, about 50 percent of NYSE volume comes from block trading by institutions. The exchange can determine whether the price change that accompanied a particular block trade was higher or lower than the price of the prior transactions. A block trade price above the prior transaction price, is referred to as an uptick and is assumed to be initiated by a buyer; a block trade price below the prior transaction price is referred to as a downtick and assumed to be initiated by a seller. This led to the development of the uptick (buyers)-downtick (sellers) ratio, which indicates institutional investor sentiment. This ratio generally has fluctuated in the range of .70, which indicates an oversold condition that is bullish, to about 1.10, which indicates an overbought environment and a bearish sentiment.

Stock Price and Volume Techniques In the introduction to this chapter, we examined a hypothetical stock price chart that demonstrated market peaks and troughs, along with rising and declining trend channels and breakouts from channels that signal new price trends or reversals of the price trends. While price patterns alone are important, most technical trading rules consider both stock price and corresponding volume movements.

The Dow Theory Any discussion of technical analysis using price and volume data should begin with a consideration of the Dow Theory because it was among the earliest work on this topic and remains the basis for many technical indicators.[5] Dow described stock prices as moving in trends analogous to the movement of water. He postulated three types of price movements over time: (1) major trends that are like tides in the ocean, (2) intermediate trends that resemble waves, and (3) short-run movements that are like ripples. Followers of the Dow Theory attempt to detect the direction of the major price trend (tide), recognizing that intermediate movements (waves) may occasionally move in the opposite direction. They recognize that a major market advance does not go straight up but, rather, includes small price declines as some investors decide to take profits.

Exhibit 16.8 shows the typical bullish pattern. The technician would look for every recovery to reach a new peak above the prior peak, and this price rise should be accompanied by heavy trading volume. Alternatively, each profit-taking reversal that follows an increase to a new peak

---

[5]A study that discusses and provides support for the Dow Theory is David A. Glickstein and Rolf E. Wubbels, "Dow Theory Is Alive and Well," *Journal of Portfolio Management* 9, no. 3 (Spring 1983): 28–32.

EXHIBIT 16.8 *SAMPLE BULLISH PRICE PATTERN*

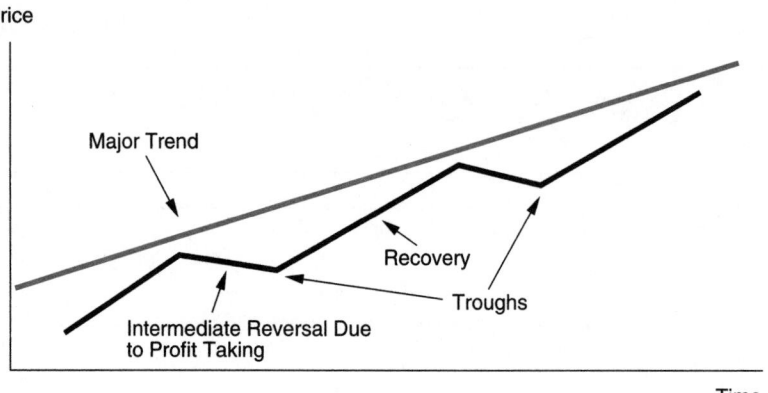

should have a trough above the prior trough, with relatively light trading volume during the profit-taking reversals. When this pattern of price and volume movements changes, the major trend may be entering a period of consolidation or a major reversal.

Importance of Volume As noted in the description of the Dow Theory, technicians watch volume changes along with price movements as an indicator of changes in supply and demand. A price movement in one direction means that the net effect on price is in that direction, but the price change alone does not indicate the breadth of the excess demand or supply. Therefore, the technician looks for a price increase on heavy volume *relative to the stock's normal trading volume* as an indication of bullish activity. Conversely, a price decline with heavy volume is bearish. A generally bullish pattern would be when price increases are accompanied by relatively heavy volume and small price reversals occur with light trading volume.

Technicians also use a ratio of upside-downside volume as an indicator of short-term momentum for the aggregate stock market. Each day the stock exchanges announce the volume of trading in stocks that experienced an increase divided by the volume of trading in stocks that declined. These data are reported daily in *The Wall Street Journal* and weekly in *Barron's*. This ratio is used as an indicator of investor sentiment. Specifically, technicians believe that a value of 1.50 or more indicates an overbought position that is bearish. Alternatively, a value of 0.75 and lower supposedly reflects an oversold position and is considered bullish.

Support and Resistance Levels A **support level** is the price range at which the technician would expect a substantial increase in the demand for a stock. Generally, a support level will develop after a stock has enjoyed a meaningful price increase and the stock experiences profit taking. Technicians reason that, at some price below the recent peak, other investors who did not buy during the first price increase and have been waiting for a small reversal to get into the stock. When the price reaches this support price, demand surges and price and volume begin to increase again.

A **resistance level** is the price range at which the technician would expect an increase in the supply of stock and a price reversal. A resistance level develops after a steady decline from a higher price level—that is, the decline in price leads some investors who acquired the stock at a higher price to look for an opportunity to sell it near their breakeven points. Therefore, the sup-

EXHIBIT 16.9 ▶ *DAILY STOCK PRICES FOR STRYKER CORP. WITH INDICATIONS OF SUPPORT AND RESISTANCE LEVELS*

Source: Created by the authors using data from Telerate.

ply of stock owned by these investors is *overhanging* the market. When the price rebounds to the target price set by these investors, this overhanging supply of stock comes to the market and there is a price decline on heavy volume. It is also possible to envision a rising trend of support and resistance levels for a stock. For example, the rising support prices would be a set of higher prices where investors over time would see the price increase and would look for the opportunity to acquire the stock when there is profit taking at higher and higher prices. In such a case, there would be a succession of higher support and resistance levels over time within a rising channel.

Exhibit 16.9 contains the daily stock prices for Stryker Corp. with support and resistance lines that show a rising pattern since Stryker has experienced strong price increases during this period. At the most recent point on the chart, the resistance level is about 60 and rising, while the support level is about 53 and also rising. The bullish technician would look for future prices to rise in line with this channel. If prices fell below the support line, this would be a bearish signal.

Moving-Average Lines   Earlier, we discussed how technicians use a moving average of past stock prices as an indicator of the long-run trend and how they examine current prices relative to this trend for signals of a change. We also noted that a 200-day moving average is a relatively popular measure for individual stocks and the aggregate market. In this discussion, we want to add a 50-day moving-average price line and consider trading volume.

EXHIBIT 16.10 ▶ *DAILY STOCK PRICES FOR CONCORD EFS WITH 50-DAY AND 200-DAY MOVING AVERAGE LINES AND A 14-DAY RELATIVE STRENGTH INDEX COMPARED TO THE S&P 500 INDEX*

Source: Telerate.

Exhibit 16.10 is a daily stock price chart from the Bridge System for Concord EFS for the 1,000 days from July 1997 into June 2001. It also contains a 50-day and 200-day moving-average (MA) line. As noted, MA lines are meant to reflect the overall trend for the price series, with the shorter MA series (50-day versus 200-day) reflecting shorter trends. Two comparisons involving the MA series are considered important. The first comparison is the specific prices to the shorter run 50-day MA series. If the overall price trend of a stock or the market has been down, the moving-average price line generally would lie above current prices. If prices reverse and break through the moving-average line *from below* accompanied by heavy trading volume, most technicians would consider this a strong *positive* change and speculate that this breakthrough signals a reversal of the declining trend. In contrast, if the price of a stock had been rising, the moving-average line would also be rising, but it would be below current prices. If current prices broke through the moving-average line *from above* accompanied by heavy trading volume, this would be considered a bearish pattern that would signal a reversal of the long-run rising trend.

The second comparison is between the 50- and 200-day MA lines. Specifically, when these two lines cross, it signals a change in the overall trend. Specifically, if the 50-day MA line crosses the 200-day MA line from below on good volume, this would be a bullish indicator (buy signal) because it signals a reversal in trend from negative to positive. In contrast, when the 50-day line crosses the 200-day line from above, it signals a change to a negative trend and would be a sell signal. As shown in Exhibit 16.10, there was a bearish crossing in late January 2000, but it was reversed in June 2000 when there was a bullish crossing. Following this bullish crossing, the 50-day line has been consistently above the 200-day line as prices have gone from the high 20s to over 50.

Overall, for a *bullish* trend, the 50-day MA line should be above the 200-day MA line as it is for Concord EFS since mid-2000. Notably, if this positive gap gets too large (which happens with a fast run up in price) a technician might consider this an indication that the stock is temporarily overbought. A *bearish* trend is when the 50-day MA is always below the 200-day MA line. If the gap was large on the downside, it might be considered a signal of an oversold stock, which is bullish for the short run.

Relative Strength   Technicians believe that once a trend begins, it will continue until some major event causes a change in direction. They believe this is also true of *relative* performance. If an individual stock or an industry group is outperforming the market, technicians believe it will continue to do so.

Therefore, technicians compute weekly or monthly **relative-strength (RS) ratios** for individual stocks and industry groups. The ratio is equal to the price of a stock or an industry index relative to the value for some stock market series such as the S&P 500. If this ratio increases over time, it shows that the stock or industry is outperforming the market, and a technician would expect this superior relative performance to continue. Relative-strength ratios work during declining as well as rising markets. In a declining market, if a stock's price declines less than the market does, the stock's relative-strength ratio will continue to rise. Technicians believe that if this ratio is stable or increases during a bear market, the stock should do well during the subsequent bull market. The bottom section in Exhibit 16.10 shows that the RS line for Concord EFS has been generally increasing for the past three months, which confirms the bullish MA line analysis.

Merrill Lynch publishes relative-strength charts for industry groups. Exhibit 16.11 describes how to read the charts. Further, some technicians construct graphs of stocks relative to their industry in addition to those relative to the market.

Bar Charting   Technicians use charts that show daily, weekly, or monthly time series of stock prices. For a given interval, the technical analyst plots the high and low prices and connects the two points vertically to form a bar. Typically, he or she will also draw a small horizontal line across this vertical bar to indicate the closing price. Finally, almost all bar charts include the volume of trading at the bottom of the chart so that the technical analyst can relate the price and volume movements. A typical bar chart in Exhibit 16.12 shows data for the DJIA from *The Wall Street Journal* along with volume figures for the NYSE.

Multiple Indicator Charts   Exhibit 16.10 is a fairly typical technical chart that contains several indicators that can be used together like the two MA lines (50 and 200 day) and the RS line, which can provide added support to the analysis. Technicians include as many price and

EXHIBIT 16.11 *HOW TO READ INDUSTRY GROUP CHARTS*

The industry group charts in this report display the following elements:

1. A line chart of the weekly close of the Standard & Poor's Industry Group Index for the past 9½ years, with the index range indicated to the left.
2. A line of the 75-week moving average of the Standard & Poor's Industry Group Index.
3. A relative-strength line of the Standard & Poor's Industry Group Index compared with the New York Stock Exchange Composite Index.
4. A 75-week moving average of relative strength.
5. A volatility reading that measures the maximum amount by which the index has outperformed (or underperformed) the NYSE Composite Index during the time period displayed.

Source: *Technical Analysis of Industry Groups* (New York: Merrill Lynch, monthly). Reprinted by permission of Merrill Lynch. All Rights Reserved.

volume series as are reasonable on one chart. Notably, based on the performance of *several* technical indicators, they try to arrive at a consensus about the future movement for the stock.

Point-and-Figure Charts Another graph that is popular with technicians is the point-and-figure chart. Unlike the bar chart, which typically includes all ending prices and volumes to show a trend, the point-and-figure chart includes only significant price changes, regardless of their timing. The technician determines, based on the characteristics of the stock, what price interval to record as significant (one point, two points, and so on) and when to note price reversals.

EXHIBIT 16.12   *A TYPICAL BAR CHART*

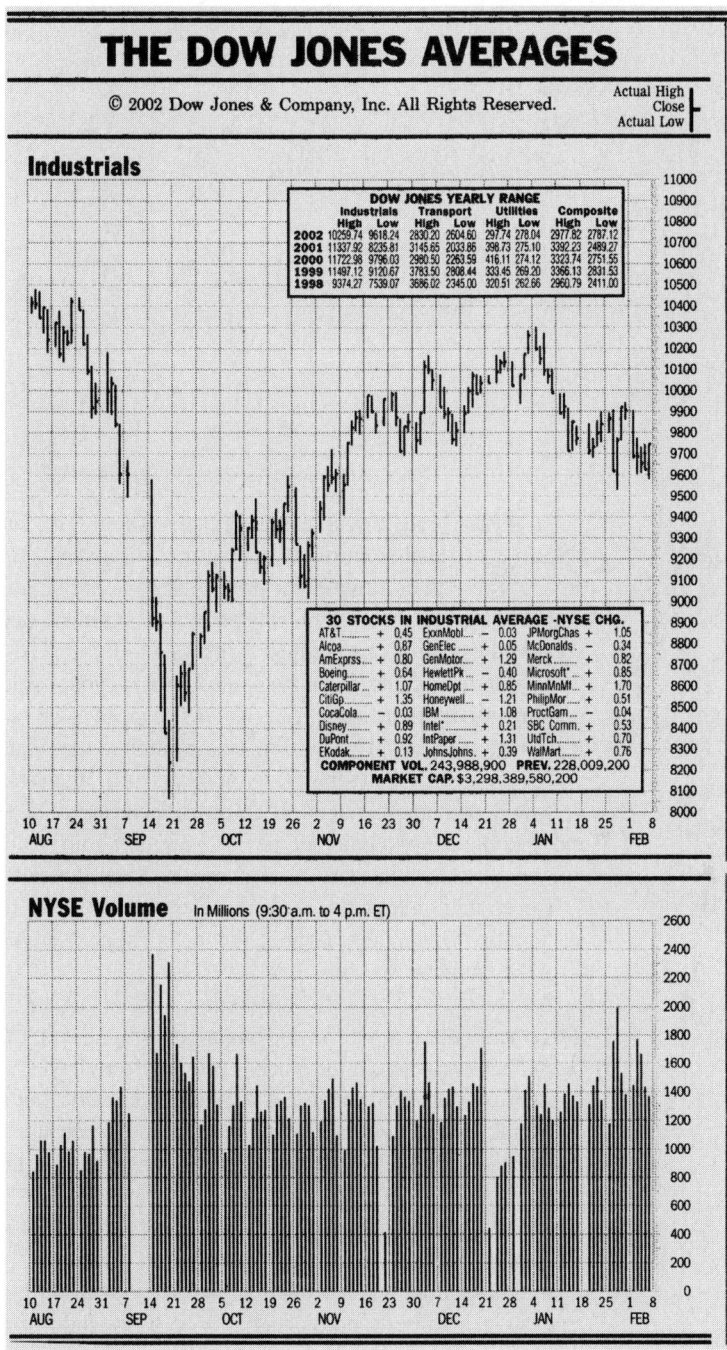

Source: "The Dow Jones Averages," *The Wall Street Journal,* 11 February 2002. Printed with permission from *The Wall Street Journal,* Dow Jones & Co. Inc.

EXHIBIT 16.13 *SAMPLE POINT-AND-FIGURE CHART*

50										
48										
46			X							
44			X							
42	X	X	X							
40	X	X	X							
38		X	X							
36		X	X							
34		X	X							
32										
30										

To demonstrate how a technical analyst would use such a chart, assume you want to chart a volatile stock that is currently selling for $40 a share. Because of its volatility, you believe that anything less than a two-point price change is not significant. Also, you consider anything less than a four-point reversal, meaning a movement in the opposite direction, quite minor. Therefore, you would set up a chart similar to the one in Exhibit 16.13, which starts at 40 and progresses in two-point increments. If the stock moves to 42, you would place an X in the box above 40 and do nothing else until the stock rose to 44 or dropped to 38 (a four-point reversal from its high of 42). If it dropped to 38, you would move a column to the right, which indicates a reversal in direction, and begin again at 38 (fill in boxes at 42 and 40). If the stock price dropped to 34, you would enter an X at 36 and another at 34. If the stock then rose to 38 (another four-point reversal), you would move to the next column and begin at 38, going up (fill in 34 and 36). If the stock then went to 46, you would fill in more Xs as shown and wait for further increases or a reversal.

Depending on how fast the prices rise and fall, this process might take anywhere from two to six months. Given these figures, the technical analyst would attempt to determine trends just as with the bar chart.

As always, you look for breakouts to either higher or lower price levels. A long horizontal movement with many reversals but no major trends up or down would be considered *a period of consolidation,* wherein the stock is moving from buyers to sellers and back again with no strong consensus about its direction. Once the stock breaks out and moves up or down after a period of consolidation, analysts anticipate a major move because previous trading has set the stage for it. In other words, the longer the period of consolidation, the larger the subsequent move.

Point-and-figure charts provide a compact record of movements because they only consider significant price changes for the stock being analyzed. Therefore, some technicians contend they are easier to work with and give more vivid pictures of price movements.

In this section, we discussed numerous widely used technical indicators. As noted, technical analysts generally do not concentrate on a few indicators but seek to derive an overall feel for the direction of change based on a *consensus of numerous technical indicators.*

Technical Analysis of Foreign Markets

Our discussion thus far has concentrated on U.S. markets, but analysts have discovered that these techniques apply to foreign markets as well. Merrill Lynch, for instance, prepares separate technical analysis publications for individual countries such as Japan, Germany, and the United

EXHIBIT 16.14   *MERRILL LYNCH GRAPH OF NIKKEI 225 INDEX OF JAPANESE STOCK MARKET AND SUMMARY COMMENTS ON THE MARKET*

Nikkei 225

	Japan (Nikkei 225: 10144.14)
Support:	10,000–10,200; 9,383–9,477
Resistance:	11,000–11,200; 11,530–12,400
52-Week Range:	9,504–14,529
Near Term:	Down
Medium Term:	Neutral, Deteriorating

Source: *The Global Technician* (New York: Merrill Lynch, January 28, 2002).

 Kingdom as well as a summary of all world markets. The examples that follow show that, when analyzing non-U.S. markets, many techniques are limited to price and volume data rather than the more detailed U.S. market information because the more detailed information that is available on the U.S. market through the SEC, the stock exchanges, the Nasdaq system, and various investment services is not always available in other countries.

Foreign Stock Market Series   Exhibit 16.14 contains the daily time-series plot of the Japanese Nikkei Index. This chart shows the generally declining trend by the Japanese stock market during the period 1996–May 2001.

In the written analysis, the market analyst at Merrill Lynch estimated support and resistance levels for the Japanese Stock Exchange series and commented on the medium-term outlook for this market.

Merrill Lynch publishes similar charts for 10 other countries and compares the countries and ranks them by stock and currency performance. The next section discusses the technical analysis of currency markets.

EXHIBIT 16.15 *TIME-SERIES PLOT OF U.S. DOLLAR TRADE-WEIGHTED EXCHANGE RATES*

Source: *The Global Technician* (New York: Merrill Lynch, January 28, 2002).

Technical Analysis of Foreign Exchange Rates   On numerous occasions, we have discussed the importance of changes in foreign exchange rates on the rates of return on foreign securities. Because of the importance of these relationships, bond and stock traders, in world markets examine the time-series data of various currencies such as the British pound. They also analyze the spread between currencies such as the difference between the Japanese yen (¥) and the British pound. Finally, an analysis of the composite dollar performance over time, as shown in Exhibit 16.15, is useful.

Technical Analysis of Bond Markets   Thus far, we have emphasized the use of technical analysis in stock markets although, these techniques can also be applied to the bond market. The theory and rationale for technical analysis of bonds are the same as for stocks, and many of the same trading rules are used. A major difference is that it is generally not possible to consider the volume of trading of bonds because most bonds are traded OTC, where volume is not reported.

Exhibit 16.16 demonstrates the use of technical analysis techniques applied to bond-yield series. Specifically, the two graphs contain time-series plots of yields for world bond yields based upon a seven-country composite. The top graph shows the yield series with the 55-day moving average. As shown, yields declined steadily until a trough in late March, followed by a strong recovery. The bottom graph that contains a plot of the 14-day RSI generally confirms this, although it shows weakness at the end of the time period. This set of technical graphs provides important insights to a global bond portfolio manager interested in adjusting his or her global bond portfolio. These examples show how technical analysis is applied to the bond market as well as the stock market.

| EXHIBIT 16.16 | *TECHNICAL ANALYSIS OF WORLD BOND YIELDS (SEVEN-COUNTRY COMPOSITE) INCLUDING THE YIELD SERIES, A 55-DAY MOVING AVERAGE, AND A 14-DAY RELATIVE-STRENGTH INDEX (RSI)* |

World Bond Yields   **6-6-01**

Source: *The Global Technician* (New York: Merrill Lynch, June 6, 2001).

The Internet *Investments Online*

By its nature, technical analysis uses charts and graphs, and many Web sites offer them for use by investors and analysts; some are free, but some of the sites for more sophisticated users require payment for access. Here are several interesting sites:

http://www.mta-usa.org The home page of the Market Technicians Association, a professional group of chartists whose goal is to enhance technical analysis and educate investors about its role. The group sponsors the Chartered Market Technician (CMT) designation. This site features news groups, investment links, training and education sources, and links to a variety of technical analysis charts.

http://www.bigcharts.com This site offers free intraday and historical charts and price quotes. Its database includes stocks, mutual funds, and indexes. Users can learn which stocks have the largest percentage gain (loss) in price and volume and which stocks are hitting new 52-week highs (lows). Other features include momentum charts, stocks with the largest short interest, and a variety of other charts of interest to technicians.

http://www.equis.com/ A Reuters company, Equis sells software used by market technicians. Their web site contains links to free downloads, education, and information about technical analysis.

http://www.investools.com The INVESTools home page offers news, reports, data, links to a variety of charts, investment newsletter links, and insights from featured advisors.

http://www.esignal.com It has information about equity securities, news, research resources, and market updates on indexes, options, and earnings; offers technical charting.

http://www.bocm.com/ A number of investment and banking firms offering technical analysis research and services. BankOne Capital Markets' page includes links to technical analyses of international markets as well as analysis and forecasts for equity and fixed income markets.

http://www.dailystocks.com This site contains information of interest to both technicians and fundamentalists. It has several stock screening features, market commentary sources, and information on earnings, insider trading, and many more links.

Summary

- Whether you want to base your investment decisions on fundamental analysis, technical analysis, or a belief in efficient markets, you should be aware of the principles and practice of technical analysis. Numerous investors believe in and use technical analysis, the large investment houses provide extensive support for technical analysis, and a large proportion of the discussion related to securities markets in the media is based on a technical view of the market. Now that you are aware of technical analysis principles, techniques, and indicators, you will recognize this tendency of security market commentators.
- Two main differences separate technical analysts and efficient market advocates. First is the information dissemination process—that is, does everybody get the information at about the same time? Second, how quickly do investors adjust security prices to reflect new information? Technical analysts believe that news takes time to travel from the insider and expert to the individual investor. They also believe that price adjustments are not instantaneous. As a result, they contend that security prices move in trends that persist and, therefore, past price trends and volume information along with other market indicators can help you determine future price trends.
- We discussed technical trading rules under four general categories: contrary-opinion rules, follow-the-smart-money tactics, other market indicators, and stock price and volume techniques. These techniques and trading rules also can be applied to foreign markets and to the analysis of currency exchange rates, and can be used to determine the prevailing sentiment in the bond market.
- Most technicians follow several indicators and attempt to derive a cosensus decision to buy, sell, or do nothing.[6]

---

[6]An analysis using numerous indicators is Jerome Baesel, George Shows, and Edward Thorp, "Can Joe Granville Time the Market?" *Journal of Portfolio Management* 8, no. 3 (Spring 1982): 5–9.

Questions
1. Technical analysts believe that investors can use past price changes to predict future price changes. How do they justify this belief?
2. Technicians contend that stock prices move in trends that persist for long periods of time. What do technicians believe happens in the real world to cause these trends?
3. Briefly discuss the problems related to fundamental analysis that are considered advantages for technical analysis.
4. Discuss some disadvantages of technical analysis.
5. If the mutual fund cash position were to increase close to 10 percent, would a technician consider this cash position bullish or bearish? Give two reasons why the technical analyst would think this way.
6. Assume a significant decline in credit balances at brokerage firms. Discuss why a technician would consider this bearish.
7. If the bearish sentiment index of advisory service opinions were to increase to 61 percent, discuss why a technician would consider this bullish or bearish.
8. Why is an increase in debit balances considered bullish?
9. Describe the Dow Theory and its three components. Which component is most important? What is the reason for an intermediate reversal?
10. Describe a bearish price and volume pattern, and discuss why it is considered bearish.
11. Discuss the logic behind the breadth of market index. How is it used to identify a peak in stock prices?
12. During a 10-day trading period, the cumulative net advance series goes from 1,572 to 1,053. During this same period of time, the DJIA goes from 11,200 to 12,100. As a technician, discuss what this set of events would mean to you.
13. Explain the reasoning behind a support level and a resistance level.
14. What is the purpose of computing a moving-average line for a stock? Describe a bullish pattern using a 50-day moving-average line and the stock volume of trading. Discuss why this pattern is considered bullish.
15. Assuming a stock price and volume chart that also contains a 50-day and a 200-day MA line, describe a bearish pattern with the two MA lines and discuss why it is bearish.
16. Explain how you would construct a relative-strength series for an individual stock or an industry group. What would it mean to say a stock experienced good relative strength during a bear market?
17. Discuss why most technicians follow several technical rules and attempt to derive a consensus.

Problems
1. Select a stock on the NYSE and construct a daily high, low, and close bar chart for it that includes its volume of trading for 10 trading days.
2. Compute the relative-strength ratio for the stock in Problem 1 relative to the S&P 500 Index. Prepare a table that includes all the data and indicates the computations as follows:

	CLOSING PRICE		RELATIVE-STRENGTH RATIO
Day	Stock	S&P 500	Stock Price/S&P 500

3. Plot the relative-strength ratio computed in Problem 2 on your bar chart. Discuss whether the stock's relative strength is bullish or bearish.
4. Currently, Charlotte Art Importers is selling at $32 per share. Although you are somewhat dubious about technical analysis, you want to know how technicians who use point-and-figure charts would

view this stock. You decide to note one-point movements and three-point reversals. You gather the following historical price information:

Date	Price	Date	Price	Date	Price
4/1	23 ½	4/18	33	5/3	27
4/4	28 ½	4/19	35 ⅜	5/4	26 ½
4/5	28	4/20	37	5/5	28
4/6	28	4/21	38 ½	5/6	28 ¼
4/7	29 ¾	4/22	36	5/9	28 ⅛
4/8	30 ½	4/25	35	5/10	28 ¼
4/11	30 ½	4/26	34 ¼	5/11	29 ⅛
4/12	32 ⅛	4/27	33 ⅛	5/12	30 ¼
4/13	32	4/28	32 ⅞	5/13	29 ⅞

Plot the point-and-figure chart using Xs for uptrends and Os for downtrends. How would a technician evaluate these movements? Discuss why you would expect a technician to buy, sell, or hold the stock based on this chart.

5. Assume the following daily closings for the Dow Jones Industrial Average:

Day	DJIA	Day	DJIA
1	12,010	7	12,220
2	12,100	8	12,130
3	12,165	9	12,250
4	12,080	10	12,315
5	12,070	11	12,240
6	12,150	12	12,310

a. Calculate a four-day moving average for Days 4 through 12.
b. Assume that the index on Day 13 closes at 12,300. Would this signal a buy or sell decision?

6. The cumulative advance-decline line reported in *Barron's* at the end of the month is 21,240. During the first week of the following month, the daily report for the *Exchange* is as follows:

	DAY				
	1	**2**	**3**	**4**	**5**
Issues traded	3,544	3,533	3,540	3,531	3,521
Advances	1,737	1,579	1,759	1,217	1,326
Declines	1,289	1,484	1,240	1,716	1,519
Unchanged	518	470	541	598	596

a. Compute the daily net advance-decline line for each of the five days.
b. Compute the cumulative advance-decline line for each day and the final value at the end of the week.

References

Benning, Carl J. "Prediction Skills of Real-World Market Timers," *The Journal of Portfolio Management* 23, no. 2 (Winter 1997).

Blume, Lawrence, David Easley, and Maureen O'Hara. "Market Statistics and Technical Analysis: The Role of Volume." *Journal of Finance* 49, no. 1 (March 1994).

Brown, David P., and Robert H. Jennings. "On Technical Analysis." *The Review of Financial Studies* 2, no. 4 (October 1989).

Colby, Robert W., and Thomas A. Mayers. *The Encyclopedia of Technical Market Indicators.* Homewood, Ill: Dow Jones–Irwin, 1988.

DeMark, Thomas R. *The New Science of Technical Analysis.* New York: John wiley & Sons, 1999.

Edwards, R. D., and John Magee, Jr. *Technical Analysis of Stock Trends,* 6th ed. Boston, Mass.: New York Institute of Finance, 1992.

Farinella, Joseph A., Edward Graham, and Cynthia McDonald. "Does High Short Interest Lead Underperformance?" *Journal of Investing* 10, no. 2 (Summer 2001).

Jagadeesh, Narasimhan. "Evidence of Predictable Behavior of Security Returns." *Journal of Finance* 45, no. 3 (July 1990).

Lo, Andrew W., Harry Mamasky, and Jiang Wang. "Foundations of Technical Analysis: Computational Algorithms, Statistical Inference, and Empirical Implementation." *Journal of Finance* 55, no. 4 (August 2000).

Lo, Andrew W., and A. Craig MacKinley. *A Non-Random Walk Down Wall Street* (Princeton, N.J.: Princeton University Press, 1999).

Meyers, Thomas A. *The Technical Analysis Course.* Chicago: Probus, 1989.

Pring, Martin J. *Technical Analysis Explained,* 3d ed. New York: McGraw-Hill, 1991.

Pruitt Stephen, and Robert White. "The CRISMA Trading System: Who Says Technical Analysis Can't Beat the Market?" *Journal of Portfolio Management* 14, no. 3 (Spring 1988).

Shaw, Alan R. "Market Timing and Technical Analysis." In *The Financial Analysts Handbook,* 2d ed., edited by Sumner N. Levine. Homewood, Ill.: Dow Jones–Irwin, 1988.

Sweeney, Richard J. "Some New Filter Rule Tests: Methods and Results." *Journal of Financial and Quantitative Analysis* 23, no. 3 (September 1988).

Zweig, Martin E. *Winning on Wall Street.* New York: Warner Books, 1986.

Chapter 17 ▶ Equity Portfolio Management Strategies

After you read this chapter, you should be able to answer the following questions:

➤ What are the two generic equity portfolio management styles?
➤ What are three techniques for constructing a passive index portfolio?
➤ How does the goal of a passive equity portfolio manager differ from the goal of an active manager?
➤ What is a portfolio's tracking error and how is it useful in the construction of a passive equity investment?
➤ What is the difference between an index mutual fund and an exchange-traded fund?
➤ What are the three themes that active equity portfolio managers can use?
➤ What stock characteristics differentiate value-oriented and growth-oriented investment styles?
➤ What is style analysis and what does it indicate about a manager's investment performance?
➤ What techniques are used by active managers in an attempt to outperform their benchmark?
➤ What are the differences between the integrated, strategic, tactical, and insured approaches to asset allocation?
➤ How can futures and options be used to help manage an equity portfolio?

Recent chapters have reviewed how to analyze industries and companies, how to estimate a stock's intrinsic value, and how technical analysis can assist in stockpicking. Some equity portfolios are constructed one stock at a time. Research staffs analyze the economy, industries, and companies; evaluate firms' strategies and competitive advantages; and recommend individual stocks for purchase or for sale.

Other equity portfolios are constructed using computer-intensive, rather than analyst-intensive, methods. Computers analyze relationships between stocks and market sectors to identify undervalued stocks. Quantitative "screens" and factor models are used to construct portfolios of stocks with such attributes as low *P/E* ratios, low price/book ratios, small capitalization, or high dividend yield; those neglected by analysts; or stocks whose returns are strongly correlated with economic variables, such as interest rates. Computer programs detect trading patterns and place buy-and-sell orders depending on past price movements. Computers also examine pricing relationships between the stock, options, and futures markets and place orders across these markets to arbitrage small price differences.

Managers of equity portfolios do not need to focus on the security selection process to produce superior investment returns. They can also increase an investor's wealth through their asset allocation decisions. For example, a manager acting as a market timer might split his funds into two index portfolios—one containing stocks and the other containing bonds—and then shift the allocation between these portfolios depending on which asset class he believes will perform the best during the coming period. The benefit of this strategy, which is formally known as *tactical* asset allocation, comes from correctly predicting broad market movements rather than trends for individual companies. Similarly, *insured* asset allocation is an attempt to limit investment losses by shifting funds between an existing equity portfolio and a risk-free security depending on changing market conditions.

Finally, equity portfolio return profiles can be modified by the use of futures and options. It is possible to trade futures contracts on major indexes, as well as acquire options on stock market indexes, on selected industry groups, and on individual stocks. These derivative securities can assist the portfolio manager in shifting a portfolio's exposure to systematic and unsystematic risk.

PASSIVE VERSUS ACTIVE MANAGEMENT

Equity portfolio management styles fall into either a passive or an active category. Unlike the immunization of bond portfolios, no middle ground exists between active and passive equity management strategies. Some argue that "hybrid" active/passive equity portfolio management styles exist (e.g. enhanced indexing), but such styles really are variations of active management philosophies. Similar to traditional active management, hybrid-style managers invest to find undervalued sectors or securities. The following discussion reviews the traditional meaning of the terms *passive* and *active* portfolio management.

Passive equity portfolio management is a long-term buy-and-hold strategy. Usually, stocks are purchased so the portfolio's returns will track those of an index over time. Because of the goal of tracking an index, this approach to investing is generally referred to as *indexing*. Occasional rebalancing is needed as dividends must be reinvested and because stocks merge or drop out of the target index and other stocks are added. Notably, the purpose of an indexed portfolio is not to "beat" the target index but to match its performance. A manager of an equity index portfolio is judged on how well he or she tracks the target index—that is, minimizes the deviation between portfolio and index returns similar to the bond index portfolio manager.

Active equity portfolio management is an attempt by the manager to outperform, on a risk-adjusted basis, a passive benchmark portfolio. A *benchmark portfolio* is a passive portfolio whose average characteristics (including such factors as beta, dividend yield, industry weighting, and firm size) match the risk-return objectives of the client.

When deciding whether to follow an active or a passive strategy (or some combination of the two), an investor must assess the trade-off between the low-cost but less-exciting alternative of indexing versus the higher-cost but potentially more lucrative alternative of active management. Not surprisingly, Sorensen, Miller, and Samak have noted that the critical factor in this evaluation is the stockpicking skill of the portfolio manager. Using pension fund performance data from the 1985–1997 period, they showed that the optimal allocation to indexing declines as managerial skill increases. However, they also conclude that some indexing is appropriate for funds in most risk objective classes.[1]

Exhibit 17.1 reports the amount of money invested in the U.S. equity and fixed-income markets using active and indexed strategies for two recent years. The data are compiled from a survey of the strategies employed by more than 2,500 professional money management firms on behalf of their clients. Three conclusions are notable. First, active management strategies dominate indexed portfolios in terms of the total amount of money controlled by the investment management industry. Second, the indexed sector of the industry is growing quite rapidly, a trend driven in part by the lower management fees charged for passive portfolios. Third, although the

---

[1]Eric H. Sorensen, Keith L. Miller, and Vele Samak, "Allocating between Active and Passive Management," *Financial Analysts Journal* 54, no. 4 (September/October 1998): 18–31.

ACTIVE AND PASSIVE INVESTMENT IN THE U.S. EQUITY AND FIXED-INCOME MARKETS

STRATEGY	1995 (BILLIONS)	1994 (BILLIONS)	% CHANGE
Active equity	$1,945.10	$1,338.01	45.4
Indexed equity	275.22	135.54	103.1
Active fixed income	1,677.45	1,370.63	22.4
Indexed fixed income	82.73	32.69	153.3

Source: Nelson Investment Management Network.

amount of money managed in active equity and fixed-income strategies is roughly comparable, equity indexing is far more popular than fixed-income indexing.

In the following sections, we examine more closely the mechanics of passive and active equity portfolio management.

AN OVERVIEW OF PASSIVE EQUITY PORTFOLIO MANAGEMENT STRATEGIES

Passive equity portfolio management attempts to design a portfolio to replicate the performance of a specific index. The key word here is *replicate*. As discussed in Chapter 2, the portfolio manager who earns higher returns by violating the client's policy statement should be fired; a passive manager who isn't really passive should likewise be dismissed. A passive manager earns his or her fee by constructing a portfolio that closely tracks the performance of a specified equity index (referred to as the *benchmark index*) that meets the client's needs and objectives. If the manager attempts to outperform the index selected, he or she violates the passive premise of the portfolio.

In Chapter 6, we presented several reasons for investing in a passive equity portfolio. Strong evidence indicates that the stock market is fairly efficient. For most active managers, the costs of actively managing a portfolio (1 to 2 percent of the portfolio's assets) are difficult to overcome. As we saw earlier, the S&P 500 index typically outperforms most equity mutual funds on an annual basis. Note that, although the S&P 500 is the most popular index to track, a client can choose from among about 30 different indexes.[2]

Chapter 5 contained a summary description of many different market indexes. Domestic U.S. equity indexes include the S&P 500, Industrials, and 100; the Major Market index; the Nasdaq composite index; and the Wilshire 5000. *The Wall Street Journal* publishes the daily values of indexes for the organized exchanges, the OTC market, and various industry groups. Indexes exist for small capitalization stocks (Russell 2000); for value- or growth-oriented stocks (Russell Growth index and the Russell Value index); and for numerous world regions (such as the EAFE index); as well as for smaller regions, individual countries, and types of countries (emerging markets). As passive investing has grown in popularity, money managers have created an index fund for virtually every broad market category.[3]

---

[2]The growing popularity of index funds is discussed in Jeffrey M. Laderman, "The Stampede to Index Funds," *Business Week,* 1 April 1996, 78–79.

[3]See, for example, Robert Fernholz, Robert Garvy, and John Hannon, "Diversity-Weighted Indexing," *Journal of Portfolio Management* 24, no. 2 (Winter 1998): 74–82; and Ajay Khorana, Edward Nelling, and Jeffrey J. Trester, "The Emergence of Country Index Funds," *Journal of Portfolio Management* 24, no. 4 (Summer 1998): 78–84.

The goal of a passive portfolio is to match the returns to the index as closely as possible; but, because of cash inflows and outflows and company mergers and bankruptcies, securities must be bought and sold, which means that there inevitably will be differences between portfolio and benchmark returns over time. In addition, even though index funds generally attempt to minimize turnover and the resultant transactions fees, they necessarily have to do some rebalancing, which means that the long-run return performance of index funds will lag the benchmark index. Certainly, substantial or prolonged deviations of the portfolio's returns from the index's returns would be a cause for concern.

Index Portfolio Construction Techniques

There are three basic techniques for constructing a passive index portfolio: full replication, sampling, and quadratic optimization or programming. The most obvious technique is **full replication**, wherein all the securities in the index are purchased in proportion to their weights in the index. This technique helps ensure close tracking, but it may be suboptimal for two reasons. First, the need to buy many securities will increase transaction costs that will detract from performance. Second, the reinvestment of dividends will also result in high commissions when many firms pay small dividends at different times in the year.

The second technique, **sampling**, addresses the problem of numerous stock issues. Statistical theory teaches us that we don't need to ask everyone in the United States for his or her opinion to determine who may win an election. Thus, opinion pollsters query only a small sample of the population to gauge public sentiment. Sampling techniques also can be applied to passive portfolio management. With sampling, a portfolio manager would only need to buy a representative sample of stocks that comprise the benchmark index. Stocks with larger index weights are purchased according to their weight in the index; smaller issues are purchased so their aggregate characteristics (e.g., beta, industry distribution, and dividend yield) approximate the underlying benchmark. With fewer stocks to purchase, larger positions can be taken in the issues acquired, which should lead to proportionately lower commissions. Further, the reinvestment of dividend cash flows will be less problematic because fewer securities need to be purchased to rebalance the portfolio. The disadvantage of sampling is that portfolio returns will almost certainly not track the returns for the benchmark index as closely as with full replication.

Rather than obtaining a sample based on industry or security characteristics, **quadratic optimization** or programming techniques can be used to construct a passive portfolio. With quadratic programming, historical information on price changes and correlations between securities are input to a computer program that determines the composition of a portfolio that will minimize tracking error with the benchmark. A problem with this technique is that it relies on *historical* price changes and correlations, and, if these factors change over time, the portfolio may experience very large tracking errors.

Some passive portfolios are not based on a published index. Sometimes customized passive portfolios, called **completeness funds**, are constructed to complement active portfolios that do not cover the entire market. For example, a large pension fund may allocate some of its holdings to active managers expected to outperform the market. Many times, these active portfolios are overweighted in certain market sectors or stock types. In this case, the pension fund sponsor may want the remaining funds to be invested passively to "fill the holes" left vacant by the active managers. The performance of the completeness fund will be compared to a customized benchmark that incorporates the characteristics of the stocks not covered by the active managers.

For example, suppose a pension fund hires three active managers to invest part of the fund's money. One manager emphasizes small-capitalization U.S. stocks, the second invests only in Pacific Rim countries, and the third invests in U.S. stocks with low *P/E* ratios. To ensure adequate diversification, the pension fund may want to passively invest the remaining assets in a completeness fund that will have a customized benchmark that includes large- and mid-capitalization U.S. stocks, U.S. stocks with normal to high *P/E* ratios, and international stocks outside the Pacific Rim.

Still other passive portfolios and benchmarks exist for investors with certain unique needs and preferences.[4] Some investors may want their funds to be invested only in stocks that pay dividends or in a company that produces a product or service that the investor deems socially responsible. Benchmarks can be produced that reflect these desired attributes, and passive portfolios can be constructed to track the performance of the customized benchmark over time so investors' special needs can be satisfied.[5]

Tracking Error and Index Portfolio Construction

If the goal of forming a passive portfolio is to replicate the essence of a particular equity index, the success of constructing such an investment fund lies not in the absolute returns it produces but, rather, in how closely its returns match those of the benchmark (e.g., the Standard & Poor's 500 index). That is, the goal of the passive manager should be to minimize the portfolio's return volatility relative to the benchmark. Said differently, the manager should try to minimize **tracking error**.

Tracking error can be defined as the extent to which return fluctuations in the managed portfolio are *not correlated* with return fluctuations in the benchmark. A flexible and straightforward way of measuring tracking error can be developed as follows. Recalling the notation from Chapter 7, let

W_i = **investment weight of asset** i **in the managed portfolio**
R_{it} = **return to asset** i **in period** t
R_{bt} = **return to the benchmark portfolio in period** t

With these definitions, we can define the Period t return to managed portfolio as

$$R_{pt} = \sum_{i=1}^{N} w_i R_{it}$$

where:

N = **number of assets in the managed portfolio**

With these definitions, we can then specify the Period t *return differential* between the managed portfolio and the benchmark as

➤17.1
$$\Delta_t = \sum_{i=1}^{N} w_i R_{it} - R_{bt} = R_{pt} - R_{bt}$$

Notice that, given the returns to the N assets in the managed portfolio and the benchmark, Δ is a function of the investment weights that the manager selects and that not all of the assets in the benchmark need be included in the managed portfolio (i.e., $w = 0$ for some assets).

---

[4]Recall our discussion in Chapter 2 on investors' objectives and constraints; two of the constraints were legal and regulatory requirements and unique needs and preferences.

[5]See Sharmin Mossavar-Rahmani, "Customized Benchmarks in Structured Management," *Journal of Portfolio Management* 13, no. 4 (summer 1988): 65–68; and Chris P. Dialynas, "The Active Decisions in the Selection of Passive Management and Performance Bogeys," in *The Handbook of Fixed Income Securities,* 5th ed., ed. Frank Fabozzi (Chicago, Ill.: Irwin Professional Publishing, 1997).

For a sample of T return observations, the variance of Δ can be calculated as follows:

➤ 17.2
$$\sigma_\Delta^2 = \frac{\sum_{t=1}^{T}(\Delta_t - \overline{\Delta})^2}{(T-1)}$$

Finally, the standard deviation of the return differential is

$$\sigma_\Delta = \sqrt{\sigma_\Delta^2} = \text{periodic tracking error}$$

so that *annualized tracking error (TE)* can be calculated as

➤ 17.3
$$TE = \sigma_\Delta \sqrt{P}$$

where P is the number of return periods in a year (e.g., $P = 12$ for monthly returns, $P = 252$ for daily returns).

Suppose an investor has formed a portfolio designed to track a particular benchmark. Over the last eight quarters, the returns to this portfolio, as well as the index returns and the return difference between the two, were:

PERIOD	MANAGER	INDEX	DIFFERENCE (Δ)
1	2.3%	2.7%	–0.4%
2	–3.6	–4.6	1.0
3	11.2	10.1	1.1
4	1.2	2.2	–1.0
5	1.5	0.4	1.1
6	3.2	2.8	0.5
7	8.9	8.1	0.8
8	–0.8	0.6	–1.6

The periodic average and standard deviation of the manager's return differential (i.e., "delta") relative to the benchmark are

$$\text{Average } \Delta = [-0.4 + 1.0 + \ldots + 0.8 - 1.6] \div 10 = 0.2\%$$
$$\sigma_\Delta = \sqrt{(-0.4 - 0.2)^2 + (1.0 - 0.2)^2 + \ldots + (-1.6 - 0.2)^2} \div (10-1) = 1.0\%$$

Thus, the manager's annualized tracking error for this two-year period is 2.0 percent (= 1.0 percent $\times \sqrt{4}$).

Generally speaking, there is an inverse relationship between a passive portfolio's tracking error relative to its index and the time and expense necessary to create and maintain the portfolio. For example, full replication of the S&P 500 would have virtually no tracking error but would necessitate positions in 500 different stocks and require frequent rebalancing. As smaller samples are used to replicate the S&P index's return performance, the expense of forming the managed portfolio would decline but the potential tracking error is likely to increase. Thus, the art of being a manager of a passive equity portfolio lies in balancing the costs (larger tracking error) and the benefits (easier management, lower trading commissions) of using smaller samples. Exhibit 17.2 estimates the tracking error that occurs from such sampling.

EXHIBIT 17.2

EXPECTED TRACKING ERROR BETWEEN THE S&P 500 INDEX AND PORTFOLIOS COMPRISED OF SAMPLES OF FEWER THAN 500 STOCKS

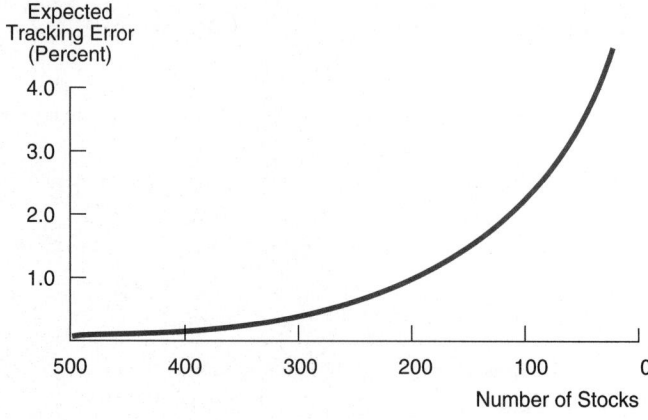

Methods of Index Portfolio Investing

Although investors can construct their own passive investment portfolios that mimic a particular equity index, there are at least two "pre-packaged" ways of accomplishing this goal that are typically more convenient and less expensive for the small investor. These are (1) buying shares in an *index mutual fund* or (2) buying shares in an *exchange-traded fund* (ETF).

Index Funds   As we discuss in Chapter 25, mutual funds represent established security portfolios managed by professional investment companies (e.g., Fidelity, Vanguard, Putnam, AIM) in which investors can participate. The investment company is responsible for deciding how the fund is managed. For an indexed portfolio, the fund manager will typically attempt to replicate the composition of the particular index exactly, meaning that he or she will buy the exact securities comprising the index in their exact weights and then alter those positions anytime the composition of the index itself is changed. Since changes to most equity indexes occur infrequently, index funds tend to generate low trading and management expense ratios. A prominent example of an index fund is Vanguard's 500 Index Fund (VFINX), which is designed to mimic the S&P 500 index. Exhibit 17.3 provides a descriptive overview of this fund and indicates that its historical return performance is virtually indistinguishable from that of the benchmark.

The advantage of index mutual funds is that they provide an inexpensive way for investors to acquire a diversified portfolio that emphasizes the desired market or industry within the context of a traditional money management product. As with any mutual fund, the disadvantages are that investors can only liquidate their positions at the end of the trading day (i.e., no intraday trading), usually cannot short sell, and may have unwanted tax repercussions if the fund has an unforeseen need to sell a portion of its holdings, thereby realizing capital gains.

Exchange-Traded Funds   ETFs are a more recent development in the world of indexed investment products than index mutual funds. Essentially, ETFs are depository receipts that give investors a pro rata claim on the capital gains and cash flows of the securities that are held in deposit by the financial institution that issued the certificates. That is, a portfolio of securities is placed on deposit at a financial institution or into a unit trust, which then issues a single type of certificate representing ownership of the underlying portfolio. In that way, ETFs are similar to the American depository receipts (ADRs) described in Chapter 3.

EXHIBIT 17.3 ▶ *DETAILS OF THE VANGUARD 500 INDEX TRUST MUTUAL FUND*

A. Description

VANGUARD 500 INDEX FUND–INV   **OBJECTIVE–INDEX FUND–LARGE CAP**

Vanguard 500 Index Fund is an open-end fund incorporated in the United States. The Fund's objective is to match the performance of the Standard & Poor's 500 Index, which is dominated by the stocks of large U.S. companies. The Fund invests all or substantially all of its assets in the stocks that make up the Index.

BLOOMBERG CLASSIFICATION DATA

Asset Class	Equity
Style	Index Fund
Market Cap Focus	Large Cap
Geographic Focus	U.S.

CURRENT/OPERATIONAL DATA

1) GP NAV		$ 105.85
Assets(mil)	12/31/01	$ 86,000.00
Inception Date	8/31/76	

1 Yr Performance vs. Benchmark Indexes

PERFORMANCE RANKING

AS OF 3/28/02		RETURN	%ALL	%OBJ
3) TRA	1 Month	3.74	51	72
	YTD	.24	50	86
	1 Year	.69	39	86
	5 Year	9.64	81	91
	2001	−12.02	34	86

B. Historical Returns

CURRENT			RETURN			PERCENTILE	
AS OF 3/28/02		FUND	SPX	DIFFERENCE		ALL	OBJECTIVE
3) TRA	1 Week	−.53	−.52	−.01		24	59
	1 Month	3.74	3.76	−.02		51	72
	3 Month	−.88	−.84	−.04		31	84
4) COMP	YTD	.24	.27	−.03		50	86
	1 Year	.69	.87	−.18		39	86
	3 Year	−2.47	−2.43	−.04		19	84
9) HRH	5 Year	9.64	9.68	−.04		81	91
	HISTORICAL	FUND	SPX	DIFFERENCE		ALL	OBJECTIVE
	2001	−12.02	−11.89	−.13		34	86
	2000	−9.06	−9.10	.04		27	87
	1999	21.07	21.04	.03		68	92
	1998	28.61	28.58	.03		92	81
	1997	33.21	33.38	−.17		95	88
	1996	22.86	22.96	−.10		89	89
	1995	37.45	37.62	−.17		94	89
	1994	1.18	1.33	−.15		86	74
	1993	9.89	10.06	−.17		33	82
	1992	7.45	7.62	−.17		48	n.a.

There are several notable example of ETFs, including (1) Standard & Poor's 500 Depository Receipts (SPDRs or "spider" as they are sometimes called), which are based on a basket of all the securities held in that index; (2) iShares, which recreate indexed positions in several global developed and emerging equity markets, including countries such as Australia, Mexico, Malaysia, the United Kingdom, France, Germany, Japan, and China; and (3) sector ETFs, which invest in baskets of stocks from specific industry sectors, including consumer services, industrial, technology, financial services, energy, utilities, and cyclicals/transportation. Exhibit 17.4 shows descriptive and return data for the SPDR Trust certificates. Notice once again how closely the returns to these shares track the overall index.

A significant advantage of ETFs over index mutual funds is that they can be bought and sold (and short sold) like common stock through an organized exchange or in an over-the-counter market. Further, they are backed by a sponsoring organization (e.g., for SPDRs, the sponsor is PDR Services LLC, a limited liability company whose sole member is the American Stock Exchange where SPDR shares trade) who can alter the composition of the underlying portfolio to reflect changes in the composition of the index. Other advantages relative to index funds include no payment of a management fee, the ability for continuous trading while markets are open, and the ability to time capital gain tax realizations. ETF disadvantages include the brokerage commission and the inability to reinvest dividends except on a quarterly basis.

AN OVERVIEW OF ACTIVE EQUITY PORTFOLIO MANAGEMENT STRATEGIES

The goal of active equity management is to earn a portfolio return that exceeds the return of a passive benchmark portfolio, net of transaction costs, on a risk-adjusted basis. The job of an active equity manager is not easy. If transaction costs and fees total 1.5 percent of the portfolio's assets annually, the portfolio has to earn a return 1.5 percentage points above the passive benchmark just to keep pace with it. Further, if the manager's strategy involves overweighting specific market sectors in anticipation of price increases, the risk of the active portfolio may well exceed that of the passive benchmark, so the active portfolio's return will have to exceed the benchmark by an even wider margin to compensate for its higher risk.

Exhibit 17.5 provides a broad overview of the different strategies that investment managers might adopt in forming their portfolios, as well as the investment "philosophy" that underlies each strategy. Notice, first of all, that the passive strategies we just considered are based (at least implicitly) on the notion that capital markets are efficient and so equity portfolios should be invested to mimic broad indexes and not traded actively. The realm of active management, however, is one in which managers are effectively "betting" against markets being perfectly efficient. For convenience, Exhibit 17.5 characterizes these bets as falling into three general categories: (1) fundamental, (2) technical, and (3) market anomalies and security attributes.

Fundamental Strategies

As we saw in Chapter 11, the three-step investment process begins at the top with an analysis of broad country and asset class allocations and progresses down through sector allocation decisions to the bottom level where individual securites are selected. The alternative to this "top-down" approach to investing was a "bottom-up" process that simply emphasized the selection of securities without any initial market or sector analysis. In similar fashion, active equity management based on fundamental analysis can start from either direction, depending on what exactly the manager thinks is mispriced relative to his or her valuation models. Generally, active managers use three generic themes in an attempt to add value to their portfolios relative to the benchmark. First, they can try to time the equity market by shifting funds into and out of stocks, bonds, and T-bills depending on broad market forecasts and estimated risk premiums. Second, they can shift funds among different equity sectors and industries (e.g., financial stocks, technology

EXHIBIT 17.4 ▶ *DETAILS OF THE SPDR EXCHANGE-TRADED FUND*

A. Description

SPDR TRUST SERIES 1   **OBJECTIVE—INDEX FUND—LARGE CAP**

SPDR Trust Series 1 issues exchange-traded funds called Standard & Poor's Depositary Receipts or "SPDRs." The SPDR Trust holds all of the common stocks of the Standard & Poor's 500 Composite Stock Price Index and is intended to provide investment results that, before expenses, generally correspond to the price and yield performance of the S&P 500 Index.

BLOOMBERG CLASSIFICATION DATA

Asset Class	Equity	Style	Index Fund
Market Cap Focus	Large Cap	Geographic Focus	U.S.

CURRENT DATA

Underlying Index	12) SPX		
1) GP	Price		$114.52
	52Wk Hi	5/22	$132.090
	52Wk Lo	9/21	$ 93.800
	NAV	3/28	$114.72
	INAV		$115.00
%Premium		n.a.	
Shares Out (×000)	3/28/02	250783.0	
Market cap(mil)		$28719.67	

1 Yr Performance vs. Benchmark Indexes

SPDRs are designed to provide a security whose market value approximates 1/10 the value of the underlying S&P 500 Index.

B. Historical Returns

CURRENT				RETURN		PERCENTILE	
AS OF 3/28/02		FUND	SPX	DIFFERENCE		ALL	OBJECTIVE
3) TRA	1 Week	−.67	−.52	−.15		31	50
	1 Month	3.32	3.76	−.44		68	30
	3 Month	−1.00	−.84	−.16		22	52
4) COMP	YTD	.48	.27	.21		39	54
	1 Year	.84	.87	−.03		25	56
	3 Year	−2.66	−2.43	−.23		11	16
9) HRH	5 Year	9.59	9.68	−.09		82	n.a.
	HISTORICAL	FUND	SPX	DIFFERENCE		ALL	OBJECTIVE
	2001	−11.75	−11.89	.14		22	62
	2000	−9.73	−9.10	−.63		17	42
	1999	20.39	21.04	−.65		80	54
	1998	28.69	28.58	.11		94	n.a.
	1997	33.48	33.38	.10		90	n.a.
	1996	22.55	22.96	−.41		87	n.a.
	1995	38.05	37.62	.43		94	n.a.
	1994	.40	1.33	−.93		95	n.a.
	1993	n.a.	10.06	n.a.		n.a.	n.a.
	1992	n.a.	7.62	n.a.		n.a.	n.a.

EXHIBIT 17.5 ▸ *EQUITY PORTFOLIO INVESTMENT PHILOSOPHIES AND STRATEGIES*

Passive Management Strategies

1. EFFICIENT MARKETS HYPOTHESIS

Buy and hold

Indexing

Active Management Strategies

2. FUNDAMENTAL ANALYSIS

"Top down" (e.g., asset class rotation, sector rotation)

"Bottom up" (e.g., stock undervaluation/overvaluation)

3. TECHNICAL ANALYSIS

Contrarian (e.g., overreaction)

Continuation (e.g., price momentum)

4. ANOMALIES AND ATTRIBUTES

Calendar effects (e.g. weekend, January)

Security characteristics (e.g., *P/E, P/B,* earnings momentum, firm size)

Investment style (e.g., value, growth)

---

stocks, consumer cyclicals, durable goods) or among investment styles (e.g., large capitalization, small capitalization, value, growth) to catch the next "hot" concept before the rest of the market does. Third, equity managers can do stockpicking, looking at individual issues in an attempt to find undervalued stocks—that is, to buy low and sell high.

An asset class rotation strategy is one that shifts funds in and out of the stock market depending on the manager's perception of how the stock market is valued compared to the various alternative asset classes. Formally, such a strategy is called **tactical asset allocation** and will be described in more detail later in the chapter. Alternatively, a **sector rotation strategy** involves positioning the portfolio to take advantage of the market's next move. Often, this means emphasizing or overweighting (relative to the benchmark portfolio) certain economic sectors or industries in response to the next expected phase of the business cycle. Exhibit 17.6 contains suggestions on how sector rotators may position their portfolios to take advantage of stock market trends during the economic cycle.

In general, asset and sector rotation strategies can be extremely profitable but also very risky for a manager to follow. This is shown in Exhibit 17.7, which lists the annual returns in each of several asset and sector classes from 1981 to 2000. The chart documents the tremendous volatility that existed during this period. For instance, bonds, which was the best-performing asset class in 1990, was the next-to-worst class in the following year. Conversely, large-cap growth stocks were the single best place to invest funds for six years (i.e., 1994–1999) but this period was bracketed by years when this sector performed quite poorly. The message from this display is clear: While there are impressive gains to be made by correctly timing the "hottest" (or the "coldest") market sectors, a manager must be right substantially more than he or she is wrong. Because this is an extremely difficult thing to do consistently, many investors choose to interpret Exhibit 17.7 as ultimately extolling the virtue of asset and sector class diversification.

Finally, a fundamental stock-picker operating on a pure "bottom-up" basis will form a portfolio of equities that can be purchased at a substantial discount to what his or her valuation model indicates they are worth. As we discussed in Chapter 15, these valuation models might be based on absolute judgments about the future of the company (i.e., discounted cash flow) or relative

EXHIBIT 17.6   *THE STOCK MARKET AND THE BUSINESS CYCLE*

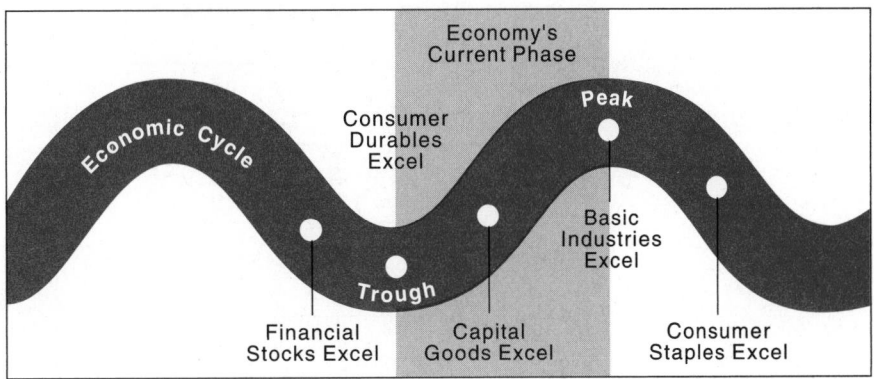

Source: Susan E. Kuhn, "Stocks Are Still Your Best Buy," *Fortune,* 21 March 1994, 140. © 1994 Time Inc. All Rights Reserved.

assessments of how attractive the stock is compared with shares in otherwise similar firms that might be acquired (i.e., relative price multiples). In either case, it is usually true that the active manager will find stockpicking to be a more reliable, although less profitable, way to add value to a client than through market timing.

Technical Strategies   In Chapter 16, we discussed the role that technical analysis plays in the stock evaluation process. As we saw, assessing past stock price trends in an effort to surmise what information they imply about future price movements was one of the primary tools of this analytical approach. Active managers can form equity portfolios on the basis of past stock price trends by assuming that one of two things will happen: (1) past stock price trends will continue in the same direction, or (2) they will reverse themselves.

A **contrarian** investment strategy is based on the belief that the best time to buy (sell) a stock is when the majority of other investors are the most bearish (bullish) about it. In this way, the contrarian investor will attempt to always purchase the stock when it is near its lowest price and sell it (or even short sell it) when it nears its peak. Implicit in this approach is the belief that stock returns are *mean reverting,* indicating that, over time, stocks will be priced so as to produce returns consistent with their risk-adjusted expected (i.e., mean) returns. DeBondt and Thaler demonstrated the potential benefits of forming active portfolios based on this notion.[6] Specifically, they showed that investing on an *overreaction hypothesis* could provide consistently superior returns. Exhibit 17.8 illustrates a summary of their experiment in which they measured returns to a portfolio of stocks that had had the worst market performance over the prior three years (i.e., "losers") and a portfolio of stocks with the best past performance (i.e., "winners"). If investors overreacted to either bad news or good news about companies, as DeBondt and Thaler contended, we should see subsequent abnormal returns move in the opposite direction. The cumulative abnormal returns (CARs) shown in the display appear to support this notion, although the evidence is stronger for losers than for winners.

[6]Werner F. M. DeBondt and Richard Thaler, "Does the Stock Market Overreact?" *Journal of Finance* 40, no. 3 (July 1985): 793–805.

EXHIBIT 17.7

ASSET AND SECTOR CLASS RETURN PERFORMANCE: 1981–2000

1981	1982	1983	1984	1985	1986	1987	1988	1989	1990	1991	1992	1993	1994	1995	1996	1997	1998	1999	2000
SV 14.85%	B 32.65%	SV 38.63%	B 15.15%	F 56.14%	F 69.46%	F 24.64%	SV 29.47%	LG 36.40%	B 8.96%	SG 51.18%	SV 29.15%	F 32.57%	F 7.78%	LG 38.13%	LG 23.97%	LG 36.52%	LG 42.16%	SG 43.09%	SV 22.83%
B 6.26%	SV 28.52%	S 29.13%	LV 10.52%	LG 33.31%	LV 21.67%	LG 6.50%	F 28.26%	L 31.69%	LG 0.20%	S 46.05%	S 18.42%	SV 23.86%	LG 3.14%	L 37.58%	L 22.96%	L 33.36%	L 28.58%	LG 28.25%	B 11.63%
S 2.03%	S 24.95%	LV 28.89%	F 7.41%	L 31.73%	L 18.67%	L 5.25%	S 24.89%	LV 26.13%	L -3.11%	SV 41.70%	LV 10.52%	S 18.89%	L 1.32%	LV 36.99%	LV 22.00%	SV 31.78%	LV 20.00%	F 26.96%	LV 6.08%
LV 0.02%	LV 22.03%	F 23.69%	L 6.27%	S 31.04%	B 15.30%	LV 3.68%	LV 21.67%	SG 20.16%	LV -6.85%	LG 38.37%	SG 7.77%	LV 18.61%	LV -0.64%	SG 31.04%	LG 21.37%	LV 29.98%	LV 14.69%	S 21.26%	S -3.02%
F -2.27%	L 21.55%	L 22.56%	LG 2.33%	SV 31.01%	LG 14.50%	B 2.75%	SG 20.38%	S 16.25%	SG -17.42%	L 30.47%	L 7.62%	SG 13.37%	SV -1.55%	S 28.44%	S 16.53%	S 22.36%	B 8.70%	L 21.04%	L -9.11%
L -4.92%	LV 21.04%	SG 20.14%	SV 2.27%	SG 30.97%	SV 7.41%	SV -7.12%	L 16.61%	B 14.53%	S -19.50%	LV 22.56%	B 7.40%	L 10.08%	S -1.81%	SV 25.75%	SG 11.32%	SG 12.93%	SG 1.23%	LV 12.72%	F -13.96%
SG -9.23%	SG 20.99%	LG 16.24%	S -7.13%	LV 29.68%	S 5.69%	S -8.76%	LG 11.95%	SV 12.43%	SV -21.77%	B 16.00%	LG 5.06%	B 9.75%	SG -2.44%	B 18.46%	F 6.05%	B 9.64%	S -2.25%	B -0.82%	LG -22.08%
LG -9.81%	F -1.86%	B 8.19%	SG -15.84%	B 22.13%	SG 3.59%	SG -10.48%	B 7.89%	F 10.53%	F -23.45%	F 12.14%	F -12.18%	LG 1.68%	B -2.92%	F 11.21%	B 3.64%	F 1.78%	F -6.46%	SV -1.48%	SG -22.43%

Legend: **L**   = *large stocks* (Standard & Poor's 500 Index)
LG = *large-growth stocks* (S&P 500/BARRA Growth Index)
LV = *large-value stocks* (S&P 500/BARRA Value Index)
S   = *small stocks* (Russell 2000 Index)
SG = *small-growth stocks* (Russell 2000 Growth Index)
SV = *small-value stocks* (Russell 2000 Value Index)
F   = *foreign stocks* (MSC EAFE Index)
B   = *bonds* (Lehman Brothers Aggregate Bond Index)

Source: Standard & Poor's, Franklin Templeton Investments.

EXHIBIT 17.8   *ABNORMAL RETURNS TO A MARKET OVERREACTION INVESTMENT STRATEGY*

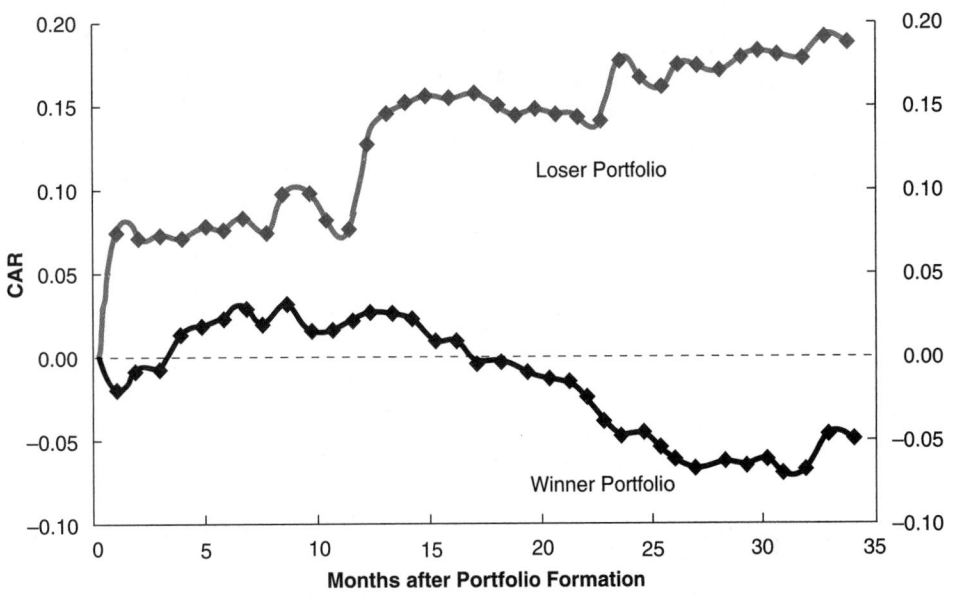

Source: Werner F. M. DeBondt and Richard Thaler, "Does the Stock Market Overreact?" *Journal of Finance* 40, no. 3 (July 1985): 793–805. Reprinted with permission of Blackwell Publishing.

At the other extreme, active portfolios can also be formed on the assumptions that recent trends in past prices will continue. A **price momentum** strategy, as it is more commonly called, assumes that stocks that have been hot will stay hot, while cold stocks will also remain so. Although there may well be sound economic reasons for these trends to continue (e.g., company revenues and earnings that continue to grow faster than expected), it may also simply be the case that investors periodically *underreact* to the arrival of new information. Thus, a pure price momentum strategy focuses just on the trend of past prices alone and makes purchase and sale decisions accordingly. Chan, Jegadeesh, and Lakonishok investigated the profitability of this approach. They divided all of the stocks traded in U.S. markets over the period 1994–1998 into 10 different portfolios based on their past six-month price movements and calculated returns over the following year.[7] Panel A of Exhibit 17.9 shows these annualized returns for each of the portfolios, from the one with the most positive past price trend (#10) to the worst price trend (#1). The data appear to justify the price momentum strategy in that the portfolios with the highest (lowest) level of price momentum generated the highest (lowest) subsequent returns. Also, the last column of the display shows that a momentum-based hedge fund that is long in the best-trend portfolio and short in the worst-trend one would also have been quite profitable.

Anomalies and Attributes   The price momentum strategies just discussed could either be based on pure price trend analysis or supported by the underlying economic fundamentals of the company. An **earnings momentum** strategy is a somewhat more formal active portfolio approach that purchases and

[7]Louis K. C. Chan, Narasimhan Jegadeesh, and Josef Lakonishok, "The Profitability of Momentum Strategies," *Financial Analysts Journal* 55, no. 6 (November/December 1999): 80–90.

EXHIBIT 17.9 ▶ *PROFITABILITY OF MOMENTUM STRATEGIES: 1994–1998*

	1 (LOW)	2	3	4	5	6	7	8	9	10 (HIGH)	10–1 (PPS)
A. Classification Based on Prior Six-Month Return											
1994	−12.00	−6.10	0.40	2.10	0.50	−0.90	−1.80	3.10	−4.50	−6.40	5.60
1995	35.70	27.40	32.30	35.00	32.30	32.20	30.30	36.70	35.30	42.10	6.40
1996	11.90	15.60	17.90	20.20	27.90	22.50	22.00	21.90	20.40	15.30	3.40
1997	7.20	05.70	14.80	20.80	26.60	32.80	35.60	37.30	37.50	23.80	16.60
1998	−2.30	−4.40	−7.00	−3.30	−0.40	0.00	04.50	0.10	−0.80	04.40	6.70
1994–98 average	8.10	7.64	11.68	14.96	17.38	17.32	18.12	19.82	17.58	15.84	7.74
B. Classification Based on Standardized Unexpected Earnings											
1994	−2.30	−2.40	−6.80	−1.00	−4.60	−1.20	−0.10	−3.30	0.90	−2.00	0.30
1995	36.70	25.40	27.80	31.00	33.40	27.50	36.10	36.90	38.60	40.60	3.90
1996	16.30	17.90	19.20	16.30	21.90	19.60	23.10	22.70	24.70	18.40	2.10
1997	25.50	21.70	23.50	22.80	24.10	24.50	25.20	28.40	29.60	28.10	2.60
1998	−3.20	−5.20	−1.30	04.40	−0.60	5.00	−0.10	−0.60	0.00	−6.20	−3.00
1994–98 average	14.60	11.48	12.48	14.70	14.84	15.08	16.84	16.82	18.76	15.78	1.18

holds stocks that have accelerating earnings and sells (or short sells) stocks with disappointing earnings. The notion behind this strategy is that, ultimately, a company's share price will follow the direction of its earnings, which is one "bottom line" measure of the firm's economic success. In judging the degree of momentum in a firm's earnings, it is often the case in practice that investors will compare the company's actual EPS to some level of what was expected. Two types of expected earnings are used most frequently: (1) those generated by a statistical model and (2) the consensus forecast of professional stock analysts. Panel B of Exhibit 17.9 shows that, over the 1994–1998 period, earnings momentum strategies were generally successful as well, although surprisingly not to the same degree as price momentum strategies.

In our examination of market efficiency in Chapter 6, we saw several anomalies that suggested a role for active equity management. Two of these—the weekend effect and the January effect—involved investing during particular times of the year. While conceptually viable, the limitations inherent in these anomalies do not produce particularly effective portfolio strategies. That is, managers investing in stocks only in January are not likely to be able to justify their annual fees, while the number of transactions implied by the weekend effect (i.e., buy every Monday, sell every Friday) generally makes for a cost-ineffective portfolio. Remember, however, that whether or not these calendar-related anomalies produce successful active portfolios, they still are useful rules for trades that an investor plans to make anyway.

A more promising approach to active anomaly investing involves forming portfolios based on various characteristics of the companies themselves. Two such characteristics we have seen to matter in the stock market are the total capitalization of the firm's outstanding equity (i.e., firm size) and the financial position of the firm, as indicated by its various financial ratios (e.g., *P/E, P/BV*). The studies we saw in Chapter 6 came to two general conclusions about these firm characteristics. First, over time, firms with smaller market capitalizations produce bigger risk-adjusted returns than those with large market capitalizations. Second, over time, firms with lower *P/E* and *P/BV* ratios produce bigger risk-adjusted returns than those with higher levels of those ratios. In fact, we saw in Chapter 9 that low and high levels of these ratios are used in practice to define value and growth stocks, respectively.

To see another reason why these firm-specific attributes may be important to active investors, recognize that the term *sector* considered earlier in the context of rotation strategies also can be defined by different stock attributes. Thus, because the market seems to favor some attributes more than others over time, sector rotation may involve overweighting stocks with certain characteristics, such as small- or large-capitalization stocks, high or low *P/E* stocks, or stocks classified more generally as value or growth stocks. For example, Panel A of Exhibit 17.10 shows the difference in returns to portfolios invested in small- and large-cap stocks on a monthly basis from 1979–1999. The graph shows the large-cap portfolio return minus the small-cap return, so any net return above the horizontal axis indicates a period when the former outperformed the latter. Notice in particular the sizable firm size rotation and spread in returns that occurred in this period; in given months, both large- and small-cap stocks outperformed the other by over 30 percent. An important point to keep in mind, however, is that small-cap stocks are almost always riskier than large-cap stocks. This is shown in Panel B of Exhibit 17.10, which reports the difference in the standard deviations of the large- and small-cap portfolios.

Similar analysis reveals the potential benefits of forming active global portfolios around financial ratios. For the period spanning 1975–1995, Fama and French divided the stocks in 13 world markets using several different ratios, including *P/E* and *P/BV*.[8] They formed portfolios of stocks based on the highest and lowest 30 percent of each ratio and measured returns and standard deviations over the entire 20-year period. Exhibit 17.11 summarizes their findings. For each country and each ratio, the display reports the average annual return differential between the lowest-ratio portfolio and the high-ratio portfolio, as well as difference in standard deviation for those two portfolios. Two facts are clear from these results. First, over time, portfolios with the lowest *P/E* and *P/BV* ratios produced the highest returns everywhere in the world except Italy. Second, those low-ratio portfolios also tended to be more volatile, although this finding was far less uniform across countries. As we will see shortly, these results are important for understanding the differences between the value and growth investment styles.

| **Miscellaneous Issues** | Regardless of which broad philosophical approach they adopt, an important issue for active managers and their clients to resolve is the selection of an appropriate benchmark (sometimes called a "normal" portfolio). The benchmark should incorporate the average qualities of the portfolio strategy of the client. Thus, an active portfolio manager who invests mainly in small-capitalization stocks with low *P/E* ratios because the client specified this strategy should not have his or her performance compared to a broad market index, such as the S&P 500. Similarly, a global equity manager will not want to have his or her performance compared to a portfolio of stocks drawn from a single country, or even a single region in the world. |

Active managers must overcome two difficulties relative to the benchmark. First, an actively managed portfolio will almost always have higher transaction costs. Second, active portfolios can often also have higher risk than the passive benchmark. One key to success is for active managers to *be consistent* in their area of expertise. Market gyrations occur, and investment styles go in and out of favor. Successful long-term investing requires that you maintain your investment philosophy and composure while others are deviating from theirs. Another key to success is to *minimize the trading activity* of the portfolio. Attempts to time price movements over short horizons will result in lower profits because of growing commissions.

Finally, notice that most active equity strategies are inherently quantitative in nature. This suggests that computer-assisted portfolio formation procedures can be quite useful. In fact, the

---

[8]Eugene F. Fama and Kenneth R. French, "Value versus Growth: The International Evidence," *Journal of Finance* 53, no. 6 (December 1998): 1975–1999.

EXHIBIT 17.10 *PERFORMANCE LARGE- AND SMALL-CAP PORTFOLIOS: 1979–1999*

A. Rotation of Large-Cap and Small-Cap Returns

B. Rotation of Large-Cap and Small-Cap Standard Deviations

Source: Fidelity Management and Research. Data based on relative rolling 12-month returns to Russell 1000 and Russell 2000 indexes.

EXHIBIT 17.11 PERFORMANCE OF RATIO-BASED STOCK PORTFOLIOS: 1975–1995

	P/E RATIO		P/BV RATIO	
COUNTRY	(LOW–HIGH) RETURN %	(LOW–HIGH) STD DEV %	(LOW–HIGH) RETURN %	(LOW–HIGH) STD DEV %
United States	6.71	2.87	6.79	1.13
Japan	7.47	−1.52	9.85	−2.75
United Kingdom	2.65	5.32	4.62	2.09
France	6.98	4.70	7.64	5.72
Germany	0.55	−10.20	2.75	−2.40
Italy	−5.37	−12.32	−5.99	−15.12
The Netherlands	5.11	0.59	2.30	12.06
Belgium	2.22	2.59	4.39	0.99
Switzerland	1.54	2.63	3.49	1.43
Sweden	8.19	17.67	8.02	12.05
Australia	9.67	−0.70	12.32	3.71
Hong Kong	4.99	4.02	7.16	8.47
Singapore	2.09	−5.13	9.67	9.18

Source: Eugene F. Fama and Kenneth R. French, "Value versus Growth: The International Evidence," *Journal of Finance* 53, no.6 (December 1998): 1975–1999. Reprinted with permission of Blackwell Publishing.

existence of computer databases has encouraged the use of computer screening and other quantitatively based methods of evaluating stocks. These screening methods search for portfolios of stocks with certain characteristics rather than examining individual stocks to determine whether they are underpriced. The simplest computer screens identify groups of stocks based on a set of attributes. Screens also are used to narrow the list of thousands of stocks to a manageable few that can then be evaluated using more traditional analytical means. Indeed, some managers let the computers do all the work. For example, *neural networks* are computer programs that attempt to imitate the thinking patterns of the human brain. They use vast databases and artificial intelligence capabilities to find cause-and-effect patterns in stock returns.[9] The computer attempts to discover undervalued securities by identifying abnormal risk-adjusted return patterns and "learning" what stock attributes drive the market.

More complicated quantitative strategies are available that are comparable in some ways to sector rotation. Factor models, similar to those based on the APT, can identify stocks whose earnings or prices are sensitive to economic variables, such as exchange rates, inflation, interest rates, or consumer sentiment. With this information, portfolios can be "tilted" by trading those stocks most sensitive to the analyst's economic forecast. The manager can try to improve the portfolio's relative performance in a recession by purchasing stocks that are *least* sensitive to the analyst's pessimistic forecast.[10]

Some quantitatively oriented portfolio managers use what is called a "long-short" approach to investing. In the long-short approach, stocks are passed through a number of screens and assigned a rank. Stocks at the top of the ranking are purchased; stocks at the bottom are sold

[9]See, for instance, George S. Swales, Jr., and Young Yoon, "Applying Artificial Neural Networks to Investment Analysis," *Financial Analysts Journal* 48, no. 4 (September/October 1992): 78–80.

[10]Richard Roll and Stephen A. Ross, "The Arbitrage Pricing Theory Approach to Strategic Portfolio Planning," *Financial Analysts Journal* 51, no. 1 (January/February 1995): 122–131.

short. Such a strategy can be neutral on the overall market, since the value and systematic risk exposure of the long position can approximate that of the short position. The performance of the top-ranked stocks is expected to exceed that of the lower-ranked stocks, regardless of whether the overall stock market rises, falls, or trades in a narrow range.

How do managers know that these quantitative models have the potential to offer above-average risk-adjusted returns? The answer is that they hope the future will be similar to the past because these quantitative strategies have been **backtested**. This involves using computers to examine the composition and returns of portfolios based on historical data to determine if the strategy would have worked successfully in the past. The risk of testing an investment strategy in this way is that relationships that existed in the past are not guaranteed to hold in the future.

VALUE VERSUS GROWTH INVESTING: A CLOSER LOOK

One of the most important developments in active equity management during the last several years has been the creation of portfolio strategies based on value- and growth-oriented investment styles. Indeed, it is now common for money management firms to define themselves as "value stock managers" or "growth stock managers" when selling their services to clients. Exhibit 17.12 indicates how pervasive these styles have become. Using the classifications of Morningstar, Inc., a leading provider of investment analysis in the mutual fund industry, the number of available growth- and value-oriented funds grew dramatically during the last decade of the 20th century. The chart shows that the available number of growth fund products expanded by almost 20 percent per year over this period, with large-cap portfolios being the most prevalent. Value fund availability did not increase quite as much but still expanded by more than 17 percent annually.

The distinction between value and growth investing can be best appreciated by considering the thought process of a representative manager for each style.[11] In Chapter 11, we saw that the price-earnings ratio for any company can be expressed as:

EXHIBIT 17.12   *NUMBER OF GROWTH AND VALUE MUTUAL FUNDS: 1991–2000*

	2000	1995	1991
Growth-Oriented Funds			
Large cap	549	178	118
Mid cap	333	106	79
Small cap	309	78	42
Total	1,191	362	239
Annual % increase (1991–2000)	19.5%		
Value-Oriented Funds			
Large cap	564	215	135
Mid cap	199	69	60
Small/cap	162	47	25
Total	925	331	220
Annual % increase (1991–2000)	17.3%		

Source: Morningstar, Inc.

---

[11]This motivation is based on an excellent overview of value, and growth-oriented investment styles that can be found in Jon A. Christopherson and C. Nola Williams, "Equity Style: What It Is and Why It Matters," in *The Handbook of Equity Style Management,* eds. T. Daniel Coggin and Frank J. Fabozzi (New Hope, Pa.: Frank J. Fabozzi Associates, 1995).

$$\blacktriangleright 17.4 \qquad P/E \text{ Ratio} = \frac{\text{(Current Price Per Share)}}{\text{(Earnings Per Share)}}$$

where the earnings per share *(EPS)* measure can be based on either current or future (i.e., fore-casted) firm performance. In broad terms, value and growth managers will focus on different aspects of this equation when deciding whether a stock should be added to an existing portfolio. Specifically, a growth-oriented investor will

➤ focus on the *EPS* component (i.e., the denominator) of the *P/E* ratio and its economic determinants;
➤ look for companies that he or she expects to exhibit rapid *EPS* growth in the future; and
➤ often implicitly assume that the *P/E* ratio will remain constant over the near term, meaning that the stock price will rise as forecasted earnings growth is realized.

On the other hand, a value-oriented investor will

➤ focus on the price component (i.e., the numerator) of the *P/E* ratio; he or she must be convinced that the price of the stock is "cheap" by some means of comparison;
➤ not care a great deal about current earnings or the fundamental drivers of earnings growth; and
➤ often implicitly assume that the *P/E* ratio is below its natural level and that the market will soon "correct" this situation by increasing the stock price with little or no change in earnings.

In summary, a growth investor focuses on the current and future economic "story" of a company, with less regard to share valuation. The value investor, on the other hand, focuses on share price in anticipation of a market correction and, possibly, improving company fundamentals.

The conceptual difference between value and growth investing may be reasonably straightforward, but classifying individual stocks into the appropriate style is not always simple in practice. Since detailed company valuations are time-consuming to produce, most analysts rely on more easily obtained financial indicators—such as *P/E* and *P/B* ratios, dividend yields, and *EPS* growth rates—to define both an individual equity holding as well as the style benchmark portfolio. Exhibit 17.13 shows one approach along these lines for classifying firms according to style

EXHIBIT 17.13 ▶ *CHARACTERISTICS OF GROWTH AND VALUE STOCKS*

EXHIBIT 17.14 ▶ *TOP STOCK HOLDINGS OF GROWTH AND VALUE MUTUAL FUNDS*

A. Babson Growth Fund (BABSX)

Company	Ticker	Market Cap ($ Bil)	P/E	P/BV	East Growth EPS (%)	Div Yld (%)	Beta
Fed Home Loan Mtg	FRE	45.0	15.39	4.18	14.48	1.36	0.51
Pfizer	PFE	249.3	30.37	13.65	19.53	1.31	0.67
Kinder Morgan	KMI	6.2	25.35	2.74	19.89	0.40	0.55
Citigroup	C	254.1	17.57	3.20	14.39	1.29	1.16
American Intl Group	AIG	189.7	28.79	3.64	14.18	0.23	0.79
Exxon Mobil	XOM	301.8	19.75	4.14	7.45	2.07	0.61
Medtronic	MDT	53.7	37.85	8.72	17.17	0.52	0.88
Microsoft	MSFT	314.0	32.39	6.08	15.79	0.00	1.12
Symantec	SYMC	5.7	33.04	4.50	20.08	0.00	1.27
Paychex	PAYX	14.5	53.78	16.44	20.49	1.14	0.86
	Average:	*143.4*	*29.43*	*6.73*	*16.35*	*0.83*	*0.84*

B. T. Rowe Price Value Fund (TRVLX)

Company	Ticker	Market Cap ($ Bil)	P/E	P/BV	Est Growth EPS (%)	Div Yld (%)	Beta
Honeywell Intl	HON	31.3	18.73	3.41	13.20	1.95	1.27
Bank One	ONE	48.7	17.18	2.41	11.30	2.01	0.93
RadioShack	RSH	5.1	19.25	7.25	15.21	0.75	1.31
Schering-Plough	SGP	43.9	18.95	6.16	11.64	2.14	0.53
American Express	AXP	53.6	30.30	4.42	12.62	0.80	1.30
Exxon Mobil	XOM	301.8	19.75	4.14	7.45	2.07	0.61
Allstate	ALL	26.8	17.83	1.56	10.23	2.23	0.76
Burlington Resources	BR	8.4	12.94	2.37	21.30	1.32	0.58
Bristol-Myers Squib	BMY	74.3	15.39	6.92	10.36	2.92	0.55
May Dept Stores	MAY	10.0	15.50	2.62	9.65	2.76	0.79
	Average:	*60.4*	*18.58*	*4.13*	*12.30*	*1.90*	*0.86*

and market capitalization. Notice that value stocks are defined as those that are relatively cheap (e.g., low *P/B,* high yield) and with modest growth opportunities (e.g., regulated firms) while growth stocks tend to be more expensive, reflecting their superior earnings potential (e.g., technology firms).

To get a better feel for the types of stock portfolios these two investment styles might produce, Exhibit 17.14 lists representative samples of the top holdings for the Babson Growth (BABSX) mutual fund and the T. Rowe Price Value (TRVLX) mutual fund as of December 31, 2001. Both of these funds emphasize large-cap companies; but, as the chart shows, they differ in their approach in other important ways. Notably, BABSX's biggest holdings include technology (Microsoft, Symantec) and health care firms (Pfizer, Medtronic) while TRVLX invests more on the retail (RadioShack) and financial (Bank One) side. On average, the stocks in the BABSX portfolio tend to have higher *P/E* and *P/BK* ratios and greater future growth potential than those in TRVLX. On the other hand, notice that there is no real difference in the average level of systematic risk in these funds. Interestingly, both funds hold Exxon Mobil, which

EXHIBIT 17.15 *RUSSELL 1000 GROWTH AND VALUE INDEX CUMULATIVE PERFORMANCE: JUNE 1995–DECEMBER 2001*

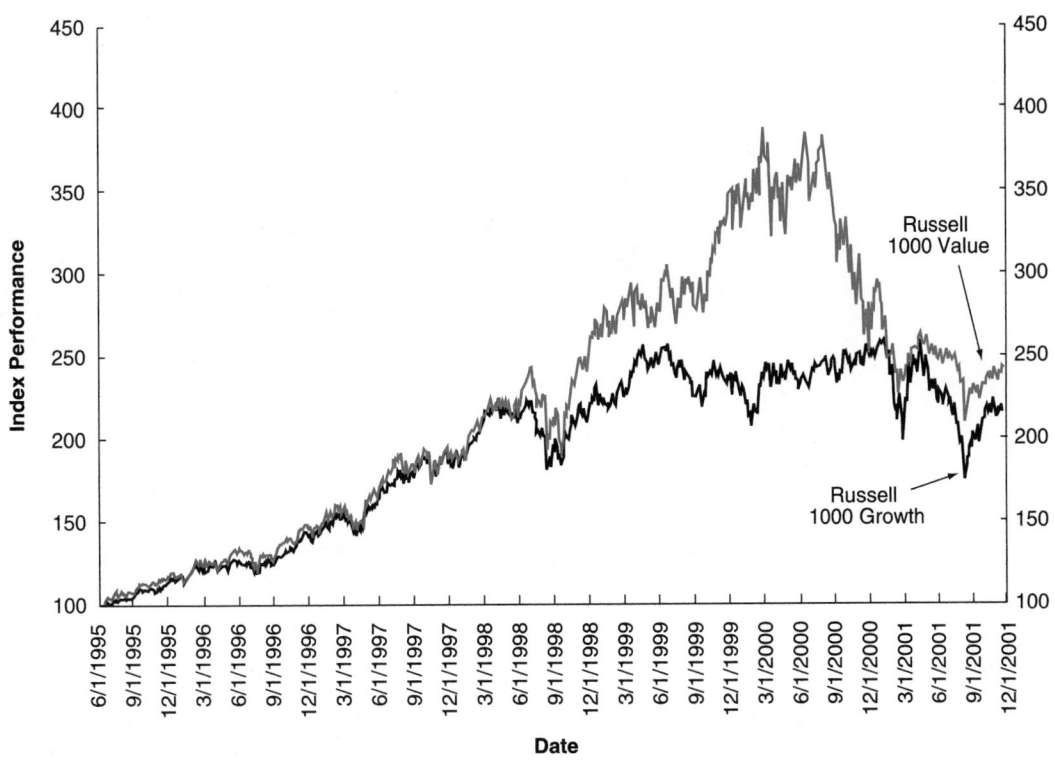

Note: June 1, 1995 = 100.

Copyright Frank Russell Company. Reprinted with permission from Frank Russell Company, Tacoma, WA.

underscores the room for investor judgment involved in classifying stocks along the value-growth style dimension.

Although investors appear to pay somewhat more attention to growth-oriented strategies, research has shown that a value approach to portfolio management tends to provide superior returns. In particular, Capaul, Rowley, and Sharpe studied the performance of value and growth portfolios (defined by relative *P/B* ratios) in six countries: the United States, the United Kingdom, Japan, France, Germany, and Switzerland.[12] Over a 10-year period ending in June 1992, they demonstrated that global value stocks outperformed global growth stocks by an average of 3.3 percent per year. Further, value stocks outperformed growth stocks in each of the six countries considered separately. Exhibit 17.15, which shows the cumulative performance of a large-cap growth index (Russell 1000 Growth) and a large-cap value index (Russell 1000 Value), indicates that this performance advantage persisted in the U.S. market over a shorter, more recent time period. This is all the more notable for the fact that much of this brief period was a particularly good time for the large-cap growth investment style.

[12]Carlo Capaul, Ian Rowley, and William F. Sharpe, "International Value and Growth Stock Returns," *Financial Analysts Journal* 49, no.1 (January/February 1993): 27–36.

EXHIBIT 17.16   *PERFORMANCE VALUE AND GROWTH PORTFOLIOS: 1979–1999*

A. Rotation of Value and Growth Returns

B. Rotation of Value and Growth Standard Deviations

Source: Fidelity Management and Research. Data based on relative rolling 12-month returns to Russel 1000 Value and Growth indexes.

It is tempting to conclude that value is unambiguously superior to growth as an investment style. However, it is important to note that, although value investing produces higher average returns than growth investing, this does not occur with much consistency from one investment period to another. In fact, Panel A of Exhibit 17.16 shows that there are significant differences in the value-growth return spread (based on the rolling annual performance of the Russell 1000 Value and Growth indexes) over time. During this analysis, the spread ranged from almost 20 percent in favor of value investing to almost 20 percent to the advantage of the growth style. Conversely, Panel B of the exhibit illustrates that the spread between value and growth return standard deviations, while itself volatile, is consistently negative, meaning that the growth strategy is consistently riskier than the value approach.

EXHIBIT 17.17 ▶ *A STYLE ANALYSIS GRID*

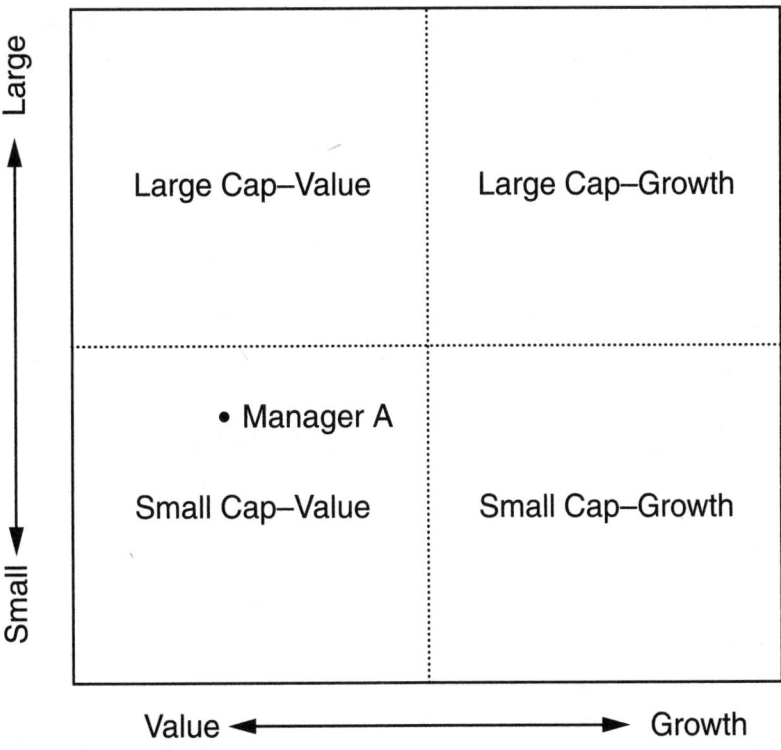

Source: Fidelity Management and Research Company.

AN OVERVIEW OF STYLE ANALYSIS

As we have seen, there are many approaches to managing a portfolio of equity securities. The different styles that have evolved over the years include forming portfolios around stock characteristics, such as market capitalization, leverage, industry sector, relative valuation, and growth potential. Returns-based **style analysis** is an attempt to explain the variability in the observed returns to a security portfolio in terms of the movements in the returns to a series of benchmark portfolios designed to capture the essence of a particular security characteristic. Effectively, style analysis determines the combination of long positions in a collection of passive indexes that best mimics the past performance of a security portfolio.

The process of returns-based style analysis involves using the past returns to a manager's portfolio along with those to a series of indexes representing different investment styles in an effort to determine the relationship between the fund and those specific styles. Generally speaking, the more highly correlated a fund's returns are with a given style index, the greater the weighting that style is given in the statistical assessment. The goals of the analysis are to better understand the underlying influences responsible for the portfolio's performance and to properly classify the manager's strategy when comparing his or her investment prowess with that of other managers. Thus, regardless of whatever investment objective a manager might profess to follow, style analysis allows the portfolio to "speak for itself."

Exhibit 17.17 shows a simple **style grid** that could be used to classify a manager's performance along two dimensions: firm size (large cap, small cap) and value-growth characteristics.

EXHIBIT 17.18 *INVESTMENT STYLE OF POPULAR STOCK MARKET INDICATORS*

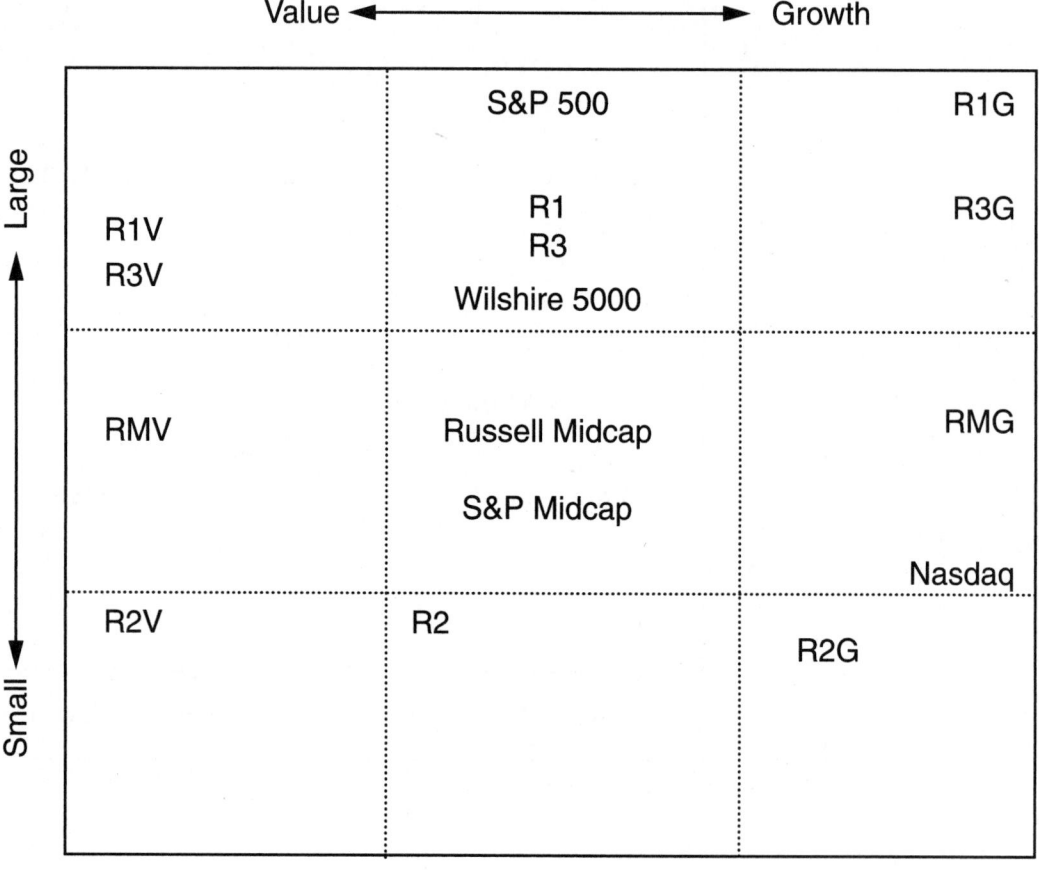

Source: Fidelity Management and Research Company.

An investor whose portfolio produced returns best mimicked by the returns to indexes representing a small-cap value style (such as Manager A) would be plotted in the lower left quadrant of the grid. These grids are also useful in establishing the implicit investment style for any of the popular stock market indicators described in Chapter 5. For example, Exhibit 17.18 shows the style plot points for the S&P 500, S&P Midcap, Wilshire 5000, Nasdaq Composite, Russell 3000 (R3), Russell 2000 (R2), and Russell 1000 (R1), among others.[13] One interesting result in this display is that the S&P 500 can be characterized as a large-cap, "blended" (i.e., between value and growth) fund. As such, it may not be the appropriate performance benchmark for someone managing a mid-cap, growth-oriented portfolio.

Formally, style analysis relies on the *constrained least squares* procedure, with the returns to the manager's portfolio designated as the dependent variable and the returns to the style index

---

[13]Exhibit 17.18 also plots the investment style for various subsets of the Russell indexes. For example, R1V and R1G are, respectively, the value and growth "halves" of the Russell 1000. They are created by ranking the 1,000 companies in the index by their price-to-book ratios and assigning those with the lowest (highest) ratios to the value (growth) subindex.

portfolios as the independent variables. In practice, there are often three constraints employed: (1) no intercept term is specified, (2) the coefficients must sum to one, and (3) all the coefficients must be non-negative. As developed by William Sharpe, returns-based style analysis is simply an application of an asset class factor model:[14]

➤ **17.5** $$R_{pt} = [b_{p1} F_{1t} + b_{p2} F_{2t} + \ldots + b_{pn} F_{nt}] + e_{pt}$$

where:

> R_{pt} = **the tth period return to the portfolio of manager p**
> F_{jt} = **the tth period return to the jth style factor**
> b_{pj} = **the sensitivity of portfolio p to style factor j**
> e_{pt} = **the portion of the return variability in portfolio p not explained by variability in the set of factors**

As with any regression equation, the coefficient of determination can be defined as

➤ **17.6** $$R^2 = 1 - [\sigma^2 (e_p)/\sigma^2 (R_p)]$$

Because of the way the factor model is designed, R^2 can be interpreted as the percentage of manager p's return variability due to the portfolio's *style,* with $(1 - R^2)$ due to his or her *selection* skills.

The benchmark portfolios that are selected as style analysis factors should be consistent with the manager's pronounced style. This suggests that a different set of indexes might be specified for a domestic equity fund than for an international bond fund. Also, an effective benchmark portfolio should be easy to measure, available as a realistic investment alternative to an actively managed portfolio, and as uncorrelated as possible with the other style indexes. Within these broad guidelines, there are a virtually unlimited number of different benchmarks that could be used in practice. Three popular approaches are:

➤ *Sharpe:* Uses portfolios of T-bills, intermediate-term government bonds, long-term government bonds, corporate bonds, mortgage-related securities, large-capitalization value stocks, large-capitalization growth stocks, medium-capitalization stocks, small-capitalization stocks, non-U.S. bonds, European stocks, and Japanese stocks.

➤ *BARRA:* Uses portfolios formed around 13 different security characteristics, including riability in markets, past firm success, firm size, trading activity, growth orientation, earnings-to-price ratio, book-to-price ratio, earnings variability, financial leverage, foreign income, labor intensity, yield, and low capitalization.[15]

➤ *Ibbotson Associates:* In its simplest style model, uses portfolios formed around five different characteristics: cash (i.e., T-bills), large-capitalization growth, small-capitalization growth, large-capitalization value, and small-capitalization value.[16]

---

[14]William F. Sharpe, "Asset Allocation: Management Style and Performance Measurement," *Journal of Portfolio Management* 18, no. 2 (Winter 1992): 7–19.

[15]For more on the conceptual development of the BARRA style factors, see Richard Grinold and Ronald N. Kahn, "Multiple-Factor Models for Portfolio Risk," in *A Practitioner's Guide to Factor Models,* ed. John Peavy (Charlottesville, Va.: Research Foundation of the Institute of Chartered Financial Analysts, 1994).

[16]See R. Cummisford and Scott Lummer, "Controlling the Limitations of Style Analysis," *Journal of Financial Planning* 9, no. 5 (October 1996): 70–76.

To illustrate how this process can be implemented, Sharpe measured the investment styles of two large institutional equity portfolios—Vanguard Trustee's U.S. Fund and Fidelity Magellan Fund—over a recent five-year interval. Both portfolios performed well during the period, generating respective average annual returns of 15.5 percent and 20.6 percent. However, Exhibit 17.19 shows that the managers of these portfolios followed very different styles. The bar charts indicate the extent to which each portfolio's returns were correlated with the underlying style factors. Accordingly, the Trustees' Fund is best thought of as being a small-cap value fund over this period while the Magellan Fund was a small-to-mid-cap growth portfolio with some global exposure. Also, security selection accounted for a relatively small amount of Magellan's return variability (2.7 percent) but was more of a consideration (7.8 percent) in the Trustees' portfolio.

Finally, style analysis can also be used to determine whether a manager is able to maintain a consistent investment style over time. This can be accomplished by reestimating the optimal combination of mimicking style indexes as additional performance data become available and then overlaying the plot points on the same grid. Exhibit 17.20 shows the connected sequence of plot points—or "snail trails" as they are sometimes called—for four different mutual funds managed by a leading investment company. Two of these funds (I and II) have well-defined style mandates and have been able to achieve relatively stable investment policies. The other two—III and IV—have exhibited considerable *style drift,* which in both cases is consistent with their flexible investment missions. Of course, an investor needs to be cautious about a manager whose portfolio exhibits unintentional style drift.

ASSET ALLOCATION STRATEGIES

An equity portfolio does not stand in isolation; rather, it is part of an investor's overall investment portfolio. Many times the equity portfolio is part of a balanced portfolio that contains holdings in various long- and short-term debt securities (such as bonds and Treasury bills) in addition to equities.

In such situations, the portfolio manager must consider more than just the composition of the equity or the bond component of the portfolio. The manager also must determine the appropriate mix of asset categories in the entire portfolio. There are four general strategies for determining the asset mix of a portfolio: the integrated, strategic, tactical, and insured asset allocation methods.

Integrated Asset Allocation

The integrated asset allocation strategy separately examines (1) capital market conditions and (2) the investor's objectives and constraints. These factors are then combined to establish the portfolio asset mix that offers the best opportunity for meeting the investor's needs given the capital market forecast. The actual returns from the portfolio are then used as inputs to an iterative process in which changes over time in the investor's objectives and constraints are noted along with changes in capital market expectations. The optimal portfolio is then revised based on this update of investor needs and capital market expectations.

This integrated approach to portfolio formation is illustrated in Exhibit 17.21. As described by Sharpe, there are three key steps to integrated asset allocation.[17] First, both capital market conditions and investor-specific objectives and constraints (e.g., risk tolerance, investment horizon, tax status) are summarized before the asset mix is determined. The processes by which the

---

[17]William F. Sharpe, "Integrated Asset Allocation," *Financial Analysts Journal* 43, no. 5 (September/October 1987): 25–32. An expanded discussion on this topic by the same author can be found in "Asset Allocation," in *Managing Investment Portfolios,* 2d ed., ed. John L. Maginn and Donald L. Tuttle (Boston, Mass.: Warren, Gorham & Lamont, 1990).

EXHIBIT 17.19   *STYLE ANALYSIS FOR TWO MUTUAL FUNDS*

A. Vanguard Trustee's U.S. Fund

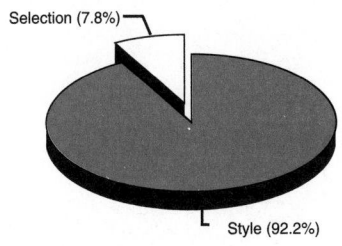

B. Fidelity Magellan Fund

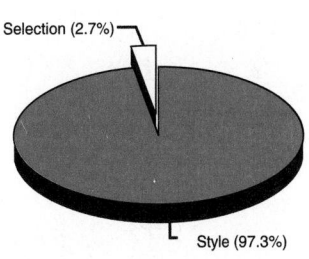

Source: William F. Sharpe, "Asset Allocation: Management Style and Performance Measurement," *Journal of Portfolio Management* 18, no. 2 (Winter 1992): 7–19.

EXHIBIT 17.20   *MUTUAL FUND STYLES OVER TIME*

A. Style Consistency

B. Style Flexibility

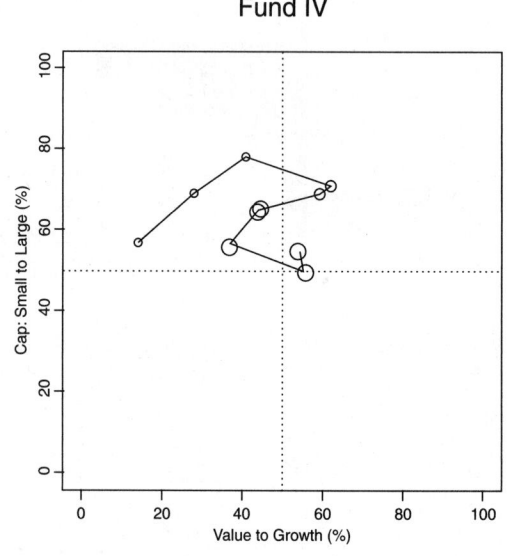

EXHIBIT 17.21   *INTEGRATED ASSET ALLOCATION*

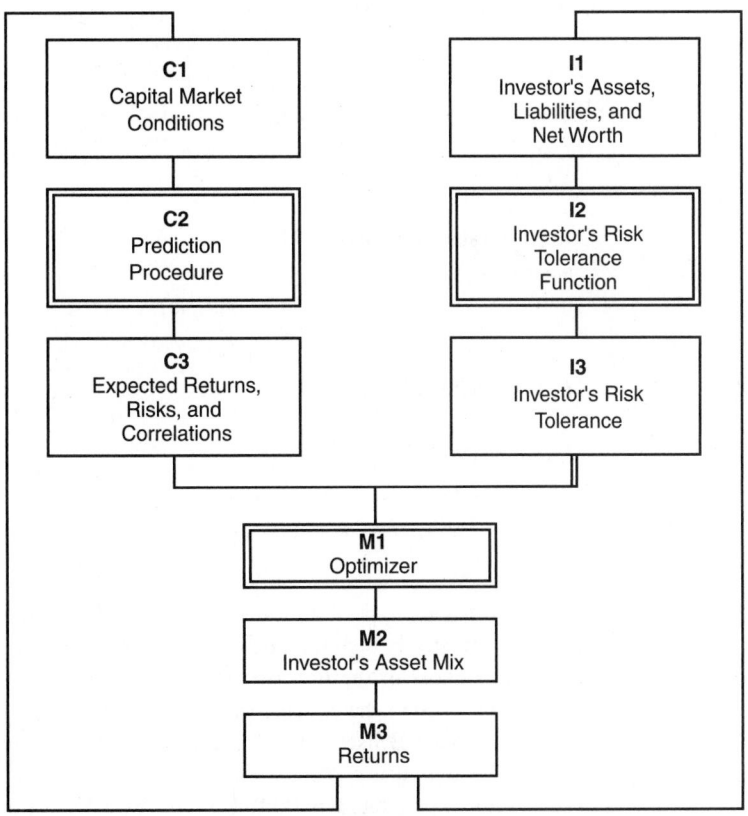

capital market and investor-specific data are summarized are shown in boxes C2 and I2, respectively, with the outcomes of those processes in boxes C3 and I3. An example of C3 might be the Markowitz efficient frontier containing portfolios of optimal risk–expected return combinations; the end product of I3 might be captured in an investment policy statement.

The second step in the integrated asset allocation process is to combine the information from the first step in order to select the single best portfolio for the investor in question. This is captured by the optimizer box in M1, with the resulting asset mix being shown in M2. One simple way of seeing how M1 might work would be to calculate the *expected utility (EU)* of each prospective asset mix using the following formula:

➤17.7
$$EU_{pk} = ER_p - \left(\frac{\sigma_p^2}{RT_k} \right) = ER_p - (\text{Risk Penalty})$$

where ER_p and σ_p^2 are the expected return and variance for Portfolio p (which come from C3) and RT_k is the risk-tolerance factor for Investor k (which comes from I3). The risk-tolerance factor is an estimate intended to capture the essence of an investor's attitude toward risk bearing. Notice that the higher this number, the more risk tolerant the investor is and, hence, the less

EXHIBIT 17.22 ▶ *OPTIMAL PORTFOLIO SELECTION: AN EXAMPLE*

A. Prospective Efficient Portfolios (C3)

PORTFOLIO	ASSET MIX STOCK	ASSET MIX BOND	ER	σ^2
A	20%	80%	7%	7%
B	50	50	8	13
C	80	20	9	20

B. Risk-Tolerance Factors (I3)

INVESTOR	RT	
1	5	(i.e., *less* tolerant)
2	40	(i.e., *more* tolerant)

C. Expected Utility Results (M2)

	A	B	C
Investor #1 *EU:*	**5.6**	5.4	5.0
Investor #2 *EU:*	6.8	7.8	**8.5**

Portfolio *p* has its expected return "penalized" by its risk level. The optimal asset mix for any particular investor is then the one that generates the highest level of expected utility.

As an example of the first two stages of the integrated asset allocation process, Panel A of Exhibit 17.22 shows the expected returns and variances for three different potential asset mixes (C3), while Panel B lists risk-tolerance factors for two investors (I3). Panel C shows the result of the expected utility calculations that combine this information (M2). For instance, the expected utility generated by Portfolio A for Investor 1 is 5.6 (= 7 – 7/5), which is the largest value of the three potential allocations and therefore his optimal asset mix. Conversely, Investor 2 is more tolerant of risk and finds that Portfolio 3, which generates an expected utility level of 8.5 (= 9 – 20/40), is her optimal allocation. Notice that the risk-tolerance factor effectively deflates the risk penalty, allowing more risk-tolerant investors to pursue more volatile portfolios with higher expected returns.

The third stage of the integrated portfolio process occurs after enough time has passed that the optimal portfolio's actual performance can be compared with the manager's original expectations. This evaluation process is represented by Box M3 in Exhibit 17.21. Following this assessment, the manager can then make adjustments to the portfolio by including any new information into the optimization process. Adjustments to the initial asset mix can result from either a fundamental change in capital market conditions (e.g., increased inflation) or a change in the investor's circumstances (e.g., increased risk tolerance). It is this "feedback loop" that makes portfolio management a *dynamic* process.

Strategic Asset Allocation

Strategic asset allocation is used to determine the long-term policy asset weights in a portfolio. Typically, long-term average asset returns, risk, and covariances are used as estimates of future capital market results. Efficient frontiers are generated using this historical return information, and the investor decides which asset mix is appropriate for his or her needs during the planning horizon. This results in a *constant-mix* asset allocation with periodic rebalancing to adjust the portfolio to the specified asset weights.

One way to think of the strategic allocation process is as being equivalent to the integrated asset allocation process shown in Exhibit 17.21 but without the feedback loops. That is, as just described, the manager will determine the long-term asset allocation that is best suited for a particular investor by optimizing information from both the capital market and that investor. However, once this asset mix is established, the manager does not constantly attempt to adjust the allocation according to temporary changes in market and investor circumstances. Thus, the strategic allocation should define the basic nature of the trade-off between opportunity and safety that confronts the investor.[18]

As an example of strategic asset allocation, Exhibit 17.23 shows the asset mixes for both large (Panel A) and small-to-midsize (Panel B) defined-benefit pension plans. The display lists average allocations for corporate, union, and public sector plans as of both 1997 and 2000. There are several interesting things to note. First, regardless of type, large plans appear to invest more heavily in equities than do smaller plans. Second, regardless of size, corporate and public funds invest more heavily in equities than do union funds, which allocate far more of their capital to fixed-income and cash equivalent securities. (Generally speaking, portfolios tilted more toward stocks than bonds and cash are considered to be riskier.) Third, no fund takes a particularly big position in foreign securities, although union plans make by far the smallest global allocations. Finally, consistent with the idea of a strategic allocation as a long-term view, these asset mixes remained relatively stable over the two years in question.

Tactical Asset Allocation

Unlike an investor's strategic allocation, which is set with a long-term focus and modified infrequently, a tactical approach to asset allocation constantly adjusts the asset class mix in the portfolio in an attempt to take advantage of changing market conditions. With tactical asset allocation, these adjustments are driven solely by perceived changes in the relative values of the various asset classes; the investor's risk tolerance and investment constraints are assumed to be constant over time. In Exhibit 17.21, it is equivalent to an integrated approach to asset allocation that removes the feedback loop involving investor-specific information (i.e., I2).

Tactical asset allocation is frequently based on the premise of *mean reversion,* which, as we have seen, holds that whatever a security's return has been in the recent past, it will eventually revert to its long-term average (mean) value. This assessment is usually done on a comparative basis. For instance, suppose that the ratio of stock and bond returns is normally 1.2, reflecting the greater degree of risk in the equity market. Then, if in the most recent investment period, stock returns were double those of bond returns, the tactical investor might determine that bonds were now undervalued relative to stock and most likely to be the best-performing asset class in the coming period. Accordingly, he should then overweight the fixed-income component of his portfolio, shifting, say, from a 60–40 percent initial mix of stocks and bonds to a 50–50 percent split.

For the preceding description, notice that tactical asset allocation is an inherently *contrarian* method of investing. That is, the investor adopting this approach will always be buying the asset class that is currently out of favor—on a relative basis, at least—and selling the asset class with the highest market value. In the preceding example, this was the case when the investor underweighted his stock allocation after stock prices rose substantially compared to bond prices. How frequently the investor chooses to adjust the asset class mix in the portfolio will depend on several factors, such as the general level of volatility in the capital markets, the relative size of the equity and fixed-income risk premiums, and changes in the fundamental macroeconomic environment.[19]

---

[18]See D. Don Ezra, "Strategic Asset Allocation and Total Portfolio Returns," in *Asset Allocation in a Changing World,* ed. T. Burns (Charlottesville, Va.: Association for Investment Management and Research, 1998).

[19]A good overview of these strategies can be found in Charles H. DuBois, "Tactical Asset Allocation: A Review of Current Techniques," in *Active Asset Allocation,* ed. R. Arnott and F. Fabozzi (Chicago, Ill.: Probus Publishing, 1992).

EXHIBIT 17.23 ▸ *STRATEGIC ASSET ALLOCATIONS FOR DEFINED-BENEFIT PENSION PLANS*

A. Sponsors of Over $100 Million

ASSET CLASS	CORPORATE 2000	CORPORATE 1997	UNION 2000	UNION 1997	PUBLIC 2000	PUBLIC 1997
Cash/Equivalents	4.1%	4.7%	5.3%	5.9%	2.4%	2.7%
U.S. Equity	44.1	46.9	37.6	35.1	45.9	43.8
International Equity	6.2	6.8	0.7	1.0	8.4	7.6
U.S. Fixed Income	27.0	30.0	40.5	42.0	33.9	35.4
Int'l Fixed Income	0.7	0.8	0.1	0.3	1.3	1.7
U.S. Balanced Accounts	1.9	2.3	2.2	2.5	2.1	3.4
Int'l Balanced Accounts	0.1	0.2	n/a	n/a	n/a	n/a
Equity Real Estate	1.1	1.5	2.0	2.0	2.1	2.3
Mortgages	0.2	0.2	1.7	2.4	0.2	0.6
Company's Own Stock	0.8	0.9	0.1	0.2	n/a	n/a
Convertibles	0.1	0.1	n/a	n/a	0.1	n/a
GIC's	0.9	1.2	0.6	1.3	0.4	0.6
Venture Capital	0.4	0.3	n/a	0.1	0.7	0.5
Gen'l Insurance Account	2.0	2.0	3.2	3.6	0.3	0.1
Other	7.1	1.9	5.2	3.6	1.2	1.1

B. Sponsors of $10 Million to $100 Million

ASSET CLASS	CORPORATE 2000	CORPORATE 1997	UNION 2000	UNION 1997	PUBLIC 2000	PUBLIC 1997
Cash/Equivalents	8.9%	9.1%	6.0%	7.5%	5.2%	6.1%
U.S. Equity	32.9	36.2	38.0	29.1	39.5	38.3
International Equity	0.4	2.4	n/a	0.3	2.4	2.5
U.S. Fixed Income	23.8	30.6	38.6	44.5	42.7	45.5
Int'l Fixed Income	0.1	0.5	n/a	0.1	0.6	0.2
U.S. Balanced Accounts	0.6	2.9	n/a	0.6	3.2	3.5
Int'l Balanced Accounts	n/a	0.1	n/a	n/a	n/a	n/a
Equity Real Estate	0.2	0.3	0.5	0.8	0.6	0.9
Mortgages	0.1	0.3	0.4	0.6	n/a	0.1
Company's Own Stock	0.5	0.6	n/a	0.1	n/a	n/a
Convertibles	n/a	0.2	n/a	0.1	n/a	n/a
GIC's	0.1	2.1	0.2	1.7	0.9	1.1
Venture Capital	0.2	0.2	0.1	n/a	0.0	0.3
Gen'l Insurance Account	7.4	10.1	4.6	9.4	0.2	0.3
Other	9.3	4.3	7.3	5.0	1.2	1.2

Source: Nelson Investment Management Network.

Insured Asset Allocation

Insured asset allocation likewise results in continual adjustments in the portfolio allocation. Insured asset allocation assumes that expected market returns and risks are constant over time, while the investor's objectives and constraints change as his or her wealth position changes. For example, rising portfolio values increase the investor's wealth and consequently his or her ability to handle risk, which means the investor can increase his or her exposure to risky assets. Declines in the portfolio's value lower the investor's wealth, consequently decreasing his or her ability to handle risk, which means the portfolio's exposure to risky assets must decline. Often, insured asset allocation involves only two assets, such as common stocks and T-bills. As stock prices rise, the asset allocation increases the stock component. As stock prices fall, the stock component of the mix falls while the T-bill component increases. This is opposite of what would happen under tactical asset allocation. Insured asset allocation is like the integrated approach without the feedback loop on the capital market side (i.e., C2 in Exhibit 17.21). It is sometimes called a *constant proportion* strategy because of the shifts that occur as wealth changes.

Selecting an Active Allocation Method

Which asset allocation strategy is used depends on the perceptions of the variability in the client's objectives and constraints and the perceived relationship between past and future capital market conditions. If you believe that capital market conditions are relatively constant over time, you might use insured asset allocation. If you believe that the client's goals, risk preferences, and constraints are constant, you likewise might use tactical asset allocation. Integrated asset allocation assumes that both the investor's needs and capital market conditions are variable and therefore must be constantly monitored. Under these conditions, the portfolio mix must be updated constantly to reflect current changes in these parameters.

USING FUTURES AND OPTIONS IN EQUITY PORTFOLIO MANAGEMENT: AN OVERVIEW

There has been growing recognition that derivative instruments such as futures and options are ideal tools for accomplishing myriad changes in a portfolio irrespective of the specific strategy of the manager. For example, the systematic and unsystematic risk of equity portfolios can be modified by using futures and options derivatives, as can the portfolio mix between equities and other assets. Cash inflows and outflows can be hedged through appropriate derivative strategies. Due to the cost, risk, and restrictions of short selling, shorting futures contracts and purchasing puts are attractive alternatives to short selling for long-short managers. Although a formal analysis of how investors use derivatives in portfolio management can be found in Chapter 21 through Chapter 24, it is useful to introduce a few basic ideas as we conclude this chapter.

Modifying Portfolio Risk and Return: An Introduction

Futures and options can affect the risk and return distribution for a portfolio. Generally, a dollar-for-dollar relationship exists between the changes in the price of the underlying security and the price of the corresponding futures contract. In effect, being long (short) in futures is identical to subtracting (adding) cash from (to) the portfolio. Long futures positions have the effect of increasing the exposure of the portfolio to the asset; shorting futures decreases the portfolio's exposure. Suppose Panel A of Exhibit 17.24 represents a portfolio's probability distribution of returns. Long positions in futures on the portfolio's underlying asset *increase* the portfolio's exposure (or sensitivity) to price changes of the asset. As shown in Panel B of Exhibit 17.24, as a result, the return distribution widens, indicating a larger return variance. Shorting futures has the effect of decreasing the portfolio's sensitivity to the underlying asset. Panel C of Exhibit 17.24 shows the effect on the portfolio if futures are sold. In this case, the variance of returns declines, causing a "narrower" return distribution.

EXHIBIT 17.24 *HOW RETURN DISTRIBUTIONS ARE MODIFIED WHEN FUTURES CONTRACTS ARE PURCHASED OR SOLD*

A.

$\bar{R}$

Portfolio without Futures

B.

$\bar{R}$

Portfolio and Long Futures

C.

$\bar{R}$

Portfolio and Short Futures

Exhibit 17.24 illustrates that futures have a symmetrical impact on portfolio returns, since their impact on the portfolio's upside and downside return potential is the same. This is because of the close relationship between changes in the price of the futures contract and changes in the price of the underlying asset.

In contrast, options give their owner the right (but not the obligation) to buy or sell the underlying asset. Because options provide this choice of whether or not to exercise the option, it means that options do not have a symmetrical impact on returns. For example, as will be shown in Chapter 23, buying a call option limits losses; buying a put when the investor owns the underlying security has the effect of controlling downside risk, as shown in Exhibit 17.25, Panel B. Writing a covered call, on the other hand, limits upside returns while not appreciably affecting loss potential, as seen in Exhibit 17.25, Panel C; writing a put option has the same effect.

Using Derivatives in Passive Equity Portfolio Management

A passive investment strategy generally seeks to buy and hold a portfolio of equity securities. With a passive investment strategy, the manager is expected to manage cash inflows and outflows without harming the ability of the portfolio to track its target index. Instead of investing all cash inflows in the index or a subsample of the index, the manager can purchase an appropriate number of futures contracts to maintain the portfolio's structure and reduce the portfolio's tracking error relative to the index during the time period when the manager invests the funds in the index stocks. Similarly, anticipated cash outflows can be hedged when the portfolio manager is liquidating part of the portfolio over time. The hedge maintains the portfolio's exposure to the market through the use of futures contracts.

Options can be used to a limited extent in passive management. When cash rebalancing is imperfect and an index fund becomes overweighted in a sector or in individual stocks relative to its index, it is possible to sell call options on the individual stocks or on industry groups to correct the portfolio's weights.

Using Derivatives in Active Equity Portfolio Management

Active management often attempts to adjust the portfolio's systematic risk, unsystematic risk, or both.

Modifying Systematic Risk An equity portfolio's systematic risk is the sensitivity of the portfolio's value to changes in the benchmark index measured by the portfolio's beta. If a rising market is expected, active portfolio managers will want to increase their portfolio's beta while expectations of a falling market will invite managers to reduce their portfolio's betas.

Traditionally, when the market was expected to rise, active managers would sell low-beta stocks and buy high-beta stocks to raise the portfolio's weighted average beta. Alternatively, the use of futures provides a quicker and cheaper way to change the portfolio's beta with less disruption to the traits of the portfolio. As we will see formally in Chapter 21, long or short positions in futures contracts allow the manager to increase or decrease a portfolio's beta.

Modifying Unsystematic Risk Opportunities exist for controlling the unsystematic risk in an equity portfolio. Futures and options on futures exist for a limited number of sectors, while there are options for numerous components of the equity market. There are option contracts on market indexes, such as the S&P 100 and S&P 500; for stock groups, such as consumer goods and cyclicals; and for selected industries, such as banks, utilities, pharmaceuticals, and mining. There are also options on over 1,400 individual stocks. Thus, portfolio managers can buy or sell derivative contracts to modify their firms and sector-specific exposures.

For example, a manager can buy call options when anticipating a rise in the market, in a sector or industry, or in a group of individual stocks. The lower call premiums can provide more leverage than using futures, and options contracts can allow greater precision in targeting sectors of the market rather than an entire index. The maximum loss for such strategies is limited to the call premium.

EXHIBIT 17.25 *EXAMPLES OF TRUNCATED RETURN DISTRIBUTIONS WHEN OPTIONS ARE USED TO MODIFY PORTFOLIO RISK*

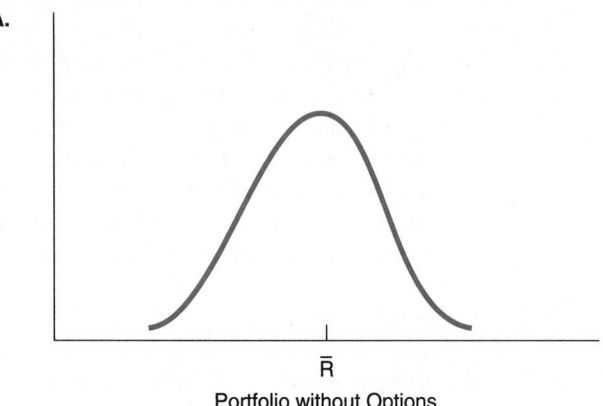

A.

$\bar{R}$

Portfolio without Options

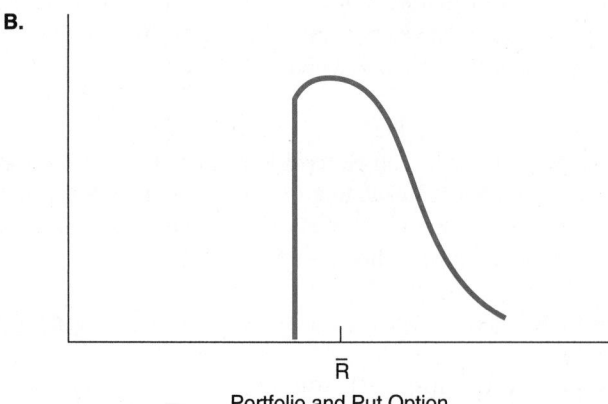

B.

$\bar{R}$

Portfolio and Put Option

C.

$\bar{R}$

Portfolio and Written Call Option

Similarly, investors can buy put options on an index future, a sector, or group of stocks in anticipation of a decline in value. Calls can be written on the market and subsets of the market when declining or stable values are forecast. Writing put options on the market and its subsectors can generate income when the portfolio managers expect the value of the market or subsectors to be stable or to rise.

The Internet *Investments Online*

Equity portfolio management is the "how-to"—it applies what we know of stock selection and portfolio theory to the practice of constructing, monitoring, and updating equity portfolios to meet the needs of individual or institutional clients. Several professional money managers describe their services on the Internet, and here's a sampling of some of them:

http://www.russell.com The home page of Frank Russell and Company contains descriptions of Russell's many services. Of special interest to us are the links to Russell's indexes, including its various style indexes, for the United States and several other countries. Reading through this site and the array of services that Russell offers will show the importance and practical nature of topics discussed in this and the other portfolio management chapters.

http://www.firstquadrant.com First Quadrant is a leader in the application of quantitative investment techniques to equity portfolio management. The product section of this site features a description of its quantitative perspective of style management. Other sections allow users to order copies of research monographs and published articles by First Quadrant personnel.

http://www.wilshire.com Wilshire Associates, Inc., offers indexes, consulting, and other services to investors. This home page offers links to a market environment commentary and to information about its indexes (the Wilshire 5000 is a widely used benchmark to represent the total equity market in the United States). The site offers a description of each Wilshire index, including such helpful information as the fundamental characteristics of each index and their exposure to different stock market sectors.

http://www.fool.com Home of The Motley Fool, a popular Web site for stock and portfolio analysis. The home page also has links to investment discussion groups and allows users to track their own portfolios. A limited number of portfolio strategies are also discussed on the Web site.

http://www.dailystocks.com The Web site contains a wealth of fundamental and technical data on individual equities, including price and earnings momentum indicators. The site also contains links to model equity portfolios assembled and maintained by professional analysts and money managers.

Summary

- Passive equity portfolios attempt to track the returns of an established benchmark, such as the S&P 500, or some other benchmark that meets the investor's needs. Active portfolios attempt to add value relative to their benchmark by market timing and/or by seeking to buy undervalued stocks. Index mutual funds and exchange-traded funds are popular ways for small investors to make passive investments.

- There are several methods for constructing and managing a passive portfolio, including full replication of a benchmark or sampling. Also, several active management strategies exist, including sector rotation, the use of factor models, quantitative screens, and linear programming methods. Value- and growth-oriented strategies have become particularly popular in recent years, and style analysis helps the investor determine the exact investment style the manager is using.

- Since equity portfolios typically are used with other assets in an investor's overall portfolio, we reviewed several common asset allocation strategies, including integrated asset allocation, strategic asset allocation, tactical asset allocation, and insured asset allocation. The basic difference between these strategies is whether they rely on current market expectations or long-run projections, and whether the investor's objectives and constraints remain constant over the planning horizon or change with market conditions.

- We also examined the use of derivative securities in equity portfolio management. Futures can be used to hedge against portfolio cash inflows and outflows; to keep a passive portfolio fully invested and help minimize tracking error; and to change an actively managed portfolio's beta. Alternatively, options can be used to modify a portfolio's unsystematic risk.

Questions

1. Why have passive portfolio management strategies increased in use over time?
2. What is meant by an indexing portfolio strategy and what is the justification for this strategy? How might it differ from another passive portfolio?
3. Briefly describe four techniques considered active equity portfolio management strategies.
4. Describe several techniques for constructing a passive portfolio.
5. Discuss three strategies active managers can use to add value to their portfolios.
6. How do trading costs and market efficiencies affect the active manager? How may an active manager try to overcome these obstacles to success?
7. Discuss how the four asset allocation strategies differ from one another.
8. *CFA Examination Level III*
   Recent empirical research has suggested that holding portfolios of stocks classified as "value" (low price/book ratio) as opposed to "growth" (high price/book ratio) in both U.S. and international markets has resulted in enhanced risk-adjusted returns. Critique the efficient market hypothesis in light of these findings.
9. Describe the difference between a price momentum strategy and an earnings momentum strategy. Under what conditions would you expect the two approaches to produce similar portfolios?
10. What are the trade-offs involved when constructing a portfolio using a full replication versus a sampling method?
11. Because of inflationary expectations, you expect natural resource stocks, such as mining companies and oil firms, to perform well over the next three to six months. As an active portfolio manager, describe the various methods available to take advantage of this forecast.

Problems

1. You have a portfolio with a market value of $50 million and a beta (measured against the S&P 500) of 1.2. If the market rises 10 percent, what value would you expect your portfolio to have?
2. Given the monthly returns that follow, how well did the passive portfolio track the S&P 500 benchmark? Find the R^2, alpha, and beta of the portfolio. Compute the average return differential with and without sign.

Month	Portfolio Return	S&P 500 Return
January	5.0%	5.2%
February	–2.3	–3.0
March	–1.8	–1.6
April	2.2	1.9
May	0.4	0.1
June	–0.8	–0.5
July	0.0	0.2
August	1.5	1.6
September	–0.3	–0.1
October	–3.7	–4.0
November	2.4	2.0
December	0.3	0.2

3. Using the Ibbotson data on asset returns from Chapter 3 (Exhibit 3.11), what percentage of the equity risk premium is consumed by trading costs of 1.5 percent? Assuming a normal distribution of returns, what is the probability that an active manager can earn a return that will overcome these trading costs?
4. *CFA Examination Level III*
   Global Advisers Company (GAC) is a SEC-registered investment counseling firm solely involved in managing international securities portfolios. After much research on the developing economy and capital markets of the country of Otunia, GAC has decided to include an investment in the Otunia stock market in its Emerging Market Commingled Fund. However, GAC has not yet decided whether

to invest actively or by indexing. Your opinion on the active versus indexing decision has been solicited. A summary of the research findings follows.

Otunia's economy is fairly well diversified across agricultural and natural resources, manufacturing (both consumer and durable goods), and a growing finance sector. Transaction costs in securities markets are relatively large in Otunia because of high commissions and government "stamp taxes" on securities trades. Accounting standards and disclosure regulations are quite detailed, resulting in wide public availability of reliable information about companies' financial performance.

Capital flows into and out of Otunia and foreign ownership of Otunia securities are strictly regulated by an agency of the national government. The settlement procedures under these ownership rules often cause long delays in settling trades made by nonresidents. Senior finance officials in the government are working to deregulate capital flows and foreign ownership, but GAC's political consultant believes that isolationist sentiment may prevent much real progress in the short run.

a. Briefly discuss four aspects of the Otunia environment that favor investing actively and four aspects that favor indexing.
b. Recommend whether GAC should invest in Otunia actively or by indexing and justify your recommendation based on the factors identified in Part a.

 5. *CFA Examination Level III*
Betty Black's investment club wants to buy the stock of either NewSoft Inc. or Capital Corp. In this connection, Black has prepared the following table. You have been asked to help her interpret the data, based on your forecast for a healthy economy and a strong market over the next 12 months.

	NewSoft Inc.	Capital Corp.	S&P 500 Index
Current price	$30	$32	n/a
Industry	Computer Software	Capital Goods	n/a
P/E ratio (current)	25×	14×	16×
P/E ratio (5-yr avg)	27×	16×	16×
P/B ratio (current)	10×	3×	3×
P/B ratio (5-yr avg)	12×	4×	2×
Beta	1.5	1.1	1.0
Dividend yield	0.3%	2.7%	2.8%

NewSoft's shares have higher price/earnings (*P/E*) and price/book (*P/B*) ratios than those of Capital Corp. Identify and briefly discuss three reasons why the disparity in ratios may not indicate that NewSoft's shares are overvalued relative to the shares of Capital Corp. Answer the question in terms of the two ratios, and assume that there have been no extraordinary events affecting either company.

6. As the chief investment officer for a money management firm specializing in taxable individual investors, you are trying to establish a strategic asset allocation for two different clients. You have established that Ms. A has a risk-tolerance factor of 8 while Mr. B's risk-tolerance factor is 27. The characteristics for four model portfolios follow:

	ASSET MIX			
Portfolio	Stock	Bond	ER	σ^2
1	5%	95%	8%	5%
2	25	75	9	10
3	70	30	10	16
4	90	10	11	25

a. Calculate the expected utility of each prospective portfolio for each of the two clients.
b. Which portfolio represents the optimal strategic allocation for Ms. A? Which portfolio is optimal for Mr. B? Explain why there is a difference in these two outcomes.
c. For Ms. A, what level of risk tolerance would leave her indifferent between having Portfolio 1 or Portfolio 2 as her strategic allocation? Demonstrate.

7. *CFA Examination Level II*

Briefly discuss whether active asset allocation among countries could consistently outperform a world market index. Include a discussion of the implications of *integration versus segmentation* of international financial markets as it pertains to portfolio diversification, but ignore the issue of stock selection.

8. *CFA Examination Level III*

Giselle Donovan is the newly appointed Chief Financial Officer of Bontemps International (BI), an import/export firm conducting a worldwide trading business from its principal office in New York. BI is a financially healthy, rapidly growing firm with a young workforce. All liabilities are denominated in U.S. dollars. Its ERISA-qualified defined-benefit pension plan is structured as follows:

		Percent Allocation	Prior Year Total Return
Higher-Risk Asset Classes			
U.S. equities (large capitalization)		35%	10.0%
U.S. equities (small capitalization)		10	12.0
International equities		5	7.0
Total equities		50%	
Lower-Risk Asset Classes			
U.S. Treasury bills (1-year duration)		10%	4.5
U.S. intermediates and mortgage-backed securities (4-year duration)		39	1.0
U.S. long-term bonds (10-year duration)		1	19.0*
Total fixed income		50%	
Total		100%	10.0%
Present value of plan liabilities	$298 million		
Market value of plan assets	$300 million		
Surplus	$ 2 million		
Duration of liabilities	10 years		
Actuarial return assumption	7.0%		
BI Board's long-term total return objective	9.0%		

*Income element 7.0%, gain element 12.0%.

The Board is concerned about the pension portfolio's downside risk and wants to adopt a formal policy for rebalancing the plan's assets in response to fluctuations in market values. Donovan asks you to review the major strategies that the Board should consider. You are aware of three strategies used to reallocate between higher-risk and lower-risk assets: "Constant Mix," "Constant Proportion," and "Buy and Hold."

a. Describe the primary characteristics of each of these three strategies as they relate to changes in market values. Identify the market environment in which each strategy should provide the best relative performance.

b. Recommend one strategy for the Board's consideration, taking their concerns into account. Justify your choice.

9. *CFA Examination Level III*

Futures contracts and options on futures contracts can be used to modify risk.

a. Identify the fundamental distinction between a futures contract and an option on a futures contract, and briefly explain the difference in the manner that futures and options modify portfolio risk.

b. The risk or volatility of an individual asset can be reduced either by writing a covered call option against the asset or by purchasing a put option on the asset. Explain the difference in the extent to which each of these two option strategies modifies an individual asset's risk. In your answer, describe the effect of each strategy on the potential upside and downside performance of the asset.

10. Consider the annual returns produced by two different active equity portfolio managers (A and B) as well as those to the stock index with which they are both compared:

Period	Manager A	Manager B	Index
1	12.8%	13.9%	11.8%
2	−2.1	−4.2	−2.2
3	15.6	13.5	18.9
4	0.8	2.9	−0.5
5	−7.9	−5.9	−3.9
6	23.2	26.3	21.7
7	−10.4	−11.2	−13.2
8	5.6	5.5	5.3
9	2.3	4.2	2.4
10	19.0	18.8	19.7

a. Did either manager outperform the index, based on the average annual return differential that he or she produced relative to the benchmark? Demonstrate.

b. Calculate the tracking error for each manager relative to the index. Which manager did a better job of limiting his or her client's unsystematic risk exposure? Explain.

References

Ammann, Manuel, and Heinz Zimmermann. "Tracking Error and Tactical Asset Allocation." *Financial Analysts Journal* 57, no. 2 (March/April 2001): 32–43.

Bernstein, Richard. *Style Investing: Unique Insight into Equity Management.* New York: John Wiley & Sons, 1995.

Burns, Terrence E. *Asset Allocation in a Changing World.* Charlottesville, Va.: Association for Investment Management and Research, 1998.

Dreman, David M. *Contrarian Investment Strategies: The Next Generation.* New York: Simon & Schuster, 1998.

Erb, Claude B., Campbell R. Harvey, and Tadas E. Viskanta. *Country Risk in Global Financial Management.* Charlottesville, Va.: Research Foundation of the Institute of Chartered Financial Analysts, 1997.

Grossman, Sanford J. "Dynamic Asset Allocation and the Informational Efficiency of Markets." *Journal of Finance* 50, no. 3 (July 1995): 773–787.

Hopkins, Peter J. B. and C. Hayes Miller. *Country, Sector, and Company Factors in Global Equity Portfolios.* Charlottesville, Va.: Research Foundation of AIMR, 2001.

Klein, Robert A., and Jess Lederman, eds. *Equity Style Management.* Chicago, Ill.: Irwin Professional Publishing, 1995.

Maginn, John L., and Donald L. Tuttle, eds. *Managing Investment Portfolios,* 2d ed. Boston, Mass.: Warren, Gorham, and Lamont, 1990.

Michaud, Richard O. *Investment Styles, Market Anomalies, and Global Stock Selection.* Charlottesville, Va.: Research Foundation of AIMR, 1999.

Squires, Jan R., ed. *Value and Growth Styles in Equity Investing.* Charlottesville, Va.: Association for Investment Management and Research, 1995.

Part 5

Analysis and Management of Bonds

*F*or most investors, bonds receive limited attention and very little respect. This is surprising when one considers that the total market value of the bond market in the United States and in most other countries is substantially larger than the market value of the stock market. For example, by the end of 2001, the U.S. market value of all publicly issued bonds was more than $16 trillion, while the market value of all stocks was about $14 trillion. On a global basis, the values are about $32 trillion for bonds versus $29 trillion for stocks. Beyond the size factor, bonds have a reputation for low, unexciting rates of return. Although this may have been true 40 or 50 years ago, it certainly has not been true during the past 15 to 20 years. Specifically, the average annual compound rate of return on government/corporate bonds for the period 1980–2000 was slightly over 10 percent versus about 16 percent for common stocks. These rates of return along with corresponding standard deviations (8 percent for bonds versus 13 percent for stocks) and the relatively low correlation between stocks and bonds (about 0.35) indicate that there are substantial opportunities in bonds for individual and institutional investors to enhance their risk-return performance.

The chapters in this section are intended to provide (1) a basic understanding of bonds and the bond markets around the world, (2) background on analyzing returns and risks in the bond market, (3) insights regarding the valuation of bonds, including numerous new fixed-income securities with very unusual cash flow characteristics, and (4) an understanding of either active or passive bond portfolio management.

Chapter 18 describes the global bond market in terms of country participation and the makeup of the bond market in major countries. Also, we examine characteristics of bonds in alternative categories, such as government, corporate, and municipal. We also discuss the many new corporate bond instruments developed in the United States, such as asset-backed securities, zero coupon bonds, high-yield bonds, and inflation protection securities. While the use of these securities has generally been limited to the large developed markets, it is certain that they will eventually be used around the world. Finally, we consider sources of price information needed by bond investors.

Chapter 19 is concerned with the analysis and valuation of bonds. This includes a detailed discussion of how one values a bond using a single discount rate or using spot rates. We also evaluate alternative rate of return measures for bonds. Subsequently, we consider what factors affect yields on bonds and what characteristics influence the volatility of bond returns including the very important concept of bond duration, which is a measure of bond price volatility that is important in active and passive bond portfolio management. We also consider bond convexity and the impact it has on bond price volatility. Notably, these concepts are examined for option-free securities as well as for how they apply to a growing set of securities with embedded options.

Chapter 20 considers how to use the background provided in Chapter 18 and Chapter 19 to create and manage a bond portfolio. We consider three major categories of portfolio strategies in detail. The first is passive portfolio management strategies, which include either a simple buy-and-hold strategy or indexing to one of the major benchmarks. The second category includes active management strategies that can involve one of five alternatives: interest rate anticipation, valuation analysis, credit analysis, yield spread analysis, or bond swaps. The third category includes matched funding strategies, which include constructing dedicated portfolios, constructing classical or contingent immunization portfolios, or horizon matching.

The fact that three fairly long chapters are devoted to the study of bonds attests to the importance of the topic and the extensive research done in this area. During the past 20 years, there have been more developments related to the valuation and portfolio management of bonds than of stocks. This growth of the fixed-income sector does not detract from the importance of equities but certainly enhances the significance of fixed-income securities. Finally, readers should keep in mind that this growth in size, sophistication, and specialization of the bond market implies numerous and varied career opportunities in the bond area, including trading these securities, valuation, credit analysis, and domestic and global portfolio management.

Chapter 18 › Bond Fundamentals*

After you read this chapter, you should be able to answer the following questions:

➤ What are some of the basic features of bonds that affect their risk, return, and value?

➤ What is the current country structure of the world bond market and how has the makeup of the global bond market changed in recent years?

➤ What are the major components of the world bond market and the international bond market?

➤ What are bond ratings and what is their purpose? What is the difference between investment-grade bonds and high-yield (junk) bonds?

➤ What are the characteristics of bonds in the major bond categories, such as governments (including TIPS), agencies, municipalities, and corporates?

➤ How does the makeup of the bond market differ in major countries, such as the United States, Japan, the United Kingdom, and Germany?

➤ What are the important characteristics of corporate bond issues developed in the United States during the past decade, such as mortgage-backed securities, other asset-backed securities, zero coupon and deep discount bonds, high-yield bonds, and structured notes?

➤ How do you read the quotes available for the alternative bond categories (e.g., governments, municipalities, corporates)?

The global bond market is large and diverse and represents an important investment opportunity. This chapter is concerned with publicly issued, long-term, nonconvertible debt obligations of public and private issuers in the United States and major global markets. In later chapters, we consider preferred stock and convertible bonds. An understanding of bonds is helpful in an efficient market because U.S. and foreign bonds increase the universe of investments available for the creation of a diversified portfolio.[1]

In this chapter, we review some basic features of bonds and examine the structure of the world bond market. The bulk of the chapter involves an in-depth discussion of the major fixed-income investments. The chapter ends with a brief review of the price information sources for bond investors. Chapter 19 discusses the valuation of bonds and considers several factors that influence bond value and bond price volatility.

---

*Material on bonds and world bond markets in this chapter is based on information from "Size and Structure of the World Bond Market: 2001," ed. Dave Mozina, International Fixed Income Research, Merrill Lynch & Co., April 2001. Reprinted by permission.

[1]Meir Statman and Neal L. Ushman, "Bonds versus Stocks: Another Look," *Journal of Portfolio Management* 13, no. 3 (Winter 1987): 33–38.

BASIC FEATURES OF A BOND

Public bonds are long-term, fixed-obligation debt securities packaged in convenient, affordable denominations for sale to individuals and financial institutions. They differ from other debt, such as individual mortgages and privately placed debt obligations, because they are sold to the public rather than channeled directly to a single lender. Bond issues are considered fixed-income securities because they impose fixed financial obligations on the issuers. Specifically, the issuer agrees to

1. Pay a fixed amount of *interest periodically* to the holder of record
2. Repay a fixed amount of *principal* at the date of maturity

Normally, interest on bonds is paid every six months, although some bond issues pay in intervals as short as a month or as long as a year. The principal is due at maturity; this *par value* of the issue is rarely less than $1,000. A bond has a specified term to maturity, which defines the life of the issue. The public debt market typically is divided into three time segments based on an issue's original maturity:

1. Short-term issues with maturities of one year or less. The market for these instruments is commonly known as the **money market**.
2. Intermediate-term issues with maturities in excess of 1 year but less than 10 years. These instruments are known as **notes**.
3. Long-term obligations with maturities in excess of 10 years, called *bonds*.

The lives of debt obligations change constantly as the issues progress toward maturity. Thus, issues that have been outstanding in the secondary market for any period of time eventually move from long-term to intermediate to short-term. This change in maturity is important because a major determinant of the price volatility of bonds is the remaining life (maturity) of the issue.

Bond Characteristics   A bond can be characterized based on (1) its intrinsic features, (2) its type, (3) its indenture provisions, or (4) the features that affect its cash flows and/or its maturity.

Intrinsic Features   The coupon, maturity, principal value, and the type of ownership are important intrinsic features of a bond. The **coupon** of a bond indicates the income that the bond investor will receive over the life (or holding period) of the issue. This is known as *interest income, coupon income,* or *nominal yield.*

The **term to maturity** specifies the date or the number of years before a bond matures (or expires). There are two different types of maturity. The most common is a **term bond**, which has a single maturity date. Alternatively, a **serial obligation bond** issue has a series of maturity dates, perhaps 20 or 25. Each maturity, although a subset of the total issue, is really a small bond issue with generally a different coupon. Municipalities issue most serial bonds.

The **principal**, or **par value**, of an issue represents the original value of the obligation. This is generally stated in $1,000 increments from $1,000 to $25,000 or more. Principal value is *not* the same as the bond's market value. The market prices of many issues rise above or fall below their principal values because of differences between their coupons and the prevailing market rate of interest. If the market interest rate is above the coupon rate, the bond will sell at a discount to par. If the market rate is below the bond's coupon, it will sell at a premium above par. If the coupon is comparable to the prevailing market interest rate, the market value of the bond will be close to its original principal value.

Finally, bonds differ in terms of ownership. With a **bearer bond**, the holder, or bearer, is the owner, so the issuer keeps no record of ownership. Interest from a bearer bond is obtained by clipping coupons attached to the bonds and sending them to the issuer for payment. In contrast, the issuers of **registered bonds** maintain records of owners and pay the interest directly to them.

Types of Issues   In contrast to common stock, companies can have many different bond issues outstanding at the same time. Bonds can have different types of collateral and be either senior, unsecured, or subordinated (junior) securities. **Secured (senior) bonds** are backed by a legal claim on some specified property of the issuer in the case of default. For example, mortgage bonds are secured by real estate assets; equipment trust certificates, which are used by railroads and airlines, provide a senior claim on the firm's equipment.

Unsecured bonds (debentures) are backed only by the promise of the issuer to pay interest and principal on a timely basis. As such, they are secured by the general credit of the issuer. **Subordinate (junior) debentures** possess a claim on income and assets that is subordinated to other debentures. Income issues are the most junior type because interest on them is paid only if it is earned. Although income bonds are unusual in the corporate sector, they are very popular municipal issues, where they are referred to as **revenue bonds.** Finally, **refunding issues** provide funds to prematurely retire another issue.

The type of issue has only a marginal effect on comparative yield because it is the credibility of the issuer that determines bond quality. A study of corporate bond price behavior found that whether the issuer pledged collateral did not become important until the bond issue approached default.[2] The collateral and security characteristics of a bond influence yield differentials only when these factors affect the bond's quality ratings.

Indenture Provisions   The *indenture* is the contract between the issuer and the bondholder specifying the issuer's legal requirements. A trustee (usually a bank) acting on behalf of the bondholders ensures that all the indenture provisions are met, including the timely payment of interest and principal. All the factors that dictate a bond's features, its type, and its maturity are set forth in the indenture.

Features Affecting Bond's Maturity   Investors should be aware of the three alternative call option features that can affect the life (maturity) of a bond. One extreme is a *freely callable* provision that allows the issuer to retire the bond at any time with a typical notification period of 30 to 60 days. The other extreme is a *noncallable* provision wherein the issuer cannot retire the bond prior to its maturity.[3] Intermediate between these is a *deferred call* provision, which means the issue cannot be called for a certain period of time after the date of issue (e.g., 5 to 10 years). At the end of the deferred call period, the issue becomes freely callable. Callable bonds have a **call premium**, which is the amount above maturity value that the issuer must pay to the bondholder for prematurely retiring the bond.

A *nonrefunding provision* prohibits a call and premature retirement of an issue from the proceeds of a lower-coupon refunding bond. This is meant to protect the bondholder from a typical refunding, but it is not foolproof. An issue with a nonrefunding provision can be called and retired prior to maturity using other sources of funds, such as excess cash from operations, the sale of assets, or proceeds from a sale of common stock. This occurred on several occasions

---

[2]W. Braddock Hickman, *Corporate Bond Quality and Investor Experience* (Princeton, N.J.: Princeton University Press, 1958).

[3]The main issuer of noncallable bonds between 1985 and 2002 was the U.S. Treasury. Corporate long-term bonds typically have contained some form of call provision, except during periods of relatively low interest rates (e.g., 1994–2001) when the probability of exercising the option was very low. We discuss this notion in more detail in Chapter 19 in connection with the analysis of embedded options.

during the 1980s and 1990s when many issuers retired nonrefundable high-coupon issues early because they could get the cash from one of these other sources and felt that this was a good financing decision.

Another important indenture provision that can affect a bond's maturity is the **sinking fund**, which specifies that a bond must be paid off systematically over its life rather than only at maturity. There are numerous sinking-fund arrangements, and the bondholder should recognize this as a feature that can change the stated maturity of a bond. The size of the sinking fund can be a percentage of a given issue or a percentage of the total debt outstanding, or it can be a fixed or variable sum stated on a dollar or percentage basis. Similar to a call feature, sinking fund payments may commence at the end of the first year or may be deferred for 5 or 10 years from date of the issue. The amount of the issue that must be repaid before maturity from a sinking fund can range from a nominal sum to 100 percent. Like a call, the sinking-fund feature typically carries a nominal premium but is generally smaller than the straight call premium (e.g., 1 percent). For example, a bond issue with a 20-year maturity might have a sinking fund that requires that 5 percent of the issue be retired every year beginning in year 10. By year 20, half of the issue has been retired and the rest is paid off at maturity. Sinking-fund provisions have a small effect on comparative yields at the time of issue but have little subsequent impact on price behavior.

A sinking-fund provision is an obligation and must be carried out regardless of market conditions. Although a sinking fund allows the issuer to call bonds on a random basis, most bonds are retired for sinking-fund purposes through direct negotiations with institutional holders. Essentially, the trustee negotiates with an institution to buy back the necessary amount of bonds at a price slightly above the current market price.

Rates of Return on Bonds   The rate of return on a bond is computed in the same way as the rate of return on stock or any asset. It is determined by the beginning and ending price and the cash flows during the holding period. The major difference between stocks and bonds is that the interim cash flow on bonds (i.e., the interest) is contractual and accrues over time as discussed subsequently, whereas the dividends on stock may vary. Therefore, the holding period return (HPR) for a bond will be

➤18.1
$$HPR_{i,t} = \frac{P_{i,t+1} + Int_{i,t}}{P_{i,t}}$$

where:

    $HPR_{i,t}$ = **the holding period return for bond i during period t**
    $P_{i,t+1}$ = **the market price of bond i at the end of period t**
    $P_{i,t}$ = **the market price of bond i at the beginning of period t**
    $Int_{i,t}$ = **the interest paid or accrued on bond i during period t. Because the interest payment is contractual, it accrues over time and if a bond owner sells the bond between interest payments, the sale price includes accrued interest[4]**

The holding period yield (HPY) is:

➤18.2
$$HPY = HPR - 1$$

Note that the only contractual factor is the amount of interest payments. The beginning and ending bond prices are determined by market forces, as discussed in Chapter 11. Notably, the ending price is determined by market forces unless the bond is held to maturity, in which case the

---

[4]The concept of accrued interest will be discussed further in Chapter 19 when we consider the valuation of bonds.

investor will receive the par value. These price variations in bonds mean that investors in bonds can experience capital gains or losses. Interest rate volatility has increased substantially since the 1960s, and this has caused large price fluctuations in bonds.[5] As a result, capital gains or losses have become a major component of the rates of return on bonds.

THE GLOBAL BOND MARKET STRUCTURE[6]

The market for fixed-income securities is substantially larger than the listed equity exchanges (NYSE, TSE, LSE) because corporations tend to issue bonds rather than common stock. Federal Reserve figures indicate that in the United States during 2001, 20 percent of all new security issues were equity, which included preferred as well as common stock. Corporations issue less common or preferred stock because firms derive most of their equity financing from internally generated funds (i.e., retained earnings). Also, although the equity market is strictly corporations, the bond market in most countries has four noncorporate sectors: the pure government sector (e.g., the Treasury in the United States), government agencies (e.g., FNMA), state and local government bonds (municipals), and international bonds (e.g., Yankees and Eurobonds in the United States).

The size of the global bond market and the distribution among countries can be gleaned from Exhibit 18.1, which lists the dollar value of debt outstanding and the percentage distribution for the major bond markets for the years 1998–2000. There has been substantial overall growth, including an 11 percent increase in the total in 2000 compared with 1998. Also, the country trends are significant. Specifically, the U.S. market went from about 48 percent of the total world bond market in 1998 to almost 52 percent in 2000. In contrast, Japan went from almost 20 percent in 1999 to less than 19 percent in 2000. The other significant change is the creation of the Euroland sector, which includes a large part of Europe (i.e., Germany, Italy, France) with the significant exception of the United Kingdom.

Participating Issuers
There are generally five different issuers in a country: (1) the federal government (e.g., the U.S. Treasury), (2) agencies of the federal government, (3) various state and local political subdivisions (known as municipalities), (4) corporations, and (5) international issues. The division of bonds among these five types for the three largest markets and the United Kingdom during 1998–2000 is contained in Exhibit 18.2.

Government The market for government securities is the largest sector in Japan. It involves a variety of debt instruments issued to meet the growing needs of this government. In Germany, the government sector is smaller but is growing in size due to deficits related to reunification of the country.

Government Agencies Agency issues have become a major segment in the U.S. market (over 25 percent) but are a smaller proportion in other countries (e.g., about 18 percent in Japan and nonexistent in the United Kingdom). These agencies represent political subdivisions of the government, although the securities are *not* typically direct obligations of the government. The

---

[5]The analysis of bond price volatility is discussed in detail in Chapter 19.

[6]For a further discussion of global bond markets, see Christopher Steward and Adam M. Greshin, "International Bond Markets and Instruments"; Christopher Steward and Adam Greshin, "International Bond Investing and Portfolio Management"; and Michael R. Rosenberg, "International Fixed Income Investing: Theory and Practice," all in *The Handbook of Fixed-Income Securities,* 6th ed., ed. Frank J. Fabozzi (New York: McGraw-Hill, 2000).

EXHIBIT 18.1

THE SIZE AND STRUCTURE OF THE WORLD BOND MARKET:* 1998–2000
(NOMINAL VALUE OUTSTANDING IN BILLIONS OF U.S. DOLLARS)

COUNTRY	2000	%	1999	%	1998	%
United States	15,417.5	51.7	14,283.6	50.0	12,803.8	47.7
Japan	5,549.3	18.6	5,668.9	19.8	4,884.4	18.2
Germany					2,704.1	10.1
Euroland	6,223.8	20.9	6,140.8	21.5	—	—
Italy					1,474.4	5.5
United Kingdom	1,065.3	3.6	939.2	3.3	891.1	3.3
France					1,160.4	4.3
Canada	540.6	1.8	548.4	1.9	502.4	1.9
Belgium					375.6	1.4
The Netherlands					420.1	1.6
Spain					301.3	1.1
Switzerland	277.5	0.9	269.3	0.9	284.5	1.1
Denmark	254.8	0.9	263.6	0.9	300.5	1.1
Australia	182.1	0.6	197.8	0.7	163.2	0.6
Sweden	155.3	0.5	188.1	0.7	208.0	0.8
Austria					150.1	0.6
Greece	72.3	0.2	—	—	—	—
Norway	46.9	0.2	51.3	0.2	56.1	0.2
Finland					64.1	0.2
Portugal					57.7	0.2
Ireland					34.0	0.1
New Zealand	18.7	0.1	23.2	0.1	22.4	0.1
Total	**29,804.1**	100.0	**28,574.2**	100.0	**26,858.2**	100.0
Annual Growth %	*4.3*		*6.4*			

*Excludes emerging/converging markets.

For 1999 and 2000, only the total for Euroland is displayed. Prior to 1999, data for the component countries are displayed. Greece was added to this table in 2000, as it is no longer considered a converging market.

Source: "Size and Structure of the World Bond Market: 2001," Merrill Lynch International Fixed Income Research, April 2001.

U.S. agency market has two types of issuers: government-sponsored enterprises and federal agencies. The proceeds of agency bond issues are used to finance many legislative programs. In most countries, the market yields of agency obligations generally exceed those from pure government bonds. Thus, they represent a way for investors to increase returns with only marginally higher risk.

Municipalities   Municipal debt includes issues of states, school districts, cities, or other political subdivisions. Unlike government and agency issues, the interest income on municipal bonds in the United States is not subject to federal income tax, although capital gains are taxable. Moreover, these bonds are exempt from state and local taxes when they are issued by the investors' home state.

EXHIBIT 18.2 ▶ *MAKEUP OF BONDS OUTSTANDING IN THE UNITED STATES, JAPAN, GERMANY, AND THE UNITED KINGDOM: 1998–2000*

	2000		1999		1998	
	TOTAL VALUE	PERCENT OF TOTAL	TOTAL VALUE	PERCENT OF TOTAL	TOTAL VALUE	PERCENT OF TOTAL
A. United States (Dollars in Billions)						
Government	2,305.0	15.0	2,492.9	17.5	2,649.5	20.7
Federal agency	4,344.0	28.2	3,912.3	27.4	3,320.5	25.9
Municipal	1,376.9	8.9	1,350.4	9.5	1,296.3	10.1
Corporate	4,515.9	29.3	4,129.0	28.9	3,679.0	28.7
International	2,875.7	18.7	2,399.0	16.8	1,858.5	14.5
Total	15,417.5	100.0	14,283.6	100.0	12,803.8	100.0
B. Japan (Yen in Trillions)						
Government—JGBs	329.7	52.0	296.5	50.6	265.5	48.1
Government associated organization	111.1	17.5	108.6	18.5	104.6	19.0
Municipal	16.1	2.5	14.6	2.5	13.2	2.4
Corporate—Nonfinancial	61.6	9.7	59.0	10.1	57.6	10.4
Corporate—financial	49.7	7.8	56.7	9.7	56.9	10.3
International	66.4	10.5	50.8	8.7	53.7	9.7
Total	634.6	100.0	586.2	100.0	551.5	100.0
C. Germany (Billions of Marks; Euros)*						
Government	805.8	35.6	768.8	36.6	1,431.6	31.8
Corporate—ex bank	996.9	44.0	959.4	45.7	1,657.1	36.8
Bank	462.5	20.4	369.8	17.6	605.5	13.4
International	—	—ˇ	—	—	808.6	18.0
Total	2,265.2	100.0	2,098.0	100.0	4,502.8	100.0
D. United Kingdom (Billions of British Pounds)						
Government	278.6	39.1	289.4	49.2	281.8	52.3
Corporate	47.2	6.6	30.4	5.2	21.8	4.0
International	386.5	54.3	268.6	45.6	235.7	43.7
Total	712.3	100.0	588.3	100.0	539.3	100.0

*1998 in marks; 1999 and 2000 in euros.

Source: "Size and Structure of the World Bond Market: 2001," Merrill Lynch International Fixed Income Research, April 2001.

As shown in Exhibit 18.2, the municipal bond market has declined in the United States from 10 percent to 9 percent. In Japan, the municipal bond market has declined to less than 3 percent. It is nonexistent in the United Kingdom. Also, although each country has unique tax laws, the income from a non-U.S. municipal bond typically would not be exempt for a U.S. investor.

Corporations   The major nongovernmental issuer of debt is the corporate sector. The importance of this sector differs dramatically among countries. It is a stable factor in the United States; a small sector in Japan where it is supplemented by bank debentures; and a small proportion of the U.K. market. Finally, it is a growing part of the German market as more German firms get their financing through the public market rather than from banks.

The market for corporate bonds is commonly subdivided into several segments: industrials, public utilities, transportation, and financial issues. The specific makeup varies between countries. Most U.S. issuers are industrials and utilities.

The corporate sector in the United States provides the most diverse issues in terms of type and quality. In effect, the issuer can range from the highest investment-grade firm, such as American Telephone and Telegraph or IBM, to a relatively new, high-risk firm that issues bonds rated noninvestment grade (i.e., high yield).[7]

International   The international sector has two components: (1) foreign bonds, such as Yankee bonds and Samurai bonds; and (2) Eurobonds, including Eurodollar, Euroyen, Eurodeutschemark, and Eurosterling bonds.[8] Although the relative importance of the international bond sector varies by country (from a low of 10 percent in Japan to a high of over 54 percent in the United Kingdom), it has grown in both absolute and relative terms in all these countries. Although Eurodollar bonds have historically made up over 50 percent of the Eurobond market, the proportion has declined as investors have attempted to diversify their Eurobond portfolios. Specifically, Eurodollar bonds constituted about 85 percent of the market in 1984, but only 50 percent in 2001. Clearly, the desire for diversification changes with the swings in the value of the U.S. dollar.

Participating Investors   Numerous individual and institutional investors with diverse investment objectives participate in the bond market. Individual investors are a minor portion because of the market's complexity and the high minimum denominations of most issues. Institutional investors typically account for 90 to 95 percent of the trading, although different segments of the market are more institutionalized than others. For example, institutions are involved heavily in the agency market, but they are less active in the corporate sector.

A variety of institutions invest in the bond market. Life insurance companies invest in corporate bonds and, to a lesser extent, in Treasury and agency securities. Commercial banks invest in municipal bonds and government and agency issues. Property and liability insurance companies concentrate on municipal bonds and Treasuries. Private and government pension funds are heavily committed to corporates and invest in Treasuries and agencies. Finally, fixed-income mutual funds have grown substantially in size and their demand spans the full spectrum of the market as they develop bond funds that meet the needs of a variety of investors. As we will discuss in Chapter 25, municipal bond funds and corporate bond funds (including high-yield bonds) have experienced significant growth.

Alternative institutions tend to favor different sectors of the bond market based on two factors: (1) the tax code applicable to the institution and (2) the nature of the institution's liability structure. For example, because commercial banks are subject to normal taxation and have fairly short-term liability structures, they favor short- to intermediate-term municipals. Pension funds are virtually tax-free institutions with long-term commitments, so they prefer high-yielding, long-term government or corporate bonds. Such institutional investment preferences can affect the short-run supply and demand of loanable funds and impact interest rate changes.

---

[7]This sector of the bond market is described in more detail later in this chapter. It is possible to distinguish another sector that exists in the United States but not in other countries—institutional bonds. These are corporate bonds issued by a variety of *private, nonprofit institutions,* such as schools, hospitals, and churches. They are not broken out because they are only a minute part of the U.S. market and do not exist elsewhere.

[8]These bonds will be discussed in more detail later in this chapter.

Bond Ratings   Agency ratings are an integral part of the bond market because most corporate and municipal bonds are rated by one or more of the rating agencies. The exceptions are very small issues and bonds from certain industries, such as bank issues. These are known as *nonrated bonds.* There are three major rating agencies: (1) Fitch Investors Service, (2) Moody's, and (3) Standard and Poor's.

Bond ratings provide the fundamental analysis for thousands of issues. The rating agencies analyze the issuing organization and the specific issue to determine the probability of default and inform the market of their analyses through their ratings.[9]

The primary question in bond credit analysis is whether the firm can service its debt in a timely manner over the life of a given issue. Consequently, the rating agencies consider expectations over the life of the issue, along with the historical and current financial position of the company. We consider default estimation further when we discuss high-yield (junk) bonds.

Several studies have examined the relationship between bond ratings and issue quality as indicated by financial variables. The results clearly demonstrated that bond ratings were positively related to profitability, size, and cash flow coverage, and they were inversely related to financial leverage and earnings instability.[10]

The original ratings assigned to bonds have an impact on their marketability and effective interest rate. Generally, the three agencies' ratings agree. When they do not, the issue is said to have a *split rating.*[11] Seasoned issues are regularly reviewed to ensure that the assigned rating is still valid. If not, revisions are made either upward or downward. Revisions are usually done in increments of one rating grade. The ratings are based on both the company and the issue. After an evaluation of the creditworthiness of the total company is completed, a company rating is assigned to the firm's most senior unsecured issue. All junior bonds receive lower ratings based on indenture specifications. Also, an issue could receive a higher rating than justified because of credit-enhancement devices, such as the attachment of bank letters of credit, surety, or indemnification bonds from insurance companies.

The agencies assign letter ratings depicting what they view as the risk of default of an obligation. The letter ratings range from AAA (Aaa) to D. Exhibit 18.3 describes the various ratings assigned by the major services. Except for slight variations in designations, the meaning and interpretation are basically the same. The agencies modify the ratings with + and – signs for Fitch and S&P or with numbers (1-2-3) for Moody's. As an example, an A+ (A1) bond is at the top of the A-rated group.

The top four ratings—AAA (or Aaa), AA (or Aa), A, and BBB (or Baa)—are generally considered to be *investment-grade securities.* The next level of securities is known as *speculative bonds* and includes the BB- and B-rated obligations. The C categories are generally either income obligations or revenue bonds, many of which are trading flat. (Flat bonds are in arrears

---

[9]For a detailed listing of rating classes and a listing of factors considered in assigning ratings, see "Bond Ratings" in *The Financial Analysts Handbook,* 2d ed., ed. Sumner N. Levine (Homewood, Ill.: Dow Jones–Irwin, 1988). For a study that examines the value of two bond ratings, see L. Paul Hsueh and David S. Kidwell, "Bond Ratings: Are Two Better Than One?" *Financial Management* 17, no. 1 (Spring 1988): 46–53. An analysis of the bond rating industry is contained in Richard Cantor and Frank Packer. "The Credit Rating Industry," *Journal of Fixed Income* 5, no 3 (December 1995): 10–34.

[10]See, for example, Ahmed Belkaoui, "Industrial Bond Ratings: A New Look," *Financial Management* 9, no. 3 (Fall 1980): 44–52; and James A. Gentry, David T. Whitford, and Paul Newbold, "Predicting Industrial Bond Ratings with a Probit Model and Funds Flow Components," *The Financial Review* 23, no. 3 (August 1988): 269–286.

[11]Split ratings are discussed in R. Billingsley, R. Lamy, M. Marr, and T. Thompson, "Split Ratings and Bond Reoffering Yields," *Financial Management* 14, no. 2 (Summer 1985): 59–65; L. H. Ederington, "Why Split Ratings Occur," *Financial Management* 14, no. 1 (Spring 1985): 37–47; and P. Liu and W. T. Moore, "The Impact of Split Bond Ratings on Risk Premia," *The Financial Review* 22, no. 1 (February 1987).

EXHIBIT 18.3 ▸ *DESCRIPTION OF BOND RATINGS*

	FITCH	MOODY'S	STANDARD & POOR'S	DEFINITION
High grade	AAA	Aaa	AAA	The highest rating assigned to a debt instrument, indicating an extremely strong capacity to pay principal and interest. Bonds in this category are often referred to as *gilt edge securities.*
	AA	Aa	AA	High-quality bonds by all standards with strong capacity to pay principal and interest. These bonds are rated lower primarily because the margins of protection are less strong than those for Aaa and AAA bonds.
Medium grade	A	A	A	These bonds possess many favorable investment attributes, but elements may suggest a susceptibility to impairment given adverse economic changes.
	BBB	Baa	BBB	Bonds are regarded as having adequate capacity to pay principal and interest, but certain protective elements may be lacking in the event of adverse economic conditions that could lead to a weakened capacity for payment.
Speculative	BB	Ba	BB	Bonds regarded as having only moderate protection of principal and interest payments during both good and bad times.
	B	B	B	Bonds that generally lack characteristics of other desirable investments. Assurance of interest and principal payments over any long period of time may be small.
Default	CCC	Caa	CCC	Poor-quality issues that may be in default or in danger of default.
	CC	Ca	CC	Highly speculative issues that are often in default or possess other marked shortcomings.
	C			The lowest-rated class of bonds. These issues can be regarded as extremely poor in investment quality.
		C	C	Rating given to income bonds on which no interest is being paid.
	DDD, DD, D		D	Issues in default with principal or interest payments in arrears. Such bonds are extremely speculative and should be valued only on the basis of their value in liquidation or reorganization.

Sources: *Bond Guide* (New York: Standard & Poor's, monthly); *Bond Record* (New York: Moody's Investors Services, Inc., monthly); *Rating Register* (New York: Fitch Investors Service, Inc., monthly).

on their interest payments.) In the case of D-rated obligations, the issues are in outright default, and the ratings indicate the bonds' relative salvage values.[12]

ALTERNATIVE BOND ISSUES

We have described the basic features available for all bonds and the overall structure of the global bond market in terms of the issuers of bonds and investors in bonds. In this section, we provide a detailed discussion of the bonds available from the major issuers of bonds. The presentation is longer than you would expect because when we discuss each issuing unit,

---

[12]Bonds rated below investment grade are also referred to as "high-yield bonds" or "junk" bonds. These high-yield bonds are discussed in the subsequent section on corporate bonds.

such as governments, municipalities, or corporations, we briefly consider the bonds available in several of the major world financial centers, such as Japan, Germany, and the United Kingdom.

Domestic Government Bonds

United States As shown in Exhibit 18.2, a significant percent of the U.S. fixed-income market is U.S. Treasury obligations. The U.S. government, backed by the full faith and credit of the U.S. Treasury, issues Treasury bills (T-bills), which mature in less than one year, and two forms of long-term obligations: government notes, which have maturities of 10 years or less, and Treasury bonds, with maturities of 10 to 30 years. Current Treasury obligations come in denominations of $1,000 and $10,000. The interest income from the U.S. government securities is subject to federal income tax but exempt from state and local levies. These bonds are popular because of their high credit quality, substantial liquidity, and noncallable feature.

Short-term T-bills differ from notes and bonds because they are sold at a discount from par to provide the desired yield. The return is the difference between the purchase price and the par at maturity. In contrast, government notes and bonds carry semiannual coupons that specify the nominal yield of the obligations.

Government notes and bonds have unusual call features. First, the period specified for the deferred call feature on Treasury issues is very long and is generally measured relative to the maturity date rather than from date of issue. They generally cannot be called until five years prior to their maturity date. Notably, *all* U.S. Treasury issues since 1989 have been noncallable.

Treasury Inflation Protected Securities (TIPS)[13] The Treasury began issuing these inflation-indexed bonds in January 1997 to appeal to investors who wanted or needed a *real* default-free rate of return. To ensure the investors will receive the promised yield in real terms, the bond principal and interest payments are indexed to the *Consumer Price Index for All Urban Consumers (CPI-U)* published by the Bureau of Labor Statistics. Because inflation is generally not known until several months after the fact, the index value used has a three-month lag built in—for example, for a bond issued on June 30, 2003, the beginning base index value used would be the CPI value as of March 30, 2003. Following the issuance of a TIPS bond, its principal value is adjusted every six months to reflect the inflation since the base period. In turn, the interest payment is computed based on this adjusted principal—that is, the interest payments equal the original coupon times the adjusted principal. The example in Exhibit 18.4 demonstrates how the principal and interest payments are computed. As shown in this example, both the interest payments and the principal payments are adjusted over time to reflect the prevailing inflation, thereby ensuring that the investor receives a *real* rate of return on these bonds of 3.50 percent.

Notably, these bonds can also be used to derive the prevailing market estimate of the expected rate of inflation during the remaining maturity of the TIPS bond. For example, if we assume that when the bond is issued on July 15, 2003, it sells at par for a YTM of 3.50 percent, while a nominal Treasury note of equal maturity is sold at a YTM of 5.75 percent. This differential implies that investors expect an average annual rate of inflation of 2.25 percent during this five-year period. If, a year later, the spread increased to 2.45 percent, it would indicate that investors expect a further increase in the inflation rate during the next four years.

---

[13]This section draws heavily from the following excellent article: Pu Shen, "Features and Risks of Treasury Inflation Protection Securities," Federal Reserve Bank of Kansas City *Economic Review* (First Quarter 1998): 23–38. Other brief articles on the topic are: William R. Emmons, "Indexed Bonds and Falling Inflation Expectations," *Monetary Trends* (Federal Reserve Bank of St. Louis, September 1997); and Frank A. Schmid, "Extracting Inflation Expectations from Bond Yields," *Monetary Trends* (Federal Reserve Bank of St. Louis, April 1999).

EXHIBIT 18.4 ▶ *PRINCIPAL AND INTEREST PAYMENT FOR A TREASURY INFLATION PROTECTED SECURITY (TIPS)*

Par Value—$1,000
Issued on July 15, 2003
Maturity on July 15, 2008
Coupon—3.50%
Original CPI Value—185.00

DATE	INDEX VALUE[a]	RATE OF INFLATION	ACCRUED PRINCIPAL	INTEREST PAYMENT[b]
7/15/03	185.00	—	$1,000.00	—
1/15/04	187.78	0.015	1,015.00	$17.76
7/15/04	190.59	0.015	1,030.22	18.03
1/15/05	193.83	0.017	1,047.74	18.34
7/15/05	197.51	0.019	1,067.65	18.68
1/15/06	201.46	0.020	1,089.00	19.06
7/15/06	205.49	0.020	1,110.78	19.44
1/15/07	209.19	0.018	1,130.77	19.79
7/15/07	212.96	0.018	1,151.13	20.14
1/15/08	217.22	0.020	1,174.15	20.55
7/15/08	222.65	0.025	1,203.50	21.06

[a]The CPI index value is for the period three months prior to the date.
[b]Semiannual interest payment equals 0.0175 (accrued principal).

Japan[14]   The second-largest government bond market in the world is Japan's. It is controlled by the Japanese government and the Bank of Japan (Japanese Central Bank). Japanese government bonds (JGBs) are an attractive investment vehicle for those favoring the Japanese yen because their quality is equal to that of U.S. Treasury securities (they are guaranteed by the government of Japan) and they are very liquid. There are three maturity segments: medium-term (2, 3, or 4 years), long-term (10 years), and super-long (private placements for 15 and 20 years). Bonds are issued in both registered and bearer form, although registered bonds can be converted to bearer bonds through the registrar at the Bank of Japan.

Medium-term bonds are issued monthly through a competitive auction system similar to that of U.S. Treasury bonds. Long-term bonds are authorized by the Ministry of Finance and issued monthly by the Bank of Japan through an underwriting syndicate consisting of major financial institutions. Most super-long bonds are sold through private placement to a few financial institutions. Very liquid federal government bonds account for over 50 percent of the Japanese bonds outstanding and over 80 percent of total bond trading volume in Japan.

At least 50 percent of the trading in Japanese government bonds will be in the so-called *benchmark issue* of the time. The benchmark issue is selected from 10-year coupon bonds. (As of early 2002, the benchmark issue was a 1.50 percent coupon bond maturing in 2011.) The designation of a benchmark issue is intended to assist smaller financial institutions in their trading

---

[14]For additional discussion, see Aron Viner, *Inside Japanese Financial Markets* (Homewood, Ill.: Dow Jones-Irwin, 1988); Edwin J. Elton and Martin J. Gruber, eds., *Japanese Capital Markets* (New York: Harper & Row, 1990); and Frank J. Fabozzi, ed., *The Japanese Bond Markets* (Chicago: Probus Publishing, 1990).

of government bonds by ensuring these institutions that they would have a liquid market in this particular security. Compared to the benchmark issue, the comparable most active U.S. bond within a class accounts for only about 10 percent of the volume.

The yield on this benchmark bond is typically about 30 basis points below other comparable Japanese government bonds, reflecting its superior marketability. The benchmark issue changes when a designated issue matures or because of a decision by the Bank of Japan.

Germany[15]   The third-largest bond market in the world is the German market, although the government segment of this market is relatively small. Exhibit 18.2 showed that approximately 40 percent of domestic deutschemark bonds are issued by the nonbank corporations, whereas the federal government issues about 36 percent through the German Central Bank.

Bonds issued by the Federal Republic of Germany, referred to as *bund* bonds, are issued in amounts up to DM 4 billion (4 billion deutschemarks) with a minimum denomination of DM 100. Original maturities are normally 10 or 12 years, although 30-year bonds have been issued.

Although bonds are issued as bearer bonds, individual bonds do not exist. A global bond is issued and held in safekeeping within the Germany Securities Clearing System (the *Kassenverein*). Contract notes confirming the terms and ownership of each issue are then distributed to individual investors. Sales are based on these contract notes. These government bunds are very liquid because the Bundesbank makes a market at all times. They also are the highest credit quality because they are guaranteed by the German government. Although listed on the exchanges, government bonds are primarily traded over the counter and interest is paid annually.

United Kingdom[16]   The U.K. government bond market is made up of jobbers and brokers who act as principals or agents with negotiated commission structures. In addition, there are 27 primary dealers similar to the U.S. Treasury market.

Maturities in this market range from short gilts (maturities of less than 5 years) to medium gilts (5 to 15 years) to long gilts (15 years and longer). Government bonds either have a fixed redemption date or a range of dates with redemption at the option of the government after giving appropriate notice. Alternatively, some bonds are redeemable on a given date or at any time afterward at the option of the government. Government bonds are normally registered, although bearer delivery is available.

Gilts are issued through the Bank of England (the British central bank) using the tender method, whereby prospective purchasers tender offering prices at which they hope to be allotted bonds. The price cannot be less than the minimum tender price stated in the prospectus. If the issue is oversubscribed, allotments are made first to those submitting the highest tenders and continue until a price is reached where only a partial allotment is required to fully subscribe the issue. All successful allottees pay the lowest allotment prices.

These issues are extremely liquid and are highly rated because they are guaranteed by the British government. All gilts are quoted and traded on the London Stock Exchange and pay interest semiannually.

Government Agency Issues   In addition to pure government bonds, the federal government in each country can establish agencies that have the authority to issue their own bonds. The size and importance of these agencies differ among countries. They are a large and growing sector of the U.S. bond market, a much smaller component of the bond markets in Japan and Germany, and nonexistent in the United Kingdom.

---

[15]For additional information on the German bond market, see *The European Bond Markets,* ed. The European Bond Commission (Chicago: Probus Publishing, 1989).

[16]For further discussion, see *The European Bond Markets.*

EXHIBIT 18.5	AGENCY ISSUES: SELECTED CHARACTERISTICS

TYPE OF SECURITY	MINIMUM DENOMINATION	FORM	LIFE OF ISSUE	TAX STATUS		HOW INTEREST IS EARNED
Government Sponsored						
Banks for cooperatives (co-ops)	$ 5,000	B,BE	No longer issued	Federal: State: Local:	Taxable Exempt Exempt	Semiannual interest, 360-day year
Federal farm credit banks Consolidated systemwide notes	50,000	BE	5 to 365 days	Federal: State: Local:	Taxable Exempt Exempt	Discount actual, 360-day year
Consolidated systemwide bonds	5,000	BE	6 and 9 months	Federal: State: Local:	Taxable Exempt Exempt	Interest payable at maturity, 360-day year
	1,000	BE	13 months to 15 years	Federal: State: Local:	Taxable Exempt Exempt	Semiannual interest
Federal Home Loan Bank						
Consolidated discount notes	100,000	BE	30 to 360 days	Federal: State: Local:	Taxable Exempt Exempt	Discount actual, 360-day year
Consolidated bonds	10,000[a]	B, BE	1 to 20 years	Federal: State: Local:	Taxable Exempt Exempt	Semiannual interest, 360-day year
Federal Home Loan Mortgage						
Corporation debentures	10,000[a]	BE	18 to 30 years	Federal: State: Local:	Taxable Taxable Taxable	Semiannual interest, 360-day year
Participation certificates	100,000	R	30 years (12-year average life)	Federal: State: Local:	Taxable Taxable Taxable	Monthly interest and principal payments
Federal interstate credit banks	5,000	B, BE	No longer issued	Federal: State: Local:	Taxable Exempt Exempt	Semiannual interest, 360-day year
Federal National Mortgage Association discount notes	50,000[a]	B	30 to 360 days	Federal: State: Local:	Taxable Taxable Taxable	Discount actual, 360-day year
Debentures	10,000[a]	B, BE	1 to 30 years	Federal: State: Local:	Taxable Taxable Taxable	Semiannual interest, 360-day year

(continued)

United States Agency securities are obligations issued by the U.S. government through either a government agency or a government-sponsored corporation. Six government-sponsored enterprises and over two dozen federal agencies issue these bonds. Exhibit 18.5 lists selected characteristics of the more popular government-sponsored and federal agency obligations.[17]

---

[17]We will no longer distinguish between federal agency and government-sponsored obligations; instead, the term *agency* shall apply to either type of issue.

EXHIBIT 18.5 *(continued)*

TYPE OF SECURITY	MINIMUM DENOMINATION	FORM	LIFE OF ISSUE	TAX STATUS		HOW INTEREST IS EARNED
Government National Mortgage Association						
Mortgage-backed bonds	25,000	B, R	1 to 25 years	Federal: State: Local:	Taxable Taxable Taxable	Semiannual interest, 360-day year
Modified pass-throughs	25,000[a]	R	12 to 40 years (12-year average)	Federal: State: Local:	Taxable Taxable Taxable	Monthly interest and principal payments
Student Loan Marketing Association discount notes	100,000	B	Out to 1 year	Federal: State: Local:	Taxable Exempt Exempt	Discount actual, 360-day year
Notes	10,000	R	3 to 10 years	Federal: State: Local:	Taxable Exempt Exempt	Semiannual interest, 360-day year
Floating rate notes	10,000[a]	R	6 months to 10 years	Federal: State: Local:	Taxable Exempt Exempt	Interest rate adjusted weekly to an increment over the average auction rate of 91-day Treasury bills and payable quarterly
Tennessee Valley Authority (TVA)	1,000	R, B	5 to 25 years	Federal: State: Local:	Taxable Exempt Exempt	Semiannual interest, 360-day year
U.S. Postal Service	10,000	R, B	25 years	Federal: State: Local:	Taxable Exempt Exempt	Semiannual interest, 360-day year

Notes: Form B = Bearer; R = Registered; BE = Book entry form. Debt issues sold subsequent to December 31, 1982, must be in registered form.
[a]Minimum purchase with increments in $5,000.

Source: *United States Government Securities* (New York: Merrill Lynch Government Securities, Inc., 1996).

Agency issues usually pay interest semiannually, and the minimum denominations vary between $1,000 and $10,000. These obligations are not direct Treasury issues, yet they carry the full faith and credit of the U.S. government. Moreover, some of the issues are subject to state and local income tax, whereas others are exempt.[18]

One agency issue offers particularly attractive investment opportunities: GNMA *(Ginnie Mae)* pass-through certificates, which are obligations of the Government National Mortgage Association.[19] These bonds represent an undivided interest in a pool of federally insured mortgages. The bondholders receive monthly payments from Ginnie Mae that include both principal and interest because the agency "passes through" mortgage payments made by the original borrower (the mortgagee) to Ginnie Mae.

[18]Federal National Mortgage Association (Fannie Mae) debentures, for example, are subject to state and local income tax, whereas the interest income from Federal Home Loan Bank bonds is exempt. In fact, a few issues are exempt from federal income tax as well (e.g., public housing bonds).

[19]For a further discussion of mortgage-backed securities, see Frank J. Fabozzi and Chuck Ramsey, "Mortgages and Overview of Mortgage-Backed Securities"; Lakhbir S. Hayre, Cyrus Mohebbi, and Thomas A. Zimmerman, "Mortgage Pass-Through"; and Lehman Bros., Inc, "Collateralized Mortgage Obligations," all in *The Handbook of Fixed-Income Securities,* 6th ed., ed. Frank J. Fabozzi (New York: McGraw-Hill, 2001).

The coupons on these pass-through securities are related to the interest charged on the pool of mortgages. The portion of the cash flow that represents the repayment of the principal is tax-free, but the interest income is subject to federal, state, and local taxes. The issues have minimum denominations of $25,000 with maturities of 25 to 30 years but an average life of only 12 years because, as mortgages in the pool are paid off, payments and prepayments are passed through to the investor. Therefore, unlike most bond issues, the monthly payment is not fixed because of the prepayment schedule that can vary dramatically over time when interest rates change.

As we will note in Chapter 19 in connection with the valuation of bonds with embedded options, mortgages generally have a call option whereby the homeowner has the option to pre-pay the mortgage. There are prepayments on these securities for two reasons: (1) because home-owners pay off their mortgages when they sell their homes and (2) because owners refinance their homes when mortgage interest rates decline as they did in 1997 and 2001. Therefore, a major disadvantage of GNMA issues is that their *maturities are very uncertain.*

Japan   The agencies in Japan, referred to as *government associate organizations,* account for about 17 percent of the total Japanese bond market. This agency market includes public debt, but almost twice as much is privately placed with major financial institutions. Public agency debt is issued like government debt.

Germany   The agency market in Germany finances about 5 percent of the public debt. The major agencies are the Federal Railway and the Federal Post Office. These Bahns are issued up to DM 2 billion. The issue procedure is similar to that used for regular government bonds and are relatively liquid, although less liquid than government bunds. These agency issues are implicitly guaranteed by the government.

United Kingdom   As shown in Exhibit 18.2, there are no agency bonds in the United Kingdom.

Municipal Bonds   Municipal bonds are issued by states, counties, cities, and other political subdivisions. Again, the size of the municipal bond market (referred to as *local authority* in the United Kingdom) varies substantially among countries. It is about 10 percent of the total U.S. market, compared to about 3 percent in Japan, 15 percent in Germany, and nonexistent in the United Kingdom. Because of the size and popularity of this market in the United States, we will discuss only the U.S. munic-ipal bond market.

Municipalities in the United States issue two distinct types of bonds: general obligation bonds and revenue issues. **General obligation bonds (GOs)** are essentially backed by the full faith and credit of the issuer and its entire taxing power. **Revenue bonds,** in turn, are serviced by the income generated from specific revenue-producing projects of the municipality, such as bridges, toll roads, hospitals, municipal coliseums, and waterworks. Revenue bonds generally provide higher returns than GOs because of their higher default risk. Should a municipality fail to gen-erate sufficient income from a project designated to service a revenue bond, it has no legal debt service obligation until the income becomes sufficient.

GO municipal bonds tend to be issued on a serial basis so that the issuer's cash flow require-ments will be steady over the life of the obligation. Therefore, the principal portion of the total debt service requirement generally begins at a fairly low level and builds up over the life of the obligation. In contrast, most municipal revenue bonds are term issues, so the principal value is not due until the final maturity date.[20]

---

[20]For a more detailed discussion of the municipal bond market, see Sylvan G. Feldstein, Frank J. Fabozzi, and Patrick M. Kennedy, "Municipal Bonds." For discussion of the credit analysis of these bonds, see Sylvan G. Feldstein, "Guide-lines in the Credit Analysis of General Obligation and Revenue Municipal Bonds." Both chapters are in *The Handbook of Fixed-Income Securities.* 6th ed.

The most important feature of municipal obligations is that the interest payments are exempt from federal income tax and from taxes in the locality and state in which the obligation was issued. This means that their attractiveness varies with the investor's tax bracket.

You can convert the tax-free yield of a municipal to an equivalent taxable yield (ETY) using the following equation:

➤18.3
$$ETY = \frac{i}{(1-t)}$$

where:

ETY = equivalent taxable yield
  i = coupon rate of the municipal obligations
  t = marginal tax rate of the investor

An investor in the 35 percent marginal tax bracket would find that a 5 percent yield on a municipal bond selling close to its par value is equivalent to a 7.69 percent fully taxable yield according to the following calculation:

$$ETY = \frac{0.05}{(1-0.35)} = 0.0769$$

Because the tax-free yield is the major benefit of municipal bonds, an investor's marginal tax rate is a primary concern in evaluating them. As a rough rule of thumb, using the tax rates expected in 2002, an investor must be in the 28 to 30 percent tax bracket before the lower yields available in municipal bonds are competitive with those from fully taxable bonds. However, although the interest payment on municipals is tax-free, any capital gains are not (which is why the ETY formula is correct only for a bond selling close to its par value).

Municipal Bond Insurance   A significant feature of the U.S. municipal bond market is *municipal bond insurance,* which provides that an insurance company will guarantee to make principal and interest payments in the event that the issuer of the bonds defaults. The insurance is placed on the bond at date of issue and is *irrevocable* over the life of the issue. The issuer purchases the insurance for the benefit of the investor, and the municipality benefits from lower interest costs due to lower default risk, which causes an increase in the rating on the bond and increased marketability. Those who would benefit from the insurance are small government units not widely known and bonds with a complex security structure.

As of 2002, approximately 40 percent of all new municipal bond issues were insured. There are six private bond insurance firms: The Municipal Bond Investors Assurance (MBIA), American Municipal Bond Assurance Corporation (AMBAC), the Financial Security Assurance (FSA), the Financial Guaranty Insurance Company (FGIC), Capital Guaranty Insurance Company (CGIC), and Connie Lee Insurance Company. These firms will insure either general obligation or revenue bonds. To qualify for private bond insurance, the issue must initially carry an S&P rating of BBB or better. Currently, the rating agencies will give an AAA (Aaa) rating to bonds insured by these firms because all the insurance firms have AAA ratings. Issues with these private guarantees have enjoyed a more active secondary market and lower required yields.[21]

---

[21]For a discussion of municipal bond insurance, see Sylvan Feldstein, Frank J. Fabozzi, and Patrick M. Kennedy, "Municipal Bonds," in *The Handbook of Fixed-Income Securities;* 6th ed. and D. S. Kidwell, E. H. Sorenson, and J. M. Wachowicz, "Estimating the Signaling Benefits of Debt Insurance: The Case of Municipal Bonds," *Journal of Financial and Quantitative Analysis* 22, no. 3 (September 1987): 299–313.

Corporate Bonds   Again, the importance of corporate bonds varies across countries. The absolute dollar value of corporate bonds in the United States is substantial and has grown overall and as a percentage of U.S. long-term capital. At the same time, corporate debt as a percentage of total U.S. debt has stabilized at about 30 percent because of the faster growth of agency debt. The pure corporate sector in Japan is small and declining and the pure corporate sector in Germany has grown to be about 44 percent. The proportion of corporate debt in the United Kingdom is in the 5 to 6 percent range.

U.S. Corporate Bond Market

Utilities dominate the U.S. corporate bond market. Other important segments include industrials, rail and transportation issues, and financial issues. This market is very diverse and includes debentures, first-mortgage issues, convertible obligations, bonds with warrants, subordinated debentures, income bonds (similar to municipal revenue bonds), collateral trust bonds backed by financial assets, equipment trust certificates, and asset-backed securities (ABS) including mortgage-backed bonds.

If we ignore convertible bonds and bonds with warrants, the preceding list of obligations varies by the type of collateral behind the bond. Most bonds have semiannual interest payments, sinking funds, and a single maturity date. Maturities range from 25 to 40 years, with public utilities generally on the longer end and industrials preferring the 25- to 30-year range. Most corporate bonds provide for deferred calls after 5 to 10 years. The deferment period varies directly with the level of the interest rates. Specifically, during periods of higher interest rates, bond issues typically will carry a 7- to 10-year deferment, while during periods of lower interest rates, the deferment periods decline.

On the other hand, corporate notes—with maturities of five to seven years—are generally noncallable. Notes become popular when interest rates are high because issuing firms prefer to avoid long-term obligations during such periods. In contrast, during periods of low interest rates, such as 1997 and 2001, most corporate issues did not include a call provision because corporations did not believe that they would be able to exercise the call option and did not want to pay the required higher yield.

Generally, the average yields for industrial bonds will be the lowest of the three major sectors, followed by utility returns. The difference in yield between utilities and industrials occurs because utilities have the largest supply of bonds, so yields on their bonds must be higher to increase the demand for these bonds.[22]

Mortgage Bonds   The issuer of a mortgage bond has granted to the bondholder a first-mortgage lien on some piece of property or possibly all the firm's property. Such a lien provides greater security to the bondholder and a lower interest rate for the issuing firm.

Equipment Trust Certificates   Equipment trust certificates are issued by railroads (the biggest issuers), airlines, and other transportation firms with the proceeds used to purchase equipment (freight cars, railroad engines, and airplanes), which serves as the collateral for the debt. Maturities range from 1 to about 15 years. The fairly short maturities reflect the nature of the collateral, which is subject to substantial wear and tear and tends to deteriorate rapidly.

Equipment trust certificates are appealing to investors because of their attractive yields, low default record, and fairly liquid secondary market.

Collateral Trust Bonds   As an alternative to pledging fixed assets or property, a borrower can pledge financial assets, such as stocks, bonds, or notes, as collateral. These bonds are termed *collateral trust bonds*. These pledged assets are held by a trustee for the benefit of the bondholder.

---

[22]For a further discussion, see Frank J. Fabozzi, Richard Wilson, and Richard Todd, "Corporate Bonds," in *The Handbook of Fixed-Income Securities,* 6th ed.

Collateralized Mortgage Obligations (CMOs)[23]   Earlier we discussed mortgage bonds backed by pools of mortgages. You will recall that the pass-through monthly payments are necessarily both interest and principal and that the bondholder is subject to early retirement if the mortgagees prepay because the house is sold or the mortgage refinanced. Therefore, when you acquire the typical mortgage pass-through bonds, you would be uncertain about the size and timing of the payments.

Collateralized mortgage obligations (CMOs) were developed in the early 1980s to offset some of the problems with the traditional mortgage pass-throughs. The main innovation of the CMO instrument is the segmentation of irregular mortgage cash flows to create short-term, medium-, and long-term securities. Specifically, CMO investors own bonds that are serviced with the cash flows from mortgages; but, rather than the straight pass-through arrangement, the CMO substitutes a *sequential distribution process* that creates a series of bonds with varying maturities to appeal to a wider range of investors.

The prioritized distribution process is as follows:

➤ Several classes of bonds (these are referred to as *tranches*) are issued against a pool of mortgages, which are the collateral. For example, assume a CMO issue with four classes (tranches) of bonds. In such a case, the first three (e.g., Classes A, B, C) would pay interest at their stated rates beginning at their issue date and the fourth class would be an accrual bond (referred to as a *Z bond*).[24]

➤ The cash flows received from the underlying mortgages are applied first to pay the interest on the bonds and then to retire these bonds.

➤ The classes of bonds are retired sequentially. All principal payments are directed first to the shortest-maturity class A bonds until they are completely retired. Then all principal payments are directed to the next shortest-maturity bonds (i.e., the class B bonds). The process continues until all the classes have been paid off.

➤ During the early periods, the accrual bonds (the class Z bonds) pay no interest, but the interest accrues as additional principal, and the cash flow from the mortgages that collateralize these bonds is used to pay interest on and retire the bonds in the other classes. Subsequently, all remaining cash flows are used to pay off the accrued interest, pay any current interest, and then to retire the Z bonds.

This prioritized sequential pattern means that the A-class bonds are fairly short term and each subsequent class is a little longer term until the Z-class bond, which is a long-term bond. It also functions like a zero coupon or PIK bond for the initial years.

Besides creating bonds that pay interest in a more normal pattern (quarterly or semiannually) and that have more predictable maturities, these bonds are considered very high quality securities (AAA) because of the structure and quality of the collateral. To obtain an AAA rating, CMOs are structured to ensure that the underlying mortgages will always generate enough cash to support the bonds issued, even under the most conservative prepayment and reinvestment rates. In fact, most CMOs are overcollateralized.

Further, the credit risk of the collateral is minimal because most are backed by mortgages guaranteed by a federal agency (GNMA, FNMA) or by the FHLMC. Those mortgages that are

---

[23]For a detailed discussion, see Lehman Bros., "Collateralized Mortgage Obligations," in *The Handbook of Fixed-Income Securities,* 6th ed.

[24]The four-class CMO was the typical configuration during the 1980s and is used here for demonstration purposes. By 2001, CMOs were issued with 18 to 20 classes. More advanced CMOs are referred to as REMICs, which are intended to provide greater certainty regarding the cash flow patterns for various components of the pool or some of those investing in the pool.

not backed by agencies carry private insurance for principal and interest and mortgage insurance. Notably, even with this AAA rating, the yield on these CMOs typically has been higher than the yields on AA industrials. This premium yield has, of course, contributed to their popularity and growth.

Asset-Backed Securities (ABSs)   A rapidly expanding segment of the securities market is that of *asset-backed securities (ABSs),* which involve *securitizing debt.* This is an important concept because it substantially increases the liquidity of these individual debt instruments, whether they be individual mortgages, car loans, or credit card debt. This general class of securities was introduced in 1983. Since then, more than $700 billion in asset-backed securities have been issued. Beyond the mortgage securities, this market is dominated by securities backed by automobile loans and credit card receivables.

Certificates for Automobile Receivables (CARs)   CARs are securities collateralized by loans made to individuals to finance the purchase of cars. Auto loans are self-amortizing, with monthly payments and relatively short maturities (i.e., two to five years). These auto loans can either be direct loans from a lending institution or indirect loans that are originated by an auto dealer and sold to the ultimate lender. CARs typically have monthly or quarterly fixed interest and principal payments, and expected weighted average lives of one to three years with specified maturities of three to five years. The expected actual life of the instrument typically is shorter than the specified maturity because of early payoffs when cars are sold or traded in. The cash flows of CARs are comparable to short-term corporate debt. They provide a significant yield premium over General Motors Acceptance Corporation (GMAC) commercial paper, which is the most liquid short-term corporate alternative. The popularity of these collateralized securities makes them important not only by themselves but also as an indication of the potential for issuing additional collateralized securities backed by other assets and/or other debt instruments.[25]

Credit Card Receivables   Since 1992, the fastest-growing segment of the ABS market has been securities supported by credit card loans. Credit card receivables are considered to be a revolving credit ABS, in contrast to auto loan receivables that are referred to as an installment contract ABS—because of the nature of the loan. Specifically, whereas the mortgaged-backed and auto loan securities amortize principal, the principal payments from credit card receivables are not paid to the investor but are retained by the trustee to reinvest in additional receivables. This allows the issuer to specify a maturity for the security that is consistent with the needs of the issuer and the demands of the investors.

When buying a credit card ABS, the indenture specifies (1) the intended maturity for the security; (2) the "lockout period" during which no principal will be paid; and (3) the structure for repaying the principal, which can be accomplished through a single-bullet payment, such as a bond, or distributed monthly with the interest payment over a specified amortization period. For example, a 5-year credit card ABS could have a lockout period of 4 years followed by a 12-month amortization of the principal.

Beyond this standard arrangement, revolving credit securities are protected by early amortization events that can force early repayment if specific payout events occur that are detrimental to the investor (e.g., if there is an increase in the loss rate or if the issuer goes into bankruptcy or receivership). Although this early amortization feature protects the investor from credit problems, it causes an early payment that may not be desirable for the investor.[26]

---

[25]For further discussion, see W. Alexander Roever, John McElravey, and Glenn Schultz, "Securities Backed by Automobile Loans," in *The Handbook of Fixed-Income Securities,* 6th ed.

[26]For further discussion, see John N. McElravey, "Securities Backed by Credit Card Receivables; in *The Handbook of Fixed-Income Securities,* 6th ed.

Variable-Rate Notes Introduced in the United States in the mid-1970s, **variable-rate notes** became popular during periods of high interest rates. The typical variable-rate note possesses two unique features:

1. After the first 6 to 18 months of the issue's life, during which a minimum rate is often guaranteed, the coupon rate floats, so that every six months it changes to follow some standard. Usually it is pegged 1 percent above a stipulated short-term rate. For example, the rate might be the preceding three weeks' average 90-day T-bill rate.
2. After the first year or two, the notes are redeemable at par, at the *holder's* option, usually at six-month intervals.

Such notes represent a long-term commitment on the part of the borrower yet provide the lender with all the characteristics of a short-term obligation. They typically are available to investors in minimum denominations of $1,000. However, although the six-month redemption feature provides liquidity, the variable rates can cause these issues to experience wide swings in semiannual coupons.[27]

Zero Coupon and Deep Discount Bonds The typical corporate bond has a coupon and maturity. In turn, the value of the bond is the present value of the stream of cash flows (interest and principal) discounted at the required yield to maturity (YTM). Alternatively, some bonds do not have any coupons or have coupons that are below the market rate at the time of issue. Such securities are referred to as *zero coupon* or *minicoupon bonds* or *original-issue discount (OID) bonds*. A zero coupon discount bond promises to pay a stipulated principal amount at a future maturity date, but it does not promise to make any interim interest payments. Therefore, the price of the bond is the present value of the principal payment at the maturity date using the required discount rate for this bond. The return on the bond is the difference between what the investor pays for the bond at the time of purchase and the principal payment at maturity.

Consider a zero coupon, $10,000 par value bond with a 20-year maturity. If the required rate of return on bonds of equal maturity and quality is 8 percent and we assume semiannual discounting, the initial selling price for this bond would be $2,082.89 because the present-value factor at 8 percent compounded semiannually for 20 years is 0.208289. From the time of purchase to the point of maturity, the investor would not receive any cash flow from the firm. Notably, the investor must pay taxes, however, on the implied interest on the bond, although no cash is received. Because an investor subject to taxes would experience severe negative cash flows during the life of these bonds, they are primarily of interest to investment accounts not subject to taxes, such as pensions, IRAs, or Keogh accounts.[28]

A modified form of zero coupon bond is the OID bond where the coupon is set substantially below the prevailing market rate, for example, a 5 percent coupon on a bond when market rates are 12 percent. As a result, the bond is issued at a deep discount from par value. Again, taxes must be paid on the implied 12 percent return rather than the nominal 5 percent, so the cash flow disadvantage of zero coupon bonds, though lessened, remains.

High-Yield Bonds A segment of the corporate bond market that has grown in size, importance, and controversy is **high-yield bonds**, also referred too as *speculative-grade bonds* and *junk bonds*. These are corporate bonds that have been assigned a bond rating as noninvestment grade, that is, they have a rating below BBB or Baa. The title of speculative-grade bonds is prob-

---

[27]For an extended discussion, see Richard S. Wilson, "Domestic Floating-Rate and Adjustable-Rate Debt Securities," in *The Handbook of Fixed-Income Securities,* 6th ed.

[28]These bonds will be discussed further in Chapter 19 in the section on volatility and duration and in Chapter 20 when we consider immunization.

ably the most objective because bonds that are not rated investment grade are speculative grade. The designation of *high-yield bonds* was by Drexel Burnham Lambert (DBL) as an indication of the returns available for these bonds relative to Treasury bonds and investment-grade corporate bonds. The *junk bond* designation is obviously somewhat derogatory and refers to the low credit quality of the issues.

Brief History of the High-Yield Bond Market   Based on a specification that bonds rated below BBB make up the high-yield market, this segment has existed as long as there have been rating agencies. Prior to 1980, most of the high-yield bonds were referred to as *fallen angels,* which means they were bonds that were originally issued as investment-grade securities, but because of changes in the firm over time, the bonds were downgraded into the high-yield sector (BB and below).

The market changed in the early 1980s when DBL began aggressively underwriting high-yield bonds for two groups of clients: (1) small firms that did not have the financial strength to receive an investment-grade rating by the rating agencies, and (2) large and small firms that issued high-yield bonds in connection with leveraged buyouts (LBOs). As a result, the high-yield bond market went from a residual market that included fallen angels to a new-issue market where bonds were underwritten and issued with below-investment-grade ratings.

As a result, the high-yield bond market exploded in size and activity beginning in 1983. As shown in Exhibit 18.6, there were a limited number of new high-yield issues in the late 1970s, and they were not very large issues. Beginning in 1983, more large issues became common (the average size of an issue currently is over $250 million), and high-yield issues became a significant percentage of the total new-issue bond market (typically between 15 and 20 percent). As of 2002, the total outstanding high-yield debt constituted about 20 percent of outstanding corporate debt in the United States.[29]

An important point bears repeating: Although the high-yield debt market has existed for many years, its real emergence as a major component of the U.S. capital market did not occur until 1983. This is relevant when considering the liquidity and default experience for these securities.

Distribution of High-Yield Bond Ratings   Exhibit 18.7 contains the distribution of ratings for all the bonds contained in the Lehman Brothers High-Yield Bond Index as of December 31, 1987–2001. As shown, the heavy concentration by market value is typically in the B class, which contains almost half of all value. There was a strong increase in the BB category that grew from 17 percent in 1987 to over 48 percent in 1995, then declined to less than 34 percent in 1999 prior to an increase to over 46 percent in 2001.

Ownership of High-Yield Bonds   The major owners of high-yield bonds have been mutual funds, insurance companies, and pension funds. As of the end of 2001, over 100 mutual funds were either exclusively directed to invest in high-yield bonds or included such bonds in their portfolio. Notably, there has been a shift of ownership away from insurance companies and savings and loans toward mutual funds. This shift occurred during the late 1980s when regulators "encouraged" the insurance companies and S&Ls to reduce or eliminate high-yield bonds from their portfolios.

---

[29]Almost everyone would acknowledge that the development of the high-yield debt market has had a positive impact on the capital-raising ability of the economy. For an analysis of this impact, see Kevin J. Perry and Robert A. Taggart, Jr., "The Growing Role of Junk Bonds in Corporate Finance," *Journal of Applied Corporate Finance* 1, no. 1 (Spring 1988): 37–45. An update on its characteristics is contained in Martin S. Fridson. "The State of the High-Yield Bond Market: Overshooting or Return to Normalcy," *Journal of Applied Corporate Finance* 7, no. 1 (Spring 1994): 85–97; Edward I. Altman, "Revisiting the High-Yield Bond Market," *Financial Management* 21, no. 2 (Summer 1992): 78–92; and Frank K. Reilly and David J. Wright, "Unique Risk-Return Characteristics of High-Yield Bonds, "*The Journal of Fixed Income* 11, no. 2 (September 2001): 65–82.

EXHIBIT 18.6 ▶ *HIGH-YIELD BONDS—NEW-ISSUE VOLUME: 1977–2001*

	PUBLIC		144A		TOTAL		
YEAR	NUMBER OF ISSUES	PRINCIPAL AMOUNT ($ MILLIONS)	NUMBER OF ISSUES	PRINCIPAL AMOUNT ($ MILLIONS)	NUMBER OF ISSUES	PRINCIPAL AMOUNT ($ MILLIONS)	AVERAGE ISSUE SIZE ($ MILLIONS)
1977	61	$ 1,040.2			61	$ 1,040.2	17.05
1978	82	1,578.5			82	1,578.5	19.25
1979	56	1,399.8			56	1,399.8	25.00
1980	45	1,429.3			45	1,429.3	31.76
1981	34	1,536.3			34	1,536.3	45.19
1982	52	2,691.5			52	2,691.5	51.76
1983	95	7,765.2			95	7,765.2	81.74
1984	131	15,238.9			131	15,238.9	116.33
1985	175	15,684.8			175	15,684.8	89.63
1986	226	33,261.8			226	33,261.8	147.18
1987	190	30,522.2			190	30,522.2	160.64
1988	160	31,095.2			160	31,095.2	194.34
1989	130	28,753.2			130	28,753.2	221.18
1990	10	1,397.0			10	1,397.0	139.70
1991	48	9,967.0			48	9,967.0	207.65
1992	245	39,755.2	29	$ 3,810.8	274	43,566.0	159.00
1993	341	57,163.7	95	15,096.8	436	72,260.5	165.74
1994	191	34,598.8	81	7,733.5	272	42,332.3	155.63
1995	152	30,139.1	94	14,242.0	246	44,381.1	180.41
1996	142	30,739.4	217	35,172.9	359	65,912.3	183.60
1997	103	19,822.0	576	98,885.0	679	118,707.0	174.83
1998	116	29,844.0	604	111,044.7	720	140,888.7	195.68
1999	60	16,520.0	357	83,157.0	417	99,677.0	239.00
2000	32	10,621.1	149	39,593.6	181	50,214.7	277.40
2001	42	14,385.6	267	69,109.6	309	83,495.2	270.20

Note: Includes nonconvertible, corporate debt rated below investment grade by Moody's or Standard & Poor's. Excludes mortgage- and asset-backed issues, as well as non-144a private placements.

Source: Merrill Lynch & Co.; Securities Data Company.

The purpose of this discussion has been to introduce you to high-yield bonds because of the growth in size and importance of this segment of the market for individual and institutional investors. We revisit this topic in Chapter 20 on bond portfolio management, where we review the historical rates of return and alternative risk factors, including the default experience for these bonds. All of this must be considered by potential investors in these securities.[30]

---

[30]For additional discussion of these bonds, see Edward I. Altman, ed., *The High-Yield Debt Market* (Homewood, Ill.: Dow Jones–Irwin, 1990); Frank J. Fabozzi, ed., *The New High-Yield Debt Market* (New York: Harper Business, 1990); and Martin S. Fridson, *High-Yield Bonds* (Chicago: Probus Publishing, 1989).

EXHIBIT 18.7

HIGH YIELD INDEX COMPOSITION BY CREDIT QUALITY: 1987–2001 (PERCENTAGE OF MARKET VALUE)

	BB	B	CCC/Unrated
1987	17.41	68.61	13.99
1988	16.26	69.09	14.64
1989	18.02	63.53	18.46
1990	15.92	67.17	16.91
1991	21.41	56.72	21.87
1992	27.86	56.70	15.44
1993	42.78	49.37	7.85
1994	42.61	48.00	9.38
1995	48.32	44.60	7.08
1996	45.67	47.36	6.97
1997	38.19	51.07	10.74
1998	35.28	52.04	12.68
1999	33.83	55.82	10.34
2000	36.63	53.94	9.43
2001	46.04	42.35	11.61

Source: Lehman Brothers, *Global Family of Indices.* (New York: Lehman Brothers, Annual).

Japanese Corporate Bond Market   The corporate bond market in Japan is made up of two components: (1) bonds issued by industrial firms or utilities and (2) bonds issued by banks to finance loans to corporations. As noted in connection with Exhibit 18.2, the pure corporate bond sector has declined in relative size over time to less than 10 percent of the total. In contrast, the dollar amount of bank debentures is over 18 percent of the total.

Japanese corporate bonds are regulated by the *Kisaikai,* a council composed of 22 bond-related banks and seven major securities companies. It operates under the authority of the Ministry of Finance (MOF) and the Bank of Japan (BOJ) to determine bond-issuing procedures, including specifying the coupons on corporate bonds in relation to coupons on long-term government bonds in order to prevent any competition with the government bond market.

Because of numerous bankruptcies during the 1930s depression, the government mandated that all corporate debt be secured. This requirement was abolished in 1988. The issuance of unsecured debt led to the birth of bond-rating agencies, which were not needed with completely secured debt. Currently, there are five major bond-rating agencies.

The Ministry of Finance specifies minimum issuing requirements and controls the issuance system that specifies who can issue bonds and when they can be issued. In addition, lead-underwriting managers are predetermined in accordance with a lead manager rotating system that ensures balance among the major securities firms in Japan.

Bank Bonds   The substantial issuance of bank bonds is because of the banking system in Japan, which is segmented into the following components:

➤ Commercial banks (13 big-city banks and 64 regional banks)
➤ Long-term credit banks (3)
➤ Mutual loan and savings banks (6)
➤ Specialized financial institutions

During the post–World War II reconstruction, several banks were permitted to obtain funding by issuing medium- and long-term debentures at rates above yields on government bonds. These funds were used to make mortgage loans to firms in the industrial sector to rebuild plants and equipment. Currently, these financial institutions sell five-year coupon debentures and one-year discount debentures directly to individual and institutional investors. The long-term credit banks are not allowed to take deposits and thus depend on the debentures to obtain funds. These bonds are traded in the OTC market.[31]

German Corporate Bond Market   Germany likewise has a combination sector in corporates that includes pure corporate bonds and bank bonds. Bank bonds may be issued in collateralized or uncollateralized form. For the collateralized bonds, the largest categories are mortgage bonds and commercial bonds.

German mortgage bonds are collateralized bonds of the issuing bank backed by mortgage loans. Due to the supervision of these bonds and the mortgage collateral, these bonds are very high quality. They are issued in bearer or registered form. Most registered bonds are sold to domestic institutions and cannot be listed on a stock exchange because they are not considered securities. Alternatively, the bearer bonds, which are transferred by book entry, are sold in small denominations, are traded on the exchanges, and enjoy an active secondary market.

German commercial bonds are subject to the same regulation and collateralization as mortgage bonds. The difference is that the collateral consists of loans to or guarantees by a German public-sector entity rather than a first mortgage. Possible borrowers include the federal government, its agencies (the federal railway or the post office), federal states, and agencies of the European Economic Community (EEC). The credit quality of these loans is excellent. Mortgage and commercial bonds have identical credit standing and trade at very narrow spreads.

Schuldscheindarlehen are private loan agreements between borrowers and large investors (usually a bank) who make the loans but who can (with the borrower's permission) sell them or divide the loans among several investors. These instruments are like a negotiable loan participation. All participants receive a copy of the loan agreement, and a letter of assignment gives the participant title to a share of principal and interest, although the bank acts as the agent. These loan agreements, which come in various sizes, account for a substantial proportion of all funds raised in Germany. A large volume of these private loan agreements exists, but because the market is not very liquid they typically are used for the investment of large sums to maturity.

U.K. Corporate Bond Market   Corporate bonds in the United Kingdom are available in three forms: debentures, unsecured loans, and convertible bonds. The value of securities in each class are about equal. The maturity structure of the corporate bond market is fairly wide because during the 1980s, the preference of investors shifted toward long-maturity bonds. The coupon structure of corporate bonds also is broad with high-coupon bonds issued during the 1980s. The higher end of the coupon range, which goes from 10 to 14 percent, is due to the unsecured segment of this market. In contrast, convertible bonds have the low coupons. Almost all U.K. corporate bonds are callable term bonds.

Corporate bonds in the United Kingdom have been issued through both public offerings and private placements. Subsequently, primary dealers have begun trading corporate bonds directly with each other. All corporate bonds are issued in registered form.

---

[31]For further discussion of this market, see Aron Viner, *Inside Japanese Financial Markets* (Homewood, Ill.: Dow Jones–Irwin, 1988), Chapters 5 and 6; and Frank J. Fabozzi, ed., *The Japanese Bond Markets* (Chicago: Probus Publishing, 1990.

International Bonds

Each country's international bond market has two components. The first, *foreign bonds,* are issues sold primarily in one country and currency by a borrower of a different nationality. An example would be U.S. dollar–denominated bonds sold in the United States by a Japanese firm. (These are referred to as *Yankee bonds.*) Second are *Eurobonds,* which are bonds underwritten by international bond syndicates and sold in several national markets. An example would be Eurodollar bonds that are securities denominated in U.S. dollars, underwritten by an international syndicate, and sold to non-U.S. investors outside the United States. The relative size of these two markets (foreign bonds versus Eurobonds) varies by country.

United States   The Eurodollar bond market has been much larger than the Yankee bond market (about $635 billion versus $220 billion). However, because the Eurodollar bond market is heavily affected by changes in the value of the U.S. dollar, it has experienced slower growth during periods when the dollar was weak. Such periods have created a desire for diversification by investors.

Yankee bonds are issued by foreign firms who register with the SEC and borrow U.S. dollars, using issues underwritten by a U.S. syndicate for delivery in the United States. These bonds are traded in the United States and pay interest semiannually. Over 60 percent of Yankee bonds are issued by Canadian corporations and typically have shorter maturities and longer call protection than U.S. domestic issues. These features increase their appeal.

The Eurodollar bond market is dominated by foreign investors, and the center of trading is in London. Eurodollar bonds pay interest annually. The Eurodollar bond market currently comprises almost 40 percent of the total Eurobond market.

Japan   Before 1985, the Japanese international bond market was dominated (over 90 percent) by foreign bonds (Samurai bonds) with the balance in Euroyen bonds. After the issuance requirements for Euroyen bonds were liberalized in 1985, the ratio of issuance swung heavily in favor of Euroyen bonds.

Samurai bonds are yen-denominated bonds sold by non-Japanese issuers and mainly sold in Japan. The market is fairly small and has limited liquidity. The market has experienced very little growth in terms of yen but substantial growth in U.S. dollar terms because of changes in the exchange rate.

Euroyen bonds are yen-denominated bonds sold in markets outside Japan by international syndicates. This market has grown substantially because of the liberal issue requirements. Its appeal over time is determined by the strength or weakness of the yen relative to other currencies.

Germany   All deutschemark bonds of foreign issuers can be considered Eurobonds. This is because the stability of German currency reduces the importance of the distinction between foreign bonds (DM-denominated bonds sold in Germany by non-German firms) and Euro-DM bonds (DM bonds sold outside Germany). Both types of bonds share the same primary and secondary market procedures, are free of German taxes, and have similar yields; and the amount outstanding is almost equal.

United Kingdom   U.K. foreign bonds, referred to as *bulldog bonds,* are sterling-denominated bonds issued by non-English firms and sold in London. Eurosterling bonds are sold in markets outside London by international syndicates.

Similar to other countries, the U.K. international bond market has become dominated by the Eurosterling bonds. As of 2001, the ratio of Eurobonds versus foreign bonds (bulldogs) had grown to 25-to-1. The procedure for issuing and trading Eurosterling bonds is similar to that of other Eurobonds.

As might be expected, the price information needs of bond investors are considerably different from those of stockholders. We know that there is substantial up-to-the-minute information on numerous listed and OTC stocks based on recent transactions. In sharp contrast, almost all bond trading (in dollar volume) is done on the OTC market, and these transactions are not reported. As a result, almost all prices reported are based upon self-reporting of yield estimates by bond dealers who trade government, corporate, or municipal bonds. There was some discussion of this in Chapter 5 when we considered the creation and maintenance of bond indexes. Given this background, the following discussion considers how investors read and interpret bond price information reported in newspapers and quote sheets.

Interpreting Bond Quotes

Essentially, all bonds are quoted on the basis of either yield or price. Price quotes are always interpreted as a *percentage of par.* For example, a quote of 98½ is interpreted not as $98.50 but 98½ percent of par. The dollar price is derived from the quote, given the par value. If the par value is $5,000 on a municipal bond, then the price of an issue quoted at 98½ would be $4,925. Actually, the market follows three systems of bond pricing: one system for corporates, another for governments (both Treasury and agency obligations), and a third for municipals.

Corporate Bond Quotes Exhibit 18.8 is a listing of U.S. Exchange corporate bond quotes that appeared in *The Wall Street Journal* on February 27, 2002. The data pertain to trading activity on February 26, 2002. Several quotes have been designated for illustrative purposes. The first issue designated in Column 1 is an American Telephone and Telegraph (ATT) issue and is representative of most corporate prices. In particular, the 8⅛22 indicates the coupon and maturity of the obligation; in this case, the ATT issue carries an 8.125 percent coupon and matures in 2022. The next column provides the *current* yield of the obligation and is found by comparing the coupon to the current market price. For example, a bond with an 8.125 percent coupon selling for 99.750 would have an 8.1 percent current yield. This is *not* the YTM or even necessarily a good approximation to it. Both of these yields will be discussed in Chapter 19.

The next column gives the volume of $1,000 par value bonds traded that day (in this case, 308 bonds were traded). The next column indicates closing quotes, followed by the column for the net change in the closing price from the last day the issue was traded. In this case, ATT closed at 99.750, which was up ¼ from the prior day ($25).

The second example in Column 1 is Anixter, which refers to an Anixter Corp. zero coupon bond ("zr") due in 2020. As discussed, zero coupon securities do not pay interest but are redeemed at par at maturity. Because there is no coupon, they sell at a deep discount, which implies a yield. Again, since there are no coupon payments, they do not report a current yield.

Finally, the third example in Column 2 is a convertible ("cv") bond from Coeur that has a 13.375 percent coupon and is due in 2003. The conversion feature means that the bond is convertible into the common stock of the company. The letters "dc" before the coupon mean "deep discount" and indicate that the original coupon for this bond was set below the going rate at the time of issue. An example of such a bond would be a 5 percent coupon bond issued when market rates were 9 or 10 percent. Alternatively, "vj" in front of a bond issue means that the firm is in receivership or bankruptcy. The small letter "f" that will usually follow the maturity date of such a bond means that the issue is trading *flat,* which means the issuer is not meeting its interest payments. Therefore, the coupon of the obligation is inconsequential and there is a dash in the current yield column because there are no coupon payments. An example of such a bond in Column 1 is BethS (Bethlehem Steel).

All fixed-income obligations, with the exception of preferred stock, are traded on an *accrued interest basis.* The prices pertain to the value of all *future* cash flows from the bond and exclude

EXHIBIT 18.8   *SAMPLE CORPORATE BOND QUOTATIONS*

U.S. EXCHANGE BONDS

Tuesday, February 26, 2002
Quotations as of 4 p.m. Eastern Time

DOW JONES BOND AVERAGES

	2001 HIGH	2001 LOW	2002 HIGH	2002 LOW		2002 CLOSE	2002 CHG	%YLD	2001 CLOSE	2001 CHG
	104.66	97.85	103.67	102.13	20 Bonds	102.33	+ 0.04	7.33	101.16	+ 0.87
	102.87	96.85	102.03	100.92	10 Utilities	101.68	− 0.07	6.92	98.93	+ 0.52
	106.89	98.86	105.71	102.29	10 Industrials	102.98	+ 0.15	7.74	103.39	+ 1.21

VOLUME

Total New York	$15,246,000
Corporation Bonds	$10,724,000
Foreign Bonds	$522,000
Amex Bonds	$233,000

SALES SINCE JAN. 1

New York

2002	$412,667,000
2001	$462,172,000
2000	$410,038,000

AMEX

2002	$19,830,000
2001	$68,422,000
2000	$25,986,000

DIARIES

	DOMESTIC TUE.	DOMESTIC MON.	ALL ISSUES TUE.	ALL ISSUES MON.
New York				
Issues Traded	126	146	134	155
Advances	60	64	65	71
Declines	42	51	45	52
Unchanged	24	31	24	32
New highs	4	2	6	4
New lows	2	5	2	5

	ALL ISSUES TUE.	MON.	FRI.	THU.
AMEX				
Issues Traded	10	11	16	9
Advances	4	6	3	3
Declines	3	3	12	5
Unchanged	3	1	1	1
New highs	0	0	0	0
New lows	0	3	5	1

NEW YORK BONDS
Corporation Bonds

BONDS	CUR YLD	VOL	CLOSE	NET CHG.
AES Cp 4½05	cv	220	46½	+ 1½
AES Cp 8s8	12.3	210	65	+ 5
AMR 9s16	9.3	40	96⅝	+ ⅝
ATT 6½02	6.4	10	101½	− ¹⁵⁄₃₂
ATT 6¾04	6.6	10	102⅞	+ ⅞
ATT 5⅞04	5.6	1164	100⅜	...
ATT 7¾07	7.4	119	104⅛	...
ATT 6s09	6.4	200	94¾	+ ¾
ATT 8½22	8.1	308	99¾	+ ¼
ATT 8⅛24	8.2	170	99½	+ ¼
ATT 8.35s25	8.3	25	101	− ½
ATT 6½29	7.7	318	84⅛	+ ½
ATT 8⅝31	8.5	20	101½	− ½
AForP 5s30	8.3	2	60	+ ½
AmFnGp 7⅛07	7.9	47	90	+ 2
Anixter zr20	...	11	27	− 1½
BPAmer 7⅞02	7.9	10	100⅜	...
BayView 9s07	9.2	95	98	...
Bellso 6⅞28	6.6	20	96⅜	...
BellsoT 6¼03	6.0	10	103¾	+ ⅛
BellsoT 5⅞09	5.8	206	101	+ ¼
BellsoT 7s25	6.8	22	103¾	...
BellsoT 7⅞32	7.5	34	104½	+ ⅛
BellsoT 7⅛33	7.3	15	102½	+ ⅛
BellsoT 6¾33	6.9	10	97⅞	...
vjBethS8.45s05f	...	1	14	+ 1½
Bordn 8⅜16	11.4	42	73¾	+ ⅛
BurN 6.55s20 O	6.9	10	95	+ 2⅞

BONDS	CUR YLD	VOL	CLOSE	NET CHG.
Capstar 4¾04	cv	3	86	− 1½
Caterplnc 6s07	5.9	5	101⅝	+ ⅛
ChespkE 7⅞04	7.8	10	100½	...
vjChiqa 10s09t	...	50	85	+ 1
ClrkOil 9½04	9.5	10	100	+ ¼
Coeur 13⅜03	cv	128	102¼	+ 1¾
Coeur 6⅞04	cv	1	47½	− ½
Consec 8⅛03	9.0	87	90	− ¾
Conseco 10½04	11.9	143	88½	− ½
Conseco 10½02	10.2	496	100½	...
ConNG 6s10	6.1	10	99	+ ¾
CrownC 7⅛02	8.8	90	81¼	+ 1¼
CrwnCk 7⅞26	13.2	20	56	...
DR Hrtn 10s06	9.6	66	103⅞	− ⅛
DVI 9¾04	9.9	30	100	+ ½
DelcoR 8⅞07	8.9	10	97½	− ½
DevonE 4.9s08	cv	254	99½	+ 1¼
DevonE 4.95s08	cv	45	99¼	...
Dole 7s03	6.9	12	101½	+ ¼
Dole 7⅞13	7.6	35	103	+ ¼
DukeEn 6⅞23	7.0	12	98¾	− ¾
DukeEn 6¼25	6.8	65	98¾	+ ¼
FedDS 8½03	8.3	25	102⅛	− ⅛
Florsh 12¾02	70.8	30	18	+ 3⅛
FstData 2s08	cv	8	118½	+ 6⅞
FordCr 6¾08	6.7	10	95⅜	− ¾
GElCap 7⅞06	7.0	121	112⅝	...
GMA 7s02	6.9	15	101⅜	− ⅛
GMA 5⅞03	5.8	55	101⅜	− ⅜
GMA zr12	...	44	44⅜	+ 2
GMA zr15	...	29	36⅜	+ 1⅞
Hilton 5s06	cv	89	92¼	+ ⅝
HousF 6¾11	6.8	10	98¾	+ 1½
HuntPly 11¾04f	...	10	33	...
IBM 7¼02	7.0	30	103⅛	...
IBM 6.45s07	6.0	17	106¾	− 1¼
IBM 5⅜09	5.4	20	99¾	+ ⅜
IBM 7½13	6.6	10	113⅛	− ⅞
JCPL 7¼04	7.1	110	100¾	− ¼
JCP 6¾25	7.0	11	97	+ ¼
K&B Hm 7¾04	7.4	60	101⅜	− ⅛
K&B Hm 9⅝06	9.2	40	104⅛	+ ⅛
Leucadia 7¾13	7.5	7	104	− ¾

BONDS	CUR YLD	VOL	CLOSE	NET CHG.
Loews 3⅛07	cv	62	87½	+ 1
LgIsLt 8.2s23	7.9	30	104	− ¼
Lucent 7¼06	8.8	304	82⅝	+ 1¼
Lucent 5½08	7.6	115	72½	+ 1½
Lucent 6½28	10.1	182	64⅛	− 2¼
Lucent 6.45s29	10.2	43	63⅝	− 1⅜
MBNA 8.28s26	8.5	187	96⅞	+ ⅜
Masco zr31	cv	18	42	+ 1⅞
McDnl 8 11	7.5	3	119	+ ½
McDnl 7⅝33	7.1	14	103¼	+ 2½
MPac 4¼05	4.4	30	96⅛	− ¾
MPac 5s45f	...	8	59⅛	+ ½
NatData 5s03	cv	10	107½	...
NRurU 6⅛05	6.1	5	100⅞	− 1¼
NRurU 6.2s08	6.3	125	99⅛	...
NStl 8⅜06	29.9	1	28	+ 4
NJBTl 7⅜12	7.3	12	101¼	− ¼
NYTel 7⅝23	7.4	100	103⅛	+ ¾
NYTel 7s25	7.1	54	98⅞	− ⅝
Noram 6s12	cv	10	88½	+ ⅝
OreStl 11s03	11.0	25	99⅝	+ ⅛
ParkerD 5½04	cv	5	89	− 1½
PhilP 7⅛28	7.1	5	101	+ 1
PrmHsp 9¼06	9.1	10	102	+ ½
ReynTob 7¾03	7.5	50	101⅝	...
ReynTob 8¾04	8.4	10	104½	...
ReynTob 8¾07	8.3	21	106	+ ½
RoyCarib zr21	...	31	32	+ 1
Ryder 9s16	8.3	35	109	+ 3
Safwy 9.65s04	8.9	25	108	...
SallM zr22	...	5	25	+ 1⅞
Sequa 9s09	9.1	120	99	+ ½
SvcCorp 6⅞04	cv	61	94	− 1
SilicnGr 5¼04	cv	128	68¾	+ ¾
Solectrn zrM20	...	6	54½	− 1¼
StdCmcl 07	cv	100	93	+ 1
StdPac 8½07	8.4	33	101½	− 2¼
TVA 8½42	7.2	20	114¾	− 5¼
TVA 7¼43	7.0	62	104¼	− ¼
Tenet 6s05	cv	10	98	...
TmeWar 8.18s07	7.6	2	108	+ 1⅞
TmeWE 7⅝08	7.1	66	102	− ⅞
TmeWar 9⅛13	7.9	25	115⅛	− ⅞
TolEd 8s03	7.9	10	101⅝	+ 1
THilfig 6½03	6.6	7	98½	+ 1⅜
THilfig 6.85s08	7.6	8	90	...
US Timb 9⅜07	14.2	250	68	...
UtdAir 10.67s04	15.0	1223	70¾	− ⅝
UtdAir 11.21s14	15.2	65	73⅞	...
Webb 10¼10	9.2	425	111¾	...
WebbDel 9⅞09	8.8	40	106½	− ⅝
Weirton 11⅜04f	...	15	11	− 3
Weirton 10⅞05f	...	70	15¾	+ 1⅞

Foreign Bonds

BONDS	CUR YLD	VOL	CLOSE	NET CHG.
Inco 7¾16	cv	68	98⅝	− ⅝
SeaCnt 12½04A	14.4	198	86⅞	+ ½
SeaCnt 12½04B	14.6	15	85⅞	+ 1⅞
SeaCnt 10½03	11.2	75	94	+ 2
SeaCnt 9½03	10.1	75	94	+ ⅝
TelMex 4¼04	cv	6	132	+ 4⅞
TelArg 11⅞04	18.6	60	64	− 1
TrnMarMx 03	...	39	88½	− ½
TrnMarMx 06	cv	50	83	+ 2½

AMEX BONDS

BONDS	CUR YLD	VOL	CLOSE	NET CHG.
ABN C 11.25s02	cv	5	97¼	...
ABN PFE11s02	cv	5	100	+ 1
ABN T 11½03	cv	5	99½	+ 2
JPMCh CPI10	...	16	131	− 1
Leh Prudents04	...	7	90¾	− ¼
SalSB PFE08	...	10	96½	...
Simula s04	cv	57	70	+ ½
TrnsLux 7½06	cv	10	86	− 2
Trump 11¾03f	...	109	77¼	+ ¼
Trump 13⅜05f	...	9	50	...

NASDAQ BONDS

BONDS	CUR YLD	VOL	CLOSE	NET CHG.
BankAtl07	cv	24	107¾	+ ¼
Kaman 6s12	cv	10	91	− 3

EXPLANATORY NOTES

(For New York and American Bonds)

Yield is Current yield. Volume is in thousands.

cv-Convertible bond. **cf**-Certificates. **cld**-Called. **dc**-Deep discount. **ec**-European currency units. **f**-Dealt in flat. **ll**-Italian lire. **kd**-Danish kroner. **m**-Matured bonds, negotiability impaired by maturity. **na**-No accrual. **r**-Registered. **rp**-Reduced principal. **st, sd**-Stamped. **t**-Floating rate. **wd**-When distributed. **ww**-With warrants. **x**-Ex interest. **xw**-Without warrants. **zr**-Zero coupon. **vj**-In bankruptcy or receivership or being reorganized under the Bankruptcy Act, or securities assumed by such companies.

Source: The Wall Street Journal, 27 February 2002. Reprinted with permission from *The Wall Street Journal,* Dow Jones Co. Inc.

interest that has accrued to the holder since the last interest payment date. The actual price of the bond will exceed the quote listed because accrued interest must be added. Assume a bond with a 7⅛ percent coupon. If two months have elapsed since interest was paid, the current holder of the bond is entitled to ⅔ or one-third of the bond's semiannual interest payment that will be paid in four months. More specifically, the 7⅛ percent coupon provides semiannual interest income of $35.625. The investor who held the obligation for two months beyond the last interest payment date is entitled to one-third (⅓) of that $35.625 in the form of accrued interest. Therefore, whatever the current price of the bond, an accrued interest value of $11.87 will be added. If a bond is trading "flat" as already discussed, accrued interest would not be added.

> **EXHIBIT 18.9** *SAMPLE QUOTES FOR TREASURY BONDS, NOTES, AND BILLS*

TREASURY BONDS, NOTES & BILLS

Monday, March 4, 2002

Representative Over-the-Counter quotation based on transactions of $1 million or more.

Treasury bond, note and bill quotes are as of mid-afternoon. Colons in bid-and-asked quotes represent 32nds; 101:01 means 101 1/32. Net changes in 32nds. n-Treasury note. i-Inflation-Indexed issue. Treasury bill quotes in hundredths, quoted on terms of a rate of discount. Days to maturity calculated from settlement date. All yields are to maturity and based on the asked quote. Latest 13-week and 26-week bills are boldfaced. For bonds callable prior to maturity, yields are computed to the earliest call date for issues quoted above par and to the maturity date for issues below par. *-When issued.

Source: eSpeed/Cantor Fitzgerald

U.S. Treasury strips as of 3 p.m. Eastern time, also based on transactions of $1 million or more. Colons in bid-and-asked quotes represent 32nds; 99:01 means 99 1/32. Net changes in 32nds. Yields calculated on the asked quotation. ci-stripped coupon interest. bp-Treasury bond, stripped principal. np-Treasury note, stripped principal. For bonds callable prior to maturity, yields are computed to the earliest call date for issues quoted above par and to the maturity date for issues below par.

Source: Bear, Stearns & Co. via Street Software Technology Inc.

GOVT. BOND & NOTES

RATE	MATURITY MO/YR	BID	ASKED	CHG.	ASKED YLD.
6½	Mar 02n	100:10	100:11	....	1.64
6¾	Mar 02n	100:10	100:11	−1	1.54
6⅜	Apr 02n	100:22	100:23	−1	1.58
6⅜	Apr 02n	100:23	100:24	−1	1.63
7½	May 02n	101:03	101:04	....	1.71
6½	May 02n	101:04	101:05	....	1.62
6¾	May 02n	101:04	101:05	−1	1.67
6¼	Jun 02n	101:13	101:14	−1	1.71
6⅜	Jun 02n	101:14	101:15	−1	1.74
3⅜	Jul 02i	101:13	101:14	....	0.04
① → 6	Jul 02n	101:22	101:23	−1	1.76
6¼	Jul 02n	101:24	101:25	−1	1.81
6⅜	Aug 02n	102:00	102:00	−1	1.86
6¼	Aug 02n	102:00	102:01	....	1.91
6¼	Aug 02n	102:01	102:02	−1	1.94
5¼	Sep 02n	102:06	102:07	−1	1.95

RATE	MATURITY MO/YR	BID	ASKED	CHG.	ASKED YLD.
5½	Feb 08n	104:12	104:13	−6	4.64
5⅝	May 08n	104:26	104:27	−7	4.71
8⅜	Aug 08	107:20	107:21	−7	n.a.
4¾	Nov 08n	99:23	99:24	−7	4.79
8¾	Nov 08	109:06	109:07	−2	n.a.
3⅜	Jan 09i	104:06	104:07	−2	3.19
5½	May 09n	103:25	103:26	−7	4.86
9⅛	May 09	111:28	111:29	−4	n.a.
6	Aug 09n	106:20	106:21	−8	4.92
10⅜	Nov 09	116:25	116:26	−6	n.a.
4¼	Jan 10i	106:27	106:28	−3	3.25
6½	Feb 10n	109:26	109:27	−8	4.98
11¾	Feb 10	121:21	121:22	−5	n.a.
10	May 10	117:21	117:22	−4	n.a.
5¾	Aug 10n	104:30	104:31	−9	5.02
12¾	Nov 10	129:03	129:04	−6	n.a.
3½	Jan 11i	101:26	101:27	−3	3.26
5	Feb 11n	99:22	99:23	−8	5.04

U.S. TREASURY STRIPS

MATURITY	TYPE	BID	ASKED	CHG.	ASKED YLD.
May 02	ci	99:23	99:23	....	1.40
May 02	np	99:21	99:21	....	1.72
Aug 02	ci	99:10	99:10	....	1.55
Aug 02	np	99:06	99:06	....	1.82
Nov 02	ci	98:28	98:29	....	1.61
Feb 03	ci	97:28	97:29	−1	2.24
Feb 03	np	97:26	97:26	−1	2.34
May 03	ci	97:06	97:07	−1	2.39
Jul 03	ci	96:17	96:17	−2	2.60
Aug 03	ci	96:08	96:09	−2	2.64
Aug 03	np	96:02	96:03	−2	2.77
Nov 03	ci	95:22	95:23	−2	2.60
Nov 03	np	95:03	95:04	−2	2.97
Jan 04	ci	94:14	94:15	−2	3.08
Feb 04	ci	94:03	94:04	−2	3.13
Feb 04	np	94:01	94:02	−2	3.16
May 04	ci	93:00	93:01	−2	3.32
May 04	np	92:29	92:31	−2	3.36
Jul 04	ci	92:12	92:13	−2	3.37
Aug 04	ci	92:00	92:01	−2	3.42
Aug 04	np	91:27	91:28	−2	3.49
Nov 04	ci	90:23	90:24	−2	3.63
Nov 04	bp	90:14	90:16	−2	3.75
Nov 04	np	90:18	90:19	−2	3.70
Jan 05	ci	90:01	90:02	−2	3.69
② → Feb 05	ci	89:19	89:21	−2	3.74
Feb 05	np	89:17	89:19	−2	3.76
May 05	ci	88:13	88:14	−2	3.88
May 05	bp	88:05	88:06	−2	3.97
May 05	np	88:09	88:11	−2	3.92
May 05	np	88:12	88:14	−2	3.88
Jul 05	ci	87:27	87:28	−3	3.88
Aug 05	ci	87:13	87:15	−3	3.92
Aug 05	bp	86:26	86:28	−3	4.13
Aug 05	np	87:05	87:07	−3	4.00
Nov 05	ci	86:22	86:24	−3	3.88
Nov 05	np	85:29	85:31	−3	4.13
Nov 05	np	86:00	86:02	−3	4.10
Jan 06	ci	85:17	85:19	−1	4.07
Feb 06	ci	85:01	85:03	−1	4.13
Feb 06	bp	84:14	84:17	−3	4.31
Feb 06	np	84:25	84:28	−3	4.20

TREASURY BILLS

MATURITY	DAYS TO MAT.	BID	ASKED	CHG.	ASKED YLD.
Mar 07 '02	2	1.74	1.73	+0.01	1.75
Mar 14 '02	9	1.73	1.72	+0.01	1.74
Mar 21 '02	16	1.74	1.73	....	1.76
Mar 28 '02	23	1.74	1.73	....	1.76
Apr 04 '02	30	1.74	1.73	+0.01	1.76
Apr 11 '02	37	1.72	1.71	....	1.74
Apr 18 '02	44	1.74	1.73	+0.02	1.76
Apr 25 '02	51	1.74	1.73	+0.01	1.76
May 02 '02	58	1.75	1.74	+0.01	1.77
May 09 '02	65	1.75	1.74	+0.01	1.77
May 16 '02	72	1.75	1.74	+0.01	1.77
May 23 '02	79	1.76	1.75	+0.02	1.78
May 30 '02	**86**	**1.76**	**1.75**	**+0.01**	**1.78**
Jun 13 '02	100	1.76	1.75	+0.01	1.78
Jun 13 '02	100	1.76	1.75	+0.01	1.78
Jun 20 '02	107	1.76	1.75	....	1.78
Jun 27 '02	114	1.75	1.74	....	1.77
Jul 05 '02	122	1.77	1.76	....	1.80
Jul 11 '02	128	1.79	1.78	+0.02	1.82
Jul 18 '02	135	1.79	1.78	+0.01	1.82
Jul 25 '02	142	1.79	1.78	....	1.82
Aug 01 '02	149	1.81	1.80	....	1.84
Aug 08 '02	156	1.84	1.83	+0.01	1.87
Aug 15 '02	163	1.85	1.84	+0.02	1.88
Aug 22 '02	170	1.85	1.84	....	1.88
Aug 29 '02	**177**	**1.86**	**1.85**	**....**	**1.89**

INFLATION-INDEXED TREASURY SECURITIES

RATE	MAT.	BID/ASKED	CHG.	*YLD.	ACCR. PRIN.
3.625	07/02	101-13/14	....	0.040	1104
3.375	01/07	102-16/17	−2	2.814	1116 ③
3.625	01/08	103-05/06	−2	3.027	1094
3.875	01/09	104-06/07	−2	3.185	1081
4.250	01/10	106-27/28	−3	3.252	1054
3.500	01/11	101-26/27	−3	3.258	1015
3.375	01/12	100-29/30	−3	3.262	995
3.625	04/28	103-16/17	−1	3.419	1093
3.875	04/29	108-00/01	−4	3.418	1079
3.375	04/32	100-30/31	−4	3.324	999

*-Yld. to maturity on accrued principal.

Source: *The Wall Street Journal*, 5 March 2002. Reprinted with permission from *The Wall Street Journal*, Dow Jones Co. Inc.

Treasury and Agency Bond Quotes Exhibit 18.9 illustrates the quote system for Treasury and agency issues. These quotes resemble those used for OTC securities because they contain both bid and ask prices rather than high, low, and close. For U.S. Treasury bond quotes, a small "n" behind the maturity date indicates that the obligation is a Treasury *note*. A small "p" indicates it is a Treasury note on which nonresident aliens are exempt from withholding taxes on the interest.

All other obligations in this section are Treasury bonds. The security identification is different because it is not necessary to list the issuer. Instead, the usual listing indicates the coupon, the month and year of maturity, and information on a call feature of the obligation. For example, if a quote carried a maturity of 2005–2010, this would mean that the issue has a deferred call feature until 2005 (and is thereafter freely callable) and a (final) maturity date of 2010. The bid-ask figures provided are stated as a percentage of par. The yield figure provided is yield to maturity, or *promised* yield based on the asking price. This system is used for Treasuries, agencies, and municipals.

Quote 1 is a 6 percent obligation of 2002 that demonstrates the basic difference in the price system of government bonds (i.e., Treasuries and agencies). The bid quote is 101:22, and the ask is 101:23. Governments are traded in thirty-seconds of a point (rather than eighths), and the figures to the right of the colons indicate the number of thirty-seconds in the fractional bid or ask. In this case, the bid price is actually 101.6875 percent of par. These quotes also are notable in terms of the bid-ask spread, which typically is 1 or 2 thirty-seconds, or about one-half the size of the spread for most stocks. This small spread reflects the outstanding liquidity and low transaction costs for Treasury securities.

The third column contains quotes for U.S. Treasury securities that have been "stripped." Specifically, the typical bond promises a series of coupon payments and its principal at maturity. A "stripped" security is created by dividing into separate units each coupon payment and principal payment, which are treated like a zero coupon bond that matures on that date. The security labeled ② was originally a coupon that was to be paid in February 2005. The asking yield (3.74) is referred to as the spot rate for this maturity (spot rate will be discussed in Chapter 19). The coupon interest payment with no principal is designated as "ci" (stripped coupon interest), while the other strip for February 2005 containing only the principal payment is designated "np" (Treasury note, stripped principal).

The securities listed in the Treasury strip and Treasury bill section only report dates and days to maturity and no coupons. This is because these are pure discount securities, that is, the return is the difference between the price you pay and par at maturity.[32]

The final section contains Treasury Inflation Protection Securities (TIPS) discussed earlier. Notice the accrued principal in the last column that reflects the inflation since the bond was issued. The bond designated ③ was the original bond issued in January 1997, so it has the highest accrued principal value of 1,116, and its yield to maturity is computed using this as the principal amount to be paid at maturity.

Municipal Bond Quotes Exhibit 18.10 contains municipal bond quotes from *The Blue List of Current Municipal Offerings*. These are ordered according to states and then alphabetically within states. Each issue gives the amount of bonds being offered (in thousands of dollars), the name of the security, the purpose or description of the issue, the coupon rate, the maturity (which includes month, day, and year), the yield or price, and the dealer offering the bonds. Bond quote 1 is for $200,000 of Indiana State Office Building bonds. The letters MBIA indicate that the bonds are guaranteed by the Municipal Bond Insurance Association (MBIA). These are zero (0.000) coupon bonds due July 1, 2005. In this instance, the yield to maturity is given (5.60 percent). To determine the price, compute the discount value or look up in a yield book the price of a zero coupon bond, due in 2005 to yield 5.60 percent. The dealer offering the bonds is Bearster. A list in the back of the publication gives the name and phone number of the firm.

The second bond is for $115,000 of Indiana State Toll Road bonds with a 9 percent coupon. These bonds have an M/S/F (mandatory sinking fund) that becomes effective in 2011, although the bond matures in 2015. The letters ETM mean that the sinking fund is put into "escrow till

---

[32]For a discussion of calculating yields, see Bruce D. Fielitz, "Calculating the Bond Equivalent Yield for T-Bills." *Journal of Portfolio Management* 9, no. 3 (Spring 1983): 58–60.

EXHIBIT 18.10 *QUOTES FOR MUNICIPALS*

INDIANA

No. of Bonds Offered	Municipal Issuer	Special Characteristics	Coupon	Maturity	Price/YTM	Broker	
100	INDIANA BD BK REV (Hoosier) EQUIP	*B/E*	4.300	01/01/96N/C	100	NORWESMN	
550	INDIANA HEALTH FAC FING AUTH	METHODIST	5.625	09/01/02N/C	101	PRUBACG	
45	INDIANA HEALTH FAC FING AUTH	P/R @ 102	7.750	08/15/20C00	5.25	EQUITSEC	
200	INDIANA PORT COMMN PORT REV		6.750	07/01/10	993/4	NOYESDAV	
3115	INDIANA ST OFFICE BLDG COMMN	P/R @ 102	8.200	07/01/01C97	4.60	MORGANNT	
200	INDIANA ST OFFICE BLDG COMMN	MBIA	0.000	07/01/05	5.60	BEARSTER	←①
335	INDIANA ST RECREATIONAL DEV		6.050	07/01/14	6.45	SMITHBCH	
115	INDIANA ST TOLL RD COMMN TOLL	M/S/F 11	9.000	01/01/15ETM	6.30	DRIZOS	←②
95	INDIANA ST TOLL RD COMMN TOLL		9.000	01/01/15ETM	6.30	EMMET	
1000	INDIANA ST TOLL RD COMMN TOLL	N/C S/F 11	9.000	01/01/15ETM	6.00	WILLIAMA	
100	ELKHART CNTY IND HOSP AUTH REV (ELKHART GEN HOSP)	*B/E* RFDG	6.200	07/01/01N/C	5.40	BLAIRWM	
45	FORT WAYNE IND HOSP AUTH HOSP	S/F 97	6.875	01/01/02ETM	5.85	EMMET	
100	FORT WAYNE IND HOSP AUTH HOSP	P/R @ 102	9.125	07/01/15C95	3.80	GABRIELE	
55	GOSHEN IND CMNTY SCHS		6.600	07/01/97	4.75	NBDBKIND	
10	INDIANAPOLIS IND ARPT AUTH REV (CA @ 102.01)	US AIR	7.500	07/01/09C97	100	HSH	←③
15	INDIANAPOLIS IND ARPT AUTH REV	US AIR	7.500	07/01/19	8.25	STERLING	
500	INDIANAPOLIS IND GAS UTIL REV		4.300	06/01/98	5.00	CITYSEC	
60	INDIANAPOLIS IND LOC PUB IMPT		0.000	08/01/07N/C	8.10	SAPNY	
25	INDIANAPOLIS IND LOC PUB IMPT		6.750	02/01/20	100	COUGHLIN	
200	LAKE CENTRAL IND MULTI-		6.000	01/15/02ETM	5.25	CREWASSC	
300	MICHIGAN CITY IND SEW WKS REV		5.200	08/01/07	5.70	NOYESDAV	
	Thursday May 28, 1994				PAGE 15.A		

maturity." The market yield on these bonds is 6.30 percent, which means the bond would be selling at a premium.

Bond quote 3 refers to $10,000 of Indianapolis, Indiana, Airport Authority revenue bonds that are backed by a contract with US Air. Although the bonds mature in 2009, they are callable beginning in 1997 (C97) at 102 of par. The coupon is 7.50 percent and, in this case, the price of the bond is listed (100), which means its market yield also is 7.50 percent. Such bonds are called *dollar bonds.*

The "+" in the far left column indicates a new item since the prior issue of *The Blue List*. A "#" in the column prior to the yield to maturity or the price indicates that the price or yield has changed since the last issue. It is always necessary to call the dealer to determine the current yield/price because these quotes are at least one day old when they are published.

The Internet *Investments Online*

This chapter discusses some of the basics of bonds—terminology, ratings, and the differences between corporate and municipal bonds. Bonds are much simpler to evaluate than stocks, since they are debt, not ownership claims, and they (usually) have a fixed time to maturity and known cash flows to the investor (barring default). But bonds are an important part of many individual and institutional portfolios, and here are some helpful Web sites for bond information:

http://www.bonds-online.com This Web site covers the gamut of bonds. It offers information and price quotes on a wide variety of instruments, including treasuries, savings bonds, corporates, munis, inflation-indexed bonds, and zero coupon bonds. It features a "bond professor" that answers queries about fixed income securities, and site visitors can submit their own questions. Other information includes a capital markets commentary and a savings bond calculator.

http://www.prudential.com Prudential Securities' Market Commentaries is one of the brokerage house's sites that focuses on bonds. It features daily market commentaries on topics such as the financial markets, including treasuries, corporates, and the stock market. Some commentaries span the trading day, starting with pre-opening thoughts, a mid-day update, and after-the-close summary of what happened during the day.

Three bond ratings firms with interesting Web sites are Fitch's Investor's Service LP (**http://www.fitchinv.com**), Moody's Investor Services (**http://www.moodys.com**), and **http://www.standardandpoors.com/ratings.** These sites feature ratings, research, products and services. Moody's includes economic commentary, a discussion of its rating track record, and an overview of its rating process. In addition to featuring bond ratings, Moody's site also offers country sovereign risk ratings. Standard & Poor's site offers selected research reports, ratings, and their rating criteria.

http://www.bradynet.com This is a good information source for emerging markets' fixed income securities. This site features bond prices and indexes as well as analysis and research.

http://www.bondmarkets.com This is an issues and information-oriented site. It has information and updates on legislative and regulatory issues affecting the bond market, including sectors such as corporate, mortgage, and municipal bond markets.

Summary

- We considered the basic features of bonds: interest, principal, and maturity. Certain key relationships affect price behavior. Price is essentially a function of coupon, maturity, and prevailing market interest rates. Bond price volatility depends on coupon and maturity. As will be demonstrated in Chapter 19, bonds with longer maturities and/or lower coupons respond most vigorously to a given change in market rates.
- Each bond has unique intrinsic characteristics and can be differentiated by type of issue and indenture provisions. Major benefits to bond investors include high returns for nominal risk, the potential for capital gains, certain tax advantages, and possibly additional returns from active trading of bonds. Aggressive bond investors must consider market liquidity, investment risks, and interest rate behavior. We considered high-yield (junk) bonds because of the growth in size and status of this segment of the bond market.
- The global bond market includes numerous countries. The non-U.S. markets have experienced strong relative growth, whereas the U.S. market has been stable and constitutes about half the world bond market. The four major bond markets (the United States, Japan, Germany, and the United Kingdom) have a different makeup in terms of the proportion of governments, agencies, municipals, corporates,

and international issues. The various market sectors also are unique in terms of liquidity, yield spreads, tax implications, and operating features.

- To gauge default risk, most bond investors rely on agency ratings. For additional information on the bond market, prevailing economic conditions, and intrinsic bond features, individual and institutional investors rely on a host of readily available publications. Although extensive up-to-date quotes are available on Treasury bonds and notes, trading and price information for corporates and municipals is relatively difficult to find and is expensive.
- The world bond market is large and is continuing to grow due to government deficits around the world and the need for capital by corporations. It is also very diverse in terms of country alternatives and issuers within countries. This chapter provides the fundamentals that will allow us to consider the valuation of individual bonds in Chapter 19 and the alternative bond portfolio techniques in Chapter 20.

Questions

1. Explain the difference between calling a bond and a bond refunding.
2. Identify the three most important determinants of the price of a bond. Describe the effect of each.
3. Given a change in the level of interest rates, discuss how two major factors will influence the relative change in price for individual bonds.
4. Briefly describe two indenture provisions that can affect the maturity of a bond.
5. Explain the differences in taxation of income from municipal bonds, from U.S. Treasury bonds, and from corporate bonds.
6. For several institutional participants in the bond market, explain what type of bond each is likely to purchase and why.
7. Why should investors be aware of the trading volume for bonds in their portfolio?
8. What is the purpose of bond ratings?
9. Based on the data in Exhibit 18.1, which is the fastest-growing bond market in the world? Which markets are losing market share?
10. Based on the data in Exhibit 18.2, discuss the makeup of the German bond market and how and why it differs from the U.S. market.
11. Discuss the positives and negatives of investing in a government agency issue rather than a straight Treasury bond.
12. Discuss the difference between a foreign bond (e.g., a Samurai) and a Eurobond (e.g., a Euroyen issue).
13. *CFA Examination Level I*
    List *three* differences between Eurodollar and Yankee bonds.

Problems

1. An investor in the 28 percent tax bracket is trying to decide which of two bonds to purchase. One is a corporate bond carrying an 8 percent coupon and selling at par. The other is a municipal bond with a 5½ percent coupon, and it, too, sells at par. Assuming all other relevant factors are equal, which bond should the investor select?
2. What would be the initial offering price for the following bonds (assume semiannual compounding):
   a. A 15-year zero coupon bond with a yield to maturity (YTM) of 12 percent.
   b. A 20-year zero coupon bond with a YTM of 10 percent.
3. An 8.4 percent coupon bond issued by the state of Indiana sells for $1,000. What coupon rate on a corporate bond selling at its $1,000 par value would produce the same after-tax return to the investor as the municipal bond if the investor is in
   a. the 15 percent marginal tax bracket?
   b. the 25 percent marginal tax bracket?
   c. the 35 percent marginal tax bracket?

4. The Shamrock Corporation has just issued a $1,000 par value zero coupon bond with an 8 percent yield to maturity, due to mature 15 years from today (assume semiannual compounding).
   a. What is the market price of the bond?
   b. If interest rates remain constant, what will be the price of the bond in three years?
   c. If interest rates rise to 10 percent, what will be the price of the bond in three years?
5. Complete the information requested for each of the following $1,000 face value, zero coupon bonds, assuming semiannual compounding.

Bond	Maturity (Years)	Yield (Percent)	Price ($)
A	20	12	?
B	?	8	601
C	9	?	350

References

Altman, Edward I., ed. *The High-Yield Debt Market.* Homewood, Ill.: Dow Jones–Irwin, 1990.

Barnhill, Theodore M., William F. Maxwell, and Mark R. Shenkman, eds. *High-Yield Bonds.* New York: McGraw-Hill, 1999.

Elton, Edwin J., and Martin J. Gruber, eds. *Japanese Capital Markets.* New York: Harper & Row, 1990.

European Bond Commission. *European Bond Markets.* Chicago: Probus Publishing, 1989.

Fabozzi, Frank J., ed. *Advances and Innovations in the Bond and Mortgage Markets.* Chicago: Probus Publishing, 1989.

Fabozzi, Frank J., ed. *The Japanese Bond Market.* Chicago: Probus Publishing, 1990.

Fabozzi, Frank J., ed. *The New High-Yield Debt Market.* New York: Harper Business, 1990.

Fabozzi, Frank J. *Fixed-Income Analysis.* New Hope, Penn.: Frank J. Fabozzi Associates, 2000.

Fabozzi, Frank J., ed. *The Handbook of Fixed-Income Securities,* 6th ed. New York: McGraw-Hill. 2001.

Fridson, Martin S. *High-Yield Bonds.* Chicago: Probus Publishing, 1989.

Howe, Jane Tripp. *Junk Bonds: Analysis and Portfolio Strategies.* Chicago: Probus Publishing, 1988.

Livingston, Douglas G. *The Fixed-Income Almanac.* Chicago: Probus Publishing, 1993.

Norton, Joseph, and Paul Spellman, eds. *Asset Securitization.* Cambridge, Mass.: Basil Blackwell, Inc., 1991.

Sundaresan, Suresh. *Fixed-Income Markets and Their Derivatives,* 2d ed. Cincinnati: South-Western, 2002.

Van Horne, James C. *Financial Market Rates and Flows,* 5th ed. Englewood Cliffs, N.J.: Prentice Hall, 1998.

Viner, Aron. *Inside Japanese Financial Markets.* Homewood, Ill.: Dow Jones–Irwin, 1988.

Wilson, Richard S., and Frank J. Fabozzi. *The New Corporate Bond Market.* Chicago: Probus Publishing, 1990.

Yago, Glenn. *Junk Bonds.* New York: Oxford University Press, 1991.

Chapter 19 > The Analysis and Valuation of Bonds

After you read this chapter, you should be able to answer the following questions:

➤ How do you determine the value of a bond based on the present value formula?
➤ What are the alternative bond yields that are important to investors?
➤ How do you compute the following major yields on bonds: current yield, yield to maturity, yield to call, and compound realized (horizon) yield?
➤ What are spot rates and forward rates and how do you calculate these rates from a yield to maturity curve?
➤ What are the spot rate yield curve and the forward rate curve?
➤ How and why do you use the spot rate curve to determine the value of a bond?
➤ What are the alternative theories that attempt to explain the shape of the term structure of interest rates?
➤ What factors affect the level of bond yields at a point in time?
➤ What economic forces cause changes in bond yields over time?
➤ When yields change, what characteristics of a bond cause differential percentage price changes for individual bonds?
➤ What is meant by the duration of a bond, how do you compute it, and what factors affect it?
➤ What is modified duration and what is the relationship between a bond's modified duration and its price volatility?
➤ What is the convexity for a bond, how do you compute it, and what factors affect it?
➤ Under what conditions is it necessary to consider both modified duration and convexity when estimating a bond's price volatility?
➤ What happens to the duration and convexity of bonds that have embedded call options?
➤ What are effective duration and effective convexity and when are they useful?
➤ What is empirical duration and how is it used with common stocks and other assets?
➤ What are the static yield spread and the option-adjusted spread?

In this chapter, we apply the valuation principles that were introduced in Chapter 11 to the valuation of bonds. This chapter is concerned with how one goes about finding the value of bonds using the traditional single yield to maturity rate and using multiple spot rates. We will also come to understand the several measures of yields for bonds. It is important to understand why these bond values and yields change over time. To do this, we begin with a review of value estimation for bonds using the present value model introduced in Chapter 11. This background on valuation allows us to understand and compute the expected rates of return on bonds.

After mastering the measurement of bond yields, we consider what factors influence the level of bond yields and what economic forces cause changes in yields over time. This is followed by a consideration of the alternative shapes of the yield curve and the alternative theories that explain changes in its shape. We discuss the effects of various characteristics and indenture provisions that affect the required returns and, therefore, the value of specific bond issues. This includes such factors as time to maturity, coupon, callability, and sinking funds.

We return to the consideration of bond value and acknowledge that, when yields change, all bond prices do not change in the same way. An understanding of the factors that affect the price changes for bonds has become more important because the price volatility of bonds has increased substantially. Before 1950, the yields on bonds were fairly low and both yields and prices were stable. In this environment, bonds were considered a very safe investment and most investors in bonds intended to hold them to maturity. During the last several decades, however, the level of interest rates has increased substantially because of inflation, and interest rates have also become more volatile because of changes in the rate of inflation and monetary policy. As a result, bond prices and rates of return on bonds have been much more volatile and the rates of return on bond investments have increased. Although this increase in interest rate volatility has affected all bonds, the impact is more significant on bonds with embedded options, such as call features.

THE FUNDAMENTALS OF BOND VALUATION

The value of bonds can be described in terms of dollar values or the rates of return they promise under some set of assumptions. In this section, we describe both the present value model, which computes a specific value for the bond using a single discount value, and the yield model, which computes the promised rate of return based on the bond's current price.

The Present Value Model

In our introduction to valuation theory in Chapter 11, we saw that the value of a bond (or any asset) equals the present value of its expected cash flows. The cash flows from a bond are the periodic interest payments to the bondholder and the repayment of principal at the maturity of the bond. Therefore, the value of a bond is the present value of the semiannual interest payments plus the present value of the principal payment. Notably, the standard technique is to use a single interest rate discount factor, which is the required rate of return on the bond. We can express this in the following present value formula that assumes semiannual compounding.[1]

➤ 19.1

$$P_m = \sum_{t=1}^{2n} \frac{C_i/2}{(1+i/2)^t} + \frac{P_p}{(1+i/2)^{2n}}$$

where:

P_m = **the current market price of the bond**
n = **the number of years to maturity**
C_i = **the annual coupon payment for bond i**
i = **the prevailing yield to maturity for this bond issue**
P_p = **the par value of the bond**

The value computed indicates what an investor would be willing to pay for this bond to realize a rate of return that takes into account expectations regarding the *RFR,* the expected rate of inflation, and the risk of the bond. The standard valuation technique assumes holding the bond to the maturity of the obligation. In this case, the number of periods would be the number of years to the maturity of the bond (referred to as its *term to maturity*). In such a case, the cash flows would include all the periodic interest payments and the payment of the bond's par value at the maturity of the bond.

---

[1]Almost all U.S. bonds pay interest semiannually so it is appropriate to use semiannual compounding wherein you cut the annual coupon rate in half and double the number of periods. To be consistent, you should also use semiannual compounding when discounting the principal payment of a coupon bond or even a zero coupon bond. All our present value calculations assume semiannual compounding.

We can demonstrate this formula using an 8 percent coupon bond that matures in 20 years with a par value of $1,000. This calculation implies that an investor who holds this bond to maturity will receive $40 every 6 months (one half of the $80 coupon) for 20 years (40 periods) and $1,000 at the maturity of the bond in 20 years. If we assume a prevailing yield to maturity for this bond of 10 percent (the market's required rate of return on the bond), the value for the bond using Equation 19.1 would be:

$$P_m = \sum_{t=1}^{40} \frac{80/2}{(1+.10/2)^t} + \frac{\$1,000}{(1+.10/2)^{40}}$$

We know that the first term is the present value of an annuity of $40 every 6 months for 40 periods at 5 percent, while the second term is the present value of $1,000 to be received in 40 periods at 5 percent. This can be summarized as follows:

Present value of interest payments		
$40 × 17.1591	=	$686.36
Present value of principal payment		
$1,000 × 0.1420	=	142.00
Total value of bond at 10%		$828.36

As expected, the bond will be priced at a discount to its par value because the market's required rate of return of 10 percent is greater than the bond's coupon rate, that is $828.36 or 82.836 percent of par.

Alternatively, if the market's required rate was 6 percent, the value would be computed the same way except we would compute the present value of the annuity at 3 percent for 40 periods and the present value of the principal at 3 percent for 40 periods as follows:

Present value of interest payments		
$40 × 23.1148	=	$ 924.59
Present value of principal payment		
$1,000 × 0.3066	=	306.60
Total value of bond at 6%		$1,231.19

Because the bond's discount rate is lower than its coupon, the bond would sell at a premium above par value—that is, $1,231.19 or 123.119 of par.

The Price-Yield Curve When you know the basic characteristics of a bond in terms of its coupon, maturity, and par value, the only factor that determines its value (price) is the market discount rate—its required rate of return. As has been shown, as we increase the required rate, the price declines. It is possible to demonstrate the specific relationship between the price of a bond and its yield by computing the bond's price at a range of yields as shown in Exhibit 19.1.

A graph of this relationship between the required return (yield) on the bond and its price is referred to as the price-yield curve, as shown in Exhibit 19.2. Besides demonstrating that price moves inverse to yield, it shows three other important points:

1. When the yield is below the coupon rate, the bond will be priced at a **premium** to its par value.

| EXHIBIT 19.1 | PRICE-YIELD RELATIONSHIP FOR A 20-YEAR, 8 PERCENT COUPON BOND ($1,000 PAR VALUE) |

REQUIRED YIELD	PRICE OF BOND
2	$1,985.09
4	1,547.12
6	1,231.19
8	1,000.00
10	828.36
12	699.05
14	600.07
16	522.98

| EXHIBIT 19.2 | THE PRICE-YIELD CURVE FOR A 20-YEAR, 8 PERCENT COUPON BOND |

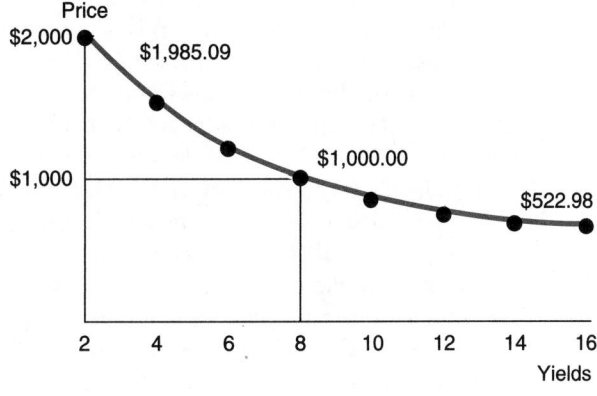

2. When the yield is above the coupon rate, the bond will be priced at a discount to its par value.
3. The price-yield relationship is not a straight line; rather, it is *convex*. As yields decline, the price increases at an increasing rate; and, as the yield increases, the price declines at a declining rate. This concept of a convex price-yield curve is referred to as *convexity* and will be discussed further in a later section.

The Yield Model   Instead of determining the value of a bond in dollar terms, investors often price bonds in terms of yields—the promised rates of return on bonds under certain assumptions. Thus far, we have used cash flows and our required rate of return to compute an estimated value for the bond. To compute an expected yield, we use the current market price (P_m) and the expected cash flows to *compute the expected yield on the bond*. We can express this approach using the same present value model. The difference is that in Equation 19.1, it was assumed that we knew the appropriate discount rate (the required rate of return), and we computed the estimated value (price) of the bond. In this case, we still use equation 19.1, but it is assumed that we know the price of the bond and we compute the discount rate (yield) that will give us the current market price (P_m).

$$P_m = \sum_{t=1}^{2n} \frac{C_i/2}{(1+i/2)^t} + \frac{P_p}{(1+i/2)^{2n}}$$

where the variables are the same as previously, except

i = **the discount rate that will discount the expected cash flows to equal the current market price of the bond**

This i value gives the expected ("promised") yield of the bond under various assumptions to be noted, assuming you pay the price P_m. In the next section, we will discuss several types of bond yields that arise from the assumptions of the valuation model.

Approaching the investment decision stating the bond's value as a yield figure rather than a dollar amount, you consider the relationship of the computed bond yield to your required rate of return on this bond. If the computed promised bond yield is equal to or greater than your required rate of return, you should buy the bond; if the computed promised yield is less than your required rate of return, you should not buy the bond.

These approaches to pricing bonds and making investment decisions are similar to the two alternative approaches by which firms make investment decisions. We referred to one approach, the **net present value (NPV)** method, in Chapter 11. With the NPV approach, you compute the present value of the net cash flows from the proposed investment at your cost of capital and subtract the present value cost of the investment to get the net present value (NPV) of the project. If this NPV is positive, you consider accepting the investment; if it is negative, you reject it. This is basically the way we compared the value of an investment to its market price.

The second approach is to compute the **internal rate of return (IRR)** on a proposed investment project. The IRR is the discount rate that equates the present value of cash outflows for an investment with the present value of its cash inflows. You compare this discount rate, or IRR (which is also the estimated rate of return on the project), to your cost of capital, and accept any investment proposal with an IRR equal to or greater than your cost of capital. We do the same thing when we price bonds on the basis of yield. If the estimated ("promised") yield on the bond (yield to maturity, yield to call, or horizon yield) is equal to or exceeds your required rate of return on the bond, you should invest in it; if the estimated yield is less than your required rate of return on the bond, you should not invest in it.

COMPUTING BOND YIELDS

Bond investors traditionally have used five yield measures for the following purposes:

YIELD MEASURE	PURPOSE
Nominal yield	Measures the coupon rate.
Current yield	Measures the current income rate.
Promised yield to maturity	Measures the estimated rate of return for bond held to maturity.
Promised yield to call	Measures the estimated rate of return for bond held to first call date.
Realized (horizon) yield	Measures the estimated rate of return for a bond likely to be sold prior to maturity. It considers specific reinvestment assumptions and an estimated sales price. It also can measure the actual rate of return on a bond during some past period of time.

Nominal and current yields are mainly descriptive and contribute little to investment decision making. The last three yields are all derived from the present value model as described previously.

To measure an estimated realized yield (also referred to as the horizon yield or total return), a bond investor must estimate a bond's future selling price. Following our presentation of bond yields, we present the procedure for finding these prices. We conclude the valuation segment with a demonstration of valuing bonds using spot rates, which is becoming more prevalent.

Nominal Yield   **Nominal yield** is the coupon rate of a particular issue. A bond with an 8 percent coupon has an 8 percent nominal yield. This provides a convenient way of describing the coupon characteristics of an issue.

Current Yield   **Current yield** is to bonds what dividend yield is to stocks. It is computed as

➤19.2 $$CY = C_i/P_m$$

where:

> CY = **the current yield on a bond**
> C_i = **the annual coupon payment of bond** i
> P_m = **the current market price of the bond**

Because this yield measures the current income from the bond as a percentage of its price, it is important to income-oriented investors who want current cash flow from their investment portfolios. An example of such an investor would be a retired person who lives on this investment income. Current yield has little use for investors who are interested in total return because it excludes the important capital gain or loss component.

Promised Yield to   **Promised yield to maturity** is the most widely used bond yield figure because it indicates the
Maturity   fully compounded rate of return promised to an investor who buys the bond at prevailing prices, *if two assumptions hold true.* Specifically, the *promised* yield to maturity will be equal to the investor's *realized* yield *if* these assumptions are met. The first assumption is that the investor holds the bond to maturity. This assumption gives this value its shortened name, *yield to maturity* (YTM). The second assumption is implicit in the present value method of computation. Referring to Equation 19.1, recall that it related the current market price of the bond to the present value of all cash flows as follows:

$$P_m = \sum_{t=1}^{2n} \frac{C_i/2}{(1+i/2)^t} + \frac{P_p}{(1+i/2)^{2n}}$$

To compute the YTM for a bond, we solve for the rate i that will equate the current price (P_m) to all cash flows from the bond to maturity. As noted, this resembles the computation of the internal rate of return (IRR) on an investment project. Because it is a present value–based computation, it implies a reinvestment rate assumption because it discounts the cash flows. That is, the equation assumes that *all interim cash flows (interest payments) are reinvested at the computed YTM.* This is referred to as a *promised* YTM because the bond will provide this computed YTM *only if* you meet its conditions:

1. You hold the bond to maturity.
2. You reinvest all the interim cash flows at the computed YTM rate.

If a bond promises an 8 percent YTM, you must reinvest coupon income at 8 percent to realize that promised return. If you spend (do not reinvest) the coupon payments or if you cannot find opportunities to reinvest these coupon payments at rates as high as its promised YTM, then the actual realized yield you earn will be less than the promised yield to maturity. As will be demonstrated in the section on realized return, if you can reinvest cash flows at rates above the YTM, your realized (horizon) return will be greater than the promised YTM. The income earned on this reinvestment of the interim interest payments is referred to as **interest-on-interest**.[2]

The impact of the reinvestment assumption (i.e., the interest-on-interest earnings) on the actual return from a bond varies directly with the bond's coupon and maturity. A higher coupon and/or a longer term to maturity will increase the loss in value from failure to reinvest the coupon cash flow at the YTM. Put another way, a higher coupon or a longer maturity makes the reinvestment assumption more important.

Exhibit 19.3 illustrates the impact of interest-on-interest for an 8 percent, 25-year bond bought at par to yield 8 percent. If you invested $1,000 today at 8 percent for 25 years and reinvested all the coupon payments at 8 percent, you would have approximately $7,100 at the end of 25 years. We will refer to this money that you have at the end of your investment horizon as your **ending-wealth value**. To prove that you would have an ending-wealth value of $7,100, look up the compound interest factor for 8 percent for 25 years (6.8493) or 4 percent for 50 periods (which assumes semiannual compounding and is 7.1073). In the case of U.S. bonds, the semiannual compounding is the appropriate procedure because almost all U.S. bonds pay interest every six months.

EXHIBIT 19.3   *THE EFFECT OF INTEREST-ON-INTEREST ON TOTAL REALIZED RETURN*

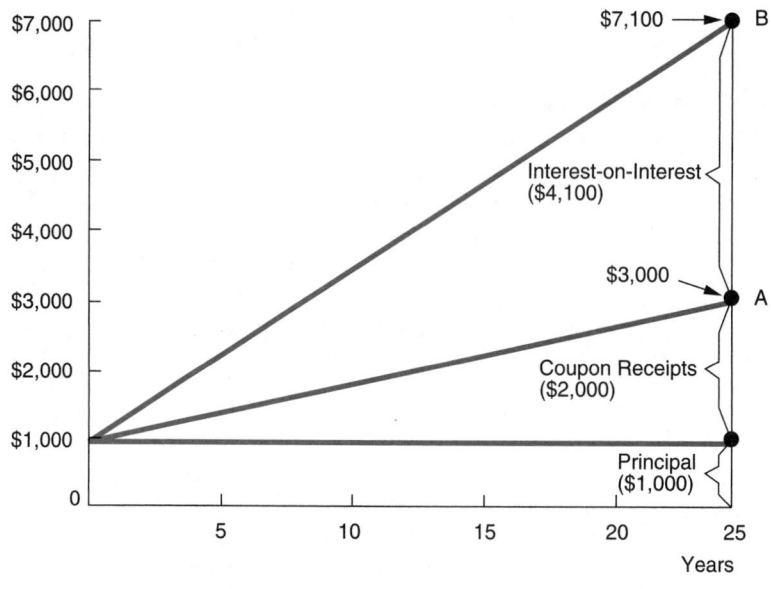

Promised yield at time of purchase: 8.00%
Realized yield over the 25-year investment horizon with no coupon reinvestment (A): 4.50%
Realized yield over the 25-year horizon with coupons reinvested at 8% (B): 8.00%

---

[2]This concept is developed in Sidney Homer and Martin L. Leibowitz. *Inside the Yield Book* (Englewood Cliffs, N.J.: Prentice-Hall, 1972), Chapter 1.

Exhibit 19.3 shows that this $7,100 is made up of $1,000 principal return, $2,000 of coupon payments over the 25 years ($80 a year for 25 years), and $4,100 in interest earned on the semi-annual coupon payments reinvested at 4 percent semiannually. If you never reinvested any of the coupon payments, you would have an ending-wealth value of only $3,000. This ending-wealth value of $3,000 derived from the beginning investment of $1,000 gives you an actual (realized) yield to maturity of only 4.5 percent. That is, the rate that will discount $3,000 back to $1,000 in 25 years is 4.5 percent. Reinvesting the coupon payments at some rate between 0 and 8 percent would cause your ending-wealth position to be above $3,000 and below $7,100; therefore, your actual rate of return would be somewhere between 4.5 percent and 8 percent. Alternatively, if you managed to reinvest the coupon payments at rates consistently above 8 percent, your ending-wealth position would be above $7,100, and your realized (horizon) rate of return would be above 8 percent.

Interestingly, during periods of very high interest rates, you often hear investors talk about "locking in" high yields. Many of these people are subject to **yield illusion** because they do not realize that attaining the high *promised* yield requires that they reinvest all the coupon payments at the very high *promised* yields. For example, if you buy a 20-year bond with a promised yield to maturity of 15 percent, you will actually realize the promised 15 percent yield *only* if you are able to reinvest all the coupon payments at 15 percent over the next 20 years.

Computing the Promised Yield to Maturity The promised yield to maturity can be computed by using the present value model with semiannual compounding. The present value model gives the investor an accurate result and is the technique used by investment professionals.

The present value model equation—Equation 19.1—shows the promised yield valuation model:

$$P_m = \sum_{t=1}^{2n} \frac{C_i/2}{(1+i/2)^t} + \frac{P_p}{(1+i/2)^{2n}}$$

All variables are as described previously. This model is somewhat complex because the solution requires iteration. As noted, the present value equation is a variation of the internal rate of return (IRR) calculation where we want to find the discount rate, i, that will equate the present value of the cash flows to the market price of the bond (P_m). Using the prior example of an 8 percent, 20-year bond, priced at $900, the equation gives us a semiannual promised yield to maturity of 4.545 percent, which implies an annual promised YTM of 9.09 percent.[3]

$$900 = 40 \sum_{t=1}^{40} \left(\frac{1}{(1.04545)^t} \right) + 1000 \left(\frac{1}{(1.04545)^{40}} \right)$$
$$= 40(18.2574) + 1,000(0.1702)$$
$$= 900$$

The values for $1/(1+i)$ were taken from the present value interest factor tables in the appendix at the back of the book using interpolation.

---

[3]You will recall from your corporate finance course that you start with one rate (e.g., 9 percent or 4.5 percent semiannual) and compute the value of the stream. In this example, the value would exceed $900, so you would select a higher rate until you had a present value for the stream of cash flows of less than $900. Given the discount rates above and below the true rate, you would do further calculations or interpolate between the two rates to arrive at the correct discount rate that would give you a value of $900.

YTM for a Zero Coupon Bond   In several instances, we have discussed the existence of zero coupon bonds that only have the one cash inflow at maturity. This single cash flow means that the calculation of YTM is substantially easier as shown by the following example.

Assume a zero coupon bond maturing in 10 years with a maturity value of $1,000 selling for $311.80. Because you are dealing with a zero coupon bond, there is only the one cash flow from the principal payment at maturity. Therefore, you simply need to determine what the discount rate is that will discount $1,000 to equal the current market price of $311.80 in 20 periods (10 years of semiannual payments). The equation is as follows:

$$\$311.80 = \frac{\$1000}{(1+i)^{20}}$$

You will see that $i = 6$ percent, which implies an annual rate of 12 percent. For future reference, this yield also is referred to as the 10-year spot rate, which is the discount rate for a single cash flow to be received in 10 years.

Promised Yield to Call

Although investors use promised YTM to value most bonds, they must estimate the return on certain callable bonds with a different measure—the **promised yield to call (YTC)**. Whenever a bond with a call feature is selling for a price above par (that is, at a premium) equal to or greater than its call price, a bond investor should consider valuing the bond in terms of YTC rather than YTM. This is because the marketplace uses the lowest, most conservative yield measure in pricing a bond. When bonds are trading at or above a specified **crossover price**, which is approximately the bond's call price plus a small premium that increases with time to call, the yield to call will provide the lowest yield measure.[4] The crossover price is important because at this price the YTM and the YTC are equal—this is the *crossover yield*. When the bond rises to this price above par, the computed YTM becomes low enough that it would be profitable for the issuer to call the bond and finance the call by selling a new bond at this prevailing market interest rate.[5] Therefore, the YTC measures the promised rate of return the investor will receive from holding this bond until it is retired at the first available call date, that is, at the end of the deferred call period. Note that if an issue has multiple call dates at different prices (the call price will decline for later call dates), it will be necessary to compute which of these scenarios provides the *lowest* yield—this is referred to as computing **yield to worst**. Investors must consider computing the YTC for their bonds after a period when numerous high-yielding, high-coupon bonds have been issued. Following such a period, interest rates will decline, bond prices will rise, and the high-coupon bonds will subsequently have a high probability of being called—that is, their yields will fall below the crossover yield.

Computing Promised Yield to Call   Again, the present value method assumes that you hold the bond until the first call date and that you reinvest all coupon payments at the YTC rate.

---

[4]For a discussion of the crossover price and yield, see Homer and Leibowitz, *Inside the Yield Book,* Chapter 4.

[5]Extensive literature exists on the refunding of bond issues, including W. M. Boyce and A. J. Kalotay, "Optimum Bond Calling and Refunding," *Interfaces* (November 1979): 36–49; R. S. Harris, "The Refunding of Discounted Debt: An Adjusted Present Value Analysis," *Financial Management* 9, no. 4 (Winter 1980): 7–12; A. J. Kalotay, "On the Structure and Valuation of Debt Refundings," *Financial Management* 11, no. 1 (Spring 1982): 41–42; and John D. Finnerty, "Evaluating the Economics of Refunding High-Coupon Sinking-Fund Debt." *Financial Management* 12, no. 1 (Spring 1983): 5–10.

Yield to call is calculated using a variation of Equation 19.1. To compute the YTC by the present value method, we would adjust the semiannual present value equation to give

➤19.3
$$P_m = \sum_{t=1}^{2nc} \frac{C_i/2}{(1+i/2)^t} + \frac{p_c}{(1+i/2)^{2nc}}$$

where

P_m = **the current market price of the bond**
C_i = **the annual coupon payment of bond** i
nc = **the number of years to first call date**
P_c = **the call price of the bond**

Following the present value method, we solve for i, which typically requires several computations or interpolations to get the exact yield.

Realized (Horizon) Yield   The final measure of bond yield, realized yield or horizon yield (i.e., the actual return over a horizon period) measures the expected rate of return of a bond that you expect to sell prior to its maturity. In terms of the equation, the investor has a holding period *(hp)* or investment horizon that is less than n. Realized (horizon) yield can be used to estimate rates of return attainable from various trading strategies. Although it is a very useful measure, it requires several additional estimates not required by the other yield measures. Specifically, the investor must estimate the expected future selling price of the bond at the end of the holding period. Also, this measure requires a specific estimate of the reinvestment rate for the coupon flows prior to the liquidation of the bond. This technique also can be used by investors to measure their actual yields after selling bonds.

Computing Realized (Horizon) Yield   The realized yields over a horizon holding period are variations on the promised yield equations. The substitution of P_f and hp into the present value model (Equation 19.1) provides the following realized yield model:

➤19.4
$$P_m = \sum_{t=1}^{2hp} \frac{C_t/2}{(1+i/2)^t} + \frac{P_f}{(1+i/2)^{2hp}}$$

Again, this present value model requires you to solve for the i that equates the expected cash flows from coupon payments and the estimated selling price to the current market price.

You will note from the present value realized yield formula in Equation 19.4 that the coupon flows are implicitly discounted at the computed realized (horizon) yield. In many cases, this is an inappropriate assumption because available market rates might be very different from the computed realized (horizon) yield. Therefore, to derive a realistic estimate of the estimated realized yield, you also need to *estimate your expected reinvestment rate during the investment horizon.* We will demonstrate this in a subsequent subsection.

Therefore, to complete your understanding of computing estimated realized yield for alternative investment strategies, the next section considers the calculation of future bond prices. This is followed by a section on calculating a realized (horizon) return with different reinvestment rates.

CALCULATING FUTURE BOND PRICES

Dollar bond prices need to be calculated in two instances: (1) when computing realized (horizon) yield, you must determine the future selling price (P_f) of a bond if it is to be sold before maturity or first call, and (2) when issues are quoted on a promised yield basis, as with municipals. You can easily convert a yield-based quote to a dollar price by using Equation 19.1, which does not require iteration. (You need only solve for P_m.) The coupon (C_i) is given, as is par value (P_p) and the promised YTM, which is used as the discount rate.

Consider a 10 percent, 25-year bond with a promised YTM of 12 percent. You would compute the price of this issue as

$$P_m = 100/2 \sum_{t=1}^{50} \frac{1}{\left(1 + \dfrac{0.120}{2}\right)^t} + 1,000 \frac{1}{\left(1 + \dfrac{0.120}{2}\right)^{50}}$$

$$= 50(15.7619) + 1,000(0.0543)$$

$$= \$842.40$$

In this instance, we are determining the prevailing market price of the bond based on the current market YTM. These market figures indicate the consensus of all investors regarding the value of this bond. An investor with a required rate of return on this bond that differs from the market YTM would estimate a different value for the bond.

In contrast to the current market price, you will need to compute a future price (P_f) when estimating the expected realized (horizon) yield performance of alternative bonds. Investors or portfolio managers who consistently trade bonds for capital gains need to compute expected realized (horizon) yield rather than promised yield. They would compute P_f through the following variation of the realized yield equation:

►19.5
$$P_f = \sum_{t=1}^{2n-2hp} \frac{C_i/2}{(1+i/2)^t} + \frac{P_p}{(1+i/2)^{2n-2hp}}$$

where:

P_f = the future selling price of the bond
P_p = the par value of the bond
n = the number of years to maturity
hp = the holding period of the bond (in years)
C_i = the annual coupon payment of bond i
i = the expected market YTM at the end of the holding period

This equation is a version of the present value model that is used to calculate the expected price of the bond at the end of the holding period *(hp)*. The term $2n - 2hp$ equals the bond's remaining term to maturity at the end of the investor's holding period, that is, the number of six-month periods remaining after the bond is sold. Therefore, the determination of P_f is based on four variables: two that are known and two that must be estimated by the investor.

Specifically, the coupon (C_i) and the par value (P_p) are given. The investor must forecast the length of the holding period and, therefore, the number of years remaining to maturity at the time the bond is sold ($n - hp$). The investor also must forecast the expected market YTM at the time of sale *(i)*. With this information, you can calculate the future price of the bond. The real difficulty (and the potential source of error) in estimating P_f lies in predicting hp and i.

Assume you bought the 10 percent, 25-year bond just discussed at $842, giving it a promised YTM of 12 percent. Based on an analysis of the economy and the capital market, you expect this bond's market YTM to decline to 8 percent in five years. Therefore, you want to compute its future price (P_f) at the end of year 5 to estimate your expected rate of return, assuming you are correct in your assessment of the decline in overall market interest rates. As noted, you estimate the holding period (5 years), which implies a remaining life of 20 years, and the market YTM of 8 percent. Using Equation 19.5 gives a future price:

$$P_f = 50 \sum_{t=1}^{40} \frac{1}{(1.04)^t} + 1,000 \frac{1}{(1.04)^{40}}$$
$$= 50(19.7928) + 1,000(0.2083)$$
$$= 989.64 + 208.30$$
$$= \$1,197.94$$

Subsequently, we will use this estimate of the selling price in our calculation of the realized (horizon) yield on this investment.

Realized (Horizon) Yield with Differential Reinvestment Rates

The realized yield equation—Equation 19.4—is the standard present value formula with the changes in holding period and ending price. As such, it includes the implicit reinvestment rate assumption that all cash flows are reinvested at the computed i rate. There may be instances where such an implicit assumption is not appropriate, given your expectations for future interest rates. Assume that current market interest rates are very high and you invest in a long-term bond (e.g., a 20-year, 14 percent coupon) to take advantage of an expected decline in rates from 14 percent to 10 percent over a 2-year period. Computing the future price (equal to $1,330.95) and using the realized yield equation to estimate the realized (horizon) yield, we will get the following fairly high realized rate of return:

$$P_m = \$1,000$$
$$hp = 2 \text{ Years}$$
$$P_f = \sum_{t=1}^{36} 70/(1+0.05)^t + \$1,000/(1.05)^{36}$$
$$= \$1,158.30 + \$172.65$$
$$= \$1,330.95$$
$$\$1,000 = \sum_{t=1}^{4} \frac{70}{(1+i/2)^t} + \frac{1,330.95}{(1+i/2)^4}$$
$$i = 27.5\%$$

As noted, this calculation assumes that all cash flows are reinvested at the computed i (27.5 percent). However, it is unlikely that during a period when market rates are going from 14 percent to 10 percent, you could reinvest the coupon at 27.5 percent. It is more appropriate and realistic to *explicitly estimate the reinvestment rates* and calculate the realized yields based on your *ending-wealth position.* This procedure is more precise and realistic, and it is easier because it does not require iteration.

The basic technique calculates the value of all cash flows at the end of the holding period, which is the investor's ending-wealth value. We compare this ending-wealth value to our *beginning-wealth value* to determine the *compound rate of return that equalizes these two values.* Adding to our prior example, assume we have the following cash flows:

$$P_m = \$1,000$$

$$i = \text{Interest Payments of } \$70 \text{ in } 6, 12, 18, \text{ and } 24 \text{ Months}$$

$$P_f = \$1,330.95 \text{ (the Ending Market Value of the Bond)}$$

The ending value of the four interest payments is determined by our assumptions regarding specific reinvestment rates. Assume each payment is reinvested at a different declining rate that holds for its time period (that is, the first three interest payments are reinvested at progressively lower rates and the fourth interest payment is received at the end of the holding period).

$$i_1 \text{ at } 13\% \text{ for } 18 \text{ Months} = \$70 \times (1 + 0.065)^3 = \$\ 84.55$$

$$i_2 \text{ at } 12\% \text{ for } 12 \text{ Months} = \$70 \times (1 + 0.06)^2 = \ \ 78.65$$

$$i_3 \text{ at } 11\% \text{ for } \ \ 6 \text{ Months} = \$70 \times (1 + 0.055) = \ \ 73.85$$

$$i_4 \text{ Not Reinvested} \ \ \ \ \ \ = \$70 \times (1.0) \ \ \ \ \ = \ \ 70.00$$

$$\text{Future Value of Interest Payments} = \$307.05$$

Therefore, our total ending-wealth value is

$$\$1,330.95 + \$307.05 = \$1,638.00$$

The compound realized (horizon) rate of return is calculated by comparing our ending-wealth value ($1,638) to our beginning-wealth value ($1,000) and determining what interest rate would equalize these two values over a two-year holding period. To find this, compute the ratio of ending wealth to beginning wealth (1.638). Find this ratio in a compound value table for four periods (assuming semiannual compounding). Table C.3 at the end of the book indicates that the realized rate is somewhere between 12 percent (1.5735) and 14 percent (1.6890). Interpolation gives an estimated semiannual rate of 13.16 percent, which indicates an annual rate of 26.32 percent. Using a calculator or computer, it is equal to $(1.638)^{1/4} - 1$. This compares to an estimate of 27.5 percent when we assume an implicit reinvestment rate of 27.5 percent.

This realized (horizon) yield computation specifically states the expected reinvestment rates as contrasted to assuming the reinvestment rate is equal to the computed realized yield. The actual assumption regarding the reinvestment rate can be very important.

The steps to calculate an expected realized (horizon) yield can be summarized as follows:

1. Calculate the future value at the horizon date of all coupon payments reinvested at estimated rates.
2. Calculate the expected sales price of the bond at your expected horizon date based on your estimate of the required yield to maturity at that time.
3. Sum the values in (1) and (2) to arrive at the total ending-wealth value.
4. Calculate the ratio of the ending-wealth value to the beginning value (the purchase price of the bond). Given this ratio and the time horizon, compute the compound rate of interest that will grow to this ratio over this time horizon.

$$\left(\frac{\text{Ending - Wealth Value}}{\text{Beginning Value}} \right)^{\frac{1}{2n}} - 1$$

5. If all calculations assume semiannual compounding, double the interest rate derived from (4).

Price and Yield Determination on Noninterest Dates

So far, we have assumed that the investor buys (or sells) a bond precisely on the date that interest is due, so the measures are accurate only when the issues are traded on coupon payment dates.

However, when the semiannual model is used, and when more accuracy is necessary, another version of the price and yield model must be used for transactions on noninterest payment dates. Fortunately, the basic models need be extended only one more step because the value of an issue that trades X years, Y months, and so many days from maturity is found by extrapolating the bond value (price or yield) for the month before and the month after the day of transaction. Thus, the valuation process involves full months to maturity rather than years or semiannual periods.[6]

Accrued Interest   Having computed a value for the bond at a noninterest payment date, it is also necessary to consider the notion of *accrued interest*. Because the interest payment on a bond, which is paid every six months, is a contractual promise by the issuer, the bond investor has the right to receive a portion of the semiannual interest payment if he/she held the bond for some part of the six-month period. For example, assume an 8 percent, $1,000 par value bond that pays $40 every six months. If you sold the bond two months after the prior interest payment, you have held it for one-third of the six-month period and would have the right to one-third of the $40 ($13.33). This is referred to as the accrued interest on the bond. Therefore, when you sell the bond, there is a calculation of the bond's remaining value until maturity, that is, its price. What you receive is this price *plus* the accrued interest ($13.33).

Yield Adjustments for Tax-Exempt Bonds

Municipal bonds, Treasury issues, and many agency obligations possess one common characteristic: Their interest income is partially or fully tax-exempt. This tax-exempt status affects the valuation of taxable versus nontaxable bonds. Although you could adjust each present value equation for the tax effects, it is not necessary for our purposes. We can envision the approximate impact of such an adjustment, however, by computing the fully taxable equivalent yield, which is one of the most often cited measures of performance for municipal bonds.

The **fully taxable equivalent yield (FTEY)** adjusts the promised yield computation for the bond's tax-exempt status. To compute the FTEY, we determine the promised yield on a tax-exempt bond using one of the yield formulas and then adjust the computed yield to reflect the rate of return that must be earned on a fully taxable issue. It is measured as

➤19.6
$$FTEY = \frac{i}{1 - T}$$

where:

   i = **the promised yield on the tax-exempt bond**
   T = **the amount and type of tax exemption. (i.e., the investor's marginal tax rate)**

For example, if the promised yield on the tax-exempt bond is 6 percent and the investor's marginal tax rate is 30 percent, the taxable equivalent yield would be

$$FTEY = \frac{0.06}{1 - 0.30} = \frac{0.06}{0.70} = 0.0857$$
$$= 8.57\%$$

---

[6]For a detailed discussion of these calculations, see Chapter 4 in Frank J. Fabozzi, ed., *The Handbook of Fixed-Income Securities,* 6th ed. (New York: McGraw-Hill, 2001).

The FTEY equation has some limitations. It is applicable only to par bonds or current coupon obligations, such as new issues, because the measure considers only interest income, ignoring capital gains, which are not tax-exempt. Therefore, we cannot use it for issues trading at a significant variation from par value (premium or discount).

Bond Yield Books Bond value tables, commonly known as *bond books* or *yield books,* can eliminate most of the calculations for bond valuation. A bond yield table is like a present value interest factor table in that it provides a matrix of bond prices for a stated coupon rate, various terms to maturity (on the horizontal axis), and promised yields (on the vertical axis). Such a table allows you to determine either the promised yield or the price of a bond.

As might be expected, access to sophisticated calculators or computers has substantially reduced the need for and use of yield books. In addition, to truly understand alternative yield measures, you must master the present value model and its variations that generate values for promised YTM, promised YTC, realized (horizon) yield, and bond prices.

BOND VALUATION USING SPOT RATES

Thus far, we have used the valuation model, which assumes that we discount all cash flows by one common yield, reflecting the overall required rate of return for the bond. Similarly, we compute the yield on the bond (YTM, YTC, horizon yield) as the single interest rate that would discount all the flows from the bond to equal the current market price of the bond. It was noted in the YTM calculations that this was a "promised" yield that depended on two assumptions: holding the bond to maturity and reinvesting all cash flows at the computed YTM (the IRR assumption). Notably, this second assumption often is very unrealistic because it requires a flat, constant yield curve. We know that it is extremely rare for the yield curve to be flat, much less remain constant for any period of time. The yield curve typically is upward sloping for several reasons, which we discuss in a later section. Investors at any point in time require *a different rate of return for flows at different times.* For example, if investors are buying alternative zero coupon bonds (promising a single cash flow at maturity), they will almost always require different rates of return if they are offered a bond that matures in 2 years, 5 years, or 10 years.

As mentioned earlier, the rates used to discount a cash flow at a point in time are called spot rates. It is possible to demonstrate the desire for different rates by examining the rates on government discount notes with different maturities (i.e., spot rates) as of early 2002 as shown in Exhibit 19.4. These rates indicate that investors require 2.91 percent for a cash flow in 2 years, 4.28 percent for the cash flow in 5 years, and 4.85 percent for the cash flow in 10 years. These differences in required rates for alternative maturities are very noticeable. The difference in yield between the 1-year bond (2.14 percent) and the 30-year bond (5.40 percent) (referred to as the *maturity spread*) was 326 basis points in early 2002, which is a very large spread historically.

Because of these differences in spot rates across maturities, bond analysts and bond portfolio managers recognize that it is inappropriate to discount all the flows for a bond at one single rate where the rate used is often based on the yield to maturity for a government bond with a single maturity. For example, when asked about the value of a particular 20-year bond rated AA, a bond trader typically will respond that the bond should trade a certain number of basis points higher than comparable maturity Treasury bonds (e.g., "plus 70 basis points"). This means that if 20-year Treasury bonds are currently yielding 5.58 percent, this AA-rated bond should trade at about a 6.28 percent yield. Notably, this rate would determine the price for the bond with no con-

EXHIBIT 19.4 ▶ *YIELDS ON U.S. TREASURY STRIPS WITH ALTERNATIVE MATURITIES*

MATURITY	YIELD
1 Year	2.14
2 Years	2.91
3 Years	3.53
4 Years	4.01
5 Years	4.28
6 Years	4.48
7 Years	4.65
8 Years	4.82
9 Years	4.88
10 Years	4.85
12 Years	5.25
14 Years	5.39
16 Years	5.47
18 Years	5.54
20 Years	5.58
25 Years	5.60
30 Years	5.40

Source: *The Wall Street Journal,* 6 March 2002. Reprinted with permission from *The Wall Street Journal,* Dow Jones Co. Inc.

sideration given to the specific cash flows of this security (i.e., high or low coupon). Therefore, there is a growing awareness that the valuation formula should be specified such that *all cash flows should be discounted at spot rates consistent with the timing of the flows* as follows:

▶ **19.7**

$$P_m = \sum_{t=1}^{2n} \frac{C_t}{(1 + i_t/2)^t}$$

where:

    P_m = the market price for the bond
    C_t = the cash flow at time t
    n = the number of years
    i_t = the spot rate for Treasury securities at maturity t

Note that this valuation model requires a different discount rate for each flow so it is not possible to use the annuity concept. Also, the principal payment at the end of the year n is no different from the interest coupon flow at year n.

To demonstrate the effect of this procedure, consider the following hypothetical spot rate curve for the next five years (in Exhibit 19.5) and three example bonds with equal maturities of five years, but with very different cash flows.

Beyond the differences in value because of the differences in cash flows and the rising spot rate curve, a significant comparison is the value that would be derived using a single discount

| EXHIBIT 19.5 | DEMONSTRATION OF DIFFERENT VALUATION OF ALTERNATIVE FIVE-YEAR MATURITY BONDS WITH UNIQUE CASH FLOWS, DISCOUNTED USING THE SPOT RATE CURVE |

| | | | CASH FLOWS | | | | | |
| | | | BOND A | | BOND B | | BOND C | |
MATURITY (YEARS)	SPOT RATE	DISCOUNT FACTOR	$	PV	$	PV	$	PV
0.5	5.00	0.9756	60	$ 58.536	30	$ 29.268	—	—
1.0	5.20	0.9499	60	56.994	30	28.497	—	—
1.5	5.50	0.9218	60	55.308	30	27.654	—	—
2.0	5.70	0.8937	60	53.622	30	26.811	—	—
2.5	5.80	0.8668	60	52.008	30	26.004	—	—
3.0	5.90	0.8399	60	50.394	30	25.197	—	—
3.5	6.10	0.8103	60	48.618	30	24.309	—	—
4.0	6.30	0.7803	60	46.818	30	23.409	—	—
4.5	6.40	0.7532	60	45.192	30	22.596	—	—
5.0	6.50	0.7270	1,060	770.620	1,030	748.810	1,000	727.00
Total present value				$1,238.110		$982.555		$727.00

rate based on the five-year maturity of all three bonds. If we assume two alternative yields to maturity of 6 percent and 6.5 percent for five-year bonds, the values for the three bonds are:

	6%	6.5%
Bond A	$ 60 × 8.5302 = $ 511.81	$ 60 × 8.4254 = $ 505.52
	$1,000 × 0.7441 = 744.10	$1,000 × 0.7270 = 727.00
	Total Value = $1,255.91	= $1,232.52
Bond B	$ 30 × 8.5302 = $ 255.90	$ 30 × 8.4254 = $ 252.76
	$1,000 × 0.7441 = 744.10	$1,000 × 0.7270 = 727.00
	Total Value = $1,000.00	= $ 979.76
Bond C	$1,000 × 0.7441 = $ 744.10	$1,000 × 0.7270 = $ 727.00
	Total Value = $ 744.10	= $ 727.00

Because there is a rising spot-yield curve, we know the YTM would be somewhere between these two values. The point is, under these conditions valuing the bonds with a single high rate tends to generate a value that is lower than that derived from the spot rate curve. This implies that a single-rate valuation technique would typically misvalue these bonds relative to the more appropriate technique that considers each flow as a single bond discounted by its own spot rate.

WHAT DETERMINES INTEREST RATES?

Now that we have learned to calculate various yields on bonds and to determine the value of bonds using yields and spot rates, the question arises as to what causes differences and changes in yields over time. Market interest rates cause these effects because the interest rates reported in the media are simply the prevailing YTMs for the bonds being discussed. For example, when you hear that the interest rate on long-term government bonds declined from 6.80 percent to 6.70 percent, this means that the price of this particular bond increased such that the computed YTM at the former price was 6.80 percent, but the computed YTM at the new, higher price is 6.70 percent. Yields and interest rates are the same. They are different terms for the same concept.

We have discussed the inverse relationship between bond prices and interest rates. When interest rates decline, the prices of bonds increase; when interest rates rise, there is a decline in bond prices. It is natural to ask which of these is the driving force—bond prices or bond interest rates? It is a simultaneous change, and you can envision either factor causing it. Most practitioners probably envision the changes in interest rates as causes because they constantly use interest rates to describe changes. They use interest rates because they are comparable across bonds, whereas the price of a bond depends not only on the interest rate but also on the bond's specific characteristics, including its coupon and maturity. The point is, as demonstrated in Exhibit 19.1 and Exhibit 19.2, when you change the interest rate (yield) on a bond, you simultaneously change its price in the opposite direction. Later in the chapter we will discuss the specific price-yield relationship for individual bonds and demonstrate that this price-yield relationship differs among bonds based on their particular coupon and maturity.

Understanding interest rates and what makes them change is necessary for an investor who hopes to maximize returns from investing in bonds. Therefore, in this section we review our prior discussion of the following topics: what causes overall market interest rates to rise and fall, why alternative bonds have different interest rates, and why the difference in rates (i.e., the yield spread) between alternative bonds changes over time. To accomplish this, we begin with a general discussion of what influences interest rates and then consider the **term structure of interest rates** (shown by yield curves), which relates the interest rates on a set of comparable bonds to their terms to maturity. The term structure is important because it implies a set of spot rates that can be used in the valuation of bonds. In addition, it reflects what investors expect to happen to interest rates in the future and it dictates their current risk attitude. In this section, we specifically consider the calculation of spot rates and forward rates from the reported yield curve. Finally, we turn to the concept of *yield spreads,* which measure the differences in yields between alternative bonds. We describe various yield spreads and explore changes in them over time.

Forecasting Interest Rates   As discussed, the ability to forecast interest rates and changes in these rates is critical to successful bond investing. Later, we consider the major determinants of interest rates, but for now you should keep in mind that interest rates *are the price for loanable funds.* Like any price, they are determined by the supply and demand for these funds. On the one side, investors are willing to provide funds (the supply) at prices based on their required rates of return for a particular borrower. On the other side, borrowers need funds (the demand) to support budget deficits (government), to invest in capital projects (corporations), or to acquire durable goods (cars, appliances) or homes (individuals).

Although lenders and borrowers have some fundamental factors that determine supply and demand curves, the prices for these funds (interest rates) also are affected for short periods by events that shift the curves. Examples include major government bond issues that affect demand for funds, or significant changes in Federal Reserve monetary policy that affect the supply of money.

Our treatment of interest rate forecasting recognizes that you must be aware of the basic determinants of interest rates and monitor these factors. We also recognize that detailed forecasting of interest rates is a very complex task that is best left to professional economists. Therefore, our goal as bond investors and bond portfolio managers is to monitor current and expected interest rate behavior. We should attempt to continuously assess the major factors that affect interest rate behavior but also rely on others—such as economic consulting firms, banks, or investment

| EXHIBIT 19.6 | *YIELDS OF INTERNATIONAL LONG-TERM GOVERNMENT BONDS: QUARTERLY 1993–2001* |

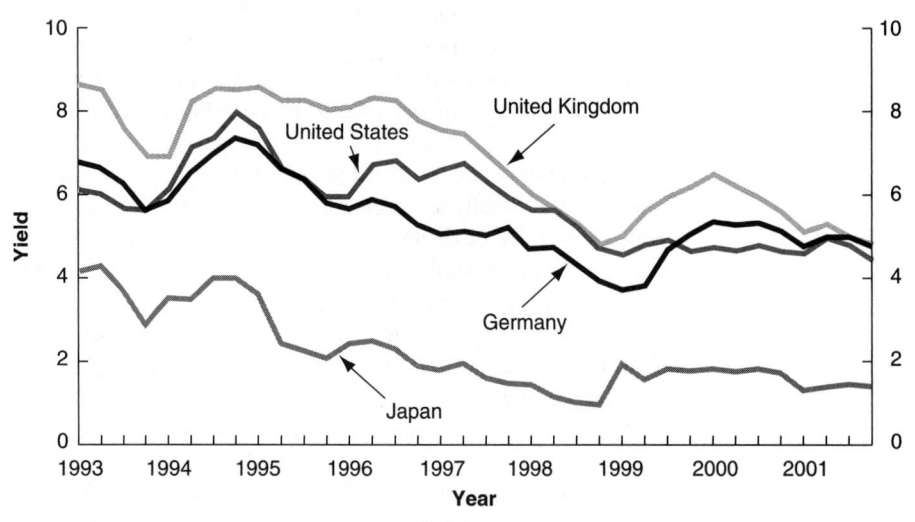

Source: International Monetary Fund, *International Financial Statistics.*

banking firms—for detailed insights on such topics as the real *RFR* and the expected rate of inflation.[7] This is precisely the way most bond portfolio managers operate.

Fundamental Determinants of Interest Rates

As shown in Exhibit 19.6, average interest rates (yields) for long-term (10-year) U.S. government bonds during the period from 1993 through 2001, went from about 6.20 percent to less than 5 percent. These results were midway between those of the United Kingdom and Germany. U.K. bonds went from about 8.70 percent to almost 4 percent, while the rate on Japanese government bonds declined from 4 percent to 1.5 percent. As a bond investor, you should understand *why* these differences exist and *why* interest rates changed.

As you know from your knowledge of bond pricing, bond prices increased dramatically during periods when market interest rates dropped, and some bond investors experienced very attractive returns. In contrast, some investors experienced substantial losses during periods when interest rates increased. A casual analysis of this chart, which covers about nine years, indicates the need for monitoring interest rates. Essentially, the factors causing interest rates *(i)* to rise or fall are described by the following model:

➤19.8
$$i = RFR + I + RP$$

where:

 RFR = **the real risk-free rate of interest**
  I = **the expected rate of inflation**
 RP = **the risk premium**

---

[7]Sources of information on the bond market and interest rate forecasts would include Merrill Lynch's *Fixed Income Weekly* and *World Bond Market Monitor;* Goldman Sach's *Financial Market Perspectives* and *The Pocket Chartroom;* and the Federal Reserve Bank of St. Louis, *Monetary Trends.*

The relationship shown in this equation should be familiar from our presentations in Chapter 1 and Chapter 11. It is a simple but complete statement of interest rate behavior. The more difficult task is estimating the *future* behavior of such variables as real growth, expected inflation, and economic uncertainty. In this regard, interest rates, like stock prices, are extremely difficult to forecast with any degree of accuracy.[8] Alternatively, we can visualize the source of changes in interest rates in terms of the economic conditions and issue characteristics that determine the rate of return on a bond:

➤**19.9**
$$i = f \text{ (Economic Forces + Issue Characteristics)}$$
$$= (RFR + I) + RP$$

This rearranged version of the previous equation helps isolate the determinants of interest rates.[9]

Effect of Economic Factors   The real risk-free rate of interest *(RFR)* is the economic cost of money, that is, the opportunity cost necessary to compensate individuals for forgoing consumption. It is determined by the real growth rate of the economy with short-run effects due to ease or tightness in the capital market.

The expected rate of inflation is the other economic influence on interest rates. We add the expected level of inflation *(I)* to the real risk-free rate *(RFR)* to specify the nominal *RFR,* which is a market rate like the current rate on government T-bills. Given the stability of the real *RFR,* it is clear that the wide swings in nominal risk-free interest rates during the years covered by Exhibit 19.6 occurred because of expected inflation.[10] Besides the unique country and exchange rate risk that we discuss in the section on risk premiums, differences in the rates of inflation between countries have a major impact on their level of interest rates.

To sum up, one way to estimate the nominal *RFR* is to begin with the real growth rate of the economy, adjust for short-run ease or tightness in the capital market, and then adjust this real rate of interest for the expected rate of inflation.

Another approach to estimating the nominal rate or changes in the rate is the macroeconomic view, where the supply and demand for loanable funds are the fundamental economic determinants of *i.* As the supply of loanable funds increases, the level of interest rates declines, other things being equal. Several factors influence the supply of funds. Government monetary policies imposed by the Federal Reserve have a significant impact on the supply of money. The savings patterns of U.S. and non-U.S. investors also affect the supply of funds. Non-U.S. investors have become a stronger influence on the U.S. supply of loanable funds during recent years, as shown by the significant purchases of U.S. securities by non-U.S. investors. It is widely acknowledged that this foreign supply of funds to the U.S. bond market has been very beneficial to the United States because it has helped reduce interest rates and the cost of capital.

Interest rates increase when the demand for loanable funds increases. The demand for loanable funds is affected by the capital and operating needs of the U.S. government, federal agencies, state and local governments, corporations, institutions, and individuals. Federal budget deficits increase the Treasury's demand for loanable funds. Likewise, the level of consumer demand for funds to buy houses, autos, and appliances affects rates, as does corporate demand

---

[8]For an overview of interest rate forecasting, see Frank J. Fabozzi, "The Structure of Interest Rates," in *The Handbook of Fixed-Income Securities,* 6th ed., ed. Frank J. Fabozzi (New York: McGraw-Hill, 2001).

[9]For an extensive exploration of interest rates and interest rate behavior, see James C. Van Horne, *Financial Market Rates and Flows,* 5th ed. (Englewood Cliffs, N.J.: Prentice-Hall, 1998).

[10]In this regard, see C. Alan Garner, "How Useful Are Leading Indicators of Inflation?" Federal Reserve Bank of Kansas City *Economic Review* 80, no. 2 (Second Quarter 1995): 5–18.

for funds to pursue investment opportunities. The total of all groups determines the aggregate demand and supply of loanable funds and the level of the nominal *RFR*.[11]

The Impact of Bond Characteristics   The interest rate of a specific bond issue is influenced not only by all the factors that affect the nominal *RFR* but also by the unique issue characteristics of the bond. These issue characteristics influence the bond's risk premium *(RP)*. The economic forces that determine the nominal *RFR* affect all securities, whereas issue characteristics are unique to individual securities, market sectors, or countries. Thus, the differences in the yields of corporate and Treasury bonds are caused not by economic forces but, rather, by different issue characteristics that cause differences in the risk premiums.

Bond investors separate the risk premium into four components:

1. The quality of the issue as determined by its risk of default relative to other bonds
2. The term to maturity of the issue, which can affect price volatility
3. Indenture provisions, including collateral, call features, and sinking-fund provisions
4. Foreign bond risk, including exchange rate risk and country risk

Of the four factors, quality and maturity have the greatest impact on the risk premium for domestic bonds, while exchange rate risk and country risk are important components of risk for non-U.S. bonds.

The credit quality of a bond reflects the ability of the issuer to service outstanding debt obligations. This information is largely captured in the ratings issued by the bond rating firms. As a result, bonds with different ratings have different yields. For example, AAA-rated obligations possess lower risk of default than BBB obligations, so they can provide lower yield.

Notably, the risk premium differences between bonds of different quality levels have changed dramatically over time, depending on prevailing economic conditions. When the economy experiences a recession or a period of economic uncertainty, the desire for quality increases, and investors bid up prices of higher-rated bonds, which reduces their yields. This difference in yield is referred to as the *quality spread*. It also has been suggested by Dialynas and Edington that this yield spread is influenced by the volatility of interest rates.[12] This variability in the risk premium over time was demonstrated and discussed in Chapter 1 and Chapter 11. The U.S. market experienced dramatic demonstrations of short-run risk premium explosions in August 1998 in response to Russia defaulting on its debt and following the terrorist attacks on September 11, 2001.

Term to maturity also influences the risk premium because it affects the price volatility of the bond. In the section on the term structure of interest rates, we will discuss the typical positive relationship between the term to maturity of a bond issue and its interest rate.

As discussed in Chapter 18, indenture provisions indicate the collateral pledged for a bond, its callability, and its sinking-fund provisions. Collateral gives protection to the investor if the issuer defaults on the bond because the investor has a specific claim on some assets in case of liquidation.

Call features indicate when an issuer can buy back the bond prior to its maturity. A bond is called by an issuer when interest rates have declined, so it is not to the advantage of the investor who must reinvest the proceeds at a lower interest rate. Obviously, an investor will charge the

---

[11]For an example of an estimate of the supply and demand for funds in the economy, see *Prospects for Financial Markets in 1999* (New York: Salomon Bros. Smith Barney, 1998). This is an annual publication of Salomon Brothers Smith Barney that gives an estimate of the flow of funds in the economy and discusses its effect on various currencies and interest rates.

[12]Chris P. Dialynas and David H. Edington, "Bond Yield Spreads: A Postmodern View," *Journal of Portfolio Management* 19, no. 1 (Fall 1992): 68–75.

issuer for including the call option, and the cost of the option (which is a higher yield) will increase with the level of interest rates. Therefore, more protection against having the bond called reduces the risk premium. The significance (value) of call protection increases during periods of high interest rates. The point is, when you buy a bond with a high coupon, you want protection from having it called away when rates decline.[13]

A sinking fund reduces the investor's risk and causes a lower yield for several reasons. First, a sinking fund reduces default risk because it requires the issuer to reduce the outstanding issue systematically. Second, purchases of the bond by the issuer to satisfy sinking-fund requirements provide price support for the bond because of the added demand. These purchases by the issuer also contribute to a more liquid secondary market for the bond because of the increased trading. Finally, sinking-fund provisions require that the issuer retire a bond before its stated maturity, which causes a reduction in the issue's average maturity. The decline in average maturity tends to reduce the risk premium of the bond much as a shorter maturity would reduce yield.[14]

We know that foreign currency exchange rates change over time and that this increases the risk of global investing. The variability of exchange rates vary among countries because the trade balances and rates of inflation differ. Volatile trade balances, and inflation rates make exchange rates more volatile, which adds to the uncertainty of future exchange rates and increases the exchange rate risk premium.

In addition to changes in exchange rates, investors also are concerned with the political and economic stability of a country. If investors are unsure about the political environment or the economic system in a country, they will increase the required risk premium to reflect this country risk.[15]

Term Structure of Interest Rates

The term structure of interest rates (or the *yield curve,* as it is more popularly known) is a static function that relates the term to maturity to the yield to maturity for a sample of bonds at *a given point in time.*[16] Thus, it represents a cross section of yields for a category of bonds that are comparable in all respects but maturity. Specifically, the quality of the issues should be constant, and ideally you should have issues with similar coupons and call features within a single industry category. You can construct different yield curves for Treasuries, government agencies, prime-grade municipals, AAA utilities, and so on. The accuracy of the yield curve will depend on the comparability of the bonds in the sample.

As an example, Exhibit 19.7 shows yield curves for a sample of U.S. Treasury obligations. It is based on the yield to maturity information for a set of comparable Treasury issues from a publication such as the *Federal Reserve Bulletin* or *The Wall Street Journal.* These promised yields were plotted on the graph, and a yield curve was drawn that represents the general configuration of rates. These data represent yield curves at four different points in time to demonstrate the changes in yield levels and in the shape of the yield curve over time.

---

[13]William Marshall and Jess B. Yawitz, "Optimal Terms of the Call Provision on a Corporate Bond," *Journal of Financial Research* 3, no. 3 (Fall 1980): 203–211; Bryan Stanhouse and Duane Stock, "How Changes in Bond Call Features Affect Coupon Rates," *Journal of Applied Corporate Finance* 12, no. 1 (Spring 1999): 92–99.

[14]For a further discussion of sinking funds, see A. J. Kalotay, "On the Management of Sinking Funds," *Financial Management* 10, no. 2 (Summer 1981): 34–40; and A. J. Kalotay, "Sinking Funds and the Realized Cost of Debt," *Financial Management* 11, no. 1 (Spring 1982): 43–54.

[15]In this regard, see Allen A. Vine, "High-Yield Analysis of Emerging Markets Debt," in *The Handbook of Fixed-Income Securities,* 6th ed.

[16]For a discussion of the theory and empirical evidence, see Suresh Sundaresan, *Fixed-Income Markets and Their Derivatives,* 2d ed. (Cincinnati, Ohio: South-Western, 2002), Chapter 6.

EXHIBIT 19.7 ▶ *YIELD ON U.S. TREASURY STRIPS WITH ALTERNATIVE MATURITIES*

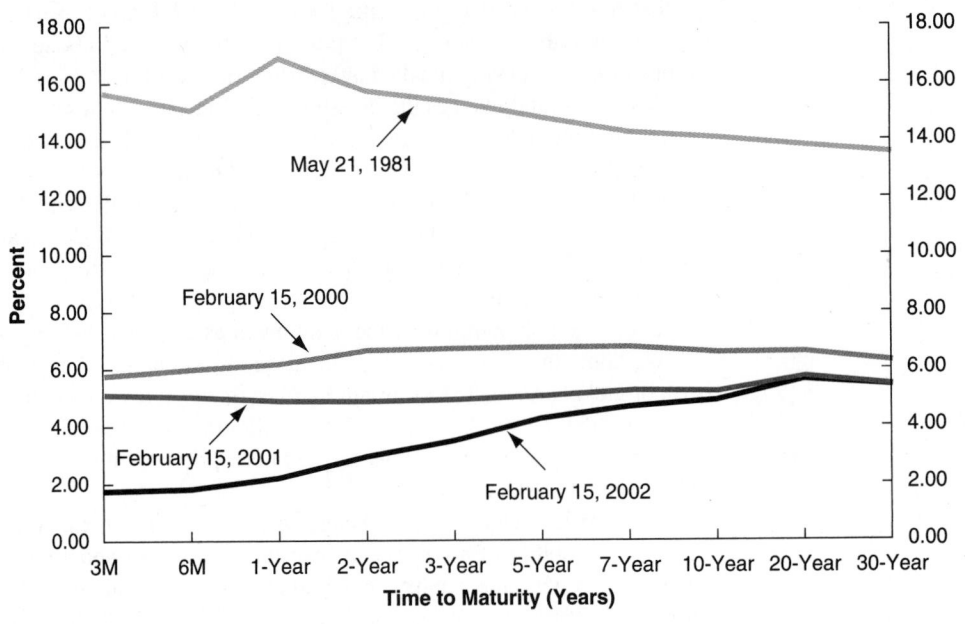

Source: Federal Reserve System Statistics.

All yield curves, of course, do not have the same shape as those in Exhibit 19.7. Although individual yield curves are static, their behavior over time is quite fluid. As shown, the level of the curve decreased from May 1981 to February 2000 and then declined further by February 2001, and the short end of the curve declined further by February 2002. Also, the shape of the yield curve can undergo dramatic alterations, following one of the four patterns shown in Exhibit 19.8. The rising yield curve is the most common and tends to prevail when interest rates are at low or modest levels. The declining yield curve tends to occur when rates are relatively high. The flat yield curve rarely exists for any period of time. The humped yield curve prevails when extremely high rates are expected to decline to more normal levels. Note that the slope of the yield curve tends to level off after 15 years.

Why does the term structure assume different shapes? Three major theories attempt to explain this: the expectations hypothesis, the liquidity preference hypothesis, and the segmented market hypothesis.

Before we discuss these three alternative hypotheses, we must first discuss two previously noted rates that not only are an integral part of the term structure but also are important in the valuation of bonds. The next two subsections will deal with the specification and computation of *spot rates* and *forward rates*. Earlier, we discussed and used spot rates to value bonds with the idea that any coupon bond can be viewed as a collection of zero coupon securities.

Creating the Theoretical Spot Rate Curve[17]   Earlier in the chapter, we discussed the notion that the yield on a zero coupon bond for a given maturity is the spot rate for the maturity.

---

[17]This discussion of the theoretical spot rate curve and the subsequent presentation on calculating forward rates draw heavily from Frank J. Fabozzi, "The Structure of Interest Rates," in *The Handbook of Fixed-Income Securities*, 6th ed.

EXHIBIT 19.8 ▶ *TYPES OF YIELD CURVES*

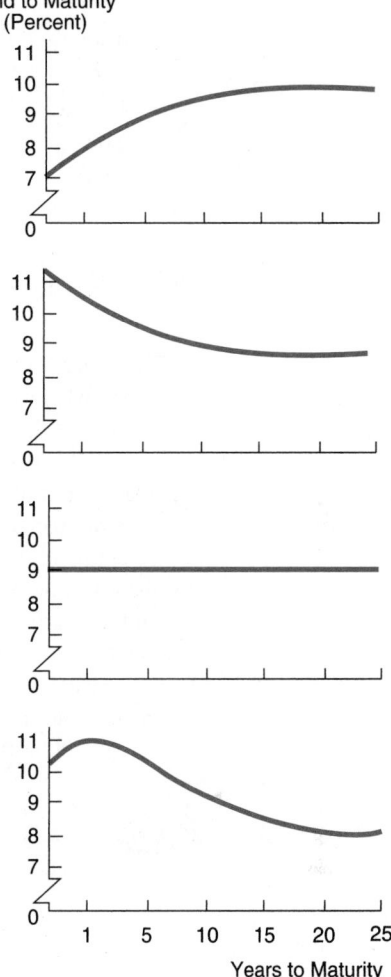

A rising yield curve is formed when the yields on short-term issues are low and rise consistently with longer maturities and flatten out at the extremes.

A declining yield curve is formed when the yields on short-term issues are high and yields on subsequently longer maturities decline consistently.

A flat yield curve has approximately equal yields on short-term and long-term issues.

A humped yield curve is formed when yields on intermediate-term issues are above those on short-term issues and the rates on long-term issues decline to levels below those for the short term and then level out.

Specifically, the **spot rate** is defined as the discount rate for a cash flow at a specific maturity. At that time, we used the rates on a series of zero coupon government bonds created by stripping coupon government bonds.

In this case, we will construct a theoretical spot rate curve from the observable yield curve that is based on the existing yields of Treasury bills and the most recent Treasury coupon securities (referred to as *on-the-run* Treasury issues). One might expect the theoretical spot rate curve and the spot rate curve derived from the stripped zero coupon bonds used earlier to be the same. The fact is, while they are close, they will not be exactly the same because the stripped zero coupon bonds will not be as liquid as the on-the-run issues. In addition, there are instances where institutions will have a strong desire for a particular spot maturity and this preference will distort the term structure relationship. Therefore, while it is possible to use the stripped zero coupon curve for a general indication, if you are going to use the spot rates for significant valuation, you would want to use the theoretical spot rate curve.

EXHIBIT 19.9   *MATURITY AND YIELD TO MATURITY FOR HYPOTHETICAL TREASURY SECURITIES*

MATURITY (YEARS)	COUPON RATE	PRICE	YIELD TO MATURITY
0.50	0.0000	96.15	0.0800
1.00	0.0000	92.19	0.0830
1.50	0.0850	99.45	0.0890
2.00	0.0900	99.64	0.0920
2.50	0.1100	103.49	0.0940
3.00	0.0950	99.49	0.0970

Sources: Federal Reserve Bulletin; Mergent Bond Record. Reprinted with permission.

The process of creating a theoretical spot rate curve from coupon securities is called *boot-strapping* wherein it is assumed that the value of the Treasury coupon security should be equal to the value of the package of zero coupon securities that duplicates the coupon bond's cash flow. Exhibit 19.9 lists the maturity and YTM for six hypothetical Treasury bonds that will be used to calculate the initial spot rates.

Consider the six-month Treasury bill in Exhibit 19.9. As discussed earlier, a Treasury bill is a zero coupon instrument so its annualized yield of 8 percent is equal to the spot rate. Similarly, for the one-year Treasury bill, the cited yield of 8.3 percent is equal to the one-year spot rate. Given these two spot rates, we can compute the spot rate for a theoretical 1.5-year zero coupon Treasury. The price for this 1.5-year security should equal the present value of three cash flows from an actual 1.5-year coupon Treasury, where the yield used for discounting a specific coupon payment is the spot rate corresponding to the cash flow.

Using $100 as par, the *cash flow* for the 1.5-year, 8.50 percent coupon Treasury is as follows:

0.5 years	$0.085 \times \$100 \times 0.5$	=	$ 4.25
1.0 years	$0.085 \times \$100 \times 0.5$	=	$ 4.25
1.5 years	$0.085 \times \$100 \times 0.5 + \$100$	=	$104.25

The present value of the cash flows discounted at the appropriate spot rates is then

$$\frac{4.25}{(1+z_1)^1} + \frac{4.25}{(1+z_2)^2} + \frac{104.25}{(1+z_3)^3}$$

where:

z_1 = **one-half the annualized six-month theoretical spot rate**
z_2 = **one-half the one-year theoretical spot rate**
z_3 = **one-half the 1.5-year theoretical spot rate**

Because the six-month spot rate and one-year spot rate are 8.0 percent and 8.3 percent, respectively, we know that

$$z_1 = 0.04 \quad and \quad z_2 = 0.0415$$

We can compute the present value of the 1.5-year coupon Treasury security as

$$\frac{4.25}{(1.0400)^1} + \frac{4.25}{(1.0415)^2} + \frac{104.25}{(1+z_3)^3}$$

Because the price of the 1.5-year coupon Treasury security (from Exhibit 19.9) is $99.45, the following relationship must hold:

$$99.45 = \frac{4.25}{(1.0400)^1} + \frac{4.25}{(1.0415)^2} + \frac{104.25}{(1+z_3)^3}$$

We can solve for the theoretical 1.5-year spot rate as follows:

$$99.45 = 4.08654 + 3.91805 + \frac{104.25}{(1+z_3)^3}$$

$$91.44541 = \frac{104.25}{(1+z_3)^3}$$

$$\frac{104.25}{91.44541} = (1+z_3)^3$$

$$(1+z_3)^3 = 1.140024$$

$$z_3 = 0.04465$$

Doubling this yield, we obtain the bond-equivalent yield of 0.0893 or 8.93 percent, which is the theoretical 1.5-year spot rate. That rate is the rate that the market would apply to a 1.5-year zero coupon Treasury, if such a security existed.

Given the theoretical 1.5-year spot rate, we can obtain the theoretical 2-year spot rate. The cash flow for the 2-year, 9.0 percent coupon Treasury in Exhibit 19.9 is

0.5 years	$0.090 \times \$100 \times 0.5$	=	\$ 4.50
1.0 years	$0.090 \times \$100 \times 0.5$	=	\$ 4.50
1.5 years	$0.090 \times \$100 \times 0.5$	=	\$ 4.50
2.0 years	$0.090 \times \$100 \times 0.5 + 100$	=	\$104.50

The present value of the cash flow is then

$$\frac{4.50}{(1+z_1)^1} + \frac{4.50}{(1+z_2)^2} + \frac{4.50}{(1+z_3)^3} + \frac{104.50}{(1+z_4)^4}$$

where:

z_4 = **one-half the two-year theoretical spot rate**

Because the 6-month, 1-year, and 1.5-year spot rates are 8 percent, 8.3 percent, and 8.93 percent, respectively, then

$$z_1 = 0.04 \quad z_2 = 0.0415 \quad and \quad z_3 = 0.04465$$

EXHIBIT 19.10 ▸ *THEORETICAL SPOT RATES*

Maturity (Years)	Yield to Maturity	Theoretical Spot Rate
0.50	0.0800	0.08000
1.00	0.0830	0.08300
1.50	0.0890	0.08930
2.00	0.0920	0.09247
2.50	0.0940	0.09468
3.00	0.0970	0.09787

Therefore, the present value of the two-year coupon Treasury security is

$$\frac{4.50}{(1.0400)^1} + \frac{4.50}{(1.0415)^2} + \frac{4.50}{(1.04465)^3} + \frac{104.50}{(1+z_4)^4}$$

Because the price of the two-year, 9.0 percent coupon Treasury security is $99.64, the following relationship must hold:

$$99.64 = \frac{4.50}{(1.0400)^1} + \frac{4.50}{(1.0415)^2} + \frac{4.50}{(1.04465)^3} + \frac{104.50}{(1+z_4)^4}$$

We can solve for the theoretical two-year spot rate as follows:

$$99.64 = 4.32692 + 4.14853 + 3.94730 + \frac{104.50}{(1+z_4)^4}$$

$$87.21725 = \frac{104.50}{(1+z_4)^4}$$

$$(1+z_4)^4 = 1.198158$$

$$z_4 = 0.046235$$

Doubling this yield, we obtain the theoretical two-year spot rate bond-equivalent yield of 9.247 percent.

One can follow this approach sequentially to derive the theoretical 2.5-year spot rate from the calculated values of z_1, z_2, z_3, z_4 (the 6-month, 1-year, 1.5-year, and 2-year spot rates), and the price and the coupon of the bond with a maturity of 2.5 years. Subsequently, one could derive the theoretical spot rate for three years. The spot rates thus obtained are shown in Exhibit 19.10. They represent the term structure of spot interest rates for maturities up to three years, based on the prevailing bond price quotations.

As shown, with a rising YTM curve, the theoretical spot rate will increase at a faster rate such that the difference increases with maturity (i.e., the theoretical spot rate curve will be above a positively sloped YTM curve).

◂ CALCULATING FORWARD RATES FROM THE SPOT RATE CURVE ▸

Now that we have derived the theoretical spot rate curve, it is possible to determine what this curve implies regarding the market's expectation of *future* short-term rates, which are referred to as *forward rates.* The following illustrates the process of extrapolating this information about expected future interest rates.

Consider an investor who has a one-year investment horizon and is faced with the following two alternatives:

Alternative 1: Buy a one-year Treasury bill.

Alternative 2: Buy a six-month Treasury bill and, when it matures in six months, buy another six-month Treasury bill.

The investor will be indifferent between the two alternatives *if* they produce the same return on the one-year investment horizon. The investor knows the spot rate on the six-month Treasury bill and the one-year Treasury bill. However, she does not know what yield will be available on a six-month Treasury bill six months from now. The yield on a six-month Treasury bill six months from now is called a **forward rate**. Given the spot rate for the six-month Treasury bill and the one-year bill, we can determine the forward rate on a six-month Treasury bill *that will make the investor indifferent between the two alternatives.*

At this point, however, we need to digress briefly and recall several present value and investment relationships. First, if you invested in a one-year Treasury bill, you would receive $100 at the end of one year. The price of the one-year Treasury bill would be

$$\frac{100}{(1+z_2)^2}$$

where:

z_2 = **one-half the bond-equivalent yield of the theoretical one-year spot rate**

Second, suppose you purchased a six-month Treasury bill for $X. At the end of six months, the value of this investment would be

$$\$X(1 + z_1)$$

where:

z_1 = **one-half the bond-equivalent yield of the theoretical six-month spot rate**

Let $_{t+0.5}\,r_{0.5}$ represent one-half the forward rate (expressed as a bond-equivalent yield) on a six-month Treasury bill (0.5) available six months from now ($t + 0.5$). If the investor were to renew her investment by purchasing that bill at that time, then the future dollars available at the end of the year from the $X investment would be

$$X(1 + z_1)\,(1 + _{t+0.5}\,r_{0.5}) = 100$$

Third, it is easy to use that formula to find out how many dollars the investor must invest in order to get $100 one year from now. This can be found as follows:

$$X(1 + z_1)\,(1 + _{t+0.5}\,r_{0.5}) = 100$$

which gives us

$$X = \frac{100}{(1+z_1)(1+_{t+0.5}r_{0.5})}$$

We are now prepared to return to the investor's choices and analyze what that situation says about forward rates. The investor will be indifferent between the two alternatives confronting her if she makes the same dollar investment and receives $100 from both alternatives at the end of one year. That is, the investor will be indifferent if

$$\frac{100}{(1+z_2)^2} = \frac{100}{(1+z_1)(1+_{t+0.5}r_{0.5})}$$

Solving for $_{t+0.5}r_{0.5}$ we get

$$_{t+0.5}r_{0.5} = \frac{(1+z_2)^2}{(1+z_1)} - 1$$

Doubling r gives the bond-equivalent yield for the six-month forward rate six months from now.

We can illustrate the use of this formula with the theoretical spot rates shown in Exhibit 19.10. From that table, we know that

Six-month bill spot rate = 0.080   so $z_1 = 0.0400$
One-year bill spot rate = 0.083   so $z_2 = 0.0415$

Substituting into the formula, we have

$$_{t+0.5}r_{0.5} = \frac{(1.0415)^2}{(1.0400)} - 1$$
$$= 0.043$$

Therefore, the forward rate six months from now $(t + 0.5)$ on a six-month Treasury security, quoted annually, is 8.6 percent (0.043×2). Let us confirm our results. The price of a one-year Treasury bill with $100 maturity is

$$\frac{100}{(1.0415)^2} = 92.19$$

If $92.19 is invested for six months at the six-month spot rate of 8 percent, the amount at the end of six months would be

$$92.19(1.0400) = 95.8776$$

If $95.8776 is reinvested for another six months in a six-month Treasury bill offering 4.3 percent for six months (8.6 percent annually), the amount at the end of one year would be

$$95.8776(1.043) = 100$$

Both alternatives will have the same $100 payoff if the six-month Treasury bill yield six months from now is 4.3 percent (8.6 percent on a bond-equivalent basis). This means that, if an investor is guaranteed a 4.3 percent yield on a six-month Treasury bill six months from now, she will be indifferent between the two alternatives.

We used the theoretical spot rates to compute the forward rate. The resulting forward rate is called the *implied forward rate*.

It is possible to use the yield curve to calculate the implied forward rate for any time in the future for any investment horizon. This would include six-month or one-year forward rates for each year in the future. The one-year forward rates would be designated as follows:

$_{t+1}r_1$ = **the one-year forward rate, one year from now** $(t + 1)$
$_{t+2}r_1$ = **the one-year forward rate, two years from now** $(t + 2)$
$_{t+3}r_1$ = **the one-year forward rate, three years from now** $(t + 3)$

Given the calculations, it is clear that with a rising spot rate curve, the forward rate curve would be above the spot rate curve. From Exhibit 19.10, we have the following one-year spot rates, which imply the following one-year forward rates:

MATURITY (YEARS)	SPOT RATES	ONE–YEAR FORWARD RATES
1.0	0.08300	
2.0	0.09247	0.1020
3.0	0.09787	0.1087

Therefore:

$$_{t+1}r_1 = \frac{(1.09247)^2}{(1.08300)} - 1 = \frac{1.19349}{1.08300} - 1 = 0.1020$$

$$_{t+2}r_1 = \frac{(1.09787)^3}{(1.09247)^2} - 1 = \frac{1.32328}{1.19349} - 1 = 0.1087$$

Specifically, the one–year forward rate that is expected one year from now $(_{t+1}r_1)$ is 10.20 percent, while the one-year forward rate that is expected two years from now $(_{t+2}r_1)$ is 10.87 percent.

TERM-STRUCTURE THEORIES

Expectations Hypothesis

According to the expectations hypothesis, the shape of the yield curve results from the interest rate expectations of market participants. More specifically, it holds that *any long-term interest rate simply represents the geometric mean of current and future one-year interest rates expected to prevail over the maturity of the issue.* In essence, the term structure involves a series of intermediate and long-term interest rates, each of which is a reflection of the geometric average of current and expected one-year interest rates. Under such conditions, the equilibrium long-term rate is the rate the long-term bond investor would expect to earn through successive investments in short-term bonds over the term to maturity of the long-term bond.

Generally, this relationship can be formalized as follows:

➤ **19.10** $(1 + _tR_n) = [(1 + _tR_1)(1 + _{t+1}r_1) \ldots (1 + _{t+n-1}r_1)]^{1/N}$

where:

R_n = **the actual long-term rate**
N = **the term to maturity (in years) of long issue**
R = **the current one-year rate**
$_{t+i}r_1$ = **the expected one-year yield during some future period,** $t + i$ **(these future one-year rates are referred to as** *forward rates*)

Given the relationship set forth in this equation, the formula for computing the one-period forward rate beginning at time $t + n$ and implied in the term structure at time t is

$$1 + {}_{t+n}r_{1t} = \frac{(1 + {}_tR_{1t})(1 + {}_{t+1}r_{1t})(1 + {}_{t+2}r_{1t})...(1 + {}_{t+n-1}r_{1t})(1 + {}_{t+n}r_{1t})}{(1 + {}_tR_{1t})(1 + {}_{t+1}r_{1t})...(1 + {}_{t+n-1}r_{1t})}$$

$$= \frac{(1 + {}_tR_{n+1})^{n+1}}{(1 + {}_tR_n)^n}$$

➤19.11 $${}_{t+n}r_{1t} = \frac{(1 + {}_tR_{n+1})^{n+1}}{(1 + {}_tR_n)^n} - 1$$

where ${}_{t+n}r_{1t}$ is the one-year forward rate prevailing at $t + n$, using the term structure at time t.

Assume that the five-year spot rate is 10 percent (${}_tR_5 = 0.10$) and the four-year spot rate is 9 percent (${}_tR_4 = 0.09$). The forward one-year rate four years from now implied by these spot rates can be calculated as follows:

$$\begin{aligned} {}_{t+4}r_{1t} &= \frac{(1 + {}_tR_5)^5}{(1 + {}_tR_4)^4} - 1 \\ &= \frac{(1 + 0.10)^5}{(1 + 0.09)^4} - 1 \\ &= \frac{1.6105}{1.4116} - 1 \\ &= 1.1409 - 1 = 0.1409 = 14.09\% \end{aligned}$$

The term structure at time t implies that the one-year spot rate four years from now (during Year 5) will be 14.09 percent. This concept and formula can be used to derive future rates for multiple years. Thus, the two-year spot rate that will prevail three years from now could be calculated using the three-year spot rate and the five-year spot rate. The general formula for computing the j-period forward rate beginning at time $t + n$ as of time t is

➤19.12 $${}_{t+n}r_{jt} = \sqrt[j]{\frac{(1 + {}_tR_{n+j})^{n+j}}{(1 + {}_tR_n)^n}} - 1$$

As a practical approximation of Equation 19.10, it is possible to use the *arithmetic* average of one-year rates to generate long-term yields.

The expectations theory can explain any shape of yield curve. Expectations for rising short-term rates in the future cause a rising yield curve; expectations for falling short-term rates in the future will cause long-term rates to lie below current short-term rates, and the yield curve will decline. Similar explanations account for flat and humped yield curves.

Consider the following explanation by the expectations hypothesis of the shape of the term structure of interest rates using arithmetic averages:

${}_tR_1 = 5\frac{1}{2}$ **percent the one-year rate of interest prevailing now (period t)**

${}_{t+1}r_1 = 6$ **percent the one-year rate of interest expected to prevail next year (period $t + 1$)**

${}_{t+2}r_1 = 7\frac{1}{2}$ **percent the one-year rate of interest expected to prevail two years from now (period $t + 2$)**

${}_{t+3}r_1 = 8\frac{1}{2}$ **percent the one-year rate of interest expected to prevail three years from now (period $t + 3$)**

Using these values and the known rate on a one-year bond, we compute rates on two-, three-, or four-year bonds (designated R_2, R_3, and R_4) as follows:

$_tR_1 = 5\frac{1}{2}$ **percent**
$_tR_2 = (0.055 + 0.06)/2 = 5.75$ **percent**
$_tR_3 = (0.055 + 0.06 + 0.075)/3 = 6.33$ **percent**
$_tR_4 = (0.055 + 0.06 + 0.075 + 0.085)/4 = 6.88$ **percent**

In this illustration (which uses the arithmetic average as an approximation of the geometric mean), the yield curve is upward sloping because, at present, investors expect future short-term rates to be above current short-term rates. This is not the formal method for constructing the yield curve. Rather, the yield curve is constructed on the basis of the prevailing promised yields for bonds with different maturities.

The expectations hypothesis attempts to explain *why* the yield curve is upward sloping, downward sloping, humped, or flat by explaining the expectations implicit in yield curves with different shapes. The evidence is fairly substantial and convincing that the expectations hypothesis is a workable explanation of the term structure. Because of the supporting evidence, its relative simplicity, and the intuitive appeal of the theory, the expectations hypothesis of the term structure of interest rates is rather widely accepted.

Consistent Investor Actions   Besides the theory and empirical support, it is also possible to present a scenario wherein investor actions will cause the yield curve postulated by the theory. The expectations hypothesis predicts a declining yield curve when interest rates are expected to fall in the future rather than rise. In a case of expected falling rates, long-term bonds would be considered attractive investments because investors would want to lock in prevailing higher yields (which are not expected to be as high in the future) or they would want to capture the increase in bond prices (as capital gains) that will accompany a decline in rates. By the same reasoning, investors will avoid short-term bonds or sell them and reinvest the funds in long-term bonds that will experience larger price increases if rates decline. The point is, investor expectations will reinforce the declining shape of the yield curve as they bid up the prices of long-maturity bonds (forcing yields to decline) and short-term bond issues are avoided or sold (so prices decline and yields rise). At the same time, there is confirming action by suppliers of bonds. Specifically, government or corporate issuers will avoid selling long bonds at the current high rates, waiting until the rates decline. In the meantime, they will issue short-term bonds, if needed, while waiting for lower rates. Therefore, in the long-term market, you will have an increase in demand and a decline in the supply and vice versa in the short-term market. These shifts between long- and short-term maturities will continue until equilibrium occurs or expectations change.

Liquidity Preference Hypothesis

The theory of liquidity preference holds that long-term securities should provide higher returns than short-term obligations because investors are willing to sacrifice some yields to invest in short-maturity obligations to avoid the higher price volatility of long-maturity bonds. Another way to interpret the liquidity preference hypothesis is to say that lenders prefer short-term loans, and, to induce them to lend long term, it is necessary to offer higher yields.

The liquidity preference theory contends that uncertainty and volatility cause investors to favor short-term issues over bonds with longer maturities because short-term bonds are less volatile and can easily be converted into predictable amounts of cash should unforeseen events occur. This theory argues that the yield curve should slope upward and that any other shape should be viewed as a temporary aberration.

This theory can be considered an extension of the expectations hypothesis because the formal liquidity preference position contends that the liquidity premium inherent in the yields for longer maturity bonds should be added to the expected future rate in arriving at long-term yields. Specifically, the liquidity premium *(L)* compensates the investor in long-term bonds for the added volatility inherent in long-term bonds compared to short-maturity securities. Because the liquidity premium *(L)* is provided to compensate the long-term investor, it is simply a variation of Equation 19.10 as follows:

$$(1 + {}_tR_N) = [(1 + {}_tR_1)(1 + {}_{t+1}r_1 + L_2) \ldots (1 + {}_{t+N-1}r_1 + L_n)]^{1/N}$$

In this specification, the *L*s are not the same but would be expected to increase with maturity because the price volatility increases with maturity. The liquidity preference theory has been found to possess some strong empirical support.[18]

To see how the liquidity preference theory predicts future yields and how it compares with the pure expectations hypothesis, let us predict future long-term rates from a single set of one-year rates: 6 percent, 7.5 percent, and 8.5 percent. The liquidity preference theory suggests that investors add increasing liquidity premiums to successive rates to derive actual market rates. As an example, they might arrive at rates of 6.3 percent, 7.9 percent, and 9.0 percent.

As a matter of historical fact, the yield curve shows an upward bias, which implies that some combination of the expectations theory and the liquidity preference theory will more accurately explain the shape of the yield curve than either of them alone. Specifically, actual long-term rates consistently tend to be above what is envisioned from the price expectations hypothesis. This tendency implies the existence of a liquidity premium.

Segmented Market Hypothesis

Despite meager empirical support, a third theory for the shape of the yield curve is the segmented market hypothesis, which enjoys wide acceptance among market practitioners. Also known as the *preferred habitat,* the *institutional theory,* or the *hedging pressure theory,* it asserts that different institutional investors have different maturity needs that lead them to confine their security selections to specific maturity segments. That is, investors supposedly focus on short-, intermediate-, or long-term securities. This theory contends that the shape of the yield curve ultimately is a function of these investment policies of major financial institutions.

As noted in Chapter 18, financial institutions tend to structure their investment policies in line with such factors as their tax liabilities, the types and maturity structure of their liabilities, and the level of earnings demanded by depositors. For example, because commercial banks are subject to normal corporate tax rates and their liabilities are generally short- to intermediate-term time and demand deposits, they consistently invest in short- to intermediate-term municipal bonds.

The segmented market theory contends that the business environment, along with legal and regulatory limitations, tends to direct each type of financial institution to allocate its resources to particular types of bonds with specific maturity characteristics. In its strongest form, the segmented market theory holds that the maturity preferences of investors and borrowers are so strong that investors never purchase securities outside their preferred maturity range to take advantage of yield differentials. As a result, the short- and long-maturity portions of the bond market are effectively segmented, and yields for a segment depend on the supply and demand *within* that maturity segment.

---

[18]See Reuben A. Kessel, "The Cyclical Behavior of the Term Structure of Interest Rates," Occasional Paper 91, National Bureau of Economic Research, 1965; Phillip Cagan, *Essays on Interest Rates* (New York: Columbia University Press for the National Bureau of Economic Research, 1969); and J. Huston McCulloch, "An Estimate of the Liquidity Premium," *Journal of Political Economy* 83, no. 1 (January–February 1975): 95–119.

Trading Implications of the Term Structure

Information on maturity yields can help you formulate yield expectations by simply observing the shape of the yield curve. If the yield curve is declining sharply, historical evidence suggests that interest rates will probably decline. Expectations theorists would suggest that you need to examine only the prevailing yield curve to predict the direction of interest rates in the future.

Based on these theories, bond investors use the prevailing yield curve to predict the shapes of future yield curves. Using this prediction and knowledge of current interest rates, investors can determine expected yield volatility by maturity sector. In turn, the maturity segments that are expected to experience the greatest yield changes give the investor the largest potential price change opportunities.[19]

Yield Spreads

Another technique that helps bond investors make profitable trades is the analysis of *yield spreads*—the differences in promised yields between bond issues or segments of the market at any point in time. Such differences are specific to the particular issues or segments of the bond market. Thus they add to the rates determined by the basic economic forces (*RFR + I*).

There are four major yield spreads:

1. Different *segments* of the bond market may have different yields. For example, pure government bonds will have lower yields than government agency bonds, and government bonds have much lower yields than corporate bonds.
2. Bonds in different *sectors* of the same market segment may have different yields. For example, prime-grade municipal bonds will have lower yields than good-grade municipal bonds; you will find spreads between AA utilities and BBB utilities, or between AAA industrial bonds and AAA public utility bonds.
3. Different *coupons* or *seasoning* within a given market segment or sector may cause yield spreads. Examples include current coupon government bonds versus deep-discount governments or recently issued AA industrials versus seasoned AA industrials.
4. Different *maturities* within a given market segment or sector also cause differences in yields. You will see yield spreads between short-term agency issues and long-term agency issues, or between 3-year prime municipals and 25-year prime municipals.

The differences among these bonds cause yield spreads that may be either positive or negative. More important, *the magnitude or the direction of a spread can change over time.* These changes in size or direction of yield spreads offer profit opportunities. We say that the spread narrows whenever the differences in yield become smaller; it widens as the differences increase. Exhibit 19.11 contains data on a variety of past yield spreads that have changed over time.

As a bond investor, you should evaluate yield spread changes because these changes influence bond price behavior and comparative return performance. You should attempt to identify (1) any normal yield spread that is expected to become abnormally wide or narrow in response to an anticipated swing in market interest rates, or (2) an abnormally wide or narrow yield spread that is expected to become normal.

Economic and market analyses will help you develop expectations regarding the potential for yield spreads to change. Taking advantage of these changes requires a knowledge of historical spreads, an ability to *predict* future total market changes, and an understanding of why and when specific spreads will change.[20]

---

[19]Gikas A. Hourdouvelis, "The Predictive Power of the Term Structure during Recent Monetary Regimes," *Journal of Finance* 43, no. 2 (June 1988): 339–356.

[20]An article that identifies four determinants of relative market spreads and suggests scenarios when they will change is Chris P. Dialynas and David H. Edington, "Bond Yield Spreads: A Postmodern View," *Journal of Portfolio Management* 19, no. 1 (Fall 1992): 68–75.

EXHIBIT 19.11   *SELECTED MEAN YIELD SPREADS (REPORTED IN BASIS POINTS)*

COMPARISONS	1995	1996	1997	1998	1999	2000	2001
1. Long Governments – Short Governments	80	89	37	67	109	–6	201
2. Long Aaa Corporates – Long Governments	79	45	72	95	118	168	159
3. Long Aaa Corporates – Long Aaa Municipals	132	169	167	160	177	204	257
4. Long Baa Municipals – Long Aaa Municipals	26	30	14	21	42	61	73
5. Utilities – Industrials	15	13	7	–1	8	1	4
6. Industrials – Financials	29	38	24	20	27	31	34
7. Long CCC Corporates – Long BB Corporates	720	624	573	682	898	1,343	1,250

Note: Yield spreads are equal to the yield on the first bond minus the yield on the second bond—for example, the yield on long governments minus the yield on short governments.

Sources: *Federal Reserve Bulletin;* Lehman Brothers Fixed Income Research, *Global Family of Indices;* Merrill Lynch Fixed Income Research.

WHAT DETERMINES THE PRICE VOLATILITY FOR BONDS?

In this chapter, we have learned about alternative bond yields, how to calculate them, what determines bond yields (interest rates), and what causes them to change. Now that we understand why yields change, we can logically ask, What is the effect of these yield changes on the prices and rates of return for different bonds? We have discussed the inverse relationship between changes in yields and the price of bonds, so we can now discuss *the specific factors that affect the amount of price change for a yield change* in different bonds. This can also be referred to as the *interest rate sensitivity* of a bond. This section lists the specific factors that affect bond price changes for a given change in interest rates (i.e., the interest rate sensitivity of a bond) and demonstrates the effect for different bonds.

A given change in interest rates can cause vastly different percentage price changes for alternative bonds, which implies different interest rate sensitivity. This section will help you understand what causes these differences in interest rate sensitivity. To maximize your rate of return from an expected decline in interest rates, for example, you need to know which bonds will benefit the most from the yield change. This section helps you make this bond selection decision.

Throughout this section, we talk about bond price changes or bond price volatility interchangeably. A bond price change is measured as the percentage change in the price of the bond, computed as follows:

$$\frac{EPB}{BPB} - 1$$

where:

EPB = the ending price of the bond
BPB = the beginning price of the bond

Bond price volatility also is measured in terms of percentage changes in bond prices. A bond with high price volatility or high interest rate sensitivity is one that experiences a relatively large percentage price change for a give change in yields.

Bond price volatility is influenced by more than yield behavior alone. Malkiel used the bond valuation model to demonstrate that the market price of a bond is a function of four factors: (1) its par value, (2) its coupon, (3) the number of years to its maturity, and (4) the prevailing

EXHIBIT 19.12 *EFFECT OF MATURITY ON BOND PRICE VOLATILITY*

PRESENT VALUE OF AN 8 PERCENT BOND ($1,000 PAR VALUE)

TERM TO MATURITY	1 YEAR		10 YEARS		20 YEARS		30 YEARS	
Discount rate (YTM)	7%	10%	7%	10%	7%	10%	7%	10%
Present value of interest	$ 75	$ 73	$ 569	$498	$ 858	$686	$1,005	$757
Present value of principal	934	907	505	377	257	142	132	54
Total value of bond	$1,009	$980	$1,074	$875	$1,115	$828	$1,137	$811
Percentage change in total value	−2.9		−18.5		−25.7		−28.7	

market interest rate.[21] Malkiel's mathematical proofs showed the following relationships between yield (interest rate) changes and bond price behavior:

1. Bond prices move inversely to bond yields (interest rates).
2. For a given change in yields (interest rates), longer-maturity bonds post larger price changes; thus, bond price volatility is *directly* related to term to maturity.
3. Bond price volatility (percentage of price change) increases at a diminishing rate as term to maturity increases.
4. Bond price movements resulting from equal absolute increases or decreases in yield are *not* symmetrical. A decrease in yield raises bond prices by more than an increase in yield of the same amount lowers prices.
5. Higher coupon issues show smaller percentage price fluctuation for a given change in yield; thus, bond price volatility is *inversely* related to coupon.

Homer and Leibowitz showed that the absolute level of market yields also affects bond price volatility.[22] As the level of prevailing yields rises, the price volatility of bonds increases, *assuming a constant percentage change in market yields*. It is important to note that if you assume a constant percentage change in yield, the basis-point change will be greater when rates are high. For example, a 25 percent change in interest rates when rates are at 4 percent will be 100 basis points; the same 25 percent change when rates are at 8 percent will be a 200 basis-point change. In the discussion of bond duration, we will see that this difference in basis point change is important.

Exhibit 19.12, Exhibit 19.13, and Exhibit 19.14 demonstrate these relationships assuming semiannual compounding. Exhibit 19.12 demonstrates the effect of maturity on price volatility. In all four maturity classes, we assume a bond with an 8 percent coupon and assume that the discount rate (YTM) changes from 7 percent to 10 percent. The only difference among the four cases is the maturities of the bonds. The demonstration involves computing the value of each bond at a 7 percent yield and at a 10 percent yield and noting the percentage change in price. As shown, this change in yield caused the price of the one-year bond to decline by only 2.9 percent; the 30-year bond declined by almost 29 percent. Clearly, the longer-maturity bond experienced the greater price volatility.

Also, price volatility increased at a decreasing rate with maturity. When maturity doubled from 10 years to 20 years, the percent change in price increased by less than 50 percent (from

[21]Burton G. Malkiel, "Expectations, Bond Prices, and the Term Structure of Interest Rates," *Quarterly Journal of Economics* 76, no. 2 (May 1962): 197–218.

[22]Sidney Homer and Martin L. Leibowitz, *Inside the Yield Book* (Englewood Cliffs, N.J.: Prentice-Hall, 1972).

EXHIBIT 19.13   *EFFECT OF COUPON ON BOND PRICE VOLATILITY*

PRESENT VALUE OF 20-YEAR BOND ($1,000 PAR VALUE)

	0 PERCENT COUPON		3 PERCENT COUPON		8 PERCENT COUPON		12 PERCENT COUPON	
Discount rate (YTM)	7%	10%	7%	10%	7%	10%	7%	10%
Present value of interest	$ 0	$ 0	$322	$257	$ 858	$686	$1,287	$1030
Present value of principal	257	142	257	142	257	142	257	142
Total value of bond	$257	$142	$579	$399	$1,115	$828	$1,544	$1,172
Percentage change in total value	−44.7		−31.1		−25.7		−24.1	

EXHIBIT 19.14   *EFFECT OF YIELD LEVEL ON BOND PRICE VOLATILITY*

PRESENT VALUE OF 20-YEAR, 4 PERCENT BOND ($1,000 PAR VALUE)

	(1)		(2)		(3)		(4)	
			INTERMEDIATE				100 BASIS-POINT CHANGE AT	
	LOW YIELDS		YIELDS		HIGH YIELDS		HIGH YIELDS	
Discount rate (YTM)	3%	4%	6%	8%	9%	12%	9%	10%
Present value of interest	$ 602	$ 547	$ 462	$396	$370	$301	$370	$343
Present value of principal	562	453	307	208	175	97	175	142
Total value of bond	$1,164	$1,000	$ 769	$604	$545	$398	$545	$485
Percentage change in total value	−14.1		−21.5		−27.0		−11.0	

18.5 percent to 25.7 percent). A similar change occurred when going from 20 years to 30 years. Therefore, Exhibit 19.12 demonstrates the first three of our price-yield relationships: (1) bond price is inversely related to yields, (2) bond price volatility is positively related to term to maturity, and (3) bond price volatility increases at a decreasing rate with maturity.

It also is possible to demonstrate the fourth relationship with this exhibit. Using the 20-year bond for demonstration purposes, if you computed the percentage change in price related to an *increase* in rates (e.g., from 7 percent to 10 percent), you would get the answer reported—a 25.7 percent decrease. In contrast, if you computed the effect on price of a *decrease* in yields from 10 percent to 7 percent, you would get a 34.7 percent increase in price (from $828 to $1,115). This demonstrates that prices change more in response to a decrease in rates (from 10 percent to 7 percent) than to a comparable increase in rates (from 7 percent to 10 percent).

Exhibit 19.13 demonstrates the coupon effect. In this set of examples, all the bonds have equal maturity (20 years) and experience the same change in YTM (from 7 percent to 10 percent). The exhibit shows the *inverse* relationship between coupon rate and price volatility: The smallest coupon bond (the zero) experienced the largest percentage price change (almost 45 percent) versus a 24 percent change for the 12 percent coupon bond.

Exhibit 19.14 demonstrates the yield level effect. In these examples, all the bonds have the same 20-year maturity and the same 4 percent coupon. In the first three cases, the YTM changed by a constant 33.3 percent (i.e., from 3 percent to 4 percent, from 6 percent to 8 percent, and from 9 percent to 12 percent). Note that the first change is 100 basis points, the second is 200 basis points, and the third is 300 basis points. The results in the first three columns confirm the statement that when rates change by a *constant percentage,* the change in the bond price is larger when the rates are at a higher level.

The fourth column shows that if you assume a *constant basis-point change in yields,* you get the opposite results. Specifically, a 100 basis-point change in yields from 3 percent to 4 percent provides a price change of 14.1 percent, while the same 100 basis-point change from 9 percent to 10 percent results in a price change of only 11 percent. Therefore, the yield level effect can differ, depending on whether the yield change is specified as a constant percentage change or a constant basis-point change.

Thus, the price volatility of a bond for a given change in yield (i.e., its interest rate sensitivity) is affected by the bond's coupon, its term to maturity, the level of yields (depending on what kind of change in yield), and the direction of the yield change. However, although both the level and direction of change in yields affect price volatility, they cannot be used for trading strategies. When yields change, the two variables that have a dramatic effect on a bond's interest rate sensitivity are coupon and maturity.

Trading Strategies Knowing that coupon and maturity are the major variables that influence a bond's interest rate sensitivity, we can develop some strategies for maximizing rates of return when interest rates change. Specifically, if you expect a major *decline* in interest rates, you know that bond prices will increase, so you want a portfolio of bonds with the *maximum interest rate sensitivity* so that you will enjoy maximum price changes (capital gains) from the change in interest rates. In this situation, the previous discussion regarding the effect of maturity and coupon indicates that you should attempt to build a portfolio of long-maturity bonds with low coupons (ideally a long-term zero coupon bond). A portfolio of such bonds should experience the maximum price appreciation for a given decline in market interest rates.

In contrast, if you expect an *increase* in market interest rates, you know that bond prices will decline, and you want a portfolio with *minimum interest rate sensitivity* to minimize the capital losses caused by the increase in rates. Therefore, you would want to change your portfolio to short-maturity bonds with high coupons. This combination should provide minimal price volatility for a change in market interest rates.

Duration Measures Because the price volatility (interest rate sensitivity) of a bond varies inversely with its coupon and directly with its term to maturity, it is necessary to determine the best combination of these two variables to achieve your objective. This effort would benefit from a composite measure that considered both coupon and maturity.

A composite measure of the interest rate sensitivity of a bond is referred to as **duration**. This concept and its development as a tool in bond analysis and portfolio management have existed for over 60 years. Notably, several specifications of duration have been derived over the past 20 years. First, **Macaulay duration**, developed over 60 years ago by Frederick Macaulay, is a measure of the time flow of cash from a bond.[23] A modified version of Macaulay duration can be used under certain conditions to indicate the price volatility of a bond in response to interest rate changes. Second, **modified duration** is derived by making a small adjustment (modification) to the Macaulay duration value. As already noted, under certain restrictive conditions (most important, there are no embedded options), modified duration can provide an approximation to the interest rate sensitivity of a bond (or any financial asset). Third, **effective duration** is a direct measure of the interest rate sensitivity of a bond (or any financial instrument) in cases where it is possible to estimate price changes for an asset using a valuation model. Finally,

---

[23]Frederick R. Macaulay, *Some Theoretical Problems Suggested by the Movements of Interest Rates, Bond Yields, and Stock Prices in the United States since 1856* (New York: National Bureau of Economic Research, 1938).

empirical duration measures directly the percentage price change of an asset for an actual change in interest rates. This measure can be used as an estimate for an asset when there is no exact valuation model available. Because of the development of many new financial instruments, which have very unique cash flows *that change with interest rates,* effective duration and empirical duration have become widely used because of their flexibility and ability to provide a useful measure of interest rate sensitivity—the primary goal of duration. Therefore, in this section, we discuss and demonstrate these four duration measures, including their limitations.

Macaulay Duration   Macaulay showed that the duration of a bond was a more appropriate measure of time characteristics than the term to maturity of the bond because duration considers both the repayment of capital at maturity and the size and timing of coupon payments prior to final maturity. Using annual compounding, duration *(D)* is

►19.13

$$D = \frac{\sum_{t=1}^{n} \frac{C_t(t)}{(1+i)^t}}{\sum_{t=1}^{n} \frac{C_t}{(1+i)^t}}$$

where:

t = **the time period in which the coupon or principal payment occurs**
C_t = **the interest or principal payment that occurs in period** t
i = **the yield to maturity on the bond**

The denominator in this equation is the price of a bond as determined by the present value model. The numerator is the present value of all cash flows *weighted according to the time to cash receipt.* The following example, which demonstrates the specific computations for two bonds, shows the procedure and highlights some of the properties of Macaulay duration. Consider the following two sample bonds:

	BOND A	BOND B
Face value	$1,000	$1,000
Maturity	10 years	10 years
Coupon	4%	8%

Assuming annual interest payments and an 8 percent yield to maturity on the bonds, duration is computed as shown in Exhibit 19.15.[24] If duration is computed by discounting flows using the yield to maturity of the bond, it is called *Macaulay duration.*

Characteristics of Macaulay Duration   This example illustrates several characteristics of Macaulay duration. First, the Macaulay duration of a bond with coupon payments always will be less than its term to maturity because duration gives weight to these interim interest payments.

Second, there is *an inverse relationship between coupon and duration.* A bond with a larger coupon will have a shorter duration because more of the total cash flows come earlier in the form

---

[24]We assume annual interest payments to reduce the space requirements and computations. In practice you would assume semiannual payments that would cause a slightly shorter duration since you receive half the payments earlier.

EXHIBIT 19.15 ▶ *COMPUTATION OF MACAULAY DURATION (ASSUMING 8 PERCENT MARKET YIELD)*

BOND A

(1) YEAR	(2) CASH FLOW	(3) PV AT 8%	(4) PV OF FLOW	(5) PV AS % OF PRICE	(6) (1) × (5)
1	$ 40	0.9259	$ 37.04	0.0506	0.0506
2	40	0.8573	34.29	0.0469	0.0938
3	40	0.7938	31.75	0.0434	0.1302
4	40	0.7350	29.40	0.0402	0.1608
5	40	0.6806	27.22	0.0372	0.1860
6	40	0.6302	25.21	0.0345	0.2070
7	40	0.5835	23.34	0.0319	0.2233
8	40	0.5403	21.61	0.0295	0.2360
9	40	0.5002	20.01	0.0274	0.2466
10	1,040	0.4632	481.73	0.6585	6.5850
Sum			$ 731.58	1.0000	8.1193

Duration = 8.12 Years

BOND B

1	$ 80	0.9259	$ 74.07	0.0741	0.0741
2	80	0.8573	68.59	0.0686	0.1372
3	80	0.7938	63.50	0.0635	0.1906
4	80	0.7350	58.80	0.0588	0.1906
5	80	0.6806	54.44	0.0544	0.2720
6	80	0.6302	50.42	0.0504	0.3024
7	80	0.5835	46.68	0.0467	0.3269
8	80	0.5403	43.22	0.0432	0.3456
9	80	0.5002	40.02	0.0400	0.3600
10	1,080	0.4632	500.26	0.5003	5.0030
Sum			$1,000.00	1.0000	7.2470

Duration = 7.25 Years

of interest payments. As shown in Exhibit 19.15, the 8 percent coupon bond has a shorter duration than the 4 percent coupon bond.

A zero coupon bond or a pure discount bond, such as a Treasury bill, will have *duration equal to its term to maturity*. In Exhibit 19.15, if you assume a single payment at maturity, duration will equal term to maturity because the only cash flow comes in the final (maturity) year—that is, you receive 100 percent of cash flows in year *n*.

Third, there is *generally a positive relationship between term to maturity and Macaulay duration*, but duration increases at a decreasing rate with maturity. Therefore, a bond with longer term to maturity almost always will have a higher duration. The relationship is not direct because as maturity increases the present value of the principal declines in value.

As shown in Exhibit 19.16, the shape of the duration-maturity curve depends on the coupon and the yield to maturity. The curve for a zero coupon bond is a straight line, indicating that duration equals term to maturity. In contrast, the curve for a low-coupon bond selling at a deep

EXHIBIT 19.16   *DURATION VERSUS MATURITY*

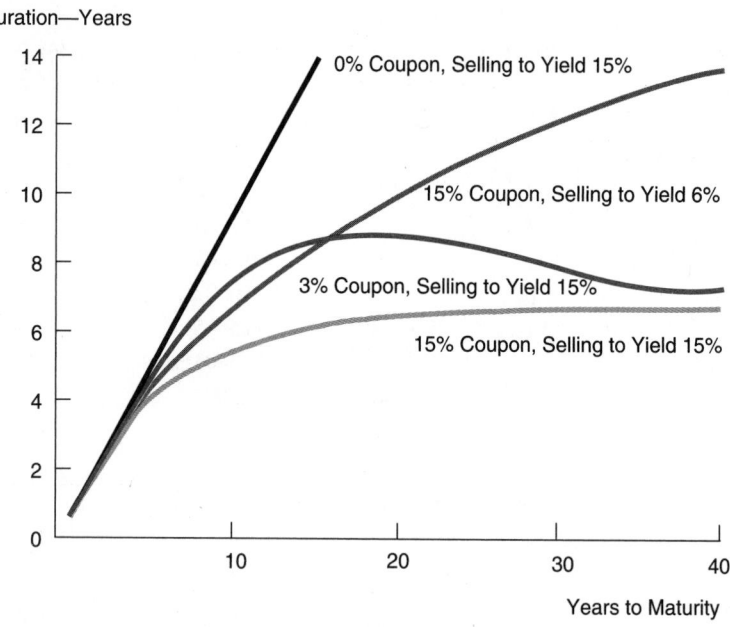

discount (due to a high YTM) will turn down at long maturities, which means that under these conditions, the longer-maturity bond will have lower duration because the discounted value of the principal payment becomes insignificant, which shifts the weight to the early interest payments, causing a decline in Macaulay duration.

Fourth, all else the same, there is an *inverse relationship between YTM and duration.* A higher yield to maturity of a bond reduces its duration. As an example, in Exhibit 19.15, if the yield to maturity had been 12 percent rather than 8 percent, the duration for the 4 percent bond would have gone from 8.12 to 7.75, and the duration of the 8 percent bond would have gone from 7.25 to 6.80.[25] The combined effect of the inverse relationships between duration and both coupon and yield can be seen with the curve for the 15 percent coupon and yield bond where the duration tops out at about six years. The real-world example of such a bond would be a high-yield bond.

Finally, sinking funds and call provisions can have a dramatic effect on a bond's duration. They can change the total cash flows for a bond and, therefore, significantly change its duration. Between these two factors, the characteristic that causes the greatest uncertainty is the call feature—it is difficult to estimate when the call option will be exercised since it is a function of changes in interest rates. We consider this further when we discuss the effect of embedded options on the duration and convexity of a bond.

A summary of Macaulay duration characteristics is as follows:

➤ The duration of a zero coupon bond will *equal* its term to maturity.
➤ The duration of a coupon bond always will be less than its term to maturity.
➤ There is an *inverse* relationship between coupon and duration.

---

[25]These properties are discussed and demonstrated in Frank K. Reilly and Rupinder Sidhu, "The Many Uses of Bond Duration," *Financial Analysts Journal* 36, no. 4 (July–August 1980): 58–72; and Frank J. Fabozzi, Gerald W. Buetow, and Robert R. Johnson, "Measuring Interest Rate Risk," in *The Handbook of Fixed-Income Securities,* 6th ed.

➤ There is generally a *positive* relationship between term to maturity and duration. Note that the duration of a coupon bond increases at a decreasing rate with maturity and the shape of the duration/maturity curve will depend on the coupon and YTM of the bond. Also, the duration of a deep discount bond will decline at very long maturities (over 20 years).

➤ There is an *inverse* relationship between yield to maturity and duration.

➤ Sinking funds and call provisions can cause a dramatic change in the duration of a bond. The effect of embedded options is discussed in a subsequent section.

Modified Duration and Bond Price Volatility

An adjusted measure of duration called *modified duration* can be used to approximate the interest rate sensitivity of an option-free (straight) bond. Modified duration equals Macaulay duration (computed in Exhibit 19.15) divided by 1 plus the current yield to maturity divided by the number of payments in a year. As an example, a bond with a Macaulay duration of 10 years, a yield to maturity (*i*) of 8 percent, and semiannual payments would have a modified duration of

$$D_{mod} = 10/\left(1 + \frac{0.08}{2}\right)$$
$$= 10/(1.04) = 9.62$$

It has been shown, both theoretically and empirically, that price movements of option-free bonds *will vary proportionally* with modified duration for *small changes in yields*.[26] Specifically, as shown in the following equation, an estimate of the percentage change in bond price equals the change in yield times modified duration:

➤19.14

$$\frac{\Delta P}{P} \times 100 = -D_{mod} \times \Delta i$$

where:

ΔP = the change in price for the bond
P = the beginning price for the bond
$-D_{mod}$ = the modified duration of the bond
Δi = the yield change in basis points divided by 100. For example, if interest rates go from 8.00 to 8.50 percent, $\Delta i = 50/100 = 0.50$.

Consider a bond with Macaulay $D = 8$ years and $i = 0.10$. Assume that you expect the bond's YTM to decline by 75 basis points (e.g., from 10 percent to 9.25 percent). The first step is to compute the bond's modified duration as follows:

$$D_{mod} = 8/\left(1 + \frac{0.10}{2}\right)$$
$$= 8/(1.05) = 7.62$$

---

[26]A generalized proof of this is contained in Michael H. Hopewell and George Kaufman, "Bond Price Volatility and Term to Maturity: A Generalized Respecification," *American Economic Review* 63, no. 4 (September 1973): 749–753. The importance of the specification "for small changes in yields" will become clear when we discuss convexity in the next section. Because modified duration is an approximate measure of interest rate sensitivity, the "years" label is not appropriate.

EXHIBIT 19.17 ▸   *BOND DURATION IN YEARS FOR BOND YIELDING 6 PERCENT UNDER DIFFERENT TERMS*

	COUPON RATES			
YEARS TO MATURITY	0.02	0.04	0.06	0.08
1	0.995	0.990	0.985	0.981
2	4.756	4.558	4.393	4.254
10	8.891	8.169	7.662	7.286
20	14.981	12.980	11.904	11.232
50	19.452	17.129	16.273	15.829
100	17.567	17.232	17.120	17.064
∞	17.167	17.167	17.167	17.167

Source: L. Fisher and R. L. Weil, "Coping with the Risk of Interest Rate Fluctuations: Returns to Bondholders from Naive and Final Strategies," *Journal of Business* 44, no. 4 (October 1971): University of Chicago Press. Reprinted by permission of The University of Chicago Press.

The estimated percentage change in the price of the bond using Equation 19.14 is:

$$\% \Delta P = -(7.62) \times \frac{-75}{100}$$
$$= (-7.62) \times (-0.75)$$
$$= 5.72$$

This indicates that the bond price should increase by approximately 5.72 percent in response to the 75 basis-point decline in YTM. If the price of the bond before the decline in interest rates was $900, the price after the decline in interest rates should be approximately $900 \times 1.0572 = \$951.48$.

The modified duration is always a negative value for a noncallable bond because of the inverse relationship between yield changes and bond price changes. Also, remember that this formulation provides an *estimate* or *approximation* of the percent change in the price of the bond. The following section on convexity shows that this formula that uses only modified duration provides an exact estimate of the percentage price change only for very small changes in yields of option-free securities.

Trading Strategies Using Modified Duration   We know that the longest duration security provides the maximum price variation. Exhibit 19.17 demonstrates that numerous ways exist to achieve a given level of duration. The following discussion indicates that an active bond investor who wants to adjust his/her portfolio for anticipated interest rate changes can use this measure of interest rate sensitivity to structure a portfolio to take advantage of changes in market yields.

If you expect a *decline* in interest rates, you should *increase* the average modified duration of your bond portfolio to experience maximum price volatility. If you expect an *increase* in interest rates, you should *reduce* the average modified duration of your portfolio to minimize your price decline. Note that the modified duration of your portfolio is the market-value-weighted average of the modified durations of the individual bonds in the portfolio.

Bond Convexity   Modified duration allows us to estimate bond price changes for a change in interest rates. However, the equation we used to make this calculation (Equation 19.14) is accurate only for *very small changes* in market yields. We will see that the accuracy of the estimate of the price change

| EXHIBIT 19.18 | PRICE-YIELD RELATIONSHIPS FOR ALTERNATIVE BONDS |

A. 12 PERCENT, 20 YEAR		B. 12 PERCENT, 3 YEAR		C. ZERO COUPON, 30 YEAR	
YIELD	PRICE	YIELD	PRICE	YIELD	PRICE
1.0%	$2,989.47	1.0%	$1,324.30	1.0%	$741.37
2.0	2,641.73	2.0	1,289.77	2.0	550.45
3.0	2,346.21	3.0	1,256.37	3.0	409.30
4.0	2,094.22	4.0	1,224.06	4.0	304.78
5.0	1,878.60	5.0	1,192.78	5.0	227.28
6.0	1,693.44	6.0	1,162.52	6.0	169.73
7.0	1,533.88	7.0	1,133.21	7.0	126.93
8.0	1,395.86	8.0	1,104.84	8.0	95.06
9.0	1,276.02	9.0	1,077.37	9.0	71.29
10.0	1,171.59	10.0	1,050.76	10.0	53.54
11.0	1,080.23	11.0	1,024.98	11.0	40.26
12.0	1,000.00	12.0	1,000.00	12.0	30.31

deteriorates with larger changes in yields because the modified duration calculation is a *linear* approximation of a bond price change that follows a *curvilinear* (convex) function. To understand the effect of this **convexity**, we must consider the price-yield relationship for alternative bonds.[27]

The Price-Yield Relationship for Bonds

Because the price of a bond is the present value of its cash flows at a particular discount rate, if you are given the coupon, maturity, and a yield for a bond, you can calculate its price at a point in time. The price-yield curve provides a set of prices for a specific maturity/coupon bond at a point in time using a range of yields to maturity (discount rates). As an example, Exhibit 19.18 lists the computed prices for a 12 percent, 20-year bond assuming yields from 1 percent to 12 percent. The exhibit shows that if you discount the flows from this bond at a yield of 1 percent, you would get a price of $2,989.47; discounting these same flows at 10 percent gives a price of $1,171.59. The graph of these prices relative to the yields that produced them (Exhibit 19.19) indicates that the price-yield relationship for this bond is not a straight line but a curvilinear relationship. That is, it is convex.

Two points are important about the price-yield relationship:

1. This relationship can be applied to a single bond, a portfolio of bonds, or any stream of future cash flows.
2. The convex price-yield relationship will differ among bonds or other cash flow streams, depending on the nature of the cash flow stream, that is, its coupon and maturity. For example, the price-yield relationship for a high-coupon, short-term security will be almost a straight line because the price does not change as much for a change in yields (e.g., the 12 percent, three-year bond in Exhibit 19.18). In contrast, the price-yield relationship for a low-coupon, long-term bond will curve radically (i.e., be very convex), as shown by the

---

[27]For a further discussion of this topic, see Mark L. Dunetz and James M. Mahoney, "Using Duration and Convexity in the Analysis of Callable Bonds," *Financial Analysts Journal* 44, no. 3 (May–June 1988): 53–73; and Fabozzi, Buetow, and Johnson," Measuring Interest Rate Risk," in *The Handbook of Fixed-Income Securities,* 6th ed.

EXHIBIT 19.19 PRICE-YIELD RELATIONSHIP AND MODIFIED DURATION AT 4 PERCENT YIELD

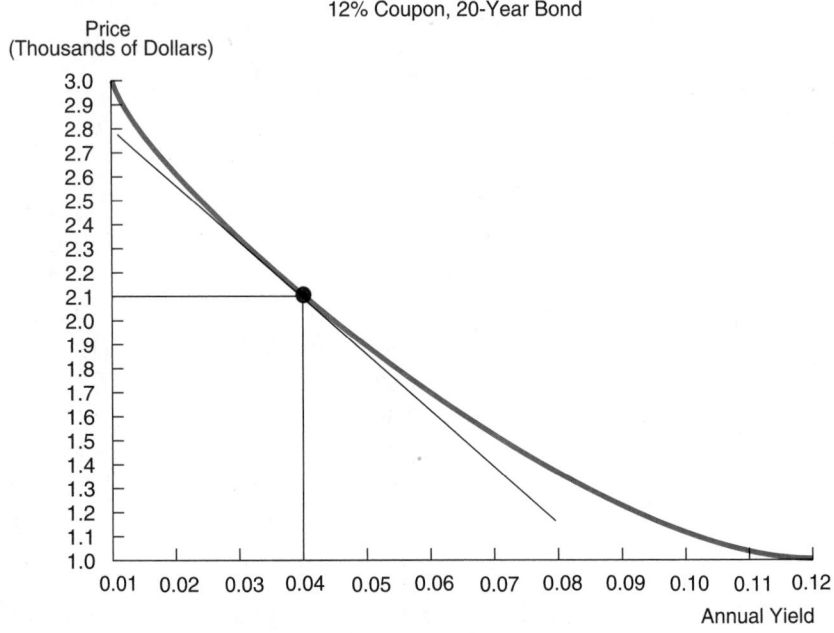

zero coupon, 30-year bond in Exhibit 19.18. These differences in convexity are shown graphically in Exhibit 19.20. The curved nature of the price-yield relationship is referred to as the bond's *convexity*.

The Desirability of Convexity   As shown by the graph in Exhibit 19.20, because of the convexity of the price-yield relationship, as yield increases, the rate at which the price of the bond declines becomes slower. Similarly, when yields decline, the rate at which the price of the bond increases becomes faster. Therefore, convexity is considered a desirable trait. Specifically, if you have two bonds with equal duration but one has greater convexity, you would want the bond with greater convexity because it would have better price performance whether yields rise (the bond price declines less) or yields fall (the bond price increases more).

Given this price-yield curve, modified duration is the percentage change in price for a nominal change in yield as follows:[28]

➤**19.15**
$$D_{mod} = \frac{\dfrac{dP}{di}}{P}$$

Notice that the *dP/di* line is tangent to the price-yield curve *at a given yield* as shown in Exhibit 19.21. For *small* changes in yields (i.e., from y^* to either y_1 or y_2), this tangent straight line gives a good estimate of the actual price changes. In contrast, for larger changes in yields (i.e., from y^* to either y_3 or y_4), the straight line will estimate the new price of the bond at less

---

[28]In mathematical terms, modified duration is the first differential of this price-yield relationship with respect to yield.

EXHIBIT 19.20   *PRICE-YIELD CURVES FOR ALTERNATIVE BONDS*

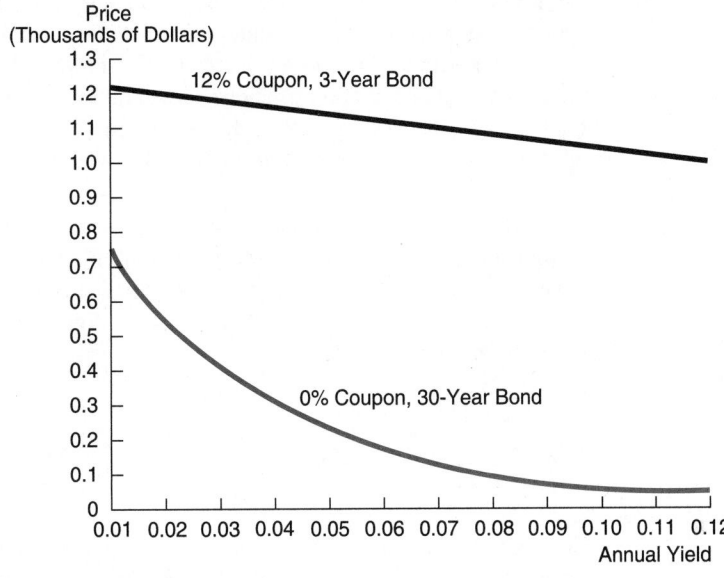

EXHIBIT 19.21   *PRICE APPROXIMATION USING MODIFIED DURATION*

Source: Frank J. Fabozzi, Gerald Buetow, and Robert R. Johnson, "Measuring Interest Rate Risk" in the *Handbook of Fixed-Income Securities,* 6th ed. (New York: McGraw-Hill, 2001). Reproduced with permission from The McGraw-Hill Companies.

than the actual price shown by the price-yield curve. This misestimate arises because the modified-duration line is a linear estimate of a curvilinear relationship. Specifically, the estimate using only modified duration will *underestimate* the actual price *increase* caused by a yield decline and *overestimate* the actual price *decline* caused by an increase in yields. This graph, which demonstrates the convexity effect, also shows that price changes are *not* symmetric when yields increase or decrease. As shown, when rates decline, there is a larger price error than when rates increase because, due to convexity, when yields decline prices rise at an *increasing* rate, while prices decline at a *decreasing* rate when yields rise.

Determinants of Convexity Convexity is a measure of the curvature of the price-yield relationship. In turn, because modified duration is the slope of the curve at a given yield, convexity indicates changes in duration. Mathematically, convexity is the second derivative of price with respect to yield (d^2P/di^2) divided by price. Specifically, convexity is the percentage change in dP/di for a given change in yield:

➤19.16
$$\text{Convexity} = \frac{\dfrac{d^2P}{di^2}}{P}$$

Convexity is a measure of how much a bond's price-yield curve deviates from the linear approximation of that curve. As indicated by Exhibit 19.19 and Exhibit 19.21 for *noncallable* bonds, convexity always is a positive number, implying that the price-yield curve lies above the modified-duration (tangent) line. Exhibit 19.20 illustrates the price-yield relationship for two bonds with very different coupons and maturities. (The yields and prices are contained in Exhibit 19.18)

These graphs demonstrate the following relationship between these factors and the convexity of a bond:

➤ There is an *inverse* relationship between coupon and convexity (yield and maturity constant)—that is, lower coupon, higher convexity.
➤ There is a *direct* relationship between maturity and convexity (yield and coupon constant)—that is, longer maturity, higher convexity.
➤ There is an *inverse* relationship between yield and convexity (coupon and maturity constant). This means that the price–yield curve is more convex at its lower-yield (upper left) segment.

Therefore, a short-term, high-coupon bond, such as the 12 percent coupon, three-year bond in Exhibit 19.20, has very low convexity—it is almost a straight line. In contrast, the zero-coupon, 30-year bond has high convexity.

Notably, the determinants of duration and convexity for option-free bonds are very similar. Specifically, the three factors are the same—maturity, coupon, and yield—and the direction of impact is the same—that is, maturity is direct and both coupon and yield are inverse. Therefore, high-duration bonds have high convexity.

The Modified-Duration–Convexity Effects In summary, the change in a bond's price resulting from a change in yield can be attributed to two sources: the bond's modified duration and its convexity. The relative effect of these two factors on the price change will depend on the characteristics of the bond (i.e., its convexity) and the size of the yield change. For example, if you are estimating the price change for a 300 basis-point change in yield for a zero coupon, 30-year bond, the convexity effect would be fairly large because this bond would have high convexity, and a 300 basis-point change in yield is relatively large. In contrast, if you are dealing with only a 10 basis-point change in yields, the convexity effect would be minimal because it is a small change in yield. Similarly, the convexity effect would likewise be small even if you assume a larger yield change if you are dealing with a bond with small convexity (i.e., a high-coupon, short-maturity bond) because the price-yield curve for such a bond is almost a straight line.

In conclusion, modified duration can help you derive an *approximate* percentage bond price change for a given change in interest rates, but you must remember that it is only a good estimate when you are considering small yield changes. The point is, you must also consider the convexity effect on price change when you are dealing with large yield changes and/or when the securities or cash flows have high convexity.

Computation of Convexity   Again, the formula for computing the convexity of a stream of cash flows looks fairly complex, but it can be broken down into manageable steps. You will recall from our convexity equation (19.16) that

$$\text{Convexity} = \frac{\dfrac{d^2 P}{di^2}}{P}$$

In turn,

➤19.17

$$\frac{d^2 P}{di^2} = \frac{1}{(1+i)^2} \left[\sum_{t=1}^{n} \frac{CF_t}{(1+i)} (t^2 + t) \right]$$

Exhibit 19.22 contains the computations related to this calculation for a three-year bond with a 12 percent coupon and 9 percent YTM assuming annual flows.

The convexity for this bond is very low because it has a short maturity, high coupon, and high yield. Note that the *convexity of a security will vary along the price-yield curve.* You will get a

EXHIBIT 19.22   *COMPUTATION OF CONVEXITY*

$$\text{Convexity} = \frac{d^2 P/di^2}{PV \text{ of Cash Flows}} = \frac{d^2 P/di^2}{\text{Price}}$$

$$\frac{d^2 P}{di^2} = \frac{1}{(1+i)^2} \left[\sum_{t=1}^{n} (t^2 + t) \frac{CF_t}{(1+i)^t} \right]$$

$$\text{Convexity} = \frac{d^2 P/di^2}{\text{Price}}$$

Example: 3-Year Bond, 12% Coupon, 9% YTM

(1) YEAR	(2) CF_t	(3) PV @ 9%	(4) PV CF	(5) $t^2 + t$	(4) × (5)
1	120	0.9174	$ 110.09	2	$ 220.18
2	120	0.8417	101.00	6	606.00
3	120	0.7722	92.66	12	1,111.92
3	1,000	0.7722	772.20	12	9,266.40
			Price = $1,075.95		$11,204.50

$$\frac{1}{(1+i)^2} = \frac{1}{(1.09)^2} = \frac{1}{1.19} = 0.84$$

$$\$11,204.50 \times 0.84 = \$9,411.78$$

$$\text{Convexity} = \frac{9,411.78}{1,075.95} = 8.75$$

different convexity at a 3 percent yield that at a 12 percent yield. In terms of the computation, the maturity and coupon will be the same, but you will use a different discount rate that reflects where you are on the curve. This is similar to the earlier observation that *you will get a different modified duration at different points on the price-yield curve* because the slope varies along the curve. You also can see this mathematically because, depending on where you are on the curve, you will be using a different market yield, and the Macaulay and modified durations are inverse to the discount rate.[29]

To compute the price change attributable to the convexity effect after you know the bond's convexity, use this equation:

➤ **19.18**   Price Change Due to Convexity $= \frac{1}{2} \times$ Price $\times$ Convexity $\times (\Delta$ in Yield$)^2$

Exhibit 19.23 shows the change in bond price considering the duration effect and the convexity effect for an 18-year bond with a 12 percent coupon and 9 percent YTM. For demonstration purposes, we assumed a decline of 100 and 300 basis points (BP) in rates (i.e., 9 percent to 8 percent and 9 percent to 6 percent).

With the 300 BP change, if you considered only the modified-duration effect, you would have *estimated* that the bond went from 126.50 to 158.30 (a 25.14 percent increase), when, in fact, the actual price is closer to 164.41, which is about a *30 percent increase.*

Duration and Convexity for Callable Bonds

The discussion and presentation thus far regarding Macaulay and modified durations and convexity have been concerned with option-free bonds. A callable bond is different because it provides the issuer with an option to call the bond under certain conditions and pay it off with funds from a new issue sold at a lower yield. Observers refer to this as a bond with an *embedded option.* We noted earlier that the duration of a bond can be seriously affected by an embedded call option if interest rates decline substantially below a bond's coupon rate. In such a case, the issuer will likely call the bond, which will dramatically change the maturity and the duration of the bond. For example, assume a firm issues a 30-year bond with a 9 percent coupon with a deferred call provision whereby the bond can be called in six years at 109 percent of par. If the bond is issued at par, its original *duration to maturity* will be about 11 years. A year later, if rates decline to about 7 percent, its duration to maturity will still be over *10 years* because duration is inversely related to yield and yields have declined. Notably, at a yield of 7 percent, this bond will probably trade at *yield to call* because at a 7 percent yield the firm will likely exercise its option and call the bond in five years. Notably, the bond's *duration to first call* would be about *four years.* Clearly, there is a significant difference between duration to maturity (over 10 years) and duration to first call (about 4 years).

To understand the impact of the call feature on the duration and convexity of a bond, it is important to consider what determines the price of a callable bond. A callable bond is a combination of a noncallable bond plus a *call option* that was *sold to the issuer,* which allows the issuer to call the bond under the conditions discussed earlier. Because the call option is owned by the issuer, it has negative value for the investor in the bond. Thus the bondholder's position is

➤ **19.19** Long a Callable Bond = Long a Noncallable Bond + A Short Position in a Call Option

Therefore, the value (price) of a callable bond is equal to

➤ **19.20**   Callable Bond Price = Noncallable Bond Price – Call Option Price

---

[29]Exhibit 19A.1 in the appendix to this chapter is a table that combines the computation of Macaulay and modified duration and convexity using semiannual cash flows.

EXHIBIT 19.23 | *ANALYSIS OF BOND PRICE CHANGE CONSIDERING DURATION AND CONVEXITY*

Example: 18-Year Bond, 12% Coupon, 9% YTM
Price: 126.50
Modified Duration:8.38 ($D*$)
Convexity: 107.70
Estimate of Price Change Using duration:
  Percent Δ Price = $D*$ (Δ in YLD/100)
Estimate of Price change from Convexity:
  Price Change = $\frac{1}{2} \times$ Price $\times$ Convexity $\times$ (Δ in YLD)^2

A. Change in Yield: −100 BP

  Duration Change: $-8.38 \times \left(\dfrac{-100}{100} \right) = +8.38\%$

                                    $+8.38\% \times 126.50 = +10.60$

  Convexity Change: $\dfrac{1}{2} \times (126.50) \times 107.70 \times (0.01)^2$

                                    $= 63.25 \times 107.70 \times 0.0001$

                                    $= 6,812.03 \times 0.0001 = 0.68$

  Combined Effect: 126.50
                                    + 10.60 (Duration)
                                    137.10
                                    + 0.68 (Convexity)
                                    137.78

B. Change in Yield: −300 BP

  Duration Change: $-8.38 \times \left(\dfrac{-300}{100} \right) = +25.14\%$

                                    $126.50 \times 1.2514 = 158.30(+31.80)$

  Convexity Effect: $\dfrac{1}{2} \times (126.50) \times 107.70 \times (0.03)^2$

                                    $6,812.03 \times 0.0009 = 6.11$

  Combined Effect: 126.50
                                    + 31.80 (Duration)
                                    158.30
                                    + 6.11 (Convexity)
                                    164.41

Given this valuation, anything that increases the value of the call option will reduce the value of the callable bond.[30] The point is, when interest rates decline, the right-hand side of this equation experiences a conflict between the value of the noncallable bond that increases in value, and the negative effect of the call option that also increases. Notably, if the value of the call option increases faster than the value of the noncallable bond, the overall value of the callable bond will *decline* when interest rates decline and this is referred to as *negative duration*—that is, in

[30]For a further discussion of the effect of these embedded options, see Frank J. Fabozzi, Gerald W. Buetow, and Robert R. Johnson," Measuring Interest Rate Risk"; and Frank J. Fabozzi, Andrew J. Kalotay, and George O. Williams, "Valuation of Bonds with Embedded Options." Both are in *The Handbook of Fixed-Income Securities,* 6th ed. Also see Kurt Winkelmann, "Uses and Abuses of Duration and Convexity," *Financial Analysts Journal* 45, no. 5 (September–October 1989): 72–75.

contrast to the usual inverse relationship between yield changes and bond price changes, in this case yield changes and price changes both decline.

Option-Adjusted Duration[31]

Given these two extreme values of (1) duration to maturity and (2) duration to first call, the investment community derives a duration estimate that is referred to as an option-adjusted or call-adjusted duration based on *the probability that the issuing firm will exercise its call option* for the bond when the bond becomes freely callable. This option-adjusted duration will be somewhere between these two extreme values. Specifically, when interest rates are substantially above the coupon rate, the probability of the bond being called is very small (i.e., the call option has very little value) and the option-adjusted duration will approach the duration to maturity. In contrast, if interest rates decline to levels substantially below the coupon rate, the probability of the bond being called at the first opportunity is very high (i.e., the call option is very valuable and will probably be exercised) and the option-adjusted duration will approach the duration to first call. In summary, the bond's option-adjusted duration will be somewhere between these two extremes with the exact option-adjusted duration depending on the level of interest rates relative to the bond's coupon rate.

The option-adjusted duration can also be envisioned or computed based on the duration of the two components, as follows:

➤19.21   Option-Adjusted Duration = Duration of the Noncallable Bond – Duration of the Call Option

If one conceives of duration as interest rate sensitivity, we know that at high interest rates a change in yield will have little if any impact on the value of the option. Thus the duration (i.e., interest rate sensitivity) of the option would be close to zero and the option-adjusted duration would equal that of a noncallable bond. In contrast, when yields decline below the coupon yield, the call option will be very interest rate sensitive since the option will experience a large increase in value at low yields. Thus, the duration (i.e., the interest rate sensitivity) of the option will be fairly high and have a large impact on the callable bond's option-adjusted duration—it will drive the duration of the callable bond toward the duration to first call. In fact, it is possible to conceive of an option that is very leveraged such that it is extremely interest rate sensitive (i.e., has a very large duration that exceeds the duration of the noncallable bond) resulting in a *negative option-adjusted duration*. An example is a mortgage-backed security that might *decline* in price when there is a *decline* in interest rates.

Convexity of Callable Bonds

Exhibit 19.24 shows what happens to the price of a callable bond versus the value of a noncallable bond when interest rates increase or decline. Starting from yield y^* (which is close to the par value yield), if interest *rates increase,* the value of the call option declines because, at market interest rates that are substantially above the coupon rate, it is unlikely the issuer will want to call the issue. Therefore, the call option has very little value and the price of the callable bond will be similar to the price of a noncallable bond. In contrast, when interest rates *decline* below y^*, there is an increase in the probability that the issuer will want to use the call option—that is, the value of the call option increases. As a result, the value of the callable bond will deviate from the value of the noncallable bond—that is, the price of the callable bond will initially not increase as fast as the noncallable bond price and eventually will not increase at all. This is what is shown in curve *a–b.*

---

[31]The discussion in this subsection will consider the option-adjusted duration on a conceptual and intuitive basis. For a detailed mathematical treatment, see Dunetz and Mahoney, "Using Duration and Convexity in the Analysis of Callable Bonds."

EXHIBIT 19.24 ▶ *NONCALLABLE AND CALLABLE BOND PRICE-YIELD RELATIONSHIP*

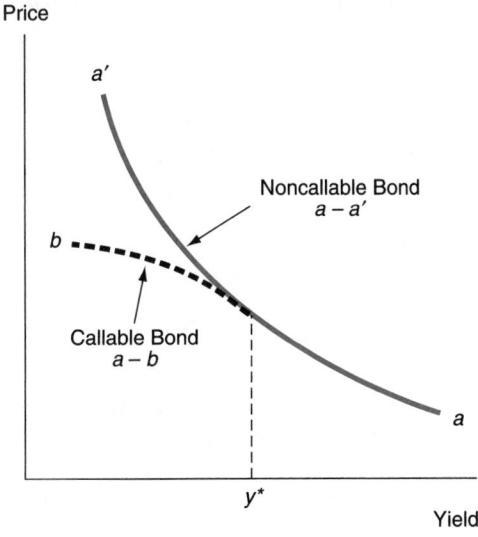

Source: Frank J. Fabozzi, Gerald W. Buetow, and Robert R. Johnson, "Measuring Interest Rate Risk," in the *Handbook of Fixed-Income Securities,* 6th ed. (New York: McGraw-Hill, 2001). Reprinted by permission of the McGraw-Hill Companies.

In the case of the noncallable bond, we indicated that it had *positive convexity* because as yields declined, the price of the bond increased at a *faster* rate. With the callable bond, when rates decline, the price increases at a *slower* rate and eventually does not change at all. This pattern of price-yield change for a callable bond when yields decline is referred to as *negative convexity.*

Needless to say, this price pattern (negative convexity) is one of the risks of a callable bond versus a noncallable bond when interest rates decline.

Limitations of Macaulay and Modified Duration

It is important to understand Macaulay and modified duration because of the perspective they provide regarding factors that affect the volatility and interest rate sensitivity of bonds. However, it also is important for bond analysts and portfolio managers to recognize the serious limitations of these measures in the real world. The major limitations are as follows.

First, as noted in the discussion of convexity, the percent change estimates using modified duration are good only for small-yield changes. This was demonstrated in Exhibit 19.21. As a result, two bonds with equal duration may experience different price changes for large-yield changes—depending on *differences in the convexity* of the bonds.

Second, it is difficult to determine the interest rate sensitivity of a portfolio of bonds when there is a change in interest rates and the yield curve experiences a *nonparallel shift.* It was noted earlier that the duration of a portfolio is the weighted average of the durations of the bonds in the portfolio. Everything works well as long as all yields change by the same amount—that is, there is a parallel shift of the yield curve. However, when yields change, the yield curve *seldom* experiences a parallel shift. Assuming a nonparallel shift, which yield do you use to describe the change—the short-, intermediate-, or long-maturity yield? Two port-folios that begin the period with the same duration can have different ending durations and perform very differently, depending on how the yield curve changed (i.e., did it steepen or flatten?) and the composition of the portfolio (i.e., relative to its duration, was it a bullet or a barbell?). Consider the following simple example for two portfolios that have a duration of 4.50 years:

Bond	Coupon	Maturity (Years)	Yield	Modified Duration	Weights
Portfolio A					
A	7.00	4	7.00	2.70	0.555
B	9.00	20	9.00	6.75	0.445
Portfolio B					
C	8.00	10	8.00	4.50	1.000

As shown, the modified durations are equal at the initiation of the portfolio. Assume a nonparallel change in yields where the *yield curve steepens.* Specifically, 4-year yields decline to 6 percent, 10-year yields do not change, and 20-year yields rise to 10 percent. Portfolio B would experience a very small change in value because of stability in yield for 10-year bonds. In contrast, the price for 4-year bonds will experience a small increase (because of small duration) and the value of 20-year bonds will experience a large decline. Overall, the value of Portfolio A will decline because of the weight of Bond B in the portfolio and its large decline in value due to its large modified duration. Obviously, if the yield curve had flattened or inverted, the barbell portfolio would have benefited from the change. This differential performance because of the change in the shape of the yield curve (i.e., it did not experience a parallel shift) is referred to as *yield curve risk,* which cannot be captured by the traditional duration-convexity presentation.

The third limitation of Macaulay and modified durations involves our initial calculation. We assumed that cash flows from the bond *were not affected by yield changes*—that is, we assumed option-free bonds. Later, we saw the effect on the computed duration and convexity when we considered the effect of an embedded call option in Exhibit 19.24. Specifically, we saw that the option-adjusted duration would be some value between the duration to maturity and duration to first call and the specific value would depend on the current market yield relative to the bond's coupon. Further, we saw that when interest rates declined with an embedded call option, the convexity of the bond went from some positive value to *negative* convexity because the price of the callable bond increased at a slower rate or it did not change when the yields declined (i.e., there is *price compression*).

Because of these limitations, practitioners have developed a way to approximate the duration of a bond or any security that can be impacted by a change in interest rates. This is referred to as *effective duration,* which is discussed in the following section.

Effective Duration[32]   As noted previously, the purpose of duration is to indicate the price change of an asset to a change in yield—that is, it is *a measure of the interest rate sensitivity of an asset.* Because modified duration is based on Macaulay duration, it can provide a reasonable approximation of the interest rate sensitivity of a bond that experiences a small-yield change and one that is option free—if yield changes do not change the cash flows for the bond. Unfortunately, the Macaulay and modified-duration measures cannot be used (1) for large-yield changes; (2) for assets with embedded options; or (3) for assets that are affected by variables other than interest rates, such as common stocks or real estate.

---

[32]This section benefited substantially from the very thorough presentation in Frank J. Fabozzi, Gerald W. Buetow, Jr., and Robert R. Johnson, "Measuring Interest Rate Risk," *Handbook of Fixed-Income Securities,* 6th ed.

To overcome these limitations, practitioners use *effective duration,* a direct measure of the interest rate sensitivity of a bond or any asset where it is possible to use a pricing model to estimate the market prices surrounding a change in interest rates. As we will demonstrate, using this measure it is possible to derive negative durations (which is not mathematically possible with Macaulay) or durations that are longer than the maturity of the asset (likewise not possible with Macaulay). Specifically, effective duration measures the interest rate sensitivity of a bond taking into consideration that the cash flows of the bond can change when yields change due to the existence of embedded options (e.g., call or put options). It is also possible to calculate the effective duration for an option-free bond, in which case the computed duration value will be equal to what would be derived for small-yield changes using modified duration.

Notably, to implement the effective duration formula, it is necessary to use an interest rate model and a corresponding pricing model that will provide price estimates for the asset when interest rates and cash flows change. The formulas for calculating effective duration and effective convexity are:

➤19.22
$$\text{Effective Duration } (D_{Eff}) = \frac{(P_-) - (P_+)}{2PS}$$

➤19.23
$$\text{Effective Convexity } (C_{Eff}) = \frac{(P_-) + (P_+) - 2P}{PS^2}$$

where:

P_- = the estimated price of the asset after a downward shift in interest rates
P_+ = the estimated price of the asset after an upward shift in interest rates
P = the current price of the asset (before any interest rate shifts)
S = the assumed shift in the term structure

The formulas are implemented by assuming small changes in yield (10 basis points) both down and up and using a pricing model to estimate the expected market prices (both P_- and P_+) at the new yields. Everything else in the formulas is given. Consider the following bond that we will initially assume is option free:

Par value	$1,000
Coupon	6%
Maturity	8 years
Initial YTM	6%
Initial price (P)	100

Given this initial scenario, we assume a change in yields of 10 basis points. The prices for the bond at yields to maturity of 5.90 percent (P_-) and 6.10 percent (P_+) are:

$$0.0590 \ (P_-) = 100.42760054$$
$$0.0610 \ (P_+) = \underline{99.57457612}$$
$$(P_-) - (P_+) = 0.85302442$$
$$2PS = (2)(100)(0.001) = 0.20$$

$$D_{Eff} = \frac{0.85302442}{0.20} = 4.265122$$

Because this is a noncallable bond (option free), we know that this effective duration equals the modified duration we would derive based upon the Macaulay duration of 4.39.

$$D_{mod} \frac{4.39}{\left(1 + \dfrac{0.06}{2}\right)} = \frac{4.39}{1.03} = 4.262$$

The difference is due to the rounding of the Macaulay duration.

The bond's effective convexity would equal

$$
\begin{aligned}
C_{Eff} &= \frac{(P_-) + (P_+) - 2P}{PS^2} \\
&= \frac{100.42760054 + 99.57457612 - 200}{(100)(0.001)^2} \\
&= \frac{200.00217666 - 200}{0.0001} \\
&= \frac{0.00217666}{0.0001} = 21.766
\end{aligned}
$$

We know from our earlier discussion that, at a lower yield, the duration would be higher. Specifically, if we assumed a YTM of 4 percent, the effective and modified durations would be about 4.34 compared to about 4.26 at 6 percent.

Let us now assume that the bond is callable at 106 of par after 3 years. Using the Black, Derman, and Toy no-arbitrage binomial model to estimate prices for this bond beginning at a yield of 4 percent, we derive the following prices:[33]

$$0.0390 \ (P_-) = 108.55626094$$
$$0.0410 \ (P_+) = 107.92318176$$
$$0.04 \ (P) = 108.24082177$$

$$
\begin{aligned}
D_{Eff} &= \frac{108.55626094 - 107.92318176}{(2)(108.24082177)(0.001)} \\
&= 2.92
\end{aligned}
$$

As expected, because of the embedded call option that would have increased in value with a decline in yields, this duration value (2.92) would be lower than the duration for the option-free bond discussed earlier (4.34). In contrast, the effective durations for callable bonds at higher yields would be equal to the durations for option-free bonds because the value of the option approaches zero.

The effective convexity of this callable bond at 4 percent would be

$$
\begin{aligned}
C_{Eff} &= \frac{108.55626094 + 107.92318176 - [2(108.24082177)]}{(108.24082177)(0.001)^2} \\
&= -20.33
\end{aligned}
$$

---

[33]F. Black, E. Derman, and Wo Toy, "A One-Factor Model of Interest Rates and Its Application to Treasury Bond Options," *Financial Analysts Journal* 46, no. 1 (January–February 1990): 33–39.

As discussed, this is an example of negative convexity because the price increase is limited because of the increasing value of the call option. For comparison purposes, the convexity of the option-free bond at 4 percent is 23.76, which is, as expected, slightly higher than its convexity of 21.77 at 6 percent (recall that both duration and convexity are inversely related to yield).

Putable Bonds   Although it is not feasible to discuss in detail the properties of bonds with put options (putable bonds), it is possible to envision the effects if one considers the basic value of a putable bond as follows:

➤19.24   Value of Putable Bond = Value of Nonputable Bond + Value of the Put Option

In this instance, the investor owns the option, which means it has a positive impact on the value of the bond and this option *increases* in value when interest rates *increase.* Therefore, when rates increase, the price of the bond does not decline as much as an option-free bond, but when rates decline, its price pattern is similar to that of an option-free bond because the value of the put option approaches zero.

A visual presentation of the effect of the call option on the price-yield curve was contained in Exhibit 19.24. Alternatively Exhibit 19.25 and Exhibit 19.26 contain the effective duration-yield curves and the effective convexity–yield curves, which show the significant impact of embedded options on the effective duration and convexity of fixed-income securities.

Effective Duration Greater than Maturity   Because effective duration is simply interest rate sensitivity, it is possible to have an asset that is highly levered such that its interest rate sensitivity exceeds its maturity. For example, there are five-year, collateralized mortgage obligations (CMOs) that are highly levered and their prices will change by 15 percent to 20 percent when interest rates change by 100 basis points. Using the formula discussed (Equation 19.22), you would compute an effective duration of 15 or 20 for a five-year maturity security.

Negative Effective Duration   We know from the formula for Macaulay duration that it is not possible to compute a negative duration. Further, in the calculation for price volatility where we use modified duration, we use $-D^*$ to reflect the negative relationship between price changes and interest rate changes for *option-free bonds.* At the same time, we know that when we leave the world of option-free bonds and consider bonds with embedded options, it is possible to envision cases where bond prices move in the same direction as yields, which implies negative duration. A prime example would be mortgage-backed securities where a significant decline in interest rates will cause a substantial increase in refinancing prepayments by homeowners, which will reduce the value of these bonds to holders. Therefore, you would see a decline in interest rates *and* a decline in the price of these mortgage-backed bonds, which implies *negative duration.* Another way to explain a price decline with lower interest rates is the value formula (Equation 19.20)—that is, with lower interest rates, the value of the call option increases in value by more than the increase in value of the noncallable bond, which causes a decline in the value of the callable bond.

Empirical Duration[34]   In the preceding discussion of effective duration, the point was made that these computations required the use of an interest rate model and a bond pricing model that considered cash flow changes when yields changed and generated market price estimates that were inputs into the effective duration and effective convexity formulas. The question arises regarding what happens when you want to estimate interest rate sensitivity for an asset class

---

[34]The discussion in this section considered the analysis in Lakhbir Hayre and Hubert Chang, "Effective and Empirical Durations of Mortgage Securities," *Journal of Fixed Income* 6, no. 4 (March 1997): 17–33.

EXHIBIT 19.25 *EFFECTIVE DURATION–YIELD CURVES*

A. Effective Duration–Yield Curve for 8-year, 6% Option-Free Bond

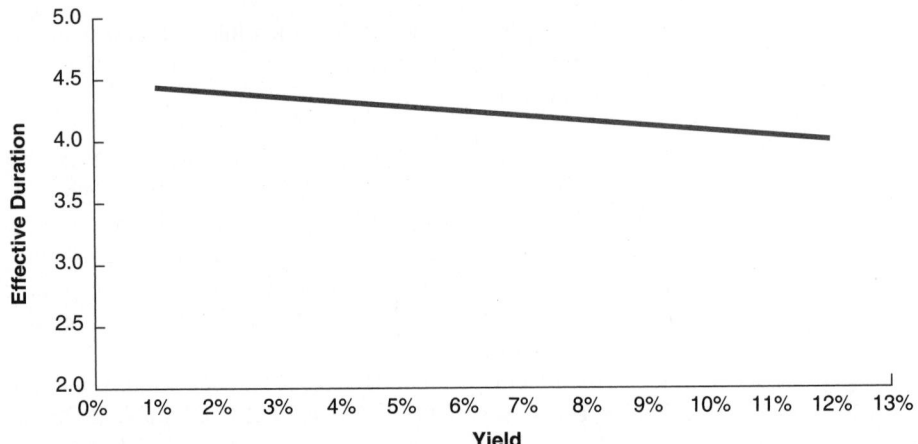

B. Effective Duration–Yield Curve for 8-year, 6% Callable Bond after 3 Years

C. Effective Duration–Yield Curve for 8-year, 6% Putable Bond after 3 Years

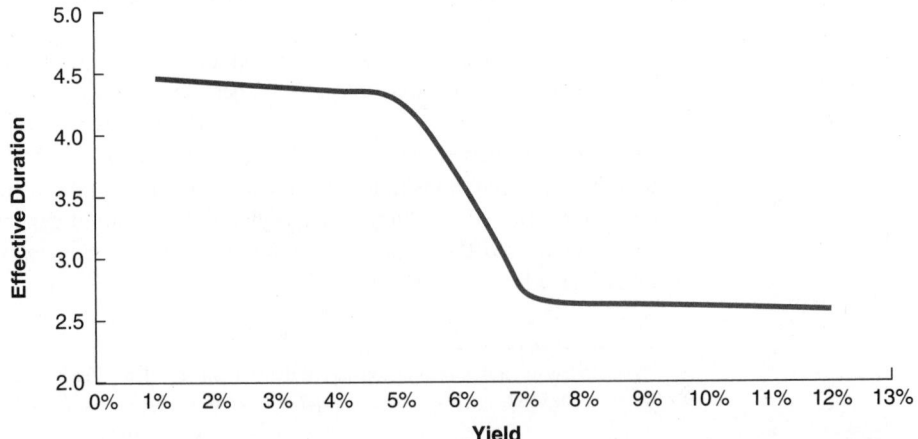

EXHIBIT 19.26   *EFFECTIVE CONVEXITY–YIELD CURVES*

A. Effective Convexity–Yield Curve for 8-year, 6% Option-Free Bond

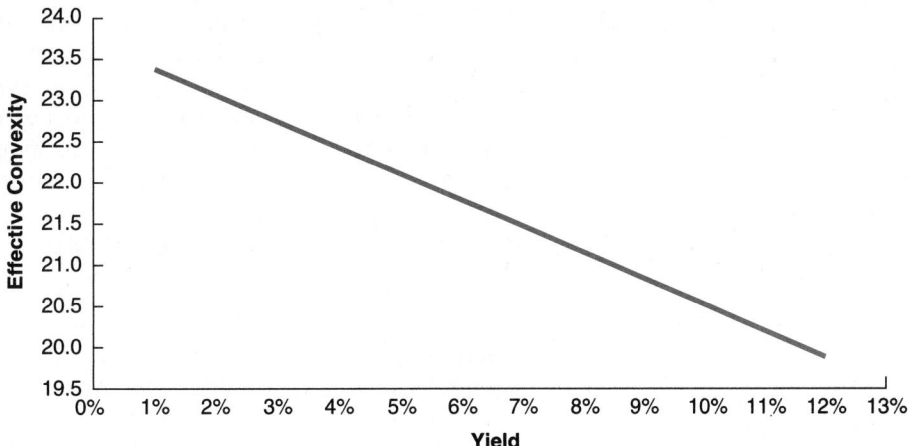

B. Effective Convexity–Yield Curve for 8-year, 6% Callable Bond after 3 Years

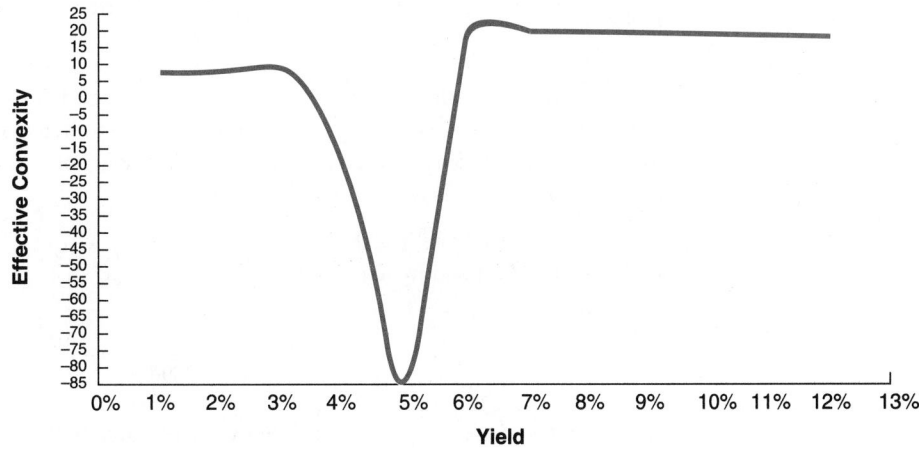

C. Effective Convexity–Yield Curve for 8-year, 6% Putable Bond after 3 Years

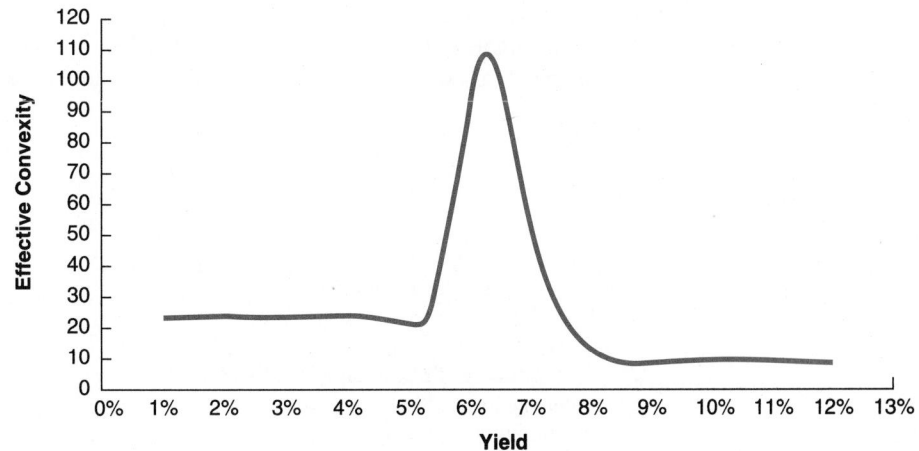

where it is not possible to generate well-specified market price estimates in response to yield changes. The classic example would be common stocks where there is an impact on price when interest rates change, but the interest rate effect can be overpowered by the growth rate effect that is likewise unknown. The other obvious example would be bonds with exotic embedded options (including mortgage-backed bonds) where prices can change based upon the value of the exotic option that is difficult to price. In order to derive some estimate of interest rate sensitivity under such circumstances, analysts and portfolio managers employ **empirical duration**, which is the actual percentage price change for an asset in response to a change in yield during a specified time period. The concept is best described by recalling the formula in Equation 19.14 used to determine the percentage price change for a bond using modified duration as follows:

$$\%\Delta Price = -D_{mod} \times (\Delta i)$$

where:

> D_{mod} = the modified Macaulay duration
> Δi = the change in interest rates in basis points divided by 100

The typical assumption is that we know D_{mod} and Δi and can solve for the approximate percentage price change. Alternatively, given this relationship, we can solve for D_{mod} as follows:

➤19.25
$$-D_{mod} = \frac{\%\Delta Price}{\Delta i}$$

When we solve for it this way, it is no longer D_{mod} (modified duration), but D_{emp}—empirical duration. Given this formulation, if you observe a change in interest rates (Δi) and the change in the price of an asset during the same time period, you can solve for the empirical duration of the asset. Consider the following simple example:

➤ Interest rates decline by 200 BP.
➤ The price of a bond increases by 10 percent.

$$D_{emp} = -\frac{10}{-200/100} = -\frac{10}{-2}$$

Therefore, the change in price coincident with a change in interest rates indicates that this bond has an empirical duration (D_{emp}) of 5. This is a direct measure of the bond's interest rate sensitivity. You should think of it as *the approximate percentage change in price for a 100-basis-point change in interest rates.*

While this simple example indicates the concept of empirical duration, the technique that is generally suggested for estimating empirical duration is to employ the following regression model:

➤19.26
$$\frac{\Delta P}{P} = \alpha + D^{**}\Delta Y + u$$

where:

> $\underline{\Delta P}$ = percentage change in price
> P
> α = constant term
> D^{**} = an estimate of D_{emp} (empirical duration)
> ΔY = change in yield in basis points
> u = random error term

The time interval for the data and the time period considered can vary based upon the asset and purpose of the analysis. When working with bonds, some analysts employ daily data for short time periods (months), while investigators using the concept for stocks or real estate (to be discussed) have employed weekly and monthly data for longer time periods (quarters or years).

Empirical Duration for Common Stock

If one considers the Macaulay duration of common stock, it is possible to envision a fairly high number because you are dealing with a perpetuity, and some growth stocks pay low dividends for many years. The values derived by Reilly and Sidhu, using various assumptions of price and growth, ranged from 10 years to 20 years.[35] In contrast, using empirical duration, one gets very different results.

Because we are dealing with the interest rate sensitivity of an asset, it is possible to compute an empirical duration for common stock that is much lower than what is implied by Macaulay duration and it is more variable. Observing a change in interest rates and the accompanying percentage change in stock prices would indicate the interest rate sensitivity of stocks. Leibowitz conducted such an analysis and derived a rolling, one-year effective duration for the S&P 500 that ranged *from about zero to almost seven*.[36] When measuring the interest rate sensitivity of common stocks over time, you would expect changes because the correlation between stock and bond returns varies substantially over time.[37] In addition, you might anticipate significant differences in the effective duration for alternative stocks. For example, you would expect a large difference in the interest rate sensitivity (empirical duration) of a banking or utility stock (which is very interest rate sensitive) compared to the empirical duration of a small-cap or technology stock where its value is based more on changes in its specific growth expectations than interest rates.

YIELD SPREADS WITH EMBEDDED OPTIONS

Earlier in the chapter, we discussed the analysis of yield spread as a technique to enhance bond investments or bond trades. At this point, it is necessary to revisit the concept of yield spreads, keeping in mind the term structure of interest rates but, more important, with an awareness of the significant impact that interest rate volatility has on the value of embedded options in bonds. In this revisitation, we will consider two spreads: (1) **static yield spreads** that consider the total term structure and (2) **option-adjusted spreads** that consider changes in the term structure and alternative estimates of the volatility of interest rates.

Static Yield Spreads You will recall that the traditional yield spread compares the yields between two bonds with similar coupons and equal maturities as follows:

8%—20-Year AA Corporate Bond 8.20%

8%—20-Year Treasury Bond   7.10%

Yield Spread   1.10%

110 bp

---

[35]Frank K. Reilly and Rupinder Sidhu, "The Many Uses of Bond Duration," *Financial Analysts Journal* 36, no. 4 (July–August 1980): 58–72.

[36]Martin L. Leibowitz, *New Perspectives on Asset Allocation* (Charlottesville, Va.: The Research Foundation of the Institute of Chartered Financial Analysts, 1987).

[37]For a specific analysis of the intertemporal correlation between stock returns and Treasury bond returns (which implies the relationship with interest rates), see Frank K. Reilly, David J. Wright, and Kam C. Chan, "Bond Market Volatility Compared to Stock Market Volatility" *Journal of Portfolio Management* 27, no. 1 (Fall 2000): 82–92.

There are three problems with this "traditional" yield spread:

➤ The two yields do not consider the prevailing term structures of interest rates but only consider the yield spread at the one point on the curve (at 20 years).
➤ The analysis does not consider the fact that the corporate bond could have an embedded option (put or call), whereby expected interest rate volatility may alter the cash flow for this bond.
➤ While not true in this example, it is possible that investors would compare two bonds with equal maturities but different coupon cash flow (e.g., a zero coupon bond versus a coupon bond).

The first concern (neglect of the term structure) suggests the consideration of the *static spread*. It is contended that the proper way to compare non-Treasury bonds of the same maturity but with different coupon rates is to compare them to a portfolio of Treasury securities that have the same cash flow. The way to do this, if there is not an existing Treasury bond with the specified flows, is to discount the corporate bond's cash flow as if the flows were risk free. Specifically, discount them using the prevailing Treasury spot rates for the life of the corporate bond. Consider the following example:

Corporate Bond—8%, Five-Year Bond

If we discount this bond's flows using the hypothetical Treasury spot rate curve contained in Exhibit 19.27, the price would be $1,040.56, which is what this bond would sell at if it were a Treasury bond. In fact, the bond is priced at $1,006.70. The *static spread* (also called the *zero volatility spread*) is the spread that will make the present value of the cash flows from the corporate bond when discounted at the Treasury spot rate plus the static spread, equal to the corporate bond's market price. To put it another way, how much of a static spread across all points on the Treasury spot rate curve is required to generate the current market price for this bond? Adding 70 basis points to every spot rate generates a price above $1,006.70, which indicates that we need to consider a larger spread. As shown in Exhibit 19.28, using a spread of 80 basis points generates a price of $1,006.70, which equals the current price of the corporate bond, which indicates that there is a static (zero volatility) spread for the bond of 80 basis points or 0.80 percent.

Option-Adjusted Spread

As noted, the traditional spread was a problem because it did not consider the full-term structure or the impact of interest rate volatility. The term structure problem was addressed by estimating the static spread.

The interest rate volatility factor is considered by the option-adjusted spread (OAS) analysis. Why is interest rate volatility a problem? The point is, as discussed earlier in the chapter, if a bond has an embedded call option, this option can affect the bond's expected cash flow. The likelihood of the call being exercised will depend on future interest rates, the remaining maturity of the bond, the call price, and other costs of a call and new issue.

The goal of the OAS is similar to the static spread except that the technique allows for a *change in the term structure* over time based on some estimates of interest rate volatility.

The concept of OAS is best understood by a presentation of the steps involved in estimating the OAS for a specific bond as follows:

1. Based upon the prevailing Treasury yield curve, estimate the term structure of interest rates (i.e., the prevailing Treasury spot rate curve) and the implied short-term forward rates derived from the spot rates.
2. Select a probability distribution for short-term Treasury spot rates. This should be based on the current term structure and the historical behavior of interest rates. The significant

EXHIBIT 19.27 CALCULATION OF THE PRICE OF A FIVE-YEAR, 8 PERCENT COUPON BOND USING TREASURY SPOT RATES

PERIOD	CASH FLOW	TREASURY SPOT RATE	PRESENT VALUE
1	$ 40	6.20	$ 38.80
2	40	6.30	37.60
3	40	6.40	36.40
4	40	6.50	35.20
5	40	6.60	34.00
6	40	6.70	32.84
7	40	6.80	31.64
8	40	6.90	30.48
9	40	7.00	29.36
10	1040	7.10	734.24
		Theoretical price	$1040.56

EXHIBIT 19.28 CALCULATION OF THE STATIC SPREAD FOR A FIVE-YEAR, 8 PERCENT COUPON CORPORATE BOND

PERIOD	CASH FLOW	TREASURY SPOT RATE	80 BP SPREAD SPOT RATE	PRESENT VALUE
1	$ 40	6.20	7.00	$ 38.64
2	40	6.30	7.10	37.30
3	40	6.40	7.20	35.98
4	40	6.50	7.30	34.66
5	40	6.60	7.40	33.36
6	40	6.70	7.50	32.07
7	40	6.80	7.60	30.81
8	40	6.90	7.70	29.57
9	40	7.00	7.80	28.35
10	1040	7.10	7.90	705.95
			Present Value	$1006.70

estimate is the volatility of interest rates—that is, how much will the forward rates change each period?

3. Using the probability distribution specified in Step 2 and Monte Carlo simulation, it is possible to randomly generate a large number of interest rate paths (e.g., 1,000).

4. For bonds with embedded options (such as callable bonds), develop rules for determining when the option will be exercised. For example, given the coupon, maturity, and call option, at what interest rate will the issue be called?

5. For each path generated in Step 3, determine the cash flows from the bond, given (a) the information about the bond (i.e., its call provision) and (b) the rules established in Step 4 for calling the bond.

6. For an assumed spread relative to the Treasury term structure of spot rates along a path, calculate a present value for all paths created in Step 3.

7. Calculate the *average* present value for all the interest rate paths.
8. Compare the average present value calculated in Step 7 to the market price of the bond. If they are equal, the assumed spread used in Step 6 is the option-adjusted spread. If they are not, try another spread and repeat Steps 6, 7, and 8.

The computed option-adjusted spread (OAS) is the average spread over the Treasury spot rate curve based on the potential paths that can be realized in the future for interest rates. The reason it is referred to as "option adjusted" is because the potential paths of cash flow are adjusted to reflect the effect of the options embedded in the bonds.

The following are some technical issues that an analyst should be aware of when attempting to estimate the OAS and also factors that can cause differences in an estimate of the OAS for a bond by alternative dealers.

➤ It is necessary to have a large number of paths for the simulation.
➤ The estimate of the probability distribution, which includes the volatility, is crucial. Notably, if alternative firms differ in this estimate of expected interest rate volatility, it can cause differences in the OAS estimate.
➤ It is necessary to determine the relationship between short-term rates and refinancing rates. Specifically, how much more does the firm have to pay above the short-term forward rate (i.e., the refinancing rate is a long-term rate)? Empirically, what is this relationship?
➤ A call rule must be specified. This depends upon the coupon rate for the bond and other costs. It has been assumed to be almost 300 BP below the coupon rate (e.g., 5.0 percent with at least three years to maturity).

As noted, different assumptions regarding these technical issues can cause different estimates of the OAS by alternative dealers. The critical estimate is the expected interest rate volatility and this can vary between dealers; and, also, individual dealers can change their estimates over time.

The Internet   *Investments Online*

Bond valuation focuses on bond mathematics, the term structure, and bond features that add to the yield (such as callability) or lead to lower yields (such as putability). Bonds are normally easier to evaluate than stocks, given their stated life, cash flows, and discount rates, which can be read from the term structure. Nonetheless, bond pricing can become quite complicated if the bond has complex options or attributes. It is not surprising that bond market commentary typically focuses on interest rate trends and factors that can favorably or unfavorably affect credit quality.

http://www.bondcalc.com This site discusses a software pricing system for fixed income securities. It includes a description of basic and sophisticated bond analyses.

http://www.kalotay.com The Web site of Andrew Kalotay Associates offers research on bond analytics, for-purchase software for bond valuation and analysis, and freeware for valuing bonds and mortgage-backed securities.

Many brokerage houses offer bond market commentaries and analysis. For example, see **http://www.salomonsmithbarney.com/research** or **http://www.leggmason.com/capitalmarkets/research/commentary/daily_bond_market.asp**. Smartmoney's "living yield curve" feature shows the changes in the yield curve over time: **http://www.smartmoney.com/onebond/index.cfm?story=yieldcurve.**

Summary

- The value of a bond equals the present value of all future cash flows accruing to the investor. Cash flows for the conservative bond investor include periodic interest payments and principal return; cash flows for the aggressive investor include periodic interest payments and the capital gain or loss when the bond is sold prior to its maturity. Bond investors can maximize their portfolio rates of return by accurately estimating the level of interest rates and, more importantly, by estimating changes in interest rates, yield spreads, and credit quality. Similarly, they must compare coupon rates, maturities, and call features of alternative bonds.

- There are five bond yield measures: nominal yield, current yield, promised yield to maturity, promised yield to call, and realized (horizon) yield. The promised YTM and promised YTC equations include the interest-on-interest (or coupon reinvestment) assumption. For the realized (horizon) yield computation, the investor estimates the reinvestment rate and the future selling price for the bond. The fundamental determinants of interest rates are a real risk-free rate, the expected rate of inflation, and a risk premium.

- The yield curve (or the term structure of interest rates) shows the relationship between the yields on a set of comparable bonds and the term to maturity. Based upon this yield curve, it is possible to derive a theoretical spot rate curve. In turn, these spot rates can be used to value bonds using an individual spot rate for each cash flow. This valuation approach is becoming more useful in a world where bonds have very different cash flows. In addition, these spot rates imply investor expectations about future rates referred to as forward rates. Yield curves exhibit four basic patterns. Three theories attempt to explain the shape of the yield curve: the expectations hypothesis, the liquidity preference (term premium) hypothesis, and the segmented market hypothesis.

- It is important to understand what causes changes in interest rates and how these changes in rates affect the prices of bonds. Differences in bond price volatility are mainly a function of differences in yield, coupon, and term to maturity. There are four duration measures that have been used as measures of bond price volatility or interest rate sensitivity. The Macaulay duration measure incorporates coupon, maturity, and yield in one measure. In turn, modified duration (which is directly related to Macaulay duration) provides an estimate of the response of bond prices to changes in interest rates under certain assumptions. Because modified duration provides a straight-line estimate of the curvilinear price-yield function, you must consider modified duration together with the convexity of a bond for large changes in yields and/or when dealing with securities that have high convexity. Notably, an embedded call option feature on a bond can have a significant impact on its duration (the call feature can shorten it dramatically) and on its convexity (the call feature can change the convexity from a positive value to a negative value). Following a discussion of some of the limitations of Macaulay and modified durations as measures of interest rate sensitivity, effective duration is introduced as a direct measure of interest rate sensitivity—that is, it is the estimated percentage change in price for a 100-basis-point change in interest rates and allows for repricing due to changes in cash flow caused by changes in interest rates. Notably, with effective duration, it is necessary to have a valid bond pricing model and it is possible to have durations longer than maturity as well as negative duration.

- Finally, there are instances when it is very difficult to estimate the price when there is a change in interest rates as required for effective duration—such as with some mortgage-backed securities, common stock, and real estate. In these instances, analysts consider estimating empirical duration, which is based on the analysis of historical data on price changes that accompany interest rate changes. While it is possible to derive such estimates for a range of assets, it is important to remember that the duration values derived can vary dramatically and are notoriously unstable.

- We concluded the chapter with a revisitation to yield spreads for bonds with embedded options. To take account of the spread across the total term structure of interest rates, we described and demonstrated the static spread. In order to consider the impact of interest rate volatility on the embedded options, we discussed and described the steps to estimate the option-adjusted spread (OAS) for these bonds.

Given the background in bond valuation and the factors that influence bond value and bond return volatility, we are ready to consider how to build a bond portfolio that is consistent with our goals and objectives. Bond portfolio analysis is the topic for Chapter 20.

Questions

1. Why does the present value equation appear to be more useful for the bond investor than for the common stock investor?
2. What are the important assumptions made when you calculate the promised yield to maturity? What are the assumptions when calculating promised YTC?
3. a. Define the variables included in the following model:

$$i = (RFR, I, RP)$$

   b. Assume that the firm whose bonds you are considering is not expected to break even this year. Discuss which factor will be affected by this information.
4. We discussed three alternative hypotheses to explain the term structure of interest rates. Briefly discuss the three hypotheses and indicate which one you think best explains the alternative shapes of a yield curve.

5. *CFA Examination Level I*
   a. Explain what is meant by *structure of interest rates*. Explain the theoretical basis of an upward-sloping yield curve [8 minutes]
   b. Explain the economic circumstances under which you would expect to see the inverted yield curve prevail. [7 minutes]
   c. Define "real" rate of interest. [2 minutes]
   d. Discuss the characteristics of the market for U.S. Treasury securities. Compare it to the market for AAA corporate bonds. Discuss the opportunities that may exist in bond markets that are less than efficient. [8 minutes]
   e. Over the past several years, fairly wide yield spreads between AAA corporates and Treasuries have occasionally prevailed. Discuss the possible reasons for this. [5 minutes]

6. *CFA Examination Level III*
   As the portfolio manager for a large pension fund, you are offered the following bonds:

	Coupon	Maturity	Price	Call Price	Yield to Maturity
Edgar Corp. (new issue)	14.00%	2012	$101.3/4	$114	13.75%
Edgar Corp. (new issue)	6.00	2012	48.1/8	103	13.60
Edgar Corp. (2000 issue)	6.00	2012	48.7/8	103	13.40

   Assuming that you expect a decline in interest rates over the next three years, identify and justify which of these bonds you would select. [10 minutes]

7. You expect interest rates to decline over the next six months.
   a. Given your interest rate outlook, state what kinds of bonds you want in your portfolio in terms of duration and explain your reasoning for this choice.
   b. You must make a choice between the following three sets of noncallable bonds. For each set, select the bond that would be best for your portfolio given your interest rate outlook and the consequent strategy set forth in Part a. In each case briefly discuss why you selected the bond.

		Maturity	Coupon	Yield to Maturity
Set 1:	Bond A	15 years	10%	10%
	Bond B	15 years	6%	8%
Set 2:	Bond C	15 years	6%	10%
	Bond D	10 years	8%	10%
Set 3:	Bond E	12 years	12%	12%
	Bond F	15 years	12%	8%

8. At the present time, you expect a decline in interest rates and must choose between two portfolios of bonds with the following characteristics:

	Portfolio A	Portfolio B
Average maturity	10.5 years	10.0 years
Average YTM	7%	10%
Modified duration	5.7 years	4.9 years
Modified convexity	125.18	40.30
Call features	Noncallable	Deferred call features that range from 1 to 3 years

Select one of the portfolios and discuss three factors that would justify your selection.

9. The Chartered Finance Corporation has issued a bond with the following characteristics:

> Maturity—25 years
> Coupon—9%
> Yield to maturity—9%
> Callable—after 3 years @ 109
> Duration to maturity—8.2 years
> Duration to first call—2.1 years

a. Discuss the concept of call-adjusted duration and indicate the approximate value (range) for it at the present time.

b. Assuming interest rates increase substantially (i.e., to 13 percent), discuss what will happen to the call-adjusted duration and the reason for the change.

c. Assuming interest rates decline substantially (i.e., they decline to 4 percent), discuss what will happen to the bond's call-adjusted duration and the reason for the change.

d. Discuss the concept of negative convexity as it relates to this bond.

10. *CFA Examination Level I*

Duration may be calculated by *two* widely used methods. Identify these *two* methods, and briefly discuss the primary differences between them. [5 minutes]

11. *CFA Examination Level II*

Option-adjusted duration and *effective duration* are alternative measures used by analysts to evaluate fixed-income securities with embedded options.

Briefly describe *each* measure and how to apply *each* to the evaluation of fixed-income securities with embedded options. [8 minutes]

12. *CFA Examination Level II*

As a portfolio manager, during a discussion with a client, you explain that historical return and risk premia of the type presented in the following table are frequently used in forming estimates of future returns for various types of financial assets. Although such historical data are helpful in forecasting returns, most users know that history is an imperfect guide to the future. Thus, they recognize that there are reasons why these data should be adjusted if they are to be employed in the forecasting process.

U.S. HISTORICAL RETURN AND RISK PREMIA (1926–1994)	
	Per Year
Inflation rate	3.0%
Real interest rate on Treasury bills	0.5%
Maturity premium of long Treasury bonds over Treasury bills	0.8%
Default premium of long corporate bonds over long Treasury bonds	0.6%
Risk premium on stock over long Treasury bonds	5.6%
Return on Treasury bills	3.5%
Return on long corporate bonds	4.9%
Return on large-capitalization stocks	9.9%

a. As shown in the table, the historical real interest rate for Treasury bills was 0.5 percent per year and the maturity premium on Treasury bonds over Treasury bills was 0.8 percent. Briefly describe and justify *one* adjustment to *each* of these two data items that should be made before they can be used to form expectations about future real interest rates and Treasury bond maturity premia. [6 minutes]

b. You recognize that even adjusted historical economic and capital markets data may be of limited use when estimating future returns. Independent of your Part a response, briefly describe *three* key circumstances that should be considered when forming expectations about future returns. [8 minutes]

13. *CFA Examination Level I*

A portfolio manager at Superior Trust Company is structuring a fixed-income portfolio to meet the objectives of a client. This client plans on retiring in 15 years and wants a substantial lump sum at that time. The client has specified the use of AAA-rated securities.

The portfolio manager compares coupon U.S. Treasuries with zero coupon stripped U.S. Treasuries and observes a significant yield advantage for the stripped bonds.

Maturity	Coupon U.S. Treasuries	Zero Coupon Stripped U.S. Treasuries
3 year	5.50%	5.80%
5 year	6.00%	6.60%
7 year	6.75%	7.25%
10 year	7.25%	7.60%
15 year	7.40%	8.80%
30 year	7.75%	7.75%

Briefly discuss *two* reasons why zero coupon stripped U.S. Treasuries could yield more than coupon U.S. Treasuries with the same final maturity. [5 minutes]

14. *CFA Examination Level II*

a. In terms of option theory, explain the impact on the offering yield of adding a call feature to a proposed bond issue. [5 minutes]

b. Explain the impact on *both* bond duration and convexity of adding a call feature to a proposed bond issue. [10 minutes]

Assume that a portfolio of corporate bonds is managed to maintain targets for modified duration and convexity.

c. Explain how the portfolio could include *both* callable and noncallable bonds while maintaining the targets. [5 minutes]

d. Describe *one* advantage and *one* disadvantage of including callable bonds in this portfolio. [5 minutes]

15. *CFA Examination Level II*

The shape of the U.S. Treasury yield curve appears to reflect two expected Federal Reserve reductions in the Federal Funds rate. The first reduction of approximately 50 basis points (BP) is expected six months from now, and the second reduction of approximately 50 BP is expected one year from now. The current U.S. Treasury term premiums are 10 BP per year for each of the next three years (out through the three-year benchmark.)

You agree that the two Federal Reserve reductions described will occur. However, you believe that they will be reversed in a single 100 BP increase in the Federal Funds rate 2 1/2 years from now. You expect term premiums to remain 10 BP per year for each of the next three years (out through the three-year benchmark.)

a. Describe *or* draw the shape of the Treasury yield curve out through the three-year benchmark. (*Note to Candidates:* Be sure to label your axes and relevant data points carefully.) [4 minutes]

b. State which term structure theory supports the shape of the U.S. Treasury yield curve described in Part a. Justify your choice. [6 minutes]

Kent Lewis, an economist, also expects two Federal Reserve reductions in the Federal Funds rate but believes that the market is too optimistic about how soon they will occur. Lewis believes that the first 50 BP reduction will be made 1 year from now and that the second 50 BP reduction will be made 1½ years from now. He expects these reductions to be reversed by a single 100 BP increase 2½ years from now. He believes that the market will adjust to reflect his beliefs when new economic data are released over the next two weeks.

Assume you are convinced by Lewis's argument and are authorized to purchase either the two-year benchmark U.S. Treasury or a Cash/three-year benchmark U.S. Treasury barbell weighted to have the same duration as the two-year U.S. Treasury.

c. Select an investment in *either* the two-year benchmark U.S. Treasury (bullet) *or* the Cash/three-year benchmark U.S. Treasury barbell. Justify your choice. [5 minutes]

16. *CFA Examination Level II*

Beth Goetz, CFA, has decided to add some asset-backed securities (ABS) to her fixed-income portfolio. She has narrowed the choice to an automobile ABS and a fixed-rate home equity loan (second mortgage) ABS.

Automobile ABS are available at a pricing spread of 75 basis points over comparable-maturity Treasuries, with a zero volatility spread of 67 basis points. Home equity loan ABS are available at a pricing spread of 85 basis points over comparable-maturity Treasuries, with an option-adjusted spread of 60 basis points.

a. Explain why pricing spread is not an appropriate measure of yield advantage for ABS. [3 minutes]

b. Describe the concepts of

(1) Zero volatility spread

(2) Option-adjusted spread [8 minutes]

c. Explain why option-adjusted spread is the appropriate measure of yield for a second mortgage ABS. [4 minutes]

17. *CFA Examination Level II*

The asset-backed securities (ABS) market has grown in the past few years partly as a result of credit enhancements to ABS.

a. Describe a "letter of credit" and the risk to the investor associated with relying exclusively on this type of credit enhancement. [6 minutes]

b. Describe "early amortization" and the risk to the investor associated with relying exclusively on this type of credit enhancement. [6 minutes]

18. *CFA Examination Level II*

Rachel Morgan owns a newly issued U.S. government agency fixed-rate pass-through mortgage-backed security (MBS) and wants to evaluate the sensitivity of its principal cash flow to the following interest rate scenario:

- Interest rates instantaneously decline by 250 basis points for all maturities, remain there for one year, and then,
- Interest rates instantaneously increase 350 basis points for all maturities and remain there for the next year.

Currently, the MBS is priced close to par and the yield curve is "flat." Morgan does not expect the shape of the yield curve to change during her interest rate scenario.

a. (1) State whether, in the interest rate scenario described, the MBS principal cash flows

- Increase or decrease in the first year
- Increase or decrease in the second year

(2) Discuss the reason why principal cash flows change. [6 minutes]

Morgan also wants to evaluate the price sensitivity of her MBS to changes in interest rates. She knows that modified duration and effective duration are two possible measures she could use to evaluate price sensitivity.

b. Select *and* justify with *one* reason which duration measure Morgan should use to evaluate the price sensitivity of her MBS. [6 minutes]

Morgan also owns a newly issued U.S. government agency collateralized mortgage obligation interest-only (IO) security.

c. State whether the IO security price increases or decreases in the first year of the interest rate scenario described. Justify your response. [6 minutes]

19. *CFA Examination Level III*

One common goal among fixed-income portfolio managers is to earn high incremental returns on corporate bonds versus government bonds of comparable durations. The approach of some corporate bond portfolio managers is to find and purchase those corporate bonds having the largest initial spreads over comparable-duration government bonds. John Ames, HFS's fixed-income manager, believes that a more rigorous approach is required if incremental returns are to be maximized.

The following table presents data relating to one set of corporate/government spread relationships present in the market at a given date:

CURRENT AND EXPECTED SPREADS AND DURATIONS OF HIGH-GRADE CORPORATE BONDS (ONE-YEAR HORIZON)

Bond Rating	Initial Spread over Governments	Expected Horizon Spread	Initial Duration	Expected Duration One Year from Now
Aaa	31 BP	31 BP	4 years	3.1 years
Aa	40 BP	50 BP	4 years	3.1 years

a. Recommend purchase of *either* Aaa *or* Aa bonds for a one-year investment horizon given a goal of maximizing incremental returns. Show your calculations. (Base your decision *only* on the information presented in the preceding table.) [6 minutes]

Ames chooses not to rely *solely* on initial spread relationships. His analytical framework considers a full range of other key variables likely to impact realized incremental returns, including

- call provisions, and
- potential changes in interest rates.

b. Describe *two* variables, *in addition to those identified,* that Ames should include in his analysis *and* explain how *each* of these *two* variables could cause realized incremental returns to differ from those indicated by initial spread relationships. [10 minutes]

20. *CFA Examination Level III*

Charles Investment Management, Inc., a fixed-income manager of U.S.-only portfolios, has provided significant excess returns for its clients through duration and sector management. The firm defines sectors as either government bonds or corporate bonds. Several of the manager's clients have asked the firm about the possibility of investing in international fixed-income markets. These clients mention the favorable performance of these markets, as exemplified by the "international fixed-income aggregate index" in the accompanying table. The clients are asking Charles to transfer the same management techniques that it has successfully applied in the U.S. market to international fixed-income markets.

ANNUALIZED RATES OF RETURN

Bond Index	One Year	Five Years
International fixed-income aggregate index, unhedged	1.0%	15.9%
International fixed-income aggregate index, hedged	6.5	7.2

a. Infer from the table the effect of changes in the U.S. dollar on international fixed-income returns for U.S. investors in the past one-year *and* five-year periods. [6 minutes]

b. Explain why the firm's techniques to generate excess returns through duration *and* sector management in U.S. fixed-income markets may not be transferrable to international fixed-income markets. [6 minutes]

21. *CFA Examination Level II*

On May 30, 1999, Janice Kerr is considering purchasing one of the following newly issued 10-year AAA corporate bonds shown in the following exhibit. Kerr notes that the yield curve is currently flat and assumes that the yield curve shifts in an instantaneous and parallel manner.

BOND CHARACTERISTICS

Description	Coupon	Price	Callable	Call Price
Sentinel due May 30, 2009	6.00%	100.00	Noncallable	Not applicable
Colina due May 30, 2009	6.20%	100.00	Currently callable	102.00

a. Contrast the effect on the price of *both* bonds if yields decline more than 100 basis points. (No calculation is required). [6 minutes]

b. State and explain under which *two* interest rate forecasts Kerr would prefer the Colina bond over the Sentinel bond. [6 minutes]

c. State the directional price change, if any, assuming interest rate volatility increases, for *each* of the following: [6 minutes]
   (1) The Sentinel bond
   (2) The Colina bond

Problems

1. Four years ago, your firm issued $1,000 par, 25-year bonds, with a 7 percent coupon rate and a 10 percent call premium.
   a. If these bonds are now called, what is the *approximate* yield to call for the investors who originally purchased them?
   b. If these bonds are now called, what is the *actual* yield to call for the investors who originally purchased them at par?
   c. If the current interest rate is 5 percent and the bonds were not callable, at what price would each bond sell?

2. Assume that you purchased an 8 percent, 20-year, $1,000 par, semiannual payment bond priced at $1,012.50 when it has 12 years remaining until maturity. Compute:
   a. Its promised yield to maturity
   b. Its yield to call if the bond is callable in three years with an 8 percent premium.

3. Calculate the duration of an 8 percent, $1,000 par bond that matures in three years if the bond's YTM is 10 percent and interest is paid semiannually.
   a. Calculate this bond's modified duration.
   b. Assuming the bond's YTM goes from 10 percent to 9.5 percent, calculate an estimate of the price change.

4. Two years ago, you acquired a 10-year zero coupon, $1,000 par value bond at a 12 percent YTM. Recently you sold this bond at an 8 percent YTM. Using semiannual compounding, compute the annualized horizon return for this investment.

5. A bond for the Webster Corporation has the following characteristics:

Maturity—12 years
Coupon—10%
Yield to maturity—9.50%
Macaulay duration—5.7 years
Convexity—48
Noncallable

a. Calculate the approximate price change for this bond using only its duration assuming its yield to maturity increased by 150 basis points. Discuss the impact of the calculation, including the convexity effect.

b. Calculate the approximate price change for this bond (using only its duration) if its yield to maturity declined by 300 basis points. Discuss (without calculations) what would happen to your estimate of the price change if this was a callable bond.

6. *CFA Examination Level I*

The following table shows selected data on a German government bond (payable in Deutschemarks) and a U.S. government bond. Identify the components of return and calculate the total return in U.S. dollars for both of these bonds for the year 1991. Show the calculations for *each* component. (Ignore interest on interest in view of the short time period.) [8 minutes]

| | | MARKET YIELD | | | EXCHANGE RATE (DM/$U.S.) | |
	Coupon	1/1/91	1/1/92	Modified Duration	1/1/91	1/1/92
German government bond	8.50%	8.50%	8.00%	7.0	1.55	1.50
U.S. government bond	8.00%	8.00%	6.75%	6.5	—	—

7. *CFA Examination Level I*

Philip Morris has issued bonds that pay semiannually with the following characteristics:

Coupon	Yield to Maturity	Maturity	Macaulay Duration
8%	8%	15 years	10 years

a. Calculate modified duration using the preceding information. [5 minutes]

b. Explain why modified duration is a better measure than maturity when calculating the bond's sensitivity to changes in interest rates. [5 minutes]

c. Identify the direction of change in modified duration if
   (1) the coupon of the bond were 4 percent, not 8 percent.
   (2) the maturity of the bond were 7 years, not 15 years. [5 minutes]

d. Define convexity and explain how modified duration *and* convexity are used to approximate the bond's percentage change in price, given a change in interest rates. [5 minutes]

8. *CFA Examination Level I*

You are a U.S. investor considering purchase of one of the following securities. Assume that the currency risk of the German government bond will be hedged, and the six-month discount on Deutschemark forward contracts is –0.75 percent versus the U.S. dollar.

Bond	Maturity	Coupon	Price
U.S. government	June 1, 2003	6.50%	100.00
German government	June 1, 2003	7.50%	100.00

Calculate the expected price change required in the German government bond that would result in the two bonds having equal total returns in U.S. dollars over a six-month horizon. [8 minutes]

9. *CFA Examination Level II*

The following are the average yields on U.S. Treasury bonds at two different points in time:

	YIELD TO MATURITY	
Term to Maturity	**January 15, 19XX**	**May 15, 19XX**
1 year	7.25%	8.05%
2 years	7.50%	7.90%
5 years	7.90%	7.70%
10 years	8.30%	7.45%
15 years	8.45%	7.30%
20 years	8.55%	7.20%
25 years	8.60%	7.10%

a. Assuming a pure expectations hypothesis, define a forward rate. Describe how you would calculate the forward rate for a three-year U.S. Treasury bond two years from May 15, 19XX, using the actual term structure provided. [3 minutes]

b. Discuss how *each* of the *three* major term structure hypotheses could explain the January 15, 19XX, term structures shown. [6 minutes]

c. Discuss what happened to the term structure over the time period and the effect of this change on U.S. Treasury bonds of 2 years *and* 10 years. [5 minutes]

d. Assume that you invest solely on the basis of yield spreads and, in January 19XX, acted upon the expectation that the yield spread between 1-year and 25-year U.S. Treasuries would return to a more typical spread of 170 basis points. Explain what you would have done on January 15, 19XX, and describe the result of this action based upon what happened between January 15, 19XX, and May 15, 19XX. [7 minutes]

10. *CFA Examination Level II*

a. Using the information in the following table, calculate the projected price change for Bond B if the yield to maturity for this bond falls by 75 basis points. [7 minutes]

b. Describe the shortcoming of analyzing Bond A strictly to call or to maturity. Explain an approach to remedy this shortcoming. [6 minutes]

MONTICELLO CORPORATION BOND INFORMATION		
	Bond A (Callable)	**Bond B** (Noncallable)
Maturity	2012	2012
Coupon	11.50%	7.25%
Current price	125.75	100.00
Yield to maturity	7.70%	7.25%
Modified duration to maturity	6.20	6.80
Convexity to maturity	0.50	0.60
Call date	2006	—
Call price	105	—
Yield to call	5.10%	—
Modified duration to call	3.10	—
Convexity to call	0.10	—

11. *CFA Examination Level II*

U.S. Treasuries represent a significant holding in Monticello's pension portfolio. You decide to analyze the yield curve for U.S. Treasury Notes.

a. Using the data in the following table, calculate the five-year spot and forward rates assuming annual compounding. Show calculations. [8 minutes]

U.S. TREASURY NOTE YIELD CURVE DATA

Years to Maturity	Par Coupon Yield to Maturity	Calculated Spot Rates	Calculated Forward Rates
1	5.00	5.00	5.00
2	5.20	5.21	5.42
3	6.00	6.05	7.75
4	7.00	7.16	10.56
5	7.00	❐	❐

b. Define and describe *each* of the following *three* concepts:

- Yield to maturity
- Spot rate
- Forward rate

Explain how these *three* concepts are related. [9 minutes]

c. You are considering the purchase of a zero coupon U.S. Treasury Note with four years to maturity. Based on the preceding yield curve analysis, calculate *both* the expected yield to maturity and the price for the security. Show calculations. [8 minutes]

12. *CFA Examination Level III*

Emily Maguire, manager of the actively managed nongovernment bond portion of PTC's pension portfolio, has received a fact sheet containing data on a new security offering. It will be a bond issued by a U.S. corporation but denominated in Australian dollars (A$), with both principal and interest payable in that currency.

The terms of the offering made in June 1992 are as follows:

- Issuer—Student Loan Marketing Association (SLMA—a U.S. government sponsored corporation)
- Rating—AAA
- Coupon Rate—8.5 percent payable quarterly
- Price—par
- Maturity—June 30, 1997 (noncallable)
- Principal and interest payable in Australian dollars (A$)

As an alternative, Maguire finds that five-year U.S. dollar pay notes issued by SLMA yield 6.75 percent.

She prepares an analysis directed at several specific questions, beginning with the following table of economic data for Australia and the United States.

Major Economic Indicators	UNITED STATES			AUSTRALIA		
	1990	1991	1992E	1990	1991	1992E
Real GNP (annual change)	1.1%	−0.5%	2.2%	1.6%	−0.5%	3.0%
Consumer expenditures (annual change)	0.9%	0.0%	1.0%	1.1%	−0.2%	2.0%
Inflation (annual change)	5.4%	4.2%	3.4%	7.3%	3.2%	3.9%
Long-bond yield (end of year)	8.1%	7.2%	7.0%	9.8%	10.0%	10.2%
Trade balance (U.S. $ billions)	−100	−83	−80	−30	−20	−75

Assuming that interest rates fall 100 basis points in both the U.S. and Australian markets over the next year, identify which of these two bonds will increase the most in value, and justify your answer. [7 minutes]

13. *CFA Examination Level II*

The following table shows yields to maturity on U.S Treasury securities as of January 1, 1993:

Term to Maturity	Yield to Maturity
1 year	3.50%
2 years	4.50%
3 years	5.00%
4 years	5.50%
5 years	6.00%
10 years	6.60%

a. Based on the data in the table, calculate the implied forward one-year rate of interest at January 1, 1996. [5 minutes]

b. Describe the conditions under which the calculated forward rate would be an unbiased estimate of the one-year spot rate of interest at January 1, 1996. [5 minutes]

Assume that one year earlier, at January 1, 1992, the prevailing term structure for U.S. Treasury securities was such that the implied forward one-year rate of interest at January 1, 1996, was significantly higher than the corresponding rate implied by the term structure at January 1, 1993.

c. On the basis of the pure expectations theory of the term structure, briefly discuss two factors that could account for such a decline in the implied forward rate. [8 minutes]

Multiple scenario forecasting frequently makes use of information from the term structure of interest rates.

d. Briefly describe how the information conveyed by this observed decrease in the implied forward rate for 1996 could be used in making a multiple scenario forecast. [5 minutes]

14. *CFA Examination Level III*

TMP is working with the officer responsible for the defined-benefit pension plan of a U.S. company. She has come to the firm for advice on what she calls "the key elements of non-U.S. dollar fixed-income investing."

The following information, based on TMP's assessment of the Italian market, has been developed to illustrate the process by which market and currency expectations are integrated.

ITALIAN GOVERNMENT SECURITIES DATA

Security	Modified Duration	Current Price	Current Yield to Maturity	Expected Yield to Maturity in Three Months
Bill	0.25	100.00	12.50%	12.50%
Note	6.00	100.00	10.00%	9.00%

LIRA/$(US) EXCHANGE RATE

Current Rate	Expected Rate in three Months
L1500/$1.00 (US)	L1526/$1.00 (US)

Based on the information provided, calculate the expected return (in U.S. dollars) on *each* security over the three-month period. [9 minutes]

15. *CFA Examination Level I*

    Bonds of Zello Corporation with a par value of $1,000 sell for $960, mature in five years, and have a 7 percent annual coupon rate paid semiannually.

    a. Calculate the
       (1) current yield;
       (2) yield to maturity (to the nearest whole percent, i.e., 3 percent, 4 percent, 5 percent, etc.); *and*
       (3) horizon yield (also called realized or total return) for an investor with a three-year holding period and a reinvestment rate of 6 percent over the period. At the end of three years, the 7 percent coupon bonds with two years remaining will sell to yield 7 percent.
       Show your work. [9 minutes]

    b. Cite *one* major shortcoming for *each* of the following fixed-income yield measures:
       (1) current yield;
       (2) yield to maturity; *and*
       (3) horizon yield (also called realized or total return). [6 minutes]

16. *CFA Examination Level I*

    During 1990, Disney issued $2.3 billion face value of zero coupon subordinated notes that resulted in gross proceeds of $965 million. The notes

    • mature in 2005;
    • can be exchanged for cash by the note holder at any time for the U.S. dollar equivalent of the current market value of 19.651 common shares of Euro Disney per $1,000 face value of notes; and
    • are callable at any time at their issuance price plus accrued interest.

    On March 11, 1993, Disney called the notes at a price of $483.50, which is equivalent to a yield to maturity of 6 percent. On the call date, Euro Disney common stock traded at a price of 86.80 French francs per share and the currency exchange rate for U.S. dollars ($US) to French francs (Ffr) was:

	$US/FFR	FFR/$US
Exchange rate	.1761	5.6786

    a. Calculate, as of the call date,
       (1) the price of a share of Euro Disney expressed in U.S. dollars; *and*
       (2) the exchange value (conversion value) of a $1,000 face value note in U.S. dollars. [6 minutes]

    b. On July 21, 1993, Disney issued, at par, $300 million of 100-year bonds with a coupon rate of 7.55 percent. The bonds are callable in 30 years at 103.02. From Disney's point of view, state *three* disadvantages of calling the zero coupon notes and effectively replacing part of that debt capital with the issue of 100-year bonds. [8 minutes]

17. *CFA Examination Level II*

    Table 1 shows the characteristics of two annual pay bonds from the same issuer with the same priority in the event of default, and Table 2 displays spot interest rates. Neither bond's price is consistent with the spot rates.

    Using the information in Tables 1 and 2, recommend *either* Bond A *or* Bond B for purchase. Justify your choice. [10 minutes]

TABLE 1 ▶ *BOND CHARACTERISTICS*

	Bond A	Bond B
Coupons	Annual	Annual
Maturity	3 years	3 years
Coupon rate	10%	6%
Yield to maturity	10.65%	10.75%
Price	98.40	88.34

TABLE 2 ▶ SPOT INTEREST RATES

Term	Spot Rates (Zero Coupon)
1 year	5%
2 year	8%
3 year	11%

18. *CFA Examination Level II*
    You ran a regression of the yield of KC Company's 10-year bond on the 10-year U.S. Treasury benchmark's yield using month-end data for the past year. You found the following result:

$$\text{Yield}_{KC} = 0.54 + 1.22\,\text{Yield}_{Treasury}$$

where Yield_{KC} is the yield on the KC bond and $\text{Yield}_{Treasury}$ is the yield on the U.S. Treasury bond.
    The modified duration on the 10-year U.S. Treasury is 7.0 years, and modified duration on the KC bond is 6.93 years.
    a. Calculate the percentage change in the price of the 10-year U.S. Treasury, assuming a 50-basis-point change in the yield on the 10-year U.S. Treasury. [3 minutes]
    b. Calculate the percentage change in the price of the KC bond, using the regression equation, assuming a 50-basis-point change in the yield on the 10-year U.S. Treasury. [6 minutes]

19. *CFA Examination Level II*
    Table 3 shows prices as a function of yields for four tranches of a collateralized mortgage obligation (CMO).

TABLE 3 ▶ PRICES FOR FOUR CMO TRANCHES AT SELECTED YIELDS

| CMO Tranche | YIELD (%) | | | | |
	6.0	6.5	7.0	7.5	8.0
T-1	111.5	105.5	100.0	95.0	90.5
T-2	107.5	104.0	100.0	95.5	90.5
T-3	112.0	105.5	100.0	95.5	92.0
T-4	104.5	102.0	100.0	98.5	97.5

    a. Calculate the effective duration of Tranche T-3. Assume that the relevant current yield is 7.0 percent. Show your work. [5 minutes]
    b. Identify the tranche with the negative convexity. Calculate the effective convexity of this tranche. Show your work. [5 minutes]
    Table 4 shows the option-adjusted spread for four different mortgage pass-through securities.

TABLE 4 ▶ MORTGAGE PASS-THROUGH OPTION-ADJUSTED SPREADS (ASSUMING INTEREST RATE VOLATILITY OF 8 PERCENT)

Security	Option-Adjusted Spread (in Basis Points)
A	43
B	70
C	89
D	99

c. Identify which of the patterns of option-adjusted spreads shown in Table 5 is plausible if the assumed interest rate volatility is 12 percent rather than the 8 percent assumed in Table 4. Justify your choice. [5 minutes]

TABLE 5 → *MORTGAGE PASS-THROUGH OPTION-ADJUSTED SPREADS (ASSUMING INTEREST RATE VOLATILITY OF 12 PERCENT)*

Security	OPTION-ADJUSTED SPREAD (IN BASIS POINTS)	
	Pattern A	Pattern B
A	–13	103
B	20	120
C	49	129
D	69	129

20. *CFA Examination Level II*

Patrick Wall is considering the purchase of one of the two bonds described in the following table. Wall realizes his decision will depend primarily on effective duration, and he believes that interest rates will decline by 50 basis points at all maturities over the next six months.

BOND DESCRIPTIONS		
Characteristic	CIC	PTR
Market price	101.75	101.75
Maturity date	June 1, 2008	June 1, 2008
Call date	Noncallable	June 1, 2003
Annual coupon	6.25%	7.35%
Interest payment	Semiannual	Semiannual
Effective duration	7.35	5.40
Yield to maturity	6.02%	7.10%
Credit rating	A	A

a. Calculate the percentage price change forecasted by effective duration for *both* the CIC and PTR bonds if interest rates decline by 50 basis points over the next six months. Show your work. [6 minutes]

b. Calculate the six-month horizon return (in percent) for *each* bond, if the actual CIC bond price equals 105.55 and the actual PTR bond price equals 104.15 at the end of six months. Assume you purchased the bonds to settle on June 1, 1998. Show your work. [6 minutes]

Wall is surprised by the fact that although interest rates fell by 50 basis points, the actual price change for the CIC bond was greater than the price change forecasted by effective duration, whereas the actual price change for the PTR bond was less than the price change forecasted by effective duration.

c. Explain why the actual price change would be greater for the CIC bond and the actual price change would be less for the PTR bond. [6 minutes]

21. *CFA Examination Level II*

a. Discuss how *each* of the following theories for the term structure of interest rates could explain an upward slope of the yield curve:

(1) Pure expectations (unbiased)

(2) Uncertainty and term premiums (liquidity preference)

(3) Market segmentation [9 minutes]

The following are the current coupon yields to maturity and spot rates of interest for six U.S. Treasury securities. Assume all securities pay interest annually.

YIELDS TO MATURITY AND SPOT RATES OF INTEREST

Term to Maturity	Current Coupon Yield to Maturity	Spot Rate of Interest
1-year Treasury	5.25%	5.25%
2-year Treasury	5.75	5.79
3-year Treasury	6.15	6.19
5-year Treasury	6.45	6.51
10-year Treasury	6.95	7.10
30-year Treasury	7.25	7.67

b. Compute, under the pure expectations theory, the two-year implied forward rate three years from now, given the information provided in preceding table. State the assumption underlying the calculation of the implied forward rate. [6 minutes]

References

Fabozzi, Frank J. *Fixed-Income Mathematics.* Chicago: Probus Publishing, 1988.

Fabozzi, Frank J. *Fixed-Income Analysis for the Chartered Financial Analyst Program.* New Hope, Penn.: Frank J. Fabozzi Associates, 2000.

Fabozzi, Frank J., ed. *The Handbook of Fixed-Income Securities,* 6th ed. New York: McGraw-Hill, 2001.

Fama, Eugene F. "Forward Rates as Predictors of Future Spot Rates." *Journal of Financial Economics* 3, no. 4 (October 1976).

Sundaresan, Suresh. *Fixed-Income Markets and Their Derivatives,* 2d ed. Cincinnati, Ohio: South-Western College Publishing, 2001.

Tuckman, Bruce. *Fixed-Income Securities.* 2nd ed. New York: John Wiley & Sons, 2002.

Van Horne, James C. *Financial Market Rates and Flows,* 5th ed. Englewood Cliffs, N.J.: Prentice-Hall, 1998.

APPENDIX
Chapter 19

EXHIBIT 19A.1

CALCULATION OF DURATION AND CONVEXITY FOR AN 8 PERCENT FIVE-YEAR BOND SELLING TO YIELD 6 PERCENT

Period	Cash Flow	Discount Factor	PV	PV × t	PV × t × (t + 1)
1	40.00	0.9709	38.83	38.83	77.67
2	40.00	0.9426	37.70	75.41	226.22
3	40.00	0.9151	36.61	109.82	439.27
4	40.00	0.8885	35.54	142.16	710.79
5	40.00	0.8626	34.50	172.52	1,035.13
6	40.00	0.8375	33.50	201.00	1,406.97
7	40.00	0.8131	32.52	227.67	1,821.32
8	40.00	0.7894	31.58	252.61	2,273.50
9	40.00	0.7664	30.66	275.91	2,759.10
10	1,040.00	0.7441	773.86	7,738.58	85,124.34
		Total	1,085.30	9,234.50	95,874.32

$$\text{Macaulay Duration} = \frac{9,234.50}{2 \times 1,085.30} = 4.25$$

$$\text{Modified Duration} = \frac{4.25}{1.03} = 4.13$$

$$\text{Convexity} = \frac{95,874.32}{(1.03)^2 \times 2^2 \times 1,085.30} = 20.82$$

chapter 20 Bond Portfolio Management Strategies

After you read this chapter, you should be able to answer the following questions:

➤ What are the four major alternative bond portfolio management strategies available?
➤ What are the two passive portfolio management strategies available?
➤ What are the five alternative active bond portfolio management strategies available?
➤ What is meant by core-plus bond management and what are some plus strategies?
➤ What is meant by matched-funding techniques and what are the four specific strategies?
➤ What are the major contingent procedure strategies that are referred to as structured active management strategies?
➤ What are the implications of capital market theory for those involved in bond portfolio management?
➤ What is the evidence on the efficient market hypothesis as it relates to bond markets?
➤ What are the implications of efficient market studies for bond portfolio managers?

In this chapter, we shift attention from bond valuation and analysis to the equally important bond portfolio management strategies. Initially, we discuss the five alternative bond portfolio management strategies: passive management, active management, core-plus bond management, matched-funding techniques, and structured active management. Next, we consider the implications of capital market theory and bond market efficiency on bond portfolio management.

ALTERNATIVE BOND PORTFOLIO STRATEGIES

Bond portfolio management strategies can be divided into five groups:[1]

1. Passive portfolio strategies
   a. Buy and hold
   b. Indexing
2. Active management strategies
   a. Interest rate anticipation
   b. Valuation analysis
   c. Credit analysis
   d. Yield spread analysis
   e. Bond swaps
3. Core-plus management strategy

---

[1]This breakdown benefited from the discussion in Martin L. Leibowitz, "The Dedicated Bond Portfolio in Pension Funds—Part I: Motivations and Basics," *Financial Analysts Journal* 42, no 1 (January–February 1986): 61–75.

   4. Matched-funding techniques
      a. Dedicated portfolio, exact cash match
      b. Dedicated portfolio, optimal cash match and reinvestment
      c. Classical ("pure") immunization
      d. Horizon matching
   5. Contingent procedures (structured active management)
      a. Contingent immunization
      b. Other contingent procedures

We discuss each of these alternatives because they are all viable for certain portfolios with different needs and risk profiles. Prior to the 1960s, only the first two groups were available, and most bond portfolios were managed on the basis of buy and hold. The early 1970s saw growing interest in alternative active bond portfolio management strategies, while the late 1970s and early 1980s were characterized by record-breaking inflation and interest rates as well as extremely volatile rates of return in bond markets. This led to the introduction of many new financial instruments in response to the increase in return volatility. Since the mid-1980s, matched-funding techniques or contingent portfolio management techniques have been developed to meet the emerging needs of institutional clients.

Passive Management Strategies

Two specific passive portfolio management strategies exist. First is a **buy-and-hold strategy** in which a manager selects a portfolio of bonds based on the objectives and constraints of the client with the intent of holding these bonds to maturity. In the second passive strategy—**indexing**—the objective is to construct a portfolio of bonds that will equal the performance of a specified bond index, such as the Lehman Brothers Corporate/Government Bond Index.

Buy-and-Hold Strategy   The simplest portfolio management strategy is to buy and hold. Obviously not unique to bond investors, it involves finding issues with desired quality, coupon levels, term to maturity, and important indenture provisions, such as call features. Buy-and-hold investors do not consider active trading to achieve attractive returns but, rather, look for vehicles whose maturities (or duration) approximate their stipulated investment horizon to reduce price and reinvestment risk. Many successful bond investors and institutional portfolio managers follow a modified buy-and-hold strategy wherein an investment is made in an issue with the intention of holding it until the end of the investment horizon. However, they still actively look for opportunities to trade into more desirable positions.[2]

   Whether the investor follows a strict or modified buy-and-hold approach, the key ingredient is finding investment vehicles that possess attractive maturity and yield features. The strategy does not restrict the investor to accept whatever the market has to offer, nor does it imply that selectivity is unimportant. Attractive high-yielding issues with desirable features and quality standards are actively sought. For example, these investors recognize that agency issues generally provide incremental returns relative to Treasuries with a little sacrifice in quality, that utilities provide higher returns than comparable rated industrials, and that various call features affect the risk and realized yield of an issue. Thus, successful buy-and-hold investors use their knowledge of markets and issue characteristics to seek out attractive realized yields. Aggressive buy-and-hold investors also incorporate timing considerations by using their knowledge of market rates and expectations.

Indexing Strategy   As discussed in the chapter on efficient capital markets, numerous empirical studies have demonstrated that the majority of money managers have not been able to

---

[2]Obviously, if the strategy becomes too modified, it becomes one of the active strategies.

match the risk-return performance of common stock or bond indexes. As a result, many clients have opted to index some part of their bond portfolios, which means that the portfolio manager builds a portfolio that will match the performance of a selected bond market index, such as a Lehman Brothers Index, Merrill Lynch Index, or Salomon Brothers Index. In such a case, the portfolio manager is judged not on the basis of risk and return compared to an index but by how closely the portfolio *tracks* the designated index. Specifically, the analysis of performance involves examining the **tracking error**, which equals the difference between the rate of return for the portfolio and the rate of return for the bond market index. For example, if the portfolio experienced an annual rate of return of 8.2 percent during a period when the index had a rate of return of 8.3 percent, the tracking error would be minus 10 basis points (8.20 − 8.30 = −0.10).

When initiating an indexing strategy, the selection of the appropriate market index is very important because it directly determines the client's risk-return results. As such, it is necessary to be very familiar with all the characteristics of the index.[3] For bond indexes, it also is important to be aware of how the aggregate bond market and the indexes change over time.[4] Reilly and Wright demonstrated that the market has experienced significant changes in composition, maturity, and duration since 1975. After the appropriate bond index is selected, several techniques are available to accomplish the actual tracking.[5]

Active Management Strategies[6]

Five active management strategies are available, including interest rate anticipation, which involves economic forecasting, as well as valuation analysis and credit analysis, which require detailed bond and company analysis. Alternatively, yield spread analysis and bond swaps, which require economic and market analysis, are also available.

Interest Rate Anticipation **Interest rate anticipation** is perhaps the riskiest active management strategy because it involves relying on uncertain forecasts of future interest rates. The idea is to preserve capital when an increase in interest rates is anticipated and achieve attractive capital gains when interest rates are expected to decline. Such objectives usually are attained by altering the maturity (duration) structure of the portfolio (i.e., reducing portfolio duration when

---

[3]Two articles that discuss how the characteristics of indexes affect their performance in different interest rate environments are Chris P. Dialynas, "The Active Decisions in the Selection of Passive Management and Performance Bogeys"; and Kenneth E. Volpert, "Managing Indexed and Enhanced Indexed Bond Portfolios." Both are in *The Handbook of Fixed-Income Securities,* 6th ed., ed. Frank J. Fabozzi (New York: McGraw-Hill, 2001). For an analysis of a new comprehensive Treasury bond index, see Frank K. Reilly and David J. Wright, "Introducing a Comprehensive U.S. Treasury Bond Market Benchmark," in *Yield Curve Dynamics,* ed. Ronald J. Ryan (Chicago: Glenlake Publishing, 1997).

[4]An article that describes the major bond market indexes, analyzes the relationship among them, and examines how the aggregate bond market has changed is Frank K. Reilly and David J. Wright, "Bond Market Indexes," in the *Handbook of Fixed-Income Securities,* 6th ed., ed. Frank J. Fabozzi (New York: McGraw-Hill, 2001). A similar study for high-yield indexes is Frank K. Reilly and David J. Wright, "An Analysis of High-Yield Bond Benchmarks," *Journal of Fixed Income* 3, no. 4 (March 1994): 6–25.

[5]For a detailed discussion of the alternative tracking techniques available, see Sharmin Mossavar-Rahmani, *Bond Index Funds* (Chicago: Probus Publishing, 1991); and Frank J. Fabozzi, *Bond Markets, Analysis and Strategies,* 3d ed. (Upper Saddle River, N.J.: Prentice-Hall, 1996), Chapter 18.

[6]For further discussion on this topic, see H. Gifford Fong, "Bond Management: Past, Current and Future," *The Handbook of Fixed-Income Securities,* 6th ed. edited Frank J. Fabozzi; Thomas Vock, "Managing Global Fixed-Income Portfolios," in *Global Portfolio Management,* ed. Jan R. Squires (Charlottesville, Va.: Association for Investment Management and Research, 1996); and Jack Malvey, "Global Corporate Bond Portfolio Management," in *The Handbook of Fixed-Income Securities,* 6th ed. For a set of readings, see *Global Bond Management,* ed. Jan R. Squires (Charlottesville, Va.: Association for Investment Management and Research, 1997); and Dwight Churchill, ed., *Fixed-Income Management: Techniques and Practices* (Charlottesville, Va.: Association for Investment Management and Research, 1994).

interest rates are expected to increase and increasing the portfolio duration when a decline in yields is anticipated). Thus, the risk in such portfolio restructuring is largely a function of these duration (maturity) alterations. When maturities are shortened to preserve capital, substantial income could be sacrificed and the opportunity for capital gains could be lost if interest rates decline rather than rise. Similarly, the portfolio shifts prompted by anticipation of a decline in rates are very risky. Specifically, if we assume that we are at a peak in interest rates, it is likely that the yield curve is downward sloping, which means that bond coupons will decline with maturity. Therefore, the investor is sacrificing current income by shifting from high-coupon short bonds to longer-duration bonds. At the same time, the portfolio is purposely exposed to greater price volatility that could work against the portfolio if an unexpected increase in yields occurs. Note that the portfolio adjustments prompted by anticipation of an increase in rates involve less risk of an absolute capital loss. When you reduce the maturity, the worst that can happen is that interest income is reduced and/or capital gains are forgone (opportunity cost).

Once future (expected) interest rates have been determined, the procedure relies largely on technical matters. Assume that you expect an increase in interest rates and want to preserve your capital by reducing the duration of your portfolio. A popular choice would be high-yielding, short-term obligations, such as Treasury bills. Although your primary concern is to preserve capital, you would nevertheless look for the best return possible given the maturity constraint. Liquidity also is important because, after interest rates increase, yields may experience a period of stability before they decline, and you would want to shift positions quickly to benefit from the higher income and/or capital gains.

One way to shorten maturities is to use a *cushion bond*—a high-yielding, long-term obligation that carries a coupon substantially above the current market rate and that, due to its current call feature and call price, has a market price lower than what it should be given current market yields. As a result, its yield is higher than normal. An example would be a 10-year bond with a 12 percent coupon, currently callable at 110. If current market rates are 8 percent, this bond (if it were noncallable) would have a price of about 127; because of its call price, however, it will stay close to 110, and its yield will be about 10 percent rather than 8 percent. Bond portfolio managers look for cushion bonds when they expect a modest increase in rates because such issues provide attractive current income *and* protection against capital loss. Because these bonds are trading at an abnormally high yield, market rates would have to rise to that abnormal level before their price would react.

The portfolio manager who anticipates higher interest rates, therefore, has two simple strategies available: shorten the duration of the portfolio and/or look for an attractive cushion bond.[7] In either case, you would want very liquid issues.

A totally different posture is assumed by investors who anticipate a decline in interest rates. The significant risk involved in restructuring a portfolio to take advantage of a decline in interest rates is balanced by the potential for substantial capital gains and holding period returns. When you expect lower interest rates, you will recall that you should increase the duration of the portfolio because the longer the duration, the greater the positive price volatility. Also, liquidity is important because you want to be able to close out the position quickly when the drop in rates has been completed.

Notably, because interest rate sensitivity is critical, it is important to recall that the higher the quality of an obligation, the more sensitive it is to interest rate changes. Therefore, high-grade securities should be used, such as Treasuries, agencies, or corporates rated AAA through BAA. Finally, you want to concentrate on noncallable issues or those with strong call protection

---

[7]For an extended discussion of cushion bonds, see Sidney Homer and Martin L. Leibowitz, *Inside the Yield Book* (Englewood Cliffs, N.J.: Prentice-Hall, 1972), Chapter 5.

because of the substantial call risk discussed in Chapter 19 in connection with the analysis of duration and convexity.

Valuation Analysis With **valuation analysis**, the portfolio manager attempts to select bonds based on their intrinsic value, which is determined based on their characteristics and the average value of these characteristics in the marketplace. As an example, a bond's rating will dictate a certain spread relative to comparable Treasury bonds: long maturity might be worth an added 60 basis points relative to short maturity (i.e., the maturity spread); a given deferred call feature might require a higher or lower yield; a specified sinking fund would likewise mean higher or lower required yields. Given all the characteristics of the bond and the normal cost of the characteristics in terms of yield, you would determine the bond's required yield and, therefore, its implied intrinsic value. After you have done this for a number of bonds, you would compare these derived bond values to the prevailing market prices to determine which bonds are undervalued or overvalued. Based on your confidence in the characteristic costs, you would buy the undervalued issues and ignore or sell the overvalued issues.

Success in valuation analysis is based on understanding the characteristics that are important in valuation and being able to accurately *estimate* the yield cost of these characteristics over time.

Credit Analysis A **credit analysis** strategy involves detailed analysis of the bond issuer to determine expected changes in its default risk. This involves attempting to project changes in the credit ratings assigned to bonds by the three rating agencies discussed in Chapter 18.[8] These rating changes are affected by internal changes in the entity (e.g., changes in important financial ratios) and by changes in the external environment (i.e., changes in the firm's industry and the economy). During periods of strong economic expansion, even financially weak firms may survive and prosper. In contrast, during severe economic contractions, normally strong firms may find it very difficult to meet financial obligations. Therefore, historically there has been a strong cyclical pattern to rating changes: typically, downgradings increase during economic contractions and decline during economic expansions.

To use credit analysis as a portfolio management strategy, it is necessary to project rating changes prior to the announcement by the rating agencies. As the subsequent discussion on bond market efficiency notes, the market adjusts rather quickly to bond rating changes—especially downgradings. Therefore, you want to acquire bond issues expected to experience upgradings and sell or avoid those bond issues expected to be downgraded.

Credit Analysis of High-Yield (Junk) Bonds One of the most obvious opportunities for credit analysis is the analysis of high-yield (junk) bonds. As demonstrated by several studies, the yield differential between junk bonds that are rated below BBB and Treasury securities ranges from about 200 basis points to over 1,000 basis points. Notably, these yield differentials vary substantially over time as shown by a time-series plot in Exhibit 20.1. Specifically, the average yield spread ranged from a low of less than 300 basis points in 1985 and 1997 to a high of over 900 basis points during early 1991 and late 2001.

---

[8]For a discussion of changes in the aggregate financial risk of U.S. corporations and the opportunities this has created, see Frank K. Reilly, "The Growing Importance of Credit Analysis," working paper, University of Notre Dame (April 2002). For a presentation on credit analysis that emphasizes changes in credit ratings, see Jane Tripp Howe, "Credit Analysis for Corporate Bonds," in *The Handbook of Fixed-Income Securities, 6th ed.* For a set of readings on global credit analysis, see ed. Jan R. Squires, *Credit Analysis Around the World* (Charlottesville, Va.: Association for Investment Management and Research, 1998).

EXHIBIT 20.1 *YIELD SPREAD HISTORY, MERRILL LYNCH HIGH-YIELD MASTER INDEX VERSUS 10-YEAR TREASURY: MONTHLY, 1985–2001*

Source: Merrill Lynch & Co. Martin S. Fridson, Chief High-Yield Strategist, Merrill Lynch, "This Year in High Yield—2001." Reprinted by permission. Copyright © 2002 Merrill Lynch, Pierce, Fenner & Smith Incorporated.

Although the spreads have changed, a study indicated that the average credit quality of high-yield bonds also changed over time.[9] As an example, interest coverage tends to fluctuate with the business cycle. In addition, the credit quality of bonds *within* rating categories tends to change over the business cycle.[10]

These changes in credit quality will make credit analysis of high-yield bonds not only more important but also more difficult. This means that bond analysts–portfolio managers need to engage in detailed credit analysis to select bonds that will survive. Given the spread in promised yields, if a portfolio manager can—through rigorous credit analysis—avoid bonds with a high probability of default, high-yield bonds will provide substantial rates of return for the investor.[11]

In summary, substantial rates of return can be derived by investing in high-yield bonds if you do the credit analysis required to avoid defaults, which occur with these bonds at substantially higher rates than the overall bond market. Several recent studies have shown that the average cumulative

---

[9]Barrie A. Wigmore, "The Decline in Credit Quality of New Issue Junk Bonds," *Financial Analysts Journal* 46, no. 5 (September–October 1990): 53–62.

[10]These changes are demonstrated in Reilly, "The Growing Importance of Credit Analysis."

[11]For a discussion regarding the analysis of high-risk bonds, see Jane Tripp Howe, "Credit Considerations in Evaluating High-Yield Debt"; Jane Tripp Howe, "Investing in Chapter 11 and other Distressed Companies"; and Allen A. Vine, "High-Yield Analysis of Emerging Markets Debt." All of these are in *The Handbook of Fixed-Income Securities,* 6th ed.

default rate for high-yield bonds after 10 years is between 30 percent and 35 percent. For example, of the high-yield bonds sold in 1988, about 33 percent had defaulted by 1998.[12]

Exhibit 20.2 lists the results for a study that considers the full spectrum of bonds. It shows substantial differences in cumulative default rates for bonds with different ratings for the periods 5 and 10 years after issue. Over 10 years—the holding period that is widely discussed—the default rate for BBB investment-grade bonds is only 4.66 percent, but the default rate increases to over 17 percent for BB-rated, to almost 33 percent for B-rated bonds, and to over 52 percent for CCC-rated bonds.

These default rates do not mean that investors should avoid high-yield bonds, but they do indicate that extensive credit analysis is a critical component for success within this sector. Given the substantial yield spreads over Treasuries, you may experience high returns *if* you can avoid owning bonds that default or are downgraded. The route to avoiding such bond issues is through rigorous, enlightened credit analysis.

Investing in Defaulted Debt   Beyond high-yield bonds that have high credit risk and high default rates, a new set of investment opportunities has evolved—investing in defaulted debt. While this sector requires an understanding of legal procedures surrounding bankruptcy as well as economic analysis, the returns have generally been consistent with the risk—that is, between high-yield debt and common stock.[13]

Credit Analysis Models   The credit analysis of high-yield bonds can use a statistical model or basic fundamental analysis that recognizes some of the unique characteristics of these bonds. The Altman-Nammacher book suggests that a modified *Z-score model* used to predict bankruptcy can also be used to predict default for these high-yield bonds or as a gauge of changes in credit quality. The Z-score model combines traditional financial measures with a multivariate technique known as *multiple discriminant analysis* to derive a set of weights for the specified variables. The result is an overall credit score (zeta score) for each firm.[14] The model is of the form

$$\text{Zeta} = a_0 + a_1 X_1 + a_2 X_2 + a_3 X_3 + \ldots + a_n X_n$$

where:

> **Zeta = the overall credit score**
> $X_1 \ldots X_n$ **= the explanatory variables (ratios and market measures)**
> $a_0 \ldots a_n$ **= the weightings or coefficients**

---

[12]Although the details of the analysis differ, the overall results for cumulative defaults are quite consistent. See Edward I. Altman, "Measuring Corporate Bond Mortality and Performance," *Journal of Finance* 44, no. 4 (September 1989): 909–922; and Paul Asquith, David W. Mullins, Jr., and Eric D. Wolff, "Original-Issue High-Yield Bonds: Aging Analysis of Defaults, Exchanges, and Calls," *Journal of Finance* 44, no. 4 (September 1989): 929–952. Another review of these studies is Edward I. Altman, "Revisiting the High-Yield Bond Market," *Financial Management* 21, no 2 (Summer 1992): 78–92. For a recent update, see Martin S. Fridson. "This Year in High Yield—2001," *Extra Credit* (New York: Merrill Lynch, January–February 2002). For a recent analysis of the market performance of high-yield bonds, see Frank K. Reilly and David J. Wright, "The Unique Risk-Return Characteristics of High-Yield Bonds," *Journal of Fixed Income* 11, no. 2 (September 2001): 65–82.

[13]For a discussion of the legal and economic analysis, see Edward I. Altman, *Corporate Financial Distress and Bankruptcy,* 2d ed. (New York: John Wiley & Sons, 1993). For an analysis of the investment performance, see Edward I. Altman, "Defaulted Bonds: Demand, Supply, and Performance, 1987–1992," *Financial Analysts Journal* 49, no 3 (May–June 1993): 55–60; Edward I. Altman and Babe E. Simon, "The Investment Performance of Defaulted Bonds for 2000 and 1987–2000," New York University, Salomon Center (February 2001); David J. Ward and Gary L. Griepentrog, "Risk and Return in Defaulted Bonds," *Financial Analysts Journal* 49, no. 3 (May–June 1993): 61–65; and Frank K. Reilly, David J. Wright, and Edward I. Altman, "Including Defaulted Bonds in the Capital Markets Asset Spectrum," *Journal of Fixed Income* 8, no. 3 (December 1998): 33–48.

[14]Edward I. Altman and Scott A. Nammacher, *Investing in Junk Bonds* (New York: John Wiley & Sons, 1987).

EXHIBIT 20.2 | *AVERAGE CUMULATIVE DEFAULT RATES FOR CORPORATE BONDS: 1978–2001*

	YEARS SINCE ISSUE		
RATINGS	5	10	15
AAA	0.10%	0.52%	0.52%
AA	0.26	0.83	1.31
A	0.57	1.58	2.32
BBB	2.16	4.66	6.64
BB	10.59	17.40	19.52
B	25.06	32.61	35.76
CCC	46.87	52.22	54.38

Source: *Rating Performance 2002* (New York: Standard & Poor's, February 2002): 8. Reprinted with permission.

The final model used in this analysis included the following seven financial measures:

X_1 = profitability: earnings before interest and taxes (EBIT)/total assets (TA)

X_2 = stability of profitability measure: the standard error of estimate of EBIT/TA (normalized for 10 years)

X_3 = debt service capabilities (interest coverage): EBIT/interest charges

X_4 = cumulative profitability: retained earnings/total assets

X_5 = liquidity: current assets/current liabilities

X_6 = capitalization levels: market value of equity/total capital (five-year average)

X_7 = size: total tangible assets (normalized)

The weightings, or coefficients, for the variables were not reported.[15]

In contrast to using a model that provides a composite credit score, most analysts simply adapt their basic corporate bond analysis techniques *to the unique needs of high-yield bonds,* which have characteristics of common stock.[16] Howe claims that the analysis of high-yield bonds is the same as with any bond except that the following five areas of analysis should be expanded.[17]

1. What is the firm's *competitive position* in terms of cost and pricing? This can be critical to a small firm.
2. What is the firm's *cash flow* relative to cash requirements for interest, research, growth, and periods of economic decline? Also, what is the firm's *borrowing capacity* that can serve as a safety net and provide flexibility?
3. What is the *liquidity value of the firm's assets?* Are these assets available for liquidation (are there any claims against them)? In many cases, asset sales are a critical part of the strategy for a leveraged buyout.

---

[15]The following studies have examined the aggregate default rate for high-yield bonds: Jon G. Jonsson and Martin S. Fridson, "Forecasting Default Rates on High-Yield Bonds," *Journal of Fixed Income* 6, no. 1 (June 1996): 69–77; Jean Helwege and Paul Kleiman, "Understanding Aggregate Default Rates of High-Yield Bonds," *Journal of Fixed Income* 7, no. 1 (June 1997): 55–61; and Martin S. Fridson, M. Christopher Garman, and Sheng Wu, "Real Interest Rates and the Default Rate on High-Yield Bonds," *Journal of Fixed Income* 7, no. 2 (September 1997): 29–34.

[16]For an analysis that shows the relationship of high-yield bonds to investment-grade bonds and common stock, see Frank K. Reilly and David J. Wright, "An Analysis of High-Yield Bond Benchmarks," *Journal of Fixed Income* 3, no. 4 (March 1994): 6–25. An updated version is in Theodore M. Barnhill, Jr., William F. Maxwell, and Mark R. Shenkman, eds., *High-Yield Bonds* (New York: McGraw-Hill, 1999).

[17]Jane Tripp Howe, "Credit Considerations in Evaluating High-Yield Bonds," in *The Handbook of Fixed-Income Securities,* 6th ed.

4. How good is the *total management team?* Is the management team committed to and capable of operating in the high-risk environment of this firm?
5. What is the firm's *financial leverage* on an absolute basis and on a market-adjusted basis (using market value of equity and debt)?

Hynes suggests that the following areas require additional analysis as part of the process of evaluating cash flows when analyzing a leveraged buyout (which typically involves the issuance of high-yield debt).[18]

➤ Inherent business risk
➤ Earnings growth potential
➤ Asset redevelopment potential
➤ Refinancing capability

In addition to the potentially higher financial risk, an increase in business risk may exist if the firm sells off some operations that have favorable risk characteristics with the remaining operations—that is, business risk would increase if the firm sells a division or a company that has low correlation of earnings with other units of the firm. Further, a change in management operating philosophy could have a negative impact on operating earnings. The managements of leveraged buyout (LBO) firms are known for making optimistic growth estimates related to sales and earnings, so the analyst should evaluate these estimates very critically. Asset divestiture plans often are a major element of an LBO because they provide necessary capital that is used to reduce the substantial debt taken on as part of the buyout. Therefore, it is important to examine the liquidity of the assets, their estimated selling values, and the timing of these programs. You must ascertain whether the estimated sales prices for the assets are reasonable and whether the timing is realistic. In contrast, if the divestiture program is successful wherein the prices received are above normal expectations and the assets are sold ahead of schedule, this can be grounds for upgrading the debt. Finally, it is necessary to constantly monitor the firm's refinancing flexibility. Specifically, what refinancing will be necessary, what does the schedule look like, and will the capital suppliers be receptive to the refinancing?[19]

The substantial increase in high-yield bonds issued and outstanding has been matched by an increase in research and credit analysis. The credit analysis of these bonds is similar to that of investment-grade bonds with an emphasis on the following factors: (1) *the use of cash flows* compared to debt obligations under very conservative assumptions; (2) the detailed analysis of *potential asset sales,* including a conservative estimate of sales prices, the asset's true liquidity, the availability of the assets, and a consideration of the timing of the sales; and (3) the recognition that high-yield bonds have many characteristics of common stock, which means that many equity analysis techniques are appropriate. An in-depth analysis of high-yield bonds is critical because of the number of issues, the wide diversity of quality within the high-yield bond universe, and the growing complexity of these issues.

High-Yield Bond Research Because of the growth of high-yield bonds, several investment houses have developed specialized high-yield groups that examine high-yield bond issues and monitor high-yield bond spreads.

---

[18]Joseph Hynes, "Key Risk Factors for LBOs," *Speculative Grade Debt Credit Review* (New York: Standard & Poor's Corporation, June 15, 1987).

[19]For a set of presentations on credit analysis including distressed securities, see Ashwinpaul C. Sondhi, ed., *Credit Analysis of Nontraditional Debt Securities* (Charlottesville, Va.: Association for Investment Management and Research, 1995); and Jan R. Squires, ed., *Credit Analysis Around the World* (Charlottesville, Va.: Association of Investment Management and Research, 1998).

Merrill Lynch's monthly publication, *High Yield,* provides an overview of the market and reviews several individual industries and firms within these main industries (e.g., retail, steel, building products, and telecommunications). It also contains reports of research done by the firm regarding the high-yield market. As noted earlier, the January/February issue of *High Yield* always contains a detailed annual review of the market with extensive historical tables.

Merrill Lynch's weekly publication, *This Week in High Yield,* discusses current events in the high-yield market. This includes weekly yields and yield spreads for the various sectors of the market and news highlights for specific companies and issues.

High-Yield Market Update, a Salomon Brothers Smith Barney monthly publication, presents monthly and cumulative long-term returns for its high-yield indexes (long-term and intermediate-term corporates, long-term utilities), as well as spreads between rating categories relative to appropriate Treasuries. The publication also features commentary on timely topics within the high-yield market.

The high-yield research group at First Boston publishes *Monthly Market Review,* which contains an extensive performance review of the HY (high-yield) bond market that examines returns by sectors and industries as well as considering yield spreads and changing volatility for these bonds. First Boston also publishes an annual *High Yield Handbook,* which reviews annual events and considers every aspect of risk, return, and correlation of high-yield bonds with other asset classes. There also is a very helpful listing of new issues, retirements, and defaults.

Lehman Brothers publishes a weekly review, *High-Yield Portfolio Advisor,* which analyzes the performance of the firm's high-yield bond indexes and has detailed comments on news events that affect prominent industries in the high-yield market. The firm also publishes a monthly *High-Yield Bond Market Report* that briefly discusses the returns and new issues for the month, contains extensive data on returns for all components of the HY market (BB, B, CCC, CC-D, nonrated, default), and contains descriptive statistics regarding bonds in the composite index and various subindexes, such as average coupon, maturity, duration to worst, modified adjusted duration, price, and yield.

In addition, several bond-rating firms conduct research on these industries and firms. Standard & Poor's publication, *Speculative Grade Debt Credit Review,* discusses the credit analysis of high-yield bonds. The publication also includes a review of several major industries and specific comments on outstanding issues.

Yield Spread Analysis   As discussed in Chapter 19, spread analysis assumes normal relationships exist between the yields for bonds in alternative sectors (e.g., the spread between high-grade versus low-grade industrial or between industrial versus utility bonds). Therefore, a bond portfolio manager would monitor these relationships and, when an abnormal relationship occurs, execute various sector swaps. The crucial factor is developing the background to know the normal yield relationship and to evaluate the liquidity necessary to buy or sell the required issues quickly enough to take advantage of the temporary yield abnormality.

The analysis of yield spreads has been enhanced by a paper by Dialynas and Edington that considers several specific factors that affect the aggregate spread.[20] It is acknowledged that the generally accepted explanation of changes in the yield spread is that it is related to the economic environment. Specifically, the spread widens during periods of economic uncertainty and recession because investors require larger risk premiums (i.e., larger spreads). In contrast, the spread will decline during periods of economic confidence and expansion. Although not denying the existence of such a relationship, the authors contend that a more encompassing factor is the

---

[20]Chris P. Dialynas and David H. Edington, "Bond Yield Spreads—A Postmodern View," *Journal of Portfolio Management* 19, no. 1 (Fall 1992): 60–75.

impact of interest rate (yield) volatility. They contend that yield volatility will affect the spread via three effects: (1) yield volatility and the behavior of embedded options, (2) yield volatility and transactional liquidity, and (3) the effect of yield volatility on the business cycle.

Recall that the value of callable bonds is equal to the value of a noncallable bond minus the value of the call option. Obviously, if the value of the option goes up, the value of the callable bond will decline and its yield will increase. When yield volatility increases, the value of the call option increases, which causes a decline in the price of the callable bond and a rise in the bond's yield and its yield spread relative to Treasury bonds. Similarly, an increase in yield volatility will raise the uncertainty facing bond dealers and cause them to increase their bid-ask spreads that reflect the transactional liquidity for these bonds. This liquidity will have a bigger effect on non-government bonds, so their yield spread relative to Treasury bonds will increase. Finally, interest rate volatility causes uncertainty for business executives and consumers regarding their cost of funds. This typically will precede an economic decline that will, in turn, lead to an increase in the yield spread. It is demonstrated that it is possible to have a change in yield spread for reasons other than economic uncertainty. If there is a period of greater yield volatility that is not a period of economic uncertainty, the yield spread will increase due to the embedded option effect and the transactional liquidity effect. This analysis implies that when examining yield spreads, you should pay particular attention to interest rate (yield) volatility.

Bond Swaps   **Bond swaps** involve liquidating a current position and simultaneously buying a different issue in its place with similar attributes but having a chance for improved return. Swaps can be executed to increase current yield, to increase yield to maturity, to take advantage of shifts in interest rates or the realignment of yield spreads, to improve the quality of a portfolio, or for tax purposes. Some swaps are highly sophisticated and require a computer for calculation. However, most are fairly simple transactions with obvious goals and risk. They go by such names as *profit takeouts, substitution swaps, intermarket spread swaps,* or *tax swaps.* Although many of these swaps involve low risk (such as the pure yield pickup swap), others entail substantial risk (the rate anticipation swap). Regardless of the risk involved, all swaps have one basic purpose: portfolio improvement.

Most swaps involve several different types of risk. One obvious risk is that the market will move against you while the swap is outstanding. Interest rates may move up over the holding period and cause you to incur a loss. Alternatively, yield spreads may fail to respond as anticipated. Possibly the new bond may not be a true substitute and so, even if your expectations and interest rate formulations are correct, the swap may be unsatisfactory because the wrong issue was selected. Finally, if the work-out time is longer than anticipated, the realized yield might be less than expected. You must be willing to accept such risks to improve your portfolio. The following subsections consider three of the more popular bond swaps.[21]

Pure Yield Pickup Swap   The pure yield pickup involves swapping out of a low-coupon bond into a comparable higher-coupon bond to realize an automatic and instantaneous increase in current yield and yield to maturity. Your risks are (1) that the market will move against you and (2) that the new issue may not be a viable swap candidate. Also, because you are moving to a higher-coupon obligation, there could be greater call risk.

An example of a pure yield pickup swap would be an investor who currently holds a 30-year, Aa-rated 10 percent issue that is trading at an 11.50 percent yield. Assume that a comparable 30-year, Aa-rated obligation bearing a 12 percent coupon priced to yield 12 percent becomes

---

[21]For additional information on these and other types of bond swaps, see Sidney Homer and Martin L. Leibowitz, *Inside the Yield Book* (Englewood Cliffs, N.J.: Prentice-Hall, 1972); Anand K. Bhattacharya and Frank J. Fabozzi, "Interest Rate Swaps," in *The Handbook of Fixed-Income Securities,* 6th ed.

EXHIBIT 20.3	A PURE YIELD PICKUP SWAP

Pure yield pickup swap: A bond swap involving a switch—from a low-coupon bond to a higher-coupon bond of similar quality and maturity—in order to pick up higher current yield and a better yield to maturity.

Example: Currently hold: 30-yr., 10.0% coupon priced at 874.12 to yield 11.5%
        Swap candidate: 30-yr., Aa 12% coupon priced at $1,000 to yield 12.0%

	CURRENT BOND	CANDIDATE BOND
Dollar investment	$874.12	$1,000.00[a]
Coupon	100.00	120.00
i on one coupon (12.0% for 6 months)	3.000	3.600
Principal value at year end	874.66	1,000.00
Total accrued	977.66	1,123.60
Realized compound yield	11.514%	12.0%

Value of swap: 48.6 basis points in one year (assuming a 12.0% reinvestment rate).

The rewards for a pure yield pickup swap are automatic and instantaneous in that both a higher-coupon yield and a higher yield to maturity are realized from the swap.

Other advantages include:

1. No specific work-out period needed because the investor is assumed to hold the new bond to maturity
2. No need for interest rate speculation
3. No need to analyze prices for overvaluation or undervaluation

A major disadvantage of the pure yield pickup swap is the book loss involved in the swap. In this example, if the current bond were bought at par, the book loss would be $125.88 ($1,000 − 874.12).

Other risks involved in the pure yield pickup swap include:

1. Increased risk of call in the event interest rates decline
2. Reinvestment risk is greater with higher-coupon bonds.

---

[a]Obviously, the investor can invest $874.12—the amount obtained from the sale of the bond currently held—and still obtain a realized compound yield of 12.0%.

Swap evaluation procedure is patterned after a technique suggested by Sidney Homer and Martin L. Leibowitz.

Source: Adapted from the book *Inside the Yield Book* by Sidney Homer and Martin L. Leibowitz, Ph.D., 1972, used by permission of the publisher, Prentice-Hall Inc., Englewood Cliffs, N.J., and New York Institute of Finance, New York, N.Y.

available. The investor would report (and realize) some book loss if the original issue was bought at par but is able to improve current yield and yield to maturity simultaneously if the new obligation is held to maturity as shown in Exhibit 20.3.

The investor need not predict rate changes, and the swap is not based on any imbalance in yield spread. The object simply is to seek higher yields. Quality and maturity stay the same as do all other factors *except coupon.* The major risk is that future reinvestment rates may not be as high as expected, and, therefore, the total terminal value of the investment (capital recovery, coupon receipts, and interest-on-interest) may not be as high as expected or comparable to the original obligation. This reinvestment risk can be evaluated by analyzing the results with a number of reinvestment rates to determine the minimum reinvestment rate that would make the swap viable.

Substitution Swap   The substitution swap generally is short term and relies heavily on interest rate expectations. Therefore, it is subject to considerably more risk than the pure yield pickup
swaps. The procedure assumes a short-term imbalance in yield spreads between issues that are
perfect substitutes. The imbalance in yield spread is expected to be corrected in the near future.
For example, the investor might hold a 30-year, 12 percent issue that is yielding 12 percent and
be offered a comparable 30-year, 12 percent bond that is yielding 12.20 percent. Because the
issue offered will trade at a price less than $1,000 for every issue sold, the investor can buy more
than one of the offered obligations.

You would expect the yield spread imbalance to be corrected by having the yield on the offering bond decline to the level of your current issue. Thus, you would realize capital gains by
switching out of your current position into the higher-yielding obligation. This swap is described
in Exhibit 20.4.

EXHIBIT 20.4   *A SUBSTITUTION SWAP*

Substitution swap: A swap executed to take advantage of temporary market anomalies in yield
spreads between issues that are equivalent with respect to coupon, quality, and maturity.

Example: Currently hold: 30-yr., Aa 12.0% coupon priced at $1,000 to yield 12.0%
  Swap candidate: 30-yr., Aa 12% coupon priced at $984.08 to yield 12.2%
  Assumed work-out period: 1 year
  Reinvested at 12.0%

	CURRENT BOND	CANDIDATE BOND
Dollar investment	$1,000.00	$ 984.08
Coupon	120.00	120.00
i on one coupon (12.0% for 6 months)	3.60	3.60
Principal value at year end (12.0% YTM)	1,000.00	1,000.00
Total accrued	1,123.60	1,123.60
Total gain	123.60	139.52
Gain per invested dollar	0.1236	0.1418
Realized compound yield	12.00%	13.71%
Value of swap: 171 basis points in one year		

The rewards for the substitution swap are additional basis-point pickups for YTM, additional
realized compound yield, and capital gains that accrue when the anomaly in yield corrects itself.

In the substitution swap, any basis-point pickup (171 points in this example) will be realized only
during the work-out period. Thus, in our example, to obtain the 171 basis-point increase in realized
compound yield, you must swap an average of once a year and pick up an average of 20 basis points
in yield to maturity on each swap.

Potential risks associated with the substitution swap include:

1. A yield spread thought to be temporary may, in fact, be permanent, thus reducing capital gains
   advantages.
2. The market rate may change adversely.

Swap evaluation procedure is patterned after a technique suggested by Sidney Homer and Martin L. Leibowitz.

Source: Adapted from the book *Inside the Yield Book* by Sidney Homer and Martin L. Leibowitz, Ph.D., © 1972,
used by permission of the publisher, Prentice-Hall Inc., Englewood Cliffs, N.J., and New York Institute of Finance,
New York, N.Y.

Although a modest increase in current income occurs as the yield imbalance is corrected, attractive capital gains are possible, causing a differential in *realized yield.* The work-out time will have an important effect on the differential realized return. Even if the yield is not corrected until maturity, 30 years later, you will still experience a small increase in realized yield (about 10 basis points). In contrast, if the correction takes place in one year, the differential realized return is much greater, as shown in Exhibit 20.4.

After the correction has occurred, you would have additional capital for a subsequent swap or other investment. Several risks are involved in this swap. In addition to the pressure of the work-out time, market interest rates could move against you, the yield spread may not be temporary, and the issue may not be a viable swap candidate (i.e., the spread may be due to the issue's lower quality).

Tax Swap The tax swap is popular with individual investors because it is a relatively simple procedure that involves no interest rate projections and few risks. Investors enter into tax swaps due to tax laws and realized capital gains in their portfolios. Assume you acquired $100,000 worth of corporate bonds and after two years sold the securities for $150,000, implying a capital gain of $50,000. One way to eliminate the tax liability of that capital gain is to sell an issue that has a comparable long-term capital loss.[22] If you had a long-term investment of $100,000 with a current market value of $50,000, you could execute a tax swap to establish the $50,000 capital loss. By offsetting this capital loss and the comparable capital gain, you would reduce your income taxes.

Municipal bonds are considered particularly attractive tax swap candidates because you can increase your tax-free income and use the capital loss (subject to normal federal and state taxation) to reduce capital gains tax liability. To continue our illustration, assume you own $100,000 worth of New York City, 20-year, 7 percent bonds that you bought at par, but they have a current market value of $50,000. Given this tax loss, you need a comparable bond swap candidate. Suppose you find a 20-year New York City bond with a 7.1 percent coupon and a market value of 50. By selling your New York 7s and instantaneously reinvesting in the New York 7.1s, you would eliminate the capital gains tax from the corporate bond transaction. In effect, you have $50,000 of tax-free capital gains, and you have increased your current tax-free yield. The money saved by avoiding the tax liability can then be used to increase the portfolio's yield, as shown in Exhibit 20.5.

An important caveat is that *you cannot swap identical issues* (such as selling the New York 7s to establish a loss and then buying back the same New York 7s). If it is not a different issue, the IRS considers the transaction a *wash sale* and does not allow the loss. It is easier to avoid wash sales in the bond market than it is in the stock market because every bond issue, even with identical coupons and maturities, is considered distinct. Likewise, it is easier to find comparable bond issues with only modest differences in coupon, maturity, and quality. Tax swaps are common at year end as investors establish capital losses because the capital loss must occur in the same taxable year as the capital gain. This procedure differs from other bond swap transactions because it exists due to tax statutes rather than temporary market anomalies.

A Global Fixed-Income Investment Strategy

An active management strategy that considers one or several of the techniques discussed thus far should apply these techniques to a global portfolio. The optimum global fixed-income asset allocation must consider three interrelated factors: (1) the local economy in each country that includes the effect of domestic and international demand, (2) the impact of this total demand and domestic monetary policy on inflation and interest rates, and (3) the effect of the economy,

---

[22]Although this discussion is concerned with bond tax swaps, comparable strategies could be used with other types of investments.

EXHIBIT 20.5   *A TAX SWAP*

Tax swap: A swap undertaken when you wish to offset capital gains in other securities through the sale of a bond currently held and selling at a discount from the price paid at purchase. By swapping into a bond with as nearly identical features as possible, you can use the capital loss on the sale of the bond for tax purposes and still maintain your current position in the market.

Example: Currently hold: $100,000 worth of corporate bonds with current market value of $150,000
    and $100,000 in N.Y., 20-year, 7% bonds with current market value of $50,000
    Swap candidate: $50,000 in N.Y., 20-year, 7.1% bonds

A. Corporate bonds sold and long-term capital gains profit established $50,000

   Capital gains tax liability (assume you have 20% capital gains tax
   Rate) ($50,000 × 0.20) $10,000

B. N.Y. 7s sold and long-term capital *loss* established $50,000

   Reduction in capital gains tax liability ($50,000 × 0.20)   ($10,000)

   Net capital gains tax liability   0

   Tax *savings* realized $10,000

C. Complete tax swap by buying N.Y. 7.1s from proceeds of N.Y. 7s

   Sale (therefore, amount invested remains largely the *same*)[a]

   Annual tax-free interest income—N.Y. 7s $ 7,000

   Annual tax-free interest income—N.Y.7.1s $ 7,100

   Net *increase* in *annual* tax-free interest income $ 100

---

[a]N.Y. 7.1s will result in substantial capital gains when liquidated at maturity (because they were bought at deep discounts) and, therefore, will be subject to future capital gains tax liability. The swap is designed to use the capital loss resulting from the swap to offset capital gains from other investments. At the same time, your funds remain in a security almost identical to your previous holding while you receive a slight increase in both current income and YTM.

Because the tax swap involved no projections in terms of work-out period, interest rate changes, etc., the risks involved are minimal. Your major concern should be to avoid potential wash sales.

---

inflation, and interest rates on the exchange rates among countries.[23] Based on the evaluation of these factors, a portfolio manager must decide on the relative weight for each country. In addition, one might consider an allocation within each country among government, municipal, and corporate bonds. In the examples that follow, most portfolio recommendations concentrate on the country allocation and do not become more specific except in the case of the United States.

Exhibit 20.6 is from the March 31, 2002, *Quarterly Investment Strategy* by UBS Global Asset Management, a global institutional asset manager. The table's "Benchmark" column indicates what the asset allocation would be if UBS had no opinion regarding the expected bond market

---

[23]For a detailed discussion of the benefits of international bond investing as well as what is involved in the analysis, see Christopher B. Steward, "International Bond Markets and Instruments"; Michael R. Rosenberg, "International Fixed-Income Investing: Theory and Practice"; Jack Malvey, "Global Corporate Bond Portfolio Management; and Christopher B. Steward and Adam Greshin, "International Bond Investing and Portfolio Management." All four are included in *The Handbook of Fixed-Income Securities, 6th ed.* Also see Dwight D. Churchhill, ed., *Fixed-Income Management: Techniques and Practices* (Charlottesville, Va.: Association of Investment Management and Research, 1994); Jan R. Squires, ed., *Global Portfolio Management* (Charlottesville, Va.: Association of Investment Management and Research, 1996); Jan R. Squires, ed., *Global Bond Management* (Charlottesville Va.: Association of Investment Management and Research, 1997); *Managing Currency Risk* (Charlottesville, Va.: Association of Investment Management and Research, 1997); "*Global Bond Management II: The Search for Alpha*" (Charlottesville, Va.: Association for Investment Management and Research, 2000); and Katheryn Dixon Jost, ed., *Fixed-Income Management for the 21st Century* (Charlottesville, Va.: Association for Investment Management and Research, 2002).

EXHIBIT 20.6 ▶ *UBS GLOBAL BOND PORTFOLIO STRATEGY*

Market Allocation as of March 31, 2002

	GLOBAL		
	BENCHMARK	OVER/UNDER WEIGHT	MARKET STRATEGY
North America	**27.2%**	**4.4%**	**31.6%**
Canada	2.7	3.0	5.7
U.S.	24.5	1.4	25.9
EMU	**36.7**	**8.5**	**45.2**
Other Europe (except United Kingdom)	**2.5**	**0.0**	**2.5**
Denmark	1.1	−1.1	0.0
Sweden	0.9	1.7	2.6
Switzerland	0.6	−0.6	0.0
United Kingdom	**4.9**	**−3.0**	**1.9**
Japan	**28.3**	**−11.5**	**16.8**
Australia	**0.4**	**1.6**	**2.0**
	100.0%		**100.0%**

	EUROPE (EMU)		
	BENCHMARK	OVER/UNDER WEIGHT	MARKET STRATEGY
Austria	3.5%	−0.5%	3.0%
Belgium	7.0	−7.0	0.0
Finland	1.5	−1.5	0.0
France	21.8	−0.6	21.2
Germany	22.6	4.0	26.6
Greece	3.4	−3.4	0.0
Ireland	0.6	−0.6	0.0
Italy	23.3	5.5	28.8
Netherlands	5.7	−0.1	5.6
Portugal	1.8	−1.8	0.0
Spain	8.8	5.9	14.7
	100.0%	100.0%	

Currency Allocation

	GLOBAL		
	BENCHMARK	OVER/UNDER WEIGHT	MARKET STRATEGY
North America	**27.2%**	**−10.0%**	**17.2%**
Canada	2.7	2.0	4.7
U.S.	24.5	−12.0	12.5
EMU	**36.7**	**12.9**	**49.6**
Other Europe (except United Kingdom)	**2.5**	**0.0**	**2.5**
Denmanrk	1.1	0.0	1.1
Sweden	0.9	0.0	0.9
Switzerland	0.6	0.0	0.6
United Kingdom	**4.9**	**−4.9**	**0.0**
Japan	**28.3**	**−4.0**	**24.3**
Australia	**0.4**	**6.0**	**6.4**
	100.0%	**100.0%**	**100.0%**

Totals may not add to 100% due to rounding.

Source: UBS Global Asset Management, *Quarterly Investment Strategy,* 31 March 2002 (Chicago, Ill.: UBS Global Asset Management).

performance in the alternative countries. In most cases, this normal allocation is based on the country's relative market value. Here, the normal allocation is 24.5 percent for the United States, 28.3 percent for Japan, and the remaining 47.2 percent for the other countries, including 36.7 percent for the combined EMU countries. Clearly, UBS *does* have an opinion regarding these countries (as shown in its market strategy) because it has overweighted the U.S. bond market with an allocation of 25.9 percent (versus 24.5 percent) and underweighted the Japan bond market with an allocation of only 16.8 percent (versus 28.3 percent). In turn, several other countries are heavily overweighted—Canada, Sweden, and Australia—while several are clearly underweighted, including Denmark, Switzerland, and the United Kingdom. In addition, UBS does a specific currency allocation among countries that would likewise be based on the normal policy weight unless the firm had an opinion on currencies. Again, UBS has a definite opinion: it heavily underweighted the U.S. dollar, the Japanese yen, and the U.K. pound and was overweighted in the currencies of the EMU, Canada, and Australia.

In making your own allocations based on these specific expectations, you would look for U.S. securities in which yields were expected to decline relative to Treasury securities and for bond markets in foreign countries that likewise had bullish interest rate expectations. Finally, you would look for countries in which the currency was expected to be strong relative to the United States.

In summary, assuming you want to actively manage a bond portfolio, this example shows an approach to the asset allocation decision on a global scale. Similar to our discussion on equity securities, global bond allocation requires substantially more research because you must evaluate each country—individually and relative to every other country. Finally, your global fixed-income recommendation also must consider exchange rate changes—that is, you must make a currency decision for each country.

Core-Plus Bond Portfolio Management

Beyond a pure passive policy or one of the several active portfolio management styles, there has been an increase in a combination approach referred to as **core-plus bond-portfolio management**. The idea is to have a significant (core) part of the portfolio (e.g., 70 percent to 75 percent) managed passively in a widely recognized sector such as the U.S. Aggregate Sector or the U.S. Government/Corporate sector. The difference between these two sectors is that the aggregate includes the rapidly growing mortgage-backed and asset-backed sectors. It is suggested that this core of the portfolio be managed passively because these segments of the bond market are quite efficient so that it is not worth the time and cost to attempt to derive excess returns within these sectors. The rest of the portfolio would be managed actively in one or several additional "plus" sectors, where it is felt that there is a higher probability of achieving positive abnormal rates of return because of potential inefficiencies. The major areas suggested for the "plus" of the portfolio include high-yield bonds (HY bonds), foreign bonds, and emerging-market debt. These are considered good candidates for active management since they generally experience above-average rates of return; but, while they have *high total risk* as measured by their standard deviation of returns, they have relatively *low systematic risk* relative to a total bond market portfolio because they have low correlations with other fixed-income sectors. An example would be HY bonds that have *very high* standard deviations but are correlated only about 0.30 with investment-grade bonds and/or other large bond benchmarks so they have *very low* systematic risk.[24]

---

[24]Two recent conferences by the Association for Investment Management and Research consider this concept and discuss potential areas for active management. See *Global Bond Management II: The Search for Alpha* (Charlottesville, Va.: Association for Investment Management and Research, August 2000); and *Core-Plus Bond Management* (Charlottesville, Va.: Association for Investment Management and Research, March 2001).

EXHIBIT 20.7 ▸   *A PRESCRIBED SCHEDULE OF LIABILITIES*

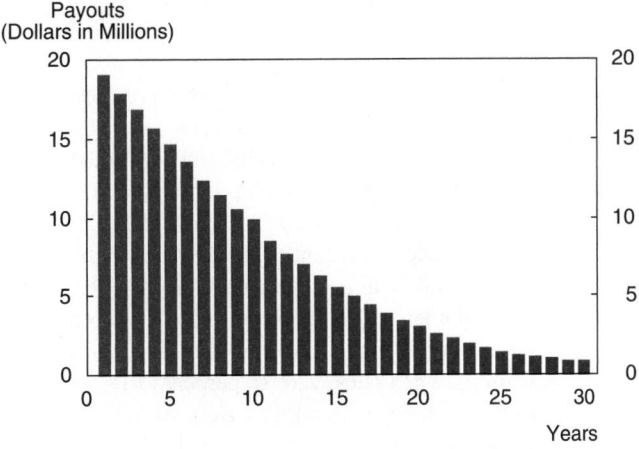

Matched-Funding Techniques[25]   As discussed previously, because of an increase in interest rate volatility and the needs of many institutional investors, there has been a growth in the use of matched-funding techniques ranging from pure cash-matched dedicated portfolios to portfolios involved in contingent immunization.

Dedicated Portfolios

Dedication refers to bond portfolio management techniques that are used to service a prescribed set of liabilities. The idea is that a pension fund has a set of future liabilities, and those responsible for administering these liabilities want a money manager to construct a portfolio of assets with cash flows that will match this liability stream. Such a "dedicated" portfolio can be created in several ways. We will discuss two alternatives.

A **pure cash-matched dedicated portfolio** is the most conservative strategy. Specifically, the objective of pure cash matching is to develop a portfolio of bonds that will provide a stream of payments from coupons, sinking funds, and maturing principal payments that will exactly match the specified liability schedules. An example of a typical liability stream for a retired-lives component of a pension system is shown in Exhibit 20.7.

The goal is to build a portfolio that will generate sufficient funds in advance of each scheduled payment to ensure that the payment will be met. One alternative is to find a number of zero coupon Treasury securities that will exactly cash match each liability. Such an exact cash match is referred to as a *total passive* portfolio because it is designed so that any prior receipts would not be reinvested (i.e., it assumes a zero reinvestment rate).

Dedication with reinvestment is the same as the pure cash-matched technique except it is assumed that the bonds and other cash flows do not have to exactly match the liability stream. Specifically, any inflows that precede liability claims can be reinvested at some reasonably conservative rate. This assumption allows the portfolio manager to consider a substantially wider set of bonds that may have higher return characteristics. In addition, the assumption of reinvestment

---

[25]An overview of these alternative strategies is contained in Martin L. Leibowitz, "The Dedicated Bond Portfolio in Pension Funds—Part I: Motivations and Basics," *Financial Analysts Journal* 42, no. 1 (January–February 1986): 68–75; and Frank J. Fabozzi and Peter F. Christensen, "Dedicated Bond Portfolios," *The Handbook of Fixed-Income Securities,* 6th ed.

within each period and between periods also will generate a higher return for the asset portfolio. As a result, the net cost of the portfolio will be lower, with almost equal safety, assuming the reinvestment rate assumption is conservative. An example would be to assume a reinvestment rate of 6 percent in an environment where market interest rates are currently ranging from 7 percent to 10 percent.

Potential problems exist with both of these approaches to a dedicated portfolio. For example, when selecting potential bonds for these portfolios, it is critical to be aware of call/prepayment possibilities (refundings, calls, sinking funds) with specific bonds or mortgage-backed securities. These prepayment possibilities become very important following periods of historically high rates. A prime example was the period 1982 to 1986, when interest rates went from over 18 percent to under 8 percent. Because of this substantial change in rates, many dedicated portfolios constructed without adequate concern for complete call protection were negatively affected when numerous bonds were called that were not expected to be called "under normal conditions." For example, bonds selling at deep discounts (which typically provide implicit call protection), when rates were 16 percent to 18 percent, went to par and above when rates declined to under 10 percent—and they were called. Obviously, the reinvestment of these proceeds at the lower rates caused many dedicated portfolios to be underfunded. Therefore, it is necessary to find bonds with complete call protection or to consider deep discount bonds under conservative interest rate conditions.

Although quality also is a legitimate concern, it is probably not necessary to invest only in Treasury bonds if the portfolio manager diversifies across industries and sectors. A diversified portfolio of AA or A industrial bonds can provide a current and total annual return of 40 to 60 basis points above Treasuries. This differential over a 30-year period can have a significant impact on the net cost of funding a liability stream.

Immunization Strategies   Instead of using a passive strategy, an active strategy, or a dedicated portfolio technique, a portfolio manager (after client consultation) may decide that the optimal strategy is to immunize the portfolio from interest rate changes. The *immunization techniques* attempt to derive a specified rate of return (generally quite close to the current market rate) during a given investment horizon regardless of what happens to market interest rates.

Components of Interest Rate Risk   A major problem encountered in bond portfolio management is deriving a given rate of return to satisfy an ending-wealth requirement at a future specific date—that is, the **investment horizon**. If the term structure of interest rates were flat and market rates never changed between the time of purchase and the horizon date when funds were required, you could acquire a bond with a term to maturity equal to the desired investment horizon, and the ending wealth from the bond would equal the promised wealth position implied by the promised yield to maturity. Specifically, the ending-wealth position would be the beginning wealth times the compound value of a dollar at the promised yield to maturity. For example, assume you acquire a 10-year, $1 million bond with an 8 percent coupon at its par value (8 percent Y_m). If conditions were as specified (there was a flat yield curve and there were no changes in the curve), your wealth position at the end of your 10-year investment horizon (assuming semiannual compounding) would be

$$\$1,000,000 \times (1.04)^{20} = \$1,000,000 \times 2.1911 = \$2,191,100$$

You can get the same answer by taking the $40,000 interest payment every six months and compounding it semiannually to the end of the period at 4 percent and adding the $1,000,000 principal at maturity. Unfortunately, in the real world, the term structure of interest rates typically is not flat and the level of interest rates is constantly changing. Consequently, the bond portfolio manager faces **interest rate risk** between the time of investment and the future target date. Interest rate risk is the uncertainty regarding the ending-wealth value of the portfolio due to changes in market interest rates between the time of purchase and the investor's horizon date. Notably, interest rate risk involves two component risks: **price risk** and **coupon reinvestment risk**.

The price risk occurs because if interest rates change before the horizon date and the bond is sold before maturity, the realized market price for the bond will differ from the *expected* price, assuming there had been no change in rates. If rates increased after the time of purchase, the realized price for the bond in the secondary market would be below expectations, whereas if rates declined, the realized price for the bond would be above expectations. Because you do not know whether interest rates will increase or decrease, you are uncertain about the bond's future price.

The coupon reinvestment risk arises because the yield to maturity computation implicitly assumes that all coupon cash flows will be reinvested at the promised yield to maturity.[26] If, after the purchase of the bond, interest rates decline, the coupon cash flows will be reinvested at rates below the promised Y_m, and the ending wealth will be below expectations. In contrast, if interest rates increase, the coupon cash flows will be reinvested at rates above expectations, and the ending wealth will be above expectations. Again, because you are uncertain about future rates, you are uncertain about these reinvestment rates.

Classical Immunization and Interest Rate Risk   The price risk and the coupon reinvestment risk caused by a change in interest rates have opposite effects on the ending-wealth position. An increase in interest rates will cause an ending price below expectations, but the reinvestment rate for interim cash flows will be above expectations. A decline in market interest rates will cause the reverse situation. Clearly, a bond portfolio manager with a specific target date (investment horizon) will attempt to eliminate these two components of interest rate risk. The process intended to eliminate interest rate risk is referred to as **immunization** and was discussed by Redington in the early 1950s.[27] It has been specified in detail by Fisher and Weil as follows:

> A portfolio of investments in bonds is *immunized* for a holding period if its value at the end of the holding period, regardless of the course of interest rates during the holding period, must be at least as large as it would have been had the interest-rate function been constant throughout the holding period.
>
> If the realized return on an investment in bonds is sure to be at least as large as the appropriately computed yield to the horizon, then that investment is immunized.[28]

Fisher and Weil found a significant difference between the *promised* yields and the *realized* returns on bonds for the period 1925 to 1968, indicating the importance of immunizing a bond portfolio. They showed that it is possible to immunize a bond portfolio if you can assume that any change in interest rates will be the same for all maturities—that is, if forward interest rates change, all rates will change by the same amount (there is a parallel shift of the yield curve). Given this assumption, Fisher and Weil proved that *a portfolio of bonds is immunized from interest rate risk if the modified duration of the portfolio is always equal to the desired investment horizon.* For example, if the investment horizon of a bond portfolio is eight years, the *modified duration* of the bond portfolio should equal eight years to immunize the portfolio. To attain a given modified duration, the weighted average modified duration (with weights equal to the

---

[26]This point was discussed in detail in Chapter 19 and in Homer and Leibowitz, *Inside the Yield Book,* Chapter 1.

[27]F. M. Redington, "Review of the Principles of Life—Office Valuations," *Journal of the Institute of Actuaries* 78 (1952): 286–340.

[28]Lawrence Fisher and Roman L. Weil, "Coping with the Risk of Interest-Rate Fluctuations: Returns to Bondholders from Naive and Optimal Strategies," *Journal of Business* 44, no. 4 (October 1971): 408–431.

proportion of value) is set at the desired length following an interest payment, and all subsequent cash flows are invested in securities *to keep the portfolio modified duration equal to the remaining investment horizon.*

Fisher and Weil showed that price risk and reinvestment rate risk are affected in opposite directions by a change in market rates and that modified duration is the time period when these two risks are of equal magnitude but opposite in direction.[29]

Application of the Immunization Principle   Fisher and Weil simulated the effects of applying the immunization concept (a duration-matched strategy) compared to a naive portfolio strategy where the portfolio's maturity was equal to the investment horizon. They compared the ending-wealth ratio for the duration-matched and for the naive strategy portfolios to a wealth ratio that assumed no change in the interest rate structure. In a perfectly immunized portfolio, the actual ending wealth should equal the expected ending wealth implied by the promised yield, so these comparisons should indicate which portfolio strategy does a superior job of immunization. The duration-matched strategy results were consistently closer to the promised yield results; however, the results were not perfect. The duration portfolio was not perfectly immunized because the basic assumption did not always hold; that is, when interest rates changed, all interest rates did not change by the same amount.

Bierwag and Kaufman pointed out several specifications of the duration measure.[30] The Macaulay duration measure, one of the duration measures discussed in Chapter 19, discounts all flows by the prevailing yield to maturity on the bond being measured.[31] Alternatively, Fisher and Weil defined duration using future one-period interest rates (forward rates) to discount the future flows.[32] Depending on the shape of the yield curve, the two definitions could give different answers. If the yield curve is flat, the two definitions will compute equal durations. Bierwag and Kaufman computed alternative measures of duration and found that, except at high coupons and long maturities, the duration values of the alternative definitions were similar, and the Macaulay definition is preferable because it is a function of the yield to maturity of the bond. This means you do not need a forecast of one-period forward rates over the maturity of the bond.[33]

Example of Classical Immunization   Exhibit 20.8 shows the effect of attempting to immunize a portfolio by matching the investment horizon and the duration of a bond portfolio using a single bond. The portfolio manager's investment horizon is eight years, and the current yield to maturity for eight-year bonds is 8 percent. Therefore, if we assumed no change in yields, the ending-wealth ratio for an investor should be 1.8509 (1.08^8) with annual compounding.[34] As noted, this also should be the ending-wealth ratio for a completely immunized portfolio.

The example considers two portfolio strategies: (1) the maturity strategy, where the portfolio manager would acquire a bond with a term to maturity of eight years, and (2) the duration strategy, where the portfolio manager sets the duration of the portfolio at eight years. For the **maturity strategy**, the portfolio manager acquires an eight-year, 8 percent bond; for the **duration**

---

[29]This also is noted and discussed in G. O. Bierwag and George G. Kaufman, "Coping with the Risk of Interest Rate Fluctuations: A Note," *Journal of Business* 50, no. 3 (July 1977): 364–370; and G. O. Bierwag, "Immunization, Duration, and the Term Structure of Interest Rates," *Journal of Financial and Quantitative Analysis* 12, no. 5 (December 1977): 725–742.

[30]Bierwag and Kaufman, "Coping with the Risk of Interest Rate Fluctuations," 364–370.

[31]Frederick R. Macaulay, *Some Theoretical Problems Suggested by the Movements of Interest Rates, Bond Yields, and Stock Prices in the United States since 1856* (New York: National Bureau of Economic Research, 1938).

[32]Fisher and Weil, "Coping with the Risk of Interest Rate Fluctuations," 408–431.

[33]Bierwag and Kaufman, "Coping with the Risk of Interest Rate Fluctuations," 367.

[34]We use annual compounding to compute the ending-wealth ratio because the example uses annual observations.

| EXHIBIT 20.8 | AN EXAMPLE OF THE EFFECT OF A CHANGE IN MARKET RATES ON A BOND (PORTFOLIO) THAT USES THE MATURITY STRATEGY VERSUS THE DURATION STRATEGY |

	RESULTS WITH MATURITY STRATEGY			RESULTS WITH DURATION STRATEGY		
YEAR	CASH FLOW	REINVESTMENT RATE	END VALUE	CASH FLOW	REINVESTMENT RATE	END VALUE
1	$ 80	.08	$ 80.00	$ 80	.08	$ 80.00
2	80	.08	166.40	80	.08	166.40
3	80	.08	259.71	80	.08	259.71
4	80	.08	360.49	80	.08	360.49
5	80	.06	462.12	80	.06	462.12
6	80	.06	596.85	80	.06	596.85
7	80	.06	684.04	80	.06	684.04
8	$1,080	.06	$1,805.08	$1,120.64[a]	.06	$1,845.72

Expected Wealth Ratio = 1.8509 or $1,850.90

[a]The bond could be sold at its market value of $1,040.64, which is the value for an 8 percent bond with two years to maturity priced to yield 6 percent.

strategy, the manager acquires a 10-year, 8 percent bond that has approximately an eight-year duration (8.12 years), assuming an 8 percent Y_m. We assume a single shock to the interest rate structure at the end of Year 4, when rates go from 8 percent to 6 percent and stay there through Year 8.

As shown, due to the interest rate change, the ending-wealth ratio for the maturity strategy bond is *below* the desired wealth ratio because of the shortfall in the reinvestment cash flow after Year 4 when the interim coupon cash flow was reinvested at 6 percent rather than 8 percent. Note that *the maturity strategy eliminated the price risk* because the bond matured at the end of Year 8. Alternatively, the duration strategy portfolio likewise suffered a shortfall in reinvestment cash flow because of the change in market rates. In contrast to the maturity strategy, this reinvestment shortfall was partially offset by an *increase* in the ending value for the bond because of the decline in market rates. This second bond is sold at the end of Year 8 at 104.06 of par because it is an 8 percent coupon bond with two years to maturity selling to yield 6 percent. Because of this partial offset due to the price increase, the duration strategy had an ending-wealth value (1,845.72) that was much closer to the expected wealth ratio (1,850.90) than the maturity strategy (1,805.08). The point is, the reinvestment rate shortfall was almost completely offset by the positive price effect in the duration strategy.

If market interest rates had increased during this period, the maturity strategy portfolio would have experienced an *excess* of reinvestment income compared to the expected cash flow and the ending-wealth ratio for this strategy would have been above expectations. In contrast, in the duration portfolio, the excess cash flow from reinvestment under this assumption would have been partially offset by a *decline* in the ending price for the bond (i.e., it would have sold at a small discount to par value). Although the ending-wealth ratio for the duration strategy would have been lower than the maturity strategy in this example, it would have been closer to the expected-wealth ratio. Although the maturity strategy would have provided a higher than expected ending value for this scenario, the whole purpose of immunization is to *eliminate uncertainty* due to interest rate changes by having the realized-wealth position equal the expected-wealth position. As shown, this is what is accomplished with the duration-matched strategy.

Another View of Immunization The prior example assumed that both bonds were acquired and held to the end of the investment horizon. An alternative way to envision what is expected to happen with an immunized portfolio is to concentrate on the specific growth path from the beginning-wealth position to the ending-wealth position and examine what happens when interest rates change.

Assume that the initial-wealth position is $1 million, your investment horizon is 10 years, and the coupon and current YTM are 8 percent. We know from an earlier computation that this implies that the expected ending-wealth value is $2,191,100 (with semiannual compounding). Exhibit 20.9A shows the compound growth rate path from $1 million to the expected ending value at $2,191,100. In Exhibit 20.9B, it is assumed that at the end of Year 2, interest rates increase 200 basis points from 8 percent to 10 percent. We know that with no prior rate changes, at the end of Year 2 the value of the portfolio would have grown at an 8 percent compound rate to $1,169,900 [$1.04^4 = 1.1699$]. Given the rate change, we know there will be two changes for this portfolio: (1) the price (value of the portfolio) will decline to reflect the higher interest rate; and (2) the reinvestment rate, which is the growth rate, will increase to 10 percent. An important question is, How much will the portfolio value decline? The answer depends on the modified duration of the portfolio when rates change. Fisher and Weil showed that *if the modified duration is equal to the remaining horizon, the price change will be such that at the new reinvestment (growth) rate (10 percent), the new portfolio value will grow to the expected-wealth position.* You can approximate the change in portfolio value using the modified duration and the change in market rates. (Recall that this will not give an exact estimate because of the convexity of the portfolio.) The approximate change in price is 16 percent based on a modified duration of eight years and a 200-basis-point change. This would imply an approximate portfolio value of $982,716 ($1,169,900 × 0.84). In fact, the actual value would be $1,003,743. (Recall that the estimated value based on using modified duration always is below the value implied by the price-yield curve.) If this new portfolio value grows at 10 percent a year for eight years, the ending-wealth value will be

$$\$1,003,743 \times 2.1829 \text{ (5\% for 16 Periods)} = \$2,191,070$$

The difference between the expected value and projected value is due to rounding. This example shows that the price decline is almost exactly offset by the higher reinvestment rate— assuming that the modified duration of the portfolio at the time of the rate change was equal to the remaining investment horizon.

What happens if the portfolio is not properly matched? If the modified duration is greater than the remaining horizon, the price change will be greater. Thus, if interest rates increase, the value of the portfolio after the rate change will be less than $1,003,743. In this case, even if the new value of the portfolio grew at 10 percent a year, it would not reach the expected ending-wealth value. This scenario is shown in Exhibit 20.9C, where it is assumed that the portfolio value declined to $950,000. If this new value grew at 10 percent a year for the remaining 8 years, its ending value would be

$$\$950,000 \times 2.1829 \text{ (5\% for 16 Periods)} = \$2,073,755$$

Therefore, the shortfall of $118,000 between the expected-wealth value and the realized-wealth value is because the portfolio was not properly duration matched (immunized) when interest rates changed.

Alternatively, if interest rates had declined, and the modified duration had been longer than eight years, the portfolio value would have increased such that the new portfolio value would have been greater than the required value. Exhibit 20.9D shows what can happen if the portfolio

EXHIBIT 20.9 *THE GROWTH PATH TO THE EXPECTED ENDING-WEALTH VALUE
AND THE EFFECT OF IMMUNIZATION*

A. *Constant 8 Percent Growth Rate*

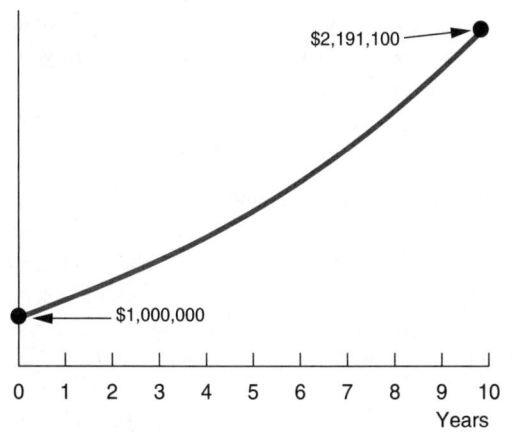

B. *Effect of Interest Rate Increase after Two
Years with Duration Equal to Investment Horizon*

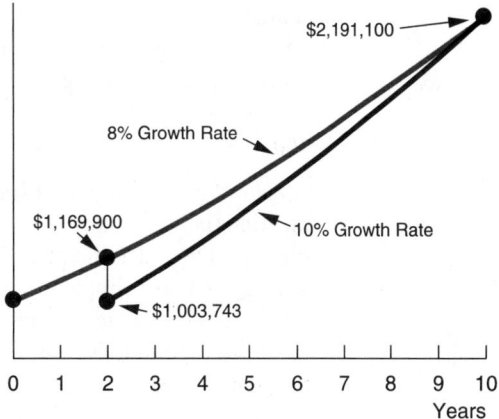

C. *Effect of Interest Rate Increase with Duration Greater
Than Investment Horizon*

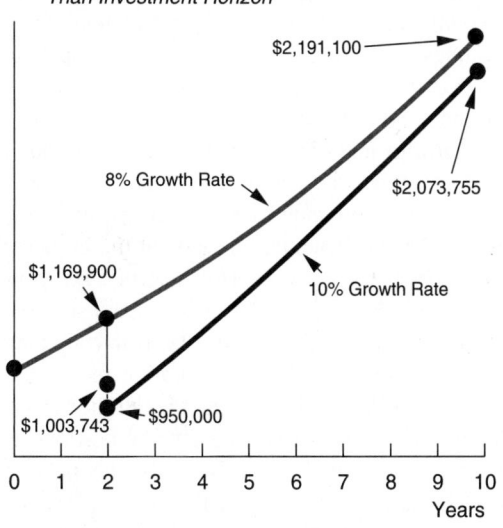

D. *Effect of Interest Rate Decline with Duration Greater
Than Investment Horizon*

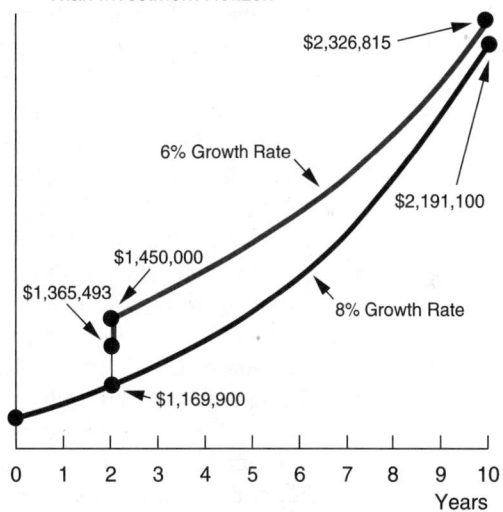

is not properly matched and interest rates decline by 200 basis points to 6 percent. First, if the
portfolio *is* properly matched, the value will increase to $1,365,493. If this new portfolio value
grows at 6 percent for eight years, its ending value will be

$$\$1,365,493 \times 1.6047 \ (3\% \text{ for } 16 \text{ Periods}) = \$2,191,207$$

Again, this deviates slightly from the expected ending-wealth value ($2,191,100) due to round-
ing. Alternatively, if the modified duration had been above eight years, the new portfolio value
would have been greater than the required current value of $1,365,493. Assume that because the

duration of the portfolio exceeded the remaining horizon, the portfolio value increased to $1,450,000. If so, the ending value would be

$$\$1,450,000 \times 1.6047 \text{ (3\% for 16 Periods)} = \$2,326,815$$

In this example, the ending-wealth value would have been greater than the expected-wealth value because you were mismatched and interest rates went in the right direction. When you are not duration matched, you are speculating on interest rate changes, and the result can be very good or very bad. The purpose of immunization is to avoid these uncertainties and to ensure the expected ending-wealth value ($2,191,100), regardless of interest rate changes.

Application of Classical Immunization   Once you understand the reasoning behind immunization (i.e., it is meant to offset the components of interest rate risk) and the general principle (you need to match modified duration and the investment horizon), you might conclude that this strategy is fairly simple to apply. You might even consider it a passive strategy; simply match modified duration and the investment horizon, and you can ignore the portfolio until the end of the horizon period. The following discussion will show that *immunization is neither a simple nor a passive strategy.*

Except for the case of a zero coupon bond, *an immunized portfolio requires frequent rebalancing* because the modified duration of the portfolio always should be equal to the remaining time horizon. The zero coupon bond is unique because it is a pure discount bond. As such, because there is no cash flow, there is *no reinvestment risk* because the discounting assumes that the value of the bond will grow at the discount rate. For example, if you discount a future value at 10 percent, the present value factor assumes that the value will grow at a compound rate of 10 percent to maturity. Also, there is *no price risk* if you set the duration at your time horizon because you will receive the face value of the bond at maturity. Also, recall that the duration of a zero coupon bond always is equal to its term to maturity. In summary, if you immunize by matching your horizon with a zero coupon bond of equal duration, you do not have to rebalance.

In contrast, if you immunize a portfolio using coupon bonds, several characteristics of duration make it impossible to set a duration equal to the remaining horizon at the initiation of the portfolio and ignore it thereafter. First, *duration declines more slowly than term to maturity, assuming no change in market interest rates.* For example, assume you have a security with a computed duration of five years at a 10 percent market yield. A year later, if you compute the duration of the security at 10 percent, you will find that it has a duration of approximately 4.2 years; that is, although the term to maturity has declined by a year, the duration has declined by only 0.8 year. This means that, assuming no change in market rates, the portfolio manager must rebalance the portfolio to reduce its duration to four years. Typically, this is not difficult because cash flows from the portfolio can be invested in short-term T-bills if necessary.

Second, *duration changes with a change in market interest rates.* In Chapter 19, we discussed the inverse relationship between market rates and duration—with higher market rates, there will be lower duration and vice versa. Therefore, a portfolio that has the appropriate modified duration at a point in time can have its duration changed immediately if market rates change. If this occurs, a portfolio manager will have to rebalance the portfolio if the deviation from the required duration becomes too large.

Third, you will recall from our initial discussion of immunization that one of the assumptions is that when market rates change, they will change by the same amount and in the same direction (i.e., there will be a parallel shift of the yield curve). Clearly, if this does not happen, it will affect the performance of a portfolio of diffuse bonds. For example, assume you own a portfolio of long- and short-term bonds with a weighted average six-year duration (e.g., 2-year duration bonds and 10-year duration bonds). Assume the term structure curve changes such that short-

EXHIBIT 20.10   *THE CONCEPT OF HORIZON MATCHING*

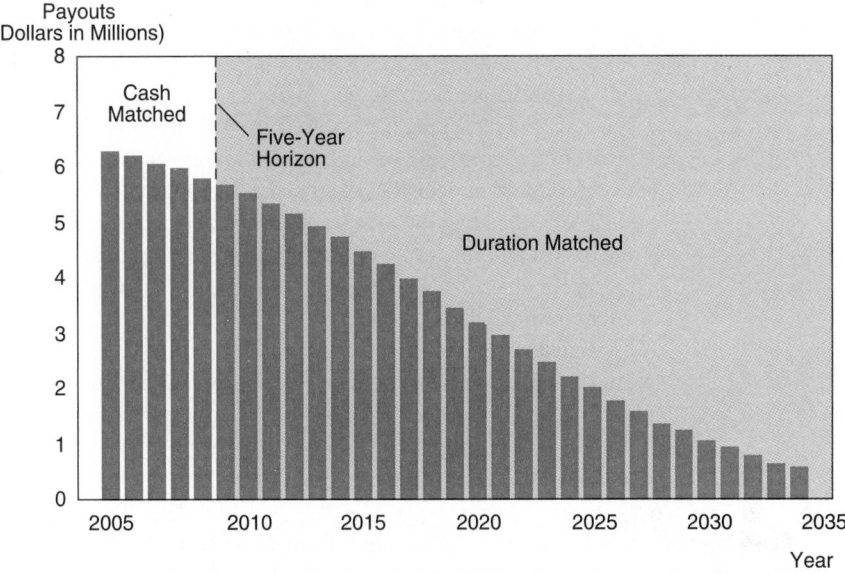

"Horizon Matching: A New Generalized Approach for Developing Minimum Cost Dedicated Portfolios." Copyright 1983 Salomon Brothers Inc. This chart was prepared for Salomon Brothers Inc. by Martin Leibowitz, a former Managing Director; Thomas E. Klaffky, Managing Director; Steven Mandel, a former Managing Director; and Alfred Weinberger, a former Director. Although the information in this chart has been obtained from sources that Salomon Brothers Inc. believed to be reliable, SSB does not guarantee their accuracy, and such information may be incomplete or condensed. All figures included in this chart constitute SSB's judgment as of the original publication date. Reprinted with permission from SalomonSmithBarney.

term rates decline and long-term rates *rise* (there is an increase in the slope of the yield curve). In such a case, you would experience a major price decline in the long-term bonds but would be penalized on reinvestment, assuming you generally reinvest the cash flow in short-term securities. This potential problem (caused by a change in the shape of the yield curve) suggests that you should attempt to bunch your portfolio selections close to the desired duration (i.e., use a bullet approach). For example, an eight-year duration portfolio should be made up of seven- to nine-year duration securities to avoid this yield curve reshaping problem.

Finally, there always can be a problem acquiring the bonds you select as optimum for your portfolio. For instance, can you buy long-duration bonds at the price you consider acceptable? In summary, it is important to recognize that classical immunization is *not a passive strategy* because it is subject to all of these potential problems.[35]

Horizon Matching   Horizon matching is a combination of two of the techniques discussed: cash-matching dedication and immunization. As shown in Exhibit 20.10, the liability stream is divided into two segments. In the first segment, the portfolio is constructed to provide a cash match for the liabilities during this horizon period (e.g., the first five years). The second segment is the remaining liability stream following the end of the horizon period—in the example, it is the 25 years after the horizon period. During this second time period, the liabilities are covered

---

[35]Several of these problems are discussed in Frank J. Fabozzi and Peter Christensen, "Bond Immunization: An Asset/ Liability Optimization Strategy," in *The Handbook of Fixed-Income Securities,* 6th ed.

by a duration-matched strategy based on immunization principles. As a result, the client receives the certainty of cash matching during the early years and the cost saving and flexibility of duration-matched flows thereafter.

The combination technique also helps alleviate one of the problems with classical immunization: the potential for nonparallel shifts in the yield curve. Most of the problems related to nonparallel shifts are concentrated in the short end of the yield curve because this is where the most severe curve reshaping occurs. Because the short end is taken care of by the cash matching, these are not of concern and we know that the long end of the yield curve tends toward parallel shifts.

An important decision when using horizon matching is the length of the horizon period. The trade-off when making this decision is between the safety and certainty of cash matching and the lower cost and flexibility of duration-based immunization. The portfolio manager should provide to the client a set of horizon alternatives and the costs and benefits of each of them and allow the client to make the decision.

It also is possible to consider *rolling out* the cash-matched segment over time. Specifically, after the first year the portfolio manager would restructure the portfolio to provide a cash match during the original Year 6, which means that you would still have a five-year horizon. The ability and cost of rolling out depends on movements in interest rates (ideally, you would want parallel shifts in the yield curve).[36]

Contingent Procedures   Contingent procedures are a form of structured active management. The procedure we discuss here is contingent immunization, which entails allowing the portfolio manager some opportunity to actively manage the portfolio with a structure that constrains the portfolio manager if he or she is unsuccessful.

Contingent Immunization

Subsequent to the development and application of classical immunization, Leibowitz and Weinberger developed a portfolio strategy called *contingent immunization*.[37] Basically, it allows a bond portfolio manager to pursue the highest returns available through active strategies, while relying on classical bond immunization techniques to ensure a given minimal return over the investment horizon—that is, it allows active portfolio management with a safety net provided by classical immunization.

To understand contingent immunization, it is necessary to recall our discussion of classical immunization. Remember that when the portfolio duration is equal to the investment horizon, a change in interest rates will cause a change in the dollar value of the portfolio such that when the new asset value is compounded at the new market interest rate, it will equal the desired ending value. This required change in value occurs *only* when the modified duration of the portfolio is equal to the remaining time horizon, which is why the modified duration of the portfolio must be maintained at the horizon value.

Consider the following example of this process. Assume that your desired ending-wealth value is $206.3 million. Given a specific ending value and the number of years to your horizon value, it is possible to determine how much you must invest today to attain that ending value if you assume a rate of return on the portfolio. Obviously, this is just the reverse of the price com-

---

[36]For a further discussion on this topic, see Martin L. Leibowitz, Thomas E. Klaffky, Steven Mandel, and Alfred Weinberger, *Horizon Matching: A New Generalized Approach for Developing Minimum-Cost Dedicated Portfolios* (New York: Salomon Brothers, 1983); and Martin L. Leibowitz, "The Dedicated Bond Portfolio in Pension Funds—Part II: Immunization, Horizon Matching, and Contingent Procedures," *Financial Analysts Journal* 42, no. 2 (March–April 1986): 47–57.

[37]Martin L. Leibowitz and Alfred Weinberger, "Contingent Immunization—Part I: Risk Control Procedures," *Financial Analysts Journal* 38, no. 6 (November–December 1982): 17–32; and Martin L. Leibowitz and Alfred Weinberger, "Contingent Immunization—Part II: Problem Areas," *Financial Analysts Journal* 39, no. 1 (January–February 1983): 35–50. This section draws heavily from these articles.

pounding exercise—that is, you compute the present value of the ending value at the expected yield for the horizon period. In this case, we assume a 5-year horizon and a 15 percent return, which means we compute the present value of $206.3 million at 15 percent for 5 years or 7.5 percent for 10 periods assuming semiannual compounding. The present value factor of 0.48473 times the $206.3 million ending value equals $100 million—that is, this is the required initial investment under these assumptions to attain the desired ending value. Assuming the five year horizon, we can do it for other interest rates as follows:

Percent	Present Value Factor[a]	Required Investment ($ Mil.)	Percent	Present Value Factor[a]	Required Investment ($ Mil.)
10	0.6139	$126.65	16	0.4632	$95.56
12	0.5584	115.20	18	0.4224	87.14
14	0.5083	104.86	20	0.3855	79.53
15	0.48473	100.00			

[a]Present value for 10 periods (5 years) at one-half the annual percent.

Exhibit 20.11 reflects these calculations—that is, the dark line indicates the required initial amount that must be invested at every yield level to attain $206.3 million in five years. Clearly, at lower yields you need a larger initial investment (e.g., $126 million at 10 percent), and it declines with higher yields (e.g., it is less than $80 million at 20 percent). The dotted line in Exhibit 20.11 indicates that the price sensitivity of a portfolio with a modified duration of five years will have almost exactly the price sensitivity required.

EXHIBIT 20.11 ▶ *CLASSICAL IMMUNIZATION*

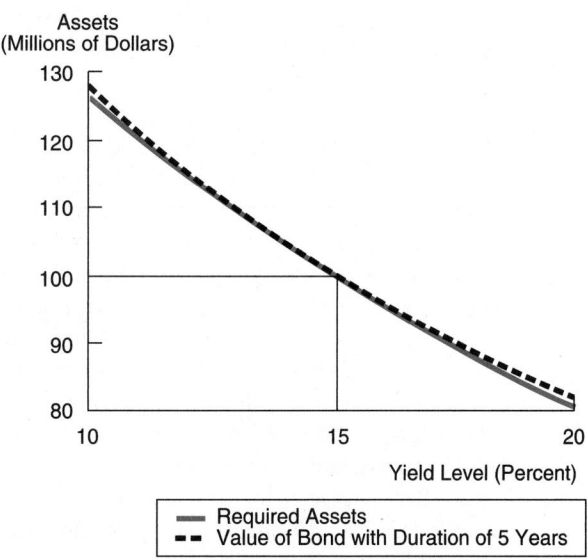

EXHIBIT 20.12 ► *PRICE BEHAVIOR REQUIRED FOR FLOOR RETURN*

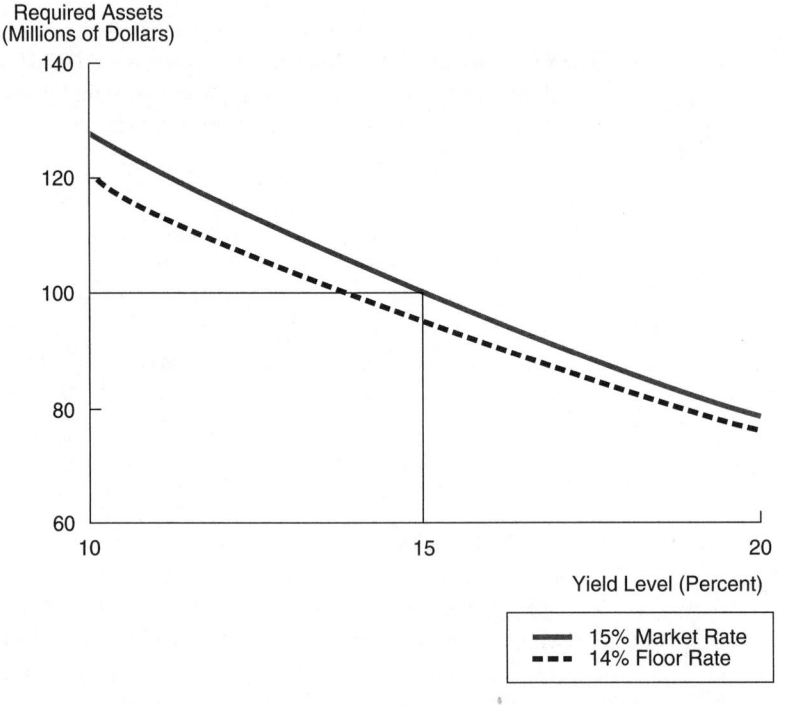

Contingent immunization requires that the client be willing to accept a potential return below the current market return, referred to as a *cushion spread*—the difference between the current market return and some floor rate. This cushion spread in required yield provides flexibility for the portfolio manager to engage in active portfolio strategies. For example, if current market rates are 15 percent, the client might be willing to accept a floor rate of 14 percent. If we assume the client initiated the fund with $100 million, the acceptance of this lower rate will mean that the portfolio manager does not have the same ending-asset requirements. Specifically, at 14 percent the required ending-wealth value would be $196.72 million (7 percent for 10 periods) compared to the $206.3 million at 15 percent. Because of this lower floor rate (and lower ending-wealth value), it is possible to experience some declines in the value of the portfolio while attempting to do better than the market through active management strategies.

Exhibit 20.12 shows the value of assets that are required at the beginning assuming a 14 percent required return and the implied ending-wealth value of $196.72 million. Notably, assuming current market rates of 15 percent, the required value of assets at the beginning would be $95.56 million, which is the present value of $196.72 million at 15 percent for 15 years. The difference between the client's initial fund of $100 million and the required assets of $95.56 million is the dollar cushion available to the portfolio manager. As noted, this dollar cushion arises because the client has agreed to a lower investment rate and, therefore, a lower ending-wealth value.

At this point, the portfolio manager can engage in various active portfolio management strategies to increase the ending-wealth value of the portfolio above that required at 14 percent. As an example, assume that the portfolio manager believes that market rates will decline. Under such

EXHIBIT 20.13 *SAFETY MARGIN FOR A PORTFOLIO OF 30-YEAR BONDS*

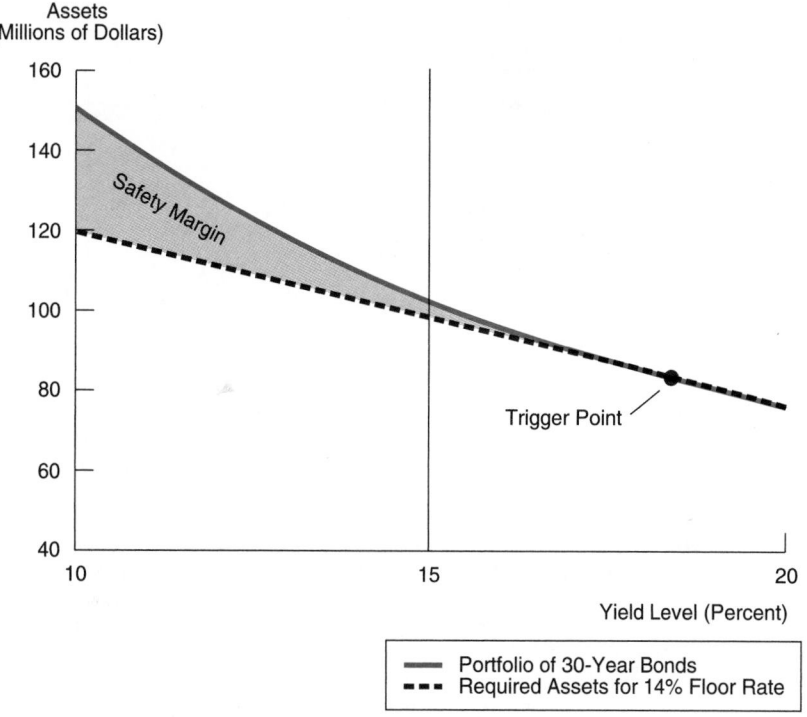

conditions, the portfolio manager might consider acquiring a 30-year bond that has a duration greater than the investment horizon of 5 years and, therefore, has greater price sensitivity to changes in market rates. Hence, if rates decline as expected, the value of the long-duration portfolio will rise above the initial value. In contrast, if rates increase, the value of the portfolio will decline rapidly. In this case, depending on how high rates go, the value of the portfolio could decline to a value below that needed to reach the desired ending-wealth value of $196.72 million.

Exhibit 20.13 shows what happens to the value of this portfolio if we assume an instantaneous change in interest rates when the fund is established. Specifically, if rates decline from 15 percent, the portfolio of long-duration, 30-year bonds would experience a large increase in value and develop a *safety margin*—a portfolio value above the required value. In contrast, if rates increase, the value of the portfolio will decline until it reaches the asset value required at 14 percent. When the value of the portfolio reaches this point of minimum return (referred to as a *trigger point*), it is necessary to stop active portfolio management and use classical immunization with the remaining assets to ensure that you attain the desired ending-wealth value (i.e., $196.72 million).

Potential Return   The concept of *potential return* is helpful in understanding the objective of contingent immunization. This is the return the portfolio would achieve over the entire investment horizon if, at any point, the assets in hand were immunized at the prevailing market rate. Exhibit 20.14 contains the various potential rates of return based on dollar asset values shown in Exhibit 20.13. If the portfolio were immediately immunized when market rates were 15 percent,

EXHIBIT 20.14	*THE POTENTIAL RETURN CONCEPT*

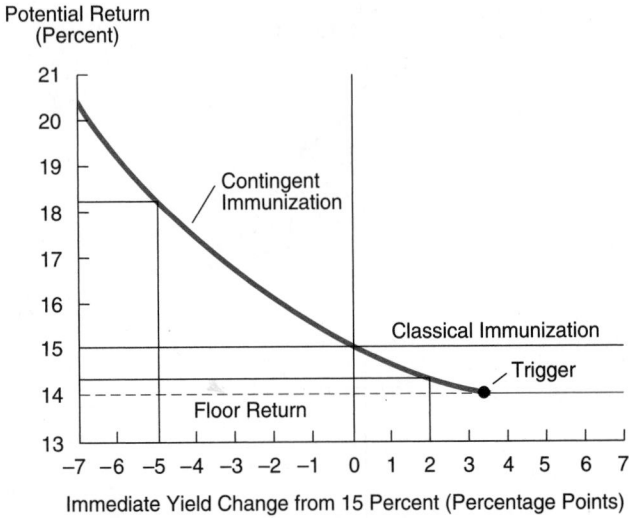

it would naturally earn the 15 percent market rate; that is, its potential return would be 15 percent. Alternatively, if yields declined instantaneously to 10 percent, the portfolio's asset value would increase to $147 million (see Exhibit 20.13). If this $147 million portfolio were immunized at the market rate of 10 percent over the remaining five-year period, the portfolio would compound at 10 percent to a total value of $239.45 million ($147 million × 1.6289, which is the compound growth factor for 5 percent and 10 periods). This ending value of $239.45 million represents an 18.25 percent realized (horizon) rate of return on the original $100 million portfolio. Consequently, as shown in Exhibit 20.14, if rates decline by 5 percent, the potential return for this portfolio at this point in time is 18.25 percent.

In contrast, if interest rates increase, the value of the portfolio will decline substantially and the potential return will decline. For example, if market rates rise to 17 percent (i.e., a yield change of 2 percent), the asset value of the 30-year bond portfolio will decline to $88 million (see Exhibit 20.13). If this portfolio of $88 million were immunized for the remaining five years at the prevailing market rate of 17 percent, the ending value would be $199 million. This ending value implies a potential return of 14.32 percent for the total period.

As Exhibit 20.13 shows, if interest rates rose to 18.50 percent, the 30-year bonds would decline to a value of $81.16 million (the trigger point) and the portfolio would have to be immunized. At this point, if the remaining assets of $81.16 million were immunized at this current market rate of 18.50 percent, the value of the portfolio would grow to $196.73 million ($81.16 × 2.424, which is the compound value factor for 9.25 percent for 10 periods). This ending value implies that the potential return for the portfolio would be exactly 14 percent as shown in Exhibit 20.14. Regardless of what happens to subsequent market rates, the portfolio has been immunized at the floor rate of 14 percent. That is a major characteristic of the contingent immunized portfolio; if there is proper monitoring, you will always know your trigger point where you must immunize and can be assured of receiving a return no less than the minimum rate of return specified.

EXHIBIT 20.15 CONTINGENT IMMUNIZATION FLOOR PORTFOLIO OVER TIME

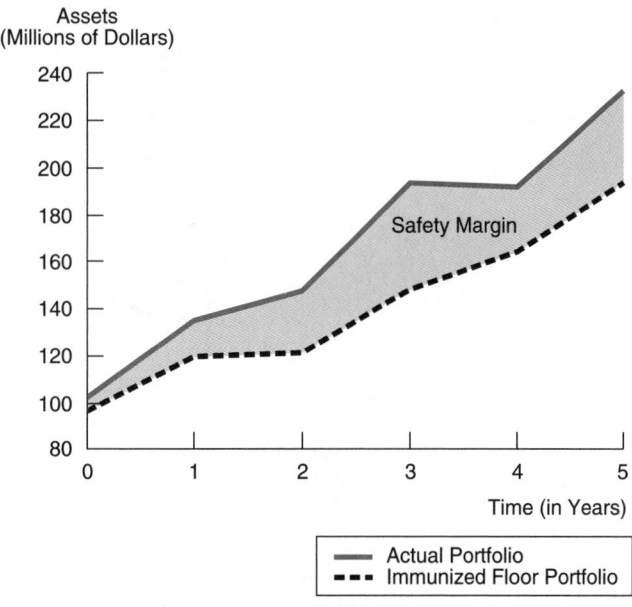

Monitoring the Immunized Portfolio Clearly, a crucial factor in managing a contingent immunized portfolio is monitoring it to ensure that if the asset value falls to the trigger point, it will be detected and the appropriate action taken to ensure that the portfolio is immunized at the floor-level rate. This can be done using a chart as in Exhibit 20.15. The top line is the current market value of the portfolio over time. The bottom line is the required value of the immunized floor portfolio. Specifically, the bottom line is *the required value of the portfolio* if we were to immunize at *today's rates* to attain the necessary ending-wealth value. This required minimum value for the portfolio is calculated by *computing the present value of the promised ending-wealth value at the prevailing market rate.*

To demonstrate how this floor portfolio would be constructed, consider our example where we derived a promised ending-wealth value in five years of $196.72 million based on an initial investment of $100 million and an acceptable floor rate of 14 percent. If one year after the initiation of the portfolio, market rates were 10 percent, you would need a minimum portfolio value of approximately $133.14 million to get to $196.72 million in four years. To compute this minimum required value, you multiply the $196.72 million (promised ending-wealth value) times the present value factor for 5 percent for eight periods, assuming semiannual compounding (.6768). The logic is that $133.14 million ($196.72 × .6768) invested (immunized) at 10 percent for four years will equal $196.72 million.

If the active manager had predicted correctly that market rates would decline and had a long-duration portfolio under these conditions, the *actual* value of the portfolio would be much higher than this *minimum required* value, and there would be a safety margin. A year later (after Year 2), you would determine the assets needed at the rate prevailing at that point in time. Assuming interest rates had increased to 12 percent, you could determine that you would need a floor portfolio of about $138.69 million. Specifically, this is the present value of the $196.72 million for

EXHIBIT 20.16 *COMPARISON OF RETURN DISTRIBUTIONS*

three years at 12 percent, assuming semiannual compounding (0.7050). Again, you would expect the actual value of the portfolio to be greater than this required floor portfolio, so you still have a safety margin. If you ever reached the point where the actual value of the portfolio was equal to the required floor value, you would stop the active management and immunize what was left *at the current market rate* to ensure that the ending value of the portfolio would be $196.72 million.

In summary, the contingent immunization strategy encompasses the opportunity for a bond portfolio manager to engage in various active portfolio strategies if the client is willing to accept a floor return (and ending-wealth value) that is below what is currently available. The graph in Exhibit 20.16 describes the trade-offs involved in contingent immunization. Specifically, by allowing for a slightly lower minimum target rate, the client is making it possible to experience a much higher potential return from active management by the portfolio manager.

IMPLICATIONS OF CAPITAL MARKET THEORY AND THE EMH ON BOND PORTFOLIO MANAGEMENT

The high level of interest rates that has prevailed since the latter part of the 1960s has provided increasingly attractive returns to bond investors, and the wide swings in interest rates that have accompanied these high market yields have provided numerous capital gains opportunities for bond portfolio managers. As a result, the average compound rates of return on bonds during the 1980s were the highest of any 10-year period in this century, and this performance continued into the 1990s. Specifically, the results contained in Exhibit 20.17 indicate that the annual returns on the aggregate of high-grade bonds during the period 1980–2001 ranged from –2.92 percent (the only negative annual return) to 32.64 percent, and the geometric mean returns of 10.04 percent were clearly impressive even compared to the average returns on common stocks of 14.69 percent. When these are compared to the long-term results since 1926 (see Exhibit 20.19), it appears that it will be difficult to continue such performance. Still, these results indicate that there are some wonderful opportunities available in bonds. An important consideration for portfolio managers, therefore, is the proper role of fixed-income securities when considering the implications of portfolio theory, capital market theory, and research related to efficient capital markets.

EXHIBIT 20.17	ANNUAL RATES OF RETURN, RISK MEASURES, AND RANGES OF RETURN FOR LEHMAN BROTHERS BOND INDEXES AND THE S&P 500 TOTAL RETURN STOCK INDEX: 1980–2001

	ARITHMETIC MEAN	GEOMETRIC MEAN	STANDARD DEVIATION	COEFFICIENT OF VARIATION[a]	HIGH YEAR	LOW YEAR
Lehman Brothers Gov./Corp.	10.21	9.95	7.84	0.77	31.10	−3.51
Lehman Brothers Government	10.03	9.81	7.23	0.72	27.74	−3.37
Lehman Brothers Corporate	10.86	10.47	9.69	0.89	39.23	−3.93
Lehman Brothers Mortgage	10.69	10.32	7.87	0.90	43.04	−1.61
Lehman Brothers Non-Corp. Inv. Gr.[b]	8.98	8.72	9.72	0.88	23.44	−4.94
Lehman Brothers Aggregate	10.30	10.04	7.89	0.77	32.64	−2.92
S&P 500	15.69	14.69	15.21	0.97	37.43	−13.04

[a]Coefficient of Variation = Standard Deviation/Arithmetic Mean Return.

[b]Data only available from 1990.

Source: *Global Family of Indices*—Historical Database 1973–2001, Lehman Brothers, Fixed Income Research. Reprinted with permission.

Bonds and Total Portfolio Theory

The performance of bonds has improved even more than indicated by returns alone because bonds offer substantial diversification benefits. In an efficient market, neither stocks nor bonds should dominate a portfolio, but some combination of them should provide a superior risk-adjusted return compared to either one taken alone (assuming low correlation between stocks and bonds). In the study by Reilly, Kao, and Wright, which showed that stock returns were superior to bond yields, they also showed that, due to the low correlation between bonds and equities (about 0.30), the combination of the stocks and bonds in a portfolio vastly improved the return per unit of risk.[38]

Bonds and Capital Market Theory

Capital market theory contends that there should be an upward-sloping market line, meaning that greater return should be accompanied by greater risk. Compared to other market vehicles, fixed-income securities were traditionally viewed as low risk and their rates of return were typically modest until the late 1970s. At that time, the inflation rate and bond yields increased. Also, during periods of high economic uncertainty, such as the recessions of 1981–1982 and 1990–1991, the risk premiums on bonds increased substantially because the risk of default for low-rated obligations increased.[39] As demonstrated earlier in the chapter (Exhibit 20.1), the risk premium on high-yield bonds has fluctuated dramatically over time.

Capital market theory also relates the risk-return behavior of fixed-income securities to other financial assets. Because fixed-income securities are considered to be relatively conservative investments, we would expect them to be on the lower end of the capital market line. A study by Reilly and Wright examined the comparative risk-return characteristics of 36 classes of long-term securities.[40] Exhibit 20.18 shows the basic findings of the study and confirms the a priori expectations. Specifically, government and high-grade corporate bonds were at the low end of the risk

[38]Frank K. Reilly, Wenchi Kao, and David J. Wright, "Alternative Bond Market Indexes," *Financial Analysts Journal* 48, no. 3 (May–June 1992): 44–58. These correlations were confirmed for the period 1980–2001 in Frank K. Reilly and David J. Wright, "An Analysis of Global Capital Market Risk-Adjusted Returns," mimeo (July 2002).

[39]For a detailed discussion on this topic that considers several studies on the subject, see James C. Van Horne, *Financial Market Rates and Flows*, 5th ed. (Englewood Cliffs, N.J.: Prentice-Hall, 1998), Chapter 6.

[40]Frank K. Reilly and David J. Wright, "An Analysis of Global Capital Market Risk-Adjusted Returns," University of Notre Dame Working Paper (July 2002).

EXHIBIT 20.18   *TOTAL RISK-RETURN COMPARISON FOR ALTERNATIVE CAPITAL MARKET ASSETS: 1980–2001*

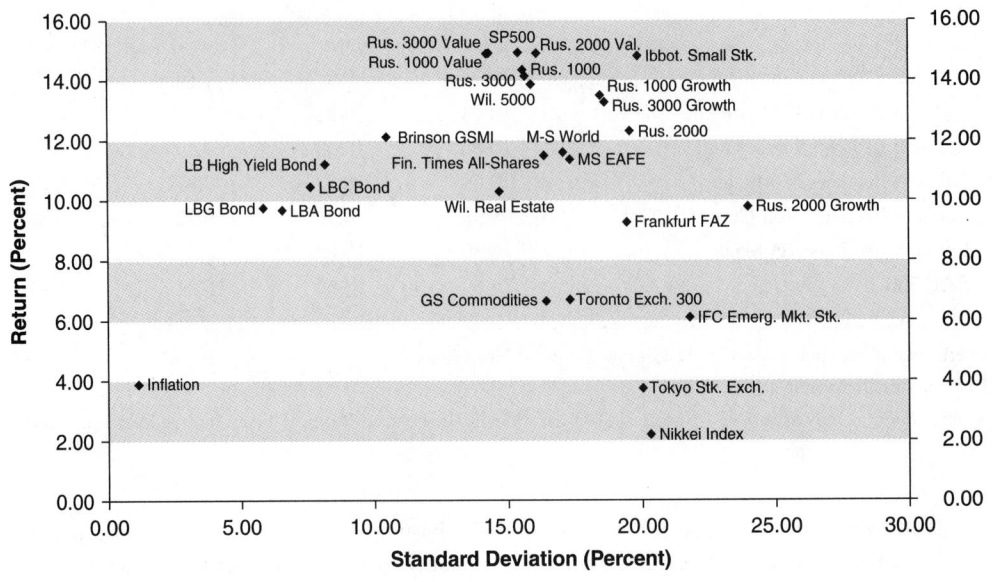

Source: Frank K. Reilly and David J. Wright, "An Analysis of Global Capital Market Risk-Adjusted Returns," University of Notre Dame Working Paper (July 2002).

spectrum, and it progressed to high-quality common stocks, small-cap stocks, foreign stocks, and, finally, emerging-market stocks. An annual analysis of capital market returns by Ibbotson Associates comparing corporate and government bonds (long- and intermediate-term) to common stocks (total NYSE and small-firm) and Treasury bill obligations indicated similar results. As Exhibit 20.19 shows, Treasury bills have the least risk and return, followed by government bonds, corporate bonds, large company common stocks, and, finally, small company common stocks.

Bond Price Behavior in a CAPM Framework   The capital asset pricing model (CAPM) is expected to provide a framework for explaining realized security returns as a function of nondiversifiable market risk. Bond returns should be linked directly to risk of default and interest rate risk. Although interest rate risk for investment-quality bonds should be nondiversifiable, some evidence exists that default risk also is largely nondiversifiable because default experience is closely related to the business cycle.[41] Therefore,

---

[41]W. Braddock Hickman, *Corporate Bond Quality and Investor Experience* (New York: National Bureau of Economic Research, 1958); Thomas R. Atkinson, *Trends in Corporate Bond Quality* (New York: National Bureau of Economic Research, 1967); Dwight M. Jaffee, "Cyclical Variations in the Risk Structure of Interest Rates," *Journal of Monetary Economics* 1, no. 2 (July 1975): 309–325; Douglas J. Lucas and John G. Lonski, "Changes in Corporate Credit Quality 1970–1990," *Journal of Fixed Income* 1, no. 4 (March 1992): 7–14; Jean Helwege and Paul Kleiman, "Understanding Aggregate Default Rates of High-Yield Bonds," *Journal of Fixed Income* 7, no. 1 (June 1997): 55–61; Martin S. Fridson, M. Christopher Garman, and Sheng Wu, "Real Interest Rates and the Default Rate on High-Yield Bonds," *Journal of Fixed Income* 7, no. 2 (September 1997): 29–34; and Chunsheng Zhon, "Credit Rating and Corporate Defaults," *Journal of Fixed Income* 11, no. 3 (December 2001): 30–40.

EXHIBIT 20.19 ▶ *MEAN RATE OF RETURN AND STANDARD DEVIATION OF RETURNS FOR COMMON STOCKS, GOVERNMENT AND CORPORATE BONDS, T-BILLS, AND INFLATION: 1926–2001*

Series	Geometric Mean	Arithmetic Mean	Standard Deviation	Distribution
Large-company stocks	11.7%	12.7%	20.2%	
Small-company stocks	12.5	17.3	33.2	*
Long-term corporate bonds	5.8	6.1	8.6	
Long-term government bonds	5.3	5.7	9.4	
Intermediate-term government bonds	5.3	5.5	5.7	
U.S. Treasury bills	3.8	3.9	3.2	
Inflation	3.1	3.1	4.4	

-90%   0%   90%

*The 1933 small-company stocks total return was 142.9 percent.

Source: *Stocks, Bonds, Bills, and Inflation*® *2002 Yearbook,* © 2002 Ibbotson Associates, Inc. Based on copyrighted works by Ibbotson and Sinquefield. All rights reserved. Used with permission.

because the major bond risks are largely nondiversifiable, this implies that we should be able to define bond returns in the context of the CAPM. Still, few studies have attempted it because of data-collection problems.

Reilly and Joehnk found that average bond betas had no significant or consistent relationships with agency ratings.[42] Because the study involved only investment-grade securities, the major factor affecting bond prices was market interest rate movements. Evidence that high-grade bond risk is almost all systematic risk is found in the Reilly-Wright study, which shows that the returns among these investment-grade bonds, regardless of sector (government, corporate, mortgages)

---

[42]Frank K. Reilly and Michael D. Joehnk, "The Association between Market-Determined Risk Measures for Bonds and Bond Ratings," *Journal of Finance* 31, no. 5 (December 1976): 1387–1403.

or ratings, were correlated 0.90 to 0.99.[43] This systematic interest rate risk has an overpowering effect on price performance and largely negates the effects of differential default risk, which is reflected in comparative agency ratings. Notably, the overpowering effect of systematic interest rate risk does *not* prevail when one considers high-yield (junk) bonds. As shown by Reilly and Wright, the correlation between high-yield bonds and investment-grade bonds is *lower* than the strong correlation between high-yield bonds and common stock, which is because both high-yield bonds and common stocks have substantial unsystematic risk.[44]

Alexander examined some of the assumptions of the market model as related to bonds and found two major problems.[45] First, the bond beta results were sensitive to the market index used.[46] Second, the results were sensitive to the time period used; the bond betas increased during periods of high bond yields.

Weinstein computed betas for bonds using several market series and related the betas to term to maturity, coupon, and bond ratings.[47] The results were likewise affected by the market indexes used. No significant relationship existed between the betas and bond ratings for the top four classes of ratings (similar to the findings of Reilly and Joehnk), but there was a weak relationship using the top six ratings. The author postulated that the risk of default becomes significant only for low ratings, which is consistent with default rates in Exhibit 20.2.

In a subsequent study, Weinstein computed bond betas and examined their stability over time.[48] He found that a bond's beta was related to firm characteristics (e.g., debt-equity ratios, and the variance of rate of return on assets) and to bond characteristics (coupon, term to maturity).

Thus, evidence on the usefulness of the CAPM as related to the bond market is mixed. Specifically, there are obvious problems regarding the appropriate market index to use, the systematic risk measure is unstable, and the risk-return relationship did not hold for the higher-quality bonds. Finally, there appears to be a relationship between the systematic risk measure and some characteristics of the firm.

Bond Market Efficiency

Two versions of the efficient market hypothesis (EMH) are examined in the context of fixed-income securities: the weak and the semistrong theories. The weak-form hypothesis contends that security price movements are independent events so historical price information is useless in predicting future price behavior. Studies of weak-form efficiency have examined the ability of investors to forecast interest rates, because if you can forecast interest rates you can forecast bond price behavior. Also, interest rate expectations are important for bond portfolio management.

Several studies[49] reached the same conclusion: interest rate behavior cannot be consistently and accurately forecast! In all cases, the most naive model, or no forecast at all, provided the best

[43]Frank K. Reilly and David J. Wright, "Bond Market Indexes" in *The Handbook of Fixed-Income Securities,* 6th ed.

[44]Frank K. Reilly and David J. Wright, "An Analysis of High-Yield Bond Indices" in *High-Yield Bonds,* ed. Theodore M. Barnhill, Jr., William F. Maxwell, and Mark R. Shenkman (New York: McGraw-Hill, 1999).

[45]Gordon J. Alexander, "Applying the Market Model to Long-Term Corporate Bonds," *Journal of Financial and Quantitative Analysis* 15, no. 5 (December 1980): 1063–1080.

[46]This is similar to the well-known work by Roll on market series.

[47]Mark I. Weinstein, "The Systematic Risk of Corporate Bonds," *Journal of Financial and Quantitative Analysis* 16, no. 3 (September 1981): 156–278.

[48]Mark I. Weinstein, "Bond Systematic Risk and the Option Pricing Model," *Journal of Finance* 38, no. 5 (December 1983): 1415–1429.

[49]See, for example, William A. Bomberger and W. J. Frazer, "Interest Rates, Uncertainty, and the Livingston Data," *Journal of Finance* 36, no. 3 (June 1981): 661–675; Stephen K. McNees, "The Recent Record of Thirteen Forecasters," *New England Economic Review,* Federal Reserve Bank of Boston (September–October 1981): 3–10; and Adrian W. Throop, "Interest Rate Forecasts and Market Efficiency," Federal Reserve Bank of San Francisco *Economic Review* (Spring 1981): 29–43.

measure of future interest rate behavior. Clearly, if it is not possible to forecast interest rates, then bond prices cannot be forecast using historical prices, all of which support the weak-form EMH.

The semistrong EMH asserts that current prices fully reflect all public knowledge and that efforts to act on public information are largely unproductive. Several studies have examined the informational value of bond rating changes. Katz examined monthly changes in bond yields surrounding ratings changes and found a significant impact of the change.[50] Weinstein examined monthly bond returns surrounding the announcement of rating changes and found an effect during the interval from 18 months to 7 months before the announcement but no effect during the period from 6 months before the announcement to 6 months after the announcement.[51]

In contrast, several studies have examined the impact of bond rating changes on stock prices and returns.[52] The results indicated either very little impact on stocks or a differential impact, depending on whether it was an upgrade or a downgrade.

The Internet *Investments Online*

Fixed-income management analytics and software are typically proprietary. The sites listed below offer some additional information about the techniques discussed in the text and will give you insight into the use of various analytical and portfolio management techniques.

http://www.ryanlabs.com Ryan Labs is a leader in the construction and analysis of fixed-income indexes. Their site offers information on its research, data, indexing, consulting, and asset/liability management skills (this latter feature is of particular importance to portfolios that must meet a stream of cash outflows, such as a pension fund). The site discusses the quantitative nature of bond-portfolio management, fixed-income index construction, and the variety of risk and reward measures used for bond investment analysis.

http://cmsbondedge.com The home page of CMS BondEdge allows users to move to sites featuring CMS's various products. CMS sells fixed-income analytical software to institutional investment managers. Research papers on fixed income security analysis are offered free of charge to users who fill out an on-line form. BondEdge is a product offering "what-if" simulations, volatility appraisals, and other analytics to fixed-income portfolio managers.

Brokerage houses offer fixed-income portfolio information and strategies with an orientation to the individual investor. See, for example, **http://www.salomonsmithbarney.com/research/fixed_income.html**.

Summary

• During the past decade, there has been a significant increase in the number and range of bond portfolio management strategies available. Bond portfolio management strategies include the relatively straightforward buy-and-hold and bond indexing strategies, several alternative active portfolio strategies, dedicated cash matching, classical immunization, horizon matching, and contingent immunization.

---

[50]Steven Katz, "The Price Adjustment Process of Bonds to Rating Reclassifications: A Test of Bond Market Efficiency," *Journal of Finance* 29, no. 2 (May 1974): 551–559.

[51]Mark I. Weinstein, "The Effect of a Rating Change Announcement on Bond Price," *Journal of Financial Economics* 5, no. 3 (December 1977): 329–350.

[52]George E. Pinches and Clay Singleton, "The Adjustment of Stock Prices to Bond Rating Changes," *Journal of Finance* 33, no. 1 (March 1978): 29–44; Paul A. Griffin and Antonio Z. Sanvicente, "Common Stock Returns and Rating Changes: A Methodological Comparison," *Journal of Finance* 37, no. 1 (March 1982): 103–119; and Robert W. Holthausen and Richard W. Leftwich, "The Effect of Bond Rating Changes on Common Stock Prices," *Journal of Financial Economics* 17, no. 1 (September 1986): 57–89.

Although you should understand the alternatives available and how to implement them, you also should recognize that the choice of a specific strategy is based on the needs and desires of the client. In turn, the success of any strategy will depend on the background and talents of the portfolio manager.

• The risk-return performance of bonds as a unique asset class has been consistent with expectations. In addition, their inclusion has generally enhanced overall portfolio performance because of their low covariance with other financial assets. The application of CAPM concepts to bonds has been mixed because it has been difficult to derive acceptable measures of systematic risk, and the risk measures derived have been unstable.

• Studies in the bond market have supported the theory of weak-form efficiency. The evidence for semi-strong efficiency has been mixed. The results that indicate a lack of efficiency could be due to the relatively inactive secondary markets for most corporate bonds, which causes pricing and adjustment problems compared to the active markets for equities.

Questions

1. What is meant by an indexing portfolio strategy and why is it used?
2. Briefly define the following bond swaps: pure yield pickup swap, substitution swap, and tax swap.
3. Briefly describe three active bond portfolio management strategies.
4. Discuss two variables you would examine very carefully if you were analyzing a high-yield bond, and indicate why they are important.
5. How would you explain to a casual observer why high-yield bond returns are more correlated to common stock returns than to investment-grade bond returns?
6. What are the advantages and difficulties of a cash-matched dedicated portfolio?
7. Describe the two components of interest rate risk.
8. What is meant by bond portfolio immunization?
9. If the yield curve were flat and did not change, how would you immunize your portfolio?
10. You begin with an investment horizon of four years and a portfolio with a duration of four years with a market interest rate of 10 percent. A year later, what is your investment horizon? Assuming no change in interest rates, what is the duration of your portfolio relative to your investment horizon? What does this imply about your ability to immunize your portfolio?
11. It has been contended that a zero coupon bond is the ideal financial instrument to use for immunizing a portfolio. Discuss the reasoning for this statement.
12. During a conference with a client, the subject of classical immunization is introduced. The client questions the fee charged for developing and managing an immunized portfolio. The client believes it is basically a passive investment strategy, so the management fee should be substantially lower. What would you tell the client to show that it is not a passive policy?
13. With contingent immunization, what do you give up and what do you gain?
14. *CFA Examination Level III*
    The ability to *immunize* a bond portfolio is very desirable for bond portfolio managers in some instances.
    a. Discuss the components of interest rate risk. Assuming a change in interest rates over time, explain the two risks faced by the holder of a bond.
    b. Define immunization and discuss why a bond manager would immunize a portfolio.
    c. Explain why a duration-matching strategy is a superior technique to a maturity-matching strategy for the minimization of interest rate risk.
    d. Explain in specific terms how you would use a zero coupon bond to immunize a bond portfolio. Discuss why a zero coupon bond is an ideal instrument in this regard.
    e. Explain how *contingent immunization,* another bond portfolio management technique, differs from *classical immunization.* Discuss why a bond portfolio manager would engage in contingent immunization. [35 minutes]
15. *CFA Examination Level III*
    During the past several years, there has been substantial growth in the dollar amount of portfolios managed using *immunization* and *dedication* techniques. Assume a client wants to know the basic differences between (1) classical immunization, (2) contingent immunization, (3) cash-matched dedication, and (4) duration-matched dedication.

a. Briefly describe each of these four techniques.

b. Briefly discuss the ongoing investment action you would have to carry out if managing an *immunized portfolio*.

c. Briefly discuss three of the major considerations involved with creating a *cash-matched dedicated* portfolio.

d. Describe two parameters that should be specified when using *contingent immunization*.

e. Select one of the four alternative techniques that you believe requires the least degree of active management and justify your selection. [20 minutes]

 16. *CFA Examination Level III*

After you have constructed a structured fixed-income portfolio (i.e., one that is dedicated, indexed, or immunized), it may be possible over time to improve on the initial optimal portfolio while continuing to meet the primary goal. Discuss three conditions that would be considered favorable for a restructuring—assuming no change in objectives for the investor—and cite an example of each condition. [10 minutes]

 17. *CFA Examination Level III*

The use of bond index funds has grown dramatically in recent years.

a. Discuss the reasons you would expect it to be easier or more difficult to construct a bond market index than a stock market index.

b. It is contended that the *operational process* of managing a corporate bond index fund is more difficult than managing an equity index fund. Discuss three examples that support this contention. [15 minutes]

 18. *CFA Examination Level III* (adapted)

Hans Kaufmann is a global fixed-income portfolio manager based in Switzerland. His clients are primarily U.S.-based pension funds. He allocates investments in the United States, Japan, Germany, and the United Kingdom. His approach is to make investment allocation decisions among these four countries based on his global economic outlook. To develop this economic outlook, Kaufmann analyzes the following five factors for each country: real economic growth, inflation, monetary policy, interest rates, and exchange rates.

When Kaufmann believes that the four economies are equally attractive for investment purposes, he equally weights investments in the four countries. When the economies are not equally attractive, he overweights the country or countries where he sees the largest potential returns.

Table 1 through Table 5 present relevant economic data and forecasts.

a. Indicate, before taking into account currency hedging, whether Kaufmann should overweight or underweight investments in each country. Justify your position. [15 minutes]

b. Briefly describe how your answer to Part a might change with the use of currency-hedging techniques. [5 minutes]

TABLE 1 ▶ *REAL GDP (ANNUAL CHANGES)*

	1996	1997	1998	1999E
United States	3.0%	2.9%	2.4%	2.7%
Japan	4.7	2.4	3.2	3.4
Germany	2.0	2.5	1.5	2.1
United Kingdom	3.4	3.0	3.4	2.3

TABLE 2 ▶ *GDP DEFLATOR (ANNUAL CHANGES)*

	1996	1997	1998	1999E
United States	3.2%	2.6%	3.3%	3.8%
Japan	1.5	2.8	3.0	3.0
Germany	2.2	3.1	2.5	2.2
United Kingdom	6.0	3.5	4.5	4.8

TABLE 3

NARROW MONEY (MI) (ANNUAL CHANGES)

	1996	1997	1998	1999E
United States	9.2%	13.4%	5.5%	7.0%
Japan	5.0	6.9	9.9	10.0
Germany	4.3	8.5	7.5	8.5
United Kingdom	7.0	8.0	6.7	5.5

TABLE 4

LONG-TERM INTEREST RATES (ANNUAL RATES)

	1996	1997	1998	1999E
United States	10.6%	7.7%	8.8%	9.0%
Japan	5.5	4.1	4.7	4.7
Germany	9.9	5.9	6.1	7.0
United Kingdom	10.6	9.9	9.8	9.5

TABLE 5

EXCHANGE RATES (CURRENCY PER U.S. DOLLARS)

	1996	1997	1998	1999E
United States (dollars)	1.00	1.00	1.00	1.00
Japan (yen)	130.10	121.50	111.40	108.35
Germany (marks)	1.95	1.80	1.60	1.52
United Kingdom (pounds)	0.67	0.60	0.58	0.59

Sources: International Monetary Fund.

19. *CFA Examination Level I*

Robert Devlin and Neil Parish are portfolio managers at the Broward Investment Group. At their regular Monday strategy meeting, the topic of adding international bonds to one of their portfolios came up. The portfolio, an ERISA-qualified pension account for a U.S. client, was currently 90 percent invested in U.S. Treasury bonds and 10 percent invested in 10-year Canadian government bonds.

Devlin suggested buying a position in 10-year German government bonds, while Parish argued for a position in 10-year Australian government bonds.

a. Briefly discuss the *three* major issues that Devlin and Parish should address in their analysis of the return prospects for German and Australian bonds relative to those of U.S. bonds. [6 minutes]

Having made no changes to the original portfolio, Devlin and Parish hold a subsequent strategy meeting and decide to add positions in the government bonds of Japan, the United Kingdom, France, Germany, and Australia.

b. Identify and discuss *two* reasons for adding a broader mix of international bonds to the pension portfolio. [9 minutes]

20. *CFA Examination Level III*

The investment committee of the money management firm of Gentry, Inc., has typically been very conservative and has avoided investing in high-yield (junk) bonds, although they have had major positions in investment-grade corporate bonds. Recently, Pete Squire, a member of the committee, suggested that they should review their policy regarding junk bonds because they currently constitute over 25 percent of the total corporate bond market.

As part of this policy review, you are asked to respond to the following questions:

a. Briefly discuss the liquidity *and* pricing characteristics of junk bonds relative to *each* of the following types of fixed-income securities:
- Treasuries
- High-grade corporate bonds
- Corporate loans
- Private placements

Briefly discuss the implications of these differences for Gentry's bond portfolio managers. The committee has learned that the correlation of rates of return between Treasuries and high-grade corporate bonds is approximately 0.98, while the correlation between Treasury/high-grade corporate bonds and junk bonds is approximately 0.45.

b. Briefly explain the reason for this difference in correlations, and briefly discuss its implications for bond portfolios.

The committee has also heard that durations at the times of issue for junk bonds are typically much shorter than for newly issued high-grade corporate bonds.

c. Briefly explain the reason for this difference in duration, and briefly discuss its implication for the volatility of high-yield bond portfolios. [15 minutes]

 21. *CFA Examination Level II*

Greg Kemp, CFA, Chief Investment Officer of Anchor Advisors, has received the following recommendation from his bond management group.

> "We believe the current environment has focused excessive pessimism on high-grade corporate bonds. Fears of 'event risk' and weakness in the junk bond market have widened yield spreads to attractive levels.
>
> "It is recommended that our employee benefit bond accounts reduce their current U.S. Treasury weightings from 75 percent to 25 percent, with this money to be invested in callable Single-A and AA utility bonds with coupon rates between 9 percent and 11 percent. The durations of the bonds purchased will be equal to those sold."

Kemp accepts the idea that yield spreads are wider than normal between U.S. Treasury bonds and corporate issues. Interest rates on long-term U.S. Treasury issues are currently 9 percent. He expects a significant (more than 100 basis points) drop in interest rates.

a. Kemp has some concerns about the volatility implications of the proposed trade in light of his understanding of the concepts of duration, convexity, and option-adjusted spreads. Given his interest rate expectations, identify and explain *two* key questions that Kemp should raise about the proposed trade. [10 minutes]

b. Recommend *two* modifications to the proposed trade that would address Kemp's concerns mentioned in Part a. [5 minutes]

22. *CFA Examination Level II*

Bond analysis often requires more than traditional credit ratio analysis. Discuss *each* of the following *three* considerations as they relate to evaluating a specific fixed-income security:

(a) Competition within the industry
(b) Liquidation value of net assets
(c) Management [6 minutes]

23. *CFA Examinaton Level III*

A consultant suggests that the weighted-average portfolio duration calculation for a global bond portfolio is the same as for a domestic bond portfolio.

a. State whether the use of portfolio duration in international bond portfolio management is more limiting than in domestic bond portfolio management. Support your conclusion with *two* reasons. [8 minutes]

The consultant recognizes that currency, duration, and investing outside the benchmark are possible sources of excess return in global bond management. He is also curious about additional methods of adding value through global bond management.

b. List and discuss *two* additional potential sources of excess return. [6 minutes]

Problems

1. You have a portfolio with a market value of $50 million and a Macaulay duration of seven years (assuming a market interest rate of 10 percent). If interest rates increase to 12 percent, what would be the estimated value of your portfolio using modified duration? Show all your computations.

2. Answer the following questions assuming that at the initiation of an investment account, the market value of your portfolio is $200 million, and you immunize the portfolio at 12 percent for six years. During the first year, interest rates are constant at 12 percent.
   a. What is the market value of the portfolio at the end of Year 1?
   b. Immediately after the end of the year, interest rates *decline* to 10 percent. Estimate the new value of the portfolio, assuming you did the required rebalancing (use only modified duration).

3. Compute the Macaulay duration under the following conditions:
   a. A bond with a five-year term to maturity, a 12 percent coupon (annual payments), and a market yield of 10 percent.
   b. A bond with a four-year term to maturity, a 12 percent coupon (annual payments), and a market yield of 10 percent.
   c. Compare your answers to Parts a and b, and discuss the implications of this for classical immunization.

4. Compute the Macaulay duration under the following conditions:
   a. A bond with a four-year term to maturity, a 10 percent coupon (annual payments), and a market yield of 8 percent
   b. A bond with a four-year term to maturity, a 10 percent coupon (annual payments), and a market yield of 12 percent
   c. Compare your answers to Parts a and b. Assuming it was an immediate shift in yields, discuss the implications of this for classical immunization.

5. A major requirement in running a contingent immunization portfolio policy is monitoring the relationship between the current market value of the portfolio and the required value of the floor portfolio. In this regard, assume a $300 million portfolio with a horizon of five years. The available market rate at the initiation of the portfolio is 14 percent, but the client is willing to accept 12 percent as a floor rate to allow you to use active management strategies. The current market values and current market rates at the end of Years 1, 2, and 3 are as follows:

End of Year	Market Value ($ Mil)	Market Yield	Required Floor Portfolio	Safety Margin (Deficiency)
1	340.00	0.12		
2	375.00	0.10		
3	360.20	0.14		

   a. What is the required ending-wealth value for this portfolio?
   b. What is the value of the required floor portfolio at the end of Years 1, 2, and 3?
   c. Compute the safety margin or deficiency at the end of Years 1, 2, and 3.

6. Evaluate the following pure yield pickup swap: You currently hold a 20-year, Aa-rated, 9.0 percent coupon bond priced to yield 11.0 percent. As a swap candidate, you are considering a 20-year, Aa-rated, 11 percent coupon bond priced to yield 11.5 percent. (Assume reinvestment at 11.5 percent.)

	Current Bond	Candidate Bond
Dollar investment	_____	_____
Coupon	_____	_____
i on one coupon	_____	_____
Principal value at year end	_____	_____
Total accrued	_____	_____
Realized compound yield	_____	_____
Value of swap: _____ basis points in one year		

7. Evaluate the following substitution swap: You currently hold a 25-year, 9.0 percent coupon bond priced to yield 10.5 percent. As a swap candidate, you are considering a 25-year, Aa-rated, 9.0 percent coupon bond priced to yield 10.75 percent. (Assume a one-year work-out period and reinvestment at 10.5 percent.)

	Current Bond	Candidate Bond
Dollar investment	_____	_____
Coupon	_____	_____
i on one coupon	_____	_____
Principal value at year end	_____	_____
Total accrued	_____	_____
Realized compound yield	_____	_____
Value of swap: _____ basis points in one year		

 8. *CFA Examination Level III*

Reinvestment risk is a major factor for bond managers to consider when determining the most appropriate or optimal strategy for a fixed-income portfolio. Briefly describe each of the following bond portfolio management strategies, and explain how each deals with reinvestment risk:
a. Active management
b. Classical immunization
c. Dedicated portfolio
d. Contingent immunization [20 minutes]

 9. *CFA Examination Level III*

A major requirement in managing a fixed-income portfolio using a contingent immunization policy is monitoring the relationship between the current market value of the portfolio and the required value of the floor portfolio. This difference is defined as the *margin of error*. In this regard, assume a $300 million portfolio with a time horizon of five years. The available market rate at the initiation of the portfolio is 12 percent, but the client is willing to accept 10 percent as a floor rate to allow use of active management strategies. The current market values and current market rates at the end of Years 1, 2, and 3 are as follows:

End of Year	Market Value ($ Mil)	Market Yield	Required Floor Portfolio ($ Mil)	Margin of Error ($ Mil)
1	$340.9	10%		
2	405.5	8		
3	395.2	12		

Table 1
Present Value Table (use tables in appendix in the back of book)
Table 2
Compound Value Table (use tables in appendix in the back of book)

Assuming semiannual compounding:
a. Calculate the required ending-wealth value for this portfolio.
b. Calculate the value of the required floor portfolios at the end of Years 1, 2, and 3.
c. Compute the margin of error at the end of Years 1, 2, and 3.
d. Indicate the action that a portfolio manager utilizing a *contingent immunization* policy would take if the margin of error at the end of any year had been zero or negative.

 10. *CFA Examination Level III*

PTC's Investment Committee has decided to allocate 50 percent of the pension plan portfolio's fixed-income investment to non-U.S. government bonds (i.e., bonds representing non-U.S. sovereign credits). For a number of reasons, BAG—the Committee's consultant—has recommended against using a pure dedication approach to management of the bonds. Instead, it has presented the committee with three alternative strategies for consideration, accompanied by the 15-year historical performance data for each strategy shown in Table 6.

a. Based on the management strategy characteristics set forth in Table 6, as well as your general knowledge, identify and explain *three* advantages of *each* strategy as an alternative for the Investment Committee to consider. In developing your response, regard yourself as a strong advocate as you explain the advantages of *each* of the three alternatives. [15 minutes]

b. Identify and explain *one* key *disadvantage* of *each* of the three strategies. [5 minutes]

TABLE 6

	15-Year Historical Universe Performance			
	Average Returns Annualized	Average Top Decile Returns[a] Annualized	Average Bottom Decile Returns[b] Annualized	Standard Deviation of Returns
Strategy Characteristics				
Active management	12.9%	15.6%	6.8%	18.6%
Duration shifts + or – 40% of Salomon WGB Index[c]				
Deviations from country allocation benchmarks in Index are unrestricted				
Transactions permitted for any management purpose				
Fee: 35 basis points/year				
Passive management	11.8%	12.8%	10.7%	16.0%
Duration shifts + or – 5% of Salomon WGB Index[c]				
Country allocation deviations limited relative to index proportions				
Transactions permitted only for replacement of deteriorating credits				
Fee: 15 basis points/year				
Indexed management	11.3%	12.0%	11.0%	14.9%
Match return of Salomon WGB Index[c]				
No duration shifts permitted				
Transactions allowed only for portfolio rebalancing				
Fee: 6 basis points/year				

[a]Top decile returns are simple average of the 10 best manager records in BAG's 100-manager universe.

[b]Bottom decile returns are a simple average of the 10 worst manager records in BAG's 100-manager universe.

[c]Salomon Brothers World Government Bond Index (WGB)

PTC has now decided to index the segment of the fixed-income portfolio to be invested in non-U.S. government bonds, using the Salomon Brothers World Government Bond Index as the benchmark portfolio. Assume this index includes the sovereign credits of nine major countries in the following proportions:

Country	Weighting
Australia	2%
Canada	8
Denmark	2
France	11
Germany	19
Japan	37
The Netherlands	8
Switzerland	2
United Kingdom	11

Several members of the Investment Committee favor use of the full replication approach to indexing the non-U.S. government bonds, while the chairman favors use of the stratified sampling approach. As the BAG representative assigned to the PTC account, you have been asked to assist the committee in choosing between the two indexing methods.

c. Describe and evaluate *each* of these two indexing alternatives for the purpose of creating and managing a bond portfolio intended to represent the Salomon Brothers World Government Bond Index benchmark. [10 minutes]

d. Evaluate the appropriateness of using the Salomon Brothers World Government Bond Index as a benchmark for purposes of monitoring PTC's non-U.S. portfolio exposures in relation to its pension benefit liability exposures. [5 minutes]

 11. *CFA Examination Level II*

PowerTool is the largest U.S. manufacturer of industrial hand tools. Its sales force is strong, but clients have complained that marketing is weak. The industrial tool business is mature, with little or no future expected growth.

PowerTool has acquired Fenton Manufacturing, a small, innovative company whose sales are entirely in the retail tool market. The retail tool market is expected to grow at a 5 percent annual rate.

Fenton recently developed a patented line of rechargeable home power tools that displayed strong potential in test markets. Fenton expects this line to generate 50 percent of its sales within five years but lacks a sales force to market this product line. Jerry Fenton, the company's founder, recently retired.

PowerTool management is highly respected and the company has experienced little management turnover. However, the Chief Executive Officer has announced her retirement after 18 years of service and will be replaced by the current Chief Operating Officer.

You are a private investor with a large investment in PowerTool bonds and wish to determine the effect of the acquisition of Fenton on PowerTool's bonds.

Table 7 presents financial ratios and debt ratings of PowerTool and Fenton prior to the merger and pro forma ratios of the combined company following the acquisition.

a. Explain how *each* of the following *three* ratios should be used to evaluate a firm's financial risk:

(1) Total debt to total capital

(2) Pretax interest coverage

(3) Operating cash flow to total debt [9 minutes]

TABLE 7 *FINANCIAL RATIOS AND DEBT RATINGS: JUNE 1, 1996*

Company	Total Debt to Total Capital	Pretax Interest Coverage	Operating Cash Flow to Total Debt	Debt Rating
PowerTool	30%	6.2 times	50%	A+
Fenton	72	2.1 times	8	Not rated
Combined	42	5.4 times	40	To be determined

TABLE 8 *BOND RATING CRITERIA: JUNE 1, 1996*

Debt Rating	Total Debt to Total Capital	Pretax Interest Coverage	Operating Cash Flow to Total Debt
AA	26%	8.8 times	75%
A	37	4.6 times	44
BBB	48	2.5 times	29

PowerTool has issued debt with the following covenants, which continue in force after its acquisition of Fenton.

Dividend Test Covenant

PowerTool may not pay any cash dividend or repurchase shares if such payment would result in a total debt-to-capital ratio in excess of 50 percent.

Put Option Covenant

If PowerTool's debt rating falls below A, bondholders have the right to redeem the bonds at a price of 105 plus accrued interest within 60 days following the change in rating.

b. Discuss the impact of *each* of the *two* debt covenants as just described on PowerTool's financial flexibility following its acquisition of Fenton:

   (1) Dividend Test covenant

   (2) Put Option Covenant [8 minutes]

Use only the information provided in the introduction in answering the following question.

c. Discuss, *from the PowerTool bondholders' point of view, two* advantages and *two* disadvantages to PowerTool of the acquisition of Fenton, with regard to the following product lines:

- Industrial tool business

- Retail tool business [12 minutes]

   PowerTool debt has not yet been re-rated following the acquisition of Fenton. PowerTool bonds are currently trading at a price comparable to A-rated bonds.

   Table 8 displays financial ratios used to determine bond ratings.

d. Recommend whether you should *hold* or *sell* the PowerTool bonds. Support your recommendations with *four* reasons drawn from the Introduction, Tables 7 and 8, and your answers to Parts a through c. [13 minutes]

 12. *CFA Examination Level II*

As a new employee at Clayton Asset Management, Emma Bennett has been assigned to evaluate the credit quality of BRT Corporation bonds. Clayton holds the bonds in its high-yield bond portfolio. The following information is provided to assist in the analysis.

   BRT Corporation is a rapidly growing company in the broadcast industry. It has grown primarily through a series of aggressive acquisitions.

   Early in 1996, BRT announced it was acquiring a competitor in a hostile takeover that would double its assets but also increase debt burdens. The credit rating of BRT debt fell from BBB to BB. The acquisition reduced the financial flexibility of BRT but increased its presence in the broadcasting industry.

Now, mid-1997, BRT has announced its merging with another large entertainment company. The merger will alter BRT's capital structure and place it as a leader in the broadcast industry. The early 1996 acquisition combined with this merger will increase the total assets of BRT by a factor of four. A large portion of the total assets are intangible, representing franchise and distribution rights.

Although the outlook for the broadcasting industry remains healthy, large telecommunication companies attempting to enter the broadcasting industry are keeping competitive pressures high. Laws and regulations also promote the competitiveness of the environment, but initial start-up costs make it difficult for new companies to enter the industry. Large capital expenditures are required to maintain and improve existing systems as well as to expand current business.

For Bennett's analysis, she has been provided with the financial data shown in Table 9 through Table 12.

a. Calculate the following ratios using the *projected 1997* financial information:
   (1) Operating income to sales
   (2) Earnings before interest and taxes to total assets
   (3) Times interest earned
   (4) Long-term debt to total assets [4 minutes]
b. Discuss the effect of the 1997 merger on the creditworthiness of BRT through an analysis of *each* of the ratios in Part a. [8 minutes]

BRT Corporation 10-year bonds are currently rated BB and are trading at a yield to maturity of 7.70 percent. The current 10-year Treasury note is yielding 6.15 percent.

c. State and justify, based on your work in Parts a and b, the information in Tables 11 and 12, and the introduction, whether Clayton should hold or sell the BRT Corporation bonds in its portfolio. Include a discussion of *two* qualitative factors. [10 minutes]

TABLE 9

BRT CORPORATION BALANCE SHEET DATA AT YEAR END— DECEMBER 31 (IN MILLIONS)

	1993	1994	1995	1996	Projected 1997
Current assets	$ 654	$ 718	$2,686	$ 2,241	$ 5,255
Net fixed assets	391	379	554	1,567	2,583
Other assets (Intangibles)	2,982	3,090	3,176	8,946	20,435
Total assets	$4,027	$4,187	$6,416	$12,754	$28,273
Current liabilities	$ 799	$ 876	$ 966	$ 1,476	$ 3,731
Long-term debt	2,537	2,321	2,378	7,142	15,701
Other liabilities	326	292	354	976	349
Total equity	365	698	2,718	3,160	8,492
Total liabilities and equity	$4,027	$4,187	$6,416	$12,754	$28,273

TABLE 10

BRT CORPORATION INCOME STATEMENT DATA—YEARS ENDING DECEMBER 31 (IN MILLIONS EXCEPT PER-SHARE DATA)

	1993	1994	1995	1996	Projected 1997
Net sales	$1,600	$1,712	$2,005	$4,103	$9,436
Operating expenses	1,376	1,400	1,620	3,683	8,603
Operating income	$ 224	$ 312	$ 385	$ 420	$ 833
Interest expense	296	299	155	270	825
Income taxes	20	42	130	131	4
Net income	$ (92)	$ (29)	$ 100	$ 19	$ 4
Earnings per share	($ 0.86)	($ 0.24)	$ 0.83	$ 0.09	$ 0.01
Average price per share	$26.30	$34.10	$ 4.90	$40.10	$40.80
Average shares outstanding	107	120	121	198	359

TABLE 11	BRT CORPORATION SELECTED FINANCIAL RATIOS

	1993	1994	1995	1996	Projected 1997
Operating income to sales (%)	14.0%	18.2%	19.2%	10.2%	*
Sales to total assets	0.39 times	0.41 times	0.31 times	0.32 times	0.33 times
Earnings before interest and taxes to total assets	5.5%	7.4%	6.0%	3.3%	*
Times interest earned	0.76 times	1.04 times	2.48 times	1.55 times	*
Long-term debt to total assets	63.0%	55.4%	37.0%	55.9%	*

TABLE 12	CLAYTON ASSET MANAGEMENT CREDIT RATING STANDARDS

	AVERAGE RATIOS BY RATING CATEGORY						
	AA	A	BBB	BB	B	CCC	CC
Financial Ratios							
Operating income to sales (%)	16.2	13.4	12.1	10.3	8.5	6.4	5.2
Sales to total assets	2.50 times	2.00 times	1.50 times	1.00 times	0.75 times	0.50 times	0.25 times
Earnings before interest and taxes to total assets	15.0%	10.0%	8.0%	6.0%	4.0%	3.0%	2.0%
Times interest earned	5.54 times	3.62 times	2.29 times	1.56 times	1.04 times	0.79 times	0.75 times
Long-term debt to total assets	19.5%	30.4%	40.2%	51.8%	71.8%	81.0%	85.4%
Bond Credit Spread Information							
Current yield spread in basis points over 10-year Treasuries	45	55	85	155	225	275	350

TABLE 13	FINANCIAL INFORMATION

Ratio	1997	1998	1999
Sturdy Machines			
Cash flow/total debt (%)	37.3	31.0	33.0
Total debt/capital (%)	38.2	40.1	41.3
Pretax interest coverage (×)	4.2	2.3	1.1
Patriot Manufacturing			
Cash flow/total debt (%)	34.6	38.0	43.1
Total debt/capital (%)	40.0	37.3	34.9
Pretax interest coverage (×)	2.7	4.5	6.1

13. *CFA Examination Level II*

Jane Berry is a fixed-income analyst at an investment management firm. She has been following the developments at two companies, Sturdy Machines and Patriot Manufacturing, which are both U.S.-based industrial companies that sell their products worldwide. Both companies operate in cyclical industries.

Sturdy Machine's profits have suffered from a rising dollar and a slump in its business. The company has said that major cuts in its operating expenses are likely to be necessary if it is to make a profit next year. On the other hand, Patriot Manufacturing has been able to maintain its profitability and enhance its balance sheet, as shown in Table 13.

Berry has been monitoring the bonds of these companies for possible purchase. She notices that a rating agency recently downgraded the senior debt of Sturdy Machines from A1 to A2 and upgraded the senior debt of Patriot Manufacturing from A3 to A2. Berry has received the following yield quotes from a broker:

- Sturdy Machines 7.50 percent due June 1, 2008, was quoted at 7.10 percent.
- Patriot Manufacturing 7.50 percent due June 1, 2008, was quoted at 7.10 percent.

Recommend which bond Berry should buy. Justify your choice with *two* factors from Table 13 and *two* qualitative factors from the preceding discussion. [16 minutes]

14. *CFA Examination Level II*

Mike Smith, CFA, an analyst with Blue River Investments, is considering buying a Montrose Cable Company Corporate bond. He has collected the following balance sheet and income statement information for Montrose as shown in Exhibit 1. He has also calculated the three ratios shown in Exhibit 2, which indicate that the bond is currently rated "A" according to the firm's internal bond-rating criteria shown in Exhibit 4.

Smith has decided to consider some off-balance-sheet items in his credit analysis, as shown in Exhibit 3. Specifically, Smith wishes to evaluate the impact of each of the off-balance-sheet items on each of the ratios found in Exhibit 2.

a. Calculate the combined effect of the *three* off-balance-sheet items in Exhibit 3 on *each* of the following *three* financial ratios shown in Exhibit 2. [9 minutes]

(1) EBITDA/interest expense.

(2) Long-term debt/equity.

(3) Current assets/current liabilities.

The bond is currently trading at a credit premium of 55 basis points. Using the internal bond-rating criteria in Exhibit 4, Smith wants to evaluate whether or not the credit yield premium incorporates the effect of the off-balance-sheet items.

b. State and justify whether or not the current credit yield premium compensates Smith for the credit risk of the bond based on the internal bond-rating criteria found in Exhibit 4. [6 minutes]

EXHIBIT 1

MONTROSE CABLE COMPANY: YEAR ENDED MARCH 31, 1999 (US$ THOUSAND)

Balance Sheet

Current assets	$ 4,735
Fixed assets	43,225
Total assets	$47,960
Current liabilities	$ 4,500
Long-term debt	10,000
Total liabilities	$14,500
Shareholder's equity	33,460
Total liabilities and shareholder's equity	$47,960

Income Statement

Revenue	$18,500
Operating and administrative expenses	14,050
Operating income	$ 4,450
Depreciation and amortization	1,675
Interest expense	942
Income before income taxes	$ 1,833
Taxes	641
Net income	$ 1,192

EXHIBIT 2

SELECTED RATIOS AND CREDIT YIELD PREMIUM DATA FOR MONTROSE

EBITDA/interest expense	4.72
Long-term debt/equity	0.30
Current assets/current liabilities	1.05
Credit yield premium over U.S. Treasuries	55 basis points

| EXHIBIT 3 | *MONTROSE OFF-BALANCE-SHEET ITEMS* |

- Montrose has guaranteed the long-term debt (principal only) of an unconsolidated affiliate. This obligation has a present value of $995,000.
- Montrose has sold $500,000 of accounts receivable with recourse at a yield of 8 percent.
- Montrose is a lessee in a new noncancelable operating leasing agreement to finance transmission equipment. The discounted present value of the lease payments is $6,144,000 using an interest rate of 10 percent. The annual payment will be $1,000,000.

| EXHIBIT 4 | *BLUE RIVER INVESTMENTS: INTERNAL BOND-RATING CRITERIA AND CREDIT YIELD PREMIUM DATA* |

Bond Rating	Interest Coverage (EBITDA/ Interest Expense)	Leverage (Long-Term Debt/Equity)	Current Ratio (Current Assets/ Current Liabilities)	Credit Yield Premium over U.S. Treasuries (in Basis Points)
AA	5.00 to 6.00	0.25 to 0.30	1.15 to 1.25	30 BPs
A	4.00 to 5.00	0.30 to 0.40	1.00 to 1.15	50 BPs
BBB	3.00 to 4.00	0.40 to 0.50	0.90 to 1.00	100 BPs
BB	2.00 to 3.00	0.50 to 0.60	0.75 to 0.90	125 BPs

References

Altman, Edward I., ed. *The High-Yield Debt Market*. Homewood, Ill.: Dow Jones–Irwin, 1990.

Barnhill, Theodore M., William F. Maxwell, and Mark R. Shenkman, eds. *High-Yield Bonds*. New York: McGraw-Hill, 1999.

Bierwag, G. O., George G. Kaufman, and Alden Toevs, eds. *Innovations in Bond Portfolio Management: Duration Analysis and Immunization*. Greenwich, Conn.: JAI Press, 1983.

Choie, Kenneth S. "A Simplified Approach to Bond Portfolio Management: DDS." *Journal of Portfolio Management* 16, no. 3 (Spring 1990).

Churchill, Dwight D., ed. *Fixed-Income Management: Techniques and Practices*. Charlottesville, Va.: Association for Investment Management and Research, 1994.

Core-Plus Bond Management. Charlottesville, Va.: Association for Investment Management and Research, 2001.

Dattatreya, Ravi E., and Frank J. Fabozzi. *Active Total Return Management of Fixed-Income Portfolios*, rev. ed. Burr Ridge, Ill.: Irwin Professional Publishing, 1995.

Fabozzi, Frank J., ed., *The Handbook of Fixed-Income Securities*, 6th ed. New York: McGraw-Hill, 2001.

Fabozzi, Frank J. *Fixed-Income Analysis for the Chartered Financial Analysts Program*. New Hope, Penn.: Frank J. Fabozzi Associates, 2000.

Fabozzi, Frank J., ed. *Fixed-Income Readings for the Chartered Financial Analysts Program*. New Hope, Penn.: Frank J. Fabozzi Associates, 2000.

Fabozzi, Frank J., ed. *The New High-Yield Debt Market*. New York: Harper Business, 1990.

Fridson, Martin. *High-Yield Bonds: Assessing Risk and Identifying Value in Speculative Grade Securities*. Chicago: Probus Publishing, 1989.

Global Bond Management II: The Search for Alpha. Charlottesville, Va.: Association for Investment Management and Research, 2000.

Howe, Jane Tripp. *Junk Bonds: Analysis and Portfolio Strategies*. Chicago: Probus Publishing, 1988.

Jost, Kathryn Dixon, ed. *Fixed-Income Management for the 21st Century*. Charlottesville, Va.: Association for Investment Management and Research, 2002.

Leibowitz, Martin L., William S. Krasker, and Ardavan Nozari. "Spread Duration: A New Tool for Bond Portfolio Management." *Journal of Portfolio Management* 16, no. 3 (Spring 1990).

Reilly, Frank K., ed. *High-Yield Bonds: Analysis and Risk Assessment.* Charlottesville, Va.: Institute of Chartered Financial Analysts, 1990.

Rosenberg, Michael R. *Currency Forecasting.* Burr Ridge, Ill.: Irwin Professional Publishing, 1996.

Ryan, Ronald J., ed. *Yield Curve Dynamics.* Chicago: Glen Lake Publishing Co. Ltd., 1997.

Squires, Jan R., ed. *Credit Analysis around the World.* Charlottesville, Va.: Association for Investment Management and Research, 1998.

Squires, Jan R., ed. *Global Bond Management.* Charlottesville, Va.: Association for Investment Management and Research, 1997.

Squires, Jan R., ed. *Global Portfolio Management.* Charlottesville, Va.: Association for Investment Management and Research, 1996.

Wilson, Richard S., and Frank J. Fabozzi. *The New Corporate Bond Market.* Chicago: Probus Publishing, 1990.

Part 6

Derivative Security Analysis

*I*n recent years, it has been difficult to read the financial press without encountering at least a passing reference to an economic scandal attributed to trading in derivative securities. Procter and Gamble's ill-fated swap transactions and the equity index futures trades that brought down Barings Bank give the casual reader the impression that derivatives are highly volatile instruments used only by those investors interested in placing speculative "bets." Of course, nothing could be further from the truth. Although it is true that the companies in these examples either miscalculated or misunderstood the nature of their investment positions, the vast majority of derivative transactions are used by individuals and institutions seeking to reduce the risk exposures generated by their other business ventures.

Derivatives, in their many forms, have become a vital part of modern security markets, trailing only stocks and bonds in terms of importance. Unlike stocks and bonds, however, their widespread use is a relatively recent phenomenon; and misconceptions still exist about how derivatives work and the proper way for investors to trade them. The chapters in this section address this concern by providing the investor with a framework for understanding how derivatives are valued and used in practice. Chapter 21 begins this process by detailing the mechanics of the two basic forms of derivative contract—*forwards* and *options*. After providing an initial description of these instruments and the markets in which they trade, we present the fundamental principles that determine their prices. The chapter concludes with several specific examples of how investors use derivatives to adjust the risk-return characteristics of their stock and bond portfolios.

Chapter 22 analyzes forward and futures contracts—the most prevalent form of derivative instrument. The similarities and differences between forward and futures contracts are described, with particular emphasis on the creation of (and subsequent adjustments to) margin accounts and the concept of basis risk. In addition, the calculation of the optimal hedge ratio and the arbitrage-free approach to determining the contract delivery price are discussed. The chapter concludes with an examination of the features of forward and futures contracts that are designed to offset financial (as opposed to commodity) risk exposures, including interest rate, equity, and currency price movements. Applications and investment strategies involving each of these contract types illustrate this discussion.

In Chapter 23, the focus turns to option contracting. The discussion begins with a consideration of how option markets are organized and how both puts and calls—the two basic types of option contracts—are quoted and traded. Several different option-based investment and hedging strategies are described as well as how these contracts can be used in conjunction with other securities to create customized payoff distributions. The chapter also includes a formal treatment of how option contracts are valued in an efficient market. Starting with the simple two-state option pricing model, which contains the essence of the basic valuation argument, the discussion progresses to include state-of-the-art approaches such as the binomial and the Black-Scholes models. In this development, special attention is paid to the role that price volatility plays in the valuation process.

Chapter 24, the last chapter of this section, considers four additional classes of derivative products. First, the rapidly developing market for swap, cap, and floor agreements is examined. After describing how these instruments are related to typical forward and option contracts, the discussion concentrates on the many ways in which investors and corporate risk managers use these products in practice. In particular, applications involving several different exposures—interest rates, exchange rates, and equity prices—are developed. Second, the fundamentals of warrants and convertible securities are described. The emphasis of this discussion is on the option-like features of these instruments and how they alter the risk-return dynamics of traditional debt and equity products. Third, we examine the market for structured notes—instruments that can be viewed as "straight" bond issues into which derivatives have been embedded. Finally, the chapter concludes with a brief discussion of how understanding *real options* can help investors value certain types of complex investments that have embedded derivative-like features, such as oil fields or gold mines.

Chapter 21

An Introduction to Derivative Markets and Securities

After you read this chapter, you should be able to answer the following questions:

➤ What distinguishes a derivative security, such as a forward, futures, or option contract, from more fundamental securities, such as stocks and bonds?

➤ What are the important characteristics of forward, futures, and option contracts, and in what sense can they be interpreted as insurance policies?

➤ How are the markets for derivative securities organized and how do they differ from other security markets?

➤ What terminology is used to describe transactions that involve forward, futures, and option contracts?

➤ How are prices for derivative securities quoted and how should this information be interpreted?

➤ What are the similarities and differences between forward and futures contracts?

➤ What do the payoff diagrams look like for investments in forward and futures contracts?

➤ What do the payoff diagrams look like for investments in put and call option contracts?

➤ How are forward contracts, put options, and call options related to one another?

➤ How can derivatives be used in conjunction with stock and Treasury bills to replicate the payoffs to other securities and create arbitrage opportunities for an investor?

➤ How can derivative contracts be used to restructure cash flow patterns and modify the risks in existing investment portfolios?

So far, we have seen several ways in which individuals and institutions can design their investments to take advantage of future market conditions. We have also seen how investors can control the volatility associated with their stock and bond positions—at least in part—by forming well-diversified portfolios of securities around a common investment theme, thereby reducing or eliminating the unsystematic component of a security's risk.

In this chapter, we begin our formal investigation of the role played by **derivative securities** in modern investment portfolios. A derivative instrument is one for which the ultimate payoff to the investor depends directly on the value of another security or commodity. Earlier in the text, we briefly described two basic types of derivatives: (1) forward and futures contracts and (2) option contracts. A call option, for example, gives its owner the right to purchase an underlying security, such as a stock or a bond, at a fixed price within a certain amount of time. Naturally, this right to purchase would most certainly be exercised only if the value of the underlying asset at the call's expiration date was greater than the contractual purchase price. In this manner, the option's ultimate value can be said to depend on—and thus derive from—that of the other (underlying) asset. Similarly, a forward contract to sell a specific bond for a fixed price at a future date will see its value to the investor rise or fall with decreases or increases in the market price of the underlying bond.

The growth of the markets in which derivative securities are created and exchanged has been nothing short of phenomenal. The last few decades have seen the emergence of forward, futures, and option contracts to trade such fundamental products as agricultural commodities, energy, precious metals, currencies, common stock, and bonds. There are even derivatives to trade hypothetical underlying assets (e.g., options and futures contracts on the Standard & Poor's stock indexes) as well as "combination" derivatives, such as option contracts that allow the investor to decide at a later date to enter into a futures contract involving another security or commodity. Interest rate swaps, which will be shown in Chapter 24 to be forward contracts on a short-term borrowing or lending rate, are a good example of the prodigious growth of these markets. Starting with the first swap in 1981, the volume of swap market activity had grown in size to the tens of trillions of dollars by the year 2000. Although this sort of rapid expansion is not typical of all new derivative products, these instruments represent one of the true legacies of the financial markets in the latter part of the 20th century.

As we will see, derivative securities can be used by investors in the same way and for the same reasons as the underlying assets; an investor believing that a certain common stock will increase in value will likely benefit from either a purchase of the stock directly or through the acquisition of an option to purchase that stock at a predetermined price. The exact returns will not be equal for these two alternatives, but both will benefit from an upward movement in the stock's price. Ultimately, however, the real key to understanding how and why derivatives are used in practice lies in their ability to modify the risk and expected return characteristics of existing investment portfolios. That is, options and futures allow investors to **hedge** (or even increase) the risk of a collection of stocks in ways that go far beyond the diversification results presented in the preceding chapters. In addition, we will see that derivative securities also allow for the convenient duplication of cash flow patterns that already exist in other forms, thereby creating the possibility of **arbitrage** if two otherwise identical series of cash flows do not carry the same current price.

The balance of this chapter describes the fundamental nature and uses of forward, futures, and option contracts on common stock and bonds. (Subsequent chapters deal with more advanced forms of these products and valuation issues.) In the next section, we describe the basic terminology associated with the forward, futures, and option markets while the second section explains the similarities and differences in the payoff structures created by each of these instruments. The third section is devoted to developing the formal relationship between forwards and options, the result of which will be a series of conditions collectively known as **put-call parity**. In the final section, we briefly introduce three of the more popular ways in which derivatives have been used in managing stock and bond portfolios, with a particular emphasis on how derivatives can adjust risk to better suit the needs of the investor.

OVERVIEW OF DERIVATIVE MARKETS

As with any financial product, derivative transactions have a specific terminology that must be understood in order to use these instruments effectively. Unlike many other securities, however, the language used to describe forward, futures, and option contracts is often a confusing blend of jargon drawn from the equity, debt, and insurance markets with some unique expressions thrown in for good measure. Thus, we begin by summarizing the most important aspects of these products and the markets in which they trade.

Before we examine the relevant details of each contract, it is useful to first consider the basic types of positions that an investor can hold in these markets. Exhibit 21.1 illustrates the possibilities. The chart reinforces the point made earlier that, at the broadest level, there are only two kinds of derivatives available: (1) forward and futures contracts, and (2) option contracts. Further, as we will explain shortly, while there need be only one forward contract for any particular maturity date and underlying asset, there must be two types of options—calls and puts—in order

EXHIBIT 21.1 *BASIC TYPES OF DERIVATIVE POSITIONS*

to offer investors a full range of choices. Finally, for each of these three general derivative arrangements (i.e., the forward contract, the call option, and the put option), an investor can enter into a transaction as either the long position (i.e., the buyer) or the short position (i.e., the seller). This leads to the six possible basic positions enumerated in the display.

It is important to recognize that every derivative arrangement that an investor might hold in his or her portfolio can be viewed in terms of one of these six positions, or as a combination of these positions. For instance, later in the chapter, we consider how an equity investor can use derivatives to protect himself or herself against general declines in the stock market. Two such strategies involve (1) shorting an equity index forward contract, and (2) buying an equity index "collar" agreement. In terms of Exhibit 21.1, we will see that the forward-based strategy represents Position 2, while the collar strategy involves a combination of the purchase of a put option (Position 5) and the sale of a call option (Position 4).

The Language and Structure of Forward and Futures Markets

To most investors, the **forward contract** is the most basic derivative product available. Generally, a forward contract gives its holder both the *right and the full obligation* to conduct a transaction involving another security or commodity—the underlying asset—at a predetermined future date and at a predetermined price. The future date on which the transaction is to be consummated is called the contract's *maturity* (or expiration) *date,* while the predetermined price at which the trade takes place is the forward **contract price**. Notice there must always be two parties (sometimes called **counterparties**) to a forward transaction: the eventual buyer (or **long position**), who pays the contract price and receives the underlying security, and the eventual seller (or **short position**), who delivers the security for the fixed price.

Forward and Spot Markets   Forward contracts are not securities in the traditional sense; they are more appropriately viewed as *trade agreements* negotiated directly between two parties for a transaction that is scheduled to take place in the future. Suppose, for example, that two investors agree at Date 0 (the present) to transfer a bond from one party to the other at the future Date *T*. To specify the full terms of this agreement, the two parties must agree on which bond and how much of it is to be exchanged, the date and location at which this exchange will take place, and the price at which the bond will be bought and sold. Consequently, the terms that must be considered in forming a forward contract are the same as those that would be necessary for a bond transaction that settled immediately (i.e., a *spot market* transaction) but with two exceptions. First, the settlement date agreed to in the contract is purposefully set to be in the future.

Second, the contract price—which we will represent as $F_{0,T}$, meaning a forward price set at Date 0 for a contract that matures at Date T—is usually different from the prevailing spot price (S_0) because of the different time frames involved. Typically, $F_{0,T}$ is chosen so that neither party needs to make an upfront payment to the other.

One important way in which spot and forward market transactions are similar is the conditions under which the long and short positions will profit. To illustrate this idea, suppose that at Date T, the long position in a bond forward contract is obligated to pay \$1,000 ($= F_{0,T}$) for a bond that is worth $S_T = \$1,050$ (i.e., the spot price at Date T). Since $F_{0,T} < S_T$, this will result in a profitable settlement for the long position in the contract since he will be able to acquire the bond for \$50 less than its current market value. On the other hand, the short position must deliver the bond at Date T and will lose \$50 on her forward position; she would have profited if S_T had been below the contract price of \$1,000. Thus, just as if the bond had been purchased at Date 0, the long position benefits when bond prices rise, at least relative to the contract price $F_{0,T}$. Conversely, the short position to the forward contract will gain from falling bond prices, just as if she had short sold the bond at Date 0. Even though the timing of the trade's settlement has shifted, "buy low, sell high" is still the way to make a profit in the forward market.

Forward and Futures Markets   Forward contracts are negotiated in the over-the-counter market. This means that forward contracts are agreements between two private parties—one of which is often a derivatives intermediary, such as a commercial or an investment bank—rather than traded through a formal security or commodity exchange. One advantage of this private arrangement is that the terms of the contract are completely flexible; they can be whatever any two mutually consenting counterparties agree to. Another desirable feature to many counterparties is that these arrangements may not require *collateral;* instead, the long and short positions sometimes trust each other to honor their respective commitments at Date T. This lack of collateral means that forward contracts involve *credit* (or *default*) *risk,* which is one reason why commercial banks are often market makers in these instruments.

One disadvantage of a forward contract is that it is quite often *illiquid,* meaning that it might be difficult or costly for a counterparty to exit the contract before it matures. Illiquidity is really a by-product of the contract's flexibility because the more specifically tailored an agreement is to the needs of a particular individual, the less marketable it will be to someone else. **Futures contracts** solve this problem by standardizing the terms of the agreement (e.g., expiration date, identity and amount of the underlying asset) to the extent that it can be exchange traded. In contrast to the forward market, both parties in a futures contract trade through a centralized market, called a *futures exchange.* Although the standardization of contracts reduces the ability of the ultimate end users to select the most desirable terms, it does create contract *homogeneity,* whereby the counterparties can always *unwind* a previous commitment prior to expiration by simply trading their existing position back to the exchange at the prevailing market price.

The *futures price* is analogous to the forward contract price and, at any time during the life of a contract, is set at a level such that a brand-new long or short position would not have to pay a premium to enter the agreement. However, the futures exchange will require both counterparties to post collateral, or *margin,* to protect itself against the possibility of default. (A futures exchange is not a credit-granting institution.) These margin accounts are held by the exchange's *clearinghouse* and are *marked to market* (i.e., adjusted for contract price movements) on a daily basis to ensure that both end users always maintain sufficient collateral to guarantee their eventual participation. A list of some of the more popular futures contracts, along with the markets where they trade, is shown in Exhibit 21.2. Although generally quite diverse, all of these underlying assets have two things in common: *volatile price movements* and *strong interest* from both buyers and sellers.

EXHIBIT 21.2 ▶ *POPULAR FUTURES CONTRACTS AND EXCHANGES*

UNDERLYING ASSET	EXCHANGE
A. Physical Commodities	
Corn, soybeans, soybean meal, soybean oil, wheat	Chicago Board of Trade
Cattle—feeder, cattle—live, hogs, pork bellies	Chicago Mercantile Exchange
Lumber	
Dairy	
Cocoa, coffee, sugar—world, sugar—domestic	Cocoa, Sugar, and Coffee Exchange
Copper, gold, silver	New York Commodity Exchange
Crude oil, heating oil, gasoline, natural gas	New York Mercantile Exchange
Platinum	
B. Financial Securities	
Yen, Euro, Canadian dollar, Swiss franc, British pound, Mexican peso, Australian dollar, Treasury bills, Eurodollar (LIBOR), S&P 500 Index, Nikkei 225 Index, Russell 2000 Index	International Monetary Market (Chicago Mercantile Exchange)
Treasury bonds, Treasury notes, Municipal bond index, federal funds	Chicago Board of Trade
Dow Jones Industrials Average	
Euro LIBOR, British gilt, German Euro govt bond	London International Financial
Canadian Bankers Acceptance, Canadian Bond	Futures and Options Exchange
FT-SE 100 Index	

Interpreting Futures Price Quotations: An Example

To illustrate how futures prices are typically quoted in financial markets, consider Exhibit 21.3, which lists spot and futures prices for contracts on the Standard and Poor's 500 index as of February 8, 2002. Recall from Chapter 5 that the S&P 500 is a value-weighted index of the relative value of a broad collection of industrial, financial, utility, and transportation companies representative of the entire U.S. stock market. At the close of trading on this particular day, the index level stood at 1,096.22, which can be considered as the spot price of one "share" of the S&P index (i.e., S_0)[1]. Exhibit 21.3 also gives futures contract prices for eight different expiration dates falling in the months of March, June, September, and December for the years 2002 and 2003.

Focusing on a specific example, consider the futures contract that expires in March 2002. The closing (or last) contract price is listed as 1,096.50 (i.e., $F_{0,T}$). This means that an investor taking a long position in this contract would be committing in February to buy a certain number of shares in the S&P 500 index—250 shares in the case of this contract—at a price of 1,096.50 per share on the expiration date in March. Conversely, the short position in this contract would be committing to sell 250 S&P shares under the same conditions. It should once again be noted that, except for the margin posted with the futures exchange (i.e., the Chicago Mercantile Exchange for this contract), no money changes hands between the long and short positions at the origination of the contract in February.

---

[1]In reality, actually purchasing the portfolio of 500 stocks comprising the S&P index would cost considerably more than $1,096.22. However, as the eventual profit or loss from a stock index futures contract is simply determined by the difference between the futures contract price and the spot price prevailing at contract expiration, this interpretation is nevertheless valid. The trading mechanics of these contracts will be described in greater detail in Chapter 22.

EXHIBIT 21.3 ▶ *STANDARD & POOR'S 500 INDEX FUTURES CONTRACT PRICE QUOTATIONS*

Session:**D**   **Contract Table**
S&P 500 FUTURE
Exchange Web Page   Pricing Date: **2/ 8/02**
Chicago Mercantile Exchange   Delayed prices   --AS REPORTED 2/8 --   **1**
Grey date = options trading   511244 78043
                 Last   **1**Change Time High **2** Low   Tic OpenInt TotVol   **Open**

		Last	Change	Time	High	Low	Tic	OpenInt	TotVol	Open
1)SPX	spot	1096.22	+16.05	16:01	1096.3	1079.9	5343	0	0	1080.17
2)SPH2	Mar02	1096.50s	+19.50	Close	1098.5	1080.0	3961	478103	73422	1083.00
3)SPM2	Jun02	1098.60s	+19.70	Close	1100.0	1082.0a	250	20982	4304	1085.50
4)SPU2	Sep02	1101.10s	+19.80	Close	1102.0b	1084.0a	104	11532	303	1094.80
5)SPZ2	Dec02	1104.80s	+19.70	Close	1107.6b	1107.6	79	454	12	1107.60
6)SPH3	Mar03	1110.80s	+20.20	Close	1113.1b	1105.3	48	61	2	1105.30
7)SPM3	Jun03	1118.80s	+20.70	Close	1120.6b	1120.6	41	92	0	1120.60
8)SPU3	Sep03	1128.30s	+20.70	Close	1130.1b	1130.1	39	6	0	1130.10
9)SPZ3	Dec03	1138.80s	+19.70	Close	1141.6b	1141.6	39	14	0	1141.60

EXHIBIT 21.4 ▶ *NET PROFIT AT EXPIRATION FROM A LONG POSITION IN AN S&P 500 FUTURES CONTRACT*

MARCH S&P 500 INDEX LEVEL	FUTURES PAYOFF AT EXPIRATION	INITIAL FUTURES PREMIUM	NET PROFIT
1,030.00	(1,030 – 1,096.5) = –66.50	0.00	–66.50
1,050.00	(1,050 – 1,096.5) = –46.50	0.00	–46.50
1,070.00	(1,070 – 1,096.5) = –26.50	0.00	–26.50
1,090.00	(1,090 – 1,096.5) = –6.50	0.00	–6.50
1,096.50	(1,096.5 – 1,096.5) = 0.00	0.00	0.00
1,110.00	(1,110 – 1,096.5) = 13.50	0.00	13.50
1,130.00	(1,130 – 1,096.5) = 33.50	0.00	33.50
1,150.00	(1,150 – 1,096.5) = 53.50	0.00	53.50
1,170.00	(1,170 – 1,096.5) = 73.50	0.00	73.50

Exhibit 21.4 summarizes the net profit for this contract from the long position's point of view assuming a hypothetical set of S&P index levels on the March expiration date (i.e., S_T). The most important thing to note about the display is that the payoff to the long position is positive when the S&P index level rises (relative to the contract price of 1,096.50), while a loss is incurred when the S&P index falls. For instance, if the expiration date level of the index is 1,110.00, the long position will receive a profit of 13.50 per share (= 1,110 – 1,096.5). In that case, the profit owes to the fact that the contract allows the investor to buy stock that is worth 1,110.00 for the predetermined price of only 1,096.50. On the other hand, if the March index level turns out to be 1,070, the futures contract still obligates the investor to purchase stock for the contract price, thus resulting in a loss of 26.50. This reinforces the fact that, as the buyer, the long position

benefits when stock prices rise and suffers when prices fall, just as would be the case for an investor purchasing stock directly in the spot market. Of course, the short position to the contract, as the seller, would have the exact opposite payoffs as those shown in Exhibit 21.4.

The data displayed in Exhibit 21.3 contain other information useful to investors. First, recognize that the spot and all of the futures contract prices listed finished higher than they had been the day before; this can be seen from the positive entries in the "Change" column in comparison with the "Last" prices. This suggests that, although they depend on other factors as well, the futures contract prices are strongly linked to the prevailing level of the underlying spot index. Second, notice that the contract prices increase the farther into the future the expiration date occurs. That is, although all nine closing prices listed (i.e., the spot and the eight futures contracts) were set on the same day and correspond to the same S&P index share, the cost of that share gets increasingly more expensive the farther forward in time the delivery date is set. We will see later that this relationship is common for some securities but not for others. Finally, the display also lists the *open interest* and *trading volume* for each contract. Open interest is the number of outstanding contracts, while trading volume is the number of those contracts that changed hands that day. Thus, it appears in this case that the nearest-term contract (i.e., March 2002) is the most abundant and that about 15 percent (= 78,043 ÷ 511,244) of the total number of S&P contracts in existence were traded on February 8, 2002.

The Language and Structure of Option Markets

An **option contract** gives its holder the right—but not the obligation—to conduct a transaction involving an underlying security or commodity at a predetermined future date and at a predetermined price. Unlike the forward contract, the option gives the long position the right to decide whether or not the trade will eventually take place. On the other hand, the seller (or *writer*) of the option must perform on his side of the agreement if the buyer chooses to exercise the option. Thus, the obligation in the option market is inherently one-sided; buyers can do as they please, but sellers are obligated to the buyers under the terms of the agreement. As a consequence, two different types of options are needed to cover all potential transactions: a **call option**—the right to buy the underlying security—and a **put option**—the right to sell that same asset.

Option Contract Terms   There are two prices that are important in evaluating an option position. The **exercise**, or striking, **price** is the price the call buyer will pay to—or the put buyer will receive from—the option seller if the option is exercised. The exercise price (represented here as X) is to an option what the contract price (i.e., $F_{0,T}$) is to a forward agreement. The second price of interest is the price that the option buyer must pay to the seller at Date 0 to acquire the contract itself. To avoid confusion, this second price is typically referred to as the **option premium**. A basic difference between options and forwards is that an option requires this up-front premium payment from buyer to seller while the forward ordinarily does not. This is because the forward contract allowed both the long and short positions to "win" at Date T (depending on where S_T settled, relative to $F_{0,T}$), but the option agreement will only be exercised in the buyer's favor; hence the seller must be compensated at Date 0, or she would never agree to the deal. Notice also that although a premium payment will be required for both puts and calls, it is quite likely that these two prices will differ. In the analysis that follows, we will define the Date 0 premium to acquire an option expiring at Date T as $C_{0,T}$ for a call and $P_{0,T}$ for a put. For example, in lieu of a long position in a bond forward contract, the investor in the previous example could have paid $20 (= $C_{0,T}$) at Date 0 for a call option that would have given him the right to buy the bond for $1,000 (= X) at Date T, but not required him to do so if $S_T < \$1,000$.

Options can be designed to provide a choice of when the contract can be exercised. **European options** can only be exercised at maturity (Date T), while **American options** can be executed any time up to expiration. For a European-style call option, the buyer will only exercise when the expiration date market value of the underlying asset that could be purchased is greater than the exercise price. On the other hand, a European-style put option will only be rationally exercised when the Date T price of the asset that could be sold is lower than X. (The decision to exercise an American-style contract is more complex and will be considered in a later chapter.)

Option Valuation Basics   Given these parameters, the Date 0 premium for an option can be divided into two components: **intrinsic value** and **time premium**. Intrinsic value represents the value that the buyer could extract from the option if she exercised it immediately. For a call, this is the greater of either zero or the difference between the price of the underlying asset and the exercise price (i.e., max $[0, S_0 - X]$). For a put, intrinsic value would be max $[0, X - S_0]$ as X would now represent the proceeds generated from the asset's sale. An option with positive intrinsic value is said to be **in the money**, while one with zero intrinsic value is **out of the money**. For the special case where $S_0 = X$, the option is **at the money**. The time premium component is then simply the difference between the whole option premium and the intrinsic component: $(C_{0,T} - \max [0, S_0 - X])$ for a call and $(P_{0,T} - \max [0, X - S_0])$ for a put. The buyer is willing to pay this amount in excess of the option's immediate exercise value because of her ability to complete the transaction at a price of X that will remain in force until Date T. Thus, the time premium is connected to the likelihood that the underlying asset's price will move in the anticipated direction by the contract's maturity.

Although a more complete discussion of valuing option premiums will be deferred until Chapter 23, several basic relationships can be seen now. First, because the buyer of a call option is never obligated to exercise, the contract should always at least be worth its intrinsic value. (The situation for put option prices or when the underlying asset pays a dividend can be more complicated and will be discussed later.) In any event, neither a call nor a put option can be worth less than zero. Second, for call options having the same maturity and based on the same underlying asset, the lower the exercise price, the higher will be the contract's intrinsic value and, hence, the greater its overall premium. Conversely, put options with higher exercise prices are more valuable than those with lower striking prices for the same reason. Third, increasing the amount of time until any option expires will increase the contract's time premium because it allows the price of the underlying security more opportunity to move in the direction anticipated by the investor (i.e., up for a call option, down for a put option). Finally, because they provide investors with more choices about exercising the agreement, American-style options are at least as valuable as otherwise comparable European-style contracts.

Option Trading Markets   Like forwards and futures, options trade both in over-the-counter markets and on exchanges. When exchange-traded, just the seller of the contract is required to post a margin account because he is the only one obligated to perform on the contract at a later date. Also, options can be based on a wide variety of underlying securities, including futures contracts or other options. Exhibit 21.5 lists the underlying assets and exchanges where a number of the most popular option contracts trade.

Interpreting Option Price Quotations: An Example   Exhibit 21.6 shows data for a variety of call and put options on the S&P 500 index as of February 8, 2002. All the contracts listed expire in March 2002, making them comparable to the S&P 500 futures contract just considered. However, unlike the futures contracts, for which there was a single contract price for a given expiration month, Exhibit 21.6 indicates that there are several March 2002 options having different exercise prices. In fact, the display lists bid and ask premium quotes for both puts and calls having striking prices ranging from 995 to 1,175.[2]

---

[2]Recall that an investor buys a security from a dealer—in this case, the options exchange—at the ask price and sells securities to the dealer at the bid price. The difference in these prices, which is the *bid-ask spread*, represents part of the compensation to the exchange for making a market in these contracts.

EXHIBIT 21.5 ▸ **POPULAR OPTION CONTRACTS AND EXCHANGES**

UNDERLYING ASSET	EXCHANGE
A. Financial Securities	
Individual Equities	Chicago Board Options
S&P 100	Exchange
Yen, Deutschemark, Canadian dollar, Swiss franc, British pound, Australian dollar, Mexican Peso	International Monetary Market (Chicago Mercantile Exchange)
S&P 500 Index	
B. Futures Options	
Cattle—feeder, cattle—live, hogs	Chicago Mercantile Exchange
Yen, Euro, Canadian dollar, Swiss franc, British pound	International Monetary Market
Eurodollar (LIBOR), 2-year Eurodollar	(Chicago Mercantile Exchange)
S&P 500 Index	
Corn, soybeans, soybean meal, soybean oil, wheat	Chicago Board of Trade
Treasury bonds, Treasury notes	
Dow Jones Industrials Average	
British gilt, GermanEuro Govt Bonds	London International Financial
EuroLIBOR	Futures and Options Exchange
FT-SE 100 Index	
Crude oil, heating oil, gasoline, natural gas	New York Mercantile Exchange
Copper, gold, silver	New York Commodity Exchange

EXHIBIT 21.6 ▸ **STANDARD & POOR'S 500 INDEX OPTION CONTRACT PRICE QUOTATIONS**

Option Monitor: S&P 500 INDEX

Center **1096.22** Number of Strikes **18** -or- **▓** % from Center   Exchange C (Composite)

		CALLS							PUTS			
Symbol	Strike	Bid	Ask	Last	Volume	Symbol	Strike	Bid	Ask	Last	Volume
SPX MAR 02	(Contract Size: 100.00)					SPX MAR 02	(Contract Size: 100.00)				
1) SXB+CS	995	106.10	108.10	99.50 y	1	19) SXB+OS	995	5.50	6.30	6.00 y	1235
2) SPQ+CE	1025	79.50	81.50	81.50 y		20) SPQ+OE	1025	8.60	9.60	8.90 y	829
3) SPQ+CJ	1050	58.80	60.80	58.00 y	951	21) SPQ+OJ	1050	12.60	13.50	12.50 y	3434
4) SPQ+CL	1060	51.10	53.10	45.00 y		22) SPQ+OL	1060	14.90	16.40	22.00 y	
5) SPQ+CN	1070	43.90	45.90	40.50 y		23) SPQ+ON	1070	17.70	19.20	19.90 y	10
6) SPQ+CO	1075	40.20	42.20	41.00 y	61	24) SPQ+OO	1075	19.00	20.50	19.20 y	507
7) SPQ+CP	1080	36.80	38.80	32.00 y	2793	25) SPQ+OP	1080	20.40	22.40	22.00 y	2514
8) SPQ+CR	1090	30.40	32.40	30.50 y	1947	26) SPQ+OR	1090	23.90	25.00	24.00 y	1810
9) SPT+CT	1100	25.00	26.50	26.50 y	3346	27) SPT+OT	1100	28.20	30.20	28.00 y	1627
10) SPT+CD	1120	15.40	16.90	14.50 y	199	28) SPT+OD	1120	38.60	40.60	41.00 y	66
11) SPT+CE	1125	13.40	14.80	14.50 y	4601	29) SPT+OE	1125	41.60	43.60	43.00 y	409
12) SPT+CF	1130	11.50	13.00	10.90 y	13	30) SPT+OF	1130	44.70	46.70	52.00 y	
13) SPT+CH	1140	8.80	9.80	6.30 y	1025	31) SPT+OH	1140	51.70	53.70	65.00 y	
14) SPT+CJ	1150	6.00	7.00	6.00 y	5366	32) SPT+OJ	1150	58.90	60.00	61.00 y	91
15) SPT+CL	1160	4.40	5.10	4.80 y		33) SPT+OL	1160	67.10	69.10	73.00 y	
16) SPT+CO	1175	2.50	3.20	2.80 y	2516	34) SPT+OO	1175	80.20	82.20	87.00 y	25

EXHIBIT 21.7 *NET PROFIT AT EXPIRATION FROM LONG POSITIONS IN S&P 500 CALL AND PUT OPTION CONTRACTS*

A. Long Call with Exercise Price of 1,100

MARCH S&P 500 INDEX LEVEL	CALL PAYOFF AT EXPIRATION	INITIAL CALL PREMIUM	NET PROFIT
1,030.00	0.00	−26.50	−26.50
1,050.00	0.00	−26.50	−26.50
1,070.00	0.00	−26.50	−26.50
1,090.00	0.00	−26.50	−26.50
1,110.00	$(1{,}110 - 1{,}100) = 10.00$	−26.50	−16.50
1,126.50	$(1{,}126.5 - 1{,}100) = 26.50$	−26.50	0.00
1,130.00	$(1{,}130 - 1{,}100) = 30.00$	−26.50	3.50
1,150.00	$(1{,}150 - 1{,}100) = 50.00$	−26.50	23.50
1,170.00	$(1{,}170 - 1{,}100) = 70.00$	−26.50	43.50

B. Long Put with Exercise Price of 1,100

MARCH S&P 500 INDEX LEVEL	PUT PAYOFF AT EXPIRATION	INITIAL PUT PREMIUM	NET PROFIT
1,030.00	$(1{,}100 - 1{,}030) = 70.00$	−30.20	39.80
1,050.00	$(1{,}100 - 1{,}050) = 50.00$	−30.20	19.80
1,069.80	$(1{,}100 - 1{,}069.8) = 30.20$	−30.20	0.00
1,070.00	$(1{,}100 - 1{,}070) = 30.00$	−30.20	−0.20
1,090.00	$(1{,}100 - 1{,}090) = 10.00$	−30.20	−20.20
1,110.00	0.00	−30.20	−30.20
1,130.00	0.00	−30.20	−30.20
1,150.00	0.00	−30.20	−30.20
1,170.00	0.00	−30.20	−30.20

Consistent with our earlier observation, notice that calls become more valuable (e.g., higher ask premiums) as the exercise price declines, with the opposite holding true for put options.

Consider the fortunes of two different investors, one of whom purchases a March S&P call struck at 1,100 (i.e., X) and the other who buys a March 1,100 put. At the origination of the transaction in February, these investors will pay their sellers the ask prices of $26.50 (i.e., $C_{0,T}$) and $30.20 (i.e., $P_{0,T}$), respectively. In return, the investor holding the call option has the right, but not the obligation, to buy one S&P share for 1,100 at the expiration date in March. Since the current (i.e., spot) price of the index is 1,096.22, this call option is out of the money and so the entire $26.50 purchase price consists of time premium. Similarly, the investor holding the put option has the right, but not the obligation, to sell one S&P share for 1,100 at the expiration date in March. The put is in the money, however, as this exercise price is higher than the current index level. Thus, the total put premium of $30.20 can be divided into an intrinsic value component of $3.78 (= 1,100 − 1,096.22) and a time premium of $26.42 (= 30.20 − 3.78).

The expiration date net payoffs to these long option positions are listed in Exhibit 21.7 for a variety of possible S&P index levels. Looking first at the call option payoffs in Panel A, notice that the investor will only exercise the contract to buy a share of the S&P index when the March S&P level is above 1,100; at index levels at or below 1,100, the investor will let the option expire worthless and simply lose his initial investment. Recognize, though, that while the call is in the money at index levels above 1,100, the investor will not realize a net profit until the March index level rises above 1,126.50, an amount equal to the exercise price plus the call premium (i.e., $X + C_{0,T}$). For the put option payoffs shown in Panel B, the holder will exercise the contract at March index levels below the exercise price, using the contract to sell for 1,100 an S&P share that is worth less than that. However, the display also documents that the put investor will not realize a positive net profit until the index level falls below 1,069.80 (i.e., $X - P_{0,T}$). For March S&P values above 1,100, the put option expires out of the money.

INVESTING WITH DERIVATIVE SECURITIES

Although the preceding section highlighted many of the differences between forward and option agreements, the two types of derivatives are quite similar in terms of the benefits they produce for investors. The ultimate difference between forwards and options lies in the way the investor must pay to acquire those benefits. This concept, along with an examination of the basic payoff structures that exist in these markets, is described in the following sections.

The Basic Nature of Derivative Investing

Consider an investor—call him Investor 1—who has decided to purchase a share of stock in SAS Corporation six months from now, a time frame that coincides with an anticipated receipt of funds. We will assume that both SAS stock forward contracts and call options are available with the market prices of $F_{0,T}$ and $C_{0,T}$ (where $T = 0.50$ year) and that the exercise price of the call option, X, is equal to $F_{0,T}$. Thus, if the investor wants to secure the price now at which the stock purchase will eventually take place, he has two alternatives: a long position in the forward or the purchase of the call option. Exhibit 21.8 compares the Date 0 and Date T cash flow exchanges for both possibilities.

The clear difference between these strategies at the time of origination is that the forward position requires no payment or receipt by either party to the transaction whereas the investor (i.e., the call buyer) must pay a cash premium to the seller of the option. As noted earlier, this front-end option payment releases the investor from the obligation to purchase SAS stock at Date T if the terms of the contract turn out to be unfavorable (i.e., $S_T < X$). This is shown in the lower panel of Exhibit 21.8. When the expiration date price of SAS stock exceeds the exercise price, the investor will exercise the call and purchase the share of stock. Notice however, that this leads to exactly the same exchange as did the long forward contract. It is only when the stock price falls below X (and $F_{0,T}$) on Date T that there is a difference between the two positions; under this condition, the right provided by the option *not* to purchase SAS stock is valuable since the investor will be required to execute his forward contract at a loss. In this sense, the call option can be viewed as the "good half" of the long forward position because it allows for the future acquisition of SAS stock at a fixed price but doesn't require the transaction to take place.

This is the critical distinction between forward and option contracts. Both the long forward and the long call positions have been structured to provide the investor with exactly the same amount of "insurance" against the price of SAS stock rising over the next six months. That is, both contracts provide a payoff of $[S_T - X] = [S_T - F_{0,T}]$ whenever S_T exceeds X, which reduces the effective purchase price for the stock back down to X. The difference in contract design can then be viewed in terms of how the investor is required to pay for that price insurance. With a forward contract, no money is paid up front, but the investor will have to make a payment at the expiration date even if the stock price falls below $F_{0,T}$. Conversely, the call option will never require a future settlement payment, but the investor will have to pay the premium at origination. Thus, for the same Date T benefit, the investor's decision between these two "insurance policies" comes down to choosing the certainty of a present premium payment (i.e., long call) versus the possibility of a future payment (i.e., long forward) that could potentially be much larger.

EXHIBIT 21.8 ▸   *EXCHANGES FOR LONG FORWARD AND LONG CALL TRANSACTIONS*

A. Exchange at Origination (i.e., Date 0)

Forward:

| Investor 1 (i.e., Long Forward) | | Short Forward |

Initial Cost: 0

Call Option:

| Investor 1 (i.e., Call Buyer) | Premium → | Call Seller |

Initial Cost: Premium > 0

B. Exchange at Contract Expiration (i.e., Date T)

Forward:

Call Option:

(*1*) If $S_T > X (= F_{0,T})$:

| Investor 1 (i.e., Long Forward) | ← Stock / $F_{0,T}$ → | Short Forward |

Net Contract Receipt: $[S_T - F_{0,T}] > 0$

| Investor 1 (i.e., Call Buyer) | ← Stock / X → | Call Seller |

Net Contract Receipt: $[S_T - X] > 0$

(*2*) If $S_T \leq X (= F_{0,T})$:

| Investor 1 (i.e., Long Forward) | ← Stock / $F_{0,T}$ → | Short Forward |

Net Contract Receipt: $[S_T - F_{0,T}] < 0$

| Investor 1 (i.e., Call Buyer) | | Call Seller |

Net Contract Receipt: 0

To see this distinction more clearly, suppose that Investor 1 plans to buy SAS stock in six months when some of the bonds in his portfolio mature. He is concerned that share values could rise substantially between now and the time he receives his investment funds, and so to hedge that risk he considers two "insurance" strategies to lock in the eventual purchase price: (1) pay nothing now to take the long position in a six-month SAS stock forward contract with a contract price of $F_{0,T} = \$45$, or (2) pay a premium of $C_{0,T} = \$3.24$ for a six-month, European-style call option with an exercise price of $X = \$45$. Assuming that at the time of his decision the price of SAS stock is $S_0 = \$40$, the call option is out of the money, meaning that its intrinsic value is zero and the entire \$3.24 is time premium. As mentioned earlier, an obvious difference between these two strategies is that the option entails a front-end expense while the forward position does not. The other difference occurs at the expiration date, depending on whether the SAS stock price is above or below \$45. If, for instance, $S_T = \$51$, both the long forward position and the call option will be worth \$6 (i.e., $51 - 45$) to the investor, reducing his net purchase price for SAS shares to \$45 ($= 51 - 6$). That is, when the stock settled above \$45 (i.e., the common value for $F_{0,T}$ and X), both the long forward and long call positions provided the same protection against rising prices. On the other hand, if $S_T = \$40.75$, the forward contract would have required that the investor pay \$4.25 ($= 40.75 - 45$) to his counterparty, which would have once again raised the net cost of his shares to \$45. With the call option, however, he could have let the contract expire without exercising it and purchased his SAS shares in the market for only \$40.75. Thus, in exchange for the option's front-end expense of \$3.24, the investor retains the possibility of paying less than \$45 for his eventual stock purchase.

EXHIBIT 21.9 *EXCHANGES FOR SHORT FORWARD AND LONG PUT TRANSACTIONS*

A. Exchange at Origination (i.e., Date 0)

Forward:

Put Option:

Investor 2 (i.e., Short Forward) → Long Forward

Initial Cost: 0

Investor 2 (i.e., Put Buyer) —Premium→ Put Seller

Initial Cost: Premium > 0

B. Exchange at Contract Expiration (i.e., Date T)

Forward:

Put Option:

(1) If $S_T > X (= F_{0,T})$:

Investor 2 (i.e., Short Forward) —Stock→ Long Forward ←$F_{0,T}$—

Net Contract Receipt: $[F_{0,T} - S_T] < 0$

Investor 2 (i.e., Put Buyer)   Put Seller

Net Contract Receipt: 0

(2) If $S_T \leq X (= F_{0,T})$:

Investor 2 (i.e., Short Forward) —Stock→ Long Forward ←$F_{0,T}$—

Net Contract Receipt: $[F_{0,T} - S_T] > 0$

Investor 2 (i.e., Put Buyer) —Stock→ Put Seller ←X—

Net Contract Receipt: $[X - S_T] > 0$

The connection between forward contracts and put options can be made in a similar fashion. Suppose a different investor—call her Investor 2—has decided to liquidate a share of SAS stock from her portfolio in six months' time. Rather than risk a falling stock price over that period, she could arrange now to sell the share at that future date for a predetermined fixed price in one of two ways: a short forward position or the purchase of a put option. Exhibit 21.9 illustrates the exchanges for these alternatives. Once again, for the same insurance against SAS stock price declines, the choice comes down to the certainty of paying the put option premium versus the possibility of making a potentially larger payment with the forward contract by having to sell her stock for $X (= F_{0,T})$ when that value is considerably less than the stock's Date T market price. Importantly, notice once again that the put option allows the investor to walk away from her obligation under the short forward position to sell her stock on the expiration date under disadvantageous conditions. Thus, in exchange for a front-end premium payment, the put option enables the investor to acquire the "good half" of the short position in a forward contract.

Basic Payoff Diagrams for Forward Contracts

Exhibit 21.8 and Exhibit 21.9 show that the respective expiration date payoffs for long and short positions in a forward contract are $[S_T - F_{0,T}]$ and $[F_{0,T} - S_T]$ and that these values could be either positive or negative depending on the spot price prevailing at Date T. These terminal payoffs are plotted against the possible expiration date values of the underlying security price in Exhibit 21.10. There are two interesting items in this display.

First, the payoffs to both long and short positions in the forward contract are *symmetric,* or two-sided, around the contract price. This, of course, is a direct result of the terms of the contract that fully obligate each party to complete the agreed-upon transaction—even at a financial

EXHIBIT 21.10 *EXPIRATION DATE PAYOFFS TO LONG AND SHORT FORWARD POSITIONS*

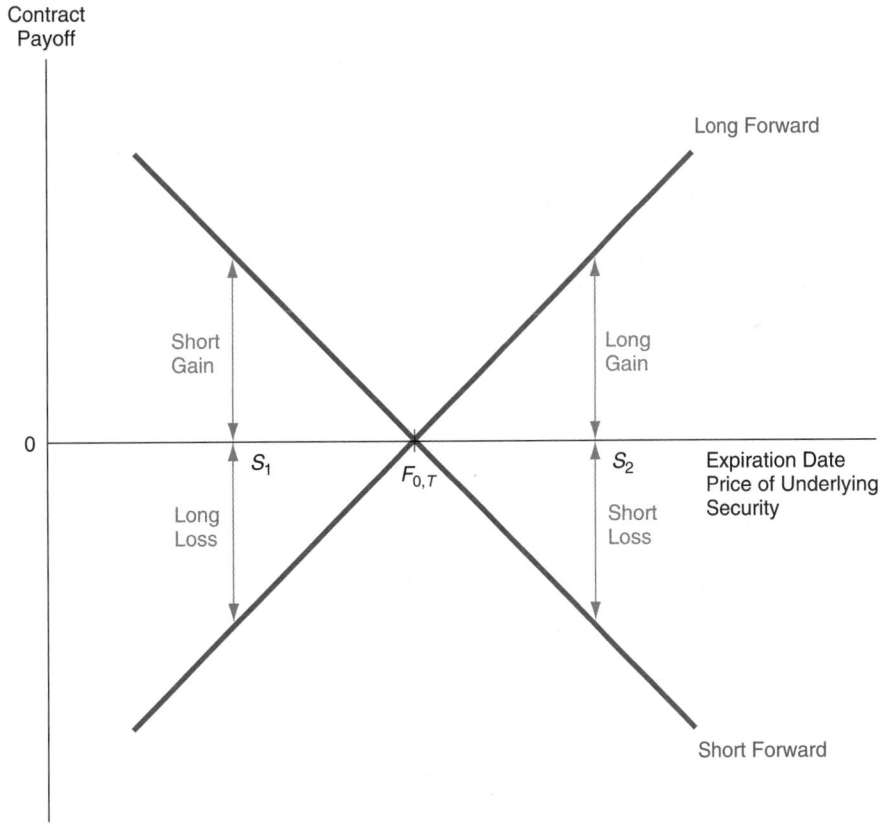

loss. For instance, in the last example, the investor holding a long position in a SAS stock forward contract with a contract price of $45 lost $4.25 when the Date T price of SAS stock was $40.75 but gained $6 when $S_T = \$51$.

Second, the Date T payoffs to the short and long positions are mirror images of each other; in market jargon, forward contracts are *zero-sum games* because the long position gains must be paid by the short position and vice versa. This illustration shows that when the Date T spot price is lower than the contract price (i.e., S_1), the short position will receive the net payoff of $[F_{0,T} - S_1]$ from the long position while the settlement is reversed at S_2, where the security price is above $F_{0,T}$. Thus, forward markets reinforce the fundamental financial tenet that long positions benefit from rising prices while short positions benefit from falling prices. Finally, notice that these gains and losses can be quite large. In fact, the short forward position has the potential for unlimited loss while the long forward position has the potential for unlimited gain since there is no theoretical limit on how high the price for the underlying security can rise. Conversely, the loss potential for the long position (and the gain potential for the short position) is limited because the price of the underlying security cannot fall below zero.

Basic Payoff Diagrams for Call and Put Options Exhibit 21.8 and Exhibit 21.9 also show that options differ from forward contracts in two fundamental ways. Most directly, the expense of purchasing either a put or a call represents a sunk cost to the investor reducing her upside return relative to the comparable forward position. In

EXHIBIT 21.11　　*EXPIRATION DATE PAYOFFS TO LONG AND SHORT CALL POSITIONS*

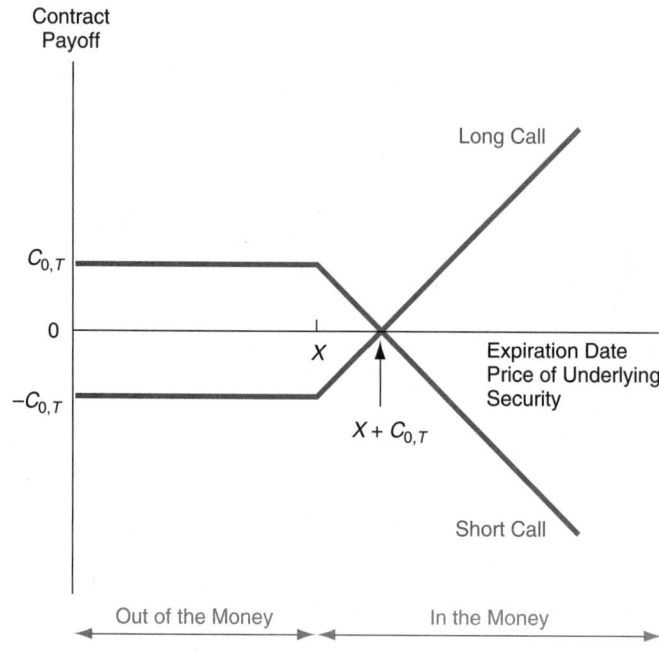

exchange for this initial fee, the investor receives expiration date payoffs that are decidedly *asymmetric,* or one-sided. Exhibit 21.11 shows the net effect these differences have on the terminal payoffs to both long and short positions in call options, while Exhibit 21.12 provides a similar illustration for put option traders. This analysis assumes that both options are European-style, and so they actually reach expiration without having been exercised prematurely.

For call option positions, notice again that the buyer of the contract still benefits whenever the terminal security price (i.e., S_T) exceeds the contract purchase (i.e., exercise) price of X. However, given that the holder had to pay an initial premium of $C_{0,T}$, the position doesn't generate a positive payoff until S_T is greater than X by the amount of the premium paid. Put another way, although the call option is in the money (and hence will be exercised) when $S_T > X$, it will not produce a capital gain for the buyer until $S_T > (X + C_{0,T})$.[3] (Recall that this result was shown for the S&P 500 index option example in Exhibit 21.7.) When $X < S_T < (X + C_{0,T})$, the option is exercised at a loss, but this loss will be less than the full cost of the option, which is what the long position would incur if the call were not exercised. In fact, when $S_T < X$, the option is out of the money and the buyer who makes the rational decision to let the contract expire will lose $C_{0,T}$.

Notice, then, that the buyer of the call option has unlimited gain potential as the security price could rise indefinitely with losses limited to the option premium no matter how far prices fall. On the other hand, the short position benefits from a terminal price for the underlying asset beneath X but only to the extent that he gets to keep the full amount of the option premium.

[3]The expiration date payoffs shown in Exhibit 21.11 and Exhibit 21.12 are somewhat inaccurate in that they show the net of the Date T value of the option and its initial cost, which was paid at Date 0. Thus, although this is an accurate way of portraying capital gains and losses from an accounting standpoint, it ignores the value differential in the timing of the two payments.

EXHIBIT 21.12 *EXPIRATION DATE PAYOFFS TO LONG AND SHORT PUT POSITIONS*

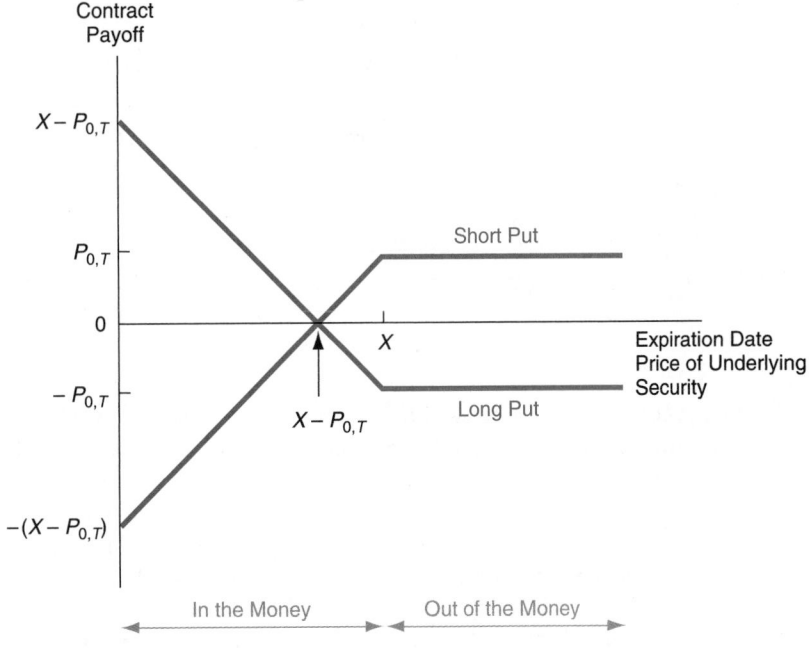

When $S_T > X$, the seller of the call has unlimited liability. Like forward contracts, the call option is a zero-sum game between the long and short positions.

For the put option positions shown in Exhibit 21.12, the buyer benefits whenever $X > S_T$ and receives a positive payoff when the Date T price of the underlying security falls below the contractual selling price, less the cost of the option. In this case, the put buyer's maximum capital gain is limited to $X - P_{0,T}$ as the underlying security itself is limited to a minimum price of zero; the best the put holder can hope for is to force the seller of the contract to buy worthless stock for X at the expiration date. On the other hand, as with the call option, the owner of an out-of-the-money put can only lose his initial investment of $P_{0,T}$, which will occur when $S_T > X$. Not surprisingly, the profit and loss opportunities for the put seller are exactly opposite of those for the put buyer. The contract seller will gain when $S_T > (X - P_{0,T})$, but this gain is limited to the amount of the option premium. A short position in a put also has limited loss potential; but, at a maximum of $X - P_{0,T}$, this can still be a large amount.

In summary, when they are held as investments, options are *directional views* on movements in the price of the underlying security. Call buyers and put sellers count on S_T to rise (or remain) above X, while put buyers and call sellers hope for S_T to fall (or remain) below the exercise price at the expiration date. However, the exact payoffs to each of these positions vary greatly for any given terminal security value. Importantly, option buyers—whether a put or a call—always have limited liability since they do not have to exercise an out-of-the-money position. This limited liability feature for option holders also means that the gain potential for the seller is limited as the two positions are mirror images of each other. For adverse price movements, though, option sellers face large potential losses, with the liability of the call writer being theoretically infinite just as if she had sold short the underlying security.

EXHIBIT 21.13   *HYPOTHETICAL STOCK AND OPTION PRICES*

INSTRUMENT	EXERCISE PRICE	MARKET PRICE	INTRINSIC VALUE	TIME PREMIUM
SAS Stock	—	$40.00	—	—
Call: 1	$35.00	8.07	$5.00	$3.07
2	40.00	5.24	0.00	5.24
3	45.00	3.24	0.00	3.24
Put: 1	35.00	1.70	0.00	1.70
2	40.00	3.67	0.00	3.67
3	45.00	6.47	5.00	1.47

Option Payoff Diagrams: An Example

Although there will only be one value of $F_{0,T}$ that allows the present value of a forward contract to be zero (i.e., does not require an initial payment from either the long or the short position), we have seen that option contracts can be designed with several different values for the exercise price. It is interesting, therefore, to consider how the choice of the exercise price affects the instrument's expiration date payoff. Extending the last example, suppose that a share of SAS stock currently sells for $40 and six different SAS options—three calls and three puts—are available to investors. The options all expire on the same date in the future and have exercise prices of either $35, $40, or $45. Current market prices for these contracts, which are assumed to be European-style, are shown in Exhibit 21.13, where they are broken down into their intrinsic value and time premium components.

Given that $S_0 = \$40$, call 1 (with $X = 35$) and Put 3 (with $X = 45$) are both $5 in the money, which leaves $3.07 and $1.47, respectively, of their value in the form of time premium. Call 3 and Put 1 are both currently $5 out of the money and so their market prices are purely time premium; someone buying either of these two contracts anticipates that stock prices will move in the desired direction by at least the option price *plus* $5. Notice that neither of the two at-the-money options, Call 2 and Put 2, have any intrinsic value, but they still sell in the market for different prices. Specifically, the call with $X = \$40$ is more valuable than the comparable put option. As we will see shortly, this occurs because of **put-call parity**, which is the formal relationship that must exist between put and call options in efficient capital markets. (In fact, for options on a stock that does not pay a dividend, this situation should always hold. However, the value of an at-the-money put can exceed that of an at-the-money call if the underlying security is a stock, a bond, or currency that does pay a cash flow.) Finally, the last column of Exhibit 21.13 shows that the time premium is largest for the at-the-money options because, at this point, the greatest amount of uncertainty exists as to whether the option will be in or out of the money (and hence valuable) at expiration.

It is instructive to compare the expiration date payoff diagrams for options on the same security with varying exercise prices but similar in every other respect. This is done for both call and put options in Exhibit 21.14. For simplicity, only the payoffs for the long positions in these contracts are shown. The call option payoffs portrayed in Panel A of the exhibit indicate that, although it is the most expensive, the deepest in-the-money contract (Call 1) becomes profitable the quickest, requiring only that S_T rise to $43.07 (= 35 + 8.07). Call 3, on the other hand, is the least expensive to purchase but requires the greatest movement in the price of the underlying stock—to $48.24 in this example—before it provides a positive payoff to the investor. The put options illustrated in Panel B tell the same story, with Put 1 (the out-of-the-money contract) cost-

EXHIBIT 21.14 ▶ *TERMINAL PAYOFFS TO OPTIONS WITH DIFFERENT EXERCISE PRICES*

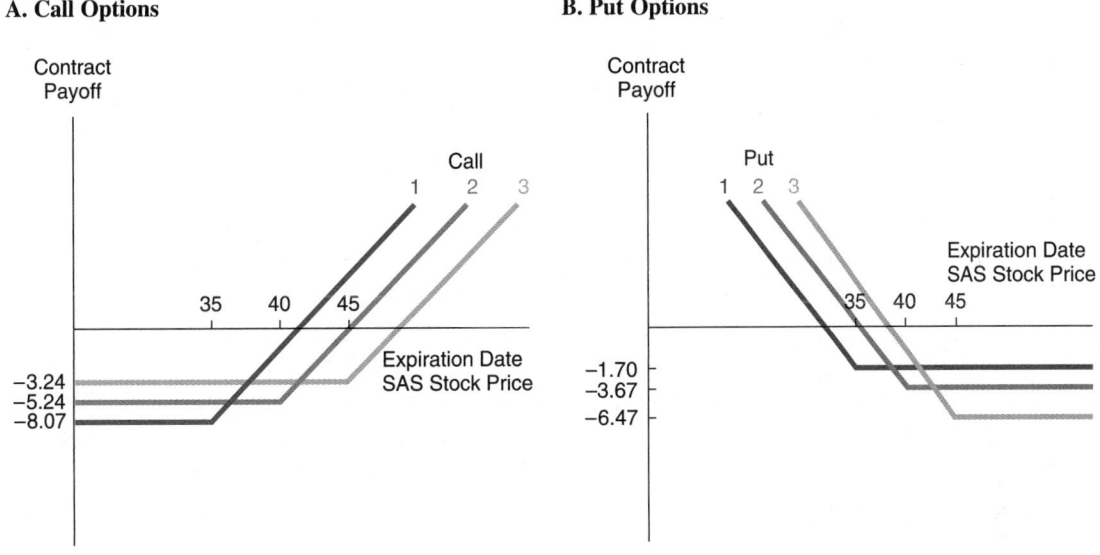

A. Call Options

B. Put Options

ing the least but needing the largest price decline to be profitable at expiration. In general, by varying the exercise price on a series of options with otherwise identical contract terms, an investor can create just as many different risk-reward trade-offs for herself. This is one of several examples of how derivatives can be used to modify investment risk and to "customize" a desired payoff structure.

Options and Leverage   As a final extension of this example, let us compare the returns to an investment in either a put or a call option with an investment (or short sale) in a share of the underlying SAS stock. To focus on the important issues, we will limit the analysis to Call 2 and Put 2, the two at-the-money contracts. Exhibit 21.15 summarizes the holding period returns for various positions assuming three different expiration date stock prices: $30, $40, and $50. Two different comparisons are made: (1) long stock versus long call and (2) short stock versus long put. In calculating the returns to the stock positions, we have measured the change in value of the SAS share as a percentage of the initial price of $40. For the option positions, the terminal payoffs of max $[0, S_T - 40]$ for the call and max $[0, 40 - S_T]$ for the put are listed relative to the contract's purchase price.

The most important thing to realize about these calculations is that both put and call options magnify the possible positive and negative returns of investing in the underlying security. In the case of the long call option position, for an initial cost of $5.24, the investor can retain the right to access the price appreciation of a share of SAS stock without spending $40 to own the share outright. This degree of financial *leverage* manifests itself in a 100 percent loss when the stock price falls by a quarter of that amount and a 91 percent gain when SAS shares increase in value from $40 to $50. Notably, if the stock price remains at $40, the owner of the share would not have lost anything while the call holder would have lost his entire investment, which was pure time premium at origination for the at-the-money contract. This suggests that in addition to anticipating the *direction* of the subsequent underlying stock price movement, the option investor also is taking a view on the *timing* of that movement. If the price of SAS stock had stayed at

EXHIBIT 21.15 ▶ *STOCK AND OPTION INVESTMENT RETURNS*

A. Long Stock versus Long Call

Terminal Stock Price	Long Stock	Long Call
30	$\dfrac{30}{40} - 1 = -25.0\%$	$\dfrac{0}{5.24} - 1 = -100.0\%$
40	$\dfrac{40}{40} - 1 = 0.0\%$	$\dfrac{0}{5.24} - 1 = -100.0\%$
50	$\dfrac{50}{40} - 1 = 25.0\%$	$\dfrac{10}{5.24} - 1 = 90.8\%$

B. Short Stock versus Long Put

Terminal Stock Price	Short Stock	Long Put
30	$1 - \dfrac{30}{40} = 25.0\%$	$\dfrac{10}{3.67} - 1 = 172.5\%$
40	$1 - \dfrac{40}{40} = 0.0\%$	$\dfrac{0}{3.67} - 1 = -100.0\%$
50	$1 - \dfrac{50}{40} = -25.0\%$	$\dfrac{0}{3.67} - 1 = -100.0\%$

$40 through Date T and then rose to $50 on the following day, the stockholder would have experienced a 25 percent gain while the buyer of the call option would have seen the instrument expire worthless.

THE RELATIONSHIP BETWEEN FORWARD AND OPTION CONTRACTS

The preceding discussion highlighted the fact that positions in forward and option contracts can lead to similar investment payoffs if the price of the underlying security moves in the anticipated direction. As we saw, the difference in the payoffs to these derivatives came when the security's price changed adversely. This similarity in payoff structures suggests that there is a tractable set of relationships between these instruments. In fact, we will see that the values of five different securities can be linked: a risk-free bond, an underlying asset, a forward contract for the future purchase or sale of that asset, a call option, and a put option. These relationships, known as **put-call parity**, specify how the put and call premiums should be set relative to one another. Further, these conditions can be expressed in terms of the connection between these two option types and either the spot or forward market price for the underlying asset. They depend on the assumption that financial markets are free from arbitrage opportunities, meaning that securities (or portfolios of securities) offering identical payoffs with identical risks must sell for the same current price. As such, put-call parity represents an important first step in understanding how derivatives are valued in an efficient capital market.[4]

---

[4]The development of the relationships linking put and call option prices is commonly attributed to Hans R. Stoll, "The Relationship between Put and Call Option Prices," *Journal of Finance* 24, no. 5 (December 1969): 801–824. It has been embellished in many interesting ways, including Robert C. Merton, "The Relationship between Put and Call Option Prices: Comment," *Journal of Finance* 28, no. 1 (March 1973): 183–184; Avraham Kamara and Thomas W. Miller, Jr., "Daily and Intradaily Tests for European Put-Call Parity," *Journal of Financial and Quantitative Analysis* 30, no. 4 (December 1995): 519–539; and Anu Bharadwaj and James B. Wiggins, "Box Spread and Put-Call Parity Tests for the S&P 500 Index LEAPS Market," *Journal of Derivatives* 8, no. 4 (Summer 2001): 62–71.

EXHIBIT 21.16   PUT-CALL-SPOT PARITY

A. Net Portfolio Investment at Initiation (Date 0)

Portfolio

Long 1 WYZ stock	S_0
Long 1 put option	$P_{0,T}$
Short 1 call option	$-C_{0,T}$
Net investment:	$S_0 + P_{0,T} - C_{0,T}$

B. Portfolio Value at Option Expiration (Date T)

Portfolio	(1) If $S_T \leq X$:	(2) If $S_T > X$:
Long 1 WYZ stock	S_T	S_T
Long 1 put option	$(X - S_T)$	0
Short 1 call option	0	$-(S_T - X)$
Net position:	X	X

Put-Call-Spot Parity

Suppose that at Date 0 (the present) an investor forms the following portfolio involving three securities related to Company WYZ:

➤ Long in a share of WYZ common stock at a purchase price of S_0,
➤ Long in a put option to deliver one share of WYZ stock at an exercise price of X on the Expiration Date T. This put could be purchased for the price of $P_{0,T}$,
➤ Short in a call option allowing the purchase of one share of WYZ stock at an exercise price of X on the Expiration Date T. This call could be sold for the price $C_{0,T}$.

In this example, both of the WYZ options are European-style and have the same expiration date and exercise price. However, the specific values of the expiration date and exercise price do not affect the conclusion of the analysis that follows. Further, we will assume initially that WYZ stock does not pay a dividend during the life of the options.

With these definitions, notice in Panel A of Exhibit 21.16 that the Date 0 investment necessary to acquire this portfolio is $(S_0 + P_{0,T} - C_{0,T})$, which is the cost of the long positions in the stock and the put option less the proceeds generated by the sale of the call option.[5] A more interesting thing to consider is the value that this portfolio will have at the expiration date of the two options. Given that the stock's value at Date T (i.e., S_T) is unknown when the investment is made at Period 0, two general outcomes are possible: (1) $S_T \leq X$ and (2) $S_T > X$. Panel B of Exhibit 21.16 shows the value of each position as well as the net value of the whole portfolio at Date T.

Notice that whenever the Date T value of WYZ stock is less than the exercise price common to the put and call options, it is best for the investor to exercise the long position in the put and sell the WYZ share for X instead of its lower market value. Under the same condition, it will not be rational for the holder of the call to pay X for a share that is worth less. Therefore, the call will expire out of the money. On the other hand, when S_T exceeds X, the holder of the call will exercise the option to purchase WYZ stock for X from the investor while the put would be out of the money. In either case, the net expiration date value of the position is X because the

---

[5]In the "arithmetic" of engineering financial portfolios, a plus ("+") sign can be interpreted as a long position and a minus ("–") sign represents a short position. Thus the portfolio investment represented by $(S_0 + P_{0,T} - C_{0,T})$ can also be expressed as (long stock) + (long put) + (short call). Donald J. Smith, "The Arithmetic of Financial Engineering," *Journal of Applied Corporate Finance* 1, no. 4 (Winter 1989): 49–58, explains this approach in more detail.

combination of options contained in the portfolio guarantees that the investor will sell the share of WYZ stock at Date T for the fixed price X. That is, at stock prices lower than X, the investor will choose to sell the share at a profit, although he will be forced to sell at a loss when WYZ trades on the market at a price higher than X. The investor has, in effect, a guaranteed contract to sell the share of stock when the long put and short call positions are held jointly.

The consequence of this result is that when the investor commits $(S_0 + P_{0,T} - C_{0,T})$ to acquire the position at Date 0, he knows that it will be worth X at Date T. Thus, this particular portfolio has a comparable payoff structure to a U.S. Treasury bill, another risk-free, zero coupon security that can be designed to have a face value of X and a maturity date T. In an arbitrage-free capital market, this means that the Date 0 value of the portfolio must be equal to that of the T-bill, which is just the face value X discounted to the present using the risk-free rate. This "no arbitrage" condition can be formalized as follows:

➤21.1
$$S_0 + P_{0,T} - C_{0,T} = \frac{X}{(1 + RFR)^T}$$

where:

> RFR = **the annualized risk-free rate**
> T = **the time to maturity (expressed in years)**

Defining $[X\ (1 + RFR)^{-T}]$ as the present value of a T-bill, this equation can be expressed in "financial arithmetic" terms as:

$$(\text{Long Stock}) + (\text{Long Put}) + (\text{Short Call}) = (\text{Long T-Bill})$$

In either form, this condition—known as the *put-call-spot* parity condition—indicates the efficient market linkages between prices for stock, T-bills, put options, and call options.

Put-Call Parity: An Example

As an example of how put-call parity might be used, suppose that WYZ stock is currently valued at \$53 and that call and put options on WYZ stock with an exercise price of \$50 sell for \$6.74 and \$2.51, respectively. Assuming that both options can only be exercised in exactly six months, Equation 21.1 suggests that we can "make" a synthetic T-bill by purchasing the stock, purchasing the put, and selling the call for a net price of \$48.77 (= 53.00 + 2.51 − 6.74). At the options' expiration date, this portfolio would have a terminal value of \$50. Thus, the risk-free rate implied by this investment can be established by solving the following equation for RFR:

$$48.77 = 50\ (1 + RFR)^{-0.5}$$

or

$$RFR = [(50 \div 48.77)^2 - 1] = 5.11\%$$

The practical application of this finding is that if the rate of return on an actual six-month T-bill with a face value of \$50 is not 5.11 percent, then an investor could exploit the difference. Suppose, for instance, that the actual T-bill rate is 6.25 percent and that there are no restrictions against using the proceeds from the short sale of any security. In such a situation, an investor wanting a risk-free investment would clearly choose the actual T-bill to lock in the higher return, while someone seeking a loan might attempt to secure a 5.11 percent borrowing rate by short-

EXHIBIT 21.17	*A PUT-CALL PARITY ARBITRAGE EXAMPLE*

A. Net Initial Investment (Date 0)

Transaction	
1. Long actual T-bill at 6.25%	−48.51
2. Short synthetic T-bill at 5.11%:	
Short WYZ stock	53.00
Short put option	2.51
Long call option	−6.74
Net receipt:	0.26

B. Position Value at Option Expiration (Date T)

Transaction	(1) If $S_T \leq 50$:	(2) If $S_T > 50$:
1. Long actual T-bill at 6.25%	50	50
2. Short synthetic T-bill at 5.11%:		
Short WYZ stock	$-S_T$	$-S_T$
Short put option	$-(50 - S_T)$	0
Long call option	0	$(S_T - 50)$
Net position:	0	0

selling the synthetic T-bill. With an arithmetic rearrangement of the parity condition in the previous equation, such an artificial short position can be obtained as

$$(\text{Short Stock}) + (\text{Short Put}) + (\text{Long Call}) = (\text{Short T-Bill})$$

With no transaction costs, a financial arbitrage could be constructed by combining a long position in the actual T-bill with a short sale of the synthetic portfolio. Given that the current value of the actual T-bill is \$48.51 [= \$50 $(1.0625)^{-0.5}$], this set of transactions would generate the cash flows shown in Exhibit 21.17 and produce a \$0.26 profit per each T-bill pair created. However, as the arbitrage trade did not require the investor to bear any risk (i.e., both the Date 0 and Date T values of the net position were known at inception) nor commit any capital, there is nothing in this example to prevent the investor from expanding the size of the trade to increasingly larger levels. Unfortunately, as additional transactions take place, the price discrepancy will disappear. In this case, the purchase of the actual T-bill and sale of the synthetic (short stock, short put, and long call) will continue until rates are equalized. This is how the markets remain efficient through arbitrage trading.

Another way of seeing this trade is

$$C_{0,T} - P_{0,T} = S_0 - X \, (1 + RFR)^{-T}$$

That is, the "no arbitrage" difference between the call and put prices should equal the difference between the stock price and the present value of the joint exercise price. The market-determined risk-free rate of 6.25 percent implies that the correct difference between the two derivatives should be \$4.49 (= 53 − 48.51), which is \$0.26 greater than the \$4.23 (= 6.74 − 2.51) actual difference. This discrepancy suggests that if you assume the actual T-bill is priced correctly, the call price is undervalued relative to the put option. Not surprisingly, then, notice that the arbitrage transaction requires the purchase of the call option while shorting the put option.

EXHIBIT 21.18 ➤ *REPLICATING A PUT OPTION*

A. Net Portfolio Investment at Initiation (Date 0)

Portfolio	
Long 1 T-bill	$X(1 + RFR)^{-T}$
Short 1 WYZ stock	$-S_0$
Long 1 call option	$C_{0,T}$
Net investment:	$X(1 + RFR)^{-T} - S_0 + C_{0,T}$

B. Portfolio Value at Option Expiration (Date T)

Portfolio	(1) If $S_T \leq X$:	(2) If $S_T > X$:
Long 1 T-bill	X	X
Short 1 WYZ stock	$-S_T$	$-S_T$
Long 1 call option	0	$(S_T - X)$
Net position:	$X - S_T$	0

Creating Synthetic Securities Using Put-Call Parity

The preceding example demonstrates that a risk-free portfolio could be created by combining three risky securities: stock, a put option, and a call option. The parity condition developed in the example can be expressed in other useful ways as well. In particular, one of the four assets represented in the first equation is always *redundant* because it can be defined in terms of the others. Three additional ways of manipulating this result are:

➤21.2
$$P_{0,T} = \frac{X}{(1 + RFR)^T} - S_0 + C_{0,T}$$

➤21.3
$$C_{0,T} = S_0 + P_{0,T} - \frac{X}{(1 + RFR)^T}$$

➤21.4
$$S_0 = \frac{X}{(1 + RFR)^T} - P_{0,T} + C_{0,T}$$

Equation 21.2 and Equation 21.3 indicate, respectively, that (1) the payoffs to a long position in a put option can be replicated by a portfolio consisting of a long position in a T-bill, a short stock position, and the purchase of a call option; and (2) a synthetic call option can be mimicked by a portfolio that is long in the stock and the put option and short in the T-bill. Equation 21.4 indicates that the payoff to the stock itself can be expressed by its derivative securities and the T-bill.

These results are useful in two ways. First, if there are not markets in either put or call options, the relationships summarized by these equations outline how investors can create the desired, but unavailable, pattern of cash flows through the appropriate "packaging" of the other three inter-related assets. Suppose, for example, that a put option on WYZ stock did not exist but a call option does. Exhibit 21.18 shows the Date 0 and Date T cash flows associated with the portfolio replicating the terminal payoff. Combining both panels of the display, an initial investment of $[X(1 + RFR)_{-T} - S_0 + C_{0,T}]$ leads to a final cash flow that is no less than zero and as large as $X - S_T$ whenever $X > S_T$. Expressed in a more traditional manner, the expiration date payoff to the synthetic put is max $[0, X - S_T]$.

Another way the alternative expressions for the put-call parity model (summarized by Equations 21.2–21.4) are used in practice is the identification of arbitrage opportunities. Even when a particular derivative instrument trades actively in the market, if its cash flows and risks can be duplicated, this leads to the possibility that the price of the actual instrument and the net cost of the replicating portfolio will differ. Using the numbers from the previous example, the Date T distribution of max $[0, 50 - S_T]$ could be acquired through the synthetic strategy at a cost of $2.25 (= 48.51 - 53 + 6.74)$ or through the purchase of the actual put for $2.51.

This is the same $0.26 price differential we saw earlier when designing an arbitrage transaction involving the actual and synthetic T-bill. The put option arbitrage would be to short the actual put while buying the replicating portfolio (i.e., long T-bill, short stock, and long call), which is the same set of transactions we used in the T-bill arbitrage. This result underscores the important point that the put-call parity model only allows us to make *relative*—rather than absolute—statements about security values. Although we can change our perspective in identifying the misvalued instrument (e.g., T-bill versus put option), the real source of the market inefficiency came from examining the *difference* between the put and call prices in relation to the stock and T-bill prices. Consequently, all four securities need to be included in the arbitrage trade.

Adjusting Put-Call-Spot Parity for Dividends

A second extension of the put-call-spot parity model involves the payment of dividends to the shareholders of WYZ stock. Suppose for simplicity that in the basic portfolio listed in Exhibit 21.16, WYZ stock pays a dividend of D_T immediately prior to the expiration of the options at Date T. Assume further that the amount of this distribution is known when the investment is initiated, a condition that is almost certainly met for values of $T \leq 0.25$ year because U.S.-based companies typically pay quarterly dividends. The result of these modifications is that the terminal value of the long stock position will be $(S_T + D_T)$. On the other hand, the terminal payoffs to the put and call options remain max $[0, X - S_T]$ and max $[0, S_T - X]$, respectively, as the holders of the two derivative contracts will not participate directly in the payment of dividends to the stockholder.[6] Thus, the net Date T value of the portfolio acquired originally for $(S_0 + P_{0,T} - C_{0,T})$ is $(X + D_T)$.

With the critical assumption that the dividend payment is known at Date 0, the portfolio long in WYZ stock, long in the put, and short in the call once again can be viewed as equivalent to a T-bill, now having a face value of $(X + D_T)$. This allows Equation 21.1 to be adapted as follows:

$$S_0 + P_{0,T} - C_{0,T} = \frac{X + D_T}{(1 + RFR)^T} = \frac{X}{(1 + RFR)^T} + \frac{D_T}{(1 + RFR)^T}$$

which can be interpreted as:

(Long Stock) + (Long Put) + (Short Call) = (Long T-Bill) + (Long Present Value of Dividends)

Alternatively, it is often more useful to rearrange this equation as follows:

$$\left\{ S_0 - \frac{D_T}{(1 + RFR)^T} \right\} + P_{0,T} - C_{0,T} = \frac{X}{(1 + RFR)^T}$$

In this form, the equation can be compared directly with the no-dividend put-call-spot parity result and shows that the current stock price must be *adjusted downward* by the present value of the dividend. With an initial stock price of $53 and an annualized risk-free rate on a six-month

---

[6]The fact that the expiration date payoff to a call option on both a dividend- and nondividend-paying stock can be expressed as max $[0, S_T - X]$ does not mean that the two will generate the same dollar amount of cash flow. This is because the stock's value will be reduced by the payment of the dividend in the former case but not in the latter. Thus, with the lower terminal payout, the call on the dividend-paying stock will be less valuable than an otherwise comparable contract on a nondividend-paying equity. We will explore this topic more fully in Chapter 23.

T-bill of 6.25 percent, a \$1 dividend paid just before the expiration of a call and a put option with an exercise price of \$50 would result in a theoretical price differential of:

$$C_{0,0.5} - P_{0,0.5} = \left\{ 53 - \frac{1}{(1 + 0.0625)^{0.5}} \right\} - \frac{50}{(1 + 0.0625)^{0.5}} = \$3.52$$

This value differs from the parity differential for options on the nondividend-paying stock, which was shown earlier to be \$4.49. Thus, the payment of the dividend has reduced the price of the call relative to the put by \$0.97, which is the discounted amount of the \$1 cash distribution.

Put-Call-Forward Parity

At this point in our analysis of the structural relationships between derivative instruments and their underlying securities, we have not explicitly included forward or futures contracts. Suppose that instead of buying the stock in the spot market at Date 0, we took a long position in a forward contract allowing us to purchase one share of WYZ stock at Date T. The price of this acquisition, $F_{0,T}$, would be established by the forward agreement at Date 0. As before, we will assume that this transaction is supplemented by the purchase of a put option and the sale of a call option, each having the same exercise price and expiration date. Exhibit 21.19 summarizes both the initial and terminal cash flows to this position.

Panel B of the exhibit reveals that this is once again a risk-free portfolio. There are, however, two important differences in its cash flow patterns. First, the net initial investment of $(P_{0,T} - C_{0,T})$ is substantially smaller than when the stock was purchased in the spot market. Second, the riskless terminal payoff of $(X - F_{0,T})$ also is smaller than before as the stock now must be purchased at Date T rather than at Date 0. This intuition leads directly to the *put-call-forward* parity condition:

➤21.5
$$P_{0,T} - C_{0,T} = \frac{X - F_{0,T}}{(1 + RFR)^T} = \frac{X}{(1 + RFR)^T} - \frac{F_{0,T}}{(1 + RFR)^T}$$

which says that for markets to be free from arbitrage, the difference between put and call prices must equal the discounted difference between the common exercise price and the contract price of the forward agreement. Just as $F_{0,T}$ did not appear in the spot market version of the parity condition, the current stock price does not appear in Equation 21.5.

EXHIBIT 21.19 ➤ *PUT-CALL-FORWARD PARITY*

A. Net Portfold Investment at Initiation (Date 0)

Portfolio

Long 1 forward contract	0
Long 1 put option	$P_{0,T}$
Shot 1 call option	$-C_{0,T}$
Net investment:	$P_{0,T} - C_{0,T}$

B. Portfolio Value at Option Expiration (Date T)

Portfolio	(1) If $S_T \le X$:	(2) If $S_T > X$:
Long 1 forward contract	$(S_T - F_{0,T})$	$(S_T - F_{0,T})$
Long 1 put option	$(X - S_T)$	0
Short 1 call option	0	$-(S_T - X)$
Net position:	$(X - F_{0,T})$	$(X - F_{0,T})$

This result implies that the only time that put and call prices should be equal to one another in an efficient market is when $X = F_{0,T}$. That is, although the put-call parity result holds for any common exercise price, there is only one value of X for which there would be no net cost to the option combination and that is the prevailing forward price. Recall, for example, that when WYZ stock did not pay a dividend, the theoretical difference between $C_{0,0.5}$ and $P_{0,0.5}$ was \$4.49 (= 53 − 48.51). This meant that an investor long in the call and short in the put with a joint \$50 exercise price would have what amounted to a forward contract to buy WYZ stock in six months at a price of \$50.[7] However, she would have to pay \$4.49 for this arrangement, suggesting that \$50 is a below-market forward price. How much below the prevailing forward contract price is \$50? By the future value of \$4.49, invested at the prevailing risk-free rate of 6.25 percent. Thus, the no-arbitrage forward price under these circumstances should be \$54.63 [= 50 + 4.49 (1 + 0.0625)$^{0.5}$].

Another way to see this result comes from combining the put-call-forward parity condition with the put-call-spot condition. Specifically, inserting the expression for ($P_{0,T} − C_{0,T}$) from the put-call-forward parity condition into the put-call-spot condition leaves

$$S_0 + \left\{ \frac{X}{(1+RFR)^T} - \frac{F_{0,T}}{(1+RFR)^T} \right\} = \frac{X}{(1+RFR)^T}$$

which simplifies to

$$S_0 = \frac{F_{0,T}}{(1+RFR)^T}$$

This equation indicates that, in the absence of dividend payments, the spot price for the share of stock should simply be the discounted value of purchasing the same security in the forward market. Equivalently, this equation can be rewritten so that $F_{0,T} = S_0 (1 + RFR)^T$. In the preceding example, this means that the market-clearing (i.e., no net initial cost) contract price for a WYZ stock forward agreement should be $F_{0,0.5} = (53) (1 + 0.0625)^{0.5} = \$54.63$. Finally, in the case where dividends are paid, the equation for the put-call-forward parity condition can be inserted into the dividend-adjusted spot parity condition to produce the more general relationship between spot and forward prices:

$$\left\{ S_0 - \frac{D_T}{(1+RFR)^T} \right\} = \frac{F_{0,T}}{(1+RFR)^T}$$

Thus, if a \$1 dividend were paid on WYZ stock just prior to the maturity of the contract in six months, the forward price would be adjusted down to $F_{0,0.5} = (53)(1 + 0.0625)^{0.5} − 1 = \$53.63$ to account for the cash distribution that would benefit the actual shareholders but not the derivative holder.

---

[7]This interpretation follows by noting that the long call position will be exercised when $S_T \le 50$ and the short put will be exercised against the investor when $S_T \le 50$. Therefore, the investor's net option position produces an identical result to holding a long position in a forward contract with a contract price of \$50. Generalizing this result, any time we have a call and a put option on the same underlying stock with a common exercise price and expiration date, the following is true: (long call at X) + (short put at X) = (long forward at X). Similarly, shorting the call and buying the put produces a synthetic short forward position.

An Introduction to the Use of Derivatives in Portfolio Management

Beyond the unique risk-reward profiles they offer as stand-alone investments, derivatives also are used widely in investment management to restructure the fundamental nature of an existing portfolio of assets. Typically, the intent of this sort of restructuring is to modify the portfolio's risk. In this section, we review three prominent derivative applications in the management of equity positions: shorting forward contracts, purchasing **protective puts**, and purchasing **equity collars**.

Restructuring Asset Portfolios with Forward Contracts

Suppose the manager of a small corporate pension fund currently has all of her investable funds committed to a well-diversified portfolio of equity securities designed to reflect the movements of a broad indicator of the stock market's performance, such as Standard & Poor's 500 index. Implicit in this investment approach is the manager's belief that she cannot "add value" by trying to select superior individual securities. She does, however, feel that it is possible to take advantage of perceived trends at a macroeconomic level by switching her funds between her current equity holding and any of several other portfolios mimicking different asset classes (e.g., fixed-income, cash equivalents), depending on her forecast of future events. Switching a portfolio's composition in an attempt to time general market movements instead of company-specific trends is known as *tactical asset allocation.*

The stock market has increased steadily over the past several months, and the pension fund has a present market value of $100 million. At this time, though, the manager has become concerned about the possibility that inflationary pressures will dampen corporate earnings and drive stock prices down. Although it is unclear now whether this concern will be realized, she feels confident that the uncertainty will be resolved in the coming quarter. Accordingly, she would like to shift her allocation from 100 percent equity to 100 percent T-bills for the next three months. There are two ways she can make this change. The most direct method would be to sell her stock portfolio and buy $100 million (less the transaction costs) of 90-day T-bills. When the T-bills mature in three months, she could then repurchase her original equity holdings.

The second approach would be to maintain her current stock holdings but convert them into a synthetic risk-free position with a three-month forward contract specifying $100 million of the stock index as the underlying asset. As we will see later, the primary benefit of this approach is that it is often more cost-effective and quicker to implement. This is a classic example of a *hedge position,* wherein the price risk of the underlying asset is offset (rather than eliminated) by a supplementary derivative transaction. The following table captures the dynamics of this hedge at a basic level.

Economic Event	Actual Stock Exposure	Desired Forward Exposure
Stock prices fall	Loss	Gain
Stock prices rise	Gain	Loss

To neutralize the risk of falling stock prices, the fund manager will need to adopt a forward position that benefits from that potential movement. Said differently, the manager requires a hedge position with payoffs that are *negatively correlated* with those of the existing exposure. As we saw in Exhibit 21.10, this requires committing to the short side of the contract. This hedging argument is identical to the point we made in the portfolio formation analysis of Chapter 7 that it is always possible to combine two perfectly negatively correlated assets to create a risk-free position.

EXHIBIT 21.20	COMPARATIVE STOCK AND STOCK FUTURES TRADING COSTS					
COST FACTOR	UNITED STATES (S&P 500)	JAPAN (NIKKEI 225)	UNITED KINGDOM (FT-SE 100)	FRANCE (CAC 40)	GERMANY (DAX)	HONG KONG (HANG SENG)
A. Stocks						
Comissions	0.12%	0.20%	0.20%	0.25%	0.25%	0.50%
Market impact	0.30	0.70	0.70	0.50	0.50	0.50
Taxes	0.00	0.21	0.50	0.00	0.00	0.34
Total	0.42%	1.11%	1.40%	0.75%	0.75%	1.34%
B. Futures						
Commissions	0.01%	0.05%	0.02%	0.03%	0.02%	0.05%
Market impact	0.05	0.10	0.10	0.10	0.10	0.10
Taxes	0.00	0.00	0.00	0.00	0.00	0.00
Total	0.06%	0.15%	0.12%	0.13%	0.12%	0.15%

The primary benefit of converting the pension fund's asset allocation using this approach is that it is far more cost-effective than the physical transformations demanded by the first solution. For instance, Exhibit 21.20 shows that when all of the costs of transaction are considered (e.g., trading commissions, market impact, taxes), the average expense of actually rebalancing a U.S. equity portfolio is about 42 basis points of the position's value, while the same trade with an equity forward contract would cost just 6 basis points. Trading expenses in other countries, though different in absolute level, reflect this same general trend.

This synthetic restructuring is best understood through the effect that it has had on the systematic risk—or beta—of the portfolio. By its original construction, we will assume that the original stock holding had a beta of one, matching the volatility of a proxy for the market portfolio. The combination of being long $100 million of stock and short a forward covering $100 million of a stock index converts the systematic portion of the portfolio into a synthetic T-bill, which by definition has a beta of zero. Once the contract matures in three months, however, the position will revert to its original risk profile. This is illustrated in Exhibit 21.21. More generally, the short forward position can be designed to allow for intermediate combinations of stock and T-bills as well. To see this, let w_s be the stock allocation so that $(1 - w_s)$ is the allocation to the risk-free asset created synthetically. The net beta for the converted portfolio is simply a weighted average of the systematic risks of its equity and T-bill portions or

➤21.6
$$\beta_P = (w_S)\,\beta_S + (1 - w_S)\,\beta_{RFR}$$

Thus, if the manager had wished to change the original allocation from 100 percent stock to a "60–40" mix of stock and T-bills, she would have shorted only $40 million of the index forward to leave her with an unhedged equity position totaling $60 million (i.e., $w_s - 0.60$ and $(1 - w_s) = 0.40$). By Equation 21.6, this in turn would leave her with an adjusted portfolio beta of $[(0.6)\,(1) + (0.4)\,(0)] = 0.6$.

Protecting Portfolio Value with Put Options

Although the manager's concern in the previous example was to protect her stock portfolio against possible share price declines over the next three months, by shorting the stock index forward contract, she has effectively committed to "selling" her equity position—even if stock

EXHIBIT 21.21 *ALTERING THE SYSTEMATIC RISK OF A STOCK PORTFOLIO SYNTHETICALLY*

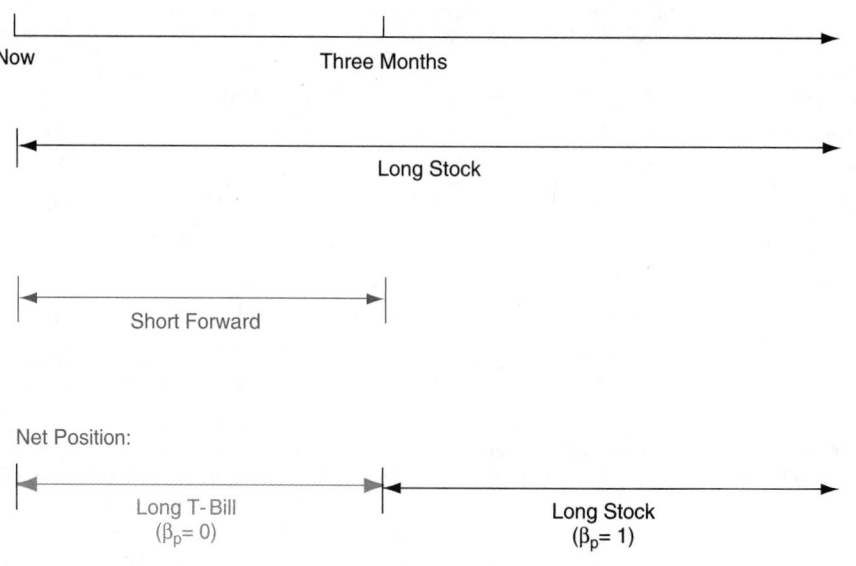

prices rise. That is, by using a derivative with a symmetric payoff structure to hedge her risk, the manager also has surrendered the upside potential of her original holding. Recognizing this, suppose instead that she attempted to design a hedge position correlated to her stock portfolio as shown in the following table.

ECONOMIC EVENT	ACTUAL STOCK EXPOSURE	DESIRED FORWARD EXPOSURE
Stock prices fall	Loss	Gain
Stock prices rise	Gain	*No loss*

In seeking an asymmetric hedge, this manager wants a derivative contract that allows her to sell stock when prices fall but keep her shares when prices rise. As we have seen, she must purchase a put option to obtain this exposure.

The purchase of a put option to hedge the downside risk of an underlying security holding is called a *protective put* position and is the most straightforward example of a more general set of derivative-based strategies known as *portfolio insurance*.[8] To see this insurance interpretation, suppose that in lieu of the short forward position, the manager purchased a three-month, at-the-money put option on her $100 million stock portfolio. Under the prevailing market conditions, let us also assume that this put cost the manager an up-front premium of $1.324 million. The value of the protective put position (net of the initial cost of the hedge) is calculated in Exhibit 21.22 for several different expiration date prices for the underlying stock portfolio. In

---

[8]The concept and use of portfolio insurance has received a great deal of scrutiny in the research literature. See, for example, the studies by Mark Rubinstein, "Alternative Paths to Portfolio Insurance," *Financial Analysts Journal* 41, no. 4 (July–August 1985): 42–52; Mark Kritzman, "What's Wrong with Portfolio Insurance?" *Journal of Portfolio Management* 13, no. 1 (Fall 1986): 13–17; and Harry M. Kat, "Portfolio Insurance: A Comparison of Alternative Strategies," *Journal of Financial Engineering* 1, no. 4 (1993): 415–442.

EXHIBIT 21.22 *EXPIRATION DATE VALUE OF A PROTECTIVE PUT POSITION*

POTENTIAL PORTFOLIO VALUE	VALUE OF PUT OPTION	COST OF PUT OPTION	NET PROTECTIVE PUT POSITION
60	(100 − 60) = 40	−1.324	(60 + 40) − 1.324 = 98.676
70	(100 − 70) = 30	−1.324	(70 + 30) − 1.324 = 98.676
80	(100 − 80) = 20	−1.324	(80 + 20) − 1.324 = 98.676
90	(100 − 90) = 10	−1.324	(90 + 10) − 1.324 = 98.676
100	0	−1.324	(100 + 0) − 1.324 = 98.676
110	0	−1.324	(110 + 0) − 1.324 = 108.676
120	0	−1.324	(120 + 0) − 1.324 = 118.676
130	0	−1.324	(130 + 0) − 1.324 = 128.676
140	0	−1.324	(140 + 0) − 1.324 = 138.676

particular, notice that with the exercise price set equal to the current portfolio value of $100 million, the put contract exactly offsets any expiration date share price decline while allowing the position to increase in value as stock prices increase. Thus, the put provides the manager with insurance against falling prices with no *deductible*.[9]

An intriguing aspect of the terminal value of the combined stock and put option portfolio shown in the last column of Exhibit 21.22 is that it resembles the payoff diagram of the long call option position illustrated earlier in Exhibit 21.11. A different way of seeing this is shown in Exhibit 21.23, which indicates that being long in the stock and long in the put generates the same net payoff as an at-the-money long call option holding "elevated" by $100 million. Given the put-call-spot parity results of the previous section, however, this should come as no surprise. Indeed, the no-arbitrage equation (Equation 21.1) can be rewritten:

$$S_0 + P_{0,T} = C_{0,T} + \frac{X}{(1 + RFR)^T}$$

This expression says that the protective put method of providing portfolio insurance generates an equivalent expiration date payoff as a long position in a call option with the same characteristics as the put and a long position in a T-bill with a face value equal to the options' common exercise price. It is this final term that provides the "elevation" to the call payoff diagram in Exhibit 21.23. Thus, the manager has two ways of providing price insurance for her current stock holding: (1) continue to hold her shares and purchase a put option, or (2) sell her shares and buy both a T-bill and a call option. Her choice between them will undoubtedly come down to specific logistic considerations, such as relative option prices and transaction costs.[10]

---

[9]In general, the deductible portion of the portfolio insurance contract can be defined as $[S_0 − X]$. For instance, with an exercise price of only 95, the manager would not receive compensation from the hedge until the portfolio value fell below $95 million; she would effectively be "self-insuring" the first $5 million of losses. Naturally, the larger this deductible amount, the lower the cost of the put option.

[10]Many authors have studied the effect that adding options to an underlying security position has on the risk of the combined portfolio. In particular, see Robert C. Merton, Myron S. Scholes, and Matthew L. Gladstein, "A Simulation of the Returns and Risk of Alternative Option Portfolio Investment Strategies," *Journal of Business* 51, no. 2 (April 1978): 183–242; and Richard M. Bookstaber and Roger G. Clarke, "Options Can Alter Portfolio Return Distributions," *Journal of Portfolio Management* 7, no. 3 (Spring 1981): 63–70. For a good nontechnical discussion of this material, see Maarten L. Nederlof, "The Comparison of Strategies Using Derivatives," in *Derivative Strategies for Managing Portfolio Risk*, ed. K. Brown (Charlottesville, Va.: Association for Investment Management and Research, 1993).

EXHIBIT 21.23 ▷ *TERMINAL PAYOFF TO AN "INSURED" STOCK POSITION*

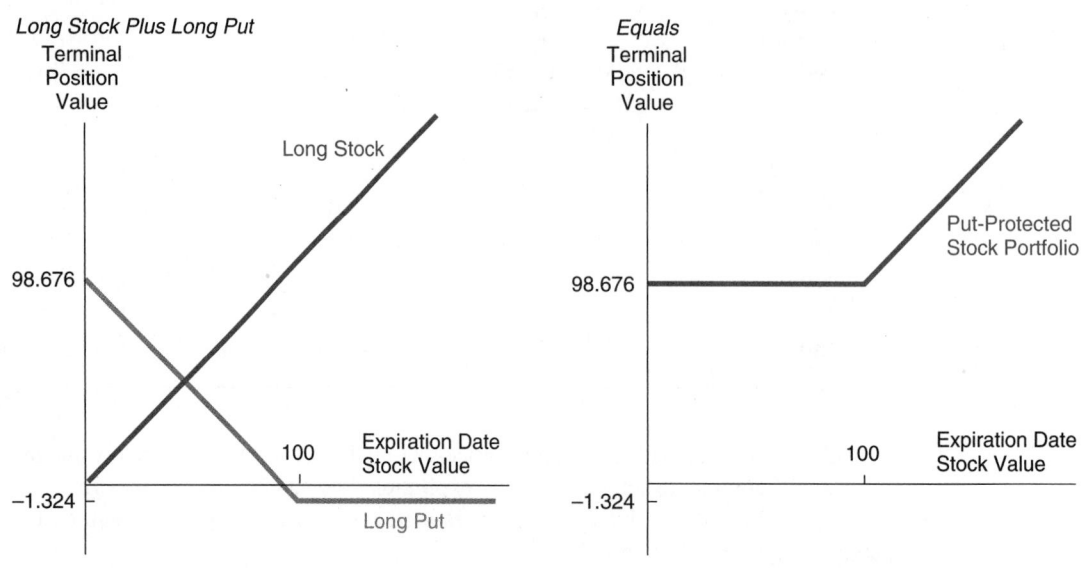

An Alternative Way to Pay for a Protective Put

In the previous two examples, we saw how a pension manager could (1) use a short position in a forward contract to convert her $100 million stock portfolio to a risk-free position with no up-front expense, or (2) protect against adverse stock price movements while retaining the upside gain potential by purchasing a put option with an up-front expense of $1.324 million. There is also a third alternative, which fits in between paying nothing for a hedge but surrendering future stock gains for the next three months (i.e., the short forward position) and keeping those potential gains in exchange for a considerable initial payment (i.e., the protective put position).

Specifically, suppose that the manager makes two simultaneous decisions that differ from those considered previously. First, she decides to purchase a three-month, out-of-the-money protective put option with an exercise price of $97 million and a commensurately lower initial cost of $0.560 million. (Notice that in purchasing an out-of-the-money contract, the manager is creating a $3 million deductible compared to her current portfolio value.) Second, she decides not to pay cash for the put option; but, instead, she sells back to the option dealer something worth an equivalent amount of money. In particular, suppose she sells back to the dealer a call option with a three-month expiration and an exercise price of $108 million that also carries an initial premium of $0.560 million. The simultaneous purchase of an out-of-the-money put and sale of an out-of-the-money call on the same underlying asset and with the same expiration date and market price is a strategy known as a **collar agreement**.

Exhibit 21.24 shows the expiration date outcomes of the manager's equity collar-protected portfolio for several different terminal stock portfolio values, while Exhibit 21.25 illustrates these outcomes graphically. There are two important things to notice from these displays. The first is that, like the forward contract hedge, there is no initial out-of-pocket expense associated with this derivative combination. Instead, the manager effectively pays for her desired portfolio insurance by surrendering an equivalent amount of the portfolio's future upside potential. That is, in exchange for being "made whole" for any stock decline below $97 million, she agrees to give up any capital gain beyond $108 million. The second thing to notice is that, like the protective put in the last example (and unlike the short forward position), she does retain some of

EXHIBIT 21.24   *EXPIRATION DATE VALUE OF AN EQUITY COLLAR-PROTECTED PORTFOLIO*

Potential Portfolio Value	Net Option Expense	Value of Put Option	Value of Call Option	Net Collar-Protected Position
60	(0.56 – 0.56) = 0	(97 – 60) = 37	0	60 + 37 = 97
70	(0.56 – 0.56) = 0	(97 – 70) = 27	0	70 + 27 = 97
80	(0.56 – 0.56) = 0	(97 – 80) = 17	0	80 + 17 = 97
90	(0.56 – 0.56) = 0	(97 – 90) = 7	0	90 + 7 = 97
97	(0.56 – 0.56) = 0	0	0	97 + 0 = 97
100	(0.56 – 0.56) = 0	0	0	100 + 0 = 100
108	(0.56 – 0.56) = 0	0	0	108 – 0 = 108
110	(0.56 – 0.56) = 0	0	(108 – 110) = –2	110 – 2 = 108
120	(0.56 – 0.56) = 0	0	(108 – 120) = –12	120 – 12 = 108
130	(0.56 – 0.56) = 0	0	(108 – 130) = –22	130 – 22 = 108
140	(0.56 – 0.56) = 0	0	(108 – 140) = –32	140 – 32 = 108

EXHIBIT 21.25   *TERMINAL PAYOFF OF A COLLAR-PROTECTED PORTFOLIO*

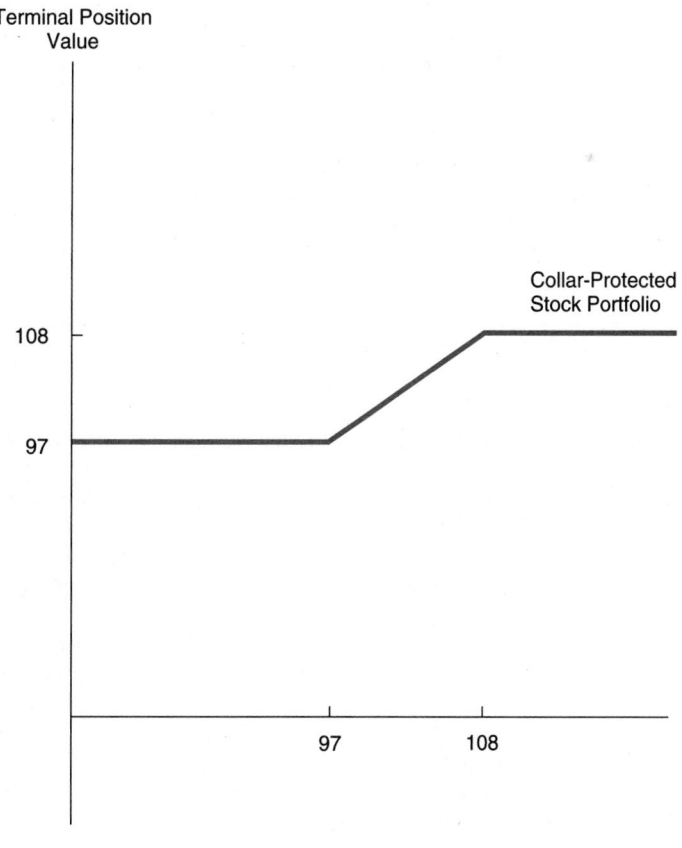

the benefit of a rising stock market. As noted, however, this upside gain potential stops at the exercise price of the call option. As best indicated in Exhibit 21.25, the manager has placed a "collar" around her portfolio for the next three months—its net value will not fall below $97 million and will not rise above $108 million. At any terminal value for the stock portfolio between these extreme levels, both of the options expire out of the money and no contract settlement payment will be required of either the manager or the dealer.

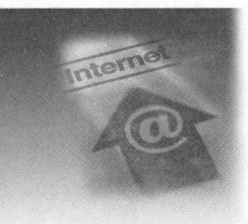

The Internet *Investments Online*

A good way to learn more about the basics of futures and options is to visit some derivative-related Web sites. Interesting futures and options exchange sites include:

http://www.cboe.com The Web site of the Chicago Board Options Exchange presents an overview of the exchange and options on equities, indexes, and LEAPS. Market data, including quotes, are available. The site offers educational materials for beginners and discussions of investment strategies. By inputting some data, users can compute the theoretical value of an option using the site's options calculator.

http://www.cbot.com The home page of the Chicago Board of Trade includes an overview of the Board, a dictionary of trading jargon, as well as price quotes and charts. The site offers government agriculture reports (since many commodities are traded on the CBOT) and weather reports (due to the effect of weather on commodity yields).

http://www.cme.com The Chicago Mercantile Exchange's Web site features similar information as the other exchanges: news, price quotes, product information, and educational resources. The Merc's site offers Web-based lessons on derivative strategies, and even offers an "Introduction to Hand Signals" **(http://www.cme.com/education/courses)** used by floor traders.

http://www.liffe.com LIFFE stands for the London International Financial Futures and Options Exchange. It trades equity and short-term interest rate contracts. It is Europe's premier derivatives exchange, and it has a goal of being one of the most technologically advanced—so keep an eye on this Web site! Users can register online for free to gain access to the site's pages, which include information on money market, bond, equity, index, and commodity trading. It contains links to many countries' futures and options exchanges.

Summary

- As their popularity in financial markets has increased over the past few decades, derivative securities have become an indispensable part of the investment manager's toolkit. Although forward, futures, and option contracts play important roles as stand-alone investments, the real advantage of derivatives is their ability to modify the risk-return characteristics of a collection of existing securities in a cost-effective manner. This use of forwards and options to restructure a portfolio synthetically has two dimensions. First, we saw that it is possible to combine derivatives with the underlying position in a way that replicates the cash flow patterns of another traded instrument. For instance, a well-diversified stock portfolio could be converted into the equivalent of a T-bill by shorting an appropriate amount of a stock index futures contract. Second, derivatives can also be used with the original portfolio to create a payoff structure that is otherwise unavailable. The use of a protective put to eliminate the downside risk of an equity holding while maintaining its upside profit potential is an example.
- At a fundamental level, forward and option contracts can be viewed as insurance policies that an investor can hold against adverse price movements in his underlying position. As forwards and options

can be structured to provide exactly the same degree of "coverage," the basic difference between these contracts lies in how the investor must pay for the desired insurance. Forwards, with symmetrical terminal payoffs, typically do not require any initial payment but do obligate the investor to the possibility of an unfavorable transaction at a future date. Conversely, with options, which provide asymmetrical terminal payoffs, the investor must pay an up-front premium but then has no further obligation to his counterparty.

- Given these similarities, it is not surprising that there are well-defined relationships that must exist in an efficient capital market between the prices of forward and option contracts. In particular, the put-call parity conditions delineated the linkages between five different securities: the underlying asset (e.g., stock), T-bills, forward contracts, call options, and put options. An important consequence of these relationships is that one of these securities is always redundant because its cash flow patterns can be replicated by the remaining instruments. This realization leads to another important use for derivatives: arbitrage investing. Through their ability to help create synthetic replicas of existing securities, derivatives provide investors with the possibility of riskless excess returns when the synthetic and actual instruments sell for different prices.

- Although this chapter provides a broad overview of the dynamics of these important financial contracts, there are several issues related to the use and management of derivative securities that remain to be addressed. Chief among these are ways in which individual positions in forwards, futures, and options are valued and the adjustments that investors need to make when designing derivatives on an underlying asset other than common stock. These topics will be considered in subsequent chapters now that we have explored the valuation and investment applications of a more basic set of securities (i.e., stocks and bonds). For now, though, it is important to appreciate these instruments for their ability to assist investors in repackaging the risks and cash flows of their portfolios.

Questions

1. Explain why the difference between put and call prices depends on whether or not the underlying security pays a dividend during the life of the contracts.

2. When comparing futures and forward contracts, it has been said that futures are more liquid but forwards are more flexible. Explain what this statement means and comment on how differences in contract liquidity and design flexibility might influence an investor's preference in choosing one instrument over the other.

3. Compare and contrast the gain and loss potential for investors holding the following positions: long forward, short forward, long call, short call, long put, and short put. Indicate what the terms *symmetric* and *asymmetric* mean in this context.

4. *CFA Examination Level III*

   The Franklin Medical Research Foundation is to be established with a gift from Mr. John Franklin in memory of his deceased wife. The foundation's grant-making and investment policy issues have been finalized. Receipt of the expected $45 million Franklin cash gift will not occur for 90 days, yet the committee believes current stock and bond prices are unusually attractive and wishes to take advantage of this perceived opportunity.

   a. Briefly describe two strategies that utilize derivative financial instruments and could be implemented to take advantage of the committee's market expectations.

   b. Evaluate whether or not it is appropriate for the foundation to undertake a derivatives-based hedge to bridge the expected 90-day time gap, considering both positive and negative factors.

5. *CFA Examination Level II*

   Robert Chen, CFA, is reviewing the characteristics of derivative securities and their use in portfolios. Chen is considering the addition of either a short position in stock index futures or a long position in stock index options to an existing well-diversified portfolio of equity securities. Contrast the way in which each of these two alternatives would affect the risk and return of the resulting combined portfolios.

6. *CFA Examination Level II*

Current equity call prices for Furniture City are contained in the following table. In reviewing these prices, Jim Smith, CFA, notices discrepancies between several option prices and basic option pricing relationships.

Closing Prices
Furniture City Equity Call Options
May 31, 1997

			Expiration Month		
Stock Close	**Strike**	**June**	**July**	**August**	**September**
119½	110	8⅞	12½	15	18
119½	120	1½	3¾	3	4¼
119½	130	1	2¼	2⅞	5

Identify three different apparent pricing discrepancies in the table. Identify which of the basic option-pricing relationships each discrepancy violates. (*Note:* The fact that option contracts do not always trade at the same time as the underlying stock should *not* be identified as a discrepancy.)

7. Explain how call and put options can represent a leveraged way of investing in the stock market and also enable investors to hedge their risk completely. Specifically, under what circumstances will the addition of an option increase the risk of an existing portfolio and under what circumstances will it decrease portfolio risk?

8. It has been said that from an investor's perspective a long position in a call option represents the "good half" of a long position in a forward contract. Explain what is meant by this statement. Also, describe what the "bad half" of the long forward position would have to be for this statement to be true.

9. Discuss the difficulties that having options in a security portfolio create for the measurement of portfolio risk. Specifically, explain why standard deviation is a deficient statistic for capturing the essence of risk in a put-protected portfolio. How could the standard deviation statistic be modified to account for this concern?

10. If the current price of a nondividend-paying stock is $32 and a one-year futures contract on that stock has a contract price of $35, explain how an investor could create an "off-market" long position in a forward contract at an exercise price of $25. Would this synthetic contract require a cash payment from either the long or short position? If so, explain which party would have to make the payment and how that payment should be calculated.

Problems

1. The common stock of Sophia Enterprises serves as the underlying asset for the following derivative securities: (1) forward contracts, (2) European-style call options, and (3) European-style put options.

   a. Assuming that all Sophia derivatives expire at the same date in the future, complete a table similar to the following for each of the following contract positions:

   (1) A long position in a forward with a contract price of $50

   (2) A long position in a call option with an exercise price of $50 and a front-end premium expense of $5.20

   (3) A short position in a call option with an exercise price of $50 and a front-end premium receipt of $5.20

Expiration Date Sophia Stock Price	Expiration Date Derivative Payoff	Initial Derivative Premium	Net Profit
25	_____	_____	_____
30	_____	_____	_____
35	_____	_____	_____
40	_____	_____	_____
45	_____	_____	_____
50	_____	_____	_____
55	_____	_____	_____
60	_____	_____	_____
65	_____	_____	_____
70	_____	_____	_____
75	_____	_____	_____

In calculating net profit, ignore the time differential between the initial derivative expense or receipt and the terminal payoff.

   b. Graph the net profit for each of the three derivative positions, using net profit on the vertical axis and Sophia's expiration date stock price on the horizontal axis. Label the breakeven (i.e., zero profit) point(s) on each graph.

   c. Briefly describe the belief about the expiration date price of Sophia stock that an investor using each of these three positions implicitly holds.

2. Refer once again to the derivative securities using Sophia common stock as an underlying asset discussed in Problem 1.

   a. Assuming that all Sophia derivatives expire at the same date in the future, complete a table similar to the following for each of the following contract positions:

     (1) A short position in a forward with a contract price of $50

     (2) A long position in a put option with an exercise price of $50 and a front-end premium expense of $3.23

     (3) A short position in a put option with an exercise price of $50 and a front-end premium receipt of $3.23

Expiration Date Sophia Stock Price	Expiration Date Derivative Payoff	Initial Derivative Premium	Net Profit
25	_____	_____	_____
30	_____	_____	_____
35	_____	_____	_____
40	_____	_____	_____
45	_____	_____	_____
50	_____	_____	_____
55	_____	_____	_____
60	_____	_____	_____
65	_____	_____	_____
70	_____	_____	_____
75	_____	_____	_____

In calculating net profit, ignore the time differential between the initial derivative expense or receipt and the terminal payoff.

b. Graph the net profit for each of the three derivative positions, using net profit on the vertical axis and Sophia's expiration date stock price on the horizontal axis. Label the breakeven (i.e., zero profit) point(s) on each graph.

c. Briefly describe the belief about the expiration date price of Sophia stock that an investor using each of these three positions implicitly holds.

3. Suppose that an investor holds a share of Sophia common stock, currently valued at $50. She is concerned that over the next few months the value of her holding might decline and she would like to hedge that risk by supplementing her holding with one of three different derivative positions, all of which expire at the same point in the future:

   (1) A short position in a forward with a contract price of $50

   (2) A long position in a put option with an exercise price of $50 and a front-end premium expense of $3.23

   (3) A short position in a call option with an exercise price of $50 and a front-end premium receipt of $5.20

   a. Using a table similar to the following, calculate the expiration date value of the investor's combined (i.e., stock and derivative) position. In calculating net portfolio value, ignore the time differential between the initial derivative expense or receipt and the terminal payoff.

Expiration Date Sophia Stock Value	Expiration Date Derivative Payoff	Initial Derivative Premium	Combined Terminal Position Value
25			
30			
35			
40			
45			
50			
55			
60			
65			
70			
75			

   b. For each of the three hedge portfolios, graph the expiration date value of her combined position on the vertical axis, with potential expiration date share prices of Sophia stock on the horizontal axis.

   c. Assuming that the options are priced fairly, use the concept of put-call parity to calculate the zero-value contract price (i.e., $F_{0,T}$) for a forward agreement on Sophia stock. Explain why this value differs from the $50 contract price used in Part a and Part b.

4. You strongly believe that the price of Breener Inc. stock will rise substantially from its current level of $137, and you are considering buying shares in the company. You currently have $13,700 to invest. As an alternative to purchasing the stock itself, you are also considering buying call options on Breener stock that expire in three months and have an exercise price of $140. These call options cost $10 each.

   a. Compare and contrast the size of the potential payoff and the risk involved in each of these alternatives.

   b. Calculate the three-month rate of return on both strategies assuming that at the option expiration date Breener's stock price has (1) increased to $155 or (2) decreased to $135.

   c. At what stock price level will the person who sells you the Breener call option break even? Can you determine the maximum loss that the call option seller may suffer, assuming that he does not already own Breener stock?

5. The common stock of Company XYZ is currently trading at a price of $42. Both a put and a call option are available for XYZ stock, each having an exercise price of $40 and an expiration date in exactly six months. The current market prices for the put and call are $1.45 and $3.90, respectively. The risk-free holding period return for the next six months is 4 percent, which corresponds to an 8 percent annual rate.

   a. For each possible stock price in the following sequence, calculate the expiration date payoffs (net of the initial purchase price) for the following positions: (1) buy one XYZ call option, and (2) short one XYZ call option:

20, 25, 30, 35, 40, 45, 50, 55, 60

   Draw a graph of these payoff relationships, using net profit on the vertical axis and potential expiration date stock price on the horizontal axis. Be sure to specify the prices at which these respective positions will break even (i.e., produce a net profit of zero).

   b. Using the same potential stock prices as in Part a, calculate the expiration date payoffs (net of the initial purchase price) for the following positions: (1) buy one XYZ put option, and (2) short one XYZ put option. Draw a graph of these payoff relationships, labeling the prices at which these investments will break even.

   c. Determine whether the $2.45 difference in the market prices between the call and put options is consistent with the put-call parity relationship for European-style contracts.

6. *CFA Examination Level III*

   On June 1, 1987, an institutional portfolio manager is managing a $1 million portfolio consisting of U.S. government bonds. Currently, the portfolio is fully invested in one bond issue—Government 8% Bonds due June 1, 2002, selling at a market price of 100.

   The manager is concerned about the outlook for interest rates over the next six months. The manager believes interest rates will move significantly with probabilities favoring a strong rise in rates, but a strong decline is also possible. For the next six-month holding period, the manager's goal is to structure a portfolio that will be substantially protected from a rate rise but that will also participate in any market advances.

   Other available investment instruments are the following:

   (1) Futures Contract on Government 8 percent Bonds, due 6/1/02

Futures expiration	12/1/87
Futures current price	$101
Contract size	$100,000

   (2) Option Contracts on Government 8 Percent Bonds, due 6/1/02 expiring 12/1/87

Option	Strike Price	Market Price	Contract Size
Calls	100	4.00	$100,000
Puts	100	2.00	$100,000

   (3) Treasury bills maturing 12/1/87, yielding 3 percent for six months.

   a. Assume that the manager wishes to maintain the current bond holding. Design an option strategy that will achieve the manager's goal of protecting against an interest rate rise while also participating in any market advances.

   b. Assume that the manager is willing to maintain or sell the current bond holding. With available instruments already listed, design two alternative portfolio structures that accomplish the same goal.

   c. Based on the following put-call parity relationship, calculate which of the two strategies designed in Part b should be implemented:

Put Price = Call Price − Bond Price + (Present Value of Exercise Price)

7. Consider Commodity Z that has both exchange-traded futures and option contracts associated with it. As you look in today's paper, you find the following put and call prices for options that expire exactly six months from now:

Exercise Price	Put Price	Call Price
40	$0.59	$8.73
45	1.93	—
50	—	2.47

a. Assuming that the futures price of a six-month contract on Commodity Z is $48, what must be the price of a put with an exercise price of $50 in order to avoid arbitrage across markets? Similarly, calculate the "no arbitrage" price of a call with an exercise price of $45. In both calculations, assume that the yield curve is flat and the annual risk-free rate is 6 percent.

b. What is the "no arbitrage" price differential that should exist between the put and call options having an exercise price of $40? Is this differential satisfied by current market prices? If not, demonstrate an arbitrage trade to take advantage of the mispricing.

8. *CFA Examination Level III*

Janice Delsing, a U.S.-based portfolio manager, manages an $800 million portfolio ($600 million in stocks and $200 million in bonds). In reaction to anticipated short-term market events, Delsing wishes to adjust the allocation to 50 percent stock and 50 percent bonds through the use of futures. Her position will be held only until "the time is right to restore the original asset allocation." Delsing determines a financial futures-based asset allocation strategy is appropriate. The stock futures index multiplier is 250, and the denomination of the bond futures contract is $100,000. Other information relevant to a futures-based strategy is given in the following exhibit.

INFORMATION FOR FUTURES-BASED STRATEGY	
Bond portfolio modified duration	5 years
Bond portfolio yield to maturity	7%
Basis point value (BPV) of bond futures	$97.85
Stock index futures price	$1,378
Stock portfolio beta	1.0

a. Describe the financial futures-based strategy needed and explain how the strategy allows Delsing to implement her allocation adjustment. No calculations are necessary.

b. Compute the number of each of the following needed to implement Delsing's asset allocation strategy:
   (1) Bond futures contracts
   (2) Stock index futures contracts

c. Discuss one advantage and one disadvantage of using each of the following for asset allocation:
   (1) Financial futures
   (2) Index put options

One month later, the yield to maturity on comparable bond portfolios has increased by 10 basis points and the stock index has risen by $28.

d. Calculate the percentage return (from price changes only) for the past month, assuming:
   (1) Delsing executed the 50/50 asset allocation strategy using futures.
   (2) Delsing did not execute the strategy but instead preserved her original long-term asset allocation.

9. *CFA Examination Level III*

Industrial Products Corp. (IPC), a publicly held company, is considering going private. It is extremely important to IPC's management that the pension fund's present surplus level be preserved pending completion of buyout financing. For the next three months (until September 1, 1990), management's goal is to sustain no loss of value in the pension fund portfolio. Today (June 1, 1990), this value is $300 million. Of this total, $150 million is invested in equities in the form of an S&P 500 Index fund, producing an annual dividend yield of 4 percent; the balance is invested in a single U.S. government bond issue, having a coupon of 8 percent and a maturity of 6/01/2005. Since the "no-loss strategy" has only a three-month time horizon, management does not wish to sell any of the present security holdings.

Assume that sufficient cash is available to satisfy margin requirements, transaction costs, and so on, and that the following market conditions exist as of June 1, 1990:

- The S&P 500 Index is at the 350 level, with a yield of 4.0 percent.
- The U.S. government 8.0 percent bonds due 6/1/2005 are selling at 100.
- U.S. Treasury bills due on 9/1/90 are priced to yield 1.5 percent for the three-month period (i.e., 6 percent annually).

Available investment instruments are the following:

Contract	Expiration	Current Contract Price	Strike Price	Contract Size
S&P 500 Index future	9/1/90	$355.00	—	$175,000
Future on U.S. government 8% bonds due 6/1/2005	9/1/90	101.00	—	100,000
S&P 500 call option	9/1/90	8.00	350	35,000
S&P 500 put option	9/1/90	7.00	350	35,000
U.S. government 8% due 6/1/2005 call option	9/1/90	2.50	100	100,000
U.S. government 8% due 6/1/2005 put option	9/1/90	4.50	100	100,000

a. Assume that the management wishes to protect the portfolio against any losses (ignoring the costs of purchasing options or futures contracts) but wishes also to participate in any stock or bond market advances over the next three months. Using the preceding instruments, design two strategies to accomplish this goal, and calculate the number of contracts needed to implement each strategy.

b. Using the put-call parity relationship and the fair value formula for futures (both follow), recommend which one of the two strategies designed in Part a should be implemented. Justify your choice.

Put Price = Call Price Minus Security Price Plus Present Value of (Exercise Price Plus Income on the Underlying Security)

Futures Price = Underlying Security Price Plus (Treasury Bill Income Minus Income on the Underlying Security)

10. a. Use combinations of payoff diagrams similar to those shown in Exhibits 21.10–21.12 to demonstrate why the "synthetic put" version of the put-call-spot parity condition must hold in an arbitrage-free capital market.

b. Once again using the appropriate payoff diagrams, provide an explanation for the put-call-forward parity relationship of the following equation:

$$S_0 = \frac{F_{0,T}}{(1 + RFR)^T}$$

11. As an option trader, you are constantly looking for opportunities to make an arbitrage transaction (i.e., a trade in which you do not need to commit your own capital or take any risk but still make a profit). Suppose you observe the following prices for options on DRKC Co. stock: $3.18 for a call with an exercise price of $60 and $3.38 for a put with an exercise price of $60. Both options expire in exactly six months, and the price of a six-month T-bill is $97.00 (for face value of $100).

    a. Using the put-call-spot parity condition, demonstrate graphically how you could synthetically recreate the payoff structure of a share of DRKC stock in six months using a combination of puts, calls, and T-bills transacted today.

    b. Given the current market prices for the two options and the T-bill, calculate the no-arbitrage price of a share of DRKC stock.

    c. If the actual market price of DRKC stock is $60, demonstrate the arbitrage transaction you could create to take advantage of the discrepancy. Be specific as to the positions you would need to take in each security and the dollar amount of your profit.

12. You are currently managing a stock portfolio worth $55 million and you are concerned that over the next four months equity values will be flat and may even fall. Consequently, you are considering two different strategies for hedging against possible stock declines: (1) buying a protective put, and (2) selling a *covered call* (i.e., selling a call option based on the same underlying stock position you hold). An over-the-counter derivatives dealer has expressed interest in your business and has quoted the following bid and offer prices (in millions) for at-the-money call and put options that expire in four months and match the characteristics of your portfolio:

	Bid	Ask
Call	$2.553	$2.573
Put	1.297	1.317

    a. For each of the following expiration date values for the unhedged equity position, calculate the terminal values for a protective put strategy.

        35, 40, 45, 50, 55, 60, 65, 70, 75

    b. Draw a graph of the protective put payoff structure in Part a and demonstrate how this position could have been constructed by using call options and T-bills, assuming a risk-free rate of 7 percent.

    c. For each of these same expiration date stock values, calculate the terminal values for a covered call strategy.

    d. Draw a graph of the covered call payoff structure in Part c and demonstrate how this position could have been constructed by using put options and T-bills, again assuming a risk-free rate of 7 percent.

13. You are a market maker in derivative instruments linked to KemCo stock. In addition to acting as a dealer in KemCo call options, put options, and forward contracts, you also spend part of your time surveying other dealers in the industry looking for arbitrage profit opportunities. Currently, the market-clearing (i.e., zero-value) contract price for a KemCo forward contract with nine months to maturity is $45. Also, an average of the last few trades involving nine-month KemCo puts with a $45 exercise price revealed a contract price of $3.22.

    a. If the nine-month T-bill is priced to yield an annual return of 6.5 percent, what bid-ask spread would you quote for a nine-month KemCo call option struck at a price of $45? In establishing this spread, first calculate the theoretical no-arbitrage price for the contract and then round this price up (or down) to the nearest one-eighth of a dollar for your ask (or bid) quote.

    b. Given the prevailing market prices for the forward and put option contracts, what should be the fair market value of KemCo stock at the present time?

c. Assuming the actual market price of KemCo stock is $41, create an arbitrage portfolio that will allow you to profit from the discrepancy. Be specific as to the positions you would need to take in each security and the dollar amount of your profit.

d. Suppose that KemCo's management has just announced that it will pay a cash dividend in exactly nine months (i.e., just before the derivative contract expiration date). To make the existing stock and forward prices arbitrage-free, what would the amount of this dividend have to be?

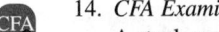

14. *CFA Examination Level III*

A stock currently sells for $77.50. Call options on the stock have an exercise price of $75 and sell for $7.75, and put options have an exercise price of $75 and sell for $4. These options will expire in three months. The three-month U.S. Treasury bill annualized yield is 5 percent. There are no transaction costs and no restrictions against using the proceeds from the short sale of any security.

a. A synthetic Treasury bill can be constructed by investing in a combination of the securities identified.
   (1) Identify the three transactions needed to construct a synthetic Treasury bill.
   (2) Calculate the synthetic Treasury bill's annualized yield.

b. An arbitrage strategy can be constructed with 75 actual and 100 synthetic Treasury bills, producing a face amount of $750,000.
   (1) State the arbitrage strategy.
   (2) Calculate the immediate incoming net cash flow.

c. Determine the net cash flow of the arbitrage strategy at the six-month expiration date if the stock price at expiration is $80. (Ignore any cash flows stemming from the original arbitrage profit.)

References

Brown, Keith C., ed. *Derivative Strategies for Managing Portfolio Risk.* Charlottesville, Va.: Association for Investment Management and Research, 1993.

Burns, Terrence E., ed. *Derivatives in Portfolio Management.* Charlottesville, Va.: Association for Investment Management and Research, 1998.

Chance, Don M. *An Introduction to Derivatives and Risk Management,* 5th ed. Fort Worth, Tex.: Harcourt College Publishers, 2001.

Clarke, Roger G. *Options and Futures: A Tutorial.* Charlottesville, Va.: The Research Foundation of the Institute of Chartered Financial Analysts, 1992.

Dubofsky, David A. *Options and Financial Futures: Valuation and Uses.* New York: McGraw-Hill, 1992.

Fabozzi, Frank J., and Gregory M. Kipnis, eds. *The Handbook of Stock Index Futures and Options.* Homewood, Ill.: Dow Jones–Irwin, 1989.

Hull, John. *Options, Futures and Other Derivatives,* 4th ed. Upper Saddle River, N.J.: Prentice-Hall, 2000.

Klemkosky, Robert C., and Bruce G. Resnick. "Put-Call Parity and Market Efficiency. *Journal of Finance* 34, no. 5 (December 1979).

Merton, Robert C., Myron S. Scholes, and Mathew I., Gladstein. "The Returns and Risks of Alternative Put-Option Portfolio Investment Strategies." *Journal of Business* 55 no. 1 (January 1982).

Moriarty, Eugene, Susan Phillips, and Paula Tosini. "A Comparison of Options and Futures in the Management of Portfolio Risk." *Financial Analysts Journal* 37, no. 1 (January–February 1981).

Rubinstein, Mark "Portfolio Insurance and the Market Crash." *Financial Analysts Journal* 44, no. 1 (January–February 1988).

Tian, Yisong. "A Reexamination of Portfolio Insurance. The Use of Index Put Options." *Journal of Futures Markets* 16, no. 2 (April 1996).

Chapter 22 ▷ Forward and Futures Contracts

After you read this chapter, you should be able to answer the following questions:

➤ What are the differences in the way forward and futures contracts are structured and traded?
➤ How are the margin accounts on a futures contract adjusted for daily changes in market conditions?
➤ How can an investor use forward and futures contracts to hedge an existing risk exposure?
➤ What is a hedge ratio and how should it be calculated?
➤ What economic functions do the forward and futures markets serve?
➤ How are forward and futures contracts valued after origination?
➤ What is the relationship between futures contract prices and the current and expected spot price for the underlying commodity or security?
➤ How can an investor use forward and futures contracts to speculate on a particular view about changing market conditions?
➤ How do agricultural futures contracts differ from those based on financial instruments, such as stock indexes, bonds, and currencies?
➤ How can forward and futures contracts be designed to hedge interest rate risk?
➤ How are implied forward rates and actual forward rates related?
➤ What is stock index arbitrage and how is it related to program trading?
➤ How can forward and futures contracts be designed to hedge foreign exchange rate risk?
➤ What is interest rate parity and how would you construct a covered interest arbitrage transaction?

As we saw in Chapter 21, forward and futures contracts are the most straightforward form of *derivative instrument* because they allow an investor to lock in the purchase or sales price of a transaction that will not be completed until a later date. Having laid the foundation for why these contracts exist and how they are used, in this chapter we continue our discussion along several lines. First, we take a closer look at the contract terms and trading mechanics of forwards and futures. In particular, we examine the important differences that exist between the two markets and describe the process by which futures contracts are **marked to market** on a daily basis. Further, we discuss how these contracts are used to hedge the price risk inherent in an existing or anticipated position and how **hedge ratios** are computed.

Second, we consider how forward and futures contracts are priced in an efficient capital market. Given that these instruments are not really securities in the same sense that stocks and bonds are, the notion of traditional security valuation is not quite appropriate in this market. Instead, valuation involves specifying the proper relationship between the forward contract price and the spot price for the underlying position. In general, we develop the "no arbitrage" result that the forward contract price should be equal to the spot price plus the cumulative costs of transporting the underlying security or commodity from the present to the future delivery date. These carrying costs can be either positive or negative; therefore, the correct forward contract price can be either higher or lower than the spot price.

Finally, we demonstrate several applications and strategies in which an investor can use forward and futures contracts. This demonstration concentrates on a class of contracts—*financial forward and futures*—that are particularly useful to investors. The underlying securities in financial futures include stock indexes, Treasury bonds, bank deposits, and foreign currencies. The use of these financial futures will be illustrated in a series of applications designed to demonstrate the connections between cash and futures markets.

AN OVERVIEW OF FORWARD AND FUTURES TRADING

Forward contracts are agreements negotiated directly between two parties in the OTC (i.e., nonexchange-traded) markets. A typical participant in a forward contract is a commercial or investment bank that, serving the role of the market maker, is contacted directly by the customer (although customers can form an agreement directly with one another). Forward contracts are individually designed agreements and can be tailored to the specific needs of the ultimate end user. Futures contracting, on the other hand, is more complicated. An investor wishing either to buy or to sell in the futures market gives his order to a broker (a *futures commission merchant*), who then passes it to a trader on the floor of an exchange (*the trading pit*). After a trade has been agreed on, details of the deal are passed to the **exchange clearinghouse**, which catalogs the transaction. The ultimate end users in a futures contract never deal with each other directly. Rather, they always transact with the clearinghouse, which is also responsible for overseeing the delivery process, settling daily gains and losses, and guaranteeing the overall transaction. Exhibit 22.1 highlights the differences in how these contracts are created.[1]

As an example, let us consider the traditional agricultural commodity futures that have been traded for more than 130 years beginning with the creation of the Chicago Board of Trade (CBT), the world's oldest and largest derivatives exchange. Futures contracts based on a wide array of commodities and securities have been created and now trade on almost 100 exchanges worldwide. Exhibit 22.2 lists the leading futures exchanges in the United States and the world, ranked by relative trading volume. Notice that two of the top three and three of the top five exchanges in the world are located in the United States. Additionally, Exhibit 22.3 shows price and trade activity data for a representative sample of commodity futures contracts; financial futures will be described in detail later in the chapter. Each of these commodity contracts is standardized in terms of the amount and type of the commodity involved and the available dates on which it can be delivered. As we will see, this standardization can lead to an important source of risk that may not exist in forward contracts.

Futures Contract Mechanics

To interpret the display in Exhibit 22.3, consider the gold futures contract traded on the Commodity Exchange (COMEX), a division of the New York Mercantile Exchange (NYM). Each contract calls for the long position to buy, and the short position to sell, 100 troy ounces of gold in the appointed months. With commodity futures, it usually is the case that delivery can take place any time during the month at the discretion of the short position. Contracts are available with settlement dates every other month for the next 16 months. An investor committing on this particular date to a long position in the June 2002 contract is obligated to buy 100 ounces of gold 4 months later for the contract price of $301.20 per ounce. The volume statistics show that

---

[1]For a more detailed discussion of the futures trading process, see Roger G. Clarke. *Options and Futures: A Tutorial* (Charlottesville, Va.: Research Foundation of the Institute of Chartered Financial Analysts, 1992). Some of this discussion is based on this book.

EXHIBIT 22.1 ▸ *FORWARD AND FUTURES TRADING MECHANICS*

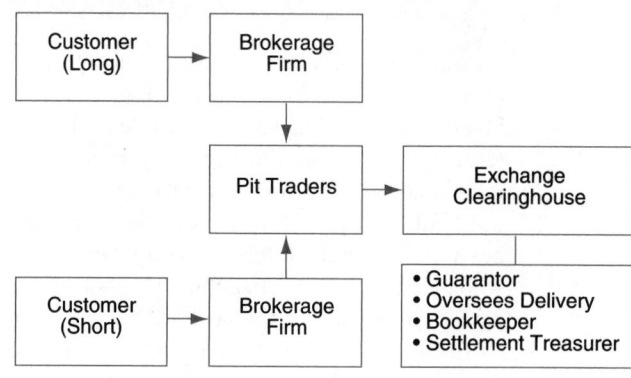

A. Forward Contracts

Customer (Long) → Market Maker ← Customer (Short)

B. Futures Contracts

Customer (Long) → Brokerage Firm

Pit Traders → Exchange Clearinghouse

Customer (Short) → Brokerage Firm

Exchange Clearinghouse:
• Guarantor
• Oversees Delivery
• Bookkeeper
• Settlement Treasurer

EXHIBIT 22.2 ▸ *LEADING FUTURES EXCHANGES RANKED BY RELATIVE TRADING VOLUME*

A. U.S. Futures Exchanges (2000 Data)

Exchange Name & Abbreviation	% of Trading Volume
Chicago Mercantile Exchange, CME	39.8%
Chicago Board of Trade, CBT	38.7
New York Mercantile Exchange, NYM	17.6
New York Board of Trade, NYBT	3.1
Kansas City Board of Trade, KC	0.5
Mid-America Commodity Exchange, MCE	0.3

B. International Futures Exchanges (2000 Data)

Exchange & Country	% of Trading Volume
EUREX, Germany & Switzerland	24.6%
CME, United States	16.5
CBT, United States	16.1
London Intl. Financial Futures Exchange, United Kingdom	9.0
NYMEX, United States	7.3
BM&F, Brazil	6.8
Paris Bourse SA, France	5.3
London Metal Exchange, United Kingdom	5.2
Tokyo Commodity Exchange, Japan	4.3
Euronext Brussels Derivative Market, Belgium	2.6
Sydney Futures Exchange, Australia	2.4

Source: Futures Industry Association. Reprinted with permission.

EXHIBIT 22.3 ▸ COMMODITY FUTURES QUOTATIONS

Corn (CBT) 5,000 bu.; cents per bu.

	OPEN	HIGH	LOW	SETTLE	CHANGE	LIFETIME HIGH	LIFETIME LOW	OPEN INT.
Mar	204¼	205	203¾	204½	+ ¼	270	203¾	227,969
May	211¼	212	211	211½	+ ½	266½	211	100,692
July	218	218¾	217¾	218¼	+ ¼	279½	210	66,715
Sept	223¾	224¼	223	223¼	+ ¼	262	210	22,066
Dec	231½	231¾	230½	231¼	....	272	230½	52,002
Mr03	238	239½	238	239	....	258½	238	6,023
July	246½	246½	246¼	246½	− ¼	272	246¼	2,659
Dec	246¾	247	245	246	−1	269	245	2,375

Est vol 39,000; vol Wed 54,653; open int 480,716, +3,755.

Oats (CBT) 5,000 bu.; cents per bu.

	OPEN	HIGH	LOW	SETTLE	CHANGE	LIFETIME HIGH	LIFETIME LOW	OPEN INT.
Mar	207	209	204¾	204¾	−	216½	114½	6,964
May	189½	193¾	186	187	−1¼	202¾	118¾	2,758
July	167¼	167½	165	165	−2	179¾	135¼	1,257
Dec	141	142¼	141	141	−1¼	153	137	1,920

Est vol 1,900; vol Wed 1,802; open int 13,055, −38.

Soybeans (CBT) 5,000 bu.; cents per bu.

	OPEN	HIGH	LOW	SETTLE	CHANGE	LIFETIME HIGH	LIFETIME LOW	OPEN INT.
Mar	427¾	432	427¼	431¼	+ 3¼	546	415¼	62,918
May	433	436	432	435¼	+ 3¼	531	419¼	50,717
July	436½	440½	436	439¼	+ 3	533	425	34,094
Aug	437	441½	436½	439¼	+ 2¾	529	425	3,909
Sept	438½	440½	438	440½	+ 1½	495	425	1,027
Nov	441½	445¼	441½	444¼	+ 2¼	561	428½	15,327

Est vol 29,500; vol Wed 45,477; open int 169,440, +4,578.

Wheat (CBT) 5,000 bu.; cents per bu.

	OPEN	HIGH	LOW	SETTLE	CHANGE	LIFETIME HIGH	LIFETIME LOW	OPEN INT.
Mar	280¼	284½	279	281	+ ¾	346	273	66,859
May	285¼	289½	284¾	287¼	+ 2	365	276½	18,283
July	288¾	293¾	288	290¼	+ 1½	365	272	21,638
Sept	293½	296¾	292¾	294	+ 1	315	284½	4,551
Dec	303	306	302½	304	+ 1	365	295	6,240

Est vol 23,500; vol Wed 21,778; open int 117,979, −1,235.

Cotton (NYCE)-50,000 lbs.; cents per lb.

	OPEN	HIGH	LOW	SETTLE	CHANGE	LIFETIME HIGH	LIFETIME LOW	OPEN INT.
Mar	37.40	38.40	37.40	38.14	+ .77	67.10	29.86	22,339
May	40.40	40.95	40.40	40.88	+ .78	68.50	30.90	15,949
July	42.25	42.70	42.25	42.85	+ .63	68.50	31.90	13,122
Oct	43.40	44.15	43.40	44.04	+ .80	65.50	33.85	464
Dec	45.10	45.65	45.10	45.65	+ .84	64.75	34.65	10,706
Mr03	47.10	47.70	47.10	47.73	+ .90	55.25	36.20	1,228
May					+ .83	54.00	38.70	1,011

Est vol 13,096; vol Wed 6,541; open int 65,123, −306.

Orange Juice (NYCE)-15,000 lbs.; cents per lb.

	OPEN	HIGH	LOW	SETTLE	CHANGE	LIFETIME HIGH	LIFETIME LOW	OPEN INT.
Mar	86.25	86.90	86.20	86.75	+ .10	103.35	84.00	10,844
May	87.50	88.20	87.50	88.20	+ .20	99.60	86.25	3,290
July	88.70	89.00	88.70	89.20	+ .30	99.60	87.80	716

Est vol 1,531; vol Wed 1,215; open int 16,878, +249.

Copper-High (Cmx.Div.NYM)-25,000 lbs.; cents per lb.

	OPEN	HIGH	LOW	SETTLE	CHANGE	LIFETIME HIGH	LIFETIME LOW	OPEN INT.
Feb	72.60	72.60	72.60	73.50	+ .85	90.00	61.20	677
Mar	72.85	73.70	72.70	73.70	+ .80	91.00	61.30	39,003
Apr	72.85	73.95	72.85	73.95	+ .75	89.70	61.50	1,778
May	73.45	74.25	73.25	74.20	+ .75	89.60	61.90	7,556
June	73.80	73.80	73.80	74.45	+ .75	89.50	62.35	1,359
July	74.10	74.80	73.95	74.70	+ .75	88.90	62.30	8,114
Sept	75.10	75.30	74.95	75.20	+ .75	88.00	62.95	7,332
Dec	75.20	76.00	75.20	75.90	+ .75	83.00	63.50	6,842

Est vol 5,000; vol Wed 4,852; open int 78,202, +114.

Gold (Cmx.Div.NYM)-100 troy oz.; $ per troy oz.

	OPEN	HIGH	LOW	SETTLE	CHANGE	LIFETIME HIGH	LIFETIME LOW	OPEN INT.
Feb	299.50	301.50	296.20	299.70	+ 2.20	308.00	248.70	1,444
Apr	301.00	302.30	296.50	300.60	+ 2.20	309.00	267.50	84,687
June	302.00	302.90	297.80	301.20	+ 2.20	385.00	264.50	13,086
Aug	302.00	302.80	301.00	301.70	+ 2.20	310.00	272.60	3,419
Oct	300.50	300.50	300.50	302.30	+ 2.20	302.30	274.00	2,683
Dc03	301.50	303.00	301.10	302.80	+ 2.10	358.00	266.10	12,741
F03	303.00	303.00	303.00	303.40	+ 2.10	307.80	286.50	5,013
Apr	304.00	304.00	304.00	304.20	+ 2.10	304.00	281.50	330
June	304.00	304.00	304.00	305.00	+ 2.00	338.00	280.00	2,480

Est vol 36,000; vol Wed 69,736; open int 136,441, −1,929.

Platinum (NYM)-50 troy oz.; $ per troy oz.

	OPEN	HIGH	LOW	SETTLE	CHANGE	LIFETIME HIGH	LIFETIME LOW	OPEN INT.
Apr	460.50	469.50	460.50	467.90	+ 11.80	489.00	407.00	5,637
July	458.00	460.90	458.00	460.90	+ 11.80	476.00	405.00	350

Est vol 980; vol Wed 868; open int 6,025, +47.

Silver (Cmx.Div.NYM)-5,000 troy oz.; cents per troy oz.

	OPEN	HIGH	LOW	SETTLE	CHANGE	LIFETIME HIGH	LIFETIME LOW	OPEN INT.
Feb	437.0	437.0	437.0	434.2	− 1.9	438.0	419.0	0
Mar	438.5	439.0	434.0	434.5	− 2.0	508.0	405.0	31,808
May	440.5	441.0	435.5	436.0	− 2.0	525.0	407.0	12,636
July	440.5	441.5	438.5	437.2	− 2.0	559.0	409.5	8,152
Sept	437.0	437.0	437.0	438.4	− 2.0	480.5	412.5	1,812
Dec	440.0	443.0	440.0	439.5	− 2.0	613.0	412.0	6,534
Jl03	446.0	446.0	446.0	441.1	− 2.0	551.0	421.0	238
Dc04	465.0	465.0	465.0	449.1	− 2.0	560.0	440.0	752

Est vol 8,500; vol Wed 14,550; open int 63,767, −2,247.

Crude Oil, Light Sweet (NYM) 1,000 bbls.; $ per bbl.

	OPEN	HIGH	LOW	SETTLE	CHANGE	LIFETIME HIGH	LIFETIME LOW	OPEN INT.
Mar	19.70	19.79	19.64	19.79	—	28.00	17.55	110,218
Apr	20.11	20.17	20.02	20.17	− .14	27.50	17.95	75,435
May	20.29	20.31	20.20	20.31	− .12	27.35	18.20	41,843
June	20.38	20.44	20.29	20.44	− .09	27.25	17.35	35,381
July	20.40	20.50	20.38	20.50	− .07	26.30	18.75	19,935
Aug	20.41	20.45	20.40	20.45	− .05	26.77	18.70	14,976
Sept	20.42	20.48	20.42	20.48	− .04	25.50	19.10	16,509
Oct	20.25	20.41	20.25	20.41	− .03	26.36	19.50	11,584
Dec	20.55	20.55	20.37	20.55	− .03	26.95	19.50	32,517
Ja03	20.37	20.48	20.37	20.48	− .02	25.75	19.90	13,934
June	20.55	20.60	20.55	20.60	+ .01	25.05	19.82	15,518
Dec	20.60	20.70	20.60	20.70	+ .03	24.44	19.92	19,039
Jul04	20.60	20.75	20.60	20.63	+ .06	20.90	20.60	1,576
Dec	20.62	20.62	20.51	20.51	+ .06	24.00	16.35	8,470
Dc05	20.30	20.36	20.30	20.36	+ .06	23.00	17.00	3,654

Est vol 159,952; vol Wed 157,175; open int 458,984, +5,478.

Natural Gas, (NYM) 10,000 MMBtu's; $ per MMBtu's

	OPEN	HIGH	LOW	SETTLE	CHANGE	LIFETIME HIGH	LIFETIME LOW	OPEN INT.
Mar	2.125	2.160	2.085	2.150	+ .049	5.730	1.960	71,620
Apr	2.170	2.230	2.160	2.222	+ .054	4.920	2.060	42,454
May	2.245	2.292	2.240	2.292	+ .054	4.775	2.160	32,801
June	2.315	2.360	2.305	2.360	+ .052	4.770	2.260	29,533
July	2.375	2.420	2.375	2.420	+ .050	4.780	2.320	22,550
Aug	2.435	2.473	2.425	2.473	+ .049	4.790	2.360	26,521
Sept	2.430	2.476	2.428	2.476	+ .048	4.785	2.375	20,225
Oct	2.465	2.502	2.455	2.502	+ .047	4.785	2.410	38,542
Nov	2.690	2.717	2.675	2.717	+ .042	4.900	2.630	26,625
Dec	2.880	2.920	2.870	2.920	+ .042	5.010	2.720	19,894
Ja03	2.975	3.010	2.970	3.010	+ .042	5.049	2.730	23,946
Feb	2.920	2.955	2.915	2.955	+ .037	4.874	2.695	17,479
Mar	2.840	2.877	2.840	2.877	+ .039	4.710	2.705	13,482
Apr	2.735	2.765	2.730	2.765	+ .037	4.520	2.610	9,018
May	2.755	2.780	2.750	2.780	+ .035	4.490	2.610	7,039
June	2.800	2.828	2.798	2.828	+ .035	4.400	2.610	9,957
July	2.850	2.866	2.835	2.866	+ .035	4.530	2.550	5,858
Aug	2.885	2.911	2.885	2.911	+ .032	4.535	2.585	12,423
Sept	2.895	2.918	2.880	2.918	+ .031	4.445	2.880	3,573
Oct	2.930	2.929	2.880	2.929	+ .031	4.455	2.905	5,583
Nov	3.070	3.100	3.070	3.100	+ .031	4.673	3.050	6,634
Dec	3.253	3.274	3.253	3.274	+ .031	4.820	3.050	7,037
Mr04	3.148	3.170	3.148	3.170	+ .052	4.510	3.250	3,241
July	3.035	3.052	3.035	3.052	+ .021	3.755	3.145	1,754

Est vol 63,157; vol Wed 64,031; open int 489,889, +11,007.

Source: *The Wall Street Journal,* 8 February 2002. Printed with permission from *The Wall Street Journal,* Dow Jones & Co. Inc.

almost 70,000 gold contracts changed hands on the last reported trading day. Open interest—the total number of outstanding contracts of any maturity—was 136,441, down 1,929 contracts from the previous day.[2]

Another important difference between forward and futures contracts is how the two types of agreements account for the possibility that a counterparty will fail to honor its obligation. Forward contracts may not require either counterparty to post collateral, in which case each is exposed to the potential default of the other during the entire life of the contract. In contrast, the futures exchange requires each customer to post an *initial* **margin account** in the form of cash or government securities when the contract is originated. (The futures exchange, as a well-capitalized corporation, does not post collateral to protect customers from its potential default.) This margin account is then adjusted, or marked to market, at the end of each trading day according to that day's price movements. All outstanding contract positions are adjusted to the **settlement price**, which is set by the exchange after trading ends to reflect the midpoint of the closing price range.

The marked-to-market process effectively credits or debits each customer's margin account for daily trading gains or losses as if the customer had closed out her position, even though the contract remains open. For example, Exhibit 22.3 indicates that the settlement price of the June 2002 gold contract increased by $2.20 per ounce from the previous trading day. This price increase benefits the holder of a long position by $220 (= $2.20 per ounce × 100 ounces). Specifically, if she had entered into the contract yesterday, she would have a commitment to buy gold for $299.00, which she could now sell for $301.20. Accordingly, her margin account will be increased by $220. Conversely, any party who is short June gold futures will have his margin account reduced by $220 per contract. To ensure that the exchange always has enough protection, collateral accounts are not allowed to fall below a predetermined *maintenance level*, typically about 75 percent of the initial level. If this $220 adjustment reduced the short position's account beneath the maintenance margin, he would receive a **margin call** and be required to restore the account to its full initial level or face involuntary liquidation.

Comparing Forward and Futures Contracts

To summarize, the main trade-off between forward and futures contracts is *design flexibility* versus *credit and liquidity risks,* as highlighted by the following comparison.

	FUTURES	FORWARDS
Design flexibility:	Standardized	Can be customized
Credit risk:	Clearinghouse risk	Counterparty risk
Liquidity risk:	Depends on trading	Negotiated exit

These differences represent extremes; some forward contracts, particularly in foreign exchange, are quite standard and liquid while some futures contracts now allow for greater flexibility in the terms of the agreement. Also, forwards require less managerial oversight and intervention—especially on a daily basis—because of the lump-sum settlement at delivery (i.e., no margin accounts or marked-to-market settlement), a feature that is often important to unsophisticated or infrequent users of these products.

---

[2]New contracts are created when a new customer comes to the exchange at a time when no existing contract holder wishes to liquidate his position. On the other hand, if an existing customer wants to close out her short position and there is not a new customer to take her place, the contract price will be raised until an existing long position is enticed to sell back his agreement, thereby canceling the contract and and reducing open interest by one.

Hedging and the Basis

The goal of a *hedge* transaction is to create a position that, once added to an investor's portfolio, will offset the price risk of another, more fundamental holding. The word "offset" is used here rather than "eliminate" because the hedge transaction attempts to neutralize an exposure that remains on the balance sheet. In Chapter 21, we expressed this concept with the following chart, which assumes that the underlying exposure results from a long commodity position:

ECONOMIC EVENT	ACTUAL COMMODITY EXPOSURE	DESIRED HEDGE EXPOSURE
Commodity prices fall	Loss	Gain
Commodity prices rise	Gain	Loss

In this case, a short position in a forward contract based on the same commodity would provide the desired negative price correlation. By virtue of holding a short forward position against the long position in the commodity, the investor has entered into a **short hedge**. A **long hedge**, on the other hand, is created by supplementing a short commodity holding with a long forward position.

The basic premise behind either a short or a long hedge is that as the price of the underlying commodity changes, so too will the price of a forward contract based on that commodity. Further, the implicit hope of the hedger is that the spot and forward prices change in a predictable way relative to one another. For instance, the short hedger in the preceding example is hoping that if commodity prices fall and reduce the value of her underlying asset, the forward contract price also will fall by the same amount to create an offsetting gain on the derivative. Thus, a critical feature that affects the quality of a hedge transaction is the way in which the spot and forward prices change over time.

Defining the Basis To understand better the relationship between spot and forward price movements, it is useful to develop the concept of the **basis**. At any Date t, the basis is the spot price minus the forward price for a contract maturing at Date T:

➤22.1
$$B_{t,T} = S_t - F_{t,T}$$

where:

S_t = **the date t spot price**
$F_{t,T}$ = **the date t forward price for a contract maturing at date T**

Potentially, a different level of the basis may exist on each trading date t. Two facts always are true, however. First, the *initial basis* at Date 0 ($B_{0,T}$) always will be known since both the current spot and forward contract prices can be observed. Second, the *maturity basis* at Date T ($B_{T,T}$) always is zero whenever the commodity underlying the forward contract matches the asset held exactly. For this to occur, the forward price must *converge* to the spot price as the contract expires ($F_{T,T} = S_T$).

Consider again the investor who hedged her long position in a commodity by agreeing to sell it at Date T through a short position in a forward contract. The value of the combined position is ($F_{0,T} - S_0$). If the investor decides to liquidate her entire position (including the hedge) prior to maturity, she will not be able to deliver the commodity to satisfy her forward obligation as originally intended. Instead, the investor will have to (1) sell her commodity position on the open market for S_t, and (2) "buy back" her short forward position for the new contract price of $F_{t,T}$.[3] The profit from the short hedge liquidated at Date t is

> **22.2**
$$B_{t,T} - B_{0,T} = (S_t - F_{t,T}) - (S_0 - F_{0,T})$$

The term $B_{t,T}$ often is called the *cover basis* because that is when the forward contract is closed out, or covered.

Understanding Basis Risk

Equation 22.2 highlights an important fact about hedging. Once the hedge position is formed, the investor no longer is exposed to the absolute price movement of the underlying asset alone. Instead, she is exposed to **basis risk** because the terminal value of her combined position is defined as the cover basis minus the initial basis. Notice, however, that only the cover basis is unknown at Date 0, and so her real exposure is to the **correlation** between future changes in the spot and forward contract prices. If these movements are highly correlated, the basis risk will be quite small. In fact, it is usually possible to design a forward contract based on a specific underlying asset and deliverable on exactly the desired future date. This sort of customized design reduces basis risk to zero, since $F_{T,T} = S_T$. Conversely, basis risk is a possibility when contract terms are standardized and is most likely to occur in the futures market where standardization is the norm.

To illustrate the concept of basis risk, suppose the investor wishes in February to hedge a long position of 100,000 pounds of cotton she is planning to sell in April. Exhibit 22.3 shows that cotton futures contracts do exist but with delivery months in either March or May. With each contract requiring the delivery of 50,000 pounds of cotton, she decides to short two of the May contracts, specifically intending to liquidate her position a month early. Suppose that on the date she initiates her short hedge, the spot cotton price was $0.3733 per pound and the May futures contract price was $0.3968 per pound. This means that her initial basis was –2.35 cents, which she hopes will move toward zero in a smooth and predictable manner. Suppose, in fact, that when she closes out her combined position in April, cotton prices have declined so that $S_t = \$0.3660$ and $F_{t,T} = \$0.3753$, leaving a cover basis of –0.93 cent. This means the basis has increased in value, or *strengthened*, which is to the short hedger's advantage. The net April selling price for her cotton is $0.3875 per pound, which is equal to the spot price of $0.3660 plus the net futures profit of $0.0215 (= 0.3968 – 0.3753). Notice that this is lower than the original futures price but considerably higher than the April spot price. Thus, the short hedger has benefited by exchanging pure price risk for basis risk.

Although it is difficult to generalize, substantial indirect evidence exists that minimizing basis risk is the primary goal of most hedgers. For example, Brown and Smith noted that the phenomenal growth of OTC products to manage interest rate risk—despite the existence of exchange-traded contracts—is a response to the desire to create customized solutions.[4] Further, a survey by Jesswein, Kwok, and Folks showed that corporate risk managers preferred to hedge their firms' foreign exchange exposure with forward contracts rather than with futures by a ratio of about five to one.[5] Finally, Edwards and Canter as well as Pirrong chronicled the severe difficulties the German firm Metallgesellschaft A. G. had in trying to hedge the energy-related positions on its balance sheet with exchange-traded futures positions.[6]

---

[3]The mechanics of liquidating a forward or futures contract prior to maturity will be described in the next section.

[4]Keith C. Brown and Donald J. Smith, *Interest Rate and Currency Swaps: A Tutorial* (Charlottesville, Va.: Research Foundation of the Institute of Chartered Financial Analysts, 1995).

[5]Kurt Jesswein, Chuck C. Y. Kwok, and William R. Folks, "What New Currency Risk Products Are Companies Using and Why?" *Journal of Applied Corporate Finance* 8, no. 3 (Fall 1995): 103–114.

[6]Franklin R. Edwards and Michael S. Canter, "The Collapse of Metallgesellschaft: Unhedgeable Risks, Poor Hedging Strategy, or Just Bad Luck?" *Journal of Applied Corporate Finance* 8, no. 1 (Spring 1995): 86–105, and Stephen C. Pirrong, "Metallgesellschaft: A Prudent Hedger Ruined or a Wildcatter on NYMEX?" *Journal of Futures Markets* 17, no. 5 (August 1997): 543–578.

Calculating the Optimal Hedge Ratio

In the preceding example, the decision to short two cotton futures contracts was a simple one because the investor held exactly twice as much of the same commodity as was covered by a single contract. In most cases, calculating the appropriate hedge ratio, or the number of futures contracts per unit of the spot asset, is not that straightforward. The approach suggested by both Johnson and Stein is to choose the number of contracts that minimizes the variance of net profit from a hedged commodity position. The determination of the required number of contracts can be established as follows.[7]

Consider the position of a short hedger who is long one unit of a particular commodity and short N forward contracts on that commodity. Rewriting Equation 22.2 for the profit from a short hedge and allowing for a variable number of contracts, the net profit (Π_t) of this position at Date t can be written

$$\Pi_t = (S_t - S_0) - (F_{t,T} - F_{0,T})\,(N) = (\Delta S) - (\Delta F)(N)$$

The variance of this value is then given as

$$\sigma_\Pi^2 = \sigma_{\Delta S}^2 + (N^2)\sigma_{\Delta F}^2 - 2(N)\mathrm{COV}_{\Delta S,\,\Delta F}$$

where:

COV = the covariance of changes in the spot and forward prices

Minimizing this expression and solving for N leaves

➤22.3
$$N^* = \frac{\mathrm{COV}_{\Delta S,\,\Delta F}}{\sigma_{\Delta F}^2} = \left(\frac{\sigma_{\Delta S}}{\sigma_{\Delta F}}\right)\rho$$

where:

ρ = the correlation coefficient between the spot and forward price changes[8]

The optimal hedge ratio (N^*) can be interpreted as the ratio of the spot and forward price standard deviations multiplied by the correlation coefficient between the two series. Recalling from Chapter 1 that standard deviation is a measure of a position's *total* risk, this means that the optimal number of contracts is determined by the ratio of total volatilities deflated by ρ to account for the *systematic* relationship between the spot and forward prices. (It is, in fact, directly comparable to the beta coefficient of a common stock.) An important implication of this is that the best contract to use in hedging an underlying spot position is the one that has the highest value of ρ. What if, for instance, a clothing manufacturer wanted to hedge the eventual purchase of a large quantity of wool, a commodity for which no exchange-traded futures contract exists? The expression for N^* suggests that it may be possible to form an effective **cross hedge** if prices for a contract based on a related commodity (e.g., cotton) are highly correlated with wool prices. In fact, the expected basis risk of such a cross hedge can be measured as $(1 - \rho^2)$. Finally, note that the value for N^* also can be calculated as the slope coefficient of a regression using ΔS and ΔF

---

[7]Leland L. Johnson, "The Theory of Hedging and Speculation in Commodity Futures," *Review of Economic Studies* 27 (1959–60): 139–160; and Jerome L. Stein, "The Simultaneous Determination of Spot and Futures Prices," *American Economic Review* 51, no. 5 (December 1961): 1012–1025.

[8]Given data for spot and forward prices, σ_Π^2 in the variance equation is a function of just one variable, N. Thus differentiating this equation with respect to N leaves $[d\sigma_\Pi^2/dN] = 2(N)\sigma_{\Delta F}^2 - 2\mathrm{COV}_{\Delta S,\,\Delta F}$, which can be set equal to zero and solved for N^*. It is easily confirmed that the second derivative of this function is positive and so N^* is a minimizing value.

as the dependent and independent variables, respectively.[9] In the regression context, ρ^2 is called the coefficient of determination or, more commonly, R^2. Some examples of these calculations are presented in subsequent sections.

FORWARD AND FUTURES CONTRACTS: BASIC VALUATION CONCEPTS

Forward and futures contracts are not securities but, rather, *trade agreements* that enable both buyers and sellers of an underlying commodity or security to lock in the eventual price of their transaction. As such, they typically require no front-end payment from either the long or short position to motivate the other's participation and, consequently, the contract's initial market value usually is zero. Once the terms of the agreement are set, however, any change in market conditions will likely increase the value of the contract to one of the participants. For example, an obligation made in November to purchase soybeans in March for $220 per ton is surely quite valuable in January if soybean prices in the spot market are already $250 and no additional harvest is anticipated in the next two months. A description of the valuation of these agreements, which is different for futures and forward contracts, follows.

Valuing Forwards and Futures

Suppose that at Date 0 you had contracted in the forward market to buy Q ounces of gold at Date T for $F_{0,T}$. At Date t, prior to the maturity date T, you decide that this long position is no longer necessary for your portfolio and you want to get rid of the future price risk it entails. Accordingly, you want to **unwind** your original obligation. One way to do this is to take a short position in a Date t forward contract designed to offset the terms of the first. That is, at Date t you would agree to sell Q ounces of gold at Date T for the price of $F_{t,T}$. This is shown in Panel A of Exhibit 22.4. Notice that because you now have contracts to buy and sell Q ounces of gold, you have no exposure to gold price movements between Dates t and T. The profit or loss on this pair of forward contracts is $(Q)[F_{t,T} - F_{0,T}]$, or the difference between the selling and purchase prices multiplied by the quantity involved. However, this amount would not be received (if $F_{t,T} > F_{0,T}$) or paid until Date T, meaning that the value of the original long forward position when it is sold on Date t (i.e., its unwind value) would be the *present value* of $(Q)[F_{t,T} - F_{0,T}]$, or

➤22.4
$$V_{t,T} = (Q)[F_{t,T} - F_{0,T}] \div (1 + i)^{(T-t)}$$

where:

i = the appropriate annualized discount rate

Equation 22.4 expresses the Date t value of a long forward contract maturing at Date t. Notice two things about this amount. First, $V_{t,T}$ can be either positive or negative depending on whether $F_{t,T}$ is greater or less than the original contract price, $F_{0,T}$. This means that any forward contract carries the potential for symmetric payoffs to both participants. Second, the value of the short side of the same contract is just $(Q)[F_{0,T} - F_{t,T}] \div (1 + i)^{(T-t)}$, reinforcing the fact that forward contracts are *zero-sum games* since whatever the long position gains, the short position loses, and vice versa. For example, if you had originally agreed to a long position in a six-month gold forward at $F_{0.05} = \$400$, and after three months the new forward contract price is $F_{0.25, 0.5} = \$415$, the value of your position would be $1,464.68 (= (100)(415 - 400) \div (1.1)^{0.25})$, assuming a 10 per-

---

[9]Some have questioned whether regression-based hedge ratios are stable enough to be useful in practice. Recent work, however, has concluded that they are stationary. See Robert Ferguson and Dean Leistikow, "Are Regression Approach Futures Hedge Ratios Stationary?" *Journal of Futures Markets* 18, no. 7 (October 1998): 851–866.

| EXHIBIT 22.4 | *UNWIND VALUES FOR FORWARD AND FUTURES CONTRACTS* |

Date 0   Date t Date T
(Origination)   (Unwind)   (Maturity)

A. Forward Contract
- Long Forward ($F_{0,T}$)   • Short Forward ($F_{t,T}$)
  - Contract Unwind Value: $V_{t,T} = (Q)[F_{t,T} - F_{0,T}] \div (1 + i)^{(T-t)}$

B. Futures Contract
- Long Futures ($F^*_{0,T}$)   • Short Futures ($F^*_{t,T}$)
  - Contract Unwind Value: $V^*_{t,T} = (Q)[F^*_{t,T} - F^*_{0,T}]$

cent discount rate. Conversely, the value of the original short position would then have to be –\$1,464.68. Finally, notice that as Date t approaches Date T, the value of the contract simply becomes $(Q)(F_{T,T} - F_{0,T})$.

Valuing a futures contract is conceptually similar to valuing a forward contract with one important difference. As we saw earlier, futures contracts are marked to market on a daily basis, and this settlement amount was not discounted to account for the temporal difference between Dates t and T. That is, the Date t value of the futures contract is simply the undiscounted difference between the futures prices at the origination and unwind (or cover) dates, multiplied by the contract quantity, as shown in panel B of Exhibit 22.4. Thus, the forward contract valuation equation can be adapted for futures as

➤ 22.5 $V^*_{t,T} = (Q)(F^*_{t,T} - F^*_{0,T})$

where:

> * = the possibility that forward and futures prices for the same commodity at the same point in time might be different

Cox, Ingersoll, and Ross showed that $F^*_{0,T}$ and $F_{0,T}$ would be equal if short-term interest rates (i in Equation 22.4) are known but need not be the same under other circumstances.[10]

Typically, for commodities and securities that support both forward and futures markets, differences between $F^*_{0,T}$ and $F_{0,T}$ exist but are relatively small. For instance, Cornell and Reinganum established few economically meaningful differences between forward and futures prices in the foreign exchange market, while Park and Chen found that certain agricultural and precious metal futures prices were significantly higher than the analogous forward prices. More recently, Grinblatt and Jegadeesh documented that the historical differences in prices for Eurodollar forward and futures contracts are due to a mispricing of the latter, although this mispricing has been eliminated over time.[11] Finally, note once again that $V^*_{t,T}$ can be either positive or negative depending on how contract prices have changed since inception.

---

[10]John Cox, Jonathan Ingersoll, and Stephen Ross, "The Relation between Forward Prices and Futures Prices," *Journal of Financial Economics* 9, no. 4 (December 1981): 321–346.

[11]Bradford Cornell and Marc R. Reinganum, "Forward and Futures Prices: Evidence from Foreign Exchange Markets," *Journal of Finance* 36, no. 5 (December 1981): 1035–1045; H. Y. Park and Andrew H. Chen, "Differences between Forward and Futures Prices: A Further Investigation of Marking to Market Effects," *Journal of Futures Markets* 5, no. 7 (February 1985): 77–88; and Mark Grinblatt and Narasimhan Jegadeesh. "Relative Pricing of Eurodollar Futures and Forward Contracts," *Journal of Finance* 51, no. 4 (September 1996): 1499–1522.

The Relationship between Spot and Forward Prices

In many respects, the relationship between the spot and forward prices at any moment in time is a more challenging question than how the contract is valued. We can understand the intuition for this relationship with an example: You have agreed at Date 0 to deliver 5,000 bushels of corn to your counterparty at Date T. What is a "fair" price ($F_{0,T}$) to charge? Recognizing that the contract price can be anything that two parties agree to, one way to look at this question is to consider how much it will cost you to fulfill your obligation. If you wait until Date T to purchase the corn on the spot market, you have a *speculative* position since your purchase price (S_T) will be unknown when you commit to a selling price.

Alternatively, suppose you buy the corn now for the current cash price of S_0 per bushel and store it until you have to deliver it at Date T. Under this scheme, the forward contract price you would be willing to commit to would have to be high enough to cover (1) the present cost of the corn and (2) the cost of storing the corn until contract maturity. In general, these storage costs, denoted here as $SC_{0,T}$, can involve several things, including commissions paid for the physical warehousing of the commodity ($PC_{0,T}$) and the cost of financing the initial purchase of the underlying asset ($i_{0,T}$) but less any cash flows received ($D_{0,T}$) by owning the asset between Dates 0 and T. Thus, in the absence of arbitrage opportunities, the forward contract price should be equal to the current spot price plus the **cost of carry** necessary to transport the asset to the future delivery date:

▶ 22.6
$$F_{0,T} = S_0 + SC_{0,T} = S_0 + (PC_{0,T} + i_{0,T} - D_{0,T})$$

Notice that even if the funds needed to purchase the commodity at Date 0 are not borrowed, $i_{0,T}$ accounts for the opportunity cost of committing one's own financial capital to the transaction.

This cost of carry model is useful in practice because it applies in a wide variety of cases. For some commodities, such as corn or cattle, physical storage is possible but the costs are enormous. Also, neither of these assets pays periodic cash flows in the traditional sense of the term. In such situations, it is quite likely that $F_{0,T} > S_0$ and the market is said to be in **contango**. On the other hand, common stock is costless to store but often pays a dividend. The presence of this cash flow sometimes makes it possible for the basis to be positive (i.e., $F_{0,T} < S_0$), meaning that $SC_{0,T}$ can be negative. There is another reason why $SC_{0,T}$ might be less than zero. For certain storable commodities that do not pay a dividend, $F_{0,T} < S_0$ can occur when there is effectively a "premium" placed on currently owning the commodity. This premium, called a **convenience yield**, results from a small supply of the commodity at Date 0 relative to what is expected at Date T after, say, a crop harvest. (Oats are a commodity that sometimes satisfies this condition, as indicated in Exhibit 22.3.) Although it is extremely difficult to quantify, the convenience yield can be viewed as a potential negative storage cost component that works in a manner similar to $D_{0,T}$. A futures market in which $F_{0,T} < S_0$ is said to be **backwardated**.

An immediate implication of Equation 22.6 is that there should be a direct relationship between contemporaneous forward and spot prices; indeed, this positive correlation is the objective of any well-designed hedging strategy. A related question involves the relationship between $F_{0,T}$ and the spot price expected to prevail at the time the contract matures (i.e., $E(S_T)$). There are three possibilities. First, the *pure expectations* hypothesis holds that, on average, $F_{0,T} = E(S_T)$, so that futures prices serve as unbiased forecasts of future spot prices. When this is true, futures prices serve an important *price discovery* function for participants in the applicable market. Conversely, $F_{0,T}$ could be less than $E(S_T)$, a situation that Keynes and Hicks argued would arise whenever short hedgers outnumber long hedgers.[12] In that case, a risk premium in the form of a lower contract price would be necessary to attract a sufficient number of long speculators.

---

[12]John Maynard Keynes, *A Treatise on Money* (London: Macmillan, 1930); and John Hicks, *Value and Capital* (Oxford: Claredon Press, 1939).

For reasons that are not entirely clear, this situation is termed *normal backwardation*. Finally, a *normal contango* market occurs when the opposite is true, specifically, when $F_{0,T} > E(S_T)$.

The existence of a risk premium in the futures market is hotly debated. Kamara surveyed the early literature on the subject and found the evidence from the commodity markets to be mixed. He concluded that although the normal backwardation hypothesis was supported, futures markets are mainly driven by risk-averse hedgers who have been able to acquire "cheap" insurance. Krehbiel and Collier examined the price behavior in the Eurodollar and Treasury bill futures markets and found evidence consistent with the existence of risk premia that were necessary to balance net hedging and net speculative positions. Finally, Brooks documented that the risk premia priced into Eurodollar futures contracts have a substantial impact on other financial securities as well. Specifically, he showed that prices for interest rate swaps—which can be viewed as portfolios of Eurodollar contracts—are biased upward, causing borrowers who use swaps to convert their variable-rate loans into synthetic fixed-rate debt to make higher payments, on average, than if they had not hedged.[13]

FINANCIAL FORWARDS AND FUTURES: APPLICATIONS AND STRATEGIES

Originally, forward and futures markets were organized largely around trading agricultural commodities, such as corn and wheat. Although markets for these products remain strong, the most significant recent developments in this area have involved the use of financial securities as the asset underlying the contract. In fact, Exhibit 22.5 shows that 9 of the 10 most heavily traded derivative contracts in the United States are based on financial securities. In this section, we take a detailed look at three different types of financial forwards and futures: interest rate, equity index, and foreign exchange.

Interest Rate Forwards and Futures

Interest rate forwards and futures were among the first derivatives to specify a financial security as the underlying asset. The earliest versions of these contracts were designed to lock in the forward price of a particular fixed-coupon bond, which in turn locks in its yield. As we will see in Chapter 24, this market has progressed to where such contracts as *forward rate agreements* and *interest rate swaps* now fix the desired interest rate directly without reference to any specific underlying security. To understand the nuances of the most popular exchange-traded instruments, it is useful to separate them according to whether they involve long- or short-term rates.

Long-Term Interest Rate Futures

Treasury Bond and Note Contract Mechanics   The U.S. Treasury bond and note contracts at the Chicago Board of Trade (CBT) are among the most popular of all the financial futures contracts; in fact, Exhibit 22.5 shows that the T-bond contract has historically been one of the most frequently traded futures contract of any kind. A smaller T-bond contract—one-half the delivery amount—is also available at the CBT. Delivery dates for both note and bond futures fall in March, June, September, and December. Exhibit 22.6 shows a representative set of quotes for these contracts.

Both the T-bond and the longer-term T-note contracts traded at the CBT call for the delivery of $100,000 face value of the respective instruments. For the T-bond contract, any Treasury bond

---

[13]See Avraham Kamara, "The Behavior of Futures Prices: A Review of Theory and Evidence," *Financial Analysts Journal* 40, no. 4 (July–August 1984): 68–75; Tim Krehbiel and Roger Collier, "Normal Backwardation in Short-Term Interest Rate Markets," *Journal of Futures Markets* 16, no. 8 (December 1996): 899–913; and Robert Brooks, *Interest Rate Modeling and the Risk Premiums in Interest Rate Swaps* (Charlottesville, Va.: Research Foundation of the Institute of Chartered Financial Analysis, 1997).

EXHIBIT 22.5 ▸ *LEADING U.S. DERIVATIVE CONTRACTS RANKED BY TRADING VOLUME*

CONTRACT, EXCHANGE, & COUNTRY	2000 VOLUME	2001 VOLUME
3-mo Eurodollar futures, CME	90,401,234	149,631,019
3-mo Eurodollar options, CME	23,019,049	69,292,451
U.S. Treasury bond futures, CBT	53,995,803	47,946,921
10-yr T-note futures, CBT	38,873,890	45,625,926
E-mini S&P 500 futures, CME	15,695,292	31,882,399
Crude oil futures, NYM	31,437,747	31,865,663
E-mini NASDAQ 100, CME	7,859,834	26,573,778
5-yr T-note futures, CBT	19,429,630	24,386,253
S&P 500 Index options, CBOE	18,530,998	19,150,977
S&P 500 Index futures, CME	18,617,638	18,662,040
Exchange-traded funds, CBOE	—	18,238,503

Source: Futures Industry Association Reprinted with permission.

EXHIBIT 22.6 ▸ *TREASURY BOND AND NOTE FUTURES QUOTATIONS*

```
Treasury Bonds (CBT)-$100,000; pts 32nds of 100%
Mar   103-25 104-00 102-30 103-10  —   12 111-16  97-11  449,639
June  102-00 102-10 101-26 102-04  —   12 110-00  96-30   41,843
Est vol 216,000; vol Wed 168,097; open int 491,837, −4,725.
Treasury Notes (CBT)-$100,000; pts 32nds of 100%
Mar   106-26 107-01 06-085 106-18  —  6.0 11-085 101-23  520,294
June  05-055 105-09 04-315 105-08  —  6.5 107-10 101-10   69,833
Est vol 306,000; vol Wed 294,167; open int 590,129, −4,876.
5 Yr Treasury Notes (CBT)-$100,000; pts 32nds of 100%
Mar   06-275 06-315 06-155 06-235  —  1.0 109-08 04-015  523,234
June  105-23 105-27 105-20 105-27  —  1.0 06-105 103-30   34,657
Est vol 155,000; vol Wed 131,960; open int 557,891, −8,814.
2 Yr Treasury Notes (CBT)-$200,000; pts 32nds of 100%
Mar   05-062 105-07 104-31 05-027  —   .2 105-27 03-255  101,355
Est vol 4,100; vol Wed 5,648; open int 101,356. −556.
```

Source: *The Wall Street Journal,* 8 February 2002. Printed with permission from *The Wall Street Journal,* Dow Jones & Co. Inc.

that has at least 15 years to the nearest call date or to maturity (if noncallable) can be used for delivery. Bonds with maturities ranging from 6.5 to 10 years and 4.25 to 5.25 years can be used to satisfy the 10-year and 5-year T-note contracts, respectively. Delivery can take place on any day during the month of maturity, with the last trading day of the contract falling seven business days prior to the end of the month.

Mechanically, the quotation process for T-bond and T-note contracts work the same way. For example, the settlement price of 103–10, for the March 2002 T-bond contract on the CBT represents $103\frac{10}{32}$ percent of the face amount, or $103,312.50. The contract price went down by 12 **ticks** (−12) from the previous day's settlement, meaning that the short side had its margin account increased by $\frac{12}{32}$ percent of $100,000—or $375—where each $\frac{1}{32}$ movement in the bond's price equals $31.25 (i.e., $1,000 \div 32$).

Although T-bond and T-note futures contracts are called interest rate futures, what the long and short positions actually agree to is the price of the underlying bond. Once that price is set, however, the yield will be locked in. When a yield is quoted, it is for reference only and typically assumes a coupon rate of 6 percent and 20 years to maturity. For the March 2002 bond contract, the settlement yield would be 5.7198 percent, which can be established by solving for the internal rate of return in the following "bond math" problem

$$\$1,033.125 = \sum_{t=1}^{40} \frac{\$30}{(1+i/2)^t} + \frac{\$1,000}{(1+i/2)^{40}}$$

This pricing formula takes into account the fact that Treasury bonds pay semiannual interest. So, a 20-year, 6 percent bond makes 40 coupon payments of 3 percent each. Thus, the long position in this contract has effectively agreed in February to buy a 20-year T-bond in March priced to yield 5.72 percent. If, in March, the actual yield on the 20-year bond is below 5.72 percent (i.e., the bond's price is greater than $103,312.50), the long position will have made a wise decision. Thus, the long position in this contract gains as prices rise and rates decrease and loses as increasing rates lead to lower bond prices.

Because the bond and note futures contracts allow so many different instruments to qualify for delivery, the seller would naturally choose to deliver the least expensive bond if there were no adjustments made for varying coupon rates and maturity dates. To account for this, the CBT uses **conversion factors** to correct for the differences in the deliverable bonds. The conversion factor is based on the price of a given bond if its yield is 6 percent at the time of delivery and the face value is $1. For example, the March 2002 conversion factor for the 9 percent T-bond maturing in November 2018 would be 1.3115, calculated as

$$1.3115 = \sum_{t=1}^{33} \frac{0.045}{(1+0.03)^t} + \frac{1}{(1+0.03)^{33}}$$

The actual delivery price, or invoice price, for that Treasury bond would be the quoted futures price, $103,312.50, times the conversion factor, $1.3115, for a total of $135,494.34 (plus accrued interest). The buyer must pay more than $103,312.50 because the seller is delivering "more valuable" bonds since their coupon rate exceeds 6 percent.

The conversion factors used by the CBT are technically correct only when the Treasury yield curve is flat at 6 percent. Therefore, there usually will be a *cheapest to deliver* bond that maximizes the difference between the invoice price (the amount received by the short) and the cash market price (the amount paid by the short to acquire the delivery bond). Market participants always know which bond is the cheapest to deliver. Therefore, the T-bond futures contract trades as if this particular security were the actual underlying delivery bond. In fact, the cheapest to deliver security usually is the T-bond with the longest duration when yields are above 6 percent, and the one with the shortest duration for yields less than 6 percent.

A Duration-Based Approach to Hedging   In Chapter 19, we stressed that the main benefit of calculating the duration statistic was its ability to link interest rate changes to bond price changes by the formula

$$\left(\frac{\Delta P}{P}\right) \approx -D\left(\frac{\Delta(1+i/n)}{(1+i/n)}\right)$$

We also saw that a more convenient way to write this expression is:

$$\left(\frac{\Delta P}{P}\right) \approx -\left(\frac{D}{(1 + i/n)}\right)\Delta(1 + i/n) = -D_{\text{mod}}\Delta(i/n)$$

where:

D_{mod} = **the bond's modified duration, combining the Macaulay duration and its periodic yield into a single measure**

Earlier in this chapter, we noted that the objective of hedging was to select a hedge ratio (N) such that $\Delta S - \Delta F(N) = 0$, where S is the current spot price of the underlying asset and F is the current futures contract price. Rewriting this leaves

$$N^* = \frac{\Delta S}{\Delta F}$$

Using the modified duration relationship, this optimal hedge ratio can now be expanded as follows:

$$N^* = \frac{\Delta S}{\Delta F} = \frac{\left(\dfrac{\Delta S}{S}\right)}{\left(\dfrac{\Delta F}{F}\right)} \times \frac{S}{F} = \frac{-D_{\text{mod}S} \times \Delta(i_S/n)}{-D_{\text{mod}F} \times \Delta(i_F/n)} \times \frac{S}{F}$$

or

➤22.7
$$N^* = \frac{D_{\text{mod}S}}{D_{\text{mod}F}} = \beta_i \times \frac{S}{F}$$

where:

β_i = **the "yield beta"**

The yield beta is also called the ratio of changes in the yields applicable to the two instruments where n is the number of payment periods per year (e.g., $n = 2$ for semiannual coupon bonds).[14]

As a general example of the duration-based approach to setting hedge ratios, consider the following fixed-income securities, each making annual payments (i.e., $n = 1$):

Instrument	Coupon	Maturity	Yield
A	8%	10 years	10%
B	10%	15 years	8%

[14]In an early study on the topic, Gerald Gay, Robert Kolb, and Raymond Chiang, "Interest Rate Hedging: An Empirical Test of Alternative Strategies," *Journal of Financial Research* 6, no. 3 (Fall 1983): 187–197, tested the duration-based hedge ratio against several other more naive approaches and found that it reduced the risk of the underlying bond position by the greatest amount.

How much of Instrument B is necessary to hedge A? This question can be answered in three steps. First, using the method shown in Chapter 19 (and summarized in Appendix 22A), the duration statistics for each position are:

$$D_A = 7.0439 \text{ so } D_{modA} = (7.0439) \div (1.10) = 6.4036 \text{ Years}$$
$$D_B = 8.8569 \text{ so } D_{modB} = (8.8569) \div (1.08) = 8.2009 \text{ Years}$$

Second, we will assume that yield beta is unity (i.e., $\beta_i = 1$). In general, this is calculated by observing historical yield curve movements across the 10- and 15-year maturities. Finally, current prices are easily confirmed to be 87.71 for Security A and 117.12 for Security B assuming par value of 100. Thus, the duration-based hedge ratio is

$$N^* = \left(\frac{6.4036}{8.2009}\right)(1)\left(\frac{87.71}{117.12}\right) = 0.5847$$

or 0.5847 unit of B short for every one unit of A held long.

Treasury Futures Applications

Hedging a Future Funding Commitment   In late July, the treasurer of a U.S.-based company begins to arrange the details of an anticipated 15-year, $100 million funding. He feels that the company will be ready to launch its new debt issue in mid- to late September but is concerned that, between July and September, interest rates may rise, thereby increasing the company's funding cost. Consequently, he decides to hedge this exposure in the T-bond futures market. In this case, he will need to take a *short* position in the futures market, which will appreciate in value if interest rates increase, thereby offsetting the higher payments that will be required on the underlying debt.

The treasurer feels that if the bond issue was placed today, the credit standing of the firm would lead to a funding cost of 8.25 percent for the 15-year period. He knows that a September T-bond futures contract is trading at a price of 83–16 to yield 7.62 percent. He is also aware that bond yields beyond 10 years to maturity tend to move in a parallel fashion to one another so he is comfortable that a yield beta of one is appropriate. Further, the treasurer is aware that T-bond futures cannot hedge for changes in the firm's risk premium over the risk-free rate; he will have to live with this source of basis risk.

If he plans to launch his new issue at par value, how many T-bond futures contracts would he need to short today? Assuming semiannual coupons for both the Treasury and corporate issues, their durations can be calculated using the closed-form equation shown in Appendix 22A:

$$D_{corp} = \frac{1.04125}{0.04125} - \frac{1.04125 + [30(0.04125 - 0.04125)]}{0.04125[(1.04125)^{30} - 1] + 0.04125} = 17.74 \text{ periods}$$

and

$$D_{trsy} = \frac{1.0381}{0.0381} - \frac{1.0381 + [40(0.03 - 0.0381)]}{0.03[(1.0381)^{40} - 1] + 0.0381} = 22.22 \text{ periods}$$

These statistics are denominated in "half years" so that the hedge ratio will be expressed in the same terms used to price the bonds. With these statistics, we can calculate the modified durations as follows: $D_{modC} = 17.04$ (= 17.74 ÷ 1.04125) and $D_{modT} = 21.40$ (= 22.22 ÷ 1.0381).

Finally, since each T-bond futures contract is standardized to a denomination of $100,000, the treasurer can calculate the optimal number of contracts to short as

$$\text{(Number of Contracts)} = \frac{(17.04)}{(21.40)} \times (1.0) \times \frac{(\$100,000,000)}{(\$83,500)} = 953.6, \text{ or 954 Contracts}$$

A T-Bond/T-Note (NOB) Futures Spread Frequently, speculators in the bond market will have a clear view on a change in the overall shape of the yield curve but be less certain as to the actual direction in future rate movements. Suppose, for instance, you think the yield curve—which is currently upward sloping across all maturities—will flatten, but you're not sure in which of several ways this might occur:

➤ Short-term rates rise and long-term rates fall.
➤ Short- and long-term rates both rise, but short-term rates rise by more.
➤ Short- and long-term rates both fall, but short-term rates fall by less.

Clearly, taking a long or short position in a single futures contract linked to a single point on the yield curve is too speculative, given your view; you could be right about the shape shift but guess wrong about direction. One way to mitigate this unwanted risk while investing (based on your view) is to go both long and short in contracts representing different points on the yield curve. This is known as the Treasury "Notes over Bond" spread (or "NOB" spread) strategy.

Suppose in mid-February you observe the following price quotes (along with their implied yields to maturity) for T-bond and T-note futures contracts maturing in June:

CONTRACT	SETTLE PRICE	IMPLIED YIELD
20-yr, 6% T-bond	103–02	5.74%
10-yr, 6% T-note	104–02	5.47%

Notice that your expectation of a flattening yield curve is identical to the view that the 27 basis point yield gap (= 0.0574 – 0.0547) between the longer- and shorter-term contracts will shrink. If you also feel this will occur by mid-June, the appropriate strategy would be:

➤ Go long in one Treasury bond futures.
➤ Go short in one Treasury note futures.

The net profit from this joint position when you close out the two contracts is calculated as the sum of the profits on the short T-note position and the long T-bond contract, or

$$\left[\frac{104.0625 - \text{June T-Note Price}}{100} + \frac{\text{June T-Bond Price} - 103.0625}{100} \right](\$100,000)$$

To see how this combined position would pay off if your view is correct, consider two scenarios in which the yield curve flattens to where there is no difference between 10- and 20-year rates by the time you close your positions in June:

1. *Rates increase to 6.00 percent by June.*
   In this case, both futures contracts will sell at par and so your net profit will be

$$\text{Net Profit} = [0.040625 - 0.030625](\$100,000) = \$1,000$$

Notice that this same calculation can be done on a "price tick" basis:

$$\text{Net Profit} = \{[(104\text{--}02) - (103\text{--}02)] - [(100\text{--}00) - (100\text{--}00)]\}(\$31.25)$$
$$= (32 \text{ Ticks})(\$31.25) = \$1,000$$

which is equivalent to the change in the number of ticks in the NOB spread multiplied by the dollar value of a tick (i.e., \$31.25).

2. *Rates decrease to 5.00 percent by June.*

   Except when both bonds trade at par, it is generally not the case that two bonds with different maturities—but the same coupon and same yield—will trade at the same price. In this scenario, the settlement prices on the two futures contracts will be

$$P_{\text{T-note}} = \sum_{t=1}^{20} \frac{\$3}{(1+0.025)^t} + \frac{\$100}{(1+0.025)^{20}} = \$107.79 \approx 107\text{--}25$$

and

$$P_{\text{T-bond}} = \sum_{t=1}^{40} \frac{\$3}{(1+0.025)^t} + \frac{\$100}{(1+0.025)^{40}} = \$112.55 \approx 112\text{--}18$$

so that the net profit from the NOB spread will be

$$\text{Net Profit} = \{[(104\text{--}02) - (103\text{--}02)] - [(107\text{--}25) - (112\text{--}18)]\}(\$31.25)$$
$$= (32 + 153)(\$31.25) = \$5,781.25$$

Interpreting this outcome differently, you made \$9,500.00 on your long position in the T-bond contract (= [(112–18) – (103–02)](31.25)), but you lost \$3,718.75 on your short T-note position (= [(104–02) – (107–25)](31.25)) for a net gain of \$5,781.25.

These results show that the futures spread allows speculators to separate their views on yield curve shape from an explicit forecast of a change in the curve's position. When using this strategy, however, the investor must be careful to recognize that, because the duration of the T-bond is greater than that of the T-note, the former will be more sensitive to a given rate change.

Short-Term Interest Rate Futures

Short-term interest rate futures have become the most rapidly expanding segment of the exchange-traded market. Currently, investors can hedge their exposures to several different money market rates (e.g., T-bill, LIBOR, Banker's Acceptance, Federal Funds) denominated in a multitude of currencies (e.g., U.S. dollar, Japanese yen, Euro). In the following analysis, we concentrate on two of these contracts: Eurodollar and Treasury bill.

Eurodollar and Treasury Bill Contract Mechanics

The Eurodollar contract traded at the International Monetary Market (IMM) on the Chicago Mercantile Exchange (CME, or "Merc") has become enormously successful since it was launched in the early 1980s. Delivery dates occur monthly for a brief period before following the March, June, September, December cycle (the so-called IMM dates) and now extend 10 years into the future. The final trading and settlement date is the second London business day before the third Wednesday of the delivery month. A representative set of quotes is shown in Exhibit 22.7. Also traded on the London International Financial Futures and Options Exchange (LIFFE) (although not shown here) are

EXHIBIT 22.7 ▶ *EURODOLLAR (LIBOR) AND TREASURY BILL FUTURES QUOTATIONS*

	OPEN	HIGH	LOW	SETTLE	CHANGE	YIELD	CHANGE	OPEN INT.
Treasury Bills (CME)-$1 mil.; pts of 100%								
Mar	....	....	....	98.28	....	1.72	....	754
Est vol 0; vol Wed 0; open int 754, unch.								
Libor-1 Mo. (CME)-$3,000,000; pts of 100%								
Feb	98.14	98.14	98.13	98.14	....	1.86	....	21,246
Mar	98.14	98.14	98.13	98.14	− .01	1.86	+.01	8,086
Apr	98.12	98.12	98.10	98.10	− .01	1.90	+.01	2,649
May	98.02	98.03	98.02	98.03	− .01	1.97	+.01	1,056
Est vol 1,197; vol Wed 3,184; open int 35,588, +1,147.								
Eurodollar (CME)-$1 Million; pts of 100%								
Feb	98.10	98.10	98.09	98.09	....	1.91	....	37,338
Mar	98.05	98.06	98.03	98.04	− .01	1.96	+.01	757,383
Apr	97.96	97.97	97.96	97.97	....	2.03	....	4,761
May	97.86	97.87	97.86	97.87	− .01	2.13	+.01	1,783
June	97.76	97.79	97.71	97.75	− .01	2.25	+.01	691,602
Sept	97.34	97.38	97.27	97.31	− .02	2.69	+.02	622,628
Dec	96.81	96.86	96.74	96.78	− .02	3.22	+.02	720,119
Mr03	96.25	96.30	96.17	96.22	− .02	3.78	+.02	413,018
June	95.70	95.72	95.64	95.66	− .04	4.34	+.04	266,486
Sept	95.31	95.31	95.21	95.25	− .02	4.75	+.02	235,095
Dec	94.91	94.92	94.85	94.90	− .02	5.10	+.02	166,061
Mr04	94.64	94.69	94.63	94.68	− .01	5.32	+.01	113,025
June	94.40	94.45	94.39	94.44	− .01	5.56	+.01	116,149
Sept	94.23	94.26	94.19	94.25	....	5.75	....	106,218
Dec	94.01	94.05	93.99	94.05	....	5.95	....	70,677
Mr05	93.92	93.98	93.91	93.97	− .01	6.03	+.01	76,664
June	93.82	93.86	93.81	93.85	− .02	6.15	+.02	68,596
Sept	93.71	93.76	93.70	93.74	− .03	6.26	+.03	76,164
Dec	93.61	93.62	93.56	93.60	− .03	6.40	+.03	56,629
Mr06	93.55	93.59	93.53	93.58	− .04	6.42	+.04	48,057
June	93.48	93.51	93.46	93.50	− .04	6.50	+.04	36,532
Sept	93.42	93.45	93.41	93.44	− .04	6.56	+.04	45,517
Dec	93.35	93.35	93.28	93.33	− .04	6.67	+.04	33,861
Est vol 732,950; vol Wed 766,691; open int 4,898,441, +15,031.								

Source: *The Wall Street Journal,* 8 February 2002. Printed with permission from *The Wall Street Journal,* Dow Jones & Co. Inc.

similar contracts for hedging Euro-IBOR (i.e., the "Euro" currency), Eurosterling, Euroyen, and Euroswiss rates.

Hypothetically, the Eurodollar contract requires the long position to make a $1,000,000, 90-day bank deposit with the short position at the maturity date. Unlike the Treasury bond and note futures just described, however, this contract requires all outstanding obligations to be settled in cash. This provision is necessary because the contract nominally requires the long position to make, and the short position to receive, a 90-day Euro-time deposit. However, that is something that the short position can't legally do unless it is a financial institution chartered for such business. The underlying interest rate is the 3-month (i.e., 90-day) LIBOR that is quoted on a 360-day bank add-on basis. As we will see, arbitrage trading should drive the sequence of Eurodollar (or LIBOR) futures rates to equal the forward rates implied by the yield curve for interbank lending in the cash market. That is, in an efficient market, the futures rates should be close to the comparable implied forward rates.

In Exhibit 22.7, the quoted contract price for the March 2003 contract is 96.22, which is not an actual purchase price but merely an index calculated as 100 minus the settlement yield of 3.78 (percent). Eurodollar futures use this settlement price index because it conveniently preserves the inverse relation between price and yield. Thus, a long position in this contract can still be thought to "win" when prices rise—and the short position wins with falling prices—even though it is the opposite movement in the underlying interest rate that matters.

The minimum price change, or "tick," for this contract is one basis point and equals a $25 change in the value of the contract. Therefore, the *basis point value* of the contract is $25

(= $1,000,000 × 0.0001 × 90/360). Thus, the two-tick (–0.02) decline in the price of the March contract means that LIBOR increased by two basis points from the prior day's settlement. This would benefit a person who acquired a short position at the close of the prior day inasmuch as he would have a locked-in borrowing cost for the 90-day period from March to June 2003 that is now two basis points lower than the market level. In fact, all sellers of this contract gained $50 per contract (i.e., $25 per tick times two ticks) in their margin accounts.

Finally, notice that Eurodollar open interest is spread over the various delivery dates to a greater extent than for the T-bond contract (shown in Exhibit 22.6). In fact, the Eurodollar contract is the "deepest" financial futures contract available with, as noted, maturities going out 10 years. This makes it possible to hedge a LIBOR-based exposure a decade into the future. Brown and Smith interpreted these trading patterns as suggesting that T-bond futures are used in the market more as a speculative trading contract and that Eurodollar futures are used more frequently as a buy-and-hold hedging instrument.[15]

Exhibit 22.7 also lists quotes for the available Treasury bill futures traded at the IMM. This contract requires the long position to buy, and the short position to sell, a 90-day Treasury bill at maturity and can be settled in cash or with a physical exchange. Similar to the Eurodollar derivative, the T-bill contract is standardized to an amount of $1,000,000 so that each basis point change in the price (or rate) is worth $25 per contract. Again, the quoted price is a price index, 100 minus the settlement discount rate. In the absence of arbitrage, the T-bill futures rates should be close to the implied forward discount rates calculated from the cash market T-bill rates.

The T-bill contract at the IMM has lost much of its market share in recent years because it is dominated by competing contracts in two important applications. First, because many more corporate and banking transactions are tied to LIBOR—which can be viewed as a risk-free rate plus a credit spread—than to the T-bill rate, more end users prefer the Eurodollar contract for hedging their interest rate exposures. Indeed, T-bill open interest is far less than that of the Eurodollar contract. Second, the T-bill contract is seldom used for speculative purposes in lieu of T-bond futures because the duration of the underlying instrument (a 3-month T-bill) in the T-bill contract is so much shorter than that of the latter (a 20-year bond), meaning that its price will increase by less if the anticipated rate change is realized. Nevertheless, the following examples will show that T-bill futures play an important (if limited) economic role in financial markets.

Short-Term Interest Rate Futures Applications

Altering Bond Duration with Futures Contracts   An investor currently holds a 6-month (i.e., 182-day) Treasury bill. Because of a fear that inflationary pressures will increase interest rates toward the end of the coming quarter, she would like to reduce her exposure by converting this position into a three-month T-bill. There are two ways to do this. First, she could sell her current holding and buy the shorter-term instrument she desires, a strategy that might entail nontrivial transaction costs. Second, she could accomplish the same change synthetically by supplementing her 6-month bill with a short position in a T-bill futures contract maturing in 92 days. This is what she decides to do.

Exhibit 22.8 shows the net effect of combining the long position in the 182-day T-bill with a short position in the T-bill futures (ignoring for simplicity the margin account on the derivative). In this illustration, the discount yield for the cash market instrument is 7.91 percent, leading to

[15]Keith C. Brown and Donald J. Smith, "Recent Innovations in Interest Rate Risk Management and the Reintermediation of Commercial Banking," *Financial Management* 17, no. 4 (Winter 1988): 45–58.

EXHIBIT 22.8 ▶ *USING INTEREST RATE FUTURES TO ADJUST DURATION*

a price of $96 (per par value of 100) Also, the futures discount yield is 8 percent; that is, the investor is committed to deliver a 90-day T-bill at a price of $98 when the contract matures. The display assumes that she settles her futures obligation by giving up the remaining 90 days of her original T-bill in exchange for $98. This indicates that the combined position is equivalent to a 92-day Treasury bill with a current price of $96 and a "face" value of $98. Thus, shorting the futures contract has effectively converted a six-month holding into a three-month instrument with an implied discount yield of 7.99 percent (= [(98 − 96) ÷ 98][360 ÷ 92]).

Because Treasury bills, as zero coupon securities, have durations equal to their maturities, a different way of interpreting this example is that the short position in a T-bill futures contract has allowed the investor to *reduce* the duration of her holding from six to three months. Conversely, although not shown in Exhibit 22.8, a long futures position can lengthen duration. For example, had the investor held a 92-day T-bill and supplemented it with a long T-bill futures contract maturing at the same date, she would have locked in her reinvestment rate for another 90-day T-bill position. Consequently, being long in the 92-day bill and long in the bill futures is equivalent to being long in a 182-day T-bill, which *increases* her investment duration from three to six months.[16]

Creating a Synthetic Fixed-Rate Funding with a Eurodollar Strip Suppose that on March 15 a senior loan officer for a large regional bank is considering an investment scheme for

---

[16]For a related discussion, see Jess B. Yawitz and William J. Marshall, "The Use of Futures in Immunized Portfolios," *Journal of Portfolio Management* 11, no. 2 (Winter 1985): 51–58.

lending $2,000,000 in temporary cash balances to a "large-cap" manufacturing firm. The plan would last for one year and have the payment rate reset on a quarterly basis at LIBOR. At the planning stage, the LIBOR yield curve appears as follows:

90-day LIBOR	5.00%
180-day LIBOR	5.10
270-day LIBOR	5.20
360-day LIBOR	5.30

Given the debt market convention that the funding rates on floating-rate deal structures always are determined in advance and paid in arrears, she knows that her loan receipt for the first 3 months would be based on the prevailing 5.00 percent rate and be receivable in 90 days. Her concern is what her receipts might be in the subsequent three quarters, and, specifically, she is worried that they may fall to an unacceptable level. Accordingly, she considers using the Eurodollar futures market to hedge her exposure.

As a prelude to checking futures contract price quotes, she calculates the forward rates implied by the current yield curve. Using money-market implied forward rate formulas shown in Appendix 22B, these computations generate:

$$_{180}IFR_{90} = \left[\frac{(0.051)(180) - (0.050)(90)}{(180 - 90)}\right]\left[\frac{1}{1 + \left(\frac{(90)(0.050)}{360}\right)}\right] = 5.14\%$$

$$_{270}IFR_{180} = \left[\frac{(0.052)(270) - (0.051)(180)}{(270 - 180)}\right]\left[\frac{1}{1 + \left(\frac{(180)(0.051)}{360}\right)}\right] = 5.27\%$$

$$_{360}IFR_{270} = \left[\frac{(0.053)(360) - (0.052)(270)}{(360 - 270)}\right]\left[\frac{1}{1 + \left(\frac{(270)(0.052)}{360}\right)}\right] = 5.39\%$$

She checks with her trading desk for quotes on the relevant Eurodollar futures contracts and receives the following information:

CONTRACT EXPIRATION	SETTLEMENT PRICE
June	94.86
September	94.73
December	94.61

The futures settlement prices indicate LIBOR contract rates that are identical to the implied forward rates, suggesting there is no arbitrage potential between the cash and futures markets on this date.

To lock in her receipts for the $2,000,000 loan, the banker would go long a *strip* of Eurodollar futures contracts. That is, she takes long positions in two June contracts, two September contracts, and two December contracts. (Recall that the long position in a Eurodollar contract gains when the price index rises with a falling LIBOR; this is the protection she is seeking.) With these positions, her quarterly interest receipts will be fixed at the following levels:

$$\text{June Receipt} = (\$2,000,000)\left[\frac{(0.0500)(90)}{360}\right] = \$25,000$$

$$\text{September Receipt} = (\$2,000,000)\left[\frac{(0.0514)(90)}{360}\right] = \$25,700$$

$$\text{December Receipt} = (\$2,000,000)\left[\frac{(0.0527)(90)}{360}\right] = \$26,350$$

$$\text{March (Next Year) Receipt} = (\$2,000,000)\left[\frac{(0.0539)(90)}{360}\right] = \$26,950$$

Although these cash inflows are fixed in advance, they clearly differ in amount from quarter to quarter. To get a better indication of her overall return, the banker asks herself the following question: What quarterly annuity payment does this sequence of receipts imply? This amount can be calculated as the solution to:

$$\frac{\$25,000}{\left[1+\frac{(0.050)(90)}{360}\right]} + \frac{\$25,700}{\left[1+\frac{(0.051)(180)}{360}\right]} + \frac{\$26,350}{\left[1+\frac{(0.052)(270)}{360}\right]} + \frac{\$26,950}{\left[1+\frac{(0.053)(360)}{360}\right]}$$

$$= \frac{\text{Annuity}}{\left[1+\frac{(0.050)(90)}{360}\right]} + \frac{\text{Annuity}}{\left[1+\frac{(0.051)(180)}{360}\right]} + \frac{\text{Annuity}}{\left[1+\frac{(0.052)(270)}{360}\right]} + \frac{\text{Annuity}}{\left[1+\frac{(0.053)(360)}{360}\right]}$$

Solving this formula for "Annuity" gives a value of $25,989.38, where the discount rates are from the prevailing cash market LIBOR curve. Finally, notice that this annuity payment, when expressed on a full 360-day percentage basis, is

$$\left[\frac{\$25,989.38}{\$2,000,000}\right]\left[\frac{360}{90}\right] = 5.198\%$$

which is a time-weighted average of the 90-day spot LIBOR and the series of three implied forward rates.

Creating a TED Spread   As noted earlier, one of the features that makes the Eurodollar futures contract such a popular hedging vehicle is the rate it is based on—three-month LIBOR. This rate can be thought of as equivalent to the three-month T-bill yield *plus* a risk premium (i.e., credit spread). Sometimes, bond traders will have a view on future movements in this credit spread; for example, a trader might believe the current difference between the LIBOR and T-bill yield is too narrow and that it will soon widen. The problem with trying to play this view with a short position in the Eurodollar contract alone, however, is even if the trader is right about the spread, the general level of interest rates could still decline by more than enough to offset any spread gains.

The solution to this dilemma is to isolate the credit spread component in LIBOR through a strategy known as the *TED* (Treasury/EuroDollar) *spread*. The TED spread is created by taking simultaneous, but opposite, positions in both a Eurodollar and T-bill futures contract having the same maturity. In the parlance of the market, we have the following definitions.

Long a TED Spread = (Long T-Bill Futures) + (Short Eurodollar Futures)

Short a TED Spread = (Short T-Bill Futures) + (Long Eurodollar Futures)

Notice that a long position in a TED spread will gain when the credit spread increases; the short TED spread benefits from a narrowing of the credit spread. Exhibit 22.9 shows how volatile the three-month TED spread has been over time.

To see how an investor can profit from this volatility, consider the following example. Suppose that in early August you observe the following prices in the Eurodollar and T-bill futures markets:

	T-BILL	EURODOLLAR	SPREAD
September contracts	95.24	94.80	44 BP
December contracts	94.68	94.11	57 BP
March contracts	94.42	93.86	56 BP

Recall that the difference between the T-bill and Eurodollar price indexes is the spread built into the Eurodollar contract for a particular maturity.

If you believe the economy will remain sluggish for an extended period of time and that credit spreads currently are too narrow in the short-term contract, you would want to take a long TED spread position (i.e., short the Eurodollar futures and buy the T-bill contract). After you establish

EXHIBIT 22.9   *TED SPREAD FOR THREE-MONTH CONTRACTS*

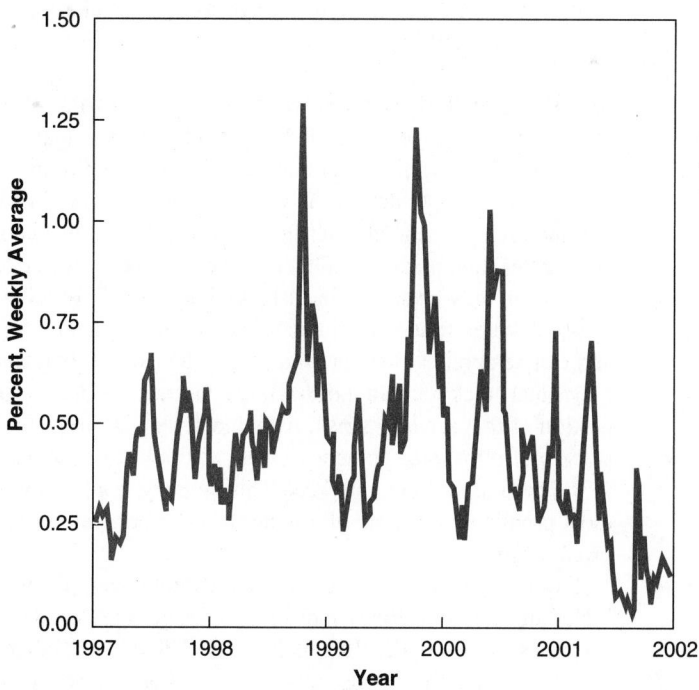

Source: Federal Reserve Bank of Cleveland.

this position using the September contracts, the Federal Reserve Board tightens rates again so that by mid-September the following prices prevail when you unwind the strategy:

New September T-bill contract	94.55
New September Eurodollar contract	93.95
New spread	0.60

This new spread is more closely aligned with the December and March contracts. The profit on your transaction is calculated as

$$\text{(New TED Spread)} - \text{(Original TED Spread)}$$

or

$$(94.55 - 93.95) - (95.24 - 94.80) = 16 \text{ Basis Points}$$

With each contract standardized so that a basis point is worth \$25, the profit per contract pair from this trade would be $(16 \times \$25) = \$400$. Another way to see this profit is that you made an 85-basis-point profit on the short position in the Eurodollar contract $(= 94.80 - 93.95)$ but lost 69 basis points on the long T-bill contract $(= 94.55 - 95.24)$. However, if both rates had declined, you still would have made money if the T-bill yield had fallen by more than LIBOR.

Stock Index Futures

Another important form of financial futures contracting specifies an equity index as the underlying asset. In this section, we consider the basics of stock index futures trading and discuss two applications for these instruments, including a popular form of computer-assisted trading known as stock index arbitrage.

Stock Index Futures Contract Fundamentals Like interest rate futures, stock index futures were originally intended to provide a hedge against movements in an underlying financial asset. We have just seen that some interest rate futures can be settled with either a cash or physical transfer. As detailed in Chapter 5 and the introductory example in Chapter 21, however, the underlying financial asset for a stock index futures contract is a hypothetical creation that does not exist in practice and therefore cannot be delivered to settle a contract. Thus, stock index futures can only be settled in cash, similar to the Eurodollar (i.e., LIBOR) contract.

Stock index futures are intended to provide general hedges against stock market movements and can be applied to either whole (i.e., diversified) portfolios or individual stocks. Hedging an individual stock with an index futures contract is done in an attempt to isolate the unsystematic portion of that security's risk. Additionally, stock index futures often are used to convert entire stock portfolios into synthetic riskless positions to exploit an apparent mispricing between stock in the cash and futures markets. This strategy, commonly called **stock index arbitrage**, is the most prominent example of a wider class of computer-assisted trading schemes known as *program trading*.

Exhibit 22.10 lists quotes for futures contracts on several U.S. and foreign stock indexes, including the Dow Jones Industrial Average, the Standard and Poor's 500, the Standard and Poor's Midcap 400, the Russell 2000, the Nikkei 225 (Japan), the CAC 40 (France), the DAX 30 (Germany), and the FT-SE 100 (England). For instance, an investor planning in February to buy stock in June can hedge against his eventual purchase price increasing with rising market prices by entering the long position of the June 2002 S&P 500 contract. With a settlement price of

EXHIBIT 22.10 *STOCK INDEX FUTURES QUOTATIONS*

DJ Industrial Average (CBOT)-$10 times average

Mar	9625	9735	9580	9593	—	52	11150	7900	28,098
June	9729	9730	9585	9598	—	52	10951	9080	613

Est vol 19,000; vol Wed 25,548; open int 28,930. −146.
Idx prl: Hi 9743.05; Lo 9624.12; Close 9625.44. −27.95.

S&P 500 Index (CME)-$250 times index

Mar	108650	109460	107650	107700	—	630	134960	94100	477,969
June	108550	109700	107800	107890	—	630	170550	95030	19,201
Sept	109650	109760	108360	108130	—	630	165670	95530	11,029

Est vol 8,301; vol Wed 83,212; open int 508,814. +1,397.
Idx prl: Hi 1094.03; Lo 1078.44; Close 1080.17. −3.34.

Mini S&P 500 (CME)-$50 times index

Mar	108625	109500	107625	107700	—	625	117850	99850	107,268

Vol Wed 344.682; open int 107,301. +1,932.

S&P Midcap 400 (CME)-$500 times index

Mar	488.50	490.00	483.00	483.50	—	5.00	560.00	412.95	13,671

Est vol 1,044; vol Wed 944; open int 13,671. +36.
Idx prl: Hi 489.11; Lo 484.75; Close 485.05. −3.99.

Nikkei 225 Stock Average (CME)-$5 times index

Mar	9560.	9630.	9550.	9565.	+	150	14620.	9245.	15.898

Est vol 795; vol Wed 1,631; open int 15,975. −26.
Idx prl: Hi 9634.79; Lo 9458.70; Close 9583.27. +162.42.

Nasdaq 100 (CME)-$100 times index

Mar	146200	146500	141300	141500	—	3650	189400	112000	51.261

Est vol 20,256; vol Wed 23,059; open int 51,274. −455.
Idx prl: Hi 1459.94; Lo 1413.42; Close 1413.86. −32.10.

Mini Nasdaq 100 (CME)-$20 times index

Mar	1461.5	1464.0	1414.0	1415.0	—	36.5	1750.0	1150.0	96,040

Vol Wed 222,911; open int 96,046. +861.

GSCI (CME)-$250 times nearby index

Feb	165.75	166.60	164.50	166.15	—	1.10	179.00	161.45	19,821

Est vol 4,242; vol Wed 107; open int 19.925. +29.
Idx prl: Hi 167.01; Lo 164.76; Close 166.53. −.46.

Russell 2000 (CME)-$500 times index

Mar	463.00	463.50	456.50	457.15	—	5.70	537.00	387.35	26,190

Est vol 2,268; vol Wed 2,290; open int 26,195. −58.
Idx prl: Hi 463.14; Lo 458.09; Close 458.40. −4.01.

U.S. Dollar Index (FINEX)-$1,000 times USDX

Mar	119.90	119.95	119.15	119.27	—	.28	120.80	112.68	9,429
June	120.42	120.42	120.04	119.80	—	.28	121.23	115.02	2,245

Est vol 1.200; vol Wed 692; open int 11,679. +36.
Idx prl: Hi 119.78; Lo 118.98; Close 119.07. −.23.

Share Price Index (SFE)-A $25 times index

Mar	3409.0	3416.0	3390.0	3415.0	+	6.0	3481.0	2907.0	141,202
June	3409.0	3427.0	3405.0	3428.0	+	6.0	3481.0	2945.0	2,177

Est vol 12.737; vol Wed 10.082; open int 144,529. +6,027.
Index Hi 3429.3; Lo 3406.6; Close 3414.5. −10.0.

CAC-40 Stock Index (MATIF)-Euro 10.00 x index

Feb	4260.0	4321.0	4236.0	4301.0	+	18.0	4737.5	4236.0	416,958
Mar	4279.5	4326.0	4275.0	4311.5	+	17.5	5527.0	3701.5	118.710
Apr	4331.0	4331.0	4327.5	4318.0	+	18.0	4498.0	4304.0	523
June	4247.5	4282.0	4220.5	4273.0	+	18.0	4980.0	4220.5	17.924

Est vol 68,693; vol Wed 78,633; open int 570.690. +18,148.

Xetra DAX (EUREX)-Euro 25 per DAX index pt.

Mar	4799.5	4892.0	4744.0	4874.0	+	54.0	6306.5	3636.5	158,471
June	4817.0	4930.0	4797.0	4918.0	+	54.5	5426.5	4036.5	9.584
Sept	4883.0	4883.0	4883.0	4960.0	+	56.0	5443.0	4883.0	2.139

Vol Thu 79,374; open int 170,194. +8.469.
Index Hi 4873.59 Lo 4730.70 Close 4862.62. +58.21.

FT-SE 100 Index (LIFFE)-£10 per index point

Mar	5045.0	5139.5	5021.5	5109.5	+	54.5	5431.5	4769.5	405.958
June	5055.5	5093.0	5040.5	5120.5	+	54.5	5447.5	4799.5	28.764
Sept	5051.0	5130.5	5051.0	5134.5	+	54.5	5371.5	5051.0	4.622

Est vol 48,830; vol Wed 46,638; open int 439,344. −789.

DJ Euro STOXX 50 Index (EUREX)-Euro 10.00 x index

Mar	3485.0	3544.0	3455.0	3527.0	+	33.0	5155.0	2794.0	808,792
June	3463.0	3518.0	3446.0	3504.0	+	34.0	3880.0	3010.0	78,656
Sept	3464.0	3529.0	3452.0	3519.0	+	32.0	3871.0	3452.0	8.051

Vol Thu 265.347; open int 895,499. +15.944.
Index Hi 3525.83; Lo 3447.01; Close 3519.93. +34.55.

DJ STOXX 50 Index (EUREX)-Euro 10.00 x index

Mar	3438.0	3496.0	3422.0	3492.0	+	43.0	4138.0	2806.0	25,290
June	3433.0	3489.0	3420.0	3486.0	+	43.0	3728.0	3289.0	2.073

Vol Thu 2,135, open int 27.363. +499.
Index Hi 3494.13; Lo 3423.92; Close 3493.28. +47.61.

Source: *The Wall Street Journal,* 8 February 2002. Printed with permission from *The Wall Street Journal,* Dow Jones & Co. Inc.

1,078.90 for this contract (shown in the display as "107890"), he has obligated himself to the theoretical purchase of 250 "shares" of the S&P 500 on the third Friday of June for $269,725 (= 1,078.90 × 250). The mininum contract price movement is 0.10 points, which equals $25. Thus, if the actual level of the S&P index on the contract settlement date turned out to be 1,081.10, the long position would gain $550, or $25 times 22 "ticks" (i.e., (1,081.10–1,078.90) ÷ 0.10), thereby reducing the net purchase price for his desired equity investment.

Stock Index Futures Valuation and Index Arbitrage   Earlier, we established that the key to understanding the pricing of futures contracts is the concept of arbitrage. To see how this works for index contracts, suppose that at Date 0 an investor takes the following positions: (1) purchases a portfolio of stock representing the underlying stock index for S_0, and (2) goes short a stock index future (with an expiration date of T) for $F_{0,T}$. Assume further that in order to avoid making any investment at Date 0, the funds for the long position are borrowed at the risk-free rate of RFR. Upon unwinding this position at Date t, the net profit (Π) is given by

$$\Pi = (F_{0,T} - F_{t,T}) + (S_t - S_0 - S_0 RFR_t + S_0 d_t) = (F_{0,T} - F_{t,T}) + [S_t - S_0(1 + RFR_t - d_t)]$$

where:

d_t = **the dividend yield accruing to the stocks comprising the index between dates 0 and t**

In other words, the profit you make on this short hedge in stock index futures will consist of two components: the net difference in the futures position and the net difference in the underlying index position (after adding borrowing costs and subtracting dividends received from the initial purchase).

Now assume the long position in the stock portpolio is held until the expiration of the futures contract (i.e., Date $t = T$). The advantage of doing this is that the cash settlement feature of the stock index futures contract ensures that the futures price and index level will converge. That is, at Date T, we will have $F_{T,T} = S_T$, which means that the short hedge profit (Π) equation can be written

$$\Pi = [F_{0,T} - S_0 - S_0(RFR_t - d_T)]$$

As before, $RFR_t - d_T$ is called the net cost of carry and represents the difference between the borrowing cost paid and the dividend received.

If the dividend yield is known at Date 0, this position is riskless and requires no initial investment. Thus, buying and selling among arbitrageurs trading in both the stock and futures markets should ensure that $\Pi = 0$. Thus, the futures price set at Date 0 will be

➤22.8
$$F_{0,T} = S_0 + S_0(RFR_t - d_T)$$

As in the cost of carry model discussed earlier, the futures price could be set below the spot level of the index (i.e., a backwardated market) if $(RFR_t - d_T) < 0$. That is, the index futures contract will be priced lower than the current level of the stock price whenever the dividends received by holding stock exceed the borrowing cost.

To see how this parity relationship helps establish the appropriate level of the stock index futures price, assume that one "share" of the S&P 500 index can be purchased for 1,250.00 and that the dividend yield and risk-free rate over the holding period are 1.5 percent and 2.5 percent, respectively. Under these conditions, the contract price on a six-month S&P 500 futures should be

$$F_{0,0.5} = 1,250 + 1,250(0.025 - 0.015) = 1,262.50$$

EXHIBIT 22.11 *STOCK INDEX FUTURES VALUATION EXAMPLE*

	S&P AT EXPIRATION IS:				
	1,220	1,240	1,260	1,280	1,300
Net futures profit	42.50	22.50	2.50	(17.50)	(37.50)
Net index profit	(30.00)	(10.00)	10.00	30.00	50.00
Dividend	18.75	18.75	18.75	18.75	18.75
Net profit	31.25	31.25	31.25	31.25	31.25

Now suppose that you construct a short hedge position by (1) purchasing the index at 1,250.00 and (2) shorting the futures at 1,262.50. If the position is held to expiration, your profit at various expiration date levels of the S&P will be as shown in Exhibit 22.11. Notice that your net profit remains constant no matter the level of the index at the expiration date. More importantly, this net profit can be expressed as

$$(31.25) \div (1{,}250) = 2.5 \text{ Percent}$$

which is the assumed cost of borrowing.

Implementing an Index Arbitrage Strategy What if the parity condition between the stock index and the stock index futures price does not hold? Could you design a portfolio to take advantage of the situation? Specifically, suppose that in the preceding example the actual contract price on a six-month S&P 500 futures was 1,265.50 (i.e., $F_{0,T} > S_0 + S_0(RFR_t - d_T)$). You could then implement the following arbitrage transaction: (1) short the stock index future at a price of 1,265.50; (2) borrow money at 2.5 percent to purchase the stock index at 1,250.00; and (3) hold the position until maturity, collecting 18.75 in dividends and then selling the stock to repay your loan. Your net profit at maturity would be

$$1{,}265.50 - 1{,}250 - 1{,}250 \,(0.025 - 0.015) = 3.00$$

However, since this strategy was riskless (i.e., the sales price of the stock and the dividends were known in advance) and none of your own capital was used, it is an arbitrage profit.

This is *stock index arbitrage,* which is possible whenever the index futures price is set at a level sufficiently different from the theoretical value for $F_{0,T}$ to account for trading costs. For example, if the actual level of $F_{0,T} < S_0 + S_0(RFR_t - d_T)$, the previous strategy could be reversed: (1) buy the stock index future at a price of $F_{0,T}$, (2) lend money at RFR_t and short the stock index at S_0, and (3) cover the position at the expiration date of the futures contract. Indeed, index arbitrage is a very popular form of trading. Exhibit 22.12 reports that about 10 percent of all computer-assisted program trading used this strategy. Further program trading accounted for about one-fifth of trading volume on the New York Stock Exchange. Both of these totals can get much higher around contract expiration dates (i.e., the so-called *triple witching days*).

One important side effect of this sort of trading activity is that stock index futures prices tend to stay close to the theoretical levels generated by the preceding valuation equation. This is because the arbitrage "prescription" for a futures settlement price that is too low (too high) is to go long (short) in the contract, which, when done in sufficient volume, adjusts the price in

EXHIBIT 22.12 ▶ *PROGRAM TRADING AND STOCK INDEX ARBITRAGE*

PROGRAM TRADING

NEW YORK—Program trading in the week ended Feb. 1 accounted for 25.5%, or an average of 348.1 million shares daily, of New York Stock Exchange volume.

Brokerage firms executed an additional 300.6 million daily shares of program trading away from the NYSE, with 12.5% of the overall total on foreign markets. Program trading is the simultaneous purchase or sale of at least 15 different stocks with a total value of $1 million or more.

Of the program total on the NYSE, 7.6% involved stock-index arbitrage. In this strategy, traders dart between stocks and stock-index options and futures to capture fleeting price differences. An additional 0.7% involved derivative product-related strategies. Index arbitrage can be executed only in a stabilizing manner when the Dow Jones Industrial Average moves 190 points or more from its previous day's close.

Some 58.9% of program trading was executed by firms for their clients, while 35.1% was done for their own accounts, or principal trading. An additional 6.0% was designated as customer facilitation, in which firms use principal positions to facilitate customer trades.

Of the five most-active firms overall for the week, **Morgan Stanley** and **UBS** AG's UBS Warburg executed most of their program trading as principal for their own accounts. Deutsche Banc Alex. Brown, a unit of **Deutsche Bank** AG and **Bear Stearns** Cos. executed most of their program trading activity for customers, as agents. **Goldman Sachs Group** Inc. split its activity between its own accounts and those of its customers.

NYSE PROGRAM TRADING
Volume in millions of shares for the week ended Feb. 1, 2002

TOP 15 FIRMS	INDEX ARBITRAGE	DERIVATIVE-RELATED*	OTHER STRATEGIES	TOTAL
Morgan Stanley	15.1	.....	280.3	295.4
Deutsche Banc Alx Brn	10.7	.....	201.2	211.9
UBS Warburg	.....	0.2	207.3	207.5
Goldman Sachs	.....	.....	140.9	140.9
Bear Stearns	22.3	.....	108.5	130.8
Interactive Brokers	.....	.....	120.6	120.6
Credit Suisse First Boston	6.0	.....	109.4	115.4
RBC Dominion	26.2	.....	74.5	100.7
BNP Paribas Brkg. Srvs.	.....	.....	98.4	98.4
Helfant Group	.....	.....	96.3	96.3
Merrill Lynch	2.7	....	85.3	88.0
Spear Leeds	0.2	.....	82.0	82.2
Salomon Smith Barney	.....	.....	63.0	63.0
Lehman Brothers	6.0	14.7	39.1	59.8
CIBC World Markets	38.1	.....	17.5	55.6
OVERALL TOTAL	**154.0**	**15.1**	**1866.5**	**2035.6**

*Other derivative-related strategies besides index arbitrage
Source: New York Stock Exchange

Source: *The Wall Street Journal,* 8 February 2002. Printed with permission from *The Wall Street Journal,* Dow Jones & Co. Inc.

the proper direction. Panel A of Exhibit 22.13 compares the actual and theoretical levels of the nearest-term future contract for several stock indexes throughout the world, including the S&P 500 (SPX), Dow Jones Industrial (INDU), and the Nikkei 225 (NKY). Notice that the pricing errors on this particular day never exceeded four-tenths of 1 percent for any contract and was much lower than that in most markets. Panel B of Exhibit 22.13 details the calculation of the theoretical level of the March 2002 S&P 500 futures price. The display shows that the actual contract price (1,107.50) was virtually identical to its theoretical value (1,107.54), which can be computed as the

EXHIBIT 22.13 ▸   *ACTUAL AND THEORETICAL STOCK INDEX FUTURES PRICES*

A. Mispricing in Stock Index Futures Contracts Throughout the World

1) North America	Cash	Future	Theo. Future	Fair Value	Spread Basis	Percent Misprice
4) SPH2vsSPX	1107.50	1108.00	1107.54	.04	.50	+.042%
5) YXH2vsNYA	571.48	571.75	571.28	−.20	.27	+.082%
6) DJH2vsINDU	9863.74	9855.00	9851.93	−11.81	−8.74	+.031%
7) MDH2vsMID	500.94	501.20	501.15	.21	.26	+.010%
8) NDH2vsNDX	1464.76	1471.00	1467.20	2.44	6.24	+.259%
9) PTH2vsSPTSE	430.47	430.00	430.21	−.26	−.47	−.048%
2) Europe						
10) Q H2vsE100	2736.74	2738.50	2736.73	−.01	1.76	+.065%
11) Z H2vsUKX	5135.70	5118.50	5119.31	−16.39	−17.20	−.016%
12) CFG2vsCAC	4337.95	4341.00	4345.18	7.23	3.05	−.096%
13) GXH2vsDAX	4884.78	4884.50	4899.71	14.93	−.28	−.310%
14) SMH2vsSMI	6253.30	6264.00	6262.83	9.53	10.70	+.019%
15) EOG2vsAEX	489.86	490.50	490.09	.23	.64	+.084%
3) Asia/Pacific						
16) NKH2vsNKY	9877.99	9840.00	9875.17	−2.82	−37.99	−.356%
17) NIH2vsNKY	9877.99	9840.00	9875.17	−2.82	−37.99	−.356%
18) TPH2vsTPX	974.10	970.00	973.88	−.22	−4.10	−.399%
19) XPH2vsAS51	3481.10	3472.00	3460.82	−20.28	−9.10	+.323%

B. Calculating the March 2002 S&P 500 Futures Contract Price

S&P 500 INDEX	Cash	Future	Theo. Future	Fair Value	Spread (Basis)	Upper Bound	Lower Bound
SPH2vsSPX	1107.50	1107.50	1107.54	.04	.00	1.20	−1.12
Risk Free:	1.89%	Expire: 3/15/02		Dividend: 1.88		Dvd Yld: 1.86%	
Implied Rate:	1.85%	Days: 33		Percent of Gross Dividend: 100.0%			

spot price (1,107.50) plus the net cost of carry (1,107.50 × (0.0189 − 0.0186) × (33/365)). These values support the notion that the market for stock index futures is an efficient one.

The empirical evidence tends to support this view, particularly after transaction costs and other trading realities are considered. Cornell, for instance, found that stock index futures prices tracked their model values more closely as the market matured, although Keim and Smirlock detected some temporal (i.e., day-of-the-week, January) pricing patterns.[17] In response to the allegation that index arbitrage caused the worldwide stock market crash of October 1987, Roll documented that countries with the greatest level of program trading activity experienced

---

[17]Bradford Cornell, "Taxes and the Pricing of Stock Index Futures: Empirical Results." *Journal of Futures Markets* 5, no. 1 (1985): 89–101; and Donald B. Keim and Michael Smirlock, "Pricing Patterns in Stock Index Futures," in *The Handbook of Stock Index Futures and Options,* ed. F. Fabozzi and G. Kipnis (Homewood, Ill.: Dow Jones–Irwin, 1989).

less-pronounced price declines.[18] This finding is consistent with the notion that index arbitrage reduces volatility by stabilizing cash and futures prices.

A Stock Index Futures Application

Isolating the Unsystematic Risk of an Individual Stock   In Chapter 21, we demonstrated how stock index futures could alter the systematic risk of an otherwise well-diversified portfolio. When the holding is an individual stock, this process can isolate the unique attributes of the company. Recall from Chapter 1 that:

$$\text{Total Stock Risk} = \text{Systematic Risk} + \text{Unsystematic Risk}$$

with the systematic component representing about 25–40 percent of the total risk for the typical firm. Thus, using stock index futures to adjust the stock's beta to zero effectively isolates the unsystematic portion of risk.

To see how this might work, suppose that in mid-August you own 75,000 shares of Merck, a multinational pharmaceutical firm. The current price of Merck stock is $46.75, and you calculate the company's beta at 0.99. You like the stock as an investment because of the quality of its management and some other unique attributes of the firm, but you are concerned that over the next few months the aggregate stock market might undergo a sizable correction that could more than offset any firm-specific gains.

To protect yourself, you decide to sell December S&P 500 futures contracts, which are currently trading at a settlement price of 1,271.10. At this price, we have seen that the implied dollar value of a single contract is $317,775. The current value of your Merck stock is $3,506,250. Since the stock's beta can be defined as $\rho[\sigma_{\Delta S} \div \sigma_{\Delta F}]$ the optional hedge ratio formula developed earlier can be adapted to provide the appropriate hedge ratio:

$$N^* = \left[\frac{\text{Market Value of Spot Position}}{\text{Value Implied by Futures Contract}} \right] \beta$$

$$= [(\$3,506,250) \div (\$317,775)](0.99) = 10.92$$

so you decide to short 11 contracts.

Now suppose that by mid-December when your futures position expires, the S&P 500 index settles at a level of 1,251.10 while the price of Merck stock has increased to 47.50. Although you have made a modest profit on your common stock holding (i.e., $56,250, or 1.60 per cent), you will also benefit from a trading profit on the futures position of $55,000 (= (11) [1,271.10 – 1,251.10](250)). As a result, your total return is $111,250, which, expressed as a percentage of your original investment of $3,506,250 is equivalent to an unsystematic appreciation in Merck's stock of 3.17 percent. Notice in this case that the difference between this amount and the gross increase of 1.60 percent in Merck stock is equal to the 1.57 percent (= [1,251.1 ÷ 1,271.1] – 1) that the stock index future position fell.

Currency Forwards and Futures

Whether in the spot or forward markets, foreign exchange (FX) transactions often involve a confusing blend of unique terminology and market conventions. Although these conventions are easily assimilated, they represent an initial barrier to understanding how FX deals work. Thus, we begin our analysis of currency derivatives with a brief overview of some of the fundamental features of these products.

---

[18]Richard Roll, "The International Crash of October 1987," *Financial Analysts Journal* 44, no. 5 (September–October 1988): 19–35.

The Mechanics of Currency Transactions

The market for foreign currency is no different than any other market in that buyer and seller negotiate for the exchange of a certain amount of a predetermined commodity at a fixed cash price. The challenge in FX transactions is that the "commodity" involved is someone else's currency. This means that the transaction can be viewed in two ways. For example, suppose that Company A agrees to pay 100 U.S. dollars to Company B in exchange for 67 British pounds. In this case, is Company A buying sterling (GBP) or selling dollars (USD)?[19] Similarly, is Company B selling pounds or buying dollars? The answer is that both are correct, depending on one's point of view.

Because of this dual interpretation, the price for all FX transactions also can be quoted in two ways. Assuming that Company A is a U.S.-based firm, it would probably think of the transaction as the purchase of 67 pounds at a cost of 100 dollars, which would yield the price of USD 1.4925/GBP (= 100/67). This method of quoting FX prices is called the *direct,* or *American,* convention. Notice that under this convention, the pound (i.e. the foreign currency from the U.S. firm's perspective) is treated as the commodity, and its price per unit is expressed in terms of dollars. On the other hand, if Company B is a British corporation, its managers would likely think of prices in terms of the amount of sterling they have to pay to acquire dollars. Here, that amount translates into a price of GBP 0.67/USD. Treating the dollar as the commodity yields the *indirect,* or *European,* quotation method. Of course, the direct and indirect quotes are just *reciprocals* of one another, as they describe the same transaction from two different perspectives.

Exhibit 22.14 shows a representative set of FX quotes. Four prices are listed beside each currency. The first two columns report the current and previous days' dollar price, respectively, for trading one unit of that currency (i.e., direct quotes). For instance, the prevailing price of a Norwegian krone on that date was USD 0.1114, which was 0.05 cent higher than the day before. The last two columns express these same prices in indirect terms (e.g., NOK 8.975/USD = 1 ÷ USD 0.1114/NOK). Thus, the terms of a spot FX transaction can be structured to meet the particular needs of the counterparties involved.

Another important aspect of the FX markets highlighted by this display is that although many currencies trade in the spot market, relatively few also quote prices for forward transactions. In this list, only the British, Canadian, Japanese, and Swiss currencies have forward contracts. These contracts, which are negotiated in the over-the-counter market with a currency dealer (such as a multinational bank), carry maturities one, three, and six months into the future. For example, an investor wishing to buy Swiss francs would pay USD 0.5918 per franc if the transaction were completed immediately, 0.5919 if the transaction were negotiated now but consummated in 30 days, and USD 0.5920 or USD 0.5925 for exchanges completed in 90 or 180 days, respectively.

In the situation where it costs increasingly more dollars to buy the same franc the farther out in the future it is delivered, the dollar is said to be trading at a **forward discount** to the franc. Conversely, the franc is at a **forward premium** to the dollar. Notice that this relationship depends on the currencies being compared. In this set of quotes, the U.S. dollar is trading at a forward discount to the Swiss franc and the Japanese yen, while it is at a forward premium to the Canadian dollar and the British pound. It should come as no surprise by now that the relationship between the spot and forward FX rates is not a random one. In fact, we will see shortly that whether a particular currency trades at a discount or a premium to another depends on the relative level of the investment rates in the two countries.

---

[19]Currency traders often use three-letter abbreviations to denote a particular currency. Some of the more common abbreviations include USD (U.S. dollars), CAD (Canadian dollars), GBP (British pounds), JPY (Japanese yen), CHF (Swiss franc), and EUR (the Euro currency). For a more complete listing, see Gary L. Gastineau and Mark P. Kritzman, *Dictionary of Financial Risk Management* (New Hope, Penn.: Frank Fabozzi Associates, 1996).

EXHIBIT 22.14 ► SPOT AND FORWARD CURRENCY QUOTATIONS

EXCHANGE RATES

The New York foreign exchange mid-range rates below apply to trading among banks in amounts of $1 million and more, as quoted at 4 p.m. Eastern time by Reuters and other sources. Retail transactions provide fewer units of foreign currency per dollar. Rates for the 12 Euro currency countries are derived from the latest dollar-euro rate using the exchange ratios set 1/1/99.

Country	U.S. $ EQUIV.		CURRENCY PER U.S. $	
	Thu	Wed	Thu	Wed
Argentina (Peso)-y	.4819	.4819	2.0750	2.0750
Australia (Dollar)	.5091	.5086	1.9641	1.9660
Austria (Schilling)	.06329	.06306	15.800	15.857
Bahrain (Dinar)	2.6525	2.6525	.3770	.3770
Belgium (Franc)	.0216	.0215	46.3198	46.4879
Brazil (Real)	.4062	.4100	2.4620	2.4390
Britain (Pound)	1.4141	1.4120	.7072	.7082
1-month forward	1.4118	1.4097	.7083	.7094
3-months forward	1.4067	1.4048	.7109	.7118
6-months forward	1.3996	1.3977	.7145	.7155
Canada (Dollar)	.6253	.6230	1.5993	1.6052
1-month forward	.6252	.6229	1.5996	1.6055
3-months forward	.6249	.6227	1.6002	1.6060
6-months forward	.6247	.6224	1.6008	1.6067
Chile (Peso)	.001455	.001454	687.15	687.95
China (Renminbi)	.1208	.1208	8.2766	8.2767
Colombia (Peso)	.0004409	.0004428	2268.00	2258.30
Czech. Rep. (Koruna)				
Commercial rate	.02740	.02729	36.499	36.649
Denmark (Krone)	.1173	.1168	8.5278	8.5595
Ecuador (US Dollar)-e	1.0000	1.0000	1.0000	1.0000
Finland (Markka)	.1465	.1459	6.8271	6.8519
France (Franc)	.1328	.1323	7.5319	7.5593
Germany (Mark)	.4453	.4437	2.2458	2.2539
Greece (Drachma)	.002556	.002547	391.22	392.59
Hong Kong (Dollar)	.1282	.1282	7.7993	7.7997
Hungary (Forint)	.003567	.003550	280.34	281.66
India (Rupee)	.02055	.02055	48.670	48.660
Indonesia (Rupiah)	.0000974	.0000969	10270	10325
Ireland (Punt)	1.1058	1.1018	.9043	.9076
Israel (Shekel)	.2144	.2160	4.6640	4.6300
Italy (Lira)	.0004498	.0004482	2223.30	2231.37
Japan (Yen)	.007480	.007480	133.69	133.69
1-month forward	.007491	.007490	133.50	133.50
3-months forward	.007514	.007513	133.08	133.09
6-months forward	.007553	.007552	132.40	132.42

Country	U.S. $ EQUIV.		CURRENCY PER U.S. $	
	Thu	Wed	Thu	Wed
Jordan (Dinar)	1.4104	1.4104	.7090	.7090
Kuwait (Dinar)	3.2468	3.2468	.3080	.3080
Lebanon (Pound)	.0006606	.0006606	1513.75	1513.75
Malaysia (Ringgit)-b	.2632	.2632	3.8000	3.8000
Malta (Lira)	2.1867	2.1820	.4573	.4583
Mexico (Peso)				
Floating rate	.1092	.1098	9.1590	9.1090
Netherlands (Guilder)	.3952	.3938	2.5304	2.5396
New Zealand (Dollar)	.4173	.4173	2.3964	2.3964
Norway (Krone)	.1114	.1109	8.9750	9.0154
Pakistan (Rupee)	.01663	.01663	60.150	60.150
Peru (new Sol)	.2869	.2870	3.4850	3.4845
Philippines (Peso)	.01953	.01951	51.200	51.250
Poland (Zloty)-d	.2363	.2334	4.2323	4.2837
Portugal (Escudo)	.004344	.004328	230.20	231.04
Russia (Ruble)-a	.03252	.03252	30.752	30.752
Saudi Arabia (Riyal)	.2666	.2666	3.7504	3.7504
Singapore (Dollar)	.5464	.5459	1.8303	1.8320
Slovak Rep. (Koruna)	.02056	.02044	48.628	48.926
South Africa (Rand)	.0884	.0870	11.3150	11.5000
South Korea (Won)	.0007615	.0007624	1313.20	1311.70
Spain (Peseta)	.005234	.005215	191.05	191.74
Sweden (Krona)	.0942	.0942	10.6127	10.6148
Switzerland (Franc)	.5918	.5896	1.6899	1.6962
1-month forward	.5919	.5896	1.6896	1.6960
3-months forward	.5920	.5899	1.6891	1.6953
6-months forward	.5925	.5903	1.6878	1.6940
Taiwan (Dollar)	.02859	.02860	34.980	34.970
Thailand (Baht)	.02281	.02275	43.840	43.965
Turkey (Lira)-f	.00000074	.00000075	1345500	1327500
United Arab (Dirham)	.2723	.2723	3.6730	3.6730
Uruguay (New Peso)				
Financial	.06885	.06920	14.525	14.450
Venezuela (Bolivar)	.001268	.001287	788.51	777.00
SDR	1.2418	1.2432	.8053	.8044
Euro	.8709	.8678	1.1482	1.1523

Special Drawing Rights (SDR) are based on exchange rates for the U.S., German, British, French, and Japanese currencies. Source: International Monetary Fund.
a-Russian Central Bank rate. b-Government rate. d-Floating rate; trading band suspended on 4/11/00. e-Adopted U.S. dollar as of 9/11/00. f-Floating rate, eff. Feb. 22. y-Floating rate.

Source: *The Wall Street Journal,* 8 February 2002. Printed with permission from *The Wall Street Journal,* Dow Jones & Co. Inc.

Exhibit 22.15 lists quotes for a sample of exchange-traded currency futures contracts. These specific instruments are traded at the International Monetary Market at the CME. Each contract follows the convention that the U.S. dollar is the native monetary unit and the foreign currency is the commodity, meaning that all prices are quoted using the direct method. Also, notice that these contracts are standardized to deliver a set number of units of the foreign currency on a specific date in the future. For instance, the March Mexican peso contract negotiated on that date required the long position to purchase—and the short position to deliver—500,000 pesos at the price of USD 0.10853 per peso. By convention, all currency futures on the IMM mature on the third Wednesday of the stated delivery month and can be settled with a wire transfer of the foreign currency. Notice that the dollar traded at a substantial forward premium to the peso at this point in time.

Interest Rate Parity and Covered Interest Arbitrage   A key concept in FX risk management is **interest rate parity**, a condition that specifies the "no-arbitrage" relationship between spot and forward FX rates (as priced into the futures contracts) and the level of interest rates in each currency. This connection is best seen through an example. Suppose that an institutional investor has USD 100,000 to invest for one year and is considering two different riskless alternatives. The first strategy entails the purchase of a U.S. Treasury bill. Assume that under current market conditions, the effective U.S. dollar risk-free interest rate is 4.50 percent per

EXHIBIT 22.15 ▶ *CURRENCY FUTURES QUOTATIONS*

```
Japan Yen (CME)-12.5 million yen; $ per yen (.00)
Mar    .7496  .7513  .7468  .7505  + .0003  .8760  .7416  107,710
June   .7538  .7545  .7506  .7540  + .0003  .8776  .7453   20,989
Est vol 5,573; vol Wed 8,654; open int 129,162, −109.
Canadian Dollar (CME)-100,000 dlrs.; $ per Can $
Mar    .6220  .6259  .6215  .6253  + .0023  .6725  .6170   62,967
June   .6233  .6256  .6213  .6251  + .0023  .6700  .6180    4,124
Sept   .6235  .6255  .6233  .6253  + .0023  .6590  .6175    1,457
Dec    .6230  .6255  .6230  .6256  + .0023  .6555  .6190    1,100
Est vol 8,476; vol Wed 9,455; open int 69,753, +1,713.
British Pound (CME)-62,500 pds.; $ per pound
Mar   1.4110 1.4120 1.4036 1.4108 + .0010 1.4700 1.3810   32,415
June  1.4014 1.4044 1.3970 1.4024 + .0010 1.4550 1.3910      162
Est vol 4,989; vol Wed 4,750; open int 32,577, −712.
Swiss Franc (CME)-125,000 francs; $ per franc
Mar    .5898  .5927  .5874  .5918  + .0015  .6370  .5540   44,478
June   .5899  .5928  .5880  .5921  + .0015  .6320  .5813      304
Est vol 5,204; vol Wed 7,334; open int 44,817, +189.
Australian Dollar (CME)-100,000 dlrs.; $ per A.$
Mar    .5072  .5080  .5040  .5068  − .0003  .5300  .4810   21,427
June   .5021  .5049  .5017  .5040  − .0003  .5218  .4885      500
Est vol 1,046; vol Wed 1,824; open int 21,953, −98.
Mexican Peso (CME)-500,000 new Mex. peso, $ per MP
Mar    .10910 .10918 .10810 .10853 − 00055 .10953 .09770   31,363
June   .10705 .10705 .10640 .10670 − 00055 .10750 .09730    2,590
Sept   .10505 .10510 .10450 .10473 − 00060 .10538 .09930    1,238
Est vol 6,729; vol Wed 6,553; open int 35,267, +801.
Euro FX (CME)-Euro 125,000; $ per Euro
Mar    .8663  .8704  .8633  .8697  + .0024  .9630  .8336  103,276
June   .8622  .8671  .8605  .8666  + .0023  .9275  .8365    4,114
Dec    .8580  .8610  .8580  .8623  + .0021  .9175  .8390      238
Est vol 14,931; vol Wed 21,615; open int 107,721, −93.
```

Source: *The Wall Street Journal,* 8 February 2002. Printed with permission from *The Wall Street Journal,* Dow Jones & Co. Inc.

annum for a one-year maturity, so that a direct T-bill investment would return USD 104,500 at the end of the 12 months.

For the second strategy, suppose that the investor also can sell the USD 100,000 in the spot market at the current exchange rate of CAD 1.70/USD (or, equivalently, USD 0.5882/CAD) to obtain a total of 170,000 Canadian dollars. We assume that that amount can then be invested in a Canadian risk-free security at an annualized rate of 7.00 percent, returning CAD 181,900 at the end of the year. Of course, to make this return comparable to the USD-denominated proceeds from the first strategy, the Canadian dollars will have to be converted back into U.S. currency. If this translation is negotiated at the end of the investment, however, the investor will be subjected to foreign exchange risk in that he will not know at Date 0 what the CAD/USD exchange rate will be at Date *T*. Thus, to make the second strategy riskless, the investor must enter into a forward contract to exchange CAD back into USD at the end of the year. The question then is, What would the exchange rate priced into a one-year forward contract have to be at Date 0 to leave the investor indifferent between these two strategies?

These investments are depicted in Exhibit 22.16. The essence of the arbitrage argument is that the one-year forward FX rate must be such that USD 104,500 equals CAD 181,900. Otherwise, an arbitrage opportunity would exist, or at least a dominating investment choice. Therefore, the forward contract rate consistent with interest rate parity is CAD 1.7407/USD (= 181,900 ÷ 104,500) on an indirect basis, or USD 0.5745/CAD quoted directly. Notice that this is a breakeven value in the sense that it allows the 4.50 percent investment return in the United States to be equal to the 7.00 percent available in Canada when the two are converted to the same currency. That is, the Canadian return must be "deflated" by 250 basis points to leave the investor indifferent between the two strategies. This reduction occurs because, to invest in the CAD-denominated security, the investor buys Canadian dollars at a price of USD 0.5882/CAD but must sell them back in the forward market at the lower price of USD 0.5745/CAD. Thus, the

EXHIBIT 22.16 *INTEREST RATE PARITY*

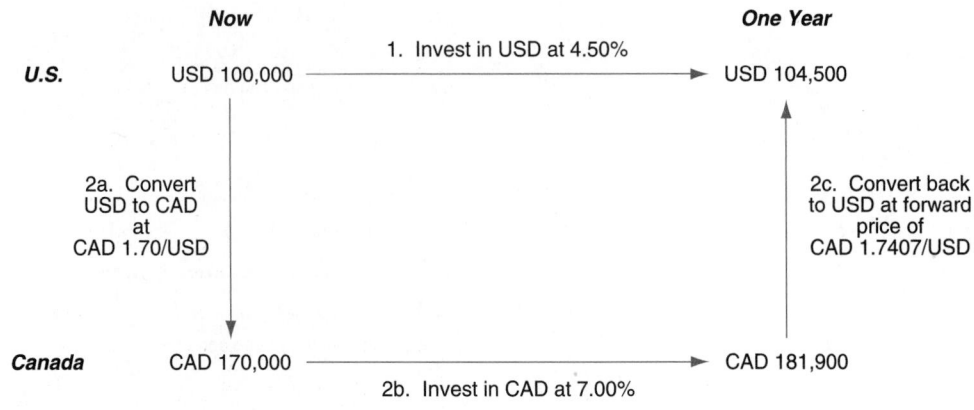

loss on the round-trip currency translation required in the second strategy adjusts its net return down to the 4.50 percent available on the direct U.S. dollar investment.[20]

If the actual one-year forward contract FX rate were higher than this breakeven level—say, for instance, CAD 1.77/USD—the currency translation loss would be greater than 250 basis points, leaving the USD-based strategy the more profitable choice. Given that there is now a difference between the returns to two otherwise comparable riskless investments, arbitrage is possible. In this case, an arbitrageur could enter the following transactions:

1. Borrow CAD 170,000 at 7.00 percent; agree to repay CAD 181,900 in one year.
2. Sell the foreign currency on the spot market at CAD 1.70/USD; receive USD 100,000.
3. Invest the USD 100,000 at 4.50 percent; receive USD 104,500 in one year.
4. Sell USD 104,500 forward at CAD 1.77/USD; agree to receive CAD 184,965.
5. Repay the CAD loan; collect net profit of CAD 3,065.

If, on the other hand, the actual one-year forward rate were lower than breakeven—for instance, CAD 1.71/USD—the arbitrageur would implement the opposite trade:

1. Borrow USD 100,000 at 4.50 percent; agree to repay USD 104,500 in one year.
2. Sell the U.S. dollars on the spot market at CAD 1.70/USD; receive CAD 170,000.
3. Invest the CAD 170,000 at 7.00 percent; receive CAD 181,900 in one year.
4. Buy USD 104,500 forward at CAD 1.71/USD; agree to pay CAD 178,695.
5. Repay the U.S. dollar loan; collect net profit of CAD 3,205.

These strategies are known as **covered interest arbitrage** because the arbitrageur will always hold the security denominated in the currency that is the least expensive to deliver in the forward market. In this sense, the arbitrage position is hedged, or covered, against adverse foreign exchange movements while receiving the largest amount of net interest income. In practice, traders involved in covered interest arbitrage strategies utilize bank rates (e.g., LIBOR) for borrowing and lending, which injects a slight amount of credit risk into the scheme. After surveying the empirical evidence, Solnik has concluded that the ability to take these arbitrage positions

---

[20]Under these conditions, the actual currency loss is calculated as $0.5745/0.5882 - 1 = -2.33$ percent. This, in turn, means the USD-denominated return to the second strategy is $(1 + 0.07) \times (1 - 0.0233) - 1 = 4.50$ percent.

keeps interest rate parity a viable description of the way spot and forward prices are set for the world's major currencies.[21]

With exchange rates quoted on an *indirect basis* (i.e., foreign currency [FC] per U.S. dollar), the general formula for the forward rate implied by interest rate parity is

$$\text{Forward} = \text{Spot} \times \left(\frac{1 + (\text{Foreign Interest Rate})\left(\dfrac{T}{365}\right)}{1 + (\text{U.S. Interest Rate})\left(\dfrac{T}{365}\right)} \right)$$

where:

T = the number of days from the joint settlement of the futures and cash positions until they mature

In the last example, $T = 365$ so that CAD 1.7407/USD = CAD 1.70/USD $\times$ (1.07/1.045). This formula also assumes that the rates in question are quoted on a 365-day basis. If U.S. money market rates such as LIBOR are used, then the equation should be adjusted to a 360-day year.

Letting S_0 and $F_{0,T}$ once again denote the current spot and forward prices for an instrument that matures at Date T, the preceding expression can be rewritten as

➤22.9

$$\frac{F_{0,T}}{S_0} = \left(\frac{1 + (RFR_{\text{FC}})\left(\dfrac{T}{365}\right)}{1 + (RFR_{\text{USD}})\left(\dfrac{T}{365}\right)} \right)$$

where:

RFR_{USD} = the annualized risk-free rate in the United States
RFR_{FC} = the annualized risk-free rate in the foreign market

Equation 22.9 defines the relationship between four different prices, all of which are determined at Date 0: spot foreign exchange rate, forward foreign exchange rate, U.S. investment rate, and foreign investment rate. Importantly, notice that, if the markets are aligned properly, $F_{0,T}$ will be greater than S_0 whenever RFR_{FC} is greater than RFR_{USD}, with the opposite holding when $RFR_{\text{FC}} < RFR_{\text{USD}}$. With indirect currency quotes, $F_{0,T} > S_0$ implies that the foreign currency is at a forward discount to the dollar. In other words, the country with the *lowest* investment rate should see its currency trade at a forward premium. The intuition behind this is that to keep investment capital from flowing to the country with the highest returns, the currency translation must adjust accordingly. Thus, the high-interest country will suffer from a weaker forward value for its currency.[22]

A Currency Futures Application

Calculating Implied World Investment Rates   Suppose that you are the cash manager for a multinational company and you have $1,000,000 in short-term balances that you can invest in

---

[21]Bruno Solnik, *International Investments,* 4th ed. (Reading, Mass.: Addison-Wesley Publishing, 1999).

[22]When using direct quotes (i.e., USD/FC), the interest rate parity condition must be adjusted by taking the reciprocal of the ratio on the left-hand side: $[S_0 \div F_{0,T}] = [(1 + RFR_{\text{FC}} (T \div 365)) \div (1 + RFR_{\text{USD}} (T \div 365))]$. In the example given, with the direct quotes for the spot and forward being USD 0.5882/CAD (= 1/1.70) and USD 0.5745/CAD, respectively, we have $S_0 =$ USD 0.5882/CAD = USD 0.5745/CAD $\times$ (1.07/1.045).

sovereign-issued paper for the next four months. On Thursday, February 7, 2002, you obtain the following quotes for both spot and futures exchange rates for several currencies:

CURRENCY	SPOT (USD/FC)	JUNE 2002 FUTURES (USD/FC)
Australian dollar	0.5091	0.5040
Japanese yen	0.007480	0.007540
Swiss franc	0.5918	0.5921
Canadian dollar	0.6253	0.6251
British pound	1.4141	1.4024
Mexican peso	0.1092	0.1067

If you enter into any of these transactions, they will settle on Monday, February 11 (i.e., two business days later). The futures contracts mature on Wednesday, June 19 2002, which leaves a 128-day investment window from settlement to maturity.

You also observe that a U.S. Treasury bill maturing at virtually the same time (i.e., June 20) pays a bond equivalent (i.e., 365-day) yield of 1.73 percent. Before checking the actual quotes for foreign-currency-denominated government paper from these other countries, you first calculate the investment rates implied by the interest rate parity relationship. Specifically, for the six countries listed, you compute:

$$\text{Implied Rate} = \left[\left(\frac{\text{Spot}}{\text{Futures}}\right)\left(1 + (\text{U.S. Interest Rate})\left(\frac{128}{365}\right)\right) - 1\right]\left(\frac{365}{128}\right)$$

which is just the parity relationship rearranged to use direct currency quotes and to isolate the foreign interest rate. Notice that the direct parity formulation is the correct one to use because of the convention prevailing in the U.S. currency futures market. For British sterling, this calculation yields an implied 128-day annualized investment rate of:

$$\left[\left(\frac{1.4141}{1.4024}\right)\left(1 + (0.0173)\left(\frac{128}{365}\right)\right) - 1\right]\left(\frac{365}{128}\right) = 0.04123 = 4.12\%$$

This means that with the current spot and futures prices for exchanging dollars and pounds, you would be indifferent between receiving a four-month investment rate of 1.73 percent in the United States or 4.12 percent in England.

Summarizing this calculation for all of the countries leaves:

COUNTRY	IMPLIED 128-DAY RATE
Australia	4.63%
Japan	−0.55
Switzerland	1.58
Canada	1.82
Great Britain	4.12
Mexico	8.45

You can now compare these figures to the actual investment rates in each of the countries to determine if a futures-based synthetic foreign bond strategy is warranted. If, for example, the actual British four-month gilt rate were 5.00 percent, you could exceed the 1.73 percent dollar-denominated T-bill return by (1) exchanging your dollars for pounds in the spot market at USD 1.4141/GBP, (2) investing for 128 days in the sterling-based security at 5.00 percent, and (3) translating your proceeds back into dollars at maturity using the futures rate of USD 1.4024/GBP.

Finally, notice that the countries with implied rates higher than 1.73 percent (i.e., Australia, Canada, Great Britain, and Mexico) are those whose currencies sold at a forward discount to the U.S. dollar over this 128-day window. Conversely, Japan and Switzerland had currencies at a forward premium to the dollar and thus had implied investment rates less than 1.73 percent. One caution necessary in interpreting these yields properly is that it is imperative that the futures and spot FX quotes were obtained simultaneously and pertain to the same investment denomination. In this example, these conditions were more than likely violated to some extent. [This, in fact, is the likely explanation for Japan's implied investment rate being negative (i.e., –0.55%), although Japan's actual short-term government rates were virtually zero at this time.]

The Internet *Investments Online*

Some sites that focus on the use of these derivative products include:

http://www.futuresmag.com *Futures Magazine*'s Web site features "hot market" analysis, technical analysis, and links to data and information about derivatives markets. It also provides free access to new, timely columns from industry experts, a Frequently Asked Questions section, a glossary of terms, and links to several articles that have appeared in the "Futures 101" section of *Futures Magazine*.

http://www.futuresbasics.com The Web site of Great Pacific Trading Company, which is a full service commodity brokerage offering services to beginning and advanced traders. Users can find links to good educational information concerning various aspects of futures trading, as well as access to economic reports and analyst opinions about current commodity futures positions.

http://www.futuresweb.com This Web site provides a broad array of fundamental and technical data about using and trading futures contracts. The "Market News" section contains timely information about commodity, currency, equity index, and interest rate contracts. Users can also find links detailing the specifications for a number of popular futures contracts as well as a glossary of useful terms.

http://tfc-charts.w2d.com The Web site of TFC Commodity Charts, a free source of daily commodity futures and financial market information. TFC tracks many commodities and financial indicators, making information available in both chart and quote form. Users are able to create their own personalized chart menu to gain quick access to the charts in which they are most interested. The site also includes futures discussion groups and many other educational materials.

Summary

• There is no question that forward and futures contracts have become an important feature of the modern investment landscape. As the most fundamental type of derivative instruments available, they greatly increase the alternatives that investors have to create and manage their portfolios and establish new trading opportunities. In this chapter, we discuss how these contracts work and the ways they are used in practice. As different mechanisms for accomplishing the same goals, forwards and futures differ primarily in the areas of design flexibility and collateralization. Specifically, forward agreements generally are more flexible but carry more credit risk, while the process of marking margin accounts to market on a daily basis makes futures contracts more secure (to the exchange, at least) even as the standardization of contract terms makes them less adaptable.

- We also show that hedging is key to understanding forward-based contracting and that the basis is the most important concept in understanding hedging. In particular, the basis, which is defined as the difference between spot and forward prices at any point in time, contains the essence of a short hedge position so that the hedger effectively trades the price risk of the underlying asset for the basis risk inherent in the spot-forward combination. This notion also leads to the calculation of an optimal hedge ratio, which specifies the appropriate number of contracts by minimizing the amount of basis (i.e., correlation) risk in the combined position.

- Although forward and futures contracts are not securities, their contract settlement prices still must follow certain regularities for these markets to remain efficient. For example, the cost of carry model suggests that in order to avoid arbitrage, the forward price should be equal to the spot price plus the cost of transporting the underlying asset to the future delivery date. These carrying costs can include commissions for physical storage, an opportunity cost for the net amount of invested capital, and a premium for the convenience of consuming the asset now. When forward prices are set in this manner, the market value of a new contract should be zero, although this value can become either positive or negative as the contract matures under changing market conditions.

- Finally, we illustrate these concepts with detailed examinations of three types of financial futures contracts: interest rate, equity index, and foreign exchange. In addition to describing the dynamics of each of these markets, we discuss different applications, including those involving hedging, speculation, and arbitrage. These applications produce some useful adaptations of the basic concepts, such as duration, and beta-based hedge ratios for interest rate and stock index futures as well as the currency futures version of the cost of carry model known as interest rate parity. Although no such list of applications could ever be complete, they should provide an understanding of why these instruments have become so important in financial markets.

Questions

1. We have futures contracts on Treasury bonds, but we do not have futures contracts on individual corporate bonds. We have cattle and hog futures but no chicken futures. Explain why the market has developed in this manner. What do you think are the most important characteristics for the success of a new futures contract concept?

2. "Hedgers trade price risk for basis risk." What is meant by this statement? In particular, explain the concept of the basis in a hedge transaction and how forward and futures contracts can be selected to minimize risk.

3. Suppose you are a derivatives trader specializing in creating customized commodity forward contracts for clients and then hedging your position with exchange-traded futures contracts. Your latest position is an agreement to deliver 100,000 gallons of unleaded gasoline to a client in three months.
   a. Explain how you can hedge your position using gasoline futures contracts.
   b. In calculating your hedge ratio, how must you account for the different valuation procedures used for forward and futures contracts? That is, what difference does it make that forward contracts are valued on a discounted basis while futures contracts are marked to market without discounting?
   c. If the only available gasoline futures contracts call for the delivery of 42,000 gallons and mature in either two or four months, describe the nature of the basis risk involved in your hedge.

4. A multinational corporation is about to embark on a major financial restructuring program. One critical stage will be the issuance of seven-year Eurobonds sometime within the next month. The CFO is concerned with recent instability in capital markets and with the particular event that market yields rise prior to issuance, forcing the corporation to pay a higher coupon rate on the bonds. It is decided to hedge that risk by selling 10-year Treasury note futures contracts. Notice that this is a classic cross hedge wherein 10-year Treasury notes are used to manage the risk of 7-year Eurobonds.

    Describe the nature of the basis risk in the hedge. In particular what specific events with respect to the shape of the Treasury yield curve and the Eurobond spread over Treasuries could render the hedge ineffective? In other words, under what circumstances would the hedge fail and make the corporation worse off?

5. *CFA Examination Level II*

   Mike Lane will have $5 million to invest in five-year U.S. Treasury bonds three months from now. Lane believes interest rates will fall during the next three months and wants to take advantage of prevailing interest rates by hedging against a decline in interest rates. Lane has sufficient bonds to pay the costs of entering into and maintaining a futures position.

   a. Describe what action Lane should take using five-year U.S. Treasury note futures contracts in protect against declining interest rates.

   Assume three months have gone by and, despite Lane's expectations, five-year cash and forward market interest rates have increased by 100 basis points compared with the five-year forward market interest rates of three months ago.

   b. Discuss the effect of higher interest rates on the value of the futures position that Lane entered into in Part a.

   c. Discuss how the return from Lane's hedged position differs from the return he could now earn if he had not hedged in Part a.

6. Eurodollar futures contracts are based on LIBOR, an add-on yield, while Treasury bill futures contracts are based on the T-bill rate, a discount yield. Despite different quotation conventions, these contracts use the same "discount" price index (100 – Yield). Explain the function of this price index and why the same design can be used for both contracts.

7. You own an equally weighted portfolio of 50 different stocks worth about $5,000,000. The stocks are from several different industries, and the portfolio is reasonably well diversified. Which do you think would provide you with the best overall hedge: a single position in an index futures or 50 different positions in futures contracts on the individual stocks? What are the most important factors to consider in making this decision.

8. *CFA Examination Level II*

   Four factors affect the value of a futures contract on a stock index. Three of these factors are: the current price of the stock index, the time remaining until the contract maturity (delivery) date, and the dividends on the stock index. Identify the fourth factor and explain how and why changes in this factor affect the value of the futures contract.

9. It is often stated that a stock index arbitrage trade is easier to implement when the stock index futures contract price is above its theoretical level than when it is below that value. What institutional realities might make this statement true? Describe the steps involved in forming the arbitrage transaction in both circumstances. To the extent that the statement is valid, what does it suggest about the ability of the stock index futures market to remain efficient?

10. *CFA Examination Level III*

    The World Ecosystem Consortium (WEC) pension trust holds $100 million in long-term U.S. Treasury bonds. To reduce interest rate risk, you, as an independent advisor to the WEC, suggest that the trust diversify by investing $30 million in German government bonds (bunds) for six months. You point out that a fixed-currency futures hedge (shorting a fixed number of contracts) could be used by WEC's pension trust to protect the $30 million in bunds against exchange rate losses over the six months.

    Explain how a fixed-currency futures hedge could be constructed for the WEC trust by shorting currency futures contracts to protect against exchange rate losses. Describe one characteristic of this hedge that WEC's investment committee might deem undesirable.

11. There are currency futures contracts that allow for the exchange of Mexican pesos and U.S. dollars, while other contracts allow for the exchange of Swiss francs and U.S. dollars. If I am an investor based in Zurich, explain how I could use these contracts to convert the payoff to a peso-denominated asset back into francs in two months.

12. Explain why the currency of Country A, whose interest rates are twice as great as those in Country B, must trade at a forward discount. If there were no difference between the spot and forward exchange rates in this interest rate environment, what arbitrage trade could be constructed to take advantage of the situation?

Problems

1. It is March 9, and you have just entered into a short position in a soybean meal futures contract. The contract expires on July 9 and calls for the delivery of 100 tons of soybean meal. Further, because this is a futures position, it requires the posting of a $3,000 initial margin and a $1,500 maintenance margin; for simplicity, however, assume that the account is marked to market on a monthly basis. Assume the following represent the contract delivery prices (in dollars per ton) that prevail on each settlement date:

March 9 (initiation)	$173.00
April 9	179.75
May 9	189.00
June 9	182.50
July 9 (delivery)	174.25

a. Calculate the equity value of your margin account on each settlement date, including any additional equity required to meet a margin call. Also compute the amount of cash that will be returned to you on July 9, and the gain or loss on your position, expressed as a percentage of your initial margin commitment.

b. Assuming that the underlying soybean meal investment pays no dividend and requires a storage cost of 1.5 percent (of current value), calculate the current (i.e., March 9) spot price for a ton of soybean meal and the implied May 9 price for the same ton. In your calculations, assume that an annual risk-free rate of 8 percent prevails over the entire contract life

c. Now suppose that on March 9 you also entered into a long forward contract for the purchase of 100 tons of soybean meal on July 9. Assume further that the July forward and futures contract prices always are identical to one another at any point in time. Calculate the cash amount of your gain or loss if you unwind both positions in their respective markets on May 9 and June 9, taking into account the prevailing settlement conditions in the two markets.

2. It is March 1, and you are a new derivatives trader making a market in forward contracts in Commodity W. One month ago (February 1), you began your operations with the following transactions, which are described from your perspective:

- With Client A: (1) Short a June 1 forward for 10,000 units at a contract price of $25.50/unit.
                  (2) Long a September 1 forward for 15,000 units at a contract price of $26.20/unit.
- With Client B: (3) Short a September 1 forward for 25,000 units at a contract price of $26.40/unit.

Your current (i.e., March 1) contract price quotes are as follows:

Contract	Bid	Ask
June	$24.95	$25.15
September	25.65	25.85

The appropriate discount is 9 percent per annum.

a. If Client A just called you wanting to unwind both of its contracts, calculate a fair cash amount that can be used in settlement today. Would you pay or receive this amount?

b. If these contracts had been exchange-traded futures contracts instead of OTC forward contracts, how would this settlement amount need to be adjusted (assuming the same March 1 contract prices)?

c. Calculate the dollar amount you would lose if Client B called you to default its contractual obligation. (Hint: Compute this amount in the same manner you calculated the net settlement in Part a.)

d. At the time you negotiated the three original agreements (i.e., February 1) did you have any price exposure on the September contracts? If so, what type of future price movements would be harmful to your net profit on the expiration date?

3. You are a coffee dealer anticipating the purchase of 82,000 pounds of coffee in three months. You are concerned that the price of coffee will rise, so you take a long position in coffee futures. Each contract covers 37,500 pounds, and so, rounding to the nearest contract, you decide to go long in two contracts. The futures price at the time you initiate your hedge is 55.95 cents per pound. Three months later, the actual spot price of coffee turns out to be 58.56 cents per pound and the futures price is 59.20 cents per pound.

   a. Determine the effective price at which you purchased your coffee. How do you account for the difference in amounts for the spot and hedge positions?

   b. Describe the nature of the basis risk in this long hedge.

4. *CFA Examination Level III*

   June Klein, CFA, manages a $100 million (market value) U.S. government bond portfolio for an institution. She anticipates a small parallel shift in the yield curve and wants to fully hedge the portfolio against any such change.

PORTFOLIO AND TREASURY BOND FUTURES CONTRACT CHARACTERISTICS

Security	Modified Duration	Basis Point Value	Conversion Factor for Cheapest to Deliver Bond	Portfolio Value/Future Contract Price
Portfolio	10 years	$100,000	Not Applicable	$100,000,000
U.S. Treasury bond futures contract	8 years	$75.32	1	94–05

   a. Discuss two reasons for using futures rather than selling bonds to hedge a bond portfolio. No calculations required.

   b. Formulate Klein's hedging strategy using only the futures contract shown. Calculate the number of futures contracts to implement the strategy. Show all calculations.

   c. Determine how each of the following would change in value if interest rates increase by 10 basis points as anticipated. Show all calculations.

      (1) The original portfolio

      (2) The Treasury bond futures position

      (3) The newly hedged portfolio

   d. State three reasons why Klein's hedging strategy might not fully protect the portfolio against interest rate risk.

   e. Describe a zero-duration hedging strategy using only the government bond portfolio and options on U.S. Treasury bond futures contracts. No calculations required.

5. The corporate treasurer of XYZ Corp. manages the firm's pension fund. On February 15, 1993, the treasurer is informed that the pension fund will be required to sell its $100 million (face value) Treasury bond portfolio on August 15, 1993, because of a pending change in the structure of the plan.

   The portfolio consists entirely of a single bond issue with a maturity date of August 2019. The bond pays coupons of 7¼ percent and is currently priced at 97–12. This corresponds to a yield of 7.479 percent. These T-bonds were originally purchased at par, so the current price reflects a modest capital loss. The treasurer is concerned that further weakness in the dollar could raise market rates and exacerbate this loss before the August sale date

   Your task is to construct a hedge using T-bond futures to offset, or at least reduce, the risk exposure. Assume an August 1993 futures contract exists with the quoted price of 101–04 and a reference yield to maturity of 7.887 percent (based on an 8 percent coupon and 20 years to maturity). To complete the task, construct a numerical example to show the optimal number of contracts necessary to provide the desired price protection.

   a. Assuming that interest rates do not change between February and August 1993, what will be the value of the T-bond portfolio? Briefly explain why this differs from the current value of $97.375 million.

b. As of August 1993, calculate the respective durations of the bond issue in the portfolio and the bond underlying the futures contract. Using the current yields to maturity, translate these into modified duration form. (Note: In your computation, recall that T-bonds pay semiannual interest.)

c. Assuming that the yield beta (β_r) between the instruments is equal to one, calculate the number of futures contracts required to form the optimal hedge. In this calculation, keep in mind that the face value of the bond underlying the futures contract is $100,000

6. A bond speculator currently has positions in two separate corporate bond portfolios: a long holding in Portfolio 1 and a short holding in Portfolio 2. All the bonds have the same credit quality. Other relevant information on these positions includes:

Portfolio	Bond	Market Value (Mil.)	Coupon Rate	Compounding Frequency	Maturity	Yield to Maturity
1	A	$ 6.0	0%	Annual	3 yrs	7.31%
	B	4.0	0	Annual	14 yrs	7.31
2	C	11.5	4.6	Annual	9 yrs	7.31

Treasury bond futures (based on $100,000 face value of 20-year T-bonds having an 8 percent semiannual coupon) with a maturity exactly six months from now are currently priced at 109–24 with a corresponding yield to maturity of 7.081 percent. The "yield betas" between the futures contract and Bonds A, B, and C are 1.13, 1.03, and 1.01, respectively. Finally, the modified duration for the T-bond underlying the futures contract is 10.355 years.

a. Calculate the modified duration (expressed in years) for each of the two bond portfolios. What will be the *approximate* percentage change in the value of each if all yields increase by 60 basis points on an annual basis?

b. Without performing the calculations, explain which of the portfolios will *actually* have its value impacted to the greatest extent (in absolute terms) by the shift yields. (Hint: This explanation requires knowledge of the concept of *bond convexity.*)

c. Assuming the bond speculator wants to hedge her *net* bond position, what is the optimal number of futures contracts that must be bought or sold? Start by calculating the optimal hedge ratio between the futures contract and the two bond portfolios separately and then combine them.

7. *CFA Examination Level II*

Susan Baker is an investor who seeks to find arbitrage pricing discrepancies in the marketplace over the next six months. She has noted the following data:

Instrument	Spot Price	Futures Price for Contract Expiring in Six Months	Income from Treasury Note for Six Months	Finance Charge for Six Months
U.S. Treasury note deliverable on the futures contract	$101	$100 (invoice price)	$4.50	$2.50

List the components of the arbitrage transaction and calculate the arbitrage profits, if any, that are available to exploit a possible pricing discrepancy. Show your calculations.

8. Consider a hypothetical Euromarket security simply called "paper" "Paper" trades and is quoted on a discount yield basis, the same as U.S. Treasury bills and commercial paper. Listed are the current rate quotes for "paper" issues of two different maturities, each having a face value of $100,000:

90-day	7.50%
180-day	7.50%

Suppose further that a futures market also exists in 90-day "paper" and that you have just obtained a quote on a contract that matures in exactly 90 days from now at 7.50 percent. Assuming you can either buy or sell any of these securities (including the futures contract) at the quoted rates, show that a financial arbitrage opportunity exists. Calculating the implied forward discount rate will be useful. Demonstrate the sequence of transactions necessary to generate this arbitrage profit and indicate how much profit you would make. In these calculations, you may ignore the marked to market effects on the futures contract, assuming the exchange will hold any long position as collateral instead of cash.

9. As a relationship officer for a money-center commercial bank, one of your corporate accounts has just approached you about a one-year loan for $1,000,000. The customer would pay a quarterly interest expense based on the prevailing level of LIBOR at the beginning of each three-month period. As is the bank's convention on all such loans, the amount of the interest payment would then be paid at the end of the quarterly cycle when the new rate for the next cycle is determined. You observe the following LIBOR yield curve in the cash market.

90-day LIBOR	4.60%
180-day LIBOR	4.75
270-day LIBOR	5.00
360-day LIBOR	5.30

a. If 90-day LIBOR rises to the levels "predicted" by the implied forward rates, what will the dollar level of the bank's interest receipt be at the end of each quarter during the one-year loan period?

b. If the bank wanted to hedge its exposure to failing LIBOR on this loan commitment, describe the sequence of transactions in the futures markets it could undertake.

c. Assuming the yields inferred from the Eurodollar futures contract prices for the next three settlement periods are equal to the implied forward rates, calculate the annuity value that would leave the bank indifferent between making the floating-rate loan and hedging it in the futures market, and making a one-year fixed-rate loan. Express this annuity value in both dollar and annual (360-day) percentage terms.

10. *CFA Examination Level III*

George Johnson is considering a possible six-month $100 million LIBOR-based, floating-rate bank loan to fund a project at the following terms. Johnson fears a possible rise in the LIBOR rate by December and wants to use the December Eurodollar futures contract to hedge this risk. The contract expires December 20, 1999, has a U.S. $1 million contract size, and a discount yield of 7.3 percent.

Johnson will ignore the cash flow implications of marking to market, initial margin requirements, and any timing mismatch between exchange-traded futures contract cash flows and the interest payments due in March.

LOAN TERMS

September 20, 1999	**December 20, 1999**	**March 20, 2000**
• Borrow $100 million at September 20 LIBOR+200 basis points (BPS) • September 20 LIBOR = 7%	• Pay interest for first three months • Roll loan over at December 20 LIBOR+200 BPS	• Pay back principal plus interest
Loan Initiated	First Loan Payment (9%) and Futures Contract Expires	Second Payment and Principal

a. Formulate Johnson's September 20 floating-to-fixed-rate strategy using the Eurodollar futures contracts discussed in the preceding text. Show that this strategy would result in a fixed-rate loan, assuming an increase in the LIBOR rate to 7.8 percent by December 20, which remains at 7.8 percent through March 20. Show all calculations.

Johnson is considering a 12-month loan as an alternative. This approach will result in two additional uncertain cash flows, as follows.

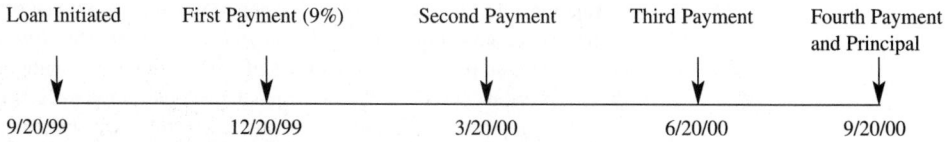

Loan Initiated	First Payment (9%)	Second Payment	Third Payment	Fourth Payment and Principal
9/20/99	12/20/99	3/20/00	6/20/00	9/20/00

b. Describe the strip hedge that Johnson could use and explain how it hedges the 12-month loan (specify number of contracts). No calculations needed.

11. Suppose that one day in early April, you observe the following prices on futures contracts maturing in June: 93.35 for Eurodollar and 94.07 for T-bill. These prices imply three-month LIBOR and T-bill settlement yields of 6.65 percent and 5.93, respectively. You think that over the next quarter the general level of interest rates will rise while the credit spread built into LIBOR will narrow. Demonstrate how you can use a TED (Treasury/Eurodollar) spread, which is a simultaneous long (short) position in a Eurodollar contract and short (long) position in the T-bill contract, to create a position that will benefit from these views.

12. An investment bank engages in stock index arbitrage for its own and customer accounts. On a particular day, the S&P index at the New York Stock Exchange is 602.25 when the futures contract for delivery in 90 days is 614.75. If the annualized 90-day interest rate is 8.00 percent and the (annualized) dividend yield is 3 percent, would program trading involving stock index arbitrage possibly take place? If so, describe the transactions that should be undertaken and calculate the profit that would be made per each "share" of the S&P 500 index used in the trade.

13. *CFA Examination Level III*

Alex Andrew, who manages a $95 million large-capitalization U.S. equity portfolio, currently forecasts that equity markets will decline soon. Andrew prefers to avoid the transactions costs of making sales but wants to hedge $15 million of the portfolio's current value using S&P 500 futures.

Because Andrew realizes that his portfolio will not track the S&P 500 index exactly, he performs a regression analysis on his actual portfolio returns versus the S&P futures returns over the past year. The regression analysis indicates a risk-minimizing beta of 0.88 with an R^2 of 0.92.

FUTURES CONTRACT DATA	
S&P 500 futures price	1,000
S&P 500 index	999
S&P 500 index multiplier	250

a. Calculate the number of futures contracts required to hedge $15 million of Andrews portfolio, using the data shown. State whether the hedge is long or short. Show all calculations.

b. Identify two alternative methods (other than selling securities from the portfolio or using futures) that replicates the feature strategy in Part a. Contract each of these methods with the futures strategy.

14. The treasurer of a middle market, import-export company has approached you for advice on how to best invest some of the firm's short-term cash balances. The company, which has been a client of the bank that employs you for a few years, has $250,000 that it is able to commit for a one-year holding period. The treasurer is currently considering two alternatives: (1) invest all the funds in a one-year U.S. Treasury bill offering a bond equivalent yield of 4.25 percent, and (2) invest all the funds in a Swiss government security over the same horizon, locking in the spot and forward currency

exchanges in the FX market. A quick call to the bank's FX desk gives you the following two-way currency exchange quotes.

	Swiss Francs per U.S. Dollar	U.S. Dollar per Swiss Franc
Spot	1.5035	0.6651
1-year CHF futures	—	0.6586

    a. Calculate the one-year bond equivalent yield for the Swiss government security that would support the interest rate parity condition

    b. Assuming the actual yield on a one-year Swiss government bond is 5.50 percent, which strategy would leave the treasurer with the greatest return after one year?

    c. Describe the transactions that an arbitrageur could use to take advantage of this apparent mispricing and calculate what the profit would be for a $250,000 transaction.

 15. *CFA Examination Level II*

Donna Doni, CFA, wants to explore potential inefficiencies in the futures market. The TOBEC stock index has a spot value of 185.00 now. TOBEC futures contracts are settled in cash, and underlying contract values are determined by multiplying $100 times the index value. The current annual risk-free interest rate is 6.0 percent.

    a. Calculate the theoretical price of the futures contract expiring six months from now, using the cost-of-carry model. Show your calculations.

      The total (round-trip) transaction cost for trading a futures contract is $15.00.

    b. Calculate the lower bound for the price of the futures contract expiring six months from now. Show your calculations.

References

Bautista, Carl, and Kris Mahabir. "Managing Risk and Capturing Opportunities with Derivative Securities." In *Fixed-Income Management: Techniques and Practices,* ed. D. Churchill. Charlottesville, Va.: Association for Investment Management and Research, 1994.

Chance, Don M. *An Introduction to Derivatives and Risk Management,* 5th ed. Fort Worth, Tex.: Harcourt College Publishers, 2001.

Duffie, Darrell. *Futures Markets.* Englewood Cliffs, N.J.: Prentice-Hall, 1989.

Hull, John C. *Options, Futures, and other Derivatives,* 4th ed. Upper Saddle River, N.J.: Prentice-Hall, 2000.

Kolb, Robert W. *Financial Derivatives.* Miami, Fla.: Kolb Publishing, 1993.

Siegel, Daniel, and Diane F. Siegel. *Futures Markets.* Hinsdale, Ill.: Dryden Press, 1990.

Smithson, Charles W., and Clifford W. Smith, Jr. *Managing Financial Risk,* 3d ed. New York: McGraw-Hill, 1998.

Telser, Lester G. "Futures Trading and the Storage of Cotton and Wheat." *Journal of Political Economy* 66 (June 1958).

Working, Holbrook. "Economic Functions of Futures Markets." In *Selected Writings of Holbrook Working.* Chicago, Ill.: Chicago Board of Trade, 1977.

APPENDIX
Chapter 22

A. A Closed-Form Equation for Calculating Duration

To calculate the duration statistic, it helps to think of a bond that pays a fixed coupon for a finite maturity as being just a portfolio of zero coupon cash flows. Duration is then the weighted average of the payment (i.e., maturity) dates of those zero coupon cash flows. What the duration statistic essentially does is convert a bond with any given coupon and maturity into what it would look like if it had been a zero coupon bond. Thus, a bond's duration is its *zero coupon equivalent maturity*.

    To see how this calculation works, consider a nonamortizing, five-year bond with a face value of $1,000 making annual coupon payments of $120 (i.e., 12 percent). Assuming a current yield to maturity

EXHIBIT 22A.1 *A DURATION CALCULATION*

Year	Cash Flow	PV at 10%	PV ÷ Price	Year × (PV ÷ Price)
1	$120	$ 109.09	0.1014	0.1014
2	120	99.17	0.0922	0.1844
3	120	90.16	0.0838	0.2514
4	120	81.96	0.0762	0.3047
5	$1,120	695.43	0.6464	3.2321
		Price = $1,075.82		Duration = 4.0740 years

of 10 percent, this bond will trade at a premium and its weighted average payment date (i.e., duration) is 4.074 years, as shown in Exhibit 22A.1. Interpreting the coupon bond as a portfolio of zero coupon cash flows, the duration of 4.0740 years is the weighted average maturity of that portfolio, where the weights are the respective shares of market value (e.g., the one-year zero coupon cash flow is 10.14 percent of the value of the portfolio, the five-year zero 64.64 percent).

This five-year coupon bond with a duration of 4.0740 years is "equivalent" in terms of price risk to a zero coupon bond having a maturity of 4.0740 years. As we saw in Chapter 19, this suggests that when the interest rate increases by 1 percent above its original level (i.e., $[\Delta (1 + i) \div (1 + i)] = 0.01$), then the price of this bond will decline by about 4.074 percent).

The Macaulay duration can be calculated with the following formula:

$$D = \dfrac{\dfrac{1 \times C}{\left(1+\dfrac{Y}{n}\right)^1} + \dfrac{2 \times C}{\left(1+\dfrac{Y}{n}\right)^2} + \dfrac{3 \times C}{\left(1+\dfrac{Y}{n}\right)^3} + \ldots + \dfrac{(n \times T) \times (C + F)}{\left(1+\dfrac{Y}{n}\right)^{n \times T}}}{\dfrac{C}{\left(1+\dfrac{Y}{n}\right)^1} + \dfrac{C}{\left(1+\dfrac{Y}{n}\right)^2} + \dfrac{C}{\left(1+\dfrac{Y}{n}\right)^3} + \ldots + \dfrac{(C + F)}{\left(1+\dfrac{Y}{n}\right)^{n \times T}}}$$

where:

> **C = the periodic coupon payment**
> **F = the face value at maturity**
> **T = the number of years until maturity**
> **n = the payments per year**
> **Y = the yield to maturity**

Note that the denominator of this equation is just P, the price of the security. The numerator is the present value of the cash flows weighted by the time the payment is made; the first by 1, the second by 2, and so forth. With some algebraic manipulation, this formula reduces to the following closed-form equation:

➤22A.1

$$D = \dfrac{1+\dfrac{Y}{n}}{\dfrac{Y}{n}} - \dfrac{1+\dfrac{Y}{n} + \left[(n \times T)\left(\dfrac{C}{F} - \dfrac{Y}{n}\right)\right]}{\dfrac{C}{F}\left[\left(1+\dfrac{Y}{n}\right)^{n \times T} - 1\right] + \dfrac{Y}{n}}$$

where

> **C/F = the coupon rate per period**

Note that the duration statistic in Equation 22A.1 is calculated on the basis of the underlying periodic cash flows even though it is often annualized when reporting the statistic by dividing it by n.

In the preceding numerical example, $Y = 0.10$, $n = 1$, $T = 5$, $C/F = 0.12$, and $Y/n = 0.10$. The bond's duration can therefore be solved as:

$$D = \frac{1+0.10}{0.10} - \frac{1+0.10+5(0.12-0.10)}{0.12[(1+0.10)^5 - 1]+0.10} = 4.0740$$

As a second example of this formula, what is the duration of a 30-year Treasury bond with a 7⅝ percent coupon and a stated yield to maturity of 7.72 percent? Here you need to recall that T-bonds pay semiannual interest and so the appropriate definitions of the variables are: $C/F = 0.38125$, $T = 30$, $n = 2$, and $Y/n = 0.0386$. Therefore:

$$D = \frac{1+0.0386}{0.0386} - \frac{1+0.0386+60(0.038125+0.0386)}{(0.038125)[(1+0.0386)^{60} - 1]+0.0386} = 24.18 \text{ Periods}$$

or 12.09 years. Although the method summarized by Exhibit 22A.1 always will work for any nonamortizing bond, the closed-form expression is considerably quicker when a large number of coupon payments are involved.

APPENDIX
Chapter 22

B. Calculating Money Market Implied Forward Rates

Implied forward rates are an essential factor in understanding how short-term interest rate futures contracts are priced. In our discussion of the expectations hypothesis of yield curve in Chapter 19, we saw that implied forward rates represented the sequence of future short-term rates that were built into the yield to maturity of a longer-term security. However, implied forward rates can have another interpretation. Consider an investor who is deciding between the following strategies for making a two-year investment: (1) buy a single two-year, zero coupon bond yielding 6 percent per annum; or (2) buy a one-year, zero coupon bond with a 5 percent yield and replace it at maturity with another one-year instrument. An implied forward rate is the answer to the following question: At what rate must the investor be able to reinvest the interim proceeds from the second strategy to exactly equal the total return from the first investment? In other words, the implied forward rate is a *breakeven* reinvestment rate. In the notation of Chapter 19, we want to solve for $_2r_1$ in the following equation:

$$(1 + 0.06)^2 = (1 + 0.05)(1 + {_2r_1})$$

or $_2r_1 = [(1 + 0.06)^2 \div (1 + 0.05)] - 1 = 7$ percent. An alternative interpretation is that investing for two years with a return of 6 percent per year is exactly the same as investing for one year at 5 percent, with the principal and interest then reinvested for a second year at 7 percent.

Implied forward money market rates can be interpreted in the same way as bond yields, but they must be calculated differently because of differences in the quotation methods for the various rates. For example, T-bill rates are quoted on a *discount yield* (DY) basis using the following pricing formula:

$$P = F - \left[F \times DY \times \frac{T}{360}\right] = F\left[1 - DY \times \frac{T}{360}\right]$$

where

    F = the face value of the underlying instrument
    P = the current price of the underlying instrument
    T = the number of days to maturity

For example, a Treasury bill with 91 days to maturity, a $10,000 face value, and a discount yield of 4.67 percent would sell for a current price of

$$P = \$10,000\left[1 - (0.0467) \times \frac{91}{360}\right] = \$9,881.95$$

On the other hand, we have seen that LIBOR is a bank *add-on yield* (AY) that is used to figure out how much money an investor will have at maturity given an initial investment of P (i.e., interest is "added on"):

$$F = P + \left[P \times AY \times \frac{T}{360} \right] = P \left[1 + AY \times \frac{T}{360} \right]$$

With this expression, a 60-day investment of $50,000 in a bank deposit paying LIBOR equal to 5.30 percent would be worth $50,441.67 at maturity. Notice that both the T-bill discount rate and LIBOR are based on a presumed 360-day year, the standard U.S. money market practice.

With these quotation conventions, Smith has shown that the implied forward rate between two money market instruments quoted on an add-on basis (e.g., LIBOR) can be calculated as

➤22B.1
$$_B AY_A = \left[\frac{(B \times AY_B) - (A \times AY_A)}{B - A} \right] \left[\frac{1}{1 + \left(\frac{A \times DY_A}{360} \right)} \right]$$

where AY_A and AY_B are add-on yields for A and B days from settlement to maturity, with $B > A$.[23] The implied forward rate ($_B AY_A$) also is on an add-on basis and has maturity of $(B - A)$ days. That is, $_B AY_A$ corresponds to the time period between Date A and Date B. For money market instruments quoted on a discount yield basis (e.g., T-bill), a slightly different formula applies:

➤22B.2
$$_B DY_A = \left[\frac{(B \times DY_B) - (A \times DY_A)}{B - A} \right] \left[\frac{1}{1 - \left(\frac{A \times DY_A}{360} \right)} \right]$$

where DY_A and DY_B are discount yields for A and B days from settlement to maturity, and $B > A$. The implied forward rate ($_A DY_B$) also is on a discount yield basis and has a maturity of $(B - A)$ days, assuming a 360-day year. Notice that these formulas have a common structure, differing only in that the add-on formula has a "plus" sign in the denominator of the second term while the discount yield has a "minus."

As an example of these calculations, consider the following short-term yield curves for T-bills and LIBOR:

Maturity	T-Bill	LIBOR
30 days	4.00%	4.15%
60 days	4.10	4.25
90 days	4.20	4.35

What is the implied forward T-bill rate between Days 30 and 60? Using $DY_A = 0.0400$, $DY_B = 0.0410$, $A = 30$ days, and $B = 60$ days for T-bills, we have:

$$_{60} DY_{30} = \left[\frac{(60 \times 0.0410) - (30 \times 0.0400)}{60 - 30} \right] \left[\frac{1}{1 - \left(\frac{30 \times 0.0400}{360} \right)} \right] = 4.21\%$$

This means that buying a 30-day T-bill at 4.00 percent and then again at 4.21 percent in another 30 days would have the same total return as the 60-day T-bill at 4.10 percent.

---

[23]Donald J. Smith, "The Calculation and Use of Money Market Implied Forward Rates," *Journal of Cash Management* 98, no. 5 (September/October 1989): 46–49.

As a second example, what is the implied forward LIBOR between Days 60 and 90? Using $AY_A = 0.0425$, $AY_B = 0.0435$, $A = 60$ days, and $B = 90$ days for LIBOR, we have:

$$_{90}AY_{60} = \left[\frac{(90 \times 0.0435) - (60 \times 0.0425)}{90 - 60} \right] \left[\frac{1}{1 - \left(\dfrac{60 \times 0.0425}{360} \right)} \right] = 4.52\%$$

That is, investing in a 60-day bank deposit at 4.25 percent and then a 30-day deposit at 4.52 percent would have the same total return (or cost of funds) as the 90-day deposit at 4.35 percent. This can be confirmed by examining the cash flows on the transactions. For example, the total return on a $100,000, 60-day deposit at 4.25 percent would be $100,708. This amount reinvested in a 30-day deposit at 4.52 percent would provide a total of $101,087, equaling the payoff on a $100,000, 90-day deposit at 4.35 percent.

Chapter 23 > Option Contracts

After you read this chapter, you should be able to answer the following questions:

➤ How are options traded on exchanges and in OTC markets?
➤ How are options for stock, stock indexes, foreign currency, and futures contracts quoted in the financial press?
➤ How can investors use option contracts to hedge an existing risk exposure?
➤ What are the three steps in establishing the fundamental "no-arbitrage" value of an option contract?
➤ What is the binomial (or two-state) option pricing model and in what way is it an extension of the basic valuation approach?
➤ What is the Black-Scholes option pricing model and how does it extend the binomial valuation approach?
➤ What is the relationship between the Black-Scholes and the put-call parity valuation models?
➤ How does the payment of a dividend by the underlying asset impact the value of an option?
➤ How can models for valuing stock options be adapted to other underlying assets, such as stock indexes, foreign currency, or futures contracts?
➤ How do American- and European-style options differ from one another?
➤ What is implied volatility and what is its role in the contract valuation process?
➤ What are exotic options and how are they valued?
➤ How do investors use options with the underlying security or in combination with one another to create payoff structures tailored to a particular need or view of future market conditions?
➤ What differentiates a spread from a straddle, a strangle, or a range forward?

Broken down to the most basic level, only two kinds of derivative contracts exist: forwards, which fix the price or rate of an underlying asset; and options, which allow holders to decide at a later date whether such a fixing is in their best interest. With our initial examination of forward and futures contracts now complete, this chapter turns our attention to issues concerning the trading and valuation of option contracts. We will develop the discussion in four parts. First, we will consider more closely the contract terms and trading mechanics for both call and put options. Options trade on exchanges as well as in the OTC dealer markets and can be based on a wide array of securities and commodities. To focus this discussion, we concentrate on options that have financial instruments as underlying securities, including options on individual stocks, stock indexes, foreign currency, and futures contracts. A formal discussion of options on interest rates is highlighted in the next chapter.

The second topic we explore is how option contracts are valued in an efficient capital market. We show that, at least intuitively, this can be viewed as a simple, three-step process: (1) creating a riskless hedge portfolio combining options with the underlying security, (2) invoking a no-arbitrage assumption about the rate of return that such a portfolio should earn, and (3) solving for the option value consistent with the first two steps. We show that several of the most widely used valuation models, including the **binomial** and the **Black-Scholes**, are consistent with this approach. In this analysis, it is important to keep in mind that we will be *valuing* options and not *pricing* them. Indeed, prices are established through the actions of buyers and sellers; investors and analysts use valuation models to estimate what those prices should be.

Third, we consider several extensions and advanced topics in option valuation. In particular, we show how the Black-Scholes model for call options on stock can be adapted to value put options, as well as the other financial assets commonly used as underlying assets. We describe how the payment of dividends affects an option's value and how the model can be adjusted accordingly. We discuss the practical differences between the European and American styles of contracting, and we also examine price or return volatility—the role it plays in the valuation process and the ways an investor can estimate it in practice. We conclude the section with an examination of **exotic options**, which are designed to have payoffs that differ from those of standard contracts.

Finally, several option-based investment and hedging strategies are examined. After describing protective put and covered call strategies, we demonstrate how options can be used in combination with one another to create risk-reward trade-offs that do not otherwise exist in financial markets. In this sense, options can be used as building blocks to help investors design customized payoff schemes. We consider three broad classes of option combination strategies: **straddles**, which involve the purchase and sale of both puts and calls; **spreads**, in which the investor simultaneously buys one call (or put) while selling another; and **range forwards** (or collars), which require the purchase of a call and the concurrent sale of a put, or vice versa.

AN OVERVIEW OF OPTION MARKETS AND CONTRACTS

In Chapter 22, we discussed the primary difference between forward and futures contracts: Futures are standardized and trade on exchanges while forward contracts have negotiable terms and therefore must be arranged in the OTC market. With the development of organized option exchanges during the past three decades, option contracts offer investors similar trading alternatives. The most important features of how these contracts are traded and quoted in the financial press are highlighted in the following sections.

Option Market Conventions

Option contracts have been traded for centuries in the form of separate agreements or embedded in other securities. Malkiel, for example, tells the story of how call options were used to speculate on flower prices during the tulip bulb frenzy in 17th-century Holland.[1] Then, and for most of the time until now, options were arranged and executed in private transactions. Collectively, these private transactions represent the OTC market for options. Like forward contracts, OTC option agreements can be structured around any terms or underlying asset to which two parties can agree. This has been a particularly useful mechanism when the underlying asset is too illiquid to support a widely traded contract. Also, credit risk is a paramount concern in this market because OTC agreements typically are not collateralized. This credit risk is one-sided with an option agreement because the buyer worries about the seller's ability to honor his obligations, but the seller has received everything he will get up front and is not concerned about the buyer's creditworthiness.

As in all security markets, OTC options ultimately are created in response to the needs and desires of the corporations and individual investors who use these products. Financial

---

[1]See Burton G. Malkiel, *A Random Walk Down Wall Street*, 7th ed. (New York: Norton, 2000).

institutions, such as money-center banks and investment banks, serve as market makers by facilitating the arrangement and execution of these deals. Over the years, various trade associations of broker-dealers in OTC options have emerged (and, in some cases, faded), including the Put and Call Brokers and Dealers Association, which helped arrange private stock option transactions, and the International Swap and Derivatives Association, which monitors the activities of market makers for interest rate and foreign exchange derivatives. These trade groups create a common set of standards and language to govern industry transactions.

In April 1973, the Chicago Board of Trade changed the dynamics of option trading when it opened the Chicago Board Options Exchange (CBOE). Specializing in stock and stock index options, the CBOE has introduced two important aspects of market uniformity. Foremost, contracts offered by the CBOE are standardized in terms of the underlying common stock, the number of shares covered, the delivery dates, and the range of available exercise prices. This standardization, which increases the possibility of basis risk, was meant to help develop a secondary market for the contracts. The rapid increase in trading volume on the CBOE and other options exchanges suggests that this feature is desirable compared to OTC contracts that must often be held to maturity due to a lack of liquidity.

The centralization of the trading function also necessitated the creation of the **Options Clearing Corporation (OCC)**, which acts as the guarantor of each CBOE-traded contract. Therefore, end users in option transactions ultimately bear the credit risk of the OCC. For this reason, even though the OCC is independent of the exchange, it demands the option seller to post margin to guarantee future performance. Again, the option buyer will not have a margin account because a future obligation to the seller is nonexistent. Finally, this central market structure makes monitoring, regulation, and price reporting much easier than in the decentralized OTC markets.

Price Quotations for Exchange-Traded Options

Equity Options   Options on the common stock of individual companies have traded on the CBOE since 1973. Several other markets, including the American (AMEX), Philadelphia (PHLX), and Pacific (PSE) Stock Exchanges, began trading their own contracts shortly afterward. The CBOE remains the largest exchange in terms of option market volume with a market share of just under 40 percent, with the AMEX second at around 25 percent. Options on each of these exchanges are traded similarly, with a typical contract for 100 shares of stock. Because exchange-traded contracts are not issued by the company whose common stock is the underlying asset, they require secondary transactions in the equity if exercised.[2]

Panel A of Exhibit 23.1 displays price quotations for a sample of equity options as well as a summary of exchange-trading volume on February 14, 2002. To interpret this exhibit, suppose that an investor wanted to buy an option on Dell Computer common stock, a quote that is highlighted on the chart. The first column indicates that Dell shares closed that day at a price of $26.40, while the next two columns list the exercise prices and expiration months for the available contracts. By convention, stock options expire on the Saturday following the third Friday of the designated month. The next two columns show the volume (number of contracts traded) and closing price, respectively, for Dell calls; the final two columns provide similar information for Dell puts.

Assume this investor wanted to buy a March 2002 Dell call with an exercise price of $25. This contract would cost a total of $260, calculated as the stated "per share" price of $2.60 multiplied by 100 shares. In exchange for that payment, the holder of this American-style call would then be able to exercise the option in mid-March—or any time before then—by paying $2,500 (= $25 × 100) and receiving 100 Dell shares from the option seller, who is obligated to make that

---

[2]Call options issued directly by the firm whose common stock is the underlying asset are called *warrants*. We discuss the use and valuation of these contracts in Chapter 24.

exchange at the buyer's request. That request will only be rational if the mid-March price of Dell is greater than $25. If that price closes below $25, the investor will simply let the call expire without acting on the option; that is her right as the derivative buyer. Finally, notice that with the February share price being $26.40, the investor could immediately recover $1.40 of the $2.60 she paid for the contract. Thus, her time premium of $1.20 (= $2.60 – $1.40) preserves her right to buy Dell stock at a price of $25 for the next month even if the market value of those shares moves higher.[3]

Consider another investor who sells the "March 25" Dell put. In return for an up-front receipt of $75 (= $0.75 × 100), he now must stand ready to buy 100 shares of stock in mid-March for $2,500 if the option holder chooses to exercise his option to sell. The stock price will, of course, have to fall from its current level before this would occur. The investor in this case has sold an out-of-the-money contract and hopes that it will stay out of the money through expiration, letting the passing of time "decay" the time premium to zero. As we saw earlier, the front-end premium is all that sellers of put or call options ever receive, and they hope to retain as much of it as possible. Like the long position in the call, the short put position benefits from an increase in Dell share prices.

Finally, notice that all the options listed in Panel A of Exhibit 23.1 expire within a few months of the quotation date. In fact, the expiration dates available for these exchange-traded contracts are the two nearest-term months (February and March for Dell) and up to two additional months from a quarterly cycle beginning in either January, February, or March. In the case of Dell options, May 2002 (which is part of the quarterly cycle beginning in February) is the additional month listed. Panel B of the figure lists quotations for long-term equity anticipation securities (LEAPS), which are simply call and put options with longer expiration dates. Like the contracts just described, LEAPS are also traded on the CBOE and have comparable terms. For instance, a Dell call with the same $25 exercise price expiring in January 2003 would cost the investor $590 (= $5.90 × 100). Thus, by extending the expiration date by ten months (i.e., from March 2002 to January 2003), the option's price increases from $2.60 to $5.90. Of course, since these two contracts had the same exercise price, this difference is purely because of additional time premium. The effect that time to expiration has on the value of an option will be examined in greater detail shortly.

Stock Index Options   As we saw in Chapter 21, options on stock indexes, such as Standard and Poor's 100 or 500, are patterned closely after equity options; however, they differ in one important way: Index options can only be settled in cash. This is because of the underlying index, which is a hypothetical portfolio that would be quite costly to duplicate in practice. First traded on the CBOE in 1983, index options are popular with investors for the same reason as stock index futures: They provide a relatively inexpensive and convenient way to take an investment or hedging position in a broad-based indicator of market performance. Index puts are particularly useful in portfolio insurance applications, such as the protective put strategy described earlier and again at the end of this chapter.

Prices for four of the more widely traded contracts are listed in Exhibit 23.2. They are interpreted in the same way as equity option prices, with each contract demanding the transfer of 100 "shares" of the underlying index. For example, the March S&P 500 index call and put contracts with an exercise price of 1,100 could be purchased for $3,810 (= $38.10 × 100) and $1,600 (= $16 × 100), respectively. On the expiration date, which will be the third Friday of the month, the

---

[3]Recall from Chapter 21 that a call option's value can be divided into two components: the *intrinsic value,* which is the greater of either zero or the stock price minus the exercise price, and the *time premium.* In this example, the Dell call is said to be *in the money* because it has positive intrinsic value, whereas an option with no intrinsic value is *out of the money.*

EXHIBIT 23.1 STOCK OPTION QUOTATIONS

A. Regular Expiration Dates

This exhibit consists of dense multi-column stock option quotation tables (columns: OPTION/STRIKE, EXP., CALL VOL., CALL LAST, PUT VOL., PUT LAST) reproduced from financial pages. The individual numeric entries are too small and densely printed to transcribe reliably.

VOLUME & OPEN INTEREST SUMMARIES

Includes all equity and index contracts

AMERICAN		
Call Vol:	454,412	Open Int: 19,010,311
Put Vol:	356,577	Open Int: 9,725,964

CHICAGO BOARD		
Call Vol:	640,595	Open Int: 46,306,913
Put Vol:	582,739	Open Int: 31,322,610

INTL SECURITIES		
Call Vol:	252,888	Open Int: 38,382,648
Put Vol:	219,041	Open Int: 25,542,275

PHILADELPHIA		
Call Vol:	222,243	Open Int: 30,481,220
Put Vol:	179,147	Open Int: 17,316,840

PACIFIC		
Call Vol:	222,413	Open Int: 42,500,000
Put Vol:	154,735	Open Int: 27,500,000

TOTAL		
Call Vol:	1,772,551	Open Int: 176,681,092
Put Vol:	1,492,239	Open Int: 111,508,889

EXHIBIT 23.1 *STOCK OPTION QUOTATIONS (CONTINUED)*

B. Long-Term Equity Anticipation Securities (LEAPS)

LEAPS – LONG TERM OPTIONS

OPTION/STRIKE	EXP	CALL VOL	CALL LAST	PUT VOL	PUT LAST
AmExpr 35	Jan 03	10	4.20	93	4.80
AppleMat 80	Jan 03	1647	4.90	20	2.20
BarnsG 20	Jan 04	1629	3.40	815	7.10
Boeing 40	Jan 03	6098	8.20		
44.77 45	Jan 03	6133	5.40	790	0.25
BrMySq 65	Jan 03	3002	0.30	1728	1.35
Celpine 10	Jan 04	1285	3.20	1675	1
Cisco 35	Jan 03	2040	1.50	184	0.45
17.46 50	Jan 03			10	13.50
CocaCola 50	Jan 03	770	2.60	72	5.20
12.50	Jan 04	1026	1.50	41	8
Corning 65	Jan 04			81	3.10
DelComr 70	Jan 03			117	1.70
26.40 96	Jan 03	49	5.90	750	12.40
eBayInc 25	Jan 04	1343	8.30	905	0.60
13.90 60	Jan 03	1125	12.60	10	2.90
EMC 17.50	Jan 03	2042	3.90	29	3
Ekodak 25	Jan 03	1825	3.50	1000	4.30
FordM 22.50					
Gap 12.50	Jan 03	1802	0.30	2043	1.05
12.79 17.50	Jan 03			161	6.40
GenElec 20	Jan 04	2001	1.30	1147	1.90
38.00 40	Jan 03	4015	1.95	1520	3.80
45	Jan 04	1113	3.40	1510	2.45
Intel 30	Jan 03	7282	5.30	2082	1.70
33.50 40	Jan 04	1283	1.60	266	2.05
33.50 45	Jan 03	462	3.20	110	6.50
IntlPapr 50	Jan 04	9	5.80	3325	3.10
Intuil 60	Jan 03	5348	1.80	125	3.90
JDS Uni 25	Jan 04	750	1.75	1159	1.90
Schlmb 50	Jan 03	3919	0.60	1564	1.10

OPTION/STRIKE	EXP	CALL VOL	CALL LAST	PUT VOL	PUT LAST
ChaseM 30	Jan 03				
30.21 35					
JnprNtw 15	Jan 04		3.10		
10.92 17.50					
10.92 20					
Lucent 10	Jan 03	2510	4.80		
5.82 7.50					
Merck 10					
59.69 60	Jan 03	1310	37.50		
59.69 60					
59.69 65					
59.69 70					
Microsft 95	Jan 03	10032	3.60		
Motorola 12.50		19	12		
13.15 15	Jan 03	2032	2.40		
13.15 15	Jan 03	3101	2.45		
13.15 17.50	Jan 03	90	7.90		
Rssl100Tr 35	Jan 03	2000	3.50		
NextelCm 5					
OmnMcom 90					
OpnwvSy 5	Jan 03	702	5		
Oracle 30	Jan 03	6255	6.50		
Pfizer 45	Jan 03	517	8.70		
PhilMor 50	Jan 03	1421	8.50		
Qualcom 45	Jan 03	6310	8.50		
QwestCm 5	Jan 03	5185	10.10		
7.49 10					
7.49 15					
7.49 25					
Schlmb 50					

OPTION/STRIKE	EXP	CALL VOL	CALL LAST	PUT VOL	PUT LAST
SemiHTr 55	Jan 04	2000	8	3253	1.85
SpmIFON 10	Jan 04	200	5.10	5017	1.40
Trycateil 10	Jan 04	1	18.20	1256	1.60
26.75 20	Jan 04	73	10.70	709	3.60
26.75 20	Jan 04	17	12.30	1045	4.40
26.75 20	Jan 04	219	6.70	4070	8.50
26.75 35	Jan 03	823	3.30		9.90
26.75 35	Jan 04	1129	2.15	3	13.60
UAL 50	Jan 03	1180	1.75	17	
11.08 5			5.50	2679	4.30
ViacomB 45		4		850	6.90
WorldCm 10	Jan 03	711	1.10	175	3.70

VOLUME & OPEN INTEREST SUMMARIES

CHICAGO BOARD

Call Vol:	64,026	Open Int:	16,681,998
Put Vol:	33,562	Open Int:	9,367,030

INTL SECURITIES

Call Vol:	29,392	Open Int:	15,998,462
Put Vol:	18,771	Open Int:	9,179,371

PACIFIC

Call Vol:	0	Open Int:	0
Put Vol:	0	Open Int:	0

TOTAL

Call Vol:	93,452	Open Int:	33,213,245
Put Vol:	53,331	Open Int:	18,966,790

Source: The Wall Street Journal, 15 February 2002. Printed with permission from The Wall Street Journal, Dow Jones & Co. Inc.

EXHIBIT 23.2 ▶ STOCK INDEX OPTION QUOTATIONS

DJ INDUS AVG(DJX)

Mon	Strike	Vol	Last	Net Chg	Open Int
Apr	68 p	1	0.20	- 0.10	2,750
Mar	80 p	5	0.10	...	18,213
Apr	80 p	20	0.65	...	2,347
May	80 p	3	1.20	- 0.30	1,623
Mar	84 c	4	16.10	- 0.90	144
Mar	84 p	11	0.05	- 0.10	20,339
Mar	88 p	503	0.25	- 0.05	8,726
Apr	88 p	10	1.15	- 0.25	5,425
Mar	90 c	3	9.80	...	189
Mar	90 p	333	0.35	+ 0.05	27,284
Apr	90 p	61	1.50	- 0.20	5,275
May	90 p	87	2.70	...	9,318
Mar	92 c	1	8.60	+ 0.50	3,614
Mar	92 p	178	0.30	- 0.20	11,086
Feb	94 c	3	5.80	- 0.10	931
Mar	94 p	580	0.65	+ 0.05	13,746
Feb	95 c	34	4.90	+ 0.20	402
Feb	96 c	200	3.90	- 0.10	11,983
Mar	96 c	402	4.80	+ 0.10	12,913
Mar	96 p	21,054	1	+ 0.10	47,183
Apr	96 c	1	7.10	+ 1.00	360
Apr	96 p	17	3	- 0.10	12,159
May	96 c	1	8.40	+ 1.80	3,387
Feb	97 c	325	3	...	3,057
Feb	97 p	10	0.05	...	3,511
Feb	98 c	843	1.75	- 0.15	10,261
Mar	98 p	1,453	0.05	- 0.05	15,350
Mar	98 c	2,511	3.30	+ 0.30	8,927
Mar	98 p	22,741	1.50	- 0.10	20,478
Apr	98 p	27	3.60	- 0.20	1,254
Feb	99 c	1,199	0.75	- 0.50	3,640
Feb	99 p	1,447	0.10	- 0.15	3,766
Feb	100 c	12,398	0.20	- 0.30	10,064
Feb	100 p	10,408	0.20	- 0.35	13,363
Mar	100 c	7,235	2	+ 0.10	14,076
Mar	100 p	5,891	2.15	- 0.05	22,373
Apr	100 c	6	4.50	+ 0.80	9,197
Apr	100 p	145	4.50	...	14,111
May	100 c	3	6	+ 1.60	440
Feb	101 c	795	0.05	- 0.10	1,753
Feb	101 p	1,714	1.10	- 0.20	1,936
Feb	102 p	35	2.25	- 0.05	2,721
Mar	102 c	2,637	1.15	+ 0.05	9,068
Mar	102 p	249	3.20	- 0.30	3,555
Apr	102 p	27	5.60	- 0.60	856
Mar	104 c	414	0.45	+ 0.05	13,278
Mar	104 p	20	4.60	...	2,813
May	104 c	50	3.90	+ 0.90	106
May	104 p	100	7.40	- 1.00	1,029
Feb	106 p	10	6.10	- 0.30	27
Feb	106 c	10	1.75	...	...
Feb	108 p	2	8.30	- 3.60	102
Mar	108 c	341	0.10	...	7,284
Mar	108 p	32	8.20	- 1.50	958
Apr	108 p	3	9.10	- 0.40	1,237
Mar	124 p	46	24	+ 1.20	85
Mar	132 p	20	32	+ 1.00	24

Call Vol. ...... 36,344 Open Int. 220,115
Put Vol. ...... 72,625 Open Int. 498,136

S & P 100(OEX)

Mon	Strike	Vol	Last	Net Chg	Open Int
Mar	440 p	20	0.30	...	1,464
Apr	440 p	15	1	...	1,567
May	440 p	6	1.90	- 1.30	76
Mar	460 c	24	0.65	+ 0.20	3,650
Mar	470 p	57	0.70	- 0.20	126
Mar	480 p	8	0.90	+ 0.10	1,918
Apr	480 p	550	2.50	...	490
Mar	490 p	2,142	1.30	+ 0.10	322
Feb	500 p	260	0.05	...	9,315
Mar	500 c	1	71.40	- 24.60	21
Mar	500 p	913	1.50	+ 0.05	3,344
Apr	500 c	1	73.50	+ 3.10	12
Apr	500 p	20	3.60	- 0.10	142
May	500 p	52	5.80	- 0.10	690
Feb	510 c	50	0.05	...	4,740
Apr	510 p	30	5	...	830
Mar	515 p	2,197	2.45	+ 0.25	164
Feb	520 c	510	0.05	...	8,414
Mar	520 p	699	2.80	+ 0.20	4,707
Mar	520 c	1	55	- 12.00	1
Apr	520 p	350	6.40	- 0.10	911
May	520 p	16	9	- 0.20	368
Feb	525 p	183	0.05	- 0.05	3,164
Mar	525 p	645	3.50	+ 0.60	91
Feb	530 p	2,460	0.05	- 0.05	5,913
Feb	530 c	8	39.80	- 4.40	100
Mar	530 p	564	3.80	+ 0.10	2,429
Mar	535 c	526	0.05	- 0.15	1,688
Mar	535 p	1	4.10	- 0.20	144
Mar	540 c	38	26	- 1.20	464
Feb	540 p	397	0.05	- 0.15	5,996
Mar	540 p	346	5	- 0.10	4,039
Mar	540 p	300	9.30	- 2.10	146
May	540 p	41	14	+ 0.80	139
Feb	545 c	26	20	- 3.00	266
Feb	545 p	2,262	0.10	- 0.20	4,757
Mar	545 p	30	6	+ 0.40	247
Mar	550 p	369	17	- 0.50	2,148
Mar	550 p	2,305	0.15	- 0.35	5,277
Mar	550 c	218	23.70	- 0.80	664
Mar	550 p	108	6.90	+ 0.10	1,315
Apr	550 c	5	13.50	+ 1.00	447
Feb	555 c	321	12.30	- 0.40	1,787
Feb	555 p	1,439	0.50	- 0.30	3,087
Mar	555 c	67	19.70	- 0.80	194
Mar	555 p	53	9	+ 0.60	276
Feb	560 c	1,539	7.50	- 1.70	4,332
Feb	560 p	5,278	0.50	- 1.20	5,924
Mar	560 c	149	16.50	...	2,474
Mar	560 p	337	10.10	+ 0.30	2,420
Mar	560 c	27	25.30	+ 1.30	602
Apr	560 p	33	16.30	- 0.40	1,033
Mar	560 p	5	20	- 0.80	60
Feb	565 c	5,186	3.50	- 2.00	3,582
Feb	565 p	8,707	1.60	- 1.40	3,856
Mar	565 c	111	14	...	391
Mar	565 p	344	11.40	- 0.10	571
Feb	570 p	8,450	0.80	- 1.70	5,445
Feb	570 p	6,820	4	- 1.00	3,149
Mar	570 p	203	11.50	+ 0.30	2,468
Mar	570 p	1,502	14.10	- 0.40	1,730
Apr	570 p	700	19.50	+ 2.30	2,801
Apr	570 p	12	19.30	- 0.70	579
Feb	575 p	3,595	0.10	- 0.70	7,392
Feb	575 p	874	8.50	...	1,902
Mar	575 p	19	9.70	+ 1.40	346
Mar	575 p	13	18	+ 0.70	163
Feb	580 c	2,139	0.10	- 0.10	6,277
Feb	580 p	192	13.10	+ 0.30	1,471
Mar	580 p	797	6.50	+ 0.10	4,393
Mar	580 p	127	20.50	+ 0.50	1,860
Apr	580 c	3	14	+ 0.50	875
Apr	580 p	4	25	- 0.50	109
May	580 p	5	29	- 10.50	3
Feb	585 c	813	0.05	- 0.05	3,987
Feb	585 p	19	18	- 1.50	396
Mar	585 c	85	4	- 0.90	828
Mar	585 p	3	23	- 1.20	22
Feb	590 p	5	20.20	- 4.30	507
Mar	590 p	888	3.50	- 0.20	2,514
Mar	590 p	17	27	+ 0.80	358
Apr	590 c	31	9.80	+ 3.30	502
Mar	595 c	126	2.30	- 0.05	518
Mar	595 p	813	31.90	+ 0.90	37
Feb	600 p	2	33.50	- 1.40	599
Mar	600 c	360	1.70	- 0.10	2,647
Apr	600 c	217	5.30	- 1.20	391
Mar	605 c	280	1.10	- 0.10	472
Feb	610 c	10	0.05	...	4,180
Mar	610 c	59	0.60	- 0.20	2,086
Apr	610 c	2	3.60	- 0.50	615
Mar	615 c	70	0.40	- 0.20	14
May	615 c	400	5.50	+ 0.10	5
Feb	620 c	65	0.35	- 0.05	2,561
Apr	620 c	103	2.50	+ 0.50	803
May	620 c	400	4.80	+ 0.80	540
Mar	630 c	25	0.15	- 0.15	1,275
Apr	630 c	350	1.45	...	625
Mar	635 c	150	0.15	+ 0.05	533
Feb	640 c	200	0.05	...	2,550
Mar	640 c	300	0.10	...	2,193
Feb	650 c	400	0.05	...	2,140
Mar	660 c	395	0.05	...	1,917
Feb	700 p	20	131.70	- 18.30	40

Call Vol. ...... 28,148 Open Int. 132,824
Put Vol. ...... 42,911 Open Int. 139,609

NASDAQ-100(NDX)

Mon	Strike	Vol	Last	Net Chg	Open Int
Mar	1050 p	11	5	- 4.00	22
Mar	1100 p	13	1.70	- 0.05	371
Mar	1150 p	2	2.40	- 0.90	321
Mar	1200 p	7	4.40	- 0.60	526
Apr	1250 p	30	7.50	- 1.00	245
Mar	1250 p	20	23	- 8.50	7
Mar	1275 p	22	8	- 3.90	5
Mar	1300 p	18	0.25	- 0.25	619
Mar	1300 p	145	12.30	- 1.70	590
Mar	1350 p	22	20	- 6.00	2,190
Mar	1400 c	5	105	+ 15.00	35
Mar	1400 p	77	0.05	- 0.55	996
Mar	1400 c	5	110	- 2.00	133
Feb	1400 p	157	32	- 1.50	860
Feb	1425 p	32	0.30	- 1.40	202
Mar	1425 p	6	30	- 15.00	1,005
Feb	1450 c	76	27	- 14.80	1,082
Mar	1450 c	353	1.95	- 2.15	1,609
Mar	1450 c	3	98	+ 13.00	1,000
Mar	1450 p	1,044	47.80	+ 2.80	4,773
Feb	1450 p	21	77	- 16.00	5
Mar	1475 p	464	10	- 10.80	453
Mar	1475 p	3,679	10	- 2.80	142
Mar	1475 p	376	62.50	- 4.50	105
Mar	1475 p	405	60	...	110
Mar	1500 c	693	2.75	- 6.65	724
Mar	1500 p	139	25	+ 2.00	618
Mar	1500 c	84	51	- 5.20	396
Mar	1500 p	427	71	- 1.00	1,127
Feb	1500 c	2	90	- 45.00	171
Feb	1525 c	1,568	2.15	- 0.75	1,164
Mar	1525 p	3	25	- 18.50	192
Feb	1525 c	14	44	- 1.70	70
Mar	1550 c	90	0.05	- 0.95	1,546
Mar	1550 p	26	70	...	945
Feb	1550 c	15	34	- 1.00	223
Feb	1550 c	3	56.50	- 6.50	200
Mar	1575 p	113	0.10	- 0.40	466
Feb	1575 c	10	0.05	- 0.25	337
Mar	1600 c	115	95	- 26.00	755
Feb	1600 c	102	17	- 4.60	1,496
Mar	1600 c	3	119	- 64.00	1,620
Feb	1600 c	10	39	- 3.90	10
Mar	1625 c	11	12.90	- 0.30	35
Mar	1650 c	5	149	- 44.00	236
Feb	1650 c	5	12	+ 2.40	494
Mar	1650 p	5	178	...	...
Feb	1675 c	18	6.10	- 1.90	155
Mar	1700 c	27	3.80	- 1.60	982
Mar	1700 c	28	23.90	+ 1.90	244
Mar	1725 c	1	4	+ 0.80	166
Mar	1750 p	4	260	- 40.00	7
Mar	1800 c	28	0.75	- 0.15	562
Mar	1850 c	3	5	...	...

Call ...... 3,230 Open Int. 28,049
Put ...... 3,419 Open Int. 37,882

S & P 500(SPX)

Mon	Strike	Vol	Last	Net Chg	Open Int
Mar	700 p	300	0.05	...	6,521
Mar	725 p	65	0.10	- 0.15	1,105
Mar	850 p	10	0.50	...	11,001
Apr	850 p	2,007	1.65	+ 0.20	136
Mar	900 c	2	213	- 5.50	65
Mar	900 p	1,058	0.90	- 0.05	18,354
Apr	900 p	224	2.65	- 0.05	728
Mar	925 p	201	1.10	- 0.05	12,891
Mar	950 c	2	165.70	- 13.30	3
Mar	950 p	3,840	1.60	+ 0.10	22,457
Apr	950 p	1,825	4.40	- 0.60	5,798
Mar	975 p	1,218	2.50	+ 0.30	15,801
Apr	975 p	2,150	6.70	+ 0.70	10,098
Feb	995 p	2	128	+ 33.00	129
Mar	995 p	1,326	0.05	- 0.05	10,575
Mar	995 c	18	130	+ 7.00	2,222
Mar	995 p	6,309	3.20	+ 0.40	30,095
Apr	995 p	1,075	8.20	+ 0.50	4,958
Feb	1025 p	25	0.05	- 0.05	14,036
Mar	1025 p	2	103	+ 4.50	3,134
Mar	1025 p	702	4.70	+ 0.40	22,973
Apr	1025 p	17	9.70	- 1.10	7,288
Feb	1050 p	31	67	- 3.00	764
Feb	1050 p	1,692	0.05	- 0.15	11,941
Mar	1050 p	146	72.50	- 3.50	10,006
Mar	1050 p	20,890	7.30	+ 0.50	25,791
Apr	1050 p	3	82.50	- 1.50	501
Apr	1050 p	175	14.90	+ 0.30	3,974
Feb	1060 c	10	62	+ 13.10	120
Feb	1060 p	204	0.10	- 0.15	2,111
Feb	1060 c	1	64	+ 19.00	1
Mar	1060 p	10	7.20	- 0.30	756
Feb	1070 p	224	10	- 1.00	499
Mar	1075 p	35	40.10	- 2.40	1,450
Feb	1075 p	447	0.05	- 0.75	7,839
Mar	1075 p	98	51	- 1.00	8,944
Mar	1075 p	2,377	10.50	+ 0.50	18,072
Feb	1075 p	2	19	- 1.00	5,743
Feb	1080 c	1	37	- 1.00	386
Feb	1080 p	1,540	0.30	- 0.20	2,299
Mar	1080 p	265	13	+ 1.80	5,237
Mar	1090 c	253	27.50	+ 8.00	1,585
Feb	1090 p	801	0.70	- 0.10	1,902
Mar	1090 c	232	42	+ 1.40	5,444
Mar	1090 p	17	16.30	+ 2.40	5,704
Feb	1100 c	8,288	18.50	- 1.80	18,475
Mar	1100 p	11,428	0.70	- 1.30	23,958
Mar	1100 p	7,363	38.10	+ 4.60	35,863
Mar	1100 p	12,970	16	- 0.50	45,667
Apr	1100 c	3	42.50	- 3.30	6,433
Mar	1100 p	3,041	28.50	+ 1.30	12,528
Apr	1110 c	1,047	7	- 4.00	2,489
Mar	1110 p	1,988	1.60	- 1.90	2,075
Feb	1120 c	1,102	1.50	- 4.20	2,228
Mar	1120 p	1,238	5.10	- 2.20	1,798
Mar	1120 c	4,420	22	...	7,296
Mar	1120 p	4,602	25	+ 2.00	7,288
Feb	1120 p	50	35	...	315
Feb	1125 c	2,371	0.50	- 2.50	8,267
Feb	1125 p	2,102	10	+ 0.40	10,597
Mar	1125 c	4,819	18	- 1.60	26,101
Mar	1125 p	11,807	28	+ 1.00	18,131
Feb	1125 c	501	31	- 1.90	8,789
Apr	1125 p	121	39.20	+ 1.70	3,237
Feb	1130 c	952	0.50	- 1.60	4,240
Feb	1130 p	648	13.50	+ 1.50	1,555
Mar	1130 c	111	15.50	- 0.90	10,964
Mar	1130 p	141	31.50	+ 1.70	11,356
Feb	1135 c	697	0.50	- 0.50	1,435
Feb	1135 p	3	21.50	- 31.30	676
Feb	1140 c	1,254	0.40	- 0.10	3,755
Feb	1140 p	444	27.30	+ 1.90	3,664
Mar	1140 p	793	13.60	+ 1.50	8,957
Mar	1140 p	32	34.50	+ 0.50	7,998
Apr	1140 p	22	45	+ 0.70	189
Feb	1150 c	1,500	0.05	- 0.10	23,048
Feb	1150 p	571	33	- 1.00	19,292
Mar	1150 c	4,970	9	- 0.20	37,087
Mar	1150 p	647	42.70	+ 2.70	44,996
Apr	1150 c	31	18.20	- 0.50	5,202
Feb	1160 p	1,045	0.60	+ 0.55	2,856
Feb	1160 c	444	5	- 0.60	20,056
Feb	1160 p	1	44.70	- 2.30	19,288
Mar	1160 c	735	14.50	- 1.20	306
Feb	1160 p	20	0.05	...	8,979
Feb	1175 p	129	59	- 1.90	1,928
Mar	1175 p	279	3.40	- 0.20	18,124
Mar	1175 p	57	56.50	- 2.50	6,161
Apr	1175 c	469	10.50	...	2,536
Feb	1175 p	15	67	- 1.00	190
Mar	1180 c	20	4	+ 1.50	2,554
Mar	1180 p	4	67	- 11.00	2
Apr	1180 c	5	9.50	+ 1.30	241
Feb	1200 c	225	86	+ 4.00	465
Mar	1200 c	1,965	1.10	...	18,958
Mar	1200 p	21	86	+ 3.50	9,019
Apr	1200 c	826	5	- 0.50	2,774
Apr	1200 p	4	84	- 4.20	433
Feb	1225 c	3	107.50	- 1.70	80
Mar	1225 c	6	0.70	- 0.50	9,284
Mar	1225 p	1	107.50	- 1.50	3,355
Apr	1225 c	10	3.50	- 0.50	5,102
Apr	1225 p	1	104	- 15.00	95
Feb	1250 p	210	136	- 2.00	242
Mar	1250 p	85	0.25	- 0.05	15,669
Mar	1250 p	199	134	- 4.00	4,688
Apr	1250 p	1,551	1.70	+ 0.60	6,250
Apr	1250 p	210	135.70	- 2.80	11

Source: *The Wall Street Journal*, 8 February 2002. Printed with permission from *The Wall Street Journal*, Dow Jones & Co. Inc.

holder of the call would exercise the contract to "buy" $110,000 worth of the index if the prevailing S&P 500 level is greater than 1,100, with the put being exercised at index levels less than 1,100.

Foreign Currency Options　Foreign currency options are structurally parallel to the currency futures contracts discussed in Chapter 22. That is, each contract allows for the sale or purchase of a set amount of foreign (i.e., non-U.S. dollar) currency at a fixed exchange (FX) rate. A currency call option is like the long position in the currency futures since it permits the contract holder to buy the currency at a later date. (Of course, unlike futures, options do not require that this exchange be made.) A currency put is therefore the option analog to being short in the futures market. These contracts exist for several major currencies, including the Euro, Australian dollars, Japanese yen, Canadian dollars, British pounds, and Swiss francs. The majority of currency options trading, which began in 1982, occurs on the PHLX. Exhibit 23.3 shows quotes from a sample of the available CAD contracts, along with the spot foreign exchange rates for the same trading day.

Like the FX futures market, all the prices are quoted from the perspective of U.S.-based investors. Consider, for example, an investor who lives in New York and holds Canadian-dollar-denominated provincial government bonds in her portfolio. It is February, and when the bonds come due in one month, she will need to convert the proceeds back into U.S. dollars, which exposes her to a possible weakening in the Canadian currency. Accordingly, she buys the March put on the Canadian dollar with an exercise price of USD 0.63/CAD for a total price of USD 345.00 (= 50,000 × 0.0069). This option would allow the holder to sell CAD 50,000 in March for a total price of USD 31,500 (= 50,000 × 0.63). Obviously, our investor will only exercise the contract if the spot USD/CAD price prevailing in March is less than 0.63 (i.e., if the Canadian dollar weakened relative to the U.S. currency). Finally, because the spot rate is USD 0.62865/CAD, this option is in the money—that is, the contract price of 0.0069 consists of 0.00135 (= 0.63 − 0.62865) of intrinsic value and 0.00555 of time premium.

Options on Futures Contracts　Although they have existed for decades in the OTC markets, options on futures contracts have only been exchange-traded since 1982. Also known as futures options, they give the holder the right, but not the obligation, to enter into a futures contract on an underlying security or commodity at a later date and at a predetermined price. Purchasing a call on a futures allows for the acquisition of a long position in the futures market, while exercising a put would create a short futures position. On the other hand, the seller of the call would be obligated to enter into the short side of the futures contract if the option holder decided to exercise the contract, while the seller of the put might be forced into a long futures position. Exhibit 23.4 lists quotations for options based on a wide variety of underlying assets, including agricultural, metal, and energy commodities; Treasury bonds and notes; foreign currencies; and stock indexes. Consistent with the trading patterns for the futures contracts we examined earlier, futures options on financial assets represent the largest part of the market.

To understand how these contracts work, consider a commodity futures option. The April call option on copper with an exercise price of $0.76 per pound would cost the buyer $0.0180 per pound of copper covered by the futures position. As each copper futures contract on the Commodity Exchange (CMX) requires the transfer of 25,000 pounds of the metal, the total purchase price for this futures call is $450 (= 25,000 × 0.018). Also, because the April copper futures price on this day was $0.7475, this contract was out of the money so that its per-ounce price of 1.80 cents was purely a time premium.

As with any call position, the holder will only exercise at the expiration date if the prevailing price of the underlying asset exceeds the exercise price; she will let it expire worthless otherwise. This payoff structure might fit the need of an electronic appliance manufacturer exposed to higher copper prices as a factor of production or a speculator bullish on copper prices. In this

EXHIBIT 23.3   *FOREIGN CURRENCY OPTION QUOTATIONS*

KEY CROSS CURRENCY RATES

	USD	EUR	JPY	GBP	CHF	CAD	AUD	NZD	HKD	DKK	SEK
SEK	10.545	9.1831	7.9292	15.057	6.1971	6.6292	5.4634	4.4489	1.3520	1.2362	....
DKK	8.5300	7.4284	6.4140	12.180	5.0129	5.3624	4.4194	3.5988	1.0937	....	.80891
HKD	7.7994	6.7921	5.8647	11.137	4.5836	4.9031	4.0409	3.2906	....	.91435	.73963
NZD	2.3702	2.0641	1.7823	3.3845	1.3929	1.4901	1.2280	....	.30390	.27787	.22477
AUD	1.9301	1.6809	1.4513	2.7560	1.1343	1.2134	....	.81432	.24747	.22628	.18304
CAD	1.5907	1.3853	1.1961	2.2714	.93483	....	.82414	.67112	.20395	.18648	.15085
CHF	1.7016	1.4818	1.2795	2.4297	....	1.0697	.88160	.71791	.21817	.19948	.16137
GBP	.70033	.60988	.52660	....	.41157	.44026	.36284	.29547	.08979	.08210	.06641
JPY	132.99	115.81	....	189.90	78.156	83.605	68.902	56.108	17.051	15.591	12.612
EUR	1.1483	....	.86345	1.6397	.67484	.72189	.59494	.48447	.14723	.13462	.10890
USD	....	.87085	.75194	1.4279	.58768	.62865	.51810	.42190	.12821	.11723	.09483

CANADIAN $ SPOT EURO M/E
Exchange :PHL
USD
Months Currently Trading
FEB02   MAR02   APR02

		CALLS						PUTS			
CDE		MAR 02Bid	Ask	Last	Volume	CDE		MAR 02Bid	Ask	Last	Volume
1)	60.00					12)	60.00	.01	.06	y	
2)	60.50					13)	60.50	.03	.08	y	
3)	61.00					14)	61.00	.06	.11	y	
4)	61.50					15)	61.50	.11	.16	y	
5)	62.00	.97	1.07			16)	62.00	.21	.26	y	
6)	62.50	.64	.74			17)	62.50	.37	.42	y	
7)	63.00	.41	.46			18)	63.00	.59	.69	y	
8)	63.50	.24	.29			19)	63.50	.91	1.01	y	
9)	64.00	.13	.18			20)	64.00				
10)	64.50	.07	.12			21)	64.50				
11)	65.00	.04	.09			22)	65.00				

EXHIBIT 23.4 ▶ FUTURES OPTION QUOTATIONS

AGRICULTURAL

Corn (CBT)
5,000 bu.; cents per bu.

STRIKE	CALLS-SETTLE			PUTS-SETTLE		
PRICE	Mar	Apr	May	Mar	Apr	May
190	....	....	....	1/8	....	7/8
200	6 3/4	....	15 1/8	1/8	3/8	1 1/8
210	7/8	6 3/8	8 3/8	4 1/8	2 3/8	4 3/8
220	1/8	2 1/4	4	13 3/8	8 1/4	10
230	1/8	....	2	23 1/4	....	17 3/4
240	1/8	1/4	7/8	33 1/4	....	26 1/2

Est vol 9,000 Wd 6,052 calls 6,341 puts
Op int Wed 282,125 calls 146,820 puts

Soybeans (CBT)
5,000 bu.; cents per bu.

STRIKE	CALLS-SETTLE			PUTS-SETTLE		
PRICE	Mar	Apr	May	Mar	Apr	May
400	36 3/8	....	41 1/4	1/8	1/4	1
420	16 1/2	....	24 3/4	1/4	1 5/8	4 3/8
440	2 7/8	9 1/4	13 1/2	6 3/4	9	13 1/4
460	1/4	2 3/4	6 5/8	24	....	26 1/2
480	1/8	3/4	3 1/4	43 3/4	....	43
500	....	....	1 3/8	60 1/4	....	61 1/4

Est vol 12,000 Wd 6,634 calls 9,293 puts
Op int Wed 136,793 calls 68,837 puts

Soybean Meal (CBT)
100 tons; $ per ton

STRIKE	CALLS-SETTLE			PUTS-SETTLE		
PRICE	Mar	May	Jly	Mar	May	Jly
140	9.00	9.00	10.50	0.10	1.60	2.50
145	4.75	5.75	7.50	0.65	3.35	4.35
150	1.50	3.55	5.00	2.75	6.00	7.00
155	0.50	2.00	3.90	6.65	9.55	10.50
160	0.20	1.15	2.85	11.40	13.65	14.35
165	0.05	0.60	2.05	16.30	18.15	....

Est vol 2,400 Wd 1,786 calls 1,040 puts
Op int Wed 22,340 calls 17,659 puts

Soybean Oil (CBT)
60,000 lbs.; cents per lb.

STRIKE	CALLS-SETTLE			PUTS-SETTLE		
PRICE	Mar	May	Jly	Mar	May	Jly
145	....	1.250	....	.005	.100	.120
150	.430	.850	....	.040	.190	.270
155	.110	.550	.820	.220	.430	.480
160	.030	.380	.600	.630	.740	.760
165	.010	.250	.450	1.120	1.100	....
170	.005	.160	.350	1.610	1.520	....

Est vol 2,100 Wd 3,409 calls 1,292 puts
Op int Wed 60,463 calls 25,106 puts

Wheat (CBT)
5,000 bu.; cents per bu.

STRIKE	CALLS-SETTLE			PUTS-SETTLE		
PRICE	Mar	May	Jly	Mar	May	Jly
260	20 3/4	28 1/4	....	1/8	1 1/4	3
270	11	20 1/4	....	1/4	3 1/4	5 5/8
280	2 7/8	13 3/4	19 1/8	2 1/8	7	9 1/2
290	5/8	9 1/4	14 1/2	9 7/8	12	14 3/4
300	1/8	6	11 1/8	19 1/4	19	21 1/4
310	1/8	3 3/4	8 1/2	29 1/4	26 1/2	....

Est vol 2,300 Wd 2,373 calls 2,363 puts
Op int Wed 70,313 calls 43,565 puts

INDEX

DJ Industrial Avg (CBOT)
$100 times premium

STRIKE	CALLS-SETTLE			PUTS-SETTLE		
PRICE	Feb	Mar	Apr	Feb	Mar	Apr
98	20.15	34.00	....	0.15	14.00	....
99	10.85	27.25	....	0.85	17.25	27.00
100	3.60	21.25	32.00	3.80	21.25	31.00
101	0.55	16.25	26.00	10.55	26.25	....
102	0.05	11.85	22.00	20.05	31.75	....
103	0.05	8.00	17.00	....	38.00	....

Est vol 1,200 Wd 477 calls 529 puts
Op int Wed 5,219 calls 8,657 puts

S&P 500 Stock Index (CME)
$250 times premium

STRIKE	CALLS-SETTLE			PUTS-SETT.		
PRICE	Feb	Mar	Apr	Feb	Mar	
1105	13.00	30.50	....	1.20	18.70	
1110	8.90	27.40	40.50	2.10	20.60	31.
1115	5.50	24.40	37.60	3.70	22.60	33.5
1120	3.00	21.50	34.70	6.20	24.70	35.6
1125	1.20	19.00	31.90	9.40	27.20	37.8
1130	0.50	16.60	29.30	13.70	29.80	....

Est vol 10,274 Wd 8,667 calls 15,084 puts
Op int Wed 78,929 calls 160,280 puts

OIL

Crude Oil (NYM)
1,000 bbls.; $ per bbl.

STRIKE	CALLS-SETTLE			PUTS-SETTLE		
PRICE	Mar	Apr	May	Mar	Apr	May
2000	1.23	2.03	2.63	0.01	0.52	0.89
2050	0.73	1.70	2.19	0.01	0.68	1.07
2100	0.23	1.40	1.91	0.01	0.88	1.28
2150	0.01	1.13	1.65	0.27	1.11	1.52
2200	0.01	0.92	1.41	0.77	1.40	1.78
2250	0.01	0.73	1.21	1.27	1.71	2.08

Est vol 46,153 Wd 36,811 calls 24,990 puts
Op int Wed 467,500 calls 491,043 puts

Heating Oil No.2 (NYM)
42,000 gal.; $ per gal.

STRIKE	CALLS-SETTLE			PUTS-SETTLE		
PRICE	Mar	Apr	May	Mar	Apr	May
54	.0263	.0402	.0491	.0101	.0219	.0298
55	.0205	.0348	.0439	.0143	.0264	.0345
56	.0155	.0299	.0390	.0193	.0315	.0396
57	.0115	.0256	.0348	.0253	.0372	.0454
58	.0084	.0219	.0309	.0322	.0434	.0514
59	.0059	.0186	.0274	.0397	.0501	....

Est vol 1,523 Wd 837 calls 1,646 puts
Op int Wed 37,030 calls 28,308 puts

Gasoline-Unlead (NYM)
42,000 gal.; $ per gal.

STRIKE	CALLS-SETTLE			PUTS-SETTLE		
PRICE	Mar	Apr	May	Mar	Apr	May
58	.0327	....	.1126	.0101	.0072	.0132
59	.0264	....	....	.0138	.0091	.0156
60	.0210	....	....	.0184	.0113	.0183
61	.0164	.0767	.0909	.0238	.0138	.0213
62	.0126	.0696	.0843	....	.0167	.0246
63	.0095	.0630	.0780	.0369	.0200	.0282

Est vol 1,880 Wd 1,745 calls 2,530 puts
Op int Wed 31,215 calls 24,756 puts

CURRENCY

Japanese Yen (CME)
12,500,000 yen; cents per 100 yen

STRIKE	CALLS-SETTLE			PUTS-SETTLE		
PRICE	Mar	Apr	May	Mar	Apr	May
7500	1.26	....	....	0.43	0.66	0.92
7550	0.94	1.51	....	0.61	0.83	1.10
7600	0.68	1.22	....	0.85	1.04	1.32
7650	0.48	0.98	....	1.15	1.30	....
7700	0.34	0.78	1.05	1.51	1.60	....
7750	0.24	0.61	....	....	1.92	....

Est vol 2,806 Wd 380 calls 1,941 puts
Op int Wed 42,805 calls 65,626 puts

Canadian Dollar (CME)
100,000 Can.$, cents per Can.$

STRIKE	CALLS-SETTLE			PUTS-SETTLE		
PRICE	Mar	Apr	Jun	Mar	Apr	Jun
6200	0.90	....	....	0.12	....	0.53
6250	0.54	0.70	0.96	0.26	....	0.72
6300	0.29	0.45	0.72	0.51	....	0.98
6350	0.13	....	0.53	0.85	....	1.28
6400	0.07	....	0.39	1.29	....	....
6450	0.04	....	0.29	1.76	....	....

Est vol 415 Wd 97 calls 4 puts
Op int Wed 20,812 calls 5,192 puts

British Pound (CME)
62,500 pounds; cents per pound

STRIKE	CALLS-SETTLE			PUTS-SETTLE		
PRICE	Mar	Apr	May	Mar	Apr	May
1410	2.20	2.08	....	0.36	0.94	....
1420	1.46	1.52	....	0.62	1.38	....
1430	0.82	1.00	....	0.98	1.86	....
1440	0.48	0.68	....	1.64	2.54	....
1450	0.24	0.46	....	....	....	....
1460	0.10	....	....	3.26	....	....

Est vol 307 Wd 228 calls 236 puts
Op int Wed 4,324 calls 6,863 puts

Euro Fx (CME)
125,000 euros; cents per euro

STRIKE	CALLS-SETTLE			PUTS-SETTLE		
PRICE	Mar	Apr	Jun	Mar	Apr	Jun
8650	1.19	....	....	0.41	0.93	....
8700	0.88	1.14	1.81	0.60	1.17	1.84
8750	0.63	....	....	0.85	....	....
8800	0.43	0.72	1.37	1.15	1.75	2.39
8850	0.29	....	....	1.51	....	....
8900	0.19	0.44	1.03	1.91	....	3.04

Est vol 1,754 Wd 1,706 calls 1,155 puts
Op int Wed 34,167 calls 19,837 puts

METALS

Copper (CMX)
25,000 lbs.; cents per lb.

STRIKE	CALLS-SETTLE			PUTS-SETTLE		
PRICE	Mar	Apr	May	Mar	Apr	May
70	4.55	5.40	6.15	0.15	0.65	1.20
72	2.90	3.95	4.80	0.45	1.20	1.80
74	1.60	2.75	3.65	1.15	2.00	2.65
76	0.70	1.80	2.70	2.25	3.05	3.70
78	0.25	1.15	1.95	3.80	4.35	4.90
80	0.10	0.65	1.35	5.65	5.90	6.30

Est vol 150 Wd 440 calls 122 puts
Op int Wed 9,888 calls 2,045 puts

Gold (CMX)
100 troy ounces; $ per troy ounce

STRIKE	CALLS-SETTLE			PUTS-SETTLE		
PRICE	Apr	May	Jun	Apr	May	Jun
290	12.10	16.00	16.30	1.90	5.30	5.50
295	8.50	13.00	13.90	3.30	7.20	8.10
300	6.50	10.40	11.40	6.30	9.60	10.60
305	4.50	8.50	9.40	9.30	12.60	13.60
310	3.50	6.90	7.30	13.30	16.00	16.50
315	3.00	5.60	6.50	17.70	19.70	20.60

Est vol 8,000 Wd 4,566 calls 1,574 puts
Op int Wed 146,319 calls 64,080 puts

Silver (CMX)
5,000 troy ounces; cts per troy ounces

STRIKE	CALLS-SETTLE			PUTS-SETTLE		
PRICE	Apr	May	Jul	Apr	May	Jul
400	54.5	55.6	58.3	0.3	1.4	3.6
425	31.2	33.6	38.7	2.0	4.5	8.8
450	12.9	17.4	23.5	8.7	13.2	18.1
475	5.1	10.2	15.7	25.9	31.0	35.3
500	2.6	6.4	10.5	48.4	52.1	54.9
525	1.6	4.6	8.0	72.4	75.1	77.1

Est vol 4,000 Wd 1,380 calls 589 puts
Op int Wed 46,689 calls 8,862 puts

INTEREST RATE

T-Bonds (CBT)
$100,000; points – 64ths of 100%

STRIKE	CALLS-SETTLE			PUTS-SETTLE		
PRICE	Mar	Apr	May	Mar	Apr	May
101	2-27	1-61	....	0-03	0-49	....
102	1-32	1-23	....	0-08	1-11	1-47
103	0-47	0-58	1-29	0-23	1-45	....
104	0-17	0-36	....	0-57	....	....
105	0-05	0-22	0-50	1-45	3-09	....
106	0-01	0-12	0-35	2-41	....	....

Est vol 63,000;
Wd vol 44,637 calls 34,362 puts
Op int Wed 353,154 calls 222,681 puts

T-Notes (CBT)
$100,000; points – 64ths of 100%

STRIKE	CALLS-SETTLE			PUTS-SETTLE		
PRICE	Mar	Apr	May	Mar	Apr	May
104	2-27	1-41	....	0-01	0-37	....
105	1-30	1-02	1-30	0-04	0-62	1-26
106	0-41	0-39	1-01	0-15	1-35	1-61
107	0-09	0-21	....	0-47	....	....
108	0-02	0-10	0-28	1-40	....	....
109	0-01	0-05	....	2-39	....	....

Est vol 100,000 Wd 68,715 calls 62,386 puts
Op int Wed 978,228 calls 563,870 puts

5 Yr Treas Notes (CBT)
$100,000; points – 64ths of 100%

STRIKE	CALLS-SETTLE			PUTS-SETTLE		
PRICE	Mar	Apr	Jun	Mar	Apr	Jun
10550	1-13	0-49	1-17	0-02	0-36	1-04
10600	0-47	0-34	1-01	0-04	0-53	1-20
10650	0-21	0-21	0-52	0-10	....	....
10700	0-07	0-13	0-40	0-28	....	....
10750	0-02	0-09	0-31	0-55	....	....
10800	0-01	0-06	0-25	1-22	....	....

Est vol 28,000 Wd 24,071 calls 13,225 puts
Op int Wed 306,597 calls 188,044 puts

Eurodollar (CME)
$ million; pts of 100%

STRIKE	CALLS-SETTLE			PUTS-SETTLE		
PRICE	Feb	Mar	Apr	Feb	Mar	Apr
9750	....	5.30	2.62	0.00	0.00	0.67
9775	2.80	2.82	1.05	0.00	0.02	1.60
9800	0.35	0.67	0.30	0.05	0.37	3.35
9825	0.00	0.07	0.10	2.20	2.27	....
9850	0.00	0.00	....	....	4.70	....
9875	....	0.00	....	....	7.20	....

Est vol 256,429;
Wd vol 259,399 calls 84,520 puts
Op int Wed 4,986,874 calls 3,896,773 puts

Source: *The Wall Street Journal*, 15 February 2002. Printed with permission from *The Wall Street Journal*, Dow Jones & Co. Inc.

example, suppose that on the expiration date of the option, the contract price of the April copper futures has risen to $0.79. At this point, the holder will exercise her option and assume a long position in an April futures with a contract price of $0.76 per pound, which will require posting a margin account. Her new position will immediately be marked to market, however, and $750 (= [0.79 − 0.76] × 25,000) will be added to her margin account. Alternatively, she may decide to unwind her "below market" futures contract immediately and take the $750 in cash.

The primary attraction of this derivative is the leverage that it provides to an investor. In this example, the call buyer has been able to control 25,000 pounds of copper for two months for an investment of $450. Had she purchased the copper, it would have cost her $18,687.50 (= 25,000 × 0.7475), assuming that the spot and futures prices were the same on this date. Further, even if it only required a 5 percent margin, a long position in the copper futures contract would necessitate a cash outlay of $934.38. Since leverage is the driving force behind this market, in most cases the option is set up to expire at virtually the same time as the underlying futures contract. This indicates that actually acquiring a futures position is not a primary concern of the option users.

THE FUNDAMENTALS OF OPTION VALUATION

Although we know that options can be used by investors to anticipate future levels of security prices, the key to understanding how they are valued comes from recognizing that they also are risk reduction tools. Specifically, in this section we show that an option's theoretical value depends on combining it with its underlying security to create a *synthetic risk-free portfolio*. That is, it always is theoretically possible to use the option as a perfect *hedge* against fluctuations in the value of the asset on which it is based.

Recall that this was essentially the same approach we used in Chapter 21 to establish the put-call parity relationships. The primary differences between put-call parity and what follows are twofold. First, the hedge portfolio implied by the put-call parity transaction did not require special calibration; it simply consisted of one stock long, one put long, and one call short—a mixture that required no adjustment prior to the expiration date. However, hedging an underlying asset position's risk with a single option position—whether it is a put or a call—often involves using multiple contracts and frequent changes in the requisite number to maintain the riskless portfolio. Second, the put-call parity paradigm did not demand a forecast of the underlying asset's future price level whereas the following analysis will. Indeed, we will see that *forecasting the volatility of future asset prices* is the most important input the investor must provide in determining option values.

The Basic Approach While the mathematics associated with option valuation can be complex, the fundamental intuition behind the process is straightforward and can be illustrated quite simply. Suppose you have just purchased a share of stock in WYZ Corp. for $50. The stock is not expected to pay a dividend during the time you plan to hold it, and you have forecast that in one year the stock price will either rise to $65 or fall to $40. This can be summarized as follows:

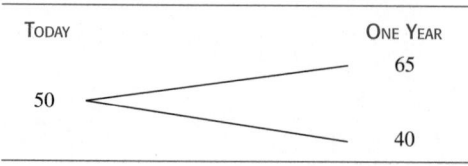

Suppose further that you can either buy or sell a call option on WYZ stock with an exercise price of $52.50. If this is a European-style contract that expires in exactly one year, it will have the following possible expiration date values:

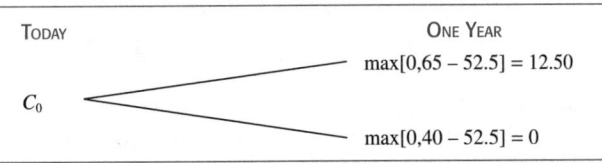

Although you do not know what the call option is worth today, you know what it is worth at expiration, given your forecast of future WYZ stock prices. The dilemma is establishing what the option should sell for today (i.e., C_0).

This question can be answered in three steps. First, design a hedge portfolio consisting of one share of WYZ stock held long and some number of call options (i.e., h), so that the combined position will be riskless. The number of call options needed can be established by ensuring that the portfolio has the same value at expiration no matter which of the two forecasted stock values occurs, or

$$65 + (h)(12.50) = 40 + (h)(0)$$

leaving

$$h = \frac{(65 - 40)}{(0 - 12.5)} = -2.00$$

There are both *direction* and *magnitude* dimensions to this number. That is, the negative sign indicates that, in order to create the necessary negative correlation between two assets that are naturally positively correlated, call options must be *sold* to hedge a long stock position. Further, given that the range of possible expiration date option outcomes (i.e., 12.5 – 0) is only half as large as the range for WYZ stock (i.e., 65 – 40), twice as many options must be sold as there is stock in the hedge portfolio. The value h is known as the *hedge ratio*.[4] Thus, the risk-free hedge portfolio can be created by purchasing one share of stock and selling two call options.

The second step in the option valuation process assumes capital markets that are free from arbitrage. Specifically, suppose no arbitrage possibilities exist in these markets so that all riskless investments are priced to earn the risk-free rate over the time until expiration. That is, the hedge portfolio costing $[50 - (2)(C_0)]$ today would "grow" to the certain value of $40 by the following formula:

$$[50 - (2.00)(C_0)](1 + RFR)^T = 40$$

where:

RFR = the annualized risk-free rate
T = the time to expiration (i.e., one year)

---

[4] In some valuation models (e.g.. Black-Scholes), the hedge ratio is expressed as the option's potential volatility divided by that for the stock. In this example, that would be $(0 - 12.5) \div (65 - 40) = -0.5$, meaning that the option is half as volatile in dollar terms as the share of stock. Of course, this alternative calculation is just the reciprocal of the value of $h = -2.00$.

Two unknown values exist in this formula: C_0 and *RFR*. Finding a suitable estimate for *RFR* seldom is a problem because the investor can use as a proxy the yield to maturity on a U.S. Treasury security of appropriate length. For example, if the one-year T-bill yield is 8 percent, the formula for C_0 can be solved as follows:

$$C_0 = \frac{50 - 40/1.08}{2.00} = \$6.48$$

This bit of algebraic manipulation is the third and final step in establishing the call's fair market value. That is, \$6.48 represents the fundamental value of a one-year call option on WYZ stock, given both the prevailing market prices for two other securities (i.e., stock and T-bills) and the investor's forecast of future share values. Of course, since the security prices are observable, the investor's forecast of future share values becomes the critical element in determining if this present value is a reasonable estimate. Finally, since the call option is currently out of the money, this amount is purely a time premium.

Improving Forecast Accuracy Because it is unrealistic to assume only two possible outcomes for future WYZ share prices, the quality of the preceding valuation is highly suspect. To improve the accuracy of this process, the expiration date forecast of stock prices can be expanded to allow for numerous possibilities. To see the consequences of this expansion in the simplest terms possible, consider a revised forecast that includes only one additional potential price falling between the previous extreme values:

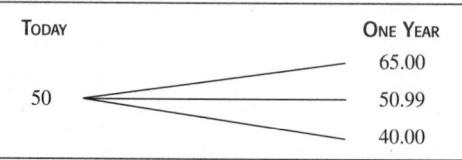

TODAY	ONE YEAR
	65.00
50	50.99
	40.00

Although the three-step riskless hedge approach to calculating C_0 is still conceptually valid, the exact methodology must be modified because it is now impossible to calculate a hedge ratio that simultaneously accounts for all three Date *T* possibilities. That is, there will be several different hedge ratios defined by each distinct pair of future share prices, which, in turn, means that it is impossible for the preceding valuation process to consider all three possible stock outcomes at once.

Creating a Stock Price Tree The solution to this problem involves dividing the time to expiration into as many *subintervals* as necessary so that at any point in time the subsequent price can only move up or down. In this example, only one additional subinterval is needed. Exhibit 23.5 shows how the WYZ stock price forecast might be embellished in this manner. This illustration, which is sometimes called a *stock price tree,* indicates that before the current stock price can reach, say, \$65 in one year, it must first move up to \$57.01 in Subperiod S1 before moving up a second time to its final value of \$65. Similarly, the lower extreme of \$40 can only be reached by two consecutive "down" price changes. On the other hand, there are two different paths to the terminal outcome in the middle: one "up" followed by one "down" or a down movement followed by an up movement both reach \$50.99.

Once the investor fills in all the details in this price tree, the call option's value can be solved by working backward on each pair of possible outcomes from the future. If, for instance, one up movement left the price of WYZ stock at \$57.01, a price change over the remaining subperiod could be characterized as:

EXHIBIT 23.5   *FORECASTED STOCK PRICE TREE (THREE TERMINAL OUTCOMES)*

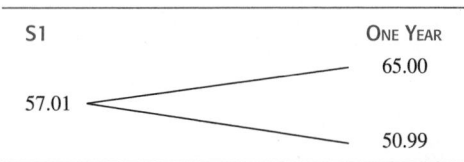

The change in the value of the call option from this uppermost state of Subinterval S1 (i.e., C_{11}) can then be shown as

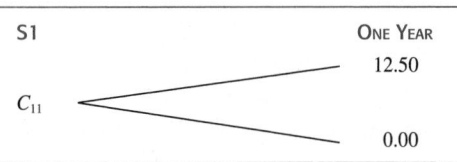

With $X = 52.50$, the call option will be in the money at expiration only if WYZ stock moves up in price again. This suggests a hedge ratio of:

$$h = \frac{(65.00 - 50.99)}{(0.00 - 12.50)} = -1.12$$

meaning that the riskless hedge portfolio at this point would contain one share of stock long and 1.12 calls short. The intermediate option value is then found by solving:

$$[57.01 - (1.12)(C_{11})](1.08)^{0.5} = [65 - (1.12)(12.50)] = 50.99$$

or

$$C_{11} = \frac{57.01 - 50.99/1.0392}{1.12} = \$7.09$$

Here the factor 1.0392 [= $(1.08)^{0.5}$] is roughly one-half the annual risk-free rate (plus one) since the original holding period was divided into two subintervals of equal length (i.e., six months each).

Valuing in Other Subintervals Having established the value for C_{11}, the value for the option corresponding to an S1 share price of $44.72 (i.e., C_{12}) can be established by the same three-step procedure with the stock and option price trees truncated as follows:

and

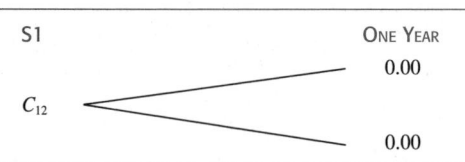

Notice that in this case the call option is certain to be out of the money at the expiration date one subinterval hence. That is, given this forecast of potential stock prices, if the WYZ stock falls in value to $44.72 after one subperiod, even a subsequent recovery to $50.99 (i.e., an up move in the second subperiod) would leave the share price below the $52.50 exercise price of the call option. Thus, it is clear that C_{12} must be $0.00; any security that is certain to be worthless in the future must also be worthless today. Further, it should also be noted that the concept of forming a riskless hedge portfolio under such circumstances is meaningless.

These intermediate calculations have little meaning to the investor who only cares about the current value of the option. They are, however, a necessary evil as C_0 cannot be established before determining C_{11} and C_{12}. With these values in hand, the relevant part of the stock price tree is

with the corresponding call option tree being given by

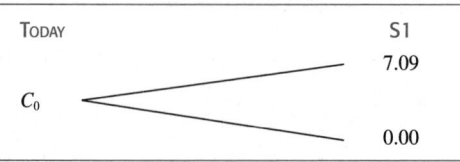

Once again applying the three-step valuation process, the initial (i.e., Date 0) hedge ratio is

$$h = \frac{(57.01 - 44.72)}{(0.00 - 7.09)} = -1.73$$

so that the riskless hedge portfolio at inception would short 1.73 calls for every share held long.

EXHIBIT 23.6 ▶ *TREE OF CALCULATED OPTION VALUES (THREE TERMINAL OUTCOMES)*

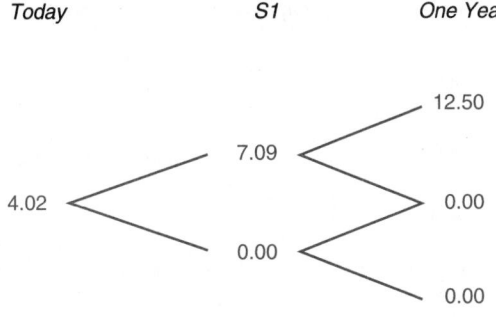

The current option value is then found by solving

$$[50.00 - (1.73)(C_0)](1.08)^{0.5} = [44.72 - (1.73)(0.00)] = 44.72$$

or

$$C_{11} = \frac{50.00 - 44.72/1.0392}{1.73} = \$4.02$$

These initial, intermediate, and terminal option values are summarized in Exhibit 23.6.

Two interesting things resulted from this expansion from two to three possible stock price outcomes. First, notice that the addition of a third potential terminal stock price had the effect of reducing the Date 0 option value from \$6.48 to \$4.02. Although this reduction was a consequence of choosing a third stock price (i.e., \$50.99) that caused the option to be out of the money—selecting a value closer to \$65.00 would have increased C_0—it does underscore once again that the option valuation process critically depends on the investor's stock price forecast. Second, notice also that the hedge ratio changes with stock price changes prior to the expiration date. That is, the composition of the riskless hedge portfolio must be rebalanced after each share price movement. For example, from the initial position of being short 1.73 calls against one share held long, an upward movement in WYZ stock from \$50.00 to \$57.01 would require buying back 0.61 (= 1.73 − 1.12) options. Thus, replicating a risk-free position with stock and call options is a *dynamic* process, a point to which we will return shortly.

Expanding the Stock Price Tree   This valuation process can become even more precise as more terminal share price outcomes are included in the forecast. Of course, as this happens, the number of pairwise calculations and the number of necessary subperiods will also increase. Consequently, although the three-step valuation method is quite flexible, there is a trade-off between realism and the volume of required calculations. To see how even seemingly minor expansions of the stock price forecast can dramatically increase the computational burden, consider the implications of including four potential expiration date stock prices:

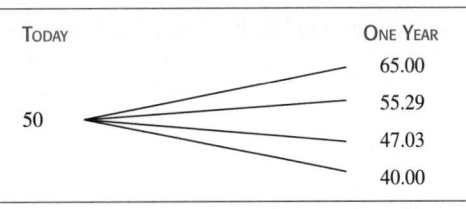

EXHIBIT 23.7 *FORECASTED STOCK PRICE TREE (FOUR TERMINAL OUTCOMES)*

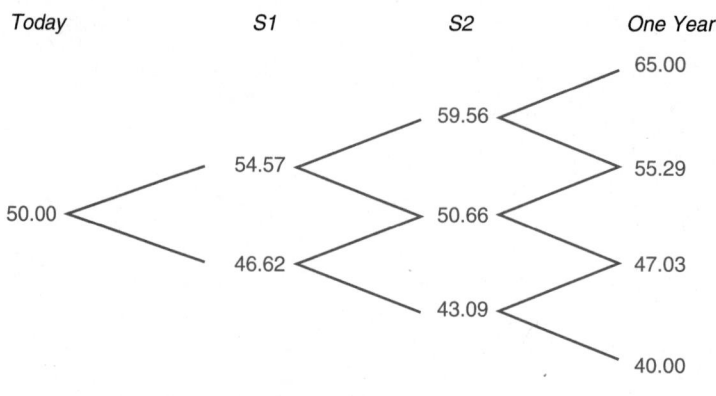

Valuing the option in this case will require the creation of two subintervals (S1 and S2) and five intermediate stock price forecasts. These are illustrated in Exhibit 23.7.

In order to compute C_0, the investor must now work recursively backward through calculations for the five intermediate option values: C_{21}, C_{22}, and C_{23} in Subperiod S2 and C_{11} and C_{12} in Subperiod 1. Of course, each of these calculations applies the same three-step riskless hedge process outlined earlier, appropriately modified for the new length of a subperiod (i.e., one-third of a year instead of six months). If, for instance, two consecutive up movements took the price of WYZ stock from \$50.00 to \$54.57 to \$59.56, a price change over the remaining subperiod could be characterized as

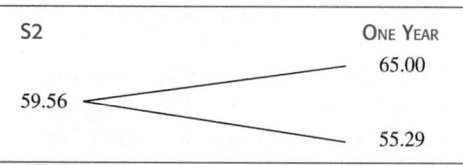

The change in the value of the call option from this uppermost state of Subinterval S2 (i.e., C_{21}) can then be shown as

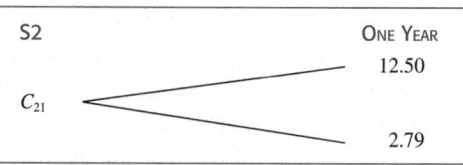

Given its exercise price of \$52.50, the call option would be certain to be in the money for both expiration date stock values. This suggests a hedge ratio of

$$h = \frac{(65.00 - 55.29)}{(2.79 - 12.50)} = -1.00$$

EXHIBIT 23.8   *TREE OF CALCULATED OPTION VALUES (FOUR TERMINAL OUTCOMES)*

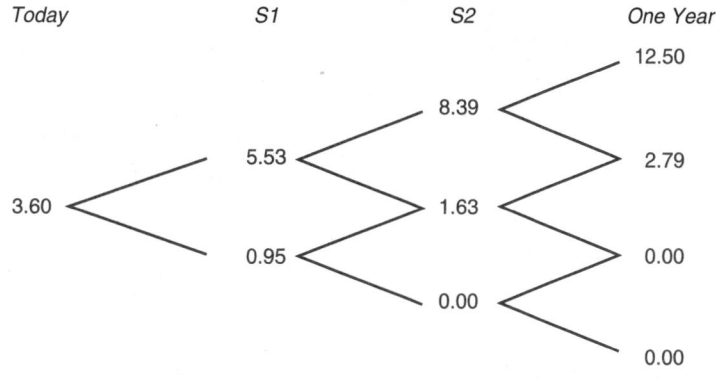

meaning that the riskless hedge portfolio at this point would contain one share of stock long and one call short. As we have seen, C_{21} can then be found by solving

$$[59.56 - (1.00)(C_{21})](1.08)^{0.33} = [65 - (1.00)(12.50)] = 52.50$$

or

$$C_{21} = \frac{59.56 - 52.50/1.026}{1.00} = \$8.39$$

Notice that the discount factor of 1.026 [$= (1.08)^{0.33}$] is now based on roughly one-third of the annual risk-free rate since the one-year option expiration period was adjusted to accommodate three subintervals of equal length. Solving for the remaining values in turn leaves the option value tree shown in Exhibit 23.8. Notice once again that the net effect of these particular forecast improvements has been to change the current value of the derivative to $3.60.

The Binomial Option Pricing Model

A crucial element of this basic approach to option valuation is that future changes in the underlying asset's price always can be simplified to one of two possibilities: an up movement or a down movement. For that reason, this analytical development is part of a more general valuation methodology known as the *two-state option pricing model*.[5] One difficulty with the preceding examples, however, is that they required the investor to specify cash amounts for each of the future potential stock prices in all the subperiods demanded by the forecast. This can be a rather daunting task as the number of terminal outcomes is allowed to grow larger with the time to expiration of the contract.

Forecasting Price Changes   To simplify this forecasting process, suppose an investor focuses her estimates on how stock prices change from one subperiod to the next, rather than on

---

[5]See Richard J. Rendleman, Jr., and Brit J. Bartter, "Two-State Option Pricing," *Journal of Finance* 34, no. 5 (December 1979): 1093–1110; and John C. Cox, Stephen A. Ross, and Mark Rubinstein, "Option Pricing: A Simplified Approach," *Journal of Financial Economics* 7, no. 3 (September 1979): 229–264.

EXHIBIT 23.9   *BINOMIAL MODEL FORECAST TREES*

A. Stock Price Forecasts

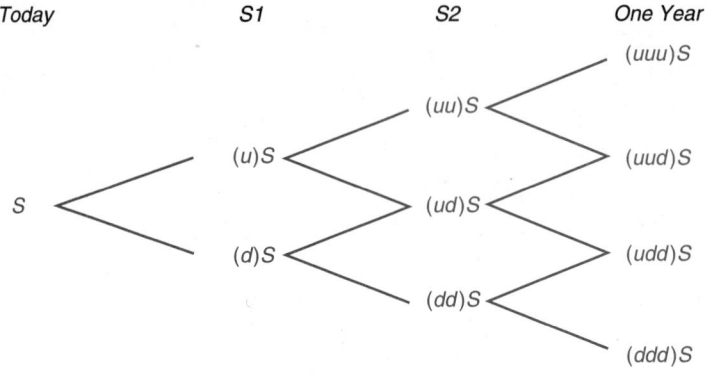

B. Option Value Forecasts

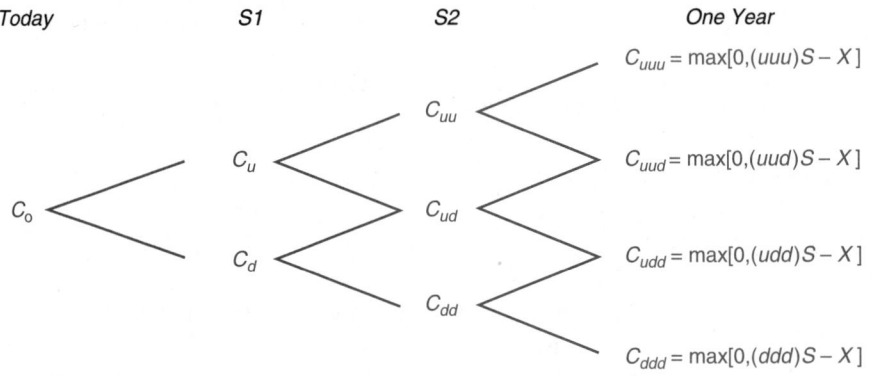

the dollar levels. That is, beginning with today's known price for a stock, for the next subperiod she forecasts: (1) one plus the percentage change associated with an up *(u)* movement, and (2) one plus the percentage change associated with a down *(d)* movement. Further, to limit the number of required forecasts, suppose she also assumes that the same values for *u* and *d* apply to every up and down price change in all subsequent subperiods. With these assumptions, the investor need only forecast three things: *u, d,* and *N*—the total number of subperiods.

Exhibit 23.9 shows the effect that these modifications—which represent the essence of the **binomial option pricing model**—have on the forecasted stock price and option value trees. Consistent with the four-outcome version of the preceding example, this illustration allows for three subperiods (i.e., $N = 3$). The upper panel of the display shows that after an up and a down movement during the first two subperiods, the initial stock price of *S* will have changed to *(ud)S*. Of course, the values *(ud)S* and *(du)S* are equal, meaning that the forecast does not depend on whether the stock price begins its journey by rising or falling. As before, once *u, d,* and *N* are determined, the expiration date payoffs to the option (i.e., C_{uuu}, C_{uud}, C_{udd}, and C_{ddd}) are established.

As before, the initial value for the call, C_0, can be solved by working backward through the tree and solving for each of the remaining intermediate option values. However, another distinct advantage of the binomial model relative to the basic three-step approach is that these intermediate values are much easier to compute. In fact, in the jth state in any subperiod, the value of the option can be calculated by

➤23.1
$$C_j = \frac{(p)C_{ju} + (1-p)C_{jd}}{r}$$

where

$$p = \frac{r-d}{u-d}$$

and

r = one plus the risk-free rate over the subperiod

If p is interpreted as the probability of an up movement in the security's price, which would then mean that $(1-p)$ is the probability of a down move, then the formula for C_j has an intuitively appealing interpretation. That is, the option's value at any point in time can be viewed as its expected value one subperiod hence discounted back to the current time. Further, although p was not an explicit part of the investor's forecast, it is nevertheless generated by the model. In this sense, p is referred to as the *implied probability* of an upward price movement. To ensure that this interpretation holds, the binomial model requires that $d < r < u,$ a condition that is quite reasonable in practice.

Generalizing the Model   Equation 23.1 can be extended to a more useful format by recognizing that the value for C_j it generates is one of the inputs for valuing the option in the preceding subperiod. Thus, the formula for an option in Subperiod t can be inserted into the right-hand side of the formula for Subperiod $t - 1$. Carrying this logic all the way back to Date 0, the binomial option valuation model becomes

➤23.2
$$C_0 = \left\{ \sum_{j=0}^{N} \frac{N!}{(N-j)!\,j!} \, p^j (1-p)^{N-j} \max[0, (u^j d^{N-j})S - X] \right\} \div r^N$$

where

$$N! = [(N)(N-1)(N-2) \ldots (2)(1)]$$

To interpret Equation 23.2, the ratio $[N! \div (N-j)!j!]$ is the "combinatorial" way of stating how many distinct paths lead to a particular terminal outcome, $p^j(1-p)^{N-j}$ is the probability of getting to that outcome, and $\max[0, (u^j d^{N-j})S - X]$ is the payoff associated with that outcome. Letting m be the smallest integer number of up moves guaranteeing that the option will be in the money at expiration (i.e., $u^m d^{N-m})S > X$), this formula can be reduced further to

➤23.3
$$C_0 = \left\{ \sum_{j=m}^{N} \frac{N!}{(N-j)!\,j!} \, p^j (1-p)^{N-j} [(u^j d^{N-j})S - X] \right\} \div r^N$$

As an example of how this model works, assume the investor has gathered contract terms and price data and has made her forecasts as follows: $S = 50.00$, $X = 52.50$, $T =$ one year, $RFR = 8$ percent (through expiration), $u = 1.09139$, $d = 0.92832$, and $N = 3$. By these forecasts, the investor has divided the one-year life of the option into three subperiods and estimated up and down moves during any subperiod as slightly greater than 9 and 7 percent, respectively. Also, the values for r and p implied by these forecasts are 1.026 (= $(1.08)^{0.33}$) and 0.599 (= $[1.026 - 0.92832] \div [1.09139 - 0.92832]$). By Equation 23.3, which ignores the two terminal option outcomes in the full binomial formula that are equal to zero, the value of a one-year European-style call option with an exercise price of $52.50 is

$$C_0 = \frac{(3)(0.599)^2(0.401)(2.79) + (1)(0.599)^3(12.50)}{(1.026)^3} = \$3.60$$

It is not surprising that this is the same value the three-step approach produced in the previous example because the forecasted stock price tree in Exhibit 23.7 was generated with these same values of u and d (e.g., $(uu)S = (1.09139)^2(50) = \$59.56$). We also can confirm that the tree of forecasted option values illustrated in Exhibit 23.8 may be replicated through repeatedly calculating the "state j" equation.[6] Finally, with this notation, the hedge ratio for any state j becomes

$$h_j = \frac{(u - d)S_j}{(C_{jd} - C_{ju})}$$

Thus, a share of stock held long could be hedged initially by shorting 1.78 call options [= $(1.09139 - 0.92832)(50) \div (0.95 - 5.53)$], a position that would be rebalanced to 1.32 calls after one subperiod if the first price change was positive.

The Black-Scholes Valuation Model

The binomial model is a *discrete* method for valuing options because it allows security price changes to occur in distinct upward or downward movements. It also can be assumed that prices change *continuously* throughout time. This was the approach taken by Black and Scholes in developing their celebrated equation for valuing European-style options.[7] This is not a more realistic assumption because it presumes that security prices change when markets are closed (e.g., at night, on weekends). The advantage of the Black-Scholes approach—identical in spirit to the basic three-step, riskless hedge method outlined earlier—is that it leads to a relatively simple, closed-form equation that is capable of valuing options accurately under a wide array of circumstances.

Specifically, the Black-Scholes model assumes that stock price movements can be described by a statistical process known as *geometric Brownian motion*. Ultimately, this process is summarized by a volatility factor, σ, which is analogous to the investor's stock price forecasts in the previous models. Formally, the stock price process assumed by Black and Scholes is

$$\frac{\Delta S}{S} = \mu[\Delta T] + \sigma\varepsilon[\Delta T]^{1/2}$$

That is, a stock's return ($\Delta S/S$) from the present through any future Period T has both an expected component ($\mu[\Delta T]$) and a "noise" component ($\sigma\varepsilon[\Delta T]^{1/2}$), where μ is the mean return and ε is the standard normally distributed random error term.[8]

---

[6]For example, $C_{uu} = [(0.599)(12.50) + (0.401)(2.79)] \div (1.026) = \$8.39$.

[7]See Fischer Black and Myron Scholes, "The Pricing of Options and Corporate Liabilities," *Journal of Political Economy* 81, no. 2 (May–June 1973): 637–654. For an interesting related discussion of this model, see Fischer Black, "How We Came Up with the Option Formula," *Journal of Portfolio Management* 15, no. 2 (Winter 1989): 4–8.

[8]For a detailed analysis of the mathematics underlying the Black-Scholes model, see John Hull, *Options, Futures, and Other Derivatives,* 4th ed. (Upper Saddle River, N.J.: Prentice-Hall, 2000).

Assuming the continuously compounded risk-free rate and the stock's variance (i.e., σ^2) remain constant until the expiration date T, Black and Scholes used the riskless hedge intuition to derive the following formula for valuing a call option on a nondividend-paying stock:

➤**23.4**
$$C_0 = SN(d_1) - X(e^{-(RFR)T})N(d_2)$$

where $e^{-(RFR)T}$ is the discount function for continuously compounded variables,

$$d_1 = [(\ln(S/X) + (RFR + 0.5\sigma^2)[T])] \div (\sigma[T]^{1/2})$$

and

$$d_2 = d_1 - \sigma[T]^{1/2}$$

with $\ln(\cdot)$ being the natural logarithm function. The variable $N(d)$ represents the cumulative probability of observing a value drawn from the standard normal distribution (i.e., one with a mean of zero and a standard deviation of one) equal to or less than d. As the standard normal distribution is symmetric around zero, a value of $d = 0$ would lead to $N(d) = 0.5000$; positive values of d would then have cumulative probabilities greater than 50 percent, with negative values of d leading to cumulative probabilities of less than one-half.

Values for $N(d)$ can be established in two ways. First, an investor can use a table of calculated values for the standard normal distribution, such as the one shown in Appendix D at the end of the book. For example, if the value of d_1 is 0.65, $N(d_1)$ could be established by finding the entry corresponding to the 0.6 row and the 0.05 column, or 0.7422. This means that 74.22 percent of the observations in the standard normal distribution have a value of 0.65 or less. Notice also that if d_1 had been -0.65, the value of $N(-d_1) = 1 - N(d_1) = 1 - 0.7422 = 0.2578$, which must be the case since the distribution is symmetric.

A second approach to calculating cumulative normal probabilities is approximating them with the following formula:

$$N(d) \approx \begin{cases} 0.5e^{-(d^2)/2 - 281/(83 - 351/d)} & \text{if } d < 0 \\ 1 - 0.5e^{-(d^2)/2 - 281/(83 + 351/d)} & \text{if } d \geq 0 \end{cases}$$

For example, with $d = 0.65$, we have an approximate probability of

$$N(0.65) \approx 1 - 0.5e^{-(0.65^2)/2 - 281/(83 + 351/0.65)} = 0.7422$$

This matches the actual value to the fourth decimal place and will likely lead to reasonable valuations.[9]

Properties of the Model   The **Black-Scholes valuation model** has several attractive features. A joint examination of the expressions for C, d_1, and d_2 reveals that the option's value is a function of five variables:

1. Current security price
2. Exercise price
3. Time to expiration

---

[9]For more on this approximation method, as well as how it can be written into a program usable on a hand-held financial calculator, see Peter Carr, "A Calculator Program for Option Values and Implied Standard Deviations," *Journal of Financial Education* 17, no. 1 (Fall 1988): 89–93.

EXHIBIT 23.10 ▶ *FACTORS AFFECTING BLACK-SCHOLES OPTION VALUES*

	WILL CAUSE AN INCREASE/DECREASE IN THE:	
AN INCREASE IN THE:	CALL VALUE	PUT VALUE
Security price (S)	Increase	Decrease
Exercise price (X)	Decrease	Increase
Time to expiration (T)	Increase	Increase or decrease
Risk-free rate (RFR)	Increase	Decrease
Security volatility (σ)	Increase	Increase

4. Risk-free rate
5. Security price volatility

Functionally, the Black-Scholes model holds that $C = f(S, X, T, RFR, \sigma)$. The first and fourth factors are observable market prices, and the second and third variables are defined by the contract itself. Thus, the only variable an investor must provide in the Black-Scholes framework is the volatility factor. As noted earlier, the estimate of σ embeds the investor's forecast of future stock prices.

The value of the call option will rise with increases in each of the five factors *except* the exercise price. Exhibit 23.10 summarizes these relationships. Specifically, the middle column of the exhibit shows what will happen to the value of the call when one of the five factors increases. The intuition behind the first three of these relationships is straightforward. In particular, an increase in the underlying asset's price (i.e., S) will increase the call's intrinsic value; a larger exercise price (i.e., X) will reduce the intrinsic value. Also, the longer the option has until it expires, the more valuable the time premium component. This is because a greater opportunity exists for the contract to finish in the money. On the other hand, the relationships between C, RFR, and σ are less obvious. An increase in RFR will increase the call's value because this reduces the present value of X, an expense that the call holder must pay at expiration to exercise the contract. Similarly, when the volatility of the underlying asset's price increases, the call becomes more valuable since this increases the probability that the option will be deeper in the money at expiration.[10]

Another useful facet of the Black-Scholes model is that the hedge ratio at any moment in time is simply $N(d_1)$, the partial derivative of the call's value with respect to the stock price (i.e., $\delta C/\delta S$). Under this interpretation, $N(d_1)$ is the change in the option's value given a one dollar change in the underlying security's price. For this reason, $N(d_1)$ often is called the option's **delta**, and it indicates the number of stock shares that can be hedged by a single call—the exact reciprocal of the previous interpretation of the hedge ratio, h. Finally, although the Black-Scholes model was developed several years before the binomial framework, the former can be viewed as an extension of the latter. Specifically, as the number of subperiods (i.e., N) is allowed to approach infinity, the up or down price movements begin to occur on a continuous basis. If the values of u and d are then set equal to $e^{\sigma[\Delta T]^{1/2}}$ and $e^{-\sigma[\Delta T]^{1/2}}$, respectively, the binomial model collapses to become the Black-Scholes formula.

---

[10]In more technical terms, these relationships can be summarized as $\delta C/\delta S > 0$, $\delta C/\delta RFR > 0$, $\delta C/\delta T > 0$, $\delta C/\delta \sigma > 0$, and $\delta C/\delta X < 0$.

EXHIBIT 23.11 ▶	*EXAMPLE OF BLACK-SCHOLES VALUATION*	

STOCK PRICE	CALL VALUE	HEDGE RATIO
$25	$0.44	0.1321
30	1.51	0.3054
35	3.53	0.5020
40	6.49	0.6736
45	10.19	0.8003
50	14.42	0.8837
55	18.98	0.9347

Note: Assumes $X = 40$, $T = 1$ year, $RFR = 9\%$, and $\sigma = 0.30$.

An Example As an example of Black-Scholes valuation, consider the following values for the five input variables: $S = 40$, $X = 40$, $T = $ one year, $RFR = 9$ percent, and $\sigma = 0.30$. To calculate the fundamental value of a European-style call option under these conditions, which again will be purely time premium, first calculate:

$$d_1 = (\ln(40/40) + (0.09 + 0.5(0.3)^2)[1]) \div (0.3[1]^{1/2}) = 0.45$$

and

$$d_2 = 0.45 - 0.3[1]^{1/2} = 0.15$$

so that

$$N(d_1) = 1 - 0.5e^{-(0.45^2)/2 - 281/(83 + 351/0.45)} = 0.6736$$

and

$$N(d_2) = 1 - 0.5e^{-(0.15^2)/2 - 281/(83 + 351/0.15)} = 0.5596.$$

Thus,

$$C_0 = (40)(0.6736) - 40(e^{-.09})(0.5596) = \$6.49.$$

$N(d_1)$ says that the call option will change in value by about 67 cents for every dollar of a change in the underlying asset, which, in turn, suggests a hedge ratio of one-and-a-half calls short for every stock share held long. Exhibit 23.11 shows how both the option's value and $N(d_1)$ change as the security's value changes—with the other factors held constant. Notably, the hedge ratios range in value from 0 to 1, and increase as stock prices increase. Therefore, the deeper in the money the option is, the closer its price movements will come to duplicating those of the stock itself. The relationship between stock prices and call option prices for this example is shown in Exhibit 23.12. The delta, or hedge ratio, associated with a given stock price is simply the slope of a line tangent to the call option price curve.

Estimating Volatility Just as the growth rate of dividends (i.e., g) was a crucial element in establishing the fundamental value of common stock using the dividend discount model, option valuation depends critically on an accurate forecast of the underlying asset's future price level. Of course, in the Black-Scholes

EXHIBIT 23.12 ▶ *BLACK-SCHOLES VALUES*

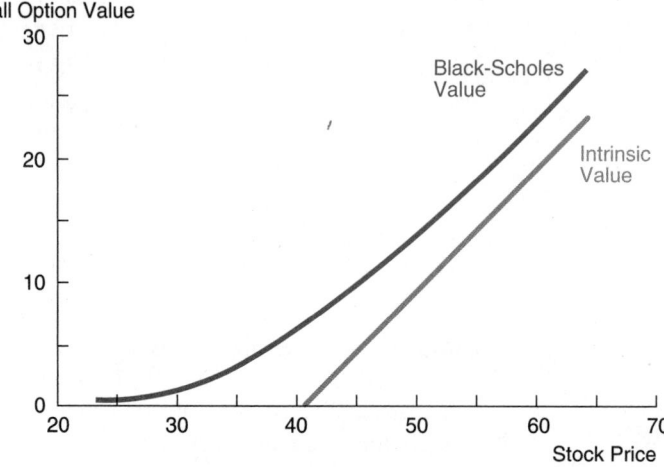

Call Option Values ($X = 40$, $T = 1$ yr, $\sigma = 0.30$, $RFR = 0.09$)

framework, this means selecting the proper σ. From the description of the geometric Brownian motion process, it should be clear that σ is equivalent to the standard deviation of returns to the underlying asset. This value can be estimated in two ways. First, it can be calculated in the traditional manner using historical returns. Specifically, calculate the Day *t price relative* as $R_t = \ln(P_t \div P_{t-1})$. If a series of price relatives are then calculated for a sequence of N days in the recent past, the mean and standard deviation of this series can be calculated as

$$\overline{R} = \left(\frac{1}{N}\right)\sum_{t=1}^{N} R_t \text{ and } \sigma^2 = \left(\frac{1}{N-1}\right)\sum_{t=1}^{N}(R_t - \overline{R})^2$$

The factor σ is expressed in terms of daily price movements. To annualize this value, σ can be multiplied by the square root of the number of trading days in the year (usually assumed to be 250), which then becomes the estimate of volatility employed in the Black-Scholes formula. The advantage of historical volatility is that it is easy to compute and requires no prior assumption about stock market efficiency; its disadvantage is its presumption that stock price behavior in the future will continue as it has in the past, a sometimes dubious assumption in a rapidly changing world.[11] Exhibit 23.13 lists 30-day historical volatilities for a representative sample of optionable stocks during November 2001.

An alternative to relying on historical price movements is a second volatility estimation approach that involves the Black-Scholes equation. Recall that if we know all five input factors—$S, X, T, RFR,$ and σ—we can solve for the value of the call option. However, because σ is the only unobservable input, and if we know the current price of the option (call it C^*) and the four other variables, we can calculate the level of σ that forces the Black-Scholes value to equal C^*. That is, the volatility implied by current market prices is established by finding σ^* such that

---

[11]For a good discussion of how stock price volatility has changed over time, see Alexander M. Ineichen, "Twentieth Century Volatility," *Journal of Portfolio Management* 27, no. 1 (Fall 2000): 93–101.

EXHIBIT 23.13 ▶ *HISTORICAL VOLATILITY ESTIMATES*

COMPANY	TICKER	30-DAY VOLATILITY ESTIMATE
Amazon.com	AMZN	96.56%
Applied Materials	AMAT	23.52
Bank of America	BAC	17.89
Cendant	CD	26.60
Cisco Systems	CSCO	21.97
Citigroup	C	19.16
Coca Cola	KO	8.71
Dell Computer	DELL	18.57
Duke Energy	DUK	25.36
eBay	EBAY	25.24
General Electric	GE	17.37
Haliburton	HAL	30.39
Intel	INTC	24.83
Merck	MRK	10.07
Oracle	ORCL	19.46
Pfizer	PFE	6.03
Philip Morris	MO	17.04
Siebel Systems	SEBL	73.32
Wal-Mart	WMT	9.40
Xerox	XRX	55.05

Source: Chicago Board Options Exchange, 15 February 2002. Provided as a courtesy by Chicago Board Options Exchange, Incorporated.

$C^* = f(S, X, T, RFR, \sigma^*)$. Accordingly, the value σ^* is known as the **implied volatility**. No simple closed-form solution exists for performing this calculation; it must be done by trial and error.

Implied volatility is advantageous because it calculates the same volatility forecast investors use to set option prices. The disadvantage of implied volatility is its presumption that markets are efficient in that the option price set in the market corresponds directly to that generated by the Black-Scholes equation. Beckers has shown that implied volatilities do a better job than historical volatilities of predicting future stock price movements; however, Figlewski cautions that σ^* can be "noisy" because it picks up not only the true level of volatility but any misestimate inherent in the valuation process.[12]

As an example of this calculation, Brown, Harlow, and Tinic estimated the volatilities implied by the S&P 500 index call option contract for the 121-day period surrounding the stock market crash in October 1987.[13] These calculations are reproduced in Exhibit 23.14. In this display, the

---

[12]See Stan Beckers, "Standard Deviations Implied in Option Prices as Predictors of Future Stock Price Variability," *Journal of Banking and Finance* 5, no. 3 (September 1981): 363–381; Stephen Figlewski, "What Does an Option Pricing Model Tell Us about Option Prices?" *Financial Analysts Journal* 45, no. 5 (September–October 1989): 12–15; and Charles J. Corrado and Thomas W. Miller, Jr., "Efficient Option-Implied Volatility Estimators," *Journal of Futures Markets* 16, no. 3 (June 1996): 247–272. For an exhaustive review of the literature on this topic, see Stewart Mayhew, "Implied Volatility," *Financial Analysts Journal* 51, no. 4 (July–August 1995): 8–20.

[13]See Keith C. Brown, W. V. Harlow, and Seha M. Tinic, "How Rational Investors Deal with Uncertainty (Or, Reports of the Death of Efficient Market Theory Are Greatly Exaggerated)," *Journal of Applied Corporate Finance* 2, no. 3 (Fall 1989): 45–58.

EXHIBIT 23.14 ▶ *IMPLIED VOLATILITIES AND THE STOCK MARKET CRASH OF 1987*

time variable is denominated relative to "Black Monday" [i.e., Day 0], which occurred on October 19, 1987. To see how much market risk changed with the crash, the *average* implied volatility measure for the period Day –60 to Day –5 (i.e., the period beginning approximately two and a half months before the crash) was 18.9 percent. The comparable statistic for the period Day +5 to Day +60 was 43.3 percent. Moreover, on Black Monday itself, the implied volatility rose to 145 percent, more than seven and a half times its pre-crash level!

Problems with Black-Scholes Valuation

The Black-Scholes option valuation model is popular with investors for at least two reasons: It is computationally convenient, and it produces reasonable values under a wide variety of conditions. There are, however, circumstances in which the model is less than desirable. The implied volatilities just described have also been useful in determining whether the fundamental values produced by Equation 23.4 match the traded prices for option contracts. In one of the earliest empirical tests of the Black-Scholes equation, MacBeth and Merville showed for a sample of six stocks that implied volatilities tended to be overly large when the associated call options were in the money and too small for out-of-the-money contracts.[14] Assuming that at-the-money options are priced fairly by the market, this suggested that in-the-money options were priced higher by investors than their Black-Scholes values, with the opposite being true for the out-of-the-money contracts. Thus, for the authors' sample of stocks, the Black-Scholes model overvalued out-of-the-money call options and undervalued in-the-money contracts. Interestingly, in two different studies, Rubinstein found evidence that both supported and contradicted these results.[15]

In general, any violation of the assumptions upon which the Black-Scholes model is based could lead to a misvaluation of the option contract. For instance, it was already noted that stock prices do not change continuously, meaning that stocks that are less actively traded might have

---

[14]See James D. MacBeth and Larry J. Merville, "An Empirical Examination of the Black-Scholes Call Option Pricing Model," *Journal of Finance* 34, no. 5 (December 1979): 1173–1186.

[15]See Mark Rubinstein, "Nonparametric Tests of Alternative Options Pricing Models Using All Reported Trades and Quotes on the 30 Most Active CBOE Options Classes from August 23, 1976, through August 31, 1978," *Journal of Finance* 40, no. 2 (June 1985): 455–480, and "Implied Binomial Trees," *Journal of Finance* 49, no. 3 (July 1994): 771–818.

options that are priced differently in the market than those stocks that trade frequently. Indeed, Figlewski has noted how such market imperfections as brokerage fees, bid-ask spreads, and inflexible position sizes can create arbitrageable differences between option values and prices.[16] He cautioned that Black-Scholes values are best viewed as approximations, best suited for comparing prices of different contracts. Further, Black has noted that other conditions of the model are almost certain to be violated in practice, such as the assumption that the risk-free rate and volatility level remain constant until the expiration date. He discusses how some of these problems can be exploited by investors.[17]

OPTION VALUATION: EXTENSIONS AND ADVANCED TOPICS

The preceding discussion has concentrated on the valuation of European-style call options having a nondividend-paying stock as the underlying asset. Many other conditions and underlying assets exist for which options need to be valued. This section explores several extensions of the basic approach as well as other important topics relevant to the valuation process.

Valuing European-Style Put Options

The put-call-spot parity model of Chapter 21 held that, in an efficient market, the value of a European-style put on a nondividend-paying security should be equivalent to a portfolio short in the security while long in both a call option and a Treasury bill having a face value equal to the common exercise price X. Converting the discounting process for the T-bill to be a continuous function, this relationship can be expressed

$$P_0 = C_0 + X(e^{-(RFR)T}) - S$$

This formula implies that if we know the prices of the security, the call option, and the T-bill, we can solve for the value of the put option. Alternatively, if the Black-Scholes value for C is inserted into this expression, we have

$$P_0 = [SN(d_1) - X(e^{-(RFR)T})N(d_2)] + X(e^{-(RFR)T}) - S$$

which can be manipulated to equal

➤23.5
$$P_0 = X(e^{-(RFR)T})N(-d_2) - SN(-d_1)$$

where all the notation is the same as before. Equation 23.5 is the Black-Scholes put option valuation model.

The comparative statics of put option valuation were shown in the final column of Exhibit 23.10. In particular, the value of the put will increase with higher levels of X but decline with an increase in S because of the effect these movements have on the contract's intrinsic value. Like the call option, the put's value benefits from an increase in σ since this increases the likelihood that the contract will finish deep in the money. Also, an increase in the risk-free rate reduces the present value of X, which hurts the holder of the put who receives the striking price if the contract is exercised. Finally, the sign of $\delta P/\delta T$ could be either positive or negative depending on the

---

[16]See Stephen Figlewski, "Options Arbitrage in Imperfect Markets," *Journal of Finance* 44, no. 5 (December 1989): 1289–1311.

[17]See Fischer Black, "How to Use the Holes in Black-Scholes," *Journal of Applied Corporate Finance* 1, no. 4 (Winter 1989): 67–73.

trade-off between the longer time over which the security price could move in the desired direction and the reduced present value of the exercise price received by the seller at expiration.

In the preceding example of a Black-Scholes call option valuation, we had the following inputs: $S = 40$, $X = 40$, T = one year, RFR = 9 percent, and $\sigma = 0.30$. With these assumptions, d_1 and d_2 still are 0.45 and 0.15, respectively, but now we need to compute $N(-0.45) = 1 - 0.6736 = 0.3264$ and $N(-0.15) = 1 - 0.5596 = 0.4404$. Thus:

$$P_0 = 40(e^{-.09})(0.4404) - 40(0.3264) = \$3.04$$

Finally, the hedge ratio for the put option in this model is $[N(d_1) - 1]$, which in this case is -0.3264 and indicates that the put option's value will *decrease* by approximately 33 cents for every dollar *increase* in S.

Valuing Options on Dividend-Bearing Securities

We learned earlier that the put-call parity relationship required an adjustment when the underlying asset common to both the put and call options paid a dividend. This adjustment is needed because the payment of the dividend reduces the asset's market value, converting the investor's return from capital appreciation to cash flow. Thus, other than the tax implications of this conversion, the underlying asset's owner should not lose any overall net worth over the payment of the dividend. On the other hand, the problem for the prospective call option owner is that he will not receive the dividend; therefore, the reduction in the present value of the stock will reduce the value of his derivative contract. Being rational, he will reduce the price he is willing to pay for the call option on the dividend-bearing security. Consequently, dividends become a sixth factor in the option valuation process.

The original Black-Scholes valuation model can be modified to incorporate dividend payments in two ways. The most straightforward and most accurate approach is reducing the current share price by the present value of the dividends paid during the option's life and then using this amount in place of the actual stock price. That is, replace S in the model with $S' = S - PV$ (dividends). For example, for the case of the one-year, at-the-money call option with an exercise price of $40 that we saw earlier, assume that a dividend payment of $1 is made in six months, with another $1 paid just prior to expiration. Recalling that the continuously compounded risk-free rate and volatility factors were 9 percent and 30 percent, respectively, we would then have

$$S' = 40 - (1)e^{-(0.09)(0.5)} - (1)e^{-(0.09)(1.0)} = 38.13$$

When inserted into the formulas for d_1 and d_2, this S' would generate values of 0.29 and -0.01, respectively.

With these inputs, the Black-Scholes valuation then becomes

$$C_0 = (38.13)N(0.29) + (40)e^{-0.09}N(0.01) = (38.13)(0.6141) - (36.56)(0.4960) = \$5.28$$

This amount can be compared to the $6.49 contract value for an otherwise identical call on a nondividend-paying share that we estimated earlier. In particular, the reduction in option value (i.e., $1.21) is not as great as the present value of the dividends (i.e., $1.87). This is due to the possibility that the option would have expired out of the money even without the dividend payment, meaning that the dividend-induced stock price reduction will not always affect the contract's terminal payoff. Also, the hedge ratio in the formula is reduced from its original level of 0.6736 to 0.6141.

The second approach to adjusting the option valuation process for dividend payments involves modifying the model itself rather than the stock price input. This requires expressing the dividend in *yield* form, defined as the annual payment divided by the current stock price, and assuming that this yield is paid continuously. Merton first showed that the Black-Scholes model can be rewritten as

$$C_0 = (e^{-(D)T})SN(d_1) - X(e^{-(RFR)T})N(d_2)$$

with

$$d_1 = [\ln((e^{-(D)T})S/X) + (RFR + 0.5\sigma^2)[T]] \div (\sigma[T]^{1/2})$$

and

$$d_2 = d_1 - \sigma[T]^{1/2}$$

where:

D = the annualized dividend yield[18]

The yield appears as a "discount" factor to the current stock value in two places in these equations. If we set $S' = (e^{-(D)T})S$, this second dividend adjustment is seen as just a continuous version of the first.

Extending the original example, we now have six factors to include: $S = 40$, $X = 40$, $T =$ one year, $RFR = 9$ percent, $\sigma = 30$ percent, and $D = (2/40) = 5$ percent. Plugging these into the model, we get values of 0.28 for d_1 and -0.02 for d_2 so that

$$C_0 = (e^{-0.05})(40)N(0.28) - (e^{-0.09})(40)N(-0.02)$$
$$= (38.05)(0.6103) - (36.56)(0.4920) = \$5.23$$

This amount differs from the first adjustment process amount because the assumption of a continuous dividend stream does not match the reality of how these payments are made. However, by modifying the model's structure instead of the input level, this approach is often much more convenient.

Valuing American-Style Options
The preceding valuation discussion assumed European-style options. If the contract had been American-style—that is, its exercise is not limited to the expiration date—how would the valuation process change? The uncertainty over the possibility of early exercise makes the derivation of an exact closed-form analog to the Black-Scholes equation an elusive goal. Instead Roll, Geske, and Whaley have designed elaborate approximation procedures for estimating the value of American-style calls, which have proven quite useful in practice.[19] Further, Johnson and

---

[18]See Robert C. Merton, "Theory of Rational Option Pricing," *Bell Journal of Economics and Management* 4, no. 1 (Spring 1973): 141–183.

[19]The development of what is commonly called the Roll-Geske-Whaley model can be found in three separate articles: Richard Roll, "An Analytic Valuation Formula for Unprotected American Call Options on Stocks with Known Dividends," *Journal of Financial Economics* 5, no. 2 (November 1977): 251–258; Robert Geske, "A Note on an Analytical Valuation Formula for Unprotected American Call Options on Stocks with Known Dividends," *Journal of Financial Economics* 7, no. 4 (June 1979): 375–380; and Robert E. Whaley, "On the Valuation of American Call Options on Stocks with Known Dividends," *Journal of Financial Economics* 9, no. 2 (June 1981): 207–212.

Barone-Adesi and Whaley, among others, have taken different approaches to address the issue of American put valuation.[20]

A formal summary of these models is beyond the scope of this discussion; however, we can consider several fundamental properties. Most important is that an American put or call has to be at least as valuable as its European-style counterpart because, by definition, the American option gives the holder more choices than the simpler contract. In other words, the American contract holder can exercise at the same time as the European option owner (i.e., at expiration) as well as any point prior to that terminal date. Since we have seen that an option's value ultimately derives from the choice to exercise the agreement or not, a better set of terms for that decision means a more valuable contract. Letting C_a and C_e represent the values of American and European calls, this relationship can be expressed as

$$S \geq C_a(S,T,X) \geq C_e(S,T,X) \geq \max[0, S - Xe^{-(RFR)T}] \geq \max[0, S - X] \geq 0$$

This expression says that (1) the American call is at least as valuable as the European contract, (2) neither call can be more valuable than the underlying stock, and (3) both contracts are at least as valuable as their intrinsic values, expressed on both a nominal and discounted basis. For puts, a similar boundary condition would be

$$X \geq P_a(S,T,X) \geq P_e(S,T,X) \geq \max[0, Xe^{-(RFR)T} - S] \geq 0^{[21]}$$

For a stock that does not pay dividends, C_a and C_e will be equal to one another. At any point prior to expiration, the preceding relationship shows that $C_a(S,T,X) - \max[0, S - X] > 0$, and $\max[0, S - X]$ is the value the investor would extract from the option's exercise. Therefore, without the depression in the stock's price caused by the dividend payment, an investor wishing to liquidate his American call position would sell it rather than exercise it so as not to surrender the contract's time premium. Thus, in the absence of dividends to consider during the life of the option, the American call offers choices that the investor neither wants nor will be willing to pay for. This result implies that the Black-Scholes model for C_e can be used to value C_a as well.

When the stock pays dividends, however, this situation changes. Suppose an investor holds an American call option on a stock just prior to its ex-dividend date. On the ex-date—call it Date t—the value of the stock will decline by about the dividend amount, leaving $S_t = S_{t-1} - (\text{dividend})_t$ assuming no other new information impacted the share's value from the previous day. The value of the option will decline accordingly, from $C(S_{t-1})$ to $C(S_t)$. Of course, selling the contract on the day prior to the ex-date will not be possible since rational buyers will know what will happen the following day. Therefore, the investor must decide on Date $t - 1$ whether he should exercise his contract and receive only the intrinsic value of $\max[0, S_{t-1} - X]$. This will be the proper choice if the loss of the option's time premium is less than $C(S_{t-1}) - C(S_t)$, which will likely occur when the option is close to maturity (and, hence, the time premium is low) and the stock's dividend is large. Because the American option allows the investor the possibility of preserving value when the European contract cannot, we must have $C_a > C_e$ for almost all cases.

---

[20]See H. E. Johnson, "An Analytic Approximation for the American Put Price," *Journal of Financial and Quantitative Analysis* 18, no. 1 (March 1983): 143–151; and Giovanni Barone-Adesi and Robert E. Whaley, "The Valuation of American Call Options and the Expected Ex-Dividend Stock Price Declines," *Journal of Financial Economics* 17, no. 1 (September 1986): 91–112.

[21]For a complete development of these boundary conditions, see Don M. Chance, *Introduction to Derivatives and Risk Management,* 5th ed. (Fort Worth, Tex.: Harcourt College Publishers, 2001).

EXHIBIT 23.15 *COMPARING AMERICAN AND EUROPEAN PUT VALUES*

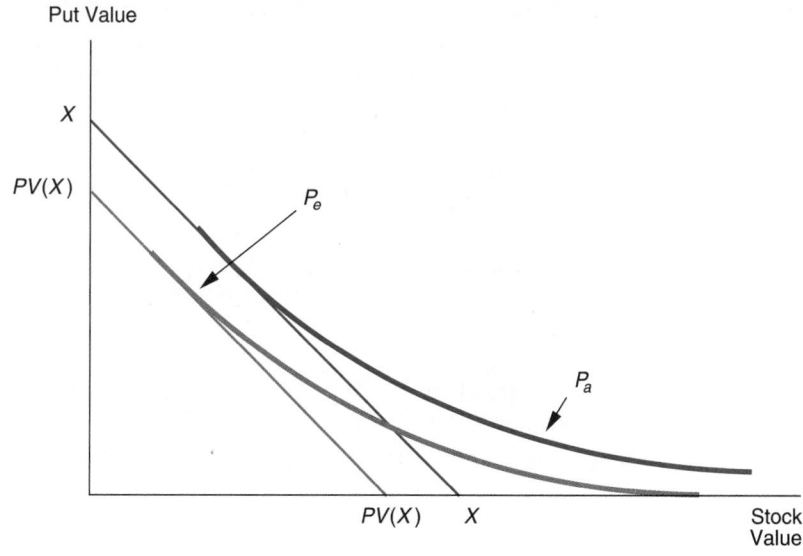

Deciding to exercise a put prior to maturity does not depend on the presence of dividends. Indeed, dividend payments increase a put's value because they reduce the underlying common stock's value without an offset in the exercise price. Instead, the relevant issue is the limited liability of the stock itself. For example, suppose an investor holds an American put on a nearly bankrupt company. The contract, which is struck at $50, has three more months before it expires, and the stock is currently selling for $1. In this case, the option holder would evaluate the trade-off between exercising the contract today to capture the $49 intrinsic value or waiting three months and hoping the stock becomes worthless. That is, she must decide whether she would rather have $49 now or the present value of the possibility of receiving $50. Depending on the discount rate and the estimated recovery probability, it is quite likely that she will exercise now.

On the other hand, the European put does not offer the investor this choice. Further, since the stock's expected return is positive, an efficient capital market would predict that the price of the nondividend-paying stock will be higher in three months, thereby reducing the expiration date value of the contract below $49. Consequently, without the ability to exercise the put prior to expiration, the European put sometimes can be worth less than its intrinsic value—unadjusted for the time value of money—which always is a lower bound for the American contract. Thus, P_e can be either greater or less than max[0, $X - S$], with the latter situation most likely to occur at extremely low values of S and large values of T. The preceding boundary condition shows that P_e must only be greater than the discounted version of the intrinsic value formula, or max[0, $Xe^{-(RFR)T} - S$]. These relationships are illustrated in Exhibit 23.15.

Other Extensions of the Black-Scholes Model

The dividend-adjusted Black-Scholes model is also quite useful in valuing options for underlying assets other than common stock. Three of the more important applications along these lines follow.

Stock Index Options As we have discussed, stock index options are fundamentally no different than regular stock options. That is, it is reasonable to assume that the index levels follow geometric Brownian motion just as the stock itself does. The primary difference is that, as a hypothetical creation, the stock index cannot be delivered to settle the contract and so it must be settled in cash. Beyond that, because it is a well-diversified portfolio, the volatility of the stock index's price usually is quite a bit lower than the typical stock. Finally, the applicable dividend yield can be assumed to be the average annualized yield on the index during the option's life, which is likely to be known to investors at least one calendar quarter into the future.

Suppose the Standard and Poor's 100 currently is at a level of 601.40 and a call option on the index with an exercise price of 600 is being offered at a price of $17.75. An investor wants to determine whether the fair value of this contract is above or below the market price. The option is set to expire in exactly 61 days, which translates to 0.1671 (= 61/365) year. The dividend yield on the S&P 100 is 2.00 percent, and the annualized yield on a 61-day Treasury bill is 5.70 percent. The investor forecasts the index's volatility to be 18 percent, and establishes that

$$d_1 = [\ln(601.40e^{-(0.02)0.1671}/600) + (0.057 + 0.5(0.18)^2)[0.1671]] \div (0.18[0.1671]^{1/2}) = 0.1525$$

and

$$d_2 = 0.1525 - 0.18[0.1671]^{1/2} = 0.0789$$

Using the cumulative normal probability approximation function, this leads to $N(d_1) = 0.5607$ and $N(d_2) = 0.5315$. Thus, she estimates the call's value to be

$$C_0 = (599.39)(0.5607) - (600)(e^{-(0.057)0.1671})(0.5315) = \$20.20$$

Since this is higher than the market price of the option (i.e., $17.75), the contract appears undervalued. This is not necessarily an arbitrage opportunity, however, as the investor's valuation was based on two assumptions that may not match the consensus view of other market participants: (1) the Black-Scholes framework is appropriate, and (2) the index's volatility is 18 percent and not something lower. This, of course, is always the challenge confronting investors in an uncertain world.

Foreign Currency Options Recall that prices for exchange-traded currency options are quoted in U.S. cents per unit of foreign currency, reflecting that a call option is the right to buy a fixed amount of foreign currency with U.S. dollars. Let RFR_f and RFR_d be the risk-free rates in the foreign and U.S. domestic markets, respectively. Further, let σ be the volatility of the exchange rate between the United States and the foreign country, denominated in USD per unit of FC. Garman and Kohlhagen showed that the Black-Scholes model for European-style calls and puts under these conditions can be written as[22]

$$C_0 = (e^{-(RFR_f)T})SN(d_1) - X(e^{-(RFR_d)T})N(-d_2)$$
$$P_0 = X(e^{-(RFR_d)T})N(d_2) - (e^{-(RFR_f)T})SN(-d_1)$$

[22]See Mark B. Garman and Steven W. Kohlhagen, "Foreign Currency Option Values," *Journal of International Money and Finance* 2, no. 3 (December 1983): 231–237; as well as Nahum Biger and John Hull, "The Valuation of Currency Options," *Financial Management* 12, no. 1 (Spring 1983): 24–28; and Seungmook Choi and Michael D. Mascozzi, "A Numerical Approach to American Currency Option Valuation," *Journal of Derivatives* 9, no. 2 (Winter 2001): 19–29.

where:

$d_1 = [\ln(e^{-(RFR_f)T})S/X) + (RFR_d + 0.5\sigma^2)\,[T]] \div (\sigma[T]^{1/2})$

$d_2 = d_1 - \sigma[T]^{1/2}$

S = **the spot exchange rate quoted on a direct (i.e., USD/FC) basis**

Again, this formula is equivalent to the dividend-adjusted Black-Scholes model for stock options when RFR_f is interpreted as the "dividend yield" on the foreign currency. As an example of valuing FX options, suppose the spot exchange rate between the U.S. dollar and the British pound is USD 1.50/GBP, and the risk-free rates in the United States and England are 4.5 percent and 9 percent, respectively. With these market conditions, interest rate parity holds that the dollar should trade at a forward premium relative to the pound. To the extent that forward FX rates "predict" future spot rates, this suggests that the dollar price of sterling will fall. Thus, an at-the-money put option should be more valuable to an investor than an at-the-money sterling call. To see if this is the case, consider the valuation of six-month contracts where $S = 1.50$, $X = 1.50$, $RFR_d = 4.5$ percent, $RFR_f = 9$ percent, $\sigma = 13$ percent, and $T = 0.5$. With these inputs, $S' = S(e^{-(.09)0.5}) = 1.434$ so that

$$d_1 = [\ln(1.434/1.50) + (0.045 + 0.5(0.13)^2)[0.5]] \div (0.13[0.5]^{1/2}) = -0.20$$

and

$$d_2 = -0.20 - 0.13[0.5]^{1/2} = -0.29$$

Therefore, the option values are

$$C_0 = (1.434)(0.4207) - (1.50)(e^{-(0.045)0.5})(0.3859) = \$0.037$$

and

$$P_0 = (1.50)(e^{-(0.045)0.5})(0.6141) - (1.434)(0.5793) = \$0.070$$

as expected.

Futures Options   In the preceding chapter, we showed that in the absence of physical storage costs or dividends, the futures contract price (F) should simply be the spot price (S) of the underlying asset carried forward to date T at the risk-free rate. With continuous yields, this can be written as $F = Se^{(RFR)T}$. Black showed that substituting F for S in the Black-Scholes formula for call options leaves[23]

$$C_0 = [e^{-(RFR)T}]FN(d_1) - (e^{-(RFR)T})XN(d_2)$$
$$= (e^{-(RFR)T})[FN(d_1) - XN(d_2)]$$

where:

$d_1 = (\ln(F/X) + 0.5\sigma^2[T]) \div (\sigma[T]^{1/2})$

$d_2 = d_1 - \sigma[T]^{1/2}$

---

[23]See Fischer Black, "The Pricing of Commodity Contracts," *Journal of Financial Economics* 3, no. 1/2 (January–March 1976): 167–179.

In the expressions for d_1 and d_2, the risk-free rate factor drops out because a risk-free hedge portfolio with futures and call options requires no initial investment since futures contracts require no front-end payment. Also, here σ represents the futures price volatility, which normally is assumed to be equal to the underlying asset volatility. Put options on futures contracts can then be valued like the call options already described.

Exotic Options   Throughout the chapter, we have seen that the terminal payoff to a standard call option that has an exercise price of X and expires at Date T can be written $\max[0, S_T - X]$. As investors have become comfortable with how these contracts work, a growing market has developed for options offering variations on this basic payoff scheme. Three such nonstandard, or *exotic,* contracts that are particularly popular in practice are *Asian, lookback,* and *digital* options. The payoff formulas for these exotic contracts can be summarized as follows:

Asian call:	$\max[0, \text{Average}(S) - X]$
Lookback call:	$\max[0, \text{Max}(S) - X]$
Digital call:	$\$Q$ if $S_T > X$ or $\$0$ if $S_T \leq X$

To see the impact of these nonstandard payoffs on option valuation, let us return to the simple binomial model described by Exhibit 23.5 and Exhibit 23.6. In that example, the European-style call option expiring in two subperiods had an exercise price of $52.50, and the risk-free rate was 3.92 percent per subperiod. For convenience, the stock price and option value trees have been reproduced in a slightly modified form in Exhibit 23.16. From the stock price forecasts in Panel A, the values for up and down movements can be calculated as $u = 1.1402$ (= 57.01/50 = 65/57.01) and $d = 0.8944$ (= 44.72/50 = 40/44.72), so that the implied probability of an upward price move is 0.5891 (= [1.0392 − 0.8944]/[1.1402 − 0.8944]). With these conditions, we saw that the value of the regular call option is $4.02.

Asian Options   As indicated previously, Asian options are contracts whose terminal payoffs are determined by the *average price* of the underlying security during the life of the contract. The effect of this averaging process is shown in Panel A of Exhibit 23.17. Notice that for a terminal stock price of $50.99, the payoff for the Asian call will be different depending on whether the Subperiod S1 share price was $57.01 or $44.72. That is, the payoff to the Asian call is *path dependent* in that how the price of the underlying security arrived at its terminal level (i.e., "up" then "down" versus "down" then "up") will affect the payoff. On the other hand, notice that standard call options are *path independent;* all that matters is the terminal share price and not how it got there.[24]

Once the expiration date payoffs are established, valuing the Asian contract proceeds in the same manner as for the standard option. That is, using the probabilities implied by $u, d,$ and $r,$ we can establish C_{11} as

$$C_{11} = \frac{(0.5891)(8.51) + (0.4109)(1.50)}{1.0392} = \$5.42$$

---

[24]For more analysis of path dependent option contracts, see S. Eckl, J. N. Robinson, and D. C. Thomas, *Financial Engineering* (Cambridge, Mass.: Blackwell Publishing, 1991); and Yue Kuen Kwok and Ka Wo Lau, "Pricing Algorithms for Options with Exotic Path Dependence," *Journal of Derivatives* 9, no. 1 (Fall 2001): 28–38.

EXHIBIT 23.16 FORECASTED STOCK PRICE AND REGULAR CALL VALUE TREES

A. Forecasted Stock Prices

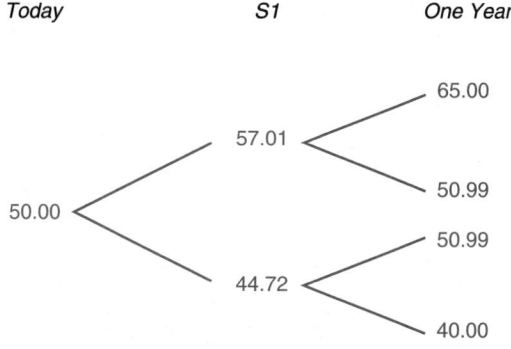

B. Regular Call Option Value ($X = 52.50$)

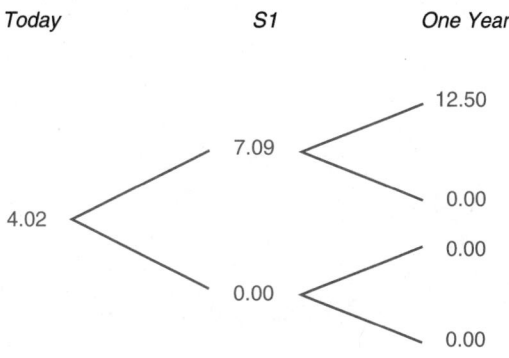

so that

$$C_0 = \frac{(0.5891)(5.42) + (0.4109)(0.00)}{1.0392} = \$3.07$$

Notice that the value for the Asian call is lower than that for the regular contract, a consequence of the fact that the averaging process *reduces* the volatility of the stock price movement.

Asian options are especially useful when an investor is trying to hedge an inventory of commodities or securities, rather than a single position. For instance, an oil importer who makes frequent purchases may want to hedge against price increases on all of his acquisition dates over the next three months. However, because there is no single purchase date, he may prefer that the contract be based on his average purchase price during the quarter. Thus, an Asian call option would be appropriate.

Lookback Options As another example of a path-dependent payoff, lookback options guarantee the holder a distribution based on the maximum price the underlying security achieves during the life of the contract. Panel B of Exhibit 23.17 shows that even if the terminal price of the stock is $50.99, the lookback call would still pay $4.51 (= 57.01 − 52.50) if the S1 price had been $57.01.

EXHIBIT 23.17 *EXOTIC CALL OPTION VALUES*

A. Asian Call Option (*X* = 52.50)

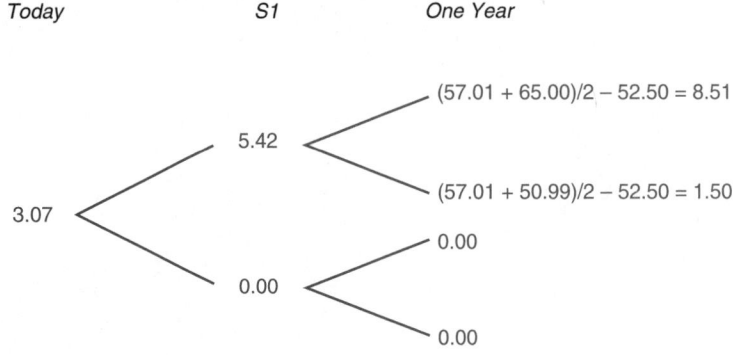

B. Lookback Call Option (*X* = 52.50)

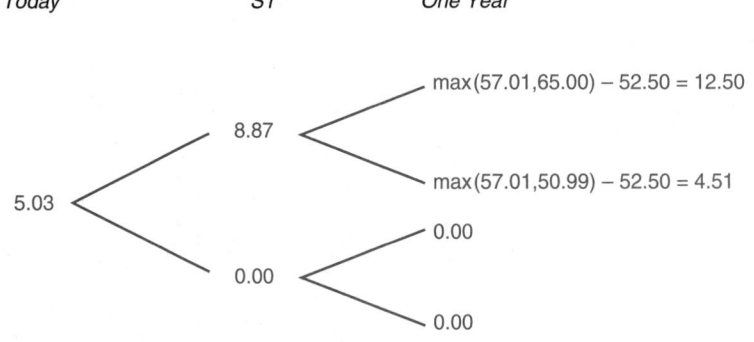

C. Digital Call Option (*X* = 52.50)

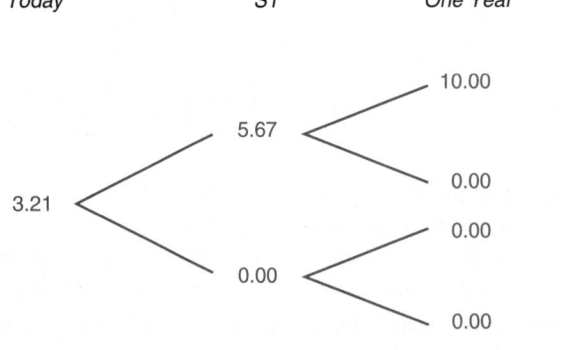

However, if the share price had initially fallen to \$44.72 before rising to \$50.99, the lookback option would be out of the money since neither of these values is greater than the exercise price of \$52.50. Like the Asian option, once these terminal payoffs are established, the current value of the lookback contract can be established as

$$C_{11} = \frac{(0.5891)(12.50) + (0.4109)(4.51)}{1.0392} = \$8.87$$

and

$$C_0 = \frac{(0.5891)(8.87) + (0.4109)(0.00)}{1.0392} = \$5.03$$

Notice that the value of the lookback option ($5.03) is greater than that of the regular call option. This increased value is a direct result of the lookback contract *preserving* volatility by basing the payoff on the highest stock price regardless of when that value occurred during the option's life. For this reason, lookback options are always designed to be European-style; there is no need to have the exercise flexibility that an American-style contract provides if you are guaranteed the highest price no matter what happens by the expiration date. Of course, the buyer pays for this desirable feature in the form of a higher front-end premium. As such, lookback options represent a way of making a speculative bet against the stock price forecast assumed by the market as a whole.

Digital Options   The payoff to a digital, or binary, option is a fixed amount regardless of how deep in the money the contract is at expiration. It is not path dependent because, as with the standard format, the payoff depends only on the terminal stock price. Panel C of Exhibit 23.17 assumes a digital payoff of $10 for an in-the-money option. In this case, the current value of the digital call is

$$C_0 = \frac{(0.5891)(5.67)}{1.0392} = \frac{(0.5891)^2 (10.00)}{(1.0392)^2} = \$3.21$$

Although this amount is lower than the regular call value of $4.02, there is no way to generalize this result because the $10 payoff was selected by the buyer rather than determined by market forces. For instance, if the digital payoff had been $15, the value of the contract would be $4.82 (= $15 \times (0.5891)^2 \div (0.0392)^2$). In fact, the value of this exotic option is simply the present value of the fixed payoff ($9.26 = $10 \div (1.0392)^2$ in this example) multiplied by the probability that the contract finishes in the money (34.70 percent = $(0.5891)^2$). Digital options are often used by investors who have a very specific view about the expiration date trading range of the underlying security.

OPTION TRADING STRATEGIES

The introductory analysis in Chapter 21 highlighted two ways in which investors use options. First, we saw that the asymmetrical payoff structures they possess as stand-alone positions allowed investors to isolate the benefits of an anticipated change in the value of an underlying security while limiting the downside risk of an adverse price movement. Options are a leveraged alternative to making a direct investment in the asset on which the contract is based. Second, we also saw that put options could be used in conjunction with an existing portfolio to limit the portfolio's loss potential. After revisiting this protective put application in the context of individual stock holdings, in this section we will consider a **covered call** option strategy as another method for modifying the risk or enhancing the return of an existing equity position. Specifically, we will see that selling a call option while holding the underlying security can generate income for the investor in an otherwise static market environment.

This section also emphasizes a third way in which options are used: in *combination* with one another to create customized payoff distributions that do not exist in more fundamental securities, like stocks or bonds. The equity collar example that concluded Chapter 21 is a good example of this type of option strategy. In designing such combinations, the investor usually attempts

EXHIBIT 23.18 *HYPOTHETICAL SAS CORPORATION STOCK AND OPTION PRICES*

Instrument		Exercise Price	Market Price	Intrinsic Value	Time Premium
Stock:		—	$40.00	—	—
Call:	#1	$35.00	8.07	$5.00	$3.07
	#2	40.00	5.24	0.00	5.24
	#3	45.00	3.24	0.00	3.24
Put:	#1	35.00	1.70	0.00	1.70
	#2	40.00	3.67	0.00	3.67
	#3	45.00	6.47	5.00	1.47

to exploit a very specific view about future economic conditions. For example, he may feel that a particular company's stock returns will be extraordinarily volatile but have no clear impression about the price movement direction. On the other hand, he may feel that another company's shares will trade within a very narrow range around their current price during the next few months. In developing all these strategies, we will return to the hypothetical example of SAS Corporation, which has exchange-traded common stock as well as call and put options. Current prices for SAS stock and six different derivatives, all of which expire at the same time, are reproduced in Exhibit 23.18.

Protective Put Options

Although we have seen that the protective put strategy is most often used to provide insurance for price declines in entire portfolios, Brown and Statman have noted that the technique can also be employed with individual equity positions.[25] To see how this "insured stock" concept works, consider an investor who holds SAS stock in her portfolio but is concerned that an unexpected downturn in the company's product sales may lead to a decline in the value of her position in the coming months. To hedge against this firm-specific exposure, she decides to purchase an at-the-money put option on SAS shares. From Exhibit 23.18, this would mean that she would spend $3.67 to buy put #2 with an exercise price of $40. If at expiration the price of SAS had declined below $40, the put option would pay her the difference.

The effect of this acquisition is shown in Exhibit 23.19, which lists the expiration date value of the combined protective put position for a range of possible SAS prices. As noted earlier, the primary benefit of the insured stock strategy is that it creates a combined payoff equivalent to holding a call option on SAS stock. That is, the protective put holding preserves the investor's upside potential from rising share prices but limits her losses when share prices fall. In this case, the at-the-money put insures her against any losses beyond the $3.67 initial put premium. This is the same outcome the investor would have if instead of the put-protected SAS shares, she had held an at-the-money SAS call option and a T-bill; the risk-free security provides the safety and the call option provides the potential for price appreciation. Recall from the put-call parity model of Chapter 21 that this result was shown as

$$S_0 + P_{0,T} = C_{0,T} + PV(X)$$

which can be rewritten as follows:

$$(\text{Long Stock}) + (\text{Long Put}) = (\text{Long Call}) + (\text{Long T-bill})$$

---

[25]See Keith C. Brown and Meir Statman, "The Benefits of Insured Stocks for Corporate Cash Management," *Advances in Futures and Options Research* 2 (1987): 243–261.

EXHIBIT 23.19 *EXPIRATION DATE VALUE OF A PROTECTIVE PUT POSITION*

Potential SAS Stock Value	Value of Put Option	Cost of Put Option	Net Protective Put Position
20	(40 − 20) = 20	−3.67	(20 + 20) − 3.67 = 36.33
25	(40 − 25) = 15	−3.67	(25 + 15) − 3.67 = 36.33
30	(40 − 30) = 10	−3.67	(30 + 10) − 3.67 = 36.33
35	(40 − 35) = 5	−3.67	(35 + 5) − 3.67 = 36.33
40	0	−3.67	(40 + 0) − 3.67 = 36.33
45	0	−3.67	(45 + 0) − 3.67 = 41.33
50	0	−3.67	(50 + 0) − 3.67 = 46.33
55	0	−3.67	(55 + 0) − 3.67 = 51.33
60	0	−3.67	(60 + 0) − 3.67 = 56.33

EXHIBIT 23.20 *TERMINAL NET PAYOFFS TO THREE PROTECTIVE PUT POSITIONS*

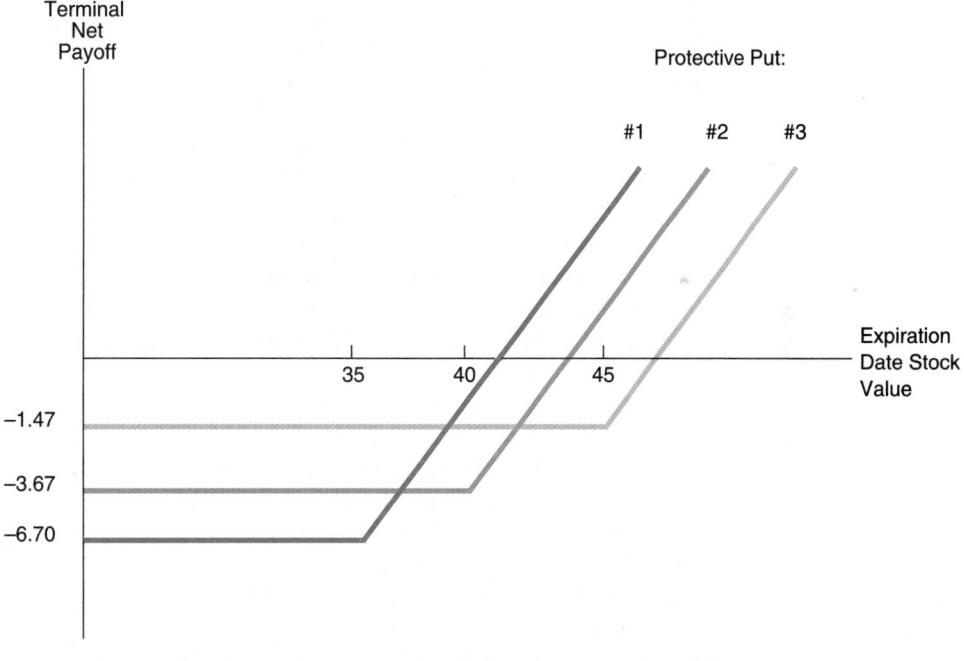

To extend the insurance interpretation of the protective put, Exhibit 23.20 shows the expiration date payoffs (net of the initial $40 purchase price for the investor's SAS shares) for using each of three put options available to her. To interpret this display, if SAS shares are priced at $40 on the expiration date, for protective put #2 (i.e., the at-the-money contract), the investor's combined position will be worth $36.33, giving her a net loss of $3.67. The main thing about this illustration is the trade-off it shows between the risk and reward potential of the various positions. Put #1 has the smallest front-end expense, but its $35 exercise price forces the investor to bear the first $5 of SAS stock price declines; this $5 "deductible" leads to the largest potential

EXHIBIT 23.21 ▶ *EXPIRATION DATE VALUE OF A COVERED CALL POSITION*

POTENTIAL SAS STOCK VALUE	VALUE OF CALL OPTION	PROCEEDS FROM CALL OPTION	NET COVERED CALL POSITION
20	0	5.24	$(20 - 0) + 5.24 = 25.24$
25	0	5.24	$(25 - 0) + 5.24 = 30.24$
30	0	5.24	$(30 - 0) + 5.24 = 35.24$
35	0	5.24	$(35 - 0) + 5.24 = 40.24$
40	0	5.24	$(40 - 0) + 5.24 = 45.24$
45	$-(45 - 40) = -5$	5.24	$(45 - 5) + 5.24 = 45.24$
50	$-(50 - 40) = -10$	5.24	$(50 - 10) + 5.24 = 45.24$
55	$-(55 - 40) = -15$	5.24	$(55 - 15) + 5.24 = 45.24$
60	$-(60 - 40) = -20$	5.24	$(60 - 20) + 5.24 = 45.24$

loss of three positions at $6.70 (= 1.70 + 5.00). However, for this degree of self-insuring on the part of the investor, protective put #1 has, at $41.70 (= 35.00 + 6.70), the smallest breakeven price. Conversely, Put #3, with an exercise price above the current share value, does not break even until SAS prices reach $46.47 but has a maximum possible loss of only $1.47 and therefore provides the best downside protection.

Covered Call Options

Another popular way in which derivatives are used to alter the payoff structure of an equity position involves the sale of call options. When investors sell call options based on an underlying position they own, they are said to be *writing* covered calls. Usually, the purpose of this strategy is to generate additional income for a stock holding that is not expected to change in value much over the near term. By selling a call in such a situation, an investor receives the premium from the option contract to bolster an otherwise small (or negative) return. The danger, of course, is that the value of the stock position rises above the exercise price by the end of the contract's life causing the shares to be called away at the lower price.[26]

For example, suppose now that our investor believes that over the next few months the value of her SAS stock will neither rise nor fall by an appreciable amount. Accordingly, she decides not to insure her position against losses but, instead, to increase the cash flow of the investment by selling an at-the-money call option (Call #2). In exchange for granting the contract buyer the right to purchase her stock for $40 at the expiration date, she receives an immediate payment of $5.24. Using the same potential stock prices as before, the expiration date values for the covered call position are listed in Exhibit 23.21. The construction of the terminal payoff diagram—once again net of the current SAS share price—is depicted in Exhibit 23.22 (which is comparable to Exhibit 21.23 in Chapter 21 for a protective put option position).

Both the numbers and the pictures from these displays indicate that the expiration date payoff to the covered call position is comparable in form to that of a short position in a put option. Once again, this can be seen directly by adjusting the put-call parity condition as follows:

$$(\text{Long Stock}) + (\text{Short Call}) = (\text{Long T-bill}) + (\text{Short Put})$$

---

[26]See James W. Yates, Jr., and Robert W. Kopprasch, Jr., "Writing Covered Call Options: Profits and Risks," *Journal of Portfolio Management* 7 (Fall 1980), for more analysis of the covered call strategy.

EXHIBIT 23.22 ▶ *TERMINAL NET PAYOFF TO A COVERED CALL POSITION*

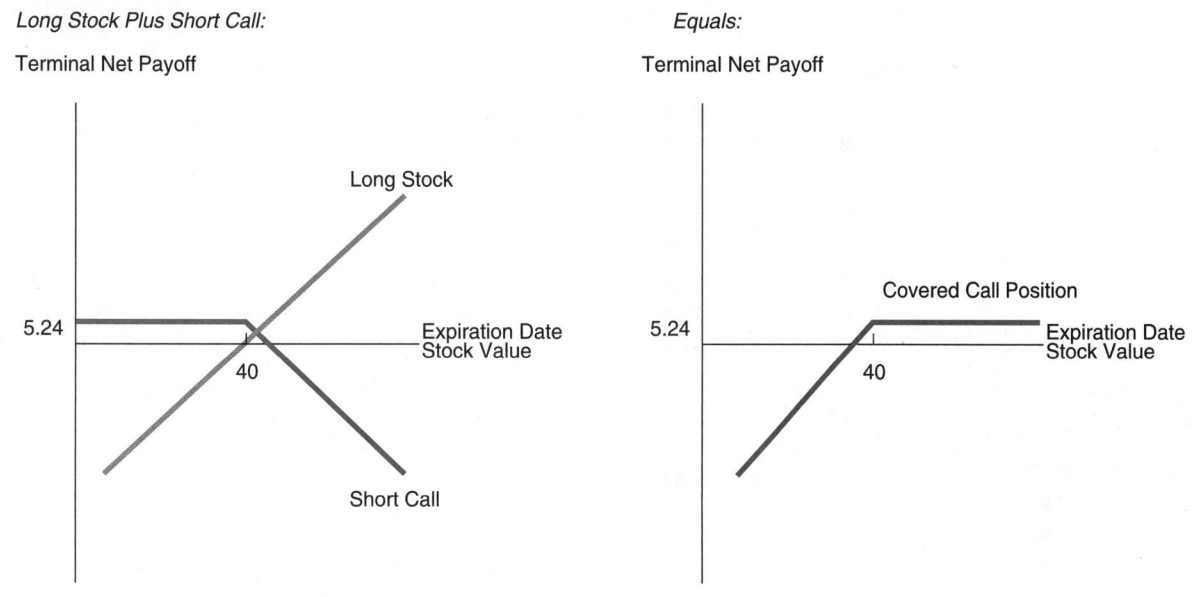

Long Stock Plus Short Call:

Terminal Net Payoff

Equals:

Terminal Net Payoff

Notice from Exhibit 23.22 that there are two dimensions to the price risk inherent in this strategy. First, if by the option expiration date, SAS stock has risen above $40, the investor will be forced to sell her shares for less than they are actually worth. However, this will represent a lost opportunity only at prices above $45.24, an amount equal to the exercise price plus the initial call premium. Second, if SAS stock experiences a decline in value, her potential loss is not hedged beyond the $5.24 in premium income that she received for selling the call; after prices fall beyond $31.09 (= $40 − $5.24 − $3.67), she would have been better off purchasing the at-the-money protective put option. Thus, to be profitable, the covered call strategy requires that the investor guess correctly that share values will remain in a reasonably narrow band around their present levels.

Straddles, Strips, and Straps

A *straddle* is the simultaneous purchase (or sale) of a call and a put option with the same underlying asset, exercise price, and expiration date. More precisely, a long straddle requires the purchase of the put and the call, while a short straddle sells both contracts. The long straddle takes positions in both a call and a put, giving the investor a combination that will appreciate in value whether stock prices rise or fall in the future. Buying two options increases the initial cost; that is, to profit from this investment, stock price movements must be more pronounced than if the investor had predicted changes in a single direction. In this sense, a straddle is a *volatility* play; the buyer expects stock prices to move strongly one way or the other, while the seller hopes for lower-than-normal volatility.

To illustrate this combination, suppose an investor (who does not hold SAS stock) purchases a put and a call, each with an exercise price of $40. The cost of this purchase will be the combined prices of Call #2 and Put #2, or $8.91 (= $5.24 + $3.67). Recalling that the terminal values of the options are max[0, S_T − 40] and max[0, 40 − S_T], respectively, the expiration date payoffs to the straddle position (net of the initial cost, unadjusted for the time value differential) are shown in Exhibit 23.23. These are illustrated in Exhibit 23.24, which also depicts the payoff to

EXHIBIT 23.23 ▶ *EXPIRATION DATE PAYOFFS TO A LONG STRADDLE POSITION*

SAS STOCK PRICE AT EXPIRATION	VALUE OF CALLS	VALUE OF PUTS	COST OF OPTIONS	NET PROFIT
$20.00	$ 0.00	$20.00	$–8.91	$11.09
25.00	0.00	15.00	–8.91	6.09
30.00	0.00	10.00	–8.91	1.09
35.00	0.00	5.00	–8.91	–3.91
40.00	0.00	0.00	–8.91	–8.91
45.00	5.00	0.00	–8.91	–3.09
50.00	10.00	0.00	–8.91	1.09
55.00	15.00	0.00	–8.91	6.09
60.00	20.00	0.00	–8.91	11.09

EXHIBIT 23.24 ▶ *THE STRADDLE ILLUSTRATED*

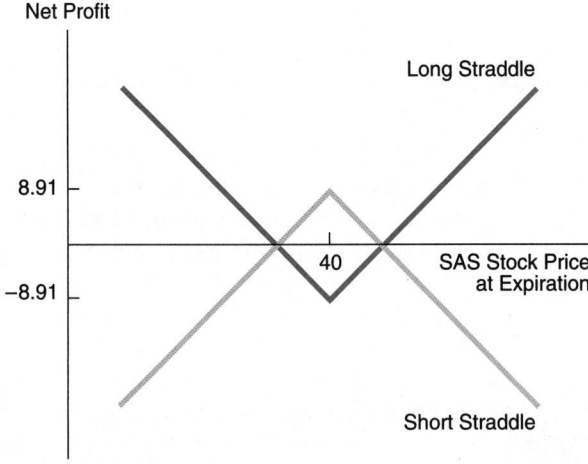

the seller of the straddle. The breakeven points on this graph occur at $31.09 (= $40 – $8.91) and $48.91 (= $40 + $8.91).

Not surprisingly, the expiration date values to the long and short positions are mirror images of each other; if the individual options themselves are zero-sum games, so too must be any combination of contracts. In particular, the buyer of the straddle is hoping for a dramatic event—such as a company-specific technological breakthrough or the impending judgment in a major lawsuit—that will either increase or decrease the stock price from its present $40 by at least $8.91. Conversely, the best result for the straddle seller is for SAS stock to continue to trade at its current price through the expiration date (i.e., no volatility at all) so that both options expire worthless. The seller's position is particularly interesting because it demonstrates that it is possible to make money in the stock market even when prices do not change.

The long straddle position assumes implicitly that the investor has no intuition about the likely direction of future stock price movements. A slight modification of this format is over-weighting either the put or call position to emphasize a directional belief while maintaining a

EXHIBIT 23.25 ▶ *EXPIRATION DATE PAYOFFS TO LONG STRAP AND LONG STRIP POSITIONS*

A. Strap Position (Two Calls and One Put)

SAS STOCK PRICE AT EXPIRATION	VALUE OF CALLS	VALUE OF PUTS	COST OF OPTIONS	NET PROFIT
$20.00	$ 0.00	$20.00	$–14.15	$ 5.85
25.00	0.00	15.00	–14.15	0.85
30.00	0.00	10.00	–14.15	–4.15
35.00	0.00	5.00	–14.15	–9.15
40.00	0.00	0.00	–14.15	–14.15
45.00	10.00	0.00	–14.15	–4.15
50.00	20.00	0.00	–14.15	5.85
55.00	30.00	0.00	–14.15	15.85
60.00	40.00	0.00	–14.15	25.85

B. Strip Position (Two Puts and One Call)

SAS STOCK PRICE AT EXPIRATION	VALUE OF CALLS	VALUE OF PUTS	COST OF OPTIONS	NET PROFIT
$20.00	$ 0.00	$40.00	$–12.58	$ 27.42
25.00	0.00	30.00	–12.58	17.42
30.00	0.00	20.00	–12.58	7.42
35.00	0.00	10.00	–12.58	–2.58
40.00	0.00	0.00	–12.58	–12.58
45.00	5.00	0.00	–12.58	–7.58
50.00	10.00	0.00	–12.58	–2.58
55.00	15.00	0.00	–12.58	2.42
60.00	20.00	0.00	–12.58	7.42

contract that would profit from a price movement the other way. A long *strap* position is the purchase of two calls and one put with the same exercise price, suggesting an investor who thinks stock prices are more likely to increase. An investor with a more "bearish" view could create a long *strip* position by purchasing two puts and only one call. The terminal payoffs to both of these combinations are listed in Exhibit 23.25, which again assumes the use of the two at-the-money SAS contracts.

Panel A of the exhibit shows that for the higher up-front payment of $14.15 (= (2 × $5.24) + $3.67), the strap will accelerate the payoff in a rising market relative to the straddle. The settlement payment when SAS stock finishes above $40 on the expiration date is twice as great because the strap has doubled the investor's number of calls. The gross payoff when the price falls below $40 remains the same; however, the net amount received is considerably lower because the extra contract the investor purchased would then be out of the money. The net terminal value of the strip position tells a similar story, only with the acceleration of the profit generated by falling stock prices. The strap is more expensive than the strip under these conditions because SAS is a nondividend-paying common stock that is expected to increase in price to provide the investor with a positive expected return.

Strangles   One final variation on the straddle theme is an option combination known as a *strangle*. Like the straddle, a strangle is the simultaneous purchase or sale of a call and a put on the same underlying

EXHIBIT 23.26 ▶ *COMPARING THE LONG STRANGLE AND LONG STRADDLE POSITIONS*

security with the same expiration date. Unlike the straddle, however, the options used in the strangle do not have the same exercise price; instead, they are chosen so that both are out of the money. By buying two out-of-the-money contracts, the investor reduces the original straddle position's initial cost. Offsetting this reduced cost, though, is that stock prices will have to change in either direction by a greater amount before the strangle becomes profitable. Thus, the strangle can be viewed as having a more modest risk-reward structure than the straddle.

As an example, suppose the investor purchased Call #3 and Put #1 for a combined price of $4.94 (= $3.24 + $1.70). If the price of SAS stock remained between the put exercise price of $35 and the call exercise price of $45, both contracts would expire worthless and the investor would lose his entire initial investment. Accordingly, prices would have to decline to $30.06 (= $35 – $4.94) or increase to $49.94 (= $45 + $4.94) before the investor would break even on the position. Exhibit 23.26 shows that these breakeven points for the strangle are outside those for the straddle described earlier. Thus, among the set of "volatility bets," the strangle costs less to implement than the straddle but requires greater movement in the underlying security's price before it generates a positive return. Finally, by varying the exercise prices on the two options—which is possible in the OTC market—the investor can create a strangle position that offers the exact trade-off between initial cost and future expected profit that he desires.

Chooser Options

The straddle is a special case of a wider class of option contracts sometimes called *chooser* options. With a chooser option, the investor selects an exercise price and expiration date but doesn't have to decide if the option should be a put or a call until after the contract is purchased. That is, the straddle is just a chooser option for which the decision can be deferred until the expiration date. Rubinstein has shown that the value of a chooser option will depend on when the investor has to make the put or call choice.[27]

At one extreme, if the decision has to be made immediately, the buyer will select the option most likely to be in the money at expiration. In the previous example, with $X = 40$, we have seen

---

[27]See Mark Rubinstein, "Options for the Undecided," in *From Black-Scholes to Black Holes* (London, England: Risk Magazine, 1992).

| EXHIBIT 23.27 | EXPIRATION DATE PAYOFFS TO A BULL MONEY SPREAD POSITION |

SAS STOCK PRICE AT EXPIRATION	VALUE OF CALL #1	VALUE OF CALL #3	COST OF OPTIONS	NET PROFIT
$20.00	0.00	$ 0.00	$–4.83	$–4.83
25.00	0.00	0.00	–4.83	–4.83
30.00	0.00	0.00	–4.83	–4.83
35.00	0.00	0.00	–4.83	–4.83
40.00	5.00	0.00	–4.83	0.17
45.00	10.00	0.00	–4.83	5.17
50.00	15.00	–5.00	–4.83	5.17
55.00	20.00	–10.00	–4.83	5.17
60.00	25.00	–15.00	–4.83	5.17

that this will be the call. Thus, a chooser option in this case is worth $5.24. At the other extreme, a chooser option that allows the holder to defer the decision until expiration is, as already noted, equivalent to holding both a put and a call for the entire time to expiration. Consequently, the straddle price of $8.91 is the upper bound of the chooser option value struck at $40. The usual design for the chooser contract requires the holder to make a choice after the initial purchase but before expiration, which would create a position worth somewhere between $5.24 and $8.91.

Spreads   As described by Black, option spreads are the purchase of one contract and the sale of another, where the options are alike in all respects except for one distinguishing characteristic.[28] For example, in a *money* spread, the investor would sell an out-of-the-money call and purchase an in-the-money call on the same stock and expiration date. Alternatively, a *calendar* (or time) spread requires the purchase and sale of two calls—or two puts—with the same exercise price but different expiration dates. Option spreads are often used when one contract is perceived to be misvalued relative to the other. For instance, if an investor determines that a call option with an exercise price of X_1 and an expiration date T is selling at too high a price in the market, he can short it, thereby speculating on an eventual correction. However, if a broad-based increase in the stock market occurs before this contract-specific correction, he stands to lose a great deal because the short call position has unlimited liability. Thus, when he sells the first option, he can hedge some or all of the risk by buying a call with an exercise price of X_2 expiring at T.

Returning to the data for SAS options, suppose the investor purchases the in-the-money call (Call #1) and sells the contract that is out of the money (Call #3). In this case, the option he buys is more valuable than the one he sells, leading to a net cash outlay of $4.83 (= $8.07 – $3.24). At the common expiration date, three price ranges should be considered. If SAS stock settles below $35, both options will expire worthless and the investor will lose all of his initial investment. With an SAS price above $45, both contracts will be exercised, meaning that the investor must sell at $45 the share he bought for $35, leaving a $10 gross profit. Finally, if SAS prices fall between the two exercise prices, the investor's option will be in the money while the contract he sold will not. This situation is summarized by the net payoff calculations shown in Exhibit 23.27.

---

[28]See Fischer Black, "Fact and Fantasy in the Use of Options," *Financial Analysis Journal* 31, no. 4 (July–August 1975): 36–41, 61–72.

EXHIBIT 23.28   COMPARING THE BULL MONEY SPREAD AND LONG CALL POSITIONS

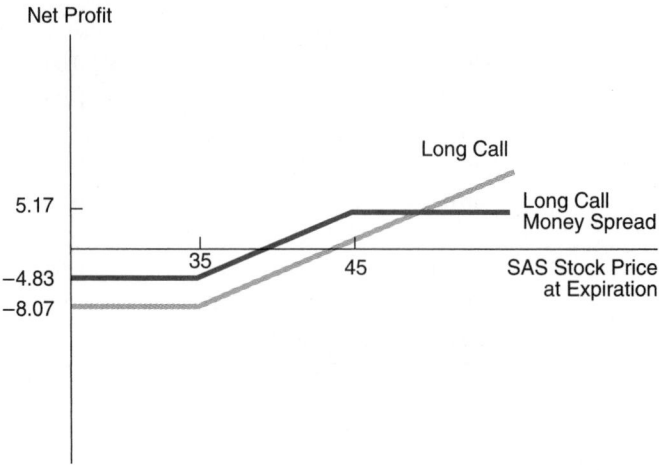

This combination is sometimes called a *bull* money spread because it will be profitable when stock prices rise. Specifically, with the initial cost of $4.83, the investor's breakeven point occurs when the stock price rises to $39.83 (= $35 + $4.83). His benefit stops increasing if SAS shares reach $45 since this is where the short position in Call #3 becomes a liability. Exhibit 23.28 contrasts this situation with the outright purchase of the in-the-money call. This contract would cost $8.07 initially, leading to the higher breakeven price of $43.07. It would not have a constraint on the upside profit potential, however, so once a share price of $48.24 is reached (= 45 + (8.07 − 4.83)), it would become the preferable alternative. Thus, in exchange for a lower initial purchase price, the bull spread investor is giving up the benefits of rising SAS prices after some point—a strategy that makes sense only if he expects the share price to settle within a fairly narrow range.

The profit for a *bear* money spread (the purchase of Call #3 and the sale of Call #1) is the opposite of that for the bull money spread. That is, buying a bear spread is equivalent to selling a bull spread. Consequently, a long bear spread position might be used by an investor who believed stock prices might decline but did not want to be short in the stock. Notice that a spread transaction also can be created using put options. For instance, suppose a new investor undertakes the simultaneous purchase of Put #3 and sale of Put #1. Her net cost to acquire the position would be $4.77 (= $6.47 − $1.70), which would then generate the terminal payoffs displayed in Exhibit 23.29. If SAS stock settled at $45 or higher, both puts would be worthless and the investor would lose all of her initial investment. If the expiration date share price was $35 or less, both options would be in the money, leaving the investor with a net position of $5.23 (= $45 − $35 − $4.77). Thus, this is the put option version of a bear money spread.

A final extension of this concept is the *butterfly* spread. Suppose an investor designed the following portfolio of SAS options: long one call #1, short two calls #2, and long one call #3. This position is equivalent to holding

➤ a bull money spread (i.e., buy Call #1 and sell Call #2), *and*
➤ a bear money spread (i.e., buy Call #3 and sell Call #2).

The net purchase price for these transactions is $0.83 (= ($8.07 − $5.24) + ($3.24 − $5.24)). The expiration date payoffs are listed in Exhibit 23.30 and show that the value of the position peaks at a stock price of $40 and that the investor can lose, at most, her initial investment. The

EXHIBIT 23.29   *A BEAR MONEY SPREAD WITH PUT OPTIONS*

EXHIBIT 23.30   *EXPIRATION DATE PAYOFFS TO A BUTTERFLY SPREAD*

SAS STOCK PRICE AT EXPIRATION	VALUE BULL SPREAD	VALUE BEAR SPREAD	COST OF OPTIONS	NET PROFIT
$20.00	$0.00	$ 0.00	$–0.83	$–0.83
25.00	0.00	0.00	–0.83	–0.83
30.00	0.00	0.00	–0.83	–0.83
35.00	0.00	0.00	–0.83	–0.83
40.00	5.00	0.00	–0.83	4.17
45.00	5.00	–5.00	–0.83	–0.83
50.00	5.00	–5.00	–0.83	–0.83
55.00	5.00	–5.00	–0.83	–0.83
60.00	5.00	–5.00	–0.83	–0.83

breakeven stock prices are $35.83 and $44.17. This form of the butterfly spread is equivalent to a hedged version of a short straddle position. That is, in exchange for receiving a smaller potential payoff (i.e., $4.17 versus $8.91) from a view on low volatility, the investor has limited her losses if SAS's stock price is more explosive than she expected. This trade-off is shown in Exhibit 23.31.

Range Forwards

In Chapter 21, we discussed an *equity collar* as a way that an investor could protect her stock portfolio from adverse movements while allowing for some upside gain potential. We saw that although the equity collar had some of the same attributes as a forward contract (e.g., no up-front premium expense), it was actually a combination of two options—the purchase of an out-of-the-money put and sale of an out-of-the-money call in this case. Equity collars are an example of a wider class of option combinations known as **range** (or "flexible") **forwards**, and they are used widely to manage the risk of underlying assets other than equity as well.

EXHIBIT 23.31 COMPARING THE BUTTERFLY SPREAD AND SHORT STRADDLE POSITIONS

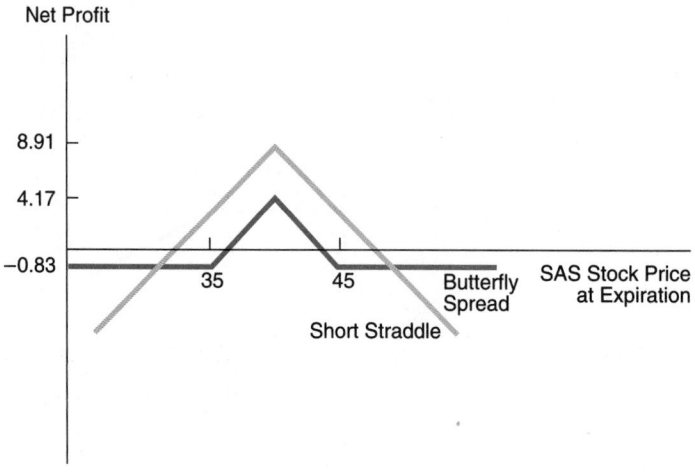

EXHIBIT 23.32 HYPOTHETICAL CHF DERIVATIVE PRICES AND TERMS

Derivative	Contract/Exercise Price (USD/CHF)	Expiration	CHF Amount	Price (USD/CHF)
Forward:	$0.67	3 months	1,000,000	—
Calls:	0.64	3 months	1,000,000	0.034
	0.67	3 months	1,000,000	0.015
	0.70	3 months	1,000,000	0.004
Puts:	0.64	3 months	1,000,000	0.004
	0.67	3 months	1,000,000	0.015
	0.70	3 months	1,000,000	0.034

To see how range forward positions might be used in a different context, suppose that the treasurer of a U.S. multinational corporation knows today that he will have a bill for imported goods that must be paid in three months. This bill, denominated in Swiss francs and requiring payment of CHF 1,000,000, presents a challenge for a dollar-based company because it must buy the francs it needs rather than generate them in the natural flow of business. As shown in Chapter 22, this is a classic opportunity to use derivatives to hedge the firm's FX exposure.[29]

After contacting a number of dealers in the OTC market, the treasurer establishes prices and terms for several CHF forward and option contracts. These are listed in Exhibit 23.32, which states prices on a direct (i.e., USD/CHF) basis. The treasurer could lock in a three-month for-

---

[29]For a good discussion of currency risk management strategies such as the range forward position, see Roger G. Clarke and Mark P. Kritzman, *Currency Management: Concepts and Practices* (Charlottesville, Va.: Research Foundation of the Institute of Chartered Analysts, 1996).

EXHIBIT 23.33 COMPARING LONG POSITIONS IN REGULAR AND RANGE FORWARDS

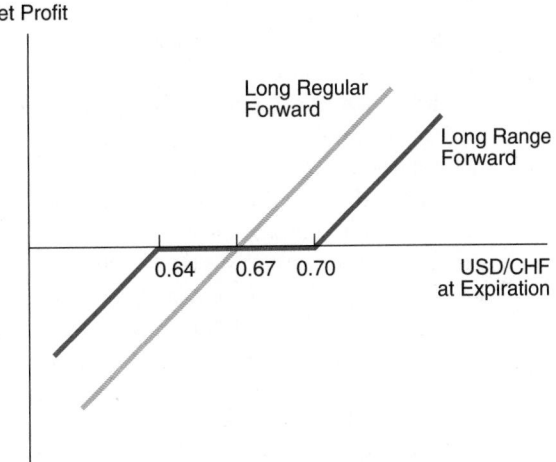

ward rate of USD 0.67/CHF without cost in two ways. First, he could commit to a long position in the CHF forward with a contract amount of CHF 1,000,000. Second, he could buy the CHF call option struck at USD 0.67/CHF and pay for it by selling the CHF put at the same exercise rate. As shown in Chapter 21, the put-call parity model indicates that buying a call and selling a put with the same exercise rate are equivalent to a long forward position. Further, this second strategy would generate a zero-cost forward (i.e., $C_0 = P_0$) only when the common exercise rate is set equal to the prevailing forward rate.

As a third alternative, what if the treasurer (1) bought the 0.70 call for USD $0.004 per franc and (2) sold the 0.64 put for the same price? Once again, this would be a costless combination of options; however, since the two options do not have a common exercise price, this combination is not equivalent to the actual forward—it is a range forward. At the expiration date, one of three things will happen: (1) if the spot FX rate is greater than USD 0.70/CHF, the treasurer will exercise his call and buy francs at that level; (2) if the spot FX rate is less than USD 0.64/CHF, the dealer to whom the treasurer sold the put will force him to buy francs for USD 0.64 per franc, and (3) if the spot FX rate is in between these extremes, both options will finish out of the money and the treasurer will buy the required currency at the regular market price. This payoff scheme is contrasted with the regular contract in Exhibit 23.33.

If the treasurer takes a long position in the regular forward contract, he will buy his francs at USD 0.67/CHF, whether or not the prevailing exchange rate in three months is above or below this level. Thus, although he is protected against a weakening dollar, he cannot benefit if the domestic currency strengthens. With a long position in the range forward, though, in exchange for worse FX "insurance"—namely, a maximum purchase USD 0.70/CHF—he could pay as little as USD 0.64/CHF if the dollar gets stronger. Finally, many zero-cost range forwards could be created; for any desired out-of-the money call option, there will be an out-of-the-money put at some exercise price that has the same premium. In fact, the actual forward contract can be viewed as a zero-cost range forward for which the put and the call options are both struck at USD 0.67/CHF.

The Internet *Investments Online*

Additional information on option contracts and strategies can be found at:

http://www.cboe.com The Chicago Board Options Exchange Web site, which features detailed descriptions of all of the various products they trade including individual and index equity options and FLEX options. Also included at the site are pages containing historical data on contract trading volume and price volatility for underlying equity securities. The CBOE site features links to an online learning center that contains a series of self-guided tutorials designed to teach and reinforce the basics of puts and calls.

http://www.optionmax.com This is a site of a software seller, but some of the pages here are quite useful and do not require a subscription to any paid service. In particular, the site contains links to descriptions of several different option-based trading strategies, from simple to complex, and includes charts of the resulting payoff patterns. There are also calculators for determining the profitability of various option positions.

http://finance.wat.ch/cbt/options This is a link off the Web site for the International Finance and Commodities Institute, which is a nonprofit organization with the objective of promoting global understanding of commodity trading as well as financial futures and options. Among other things available here, you will find an excellent series of online tutorials in the fundamentals of option contracting, valuation, and trading.

http://www.coveredcall.com This somewhat specialized Web site was created as a forum for investors to acquire new ideas and exchange information about trading covered call options. As its name implies, this site concentrates on the various data many covered call writers deem as "required reading" and has quick links to other critical data fields all presented in an extremely easy to read and use format.

Summary

- Along with forwards and futures, options represent another basic form of derivative contracting. Like the forward positions to which they are linked, puts and calls are used as either stand-alone investments or as supplements to an existing collection of assets. In the latter application, they provide investors with a convenient and inexpensive way to restructure the risk-reward trade-off in a portfolio. The flexibility of this form of contracting permits investors to create unique payoff structures by combining different options in various ways. Option straddles, for instance, allow the holder to take advantage of a view on the underlying asset's volatility while remaining neutral about the direction of future price movements. Forward contracts can be viewed as a specifically chosen pair of options; and these contracts are special cases of option combinations known as range forwards (or collars).

- We consider how option contracts are valued in an efficient market. Although the mathematics of some valuation models can be formidable, the intuition behind the process is not. Each of three models we discuss—the two-state, the binomial, and the Black-Scholes—is based on the same three-step evolution. The first step is combining options with the underlying asset in order to create a riskless position. Invariably, this synthetic risk-free portfolio requires the sale (purchase) of multiple calls (puts) to offset to the full cash exposure of a single share of stock held long. This hedge ratio changes with movements in the underlying asset's price and the passage of time; therefore, the riskless hedge portfolio needs to be rebalanced frequently. Once it is formed, however, the option's value can be established by assuming that the hedge portfolio should earn the risk-free rate (i.e., the "no-arbitrage" condition) and solving for the option value that makes this assumption true.

- The Black-Scholes model is extremely flexible. Although originally created for European-style call options on nondividend-bearing stock, this model extends easily to valuing put options and options on dividend-paying stocks. The payment of dividends decreases the value of an otherwise identical call option but not by the amount of the dividend itself. We also discuss how volatility, the only user-provided variable in the valuation model, is either estimated directly from a historical series of asset prices or implied from option prices themselves.

• We discuss the process for valuing American-style puts and calls and how this differs from the valuation of their European counterparts. Further, we explain how the Black-Scholes model could be adapted to value options on other underlying assets, such as stock indexes, foreign currency, or commodity futures contracts. An introduction to the use and valuation of several exotic options having nonstandard payoffs is also offered.

Questions

1. Straddles have been described as "volatility plays." Explain what this means for both long and short straddle positions. Given the fact that volatility is a primary factor in how options are priced, under what conditions might an investor who believes that markets are efficient ever want to create a straddle?

2. Put-call-forward parity and range forward positions both involve the purchase of a call option and the sale of a put option (or vice versa) on the same underlying asset. Describe the relationship between these two trading strategies. Is one a special case of the other?

3. *CFA Examination Level II*

   Michelle Industries issued a Swiss-franc denominated five-year discount note for CHF 200 million. The proceeds were converted to U.S. dollars to purchase capital equipment in the United States. The company wants to hedge this currency exposure and is considering the following alternatives:

   (a) At-the-money Swiss Franc call options

   (b) Swiss franc forwards

   (c) Swiss franc futures

   Contrast the essential characteristics of each of these three derivative instruments. Evaluate the suitability of each in relation to Michelle's hedging objective, including both advantages and disadvantages.

4. *CFA Examination Level III*

   Six factors affect the value of call options on stocks. Three of these factors are: the current price of the stock, the time remaining until the option expires, and the dividend on the stock. Identify the other three factors and explain how and why changes in each of these three factors affect the value of call options.

5. "Although options are risky investments, they are valued by virtue of their ability to convert the underlying asset into a synthetic risk-free security." Explain what this statement means, being sure to describe the basic three-step process for valuing option contracts.

6. In valuing currency options with the Black-Scholes model, we saw that the risk-free rate on the foreign currency was equivalent to the dividend yield when an individual stock or stock index was the underlying asset. Discuss the appropriateness of this analogy. What sort of transaction involving foreign currency would be required to make this parallel exact?

7. Describe the condition under which it would be rational to exercise both an American-style put and call stock option before the expiration date. In both cases, comment specifically on the role that dividends play.

8. Explain why a change in the time to expiration (i.e., T) can have either a positive or negative impact on the value of a European-style put option. In this explanation, it will be useful to contrast the put's reaction with that of a European-style call, for which an increase in T has an unambiguously positive effect.

9. Currency option traders often speak of "buying low volatility (or 'vol') and selling high vol" rather than buying or selling the option itself. What does this mean exactly? From this perspective, what is the real underlying asset: volatility or foreign currency?

10. It has been shown empirically that stock volatility decreases as a stock's price increases. Comment on how this phenomenon would tend to bias the call and put option values generated by the Black-Scholes model, which assumes that volatility remains constant.

11. On October 19, 1987, the stock market (as measured by the Dow Jones Industrial Average) lost almost one-quarter of its value in a single day. Nevertheless, some traders made a profit buying call options on the stock index and then liquidating their positions before the market closed. Explain how this is possible, assuming that it was not a case of the traders taking advantage of spurious upward "ticks" in stock prices.

Problems

1. *CFA Examination Level III*

   You are considering the sale of a call option with an exercise price of $100 and one year to expiration. The underlying stock pays no dividends, its current price is $100, and you believe it will either increase to $120 or decrease to $80. The risk-free rate of interest is 10 percent.

   a. Describe the specific steps involved in applying the binomial option pricing model to calculate the option's value.

   b. Compare the binomial option pricing model to the Black-Scholes option pricing model.

2. *CFA Examination Level III*

   You have decided to buy protective put options to protect the U.S. stock holdings of one of Global Advisers Company's (GAC) portfolios from a potential price decline over the next three months. You have researched the stock index options available in the United States and have assembled the following information:

Stock Index Option	Current Index Value	Underlying Value of One Put	Strike Price of Put	Put Premium	Average Daily Trading Volume of Puts
S&P 100	$365.00	$100 times index	365	$10.25	10,000
S&P 500	390.00	$100 times index	390	11.00	4,000
NYSE	215.00	$100 times index	215	6.25	1,000

(For each stock index option, the total cost of one put is the put premium times 100.)

	Beta vs. S&P 500	Correlation with Portfolio
Portfolio	1.05	1.00
S&P 100	0.95	0.86
S&P 500	1.00	0.95
NYSE	1.03	0.91

   a. Using all relevant data from the preceding tables, calculate for each stock index option both the number and cost of puts required to protect a $7,761,700 diversified equity portfolio from loss. Show all calculations.

   b. Recommend and justify which stock index option to use to hedge the portfolio, including reference to two relevant factors other than cost.

   You know that it is very unlikely that the current stock index values will be exactly the same as the put strike prices at the time you make your investment decision.

   c. Explain the importance of the relationship between the strike price of the puts and the current index values as it affects your investment decision.

   d. Explain how an option pricing model may help you make an investment decision in this situation.

3. *CFA Examination Level II*

   Joel Franklin is a portfolio manager responsible for derivatives. Franklin observes an American-style option and a European-style option with the same strike price, expiration, and underlying stock. Franklin believes that the European-style option will have a higher premium than the American-style option.

a. Critique Franklin's belief that the European-style option will have a higher premium.
Franklin is asked to value a one-year European-style call option for Abaco Ltd. Common stock, which last traded at $43.00. He has collected the following information:

Closing stock price	$43.00
Call and put option exercise price	45.00
One-year put option price	4.00
One-year Treasury bill rate	5.50%
Time to expiration	One year

b. Calculate, using put-call parity and the information provided, the European-style call option value.
c. State the effect, if any, of each of the following three variables on the value of a call option: (1) an increase in short-term interest rate, (2) an increase in stock price volatility, and (3) a decrease in time to option expiration.

4. Assuming that a one-year call option with an exercise price of $38 is available for the stock of the DEW Corp., consider the following price tree for DEW stock over the next year:

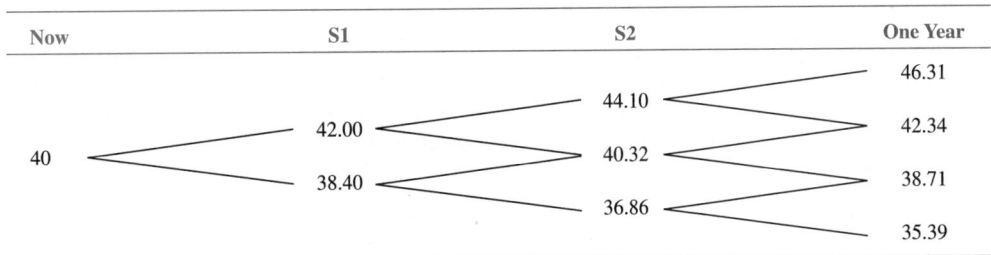

Now	S1	S2	One Year
			46.31
		44.10	
	42.00		42.34
40		40.32	
	38.40		38.71
		36.86	
			35.39

a. If the sequence of stock prices that DEW stock follows over the year is 40.00, 42.00, 40.32, and 38.71, describe the composition of the initial riskless portfolio of stock and options you would form and all the subsequent adjustments you would have to make to keep this portfolio riskless. Assume the one-year risk-free rate is 6 percent.
b. Given the initial DEW price of $40, what are the probabilities of observing each of the four terminal stock prices in one year? (Hint: In arriving at your answer, it will be useful to consider (1) the number of different ways that a particular terminal price could be achieved and (2) the probability of an up or down movement.)
c. Use the binomial option model to calculate the present value of this call option.
d. Calculate the value of a one-year put option on DEW stock having an exercise price of $38; be sure your answer is consistent with the correct response to Part c.

 5. *CFA Examination Level II*
A stock index is currently trading at 50.00. The annual index standard deviation is 20 percent. Paul Tripp, CFA, wants to value two-year index options using the binomial model. To correctly value the options, he needs the following formulas. The annual risk-free interest rate is 6 percent. Assume no dividends are paid on any of the underlying securities in the index.

FORMULAS FOR OPTION VALUATION

$$U = e^{\sigma\sqrt{\Delta t}}$$

where:

$$U = 1.2214$$

$$D = \frac{1}{U}$$

$$\pi_u = \frac{e^{r\Delta t} - D}{U - D}$$

where:

$$e^{r\Delta t} = 1.06184$$

Where:

U = up movement factor
D = down movement factor
Π_u = probability of an upward price movement

DISCOUNT FACTORS

	5.00 Percent	6.00 Percent	7.00 Percent
Period 1	0.95123	0.94176	0.93239
Period 2	0.90484	0.88692	0.86936
Period 3	0.86071	0.83527	0.81058

---

a. Construct a two-period binomial price tree for the stock index.
b. Calculate the value of a European-style index call option with an exercise price of 60.00.
c. Calculate the value of a European-style index put option with an exercise price of 60.00.

6. Following is a two-period price tree for a share of stock in SAB Corp.:

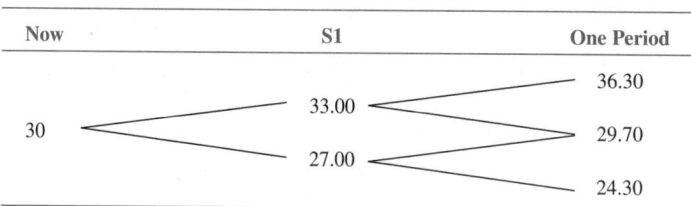

Now	S1	One Period
		36.30
	33.00	
30		29.70
	27.00	
		24.30

a. Using the binomial model, calculate the current fair value of a regular call option on SAB stock with the following characteristics: $X = 28$, $RFR = 5$ percent (per subperiod). You should also indicate the composition of the implied riskless hedge portfolio at the valuation date.
b. Using the same stock price tree, and assuming that the values of X and RFR remain the same, calculate: (1) the value of an Asian-style (i.e., average price) call option, (2) the value of a lookback call option, and (3) the value of a digital call option with a fixed payout of $Q = 5$.

7. Consider the following questions on the pricing of options on the stock of ARB Inc.:
a. A share of ARB stock sells for $75 and has a standard deviation of returns equal to 20 percent per year. The current risk-free rate is 9 percent and the stock pays two dividends: (1) a $2 dividend just prior to the option's expiration day, which is 91 days from now (i.e., exactly one quarter of a year); and (2) a $2 dividend 182 days from now (i.e., exactly one-half year). Calculate the Black-Scholes value for a European-style call option with an exercise price of $70.
b. What would be the price of a 91-day European-style put option on ARB stock having the same exercise price?
c. Calculate the change in the call option's value that would occur if ARB's management suddenly decided to suspend dividend payments and this action had no effect on the price of the company's stock.
d. Briefly describe (without calculations) how your answer in Part a would differ under the following separate circumstances: (1) the volatility of ARB stock increases to 30 percent, and (2) the risk-free rate decreases to 8 percent.

8. Consider the following data relevant to valuing a European-style call option on a nondividend-paying stock: $X = 40$, $RFR = 9$ percent, $T = $ six months (i.e., 0.5), and $\sigma = 0.25$.
   a. Compute the Black-Scholes option and hedge ratio values for the series of hypothetical current stock price levels shown in Exhibit 23.11.
   b. Explain why the values in Part a differ from those shown in Exhibit 23.11.
   c. For $S = 40$, calculate the Black-Scholes value for a European-style put option. How much of this value represents time premium?

9. Suppose the current contract price of a futures contract on Commodity Z is $46.50 and the expiration date is in exactly six months (i.e., $T = 0.5$). The annualized risk-free rate over this period is 5.45 percent and the volatility of futures price movement is 23 percent, which is equal to that of the underlying commodity.
   a. Calculate the values for both a call option and a put option for this futures contract, assuming both have an exercise price of $46.50 and a six-month expiration date.
   b. Suppose the market prices for these contracts agree with the values you computed in Part a. You decide to buy the call option and sell the put option. What sort of position have you just created? Under what circumstances (i.e., for what view of subsequent market conditions) would it make sense for an investor to create such a position?

10. Suppose the current value of the Standard and Poor's 500 index is 653.50 and the dividend yield on the index is 2.8 percent. Also, the yield curve is flat at a continuously compounded rate of 5.5 percent.
   a. If you estimate the volatility factor for the index to be 16 percent, calculate the value of an index call option with an exercise price of 670 and an expiration date in exactly three months.
   b. If the actual market price of this option is $17.40, calculate its implied volatility coefficient.
   c. Besides volatility estimation error, explain why your valuation and the option's traded price might differ from one another.

11. Consider the following price data for TanCo stock in two different subperiods:

    Subperiod A: 168.375; 162.875; 162.5; 161.625; 160.75; 157.75; 157.25; 157.75; 161.125; 162.5; 157.5; 156.625; 157.875; 155.375; 150.5; 155.75; 154.25; 155.875; 156; 152.75; 150.5; 150.75
    Subperiod B: 122.5; 124.5; 121.875; 120.625; 119.5; 118.125; 117.75; 119.25; 122.25; 121.625; 120; 117.75; 118.375; 115.625; 117.75; 117.5; 118.5; 117.625; 114.625; 110.75

    a. For each subperiod, calculate the annualized historical measure of stock volatility that could be used in pricing an option for TanCo. In your calculations, you may assume that there are 250 trading days in a year.
    b. Suppose now that you decide to gather additional data for each subperiod. Specifically, you obtain information for a call option with a current price of $12.25 and the following characteristics: $X = 115$; $S = 120.625$; time to expiration $= 62$ days; $RFR = 7.42$ percent; and dividend yield $= 3.65$ percent. Here the risk-free rate and dividend yields are stated on an annual basis. Use the volatility measure from Subperiod B and the Black-Scholes model to obtain the "fair value" for this call option. Based on your calculations, is the option currently priced as it should be? Explain.

12. In March, a derivatives dealer offers you the following quotes for June British pound option contracts (expressed in U.S. dollars per GBP):

		MARKET PRICE OF CONTRACT	
Contract	Strike Price	Bid	Offer
Call	USD 1.40	0.0642	0.0647
Put		0.0255	0.0260
Call	1.44	0.0417	0.0422
Put		0.0422	0.0427
Call	1.48	0.0255	0.0260
Put		0.0642	0.0647

a. Assuming each of these contracts specifies the delivery of GBP 31,250 and expires in exactly three months, complete a table similar to the following (expressed in dollars) for a portfolio consisting of the following positions:

(1) Long a 1.44 call
(2) Short a 1.48 call
(3) Long a 1.40 put
(4) Short a 1.44 put

June USD/GBP	Net Initial Cost	Call 1.44 Profit	Call 1.48 Profit	Put 1.40 Profit	Put 1.44 Profit	Net Profit
1.36	—	—	—	—	—	—
1.40	—	—	—	—	—	—
1.44	—	—	—	—	—	—
1.48	—	—	—	—	—	—
1.52	—	—	—	—	—	—

b. Graph the total net profit (i.e., cumulative profit less net initial cost, ignoring time value considerations) relationship using the June USD/GBP rate on the horizontal axis (be sure to label the breakeven point(s)). Also, comment briefly on the nature of the currency speculation represented by this portfolio.

c. If in exactly one month (i.e., in April) the spot USD/GBP rate falls to 1.385 and the effective annual risk-free rates in the United States and England are 5 percent and 7 percent, respectively, calculate the equilibrium price differential that should exist between a long 1.44 call and a short 1.44 put position. (Hint: Consider what sort of forward contract this option combination is equivalent to and treat the British interest rate as a dividend yield.)

13. *CFA Examination Level II*

Linda Morgan is evaluating option strategies that will allow her to profit from large moves in a stock's price, either up or down. She believes that a combination of a long put and a long call option with the same expiration and exercise price (straddle) would meet her objective.

Price information on APEX stock and options follows. (Assume it is June 1999.)

APEX STOCK AND OPTION CURRENT MARKET PRICES

APEX stock: $50
Call option with an exercise price of $50 expiring December 1999: $4
Put option with an exercise price of $50 expiring December 1999: $3
No transactions costs or taxes exist

---

a. Draw a net-profit-and-loss diagram at expiration for the straddle, using the preceding information. Calculate and label the following on a graph:

- Maximum loss
- The breakeven points of the position

Morgan is considering a lower-cost strategy that would allow her to profit from large changes in the stock's price.

APEX STOCK AND OPTION CURRENT MARKET PRICES

APEX stock: $50
Call option with an exercise price of $55 expiring December 1999: $2.50
Put option with an exercise price of $45 expiring December 1999: $2.00
No transactions costs or taxes exist

---

b. Draw a net-profit-and-loss diagram at expiration for the alternative option strategy, using this additional information. Calculate and label the following on a graph:

- Maximum loss
- The breakeven points of the position

14. In mid-May, there are two outstanding call option contracts available on the stock of ARB Co.:

Call #	Exercise Price	Expiration Date	Market Price
1	$50	August 19	$8.40
2	60	August 19	3.34

a. Assuming that you form a portfolio consisting of *one* Call #1 held long and *two* Calls #2 held short, complete the following table showing your intermediate steps. In calculating net profit, be sure to include the net initial cost of the options.

Price of ARB Stock at Expiration	Profit on Call #1 Position	Profit on Call #2 Position	Net Profit on Total Position
$40	—	—	—
45	—	—	—
50	—	—	—
55	—	—	—
60	—	—	—
65	—	—	—
70	—	—	—
75	—	—	—

b. Graph the net profit relationship in Part a, using stock price on the horizontal axis. What is (are) the breakeven stock price(s)? What is the point of maximum profit?

c. Under what market conditions will this strategy (which is known as a *call ratio spread*) generally make sense? Does the holder of this position have limited or unlimited liability?

15. In developing the butterfly spread position, we showed that it could be broken down into two call option money spreads. Using the price data for SAS stock options from Exhibit 23.18, demonstrate how a butterfly payoff structure similar to that shown in Exhibit 23.31 could be created using put options. Be specific as to the contract positions involved in the trade and show the expiration date net payoffs for the combined transaction.

16. *CFA Examination Level III*

Ken Webster manages a $100 million equity portfolio benchmarked to the S&P 500 index. Over the past two years, the S&P 500 index has appreciated 60 percent. Webster believes the market is overvalued when measured by several traditional fundamental/economic indicators. He is concerned about maintaining the excellent gains the portfolio has experienced in the past two years but recognizes that the S&P index could still move above its current 668 level. Webster is considering the following *option collar* strategy:

- Protection for the portfolio can be attained by purchasing an S&P 500 index put with a strike price of 665 (just out of the money).
- The put can be financed by selling two 675 calls (farther out of the money, for every put purchased).
- Because the combined delta of the two calls is less than 1 (that is, $2 \times 0.36 = 0.72$), the options will not lose more than the underlying portfolio advances.

The information in the following table describes the two options used to create the collar.

OPTIONS TO CREATE THE COLLAR

Characteristics	675 Call	665 Put
Option price	$4.30	$8.05
Option implied volatility	11.00%	14.00%
Option's delta	0.36	0.44
Contracts needed for collar	602	301

Notes:

- Ignore transaction costs
- S&P 500 historical 30-day volatility = 12.00%
- Time to option expiration = 30 days

a. Describe the potential returns of the combined portfolio (the underlying portfolio plus the option collar) if after 30 days the S&P 500 index has (1) risen approximately 5 percent to 701.00, (2) remained at 668 (no change), and (3) declined by approximately 5 percent to 635.

b. Discuss the effect on the hedge ratio (delta) of each option as the S&P 500 approaches the level for each of the potential outcomes listed in Part a.

c. Evaluate the pricing of each of the following in relation to the volatility data provided: (1) the put, (2) the call, and (3) the collar.

d. Explain the term *wasting asset* in the context of the suggested collar strategy and discuss its effect on Webster's management of the portfolio.

References

Bookstaber, Richard M. *Option Pricing and Investment Strategies,* 3d ed. Chicago, Ill.: Probus Publishing, 1991.

Brenner, Menachem, Georges Courtadon, and Marti Subrahmanyam. "Options on the Spot and Options on Futures." *Journal of Finance* 40, no. 5 (December 1985).

Briys, Eric, Mondher Bellalah, Huu Minh Mai, and Francois De Varenne. *Options, Futures, and Exotic Derivatives.* New York: John Wiley and Sons, 1998.

Cheng, Wai-Yan, and Shuguang Zhang. "The Analytics of Reset Options." *Journal of Derivatives* 8, no. 1 (Fall 2000): 59–71.

Cox, John C., and Mark Rubinstein. *Option Markets.* Englewood Cliffs, N.J.: Prentice-Hall, 1985.

Gastineau, Gary. *The Options Manual,* 3d ed. New York: McGraw-Hill, 1988.

Jarrow, Robert, and Stuart Turnbull. *Derivative Securities,* 2d ed. Cincinnati, Ohio: Thomson Learning, 2000.

Kolb, Robert W. *Options,* 3d ed. Cambridge, Mass.: Blackwell Publishers, 1997.

McMillan, Lawrence G. *Options as a Strategic Investment,* 3d ed. Upper Saddle River, N.J.: Prentice-Hall, 1992.

Shastri, Kuldeep, and Kishore Tandon. "Options on Futures Contracts: A Comparison of European and American Pricing Models." *Journal of Futures Markets* 6, no. 4 (Winter 1986).

Smith, Clifford W., Jr. "Option Pricing: A Review." *Journal of Financial Economics* 3, no. 1/2 (January–March 1976).

Chapter 24 ▶ Swap Contracts, Convertible Securities, and Other Embedded Derivatives

After you read this chapter, you should be able to answer the following questions:

➤ What are forward rate agreements and how can they be used to reduce the interest rate exposure of a borrower or an investor?

➤ What are interest rate swaps and how can they transform the cash flows of a fixed or floating rate security?

➤ How does the swap market operate and how are swap contracts quoted and priced?

➤ How can swaps be interpreted as a pair of capital market transactions and how does this aid in the swap valuation process?

➤ How is credit risk measured in the interest rate swap market?

➤ What are interest rate caps and floors and how are they related to interest rate swaps?

➤ How does a currency swap differ from a "plain vanilla" interest rate swap and what is it used for?

➤ How can the swap contracting concept be adapted to manage equity price risk?

➤ How do the derivatives in convertible securities and warrant issues differ from traditional exchange-traded products?

➤ What are the similarities and differences between convertible preferred stock and convertible bonds?

➤ What are structured notes and what factors make their existence possible?

➤ How can securities with embedded derivatives reduce the funding cost of a corporate borrower?

➤ What are real options and how can an investor use them to value company flexibility?

Although derivatives only come in two basic "flavors"—forwards and options—the preceding chapters have shown that they can be used in a virtually unlimited number of situations by simply changing the contract terms or the nature of the underlying asset. In this chapter, we discuss several more ways in which these instruments can be modified to the specific needs of a particular end user. Invariably, these modifications involve combining derivatives with other assets or liabilities to create the most highly valued cash flow pattern. We look at two general approaches to forming these combinations: "packages" of derivatives, such as **interest rate swaps**, caps, and floors; and derivatives that have been "embedded" in more fundamental assets, such as equity or debt issues.

To begin, we consider the market for OTC interest rate agreements—one of the fastest-growing segments of the derivatives industry in the past 20 years. In this examination, we once again focus on the differences between forward-based and option-based agreements while exploring the connection between the two. We then extend our discussion of swap contracting to include agreements based on foreign exchange and equity price movements. Next, we provide an overview of the myriad ways in which forwards and options are incorporated into other financial instruments. This includes an analysis of convertible securities, **warrants**, and **structured notes**. These innovations allow investors to acquire any of four different exposures—interest rate, currency, equity, or commodity price risk—in a creative and cost-effective manner. We conclude with a discussion of how investors can value the options embedded in real assets.

OTC INTEREST RATE AGREEMENTS

In addition to futures and options contracts, an extremely active OTC market exists for products designed to manage an investor's or an issuer's interest rate risk. In describing strategies involving these instruments, it is useful to classify them as either forward-based or option-based contracts.[1]

Forward-Based Interest Rate Contracts

Forward Rate Agreements   The **forward rate agreement (FRA)** is the most basic of the OTC interest rate contracts. In an FRA, two parties agree today to a future exchange of cash flows based on two different interest rates. One of the cash flows is tied to a yield that is fixed at the deal's origination (the fixed rate); the other is determined at some later date (the floating rate). On the contract's settlement date, the difference between the two interest rates is multiplied by the FRA's **notional principal** (the "scale" of the transaction) and prorated to the length of the holding period. As the London Interbank Offer Rate (LIBOR) is frequently used as the floating rate index, FRAs are the OTC equivalent of the Eurodollar futures contracts traded at the Chicago Mercantile Exchange with two important exceptions: (1) FRAs typically require no collateral account, and (2) they are not marked to market on a daily basis.

An FRA's settlement date and maturity are defined by its name: a 3×6 FRA allows the investor to lock in three-month LIBOR, three months forward; a 12×18 FRA locks in six-month LIBOR, one year forward, and so forth. FRA market makers quote a bid-offer spread on a rate basis. For example, suppose the FRA rates for three-month LIBOR shown in Exhibit 24.1 prevail in the market at Date 0, with current three-month LIBOR assumed to be 4.50 percent. This means that on a 3×6 FRA, the market maker is prepared to pay a fixed rate of 4.81 percent for receipt of three-month LIBOR and to receive a fixed rate of 4.85 percent for payment of LIBOR. In either case, there will be no payment until LIBOR is revealed in Month 3. Settlement can then be made in arrears at Month 6 or in advance at Month 3. If in arrears, the settlement flow will be adjusted to the actual number of days in the holding period and calculated by the following formula:

➤**24.1** $$\left[\text{LIBOR} - \text{Fixed Rate}\right] \times \left[\text{Notional Principal}\right] \times \left[\frac{\text{Number of Days}}{360}\right]$$

recalling that, in the U.S. market, LIBOR is based on a 360-day year. The advance settlement amount is calculated as the present value of the in-arrears amount, using the prorated level of the realized LIBOR as the discount rate. Notice that this settlement occurs on a net basis—that is, only a single check for the rate differential will be written.

To see how an FRA might be used, suppose that Company Z decides to borrow financial capital for a six-month period, in two three-month installments. Because of the "set in advance, pay in arrears" convention for interest rate determination used in most debt markets, the firm finds itself exposed to rising interest rates over the next three months because the level of its second

---

[1]Some of the discussion in this section is based on Keith C. Brown and Donald J. Smith, *Interest Rate and Current Swaps: A Tutorial* (Charlottesville, Va.: Research Foundation of the Institute of Chartered Financial Analysts, 1995).

EXHIBIT 24.1   *INDICATIVE BID-OFFER QUOTES ON THREE-MONTH FORWARD RATE AGREEMENTS*

PERIOD	BID	OFFER
3×6	4.81%	4.85%
6×9	5.20	5.24
9×12	5.64	5.68
12×15	6.37	6.41
15×18	6.78	6.82
18×21	7.10	7.14
21×24	7.36	7.40

EXHIBIT 24.2   *A MATCHED PAIR OF 3 × 6 FRA TRANSACTIONS*

interest payment will not be established until the end of that period. (The amount of Company Z's first three-month payment would be known at origination.) To solve this problem, the firm can acquire a 3 × 6 FRA whereby it pays the dealer's quoted fixed rate of 4.85 percent in exchange for receiving three-month LIBOR at the settlement date. This is illustrated on the right-hand side of Exhibit 24.2, which depicts both the borrowing and derivative transactions.

Once the dealer has committed to the FRA with Company Z, two things occur. First, Company Z no longer is exposed to a rising funding cost because it now has a forward contract that obligates the dealer to "sell" it the LIBOR it needs in Month 3 at a "price" of 4.85 percent. Second, the dealer now is exposed to rising LIBOR because it will be obligated to make the net settlement payment if LIBOR exceeds 4.85 percent three months from now. That is, Company Z has effectively used the FRA to transfer its interest rate exposure to the dealer. Unless the dealer wishes to hold this position as a speculation that rates will subsequently fall, the exposure can be hedged by "buying" LIBOR from another counterparty for its bid rate of 4.81 percent. This alternative is shown on the left-hand-side of Exhibit 24.2 as a second FRA with Company Y, which is assumed to be an investor in a variable-rate asset who is naturally concerned about falling rates.

Now suppose that three-month LIBOR is 5.00 percent on the rate-determination date in Month 3 and that the agreements with Companies Y and Z were negotiated to have a notional principal of $10 million. If its contract specified settlement in arrears at Month 6, Company Y would be obligated to pay the market maker $4,750, calculated as

$$[0.0500 - 0.0481] \times [10,000,000] \times \left[\frac{90}{360}\right]$$

assuming there are 90 days between Months 3 and 6. If settled in advance, the Month 3 payment would be

$$4,750 \div \left[1 + \frac{90 \times 0.0500}{360}\right] = \$4,691,36$$

Similarly, the payment from the dealer to Company Z would be $3,750 (= [0.0500 − 0.0485] × [10,000,000] × [90/360]) in Month 6, or $3,703.70 if accelerated to Month 3. By matching the FRAs, the market maker is fully hedged from interest rate risk. Its spread of four basis points, which translates into $1,000, compensates for the costs (e.g., transaction costs, credit risk) of making a market in these contracts.

Finally, although the terms "buy" and "sell" are awkward, they are commonly used when describing FRA transactions. Since the FRA has an initial value of zero and therefore is neither an asset nor a liability, a counterparty doesn't really buy or sell anything. Instead, the parties to the transaction enter into a contract that may obtain a positive or a negative value—depending on the direction of future interest rate level changes. Nevertheless, this language is consistent with interpreting LIBOR as the "commodity" involved in the deal. In that case, the fixed rate is then the price paid or received in exchange for LIBOR, so that the payer of the fixed rate (Company Z) is said to be buying LIBOR, with the fixed-rate receiver (Company Y) selling LIBOR.

Interest Rate Swaps Although FRAs are quite useful, they represent a "one time only" solution to an interest rate risk management problem since they have a single settlement date. In fact, both investors and borrowers are routinely exposed to interest rate movements at regular intervals over an extended period of time, such as for the buyer and seller of a **floating-rate note (FRN)** that resets its coupon rate twice annually for several years according to movements in six-month LIBOR.[2] In that case, several "exposure dates" would need to be hedged, which could be accomplished with a series of FRAs. For example, suppose that an investor holding a one-year FRN paying quarterly coupons of three-month LIBOR becomes concerned that rates may fall in the future, thereby depressing the level of her last three coupons. (Recall that by convention her first coupon, payable in three months, is based on current LIBOR, which was assumed to be 4.50 percent.) Accordingly, she offsets this exposure by agreeing to receive the fixed rate on three separate FRA contracts: the 3 × 6, the 6 × 9, and the 9 × 12. Given the bid rates quoted in Exhibit 24.1, these positions transform the cash flows on the floating-rate asset as shown in Exhibit 24.3.

This series of FRAs locks in the coupon levels, but they are at different fixed rates and require three separate contracts. This may be inconvenient to the investor, who might prefer a single contract that covers all the future coupon dates using the same fixed rate. This is exactly what an

---

[2] As we discussed briefly in Chapter 18, a floating- (or variable) rate note is a debt instrument that is similar to a fixed-income bond in that it pays coupons at regular (e.g., semiannual) dates during its life. The difference is that the floating-rate note, or FRN, pays a coupon that is adjusted in a predetermined way with changes in some reference rate. For instance, a typical payment formula might be to reset the coupon every six months at LIBOR + 0.25 percent, meaning that the coupon amount would vary directly with LIBOR. Do not confuse the two acronyms FRA and FRN: The former is an over-the-counter forward contract; the latter is a bond.

EXHIBIT 24.3 ▸ *CONVERTING A FLOATING-RATE NOTE WITH A SERIES OF FRAS*

A. Long One-Year FRN Paying LIBOR Quarterly

B. Series of Receive-Fixed FRAs

C. Combined Position

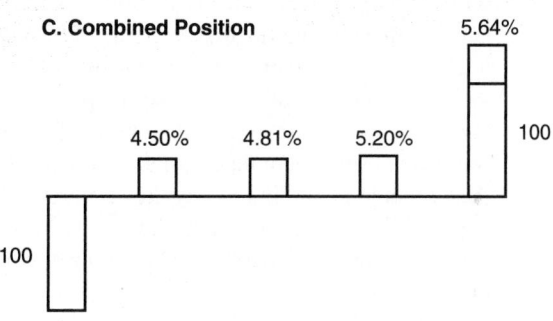

interest rate swap does. Specifically, the swap contract can be viewed as a prepackaged series of forward contracts to buy or sell LIBOR (i.e., FRAs) at the same fixed rate. Alternatively, an FRA can be viewed as a one-date interest rate swap. Of course, for the swap and FRA markets to remain efficient, the single fixed rate on the swap would have to be the appropriate average of 4.50 percent, 4.81 percent, 5.20 percent, and 5.64 percent. For simplicity, assume that each quarterly settlement period is exactly 0.25 year. This average can be approximated by solving for the internal rate of return on the hedged FRN:

$$100 = \frac{4.50 \times (0.25)}{(1 + IRR)^1} + \frac{4.81 \times (0.25)}{(1 + IRR)^2} + \frac{5.20 \times (0.25)}{(1 + IRR)^3} + \frac{100 + \left[5.64 \times (0.25)\right]}{(1 \times IRR)^4}$$

or *IRR* = 1.258 percent. Thus, 5.03 percent (1.258 × 4) would be the fixed rate on a one-year, receive-fixed swap consistent with the forward rate agreements listed in Exhibit 24.1. Notice that this *IRR* calculation is a very accurate approximation for the forward rate "annuitization" process we saw in Chapter 22. Specifically, a more general way to determine the swap fixed rate *(SFR)* that represents the appropriate average of this sequence of spot and forward LIBOR would be to solve the following equation:

$$\frac{(4.50)(0.25)(NP)}{\left[1+\dfrac{i_{0.3}}{4}\right]^{1}} + \frac{(4.81)(0.25)(NP)}{\left[1+\dfrac{i_{0.6}}{4}\right]^{2}} + \frac{(5.20)(0.25)(NP)}{\left[1+\dfrac{i_{0.9}}{4}\right]^{3}} + \frac{(5.64)(0.25)(NP)}{\left[1+\dfrac{i_{0.12}}{4}\right]^{4}}$$

$$=$$

$$\frac{(SFR)(0.25)(NP)}{\left[1+\dfrac{i_{0.3}}{4}\right]^{1}} + \frac{(SFR)(0.25)(NP)}{\left[1+\dfrac{i_{0.6}}{4}\right]^{2}} + \frac{(SFR)(0.25)(NP)}{\left[1+\dfrac{i_{0.9}}{4}\right]^{3}} + \frac{(SFR)(0.25)(NP)}{\left[1+\dfrac{i_{0.12}}{4}\right]^{4}}$$

where *NP* is the swap's notional principal and $i_{0,t}$ is the spot discount rate for a cash flow received or paid at a Date *t* months in the future. For a given interest rate term structure and contract notional principal, *SFR* is the only unknown element in this equation and can be solved for accordingly.[3]

Although interest rate swaps are priced off the LIBOR forward yield curve, they are quoted off the Treasury bond yield curve. That is, the fixed rate side of a U.S. dollar–based swap generally is broken down to two components for trading purposes: (1) the yield of a Treasury bond with a maturity comparable to that of the swap; and (2) a risk premium term known as the **swap spread**. Because the floating-rate side of the agreement typically is based on LIBOR "flat" (i.e., without any adjustment), the swap dealer can incorporate his bid-ask profit margin directly into this swap spread. Exhibit 24.4 lists a representative set of fixed-rate quotes for U.S. dollar swaps, both in absolute and swap spread terms. Each of the swaps represented in this exhibit assumes semiannual settlement dates with six-month LIBOR as the floating rate. For example, the swap dealer would be willing to pay the fixed rate of 4.82 percent on a five-year contract, a rate that is 63 basis points greater than the five-year T-bond yield. Notice that swaps with maturities as long as 30 years are quoted, although most contracts are transacted with maturities of 10 years or less.

With the fixed rate on the swap linked to a bond (i.e., [30/360] day count) yield and the floating rate as a money market (i.e., actual/360] day count in the U.S. market) yield, the swap settlement cash flows are calculated in a slightly different manner than for FRAs. Specifically, while the swap is still a net settlement contract, the Date *t* fixed- and floating-rate payments are determined separately as

$$(\text{Fixed-Rate Payment})_t = (\text{Swap Fixed Rate}) \times \left(\frac{\text{Number of "30/360" Days}}{360}\right) \times (\text{Notional Principal})$$

and

$$(\text{Floating-Rate Payment})_t = (\text{Reference Rate})_{t-1} \times \left(\frac{\text{Number of Days}}{360}\right) \times (\text{Notional Principal})$$

[3]See Vipul S. Bansal, M. E. Ellis, and John F. Marshall, "The Pricing of Short-Dated and Forward Interest Rate Swaps," *Financial Analysts Journal* 49, no. 2 (March–April 1993): 82–87; and Robert Brooks, *Interest Rate Modeling and the Risk Premiums in Interest Rate Swaps* (Charlottesville, Va.: Research Foundation of the Institute of Chartered Financial Analysts, 1997).

EXHIBIT 24.4 *INTEREST RATE SWAP AND SWAP SPREAD QUOTES*

SECURITY	Bid	Ask	CHANGE	SECURITY	Bid	Ask	CHANGE
US Semi 30/360				US Spreads 30/360			
3)2 YR	3.3400	3.3600	+.0100	23)2YR	40.00	42.00	+.50
4)3 YR	4.0200	4.0400	-.0090	24)3YR	67.00	69.00	-.50
5)4 YR	4.4900	4.5100	+.0040	25)4YR	71.50	73.50	-.50
6)5 YR	4.8200	4.8400	+.0110	26)5YR	63.00	65.00	--
7)6 YR	5.0600	5.0800	+.0290	27)6YR	73.00	75.00	+.50
8)7 YR	5.2400	5.2600	+.0190	28)7YR	77.50	79.50	+.25
9)8 YR	5.3800	5.4000	+.0220	29)8YR	77.50	79.50	--
10)9 YR	5.4800	5.5000	+.0250	30)9YR	74.00	76.00	+.50
11)10 YR	5.5800	5.6000	+.0240	31)10YR	70.00	72.00	+.50
12)15 YR	5.9000	5.9200	+.0370	32)15YR	88.75	90.75	+.50
13)20 YR	6.0100	6.0300	+.0300	33)20YR	87.25	89.25	+.25
14)30 YR	6.0500	6.0700	+.0205	34)30YR	66.00	68.00	--

In these equations, the fixed rate never changes and the floating-rate reference rate (i.e., LIBOR) always is determined at the beginning of a given settlement period.

As an example of these calculations, assume that Counterparty A is an institutional investor who currently holds a three-year bond paying a semiannual coupon of 5.00 percent. He feels that interest rates are likely to rise in the near term and, although he does not want to sell this position, he is concerned about a reduction in the bond's value. Consequently, the investor decides to convert his investment into a synthetic floating-rate note whose coupons will rise with future LIBOR increases. Specifically, he accomplishes this by agreeing to pay the fixed rate on a three-year interest rate swap contract with Counterparty B (i.e., the swap dealer). The terms of this agreement would be summarized as follows:

➤ Origination date: February 19, 2002
➤ Maturity date: February 19, 2005
➤ Notional principal: $30 million
➤ Fixed-rate payer: Counterparty A (i.e., the investor)
➤ Swap fixed rate: 4.04 percent (semiannual, 30/360 bond basis)
➤ Fixed-rate receiver: Counterparty B (i.e., the swap dealer)
➤ Floating rate: Six-month LIBOR (money market basis)
➤ Settlement dates: February 19 and August 19 of each year
➤ LIBOR determination: Set in advance, paid in arrears

This "fixed-for-floating" transaction—the most basic form of a swap—is often called a *plain vanilla* agreement. Exhibit 24.5 illustrates the approximate effect (ignoring slight day count differentials) of combining the swap with the underlying bond position, while Exhibit 24.6 lists the precise settlement cash flows from the investor's perspective for a hypothetical time series of six-month LIBOR. In this display, the fixed-rate payer makes the net settlement payment when the day count-adjusted level of LIBOR is less than 4.04 percent; the fixed-rate receiver makes the settlement payment when LIBOR exceeds 4.04 percent.

EXHIBIT 24.5 *CONVERTING CASH FLOWS FROM A FIXED-RATE BOND ISSUE WITH A SWAP AGREEMENT*

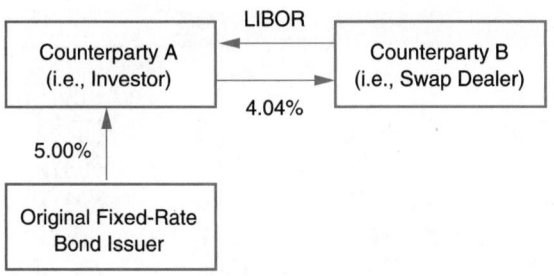

$$\text{Net Interest Income} = 5.00\% + [\text{LIBOR} - 4.04\%]$$
$$= \text{LIBOR} + 0.96\%$$

EXHIBIT 24.6 *SETTLEMENT CASH FLOWS FOR A THREE-YEAR "PLAIN VANILLA" INTEREST RATE SWAP (FIXED-PAYER'S PERSPECTIVE)*

SETTLEMENT DATE	NUMBER OF ACTUAL DAYS	NUMBER OF "30/60" DAYS	CURRENT LIBOR	FIXED-RATE PAYMENT	FLOATING-RATE RECEIPT	NET PAYMENT (RECEIPT)
2/19/2002	—	—	3.60%	—	—	—
8/19/2002	181	180	3.90	606,000	543,000	63,000
2/19/2003	184	180	4.45	606,000	598,000	8,000
8/19/2003	181	180	4.60	606,000	671,208	(65,208)
2/19/2004	184	180	4.20	606,000	705,333	(99,333)
8/19/2004	182	180	3.95	606,000	637,000	(31,000)
2/19/2005	184	180	4.05	606,000	605,667	333

Plain vanilla swaps are generally used for the same reason as FRAs: namely, to restructure the cash flows of an interest-sensitive asset or liability. In this example, the investor has reduced the price sensitivity (i.e., duration) of his asset by converting the fixed-rate coupon into one that adjusts to shifting market conditions. We saw in Chapter 21 that making this change synthetically with derivatives—rather than through a physical rebalancing of the portfolio—is the more cost-effective method. Given A's original coupon rate of 5 percent, the net annualized cash flow he will receive after accounting for the swap position will be (again ignoring day count differentials):

Fixed-Rate Bond Coupon Receipt	=	5.00%
Swap: (1) LIBOR Receipt	=	LIBOR
(2) Fixed Payment	=	(4.04%)
Net Interest Income:	=	LIBOR + 0.96%

EXHIBIT 24.7   *A CAPITAL MARKET INTERPRETATION OF AN INTEREST RATE SWAP*

Long in a Par-Value FRN and Short in a Par-Value, 4.04% Coupon Bond:

Equals a "Pay-Fixed, Receive-Floating" Plain Vanilla Swap:

Thus, the net impact of combining the swap with the fixed-rate bond is to convert that security into a variable-rate asset paying a coupon of LIBOR plus 96 basis points.

There is another important way of viewing this swap transaction. With the swap agreement, Counterparty A is effectively paying the fixed-rate coupons he receives from his bond in exchange for receiving floating-rate coupons. That is, the pay-fixed swap position can be viewed as equivalent to holding a portfolio consisting of (1) a long position in a par-value FRN paying semiannual coupons of LIBOR, and (2) a short position in a par-value fixed-rate note paying semiannual coupons of 4.04 percent. This capital market interpretation is illustrated in Exhibit 24.7. Notice that by essentially buying and selling two different par-value instruments, no net principal amount exists at origination or maturity; this is what allows the swap's principal to be notional (i.e., not actually exchanged). Thus, all the swap agreement really does is transform the nature of the coupon payments.

The immediate consequence of this interpretation is that at any point in time the value of the pay-fixed swap position can be calculated as the present value of the floating-rate cash flows held as an asset minus the present value of the fixed-rate bond cash flow that is a liability, or

$$(PV \text{ of Pay-Fixed Swap}) = (PV \text{ of } FRN \text{ Paying LIBOR}) - (PV \text{ of Fixed-Rate Bond Paying } 4.04\%)$$

For example, suppose that one year after this swap was originated, yields have generally risen so that the fixed rate on a new two-year swap (i.e., the remaining time until the original maturity) is 5.04 percent. The value of this swap under these conditions can be established in two steps. First, on any settlement date, the FRN will be valued at par since its coupon always is reset according to current market conditions. Second, the market value of a bond paying a coupon of only 4.04 percent will fall, which benefits Counterparty A to whom this is a liability. Thus, using the new swap rate as a discount factor, A's position in the agreement (which as a forward contract had no value at origination) is now worth

$$100 - \left[\sum_{t=1}^{4} \frac{(4.04/2)}{(1+0.0504/2)^t} + \frac{100}{(1+0.0504/2)^4} \right] = 1.8801$$

or 1.8801 percent of notional principal. Therefore, if Counterparty A chose to unwind his contract at this time, the dealer would be willing to pay as much as $564,030 (= 0.018801 × $30 million) and then find a new swap counterparty who would pay the now current fixed rate of 5.04 percent. The $564,030 is considered to be the *marked-to-market value* of the swap. Given that interest rates have risen since inception, the original contract is now an asset to the fixed-rate payer (i.e., Counterparty A) and a liability to the fixed-rate receiver (i.e., the dealer).

An important characteristic of the swap agreement is that it becomes an *asset* to one participant and a *liability* to the other as soon as market conditions change after the terms of the contract are set. This means that swaps entail credit risk. To see why, consider what would happen to Counterparty A if, on a particular settlement date when LIBOR was 8 percent, the swap dealer was unable to make the net settlement payment. In that case, the investor would receive only the 5 percent coupon from his bond rather than the 8.96 percent (= LIBOR + 0.96 percent) coupon he expected from his synthetic FRN. The possibility that the swap counterparty either cannot or will not honor its obligation means that the synthetic floating-rate note carries *more* credit risk than the original fixed-rate bond. Further, notice that the swap dealer also will be concerned about the ability of Counterparty A to perform on the agreement when LIBOR is less than 4.04 percent. Thus, like any forward arrangement, the credit risk on a swap runs two ways.

What would it cost Counterparty A if, with exactly two years remaining on the contract described, the swap dealer suffered bankruptcy and defaulted on the remainder of the agreement? To retain his synthetic FRN, the investor would have to find a new swap dealer to replace the old contract. Unfortunately, with the change in market conditions, Counterparty A will now have to pay 5.04 percent to receive LIBOR over the next two years, implying an additional cost of 50 basis points (times 30 million) each settlement period. Thus, the economic consequence to A of the dealer's default can be measured as

$$\sum_{t=1}^{4} \frac{[(0.0504/2) - (0.0404/2)] \times (30,000,000)}{(1+0.0504/2)^t} = \$564,030$$

which, of course, is the same amount as the marked-to-market value of the swap. Thus, this figure represents the current potential default loss for the counterparty to whom the swap is an asset.[4]

Interest rate swaps have been in existence since 1981, and some empirical evidence exists on how they are priced in the marketplace. The available evidence includes Kim and Koppenhaver's investigation of commercial bank activity in the swap market; Sun, Sundaresan, and Wang, who examined the consistency of bid-ask quotes issued by two swap dealers with different credit

---

[4]For an interesting discussion of credit risk in the swap market, see Eric H. Sorensen and Thierry F. Bollier, "Pricing Interest Rate Swap Default Risk," *Financial Analysts Journal* 50, no. 3 (May–June 1994): 23–33.

grades; and Brown, Harlow, and Smith, as well as Minton, who tested several theoretical relationships designed to explain the historical pattern of variation in the swap spread component.[5] Although each of the studies examined a different aspect of the swap contracting process, the collective evidence they present is consistent with the notion that this market works in an orderly and efficient manner. Further, the mechanics of swap pricing, which have matured over time, seem to be integrated with other affiliated securities, such as Treasury notes and bills and Eurodollar futures contracts.

Option-Based Interest Rate Contracts

In this section, we discuss two types of OTC interest rate option arrangements as well as their relationship with interest rate swaps: (1) caps and floors, the two most basic option-based products; and (2) collars, special combinations of caps and floors.

Caps and Floors

Interest rate cap and floor agreements are equivalent to portfolios of interest rate option contracts, with each contract corresponding to a different settlement period. A **cap agreement** is a series of cash settlement interest rate options, typically based on LIBOR. The seller of the cap, in return for the option premium that is usually paid at origination, is obliged to pay the difference between LIBOR and the exercise, or cap, rate (times the fraction of the year, times the notional principal) whenever that difference is positive. The seller of a **floor agreement** makes settlement payments only when LIBOR is below the floor rate. No payment is made if LIBOR is above the floor or below the cap rate. As with swaps and FRAs, settlement can be either in advance or in arrears. Payment in arrears is more common because these contracts usually are used to hedge exposure to floating-rate bank loans and notes, which typically settle in arrears.

From these descriptions, the Date t settlement payments on cap and floor agreements can be written as follows:

➤**24.2** *Cap Settlement*: $\text{(Notional Principal)} \times \left(\dfrac{\text{Number of Days}}{360} \right) \times \max\left[\text{LIBOR}_{t-1} - X_c, 0 \right]$

and

➤**24.3** *Floor Settlement*: $\text{(Notional Principal)} \times \left(\dfrac{\text{Number of Days}}{360} \right) \times \max\left[X_f - \text{LIBOR}_{t-1}, 0 \right]$

where:

    X_c = **the cap exercise rate**
    X_f = **the floor exercise rate**

(Recall once again that a 360-day year is used because of the quotation convention for U.S. dollar LIBOR.) For example, consider a three-year, semiannual settlement, 8 percent cap on six-month LIBOR. The buyer of the cap pays the writer an up-front premium, quoted as a percentage of the notional principal. Assuming the cost is 120 basis points and the notional principal is

[5]See Sung-Hwa Kim and Gary D. Koppenhaver, "An Empirical Analysis of Bank Interest Rate Swaps," *Journal of Financial Services Research* 7, no. 1 (January 1993): 57–72; Tong-sheng Sun, Suresh Sundaresan, and Ching Wang, "Interest Rate Swaps: An Empirical Investigation," *Journal of Financial Economics* 34, no. 1 (August 1993): 77–99; Keith C. Brown, W. V. Harlow, and Donald J. Smith, "An Empirical Analysis of Interest Rate Swap Spreads," *Journal of Fixed Income* 3, no. 3 (March 1994): 61–78; and Bernadette A. Minton, "An Empirical Examination of Basic Valuation Models for Plain Vanilla U.S. Interest Rate Swaps," *Journal of Financial Economics* 44, no. 2 (May 1997): 251–277.

EXHIBIT 24.8 *PAYOFF DIAGRAMS FOR BUYING AND WRITING AN INTEREST RATE CAP AND FLOOR*

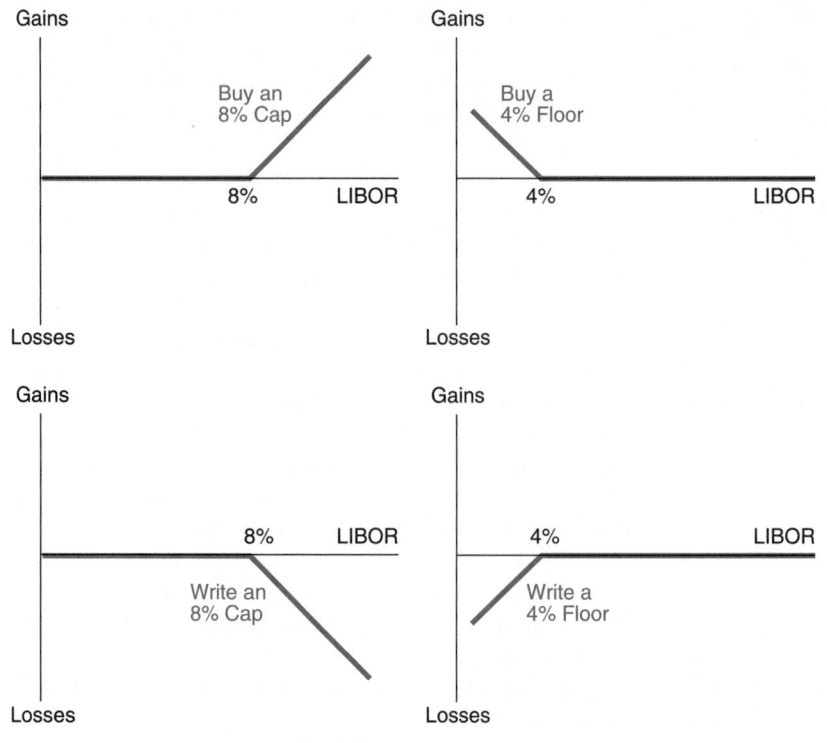

$100 million, the cost of the cap is $1,200,000.[6] Suppose that settlement dates are on the 15th of May and November of each year and that LIBOR on one particular May 15th is 9⅛ percent. The holder of the cap will receive settlement in arrears the following November in the amount of $575,000, calculated as (9.125 percent − 8 percent) × $100 million × (184/360).

The payoff relationships for caps and floors can be illustrated using traditional, option-style diagrams. Exhibit 24.8 portrays an 8 percent cap and a 4 percent floor on LIBOR. Notice that the payoff diagram for the cap looks like a typical call option on a commodity and the floor takes the form of a put option. Indeed, following the convention where LIBOR is the commodity, caps are referred to as "calls on LIBOR" and floors as "puts on LIBOR." Alternatively, a cap agreement on LIBOR is a series of put options on an underlying Eurodollar time deposit. In effect, the owner of the option has the right, but not the obligation, to sell to the cap writer a time deposit having a coupon rate equal to the cap rate in the amount of the notional principal of the contract. The owner exercises that option if current LIBOR exceeds the cap rate, thus selling a relatively low coupon deposit at par value. The proceeds of that sale can then be used to buy a time deposit

---

[6]In practice, interest rate caps and floors are quoted by market makers on a volatility basis, for instance, 18.5 percent bid and 19.5 percent offered. That measure of volatility (stated as a standard deviation), plus the exercise rate, the current term structure of interest rates, and the time frame for the contract, are then entered into an option pricing model to obtain the actual amount of the premium. Hull has shown that this amount can be established by adapting Black's model for valuing futures options to price each separate option in the contract (i.e., "caplets" and "floorlets"), and then summing them across all settlement dates. See John C. Hull, *Options, Futures, and Other Derivatives.* 4th ed. (Upper Saddle River, N.J.: Prentice-Hall, 2000).

that earns the higher market rate. The gain on those hypothetical transactions is equivalent to the payoff on the cap agreement. Whether one interprets a cap as a call on LIBOR or a put on a time deposit (and, similarly, a floor as a put on LIBOR or a call on a time deposit) is purely a matter of semantic preference.[7]

Collars   In Chapter 21, we saw that an equity collar arrangement consisted of a long position in an equity put option that was paid for with a short position in a call option on the same stock. Similarly, an **interest rate collar** is a combination of a cap and a floor, a long position in one and a short position in the other. To buy a 4 percent–8 percent collar on LIBOR is to buy an 8 percent cap and to write a 4 percent floor. The buyer will receive cash payments when LIBOR exceeds 8 percent, make payments when LIBOR is below 4 percent, and neither receive nor pay if LIBOR is between 4 percent and 8 percent. Often the motive for a firm to buy a collar is to reduce the initial cost of acquiring the protection from higher levels of LIBOR, as the up-front receipt from selling the floor can be used to offset the cost of buying the cap.

A special interest rate collar occurs when the initial premiums on the cap and the floor are equal and therefore offset each other. For instance, suppose that the premium on a three-year, 4 percent floor is 120 basis points, which matches the premium on the 8 percent cap. The combination is known as *zero-cost,* or zero-premium, collar. This is a useful concept because it is easy to show that an interest rate swap is just a special case of a zero-cost interest rate collar. To see this, consider again the 4 percent–8 percent zero-cost collar on LIBOR that was constructed from buying the 8 percent cap and selling the 4 percent floor. Now tighten the collar by lowering the cap rate to 7 percent. The up-front premium paid by the buyer must go up; an insurance policy providing protection whenever LIBOR exceeds 7 percent has to cost more than a policy that pays off only when LIBOR moves above 8 percent. Suppose that premium is 200 basis points (times the notional principal). To keep the collar at a zero initial cost, the written floor must then generate additional premium for the seller as well. This will require a higher floor rate because a contract in which the seller makes settlement payments whenever LIBOR is less than 5 percent certainly will be worth more than one with a floor rate of 4 percent. If we keep tightening the collar at some exercise rate common to both the cap and the floor, say 6 percent, the combination will be zero cost. That will be the pay-fixed swap fixed rate that prevails in the market. This is illustrated in Exhibit 24.9.

To summarize, buying a 6 percent cap and writing a 6 percent floor on LIBOR are equivalent in terms of settlement cash flows to an interest rate swap paying a fixed rate of 6 percent and receiving LIBOR. When LIBOR is above 6 percent, the net settlement receipt on the swap is the same as the receipt on the in-the-money cap that is owned. When LIBOR is below 6 percent, the net settlement payment on the swap is the same as the payment on the in-the-money floor that has been sold. Similarly, writing a cap and buying a floor at the same exercise rate are identical to a receive-fixed interest rate swap. Notice that a cap-floor combination at the same exercise rate always has the same payoffs as a swap contract. However, only when the combination also nets to a zero initial cost does that common rate match the prevailing swap fixed rate. This relationship is known as *cap-floor-swap parity* and is the swap market analog to the put-call-forward parity formula first discussed in Chapter 21 and extended to the range forward strategy in Chapter 23.

Along with the "portfolio of FRAs" and "pair of bonds" ways of viewing a swap contract, cap-floor-swap parity shows that a third interpretation exists: The swap can be viewed as a pair of option positions. This can be used to test the internal consistency of credit risk and valuation models for swaps. For example, because selling a cap and buying a floor at the same exercise

---

[7]A good review of these instruments can be found in Peter A. Abken, "Interest Rate Caps, Collars, and Floors," Federal Reserve Bank of Atlanta *Economic Review* 74 (November–December 1989): 2–24.

EXHIBIT 24.9 *AN ILLUSTRATION OF CAP-FLOOR-SWAP PARITY*

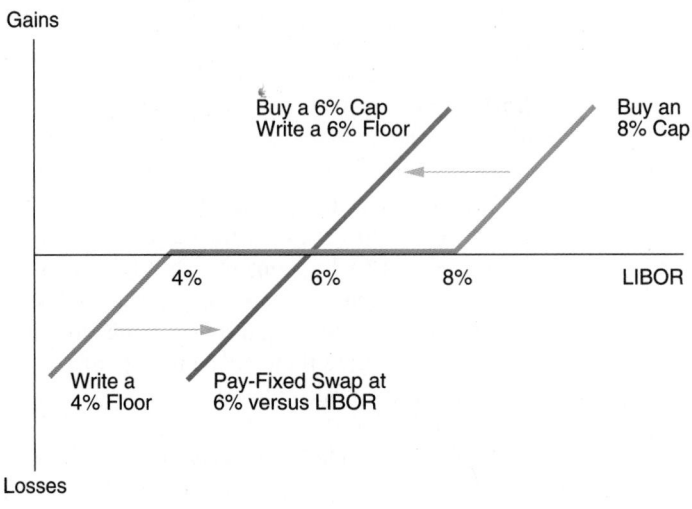

rate can offer the same cash flows as a receive-fixed swap, the projected credit risk on the swap must be comparable to the credit risk on the floor agreement. (Note that a firm bears the counterparty's credit risk on purchased options and not on written options, because only with purchased options is the firm relying on the other party's future performance.) This parity relationship also implies that variations of the option valuation models discussed in Chapter 23 can be used in the valuation of swap contracts.[8]

SWAP CONTRACTING EXTENSIONS

Although interest rate swaps are by far the most prevalent OTC rate contract, two other extensions of this concept that are important for portfolio managers have developed recently. All these agreements, which preserve the essential feature of a swap contract by exchanging cash flows based on two different rates or prices, include (1) currency (i.e., foreign exchange) swaps and (2) equity index-linked swaps.

Currency Swaps

Like the plain vanilla swap agreements, a **currency swap** is an agreement wherein two counterparties make periodic cash flow exchanges based on two different interest rates.[9] These contracts, also known as cross-currency swaps, differ from the single-currency version in two ways. First, because the associated cash flows are denominated in different monetary units, the principal

[8]The relationship between swap, cap, and floor agreements is described in Rudy Yaksick, "Swaps, Caps, and Floors: Some Parity and Price Identities," *Journal of Financial Engineering* 1, no. 1 (1992): 105–115.

[9]A good collection of readings on both the currency swap market and applications of these instruments can be found in Carl R. Beidleman, ed., *Cross Currency Swaps* (Homewood, Ill.: Business One–Irwin, 1992). Also, Christopher Géczy, Bernadette A. Minton, and Catherine Schrond, "Why Firms Use Currency Derivatives," *Journal of Finance* 52, no. 4 (September 1997): 1323–1354, provide a good overview of corporate uses of these contracts. For a more general discussion of derivative-based currency risk management, see Gregory W. Brown, "Managing Foreign Exchange Risk with Derivatives," *Journal of Financial Economics* 60, nos. 2–3 (May/June 2001): 401–448.

EXHIBIT 24.10 ▸ *A BASIC CURRENCY SWAP TRANSACTION*

A. At Origination

Foreign Currency
Principal

| Counterparty D | ◂ | Counterparty E |

U.S. Dollar
Principal

B. On Each Settlement Date (Including Maturity)

Foreign Currency
Fixed-Coupon Rate

| Counterparty D | ▸ | Counterparty E |
| | ◂ | |

U.S. Dollar
LIBOR

C. At Maturity

Foreign Currency
Principal

| Counterparty D | ▸ | Counterparty E |
| | ◂ | |

U.S. Dollar
Principal

amounts usually are exchanged at the origination and maturity dates of the contract. Second, because there are two currencies involved, the interest rates defining the transaction can be expressed on either a fixed- or floating-rate basis in either or both currencies. Assuming that the U.S. dollar is one of the currencies involved in the deal, this leaves the following four possibilities: (1) a fixed rate in the foreign currency versus a fixed rate in U.S. dollars, (2) a fixed rate in the foreign currency versus a floating rate in U.S. dollars, (3) a floating rate in the foreign currency versus a fixed rate in U.S. dollars, and (4) a floating rate in the foreign currency versus a floating rate in U.S. dollars. Although all of these formats are available, the predominant currency swap exchanges a fixed rate in the foreign currency for U.S. dollar LIBOR. This structure is shown in Exhibit 24.10.

This diagram shows that two distinct types of exchanges exist: principal at both origination and maturity and coupon interest on all the settlement dates. It is customary that both principal exchanges be executed at the spot foreign exchange (FX) rate prevailing at the initiation date, regardless of subsequent market FX rates. Further, similar to interest rate swap, the floating-rate side of the coupon exchanges in the standard currency swap usually is quoted flat. Thus, the dollar cash flow paid by Counterparty E on each settlement date is determined by multiplying the relevant LIBOR (which would have been determined at the previous settlement date) by the U.S. dollar principal amount, adjusted by the day count factor. The periodic cash flow that Counterparty D is obligated to pay is the product of the quoted fixed rate and the foreign currency–based principal amount. Because the cash flows differ in denomination, currency swaps do not settle on a net basis.

EXHIBIT 24.11 ▶ SETTLEMENT CASH FLOWS FOR A U.S. DOLLAR/BRITISH POUND CURRENCY SWAP

SETTLEMENT DATE	NUMBER OF DAYS	ASSUMED CURRENT LIBOR	FIXED-RATE PAYMENT	FLOATING-RATE RECEIPT
A. Initial Exchange of Principal				
11/15/00	—	5.75%	USD 34.400	GBP 20.000
B. Coupon Exchanges				
5/15/01	181	6.00%	GBP 0.858	USD 0.994
11/15/01	184	6.25%	0.872	1.055
5/15/02	181	6.70%	0.858	1.087
11/15/02	184	7.25%	0.872	1.178
5/15/03	181	7.00%	0.858	1.254
11/15/03	184	6.75%	0.872	1.187
5/15/04	182	5.50%	0.863	1.167
C. Final Coupon and Principal Exchange				
11/15/04	184	5.75%	GBP 0.872 and GBP 20.000	USD 0.967 and USD 34.400

To see how these conventions translate into cash flows, suppose Counterparty D has agreed to pay Counterparty E 8.65 percent on a four-year, British pound swap. Assume further that the transaction can be summarized as follows:

➤ Origination date: November 15, 2000
➤ Maturity date: November 15, 2004
➤ Notional principal: GBP 20 million and USD 34.4 million
➤ Fixed-rate payer: Counterparty D
➤ Swap fixed rate: 8.65 percent in pounds sterling (Actual/365 day count)
➤ Fixed-rate receiver: Counterparty E
➤ Floating rate: Six-month LIBOR in U.S. dollars (Actual/360 day count)
➤ Settlement dates: November 15 and May 15 of each year
➤ LIBOR determination: Set in advance, paid in arrears

The initial and ultimate principal exchanges are based on the spot exchange rate of USD 1.72/GBP that is assumed to have prevailed at the swap origination date. Given the rate conventions in each country, the pound-denominated coupon settlement payments are computed as [0.0865 × (Number of Days ÷ 365) × GBP 20 Million] while the dollar-based cash flows are determined by [LIBOR × (Number of Days ÷ 360) × USD 34.4 Million]. These amounts are shown in Exhibit 24.11 from the perspective of Counterparty D (i.e., the fixed-rate payer).[10]

---

[10]Although the most typical form of a currency swap is this fixed foreign currency/floating dollar structure, that is not always the most useful way to package cash flows. If, for instance, Counterparty D had wanted to pay a fixed rate in U.S. dollars (USD), instead of LIBOR, in exchange for fixed sterling (GBP) receipts, the standard fixed/floating currency swap can be easily repackaged by combining it with a floating/fixed U.S. dollar interest rate swap. As a practical matter, if both of these transactions were executed simultaneously with the same market maker, the corporate end user (i.e., Counterparty D) would not undertake two separate transactions. Rather, to minimize the requisite documentation and bookkeeping, the swap intermediary in this case would undoubtedly offer the counterparty a direct, blended quote of "receive fixed USD, pay fixed GBP," leaving LIBOR out altogether. These fixed/fixed swaps were once known as CIRCUS swaps, standing for "combined interest rate and currency swaps."

EXHIBIT 24.12   *TRANSFORMING A BOND INVESTMENT WITH A CURRENCY SWAP*

A. Purchase USD Floating-Rate Note

LIBOR x (1/2) x (USD 34.4)

USD 34.4

USD 34.4

B. Enter Pay USD Floating, Receive GBP Fixed-Currency Swap

USD 34.4

(0.0865) x (1/2) x (GBP 20.0)

GBP 20.0

USD 34.4

LIBOR x (1/2) x (USD 34.4)

GBP 20.0

C. Net Position

(0.0865) x (1/2) x (GBP 20.0)

GBP 20.0

GBP 20.0

As an example of why such a transaction might be used, suppose that Counterparty E is a British pension fund that would like to invest GBP 20 million in a fixed-rate note making semi-annual coupon payments for the next four years. Given the current pricing in the market, however, the coupon on sterling-denominated, par-value fixed-rate bonds issued by companies with an acceptable Aa credit rating is 8.40 percent. Suppose, on the other hand, that the pension fund buys a four-year floating rate note from an Aa-rated American corporation paying LIBOR flat for USD 34.4 million. In this case, the pension manager could purchase the dollar-denominated FRN and enter into the "pay USD floating/receive GBP fixed" swap outlined previously. The combination of these two transactions, shown in Exhibit 24.12, would leave the investor with the equivalent of owning a pound-denominated bond paying a fixed rate of 8.65 percent in sterling, a yield "pickup" of 25 points relative to the direct issue market. Thus, by using the swap to transform both the rate sensitivity and currency denomination of the dollar FRN, the pension fund has created a more desirable package of cash flows than was otherwise available. In this sense, we can view any financial security as a substitute for any other financial security, once the appropriate repackaging has been accomplished.[11]

As with plain vanilla interest rate swaps, currency swaps can be viewed as a pair of bond transactions. Specifically, Panel B of Exhibit 24.12 shows that, from Counterparty E's perspective, the swap can be interpreted as a portfolio containing (1) a long position in a fixed-rate, pound-denominated bond; and (2) a short position in a USD FRN. This intuition is useful in calculating the value of the agreement after origination, which is

$$\text{Value of Currency Swap (in GBP)} = (PV \text{ of GBP Fixed Cash Flows}) \\ - [(PV \text{ of USD FRN}) \div (\text{Spot USD/GBP})]$$

There are two important features of this equation. First, the swap's value depends on changes in three fundamental factors: British interest rates, U.S. interest rates, and the USD/GBP exchange rate. Second, on any given settlement date, the floating-rate note should once again be valued at par, which assumes no change in counterparty creditworthiness. This simplifies the swap valuation calculation tremendously.

Suppose, for example, that exactly two years (i.e., four settlement dates) after this agreement was originated, the fixed rate on a new two-year "receive GBP fixed, pay USD LIBOR" swap has fallen to 7.65 percent while the prevailing exchange rate has moved to USD 1.82/GBP. Assuming, for the ease of computation, that all the remaining GBP cash flows on the existing contract are 0.865 million (= $(0.0865) \times (1/2) \times (20.0 \text{ million})$), Counterparty E's position in the swap is worth:

$$\left[\sum_{t=1}^{4} \frac{\text{GBP } 0.865}{(1 + 0.0765/2)^t} + \frac{\text{GBP } 20.0}{(1 + 0.0765/2)^4} \right] - \frac{\text{USD } 34.4}{(\text{USD } 1.82/\text{GBP})}$$

$$= (20.364) - (18.901) = \text{GBP } 1.463 \text{ Million}$$

Of course, this amount also represents a liability to Counterparty D; like any derivative, a currency swap is a zero-sum game. Finally, notice that both the GBP rate decline and the exchange rate increase have changed the swap's value in the same direction by increasing the value of the pound-denominated asset and reducing the translated value of the dollar liability, respectively. Thus, even though the swap was originally negotiated to have no net value to either counterparty, it will become an asset to one and a liability to the other as soon as market conditions change.

Equity Index-Linked Swaps

Similar in form to interest rate swaps, equity-index-linked swaps or **equity swaps**, are equivalent to portfolios of forward contracts calling for the exchange of cash flows based on two different investment rates: (1) a variable-debt rate (e.g., three-month LIBOR) and (2) the return to an equity index (e.g., Standard and Poor's 500). The index-linked payment is based on either the total return (i.e., dividends plus capital gain or loss) or just the percentage index change for the settlement period plus a fixed spread adjustment, which is expressed in basis points and can be negative. The floating-rate payments typically are based on LIBOR flat. Like interest rate and currency swaps, equity swaps are traded in the OTC markets and can have maturities out to 10 years or beyond.

---

[11]An important mitigating factor that must once again be considered with any swap-based investment scheme is the credit risk of the swap counterparty. Whether the presence of this additional exposure in this case explains the 25 BP investment advantage would, of course, depend on an assessment of the likelihood that Counterparty D would default on the swap agreement under adverse market conditions. For discussions on this topic, see Ian A. Cooper and Antonio S. Mello, "The Default Risk of Swaps," *Journal of Finance* 46, no. 2 (June 1991): 597–620; and Wai-Yan Cheng, "Recent Advances in Default Swap Valuation, "*Journal of Derivatives* 9, no. 1 (Fall 2001): 18–27.

In addition to the S&P 500, equity swaps can be structured around foreign indexes, such as TOPIX (Japan), FT-SE 100 (Great Britain), DAX (Germany), CAC 40 (France), TSE 35 (Canada), and Hang Seng (Hong Kong). These agreements also can be designed so that the cash flows are denominated in the same currency or in two different currencies. The equity-index-based cash flow typically is denominated in the currency of the index's country of origination, but the swap can be designed so that this payment is automatically hedged into a different currency. Further, these agreements specify a notional principal that is not exchanged at origination but serves the purpose of converting percentage returns into cash flows. This notional principal can either be variable or fixed during the life of the agreement, but the same notional principal applies to both sides of the transaction.

The equity swap market has developed for several reasons. First, these agreements allow investors to take advantage of overall price movements in a specific country's stock market without having to purchase the equity securities directly.[12] This has the advantage of reducing both the transaction costs and tracking errors associated with assembling a portfolio that mimics the index as well as allowing the investor to avoid dividend withholding taxes normally associated with cross-border investing. Second, creating a direct equity investment in a foreign country may be difficult for some companies where prohibited by law or operating policy. Finally, an investment fund wanting to accumulate foreign index returns denominated in their domestic currency may not be able or legally permitted to obtain sufficient exchange-traded futures or option contracts to hedge a direct equity investment. The equity swap can be structured so that there is no need for separate hedging transactions.

The most common application for an equity swap involves a counterparty that receives the index-based payment in exchange for making the floating-rate payment. For example, consider a pension fund that currently has a substantial portion of its asset portfolio invested in floating-rate notes paying quarterly coupons based on LIBOR. If the manager of this fund wants to alter her existing asset allocation by converting some of these debt-based cash flows into equity-based receipts, she has two ways to do so. First, she can sell the existing floating-rate notes and purchase a portfolio of equities directly in the market. Alternatively, the manager can enter into an equity swap with an initial notional principal equal to the amount of the existing debt holdings she wants to convert. As we have seen, from the standpoint of reducing transaction costs, the second alternative is clearly preferable. The mechanics of this arrangement are illustrated in Exhibit 24.13.

EXHIBIT 24.13 *ALTERING AN ASSET ALLOCATION POSITION WITH AN EQUITY SWAP*

---

[12]For a more detailed analysis of the uses and development of this product, see Julie A. Allen and Janet L. Showers, "Equity-Index-Linked Derivatives: A User's Guide" (New York: Salomon Brothers, 1991).

The net return to the fund in this example is simply the return on the equity index plus the spread adjustment. Further, if the floating-rate notes held as an asset yield more than LIBOR, this incremental amount would increase the overall net return. Assuming that both cash flows are denominated in the same currency, the net settlement payment on the equity swap from the company's standpoint can be calculated as the difference between the variable-rate outflow and the equity-linked inflow, where

➤ **24.4** $$\text{Payment} = \left[\text{LIBOR} - \text{Spread}\right] \times \left[\text{Notional Principal}\right] \times \left[\frac{(\text{Number of Days})}{360}\right]$$

and

$$\text{Receipt} = \left[\frac{\text{Index}_{new} - \text{Index}_{old}}{\text{Index}_{old}}\right] \times \left[\text{Notional Principal}\right]$$

where Index_{new} and Index_{old} represent the index levels occurring on the current and immediate past settlement dates, assuming all dividends are reinvested. Notice here that to minimize calculations, the settlement payment is computed using (LIBOR – Spread) rather than adding a separate inflow for the equity spread itself. Gastineau investigated indicative spread quotes for various indexes throughout the world and found that, while some were positive (e.g., 90 BP for DAX, 25 BP for FT-SE), others were negative (e.g., –10 BP for S&P 500, –60 BP for Hang Seng).[13] However, he noted that the equity swap quotations methods are not standardized across all dealers; therefore, the quoted values may not be directly comparable.

Another way to view the effect of this swap-based cash flow transformation is shown in Exhibit 24.14. Here, it should be clear that equity swaps differ from interest rate and currency swaps in one important way. Specifically, because there is no guarantee that the equity index will appreciate in value from one settlement period to the next, it is possible that the company receiving the equity index will have to make a double payment. First, the usual debt-related cash flow, based on LIBOR, will have to be paid. Second, whenever Index_{new} is less than Index_{old}, the company will make an equity-index-based payment to (i.e., "receive" a negative payment from) its counterparty. Thus, rather than netting one cash flow against the other, the company will pay both when the value of the equity index declines. (Examples of this situation are represented by the third and fifth payments in the exhibit.)

WARRANTS AND CONVERTIBLE SECURITIES

A popular investment strategy in recent years has involved the creation of security "packages" in which derivatives are combined with, or embedded into, more basic instruments, such as stock shares or bonds. In this section, we take a detailed look at two important variations on this theme: (1) bonds with warrants that give the investor the right to buy additional shares of the company's common stock; and (2) securities, such as debt or preferred stock, that the investor can convert into other securities.

---

[13]See Gary L. Gastineau, "Using Swaps in Equity Portfolios," in *Derivative Strategies for Managing Portfolio Risk,* ed. K. Brown (Charlottesville, Va.: Association for Investment Research and Management, 1993). See also Don Chance and Don Rich, "The Pricing of Equity Swaps and Swaptions," *Journal of Derivatives* 5, no. 2 (Summer 1998): 19–31.

EXHIBIT 24.14   *CONVERTING A BOND WITH AN EQUITY SWAP*

Purchase an FRN:

Equity Swap (Receive Equity Index, Pay LIBOR):

Net Transaction:

☐ Principal cash flows
■ LIBOR-based cash flows
▨ Equity-index-linked cash flows

Warrants   By its most commonly used definition, a **warrant** is an equity call option issued directly by the company whose stock serves as the underlying asset. The key feature that distinguishes it from an ordinary call option is that, if exercised, the company will create new shares of stock to give to the warrantholder. Thus, the exercise of a warrant will increase the total number of outstanding shares, which reduces the value of each individual share. Because of this dilutive effect, the warrant will not be as valuable as an otherwise comparable option contract. Indeed, the valuation of warrants is complicated by many factors, such as how and when the number of outstanding warrants will be exercised, what the company's current capital structure looks like, and what the company plans to do with the new capital it will receive if and when the warrant is exercised.

Galai and Schneller proposed a simple warrant valuation model in which a firm is presently financed with all equity and the warrants it issues are European-style.[14] On its expiration date T, the warrant will be worth

$$W_T = \max\left[\frac{V_T + N_W X}{N + N_W} - X, 0\right]$$

where:

N = the current number of outstanding shares
N_W = the number of new shares created if the warrants are exercised
V_T = the value of the firm before the warrants are exercised
X = the exercise price

They show that this terminal value can be rewritten as

➤24.5
$$W_T = \left[\frac{1}{1 + (N_W/N)}\right] C_T$$

where:

C_T = the expiration date value of a regular call option with otherwise identical terms as the warrant

Consequently, at any point prior to expiration, the value of the warrant should be equal to the value of the call deflated (i.e., diluted) by the factor $[1 + (N_w/N)]^{-1}$.

Although warrants can be issued as stand-alone instruments, more frequently a company will attach them to a bond issue to lower its initial funding cost. Warrants created in this manner usually can be detached from the debt instrument by the buyer and traded separately. Suppose, for example, a firm with 1,000,000 shares of common stock outstanding at a current share price of $100 attempts to raise an additional $10 million by issuing a 10-year bond paying annual coupons. Given its current credit rating, assume further that the yield it would have to pay for a straight debt issue is 8.50 percent. The firm could lower this borrowing cost by attaching to the bond European-style equity warrants that mature in exactly one year and have an exercise price of $115 per share. Assuming the firm eventually hopes to raise an additional $5.75 million with these warrants, it will have to create new derivative contracts to cover 50,000 shares ($5.75 million ÷ $115).

Assuming that the one-year risk-free rate is 7 percent and the volatility of the firm's common stock is 25 percent, the Black-Scholes value for a one-year call option to buy one share at $X =$ $115 can be calculated as $7.09. By Equation 24.5, this means that the warrants are worth $6.75 (= 7.09 ÷ [1 + (50,000/1,000,000)]) per share. If each warrant allows for the purchase of one share and the face value of a single bond is $1,000, the firm will issue 10,000 bonds with five warrants attached to each. Assuming it pays an 8.50 percent coupon, the total proceeds it would generate from the sale of each bond with the warrants attached would be $1,033.75, or $1,000 for the bond and $33.75 (= 5 × $6.75) for the warrants. Thus, the firm can reduce its funding cost to 8.00 percent—the solution to the yield to maturity in the following bond calculation:

---

[14]See Dan Galai and Meir I. Schneller, "Pricing Warrants and the Value of the Firm," *Journal of Finance* 33, no. 5 (December 1978): 1333–1342. Also, the implications of altering the terms of a warrant are considered in John S. Howe and Tie Su, "Discretionary Reductions in Warrant Exercise Prices," *Journal of Financial Economics* 61, no. 2 (August 2001): 227–252.

$$1033.75 = \sum_{t=1}^{10} \frac{85}{(1+y)^t} + \frac{1000}{(1+y)^{10}}$$

Packaging warrants with bonds to reduce debt expenses for the issuer and enhance return potential for the investor can be done in a variety of ways. In particular, a recent trend in financial markets is for a firm to attach to its bonds an option that is based on an underlying asset other than the company's own stock. To date, alternative structures have included foreign exchange and stock index transactions. For instance, Rogalski and Seward detail the development of the market for *foreign currency exchange warrants,* which give the holder the right, but not the obligation, to purchase a predetermined number of U.S. dollars for a price denominated in a foreign currency.[15] Although called warrants, these contracts are closer in form to traditional call options on the dollar (or, equivalently, put options on the foreign currency) because they do not result in any direct change to the issuing firm's capital structure. That is, no dilutive valuation effect exists for these derivatives since there are no new shares of stock issued. Beyond that, these instruments generally can be settled only in cash but can be detached and traded separately from the original bond.[16]

Convertible Securities

A convertible security gives its owner the right, but not the obligation, to convert the existing investment into another form. Typically, the original security is either a bond or a share of preferred stock, which can be exchanged into common stock according to a predetermined formula. From this description, it should be clear that a convertible security is a hybrid issue consisting of a regular bond or preferred stock holding and a call option that allows for the conversion. Similar to warrants, they have been popular with issuers because they generally lead to a lower initial borrowing cost and represent a future supply of equity capital. In fact, Pinches noted that these securities often are used in connection with mergers because they generate capital without immediately diluting the equity base of the acquiring firm.[17] On the other hand, investors in convertibles gain the upside potential of common stock while actually holding a less-risky asset.

Convertible Preferred Stock

To see how convertible securities work, let us consider the dynamics of convertible preferred stock. As previously suggested, owning a share of convertible preferred is equivalent to holding a portfolio long in a normal share of preferred stock and long in a call option on the firm's common stock that can be exercised by surrendering the preferred stock. There generally is no waiting period before the conversion can be made, and the conversion privilege usually never expires. This means that the *minimum value of the convertible* issue must be:

max[Preferred Stock Value, Conversion Value]

where the **conversion value** is the value of the common stock into which the preferred issue can be exchanged.

---

[15]See Richard J. Rogalski and James K. Seward, "Corporate Issues of Foreign Currency Warrants," *Journal of Financial Economics* 30, no. 2 (December 1991): 347–366.

[16]For several additional discussions about how warrants are used in capital markets, see Jack Clark Francis, William W. Toy, and J. Gregg Whittaker, *The Handbook of Equity Derivatives* (Chicago, Ill.: Irwin Professional Publishing, 1995).

[17]See George E. Pinches, "Financing with Convertible Preferred Stock, 1960–1967," *Journal of Finance* 25, no. 1 (March 1970): 56–63. See also S. R. McGuire, *The Handbook of Convertibles* (New York: Simon & Schuster, 1991).

EXHIBIT 24.15

MINIMUM CONVERTIBLE PREFERRED STOCK VALUES AS A FUNCTION OF REGULAR PREFERRED YIELDS AND COMMON STOCK PRICES

		COMMON STOCK PRICES		
		15	20	25
Yield	*8%:*	37.50	37.50	43.75
	10%:	30.00	35.00	43.75
	12%:	26.25	35.00	43.75

Suppose that for a $1,000,000 investment, an institutional investor could purchase 25,000 shares of a convertible preferred issue with the following terms (per share):

➤ Current convertible share price: $40.00
➤ Annual convertible dividend: $ 3.00
➤ Convertible yield: 7.50% (= $3 ÷ $40)
➤ Regular preferred yield: 10.00%
➤ Current common stock price: $20.00
➤ Conversion ratio: 1.75

With these conditions, the share value of a regular preferred stock issue paying a $3 dividend would be $30.00 (= $3 ÷ 0.10 percent), or the perpetual dividend amount divided by the prevailing regular yield. This means that the convertible issue sells at a 33 percent premium to the regular preferred. Also, given the **conversion ratio** of 1.75 shares of common to each share of preferred, the conversion value of the convertible issue is $35 (= 1.75 × $20). Thus, the minimum price of the convertible security would be $35, the greater of the regular preferred price and the conversion value. Since the market price of the convertible still is above this level, this implies a **conversion premium** of 14.29 percent (= [$40 − $35] ÷ $35), meaning that the convertible currently is selling based on its option value.

The future value of the convertible issue will depend on two events: (1) interest rate movements, which directly affect the yield on the regular preferred stock component, and (2) changes in common stock prices, given the 1.75 conversion ratio. Consider the matrix of minimum values for various levels of these two variables, shown in Exhibit 24.15. In this situation, the value of the convertible preferred stock will likely be driven by its conversion value when interest rates and common stock prices are high and by its preferred stock value when rates and share prices are low.

Convertible Bonds   Like convertible preferred stock, a convertible bond can be viewed as a prepackaged portfolio containing two distinct securities: a regular bond and an option to exchange the bond for a prespecified number of shares of the issuing firm's common stock. Thus, a convertible bond represents a hybrid investment involving elements of both the debt and equity markets. From the investor's standpoint, there are both advantages and disadvantages to this packaging. Specifically, although the buyer receives equity-like returns with a "guaranteed" terminal payoff equal to the bond's face value, he or she must also pay the option premium, which, as we will see shortly, is embedded in the price of the security.[18] Conversely, the issuer of a convertible bond increases the company's leverage while providing a potential source of equity financing in the future. Exhibit 24.16 shows a portion of a page from *Mergent Bond Record* summarizing the pertinent details of a sample of outstanding convertible bonds issued by U.S.-based companies.

---

[18]In fact, some authors have argued that the risk–return dynamics that convertible bonds offer to investors are sufficiently unique as to merit their own asset class. See Scott L. Lummer and Mark W. Riepe, "Convertible Bonds as an Asset Class: 1957–1992," *Journal of Fixed Income* 3, no. 2 (September 1993): 47–56.

EXHIBIT 24.16 ▶ CONVERTIBLE BOND INFORMATION SUMMARY

CUSIP	ISSUE	MOODY'S® RATING	INT. DATES	ANN. S.F. THOUS.	CURR. CALL PRICE	AMT. OUTS. MILL.	CONV. PRICE‡	SHS. $1,000 DEB.	CURRENT PRICE COM.	CURRENT PRICE DEB.	DEB. YIELDS CURR.	DEB. YIELDS MAT.	DEB. CONV. VALUE	ANTIC. COM. PRICE	2001 PRICE RANGE COM.		2001 PRICE RANGE DEB.		LAT ANN. PER EARNS	COM. ANN. DIV. / RATE
00253AAE	Aames Financial Corp. sub cv deb 5.50 2006	Ca	M&S 15	None		115	—	—	—	23⅛	—	10.6	—	—	—	·	25⅛	-23⅛	d21.02	0.24
00651FAC	Adaptec Inc. sub cv nt 4.75 2004	B1	F&A 1	None		230	—	—	—	82¼	—	9.8	—	—	—	·	82⅞	-79¾	1.65	Nil
000945AC	•ADT Operations, Inc. LYONS 0.00 2010[1]	Baa1r		None	599.46	776.25	—	—	—	—	—	—	—	—	—	·	—	—	—	Nil
00738VAA	Advance Agro Public Co Ltd global deb 3.50 2001[2]	Caa1	JUN 14	None		60.0	—	—	—	—	—	—	—	—	—	·	—	—	—	Nil
007903AC	Advanced Micro Devices Inc sub cv nt 6.00 2005	Caa1	M&N 15	None		450	—	—	—	141	—	2.5	—	—	—	·	141	-92½	d0.3	Nil
00130HAA	AES Corp. sub cv deb 6.50 2002	B1	M&S 13	None		50.0	—	—	—	—	—	6.5	—	—	—	·	—	—	1.19	Nil
00130HAN	• jr sub cv deb 4.50 2005	B1	F&A 15	None	102.57	150	54.00	18.52	•57¾	—	—	4.5	100	0	12½	-5¼	—	—	1.19	Nil
008190AD	Affiliated Computer Srcs Inc sub cv nt 4.00 2005	Baa3	M&S 15	None		230	—	—	—	158⅞	—	0.5	—	—	—	·	158⅞	-140¾	2.22	Nil
008474AA	Agnico-Eagle Mines Ltd. sr cv nt 3.50 2004	B2	J&J 27	None	958.06	110	17.93	55.76	•6⅛	71	3.9	8.6	78⅛	12¾	20½	-12⅝	73	-68¼	—	0.02
018490AA	Allergan, Inc. LYONS 0.00 2020	Baa1		None	655.49	657.451	105.60	5.76	•81¾	64¼	—	—	100	67⅞	21	-15	65¼	—	1.42	0.36
022615AC	•ALZA Corp. LYONS 0.00 2014	Baa3r	N.P.	None	509.82	825	—	12.99	•41¾	110	—	—	100	—	18	-12	110	—	0.45	Nil
02261WAB	Alza Corp. zero cpn deb 0.00 2020[3]	Baa3		None	602.77			39.30	14.03	—	69¼	—	—	100	27¼	7½	-0⅛	69⅜	-64¼	—	Nil
023135AF	Amazon.com Inc. sr sub cv nt 4.75 2009[4]	Caa3	F&A 1	None	103.33			156.06	3.20	17¾	43	—	9.8	50	67¼	5½	-1¼	45½	-35¼	d2.2	Nil
02364JAB	America OnLine Inc. (DE) sub cv nt 4.00 2002	Baa2	M&N 15	None		350	—	—	—	777¾	—	0.5	—	—	—	·	777¾	-777¾	—	0.60
029912AB	American Tower Corp. cv nt 6.25 2009	B3	A&O 15	None	103.13	300	24.40	400.98	•36¼	162¾	—	2.7	100	39⅝	29⅝	-13¼	177¾	-162¼	d0.34	Nil
029912AD	cv nt 2.25 2009	B3	A&O 15	None	802.93	425.5	24.00	29.38	•36¼	118½	—	0.0	141¾	28½	29⅝	-13¼	127	-115¾	d0.34	Nil
03071PAB	AmeriSource Health Corp. sub cv nt 0.00 2007[3]	Baa3		None		200	—	—	—	114¼	—	—	—	—	—	·	117⅛	-104⅛	1.92	Nil
030955AG	Ameritech Capital Funding gtd nt 6.125 2001[5]	Aa3 r	A&O·15	None	N.C.	200	—	—	—	100⅝	—	5.5	—	—	—	·	100⅝	-100	—	Nil
03113VAB	AMF Bowling, Inc. zero cpn nt 0.00 2018[6]	C		None	100.00			115.30	—	0⅛	0½	—	—	7⅛	0⅛	25¼	-20	0½	-0½	d2.32	Nil
031652AA	Amkor Technology Inc. sub cv nt 5.75 2003	B2	M&N 1	None		207	—	—	—	170¼	—	2.2	—	—	—	·	171¼	-121	0.64	Nil
032511AP	Anadarko Petroleum Corp. cv deb 0.00 2020	Baa1		None	554.41	600	85.99	11.63	•56⅞	74⅝	—	—	100	64⅛	34½	-23⅜	88	-74⅝	0.25	0.20
036115AC	AnnTaylor Stores Corp. gtd sub cv deb 0.00 2019[7]	B2	J&D 18	None	635.42	199.072	82.80	12.08	•29⅜	50⅛	—	4.5	100	41¾	24¼	-9¼	50½	-45¼	2.22	Nil
03664PAB	ANTEC Corp. sub cv nt 4.50 2003	B2	M&N 15	None	100			16.15	—	76⅞	—	9.6	—	—	—	·	76⅞	-52¾	1.49	2.25
00202NAA	•APP Finance VI Mauritius LYONS 0.00 2012[8]	B3		None				16.15	—	7⅞	—	—	100	1¼	13⅛	-7¾	12½	-7⅛	—	Nil
00202PAA	APP Finance VII Mauritius Ltd gtd cv global nt 3.50 2003[2]	B3	A&O 30	None		500	—	—	—	30	—	8.6	—	—	—	·	34½	-30	—	Nil
038522AE	ARAMARK Services, Inc. gtd sub cv nt 7.25 2007[3]	Baa3	J&D 18	None		31.2	—	—	—	—	—	7.3	—	—	—	·	—	—	—	Nil
045327AB	Aspen Technology, Inc. sub cv deb 5.25 2005	B2 r	J&D 15	None	100.00	86.25	52.97	—	39¼	96	—	6.3	35⅜	50¾	42½	-15¾	96	-74¼	0.19	Nil
045919AF	At Home Corp. sub cv nt 4.75 2006	B3	J&D 15	None	102.71	500	56.52	17.69	6⅛	58¾	—	9.8	100	33¼	16	-9	60½	-50⅛	d4.61	Nil
045919AC	sub cv deb 0.525 2018	B3	J&D 28	None	100.00	437	76.34	—	6⅛	39¼	—	5.6	17⅛	30	16	-9	40¼	-30¼	d4.61	Nil
	Atlantic Coast Airlines, Inc. sub cv nt 7.00 2004[3]	Caa1	J&D 1	None		57.5	—	—	—	—	—	7.0	—	—	—	·	—	—	—	Nil
050757AA	Audiovox Corp sr cv deb 6.25 2001	Caa	M&S 15	None	100.00	65.0	17.70	55.49	13¼	—	9.6	6.3	0	—	7½	-4	—	—	1.43	Nil
053015AC	•Automatic Data Processing Inc LYONS 0.00 2012	Aa1		None	627.25	700	—	—	—	154	—	—	—	—	—	·	154	—	1.34	Nil
053494AD	Avatar Holdings Inc. sub cv nt 0.00	Caa3	A&O 1	None	104.00	100	—	—	—	94½	—	—	—	—	—	·	96½	-87	9.64	Nil
054303AN	Avon Products, Inc. sub cv zero cpn nt 0.00 2020[8]	A3	&	None	100.00	350	57.50	—	•42¼	48¾	—	—	100	28	29¾	-18¼	51⅜	-48¾	1.18	0.76
057232AA	Baker (J.), Inc. sub cv nt 7.00 2002	B3		None		65.0	—	—	—	83	—	—	—	—	—	·	85	-75½	0.63	Nil
057224AH	•Baker Hughes Inc. LYONS 0.00 2008	A2	N.P.	None	81.21	385.25	—	—	—	89½	—	—	—	—	—	·	90	-87	0.1	0.76
08160HAC	Benchmark Electronics, Inc. sub cv nt 6.00 2006	B2 r	F&A 15	None	103.43	125	40.20	24.88	• 29	91½	—	7.9	100	36¾	17¼	-12⅛	93½	-72⅞	0.85	Nil
083739AC	•Bergen Brunswig Corp. sub exch nts 6.875 2011	B2	J&J 15	2150-'96	100.00	10.6	—	—	—	95	7.4	7.6	—	—	—	·	95	-93	0.6	Nil
09067J20	•Biovail Corp sub cv deb 6.75 2025	B2	MJ&SD 31	None	0.00	300	60.36	0.82	•43¼	—	—	6.8	100¼	0	45¼	-19¼	—	—	—	Nil
09067JAA	sub cv deb 0.00 2025	B2	M&S 31	None			—	—	—	—	—	—	—	—	—	·	—	—	—	Nil
096231AA	Bluegreen Corp. sub cv deb 8.25 2012	Caa1	M&N 21	None		40.0	—	—	—	60½	—	13.3	—	—	—	·	62	-60	0.29	0.50
097689AA	•Boca Research & Newman, Inc. sub cv deb 6.30 2012[3]	B3 r	A&O 1	5%-'98	73.95	30.00	33.33	—	—	96	4.2	6.0	0	—	—	·	—	—	—	Nil
098904AA	Bonneville Pacific Corp. sub cv deb 7.75 2009	Caa1		10'02/15/1992	5%-'98	55.0	11.59	86.28	—	—	—	—	0	—	—	·	—	—	—	Nil
109473AC	Brightpoint Inc. LYONS 0.00 2018[8]	B2		None	552.07	380	—	19.11	4⅞	28⅝	—	—	—	—	12¼	-3⅛	28⅝	-26½	d1.75	Nil
119003AD	Budget Group, Inc. jr sub cv deb 6.25 2008	Caa3	MJ&SD 15	None		300	—	—	—	—	—	6.3	—	—	—	·	—	—	—	d1.77	Nil
129466AF	CalEnergy Co., Inc. (DE) jr sub cv deb 6.50 2027[3]	Baa3 r	MJ&SD 1	None	51.00	231.959	47.75	—	•	—	—	6.5	0	0	35	-18¾	—	—	—	Nil
131347AQ	Calpine Corp. sub cv deb nt 5.75 2009[3]	Baa3		None	105.72	240	—	—	—	—	—	—	—	—	—	·	—	—	0.455	Nil
133131AA	•Camden Property Trust sub cv deb 7.33 2001	Baa3 r	A&O 1	None	N.C.	44.0	24.00	41.66	•33¼	144	6.8	3.9	119¼	34½	29¼	-21¾	144	-144	1.27	2.25
140918AC	•CapStar Hotel Co. sub cv nt 4.75 2004	B1	A&O 15	None	102.71	150	—	23.26	—	90	—	7.7	—	—	—	·	90	-77	0.23	Nil
143898AA	•Carolina Freight Corp. sub cv deb 6.25 2011	B2 r	A&O 15	None	100.00	50.0	—	—	—	—	—	6.3	—	—	—	·	—	—	—	Nil
15101QAA	Celestica, Inc. LYONS 0.00 2020	Ba3		None			—	—	—	52½	—	—	—	—	—	·	52½	—	—	Nil
150925AC	CellStar Corp. sub cv nt 5.00 2002	B2	A&O 15	None		150	—	—	—	25½	—	10.1	—	—	—	·	25½	-25½	1.16	Nil
150918AE	Cellular Communications Intl sub cv nt 6.00 2005	Caa1	A&O 1	None		86.25	—	—	—	200¼	—	2.5	—	—	—	·	200¼	-200¼	d1.94	Nil
	Centerpoint Properties Trust sub cv nt 8.22 2004	Baa3	J&J 15	None	100.00	58.5	18.25	54.79	—	—	—	8.2	119½	0	—	·	—	—	—	Nil
152007AA	Cendant Bancorporation sub cv deb 6.25 2011	A1 r	M&N 1	None	N.C.	30.0	15.71	59.84	—	—	1.6	6.3	386	0	68	-37¼	—	—	—	Nil
153527AC	Central Garden & Pet Co. sub cv nt 6.00 2003	B3	M&S 15	None	101.71	115	28.00	35.71	8⅜	69¾	—	11.1	100	19½	26⅜	-7	70½	-65	d0.63	Nil
154785AA	Central Parking Corp. sub cv deb 5.25 2028[8]	B1	A&O 1	None		100	—	—	—	54	—	5.3	—	—	—	·	—	-1	1	Nil
161133AA	Charming Shoppes, Inc. sub cv nt 7.50 2006	B2	J&J 15	None	102.50	120	7.46	134.04	7	102¾	—	6.9	67⅞	7⅜	8¼	-2½	102¾	-93½	0.46	Nil
16117MAA	Charter Communications Inc. cv nt 7.00 2002	B3		None		750	—	—	—	123¾	—	—	—	—	—	·	126⅝	-118½	—	Nil
170032AH	Chiquita Brands International sub cv nt 7.00 2001	C	M&S 28	None		138	—	—	—	7	—	12.1	—	—	—	·	87½	-7	d1.15	Nil
171870AM	Cincinnati Bell, Inc. sub cv nt 6.75 2009[3]	B1	J&J 21	None	103.38	400	29.89	33.46	—	—	—	6.8	100	0	30¾	-15¾	—	—	—	Nil
172082AB	Cincinnati Financial Corp. sr cv deb 5.50 2002	A2	M&N 1	None	100.00	75.0	49.20	21.34	35⅜	263½	3.9	2.0	131¾	129¾	21¾	-17¾	290	-220	1.55	0.76
12561EAA	CKE Restaurants, Inc. cv nt 4.25 2004[3]	Caa2	M&S 15	None	171.5			—	—	50	—	9.3	—	—	—	·	50	-40½	d0.56	Nil
184502AE	Clear Channel Communications cv nt 1.50 2002	Baa3	J&D 1	None		600	105.78	9.45	•65¼	96	—	3.6	100	101½	22½	-10¼	96	-89	0.23	Nil
184502AB	sr cv nt 2.625 2003	Baa3	A&O 1	None	101.05	500	123.90	8.07	•65¼	114⅜	—	—	100	142	22½	-10¼	114⅛	-100¼	0.23	Nil
125896AN	CMS Energy Corp. jr sub cv deb 3.75 2004	B2	JAJ&O 1	None	N.C.	345.01	—	—	—	—	—	8.8	—	—	—	·	—	—	2.18	Nil
126126AB	CNB Bancshares Inc. jr sub cv deb 6.00 2028	A1	MJ&SD 30	None		150	—	—	—	—	—	6.0	—	—	—	·	—	—	1.74	0.76
192108AB	Coeur D'Alene Mines Corp. sub cv deb 6.00 2002	Caa2	JUN 10	None		50.0	—	—	—	33	—	—	—	—	—	·	42	-33	d1.61	Nil
192108AE	• sub cv deb 6.375 2004	Caa2	J&J 31	None		100	26.19	38.17	• 1½	37⅜	6.8	11.5	57¾	9¾	25¼	-13¼	37⅜	-31	d1.61	Nil
192108AF	• sub cv deb 7.25 2005[5]	Caa2	A30&O 31	None	143.75			—	—	42¾	—	12.3	—	—	—	·	42¾	-42¾	d1.61	Nil
196879AJ	Coltec Industries Inc jr sub cv deb 5.25 2028[13]	Baa3	JAJ&O 15	None		150	—	—	—	—	—	5.3	—	—	—	·	—	—	1.81	0.24
200300BH	Comcast Corp. zero cpn cv deb 0.00 2020[19]	Baa3		None	829.52			54.67	14.26	42⅞	82¾	—	—	100	45¼	11	-6⅞	84¼	-80⅛	1.38	Nil
203372AB	Commscope, Inc. sub cv nt 4.00	Baa3	J&D 15	None		172.5	48.19	20.75	•20¼	79	—	—	100	38¼	19	-10¼	80¼	-71¾	1.34	Nil
20589TAA	Concentra Managed Care Inc. sub cv nt 6.00 2001	Caa1	J&D 15	None		97.75	—	—	—	99½	—	6.5	—	—	—	·	99½	-99½	0.48	Nil
20589TAC	sub cv nt 4.50 2003	Caa1	M&S 15	None		230	—	—	—	99½	—	4.7	—	—	—	·	99½	-99½	0.48	Nil
219350AJ	Corning, Inc. zero cpn cv deb 0.00 2015[20]	A2		None	819.54			89.06	8.33	•56¾	74¾	—	—	100	66⅝	15¾	-9¼	81¼	-70½	0.6667	0.24
222814AN	Covad Communications Group ln sr cv nt 0.00[3]	Caa1		None		500	—	—	—	34½	—	—	—	—	—	·	34½	-20½	d1.8267	Nil
225224AA	•Cray Research Inc. sub cv deb 6.125 2011[3]	Baa2r	F&A 1	5%-'97	100.00	125	78.00	12.82	—	41½	7.7	11.2	0	32⅛	29¾	·	41½	-41¾	d8.95	Nil
126545AD	CUC International Inc. sub cv nt 3.00 2002[8]	Baa2	F&A 15	None		550	—	—	—	94¼	—	8.1	—	—	—	·	94½	-93	—	Nil
232806AE	•Cypress Semiconductor sub cv nt 4.00 2005	B1	F&A I	None	101.00	250	46.25	21.62	•27¾	92	—	6.3	100	42½	16½	-9¼	100	·	0.87	Nil
235851AD	Danaher Corp. cv nt 0.00 2021[8]	A2		None	721.59			—	—	62¾	—	—	—	—	—	·	62¾	—	1.84	0.50
237823AA	Data Processing Res Corp. sub cv nt 5.25 2005	B2		None	103.00	115	35.50	—	—	99½	—	5.4	100	35¾	29½	-15½	99½	-99¼	1	0.50
238100AB	Datapoint Corp. sub cv deb 8.875 2006	Ca r	J&D 1	5000-'91	100.00	71.0	22.53	44.37	—	37f	17	flat	5	8⅞	1⅛	-1	37	-37	—	Nil
25271CAA	Diamond Offshore Drilling Inc sub cv nt 3.75 2007	Baa1r	F&A 15	None	102.08	350	81.00	12.35	•40½	109¼	—	2.0	0	88¼	32½	-16½	111¾	-101¾	1.15	0.50
25271CAC	zero cpn deb 0.00 2020	A3		None	594.25	805	58.04	8.61	•40½	51¼	—	—	100	29¾	32½	-16½	51½	-48¼	1.15	0.50
255579AA	Dixie Yarns, Inc. sub cv deb 7.00 2012	B3 r	M&N 15	5%-'98		50.0	32.20	31.06	—	—	—	9.1	7.0	24⅛	0	8½	·	—	—	—	Nil

[1] Gtd. by Tyco International Ltd [2] Partial 144A [3] Amt. outstg. 1.09 billion. [4] Amt. outstg. 1.25 billion. [5] Private placement. [6] Gtd. by Ameritech Corp. Amt. outstg. 1.125 billion. Interest accrues [8] Amt. outstg. 1.25 billion. Gtd. by Asia Pulp & Paper Company Ltd. [9] name change BBN Corp. [10] Due 08-15-09. Co. filed for Chap. 11 [11] Interest accrues Conditional right to shorten maturity. Now MidAmerican Energy Holdings Co. (Iowa) [12] name change Worldway Corp. [14] Amt. outstg. 1.8135 billion. [15] Formerly CenterPoint Properties Corp. [16] Callable at the holder's option. Acq by Boatmen's Bancshares then NationsBank, name chg Bank of America [17] Name changed to Broadwing Inc. [18] merged Goodrich (BF) Co

[19] Amt. outstg. 1.285 billion. [20] Amt. outstg. 2.712546 billion. [21] Co. operating under Chap. 11. merged Silicon Graphics Inc. [22] Gtd. by Cendant Corp. Assumed by Cendant Corp., name chg Cedant Corp

Notes: Moody's® ratings are subject to change. Because of the possible time lapse between Moody's® assignment or change of a rating and your use of this monthly publication, we suggest you verify the current rating of any security or issuer in which you are interested. For standard abbreviations and symbols, see page 2.

Source: *Mergent Bond Record*, February 2001.

As an example of how one such issue is structured and priced, consider the 4.00 percent coupon convertible subordinated notes ("sub cv nt") issued by a NYSE-traded company, Cypress Semiconductor Corporation. Cypress Semiconductor designs, develops, manufactures, and markets a broad line of high-performance digital and mixed-signal integrated circuits for a range of markets, including data communications, telecommunications, computers, and instrumentation systems. The listing for this issue, which is scheduled to mature in February 2005, is shown on the seventh line from the bottom of Exhibit 24.16. After showing the issue's CUSIP identifier, contract terms, and default rating, (i.e., B1), the entry in the fourth column indicates that this bond pays interest semiannually on February 1 and August 1. The bond issue has $250 million outstanding and is callable at 101 percent of par. At the time of this report (i.e., February 2001), the listed price of the note was 92 percent of par and the price of Cypress Semiconductor common stock was 27.375. Additional details of this security are shown in Exhibit 24.17, which was generated by Bloomberg.

As spelled out at the top of Exhibit 24.17—and approximated in the ninth column of Exhibit 24.16—each $1,000 face value of this bond can be converted into 21.6216 shares of Cypress Semiconductor common stock. As in the convertible preferred example, this statistic is called the instrument's **conversion ratio**. At the listed share price of $27.375, an investor exercising her conversion option would have received only $591.89 (= $27.375 × 21.6216) worth of stock, an amount considerably below the current market value of the bond. In fact, the **conversion parity**

EXHIBIT 24.17 ▶ *DETAILS OF CYPRESS SEMICONDUCTOR CORP.'S CONVERTIBLE BOND ISSUE*

```
CYPRESS SEMICON  CY 4 02/01/05
CONV TO         21.6216 SHRS(PER    1000.0)CY    (NY ) $21.53 (         )
CONVERTIBLE UNTIL  2/ 1/ 5          ┌─ISSUER INFORMATION──────────────┐
┌─SECURITY INFORMATION────────┐     │NAME    CYPRESS SEMICONDUCTOR     │
│ CPN FREQ       SEMI-AN       │     │TYPE    INDUSTRIAL                │
│ CPN TYPE       FIXED         │    ┌─IDENTIFICATION #'s──┬─REDEMPTION INFO──┐
│ MTY/REFUND TYP CONV/CALL     │    │CUSIP    232806AE9   │MATURITY DT   2/ 1/05│
│ CALC TYP ( 49)CONVERTIBLE    │    │MLNUM 99999          │REFUNDING DT         │
│ DAY COUNT( 5) 30/360         │    │                     │NEXT CALL DT  2/ 5/03│
│ MARKET ISS     US DOMESTIC   │    │COMMON     010718309 │WORKOUT DT    2/ 1/05│
│ COUNTRY/CURR   US /USD       │    │                     │RISK FACTOR   3.0702 │
│ COLLATERAL TYP SUB NOTES     │    ├─ISSUANCE INFO───────┴─────────────────┤
│ AMT ISSUED        283,000(M) │    │ANNOUNCE DT    1/20/00 ┌──RATINGS──────┐ │
│ AMT OUTSTAND      283,000(M) │    │1ST SETTLE DT  1/25/00 │MOODY   B1     │ │
│ MIN PC/INC   1,000/    1,000 │    │1ST CPN DT     8/ 1/00 │S & P   B+     │ │
│ PAR AMT          1,000.00    │    │INT ACCRUE DT  1/25/00 │COMP    B1     │ │
│ LEADMGR/UWRTR CSFB           │    │PRICE @ ISSUE  100     │               │ │
│ EXCHANGE       NEW YORK      │    └───────────────────────│FI      NA     │ │
├──────────────────────────────┘                           └───────────────┘ 
Hit 1 <GO> to See Other Avail Info
NOTES  HAVE PROSPECTUS, DTC, BOOKENTRY
PRX/SHR=US$46.25. INIT CVR PREM=28.5%. UNSEC'D. POISON PUT. LONG 1ST CPN.
```

price (i.e., the common stock price at which immediate conversion would make sense) is equal to $42.55, which is the bond price of $920 divided by the conversion ratio of 21.6216. The prevailing market price of 27.375 is far below this parity level, meaning that the conversion option is currently out of the money. Of course, if the conversion parity price ever fell below the market price for the common stock, an astute investor could buy the bond and immediately exchange it into stock with a greater market value.

As indicated in the sixth column of Exhibit 24.16, most convertible bonds are also callable by the issuer. Of course, a firm will never call a bond selling for less than its call price (which is the case with the Cypress Semiconductor note). In fact, firms often wait until the bond is selling for significantly more than its call price before calling it.[19] If the company calls the bond under these conditions, investors will have an incentive to convert the bond into the stock that is worth more than they would receive from the call price; the situation is referred to as *forcing conversion.* Two other factors also increase the investors' incentive to convert their bonds. First, some instruments have conversion prices that step up over time according to a predetermined schedule. Since a stepped-up conversion price leads to a lower number of shares received, it becomes more likely that investors will exercise their option just before the conversion price increases. Second, a firm can help to encourage conversion by increasing the dividends on the stock, thereby making the income generated by the shares more attractive relative to the income from the bond.

Another important characteristic when evaluating convertible bonds is the **payback** or *break-even time,* which measures how long the higher interest income from the convertible bond (compared to the dividend income from the common stock) must persist to make up for the difference between the price of the bond and its conversion value (i.e., the conversion premium). The calculation is as follows:

$$\text{Payback} = \frac{\text{Bond Price} - \text{Conversion Value}}{\text{Bond Income} - \text{Income from Equal Investment in Common Stock}}$$

For instance, the annual coupon yield payment on the Cypress Semiconductor convertible bond is $40, while the firm's dividend yield is zero. Thus, assuming you sold the bond for $920 and used the proceeds to purchase 33.607 shares (= $920/$27.375) of Cypress Semiconductor stock, the payback period would be

$$\frac{\$920.00 - \$591.89}{\$40.00 - \$0.00} = 8.20 \text{ Years}$$

It is also possible to calculate the combined value of the investor's conversion option and issuer's call feature that are embedded in the note. In the Cypress Semiconductor example, with a market price of $920, the convertible's yield to maturity can be calculated as the solution to

$$\$920 = \sum_{t=1}^{8} \frac{20}{(1 + y/2)^t} + \frac{1,000}{(1 + y/2)^8}$$

or $y = 6.29$ percent (reported as 6.3 percent in the thirteenth column of Exhibit 24.16). This computation assumes eight semiannual coupon payments of $20 (= 40 ÷ 2). Since the yield on a Cypress Semiconductor debt issue with no embedded options and the same (B1) credit rating

---

[19]An empirical study of this issue revealed that almost all of the convertible securities studied were called later than the theoretically optimal time. See Jonathan E. Ingersoll, Jr., "An Examination of Corporate Call Policies on Convertible Securities," *Journal of Finance* 32, no. 2 (May 1977): 463–478.

and maturity was 8.50 percent, the present value of a "straight" fixed-income security with the same cash flows would be

$$\$850.06 = \sum_{t=1}^{8} \frac{20}{(1+0.0425)^t} + \frac{1,000}{(1+0.0425)^8}$$

This means that the net value of the combined options is $69.94, or $920 minus $850.06. Using the Black-Scholes valuation model, it is easily confirmed that a four-year call option to buy *one* share of Cypress Semiconductor stock—which does not pay a dividend—at an exercise price of $42.55 (i.e., the conversion parity value) is equal to $6.35.[20] Thus, the value of the investor's conversion option—which allows for the acquisition of 21.6216 shares—must be $137.26 (= 21.6216 × $6.35). This means that the value of the issuer's call feature under these conditions must be $67.32 (= $137.26 – $69.94).

Exhibit 24.18 illustrates the value of a convertible bond in a more general way. The horizontal axis plots the value of the firm, which establishes an upper bound for the value of a convertible since it cannot sell for more than the firm's assets. Thus, there is a firm value line that bisects the plane and the value of the convertible must be below that line. Note that the line for the bond value is relatively flat for a wide range of firm values because higher firm values do not increase the value of the bond since bondholders receive only their promised payments. In contrast, at fairly low firm values, the value of the bond drops off as bankruptcy becomes more likely. Conversion value rises directly with the value of the firm. The exhibit shows that for low firm values, the bond value will be the minimum value of the convertible, whereas the convertible's price will be driven by its conversion potential for high firm values. Finally, the line for the value of the convertible shows that when the firm value is low, the convertible will act more like a bond, trading for only a slight pre-

EXHIBIT 24.18   *ILLUSTRATING THE VALUE OF A CONVERTIBLE BOND*

---

[20]This calculation assumes the following input values: $S = 27.375$, $X = 42.55$, $T = 4$, $RFR = 0.05$, $\sigma = 0.40$, and $D = 0.00$.

mium over the bond value (as is the case with the Cypress Semiconductor note discussed earlier). Alternatively, when firm values are high, the convertible will act more like a stock, selling for only a slight premium over the conversion value. In the fairly wide middle range, the convertible will trade as the hybrid security that acts somewhat like a bond and somewhat like a stock.

OTHER EMBEDDED DERIVATIVES

For many years, the nature of borrowing and lending in securitized capital markets remained quite stable, with companies typically issuing bonds at par value and paying either a fixed or floating rate of interest in the same currency in which the money was borrowed. With few exceptions, the choice of maturity or coupon structure was driven by the economic situation faced by the borrower, rather than the investor. Over the past decade, however, this scenario has greatly changed with the development of the *structured note* market. Generally speaking, structured notes are debt issues that have their principal or coupon payments linked to some other underlying variable. Examples include bonds whose coupons are tied to the appreciation of an equity index, such as the S&P 500, or a zero coupon bond with a principal amount tied to the appreciation of an oil price index.

Crabbe and Argilagos have pointed out several common features that distinguish structured notes from regular fixed-income securities, two of which are important for our discussion.[21] First, structured notes are designed for and targeted to a specific investor with a very particular need. That is, these are not "generic" instruments but products tailored to address an investor's special constraints, which often are themselves created by tax, regulatory, or institutional policy restrictions. Second, after structuring the financing to meet the investor's needs, the issuer typically will hedge that unique exposure with swaps or exchange-traded derivatives. Inasmuch as the structured note most likely required an embedded derivative to create the desired payoff structure for the investor, this unwinding of the derivative position by the issuer generates an additional source of profit opportunity for the bond underwriter.

The growth of this market has been quite rapid. From its ostensible origin in the mid-1980s, more than $100 billion of these notes were issued annually by the end of the last century. Equally impressive is the wide variety of economic risks that have been embedded and the maze of new acronyms that has accompanied these innovations (e.g., FLAG, LYON, SPEL, STEER, PERCS, and ICON). We will take a detailed look at four such structures representative of the major exposures an investor might desire: currency, equity, commodity, and interest rates.

Dual Currency Bonds

A dual currency bond is a debt instrument that has coupons denominated in a different currency than its principal amount. They have been popular funding instruments, particularly in the Euromarkets, for more than a decade and have been designed to include virtually all the world's major currencies. These bonds can be viewed as a combination of two simpler financial instruments: (1) a single-currency fixed-coupon bond, and (2) a forward contract to exchange the bond's principal into a predetermined amount of a foreign currency. They often are sold to investors who are willing to "take a view" over the longer term in the foreign exchange markets. By having the currency forward attached to the bond, fixed-income portfolio managers who might otherwise be restricted from trading in FX have the potential to enhance their performance if their beliefs about future market conditions prove correct.

[21]See Leland E. Crabbe and Joseph D. Argilagos, "Anatomy of the Structured Note Market," *Journal of Applied Corporate Finance* 7, no. 3 (Fall 1994): 85–98. Also see Ira G. Kawaller, "Understanding Structured Notes," *Derivatives Quarterly* 1, no. 3 (Spring 1995).

EXHIBIT 24.19   *CASH FLOWS FOR A DUAL CURRENCY BOND FROM INVESTORS' PERSPECTIVE*

	YEAR					
	0	1	2	3	4	5
Transaction						
1. Long 9% USD bond	−USD 1,000	+ USD 90	+ USD 90	+ USD 90	+ USD 90	+ USD 1,090
2. Long yen forward (pay USD, receive JPY)	−USD 20	—	—	—	—	+JPY 110,000 and −USD 1,000
3. Long dual currency bond (Transaction 1 + Transaction 2)	−USD 1,020	+ USD 90	+ USD 90	+ USD 90	+ USD 90	+JPY 110,000 −and +USD 90

Source: *Mergent Bond Record,* February 2001.

To demonstrate a structure typical of these products, consider a five-year bond paying an annual coupon of 9 percent in U.S. dollars and redemption amount of JPY 110,000. The initial price of the bond is USD 1,020, relative to a par value of USD 1,000. Assuming further that a regular five-year, dollar-denominated bond of comparable risk yielding 9 percent could have been issued at par, this means that the forward contract portion of the dual currency instrument is "off market" because it carries a present value of USD 20. Exhibit 24.19 shows the cash flows for this structure from the investor's point of view. It also demonstrates how it can be assembled from its more basic component parts.

Notice that the embedded forward contract allows the bondholder to exchange the USD 1,000 for JPY 110,000, generating an implied *nominal* exchange rate of JPY 110/USD (or, equivalently, USD 0.0091/JPY). However, given that the investor has to pay an additional USD 20 today for this future transaction, this is not the *effective* exchange rate that the investor faces. Indeed, the fact that the investor is willing to pay the additional USD 20 suggests that JPY 110/USD is a favorable price to purchase yen forward. The effective exchange rate built into this transaction can be established by dividing JPY 110,000 by the sum of USD 1,000 and the future value (in Year 5) of USD 20. Calculating this latter amount as 30.77 (= $20 \times (1.09)^5$), the effective exchange rate becomes JPY 106.72/USD (= 110,000 ÷ (1,000 + 30.77)).

There are at least two reasons why this dual currency bond might trade at a premium over a single-currency 9 percent coupon bond of comparable creditworthiness. First, it is possible that the five-year forward exchange rate between yen and dollars is JPY 106.72/USD, meaning that at USD 1,020, the bond is priced properly. The more likely possibility, though, is that the five-year forward rate actually is JPY 110/USD and that investors are "paying up" for a desirable FX exposure that they cannot acquire in any other way. If this is true, the issuer—who is effectively short the regular dollar bond and short in the yen forward—can unwind its derivative position at a profit, thereby reducing its funding cost below 9 percent. That is, the issuer's commitment to "sell" JPY 110,000 to the investor in Year 5 can be offset by a long position in a separate yen forward (which, once again, is usually done with the bond's underwriter as the counterparty) at the market forward exchange rate of JPY 110/JSD. Thus, the issuer's net borrowing cost can be calculated by solving for the yield as follows:

$$1,020 = \sum_{t=1}^{5} \frac{90}{(1+y)^t} + \frac{1,000}{(1+y)^5}$$

or $y = 8.49$ percent. This 51-basis-point differential from the "plain vanilla" borrowing rate of 9 percent represents the issuer's compensation for creating an investment vehicle that is tailored to the needs of the investor.

Equity-Index-Linked Notes

In September 1997, Merrill Lynch & Co. raised $167,500,000 by issuing 16,750,000 units of a Russell 2000 Market Index Target-Term Security (MITTS) at a price of $10 per unit.[22] For several years, Merrill Lynch had been successful raising funds by issuing MITTS based on a wide variety of equity indexes, including the S&P 500, the Dow Jones Industrial Average, and the Nikkei 225. These particular MITTS units had a maturity date of September 30, 2004, making them comparable in form to a seven-year bond even though they traded on the American Stock Exchange. Indeed, Merrill Lynch issued them as the equivalent of a series of Senior Debt Securities making no coupon payments prior to maturity. At maturity, a unitholder received the original issue price plus a "supplemental redemption amount," the value of which depended on where the Russell 2000 index (which is a prominent indicator of the performance of "small-cap" stocks) settled relative to a predetermined initial level. Given that this supplemental amount could not be less than zero, the total payout to the investor at maturity can be written:

$$10 + \max\left[0, \left\{10 \times \left(\frac{\text{Final RUT Value} - \text{Initial RUT value}}{\text{Initial RUT Value}}\right)\right\}\right]$$

where the initial Russell 2000 (i.e., RUT) index value was specified as 494.36.

From the preceding description, recognize that the MITTS structure combines a seven-year, zero coupon bond with a RUT index call option, both of which were issued by Merrill Lynch. Thus, the MITTS investor essentially owns a "portfolio" that is (1) long in a bond and (2) long in an index call option position. This particular security was designed primarily for those investors who wanted to participate in the small-cap portion of the equity market but, for regulatory or taxation reasons, were not permitted to do so directly. For example, the manager of a fixed-income mutual fund might be able to enhance her return performance by purchasing this "bond" and then hoping for an appreciating stock market. Notice that the use of the call option in this design makes it fairly easy for Merrill Lynch to market to its institutional customers in that it is a "no lose" proposition; the worst-case scenario for the investor is that she simply gets her money back without interest in seven years. (Of course, the customer does carry the company's credit risk for this period.) Thus, unlike the dual currency bond where the investor could either gain or lose from changing exchange rates, at origination the MITTS issue had no downside exposure to stock price declines.

The call option embedded in this structure is actually a partial position. To see this, we can rewrite the option portion of the note's redemption value as

$$\max\left[0, \left\{10 \times \left(\frac{\text{Final RUT} - 494.36}{494.36}\right)\right\}\right] = \max\left[0, \left\{\left(\frac{10}{494.36}\right)(\text{Final RUT} - 494.36\right\}\right]$$

or

$$(0.0202)\ \{\max[0,\ (\text{Final RUT} - 494.36)]\}$$

Thus, given that a regular index option would have a terminal payoff of $\max[0, (\text{Final RUT} - X]$, where X is the exercise price, the derivative in the MITTS represent 2.02 percent of this amount. The terminal payoffs to the MITTS embedded option are shown in Exhibit 24.20, along with those to a regular index call option for several potential September 2004 levels of the Russell 2000 index. Notice that although the MITTS and regular options become in the money at the same point

---

[22]We would like to thank Jim Spilman and Scott Soules of Merrill Lynch for their insights into the creation and trading of this security.

EXHIBIT 24.20 ▶ *TERMINAL PAYOFFS TO MITTS EMBEDDED CALL OPTION AND REGULAR INDEX CALL OPTION (X = 494.36)*

TERMINAL RUT VALUE	REGULAR INDEX CALL	MITTS CALL
420	0.00	0.00
440	0.00	0.00
460	0.00	0.00
480	0.00	0.00
500	5.64	0.11
520	25.64	0.52
540	45.64	0.92
560	65.64	1.33
580	85.64	1.73
600	105.64	2.13
620	125.64	2.54
640	145.64	2.94
660	165.64	3.35
680	185.64	3.75
700	205.64	4.15
720	225.64	4.56
740	245.64	4.96
760	265.64	5.37
780	285.64	5.77
800	305.64	6.17
820	325.64	6.58
840	345.64	6.98

(i.e., 494.36), only the latter produces a "dollar-for-dollar" payoff with increasing values of the index beyond this point. The payoff call feature in the structured note still rises for any Russell 2000 level above 494.36 but gains only $0.0202 for every one point gained by the index.

Rewriting the redemption value in this fashion also makes valuing the MITTS issue a more transparent process. This can be accomplished by recognizing that the value of the entire structure simply should be the value of the bond portion plus the value of the option component; any price "synergy" for the packaging will be a market-driven phenomenon. Specifically, on January 1, 2002, the closing price for this MITTS issue (ticker symbol: RUM) was $10.34, while the Russell 2000 index closed at 488.50. Further, the semiannually compounded yield of a zero coupon (i.e., "stripped") Treasury bond on this date was 3.77 percent while a Merrill Lynch bond maturing at the same time as the MITTS issue carried yield of 4.28 percent. (This 51-basis-point credit spread was appropriate for Merrill Lynch's credit rating of AA and Aa3—by Standard & Poor's and Moody's, respectively.) Given the remaining time to maturity (i.e., two years and nine months, or 5.5 half-years), the bond portion of the MITTS issue should be worth:

$$\text{MITTS Bond Value} = \frac{10}{\left(1 + \dfrac{.0428}{2}\right)^{5.5}} = \$8.90$$

This means that the investor is paying $1.44 (= $10.34 − $8.90) for the embedded index call.

Whether $1.44 represents a fair price for the MITTS call depends on the value of the regular index option, which, as we saw in Chapter 23, can be calculated with the dividend yield-adjusted version of the Black-Scholes model. To perform this computation, some additional inputs are needed. First, the Russell 2000 dividend yield on January 1, 2002, was 1.3 percent. Second, the number of days between January 1, 2002, and September 30, 2004, is 1,003. Third, the continuously compounded equivalent of the quoted risk-free rate is 3.73 percent.[23] Finally, the volatility of Russell 2000 index returns over the time to MITTS issue's maturity is assumed to be 22.90 percent, a level approximated from the prevailing implied volatilities for traded index options on that date.

The value of an index call option with an exercise price of 494.36 can now be generated by the Black-Scholes formula using the following inputs: $S = 488.50$, $X = 494.36$, $T = 2.748$ ($= 1,003/365$), $RFR = 0.0373$, $D = 0.013$, and $\sigma = 0.229$. Under these conditions we have

$$d_1 = [\ln(488.5e^{-(.013)2.748}/494.36) + (.0373 + 0.5(.229)^2)(2.748)] \div (.229[2.748]^{1/2}) = 0.334$$

and

$$d_2 = 0.334 - .229[2.748]^{1/2} = -0.045$$

so that $N(d_1) = 0.6310$ and $N(d_2) = 0.4819$. Thus the index call's Black-Scholes value is

$$C_0 = (488.5)(e^{-(.013)2.748})(0.6310) - (494.36)(e^{-(.0373)2.748})(0.4819) = 82.43$$

The value of the embedded MITTS call is then established by multimplying 82.43 by 0.0202, which leaves a value of $1.67. Therefore, on this particular date, the MITTS issue was priced in the market $0.23 ($= 1.67 - 1.44$) below its theoretical value, presenting investors with a potential buying opportunity depending on their transaction costs. Finally, notice that since the January 1, 2002, index value (i.e., 488.50) was less than the initial (i.e., exercise) level, the MITTS call feature is out of the money and the entire option value represents a time premium.

Commodity-Linked Bull and Bear Bonds

Besides linking their payoffs to currency or equity indexes, fixed-income securities can be designed to give an investor exposure to commodity price movements as well. As with the swap contracts we saw earlier, the commodities involved in these structures are seldom exchanged but instead represented in the form of "cash settlement only" derivatives. Thus, virtually no theoretical limit exists to the number of different underlying assets that can be embedded into a bond issue. However, recall that innovation in the structured note market is dictated by investor demands, which to date have tended to concentrate on either oil or precious metals. As in the previous examples, the primary attractions to the investor of gaining the desired exposure through the purchase of structured notes are their convenience and their ability to avoid restrictions on taking commodity positions directly.

A particularly interesting form of the commodity-linked bond is the so-called bull and bear note. This structure gets its name from a bond that is issued in two portions: a bull tranche, whose

---

[23]This value can be established by solving for r in the following equation:

$$e^r = (1 + (.0377/2))^2$$

or

$$r = \ln[(1 + (.0377/2))^2] = 0.0373$$

principal redemption amount increases directly with the price of the designated commodity; and a bear tranche, whose principal refunding declines with increasing commodity prices. One of the first issues of this kind occurred in October 1986 when the Kingdom of Denmark raised $120 million in two separate $60 million tranches, each having a different payoff structure depending on the movement of an index of gold prices.[24] Both of these gold-linked note tranches had a seven-year maturity, paid an annual coupon of 3 percent, and were issued at a price of 100.125 percent of par value. The principal redemptions for each $1,000 of face value for the two tranches were:

Bull Redemption: ($1,000) × [1.158 × (Index at Redemption ÷ Initial Index)]

and

Bear Redemption: ($1,000) × {2.78 − [1.158 × (Index at Redemption ÷ Initial Index)]}

Finally, for both tranches, maximum and minimum redemption levels of $2,280 and $500, respectively, were set.

Exhibit 24.21 shows the redemption amount that the Kingdom of Denmark is obligated to pay on each tranche for a series of gold index levels relative to the initial level, which was set at 426.50. The final column of this display shows what the average redemption value is when the two tranches are considered together. Notice that this average amount does not vary—that is, *the issuer has no net exposure to gold price movements.* Unlike the dual currency bond example considered earlier, which required the issuer to adopt an additional derivative position to offset the instrument's inherent FX exposure, the virtue of this two-tranche approach is that the commodity exposure is neutralized internally. That is, the Kingdom of Denmark is effectively both long and short gold in equal amounts across the bear and bull segments, respectively. An immediate consequence of this is that they have a fixed funding cost for the full $120 million issue, calculated by solving:

$$1,001.25 = \sum_{t=1}^{7} \frac{30}{(1+y)^t} + \frac{1,390}{(1+y)^7}$$

or $y = 7.42$ percent. At the time this deal was launched, a regular seven-year, par-value debt issue would have required a yield of about 8 percent, a fact that underscores the Kingdom of Denmark's incentive to create this structure in the first place.

The attraction for the investors, of course, is the ability to purchase a fixed-income security that also allows for participation in gold price movements. In exchange for accepting a lower-than-market coupon, buyers of the bull (bear) tranche will receive a redemption value that exceeds their purchase price if the gold index increases (declines). Exhibit 24.22, which shows the redemption values for the two tranches in a graphical form, suggests that the commodity derivatives embedded in this transaction are not simple forward or option positions. Rather, the minimum and maximum principal payoffs effectively convert the gold exposure into a call option money spread—a bull spread for the bull tranche, a bear for the bear—as described in Chapter 23. The investors, who undoubtedly will be different people for the two positions, pay for this spread position through a reduction in their average yield to maturity relative to the regular bond.

---

[24]Additional details of this bull-and-bear structure are explained in Julian Walmsley, *The New Financial Instruments,* 2d ed. (New York: John Wiley & Sons, 1998), which also contains descriptions of an exhaustive set of such deals. It is recommended reading for anyone wishing to learn more about the development of these innovative products.

REDEMPTION VALUES FOR THE "BULL AND BEAR" GOLD-LINKED NOTE (IN U.S. DOLLARS)

TERMINAL GOLD INDEX	BULL TRANCHE	BEAR TRANCHE	AVERAGE
100	500	2,280	1,390
150	500	2,280	1,390
200	543	2,237	1,390
250	679	2,101	1,390
300	815	1,965	1,390
350	950	1,830	1,390
400	1,086	1,694	1,390
450	1,222	1,558	1,390
500	1,358	1,422	1,390
550	1,493	1,287	1,390
600	1,629	1,151	1,390
650	1,765	1,015	1,390
700	1,901	879	1,390
750	2,036	744	1,390
800	2,172	608	1,390
850	2,280	500	1,390
900	2,280	500	1,390

REDEMPTION VALUES FOR THE "BULL AND BEAR" GOLD-LINKED NOTE

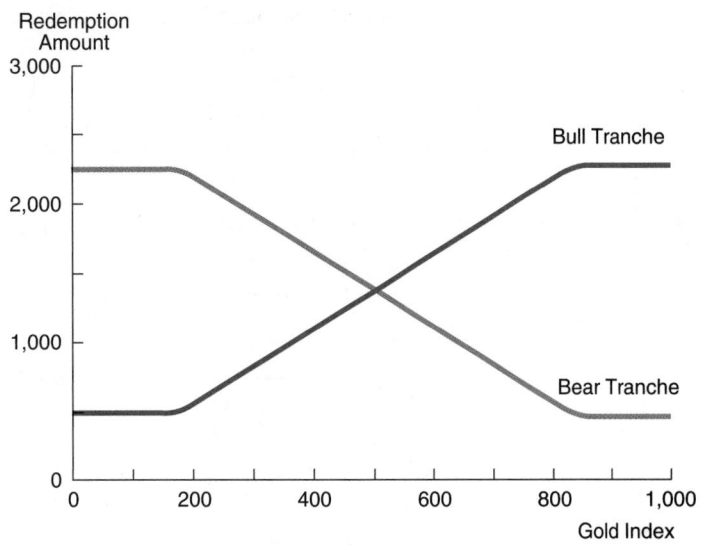

Swap-Linked Notes

As we have seen, interest rate swaps are efficient mechanisms for transforming the cash flows of existing debt issues. They also are quite useful in the new-issue market when the desired rate exposures of the borrower and lender do not coincide naturally. Imagine, for example, that Company LMN wishes to raise $50 million by issuing a fixed-rate note with semiannual coupon payments over a three-year period. Having launched a similar issue in the capital markets recently, however, LMN finds that little "appetite" exists for another one of its fixed-rate notes. On the other hand, a large institutional investor is willing to accept LMN's credit risk on a privately placed loan, providing that the deal can be structured to its satisfaction. In particular, the fund manager for this investment company thinks that interest rates are going to decline substantially over the next few years and wants to design the loan contract to take advantage of that possibility. Accordingly, she wants the semiannual coupon on the note to move inversely with the level of some variable interest rate index, such as LIBOR. This sort of arrangement is known as a *reverse floating-rate* contract; the coupon rate changes as the general level of interest rates moves but in the opposite direction.

Suppose the specific structure that LMN and the investor agree on resets the coupon on a semiannual basis at a level equal to 12 percent minus LIBOR. Thus, if six-month LIBOR on a particular settlement date is 7.5 percent, the coupon payment will be 4.5 percent (times one-half times $50 million). Conversely, a LIBOR of only 3.75 percent would generate a coupon of 8.25 percent. In this way, the investor gains the desired benefit from falling rates and does so in a convenient form that entails less credit risk than if it had transformed a regular bond issue with a derivative on its own. In addition, the reverse floater will actually benefit more from a rate decline than would a fixed-rate note of identical maturity. Specifically, while the price of a fixed-rate bond paying constant coupons will appreciate when yields fall, the reverse floater will increase the investor's periodic cash flow as well.

Unfortunately, although this design satisfies the investor's requirements, it does not do the same for the issuer. This discrepancy can be easily remedied, though, by combining Company LMN's debt position with a swap in which it receives the fixed rate and pays LIBOR. This is illustrated in Exhibit 24.23, assuming a three-year fixed swap rate of 6.5 percent against six-month LIBOR. One helpful way to see how a swap must be written to fix the coupon on this reverse rate structure is to notice that paying a coupon of 12 percent minus LIBOR is equivalent to paying a coupon of 12 percent and receiving one of LIBOR. Thus, to neutralize LMN's floating-rate exposure, it must pay out LIBOR on the swap.

Exhibit 24.23 also shows that the net synthetic fixed-rate funding cost to Company LMN is 5.5 percent (assuming the swap fixed rate has been converted to an actual/360 basis). This will

EXHIBIT 24.23 ▶ *CONVERTING A RESERVE FLOATING-RATE NOTE WITH A SWAP*

LMN's Net Funding Cost:

[12% − LIBOR] + [LIBOR − 6.5%] = 5.5%

only be true, however, whenever LIBOR does not exceed 12 percent. If LIBOR is greater than 12 percent, the benefit from paying lower coupons to the investor will stop—the coupon rate can never go negative—but LMN will continue having to make the higher net settlement payment on the swap, which raises the effective borrowing cost above 5.5 percent. Consequently, because there is an implicit cap on LIBOR built into the reverse floating-rate loan, Company LMN will need to offset this by purchasing an actual cap agreement with an exercise rate of 12 percent and a notional principal of $50 million. This option will not be expensive because it is quite far out of the money but it will not be free, which means the net funding cost will be somewhat greater than 5.5 percent.

Earlier in the chapter, we saw that an interest rate swap can be interpreted as a pair of capital market transactions. In this particular case, a "receive 6.5 percent fixed, pay LIBOR" swap can be viewed as a portfolio long in a fixed-rate note paying 6.5 percent and short in a LIBOR-based floating-rate note. Recalling that "+" represents a long position and "–" represents a short position, the synthetic fixed-rate issue from Company LMN's perspective can be written as follows:

$$- \text{(Synthetic Fixed Rate Bond at 5.5\%)} = - \text{(Reverse Floater at 12\% − LIBOR)}$$
$$+ \text{(Receive 6.5\%, Pay LIBOR Swap)}$$
$$+ \text{(Cap at 12\% Exercise Rate)}$$
$$= - \text{(Reverse Floater at 12\% − LIBOR)}$$
$$- \text{(FRN at LIBOR)} + \text{(Fixed Rate Bond at 6.5\%)}$$
$$+ \text{(Cap at 12\% Exercise Rate)}$$

As in the previous examples, this sort of structured solution would only make sense to the issuer if it could ultimately obtain funding cost that was lower than a direct fixed-rate loan. The biggest reason for this is that while a direct fixed-rate loan would carry no credit risk for Company LMN, the structured loan would because of the swap and cap positions. Thus, the swap-based borrowing is never as good as a direct approach and, therefore, requires a lower cost to entice the issuer.

As a final extension of this concept, consider what would have happened if the institutional investor decided to take an even more aggressive view of falling interest rates and requested that the coupon reset the formula to 18.4 percent minus $(2 \times \text{LIBOR})$. Such a design is called a *leveraged* reverse floating-rate note, with the leverage coming from the fact that the coupon increases twice as fast as the decline in yields. Exhibit 24.24 indicates that to convert this to a fixed-rate

EXHIBIT 24.24 ▶ *CONVERTING A LEVERAGED RESERVE FLOATER WITH TWO SWAPS*

LMN's Net Funding Cost:

$$[18.4\% - (2 \times \text{LIBOR})] + ([2 \times \text{LIBOR}] - (2 \times 6.5\%)) = 5.4\%$$

issue, Company LMN would have to enter into two $50 million receive-fixed swaps (or, more practically, one contract with a notional principal of $100 million). As before, to fix its funding cost completely, it also would have to purchase two $50 million cap agreements with a cap rate of 9.2 percent (= 18.4 percent ÷ 2). This converted position, which would have a net funding cost of 5.4 percent before factoring in the cost of the caps, can be represented as

$$- \text{(Synthetic Fixed-Rate Bond at 5.4\%)} = - \text{(Reverse Floater at } 18.4\% - 2 \times \text{LIBOR)}$$
$$+ \text{(2 Receive 6.5\%, Pay LIBOR Swaps)}$$
$$+ \text{(2 Caps at 9.2 \% Exercise Rate)}$$
$$= - \text{(Reverse Floater at } 18.4\% - 2 \times \text{LIBOR)}$$
$$- \text{(2 FRNs at LIBOR)} + \text{(2 Fixed-Rate Bonds at 6.5\%)}$$
$$+ \text{(2 Caps at 9.2\% Exercise Rate)}$$

Although the net coupon on this swapped leveraged structure is lower than on the swapped unleveraged reverse floater, the cost of the required options will be more than twice as expensive since two contracts must be purchased at a lower cap rate.[25]

VALUING FLEXIBILITY: AN INTRODUCTION TO REAL OPTIONS

Recently, energy companies have begun to open gas-fired power plants that generate electricity at an expense 50 percent to 70 percent greater than those of other, more cost-effective plants.[26] These new, "inefficient" plants are intended to operate only when the price of electricity is high enough to justify the cost. The energy firms hope to make a profit on the new plants because power prices have become increasingly volatile and the new plants—although they cost more to run—are much less costly to fire up and shut down on short notice than traditional plants. Although these so-called "peaking" plants are also cheaper to build, their main attraction lies in their *flexibility*. That is, they allow energy companies to supply more electricity when prices are high and to cease production almost immediately when electricity prices have dropped.

How should investors value companies that possess this sort of operational flexibility? Conventional net present value calculations ignore the benefits of flexibility and may therefore undervalue projects that allow companies to react rapidly to changing circumstances. For example, the fact that these new power plants are expected to run only part of the year is easily incorporated into a standard value calculation. However, predicting the future cash flows based on factors like expected running time, expected electricity prices, or expected production costs will fail to capture the most valuable feature of these plants: namely, that they will only be generating electricity when the price of a megawatt-hour of electricity exceeds the cost of producing it. This is in contrast to conventional plants that produce electricity more cheaply overall but are sometimes forced to sell below-cost power because shutting down and then restarting the facility would be prohibitively expensive.

As we have seen earlier, options give their holders the right, but not the obligation, to trade an asset at a predetermined exercise price by a prespecified future date. So far, the derivative

---

[25]For a more complete examination of how swaps can be used to create structured investment payoffs, see Keith C. Brown and Donald J. Smith, "Structured Swaps," in *Yearbook of Fixed Income Investing,* ed. J. Finnerty and M. Fridson (Burr Ridge, Ill.: Irwin Professional Publishing, 1995).

[26]See Peter Coy, "Exploiting Uncertainty: The 'Real Options' Revolution in Decision Making," *Business Week Online,* 7 June 1999.

contracts we have discussed are exchanged in financial markets and the asset underlying the derivative contract is often another financial instrument (such as a share of common stock, a government bond, or a futures contract). However, options are also embedded in real assets owned by firms; these are known as **real options**. A pharmaceutical company, for instance, owns valuable options in the form of its collection of drug patents. The firm has the right, but not the obligation, to develop marketable drugs based on its patents and will do so if the value of those drugs (in terms of discounted present value) exceeds the cost of development and regulatory approval. In the language of derivative contracting, these costs can be considered as the strike price for the development option. For the energy example, the peaking plant in effect gives the firm the right but not the obligation to "buy" Y megawatt-hours of electricity at an exercise price X, where Y is the total capacity of the plant and X is the generating cost per megawatt-hour.

Although real options have existed ever since man walked the earth—for instance, storing food and other necessities gave people a valuable option, allowing them to consume more (or less) than the amount produced in a given time period—a number of recent changes have made understanding them more important than ever. These factors include: (1) the *pace of technological innovation,* which has made a company's long-term planning more difficult to assess for managers and investors alike; (2) *deregulation and privatization,* which has created new incentives for firms to analyze and use real options in order to gain a competitive advantage; and (3) *advances in derivatives pricing theory* and *decreases in the computing costs,* making it easier to interpret and value real options, which are often quite complex in practice.

Company Valuation with Real Options

To highlight the advantages of the "real options" derivative-based approach over traditional company valuation methods, we present the case of the fictional GoldFlex Corporation.[27] One of GoldFlex's assets is a lease on a gold mine, which expires in February 2003, exactly one year from now. GoldFlex geologists estimate that the mine—which is currently idle—holds 100,000 Troy ounces of gold and that extraction costs are $260/ounce. The February 2002 (i.e., current) spot price of an ounce of gold is $264.40, while the February 2003 forward contract price equals $268.40. For simplicity, we will assume that all the gold is extracted at the end of the year. To be able to mine gold in a year, the company must spend $1,000,000 today to restore the mining facilities to working order. Suppose further that the spot price of gold in one year will be either $290 or $240 and that the one-year risk-free rate is 5 percent. How should an investor establish the value of GoldFlex's mining lease?

To see the issues, first recognize that GoldFlex could sell all of its gold at the current forward price. Since the resulting sales proceeds a year from now would then be known, assuming that extraction costs and the quantity of gold are known with certainty, the appropriate discount rate is the one-year T-bill (i.e., risk-free) yield. Thus, the value of the mine calculated using a traditional net present value approach would be

$$NPV = \{[268.40 - 260) \times 100,000] \div (1.05)\} - 1,000,000 = -\$200,000$$

Of course, this calculation suggests that the lease has no value because opening the mine would be a money-losing project. However, the traditional approach ignores the value of flexibility: If gold prices decline in the future, management can shut down production and leave the gold in the ground. Once we consider the possibility of shutting down, the cash flows from the mine can be viewed in a different and more realistic manner.

---

[27]This example follows a greatly simplified approach based on the valuation method first introduced by Michael J. Brennan and Eduardo S. Schwartz, "Evaluating Natural Resource Investments," *Journal of Business* 58, no. 2 (April 1985): 135–158.

The main premise behind the derivatives-based approach to valuing a real asset with embedded timing options (such as the mine) is that it is possible for an investor to assemble a portfolio of financial securities that will have the same pattern of future cash flows with the same level of risk. Specifically, such an investor could value the potential future cash flows by creating a hypothetical portfolio consisting of risk-free, one-year T-bills and gold forward contracts that would exactly mimic the mining operation. This *replicating portfolio* will have the same possible cash flows as the gold mine, so its value in an efficient capital market should also be the same. For example, we can use the "two-state" framework from Chapter 23 to view the valuation question as follows:

TODAY (FEBRUARY 2002):	IN ONE YEAR (FEBRUARY 2003):	
	Gold Price	Cash Flow
Spend $1 Million to Reopen Mine?	$290	$3,000,000 (= (290 – 260) × 100,000))
	$240	$0 (No Production)

How many forward contracts are necessary to build a security position that duplicates these cash flows? Notice that the other asset involved in this process is risk free, so all the variation in the cash flows of the replicating portfolio must come from the payoff to the forward contract. With the assumed February 2003 gold price forecasts, a long position in a one-year gold forward contract will leave the investor with either a profit of $21.60 (= $290 – $268.40) or a loss of –$28.40 (= $240 – $268.40) per ounce. The difference between these two payoffs equals $50 (= 21.6 – (–28.4)), while the difference between the two possible cash flows from the mine is 3,000,000. Therefore, the number of forward contracts necessary to form a replicating portfolio equals (where each contract stipulates the delivery of one ounce of gold):

$$(3,000,000) \div (50) = 60,000$$

To find the amount of the T-bill investment needed in the replicating portfolio, notice that if the price of gold drops to $240 in one year, the holder of 60,000 forward contracts will lose $1,704,000 (= 28.4 × 60,000) while the cash flow from the mine would be zero. The payoff from the risk-free investment must make up for the difference, so the amount that must be invested in one-year T-Bills in order to form a "synthetic mine" is

$$(1,704,000) \div (1.05) = \$1,622.857$$

Exhibit 24.25 summarizes the process of creating this replicating portfolio.

Given that this portfolio of securities has, by design, the same future cash flows as the mine with the same level of volatility, in an efficient capital market the replicating portfolio and the mine should have the same present value. This can be expressed as

[Value of Gold Forward Position] + [Value of T-bill Position] = [Value of Mine Lease]

Since we saw in Chapter 22 that the present value of an "at-market" forward contract is zero, the replicating portfolio (and therefore the lease on the mine) is worth $1,622,857, which is

| **EXHIBIT 24.25** | *CREATING A "REAL OPTIONS" REPLICATING PORTFOLIO* |

Step 1: Design a portfolio containing F forward contracts and T invested in a risk-free security that has the same future payoffs as the mine:

"Up" State (Gold Price = $290): $[F \times (290 - 268.4)] + [(1.05) \times (T)] = \$3,000,000$

"Down" State (Gold Price = $240): $[F \times (240 - 268.4)] + [(1.05) \times (T)] = \$0$

Step 2: Solve for F and T simultaneously:

a. Rewrite the "down" state cash flow equation:

$$T = F \times [(-28.4) \div (-1.05)] = F \times [(28.4) \div (1.05)]$$

b. Insert the "down" state T value into the "up" state cash flow equation:

$$[F \times (21.6)] + [(1.05) \times F \times [(28.4) \div (1.05)]] = 50 \times F = 3,000,000$$

c. Solve for F:

$$F = (3,000,000) \div 50 = 60,000$$

d. Solve for T from 2(a):

$$T = (60,000) \times [(28.4) \div (1.05)] = \$1,622,857$$

(*Note:* This is the "real options" value of the mine lease cash flows, before netting out the initial reopening expense.)

Step 3: Confirm the equality of replicating portfolio and mine future cash flows:

"Up" State: $[(60,000) \times (21.6)] + (1.05)(1,622,857) = \$3,000,000$

"Down" State: $[(60,000) \times (-28.4)] \times (\$1.05)(1,622,857) = \$0$

---

greater than the $1,000,000 required to restore the facilities. Investors using traditional discounted cash flow analysis will consider the lease worthless and ignore an important asset when valuing GoldFlex. Also, recognize that increased volatility in future gold prices will have no effect on the traditional valuation estimate, while it would increase the value of the lease when using the real options methodology since greater uncertainty generally leads to higher option values.

Of course, in practice, real options are much more complex than this example. For instance, gold production typically takes place steadily during the year, so the analysis may require either a continuous-time (e.g., Black-Scholes) option valuation model or an expansion of the prior binomial tree approach to include a large number of subintervals. Note also that extraction costs and the exact amount of the gold deposits are rarely known with certainty. The problem of having uncertain extraction costs can be solved by realizing that the lease on the mine in effect becomes an *exchange option,* a problem that was first considered by Margrabe.[28] In this context, the leaseholder effectively has an option to exchange the gold in the mine for the extraction costs (e.g., the cost of the required equipment, material and manpower).[29]

---

[28]See William Margrabe, "The Value of an Option to Exchange One Asset for Another," *Journal of Finance* 33, no. 1 (March 1978): 177–186.

[29]We would like to thank Professor Andras Marosi for his contributions to this section.

The Internet *Investments Online*

Otherwise straightforward financial instruments (e.g., bonds) can become quite complex when they have swap agreements attached or when they contain embedded options, such as convertible and call features or warrants. Several Web sites can help students and investors learn more about these advanced applications of derivatives:

http://www.isda.org The Web site of the International Swaps and Derivatives Association, which is the leading trade organization representing over-the-counter derivative market makers. Among other things, ISDA is committed to advancing the understanding and treatment of derivatives and risk management from public policy and regulatory capital perspectives. Their Web site contains a wealth of information about the nature and use of swap contracts.

http://www.numa.com This is the Web site of Numa Financial Systems. It provides access to a substantial amount of educational and strategic information concerning derivative securities. Of particular note is the availability of financial calculators for computing the value of options, multiple options, warrants, and convertible bonds.

http://www.goldmansachs.com/qs A page on the Goldman Sachs Web site that features research papers on quantitative strategies by Goldman analysts, many of which involve derivative applications.

http://www.calamos.com Calamos Investments specializes in research, investment, and management of convertible securities. This site features descriptions of convertibles, including their characteristics and uses, and their benefits to issuers and investors. A chart shows the relative performance of convertibles compared to a variety of other bonds. In addition, news, analysis, and market updates are available here, as are several good FAQs (frequently asked questions) about convertibles and their place in the portfolio.

http://www.dir.co.jp/InfoManage/datarsc.html The site of the Daiwa Warrant Index includes data and information on how the index is constructed.

http://www.optionscentral.com The Options Clearing Corporation is the issuer and guarantor of all exchange-traded options contracts in the United States. Its home page allows users to download free software and videos. If features a "Strategy of the Month" for options trading and has a number of resource links to exchanges that trade options.

http://www.amex.com/structuredeq A link on the Web site of the American Stock Exchange, which contains details of several structured products, such as the MITTS equity-index-linked notes.

Summary

- The genius of modern financial markets is that they continuously provide new products and strategies to meet the constantly changing needs of anyone willing to pay the required price. In this chapter, we explore several ways in which derivatives can aid in that development process. In particular, we see that innovation sometimes takes the form of creating a new set of instruments, such as interest rate and currency swaps, while at other times it involves packaging existing securities in a creative way. Structured notes, which combine bonds with a derivative position based on a different sort of underlying asset, are a good example of this latter approach. It is important to keep in mind that the ultimate purpose of this financial engineering is to help borrowers and lenders manage one of four types of potential exposures: interest rate, currency, equity, or commodity price risk.

- We began our discussion with an examination of the market for OTC interest rate agreements. Although forward rate agreements are the most basic product in this category, interest rate swaps are the most popular. Swap contracts can be interpreted in three unique ways: as a series of FRAs, as a portfolio of bond positions, or as a zero-cost collar, which consists of a pair of cap and floor agreements. We then extended the "plain vanilla" swap concept to include contracts designed to handle other exposures, such as currency and equity swaps. Since all of these agreements are traded off of the organized exchanges, they are extremely flexible in the terms available—the primary appeal to investors and issuers.

- We conclude with an analysis of several ways in which derivatives can be embedded into other securities to create customized payoff distributions. Because these hybrid structures often are designed to the specific needs of a particular investor, the investor must "pay up" for the customization. Warrants, which are call options on common stock issued directly by the company itself, can be attached to a debt issue to offer investors the upside potential of equity with the safety of a bond. Further, bonds and preferred stock issues can be set up to allow for conversion into common stock at the investor's option. In both cases, the issuing firm will likely end up with a lower front-end funding cost because of the options it has implicitly sold. Finally, a class of instruments known as structured notes carries this concept even further by embedding into bonds derivatives that often are based on exposures that may not appear on the issuer's balance sheet. These instruments epitomize how much value derivatives can add when they are used properly, and are indicative of the ways in which investors are likely to see them appear in the market for years to come. Finally, we discuss how the option features embedded in physical assets (i.e., real options) can be used by investors to value companies.

Questions

1. *CFA Examination Level III*

    Several Investment Committee members for the pension fund you work for have asked about interest rate swap agreements and how they are used in the management of domestic fixed-income portfolios.

    a. Define an interest rate swap and briefly describe the obligation of each party involved.

    b. Cite and explain two examples of how interest rate swaps could be used by a fixed-income portfolio manager to control risk or improve return.

2. Explain how an interest rate swap can be viewed as either a series of forward rate agreements, a pair of bond transactions, or a pair of option agreements. To make your description more precise, take the point of view of the fixed-rate receiver in the swap.

3. "When the yield curve is upward sloping, the fixed rate on a multiyear swap must be higher than the current level of LIBOR. With a downward-sloping yield curve, the opposite will occur." Explain what is meant by this statement and why it must be true.

4. Three years ago, you entered into a five-year interest rate swap agreement by agreeing to pay a fixed rate of 7 percent in exchange for six-month LIBOR. If your counterparty were to default today when the fixed rate on a new two-year swap is 6.5 percent, would you experience an economic loss? Explain.

5. If the fixed rate on a five-year, plain vanilla swap is currently 8 percent, what would happen if you (a) bought a five-year cap agreement with an exercise rate of 7 percent and (b) sold a five-year, 7 percent floor agreement? Use the concept of cap-floor-swap parity to describe the kind of position you have created and discuss whether or not a front-end cash payment would be necessary and whether you or your counterparty would receive it.

6. *CFA Examination Level III*

    The manager of Bontemps International (BI) defined-benefit pension plan's fixed-income portfolio has shown exceptional security selection skills and has produced returns consistently above those on BI's fixed-income benchmark portfolio. The Board wants to allocate more money to this manager to enhance further the fund's alpha. This action would increase the proportion allocated to fixed income and decrease the proportion in equities. However, the Board wants to keep the present fixed-income/equity proportions unchanged.

    a. Identify two distinct strategies using derivative financial instruments that the Board could use to increase the fund's allocation to the fixed-income manager without changing the present fixed-income/equity proportions. Briefly explain how each of these two strategies would work. (Note: Make sure that equity swaps are one of the two strategies that you choose.)

    b. Briefly discuss one advantage and one disadvantage of each of the strategies you identified in Part a. Present your discussion in terms of the effect(s) of these advantages and disadvantages on the portfolio's

        (1) risk characteristics and

        (2) return characteristics.

7. *CFA Examination Level III*

The Board of Bontemps International (BI) will substantially increase the company's defined-benefit pension fund's allocation to international equities in the future. However, the Board wants to retain the ability to reduce temporarily this exposure without making the necessary transactions in the cash markets. You develop a way to meet the Board's condition:

"BI enters into a swap arrangement with Bank A for a given notional amount and agrees to pay the EAFE (Europe, Australia, and Far East) Index return (in U.S. dollars) in exchange for receiving the LIBOR interest rate plus 0.2 percent (20 basis points).

On the same notional amount, BI arranges another swap with Bank B under which BI receives the return on the S&P 500 Index (in U.S. dollars) in exchange for paying the interest rate on the U.S. Treasury bill plus 0.1 percent (10 basis points).

Both swaps would be for a one-year term."

From BI's perspective, identify and briefly describe
(a) the major risk that this transaction would eliminate,
(b) the major risk that this transaction would not eliminate (i.e., retain), and
(c) three risks that this transaction would create.

8. *CFA Examination Level III*

A pension plan is currently underfunded by about $400 million. This situation will be resolved soon when the plan sponsor issues a $400 million private placement two-year floater bond that will be placed into the plan under a stipulation that it will be held to maturity. This bond will carry an interest rate of 50 basis points (or 0.5 percent) above the rate of U.S. Treasury bills.

The actual, as well as desired, asset allocation is 50 percent bonds and 50 percent domestic equities. When the bond is added, the portfolio will become significantly overweighted in fixed-income instruments. In addition, the overall duration will be decreased for the next two years. When the bond matures, the proceeds can be used to buy equities and liquid bonds with longer maturities. One Board member has suggested that futures or swaps could be used to keep the portfolio allocation in line with the desired asset allocation during the two-year period before the floater's maturity.

a. Describe the transactions needed to restore the desired 50 percent/50 percent portfolio allocation using each of the following two derivative instruments: (1) futures, and (2) swaps.

b. Discuss one advantage and one disadvantage of using futures instead of swaps to implement this strategy.

9. We have seen that equity warrants are not as valuable as an otherwise identical call option on the stock of the same company. Explain why this must be the case. Also, what is the incentive for a firm to issue a warrant rather than issuing stock directly?

10. Bonds and preferred stock that are convertible into common stock are said to provide investors with both upside potential and downside protection. Explain how one security can possess both attributes. What implications do these features have for the way a convertible security is priced?

11. *CFA Examination Level II*

Martin Bowman is preparing a report distinguishing traditional debt securities from structured note securities.

a. Discuss how the following structured note securities differ from a traditional debt security with respect to coupon and principal payments:
  (1) Equity-index-linked notes
  (2) Commodity-linked bear bond

Bowman is also analyzing a dual currency bond (USD/CHF) as a possible addition to his bond portfolio. Bowman is a USD-based investor and believes the CHF will appreciate against the USD over the life of the bond.

b. (1) Describe the principal and coupon components of a dual currency bond.
  (2) State one reason why a dual currency bond might trade at a premium over an otherwise identical single currency bond.
  (3) Discuss whether there is an impact on a dual currency bond's interest payments and principal payments if the CHF appreciates against the USD over the life of the bond.

Problems

1. With the interest rate swap quotations shown in Exhibit 24.4, calculate the swap cash flows from the point of view of the fixed-rate receiver on a two-year swap with a notional principal of $22.5 million. You may assume the relevant part of the settlement date pattern and the realized LIBOR path shown in Exhibit 24.6 for the three-year agreement. Also, calculate the fixed-rate payment on a 30/360 day count and the floating-rate payments on an actual/360 day basis.

2. Suppose that on February 19, 2002, the treasurer for Company W wishes to restructure the coupon payments of one of her outstanding debt issues. The bond in question is scheduled to pay semiannual interest on February 19 and August 19 each year until February 19, 2007, and has a coupon rate of 5.50 percent with a face value of $35 million. On the same day, the treasurer for Company X wants to restructure the interest payments on his $50 million, four-year floating-rate note having its coupon reset each February 19 and August 19 to a reference rate of LIBOR flat. The maturity of this floating-rate bond is February 19, 2006.

   a. Using the plain vanilla interest rate swap quotes in Exhibit 24.4, describe how both treasurers, working with a dealer, can use a swap agreement to alter synthetically their current cash flow obligations. Specifically, assume that Company W wishes to wind up with floating-rate exposure while Company X desires fixed-rate debt.

   b. Assuming that the dealer negotiates these swap transactions simultaneously, will they represent a matched book? If not, describe two remaining sources of market exposure that the dealer still faces.

3. The treasurer of a British brewery is planning to enter a plain vanilla, three-year, quarterly settlement interest rate swap to pay a fixed rate of 8 percent and to receive three-month sterling LIBOR. But first he decides to check various cap-floor combinations to see if any might be preferable. A market maker in British pound sterling OTC options presents the treasurer with the following price list for three-year, quarterly settlement caps and floors:

	INTEREST RATE CAPS		INTEREST RATE FLOORS	
Strike Rate	Buy	Sell	Buy	Sell
7%	582 BP	597 BP	320 BP	335 BP
8	398	413	401	416
9	205	220	502	517

The prices are in basis points, which when multiplied by the notional principal give the actual purchase or sale price in pounds sterling. These quotes are from the perspective of the market maker, not the firm. That is, the treasurer could buy a 9 percent cap from the market maker for 220 BP, or sell one for 205 BP. The strike rates are quoted on a 365-day basis, as is sterling LIBOR.

   In financial analysis of this sort, the treasurer assumes that the three-year cost of funds on fully amortizing debt would be about 8.20 percent (for quarterly payments). Should another structure be considered in lieu of the plain vanilla swap?

4. Corporation XYZ seeks USD 100 million, five-year fixed-rate funding. The firm is confident that it can issue a 6 1/2 percent coupon bond (semiannual payments) at par value. Since the five-year, on-the-run U.S. Treasury issue yields 6.00 percent, this funding could be attained at 50 basis points over Treasuries—a reasonable spread given XYZ's strong credit rating. The corporate treasurer would like to explore the possibility of issuing a floating-rate note (FRN), possibly a structured note, and use the interest rate swap market to create synthetic fixed-rate funding.

   As the bank relationship officer working with the treasurer, you check with your Capital Markets Group to determine that in the current market the following FRNs could be launched for XYZ at par value:

Type	Reset Formula	LIBOR = 5.75%: Initial Coupon
"Straight floater"	LIBOR + 0.10%	5.85%
"Bull floater"	12.75% − LIBOR	7.00
"Bear floater"	(2 × LIBOR) − 6.40%	5.10

The FRNs are each based on six-month USD LIBOR and make semiannual coupon payments in arrears. Assume that the flotation costs for the fixed-rate bond and various FRNs are the same (and can therefore be ignored in the comparison). Also, assume that all rates are quoted on a semiannual bond basis so that no day-count conversions need be made.

You also check with the Derivatives Group to ascertain the rates at which XYZ could execute five-year, semiannual settlement plain vanilla swaps:

Bank's Bid	Bank's Offer
TSY + 34 BP	TSY + 38 BP
where TSY = 6.00%	

a. What specific swap transactions are needed to transform each of the FRNs into a *synthetic fixed rate?*

b. What synthetic fixed rate can be attained by each of the structures? For which possible levels of LIBOR is a fixed-rate attained?

c. What other derivative instrument(s) would be needed to obtain a truly fixed rate?

d. Which structure would you recommend for XYZ?

e. What types of investors might be interested in acquiring a bear floater? If an investor's motive was to hedge exposure to LIBOR, what might its balance sheet look like?

5. As a swap dealer, you have just been contacted by a prospective corporate counterparty who wishes to do a three-year "fixed/fixed" yen/sterling currency swap. In particular, the corporation needs to pay a fixed interest rate in Japanese yen and to receive a fixed rate in British pound sterling. Your current spot FX and three-year currency swap quotes (versus six-month U.S. dollar LIBOR) are as follows:

		Japanese Yen	British Pound Sterling
Spot exchange rate		JPY 127.47/USD	USD 1.82/GBP
Currency swap:	Bid	4.85%	9.83%
	Offer	4.92	9.93

These quotes imply that you would be willing to pay 4.85 percent in yen to receive U.S. dollar LIBOR, but you would need to receive 4.92 percent in yen when paying LIBOR. Your bid-offer spread is seven basis points in yen. Note that the bid-offer spread is higher in sterling because each basis point is not worth as much (since sterling would be at a forward discount to yen).

a. Describe the sequence of transactions necessary to construct this swap from the counterparty's perspective, including your quotes for both of the fixed rates.

b. Construct a chart similar to Exhibit 24.11 summarizing the cash flow exchanges on each exchange date, again adopting the end user's viewpoint. In this analysis, assume that the deal is to be scaled to a transaction size of USD 25 million and that the number of days in the settlement payments alternates between 182 and 183, starting with 183 days between the origination date and the first settlement date.

6. *CFA Examination Level II*

Ashton Bishop is debt manager for World Telephone, which needs Euro 3.33 billion of financing for its operations. Bishop is considering the choice between issuance of debt denominated in

- Euros (EUR), or
- U.S. dollars (USD), accompanied by a combined interest rate and currency swap.

a. Explain one risk World Telephone would assume by entering into the combined interest rate and currency swap.

Bishop believes that issuing the U.S. dollar debt and entering into the swap can lower World's cost of debt by 45 basis points. Immediately after selling the debt issue, World would swap the U.S. dollar payments for Euro payments throughout the maturity of the debt. She assumes a constant currency exchange rate throughout the tenor of the swap.

The following charts give the details for the two alternative debt issues and current information about spot currency exchange rates and the three-year tenor EUR/USD currency and interest rate swap.

WORLD TELEPHONE DEBT DETAILS

Characteristic	Euro Currency Debt	U.S. Dollar Currency Debt
Par value	EUR 3.33 billion	USD 3 billion
Term to maturity	3 years	3 years
Fixed interest rate	6.25%	7.75%
Interest payment	Annual	Annual

CURRENCY EXCHANGE RATE AND SWAP INFORMATION

Spot currency exchange rate	USD0.90 per EUR (USD0.90/EUR 1.00)
3-year tenor EUR/USD fixed interest rates	5.80% EUR/7.30% USD

b. Show the notional principal and interest payment cash flows of the combined interest rate and currency swap. Note: Your response should show both the correct currency (USD or EUR) and amount for *each* cash flow.

c. State whether or not World would reduce its borrowing cost by issuing the debt denominated in U.S. dollars, accompanied by the combined interest rate and currency swap. Justify your response with *one* reason.

7. On December 2, the manager of a tactical asset allocation fund that is currently invested entirely in floating-rate debt securities decides to shift a portion of her portfolio to equities. To effect this change, she has chosen to enter into the "receive equity index" side of a one-year equity swap based on movements in the S&P 500 index plus a spread of 10 basis points. The swap is to have quarterly settlement payments with the floating-rate side of the agreement pegged to three-month LIBOR denominated in U.S. dollars. At the origination of the swap, the value of the S&P 500 index was 463.11 and three-month LIBOR was 3.50 percent. The notional principal of the swap is set for the life of the agreement at $50 million, which matches the amount of debt holdings in the fund that she would like to convert to equity.

a. Calculate the net cash receipt or payment—from the fund manager's perspective—on each future settlement date, assuming the value for the S&P 500 index (with all dividends reinvested) and LIBOR are as follows:

Settlement Date	Number of Days	S&P Level	LIBOR Level
December 2 (initial year)	—	463.11	3.50%
March 2 (following year)	90	477.51	3.25
June 2	92	464.74	3.75
September 2	92	480.86	4.00
December 2	91	482.59	—

b. Explain why the fund manager might want the notional principal on this swap to vary over time and what the most logical pattern for this variation would be.

8. *CFA Examination Level III*

On June 30, 1996, Help for Students (HFS) Foundation owns $10 million (face amount) of 6 percent coupon SteelCo. bonds, currently priced at par, which it must hold to maturity on June 30, 1998, two years from now. John Ames, HFS's fixed-income manager, expects that the yield curve, now normal in shape (i.e., positively sloped), will undergo an upward shift and invert sometime prior to maturity. He wishes to enter into a swap on the $10 million notional amount of the holding to take advantage of this yield curve forecast. Assume that HFS's policy permits such action.

Selected June 30, 1996, Market Data		
	Price	Yield
September 1996 Eurodollar future	94.9	5.1%
2-year swap fixed rate	n/a	5.5

a. Identify and explain an interest rate swap arrangement that could achieve Ames's goal in this particular instance. Base your response on the preceding data and assume quarterly cash flows.

b. Describe the direction and calculate the amount of the first quarterly cash flow (on September 30, 1996) under this arrangement. (*Note: Assume that 90-day spot LIBOR on June 30, 1996, equals the September 1996 Eurodollar futures contract settlement yield.*)

c. Explain the effect of the interest rate swap created in Part a on the sensitivity of HFS's portfolio value to interest rate changes.

d. Describe the role of the Eurodollar forward rate curve in pricing the fixed-rate payment side of the interest rate swap created in Part a.

e. Identify a strategy that would use options to replicate the position of a fixed-rate payer in a swap and explain how this strategy would accomplish its purposes. (Assume no transaction costs.)

9. A Spanish pension fund is considering buying a five-year floating-rate note named "El Oso Grande." El Oso Grande would have a coupon reset formula of three times six-month (Spanish peseta) LIBOR minus 24 percent, subject to a minimum coupon rate of 0 percent if peseta LIBOR were to fall below 8 percent. Currently, six-month peseta LIBOR is 11.20 percent, so the initial coupon would be based on a rate of 9.60 percent. The five-year, semiannual payment, 100 million peseta floating-rate note can be bought at par value. The pension fund intends to use derivative instruments to convert El Oso Grande into a synthetic fixed-rate asset. Quotes for five-year, semiannual settlement interest rate swaps, caps, and floors on six-month Spanish peseta LIBOR are obtained from a Madrid commercial bank specializing in derivative products.

Interest Rate Swaps: The pension fund can pay a fixed rate of 13.50 percent and receive six-month peseta LIBOR, or the fund can receive a fixed rate of 13.35 percent and pay six-month peseta LIBOR.

Interest Rate Caps:

Strike Rate	The Fund Buys the Cap	The Fund Writes the Cap
24%	125 BP	90 BP

Interest Rate Floors:

Strike Rate	The Fund Buys the Floor	The Fund Writes the Floor
8%	175 BP	140 BP

(Recall that the premiums on the caps and floors are quoted as a percentage of the notional principal.)

a. Indicate the specific combination of transactions that provides a synthetic fixed-rate asset to the pension fund.

b. Calculate the "all-in," fixed rate of return. Assume that Spanish peseta LIBOR, the coupon rate on El Oso Grande, the swap fixed rate, and the strike rate on the caps and floors are all stated on a semiannual bond basis.

10. You are considering the purchase of a convertible bond issued by Bildon Enterprises, a non-investment-grade medical service firm. The issue has seven years to maturity and pays a semiannual coupon rate of 7.625 percent (i.e., 3.8125 percent per period). The issue is callable by the company at par and can be converted into 48.852 shares of Bildon common stock. The bond currently sells for $965 (relative to par value of $1,000), and Bildon stock trades at $12.125 a share.

a. Calculate the current conversion value for the bond. Is the conversion option embedded in this bond in the money or out of the money? Explain.

b. Calculate the conversion parity price for Bildon stock that would make conversion of the bond profitable.

c. Bildon does not currently pay its shareholders a dividend, having suspended these distributions six months ago. What is the payback (i.e., break-even time) for this convertible security and how should it be interpreted?

d. Calculate the convertible's current yield to maturity. If a "straight" Bildon fixed-income issue with the same cash flows would yield 9.25 percent, calculate the net value of the combined options (i.e., the issuer's call and the investor's conversion) embedded in the bond.

11. *CFA Examination Level II*

Rajiv Singh, a bond analyst, is analyzing a convertible bond. The characteristics of the bond and the underlying common stock follow.

CONVERTIBLE BOND AND UNDERLYING STOCK CHARACTERISTICS	
Convertible Bond Characteristics	
Par Value	$1,000
Annual coupon rate (annual pay)	6.5%
Conversion ratio	22
Market price	105% of par value
Straight value	99% of par value
Underlying Stock Characteristics	
Current market price	$40 per share
Annual cash dividend	$1.20 per share

a. Compute the bond's

(1) Conversion value

(2) Market conversion price

(3) Premium payback period

b. Determine whether the value of a callable convertible bond will increase, decrease, or remain unchanged in response to each of the following changes, and justify each of your responses with one reason:

(1) An increase in stock price volatility

(2) An increase in interest rate volatility

12. On May 26, 1991, Svensk Exportkredit (SEK), the Swedish export credit corporation, issued a Bull Indexed Silver Opportunity Note (BISON). Consider an extended version of this BISON issue that has the following terms:

Maturity:	May 26, 1993
Coupon:	6.50%, paid annually in arrears
Face value:	USD 30 million
Purchase price:	100.125% of par value

Additionally, this BISON includes a redemption feature that, for each USD 1,000 of face value held at maturity, repays the investor's principal according to the following formula:

$$\text{USD } 1,000 + [(\text{Spot Silver Price per Ounce} - \text{USD } 4.46) \times (\text{USD } 224.21525)]$$

a. Demonstrate that, from SEK's perspective, the BISON represents a combination of a straight debt issue priced at a small premium and a derivative contract. Be explicit as to the type of derivative contract and the underlying asset on which it is based. What implicit speculative position are the investors who buy these bonds taking?

b. Calculate the yield to maturity for an investor holding USD 10,000 in face value of these BISON if the May 1993 spot price for silver is (1) USD 4.96 per ounce, or (2) USD 3.96 per ounce.

c. In May 1991 (i.e., when the BISON were used), the prevailing delivery price on a two-year silver futures contract was USD 4.35 per ounce. If SEK wanted to hedge its BISON-related exposure to silver prices with an offsetting futures position at this price, what type of position would need to be entered? Ignoring margin accounts and underwriting fees, calculate SEK's average annualized borrowing cost of funds for the resulting synthetic straight bond.

13. In July 1986, Guinness Finance B.V. placed a three-year, $100 million Eurobond issue known as *Stock Performance Exchange Linked* (SPEL) bonds. The concept of the SPEL is that the bond has its principal redemption amount tied to the level of the NYSE composite index at maturity (i.e., NY_3) by the following formula:

$$\text{Variable Redemption Amount} = \max \{100, 100 \times (1 + [(NY_3 - 166) \div 166])\}$$

Notice that the investor is guaranteed redemption at par as a minimum. The bond also pays an annual coupon of 3 percent, which is 0.5 percent below the average annual dividend yield of shares on the NYSE. At the time the SPEL was launched, the NYSE composite index stood at 134.

a. Demonstrate that the SPEL is a combination of a regular debt issue and an equity option by analyzing the pattern of annual cash flows generated by the issue. In your work, assume a par value of 100.

b. The SPEL bonds were issued at a price of 100.625. Assuming that Guinness would ordinarily have to pay a borrowing cost of 7.65 percent on a three-year "straight" bond (i.e., one with no attached options), calculate the implicit dollar price of the equity index option embedded in this issue. How much of this amount represents intrinsic value and how much is time premium?

14. A firm has 100,000 shares of stock outstanding priced at $35 per share. The firm has no debt and does not pay a dividend. To raise more capital, it plans to issue 10,000 warrants, each allowing for the purchase of one share of stock at a price of $50. The warrants are European-style and expire in five years. The standard deviation of the firm's common stock is 34 percent and the continuously compounded, five-year risk-free rate is 5.2 percent.

a. Estimate the fair value of the warrants, first using the relevant information to calculate the Black-Scholes value of an analogous call option.

b. Determine the stock price at expiration, assuming the warrants are exercised if the value of the firm is at least $5,200,000.

c. Using the information in Parts a and b about initial and terminal warrant and stock prices, discuss the relative merits of these two ways of making an equity investment in the firm.

15. You are an investor trying to value a gold mining company's lease on a gold mine that is currently not operating. It would cost $1,000,000 for the company to reopen the mine, and it is expected to produce 100,000 ounces of gold at the end of next year. The forward contract price on a one-year gold forward contract is $268.40/ounce and the current one-year risk-free rate is 5 percent. Extraction costs are estimated to be $260/ounce.

   a. Assuming the per-ounce gold price in the spot market one year from now is forecasted to be either $300 or $230, calculate (1) the composition of a portfolio of T-bills and gold forward contracts that would replicate the cash flows from the mine and (2) the "real options" value of the mine lease.

   b. Assuming the per-ounce gold price in the spot market one year from now is forecasted to be either $280 or $250, calculate (1) the composition of a portfolio of T-bills and gold forward contracts that would replicate the cash flows from the mine, and (2) the "real options" value of the mine lease.

   c. What do your answers in Parts a and b tell you about the effect that the volatility of future gold prices has on the current value of the mine lease?

References

Beidleman, Carl R., ed. *Interest Rate Swaps.* Homewood, Ill.: Business One–Irwin, 1991.

Bicksler, James, and Andrew H. Chen. "An Economic Analysis of Interest Rate Swaps." *Journal of Finance* 41, no. 3 (July 1986).

Braham, Lewis. "MITTS: Stock Plays for Chickens." *Business Week On-Line,* 9 April 2001.

Buetow, Gerald W. Jr., and Frank J. Fabozzi. *Valuation of Interest Rate Swaps and Swaptions.* New York: John Wiley, 2000.

Chance, Don M., and Pamela P. Peterson. *Real Options and Investment Valuation.* Charlottesville, VA: Research Foundation of AIMR, 2002.

Constantinides, George M. "Warrant Exercise and Bond Conversion in Competitive Markets." *Journal of Financial Economics* 13, no. 3 (September 1984).

Dattatreya, Ravi E., Raj E. S. Venkatesh, and Vijaya Venkatesh. *Interest Rate and Currency Swaps.* Chicago, Ill.: Probus Publishing, 1994.

Duffie, Darrell, and Kenneth J. Singleton. "An Econometric Model of the Term Structure of Interest-Rate Swap Yields." *Journal of Finance* 52, no. 4 (September 1997): 1287–1321.

Eckl, S., J. N. Robinson, and D. C. Thomas. *Financial Engineering: A Handbook of Derivative Products.* Cambridge, Mass.: Basil Blackwell, 1991.

Finnerty, John D. "An Overview of Corporate Securities Innovation." *Journal of Applied Corporate Finance* 4, no. 4 (Winter 1992).

Ingersoll, Jonathan E., Jr. "A Contingent Claims Valuation of Convertible Securities." *Journal of Financial Economics* 4, no. 3 (May 1977).

Litzenberger, Robert H. "Swaps: Plain and Fanciful." *Journal of Finance* 47, no. 3 (July 1992).

Trigeorgis, Lenos. *Real Options.* Cambridge, Mass.: MIT Press, 1996.

Wall, Larry D., and John J. Pringle. "Alternative Explanations of Interest Rate Swaps: A Theoretical and Empirical Analysis." *Financial Management* 18, no. 2 (Summer 1989).

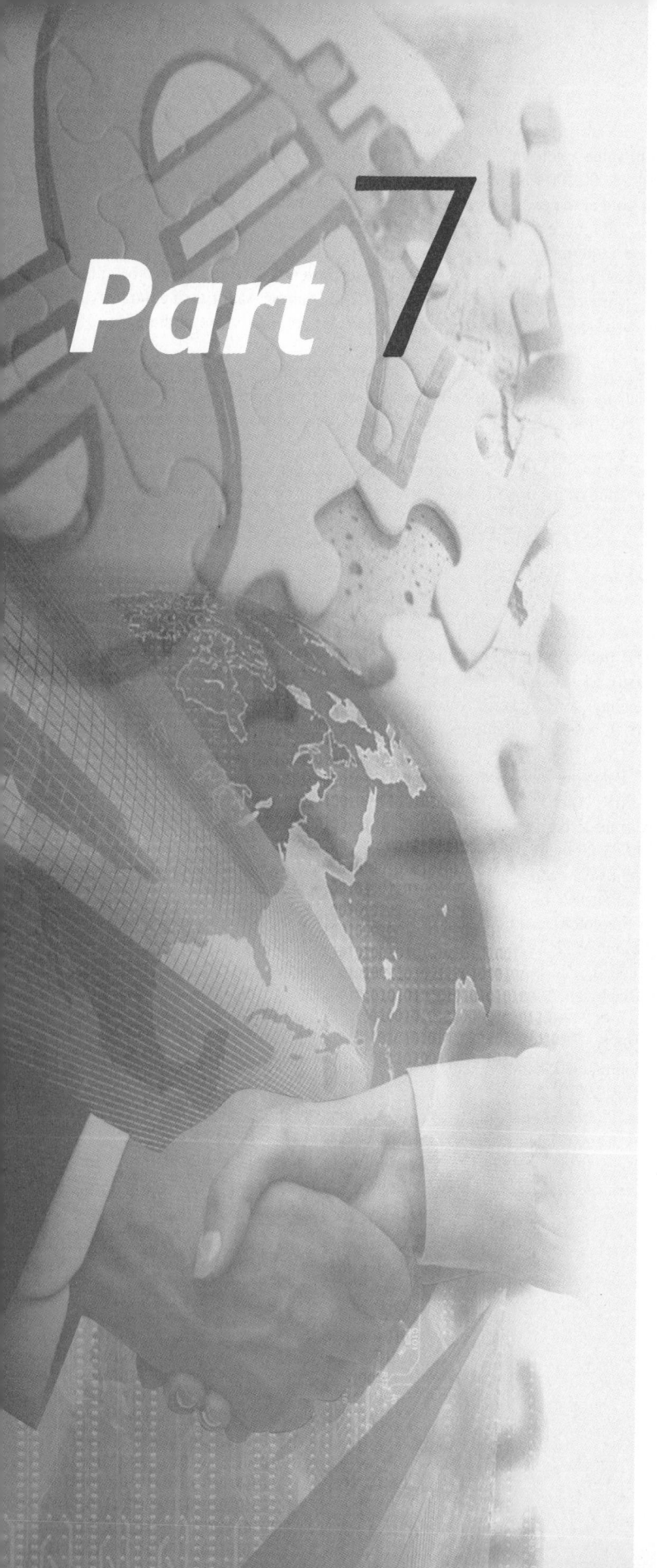

Part 7

Specification and Evaluation of Asset Management

This final section of the book contains two chapters: the first deals with professional asset management, and the second is concerned with the evaluation of portfolio performance. The asset management chapter is mainly of concern to individual investors, while both individual and institutional investors need to be aware of how one evaluates the performance of a portfolio.

Because many investors employ professional asset managers to manage their assets, Chapter 25 is an important wrap-up to their asset allocation and portfolio construction process. After a broad overview of the different ways that professional asset management firms can be organized, the chapter describes how the asset management industry has changed over time and how professional managers are compensated for their expertise. Particular emphasis is paid to the role of *investment companies* (also more commonly called *mutual funds*), which manage the majority of assets held by individual investors. The discussion includes a description of the major forms of investment companies and the general types of funds available, such as money market, growth, aggressive growth, income, balanced, and bond funds. It is argued that almost any investment objective can be met by investing in one or several investment companies.

There is also a discussion of ethical and regulatory issues that arise when hiring a professional asset manager. Two issues that are of special concern are designing compensation contracts to provide managers with the proper incentives to act in the investor's best interest and the proper use of trading commission fees. The chapter ends with an extensive analysis of the data sources available to investors about investment companies and the performance of these professional managers over time. The results of the research into fund performance indicate that, on average, investment companies have not been able to consistently outperform the aggregate market, although there is some recent evidence of performance persistence. However, it is noted that, even with the average performance shortfall, investment companies are capable of fulfilling a number of functions that are important to investors.

We conclude the book with a chapter dealing with the evaluation of portfolio performance. Perhaps the most important concept to understand from this discussion is that any meaningful evaluation of an investment manager's performance must consider both the return and the riskiness of the portfolio. Thus, after a discussion of what is required of a portfolio manager, we review in detail the major *risk-adjusted* portfolio performance models, including a recent performance attribution model that, in turn, is capable of evaluating a global portfolio that necessarily includes the effect of currency allocation. We also consider how the alternative models relate to each other. This is followed by a demonstration of their use with a sample of mutual funds.

As always, it is important to understand potential problems with a technique or models. Therefore, we consider potential problems with the performance measures including a review of Roll's benchmark problem and its effect on these performance models. It is demonstrated that this benchmark problem has become more significant with the growth of global investing. Also, because the factors that determine success in bonds differ from what is important in equities, we review and evaluate several alternative models used to evaluate the performance of bond portfolio managers. Chapter 26 ends with a consideration of how investment performance results should be presented so as to be consistent with industry practice.

chapter 25 Professional Asset Management

After you read this chapter, you should be able to answer the following questions:

➤ What are the different ways that professional asset management firms can be organized?
➤ How has the structure of the asset management industry changed over time?
➤ How are managers at investment advisory firms compensated?
➤ Who manages the investment company portfolio and how are its managers compensated?
➤ How do you compute the net asset value (NAV) for investment companies?
➤ What is the difference between closed-end and open-end investment companies?
➤ What is the difference between the NAV and the market price for a closed-end fund?
➤ What are load fees, 12b-1 fees, and management fees and how do they influence investment company performance?
➤ What are the two major means of fund distribution and what has been the trend for each approach?
➤ Given the breakdown of all funds by investment objectives, which groups have experienced relative growth or decline?
➤ Given a desire to have a personal portfolio manager perform certain functions for you, how do investment companies help fulfill this need?
➤ What are the ethical dilemmas involved in the professional asset management industry?
➤ What has been the risk-adjusted performance of mutual funds relative to alternative market indexes?

So far, we have discussed how to analyze the aggregate market, alternative industries, and individual companies as well as their stocks and bonds in order to build a portfolio that is consistent with your investment objectives. Part 6 centered on alternative investment vehicles, such as options, warrants, convertibles, and futures, that provide additional risk-return possibilities beyond those available from a straight stock-bond portfolio. This chapter introduces another possibility: entrusting your money to a professional portfolio manager. As we will see, using a professional money manager can entail establishing a private account with an investment advisor or purchasing shares of an established security portfolio managed by an investment company. In either form, professionally managed investments often represent a substantial portion of an individual's total holdings.

The efficient market studies we have seen indicated that few individual investors outperform the aggregate market averages. This makes using professional asset managers a potentially appealing alternative for several reasons, including the additional services they provide. For example, it is often the case that an investment company offers an investor a cost-effective way to choose among a wide variety of diversified portfolios spanning the risk-return spectrum. However, this relationship also creates potential conflicts between the goals of the investor and the goals of the manager; we will consider some ethical implications of the investor-manager contract as well.

The initial sections of this chapter explain the two ways in which asset management firms are typically organized and charge for their services. In this discussion, we will pay particular attention to investment companies, which are the most prevalent way in which individual investors employ professional investment counsel. Subsequently, we describe how investment company shares are traded in the secondary market and how these companies can be divided into classes based on investment objectives and the types of securities in their portfolios. One important classification that we will see focuses on investment companies that invest in stocks and bonds from around the world.

To choose among the approximately 8,000 investment companies available, you need to understand how to access and interpret publicly available data and then to evaluate performance. We continue our discussion with a presentation of some sources of information on investment companies that can help you make decisions of an increasingly global nature. We then conclude with a consideration of the results from some major studies of investment company performance and the implications of these findings for investors.

THE ASSET MANAGEMENT INDUSTRY: STRUCTURE AND EVOLUTION

At the most basic level, there are two ways in which professional asset management firms are organized. In arguably the most straightforward structure, individuals as well as institutional investors, such as the sponsors of pension and endowment funds, make contracts directly with a **management and advisory firm** for its services. These services can range from providing standard banking transactions (savings accounts, personal loans) to advising clients on structuring their own portfolios to actually managing the investment funds themselves. Although banking and financial advice were once the main services these firms offered, the last several decades have seen a dramatic shift toward the *assets under management* (AUM) approach. In that arrangement, the management firm becomes the custodian of the investor's capital, usually with full discretion as to how those funds are invested. An important feature of this structure is that each client of the management firm has a *separate account*. That is, even if investors select the firm because of its expertise in a particular niche—say, selecting small-capitalization growth stocks—the assets of each client will be accounted for separately regardless of whether the firm employs a single "model" portfolio. This situation is illustrated in Panel A of Exhibit 25.1.

A second general approach to asset management involves the *commingling* of investment capital from several clients. An **investment company** invests a pool of funds belonging to many individuals in a single portfolio of securities. In exchange for this commitment of capital, the investment company issues to each investor new shares representing his or her proportional ownership of the mutually held securities portfolio, which is commonly known as a *fund*. For example, suppose an investment company sells 10 million shares to the public at $10 a share, thereby raising $100 million. If the fund's purpose is to emphasize blue-chip common stocks, the manager would invest the proceeds of the fund share sale ($100 million less any brokerage fees) in the stock of such companies as AT&T, IBM, Xerox, and General Electric. Each investor who bought shares of the investment company would then own the appropriate percentage of the overall fund, rather than any portion of the shares in the portfolio themselves. Panel B of Exhibit 25.1 shows how this structure might work.

There are important differences between these two organizational forms. Private management and advisory firms typically develop a personal relationship with their clients, getting to know the specific investment objectives and constraints of each. The collection of assets held in the various separate accounts can then be tailored to these special needs, even if a general

EXHIBIT 25.1   *OPERATING STRUCTURES OF ASSET MANAGEMENT COMPANIES*

A. Private Management Firms

B. Investment (Fund) Companies

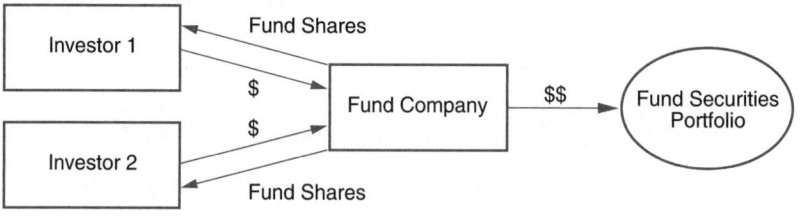

"blueprint" portfolio is used for all clients. Of course, special attention comes at a cost, and for this reason private management firms are used mainly by investors with substantial levels of capital, such as pension fund sponsors and high net worth individuals. Conversely, a mutual fund offered by an investment company is formed as a general solution to an investment problem and then marketed to investors who might fit that profile. Not surprisingly, the primary clients who seek professional asset management through investment companies are individual investors with relatively small pools of capital. In fact, the Investment Company Institute (a nonprofit industry trade association) reported that in 2000 about 80 percent of mutual fund shares were held by households with only 10 percent being held by business organizations.[1]

It is not unusual for professional asset management firms to combine these two structures by offering private advisory services as well as publicly traded funds. For instance, consider T. Rowe Price Associates, a multi-asset, independent advisory firm located in Baltimore, Maryland. Founded in 1937, T. Rowe Price has seen its business grow to the point where it managed over $156 billion by the end of 2001, compared with less than $54 billion AUM just seven years earlier. The majority of this capital is invested in the firm's various public mutual fund portfolios, but T. Rowe Price also has several hundred private clients, including corporate retirement funds, public funds and unions, foundations and endowments, and individual investors.[2]

The AUM growth that T. Rowe Price has experienced during the past few years has been typical for the entire industry. Exhibit 25.2 charts the top 50 asset management companies as of the end of 1994 and 2001. A striking feature of these lists is the rapid increase in the number of large asset management firms, defined as those organizations with AUM of more than $100 billion. In 1994, there were only 10 such firms; by 2001, there were 48. Much of this asset growth can be explained by the strong performance of the U.S. equity market during this period, but another

---

[1]See Chapter 4 of *2001 Mutual Fund Fact Book* (Washington, D.C.: Investment Company Institute).

[2]This, and much more, information is available from T. Rowe Price's public home page at http://www.troweprice.com.

EXHIBIT 25.2 ▶ *ASSETS UNDER MANAGEMENT (AUM) FOR LEADING FIRMS*

	DECEMBER 31, 2001		DECEMBER 31, 1994	
RANK	FIRM	AUM ($MM)	FIRM	AUM ($MM)
1	Fidelity Investments	$883,400	Fidelity Management & Research	$314,543
2	State Street Global Advisors	785,421	Bankers Trust Company	186,797
3	Barclays Global Investors	769,219	Merrill Lynch Asset Management Group	163,822
4	JPMorgan Fleming Management	598,760	Capital Group	162,634
5	The Vanguard Group	557,834	Wells Fargo/BMZ	158,392
6	Fleming Asset Management	537,170	State Street Global Advisors	140,413
7	Merrill Lynch Investment Managers	528,701	Alliance Capital Management	121,290
8	Deutsche Asset Management	512,440	Franklin/Templeton Group	114,100
9	Metropolitan Life Insurance Co.	423,200	J.P. Morgan Investment Management	111,983
10	AllianceBernstein Institutional Investment Mgmt.	421,402	American Express Financial/IDS	102,128
11	Citigroup Asset Management	416,881	Putnam Investments	95,182
12	**Brinson Partners/UBS**	**405,079**	INVESCO	94,066
13	Morgan Stanley Investment Management Inc.	403,102	Scudder Stevens & Clark	91,253
14	Capital Research & Management Company	367,055	The Northern Trust Company	82,353
15	Zurich Scudder Investments, Inc.	345,240	Wellington Management Company	81,970
16	Putnam Investments	314,566	The Vanguard Group	81,743
17	Wellington Management Company, LLP	307,212	Citibank Global Asset Management	73,999
18	AIG Global Investment Group	303,161	Pacific Investment Management Company (PIMCO)	72,175
19	Prudential Investment Management, Inc.	287,797	Smith Barney Capital	69,114
20	Credit Suisse Asset Management, LLC	279,973	Kemper Financial Services	62,748
21	Goldman Sachs Asset Management	273,125	Dreyfus Corp.	62,055
22	American Express Retirement Services	253,297	New England Investment Cos.	56,609
23	Pacific Investment Management Co. (PIMCO)	241,289	PNC Asset Management Group	56,422
24	BlackRock	238,584	**T. Rowe Price Associates**	**53,705**
25	Chase Asset Management	213,203	Dean Witter InterCapital	51,197
26	Evergreen Investments	210,688	Federated Investors	50,743
27	Banc of America Capital Management, LLC	183,058	Van Kampen American Capital	46,699
28	Janus Capital Corporation	181,645	John Nuveen Co.	46,497
29	Federated Investors Inc.	176,237	Chase Manhattan Corp.	44,839
30	A I M Management Group Inc.	170,211	Bank of New York	42,599
31	Northern Trust Global Investment Services	162,057	TCW Group	41,981
32	**T. Rowe Price Group Inc.**	**156,340**	Sun Trust Banks	41,811
33	BNP Paribas Asset Management, Inc.	155,919	Chemical Bank Portfolio Group	41,725
34	SG Asset Management	150,922	Bank of America Investment Mgmt Services	41,328
35	Henderson Global Investors	138,701	NationsBank	40,771
36	MFS Institutional Advisors	137,238	**Union Bank of Switzerland**	**38,685**

EXHIBIT 25.2 *CONTINUED*

	DECEMBER 31, 2001		DECEMBER 31, 1994	
RANK	FIRM	AUM ($MM)	FIRM	AUM ($MM)
37	OppenheimerFunds, Inc.	126,589	GE Investments	38,230
38	John Hancock Financial Services, Inc.	123,292	Goldman Sachs Asset Management	37,400
39	U.S. Bancorp Asset Management, Inc.	121,194	**Brinson Partners**	**36,540**
40	Capital Guardian Trust Company	120,031	Boatmen's Trust Co.	36,420
41	Scottish Widows Investment Partnership	118,100	Morgan Stanley Asset Management	35,678
42	INVESCO Institutional	116,834	National Bank of Detroit	35,590
43	Franklin/FTI Institutional	114,389	Mitchell Hutchins Asset Management	34,394
44	General Motors Asset Management	111,000	Harris Bankcorp.	33,827
45	Banc One Investment Advisors Corp.	108,740	Massachusetts Financial Services	33,432
46	Wells Capital Management	106,107	U.S. Trust Company of New York	33,032
47	Nikko Global Asset Management (U.S.A.)	103,387	Mellon Capital Management	31,910
48	GE Asset Management	100,706	Bank One Investment Corp.	31,537
49	Fleet Investment Advisors	96,572	HSBC Asset Management	30,488
50	AXA Investment Managers New York	96,000	Fiduciary Trust Co. Int'l	29,903

Source: *Nelson's Directory of Investment Managers.*

important contributing factor was the consolidation trend that marked the industry. Typical of this phenomenon was the merger of the asset management groups Union Bank of Switzerland and Brinson Partners (ranked 36 and 39 on the 1994 list, respectively) to become Brinson Partners/UBS (ranked 12 on the 2001 list). This consolidation trend is likely to continue as the competition among existing asset management firms for the flow of new investment capital is expected to increase significantly.[3]

> ## PRIVATE MANAGEMENT AND ADVISORY FIRMS

Despite the notable movement toward larger management companies that offer a broader range of services and products, the majority of private management and advisory firms are still much smaller and more narrowly focused on a particular niche of the market. To examine one fairly typical organization in greater detail, we will consider Prudent Capital Management (PCM),[4] a growth-oriented equity and fixed-income manager located in Southern California. PCM utilizes a "bottom-up" security selection process with its portfolio managers looking for companies that have exceptional profitability, market share, return on equity, and earnings growth. PCM's

---

[3]A good economic analysis of the professional asset management business can be found in M. Hurley, S. Meers, B. Bornstein, and N. Struminghr, *The Coming Evolution of the Investment Management Industry: Opportunities and Strategies* (New York: Goldman, Sachs & Co., October 1995). See also G. Brinson, "Investment Management in the 21st Century," and B. Putnam, "Thoughts about the Asset Management Industry of the Future," both in *The Future of Investment Management* (Charlottesville, Va.: Association for Investment Management and Research, 1998).

[4]Prudent Capital Management is a pseudonym for a real firm whose name has been changed by request. However, all of the subsequent information reported is real.

EXHIBIT 25.3 ▶ *REPRESENTATIVE PRIVATE MANAGEMENT FIRM INVESTMENT PRODUCTS*

	LARGE CAP	MID CAP	SMALL CAP
Equity:	$5 million	$5 million	
	$2 million Commingled fund (Delaware Business Trust)	$5 million Commingled fund (Delaware Business Trust)	$10 million Commingled fund (closed)
	$2 million for sponsored program affiliates	$2 million for sponsored program affiliates	
Balanced:	$5 million		
	$2 million for sponsored program affiliates		
Concentrated:	$5 million		
	$2 million for sponsored program affiliates		
Tax-Sensitive Management:	$5 million Equity, balanced, fixed		
	$2 million for sponsored program affiliates Equity, balanced, fixed		
Concentrated Tax-Sensitive Management:	$5 million $2 million for sponsored program affiliates		
Active Fixed Income:	$5 million Separately managed		
	$2 million for sponsored program affiliates		

clients include both institutional investors and high net worth individuals (with between $2 million and $5 million in assets) in both separate and commingled accounts. The firm offers management of both taxed and nontaxed products. Exhibit 25.3 shows the myriad investment products that PCM offers, along with the minimum investment accepted in each.

Like the industry as a whole, PCM saw the assets under its management increase steadily over the past several years. Panel A of Exhibit 25.4 reports that between December 1994 and December 1999, the firm's AUM grew by almost 80 percent, from $11.8 billion to $21.2 billion. During the same period, the median separate account size jumped from $24.8 million to over $39 million. This account size suggests that PCM's clients tend to be institutional investors, and the client profile summarized in Panel B of Exhibit 25.4 shows this to be true. Indeed, the company offers services to more than 350 clients, but the majority of these are—and the vast majority of the assets come from—institutional investors. Perhaps because of the minimum investment restrictions, relatively few of the clients are individual investors and the assets they represent are slightly less than 3 percent (535 ÷ 21,165) of PCM's business.

Panel C of Exhibit 25.4 shows fee schedules representative of both the equity and fixed-income management services that PCM offers. Typical of the entire industry, these fees are not flat amounts but are expressed as percentages of invested capital on an annual basis. Further, they are also graduated on a declining scale so that the more capital an investor commits to the firm, the lower his or her average cost would be. For example, an individual with $15 million would

| EXHIBIT 25.4 | *REPRESENTATIVE PRIVATE MANAGEMENT FIRM: AUM, CLIENTS, AND FEES* |

A. Assets under Management

DATE	ASSETS MANAGED ($ MIL.)	NO. OF INSTITUTIONAL CLIENTS	ACCOUNT SIZE AVERAGE ($ MIL.)	ACCOUNT SIZE MEDIAN ($ MIL.)
12/99	21,165.0	207	97.5	39.3
12/98	18,441.0	206	85.1	34.9
12/97	17,608.0	226	74.2	30.6
12/96	17,808.0	233	72.3	30.4
12/95	14,578.0	237	61.5	27.8
12/94	11,833.0	230	51.4	24.8

B. Clients

	NO. OF CLIENTS	ASSETS ($ MIL.)
Corp. retirement funds	126	7,937.0
Public funds	35	3,881.0
Unions (Taft-Hartley)	18	1,442.0
Found., endow., assns.	66	1,656.0
Commingled funds	4	1,682.0
General insurance accounts	NA	NA
Limited partnership	NA	NA
Mutual funds	18	3,411.0
Individuals: IRAs & other	75	535.0
Other	5	186.0
Taxable corporate	17	435.0

C. Fee Schedule

LARGE-CAP GROWTH EQUITY ACCOUNTS
- 1.00% on the first $10,000,000
- 0.75% on the next $10,000,000
- 0.50% above $20,000,000

FIXED-INCOME ACCOUNTS
- 0.375% on the first $25,000,000
- 0.30% over $25,000,000

Source: *Nelson's Directory of Investment Managers.*

pay annual fees of $137,500 (10,000,000 × 0.01 + 5,000,000 × 0.0075), or 0.92 percent of total invested capital. On the other hand, the fee paid by a pension fund with $115 million under management would be $650,000 (10,000,000 × 0.01 + 10,000,000 × 0.0075 + 95,000,000 × 0.005), or 0.57 percent. Of course, one advantage to the investor of having the fee schedule tied directly to AUM is that, as the management firm performs better for the client, its fees will increase. This reward system helps to align the incentives of the investor and the manager.

Investment Strategy at a Private Money Management Firm

The schematic representation of a private money management firm shown in Panel A of Exhibit 25.1 indicated that each client's assets were held in a separate account. It was also noted, however, that the security portfolios formed for each client are likely to be guided by the firm's overall investment philosophy. Indeed, it is this investment philosophy—along with the returns it produces—that attracts clients to a particular money manager in the first place. Exhibit 25.5

EXHIBIT 25.5 ▶ *INVESTMENT STRATEGY AT A REPRESENTATIVE PRIVATE MANAGEMENT FIRM*

A. Large-Cap Growth Equity Portfolio

Investment Approach:

"Our focused, fundamental research process is primarily based on the ideas from our in-house analysts. Our analysts operate as specialists. They direct their expertise on specific industries and sectors covering seven key growth sectors: technology/components, technology/systems, telecom, healthcare, retail, consumer, and finance.

"Our investment process seeks out companies that have at least one or more catalysts for growth. The catalysts may be identified as: new products, exploitation of demographic trends, proprietary products, gaining market share, and/or changing cost structure, in order to attain or maintain very strong earnings per share growth.

"We search for companies that have: significant management ownership, well-thought-out management goals and growth plans supported by stringent controls, and a commitment to enhancing shareholder value. We also seek out companies with a proven track record (at least three to five years) of superior revenue and earnings growth, strong pretax margins, low levels of debt, exceptional profitability, market share, high return on equity, high reinvestment rates, and attractive valuations relative to their industry and the market in general."

Largest Holdings:			
	1. Microsoft	6.	Motorola
	2. Nokia	7.	Sun Microsystems
	3. Cisco Systems	8.	EMC
	4. MCI Worldcom	9.	Amgen
	5. Lucent Technologies	10.	Solectron

Benchmark Used: Russell 1000 Growth index

B. Active Fixed Income

Investment Approach:

"We believe that superior risk-adjusted returns can be achieved by capturing changes in relative value through active yield curve management, sector rotation and prudent security selection. We follow a disciplined process designed to add incremental value over long periods of time by taking advantage of relative value opportunities without accepting excessive interest rate risk. Our process is not dependent on forecasts of future interest rates or economic events. Rather our decisions are based on current conditions, analyzed in the context of historical relationships. Our performance record has been built employing this process. We expect that in the future market conditions will offer similar opportunities. While markets will change our process will not."

Largest Holdings:		
	1.	A–Baa rated corporates (56.9%)
	2.	Treasury/agencies (33.6%)
	3.	Aaa–Aa rated corporates (9.5%)

Benchmark Used: Lehman Government/Corporate index

Source: *Nelson's Directory of Investment Managers–2000.*

reproduces the investment strategy and major holdings for two of PCM's model portfolios, one in equities and one in fixed-income securities.

The investment approach expressed in Panel A of Exhibit 25.5 makes it clear that clients choosing to invest in PCM's large-cap growth stock product will have their money invested primarily in technology companies. While the specific stock allocations might vary from one client to another, the same fundamental orientation toward stock selection will be applied to all accounts. Similarly, a client choosing to invest in PCM's core fixed-income product will end up holding a portfolio of bonds split between government and investment-grade corporate names. Finally, notice that the stated investment process at PCM requires extensive interaction between the firm's portfolio managers and security analysts. At the time in question, PCM employed 11 equity portfolio managers, 10 equity analysts, 3 equity traders, and 6 additional manager/analysts.

MANAGEMENT OF INVESTMENT COMPANIES

As noted earlier, an investment company typically is a corporation that has as its major assets the portfolio of marketable securities referred to as a fund. The management of the portfolio of securities and most of the other administrative duties are handled by a separate **investment management company** hired by the board of directors of the investment company. This legal description oversimplifies the typical arrangement. The actual management usually begins with an investment advisory firm that starts an investment company and selects a board of directors for the fund. Subsequently, this board of directors hires the investment advisory firm as the fund's portfolio manager.

The contract between the investment company (the portfolio of securities) and the investment management company indicates the duties and compensation of the management company. The major duties of the investment management company include investment research, the management of the portfolio, and administrative duties, such as issuing securities and handling redemptions and dividends. The management fee is generally stated as a percentage of the total value of the fund and typically ranges from one-quarter to one-half of 1 percent, with a sliding scale as the size of the fund increases.

To achieve economies of scale, many management companies start numerous funds with different characteristics. The variety of funds allows the management group to appeal to many investors with different risk-return preferences. In addition, it allows investors to switch among funds as economic or personal conditions change. This "family of funds" promotes flexibility and increases the total capital managed by the investment firm.

VALUING INVESTMENT COMPANY SHARES

When clients have their invested capital held in separate accounts, as is typical in a private management and advisory firm, the value of any given account can be calculated by simply totaling the market value of the securities held in the portfolio less fees. When the securities are held jointly, as they are in an investment company, the appropriate way to value a client's investment is to multiply the number of shares in the fund he or she owns by the per-share value of the entire security fund. This per-share value is known as the **net asset value (NAV)** of the investment company. It equals the total market value of all the firm's assets divided by the total number of fund shares outstanding, or

$$\text{Fund NAV} = \frac{(\text{Total Market Value of Fund Portfolio}) - (\text{Fund Expenses})}{(\text{Total Fund Shares Outstanding})}$$

Notice that the NAV for an investment company is analogous to the share price of a corporation's common stock; like common stock, the NAV of the fund shares will increase as the value of the underlying assets (the fund security portfolio) increases.

In an earlier example, we saw that an investment company with a $100 million blue-chip stock portfolio and 10 million outstanding shares would have an NAV of $10. What would happen, however, if during a holding period the value of the stock portfolio increased to $112.5 million while the fund incurred $0.1 million in trading expenses and management fees? If no new shares were sold during the period, the net value of the total investment company is $112.4 million, which leaves a net asset value for each existing fund share of $11.24 ([112,500,000 − 100,000] ÷ 10,000,000). Thus, the NAV provides an immediate reflection of the investment company's market value net of operating expenses. Also, had the investment company made any capital gain or dividend distributions to its investors, these too would be reflected in the NAV calculation because they would reduce the value of the fund portfolio. For publicly traded funds, NAVs are calculated and reported on a daily basis.

CLOSED-END VERSUS OPEN-END INVESTMENT COMPANIES

Investment companies begin like any other company—someone sells an issue of common stock to a group of investors. An investment company, however, uses the proceeds to purchase the securities of other publicly held companies rather than buildings and equipment. An open-end investment company (often referred to as a **mutual fund**) differs from a closed-end investment company (typically referred to as a *closed-end fund*) in the way each operates *after* the initial public offering.

Closed-End Investment Companies

A **closed-end investment company** operates like any other public firm. Its stock trades on the regular secondary market, and the market price of its shares is determined by supply and demand. The typical closed-end investment company offers no further shares and does not repurchase the shares on demand. Thus, if you want to buy or sell shares in a closed-end fund, you must make transactions in the public secondary market. The shares of many of these funds are listed on the NYSE. No new investment dollars are available for the investment company unless it makes another public sale of securities. Similarly, no funds can be withdrawn unless the investment company decides to repurchase its stock, which is quite unusual.

The closed-end investment company's NAV is computed twice daily based on prevailing market prices for the portfolio securities. The *market price* of the investment company shares is determined by the relative supply and demand for the investment company stock in the public secondary market. When buying or selling shares of a closed-end fund, you pay or receive this market price plus or minus a regular trading commission. You should recognize that *the NAV and the market price of a closed-end fund are almost never the same!* Over the long run, the market price of these shares has historically been from 5 to 20 percent below the NAV (i.e., closed-end funds typically sell at a discount to NAV). Exhibit 25.6 is a list of closed-end stock funds, including general equity funds; specialized equity funds; convertible securities, dual-purpose funds; and world equity funds as quoted in *Barron's.* The display also contains a listing of closed-end bond funds, including loan participation funds, high-yield bond funds, world income funds, national municipal bond funds, and single state municipal bond funds. Exhibit 25.7 breaks down the number of closed-end funds by category and AUM and indicates that a total of more than 600 such portfolios traded on U.S. exchanges by early 2002.

At the time of the quotes in Exhibit 25.6, most of the funds were selling at discounts to their NAV. This typical relationship has prompted questions from investors: Why do these funds sell at a discount? Why do the discounts differ between funds? What are the returns available to investors from funds that sell at large discounts? This final question arises because an investor who acquires a portfolio at a price below market value (i.e., below NAV) expects an above-average dividend yield. Still, the total rate of return on the fund depends on what happens to the discount during the holding period. If the discount relative to the NAV declines, the investment

EXHIBIT 25.6 ▶ *CLOSED-END FUNDS: PRICE QUOTATIONS*

CLOSED-END FUNDS

Closed-end funds sell a limited number of shares and invest in securities. Unlike open-end funds, closed-ends generally do not buy their shares back from investors who wish to sell. Instead, shares trade on a stock exchange. The following list, provided by Lipper, shows the ticker symbol and exchange where a fund trades (A: American; C: Chicago; N: NYSE; O: Nasdaq; T: Toronto; z: does not trade on an exchange). The data also include the fund's most recent net asset value (NAV), share prices and the percentage difference between the market price and the NAV (the premium or discount), unless indicated by a footnote otherwise. For equity funds, the final column provides 52-week returns based on market prices plus dividends; for bond funds, the

past 12 months' income distributions as a percentage of the market price at last month's end. Footnotes: a: the Net Asset Value and the market price are ex dividend. b: the NAV is fully diluted. c: NAV is as of Thursday's close. d: NAV as of Wednesday's close. e: NAV assumes rights offering is fully subscribed. v: NAV is converted at the commercial Rand rate. y: NAV and market price are in Canadian dollars. NA: Information is not available or not applicable. NS: Fund not in existence for whole period. ♣ Free annual or semiannual reports are available by phoning 1-800-965-2929 or faxing 1-800-747-9384. Daily closed-end listings are available in The Wall Street Journal Interactive Edition at http://wsj.com on the Internet's World Wide Web.

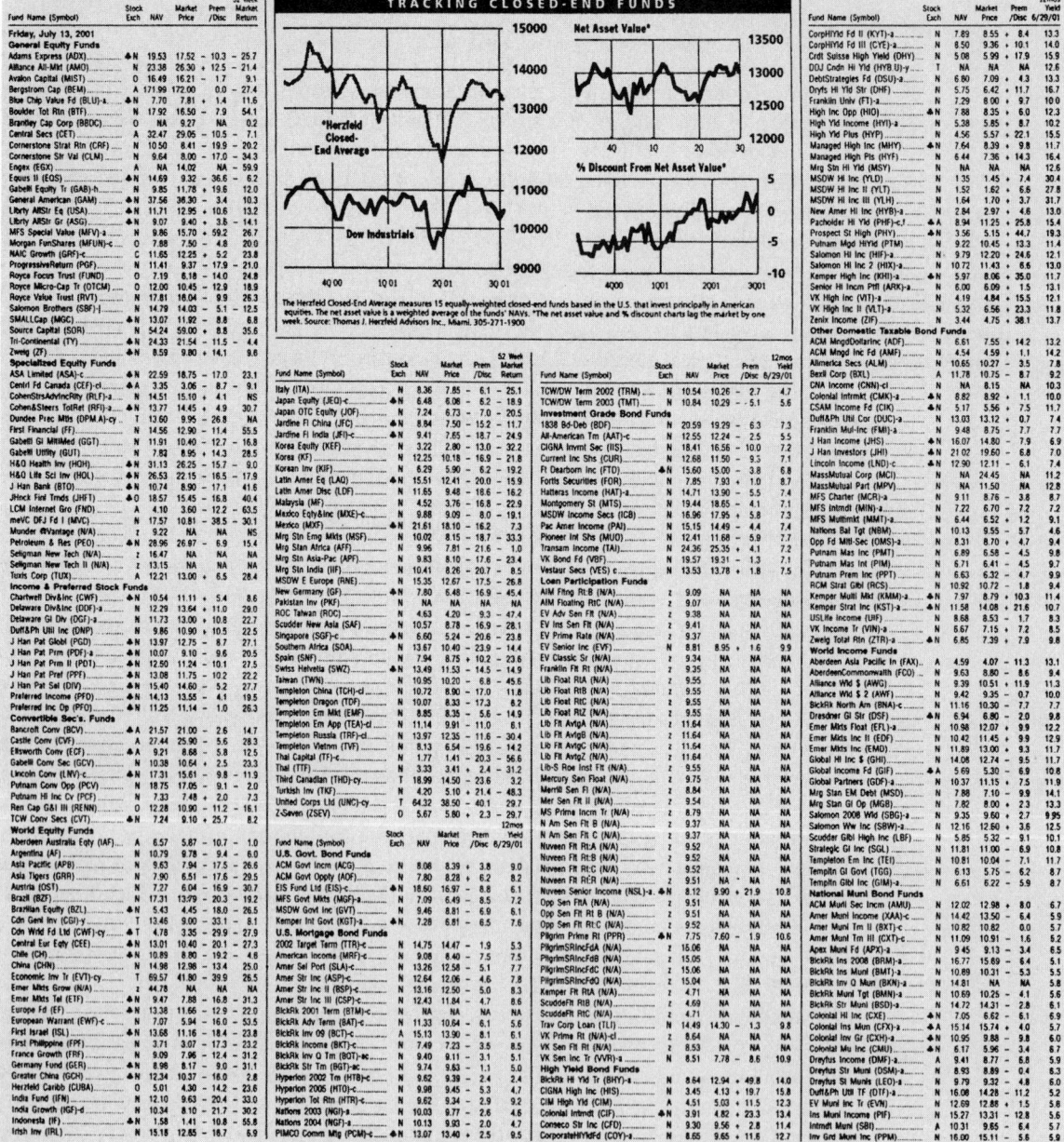

Source: *Barron's,* 21 July 2001, Dow Jones & Co., Inc. Reprinted with permission.

1076

EXHIBIT 25.7 ▶ *CLOSED-END FUNDS: CATEGORIES AND AUM*

Statistic	Value
Total number of closed-end funds (U.S. exchanges only):	606
Total Assets*:	123,370.37

ASSETS BY CLASSIFICATION			
Category	Abbrev	Funds	Assets*
Corporate—High yield	CHY	33	$7,351.89
Corporate—Investment grade	CIG	4	$643.78
Emerging-market equity	EME	4	$821.26
Emerging-market income	EMI	7	$1,355.65
Equity income	EQI	10	$1,085.56
General bd—Investment grade	BDI	11	$1,593.24
General mortgage	MTG	18	$9,025.49
Global equity	GLE	9	$562.75
Global income	GLI	27	$8,803.12
Government bond	GOV	5	$2,463.79
Growth & income	GCI	31	$11,549.06
Growth—Domestic	GRD	82	$6,779.38
Loan participation	LPF	5	$3,015.69
Multisector bond	MLT	12	$5,031.71
Municipal—High yield	MHY	4	$1,218.53
Municipal—National	MNL	104	$31,292.02
Municipal single state	MSS	129	$13,936.36
Non-US equity	FOR	82	$11,562.27
Sector—Energy/natural res	ENR	6	$474.82
Sector—Financial services	FIN	8	$1,363.07
Sector—Health/biotechnology	HLT	7	$844.27
Sector—Precious metals	GPM	3	$376.99
Sector—Utilities	UTL	5	$2,219.65

*Assets are net assets, expressed in millions, and exclude leveraged capital (preferred stock, debt, etc.), which totals about $28 billion.

Source: Closed-End Fund Association, 22 February 2002. Reprinted with permission.

should generate positive excess returns. If the discount increases, the investor will likely experience negative excess returns. The analysis of these discounts remains a major question of modern finance.[5]

---

[5]Studies over the years include Charles Lee, Andrei Shleifer, and Richard Thaler, "Investor Sentiment and the Closed-End Fund Puzzle," *Journal of Finance* 46, no. 1 (March 1991): 76–110; Michael Barclay, Clifford Holderness, and Jeffrey Pontiff, "Private Benefits from Block Ownership and Discounts on Closed-End Funds," *Journal of Financial Economics* 33, no. 3 (June 1993): 263–292; Burton Malkiel, "The Structure of Closed-End Fund Discounts Revisited," *Journal of Portfolio Management* 21, no. 4 (Summer 1995): 32–38; and Peter Klibanoff, Owen Lamont, and Thierry A. Wizman, "Investor Reaction to Salient News in Closed-End Country Funds," *Journal of Finance* 53, no. 2 (April 1998): 673–699. For a discussion of bond funds, see Malcolm Richards, Donald Fraser, and John Groth, "The Attractions of Closed-End Bond Funds," *Journal of Portfolio Management* 8, no. 2 (Winter 1982): 56–61.

EXHIBIT 25.8 ► OPEN-END INVESTMENT COMPANIES: NUMBER AND VALUE OF ASSETS: 1945–2000

	NUMBER OF REPORTING FUNDS	ASSETS ($ BILLIONS)		NUMBER OF REPORTING FUNDS	ASSETS ($ BILLIONS)
1950	98	2.5	1988	2,127	471.4
1955	125	7.8	1989	2,262	552.6
1960	161	17.0	1990	2,338	566.8
1965	170	35.2	1991	2,583	850.7
1970	361	47.6	1992	2,960	1,096.3
1975	390	42.2	1993	3,614	1,504.6
1980	458	58.4	1994	4,362	1,544.3
1981	486	55.2	1995	4,728	2,058.3
1982	539	76.9	1996	5,260	2,624.0
1983	653	113.6	1997	5,671	3,409.3
1984	818	137.1	1998	6,288	4,173.5
1985	1,068	251.6	1999	6,746	5,233.2
1986	1,348	423.5	2000	7,116	5,119.4
1987	1,769	453.1	2001	7,292	4,689.6

Note: Does not include money market and short-term bond funds.

Source: *2002 Mutual Fund Fact Book,* Copyright © 2002 Investment Company Institute. Reprinted by permission of Investment Company Institute (www.ici.org).

The interest in closed-end funds has led Thomas J. Herzfeld Advisors, a firm that specializes in closed-end funds, to create an index that tracks the market price performance of a sample of U.S. closed-end funds that invest principally in U.S. equities. The price-weighted series is based on fund market values rather than on NAVs. In addition to its market price index, Herzfeld also computes the average discount from NAV. The graph in Exhibit 25.6 indicates that the average discount from NAV changes over time and has a major impact on the market performance of the index. For example, from the third quarter of 2000 to the third quarter of 2001, this value changed from a discount of 7 percent to a premium of about three percent. Despite this, the performance of the Herzfeld closed-end average at the end of this period was ahead of the DJIA.

Open-End Investment Companies

Open-end investment companies, or mutual funds, continue to sell and repurchase shares after their initial public offerings. They stand ready to sell additional shares of the fund at the NAV, with or without sales charge, or to buy back (redeem) shares of the fund at the NAV, with or without redemption fees.

Open-end investment companies have enjoyed substantial growth since World War II, as shown by the figures in Exhibit 25.8. Clearly, open-end funds account for a substantial portion of invested assets, and they provide a very important service for almost 200 million accounts.

Load versus No-Load Open-End Funds One distinction of open-end funds is that some charge a sales fee for share sales. The offering price for a share of a *load fund* equals the NAV of the share plus a sales charge, which can be as large as 7.5 to 8.0 percent of the NAV. A fund with an 8 percent sales charge (load) would give an individual who invested $1,000 in the fund shares that are worth only $920. Such funds generally charge no redemption fee, which means the shares can be redeemed at their NAV. These funds typically are quoted with an NAV and an offering price. The NAV price is the redemption (bid) price, and the offering (ask) price equals the NAV divided by 1.0 minus the percent load. For example, if the NAV of a fund with an 8 percent load is $8.50 a share, the offering price would be $9.24 ($8.50/0.92). The 74-cent differential is really 8.7 percent of the NAV. The load percentage typically declines with the size of the order.

A **no-load fund** imposes no initial sales charge so it sells shares at their NAV. Some of these funds charge a small redemption fee of about one-half of 1 percent. In *The Wall Street Journal,* quotes for these no-load funds list bid prices as the NAV with the designation "NL" (no load) for the offering price—that is, the bid and offer are the same. The number of no-load funds has increased substantially in recent years. *The Wall Street Journal* lists more than 350 no-load funds, and *Barron's* lists more than 800.

Between the full-load fund and the pure no-load fund, several important variations exist. The first is the **low-load fund**, which imposes a front-end sales charge when the fund is bought, but it is typically in the 3 percent range rather than 7 to 8 percent. Generally, low-load funds are used for bond funds or equity funds offered by management companies that also offer no-load funds. For example, most Fidelity Management funds were no load prior to 1985, but several of their newer funds have carried a low load of 3 percent. Alternatively, some funds—previously charging full loads—have reduced their loads.

The second major innovation is the **12b-1 plan**, named after a 1980 SEC ruling. This plan permits funds to deduct as much as 0.75 percent of average net assets *per year* to cover distribution costs, such as advertising, brokers' commissions, and general marketing expenses. A large and growing number of no-load funds are adopting these plans, as are a few low-load funds. You can determine if a fund has a 12b-1 plan only by reading the prospectus or using an investment service that reports charges in substantial detail.

Finally, some funds have instituted **contingent, deferred sales loads** in which a sales fee is charged when the fund is sold if it is held for less than some time period, perhaps three or four years.

Fund Management Fees

In addition to selling charges (loads or 12b-1 charges), all investment firms charge annual **management fees** to compensate professional managers of the fund. Similar to the compensation structure for private management firms, such a fee typically is a percentage of the average net assets of the fund varying from about 0.25 to 1.00 percent. Most of these management fees are on sliding scales that decline with the size of the fund. For example, a fund with assets under $1 billion might charge 1 percent, funds with assets between $1 billion and $5 billion might charge 0.50 percent, and those over $5 billion would charge 0.25 percent.

These management fees are a major factor driving the creation of new funds. More assets under management generate more fees, but the costs of management do not increase at the same rate as the managed assets because substantial economies of scale exist in managing financial assets. Once the research staff and management structure have been established, the incremental costs do not rise in line with the assets under management. For example, the cost of managing $1 billion of assets is *not* twice the cost of managing $500 million. Finally, one consequence of the industry consolidation we discussed earlier is that mutual fund fees have been declining. For instance, the Investment Company Institute reported that between 1980 and 1998 total shareholder costs to equity fund investors decreased by 40 percent, from 2.25 to 1.35 percent of average fund AUM.

TYPES OF INVESTMENT COMPANIES BASED ON PORTFOLIO MAKEUP

Common Stock Funds

Some funds invest almost solely in common stocks; others invest in preferred stocks, bonds, and so forth. Within common stock funds, wide differences are found in emphasis, including funds that focus on growth companies, small-cap stocks, companies in specific industries (e.g., Chemical

Fund, Oceanography Fund), certain classes of industry (e.g., Technology Fund), or even geographic areas (such as the Northeast Fund or international funds). Different common stock funds can suit almost any taste or investment objective. Therefore, you must decide whether you want a fund that invests only in common stock; then you must consider the type of common stock you desire. Exhibit 25.9 provides a list of some of the more popular mutual fund objectives and definitions for those objectives.

Hybrid Funds

Balanced funds diversify outside the stock market by combining common stock with fixed-income securities, including government bonds, corporate bonds, convertible bonds, or preferred stock. The ratio of stocks to fixed-income securities will vary by fund, as stated in each fund's prospectus. **Flexible portfolio** (or *asset allocation*) **funds** seek high total returns by investing in a mix of stocks, bonds, and money-market securities.

Bond Funds

Bond funds concentrate on various types of bonds to generate high current income with minimal risk. They are similar to common stock funds; however, their investment policies differ. Some funds concentrate on U.S. government or high-grade corporate bonds, others hold a mixture of investment-grade bonds, and some concentrate on high-yield (junk) bonds. Management strategies also can differ, ranging from buy and hold to extensive trading of the portfolio bonds.

In addition to government, mortgage, and corporate bond funds, a change in the tax law in 1976 caused the creation of numerous municipal bond funds. These funds provide investors with monthly interest payments that are exempt from federal income taxes, although some of the interest may be subject to state and local taxes. To avoid the state tax, some municipal bond funds concentrate on bonds from specific states, such as the New York Municipal Bond Fund, which allows New York residents to avoid most state taxes on the interest income.

Money Market Funds

Money market funds were initiated during 1973 when short-term interest rates were at record levels. These funds attempt to provide current income, safety of principal, and liquidity by investing in diversified portfolios of short-term securities, such as Treasury bills, banker certificates of deposit, bank acceptances, and commercial paper. They typically are no-load funds and impose no penalty for early withdrawal. Also, they generally allow holders to write checks against their account.[6] Exhibit 25.10 documents the significant growth of these funds. Changes in their growth rate usually are associated with investor attitudes toward the stock market. When investors are bullish toward stocks, they withdraw funds from their money market accounts to invest; when they are uncertain, they shift from stocks to the money funds.

Breakdown by Fund Characteristics

Exhibit 25.11 groups funds by their method of sale and by investment objectives. The two major means of distribution are (1) by a sales force and (2) by direct purchase from the fund or direct marketing. Sales forces would include brokers, such as Merrill Lynch; commission-based financial planners; or dedicated sales forces, such as those of American Express Retirement Services. Almost all mutual funds acquired from these individuals charge sales fees (loads) from which salespeople are compensated.

Investors typically purchase shares of directly marketed funds through the mail, telephone, bankwire, or an office of the fund. These direct sales funds usually impose a low sales charge or none at all. In the past, because they had no sales fee, they had to be sold directly because a

---

[6]For a list of names and addresses of money market funds, write to Investment Company Institute, 1775 K Street N.W., Washington, DC 20006.

EXHIBIT 25.9 ▶ *MUTUAL FUND OBJECTIVES*

Equity Funds

Capital Appreciation Funds seek capital appreciation; dividends are not a primary consideration

- *Aggressive growth funds* invest primarily in common stocks of small, growth companies.
- *Growth funds* invest primarily in common stocks of well-established companies.
- *Sector funds* invest primarily in companies in related fields.

Total Return Funds seek a combination of current income and capital appreciation.

- *Growth and income funds* invest primarily in common stocks of established companies with the potential for growth and a consistent record of dividend payments.
- *Income equity funds* invest primarily in equity securities of companies with a consistent record of dividend payments. They seek income more than capital appreciation.

World Equity Funds invest primarily in stocks of foreign companies.

- *Emerging market funds* invest primarily in companies based in developing regions of the world.
- *Global equity funds* invest primarily in equity securities traded worldwide, including those of U.S. companies.
- *International equity funds* invest primarily in equity securities of companies located outside the United States.
- *Regional equity funds* invest in companies based in a specific part of the world.

Hybrid Funds

Hybrid Funds may invest in a mix of equities, fixed-income securities, and derivative instruments.

- *Asset allocation funds* invest in various asset classes including, but not limited to, equities, fixed-income securities, and money market instruments. They seek high total return by maintaining precise weightings in asset classes. Global asset allocation funds invest in a mix of equity and debt securities issued worldwide.
- *Balanced funds* invest in a mix of equity securities and bonds with the three-part objective of conserving principal, providing income, and achieving long-term growth of both principal and income. These funds maintain target percentages in asset classes.
- *Flexible portfolio funds* invest in common stocks, bonds, other debt securities, and money market securities to provide high total return. These funds may invest up to

100 percent in any one type of security and may easily change weightings depending upon market conditions.

- *Income-mixed funds* invest in a variety of income-producing securities, including equities and fixed-income instruments. These funds seek a high level of current income without regard to capital appreciation.

Taxable Bond Funds

Corporate Bond Funds seek current income by investing in high-quality debt securities issued by U.S. corporations.

- *Corporate bond funds—general* invest two-thirds or more of their portfolios in U.S. corporate bonds with no explicit restrictions on average maturity.
- *Corporate bond funds—intermediate-term* invest two-thirds or more of their portfolios in U.S. corporate bonds with an average maturity of five to 10 years. These funds seek a high level of income with less price volatility than longer-term bond funds.
- *Corporate bond funds—short-term* invest two-thirds or more of their portfolios in U.S. corporate bonds with an average maturity of one to five years. These funds seek a high level of income with less price volatility than intermediate-term bond funds.

High-Yield Funds invest two-thirds or more of their portfolios in lower-rated U.S. corporate bonds (Baa or lower by Moody's and BBB or lower by Standard and Poor's rating service.)

World Bond Funds invest in debt securities offered by foreign companies and governments. They seek the highest level of current income available worldwide.

- *Global bond funds—general* invest in worldwide debt securities with no stated average maturity or an average maturity of five years or more. These funds may invest up to 25 percent of assets in companies located in the United States.
- *Global bond funds—short-term* invest in debt securities worldwide with an average maturity of one to five years. These funds may invest up to 25 percent of assets in companies located in the United States.
- *Other world bond funds,* such as international bond and emerging market debt funds, invest in foreign government and corporate debt instruments. Two-thirds of an international bond funds portfolio must be invested outside the United States. Emerging market debt funds invest primarily in debt from underdeveloped regions of the world.

Government Bond Funds invest in U.S. government bonds of varying maturities. They seek high current income.

- *Government bond funds—general* invest two-thirds or more of their portfolios in U.S. government securities of no stated average maturity. Securities utilized by investment managers may change with market conditions.
- *Government bond funds—intermediate-term* invest two-thirds or more of their portfolios in U.S. government securities with an average maturity of five to 10 years. Securities utilized by investment managers may change with market conditions.
- *Government bond funds—short-term* invest two-thirds or more of their portfolios in U.S. government securities with an average maturity of one to five years. Securities utilized by investment managers may change with market conditions.
- *Mortgage-backed* funds invest two-thirds or more of their portfolios in pooled mortgage-backed securities.

Strategic Income Funds invest in a combination of U.S. fixed-income securities to provide a high level of current income.

Tax-Free Bond Funds

State Municipal Bond Funds invest primarily in municipal bonds issued by a particular state. These funds seek high after-tax income for residents of individual states.

- *State municipal bond funds—general* invest primarily in single-state municipal bonds with an average maturity of greater than five years or no specific stated maturity. The income from these funds is largely exempt from federal as well as state income tax for residents or the state.
- *State municipal bond funds—short-term* invest primarily in single-state municipal bonds with an average maturity of one to five years. The income of these funds is largely exempt from federal as well as state income tax for residents of the state.

National Municipal Bond Funds invest primarily in the bonds of various municipal issuers in the United States. These funds seek high current income free from federal tax.

- *National municipal bond funds—general* invest primarily in municipal bonds with an average maturity of more than five years or no specific stated maturity.
- *National municipal bond funds—short-term* invest primarily in municipal bonds with an average maturity of one to five years.

EXHIBIT 25.10 ► *TAXABLE MONEY MARKET FUNDS (MILLIONS OF DOLLARS)*

YEAR	NUMBER OF FUNDS	TOTAL ACCOUNTS OUTSTANDING	AVERAGE MATURITY (DAYS)	TOTAL NET ASSETS	YEAR	NUMBER OF FUNDS	TOTAL ACCOUNTS OUTSTANDING	AVERAGE MATURITY (DAYS)	TOTAL NET ASSETS
1976	48	180,676	110	$ 3,685.8	1989	470	20,173,265	40	$ 358,719.2
1977	50	177,522	76	3,887.7	1990	506	21,577,559	47	414,733.3
1978	61	467,803	42	10,858.0	1991	553	21,863,352	56	452,559.2
1979	76	2,307,852	34	45,214.2	1992	585	21,770,693	58	451,353.4
1980	96	4,745,572	24	74,447.7	1993	628	21,586,862	59	461,903.9
1981	159	10,282,095	34	181,910.4	1994	646	23,339,838	38	500,635.5
1982	281	13,101,347	37	206,607.5	1995	674	27,859,258	57	629,985.8
1983	307	12,276,639	37	162,549.5	1996	666	29,907,471	54	761,989.0
1984	329	13,556,180	43	209,731.9	1997	682	32,960,628	55	898,083.1
1985	348	14,435,386	42	207,535.3	1998	685	36,442,150	56	1,163,166.7
1986	360	15,653,595	45	228,345.8	1999	702	41,177,138	49	1,408,731.0
1987	389	16,832,666	34	254,676.4	2000	703	45,479,697	51	1,607,248.2
1988	434	17,630,528	31	272,293.3	2001	689	44,414,701	58	2,012,949.4

Source: *1996 and 2002 Mutual Fund Fact Books,* Copyright © 1996 and 2002 Investment Company Institute. Reprinted by permission of the Investment Company Institute (www.ici.org).

broker had no incentive to sell a no-load fund. This has changed recently because some broker-age firms, most notably Charles Schwab & Co., have developed agreements with specific no-load funds whereby they will sell these funds to their clients and collect a fee from the fund. As of March 2002, Schwab had a list of more than 1,100 no-load funds that they would sell through their OneSource service. As seen in the most recent figures available in Exhibit 25.11, the division between these two major distribution channels is currently about 60 to 40 percent in favor of the sales force method, although there has been a steady shift toward direct institutional marketing. Given the investor preference for no-load funds and the increasing availability through firms like Charles Schwab, this trend toward direct marketed funds should continue.

The breakdown by investment objective indicates the investment companies' response to a shift in investor emphasis. The growth of an alternative investment objective category reflects not only the overall growth of the industry but also the creation of new funds in response to the evolving demands of investors. For example, aggressive growth, growth, and growth and income funds have continued to grow and generally increased their percentages. Finally, the growing desire for international diversification is reflected in the ongoing popularity of world equity funds. This trend is discussed more thoroughly in the next section.

GLOBAL INVESTMENT COMPANIES

As discussed throughout this text, serious thought should be given to global diversification of your investment portfolio. Funds that invest in non-U.S. securities are generally called *foreign funds.* More specific designations include either *international funds* or *global funds.* International funds include only non-U.S. stocks from such countries as Germany, Japan, Singapore, and Korea. Global funds contain both U.S. and non-U.S. securities. Ideally, a global fund should invest in a

EXHIBIT 25.11 ▸ *TOTAL NET ASSETS BY FUND CHARACTERISTICS ($ MILLIONS)*

	2001		1995	
	DOLLARS	PERCENT	DOLLARS	PERCENT
Total Net Assets	$4,689,628.0	100.0%	$2,067,337.3	100.0%
Method of Sale:				
Third Party/Institutional—Sales Force	—	60.0	—	59.0
Third Party/Institutional—Direct Market	—	25.0	—	20.0
Retail—Direct Sales	—	15.0	—	21.0
Investment Objective:				
Aggressive growth	576,241.9	12.3	190,822.3	9.2
Growth	1,047,517.4	22.3	354,235.0	17.1
Growth & income	1,066,633.4	22.7	429,202.7	20.8
World equity	428,796.3	9.1	196,737.9	9.5
Income equity	125,382.1	2.7	93,314.1	4.5
Flexible & Asset allocation	115,284.5	2.5	52,435,9	2.5
Balanced	179,659.3	3.8	81,288.0	3.9
Income—mixed	51,386.8	1.1	77,404.4	3.7
Corporate bond	160,968.3	3.4	31,731.9	1.5
High-yield bond	94,275.7	2.0	59,715.9	2.9
World bond	19,066.3	0.4	33,412.3	1.6
Government bond	90,875.4	1.9	87,926.7	4.3
Govt. bond—mortgage-backed	73,367.6	1.6	55,257.0	2.7
Strategic income—bond	191,552.9	4.1	66,111.2	3.2
State municipal bond	140,990.5	3.0	117,225.5	5.7
National municipal bond	154,027.4	3.3	135,789.0	6.6
Other (e.g., Sector, Metals)	173,602.2	3.7	4,727.5	0.2

Source: Adapted from the *1996 and 2002 Mutual Fund Fact Books,* by permission of the Investment Company Institute (www.ici.org). Copyright © 1996 and 2002 Investment Company Institute.

large number of countries. Both international and global funds fall into familiar categories: money funds, long-term government and corporate bond funds, and equity funds. In turn, an international equity fund might limit its focus to a segment of the non-U.S. market, such as the European Fund or Pacific Basin Fund, or to a single country, such as Germany, Italy, Japan, or Korea. In the chapter on global investing, there was an extensive discussion about investing in emerging markets. Given the need to invest in a diversified portfolio of emerging markets, an emerging market mutual fund that contains a number of them is an ideal vehicle for this asset allocation.

Although most global or international funds are open-end funds (either load or no load), a significant number are closed-end funds, including most of the single country and the emerging-market funds. These funds have opted to be closed end so that they are not subject to major investor liquidations that require the sale of stocks in the portfolio on an illiquid foreign stock exchange. Because of the growth and popularity of foreign funds, most sources of information include separate sections on foreign stock or bond funds.

A final alternative that all investors—particularly those in the United States—should appreciate is the large number of non-U.S. investment companies that offer both domestic and global products in their local markets. In fact, the Investment Company Institute reported that of $12,152,533 million invested worldwide in open-end investment companies at the end of 2000, over 40 percent of these assets were controlled by firms located outside the United States. In order, the largest concentrations of these AUM occurred in France, Luxembourg, Japan, Italy, Canada, Australia, and Germany. Further, of the 53,450 investment companies in operation during 2000, slightly more than 8,000 were domiciled in the United States. From these statistics, it is reasonable to assume that no single region of the world has a monopoly on investment management skill.

SOURCES OF INFORMATION

Because a wide variety of funds are available, you should examine the performance of various funds over time to understand their goals and management philosophies. Daily quotations for numerous open-end funds appear in *The Wall Street Journal*. These quotations and the information provided have been enhanced dramatically since 1992, and *The Journal* now provides a comprehensive listing of historical returns and rankings on a monthly basis. (A description of the performance data provided is shown in Exhibit 25.12.)

A major source of comprehensive historical information is *Investment Companies,* an annual publication issued by Thomson Financial, parent company of Wiesenberger, a leading provider of mutual fund analysis. This book contains statistics for over 600 mutual funds. Arranged alphabetically, it describes each major fund, including a brief history, investment objectives and portfolio analysis, statistical history, special services available, personnel, advisors and distributors, sales charges, and a chart of the value of a hypothetical $10,000 investment over 10 years. Exhibit 25.13 shows a sample page for the Warburg Pincus Emerging Growth Fund. The Thomson Financial book also contains a summary list with annual rates of return and price volatility measures for a number of additional funds.

Thomson Financial also offers several other services, in both print and software formats. *Mutual Funds Update* and *Mutual Funds Report* are monthly publications with information on more than 9,500 funds, as well as commentary on the industry. *Closed-End Weekly Review* provides information about the weekly performance of closed-end funds, and *FundEdge* is analytical software for investors in the closed-end fund industry.

Another source of analytical historical information funds is *Forbes*. This biweekly financial publication typically discusses individual companies and their investment potential. In addition, the magazine's August issue contains an annual survey of mutual funds. A sample page in Exhibit 25.14 demonstrates the survey reports on annual average 10-year returns and last-12-month returns. The survey also provides information regarding each fund's yield, its sales charge, and its annual expense ratio. Notably, the survey also includes a separate section on foreign stock funds.

Business Week publishes a "Mutual Fund Scoreboard." Exhibit 25.15 contains a sample of this scoreboard for open-end equity funds. The magazine publishes a comparable one for closed-end, fixed-income funds and equity funds. Besides information on performance (both before-tax and after-tax returns for 1–3–5–10 years), sales charges (including those for 12b-1 plans), expenses, portfolio yield, and rank within objective, the table also contains portfolio information and telephone numbers for all the funds.

EXHIBIT 25.12   *DESCRIPTION OF MUTUAL FUND QUOTATIONS IN THE WALL STREET JOURNAL*

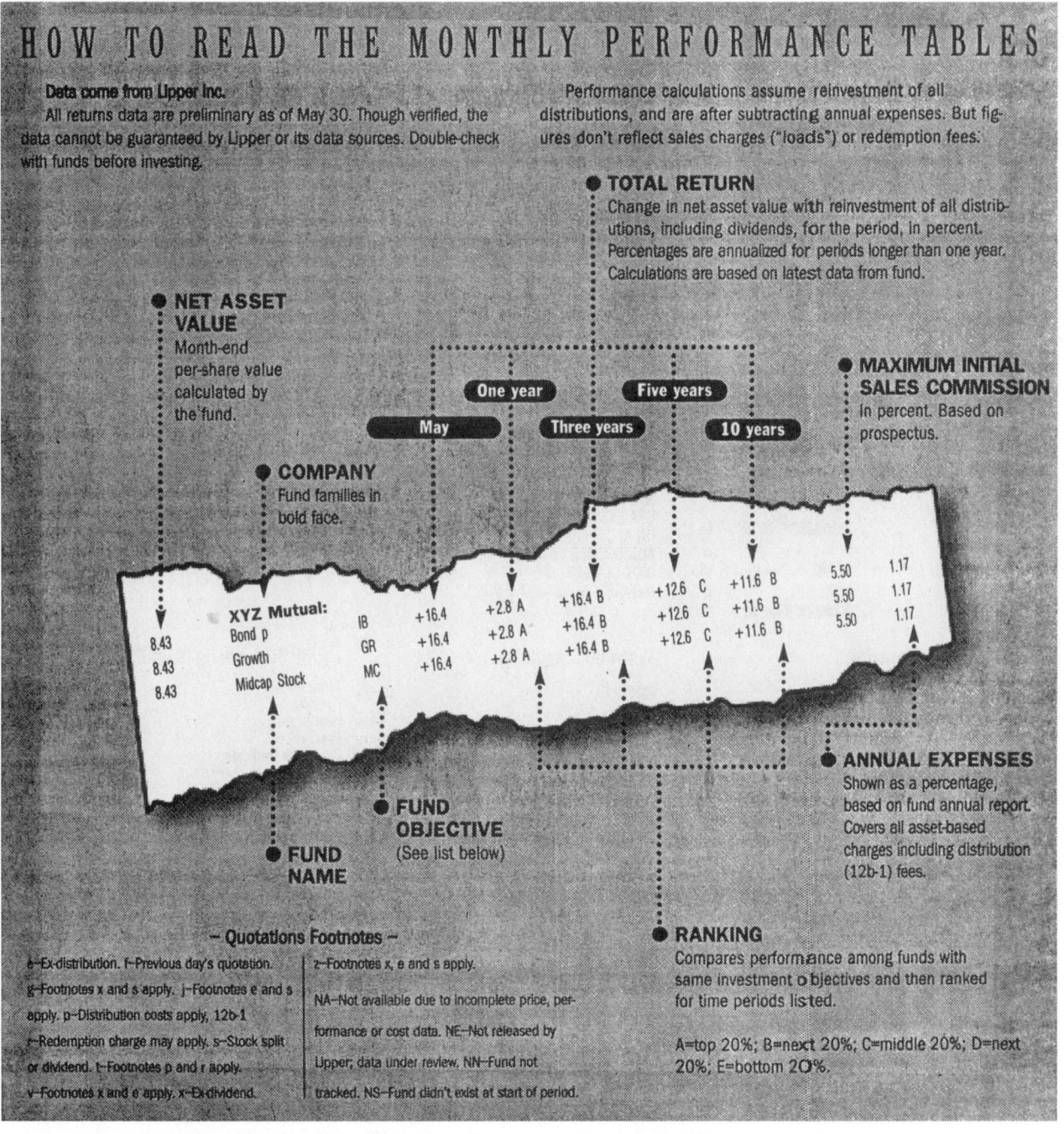

HOW TO READ THE MONTHLY PERFORMANCE TABLES

Data come from Lipper Inc.
All returns data are preliminary as of May 30. Though verified, the data cannot be guaranteed by Lipper or its data sources. Double-check with funds before investing.

Performance calculations assume reinvestment of all distributions, and are after subtracting annual expenses. But figures don't reflect sales charges ("loads") or redemption fees.

● **TOTAL RETURN**
Change in net asset value with reinvestment of all distributions, including dividends, for the period, in percent. Percentages are annualized for periods longer than one year. Calculations are based on latest data from fund.

● **NET ASSET VALUE**
Month-end per-share value calculated by the fund.

One year   **Five years**

May   **Three years**   **10 years**

● **MAXIMUM INITIAL SALES COMMISSION**
In percent. Based on prospectus.

● **COMPANY**
Fund families in bold face.

	XYZ Mutual:									
8.43	Bond p	IB	+16.4	+2.8 A	+16.4 B	+12.6 C	+11.6 B	5.50	1.17
8.43	Growth	GR	+16.4	+2.8 A	+16.4 B	+12.6 C	+11.6 B	5.50	1.17
8.43	Midcap Stock	MC	+16.4	+2.8 A	+16.4 B	+12.6 C	+11.6 B	5.50	1.17

● **FUND NAME**

● **FUND OBJECTIVE**
(See list below)

● **ANNUAL EXPENSES**
Shown as a percentage, based on fund annual report. Covers all asset-based charges including distribution (12b-1) fees.

– Quotations Footnotes –

e–Ex-distribution. f–Previous day's quotation.
g–Footnotes x and s apply. j–Footnotes e and s apply. p–Distribution costs apply, 12b-1
r–Redemption charge may apply. s–Stock split or dividend. t–Footnotes p and r apply.
v–Footnotes x and e apply. x–Ex-dividend.

z–Footnotes x, e and s apply.

NA–Not available due to incomplete price, performance or cost data. NE–Not released by Lipper; data under review. NN–Fund not tracked. NS–Fund didn't exist at start of period.

● **RANKING**
Compares performance among funds with same investment objectives and then ranked for time periods listed.

A=top 20%; B=next 20%; C=middle 20%; D=next 20%; E=bottom 20%.

Source: *The Wall Street Journal,* 4 June 2001. Reprinted with permission from *The Wall Street Journal,* Dow Jones Co. Inc.

EXHIBIT 25.13 *SAMPLE PAGE FROM THOMSON FINANCIAL 2001 INVESTMENT COMPANIES YEARBOOK*

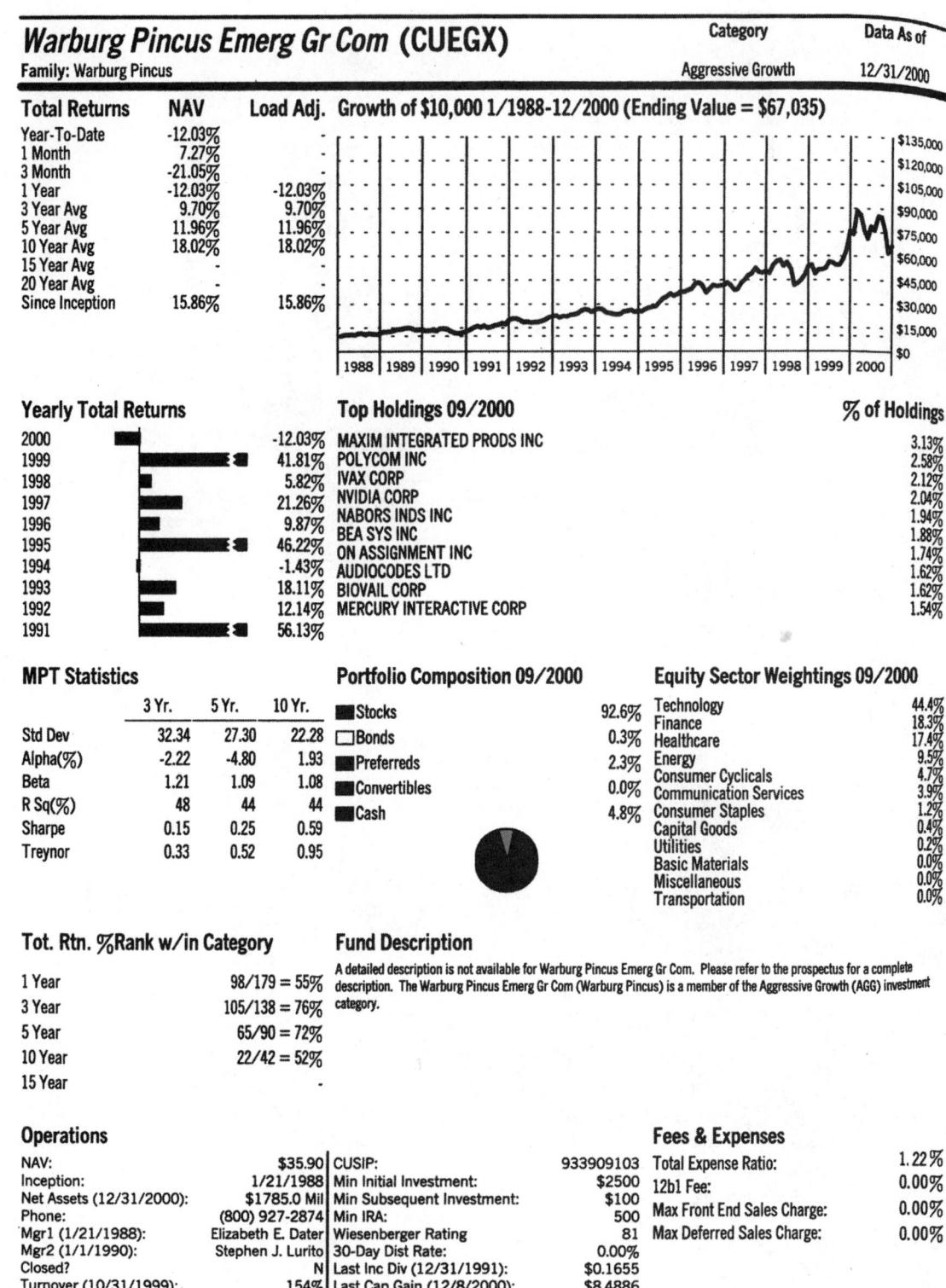

Warburg Pincus Emerg Gr Com (CUEGX)

Family: Warburg Pincus

		Category	Data As of
		Aggressive Growth	12/31/2000

Total Returns

	NAV	Load Adj.
Year-To-Date	-12.03%	-
1 Month	7.27%	-
3 Month	-21.05%	-
1 Year	-12.03%	-12.03%
3 Year Avg	9.70%	9.70%
5 Year Avg	11.96%	11.96%
10 Year Avg	18.02%	18.02%
15 Year Avg	-	-
20 Year Avg	-	-
Since Inception	15.86%	15.86%

Growth of $10,000 1/1988-12/2000 (Ending Value = $67,035)

Yearly Total Returns

Year	Return
2000	-12.03%
1999	41.81%
1998	5.82%
1997	21.26%
1996	9.87%
1995	46.22%
1994	-1.43%
1993	18.11%
1992	12.14%
1991	56.13%

Top Holdings 09/2000

	% of Holdings
MAXIM INTEGRATED PRODS INC	3.13%
POLYCOM INC	2.58%
IVAX CORP	2.12%
NVIDIA CORP	2.04%
NABORS INDS INC	1.94%
BEA SYS INC	1.88%
ON ASSIGNMENT INC	1.74%
AUDIOCODES LTD	1.62%
BIOVAIL CORP	1.62%
MERCURY INTERACTIVE CORP	1.54%

MPT Statistics

	3 Yr.	5 Yr.	10 Yr.
Std Dev	32.34	27.30	22.28
Alpha(%)	-2.22	-4.80	1.93
Beta	1.21	1.09	1.08
R Sq(%)	48	44	44
Sharpe	0.15	0.25	0.59
Treynor	0.33	0.52	0.95

Portfolio Composition 09/2000

■Stocks	92.6%
□Bonds	0.3%
■Preferreds	2.3%
■Convertibles	0.0%
■Cash	4.8%

Equity Sector Weightings 09/2000

Technology	44.4%
Finance	18.3%
Healthcare	17.4%
Energy	9.5%
Consumer Cyclicals	4.7%
Communication Services	3.9%
Consumer Staples	1.2%
Capital Goods	0.4%
Utilities	0.2%
Basic Materials	0.0%
Miscellaneous	0.0%
Transportation	0.0%

Tot. Rtn. %Rank w/in Category

1 Year	98/179 = 55%
3 Year	105/138 = 76%
5 Year	65/90 = 72%
10 Year	22/42 = 52%
15 Year	-

Fund Description

A detailed description is not available for Warburg Pincus Emerg Gr Com. Please refer to the prospectus for a complete description. The Warburg Pincus Emerg Gr Com (Warburg Pincus) is a member of the Aggressive Growth (AGG) investment category.

Operations

NAV:	$35.90
Inception:	1/21/1988
Net Assets (12/31/2000):	$1785.0 Mil
Phone:	(800) 927-2874
Mgr1 (1/21/1988):	Elizabeth E. Dater
Mgr2 (1/1/1990):	Stephen J. Lurito
Closed?	N
Turnover (10/31/1999):	154%

CUSIP:	933909103
Min Initial Investment:	$2500
Min Subsequent Investment:	$100
Min IRA:	500
Wiesenberger Rating	81
30-Day Dist Rate:	0.00%
Last Inc Div (12/31/1991):	$0.1655
Last Cap Gain (12/8/2000):	$8.4886

Fees & Expenses

Total Expense Ratio:	1.22%
12b1 Fee:	0.00%
Max Front End Sales Charge:	0.00%
Max Deferred Sales Charge:	0.00%

EXHIBIT 25.14 ▶ *SAMPLE FUND RATING PAGE FROM FORBES*

Fund Survey

Stock Funds

U.S. equity funds are rated through four market cycles beginning with the Oct. 31, 1990 upward move in the S&P 500. To qualify for this issue, stock funds must have four full cycles of bull and bear market performance history and at least $100 million in assets.

Pay close attention to the DOWN market grade. Although the four bearish cycles since 1990 were short in duration (only 18 months out of a total of 122), this grade gives a good indication of how a fund is likely to perform in future market dips.

Our tables show pretax and theoretical aftertax returns on each fund over the last five years. Assumptions: Income dividends and capital gains are reinvested in the fund; the fund is not redeemed after the five-year period; an investor is in an upper-middle-income bracket.

See www.forbes.com/fundsurvey for updated grades on 2,000 funds as well as individual reports on 6,000 funds.

MARKET PERFORMANCE			ANNUALIZED TOTAL RETURN 10/31/90 to 12/31/00	Pretax 5-year	Aftertax 5-year	Assets 11/30/00 ($mil)	Weighted average P/E	Median market cap ($bil)	Maximum sales charge	Annual expenses per $100
UP	DOWN	FUND/800 number								
▲	▼	Standard & Poor's 500 stock average	18.1%	18.2%						
		Forbes stock fund composite	17.9%	16.2%			30.7	$29.8		$1.06
C	B	AAL Capital Growth Fund-A/553-6319	17.7%	20.4%	19.1%	$4,198	31.3	$53.5	4.00%	$0.90
D	B	Activa Value Fund-A/346-2670	14.1	12.0	8.6	162	22.6	22.5	none	1.00
B	D	Advance Capital I–Equity Growth/345-4783	16.8	20.9	19.7	125	32.7	4.7	none	1.02
F	B	AIM Advisor–Flex Portfolio-A/347-1919	12.0	9.2	5.9	278	20.8	42.3	5.50	1.13
C	C	AIM Blue Chip-A/347-1919	17.3	19.4	18.1	6,168	36.9	88.9	5.50	1.19
A+	D	AIM Equity–Aggressive Growth/347-1919	25.9	15.0	12.2	4,055	34.8	1.6	5.50	1.09
B	D	AIM Equity–Charter-A/347-1919	16.1	16.7	14.2	8,021	34.4	68.7	5.50	1.05
A	D	AIM Equity–Constellation-A/347-1919	21.9	15.1	12.3	17,066	40.9	15.3	5.50	1.10
B	D	AIM Equity–Weingarten-A/347-1919	16.3	16.2	12.4	9,221	39.6	38.3	5.50	1.03
C	B	AIM Mid Cap Equity-A/347-1919	17.9	15.4	12.3	444	25.0	2.8	5.50	1.46
B	D	AIM Select Growth-A/347-1919	17.2	20.2	17.8	1,217	43.1	13.8	5.00	1.09
B	D	AIM Summit Fund/347-1919	19.3	20.8	16.8	2,801	39.7	18.3	plan [2]	0.67
B	D	AIM Value Fund-A/347-1919	20.0	15.8	13.2	24,903	27.4	28.9	5.50	1.00
A	D	Alger Fund–LargeCap Growth-A[1]/992-3863	20.1	17.4	14.2	1,098	36.7	51.7	4.75	1.21
B	F	Alger Fund–Small Capitalization-A/992-3863	11.7	0.2	–3.1	336	42.8	1.1	4.75	1.38
B	D	Alliance Fund-A/227-4618	16.2	11.9	8.0	959	20.6	4.5	4.25	1.06
C	B	Alliance Growth & Income-A/227-4618	17.5	19.5	15.9	5,328	21.3	21.5	4.25	0.93
A	D	Alliance Growth Fund-A/227-4618	21.3	15.5	12.8	6,486	23.9	28.3	4.25	1.18
C	C	Alliance Quasar Fund-A/227-4618	14.8	10.8	8.2	845	34.6	1.3	4.25	1.69
A+	D	Alliance Technology Fund-A/227-4618	28.7	21.4	20.1	8,588	42.1	15.4	4.25	1.68
C	B	Amcap Fund-A/421-4120	19.4	20.5	16.0	7,334	31.9	14.7	5.75	0.68
A+	F	American Century–Giftrust/345-2021	20.9	7.3	5.2	1,424	45.5	6.3	none	1.00
B	D	American Century–Growth Fund-I/345-2021	17.4	18.5	14.4	8,591	46.2	103.5	none	1.00
B	C	American Century–Heritage Fund-I/345-2021	18.3	19.5	15.5	1,750	36.6	4.7	none	1.00
C	C	American Century–Select Fund-I/345-2021	14.9	19.0	14.9	6,545	36.5	94.2	none	1.00
A	D	American Century–Ultra Fund-I/345-2021	22.5	16.4	13.0	33,734	46.3	73.8	none	1.00

Five-year return 12/31/95 through 12/31/00. [1]Formerly Alger Fund-Growth-A. [2]Available only through monthly contractual plan. *Sources: Forbes; Lipper Inc.; Morningstar, Inc.*

EXHIBIT 25.15 ▶ *BUSINESS WEEK'S MUTUAL FUND SCOREBOARD*

MUTUAL FUND SCOREBOARD

How to Use the Tables

B	ABOVE AVERAGE
C	AVERAGE
C−	BELOW AVERAGE
D	POOR
F	VERY POOR

BUSINESS WEEK RATINGS

Overall ratings are based on five-year, risk-adjusted returns. They are calculated by subtracting a fund's risk-of-loss factor (see RISK) from historical pretax total return. Category ratings are based on risk-adjusted returns of the funds in that category. The ratings are as follows:

A	SUPERIOR
B+	VERY GOOD

MANAGEMENT CHANGES

ᖯ indicates the fund's manager has held the job at least 10 years; ɑ indicates a new manager since Dec. 31, 1999.

S&P 500 COMPARISON

The pretax total returns for the S&P 500 are as follows: 2000, −9.1%; three-year average (1998-2000), 12.3%; five-year average (1996-2000), 18.3%; 10-year average (1991-2000), 17.4%.

CATEGORY

Each U.S. diversified fund is classified by market capitalization of the stocks in the portfolio and by the nature of those stocks. If the average market cap is greater than $10 billion, the fund is large-cap; from $2 billion to $10 billion, mid-cap; and less than $2 billion, small-cap. All cap funds are those that don't follow a fixed-capitalization policy. "Value" funds are those whose stocks have price-to-earnings and price-to-book ratios lower than the average of the stocks in their market capitalizations. "Growth" funds have higher than average p-e and p-b ratios. "Blend" funds are those in which the ratios are about average. Hybrids mix stocks and bonds, and possibly other assets. World funds generally include U.S. stocks; foreign funds do not. Sector and regional foreign funds are as indicated.

FUND	OVERALL RATING (COMPARES RISK-ADJUSTED PERFORMANCE OF EACH FUND AGAINST ALL FUNDS)	CATEGORY (COMPARES RISK-ADJUSTED PERFORMANCE OF FUND WITHIN CATEGORY)	RATING	SIZE ASSETS $MIL.	% CHG. 1999-2000	FEES SALES CHARGE (%)	FEES EXPENSE RATIO (%)	2000 RETURNS (%) PRE-TAX	2000 RETURNS (%) AFTER-TAX	2000 RETURNS (%) YIELD
AIM AGGRESSIVE GROWTH A	D	Small-cap Growth	C	3625.2	20	5.50**	1.09†	3.0	−1.3	0.0
AIM BALANCED A	B	Domestic Hybrid	C−	2435.7	47	4.75**	0.94†	−4.2	−5.2	2.5
AIM BLUE CHIP A	B	Large-cap Blend	B	2931.3	22	5.50**	1.19†	−9.3	−9.3	0.0
AIM CAPITAL DEVELOPMENT A		Small-cap Growth		672.9	8	5.50**	1.38†	9.8	6.8	0.0
AIM CHARTER A	C	Large-cap Growth	C	4980.3	−3	5.50**	1.05†	−14.7	−15.6	0.0
AIM CONSTELLATION A	C−	Mid-cap Growth	D	15607.8	1	5.50**	1.10†	−10.4	−14.0	0.0
AIM DENT DEMOGRAPHIC TRENDS B		Large-cap Blend		626.0	170	0.00**	2.24†	−17.8	−17.8	0.0
AIM GLOBAL AGGRESSIVE GROWTH B	D	World	D	967.8	−10	0.00**	2.37†	−22.4	−25.7	0.0
AIM GLOBAL GROWTH B	C	World	C	687.3	45	0.00**	2.23†	−22.6	−22.6	0.0
AIM GLOBAL TELECOMM. & TECH. A	D	Communications	F	1050.4	−14	4.75**	1.77†	−38.9	−40.8	0.0
AIM INTERNATIONAL EQUITY A	C−	Foreign	C−	2086.4	−10	5.50**	1.48†	−25.7	−26.8	0.0
AIM SELECT GROWTH B	C	Large-cap Growth	C	644.6	23	0.00**	1.90†	−2.5	−4.9	0.0
AIM SUMMIT I	C	Large-cap Growth	C−	2800.9	−3	8.50	0.67	−14.7	−18.0	0.0
AIM VALUE B	C	Large-cap Growth	C	12450.1	−7	0.00**	1.79†	−15.6	−17.3	0.0
AIM WEINGARTEN A ᖯ	C−	Large-cap Growth	D	7362.0	−15	5.50**	1.03†	−20.4	−22.7	0.0
ALGER CAPITAL APPRECIATION B	C−	Large-cap Growth	D	879.7	28	0.00**	2.12†	−31.0	−31.1	0.0
ALGER LARGE CAP GROWTH B (a) ᖯ	C	Large-cap Growth	C−	783.6	−1	0.00**	1.96†	−15.7	−17.0	0.0
ALLEGHANY/MONTAG & CALDWELL GROWTH I		Large-cap Growth		1309.1	−10	No load	0.76	−6.9	−9.4	0.0
ALLIANCE A	D	Mid-cap Blend	D	856.9	−25	4.25**	1.06†	−15.9	−16.7	0.0
ALLIANCE GROWTH & INCOME B	B+	Large-cap Value	B+	2458.8	30	0.00**	1.70†	12.8	11.2	0.4
ALLIANCE GROWTH B ᖯ	C	Large-cap Growth	C−	4300.3	−23	0.00**	1.90†	−19.1	−21.7	0.0
ALLIANCE PREMIER GROWTH B	C	Large-cap Growth	C	8802.3	8	0.00**	2.18†	−20.4	−21.9	0.0
ALLIANCE TECHNOLOGY B	C−	Technology	C−	4705.4	20	0.00**	2.39†	−25.2	−26.2	0.0
AMCAP A ᖯ	A	Large-cap Blend	A	7333.7	9	5.75**	0.68†	7.5	4.8	0.5
AMER. CENTURY BALANCED INV.	C	Domestic Hybrid	C−	789.6	−14	No load	1.00	−2.7	−4.1	2.7
AMER. CENTURY EQUTIY GROWTH INV.	B	Large-cap Blend	B	1906.3	−13	No load	0.68	−11.0	−12.2	0.6
AMER. CENTURY GIFTRUST INV. ᖯ	F	Small-cap Growth	F	1424.0	−2	No load	1.00	−16.4	−20.9	0.0
AMER. CENTURY GROWTH INV.	C	Large-cap Growth	C	8591.1	−3	No load	1.00	−14.7	−16.9	0.0
AMER. CENTURY HERITAGE INV.	B	Small-cap Growth	A	1749.7	57	No load	1.00	17.4	12.5	0.0
AMER. CENTURY INCOME & GROWTH INV. ᖯ	B	Large-cap Blend	C	5385.1	−10	No load	0.68	−10.5	−10.8	1.0
AMER. CENTURY INTL. DISCOVERY INV.	A	Foreign	A	1570.4	12	0.00*	1.55	−14.2	−16.1	0.0
AMER. CENTURY INTL. GROWTH INV.	B	Foreign	B+	4479.1	21	No load	1.27	−15.0	−17.4	0.0
AMER. CENTURY NEW OPPORT. INV.		Small-cap Growth		591.5	4	0.00*	1.50	−18.2	−23.5	0.0
AMER. CENTURY SELECT INV.	B+	Large-cap Growth	B+	6544.7	−26	No load	1.00	−8.7	−9.8	0.0
AMER. CENTURY ULTRA INV.	C−	Large-cap Growth	D	33733.8	−10	No load	1.00	−19.9	−21.8	0.0
AMER. CENTURY VALUE INV.	C	Mid-cap Value	C	1409.8	−16	No load	1.00	18.3	17.6	1.5
AMER. CENTURY VISTA INV.	D	Small-cap Growth	C−	1894.9	40	No load	1.00	−1.0	−7.0	0.0
AMERICAN BALANCED A ᖯ	B+	Domestic Hybrid	B+	5682.5	−6	5.75**	0.66†	15.9	13.6	3.3
AMERICAN MUTUAL A ᖯ	B	Large-cap Value	C	8163.9	−20	5.75**	0.57†	9.1	6.9	2.8
AMERICAN NEW WORLD A		Diversified Emerging Markets		1208.9	43	5.75**	0.52†	−20.9	−21.3	1.6
ARMADA EQUITY GROWTH I	B+	Large-cap Growth	B+	1145.4	−13	No load	0.90†	−5.2	−6.0	0.0
ARMADA EQUITY INCOME I	C	Large-cap Value	C	648.3	29	No load	0.92†	11.6	10.5	1.7
ARMADA INTERNATIONAL EQUITY I		Foreign		621.6	99	No load	1.43†	−16.9	−17.9	0.0
ARTISAN INTERNATIONAL	A	Foreign	A	4438.0	102	No load	1.27	−10.6	−13.1	0.0
ARTISAN MID CAP		Mid-cap Growth		596.8	755	No load	1.40	27.2	26.3	0.0

*Includes redemption fee. **Includes deferred sales charge. †12(b)-1 plan in effect. ‡Not currently accepting new accounts. §Less than 0.5% of assets. NA=Not available. NM=Not meaningful. (a) Formerly Alger Fund:Growth Portfolio B.

EXHIBIT 25.15 ▶ *CONTINUED*

SALES CHARGE
The cost of buying a fund. Many funds take this "load" out of the initial investment, and for ratings purposes, returns are reduced by these charges. Loads may be levied on withdrawals.

EXPENSE RATIO
Expenses as a percentage of average net assets for the fund's most recent fiscal year. It's a measure of how much shareholders pay for management. Footnotes indicate if the ratio includes a 12(b)-1 plan, which spends shareholder money on marketing. The average is 1.42%.

PRETAX TOTAL RETURN
A fund's net gain to investors, including reinvestment of dividends and capital gains at month-end prices.

AFTERTAX TOTAL RETURN
Pretax return adjusted for federal taxes. Assumes ordinary income is taxed at the 31% tax rate. Capital gains are assumed to be long-term, and taxed at 20%.

YIELD
Income distributions as a percent of net asset value, adjusted for capital-gains distributions.

HISTORY
A fund's returns relative to all other equity funds for five one-year periods, which from left to right are: 1996, 1997, 1998, 1999 and 2000. The numbers designate which quintile the fund was in during the period: ∎ for the top quintile; ∎ for the second quintile; ∎ for the third quintile; ∎ for the fourth quintile and ∎ for the bottom quintile. No number indicates no data for that period.

TURNOVER
Trading activity, the lesser of purchases or sales divided by average monthly assets.

CASH
Portion of fund assets not invested in stocks or bonds. A negative number means the fund has borrowed to buy securities.

UNTAXED GAINS
Percentage of assets in portfolio that are unrealized and undistributed capital gains. A negative figure indicates losses that may offset future gains.

TOP 10 STOCKS
The percentage of fund assets that represents the 10 largest holdings. The higher the number, the more concentrated the fund and more dependent on the performance of a relatively small number of stocks.

LARGEST HOLDING
Comes from the latest available fund reports.

RISK
Potential for losing money in a fund, or risk-of-loss factor. For each fund, the three-month Treasury bill return is subtracted from the monthly total return for each of the 60 months in the ratings period. When a fund has not performed as well as Treasury bills, the monthly result is negative. The sum of these negative numbers is divided by the number of months. The result is a negative number, and the greater its magnitude, the higher the risk of loss. This number is the basis for BW ratings, category ratings, and the RISK column.

BEST & WORST QUARTERS
The fund's highest and lowest quarterly returns of the past five years.

AVERAGE ANNUAL TOTAL RETURNS (%)						HISTORY	PORTFOLIO DATA				LARGEST HOLDING	RISK		BEST		WORST		TELEPHONE
3 YEARS		5 YEARS		10 YEARS		RESULTS VS.	TURNOVER	CASH	UNTAXED	TOP 10		LEVEL	QTR	% RET	QTR	% RET	
PRETAX	AFTERTAX	PRETAX	AFTERTAX	PRETAX	AFTERTAX	ALL FUNDS		%	GAINS %	STKS. %	COMPANY (% ASSETS)						
16.2	13.7	15.0	12.9	24.2	22.3	5 5 4 2 3	Low	7	22	16	Microchip Technology (2)	High	IV 99	31.4	III 98	−22.8	800-347-4246
8.6	7.7	13.7	12.4	16.0	14.8	3 3 4 4 3	Average	7	10	11	InfoSpace (2)	Low	IV 99	16.2	III 98	−8.9	800-347-4246
14.1	14.1	19.4	18.2	16.7	15.6	3 2 2 3 4	Low	4	16	29	Cisco Systems (5)	Average	IV 98	24.5	IV 00	−11.1	800-347-4246
13.6	12.6	NA	NA	NA	NA	3 4 3 2	Average	7	29	12	Osicom Technologies (1)		IV 99	30.9	III 98	−20.9	800-347-4246
13.1	11.8	16.7	14.6	15.6	13.8	3 3 2 2 4	High	5	22	35	Tyco International (5)	Average	IV 98	26.1	IV 00	−16.4	800-347-4246
15.4	13.0	15.1	12.9	20.3	19.0	4 5 3 2 4	Low	7	24	19	Veritas Software (3)	High	IV 99	36.6	IV 00	−22.1	800-347-4246
NA	NA	NA	NA	NA	NA	4	Low	6	−10	27	Warner-Lambert (4)		IV 99	38.6	IV 00	−23.9	800-347-4246
10.8	8.8	11.6	10.4	NA	NA	1 5 4 1 5	Average	9	17	21	JDS Uniphase (6)	High	IV 99	49.1	III 98	−20.9	800-347-4246
12.5	11.8	14.0	13.4	NA	NA	2 4 2 1 5	Average	7	7	19	EMC (3)	Average	IV 99	37.8	IV 00	−17.1	800-347-4246
14.5	12.4	12.4	10.1	NA	NA	5 4 3 1 5	Average	4	−1	31	JDS Uniphase (6)	Very High	IV 99	62.2	IV 00	−39.4	800-347-4246
9.3	8.4	10.4	9.7	NA	NA	4 5 4 2 5	Average	8	17	23	Vodafone AirTouch ADR (5)	Average	IV 99	43.1	III 98	−14.6	800-347-4246
19.9	18.4	19.2	17.2	NA	NA	2 3 1 2 3	Low	11	27	27	PMC-Sierra (5)	High	IV 99	30.2	IV 00	−20.1	800-347-4246
20.0	16.9	20.8	17.7	18.6	15.8	4 4 2 2 5	Average	3	21	29	JDS Uniphase (6)	High	IV 99	37.1	IV 00	−22.9	800-347-4246
12.7	11.0	14.9	12.8	NA	NA	3 2 1 2 4	Average	11	11	44	Nokia ADS (7)	Average	IV 99	27.1	III 98	−12.3	800-347-4246
12.6	10.3	16.2	13.1	15.4	12.9	4 3 1 2 5	High	9	12	30	Intel (4)	High	IV 98	28.0	IV 00	−22.6	800-347-4246
17.9	16.3	17.5	16.1	NA	NA	3 3 1 1 5	Very High	6	−22	35	eBay (4)	High	IV 99	40.3	IV 00	−26.6	800-992-3863
17.2	14.6	17.3	14.7	19.2	17.0	4 2 1 2 4	Very High	7	−20	39	Cisco Systems (5)	High	IV 98	25.0	IV 00	−14.9	800-992-3863
14.8	13.2	NA	NA	NA	NA	1 1 3 3	Low	2	13	43	Pfizer (5)		IV 98	27.1	III 98	−14.2	800-992-8151
3.1	1.7	11.9	8.5	15.0	11.4	4 1 5 2 4	Average	1	14	46	NTL (6)	High	IV 99	26.4	III 98	−24.3	800-824-1916
14.3	12.6	18.6	15.8	NA	NA	1 1 2 4 1	Average	4	11	36	United Technologies (5)	Average	IV 98	22.9	III 98	−14.1	800-824-1916
8.7	5.8	14.7	12.1	19.1	16.5	2 2 1 3 4	Average	0	5	39	Vodafone AirTouch ADR (11)	Average	IV 98	28.6	III 98	−16.4	800-824-1916
14.8	13.4	19.7	17.9	NA	NA	1 1 1 2 6	Average	1	−12	43	Nokia Corp ADS (6)	High	IV 98	30.8	IV 00	−16.1	800-824-1916
27.4	25.9	20.5	19.6	NA	NA	2 5 1 1 5	Average	4	11	38	Cisco Systems (6)	Very High	IV 99	44.3	IV 00	−27.5	800-824-1916
19.4	16.2	20.5	16.8	18.2	15.0	5 2 2 3 2	Average	19	29	22	Medtronic (3)	Low	IV 98	22.0	III 98	−8.6	800-345-2021
7.6	4.9	10.4	7.4	11.4	9.2	4 3 2 4 3	High	1	7	17	Microsoft (3)	Low	II 97	12.3	III 98	−6.9	800-345-2021
9.8	8.6	18.1	15.7	NA	NA	1 1 1 1 3 4	High	3	11	28	Microsoft (5)	Average	IV 98	23.1	III 98	−13.9	800-345-2021
10.8	8.8	7.3	5.7	20.4	18.2	5 5 5 1 4	Average	3	4	39	Gemstar Intl. Group (7)	Very High	IV 99	56.3	IV 00	−35.1	800-345-2021
16.3	13.0	18.5	15.4	16.6	13.7	3 1 1 2 4	Average	5	12	42	Cisco Systems (7)	High	IV 99	23.6	IV 00	−16.8	800-345-2021
21.0	18.5	19.5	16.2	18.0	15.5	3 3 4 1 1	Average	6	20	29	Gemstar Intl. Group (6)	Average	IV 99	40.4	III 98	−21.2	800-345-2021
10.4	9.7	17.6	15.8	17.7	15.9	1 1 1 3 4	Average	2	14	24	Microsoft (4)	Average	IV 98	22.2	III 98	−11.3	800-345-2021
24.0	22.6	24.1	22.5	NA	NA	1 3 2 1 4	High	11	21	21	Marscholek VZ (4)	Average	IV 99	50.9	III 98	−19.9	800-345-2021
18.5	16.8	17.9	15.3	NA	NA	3 3 2 1 4	High	6	11	22	Vodafone AirTouch ADR (4)	Average	IV 99	48.2	III 98	−17.9	800-345-2021
32.0	28.3	NA	NA	NA	NA	5 3 1 4	Average	0	−1	38	Pinnacle Systems (7)		IV 99	77.3	IV 00	−36.6	800-345-2021
14.8	12.3	19.0	15.7	14.5	11.6	2 1 1 3 3	High	2	24	35	General Electric (6)	Average	IV 99	22.4	IV 00	−9.8	800-345-2021
15.1	13.3	16.4	13.5	20.6	18.9	3 2 1 2 5	Low	2	27	46	Qualcomm (7)	High	IV 99	32.1	IV 00	−16.9	800-345-2021
7.2	5.0	14.0	10.9	NA	NA	1 2 4 5 1	High	2	1	39	FPL Group (5)	Average	II 99	18.5	III 99	−11.0	800-345-2021
23.0	20.1	12.8	10.3	17.5	15.3	5 5 5 1 2	High	4	7	47	JDS Uniphase (13)	Very High	IV 99	72.2	III 98	−27.5	800-345-2021
10.0	7.5	12.8	9.9	13.5	10.8	5 4 4 5 1	Average	9	10	14	U.S. Treas. Infl. 3.756 7/02 (2)	Very Low	II 97	10.0	III 98	−5.2	800-421-0180
7.7	4.6	12.9	9.7	13.8	10.8	4 3 3 5 2	Average	21	16	16	Sprint (FON Group) (2)	Low	IV 98	12.4	III 99	−7.6	800-421-0180
NA	NA	NA	NA	NA	NA	5		13	−16	19	Samsung Electronics (3)		IV 99	25.2	II 00	−9.4	800-421-0180
14.6	13.9	19.9	17.3	16.4	14.7	2 1 1 3 3	Low	3	34	15	Cisco Systems (2)	Average	IV 98	22.9	III 98	−9.0	800-451-8377
7.1	5.9	13.4	11.8	NA	NA	2 1 3 5 1	Average	1	17	12	Exxon Mobil (2)	Low	II 97	12.6	III 99	−9.2	800-451-8377
14.4	13.8	NA	NA	NA	NA	2 2 4	High	2	0	10	NTT Mobile Communs. (2)		IV 99	36.2	III 98	−15.6	800-451-8377
28.9	27.3	24.4	22.7	NA	NA	1 5 1 1 4	High	4	−9	24	AT&T Canada B (4)	Average	IV 99	49.1	III 98	−18.8	800-344-1770
38.9	37.2	NA	NA	NA	NA	1 1 1	High	5	5	29	Kinder Morgan (5)		IV 99	37.7	III 98	−10.5	800-344-1770

Source: *Business Week,* 29 January 2001.

EXHIBIT 25.16 ▸ *SAMPLE PAGE FROM MORNINGSTAR MUTUAL FUNDS*

Fidelity Magellan

Ticker	Load	NAV	Yield	Total Assets	Mstar Category
FMAGX	Closed	$113.90	0.3%	$88,173.1 mil	Large Blend

Prospectus Objective: Growth

Fidelity Magellan Fund seeks capital appreciation.

The fund invests primarily in common stocks and convertible securities. It features domestic corporations operating primarily in the United States, domestic corporations that have significant activities and interests outside the U.S., and foreign companies. No limitations are placed on total foreign investment, but no more than 40% of assets may be invested in companies operating exclusively in one foreign country.

The fund closed to new investment in 1965 and reopened in 1981. It closed again in 1997.

Historical Profile
Return: Above Avg
Risk: Average
Rating: ★★★★ Above Avg

Investment Style: Equity — Average Stock %

▼ Manager Change
▽ Partial Manager Change

Fund Performance vs. Category Average
■ Quarterly Fund Return
+/– Category Average
— Category Baseline

Performance Quartile (within Category)

Portfolio Manager(s)

Robert E. Stansky, CFA. Since 6-96. BA'78 Nichols C.; MBA'83 New York U.

	1990	1991	1992	1993	1994	1995	1996	1997	1998	1999	2000	05-01	History
	53.93	68.61	63.01	70.85	66.80	85.98	80.65	95.27	120.82	136.63	119.30	113.90	NAV
	–4.51	41.03	7.02	24.66	–1.81	36.82	11.69	26.59	33.63	24.05	–9.29	–3.74	Total Return %
	–1.39	10.54	–0.60	14.60	–3.13	–0.71	–11.26	–6.76	5.05	3.01	–0.19	0.63	+/– S&P 500
	–0.48	8.59	–0.64	14.82	–2.26	–0.78	–10.48	–6.43	4.99	2.22	1.66	1.52	+/– Wilshire Top 750
	1.42	2.46	1.93	1.22	0.18	0.88	1.41	1.57	0.72	0.63	0.20	0.12	Income Return %
	–5.93	38.57	5.09	23.43	–1.99	35.94	10.28	25.03	32.91	23.42	–9.49	–3.86	Capital Return %
	64	12	54	5	66	21	97	64	4	27	56	25	Total Rtn % Rank Cat
	0.83	1.30	1.25	0.75	0.13	0.59	1.10	1.25	0.67	0.73	0.27	0.14	Income $
	2.42	5.43	8.82	6.50	2.64	4.69	12.85	5.21	5.15	11.39	4.69	0.80	Capital Gains $
	1.03	1.06	1.05	1.00	0.99	0.96	0.92	0.64	0.61	0.60	0.74	—	Expense Ratio %
	2.54	2.47	1.57	2.11	1.07	0.39	0.95	1.75	0.77	0.66	0.46	—	Income Ratio %
	82	135	172	155	132	120	155	67	34	37	28	—	Turnover Rate %
	12,325.7	19,257.1	22,268.9	31,705.1	36,441.5	53,702.3	53,988.7	63,766.2	83,552.1	105,938.5	93,066.9	88,173.1	Net Assets $mil

Performance 05-31-01

	1st Qtr	2nd Qtr	3rd Qtr	4th Qtr	Total
1997	–0.56	16.55	9.67	–0.40	26.59
1998	14.22	3.37	–11.05	27.22	33.63
1999	7.39	5.93	–5.97	15.97	24.05
2000	4.85	–3.96	–0.58	–9.40	–9.29
2001	–12.41	—	—	—	—

Trailing	Total Return%	+/– S&P 500	+/– Wil Top 750	% Rank All	% Rank Cat	Growth of $10,000
3 Mo	2.86	1.25	1.50	20	12	10,286
6 Mo	–2.93	0.96	1.31	68	33	9,707
1 Yr	–9.95	0.60	2.69	69	40	9,005
3 Yr Avg	8.52	2.37	3.08	18	18	12,779
5 Yr Avg	14.74	–0.39	0.39	11	28	19,885
10 Yr Avg	15.03	0.19	0.53	12	17	40,546
15 Yr Avg	14.90	0.55	1.00	8	11	80,302

Tax Analysis	Tax-Adj Ret%	%Rank Cat	%Pretax Ret	%Rank Cat
3 Yr Avg	7.11	16	83.4	37
5 Yr Avg	13.19	25	89.5	27
10 Yr Avg	12.21	35	81.2	51

Potential Capital Gain Exposure: 34% of assets

Risk Analysis

Time Period	Load-Adj Return %	Risk %Rank¹ All	Risk %Rank¹ Cat	Morningstar Return	Morningstar Risk	Morningstar Risk-Adj Rating
1 Yr	–12.65					
3 Yr	7.42	68	57	0.42²	0.93	★★★
5 Yr	14.04	70	60	1.46	0.91	★★★★
10 Yr	14.68	74	67	1.24	0.95	★★★★

Average Historical Rating (186 months): 4.6★s

¹1=low, 100=high ² T-Bill return substituted for category avg.

Category Rating (3 Yr)

Worst				Best
1	2	3	4	5

Return: Above Avg
Risk: Average

Other Measures	Standard Index S&P 500	Best Fit Index S&P 500
Alpha	2.4	2.4
Beta	1.06	1.06
R-Squared	97	97
Standard Deviation	22.42	
Mean	8.52	
Sharpe Ratio	0.16	

Analysis by Scott Cooley 05-23-01

Fidelity Magellan Fund still makes an excellent core holding.

This isn't the world-beater it was years ago, when it was considerably smaller, but manager Bob Stansky has found a style that works well at this behemoth. Stansky has excelled when buying stocks that are at least mildly out of favor and then holding them until he can sell into strength. In the past, that has produced well-timed forays into technology and health-care stocks. More recently, Stansky bought retail, media, and brokerage stocks in the first quarter, when they were beaten down. Each of those areas has rebounded strongly in recent months. Stansky moved into those areas to play a rebound in the U.S. economy, and so far, that wager has paid off. Those stocks have rebounded sharply, giving the fund a big lift. For the year to date through May 21, 2001, the fund's slight gain puts it ahead of more than two thirds of its rivals, and 33 basis points

(0.33%) in front of its S&P 500 benchmark.

Although Stansky's foray into economically sensitive areas has been at least a short-term winner, he has mixed feelings about those stocks' performances. They have rallied so strongly that Stansky is concerned about their valuations. He said that although their share prices had improved dramatically, few tangible signs of improvement in the firms' operations existed. However, he's more bullish on the prospects for energy firms, thanks to an attractive supply/demand picture.

Stansky's opportunistic purchases and attention to valuations have produced an admirable record here over the past few years. Indeed, the fund's three-year return tops the index's by more than two percentage points annually. Stansky isn't likely to blow the index out of the water in any given year, but we see no reason why he cannot continue to generate solidly above-average long-term results.

Portfolio Analysis 09-30-00

Share change since 03–00 Total Stocks: 317

Sector	PE	YTD Ret%	% Assets
⊕ General Elec	Industrials	38.3	2.58	5.09
⊕ Citigroup	Financials	20.3	0.89	3.04
⊕ Cisco Sys	Technology	—	–49.60	2.93
⊕ ExxonMobil	Energy	16.2	3.13	2.52
⊖ Home Depot	Retail	44.8	7.99	2.40
⊕ Tyco Intl	Industrials	9.8	3.54	2.06
⊕ EMC	Technology	38.5	–51.50	2.01
⊕ Viacom Cl B	Services	—	—	2.00
⊕ American Intl Grp	Financials	32.5	–17.70	1.87
⊕ Sun Microsystems	Technology	26.1	–40.90	1.78
⊖ Pfizer	Health	46.6	–6.30	1.75
⊕ Intel	Technology	22.5	–10.00	1.73
⊖ Microsoft	Technology	39.8	59.49	1.58
⊖ Time Warner	Services	—	–27.50	1.53
⊕ Oracle	Technology	13.8	–47.30	1.50
⊕ IBM	Technology	24.4	31.83	1.38
⊕ Texas Instruments	Technology	21.1	–27.90	1.33
⊕ Wal–Mart Stores	Retail	36.7	–2.45	1.33
⊕ Eli Lilly	Health	30.7	–8.36	1.31
⊕ Fannie Mae	Financials	19.2	–4.22	1.19
⊖ Wells Fargo	Financials	19.8	–14.60	1.07
⊖ Merck	Health	24.6	–21.30	1.03
⊖ Morgan Stanley/Dean Witter	Financials	15.2	–17.30	0.98
⊖ Schering–Plough	Health	28.2	–25.50	0.93
⊕ Nortel Networks	Technology	—	–58.30	0.93

Current Investment Style

Style: Value Blend Growth — Large Mid Small

	Stock Port Avg	Relative S&P 500 Current	Relative S&P 500 Hist	Rel Cat
Price/Earnings Ratio	30.1	1.02	1.15	1.03
Price/Book Ratio	6.8	1.05	1.20	1.03
Price/Cash Flow	23.7	1.11	1.08	1.07
3 Yr Earnings Growth	20.1	1.17	1.30	1.08
1 Yr Earnings Est%	6.1	0.98	—	0.71
Med Mkt Cap $mil	74,099		1.2 1.7	1.49

Special Securities % assets 09-30-00

Restricted/Illiquid Secs	0
Emerging–Markets Secs	Trace
Options/Futures/Warrants	No

Composition % assets 09-30-00

		Market Cap	
		Giant	61.2
Cash	4.1	Large	30.5
Stocks*	95.9	Medium	7.9
Bonds	0.0	Small	0.4
Other	0.0	Micro	0.0
*Foreign (% stocks)	4.5		

Sector Weightings

	% of Stocks	Rel S&P	5-Year High	Low
Utilities	0.0	0.0	9	0
Energy	8.1	1.1	25	1
Financials	15.2	0.9	17	7
Industrials	11.1	1.0	31	10
Durables	1.5	0.8	16	2
Staples	2.9	0.4	10	0
Services	12.7	1.1	17	10
Retail	8.0	1.2	11	2
Health	11.0	0.8	15	2
Technology	29.5	1.5	42	4

Address:	82 Devonshire Street Boston, MA 02109 800–544–8888	Minimum Purchase:	Closed	Add: $250	IRA: —
		Min Auto Inv Plan:	Closed	Add: $100	
		Sales Fees:	3.00%L		
Web Address:	www.fidelity.com	Management Fee:	.57%+.52% mx./.27% mn.(G)+(–).20%P		
Inception:	05-02-63	Actual Fees:	Mgt: 0.57%	Dist: —	
Advisor:	Fidelity Mgmt. & Research	Expense Projections:	3Yr: $532	5Yr: $704	10Yr: $1202
Subadvisor:	FMR (U.K.)/FMR (Far East)	Avg Brok Commission:	—	Income Distrib: Semi-Ann.	
NTF Plans:	Fidelity Inst.	**Total Cost** (relative to category):		Below Avg	

 M⊙RNINGSTAR Mutual Funds

| EXHIBIT 25.17 | *MUTUAL FUND INFORMATION FROM BLOOMBERG AND BRIDGE INFORMATION SERVICES* |

A. Bloomberg

DGAGX US
DREYFUS APPRECIATION FD INC   Objective – Blue Chip

Dreyfus Appreciation Fund, Inc. is an open-end fund incorporated in the USA. The Fund's objective is long-term capital growth consistent with the preservation of capital. Its secondary goal is current income. The Fund invests at least 80% of its net assets in the common stock of large-cap U.S. and foreign blue-chip companies.

Bloomberg Classification Data

Asset Class	Equity
Style	Blue Chip
Market Cap Focus	Large-cap
Geographic Focus	Global

Current / Operational Data

1)GP NAV		$	38.74
Assets(mil)	2/28/02	$	3422.63
Inception Date		1/18/84	

Performance Ranking

as of 3/25/02	Return	%All	%Obj.
3)TRA 1 Month	1.79	42	39
YTD	1.89	81	95
1 Year	5.46	78	97
5 Year	9.66	83	94
2001	-10.75	37	89

1 Yr Performance vs. Benchmark Indices

DGAGX
SPX

30MAR01 31MAY 31JUL 28SEP 30NOV 31JAN02

B. Telerate

us;DGAGX   Name: Dreyfus Appreciation Fund Inc   Cusip: 261970-10-7
    Objective: GRD Growth - Domestic   NAV: 38.74
                         Load: 0.00%   Offer Pr: 38.74

Perf. as of 28-Feb-02	Total Return	SEC 482 Return	Percentile Rank in Obj	Net Assets: 3,427 M (as of 31-Dec-01)	
1 month	-0.24%		10	Equities	: 95.3
3 month	-0.27%		20	Convertibles	:
YTD	-0.08%		6	Preferred	: 0.6
1 year	-6.46%	-10.75%	20	Bonds	:
2 year - ann	-0.82%		21	Cash	: 4.1
3 year - ann	-0.21%		39		
5 year - ann	9.12%	10.82%	30		
10 year - ann	12.39%	12.20%	20		

Last 12 Mos.		Beta	
Yield:	0.80%	1 Year	0.696
Income Divs:	0.30	3 Year	0.675
Cap Gain Divs:		5 Year	0.807
Expense Ratio:	0.88	10 Year	0.841
Port Turnover:	4.28		

dgagx/fnd   26-Mar-02 10:45 NYC   (c)BRIDGE

Morningstar is a well-regarded information service for mutual funds. Its basic service is available online and provides an informative one-page sheet that evaluates the performance of open-end mutual funds. An example sheet for a fund is included as Exhibit 25.16. This sheet provides up-to-date information on the fund's objective, investment style, and its risk-adjusted performance relative to an appropriate benchmark. There is also an analysis of performance and investment strategy based on an interview with the fund manager. A similar service evaluates several hundred closed-end funds.

One of the most useful features of the information provided by *Morningstar* is a performance and risk rating system. *Morningstar* gives each fund between one and five stars based on the fund's weighted risk-adjusted return performance over several time periods. The star ratings are interpreted as follows: Lowest Rating (1), Below Average (2), Neutral (3), Above Average (4), and Highest Rating (5). The Fidelity Magellan fund summarized in Exhibit 25.16 received an overall four-star rating in this assessment. *Morningstar* also gave Magellan an "above average risk" rating when comparing it to other funds in the same objective class.

Finally, investors should be aware of the tremendous amount of investment data that is now available over the Internet and from other online sources. In fact, virtually all private and public asset management companies now have their own Web sites that are easily reached through standard search engines. [We saw earlier that Nelson's Investment Manager Network (http://www. nelnet.com) is a particularly good site for information about private advisory and management firms.] Further, Bloomberg and Bridge Information Services, two of the more popular online information services, provide investors with a combination of both unique information and data gathered from other sources. Exhibit 25.17 shows representative pages from both Bloomberg and Telerate for the Dreyfus Appreciation fund, another growth-oriented equity portfolio.

ETHICS AND REGULATION IN THE PROFESSIONAL ASSET MANAGEMENT INDUSTRY

The issue of ethical behavior arises any time one person is hired to perform a service for or look after the interests of another. This topic is particularly important for the asset management business because the entire industry is based on handling someone else's money. Not surprisingly, then, the investment industry is highly regulated to ensure a minimum level of acceptable practice. Exhibit 25.18 describes the four principal securities laws that govern investment companies, including the Investment Company Act of 1940, the Securities Act of 1933, the Securities Exchange Act of 1934, and the Investment Advisers Act of 1940. Notice that a primary intention of these regulations is to guarantee that investment companies keep accurate and detailed transaction records and that account information is reported to investors in a fair and timely manner. The primary federal regulation governing the management of private pension funds is the Employee Retirement Income Security Act (ERISA), which was enacted in 1974.[7]

Investors are well aware of the securities scandals of the 1980s that made such individuals as Ivan Boesky and Michael Milken household names. Unfortunately, transgressions of this nature attest to the fact that, although regulations can punish those found in violation of the law, they cannot prevent all such abuses from occurring. Absolute prevention requires self-regulation on

---

[7]The main feature of ERISA is the *prudent man* statute, which outlines the level of fiduciary care that the manager is required to provide to the investor. For a good discussion of this topic, see Diane Del Guerico, "The Distorting Effect of the Prudent-Man Laws on Institutional Equity Investments," *Journal of Financial Economics* 40, no. 1 (January 1996): 31–62.

EXHIBIT 25.18 *PRINCIPAL SECURITIES LAWS FOR THE ASSET MANAGEMENT INDUSTRY*

- **The Investment Company Act of 1940** regulates the structure and operations of mutual funds and other investment companies. Among other things, the 1940 Act requires mutual funds to maintain detailed books and records, safeguard their portfolio securities, and file semiannual reports with the U.S. Securities and Exchange Commission (SEC).
- **The Securities Act of 1933** requires the federal registration of all public offerings of securities, including mutual fund shares. The 1933 Act also requires that all prospective investors receive a current prospectus describing the fund.
- **The Securities Exchange Act of 1934** regulates broker-dealers, including mutual fund principal underwriters and others who sell mutual fund shares, and requires them to register with the SEC. Among other things, the 1934 Act requires registered broker-dealers to maintain extensive books and records, segregate customer securities in adequate custodial accounts, and file detailed, annual financial reports with the SEC.
- **The Investment Advisers Act of 1940** requires federal registration of all investment advisers to mutual funds. The Advisers Act contains various antifraud provisions and requires fund advisers to meet recordkeeping, reporting, and other requirements.

Source: *2002 Mutual Fund Fact Book,* Copyright © 2002 Investment Company Institute. Reprinted by permission of the Investment Company Institute (www.ici.org).

the part of the asset manager in the form of a strict set of personal ethical standards. Avera has outlined four general principles that should form the cornerstone of the standards of conduct in the profession.[8] First, managers must conduct themselves with integrity and dignity and act in an ethical manner in all dealings. Second, they should perform financial analysis in a professional and ethical manner that reflects credit on the profession. Third, managers should act with competence and strive to maintain and improve competence in themselves. Finally, they should always use proper care and exercise independent professional judgment.

The Association for Investment Management and Research (AIMR) has developed for its worldwide membership of security analysts and money managers a rigorous *Code of Ethics and Standards of Professional Conduct* based on these principles. The *Code of Ethics* contains four primary themes and can be stated as follows:

> Members of the Association for Investment Management and Research shall
> - Act with integrity, competence, dignity, and in an ethical manner when dealing with the public, clients, prospects, employers, employees, and fellow members.
> - Practice and encourage others to practice in a professional and ethical manner that will reflect credit on members and their profession.
> - Strive to maintain and improve their competence and the competence of others in the profession.
> - Use reasonable care and exercise independent professional judgment.

The specific standards of practice suggested by these ethical mandates are summarized in Appendix B. These standards provide asset managers with precisely defined conduct and actions

---

[8]William F. Avera, "Definition of Industry Ethics and Development of a Code," in *Good Ethics: The Essential Element of a Firm's Success,* ed. K. Baker (Charlottesville, Va.: Association for Investment Management and Research, 1994). For an interesting discussion of the investing public's perception of ethics in the asset management industry, see also Scott L. Lummer, "Public Perception of the Investment Industry: Trends and Counteractions," in the same volume.

that are acceptable (or, more to the point, unacceptable) in daily practice. For example, the general principle that managers should use proper care becomes a specific requirement that they must be able to justify the suitability of any investment decision made on behalf of a particular client. AIMR expects all of its members, which includes everyone holding the Chartered Financial Analyst (CFA) designation, to uphold these standards on a voluntary basis. Violations deemed severe enough can result in the loss of a manager's charter.

Many ethical lapses, such as plagiarizing research reports or falsifying performance statements, are unambiguously wrong. Others, however, are not as clear-cut. We will conclude this section with a discussion of two examples of how possible conflicts between the manager and the investor can arise from accepted business practices. The first example is related to the way in which managers are compensated for their service. We saw earlier in the chapter that asset management companies—both public and private—typically receive fees based on AUM. The managers at these companies, in turn, are often compensated with a base salary and a bonus that depends on the performance of their portfolios relative to those of their peers. Brown, Harlow, and Starks argued that this arrangement is analogous to a golf or tennis tournament where the players with the best relative performance at the end of the competition receive the largest payoffs.[9] They documented that managers with the worst relative performance midway through a compensation period were more likely to increase the risk of the portfolio in an effort to increase their final standing. Of course, altering fund risk to enhance their own compensation suggests that some managers may not always act in their clients' best interest.

A second potential ethical dilemma for professional asset managers involves the use of **soft dollars**. Soft dollars are generated when a manager commits the investor to paying a brokerage commission that is higher than the simple cost of executing a stock trade in exchange for the manager receiving additional bundled services from the broker. A typical example of this practice would be for a manager to route her trades through a nondiscount broker in order to receive security research reports that the brokerage firm produces. It may not be hard for the manager to justify how this additional research benefits the investor—who, of course, is ultimately paying for the service—but the story is quite different if instead of research the manager receives from the broker "perks," such as office equipment, secretarial services, or even personal travel. Several authors have argued that this practice can result in an expropriation of investor wealth by the manager, although Horan and Johnsen document that the use of soft dollars is actually a cost-effective way for investors to monitor a manager's behavior.[10] In May 1998, AIMR adopted a comprehensive set of voluntary standards designed to give its members guidance on the permissible uses of soft dollar arrangements.

In summary, it is important for investors to recognize that potential ethical conflicts will exist any time they hire a professional investment manager. Investors are protected by the series of regulations that govern the security industry as well as the strict standards imposed by trade associations, such as AIMR. Of course, perhaps the best protection that investors have is that the vast majority of the thousands of investment advisors and managers throughout the world are unwilling to do anything that would jeopardize their personal and professional reputations.

---

[9]Keith C. Brown, W. V. Harlow, and Laura T. Starks, "Of Tournaments and Temptations: An Analysis of Managerial Incentives in the Mutual Fund Industry," *Journal of Finance* 51, no. 1 (March 1996).

[10]Stephen M. Horan and D. Bruce Johnsen, *The Welfare Effects of Soft Dollar Brokerage: Law and Economics* (Charlottesville, Va.: The Research Foundation of the Institute of Chartered Financial Analysts, 2000). See also Marshall E. Blume, "Soft Dollars and the Brokerage Industry," *Financial Analysts Journal* 49, no. 2 (March–April 1993): 36–44.

PERFORMANCE OF INVESTMENT COMPANIES

Investment company performance has been one of the most widely studied topics in all of finance. There are two primary reasons for this: (1) These funds reflect the performance of professional money managers, and (2) fund data have been available for a long time. Although a more complete discussion of performance measurement techniques will be presented in Chapter 26, it is useful to conclude this chapter with a summary of some of what has been written on mutual fund investing.

Analysis of Overall Performance

When Sharpe evaluated the overall performance of mutual funds, only 32 percent of the funds outperformed the DJIA.[11] Further, comparing the ranks of the funds between the first and second halves of the sample period led Sharpe to conclude that past performance was not the best predictor of future performance.

An examination of the relationship between performance and the expense ratio indicated that good performance was associated with low expense ratios. Finally, analysis of *gross* performance, with expenses added back to the returns, indicated that 56 percent of the funds did better than the DJIA. Therefore, Sharpe concluded that the average mutual fund manager selected a portfolio at least as good as the DJIA; but, after deducting the operating costs of the fund, most achieved *net* returns below those of the DJIA.

The results of a study by Jensen indicated that on average the funds earned 1.1 percent less per year than they should have earned for their level of risk.[12] Analysis of gross returns with expenses added back indicated that 42 percent did better than the overall market on a risk-adjusted basis, whereas the analysis of net returns indicated that only 34 percent of the funds outperformed the market. The gross returns indicate the forecasting ability of the funds because these results do not penalize the funds for operating expenses (only brokerage commissions). Jensen concluded that on average these funds could not beat a buy-and-hold policy.

Carlson examined the overall performance of mutual funds with emphasis on the effects of the market series used for comparison and the time period.[13] The results depended heavily on which market series were used: the S&P 500, the NYSE composite, or the DJIA. For the total period, most fund groups outperformed the DJIA, but only a few had gross returns better than the S&P 500 or the NYSE composite. Using net returns, *none* of the groups outperformed the S&P 500 or the NYSE composite. Analysis of the performance factors indicated consistency over time for return or risk alone but no consistency in the risk-adjusted performance. Less than one-third of the funds that performed above average during the first half did so in the second half. Lehmann and Modest likewise found substantial differences between benchmarks but also concluded that average performance was consistently inferior to the overall market performance.[14] A study by Grinblatt and Titman examined performance using portfolio holdings, which does not require a market benchmark.[15] Notably, using this technique, they find that portfolio managers who manage aggressive growth stocks earned significantly positive risk-adjusted returns during 1976–1985.

[11]William F. Sharpe, "Mutual Fund Performance," *Journal of Business* 39, no. 1, part 2 (January 1966): 119–138.

[12]Michael C. Jensen, "The Performance of Mutual Funds in the Period 1945–1964," *Journal of Finance* 23, no. 2 (May 1968): 389–416.

[13]Robert S. Carlson, "Aggregate Performance of Mutual Funds, 1948–1967," *Journal of Financial and Quantitative Analysis* 5, no. 1 (March 1970): 1–32.

[14]Bruce N. Lehmann and David M. Modest, "Mutual Fund Performance Evaluations: A Comparison of Benchmarks and Benchmark Comparisons," *Journal of Finance* 42, no. 2 (June 1987): 233–265.

[15]Mark Grinblatt and Sheridan Titman, "Performance Measurement without Benchmarks: An Examination of Mutual Fund Returns," *Journal of Business* 66, no. 1 (January 1993): 47–68.

All the early studies were concerned with evaluating the performance of U.S. equity funds. Given the growing tendency toward global stock and bond investing, several authors have examined the performance of international equity and fixed-income funds.

Cumby and Glen examined the performance of international funds compared to the Morgan Stanley world equity index and a U.S. index.[16] Using two risk-adjusted performance measures, they found no evidence that the performance of the funds surpassed that of a broad international index during the sample period. Bailey and Lim examined the performance of country funds (e.g., France, Germany, Korea, Spain) to see if these funds helped investors attain international diversification.[17] They found that country fund returns often resembled domestic U.S. stock returns more than returns from foreign stock portfolios—that is, these funds would not provide the expected benefits of diversification. Cai, Chan, and Yamada showed that Japanese mutual funds tend to underperform their benchmarks.[18]

Blake, Elton, and Gruber examined the performance of bond mutual funds and found that the bond funds generally underperformed relevant bond indexes.[19] Because the underperformance was about equal to the management fees, it is suggested that these funds performed about equal to the indexes—before expenses. They also found no evidence that past performance could predict future performance.

Investment Style and the Classification of Mutual Funds

From the inception of the industry, mutual funds have attempted to inform potential investors about their intended investment strategy by committing to a specific objective classification. As we have seen, these investment objectives are listed in the fund's prospectus and include such categories as aggressive growth, growth, growth and income, balanced, global, and income. Prior to the advances that have been made in defining investment style during the last several years, researchers and investors alike often used these objective classes as surrogates for the risk-expected return trade-off a given fund was likely to produce. McDonald produced one of the earliest studies along these lines, showing that the returns generated by a sample of mutual funds segmented by their stated objectives.[20] In particular, he finds that measures of both risk and return increased as the fund objective became more aggressive and that risk-adjusted performance of the more aggressive funds dominated that of the more conservative funds during the sample period. More recently, Malkiel offers evidence that a fund's ability to outperform a benchmark such as the S&P 500 was also related to its objective classification; and Bogle shows that low-cost, passively managed index funds have generally delivered the highest risk-adjusted returns in each category.[21]

Despite their documented connections with risk and performance, traditional fund objective categories appear to have fallen out of favor as methods of classifying funds. One reason for this is that the selection process for these objectives can be subjective and might not always repre-

[16]Robert E. Cumby and Jack D. Glen, "Evaluating the Performance of International Mutual Funds," *Journal of Finance* 45, no. 2 (June 1990): 497–522.

[17]Warren Bailey and Joseph Lim, "Evaluating the Diversification Benefits of the New Country Funds," *Journal of Portfolio Management* 18, no. 3 (Spring 1992): 74–80.

[18]J. Cai, K. C. Chan, and T. Yamada, "The Performance of Japanese Mutual Funds," *Review of Financial Studies* 10, no. 2 (Summer 1997): 237–274.

[19]Christopher R. Blake, Edwin J. Elton, and Martin J. Gruber, "The Performance of Bond Mutual Funds," *Journal of Business* 66, no. 3 (July 1993): 371–403.

[20]John G. McDonald, "Objectives and Performance of Mutual Funds, 1960–1969," *Journal of Financial and Quantitative Analysis* 9, no. 3 (June 1974): 311–333.

[21]Burton G. Malkiel, "Returns from Investing in Equity Mutual Funds: 1971–1991," *Journal of Finance* 50, no. 2 (June 1995): 549–572; and John C. Bogle, "The Implications of Style Analysis for Mutual Fund Performance Evaluation," *Journal of Portfolio Management* 24, no. 4 (Summer 1998): 34–42.

sent a fund's actual holdings very well. More typical of current fund classification methods is the effort to define a portfolio's investment style directly by a decomposition of its security characteristics. Not surprisingly, a consequence of such efforts has been the finding that funds are often classified improperly using the traditional categories. Brown and Goetzmann develop an entirely new classification system based on style factors that is superior to the conventionally defined categories in predicting future fund returns.[22] Further, diBartolomeo and Witkowski use a multifactor decomposition of fund security holdings to conclude that 40 percent of the 748 equity funds in their sample were misclassified, a problem they attribute primarily to the ambiguity of the current objective classification system.[23]

Investment Style and Performance Persistence

Although analyzing overall performance has been the primary focus of the fund performance literature, a related topic that has received considerable recent attention has been the persistence of that performance—whether good or bad—over time. Against the backdrop of Jensen's original finding that managers generally are not able to sustain superior performance, much of the more current research reports data supporting persistence. Some of these studies, such as Hendricks, Patel, and Zeckhauser, as well as Brown and Goetzmann, document a short-run, positive correlation between abnormal returns in successive years. This phenomenon is attributed to managers with "hot hands," but the evidence in both studies appears to be driven by those funds sustaining poor performance (i.e., "icy hands").[24] Additionally, Grinblatt and Titman and Elton, Gruber, and Blake find that past risk-adjusted performance is predictive of future performance over periods as long as three years, although these results appear to be sample-period dependent.[25] Finally, Carhart and Wermers document that the dominance of past winner funds over past losers is largely driven by momentum investing and is most pronounced in growth-oriented portfolios.[26]

Obviously, an important issue in establishing persistence is how abnormal performance is measured. In these studies, risk-adjusted performance is typically measured in terms of a multifactor return generating process designed to capture the essence of the fund's style in either an implicit or explicit fashion. Some, like Carhart, use variations of the Fama-French characteristic-based model; while others, such as Grinblatt and Titman, use a multiple benchmark portfolio model. While nominally a study of the performance of private asset managers rather than the public fund industry, Christopherson, Ferson, and Glassman extend this literature in two interesting ways while corroborating the finding that bad performance persists.[27] First, they calculate abnormal performance directly against returns to specific (i.e., Russell) style indexes. Second, the authors exploit a statistical technique that allows them to assess performance conditioned on the myriad macroeconomic information that was publicly available at the time the returns were generated.

---

[22]Stephen J. Brown and William N. Goetzmann, "Mutual Fund Styles," *Journal of Financial Economics* 43, no. 1 (March 1997): 373–399.

[23]Dan diBartolomeo and Erik Witkowski, "Mutual Fund Misclassification: Evidence Based on Style Analysis, *Financial Analysts Journal* 53, no. 5 (September/October 1997): 32–43.

[24]Darryl Hendricks, Jayendu Patel, and Richard Zeckhauser, "Hot Hands in Mutual Funds: Short-Run Persistence of Relative Performance, 1974–1988," *Journal of Finance* 48, no. 1 (March 1993): 93–130; and Stephen J. Brown and William N. Goetzmann, "Performance Persistence," *Journal of Finance* 50, no. 2 (June 1995): 679–698.

[25]Mark Grinblatt and Sheridan Titman, "The Persistence of Mutual Fund Performance," *Journal of Finance* 47, no. 5 (June 1992): 1977–1984; and Edwin Elton, Martin J. Gruber, and Christopher Blake, "The Persistence of Risk-Adjusted Mutual Fund Performance," *Journal of Business* 69, no. 2 (April 1996): 133–157.

[26]Mark M. Carhart, "On Persistence in Mutual Fund Performance," *Journal of Finance* 52, no. 1 (March 1997): 57–82; and Russ Wermers, "Mutual Fund Performance: An Empirical Decomposition Into Stock-Picking Talent, Style, Transaction Costs, and Expenses," *Journal of Finance* 55, no. 4 (August 2000): 1655–1695.

[27]Jon A. Christopherson, Wayne E. Ferson, and Debra A. Glassman, "Conditioning Manager Alphas on Economic Information: Another Look at the Persistence of Performance," *Review of Financial Studies* 11, no. 1 (Spring 1998): 111–142.

What Performance Studies Mean to You

What functions would you want your own personal portfolio manager to perform for you? The list would probably include:

1. Determine your risk-return preferences and develop a portfolio that is consistent with them.
2. Diversify your portfolio to eliminate unsystematic risk.
3. Maintain your portfolio diversification and your desired risk class while allowing flexibility so you could shift between alternative investment instruments as desired.
4. Attempt to achieve a risk-adjusted performance that is superior to aggregate market performance. Some investors may be willing to sacrifice diversification for superior returns in limited segments of their portfolios.
5. Administer the account, keep records of costs, provide timely information for tax purposes, and reinvest dividends if desired.

Although the performance studies typically reviewed only risk-adjusted performance, all of these functions should be considered to put performance into perspective. Therefore, let us consider each of these functions and discuss how mutual funds fulfill them.

Mutual funds do not determine your risk preference. However, once you determine your risk-return preferences, you can choose a mutual fund from a large and growing variety of alternative funds designed to meet almost any investment goal. Recall that the empirical studies indicated that the funds generally were consistent in meeting their stated goals for investment strategies, risk, and returns.

Diversifying your portfolio to eliminate unsystematic risk is one of the major benefits of mutual funds. Many funds provide *instant diversification.* This is especially beneficial to small investors who do not have the resources to acquire 100 shares of 12 or 15 different issues required to reduce unsystematic risk. By initiating an investment in a fund with about $1,000, you can participate in a portfolio of securities that is correlated about 0.90 with the market portfolio, which means that it is about 90 percent diversified. Although diversification varies among funds, typically about three-quarters of the funds have a correlation with the market above 0.90. Therefore, most funds provide excellent diversification, especially if they state this as an objective.

The third function of your portfolio manager is to maintain the diversification and your desired risk class. It is not too surprising that mutual funds have generally maintained the stability of their correlation with the market because few change the makeup of reasonably well-diversified portfolios substantially. Strong evidence exists regarding the consistency of the risk class for individual funds even when there was inconsistency in risk-adjusted performance.

Mutual funds have met the desire for flexibility to change investment instruments by the initiation of numerous funds within a given management company. Typically, investment groups, such as T. Rowe Price or Fidelity Investments, will allow you to shift among their funds without a charge simply by calling the fund. Therefore, you can shift among an aggressive stock fund, a money market fund, and a bond fund for much less than it would cost you in time and money to buy and sell numerous individual issues.

The fourth function of your portfolio manager is to provide risk-adjusted performance that is superior to the aggregate market, which implies that it is superior to a naive buy-and-hold policy. As indicated in the prior discussion, the majority of empirical evidence indicates that, on average, fund managers' results in selecting undervalued securities are about as good as, or only slightly better than, the results of a naive buy-and-hold policy. This conclusion is based on *gross* returns. Unfortunately, the evidence from *net* returns, after research and trading costs, indicates that most funds do not do as well as a naive buy-and-hold policy. Notably, some recent studies indicate that there is some persistence in performance. The shortfall in performance of about 1 percent a year roughly matches the average cost of research and trading commissions.

In response to these findings, several investment management firms have started index funds based on the philosophy, "if you can't beat 'em, join 'em." These *Market-wide and Sector-specific index funds* do not attempt to beat the market but merely try to match the composition and, therefore, the performance of some specified market index, such as the S&P 500 index. Because these index funds have no research costs and minimal trading expenses, their returns typically have correlated with the chosen indexes at rates in excess of 0.99 with very low expenses. Also, their management fees are substantially below those charged by active managers.

The final function of a portfolio manager is account administration. This is another significant benefit of most mutual funds because they allow automatic reinvestment of dividends with no charge and consistently provide records of total cost. Further, each year they supply statements of dividend income and capital gain distribution that can be used to prepare tax returns.

In summary, as an investor, you probably want your portfolio manager to perform a set of functions. Typically, mutual funds can help you accomplish four of the five functions at a lower cost in terms of time and money than doing the work on your own. This convenience and service have, on average, cost about 1 percent a year in terms of performance.

Finally, assuming that you decide to build your portfolio with mutual funds, it is important to minimize your trading. A study by Nesbitt showed that individual investors who attempt to select undervalued securities generally buy into asset categories near their peaks and sell after they level off or fall.[28] This results in an underperformance of about 1 percent a year.

The Internet *Investments Online*

As mutual funds have grown in popularity as a means to gain instant diversification and professional management, so have the number of Web sites devoted to some aspect of mutual fund investing. Any of the major fund companies (Fidelity, T. Rowe Price, Vanguard, Scudder, and so on) will have interesting Web sites to visit. Here are some others:

http://www.investools.com This is a site with links to several publications. The All Star Fund Trader site is a newsletter on sector and equity funds. This site offers descriptions of the newsletter's features. A sample copy can be viewed online.

http://www.wiesenberger.com The home page of Wiesenberger offers an overview of the firm's various investment products. Both closed-end and open-end investment company data, analysis, and software can be purchased, hard

copy or online, from this firm. This site has a page with links to many mutual fund sites, including mutual fund families and variable annuity firms.

http://www.brill.com The Mutual Funds Interactive Web site offers basic information about mutual fund investing, via charts, market commentary, and fund price quotes. It has a number of educational features, including a Q&A section, a manager profile, and discussions of various investment topics and of the different types of mutual funds.

http://www.mfea.com A good place to start if you want to learn more about mutual funds is this home page for the Mutual Fund Education Alliance. This site, called the Mutual Fund Investor's Center, offers a great deal of information. The Fund Center allows users to research, track, and customize their own fund portfolio from

(continued)

---

[28]Stephen L. Nesbitt, "Buy High, Sell Low: Timing Errors in Mutual Fund Allocations," *Journal of Portfolio Management* 22, no. 1 (Fall 1995): 57–60.

The Internet *Investments Online (cont.)*

a list of over 1,000 funds. Investors can search by a specific fund's name or search for funds by their characteristics, including investment category, level of 12b-1 fee, expense ratio, and sales charge. Investors can also discover the three top-performing funds year-to-date in different investment categories and find the lowest-cost fund by investment category. The Education Center page deals with the basics of mutual fund investing, while the Planning and Retirement Center page covers information and investment strategies for retirement, future education, and children. The site has links to a number of fund families.

http://www.investorguide.com/funds.htm
This page from that Web site focuses on mutual fund investing and has links to a variety of mutual-fund-related sites. Topics include learning about mutual funds, getting performance data and ratings, screening mutual funds, and obtaining a mutual fund prospectus.

http://www.stocksmart.com/tr/tmf.html
This site ranks the current performance of over 7,400 mutual funds and compares their relative performance to that of the S&P 500 and to a peer comparison group. It includes, as well, some data of interest to stock and bond investors.

http://www.morningstar.com *Morningstar* is a leading provider of mutual fund information. The site features much information and many links of interest to mutual fund investors. Items on the Web site include news, analysis, and columns by several *Morningstar* writers, and an interview with a fund manager. Past articles are available in an archive. The site also features sections dealing with learning, planning, and researching about mutual funds. A mutual fund screen allows users to find funds from *Morningstar*'s database that meet certain investment category, return, rating, and volatility criteria.

http://www.mfmag.com The Web site of Mutual Funds Online is a subscription service offering fund price quotes, a variety of performance rankings, profiles on over 10,000 funds, and access to a variety of screens that help investors find the funds that best suit their needs.

http://www.ici.org The Investment Company Institute is a mutual fund trade organization. Visitors to their home page can view issues of their annual publication, *Mutual Fund Handbook*, learn mutual fund facts and figures, read ICI's newsletter, and get information about financial market and mutual fund regulation issues.

Summary

- There are two primary types of professional asset management companies. Management and advisory firms hold the assets of both individual and institutional investors in separate accounts, which allows for the possibility of managing each client's portfolio in a unique manner. Conversely, investment companies, such as closed- and open-end funds, are pools of assets that are managed collectively. Investors in these funds receive shares representing their proportional ownership in the underlying portfolio of stocks, bonds, or other securities. These fund shares can either be traded in the secondary market (closed-end) or sold directly back to the investment company (mutual fund) at the prevailing net asset value. A wide variety of funds are available, so you can find one to match almost any investment objective or combination of investment objectives.

- In recent years, the professional asset management industry has undergone considerable structural change. Most notably, there has been a trend toward consolidating assets under management (AUM) in large, multiproduct firms. This trend has had a beneficial effect for investors of reducing management fees, which are usually charged on a declining percentage of AUM. Investment companies also often charge fees for marketing their shares. These sales charges can take the form of front-end fees, annual

12b-1 fees, or back-end load fees. A substantial amount of publicly available information exists on mutual fund investment practices and performance to help investors make decisions that are appropriate for their circumstances.

- Issues of ethical behavior arise any time one person is hired to perform a service for another. The professional asset management industry protects investors through a series of government regulations and voluntary standards of practice imposed by trade associations on their members. The primary purpose of these regulations and standards is to ensure that managers deal with all investors fairly and equitably and that information about investment performance is accurately reported. Two areas of particular concern in the investment community involve manager compensation arrangements and the use of soft dollars.

- Numerous studies have examined the historical performance of mutual funds. Most found that less than half the funds matched the risk-adjusted net returns of the aggregate market. The results with gross returns generally indicated average risk-adjusted returns about equal to those of the market, with about half the funds (more than half for some studies) outperforming the market. Interestingly, some recent studies have found evidence of performance persistence.

- Although the returns received by the average individual investor on funds managed by investment companies will probably not be superior to the average results for a specific U.S. or international market, several other important services are provided by investment companies. Therefore, you should give serious consideration to these funds as an important alternative to investing in individual stocks and bonds in the United States or worldwide. For the vast majority of investors, the ideal way to invest internationally is through mutual funds for a country, a region, or a sector of the world (e.g., emerging markets).

Questions

1. What are the differences between a management and advisory firm and an investment company? Describe the approach toward portfolio management adopted by each organization.
2. It has been suggested that the professional asset management community is rapidly becoming dominated by a fairly small number of huge, multiproduct firms. Discuss whether the data presented in Exhibit 25.2 support that view.
3. Closed-end funds generally invest in securities and financial instruments that are relatively illiquid whereas most mutual funds invest in widely traded stocks and bonds. Explain the difference between closed-end and open-end funds and why this liquidity distinction matters.
4. What is the difference between a load fund and a no-load fund?
5. Should you care about how well a mutual fund is diversified? Why or why not?
6. As an investigator evaluating how well mutual fund managers select undervalued stocks or project market returns, discuss whether net or gross returns are more relevant.
7. Based on the numerous tests of mutual fund performance, you believe that only about half the funds do better than a naive buy-and-hold policy. Does this mean you would forget about investing in investment companies? Why or why not?
8. You are told that Fund X experienced *above-average* performance over the past two years. Do you think it will continue over the next two years? Why or why not?
9. Most money managers have a portion of their compensation tied to the performance of the portfolios they manage. Explain how this arrangement can create an ethical dilemma for the manager.
10. What are soft dollar arrangements? Describe one potential way they can be used to transfer wealth from the investor to the manager.
11. You see advertisements for two mutual funds indicating that they have investment objectives that are consistent with yours.
    a. How would you get a quick view of these two funds' performance over the past two or three years?
    b. Where would you find longer-term and more in-depth information on the funds?

Problems

1. Suppose ABC Mutual fund had no liabilities and owned only four stocks as follows:

Stock	Shares	Price	Market Value
W	1,000	$12	$12,000
X	1,200	15	18,000
Y	1,500	22	33,000
Z	800	16	12,800
			$75,800

The fund began by selling $50,000 of stock at $8.00 per share. What is its NAV?

2. Suppose you are considering investing $1,000 in a load fund that charges a fee of 8 percent, and you expect your investment to earn 15 percent over the next year. Alternatively, you could invest in a no-load fund with similar risk that charges a 1 percent redemption fee. You estimate that this no-load fund will earn 12 percent. Given your expectations, which is the better investment and by how much?

3. Consider the recent performance of the Closed Fund, a closed-end fund devoted to finding undervalued, thinly traded stocks:

Period	NAV	Premium/Discount
0	$10.00	0.0%
1	11.25	−5.0
2	9.85	+2.3
3	10.50	−3.2
4	12.30	−7.0

Here price premiums and discounts are indicated by pluses and minuses, respectively, and Period 0 represents Closed Fund's initiation date.

a. Calculate the average return per period for an investor who bought 100 shares of the Closed Fund at the initiation and then sold her position at the end of Period 4.

b. What was the average periodic growth rate in NAV over that same period?

c. Calculate the periodic return for another investor who bought 100 shares of Closed Fund at the end of Period 1 and sold his position at the end of Period 2.

d. What was the periodic growth rate in NAV between Periods 1 and 2?

4. CMD Asset Management has the following fee structure for clients in its equity fund:

> 1.00% of first $5 million invested
> 0.75% of next $5 million invested
> 0.60% of next $10 million invested
> 0.40% above $20 million

a. Calculate the annual dollar fees paid by Client 1, which has $27 million under management, and Client 2, which has $97 million under management.

b. Calculate the fees paid by both clients as a percentage of their assets under management.

c. What is the economic rationale for a fee schedule that declines (in percentage terms) with increases in assets under management?

5. *CFA Examination Level II*

Describe a potential conflict of interest in each of the following four situations:

a. An investment advisor whose compensation is based on commissions from client trades

b. An investment manager's use of client brokerage ("soft dollars") to purchase research or other services

c. A portfolio manager of a mutual fund who purchases, for the fund, a substantial amount of stock in a small-capitalization company whose warrants the manager owns

d. A research analyst who accepts reimbursement for food, lodging, and air transportation expenses for a site visit from the company on which she is writing a research report

> (*Note:* In formulating your answers, you should consider AIMR's *Code of Ethics and Standards of Professional Conduct.*)

6. Suppose that at the start of the year, a no-load mutual fund has a net asset value of $27.15 per share. During the year, it pays its shareholders a capital gain and dividend distribution of $1.12 per share and finishes the year with an NAV of $30.34.
   a. What is the return to an investor who holds 257.876 shares of this fund in his (nontaxable) retirement account?
   b. What is the after-tax return for the same investor if these shares were held in an ordinary savings account? Assume that the investor is in the 30 percent tax bracket.
   c. If the investment company allowed the investor to automatically reinvest his cash distribution in additional fund shares, how many additional shares could the investor acquire? Assume that the distribution occurred at year end and that the proceeds from the distribution can be reinvested at the year-end NAV.

7. The Focus Fund is a mutual fund that holds long-term positions in a small number of nondividend-paying stocks. Their holdings at the end of two recent years are as follows:

Stock	YEAR 1 Shares	YEAR 1 Price	YEAR 2 Shares	YEAR 2 Price
A	100,000	$45.25	100,000	$48.75
B	225,000	25.38	225,000	24.75
C	375,000	14.50	375,000	12.38
D	115,000	87.13	115,000	98.50
E	154,000	56.50	154,000	62.50
F	175,000	63.00	175,000	77.00
G	212,000	32.00	212,000	38.63
H	275,000	15.25	275,000	8.75
I	450,000	9.63	450,000	27.45
J	90,000	71.25	90,000	75.38
K	87,000	42.13	87,000	49.63
L	137,000	19.88	0	27.88
M	0	17.75	150,000	19.75
Cash		$3,542,000		$2,873,000
Expenses		$ 730,000		$ 830,000

At the end of both years, Focus Fund had 5,430,000 shares outstanding.
   a. Calculate the net asset value for a share of the Focus Fund at the end of Year 1, being sure to include the cash position in the net total portfolio value.
   b. Immediately after calculating its Year 1 NAV, Focus Fund sold its position in Stock L and purchased its position in Stock M (both transactions were done at Year 1 prices). Calculate the Year 2 NAV for Focus Fund and compute the growth rate in the fund share value on a percentage basis.
   c. At the end of Year 2, how many fund shares of the Focus Fund could the manager redeem without having to liquidate her stock positions (i.e., using only the cash account)?
   d. If immediately after calculating the Year 2 NAV the manager received investor redemption requests for 500,000 shares, how many shares of each stock would she have to sell in order to

maintain the same proportional ownership position in each stock? Assume that she liquidates the entire cash position before she sells any stock holdings.

8. Mutual funds can effectively charge sales fees in one of three ways: front-end load fees, 12b-1 (i.e., annual) fees, or deferred (i.e., back-end) load fees. Assume that the SAS Fund offers its investors the choice of the following sales fee arrangements: (1) a 3 percent front-end load, (2) a 0.50 percent annual deduction, or (3) a 2 percent back-end load, paid at the liquidation of the investor's position. Also, assume that SAS Fund averages NAV growth of 12 percent per year.

a. If you start with $100,000 in investment capital, calculate what an investment in SAS would be worth in three years under each of the proposed sales fee schemes. Which scheme would you choose?

b. If your investment horizon were 10 years, would your answer in Part a change? Demonstrate.

c. Explain the relationship between the timing of the sales charge and your investment horizon. In general, if you intend to hold your position for a long time, which fee arrangement would you prefer?

9. *CFA Examination Level II*

Clark & Kerns (C&K), a U.S. pension fund manager for more than 20 years, plans to establish offices in a European and a Pacific Rim country in order to manage pension funds located in those countries and invested in their local stock markets. Tony Clark, CFA, managing partner, learns that investment organizations and their affiliates in the European country perform three functions:

- consult with corporate pension sponsors on how the pension fund should be managed and by whom;
- manage their portfolios; and
- execute securities transactions as a broker for the funds.

Common practice in this country is to withhold disclosure of the ownership of business organizations. Clark believes that C&K must provide all three functions to compete effectively. He therefore decides to establish offices in Europe to offer all three services to prospective pension fund clients, through local organizations owned by C&K. The pension consulting organization will be Europension Group; the portfolio management firm will be C&K International; and the broker-dealer operation will be Alps Securities.

a. Briefly describe two AIMR Standards of Professional Conduct that apply to Clark, if C&K provides all three functions on a combined basis. Describe the specific duty Clark is required to perform to comply with these Standards.

Clark learns that a customary practice in the European country is to allocate at least 80 percent of pension fund assets to fixed-income securities.

b. Identify and briefly explain two AIMR Standards of Professional Conduct that apply to this situation. Clark observes that portfolio managers in the Pacific Rim country frequently use insider information in their investment decisions. Because the pension fund management industry is performance oriented, Clark decides to adopt local investment practices as the only way to attract and retain local corporate clients in that country.

c. Identify and briefly explain two AIMR Standards of Professional Conduct that apply to this situation.

10. *CFA Examination Level III*

Peter and Andrea Mueller have built up their $600,000 investment portfolio over many years through regular purchases of mutual funds holding only U.S. securities. Each purchase was based on personal research but without consideration of their other holdings. They would now like advice on their total portfolio, which follows:

	Type	Market Sector	Beta	Percent of Total
Andrea's company stock	Stock	Small-cap growth	1.40	35
Blue-chip growth fund	Stock	Large-cap growth	1.20	20
Super beta fund	Stock	Small-cap growth	1.60	10
Conservative fund	Stock	Large-cap value	1.05	2
Index fund	Stock	Large-cap index	1.00	3
No dividend fund	Stock	Large-cap growth	1.25	25
Long-term zero coupon fund	Bond	Government	—	5

Evaluate the Mueller's portfolio in terms of the following criteria:
a. Preference for "minimal volatility"
b. Equity diversification
c. Asset allocation (including cash flow needs)

11. You have been asked to evaluate the investment performance of three different professional asset managers relative to each other and to the Standard and Poor's 500 index. After gathering quarterly return data over the past five years, you compute the following statistics:

Portfolio	Average Annual Return	Beta	Diversification Level
A	10.2%	0.82	86%
B	15.4	1.36	63
C	13.2	0.99	98
S&P	13.3	1.00	100

a. Based on this data, can you conclude that Manager A underperformed the market and Manager B outperformed the market? Why or why not?
b. What additional information do you think you would require in order to perform a compelling analysis of the investment performance of these managers?
c. What was the most likely investment objective followed by Portfolio Manager C? By Manager A?
d. What might explain the fact that Manager B's portfolio is so much less diversified than those run by Managers A and C?

References

Association for Investment Management and Research. *Standards of Practice Handbook,* 8th ed. Charlottesville, Va.: AIMR, 1999.

Bekaert, Geert, and Michael S. Urias. "Diversification, Integration, and Emerging Market Closed-End Funds." *Journal of Finance* 51, no. 3 (July 1996).

Caccese, Michael S. "Ethics and the Financial Analyst." *Financial Analysts Journal* 53, no. 1 (January/February 1997).

Chordia, Tarun. "The Structure of Mutual Fund Charges." *Journal of Financial Economics* 41, no. 1 (May 1996): 3–39.

Edelen, Roger M. "Investor Flows and the Assessed Performance of Open-End Fund Managers." *Journal of Financial Economics* 53, no. 3 (September 1999): 439–466.

Ferson, Wayne E., and Rudi W. Schadt. "Measuring Fund Strategy and Performance in Changing Economic Conditions." *Journal of Finance* 51, no. 2 (June 1996).

Lakonishok, Josef, Andrei Shleifer, and Robert W. Vishny. "The Structure and Performance of the Money Management Industry." In *Brookings Papers on Economic Activity.* Washington, D.C.: Brookings Institute, 1992.

Peavy, John W. *Investment Counsel for Private Clients.* Charlottesville, Va.: Association for Investment Management and Research, 1993.

Porter, Gary E., Rodney L. Roenfeldt, and Neil W. Sicherman. "The Value of Open Market Repurchases of Closed-End Fund Shares." *Journal of Business* 72, no.2 (April 1999): 251–276.

Pozen, Robert C. *The Mutual Fund Business,* 2d ed. Boston, Mass.: Houghton Mifflin, 2001.

Chapter 26 › Evaluation of Portfolio Performance

After you read this chapter, you should be able to answer the following questions:

➤ What major requirements do clients expect from their portfolio managers?

➤ What can a portfolio manager do to attain superior performance?

➤ What is the peer group comparison method of evaluating an investor's performance?

➤ What is the Treynor portfolio performance measure?

➤ What is the Sharpe portfolio performance measure?

➤ What is the critical difference between the Treynor and Sharpe portfolio performance measures?

➤ What is the Jensen portfolio performance measure and how can it be adapted to include multifactor models of risk and expected return?

➤ What is the information ratio and how is it related to the other performance measures?

➤ When evaluating a sample of portfolios, how do you determine how well diversified they are?

➤ What is the bias found regarding the composite performance measures?

➤ What is the Fama portfolio performance measure and what information does it provide beyond other measures?

➤ What is attribution analysis and how can it be used to distinguish between a portfolio manager's market timing and security selection skills?

➤ What is the Roll benchmark error problem and what are the two factors that are affected when computing portfolio performance measures?

➤ What is the impact of global investing on the benchmark error problem?

➤ What are customized benchmarks?

➤ What are the important characteristics that any benchmark should possess?

➤ How do bond portfolio performance measures differ from equity portfolio performance measures?

➤ In the Wagner and Tito bond portfolio performance measure, what is the measure of risk used?

➤ What are the components of the Dietz, Fogler, and Hardy bond portfolio performance measure?

➤ What are the sources of return in the Fong, Pearson, and Vasicek bond portfolio performance measure?

➤ What are time-weighted and dollar-weighted returns and which should be reported under AIMR's Performance Presentation Standards?

Investors always are interested in evaluating the performance of their portfolios. It is both expensive and time consuming to analyze and select securities for a portfolio, so an individual, company, or institution must determine whether this effort is worth the time and money invested in it. Investors managing their own portfolios should evaluate their performance as should those who pay one or several professional money managers. In the latter case, it is imperative to determine whether the investment performance justifies the service's cost.

This chapter outlines the theory and practice of evaluating the performance of an investment portfolio. In the first section, we consider what is required of a portfolio manager. We pinpoint what to look for before we discuss techniques to evaluate portfolio managers.

In section two, we briefly discuss how performance was evaluated before portfolio theory and the CAPM were developed. The rest of the section contains a detailed discussion of four portfolio performance evaluation techniques (referred to as *composite performance measures*) that consider return and risk.

The third section applies these composite measures to gauge the performance of a selected sample of mutual funds. This demonstration analyzes how these measures relate to each other. Although some redundancy exists among the measures, each of them provides unique perspectives, so they are best viewed as complementary measures. We also consider a fifth measure that evaluates the components of performance. Because some observers have contended that these composite measures of performance are biased in favor of low-risk portfolios, we examine their arguments and the evidence for and against these contentions. The section concludes with an examination of attribution analysis, a measurement technique designed to establish the source of a portfolio manager's skill.

Section four identifies factors to consider when applying these measures. This includes the work of Roll, which questioned any evaluation technique that depends on the CAPM and a market portfolio. This controversy is referred to as the *benchmark problem*. We also discuss why this benchmark problem becomes larger when you begin investing globally. Notably, it affects both your measures of risk and your portfolio performance measures. The section concludes with a description of studies that have evaluated how reliable the composite measures are at predicting future performance.

In the fifth section, we discuss how factors that determine the performance of a bond portfolio differ from those that affect common stocks. Therefore, we consider several models developed to evaluate the performance of bond portfolios. Finally, we examine industry standards for calculating returns and reporting portfolio performance to investors.

WHAT IS REQUIRED OF A PORTFOLIO MANAGER?

There are two major requirements of a portfolio manager:

1. The ability to derive above-average returns for a given risk class
2. The ability to diversify the portfolio completely to eliminate all unsystematic risk, relative to the portfolio's benchmark

In terms of return, the first requirement is obvious, but the need to consider *risk* in this context was generally not apparent before the 1960s, when work in portfolio theory showed its significance. In modern theory, superior risk-adjusted returns can be derived through *either* superior timing or superior security selection.

An equity portfolio manager who can do a superior job of predicting the peaks or troughs of the equity market can adjust the portfolio's composition to anticipate market trends, holding a completely diversified portfolio of high-beta stocks through rising markets and favoring low-beta stocks and money market instruments during declining markets. Bigger gains in rising markets and smaller losses in declining markets give the portfolio manager above-average risk-adjusted returns.

A fixed-income portfolio manager with superior timing ability changes the portfolio's duration in anticipation of interest rate changes by increasing the duration of the portfolio in anticipation of failing interest rates and reducing the duration of the portfolio when rates are expected to rise. If properly executed, this bond portfolio management strategy likewise provides superior risk-adjusted returns.

As an alternative strategy, a portfolio manager and his or her analysts may try consistently to select undervalued stocks or bonds for a given risk class. Even without superior market timing, such a portfolio would likely experience above-average risk-adjusted returns.

The second factor to consider in evaluating a portfolio manager is the ability to diversify completely. As noted in Chapter 8, on average the market rewards investors only for bearing systematic (market) risk. Unsystematic risk is not considered when determining required returns because it can be eliminated in a diversified market portfolio. Because they can expect no reward for bearing this uncertainty, investors often want their portfolios completely diversified, which means they want the portfolio manager to eliminate most or all unsystematic risk. The level of diversification can be judged on the basis of the correlation between the portfolio returns and the returns for a market portfolio or some other benchmark index. A completely diversified portfolio is perfectly correlated with the fully diversified benchmark portfolio.

These two requirements of a portfolio manager are important because some portfolio evaluation techniques take into account one requirement but not the other. Other techniques implicitly consider both factors but do not differentiate between them.

COMPOSITE PORTFOLIO PERFORMANCE MEASURES

Portfolio Evaluation before 1960

At one time, investors evaluated portfolio performance almost entirely on the basis of the rate of return. They were aware of the concept of risk but did not know how to quantify or measure it, so they could not consider it explicitly. Developments in portfolio theory in the early 1960s showed investors how to quantify and measure risk in terms of the variability of returns. Still, because no single measure combined both return and risk, the two factors had to be considered separately as researchers had done in several early studies.[1] Specifically, the investigators grouped portfolios into similar risk classes based on a measure of risk (such as the variance of return) and then compared the rates of return for alternative portfolios directly within these risk classes.

This section describes in detail the four major composite equity portfolio performance measures that combine risk and return performance into a single value. We describe each measure and its intent and then demonstrate how to compute it and interpret the results. We also compare the measures and discuss how they differ and why they rank portfolios differently.

Peer Group Comparisons

Before examining measures of portfolio performance that adjust an investor's return for the level of investment risk, we first consider the concept of a **peer group comparison**. This method, which Kritzman describes as the most common manner of evaluating portfolio managers, collects the returns produced by a representative universe of investors over a specific period of time and displays them in a simple boxplot format.[2] To aid the comparison, the universe is typically divided into percentiles, which indicate the relative ranking of a given investor. For instance, a portfolio manager that produced a one-year return of 12.4 percent would be in the 10th percentile if only nine other portfolios in a universe of 100 produced a higher return. Although these comparisons can get quite detailed, it is common for the boxplot graphic to include the maximum and minimum returns, as well as the returns falling at the 25th, 50th (i.e., the median), and 75th percentiles.

---

[1]Irwin Friend, Marshall Blume, and Jean Crockett, *Mutual Funds and Other Institutional Investors* (New York: McGraw-Hill, 1970).

[2]See Mark P. Kritzman, "Quantitative Methods in Performance Measurement," in *Quantitative Methods for Financial Analysis,* 2d ed., ed. S. Brown and M. Kritzman (Homewood, Ill.: Dow Jones–Irwin, 1990).

Exhibit 26.1 shows the returns from periods of varying length for a representative investor—labeled here as "U.S. Equity with Cash"—relative to its peer universe of other U.S. domestic equity managers.[3] Also included in the comparison are the periodic returns to three indexes of the overall market: Standard and Poor's 500, Russell 1000, and Russell 3000. The display shows return quartiles for investment periods ranging from 5 to 10 years. In this example, the investor in question (indicated by the large dot) performed admirably, finishing above the median in each of the comparison periods. Indeed, the manager of this portfolio produced the largest nine-year return (16.5 percent), well above the median return of 13.0 percent. Notice, however, that although the investor's 10-year average return exceeds the 9-year level (16.6 percent), it falls below the fifth percentile, which, while still laudable, is no longer the best.

There are several potential problems with the peer group comparison method of evaluating an investor's performance. First, and foremost, the boxplots shown in Exhibit 26.1 do not make any explicit adjustment for the risk level of the portfolios in the universe. In fact, investment risk is only *implicitly* considered to the extent that all the portfolios in the universe have essentially the same level of volatility. This is not likely to be the case for any sizable peer group, particularly if the universe mixes portfolios with different investment styles. A second, related point is that it is almost impossible to form a truly comparable peer group that is large enough to make the percentile rankings valid and meaningful. Finally, by focusing on nothing more than relative returns, such a comparison loses sight of whether the investor in question—or any in the universe, for that matter—has accomplished his individual objectives and satisfied his investment constraints.

Treynor Portfolio Performance Measure

Treynor developed the first **composite measure** of portfolio performance that included risk.[4] He postulated two components of risk: (1) risk produced by general market fluctuations and (2) risk resulting from unique fluctuations in the portfolio securities. To identify risk due to market fluctuations, he introduced the *characteristic line,* which defines the relationship between the rates of return for a portfolio over time and the rates of return for an appropriate market portfolio, as we discussed in Chapter 8. He noted that the characteristic line's slope measures the *relative volatility* of the portfolio's returns in relation to returns for the aggregate market. As we also know from Chapter 8, this slope is the portfolio's beta coefficient. A higher slope (beta) characterizes a portfolio that is more sensitive to market returns and that has greater market risk.

Deviations from the characteristic line indicate unique returns for the portfolio relative to the market. These differences arise from the returns on individual stocks in the portfolio. In a completely diversified portfolio, these unique returns for individual stocks should cancel out. As the correlation of the portfolio with the market increases, unique risk declines and diversification improves. Because Treynor was not concerned about this aspect of portfolio performance, he gave no further consideration to the diversification measure.

Treynor's Composite Performance Measure

Treynor was interested in a measure of performance that would apply to all investors—regardless of their risk preferences. Building on developments in capital market theory, he introduced a risk-free asset that could be combined with different portfolios to form a straight portfolio possibility line. He showed that rational,

---

[3]This example comes from Brian Singer, "Valuation of Portfolio Performance: Aggregate Return and Risk Analysis," *Journal of Performance Measurement* 1, no. 1 (Fall 1996): 6–16, and was based on data from the Frank Russell Company.

[4]Jack L. Treynor, "How to Rate Management of Investment Funds," *Harvard Business Review* 43, no. 1 (January–February 1965): 63–75.

EXHIBIT 26.1 AN ILLUSTRATIVE PEER GROUP COMPARISON

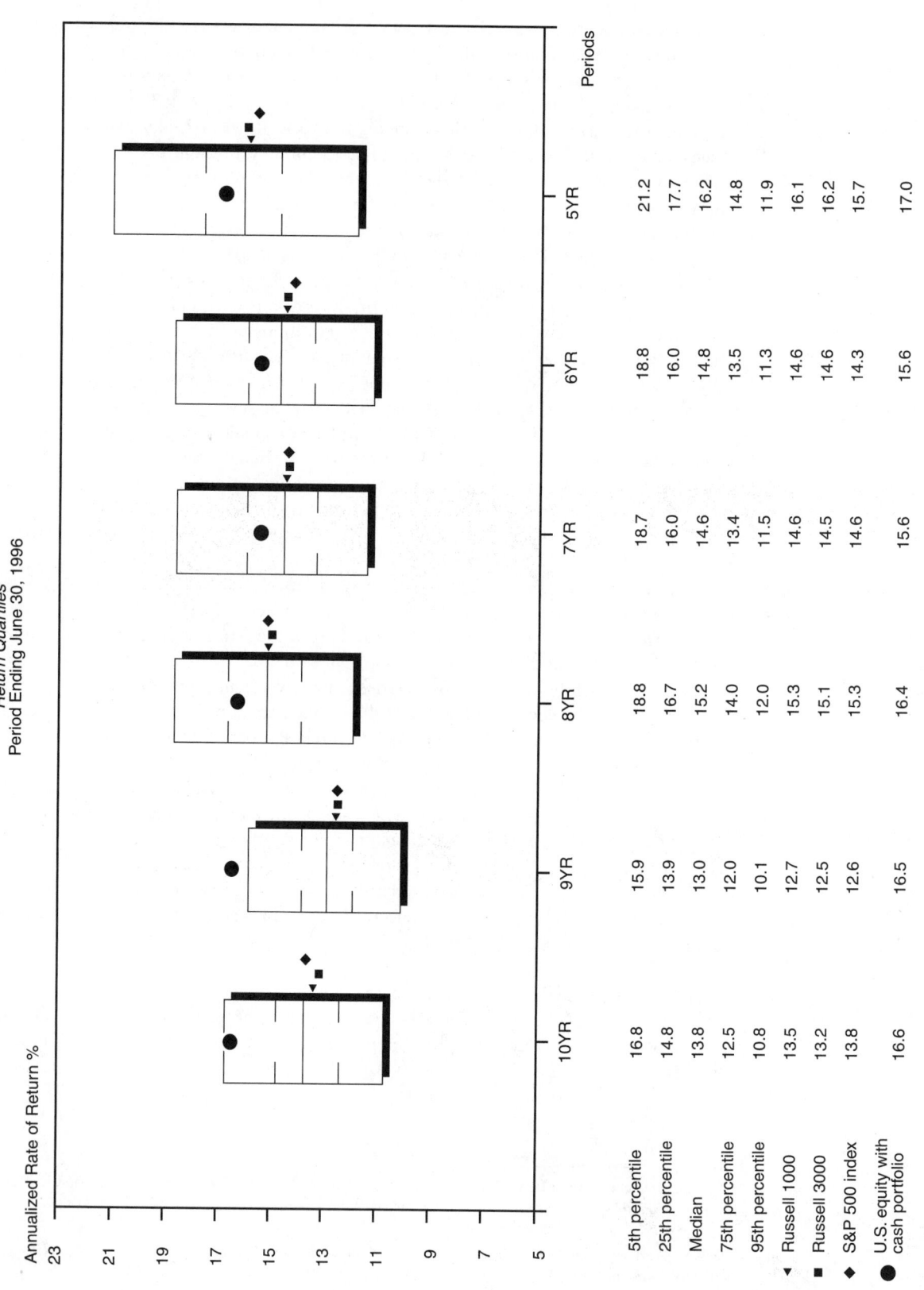

Return Quartiles
Period Ending June 30, 1996

	5YR	6YR	7YR	8YR	9YR	10YR
5th percentile	21.2	18.8	18.7	18.8	15.9	16.8
25th percentile	17.7	16.0	16.0	16.7	13.9	14.8
Median	16.2	14.8	14.6	15.2	13.0	13.8
75th percentile	14.8	13.5	13.4	14.0	12.0	12.5
95th percentile	11.9	11.3	11.5	12.0	10.1	10.8
▼ Russell 1000	16.1	14.6	14.6	15.3	12.7	13.5
■ Russell 3000	16.2	14.6	14.5	15.1	12.5	13.2
◆ S&P 500 index	15.7	14.3	14.6	15.3	12.6	13.8
● U.S. equity with cash portfolio	17.0	15.6	15.6	16.4	16.5	16.6

Source: Brian Singer, "Valuation of Portfolio Performance: Aggregate Return and Risk Analysis," *Journal of Performance Measurement* 1, no. 1 (Fall 1996): 6–16.

risk-averse investors would always prefer portfolio possibility lines with larger slopes because such high-slope lines would place investors on higher indifference curves. The slope of this portfolio possibility line (designated T) is equal to[5]

➤26.1
$$T = \frac{\overline{R}_i - \overline{RFR}}{\beta_i}$$

where:

$\overline{R}_i$ = the average rate of return for portfolio i during a specified time period
$\overline{RFR}$ = the average rate of return on a risk-free investment during the same time period
β_i = the slope of the fund's characteristic line during that time period (this indicates the portfolio's relative volatility)

As noted, a larger T value indicates a larger slope and a better portfolio for all investors (regardless of their risk preferences). Because the numerator of this ratio ($\overline{R}_i - \overline{RFR}$) is the *risk premium* and the denominator is a measure of risk, the total expression indicates the portfolio's *risk premium return per unit of risk*. All risk-averse investors would prefer to maximize this value. Note that the risk variable beta measures systematic risk and tells us nothing about the diversification of the portfolio. It *implicitly assumes* a completely diversified portfolio, which means that systematic risk is the relevant risk measure.

Comparing a portfolio's T value to a similar measure for the market portfolio indicates whether the portfolio would plot above the SML. Calculate the T value for the aggregate market as follows:

$$T_M = \frac{\overline{R}_M - \overline{RFR}}{\beta_M}$$

In this expression, β_M equals 1.0 (the market's beta) and indicates the slope of the SML. Therefore, a portfolio with a higher T value than the market portfolio plots above the SML, indicating superior risk-adjusted performance.

Demonstration of Comparative Treynor Measures To understand how to use and interpret this measure of performance, suppose that during the most recent 10-year period, the average annual total rate of return (including dividends) on an aggregate market portfolio, such as the S&P 500, was 14 percent ($\overline{R}_M = 0.14$) and the average nominal rate of return on government T-bills was 8 percent ($\overline{RFR} = 0.08$). Assume that, as administrator of a large pension fund that has been divided among three money managers during the past 10 years, you must decide whether to renew your investment management contracts with all three managers. To do this, you must measure how they have performed.

Assume you are given the following results:

INVESTMENT MANAGER	AVERAGE ANNUAL RATE OF RETURN	BETA
W	0.12	0.90
X	0.16	1.05
Y	0.18	1.20

[5]The terms used in the formula differ from those used by Treynor but are consistent with our earlier discussion. Also, our discussion is concerned with general *portfolio* performance rather than being limited to mutual funds.

You can compute T values for the market portfolio and for each of the individual portfolio managers as follows:

$$T_M = \frac{0.14 - 0.08}{1.00} = 0.060$$

$$T_W = \frac{0.12 - 0.08}{0.90} = 0.044$$

$$T_X = \frac{0.16 - 0.08}{1.05} = 0.076$$

$$T_Y = \frac{0.18 - 0.08}{1.20} = 0.083$$

These results indicate that Investment Manager W not only ranked the lowest of the three managers but did not perform as well as the aggregate market. In contrast, both X and Y beat the market portfolio, and Manager Y performed somewhat better than Manager X. In terms of the SML, both of their portfolios plotted above the line, as shown in Exhibit 26.2.

Very poor return performance or very good performance with very low risk may yield negative T values. An example of poor performance is a portfolio with both an average rate of return below the risk-free rate and a positive beta. For instance, in the preceding case, assume that a fourth portfolio manager, Z, had a portfolio beta of 0.50 but an average rate of return of only 0.07. The T value would be

$$T_Z = \frac{0.07 - 0.08}{0.50} = -0.02$$

Obviously, this performance would plot below the SML in Exhibit 26.2.

EXHIBIT 26.2   *PLOT OF PERFORMANCE ON SML (T MEASURE)*

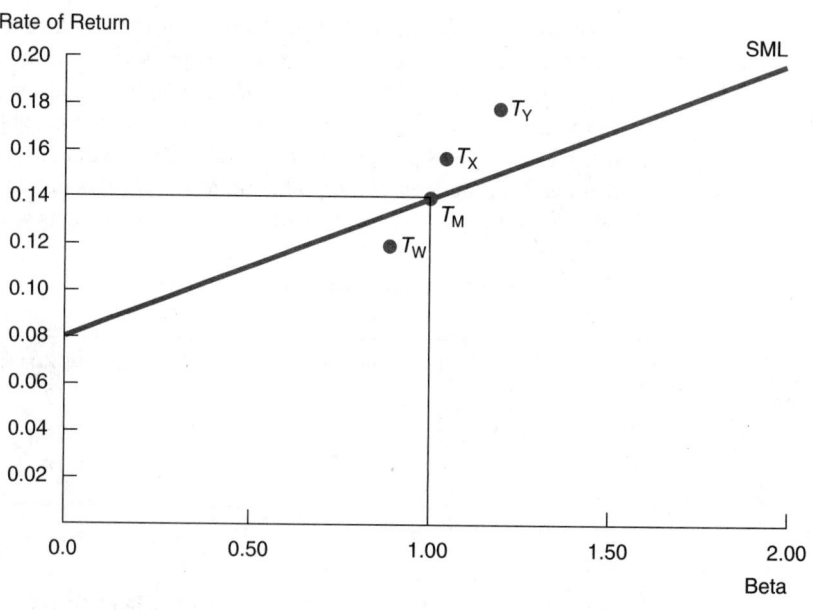

A portfolio with a *negative* beta and an average rate of return above the risk-free rate of return would likewise have a negative T value. In this case, however, it indicates exemplary performance. As an example, assume that Portfolio Manager G invested heavily in gold mining stocks during a period of great political and economic uncertainty. Because gold often has a negative correlation with most stocks, this portfolio's beta could be negative. Assume that our gold portfolio G had a beta of –0.20 and yet experienced an average rate of return of 10 percent. The T value for this portfolio would then be

$$T_G = \frac{0.10 - 0.08}{-0.20} = -0.100$$

Although the T value is –0.100, if you plotted these results on a graph, it would indicate a position substantially above the SML in Exhibit 26.2.

Because negative betas can yield T values that give confusing results, it is preferable either to plot the portfolio on an SML graph or to compute the expected return for this portfolio using the SML equation and then compare this expected return to the actual return. This comparison will reveal whether the actual return was above or below expectations. In the preceding example for Portfolio G, the expected return would be

$$E(R_G) = RFR + \beta_i(R_M - RFR)$$
$$= 0.08 + (-0.20)(0.06)$$
$$= 0.08 - 0.012$$
$$= 0.068$$

Comparing this expected (required) rate of return of 6.8 percent to the actual return of 10 percent shows that Portfolio Manager G has done a superior job.

Sharpe Portfolio Performance Measure

Sharpe likewise conceived of a composite measure to evaluate the performance of mutual funds.[6] The measure followed closely his earlier work on the capital asset pricing model (CAPM), dealing specifically with the capital market line (CML).

The **Sharpe measure** of portfolio performance (designated S) is stated as follows:

➤26.2
$$S_i = \frac{\overline{R}_i - \overline{RFR}}{\sigma_i}$$

where:

$\overline{R}_i$ = the average rate of return for portfolio i during a specified time period
$\overline{RFR}$ = the average rate of return on risk-free assets during the same time period
σ_i = the standard deviation of the rate of return for portfolio i during the time period

This composite measure of portfolio performance clearly is similar to the Treynor measure; however, it seeks to measure the *total risk* of the portfolio by including the standard deviation of returns rather than considering only the systematic risk summarized by beta. Because the numerator is the portfolio's risk premium, this measure indicates the *risk premium return earned per*

[6]William F. Sharpe, "Mutual Fund Performance," *Journal of Business* 39, no. 1, part 2 (January 1966): 119–138. For a more recent interpretation of this measure, also see William F. Sharpe, "The Sharpe Ratio," *Journal of Portfolio Management* 21, no. 1 (Fall 1994): 49–59.

unit of total risk. In terms of capital market theory, this portfolio performance measure uses total risk to compare portfolios to the CML, whereas the Treynor measure examines portfolio performance in relation to the SML. Finally, notice that in practice the standard deviation can be calculated using either total portfolio returns or portfolio returns in excess of the risk-free rate.

Demonstration of Comparative Sharpe Measures   The following examples use the Sharpe measure of performance. Again, assume that $\overline{R}_M = 0.14$ and $\overline{RFR} = 0.08$. Suppose you are told that the standard deviation of the annual rate of return for the market portfolio over the past 10 years was 20 percent ($\sigma_M = 0.20$). Now you want to examine the performance of the following portfolios:

PORTFOLIO	AVERAGE ANNUAL RATE OF RETURN	STANDARD DEVIATION OF RETURN
D	0.13	0.18
E	0.17	0.22
F	0.16	0.23

The Sharpe measures for these portfolios are as follows:

$$S_M = \frac{0.14 - 0.08}{0.20} = 0.300$$

$$S_D = \frac{0.13 - 0.08}{0.18} = 0.278$$

$$S_E = \frac{0.17 - 0.08}{0.22} = 0.409$$

$$S_F = \frac{0.16 - 0.08}{0.23} = 0.348$$

The D portfolio had the lowest risk premium return per unit of total risk, failing even to perform as well as the aggregate market portfolio. In contrast, Portfolios E and F performed better than the aggregate market: Portfolio E did better than Portfolio F.

Given the market portfolio results during this period, it is possible to draw the CML. If we plot the results for Portfolios D, E, and F on this graph, as shown in Exhibit 26.3, we see that Portfolio D plots below the line, whereas the E and F portfolios are above the line, indicating superior risk-adjusted performance.

Treynor versus Sharpe Measure   The Sharpe portfolio performance measure uses the standard deviation of returns as the measure of total risk, whereas the Treynor performance measure uses beta (systematic risk). The Sharpe measure, therefore, evaluates the portfolio manager on the basis of both rate of return performance and diversification.

For a completely diversified portfolio, one without any unsystematic risk, the two measures give identical rankings because the total variance of the completely diversified portfolio is its systematic variance. Alternatively, a poorly diversified portfolio could have a high ranking on the basis of the Treynor performance measure but a much lower ranking on the basis of the Sharpe performance measure. Any difference in rank would come directly from a difference in diversification.

Therefore, these two performance measures provide complementary yet different information, and both measures should be used. If you are dealing with a group of well-diversified portfolios, as many mutual funds are, the two measures provide similar rankings.

EXHIBIT 26.3 ▶ *PLOT OF PERFORMANCE ON CML (S MEASURE)*

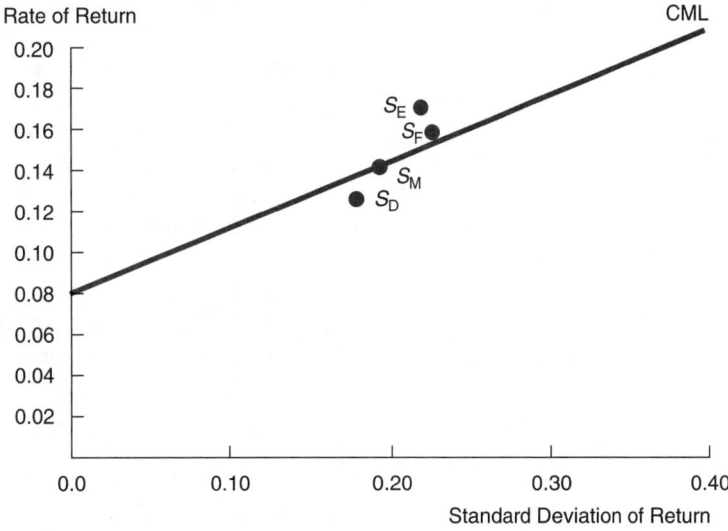

A disadvantage of the Treynor and Sharpe measures is that they produce relative, but not absolute, rankings of portfolio performance. That is, the Sharpe measures for Portfolios E and F illustrated in Exhibit 26.3 show that both generated risk-adjusted returns above the market. Further, E's risk-adjusted performance measure is larger than F's. What we cannot say with certainty, however, is whether any of these differences are statistically significant.

Jensen Portfolio Performance Measure

The **Jensen measure** is similar to the measures already discussed because it is based on the capital asset pricing model (CAPM).[7] All versions of the CAPM calculate the expected one-period return on any security or portfolio by the following expression:

▶ **26.3**
$$E(R_j) = RFR + \beta_j[E(R_M) - RFR]$$

where:

$E(R_j)$ = **the expected return on security or portfolio** j
RFR = **the one-period risk-free interest rate**
β_j = **the systematic risk (beta) for security or portfolio** j
$E(R_M)$ = **the expected return on the market portfolio of risky assets**

The expected return and the risk-free return vary for different periods. Consequently, we are concerned with the time series of expected rates of return for Security or Portfolio j. Moreover, assuming the asset pricing model is empirically valid, you can express Equation 26.3 in terms of *realized* rates of return as follows:

$$R_{jt} = RFR_t + \beta_j[R_{mt} - RFR_t] + e_{jt}$$

[7]Michael C. Jensen, "The Performance of Mutual Funds in the Period 1945–1964," *Journal of Finance* 23, no. 2 (May 1968): 389–416.

This equation states that the realized rate of return on a security or portfolio during a given time period should be a linear function of the risk-free rate of return during the period, plus a risk premium that depends on the systematic risk of the security or portfolio during the period plus a random error term (e_{jt}).

Subtracting the risk-free return from both sides, we have

$$R_{jt} - RFR_t = \beta_j[R_{mt} - RFR_t] + e_{jt}$$

This shows that the risk premium earned on the jth portfolio is equal to β_j times a market risk premium plus a random error term. In this form, an intercept for the regression is not expected if all assets and portfolios were in equilibrium.

Alternatively, superior portfolio managers who forecast market turns or consistently select undervalued securities earn higher risk premiums than those implied by this model. Specifically, superior portfolio managers have consistently positive random error terms because the actual returns for their portfolios consistently exceed the expected returns implied by this model. To detect and measure this superior performance, you must allow for an intercept (a nonzero constant) that measures any positive or negative difference from the model. Consistent positive differences cause a positive intercept, whereas consistent negative differences (inferior performance) cause a negative intercept. With an intercept or nonzero constant, the earlier equation becomes

➤26.4
$$R_{jt} - RFR_t = \alpha_j + \beta_j[R_{mt} - RFR_t] + e_{jt}$$

In Equation 26.4, the α_j value indicates whether the portfolio manager is superior or inferior in market timing and/or stock selection. A superior manager has a significant positive α (or "alpha") value because of the consistent positive residuals. In contrast, an inferior manager's returns consistently fall short of expectations based on the CAPM model giving consistently negative residuals. In such a case, α is a significant negative value.

The performance of a portfolio manager with no forecasting ability but not clearly inferior equals that of a naive buy-and-hold policy. In the equation, because the rate of return on such a portfolio typically matches the returns you expect, the residual returns generally are randomly positive and negative. This gives a constant term that differs insignificantly from zero, indicating that the portfolio manager basically matched the market on a risk-adjusted basis.

Therefore, the α represents how much of the rate of return on the portfolio is attributable to the manager's ability to derive above-average returns adjusted for risk. Superior risk-adjusted returns indicate that the manager is good at either predicting market turns, or selecting undervalued issues for the portfolio, or both.

Applying the Jensen Measure   The Jensen measure of performance requires using a different *RFR* for each time interval during the sample period. For example, to examine the performance of a fund manager over a 10-year period using yearly intervals, you must examine the fund's annual returns less the return on risk-free assets for each year and relate this to the annual return on the market portfolio less the same risk-free rate. This contrasts with the Treynor and Sharpe composite measures, which examine the *average* returns for the total period for all variables (the portfolio, the market, and the risk-free asset).

Also, like the Treynor measure, the Jensen measure does not directly consider the portfolio manager's ability to diversify because it calculates risk premiums in terms of systematic risk. As noted earlier, to evaluate the performance of a group of well-diversified portfolios such as mutual funds, this is likely to be a reasonable assumption. Jensen's analysis of mutual fund performance showed that complete diversification was a fairly reasonable assumption because the funds typically correlated with the market at rates above 0.90.

Jensen Measure and Multifactor Models

The Jensen composite measure of performance has several advantages over the Treynor and Sharpe. First, it is easier to interpret in that an alpha value of 0.02 indicates that the manager generated a return of 2 percent per period more than what was expected given the portfolio's risk level. Second, because it is estimated from a regression equation, it is possible to make statements about the statistical significance of the manager's skill level, or the difference in skill levels between two different managers.

A third advantage of the Jensen performance measure is that it is flexible enough to allow for alternative models of risk and expected return than the CAPM. Specifically, risk-adjusted performance (i.e., a) can be computed relative to any of the multifactor models discussed in Chapter 9 as follows:

➤26.5
$$R_{jt} - RFR_t = \alpha_j + [b_{j1} F_{1t} + b_{j2}F_{2t} + \ldots + b_{jk}F_{kt}] + e_{jt}$$

where F_{kt} represents the Period t return to the kth common risk factor. Notice that the Sharpe measure, which focuses on total risk, ignores the specific form of the return-generating process altogether, while the Treynor measure requires a single measure of systematic risk.

The Information Ratio Performance Measure

Closely related to the statistics just presented is another widely used performance measure: the **information ratio**. Also known as an *appraisal ratio,* this statistic measures a portfolio's average return in excess of that of a comparison or **benchmark portfolio** divided by the standard deviation of this excess return. Formally, the information ratio (IR) is calculated as:

➤26.6
$$IR_j = \frac{\overline{R}_j - \overline{R}_b}{\sigma_{ER}} = \frac{\overline{ER}_j}{\sigma_{ER}}$$

where:

> IR_j = the information ratio for portfolio j
> R_j = the average return for portfolio j during the specified time period
> R_b = the average return for the benchmark portfolio during the period
> σ_{ER} = the standard deviation of the excess return during the period

To interpret IR, notice that the mean excess return in the numerator represents the investor's ability to use her talent and information to generate a portfolio return that differs from that of the benchmark against which her performance is being measured (e.g., the Standard and Poor's 500 index). Conversely, the denominator measures the amount of residual (unsystematic) risk that the investor incurred in pursuit of those excess returns. The coefficient σ_{ER} is sometimes called the *tracking error* of the investor's portfolio and it is a "cost" of active management in the sense that fluctuations in the periodic ER_j values represent random noise beyond an investor's control that could hurt performance. Thus, the IR can be viewed as a benefit-to-cost ratio that assesses the quality of the investor's information deflated by unsystematic risk generated by the investment process.

Goodwin has noted that the Sharpe ratio is a special case of the IR where the risk-free asset is the benchmark portfolio, despite the fact that this interpretation violates the spirit of a statistic that should have a value of zero for any passively managed portfolio.[8] More importantly, he

---

[8]See Thomas H. Goodwin, "The Information Ratio," *Financial Analysts Journal* 54, no. 4 (July–August 1998): 34–43.

also showed that if excess portfolio returns are estimated with historical data using the same single-factor regression equation used to compute Jensen's alpha, the *IR* simplifies to

$$IR_j = \frac{\alpha_j}{\sigma_e}$$

where:

σ_e = the standard error of the regression[9]

Finally, he showed that one way an information ratio based on periodic returns measured *T* times per year could be annualized is as follows:

$$\text{Annualized } IR = \frac{(T)\alpha_j}{\sqrt{T}\sigma_e} = \sqrt{T}\,(IR)$$

For instance, an investor that generated a quarterly ratio of 0.25 would have an annualized *IR* of 0.50 $(= \sqrt{4} \times 0.25)$.

Grinold and Kahn have argued that reasonable information ratio levels should range from 0.50 to 1.00, with an investor having an *IR* of 0.50 being good and one with an *IR* of 1.00 being exceptional.[10] These, however, appear to be exceptionally difficult hurdles to clear. Goodwin studied the performance of more than 200 professional equity and fixed-income portfolio managers with various investment styles over a 10-year period. He found that the *IR* of the median manager in each style group was positive but that the ratio never exceeded 0.50. Thus, although the average manager appears to add value to investors—α (and hence *IR*) is greater than zero— she doesn't qualify as "good." Further, no style group had more than 3 percent of its managers deliver an *IR* in excess of 1.00. Information ratio histograms summarizing this research are shown in Exhibit 26.4.

APPLICATION OF PORTFOLIO PERFORMANCE MEASURES

To apply these measures, we selected 20 open-end mutual funds and used monthly data for the five-year period from July 1995 to June 2000. The monthly rates of return for the first fund (Aim Constellation Fund) and the S&P 500 are contained in Exhibit 26.5. The total rate of return for each month is computed as follows:

$$R_{it} = \frac{EP_{it} + Div_{it} + Cap.Dist._{it} - BP_{it}}{BP_{it}}$$

where:

R_{it} = the total rate of return on fund *i* during month *t*
EP_{it} = the ending price for fund *i* during month *t*
Div_{it} = the dividend payments made by fund *i* during month *t*
$Cap.Dist._{it}$ = the capital gain distributions made by fund *i* during month *t*
BP_{it} = the beginning price for fund *i* during month *t*

---

[9]The development of this form of the information ratio is credited to Jack L. Treynor and Fischer Black, "How to Use Security Analysis to Improve Security Selection," *Journal of Business* 46, no. 1 (January 1973): 66–86.

[10]See Richard C. Grinold and Ronald N. Kahn, *Active Portfolio Management* (Chicago, Ill.: Probus Publishing, 1995).

EXHIBIT 26.4 ▸ *INFORMATION RATIOS FOR SIX INVESTMENT STYLES: 1986:Q1 TO 1995:Q4*

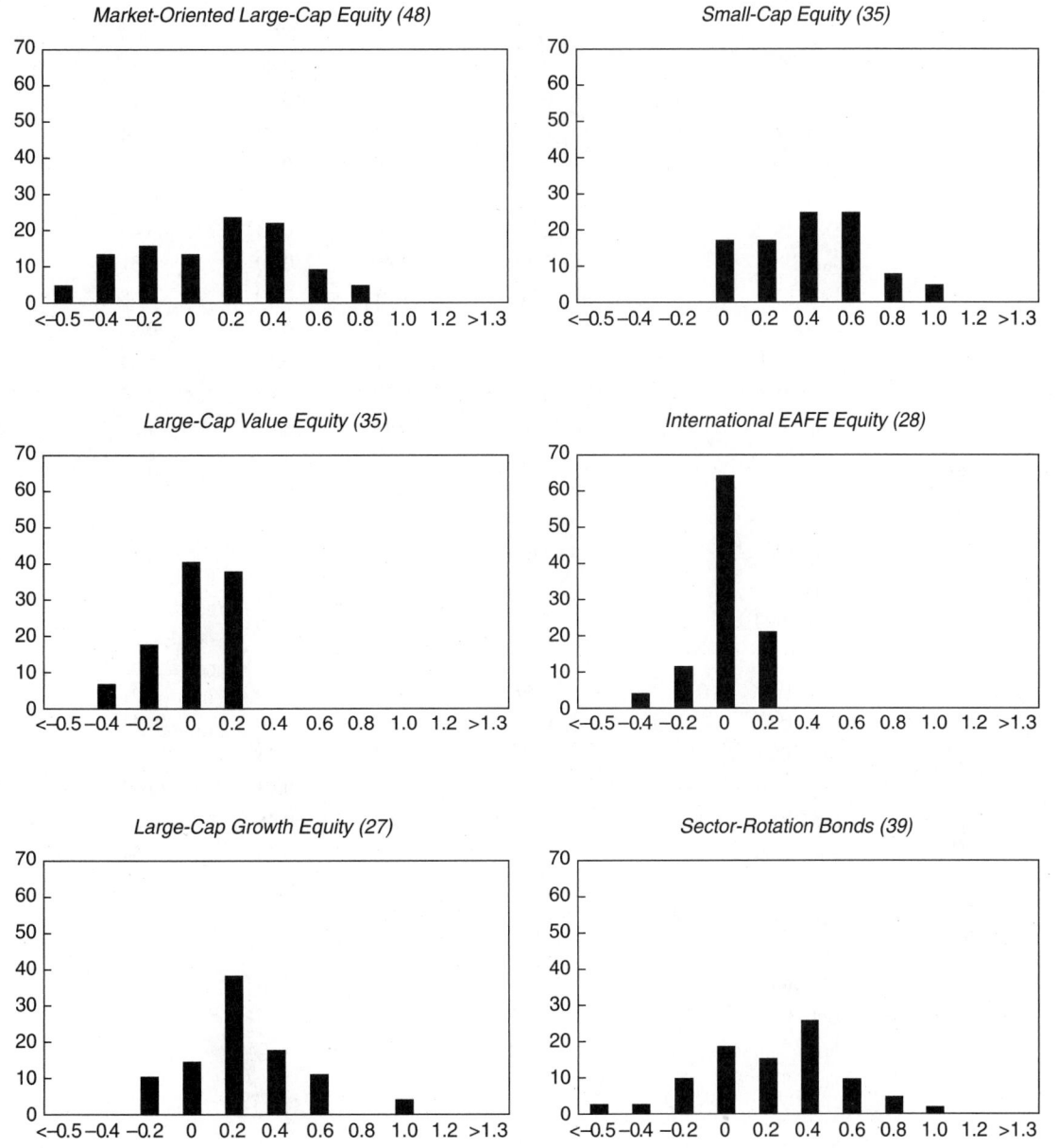

Note: Midpoints of ranges. Information ratios are on the *x*-axes; relative frequencies, in percentages, are on the *y*-axes.

These return computations do not take into account any sales charges by the funds. Given the monthly results for the fund and the aggregate market (as represented by the S&P 500), you can compute the composite measures presented in Exhibit 26.5.

The arithmetic average annual rate of return for Aim Constellation Fund was 22.30 percent versus 22.96 percent for the market, and the fund's beta was greater than 1.00 (1.086). Using the average annual rate of T-bills of 5.28 percent as the $\overline{RFR}$, the Treynor measure for the Aim

EXHIBIT 26.5

EXAMPLE OF PORTFOLIO EVALUATION MEASURES COMPUTATION USING AIM CONSTELLATION FUND

	R_{it}	R_{Mt}	RFR_t	$R_{it}-RFR_t$	$R_{Mt}-RFR_t$
Jul. 1995	9.79	3.34	0.49	9.31	2.85
Aug. 1995	0.69	0.35	0.51	0.18	−0.16
Sep. 1995	3.58	4.21	0.43	3.14	3.78
Oct. 1995	−2.59	−0.34	0.48	−3.07	−0.83
Nov. 1995	1.22	4.40	0.45	0.78	3.96
Dec. 1995	−2.90	1.76	0.54	−3.44	1.22
Jan. 1996	0.80	3.49	0.49	0.31	3.00
Feb. 1996	4.98	1.01	0.40	4.58	0.61
Mar. 1996	−0.13	0.96	0.37	−0.50	0.59
Apr. 1996	6.09	1.51	0.46	5.64	1.06
May. 1996	3.17	2.52	0.44	2.73	2.08
Jun. 1996	−3.84	0.41	0.41	−4.25	0.00
:	:	:	:	:	:
:	:	:	:	:	:
:	:	:	:	:	:
Jul. 1999	−3.01	−3.01	0.41	−3.43	−3.43
Aug. 1999	−0.53	−0.50	0.42	−0.95	0.91
Sep. 1999	0.78	−2.78	0.46	0.32	−8.23
Oct. 1999	7.41	6.43	0.39	7.01	6.04
Nov. 1999	8.80	2.10	0.43	8.37	1.67
Dec. 1999	16.88	6.27	0.46	16.43	5.81
Jan. 2000	−1.78	−4.94	0.43	−2.21	−5.37
Feb. 2000	13.27	−1.76	0.43	12.84	−2.19
Mar. 2000	2.75	9.88	0.48	2.27	9.40
Apr. 2000	−8.01	−3.19	0.49	−8.51	−3.68
May. 2000	−5.75	−2.24	0.62	−6.37	−2.86
Jun. 2000	9.79	2.63	0.43	9.35	2.20
Average (annual)	22.30	22.96	5.28		
Standard deviation	21.68	14.95	0.18		
Beta	1.086				
S_i	0.785				
S_M	1.182				
T_i	15.665				
T_M	17.682				
Jensen alpha (1 factor)	−0.184				
R^2_{iM}	0.561				

Constellation Fund (T_i) was substantially smaller than the comparable measure for the market (T_M) (15.665 versus 17.682). Likewise, the standard deviation of returns for Aim Constellation was greater than the market's (21.68 versus 14.95). Partly because of the higher standard deviation, the Sharpe measure for the fund (S_i) was smaller than the measure for the market (S_M) (0.785 versus 1.182).

EXHIBIT 26.6 ▶ *PERFORMANCE MEASURES FOR 20 SELECTED MUTUAL FUNDS*

	AVERAGE ANNUAL RATE OF RETURN	STANDARD DEVIATION	BETA	R^2	TREYNOR		SHARPE		JENSEN (1 FACTOR)	
AIM Constellation Fund A	22.30	21.68	1.086	0.561	15.665	(10)	0.785	(10)	−0.184	(11)
AXP Invest Series: Mutual A	10.81	9.12	0.558	0.836	9.911	(19)	0.006	(19)	−0.361[a]	(17)
Dreyfus Growth Opportunity Fund	16.14	16.15	1.010	0.874	10.750	(18)	0.672	(16)	−0.584[a]	(19)
Fasciano Fund	14.40	14.22	0.694	0.534	13.122	(14)	0.641	(18)	−0.263	(15)
Fidelity Magellan Fund	20.30	15.77	1.004	0.906	14.953	(11)	0.952	(8)	−0.229	(13)
Fidelity Puritan Fund	13.00	9.66	0.605	0.878	12.758	(15)	0.799	(9)	−0.247	(14)
Gabelli Asset Fund	19.67	13.41	0.815	0.826	17.652	(9)	1.073	(4)	−0.003	(9)
Guardian Park Avenue Fund A	24.27	17.32	0.935	0.652	20.303	(5)	1.096	(3)	0.202	(6)
Income Fund of America	11.30	8.07	0.454	0.709	13.247	(13)	0.746	(13)	−0.167	(10)
Investment Company of America	19.73	12.59	0.817	0.943	17.670	(8)	1.147	(2)	0.000	(8)
Janus Investment Fund: Venture Fund	29.47	31.92	1.010	0.224	23.949	(4)	0.758	(12)	0.523	(3)
Kemper Technology Fund A	36.61	30.71	1.300	0.401	24.100	(2)	1.020	(6)	0.693	(1)
Lindner Asset Allocation Fund Investor	5.57	9.89	0.470	0.505	0.606	(20)	0.029	(20)	−0.669[a]	(20)
Morgan Stanley Dean Witter Devel Gr Sec B	27.05	32.29	1.083	0.251	20.095	(6)	0.674	(15)	0.214	(5)
Oppenheimer Growth Fund A	24.01	17.53	0.779	0.442	24.036	(3)	1.068	(5)	0.410	(4)
Putnam Fund for Growth and Income A	14.68	14.58	0.857	0.772	10.963	(17)	0.644	(17)	−0.479	(18)
T Rowe Price Growth Stock Fund	22.73	14.74	0.933	0.896	18.696	(7)	1.183	(1)	0.079	(7)
Templeton World Fund A	15.41	14.82	0.804	0.659	12.586	(16)	0.683	(14)	−0.342	(16)
Value Line Special Situations Fund	28.29	23.32	0.920	0.348	25.019	(1)	0.987	(7)	0.560	(2)
Vanguard Wellington Fund	13.09	10.25	0.587	0.733	13.307	(12)	0.762	(11)	−0.212	(12)
Average fund	19.44	16.90	0.836	0.647	15.969		0.816		−0.053	
S&P 500	22.96	14.95	1.000	1.000	17.682		1.182		0.000	
90-day T-bill rate	5.28	0.18								

[a]Significant at the 0.05 level.

Finally, a one-factor regression of the fund's annual risk premium ($R_{it} - RFR_t$) and the market's annual risk premium ($R_{Mt} - RFR_t$) indicated a negative intercept (constant) value of −0.184 but was not statistically significant. If this intercept value had been significant, Aim Constellation's risk-adjusted annual rate of return would have averaged about 0.18 percent below the market on a reliable basis.

Total Sample Results The overall results in Exhibit 26.6 generally are consistent with the findings of earlier studies. Our sample was rather casually selected because we intended it for demonstration purposes only. The mean annual return for all the funds was below the market return (19.44 versus 22.96). Considering only the rate of return, 6 of the 20 funds outperformed the market.

The R^2 for a portfolio with the market can serve as a measure of diversification. The closer the R^2 is to 1.00, the more completely diversified the portfolio. The average R^2 for our sample was not very high at 0.647, and the range was quite large, from 0.224 to 0.943. This indicates that many of the funds were not well diversified. Of the 20 funds, 12 had R^2 values less than 0.75.

The two risk measures (standard deviation and beta) also show a wide degree of dispersion but generally are consistent with expectations. Specifically, 9 of the 20 funds had larger standard deviations than the market, and the mean standard deviation was larger (16.90 versus 14.95). Only six of the funds had a beta above 1.00; the average beta was 0.836.

Alternative measures ranked the performance of individual funds somewhat differently. (These rankings are listed in parentheses beside each measure). Using the Treynor measure, 7 of the 20 funds had a value better than that of the market; only one fund had a Sharpe measure as large as that of the market. The Jensen measure using the Single-Index Market Model indicated that 8 of the 20 had positive intercepts, but none of these was statistically significant (three of the negative intercepts were significant). The mean values for the Sharpe and Treynor measures were smaller than the aggregate market figure. These results indicate that, on average, and without considering transaction costs, this sample of funds had essentially worse risk-adjusted results than the market during this time period.

You should analyze the individual funds and consider each of the components: rate of return, risk (both standard deviation and beta), and the R^2 as a measure of diversification. One might expect the best performance by funds with low diversification because they apparently are attempting to beat the market by being unique in their selection or timing. This seems to be true for some of the top-performing funds, such as Janus Venture Fund and Kemper Technology Fund, as well as some unsuccessful funds that had poor diversification but low returns, such as the Lindner Asset Allocation Fund.

Exhibit 26.7 reports information ratios for these 20 funds. To interpret the display, consider that the Value Line Special Situations had a monthly *IR* value of 0.101, which was calculated by dividing its alpha (0.560) by its regression standard error (5.528). This statistic is then annualized to 0.351 by multiplying the monthly *IR* by the square root of 12. Notice that 7 of the 20 funds had positive *IR* levels, which follows directly from the number of funds that had a positive value for Jensen's alpha measure. The mean annualized *IR* for the sample was –0.290, well below the Grinold-Kahn standard for "good" performance of 0.500. Thus, on average and after accounting for tracking error costs, this collection of funds did not add value to their investors.

Potential Bias of One-Parameter Measures   Friend and Blume pointed out that, theoretically, the composite measures of performance should be independent of alternative measures of risk because they are *risk-adjusted* measures.[11] An analysis of the relationship between the composite measures of performance and two measures of risk (standard deviation and beta) for 200 random portfolios from the NYSE indicated a significant *inverse* relationship (the risk-adjusted performance of low-risk portfolios was better than the comparable performance for high-risk portfolios).

Subsequently, Klemkosky examined the relationship between composite performance measures and risk measures using actual mutual fund data in contrast to the random portfolio data used by Friend and Blume.[12] Beyond the preceding risk-adjusted performance measures, the author derived two statistics that computed the excess return above the risk-free rate relative to the semistandard deviation and relative to the mean absolute deviation as risk measures. The results indicated a *positive* bias—that is, a *positive* relationship between the composite performance measures and the risk involved. This was especially true for the Treynor and Jensen measures. The performance measures that used the mean absolute deviation and the semistandard

---

[11]Irwin Friend and Marshall Blume, "Measurement of Portfolio Performance under Uncertainty," *American Economic Review* 60, no. 4 (September 1970): 561–575.

[12]Robert C. Klemkosky, "The Bias in Composite Performance Measures," *Journal of Financial and Quantitative Analysis* 8, no. 3 (June 1973): 505–514.

EXHIBIT 26.7	INFORMATION RATIOS FOR 20 MUTUAL FUNDS				
	ALPHA	STANDARD ERROR	IR	ANNUALIZED IR	RANK
AIM Constellation Fund A	−0.184	4.216	−0.044	−0.151	(10)
AXP Invest Series: Mutual A	−0.361	1.083	−0.334	−1.155	(19)
Dreyfus Growth Opportunity Fund	−0.584	1.682	−0.347	−1.202	(20)
Fasciano Fund	−0.263	2.849	−0.092	−0.320	(11)
Fidelity Magellan Fund	−0.229	1.418	−0.162	−0.560	(15)
Fidelity Puritan Fund	−0.247	0.986	−0.251	−0.869	(17)
Gabelli Asset Fund	−0.003	1.644	−0.002	−0.006	(9)
Guardian Park Avenue Fund A	0.202	3.000	0.067	0.234	(4)
Income Fund of America	−0.167	1.270	−0.131	−0.454	(12)
Investment Company of America	0.000	0.881	0.000	−0.001	(8)
Janus Investment Fund: Venture Fund	0.523	8.255	0.063	0.219	(5)
Kemper Technology Fund A	0.693	6.978	0.099	0.344	(3)
Lindner Asset Allocation Fund Investor	−0.669	2.043	−0.327	−1.134	(18)
Morgan Stanley Dean Witter Devel Gr Sec B	0.214	8.203	0.026	0.090	(7)
Oppenheimer Growth Fund A	0.410	3.847	0.107	0.369	(1)
Putnam Fund for Growth and Income A	−0.479	2.042	−0.234	−0.812	(16)
T Rowe Price Growth Stock Fund	0.079	1.397	0.056	0.195	(6)
Templeton World Fund A	−0.342	2.542	−0.135	−0.466	(13)
Value Line Special Situations Fund	0.560	5.528	0.101	0.351	(2)
Vanguard Wellington Fund	−0.212	1.550	−0.137	−0.474	(14)
Mean:	−0.053	3.071	−0.084	−0.290	
Median:	−0.175	2.042	−0.068	−0.235	

deviation as risk proxies were less biased than the three standard performance measures. He concluded that although a bias might exist, one could not be certain of its direction. More recently, Leland has shown that alpha can be biased downward for those portfolios designed to limit downside risk.[13]

Measuring Performance with Multiple Risk Factors Equation 26.5 showed how the Jensen composite measure could be estimated relative to multifactor models of risk and expected return. Exhibit 26.8 shows the Jensen measures calculated for the 20 mutual funds compared to the Fama-French three-factor model discussed at length in Chapter 9.[14] The form of this estimation equation is

$$R_{jt} - RFR_t = \alpha_j + [b_{j1}(R_{Mt} - RFR_t) + b_{j2}SMB_t + b_{j3}HML_t] + e_{jt}$$

---

[13]Hayne E. Leland, "Beyond Mean-Variance: Performance Measurement in a Nonsymmetrical World," *Financial Analysts Journal* 55, no. 1 (January–February 1999): 27–36.

[14]See Eugene F. Fama and Kenneth R. French, "Common Risk Factors in the Returns on Stocks and Bonds," *Journal of Financial Economics* 33, no. 1 (January 1993): 3–56. Also, the data for this analysis came from Professor Kenneth French's Web site at http://mba.tuck.dartmouth.edu/pages/faculty/ken.french

EXHIBIT 26.8 *PERFORMANCE MEASURES FOR 20 FUNDS USING A THREE-FACTOR MODEL*

| | FACTOR BETAS | | | | |
	R_M-RFR	SMB	HML	JENSEN ALPHA (3-FACTOR)	RANK
AIM Constellation Fund A	1.030	0.228	−0.376	−0.118	(10)
AXP Invest Series: Mutual A	0.652	−0.089	0.268	−0.304[a]	(17)
Dreyfus Growth Opportunity Fund	1.004	−0.100	−0.057	−0.493[a]	(19)
Fasciano Fund	0.938	0.255	0.552	−0.231	(15)
Fidelity Magellan Fund	0.974	−0.158	−0.101	−0.131	(12)
Fidelity Puritan Fund	0.669	−0.107	0.197	−0.179	(14)
Gabelli Asset Fund	0.957	0.070	0.304	0.050	(9)
Guardian Park Avenue Fund A	0.899	0.143	−0.233	0.281	(5)
Income Fund of America	0.602	0.013	0.392	−0.127	(11)
Investment Company of America	0.889	−0.079	0.193	0.080	(8)
Janus Investment Fund: Venture Fund	0.800	0.458	−1.047	0.525	(3)
Kemper Technology Fund A	0.872	0.061	−1.374	0.826	(1)
Lindner Asset Allocation Fund Investor	0.626	0.207	0.325	−0.643[a]	(20)
Morgan Stanley Dean Witter Devel Gr Sec B	0.951	0.747	−0.841	0.243	(6)
Oppenheimer Growth Fund A	0.673	0.209	−0.449	0.482	(4)
Putnam Fund for Growth and Income A	1.018	−0.176	0.485	−0.400[a]	(18)
T Rowe Price Growth Stock Fund	0.946	−0.039	−0.024	0.160	(7)
Templeton World Fund A	0.952	0.141	0.305	−0.289	(16)
Value Line Special Situations Fund	0.909	0.521	−0.361	0.592	(2)
Vanguard Wellington Fund	0.721	−0.078	0.394	−0.151	(13)
Mean	0.854	0.111	−0.072	0.009	

[a]Significant at the 0.05 level.

where, in addition to the excess return on the market portfolio, two additional common risk factors are included: *SMB,* based on the return differential between portfolios of small-cap and large-cap stocks, and *HML,* based on the return differential between portfolios of stocks with high book-to-market ratios (i.e., "value" stocks) and low book-to-market ratios (i.e., "growth" stocks).

Although not listed in Exhibit 26.8, the average annual returns (i.e., risk premia) for the *SMB* and *HML* factors were −1.44 percent and −5.40 percent, respectively. This indicates that in the stock market as a whole over the July 1995 to June 2000 investment period, large stock outperformed small stocks (i.e., a negative mean *SMB* return) and growth stocks outperformed value stocks (i.e., a negative mean *HML* return). For this particular collection of 20 funds, the mean factor betas—0.854 for the market factor, 0.111 for the *SMB* factor, and −0.072 for the *HML* factor—indicate that the average fund has less systematic market risk than average and is oriented more toward small, growth stocks.

The Jensen alpha results for the three-factor model show some important differences with the comparable findings from the one-factor model reported in Exhibit 26.6. In particular, the mean value for alpha (0.009) is now positive. Also, nine (rather than eight) of the funds had positive alpha values, but four (rather than three) of the funds with negative alphas had statistically significant underperformance. This highlights the fact that the one-factor and three-factor Jensen measures produce similar but distinct performance rankings and should therefore be considered as different from one another as the Sharpe and Treynor measures.

Components of Investment Performance

Following the work of Treynor, Sharpe, and Jensen, Fama suggested a somewhat finer breakdown of performance.[15] The basic premise for Fama's technique is that *overall performance* of a portfolio, which is its return in excess of the risk-free rate, can be decomposed into measures of risk-taking and security selection skill. That is,

Overall Performance = Excess Return = (Portfolio Risk) + (Selectivity)

Further, if there is a difference between the risk level specified by the investor and the actual risk level adopted by the portfolio manager (in cases where these are separate people), this calculation can be further refined to

Overall Performance = [(Investor's Risk) + (Manager's Risk)] + (Selectivity)

Notice that the *selectivity* component represents the portion of the portfolio's actual return beyond that available to an unmanaged portfolio with identical systematic risk. Thus, this selectivity measure is used to assess the manager's investment prowess.

As with the preceding performance statistics, Fama's evaluation model assumes that returns to managed portfolios can be compared to those of naively selected portfolios with similar risk levels. The technique is based on the *ex ante* market line summarizing the equilibrium relationship between expected return and risk for Portfolio j:

$$E(\hat{R}_j) = RFR + \left[\frac{E(\hat{R}_M) - RFR}{\sigma(\hat{R}_M)} \right] \frac{\mathrm{Cov}(\hat{R}_j, \hat{R}_M)}{\sigma(\hat{R}_M)}$$

$\mathrm{Cov}(R_j, R_M)$ is the covariance between the returns for Portfolio j and the return on a single market portfolio. This equation indicates that the expected return on Portfolio j is the riskless rate of interest, *RFR*, plus a risk premium that is $[E(\tilde{R}_M) - RFR]/\sigma(\tilde{R}_M)$, called the *market price per unit of risk,* times the risk of Asset j, which is $[\mathrm{Cov}(\tilde{R}_j, \tilde{R}_M)]/\sigma(\tilde{R}_M)$.

If a portfolio manager believes that the market is not completely efficient and that she can make better judgments than the market, then an *ex post* version of this market line can provide a benchmark for the manager's performance. Given that the risk variable, $\mathrm{Cov}(R_j, R_M)/\sigma(R_M)$, can be denoted β_x, the *ex post* market line is as follows:

$$R_x = RFR + \left(\frac{R_M - RFR}{\sigma(R_M)} \right) \beta_x$$

This *ex post* market line provides the benchmark used to evaluate managed portfolios in a sequence of more complex measures.

Evaluating Selectivity   Formally, you can measure the return due to selectivity as follows:

$$\text{Selectivity} = R_a - R_x(\beta_a)$$

[15]Eugene F. Fama, "Components of Investment Performance," *Journal of Finance* 27, no. 3 (June 1972): 551–567.

where:

R_a = **the actual return on the portfolio being evaluated**

$R_x(\beta_a)$ = **the return on the combination of the riskless asset and the market portfolio M that has risk β_x equal to β_a, the risk of the portfolio being evaluated**

As shown in Exhibit 26.9, selectivity measures the vertical distance between the actual return and the *ex post* market line and is quite similar to Treynor's measure.

As already noted, you can examine overall performance in terms of selectivity and the returns from assuming risk as follows:

➤26.7
$$
\begin{array}{ccc}
& \text{Overall} & \\
\text{Performance} = & \text{Selectivity} + & \text{Risk} \\
[R_a - RFR] = [R_a - R_x(\beta_a)] + [R_x(\beta_a) - RFR]
\end{array}
$$

Exhibit 26.9 shows that overall performance is the total return above the risk-free return and includes the return that *should* have been received for accepting the portfolio risk (β_a). This expected return for accepting risk (β_a) is equal to $[R_x(\beta_a) - RFR]$. Any excess over this expected return is due to selectivity.

Evaluating Diversification The selectivity component in Equation 26.7 can also be broken down into two parts. If a portfolio manager attempts to select undervalued stocks and in the process gives up some diversification, it is possible to measure the added return necessary to justify this diversification decision. The portfolio's *gross selectivity* is made up of *net selectivity* plus *diversification* as follows:

$$
\begin{array}{cc}
\text{Selectivity} & \text{Diversification} \\
R_a - R_x(\beta_a) = \text{Net Selectivity} + [R_x(\sigma(R_a)) - R_x(\beta_a)]
\end{array}
$$

EXHIBIT 26.9 ▶ *AN ILLUSTRATION OF THE PERFORMANCE MEASURES*

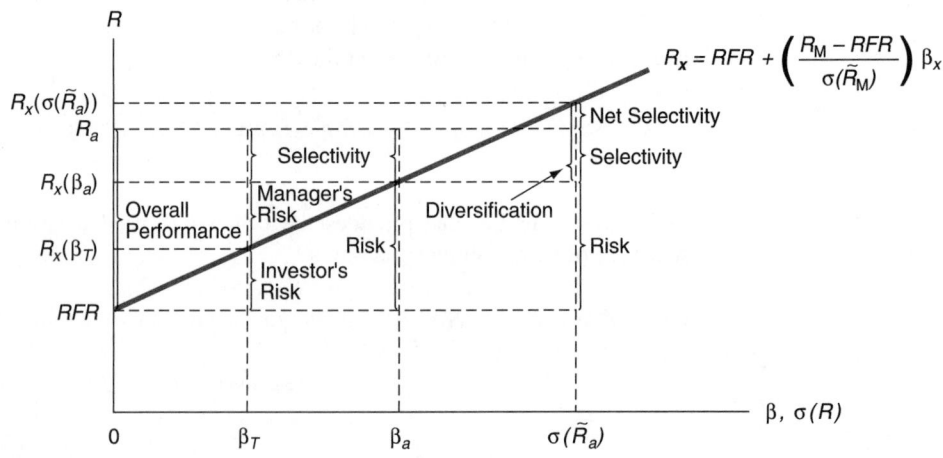

Source: Eugene F. Fama, "Components of Investment Performance," *Journal of Finance* 27, no. 3 (June 1972): 588. Reprinted with permission of Blackwell Publishing.

or

➤26.8

$$\text{Net Selectivity} = R_a - R_x(\beta_a) - [R_x(\sigma(R_a)) - R_x(\beta_a)]$$

$$\overset{\text{Selectivity} -}{} \qquad \overset{\text{Diversification}}{}$$

$$= R_a - R_x(\sigma(R_a))$$

where:

$R_x(\sigma(R_a))$ = the return on the combination of the riskless asset and the market portfolio that has return dispersion equivalent to that of the portfolio being evaluated

Therefore, the diversification measure in Equation 26.8 indicates the *added return* required to justify any loss of diversification in the portfolio. The term emphasizes that diversification is the elimination of all unsystematic variability. If the portfolio is completely diversified so that total risk (σ) is equal to systematic risk (β), then the $R_x(\sigma(R_a))$ would be the same as $R_x(\beta_a)$, and the diversification term would equal zero.

Because the diversification measure always is nonnegative, net selectivity will always be equal to or less than gross selectivity. The two will be equal when the portfolio is completely diversified. If the investor is not concerned with the diversification of the portfolio, this particular breakdown will not be important, and only selectivity will be considered.[16]

Evaluating Risk   Assuming the investor has a target level of risk for the portfolio equal to β_T, the portion of overall performance due to risk (the total return above the risk-free return) can be assessed as follows:

$$\text{Risk} \qquad = \text{Manager's Risk} + \text{Investor's Risk}$$

$$[R_x(\beta_a) - RFR] = [R_x(\beta_a) - R_x(\beta_T)] + [R_x(\beta_T) - RFR]$$

where:

$R_x(\beta_T)$ = the return on the naively selected portfolio with the target level of market risk (β_T)

If the portfolio risk is equal to the target risk ($\beta_a = \beta_T$), then the manager's risk does not exist. If there is a difference between β_a and β_T, then the manager's risk is the return she must earn due to the decision to accept risk (β_a), which is different from the risk desired by the investor (β_T). The investor's risk is the return expected because the investor stipulated some positive level of risk. This evaluation is possible only if the client has specified a desired level of market risk, which is typical of pension funds and profit-sharing plans. Generally, it is not possible to compute this measure for *ex post* evaluations because the desired risk level is typically not available.

Application of Fama Measures   Several of these performance components can be used in *ex post* evaluation, as shown in Exhibit 26.10. Overall performance is the return derived above the risk-free return (i.e., the return above 5.28 percent as shown in Exhibit 26.6). All of these mutual funds experienced positive overall performance. Next, determine how much the

---

[16]Franco Modigliani and Leah Modigliani, "Risk-Adjusted Performance," *Journal of Portfolio Management* 23, no. 2 (Winter 1997): 45–54, presents a performance measure (dubbed M^2) that is a variation of both the Sharpe measure and Fama's $R_x[\sigma(R_a)]$ component.

EXHIBIT 26.10 COMPONENTS OF PERFORMANCE FOR 20 SELECTED MUTUAL FUNDS

	Average Rate of Return	Standard Deviation	Beta	R^2	Overall Performance	Risk	Selectivity	Diversification	Net Selectivity
AIM Constellation Fund A	22.30	21.68	1.086	0.561	17.02	19.21	-2.19	6.43	-8.62 (17)
AXP Invest Series: Mutual A	10.81	9.12	0.558	0.836	5.53	9.86	-4.34	0.92	-5.26 (12)
Dreyfus Growth Opportunity Fund	16.14	16.15	1.010	0.874	10.85	17.85	-7.00	1.24	-8.24 (16)
Fasciano Fund	14.40	14.22	0.694	0.534	9.11	12.28	-3.17	4.53	-7.70 (14)
Fidelity Magellan Fund	20.30	15.77	1.004	0.906	15.01	17.75	-2.74	0.90	-3.64 (7)
Fidelity Puritan Fund	13.00	9.66	0.605	0.878	7.72	10.70	-2.98	0.72	-3.70 (8)
Gabelli Asset Fund	19.67	13.41	0.815	0.826	14.39	14.41	-0.02	1.45	-1.47 (3)
Guardian Park Avenue Fund A	24.27	17.32	0.935	0.652	18.99	16.54	2.45	3.94	-1.49 (4)
Income Fund of America	11.30	8.07	0.454	0.709	6.02	8.03	-2.01	1.51	-3.52 (6)
Investment Company of America	19.73	12.59	0.817	0.943	14.44	14.45	-0.01	0.43	-0.44 (2)
Janus Investment Fund: Venture Fund	29.47	31.92	1.010	0.224	24.19	17.86	6.33	19.88	-13.55 (19)
Kemper Technology Fund A	36.61	30.71	1.300	0.401	31.33	22.99	8.34	13.33	-4.98 (11)
Lindner Asset Allocation Fund Investor	5.57	9.89	0.470	0.505	0.28	8.31	-8.02	3.39	-11.41 (18)
Morgan Stanley Dean Witter Devel Gr Sec B	27.05	32.29	1.083	0.251	21.76	19.15	2.61	19.04	-16.42 (20)
Oppenheimer Growth Fund A	24.01	17.53	0.779	0.442	18.72	13.77	4.95	6.95	-2.00 (5)
Putnam Fund for Growth and Income A	14.68	14.58	0.857	0.772	9.39	15.15	-5.76	2.09	-7.84 (15)
T Rowe Price Growth Stock Fund	22.73	14.74	0.933	0.896	17.45	16.50	0.95	0.93	0.01 (1)
Templeton World Fund A	15.41	14.82	0.804	0.659	10.12	14.22	-4.10	3.30	-7.40 (13)
Value Line Special Situations Fund	28.29	23.32	0.920	0.348	23.01	16.26	6.75	11.31	-4.56 (10)
Vanguard Wellington Fund	13.09	10.25	0.587	0.733	7.81	10.37	-2.57	1.75	-4.31 (9)
S&P 500	22.96	14.95							
90-day T-bill rate	5.28	0.18							

portfolio (fund) *should* receive for its systematic risk using the following expected return equation for this period (22.96 percent is the return on the S&P 500 during this period, as shown in Exhibit 26.6):

$$E(R_i) = 5.28 + \beta_i(22.96 - 5.28)$$
$$= 5.28 + \beta_i(17.68)$$

The required return for risk simply is the latter term in this expression: $\beta_i(17.68)$. The required return for risk for Gabelli Asset Fund was $0.815(17.68) = 14.41$ percent (its total required return is $(5.28 + 14.41 = 19.69)$. The return for selectivity is the difference between overall performance $(19.67 - 5.28 = 14.39)$ and the required return for risk (14.41). If the overall performance exceeds the required return for risk, the portfolio has experienced a positive return for selectivity. The results indicate that Gabelli Asset actually had an average annual return of -0.02 percent for selectivity $(14.39 - 14.41)$. Seven funds had positive returns for selectivity (e.g., Kemper Technology Fund). In contrast, several funds had positive overall performance, but their required return for risk exceeded this figure, giving them negative returns for selectivity.

The next two columns in Exhibit 26.10 indicate the effect of diversification on performance. The diversification term indicates the required return for not being completely diversified (i.e., having total risk above systematic risk). If a fund's total risk is equal to its systematic risk, then the ratio of its total risk to the market's total risk will equal its beta. If this is not the case, then the ratio of the fund's total risk for the fund relative to the market will be greater than its beta, which implies an added return required because of incomplete diversification. For Gabelli Asset, the ratio of total risk was

$$\frac{\sigma_i}{\sigma_M} = \frac{13.41}{14.95} = 0.897$$

This total risk ratio compares to the fund's beta of 0.815, indicating that the fund is not completely diversified, which is consistent with its R^2 of 0.826. The fund's required return, given its standard deviation, is

$$R_i = 5.28 + 0.897(17.68)$$
$$= 21.14$$

Recall that the fund's required return for systematic risk was 19.69 [$= 5.28 + 0.815(17.68)$]. The difference of 1.45 ($= 21.14 - 19.69$) is the added return required because of less than perfect diversification. This moderate required return for diversification is in contrast to Morgan Stanley Growth Fund, which has an R^2 with the market of 0.251 and a required return for diversification of 19.04 percent.

This required return for diversification is subtracted from the selectivity return to arrive at net selectivity. Gabelli Asset had a return for selectivity of -0.02 percent and net selectivity of -1.47 percent. This indicates that, after accounting for the added cost of incomplete diversification, the fund's performance was below the market line. Only one fund had a nonnegative net selectivity return.

Relationship among Performance Measures   Exhibit 26.11 contains the matrix of rank correlation coefficients among the Treynor, Sharpe, Jensen (both one-factor and three-factor), Information Ratio, and Fama net selectivity measures. The striking feature of the display is that all of these statistics are positively correlated with one another, but not perfectly so

EXHIBIT 26.11	CORRELATIONS AMONG ALTERNATIVE PORTFOLIO PERFORMANCE MEASURES					
	TREYNOR	SHARPE	JENSEN (1 FACTOR)	JENSEN (3 FACTOR)	INFORMATION RATIO	NET SELECTIVITY
Treynor	—					
Sharpe	0.72	—				
Jensen (1 factor)	0.98	0.68	—			
Jensen (3 factor)	0.99	0.71	0.99	—		
Information ratio	0.95	0.67	0.94	0.94	—	
Net selectivity	0.29	0.78	0.29	0.30	0.30	—

(particularly the Net Selectivity measure). This suggests that, although the measures provide a generally consistent assessment of portfolio performance when taken as a whole, they remain distinct at an individual level. This reinforces our earlier point that it is best to consider these composites collectively and that the user must understand what each means.

PERFORMANCE ATTRIBUTION ANALYSIS

As noted earlier, portfolio managers can add value to their investors in either of two ways: selecting superior securities or demonstrating superior market timing skills by allocating funds to different asset classes or market segments. **Attribution analysis** attempts to distinguish which of these factors is the source of the portfolio's overall performance. Specifically, this method compares the total return to the manager's actual investment holdings to the return for a predetermined benchmark portfolio and decomposes the difference into an *allocation effect* and a *selection effect*. The most straightforward way to measure these two effects is as follows:

➤ 26.9
$$\text{Allocation Effect} = \sum_i [(w_{ai} - w_{pi}) \times (R_{pi} - R_p)]$$
$$\text{Selection Effect} = \sum_i [(w_{ai}) \times (R_{ai} - R_{pi})]$$

where:

w_{ai}, w_{pi} = the investment proportions given to the *i*th *market segment* (e.g., asset class, industry group) in the manager's actual portfolio and the benchmark portfolio, respectively

R_{ai}, R_{pi} = the investment return to the *i*th market segment in the manager's actual portfolio and the benchmark portfolio, respectively

R_p = the total return to the benchmark portfolio

With Equation 26.9, the allocation effect measures the manager's decision to over- or underweight a particular market segment (i.e., $[w_{ai} - w_{pi}]$) in terms of that segment's return performance relative to the overall return to the benchmark (i.e., $[R_{pi} - R_p]$). Good timing skill is therefore a matter of investing more money in those market segments that end up producing greater than average returns. The selection effect measures the manager's ability to form specific market segment portfolios that generate superior returns relative to the way in which the comparable market segment is defined in the benchmark portfolio (i.e., $[R_{ai} - R_{pi}]$), weighted by the manager's actual market segment investment proportions. When constructed in this manner, the manager's total value-added performance is the sum of the allocation and selection effects.[17]

Asset Class Attribution Analysis: An Example

As an example of this process, consider an investor whose top-down portfolio strategy consists of two dimensions. First, he decides on a broad allocation of his investment dollars across three asset classes: U.S. stocks, U.S. long-term bonds, and cash equivalents, such as U.S. Treasury bills or certificates of deposit. Once this judgment is made, the investor's second general decision is choosing which specific stocks, bonds, and cash instruments to buy. As a benchmark, he selects a hypothetical portfolio with a 60 percent allocation to the Standard and Poor's 500 index, a 30 percent investment in the Lehman Corporate Long Bond index, and a 10 percent allocation to three-month Treasury bills.

Suppose that at the start of the investment period, the investor believes equity values are somewhat inflated and is not optimistic about the near-term performance of the stock market. Compared to the benchmark, he therefore decides to underweight stocks and overweight bonds and cash in his actual portfolio. The investment proportions he chooses are 50 percent in equity, 38 percent in bonds, and 12 percent in cash. Further, instead of selecting a broad portfolio of equities, he decides to concentrate on the interest rate–sensitive sectors, such as utilities and financial companies, while deemphasizing the technology and consumer durables sectors. Finally, he resolves to buy shorter duration bonds of a higher credit quality than are contained in the benchmark bond index and to buy commercial paper rather than Treasury bills.

In this example, the manager has made active investment decisions involving both the allocation of assets and the selection of individual securities. To determine if either (or both) of these decisions proved to be wise ones, at the end of the investment period he can calculate his overall and segment-specific performance. Exhibit 26.12 summarizes these hypothetical returns for the investor's actual and benchmark asset class portfolios as well as the investment weightings for each. The overall actual and benchmark returns can be computed as follows:

$$\text{Overall Actual Return} = (0.50 \times 0.097) + (0.38 \times 0.091) + (0.12 \times 0.056)$$
$$= 8.98\%$$

and

$$\text{Overall Benchmark Return} = (0.60 \times 0.086) + (0.30 \times 0.092) + (0.10 \times 0.054)$$
$$= 8.46\%$$

Thus, the manager beat the benchmark by 52 basis points (= 0.0898 − 0.0846) over this particular investment horizon.

---

[17]Wainscott has argued that a better way to measure the selection effect is to multiply the market segment return differential by the benchmark for that segment, or $\Sigma_i(w_{pi}) \times (R_{ai} - R_{pi})]$. A drawback of this approach, however, is that the allocation and selection effects no longer sum to the total value-added return. To balance the equation, he calculates an *interaction effect* as $\Sigma_i[(w_{ai} - w_{pi}) \times (R_{ai} - R_{pi})]$ to measure the residual performance. See Craig B. Wainscott, "Attribution Analysis for Equities," in *Performance Evaluation, Benchmarks, and Attribution Analysis,* ed. J. Squires (Charlottesville, Va.: Association for Investment Management and Research, 1995).

EXHIBIT 26.12   *ASSET CLASS PERFORMANCE ATTRIBUTION ANALYSIS*

ASSET CLASS	INVESTMENT WEIGHTS			RETURNS		
	ACTUAL	BENCHMARK	EXCESS	ACTUAL	BENCHMARK	EXCESS
Stock	0.50	0.60	−0.10	9.70%	8.60%	1.10%
Bonds	0.38	0.30	0.08	9.10	9.20	−0.10
Cash	0.12	0.10	0.02	5.60	5.40	0.20

The goal of attribution analysis is to isolate the reason for this value-added performance. The manager's allocation effect can be computed by multiplying the excess asset class weight by that class's relative investment performance:

$$[(-0.10) \times (0.086 - 0.0846)] + [(0.08) \times (0.092 - 0.0846)] +$$
$$[(0.02) \times (0.054 - 0.0846)] = -0.02\%$$

This shows that if the investor had made just his market timing decisions and not picked different securities than those represented in the benchmark, his performance would have lagged the target return by two basis points. This total allocation effect can be broken down further into an equity allocation return of −2 basis points (= $[(-0.10) \times (0.086 - 0.0846)]$), a bond allocation return of 6 basis points (= $[(0.08) \times (0.092 - 0.0846)]$), and a cash allocation return of −6 basis points (= $[(0.02) \times (0.054 - 0.0846)]$). Therefore, the decision to underweight stock and overweight cash (asset classes that generated returns above and below the benchmark, respectively) resulted in diminished performance that was more than enough to offset the benefit of emphasizing bonds.

Since the investor knows that he outperformed the benchmark overall, a negative allocation effect necessarily implies that he exhibited positive security selection skills. His selection effect can be computed as

$$[(0.50) \times (0.097 - 0.086)] + [(0.38) \times (0.091 - 0.092)] + [(0.12) \times (0.056 - 0.054)] = 0.54\%$$

In this example, the investor formed superior stock and cash portfolios, although his bond selections did not perform quite as well as the Lehman Long Bond index. One important caveat in this analysis is that, because the returns are not risk-adjusted, it is possible that the asset class portfolios formed by the investor are riskier than their benchmark counterparts. If this is the case, which is almost certainly true for a cash portfolio that holds short-term corporate debt obligations instead of Treasury bills, the investor should expect a higher return that has nothing to do with his skill. Finally, notice that the investor's total incremental return of 52 basis points can be decomposed as

Total Value Added = Allocation Effect + Selection Effect
$$= (-0.02\%) + (0.54\%) = 0.52\%$$

Using a procedure similar to the one just described, Brinson, Hood, and Beebower examined the return performance of a group of 91 large U.S. pension plans over the decade from 1974 to 1983.[18]

---

[18]Gary P. Brinson, L. Randolph Hood, and Gilbert L. Beebower, "Determinants of Portfolio Performance," *Financial Analysts Journal* 42, no. 4 (July–August 1986): 39–44.

They established that the mean annual return for this sample was 9.01 percent, compared to 10.11 percent for their benchmark. Thus, they documented that active management cost the average plan 110 basis points of return per year. This "value subtracted" return increment consisted of a –77-basis-point allocation effect and a –33-basis-point selection effect. Further, they concluded that a plan's initial strategic asset allocation choice, rather than any of its active management decisions, was the primary determinant of portfolio performance. In a follow-up study, Brinson, Singer, and Beebower reached a similar conclusion for a different group of 82 pension plans over the 1977–1987 period.[19] For this new sample, however, they showed that the total active return shortfall had fallen to –7 basis points, which was divided into an 18-basis-point selection effect and a –25-basis-point allocation effect.

Performance Attribution Extensions

Although the preceding example concentrated partly on an investor's ability to time broad asset class movements, the attribution methodology can be used to distinguish security selection skills from any of several other decisions that an investor might make. For instance, the manager of a broad-based, all-equity portfolio must decide what economic sectors (e.g., basic materials, consumer nondurables, transportation) to under- and overweight before she can choose her preferred companies in those sectors. In such cases, performance attribution analysis is still applicable, with a "sector rotation" effect replacing the market timing effect. To see how this might work, Exhibit 26.13 summarizes the performance of the growth-oriented stock portfolio managed by The MBA Investment Fund, L.L.C., a privately funded investment management company run by a group of graduate students at the University of Texas. During the time of this analysis, which covered the first full one-year period of the Fund's existence, the managers were restricted to investing in U.S.-traded equities and ADRs only. Because the Fund's investment mandate was to beat the return on the Standard and Poor's 500, the managers had two basic decisions to make: which sectors to emphasize and which individual stocks to buy within those sectors.

Over the course of the year, the overall returns to the S&P 500 and the Fund were 29.63 percent and 29.54 percent, respectively. The second and third columns of Exhibit 26.13 document the actual and benchmark weights for the 10 economic sectors comprising the S&P 500 index, with the Fund's excess weightings (i.e., $[w_{ai} - w_{pi}]$) listed in the fourth column. The entries in the last column show the benchmark sector return relative to the overall S&P return (i.e., $[R_{pi} - R_p]$). Thus, the sector allocation effect can be calculated by summing the product of the entries in the last two columns:

$$[(-0.0339) \times (-0.1515)] + [(0.0703) \times (-0.0331)]$$
$$+ \ldots + [(-0.0242) \times (-0.1315)] = -0.28\%$$

With an overall return difference of –9 basis points (= 0.2954 – 0.2963), this means that the Fund's managers generated a security selection effect of 19 basis points (= (–0.0009) – (–0.0028)). Consequently, although the student managers virtually matched the strong performance of the entire stock market, it appears they were better at picking stocks than forecasting broader economic trends.

This general attribution analysis methodology has been extended to other specific asset classes as well. Kuberek showed that producing fixed-income attributions for bond portfolio managers is quite straightforward once the relevant decision variables have been specified.[20] He

[19]Gary P. Brinson, Brian D. Singer, and Gilbert L. Beebower, "Determinants of Portfolio Performance II: An Update," *Financial Analysts Journal* 47, no. 3 (May–June 1991): 40–48.

[20]Robert C. Kuberek, "Attribution Analysis for Fixed Income," in *Performance Evaluation, Benchmarks, and Attribution Analysis,* ed. J. Squires (Charlottesville, Va.: Association for Investment Management and Research, 1995).

EXHIBIT 26.13 ▶ *MBA INVESTMENT FUND SECTOR PERFORMANCE ATTRIBUTION ANALYSIS*

	INVESTMENT WEIGHTS			EXCESS RETURNS
S&P 500 SECTOR	ACTUAL	S&P 500	EXCESS	S&P SECTOR–OVERALL S&P
Basic materials	0.0331	0.0670	–0.0339	–15.15%
Capital equipment and technology	0.2544	0.1841	0.0703	–3.31
Consumer services	0.0208	0.0692	–0.0484	6.95
Consumer durables	0.0588	0.0353	0.0235	–21.34
Consumer nondurables	0.2752	0.2851	–0.0099	5.85
Energy	0.1170	0.0935	0.0235	–7.08
Financial	0.1619	0.1249	0.0370	7.15
Transportation	0.0199	0.0172	0.0027	–1.72
Utilities	0.0590	0.1000	–0.0410	1.91
Miscellaneous	0.0000	0.0242	–0.0242	–13.15

noted that these decision variables might include allocations to different countries, foreign exchange effects, individual bond selections, and other risk factors, such as the portfolio's term structure positioning. Karnosky and Singer have developed a comprehensive, unified framework for attributing performance in a global asset management context.[21] In particular, they have added both active and hedged currency allocation returns to the single-currency attribution model of Brinson, Hood, and Beebower to allow for the intricacies of cross-border investing. In a comparison of the performance of one of their global investment portfolios relative to the MSCI World Equity Index during 1989, they demonstrated that the combined effect of the currency selection decision accounted for 563 basis points of the 7.66 percent return advantage that the portfolio enjoyed.

◀ *MEASURING MARKET TIMING SKILLS* ▶

As we saw in Chapter 17, tactical asset allocation (TAA) is a portfolio management strategy in which a manager attempts to produce active value-added returns solely through allocation decisions. Specifically, instead of trying to pick superior individual securities, TAA managers adjust their asset class exposures based on perceived changes in the relative valuations of those classes. A typical TAA fund shifts money between three asset classes—stocks, bonds, and cash equivalents—although many definitions of these categories (e.g., large cap versus small cap, long term versus short term) are used in practice. Of course, this means that the relevant performance measurement criterion for a TAA manager is how well he is able to time broad market movements. There are two reasons why attribution analysis is ill-suited for this task. First, by design, a TAA manager indexes his actual asset class investments and so the selection effect is not relevant. Second, a TAA approach to investing might entail dozens of changes to asset class weightings during an investment period, which could render meaningless an attribution effect computed on the average holdings. Because of these problems, many analysts consider a regression-based method for measuring timing skills to be a superior approach.

---

[21]Denis S. Karnosky and Brian D. Singer, *Global Asset Management and Performance Measurement* (Charlottesville, Va.: Research Foundation of the Institute of Chartered Financial Analysts, 1994). See also Ernest M. Ankrim and Chris R. Hensel, "Multicurrency Performance Attribution," *Financial Analysts Journal* 50, no. 2 (March–April 1994): 29–35.

Weigel tested the market timing skills of a group of 17 U.S.-based managers using the TAA approach.[22] His methodology was motivated by the pioneering work of Merton and Hendriksson and assumed that perfect market timing ability was equivalent to owning a lookback call option that pays at expiration the return to the best-performing asset class.[23] That is, for any given Investment Period t, a manager with perfect market timing skills would have a return (R_{pt}) equal to

$$R_{pt} = RFR_t + \max[R_{st} - RFR_t, R_{bt} - RFR_t, 0]$$

where R_{st} and R_{bt} are the Period t returns to the stock and bond benchmark portfolios, respectively. Thus, controlling for stock and bond price movements in a manner comparable to Jensen's method, the following regression equation can be calculated:

$$(R_{pt} - RFR_t) = \alpha + \beta_b(R_{bt} - RFR_t) + \beta_s(R_{st} - RFR_t)$$
$$+ \gamma\{\max[R_{st} - RFR_t, R_{bt} - RFR_t, 0]\} + e_t$$

Weigel showed that the samplewide average value for γ, which measures the proportion of the perfect timing option that the TAA managers were able to capture, was 0.30. This value was statistically significant, meaning that this group of managers had reliable, although not perfect, market timing skills. He also demonstrated that the average alpha was –0.5 percent per quarter, indicating that these same managers had negative nonmarket timing skills (e.g., hedging strategies).

Many other studies have examined the market timing ability of portfolio managers who are not exclusively TAA practitioners. Several investigations, as typified by Kon and Chang and Lewellen, concluded that mutual fund managers generally possess negative market timing skills.[24] Coggin, Fabozzi, and Rahman carried this analysis further by looking at both the timing and selectivity skills of a group of U.S. equity pension fund managers.[25] Using a regression-based model with monthly return data for an eight-year period ending in December 1990, they demonstrated that their sample of managers possessed positive, but small, selection skills and negative timing skills. From these studies, it is reasonable to conclude that only those managers explicitly trying to time market movements have a chance of doing so.

FACTORS THAT AFFECT USE OF PERFORMANCE MEASURES

All the performance measures just described are only as good as their data inputs. You must be careful when computing the rates of return to take proper account of all inflows and outflows. More importantly, you should use judgment and be patient in the evaluation process. It is not pos-

---

[22]Eric J. Weigel, "The Performance of Tactical Asset Allocation," *Financial Analysts Journal* 47, no. 5 (September–October 1991): 63–70.

[23]Robert C. Merton, "On Market Timing and Investment Performance: An Equilibrium Theory of Value for Market Forecasts," *Journal of Business* 54, no. 3 (July 1981): 363–406; and Roy D. Hendriksson and Robert C. Merton, "On Market Timing and Investment Performance: Statistical Procedures for Evaluating Forecasting Skills," *Journal of Business* 54, no. 4 (October 1981): 513–534. See also Carl R. Chen, Anthony Chan, and Nancy J. Mohan, "Asset Allocation Managers' Investment Performance," *Journal of Fixed Income* 3, no. 3 (December 1993): 46–53, for another application of this methodology.

[24]Stanley J. Kon, "The Market-Timing Performance of Mutual Fund Managers," *Journal of Business* 56, no. 3 (July 1983): 323–347; and Eric C. Chang and Wilbur G. Lewellen, "Market Timing and Mutual Fund Investment Performance," *Journal of Business* 57, no. 1 (1984): 57–72.

[25]T. Daniel Coggin, Frank J. Fabozzi, and Shafiqur Rahman, "The Investment Performance of U.S. Equity Pension Fund Managers: An Empirical Investigation," *Journal of Finance* 48, no. 3 (July 1993): 1039–1055.

sible to evaluate a portfolio manager on the basis of a quarter or even a year. Your evaluation should extend over several years and cover at least a full market cycle. This will allow you to determine whether the manager's performance differs during rising and declining markets.[26] Beyond these general cautions, several specific factors should be considered when using these measures.

Most of the equity portfolio performance measures we have discussed are derived from the CAPM and assume the existence of a market portfolio at the point of tangency on the Markowitz efficient frontier. Theoretically, the market portfolio is an efficient, completely diversified portfolio because it is on the efficient frontier. As we discussed in Chapter 8, this market portfolio must contain all risky assets in the economy, so that it will be completely diversified, and all components must be market-value weighted. The problem arises in finding a realistic proxy for this theoretical market portfolio. As noted previously, analysts typically use the Standard and Poor's 500 Index as the proxy for the market portfolio because it contains a fairly diversified portfolio of stocks, and the sample is market-value weighted. Unfortunately, it does not represent the true composition of the market portfolio. Specifically, it includes only common stocks and most of them are listed on the NYSE. Notably, it excludes many other risky assets that theoretically should be considered, such as numerous AMEX and OTC stocks, foreign stocks, foreign and domestic bonds, real estate, coins, precious metals, stamps, and antiques.

This lack of completeness was highlighted in several articles by Roll, who detailed the problem with the market proxy and pointed out its implications for measuring portfolio performance.[27] Although a detailed discussion of Roll's critique will not be repeated here, we need to consider his major problem with the measurement of the market portfolio, which he refers to as a **benchmark error**. He showed that if the proxy for the market portfolio is not a truly efficient portfolio, then the SML using this proxy may not be the true SML—the true SML could have a higher slope. In such a case, a portfolio plotted above the SML and derived using a poor benchmark could actually plot below the SML that uses the true market portfolio.

Another problem is that the beta could differ from that computed using the true market portfolio. For example, if the true beta were larger than the beta computed using the proxy, the true position of the portfolio would shift to the right. In an empirical test, Brown and Brown documented a considerable amount of "ranking reversal" when the definition of the market portfolio was changed in a Jensen's alpha analysis of a sample of well-established mutual funds.[28] In efforts to address this problem, Grinblatt and Titman attempted to avoid the conflict altogether by introducing a performance measurement process that did not require benchmarks while Daniel, Grinblatt, Titman, and Wermers developed benchmarks based on the characteristics of the stock held, such as firm size and book-to-market ratios.[29] Terhaar shows how the benchmark error problem can also affect attribution analysis.[30]

---

[26]For a good discussion of how performance measurement can be affected by market cycles, see Wayne E. Ferson and Rudi W. Schadt, "Measuring Fund Strategy and Performance in Changing Economic Conditions," *Journal of Finance* 52, no. 2 (June 1996): 425–461.

[27]Richard Roll, "A Critique of the Asset Pricing Theory's Tests," *Journal of Financial Economics* 4, no. 4 (March 1977): 129–176; Richard Roll, "Ambiguity When Performance Is Measured by the Securities Market Line," *Journal of Finance* 33, no. 4 (September 1978): 1051–1069; Richard Roll, "Performance Evaluation and Benchmark Error I," *Journal of Portfolio Management* 6, no. 4. (Summer 1980): 5–12; and Richard Roll, "Performance Evaluation and Benchmark Error II," *Journal of Portfolio Management* 7, no. 2 (Winter 1981): 17–22.

[28]Keith C. Brown and Gregory D. Brown, "Does the Composition of the Market Portfolio Really Matter?" *Journal of Portfolio Management* 13, no. 2 (Winter 1987): 26–32.

[29]See Mark Grinblatt and Sheridan Titman, "Performance Measurement without Benchmarks: An Examination of Mutual Fund Returns," *Journal of Business* 66, no. 1 (January 1993): 47–68; and Kent Daniel, Mark Grinblatt, Sheridan Titman, and Russ Wermers, "Measuring Mutual Fund Performance with Characteristics-Based Portfolios," *Journal of Finance* 52, no. 3 (July 1997): 1035–1058.

[30]Kevin Terhaar, "Return, Risk, and Performance Attribution," in *Benchmarks and Attribution Analysis,* ed. Katrina Sherrerd (Charlottesville, Va.: AIMR, 2001).

A Demonstration of the Global Benchmark Problem

To illustrate the impact of the benchmark problem in an environment of global capital markets, consider what happens to the individual measures of risk (beta) and the SML when the world equity market is employed. Exhibit 26.14 contains the parameters of the characteristic line for the 30 stocks in the Dow Jones Industrial Average (DJIA) using the S&P 500, which is the typical proxy, and the Morgan Stanley Capital International (MSCI) World Stock Index, which is a market-value-weighted index that contains stocks from around the world. These findings were

EXHIBIT 26.14 ▶ *PARAMETERS OF THE CHARACTERISTIC LINE FOR THE DOW JONES INDUSTRIALS: 1996–2000*

		S&P 500			WORLD		
Stock	Standard Deviation	Intercept	Beta	R^2	Intercept	Beta	R^2
ALCOA	0.113	0.006	1.111	0.210	0.009	1.339	0.240
American Express	0.080	0.010	1.202	0.481	0.015	1.278	0.430
AT&T	0.105	−0.019	1.076	0.228	−0.013	0.990	0.153
Boeing	0.084	0.004	0.566	0.098	0.008	0.487	0.057
Caterpillar	0.095	0.001	0.777	0.144	0.004	0.840	0.133
Citigroup	0.101	0.011	1.503	0.474	0.017	1.563	0.405
Coca Cola	0.090	0.003	0.675	0.121	0.006	0.685	0.099
Du Pont	0.081	−0.002	0.765	0.193	0.001	0.836	0.182
Eastman Kodak	0.082	−0.012	0.450	0.064	−0.010	0.515	0.067
Exxon Mobil	0.049	0.008	0.384	0.132	0.010	0.395	0.110
General Electric	0.073	0.008	1.243	0.623	0.013	1.346	0.577
General Motors	0.098	−0.008	1.118	0.282	−0.002	1.098	0.215
Hewlett-Packard	0.131	−0.002	1.465	0.270	0.003	1.728	0.296
Home Depot	0.091	0.015	0.950	0.233	0.017	1.277	0.333
Honeywell International	0.115	0.004	0.972	0.154	0.008	1.043	0.140
IBM	0.097	0.009	1.218	0.336	0.016	1.177	0.248
Intel	0.133	0.013	1.444	0.254	0.021	1.378	0.183
International Paper	0.109	−0.008	1.053	0.202	−0.003	1.100	0.174
J.P. Morgan Chase	0.096	0.000	1.200	0.338	0.005	1.195	0.264
Johnson & Johnson	0.076	0.009	0.653	0.158	0.013	0.537	0.084
McDonald's	0.074	−0.001	0.743	0.218	0.002	0.773	0.186
Merck	0.090	0.014	0.567	0.085	0.018	0.373	0.029
Microsoft	0.134	0.006	1.828	0.401	0.015	1.844	0.322
Minnesota M&M	0.071	0.007	0.430	0.079	0.008	0.492	0.082
Philip Morris	0.097	0.006	0.324	0.024	0.010	0.162	0.005
Procter & Gamble	0.086	0.010	0.355	0.037	0.011	0.385	0.034
SBC Communications	0.081	0.002	0.658	0.143	0.006	0.570	0.084
United Technologies	0.088	0.006	1.299	0.470	0.010	1.535	0.518
Wal-Mart	0.091	0.018	0.880	0.203	0.019	1.169	0.283
Walt Disney	0.089	−0.003	0.940	0.238	0.002	0.889	0.168
Mean	0.093	0.004	0.928	0.230	0.008	0.967	0.203

calculated using monthly returns from the five-year period from 1996–2000. The major differences are reflected in the betas and the R^2 of the regression lines. Specifically in the majority of cases, the beta was larger when measured against the world index than against the S&P 500 index, and the average beta (0.928 versus 0.967) was about 5 percent higher. The impact also is reflected in the R^2, which was often lower with the world index and had an average (0.230 versus 0.203) that was 13 percent smaller. These results imply a fairly significant impact on the individual measures of risk with a clear tendency for a decline in the measure.

Reilly and Akhtar examined the effect of the choice of a benchmark on global performance measurement.[31] Their results are summarized in Exhibit 26.15, which plots the SMLs for six different indexes over three time horizons: 1983–1988, 1989–1994, and 1983–1994. Four country-specific benchmarks—the S&P 500 (United States), the Nikkei (Japan), the FT-All Shares (England), and the FAZ (Germany)—and two aggregate benchmarks—M-S World and Brinson GSMI—were used in the analysis. The results indicate that using alternative market proxies for different countries or alternative composite series will generate SMLs that differ substantially during a given time period and that these SMLs tend to be very unstable over time. For instance, the Nikkei SML goes from the largest risk premium during 1983–1988 to a negative risk premium during 1989–1994, which clearly is contrary to capital market theory. Notice, however, that this volatility would be masked by anyone looking at Japanese performance over the entire 1983–1994 period, during which the Nikkei SML assumed a more "normal" shape. Finally, the S&P 500 provided investors with the biggest performance hurdle over the whole sample period, which was mostly due to the high risk premiums in the United States during 1989–1994.

Implications of the Benchmark Problems

Several points are significant regarding this benchmark criticism. First, the benchmark problems noted by Roll, which are increased with global investing, do not negate the value of the CAPM as a *normative* model of equilibrium pricing; the theory is still viable. The problem is one of *measurement* when using the theory to evaluate portfolio performance.

You need to find a better proxy for the market portfolio or to adjust measured performance for benchmark errors. In fact, Roll made several suggestions to help overcome this problem.[32] From Chapter 5, we know that new comprehensive stock market and bond market series are being developed that will be available as market portfolio proxies. Finally, the multiple markets index (MMI), developed by Brinson, Diermeier, and Schlarbaum, is a major step toward a truly comprehensive world market portfolio.[33]

Alternatively, you might consider giving greater weight to the Sharpe portfolio performance measure because it does not depend heavily on the market portfolio. Recall that this measure relates excess return to the *standard deviation* of return—that is, to total risk. Although this evaluation process generally uses a benchmark portfolio as an example of an unmanaged portfolio for comparison purposes, the risk measure for the portfolio being evaluated does not directly depend on a market portfolio. Also, recall that the portfolio rank from the Sharpe measure typically correlates highly with the ranks derived from alternative performance measures (see Exhibit 26.11).

---

[31]Frank K. Reilly and Rashid A. Akhtar, "The Benchmark Error Problem with Global Capital Markets," *Journal of Portfolio Management* 22, no. 1 (Fall 1995): 33–52.

[32]Richard Roll, "Performance Evaluation and Benchmark Error II," *Journal of Portfolio Management* 7, no. 2 (Winter 1981): 17–22. Also see Richard C. Grinold, "Are Benchmark Portfolios Efficient?" *Journal of Performance Management* 19, no. 1 (Fall 1992): 34–40.

[33]Gary P. Brinson, Jeffrey J. Diermeier, and G.G. Schlarbaum, "A Composite Portfolio Benchmark for Pension Plans," *Financial Analysts Journal* 42, no. 2 (March–April 1986): 15–24.

SECURITY MARKET LINES FOR S&P 500, NIKKEI, FT-ALL SHARES, FAZ, M-S WORLD, AND BRINSON GSMI INDEXES

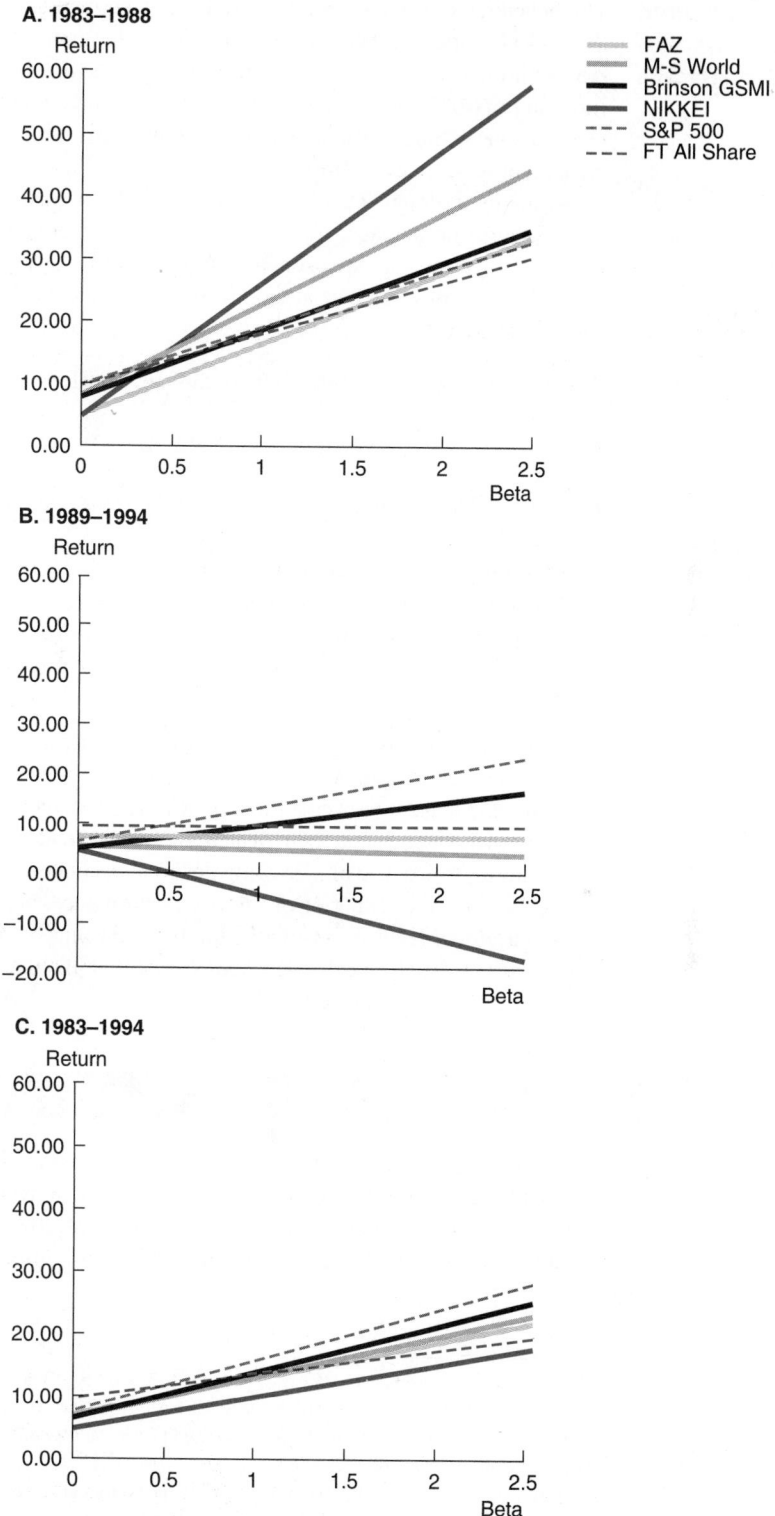

Source: Frank K. Reilly and Rashid A. Akhtar, "The Benchmark Error Problem with Global Capital Markets," *Journal of Portfolio Management* 22, no. 1 (Fall 1995): 33–52.

Required Characteristics of Benchmarks

The benchmark problem just discussed was described as being related to finding a proxy for the theoretical market portfolio, especially given the trend toward global capital markets. Concurrent with this search for a global market portfolio, there has also been a search for appropriate **normal portfolios,** which are customized benchmarks that reflect the specific styles of alternative managers. Bailey, Richards, and Tierney consider this a critical need of pension plans and endowments who hire multiple managers with widely divergent styles.[34] They point out that if a broad market index is used rather than a specific benchmark portfolio, it is implicitly assumed that the portfolio manager does not have an investment style, which is quite unrealistic. Also, it does not allow the plan sponsors to determine if the money manager is consistent with his or her stated investment style. The authors contend that any useful benchmark should have the following characteristics:

➤ *Unambiguous.* The names and weights of securities comprising the benchmark are clearly delineated.
➤ *Investable.* The option is available to forgo active management and simply hold the benchmark.
➤ *Measurable.* It is possible to calculate the return on the benchmark on a reasonably frequent basis.
➤ *Appropriate.* The benchmark is consistent with the manager's investment style or biases.
➤ *Reflective of current investment opinions.* The manager has current investment knowledge (be it positive, negative, or neutral) of the securities that make up the benchmark.
➤ *Specified in advance.* The benchmark is constructed prior to the start of an evaluation period.

If a benchmark does not possess all of these properties, it is considered flawed as an effective management tool. One example of a flawed benchmark is the use of the median manager from a broad universe of managers or even a limited universe of managers. This criticism is spelled out in detail by Bailey, who argues that the manager universe is inadequate on almost every characteristic.[35]

In summary, because of a growing desire to evaluate aggregate performance and identify what factors contribute to superior or inferior performance, benchmarks must be selected at two levels: (1) a *global* level that contains the broadest mix of risky assets available from around the world and (2) a fairly specific level consistent with the management style of an individual money manager (i.e., a customized benchmark).

EVALUATION OF BOND PORTFOLIO PERFORMANCE

As discussed, the analysis of risk-adjusted performance for equity portfolios began in the late 1960s following the development of portfolio theory and the CAPM. The common stock risk measures have been fairly simple—either total risk (the standard deviation of returns) or systematic risk (betas). No such development has simplified analysis for the bond market, where

---

[34]Jeffrey V. Bailey, Thomas M. Richards, and David E. Tierney, "Benchmark Portfolios and the Manager/Plan Sponsor Relationship," *Current Topics in Investment Management* (New York: Harper & Row, 1990). See also Thomas M. Richards, "Alternatives in Broad Market Indexes," in *Benchmarks and Attribution Analysis,* ed. Katrina Sherrerd (Charlottesville, Va.: AIMR, 2001).

[35]Jeffrey V. Bailey, "Are Manager Universes Acceptable Performance Benchmarks?" *Journal of Portfolio Management* 18, no. 3 (Spring 1992): 9–13. For a discussion of fixed-income benchmarks, see Chris P. Dialynas, "The Active Decisions in the Selection of Passive Management and Performance Bogeys," in *The Handbook of Fixed-Income Securities,* 6th ed., ed. Frank J. Fabozzi (New York: McGraw-Hill, 2001).

numerous and complex factors can influence portfolio returns. One reason for this lack of development of bond portfolio performance measures was that, prior to the 1970s, most bond portfolio managers followed buy-and-hold strategies, so their performance probably did not differ much. In this era, interest rates were relatively stable, so one could gain little from the active management of bond portfolios.

The environment in the bond market changed considerably in the late 1970s and especially in the 1980s when interest rates increased dramatically and became more volatile. This created an incentive to trade bonds, and this trend toward more active management led to substantially more dispersed performance by bond portfolio managers. This dispersion in performance in turn created a demand for techniques that would help investors evaluate the performance of bond portfolio managers.

As with attribution analysis in the equity market, the critical questions are: (1) How did performance among portfolio managers compare to the overall bond market? and (2) What factors explain or contribute to superior or inferior bond portfolio performance? In this section, we present various attempts to develop bond portfolio performance evaluation systems that consider multiple-risk factors.[36]

A Bond Market Line

Wagner and Tito attempted to apply asset pricing techniques to the evaluation of bond portfolio performance.[37] A prime factor needed to evaluate performance properly is a measure of risk, such as the beta coefficient for equities. This is difficult to achieve because a bond's maturity and coupon have a significant effect on the volatility of its prices. The bond's *duration* statistic captures the net effect of this volatility.

Using this as a measure of risk, the authors derived a bond market line much like the security market line used to evaluate equity performance. Duration simply replaces beta as the risk variable. The bond market line in Exhibit 26.16 is drawn from points defined by returns on Treasury bills to the Lehman Brothers Government–Corporate Bond Index rather than the S&P 500 index.[38] The Lehman Brothers Index gives the market's average annual rate of return during some common period, and the duration for the index is the value-weighted duration for the individual bonds in the index.

Given the bond market line, this technique divides the portfolio return that differs from the return on the Lehman Brothers Index into four components: (1) a **policy effect**, (2) a **rate anticipation effect**, (3) an **analysis effect**, and (4) a **trading effect**. When the latter three effects are combined, they are referred to as the **management effect**. These effects are portrayed in Exhibit 26.17.

The policy effect measures the difference in the expected return for a given portfolio because of a difference in policy regarding the duration of this portfolio compared to the duration of the index.[39] The duration of a portfolio being evaluated that differs from the index duration indicates a basic policy decision regarding relative risk (measured by duration), and there should be a

---

[36]An overview of this area and a discussion of the historical development are contained in H.Gifford Fong, "Bond Management: Past, Current, and Future," in *The Handbook of Fixed-Income Securities,* 6th ed., ed. Frank J. Fabozzi (New York: McGraw-Hill, 2001).

[37]Wayne H. Wagner and Dennis A. Tito, "Definitive New Measures of Bond Performance and Risk," *Pension World* (May 1977): 17–26; and Dennis A. Tito and Wayne H. Wagner, "Is Your Bond Manager Skillful?" *Pension World* (June 1977): 10–16.

[38]We saw in Chapter 5 that it would be equally reasonable to use a comparable bond market index series from Merrill Lynch, Salomon Brothers, or the Ryan Index.

[39]Notably, the duration of the various bond market indexes has changed over time (i.e., the duration of the corporate bond series has declined, whereas the duration of the government bond series has increased slightly). For a presentation and discussion of this phenomenon, see Frank K. Reilly, and David J. Wright, "Bond Market Indexes," in *The Handbook of Fixed-Income Securities,* 6th ed., ed. Frank J. Fabozzi (New York: McGraw-Hill, 2001).

EXHIBIT 26.16 ▶   *SPECIFICATION OF BOND MARKET LINE USING LEHMAN BROTHERS BOND INDEX*

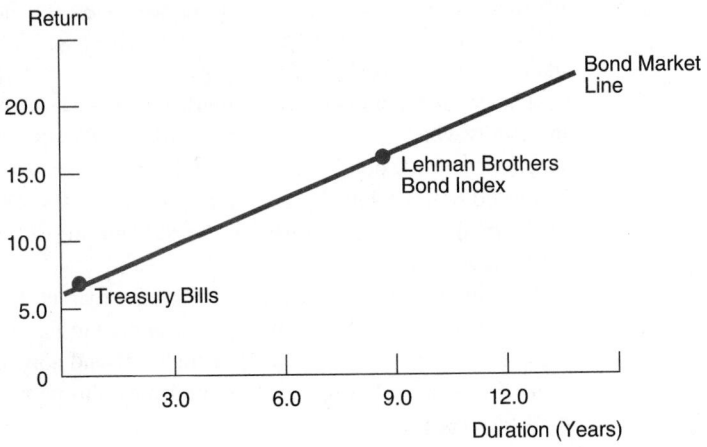

Source: Wayne H. Wagner and Dennis A. Tito, "Definitive New Measures of Bond Performance and Risk." *Pension World* (May 1977): 17–26.

EXHIBIT 26.17 ▶   *GRAPHIC DISPLAY OF BOND PORTFOLIO PERFORMANCE BREAKDOWN*

Management effect is the improvement in investment performance of a passive strategy through active bond management. It is the difference between total bond portfolio return and the expected return at the long-term average duration.

Trading effect is the result of the current quarter's trading, either through effective trade-desk operation or short-term selection abilities. It is the difference between total management effect and the effects attributable to analysis and interest rate anticipation.

Policy effect is the difference between long-term duration of a bond portfolio and the duration of a bond market index resulting from long-term investment policy. Measured as the return at the long-term average less the return on the Lehman Brothers Index.

Analysis effect, attributable to the selection of issues with better-than-average long-term prospects, is the difference between the actual return of the buy-and-hold portfolio at the beginning of the quarter and the expected return of that buy-and-hold portfolio.

Bond market line is a straight line drawn through the return/duration of Treasury bills and the return/duration of the Lehman Brothers Index.

Interest rate anticipation effect is attributable to changes in portfolio duration resulting from attempts to profit from and ability to predict bond market movements. It is the difference between the expected return at the actual portfolio duration and the expected return at the long-term duration.

Buy-and-hold portfolio is the composition of the portfolio at the beginning of the quarter. Used to differentiate between trading gains secured within a quarter and long-term analysis gains.

Duration is a measure of the average time to receipt of cash flows from an investment. It is a measure of the sensitivity of a bond's price to changes in interest rates.

Source: Wayne H. Wagner and Dennis A. Tito, "Definitive New Measures of Bond Performance and Risk," *Pension World* (May 1977): 17–26.

difference in expected return consistent with that risk policy decision. For example, assume the duration and return for the Lehman Brothers Index is 9.0 years and 8.25 percent, respectively. If your portfolio has a duration of 9.5 years, according to the prevailing bond market line, your return should be about 8.60 percent. In this example, the policy effect is 0.5 year and 0.35 percent (35 basis points). Specifically, the higher duration implies that your portfolio should have a higher average return of 0.35 percent (this positive relationship assumes the typical upward-sloping yield curve).

Given the expected return and duration for this long-term portfolio, all deviations from the index portfolio are attributable to the remaining management effect components. The interest rate anticipation effect attempts to measure the differential return from changing the duration during this period compared to the portfolio's long-term duration. Hopefully, the manager would increase the duration of the portfolio during periods of declining interest rates to increase the price appreciation of your portfolio and reduce duration during periods of rising interest rates to minimize the price decline. Therefore, you would determine the duration of the actual portfolio during the period and compare this to the duration of the long-term portfolio. Then you would determine the difference in expected return for these portfolios and their two durations using the bond market line. For example, assume the duration for the long-term portfolio is 9.5 years, which implies an expected return of 8.60 percent, and that the prevailing duration for the portfolio being evaluated is 10.0 years, which implies an expected return of 9.00 percent using the bond market line. Therefore, the rate anticipation effect during this period is 0.40 percent (9.00–8.60).

The difference between this expected return based on the portfolio's duration and the actual return for the portfolio during this period is a combination of an analysis effect and a trading effect. The analysis effect is the differential return attributable to acquiring bonds that are temporarily mispriced relative to their risk level. To measure the analysis effect, compare the *expected* return for the portfolio held at the beginning of the period (using the bond market line) to the *actual* return of this same portfolio. If the actual return is greater than the expected return, it implies that the portfolio manager acquired some underpriced issues that became properly priced and thus provided excess returns during the period. For example, if the portfolio at the beginning of the period had a duration of 10 years, this might indicate that the portfolio's expected return was 9.00 percent for the period. In turn, if the actual return for this buy-and-hold portfolio was 9.40 percent, it would indicate an analysis effect of 40 basis points.

Finally, the trading effect occurs because of short-run changes in the portfolio during the period. It is measured as the residual after taking account of the analysis effect from the total excess return based on duration. For example, assume the total actual return is 10.50 percent with a duration of 10.0 years. The prevailing bond market line indicates an expected return of 9 percent for a portfolio with a 10-year duration. Thus, the combination of the analysis and trading effects is 1.50 percent (= 10.50–9.00). Previously, we determined that the analysis effect was 0.40 percent, so the trading effect must be 1.10 percent. In summary, for this portfolio manager, the actual return was 10.50 percent, compared to a return for the Lehman Brothers Index of 8.25 percent. This total excess of 2.25 percent would be divided as follows:

➤ 0.35 percent policy effect due to higher long-term duration
➤ 0.40 percent interest rate anticipation effect due to increasing the duration of the current portfolio above the long-term portfolio duration
➤ 0.40 percent analysis effect—the impact of superior selection of individual issues in the beginning portfolio
➤ 1.10 percent trading effect—the impact of trading the issues *during* the period

This technique breaks down the return based on the duration as a comprehensive risk measure. The only concern is that *it does not consider differences in the risk of default.* Specifically, the technique does not differentiate between an Aaa bond with a duration of eight years and a Baa bond with the same duration. This could clearly affect the performance. A portfolio manager that invested in Baa bonds, for example, could experience a very positive analysis effect simply because the bonds were lower quality than the average quality implicit in the Lehman Brothers Index. The only way to avoid this would be to construct differential market lines for alternative ratings or construct a benchmark line that matches the quality makeup of the portfolio being evaluated.[40]

Decomposing Portfolio Returns

Dietz, Fogler, and Hardy developed a technique to decompose the bond portfolio returns into maturity, sector, and quality effects.[41] The total return for a bond during a period of time is composed of a known **income effect** (due to normal yield to maturity factors) and an unknown **price change effect** (due to an interest rate effect, a sector/quality effect, and a residual effect). It is graphed as follows:

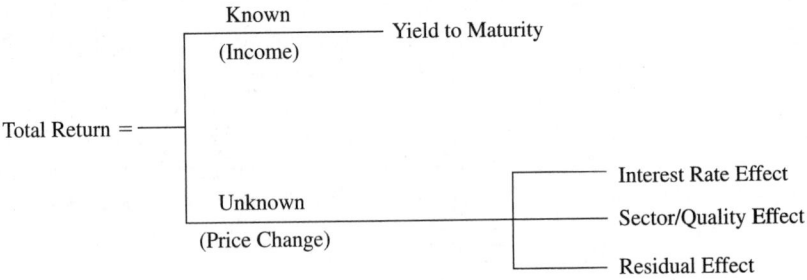

The yield to maturity (income) effect is the return an investor would receive if nothing had happened to the yield curve during the period. That is, the investor would receive the interest income and any price change due to the passage of time and the shape of the yield curve.

The **interest rate effect** measures what happened to each issue because of changes in the term structure of interest rates during the period. Each bond is valued based on the Treasury yield curve at its maturity and takes account of its normal premium relative to Treasury yields. Assume a normal risk premium spread of 30 basis points and that yields on Treasury bonds with the maturity of your bond go from 8.50 percent to 9.25 percent. To determine the interest rate effect, you would compute the value of your bond at 8.80 percent (8.50 + 0.30) and at 9.55 percent (9.25 + 0.30) and then compute the price change. This is the price change caused by a change in market interest rates.

The **sector/quality effect** measures the expected impact on the returns because of the sector of the bonds (corporates, agencies, etc.) and also the quality of the bonds (Aaa, Aa, A, Baa). Given this breakdown, you can determine what happened to bonds in each sector after taking account of the yield to maturity and the interest rate effect. As an example, during a given period you might find that an average Aa utility had negative excess returns of −0.50 percent after taking account of the yield to maturity and the interest rate effect, whereas an A-rated corporate bond experienced a comparable positive excess return of 0.30 percent. Therefore, the sector/quality effect would be −0.50 and 0.30 for these sets of bonds.

---

[40]This problem is briefly discussed in Frank K. Reilly and Rupinder Sidhu, "The Many Uses of Bond Duration," *Financial Analysts Journal* 36, no. 4 (July–August 1980): 58–72. See also Arthur Gudikunst and Joseph McCarthy, "Determinants of Bond Mutual Fund Performance," *Journal of Fixed Income* 2, no. 1 (June 1992): 95–101.

[41]Peter O. Dietz, H. Russell Fogler, and Donald J. Hardy, "The Challenge of Analyzing Bond Portfolio Returns," *Journal of Portfolio Management* 6, no. 3 (Spring 1980): 53–58.

The **residual effect** is what remains after taking account of the three prior factors—yield to maturity, interest rate effect, and the sector/quality effect. It is computed as follows:

$$\text{Total Return} - \text{Yield to Maturity Effect} - \text{Interest Rate Effect} - \text{Sector/Quality Effect} = \text{Residual}$$

The presence of a consistently large positive residual would indicate superior bond selection capabilities. Specifically, a positive residual indicates that after taking account of all market effects from interest rate changes and sector/quality, it is still possible the bond manager has helped provide positive returns due to bond selection. Alternatively, large positive interest rate effects during periods of declining interest rates and small negative interest rate effects during periods of rising interest rates would indicate a bond manager with good skills at interest rate anticipation. Consistently positive sector/quality effects would indicate the ability to make proper allocations and to anticipate shifts in this area over time.

Layard-Liesching used the information ratio performance measure to assess the relative impact of each possible decision that a bond manager could make on the return to the overall portfolio. His analysis showed that while large-scale duration "bets" could certainly be taken, their payoffs were likely to be low once the high degree of tracking error they created was taken into account. On the other hand, he also argued that credit quality bets were more likely to be fruitful, particularly as the global movement to privatizing companies that were previously under governmental control continues to create new investment opportunities.[42]

Analyzing Sources of Return

Fong, Pearson, and Vasicek proposed a performance evaluation technique that likewise divides the total returns into several components that affect bond returns.[43] Their intent was to measure total realized return and attribute the return to its sources (i.e., what factors contributed to the total return). The first breakdown divides the total return *(R)* between the effect of the external interest rate environment *(I),* which is beyond the control of the portfolio manager, and the contribution of the management process *(C).* Thus:

$$R = I + C$$

In turn, *I* is broken down into two parts. The first is the *expected* rate of return *(E)* on a portfolio of default-free securities, assuming no change in forward rates (i.e., no change in future one-period rates). This expected return also is referred to as the *market's implicit forecast.* The second component of *I* is *U,* the *unexpected* return on the Treasury index that is due to actual changes in forward rates. Thus:

$$I = E + U$$

For example, assume that at the beginning of a quarter, the expected annual return on a portfolio of Treasury bonds is 11 percent. (This expected return assumes no change in the term

[42]Ronald Layard-Liesching, "Exploiting Opportunities in Global Bond Markets," in *Core-Plus Bond Management,* ed. Katrina Sherrerd (Charlottesville, Va.: AIMR, 2001.)

[43]Gifford Fong, Charles Pearson, and Oldrich Vasicek, "Bond Performance: Analyzing Sources of Return," *Journal of Portfolio Management* 9, no. 3 (Spring 1983): 46–50.

structure of bonds during this year.) At the end of the year, you determine that the actual return on this portfolio of Treasury bonds was 11.75 percent. This would imply an E of 11 percent and a U of 0.75 percent.

In turn, C (the management contribution) is composed of three factors:

- M = return from maturity management
- S = return from spread/quality management
- B = return attributable to the selection of specific securities

The return from *maturity management, M,* is determined by how well the portfolio manager changes maturity (duration) in anticipation of interest rate changes. The component is measured by computing the default-free price of every security (at the beginning and end of the period) based on the spot rate for its maturity, as indicated by the Treasury yield curve. The total return over the evaluation period is derived from these prices, while maintaining all actual trading activity. Given this total return based on maturity yields, subtract the actual return on the Treasury index (assumed earlier to be 11.75 percent) to arrive at the maturity return. For example, if the total return for the portfolio based on the pricing computations was 12.25 percent, the maturity management return would be 0.50 percent, assuming the Treasury index return of 11.75 percent.[44]

The *spread/quality management* component indicates the effect on return due to the manager's selection of bonds from various sectors and qualities. It is measured by pricing each bond at the beginning and end of the period using yields appropriate for its specific sector and quality and then computing the rate of return given these prices. This total return less the return for Treasury bonds, considering the maturity effect (assumed to be 12.25 percent), indicates the return attributable to sector/quality selection. If this sector/quality pricing indicates a total return of 12.0 percent, it would imply a negative 0.25 percent for sector/quality management (12.00 – 12.25).

The *selectivity component (B)* is the remaining return. It is attributable to the selection of specific bonds after considering the maturity and sector/quality decisions—specifically, what individual bonds were selected to carry out these decisions? It is measured as the difference between the actual total return on the portfolio and the prior total return that considered maturity and sector/quality. Continuing our example, if the actual total return on the portfolio was 13.00 percent, the selectivity component would be 1.00 percent because the preceding return for maturity and sector/quality was 12.00 percent. To summarize the results:

$$R = \quad I \quad + \quad C$$
$$= (E + U) + (M + S + B)$$

where:

E = expected Treasury yield	11.00
U = unexpected Treasury yield	0.75
M = maturity management	0.50
S = spread/quality management	(0.25)
B = selectivity	1.00
Total return	**13.00**

---

[44]A subsequent article suggests a possible refinement of the maturity management effect by considering the separate effects of duration, convexity, and yield curve "twist." See Gifford Fong, Charles Pearson, Oldrich Vasicek, and Theresa Conroy, "Fixed-Income Portfolio Performance: Analyzing Sources of Returns," in *The Handbook of Fixed-Income Securities,* 3d ed., edited by Frank J. Fabozzi (Homewood, Ill.: Business One Irwin, 1991).

This analysis indicates that the portfolio manager was quite good at maturity (duration) decisions and at selecting individual bonds but did not do well in terms of sector/quality decisions. As before, you should do a similar breakdown for some market index series as a basis of comparison to an unmanaged portfolio. Also, examine these components over time to determine any consistent strengths or weaknesses for the portfolio manager.

Consistency of Performance

Numerous investigators have documented performance inconsistency for managers of equity portfolios. Kritzman considered this question for bond managers by examining the ranking for 32 bond managers employed by AT&T.[45] He divided a 10-year period into two 5-year periods, determined each manager's percentile ranking in each period, and correlated the rankings. The results revealed *no relationship* between performance in the two periods. A further test also revealed *no relationship* between past and future performance even among the best and worst performers. Based on these results, Kritzman concluded that it would be necessary to examine something besides past performance to determine superior bond portfolio managers.

REPORTING INVESTMENT PERFORMANCE

The performance measures just described represent the essential elements of how any investor's performance should be evaluated. However, before the various composite statistics can be calculated, a more fundamental question must be addressed: How should the returns upon which the performance measures are based be reported to the investor? We conclude the chapter by exploring two dimensions of this problem. First, we consider the issue of how returns should be computed for a portfolio that experiences infusions and withdrawals of cash during the investment period. Second, we will briefly summarize the **performance presentation standards (PPS)** created by the Association for Investment Management and Research (AIMR), an international organization of over 50,000 investment practitioners and educators in more than 100 countries.

Time-Weighted and Dollar-Weighted Returns

As we saw in Chapter 1, the holding period yield (HPY) for any investment position was determined by that position's market value at the end of the period divided by its initial value:

$$HPY = \frac{\text{Ending Value of Investment}}{\text{Beginning Value of Investment}} - 1$$

For any security or portfolio of securities, we also saw that there are two basic reasons why the ending and beginning values could differ: the receipt of cash payments (e.g., dividends) or a change in price (e.g., capital gains) during the period. Thus, for most investment positions, calculating returns during any given time frame is a reasonably straightforward matter.

For professional money managers and management companies, however, there is another reason why the beginning and ending value of a portfolio can differ, and it has nothing to do with the manager's investment prowess. Specifically, if the investor either withdraws or adds to her

---

[45]Mark Kritzman, "Can Bond Managers Perform Consistently?" *Journal of Portfolio Management* 9, no. 4 (Summer 1983): 54–56.

initial investment capital during the period, the ending value of the position will reflect these changes. Of course, it would be unfair to credit the manager with having produced high returns that were due to additional capital commitments. Similarly, it would be equally unfair to penalize him for reductions in the ending value of the investment that were caused by the investor removing funds from her account. Consequently, an evaluation of the manager's true performance must take these contributions and withdrawals into account.

To see the potential problem more clearly, consider two portfolio managers (A and B) who have exactly identical investment styles and stockpicking abilities. Indeed, we will assume further that over a two-period investment horizon, they produce exactly the same capital gains with the investment capital entrusted to them: 25 percent in Period 1 and 5 percent in Period 2. Further, suppose that each manager receives from his respective investor $500,000 to invest. The difference is that Manager A receives all of these funds immediately whereas Manager B's investor commits only $250,000 initially and the remaining $250,000 at the end of the first period.

The immediate effect of this investment timing discrepancy can be seen by calculating the terminal (Period 2) value of each portfolio:

$$\text{Portfolio A: } 500,000 \ [(1 + 0.25)(1 + (0.05)] = \$656,250$$

and

$$\text{Portfolio B: } 250,000[(1 + 0.25)(1 + 0.05)] + 250,000(1 + 0.05) = \$590,625$$

Obviously, Manager B's portfolio is worth less than Manager A's, but this is a result of the way the investment funds were committed rather than of any real differences in the performance of the two managers. Accordingly, the managers' performance evaluation should not be affected by the investors' decisions concerning the timing of their capital commitments. In other words, Manager B should not be held accountable for the fact that Investor B did not have all of her funds invested during the high-return environment of the first period.

One common method of computing average returns that we have seen is to use a discounted cash flow approach to calculate an investment's internal rate of return. For the two managers in this example, these calculations generate the following returns:

$$\text{Manager A: } 500,000 = \frac{656,250}{(1 + r_{dA})^2}, \text{ or } r_{dA} = 14.56 \text{ percent}$$

and

$$\text{Manager B: } 250,000 = \frac{-250,000}{(a + r_{dB})^1} = \frac{590,625}{(1 + r_{dB})^2}, \text{ or } r_{dB} = 11.63 \text{ percent}$$

These returns (r_{dA} and r_{dB}) are sometimes called *dollar-weighted* returns because they are the discount rates that set the present value of future cash flows (including future investment contributions and withdrawals) equal to the level of the initial investment. Unfortunately, in this case, dollar-weighted returns give an inaccurate impression of Manager B's ability; he did not actually perform 2.93 percent (= 0.1456 – 0.1163) "worse" than Manager A. Thus, while this internal rate of return method gives an accurate assessment of *Investor* B's return, it is a misleading measure of *Manager* B's talent.

A better way of evaluating a manager's performance would be to consider how well he did regardless of the size or timing of the investment funds involved. For both managers in this example, the *time-weighted* average return is simply the geometric average of (one plus) the periodic returns:

$$r_{tA} = r_{tB} = \sqrt[2]{(1 + 0.25)(1 + 0.05)} - 1 = 14.56\%$$

Notice that dollar-weighted and time-weighted returns are only the same when there are no interim investment contributions within the evaluation period. This was the case for Manager A. For Manager B, on the other hand, the dollar-weighted return understates the true (time-weighted) performance because of the way the investor deployed her funds. When there are contributions, Dietz has suggested a method for adjusting holding period yields:

$$\text{Adjusted HPY} = \frac{\text{Ending Value of Investment} - (1 - DW)(\text{Contribution})}{\text{Beginning Value of Investment} + (DW)(\text{Contrituion})} - 1$$

where the contribution can be either positive (a new commitment) or negative (a withdrawal).[46] This adjustment process alters the initial and terminal values of the portfolios by the weighted amount of the contribution made during the holding period. In this calculation, the day-weight *(DW)* factor represents the portion of the period that the contribution is actually held in the account. For example, if a contribution were placed in the portfolio halfway through a 30-day month, *DW* would be 0.5 (= (30 − 15)/30).

Performance Presentation Standards

The preceding example underscores the fact that there may not always be a single answer to a seemingly simple question. For instance, although Portfolio B had an internal rate of return of 11.63 percent, its manager generated an average return of 14.56 percent. Which should be reported to the investor? Although Security and Exchange Commission regulations guard against the publication of outright fraudulent claims, only recently has the investment community begun to demand the adoption of a more rigorous set of reporting guidelines. In an effort to fulfill the call for uniform, accurate, and consistent performance reporting, AIMR has developed a comprehensive set of performance presentation standards (PPS). As the organization states its mission:

> The investment community's need for a common, accepted set of guidelines to promote fair representation and full disclosure in every firm's presentation of its performance results to clients and prospective clients has guided the development of the AIMR-PPS. The Standards are the manifestation

---

[46]Peter O. Dietz and Jeannette R. Kirschman, "Evaluating Portfolio Performance," in *Managing Investment Portfolios,* 2d ed., ed. J. Maginn and D. Tuttle (Boston: Warren, Gorham, & Lamont, 1990).

of a set of guiding ethical principles and should be interpreted as *minimum* standards for presenting investment performance. The standards have been designed to meet the following four goals:

- achieve greater uniformity and comparability among performance presentations;
- improve the service offered to investment management clients;
- enhance the professionalism of the industry;
- bolster the notion of self-regulation.

The Standards set expectations and provide an industry yardstick for evaluating fairness and accuracy in investment performance presentation.[47]

Introduced in 1987 and formally adopted in 1993, the AIMR-PPS have become the accepted practice within the investment management community. Although a detailed analysis of these standards (which are frequently revised) is beyond our current scope, it is worth noting several of the fundamental principles on which the PPS are based:

➤ Total return, including realized and unrealized gains plus income, must be used when calculating investment performance.

➤ Time-weighted rates of return must be used.

➤ Portfolios must be valued at least monthly, and periodic returns must be geometrically linked.

➤ If composite return performance is presented, this composite must contain all actual fee-paying accounts, including all terminated accounts for periods up through the last full reporting period the account was under management. Composite results may not link simulated or model portfolios with actual performance.

➤ Performance must be calculated after the deduction of trading expenses (e.g., broker commissions and SEC fees), if any.

➤ For taxable clients, taxes on income and realized capital gains must be recognized in the same period they were incurred and must be subtracted from results regardless of whether taxes are paid from assets outside the account.

➤ Annual returns for all years must be presented. Performance of less than one year must not be annualized. A 10-year performance record (or a record for the period since firm inception if less than 10 years) must be presented.

➤ Performance presentation must disclose whether performance results are calculated gross or net of investment management fees and what the firm's fee schedule is. Presentation should also disclose any use of leverage (including derivatives) and any material change in personnel responsible for investment management.

In addition to the preceding requirements, AIMR also encourages managers to disclose the volatility of the aggregate composite return and to identify benchmarks that parallel the risk or investment style the composite is expected to track. Exhibit 26.18 shows a checklist of many of the points necessary to ensure compliance with the PPS, while Exhibit 26.19 shows a sample performance presentation that is in compliance with the Standards.

---

[47]A complete discussion of these standards can be found in *AIMR Performance Presentation Standards Handbook,* 2d ed. (Charlottesville, Va.: AIMR, 1997), as well as *Performance Reporting for Investment Managers* (Charlottesville, Va.: AIMR, 1991).

EXHIBIT 26.18 ▶ *A CHECKLIST FOR AIMR'S PERFORMANCE PRESENTATION STANDARDS*

This checklist for investment managers, their clients and prospects, and for consultants, is meant to assure proper conformance to the AIMR Performance Presentation Standards.

I. Performance Calculations

☐ A. Performance results have been calculated on a time-weighted basis.

☐ B. Returns combine income and current market valuations (thus, presenting so-called total returns).

☐ C. Manager fee levels have been disclosed along with performance records so that after-fee results can be measured.

☐ D. Performance results of broad security classes, such as equities or fixed income, have been included with cash or substitute securities included. If cash has been excluded from the calculations, then returns with cash have been presented with the statement that AIMR Standards consider performance with cash to be most representative of managerial results and most representative for comparisons with other managers.

☐ E. All exclusions from performance calculations and presentation by the manager have been disclosed.

☐ F. The method of linking interim performance results (daily, monthly, quarterly) has been explained. AIMR Standard is for monthly linking.

☐ G. Balanced account performance.

    ☐ 1. The manager has assigned cash and substitute securities to the specific asset category to which they belong, thereby allowing a clear division of the performance record for each asset managed.

    ☐ 2. If cash and substitute securities are not assigned to a separate asset, comparisons should not be made against other managers' performance figures for assets where cash returns have been included.

    ☐ 3. The manager has supplied information on risk, volatility, and/or other measures that allows for reasonable performance evaluation.

☐ H. Convertible securities have been consistently assigned to either equities or fixed income and have not been shifted without notice being given to clients concurrent or prior to such shift.

☐ I. Managers have provided the indexes against which their submitted performance records have normally been compared.

☐ J. If managers' assets have been leveraged, and performance returns calculated on this basis, results on an all-cash (unleveraged) basis have been provided.

II. Investment Manager Composites of Performance Results

☐ A. The manager has submitted a composite of all accounts managed for each period submitted; the composite includes results from any and all accounts no longer clients of the firm.

☐ B. If a manager has separate composites, all have been submitted. A prospect should be able to account for the performance of all the manager's assets managed.

☐ C. Composites are not "survivors only" compilations; they include results of all accounts ever managed, including those of clients no longer with the firm.

☐ D. All performance results contained in the composite include cash and substitutable securities, as per I.D. above.

☐ E. All individual years and cumulative performance results for all periods have been supplied. The composite covers every year of the past 10 years, along with longer-term results if the manager has been in the business this long.

☐ F. Compound annualized returns have been provided for all periods.

☐ G. A clear statement from manager indicates that no selectivity of account results for partial periods exists.

☐ H. Composite or other data have not been altered for reasons of personnel changes or any other reasons.

☐ I. Composite results are:

    ☐ 1. Weighted for the dollars under management (the AIMR Standard).

    ☐ 2. Presented on a median (unweighted) basis (recommended only as additional information, not as the primary disclosure).

☐ J. Data includes:

    ☐ 1. Number of client relationships in the composite.

    ☐ 2. Assets under management for each period.

    ☐ 3. Average and median size of accounts in the composite.

    ☐ 4. Assets shown as a percentage of the manager's total accounts, which share very comparable investment guidelines and risks; and as a percentage of the manager's total funds under management. (All clients and related performance data for this asset type can be accounted for.)

☐ K. Fee information is clear, so that pre- and post-fee results can be determined.

☐ L. Composites include typical indexes against which the manager has been judged.

☐ M. Alpha, beta, standard deviation of returns, and other measures of risk, quality, variability, etc., within the composite for each year have been indicated.

☐ N. Other information provided.

III. Verification of Performance Data.

☐ A. Results have been audited by reputable auditors.

☐ B. Results are not audited but include statements that calculations and presentation of individual accounts and composites conform to AIMR Standards.

☐ C. Neither A. nor B. above.

EXHIBIT 26.19 ▶ *A SAMPLE PERFORMANCE PRESENTATION*

XYZ INVESTMENT FIRM PERFORMANCE RESULTS: U.S. BALANCED COMPOSITE
JANUARY 1, 1990, THROUGH DECEMBER 31, 2001

YEAR	TOTAL RETURN (%)	BENCHMARK RETURN (%)	NUMBER OF PORTFOLIOS	COMPOSITE DISPERSION (%)	TOTAL ASSETS OF END OF PERIOD (USD MILLIONS)	PERCENTAGE OF FIRMS ASSETS	PERCENTAGE OF NON-FEE-PAYING PORTFOLIOS	TOTAL FIRM ASSETS (USD MILLIONS)
1990	12.1	9.4	6	3.2	50	80	15	63
1991	24.2	26.4	10	5.4	85	82	15	104
1992	17.0	16.4	15	3.8	120	78	12	154
1993	−3.3	−1.7	14	1.2	100	80	10	125
1994	15.8	12.8	18	4.3	124	75	10	165
1995	16.0	14.1	26	4.5	165	70	0	236
1996	2.2	1.8	32	2.0	235	68	0	346
1997	22.4	24.1	38	5.7	344	65	0	529
1998	7.1	6.0	45	2.8	445	64	0	695
1999	8.5	8.0	48	3.1	520	62	0	839
2000	−1.9	−3.7	56	4.2	681	65	0	1,036
2001	2.6	3.4	66	5.4	820	76	0	1,077

XYZ Investment Firm has prepared and presented this report in compliance with the Performance Presentation Standards of the Association for Investment Management and Research (AIMR-PPS®), the U.S. and Canadian version of the Global Investment Performance Standards (GIPS®). AIMR has not been involved in the preparation or review of this report.

Notes:

1. XYZ Investment Firm is an independent investment management firm established in 1989. XYZ Investment Firm manages a variety of equity, fixed-income, and balanced assets for primarily U.S. and Canadian institutional clients.

2. These results have been prepared and presented in compliance with the AIMR-PPS only for the period January 1, 1993, through December 31, 2001. The full period is not in compliance. Prior to January 1, 1993, not all fully discretionary portfolios were represented in appropriate composites. Composite results for the years 1990 through 1992 include the five largest institutional portfolios that were managed in accordance with the balanced strategy. These five accounts are consistently represented in the composite for the full period from 1990 through 2001.

3. The benchmark: 60 percent S&P 500 Index; 40 percent Lehman Intermediate Aggregate Index—rebalanced monthly. Annualized compound composite return = 11.0 percent; annualized compound benchmark return = 9.9 percent.

4. Valuations and returns are computed and stated in U.S. Dollars.

5. The dispersion of annual returns is measured by the standard deviation across asset-weighted portfolio returns represented within the composite for the full year.

6. Performance results are presented before management and custodial fees but after all trading commissions. The management fee schedule is as follows:

   $5,000,000–$25,000,000   0.75%
   $25,000,000–$50,000,000   0.50%
   $50,000,000–and above   0.35%

7. This composite was created in February 1997.

8. The minimum portfolio size for the U.S. Balanced Composite is $5,000,000.

9. Settlement-date accounting was used prior to 1992.

10. A complete list of firm composites and performance results is available upon request.

The Internet   *Investments Online*

Mutual fund performance is a matter of public knowledge, but performance for the vast variety of pension funds, endowments, insurance company portfolios, trust portfolios, and other private investment pools may not be public. Investors will have to use the tools discussed in this chapter to evaluate the performance of nonpublic portfolios. Many investor consultant and software firms have proprietary databases and products, and they try to sell their services to individual and institutional investors as a means of evaluating portfolio performance. Consultants who evaluate money managers for clients will not offer the proprietary results of that research for free on the Internet. Nonetheless, some sites are helpful in showing applications of the material covered in this chapter.

http://www.nelnet.com The Web site of the Nelson Investment Manager database calls itself the "World's Best Money Managers" page. Nelson has a database of over 2,500 investment managers. After registering at the site, users can specify investment categories and obtain ranking performance data in a variety of formats. The site offers links to industry analysis and news as well as to investment managers' home pages and to sites of institutional investment managers.

http://www.styleadvisor.com Zephyr Associates, Inc.'s Web site features information about StyleADVISOR. StyleADVISOR is a returns-based style and performance analysis software package.

It uses Sharpe's techniques of performance analysis and attribution. Pages offer visitors the chance to learn about StyleADVISOR and to view sample reports. Visitors can view past newsletters, which give analysis and insights into portfolio performance attribution issues.

http://www.morningstar.com This site, mentioned in Chapter 25, allows users to obtain summary reports on funds. "Quicktake" reports offer information on returns, the *Morningstar* rating, graphs of fund performance versus a benchmark, and the sector weightings of a fund's investments. The report gives the fund's style, as well, using *Morningstar*'s 3×3 style box.

http://www.valueline.com This site is mentioned again as subscribers can obtain useful mutual fund performance information, including charts, both absolute and relative-to-peer-group return performance, and the fund's style, using Value Line's style box.

http://www.aimr.org First mentioned in Chapter 2, the Association for Investment Management and Research's home page offers a link to information about the AIMR Performance Presentation Standards. These are a set of ethical principles and guidelines to help ensure fair representation, full disclosure, and comparability in reported portfolio performance results. The site provides links to resources for training and for library information on the standards.

Summary:

- The first major goal of portfolio management is to derive rates of return that equal or exceed the returns on a naively selected portfolio with equal risk. The second goal is to attain complete diversification relative to a suitable benchmark. Several techniques have been derived to evaluate equity portfolios in terms of both risk and return (composite measures). The Treynor measure considers the excess returns earned per unit of systematic risk. The Sharpe measure indicates the excess return per unit of total risk. The Jensen and Information Ratio measures likewise evaluate performance in terms of the systematic risk involved and show how to determine whether the difference in risk-adjusted performance (good or bad) is statistically significant. Additional work in equity portfolio evaluation has been concerned with models that indicate what components of the management process contributed to the results. A model by Fama divided the composite return into measures related to total risk, systematic risk, diversification, and selectivity, in addition to measuring overall performance. Finally, attribution analysis seeks to establish whether market timing or security selection skills (or both) are the source of a manager's performance.

- Roll challenged the validity of all techniques that assume a market portfolio that theoretically includes all risky assets when actual investigators use a proxy such as the S&P 500 that is limited to U.S. common stocks. This criticism does not invalidate the normative asset pricing model, only its application because of measurement problems related to the proxy for the market portfolio. It is demonstrated that the measurement problem is increased in an environment where global investing is the norm. The good news is that more comprehensive indexes are feasible and are constantly being developed.

- Although the techniques for evaluating equity portfolio performance have been in existence for almost 40 years, comparable techniques for examining bond portfolio performance were initiated more recently. Notably, the evaluation models for bonds typically consider separately the several important decision variables related to bonds: the overall market factor, the impact of maturity-duration decisions, the influence of sector and quality factors, and the impact of individual bond selection. A study indicated a lack of consistency over time for a sample of bond managers similar to results for equity managers.

- In conclusion, investors need to evaluate their own performance and the performance of hired managers. The various techniques we discuss provide theoretically justifiable measures that differ slightly. Although there is high rank correlation among the alternative measures, *all the measures should be used* because they provide different insights regarding the performance of managers. Finally, an evaluation of a portfolio manager should be done many times over different market environments before a final judgment is reached regarding the strengths and weaknesses of a manager.

Questions

1. Describe two major factors that a portfolio manager should consider before designing an investment strategy. What types of decisions can a manager make to achieve these goals?

2. Compare and contrast four prominent approaches to measuring investment performance on a risk-adjusted basis. In developing your answer, comment on the conditions under which each measure will be most useful.

3. The Sharpe and Treynor performance measures both calculate a portfolio's average excess return per unit of risk. Under what circumstances would it make sense to use both measures to compare the performance of a given set of portfolios? What additional information is provided by a comparison of the rankings achieved using the two measures?

4. Describe how the Jensen measure of performance is calculated. Under what conditions should it give a similar set of portfolio rankings as the Sharpe and Treynor measures? Is it possible to adjust the Jensen measure so that a portfolio's alpha value is measured relative to an empirical form of the arbitrage pricing theory rather than the capital asset pricing model? Explain.

5. The information ratio *(IR)* has been described as a benefit-cost ratio. Explain how the *IR* measures portfolio performance and whether this analogy is appropriate.

6. A fund had an overall performance value of –0.50 percent using the Fama performance technique. Discuss whether the manager of this fund could have experienced a positive selectivity value and under what conditions that value might have occurred.

7. A portfolio has an R^2 with the market of 0.95 and a selectivity value of 2.5 percent. Would you expect this portfolio to have a positive or a negative net selectivity value? Explain.

8. *CFA Examination Level I*
   a. Explain why the asset allocation decision is the primary determinant of total portfolio performance over time.
   b. Describe three reasons why successful implementation of asset allocation decisions is even more difficult in practice than in theory.

9. Performance attribution analysis is an attempt to divide a manager's "active" residual return into an allocation effect and a selection effect. Explain how these two effects are measured and why their sum must equal the total value-added return for the manager. Is this analysis valid if the actual portfolio in question is riskier than the benchmark portfolio to which it is being compared?

10. *CFA Examination Level III*
    During the annual review of Acme's pension plan, several trustees questioned Lucy Graham, a pension consultant, about various aspects of performance measurement and risk assessment. In particular, one trustee asked about the appropriateness of using each of the following benchmarks:

    - Market index
    - Benchmark normal portfolio
    - Median of the manager universe

a. Explain *two* different weaknesses of using each of the three benchmarks to measure the performance of a portfolio.

Another trustee asked how to distinguish among the following performance measures:

- The Sharpe ratio
- The Treynor measure
- Jensen's alpha

b. (1) Describe how *each* of the three performance measures is calculated.
(2) State whether *each* measure assumes that the relevant risk is systematic, unsystematic, or total. Explain how each measure relates excess return and the relevant risk.

11. *CFA Examination Level III*

Richard Roll, in an article on using the capital asset pricing model (CAPM) to evaluate portfolio performance, indicated that it may not be possible to evaluate portfolio management ability if there is error in the benchmark used.

a. In evaluating portfolio performance, describe the general procedure, with emphasis on the benchmark employed.
b. Explain what Roll meant by the benchmark error and identify the specific problem with this benchmark.
c. Draw a graph that shows how a portfolio that has been judged as superior relative to a "measured" security market line (SML) can be inferior relative to the "true" SML.
d. Assume that you are informed that a given portfolio manager has been evaluated as superior when compared to the DJIA, the S&P 500, and the NYSE Composite Index. Explain whether this consensus would make you feel more comfortable regarding the portfolio manager's true ability.
e. While conceding the possible problem with benchmark errors as set forth by Roll, some contend this does not mean the CAPM is incorrect, but only that there is a measurement problem when implementing the theory. Others contend that because of benchmark errors, the whole technique should be scrapped. Take and defend one of these positions.

12. It has been contended that the derivation of an appropriate model for evaluating the performance of a bond manager is more difficult than an equity portfolio evaluation model because more decisions are required. Discuss some of the specific decisions that need to be considered when evaluating the performance of a bond portfolio manager.

13. *CFA Examination Level III*

During a quarterly review session, a client of Fixed Income Investors, a pension fund advisory firm, asks Fred Raymond, the portfolio manager for the company's account, if he could provide a more detailed analysis of their portfolio performance than simply total return. Specifically, the client had recently seen a copy of an article by Dietz, Fogler, and Hardy on the analysis of bond portfolio returns that attempted to decompose the total return into the following four components:

a. Yield to maturity effect
b. Interest rate effect
c. Sector/quality effect
d. Residual

Although he does not expect you to be able to provide such an analysis this year, he asks you to explain each of these components to him so he will be better prepared to understand such an analysis when you do it for his company's portfolio next year. Explain each of these components.

Problems

1. *CFA Examination Level III*

You have been asked to evaluate the performance of two portfolios: Good Samaritan Hospital's endowment assets and estate fund of the recently deceased Mrs. Mary Atkins, which has just been transferred in a bequest to Good Samaritan. The existing Good Samaritan endowment assets (excluding the Atkins estate) have been managed by an investment counseling firm with an income objective of approximately 5 percent annually. The returns from this portfolio and from Mrs. Atkins' portfolio are shown in the following table:

	Latest Fiscal Year Total Return	Beta
Good Samaritan existing endowment assets		
—Equity only	11.8%	1.20
—Total portfolio	8.4	
Mrs. Atkins' portfolio		
—Equity only	10.7%	1.05
—Total portfolio	5.1	
S&P 500 Index	9.9%	
Lehman Bond Index	3.4	
90-day Treasury bills	7.8	
Municipal Bond Index	1.4	

   a. Calculate the risk-adjusted return of each of the two equity-only portfolios. Compare these returns to each other and to the S&P 500, and explain the significance of any differences.

   b. List and briefly comment on three factors that could account for the difference in reported performance between Mrs. Atkins' and Good Samaritan's total portfolios.

2. The following portfolios are being considered for investment. During the period under consideration, $RFR = 0.07$.

Portfolio	Return	Beta	σ_i
P	0.15	1.0	0.05
Q	0.20	1.5	0.10
R	0.10	0.6	0.03
S	0.17	1.1	0.06
Market	0.13	1.0	0.04

   a. Compute the Sharpe measure for each portfolio and the market portfolio.

   b. Compute the Treynor measure for each portfolio and the market portfolio.

   c. Rank the portfolios using each measure, explaining the cause for any differences you find in the rankings.

 3. *CFA Examination Level II*

An analyst wants to evaluate Portfolio X, consisting entirely of U.S. common stocks, using both the Treynor and Sharpe measures of portfolio performance. The following table provides the average annual rate of return for Portfolio X, the market portfolio (as measured by the Standard and Poor's 500 Index), and U.S. Treasury bills (T-bills) during the past eight years.

	Annual Average Rate of Return	Standard Deviation of Return	Beta
Portfolio X	10%	18%	0.60
S&P 500	12	13	1.00
T-bills	6	n/a	n/a

n/a = not applicable

   a. Calculate both the Treynor measure and the Sharpe measure for both Portfolio X and the S&P 500. Briefly explain whether Portfolio X underperformed, equaled, or outperformed the S&P 500 on a risk-adjusted basis using both the Treynor measure and the Sharpe measure.

b. Based on the performance of Portfolio X relative to the S&P 500 calculated in Part a, briefly explain the reason for the conflicting results when using the Treynor measure versus the Sharpe measure.

4. You have been assigned the task of comparing the investment performance of five different pension fund managers. After gathering 60 months of excess returns (i.e., returns in excess of the monthly risk-free rate) on each fund as well as the monthly excess returns on the entire stock market, you perform the regressions of the form:

$$(R_{fund} - RFR)_t = \alpha + \beta(R_{mkt} - RFR)_t + e_t$$

You have prepared the following summary of the data, with the standard errors for each of the coefficients listed in parentheses.

	REGRESSION DATA:			$(R_{FUND} - RFR)$:	
Portfolio	α	β	R^2	**Mean**	σ
ABC	0.192	1.048	94.1%	1.022%	1.193%
	(0.11)	(0.10)			
DEF	−0.053	0.662	91.6	0.473	0.764
	(0.19)	(0.09)			
GHI	0.463	0.594	68.6	0.935	0.793
	(0.19)	(0.07)			
JKL	0.355	0.757	64.1	0.955	1.044
	(0.22)	(0.08)			
MNO	0.296	0.785	94.8	0.890	0.890
	(0.14)	(0.12)			

a. Which fund had the highest degree of diversification over the sample period? How is diversification measured in this statistical framework?

b. Rank these funds' performance according to the Sharpe, Treynor, and Jensen measures.

c. Since you know that according to the CAPM the intercept of these regressions (i.e., alpha) should be zero, this coefficient can be used as a measure of the value added provided by the investment manager. Which funds have statistically outperformed and underperformed the market using a two-sided 95 percent confidence interval? (Note: The relevant t-statistic using 60 observations is 2.00.)

5. You have just gathered the following performance data for three different money managers, based on a regression of their excess returns relative to those for the S&P 500 index. Each manager's performance was measured over the same three-year period, but the return period for each was different.

Manager	**Alpha**	**Beta**	**Std. Error of Regression**	**Return Period**
A	0.058%	0.95	0.533%	Weekly
B	0.115	1.12	5.884	Biweekly
C	0.250	0.78	2.165	Monthly

a. Calculate the information ratio for each manager, ignoring the difference in return reporting periods.

b. Calculate the annualized information ratio for each manager.

c. Rank the managers' performance according to your answers in Parts a and b. Which manager performed the best? Explain.

6. You have decided to undertake an evaluation of the performance of the Cirrus International Fund (CIF) for your investment club. After collecting the following data:

$$R_a = 0.15$$
$$RFR = 0.05$$
$$\beta_a = 1.20$$
$$R_M = 0.10$$

a. Draw the security market line.
b. Calculate CIF's overall performance.
c. Calculate CIF's selectivity.
d. Calculate CIF's risk.

7. Consider the following historical performance data for two different portfolios, the Standard and Poor's 500, and the 90-day T-bill.

Investment Vehicle	Average Rate of Return	Standard Deviation	Beta	R^2
Fund 1	26.40%	20.67%	1.351	0.751
Fund 2	13.22	14.20	0.905	0.713
S&P 500	15.71	13.25		
90-day T-bill	6.20	0.50		

a. Calculate the Fama overall performance measure for both funds.
b. What is the return to risk for both funds?
c. For both funds, compute the measures of (1) selectivity, (2) diversification, and (3) net selectivity.
d. Explain the meaning of the net selectivity measure and how it helps you evaluate investor performance. Which fund had the best performance?

8. *CFA Examination Level III*
Your discussion with a client has turned to the measurement of investment performance, particularly with respect to international portfolios.

PERFORMANCE AND ATTRIBUTION DATA: ANNUALIZED RETURNS FOR 5 YEARS ENDED 12/31/94

International Manager/Index	Total Return	Country/Security Return	Currency Return
Manager A	−6.0%	2.0%	−8.0%
Manager B	−2.0	−1.0	−1.0
EAFE Index	−5.0	0.2	−5.2

a. Assume that the data in the table for Manager A and Manager B accurately reflect their investment skills and that both managers actively manage currency exposure. Briefly describe one strength and one weakness for each manager.
b. Recommend and justify a strategy that would enable the Fund to take advantage of the strengths of each of the two managers while minimizing their weaknesses.

9. Consider the following performance data for two portfolio managers (A and B) and a common benchmark portfolio:

	BENCHMARK		MANAGER A		MANAGER B	
	Weight	Return	Weight	Return	Weight	Return
Stock	0.6	–5.0%	0.5	–4.0%	0.3	–5.0%
Bonds	0.3	–3.5	0.2	–2.5	0.4	–3.5
Cash	0.1	0.3	0.3	0.3	0.3	0.3

a. Calculate: (1) the overall return to the benchmark portfolio; (2) the overall return to Manager A's actual portfolio; and (3) the overall return to Manager B's actual portfolio. Briefly comment on whether these managers have under- or outperformed the benchmark fund.

b. Using attribution analysis, calculate (1) the *selection effect* for Manager A, and (3) the *allocation effect* for Manager B. Using these numbers in conjunction with your results from Part a, comment on whether these managers have added value through their selection skills, their allocation skills, or both.

10. *CFA Examination Level III*

A U.S. pension plan hired two off-shore firms to manage the non-U.S. equity portion of its total portfolio. Each firm was free to own stocks in any country market included in Morgan Stanley/Capital International's Europe, Australia, and Far East Index (EAFE) and free to use any form of dollar and/or nondollar cash or bonds as an equity substitute or reserve. After three years had elapsed, the records of the managers and the EAFE Index were as follows:

SUMMARY: CONTRIBUTIONS TO RETURN

	Currency	Country Selection	Stock Selection	Cash/Bond Allocation	Total Return Recorded
Manager A	(9.0%)	19.7%	3.1%	0.6%	14.4%
Manager B	(7.4)	14.2	6.0	2.81	5.6
Composite of A & B	(8.2)	16.9	4.5	1.71	5.0
EAFE Index	(12.9)	19.9	—	—	7.0

You are a member of the plan sponsor's Pension Committee, which will soon meet with the plan's consultant to review manager performance. In preparation for this meeting, you go through the following analysis:

a. Briefly describe the strengths and weaknesses of each manager, relative to the EAFE Index data.

b. Briefly explain the meaning of the data in the "Currency" column.

11. Reggie Portmus has made a performance evaluation of his bond holdings. He has misplaced some of the values and has asked for your help in calculating the remaining ones. At present, he holds 10-year AA, 5-year A, and 25-year B bonds, and the following information has been recovered:

I = external interest rate environment:	11.00
E = expected return:	10.00
U = unexpected return:	?
M = maturity:	0.2%/year in the first 5 years, 0.1%/year thereafter
S = spread/quality:	–0.2%/rank (AAA, AA, A, BBB, etc.)
B = specific selection:	0.25, 0.50, 0.75, respectively
C:	?
R:	?

12. *CFA Examination Level III*

To illustrate for the Investment Committee of the profit-sharing plan to which you are a consultant on some of the issues that arise in measuring performance, you have identified three U.S. fixed-income management firms whose investment approaches are representative of general practice. Each firm's approach follows.

Firm A: An enhanced index fund manager that seeks to add value by superior security selection while maintaining portfolio duration and sector weights equal to the overall bond market.
Firm B: An active duration manager investing only in the government and corporate bond sectors. The firm uses futures to manage portfolio duration.
Firm C: An active manager seeking to add value by correctly anticipating changes in the shape of the yield curve, while maintaining portfolio duration and sector weights roughly equal to the overall bond market.

You have provided the Committee with the following additional information about these firms, derived from a consultant's database.

ANNUALIZED TOTAL RETURN DATA (PAST FIVE YEARS)			
	Firm A	Firm B	Firm C
Reported Returns	9.2%	9.3%	9.0%

		INDEX SECTORS			
	Aggregate Index	Governments	Corporates	Government/ Corporate	Mortgages
Index Return	8.7%	9.0%	9.8%	9.5%	8.3%

	CONSULTANT'S MANAGER UNIVERSE		
	All Managers	Managers Using the Aggregate Index as Their Benchmark	Managers Using the Govt./Corp. Sector as Their Benchmark
Return 5th percentile	6.0%	7.7%	8.4%
25th percentile	7.1	8.1	8.9
50th percentile	8.0	8.6	9.4
75th percentile	8.6	9.1	9.9
95th percentile	9.3	13.1	13.9

a. Evaluate the performance of each of these three firms relative to its appropriate Index and to the manager universe. Use only the data from the descriptions and the preceding table, even though other information would be required for a more complete and accurate appraisal.

To provide additional guidance to the Committee, you decide to do an attribution analysis on the returns produced by Firm A and Firm C and have prepared the following table:

PERFORMANCE ATTRIBUTION ANALYSIS (PAST FIVE YEARS—ANNUALIZED TOTAL RETURNS)

	Total Return	=	Duration Decisions	+	Yield Curve Decisions	+	Sector Weighting Decisions	+	Security Selection Decisions & Residuals
Firm A									
Total return	9.20%		8.00%		0.80%		0.00%		0.40%
Benchmark index return	8.70		7.00		0.50		0.70		0.50
Difference	0.50		1.00		0.30		−0.70		−0.10
Firm C									
Total return	9.00%		7.03%		0.80%		0.71%		0.46%
Benchmark index return	8.70		7.00		0.50		0.70		0.50
Difference	0.30		0.03		0.30		0.01		−0.04

    b. Evaluate the performance of Firm A and of Firm C based on all the information previously provided and your interpretation of the data in this new table.

    c. Based solely on the attribution analysis you performed in Part b, state which firm produced the better result and justify your conclusion.

13. For each of the last six quarters, Managers L and M have provided you with the total dollar value of the funds they manage, along with the quarterly contributions or withdrawals made by their clients. (*Note:* Contributions are indicated by positive numbers, withdrawals by negative numbers.)

	MANAGER L		MANAGER M	
Quarter	Total Funds Under Management	Contributions/ Withdrawals	Total Funds Under Management	Contributions/ Withdrawals
Initial	$500,000	—	$700,000	—
1	527,000	12,000	692,000	−35,000
2	530,000	7,500	663,000	−35,000
3	555,000	13,500	621,000	−35,000
4	580,000	6,500	612,000	−35,000
5	625,000	10,000	625,000	−35,000

For each manager, calculate:

    a. her dollar-weighted return;

    b. her time-weighted return; and

    c. estimates of her quarterly performance returns using the Dietz approximation method, assuming contributions/withdrawals are made exactly halfway through the quarter.

References

Barber, Brad M., and Terrance Odean. "Too Many Cooks Spoil the Profits: Investment Club Performance." *Financial Analysts Journal* 56, no. 1 (January–February 2000): 17–25.

Brown, Stephen J., William Goetzmann, Roger G. Ibbottson, and Stephen A. Ross. "Survivorship Bias in Performance Studies." *Review of Financial Studies* 5, no. 4 (December 1992).

Christopherson, Jon A., Wayne E. Ferson, and Andrew L. Turner. "Performance Evaluation Using Conditional Alphas and Betas." *Journal of Portfolio Management* 26, no. 1 (Fall 1999): 59–72.

DeFusco, Richard A., Dennis W. McLeavey, Jerald E. Pinto, and David E. Runkle. *Quantitative Methods for Investment Analysis.* Baltimore, Md: AIMR, 2001.

Dybvig, Philip H., and Stephen A. Ross. "The Analytics of Performance Measurement Using a Security Market Line." Journal of Finance 40, no. 2 (June 1985).

Fabozzi, Frank J. *Bond Markets, Analysis and Strategies,* 4th ed. Upper Saddle River, N.J.: Prentice-Hall, 2000.

Grinblatt, Mark, and Sheridan Titman. "Performance Evaluation." In R. Jarrow et al., eds., *Handbook in Operations Research and Management Science.* New York: Elsevier Science B.V., 1995.

Sharpe, William F. "Asset Allocation: Management Style and Performance Measurement." *Journal of Portfolio Management* 18, no. 2 (Winter 1992).

Sherrerd, Katrina F., ed. *Benchmarks and Attribution Analysis.* Charlottesville, Va: Association for Investment Management and Research, 2001.

Shulka, Ray, and Charles Trzcinka. "Performance Measurement of Managed Portfolios." In *Financial Markets, Institutions, and Investments* 1, no. 4. New York: New York University Salomon Center, 1992.

Squires, Jan, ed. *Performance Evaluation, Benchmarks, and Attribution Analysis.* Charlottesville, Va.: Association for Investment Management and Research, 1995.

APPENDIX A   How to Become a CFA® Charterholder

As mentioned in the section on career opportunities, the professional designation of Chartered Financial Analyst (CFA) is becoming a significant requirement for a career in investment analysis and/or portfolio management. For that reason, this section presents the history and objectives of the Association for Investment Management and Research (AIMR®) and general guidelines for acquiring the CFA designation. If you are interested in the program, you can write or email AIMR for more information.

The CFA examinations were first offered in 1963 by the Institute of Chartered Financial Analysts (ICFA) which was formed in 1959 to enhance the professionalism of those involved in various aspects of the investment decision-making process and to recognize those who achieve a high level of professionalism. The ICFA combined with the Financial Analysts Federation in 1990 to form AIMR.

AIMR's mission is to advance the interests of the global investment community by establishing and maintaining the highest standards of education and professional practice. As applied to the CFA program, AIMR's focus is:

- To develop and keep current a "body of knowledge" applicable to the investment decision-making process. The principal components of this knowledge are financial accounting, economics, both debt and equity securities analysis, portfolio management, ethical and professional standards, and quantitative techniques.
- To administer a study and examination program for eligible candidates, the primary objectives of which are to assist the candidate in mastering and applying the body of knowledge and to test the candidate's competency in the knowledge gained.
- To award the professional CFA designation to those candidates who have passed three examination levels (encompassing a total of 18 hours of testing over a minimum of three years), who meet stipulated standards of professional conduct, and who otherwise are eligible for membership in AIMR.
- AIMR also provides a useful and informative program of continuing education through seminars, publications, and other formats that enable members, candidates, and others in the investment constituency to be more aware of and to better utilize the changing and expanding body of knowledge.
- Importantly, AIMR also sponsors and enforces a Code of Ethics and Standards of Professional Conduct that apply to enrolled candidates and to all members.

To enter the CFA program an applicant must have a bachelor's degree (or the equivalent work experience). An applicant must receive a bachelor's degree no later than December 31 of the current exam year in order to qualify for entrance. A candidate may sit for all three examinations without having had investment experience *per se* or having joined a member society or chapter of AIMr. However, after passing the three examination levels, the CFA Charter will not be awarded unless or until the candidate:

- has at least three years of experience as a financial analyst, which is defined as a person who has spent and/or is spending a substantial portion of his/her professional time collecting, evaluating, and applying financial, economic, and related data to the investment decision-making process; and
- has applied for membership or is a member of an affiliated member society or chapter of AIMR, if such a society/chapter exists within 50 miles of the candidate's principal place of business.

The curriculum of the CFA study program covers:

1. Ethical and Professional Standards
2. Quantitative Techniques
3. Economics
4. Financial Statement Analysis
5. Corporate Finance
6. Analysis of Debt Investments
7. Analysis of Equity Investments
8. Analysis of Derivatives
9. Analysis of Alternative Investments
10. Portfolio Management
11. PERFORMANCE MEASUREMENT AND PRESENTATION

Members and candidates are typically employed in the investment field. From 1963 to May 2002, over 50,000 charters have been awarded. More than 100,000 individuals were enrolled in the 2002 CFA Candidate Program. If you are interested in learning more about the CFA Program, AIMR has a booklet that describes the program and includes an application form. The address is: AIMR, Attn: Information Central, PO Box 3668, Charlottesville, Virginia, 22903, USA. You may also request a booklet by email to info@aimr.org.

APPENDIX B

Association for Investment Management and Research (AIMR): The Code of Ethics and Standards of Professional Conduct

The Code of Ethics

Members of the Association for Investment Management and Research shall:

- Act with integrity, competence, dignity, and in ethical manner when dealing with the public, clients, prospects, employers, employees, and fellow members.
- Practice and encourage others to practice in a professional and ethical manner that will reflect credit on members and their profession.
- Strive to maintain and improve their competence and the competence of others in the profession.
- Use reasonable care and exercise independent professional judgment.

Standards of Professional Conduct

Standard I: Fundamental Responsibilities

Members shall:

A. Maintain knowledge of and comply with applicable laws, rules, and regulations (including AIMR's Code of Ethics and Standards of Professional Conduct) of any government, governmental agency, regulatory organization, licensing agency, or professional association governing the members' professional activities.

B. Not knowingly participate or assist in any violation of such laws, rules, or regulations.

Standard II: Relationships with and Responsibilities to the Profession

A. **Use of Professional Designation.**

1. AIMR members may reference their membership only in a dignified and judicious manner. The use of the reference may be accompanied by an accurate explanation of the requirements that have been met to obtain membership in these organizations.

2. Those who have earned the right to use the Chartered Financial Analyst designation may use the marks "Chartered Financial Analyst" or "CFA" and are encouraged to do so, but only in a proper, dignified, and judicious manner. The use of the designation may be accompanied by an accurate explanation of the requirements that have been met to obtain the right to use the designation.

3. Candidates in the CFA Program, as defined in the AIMR Bylaws, may reference their participation in the CFA Program, but the reference must clearly state that an individual is a candidate in the CFA Program and cannot imply that the candidate has achieved any type of partial designation.

B. **PROFESSIONAL MISCONDUCT.**

1. Members shall not engage in any professional conduct involving dishonesty, fraud, deceit, or misrepresentation or commit any act that reflects adversely on their honesty, trustworthiness, or professional competence.

2. Members and candidates shall not engage in any conduct or commit any act that compromises the integrity of the CFA designation or the integrity or validity of examinations leading to the award of the right to use the CFA designation.

C. **Prohibition against Plagiarism.** Members shall not copy or use, in substantially the same form as the original, material prepared by another without acknowledging and identifying the name of the author, publisher, or source of each material. Members may use, without acknowledgement, factual information published by recognized financial and statistical reporting services or similar sources.

Standard III: Relationships with and Responsibilities to the Employer

A. **Obligation to Inform Employer of Code and Standards.** Members shall:

1. Inform their employer in writing, through their direct supervisor, that they are obligated to comply with the Code of Standards and are subject to disciplinary sanctions for violations thereof.

2. Deliver a copy of the Code of Standards to their employer if the employer does not have a copy.

B. **Duty to Employer.** Members shall not undertake any independent practice that could result in compensation or other benefit in competition with their employer unless they obtain written consent from both their employer and the persons or entities for whom they undertake independent practice.

C. **Disclosure of Conflicts to Employer.** Members shall:

1. Disclose to their employer all matters, including beneficial ownership of securities or other investments, that reasonably could be expected to interfere with their duty to their employer or ability to make unbiased and objective recommendations.

2. Comply with any prohibitions on activities imposed by their employer if a conflict of interest exists.

D. **Disclosure of Additional Compensation Arrangements.** Members shall disclose to their employer in writing all monetary compensation or other benefits that they receive for their services that are in addition to compensation or benefits conferred by a member's employer.

E. **Responsibilities of Supervisors.** Members with supervisory responsibility, authority, or the ability to influence the conduct of others shall exercise reasonable supervision over those subject to their supervision or authority to prevent any violation of applicable statutes, regulations, or provisions of the Code of Standards. In so doing, members are entitled to rely on reasonable procedures designed to detect and prevent such violations.

Standard IV: Relationships with and Responsibilities to Clients and Prospects

A. Investment Process.

A.1 Reasonable Basis and Representations. Members shall:

   a. Exercise diligence and thoroughness in making investment recommendations or in taking investment actions.

   b. Have a reasonable and adequate basis, appointed by appropriate research and investigation, for such recommendations or actions.

   c. Make reasonable and diligent efforts to avoid any material misrepresentation in any research report or investment recommendation.

   d. Maintain appropriate records to support the reasonableness of such recommendations or actions.

A.2 RESEARCH REPORTS. Members shall:

   a. Use reasonable judgment regarding the inclusion or exclusion of relevant factors in research reports.

   b. Distinguish between facts and opinions in research reports.

   c. Indicate the basic characteristics of the investment involved when preparing for publication a research report that is not directly related to a specific portfolio or client.

A.3 Independence and Objectivity. Members shall use reasonable care and judgment to achieve and maintain independence and objectivity in making investment recommendations or taking investment action.

B. Interactions with Clients and Prospects.

B.1 Fiduciary Duties. In relationships with clients, members shall use particular care in determining applicable fiduciary duty and shall comply with such duty as to those persons and interests to whom the duty is owed. Members must act for the benefit of their clients and place their clients' interests before their own.

B.2 Portfolio Investment Recommendations and Actions. Members shall:

   a. Make a reasonable inquiry into a client's financial situation, investment experience, and investment objectives prior to making any investment recommendations and shall update this information as necessary, but no less frequently than annually, to allow the member to adjust their investment recommendations to reflect changed circumstances.

   b. Consider the appropriateness and suitability of investment recommendations or actions for each portfolio or client. In determining appropriateness and suitability, members shall consider applicable relevant factors, including the needs and circumstances of the portfolio or client, the basic characteristics of the investment involved, and the basic characteristics of the total portfolio. Members shall not make a recommendation unless they reasonably determine that the recommendation is suitable to the client's financial situation, investment experience, and investment objectives.

   c. Distinguish between facts and opinions in the presentation of investment recommendations.

   d. Disclose to clients and prospects the basic format and general principles of the investment processes by which securities are selected and portfolios are constructed and shall promptly disclose to clients and prospects any changes that might significantly affect those processes.

B.3 Fair Dealing. Members shall deal fairly and objectively with all clients and prospects when disseminating investment recommendations, disseminating material changes in prior investment recommendations, and taking investment action.

B.4 Priority of Transactions. Transactions for clients and employers shall have priority over transactions in securities or other investments of which a member is the beneficial owner so that such personal transactions do not operate adversely to their clients' or employer's interests. If members make a recommendation regarding the purchase or sale of a security or other investment, they shall give their clients and employer adequate opportunity to act on the recommendation before acting on their own behalf. For purposes of standards, a member is a "beneficial owner" if the member has

   a. a direct or indirect pecuniary interest in the securities;

   b. the power to vote or direct the voting of the shares of the securities or investments;

   c. the power to dispose or direct the disposition of the security or investment.

B.5 Preservation of Confidentiality. Members shall preserve the confidentiality of information communicated by clients, prospects, or employers concerning matters within the scope of the client-member, prospect-member, or employer-member relationship unless the member receives information concerning illegal activities on the part of the client, prospect, or employer.

B.6 Prohibition against Misrepresentation. Members shall not make any statements, orally or in writing, that misrepresent

   a. the services that they or their firms are capable of performing;

   b. their qualifications or the qualifications of their firm;

   c. the member's academic or professional credentials. Members shall not make or imply, orally or in writing, any assurances or guarantees regarding any investment except to communicate accurate information regarding the terms of the investment instrument and the issuer's obligations under the instrument.

B.7 Disclosure of Conflicts to Clients and Prospects. Members shall disclose to their clients and prospects all matters, including beneficial ownership of securities or other investments, that reasonably could be expected to impair the member's ability to make unbiased and objective recommendations.

B.8 Disclosure of Referral Fees. Members shall disclose to clients and prospects any consideration or benefit received by the member or delivered to others for the recommendation of any services to the client or prospect.

Standard V: Relationships with and Responsibilities to the Investing Public

A. **Prohibition against Use of Material Nonpublic Information.** Members who possess material nonpublic information related to the value of a security shall not trade or cause others to trade in that security if such trading would breach a duty or if the information was misappropriated or relates to a tender offer. If members receive material nonpublic information in confidence, they shall not breach that confidence by trading or causing others to trade in securities to which such information relates. Members shall make reasonable efforts to achieve public dissemination of material nonpublic information disclosed in breach of a duty.

B. **Performance Presentation.**
1. MEMBERS SHALL NOT MAKE ANY STATEMENTS, ORALLY OR IN WRITING, THAT MISREPRESENT THE INVESTMENT PERFORMANCE THAT THEY OR THEIR FIRMS HAVE ACCOMPLISHED OR CAN REASONABLY BE EXPECTED TO ACHIEVE.
2. If members communicate individual or firm performance information directly or indirectly to clients or prospective clients, or in a manner intended to be received by clients or prospective clients, members shall make every reasonable effort to assure that such performance information is a fair, accurate, and complete presentation of such performance.

APPENDIX C   Interest Tables

TABLE C.1 Present Value of $1: PVIF $= 1/(1 + k)^t$

Period	1%	2%	3%	4%	5%	6%	7%	8%	9%	10%	12%	14%	15%	16%	18%	20%	24%	28%	32%	36%
1	.9901	.9804	.9709	.9615	.9524	.9434	.9346	.9259	.9174	.9091	.8929	.8772	.8696	.8621	.8475	.8333	.8065	.7813	.7576	.7353
2	.9803	.9612	.9426	.9246	.9070	.8900	.8734	.8573	.8417	.8264	.7972	.7695	.7561	.7432	.7182	.6944	.6504	.6104	.5739	.5407
3	.9706	.9423	.9151	.8890	.8638	.8396	.8163	.7938	.7722	.7513	.7118	.6750	.6575	.6407	.6086	.5787	.5245	.4768	.4348	.3975
4	.9610	.9238	.8885	.8548	.8227	.7921	.7629	.7350	.7084	.6830	.6355	.5921	.5718	.5523	.5158	.4823	.4230	.3725	.3294	.2923
5	.9515	.9057	.8626	.8219	.7835	.7473	.7130	.6806	.6499	.6209	.5674	.5194	.4972	.4761	.4371	.4019	.3411	.2910	.2495	.2149
6	.9420	.8880	.8375	.7903	.7462	.7050	.6663	.6302	.5963	.5645	.5066	.4556	.4323	.4104	.3704	.3349	.2751	.2274	.1890	.1580
7	.9327	.8706	.8131	.7599	.7107	.6651	.6227	.5835	.5470	.5132	.4523	.3996	.3759	.3538	.3139	.2791	.2218	.1776	.1432	.1162
8	.9235	.8535	.7894	.7307	.6768	.6274	.5820	.5403	.5019	.4665	.4039	.3506	.3269	.3050	.2660	.2326	.1789	.1388	.1085	.0854
9	.9143	.8368	.7664	.7026	.6446	.5919	.5439	.5002	.4604	.4241	.3606	.3075	.2843	.2630	.2255	.1938	.1443	.1084	.0822	.0628
10	.9053	.8203	.7441	.6756	.6139	.5584	.5083	.4632	.4224	.3855	.3220	.2697	.2472	.2267	.1911	.1615	.1164	.0847	.0623	.0462
11	.8963	.8043	.7224	.6496	.5847	.5268	.4751	.4289	.3875	.3505	.2875	.2366	.2149	.1954	.1619	.1346	.0938	.0662	.0472	.0340
12	.8874	.7885	.7014	.6246	.5568	.4970	.4440	.3971	.3555	.3186	.2567	.2076	.1869	.1685	.1372	.1122	.0757	.0517	.0357	.0250
13	.8787	.7730	.6810	.6006	.5303	.4688	.4150	.3677	.3262	.2897	.2292	.1821	.1625	.1452	.1163	.0935	.0610	.0404	.0271	.0184
14	.8700	.7579	.6611	.5775	.5051	.4423	.3878	.3405	.2992	.2633	.2046	.1597	.1413	.1252	.0985	.0779	.0492	.0316	.0205	.0135
15	.8613	.7430	.6419	.5553	.4810	.4173	.3624	.3152	.2745	.2394	.1827	.1401	.1229	.1079	.0835	.0649	.0397	.0247	.0155	.0099
16	.8528	.7284	.6232	.5339	.4581	.3936	.3387	.2919	.2519	.2176	.1631	.1229	.1069	.0930	.0708	.0541	.0320	.0193	.0118	.0073
17	.8444	.7142	.6050	.5134	.4363	.3714	.3166	.2703	.2311	.1978	.1456	.1078	.0929	.0802	.0600	.0451	.0258	.0150	.0089	.0054
18	.8360	.7002	.5874	.4936	.4155	.3503	.2959	.2502	.2120	.1799	.1300	.0946	.0808	.0691	.0508	.0376	.0208	.0118	.0068	.0039
19	.8277	.6864	.5703	.4746	.3957	.3305	.2765	.2317	.1945	.1635	.1161	.0829	.0703	.0596	.0431	.0313	.0168	.0092	.0051	.0029
20	.8195	.6730	.5537	.4564	.3769	.3118	.2584	.2145	.1784	.1486	.1037	.0728	.0611	.0514	.0365	.0261	.0135	.0072	.0039	.0021
25	.7798	.6095	.4776	.3751	.2953	.2330	.1842	.1460	.1160	.0923	.0588	.0378	.0304	.0245	.0160	.0105	.0046	.0021	.0010	.0005
30	.7419	.5521	.4120	.3083	.2314	.1741	.1314	.0994	.0754	.0573	.0334	.0196	.0151	.0116	.0070	.0042	.0016	.0006	.0002	.0001
40	.6717	.4529	.3066	.2083	.1420	.0972	.0668	.0460	.0318	.0221	.0107	.0053	.0037	.0026	.0013	.0007	.0002	.0001	*	*
50	.6080	.3715	.2281	.1407	.0872	.0543	.0339	.0213	.0134	.0085	.0035	.0014	.0009	.0006	.0003	.0001	*	*	*	*
60	.5504	.3048	.1697	.0951	.0535	.0303	.0173	.0099	.0057	.0033	.0011	.0004	.0002	.0001	*	*	*	*	*	*

*The factor is zero to four decimal places.

TABLE C.2   Present Value of an Annuity of $1 Per Period for n Periods:

$$PVIFA = \sum_{t=1}^{n}\frac{1}{(1+k)^t} = \frac{1 - \dfrac{1}{(1+k)^n}}{k}$$

Number of Payments	1%	2%	3%	4%	5%	6%	7%	8%	9%	10%	12%	14%	15%	16%	18%	20%	24%	28%	32%
1	0.9901	0.9804	0.9709	0.9615	0.9524	0.9434	0.9346	0.9259	0.9174	0.9091	0.8929	0.8772	0.8696	0.8621	0.8475	0.8333	0.8065	0.7813	0.7576
2	1.9704	1.9416	1.9135	1.8861	1.8594	1.8334	1.8080	1.7833	1.7591	1.7355	1.6901	1.6467	1.6257	1.6052	1.5656	1.5278	1.4568	1.3916	1.3315
3	2.9410	2.8839	2.8286	2.7751	2.7232	2.6730	2.6243	2.5771	2.5313	2.4869	2.4018	2.3216	2.2832	2.2459	2.1743	2.1065	1.9813	1.8684	1.7663
4	3.9020	3.8077	3.7171	3.6299	3.5460	3.4651	3.3872	3.3121	3.2397	3.1699	3.0373	2.9137	2.8550	2.7982	2.6901	2.5887	2.4043	2.2410	2.0957
5	4.8534	4.7135	4.5797	4.4518	4.3295	4.2124	4.1002	3.9927	3.8897	3.7908	3.6048	3.4331	3.3522	3.2743	3.1272	2.9906	2.7454	2.5320	2.3452
6	5.7955	5.6014	5.4172	5.2421	5.0757	4.9173	4.7665	4.6229	4.4859	4.3553	4.1114	3.8887	3.7845	3.6847	3.4976	3.3255	3.0205	2.7594	2.5342
7	6.7282	6.4720	6.2303	6.0021	5.7864	5.5824	5.3893	5.2064	5.0330	4.8684	4.5638	4.2883	4.1604	4.0386	3.8115	3.6046	3.2423	2.9370	2.6775
8	7.6517	7.3255	7.0197	6.7327	6.4632	6.2098	5.9713	5.7466	5.5348	5.3349	4.9676	4.6389	4.4873	4.3436	4.0776	3.8372	3.4212	3.0758	2.7860
9	8.5660	8.1622	7.7861	7.4353	7.1078	6.8017	6.5152	6.2469	5.9952	5.7590	5.3282	4.9464	4.7716	4.6065	4.3030	4.0310	3.5655	3.1842	2.8681
10	9.4713	8.9826	8.5302	8.1109	7.7217	7.3601	7.0236	6.7101	6.4177	6.1446	5.6502	5.2161	5.0188	4.8332	4.4941	4.1925	3.6819	3.2689	2.9304
11	10.3676	9.7868	9.2526	8.7605	8.3064	7.8869	7.4987	7.1390	6.8052	6.4951	5.9377	5.4527	5.2337	5.0286	4.6560	4.3271	3.7757	3.3351	2.9776
12	11.2551	10.5753	9.9540	9.3851	8.8633	8.3838	7.9427	7.5361	7.1607	6.8137	6.1944	5.6603	5.4206	5.1971	4.7932	4.4392	3.8514	3.3868	3.0133
13	12.1337	11.3484	10.6350	9.9856	9.3936	8.8527	8.3577	7.9038	7.4869	7.1034	6.4235	5.8424	5.5831	5.3423	4.9095	4.5327	3.9124	3.4272	3.0404
14	13.0037	12.1062	11.2961	10.5631	9.8986	9.2950	8.7455	8.2442	7.7862	7.3667	6.6282	6.0021	5.7245	5.4675	5.0081	4.6106	3.9616	3.4587	3.0609
15	13.8651	12.8493	11.9379	11.1184	10.3797	9.7122	9.1079	8.5595	8.0607	7.6061	6.8109	6.1422	5.8474	5.5755	5.0916	4.6755	4.0013	3.4834	3.0764
16	14.7179	13.5777	12.5611	11.6523	10.8378	10.1059	9.4466	8.8514	8.3126	7.8237	6.9740	6.2651	5.9542	5.6685	5.1624	4.7296	4.0333	3.5026	3.0882
17	15.5623	14.2919	13.1661	12.1657	11.2741	10.4773	9.7632	9.1216	8.5436	8.0216	7.1196	6.3729	6.0472	5.7487	5.2223	4.7746	4.0591	3.5177	3.0971
18	16.3983	14.9920	13.7535	12.6593	11.6896	10.8276	10.0591	9.3719	8.7556	8.2014	7.2497	6.4674	6.1280	5.8178	5.2732	4.8122	4.0799	3.5294	3.1039
19	17.2260	15.6785	14.3238	13.1339	12.0853	11.1581	10.3356	9.6036	8.9501	8.3649	7.3658	6.5504	6.1982	5.8775	5.3162	4.8435	4.0967	3.5386	3.1090
20	18.0456	16.3514	14.8775	13.5903	12.4622	11.4699	10.5940	9.8181	9.1285	8.5136	7.4694	6.6231	6.2593	5.9288	5.3527	4.8696	4.1103	3.5458	3.1129
25	22.0232	19.5235	17.4131	15.6221	14.0939	12.7834	11.6536	10.6748	9.8226	9.0770	7.8431	6.8729	6.4641	6.0971	5.4669	4.9476	4.1474	3.5640	3.1220
30	25.8077	22.3965	19.6004	17.2920	15.3725	13.7648	12.4090	11.2578	10.2737	9.4269	8.0552	7.0027	6.5660	6.1772	5.5168	4.9789	4.1601	3.5693	3.1242
40	32.8347	27.3555	23.1148	19.7928	17.1591	15.0463	13.3317	11.9246	10.7574	9.7791	8.2438	7.1050	6.6418	6.2335	5.5482	4.9966	4.1659	3.5712	3.1250
50	39.1961	31.4236	25.7298	21.4822	18.2559	15.7619	13.8007	12.2335	10.9617	9.9148	8.3045	7.1327	6.6605	6.2463	5.5541	4.9995	4.1666	3.5714	3.1250
60	44.9550	34.7609	27.6756	22.6235	18.9293	16.1614	14.0392	12.3766	11.0480	9.9672	8.3240	7.1401	6.6651	6.2402	5.5553	4.9999	4.1667	3.5714	3.1250

TABLE C.3   Future Value of $1 at the End of n Periods: $FVIF_{k,n} = (1 + k)^n$

Period	1%	2%	3%	4%	5%	6%	7%	8%	9%	10%	12%	14%	15%	16%	18%	20%	24%	28%	32%	36%
1	1.0100	1.0200	1.0300	1.0400	1.0500	1.0600	1.0700	1.0800	1.0900	1.1000	1.1200	1.1400	1.1500	1.1600	1.1800	1.2000	1.2400	1.2800	1.3200	1.3600
2	1.0201	1.0404	1.0609	1.0816	1.1025	1.1236	1.1449	1.1664	1.1881	1.2100	1.2544	1.2996	1.3225	1.3456	1.3924	1.4400	1.5376	1.6384	1.7424	1.8496
3	1.0303	1.0612	1.0927	1.1249	1.1576	1.1910	1.2250	1.2597	1.2950	1.3310	1.4049	1.4815	1.5209	1.5609	1.6430	1.7280	1.9066	2.0972	2.3000	2.5155
4	1.0406	1.0824	1.1255	1.1699	1.2155	1.2625	1.3108	1.3605	1.4116	1.4641	1.5735	1.6890	1.7490	1.8106	1.9388	2.0736	2.3642	2.6844	3.0360	3.4210
5	1.0510	1.1041	1.1593	1.2167	1.2763	1.3382	1.4026	1.4693	1.5386	1.6105	1.7623	1.9254	2.0114	2.1003	2.2878	2.4883	2.9316	3.4360	4.0075	4.6526
6	1.0615	1.1262	1.1941	1.2653	1.3401	1.4185	1.5007	1.5869	1.6771	1.7716	1.9738	2.1950	2.3131	2.4364	2.6996	2.9860	3.6352	4.3980	5.2899	6.3275
7	1.0721	1.1487	1.2299	1.3159	1.4071	1.5036	1.6058	1.7138	1.8280	1.9487	2.2107	2.5023	2.6600	2.8262	3.1855	3.5832	4.5077	5.6295	6.9826	8.6054
8	1.0829	1.1717	1.2668	1.3686	1.4775	1.5938	1.7182	1.8509	1.9926	2.1436	2.4760	2.8526	3.0590	3.2784	3.7589	4.2998	5.5895	7.2058	9.2170	11.703
9	1.0937	1.1951	1.3048	1.4233	1.5513	1.6895	1.8385	1.9990	2.1719	2.3579	2.7731	3.2519	3.5179	3.8030	4.4355	5.1598	6.9310	9.2234	12.166	15.916
10	1.1046	1.2190	1.3439	1.4802	1.6289	1.7908	1.9672	2.1589	2.3674	2.5937	3.1058	3.7072	4.0456	4.4114	5.2338	6.1917	8.5944	11.805	16.059	21.646
11	1.1157	1.2434	1.3842	1.5395	1.7103	1.8983	2.1049	2.3316	2.5804	2.8531	3.4785	4.2262	4.6524	5.1173	6.1759	7.4301	10.657	15.111	21.198	29.439
12	1.1268	1.2682	1.4258	1.6010	1.7959	2.0122	2.2522	2.5182	2.8127	3.1384	3.8960	4.8179	5.3502	5.9360	7.2876	8.9161	13.214	19.342	27.982	40.037
13	1.1381	1.2936	1.4685	1.6651	1.8856	2.1329	2.4098	2.7196	3.0658	3.4523	4.3635	5.4924	6.1528	6.8858	8.5994	10.699	16.386	24.758	36.937	54.451
14	1.1495	1.3195	1.5126	1.7317	1.9799	2.2609	2.5785	2.9372	3.3417	3.7975	4.8871	6.2613	7.0757	7.9875	10.147	12.839	20.319	31.691	48.756	74.053
15	1.1610	1.3459	1.5580	1.8009	2.0789	2.3966	2.7590	3.1722	3.6425	4.1772	5.4736	7.1379	8.1371	9.2655	11.973	15.407	25.195	40.564	64.358	100.71
16	1.1726	1.3728	1.6047	1.8730	2.1829	2.5404	2.9522	3.4259	3.9703	4.5950	6.1304	8.1372	9.3576	10.748	14.129	18.488	31.242	51.923	84.953	136.96
17	1.1843	1.4002	1.6528	1.9479	2.2920	2.6928	3.1588	3.7000	4.3276	5.0545	6.8660	9.2765	10.761	12.467	16.672	22.186	38.740	66.461	112.13	186.27
18	1.1961	1.4282	1.7024	2.0258	2.4066	2.8543	3.3799	3.9960	4.7171	5.5599	7.6900	10.575	12.375	14.462	19.673	26.623	48.038	85.070	148.02	253.33
19	1.2081	1.4568	1.7535	2.1068	2.5270	3.0256	3.6165	4.3157	5.1417	6.1159	8.6128	12.055	14.231	16.776	23.214	31.948	59.567	108.89	195.39	344.53
20	1.2202	1.4859	1.8061	2.1911	2.6533	3.2071	3.8697	4.6610	5.6044	6.7275	9.6463	13.743	16.366	19.460	27.393	38.337	73.864	139.37	257.91	468.57
21	1.2324	1.5157	1.8603	2.2788	2.7860	3.3996	4.1406	5.0338	6.1088	7.4002	10.803	15.667	18.821	22.574	32.323	46.005	91.591	178.40	340.44	637.26
22	1.2447	1.5460	1.9161	2.3699	2.9253	3.6035	4.4304	5.4365	6.6586	8.1403	12.100	17.861	21.644	26.186	38.142	55.206	113.57	228.35	449.39	866.67
23	1.2572	1.5769	1.9736	2.4647	3.0715	3.8197	4.7405	5.8715	7.2579	8.9543	13.552	20.361	24.891	30.376	45.007	66.247	140.83	292.30	593.19	1178.6
24	1.2697	1.6084	2.0328	2.5633	3.2251	4.0489	5.0724	6.3412	7.9111	9.8497	15.178	23.212	28.625	35.236	53.108	79.496	174.63	374.14	783.02	1602.9
25	1.2824	1.6406	2.0938	2.6658	3.3864	4.2919	5.4274	6.8485	8.6231	10.834	17.000	26.461	32.918	40.874	62.668	95.396	216.54	478.90	1033.5	2180.0
26	1.2953	1.6734	2.1566	2.7725	3.5557	4.5494	5.8074	7.3964	9.3992	11.918	19.040	30.166	37.856	47.414	73.948	114.47	268.51	612.99	1364.3	2964.9
27	1.3082	1.7069	2.2213	2.8834	3.7335	4.8223	6.2139	7.9881	10.245	13.110	21.324	34.389	43.535	55.000	87.259	137.37	332.95	784.63	1800.9	4032.2
28	1.3213	1.7410	2.2879	2.9987	3.9201	5.1117	6.6488	8.6271	11.167	14.421	23.883	39.204	50.065	63.800	102.96	164.84	412.86	1004.3	2377.2	5483.8
29	1.3345	1.7758	2.3566	3.1187	4.1161	5.4184	7.1143	9.3173	12.172	15.863	26.749	44.693	57.575	74.008	121.50	197.81	511.95	1285.5	3137.9	7458.0
30	1.3478	1.8114	2.4273	3.2434	4.3219	5.7435	7.6123	10.062	13.267	17.449	29.959	50.950	66.211	85.849	143.37	237.37	634.81	1645.5	4142.0	10143.
40	1.4889	2.2080	3.2620	4.8010	7.0400	10.285	14.974	21.724	31.409	45.259	93.050	188.88	267.86	378.72	750.37	1469.7	5455.9	19426.	66520.	•
50	1.6446	2.6916	4.3839	7.1067	11.467	18.420	29.457	46.901	74.357	117.39	289.00	700.23	1083.6	1670.7	3927.3	9100.4	46890.	•	•	•
60	1.8167	3.2810	5.8916	10.519	18.679	32.987	57.946	101.25	176.03	304.48	897.59	2595.9	4383.9	7370.1	20555.	56347.	•	•	•	•

*FVIFA > 99,999

TABLE C.4 Sum of an Annuity of $1 Per Period for n Periods:

$$FVIFA_{k,n} = \sum_{t=1}^{n}(1+k)^{t-1} = \frac{(1+k)^n - 1}{k}$$

Number of Periods	1%	2%	3%	4%	5%	6%	7%	8%	9%	10%	12%	14%	15%	16%	18%	20%	24%	28%	32%	36%
1	1.0000	1.0000	1.0000	1.0000	1.0000	1.0000	1.0000	1.0000	1.0000	1.0000	1.0000	1.0000	1.0000	1.0000	1.0000	1.0000	1.0000	1.0000	1.0000	1.0000
2	2.0100	2.0200	2.0300	2.0400	2.0500	2.0600	2.0700	2.0800	2.0900	2.1000	2.1200	2.1400	2.1500	2.1600	2.1800	2.2000	2.2400	2.2800	2.3200	2.3600
3	3.0301	3.0604	3.0909	3.1216	3.1525	3.1836	3.2149	3.2464	3.2781	3.3100	3.3744	3.4396	3.4725	3.5056	3.5724	3.6400	3.7776	3.9184	4.0624	4.2096
4	4.0604	4.1216	4.1836	4.2465	4.3101	4.3746	4.4399	4.5061	4.5731	4.6410	4.7793	4.9211	4.9934	5.0665	5.2154	5.3680	5.6842	6.0156	6.3624	6.7251
5	5.1010	5.2040	5.3091	5.4163	5.5256	5.6371	5.7507	5.8666	5.9847	6.1051	6.3528	6.6101	6.7424	6.8771	7.1542	7.4416	8.0484	8.6999	9.3983	10.146
6	6.1520	6.3081	6.4684	6.6330	6.8019	6.9753	7.1533	7.3359	7.5233	7.7156	8.1152	8.5355	8.7537	8.9775	9.4420	9.9299	10.980	12.135	13.405	14.798
7	7.2135	7.4343	7.6625	7.8983	8.1420	8.3938	8.6540	8.9228	9.2004	9.4872	10.089	10.730	11.066	11.413	12.141	12.915	14.615	16.533	18.695	21.126
8	8.2857	8.5830	8.8923	9.2142	9.5491	9.8975	10.259	10.636	11.028	11.435	12.299	13.232	13.726	14.240	15.327	16.499	19.122	22.163	25.678	29.731
9	9.3685	9.7546	10.159	10.582	11.026	11.491	11.978	12.487	13.021	13.579	14.775	16.085	16.785	17.518	19.085	20.798	24.712	29.369	34.895	41.435
10	10.462	10.949	11.463	12.006	12.577	13.180	13.816	14.486	15.192	15.937	17.548	19.337	20.303	21.321	23.521	25.958	31.643	38.592	47.061	57.351
11	11.566	12.168	12.807	13.486	14.206	14.971	15.783	16.645	17.560	18.531	20.654	23.044	24.349	25.732	28.755	32.150	40.237	50.398	63.121	78.998
12	12.682	13.412	14.192	15.025	15.917	16.869	17.888	18.977	20.140	21.384	24.133	27.270	29.001	30.850	34.931	39.580	50.894	65.510	84.320	108.43
13	13.809	14.680	15.617	16.626	17.713	18.882	20.140	21.495	22.953	24.522	28.029	32.088	34.351	36.786	42.218	48.496	64.109	84.852	112.30	148.47
14	14.947	15.973	17.086	18.291	19.598	21.015	22.550	24.214	26.019	27.975	32.392	37.581	40.504	43.672	50.818	59.195	80.496	109.61	149.23	202.92
15	16.096	17.293	18.598	20.023	21.578	23.276	25.129	27.152	29.360	31.772	37.279	43.842	47.580	51.659	60.965	72.035	100.81	141.30	197.99	276.97
16	17.257	18.639	20.156	21.824	23.657	25.672	27.888	30.324	33.003	35.949	42.753	50.980	55.717	60.925	72.939	87.442	126.01	181.86	262.35	377.69
17	18.430	20.012	21.761	23.697	25.840	28.212	30.840	33.750	36.973	40.544	48.883	59.117	65.075	71.673	87.068	105.93	157.25	233.79	347.30	514.66
18	19.614	21.412	23.414	25.645	28.132	30.905	33.999	37.450	41.301	45.599	55.749	68.394	75.836	84.140	103.74	128.11	195.99	300.25	459.44	700.93
19	20.810	22.840	25.116	27.671	30.539	33.760	37.379	41.446	46.018	51.159	63.439	78.969	88.211	98.603	123.41	154.74	244.03	385.32	607.47	954.27
20	22.019	24.297	26.870	29.778	33.066	36.785	40.995	45.762	51.160	57.275	72.052	91.024	102.44	115.37	146.62	186.68	303.60	494.21	802.86	1298.8
21	23.239	25.783	28.676	31.969	35.719	39.992	44.865	50.422	56.764	64.002	81.698	104.76	118.81	134.84	174.02	225.02	377.46	633.59	1060.7	1767.3
22	24.471	27.299	30.536	34.248	38.505	43.392	49.005	55.456	62.873	71.402	92.502	120.43	137.63	157.41	206.34	271.03	469.05	811.99	1401.2	2404.6
23	25.716	28.845	32.452	36.617	41.430	46.995	53.436	60.893	69.531	79.543	104.60	138.29	159.27	183.60	244.48	326.23	582.62	1040.3	1850.6	3271.3
24	26.973	30.421	34.426	39.082	44.502	50.815	58.176	66.764	76.789	88.497	118.15	158.65	184.16	213.97	289.49	392.48	723.46	1332.6	2443.8	4449.9
25	28.243	32.030	36.459	41.645	47.727	54.864	63.249	73.105	84.700	98.347	133.33	181.87	212.79	249.21	342.60	471.98	898.09	1706.8	3226.8	6052.9
26	29.525	33.670	38.553	44.311	51.113	59.156	68.676	79.954	93.323	109.18	150.33	208.33	245.71	290.08	405.27	567.37	1114.6	2185.7	4260.4	8233.0
27	30.820	35.344	40.709	47.084	54.669	63.705	74.483	87.350	102.72	121.09	169.37	238.49	283.56	337.50	479.22	681.85	1383.1	2798.7	5624.7	11197.9
28	32.129	37.051	42.930	49.967	58.402	68.528	80.697	95.338	112.96	134.20	190.69	272.88	327.10	392.50	566.48	819.22	1716.0	3583.3	7425.6	15230.2
29	33.450	38.792	45.218	52.966	62.322	73.639	87.346	103.96	124.13	148.63	214.58	312.09	377.16	456.30	669.44	984.06	2128.9	4587.6	9802.9	20714.1
30	34.784	40.568	47.575	56.084	66.438	79.058	94.460	113.28	136.30	164.49	241.33	356.78	434.74	530.31	790.94	1181.8	2640.9	5873.2	12940.	28172.2
40	48.886	60.402	75.401	95.025	120.79	154.76	199.63	259.05	337.88	442.59	767.09	1342.0	1779.0	2360.7	4163.2	7343.8	22728.	69377.	•	•
50	64.463	84.579	112.79	152.66	209.34	290.33	406.52	573.76	815.08	1163.9	2400.0	4994.5	7217.7	10435.	21813.	45497.	•	•	•	•
60	81.669	114.05	163.05	237.99	353.58	533.12	813.52	1253.2	1944.7	3034.8	7471.6	18535.	29219.	46057.	•	•	•	•	•	•

*FVIF > 99,999

APPENDIX D   Standard Normal Probabilities

z	0.00	0.01	0.02	0.03	0.04	0.05	0.06	0.07	0.08	0.09
0.0	.5000	.5040	.5080	.5120	.5160	.5199	.5239	.5279	.5219	.5359
0.1	.5398	.5438	.5478	.5517	.5557	.5596	.5636	.5675	.5714	.5753
0.2	.5793	.5832	.5871	.5910	.5948	.5987	.6026	.6064	.6103	.6141
0.3	.6179	.6217	.6255	.6293	.6331	.6368	.6406	.6443	.6480	.6517
0.4	.6554	.6591	.6628	.6664	.6700	.6736	.6772	.6808	.6844	.6879
0.5	.6915	.6950	.6985	.7019	.7054	.7088	.7123	.7157	.7190	.7224
0.6	.7257	.7291	.7324	.7357	.7389	.7422	.7454	.7486	.7517	.7549
0.7	.7580	.7611	.7642	.7673	.7704	.7734	.7764	.7794	.7823	.7852
0.8	.7881	.7910	.7939	.7967	.7995	.8023	.8051	.8078	.8106	.8133
0.9	.8159	.8186	.8212	.8238	.8264	.8289	.8315	.8340	.8365	.8389
1.0	.8413	.8438	.8461	.8485	.8508	.8531	.8554	.8577	.8599	.8621
1.1	.8643	.8665	.8686	.8708	.8729	.8749	.8770	.8790	.8810	.8830
1.2	.8849	.8860	.8888	.8907	.8925	.8943	.8962	.8980	.8997	.9015
1.3	.9032	.9049	.9066	.9082	.9099	.9115	.9131	.9147	.9162	.9177
1.4	.9192	.9207	.9222	.9236	.9251	.9265	.9279	.9292	.9306	.9319
1.5	.9332	.9345	.9357	.9370	.9382	.9394	.9406	.9418	.9429	.9441
1.6	.9452	.9463	.9474	.9484	.9495	.9505	.9515	.9525	.9535	.9545
1.7	.9554	.9564	.9573	.9582	.9591	.9599	.9608	.9616	.9625	.9633
1.8	.9641	.9649	.9656	.9664	.9671	.9678	.9686	.9693	.9699	.9706
1.9	.9713	.9719	.9726	.9732	.9738	.9744	.9750	.9756	.9761	.9767
2.0	.9772	.9778	.9783	.9788	.9793	.9798	.9803	.9808	.9812	.9817
2.1	.9821	.9826	.9830	.9834	.9838	.9842	.9846	.9850	.9854	.9857
2.2	.9861	.9864	.9868	.9871	.9875	.9878	.9881	.9884	.9887	.9890
2.3	.9893	.9896	.9898	.9901	.9904	.9906	.9909	.9911	.9913	.9916
2.4	.9918	.9920	.9922	.9925	.9927	.9929	.9931	.9932	.9934	.9936
2.5	.9938	.9940	.9941	.9943	.9945	.9946	.9948	.9949	.9951	.9952
2.6	.9953	.9955	.9956	.9957	.9959	.9960	.9961	.9962	.9963	.9964
2.7	.9965	.9966	.9967	.9968	.9969	.9970	.9971	.9972	.9973	.9974
2.8	.9974	.9975	.9976	.9977	.9977	.9978	.9979	.9979	.9980	.9981
2.9	.9981	.9982	.9982	.9983	.9984	.9984	.9985	.9985	.9986	.9986
3.0	.9987	.9987	.9987	.9988	.9988	.9989	.9989	.9989	.9990	.9990

GLOSSARY

Abnormal rate of return The amount by which a security's return differs from its expected rate of return based on the market's rate of return and the security's relationship with the market.

Accumulation phase Phase in the investment life cycle during which individuals in the early-to-middle years of their working career attempt to accumulate assets to satisfy short-term needs and longer-term goals.

Actuarial rate of return The discount rate used to find the present value of a defined benefit pension plan's future obligations and thus determine the size of the firm's annual contribution to the plan.

American Depository Receipts (ADRs) Certificates of ownership issued by a U.S. bank that represent indirect ownership of a certain number of shares of a specific foreign firm. Shares are held on deposit in a bank in the firm's home country.

American option An option contract that can be exercised at any time until its expiration date.

Analysis effect The difference in performance of a bond portfolio from that of a chosen index due to acquisition of temporarily mispriced issues that then move to their correct prices.

Anomalies Security price relationships that appear to contradict a well-regarded hypothesis; in this case, the efficient market hypothesis.

Arbitrage A trading strategy designed to generate a guaranteed profit from a transaction that requires no capital commitment or risk bearing on the part of the trader. A simple example of an arbitrage trade would be the simultaneous purchase and sale of the same security in different markets at different prices.

Arbitrage pricing theory (APT) A theory that posits that the expected return to a financial asset can be described by its relationship with several common risk factors. The APT can be contrasted with the single-factor CAPM.

Arithmetic mean (AM) A measure of mean annual rates of return equal to the sum of annual holding period rates of return divided by the number of years.

Asset allocation The process of deciding how to distribute an investor's wealth among different asset classes for investment purposes.

Asset class Securities that have similar characteristics, attributes, and risk/return relationships.

Assets under management (AUM) The total market value of the assets managed by an investment firm.

At the money A special case of an option where the exercise price and the price of the underlying asset are identical.

Attribution analysis An assessment technique designed to establish whether a manager's performance relative to a benchmark resulted from market timing or security selection skills.

Autocorrelation test A test of the efficient market hypothesis that compares security price changes over time to check for predictable correlation patterns.

Average tax rate A person's total tax payment divided by his or her total income.

Backtest A method of testing a quantitative model in which computers are used to examine the composition and returns of portfolios based on historical data to determine if the selected strategy would have worked in the past.

Backwardated A situation in a futures market where the current contract price is less than the current spot price for the underlying asset.

Balance sheet A financial statement that shows what assets the firm controls at a fixed point in time and how it has financed these assets.

Balanced fund A mutual fund with, generally, a three-part investment objective: (1) to conserve the investor's principal, (2) to pay current income, and (3) to increase both principal and income. The fund aims to achieve this by owning a mixture of bonds, preferred stocks, and common stocks.

Basis The difference between the spot price of the underlying asset and the futures contract price at any point in time (e.g., the *initial* basis at the time of contract origination, the *cover* basis at the time of contract termination).

Basis of an asset For tax purposes, the cost of an asset.

Basis risk The residual exposure to the price volatility of an underlying asset that results from a cross hedge transaction.

Bearer bond An unregistered bond for which ownership is determined by possession. The holder receives interest payments by clipping coupons attached to the security and sending them to the issuer for payment.

Behavioral finance Involves the analysis of various psychological traits of individuals and how these traits affect how they act as investors, analysts, and portfolio managers.

Benchmark error Situation where an inappropriate or incorrect benchmark is used to compare and assess portfolio returns and management.

Benchmark portfolio A comparison standard of risk and assets included in the policy statement and similar to the investor's risk preference and investment needs, which can be used to evaluate the investment performance of the portfolio manager.

Beta A standardized measure of systematic risk based upon an asset's covariance with the market portfolio.

Binomial option pricing model A valuation equation that assumes the price of the underlying asset changes through a series of discrete upward or downward movements.

Black-Scholes option pricing model A valuation equation that assumes the price of the underlying asset changes continuously through the option's expiration date by a statistical process known as *geometric Brownian motion.*

Bond price volatility The percentage changes in bond prices over time.

Bond swap An active bond portfolio management strategy that exchanges one position for another to take advantage of some difference between them.

Business risk The variability of operating income arising from the characteristics of the firm's industry. Two sources of business risk are sales variability and operating leverage.

Buy-and-hold strategy A passive portfolio management strategy in which bonds are bought and held to maturity.

Call market A market in which trading for individual stocks only takes place at specified times. All the bids and asks available at the time are combined and the market administrators specify a single price that will possibly clear the market at that time.

Call option Option to buy an asset within a certain period at a specified price called the *exercise price.*

Call premium Amount above par issuer must pay to bondholder for retiring the bond before its stated maturity.

Call provisions Specifies when and how a firm can issue a call for bonds outstanding prior to their maturity.

Cap agreement A contract that on each settlement date pays the holder the greater of the difference between the reference rate and the cap rate or zero; it is equivalent to a series of call options on the reference rate.

Capital appreciation A return objective in which the investor seeks to increase the portfolio value, primarily through capital gains, over time to meet a future need rather than dividend yield.

Capital asset pricing model (CAPM) A theory concerned with deriving the expected or required rates of return on risky assets based on the assets' systematic risk levels.

Capital market instruments Fixed-income or equity investments that trade in the secondary market.

Capital market line (CML) The line from the intercept point that represents the risk-free rate tangent to the original efficient frontier; it becomes the new efficient frontier since investments on this line dominate all the portfolios on the original Markowitz efficient frontier.

Capital preservation A return objective in which the investor seeks to minimize the risk of loss; generally a goal of the risk-averse investor.

Certificates of deposit (CDs) Instruments issued by banks and S&Ls that require minimum deposits for specified terms and that pay higher rates of interest than deposit accounts.

Characteristic line Regression line that indicates the systematic risk of a risky asset.

Closed-end investment company An investment company that issues only a limited number of shares, which it does not redeem (buy back). Instead, shares of a closed-end fund are traded in securities markets at prices determined by supply and demand.

Coefficient of variation (CV) A measure of relative variability that indicates risk per unit of return. It is equal to: standard deviation divided by the mean value. When used in investments, it is equal to: standard deviation of returns divided by the expected rate of return.

Coincident indicators A set of economic variables whose values reach peaks and troughs at about the same time as the aggregate economy.

Collar agreement A hedging arrangement where an underlying asset is protected against decreases in value by the simultaneous purchase of a put option and sale of a call option.

Collateral trust bonds A mortgage bond wherein the assets backing the bond are financial assets like stocks and bonds.

Collateralized mortgage obligation (CMO) A debt security based on a pool of mortgage loans that provides a relatively stable stream of payments for a relatively predictable term.

Commission brokers Employees of a member firm who buy or sell securities for the customers of the firm.

Common stock An equity investment that represents ownership of a firm, with full participation in its success or failure. The firm's directors must approve dividend payments.

Common-size statements The normalization of balance sheet and income statement items to allow for more meaningful comparison of different-size firms. Balance sheet items are divided by total assets; income statement items are divided by total sales.

Competitive bid An underwriting alternative wherein an issuing entity (governmental body or a corporation) specifies the type of security to be offered (bonds or stocks) and the general characteristics of the issue, and the issuer solicits bids from competing investment banking firms with the understanding that the issuer will accept the highest bid from the bankers.

Competitive environment The level of intensity of competition among firms in an industry, determined by an examination of five competitive forces. ·

Competitive strategy The search by a firm for a favorable competitive position within an industry, which affects evaluation of the industry's prospects.

Completely diversified portfolio A portfolio in which all unsystematic risk has been eliminated by diversification.

Completeness fund A specialized index used to form the basis of a passive portfolio whose purpose is to provide diversification to a client's total portfolio by excluding those segments in which the client's active managers invest.

Composite measure An investment performance statistic that considers both the return and risk associated with a portfolio (e.g., Sharpe measure, Treynor measure, Jensen measure).

Consolidation phase Phase in the investment life cycle during which individuals who are typically past the midpoint of their career have earnings that exceed expenses and invest them for future retirement or estate planning needs.

Construct the portfolio Given the strategy and economic outlook, what specific stocks and/or bonds will be put into the portfolio at the present time that are consistent with the client's policy statement.

Contango A situation in a futures market where the current contract price is greater than the current spot price for the underlying asset.

Contingent deferred sales load A mutual fund that imposes a sales charge when the investor sells or redeems shares. Also referred to as *rear-end loads* or *redemption charges.*

Continual monitoring This involves constant evaluation of the economic environment, the policy statement, and the portfolio to ensure that it is consistent with the policy statement. Also involves evaluating performance to determine if changes are required in the portfolio, the strategy, or the policy statement.

Continuous market A market where stocks are priced and traded continuously by an auction process or by dealers when the market is open.

Contract price The transaction price specified in a forward or futures contract.

Contrarian An investment strategy that attempts to buy (sell) securities on which the majority of other investors are bearish (bullish).

Convenience yield An adjustment made to the theoretical forward or futures contract delivery price to account for the preference that consumers have for holding spot positions in the underlying asset.

Conversion factors The adjustments made to Treasury bond futures contract terms to allow for the delivery of an instrument other than the standardized underlying asset.

Conversion parity price The price at which common stock can be obtained by surrendering the convertible instrument at par value.

Conversion premium The excess of the market value of the convertible security over its equity value if immediately converted into common stock. Typically expressed as a percentage of the equity value.

Conversion ratio The number of shares of common stock for which a convertible security may be exchanged.

Conversion value The value of the convertible security if converted into common stock at the stock's current market price

Convertible bonds A bond with the added feature that the bondholder has the option to turn the bond back to the firm in exchange for a specified number of common shares of the firm.

Convexity A measure of the degree to which a bond's price-yield curve departs from a straight line. This characteristic affects estimates of a bond's price volatility for a given change in yields.

Core-plus bond portfolio management This is a combination approach to bond portfolio management wherein a significant (core) part of the portfolio (e.g., 70–75 percent) of the portfolio is managed passively in a widely recognized sector of the bond market, such as an aggregate bond index or a U.S. Government/corporate sector. The rest of the portfolio would be actively managed in one or several "plus" sectors that are less efficient than the core component—for example, high-yield bonds, foreign bonds, or emerging market debt.

Correlation coefficient A standardized measure of the relationship between two variables that ranges from −1.00 to +1.00.

Cost of carry The net amount that would be required to store a commodity or security for future delivery, usually calculated as physical storage costs plus financial capital costs less dividends paid to the underlying asset.

Counterparty A participant to a derivative transaction.

Country risk Uncertainty due to the possibility of major political or economic change in the country where an investment is located. Also called *political risk.*

Coupon Indicates the interest payment on a debt security. It is the coupon rate times the par value that indicates the interest payments on a debt security.

Coupon reinvestment risk The component of interest rate risk due to the uncertainty of the rate at which coupon payments will be reinvested.

Covariance A measure of the degree to which two variables, such as rates of return for investment assets, move together over time relative to their individual mean returns.

Covered call A trading strategy in which a call option is sold as a supplement to a long position in an underlying asset or portfolio of assets.

Covered interest arbitrage A trading strategy involving borrowing money in one country and lending it to another designed to exploit price deviations from the interest rate parity model.

Credit analysis An active bond portfolio management strategy designed to identify bonds that are expected to experience changes in rating. This strategy is critical when investing in high-yield bonds.

Cross hedge A trading strategy in which the price volatility of a commodity or security position is hedged with a forward or futures contract based on a different underlying asset or different settlement terms.

Crossover price The price at which the yield to maturity equals the yield to call. Above this price, yield to call is the appropriate yield measure; below this price, yield to maturity is the appropriate yield measure.

Cross-sectional analysis An examination of a firm's performance in comparison to other firms in the industry with similar characteristics to the firm being studied.

Cross-sectional return studies Studies wherein investigators look for public information regarding individual stocks that predict the cross-sectional distribution of risk-adjusted returns—e.g., is there an inverse relationship between market-value size of a firm and future risk-adjusted rates of return for its stock?

Currency swap A swap transaction in which the cash flows, which can be either fixed or variable, are denominated in different currencies.

Current income A return objective in which the investor seeks to generate income rather than capital gains; generally a goal of an investor who wants to supplement earnings with income to meet living expenses.

Current yield A bond's yield as measured by its current income (coupon) as a percentage of its market price.

Cyclical change An economic trend arising from the ups and downs of the business cycle.

Cyclical company A firm whose earnings rise and fall with general economic activity.

Cyclical stock A stock with a high beta; its gains typically exceed those of a rising market and its losses typically exceed those of a falling market.

Debentures Bonds that promise payments of interest and principal but pledge no specific assets. Holders have first claim on the issuer's income and unpledged assets. Also known as *unsecured bonds*.

Declining trend channel The range defined by security prices as they move progressively lower.

Dedication A portfolio management technique in which the portfolio's cash flows are used to retire a set of liabilities over time.

Dedication with reinvestment A dedication strategy in which portfolio cash flows may precede their corresponding liabilities. Such cash flows can be reinvested to earn a return until the date the liability is due to be paid.

Defensive company Firms whose future earnings are likely to withstand an economic downturn.

Defensive competitive strategy Positioning the firm so that its capabilities provide the best means to deflect the effect of the competitive forces in the industry.

Defensive stock A stock whose return is not expected to decline as much as that of the overall market during a bear market.

Defined benefit pension plan A pension plan to which the company contributes a certain amount each year and that pays employees an income after they retire. The benefit size is based on factors such as workers' salary and time of employment.

Defined contribution pension plan A pension plan in which worker benefits are determined by the size of employees' contributions to the plan and the returns earned on the fund's investments.

Delta The change in the price of the option with respect to a one dollar change in the price of the underlying asset; this is the option's *hedge ratio,* or the number of units of the underlying asset that can be hedged by a single option contract.

Derivative security An instrument whose market value ultimately depends upon, or derives from, the value of a more fundamental investment vehicle called the underlying asset or security.

Diffusion index An indicator of the number of stocks rising during a specified period of time relative to the number of stocks declining and not changing price.

Discount A bond selling at a price below par value due to capital market conditions.

Dividend discount model (DDM) A technique for estimating the value of a stock issue as the present value of all future dividends.

Dollar-weighted return The discount rate that sets the present value of a future set of cash flows equal to the investment's current value; also known as the *internal rate of return.*

Downtick A price decline in a transaction price compared to the previous transaction price.

DuPont system A method of examining ROE by breaking it down into three component parts: (1) profit margin, (2) total asset turnover, and (3) financial leverage.

Duration A measure of the interest rate sensitivity of a bond's market price taking into consideration its coupon and term to maturity.

Duration strategy A portfolio management strategy employed to reduce the interest rate risk of a bond portfolio by matching the modified duration of the portfolio with its investment horizon. For example, if the investment horizon is 10 years, the portfolio manager would construct a portfolio that has a modified duration of 10 years. This strategy is referred to as *immunization of the portfolio.*

Earnings momentum A strategy in which portfolios are constructed of stocks of firms with rising earnings.

Earnings multiplier Also known as the price/earnings ratio, it is a measure of the relationship between a company's, or the aggregate stock market's, stock prices and earnings.

Earnings multiplier model A technique for estimating the value of a stock issue as a multiple of its earnings per share.

Earnings surprise A company announcement of earnings that differ from analysts' prevailing expectations.

Economic value added (EVA) Internal management performance measure that compares net operating profit to total cost of capital. Indicates how profitable company projects are as a sign of management performance.

Effective duration Direct measure of the interest rate sensitivity of a bond (or any financial instrument) based upon price changes derived from a pricing model.

Efficient capital market A market in which security prices rapidly reflect all information about securities.

Efficient frontier The set of portfolios that has the maximum rate of return for every given level of risk, or the minimum risk for every potential rate of return.

Empirical duration Measures directly the interest rate sensitivity of an asset by examining the percentage price change for an asset in response to a change in yield during a specified period of time.

Ending-wealth value The total amount of money derived from investment in a bond until maturity, including principal, coupon payments, and income from reinvestment of coupon payments.

Equipment trust certificates Mortgage bonds that are secured by specific pieces of transportation equipment like boxcars and planes.

Equity collar An option-based hedging strategy that protects a stock position from price declines by purchasing a put option that is paid for by the sale of a call option.

Equity swap A swap transaction in which one cash flow is tied to the return to an equity portfolio position, often an index such as the Standard and Poor's 500, while the other is based on a floating-rate index.

Estimated rate of return The rate of return an investor anticipates earning from a specific investment over a particular future holding period.

Eurobonds Bonds denominated in a currency not native to the country in which they are issued.

European option An option contract that can only be exercised on its expiration date.

Event study Research that examines the reaction of a security's price to a specific company, world event, or news announcement.

Exchange clearinghouse The functional unit attached to a futures exchange that guarantees contract performance, oversees delivery, serves as a bookkeeper, and calculates settlement transactions.

Exchange rate risk Uncertainty due to the denomination of an investment in a currency other than that of the investor's own country.

Exercise price The transaction price specified in an option contract; also known as the *strike price.*

Exotic option Designed to have payoffs that differ from those of standard contract options. Three such nonstandard contracts are *Asian, lookback,* and *digital* options.

Expected rate of return The return that analysts' calculations suggest a security should provide, based on the market's rate of return during the period and the security's relationship to the market.

Expiry The expiration date of a derivative security.

External efficiency When prices reflect all available information about an asset, which implies that prices adjust quickly to new information regarding supply or demand. Also referred to as *informational efficiency.*

Fiduciary A person who supervises or oversees the investment portfolio of a third party, such as in a trust account, and makes investment decisions in accordance with the owner's wishes.

Filter rule A trading rule that recommends security transactions when price changes exceed a previously determined percentage.

Financial risk The variability of future income arising from the firm's fixed financing costs, for example, interest payments. The effect of fixed financial costs is to magnify the effect of changes in operating profit on net income or earnings per share.

Fixed-income investments Loans with contractually mandated payment schedules from investors to firms or governments.

Flat trend channel The range defined by security prices as they maintain a relatively steady level.

Flexible portfolio fund Mutual fund that allows managers to shift assets between stocks, bonds, and cash acccording to changing market conditions; also known as *asset allocation* fund.

Floating-rate note (FRN) Short- to intermediate-term bonds with regularly scheduled coupon payments linked to a variable interest rate, most often LIBOR.

Floor agreement A contract that on each settlement date pays the holder the greater of the difference between the floor rate and the reference rate or zero; it is equivalent to a series of put options on the reference rate.

Floor brokers Independent members of an exchange who act as brokers for other members.

Forward contract An agreement between two counterparties that requires the exchange of a commodity or security at a fixed time in the future at a predetermined price.

Forward discount A situation where, from the perspective of the domestic country, the spot exchange rate is smaller than the forward exchange rate with a foreign country.

Forward premium A situation where, from the perspective of the domestic country, the spot exchange rate is larger than the forward exchange rate with a foreign country.

Forward rate A short-term yield for a future holding period implied by the spot rates of two securities with different maturities.

Forward rate agreement (FRA) A transaction in which two counterparties agree to a single exchange of cash flows based on a fixed and floating rate, respectively.

Fourth market Direct trading of securities between owners, usually institutions, without any broker intermediation.

Franchise factor A firm's unique competitive advantage that makes it possible for a firm to earn excess returns (rates of return above a firm's cost of capital) on its capital projects. In turn, these excess returns and the franchise factor cause the firm's stock price to have a *P/E* ratio above its base *P/E* ratio that is equal to $1/k$.

Free cash flow This cash flow measure equals cash flow from operations minus capital expenditures and debt payments.

Full replication A technique for constructing a passive index portfolio in which all securities in an index are purchased in proportion to their weights in the index.

Fully taxable equivalent yield (FTEY) A yield on a tax-exempt bond that adjusts for its tax benefits to allow comparisons with taxable bonds.

Futures contract An agreement that provides for the future exchange of a particular asset at a specified delivery date in exchange for a specified payment at the time of delivery.

General obligation bond (GO) A municipal issue serviced from and guaranteed by the issuer's full taxing authority.

Generally accepted accounting principles (GAAP) Accounting principles formulated by the Financial Accounting Standards Board and used to construct financial statements.

Geometric mean (GM) The *n*th root of the product of the annual holding period returns for *n* years minus 1.

Gifting phase Phase in the investment life cycle during which individuals use excess assets to financially assist relatives or friends, establish charitable trusts, or construct trusts to minimize estate taxes.

Growth company A company that consistently has the opportunities and ability to invest in projects that provide rates of return that exceed the firm's cost of capital. Because of these investment opportunities, it retains a high proportion of earnings, and its earnings grow faster than those of average firms.

Growth stock A stock issue that generates a higher rate of return than other stocks in the market with similar risk characteristics; usually identified by high *P/E* or high price-to-book ratios.

Hedge A trading strategy in which derivative securities are used to reduce or completely offset a counterparty's risk exposure to an underlying asset.

Hedge ratio The number of derivative contracts that must be transacted to offset the price volatility of an underlying commodity or security position.

High-yield bond A bond rated below investment grade. Also referred to as *speculative-grade bonds* or *junk bonds.*

Holding period return (HPR) The total return from an investment, including all sources of income, for a given period of time. A value of 1.0 indicates no gain or loss.

Holding period yield (HPY) The total return from an investment for a given period of time stated as a percentage.

Immunization A bond portfolio management technique of matching modified duration to the investment horizon of the portfolio to eliminate interest rate risk.

Implied volatility The standard deviation of changes in the price of the underlying asset that can be inferred from an option's market price in relation to a specific valuation model.

In the money An option that has positive intrinsic value.

Income bonds Debentures that stipulate interest payments only if the issuer earns the income to make the payments by specified dates.

Income effect The known component of the total return for a bond during a period of time if the shape and position of the yield curve did not change.

Income statement A financial statement that shows the flow of the firm's sales, expenses, and earnings over a period of time.

Indenture The legal agreement that lists the obligations of the issuer of a bond to the bondholder, including payment schedules, call provisions, and sinking funds.

Indexing A passive bond portfolio management strategy that seeks to match the composition, and therefore the performance, of a selected market index.

Industry life cycle analysis An analysis that focuses on the industry's stage of development.

Information An attribute of a good market that includes providing buyers and sellers with timely, accurate information on the volume and prices of past transactions and on all currently outstanding bids and offers.

Information ratio Statistic used to measure a portfolio's average return in excess of a comparison, benchmark portfolio divided by the standard deviation of this excess return.

Informationally efficient market A more technical term for an efficient capital market that emphasizes the role of information in setting the market price.

Initial public offering (IPO) A new issue by a firm that has no existing public market.

Interest rate anticipation An active bond portfolio management strategy designed to preserve capital or take advantage of capital gains opportunities by predicting interest rates and their effects on bond prices.

Interest rate collar The combination of a long position in a cap agreement and a short position in a floor agreement, or vice versa; it is equivalent to a series of range forward positions.

Interest rate effect The return on a bond portfolio caused by changes in the term structure of interest rates during a period that affect both bond prices and reinvestment rates.

Interest rate parity The relationship that must exist in an efficient market between the spot and forward foreign exchange rates between two countries and the interest rates in those countries.

Interest rate risk The uncertainty of returns on an investment due to possible changes in interest rates over time.

Interest rate swap An agreement calling for the periodic exchange of cash flows, one based on an interest rate that remains fixed for the life of the contract and the other that is linked to a variable-rate index.

Interest-on-interest Bond income from reinvestment of coupon payments.

Internal liquidity (solvency) ratios Financial ratios that measure the ability of the firm to meet future short-term financial obligations.

Internal rate of return (IRR) The discount rate at which cash outflows of an investment equal cash inflows.

International domestic bonds Bonds issued by a foreign firm, denominated in the firm's native currency, and sold within its own country.

Intrinsic value The portion of a call option's total value equal to the greater of either zero or the difference between the current value of the underlying asset and the exercise price; for a put option, intrinsic value is the greater of either zero or the exercise price less the underlying asset price. For a stock, it is the value derived from fundamental analysis of the stock's expected returns or cash flows.

Investment The current commitment of dollars for a period of time in order to derive future payments that will compensate the investor for the time the funds are committed, the expected rate of inflation, and the uncertainty of future payments.

Investment company A firm that sells shares of the company and uses the proceeds to buy portfolios of stock, bonds, or other financial instruments.

Investment decision process Estimation of value for comparison with market price to determine whether or not to invest.

Investment horizon The time period used for planning and forecasting purposes or the future time at which the investor requires the invested funds.

Investment management company A company separate from the investment company that manages the portfolio and performs administrative functions.

Investment strategy A decision by a portfolio manager regarding how he or she will manage the portfolio to meet the goals and objectives of the client. This will include either active or passive management and, if active, what style in terms of top-down or buttom-up or fundamental versus technical.

January effect A frequent empirical anomaly where risk-adjusted stock returns in the month of January are significantly larger than those occurring in any other month of the year.

Jensen measure An absolute measure of a portfolio's risk-adjusted performance, computed as the intercept in a regression equation where the excess returns to a manager's portfolio and the market index are, respectively, the dependent and independent variables.

Lagging indicators A set of economic variables whose values reach peaks and troughs after the aggregate economy.

Leading indicators A set of economic variables whose values reach peaks and troughs in advance of the aggregate economy.

Limit order An order that lasts for a specified time to buy or sell a security when and if it trades at a specified price.

Liquid Term used to describe an asset that can be quickly converted to cash at a price close to fair market value.

Liquidity The ability to buy or sell an asset quickly and at a reasonable price.

Liquidity risk Uncertainty due to the ability to buy or sell an investment in the secondary market.

Long hedge A long position in a forward or futures contract used to offset the price volatility of a short position in the underlying asset.

Long position The buyer of a commodity or security or, for a forward contract, the counterparty who will be the eventual buyer of the underlying asset.

Long-term, high-priority goal A long-term financial investment goal of personal importance that typically includes achieving financial independence, such as being able to retire at a certain age.

Lower-priority goal A financial investment goal of lesser personal importance, such as taking a luxurious vacation or buying a car every few years.

Low-load fund A mutual fund that imposes a moderate front-end sales charge when the investor buys the fund, typically about 3 to 4 percent.

Macaulay duration A measure of the time flow of cash from a bond where cash flows are weighted by present values discounted by the yield to maturity.

Maintenance margin The required proportion that the investor's equity value must be to the total market value of the stock. If the proportion drops below this percent, the investor will receive a margin call.

Management and advisory firm A firm that provides a range of services from standard banking transactions (savings accounts, personal loans) to advising individual and institutional investors on structuring their portfolios and managing investment funds.

Management effect A combination of the interest rate anticipation effect, the analysis effect, and the trading effect.

Management fee The compensation an investment company pays to the investment management company for its services. The average annual fee is about 0.5 percent of fund assets.

Margin The percent of cost a buyer pays in cash for a security, borrowing the balance from the broker. This introduces leverage, which increases the risk of the transaction.

Margin account The collateral posted with the futures exchange clearinghouse by an outside counterparty to insure its eventual performance; the *initial* margin is the deposit required at contract origination while the *maintenance* margin is the minimum collateral necessary at all times.

Margin call A request by an investor's broker for additional capital for a security bought on margin if the investor's equity value declines below the required maintenance margin.

Marginal tax rate The part of each additional dollar in income that is paid as tax.

Marked to market The settlement process used to adjust the margin account of a futures contract for daily changes in the price of the underlying asset.

Market The means through which buyers and sellers are brought together to aid in the transfer of goods and/or services.

Market order An order to buy or sell a security immediately at the best price available.

Market portfolio The portfolio that includes all risky assets with relative weights equal to their proportional market values.

Market risk premium The amount of return above the risk-free rate that investors expect from the market in general as compensation for systematic risk.

Market value added (MVA) External management performance measure to compare the market value of the company's debt and equity with the total capital invested in the firm.

Market-value-weighted series An indicator series calculated as the total market value of the securities in the sample.

Maturity strategy A portfolio management strategy employed to reduce the interest rate risk of a bond portfolio by matching the maturity of the portfolio with its investment horizon. For example, if the investment horizon is 10 years, the portfolio manager would construct a portfolio that will mature in 10 years.

Mean rates of return The average of an investment's returns over an extended period of time.

Modified duration A measure of Macaulay duration divided by one plus the bond's periodic yield used to approximate the bond's price volatility.

Money market The market for short-term debt securities with maturities of less than one year.

Money market mutual fund A fund that invests in short-term securities sold in the money market. (Large companies, banks, and other institutions also invest their surplus cash in the money market for short periods of time.) In the entire investment spectrum, these are generally the safest, most stable securities available. They include Treasury bills, certificates of deposit of large banks, and commercial paper (short-term IOUs of large corporations).

Mortgage bonds Bonds that pledge specific assets such as buildings and equipment. The proceeds from the sale of these assets are used to pay off bondholders in case of bankruptcy.

Moving average The continually recalculating average of security prices for a period, often 200 days, to serve as an indication of the general trend of prices and also as a benchmark price.

Multifactor model An empirical version of the APT where the investor chooses the exact number and identity of the common risk factors used to describe an asset's risk-return relationship. Risk factors are often designated as *macroeconomic* variables (e.g., inflation, changes in gross domestic product) or *microeconomic* variables (e.g., security-specific characteristics like firm size or book-to-market ratios).

Mutual fund An investment company that pools money from shareholders and invests in a variety of securities, including stocks, bonds, and money market securities. A mutual fund ordinarily stands ready to buy back (redeem) its shares at their current net asset value, which depends on the market value of the fund's portfolio of securities at the time. Mutual funds generally continuously offer new shares to investors.

National Association of Securities Dealers Automated Quotation (Nasdaq) system An electronic system for providing bid-ask quotes on OTC securities.

Near-term, high-priority goal A short-term financial investment goal of personal importance, such as accumulating funds for making a house down payment or buying a car.

Negotiated sales An underwriting arrangement wherein the sale of a security issue by an issuing entity (governmental body or a corporation) is done using an investment banking firm that maintains an ongoing relationship with the issuer. The characteristics of the security issue are determined by the issuer in consultation with the investment banker.

Net asset value (NAV) per share The market value of an investment company's assets (securities, cash, and any accrued earnings) after deducting liabilities, divided by the number of shares outstanding.

Net present value (NPV) A measure of the excess cash flows expected from an investment proposal. It is equal to the present value of the cash *inflows* from an investment proposal, discounted at the required rate of return for the investment, minus the present value of the cash *outflows* required by the investment, also discounted at the investment's required rate of return. If the derived net present value is a positive value (i.e., there is an excess net present value), the investment should be acquired since it will provide a rate of return above its required returns.

New issue Common stocks or bonds offered by companies for public sale.

No-load fund A mutual fund that sells its shares at net asset value without adding sales charges.

Nominal yield A bond's yield as measured by its coupon rate.

Normal portfolio A specialized or customized benchmark constructed to evaluate a specific manager's investment style or philosophy.

Notes Intermediate-term debt securities with maturities longer than 1 year but less than 10 years.

Notional principal The principal value of a swap transaction, which is not exchanged but is used as a scale factor to translate interest rate differentials into cash settlement payments.

Objectives The investor's goals expressed in terms of risk and return and included in the policy statement.

Offensive competitive strategy A strategy whereby a firm attempts to use its strengths to affect the competitive forces in the industry and, in so doing, improves the firm's relative position in the industry.

Open-end investment company The more formal name for a mutual fund, which derives from the fact that it continuously offers new shares to investors and redeems them (buys them back) on demand.

Operating efficiency ratios Financial ratios intended to indicate how efficiently management is utilizing the firm's assets in terms of dollar sales generated per dollar of assets. Primary examples would be: total asset turnover, fixed asset turnover, or equity turnover.

Operating leverage The use of fixed-production costs in the firm's operating cost structure. The effect of fixed costs is to magnify the effect of a change in sales on operating profits.

Operating profitability ratios Financial ratios intended to indicate how profitable the firm is in terms of the percent of profit generated from sales. Alternative measures would include: operating profit (EBIT)/net sales; pretax profit (EBT)/net sales; and net profit/sales.

Optimal portfolio The portfolio on the efficient frontier that has the highest utility for a given investor. It lies at the point of tangency between the efficient frontier and the curve with the investor's highest possible utility.

Options Clearing Corporation (OCC) A company designed to guarantee, monitor margin accounts, and settle exchange-traded option transactions.

Option contract An agreement that grants the owner the right, but not the obligation, to make a future transaction in an underlying commodity or security at a fixed price and within a predetermined time in the future.

Option premium The initial price that the option buyer must pay to the option seller to acquire the contract.

Option-adjusted spread A type of yield spread that considers changes in the term structure and alternative estimates of the volatility of interest rates.

Out of the money An option that has no intrinsic value.

Overfunded plan A defined benefit pension plan in which the present value of the pension liabilities is less than market value of the plan's assets.

Overweighted A condition in which a portfolio, for whatever reason, includes more of a class of securities than the relative market value alone would justify.

Par value *See* Principal.

Payback The time required for the added income from the convertible security relative to the stock to offset the conversion premium.

Peak The culmination of a bull market when prices stop rising and begin declining.

Peer group comparison A method of measuring portfolio performance by collecting the returns produced by a representative universe of investors over a specific period of time and displaying them in a simple boxplot format.

Performance presentation standards (PPS) A comprehensive set of reporting guidelines created by the Association for Investment Management and Research (AIMR), in an effort to fulfill the call for uniform, accurate, and consistent performance reporting.

Perpetuity An investment without any maturity date. It provides returns to its owner indefinitely.

Personal trust An amount of money set aside by a grantor and often managed by a third party, the trustee. Often constructed so one party receives income from the trust's investments and another party receives the residual value of the trust after the income beneficiaries' death.

Policy effect The difference in performance of a bond portfolio from that of a chosen index due to differences in duration, which result from a fund's investment policy.

Policy statement A statement in which the investor specifies investment goals, constraints, and risk preferences.

Portfolio A group of investments. Ideally, the investments should have different patterns of returns over time.

Preferred stock An equity investment that stipulates the dividend payment either as a coupon or a stated dollar amount. The firm's directors may withhold payments.

Premium A bond selling at a price above par value due to capital market conditions.

Price change effect The unknown component of the total return for a bond portfolio during a period of time due to the interest rate effect, sector/quality effect, and residual effect.

Price continuity A feature of a liquid market in which prices change little from one transaction to the next due to the depth of the market.

Price momentum A portfolio strategy in which you acquire stocks that have enjoyed above-market stock price increases.

Price risk The component of interest rate risk due to the uncertainty of the market price of a bond caused by possible changes in market interest rates.

Price/earnings (P/E) ratio The number by which expected earnings per share is multiplied to estimate a stock's value; also called the *earnings multiplier.*

Price-weighted series An indicator series calculated as an arithmetic average of the current prices of the sampled securities.

Primary market The market in which newly issued securities are sold by their issuers, who receive the proceeds.

Principal (par value) The original value of the debt underlying a bond that is payable at maturity.

Private placement A new issue sold directly to a small group of investors, usually institutions.

Promised yield to call (YTC) A bond's yield if held until the first available call date, with reinvestment of all coupon payments at the yield-to-call rate.

Promised yield to maturity (YTM) The most widely used measure of a bond's yield that states the fully compounded rate of return on a bond bought at market price and held to maturity with reinvestment of all coupon payments at the yield to maturity rate.

Protective put A trading strategy in which a put option is purchased as a supplement to a long position in an underlying asset or portfolio of assets; the most straightforward form of *portfolio insurance.*

Public bond A long-term, fixed-obligation debt security in a convenient, affordable denomination for sale to individuals and financial institutions.

Pure cash-matched dedicated portfolio A conservative dedicated portfolio management technique aimed at developing a bond portfolio that will provide payments exactly matching the specified liability schedules.

Put options Options to sell a firm's common stock within a certain period at a specified price.

Put-call parity The relationship that must exist in an efficient market between the prices for put and call options having the same underlying asset, exercise price, and expiration date.

Quadratic optimization A technique that relies on historical correlations in order to construct a portfolio that seeks to minimize tracking error with an index.

Quality financial statements Financial statements that most knowledgeable observers (analysts, portfolio managers) would consider conservatively prepared in terms of sales, expenses, earnings, and asset valuations. The results reported would reflect reasonable estimates and indicate what truly happened during the period and the legitimate value of assets and liabilities on the balance sheet.

Range forward A trading strategy based on a variation of the put-call parity model where, for the same underlying asset but different exercise prices, a call option is purchased and a put option is sold (or vice versa).

Rate anticipation effect The difference in return because of changing the duration of the portfolio during a period as compared with the portfolio's long-term policy duration.

Real estate investment trusts (REITs) Investment funds that hold portfolios of real estate investments.

Real options Options embedded in a firm's real assets that give managers valuable decision-making flexibility, such as the right to either undertake or abandon an investment project.

Real risk-free rate (RRFR) The basic interest rate with no accommodation for inflation or uncertainty. The pure time value of money.

Realized capital gains Capital gains that result when an appreciated asset is sold; realized capital gains are taxable.

Realized yield The expected compounded yield on a bond that is sold before it matures assuming the reinvestment of all cash flows at an explicit rate. Also called *horizon yield* for the yield realized during an investment horizon period.

Refunding issue Bonds that provide funds to prematurely retire another bond issue. These bonds can be either a junior or senior issue.

Registered bond A bond for which ownership is registered with the issuer. The holder receives interest payments by check directly from the issuer.

Registered competitive market makers (RCMMs) Members of an exchange who are allowed to use their memberships to buy or sell for their own account within the specific trading obligations set down by the exchange.

Registered traders Members of the stock exchange who are allowed to use their memberships to buy and sell for their own account, which means they save commissions on their trading but they provide liquidity to the market, and they abide by exchange regulations on how they can trade.

Relative-strength (RS) ratio The ratio of a stock price or an industry index value to a market indicator series, indicating the stock's or the industry's performance relative to the overall market.

Required rate of return The return that compensates investors for their time, the expected rate of inflation, and the uncertainty of the return.

Residual effect The return on a bond portfolio after taking account of the three prior factors—yield to maturity, interest rate effect, and sector/quality effect.

Resistance level A price at which a technician would expect a substantial increase in the supply of a stock to reverse a rising trend.

Return prediction studies Studies wherein investigations attempt to predict the time series of future rates of return using public information. An example would be predicting above-average returns for the stock market based on the aggregate dividend yield—e.g., high dividend yield indicates above average future market returns.

Revenue bond A bond that is serviced by the income generated from specific revenue-producing projects of the municipality.

Rising trend channel The range defined by security prices as they move progressively higher.

Risk The uncertainty that an investment will earn its expected rate of return.

Risk averse The assumption about investors that they will choose the least risky alternative, all else being equal.

Risk premium (RP) The increase over the nominal risk-free rate that investors demand as compensation for an investment's uncertainty.

Risk-free asset An asset with returns that exhibit zero variance.

Risky asset An asset with uncertain future returns.

Runs test A test of the weak-form efficient market hypothesis that checks for trends that persist longer in terms of positive or negative price changes than one would expect for a random series.

Sampling A technique for constructing a passive index portfolio in which the portfolio manager buys a representative sample of stocks that comprise the benchmark index.

Seasoned equity issues New equity shares offered by firms that already have stock outstanding.

Secondary market The market in which outstanding securities are bought and sold by owners other than the issuers.

Sector rotation strategy An active strategy that involves purchasing stocks in specific industries or stocks with specific characteristics (low *P/E*, growth, value) that are anticipated to rise in value more than the overall market.

Sector/quality effect The return on a bond portfolio caused by changing yield spreads between bonds in different sectors and with different quality ratings.

Secured (senior) bond A bond backed by a legal claim on specified assets of the issuer.

Security market indicator series An index created as a statistical measure of the performance of an entire market or segment of a market based on a sample of securities from the market or segment of a market.

Security market line (SML) The line that reflects the combination of risk and return of alternative investments. In CAPM risk is measured by systematic risk (beta).

Semistrong-form efficient market hypothesis The belief that security prices fully reflect all publicly available information, including information from security transactions and company, economic, and political news.

Separation theorem The proposition that the investment decision, which involves investing in the market portfolio on the capital market line, is separate from the financing decision, which targets a specific point on the CML based on the investor's risk preference.

Serial obligation bond A bond issue that has a series of maturity dates.

Settlement price The price determined by the exchange clearinghouse with which futures contract margin accounts are marked to market.

Sharpe measure A relative measure of a portfolio's benefit-to-risk ratio, calculated as its average return in excess of the risk-free rate divided by its standard deviation.

Short hedge A short position in a forward or futures contract used to offset the price volatility of a long position in the underlying asset.

Short position The seller of a commodity or security or, for a forward contract, the counterparty who will be the eventual seller of the underlying asset.

Short sale The sale of borrowed securities with the intention of repurchasing them later at a lower price and earning the difference.

Sinking fund Bond provision that requires the issuer to redeem some or all of the bond systematically over the term of the bond rather than in full at maturity.

Small-firm effect A frequent empirical anomaly where risk-adjusted stock returns for companies with low market capitalization (i.e., share price multiplied by number of outstanding shares) are significantly larger than those generated by high market capitalization firms.

Soft dollars A form of compensation to a money manager generated when the manager commits the investor to paying higher brokerage fees in exchange for the manager receiving additional services (e.g., stock research) from the broker.

Specialist The major market maker on U.S. stock exchanges who acts as a broker or dealer to ensure the liquidity and smooth functions of the secondary stock market.

Speculative company A firm with a great degree of business and/or financial risk, with commensurate high earnings potential.

Speculative stock A stock that appears to be highly overpriced compared to its reasonable valuation.

Spending phase Phase in the investment life cycle during which individuals' earning years end as they retire. They pay for expenses with income from social security and returns from prior investments and invest to protect against inflation.

Spot rate The required yield for a cash flow to be received at some specific date in the future—for example, the spot rate for a flow to be received in one year, for a cash flow in two years, and so on.

Spread A trading strategy where long and short positions in two call (or two put) option contracts having the same underlying asset but different exercise prices or expiration dates are combined to create a customized return distribution.

Standard deviation A measure of variability equal to the square root of the variance.

Statement of cash flows A financial statement that shows the effects on the firm's cash flow of income flows and changes in its balance sheet.

Static yield spread Yield spreads that consider a spread over the total term structure.

Stock index arbitrage A trading strategy involving a long position in a stock portfolio and a short position in a stock index futures contract (or vice versa) designed to exploit a mispricing in the futures contract relative to the underlying index.

Straddle A trading strategy requiring the simultaneous purchase of a call option and a put option having the same exercise price, underlying asset, and expiration date. Variations of this theme include *strips, straps, strangles,* and *chooser options.*

Strong-form efficient market hypothesis The belief that security prices fully reflect all information from both public and private sources.

Structural change Economic trend occurring when the economy is undergoing a major change in organization or in how it functions.

Structured note A bond with an embedded derivative designed to create a payoff distribution that satisfies the needs of a specific investor clientele.

Style analysis An attempt to explain the variability in the observed returns to a security portfolio in terms of the movements in the returns to a series of benchmark portfolios designed to capture the essence of a particular security characteristic such as size, value, and growth.

Style grid A graph used to classify and display the investment style that best defines the nature of a security portfolio.

Subordinate (junior) bonds Debentures that, in case of default, entitle holders to claims on the issuer's assets only after the claims of holders of senior debentures and mortgage bonds are satisfied.

Support level A price at which a technician would expect a substantial increase in price and volume for a stock to reverse a declining trend that was due to profit taking.

Sustainable growth rate A measure of how fast a firm can grow using internal equity and debt financing and a constant capital structure. Equal to retention rate × ROE.

Swap spread A measure of the risk premium for an interest rate swap, calculated as the difference between the agreement's fixed rate and the yield on a Treasury bond with the same maturity.

SWOT analysis An examination of a firm's *S*trengths, *W*eaknesses, *O*pportunities, and *T*hreats. This analysis helps an analyst evaluate a firm's strategies to exploit its competitive advantages or defend against its weaknesses.

Systematic risk The variability of returns that is due to macroeconomic factors that affect all risky assets. Because it affects all risky assets, it cannot be eliminated by diversification.

Tactical asset allocation An investment strategy that adjusts the investor's mix of stocks and bonds by increasing the allocation to the asset class that is relatively undervalued.

Technical analysis Estimation of future security price movements based on past price and volume movements.

Term bond A bond that has a single maturity date.

Term structure of interest rates The relationship between term to maturity and yield to maturity for a sample of comparable bonds at a given time. Popularly known as the *yield curve.*

Term to maturity Specifies the date or the number of years before a bond matures or expires.

Third market Over-the-counter trading of securities listed on an exchange.

Tick The minimum price movement for the asset underlying a forward or futures contract; for Treasury bonds, one tick equals 1/32 of 1 percent of par value.

Time premium The difference between an option's total market value and its intrinsic value.

Time-series analysis An examination of a firm's performance data over a period of time.

Time-weighted return The geometric average of (one plus) the *holding period yields* to an investment portfolio.

Total return A return objective in which the investor wants to increase the portfolio value to meet a future need by both capital gains and current income reinvestment.

Tracking error The standard deviation of the difference in returns between an active investment portfolio and its benchmark porfolio; also called *tracking error volatility.*

Trading effect The difference in performance of a bond portfolio from that of a chosen index due to short-run changes in the composition of the portfolio.

Trading rule A formula for deciding on current transactions based on historical data.

Trading turnover The percentage of outstanding shares traded during a period of time.

Transaction cost The cost of executing a trade. Low costs characterize an operationally efficient market.

Treasury bill A negotiable U.S. government security with a maturity of less than one year that pays no periodic interest but yields the difference between its par value and its discounted purchase price.

Treasury bond A U.S. government security with a maturity of more than 10 years that pays interest periodically.

Treasury note A U.S. government security with maturities of 1 to 10 years that pays interest periodically.

Treynor measure A relative measure of a portfolio's benefit-to-risk ratio, calculated as its average return in excess of the risk-free rate divided by its beta coefficient.

Trough The culmination of a bear market at which prices stop declining and begin rising.

12b-1 plan A fee charged by some funds, named after the SEC rule that permits it. Such fees pay for distribution costs, such as advertising, or for brokers' commissions. The fund's prospectus details any 12b-1 charges that apply.

Underfunded plan A defined benefit pension plan in which the present value of the fund's liabilities to employees exceeds the value of the fund's assets.

Underweighted A condition in which a portfolio, for whatever reason, includes less of a class of securities than the relative market value alone would justify.

Unrealized capital gains Capital gains that reflect the price appreciation of currently held unsold assets; taxes on unrealized capital gains can be deferred indefinitely.

Unsecured bonds Bonds that promise payments of interest and principal but pledge no specific assets. Holders have first claim on the issuer's income and unpledged assets. Also known as *debentures*.

Unsystematic risk Risk that is unique to an asset, derived from its particular characteristics. It can be eliminated in a diversified portfolio.

Unweighted index An indicator series affected equally by the performance of each security in the sample regardless of price or market value. Also referred to as an *equal-weighted series.*

Unwind The negotiated termination of a forward or futures position before contract maturity.

Uptick An incremental movement upward in a transaction price over the previous transaction price.

Uptick-downtick ratio A ratio of the number of uptick block transactions (indicating buyers) to the number of downtick block transactions (indicating sellers of blocks). An indicator of institutional investor sentiment.

Valuation analysis An active bond portfolio management strategy designed to capitalize on expected price increases in temporarily undervalued issues.

Valuation process Part of the investment decision process in which you estimate the value of a security.

Value stocks Stocks that appear to be undervalued for reasons besides earnings growth potential. These stocks are usually identified based on high dividend yields, low *P/E* ratios, or low price-to-book ratios.

Variable-rate note A debt security for which the interest rate changes to follow some specified short-term rate, for example, the T-bill rate; see *floating rate note.*

Variance A measure of variability equal to the sum of the squares of a return's deviation from the mean, divided by the total number of returns.

Warrant An instrument that allows the holder to purchase a specified number of shares of the firm's common stock from the firm at a specified price for a given period of time.

Weak-form efficient market hypothesis The belief that security prices fully reflect all security market information.

Yankee bonds Bonds sold in the United States and denominated in U.S. dollars but issued by a foreign firm or government.

Yield The promised rate of return on an investment under certain assumptions.

Yield illusion The erroneous expectation that a bond will provide its stated yield to maturity without recognizing the implicit reinvestment assumption related to coupon payments.

Yield spread The difference between the promised yields of alternative bond issues or market segments at a given time relative to yields on treasury issues of equal maturity.

Yield to worst Given a bond with multiple potential maturity dates and prices due to embedded call options, the practice is to calculate a yield to maturity for each of the call dates and prices and select the lowest yield (the most conservative possible yield) as yield to worst.

Zero coupon bond A bond that pays its par value at maturity but no periodic interest payments. Its yield is determined by the difference between its par value and its discounted purchase price. Also called *original issue discount (OID) bonds.*

NAME AND COMPANY INDEX

SUBJECT INDEX